CAMBRIDGE Academic Content Dictionary

CAMBRIDGE
UNIVERSITY PRESS

32 Avenue of the Americas, New York, NY 10013-2473, USA

Cambridge University Press is part of the University of Cambridge.

It furthers the University's mission by disseminating knowledge in the pursuit of
education, learning and research at the highest international levels of excellence.

www.cambridge.org
Information on this title: www.cambridge.org/9780521691963

First edition 2009
6th printing 2014

Printed in Hong Kong, China, by Golden Cup Printing Company, Limited

A catalogue record for this publication is available from the British Library

Library of Congress Cataloging-in-Publication Data

Cambridge academic content dictionary.
p. cm.
ISBN 978-0-521-87143-3 (hardback ; alk. paper) — ISBN 978-0-521-69196-3 (pbk. with cd-rom : alk. paper)
1. English language — Dictionaries. 2. Vocabulary. I. Cambridge University Press. II. Title: Academic
content dictionary.

PE1628.C215 2008
423 — dc22

2007049860

ISBN 978-0-521-69196-3 paperback with CD-ROM (Windows, Mac)
ISBN 978-0-521-87143-3 hardback

Editorial and production team

COMMISSIONING EDITOR
Paul Heacock

MANAGING EDITOR
Carol-June V. Cassidy

SENIOR EDITORS
John K. Bollard, Ph.D.
Julie Plier

LEXICOGRAPHERS
Grant Barrett
Orin Hargraves

PRONUNCIATIONS
John K. Bollard, Ph.D.

EDITORIAL REVIEW
Sylvia P. Bloch
Allene Feldman

PROOFREADERS
Katherine M. Isaacs
Linda M. LiDestri
Tyler Cassidy-Heacock

ILLUSTRATIONS
Vilma Ortiz-Dillon
Steve Cancel

CONTENT MANAGEMENT SYSTEM
Stephen F. Perkins, dataformat.com

DESIGN AND COMPOSITION
Jane Tenenbaum, Tenenbaum Design
Chris Cott, Grapevine Publishing Services LLC
Daniel Grossberg, Grapevine Publishing Services LLC

SOFTWARE SUPPORT
Dominic Glennon

CAMBRIDGE INTERNATIONAL CORPUS
Ann Fiddes, Corpus Manager
Julie Sontag, Corpus Administrator
Robert Fairchild, Systems Developer

SMARTTHESAURUS CODING (CD-ROM)
Mary Coe, Potomac Indexing
John K. Bollard, Ph.D.

DATABASE DEVELOPMENT
Walter Friedman

Based on the *Cambridge Dictionary of American English,* Second Edition

Contents

Preface

Mastering school subjects is hard work. Understanding the *Fundamental Counting Principle* or knowing what a *polis* was or what a *nuclease* does are not things that just happen – acquiring this knowledge requires effort. One tool for acquiring and retaining knowledge is a good dictionary, which will explain all the important words and phrases used in school subjects. The *Cambridge Academic Content Dictionary* does that, and more.

This book includes the important vocabulary for twenty different content areas, from algebra to world history. The subject vocabulary defined in this book is taken from state standards and standardized tests. We have also included vocabulary from the National Assessment of Educational Progress (NAEP) subject area assessments.

In addition, the *Cambridge Academic Content Dictionary* includes the words from the Academic Word List: 570 words and their derivatives, or word families, that are used frequently in academic texts. Words in the Academic Word List – like *authority*, *method*, and *significant* – are not specific to one subject; they are used across many different subject areas. (See page ix for a full list of the content areas covered in this dictionary and more information about the Academic Word List.)

You should not have to work hard to understand the explanations given in a dictionary. That is why the definitions in the *Cambridge Academic Content Dictionary* are written using the Cambridge Defining Vocabulary, a list of about 2,500 very common words that students already know. The Cambridge Defining Vocabulary was developed using the American English portions of the Cambridge International Corpus, a database of more than 1 billion words of written and spoken English.

The corpus was also used to help editors decide which words and phrases to include in the dictionary, which meanings to define, and what examples should be included. This means that the entries in this dictionary show how English is really used by writers and speakers of American and Canadian English today.

There are many more features in the *Cambridge Academic Content Dictionary* that you will find helpful, especially in your writing. The following pages – **Finding your way around the dictionary** – describe how to use them. We hope you will agree that they make this the most useful dictionary available for students, one that will prepare you for success in high school and beyond.

Paul Heacock
Commissioning Editor
August 2008

Academic content

Subject area words and meanings

Words and meanings in this dictionary are labeled if they are used in particular academic subjects. Be sure to look at all the guidewords for a particular word when you are looking for subject-area meanings. Some words have different meanings that are used in different subjects – for example, **altitude** has one meaning (HEIGHT) that is used in *earth science* and another meaning (LINE) that is used in *geometry*. Sometimes, a single meaning of a word will have uses in two different subjects, such as **assymetry**, which is used in both *geometry* and *art*.

The subject areas that are covered in this dictionary are:

- algebra
- art
- biology
- chemistry
- earth science
- English
- geometry
- grammar
- literature
- mathematics
- music
- physics
- politics & government
- science
- social studies
- trigonometry
- US history
- world history
- writing

General academic words

There are hundreds of words that are used more often in academic writing than they are used in other types of written material. Research by Averil Coxhead has identified these words as the Academic Word List. Words that are part of the Academic Word List are marked with an Ⓐ in this book. You can find out more about the Academic Word List at http://language.massey.ac.nz/staff/awl/awlinfo.shtml.

Finding your way around the dictionary

How do I find the word I'm looking for?

The first meaning of a word is shown with a bold green **headword**. If there is more than one meaning, the headword is followed by a guideword.

Words that are closely related to the headword are grouped with it.

culture Ⓐ WAY OF LIFE /ˈkʌl·tʃər/ *n* [C/U] *social studies* the way of life of a particular people, esp. as shown in their ordinary behavior and habits, their attitudes toward each other, and their moral and religious beliefs ○ [U] *He studied the culture of the Sioux Indians.*

cultural Ⓐ /ˈkʌl·tʃə·rəl/ *adj* relating to the way of life of a country or a group of people ○ *The country has a rich cultural heritage.*

culturally Ⓐ /ˈkʌl·tʃə·rə·li/ *adv*

Common phrases in which a word is used are shown in **bold**.

cross-purposes /ˈkrɔːˈspɜr·pə·səz/ *pl n* If two people or groups are **at cross-purposes** they do not understand each other because they have different intentions ○ *They're talking at cross-purposes without realizing it.*

Idioms follow the main meanings of the word. They are listed separately at the first important word in the idiom.

IDIOM with crying

• **a crying shame** a great misfortune ○ *It's a crying shame that new mothers have to go back to work after six weeks.*

Phrasal verbs follow all the other uses of a word.

PHRASAL VERB with cut

• **cut across** *something* to include several things that usually are separated from each other ○ *Iron deficiency in women cuts across all socioeconomic levels.*

Compound words – two or more words used together to make a word – have their own entries, in alphabetical order.

day-to-day *adj* ordinary and regular ○ *Your day-to-day responsibilities will include sorting the mail and making appointments.*

day trip *n* [C] a visit to a place in which you return home or to your hotel on the same day

day-tripper *n* [C] ○ *A lot of the people on the beach are day-trippers.*

How do I find content-area and academic words?

Content labels appear just before the meaning that applies to that subject.

genus /ˈdʒiː·nəs/ *n* [C] *pl* **genera** *biology* a group of animals or plants that share some characteristics in a larger biological group

geography /dʒiːˈɑg·rə·fi/ *n* [U] *social studies* the study of the features and systems of the earth's surface, including continents, mountains, seas, weather, and plant life, and of the ways in which countries and people organize life within an area

Words that are more common in academic writing than in other types of writing and that are used across many different subject areas are marked with an Ⓐ.

hierarchy Ⓐ /ˈhɑɪ·əˌrɑr·ki, ˈhɑɪˌrɑr-/ *n* [C] *social studies* a system in which people or things are put at various levels or ranks according to their importance ○ *He rapidly rose in the corporate hierarchy.*

What does the word mean?

When a word has more than one main meaning, each meaning has a green-shaded **GUIDEWORD**. Guidewords are a fast way of finding the meaning you are looking for.

highlight Ⓐ **EMPHASIZE** /ˈhɑɪ·lɑɪt/ *v* [T] to attract attention to or emphasize something important ○ *The report highlights the need for increased funding.*

BEST PART /ˈhɑɪ·lɑɪt/ *n* [C] the best, most important, or most interesting part ○ *The highlight of our trip to New York was going to the top of the Empire State Building.*

BRIGHT AREA /ˈhɑɪ·lɑɪt/ *n* [C usually pl] a bright or lighter-colored area on the surface of something, esp. on a painting

Smaller differences in meaning are shown by separate numbered definitions.

house **HOME** /hɑʊs/ *n* [C] *pl* **houses** **1** a building in which people, usually one family, live ○ *to buy/rent a house* ○ *a brick/clapboard house* ○ *my/your/grandma's house* **2** A house can also be a building where animals are kept: *a dog house* **3** A house (also **household**) can also be all the people living in a house: *Try not to wake the whole house when you come in!*

Definitions are written using the Cambridge Defining Vocabulary, a list of about 2,500 very common words that students already know.

A word in the definition that is not in the Cambridge Defining Vocabulary is printed in SMALL CAPITALS and has its own entry in the dictionary.

horsepower /ˈhɔːrˌspɑʊ·ər/ *n* [C/U] *pl* **horsepower** a unit for measuring the power of an engine ○ [C] *a 170-horsepower engine*

horseradish /ˈhɔːrsˌræd·ɪʃ/ *n* [U] a plant with a long, white root that has a strong taste

horseshoe /ˈhɔːrs·ʃuː/ *n* [C] a U-shaped metal object that is attached to the bottom of a horse's HOOF (= foot) to protect it

How do I pronounce the word?

Pronunciations of a word are shown after the headword. These are written using the International Phonetic Alphabet (IPA). For more information, see page xviii. A pronunciation guide appears at the bottom of the dictionary pages.

icon REPRESENTATION /ˈɑɪ·kɑn/ *n* [C] a famous person or thing that represents something of importance ○ *The US Capitol building is an American icon.*
iconic /ɑɪˈkɑn·ɪk/ *adj* ○ *Scenes of Parisians dancing in the streets remain iconic images from World War II.*

If more than one pronunciation or stress pattern is common, a variant is given.

influence /ˈɪn,fluː·əns, *Southern also* ɪnˈfluː-/ *v* [T] to cause someone to change their behavior or the way they think about something, or to cause

How is the word used?

The part of speech is shown with an *italic* abbreviation.

Plural forms, verb forms, and comparatives and superlatives are shown if they do not obey the usual rules for changing word endings.

The grammar of a word is shown in square brackets. When the grammar information is given after the part of speech, it relates to all meanings in that entry.

gallop /ˈgæl·əp/ *v* [I/T] (of a horse) to run fast so that all four feet come off the ground together in each act of forward movement
gallop /ˈgæl·əp/ *n* [C] ○ *The horse suddenly broke into a gallop.*
galloping /ˈgæl·ə·pɪŋ/ *adj* [not gradable] increasing or developing at a very fast and often uncontrollable rate ○ *galloping inflation*

gallows /ˈgæl·oʊz/ *n* [C] *pl* **gallows** a raised, wooden structure used, esp. in the past, for hanging and killing criminals as a punishment

galore /gəˈlɔːr, -ˈloʊr/ *adj* [only after n] [not gradable] in great amounts or numbers ○ *Down South you get biscuits and gravy and fried foods galore.*

galoshes /gəˈlɑʃ·əz/ *pl n* large, waterproof shoes, usually made of rubber, for wearing over ordinary shoes esp. during snowy weather

galvanize /ˈgæl·və,nɑɪz/ *v* [T] to cause someone to suddenly take action, esp. by shocking or exciting them in some way ○ *Why not use the media to galvanize the community into action?*

When the grammar information is given before a definition or example, it relates only to that meaning or example.

gamble /ˈgæm·bəl/ *v* **1** to risk losing money in the hope of winning a lot more money, esp. if the result of a future event happens as you hope ○ [I] *She spent her day gambling at the slot machines in a Las Vegas casino.* ○ [M] *He gambled away most of his money.* **2** To gamble is also to do something that you think is worth doing although it might not succeed or you might lose money: [+ *that* clause] *We're gambling that enough people will show up at the concert to cover our expenses.*

Labels in *italics* show when a word or meaning expresses a particular attitude or may not be acceptable in certain situations.

kinda /ˈkɑɪn·də/ *adv* [not gradable] *not standard* (spelled the way it is often spoken) kind of (= slightly) ○ *I was kinda sorry to see him go.*

medic /ˈmed·ɪk/ *n* [C] *infml* a person who belongs to the part of the armed forces that gives medical help to soldiers

Usage notes give more information about how a word is used.

IDIOMS with matter

• **a matter of** *something* only; just ○ *In a matter of seconds, the building was in flames.* ◊ **USAGE:** Used to emphasize that an amount is small.

Note boxes give useful information to help you avoid mistakes when you speak and write English.

CONFUSABLES

advice or **advise**?

Be careful not to confuse the noun **advice** with the verb **advise**.

I advise you to see a lawyer.

~~*I advice you to see a lawyer.*~~

Word Choices boxes offer other words to use in writing and explain the differences among these related words.

WORD CHOICES medicine

A common alternative to "medicine" is **drug**.

Scientists have developed a new ***drug*** *for treating breast cancer.*

Medication is a medicine or set of medicines for a particular illness or condition.

He's currently on ***medication*** *for his heart.*

A small solid piece of medicine is a **pill** or **tablet**.

He takes a sleeping ***pill*** *at night.*

Do you take any vitamin ***tablets****?*

Ointment is medicine in the form of a cream that you rub into your skin.

Apply the ***ointment*** *to the sore area.*

Drops are a type of medicine that you put into your eyes, ears, or nose in small drops.

These eye ***drops*** *should clear up the infection.*

Word Family boxes show the different words related to a particular entry.

WORD FAMILY magic

Nouns	magic	*Adjectives*	magical
	magician	*Adverbs*	magically

Cross-references point to related words and information given at other entries.

monastery /ˈmɑn·əˌster·i/ *n* [C] a building or group of buildings in which MONKS (= religious men) live and worship ◊ Compare CONVENT

Words that are used in Canadian or British English are shown with the label *Cdn* or *Br*.

First Nation *n* [C] *esp. Cdn* one of the groups of people whose ANCESTORS lived in North America before the arrival of Europeans

Spellings that are used in Canadian or British English are shown following the main entry word with the label *Cdn* or *Br*.

flavor, *Cdn, Br* **flavour** /ˈfleɪ·vər/ *n* [C/U] the particular way a substance, esp. food or drink, is recognized from its taste and smell ○ [C] *We sell 32 different flavors of ice cream.* ○ [U] *This soup doesn't have much flavor.* ○ [U] *(fig.) This brief description should give you a flavor of what the book is like* (= show you the character of the book).

Usage labels

Usage labels are a guide that helps you decide if a term would be suitable in a particular situation. Most words in the English language can be used in any context. But some words will not be appropriate or will seem strange when used in a particular way or at a particular time. The following labels are used in this dictionary before definitions or examples to provide additional usage information.

Words that are suitable for some people or in some situations

fml (formal)	terms used in specialized written English or in formal speech, but not in ordinary written or spoken English
infml (informal)	terms that can be used in speaking and writing to friends, but not in writing for school or work
slang	very informal terms used among friends, by people of the same age group, or by people who share a particular interest

Words from the past

dated	terms used more often before the 1970s
old use	terms used before the twentieth century

Words used among some groups

law	terms used by lawyers, judges, and people involved in legal matters
medical	terms used by doctors, nurses, and people talking about medical care
trademark	a product name or term that is owned by a company

Words used only for women or only for men

female	terms applied only to females
male	terms applied only to males

Words used in some places

Br	British English term
Cdn	Canadian English term
regional	terms used only in parts of the US

Words that express an attitude

approving	terms that show a good opinion of someone or something
disapproving	terms that show a bad opinion of someone or something
a child's word	terms that are suitable for use to or by children
fig. (figurative)	terms that are not used with their basic meaning but suggest part of that meaning
humorous	terms that are used to show an amused attitude toward something

Shortened forms and special symbols

abbreviation	a shortened form of a word, or a shortened form of a phrase usually taken from the first letter of each word in the phrase
contraction	a combination of two words that leaves out one or more letters
short form	a word taken from the first or last part of a longer word
symbol	a sign that represents a word

Qualifiers for other labels

esp. (especially)	a term that is particularly used this way or in this variety of English, but may be used in others
often	a term that is frequently used this way, but may be used in other ways
usually	a term that is almost always used in a particular way, although it can be used in other ways as well

Grammar codes

Grammar codes give additional information about how words with different parts of speech can be used. A grammar code is given at the beginning of each part of an entry. If more than one pattern is possible, examples are coded for the pattern being shown.

Nouns

C	a COUNTABLE noun that can be used in both singular and plural forms
C usually pl	a countable noun usually used in its plural form
C usually sing	a countable noun usually used in its singular form
U	an UNCOUNTABLE noun that does not have a plural form, and cannot be used with the indefinite articles *a* or *an*
C/U	a noun that has both countable and uncountable uses
pl	a noun that is usually uncountable but is plural in a particular meaning, and takes the plural form of a verb

Verbs

I	an INTRANSITIVE verb that does not have a direct object in the sentence identifying the person or thing being acted on
T	a TRANSITIVE verb that has a direct object in the sentence identifying the person or thing being acted on
I/T	a verb that can be intransitive or transitive
always + adv/ prep	a verb that can be transitive, intransitive, or both, but which must always be followed by an adverb or preposition
M	a phrasal verb that takes an object which can come before or after the adverb or preposition
L	a LINKING VERB that connects the subject of the sentence to an adjective or noun that describes it
past part.	a PAST PARTICIPLE form of a verb
past simp.	a PAST SIMPLE form of a verb
pres. part.	a PRESENT PARTICIPLE form of a verb

Adjectives and Adverbs

only after n	an adjective used only after a noun
-er/-est only	an adjective that is used with *-er* to form a comparative and with *-est* to form a superlative but cannot be used with *more* and *most*
not gradable	an adjective or adverb that does not have a comparative or superlative form

Complements

These codes show that a verb, adjective, or noun is used in combination with particular types of words or phrases.

+ *that* clause	a clause beginning with *that* can immediately follow the word
+ (*that*) clause	a clause can immediately follow the word; it can begin with the word *that* but does not have to
+ *to* infinitive	a *to* infinitive immediately follows the word
+ question word	a question word – *who, what, why, when, where, how,* or *whether* – immediately follows the word

Parts of speech

adj (adjective)
adv (adverb)
auxiliary verb
comparative
conjunction
definite article
exclamation
indefinite article
modal verb
n (noun)
number
phrasal verb
pl n (plural noun)
prefix
prep (preposition)
pronoun
suffix
superlative
v (verb)

Pronunciation symbols

The lists below show how the symbols of the *International Phonetic Alphabet* are used in this dictionary to indicate the pronunciation of an entry word. Next to each symbol are one or two English words in which a particular sound occurs.

As is the case with any dictionary, the pronunciation system used in the *Cambridge Academic Content Dictionary* provides a guide to pronunciation to help the user who does not know how a word is pronounced, but does not impose a "correct" pronunciation. In the US, pronunciation often varies from one region to another, just as pronunciations vary from person to person. The goal for any speaker is to be understood, and the pronunciations in this dictionary are designed to help the student of English reach that point.

Vowel symbols

æ bat, hand
ɑ hot, barn
ɑː **a**unt, tom**a**to (*variant pronunciations*)
ɑ̃ g**en**re (*variant pronunciation*)
ɑɪ bite, sky
ɑʊ house, now
e bet, head
eɪ late, play
ɪ fit, bid
iː feet, please
i *either* /iː/ *or* /ɪ/
ɔː saw, dog
ɔ̃ː sal**on** (*variant pronunciation*)
ɔɪ boy, join
oʊ go, boat
ʊ put, good
uː rude, boot
ʌ cut, love
ʌ̃ **Huh**
ɜ bird, fur (*used only before* /r/ *in stressed syllables*)
ə sitter, alone

Other symbols

ˈ *Stress mark placed before a syllable with the heaviest stress, as before the first syllable of* **business** / ˈbɪz·nəs/
ˌ *Stress mark placed before a syllable with lighter stress, as before the last syllable of* **businesslike** / ˈbɪz·nəs ˌlɑɪk/
· *The raised dot separates syllables.*
\- *The hyphen shows that only part of a variant pronunciation is given.*

Consonant symbols

b **b**id, jo**b**
d **d**o, la**d**y
dʒ **j**ump, bri**dge**
f **f**oot, sa**f**e
g **g**o, do**g**
h **h**ome, be**h**ind
hw **wh**ich, **wh**ere (*many people say* /w/ *instead of* /hw/)
j **y**es, oni**o**n
k **k**iss, **c**ome
l **l**ook, poo**l**
əl litt**le**, met**al** (*used in a syllable with no vowel sound*)
m **m**any, so**m**e
əm h**m** (*used in a syllable with no vowel sound*)
n **n**eed, ope**n**
ən hidd**en**, cott**on** (*used in a syllable with no vowel sound*)
ŋ si**ng**, si**n**k
p **p**en, ho**p**e
r **r**oad, ca**r**d
s **s**ee, re**c**ent
ʃ **sh**oe, na**t**ion
t **t**eam, mee**t**
ţ mee**t**ing, la**tt**er
θ **th**ink, bo**th**
ð **th**is, fa**th**er
tʃ **ch**oose, ri**ch**
v **v**isit, sa**v**e
w **w**atch, a**w**ay
x **Ch**anukah (*variant pronunciation*)
z **z**oo, the**s**e
ʒ bei**g**e, mea**s**ure

A a

A **LETTER**, **a** /eɪ/ *n* [C] *pl* **A's, a's** the first letter of the English alphabet

MUSICAL NOTE /eɪ/ *n* [C/U] *pl* **A's, As** ***music*** in Western music, the sixth note in the SCALE (= series of notes) that begins on the note C, or a set of notes based on this note

MARK /eɪ/ *n* [C] *pl* **A's, As** a mark that means excellent, given to something of the highest quality, esp. school work ○ *The teacher gave me an A for my essay.*

a **GENERAL THING** /ə, eɪ/, **an** *indefinite article* **1** used before nouns to refer generally to someone or something that has not been mentioned before ○ *This is a very mild cheese.* ○ *Can I have a banana, please?* ○ *There was a sudden loud noise.* ○ *Is he a friend of yours?* ○ *My birthday is on a Friday this year.* **2** You can also use "a" before some words expressing an amount: *a few days* ○ *a great number* ○ *a lot of money*

PARTICULAR THING /ə, eɪ/, **an** *indefinite article* **1** used before nouns to refer to someone or something specific that has not been mentioned before ○ *I'd love a soda.* **2** "A" can be used to mean a work created by someone: *Experts think that the painting may be a Picasso.* **3** "A" can also be used to mean any person or thing of a specific type: *A cheetah can run faster than a lion.* ○ *She wants to be a doctor when she grows up.* **4** "A" in front of a name means you are referring to a particular person: *Do you know a Julio Perez?*

ONE /ə, eɪ/, **an** *indefinite article* one ○ *a hundred/million/dozen* ○ *a quarter of an hour*

EACH OR EVERY /ə/ *prep* in or for each or every; PER ○ *Take one tablet three times a day.* ○ *These shoes cost $30 a pair.*

abacus /'æb·ə·kəs, ə'bæk·əs/ *n* [C] a frame that holds thin metal rods with balls that slide on them, used for counting, adding, and subtracting

abandon Ⓐ /ə'bæn·dən/ *v* [T] to leave behind or run away from someone or something, or to give up something ○ *Air attacks forced the villagers to abandon their homes.* ○ *The weather was so bad, we abandoned our plans for a picnic.*

abandoned Ⓐ /ə'bæn·dənd/ *adj* ○ *Shelters are full of abandoned pets.* ○ *The fire started in an abandoned warehouse.*

abandonment Ⓐ /ə'bæn·dən·mənt/ *n* [U] ○ *Archeologists don't know what could have caused a mass abandonment of the area.*

abate /ə'beɪt/ *v* [I/T] to become less strong, or to make something less strong ○ *Our desire for consumer goods has not abated.*

abbey /'æb·i/ *n* [C] a building for MONKS (= religious men) or NUNS (= religious women) to live in

abbreviation /əˌbriː·viː'eɪ·ʃən/ *n* [C] a shortened form esp. of a word or phrase ○ *UN is the abbreviation for the United Nations.* ○ *I.e. is an abbreviation of a Latin phrase that means "that is."*

abbreviate /ə'briː·viːˌeɪt/ *v* [T] to shorten a word or words, or to make something shorter ○ *We had to abbreviate the names of the states.*

abbreviated /ə'briː·viːˌeɪţ·əd/ *adj* [not gradable] ○ *An abbreviated version was published last year.*

ABCs /ˌeɪ·biː'siːz/ *pl n infml* **1** the alphabet **2** The ABCs of something is basic information about it: *I need a book that covers the ABCs of gardening.*

abdicate /'æb·dəˌkeɪt/ *v* [I/T] *fml* to give up a position as king, or to fail to take responsibility for something ○ [T] *Edward VIII abdicated the British throne in 1936.* ○ *The administration has abdicated its leadership on this critical issue.*

abdication /ˌæb·də'keɪ·ʃən/ *n* [C/U] ○ [U] *I think it's an abdication of your responsibility if you don't vote.*

abdomen /'æb·də·mən/ *n* [C] the part of the body that contains the stomach, bowels, and other organs in a person or animal ➤ Picture: **insect; spider**

abdominal /æb'dɑm·ən·əl, əb-/ *adj* [not gradable] ○ *This virus causes terrible abdominal pain.*

abduct /æb'dʌkt, əb-/ *v* [T] to take a person away by force ○ *Kidnappers abducted the child from the playground.*

abduction /æb'dʌk·ʃən, əb-/ *n* [C/U] ○ [C] *The abduction took place in front of several helpless witnesses.*

aberration /ˌæb·ə'reɪ·ʃən/ *n* [C] a change from what is typical or usual, esp. a temporary change ○ *The drop in our school's test scores was dismissed as an aberration.*

abet /ə'bet/ *v* [T] **-tt-** to help or encourage a person or thing to do something, esp. something wrong or illegal ○ *Shady lawyers abetted the company's officers in stealing the funds.*

abhor /əb'hɔːr/ *v* [T] **-rr-** to hate something or someone ○ *His opponent abhors the death penalty.*

abhorrent /əb'hɔːr·ənt, -'hɑr-/ *adj* ○ *His attitude of superiority is abhorrent.*

abhorrence /əb'hɔːr·əns, -'hɑr-/ *n* [U] ○ *She has an abhorrence of violence.*

abide **IDIOM** /ə'baɪd/

• **can't abide** to not like or accept something ○ *He can't abide laziness.*

PHRASAL VERB with abide

• **abide by** *something* to accept or obey an agreement, decision, rule, etc. ○ *Competitors must abide by the judges' decision.*

abiding /ə'baɪd·ɪŋ/ *adj* lasting for a long time ○ *Muir had an abiding interest in dogs.*

ability /ə'bɪl·əţ·i/ *n* [C/U] the mental or physical power or skill needed to do something ○ [U] *Someone with that kind of ability will do well.* ○ [C] *Her*

teammates respect her abilities. ○ Related adjective: ABLE SKILLFUL; ABLE HAVING WHAT IS NEEDED

abiotic /ˌeɪ·bɑɪ ˈɑt̬·ɪk/ *adj* ***earth science*** relating to things in the environment that are not living

abject /ˈæb·dʒekt/ *adj* extreme and without hope ○ *They live in abject poverty.* ○ *My experiment was an abject failure.*

ablaze /əˈbleɪz/ *adj* [not gradable] burning or very bright ○ *Fire spread quickly until the whole building was ablaze.* ○ *The ballroom was ablaze with lights.*

able **HAVING WHAT IS NEEDED** /ˈeɪ·bəl/ *adj* [+ *to* infinitive] having what is needed to do something, esp. the physical or mental power, skill, time, money, or opportunity ○ *I lost my job and wasn't able to afford my old apartment.* ○ *We won't be able to keep up this kind of effort much longer.* ○ Related noun: ABILITY

> **GRAMMAR**
>
> able or can/could?
>
> **Able** is used with modal and auxiliary verbs, where **can** or **could** are not grammatically possible.
>
> *I might not be able to attend the meeting.*
>
> *I've never been able to understand him.*

SKILLFUL /ˈeɪ·bəl/ *adj* good at what you do ○ *He is an able student.* ○ Related noun: ABILITY

ably /ˈeɪ·bli/ *adv* ○ *He does his job very ably.*

WORD FAMILY able

Nouns	ability disability inability	*Adjectives*	able unable disabled
Verbs	enable disable	*Adverbs*	ably

abnormal Ⓐ /æbˈnɔːr·məl, əb-/ *adj* not usual or average ○ *We had an abnormal amount of snow.* ○ *He has an abnormal heartbeat.*

abnormality /ˌæb·nɔːrˈmæl·ət̬·i, -nər-/ *n* [C/U] ○ [C] *No abnormalities showed up in the blood tests.*

abnormally Ⓐ /æbˈnɔːr·mə·li, əb-/ *adv* ○ *It was abnormally hot this summer.*

aboard /əˈbɔːrd, -ˈbourd/ *prep, adv* [not gradable] on or onto a ship, aircraft, bus, or train ○ *We finally went aboard the plane three hours later.*

abode /əˈboud/ *n* [C/U] *fml* the place where someone lives ○ [C] *He was a wanderer with no permanent abode.*

abolish /əˈbɑl·ɪʃ/ *v* [T] to put an end to something, such as an organization, rule, or custom ○ *Massachusetts voters abolished rent control.*

abolition /ˌæb·əˈlɪʃ·ən/ *n* [U] **1** the official ending of an activity or custom **2** ***US history*** Abolition also means the official end to SLAVERY in the US, which took place in 1863.

Abolitionist /ˌæb·əˈlɪʃ·ə·nəst/ *n* [C] ***US history*** a person who supported an end to SLAVERY.

abominable /əˈbɑm·ə·nə·bəl/ *adj* very bad or unpleasant ○ *The abominable working conditions made many workers sick.*

aboriginal /ˌæb·əˈrɪdʒ·ən·əl/ *adj* having lived or existed in a place since the earliest known time ○ *The exhibit was of aboriginal plants of this area.*

Aborigine /ˌæb·əˈrɪdʒ·ə·ni/ *n* [C] a member of any of the groups of people who first lived in Australia

abort **STOP** /əˈbɔːrt/ *v* [T] to stop something before it has begun or to cause something to fail before it is complete ○ *Engineers aborted the test flight at the last minute.*

abortive /əˈbɔːrt̬·ɪv/ *adj* [not gradable] ○ *An abortive uprising led to his exile.*

END PREGNANCY /əˈbɔːrt/ *v* [I/T] to end a pregnancy before a baby is fully developed

abortion /əˈbɔːr·ʃən/ *n* [C/U]

abound /əˈbɑund/ *v* [I] to exist in large numbers ○ *The streams and rivers abound in fish.*

about **CONNECTED WITH** /əˈbɑut/ *prep* on the subject of; connected with ○ *"What's that book about?" "It's about the Civil War."* ○ *I don't know what all the fuss is about.* ○ *There's something about her attitude that worries me.*

APPROXIMATELY /əˈbɑut/ *adv* [not gradable] a little more or less than a specific number; approximately ○ *He's about six feet tall.* ○ *It happened about two months ago.* ○ *I've had just about enough of your complaining* (= I do not want to hear any more).

> **WORD CHOICES** about
>
> Common alternatives to "about" are **approximately** or **around**.
>
> *The job will take **approximately** three months.*
>
> *The accident happened **around** 4 o'clock.*
>
> When you are talking about an approximate number, you can use **roughly** or the phrase **somewhere in the neighborhood of**.
>
> *There were **roughly** two hundred people at the meeting.*
>
> *She earns **somewhere in the neighborhood of** $40,000.*
>
> If you want to say "about" and possibly more than a particular number, you can use the phrase **or so** or the suffix **-odd**.
>
> *They raised $200 **or so** for charity.*
>
> *Her son must be forty-**odd** years old by now.*

IN THIS PLACE /əˈbɑut/, **around** *prep, adj, adv* [not gradable] positioned or moving in or near a place ○ *Reporters stood about, waiting for more news.*

INTENDING /əˈbɑut/ *adj* [+ *to* infinitive; not gradable] almost ready to do something, or intending to do something soon ○ *He looked as if he was about to burst into tears.* ○ *I'm not about to apologize to him.*

IDIOM with **about**

• **(it's) about time** (it is) past the time when something should have happened ○ *It's about time she got a job.* ○ Compare IT'S HIGH TIME at HIGH IDIOMS

about-face /ə'bɑʊt'feɪs/ *n* [C usually sing] **1** a complete change of direction, opinion, or way of acting **2** About-face is also an order given to soldiers to tell them to turn around and face the other way.

above /ə'bʌv/ *adv, prep* **1** higher than, more than, or at a level greater than ○ *The helicopter was hovering above the building.* ○ *Temperatures here rarely rise above freezing in winter.* ○ *Our wages are above average.* ○ *I could hardly hear him above the blare of the music.* **2** In writing, above can mean as stated higher up on this page or on a previous page: *Refer to the diagram shown above.* **3** To be above doing something is to consider yourself too important or too moral to do it: *He's not above lying to protect himself.*

above /ə'bʌv/ *pl n* those mentioned earlier ○ *All of the above are to be included.*

IDIOM with **above**

• **above all** most importantly ○ *Above all, don't forget to call when you get there.*

aboveboard /ə'bʌvˌbɔːrd, -ˌbourd/ *adj* easily seen, honest, not trying to deceive ○ *The discussions were completely open and aboveboard.*

abrasion /ə'breɪ·ʒən/ *n* [U] ***earth science*** the gradual rubbing away of the surface of rock, for example, by other rock, water, or a GLACIER (= large moving mass of ice)

abrasive ROUGH /ə'breɪ·sɪv, -zɪv/ *adj* having a rough surface that will rub off a thin layer of another surface ○ *The paint comes off with an abrasive steel-wool pad.*

UNPLEASANT /ə'breɪ·sɪv, -zɪv/ *adj* rude and unkind ○ *His abrasive style puts people off.*

abreast /ə'brest/ *adv* **1** next to another person and facing in the same direction ○ *We were running two abreast around the track.* **2** If you keep abreast of a subject, you stay informed about new developments in it: *Staying abreast of new software releases takes lots of time.*

abridge /ə'brɪdʒ/ *v* [T] to make a written text shorter

abridged /ə'brɪdʒd/ *adj* ○ *They listened to an abridged version on tape.*

abroad /ə'brɔːd/ *adv* [not gradable] in or to a foreign country or countries ○ *They used to go abroad every summer.*

abrupt SUDDEN /ə'brʌpt/ *adj* sudden and not expected, often with unpleasant results ○ *There was an abrupt change in her mood.* ○ *We came to an abrupt curve in the road.*

abruptly /ə'brʌp·tli/ *adv* ○ *They abruptly left the party.*

NOT FRIENDLY /ə'brʌpt/ *adj* not friendly or polite; showing little interest in talking to other people ○ *His abrupt manner makes me uncomfortable.*

abscess /'æb·ses/ *n* [C] a painful, swollen area in the body that contains PUS (= a thick, yellow liquid)

abscissa /æb'sɪs·ə/ *n* [C] ***mathematics*** the first number in a pair; a number on an X-AXIS (= line) that shows the COORDINATE (= place along that line) of a point ○ Compare ORDINATE

abscond /əb'skɑnd, æb-/ *v* [I] to escape and hide somewhere, esp. because you have stolen something ○ *They absconded with $100,000 of the company's money.*

absence /'æb·səns/ *n* [C/U] **1** the state of not being somewhere, or a period in which you are not somewhere ○ [C] *She has had repeated absences from school this year.* **2** An absence can also be a lack of existence: [U] *He drew attention to the absence of any solid evidence against the defendant.*

absent /'æb·sənt/ *adj* [not gradable] ○ *If Callie is absent from school, she should bring a note from home.*

absently /'æb·sənt·li/ *adv* ○ *He stared out the window, absently rubbing his cheek.*

absentee /ˌæb·sən'tiː/ *n* [C] someone who is absent

absentee ballot *n* [C] an official paper that someone who cannot be at the voting place on the day of an election can use for voting and can send in by mail

absent-minded *adj* likely to forget things, esp. because you do not give your attention to what is happening

absolute WITHOUT LIMIT /'æb·səˌluːt, ˌæb·sə'luːt/ *adj* [not gradable] without limit, very great, or to the largest degree possible ○ *She demanded absolute silence.* ○ *The day was an absolute* (= complete) *disaster.*

absolutism /ˌæb·sə'luːt̬ˌɪz·əm/ *n* [U] ***politics & government*** a political system in which a single leader controls all branches of government and has authority over everyone and everything in the country

CERTAIN /'æb·səˌluːt, ˌæb·sə'luːt/ *adj* [not gradable] certain; not to be doubted ○ *Health insurance is an absolute necessity.*

absolutely /'æb·səˌluːt·li, ˌæb·sə'luːt·li/ *adv* [not gradable] **1** completely; beyond any doubt ○ *You are absolutely right.* ○ *Are you absolutely sure that you locked the front door?* **2** Absolutely is also used in conversation to show emphasis in agreeing to something: *"Can you lend me $10 till tomorrow?" "Absolutely, it's no problem."* **3** If you say absolutely not, you are showing emphasis in not agreeing to something: *"You mean you won't sign this?" "No, absolutely not."*

absolute value *n* [C] ***mathematics*** the distance from zero of a number on a number line ○ USAGE: only a number larger than zero can have an absolute value

absolute zero *n* [U] ***chemistry*** the temperature that scientists believe is the lowest possible and at which all MOLECULES (= smallest units of a substance) stop moving

absolve /əbˈzɑlv, -ˈzɔːlv/ *v* [T] *fml* to officially remove guilt or responsibility for something wrong that someone has done or might have done ○ *He was absolved of all wrongdoing.*

absorb SUCK IN /əbˈzɔːrb, -ˈsɔːrb/ *v* [T] to take in a liquid, gas, or chemical ○ *The black clay soil around here doesn't absorb water very well.* ○ (*fig.*) *The country has absorbed millions of immigrants over the years.* ○ USAGE: Used to describe the behavior of a substance or object.
absorbent /əbˈzɔːr·bənt, -ˈsɔːr-/ *adj* able to take in liquids esp. through the surface ○ *absorbent paper towels*

TAKE ATTENTION /əbˈzɔːrb, -ˈsɔːrb/ *v* [T] **1** to completely take the attention of someone ○ *She was absorbed in listening to music.* **2** To absorb knowledge, ideas, or information is to understand them completely and store them in your memory: *It was difficult to absorb so much information.*

absorption TAKING IN /əbˈzɔːrp·ʃən, -ˈsɔːrp-/ *n* [U] ***physics*** the process by which a substance or object takes in a liquid, gas, waves, or chemical and makes it a part of itself ○ *Using a special numerical procedure, they calculated the absorption spectrum* (= the range of light waves that are left when some have been absorbed by something that they passed through).

ATTENTION /əbˈzɔːrp·ʃən, -ˈsɔːrp-/ *n* [U] the condition of giving your complete attention to something

abstain /æbˈsteɪn, əb-/ *v* [I] **1** to not do something you could do, esp. something that is unhealthy or gives you pleasure ○ *Some families abstain from eating fried food.* **2** If you abstain from voting, you do not vote although you are permitted to vote.

abstinence /ˈæb·stə·nəns/ *n* [U] the act of not doing something, esp. something that gives you pleasure

abstract Ⓐ /æbˈstrækt, ˈæb·strækt/ *adj* **1** existing as an idea, feeling, or quality, not as a material object ○ *"Humanity" is an abstract idea.* **2** ***English*** If a statement, argument, or discussion is abstract, it is general and not based on particular examples. **3** ***art*** A painting, drawing, or SCULPTURE is described as abstract if it tries to represent the qualities of objects or people but does not show their outer appearance: *abstract art*
abstract Ⓐ /æbˈstrækt, ˈæb·strækt/ *n* [C] ***writing*** a few sentences that give the main ideas in an article or a scientific paper
abstraction Ⓐ /æbˈstræk·ʃən/ *n* [C] an idea that develops by looking at or thinking about a number of different things
abstractly Ⓐ /æbˈstræk·tli/ *adv*

absurd /əbˈsɜrd, -ˈzɜrd/ *adj* ridiculous or completely unreasonable ○ [+ *to* infinitive] *It is absurd for the council to cut taxes without proposing another way to raise money.*
absurdity /əbˈsɜrd·əţ·i, -ˈzɜrd-/ *n* [C/U]

abundance /əˈbən·dəns/ *n* [C] ***chemistry*** the level of a particular ELEMENT in the outer layer of the earth

abundant /əˈbʌn·dənt/ *adj* more than enough; a lot ○ *It is a region with abundant natural resources.*
abundance /əˈbʌn·dəns/ *n* [U] ○ *We all seem to have an abundance of those plastic grocery bags.*
abundantly /əˈbʌn·dənt·li/ *adv* [not gradable] very ○ *The solution to the problem seemed abundantly clear.*

abuse /əˈbjuːs/ *n* [C/U] bad or cruel treatment of a person or animal, or the use of something in an unsuitable or wrong way ○ [U] *The rescued dogs had been victims of physical abuse.*
abuse /əˈbjuːz/ *v* [T] to treat a person or animal badly or cruelly, or to use something in the wrong way ○ *He was always welcome but he never abused the privilege by visiting us too often.*
abusive /əˈbjuː·sɪv, -zɪv/ *adj* treating someone badly or cruelly, esp. physically ○ *He was a very strict parent, but never abusive.*
abuser /əˈbjuː·zər/ *n* [C]

abysmal /əˈbɪz·məl/ *adj* very bad ○ *This experiment could help a lot of people, or it could be an abysmal failure.*

academia Ⓐ /ˌæk·əˈdiː·miː·ə/ *n* [U] the teaching, studying, and scientific work that happens in colleges and universities ○ *experts from industry, academia, and the government*

academic Ⓐ SCHOOL RELATED /ˌæk·əˈdem·ɪk/ *adj* relating to schools, esp. colleges and universities, or connected with studying and thinking and not with useful skills
academic Ⓐ /ˌæk·əˈdem·ɪk/ *n* [C] a person who teaches in a college or university
academically Ⓐ /ˌæk·əˈdem·ɪk·li/ *adv*

NOT IMPORTANT /ˌæk·əˈdem·ɪk/ *adj* not important because it is based only on possibilities ○ *Which diamond ring you like more is purely academic, because I can't afford either one.*
academically /ˌæk·əˈdem·ɪk·li/ *adv*

academics Ⓐ /ˌæk·əˈdem·ɪks/ *pl n* the subjects that you study in high school or college

academy Ⓐ /əˈkæd·ə·mi/ *n* [C] a school that teaches a particular subject or trains people for a particular job, or an organization that supports art, literature, or science ○ *a military/police academy*

Academy Award, **Oscar** *n* [C] *trademark* one of a set of prizes given each year by a US film organization to recognize the best movie and the people involved in the best movies

accelerate GO FASTER /ɪkˈsel·əˌreɪt, æk-/ *v* [I] to move more quickly, or to make something happen faster or sooner ○ [I] *He stepped on the gas and accelerated rapidly to pass a car.*
acceleration /ɪkˌsel·əˈreɪ·ʃən, æk-/ *n* [U] ○ *The car has good acceleration.*
accelerator /ɪkˈsel·əˌreɪţ·ər, æk-/ *n* [C] a PEDAL (= part worked with the foot) in a car that makes the car go faster when pressed

INCREASE RATE /ɪkˈsel·əˌreɪt, æk-/ *v* [T] ***physics*** to make something, esp. a process or a very small piece of matter, move faster
acceleration /ɪkˌsel·əˈreɪ·ʃən, æk-/ *n* [U] ***physics*** the rate of change in the speed of something over time

A

accelerator /ɪkˈsel·əˌreɪt̬·ər, æk-/, **particle accelerator** *n* [C] ***physics*** a device used to accelerate very small pieces of nuclear material for scientific experiments

accelerator /ɪkˈsel·əˌreɪt̬·ər, æk-/ *n* [C] ***chemistry*** a substance that is added to other substances to speed up a chemical reaction

accent WAY OF PRONOUNCING /ˈæk·sent/ *n* [C] **1** the way in which people in a particular area or country pronounce words ○ *She spoke with a slight southern accent.* **2** An accent is also a mark written or printed over a letter to show how to pronounce it.

EMPHASIS /ˈæk·sent/ *n* [C] a special emphasis given to a syllable in a word or to a word in a sentence ○ *In "government," the accent is on the first syllable.*

accent /ˈæk·sent, ækˈsent/ *v* [T] ○ *In Spanish, you usually accent the next-to-last syllable.*

accentuate /ɪkˈsen·tʃəˌweɪt, æk-/ *v* [T] to emphasize a particular feature of something or to make something more noticeable ○ *The short black dress accentuated her slenderness.*

accept /ɪkˈsept, æk-/ *v* [T] **1** to agree to take something, or to consider something as satisfactory, reasonable, or true ○ *She accepted the job offer.* ○ *He was accused of accepting bribes.* ○ *Do you accept credit cards?* ○ *He refuses to accept the fact that he could be wrong.* **2** If you accept an offer or an invitation, you say yes to it: *We accepted an invitation to visit China.* **3** To accept is also to allow someone to become a member of an organization or group: *He was accepted by three colleges.* **4** To accept is also to consider someone as now belonging to your group as an equal: *She never felt accepted by the other girls in her sorority.*

acceptable /ɪkˈsep·tə·bəl, æk-/ *adj* **1** satisfactory; good enough ○ *An offer that is acceptable to the union leaders might still be voted down by the union members.* **2** If behavior is acceptable, it is considered to be within the range of behavior that is permitted and is not disapproved: *In those days, it was not acceptable for men to wear shirts without ties.*

acceptance /ɪkˈsep·təns, æk-/ *n* [U] **1** *Congress opposed the president's acceptance of the international trade agreement.* **2** Acceptance of an offer or an invitation means that you say yes to it: *The White House indicated its acceptance of the offer to visit Russia.* **3** Acceptance of a person is the act of agreeing to that person's becoming a member of an organization or group, or to that person's belonging to your group as an equal.

USAGE

accept or agree?

When you **accept** an invitation, job, or offer, you say yes to something that is offered. **Accept** is never followed by another verb.

They offered me the job and I've accepted it.

~~*They offered me the job and I've accepted to take it.*~~

When you **agree** *to do something*, you say that you will do something that someone asks you to do.

They offered me the job and I agreed to take it.

WORD FAMILY accept			
Nouns	acceptance	*Verbs*	accept
Adjectives	acceptable unacceptable accepted	*Adverbs*	acceptably unacceptably

acceptor /ɪkˈsep·tər, æk-/ *n* [C] ***chemistry, physics*** an atom or MOLECULE that receives ELECTRONS to form a chemical substance

access Ⓐ /ˈæk·ses/ *n* [U] **1** the method or way of approaching a place or person, or the right to use or look at something ○ *Without an official pass, the guards will deny you access to* (= will not let you enter) *the courthouse.* **2** Access to something can also mean the opportunity or ability to use it: *Many of the families do not have access to health care.*

access Ⓐ /ˈæk·ses/ *v* [T] to get information, esp. when using a computer ○ *People now can access information from the Internet as never before.*

accessible Ⓐ /ɪkˈses·ə·bəl, æk-/ *adj* possible to approach, enter, or use ○ *The island is accessible only by ferry.* ○ *Public areas and buildings are now more accessible to people with disabilities.* ○ *By using more illustrations, he made the magazine more accessible to the public* (= easier to understand).

accessibility Ⓐ /ɪkˈses·əˈbɪl·ət̬·i, æk-/ *n* [U] ○ *Touch-screen voting machines meet the requirements for accessibility to people with disabilities.* ○ *Accessibility is one of the most important aspects of textual analysis.*

accessory EXTRA /ɪkˈses·ə·ri, æk-/ *n* [C usually pl] something extra that improves or completes the thing it is added to ○ *We sell plants, seeds, fertilizer, and gardening accessories, such as tools and gloves.*

CRIMINAL /ɪkˈses·ə·ri, æk-/ *n* [C] *law* someone who helps another person to commit a crime but does not take part in it

accident INJURY /ˈæk·səd·ənt, -səˌdent/ *n* [C] an event not intended by anyone but which has the result of injuring someone or damaging something ○ *He was killed in an automobile accident at the age of 21.*

EVENT NOT PLANNED /ˈæk·səd·ənt, -səˌdent/ *n* [C] something that happens unexpectedly and unintentionally ○ *It's no accident that* (= There are reasons that explain why) *she was chosen to be a member of the most powerful committee in Congress.*

accidental /ˌæk·səˈdent·ᵊl/ *adj* ○ *The fire began shortly after 1:30 a.m. and appears to have been accidental.*

accidentally /ˌæk·səˈdent·ᵊl·i/ *adv*

WORD FAMILY accident			
Nouns	accident	*Adverbs*	accidentally
Adjectives	accidental		

IDIOM with accident

• **by accident** without intending to ○ *She hit me with her hand, apparently by accident.*

accident-prone *adj* having or likely to have accidents frequently ○ *Sleep-deprived kids are more accident-prone.*

acclaim PRAISE /ə'kleɪm/ *n* [U] enthusiastic approval and praise ○ *Despite critical acclaim, the TV show always ran third in the ratings.*

acclaim /ə'kleɪm/ *v* [T] ○ *The orchestra was widely acclaimed as one of the best in the nation.*

ELECT /ə'kleɪm/ *v* [T] *Cdn* to elect someone without opposition ○ *Marion was acclaimed president of the club.*

acclamation /ˌæk·lə'meɪ·ʃən/ *n* [U] **1** loud and enthusiastic praise or approval **2** *Cdn* Someone who is elected by acclamation is elected without opposition.

acclimate /'æk·ləˌmeɪt/ *v* [I/T] to change to suit different conditions of life, or to cause someone to change to suit conditions ○ [I] *Apparently the zoo animals had become acclimated to the crowd noise and were no longer startled by it.*

accommodate Ⓐ FIND A PLACE FOR /ə'kɑm·əˌdeɪt/ *v* [T] to provide space or a place for a group ○ *The new dormitory will be able to accommodate an additional 200 students.*

accommodations /əˌkɑm·ə'deɪ·ʃənz/, **accommodation** /əˌkɑm·ə'deɪ·ʃən/ *pl n* a place to stay, esp. a hotel room ○ *Tour operators are advertising accommodations as low as $79 per night in first-class hotels.*

SUIT /ə'kɑm·əˌdeɪt/ *v* [T] to give what is needed to someone ○ *We certainly try to accommodate students with disabilities.*

accommodating /ə'kɑm·əˌdeɪt̬·ɪŋ/ *adj* ○ *The airline could not have been more accommodating* (= willing to help) *in getting me on a connecting flight.*

accompany Ⓐ /ə'kʌm·pə·ni/ *v* [T] **1** to go with someone or to exist at the same time as something ○ *Students cannot leave the building during class hours unless they are accompanied by an adult.* **2** ***music*** In music, to accompany is to play an instrument in support of someone who is playing an instrument or singing.

accompaniment Ⓐ /ə'kʌm·pə·ni:·mənt/ *n* [C/U] **1** something done in support of something else **2** ***music*** Accompaniment is music that supports someone who is singing or playing an instrument.

accomplice /ə'kɑm·pləs, -kʌm-/ *n* [C] a person who helps someone else to commit a crime or do something morally wrong ○ *The thieves and two accomplices made away with over $25,000 in cash.*

accomplish /ə'kɑm·plɪʃ, -'kʌm-/ *v* [T] to do or finish something successfully; achieve something ○ *On retiring from the Congress, he said he had accomplished everything he set out to do.*

accomplished /ə'kɑm·plɪʃt, -'kʌm-/ *adj* ○ *She's an accomplished* (= skilled) *violinist.*

accomplishment /ə'kɑm·plɪʃ·mənt, -'kʌm-/ *n* [C/U] ○ [U] *There's a feeling of accomplishment* (= achievement) *from having a job and all that goes with it.*

accord AGREEMENT /ə'kɔ:rd/ *n* [C/U] **1** a formal agreement, or the condition of agreeing ○ [C] *Both parties signed an accord last week in Geneva that may finally bring an end to the conflict.* **2** Accord also means agreement: *The officer acted* **in accord with** *Florida law.*

accordance /ə'kɔ:rd·ᵊns/ *n* If you do something **in accordance with** a rule, you follow or obey it: *In accordance with school rules, the teacher asked him to remove his hat when inside the building.*

GIVE /ə'kɔ:rd/ *v* [T] *fml* to give officially something desirable ○ *Reporters asked why the United States did not accord full recognition to the new government.*

accordingly /ə'kɔ:rd·ɪŋ·li/ *adv* in a way that suits the situation ○ *Surveys suggest that these shows are not what most people want to watch. Accordingly* (= Therefore), *one network is now scheduling a made-for-TV movie every Sunday night.*

according to AS STATED BY /ə'kɔ:rd·ɪŋ·tə, -ˌtʊ, -ˌtu:/ *prep* as stated by ○ *According to my mother, you have to eat three meals a day every day.*

FOLLOWING /ə'kɔ:rd·ɪŋ·tə, -ˌtʊ, -ˌtu:/ *prep* in a way that agrees with; by ○ *The teacher sorted the exams according to grade, with the A's on top and the F's on the bottom.*

accordion /ə'kɔ:rd·i:·ən/ *n* [C/U] a musical instrument with a row of keys and a folding central part that is pushed between the hands to force air through and produce notes, or this type of instrument generally

accost /ə'kɔ:st, ə'kɑst/ *v* [T] to approach or stop and speak to someone in a threatening way ○ *They were accosted at a bus stop by someone who said he needed money.* ○ **USAGE:** Usually the person who stops you or speaks to you is someone you do not know.

account FINANCIAL SERVICE /ə'kɑʊnt/ *n* [C] **1** money kept in a bank or other organization that you can add to or take back ○ *I have about $800 in my checking account.* **2** An account is also an arrangement with a store or a company that allows you to buy things and pay for them later: *Our company has accounts with all the major wholesalers.*

accountant /ə'kɑʊnt·ᵊnt/ *n* [C] someone who keeps or examines the records of money received, paid, and owed by a company or person ○ *a tax accountant*

accounting /ə'kɑʊnt·ɪŋ/ *n* [U] ○ *She is a CPA and holds a B.S. in accounting from the University of Minnesota.*

REPORT /ə'kɑʊnt/ *n* [C] a written or spoken description of an event ○ *Her account of the incident was contradicted by others.* ○ *She's sophisticated, worldly and, by her own account* (= according to her own statement), *opinionated.*

IDIOMS with account

• **on** *someone's* **account** only for or because of one person ○ *Don't cook on my account. I'm perfectly happy with a sandwich.*

• on account of *something* because of something ○ *The whole city shut down on account of two to three inches of snow.*

PHRASAL VERBS with **account**

• account for *something* **EXPLAIN** to explain the reason for something ○ *Police say they are unable to account for the increase in shoplifting.*
• account for *something* **BE** to form the total of; to be ○ *In Florida, senior citizens account for more than 25 percent of the population.*

accountable /ə'kɑʊnt·ə·bəl/ *adj* responsible for and having to explain your actions ○ *He knew he would be held accountable for any flaws in the programming.*
accountability /əˌkɑʊnt·ə'bɪl·əţ·i/ *n* [U] ○ *The Attorney General says he has a plan to ensure accountability of CEOs.*

accreditation /əˌkred·ə'teɪ·ʃən, -əţ'eɪ·ʃən/ *n* [U] official approval, esp. in order to maintain satisfactory standards ○ *The hospital was threatened with the loss of accreditation if it did not improve the quality of its care.*
accredited /ə'kred·əţ·əd/ *adj* [not gradable] ○ *Only accredited journalists are admitted to White House press conferences.*

accrue /ə'kruː/ *v* [I/T] to increase over a period of time, or to get an amount of something gradually over time ○ [I] *Interest on this savings account accrues at the rate of 4 percent.*

acculturation /əˌkəl·tʃə'reɪ·ʃən/ *n* [U] ***social studies*** changing of one culture to be more like another

accumulate Ⓐ /ə'kjuː·mjəˌleɪt/ *v* [I/T] to collect or increase something gradually, esp. over a period of time ○ [T] *We've accumulated a lot of junk over the years.* ○ [T] *He accumulated a fortune in the music business.*
accumulation Ⓐ /əˌkjuː·mjə'leɪ·ʃən/ *n* [C/U] ○ [U] *the accumulation of wealth*

accurate Ⓐ **CORRECT** /'æk·jə·rət/ *adj* correct and without any mistakes ○ *The radio will give you the accurate time.* ○ *We need accurate information before we can develop a plan of action.*
accurately Ⓐ /'æk·jə·rət·li/ *adv* ○ *Can anyone accurately predict future climate change?*
accuracy Ⓐ /'æk·jə·rə·si/ *n* [U] **1** *He challenged the accuracy of the research results.* **2** ***science*** Accuracy is also the agreement of a particular measurement with an accepted standard. ○ Compare PRECISION

EXACT /'æk·jə·rət/ *adj* exactly aimed and moving on an intended path ○ *Good golfers usually make accurate approach shots from the tee.*
accuracy /'ɑk·jə·rə·si/ *n* [U] ○ *The predawn raid was executed with pinpoint accuracy.*

WORD FAMILY **accurate**			
Nouns	accuracy inaccuracy	*Adverbs*	accurately inaccurately
Adjectives	accurate inaccurate		

accusative /ə'kjuː·zəţ·ɪv/ *adj* [not gradable] ***grammar*** having or relating to the CASE (= form) of a noun, pronoun, or adjective that is used to show that a word is the DIRECT OBJECT of a verb

accuse /ə'kjuːz/ *v* [T] to say that someone is responsible for a crime or for having done something wrong ○ *He was accused of failing to pay his taxes.* ○ *She accused me of lying.*
accusation /ˌæk·jə'zeɪ·ʃən/ *n* [C] ○ *He denied the accusation, saying he was innocent.*
accused /ə'kjuːzd/ *n* [C] *pl* **accused** *law* a person or people who may be guilty of a crime and who are being judged in a court of law

WORD FAMILY **accuse**			
Nouns	accusation accused	*Verbs*	accuse

accustom /ə'kʌs·təm/ *v* [T] to make someone familiar with new conditions ○ *It takes awhile to accustom yourself to working at night.* ○ **USAGE:** Often said about yourself.
accustomed /ə'kʌs·təmd/ *adj* ○ *She's accustomed to waking at 6 a.m.*

ace PLAYING CARD /eɪs/ *n* [C] one of the four playing cards with a single mark or spot, which have the highest or lowest value in many card games

SKILLED PERSON /eɪs/ *infml* a person who is unusually good at doing something skillful ○ *Yankee ace Chien-Ming Wang will pitch tonight's game.*

TENNIS /eɪs/ *n* [C] a SERVE (= hit of the ball that starts play) in tennis that is so strong and fast the other player cannot return the ball

ache /eɪk/ **1** a continuous pain that is unpleasant but not usually strong ○ *She has a fever, muscle aches, and a cough.* **2** Ache is often used in combination: *earache/headache/toothache*
ache /eɪk/ *v* ○ [I] *They did pushups until their arms ached.* ○ [I] (*fig.*) *Her heart ached* (= She felt very sorry) *for the people who had lost their loved ones in the plane crash.*

achieve Ⓐ /ə'tʃiːv/ *v* [T] to do or obtain something that you wanted after planning and working to make it happen ○ *She achieved her objective of qualifying for the US Olympic team.* ○ *I am hopeful that we can achieve peace eventually, but it is not going to be easy.*
achievable Ⓐ /ə'tʃiː·və·bəl/ *adj* [not gradable] ○ *Increasing sales by 5 percent is an achievable goal.*
achievement Ⓐ /ə'tʃiːv·mənt/ *n* something that you did or got after planning and working to make it happen, and that therefore gives you a feeling of satisfaction, or the act of working to make this happen ○ [C] *a scientific achievement* ○ [C] *For an actor, winning an Oscar is one of the greatest achievements you can hope for.*

WORD FAMILY **achieve**			
Nouns	achievement underachiever	*Adjectives*	achievable
		Verbs	achieve

achievement test *n* [C] a test of a student's knowledge of a subject, which can be compared

with the performance of other students taking the same test. ○ Compare INTELLIGENCE TEST

Achilles heel /əˌkɪl·iːzˈhiːl/ *n* [C usually sing] a weak point in a person or system that can result in its failure

acid /ˈæs·əd/ *n* [C/U] ***chemistry*** any of various chemical substances that can produce SALTS, some of which are able to damage whatever they touch

acid /ˈæs·əd/ *adj* **1** sour in taste ○ *The salad dressing has an acid taste.* **2** *fig.* An acid comment/remark is something said or written in strong criticism.

acidic /əˈsɪd·ɪk, æ-/ *adj* ***chemistry*** containing or having the chemical characteristics of an acid

acidity /əˈsɪd·ət̬·i, æ-/ *n* [U] ***science*** the amount of acid that is in a substance

acid rain *n* [U] rain that contains acids produced by burning fuels such as coal and oil and that can cause harm to the environment

acid test *n* [C usually sing] the proof of the value of something, or the standard that something must meet in order to prove its value ○ *In 1933, the pressurized airplane passed the acid test when it flew from Chicago to Washington at 22,000 feet above heavy storm clouds.*

acknowledge Ⓐ /ɪkˈnɑl·ɪdʒ, æk-/ *v* [T] to accept the truth or recognize the existence of something ○ *The president acknowledged his mistake in not vetoing the tax bill.* ○ *He's acknowledged as a leader in the Latino community.* ○ (*fml*) *Please acknowledge receipt of this letter* (= tell us when you receive it).

acknowledged Ⓐ /ɪkˈnɑl·ɪdʒd, æk-/ *adj* [not gradable] known or accepted by many people

acknowledgment Ⓐ, **acknowledgement** /ɪkˈnɑl·ɪdʒ·mənt, æk-/ *n* [C/U] ○ [C] *Her resignation was an acknowledgment of defeat.* ○ [C] *I applied for a grant and just received an acknowledgment* (= letter saying that my letter was received).

acknowledgments Ⓐ /ɪkˈnɑl·ɪdʒ·mənts, æk-/ *pl n* a short text at the beginning or end of a book where the writer names people who have helped in writing the book

acme /ˈæk·mi/ *n* [U] the highest point of achievement ○ *Chaplin's "City Lights" marked the acme of his filmmaking career.*

acne /ˈæk·ni/ *n* [U] a disease of the skin in which small red spots appear, usually on the face and neck, esp. in young people

acorn /ˈeɪ·kɔːrn, -kərn/ *n* [C] the fruit of the OAK tree, consisting of an oval nut with a top shaped like a cup

acoustic /əˈkuː·stɪk/ *adj* [not gradable] **1** relating to sound or hearing ○ *Scientists have developed a tiny acoustic device to improve hearing aids.* **2** An acoustic musical instrument is one that is not made louder by electrical equipment. **3** Acoustic also means designed to control sound so that you can hear only the sounds you want to hear: *acoustic tile*

acoustics /əˈkuː·stɪks/ *pl n* the way in which the structural characteristics of a place relate to how well sound can be heard in it ○ *The acoustics in the recital hall are very good.*

acquaint *someone* **with** *something* /əˈkweɪntˌwɪð, -ˌwɪθ/ *phrasal verb fml* to give someone information about something ○ *The museum offers workshops to acquaint children with the world of radio.*

acquaintance /əˈkweɪnt·ᵊns/ *n* [C/U] **1** a person whom you know but do not know well and who is therefore not exactly a friend **2** Acquaintance is also knowledge about something: [U] *The young have little acquaintance with real-life tragedy.*

acquainted /əˈkweɪnt·əd/ *adj* knowing or being familiar with someone or something ○ *"Do you know Megan?" "No, we're not acquainted."* ○ *We got acquainted when they gave us a ride home last night.*

acquiesce /ˌæk·wiːˈes/ *v* [I] to accept or agree to something, often without really wanting to ○ *The bank acquiesced to an extension of the loan.*

acquiescence /ˌæk·wiːˈes·əns/ *n* [U] ○ *His acquiescence in these policies has made it possible for him to increase his support among some voters.*

acquire Ⓐ /əˈkwaɪr/ *v* [T] to obtain or begin to have something ○ *His family acquired the property in 1985.* ○ *She acquired her love of the outdoors as a child.*

acquired taste *n* [C] something that you may not like at first, but begin to like after you have tried it ○ *You can try drinking it, although it's something of an acquired taste.*

acquisition Ⓐ /ˌæk·wəˈzɪʃ·ən/ *n* [C/U] the act of obtaining or beginning to have something, or something obtained ○ [C] *The museum has made several recent acquisitions.* ○ [U] *The acquisition of a new language requires a commitment of time and effort.*

acquit **DECIDE NOT GUILTY** /əˈkwɪt/ *v* [T] **-tt-** to decide officially in a court of law that someone is not guilty of a particular crime ○ *She was acquitted.* ○ *The jury acquitted him.* ○ Opposite: CONVICT

acquittal /əˈkwɪt̬·ᵊl/ *n* [C/U] ○ [C] *He hoped for an acquittal.*

PERFORM /əˈkwɪt/ *v* [T] **-tt-** *fml* to cause yourself to perform or behave in the stated way ○ *She acquitted herself well, finishing second.*

acre /ˈeɪ·kər/ *n* [C] a unit for measuring area, equal to 43,560 square feet or 4047 square meters ○ *They bought half an acre of land to build their house on.*

acreage /ˈeɪ·kə·rɪdʒ/ *n* [U] ○ *Forest covers half the acreage.*

acrid /ˈæk·rəd/ *adj* strong, bitter, and unpleasant ○ *The electrical fire sent thick clouds of acrid smoke through the office.* ○ **USAGE:** Used to describe a smell or taste.

acrimonious /ˌæk·rəˈmoʊ·niː·əs/ *adj* angry and including strong accusations ○ *After an acrimonious debate, the proposal was adopted.*
acrimony /ˈæk·rəˌmoʊ·ni/ *n* [U] ○ *The acrimony of a legal battle destroyed their friendship.*

acrobat /ˈæk·rəˌbæt/ *n* [C] a person who entertains people by carrying out difficult and skillful physical actions, such as walking on a wire high above the ground ○ *a circus acrobat*
acrobatic /ˌæk·rəˈbæţ·ɪk/ *adj* involving a lot of skill and energy in controlling the movement of your body to do something difficult ○ *Karate is a very acrobatic martial art.*

acronym /ˈæk·rəˌnɪm/ *n* [C] a word created from the first letters of each word in a series of words ○ *NASA is an acronym for National Aeronautics and Space Administration.*

across /əˈkrɔːs/ *prep, adv* [not gradable] **1** from one side to the other side of, or at the other side of ○ *We walked across the bridge.* ○ *She was sitting across the aisle.* ○ *He opened a store across the street from the theater.* ○ *Over 300,000 refugees fled across the border.* **2** If something is happening across the country, it is happening in all parts of the country.

across the board, **across-the-board** *adj, adv* having an effect on everyone or everything of a particular type ○ *The mayor threatened across-the-board spending cuts.*

acrylic /əˈkrɪl·ɪk/ *adj* [not gradable] of or made from a type of acid or a RESIN (= chemically produced sticky substance) which is used in making plastic, cloth, and paint ○ *acrylic paint* ○ *They used acrylic yarn for the sweaters.*
acrylic /əˈkrɪl·ɪk/ *n* [C usually pl] ○ *He paints with acrylics.*

act **DO SOMETHING** /ækt/ *v* [I] to do something for a particular purpose or in a particular way ○ [+ *to* infinitive] *The president acted quickly to bring federal aid to areas damaged by flooding.* ○ *She acted responsibly.* ○ *He acted as if he'd never seen me before.* ○ *She acted as* (= performed in the position of) *a tour guide for the group.* ○ *He said he was acting on* (= doing something as a result of) *the advice of his lawyer.*
act /ækt/ *n* [C] ○ *an act of bravery/love/madness* ○ *a selfish/senseless/thoughtless act* ○ *a criminal/illegal/terrorist act* ○ *He said any air strike would be considered an act of war.*
acting /ˈæk·tɪŋ/ *adj* [not gradable] ○ *Ms. Lopez-Smith will be the acting treasurer* (= temporarily perform those duties).

PERFORM /ækt/ *v* [I/T] to perform in a movie, play, or television show ○ [T] *He acts the part of a small-town lawyer.* ○ [I] *She has acted in lots of television sitcoms.*
act /ækt/ *n* [C] **1** one of a set of short performances that are parts of a show, or the person or group who performs one of these parts ○ *a circus act* ○ (*fig.*) *His story is just an act* (= is pretended and not sincere). **2** An act is also one of the main parts of a play or opera: *The play is presented in three acts.*
actor /ˈæk·tər/, *female* **actress** /ˈæk·trəs/ *n* [C] a person who plays the part of a character in a movie or play ○ *The play has a cast of six actors.*

LAW /ækt/ *n* [C] *law* a law made by Congress or another legislature ○ *an act of Congress*

WORD FAMILY act

Nouns	act action actor actress inaction interaction reaction transaction	*Adjectives* *Verbs*	acting act interact react

IDIOM with act

• **act** *your* **age** to behave in a way suitable for someone as old as you are ○ *Stop being silly and act your age!*

PHRASAL VERBS with act

• **act out** to behave badly because you are unhappy or upset, often in ways that you are not aware of ○ *These kids act out because their lives are a mess.*
• **act up** **BEHAVE BADLY** to behave badly ○ *The little girl was acting up, so her mother took her out of the restaurant.*
• **OPERATE BADLY** to operate badly ○ *My car is acting up again - I don't know what's wrong with it.*
• **BECOME ACTIVE** to become active ○ *Her allergies acted up when she went hiking in the woods.*

action **SOMETHING DONE** /ˈæk·ʃən/ *n* [C/U] **1** the process of doing something, or something done, esp. for a particular purpose ○ [U] *Quick action in calling the fire department saved many lives.* ○ [C] *It was a reckless action which he later came to regret.* ○ [+ *to* infinitive] *We want a leader who will take action to fix our problems.* ○ [U] *Financial advisers urged the city to take action* (= do something) *to deal with the fiscal crisis.* **2** Action is also fighting in a war: [U] *Her younger son was killed in action.* **3** In an action film/movie, there is usually a lot of violence and many exciting things happen.

MOVEMENT /ˈæk·ʃən/ *n* [C/U] the way something moves or works, or the effect it has on something else ○ [C] *The heart's action in regulating blood flow is critically important.*

LEGAL PROCESS /ˈæk·ʃən/ *n* [C/U] *law* a process in a court of law to correct a wrong by which a person or group claims to have been hurt ○ [C] *She brought an action against the hospital for negligence.*

IDIOM with action

• **actions speak louder than words** what you do is more important than what you say, because the things you do show your true intentions and feelings ○ *Team USA is not expected to win, but they believe actions speak louder than words.*

action-packed *adj* full of exciting events ○ *an action-packed movie*

activate /ˈæk·təˌveɪt/ *v* [T] **1** to cause something to start working ○ *Something activated the car alarm.* **2** In sports, to activate a player is to bring that player back to the regular team after an injury.
activation /ˌæk·təˈveɪ·ʃən/ *n* [U]

active DOING SOMETHING /ˈæk·tɪv/ *adj* **1** doing something as you usually do, or being able to do something physically or mentally ○ *He was still an active runner at 55.* ○ *She's active in state politics* (= involved in it). ○ *She intends to remain politically active.* ○ *His National Guard unit was put on active duty* (= made part of the regular fighting force). **2** An active VOLCANO is one that might begin to throw out hot gases, liquid, or rocks at any time.
actively /ˈæk·tɪv·li/ *adv* ○ *He isn't actively involved in the day-to-day management of the business anymore.*
activity /ækˈtɪv·ət̬·i/ *n* [C/U] the doing of something, or something that you are doing, have done, or could do ○ [C] *There were lots of activities for children at the museum.* ○ [C] *Her favorite activity is visiting antique shops.* ○ [U] *Carbon dioxide is also produced by human activity.*

GRAMMAR /ˈæk·tɪv/ *adj* [not gradable] ***grammar*** describing a verb or sentence in which the subject is the person or thing that does what is stated ○ *In "Alex gave me a gift," the verb "give" is active, and in "I was given a gift by Alex," "give" is passive.* ○ Compare PASSIVE GRAMMAR

WORD FAMILY active

Nouns	activity inactivity	*Adjectives*	active inactive interactive proactive
Verbs	activate		
Adverbs	actively		

active voice *n* [U] ***grammar*** the relationship between a subject and a verb in which the subject performs the action of the verb, or the verb forms which show this relationship: *In the sentence "She hit the ball," "hit" is in the active voice.* ○ Compare PASSIVE VOICE

activism /ˈæk·təˌvɪz·əm/ *n* [U] the use of direct and public methods to try to bring about esp. social and political changes that you and others want ○ *political/social activism*
activist /ˈæk·tə·vəst/ *n* [C] ○ *a civil-rights activist*

actor /ˈæk·tər/, *female* **actress** /ˈæk·trəs/ *n* [C] ○ See at ACT PERFORM

actual /ˈæk·tʃə·wəl, -ʃə·wəl/ *adj* [not gradable] real; existing in fact ○ *We expected 50 people, but the actual number was a lot higher.*
actually /ˈæk·tʃə·wə·li, -ʃə·wə·li/ *adv* [not gradable] **1** used to say that something is true, esp. when the true situation may not be known ○ *We actually had a hard time moving the sofa.* **2** Actually is often used when you want to emphasize that something is surprising or unusual: *He actually expected me to pay for his dinner.*

USAGE

actual or **current**?

Use **actual** when you mean "real."

His friends call him Jo-Jo, but his actual name is John.

Use **current** to talk about things that are happening or which exist now.

She started her current job two years ago.
the current economic situation
~~*the actual economic situation*~~

acumen /əˈkjuː·mən, ˈæk·jə·mən/ *n* [U] the ability to make correct judgments ○ *Mr. Estavez has a real business acumen.*

acupuncture /ˈæk·jəˌpʌŋ·tʃər/ *n* [U] a treatment for pain and illness in which special needles are put into the skin at particular positions

acute EXTREME /əˈkjuːt/ *adj* **1** very serious, extreme, or severe ○ *The area has an acute water shortage.* **2** In medicine, acute describes severe conditions, illnesses, or injuries that need immediate care: *Not all hospitals can provide acute care.*

ACCURATE /əˈkjuːt/ *adj* aware of or able to recognize small differences between things, or being accurate in judging something ○ *He has very acute hearing.* ○ **USAGE:** Used to describe thinking, feeling, hearing, seeing, smelling, or tasting.
acutely /əˈkjuːt·li/ *adv* ○ *I was acutely aware of their problems.*

ANGLE /əˈkjuːt/ *adj* ***geometry*** **1** (of an angle) less than 90° ➤ Picture: **angle** **2** An **acute triangle** is a triangle with three angles of less than 90°. ➤ Picture: **triangle** ○ Compare OBTUSE ANGLE

ad /æd/ *n* [C] *short form of* ADVERTISEMENT

A.D. *abbreviation for* anno Domini (= in the year of God), used to show that a year is after the year in which Jesus Christ was thought to have been born ○ *the 12th century A.D.* ○ *The Roman empire ended in A.D. 476.* ○ **USAGE:** A.D. usually appears before the year and after a century. ○ Compare B.C.

adage /ˈæd·ɪdʒ/ *n* [C] a wise saying or PROVERB ○ *He remembered the old adage, "Look before you leap."*

adamant /ˈæd·ə·mənt/ *adj* unwilling to be persuaded to change an opinion or decision ○ *She was adamant about becoming a dancer.*
adamantly /ˈæd·ə·mənt·li/ *adv* ○ *The mayor adamantly refused to consider a tax increase.*

Adam's apple /ˌæd·əm ˈzæp·əl/ *n* [C] the front part of the neck that sticks out, esp. in a man, and moves up and down when you speak or swallow

adapt Ⓐ /əˈdæpt/ *v* [I/T] to adjust to different conditions or uses, or to change to meet different situations ○ [T] *I adapted this recipe from one in an old cookbook.*
adaptability Ⓐ /əˌdæp·təˈbɪl·ət̬·i/ *n* [U] ability or willingness to change
adaptable Ⓐ /əˈdæp·tə·bəl/ *adj* able or willing to change ○ *He's pretty adaptable, and change doesn't bother him.*

adaptation Ⓐ /ˌæd·əpˈteɪ·ʃən, -ˌæp-/ *n* [C/U] **1** [C] *The movie was an adaptation of a novel.* **2** ***biology*** a characteristic of a plant or animal that makes it able to adjust to the conditions of a particular environment

adaptive Ⓐ /əˈdæp·tɪv/ *adj* **1** able to adjust ○ *These governments do not possess the adaptive capacity to endure such changes.* **2** ***biology*** able to adjust to the conditions of a particular environment

add INCREASE /æd/ *v* [I/T] to put something with something else to increase the number or amount or to make it more important ○ [T] *Beat the butter and sugar together, and then add the eggs.* ○ [T] *"Thanks for all your help!" he added as he was leaving.* ○ [I] *Factors beyond their control added to their success.*

added /ˈæd·əd/ *adj* [not gradable] ○ *He had the added disadvantage of being the only man present.*

addition /əˈdɪʃ·ən/ *n* [C/U] the joining of something to something else to make it larger or more important ○ [C] *Harold is the newest addition to our staff.*

additional /əˈdɪʃ·ən·əl/ *adj* [not gradable] ○ *There's no additional charge for children under twelve.*

CALCULATE /æd/ *v* [I/T] ***mathematics*** to calculate the total of a group of numbers ○ [T] *If you add three and four you get seven.* ○ Compare SUBTRACT; MULTIPLY CALCULATE

addition /əˈdɪʃ·ən/ *n* [U] ***mathematics*** the process of calculating the total of a group of numbers ○ [U] *We learn addition and subtraction in first and second grade.*

IDIOM with add

• **add fuel to the fire, add insult to injury** to make a bad situation worse ○ *The President said he wouldn't add fuel to the fire by commenting without knowing all the facts.* ○ *I was late and, to add insult to injury, forgot my keys.*

PHRASAL VERBS with add

• **add on** *something* [M] to include or build something extra ○ *We've added on a couple of rooms to the house.*

• **add up** INCREASE to increase gradually until there is a large amount ○ *The changes in air quality are small, but after a while they do add up and affect people's health.*

• **add up** BE REASONABLE to seem reasonable or likely ○ *Watson claimed he was at home at the time of the murder, but police said his story didn't add up.*

• **add up** *(something)* CALCULATE [M] to calculate the total of two or more numbers ○ *We added up the cost of everything we wanted to buy and divided the total between us.*

• **add up to** *something* RESULT to result in something ○ *The details don't add up to a complete picture of what caused the explosion.*

• **add up to** *something* TOTAL to make a particular total ○ *The numbers in each row add up to 25.*

WORD FAMILY add

Nouns	addition additive	*Adjectives*	added additional
Verbs	add	*Adverbs*	additionally

addiction /əˈdɪk·ʃən/ *n* [C/U] the need or strong desire to do or to have something, or a very strong liking for something ○ [U] *His addiction began with prescription drugs.* ○ [C] *I have an addiction to mystery stories.*

addict /ˈæd·ɪkt/ *n* [C] a person who is unable to stop doing or using something

addicted /əˈdɪk·təd/ *adj* ○ *She was addicted to TV.*

addictive /əˈdɪk·tɪv/ *adj* ○ *Video games can be addictive.*

addition /əˈdɪʃ·ən/ *n* ○ See at ADD INCREASE; ADD CALCULATE

addition reaction *n* [C] ***chemistry*** a chemical REACTION in which two or more substances combine to form a new substance

addition sign *n* [C] ***mathematics*** the symbol + used between two numbers to show that they should be added together

additive /ˈæd·əṭ·ɪv/ *n* [C] something added to a substance, esp. food, to improve it or to preserve it ○ *Additives keep certain foods fresh.* ○ *This paint has an additive that keeps mold from growing on it.*

additive inverse *n* [C] ***mathematics*** the opposite of a number

address PLACE /əˈdres, ˈæd·res/ *n* [C] **1** the specific place where a person, business, or organization can be found and where mail can be received ○ *What is your street address now?* ○ *I need your home and your business address.* **2** An address is also a group of letters or numbers and an @ symbol used to send electronic mail to someone: *My e-mail address is pjh17@cambridge.org.*

address /əˈdres/ *v* [T] ○ *I addressed envelopes all morning.*

SPEAK TO /əˈdres/ *v* [T] to speak or write to someone, or to direct information to someone ○ *The First Lady addressed the meeting briefly.* ○ *He was generally addressed as "Captain."*

address /əˈdres, ˈæd·res/ *n* [C] a formal speech ○ *The graduation address was very dull.*

DEAL WITH /əˈdres/ *v* [T] to give attention to or to deal with a matter or problem ○ *We'll address that question at the next meeting.*

adenine *n* [U] ***biology*** a substance that is found in DNA and RNA

adept /əˈdept/ *adj* skilled ○ *He's adept at making people feel at ease.*

adequate Ⓐ /ˈæd·ɪ·kwət/ *adj* enough or satisfactory for a particular purpose ○ *He didn't have adequate time to prepare for the exam.*

adequacy Ⓐ /ˈæd·ɪ·kwə·si/ *n* [U] ○ *We must reexamine the adequacy of our current security procedures.*

adequately Ⓐ /ˈæd·ɪ·kwət·li/ *adv* ○ *Were you adequately paid, or do you need more money?*

adhere /ədˈhɪr, æd-/ *v* [I] to stick or be attached firmly to a surface ○ *Glue won't adhere to any surface that's wet.*

adhesive /əd'hiː·sɪv, æd-, -zɪv/ *adj* ○ *The pages were held together with adhesive tape.*
adhesive /əd'hiː·sɪv, æd-, -zɪv/ *n* [C/U] glue ○ [C] *Use a water-resistant adhesive.*

PHRASAL VERB with adhere

• **adhere to** *something* to continue to obey, believe in, or support something, esp. a custom or belief ○ *College coaches have to adhere to the rules about recruiting high school students.*

adherence /əd'hɪr·əns, æd-/ *n* [U] the obeying of a rule or law ○ *He insists upon adherence to every rule, no matter how silly.*

adherent /əd'hɪr·ənt, æd-/ *n* [C] someone who strongly supports an idea, plan, person, etc. ○ *She has been an adherent of home schooling for years.*

ad hoc /æd'hɑk, -'hoʊk/ *adj, adv* for a particular purpose or need, esp. for an immediate need ○ *The ad hoc committee will meet next week.* ○ *Unfortunately, we deal with problems ad hoc.*

adiabatic /ˌeɪ·diː·ə'bæt̬·ɪk, ˌeɪˌdɑɪ·ə-/ *adj* [not gradable] ***earth science*** describes a change in temperature of air caused by EXPANSION or COMPRESSION

adjacent Ⓐ /ə'dʒeɪ·sənt/ *adj* [not gradable] **1** very near, or with nothing in between ○ *They work in adjacent buildings.* **2** ***geometry*** Two angles are adjacent if they are next to each other and share a line. ➤ Picture: **angle**

adjective /'ædʒ·ɪk·tɪv/ *n* [C] ***grammar*** a word that describes a noun or pronoun ○ *"Big," "purple," "quick," "obvious," and "silvery" are adjectives.*
adjectival /ˌædʒ·ɪk'tɑɪ·vəl/ *adj* [not gradable] ○ *an adjectival phrase*

adjoining /ə'dʒɔɪ·nɪŋ/ *adj* [not gradable] with nothing in between, or touching ○ *We had adjoining rooms in the hotel.*

adjourn /ə'dʒɜrn/ *v* [I/T] to rest or pause during a meeting or trial ○ [T] *They adjourned the meeting until after lunch.*
adjournment /ə'dʒɜrn·mənt/ *n* [C/U] ○ [C] *There was a two-day adjournment in the trial.*

adjudicate /ə'dʒuːd·əˌkeɪt/ *v* [T] to act as a judge of an argument ○ *He has adjudicated many labor disputes.*

adjunct /'ædʒ·ʌŋt/ *n* [C] **1** something added or connected to something larger or more important ○ *Canada's economy is not an adjunct to the US's but rather is expanding on its own.* **2** An adjunct is also a temporary teacher at a college or university: *adjunct professors/faculty*

adjust Ⓐ /ə'dʒʌst/ *v* [I/T] to change something slightly to make it fit, work better, or be more suitable ○ [T] *Adjust the angle of your monitor so you can easily read it.* ○ [I] *You need time to adjust to a new situation.*
adjustable /ə'dʒʌs·tə·bəl/ *adj* ○ *The height of the steering wheel is adjustable.*
adjustment Ⓐ /ə'dʒʌst·mənt/ *n* [C/U] ○ [C] *Only a few adjustments were needed to make her dress fit perfectly.*

ad-lib /'æd'lɪb/ *v* [I/T] **-bb-** to do something without preparation or planning ○ [I] *She had lost her notes, so she ad-libbed for ten minutes.*
ad-lib /'æd'lɪb/ *adj, adv* ○ *I did not want to give an ad-lib speech.*

administer MANAGE /əd'mɪn·ə·stər/, **administrate** /əd'mɪn·əˌstreɪt/ *v* [T] to manage or control the operation of something; govern ○ *The British administered Hong Kong for 99 years.*

GIVE /əd'mɪn·ə·stər/ *v* [T] to be responsible for giving something to someone ○ *Two proctors administered the exam.* ○ *She administers medicines to patients.*

administration Ⓐ /ədˌmɪn·ə'streɪ·ʃən/ *n* [C/U] **1** the management or control of an organization ○ [U] *He's studying business administration.* **2** ***politics & government*** An administration in the US is the period when a President is in office: [C] *The Clinton administration has been full of surprises.* **3** ***politics & government*** An administration is also all of the officials working in a government's EXECUTIVE BRANCH PART.
administrative Ⓐ /əd'mɪn·əˌstreɪt̬·ɪv/ *adj* [not gradable] ○ *You will do mainly administrative work.*
administrator Ⓐ /əd'mɪn·əˌstreɪt̬·ər/ *n* [C] ○ *She works as a school administrator.*
administratively Ⓐ /əd'mɪn·əˌstreɪt̬·ɪv·li, ədˌmɪn·ə'streɪt̬-/ *adv* [not gradable]

administrative assistant *n* [C] a person whose job is to help someone in charge, usually in an office

admiral /'æd·mə·rəl/ *n* [C] a naval officer of the highest rank

admire /əd'mɑɪr/ *v* [T] to respect and approve of someone or something ○ *I admire that music more than any other.*
admirable /'æd·mə·rə·bəl/ *adj* ○ *The police did an admirable job of calming down the crowd.*
admirably /'æd·mə·rə·bli/ *adv* ○ *I think she coped admirably with a very difficult situation.*
admiration /ˌæd·mə'reɪ·ʃən/ *n* [U] ○ *My admiration for her grows daily.*
admirer /əd'mɑɪr·ər/ *n* [C] ○ *Many admirers waited in the rain just to see their hero.*

WORD FAMILY admire

Nouns	admiration admirer	*Verbs*	admire
		Adverbs	admirably
Adjectives	admirable		

WORD CHOICES admire

Respect is an alternative to "admire."
I deeply ***respect*** *David for what he has achieved.*

Revere is a formal way of saying "admire very much."
Nelson Mandela is ***revered*** *for his brave fight against apartheid.*

Look up to or **think highly of** are phrases which can be used about someone whom you admire.

*He'd always **looked up to** his uncle.*
*She **thinks** very **highly of** her boss.*
If a person admires someone very much or too much, you could use the verb **idolize**.
*He **idolized** his mother.*

admissible /əd'mɪs·ə·bəl/ *adj law* able to be considered in a court of law ○ *The judge ruled that this new evidence was admissible.*

admission PERMISSION TO ENTER /əd'mɪʃ·ən/ *n* [C/U] **1** permission to study at a school or college, or permission to enter a theater or other building ○ [U] *How many students will gain admission to Yale?* ○ [U] *The club refuses admission to those under 18.* **2** Admission is also the price paid to enter a place: [C] *Museum admission is $5.*
admissions /əd'mɪʃ·ənz/ *pl n* the people allowed into a college, hospital, or other place, or the process of allowing people in ○ *The city opened admissions to all residents.* ○ *He's been director of admissions at Boston University.*

STATEMENT /əd'mɪʃ·ən/ *n* [C/U] a statement accepting the truth about something ○ [U] *There was no admission of guilt from anyone.*

admit ACCEPT /əd'mɪt/ *v* **-tt-** to recognize or accept something as true ○ [T] *He admitted his guilt.* ○ [+ (*that*) clause] *She admitted (that) she had made a mistake.*

WORD CHOICES admit

If a person admits that something is true, the verbs **accept** and **acknowledge** may be used.
*I **accept** that things should have been done differently.*
*He refuses to **acknowledge** the problem.*
The verb **concede** is used if the person admits unwillingly that something is true.
*She did eventually **concede** that the instructions were not very clear.*
If a person admits to having done something bad or illegal, the verb **confess** is often used.
*Rawlinson finally **confessed** to the robbery.*
The phrasal verbs **own up** and (*informal*) **fess up**, and the expression **come clean** can also be used when a person admits to having done something.
*I decided to **come clean** about the broken vase.*
*Come on, **own up** – who's eaten the last sandwich?*

ALLOW IN /əd'mɪt/ *v* [T] **-tt-** to allow someone or something to enter ○ *Each ticket admits one member and a guest.*
admittance /əd'mɪt·ᵊns/ *n* [U] ○ *He was refused admittance to the club.*

admonish /əd'mɑn·ɪʃ, æd-/ *v* [T] to warn someone not to do something, usually in a kind way, or to tell someone to do something ○ *His mother admonished him for eating too quickly.*

admonition /ˌæd·mə'nɪʃ·ən/, **admonishment** /əd'mɑn·ɪʃ·mənt/ *n* [C] ○ *As I left I heard my husband's admonition – "Don't be late."*

ado /ə'duː/ *n* [U] delay or unnecessary activity ○ *Without further ado, I shall introduce tonight's speaker.*

adobe /ə'doʊ·bi/ *n* [U] a mixture of wet earth and grass made into bricks and dried in the sun, used to build houses ○ *Adobe houses were common in the Southwest.*

adolescent /ˌæd·ᵊl'es·ənt/ *adj* **1** between the ages of a child and an adult ○ *The two adolescent boys made their mother very tired.* **2** If you describe an adult as adolescent, you mean that the person is behaving in a silly way.
adolescent /ˌæd·ᵊl'es·ənt/ *n* [C] ○ *I teach in a middle school, because I like young adolescents.*
adolescence /ˌæd·ᵊl'es·əns/ *n* [C/U] ○ [C] *He had an unhappy adolescence.*

adopt TAKE CHILD /ə'dɑpt/ *v* [I/T] to take another person's child legally into your own family to raise as your own child ○ [T] *They adopted Raphael last September.* ○ Compare FOSTER TAKE CARE OF
adoption /ə'dɑp·ʃən/ *n* [C/U] ○ [C] *The agency handles about a hundred adoptions a year.*
adoptive /ə'dɑp·tɪv/ *adj* [not gradable] ○ *Her adoptive parents were farmers.*

START /ə'dɑpt/ *v* [T] **1** to accept or begin to use something ○ *The new law means companies will adopt energy-saving measures.* **2** If an organization adopts a rule, it votes to accept it: *The motion to increase fees was adopted.*
adoption /ə'dɑp·ʃən/ *n* [U] ○ *The adoption of a different insurance company caused a lot of confusion.*

adore /ə'dɔːr, ə'doʊr/ *v* [T] to love and respect someone very much, or to like something very much ○ *Both girls adored their father.* ○ *I adore those shoes!*
adorable /ə'dɔːr·ə·bəl, -'doʊr-/ *adj* charming, attractive, and easily loved ○ *He was an absolutely adorable child.* ○ USAGE: said about a person or animal
adoration /ˌæd·ə'reɪ·ʃən/ *n* [U] ○ *His adoration of his wife is obvious.*

adorn /ə'dɔːrn/ *v* [T] to make something more attractive by putting something on it ○ *The bride's hair was adorned with fresh flowers.*
adornment /ə'dɔːrn·mənt/ *n* [C/U] ○ [C] *Her only adornment was a ruby necklace.*

adrenal cortex /əˌdriːn·ᵊl 'kɔːrˌteks/ *n* [C] ***biology*** the outer part of the ADRENAL GLAND

adrenal gland /ə'driːn·ᵊl ˌglænd/ *n* [C] ***biology*** either of two organs in the body that produce several chemical substances including ADRENALINE

adrenaline /ə'dren·ᵊl·ən/ *n* [U] ***biology*** a HORMONE (= chemical substance) produced by the

body when a person is frightened, angry, or excited, which makes the heart beat faster and prepares the body to react to danger

adrenal medulla /ə'driːn·əl mə'dʌl·ə/ *n* [C] ***biology*** the inner part of the ADRENAL GLAND that produces ADRENALINE

adrift /ə'drɪft/ *adj, adv* (of a boat) not fastened and moving with the sea and wind, or *fig.* not controlled and living without a clear purpose or direction ○ (*fig.*) *Hopeful actors from small towns are often adrift in New York.*

adroit /ə'drɔɪt/ *adj* very skillful and quick in the way you think or move ○ *She became adroit at dealing with difficult people.*
adroitly /ə'drɔɪt·li/ *adv* ○ *He adroitly slid the money into his pocket.*

adulation /ˌædʒ·ə'leɪ·ʃən/ *n* [U] too much admiration or praise for someone ○ *He couldn't deal with the adulation of his fans.*

adult Ⓐ /ə'dʌlt, 'æd·ʌlt/ *adj* **1** grown to full size and strength ○ *More than half of adult Americans are considered overweight.* **2** Adult also means suitable for grown people and not children: *It's a kids' show, but they sneak in some adult humor.* **3** Adult movies, magazines, shows, and books include content that is intended for adults only.
adult /ə'dʌlt, 'æd·ʌlt/ *n* [C] ○ *We invited only adults to the wedding.*
adulthood Ⓐ /ə'dʌltˌhʊd/ *n* [U] ○ *When she reached adulthood, she moved away.*

adulterate /ə'dʌl·təˌreɪt/ *v* [T] to make something weaker or of worse quality by adding something else to it ○ *Saffron is very expensive, and is often adulterated with other plants.*

adultery /ə'dʌl·tə·ri, -tri/ *n* [U] sex between a married person and someone who is not that person's wife or husband
adulterous /ə'dʌl·tə·rəs, -trəs/ *adj* ○ *an adulterous relationship*

advance MOVE FORWARD /əd'væns/ *v* [I/T] to go or move something forward, or to develop or improve something ○ [T] *Research has advanced our understanding of the virus.* ○ [I] *Tonight's winner advances to the semifinals.*
advance /əd'væns/ *n* [C/U] ○ [C] *Technological advances have changed TV news.* ○ [U] *The army's advance was halted.* ○ [C] (*fig.*) *She rejected his unwelcome advances* (= attempts to make her interested in him).
advanced /əd'vænst/ *adj* highly developed or difficult ○ *Are you taking any advanced courses?*
advancement /əd'væn·smənt/ *n* [U] ○ *They did nothing for the advancement of women.*

HAPPENING EARLY /əd'væns/ *adj* happening before an event ○ *We got no advance warning of the changes.*
advance /əd'væns/ *n* [C] money paid before something happens ○ *Most authors get an advance on royalties they'll earn later.*

IDIOM with advance

• **in advance** before something happens ○ *If you're coming to the party, please let me know in advance.*

advantage /əd'vænt·ɪdʒ/ *n* [C/U] a condition that helps you or gives you a greater chance of success ○ [C] *His long arms give him a big advantage over other boxers.* ○ [U] *Test scores show no advantage for students in the new schools.* ○ [U] *Her teacher likes her very much, which works to her advantage* (= helps her) *if she has trouble in class.*
advantageous /ˌædˌvæn'teɪ·dʒəs, -vən-/ *adj* ○ *The agreement is advantageous to both sides.*

WORD FAMILY advantage			
Nouns	advantage disadvantage	*Adjectives*	advantageous disadvantaged

advent /'æd·vent/ *n* [U] **1** the beginning of an event, the invention of something, or the arrival of a person ○ *Transportation was transformed by the advent of the internal combustion engine.* **2** For Christians, Advent is the period of four weeks before Christmas.

adventure /əd'ven·tʃər/ *n* [C/U] an unusual, exciting, and possibly dangerous activity, trip, or experience, or the excitement produced by such activities ○ [C] *She had some exciting adventures in Peru.* ○ [U] *Henry is looking for thrills and adventure.*
adventurer /əd'ven·tʃə·rər/ *n* [C] someone who enjoys and looks for dangerous and exciting experiences ○ *An intrepid adventurer, he loves exploring the wilderness.*
adventurous /əd'ven·tʃə·rəs/, **adventuresome** /əd'ven·tʃər·səm/ *adj* ○ *I'm pretty adventurous in cooking* (= willing to try new and unusual things).

adverb /'æd·vɜrb/ *n* [C] ***grammar*** a word that describes or gives more information about another word, esp. a verb, adjective, or other adverb, or about a phrase ○ *In the sentences, "She smiled cheerfully" and "He waited right outside the door," "cheerfully" and "right" are adverbs.*
adverbial /æd'vɜr·biː·əl/ *adj* [not gradable] ○ *an adverbial phrase*

adversary /'æd·vərˌser·i/ *n* [C] an enemy ○ *He saw her as his main adversary within the company.*
adversarial /ˌæd·vər'ser·iː·əl/ *adj* involving opposition or disagreement ○ *Lawyers enjoy being adversarial.*

adverse /æd'vɜrs, 'æd·vɜrs/ *adj* going against something, or causing harm ○ *Her policies may have adverse effects on the economy.*

adversity /æd'vɜr·səṭ·i/ *n* [C/U] a difficult or unlucky situation or event ○ [U] *She's cheerful in the face of adversity.*

advertise /'æd·vərˌtɑɪz/ *v* [I/T] to make something known generally or in public, esp. in order to sell it ○ [T] *He advertises his business on the Internet.* ○ [I] *I'm going to advertise for* (= put a notice in the newspaper asking for) *someone to clean my house.*
advertisement /ˌæd·vər'tɑɪz·mənt, əd'vɜrṭ·əz·mənt/, *short form* **ad** *n* [C] a paid notice that tells people about a product or service ○ *I saw an advertisement for the job in yesterday's paper.*
advertiser /'æd·vərˌtɑɪ·zər/ *n* [C] ○ *Car companies are major TV advertisers.*

A

advertising /ˈæd·vər ˌtɑɪ·zɪŋ/ *n* [U] ○ *an advertising campaign* ○ *She works in advertising.*

WORD FAMILY advertise

Nouns	ad advertisement advertiser advertising	*Verbs*	advertise

advice /ədˈvɑɪs/ *n* [U] an opinion that someone offers you about what you should do or how you should act in a particular situation ○ *She gave me some good advice.* ○ *I think I'll take your advice and go home.*

GRAMMAR

advice

Remember that this word is not countable.

She gave me lots of advice.

~~*She gave me lots of advices.*~~

If you want to use **advice** in a countable way, say **a piece of advice**.

He gave me a good piece of advice.

~~*He gave me a good advice.*~~

CONFUSABLES

advice or advise?

Be careful not to confuse the noun **advice** with the verb **advise**.

I advise you to see a lawyer.

~~*I advice you to see a lawyer.*~~

WORD FAMILY advice

Nouns	advice adviser	*Adjectives*	advisable inadvisable advisory
Verbs	advise		

advise /ədˈvɑɪz/ *v* [I/T] to give advice to someone, or to suggest something ○ [T] *I advised him to stay home.* ○ [T] *Parental supervision is advised.* ○ [T] *I wouldn't advise you to walk there alone.* ○ [I] *I'd advise against staying.* ○ [T] *Experts advised the president* (= gave information and suggested action).

advisable /ədˈvɑɪ·zə·bəl/ *adj* ○ *It's not advisable to contradict him.*

adviser, **advisor** /ədˈvɑɪ·zər/ *n* [C] ○ *She's the chief economic adviser to the president.*

advisory /ədˈvɑɪ·zə·ri/ *adj* ○ *She serves on the newspaper's advisory board.* ➤ Confusables: **advice or advise?** at ADVICE

advocate Ⓐ /ˈæd·vəˌkeɪt/ *v* [I/T] to speak in support of an idea or course of action ○ [T] *Some people advocate teaching to the test.* ○ [I] *The organization advocates for human rights.*

advocate Ⓐ /ˈæd·və·kət/ *n* [C] ○ *She's a strong advocate of women's rights.*

advocacy Ⓐ /ˈæd·və·kə·si/ *n* [U] ○ *These groups have been increasing their education advocacy.*

aerial BROADCASTING /ˈer·iː·əl, ˈær-/ *n* an ANTENNA BROADCASTING

IN AIR /ˈer·iː·əl, ˈær-/ *adj* [not gradable] of, from, or in the air ○ *Aerial photographs are used in making these maps.*

aerobic respiration *n* [U] ***biology*** a chemical process in which energy is produced in the body from food by using oxygen

aerobics /erˈoʊ·bɪks, ær-/ *n* [U] energetic physical exercises that make the heart, lungs, and muscles stronger and increase the amount of oxygen in the blood ○ *I do aerobics and weight training at the gym.*

aerobic /erˈoʊ·bɪk, ær-/ *adj* [not gradable] ○ *aerobic exercise*

aerodynamics /ˌer·oʊ·dɑɪˈnæm·ɪks, ˌær-/ *n* [U] the science that studies the movement of gases and the way solid bodies, such as aircraft, move through them

aerodynamic /ˌer·oʊ·dɑɪˈnæm·ɪk, ˌær-/ *adj* ○ *The car's design is splendidly aerodynamic.*

aeroplane /ˈer·əˌpleɪn, ˈær-/ *n* [C] *Br* AIRPLANE

aerosol /ˈer·əˌsɔːl, ˈær-, -ˌsɑl/ *n* [C] a container in which liquids are kept under pressure and forced out in a SPRAY (= mass of small drops) ○ *The gasses used in aerosols were damaging the atmosphere.*

aerospace /ˈer·oʊˌspeɪs, ær-/ *adj* [not gradable] producing or operating aircraft or spacecraft ○ *the aerospace industry*

aesthetic, **esthetic** /esˈθet̬·ɪk/ *adj* relating to the enjoyment or study of beauty, or showing great beauty ○ *Those buildings have little aesthetic appeal.*

aesthetics, **esthetics** /esˈθet̬·ɪks/ *n* [U] ***art*** the formal study of the principles of art and beauty

aesthetically, **esthetically** /esˈθet̬·ɪ·kli/ *adv* ○ *I like objects to be both functional and aesthetically pleasing.*

afar /əˈfɑr/ *adv* [not gradable] from or at a great distance ○ *He watched the proceedings from afar.*

affable /ˈæf·ə·bəl/ *adj* friendly, kind, relaxed, and easy to talk to ○ *It's hard not to like such an affable fellow.*

affair SITUATION /əˈfer, əˈfær/ *n* [C] a situation or subject that is being dealt with or considered; a matter ○ *The meeting was addressed by an expert in South American affairs.* ○ *What I do in my spare time is my own affair* (= a private matter).

RELATIONSHIP /əˈfer, əˈfær/ *n* [C] a sexual relationship, esp. a secret one

EVENT /əˈfer, əˈfær/ *n* [C] an event ○ *Their wedding was a pretty boring affair.*

affairs of state *pl n* ***politics & government*** matters that the government of a country deals with

affect Ⓐ INFLUENCE /əˈfekt/ *v* [T] to have an influence on someone or something ○ *The disease only affects cattle.* ○ *I was deeply affected by the film.*

CONFUSABLES

affect or effect?

Do not confuse the verb **affect** with the noun **effect**, which means the result of a particular influence.

Global warming is one of the most serious effects of pollution.

Do not confuse the verb **affect** with the verb **effect**, which is formal and means to make something happen.

Will the rainy weather affect the election results?

~~*Will the rainy weather effect the election results?*~~

The management wish to effect a change in company procedure.

PRETEND /ə'fekt/ *v* [T] to pretend to be or have something ○ *Since joining the band he's affected a ridiculous southern accent.*

affected Ⓐ /ə'fek·təd/ *adj* artificial and not sincere ○ *He has a very affected style of writing.*

affectation /ˌæfˌek'teɪ·ʃən/ *n* [C/U] speech or behavior that is not natural or sincere and is used to produce a certain effect ○ [C] *She has many annoying little affectations.*

affection /ə'fek·ʃən/ *n* [C/U] a feeling of liking someone or something ○ [U] *Pets should be treated with affection.* ○ [U] *Harriet felt great affection for him.*

affectionate /ə'fek·ʃə·nət/ *adj* ○ *an affectionate child*

affectionately /ə'fek·ʃə·nət·li/ *adv* ○ *He was affectionately known as "Bobo."*

affidavit /ˌæf·ə'deɪ·vət/ *n* [C] *law* a written statement made by someone who has sworn to tell the truth, which might be used in a court of law

affiliate /ə'fɪl·iːˌeɪt/ *v* [I/T] to become part of or form a close relationship with a group or organization ○ [T] *I'm not affiliated with any political party.* ○ [I] *The two schools will affiliate next year.*

affiliate /ə'fɪl·iː·ət, -ˌeɪt/ *n* [C] one part of a larger group or organization ○ *The show is broadcast on most of the network's affiliates.*

affiliation /əˌfɪl·iː'eɪ·ʃən/ *n* [C/U] ○ [C] *The group has affiliations with several organizations abroad.*

affinity /ə'fɪn·əṭ·i/ *n* [C/U] a close similarity between two things, or an attraction or sympathy for someone or something, esp. because of shared characteristics ○ [C] *Many people really feel an affinity for/with dolphins.*

affirm /ə'fɜrm/ *v* to state something is true, or to state your support for an idea, opinion, etc. ○ [T] *Applicants signed a form affirming their citizenship.* ○ [+ *that* clause] *These stories affirmed that the world is strange.*

affirmation /ˌæf·ər'meɪ·ʃən/ *n* [C/U] ○ [U] *We're looking for affirmation of the city's goal.*

affirmative /ə'fɜr·məṭ·ɪv/ *adj* positive, or showing agreement ○ *There should be an affirmative role for government in social problems.* ○ Compare NEGATIVE NO

affirmative /ə'fɜr·məṭ·ɪv/ *n* [C/U] ○ [U] *He replied in the affirmative* (= He said yes).

affirmative /ə'fɜr·məṭ·ɪv/ *adv* used to mean yes in an answer to a question, esp. in a military context ○ *"Can you hear me?" "Affirmative."*

affirmatively /ə'fɜr·məṭ·ɪv·li/ *adv* ○ *She answered affirmatively.*

affirmative action *n* [U] ***politics & government*** efforts to make education and employment available to people who have traditionally been treated unfairly, for example because of their race or sex, by giving them some advantages over people who have traditionally been more powerful ○ Compare REVERSE DISCRIMINATION

affix **ATTACH** /ə'fɪks, æ-/ *v* [T] *fml* to attach, add, or join one thing to another ○ *The sticker must be affixed to your windshield.*

WORD PART /'æ·fɪks/ *n* [C] ***grammar*** a letter or letters added at the beginning or end of a word to make a new word ○ Compare PREFIX; SUFFIX

afflict /ə'flɪkt/ *v* [T] to make someone or something suffer physically or mentally ○ *He was afflicted with severe asthma.*

affliction /ə'flɪk·ʃən/ *n* [C] ○ *Illiteracy is a serious affliction.*

affluent /'æfˌluː·ənt, ə'fluː-/ *adj* having a lot of money or possessions; rich ○ *We live in an affluent neighborhood.*

affluence /'æfˌluː·əns, ə'fluː-/ *n* [U] ○ *She makes a display of affluence.*

afford /ə'fɔːrd, ə'foʊrd/ *v* [I/T] to have enough money or time to buy, keep, or do something ○ [T] *I don't know how he can afford a new car.* ○ [I] *Can you afford to take any time off work?*

affordable /ə'fɔːrd·ə·bəl, ə'foʊrd-/ *adj* not expensive ○ *Affordable housing isn't enough – we also need job opportunities.*

GRAMMAR

afford

When **afford** is followed by a verb, it is always in the form **afford to *do something***.

We can't afford to go on vacation this year.

~~*We can't afford going on vacation this year.*~~

affront /ə'frʌnt/ *n* [C] a remark or action intended to insult or upset someone ○ *Such statements are an affront to people of conscience.*

afloat /ə'floʊt/ *adj* floating on or in water ○ *They couldn't keep the ferry afloat.* ○ (fig.) *Loan programs are aimed at keeping small businesses afloat* (= operating).

afoot /ə'fʊt/ *adj* [not gradable] happening, or being planned or prepared ○ *Big changes are afoot at Lake Utah.*

afraid **FEARFUL** /ə'freɪd/ *adj* feeling fear, or feeling anxiety about the possible results of a particular situation ○ *She was afraid, but never thought of quitting.* ○ *I've always been afraid of heights.* ○ *Dad's afraid I'll end up like my cousin.* ○ *He's not afraid of losing.*

WORD CHOICES afraid

Other common ways of saying "afraid" are **frightened** and **scared.**

If someone is extremely afraid, then you can use adjectives such as **petrified, terrified, panic-stricken,** or the informal phrase **scared to death.**

I'm ***terrified*** *of flying.*

She was ***panic-stricken*** *when her little boy disappeared.*

He's ***scared to death*** *of having the operation.*

If someone is afraid because of worrying about something, then you can use adjectives such as **anxious, concerned, nervous,** or **worried.**

I'm ***worried*** *that something will go wrong.*

All this waiting is making me feel ***anxious.***

If someone is afraid of something that might happen in the future, you can use the adjectives **apprehensive** or **uneasy.**

He's a bit ***apprehensive*** *about living away from home.*

To talk about things that make you feel uncomfortable and scared, you could use the idiom **give** *someone* **the creeps.**

Being alone in that big house ***gives me the creeps.***

To talk about something that is frightening in a shocking way, you could use the adjective **hair-raising.**

The pilots are trained to do ***hair-raising*** *stunts at low altitude.*

REGRET /əˈfreɪd/ *adj* [not gradable] feeling regret, esp. because something is not the way you think it should be ○ *A lot of those stores will cheat you, I'm afraid.*

afresh /əˈfreʃ/ *adv* [not gradable] again, esp. from a new beginning ○ *She tore up the letter and started afresh.*

African /ˈæf·rɪ·kən/ *adj, n* [C] (a person) of or from Africa

African-American *n* [C] an American who has at least some family members who were from Africa ○ Compare BLACK DARK SKIN

African Methodist Episcopal, *abbreviation* **AME** *adj, n* [U] (a member) of a Christian religious group that is one of the Protestant churches ○ *the oldest African Methodist Episcopal congregation in Orange County*

aft /æft/ *adj, adv* [not gradable] in or toward the back part of a boat ○ *There are windows aft on each side.*

after **FOLLOWING** /ˈæf·tər/ *prep* following in time, place, or order ○ *What do you want to do after breakfast?* ○ *I expect to return to work after the baby comes.* ○ *Repeat these words after me.* ○ *I'll see you the day after tomorrow.* ○ *It's ten minutes after four.* ○ *Week after week* (= For many weeks), *he's been too busy to help.*

after /ˈæf·tər/ *conjunction* ○ *The house was empty for three months after they moved out.*

after /ˈæf·tər/ *adv* [not gradable] ○ *Hilary drove up and Nick arrived soon after.*

BECAUSE /ˈæf·tər/ *prep* as a result of; because ○ *After what she did to me, I'll never trust her again.* ○ *She's named after her aunt* (= given the same name in her honor).

DESPITE /ˈæf·tər/ *prep* despite ○ *Even after everything that's happened here, his behavior seems odd.*

WANTING /ˈæf·tər/ *prep* wanting to find or have ○ *The police are after him.* ○ *He's after Jane's job.*

IDIOM with after

• **after all** **1** despite problems or doubts ○ *The rain stopped and the game went ahead after all.* **2 After all** also means for this reason: *"Of course I love her – after all, she's my sister."*

aftereffect /ˈæf·tər·ɪˌfekt/ *n* [C usually pl] a result of a condition or event ○ *Headaches are an aftereffect of this sort of accident.*

afterlife /ˈæf·tərˌlɑɪf/ *n* [C usually sing] *pl* **afterlives** the life that some people believe begins after death, esp. in heaven

aftermath /ˈæf·tərˌmæθ/ *n* [U] the period following an event, such as an accident or war, and the effects caused by the event ○ *We all worked together in the aftermath of the earthquake.*

afternoon /ˌæf·tərˈnuːn/ *n* [C/U] the period that starts at about twelve o'clock or after the meal in the middle of the day and ends at about six o'clock or when the sun goes down ○ [C] *She works three afternoons a week at the library.* ○ [U] *My baby usually sleeps in the afternoon.* ○ [U] *I spoke to her yesterday afternoon.*

USAGE

afternoon

If you talk about what happens during the afternoon, use the preposition **in.**

In the afternoon I phoned my girlfriend.

~~*At the afternoon I phoned my girlfriend.*~~

If you say a day of the week before **afternoon,** use the preposition **on.**

I'm going to the dentist on Tuesday afternoon.

~~*I'm going to the dentist in Tuesday afternoon.*~~

aftershock /ˈæf·tərˌʃɑk/ *n* [C] a sudden movement of the earth's surface that often follows an EARTHQUAKE and is less violent than the first main movement ○ (*fig.*) *There's going to be a real aftershock* (= powerful effect) *if the party loses another election.*

aftertaste /ˈæf·tərˌteɪst/ *n* [C usually sing] the flavor that a food or drink leaves in your mouth when you have swallowed it ○ *Some vinegars have a sweet aftertaste.*

afterthought /ˈæf·tərˌθɔːt/ *n* [C usually sing] an idea or plan that was not originally intended ○ *Pine included the song almost as an afterthought on his last album.*

afterward /ˈæf·tər·wərd/, **afterwards** /ˈæf·tər·wərdz/ *adv* [not gradable] after the time mentioned; later ○ *We had a swim and afterward we lay on the beach for a while.*

again /əˈgen, əˈgeɪn/ *adv* [not gradable] once more, or as before ○ *Could you spell your name again please?* ○ *Get some rest and you'll soon be well again.* ○ *Don't be late again* (= another time).

again and again *adv* many times ○ *I've told you again and again that I don't know anything about it.* ○ Compare REPEATEDLY at REPEAT

against IN OPPOSITION /əˈgenst, əˈgeɪnst/ *prep* **1** in opposition to; opposed to ○ *I know you'd like to get a more expensive car, but I'm against it.* ○ *It's against the law to throw your trash there* (= It's illegal). ○ *She voted against the tax increase.* ○ *He warned them against repeating* (= not to repeat) *the mistakes of the former administration.* **2** Against also means in competition with: *He would have to run against O'Toole for county treasurer.* **3** To go against something means to go in the opposite direction to it: *swimming against the current*

DIRECTED AT /əˈgenst, əˈgeɪnst/ *prep* directed at or toward ○ *Among the charges leveled against them were bribery and tax evasion.* ○ *There's a process for filing claims against the city.* ○ **USAGE:** Used about something negative.

TOUCHING /əˈgenst, əˈgeɪnst/ *prep* next to and touching or being supported by something ○ *It would save space if we put the bed against the wall.* ○ *He leaned his head against the back of his chair.*

IDIOMS with against

• **against** *your* **better judgment** even though you feel you are not making the best decision ○ *Against his better judgment, he gave John the job.*
• **against the clock** before a particular time, or within the allowed time ○ *I was racing against the clock, but I finished the test just before the bell.*

age TIME SPENT ALIVE /eɪdʒ/ *n* the length of time someone has been alive or something has existed ○ [C] *At age 24 he won a starring role in his first movie.* ○ [U] *She was 74 years of age when she wrote her first novel.* ○ *The program is aimed at viewers in the 18-to-30 age group.*
age /eɪdʒ/ *v* [I/T] **1** to become or appear old, or to cause someone to appear old ○ [I] *She's aged a lot since the last time we met.* ○ **USAGE:** Usually said about a person. **2** To age food or drink is to give it time to become ripe or develop a full flavor: [T] *The cheese is aged for three to six months.*
aged /eɪdʒd/ *adj* [not gradable] ○ *They have one daughter, aged three* (= three years old).
ageless /ˈeɪdʒ·ləs/ *adj* never seeming to get or look older ○ *ageless beauty*
aging, **ageing** /ˈeɪdʒ·ɪŋ/ *adj* [not gradable] ○ *Oil companies are particularly concerned about their aging fleet of deep-water rigs.*

PERIOD /eɪdʒ/ *n* [C] a particular period in time ○ *the modern/industrial/Victorian age*
ages /ˈeɪ·dʒəz/ *pl n* a very long time ○ *It's been ages since I've seen you.*

aged /ˈeɪ·dʒəd/ *adj* old ○ *an aged man*
aged /ˈeɪ·dʒəd/ *pl n* old people ○ *The apartment was built to meet the needs of the aged.*
ageism /ˈeɪˌdʒɪz·əm/ *n* [U] unfair treatment of people who are becoming old or who are old ○ *At 56, no one would hire her, and she felt she was a victim of ageism.*

agenda /əˈdʒen·də/ *n* [C] **1** a list of matters to be discussed at a meeting ○ *Among the items on the agenda were next year's budget and raising the membership dues.* **2** An agenda can also refer to any matters that have to be dealt with: *Finding a job is at the top of my agenda.* **3** *esp. disapproving* An agenda is also a particular program of action, often one that is not directly expressed: *She has a political agenda.*

agent REPRESENTATIVE /ˈeɪ·dʒənt/ *n* [C] **1** a person who acts for or represents another ○ *a travel agent* ○ *He is the agent for several of the highest paid players in baseball.* **2** An agent is also someone who works secretly for a government or other organization: *a secret agent* ○ *an undercover agent*
agency /ˈeɪ·dʒən·si/ *n* [C] **1** a business acting for or representing a person, an organization, or another business ○ *an advertising/employment agency* ○ *a real estate agency* **2** An agency is also a government organization: *federal agencies* ○ *the Environmental Protection Agency*

CAUSE /ˈeɪ·dʒənt/ *n* [C] **1** a person or thing that produces a particular effect or change ○ *a cleaning agent* **2** An agent is also a chemical substance, organism, or natural force that produces a particular effect by its action.

Age of Exploration *n* ***world history*** a period from 1400 to 1600 in which Europeans traveled the rest of the world in search of goods, raw materials, land, and trade partners

age-old *adj* very old, or having existed for a long time ○ *It's an age-old story of love and betrayal.*

aggravate MAKE WORSE /ˈæg·rəˌveɪt/ *v* [T] to make something bad worse ○ *Road repair work has aggravated the problem of traffic congestion.*

ANNOY /ˈæg·rəˌveɪt/ *v* [T] *infml* to make someone feel very annoyed and upset ○ *It really aggravates me when the car won't start, after all the money we put into it.*
aggravating /ˈæg·rəˌveɪt̬·ɪŋ/ *adj infml* ○ *It's so aggravating to have an injury like that, when you can't lift anything or bend down and tie your shoelaces.*
aggravation /ˌæg·rəˈveɪ·ʃən/ *n* [U] *infml* ○ *I won't bother returning it – it isn't worth the aggravation.*

aggregate Ⓐ /ˈæg·rɪ·gət/ *adj* [not gradable] formed by adding together several amounts or things; total ○ *The seven companies made an aggregate profit of $10.2 million.*

aggregate Ⓐ /ˌæg·rəˈgeɪt/ *v* [T] to bring different things together ○ *The company aggregates news and information from a number of sources on its website.*
aggregate Ⓐ /ˈæg·rɪ·gət/ *n* [C] ○ *The family owned over 2 million shares in the aggregate.*
aggregation Ⓐ /ˌæg·rəˈgeɪˈʃən/ *n* [C/U] ○ *the aggregation of the companies into one organization*

aggression /əˈgreʃ·ən/ *n* [U] actions or behavior that use threats or force against others ○ *We regard the presence of troops on our border as an act of aggression.*
aggressive /əˈgres·ɪv/ *adj* ○ *Jack was a large, aggressive child given to outbursts of temper.*
aggressor /əˈgres·ər/ *n* [C] a person, group, or country that starts an argument, fight, or war by attacking first ○ *He claimed that he was just defending himself, and that the other guy was the aggressor.*

aggressive /əˈgres·ɪv/ *adj* using strong, forceful methods esp. to sell or persuade ○ *The company mounted an aggressive marketing campaign.* ○ *You have to be aggressive if you want to succeed in this business.*
aggressively /əˈgres·ɪv·li/ *adv* ○ *The company is aggressively pursuing new business opportunities.*

aggrieved /əˈgriːvd/ *adj* unhappy, hurt, and angry because of unfair treatment ○ *Our hearts go out to the aggrieved families of the innocent victims.*

aghast /əˈgæst/ *adj* [not gradable] shocked or surprised in an unpleasant way ○ *Workers and union officials were aghast at the layoffs.*

agile /ˈædʒ·əl, -ɑɪl/ *adj* able to move about quickly and easily ○ *Years of ballet and modern dance had made her strong and agile.* ○ *(fig.) He has an agile mind* (= He can think quickly).
agility /əˈdʒɪl·ət̬·i/ *n* [U] ○ *A top-rated football player, he combines speed and agility.* ○ *(fig.) Her voice has the lightness and agility that Handel's music demands.*

agitate ARGUE /ˈædʒ·əˌteɪt/ *v* [I] to argue energetically, esp. in public, in order to achieve a particular type of change ○ *Telephone companies began to agitate for permission to compete in long distance services.*
agitator /ˈædʒ·əˌteɪt̬·ər/ *n* [C] ○ *They blamed the protest on political agitators.*

MAKE NERVOUS /ˈædʒ·əˌteɪt/ *v* [T] to make someone become nervous because of worry or fear that is difficult to control ○ *Any mention of his son agitated him.*
agitated /ˈædʒ·əˌteɪt̬·əd/ *adj* ○ *Gordon became visibly agitated when asked about the minimum wage issue.* ○ *Many times the private hospitals transfer their terribly aggressive, agitated patients to us because they cannot handle them.*
agitation /ˌædʒ·əˈteɪ·ʃən/ *n* [U] ○ *He arrived home in a state of agitation.*

aglow /əˈgloʊ/ *adj* bright; shining ○ *His eyes were aglow with pleasure.*

agnostic /ægˈnɑs·tɪk/ *n* [C] someone who believes that it is impossible to know whether or not God exists

ago /əˈgoʊ/ *adv* [only after n] [not gradable] back in the past; back in time from the present ○ *That was a few years ago.* ○ *Your mother called about an hour ago.* ○ *Some time ago I read a book about that.* ○ *Are you still seeing Vivian? No, we stopped seeing each other a long time ago.*

agonize /ˈæg·əˌnɑɪz/ *v* [I] to spend a lot of time trying to make a decision ○ *She agonized for days over whether she should take the job.*
agonizing /ˈæg·əˌnɑɪ·zɪŋ/ *adj* ○ *After hours of agonizing debate, the membership rejected the proposal.*

agony /ˈæg·ə·ni/ *n* [C/U] extreme physical or mental pain or suffering, or a period of such suffering ○ [U] *They put her on painkillers, but they didn't do enough, and she was in agony.*

Agrarian Revolution /əˈgrer·iː·ən/ *n* ***world history*** a big change in British AGRICULTURE in the 18th century that increased food production

agree /əˈgriː/ *v* **1** to have the same opinion, or to accept a suggestion or idea ○ [I] *I agree with you.* ○ [I] *We all agree on that point.* ○ [+ to infinitive] *In settling the dispute, he agreed to pay $60,000 in damages.* ○ [+ that clause] *Most economists agree that it would be unwise to cut taxes right now.* ○ [I] *Both sides agreed to the terms of the peace treaty.* ○ [I] *I agree with letting children learn at their own pace.* **2** If two sets of information agree, they are generally the same: [I] *Since their stories did not agree at all, he knew one of them was lying.*
agreeable /əˈgriː·ə·bəl/ *adj* **1** acceptable or satisfactory ○ *We prefer to reach a solution agreeable to all interested parties.* **2** Someone who is agreeable to doing something is willing to do it: *We can close the deal tomorrow if your client is agreeable.*
agreement /əˈgriː·mənt/ *n* [C/U] the condition of having the same opinion, or a decision or arrangement between two or more people or groups to do something or to obey the same rules ○ [C] *a new trade agreement* ○ [U] *Both sides were in agreement on the basic terms, but many details still had to be worked out.* ○ [C] *Leaders of both countries signed an agreement to exchange diplomats.* ○ [U] *Let us help you to reach agreement.*
➤ Usage: **accept or agree?** at ACCEPT

WORD FAMILY agree

Nouns	agreement disagreement	*Verbs*	agree disagree
Adjectives	agreeable disagreeable	*Adverbs*	agreeably

PHRASAL VERB with agree

• **agree with** *someone* to cause someone to feel healthy and happy ○ *You both look great – marriage must agree with you.* ○ *The fish dinner on our flight did not agree with me* (= made me feel ill).

agreeable /əˈgriː·ə·bəl/ *adj* pleasant; pleasing ○ *She has an agreeable personality.*
agreeably /əˈgriː·ə·bli/ *adv* [not gradable] with enjoyment or pleasure ○ *They were agreeably surprised to see that he'd come after all.*

agriculture /ˈæg·rəˌkʌl·tʃər/ *n* [U] the practice or work of farming ○ *Agriculture and tourism are both important to the region's economy.*
agricultural /ˌæg·rəˈkʌl·tʃə·rəl/ *adj* ○ *Chicago was an important shipping point for agricultural products and livestock.*

aground /əˈgrɑʊnd/ *adv* [not gradable] touching the ground below the water ○ *The tanker ran aground and leaked 11 million gallons of crude oil.* ○ **USAGE**: Used to describe a ship that has become stuck in the water.

ah /ɑ/ *exclamation* used to show a sudden feeling, such as one of surprise, pleasure, or understanding ○ *Ah, so that's what the problem was!*

aha /ɑˈhɑ, əˈhɑ/ *exclamation* used to express pleasure at suddenly understanding or learning the truth about something ○ *Aha! We've found the solution!*

ahead **IN FRONT** /əˈhed/ *adv* [not gradable] **1** directly in front ○ *She only had a few things in her shopping cart, so I told her she could go ahead of me in the checkout line.* **2** Ahead also means further along in development or achievement: *Sophie is way ahead of the rest of her class.*

IN THE FUTURE /əˈhed/ *adv* in or into the future ○ *We have a lot of hard work ahead of us.* ○ *You have to plan ahead when you're thinking of going to graduate school.*

IDIOMS with ahead

- **ahead of time** in advance ○ *We had a date for lunch, and I said I'd call her ahead of time to decide where.*
- **ahead of** *your* **time** having very modern ideas ○ *He was way ahead of his time in realizing the importance of being able to record sound.*

ahold **IDIOM** /əˈhoʊld/
- **get ahold of** to communicate with someone by phone ○ *I'm trying to get ahold of some of these people for our meeting tomorrow.*

aid Ⓐ /eɪd/ *n* [C/U] **1** help or support, or something that provides it ○ [U] *He gets around with the aid of a cane.* ○ [U] *She went to the aid of a man trapped in his car.* ○ [C] *A good dictionary can be a useful aid to understanding a new language.* **2** Aid is often used to refer to help given in the form of food, money, medical supplies, etc., to a country or group of people that is in need or because of an emergency: [U] *foreign aid* ○ [U] *Aid for the flood victims was on the way.*
aid Ⓐ /eɪd/ *v* [T] ○ *The project is designed to aid the homeless.* ○ *He was aided in his research by his knowledge of Greek.*

aide /eɪd/ *n* [C] a person whose job is to help someone important, such as a member of a government or a military officer of high rank ○ *The senator asked an aide to distribute copies of his speech.*

AIDS /eɪdz/ *n* [U] *abbreviation for* acquired immune deficiency syndrome (= serious disease caused by a virus that destroys the body's natural protection from infection and can result in death)

ail /eɪl/ *v* [I/T] to feel or cause someone to feel ill, unhealthy, or weak ○ [T] *I don't know what's ailing her.*
ailing /ˈeɪ·lɪŋ/ *adj* [not gradable] unhealthy or weak, and not getting any better ○ *The plan was supposed to give a boost to our ailing economy.*
ailment /ˈeɪl·mənt/ *n* [C] an illness or health problem ○ *a respiratory/stomach ailment*

aim **POINT** /eɪm/ *v* [I/T] **1** to point or direct a weapon or other object toward someone or something ○ [T] *I turned and saw a big man aiming a camera at me.* **2** To aim something is also to direct it toward someone whom you want to influence or toward achieving something: [T] *These ads are aimed at young people.*
aim /eɪm/ *n* [U] the act of pointing a weapon toward something ○ *She raised her bow, took aim, and hit the bull's-eye.*

INTEND /eɪm/ *v* [I] to plan for a specific purpose; intend ○ *The measures are aimed at preserving family life.* ○ *This book is not aimed at the serious reader.*
aim /eɪm/ *n* [C] a result that your plans or actions are intended to achieve ○ *The commission's aim was to convince workers of their extreme importance in ship production.*
aimless /ˈeɪm·ləs/ *adj* without having any clear purpose or specific reason ○ *aimless violence*
aimlessly /ˈeɪm·lə·sli/ *adv*
aimlessness /ˈeɪm·lə·snəs/ *n* [U]

WORD FAMILY aim			
Nouns	aim aimlessness	*Verbs*	aim
		Adverbs	aimlessly
Adjectives	aimless		

ain't /eɪnt/ *contraction of* am not, is not, are not, has not, or have not ○ *"Is Terry here?" "No, he ain't coming in today."* ○ **USAGE**: This word is not considered to be correct English by many people.

air **GAS** /er, ær/ *n* [U] **1** the mixture of gases that surrounds the earth and that we breathe ○ *Let's go outside for some fresh air.* **2** Air pressure is the force that air produces when it presses against any surface.
airless /ˈer·ləs, ˈær-/ *adj* having little or no air from outside, and having no movement of air ○ *My hotel room was small, airless, and uncomfortable.* ○ **USAGE**: Used to describe an inside space.

SPACE ABOVE /er, ær/ *n* [U] the space above, esp. high above, the ground ○ *Keith kicked the football high in the air.*

FLIGHT /er, ær/ *n* [U] flight above the ground, esp. in an aircraft ○ *air travel* ○ *You can get there by train, but it's faster by air.*

BROADCAST /er, ær/ *v* [I/T] to broadcast something on radio or television ○ [T] *The game will be aired at 9 p.m. tomorrow.*
air /er, ær/ *n* [U] **1** a program or a person **on the air** is broadcasting on radio or television: ○ *His show is on the air from 8:00 to 8:30 every Tuesday night.* **2** A program or person that is not broadcasting on radio or television is **off the air**.
airing /ˈer·ɪŋ, ˈær-/ *n* [C] ○ *The third airing of the miniseries will begin next week.*

MAKE KNOWN /er, ær/ *v* [T] to make your opinions or complaints known to other people ○ *The meeting gave us a chance to air our complaints.*

MANNER /er, ær/ *n* [C] a manner or appearance ○ *She had an air of confidence.*

CLEAN /er, ær/ *v* [I/T] to let air from outside come in a room or other inside space to make it smell cleaner, or to put something outside in the air to make it smell cleaner ○ [M] *Let's open some windows and air out this place.*

air bag *n* [C] a device in a vehicle that very quickly fills with air in order to protect the driver or a passenger from injury when the vehicle is involved in an accident

air base *n* [C] a place for the storage, operation, and care of military aircraft

airborne /ˈer·bɔːrn, ˈær-, -bourn/ *adj* [not gradable] in the air, or carried by air or wind or by an aircraft ○ *The plane was not yet airborne when the engine failed.*

air-conditioned *adj* cooled, or equipped with a system for cooling ○ *The restaurant is air-conditioned.* ○ **USAGE**: Used to describe a room, building, or vehicle.

air conditioner *n* [C] a machine that cools a room, building, or vehicle

air conditioning *n* [U] a system for cooling a room, building, or vehicle

aircraft /ˈer·kræft, ˈær-/ *n* [C] *pl* **aircraft** **1** any vehicle made to fly **2** An **aircraft carrier** is a large ship with a long, flat surface where military aircraft can take off and land.

airfare /ˈer·fer, ˈær·fær/ *n* [C] the price of a trip by aircraft

air force *n* [C] the part of a country's military forces using aircraft

airlift /ˈer·lɪft, ˈær-/ *n* [C] an operation organized to move supplies or people by aircraft to or from a place, esp. in a difficult or dangerous situation ○ *Officials are planning an airlift of animal feed to the area hit by early winter snowfalls.*

airlift /ˈer·lɪft, ˈær-/ *v* [T] ○ *They airlifted food and supplies to people stranded on the snow-covered mountains.*

airline /ˈer·lɑɪn, ˈær-,/ *n* [C] a business that operates regular services for carrying passengers or goods by aircraft

airliner /ˈer,lɑɪ·nər, ˈær-,/ *n* [C] a large passenger aircraft

airmail /ˈer·meɪl, ˈær-,/ *n* [U] a system of sending letters and packages by aircraft

air mass *n* [C] ***earth science*** a large area of air that has nearly the same temperature and HUMIDITY at any height

airplane /ˈer·pleɪn, ˈær-,/ *n* [C] a vehicle with wings, powered by engines and having the ability to fly

airport /ˈer·pɔːrt, ˈær-, -pourt/ *n* [C] a place where aircraft regularly take off and land, with buildings for passengers and flight management

air raid *n* [C] an attack by enemy aircraft, usually dropping bombs

airsick /ˈer·sɪk, ˈær-/ *adj* having the feeling that you will vomit because of the movement of an aircraft you are traveling in

airtight /ˈer·tɑɪt, ˈær-,/ *adj* completely shut so that no air can get in or out ○ *Put the cookies in an airtight jar to keep them fresh.*

airtime /ˈer·tɑɪm, ˈær-,/ *n* [U] the amount of time that someone or something has on television or radio ○ *The candidates complained that they weren't given enough airtime to debate the issues.*

airwaves /ˈer·weɪvz, ˈær-,/ *pl n* the radio waves used for broadcasting radio and television programs, or more generally, radio or television broadcasting ○ *The president took to the airwaves to explain the reasons for going to war.*

airy /ˈer·i, ˈær·i/ *adj* spacious and light ○ *The new offices are bright and airy.*

aisle /ɑɪl/ *n* [C] a long, narrow space between rows of seats in an aircraft, theater, church, etc., or between the rows of shelves in a store

ajar /əˈdʒɑr/ *adj* almost shut; slightly open ○ *I left the door ajar so that I could hear the baby.* ○ **USAGE**: Used to describe the position of a door.

aka /ˌeɪˌkeɪˈeɪ/ *abbreviation for* also known as (= having as another name) ○ *James Brown, aka "the Godfather of Soul," is one of my musical heroes.*

akin /əˈkɪn/ *adj* having some of the same qualities; similar ○ *They speak a language akin to French.*

à la carte /ˌæl·əˈkɑrt, ˌɑl-/ *adj, adv* [not gradable] choosing separate foods in a restaurant rather than having a complete meal ○ *You get more choices if you order à la carte.*

alacrity /əˈlæk·rət̬·i/ *n* [U] speed and interest ○ *He invited us all to visit, and we agreed with alacrity.*

à la mode /ˌæl·əˈmoud, ˌɑl-/ *adj* served with ice cream ○ *pie à la mode*

alarm **ANXIETY** /əˈlɑrm/ *n* [U] sudden anxiety and fear, esp. that something very bad or dangerous might happen ○ *Nicholas detected a note of alarm in her voice.*

alarm /əˈlɑrm/ *v* [T] ○ *Guests were sometimes alarmed to learn that we never locked the doors of the house.*

alarming /əˈlɑr·mɪŋ/ *adj* ○ *Stock prices began to rise at an alarming rate.*

alarmist /əˈlɑr·məst/ *n* [C] a person who communicates anxiety and fear, esp. unnecessarily ○ *Some in the insurance industry consider Weiss an alarmist, but others think his predictions are accurate.*

WARNING /əˈlɑrm/ *n* [C] a warning signal such as a loud noise or flashing light that gets your im-

mediate attention, or a device that produces such a signal ○ *Firefighters said the tragedy could have been avoided if the house had had smoke alarms.*

alarm clock *n* [C] a clock that you can set to make a noise at a particular time, esp. to wake you from sleep

alas /əˈlæs/ *exclamation old use* used to express sadness or regret ○ *Alas! What are we to do now?*

albeit Ⓐ /ɔːlˈbiː·ət, æl-/ *conjunction* despite the stated thing; although ○ *The nation is adapting, albeit slowly, to the new global economy.*

albino /ælˈbɑɪ·noʊ/ *n* [C] *pl* **albinos** a person or animal having a condition that causes their skin and hair to appear white or very pale

album RECORDING /ˈæl·bəm/ *n* [C] a recording of several pieces of music ○ *Her new album includes two hit singles.*

BOOK /ˈæl·bəm/ *n* [C] a book with pages for keeping photographs or other paper objects that you have collected and may want to look at in the future

alcohol /ˈæl·kəˌhɔːl/ *n* [U] **1** a liquid that is produced in making wine, beer, and LIQUOR and that can cause changes in behavior in people who drink it ○ *Most wines contain about 12% alcohol.* **2** ***chemistry*** Alcohol is also any of a group of similar chemical substances used as SOLVENTS (= substances that dissolve others) and in fuel and medicines.
alcoholic /ˌæl·kəˈhɔː·lɪk, -ˈhɑl·ɪk/ *adj* ○ *alcoholic content*
alcoholic /ˌæl·kəˈhɔː·lɪk, -ˈhɑl·ɪk/ *n* [C] a person who is unable to give up the habit of drinking too much alcohol
alcoholism /ˈæl·kəˌhɔːˌlɪz·əm, -ˌhɑlˌɪz-/ *n* [U] the condition of being unable to stop drinking too much alcohol, often causing you to be unable to live and work in society

alcove /ˈæl·koʊv/, **recess** *n* [C] a small space in a room, formed by one part of a wall being farther back than the parts on each side

aldehyde /ˈæl·dəˌhɑɪd/ *n* [C] ***chemistry*** a chemical substance that is made from alcohol

alderman /ˈɔːl·dər·mən/ *n* [C] *pl* **-men** an elected member of some city governments

ale /eɪl/ *n* [C] a type of beer, esp. one that is darker and more bitter than other beers

alert /əˈlɜrt/ *adj* quick to see, understand, and act in a particular situation ○ *When you're driving, you must stay alert.* ○ *We had to be alert to any danger signs in the economy.*
alert /əˈlɜrt/ *n* [C/U] a warning to people to get ready to deal with something dangerous ○ [U] *The police were on the alert for* (= watching carefully for) *any sign of trouble.*
alert /əˈlɜrt/ *v* [T] ○ *The auto company mailed letters to owners of that model car, alerting them of safety risks.*

alga /ˈæl·gə/ *n* [C usually pl] *pl* **algae** ***biology*** a very simple plant that grows in or near water and does not have ordinary leaves or roots

algebra /ˈæl·dʒə·brə/ *n* [U] ***mathematics*** a part of mathematics in which signs and letters represent numbers
algebraic /ˌæl·dʒəˈbreɪ·ɪk/ *adj* ***mathematics*** ○ *algebraic numbers*
algebraically /ˌæl·dʒəˈbreɪ·ɪ·kli/ *adv* ***mathematics*** ○ *Solve the equation algebraically.*

algorithm /ˈæl·gəˌrɪð·əm/ *n* [C] ***mathematics*** a list of instructions for solving a problem

alias /ˈeɪ·liː·əs/ *adv, n* [C] a false name that someone is known by ○ *He admitted that the name Rupert Sharp was an alias.* ○ *Paul Sopworth, alias* (= also known as) *Rupert Sharp, went to prison today.*

alibi /ˈæl·əˌbɑɪ/ *n* [C] **1** proof that someone who is thought to have committed a crime could not have done it, esp. the fact or claim that the person was in another place at the time the crime happened **2** An alibi is also an excuse for something: *You're late again – what's your alibi this time?*

alien /ˈeɪ·liː·ən/ *n* [C] **1** a person who lives in a country but is not a CITIZEN (= member of a country with specific rights) **2** An alien is also a creature from a planet other than Earth.
alien /ˈeɪ·liː·ən/ *adj* coming from a different country, race, or group; foreign ○ *alien customs*

alienate /ˈeɪ·liː·əˌneɪt/ *v* [T] to cause a person or people to stop supporting someone or to stop feeling welcome ○ *All these changes to the newspaper have alienated its old readers.*
alienation /ˌeɪ·liː·əˈneɪ·ʃən/ *n* [U] ○ *The alienation of young adults has lowered the number of people who vote.*

alight GET OUT /əˈlɑɪt/ *v* [I] to get out of a vehicle ○ *He helped her alight from the train.*

TO LAND /əˈlɑɪt/ *v* [I] to come down from the air and land ○ *The butterfly alighted on a flower.*

align /əˈlɑɪn/ *v* [T] to put two or more things into a straight line ○ *You need to align the numbers properly in a column.* ○ *(fig.) Business leaders are aligned with* (= agree with) *the president on this issue.*
alignment /əˈlɑɪn·mənt/ *n* [C/U] ○ [U] *You hear that noise because the wheels are out of alignment.*

alike SIMILAR /əˈlɑɪk/ *adj* similar; like each other ○ *You and your father don't look very much alike.*

EQUALLY /əˈlɑɪk/ *adv* [only after n] [not gradable] equally; both ○ *She received hundreds of letters of support from friends and strangers alike.*

alimony /ˈæl·əˌmoʊ·ni/ *n* [U] a regular amount of money that a court of law orders a person to pay to his or her partner after a DIVORCE (= marriage that has legally ended) or a legal separation

alive /əˈlɑɪv/ *adj* [not gradable] **1** living; having life; not dead ○ *I survived the accident with minor injuries, and I was happy to be alive.* **2** Alive can also mean active and energetic or exciting: *The club really comes alive on weekends.*

IDIOM with alive

• **alive and well, alive and kicking** still full of energy and activity ○ *Traditional jazz is still alive and well in Chicago.*

alkali /ˈæl·kəˌlɑɪ/ *n* [C] *pl* **alkalis, alkalies** ***chemistry*** a substance that has the opposite effect or chemical behavior of an acid
alkaline /ˈæl·kəˌlɑɪn/ *adj*

alkali metal *n* [C] ***chemistry*** any of a group of soft, white metals that are chemical elements and react easily with other substances

alkane /ˈælˌkeɪn/ *n* [C] ***chemistry*** any of a group of substances that contain only the elements carbon and HYDROGEN, which are held together by a single CHEMICAL BOND

alkene /ˈælˌkiːn/ *n* [C] ***chemistry*** any of a group of substances that contain only the elements carbon and HYDROGEN, which are held together by a CHEMICAL BOND in which two atoms share two pairs of ELECTRONS

all **EVERY ONE** /ɔːl/ *adj* every one of, or the complete number of ○ *All four of her children are under six.* ○ *Not all my friends approved of what I did.* ○ *All but the weakest plants survived the hot weather.*
all /ɔːl/ *pronoun* **1** *All of her children have graduated from high school.* **2** All also means the one thing: *Speed is all that matters.* ○ *All I need is a hot shower.*

COMPLETELY /ɔːl/ *adv* [not gradable] **1** completely ○ *This coat is all wool.* ○ *Is the milk all gone?* ○ *Did you drink it all?* ○ *Don't get all upset.* **2** All is also used after a number to mean that both teams or players in a game have equal points: *The score at halftime was 10 all.* **3** **All over** is everywhere in a place or area: *Soon the news was all over town.* ○ *There were these tiny little blue flowers growing all over.*
all /ɔːl/ *adj* [not gradable] ○ *I've been trying all day to contact you.*

USAGE

all

Do not use **the** when you use **all** followed by a period of time.

all day/morning/week/year/summer
~~*all the day/morning/week/year/summer*~~

IDIOMS with all

- **all along** from the beginning of a period of time ○ *Do you think he's been lying to us all along?*
- **all but** almost completely ○ *In some places, bus service has all but disappeared.*
- **all manner of** *fml* a great variety of ○ *He's survived all manner of difficulties.*
- **all of** only or just ○ *His book has sold all of 200 copies.* ○ **USAGE:** Used to emphasize how few or how little of something there is.
- **all of a sudden, all at once** quickly and without warning ○ *All of a sudden we heard a loud noise.*
- **not all that** not very, or not really ○ *The game of football is not all that complicated*
- **all the time in the world** lots of time, especially enough to do something fully or well ○ *Don't hurry – we have all the time in the world.*
- **all told** in total ○ *There were 550 people there all told.*
- **all too** more than is desirable ○ *The week passed all too quickly, and it was time to go back home.*
- **all very well, all well and good** good, but not good enough or not good in every situation ○ *A high-fiber diet is all very well for an adult, but it's totally wrong for a child.*
- **of all people, of all things/places** especially ○ *I thought that you, of all people, would believe me!*
- **on all fours** having both knees and hands on the ground ○ *Shirelle was on all fours, looking for her contact lens.*

Allah /ˈæl·ə, ˈɑl·ə, ɑˈlɑ/ *n* [U] the Islamic name for God

all-American /ˌɔː·ləˈmer·ɪ·kən, -ˈmær-/ *adj* having or showing the values that are typical of the US, or made up completely of the best American things or people ○ *He made the all-American team in his last two years of college.*
all-American, All-American /ˌɔː·ləˈmer·ɪ·kən, -ˈmær-/ *n* [C] ○ *He was a great athlete, and an academic all-American as well.*

all-around /ˈɔː·ləˌrɑʊnd/, **all-round** /ˈɔːl·rɑʊnd/ *adj* [not gradable] having a good variety of skills or abilities ○ *Gretzky was an all-around great hockey player.*

allay /æˈleɪ, ə-/ *v* [T] to make a negative emotion less strong or a problem less difficult ○ *I was nervous, but seeing her allayed my fears.*

allege /əˈledʒ/ *v* [T] to state that something bad is a fact without giving proof ○ *School districts are alleging the state has not continued to finance schools adequately.* ○ **USAGE:** Usually used to describe legal matters.
alleged /əˈledʒd/ *adj* [not gradable] ○ *the alleged crime/incident/wrongdoing*
allegedly /əˈledʒ·əd·li/ *adv* [not gradable] ○ *The company is being investigated for allegedly falsifying sales records.*
allegation /ˌæl·əˈgeɪ·ʃən/ *n* [C] a statement, made without giving proof, that someone has done something wrong or illegal ○ *The allegations of corruption were not true.* ○ **USAGE:** Usually used to describe legal matters.

allegiance /əˈliː·dʒəns/ *n* [C/U] support for a leader, country, group, or belief ○ [U] *For many here, allegiance to the local community comes first.*

allegory /ˈæl·əˌgɔːr·i, -ˌgoʊr·i/ *n* [C/U] ***literature*** a story, play, poem, picture, or other work in which the characters and events represent particular moral, religious, or political qualities or ideas
allegorical /ˌæl·əˈgɔːr·ɪ·kəl, -ˈgɑr-/ *adj* ○ *Apples represent people in this allegorical contest between wilderness and civilization.*

allele /əˈliːl/ *n* [C] ***biology*** one of two or more GENES (= part of a cell that controls characteristics) that is found in the same position in a CHROMOSOME (= cell structure), and so produces a particular characteristic such as eye color

allergy /ˈæl·ər·dʒi/ *n* [C] a condition that causes illness when someone eats certain foods or

touches or breathes in certain substances ○ *Your rash is caused by an allergy to peanuts.*
allergic /ə'lɜr·dʒɪk/ *adj* ○ *I'm allergic to cats.*

alleviate /ə'liː·viːˌeɪt/ *v* [T] to make pain or problems less severe ○ *The medicine did nothing to alleviate her discomfort.*

alley /'æl·i/, **alleyway** /'æl·iːˌweɪ/ *n* [C] a narrow road or path between buildings, esp. between the backs of buildings ○ *I ran down the alley and up the back stairs.*

alliance /ə'lɑɪ·əns/ *n* [C/U] ***politics & government*** a group of countries, political parties, or people who work together because of shared interests or aims, or the act of forming such a group ○ [C] *Switzerland does not belong to any military alliance.* ○ [U] *Alliance against our common enemy is our only hope for survival.*

allied /'æl·ɑɪd, ə'lɑɪd/ *adj* See at ALLY.

alligator /'æl·əˌgeɪṭ·ər/, *short form* **gator** *n* [C] a large, hard-skinned REPTILE (= type of animal) with a long nose that is shorter and slightly wider than that of a CROCODILE and which lives in and near rivers and lakes in the parts of the US and China

all-important *adj* [not gradable] more important than anything else ○ *For this sauce, fresh basil is the all-important ingredient.*

all-inclusive *adj* [not gradable] including all related things, esp. expenses ○ *an all-inclusive vacation package*

alliteration /əˌlɪṭ·ə'reɪ·ʃən/ *n* [U] ***English*** the repetition of consonants at the beginning of two or more words, as in "live and learn"

allocate Ⓐ /'æl·əˌkeɪt/ *v* [T] to give something as a share of a total amount ○ *State funds will not be allocated to the program next year.*
allocation Ⓐ /ˌæl·ə'keɪ·ʃən/ *n* [C/U] the act or process of giving out parts of a whole, or a part given out in this way ○ [U] *The allocation of space in this office is unusual.*

allot /ə'lɑt/ *v* [T] **-tt-** to give a share of something for a particular purpose ○ *The board allotted $5000 to the recreation center.*
allotted /ə'lɑṭ·əd/ *adj* [not gradable] ○ *Use only the allotted time.*
allotment /ə'lɑt·mənt/ *n* [C/U] ○ [U] *There are huge differences in the allotment of highway funds around the state.*

allotrope /'æl·əˌtroʊp/ *n* [C] ***chemistry*** one of many forms of a chemical element, for example, coal and GRAPHITE (= substance used in pencils) are different forms of carbon

allow PERMIT /ə'lɑʊ/ *v* [T] to let someone do something or let something happen; permit ○ *You're not allowed to talk during the exam.* ○ *Are you allowed in the building on weekends?* ○ *Video links allow rural schoolchildren to be taught by teachers hundreds of miles away.*
allowable /ə'lɑʊ·ə·bəl/ *adj* ○ *Our well water has nitrates above the allowable level.*

USAGE

allow or **let**?

Allow and **let** have similar meanings. **Allow** is used in both formal and informal situations, especially when talking about rules and laws. It is used in the verb pattern **allow** + *object* + **to infinitive**.

The new legislation allows companies to charge for this service.

We can't allow this situation to continue.

Let is not used in formal situations. It is only used in informal and spoken situations and is used in the verb pattern **let** + *object* + **infinitive without to**.

Dad won't let her drive his car.

She let her hair grow longer.

~~*Dad won't let her to drive his car.*~~

WORD CHOICES allow

A common alternative to the verb "allow" is **let**.

*She wanted to go but her parents wouldn't **let** her.*

A more formal word for "allow" is **permit**.

*Eating is not **permitted** in any part of the building.*

If someone in authority allows something, you can use the verb **authorize**.

*Who **authorized** this expenditure?*

You can use **go-ahead** or **green light** to say that someone in an official job allows a plan to happen.

*The city council has given the **green light** to the new shopping mall.*

*The government has given the **go-ahead** for a multibillion-dollar highway project.*

MAKE AVAILABLE /ə'lɑʊ/ *v* [T] to make it possible for something to be done or to happen ○ *He didn't allow enough time to finish the test.* ○ *Be sure to allow room in your bags for the souvenirs you'll want to bring home.*
allowance /ə'lɑʊ·əns/ *n* [C] **1** the amount of something available or needed for a particular purpose ○ *What is the recommended daily allowance of vitamin A?* **2** An allowance is also money given by parents to a child every week that the child can spend.

PHRASAL VERB with allow

• **allow for** *something* to take something into consideration; to plan for something ○ *Does your insurance allow for home nursing care?*

alloy /'ælˌɔɪ, ə'lɔɪ/ *n* [C] ***chemistry*** a metal that is made by mixing together two or more metals, or a metal and another substance

all right SATISFACTORY, *not standard* **alright** /ɔːl'rɑɪt/ *adj, adv* [not gradable] (in a way that is) satisfactory or acceptable ○ *The movie was all right*

– *not great, though.* ○ *Are you managing all right in your new job?*

SAFE, *not standard* **alright** /ɔːlˈrɑɪt/ *adj, adv* [not gradable] safe, well, or not harmed ○ *She was really sick for a while but she's all right now.*

AGREED, *not standard* **alright** /ɔːlˈrɑɪt, ˈɔːlˈrɑɪt/ *exclamation, adj* [not gradable] used to show that something is agreed, understood, or acceptable ○ *I'd rather not go to Jane's party if that's all right with you.*

CERTAINLY, *not standard* **alright** /ɔːlˈrɑɪt/ *adv* [not gradable] *infml* certainly or without any doubt ○ *"Are you sure he was the guy you saw?" "Oh, he was the guy all right."*

VERY GOOD, *not standard* **alright** /ɔːlˈrɑɪt/ *exclamation infml* used to express praise or happiness over what has been said or done ○ *"Did you hear I won that writing contest?" "All right!"*

IDIOM with all right

• **that's all right, it's all right** do not worry; everything is OK ○ *"Excuse me, I'm sorry." "That's all right."* ○ **USAGE:** Used to answer someone who has just thanked you for something or just said they are sorry for something they did.

all-star *adj* [not gradable] involving the best players or performers ○ *He has played in the last five all-star games and won six straight Gold Gloves.*

allude to *someone/something* /əˈluːd·tə, -tʊ, -ˌtuː/ *phrasal verb* to mention someone or something in a brief or indirect way ○ *He alluded to problems with the new computers.*

allure /əˈlʊr/ *n* [U] attraction, charm, or excitement ○ *The allure of the stage drew him back to acting.*
alluring /əˈlʊr·ɪŋ/ *adj* ○ *There's something alluring about motorcycles.*

allusion /əˈluː·ʒən/ *n* [C] ***literature*** a brief or indirect reference ○ *He made some allusion to the years they lived apart.*

ally /ˈæl·ɑɪ, əˈlɑɪ/ *n* [C] ***politics & government*** a country that has agreed to give help and support to another, esp. during a war, or a person who helps and supports someone else
ally /əˈlɑɪ, ˈæl·ɑɪ/ *v* [T always + adv/prep] ○ *I refused to ally myself with that mob.*
allied /ˈæl·ɑɪd, əˈlɑɪd/ *adj* connected, esp. by having many things in common ○ *allied forces* ○ *It takes a lot of enthusiasm allied with a love of children to make a good teacher.*

alma mater /ˌæl·məˈmɑt̬·ər, ˌɑl-/ *n* [C usually sing] the school, college, or university where you studied, or the official song of a school, college, or university ○ *Former students are asked to donate money to their alma mater.*

almanac /ˈɔːl·məˌnæk, ˈæl-/ *n* [C] a book published every year that contains facts and information, esp. tables showing the days, weeks, and months, important holidays, and times when the sun and moon rise, or a book containing facts and information about a particular subject ○ *a baseball almanac*

almighty /ɔːlˈmɑɪt̬·i/ *adj* [not gradable] **1** having the power to do everything ○ *the Almighty Creator* **2** Almighty also means very strong and powerful: *the almighty dollar*
Almighty /ɔːlˈmɑɪt̬·i/ *n* [U] God ○ *We asked the Almighty for mercy.*

almond /ˈɔː·mənd, ˈɔːl-; ˈɑm·ənd, ˈɑl·mənd/ *n* [C] an edible, oval nut with a hard shell, or the tree that it grows on

almost /ˈɔːl·moʊst, ɔːlˈmoʊst/ *adv* [not gradable] nearly but not quite ○ *It'll cost almost as much to repair your computer as to buy a new one.* ○ *We were bitten by mosquitoes almost every night.*

alms /ɑmz, ɑlmz/ *pl n old use* clothing, food, or money that is given to poor people

aloft /əˈlɔːft/ *adv* [not gradable] in the air or in a higher position ○ *Her kite remained aloft for hours.*

alone WITHOUT PEOPLE /əˈloʊn/ *adj, adv* without other people ○ *She decided to climb the mountain alone.* ○ *We can discuss your proposal when we're alone* (= when other people present have left).

CONFUSABLES

alone or lonely?

Alone means that no other person is with you.

I prefer working alone – I hate crowded offices.

Do not confuse with **lonely**, which means feeling sad because you are alone.

She's been feeling very lonely since her husband died.

~~*I prefer working lonely.*~~

WORD CHOICES alone

The phrase **on your own** is often used instead of "alone."

*I like living **on my own**.*

If you do something without the help of anyone else, you could use **(all) by yourself**, **single-handed**, or **unaided**.

*She had made the meal **by herself/unaided**.*

*He has raced sailboats both as part of a crew and **single-handed**.*

Unaccompanied can be used when someone goes somewhere alone.

*To everyone's great surprise, the princess arrived at the ball **unaccompanied**.*

If someone feels very sad because of being alone, you could use the words **lonely** or **isolated**.

*She felt very **lonely** without him.*

*Older people can often feel very **isolated**.*

Someone who lives alone and does not like going out or talking to people can be described as a **recluse**.

*He is a millionaire **recluse** who refuses to give interviews.*

ONLY /əˈloʊn/ *adj* [not gradable] without any others, or only ○ *I based my decision on her recommendation alone.*

along **BESIDE** /əˈlɔːŋ/ *prep* **1** in the same direction as, or beside ○ *We walked along the canal path.* **2** Along also means at a particular point or continuing to go on: *My office is the third door along the hallway on the left.*

FORWARD /əˈlɔːŋ/ *adv* [not gradable] toward a direction or goal; forward ○ *You wait ages for a bus, then three come along all at once.* ○ *How far along are you with your homework?*

WITH OTHERS /əˈlɔːŋ/ *adv* [not gradable] with the person or persons already mentioned ○ *Why don't you take him along?*

IDIOMS with along

- **along the same lines** similar ○ *My sister works in publishing, and I'm hoping to do something along the same lines.*
- **along the way** **1** during a particular period of time ○ *I've been here for thirty years, and I've picked up a lot of experience along the way.* **2** **Along the way** also means while traveling from one place to another place: *I drove from Texas to Maine, and I met a lot of interesting people along the way.*
- **along with** *someone/something* in addition to someone or something else ○ *Now we've got hospital bills along with our usual expenses.*

alongside /əˈlɔːŋˌsɑɪd/ *prep, adv* [not gradable] beside, or together with ○ *They put out cookies alongside the cake.*

aloof /əˈluːf/ *adj, adv* not taking part in things, esp. in a way that seems unfriendly ○ *Is she aloof and arrogant or just shy?* ○ *When they argued, I remained aloof.*

aloud /əˈlɑʊd/ *adv* [not gradable] in a voice loud enough to be heard ○ *I wondered aloud whether it would be worth the wait.*

alphabet /ˈæl·fəˌbet/ *n* [C] ***writing*** a set of letters arranged in a fixed order that is used for writing a language ○ *the Cyrillic/Hebrew alphabet*

alphabetical /ˌæl·fəˈbeţ·ɪ·kəl/, **alphabetic** /ˌæl·fəˈbeţ·ɪk/ *adj* [not gradable] ○ *The names are in alphabetical order.*

alphabetically /ˌæl·fəˈbeţ·ɪ·kli/ *adv* [not gradable] ○ *Recipes are arranged alphabetically by type of food.*

alphabetic *adj* [not gradable] ***writing*** An alphabetic language has a letter or combinations of letters and marks to represent each speech sound in the language.

alpha particle /ˈæl·fə/ *n* [C] ***physics*** a very small unit of matter with a positive electrical CHARGE **STORE ENERGY** that is sent out by some RADIOACTIVE substances

alpine /ˈæl·pɑɪn/ *adj* relating to high mountains, esp. the Alps (= the highest mountains in Europe) ○ *Alpine skiing* ○ *an alpine meadow*

already /ɔːlˈred·i/ *adv* [not gradable] **1** earlier than the time expected, in a short time, or before the present time ○ *Are you planning a summer trip already? It's only September!* ○ *I've already seen that movie.* **2** Already can also mean now: *It's bad enough already – don't make it any worse.*

alright /ɔːlˈrɑɪt, ˈɔːl·rɑɪt/ *exclamation, adj, adv* [not gradable] *not standard* ALL RIGHT

also /ˈɔːl·soʊ/ *adv* [not gradable] **1** in addition ○ *She's a photographer and also writes books.* **2** Also can also mean similarly: *That's funny, I'm also on a diet.*

altar /ˈɔːl·tər/ *n* [C] a type of table used in religious ceremonies

altar boy, *female* **altar girl** *n* [C] a boy or girl who helps a priest in worship services

alter Ⓐ /ˈɔːl·tər/ *v* [I/T] to change a characteristic, often slightly, or to cause this to happen ○ [T] *The coat was too long, so I took it back to the store to have it altered.*

alterable Ⓐ /ˈɔːl·tə·rə·bəl/ *adj*

alteration Ⓐ /ˌɔːl·təˈreɪ·ʃən/ *n* [C/U] ○ [C] *I had to make some alterations in my research paper.*

altercation /ˌɔːl·tərˈkeɪ·ʃən/ *n* [C] a loud argument or disagreement ○ *Phil got into an altercation with his partner.*

alternate Ⓐ /ˈɔːl·tərˌneɪt/ *v* [I/T] to cause two things to happen or exist one after the other ○ [I] *The children alternated between being excited and being tired.* ○ [T] *I like to alternate physical and intellectual activities.*

alternate Ⓐ /ˈɔːl·tər·nət/ *adj* [not gradable] every second, or every other ○ *I visit my father on alternate weekends.* ○ **USAGE:** Used only about sets of two.

alternate Ⓐ /ˈɔːl·tər·nət/ *n* [C] one that can take the place of another ○ *David was too sick to attend, so Janet served as his alternate.*

alternately /ˈɔːl·tər·nət·li/ *adv* in a manner in which two things each replace the other ○ *The movie is alternately depressing and amusing.*

alternating current *n* [U] ***physics*** a form of electricity that regularly changes direction as it flows, and that is the form of electricity used in homes and buildings

alternative Ⓐ /ɔːlˈtɜr·nəţ·ɪv/ *n* [C] something that is different, esp. from what is usual; a choice ○ *You can make it look good by comparing it to a crummy alternative.* ○ *I have no alternative but to ask you to leave.*

alternative Ⓐ /ɔːlˈtɜr·nəţ·ɪv/ *adj* [not gradable] **1** *People stay because they don't have alternative opportunities.* **2** Alternative medicine is a wide range of treatments for medical conditions that people use instead of, or with, Western medicine.

alternatively Ⓐ /ɔːlˈtɜr·nəţ·ɪv·li/ *adv* [not gradable] ○ *We could go to the Mexican restaurant, or alternatively* (= instead of that), *we could try that new Italian place.*

although /ɔːlˈðoʊ/ *conjunction* despite the fact that, or despite being ○ *He decided to go, although I begged him not to.*

altitude HEIGHT /ˈæl·təˌtuːd/ *n* [C] ***earth science*** **1** height above sea level ○ *The city of Denver is situated at an altitude of almost exactly one mile.* **2** Altitude is also the distance measured by an angle made by a point on the earth to a star and to the HORIZON (= place where earth and sky seem to meet).

LINE /ˈæl·təˌtuːd/ ***geometry*** a SEGMENT (= part of a line) that is at a 90° angle to the side to which it is drawn

alto /ˈæl·toʊ/ *n* [C] *pl* **altos** a woman's or boy's singing voice in the range lower than a SOPRANO, or a person or musical instrument with this range

altogether /ˌɔːl·təˈgeð·ər/ *adv* [not gradable] completely or in total ○ *The train slowed down and then stopped altogether.* ○ *He was altogether exhausted.* ○ *Altogether, she gave away some $60 million in her lifetime.*

altruism /ˈæl·trʊˌɪz·əm/ *n* [U] the attitude of caring about others and doing acts that help them although you do not get anything by doing those acts ○ *Nobody believes those people are donating money to the president's party purely out of altruism.*

altruistic /ˌæl·trʊˈɪs·tɪk/ *adj* ○ *altruistic motives*

aluminum /əˈluː·mə·nəm/, *Br* **aluminium** /ˌæl·jʊˈmɪn·iː·əm/ *n* [U] a light, silver-colored metal used esp. for making containers, cooking equipment, and aircraft parts

alumni /əˈlʌmˌnɑɪ/ *pl n* men and women who have completed their studies, esp. at a college or university ○ *a reunion of Yale alumni of the class of 1990* ○ *Vassar alumni* ○ **USAGE:** Alumni can be used to refer to men only, and in that case alumnae is used to refer to women only, but more often alumni is used to refer to either or both sexes where both attend the same school. The singular forms are alumnus for a man, and alumna for a woman.

always /ˈɔːl·wiːz, -weɪz/ *adv* [not gradable] **1** every time, all the time, or forever ○ *He always enjoyed having dinner with friends.* ○ *You always try to do your best.* ○ *I'll always remember her.* ○ *She's always* (= very often) *late.* **2** Always is sometimes used after can or could to suggest another possibility: *If you don't like what's on TV, you can always change the channel.*

WORD CHOICES always

If you use **always** to mean "again and again," then you could also use **constantly, continually, forever**, or the fixed expressions **time after time** or **all the time.**

*He's **constantly/forever** losing his keys.*

*I'm fed up with you making excuses **all the time**.*

The word **invariably** is a more formal way of saying **always** especially when talking about something you wish would not happen.

*The train is **invariably** late.*

Consistently is used when something happens or someone does something in the same way again and again.

*He received **consistently** high marks throughout his school years.*

The fixed expression **without fail** can be used to show that someone always does something, even when it is difficult.

*He visited her every Sunday **without fail**.*

Alzheimer's (disease) /ˈɔːltsˌhɑɪ·mərz (dɪˌziːz)/ *n* [U] a disease that results in the gradual loss of memory, speech, movement, and the ability to think clearly, and that is common esp. among older people

am /æm, əm, m/ *v* (used with I) BE ○ *I am 48 years old.* ○ *I am getting ready now.*

AM /ˈeɪˈem/ *n* [U] *abbreviation for* amplitude modulation (= one of two main types of radio waves used to broadcast in the US) ○ *Most of the talk radio programs can be found on AM stations.* ○ Compare FM

a.m., **A.M.** /eɪˈem/ *adv* [not gradable] used when referring to a time between twelve o'clock at night and twelve o'clock in the middle of the day; past the middle of the night, or in the morning ○ *We fly out of New York late in the evening and arrive in London at 7 a.m. the next morning.* ○ Compare P.M.

amalgamate /əˈmæl·gəˌmeɪt/ *v* [I/T] to join together or unite, or to cause to join together ○ [I] *The two towns amalgamated to combine their police and fire protection.* ○ **USAGE:** describes the joining of separate organizations or groups

amass /əˈmæs/ *v* [T] to gather a large amount of something, esp. money, by collecting it over a period of time ○ *By the time he was 40, he had amassed a fortune.*

amateur /ˈæm·əˌtɜr, -əˌtʃʊr, -əṭ·ər/ *adj* taking part in an activity for pleasure and not as a job, or (of an activity) done for pleasure and not as a job ○ *He was an amateur archaeologist.* ○ Compare PROFESSIONAL at PROFESSION

amateur /ˈæm·əˌtɜr, -əˌtʃʊr, -əṭ·ər/ *n* [C] **1** *The sailing competition is for wealthy amateurs.* **2** An amateur is also someone who lacks skill in doing something: *Some of the people who show up at practice shooting ranges are real amateurs.* ○ Compare PROFESSIONAL at PROFESSION

amateurish /ˌæm·əˈtɜr·ɪʃ, -ˈtʃʊr·ɪʃ/ *adj* performed without much skill ○ *The movie drags along, made even worse by amateurish acting.*

amaze /əˈmeɪz/ *v* [T] to cause someone to be extremely surprised ○ *The prices they're getting for vegetables just amaze me.* ○ *I'm amazed at how well your little girl can read.*

amazement /əˈmeɪz·mənt/ *n* [U] ○ *Much to my amazement, she liked the idea.*

amazing /əˈmeɪ·zɪŋ/ *adj* ○ *It's pretty amazing how much top athletes get paid.*

WORD FAMILY amaze			
Nouns	amazement	*Verbs*	amaze
Adjectives	amazed amazing	*Adverbs*	amazingly

ambassador /æm ˈbæs·əd·ər/ *n* [C] an official who represents his or her own country in a foreign country ○ *the US ambassador to Sweden*

ambidextrous /ˌæm·bɪ ˈdek·strəs/ *adj* able to use both your right and left hand equally well

ambience, **ambiance** /ˈæm·biː·əns, ˌɑm·biː ˈɑ̃s/ *n* [U] the character of a place or the quality it seems to have ○ *The city's ambience, particularly on the waterfront, is changing quickly.*

ambiguity Ⓐ /ˌæm·bəˈgjuː·əṭ·i/ *n* [C/U] **1** a situation or statement that is unclear because it can be understood in more than one way ○ [C] *This is a first step toward clarifying things, but there are still many ambiguities.* **2** ***literature*** **Intentional ambiguity** is the use of language or images to suggest more than one meaning at the same time, esp. in a poem.

ambiguous Ⓐ /æm ˈbɪg·jə·wəs/ *adj* having or expressing more than one possible meaning, sometimes intentionally ○ *The movie's ending is ambiguous.*

ambition /æm ˈbɪʃ·ən/ *n* [C/U] a strong desire for success, achievement, power, or wealth ○ [C] *His presidential ambitions were frustrated in the 1980s.* ○ [U] *No one ever accused him of lacking ambition.*

ambitious /æm ˈbɪʃ·əs/ *adj* **1** *Even as a young man he was ambitious and self-assured.* **2** If you describe an activity as ambitious, you mean that it involves a lot of effort or expense: *It was an ambitious project to restore the public parks.*

ambivalent /æm ˈbɪv·ə·lənt/ *adj* having two opposing feelings at the same time, or being uncertain about how you feel ○ *My wife loves the opera, but I have ambivalent feelings about it.*

ambivalence /æm ˈbɪv·ə·ləns/ *n* [U]

amble /ˈæm·bəl/ *v* [I always + adv/prep] to walk in a slow and relaxed way ○ *The couple ambled along, arm in arm.*

ambulance /ˈæm·bjə·ləns, -ˌlæns/ *n* [C] a special vehicle equipped to take people who are injured or ill to the hospital

ambulatory /ˈæm·bjə·ləˌtɔːr·i, -ˌtoʊr·i/ *adj* (of people being treated for an injury or illness) able to walk, and, when treated in a hospital, usually not staying for the night in a bed ○ *We will soon be opening two new ambulatory care facilities.*

ambush /ˈæm·bʊʃ/ *n* [C] a sudden and surprising attack on a person or group by one or more people who have been hiding and waiting for them ○ *Seven commandos were wounded in an ambush.*

ambush /ˈæm·bʊʃ/ *v* [T] ○ *The Air Cavalry was ambushed and suffered big losses.*

AME /ˌeɪ ˌem ˈiː/ *adj, n* [U] *abbreviation for* AFRICAN METHODIST EPISCOPAL ○ *First AME Church*

amen /ɑˈmen, eɪ-/ *exclamation, n* [C] **1** (said or sung at the end of some prayers or religious songs) it is so **2** You can say amen to show that you agree strongly with something that someone has just said: *"Two public service announcements will address the habit of running red lights." "Amen to that!"*

amenable /əˈmiː·nə·bəl, -ˈmen·ə-/ *adj* willing to accept or be influenced by a suggestion ○ *He was amenable to suggestion, and really worked hard to improve himself.*

amend Ⓐ /əˈmend/ *v* [T] to change the words of something written, esp. a law or a legal document ○ *The terms of the contract were amended in later years.*

amendment Ⓐ /əˈmend·mənt/ *n* [C] ***US history*** a change or addition to the US CONSTITUTION ○ *the First/Fifth/Fourteenth amendment* ○ *a constitutional amendment*

amends Ⓐ /əˈmendz/ *pl n* To **make amends** is to correct a mistake you have made, esp. in behavior.

amenity /əˈmen·əṭ·i, əˈmiː·nəṭ·i/ *n* [C usually pl] something intended to make life more pleasant or comfortable for people ○ *Straus established employee amenities such as restrooms, medical care, and a lunchroom.*

American /əˈmer·ə·kən, əˈmær-/ *adj, n* [C] (a person) of or coming from the United States, or of or coming from North America or South America

Americanize /əˈmer·ə·kəˌnɑɪz, əˈmær-/ *v* [T] to make someone or something more typical of Americans in appearance, customs, or language ○ *In the 1890s, immigrants into the U.S.A. organized a night school to help them become Americanized.*

American English *n* [C] the English language as it is spoken and written in the US

American Indian, **Native American** *n* [C] someone who belongs to one of the groups of people that originally lived in North America before the Europeans arrived

American plan *n* [C usually sing] a hotel price that includes meals in the cost of the room

Americas /əˈmer·ə·kəz, əˈmær-/ *pl n* the countries of North and South America, considered together ○ *Health workers have eliminated the virus in the Americas, Europe, and most of Asia.*

amiable /ˈeɪ·miː·ə·bəl/ *adj* pleasant and friendly ○ *He was amiable and charming, and he possessed an ability to make people feel comfortable in his presence.*

amicable /ˈæm·ɪ·kə·bəl/ *adj* friendly in attitude, or (of decisions or agreements) achieved with friendly attitudes and without unpleasant argument ○ *Wagner predicted the whole issue would be resolved in an amicable manner.*

amicably /ˈæm·ɪ·kə·bli/ *adv* ○ *They stayed together almost a year and parted amicably.*

amid /əˈmɪd/, **amidst** /əˈmɪdst, əˈmɪtst/ *prep* in the middle of or surrounded by; among ○ *We camped that night in a shallow valley amid low hills.*

amide /ˈæmˌɑɪd, ˈæm·əd/ *n* [C] ***chemistry*** a substance formed from AMMONIA by replacing a HYDROGEN atom with a metal

amine /əˈmiːn, ˈæmˌiːn/ *n* [C] ***chemistry*** any of a group of substances formed from AMMONIA by replacing HYDROGEN atoms with a group of atoms containing carbon

amino acid /əˈmiː·noʊ/ *n* [C] ***biology, chemistry*** any of the chemical substances found in plants and animals that combine to make PROTEIN (= substance necessary for the body to grow)

Amish /ˈɑm·ɪʃ, ˈæm-/ *pl n* a Christian religious group that lives in a traditional way in many rural areas, esp. in the eastern US

amiss /əˈmɪs/ *adj* not right; not suitable or as expected ○ *He suspected something was amiss.*

ammeter /ˈæmˌiːt̬·ər/ *n* [C] ***physics*** a device that measures the strength of an electric current in AMPERES

ammonia /əˈmoʊn·jə/ *n* [U] a gas or liquid with a strong smell, having various industrial uses such as in cleaning

ammonite /ˈæm·əˌnɑɪt/ *n* [C] ***earth science*** an EXTINCT (= no longer existing) sea creature often found as a FOSSIL (= animal or plant preserved in rock)

ammonoid /ˈæm·əˌnɔɪd/ *n* [C] ***earth science*** an AMMONITE

ammunition /ˌæm·jəˈnɪʃ·ən/, *infml* **ammo** /ˈæm·oʊ/ *n* [U] **1** objects such as bullets and bombs that can be shot from a weapon **2** Ammunition is also information used to attack someone or to support an argument: *The president's endorsement of the crime bill has deprived his opponents of ammunition to paint him as soft on crime.*

amnesia /æmˈniː·ʒə/ *n* [U] *medical* loss of the ability to remember

amnesty /ˈæm·nə·sti/ *n* [C/U] ***politics & government*** a decision by a government to forgive people who have committed particular illegal acts or crimes, and not to punish them ○ [C] *The state has declared an amnesty for individuals who pay their outstanding back taxes.*

amniotic fluid /ˌæm·niːˈɑt̬·ɪk/ *n* [U] ***biology*** the liquid that surrounds an EMBRYO (= growing baby) inside its mother

amoeba /əˈmiːˌbə/ *pl* **amoebas, amoebae** ***biology*** a type of organism that has one cell

amoebic *adj* ***biology*** relating to or caused by amoebas ○ *amoebic dysentery*

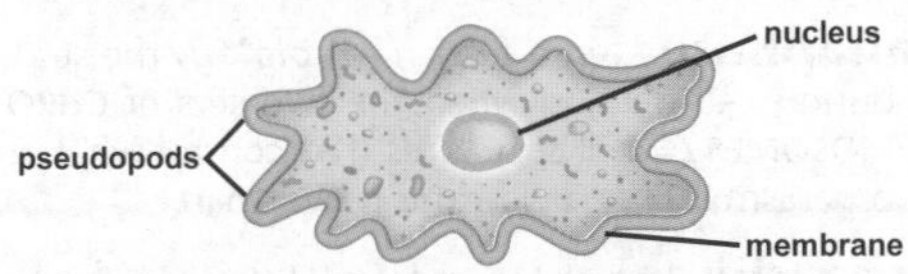

AMOEBA

among /əˈmʌŋ/, **amongst** /əˈmʌŋst/ *prep* **1** in the middle of or surrounded by ○ *She felt lonely among all these strange people.* **2** Among also means as part of a group or in the group of people or things named: *They discussed it among themselves.* ○ *Among the problems we have to deal with, improving education is probably the most difficult.*

amoral /eɪˈmɔːr·əl, -ˈmɑr-/ *adj* [not gradable] without moral principles ○ *Business is an amoral activity focused coldly on success.*

amorous /ˈæm·ə·rəs/ *adj* of or relating to romantic love

amorphous /əˈmɔːr·fəs, eɪ-/ *adj* having no fixed form or shape; not clear or not determined ○ *Plans for a 40-acre shopping center section remain so amorphous that the project has been shelved.*

amount /əˈmɑʊnt/ *n* [C] the degree to which something is a lot or a little; how much something is ○ *She's made a tremendous amount of progress since the accident.* ○ *He liked to carry a large amount of money around with him.*

USAGE

amount of or **number of?**

Amount of is used with uncountable nouns.

I should reduce the amount of coffee I drink.

Did you use the right amount of flour?

Number of is used with countable nouns.

We don't know the number of people involved yet.

They received a large number of complaints.

IDIOM with amount

• **not amount to much, not amount to anything** to not become successful or important ○ *He's lazy, and he'll never amount to anything.*

PHRASAL VERB with amount

• **amount to** *something* to add up to, be in total, be equal to, or be the same as ○ *Federal and state costs for building and operating prisons amounted to $25 billion.* ○ *The blog amounts to a critique of the U.S. news media.*

ampere /ˈæm·pɪr/, **amp** /æmp/ *n* [C] ***physics*** the standard unit of measurement for the strength of an electric current

amphetamine /æmˈfet̬·əˌmiːn, -mɪn/ *n* [C] a strong drug used as a medicine that makes the mind and body more active; a STIMULANT

amphibian /æmˈfɪb·iː·ən/ *n* [C] ***biology*** a type of animal that lives both on land and in water ○ *Frogs and turtles are amphibians.*

amphibious /æmˈfɪb·iː·əs/ *adj* [not gradable] **1** ***biology*** able to live on land and in water ○ *amphibious creatures* **2** Amphibious also means able to operate on land and in water: *We toured the harbor in an amphibious bus.*

amphipod /ˈæm·fəˌpɑd/ *n* [C] ***biology*** a small CRUSTACEAN (= animal that lives in water) that is similar in appearance to a SHRIMP but has no shell

amphiprotic /ˈˌæm·fəˈprɑt̬·ɪk/, **amphoteric** /ˌæm·fəˈter·ɪk/ *adj* [not gradable] having characteristics of both an acid and a BASE CHEMICAL

amphitheater, **amphitheatre** /ˈæm·fəˌθiː·ət̬·ər, ˈæm·pə-/ *n* [C] a circular or oval area around which rows of seats are arranged on a steep slope, esp. for watching the performance of plays and musical entertainment outside

ample /ˈæm·pəl/ *adj* enough, or more than enough, or (esp. of body size) large ○ *There will be ample opportunity for everyone here to speak.*
amply /ˈæm·pli/ *adv* ○ *The research was amply funded.*

amplify /ˈæm·pləˌfɑɪ/ *v* [T] **1** to increase the strength of a sound; make louder ○ *Electric guitars are amplified through loudspeakers.* **2** To amplify is also to add to the information given in something: *This study amplifies earlier research.*
amplification /ˌæm·plə·fəˈkeɪ·ʃən/ *n* [C/U] ○ [U] *sound amplification*
amplifier /ˈæm·pləˌfɑɪ·ər/ *n* [C] an electronic device that strengthens the electric signal used to carry sound

amplitude /ˈæm·pləˌtuːd/ *n* [C/U] **1** ***physics*** the strength of a WAVE of sound or electricity, measured at the strongest repeating part of the wave **2** ***trigonometry*** Amplitude is also the greatest height of a GRAPH (= drawing) of the relationships of a SINE or COSINE. **3** ***earth science*** Amplitude is also the height of a WAVE (= water movement) from top to bottom. ➤ Picture: **wave**

amputate /ˈæm·pjəˌteɪt/ *v* [I/T] to cut off part of the body ○ [T] *Doctors had to amputate his leg below the knee.*
amputation /ˌæm·pjəˈteɪ·ʃən/ *n* [C/U] ○ [U] *Frostbite led to the amputation of three fingers.*

Amtrak /ˈæm·træk/ *n* [U] the US national passenger railroad system

amuse ENTERTAIN /əˈmjuːz/ *v* [T] to keep the attention of someone by entertaining that person ○ *It's a relief when your child can amuse herself for a whole hour.*
amusement /əˈmjuːz·mənt/ *n* [C/U] ○ [U] *For the children's amusement, Elizabeth helped them put on a play.*

MAKE LAUGH /əˈmjuːz/ *v* [T] to make someone smile or laugh ○ *His subtle humor amused me.* ○ *Her ability to hack into computer systems did not amuse her superiors.*
amusing /əˈmjuː·zɪŋ/ *adj* ○ *One amusing story after another kept the audience laughing.*
amusement /əˈmjuːz·mənt/ *n* [C/U] ○ [U] *We watched the clown with great amusement.*

amusement park *n* [C] a place where people can go to enjoy games, rides, and other activities

amylase /ˈæm·əˌleɪs, -ˌleɪz/ *n* [U] ***biology*** an ENZYME (= substance that causes chemical change) that helps to change STARCH (= substance found in plants) into sugar

an /æn, ən/ *indefinite article* (used when the word following begins with a vowel sound) A ○ *an apple* ○ *an honest man*

anachronism /əˈnæk·rəˌnɪz·əm/ *n* [C] someone or something placed in the wrong period in history, or something that belongs to the past rather than the present ○ *For a historical drama, the movie was filled with anachronisms.*
anachronistic /əˌnæk·rəˈnɪs·tɪk/ *adj* ○ *He uses only e-mail, never anachronistic regular mail.*

anaerobic respiration /ˌæn·əˈroʊ·bɪk/ *n* [U] ***biology*** a chemical process in which energy is produced without the use of oxygen

anagram /ˈæn·əˌɡræm/ *n* [C] a word or phrase made by using the letters of another word or phrase in a different order ○ *"Neat" is an anagram of "a net."*

anal /ˈeɪn·əl/ *adj* ○ See at ANUS

analgesic /ˌæn·əlˈdʒiː·zɪk, -sɪk/ *adj* tending to reduce or prevent pain ○ *Did you know that the caffeine in coffee has analgesic qualities?*

analog, **analogue** /ˈæn·əlˌɔːɡ, -ˌɑɡ/ *adj* [not gradable] representing electronic information as a continuously varying signal ○ *Analog broadcasts, the current technology, would continue side by side with digital.* ○ Compare DIGITAL at DIGIT NUMBER

analogy Ⓐ /əˈnæl·ə·dʒi/ *n* [C/U] ***literature*** a comparison of the features or qualities of two different things to show their similarities ○ [C] *He was explaining that the mind has no form and is invisible, and that a useful analogy is of the mind being like the sky.*
analogous Ⓐ /əˈnæl·ə·ɡəs/ *adj* ○ *The stock market recorded a 0.4% annual increase that was roughly analogous to results in the late 1960s.*

analysis Ⓐ /əˈnæl·ə·səs/ *n* [C/U] *pl* **analyses 1** the process of studying or examining something in an organized way to learn more about it, or a particular study of something ○ [C] *Chemical analysis of the woman's dress revealed traces of blood.* **2** Analysis is also a short form of PSYCHOANALYSIS.
analyze Ⓐ /ˈæn·əlˌɑɪz/ *v* [T] to study something in a systematic and careful way ○ *In the article, several experienced diplomats analyzed the president's foreign policy.*
analyst Ⓐ /ˈæn·əl·əst/ *n* [C] **1** *She is a financial analyst* (= someone who studies financial investments). **2** Analyst is also a short form of PSYCHOANALYST.
analytical Ⓐ /ˌæn·əlˈɪt̬·ɪ·kəl/, **analytic** /ˌæn·əlˈɪt̬·ɪk/ *adj* involving the careful, systematic study of something ○ *An analytical approach to the problem had surprising results.*
analytically Ⓐ /ˌæn·əlˈɪt̬·ɪk·li/ *adv*

anaphase /ˈæn·əˌfeɪz/ *n* [U] ***biology*** the stage during cell division when the two sets of CHROMOSOMES (= cell structures that control what an organism is like) divide and move apart

anarchy /ˈæn·ər·ki, -ˌɑr·ki/ *n* [U] ***politics & government*** a lack of organization and control in a society or group, esp. because either there is no government or it has no power ○ *Civil war has led*

to anarchy. ○ *The crowd was restless and verging on anarchy.*
anarchist /ˈæn·ər·kəst, ˈæn ˌɑr-/ *n* [C] ***politics & government*** ○ *Belief in freedom doesn't make you an anarchist.*

anathema /əˈnæθ·ə·mə/ *n* [U] something that is considered completely wrong and offensive ○ *The idea of higher taxes is anathema to most conservatives.*

anatomy /əˈnæt̬·ə·mi/ *n* [U] the scientific study of the structure of animals or plants, or of a particular type of animal or plant ○ *You have to know something about anatomy if you want to draw the human body well.* ○ *(fig.) He was studying the anatomy of long-term relationships* (= their structure).
anatomical /ˌæn·əˈtɑm·ɪ·kəl/ *adj* [not gradable] ○ *anatomical drawings*

ANC *n* ***politics & government*** *abbreviation for* African National Congress (= a political group in South Africa that supports the rights of black people and fought for destruction of the apartheid system).

ancestor /ˈæn ˌses·tər, -səs-/ *n* [C] any member of your family from long ago, for example, the GRANDPARENTS of your grandparents ○ *He returned to Ecuador, where his mother's ancestors lived.*
ancestral /ænˈses·trəl/ *adj* [not gradable] ○ *He wanted to tour his family's ancestral homeland, Germany.*
ancestry /ˈæn ˌses·tri/ *n* [C usually sing] ○ *She was of Spanish and Iriquois ancestry.*

anchor HEAVY WEIGHT /ˈæŋ·kər/ *n* [C] **1** a heavy metal object attached to a boat by a rope or chain that, when dropped into the water and resting on the bottom, keeps the boat from moving ○ *We dropped the anchor and took out our fishing rods.* **2** An anchor is also someone or something that gives support when needed: *She's looking for a spiritual anchor.*
anchor /ˈæŋ·kər/ *v* [I/T] ○ [T] *We anchored our sailboat near the shore.*
NEWS PERSON /ˈæŋ·kər/ *n* [C] a person who reports the news and manages reports by others on a television or radio program ○ *The mayor grants frequent interviews to local news anchors.*
anchor /ˈæŋ·kər/ *v* [T] ○ *He anchored the morning news for many years.*

anchorman /ˈæŋ·kər ˌmæn/ *n* [C] *pl* **anchormen** a male ANCHOR NEWS PERSON

anchorwoman /ˈæŋ·kər ˌwʊm·ən/ *n* [C] *pl* **anchorwomen** a female ANCHOR NEWS PERSON

anchovy /ˈæn ˌtʃoʊ·vi, ænˈtʃoʊ-/ *n* [C] *pl* **anchovy, anchovies** a small fish which is usually preserved in oil with salt, giving it a strong, salty taste

ancient /ˈeɪn·tʃənt/ *adj* **1** of or from a very long time ago ○ *Archaeologists study the remains of ancient civilizations.* **2** *infml* Something that is ancient is very old: *This computer is ancient – I've got to get a new one.*

USAGE

ancient

Ancient cannot be used to refer to something or someone that existed in the recent past but not now. Use **former** or **ex-** for this meaning.

A party was organized for former students of the school.
~~*A party was organized for ancient students of the school.*~~
my ex-girlfriend
~~*my ancient girlfriend*~~

Be careful not to confuse **ancient** with **old. Ancient** means thousands or hundreds of years old.

a medical center for old/elderly people
~~*a medical center for ancient people*~~

and ALSO /ænd, ənd/ *conjunction* **1** (used to join two words, phrases, or parts of sentences) in addition to; also ○ *boys and girls* ○ *We were tired and hungry.* **2** And can be used when you add numbers: *Three and two are five.*
THEN /ænd, ənd/ *conjunction* (used to join two parts of a sentence, one part happening after or because of the other part) after that; then ○ *I met Jonathan, and we went out for a cup of coffee.*
TO /ænd, ənd/ *conjunction infml* (used after some verbs) to, or in order to ○ *Let's try and get tickets for the hockey game tonight.*
VERY /ænd, ənd/ *conjunction* (used to join two words, esp. two that are the same, to make their meaning stronger) ○ *The sound grew louder and louder.*

IDIOM with and

• **and so on, and so forth** in addition to other things of the same kind ○ *Economic growth makes us all richer, provides jobs, and so on.* ○ *I realize they're not doing a good job and so forth, but I don't really like having to fire anyone.*

and/or /ˈænˈdɔːr/ *conjunction* (used to refer to both things or either one of the two mentioned) either "and" or "or" ○ *If the game is canceled, you will get a refund and/or new tickets.*

android /ˈæn·drɔɪd/ *n* [C] a ROBOT (= mechanical device) that looks like a person ○ *He acted just like a clever android, avoiding any expression of affection.*

anecdote /ˈæn·ɪk ˌdoʊt/ *n* [C] ***literature*** a short, often amusing story about an event, usually involving a particular person ○ *He told some funny anecdotes about famous people.*
anecdotal /ˌæn·ɪkˈdoʊt̬·əl/ *adj* [not gradable] based on reports or things someone saw rather than on proven facts ○ *There is only anecdotal evidence that the medicine works.*

anemia /əˈniː·miː·ə/ *n* [U] ***biology*** a condition in which the blood cannot carry enough oxygen,

usually as a result of having too few red blood cells, causing a lack of energy

anemic /əˈniː·mɪk/ *adj* ○ *I was anemic for a while after my operation.* ○ (*fig.*) *First-quarter sales were anemic* (= weak).

anemometer /ˌæn·əˈmɑm·ət̬·ər/ *n* [C] ***earth science*** a device that measures the speed and force of wind

anesthesia /ˌæn·əsˈθiː·ʒə/ *n* [U] the condition of not feeling pain, esp. by use of special drugs ○ *The procedure is performed under general anesthesia.*

anesthetic /ˌæn·əsˈθet̬·ɪk/ *n* [C] a drug that makes the body unable to feel pain ○ *With a local anesthetic, a patient is awake during surgery.*

anesthetist /əˈnes·θət̬·əst/ *n* [C] *medical* a medical specialist who gives ANESTHESIA, esp. during an operation

anesthetize /əˈnes·θəˌtɑɪz/ *v* [T] ○ *The vet anesthetized my dog to take x-rays.*

anew /əˈnuː/ *adv* [not gradable] once more; again ○ *After a short time, their old arguments simply began anew.*

angel /ˈeɪn·dʒəl/ *n* [C] **1** in some religious traditions, a being in heaven who serves God, often represented in art as a human with wings **2** An angel is also someone who is very good or kind: *You're an angel to bring me this coffee.*

angelic /ænˈdʒel·ɪk/ *adj* belonging to an angel, or pretty and kind like an angel ○ *an angelic face/voice/choir*

angel food cake *n* [C/U] a light cake made without egg YOLKS or fat

anger /ˈæŋ·gər/ *n* [U] a feeling of fierce annoyance because of something unfair or painful that has happened ○ *When my father saw the plumber's bill, he erupted in anger.*

anger /ˈæŋ·gər/ *v* [T] ○ *His constant complaining only angered her.*

angry /ˈæŋ·gri/ *adj* ○ *an angry mob* ○ *I hope you aren't angry with me.*

angrily /ˈæŋ·grə·li/ *adv* ○ *He angrily slammed the door.*

WORD FAMILY anger

Nouns	anger	*Verbs*	anger
Adjectives	angry	*Adverbs*	angrily

WORD CHOICES anger

See also: **annoy, bad-tempered**

If someone is angry about something that has happened you can say that this person is **annoyed** or **irritated.**

*He was a bit **annoyed** with her for being late.*

*I was **irritated** that he didn't thank me.*

If someone is extremely angry, you can use adjectives such as **furious, irate,** or **livid.**

*My boss was **furious** with me.*

*Hundreds of **irate** passengers have complained to the airline.*

If you are angry with a child, you might describe yourself as **cross.**

*I'm **cross** with you for not telling me where you were going.*

The expression **up in arms** is sometimes used when people are angry about something they think is unfair.

*Local people are **up in arms** over plans to close the local swimming pool.*

If someone suddenly becomes very angry, you can use the informal expression **go crazy** or the idiom **hit the roof.**

*Dad **went crazy** when he found out we'd broken the window.*

An angry argument can be described as **heated** or **acrimonious.**

*He was involved in an **acrimonious** dispute with his neighbor.*

angle MEASUREMENT /ˈæŋ·gəl/ *n* [C] ***geometry*** **1** the space measured in degrees between two lines or surfaces from the point where they meet ○ *The angles of a square are 90 degrees.* **2** The **angle of depression** is the angle formed when viewing something from below the horizontal. **3** The **angle of elevation** is the angle formed when viewing something from above the horizontal.

VIEW /ˈæŋ·gəl/ *n* [C] a position from which something is seen, or a way of seeing something ○ *The photographer kept moving around to find the best angle for the picture.* ○ *Look at this from another angle.*

angle /ˈæŋ·gəl/ *v* [I/T] to turn, or to move something so that it is not in a straight line or in the center ○ [I] *The path angles to the left.* ○ [T] *We angled the light to take the picture.*

right angle

straight angle

adjacent angles

complementary angles

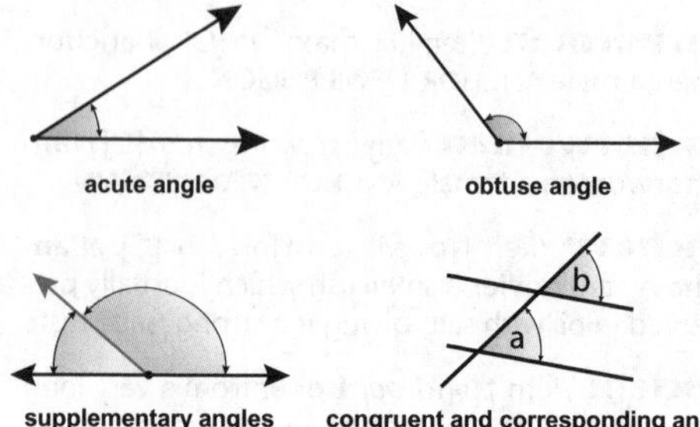

ANGLES

A

IDIOM with angle

• **at an angle** not straight ○ *The picture was hanging at an angle, so I straightened it.*

PHRASAL VERB with angle

• **angle for** *something* to try to get or achieve something, esp. without saying what your goal is ○ *The way he hangs around, he must be angling for a job.*

angle of incidence *n* [C] ***physics*** the angle that a beam of light touching a surface makes with a line vertical to that surface

Anglican /ˈæŋ·glɪ·kən/ *n* [C] a member of a Christian religious group that includes the Church of England and the Episcopal Church in the US

Anglican /ˈæŋ·glɪ·kən/ *adj* [not gradable] ○ *an Anglican bishop*

anglicize /ˈæŋ·gləˌsɑɪz/ *v* [T] to change a word or name to make it sound or look like English ○ *Lloyd is an anglicized form of the Welsh name Llwyd, meaning "gray(-haired)" or "senior."*

angling /ˈæŋ·glɪŋ/ *n* [U] the sport of trying to catch fish with a rod, LINE (= string), and hook

angler /ˈæŋ·glər/ *n* [C] ○ *Anglers line the stream, fishing for salmon.*

Anglo /ˈæŋ·gloʊ/ *n* [C] *pl* **Anglos** a white person in the US who is not from a Latin American country ○ *The students are Anglos, Latinos, and Native Americans.*

Anglo- /ˌæŋ·gloʊ/ *prefix* ENGLISH or BRITISH.

Anglo-American *adj* [not gradable] British and American ○ *There is a new Anglo-American trade agreement.*

Anglo-Canadian, **English Canadian** *n* [C] a Canadian citizen whose first language is English

angora /æŋˈgɔːr·ə, æn-, -ˈgoʊr·ə/ *n* [U] a soft wool made from the long hair of a type of goat or rabbit

angrily /ˈæŋ·grə·li/ *adv* ○ See at ANGER

angry /ˈæŋ·gri/ *adj* ○ See at ANGER

angst /ɑŋst, æŋst/ *n* [U] a feeling of extreme anxiety and unhappiness ○ *The boy's mysterious disappearance has caused angst and guilt for the family.*

anguish /ˈæŋ·gwɪʃ/ *n* [U] extreme pain or suffering ○ *Somehow we deal with the anguish of serious illness.*

anguished /ˈæŋ·gwɪʃt/ *adj* ○ *The anguished song at the end was beautiful.*

angular /ˈæŋ·gjə·lər/ *adj* thin and bony ○ *She was tall and angular.*

anhydrous /ænˈhɑɪ·drəs/ *adj* [not gradable] ***chemistry*** containing no water

animal **LIVING THING** /ˈæn·ə·məl/ *n* [C] **1** a living thing that can move and eat and react to the world through its SENSES, esp. of sight and hearing ○ *Mammals, insects, reptiles, and birds are all animals.* **2** In ordinary use, animal means all living beings except humans: *A lion is a wild animal, and a dog is a domestic animal.* ○ *Tests of the drug were done on laboratory animals.* **3** An animal is also a person who likes something or does something more than most people do: *a party animal* ○ *He's the most political animal on the city council.*

GROUP /ˈæn·ᵊ·məl/ *n* [U] ***biology*** one of five KINGDOMS (= groups) into which living things are divided, the members of which have many cells, the ability to control their own movement, and get their energy from eating rather than from the light of the sun

PHYSICAL /ˈæn·ə·məl/ *adj* [not gradable] relating to physical needs or desires, such as to eat or reproduce ○ *Animal instincts apply to all animals, including humans.*

animal rights *pl n* the idea that animals should not be treated cruelly by people

animate /ˈæn·əˌmeɪt/ *v* [T] to cause someone or something to be more active or full of life ○ *He knows exactly what to say to animate a crowd.*

animated /ˈæn·əˌmeɪt̬·əd/ *adj* **1** full of interest and energy ○ *We had a very animated discussion.* **2** An animated movie or CARTOON, is made up of a series of slightly different drawings of people, animals, and objects that make them appear to move.

animation /ˌæn·əˈmeɪ·ʃən/ *n* [U] **1** energy and enthusiasm ○ *Her voice was full of animation.* **2** Animation is also the process by which an ANIMATED movie, esp. a CARTOON, is made from drawings done by hand or by a computer.

animosity /ˌæn·əˈmɑs·ət̬·i/ *n* [C/U] a strong dislike or unfriendly feeling ○ [C/U] *I have no animosity toward him whatsoever.*

ankle /ˈæŋ·kəl/ *n* [C] the joint connecting the foot to the leg, or the thin part of the leg just above the foot

anklet /ˈæŋ·klət/ *n* [C] a short sock that reaches to the ANKLE

annals /ˈæn·ᵊlz/ *pl n* the record of an activity or organization, arranged year by year, or a history that covers a long period of time ○ *This period was one of the darkest in the annals of US history.*

annex **TAKE** /əˈneks, ˈæn·eks/ *v* [T] to take possession of an area of land or a country and add it to a larger area, usually by force ○ *The United States annexed parts of Texas and New Mexico, which belonged to Mexico.*

annexation /ˌænˌekˈseɪ·ʃən, ˌæn·ək-/ *n* [C/U] ○ [U] *the annexation of Latvia by the Soviet Union*

ADDED BUILDING /ˈæn·eks, -ɪks/ *n* [C] an addition to a building, or another building, used with an existing building ○ *The old warehouse became an annex of the main store.*

annihilate /əˈnɑɪ·əˌleɪt/ *v* [T] to destroy completely, leaving nothing ○ *The approaching tornado was annihilating everything in its path.*

annihilation /əˌnɑɪ·əˈleɪ·ʃən/ *n* [U] ○ *The annihilation of smallpox is a triumph of medicine.*

anniversary /ˌæn·əˈvɜr·sə·ri/ *n* [C] a day in a previous year on which something important happened ○ *To celebrate our wedding anniversary, we gave a big party.*

annotate /ˈæn·əˌteɪt/ *v* [T] ***writing*** **1** to add notes or remarks on a piece of writing **2** An **annotated bibliography** is a list of books or articles with notes giving additional information about each item.

announce /əˈnɑʊns/ *v* [T] to state officially or make known publicly ○ *She announced her resignation last Monday.*

announcement /əˈnɑʊn·smənt/ *n* [C] ○ *Wedding announcements were mailed a week after their marriage.*

announcer /əˈnɑʊn·sər/ *n* [C] someone who speaks on radio or television broadcasts or at a sports event ○ *He was the announcer for the Mamaroneck Tigers baseball team.*

WORD FAMILY announce

Nouns	announcement announcer	*Adjectives*	unannounced
		Adverbs	unannounced
Verbs	announce		

annoy /əˈnɔɪ/ *v* [T] to make someone slightly angry or upset ○ *I know you're doing this only to annoy me.*

annoyed /əˈnɔɪd/ *adj* ○ *He gave me an annoyed look and left without speaking.*

annoying /əˈnɔɪ·ɪŋ/ *adj* ○ *It's annoying to have to explain this a second time.*

annoyingly /əˈnɔɪ·ɪŋ·li/ *adv* ○ *Ads annoyingly interrupted the TV movie.*

annoyance /əˈnɔɪ·əns/ *n* [C/U] ○ [U] *As soon as he saw me, a look of annoyance crossed his face.*

➤ Learner error: **embarrassing or annoying?** at EMBARRASS

WORD CHOICES annoy

See also: **angry**

Irritate or **peeve** are alternatives to "annoy."

After a while her behavior really began to ***irritate*** *me.*

What ***peeved*** *her most was that he hadn't even called her.*

Bug or **aggravate** are informal ways of saying "annoy."

He's been ***bugging*** *me all morning.*

It really ***aggravates*** *me the way he never thanks me for what I've done.*

A more formal way of saying "annoy" would be to use the verb **irk**.

The negative reply to my complaint really ***irked*** *me.*

If something annoys you, especially because you can do nothing to change a situation, you could use the verb **exasperate**.

Being dependent on other people ***exasperated*** *her.*

If noise or behavior annoys you, you could say that it **grates on** you.

After a while, her voice really started to ***grate on*** *me.*

annual Ⓐ **ONE YEAR** /ˈæn·jə·wəl/ *adj* [not gradable] of or for a period of one year ○ *an annual salary* ○ *annual rainfall* ○ *Our annual costs have risen steadily.*

annual /ˈæn·jə·wəl/ *n* [C] a publication appearing once a year ○ *the "Sports Illustrated" college football annual*

annualized /ˈæn·jə·wəˌlɑɪzd/ *adj* [not gradable] calculated to represent one year, rather than some shorter or longer period ○ *The fund has returned an annualized 16% over ten years, five percentage points better than the S&P 500.*

PLANT /ˈæn·jə·wəl/ *n* [C] a plant that grows, produces seeds, and dies within one year ○ Compare BIENNIAL; PERENNIAL **PLANT**

annually /ˈæn·jə·wə·li, ˈæn·jə·li/ *adv* every year ○ *The hospital spends $1.1 million annually for its computer operations.*

annuity /əˈnuː·ət̬·i/ *n* [C] an amount of money paid to someone every year, usually until that person's death, or the INSURANCE agreement or investment that provides money that is paid this way ○ *A small annuity lets her travel.*

annul /əˈnʌl/ *v* [T] **-ll-** *law* to announce officially a law, marriage, or other contract as no longer existing ○ *The contract was finally annulled.*

annulment /əˈnʌl·mənt/ *n* [C] *law* ○ *You will need a court hearing to get an annulment.*

anode /ˈænˌoʊd/ *n* [C] ***chemistry, physics*** one of the ELECTRODES (= object that electricity moves through) in a piece of electrical equipment; the negative electrode in a BATTERY **ELECTRICAL DEVICE** and the positive electrode in most other electrical devices

anoint /əˈnɔɪnt/ *v* [T] **1** to put water or oil on someone in a religious ceremony ○ *The archbishop was anointed in a ceremony at the cathedral.* **2** Anoint also means to choose someone or something for a particular job or purpose; DESIGNATE: *He anointed his eldest son as his successor.* ○ *They anointed broadband as the Next Great Thing.*

anomaly /əˈnɑm·ə·li/ *n* [C] something that is unusual enough to be noticeable or seem strange ○ *The government does computer checks of tax returns to find anomalies that might indicate fraud.*

Anon. *n abbreviation for* ANONYMOUS (= a writer whose name is not known)

anonymity /ˌæn·əˈnɪm·ət̬·i/ a situation in which a person is not known by or spoken of by name ○ *For witnesses who may be afraid to speak out, the police have guaranteed anonymity.*

anonymous /əˈnɑn·ə·məs/ *adj* [not gradable] (made or done by someone) with a name that is not known or not made public ○ *an anonymous donor* ○ *an anonymous gift*

A

anonymously /əˈnɑn·ə·mə·sli/ *adv* ○ *The donation was made anonymously.*

anorexia (nervosa) /ˌæn·əˈrek·siː·ə (nɜr ˈvoʊ·sə)/ *n* [U] *medical* an illness often resulting in dangerous weight loss, in which a person, usually a girl or woman, refuses to eat enough over a long period of time ○ Compare BULIMIA (NERVOSA)
anorexic /ˌæn·əˈrek·sɪk/ *adj*

another **ADDITIONAL** /əˈnʌð·ər, æ-/ *adj, pronoun* one more (person or thing) or an additional (amount) ○ *We have two tickets and need another (one).* ○ *Summer will be here in another three months* (= three months in the future). ○ *We have room in the car for another if we all sit close together.*

> **USAGE**
> **another** or **other**?
> **Another** means "one other" and is used with a noun in the singular. Make sure that you write it as one word, not two words.
> *Would you like another cup of coffee?*
> ~~*Would you like other cup of coffee?*~~
> ~~*Would you like an other cup of coffee?*~~
> **Other** is used with a noun in the plural and means different things or people from the ones you are talking about.
> *She had other ambitions.*
> ~~*She had another ambitions.*~~

DIFFERENT /əˈnʌð·ər, æ-/ *adj, pronoun* a different (person or thing) ○ *Do you want to exchange this dress for another (one), or do you want your money back?* ○ *It's raining today, so we'll have to have the picnic another day.*

answer **REACTION** /ˈæn·sər/ *n* [C] **1** something said or written in reaction to a question or statement ○ *If you are asking me if I want to go into business with you, the answer is no.* ○ *I called several times, but there was no answer.* **2** An answer is also a reaction to a question asked as part of a test: *I think I got most of the answers right on the exam.*
answer /ˈæn·sər/ *v* [I/T] ○ [I] *I knocked on your door last night, but no one answered.* ○ *"I don't know," he answered.* ○ [+ *that* clause] *She answered that she couldn't arrive before nine o'clock.* ○ [T] *She refused to answer questions on whether she would run for the Senate.*

SOLUTION /ˈæn·sər/ *n* [C] a solution to a problem ○ *There is no easy answer to the problem.*

PHRASAL VERBS with answer

• **answer for** *something* to be responsible for having done something bad ○ *Companies that turn a blind eye to this practice will have a lot to answer for.*
• **answer to** *someone* to take orders from and explain your actions to someone ○ *The great thing about having your own business is that you don't have to answer to anyone.*

answering machine *n* [C] a device connected to a telephone that answers the telephone automatically and records messages

ant /ænt/ *n* [C] a small insect that lives in large and highly organized social groups

antacid /æntˈæs·əd/ *n* [C/U] a medicine you can take to reduce or prevent the uncomfortable feeling of having too much acid in the stomach

antagonism /ænˈtæg·əˌnɪz·əm/ *n* [C/U] strong dislike or opposition, or a particular example of it ○ [U] *The attorney accused the witness of antagonism toward his client.*
antagonist /ænˈtæg·ə·nəst/ *n* [C] a person who opposes or disagrees with another
antagonistic /ænˌtæg·əˈnɪs·tɪk/ *adj* expressing strong dislike or opposition ○ *He's extremely antagonistic toward critics.* ○ *You can be clear about what you need without being antagonistic.*

antagonize /ænˈtæg·əˌnɑɪz/ *v* [T] to anger someone enough to dislike and oppose you ○ *The company doesn't want to antagonize one of its biggest oil suppliers.*

Antarctic /æntˈɑrk·tɪk, -ˈɑrṭ·ɪk/ *n* [U] the very cold area around the South Pole that includes Antarctica and the surrounding seas ○ Compare ARCTIC

ante /ˈænt·i/ *n* [C usually sing] an amount of money that each person must risk in order to be part of a game, or the price of something

IDIOM with ante

• **up the ante**, **raise the ante** to increase your risks or demands in order to get a greater advantage ○ *The governor upped the ante in her war of words with the mayor, by calling him "dangerous" for the city.*

PHRASAL VERB with ante

• **ante up** *something infml* to give money in order to join or be part of something ○ *The new teams each had to ante up a huge entry fee to the major leagues.*

antecedent /ˌænt·əˈsiːd·ᵊnt/ *n* [C usually pl] **1** something existing or happening before, esp. as the cause of an event or situation ○ *The book dealt with the historical antecedents of the Civil War.* **2** ***grammar*** An antecedent is also a word or phrase that a pronoun refers to: *In the sentence, "Joe threw the ball to Wendy, and Wendy threw it back," "the ball" is the antecedent of "it."* **3** ***mathematics*** An antecedant is also the part of a CONDITIONAL statement that follows the word "if."

antelope /ˈænt·ᵊlˌoʊp/ *n* [C] a large animal that looks like a deer, with wide branching horns

antenna **INSECT** /ænˈten·ə/ *n* [C] *pl* **antennae** either of the two long, thin parts attached to the head of an insect that it uses to know what it around it ○ (*fig.*) *Her political antennae helped her answer questions without offending anyone.* ➤ Picture: **insect**

BROADCASTING /ænˈten·ə/ *n* [C] *pl* **antennas** a structure made of metal rods or wires, often positioned on top of a building or vehicle, that receives or sends radio or television signals

anthem /ˈæn·θəm/ *n* [C] a song that has special importance for a particular group of people or country, often sung on special occasions

anthology /æn ˈθɑl·ə·dʒi/ *n* [C] a collection of stories, poems, etc., by different writers

anthrax /ˈæn·θræks/ *n* [U] **1** a disease of cattle and sheep that humans can become ill with and die ○ *Humans can contract anthrax by handling products from infected animals.* **2** Anthrax is also the type of bacteria that causes the disease.

anthropology /ˌæn·θrəˈpɑl·ə·dʒi/ *n* [U] the study of the human race, its culture and society, and its physical development
anthropologist /ˌæn·θrəˈpɑl·ə·dʒəst/ *n* [C] a person who is an expert in anthropology
anthropological /ˌæn·θrə·pəˈlɑdʒ·ɪ·kəl/ *adj*

anti- /ˌænt·i, ˌænˌtɑɪ/ *prefix* opposed to or against ○ *antienvironmentalist* ○ Compare PRO- SUPPORT

antibiotic /ˌænt·i·bɑɪˈɑt̬·ɪk, ˌænˌtɑɪ-/ *n* [C] a medicine or chemical that can destroy harmful bacteria in the body or limit their growth ○ *I'm taking an antibiotic for a throat infection.*

antibody /ˈænt·iˌbɑd·i/ *n* [C] ***biology*** a PROTEIN (= type of chemical) produced in the blood to fight diseases by attacking and killing harmful bacteria

anticipate Ⓐ /ænˈtɪs·əˌpeɪt/ *v* [T] to imagine or expect that something will happen, sometimes taking action in preparation for it ○ *No job cuts are anticipated under the new ownership.* ○ [+ (that) clause] *I don't anticipate (that) we'll solve all our problems with one meeting.* ○ *We anticipate criticism but plan to go ahead anyway.* ○ [+ question word] *At this stage we can't anticipate what will happen.*
anticipation Ⓐ /ænˌtɪs·əˈpeɪ·ʃən/ *n* [U] **1** *A number of industrial companies are raising prices in anticipation of future inflation.* **2** Anticipation is also a feeling of excitement about something that is going to happen in the near future: *Skiers look forward to the first snow of winter with eager anticipation.*

anticlimactic /ˌænt·i·klɑɪˈmæk·tɪk, ˌænˌtɑɪ-/ *adj* [not gradable] causing unhappiness by being less exciting than expected or not as interesting as something that happened earlier ○ *The announcement of his resignation was anticlimactic, as we all knew he could no longer stay in the job.*

anticline /ˈænt·ɪˌklɑɪn/ *n* [C] ***earth science*** a fold in layers of rock in the earth's surface which curves up ○ Compare SYNCLINE

antics /ˈænt·ɪks/ *pl n* amusing, silly, or strange behavior ○ *The antics of the clowns amused the children.*

antidepressant /ˌænt·i·dɪˈpres·ənt, ˌænˌtɑɪ-/ *n* [C] a type of medicine that is used to reduce feelings of being unhappy and without hope

antidote /ˈænt·ɪˌdoʊt/ *n* [C] **1** a chemical, esp. a drug, that acts against the bad effects of a poison to limit the harm it can do ○ *an antidote for snake venom* **2** *fig.* An antidote is also a way of preventing or acting against something bad: *Exercise can be an antidote to depression.*

antifreeze /ˈænt·iˌfriːz/ *n* [U] a liquid that reduces the temperature at which water freezes, and that is added to the water in car engines in winter to keep it from freezing

antigen /ˈænt·ə·dʒən, -ˌdʒen/ *n* [C] ***biology*** a harmful substance that causes the body to produce ANTIBODIES (= substances that fight disease)

antihistamine /ˌænt·iˈhɪs·təˌmiːn, ˌænˌtɑɪ-, -mən/ *n* [C] a drug taken to limit the bad effect of the body's reaction to some substances ○ *I took an antihistamine for my runny nose.*

antilepton /ˈænt·əlˌepˌtɑn, ˈæn·tɑɪˌlepˌtɑn/ *n* [C] ***physics*** the ANTIPARTICLE of a LEPTON

antimatter /ˈænt·iˌmæt̬·ər, ˈæn·tɑɪ-/ *n* [U] ***physics*** matter that consists of PARTICLES (= small parts of atoms) that have the opposite electrical characteristics of the particles in regular matter

antineutrino /ˌænt·i·nuːˈtriː·noʊ, ˌænˌtɑɪ-/ *n* [C] ***physics*** the ANTIPARTICLE of a NEUTRINO

antinode /ˈænt·iˌnoʊd, ˈæn·tɑɪ-/ *n* [C] ***physics*** the point that represents the highest AMPLITUDE in a pattern of CONSTRUCTIVE INTERFERENCE

antioxidant /ˌænt·iːˈɑks·əd·ənt, ˌænˌtɑɪ-/ *n* [C] a chemical substance that prevents or slows down the damage that oxygen does to organisms or to food ○ *Vitamin C's antioxidant activity may help boost immune function and may make some people feel better.* ○ *She takes the vitamins, minerals, antioxidants, and folic acid in women's multivitamins.*

antiparticle /ˈænt·iˌpɑrt̬·ɪ·kəl, ˈæn·tɑɪ-/ *n* [C] ***physics*** a PARTICLE that makes up ANTIMATTER, containing the same amount of matter but having the opposite electrical CHARGE STORE ENERGY that a regular particle has

antipathy /ænˈtɪp·ə·θi/ *n* [U] strong dislike or opposition ○ *His letters show a deep and intense antipathy toward workers.*

antiperspirant /ˌænt·iˈpɜr·spə·rənt, ˌænˌtɑɪ-/ *n* [C] a substance that is put on the skin, esp. under the arms, in order to prevent or reduce PERSPIRATION (= the excretion of liquid through the skin)

antiproton /ˌænt·i·ˈproʊˌtɑn, ˌænˌtɑɪ-/ *n* [C] ***physics*** the ANTIPARTICLE of a PROTON

antiquark /ˈænt·iˌkwɑrk, ˈænˌtɑɪ-/ *n* [C] ***physics*** the ANTIPARTICLE of a QUARK

antiquated /ˈænt·ɪˌkweɪt̬·əd/ *adj* old-fashioned or unsuitable for modern society ○ *antiquated ideas/technology*

antique /ænˈtiːk/ *n* [C] something made in an earlier period and valued because it is old, rare, or of high quality ○ *He sold antiques for a while.*
antique /ænˈtiːk/ *adj* ○ *an antique dealer/show*

antiquity /ænˈtɪk·wət̬·i/ *n* [C/U] the past, esp. before the MIDDLE AGES (= before the sixth century), or something of great age ○ [C] *We spent some time in the museum looking at Roman antiquities.*

anti-Semitism /ˌænt·iˈsem·əˌtɪz·əm, ˌænˌtɑɪ-/ *n* [U] hate or strong dislike of Jews, or actions that express hate or dislike of Jews ○ *Nazi anti-Semitism forced him to emigrate from Germany.*
anti-Semitic /ˌænt·i·səˈmɪt̬·ɪk, ˌænˌtɑɪ-/ *adj* ○ *anti-Semitic literature*
anti-Semite /ˌænt·iˈsemˌɑɪt, ˌænˌtɑɪ-/ *n* [C] a person who hates or strongly dislikes Jews ○ *He denied that he was an anti-Semite.*

antiseptic /ˌænt·ɪˈsep·tɪk/ *n* [C] a chemical used to prevent infection from an injury, esp. by killing bacteria
antiseptic /ˌænt·ɪˈsep·tɪk/ *adj* ○ *an antiseptic ointment*

antisocial /ˌænt·iˈsoʊ·ʃəl, ˌænˌtɑɪ-/ *adj* **1** harmful to society ○ *Some critics argued that movies caused antisocial behavior.* **2** Antisocial also means not wanting to spend time with or be friendly with other people: *If you don't hang out with your friends, they'll consider you weird and antisocial.*

antithesis /ænˈtɪθ·ə·səs/ *n* [C/U] *pl* **antitheses** **1** the exact opposite, or opposition ○ [C] *The relaxed company management is the antithesis of a formal bureaucracy.* **2** ***literature*** In formal argument, the antithesis is the opposite of the THESIS (= the main idea). ○ Compare THESIS

antitrust /ˌænt·iːˈtrʌst, ˌænˌtɑɪ-/ *adj* [not gradable] involving laws or actions that are intended to make business competition fair and to prevent any company from being a MONOPOLY ○ *The government is expanding its antitrust investigation against Microsoft.*

antiwar, **anti-war** /ˈænt·iːˈwɔːr, ˈænˌtɑɪ-/ *adj* opposed to a particular war, or opposed to all wars ○ *the/an antiwar movement*

antlers /ˈænt·lərz/ *pl n* the pair of horns that grow from the head of the male of some animals, such as deer, and that look like branches

antonym /ˈænt·əˌnɪm/ *n* [C] ***grammar*** a word or phrase whose meaning is the opposite of another word or phrase ○ Compare SYNONYM

antsy /ˈænt·si/ *adj slang* anxious and excited in an unpleasant way; extremely nervous ○ *I'm as antsy as I was before my first class.*

anus /ˈeɪ·nəs/ *n* [C] the opening at the end of the INTESTINES (= tube in the body in which food is digested) through which solid excrement leaves the body
anal /ˈeɪn·əl/ *adj* [not gradable]

anxiety /æŋˈzɑɪ·ət̬·i/ *n* [C/U] an uncomfortable feeling of worry about something that is happening or might happen, or a cause of this ○ [U] *For many children, every new school year causes anxiety.* ○ [C] *Don't you have any fears or anxieties about middle age?*
anxious /ˈæŋ·ʃəs/ *adj* ○ *They exchanged anxious glances in the doctor's office.*
anxiously /ˈæŋ·ʃə·sli/ *adv* ○ *We waited anxiously by the phone.*

anxious /ˈæŋ·ʃəs/ *adj* wanting very much for something to happen; eager ○ [+ *to* infinitive] *I've been anxious to meet you.* ○ [+ *to* infinitive] *It was getting late, and I was anxious to get home.*

any SOME /ˈen·i/ *adj, pronoun* (used in negative statements and questions) some, or even the smallest amount (of) ○ *We didn't have any idea what the airfare would be.* ○ *There was hardly any snow this winter.* ○ *Is there any hope that he will recover?* ○ *Are any of the concerts on a Saturday night?* ➤ Usage: **some or any?** at SOME UNKNOWN AMOUNT

NOT IMPORTANT WHICH /ˈen·i/ *adj, pronoun* one of or each of, or a stated amount of (something that is more than one or has a number of parts), without saying which particular part is meant ○ *You can have any three items of clothing you like for $30.* ○ *Any advice that you can give me would be greatly appreciated.* ○ *They should be here any minute* (= soon). ○ *Any way you look at it, the investment was a bad idea.* ○ *I saw some beautiful cars at the auto show, any of which I'd like to have.*

AT ALL /ˈen·i/ *adv* [not gradable] at all or in the least ○ *I can't say any more.* ○ *He wasn't any smarter than I was.* ○ *If she comes any later, we'll miss the show.*

IDIOMS with any

• **at any rate** more exactly or clearly ○ *I don't think they liked my idea – at any rate, they weren't very enthusiastic.* ○ Compare AT LEAST at LEAST IDIOMS ○ **USAGE:** Used to make a statement that is obviously true after making a statement that shows uncertainty.

• **in any case** whatever happens or happened ○ *You should be able to catch a bus, but in any case you can always take a taxi home.* ○ **USAGE:** Used to say that although some facts in a situation may change, one thing does not change.

anybody /ˈen·iːˌbɑd·i, -bəd·i/ *pronoun* ANYONE ○ *Does anybody have change for a $10 bill?*

anyhow /ˈen·iːˌhɑʊ/ *adv* [not gradable] *infml* ANYWAY ○ *Anyhow, I didn't ask you to come here to talk about your business.*

anymore /ˌen·iːˈmɔːr, -ˈmoʊr/, **any more** *adv* [not gradable] **1** (used esp. in negative statements) any longer ○ *I don't know who to trust anymore.* ○ *She doesn't work here anymore.* **2** Anymore also means now or from now on, often even in positive statements: *We never go out – all we do anymore is watch TV.* ○ *I'm scared to be alone anymore.*

anyone /ˈen·iː·wən, -ˌwʌn/, **anybody** /ˈen·iːˌbɑd·i, -bəd·i/ *pronoun* any person whatever, or (esp. in negative statements and questions) a person, but without saying which person ○ *Hello, is anyone home?* ○ *If anyone calls, tell them I'm out of the office.* ○ *We didn't know anyone when we first moved here, but now we have lots of friends.* ○ *I can't think of anyone with more imagination than Maggie.*

anyplace /ˈen·iːˌpleɪs/ *adv* [not gradable] ANYWHERE ○ *There wasn't anyplace to pull off the road if your car broke down.*

anything /ˈen·iː ˌθɪŋ/ *pronoun* any event, act, or object whatever, or (esp. in negative statements or questions) something ○ *Is there anything I can do to help?* ○ *I didn't know anything about computers till I started this job.* ○ *I don't want to say anything to upset her.* ○ (*infml*) *It was a fantastic party – I wouldn't have missed it for anything* (= for any reason).

IDIOMS with anything

• **anything but** not at all or not in any way ○ *She was anything but friendly the last time I saw her.*
• **anything like** similar to ○ *The pictures on cereal boxes don't look anything like the actual stuff you eat.* ○ **USAGE**: Used in questions and negative sentences.

anytime /ˈen·iː ˌtɑɪm/ *adv* [not gradable] at any time or at a time, but without saying which time ○ *Come to see me anytime.* ○ *I'm not planning on leaving anytime soon.* ○ *Joe and his family ought to be here anytime now* (= soon).

anyway /ˈen·iː ˌweɪ/, *infml* **anyhow** *adv* [not gradable] **1** not considering other facts or conditions; considered independently, without being influenced by other things ○ *Of course I don't mind taking you home – I'm going that way anyway.* ○ *The economy was slowing down anyway, so there was no need to worry about inflation.* **2** In conversation, anyway is often used to support or explain a previous statement: *So, you're right, there are very few black quarterbacks in football, or at least that are starting anyway.* **3** In conversation, anyway is often used to change the subject, return to an earlier subject, or get to the most interesting point, and is also used to take up time so that you can decide what to say next: *So anyway, what are you going to do tonight?* ○ *Anyway, in the end we just agreed to stop seeing each other.*

anywhere /ˈen·iː ˌwer, -ˌwær/, **anyplace** *adv* [not gradable] **1** in, to, or at any place whatever or (esp. in negative statements and questions) a place, but without saying which place ○ *I can't find my scarf anywhere.* ○ *There are plants in this desert that you won't find anywhere else.* ○ *There are no reserved seats – just sit anywhere you like.* **2** Anywhere also means within the range of or approximately: *The turkey can weigh anywhere from ten to twenty pounds.*

aorta /eɪˈɔːrt̬·ə/ *n* [C] ***biology*** the main ARTERY (= large tube carrying blood from the heart) which takes blood to the other parts of the body

AP *n* [U] *trademark, abbreviation for* Advanced Placement (= a program for HIGH SCHOOL students offering courses that are equal to college courses) ○ *Students' decisions to either take or avoid AP courses have fundamental effects on their college attendance.*

apart /əˈpɑrt/ *adv* **1** separated by a distance ○ *Stand with your feet wide apart and bend from the waist.* ○ *How far apart should I put my stereo speakers?* ○ *We both travel a lot, but when we're apart we keep in touch by phone.* ○ (*fig.*) *The strike continued, and both sides remained very far apart.* **2** (esp. of a machine) Apart can also mean separated into its parts: *He had to take the hot-water pump apart to repair it.* **3** Apart can also mean separated in time: *Our two kids were born just eighteen months apart.*

IDIOM with apart

• **apart from** except for ○ *Apart from the low salary, it's not a bad job.*

apartheid /əˈpɑr ˌtɑɪt, -ˌteɪt/ *n* [U] (in the past) a political system in South Africa that legally separated people of different races

apartment /əˈpɑrt·mənt/, *abbreviation* **apt.**, *esp. Br* **flat** *n* [C] **1** a set of rooms for living in that includes a kitchen and a bathroom ○ *They lived in a six-room apartment on the eighth floor.* **2** An apartment is also an APARTMENT BUILDING.

apartment building, **apartment house** *n* [C] a building containing apartments

apathy /ˈæp·ə·θi/ *n* [U] lack of interest, or the attitude of not caring resulting from it ○ *There is a growing sense of apathy among teens and a feeling that there are no opportunities, he said.*
apathetic /ˌæp·əˈθet̬·ɪk/ *adj* ○ *apathetic voters*

ape **ANIMAL** /eɪp/ *n* [C] a mammal that has long arms and no tail or a short tail and that is related to monkeys ○ *Chimpanzees, gorillas, and orangutans are all apes.*

COPY /eɪp/ *v* [T] *often disapproving* to copy something or someone ○ *Because of snob appeal, high-priced American clothing stores ape British usage and call suspenders "braces."*

aperture /ˈæp·ər ˌtʃʊr, -tʃər/ *n* [C] a small and often narrow opening, esp. one that allows light into a camera

apex /ˈeɪ·peks/ *n* [C usually sing] the highest point or top of something ○ *the apex of a pyramid* ○ *He reached the apex of his career during that period.*

aphorism /ˈæf·əˌrɪz·əm/ *n* [C] a short saying that is intended to express a general truth

apiece /əˈpiːs/ *adv* [not gradable] each ○ *In good condition, dolls from this period sell for $500 apiece.*

apocalypse /əˈpɑk·əˌlɪps/ *n* [U] **1** an event resulting in great destruction and violent change **2** In the Bible, the Apocalypse is the total destruction of the world.

apolitical /ˌeɪ·pəˈlɪt̬·ɪ·kəl/ *adj* not interested in or connected with politics ○ *The appointment of judges, they said, should be apolitical.*

apologetic /əˌpɑl·əˈdʒet̬·ɪk/ *adj* expressing regret about having caused someone inconvenience or unhappiness ○ *He was apologetic for not returning my call.*
apologetically /əˌpɑl·əˈdʒet̬·ɪ·kli/ *adv*

apologize /əˈpɑl·əˌdʒɑɪz/ *v* [I] to tell someone that you are sorry for something that has caused inconvenience or unhappiness ○ *She apologized for her husband's rudeness.* ○ *If I offended you, I apologize.* ○ *He said he had nothing to apologize for.*

apology /ə'pɑl·ə·dʒi/ *n* [C] an act of saying that you are sorry ○ *I have an apology to make to you – I opened your letter by mistake.* ○ *He owes me an apology* (= He should say he is sorry). ○ *My apologies* (= I am sorry) *for not writing you sooner.*

apostle /ə'pɑs·əl/ *n* [C] any of the twelve men whom Jesus Christ chose to teach other people about Christianity, or someone who strongly supports a particular belief or political movement

apostrophe /ə'pɑs·trə·fi/ *n* [C] ***grammar*** a mark (') used in writing to show that a letter or a number has been omitted, or before or after s to show possession

appall /ə'pɔːl/ *v* [T] to cause someone to be extremely upset or shocked ○ *I was appalled by the condition of our facilities, especially the dirty locker room.*

appalling /ə'pɔː·lɪŋ/ *adj* ○ *I was dismayed by the President's appalling economic record.*

apparatus EQUIPMENT /ˌæp·ə'ræt̬·əs, -'reɪt̬-/ *n* [C/U] *pl* **apparatuses, apparatus** a set of equipment, tools, or a machine that is used for a particular purpose ○ [C] *The garage had an apparatus to lift cars up.*

SYSTEM /ˌæp·ə'ræt̬·əs, -'reɪt̬-/ *n* [C] *pl* **apparatuses, apparatus** a system or organization ○ *Technology has moved so fast, the old regulatory apparatus can't be made to apply to the Internet.*

apparel /ə'pær·əl/ *n* [U] clothes, esp. of a special type ○ *children's/women's apparel* ○ *riding/sports apparel*

apparent Ⓐ /ə'pær·ənt, -'per-/ *adj* **1** able to be seen or understood ○ [+ *that* clause] *It was becoming increasingly apparent that he could no longer look after himself.* **2** Apparent also means seeming to be true: *The apparent cause of death was drowning, but further tests were needed.*

apparently Ⓐ /ə'pær·ənt·li, -'per-/ *adv* according to what seems to be true or what is likely, based on what you know ○ *The computer trouble was apparently caused by a programming error.*

apparition /ˌæp·ə'rɪʃ·ən/ *n* [C] something you believe, imagine, or dream you see, esp. the form of a person; GHOST

appeal ATTRACT /ə'piːl/ *v* [I] to be interesting or attractive ○ *Such music managed to appeal to the tastes of both young and old.*

appeal /ə'piːl/ *n* [U] ○ *Eating out has lost much of its appeal.*

appealing /ə'piː·lɪŋ/ *adj* ○ *The package describing European tours certainly made them seem appealing.*

ARGUE /ə'piːl/ *v* [I/T] to request formally that a decision, esp. a legal or official one, be changed ○ [T] *The verdict was appealed to a higher court.*

appeal /ə'piːl/ *n* [C/U] ○ [U] *The decision was reversed on appeal.*

REQUEST /ə'piːl/ *v* [I] to make a serious or formal request for help, esp. in an emergency ○ *Blood supplies are running low, and the Red Cross is appealing for blood donations.*

appeal /ə'piːl/ *n* [C] ○ *Many charities issued an appeal for contributions to help victims of the earthquake.*

appear BE PRESENT /ə'pɪr/ *v* [I] **1** to become noticeable or to be present ○ *At this point the ferry boat suddenly appeared.* ○ *Her picture appeared on the front page of the newspaper.* ○ *We have to appear in court next week.* **2** To appear is also to be made available: *The interview with the president will appear next Sunday.*

appearance /ə'pɪr·əns/ *n* [C] ○ *It was his first television appearance.*

SEEM /ə'pɪr/ *v* to seem ○ [L] *The governor appeared confident of victory on the eve of the election.* ○ [+ (*that*) clause] *It appears (that) she had asked someone to drive her home from the party.* ○ [+ *to* infinitive] *There appears to be some mistake.*

appearance /ə'pɪr·əns/ *n* [U] the way a person or thing looks or seems to other people ○ *The most striking feature of his appearance was his long hair.*

appearances /ə'pɪr·ən·səz/ *pl n* what things look like or seem to be rather than what they actually are ○ *He was a far more complicated man than outward appearances suggested.*

PERFORM /ə'pɪr/ *v* [I always + adv/prep] to perform publicly in a play, movie, dance, or other similar event ○ *He is currently appearing in two movies.*

appearance /ə'pɪr·əns/ *n* [C] ○ *Her only screen appearances were in two made-for-television movies.*

WORD FAMILY appear

Nouns	appearance disappearance	*Verbs*	appear disappear

IDIOM with appear

• **put in/make an appearance** to go to an event, but only for a short time because you do not really want to be there ○ *I felt like I had to put in an appearance at the staff party, but I only stayed for an hour.*

appease /ə'piːz/ *v* [T] (in arguments or war) to prevent further disagreement by giving to the other side something that they have demanded ○ *They questioned whether, in his desire to appease the conservatives in his own party, the president was selling out to them.*

appeasement /ə'piːz·mənt/ *n* [U] **1** the action of satisfying the demands an AGGRESSIVE person, country, or organization ○ *a policy of appeasement* **2** ***world history*** Appeasement was also a policy used in the 1930s by England and France in response to Germany's military attempts to take more land.

appelate jurisdiction *n* [U] ***social studies*** the right of a court to change the decisions of a lower court ○ Compare ORIGINAL JURISDICTION

appellate /ə'pel·ət/ *adj* [not gradable] involving an attempt to get a legal decision changed ○

The mistrial ruling was upheld in 2007 by a state appellate court.

append Ⓐ /əˈpend/ *v* [T] *fml* to add something to the end of a piece of writing ○ *Several footnotes were appended to the text.*

appendage /əˈpen·dɪdʒ/ *n* [C] a smaller or less important part that is attached to something ○ *The organism has small, leaflike appendages.*

appendicitis /əˌpen·dəˈsɑɪt̬·əs/ *n* [U] a painful and serious infection of the APPENDIX, which often results in the appendix being removed by an operation

appendix Ⓐ **BOOK PART** /əˈpen·dɪks/ *n* [C] *pl* **appendices, appendixes** ***writing*** a separate part at the end of a book or report that gives additional information ○ *The appendix lists all the Olympic champions.*

BODY PART /əˈpen·dɪks/ *n* [C] *pl* **appendixes, appendices** a small, curved part attached to the INTESTINES (= tube in the body in which food is digested) which has no known use

appetite /ˈæp·əˌtɑɪt/ *n* [C] a desire or need for something, esp. food ○ *a good/healthy appetite* ○ *an appetite for adventure*

appetizing /ˈæp·əˌtɑɪ·zɪŋ/ *adj* interesting or attractive, esp. because you think it will be good to eat ○ *an appetizing dessert*

appetizer /ˈæp·əˌtɑɪ·zər/ *n* [C] a small amount of food eaten before a meal or as the first part of it

applaud **CLAP** /əˈplɔːd/ *v* [I/T] to show your enjoyment or approval of something such as a performance by clapping your hands repeatedly

PRAISE /əˈplɔːd/ *v* [T] to say that you admire and agree with a person's action or decision ○ *We applaud the family's decision to protect their privacy.*

applause /əˈplɔːz/ *n* [U] the action or sound made by a number of people clapping their hands repeatedly to show their enjoyment or approval, esp. of a performance or speech

apple /ˈæp·əl/ *n* [C/U] a round, edible fruit having a red, green, or yellow skin, or the tree on which it grows

applesauce /ˈæp·əlˌsɔːs/ *n* [U] a sweet food made from cooked apples

appliance /əˈplɑɪ·əns/ *n* [C] a device, machine, or piece of equipment, esp. an electrical one that is used in the home, such as a REFRIGERATOR or washing machine ○ *electrical/home/household/kitchen appliances*

apply **REQUEST** /əˈplɑɪ/ *v* [I] to request something, usually officially, esp. by writing or by sending in a form ○ *to apply for a job/loan* ○ *She applied for admission to law school.*

application /ˌæp·ləˈkeɪ·ʃən/ *n* [C/U] ○ [U] *a letter of application* ○ [C] *I've sent off applications for four different jobs.*

applicant /ˈæp·lɪ·kənt/ *n* [C] a person who formally requests something, such as a job or admission to a college or university

HAVE TO DO WITH /əˈplɑɪ/ *v* [I] (esp. of rules or laws) to have to do with someone or something; relate ○ *The same rules apply to everybody.*

applicable /ˈæp·lɪ·kə·bəl, əˈplɪk·ə-/ *adj* ○ *This law is only applicable to nonprofit organizations.*

PUT ON /əˈplɑɪ/ *v* [T] to spread or rub cream, paint, etc., on a surface ○ *She applied the lotion gently to her sunburned arms.*

application /ˌæp·ləˈkeɪ·ʃən/ *n* [C] ○ *Allow two hours between applications of the paint to let it dry.*

USE /əˈplɑɪ/ *v* [T] **1** to make use of something for a particular purpose ○ *As a translator, he was able to apply his knowledge of foreign languages.* ○ *The driver failed to apply his brakes in time.* **2** If you apply yourself to something, you work hard at it.

applied /əˈplɑɪd/ *adj* (of a subject of study) having a practical use rather than being only theoretical ○ *applied mathematics*

application /ˌæp·ləˈkeɪ·ʃən/ *n* [C] **1** a particular use **2** An application is a computer program that is designed for a particular purpose.

WORD FAMILY apply

Nouns	applicant application	*Adjectives*	applicable applied
Verbs	apply		

appoint /əˈpɔɪnt/ *v* [T] to choose someone officially for a job or responsibility ○ *Commissioner Curtis was appointed by President Bush.*

appointee /əˌpɔɪnˈtiː/ *n* [C] a person who is appointed to a job or position ○ *The 39-year-old is a Commerce Department political appointee* (= someone who gets a job because of support for a political party).

appointment /əˈpɔɪnt·mənt/ *n* [C/U] ○ *There were questions about Lynch's appointment to a federal post.*

appointment /əˈpɔɪnt·mənt/ *n* [C/U] a formal arrangement to meet or visit someone at a particular time and place ○ [C] *I have a doctor's appointment tomorrow.*

IDIOM with appointment

• **by appointment** happening only when a special arrangement has been made for someone to do something or see someone ○ *Visitors can see the art collection by appointment only.*

apportion /əˈpɔːr·ʃən, -ˈpoʊr-/ *v* [T] to give or share something among several people or things ○ *How should medical care be funded and apportioned?*

appraise /əˈpreɪz/ *v* [T] **1** to judge the quality, success, or needs of someone or something ○ *Social workers appraise the needs of each family.* **2** Appraise also means to judge the worth of something: *A professional appraised my jewelry.*

appraisal /əˈpreɪ·zəl/ *n* [C/U] ○ *I was pleased with the appraisal of my work.*

appreciable Ⓐ /əˈpriː·ʃə·bəl, əˈprɪʃ·ə-/ *adj* (esp. of amounts or changes) large enough to be noticed or to have an effect ○ *My little donation will not make an appreciable difference.*

appreciably Ⓐ /ə'priː·ʃə·bli, ə'prɪʃ·ə-/ *adv*

appreciate Ⓐ **VALUE** /ə'priː·ʃiː,eɪt, ə'prɪʃ·iː-/ *v* [T] **1** to be aware of something, or to understand that something is valuable ○ [+ *that* clause] *I appreciate that this is a difficult decision for you.* **2** To appreciate something also means to be grateful for something: *I appreciated your help very much.*
appreciation Ⓐ /ə,priː·ʃiː'eɪ·ʃən, ə,prɪʃ·iː-/ *n* [U] ○ *"I'd just like a little appreciation," she sobbed.*
appreciative /ə'priː·ʃət̬·ɪv, ə'prɪʃ·ət̬-/ *adj* ○ *An appreciative audience wildly applauded the performance.*
appreciatively /ə'priː·ʃət̬·ɪv·li, ə'prɪʃ·ət̬-/ *adv* ○ *She smiled appreciatively at him.*

INCREASE /ə'priː·ʃiː,eɪt, ə'prɪʃ·iː-/ *v* [I/T] to increase in value ○ [I] *Our house appreciated by 20% in two years.*
appreciation /ə,priː·ʃiː'eɪ·ʃən, ə,prɪʃ·iː-/ *n* [U] ○ *New funds are generated by the appreciation of our assets.*

WORD FAMILY appreciate

Nouns	appreciation	*Verbs*	appreciate
Adjectives	appreciable appreciative	*Adverbs*	appreciatively

apprehend /,æp·rɪ'hend/ *v* [T] to catch and put a person under police control; to ARREST ○ *Last night police apprehended the suspect.*
apprehension /,æp·rɪ'hen·tʃən/ *n* [U] ○ *There's an $8000 reward for the apprehension of the perpetrators.*

apprehension /,æp·rɪ'hen·tʃən/ *n* [U] anxiety about the future; fear of something unpleasant happening ○ *I felt great apprehension over my first day at work.*
apprehensive /,æp·rɪ'hen·sɪv/ *adj* ○ *We're all apprehensive about tomorrow's meeting.*
apprehensively /,æp·rɪ'hen·sɪv·li/ *adv* ○ *They looked apprehensively around the room.*

apprentice /ə'prent·əs/ *n* [C] someone who works for an expert to learn a particular skill or job ○ *He worked for two years as a plumber's apprentice*
apprentice /ə'prent·əs/ *v* [I/T] ○ [I] *I apprenticed with my father, who was a stonemason.*

apprise /ə'prɑɪz/ *v* [T] *fml* to tell or inform someone about something ○ *The parents were apprised of their son's injuries.*

approach **COME NEAR** /ə'proʊtʃ/ *v* [I/T] **1** to come nearer to something or someone ○ [I] *We could see the train approaching from a distance.* **2** If you approach someone, you meet or communicate directly with that person: [T] *We approached the bank manager about a loan.*
approach /ə'proʊtʃ/ *n* [C/U] ○ [U] *The approach of winter sends many birds flying south.*
approachable /ə'proʊ·tʃə·bəl/ *adj* easy to talk to; friendly ○ *Malcolm is always very approachable – talk it over with him.*

USAGE

approach

The verb **approach** is not normally followed by a preposition.

He approached the door.
~~*He approached to the door.*~~

DEAL WITH /ə'proʊtʃ/ *v* [T] to deal with something ○ *We should approach this problem logically.*
approach /ə'proʊtʃ/ *n* [C] ○ *We need to adopt a different approach to the problem.*

approbation /,æp·rə'beɪ·ʃən/ *n* [U] *fml* approval or agreement, often given by an official group; praise ○ *Kids need their fathers' approbation.*

appropriate Ⓐ **CORRECT** /ə'proʊ·priː·ət/ *adj* correct or right for a particular situation or occasion ○ *Punishment should be appropriate to the crime.* ○ *I don't have any appropriate clothes.*
appropriately Ⓐ /ə'proʊ·priː·ət·li/ *adv* ○ *Those kids aren't appropriately dressed for the cold.*
appropriateness Ⓐ /ə'proʊ·priː·ət·nəs/ *n* [U] ○ *I wonder about the appropriateness of borrowing money from my brother.*

TAKE /ə'proʊ·priː,eɪt/ *v* [T] **1** to take and use for a purpose ○ *The state appropriated funds for more clinics.* **2** Appropriate also means to steal: *He lost his job after he appropriated some of the company's money.*
appropriation /ə,proʊ·priː'eɪ·ʃən/ *n* [C] ○ *The city council approved an appropriation of $10,000 to plant trees.*

approve **AGREE WITH** /ə'pruːv/ *v* [I] to have a good opinion of someone or something ○ *I wish my mother approved of my friends.*
approval /ə'pruː·vəl/ *n* [U] ○ *She craves the approval of her classmates.*

USAGE

approve

If you are using **approve** to say that you think something is good, then you cannot say that you "approve something." You have to say that you "approve **of** something."

~~*He doesn't approve his brother's behaviour.*~~
He doesn't approve of his brother's behavior.

PERMIT /ə'pruːv/ *v* [T] to accept or allow something officially ○ *Finally the court approved the sale of the property.*
approval /ə'pruː·vəl/ *n* [U] ○ *You'll need your parents' approval to take this field trip.*

WORD FAMILY approve

Nouns	approval disapproval	*Verbs*	approve disapprove
Adverbs	approvingly		

approximate Ⓐ /ə'prɑk·sə·mət/ *adj* almost exact ○ *Can you tell me the approximate value of this watch?*
approximate Ⓐ /ə'prɑk·sə,meɪt/ *v* [T] to come near in quality, amount, value, or character ○ *The painting only approximated the mountain landscape.*
approximately Ⓐ /ə'prɑk·sə·mət·li/ *adv* ○ *The job will take approximately three weeks to do.*

approximation Ⓐ /əˌprɑk·səˈmeɪ·ʃən/ *n* [C] ○ *I only have an approximation of the size of the room.*

WORD FAMILY approximate	
Nouns approximation	*Adjectives* approximate
Verbs approximate	*Adverbs* approximately

apricot /ˈæp·rəˌkɑt, ˈeɪ·prə-/ *n* [C] a small orange fruit

April /ˈeɪ·prəl/, *abbreviation* **Apr.** *n* [C/U] the fourth month of the year, after March and before May

April Fool's Day *n* [C usually sing] April 1, a day when people deceive others for amusement and then say, "April fool".

apron /ˈeɪ·prən/ *n* [C] a piece of clothing worn over the front of other clothes to keep them clean when doing a dirty or messy job, esp. cooking

apt CORRECT /æpt/ *adj* correct or right for a particular situation ○ *Chris's apt comments summed up our opinions.*
aptly /ˈæp·tli/ *adv* ○ *He was very tall and was aptly called "Stretch."*

LIKELY /æpt/ *adj* [+ *to* infinitive] likely ○ *This old roof is apt to leak when it rains.*

apt. *n* [C] *abbreviation for* APARTMENT

aptitude /ˈæp·təˌtuːd/ *n* [C/U] natural ability or skill ○ [U] *My son has no aptitude for sports.*

aptitude test *n* [C] a test that measures your ability to succeed at something

aqua /ˈæk·wə, ˈɑk-/, **aquamarine** /ˌæk·wə·məˈriːn, ˌɑk-/ *adj, n* [U] (of) the color that is a mixture of blue and green ○ *an aqua sea* ○ [U] *You look good in aqua.*

aquarium /əˈkwer·iː·əm, əˈkwær-/ *n* [C] a glass container or pool in which small fish and other water animals and plants are kept, or a building, usually open to the public, in which many different fish and other water animals live and can be studied

Aquarius /əˈkwer·iː·əs, əˈkwær-/ *n* [C/U] the eleventh sign of the ZODIAC, covering the period January 20 to February 18 and represented by a person carrying water, or a person born during this period

aquatic /əˈkwæṭ·ɪk/ *adj* [not gradable] living in, happening in, or connected with water ○ *Water-skiing is my favorite aquatic sport.*

aqueduct /ˈæk·wəˌdʌkt/ *n* [C] a structure like a bridge for carrying water across land in pipes or an open channel

aqueous /ˈæk·wiː·əs/ *adj* [not gradable] ***chemistry*** made with or containing water

Arab /ˈær·əb/ *adj, n* [C] a person whose language is Arabic, an important language of the Middle East, or who comes from an Arabic-speaking country, esp. in the Middle East

Arabic numeral /ˌær·ə·bɪkˈnuː·mə·rəl/ *n* [C] one of the symbols (1, 2, 3, etc.) used by many people to write numbers ○ Compare ROMAN NUMERAL

arable /ˈær·ə·bəl/ *adj* (of land) used for or right for growing crops ○ *The country is rich in arable land.*

arbiter /ˈɑr·bəṭ·ər/ *n* [C] **1** a person who acts as a judge in an argument or of a subject of interest ○ *Certain magazines are arbiters of fashion.* **2** An arbiter is also an ARBITRATOR. ○ See at ARBITRATE

arbitrary Ⓐ /ˈɑr·bəˌtrer·i/ *adj* based on a desire or idea or chance rather than reason ○ *Her outfit was an arbitrary choice but was just perfect.*
arbitrarily Ⓐ /ˌɑr·bəˈtrer·ə·li/ *adv* ○ *We didn't think much about it, just arbitrarily decided to go to Italy.*
arbitrariness Ⓐ /ˌɑr·bəˈtrer·iː·nəs/ *n* [U] *disapproving* ○ *The arbitrariness of human nature infuriates me.*

arbitrate /ˈɑr·bəˌtreɪt/ *v* [I/T] to make a formal judgment to decide an argument ○ [T] *A referee was hired to arbitrate the dispute.*
arbitration /ˌɑr·bəˈtreɪ·ʃən/ *n* [U] the formal process of having an outside person, chosen by both sides to a disagreement, end the disagreement ○ *Both labor and management have agreed to arbitration.*
arbitrator /ˈɑr·bəˌtreɪṭ·ər/, **arbiter** *n* [C] ○ *The independent arbitrator has the approval of both sides in the dispute.*

arc /ɑrk/ *n* [C] ***geometry*** a part of a circle, or the shape of a curved line ○ *The ball rose in a high arc and landed beyond the fence.*

arcade /ɑrˈkeɪd/ *n* [C] **1** an area where there are many electronic or other coin-operated games for the public ○ *video-game arcades* ○ *a carnival arcade* **2** An arcade is also a covered area between buildings, esp. one with arches and columns where there are shops.

arcane /ɑrˈkeɪn/ *adj* complicated and therefore understood or known by only a few people ○ *They worked hard to negotiate New York's arcane rules for getting on presidential ballots.*

arch /ɑrtʃ/ *n* [C] **1** a structure consisting of a curved top on two supports which holds the weight of something above it, or something decorative that has this shape ○ *Two rows of arches support the roof of the building.* **2** The arch of your foot is the higher, curved part on the bottom.
arch /ɑrtʃ/ *v* [I/T] ○ [T] *Cats often arch their backs when they stretch.*
arched /ɑrtʃt/ *adj* ○ *Arched bookcases filled each end of the room.*

archaeology, **archeology** /ˌɑr·kiːˈɑl·ə·dʒi/ *n* [U] the study of ancient cultures through examination of their buildings, tools, and other objects
archaeological, **archeological** /ˌɑr·kiː·əˈlɑdʒ·ɪ·kəl/ *adj* [not gradable] ○ *I always wanted to go on an archaeological dig.*
archaeologist, **archeologist** /ˌɑr·kiːˈɑl·ə·dʒəst/ *n* [C] ○ *A marine archaeologist has uncovered the wreck of the sunken ship.*

A

archaic /ɑrˈkeɪ·ɪk/ *adj* of or belonging to the past; from an ancient period in history ○ *Some people like to show off by using archaic words.*

archbishop /ɑrtʃˈbɪʃ·əp, ˈɑrtʃˌbɪʃ-/ *n* [C] a BISHOP (= an important priest) of the highest rank, in charge of the churches and other bishops in a large area

archdiocese /ɑrtʃˈdɑɪ·ə·səs, -ˌsiːz/ *n* [C] the area of which an ARCHBISHOP is in charge

archer /ˈɑr·tʃər/ *n* [C] a person who shoots with a BOW (= long stick held bent by a string tied to the ends) and arrow, usually for sport

archery /ˈɑr·tʃə·ri/ *n* [U] the skill or sport of shooting arrows

archetype /ˈɑr·kəˌtɑɪp/ *n* [C] ***literature*** the original model or a perfect example of something

archetypal /ˌɑr·kəˈtɑɪ·pəl/ *adj* [not gradable]

archipelago /ˌɑr·kəˈpel·əˌgoʊ, ˌɑr·tʃə-/ *n* [C] *pl* **archipelagoes, archipelagos** a group of islands, or an area of sea where there are many islands ○ *The Hawaiian archipelago is made up of a number of large islands and some extremely small ones.*

architect /ˈɑr·kəˌtekt/ *n* [C] a person who designs new buildings and is responsible for how they are built ○ *(fig.) President Roosevelt was the architect of the New Deal during the Great Depression.*

architecture /ˈɑr·kəˌtek·tʃər/ *n* [U] the art and science of designing and making buildings, or the style of a building ○ *modern/classical/Gothic architecture* ○ *He studied architecture with Gropius.*

architectural /ˌɑr·kəˈtek·tʃə·rəl/ *adj* [not gradable] ○ *Framed architectural drawings hung on the walls of his office.*

archive /ˈɑr·kɑɪv/, **archives** *n* the documents showing the history of a place, organization, or family, or the place where these are kept ○ *The author's manuscripts are in the college archives.*

archival /ɑrˈkɑɪ·vəl/ *adj* [not gradable] ○ *I'm doing some archival research on my family's history.*

Arctic /ˈɑrk·tɪk, ˈɑrt̬·ɪk/ *n* [U] the large and extremely cold area around the North Pole ○ *The Arctic is not a barren wasteland.* ○ Compare ANTARCTIC

arctic /ˈɑrk·tɪk, ˈɑrt̬·ɪk/ *adj* extremely cold ○ *Arctic air stung New England with freezing temperatures.*

ardent /ˈɑrd·ᵊnt/ *adj* showing strong feelings; eager ○ *They were ardent pacifists.*

ardor, *Cdn* **ardour** /ˈɑrd·ər/ *n* [U] strong emotion, or great enthusiasm or excitement ○ *She fires off the facts, yet lets her ardor for her cause come through.* ○ *Her ardor for basketball impressed me.*

arduous /ˈɑr·dʒə·wəs/ *adj* difficult and tiring, or needing a great deal of effort ○ *In those days, a trip to the West was an arduous journey.*

are /ɑr, ər, r/ *present simple of* BE, used with you/we/they ○ *Are you hungry?* ○ *They are late.*

area Ⓐ **PLACE** /ˈer·iː·ə, ˈær-/ *n* [C] **1** a part of the earth's surface of land and water, or a particular part of a country, city, town, etc. ○ *an industrial/suburban/mountainous area* **2** An area is also a particular part of anything that takes space: *This area of the brain is called the cerebral cortex.*

SUBJECT /ˈer·iː·ə, ˈær-/ *n* [C] a particular subject or activity ○ *His area of expertise includes learning disorders.*

MEASURE /ˈer·iː·ə, ˈær-/ *n* [C/U] ***geometry*** the measure of a flat space or surface ○ [C] *You get the area of a rectangle by multiplying its length by its width.*

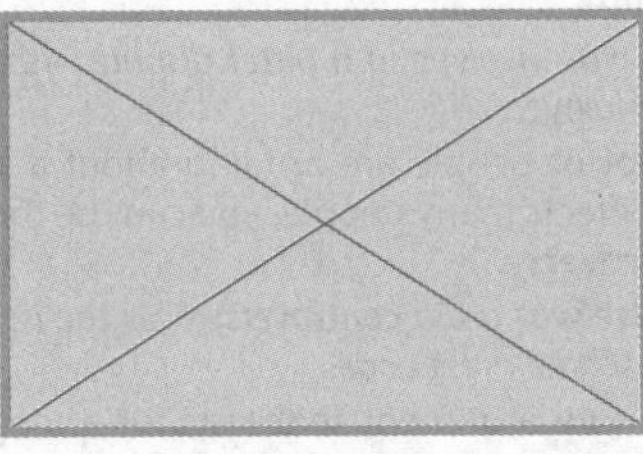

AREA

area code *n* [C] a set of three numbers, connected with a particular area, that come at the beginning of a telephone number

arena /əˈriː·nə/ *n* [C] **1** a central, level area for the performance of sports or entertainment, having raised seats around it from which people can see the activities, or a building containing the seats and performance area ○ *a sports arena* **2** An arena is also a particular activity, esp. one that involves competition and gets a lot of public attention: *She entered the political arena as a young woman.*

aren't /ɑrnt, ˈɑr·ənt/ *contraction of* are not ○ *They aren't here yet.*

IDIOM with aren't

• **aren't I?** am I not? ○ *I'm getting better at this, aren't I?* ○ *Aren't I lucky to have such a great family?* ○ **USAGE:** Used in questions.

argon /ˈɑrˌgɑn/ *n* [U] ***chemistry*** a gas, one of the chemical elements, that has no color, taste, or smell and does not combine with other elements

argue **DISAGREE** /ˈɑr·gjuː/ *v* [I] to disagree esp. strongly and sometimes angrily in talking or discussing something ○ *They argued about money.* ○ *I can't argue with you about that* (= I agree with you).

argument /ˈɑr·gjə·mənt/ *n* [C] ○ *I had an argument with my boss.*

WORD CHOICES argue

The word **disagreement** can be used as an alternative to "argument."

*There was a **disagreement** over who should pay the bill.*

If an argument involves a lot of angry feelings, you can use the word **quarrel**.

*There were bitter **quarrels** between the two neighbors.*

An argument about something that is not important can be described as a **squabble**.

*I'm always dealing with **squabbles** between the children.* ➤

A **tiff** is an informal word for a slight argument between two people.

*A **tiff** with a teammate had something to do with his leaving the game early.*

If you want to suggest that an argument is polite and not very serious, you can use the phrase **a difference of opinion.**

*There was a slight **difference of opinion** over whose turn it was to do the dishes.*

An official argument can be described as a **dispute.**

*He was involved in a bitter **dispute** with his employer.*

If a lot of people are arguing about a subject that affects many people, you can use the word **controversy.**

*There was a big **controversy** over the issue of a school dress code.*

An angry argument that lasts for a long time can be described as a **feud.**

*Relatives can't remember how the **feud** between the brothers began.*

GIVE REASONS /ˈɑr·gjuː/ *v* [I/T] **1** to give the reasons for your opinion about the truth of something or to explain why you believe something should be done ○ [I] *They argued for/against a tax cut.* **2** *law* To argue is also to represent the case of someone in a court of law.

arguable /ˈɑr·gjə·wə·bəl/ *adj* [not gradable] possible to give reasons for and against; DEBATABLE ○ *It's arguable that another route would be just as bad.*

arguably /ˈɑr·gjə·wə·bli/ *adv* [not gradable] ○ *She was, arguably, the best female basketball player of all time.*

argument /ˈɑr·gjə·mənt/ *n* [C] **1** *A good argument can be made for providing health insurance for all children.* **2** *law* An argument is a lawyer's representation of a case in a court of law.

WORD FAMILY argue			
Nouns	argument	*Verbs*	argue
Adjectives	arguable argumentative	*Adverbs*	arguably

argument /ˈɑr·gjə·mənt/ *n* [C] ***literature*** **1** the subject matter of a written work and the development of the ideas in it **2** An argument is also a brief SUMMARY of a written work.

argumentative /ˌɑr·gjəˈment·ət̬·ɪv/ *adj* quick to disagree and argue ○ *Don't be so argumentative.*

aria /ˈɑr·iː·ə/ *n* [C] a song sung by one person in an opera or in some other types of music

arid /ˈær·əd/ *adj* (of land or weather) having little rain; very dry ○ *an arid region*

Aries /ˈer·iːz, ˈer·iːˌiːz, ˈær-/ *n* [C/U] the first sign of the ZODIAC, covering the period March 21 to April 19 and represented by a RAM, or a person born during this period

arise **HAPPEN** /əˈrɑɪz/ *v* [I] *past simp.* **arose,** *past part.* **arisen** to come into existence or begin to be noticed; happen ○ *Problems arise when kids leave school.* ○ *When the opportunity arose, he decided to take it.*

GET UP /əˈrɑɪz/ *v* [I] *past simp.* **arose,** *past part.* **arisen** *fml* to get up, esp. from bed after sleeping ○ *We arose early on Saturday morning.*

aristocracy /ˌær·əˈstɑk·rə·si/ *n* [C] **1** a class of people of high social rank **2** ***politics & government*** An aristocracy is also a government ruled by or consisting of people of a high social class.

aristocrat /əˈrɪs·təˌkræt, ˈær·ə·stə-/ *n* [C] ○ *a prep-school-educated American aristocrat*

aristocratic /əˌrɪs·təˈkræt̬·ɪk, ˌær·ə·stə-/ *adj* [gradable] ○ *His aristocratic manner alienated many voters.*

arithmetic /əˈrɪθ·məˌtɪk/ *n* [U] ***mathematics*** the process of making calculations such as adding, multiplying, and dividing by using numbers, or the study of this

arithmetical /ˌer·əθˈmet̬·ɪ·kəl, ˌær-/ *adj* ***mathematics*** ○ *an arithmetical operation/progression*

arithmetically /ˌer·əθˈmet̬·ɪ·kli, ˌær-/ *adv* ***mathematics*** ○ *arithmetically equivalent numbers*

arm **BODY PART** /ɑrm/ *n* [C] **1** either of the two long parts of the upper body that are joined to the shoulders and have hands at the end ○ *Her arm was bandaged from elbow to wrist.* ○ *He held his young son in his arms* (= closely). **2** The arm of a piece of clothing or furniture is a part of it that you put your arm in or on: *the arm of a jacket/chair* **3** An arm of an organization is a part of it with particular responsibilities: *the company's investment banking arm*

armful /ˈɑrm·fʊl/ *n* [C] the amount that a person can carry in one or both arms ○ *an armful of groceries*

PROVIDE WEAPONS /ɑrm/ *v* [T] to provide yourself or others with a weapon or weapons ○ *He armed himself with a baseball bat before going outside.*

armed /ɑrmd/ *adj* [not gradable] **1** using or carrying weapons ○ *armed guards* ○ *armed robbery* **2** If you are armed with something, you know or have access to something that can be useful to you: *Kids should be armed with the facts about the disease.*

arms /ɑrmz/ *pl n* weapons and explosives used in fighting wars

IDIOMS with arm

- **arm in arm** with your arm resting in the curve of another person's arm ○ *We walked arm in arm through the park.*
- **at arm's length** as far away from your body as possible ○ *He held the snake at arm's length.*

armadillo /ˌɑr·məˈdɪl·oʊ/ *n* [C] *pl* **armadillos** a small animal found in South America, Central America, and in the southern US which has a body covered by hard, bony strips that allow it to curl into a ball to protect itself when attacked

A

armament /ˈɑr·mə·mənt/ *n* [C/U] weapons, explosives, and other military equipment ○ [C] *a seller of armaments*

armchair /ˈɑrm·tʃer, -tʃær/ *n* [C] a comfortable chair with two resting places for the arms

armed forces *pl n* a country's military forces, usually an army, navy, and air force

armistice /ˈɑr·mə·stəs/ *n* [C] ***politics & government*** an agreement between two countries or groups at war to stop fighting for a period of time, esp. to talk about possible peace

armor, *Cdn, Br* **armour** /ˈɑr·mər/ *n* [U] **1** strong covering that protects a person, animal, or vehicle ○ *samurai armor* **2** Armor is also military vehicles that are covered in strong metal.

armored, *Cdn, Br* **armoured** /ˈɑr·mərd/ *adj* **1** covered with a special material that protects against weapons ○ *an armored personnel carrier* **2** An armored military division has vehicles covered with armor.

armory, *Cdn, Br* **armoury** /ˈɑr·mə·ri/ *n* [C] **1** a place where weapons and other military equipment are stored **2** An armory is also a large building where members of local military units meet to train and where other events are sometimes held.

armored car *n* [C] a small truck that is covered with ARMOR and that is used esp. to move large amounts of money from one place to another

armpit /ˈɑrm·pɪt/ *n* [C] the hollow place under your arm where it joins your body

arms /ɑrmz/ *pl n* ○ See at ARM PROVIDE WEAPONS

arms control *n* [U] ***world history*** the international effort to limit the number and types of weapons that countries are allowed to have

arms race *n* [C] ***world history*** a situation in which two or more countries are increasing the number and strength of their weapons

army /ˈɑr·mi/ *n* [C] **1** a military force, usually belonging to a country, that has the training and equipment to fight on land ○ *She decided to join the army.* **2** An army is also any large group: *An army of bystanders watched the film crew work.*

aroma /əˈroʊ·mə/ *n* [C] a strong, usually pleasant smell ○ *the aroma of coffee and frying eggs*

aromatic /ˌær·əˈmæt̬·ɪk/ *adj* ○ *an aromatic pine forest*

arose /əˈroʊz/ *past simple of* ARISE

around IN THIS DIRECTION /əˈrɑʊnd/ *prep, adv* [not gradable] in a position or direction surrounding, along the outside of, or from one part of to another ○ *We sat around the table.* ○ *Go around to the back of the house and come in through the kitchen.* ○ *We drove around town for a while, looking for a place to park.* ○ *She turned around* (= so that she was facing in the opposite direction) *and waved goodbye.* ○ (fig.) *He built his story around the theme of spiritual loneliness.*

HERE/NEAR /əˈrɑʊnd/ *adj, adv* positioned or moving in or near a place ○ *I used to live around here.* ○ *Will you guys be around next week?*

TO ALL PARTS /əˈrɑʊnd/ *prep, adv* [not gradable] in or to many parts of or all directions ○ *Car phones are common all around the country.* ○ *People came from miles around.*

APPROXIMATELY /əˈrɑʊnd/ *adv* about; approximately ○ *Around 40 people showed up.* ○ *He arrived in Kansas City around 1984.*

IDIOMS with around

• **around and around** moving in circles ○ *The skater twirled around and around.* ○ Compare ROUND AND ROUND at ROUND IDIOMS

• **around the clock** all day and all night without stopping ○ *They're working around the clock to get it done.* ○ *around-the-clock news coverage* ○ Compare ROUND THE CLOCK at ROUND IDIOMS

• **(right/just) around the corner 1** very close to the place that you are ○ *There's a deli around the corner.* **2** A time or event that is just **around the corner** is coming very soon: *It's still cold today, but spring is just around the corner.*

arouse /əˈrɑʊz/ *v* [T] to cause someone to have a particular feeling ○ *He works hard to arouse his students' curiosity.*

arraign /əˈreɪn/ *v* [T] *law* to formally accuse someone of a particular crime in a court of law and to ask the accused to state guilt or innocence ○ *He was arraigned on a robbery charge.*

arraignment /əˈreɪn·mənt/ *n* [C] *law* ○ *They pleaded not guilty at their arraignment.*

arrange PLAN /əˈreɪndʒ/ *v* [I/T] to plan or make preparations for something or for something to happen ○ [T] *He arranged a meeting between the two leaders.* ○ [+ to infinitive] *My friends arranged to eat with me.* ○ [I] *Shelly arranged for the publication of her thesis.*

arrangement /əˈreɪndʒ·mənt/ *n* [C] a plan or preparation for something, esp. for something to happen in a particular way ○ *She had an arrangement to work at home two days a week.* ○ *Since the hotel was full, we had to make other arrangements.*

USAGE

arrange or **arrange for**?

Don't forget to use **for** when you say that you are arranging for someone to do something or for something to happen.

I will arrange for all the new trainees to visit the factory next week.

~~*I will arrange all the new trainees to visit the factory next week.*~~

We have arranged for the talk to be held on Wednesday.

~~*We have arranged the talk to be held on Wednesday.*~~

PUT IN POSITION /əˈreɪndʒ/ *v* [T] to put something in a particular order ○ *We arranged the chairs in a circle.* ○ *Books should be arranged alphabetically by author.*

arrangement /əˈreɪndʒ·mənt/ *n* [C] ○ *a flower arrangement*

WRITE MUSIC /ə'reɪndʒ/ *v* [T] to write the parts of a piece of music so that it can be played by a particular instrument or instruments
arrangement /ə'reɪndʒ·mənt/ *n* [C] ○ *an arrangement for trumpet and cello*
arranger /ə'reɪn·dʒər/ *n* [C] ○ *Ellington was a composer, arranger, and pianist.*

WORD FAMILY arrange			
Nouns	arrangement	*Verbs*	arrange rearrange

arranged marriage *n* [C] a marriage in which the parents choose the person their son or daughter will marry

array /ə'reɪ/ *n* [C] a large group of things or people, esp. when shown or positioned in an attractive way ○ *The airport shops offer a wide array of merchandise.*
array /ə'reɪ/ *v* [T] ○ *A battery of cameras was arrayed before them.*

arrest CATCH /ə'rest/ *v* [T] (of the police) to use legal authority to catch and take someone to a place where the person may be accused of a crime ○ *Kansas City police arrested a serial bank robber.*
arrest /ə'rest/ *n* [C/U] ○ [C] *FBI agents made the arrest.* ○ [U] *He was placed under arrest by federal marshals.*

STOP /ə'rest/ *v* [T] to stop or slow an activity ○ *Antibiotics arrest the development of harmful bacteria.*
arresting /ə'res·tɪŋ/ *adj* If something is arresting, it causes you to stop and notice it: *The house has an arresting view of the river.*

Arrhenius acid /ə'riː·niː·əs, ə'reɪ-/ *n* [C] a substance that reacts with water to release atoms of HYDROGEN that have a positive electrical CHARGE

Arrhenius base /ə'riː·niː·əs, ə'reɪ-/ ***chemistry*** a substance that reacts with water to release atoms of a HYDROXIDE

arrive /ə'rɑɪv/ *v* [I] **1** to come to a place, esp. after traveling ○ *What time is their plane scheduled to arrive?* **2** If someone or something arrives, it appears: *Sausages suddenly arrived on our table.* **3** *infml* Someone who has arrived has become successful: *When they sent a limo for us, I knew we'd arrived.*
arrival /ə'rɑɪ·vəl/ *n* [C/U] the act of someone or something that reaches a place or comes into existence, or a person or thing that reaches a place ○ [U] *The arrival of the railroad changed the western US.* ○ [U] *The arrival of the new year was greeted with joy.* ○ [C] *There were so many refugees that tents were needed to house new arrivals.*

USAGE
arrive

You **arrive at** a building or a part of a building.
We arrived at the theater just as the play was starting.
I arrived at the front entrance to find the door locked.
You **arrive in** a city, town, or country.
When do you arrive in Kansas City?
You **arrive home/here/there/etc.** Do not use a preposition when arrive is used before an adverb that tells where.
We arrived home yesterday.

WORD CHOICES arrive

You can use **get** instead of arrive when you arrive at a particular place.
*What time did you **get** there?*
*We **got to** the airport at six o'clock.*
If you arrive somewhere after a lot of traveling, you could use the verb **reach**.
*We won't **reach** Miami until evening.*
Come can be used instead of arrive when someone arrives at the place where you are.
*Has she **come** yet?*
If you successfully arrive somewhere when it has been difficult, in informal English, you could say **make**.
*We **made** it to the airport just in time for our flight.*
If you arrive by plane or train, or a plane or train you are traveling on arrives, you can say that you or it **gets in**.
*The train **gets in** at 6:40 p.m.*
Turn up, show up, and **roll in** are informal phrasal verbs that can be used when someone arrives at a place, especially when that person is late or was not expected.
*She **turned up** at my house late one night.*
*He finally **rolled in**, three hours late.*

PHRASAL VERB with arrive

• **arrive at** *something* to come to a decision about something after much consideration ○ *How did he arrive at this estimate?*

arrogant /'ær·ə·gənt/ *adj* proud in an unpleasant way and behaving as if you are better or more important than other people ○ *I never met a more conceited and arrogant young man.*
arrogantly /'ær·ə·gənt·li/ *adv* ○ *Lapham arrogantly claimed the land was his.*
arrogance /'ær·ə·gəns/ *n* [U] ○ *I was disgusted by his arrogance.*

arrow /'ær·oʊ/ *n* [C] **1** a long, thin stick, pointed at one end, that can be shot from a BOW **2** An arrow is also a sign (→), which points in a particular direction.

arroyo /ə'rɔɪ·ə, -ˌoʊ/ *n* [C] (in the southwestern US) a narrow channel in the ground that is usually dry but becomes a stream after heavy rain

arsenal /'ɑr·sən·əl/ *n* [C] a building or place where weapons and military equipment are made or stored, or a collection of weapons ○ *the Picatinny Arsenal in New Jersey* ○ *an arsenal of rockets*

arsenic /ˈɑr·snɪk, ˈɑr·sə·nɪk/ *n* [U] a very poisonous substance, used to kill RATS (= animals like mice, but larger) and harmful insects

arson /ˈɑr·sən/ *n* [C/U] the crime of intentionally starting a fire in order to damage or destroy something, esp. a building
arsonist /ˈɑr·sə·nəst/ *n* [C] ○ *He was a convicted arsonist.*

art /ɑrt/ *n* [U] **1** the making or doing of something whose purpose is to bring pleasure to people through their enjoyment of what is beautiful and interesting, or things often made for this purpose, such as paintings, drawings, or SCULPTURES ○ *ancient/modern art* ○ *American/French/Japanese art* ○ *an art museum/gallery* **2** An art is also a skill or ability: *He never learned the art of saying "Thank you."*
artist /ˈɑrt̬·əst/ *n* [C] **1** a person who paints, draws, or makes SCULPTURES **2** An artist is also an actor, musician, dancer, or other performer.
artistic /ɑrˈtɪs·tɪk/ *adj* **1** *These were the years of his finest artistic creativity.* **2** An artistic person has skill or ability in painting, dancing, singing, etc.
artistically /ɑrˈtɪs·tɪ·kli/ *adv* ○ *It was her most artistically impressive performance to date.*
artistry /ˈɑrt̬·ə·stri/ *n* [U] the special skills possessed by someone who has the ability to make art ○ *No American composer has topped the sheer artistry, elegance, and wit of Cole Porter.*
arts /ɑrts/ *pl n* the making, showing, or performance of painting, acting, dancing, music, etc. ○ *fine/decorative/performing arts*
arty /ˈɑrt̬·i/, **artsy** /ˈɑrt·si/ *adj infml, disapproving* trying to be like artists or dress and live in the style typical of artists, esp. while lacking any real understanding of art or the work of artists ○ *an arty crowd*

WORD FAMILY art

Nouns	art	*Adjectives*	artistic
	artist		arty
	artistry	*Adverbs*	artistically
	arts		

artery TUBE /ˈɑrt̬·ə·ri/ *n* [C] ***biology*** one of the larger tubes that carry blood from the heart to other parts of the body ○ Compare VEIN TUBE
ROAD /ˈɑrt̬·ə·ri/ *n* [C] an important road, river, or other transportation route

artesian well /ɑrˈtiː·ʒən ˈwel/ *n* [C] a WELL (= underground place for water) in which the water is forced to the surface by natural pressure

artful /ˈɑrt·fəl/ *adj* intelligent and skillful, esp. in persuading, sometimes without being completely honest ○ *His politics was an artful blend of high-minded patriotism and malicious gossip about his opponents.*
artfully /ˈɑrt·fə·li/ *adv* ○ *The machinery is artfully concealed in a polished cabinet.*

arthritis /ɑrˈθrɑɪt̬·əs/ *n* [U] a disease in which a person's joints become swollen, and in which there is some loss in the ability to move them without pain
arthritic /ɑrˈθrɪt̬·ɪk/ *adj* ○ *an arthritic knee*

arthropod /ˈɑr·θrəˌpɑd/ *n* [C] ***biology*** a member of a group of animals with no SPINE (= bone down the center of the back), a hard outer skin, legs with bones joined together, and a body divided into sections, for example a SPIDER, CRAB, or ANT

artichoke /ˈɑrt̬·əˌtʃoʊk/ *n* [C] a tall plant with a rounded edible top that is enclosed by thick, pointed leaves

article PIECE OF WRITING /ˈɑrt̬·ɪ·kəl/ *n* [C] ***writing*** a piece of writing on a particular subject in a newspaper or magazine ○ *an article on Chinese art*
OBJECT /ˈɑrt̬·ɪ·kəl/ *n* [C] a particular thing or item ○ *The police want a description of each missing article.*
SMALL WORD /ˈɑrt̬·ɪ·kəl/ *n* [C] ***grammar*** any of the English words "a," "an," and "the," or words in other languages that are used in a similar way as these ○ See also: DEFINITE ARTICLE ; INDEFINITE ARTICLE

Articles of Confederation *pl n* ***US history*** the first agreement establishing an American government in 1781, later replaced by the CONSTITUTION LAWS

articulate /ɑrˈtɪk·jə·lət/ *adj* expressing or able to express things easily and clearly ○ *The First Lady was an intelligent and articulate spokeswoman for a lot of causes.*
articulate /ɑrˈtɪk·jəˌleɪt/ *v* [T] to explain in words, esp. to express something clearly ○ *She has not yet articulated her vision of why she wants to be governor.*

articulation /ɑrˌtɪk·jəˈleɪ·ʃən/ *n* [U] ***music*** **1** the way in which words are pronounced, esp. in singing **2** Articulation is the ability to recognize and produce separate notes.

artifact /ˈɑrt̬·ɪˌfækt/ *n* [C] an object, such as a tool, that was made in the past ○ *The museum has artifacts dating back to prehistoric times.*

artificial PRODUCED /ˌɑrt̬·əˈfɪʃ·əl/ *adj* made by people, often as a copy of something natural ○ *artificial flowers* ○ *artificial grass* ○ *an artificial leg*
artificially /ˌɑrt̬·əˈfɪʃ·ə·li/ *adv* ○ *Those oranges have been artificially colored.*
artificiality /ˌɑrt̬·əˌfɪʃ·iːˈæl·ət̬·i/ *n* [U]

WORD CHOICES artificial

Something that is artificial because it is made of substances that are not natural can be described as **man-made** or **synthetic**.

Nylon is a ***man-made*** *fiber.*

Fake, **false**, and **imitation** mean the same as artificial when something is made to look exactly like something real.

fake *fur jackets*
false *eyelashes*

Bogus can be used when something is made to look like something in order to be dishonest.

If you get a call from a ***bogus*** *charity asking for money, report it to the police.*

A

NOT SINCERE /ˌɑrţ·əˈfɪʃ·əl/ *adj* not sincere; not truly intended ○ *an artificial smile*

artificial intelligence, *abbreviation* **AI** *n* [U] the use of computer programs that have some of the qualities of the human mind, such as the ability to understand language, recognize pictures, and learn from experience

artificial respiration *n* [U] the act of forcing air in and out of the lungs of a person who has stopped breathing

artillery /ɑrˈtɪl·ə·ri/ *n* [U] large guns that are moved on wheels or metal tracks, or the part of an army that uses these ○ *He served as an artillery officer.*

artisan /ˈɑrţ·ə·zən, -sən/ *n* [C] a person who does skilled work with his or her hands ○ *You will learn how eighteenth-century artisans did their work.*

artist /ˈɑrţ·əst/ *n* [C] ○ See at ART

artistic /ɑrˈtɪs·tɪk/ *adj* ○ See at ART

artistically /ɑrˈtɪs·tɪ·kli/ *adv* ○ See at ART

artistry /ˈɑrţ·ə·stri/ *n* [U] ○ See at ART

arts /ɑrts/ *pl n* ○ See at ART

arts and crafts *pl n* the skills of making objects for decoration and practical uses by hand

artwork **ARTIST'S WORK** /ˈɑrt·wɜrk/ *n* [C] an object made by an artist, esp. a picture or statue

PICTURES WITH TEXT /ˈɑrt·wɜrk/ *n* [U] the drawings and photographs that are used in books, newspapers, and magazines

arty /ˈɑrţ·i/ *adj* ○ See at ART

arugula /əˈruː·gə·lə, -gjə-/ *n* [U] a green, leafy plant that is eaten in salads

as **COMPARISON** /æz, əz/ *prep, conjunction, adv* [not gradable] used in expressions that compare two things, persons, groups, or qualities ○ *This jacket costs twice as much as that one.* ○ *They live in the same town as my parents.* ○ *She'll soon be as tall as her mother.*

BEING /æz, əz/ *prep* appearing to be, or being ○ *He went to the costume party dressed as a banana.* ○ *As a child, Miriam had lived in India.* ○ *The news came as no surprise.*

BECAUSE /æz, əz/ *conjunction* because ○ *As it was getting late, I decided to stop at a motel.*

WHEN /æz, əz/ *conjunction* while; during the time that ○ *As I was getting out of the car, my heel caught on something and I fell.*

ALTHOUGH /æz, əz/ *conjunction* although ○ *Angry as he was, he had to smile.*

THE SAME WAY /æz, əz/ *conjunction* in the way that; like ○ *Do exactly as I say.* ○ *As is often the case with children, Aimee was completely better by the time the doctor arrived.* ○ *Just as I thought, Derrick was to blame.* ○ *Use your coat as a blanket.*

IDIOMS with as

• **as a matter of fact** actually ○ *"Are you new around here?" "As a matter of fact, I've lived here for ten years."* ○ Compare IN FACT at FACT **IDIOMS** ○ **USAGE:** Used to emphasize what you are saying, often because it is surprising.

• **as a (general) rule** usually ○ *As a general rule, we don't allow children in here.*

• **as American as apple pie** considered very typical of the United States or of the people of the United States

• **as follows** the ones named here ○ *The winners were as follows – Smith, Mitchell, Glowser, and Bryce.* ○ **USAGE:** Used to introduce a list of items, often in a particular order.

• **as for** considering or speaking about ○ *As for the money, we'll talk about that later.* ○ **USAGE:** Used to begin talking about another subject which had been mentioned before.

• **as if** it is not true that ○ *He wants to get another car - as if we don't have enough cars in the driveway already!* ○ **USAGE:** Used humorously to show that what you are about to say is the opposite of what you really think.

• **as if/as though** in a way that seems to show something ○ *She acted as though she had never seen me before, when I'd just met her at lunch.*

• **as is** in the condition that something is in ○ *All merchandise is sold as is – no discounts, and no exchanges.* ○ **USAGE:** Used to warn buyers that something that is being sold is not in perfect condition.

• **as it is** already ○ *No, I'm not buying you kids anything else today – I've spent far too much money as it is.*

• **as long as** if ○ *You can have a dog as long as you promise to take care of it.*

• **as of** starting from a particular time ○ *As of next month, all the prices will go up.* ○ *We won't be living here anymore as of tomorrow.*

• **as old as the hills** very old ○ *My grandfather seemed as old as the hills to me.*

• **as opposed to** rather than; instead of ○ *The box is made of plastic, as opposed to wood.*

• **as regards** *fml* about; relating to ○ *There is no problem as regards the financial arrangements.*

• **as soon as** in the shortest possible time ○ *We'll come as soon as we can.*

• **as such** using the exact meaning of the word or phrase ○ *There weren't many vegetarian dishes as such, although there were several different kinds of cheese.*

• **as to** about; relating to ○ *I can't answer questions as to how much money Mr. Mayer is being paid.*

• **as usual** in a way that often happens and is expected ○ *As usual, she was wearing jeans.* ○ *Dan got there late, as usual.*

• **as well** also; too ○ *They advertised the new movie on television, and in newspapers as well.*

• **as well as** in addition; and also ○ *We have a responsibility to our community as well as to our families.*

asap /ˌeɪˌesˌeɪˈpiː, ˈæs·æp/ *abbreviation for* as soon as possible

asbestos /æsˈbes·təs, æz-/ *n* [U] a soft, gray-white material that does not burn and was used in buildings as a protection against fire, and as a form of INSULATION (= way of stopping heat from escaping) ○ *Inhaling asbestos fibers can make you sick.*

ascend /ə'send/ *v* [I/T] to move up or climb something ○ [T] *They slowly ascended the steep path up the mountain.* ○ [I] *A long flight of steps ascends* (= leads up) *to the door of the museum.*

ascent /ə'sent/ *n* [C] ○ [C] *She made a successful ascent* (= climb) *of Mt. McKinley last year.*

ascertain /ˌæs·ər'teɪn/ *v* [T] to discover a fact; to make certain ○ *The fire department has been unable to ascertain the cause of the fire.*

ascetic /ə'seṭ·ɪk/ *adj* avoiding physical comforts and living a simple life

ASCII, **ascii** /'æs·ki/ *n* [U] *abbreviation for* American Standard Code for Information Interchange (= a way of storing text or information on a computer) ○ *All the files are in ASCII.*

ascribe *something* **to** *someone/something* /ə'skrɑɪb·tə, -tʊ, -ˌtuː/ *phrasal verb* to consider something to be caused, created, or owned by someone or something ○ *To what do you ascribe the enormous success of your latest book?* ○ *People like to ascribe human feelings to animals* (= believe animals have human feelings).

asexual reproduction /eɪ'sek·ʃə·wəl/ *n* [U] ***biology*** a method of producing new young plants or animals from a single plant or animal without separate male and female cells joining together ○ Compare SEXUAL REPRODUCTION

ash **POWDER** /æʃ/ *n* [C/U] the soft, gray or black, powdery substance left after something has burned ○ [U] *volcanic ash* ○ [C] *We cleaned the ashes out of the fireplace.*

ashes /'æʃ·əz/ *pl n* the ash left after a dead body has been CREMATED (= burned) ○ *My grandmother's ashes were scattered over this lake.*

TREE /æʃ/ *n* [C/U] a tree that has a smooth gray BARK (= strong outer covering), or the hard wood of this tree

ashamed /ə'ʃeɪmd/ *adj* feeling bad because you are aware that others know that you or someone connected with you has done something wrong or embarrassing ○ [+ *to* infinitive] *Pedro was never ashamed to admit his mistakes.* ○ *I felt deeply ashamed for my father's impoliteness.* ○ *You have nothing to be ashamed of.* ○ [+ *to* infinitive] *She was ashamed to ask her brother for money.*

WORD CHOICES ashamed

Embarrassed is often used instead of "ashamed."

I was too ***embarrassed*** *to admit I was wrong.*

If someone feels very ashamed, you could say that person is **mortified**.

She'd be ***mortified*** *if she knew she'd upset her family.*

If you feel ashamed because you know you have done something wrong, you could use the word **guilty**.

I feel so ***guilty*** *about forgetting her birthday.*

You could use the word **humiliated** when people are so ashamed that they lose respect for themselves.

Feeling betrayed and ***humiliated****, she considered quitting her job.*

ashen /'æʃ·ən/ *adj* (of a person's face) looking pale and gray from illness, shock, or fear

ashore /ə'ʃɔːr, ə'ʃoʊr/ *adv* [not gradable] toward or onto land from an area of water, or on land after coming from an area of water ○ *Julie jumped off the boat and swam ashore.*

ashtray /'æʃ·treɪ/ *n* [C] a small container in which smokers leave ASH and cigarette ends

Asian /'eɪ·ʒən, -ʃən/ *adj, n* [C] (a person) of or coming from Asia

aside /ə'sɑɪd/ *adv* [not gradable] on or to one side ○ *I pushed aside the curtain and looked out the window.* ○ *I took her aside* (= out of hearing distance of other people) *to tell her to behave herself.* ○ *The governor wants to set aside* (= keep separate and not spend) *$50 million for emergencies.*

IDIOM with aside

• **aside from** except for; besides ○ *I don't watch any television, aside from the news.*

asinine /'æs·əˌnɑɪn/ *adj* foolish or stupid ○ *an asinine comment*

ask **QUESTION OR REQUEST** /æsk/ *v* [I/T] to state a question to someone, or to request something from someone ○ [T] *Can I ask you a question?* ○ [T] *If you are asking me if I was foolish, yes, I was foolish.* ○ [+ question word] *We kept asking why he had done it.* ○ [+ question word] *He asked how much the necklace cost.* ○ [I] *He asked for more time to repay the loan.* ○ [T] *You should ask your lawyer for advice.* ○ [T] *I'd like to ask your advice on a financial matter.* ○ [+ *to* infinitive] *I asked to see my accountant.* ○ *"How much time do we have left?" he asked.* ○ [I] *Our neighbors are selling their house, but I don't know how much they're asking for it* (= how much they want for it). ➤ Usage: **demand or ask?** at DEMAND

USAGE

ask

Remember to use the preposition **for** when you **ask for** *something* or **ask** *someone* **for** *something.*

Please do not hesitate to ask me for more details, if you need them.

~~*Please do not hesitate to ask me more details, if you need them.*~~

WORD CHOICES ask

If someone is asking for information, the word **inquire** can be used.

She called to ***inquire*** *when her car would be ready.*

The verb **consult** is often used when you are asking for advice or information from someone who knows a lot because it is their job.

Consult *your doctor if your symptoms don't improve.* ➤

If someone asks a lot of people in order to get information or help, you can use the phrasal verb **ask around.**

*I'll **ask around** and see if anyone knows of a good carpenter.*

The verb **question** is used in serious or official situations.

*The police are **questioning** him about the robbery.*

If someone asks a person questions for a television program or newspaper article, the verb **interview** is often used.

*After the race, she was **interviewed** by journalists.*

INVITE /æsk/ *v* [T] to invite someone to go somewhere ○ *"Are you going to Michelle's party?" "No, I haven't been asked."* ○ *Megan's asked us over for dinner next Friday.*

IDIOM with ask

• **asking for trouble, asking for it** behaving in a way that is likely to cause problems for you ○ *If you wear light shoes for a long walk you're asking for trouble.* ○ *He knows Mom doesn't like it when he stays out this late. He's asking for it!* ○ Compare LOOKING FOR TROUBLE at LOOK **IDIOMS**

PHRASAL VERBS with ask

• **ask around** to talk to several people in order to get or learn something ○ *If you ask around I'm sure someone there can give you directions to the museum.*

• **ask** *someone* **out** [M] to invite someone to go with you somewhere socially, esp. because you have romantic feelings for the person ○ *She said she was going to ask him out to lunch.*

askew /ə'skjuː/ *adj, adv* not straight or level ○ *His shirt was wrinkled and his tie was askew.*

asleep /ə'sliːp/ *adj* [not gradable] **1** sleeping or not awake ○ *I fell asleep* (= began to sleep) *while watching television.* ○ *I didn't hear the phone – I was fast/sound asleep* (= sleeping and not easily woken). **2** If your arm or leg is asleep, you have no feeling there because the flow of blood to that part has been reduced by being in the same position for too long.

WORD CHOICES asleep

The verbs **doze** and **snooze**, and the expression **have/take a nap** all mean "to sleep a short time."

*She's always **dozing** in front of the TV.*

*Granddad was **snoozing** in his chair.*

*Owen is really tired so he's just **taking a nap**.*

The phrasal verbs **doze off** and (*informal*) **nod off** mean to start to sleep, especially during the day.

*I must have **dozed off** after lunch.*

*She **nodded off** during the lecture.*

If you have slept for longer than you intended, you can use the verb **oversleep**.

*I **overslept** and was late for work.*

asparagus /ə'spær·ə·gəs/ *n* [U] a plant with green or white stems that are cooked and eaten as a vegetable

aspect Ⓐ /'æs·pekt/ *n* [C] a particular feature of or way of thinking about something, esp. something complicated ○ *There's another aspect of the cost of caring for old parents at home that I'd like to mention.* ○ *He knows almost every aspect of the criminal justice system.* ○ *A farmer has to handle various aspects of the business.*

USAGE

aspect

Do not use **aspect** to describe what someone looks like. It always sounds formal when it is used with this meaning, and people don't usually use it in this way. You should use the word **appearance** instead.

The author describes Caroline's physical appearance in great detail.

~~*The author describes Caroline's physical aspect in great detail.*~~

asphalt /'æs·fɔːlt/ *n* [U] a black substance mixed with small stones, sand, etc., that forms a hard surface when it dries and is commonly used as a surface for roads

asphyxiate /æs'fɪk·siː,eɪt/ *v* [I/T] to be unable to breathe, usually resulting in death, or to cause someone to be unable to breathe; SUFFOCATE ○ [T] *The men were asphyxiated by smoke.*

asphyxiation /æs,fɪk·siː'eɪ·ʃən/ *n* [U]

aspiration /,æs·pə'reɪ·ʃən/ *n* [C] a strong hope or wish for achievement or success ○ *He has political aspirations, and hopes to run for Congress some day.*

aspire to *something* /əspɑɪr·tə, -tʊ, -,tuː/ *phrasal verb* to have a strong hope to do or have something ○ *Rebecca worked as a waitress but aspired to be a dancer.*

aspirin /'æs·prən, -pə·rən/ *n* [C/U] *pl* **aspirin, aspirins** a drug taken to reduce pain, fever, and swelling

aspiring /ə'spɑɪ·rɪŋ/ *adj* [not gradable] wishing to become successful in a particular type of job ○ *Marcus is an aspiring actor.*

ass ANIMAL /æs/ *n* [C] a DONKEY (= animal like a small horse)

PERSON /æs/ *n* [C] a person who does or says stupid things ○ *a pompous ass*

assail /ə'seɪl/ *v* [T] to criticize something or someone strongly, or to cause someone to experience unpleasant thoughts or feelings ○ *Many parents assailed the proposal to lengthen the school day.* ○ *After the decision to quit his job, he was assailed by doubts.*

assailant /ə'seɪ·lənt/ *n* [C] someone who attacks another ○ *None of the witnesses could identify the assailant.*

A

assassinate /əˈsæs·əˌneɪt/ *v* [T] to murder a famous or important person, esp. for political reasons or in exchange for money ○ *President Kennedy was assassinated in Dallas, Texas, in 1963.*
assassin /əˈsæs·ən/ *n* [C] a person who murders a famous or important person, esp. for political reasons or in exchange for money
assassination /əˌsæs·əˈneɪ·ʃən/ *n* [C/U] ○ *the assassination of John Lennon*

assault /əˈsɔːlt/ *v* [T] to make a sudden, violent attack on someone
assault /əˈsɔːlt/ *n* [C/U] ○ [C] *University officials are concerned about a series of assaults on teachers and students near the campus.*

assemblage /əˈsem·blɪdʒ/ *n* [C] **1** a collection of people or things that are brought together for some reason **2** ***art*** An assemblage is also a work of art that is made of different things put together.

assemble Ⓐ /əˈsem·bəl/ *v* [I/T] to bring or come together in a single group or place, or to put together the parts of something ○ [I] *When the fire alarm rings, everyone is supposed to leave the building and assemble in the schoolyard.* ○ [T] *Workers were earning $20 an hour assembling cars.*

assembly Ⓐ **GATHERING** /əˈsem·bli/ *n* [C/U] **1** a group of people, esp. one gathered together regularly for a particular purpose **2** In the US, an assembly is one of the two parts of the government in many states that makes laws: [C] *The state assembly will vote on a death penalty bill next week.* **3** An assembly in a school is a gathering of several classes for a group activity that is usually educational.
JOINING /əˈsem·bli/ *n* [C/U] the process of putting together the parts of a machine or structure, or the thing produced by this process
assembly line *n* [C] an arrangement in a factory in which each machine or worker has a particular job to complete before the next job is started by another machine or worker

assemblyman /əˈsem·bliː·mən/ *n* [C] *pl* **-men** a man who is a member of a state ASSEMBLY GATHERING (= elected law-making group)

assemblywoman /əˈsem·bliːˌwʊm·ən/ *n* [C] *pl* **-women** a woman who is a member of a state ASSEMBLY GATHERING (= elected law-making group)

assent /əˈsent/ *n* [U] *fml* agreement to an idea, plan, or request, esp. after serious consideration ○ *He gave a nod of assent, and we knew we had a deal at last.*
assent /əˈsent/ *v* [I] *fml* ○ *At long last, the general assented to a halt in the bombing.*

assert /əˈsɜrt/ *v* [T] **1** to state an opinion or claim a right forcefully ○ [+ *that* clause] *The companies have asserted that everything they did was appropriate.* **2** To assert is also to behave in a way that shows power, authority, or control: *Several members of Congress called upon the president to assert leadership.* **3** If you assert yourself, you act forcefully in a way that expresses your confidence: *You have to learn to speak up and assert yourself at meetings, or you'll never get anywhere.*
assertion /əˈsɜr·ʃən/ *n* [C] ○ *Critics say the company forces workers to drive recklessly, an assertion the company denies.*
assertive /əˈsɜrt̬·ɪv/ *adj* behaving confidently and able to say in a direct way what you want or believe ○ *If you really want the promotion, you'll have to be more assertive.*

assess Ⓐ **JUDGE** /əˈses/ *v* [T] **1** to decide the quality or importance of something ○ *A college is going to assess a student's ability based on grades.* **2** To assess is also to judge the cost or value of something: *Government officials assessed the flood damage in the millions of dollars.*
assessment Ⓐ /əˈses·mənt/ *n* [C] ○ *This is an interesting assessment of Mark Twain's importance in American literature.*
ASK FOR MONEY /əˈses/ *v* [T] to charge someone an amount of money as a special payment ○ *In order to complete the new clubhouse, all members will be assessed an additional $200 a year.*
assessment /əˈses·mənt/ *n* [C] ○ *Co-op owners had to pay an assessment to cover the cost of the roof repair.*

asset /ˈæs·et, -ət/ *n* [C usually pl] **1** something having value, such as a possession or property, that is owned by a person, business, or organization **2** An asset is also any positive feature that gives you an advantage: *Her knowledge of Spanish and French is a real asset in her work.* ○ Compare LIABILITY

assign Ⓐ /əˈsɑɪn/ *v* [T] **1** to give to someone a job or responsibility, or to decide on a person for a particular job or responsibility ○ *We assigned Alberto the task of watching the children.* **2** Someone who is assigned to a place is sent there to do a job: *Judith was assigned to the office in Washington, D.C.* **3** If you assign things to people, you give them out in an organized way: *We're assigning seats on a first-come, first-serve basis.*
assignment Ⓐ /əˈsɑɪn·mənt/ *n* [C/U] a particular job or responsibility given to you ○ [C] *The homework assignment was to read Chapter 2 in our history book.*

IDIOM with assign

• **on assignment** doing a job, especially a job in which you are reporting news for a newspaper, television station, etc. ○ *The two journalists met while on assignment in Colombia.*

assimilate /əˈsɪm·əˌleɪt/ *v* [I/T] **1** to take in and make a part of your basic knowledge something learned from others, so that you can use it as your own ○ [T] *We hoped the students would assimilate the information contained in the lecture.* **2** People who are or become assimilated in a society become similar to others by learning and using the customs and culture of the new society: [T] *Once outsiders, they had now been assimilated into the cultural mainstream.*
assimilation /əˌsɪm·əˈleɪ·ʃən/ *n* [U] the process of becoming similar to others by taking in and us-

ing their customs and culture ○ *The assimilation of immigrants into American culture has been a constant feature of US history.*

assist Ⓐ /ə'sɪst/ *v* [I/T] to take action to help someone or support something ○ [T] *The company said it would assist workers in finding new jobs.* ○ [I] *No one knew where my grandfather was, and many came to assist in the search.*

assistance Ⓐ /ə'sɪs·təns/ *n* [U] ○ *With some financial assistance, we'll be able to start our own business.*

assistant Ⓐ /ə'sɪs·tənt/ *n* [C] a person who helps someone else to do a job or who holds a less important position in an organization ○ *an assistant coach/professor* ○ *My assistant will show you around the factory.*

associate SPEND TIME /ə'soʊ·siː,eɪt, -ʃiː-/ *v* [I always + adv/prep] to spend time with someone or have some connection with someone or something ○ *I don't want you associating with that wild crowd anymore.*

associate /ə'soʊ·siː·ət, -'ʃiː-/ *n* [C] **1** someone who is connected to another person as a business partner or companion ○ *Claire invited several business associates to dinner.* **2** An associate is also a person who has a position in a job or type of work that is just below the top position: *an associate director/professor*

association /ə,soʊ·siː'eɪ·ʃən, -ʃiː-/ *n* [C] a group of people united in an organization because of their common interests ○ *The AARP, the American Association of Retired Persons, is a huge organization with millions of members.*

CONNECT MENTALLY /ə'soʊ·siː,eɪt, -ʃiː-/ *v* [T] to think about something as being connected to something else ○ *He always associated that perfume with Lila.*

association /ə,soʊ·siː'eɪ·ʃən, -ʃiː-/ *n* [C/U] ○ [C] *French bread has pleasant associations for me because I enjoyed my trip to France so much.*

associate degree, **associate's degree** *n* [C] the level of achievement recognized for a student by a COMMUNITY COLLEGE after two years of study

associative property /ə'soʊ·ʃəţ·ɪv 'prɑp·ərţ·i/ *n* [U] ***mathematics*** the mathematical principle that the order in which three numbers are grouped when being added or mulitplied does not matter

assonance /'æs·ə·nəns/ *n* [U] ***literature*** the use of similar sounds, esp. vowels, in two or more words, as in "mellow wedding bells" ○ Compare ALLITERATION

assorted /ə'sɔːrţ·əd/ *adj* consisting of various types mixed together ○ *a box of assorted chocolates*

assortment /ə'sɔːrt·mənt/ *n* [C] a mixture or combination of different types ○ *"That's Dancing!" contains an assortment of musical numbers from famous Hollywood films.*

assume Ⓐ ACCEPT /ə'suːm/ *v* [T] to accept something as true without question or proof ○ [+ (*that*) clause] *We can't assume (that) he's innocent simply because he says he is.* ○ [+ (*that*) clause] *I assumed (that) nobody was home because the car wasn't in the driveway.*

assuming (that) Ⓐ /ə'suː·mɪŋ (ðət, ðæt)/ *conjunction* accepting something as true; if ○ *My plans include you, she said, assuming I could discover a way to interest you.*

PRETEND /ə'suːm/ *v* [T] to pretend to be someone you are not, or to express a feeling falsely ○ *During the investigation, two detectives assumed the identities of antique dealers.* ○ *Jim assumed a look of indifference.*

TAKE CONTROL /ə'suːm/ *v* [T] **1** to take control or claim authority, sometimes without the right to do so ○ *The new president assumes office in January.* **2** If you assume responsibility for something, you become responsible for it.

assumption Ⓐ ACCEPT AS TRUE /ə'sʌm·ʃən/ *n* [C] a willingness to accept something as true without question or proof ○ [+ *that* clause] *The plan was based on the assumption that the schedule could be substantially speeded up by adding more people.*

CONTROL /ə'sʌm·ʃən/ *n* [U] the act of taking control or claiming authority ○ *Her assumption of the post of ambassador was a significant development.*

assure Ⓐ PROMISE /ə'ʃʊr/ *v* [T] to promise or tell something to someone confidently or firmly, or to cause someone to feel certain by removing doubt ○ *She assured him (that) the check was in the mail.* ○ *The governor assured the voters (that) taxes would not be raised.*

assurance Ⓐ /ə'ʃʊr·əns/ *n* [C/U] **1** [C] *He gave me his assurance that he would give us an answer by the end of the week.* **2** Assurance is also a feeling of confidence in your abilities: [U] *She answered all the questions put to her with assurance and poise.*

MAKE CERTAIN /ə'ʃʊr/ *v* [T] to cause something to be certain ○ *Her future was assured when her performance drew rave reviews from all the critics.*

assuredly /ə'ʃʊr·əd·li/ *adv* ○ *These problems might not be solved by money alone, but they will assuredly* (= certainly) *not be solved without it.*

asterisk /'æs·tə,rɪsk/ *n* [C] a symbol (*) shaped like a star ○ **USAGE**: Asterisks are usually used to show that additional information is given at the bottom of a page of text.

asteroid /'æs·tə,rɔɪd/ *n* [C] ***earth science*** an object like a very large rock that goes around the sun like a planet ○ *Scientists are hoping an asteroid will clue them in about early life on earth.*

asthenosphere /,æs'θiː·nə,sfɪr/ *n* [U] ***earth science*** the thin, almost liquid, layer under the hard rock that forms the outer layer of the earth

asthma /'æz·mə/ *n* [U] a chest disease in which breathing can become difficult, often caused by an ALLERGIC reaction

astonish /ə'stɑn·ɪʃ/ *v* [T] to surprise someone very much ○ *We were astonished at how much she had aged.* ○ *It was astonishing to see the size of the crowds for the Pope.*

astonishment /ə'stɑn·ɪʃ·mənt/ *n* [U] ○ *To the astonishment of her colleagues, she turned down the award.*

astound /ə'stɑʊnd/ *v* [T] to surprise and shock someone, esp. with news of something that is completely unexpected ○ *Considering how badly they're paid and what little support they get, the dedication of these teachers astounds me.*

astray /ə'streɪ/ *adv* away from the correct path or way of doing something ○ *Our district was led astray, and as a result, we wasted valuable resources.*

astride /ə'strɑɪd/ *adv, prep* with one leg on either side (of something) ○ *He sat astride a horse.*

astrology /ə'strɑl·ə·dʒi/ *n* [U] the ancient practice of studying the movements and positions of the sun, moon, planets, and stars in the belief that they influence human behavior

astronaut /'æs·trəˌnɔːt, -ˌnɑt/ *n* [C] a person who is trained for traveling in spacecraft

astronomical /ˌæs·trə'nɑm·ɪ·kəl/ *adj* extremely large ○ *The costs were astronomical.*

astronomy /ə'strɑn·ə·mi/ *n* [U] ***science*** the scientific study of the universe as a whole and of objects that exist naturally in space, such as the stars
astronomical /ˌæs·trə'nɑm·ɪ·kəl/ *adj* [not gradable] connected with ASTRONOMY ○ *astronomical observations*
astronomer /ə'strɑn·ə·mər/ *n* [C]

astute /ə'stuːt/ *adj* quick to see how to use a situation to your advantage ○ *He was politically astute, and was soon appointed to a number of powerful committees in Congress.*

asylum **PROTECTION** /ə'sɑɪ·ləm/ *n* [U] protection or safety, or a protected and safe place, given esp. to someone who has left a country or place for political reasons ○ *The refugees have asked for political asylum.*
HOSPITAL /ə'sɑɪ·ləm/ *n* [C] *dated* a mental hospital, or any other INSTITUTION giving shelter and other help to poor or suffering people ○ *He was committed to an insane asylum in 1899.*

asymmetry /ˌeɪ'sɪm·ə·tri/ *n* [C] ***geometry, art*** the quality of having parts on either side or half that do not match or are not the same size or shape
asymmetrical /ˌeɪ·sə'me·trɪ·kəl/, **asymmetric** *adj* ***geometry*** **1** having parts on either side or half that do not match or are not the same size or shape ○ *The building's asymmetrical silhouette features a single tower on one corner.* ➤ Picture: **symmetry** **2** ***chemistry*** An asymmetrical carbon atom is one that is attached to four different atoms or groups of atoms.

asymptote /'æs·əmˌtoʊt, -əmp-/ *n* [C] ***mathematics*** a line that a GRAPH (= drawing that shows two sets of related amounts) approaches but does not INTERSECT (= cross)

at **PLACE/TIME** /æt, ət/ *prep* used to show a particular place or a particular time ○ *I'll meet you at the theater at 7:45 tonight.* ○ *Call me at work.* ○ *There's someone at the door* (= outside the door). ○ *I wasn't here to meet you because I was in Detroit at the time* (= then). ➤ Usage: **in or at?** at IN WITHIN
DIRECTION /æt, ət/ *prep* in the direction of ○ *They waved at us as we drove by.* ○ *She aimed at the target, but missed.*
CAUSE /æt, ət/ *prep* used to show the cause of something, esp. a feeling ○ *I was so happy at the news.*
CONDITION /æt, ət/ *prep* used to show a state, condition, or continuous activity ○ *The country was at peace/war.* ○ *I love watching the children at play.* ○ *She was hard at work* (= working hard).
AMOUNT /æt, ət/ *prep* used to show a price, temperature, rate, speed, etc. ○ *They're selling these coats at 30% off this week.*
JUDGMENT /æt, ət/ *prep* used to show the activity in which someone's ability is being judged ○ *I'm really not very good at math.* ○ *Sheila is really terrible at getting to places on time.*
THE MOST /æt, ət/ *prep* used before a superlative ○ *I'm afraid we can only pay you $12 an hour at (the) most.* ○ *At best you'll get to speak to some assistant – you'll never reach anyone important.*

at all /æţ'ɔːl, əţ'ɔːl, ə'tɔːl/ *adv* (used to make negatives and questions stronger) in any way or of any type ○ *I haven't been at all well recently.* ○ *He's had no food at all.* ○ *I'm not at all worried about it.*

ate /eɪt, *regional US* et/ *past simple of* EAT

atheist /'eɪ·θiː·əst/ *n* [C] someone who believes that God does not exist
atheism /'eɪ·θiːˌɪz·əm/ *n* [U] the belief that God does not exist
atheistic /ˌeɪ·θiː'ɪs·tɪk/ *adj*

athlete /'æθˌliːt, *not standard* 'æθ·əˌliːt/ *n* [C] a person who is trained or skilled in a sport and esp. one who regularly competes with others in organized events ○ *a professional athlete*
athletic /æθ'leţ·ɪk/ *adj* ○ *an athletic competition*
athletics /æθ'leţ·ɪks/ *n* [U] **1** sports and games ○ *Girls who participate in high school athletics are three times more likely to graduate than those who don't.* **2** *esp. Br* Athletics is another way of saying TRACK AND FIELD.

athlete's foot *n* [C] a disease in which the skin between the toes cracks and feels uncomfortable

atlas /'æt·ləs/ *n* [C] a book containing maps ○ *a road atlas*

ATM, **cash machine** *n* [C] *abbreviation for* automated/automatic teller machine (= a machine from which you can get money by using a special card)

atmosphere **AIR** /'æt·məˌsfɪr/ *n* [C usually sing] ***earth science*** the mixture of gases that surrounds some planets, such as the earth; the air
atmospheric /ˌæt·mə'sfɪr·ɪk, -sfer·ɪk/ *adj* [not gradable] ***earth science*** of or in the atmosphere

SPELLING

atmosphere

Many people forget the final "e" when spelling this word. One way to remember the correct spelling is that the second part of the word is "sphere."

Meteors usually burn up in the Earth's atmosphere.

MEASUREMENT /ˈæt·məˌsfɪr/ *n* [C] ***science*** a unit for measuring pressure

CHARACTER /ˈæt·məˌsfɪr/ *n* [U] **1** the character or mood of a place or situation ○ *The club provided a relaxed and friendly atmosphere for its members.* **2** ***literature*** Atmosphere is also the mood or feeling produced by a work of literature.

atom /ˈæt̬·əm/ *n* [C] ***physics*** the smallest unit of any chemical element, consisting of a positive NUCLEUS surrounded by negative ELECTRONS. Atoms can combine to form a MOLECULE.

atomic /əˈtɑm·ɪk/ *adj* ***physics*** relating to atoms or the energy that can be produced by them

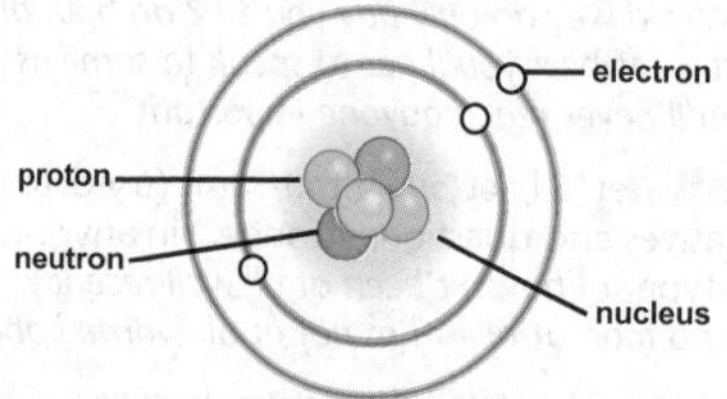

ATOM (lithium)

atomic bomb, atom bomb *n* [C] *dated* a bomb that uses the explosive power of dividing atoms

atomic mass *n* [U] ***chemistry, physics*** the total number of PROTONS and NEUTRONS in the NUCLEUS (= central part) of an atom

atomic mass unit *n* [C] ***chemistry, physics*** one-twelfth the MASS of one atom of carbon

atomic number *n* [C] ***physics*** the number of PROTONS in the NUCLEUS (= central part) of an atom of a particular chemical, used as a way of listing the chemical elements in the PERIODIC TABLE

atonal Ⓐ /eɪˈtoʊn·əl/ *adj* ***music*** (of music) not organized based on a particular note ○ Compare TONAL at TONE

atone /əˈtoʊn/ *v* [I] to do something that shows you are sorry for something bad that you did or for something that you failed to do ○ *The director of the company has expressed a wish to atone for her past sins.*

atop /əˈtɑp/ *prep* on or at the top of ○ *She and Harry toyed with the idea of living in a penthouse atop the building.*

ATP /ˌeɪˌtiːˈpiː/ *n* [U] ***biology*** *abbreviation for* adenosine triphosphate (= an important chemical in the cells of living organisms that stores energy and releases it when it is needed)

atrocious /əˈtroʊ·ʃəs/ *adj* **1** of very bad quality ○ *His Russian was atrocious, but he communicated.* **2** An action that is atrocious is extremely cruel: *an atrocious crime*

atrocity /əˈtrɑs·ət̬·i/ *n* [C/U] an extremely cruel act, or the committing of such acts ○ [C] *The commission reports that atrocities were committed by all sides during the struggle.*

attach Ⓐ /əˈtætʃ/ *v* [T] **1** to fasten or fix something in position, esp. in relation to something else ○ *You attach this device to your windshield, and it sends a signal that opens the garage door.* **2** To attach a particular quality to something is to consider it to have that quality: *If you attach a negative label to a group, you can then treat all the members of that group badly.*

attached Ⓐ /əˈtætʃt/ *adj* feeling close to emotionally, or loving ○ *She really gets attached to her cats.*

attachment Ⓐ /əˈtætʃ·mənt/ *n* [C/U] **1** a strong feeling of being emotionally close to someone or something ○ [C] *She had a special attachment to these students.* **2** An attachment is an extra piece of equipment that can be added to a machine: [C] *computer attachments*

WORD FAMILY attach

Nouns	attachment detachment	*Adjectives*	attached unattached detachable detached
Verbs	attach detach		

attaché /ˌæt̬·əˈʃeɪ, ˌæˌtæ-/ *n* [C] a person who works in an EMBASSY (= group of people representing their country in a foreign country) and has a particular area of special knowledge and responsibility ○ *a military attaché*

attaché case /ˌæˌtæˈʃeɪˌkeɪs, ˌæt̬·ə-/ *n* [C] a hard-sided, rectangular container used esp. for carrying business papers; a type of BRIEFCASE

attack **HURT** /əˈtæk/ *v* [I/T] **1** to try to hurt or defeat someone or something using violence ○ [T] *Two campers were attacked by a bear last night.* ○ [I] *Most wild animals won't attack unless they are provoked.* **2** If a disease or a chemical attacks something, it damages it: [T] *The stress hormone cortisol attacks the immune system.*

attack /əˈtæk/ *n* [C/U] **1** [C] *a missile attack* ○ [U] *The city was under attack from artillery.* **2** An attack is also a sudden, short period of illness, or a sudden feeling that you cannot control: [C] *an asthma attack* ○ [C] *How do you let your kids go without having anxiety attacks?*

attacker /əˈtæk·ər/ *n* [C]

WORD CHOICES attack

See also: **criticize**

Assault is a word that can be used instead of attack when a person is attacked. It is often used in legal contexts.

*The player was suspended for **assaulting** a referee.*

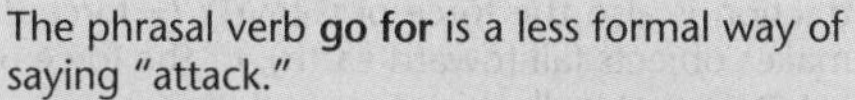

The phrasal verb **go for** is a less formal way of saying "attack."

She suddenly lost her temper and ***went for*** *me.*

If someone moves toward another person in order to attack, you could use the phrase **come at**.

He ***came at*** *me with a baseball bat.*

Mug is often used when someone is attacked in the street and the attacker steals something.

She was ***mugged*** *in broad daylight.*

If someone is attacked by someone who has been hiding and waiting, you could use the verb **ambush**.

He was ***ambushed*** *by three men on his way to work.*

Invade or **storm** are used when a large group of people such as an army attack a place.

Troops ***invaded*** *the capital.*

Soldiers ***stormed*** *the building.*

CRITICIZE /əˈtæk/ *v* [T] to criticize someone or something strongly ○ *Critics have attacked her ideas as antidemocratic.* ○ *In TV ads, he attacked his opponent's record.*

attack /əˈtæk/ *n* [C/U] ○ [U] *The more he speaks out, the more he comes under attack.*

WORD FAMILY attack

Nouns		Verbs	
	attack		attack
	attacker		counterattack
	counterattack		

IDIOM with attack

• **on the attack** to act in a strong, determined way to defeat someone or something, often in a game or competition ○ *In the second half, the Panthers went on the attack and they scored after two minutes.* ○ *The Democrats have changed their campaign strategy, and are now on the attack against the Republicans.*

attain Ⓐ /əˈteɪn/ *v* [T] to achieve something difficult to do or obtain ○ *You need financial security in order to attain emotional well-being.*

attainable Ⓐ /əˈteɪ·nə·bəl/ *adj* ○ *You need to set goals that are clear and attainable.*

attainment Ⓐ /əˈteɪn·mənt/ *n* [C/U] *fml* ○ [U] *Abiola pledged his life to the attainment of justice.*

attempt /əˈtemt/ *v* to try to make or do something ○ [T] *The team's quarterback attempted only 12 passes during the entire game.* ○ [+ *to* infinitive] *Don't attempt to do these tricks at home.*

attempt /əˈtemt/ *n* [C] **1** [+ *to* infinitive] *The pilot made several attempts to regain control of the aircraft.* **2** An attempt on someone's life is an act of trying to kill that person: *a failed attempt on the president's life*

attend /əˈtend/ *v* [I/T] to be at an event or go to a place ○ [T] *She attends classes on Tuesdays.* ○ [I] *You don't have to attend if you don't want to.*

attendance /əˈten·dəns/ *n* [U] **1** *Attendance at rehearsals is required.* **2** Attendance is also the number of people present: *Annual attendance at the museum is nearly 100,000.*

attendee /əˌtenˈdiː/ *n* [C] someone who attends a performance, meeting, speech, etc. ○ *The Manufacturing Technology Show in Chicago attracted nearly 90,000 attendees and 1,200 exhibitors.*

USAGE

attend or wait/expect?

Attend cannot be used to talk about being in a place when you know that someone or something will come there soon. For this meaning you should use **wait for** or **expect**.

Her mother was waiting for her outside in the car.

~~*Her mother was attending her outside in the car.*~~

"We're expecting a delivery at three o'clock," she said.

~~*"We're attending a delivery at three o'clock," she said.*~~

WORD CHOICES attend

Instead of the verb "attend" people usually say **come/go to**.

How many people ***came to*** *the meeting?*

He ***goes to*** *the gym regularly.*

The verb **make** is sometimes used when people are talking about whether or not they are able to attend an event.

I'm afraid I can't ***make*** *the meeting this afternoon* (= I will not be able to attend).

The expression **make it** is also used, meaning "to get to a place, even when there are problems."

The traffic was so bad we only just ***made it*** *in time for the start of the movie.*

PHRASAL VERB with attend

• **attend to** *something/someone* to manage or take care of something or someone ○ *Her company helps employees attend to elderly relatives.*

attendant /əˈten·dənt/ *n* [C] someone whose job is to help others in a particular place or situation ○ *a gas station/parking lot attendant* ○ See also: FLIGHT ATTENDANT

attention NOTICE /əˈten·tʃən/ *n* [U] the act of directing the mind to listen, see, or understand; notice ○ *In order to learn anything, you have to pay attention.* ○ *It's hard to command the attention of 23 eight-year-olds.* ○ *Let me finish this, then I'll give you my undivided attention.*

WAY OF STANDING /əˈten·tʃən/ *exclamation, n* [U] (in the armed forces) an order to stand straight and not move, with your feet together, arms by your sides, and head facing to the front, or this

way of standing ○ *Each cadet stood at attention for inspection.*

CARE /əˈten·tʃən/ *n* [U] time or effort that you are willing to give to help someone or something because you care about that person or thing ○ *It's an old house, and needs a lot of attention.*

WORD FAMILY attention			
Nouns	attention	*Adjectives*	attentive inattentive
Adverbs	attentively		

attention span *n* [C] the period during which you can stay interested or listen carefully to something

attentive /əˈtent·ɪv/ *adj* listening or watching carefully ○ *an attentive audience*

attentively /əˈtent·ɪv·li/ *adv* ○ *The children listened attentively to the story.*

attest /əˈtest/ *v* (of a person) to state with authority that something is true, or (of a situation or event) to show that something is likely to be true ○ [+ *that* clause] *As one who worked there for years, I can attest that applications are carefully reviewed.* ○ [I] *Her wealth was attested to by her fur coat and designer shoes.*

attic /ˈæt̬·ɪk/ *n* [C] a space in a house just under the roof, often used for storing things

attire /əˈtɑɪr/ *n* [U] clothes, esp. of a particular type ○ *business/formal attire*

attired /əˈtɑɪrd/ *adj* [not gradable] ○ *She was tastefully attired in a simple black dress.*

attitude Ⓐ /ˈæt̬·əˌtuːd/ *n* [C/U] **1** the way you feel about something or someone, or a particular feeling or opinion ○ [U] *Start each day with a positive attitude.* ○ [C] *People's attitudes toward family are set very early in life.* **2** *infml* If you say that someone has an attitude, you mean that the person seems unwilling to be helpful or polite.

attorney /əˈtɜr·ni/ *n* [C] a LAWYER ○ *a defense attorney* ➤ Usage: **lawyer, counsel or attorney?** at LAWYER

Attorney General /əˌtɜr·niˈdʒen·rəl/ *n* [C] *pl* **Attorneys General** the most important legal officer in a state or in the US

attract /əˈtrækt/ *v* [T] **1** to cause something to come toward something else, or to cause a person or animal to become interested in someone or something ○ *An open flame attracts moths.* ○ *The tennis championship will attract a lot of tourists to the city.* ○ *This movie is going to attract a lot of attention.* **2** If someone is attracted to someone else, he or she likes the other person or is interested in that person.

attraction /əˈtræk·ʃən/ *n* [C/U] **1** a quality or force of someone or something that tends to pull others in or create interest in the person or thing ○ [C] *The company's excellent employee benefits package is a major attraction.* ○ [U] *Sports hold little attraction for me.* **2** An attraction is also something that makes people want to go to a place: [C] *Florida has numerous tourist attractions.* **3** ***physics*** Attraction is also the force of GRAVITY (= force that makes objects fall toward earth), or the force of a MAGNET that pulls things toward it.

attractive /əˈtræk·tɪv/ *adj* causing interest or pleasure ○ *They made me a very attractive job offer.* ○ *They are an attractive family.* ○ *One of the less attractive features of California is the threat of earthquakes.*

attractively /əˈtræk·tɪv·li/ *adv* ○ *She likes to be attractively dressed.*

WORD FAMILY attract			
Nouns	attraction	*Verbs*	attract
Adjectives	attractive unattractive	*Adverbs*	attractively

WORD CHOICES attract

The verb **draw** can be used when a place or event attracts a lot of people.

*The game **drew** a crowd of 30,000.*

If someone is attracted to something by the offer of something pleasant or exciting, the verbs **entice** or **lure** can be used.

*The smell of coffee **enticed** people to enter the shop.*

*I was **lured** into the store by the smell of fresh bread.*

If something **tempts** you, you are attracted to it even though you know you do not need it or should not have it.

*I was **tempted** by the offer of a free cell phone.*

You can use the verb **seduce** when something attracts you so much that you do something you would not usually do.

*I wouldn't normally have bought this but I was **seduced** by the low price.*

When something attracts a particular person or group, you can use the verb **appeal**.

*The program is designed to **appeal** to 13- to 18-year-olds.*

attributable Ⓐ /əˈtrɪb·jət̬·ə·bəl/ *adj* caused by ○ *Her death was attributable to natural causes.* ○ **USAGE:** almost always followed by the preposition **to**.

attribute /ˈæ·trəˌbjuːt/ *n* [C] a quality or feature of a person or thing, esp. one that is an important part of its nature ○ *Self-confidence is a rare attribute in a 17-year-old.* ○ *She has the physical attributes to become a championship swimmer.*

PHRASAL VERB with attribute

• **attribute** *something* **to** *someone/something* Ⓐ to say or think that something is the result or work of something or someone else ○ *He attributed the project's success to a sophisticated computer program.* ○ *Most experts have attributed the etching to Dürer.*

attribution Ⓐ /ˌæ·trəˈbjuː·ʃən/ *n* [U] the act of saying what the origin or cause of something is ○ *He borrowed from other people's writing without attribution.*

A

attributive /ə'trɪb·jət̬·ɪv/ *adj* [not gradable] ***grammar*** of an adjective, noun, pronoun, or phrase placed before the noun it describes ○ *an attributive noun* ○ *In "a young woman," "young" is an adjective in the attributive position.*

attrition /ə'trɪʃ·ən/ *n* [U] *fml* a gradual reduction in the number of people who work for an organization that is achieved by not replacing those who leave ○ *Most of the job losses will come through attrition.*

attuned to /ə'tu:nd·tə, -tʊ, -ˌtu:/ *adj* especially able to understand or deal with ○ *People in New York seem attuned to fashion.*

atypical /eɪ'tɪp·ɪ·kəl/ *adj* not typical; different from most others of its type ○ *This game is very atypical of how we played this year.*

auburn /'ɔ:·bərn/ *adj, n* [U] (of) a red-brown color ○ *auburn hair* ○ [U] *Browns in the picture were highlighted with auburn.*

auction /'ɔ:k·ʃən/ *n* [C/U] a usually public sale of goods or property, where people make higher and higher BIDS (= offers of money) for each item, until there are no higher BIDS and it is sold for the most money offered ○ [C] *an auction of early American furniture* ○ [U] *bulls sold at auction*

auction /'ɔ:k·ʃən/ *v* [T] ○ *The artwork is being auctioned to benefit UNICEF.*

auctioneer /ˌɔ:k·ʃə'nɪr/ *n* [C] a person in charge of an auction

audacious /ɔ: 'deɪ·ʃəs/ *adj* showing an unusual willingness to take risks ○ *The car maker's audacious goal is to compete with the luxury cars of other manufacturers.*

audacity /ɔ:'dæs·ət̬·i/ *n* [U] unusually strong and esp. rude confidence in yourself ○ [+ *to* infinitive] *Our mayor has the audacity to claim credit for improvements he had nothing to do with.*

audible /'ɔ:d·ə·bəl/ *adj* loud enough to be heard ○ *Her voice was barely audible above the roar of the engines.*

audibly /'ɔ:d·ə·bli/ *adv* ○ *He sighed audibly.*

audience /'ɔ:d·i:·əns, 'ɑd-/ *n* [C] **1** the people, considered as a group, who watch or listen to a performance, movie, public event, etc., either together in one place or separately ○ *a live/television audience* ○ *The magazine is trying to reach a younger audience.* **2** ***literature*** The audience of a work of literature is the type of people the writer intended to read it. **3** An audience is also a formal meeting that you have with an important person: *an audience with the president*

audio /'ɔ:d·i:ˌoʊ/ *adj* [not gradable] of or involving sound and the recording and broadcasting of sound ○ *We lost the audio portion of the TV broadcast.* ○ Compare VIDEO

audiocassette /ˌɔ:d·i:ˌoʊ·kə'set/ *n* [C] a CASSETTE on which sound is recorded

audiotape /'ɔ:d·i:·oʊˌteɪp/ *n* [C] a thin, magnetic strip, usually made of plastic, on which sound is recorded

audiovisual /ˌɔ:d·i:·oʊ'vɪʒ·ə·wəl/, *abbreviation* **AV** *adj* [not gradable] involving both seeing and hearing ○ *The audiovisual presentation included slides of the birds and tapes of their songs.*

audit EXAMINATION /'ɔ:d·ət/ *n* [C] an official examination of records ○ *The agency is subject to regular financial audits.*

audit /'ɔ:d·ət/ *v* [T] ○ *We hired accountants to audit the company's books.*

auditor /'ɔ:d·ət̬·ər/ *n* [C] a person trained to make an official examination of financial records

audit BE AT CLASS /'ɔ:d·ət/ *v* [T] to go regularly to a class without being formally involved in it ○ *I audited some of her seminars.*

audition /ɔ:'dɪʃ·ən/ *n* [C] a short performance given by an actor, dancer, musician, or other performer that tests whether that person's skills are suitable for a particular event or group ○ *The boys' choir held rigorous auditions before each new member was admitted.*

audition /ɔ:'dɪʃ·ən/ *v* [I/T] to give, watch, or listen to a short performance that tests whether a performer's skills are suitable for a particular event or group ○ [I] *You'll have to audition for the role.* ○ [T] *They auditioned 125 dancers before choosing ten.*

auditorium /ˌɔ:d·ə'tɔ:r·i:·əm, -'toʊr-/ *n* [C] a large room with rows of seats and often a stage which is used for performances and for public events or meetings, or a building containing such a room ○ *a school/municipal auditorium*

auditory /'ɔ:d·əˌtɔ:r·i, -ˌtoʊr·i/ *adj* [not gradable] ***biology*** of or involving hearing ○ *The stroke impaired her auditory function but not her vision.*

augment /ɔ:g'ment/ *v* [T] to make something larger or fuller by adding something to it ○ *He augmented his income by taking a second job.*

august /ɔ:'gʌst/ *adj fml* having great importance and respect in society ○ *We toured the august chambers of the Supreme Court.*

August /'ɔ:·gəst/, *abbreviation* **Aug.** *n* [C/U] the eighth month of the year, after July and before September

aunt /ænt, ɑ:nt, ɑnt/ *n* [C] the sister of someone's mother or father, or the wife of someone's uncle ○ *We stopped off to visit my aunt and uncle in Boston.*

au pair /oʊ'per, -'pær/ *n* [C] *pl* **au pairs** a foreign person, usually a young woman, who lives with a family and looks after their children or cleans the house in return for meals, a room, and a small payment

aura /'ɔ:r·ə/ *n* [C] a feeling or character that a person or place seems to have ○ *The hotel had an aura of fading glamor about it.*

aural /'ɔ:r·əl/ *adj* [not gradable] relating to hearing ○ *She doesn't speak English well, but her aural comprehension is good.*

auspices /'ɔ:·spə·səz, -ˌsi:z/ *pl n* approval, support, and control ○ *Relief volunteers worked under the auspices of the Red Cross.*

auspicious /ɔː'spɪʃ·əs/ *adj* suggesting a positive and successful future ○ *Winning her first seven cases was an auspicious beginning for the young lawyer.*

austere /ɔː'stɪr/ *adj* **1** plain and without decoration, comforts, or anything extra ○ *Despite their wealth, they lead an austere life.* ○ *She depicts the austere beauty of the desert.* **2** An austere person does not seem friendly.
austerity /ɔː'ster·əṭ·i, -'stɪr-/ *n* [U] **1** *The warriors led a life of austerity.* **2** Austerity is also a bad economic condition that does not allow luxuries: *Military spending continues even in periods of austerity.*

authentic /ɔː'θent·ɪk/ *adj* being what it is claimed to be; GENUINE ○ *an authentic Goya drawing* ○ *How can we be sure the signature is authentic?* ○ *Sylvia's serves authentic soul food.*
authenticity /ˌɔːˌθen'tɪs·əṭ·i, -θən-/ *n* [U] ○ *Officials questioned the authenticity of his claim.*

author Ⓐ /'ɔː·θər/ *n* [C] a writer of a book, article, etc., or a person whose main job is writing books ○ *a talented young author* ○ *He is the author of seven books.*
author Ⓐ /'ɔː·θər/ *v* [T] ○ *Murphy authored the new legislation.*
authorship Ⓐ /'ɔː·θərˌʃɪp/ *n* [U] the origin of a written work ○ *No one would admit authorship of the memo.*

authoritarian /ɔːˌθɔːr·ə'ter·iː·ən, -ˌθɑr-/ *adj* demanding total obedience to those in positions of authority ○ *an authoritarian ruler/parent*

authority Ⓐ /ə'θɔːr·əṭ·i, ə'θɑr-/ *n* [C/U] **1** the power to control or demand obedience from others ○ [U] *The police have no legal authority in these disputes.* ○ [U] *We have to find someone in authority* (= a position of power). **2** An authority is someone with official responsibility for a particular area of activity: [C] *government/church authorities* **3** The authorities are the police or other government officials: *No attacks were reported to the authorities.* **4** An authority on a subject is an expert on it: [C] *an authority on immigration law*
authoritative Ⓐ /ə'θɔːr·əˌteɪṭ·ɪv, ə'θɑr-/ *adj* having the power of special knowledge, or (of a person) showing the confidence of having special knowledge ○ *an authoritative manner* ○ *Her opinion on the subject was considered authoritative.*
authoritatively /ə'θɔːr·əˌteɪṭ·ɪv·li, ə'θɑr-/ *adv* ○ *He spoke authoritatively about police work.*

WORD FAMILY authority			
Nouns	authority authorization	*Adjectives*	authoritarian authoritative unauthorized
Verbs	authorize		
		Adverb	authoritatively

authorize /'ɔː·θəˌrɑɪz/ *v* [T] to give official permission for something to happen, or to give someone official permission to do something ○ *The board authorized a new contract.*
authorization /ˌɔː·θə·rə'zeɪ·ʃən/ *n* [C/U] ○ [U] *I can't issue a check without authorization.*

autism /'ɔːˌtɪz·əm/ *n* [U] *medical* an illness that starts in young children and causes behavior that is unusually centered on the self while limiting development of social and communication skills
autistic /ɔː'tɪs·tɪk/ *adj* ○ *She works with autistic children.*

auto /'ɔːṭ·oʊ, 'ɑṭ-/ *n* [C] *pl* **autos** *short form of* AUTOMOBILE ○ *auto makers/manufacturers* ○ *the auto industry*

autobiography /ˌɔːṭ·ə·bɑɪ'ɑg·rə·fi/ *n* [C/U] ***literature*** the story of a person's life as written by that person, or the area of literature relating to books that describe such stories ○ [U] *The book was a mixture of family history and autobiography.* ○ Compare BIOGRAPHY
autobiographical /ˌɔːṭ·ə·bɑɪ·ə'græf·ɪ·kəl/ *adj* describing the writer or based on the writer's life ○ *an autobiographical novel*

autocracy /ɔː'tɑk·rə·si/ *n* [C/U] ***politics & government*** government by a single person or small group that has unlimited power or authority, or a country or society that has this form of government
autocratic /ˌɔːṭ·ə'kræṭ·ɪk/ *adj* ○ *an autocratic regime*

autograph /'ɔːṭ·əˌgræf/ *n* [C] a signature, esp. of a famous person ○ *He thought I was a famous actor and asked for my autograph.*
autograph /'ɔːṭ·əˌgræf/ *v* [T] to write your signature on something, often for someone else to keep

automaker /'ɔːṭ·oʊˌmeɪ·kər, 'ɑṭ-/ *n* [C] a big company that makes cars ○ *The nation's No. 3 automaker set an all-time monthly sales record in June.*

automate Ⓐ /'ɔːṭ·əˌmeɪt/ *v* [T] to make something operate automatically by using machines or computers ○ *New technologies let you automate control of your home lighting, appliances, and even heating and cooling systems.*
automated Ⓐ /'ɔːṭ·əˌmeɪ·ṭɪd/ made to operate by machines or computers in order to reduce the work done by humans ○ *an automated system* ○ *automated equipment*

automated teller machine, **automatic teller machine** *n* [C] an ATM

automatic Ⓐ **INDEPENDENT** /ˌɔːṭ·ə'mæṭ·ɪk/ *adj* able to operate independently of human control ○ *The car has a five-speed automatic transmission.*
automatically Ⓐ /ˌɔːṭ·ə'mæṭ·ɪ·kli/ *adv* ○ *The camera focuses automatically.*

NOT CONSCIOUS /ˌɔːṭ·ə'mæṭ·ɪk/ *adj* (of an action) done without thinking about it ○ *Soon enough, taking her pill every morning became automatic.*

CERTAIN /ˌɔːṭ·ə'mæṭ·ɪk/ *adj* happening according to rules that are certain to be followed, and therefore not needing a decision ○ *Citizenship is automatic for children born in the US.* ○ *People on Social Security get automatic cost-of-living increases each year.*
automatically /ˌɔːṭ·ə'mæṭ·ɪ·kli/ *adv* ○ *You get a pay increase automatically after six months.*

automation Ⓐ /ˌɔːṭ·ə'meɪ·ʃən/ *n* [U] the use of machines that operate automatically ○ *factory automation*

automobile /ˈɔːt̬·ə·moʊˌbiːl, ˌɔːt̬·ə·moʊˈbiːl/, *short form* **auto** *n* [C] a car ○ *the automobile industry*

automotive /ˌɔːt̬·əˈmoʊt̬·ɪv/ *adj* [not gradable] relating to road vehicles ○ *automotive equipment/fuels/supplies*

autonomic nervous system /ˌɔːt̬·əˈnɑm·ɪk ˈnɜr·vəs ˈsɪs·təm/ *n* [C] ***biology*** the part of the NERVOUS SYSTEM that controls automatic processes such as breathing, digestion, and the beating of the heart ○ Compare NERVOUS SYSTEM

autonomy /ɔːˈtɑn·ə·mi/ *n* [U] the right of a group of people to govern itself or to organize its own activities ○ *District officials had rebuffed a proposal to grant greater autonomy to local schools.*
autonomous /ɔːˈtɑn·ə·məs/ *adj* ○ *an autonomous region/republic*

autopsy /ˈɔːˌtɑp·si, ˈɔːt̬·əp-/ *n* [C] the act of cutting open and examining a dead body in order to discover the cause of death ○ *Police said they were awaiting the results of an autopsy.*

autumn /ˈɔːt̬·əm/ *n* [C/U] the season of the year between summer and winter, lasting from September to December north of the equator and from March to June south of the equator; fall

auxiliary /ɔːgˈzɪl·jə·ri/ *adj* giving help or support, esp. to a more important person or thing ○ *The hospital has an auxiliary power supply in case of a power failure.*

auxiliary verb *n* [C] ***grammar*** a verb that gives grammatical information that is not given by the main verb of a sentence ○ *"Has" is an auxiliary verb in the sentence "She has finished her book."*

auxin /ˈɔːk·sən/ *n* [C] ***biology*** a chemical substance that controls growth in plants

AV *adj abbreviation for* AUDIOVISUAL

avail *yourself* **of** *something* /əˈveɪl·əv, -ˌʌv, -ˌɑv/ *phrasal verb fml* to use something for your own benefit ○ *Voters should avail themselves of all the tools available to get information about the candidates.*

available Ⓐ /əˈveɪ·lə·bəl/ *adj* able to be obtained, used, or reached ○ *Her new book is available in bookstores all across America.*
availability Ⓐ /əˌveɪ·ləˈbɪl·ət̬·i/ *n* [U] ○ *I'll check on the availability of tickets.*

WORD FAMILY available	
Nouns availability	*Adjectives* available unavailable

avalanche /ˈæv·əˌlæntʃ/ *n* [C] **1** a large amount of ice, snow, dirt, or rock falling suddenly and quickly down the side of a mountain **2** *fig.* An avalanche is also the sudden arrival of too many things: *We received an avalanche of complaints.*

avant-garde /ˌɑvˌɑntˈgɑrd, ˌævˌɔːˈgɑrd/ *n* [U] the artists, writers, and musicians whose ideas, styles, and methods are highly original or modern in the period in which they live
avant-garde /ˌɑvˌɑntˈgɑrd, ˌævˌɔːˈgɑrd/ *adj* ○ *avant-garde art*

avarice /ˈæv·ə·rəs/ *n* [U] an extremely strong desire to obtain or keep wealth
avaricious /ˌæv·əˈrɪʃ·əs/ *adj* ○ *avaricious land speculators*

Ave. /æv/ *n abbreviation for* AVENUE STREET ○ *Our new address is 1366 Columbus Ave.*

avenge /əˈvendʒ/ *v* [T] to get satisfaction by harming or punishing the person responsible for something bad done to you or your family or friends ○ *In the second half of the movie, they team up to avenge the wrongs done to them.*

avenue STREET /ˈæv·əˌnuː/ *n* [C] a street, often a wide one, in a city or town ○ *Michigan Avenue in Chicago is famous for its elegant stores.*

POSSIBILITY /ˈæv·əˌnuː/ *n* [C] a method or way of doing something; a possibility ○ *China and the United States are exploring avenues of military cooperation.* ○ *Only two avenues are open to us – accept his offer or file a lawsuit.*

average USUAL STANDARD /ˈæv·rɪdʒ, -ə·rɪdʒ/ *n* [U] a standard or level that is considered to be typical or usual ○ *The quality of her work is well above average.*
average /ˈæv·rɪdʒ, -ə·rɪdʒ/ *adj* [not gradable] ○ *Janeen was of average height but had great jumping ability.* ○ *"Was the movie good?" "It wasn't great, just average."*

AMOUNT /ˈæv·rɪdʒ, -ə·rɪdʒ/ *n* [C] ***mathematics*** the result obtained by adding two or more amounts together and dividing the total by the number of amounts, or by another total ○ *I'm 35 and my brothers are 32 and 26, so the average of our ages is 31.* ○ *In his third season on the team, he raised his batting average to .270.* ○ *Interest rates rose on average to 10.05% in January.*
average /ˈæv·rɪdʒ, -ə·rɪdʒ/ *adj* [not gradable] ○ *The average sales price for a house around here is about $150,000.*
average /ˈæv·rɪdʒ, -ə·rɪdʒ/ *v* [I/T] ○ [T] *Trainees average* (= earn an average of) *$20,000 a year.* ○ [I/T] *My grades vary from year to year, but they average (out to) 3.2, or a little better than a B.*

IDIOM with average

• **on average** usually ○ *On average, a person's income is highest when they are in their mid-50s.* ○ *The city's police chief says they arrest, on average, 300 people each day.*

PHRASAL VERB with average

• **average out** to become equal or similar over a period of time ○ *The highs and lows of life tend to average out.*

averse /əˈvɜrs/ *adj* strongly disliking or opposed to ○ *Few politicians are averse to appearing on television.*

aversion /əˈvɜr·ʒən, -ʃən/ *n* [C] a feeling of strong dislike or unwillingness to do something ○ *I felt an instant aversion to his parents.* ○ *She has a deep aversion to getting up early.*

avert PREVENT /ə'vɜrt/ *v* [T] to prevent something bad from happening; avoid ○ *The last-minute agreement averted renewed fighting.*
TURN AWAY /ə'vɜrt/ *v* [T] to turn away your eyes or thoughts ○ *The shy man was standing before me, his eyes averted.*

aviation /ˌeɪ·viː'eɪ·ʃən/ *n* [U] the activity of flying aircraft, or of designing, producing, and maintaining them
aviator /'eɪ·viːˌeɪţ·ə/ *n* [C] *dated* ○ *Charles Lindbergh was the first aviator to fly nonstop across the Atlantic Ocean.*

avid /'æv·+əd/ *adj* extremely eager or interested ○ *Knowles is an avid runner and cross-country skier.*
avidly /'æv·+əd·li/ *adv* ○ *We listened avidly to the news from our secret radios.*

avocado /ˌɑv·ə'kɑd·oʊ, ˌæv-/ *n* [C] *pl* **avocados** a fruit with thick green or black skin, a large round seed at the center, and oily green or yellow flesh, which is often eaten as a vegetable in salads

avoid /ə'vɔɪd/ *v* [T] to stay away from someone or something, or prevent something from happening, or not allow yourself to do something ○ *Do you think Robert is avoiding me? I haven't seen him for a month.* ○ *I try to avoid going shopping on Saturdays because the stores are so crowded.* ○ *If you want to lose weight, avoid eating between meals.*
avoidance /ə'vɔɪd·ᵊns/ *n* [U] ○ *The avoidance of injury is more important than winning a game.*

GRAMMAR

avoid

When **avoid** is followed by a verb, the verb is always in the **-ing** form.

I avoided seeing him for several days.
~~*I avoided to see him for several days.*~~

WORD FAMILY avoid

Nouns	avoidance	*Adjectives*	unavoidable
Verbs	avoid		

avowed /ə'vɑʊd/ *adj* stated or admitted ○ *an avowed enemy*
avowedly /ə'vɑʊ·+əd·li/ *adv* ○ *an avowedly old-fashioned teacher*

await /ə'weɪt/ *v* [T] to wait for or be in the future of someone or something ○ *The two men are awaiting trial, scheduled to begin next month.* ○ *There are no jobs awaiting those farmers.*

awake /ə'weɪk/ *adj* not sleeping ○ *If I drink coffee late in the day, I can't sleep and stay awake all night.*
awake /ə'weɪk/ *v* [I/T] *past simp.* **awoke, awaked,** *past part.* **awoken** to stop sleeping, or to cause someone to stop sleeping ○ [I] *I awoke at 7, as usual.*

awaken /ə'weɪ·kən/ *v* [I/T] **1** to stop sleeping, or to cause someone to stop sleeping ○ [T] *The family was awakened by a noise.* **2** *fig.* If interest is awakened, it is made more active: [T] *His television series awakened popular interest in American architecture.*

award /ə'wɔːrd/ *v* [T] to give something valuable, such as money or a prize following an official decision ○ *Her poodle was awarded first prize in the dog show.* ○ *Their company was awarded a contract worth $40 million by the federal government.*
award /ə'wɔːrd/ *n* [C] ○ *Marion Jones won the Jesse Owens award as the outstanding athlete of the year.*

aware Ⓐ /ə'wer, ə'wær/ *adj* knowing that something exists, or having knowledge or experience of a particular thing ○ [+ (*that*) clause] *We were just not aware (that) garbage would be a problem, that we ever would need to recycle.* ○ *Are you aware of any reason why you cannot act fairly as a juror in this trial?*
awareness Ⓐ /ə'wer·nəs, ə'wær-/ *n* [U] ○ *His tragedy has brought a heightened awareness to the conditions surrounding heatstroke.*

WORD FAMILY aware

Nouns	awareness	*Adjectives*	aware unaware
Adverbs	unawares		

awash /ə'wɑʃ, ə'wɔːʃ/ *adj* **1** covered with a liquid, usually water ○ *They believe that the red planet was not only awash in water at one time, but also may have supported life.* **2** If someone or some place is awash in something that is not a liquid, there is a large amount of it: *The reason why I say that is because the country is awash in money.*

away SOMEWHERE ELSE /ə'weɪ/ *adj, adv* [not gradable] somewhere else, or to or in a different place, position, or situation ○ *Barbara is away on vacation until the end of the week.* ○ *The Jeffersons went away for the weekend, but they'll be back on Monday.*
DISTANT /ə'weɪ/ *adv* [not gradable] at a distance (from this place) ○ *How far away is the station?*
IN THE FUTURE /ə'weɪ/ *adv* [not gradable] in the future; from now ○ *The wedding is still six months away.*
INTO PLACE /ə'weɪ/ *adv* [not gradable] in or into the usual or a suitable place, esp. one that is enclosed ○ *Put the groceries away before you go out again.*
GRADUALLY /ə'weɪ/ *adv* [not gradable] gradually until mostly or completely gone ○ *The music faded away.*
CONTINUOUSLY /ə'weɪ/ *adv* [not gradable] continuously or repeatedly, or actively ○ *Chris has been working away on the car all day.*

awe /ɔː/ *n* [U] **1** a feeling of great respect, usually mixed with fear or surprise ○ *I was too much in awe of him to address him directly.* **2** If something is **awe-inspiring**, it causes you to admire or respect it a lot: *Niagara Falls is an awe-inspiring sight.*
awe /ɔː/ *v* [T] *pres. part.* **awing** ○ *The school kids were awed when Doug Flutie, the football star, entered the room.*

awesome /ˈɔː·səm/ *adj* causing feelings of great admiration, respect, or fear ○ *an awesome achievement* ○ *(slang) Your new haircut is awesome* (= extremely good).

awful /ˈɔː·fəl/ *adj* **1** very bad, unpleasant, or of low quality ○ *The weather was awful the whole time – cold and wet.* ○ *Fox TV has canceled the truly awful sitcom "Monty" after a short tryout.* **2** Awful also means very great or large: *We're spending an awful amount of money!*
awfully /ˈɔː·fliː, -fə·li/, *infml* **awful** /ˈɔː·fəl/ *adv* very or extremely ○ *Your fever is awfully high – I think we'd better call a doctor.* ○ *I'm awfully sorry, but there are no rooms in the hotel available right now.* ○ *We were awfully pleased when our daughter was named the best student in her class.*

IDIOM with awful

• **an awful lot** a very large amount ○ *That red is an awful lot brighter than the color of your house.* ○ *I don't know an awful lot about art* (= I know very little), *but I'm learning.*

awhile /əˈhwɑɪl, əˈwɑɪl/ *adv* [not gradable] for a short time ○ *I'd like to rest awhile before we continue.*

awkward DIFFICULT /ˈɔː·kwərd/ *adj* difficult to use, do, or deal with ○ *The computer came in a big box that was awkward to carry.*
ANXIOUS /ˈɔː·kwərd/ *adj* **1** causing inconvenience, anxiety, or embarrassment ○ *It was an awkward situation, because the restaurant was too expensive for us but we didn't want to just get up and walk out.* **2** Someone who feels awkward feels embarrassed or nervous: *We were the first to arrive at the party and felt a little awkward.*
awkwardly /ˈɔː·kwər·dli/ *adv* ○ *The publication of the article was awkwardly timed for the government.*
awkwardness /ˈɔː·kwərd·nəs/ *n* [U] ○ *His awkwardness with girls disappeared once he got to college.*
LACKING GRACE /ˈɔː·kwərd/ *adj* lacking grace or skill when moving ○ *He's too awkward – he'll never be a good dancer.*
awkwardly /ˈɔː·kwər·dli/ *adv* ○ *He sat awkwardly on the floor.*

awning /ˈɔː·nɪŋ/ *n* [C] a piece of material supported by a frame and used to protect part of a building from the sun or rain

awoke /əˈwoʊk/ *past simple of* AWAKE

awoken /əˈwoʊ·kən/ *past participle of* AWAKE

AWOL /ˈeɪ·wɔːl; ˌeɪˌdʌb·əl·jʊˌoʊˈel/ *adj* [not gradable] *abbreviation for* away without offical leave (= absent without permission) ○ *The corporal went AWOL, and we haven't seen him since.* ○ **USAGE:** Used esp. about soldiers.

awry /əˈrɑɪ/ *adj, adv* not in the intended manner, or out of position, or wrong ○ *There are too many people involved, and something is bound to go awry.*

ax TOOL, **axe** /æks/ *n* [C] a tool consisting of a heavy iron or steel blade at the end of a long wooden handle, used for cutting wood
STOP /æks/ *v* [T] to order someone suddenly to give up a job, or to stop or reduce something suddenly ○ *The company has already axed 14 people, and many more may lose their jobs.* ○ *Yesterday the airline axed three of its daily flights to Chicago.*
ax, axe /æks/ *n* [C usually sing] the order to give up your job, or to stop or prevent something from happening ○ *Three staff members got the ax yesterday.* ○ *If the budget is cut, educational programs will get the ax.* ○ *Everyone is scared to death wondering where the ax will fall next.*

axiom /ˈæk·siː·əm/ *n* [C] a statement or principle that is generally accepted to be true
axiomatic /ˌæk·siː·əˈmæt̬·ɪk/ *adj* obvious and not needing proof

axis /ˈæk·səs/ *n* [C] *pl* **axes** **1** a real or imaginary straight line that goes through the center of a spinning object or a line that divides a shape into two equal halves **2** ***earth science*** The earth's axis is an imaginary line that goes through the earth between the North Pole and the South Pole. **3** ***mathematics*** An axis is also a line on a GRAPH used to show the position of a point.

Axis Powers *pl n* Germany, Italy, and Japan during World War II.

axle /ˈæk·səl/ *n* [C] a bar connected to the center of a circular object such as a wheel that allows or causes it to turn, esp. one connecting two wheels of a vehicle

axon /ˈæk·sɑn/ *n* [C] ***biology*** a long thread that comes out of a nerve cell and carries signals from it

aye /ɑɪ/ *n* [C] (used esp. in voting) yes, or a vote that means yes and supports a suggestion or plan of action ○ *The ayes have it, 20 to 12, and the motion is carried.*

B b

B LETTER, **b** /biː/ *n* [C] *pl* **B's, Bs, b's, bs** the second letter of the English alphabet

MUSICAL NOTE /biː/ *n* [C/U] *pl* **B's, Bs** ***music*** in Western music, the seventh note in the SCALE (= series of notes) that begins on the note C, or a set of notes based on this note

MARK /biː/ *n* [C] *pl* **B's, Bs** a mark that means very good, given to something of satisfactory quality, esp. school work ○ *Mrs. Madden gave me a B on my essay for English.*

B.A., **A.B.** *n* [C] *abbreviation for* Bachelor of Arts (= a first college degree in an art or SOCIAL SCIENCE). ○ Compare B.S.

babble /ˈbæb·əl/ *v* [I/T] to speak quickly, in a confused, excited, or foolish way ○ [I] *She was babbling on about a robbery.*

babble /ˈbæb·əl/ *n* [U] **1** *The baby's babble would soon turn into language.* **2** Babble also means a low, continuous sound: *It was hard to talk over the babble of voices in the room.*

babe /beɪb/ *n* [C] a small baby, or *infml* an affectionate way of addressing a wife, husband, or other person you love

baboon /bæˈbuːn/ *n* [C] a PRIMATE (= animal that is most like humans) found in Africa and southern Asia that has a long nose, short tail, and is related to monkeys

baby /ˈbeɪ·bi/ *n* [C] **1** a very young child ○ *Sandra had a baby on May 29th.* ○ *My younger brother is the baby of the family.* **2** Baby can be used to refer to anything young or smaller than usual: *baby corn/lima beans* **3** *disapproving* Baby can also mean someone who is behaving childishly. ○ *She complained like a baby about her boyfriend.* **4** *infml* Baby is an affectionate way of addressing someone. **5** *infml* A baby can also be a project or job someone has a special interest in or responsibility for: *The new computer system is really Phil's baby.*

baby /ˈbeɪ·bi/ *v* [T] ○ *Some parents baby their children too much.* ○ *I like to be babied when I'm sick.*

babyish /ˈbeɪ·biː ˌɪʃ/ *adj disapproving* ○ *Aren't those toys a bit babyish for him?*

baby boom *n* [C] a large increase in the number of babies born in a particular place during a particular time

baby boomer, *infml* **boomer** *n* [C] a person born during a baby boom in the US between 1947 and 1961 ○ *Like typical baby boomers, they're making different choices than those of their parents' generation.*

baby carriage *n* [C] a small bed for carrying a baby that has four wheels and a wide handle for pushing it

baby-sit /ˈbeɪ·biː ˌsɪt/, **sit** *v* [I/T] **-tt-** to take care of a baby or child, esp. as a job ○ [I] *I'm going to baby-sit on Tuesday night.*

baby-sitter /ˈbeɪ·biː ˌsɪt̬·ər/, **sitter** *n* [C] ○ *Our baby-sitter is from the local college.*

bachelor /ˈbætʃ·ə·lər/ *n* [C] a man who is not married ○ *He remained a confirmed bachelor until he was 60.*

bachelor party *n* [C] a party with male friends and family members for a man about to be married

bachelor's (degree) /ˈbætʃ·ə·lərz (dɪˈɡriː)/ *n* [C] a first degree at a college or university; B.A. or B.S.

back RETURN /bæk/ *adv* [not gradable] **1** in, at, or toward a previous place or condition or an earlier time ○ *When you're done, please put back my scissors.* ○ *She just came back from vacation yesterday.* ○ *He looked back to see if he was being followed.* ○ *I heard from them back in January.* **2** Back can also mean in return: *Can I call you back in a few minutes?*

back /bæk/ *adj* [not gradable] ○ *She went out shopping earlier, but I think she's back.*

FARTHER AWAY /bæk/ *adv* [not gradable] farther away; to a farther place ○ *We can push the table back and have more room.* ○ *Stand back!* ○ *She lay back in the chair and napped.* ○ *Marsha always wears her hair pulled back from her face.*

back /bæk/ *v* [I/T] to move backward ○ [T] *I backed the car into a big rock.* ○ [I] *He backed away from the guy.*

FARTHEST PART /bæk/ *n* [U] **1** the part of something that is farthest from the front ○ *I found my tennis racket at the back of the closet.* ○ *We sat in the back of the bus.* **2** The back of your hand is the side opposite the PALM that has hair growing on it.

back /bæk/ *adj* [not gradable] ○ *She left the house by the back door.*

SUPPORT /bæk/ *v* [T] to give support to someone or something with money or words ○ *The board refuses to back our plan.*

backing /ˈbæk·ɪŋ/ *n* [U] ○ *If I go ahead with this project, can I count on your backing?*

backer /ˈbæk·ər/ *n* [C] ○ *We'll need financial backers to do this.*

BODY PART /bæk/ *n* [C] **1** the part of your body opposite the front, from your neck to the top of your legs ○ *He lay on his back, staring at the ceiling.* ○ *She didn't want to talk and turned her back to him.* **2** The back of a seat is the part your back leans against.

IDIOMS with back

- **back and forth** moving first in one direction and then in the opposite one ○ *She swayed back and forth to the music.*
- **back in the saddle** doing something that you stopped doing for a period of time ○ *The chairman is back in the saddle after his heart attack.*
- *someone's* **back is turned** someone is not facing you or looking at you ○ *He couldn't see her face because her back was turned.*

•**back to the drawing board** back to the beginning of a process to start it again, because it is not working ○ *With the peace accord in shreds, we must go back to the drawing board.*
•**back to basics** returning to the simple and most important things ○ *In her latest album, she has gone back to basics, using acoustic instruments with wonderful results.*
•**in back of** behind ○ *They sat in back of us on the plane.*
•**in the back of** *your* **mind, at the back of** *your* **mind** held as an idea in your mind, but not thought about frequently ○ *In the back of my mind I guess I always thought I would be a ballplayer.*
•**on the back burner, to the back burner** not being done now, but left to be considered in the future ○ *The company put the project on the back burner.* ○ *Their complaints have definitely been pushed to the back burner.*

PHRASAL VERBS with **back**

•**back down, back off** to admit you were wrong, or to stop supporting a position ○ *The mayor will not back down from his decision.*
•**back out** to refuse to do something you earlier had agreed to do ○ *You said you'd come – you can't back out now!*
•**back up** *(something)* **MOVE BACKWARD** [M] to move backward, or to drive a vehicle backward ○ *It was hard to back up in such a narrow driveway.* ○ *Back your truck up to my door.*
•**back up** *(something)* **GATHER** [M] to gradually collect or gather in one place, esp. traffic or a liquid ○ *The sink backed up.* ○ *The accident backed traffic up for miles.*
•**back up** *someone/something* **PROVIDE SUPPORT** [M] to provide support or help to someone or something ○ *The last witness backed up what other people had said happened.* ○ Related noun: BACKUP SUPPORTER
•**back up** *something* **MAKE EXTRA COPY** [M] to make a copy of information in a computer that is stored separately ○ *We back up our files every day on a disk.* ○ Related noun: BACKUP EXTRA COPY

backache /ˈbæk·eɪk/ *n* [C] a pain in your back

backbiting /ˈbækˌbɑɪt̬·ɪŋ/ *n* [U] unpleasant or unkind remarks made about a person who is not present ○ *There's a lot of backbiting and disarray among key officials.*

backboard /ˈbæk·bɔːrd, -bourd/ *n* [C] (in BASKETBALL) a board behind the metal ring that you have to throw the ball through to score ○ *He missed, and the ball bounced off the backboard.*

backbone **BODY PART** /ˈbæk·boun/ *n* [C] your SPINE

IMPORTANT PART /ˈbæk·boun/ *n* [U] the part of something that provides strength and support ○ *Newcomers are now the backbone of this team.*

CHARACTER /ˈbæk·boun/ *n* [U] strength of character or bravery ○ *The delegates had enough backbone to reject the proposal.*

backbreaking /ˈbækˌbreɪ·kɪŋ/ *adj* very tiring or needing a lot of physical energy ○ *Digging a trench is backbreaking work.*

backcountry /ˈbækˌkʌn·tri/ *n* [U] a rural or mountain area that is away from cities and has few people ○ *That night, I camped at Bee Island, one of the park's six backcountry campsites.*

backdrop /ˈbæk·drɑp/ *n* [U] **1** the things that can be seen behind something ○ *An impressive rocky coastline with a backdrop of green hills continues southward.* **2** A backdrop to an event is a situation that already exists and that influences the event: *Today we work against the backdrop of an industry in the midst of change.*

backfire **HAVE BAD RESULT** /ˈbæk·fɑɪr/ *v* [I] (of a plan) to have the opposite result from the one you intended ○ *Some hotel owners worry that the idea of attracting more visitors may backfire and make the place less attractive.*

MAKE NOISE /ˈbæk·fɑɪr/ *v* [I] (of an engine) to make a loud noise because the fuel burned too soon

backgammon /ˈbækˌgæm·ən/ *n* [U] a game for two players in which the winner is the first to move the pieces around a special board

background **THINGS BEHIND** /ˈbæk·grɑʊnd/ *n* [C/U] **1** things that appear to be farther away or behind what is nearer or in front, esp. in a picture ○ [C] *He photographed the models against different backgrounds.* ○ [U] *With so much noise in the background, I couldn't hear what she was saying.* ○ [C] *The city's skyline was our background.* **2** A background can also be whatever is happening around you but not involving you directly: *Worry was always part of the background.* **3** ***art*** In a painting or a story, the background is the people and things that are less important and not the main subject.

EXPERIENCE /ˈbæk·grɑʊnd/ *n* [C] **1** the things that have made you into the person you are, esp. family, experience, and education ○ *The school has students from many different backgrounds.* **2** An event's background is facts or history that help to explain how or why it happened: *To understand the war, we need to consider its historical and political background.*

backhand /ˈbæk·hænd/ *n* [C] (in sports such as tennis) a way of hitting the ball in which the back of the hand holding the RACKET is turned in the direction you want to hit the ball ○ *He has a fabulous backhand.* ○ Compare FOREHAND

backhanded /ˈbækˈhæn·dəd/ *adj* (of something said) not clear and usually meaning the opposite of what it seems to mean ○ *Her backhanded compliments annoyed everyone.*

backlash /ˈbæk·læʃ/ *n* [C] a strong, negative reaction to something, esp. to change ○ *The mayor foresaw no political backlash against his proposal.*

backlog /ˈbæk·lɔːg, -lɑg/ *n* [C usually sing] a large number of things waiting to be done ○ *I have a huge backlog of work on my desk.*

B

backpack /ˈbæk·pæk/, *short form* **pack** *n* [C] a bag carried on the back, usually of cloth with many pockets and straps that go over your shoulders, used to carry things

backpack /ˈbæk·pæk/ *v* [I] to walk long distances, carrying your things in a backpack ○ *We backpacked through the Colorado Rockies last summer.*

backpacker /ˈbæk·pæk·ər/ *n* [C] ○ *A string of backpackers passed us on the trail.*

back road *n* [C] a small road without much traffic, away from a main road

backseat SEAT BEHIND DRIVER /ˈbækˈsiːt/ *n* [C] the seat behind the front seat of a car

LESS IMPORTANT PLACE /ˈbækˈsiːt/ *n* [C] a position of less importance ○ *Nelson will never take a backseat to anyone.*

backseat driver *n* [C] a person who gives unwanted advice or criticism, esp. to the driver of a car

backside /ˈbæk·sɑɪd/ *n* [C] *infml* the part of the body you sit on; your buttocks

backslide /ˈbæk·slɑɪd/ *v* [I] *past* **backslid** to return to old, often bad, habits, or to a worse condition ○ *Some states have started to backslide on health care.*

backstage /ˈbækˈsteɪdʒ/ *adj, adv* [not gradable] in or to the area behind the stage of a theater ○ *We went backstage after the show to meet the actors.*

backstroke /ˈbæk·stroʊk/ *n* [U] a way of swimming while lying on your back ○ *She was a bronze medalist in the 200-meter backstroke at the 2000 Sydney Games.*

back-to-back BACKS TOUCHING *adj* [not gradable] with backs touching or toward each other ○ *We stood back-to-back to see who was taller.*

ONE AFTER ANOTHER *adj, adv* [not gradable] one following after another ○ *The soccer team won back-to-back victories last weekend.*

backtrack /ˈbæk·træk/ *v* [I] **1** to go back the same way you came, or to consider information again ○ *We need to backtrack a bit and examine the history of this problem.* **2** If you backtrack from something you previously said or agreed to do, you begin to stop supporting it: *The government backtracked on plans that would have increased taxes.*

backup SUPPORT /ˈbæk·ʌp/ *n* [C/U] support or help, or someone or something that provides support or help ○ *a backup generator* ○ *They didn't realize when they hired him that he had a backup band.* ○ *We want to have the factual backup to make our case.* ○ Related verb: BACK UP PROVIDE SUPPORT

EXTRA COPY /ˈbæk·ʌp/ *n* [C/U] an extra copy of information on a computer that is stored separately ○ *Did you make a backup of these files?* ○ Related verb: BACK UP MAKE EXTRA COPY

backward TOWARD THE BACK /ˈbæk·wərd/, **backwards** /ˈbæk·wərdz/ *adv* [not gradable] toward the direction that is opposite to the one in which you are facing or opposite to the usual direction ○ *He took a step backward.* ○ *He began counting backward: "Ten, nine, eight . . ."* ○ *She was skating around the rink, backward and forward.* ○ Compare FORWARD LEADING

backward /ˈbæk·wərd/ *adj* [not gradable] ○ *He did a terrific backward somersault.*

NOT DEVELOPED /ˈbæk·wərd/ *adj* not developed, or not modern or advanced ○ *The state needs to reform its backward election laws.*

backwardness /ˈbæk·wərd·nəs/ *n* [U] ○ *The country must first overcome its backwardness and poverty.*

backwater /ˈbækˌwɔːt̬·ər, -ˌwɑt̬-/ *n* [C] a place that does not seem to know much about the world and its ways ○ *Miami transformed from a cultural backwater to a culinary trendsetter.*

backwoods /ˈbækˈwʊdz/ *pl n* a place that is off by itself, not near to transportation or a larger town ○ *I grew up in the backwoods of North Carolina.*

backyard /ˈbækˈjɑrd/ *n* [C] the area behind a house, or more generally, an area near the place you live ○ *Residents don't want a nuclear power plant in their backyard.*

bacon /ˈbeɪ·kən/ *n* [U] salted or smoked meat from the back or sides of a pig, usually eaten sliced and fried

bacteria /bækˈtɪr·iː·ə/ *pl n singular* **bacterium** ***biology*** very small organisms that are found everywhere and are the cause of many diseases

bacterial /bækˈtɪr·iː·əl/ *adj* [not gradable] relating to or caused by bacteria

bad UNPLEASANT /bæd/ *adj comparative* **worse**, *superlative* **worst 1** not good; disappointing or unpleasant, or causing difficulties or harm ○ *We heard the bad news about Dorothy's illness.* ○ *Flights were delayed because of bad weather.* ○ *Too much salt is bad for you* (= has a harmful effect on your health). **2** Bad can also mean serious or severe: *a bad accident/storm*

badly /ˈbæd·li/, *not standard* **bad** *adv comparative* **worse**, *superlative* **worst** in an extreme way; seriously or severely ○ *His face was badly bruised and swollen after the accident.* ○ *He took the news of his sister's death badly.* ○ See also: BADLY

LOW QUALITY /bæd/ *adj comparative* **worse**, *superlative* **worst** of very low quality; not acceptable ○ *bad manners* ○ *We thought the hotel was bad and the food was terrible.* ○ *That was one of the worst movies I've ever seen.*

badly /ˈbæd·li/, *not standard* **bad** *adv* [not gradable] *comparative* **worse**, *superlative* **worst** ○ *The event was badly organized.* ○ *He behaved badly.* ○ See also: BADLY

B

EVIL /bæd/ *adj comparative* **worse**, *superlative* **worst** (of people or actions) evil or morally unacceptable ○ *He's not a bad person.*

UNHEALTHY /bæd/ *adj comparative* **worse**, *superlative* **worst** (of a person) ill or not well, or (of an illness) serious or severe ○ *a bad back/heart* ○ *a bad cough* ○ *bad health* ○ *He's in really bad shape.* ○ *He's got bad arthritis and can hardly walk.*

IDIOM with bad

• **not (too) bad** satisfactory; OK ○ *"How are you?" "Not too bad, thanks - ready for my vacation to start!"* ○ See also: TOO BAD at TOO IDIOMS; FEEL BAD at FEEL IDIOMS

bad breath *n* [U] breath that smells unpleasant

bade /bæd, beɪd/ *past simple of* BID TELL

badge /bædʒ/ *n* [C] a small piece of metal worn to show your membership in a group or your authority within an organization such as the police

badger **ANIMAL** /ˈbædʒ·ər/ *n* [C] an animal that digs holes in the ground, where it lives, and comes out at night to feed

ASK /ˈbædʒ·ər/ *v* [T] to annoy someone by repeatedly asking questions or telling the person to do something ○ *He badgered officials at the American Embassy to help.*

badlands /ˈbæd·lændz/ *pl n* a dry area without plants and with large rocks that the weather has worn into strange shapes

badly /ˈbæd·li/, *not standard* **bad** /bæd/ *adv* [not gradable] much or very much ○ *The UN sent 90 tons of badly needed food.* ○ *Texas wants very badly to be considered tops in the school system.* ○ See also: BADLY at BAD UNPLEASANT; BADLY at BAD LOW QUALITY

badminton /ˈbæd ˌmɪnt·ᵊn/ *n* [U] a sport in which two or four people hit a SHUTTLECOCK (= small, very light object with feathers) over a high net

bad-mouth /ˈbæd·mɑʊθ, -mɑʊð/ *v* [T] *esp. disapproving* to make criticisms about someone or something ○ *Why are you always bad-mouthing the medical profession?*

bad-tempered *adj* becoming annoyed or angry very easily

baffle /ˈbæf·əl/ *v* [T] to cause someone to be unable to understand or explain something ○ *Even his friends were baffled by his behavior.*

baffling /ˈbæf·lɪŋ/ *adj* ○ *a baffling mystery*

bag **OPEN CONTAINER** /bæg/ *n* [C] a container of paper or light plastic that is open at the top, used esp. to hold things you have bought ○ *a grocery/shopping bag*

bag /bæg/ *v* [T] **-gg-** to put items in a bag ○ *I'll bag your groceries for you.*

CLOSED CONTAINER /bæg/ *n* [C] **1** a container of leather, hard plastic, or cloth material with a top that can be closed, for carrying clothes or other objects, esp. when you are traveling; a SUITCASE ○ *You can leave your bags in the hotel room, and I'll send someone up for them later.* **2** A bag is also a woman's POCKETBOOK: *I carry a large shoulder bag.*

HUNT /bæg/ *v* [T] **-gg-** to hunt and capture or kill an animal or bird ○ *Only 15 percent of last year's hunters actually bagged a deer.*

IDIOMS with bag

• **bags under** *someone's* **eyes** dark circles, sometimes with loose or swollen skin, under the eyes, usually as a result of being tired or ill ○ *I'd been up late the night before , and I had huge bags under my eyes.*

• **in the bag** certain to be won, achieved, or obtained ○ *When the score got to 8 to 2 we knew the game was in the bag.*

bagel /ˈbeɪ·gəl/ *n* [C] a soft, chewy, circular piece of bread with a hole in the center

baggage **BAGS** /ˈbæg·ɪdʒ/ *n* [U] the bags that you take with you when you travel; LUGGAGE ○ *How many pieces of baggage do you have?*

FEELINGS /ˈbæg·ɪdʒ/ *n* [U] the beliefs and feelings that you have which influence how you think and behave ○ *Everybody brings their own baggage to viewing a work of art.*

baggy /ˈbæg·i/ *adj* (of clothes) hanging loosely because of being too big or having been stretched ○ *a baggy sweater*

bagpipes /ˈbæg·pɑɪps/ *pl n* a musical instrument played by blowing air into a bag and forcing it out through pipes, used esp. in Scotland

bail **MONEY** /beɪl/ *n* [U] a sum of money given to a law court by a person accused of a crime so that the person can be released until the trial, at which time the money will be returned ○ *The judge set bail at $100,000.*

REMOVE WATER /beɪl/ *v* [I/T] to remove water from a boat by using a container ○ [T] *I'd float around for hours fishing and bailing out the water leaking in.*

PHRASAL VERBS with bail

• **bail out** *something/someone* **HELP** [M] to help someone or something such as a plan or company, esp. by giving or lending money ○ *Congress passed a $15 billion Aid package to bail out the airlines.* ○ Related noun: BAILOUT

• **bail out** **JUMP** **1** to jump out of an aircraft with a PARACHUTE, esp. because the aircraft is about to have an accident ○ *The pilot barely had time to bail out.* **2** *fig.* To bail out is also to stop doing or being involved in something, esp. to avoid failure or difficulty: *The TV show triggered a number of protests, and some of the sponsors bailed out.*

bailiff /ˈbeɪ·ləf/ *n* [C] an official who is responsible for prisoners who are appearing in court

bailout /ˈbeɪ·lɑʊt/ *n* [C] the process of saving a company, plan, or other thing from failing by providing lots of money ○ *The government mounted a massive bailout of troubled savings and loan institutions.* ○ Related verb: BAIL OUT HELP

B

bait **FOOD** /beɪt/ *n* [U] **1** a small amount of food used to attract and catch a fish or animal ○ *The fishermen bought some worms to use as bait.* **2** *fig.* Bait is also anything used to persuade someone to do something: *Lawyers making the investment offering will find out today whether someone is ready to take the bait.*

bait /beɪt/ *v* [T] ○ *You can bait the mousetrap with a piece of cheese.*

MAKE ANGRY /beɪt/ *v* [T] to intentionally make someone angry by saying or doing annoying things ○ *She enjoys baiting her brother by teasing him about his girlfriend.*

bake /beɪk/ *v* [I/T] to cook inside an OVEN ○ [T] *to bake a cake/bread/cookies*

baker /ˈbeɪ·kər/ *n* [C] a person whose job is to make bread and cakes for sale

bakery /ˈbeɪ·kə·ri/ *n* [C] a place where bread, cakes, and pastries are made or sold

balance **POSITION** /ˈbæl·əns/ *n* [U] **1** the condition of someone or something in which its weight is equally divided so that it can stay in one position or be under control while moving ○ *He jumped off the porch and lost his balance when he landed on the grass, falling to the ground.* ○ *We're teaching Sue how to ride a bike, but she's still having trouble keeping her balance.* ○ *The horse jumped the fence but landed off balance and fell.* **2** ***art*** Balance in a work of art means that all the parts of it work together and no part is emphasized too much.

balance /ˈbæl·əns/ *v* [I/T] ○ [T] *He balanced the book on top of his coffee cup.*

OPPOSING FORCES /ˈbæl·əns/ *n* [U] a situation in which two opposing forces have or are given the same power ○ *He works toward a balance between extremes.* ○ *As a journalist, you try to strike a balance between serious reporting and the temptation to say clever things.*

balance /ˈbæl·əns/ *v* [T] to put opposing forces into a position in which neither controls the other ○ *I had to balance the children's needs against my own.*

balanced /ˈbæl·ənst/ *adj* **1** *The news program prided itself on its balanced reporting* (= one that considered all sides). **2** A balanced budget is a financial plan in which the amount of money spent is not greater than the amount received. **3** A balanced diet is a combination of the correct types and amounts of food.

AMOUNT /ˈbæl·əns/ *n* [C usually sing] **1** the amount of money you have in a bank account or an amount of money owed ○ *a bank balance* **2** A balance is also the amount of something that you have left after you have spent or used up the rest: *We'll go over your homework for the first half hour and use the balance of the class period to prepare for the exam.*

IDIOMS with balance

• **balance the budget** to make the amount of money spent in a BUDGET (= financial plan) equal the amount of money taken in during a particular period ○ *The government is required to balance the budget.*

• **in balance** spending no more money in a BUDGET (= financial plan) than is taken in during a particular period ○ *We want to cut the budget to get it in balance by the year 2012.*

• **on balance** after considering the power or influence of both sides of a question ○ *The job offer had some advantages, but on balance he thought he was better off where he was.* ○ See also: HANG IN THE BALANCE at HANG IDIOMS

balance of payments, **balance of trade** *n* [C usually sing] the difference between income from EXPORTS (= goods and services sold to other countries) and the cost of IMPORTS (= goods and services bought from other countries)

balance of power *n* [C usually sing] ***politics & government*** a situation in which no country is powerful enough to control the others

balance sheet *n* [C] a record of the value of things a company owns and of its debts for a particular period, usually a year

balcony /ˈbæl·kə·ni/ *n* [C] a narrow floor that is attached to the outside wall of a building above the ground, usually with sides or bars, or an area of seats at an upper level in a theater ○ *Our hotel room has a balcony that looks out over the pool.*

bald **WITHOUT HAIR** /bɔːld/ *adj* [-er/-est only] without hair on the head, or without much hair

balding /ˈbɔːl·dɪŋ/ *adj* [not gradable] beginning to lose the hair on your head ○ *He was plump and balding but very attractive to women.*

baldness /ˈbɔːld·nəs/ *n* [U]

PLAIN /bɔːld/ *adj* basic and with no unnecessary words; not detailed ○ *She just left a bald statement of resignation without any explanation.*

bale /beɪl/ *n* [C] a large amount of something such as HAY (= dry grass), paper, wool, or cloth that has been tied tightly together

balk /bɔːk/ *v* [I] to be unwilling to do something or let something happen ○ *I balked at the prospect of spending four hours on a train with him.*

ball **ROUND OBJECT** /bɔːl/ *n* [C] **1** a round object that can roll and usually bounce and that is used in many games in which it is thrown, hit, or kicked ○ *a golf/soccer/tennis ball* **2** The ball of the foot is the curved part where the big toe joins the foot.

DANCE /bɔːl/ *n* [C] **1** a large, formal occasion where people dance **2** *infml* A ball is also any very enjoyable experience: *"How was your weekend?" "We had a ball!"*

IDIOMS with ball

• **get/start the ball rolling** to make something begin or happen ○ *We have to get the ball rolling on this project soon.*

• **on the ball** aware of any changes or developments and quick to react to them ○ *We need someone who's really on the ball to answer questions from the press.*

• **take the ball and run with it**, **pick up the ball and run with it** to continue an activity or process that someone else has started, often when that

person could not finish it or make it work ○ *We had a very vague idea of what we wanted, but the marketing team just took the ball and ran with it.*
• **the ball's in** *someone's* **court** it is time for someone to deal with a problem or make a decision, because other people have already done as much as they can ○ *I've helped him in every way I can – the ball's in his court now.* ○ See also: PLAY BALL at PLAY IDIOMS

ballad /ˈbæl·əd/ *n* [C] ***literature*** a song or poem that tells a story, or a slow love song

ballerina /ˌbæl·əˈriː·nə/ *n* [C] a female BALLET dancer

ballet /bælˈeɪ/ *n* [C/U] a type of dancing in which controlled movements of the body are designed to express the beauty of physical motion, often while telling a story, or a piece of music for such dancing

ballgame **SPORTS EVENT** /ˈbɔːl·geɪm/ *n* [C] a baseball game or a similar game
CONDITIONS /ˈbɔːl·geɪm/ *n* [C] a set of conditions that control how something can be done ○ *Working for a large corporation was one thing, but now that we're in business for ourselves, it's a whole new ballgame.*

ballistic missile /bəˈlɪs·tɪk ˈmɪs·əl/ *n* [C] a MISSILE (= flying weapon) that is powered as it rises, but then falls without being controlled

ballistics /bəˈlɪs·tɪks/ *n* [U] the study of objects that are shot or thrown through the air

balloon /bəˈluːn/ *n* [C] **1** a small, thin, rubber bag that you can fill with air or another gas until it is round in shape, often used for decoration at parties or as a child's toy **2** A balloon is also a very large, round container filled with a gas that can rise in the air and carry people riding under it in an attached box.
balloon /bəˈluːn/ *v* [I] to become larger, esp. quickly ○ *The rumors soon ballooned into* (= quickly became) *a full-grown scandal.*

ballot /ˈbæl·ət/ *n* [C/U] **1** a piece of paper on which you write a secret vote **2** The ballot is also a system or occasion of secret voting: [U] *Issues need to be considered in open debate or put on the ballot.*

ballpark **PLACE FOR SPORTS** /ˈbɔːl·pɑrk/ *n* [C] a large structure enclosing a field on which games, esp. baseball games, are played
ACCEPTABLE RANGE /ˈbɔːl·pɑrk/ *n* [C] an acceptable range in the amount or number of something when you do not know or cannot agree on an exact amount or number ○ *I'd sell the house for $500,000, but his offer isn't even in the ballpark.* ○ *A ballpark figure of $3,000 would be realistic.*

ballpoint (pen) /ˈbɔːl·pɔɪnt (ˈpen)/ *n* [C] a pen with a small, metal ball at the end that rolls ink out when you press the ball against paper to write

ballroom /ˈbɔːl·ruːm, -rʊm/ *n* [C] a large room that is used for dancing or other activities

balm /bɑm, bɑlm/ *n* [C/U] an oily substance rubbed into the skin and used esp. to treat injuries or reduce pain

balmy /bɑm·i, bɑl·mi/ *adj* (of weather) pleasantly warm ○ *a balmy night*

baloney **NONSENSE** /bəˈloʊ·ni/ *n* [U] *infml* nonsense ○ *That's a lot of baloney!*
FOOD /bəˈloʊ·ni/ *n* [U] BOLOGNA

bamboo /bæmˈbuː/ *n* [C/U] a tall grass that grows in hotter regions and that has hard, hollow stems, or the stems of this plant

ban /bæn/ *v* [T] **-nn-** to forbid someone from doing something or something from being done ○ *The bill would ban drivers from using hand-held phones.*
ban /bæn/ *n* [C] ○ *The president supported a ban on assault weapons.*

banal /bəˈnæl, -nɑl; ˈbeɪn·əl/ *adj* too often used in the past and therefore not interesting ○ *He just sat there making banal remarks all evening.*

banana /bəˈnæn·ə/ *n* [C/U] a long, curved fruit with a usually yellow skin and soft, sweet flesh inside

bananas /bəˈnæn·əz/ *adj* [not gradable] *infml* very excited because of pleasure, anger, or another emotion ○ *She'll go bananas when you tell her the news.*

band **MUSICIANS** /bænd/ *n* [C] a group of musicians who play music together, esp. popular music ○ *a jazz/rock band* ○ *a marching/military band*
GROUP /bænd/ *n* [C] a group of people who have joined together for a special purpose, or a group of animals ○ *a band of outlaws*
STRIP /bænd/ *n* [C] a thin, flat strip of a material put around something to fasten or strengthen it, or a strip of color, light, etc., that is different from its surrounding area ○ *The silver band from his wristwatch left a green ring over his wrist.*

PHRASAL VERB with **band**

• **band together** to join together as a group, often for a specific purpose ○ *The workers banded together to demand better working conditions.*

bandage /ˈbæn·dɪdʒ/ *n* [C] a strip of cloth that is used to cover an injury on someone's body to protect it
bandage /ˈbæn·dɪdʒ/ *v* [T] ○ *They bandaged his wounds.*

Band-Aid **COVERING FOR CUTS** /ˈbæn·deɪd/ *n* [C] *trademark* a thin piece of cloth on a strip that sticks to the skin and is used to cover small cuts
TEMPORARY SOLUTION *n* [C] a temporary solution to a problem that is unlikely to be successful ○ *It was a Band-Aid solution for a major, long-term problem.*

bandanna, **bandana** /bænˈdæn·ə/ *n* [C] a large, colored HANDKERCHIEF that is worn around your neck or head

B

bandit /ˈbæn·dət/ *n* [C] an armed thief, esp. (in older use) one who attacks people while they are traveling ○ *Bandits attacked the travelers just outside of town.*

bandleader /ˈbændˌliːd·ər/ *n* [C] a person who leads a large group of musicians while they play, and who sometimes plays an instrument at the same time

bandwagon /ˈbænˌdwæg·ən/ *n* [C usually sing] an activity or idea that has become very popular

IDIOM with bandwagon

• **jump on the bandwagon**, **get on the bandwagon** to join an activity that has become very popular or to change your opinion to one that has become very popular so that you can share in its success ○ *After a couple of politicians won elections by promising to cut taxes, most of the others jumped on the bandwagon.*

bandwidth /ˈbænd·wɪtθ, -wɪdθ/ *n* [U] **1** the amount of information that can be sent over a network connection at one time ○ *These streaming applications swallow enormous chunks of bandwidth for long periods of time.* **2** Bandwidth is also the amount of time, information, or influence that someone has: *He has more bandwidth* (= more influence) *than any presidential adviser has ever had in history.*

bandy *something* **about** /ˈbæn·diː ·əˈbɑʊt/ *phrasal verb* to talk about something without careful consideration ○ *Wild guesses of the value of the painting were being bandied about.*

bane /beɪn/ *n* [U] something that is particularly effective in causing you trouble or worry ○ *Instead of doing his homework, my son is always playing computer games – they're the bane of my existence these days.*

bang /bæŋ/ *v* [I/T] **1** to make or cause something to make a sudden loud, usually short noise, esp. by hitting two things together ○ [T] *He banged his head on the open cupboard door.* **2** To bang out something is to do something quickly: [M] *I sat down at the piano and banged out a tune.*

bang /bæŋ/ *n* [C] ○ *She ran out of the room and slammed the door with a bang.*

IDIOM with bang

• **bang for the buck** value in return for your money ○ *They're very careful when they spend money, and they're going to insist on getting the most bang for their buck.*

PHRASAL VERB with bang

• **bang up** *someone/something* [M] to damage or injure someone or something by hitting ○ *He banged up the car backing out of the garage.*

bangs /bæŋz/ *pl n* the hair, usually cut straight across the front of the face above the eyes

bang-up /ˈbæŋ·ʌp/ *adj* [not gradable] *infml* very good; excellent ○ *She did a bang-up job.*

banish /ˈbæn·ɪʃ/ *v* [T] **1** to send someone away and forbid the person to come back ○ *He was banished from his sister's house.* **2** To banish is also to get rid of: *Their goal is to banish war forever.*

banister /ˈbæn·ə·stər/ *n* [C] a row of wooden or metal poles at the side of stairs and the bar attached to them on top

banjo /ˈbæn·dʒoʊ/ *n* [C] *pl* **banjos, banjoes** a musical instrument with four or five strings and a body like a drum that is played by pulling at the strings with the fingers or a small piece of plastic

bank ORGANIZATION /bæŋk/ *n* [C] **1** an organization that holds money belonging to others, investing and lending it to get more money, or the building in which the organization is situated **2** A bank of blood or human organs is a place that stores these things for later medical use: *a blood bank* **3** In a CASINO, the bank is money that is used to pay the players who win.

bank /bæŋk/ *v* [I/T] ○ [I always + adv/prep] *I bank at First National because it's near where I work.*

banker /ˈbæŋ·kər/ *n* [C] a person who has an important position in a bank

banking /ˈbæŋ·kɪŋ/ *n* [U] the business of operating a bank ○ *a career in international banking*

RAISED GROUND /bæŋk/ *n* [C] **1** sloping raised land, esp. along the sides of a river or lake, or a mass of something that has been piled together and has sloping sides ○ *We walked along the river bank.* **2** A bank of clouds is a group of clouds that look as if they are piled together. **3** A bank is also a row of similar objects: *A bank of computers displays the latest weather data.*

COMMON LEARNER ERROR

bank

You can sit on the bank of a river. But do not use **bank** if you mean a long seat for people to sit on (for example, in a park). The correct word for this kind of seat is **bench**.

The old man sat down on the bench to rest for a while.

~~*The old man sat down on the bank to rest for a while.*~~

TURN /bæŋk/ *v* [I] (of an aircraft) to fly with one wing higher than the other when turning ○ *We banked to make a left turn as we approached the airport.*

PHRASAL VERB with bank

• **bank on** *something* to expect something or depend on something happening ○ *You can bank on my support.*

bank account *n* [C] an arrangement in which a bank keeps your money but makes it available to you when you want it

bankrupt /ˈbæŋ·krəpt/ *adj* **1** without enough money to pay your debts ○ *If I don't find a job, I'll be bankrupt in two months.* **2** *law* When a company or person is bankrupt, a court of law gives control of the finances to someone who will arrange to pay as much as possible of what is owed.

bankrupt /ˈbæŋ·krəpt/ *v* [T] ○ *The senator said the president's plan would bankrupt the country.*

bankruptcy /ˈbæŋ·krəp·si/ *n* [C/U] the inability to pay your debts, or a particular example of this, involving the sale of your property or some other arrangement to pay as much as possible of the money you owe ○ [U] *If sales don't improve, we'll have to declare bankruptcy within a year.*

banner /ˈbæn·ər/ *n* [C] **1** a strip of material showing a name, such as of a sports team, or a message, which is often put in a place where it can be seen by many people ○ *The museum had a huge banner over its front entrance advertising its current show.* **2** A banner year is an unusually good year: *This is clearly not a banner year for Canadian poetry.*

banquet /ˈbæŋ·kwət/ *n* [C] a large formal meal for many people, often followed by speeches in honor of someone ○ *Ed Carey will receive the award at the organization's annual banquet.*

banquette /bæŋˈket, bæn-/ *n* [C] a long seat covered with cloth or similar material and put against a wall, esp. with tables and chairs facing it in a restaurant ○ *She sat on the banquette because she likes to look at everyone in the restaurant.*

banter /ˈbænt·ər/ *n* [U] conversation that is not serious and is often playful ○ *That kind of banter isn't appropriate at work.*

baptism /ˈbæpˌtɪz·əm, *Southern also* ˈbæb-/ *n* [C] a Christian ceremony in which water is poured over someone's head or the person is briefly covered completely by water, and is named as a Christian ○ *We're hoping to be able to get to Pasadena for the baptism of our grandson.*

Baptist /ˈbæp·təst/, *Southern also* /ˈbæb-/ *n* [C] a member of a Christian religious group that is one of the Protestant churches

Baptist /ˈbæp·təst/, *Southern also* /ˈbæb-/ *adj* [not gradable] ○ *the Baptist church* ○ *a Baptist minister*

baptize /bæpˈtɑɪz/, *Southern also* /bæbˈtɑɪz/ *v* [T] to name and recognize a person as a Christian during a BAPTISM ceremony ○ *She was baptized a Catholic at age 20.*

bar POLE /bɑr/ *n* [C] **1** a strong pole, esp. one made of metal, used as a support, to force something to move, or to block an opening ○ *He stuck his hand through the bars of the cage* **2** A bar is also any of various small objects having a rectangular shape: *a granola bar*

bar /bɑr/ *v* [T] **-rr-** to put a strong pole or poles across an opening ○ *We barred the windows as protection against burglars.*

PREVENT /bɑr/ *v* [T] **-rr-** to prevent someone from doing something or going somewhere ○ *Protesters tried to break into the building, but the police barred their way.*

DRINKING PLACE /bɑr/ *n* [C] a place, sometimes within a restaurant, where alcoholic drinks are served, or a long, high table in such a place along which people stand or sit while drinking ○ *He used to just sit in a bar and listen to jazz.* ○ *They sat at the bar and chatted with the bartender.*

MUSIC /bɑr/, **measure** *n* [C] **1** one of the small equal parts into which a piece of music is divided, containing a fixed number of beats ○ *He played four bars of music.* **2** A bar is also one of the vertical lines that divide a piece of music into equal parts.

LAWYERS /bɑr/ *n* [U] all lawyers considered as a group ○ *She passed the Massachusetts bar exam on her first try.*

EXCEPT /bɑr/ *prep* except for ○ *He's the greatest pitcher of all time, bar none* (= no one else is better).

barring /ˈbɑr·ɪŋ/ *prep* ○ *We were assured that, barring unexpected developments, we would get the contract.*

barb SHARP END /bɑrb/ *n* [C] the sharp part of a fish hook or arrow that makes it difficult to remove from something caught on it

barbed /bɑrbd/ *adj*

CRUEL REMARK /bɑrb/ *n* [C] an intelligent but critical remark that is intended to hurt ○ *Some of Weaver's sharpest barbs were aimed at his boss.*

barbed /bɑrbd/ *adj* ○ *a barbed comment*

barbarian /bɑrˈber·iː·ən, -ˈbær-/ *n* [C] a person who has no experience of the habits and culture of modern life, and whose behavior you therefore consider strange or offensive ○ *They thought I was some kind of barbarian because I didn't know how to use a computer.*

barbarous /ˈbɑr·bə·rəs/ *adj* **1** characteristic of people who have no experience of the habits and culture of modern life, and whose behavior you therefore consider strange **2** Barbarous also means BARBARIC.

barbaric /bɑrˈbær·ɪk/, **barbarous** /ˈbɑr·bə·rəs/ *adj* extremely cruel ○ *barbaric behavior/practices*

barbecue /ˈbɑr·bɪˌkjuː/, *abbreviation* **BBQ** *n* [C] a metal frame on which food is cooked outside over a fire, or a meal prepared using such a frame and usually eaten outside ○ *I like catfish cooked on a barbecue.* ○ *Our neighbors invited all of us to a backyard barbecue.*

barbecue /ˈbɑr·bɪˌkjuː/ *v* [T] ○ *During the summer we barbecue all the time.*

barbed wire /ˈbɑrbˈdwɑɪr, ˈbɑb-, -ˈwɑɪr/ *n* [U] a type of strong wire with sharp points on it, used to prevent people or animals from entering or leaving a place

barber /ˈbɑr·bər/ *n* [C] a person whose job is cutting hair, esp. of men and boys

barbershop, barber shop /ˈbɑr·bərˌʃɑp/ *n* [C] a place where men and boys get their hair cut

barbiturate /bɑrˈbɪtʃ·ə·rət/ *n* [C] a strong medicine that makes people calm or helps them sleep

bar code, barcode /ˌbɑr·koʊd/ *n* [C] a small rectangle of black lines of different widths that contains information that can be read by a computer

bare /ber, bær/ *adj* [-er/-est only] **1** without any clothes or not covered by anything ○ *The hot sand burned my bare feet.* ○ *Inside, the floors were bare and there was very little furniture.* **2** Bare also means the least possible or only this much of something: *They had nothing beyond the bare necessities (of life)* (= the most basic things you need).
bare /ber, bær/ *v* [T] to show something that is usually covered ○ *The dog bared its teeth and growled.*

bareback /ˈber·bæk, ˈbær-/ *adj, adv* [not gradable] without a SADDLE (= leather seat) on the back of a horse that someone is riding ○ *a bareback rider*

barefoot /ˈber·fʊt, ˈbær-/, **barefooted** /ˈber ˈfʊt̬·əd, ˈbær-/ *adj, adv* [not gradable] not wearing any shoes or socks ○ *A young barefoot girl led him away.*

bareheaded /ˈberˈhed·əd, ˈbær-/ *adj, adv* [not gradable] without any covering on your head ○ *Some of the men wore hats, and some were bareheaded.*

barely /ˈber·li, ˈbær-/ *adv* [not gradable] by the smallest amount; only just ○ *There was barely enough room for the two of them.* ○ *The dark line of the mountains was barely visible against the night sky.*

barf /bɑrf/ *v* [I] *slang* to vomit

bargain AGREEMENT /ˈbɑr·gən/ *n* [C] an agreement between two people or groups in which each promises to do something in exchange for something else ○ *He failed to carry out his side of the bargain.*
bargaining /ˈbɑr·gə·nɪŋ/ *n* [U] ○ *Harriman pressed for tougher bargaining by the American side.*
LOW PRICE /ˈbɑr·gən/ *n* [C] something sold for a price that is lower than usual or lower than its value ○ *We got tickets to the show at half-price, a real bargain.*
bargain /ˈbɑr·gən/ *v* [I] to try to reach agreement with someone in order to get a lower price ○ *You can usually bargain with antique dealers.*

PHRASAL VERB with bargain

• **bargain on** *something* to expect something to happen ○ *We hadn't bargained on an entire week of rain.*

bargain-basement *adj* [not gradable] (of prices) extremely low, or (of products) of low quality ○ *Farmers bought up the land at bargain-basement prices.*

bargaining chip *n* [C] something that one side can use to persuade the other side to reach an agreement ○ *Union leaders used the threat of a strike during the busy season as a bargaining chip.*

barge BOAT /bɑrdʒ/ *n* [C] a long boat with a flat bottom, used for carrying heavy loads
HURRY /bɑrdʒ/ *v* [I always + adv/prep] to force your way rudely or suddenly and quickly ○ *You ought to knock instead of just barging into my office.*

bar graph *n* [C] a drawing that uses rectangular boxes to show how two sets of amounts are related ➤ Picture: **graph**

baritone /ˈbær·əˌtoʊn/ *n* [C] a man's singing voice in the range lower than a TENOR, or a person or musical instrument with this range

barium /ˈbær·iː·əm, ˈber-/ *n* [U] ***chemistry*** a soft, gray-white chemical element that is a metal

bark DOG /bɑrk/ *v* [I/T] **1** to make the loud, short noise that a dog and some other animals make ○ [I] *The dog barked all night.* **2** A human who barks something shouts it suddenly and strongly: [T] *The sergeant barked orders at his troops.*
bark /bɑrk/ *n* [C] ○ *The dog gave two loud barks.*
TREE /bɑrk/ *n* [U] the hard, outer covering of a tree

IDIOMS with bark

• *someone's* **bark is worse than** *his or her* **bite** although someone says things that sound frightening, the person's actions will not be as severe as the things that were said ○ *The boss seems mean, but his bark is worse than his bite.*
• **barking up the wrong tree** trying to do something in a way that will not work ○ *His attorney suggested that the investigators might be barking up the wrong tree.*

barley /ˈbɑr·li/ *n* [U] a tall plant grown for its grain, or the grain from this plant which is used for food

bar mitzvah /bɑrˈmɪts·və/ *n* [C] a Jewish ceremony held when a boy reaches the age of 13 and has the responsibilities of an adult man

barn /bɑrn/ *n* [C] a large building on a farm in which HAY (= dried grass) and grain and often farm animals are kept

barnacle /ˈbɑr·nɪ·kəl/ *n* [C] a small sea creature with a shell that fastens itself tightly and in large numbers to rocks and the bottoms of boats

barnstorm /ˈbɑrn·stɔːrm/ *v* [I/T] to travel to many places briefly in order to give a performance or to make a political appearance ○ [I/T] *He barnstormed (through) the West.*

barnyard /ˈbɑrn·jɑrd/ *n* [C] the area around a BARN (= farm building), often fenced so that animals cannot get away

barometer /bəˈrɑm·ət̬·ər/ *n* [C] ***earth science*** a device that measures air pressure which shows when the weather is likely to change

barometric pressure /ˌber·əˈme·trɪk ˈpreʃ·ər, ˌbær-/ *n* [U] ***earth science*** the amount of force at any point on the earth's surface caused by the weight of the air

baroque /bəˈroʊk, -ˈrɑk, -ˈrɔːk/ *adj* relating to the highly decorated style in buildings, art, and music that was popular in Europe in the 17th century and the early part of the 18th century ○ *baroque architecture*

barracks /ˈbær·əks/ *n* [C] *pl* **barracks** a building or group of buildings where soldiers live ○ *The 15 tents were normally used as barracks for Marines.*

barrage /bəˈrɑʒ, -ˈrɑdʒ/ *n* [C usually sing] **1** a continuous firing of large guns, esp. to protect soldiers advancing on an enemy ○ *an artillery barrage* **2** A barrage is also a great number of complaints, criticisms, or questions suddenly directed at someone: *Morris fired off a barrage of questions about Halperin's politics.*

barrel CONTAINER /ˈbær·əl/ *n* [C] **1** a large wooden container with a flat top and bottom and curving sides that are wider in the middle **2** A barrel is also a unit of measurement of volume equal to 31.5 gallons (119 liters) or, of oil, equal to 42 gallons (159 liters).

MOVE FAST /ˈbær·əl/ *v* [I always + adv/prep] to travel or move very fast ○ *We were barreling along at 80 miles an hour.*

GUN PART /ˈbær·əl/ *n* [C] the long part of a gun that is shaped like a tube

barren /ˈbær·ən/ *adj* **1** (of land) not producing or unable to produce plants ○ *The landscape was barren, with not a tree or shrub in sight.* **2** *old use* If a woman is barren, she is unable to have a baby.

barrette /bəˈret, bɑ-/ *n* [C] a fastener, often decorative, that women and girls use to hold their hair in place

barricade /ˈbær·əˌkeɪd/ *n* [C] a large object or objects that are used to stop people from going where they want to go

barricade /ˈbær·əˌkeɪd/ *v* [T] to block anyone from reaching a place ○ *The protesting students barricaded the streets leading to the university.*

barrier /ˈbær·iː·ər/ *n* [C] anything used or acting to block someone from going somewhere or from doing something, or to block something from happening ○ *The Secret Service erected concrete barriers around the White House.* ○ *Jackie Robinson was the African-American who succeeded in breaking major league baseball's color barrier* (= use of race to block something from happening).

barring /ˈbɑr·ɪŋ/ *prep* ○ See at BAR EXCEPT

barrio /ˈbɑr·iːˌoʊ, ˈbær-/ *n* [C] *pl* **barrios** in the US, a part of a city where mainly Spanish-speaking people live

bartender /ˈbɑrˌten·dər/ *n* [C] someone who makes and serves drinks in a bar

barter /ˈbɑrt̬·ər/ *v* [I/T] to exchange goods for other things rather than for money ○ [I] *In the marketplace, you can barter for souvenirs by offering jeans and lipstick.*

baryon /ˈbær·iːˌɑn, ˈber-/ *n* [C] ***physics*** a PARTICLE (= small piece of matter that makes up an atom) that contains three QUARKS, esp. a NEUTRON or a PROTON

basalt /bəˈsɔːlt, ˈbeɪ·sɔːlt/ *n* [U] ***earth science*** a type of black rock that comes from a VOLCANO (= mountain that explodes and throws out hot rocks)

basaltic /bəˈsɔːl·tɪk/ *adj* [not countable] ***earth science*** relating to or containing basalt

base BOTTOM /beɪs/ *n* [C] **1** the bottom of an object; the part on which it rests ○ *This lamp has a heavy base so it won't tip over.* **2** ***geometry*** A **base angle** is one of the two equal angles that include the bottom of an ISOSCELES TRIANGLE.

MAIN PLACE /beɪs/ *n* [C] **1** the place from which a business operates or a person works ○ *We have an office in San Diego, but Washington is still our base.* **2** A base is also a place from which the military operates that provides weapons storage and housing: *The military has bases all over the US.*

base /beɪs/ *v* [T always + adv/prep] ○ *Where is your company based?*

SUBSTANCE /beɪs/ *n* [C] ***biology*** one of four chemical substances that make up the part of DNA and RNA that controls the structure of GENES

CHEMICAL /beɪs/ *n* [C/U] ***chemistry*** any of various chemical substances that have the opposite effect or chemical behavior as that of an acid

NUMBER /beɪs/ *n* [C] ***mathematics*** a number that is multiplied by itself ○ *In 6^3, 6 is the base and it is multiplied by 6 three times.*

MAIN PART /beɪs/ *n* [C usually sing] the main part of something, or the people or activities that form the main part of something ○ *The sauce has an olive oil base.* ○ *Tourism remains the city's economic base.* ○ *He'll need a wide base of regional support to win the election.*

WORD PART /beɪs/ *n* [C] ***grammar*** a word or word part to which prefixes and endings may be added to make new words, as in "do," the base of "redo" and "doable"

BASEBALL /beɪs/ *n* [C] (in the game of baseball) one of the four angles of a square, all of which a player must touch in order to score ○ *He reached first base on a single.*

WORD FAMILY base

Nouns	base basics basis	*Adjectives*	baseless basic
		Adverbs	basically
Verbs	base		

PHRASAL VERB with **base**

• **base** *something* **on** *something* **1** to use information to support or prove an opinion or belief ○ *We based our decision on the facts in the report.* **2** If you base a story, painting, or other work on something else, you use the other thing as the main idea for creating the story: *The book is based on the life of abolitionist John Brown.*

baseball /ˈbeɪs·bɔːl/ *n* [C/U] **1** a game with two teams of nine players in which a ball, thrown by a PITCHER, is hit by a player with a BAT (= special stick) who then tries to run around four BASES before being stopped by the other team ○ [U] *Austin never played baseball like the other kids.* **2** A baseball is the ball used in this game.

baseball cap *n* [C] a hat with a curved piece of stiff material above the eyes to give protection from the sun, originally worn by baseball players

B

base hit *n* [C] (in baseball) a play in which a player hits the ball and successfully reaches the first base

baseless /ˈbeɪ·sləs/ *adj* without supporting facts ○ *Investigation showed these were baseless accusations.*

basement /ˈbeɪ·smənt/ *n* [C] a part of a building that is below the level of the first floor ○ *The hardware department is in the basement.*

bases /ˈbeɪ·siːz/ *pl of* BASIS

bash HIT /bæʃ/ *v* [T] *infml* **1** to attack someone or something with an object ○ *He bashed his arm against a shelf.* **2** If you bash someone with words, you criticize that person severely: *Some of these countries have been bashing the United States.*

bashing /ˈbæʃ·ɪŋ/ *n* [U] ○ *The more things I do to get this union on the right track, the more of a bashing I take.*

PARTY /bæʃ/ *n* [C] *infml* a large, energetic party ○ *He had a big bash, including live music, for his 18th birthday.*

bashful /ˈbæʃ·fəl/ *adj* easily embarrassed and uncomfortable; shy ○ *She gave a bashful smile when she was introduced.*

basic /ˈbeɪ·sɪk/ *adj* most important or central to something ○ *In physics we study basic principles of force and motion.* ○ *We help with basic needs like food and shelter.*

basics /ˈbeɪ·sɪks/ *pl n* the central and most important principles of something ○ *Pablo has promised to teach me the basics of sailing.*

basically /ˈbeɪ·sɪ·kli/ *adv* [not gradable] ○ *The two cars are basically the same.*

basil /ˈbæz·əl, ˈbeɪ·zəl/ *n* [U] an herb with a strong smell that is used to flavor foods in cooking

basin /ˈbeɪ·sən/ *n* [C] **1** a large, open bowl, or the amount such a container will hold ○ *I left the napkins soaking in a basin.* **2** The basin of a river or body of water is the land that surrounds it and the streams that flow into it. **3** A basin is also a sheltered area of water deep enough for boats, or an area of land that is lower than all the surrounding land.

basis /ˈbeɪ·səs/ *n* [C] *pl* **bases 1** the most important facts or principles or ideas that support something ○ *There is no basis for their statements.* **2** A basis is also a way or method of doing something: *Mostly people work on a part-time basis.*

bask /bæsk/ *v* [I always + adv/prep] to lie or sit and enjoy warmth ○ *On top of the wall, a cat basked happily in the sun.* ○ *(fig.) Marina basked in the crowd's admiration* (= enjoyed it).

basket CONTAINER /ˈbæs·kət/ *n* [C] a container like a rounded box, often with a handle, which is used for carrying or storing things and made of woven strips of dried grass or other material, or the amount such a container holds ○ *a wicker basket* ○ *a wastepaper basket* ○ *a basket of flowers*

GOAL /ˈbæs·kət/ *n* [C] (in the game of BASKETBALL) an open net hanging from a metal ring which players must throw the ball through to score, or a successful throw through the ring ○ *She made three baskets in a row.*

COMMON LEARNER ERROR

basket or basketball?

In some languages **basketball** and **volleyball** are referred to simply as **basket** and **volley**, but in English a **basket** is the round net itself and a **volley** is the hitting of the ball. For the names of the sports you have to use **basketball** and **volleyball**.

I love basketball.

~~*I love basket.*~~

basketball /ˈbæs·kət ˌbɔːl/ *n* [C/U] a game played by two teams of five players who score points by throwing the ball through a net that hangs from a metal ring, or the ball used in this game ○ [U] *We played basketball all the time.* ➤ Learner error: **basket or basketball?** at BASKET GOAL

basket case /ˈbæs·kət ˌkeɪs/ *n* [C usually sing] *infml* someone who is made very anxious by the demands and pressures of something, esp. work ○ *I was a basket case by the end of the day.*

bas mitzvah /bɑs ˈmɪts·və/ *n* [C] BAT MITZVAH

bass MUSICAL RANGE /beɪs/ *n* [C/U] the lowest range of a voice or musical instrument, or a person or musical instrument with this range ○ [C] *The qualities of his voice make you forget he is a bass.*

FISH /bæs/ *n* [C/U] *pl* **bass** any of several related fishes found in rivers or the sea, used for food ○ [C] *striped bass*

bass clef /beɪs ˈklef/ *n* [C] ***music*** in Western music, a sign that shows the fourth line of a STAFF (= the five lines on which music is written) is the note F below middle C (= the note C near the middle of a piano keyboard) ➤ Picture: **notation**

bass fiddle, *short form* **bass** *n* [C] *infml* a DOUBLE BASS

bassoon /bəˈsuːn/ *n* [C/U] a tube-shaped musical instrument that produces low notes and is played by blowing through two REEDS (= thin pieces of wood) and pressing keys on its front to produce notes, or this type of instrument generally; a WOODWIND

baste /beɪst/ *v* [T] to put fat or meat juices on food, esp. meat, while it cooks ○ *We basted the turkey every twenty minutes.*

bat STICK /bæt/ *n* [C] a specially shaped stick of wood or metal, used for hitting the ball esp. in baseball ○ *I hear the crack of a bat and the voices of children.*

bat /bæt/ *v* [I/T] **-tt- 1** [T] *He batted the ball high into the air.* **2** If you bat at something, you hit it lightly: [I] *She batted at the air, trying to shoo the bugs.*

batter /ˈbæt̬·ər/ *n* [C] (in baseball) the player whose turn it is to hit the ball ○ See also: BATTER HIT; BATTER FOOD

ANIMAL /bæt/ *n* [C] a small, flying animal with big ears and wings of skin

MOVE EYE /bæt/ *v* [T] **-tt-** to open and close your eyes quickly several times, esp. to attract attention or admiration ○ *She smiled and batted her eyes.*

IDIOM with bat

• **at bat** taking your turn to try to hit the ball in a baseball game ○ *The bases were loaded, and Ortiz was at bat.*

batch /bætʃ/ *n* [C] people or things dealt with as a group or at the same time ○ *Mom just made a fresh batch of cookies.* ○ *I've got a whole batch of applications to read through.*

bath /bæθ/ *n* [C] **1** the activity of washing yourself or another person or an animal in a large container filled with warm water ○ *I gave the dog a bath.* **2** When describing homes, a bath can also mean a BATHROOM: *a three-bedroom, two-bath apartment*

bathe **WASH** /beɪð/ *v* [I/T] to wash someone, usually with soap and water in a BATHTUB ○ [T] *I had to change the kids' diapers and feed them and bathe them.*

COVER /beɪð/ *v* [T] to cover with a liquid, esp. as a treatment for pain or injury ○ *I bathed my foot in warm salt water.* ○ (*fig.*) *The afternoon sun bathed the city in pink and gold.*

bathing suit /ˈbeɪ·ðɪŋˌsuːt/ *n* [C] a piece of clothing for swimming; a SWIMSUIT

bath mat *n* [C] a cloth put on the floor to stand on after a bath or a piece of rubber on the bottom of a bath or SHOWER to keep someone from sliding and falling

bathrobe /ˈbæθ·roʊb/, **robe** *n* [C] a piece of clothing rather like a loose-fitting coat, worn to cover up after a bath, or before getting dressed

bathroom /ˈbæθ·ruːm, -rʊm/ *n* [C] a room with a toilet and a place to wash your hands, and often a BATHTUB and a SHOWER (= device that sprays water on a person's body) ○ *Our bathroom is the warmest room in the house.* ➤ Usage: **toilet, bathroom, or restroom?** at TOILET

bath towel *n* [C] a large TOWEL (= piece of cloth) for drying off after a bath or SHOWER

bathtub /ˈbæθ·tʌb/, *short form* **tub** *n* [C] a container large enough for a person to sit in to take a bath

batik /bəˈtiːk, bæ-/ *n* [U] a way of printing patterns on cloth by covering the design with wax and coloring the cloth that does not have wax on it with DYE

bat mitzvah /bɑtˈmɪts·və, bɑs-/, **bas mitzvah** *n* [C] a Jewish ceremony held when a girl reaches the age of 12 or 13 and has the responsibilities of an adult woman

baton /bəˈtɑn/ *n* [C] any of various specially designed sticks used in races, to lead a group of musicians, or thrown in the air by people who are marching ○ *She twirls a baton as the parade passes by.* ○ *He waves his fork like a conductor's baton.*

battalion /bəˈtæl·jən/ *n* [C] a large military unit under a single leader, consisting of three or more COMPANIES

batter **HIT** /ˈbæt̬·ər/ *v* [I/T] to hit someone or something again and again ○ [T] *Thunderstorms were battering Kansas again on Sunday.* ○ [T] (*fig.*) *He had been battered by opponents who turned public opinion against him.* ○ See also: BATTER at BAT STICK

battered /ˈbæt̬·ərd/ *adj* old and damaged, or hurt ○ *He stuffed his battered briefcase with all of his notes.*

battering /ˈbæt̬·ə·rɪŋ/ *n* [C/U] damage caused by an action or event ○ [C] *Florida is starting to recover from the battering it endured in recent hurricanes.* ○ [C usually sing] *Stock markets have taken a battering in the past week.*

battery /ˈbæt̬·ə·ri/ *n* [U] the crime of attacking and beating someone

FOOD /ˈbæt̬·ər/ *n* [U] any liquid mixture containing milk, eggs, and flour, as used to make cake, PANCAKES, or other similar food, or to cover food before frying it ○ See also: BATTER at BAT STICK

battering ram *n* [C] a long, heavy pole, used to break down doors

battery **ELECTRICAL DEVICE** /ˈbæt̬·ə·ri/ *n* [C] **1** a device that produces electricity to provide power for radios, cars, toys, etc. ○ *What size battery do you need for the alarm clock?* **2** ***physics*** A battery is also any device that produces electrical energy from chemical energy.

LARGE NUMBER /ˈbæt̬·ə·ri/ *n* [C] a number of things of a similar type ○ *You have to pass a whole battery of tests to get into that school.*

battle /ˈbæt̬·əl/ *n* [C/U] **1** a fight between armed forces, or an argument between two groups ○ [C] *the Battle of Cedar Creek* ○ [C] *a naval battle* ○ [C] *The battle between street gangs went on for years.* ○ [C] *They're in a battle with their publisher over electronic rights.* **2** A battle can also be an serious effort to change a situation: [C] *Doctors Without Borders is a group that wages battles against hunger and disease.*

battle /ˈbæt̬·əl/ *v* [I/T] ○ [I] *Congress is battling with the White House over funding.* ○ [T] *Long Horse died battling the Sioux in 1875.* ○ [I] *I thought we had the game under control, but they really battled back.*

battlefield /ˈbæt̬·əlˌfiːld/ *n* [C] a place where a BATTLE (= a fight between armed forces) is being fought or was fought ○ *We visited the Civil War battlefield at Gettysburg.*

battleground /ˈbæt̬·əlˌgrɑʊnd/ *n* [C] **1** a place where an argument or competition is happening ○ *Pennsylvania and Ohio are key battlegrounds in this year's election.* **2** A battleground is also a BATTLEFIELD.

batty /ˈbæt̬·i/ *adj infml, disapproving* foolish or crazy

bawl /bɔːl/ *v* [I] to cry or shout loudly ○ *He started bawling when the dog snatched his toy.*

B

bay **SHELTERED WATER** /beɪ/ *n* [C] an area of water sheltered by land on three sides ○ *We went sailing in Cape Cod Bay.*

SPACE /beɪ/ *n* [C] a partly enclosed space ○ *A truck in the loading bay is blocking my car.*

CALL /beɪ/ *v* [I] (of dogs and similar animals) to make a low, long, deep cry

IDIOMS with bay

• **keep** *someone* **at bay, hold** *someone* **at bay** to prevent someone from moving closer ○ *He held the police at bay for several hours.*

• **keep** *something* **at bay, hold** *something* **at bay** to control something and prevent it from causing you problems ○ *She fought to keep her unhappiness at bay.*

bay leaf /ˈbeɪ·liːf/ *n* [C] *pl* **bay leaves** the leaves of an evergreen tree, which are dried and used in cooking to add flavor

bayonet /ˈbeɪ·ə·nət, ˌbeɪ·əˈnet/ *n* [C] a long, sharp blade attached to a gun

bayonet /ˈbeɪ·ə·nət, ˌbeɪ·əˈnet/ *v* [T] **-t-, -tt-** ○ *In training, we learned to bayonet a straw dummy.*

bayou /ˈbɑɪ·uː, -oʊ/ *n* [C] (in the southern US) an area of slowly moving or still water connected to a river or lake

bazaar /bəˈzɑr/ *n* [C] **1** an open market where people sell things, or any group of small shops or people selling goods **2** A bazaar is also an event where people sell things to raise money for an organization, such as a school or hospital: *Our school is having its springtime bazaar next Saturday.*

BB gun /ˈbiː·biː ˌgʌn/ *n* [C] a gun that uses air to shoot small, round balls

BBQ *n* [C] *abbreviation for* BARBECUE

BBS *n* [C] *abbreviation for* bulletin board system (= a computer system allowing users to exchange messages and information)

B.C. *abbreviation for* before Christ, used to show that a year or century comes before the year in which Jesus Christ is thought to have been born ○ *Caesar was assassinated in 44 B.C.* ○ **USAGE:** B.C. always appears after the year. ○ Compare A.D.

B.C.E. *abbreviation for* before the Common Era, used to show that a year or century comes before the year 1 of the CALENDAR used today in much of the world, esp. in Europe and North and South America ○ *The Upanishads date from the eighth century B.C.E.* ○ *Demosthenes died in 323 B.C.E.*

be **RELATIONSHIP** /biː/ *v* **am, are, is,** *pres. part.* **being,** *past simp.* **was, were,** *past part.* **been** **1** used to connect two things or a thing with something that it has as a quality or condition ○ [L] *It is cold today.* ○ [L] *My name is Andy.* ○ [L] *She is a doctor.* ○ [L] *How old are you?* ○ [L] *These books are* (= cost) *$12.99 each.* ○ [L] *Please be patient.* **2** Be is also used to show the position of a person or thing in space or time: [I always + adv/prep] *The food was on the table.* ○ [I always + adv/prep] *Tony is in trouble again.*

EXIST /biː/ *v* [L] **am, are, is,** *pres. part.* **being,** *past simp.* **was, were,** *past part.* **been** to exist ○ *She apologized for the way things are around here.* ○ *There was no sound.*

CONTINUE /biː/ *auxiliary verb* **am, are, is,** *pres. part.* **being,** *past simp.* **was, were,** *past part.* **been** used with the present participle of other verbs to describe actions that are or were continuing ○ *You are being very selfish.* ○ *She was studying to be a lawyer.* ○ *It is raining.* ○ *I'll be coming back* (= I plan to come back).

PASSIVE /biː/ *auxiliary verb* **am, are, is,** *pres. part.* **being,** *past simp.* **was, were,** *past part.* **been** used with the past participle of other verbs to form the passive ○ *He was asked to wait.* ○ *Please be seated.* ○ *The World Trade Center was built in the early 1970s.*

POSSIBLE CONDITION /biː/ *auxiliary verb past simp.* **were, were** used to show the possibility of a condition or of something happening in the future ○ *If I were afraid of you, why would I be here?* ○ *If you were allowed to have one wish, what would it be?* ○ **USAGE:** In grammar, this form of be is called the SUBJUNCTIVE.

FUTURE /biː/ *auxiliary verb* **am, are, is,** *past simp.* **was, were** *fml* used to say what will happen ○ [+ *to* infinitive] *The president is to decide this issue very soon.*

ALLOW /biː/ *auxiliary verb* **am, are, is,** *past simp.* **was, were** *fml* used to tell people they must or should do something ○ [+ *to* infinitive] *Their mother said they were to play nearby.*

beach /biːtʃ/ *n* [C] a flat, sloping area of sand or small stones beside the sea or a lake ○ *Let's go to the beach.*

beach ball *n* [C] a large, light, brightly colored ball filled with air that people play with esp. on a beach

beacon /ˈbiː·kən/ *n* [C] **1** a light that acts as a signal or warning ○ (*fig.*) *a beacon of hope* **2** A beacon is also a device that sends a signal or information: *a radar/navigation beacon*

bead /biːd/ *n* [C] a small, often round piece of plastic, wood, glass, or other material with a hole through it, which is put on a string to make jewelry such as a NECKLACE ○ *She fingered the beads of her rosary.* ○ (*fig.*) *Beads of sweat formed on his forehead as he worked in the sun.*

beady /ˈbiːd·i/ *adj* (of eyes) small and shiny, esp. like a bird's eyes ○ *Her beady eyes stared from behind thick glasses.*

beak /biːk/ *n* [C] the hard, pointed part of a bird's mouth

beaker /ˈbiː·kər/ *n* [C] a wide glass container with a flat bottom and an edge for pouring, used in science LABORATORIES

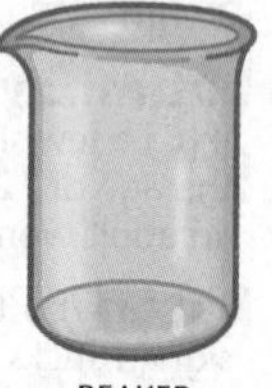
BEAKER

beam **LIGHT** /biːm/ *n* [C] a line of light coming from the sun or a bright light, esp. as seen against a darker background ○ *a beam of sunlight* ○ *A laser beam scans the disc's surface.*

beam /biːm/ *v* [I/T] ○ [I] *The sun beamed down*

on the ball field. ○ [T] *Detroit stations are beamed* (= broadcast) *to Canadian communities.*

WOOD /biːm/ *n* [C] a long, thick piece of wood, metal, or concrete, esp. one used to support weight in a building or other structure

SMILE /biːm/ *v* [I] to smile with obvious pleasure ○ *His face beamed as if he'd won a gold medal at the Olympics.*

bean /biːn/ *n* [C] a seed, or the POD (= seed container) of various plants, eaten as a vegetable ○ *string beans*

beanbag /ˈbiːn·bæg/ *n* [C] a large cloth bag filled with dried beans or some similar filling that is used for sitting on, or a small bag of the same type used as a children's toy

bean curd *n* [U] TOFU

bean sprouts *pl n* beans that have started to grow and that are eaten as vegetables

bear ANIMAL /ber, bær/ *n* [C] a large, strong mammal with thick fur that lives esp. in colder parts of the world ○ *a black/grizzly/polar bear*

CARRY /ber, bær/ *v* [T] *past simp.* **bore,** *past part.* **borne** to carry or bring something ○ *Fans bearing banners ringed the stadium.*

bearer /ˈber·ər, ˈbær·ər/ *n* [C] ○ *Stretcher bearers carried the injured across the lawn.*

SUPPORT /ber, bær/ *v* [T] *past simp.* **bore,** *past part.* **borne** to hold or support something ○ *The bridge has to be strengthened to bear heavier loads.*

ACCEPT /ber, bær/ *v past simp.* **bore,** *past part.* **borne** to accept something painful or unpleasant with determination and strength ○ [T] *Since you will bear most of the responsibility, you should get the rewards.* ○ [+ to infinitive] *He could not bear to see her suffering.*

HAVE /ber, bær/ *v* [T] *past simp.* **bore,** *past part.* **borne** to have as a quality or characteristic ○ *My life bore little resemblance to what I'd hoped for.*

PRODUCE /ber, bær/ *v* [T] *past simp.* **bore,** *past part.* **born, borne** (of mammals) to give birth to young, or of a tree or plant to give or produce fruit or flowers ○ *She bore three children in five years.* ○ USAGE: When talking about mammals, use the past participle spelling "born" to talk about a person or animal's birth, and the spelling "borne" to talk about a mother giving birth to a child: *She had borne four boys.*

TRAVEL /ber, bær/ *v* [I always + adv/prep] *past simp.* **bore,** *past part.* **borne** to travel or move in the stated direction ○ *After you pass the light, bear left until you come to a bank.*

bearings /ˈber·ɪŋz, ˈbær-/ *pl n* an understanding of directions and positions that helps you know where you are ○ *It's sometimes hard to get your bearings in the dark.* ○ See also: BEARING CONNECTION; BEARING BODY POSITION

WORD FAMILY bear

Nouns	bearer	*Verbs*	bear
Adjectives	bearable unbearable	*Adverbs*	unbearably

IDIOM with bear

• **bear fruit** to be successful especially after a lot of work or effort ○ *Some of their research is now bearing fruit, and the results are interesting.*

PHRASAL VERBS with bear

• **bear down** to put more effort into doing something ○ *I knew I had to bear down hard in order to hit the ball.*

• **bear down on** *someone/something* to move toward someone or something in a way that is threatening ○ *He leaped away from the car bearing down on him.*

• **bear out** *something/someone* [M] to support the truth of something, or to support someone's statement or claim ○ *The facts don't bear out your fears.* ○ *The evidence so far simply does not bear him out.*

• **bear up** to show bravery despite difficulties ○ *How is Carmine bearing up since his wife died?*

• **bear with** *someone/something* to be patient with someone or something ○ *Just bear with me while I finish downloading this file.*

beard /bɪrd/ *n* [C] hair that grows on the lower part of a man's face, sometimes including the hair that grows above the lips

bearded /ˈbɪrd·əd/ *adj* [not gradable] having a beard ○ *a bearded, 43-year-old truck driver*

bear hug *n* [C] the action of putting your arms around someone and holding that person against you tightly

bearing CONNECTION /ˈber·ɪŋ, ˈbær-/ *n* [U] connection to or influence on a result ○ *The fact that he was ordered to stand trial has no bearing on whether he'll be found guilty.* ○ See also: BEARINGS at BEAR TRAVEL

MANNER /ˈber·ɪŋ, ˈbær-/ *n* [U] the particular way you find it natural to hold your body or the way you appear to other people ○ *She was an imposing attorney with a dignified bearing.* ○ See also: BEARINGS at BEAR TRAVEL

bear market /ˈberˈmɑr·kət, ˈbær-/ *n* [U] a time when investments in the financial markets are generally falling in value ○ Compare BULL MARKET

beast /biːst/ *n* [C] a wild animal

beast of burden *n* [C] an animal used to perform work

beat DEFEAT /biːt/ *v* [T] *past simp.* **beat,** *past part.* **beaten, beat 1** to defeat a competitor, or to do or be better than someone or something ○ *In football, the Giants beat the 49ers, 17-3.* ○ *Most people think that the governor will beat his opponent.* ○ *The room wasn't much, but it beat driving to a hotel 20 miles away.* **2** To beat something that is going to happen is to take action that will prevent it from having an effect on you: *I leave work early to beat the traffic.* ➤ Usage: **win or beat?** at WIN

HIT /biːt/ *v* [I/T] *past simp.* **beat,** *past part.* **beaten, beat** to hit repeatedly ○ [T] *He looked as if he'd been beaten.* ○ [I] *The children were beating on the table.*

B

beating /ˈbiːt̬·ɪŋ/ *n* [C] ○ *the beating of a butterfly's wings* ○ *He escaped a beating.* ○ *(fig.) This chair has taken a beating over the years* (= been used often and damaged).

MIX /biːt/ *v* [T] *past simp.* **beat**, *past part.* **beaten**, *past part.* **beat** to mix food with a fast circular motion ○ [M] *Beat in the egg yolks.*

beater /ˈbiːt̬·ər/ *n* [C] a device used for mixing foods

RHYTHM /biːt/ *v* [I/T] *past simp.* **beat**, *past part.* **beaten, beat** to make a rhythmic sound or movement, or to hit something in rhythm to make such a sound ○ [I] *I was so nervous I could feel my heart beating.* ○ [T] *He steadily beat the drum.* ○ [I] *Without calcium, your heart could not beat correctly.*

beat /biːt/ *n* [C usually sing] ***music*** the rhythmic sound in music that repeats regularly ○ *We clapped in time to the beat.*

AREA /biːt/ *n* [C usually sing] an area for which someone, esp. a police officer, has responsibility as part of the job ○ *People are comforted to see cops on the beat.*

TIRED /biːt/ *adj infml* extremely tired ○ *I'm beat – I'm going to bed.*

WORD FAMILY beat

Nouns	beat beating	*Adjectives*	unbeatable unbeaten
Verbs	beat		

IDIOMS with beat

• **beat around the bush** to talk about lots of unimportant things because you want to avoid talking about what is really important ○ *Quit beating around the bush and say what's on your mind.*

• **beat it** *slang* leave immediately ○ *The big guy turned to me and said, "Beat it, kid – nobody wants you here."* ○ **USAGE**: Used to tell someone to leave.

• **(it) beats me** *slang* I do not know, or I do not understand ○ *"Any idea who won the pennant last year?" "Beats me."* ○ **USAGE**: Used to answer someone's question.

PHRASAL VERBS with beat

• **beat down, beaten, beat** (of sun) to shine very brightly or (of rain) to come down strongly ○ *The sun beat down, parching the already dry fields.*

• **beat out** *someone* [M] to defeat or finish before a competitor ○ *Chicago beat out Washington for the last playoff spot.*

• **beat** *someone* **to** *something* to do something before someone else ○ *I wanted to call with the news, but Steve beat me to it.*

• **beat up** *someone* [M] to hit someone hard and repeatedly ○ *Two people were arrested for beating up that man.* ○ See also: BEAT-UP

• **beat up on** *someone infml* to attack someone unfairly ○ *She didn't like being beat up on by the press.*

beat-up *adj* damaged and in bad condition ○ *He drove an old, beat-up station wagon.* ○ See also: BEAT UP SOMEONE

beautician /bjuːˈtɪʃ·ən/ *n* [C] someone who works in a BEAUTY PARLOR cutting and styling hair and improving people's appearance

beautiful /ˈbjuːt̬·ɪ·fəl/ *adj* having an attractive quality that gives pleasure to those who experience it or think about it ○ *I thought she was the most beautiful woman I'd ever seen.* ○ *The scenery around here is beautiful.* ○ *We heard beautiful music every night.* ○ *It was a beautiful plan.*

beautifully /ˈbjuːt̬·ɪ·fli, -fə·li/ *adv* ○ *She sings beautifully.*

beauty /ˈbjuːt̬·i/ *n* [C/U] **1** an attractive quality that gives pleasure to those who experience it or think about it, or a person who has this attractive quality ○ [U] *The Grand Canyon's natural beauty attracts tourists from all over.* ○ [C] *At 37 she was known as a great beauty.* **2** Beauty can also mean an attractive appearance: [U] *Women's magazines feature articles about diets and beauty tips.*

WORD CHOICES beautiful

If someone (man or woman) is beautiful, we can say that the person is **attractive** or **good-looking**. The adjective **handsome** is also sometimes used for men, and **pretty** for women.

Her husband is really ***good-looking.***

Your daughter is very ***pretty.***

If someone, especially a woman, is extremely beautiful, you can say that the person is **gorgeous** or **stunning**.

You look ***gorgeous*** *in that dress!*

I think she's ***stunning.***

The adjectives **breathtaking, lovely**, and **gorgeous** are often used to describe scenery that is very beautiful.

The view from the window is ***breathtaking.***

We drove through some ***gorgeous*** *countryside.*

The adjective **exquisite** is sometimes used to describe objects which are very beautiful and often delicate.

They make ***exquisite*** *lace.*

IDIOM with beautiful

• **the beauty of** *something* a quality of something that makes it good, easy, or worth doing ○ *One of the beauties of soccer is that you don't have to be big to play the game.*

beauty parlor, beauty salon, beauty shop *n* [C] a place where women go to have their hair cut and styled and their appearance improved

beaver /ˈbiː·vər/ *n* [C] a small mammal that lives in water esp. in rivers and lakes, and has smooth fur, sharp teeth, and a wide, flat tail

bebop /ˈbiː·bɑp/ *n* [U] BOP MUSIC

because /bɪˈkɔːz, -ˈkʌz/ *conjunction* for the reason that ○ *"Why did you throw it?" "Because Carlos told me to."* ○ *We can't go to Julia's party because we're going away that weekend.*

because of *prep* as a result of ○ *The trip was canceled because of bad weather.* ➤ Usage: **for or because?** at FOR BECAUSE

USAGE

because or because of?

Use **because of** if the next thing in the sentence is simply a noun or a noun phrase.

The flight was delayed because of technical problems.

~~*The flight was delayed because technical problems.*~~

beck IDIOM /bek/

• **at** *someone's* **beck and call** ready to do something for someone any time you are asked ○ *She was confined to a wheelchair but had a private nurse at her beck and call.*

beckon /ˈbek·ən/ *v* [I/T] to move your hand or head in a way that tells someone to come nearer ○ [I] *Fargis beckoned to the waiter.*

become BE /bɪˈkʌm/ *v* [L] *past simp.* **became**, *past part.* **become** to start to be ○ *He became a US citizen in 1955.* ○ *The days are becoming shorter.* ○ *It's becoming obvious that Dorothy doesn't like me.*

USAGE

become or get?

Become and **get** can both mean "begin to be something."

You will become dizzy if you spin around too fast.

You will get dizzy if you spin around too fast.

Use **get** if you mean receive or accept something. Do not use **become** in this way.

Of course, we got a lot of support from family and friends.

~~*Of course, we became a lot of support from family and friends.*~~

SUIT /bɪˈkʌm/ *v* [T] *past simp.* **became**, *past part.* **become** to cause someone to look attractive, or to be suitable for someone ○ *That color really becomes you.*

becoming /bɪˈkʌm·ɪŋ/ *adj* ○ *a becoming* (= attractive) *dress*

PHRASAL VERB with **become**

• **become of** *someone/something* to happen to or be a result for something or someone ○ *It's unclear exactly what will become of Bill 35 now, but the issues surrounding it aren't going away.* ○ *Whatever became of Jennie O'Hearn?* (= what happened to)

bed FURNITURE /bed/ *n* [C] a large piece of furniture with a flat surface that a person can lie on to sleep or rest ○ *He felt sick and decided to stay in bed that day.* ○ *He sat down on the bed and took off his shoes.* ○ *Some mornings it's really hard to get out of bed.* ○ *I'm really tired – I think I'll go to bed* (= get into bed in order to sleep).

BOTTOM OF THE SEA /bed/ *n* [C] ***earth science*** the bottom of a river, lake, or sea

AREA OF GROUND /bed/ *n* [C] an area of ground used for planting flowers ○ *a flower bed*

PHRASAL VERB with **bed**

• **bed down** to sleep somewhere temporarily, or to get into bed to sleep ○ *After the earthquake, more than 150 families bedded down in the lobby of City Hall.*

bed-and-breakfast, *abbreviation* **B&B** *n* [C] a small hotel or private house that rents rooms and provides a morning meal

bedclothes /ˈbed·kloʊðz, -kloʊz/ *pl n* BEDDING

bedding /ˈbed·ɪŋ/, *infml* **bedclothes** *n* [U] the sheets, BLANKETS (= covers to keep you warm), and other covers that you put on a bed ○ *The new recruits at the army base were lined up to pick up their bedding.*

bedlam /ˈbed·ləm/ *n* [U] complete disorder and confusion ○ *In the bedlam of shouting, screaming, running people, some ran toward the stage.*

bedpan /ˈbed·pæn/ *n* [C] a container serving as a toilet for people who are too ill to get out of bed

bedraggled /bɪˈdræg·əld/ *adj* (of people or their appearance) messy, dirty, and often wet ○ *We picked up four bedraggled sailors who had weathered the storm in a lifeboat.*

bedridden /ˈbed ˌrɪd·ən/ *adj* [not gradable] unable to get out of bed because of illness or injury

bedrock /ˈbed·rɑk/ *n* [U] **1** ***earth science*** the hard, solid area of rock in the ground that supports the earth above it **2** Bedrock also means the principles and ideas on which something is based: *We feel that the family is the bedrock of society.*

bedroom /ˈbed·ruːm, -rʊm/ *n* [C] a room with a bed or beds for sleeping

bedside /ˈbed·sɑɪd/ *n* [U] the place next to a bed ○ *She sat by his bedside, holding his hand.*

bedside /ˈbed·sɑɪd/ *adj* [not gradable]

bedside manner *n* [U] the way a doctor behaves toward people being treated to make them feel comfortable ○ *He's a good surgeon but he has an awful bedside manner.*

bedspread /ˈbed·spred/ *n* [C] a cover put on a bed over the sheets and BLANKETS (= covers to keep you warm)

bedtime /ˈbed·tɑɪm/ *n* [C usually sing] the time that you usually go to bed at night ○ *Come on, Joey, it's past your bedtime.*

bee /biː/ *n* [C] a flying insect that has a yellow and black body and is able to sting

beech /biːtʃ/ *n* [C/U] a tree with a smooth, gray trunk, or the wood of this tree

beef **MEAT** /biːf/ *n* [U] the flesh of cattle eaten as meat ○ *a roast beef sandwich*
beefy /ˈbiː·fi/ *adj* (of a person, esp. a man) large, heavy, and powerful looking ○ *a big, beefy football player*

COMPLAIN /biːf/ *v* [I] *slang* to complain ○ *Stop beefing about having to work late – you're not the only one.*
beef /biːf/ *n* [C] *slang* ○ *My beef is, how come I'm not making as much as you?*

PHRASAL VERB with beef

• **beef up** *something* [M] to make something stronger or more effective, esp. by adding more support ○ *The company has beefed up its e-mail service.*

beehive /ˈbiː·hɑɪv/ *n* [C] a container shaped like a box where bees are kept so that their HONEY (= the sweet substance they produce) can be collected

been /bɪn/ *past participle of* **1** BE **2** Been is also used to mean visited or traveled: *"Have you ever been to Africa?" "No, I've never been there, but I'd love to go."* ➤ Usage: **gone or been?** at GO **TRAVEL**

beep /biːp/ to make a high, brief, mechanical sound or series of sounds, or cause (a device) to make such a sound ○ [I] *The computer started beeping, so I knew something was wrong.*
beep /biːp/ *n* [C] ○ *The recording told me to leave a message after the beep.*
beeper /ˈbiː·pər/ *n* [C] a small electronic device that you carry or wear that makes a noise or shows a message to tell you that someone wants you to telephone; a PAGER

beer /bɪr/ *n* [C/U] a slightly bitter, alcoholic drink made from grain, or a serving of this drink in a glass or other container

beet /ˈbiːt/ *n* [C/U] the small, round, dark red root of a plant, which is cooked and eaten as a vegetable

beetle /ˈbiːt̬·əl/ *n* [C] any of various insects with a hard, shell-like back

befall /bɪˈfɔːl/ *v* [T] *past simp.* **befell**, *past part.* **befallen** (of something bad) to happen to a person or place ○ *Many natural disasters have befallen that region.*

befit /bɪˈfɪt/ *v* [T] **-tt-** to be suitable or right for ○ *As befits its rural mountain setting, the nine-room inn serves up a huge country breakfast.*

before **EARLIER** /bɪˈfɔːr, -ˈfoʊr/ *prep, conjunction, adv* [not gradable] **1** at or during a time earlier than (the thing mentioned) ○ *I left early because I wanted to arrive home before dark.* ○ *Before making up your mind, think about all your options.* ○ *It was another half hour before* (= until) *the ambulance finally arrived.* ○ *Less than a week before, he'd graduated from college.* **2** **Before last** means before the most recent: *Today is Monday, so the day before last was Saturday.*

IN FRONT /bɪˈfɔːr, -ˈfoʊr/ *prep* in front of ○ *It took courage to stand before a courtroom full of people.*

IDIOMS with before

• **before** *you* **know it** very soon ○ *A week seems like a long time, but Saturday will be here before you know it.*
• **before long** soon ○ *With a little exercise, you'll be back in shape before long.*

beforehand /bɪˈfɔːrˌhænd, -ˈfoʊr-/ *adv* [not gradable] earlier (than a particular time); in advance ○ *She had phoned beforehand to let me know she was coming.*

befriend /bɪˈfrend/ *v* [T] to be friendly to someone ○ *While at college, he had befriended a young student from China.*

befuddled /bɪˈfʌd·əld/ *adj* confused and unable to think clearly ○ *The director was sitting there looking somewhat befuddled.*

beg /beg/ *v* [I/T] **-gg-** **1** to ask for money, or to ask someone to do something in an urgent way ○ [I] *There are a lot of homeless people begging on the streets these days.* ○ [T] *Is your child begging you for a skateboard?* **2** If a dog begs, it sits with its front legs in the air as if to ask for something.

IDIOMS with beg

• **beg off** to ask to be excused from something that you are expected to do ○ *I had to beg off from the meeting because I had too much work to do.*
• **(I) beg your pardon** **1** could you please repeat what you just said ○ *"Are you feeling better?" "I beg your pardon?" "I said: Are you feeling better?"* **2** **(I) beg your pardon** also means I am sorry: *I beg your pardon – can I just get past you?* ○ **USAGE:** Used as a polite way to ask someone to forgive you. ○ Compare EXCUSE ME at EXCUSE **IDIOM**; PARDON ME at PARDON **IDIOM**

beggar /ˈbeg·ər/ *n* [C] a poor person who lives by asking others for money or food

begin /bɪˈgɪn/ *v* [I/T] *pres. part.* **beginning**, *past simp.* **began**, *past part.* **begun** to do or be the first part of something that continues; start ○ [T] *He begins his new job on Monday.* ○ [I] *The movie begins at seven.* ○ [I] *I began by explaining why I had come.*
beginner /bɪˈgɪn·ər/ *n* [C] a person who is just learning how to do an activity ○ *a karate class for beginners*
beginning /bɪˈgɪn·ɪŋ/ *n* [C/U] ○ [C] *She arrived late on her first day of work – it was not a good beginning.* ○ [U] *He sat down and read the story from beginning to end.*

WORD FAMILY begin

Nouns	beginner beginning	Verbs	begin

IDIOM with begin

• **to begin with** first ○ *We had an awful time! To begin with, Cameron got sick on the first day.* ○ Compare TO START WITH at START **IDIOMS**

beginner's luck *n* [U] unexpected early success

begonia /bɪˈgoʊn·jə/ *n* [C] any of a variety of plants with brightly colored flowers and decorative leaves

begrudge /bɪˈgrʌdʒ/ *v* [T] to allow or give unwillingly ○ *He's worked every weekend for the last three months, so you can't begrudge him a little time off now.*

beguile /bɪˈgɑɪl/ *v* [T] ***literature*** to charm, attract, or interest, sometimes in order to deceive ○ *I had to show I was not beguiled by his good looks.*
beguiling /bɪˈgɑɪ·lɪŋ/ *adj* ○ *a beguiling smile*

begun /bɪˈgʌn/ *past participle of* BEGIN

behalf Ⓐ **IDIOM** /bɪˈhæf/
• **on behalf of** *someone*, **on** *someone's* **behalf** done for another person's benefit or support, or because you are representing the interests of that person ○ *I'd like to say on behalf of the whole group that we wish you well in your new job.*

behave /bɪˈheɪv/ *v* [I/T] to act in a particular way, or to act in a way that is considered correct ○ [I] *The judge will instruct the jury on how it is to behave.*
behavior, *Cdn, Br* **behaviour** /bɪˈheɪ·vjər/ *n* [C/U] a particular way of acting ○ [U] *Many people complained about the behavior of some of the fans, who were loud and threatening to those around them.* ○ [C] *This approach can help identify common behaviors and their causes.*
behavioral, *Cdn, Br* **behavioural** /bɪˈheɪ·vjə·rəl/ *adj* [not gradable] expressed in or involving behavior ○ *Emotional and behavioral problems were most prevalent in school-aged children.*

WORD FAMILY behave			
Nouns	behavior misbehavior	*Verbs*	behave misbehave
Adjectives	behavioral		

behead /bɪˈhed/ *v* [T] to cut off the head of a person

behest /bɪˈhest/ *n* [U] *fml* a request ○ *Congress adopted the budget resolution at the behest of the president.*

behind **IN BACK OF** /bɪˈhɑɪnd/ *prep, adv* [not gradable] **1** in or to the back (of) ○ *The sun came out from behind the clouds.* ○ *He opened the door and went in, pulling it shut behind him.* ○ *A police car pulled up behind us.* ○ *I realized I'd left my umbrella behind* (= in the place I had left). **2** Behind can also mean responsible for or causing: *What was the motive behind the bombing?*
BODY PART /bɪˈhɑɪnd/ *n* [C] *infml* the part of the body on which a person sits; the buttocks

IDIOMS with behind

• **behind** *someone* supporting someone in what the person intends to do ○ *Her family was solidly behind her when she decided to go back to school.*
• **behind** *someone's* **back** when someone is not present ○ *What do they say about me behind my back?* ○ **USAGE:** Used to say that someone intentionally says or does something when another person is not there and cannot know about it.
• **behind bars** in prison ○ *Until the court hearing, they will remain behind bars.*
• **behind closed doors** done in a place where things can be kept secret from the public ○ *The meeting was held behind closed doors.*
• **behind-the-scenes** unknown to the public ○ *behind-the-scenes negotiations*

B

behold /bɪˈhoʊld/ *v* [T] *past* **beheld** ***literature*** to see or look at ○ *He looked up and beheld the stranger sitting across the table, smiling a secret smile.*

beholden /bɪˈhoʊl·dən/ *adj* feeling you have a duty to someone who has done something for you ○ *They do not benefit from state subsidies and therefore are not beholden to the government.*

beige /beɪʒ/ *adj, n* [U] (of) a pale, creamy, brown color

being **BE** /ˈbiː·ɪŋ/ *present participle of* BE
PERSON /ˈbiː·ɪŋ/ *n* [C/U] a person or thing that exists, or the state of existing ○ [C] *human/living beings* ○ [U] *The group came into being* (= began to exist) *to help relatives of the terminally ill.*

belabor /bɪˈleɪ·bər/ *v* [T] to explain something more than necessary ○ *I don't want to belabor the point, but I still don't think you understand.*

belated /bɪˈleɪţ·əd/ *adj* coming later than expected ○ *He did make a belated attempt to apologize.*
belatedly /bɪˈleɪţ·əd·li/ *adv*

belch /beltʃ/ **1** to have air from the stomach come out in a noisy way through the mouth **2** If something is belched or belched out, it comes out in quick, violent bursts: [I/T] *The chimney was belching (out) thick smoke.*
belch /beltʃ/ *n* [C]

beleaguered /bɪˈliː·gərd/ *adj* having so many difficulties that you feel as if you are being attacked from every direction ○ *As a candidate, she had promised tax relief for the beleaguered middle class.*

belie /bɪˈlɑɪ/ *v* [T] *pres. part.* **belying**, *past* **belied** *fml* to represent something falsely or to hide something ○ *His gruff manner belied a gentle personality.*

belief /bɪˈliːf/ *n* [C/U] the feeling of being certain that something exists or is true ○ [C] *philosophical beliefs* ○ [C] *He made no secret of his belief that she was guilty.* ○ [U] *He has strong belief in teaching as a calling to help others.*

believe /bɪˈliːv/ *v* [I/T] **1** to think that something is true or correct ○ [T] *One juror said he didn't believe the policeman's testimony.* ○ [+ (*that*) clause] *She believed (that) it was wrong to censor the text.* **2** If you believe in something, you feel that it is right: [I always + adv/prep] *I believe in giving a per-*

son a second chance. **3** If you believe in someone you have confidence in that person's abilities: [I always + adv/prep] *We just need to believe in ourselves.*

believable /bɪˈliː·və·bəl/ *adj* belonging to a type that seems real; realistic ○ *a believable character/plot/story*

believer /bɪˈliː·vər/ *n* [C] **1** a person who feels certain about the truth of a religion or religious ideas **2** A believer is also someone who has a strong opinion that something is right or good: *I'm a believer in the public's right to know.*

WORD FAMILY believe

Nouns	belief believer disbelief	*Adjectives*	believable unbelievable
		Verbs	believe
Adverbs	unbelievably		disbelieve

IDIOMS with believe

• **believe it or not** this is surprising but true ○ *Believe it or not, they got married after knowing each other only a week.* ○ **USAGE:** Used to introduce a surprising fact.

• **believe me** this is true ○ *Believe me, I was scared!* ○ **USAGE:** Used to emphasize something you say.

• **not believe** *your* **eyes, not believe** *your* **ears** to be very surprised ○ *I could not believe my eyes when I saw the garden in full bloom.*

belittle /bɪˈlɪt̬·əl/ *v* [T] to make an action or a person seem unimportant ○ *You gain nothing by belittling him and creating bad feelings.*

bell /bel/ *n* [C] **1** a hollow, cup-shaped, metal object that makes a ringing sound when a part hanging inside swings against its sides, or when it is hit by any hard object ○ *The school bell was ringing.* **2** A bell is also a DOORBELL.

bellhop /ˈbel·hɑp/ *n* [C] a person in a hotel employed to carry bags for customers and perform other services

belligerent /bəˈlɪdʒ·ə·rənt/ *adj* eager to fight or argue ○ *She was so belligerent that I gave up trying to explain.*

belligerence /bəˈlɪdʒ·ə·rəns/ *n* [U]

bellow /ˈbel·oʊ/ *v* [I/T] to shout in a loud voice ○ *"I don't believe this!" the old man bellowed.*

bellwether /ˈbel ˌweð·ər/ *n* [C] something that shows what the general future of changes or developments will probably be ○ *In Massachusetts, a bellwether state for the region, more people are buying and building houses.*

belly /ˈbel·i/ *n* [C] *infml* the stomach, or the front part of your body at the waist, between your chest and legs

belly button *n* [C] *infml* a NAVEL

belong /bɪˈlɔːŋ/ *v* [I] to be in the right place, or (of a person) to feel that you are in the right place ○ *Your shoes belong in the closet, not in the middle of the room.* ○ *Tom, it's great to see you on TV – you belong here.* ○ *The painting belongs in* (= should be in) *a modern art museum.*

belongings /bɪˈlɔːŋ·ɪŋz/ *pl n* the things that you own, esp. those that can be taken with you ○ *Fleeing the flood waters, families here packed their belongings and headed to higher land.*

PHRASAL VERBS with belong

• **belong to** *someone* **PROPERTY** to be the property of someone ○ *Does this book belong to you or to Sarah?*

• **belong to** *something* **MEMBER** to be a member of something ○ *We belong to the same softball team.*

beloved /bɪˈlʌv·əd, -ˈlʌvd/ *adj* loved very much ○ *His beloved wife died last year, and he is still grieving.*

below /bɪˈloʊ/ *prep, adv* [not gradable] **1** in a lower position (than); under ○ *The author's name was printed below the title.* ○ *There's a basement below the first floor.* **2** Below also means less in number or value: *It's been below freezing every day this week.* ○ *It's for young kids below the age of six.*

belt **STRIP** /belt/ *n* [C] **1** a strip of leather or other material worn around the waist ○ *a black leather belt* **2** A belt is also a continuous strip of material that moves as part of a machine.

HIT /belt/ *v* [T] *infml* to hit someone or something hard ○ *He belted the ball out of the park for a home run.*

AREA /belt/ *n* [C] **1** an area that is known for a particular characteristic ○ *the corn belt* (= area known for growing corn) **2** ***earth science*** A belt is also a region that has a particular type of CLIMATE WEATHER.

PHRASAL VERB with belt

• **belt out** *something* [M] *infml* to sing very loudly and with enthusiasm ○ *I knew how to belt out a song and win over an audience.*

beltway /ˈbelt·weɪ/ *n* [C] a main road that goes around the edge of a city

belying /bɪˈlɑɪ·ɪŋ/ *present participle of* BELIE

bemused /bɪˈmjuːzd/ *adj* slightly confused; not knowing what to do or how to understand something ○ *He was looking from one face to the other with an air of bemused disbelief.*

bench /bentʃ/ *n* [C] **1** a long seat for two or more people, often of wood and usually used outside ○ *a park bench* **2** The bench is a court of law, or the place where a judge or judges sit in court: *Face the bench when you are talking, Mr. Smith.*

benchmark /ˈbentʃ·mɑrk/ *n* [C] a standard for measuring or judging other things of the same type ○ *Her performances set a new benchmark for classical pianists.*

bend /bend/ *past* **bent** to change the position of your body or a part of your body so that it is no longer straight but curved or forming an angle ○ [I always + adv/prep] *She dropped her umbrella and bent down to pick it up.* ○ [T] *Bend your knees and* *keep your back straight when lifting heavy objects.* ○ See also: BENT TENDENCY; BENT ON at BENT IDIOM

bend /bend/ *n* [C] a curved path or an angle ○ *a bend in the road*

IDIOMS with **bend**

• **bend over backwards** to try very hard to do something good or helpful ○ *Mann insisted that he bent over backwards to be objective in presenting the story.* ○ Compare GO OUT OF YOUR WAY at GO IDIOMS

• **bend the rules** to break the rules in a way that you consider unimportant or not harmful ○ *You've got to know when to bend the rules a little.*

beneath /bɪˈni:θ/ *prep* in or to a lower position than; under ○ *Jerry hid the letter beneath a pile of papers.* ○ *The cool grass felt good beneath their feet.*

benediction /ˌben·əˈdɪk·ʃən/ *n* [C] a prayer asking for God's help and protection

benefactor /ˈben·əˌfæk·tər/ *n* [C] someone who gives money to help an organization, society, or person

beneficial /ˌben·əˈfɪʃ·əl/ *adj* tending to help; having a good effect ○ *Moderate exercise is really beneficial.*

beneficiary /ˌben·əˈfɪʃ·i:ˌer·i, -ˈfɪʃ·ə·ri/ *n* [C] a person or group who receives money or other benefits as a result of something else ○ *Among major beneficiaries of the new tax law will be giant telecommunications companies.*

benefit Ⓐ /ˈben·əˌfɪt/ *n* [C/U] **1** a helpful or good effect ○ [C] *It was a giveaway to the rich, he said, and not something that's a benefit to most Americans.* ○ [U] *She wanted her money to be used for the benefit of* (= to help) *poor children.* **2** ***social studies*** A benefit is also a helpful service given to employees in addition to their pay or to someone else who needs help: [C] *health/medical benefits* ○ [C] *I'm collecting unemployment benefits.* **3** A benefit is also a party or other event that has the purpose of raising money.

benefit Ⓐ /ˈben·əˌfɪt/ *v* [I/T] ○ [I] *I have benefited greatly from her wisdom.*

benevolent /bəˈnev·ə·lənt/ *adj* kind and helpful ○ *I grew up happily under the benevolent influence of my Uncle Walt.*

benevolence /bəˈnev·ə·ləns/ *n* [U]

benign /bɪˈnɑɪn/ *adj* **1** pleasant and kind; not harmful or severe ○ *a benign smile* ○ *His humor was benign, never cruel or hurtful.* **2** *medical* (of a disease or tissue growing because of a disease) not likely to result in death: *a benign tumor* ○ Compare MALIGNANT

bent **BEND** /bent/ *past simple and past participle of* BEND

TENDENCY /bent/ *n* [U] *fml* a natural tendency ○ *the philosophical bent of his mind*

IDIOM with **bent**

• **bent on** to be very determined to do something ○ *He was bent on quitting his job even though he was making a lot of money.*

benzene /ˈbenˌzi:n/ *n* [U] ***chemistry*** a colorless liquid made from PETROLEUM (= thick oil from under the ground), from which plastics and many chemical products can be made

bequeath /bɪˈkwi:θ, -ˈkwi:ð/ *v* [T] to give money or property to others after your death ○ *Her father bequeathed the business to her.*

bequest /bɪˈkwest/ *n* [C] the money or property that someone, after death, gives to someone else ○ *Her will included large bequests to charity.*

berate /bɪˈreɪt/ *v* [T] to criticize someone in an angry manner ○ *His mother berated him for making a mess.*

bereaved /bɪˈri:vd/ *adj* [not gradable] having had a close family member or friend die

bereaved /bɪˈri:vd/ *pl n* the people who are sad because someone close to them has died

bereft /bɪˈreft/ *adj* having to do without something or someone and suffering from the loss ○ *I do hope he won't leave us utterly bereft of his wit and wisdom.*

beret /bəˈreɪ/ *n* [C] a round, flat hat made of soft material

berry /ˈber·i/ *n* [C] any of various small, round fruits that grow on plants and trees

berserk /bərˈzɜrk, -ˈsɜrk/ *adj* not in control, extremely excited, or crazy ○ *He received a perfect score and the crowd went berserk.*

berth /bɜrθ/ *n* [C] a bed in a boat or train, or a place for a ship or boat to stay in a port

beryllium /bəˈrɪl·i:·əm/ *n* [U] ***chemistry*** a hard, light, gray chemical element that is a metal and is used to make strong ALLOYS (= mixtures of metals)

beset /bɪˈset/ *v* [T] *past simp.* **beset**, *pres. part.* **besetting** hurt or troubled by something bad ○ *Many problems have beset the team in recent months.*

beside /bɪˈsɑɪd/ *prep* at the side of; next to ○ *Come and sit here beside me.*

IDIOMS with **beside**

• **beside *yourself*** extremely upset ○ *He was beside himself when he found out his dog had died.*

• **beside the point** not important ○ *The exact cost is beside the point – what's important is that we get the job done.*

besides /bɪˈsɑɪdz/ *prep, adv* [not gradable] in addition to; also ○ *Do you play any other sports besides golf?* ○ *He won't mind if you're late – besides, it's not your fault.*

besiege /bɪˈsi:dʒ/ *v* [T] **1** to surround a place, esp. with an army, to prevent people or supplies from getting in or out ○ (*fig.*) *After the controversial show, the television network was besieged with complaints.* **2** A person who is besieged is surrounded: *Mick Jagger was besieged by fans at the airport.*

B

best HIGHEST QUALITY /best/ *adj, adv* **1** of the highest quality, to the greatest degree, in the most effective way, or being the most suitable or pleasing; *superlative of* GOOD or WELL ○ *He's one of our best students.* ○ *Which of the songs did you like best?* ○ *She was my best friend at school.* **2** Someone's **best bet** is the action most likely to be successful: *If you want to get to the theater on time, your best bet is to get a cab.* **3** **Best wishes** is a polite way of finishing a letter to someone.

EXCELLENCE /best/ *n* [U] the most excellent in a group of things or people ○ *As an athlete, Jim Thorpe is one of the best of all time.* ○ *I like all of Hitchcock's films, but I think "Notorious" is the best.*

DEFEAT /best/ *v* [T] to defeat someone in a fight or competition ○ *In chess, I was bested by my 13-year-old niece.*

IDIOMS with best

• **at best** even if the best possible result happens ○ *If he drops the course now, at best he'll get an incomplete, and he could fail.*

• **do** *your* **very best**, **do the best** *you* **can** to try as hard as possible ○ *We did our very best to give our kids a good education.*

bestial /ˈbes·tʃəl, ˈbiːs-/ *adj* fierce and cruel, and without any human feelings ○ *a bestial dictator*

best man *n* [C] (at a marriage ceremony) the male friend or family member who stands with the BRIDEGROOM

bestow /bɪˈstoʊ/ *v* [T] *fml* to give something as an honor or present ○ *The country's highest medal was bestowed upon him for heroism.*

best-seller, **bestseller** /ˈbestˈsel·ər/ *n* [C] a new book or other product that has sold a great number of copies

best-selling, **bestselling** /ˈbestˈsel·ɪŋ/ *adj* [not gradable] ○ *Released in February 2000, it is the best-selling computer game ever.*

bet /bet/ *v* [I/T] *pres. part.* **betting**, *past* **bet** **1** to risk a sum of money on the unknown result of an event in the hope of winning more money than you have risked ○ [T] *He went to the race track and bet $2 on a horse.* ○ [I] *I bet that the Yankees won't win the pennant this year.* **2** If you bet someone that something is true or will happen, you think it is likely: [T] *I bet (you) she missed the bus.*

bet /bet/ *n* [C] **1** *He placed a bet on the race.* **2** A bet is also a guess or opinion: *My bet is that the senator will decide not to run again.* **3** A bet is also a chance or opportunity: *Putting your savings in a high-interest account is a good bet/your best bet.*

IDIOM with bet

• **don't bet on it**, **I wouldn't bet on it** that is unlikely to be true or to happen ○ *"Do you think I'll get my money back?" "I wouldn't bet on it."*

beta particle /ˈbeɪt̬·ə ˌpɑrt̬·ɪ·kəl/ ***chemistry, physics*** an extremely small piece of matter with a positive or negative electric CHARGE, produced when an atom is broken down. A **beta (+) particle** is the same as a POSITRON; a **beta (–) particle** is an ELECTRON.

betray BE NOT LOYAL /bɪˈtreɪ/ *v* [T] to be not loyal to your country or to someone who believes you are loyal, often by doing something harmful ○ *Some lawmakers say they feel betrayed by the president.*

betrayal /bɪˈtreɪ·əl/ *n* [C/U] ○ [U] *I felt a sense of betrayal when my friends refused to lend me money.*

SHOW /bɪˈtreɪ/ *v* [T] to show your feelings or thoughts without intending to ○ *She could not help betraying her sympathy for us.*

better HIGHER STANDARD /ˈbet̬·ər/ *adj* **1** of a higher standard, or more suitable, pleasing, or effective than other things or people; *comparative of* GOOD ○ *He sat near the front to get a better view.* ○ *Relations between the two countries have never been better.* ○ *She is much better at tennis than I am.* **2** Better can also be used as the comparative to form adjectives beginning with good: *She's good-looking, and her brother is even better-looking.*

GREATER DEGREE /ˈbet̬·ər/ *adv* **1** to a greater degree, or in a more suitable, pleasing, or satisfactory way; *comparative of* WELL ○ *The next time he took the test, he was better prepared.* ○ *I like this jacket much better than the brown one.* ○ *She knows her way around the college better than I do.* ○ *She did much better* (= She was more successful) *in the second part of the exam.* **2** If you are or get better after an illness or injury, you are healthy and no longer ill.

IMPROVE /ˈbet̬·ər/ *v* [T] *fml* to improve a situation, condition, or person ○ *The organization was established to better conditions for the disabled.*

better /ˈbet̬·ər/ *n* [U] used in comparisons to show that a condition is improved ○ *The cleaner the glass is, the better you can see.*

IDIOMS with better

• **better late than never** it is better for someone to arrive or do something late than not to arrive or do it at all ○ *"Dan finally paid me the money he owed me." "Well, better late than never."*

• **better luck next time** I hope you will succeed when you try again ○ *I'm sorry you didn't get a better SAT score, but better luck next time.*

• **better off** **1** in a more satisfactory situation than you were before ○ *I know you're unhappy that the relationship ended, but you're better off without him.* **2** **Better off** also means having more money and a better level of comfort in your life than you had before, or than someone else has: *People in this country are far better off than they were ten years ago.*

• **better safe than sorry** it is wise to be careful and protect yourself against risk rather than be careless ○ *Make sure you take an umbrella – I know it's sunny now, but better safe than sorry.*

• **better still** even more satisfactory ○ *Give her a call, or better still go see her.*

• **the better part of** most of ○ *We waited there for the better part of an hour.* ○ **USAGE:** Used to emphasize that most of a period of time was spent doing something.

between SPACE /bɪˈtwiːn/, **in between** /ˌɪn·bɪˈtwiːn/ *prep, adv* [not gradable] **1** in or into the space that separates two places, people, or objects ○ *We live halfway between Toronto and Montreal.* ○ *She squeezed in between the parked cars.* **2** If something is between two amounts, it is greater than the first amount but smaller than the second: *She weighs between 55 and 60 pounds.*

TIME /bɪˈtwiːn/, **in between** /ˌɪn·bɪˈtwiːn/ *prep, adv* in the period of time that separates two different times or events ○ *There's a ten-minute break between classes.* ○ *You should arrive between 8 and 8:30.* ○ *In between sobs, he managed to tell them what had happened.*

AMONG /bɪˈtwiːn/ *prep* shared by or involving two or more people or things ○ *The money was divided equally between her three children.* ○ *Trade between the two countries has increased sharply.* ○ *There is a great deal of similarity between Caroline and her mother.* ○ *Between the three of us, we were able to afford a nice graduation gift.* ○ *You'll have to choose between dinner and a movie.* ○ *Next week's game will be between the two finalists.*

CONNECTING /bɪˈtwiːn/ *prep* connecting two or more places, things, or people ○ *There is regular train service between New York and Philadelphia.* ○ *The survey shows a link between asthma and air pollution.*

SEPARATING /bɪˈtwiːn/ *prep* separating two places or things ○ *The wall between East and West Berlin came down in 1989.* ○ *What's the difference between this $100 watch and the $500 one* (= In what way are they different)?

IDIOM with **between**

• **between you and me** what I am about to say should be kept secret ○ *Just between you and me, I think she's lying.*

beverage /ˈbev·rɪdʒ/ *n* [C] a drink of any type ○ *cool, refreshing beverages* ○ *What's your favorite beverage?*

bevy /ˈbev·i/ *n* [C] a large group ○ *a bevy of lawyers*

beware /bɪˈwer, -ˈwær/ *v* [I/T] to be very careful about something or someone ○ [I] *In grassy areas, beware of ticks.*

GRAMMAR

beware

You can only use this verb in the present tense in commands and warnings.

Beware of the dog.

Beware of giving your credit card number to register on a website.

You should beware of running into debt.

bewildered /bɪˈwɪl·dərd/ *adj* confused and uncertain ○ *He sat up in bed, bewildered, unsure of where he was.*

bewildering /bɪˈwɪl·də·rɪŋ/ *adj* ○ *Buying a car can be a bit bewildering.*

bewilderment /bɪˈwɪl·dər·mənt/ *n* [U] ○ *Parents expressed bewilderment and anger at the meeting.*

bewitched /bɪˈwɪtʃt/ *adj* extremely attracted, or completely controlled ○ *Once kids step inside a circus tent, they're bewitched.*

bewitching /bɪˈwɪtʃ·ɪŋ/ *adj* ○ *a bewitching actress*

beyond FARTHER AWAY /biːˈɑnd/ *prep, adv* [not gradable] farther away in the distance than something ○ *Beyond the river was a small town.* ○ *From the top of the hill we could see our house and the woods beyond.*

OUTSIDE A LIMIT /biːˈɑnd/ *prep, adv* [not gradable] **1** outside or after a stated limit ○ *Few people live beyond the age of a hundred.* ○ *Beyond a certain level of tiredness, it is impossible to work productively.* ○ *Tonight's performance has been cancelled due to circumstances beyond our control.* **2** Beyond also means more than: *I've got nothing to tell you beyond what I said earlier.* ○ *My job goes beyond teaching facts – my aim is to get children to think for themselves.* **3** Beyond also means at a point where something could not be: *She has changed beyond recognition.* ○ *The car was damaged beyond repair.*

IDIOMS with **beyond**

• **beyond me** *infml* not something that I can understand ○ *How they can live in such chaos is beyond me.*

• **beyond** *someone's* **wildest dreams** better or more than someone had ever thought possible ○ *Suddenly she was rich beyond her wildest dreams.*

biannual /bɑɪˈæn·jə·wəl/ *adj* [not gradable] happening twice a year ○ *a biannual report/meeting* ○ Compare BIENNIAL

bias Ⓐ /ˈbɑɪ·əs/ *n* [C/U] an unfair personal opinion that influences your judgment ○ [U] *They vowed to fight racial bias in the school.* ○ [C usually sing] *Does news coverage reflect a reporter's bias?*

bias Ⓐ /ˈbɑɪ·əs/ *v* [T] -s-, -ss- ○ *The judge withheld the information on the grounds that it would bias the jury.*

biased Ⓐ /ˈbɑɪ·əst/ *adj* showing an unreasonable preference or dislike based on personal opinion ○ *The newspapers gave a biased report of the meeting.*

bib /bɪb/ *n* [C] a cover made of cloth or plastic that is worn by young children when eating to prevent their clothes from getting dirty

Bible /ˈbɑɪ·bəl/ *n* [C/U] **1** the holy writings of the Christian religion consisting of the OLD TESTAMENT and the NEW TESTAMENT, or the holy writings of the Jewish religion consisting of the TORAH and other writings, or a book containing either of these sets of writings ○ [C] *Her parents gave her a Bible when she was young.* **2** A Bible is also the holy writings of any religion. **3** A bible is a book that gives important advice and information about a particular subject: [C] *The magazine became the bible of fashionable women.*

B

biblical /ˈbɪb·lɪ·kəl/ *adj* [not gradable] in or relating to the Bible ○ *Isaac is a biblical name.*

bibliography /ˌbɪb·liːˈɑg·rə·fi/ *n* [C] a list of the books and articles that have been used by someone when writing a book or article

bicameral legislature /bɑɪˈkæm·ə·rəl ˈledʒ·əˌsleɪ·tʃər/ *n* [C] ***politics & government*** a lawmaking body made up of two groups of elected officials

bicentennial /ˌbɑɪˌsenˈten·iː·əl, -sən-/, **bicentenary** /ˌbɑɪˌsenˈten·ə·ri, -sən-/ *n* [C] the day or year that is 200 years after a particular event, esp. an important one; a 200th ANNIVERSARY ○ *The university marked its bicentennial with a weeklong celebration.*

biceps /ˈbɑɪ·seps/ *n* [C] *pl* **biceps** the large muscle at the front of the upper arm ○ *He flexed his biceps.*

bicker /ˈbɪk·ər/ *v* [I] *disapproving* to argue about unimportant matters ○ *They were bickering over what to order and where to sit.*

bicycle /ˈbɑɪˌsɪk·əl/, **bike** *n* [C] a vehicle with two wheels and a seat for a rider whose feet push PEDALS around in circles to make the wheels turn ○ *He rides his bicycle to school.*

bicycle /ˈbɑɪˌsɪk·əl/, , *v* [I] ○ *I saw you bicycling through town yesterday.*

bid OFFER /bɪd/ *v* [I/T] *pres. part.* **bidding**, *past* **bid** **1** to offer a particular amount of money for something when competing against other people to buy it ○ [T] *A collector bid $500,000 for the portrait.* **2** People who bid for/on a job offer to do it for a particular amount of money. **3** Someone who bids to do something competes with others to do it: [I] *Paris is bidding to host the next Olympics.*

bid /bɪd/ *n* [C] **1** an offer of a particular amount of money for something that is for sale ○ *The minimum bid for these dolls is $75.* **2** A bid is also an offer to do a job for a particular price: *His bid to build the garage was too high.* **3** A bid for something is an attempt to achieve or obtain it: *Her bid for reelection was unsuccessful.*

bidder /ˈbɪd·ər/ *n* [C] a person who offers money for goods or property when competing with other people to buy it, or someone who offers to do a job for a particular price

TELL /bɪd/ *v* [T] *pres. part.* **bidding**, *past simp.* **bid, bade**, *past part.* **bidden, bid** to give a greeting to someone, or to ask someone to do something ○ *He bade us farewell.*

bidding /ˈbɪd·ɪŋ/ *n* [U] *fml* a request or an order ○ *At my grandmother's bidding, I wore my best dress.*

bide IDIOM /bɑɪd/

• **bide** *your* **time** to wait patiently for a good opportunity to do something ○ *He's just biding his time until a permanent job opens up.*

biennial /bɑɪˈen·iː·əl/ *adj* [not gradable] happening once every two years ○ *a biennial exhibit* ○ Compare BIANNUAL

biennial /bɑɪˈen·iː·əl/ *n* [C] a plant that lives for two years, producing seeds and flowers in its second year ○ Compare ANNUAL PLANT; PERENNIAL PLANT

bifocals /ˈbɑɪˌfoʊ·kəlz/ *pl n* glasses with an upper part for looking at things far away and a lower part for reading or looking at things that are near

bifocal /bɑɪˈfoʊ·kəl, ˈbɑɪˌfoʊ-/ *adj* [not gradable] ○ *bifocal lenses*

big LARGE /bɪg/ *adj* [*-er/-est* only] **-gg- 1** large in size or amount ○ *a big ant/man/building/city* ○ *Do you have these shoes in a bigger size?* ○ *He tried to impress his friends by using big words.* ○ *She got a big raise.* ○ *I had a great big slice of chocolate cake.* ○ *This is the region's biggest bicycle race.* **2** Big can also mean to a large degree: *a big spender/eater* **3** *infml* Big can also mean older: *a big sister/brother* **4** *infml* Big can also be used to add emphasis: *You're a big bully!*

biggie /ˈbɪg·i/ *n* [C] *infml* something that is large ○ *We got a new client, and it's a biggie.*

IMPORTANT /bɪg/ *adj* [*-er/-est* only] **-gg- 1** important, because of being powerful, influential, or having a serious effect ○ *He had a big decision to make about his future.* ○ *There's a big difference between starting up a business and just talking about it.* ○ *The big story in the news this week is the blizzard in the Midwest.* ○ *We just bought a house, so today's a big day for us.* **2** *infml* If a product or activity is big, it is extremely popular: *Those toys are very big in Japan.*

biggie /ˈbɪg·i/ *n* [C] *infml* something that is very important or successful ○ *Finger food is a biggie with the kids.*

IDIOMS with big

• **big deal 1** *infml* something important ○ *Going to college is still a big deal.* **2** *infml* **Big deal** also means you do not think that what someone has said or done is important or special: *"I ran five miles this morning." "Big deal! I ran ten."*

• **big on** *infml* to like very much ○ *I'm not very big on classical music.*

• **no big deal** *infml* not important ○ *I'd like to work out today, but if I can't it's no big deal.*

bigamy /ˈbɪg·ə·mi/ *n* [U] the act of marrying a person while already legally married to someone else

Big Apple *n* [U] *infml* New York City

big bang theory *n* [U] the very large explosion of a single mass of matter that many scientists believe was the beginning of the universe

Big Brother *n* [C usually sing] a government or person in authority that tries to control people's behavior and thoughts

big business *n* [U] ***politics & government*** powerful, influential businesses and financial organizations considered as a group

Big Dipper *n* [U] a group of seven bright stars that can be seen in the northern part of the world

big gun, **big shot, big wheel** *n* [C] someone who has an important or powerful position ○ *Their law-*

yer, a big gun from Detroit, commissioned a bunch of surveys to show that their products met the state's standards.

bighearted /ˈbɪɡˈhɑrţ·əd/ *adj* kind and generous

big leagues *pl n infml* the top level of a particular sport, business, or activity ○ *the big leagues of horse racing*

big name *n* [C] *infml* a famous or important person ○ *She's a big name in local politics.*

bigot /ˈbɪɡ·ət/ *n* [C] a person who has strong, unreasonable ideas, esp. about race or religion, and who thinks anyone who does not have the same beliefs is wrong ○ *Some of the townspeople are bigots who call foreigners terrible names.*
bigoted /ˈbɪɡ·əţ·əd/ *adj* ○ *He was removed from the committee for making bigoted remarks.*
bigotry /ˈbɪɡ·ə·tri/ *n* [U] ○ *racial/religious bigotry*

big time *n* [U] *infml* the state of being famous or successful ○ *You've really hit the big time now.*
big-time, big time *adj, adv* ○ *Her influence is secure even though she's had limited experience in big-time politics.* ○ *I flunked the MCP test big time* (= completely).

bigwig /ˈbɪɡ·wɪɡ/ *n* [C] *infml* an important or powerful person ○ *The network television bigwigs loved the show.*

bike /bɑɪk/ *n* [C] **1** a bicycle **2** A bike is also a MOTORBIKE or MOTORCYCLE.
bike /bɑɪk/ *v* [I] ○ *She got in the habit of biking to work when the weather was good.*
biker /ˈbɑɪ·kər/ *n* [C] someone who rides a MOTORCYCLE or bicycle

bikini /bəˈkiː·ni/ *n* [C] a two-piece SWIMSUIT (= clothing worn for swimming) for women

bilateral /bɑɪˈlæţ·ə·rəl/ *adj* [not gradable] involving two groups or countries ○ *bilateral relations* ○ *The countries signed a bilateral agreement.*

bile /bɑɪl/ *n* [U] **1** ***biology*** a bitter, yellow liquid produced by the LIVER (= organ in the body) that helps to break down fats so that you can digest them **2** Bile is also a strong feeling of anger.

bilingual /bɑɪˈlɪŋ·ɡwəl, -ɡjə·wəl/ *adj* [not gradable] able to speak or using two languages ○ *Kate is bilingual.* ○ *a bilingual dictionary* ○ Compare MONOLINGUAL

bill **REQUEST FOR PAYMENT** /bɪl/ *n* [C] **1** a list of expenses to be paid, or the total amount of costs or expenses ○ *We still have doctors' bills to pay.* **2** A bill is also a CHECK REQUEST FOR PAYMENT.
bill /bɪl/ *v* [T] to send someone a statement of what is owed ○ *Some places will bill you, but at others you have to pay right away.*

MONEY /bɪl/ *n* [C] a piece of paper money ○ *He pulled out a thick wad of bills and gave me $20.*

LAW /bɪl/ *n* [C] ***politics & government*** a formal statement of a planned new law that is discussed by a government or legislature before being voted on ○ *After a bill is passed by both houses of Congress, it becomes law when the president signs it.*

BIRD /bɪl/ *n* [C] the beak of a bird

billboard /ˈbɪl·bɔːrd, -boʊrd/ *n* [C] a very large board on which advertisements are shown, esp. at the side of a road

billfold /ˈbɪl·foʊld/ *n* [C] a small, folding case or WALLET for carrying money

billiards /ˈbɪl·jərdz/ *n* [U] a game played by two or more people on a table covered in green cloth in which a CUE (= long pole) is used to hit a ball against other balls to send them into the holes along the edge of the table

billion /ˈbɪl·jən/ *number* 1,000,000,000 ○ *Congress cut spending by $255 billion.* ○ *Four hurricanes battered Florida, causing billions of dollars in damage.*

billionaire /ˌbɪl·jəˈner, -ˈnær/ *n* [C] someone who has more than a BILLION dollars (= $1,000,000,000) in the form of property, possessions, or money

Bill of Rights *n* [U] ***US history*** a statement of the rights of US citizens, as added to the country's CONSTITUTION

billow /ˈbɪl·oʊ/ *v* [I] to spread over a large area, or (esp. of items made of cloth) to become filled with air and appear to be larger ○ *The building is draped in blue plastic sheeting that flaps and billows like a sail.*
billow /ˈbɪl·oʊ/ *n* [C usually pl] a large wave or any large, swelling mass ○ *billows of smoke*

bimonthly /bɑɪˈmʌnθ·li/ *adj, adv* [not gradable] **1** happening or appearing every two months ○ *a bimonthly report* **2** Bimonthly is sometimes used to mean twice a month.

bin /bɪn/ *n* [C] **1** a large storage container ○ *a compost/storage bin* **2** *Br* A bin is also a TRASH CAN.

binary /ˈbɑɪ·nə·ri/ *adj* [not gradable] **1** consisting of two of something **2** Binary also describes a numbering system using only two numbers, zero and one.

binary fission *n* [U] ***biology*** the process in which organisms with only one cell create new organisms by dividing

bind **TIE** /bɑɪnd/ *v* [T] *past* **bound** **1** to tie someone or something tightly, or to fasten things together ○ *The room was full of wooden boxes bound with twisted wire.* ○ (*fig.*) *The club is home to a mix of people bound together by a love of boats and boating.* **2** *fig.* To bind someone is also to force the person to keep a promise: *This contract binds the state to use this land as a park, said Judge Harry Smith.* **3** To bind a book is to fasten one edge of the pages together inside a cover to make a book.
binder /ˈbɑɪn·dər/ *n* [C] a stiff cover that can hold loose papers, often having a part that fastens them ○ *a three-ring binder*

binding /ˈbɑɪn·dɪŋ/ *n* [C] The binding of a book is the type of cover it has: *a cloth binding*

UNPLEASANT SITUATION /bɑɪnd/ *n* [U] a difficult situation in which none of the choices available are good ○ *If you lose a lot of your customers, you'll soon get in a financial bind.*

binding /ˈbɑɪn·dɪŋ/ *adj law* (esp. of an agreement) not to be avoided or broken ○ *Both sides agreed to submit the dispute to binding arbitration* (= to a decision they would have to obey).

binding energy *n* [U] ***physics*** the amount of energy necessary to break up a NUCLEUS (= central part of an atom) into its separate parts

binge /bɪndʒ/ *n* [C] **1** an occasion when an activity is done in an extreme way, esp. eating, drinking, or spending money ○ *He admits to having an occasional ice-cream binge.* **2** To go on a binge is to do a lot of something: ○ *He's on a binge, eating everything in sight.*

binge /bɪndʒ/ *v* [I] *pres. part.* **binging, bingeing** to do something in a way that is extreme and not controlled ○ *I tend to binge on ice cream when I'm lonely.*

bingo /ˈbɪŋ·goʊ/ *n* [U] a game of chance often played for prizes in which people are given cards and cover each number on their cards as it is called, with the person who is first to cover a whole line of numbers on any card being the winner ○ *Mother loved to play bingo at her church.*

binoculars /bəˈnɑk·jə·lərz, bɑɪ-/ *pl n* a device for making objects that are far away appear nearer and larger, and made of two attached tubes that you hold up to your eyes to look through ○ *a pair of binoculars*

binomial /bɑɪˈnoʊ·miː·əl/ *n* [C] ***mathematics*** an EXPRESSION (= mathematical statement) that has two TERMS (= numbers or symbols) that are not the same ○ *4x + y is a binomial.*

biochemistry /ˌbɑɪ·oʊˈkem·ə·stri/ *n* [U] ***biology*** the scientific study of the chemistry of living things, such as animals, plants, and body organs

biochemical /ˌbɑɪ·oʊˈkem·ɪ·kəl/ *adj*

bioclastic /ˌbɑɪ·oʊˈklæs·tɪk/ *adj* [not gradable] ***earth science*** describes a type of rock consisting of very small pieces of animals and plants

biodegradable /ˌbɑɪ·oʊ·dɪˈgreɪd·ə·bəl/ *adj* ***biology*** (of a substance) able to decay naturally and without harming the environment

biogeochemical /ˌbɑɪ·oʊˌdʒiː·əˈkem·ɪ·kəl/ *adj* [not gradable] ***earth science, chemistry, biology*** relating to the movement of chemical substances between organisms and the environment

biography /bɑɪˈɑg·rə·fi/ *n* [C/U] ***literature*** the story of the life of a person written by someone else, or the area of literature relating to books that describe such stories ○ [C] *He wrote a biography of Lincoln.* ○ Compare AUTOBIOGRAPHY

biographical /ˌbɑɪ·əˈgræf·ɪ·kəl/ *adj* [not gradable] ○ *The funeral elegy provides a treasure of biographical information about Shakespeare.*

biographer /bɑɪˈɑg·rə·fər/ *n* [C] someone who writes about the life of a particular person or of various people

biological warfare, **germ warfare** *n* [U] war in which BIOLOGICAL WEAPONS are used

biological weapon *n* [C] a weapon that uses living matter such as bacteria to cause damage or death to people, animals, or crops

biology /bɑɪˈɑl·ə·dʒi/ *n* [U] ***science*** the scientific study of the natural processes of living things

biologic /ˌbɑɪ·əˈlɑdʒ·ɪk/ *adj* [not gradable] relating to the natural processes of living things

biological /ˌbɑɪ·əˈlɑdʒ·ɪ·kəl/ *adj* [not gradable] **1** relating to the natural processes of living things ○ *the biological sciences* **2** Biological also means being related through birth: *the biological father/mother/parents*

biologist /bɑɪˈɑl·ə·dʒəst/ *n* [C] a scientist who studies the natural processes of living things

biomass **FUEL** /ˈbɑɪ·oʊˌmæs/ *n* [U] ***biology*** dead plant and animal material suitable for using as fuel

ORGANISMS /ˈbɑɪ·oʊˌmæs/ *n* [U] ***biology*** the total amount of living things in a particular area

biome /ˈbɑɪˌoʊm/ *n* [C] ***biology*** a region of the Earth's surface and the particular combination of weather conditions, plants, and animals that are found in it

biopsy /ˈbɑɪˌɑp·si/ *n* [C] the removal of a small number of cells from a living body in order to examine them to learn if they show signs of a disease

biosphere /ˈbɑɪ·əˌsfɪr/ *n* [U] ***biology*** the part of the Earth's environment where life exists

biotechnology /ˌbɑɪ·oʊ·tekˈnɑl·ə·dʒi/, *short form* **biotech** *n* [U] the use of living things, esp. cells and bacteria, in industrial processes

bioterrorism /ˌbɑɪ·oʊˈter·əˌrɪz·əm/ *n* [U] acts of TERRORISM that use harmful viruses or bacteria as weapons

biotic /bɑɪˈɑt̬·ɪk/ *adj* [not gradable] ***biology*** involving, caused by, or relating to living things in the environment

bipartisan /bɑɪˈpɑrt̬·ə·zən, -sən/ *adj* [not gradable] ***politics & government*** involving or having the support of both sides, esp. of political parties ○ *a bipartisan agreement*

birch /bɜrtʃ/ *n* [C] a tree with a smooth, often white BARK (= outer covering), or the wood of this tree

bird /bɜrd/ *n* [C] **1** a creature with feathers and wings, usually able to fly ○ *a flock of birds* **2** Bird is often used in combination to describe a particular type of bird: *a bluebird/hummingbird/mockingbird*

B

birdie /ˈbɜrd·i/ *n* [C] (in golf) a score for a hole that is one less than the usual score ○ *Weir faced a 30-footer for birdie, while Monty had lost his approach right of the green.*
birdie /ˈbɜrd·i/ *v* [I/T] ○ *He birdied four of his final five holes Thursday to take the first-round lead.*

bird of prey *n* [C] *pl* **birds of prey** a bird such as a HAWK or an EAGLE that kills and eats small birds and animals

birdseed /ˈbɜrd·siːd/ *n* [U] seeds for feeding birds

bird's-eye view *n* [C usually sing] the ability to look at something from a very high place so that you see a large area below you ○ *From the top of this building, you can get a bird's-eye view of the city.*

birth /bɜrθ/ *n* [C/U] **1** the occasion when a baby comes out of its mother's body ○ [C] *He remembered the birth of their first child.* ○ [U] *Their son weighed eight pounds at birth.* **2** Birth also refers to your family origin: [U] *She was Swedish by birth.* **3** When a woman gives birth, one or more babies come out of her body: [U] *She gave birth to twins.*

birth certificate *n* [C] an official document recording important facts connected with a baby's birth

birth control *n* [U] methods and devices that allow people to have sex without having children as a result

birthday /ˈbɜrθ·deɪ/ *n* [C] the day that is an exact year or number of years after a person was born ○ *Today is my mother's 49th birthday.*

birthmark /ˈbɜrθ·mɑrk/ *n* [C] a mark on a baby's skin at birth that usually stays there for life

birthplace /ˈbɜrθ·pleɪs/ *n* [C] **1** the town or other place where a person was born ○ *The town was the birthplace (1868) of black writer W.E.B. DuBois.* **2** The birthplace of something is the place where it began or first developed: *Known for its famous Mardi Gras celebrations, New Orleans is called the birthplace of jazz.*

birthrate /ˈbɜrθ·reɪt/ *n* [C] a measure of how many children are born during a period of time in a particular place ○ *Officials expressed concern over Quebec's declining birthrate.*

birthright /ˈbɜrθ·rɑɪt/ *n* [C/U] something that is received or owned esp. because of where you were born or your family or social situation, without having to be worked for or bought ○ [U] *He told them that human rights are a universal birthright.*

biscuit /ˈbɪs·kət/ *n* [C] **1** a small, soft, raised bread ○ *homemade biscuits* **2** A biscuit is also a type of hard cracker: *dog biscuits*

bisect /ˈbɑɪ·sekt, bɑɪˈsekt/ *v* [T] **1** to divide into two usually equal parts ○ *The new road would bisect a designated historic district.* **2** ***geometry*** to divide something into two CONGRUENT (= exactly equal) parts
bisector /ˈbɑɪˈsek·tər, bɑɪˈsek-/ *n* [C] ***geometry*** ○ *the bisector of an angle/segment*

bishop /ˈbɪʃ·əp/ *n* [C] **1** a priest of high rank who is in charge of the priests of lower rank in a particular area **2** In the game of CHESS, a bishop is a piece that can move only in a diagonal way along squares of the same color.

bison /ˈbɑɪ·sən/ *n* [C] *pl* **bison** a large, wild animal, similar to a cow but having a larger head and hairy shoulders, found esp. in North America ○ *Large herds of bison, popularly known as buffalo, used to live on the plains of western North America.*

bit **PIECE** /bɪt/ *n* [C] **1** a small piece or a small amount of something ○ *little bits of paper* ○ *We need every bit of evidence we can find.* ○ *We showed a little bit on videotape.* ○ *Could you talk a bit* (= for a short period) *about your childhood experiences?* **2** A bit or a little bit can mean slightly or to some degree: *We found the dinner a little bit of a disappointment.*

HORSE /bɪt/ *n* [C] a piece of metal put in a horse's mouth to allow the person riding it to control its movements

COMPUTER /bɪt/ *n* [C] the smallest unit of information in a computer, represented by either 0 or 1

TOOL /bɪt/ *n* [C] the part of a tool used to cut or DRILL (= make holes)

BITE /bɪt/ *past simple of* BITE

IDIOM with bit

• **chafing at the bit, champing/chomping at the bit** very eager to do something ○ *As soon as the kids saw the pool, they were chafing at the bit to get in.*

bitch /bɪtʃ/ *n* [C] a female dog

bite **USE TEETH** /bɑɪt/ *v* [I/T] *past* **bit**, *past part.* **bitten** **1** to use your teeth to cut into something ○ [I/T] *He bit (into) the apple.* ○ [I/T] *You have to teach your children not to bite (other kids).* **2** If an insect bites, it breaks the surface of the skin of a person and leaves a sore place: [I] *We can't eat outside tonight – the mosquitoes are biting.* **3** A fish bites when it takes a fishing hook into its mouth: [I] *We were on the lake all day, but the fish just weren't biting.*
bite /bɑɪt/ *n* [C] **1** the act of using your teeth to cut and tear something, or the piece torn away ○ *He took a few bites of the chicken and drank some water.* **2** A bite is also a sore place on the surface of your skin made by an insect: *mosquito bites* **3** In fishing, a bite is a fish taking a hook in its mouth.

HAVE AN EFFECT /bɑɪt/ *v* [I] *past* **bit**, *past part.* **bitten** to have an effect that is often unpleasant or severe ○ *When the recession began to bite, people spent less on eating out in restaurants.*
bite /bɑɪt/ *n* [C usually sing] ○ *The tax bite with a 13 percent flat tax would be a lot worse.*
biting /ˈbɑɪt̬·ɪŋ/ *adj* **1** severe and unpleasant; strong enough to hurt ○ *A cold, biting wind blew in*

B

from the north. **2** If you describe a remark as biting, you mean that it was strongly critical, often accurate, and likely to hurt someone's feelings: *He delivered a biting attack on political favoritism.*

IDIOMS with **bite**

• **a bite (to eat)** some food ○ *You'll feel better once you've had a bite to eat.*
• **bite** *someone's* **head off** to speak to someone angrily when there is no reason to ○ *I just asked if I could help – you don't have to bite my head off!*
• **bite off more than** *you* **can chew** to try to do something that is too difficult for you ○ *I think he's bitten off more than he can chew taking all those classes.*
• **bite the bullet** to force yourself to perform an unpleasant or difficult action or to be brave in a difficult situation ○ *I decided I had to bite the bullet and take a couple of math classes even though I knew they were hard.*
• **bite the dust** to die or to stop working ○ *I think our car just bit the dust.*
• **bite** *your* **tongue** to stop yourself from saying something ○ *I wanted to tell him he looked ridiculous, but I bit my tongue.*

bitter **TASTE** /ˈbɪt̬·ər/ *adj* having a slightly stinging, strong taste, not salty or sweet ○ *The coffee was bitter.*

ANGRY /ˈbɪt̬·ər/ *adj* showing or causing deep anger and pain ○ *Losing the election was a bitter disappointment.*

bitterly /ˈbɪt̬·ər·li/ *adv* [not gradable] ○ *When he couldn't have the bike, my son was bitterly disappointed.*

bitterness /ˈbɪt̬·ər·nəs/ *n* [U] ○ *She has no bitterness about the past.*

COLD /ˈbɪt̬·ər/ *adj, adv* extremely cold ○ *A bitter wind kept everyone indoors.*

bitterly /ˈbɪt̬·ər·li/ *adv* ○ *a bitterly cold day*

IDIOM with **bitter**

• **to the bitter end, until the bitter end** to the end of something difficult that will likely have a bad ending ○ *The president fought for his plan to the bitter end.*

bittersweet /ˈbɪt̬·ərˌswiːt/ *adj* containing a mixture of sadness and happiness ○ *The bittersweet end to the movie is just right.*

biweekly /bɑɪˈwiː·kli, ˈbɑɪˌwiː-/ *adj, adv* [not gradable] happening or appearing every two weeks ○ *The magazine is published biweekly.*

bizarre /bɪˈzɑr/ *adj* strange and unusual ○ *That party was too bizarre for me!*

blab /blæb/ *v* [I/T] **-bb-** *infml* to talk too much or speak without thinking ○ [T] *She just blabs to anyone who will listen.*

blabbermouth /ˈblæb·ərˌmɑʊθ/ *n* [C] *infml* a person who talks too much

black **COLOR** /blæk/ *adj, n* [U] **1** (of) the darkest color there is, like night ○ *He was dressed all in black.* **2** Black coffee or tea has no milk or cream in it.

blacken /ˈblæk·ən/ *v* [T] to make something black ○ *For miles around, trees were blackened by the fire.*

blackness /ˈblæk·nəs/ *n* [U] ○ *In such complete blackness, we couldn't see a thing.*

DARK SKIN /blæk/ *adj* [*-er/-est* only] of or belonging to a group of people having skin that is brown, esp. African-American people ○ *As a black woman, I am proud of my African-American heritage.* ○ **USAGE:** Although African-American is the word preferred by many, black is also widely used and is not offensive: *Black leaders disagreed over how to respond.* As a noun, African-American is now more commonly used, but when describing historical events, black may be used.

SAD OR BAD /blæk/ *adj* without hope, very bad, or sad ○ *The blackest time of all was when his eyes failed.*

IDIOMS with **black**

• **in black and white** in writing ○ *I had to believe it, because it was there in black and white.*
• **in the black** earning more money than you spend ○ *This year our business is in the black.* ○ Compare IN THE RED at RED **IDIOM**

PHRASAL VERBS with **black**

• **black out** *something* **NO LIGHT** [M] **1** to have a failure in the supply of electricity, causing a loss of lights ○ *The power failure blacked out all of northern Illinois.* **2** If you black out something, you prevent it from being seen: *On my copy, they blacked all the names out so I couldn't read them.* ○ Related noun: BLACKOUT **NO ELECTRICITY**
• **black out** **UNCONSCIOUS** to become unconscious ○ *I blacked out right after the accident.* ○ Related noun: BLACKOUT **NOT CONSCIOUS**

black-and-blue *adj* (of skin) have dark marks as a result of injury ○ *The fall left her leg all black-and-blue.*

black-and-white *adj* [not gradable] having no colors except black, white, and gray ○ (*fig.*) *The press has been presenting the conflict in black-and-white terms* (= as being much clearer than it is).

black belt *n* [C] someone who has reached the highest level of JUDO or KARATE (= methods of fighting) ○ *He took up karate, eventually earning a black belt, and thought about becoming a cop.*

blackboard /ˈblæk·bɔːrd, -bourd/ *n* [C] a CHALKBOARD

black box *n* [C] a FLIGHT RECORDER

black codes *pl n* ***US history*** laws intended to prevent those people who had been enslaved from using their RIGHTS

Black Death *n* ***world history*** a serious disease that killed a great many people in Africa, Asia, and Europe in the fourteenth century; the PLAGUE

B

black eye *n* [C] dark colored skin around the eye from being injured or hit ○ (*fig.*) *The controversy gave him a political black eye.*

black hole *n* [C] ***physics*** a region in space where the force of GRAVITY is so strong that nothing, not even light, can escape from it

blacklist /ˈblæk·lɪst/ *v* [T] to put someone's name on a list of people who are considered not acceptable, which keeps the person from getting jobs, going certain places, or doing particular things ○ *The industry blacklisted him for exposing its corruption.*

blacklist /ˈblæk·lɪst/ *n* [C] ○ *The blacklist destroyed his career.*

blackmail /ˈblæk·meɪl/ *n* [U] the act of threatening to harm someone or someone's reputation unless the person does as you say, or a payment made to someone who has threatened to harm you or your reputation if you fail to pay the person ○ *Reckless behavior made him an easy target for blackmail.*

blackmail /ˈblæk·meɪl/ *v* [T] ○ *The guy who blackmailed my father went to jail.*

black market *n* [C/U] an illegal trade in goods or money ○ [U] *You can sell dollars on the black market.*

blackness /ˈblæk·nəs/ *n* [U] See at BLACK COLOR.

blackout **NO ELECTRICITY** /ˈblæk·ɑʊt/ *n* [C] a period of time when electric power has failed, causing a loss of lights ○ *A blackout ended the game early.* ○ Related verb: BLACK OUT NO LIGHT

NOT CONSCIOUS /ˈblæk·ɑʊt/ *n* [C] a short period of time when you are not conscious ○ *He suffers from Parkinson's Disease and has occasionally experienced blackouts.* ○ Related verb: BLACK OUT UNCONSCIOUS

black sheep *n* [C] someone who embarrasses a group or family because the person is different or has gotten into trouble ○ *She had different interests, and we stupidly thought of her as a black sheep.*

blacksmith /ˈblæk·smɪθ/ *n* [C] a person who makes HORSESHOES (= U-shaped metal objects attached to a horse's feet) and other things from iron

blacktop /ˈblæk·tɑp/ *n* [U] the material used on the surface of most roads

bladder /ˈblæd·ər/ *n* [C] an organ inside the body that stores urine until it can be excreted

blade /bleɪd/ *n* [C] **1** the thin, flat cutting part of a tool or weapon ○ *The blade on this knife isn't very sharp.* **2** A blade is also a thin, flat leaf of grass: *The boy made a whistle from a blade of grass.*

blah /blɑ/ *adj infml* boring or ordinary ○ *I thought the show was blah.*

IDIOM with blah

• **blah, blah, blah** *infml* and other words that mean very little ○ *The critics always say, "There's no melody, the words are stupid, blah, blah, blah."* ○ USAGE: Used to represent words that have been used too many times before or you feel are not worth hearing.

blame /bleɪm/ *v* [T] **1** to make someone or something responsible for something ○ *You can't blame the government for all your troubles.* **2** If *you* **don't blame** *someone* for something, you understand and accept that person's reasons for it: *I don't blame her for not supporting the final budget agreement.*

blame /bleɪm/ *n* [U] ○ *He put the blame on everyone but himself.*

blameless /ˈbleɪm·ləs/ *adj* ○ *In this situation, no one is completely blameless.*

blanch **BECOME PALE** /blæntʃ/ *v* [I] to become pale, esp. from being surprised ○ *When he realized who was on the phone, he blanched.*

BOIL /blæntʃ/ *v* [T] to cook food, esp. vegetables, in boiling water for a very brief time ○ *Blanch the peaches before peeling them.*

bland /blænd/ *adj* [-er/-est only] lacking a strong or particular flavor; not interesting ○ *This sauce has a sharp taste and isn't bland at all.*

blank /blæŋk/ *adj* **1** having no printing, writing, or images ○ *I needed a blank form to fill in.* ○ *The computer screen suddenly went blank.* **2** A blank expression on someone's face shows no emotion.

blank /blæŋk/ *n* [C] **1** a form that has spaces to write in, or a space on a form ○ *Just fill out the order blank and fax it to me.* **2** A blank is also a CARTRIDGE (= container filled with explosive powder) that does not contain a bullet.

blankly /ˈblæŋ·kli/ *adv* without expression ○ *She stared blankly out of the window.*

PHRASAL VERB with blank

• **blank out** *something* [M] to forget something ○ *I've blanked out everything about the accident.*

blank check *n* [C usually sing] the authority and the freedom to do whatever you decide is necessary or best ○ *I was given a blank check to set up my own lab.*

blanket **COVER** /ˈblæŋ·kət/ *n* [C] a cloth cover used to keep warm, esp. on a bed ○ (*fig.*) *Congress was nearly buried under a blanket of criticism.*

blanket /ˈblæŋ·kət/ *v* [T] to cover ○ *All week, smog has blanketed much of this hot, baked countryside.*

UNLIMITED /ˈblæŋ·kət/ *adj* [not gradable] without a limit ○ *You have blanket authority to hire anyone you want.*

blank verse *n* [U] ***literature*** a style of writing poems without using RHYME (= words that end with the same sound) ○ Compare IAMBIC PENTAMETER

blare /bler, blær/ *v* [I] to make a very loud noise ○ *Music blared from a radio.*

blare /bler, blær/ *n* [U] ○ *The siren's blare was deafening.*

B

blasé /blɑˈzeɪ/ *adj* bored or not very interested ○ *How could she be so blasé about her victory?*

blasphemous /ˈblæs·fə·məs/ *adj* (of speech or writing) showing lack of respect to God or to a religion ○ *Some people believe such art is blasphemous.*

blasphemy /ˈblæs·fə·mi/ *n* [U] ○ *His writing has been condemned for blasphemy.*

blast EXPLOSION /blæst/ *n* [C] an explosion, or something sudden and violent ○ *One blast of wind blew out a couple of windows.* ○ *The symphony begins with a trumpet blast.*

blast /blæst/ *v* [I/T] to break apart or destroy by using explosives ○ [I] *To make the tunnel, engineers will have to blast through solid rock.*

CRITICIZE /blæst/ *v* [T] to criticize strongly ○ *The mayor blasted the press for not printing the facts.*

ENJOYMENT /blæst/ *n* [C usually sing] *slang* an exciting and enjoyable experience ○ *The party was a blast.*

PHRASAL VERB with **blast**

• **blast off** (esp. of a spacecraft) to take off ○ *The space shuttle blasted off on schedule.* ○ Related noun: BLASTOFF

blastoff /ˈblæsˌtɔːf/ *n* [C/U] the act of sending a spacecraft into space ○ [U] *Blastoff is scheduled for eight tonight.* ○ Related verb: BLAST OFF

blatant /ˈbleɪt·ᵊnt/ *adj* (of an action) obvious or intentional, and done without worry about what others think ○ *His behavior showed a blatant lack of respect.*

blatantly /ˈbleɪt·ᵊnt·li/ *adv* ○ *It was a blatantly unfair decision.*

blaze BURN /bleɪz/ *v* [I] **1** to burn brightly and strongly ○ *The fires blazed for days.* **2** If someone's eyes blaze, they seem to shine brightly: *Her eyes blazed with anger.*

blaze /bleɪz/ *n* [C] **1** *Three fire companies fought the blaze.* **2** A blaze is also a bright show of something: *Times Square is a blaze of lights.*

blazing /ˈbleɪ·zɪŋ/ *adj* ○ *They worked all day in the blazing sun.*

SHOW THE WAY /bleɪz/ *v* [T] to make a new path or way by marking it so that others can follow ○ *It took the Cherokee two years to blaze a trail between Texas and Kansas.* ○ *(fig.) Science blazed the trail that opened up space exploration.*

blazer /ˈbleɪ·zər/ *n* [C] a type of jacket of one color, usually with metal buttons ○ *He wore a navy blue blazer and gray pants.*

bleach /bliːtʃ/ *n* [U] a liquid or powder used to clean or make something whiter or lighter in color

bleach /bliːtʃ/ *v* [T] ○ *Her hair was bleached by the sun.*

bleachers /ˈbliː·tʃərz/ *pl n* (in a building or structure for viewing sports) seats that are usually not covered and often farthest from the action

bleak /bliːk/ *adj* [-er/-est only] **1** (esp. of a place or the weather) cold and not welcoming ○ *It was a bleak, unpleasant day in December.* **2** Bleak also means without hope: *With no job, the future looked bleak.*

bleary /ˈblɪr·i/ *adj* (of eyes) tired, red, or watery ○ *After studying all night, his eyes were bleary.*

bleat /bliːt/ *v* [I] to produce the sound made by a sheep or goat ○ *The brass section bleated like goats with bad colds.*

bleat /bliːt/ *n* [C] ○ *We could hear the bleat of sheep in the meadow.*

bleed /bliːd/ *v* [I/T] *past* **bled** to lose blood ○ [I] *Before help could reach him, the man bled to death.* ○ [T] *(fig.) Because of the taxes, our state is bleeding jobs* (= many jobs are leaving).

WORD FAMILY **bleed**			
Nouns	blood bleeding	*Adjectives*	bloodless bloody
Verbs	bleed		

bleeding heart *n* [U] *disapproving* someone who is too sympathetic about people in need ○ *He is not a typical bleeding heart, which makes his support for child care so important.*

bleep /bliːp/ *n* [C] a short, continuous, electronic sound ○ *Mobile phones now play pop tunes rather than making electronic bleeps.*

bleep /bliːp/ *v* [I/T] ○ *Offensive portions of the program were bleeped before they were broadcast.*

blemish /ˈblem·ɪʃ/ *n* [C] **1** a mark or fault that spoils the appearance of someone or something ○ *Makeup can cover up your skin blemishes.* **2** A blemish can also be a mistake or fault: *Only one blemish spoiled her school record.*

blend /blend/ *v* [I/T] to mix together or combine ○ [I] *The president's daughter hopes to blend in with the other students.*

blend /blend/ *n* [C] ○ *His books are a blend of journalism and history.*

blender /ˈblen·dər/ *n* [C] an electric machine that cuts or crushes foods into small pieces or liquids, used esp. in cooking

bless /bles/ *v* [T] to ask for God's help and protection for someone or something, or to call or make someone or something holy ○ [T] *God bless our soldiers.*

blessed /ˈbles·əd/ *adj* **1** holy ○ *a blessed day/life* **2** Blessed also means bringing happiness or comfort: *She found the routine of a regular job a blessed relief.*

blessing /ˈbles·ɪŋ/ *n* [C] **1** a prayer asking for God's help, or a prayer of thanks for God's help ○ *Before we eat, Sam will say the blessing.* **2** A blessing can mean something that is very good or lucky: *It was a blessing that nobody was hurt in the accident.* **3** A blessing also means the approval to do something: *My parents finally gave their blessing to my marriage.*

IDIOMS with bless

• **bless *your* heart** may good things happen to someone ○ *My dad, bless his heart, is 92 today.* ○ *My niece sent me the sweetest card, bless her.* ○ USAGE: Used to show affection or sympathy for someone.
• **blessed with** to have something that you feel is special or lucky ○ *I was blessed with good health.*
• **blessing in disguise** something that seems bad or unlucky at first but causes something good to happen later ○ *Being laid off was a blessing in disguise – within a month I got a much better job.*
• **(God) bless you!** may you have good health ○ *"Achoo!" "Bless you!"* ○ USAGE: Used to wish someone who has just sneezed good health.

blew /bluː/ *past simple of* BLOW

blight /blɑɪt/ *n* [C/U] **1** something that spoils or destroys or causes damage ○ [U] *The city stopped urban blight by rebuilding neighborhoods.* **2** ***biology*** A blight is also any of various deadly diseases in plants.
blight /blɑɪt/ *v* [T] ○ *Poverty and disease blighted their lives.*

blimp /blɪmp/ *n* [C] an aircraft without wings, consisting of a very large bag that is filled with gas and has a structure attached to the bottom in which people ride, which moves and turns under power provided by engines

blind NOT SEEING /blɑɪnd/ *adj* [*-er/-est* only] not able to see ○ *He began to go blind a year ago.* ○ *(fig.) She is completely blind to his faults.*
blind /blɑɪnd/ *v* [T] to make someone unable to see ○ *The sun blinded me for a moment.* ○ *(fig.) We cannot let feelings blind us to the facts.*
blindness /ˈblɑɪn·nəs/ *n* [U]
NOT THINKING /blɑɪnd/ *adj* [not gradable] not able to be influenced by thought or reason ○ *He declared that the verdict was the result of blind prejudice.*
WINDOW COVER /blɑɪnd/ *n* [C] a cover for a window, esp. a VENETIAN BLIND

blind alley *n* [C] something that leads you nowhere or is of no use ○ *All our work has only led us up a blind alley.*

blind date *n* [C] a social meeting arranged between two people who have never met before, or one of the people involved in this

blindfold /ˈblɑɪnd·fould/ *n* [C] a strip of cloth that covers someone's eyes to keep that person from seeing
blindfold /ˈblɑɪnd·fould/ *v* [T] to cover someone's eyes with a blindfold

blind spot PLACE NOT SEEN *n* [C] an area outside your car that you cannot see, esp. in your mirror, when driving
SUBJECT NOT UNDERSTOOD *n* [C] a subject or area in which someone's ability to understand is weak or lacking ○ *He was a great scientist, but he had his blind spots.*

blink /blɪŋk/ *v* [I/T] **1** to close and open the eyes quickly, once or several times ○ [I] *He stared at us without blinking.* **2** If a light blinks, it flashes off and on.

IDIOM with blink

• **on the blink** not working correctly ○ *The DVD player is on the blink again.*

blip /blɪp/ *n* [C] **1** an unexpected and unusual condition that is usually temporary ○ *The drop in sales last month was just a blip, nothing to worry about.* **2** A blip is also a small spot of light that appears on a RADAR screen and shows where a physical object is.

bliss /blɪs/ *n* [U] complete happiness ○ *Two weeks lying on a beach is my idea of absolute bliss.*

blister /ˈblɪs·tər/ *n* [C] **1** a painful swelling on the skin, often filled with a watery liquid, caused by a burn or by rubbing against something ○ *I got blisters from my new shoes.* **2** A blister is also a raised place on a painted surface.
blister /ˈblɪs·tər/ *v* [I/T] ○ [T] *Grace's feet were blistered and numb with cold.*

blistering /ˈblɪs·tə·rɪŋ/ *adj* very strong and severe ○ *The vice president launched a blistering attack on Senate Republicans.*

blithe /blɑɪð, blɑɪθ/ *adj* [*-er/-est* only] satisfied and without worry ○ *I am upset by the author's blithe indifference toward facts.*
blithely /ˈblɑɪð·li, ˈblɑɪθ-/ *adv* ○ *Without reading the contract, she blithely agreed to sign it.*

blitz /blɪts/ *n* [C] **1** a sudden and violent military attack, usually with bombs dropped from aircraft **2** A blitz is also a big and determined effort to do something, esp. in business: *That computer needs an advertising blitz to sell it.*

blizzard /ˈblɪz·ərd/ *n* [C] a severe snow storm with strong winds ○ *We didn't get out for three days after the blizzard was over.*

bloated /ˈblout̬·əd/ *adj* swollen from containing too much air, liquid, or food ○ *I feel bloated from having too much to eat.*

blob /blɑb/ *n* [C] a large, round drop, usually of something sticky or thick ○ *a blob of glue/paint*

bloc /blɑk/ *n* [C] ***politics & government*** a group of countries or people that have similar goals and work together to achieve them ○ *a powerful voting bloc*

block AREA OF A CITY /blɑk/ *n* [C] **1** the buildings next to each other between crossing streets, or the distance from one street to the next in a city or town ○ *There's a good deli on this block.* **2** A block is also an area enclosed by four streets that form a rectangle in a city or town: *The new building will take up an entire city block.*
PREVENT /blɑk/ *v* [T] to prevent movement through or past something, or to prevent something from happening or succeeding ○ *A fallen tree blocked the road.* ○ *A large man in front of me blocked my view.*

○ *Earl scored 28 points and blocked five shots.* ○ *Congress blocked US aid to the government because of its segregation and human rights policies.*

B

LUMP /blɑk/ *n* [C] **1** a solid, straight-sided lump of hard material ○ *The warehouse stores building material, including cement blocks.* **2** A block is also a child's toy, usually a set of pieces of wood that can be arranged to make structures, walls, etc.

GROUP /blɑk/ *n* [C] a group of things considered together, or an amount of something ○ *a block of tickets/seats* ○ *a block of time*

WORD FAMILY block	
Nouns block	*Verbs* block

PHRASAL VERBS with **block**

• **block out** *something* **PLAN** to arrange to have time or space for something by planning in advance ○ *She blocked out time each day to work on her book.*

• **block out** *something* **STOP RECEIVING** [M] to prevent the ability to receive or remember something ○ *Some people are able to block out every distraction.* ○ *You can program the TV, blocking out channels you don't want your children to watch.*

blockade /blɑˈkeɪd/ *n* [C] the act of using force or the threat of force to stop the movement of people or goods into or out of a country or area, or the people or objects used to prevent such movement ○ *The blockade consisted of a dozen ships surrounding the port.*

blockade /blɑˈkeɪd/ *v* [T] ○ *The army blockaded roads leading into the city.*

blockbuster /ˈblɑkˌbʌs·tər/ *n* [C] *infml* a book or movie that is very successful ○ *We all felt the movie was a potential blockbuster.*

blog /blɔːɡ, blɑɡ/ *n* [C] a WEBSITE on which one person or group puts new information regularly, often every day; WEBLOG ○ *As millions express their views on blogs, political dialogue has taken on a life of its own on the Web.*

blog /blɔːɡ, blɑɡ/ *v* [I/T] to keep a blog, or to put new information on one ○ *Earlier this week, I blogged on the gulf between printed reports about these Olympics and the experience of living here.*

blogger /blɔːɡ·ər, blɑɡ-/ *n* [C] ○ *Bloggers are expanding their influence on American politics.*

bloke /bloʊk/ *n* [C] *Br, infml* a man

blond, *usually female* **blonde** /blɑnd/ *adj* [-er/-est only] (esp. of hair) pale yellow or golden

blond, *usually female* **blonde** /blɑnd/ *n* [C] ○ *Do you think she's a natural blonde, or is her hair bleached?*

blood **LIQUID** /blʌd/ *n* [U] the red liquid that is sent around the body by the heart and that is necessary for life ○ *He lost a lot of blood in the accident.*

bloody /ˈblʌd·i/ *adj* **1** showing blood or losing blood ○ *I had a bloody nose.* **2** Bloody also means with much loss of life and many serious injuries: *The Civil War was a very bloody war.*

bloodless /ˈblʌd·ləs/ *adj* happening without the use of violence ○ *The rebel soldiers seized power in a bloodless coup.*

RELATIONSHIP /blʌd/ *n* [U] a person's relationship to a family or a nation by birth rather than by marriage ○ *They are related by blood.* ○ *She has Russian blood in her veins.*

blood /blʌd/ *adj* [not gradable] related by birth ○ *blood relatives* ○ *a blood brother*

blood bank *n* [C] a place where blood given by people is collected and stored

bloodbath /ˈblʌd·bæθ/ *n* [C] the killing of a great number of people

bloodcurdling /ˈblʌdˌkɜrd·əl·ɪŋ/ *adj* causing a feeling of extreme fear ○ *a bloodcurdling story*

bloodhound /ˈblʌd·hɑʊnd/ *n* [C] a type of dog with an unusually good ability to smell something, sometimes used for hunting animals or finding people

blood pressure *n* [U] a measure of the pressure at which the blood is sent by the heart through the body ○ *I take medicine for my high blood pressure.*

bloodshed /ˈblʌd·ʃed/ *n* [U] a great amount of killing and injury ○ *The government must find a way to restore order and end the bloodshed.*

bloodshot /ˈblʌd·ʃɑt/ *adj* (of the eyes) with the white part showing red or pink ○ *Hay fever gives me a runny nose and bloodshot eyes.*

bloodstain /ˈblʌd·steɪn/ *n* [C] a mark made by blood ○ *Savir analyzed bloodstains found on a staircase.*

bloodstream /ˈblʌd·striːm/ *n* [U] the flow of blood through the body ○ *Most medicines reach the body through the bloodstream.*

blood test *n* [C] a study of the substances in a person's blood to learn if that person has any diseases or lacks anything important

bloodthirsty /ˈblʌd·θɜr·sti/ *adj* eager to see or take part in violence ○ *a bloodthirsty tyrant/crowd*

blood type, **blood group** *n* [C] any of several types of blood that separate people into certain groups for medical purposes

blood vessel *n* [C] any of the tubes through which blood flows in the body

bloom /bluːm/ *v* [I] (of a plant or tree) to produce flowers, or (of a flower) to open or be open ○ *Alta loved watching her flowers bloom in the spring.* ○ (fig.) *Their interest suddenly bloomed when they knew they would make money out of the deal.*

bloom /bluːm/ *n* [C/U] a flower, or the condition of having flowers ○ [U] *Roses in bloom are a beautiful sight.*

blooper /ˈbluː·pər/ *n* [C] a mistake, often amusing, made by a person in public

B

blossom /ˈblɑs·əm/ *v* [I] (of a tree or plant) to produce flowers that develop into fruit ○ *The cherry tree is beginning to blossom.* ○ *(fig.) She has really blossomed recently* (= become more confident and successful).
blossom /ˈblɑs·əm/ *n* [C/U] ○ [C] *The tree was covered with white blossoms.* ○ [U] *The scent of apple blossom filled the air.*

blot MARK WITH INK /blɑt/ *v* [T] **-tt-** to spoil a letter, drawing, etc. with scattered drops of ink
blot /blɑt/ *n* [C] **1** *Ink blots covered the page.* **2** A blot is also a fault that spoils the appearance or reputation of someone or something: *This arrest is a blot on his reputation.*
DRY /blɑt/ *v* [T] **-tt-** to dry something by using a paper or cloth to absorb a liquid ○ *I've spilled some coffee – can you bring me some paper towels to blot it up?*

PHRASAL VERB with **blot**

• **blot out** *something* [M] to cause something to disappear, or to remove something unpleasant from your thoughts ○ *A dark cloud blotted out the sun.* ○ *He blots out the painful memories by keeping very busy.*

blotch /blɑtʃ/ *n* [C] an unwanted mark on a surface that is different from the surrounding area ○ *There were red blotches on her face and neck.*

blouse /blɑʊs, blɑʊz/ *n* [C] a shirt for a woman or girl ○ *a cotton blouse*

blow MAKE AIR CURRENT /bloʊ/ *v* [I/T] *past simp.* **blew**, *past part.* **blown** **1** to make a current of air, or to move something or be moved with a current of air ○ [M] *The wind blew over a garbage can* (= pushed it down on its side). ○ [M] *We brought in the birthday cake and watched Lisa blow out the candles.* **2** To blow up something is to push air inside it to make it larger: [M] *We blew 12 balloons up for Charles' party.* **3** If you blow your nose, you force air through it to push out something that is blocking it, so that you can breathe better.
DESTROY /bloʊ/ *v* [I/T] *past simp.* **blew**, *past part.* **blown** **1** to destroy something in an explosion or to be destroyed in this way ○ [T] *The gas explosion blew a huge hole in the ground.* ○ [M] *The explosion from the gas leak blew all the windows out.* **2** *infml* To blow a sum of money is to spend it in a foolish way: [T] *I blew my first paycheck on a night out with my friends.*
HIT /bloʊ/ *n* [C] **1** a hard hit with the hand or a weapon ○ *A sharp blow on the chest sent him spinning to the floor.* **2** A blow is also an unexpected, harmful event: *Her death at twenty was a terrible blow to her parents.* **3** If people come to blows, they physically fight: *The brothers almost came to blows over sharing the car.*

IDIOMS with **blow**

• **blow it, blow your chance** *infml* to lose an opportunity to do something by doing or saying the wrong thing ○ *I guess I blew it when I told my teacher I didn't care what grade she gave me.*
• **blow** *your* **mind** *slang* to find something very exciting and unusual ○ *The concert was so good, it blew my mind.*
• **blow off steam** to do or say something that helps you to get rid of strong feelings or energy ○ *Call me any time you need to blow off some steam.* ○ Compare LET OFF STEAM at LET IDIOMS
• **blow** *something* **out of proportion** to make something seem more important or serious than it really is ○ *As usual the TV news is blowing the issue all out of proportion – there's really nothing to worry about.*
• **blow the lid off** *something* to make public something that people did not know before ○ *The New York Times blew the lid off the story.*
• **blow the whistle on** to bring something to the attention of other people in order to stop something bad from happening ○ *The company stopped using certain chemicals only after some workers blew the whistle on it.*
• **soften the blow, cushion the blow** to make a bad situation less serious ○ *He lost his job, but he has enough money in the bank to soften the blow.*

PHRASAL VERBS with **blow**

• **blow away** *someone* SURPRISE [M] *slang* to surprise someone very much ○ *Winning first prize and a full scholarship blew her away.*
• **blow away** *someone* DEFEAT [M] *infml* **1** to defeat a competitor completely ○ *We just got blown away yesterday, losing 12 to 0.* **2** *slang* To blow someone away is also to shoot and kill a person.
• **blow off** *something/someone* [M] *slang* to decide not to do something you are expected to do, or not to meet someone you are expected to meet ○ *"Aren't you going to the meeting?" "No, I'm going to blow it off."*
• **blow over** to pass by or to end ○ *The storm blew over and missed our area.* ○ *We hope that this crisis will soon blow over.*
• **blow up** *something* INCREASE SIZE [M] to increase the size of something ○ *I'm going to have this photo blown up and framed.* ○ Related noun: BLOWUP
• **blow up** BECOME ANGRY *infml* to become suddenly very angry ○ *He may blow up when he finds out how much I spent.*

blow-by-blow *adj* (of explanations, reports, etc.) including every detail in the order it happened ○ *We had to sit through a blow-by-blow account of how they missed their flight to Las Vegas.*

blow-dry /ˈbloʊ·drɑɪ/ *v* [T] to dry hair with a small electric device that blows out hot air ○ *I'll be ready as soon as I blow-dry my hair.*

blowout AIR BURST /ˈbloʊ·ɑʊt/ *n* [C] a sudden bursting and release of air from a tire on a moving vehicle ○ *He narrowly averted crashing into another car after the blowout.*
SPORTS VICTORY /ˈbloʊ·ɑʊt/ *n* [C] a sports competition in which one side wins by a very large amount ○ *If the game is a blowout, fans start to leave before it's over.*

B

blowtorch /ˈbloʊ·tɔːrtʃ/ *n* [C] a tool that produces a very hot flame, used to heat metal or remove paint from a surface

blowup /ˈbloʊ·ʌp/ *n* [C] a copy of something that is made bigger ○ *We need a blowup of this picture.* ○ Related verb: BLOW UP INCREASE SIZE

blubber FAT /ˈblʌb·ər/ *n* [U] the layer of fat under the skin of sea mammals such as WHALES which keeps them warm ○ *Some of the larger whales are insulated by a two-foot layer of blubber.* ○ *(fig.) I'm on a diet, trying to lose some of this blubber around the middle.*

CRY /ˈblʌb·ər/ *v* [I] to cry in a noisy and uncontrollable way

bludgeon /ˈblʌdʒ·ən/ *v* [T] to hit someone hard and repeatedly with a heavy weapon ○ *He was bludgeoned to death.*

blue COLOR /bluː/ *adj, n* [C/U] (of) the color of the sky on a clear, bright day ○ *She has blue eyes.*

SAD /bluː/ *adj* [-*er*/-*est* only] sad; unhappy ○ *I don't know what's wrong – I just feel blue.*

IDIOM with blue

• **the blues** a mood of sadness ○ *She's got a bad case of the blues.*

blueberry /ˈbluː·ber·i/ *n* [C] the dark blue fruit of a common North American bush ○ *blueberry pie*

blue cheese *n* [U] a cheese with a strong flavor that has some blue spots within it

blue-chip /ˌbluː ˌtʃɪp/ *adj* [not gradable] **1** (of a company) considered to be a safe investment for your money because it is well-established and has performed well in the past **2** Blue-chip also means of top quality: *Even a profitable team like the Cowboys can't keep all their blue-chip players.*

blue-collar *adj* relating to people who do physical work rather than mental work, and who usually do not work in an office ○ *blue-collar workers.* ○ Compare WHITE-COLLAR

bluegrass /ˈbluː·græs/ *n* [U] a type of traditional music from the southern US that is played on instruments with strings such as guitars, BANJOS, and VIOLINS

bluejay /ˈbluː·dʒeɪ/ *n* [C] a common North American bird that is mainly blue and has a growth of feathers on the top of its head

blue jeans *pl n* pants made of blue DENIM (= strong, cotton cloth), usually worn on informal occasions

blue law *n* [C] a law that prevents or limits particular activities on Sundays, such as opening stores or selling alcoholic drinks

blueprint PLAN FOR BUILDING /ˈbluː ˌprɪnt/ *n* [C] a plan for a building or machine, printed with white lines on a blue background

PLAN FOR FUTURE /ˈbluː·prɪnt/ *n* [C] a complete plan that explains how to do or develop something ○ *The report provided a blueprint for relieving the county's crowded jail facilities.*

blue-ribbon *adj* [not gradable] expert ○ *Critics asked the president to appoint a blue-ribbon commission to investigate police practices.*

blues /bluːz/ *n* [U] a type of music that began among African-American musicians in the southern US, often with LYRICS (= words) about a difficult life or bad luck in love

bluff TRICK /blʌf/ *v* to try to trick someone into believing something, esp. in order to get an advantage over that person ○ [I] *The landlord claimed to have the right to raise his rent, but we believed he was bluffing and refused to pay it.*

bluff /blʌf/ *n* [C] an attempt to trick someone ○ *The threat to go on strike was no bluff, the union leaders insisted.*

CLIFF /blʌf/ *n* [C] (used in many names of places) a cliff or steep slope, often above a river ○ *Council Bluffs, Iowa*

blunder /ˈblʌn·dər/ *n* [C] a big mistake, especially one resulting from a lack of care or thought ○ *His failure to respond immediately to the accusations was a major political blunder.*

blunder /ˈblʌn·dər/ *v* [I] ○ *He feared he had blundered.*

blunt DIRECT IN SPEECH /blʌnt/ *adj* saying what you think without trying to be polite or caring about other people's feelings ○ *blunt criticism* ○ *Blunt and outspoken, he often quarreled with fellow officials.*

bluntly /ˈblʌnt·li/ *adv* ○ *He is, to put it bluntly, a big bore.*

NOT SHARP /blʌnt/ *adj* [-*er*/-*est* only] not having a sharp edge or point ○ *Use a blunt instrument to smash the ginger and onion into the garlic.*

blunt /blʌnt/ *v* [T] to make something less strongly felt ○ *Eating between meals will blunt your appetite.*

blur /blɜr/ *n* [U] **1** something whose shape is not clear **2** A blur is also something that you cannot remember clearly: *It all happened so long ago that it's just a blur to me now.*

blur /blɜr/ *v* [I/T] **-rr-** ○ [T] *These deals are blurring the distinction between local and long-distance telephone service.*

blurred /blɜrd/ *adj* ○ *People who develop meningitis can get a stiff neck, blurred vision, and headaches.*

blurry /ˈblɜr·i, ˈblʌ·ri/ *adj* ○ *The exhibit consisted of blurry, blown-up, black-and-white photographs.*

blurb /blɜrb/ *n* [C] a brief description of something, often intended to make it seem attractive when offered for sale ○ *The blurb on the back of the book says that "it will touch your heart."*

blurt out *something* /ˈblɜrt̬ ˈaʊt/ *phrasal verb* [M] to say something suddenly, and without thinking of the results ○ *At one point, Goetz blurted out, "The subways down there are terrible."*

blush REDDEN /blʌʃ/ *v* [I] to become redder or darker in the face, usually from embarrassment ○ *He blushed at the thought of what he'd done.*
blush /blʌʃ/ *n* [C]
MAKEUP /blʌʃ/ *n* [U] a substance, often a powder, put on the face to add a slightly red color

bluster /ˈblʌs·tər/ *n* [U] talk intended to seem important or threatening but which is not taken seriously and has little effect ○ *For all his bluster about his military adventures, McLaughlin was enormously likable.*

blustery /ˈblʌs·tə·ri/ *adj* (of the weather) stormy and windy ○ *a cold and blustery night*

blvd *n* [C] *abbreviation for* BOULEVARD

B.O. *n* [U] *abbreviation for* BODY ODOR

boa (constrictor) /ˈboʊ·ə (kənˌstrɪk·tər)/ *n* [C] a large, strong snake, found in South and Central America, that kills animals and birds by wrapping itself around them and crushing them to death

boar /bɔːr, boʊr/ *n* [C] a male pig kept for breeding on a farm, or a type of wild pig

board FLAT PIECE /bɔːrd, boʊrd/ *n* [C] **1** a thin, flat piece of hard material such as wood or plastic ○ *The floor boards of the old house squeaked as he walked across them.* **2** A board is also a flat piece of hard material that is made to be used for a particular purpose: *an ironing board* ○ *a cheese board* **3** A board can be a CHALKBOARD. **4** A board can also be a CIRCUIT BOARD
PEOPLE /bɔːrd, boʊrd/ *n* [C] the group of people who are responsible for controlling the operation of a public or private organization ○ *a community/school board* ○ *She sits on the board of several large companies.*
MEALS /bɔːrd, boʊrd/ *n* [U] meals provided when you are staying somewhere
board /bɔːrd, boʊrd/ *v* [T] to arrange for an animal to be temporarily taken care of and fed at a place other than its home ○ [T] *We board our dogs at the kennel when we go away.*
boarder /ˈbɔːrd·ər, ˈboʊrd-/ *n* [C] someone who pays for a place to sleep and meals in someone else's house
GET ON /bɔːrd, boʊrd/ *v* [I/T] to get onto or allow people to get onto an aircraft, train, or ship ○ [I] *Flight 701 to Los Angeles is now boarding at gate 14A.*
board /bɔːrd, boʊrd/ *n*

IDIOM with **board**

• **on board** on or in an aircraft, train, or ship ○ *All passengers should be on board at this time.*

PHRASAL VERB with **board**

• **board up** *something* [M] to cover doors or windows with thin, flat pieces of wood ○ *The vacant store had been boarded up for several years.*

board game *n* [C] any game in which pieces are moved in particular ways on a board marked with a pattern ○ *All our old board games like Monopoly were gathering dust in a closet.*

boarding house *n* [C] *pl* **boarding houses** a private house that a person pays to stay in and receive meals

boarding pass *n* [C] a card that a passenger must have to be allowed to enter an aircraft or ship

boarding school *n* [C] a school equipped with rooms where its students live instead of living in their own homes

boardwalk /ˈbɔːrd·wɔːk, ˈboʊrd-/ *n* [C] a path usually built of wooden boards near the sea, often raised above the back part of a beach

boast SPEAK PROUDLY /boʊst/ *v* to speak too proudly or show too much satisfaction about something or someone connected with you ○ [I] *They are always boasting about how smart their children are.* ○ [+ *that* clause] *She boasted that she had never had an accident.*
boast /boʊst/ *n* [C] ○ *It was his proud boast that he had run over 20 marathons.*
boastful /ˈboʊst·fəl/ *adj* having a tendency to praise yourself and what you have done

> **WORD CHOICES boast**
>
> An alternative to "boast" is **brag**.
>
> *She likes to* **brag** *about how much money she earns.*
>
> The verb **trumpet** can be used when someone boasts about how successful he or she has been.
>
> *He's always* **trumpeting** *his latest triumph.*
>
> If someone often boasts, you can describe that person as **boastful**.
>
> *He was* **boastful** *and arrogant.*

POSSESS /boʊst/ *v* [T] to have or possess something to be proud of ○ *New Orleans boasts great music and excellent restaurants.*

boat /boʊt/ *n* [C] a vehicle for traveling on water, esp. one that is not very large ○ *a fishing boat*
boating /ˈboʊt̬·ɪŋ/ *n* [U] the activity of traveling in a boat, esp. as a hobby or for pleasure ○ *Lake of the Ozarks is a popular boating and fishing mecca for Midwesterners.*

boat people *pl n* people who have left their country by boat, usually in the hope of finding safety in another place

bob MOVE /bɑb/ *v* [I] **-bb-** to move up and down quickly and gently ○ *Empty cans and bottles bobbed in the water of the harbor.*
HAIRSTYLE /bɑb/ *n* [C] a hairstyle that is short at the front while the other hair is cut to neck length all around the head ○ *She wears her hair in a bob.*

bobby pin /ˈbɑb·iːˌpɪn/ *n* [C] a U-shaped pin tightly bent so that the two sides touch, used esp. to keep hair in a desired way

bobcat /ˈbɑb·kæt/ *n* [C] a wild animal of North America of the cat family, having brown hair, pointed ears, and a short tail

B

bode /boʊd/ *v* [I] to be a sign of something good or bad for the future ○ *This does not bode well for the future of the peace process.*

bodega /boʊˈdeɪ·ɡə/ *n* [C] (in a neighborhood with a lot of Spanish-speaking people) a small store that sells food and other items for the house ○ *Would you run down to the bodega and pick up a quart of milk and some kitty litter?*

bodice /ˈbɑd·əs/ *n* [C] the upper part of a woman's dress

body PHYSICAL CREATURE /ˈbɑd·i/ *n* [C] **1** the whole physical structure that is a person or animal ○ *A good diet and plenty of exercise will help you keep your body healthy.* **2** Sometimes body can refer to the main, physical part of a person or animal but not include the head, or not include the head and the arms and legs. **3** A body is also a dead person: *Police found the man's body in the next room.*

bodily /ˈbɑd·əl·i/ *adj, adv* [not gradable] relating to a person's physical structure ○ *They had no intention of causing bodily harm.*

MAIN PART /ˈbɑd·i/ *n* [U] the main part of something such as a book, a large building, or a vehicle ○ *Most scientists will be less interested in the body of the article than in the detailed notes at the end.*

GROUP OF PEOPLE /ˈbɑd·i/ *n* [C] a group of people who have joined together for a particular reason ○ *Congress is a legislative body created to consider and pass laws.*

AMOUNT /ˈbɑd·i/ *n* [C] **1** an amount of something ○ *There is a growing body of evidence to support their innocence.* **2** A body of water is a large area of water, such as a lake.

bodyguard /ˈbɑd·iˌɡɑrd/ *n* [C] a person paid to protect another person from danger or attack

body language *n* [U] the movements or positions by which you show other people your feelings without using words ○ *Their body language said that they were really enjoying each other's company.*

body odor, *abbreviation* **B.O.** *n* [C usually sing] the unpleasant smell of a person's body that is caused by SWEAT (= liquid you excrete through your skin)

bog /bɑɡ, bɔːɡ/ *n* [C] an area of soft, wet earth

PHRASAL VERB with bog

• **bog down** *someone/something* [M] to prevent someone or something from moving on or progressing ○ *He's a big-picture leader and doesn't get bogged down in the details.*

bogey /ˈbʊɡ·i, ˈboʊ·ɡi, ˈbuː·ɡi/, **boogeyman** /ˈbʊɡ·iːˌmæn, ˈbuː·ɡi-/ *n* [C] something feared, esp. when the fear is not based on reason ○ *Too many economists are scared by the bogey of inflation, he says.*

boggle /ˈbɑɡ·əl/ *v* [I/T] to have difficulty imagining or accepting something as true or possible, or to give the mind such difficulty ○ [T] *It boggles the mind to think about how much money was wasted.*

bogus /ˈboʊ·ɡəs/ *adj* (of something) not what it appears or claims to be; false but made to look real ○ *He was arrested and charged with carrying a bogus passport.*

bohemian /boʊˈhiː·miː·ən/ *n* [C] a person who lives in a very informal style that is different from the way most people live

bohemian /boʊˈhiː·miː·ən/ *adj* ○ *She belonged to a West Coast group of bohemian writers and intellectuals.*

boil HEAT /bɔɪl/ *v* [I/T] **1** (of a liquid) to start to turn into a gas because of being heated, or to cause a liquid to turn into a gas in this way ○ [I] *The water is boiling.* ○ [T] *We'd better boil this water before we drink it.* **2** If you say that a container has boiled, the liquid in it has started to turn into a gas: [I] *The pot's beginning to boil.* **3** If food boils, or you boil food, it is cooked by being put in water that is heated until the water is in the process of turning into a gas: [T] *I boiled some potatoes for dinner.*

boil /bɔɪl/ *n* [U] If you bring something to a boil, or let something come to a boil, you heat it until it starts to turn into a gas: *Bring the water to a boil, then add the pasta.*

boiler /ˈbɔɪ·lər/ *n* [C] a device that heats water esp. to provide heating and hot water in a house

boiling /ˈbɔɪ·lɪŋ/ *adj* [not gradable] **1** *a pot of boiling water* **2** Boiling can also mean extremely angry: *He was boiling with rage.*

SWELLING /bɔɪl/ *n* [C] a painful, red swelling on the skin that is filled with PUS (= a yellow liquid from an infection)

WORD FAMILY boil			
Nouns	boil boiler	*Adjectives* *Verbs*	boiling boil

PHRASAL VERBS with boil

• **boil down** *something* [M] to reduce information, usually so that it contains only its most important part ○ *The boss wants me to boil down the ten-page sales report to one page.*

• **boil down to** *something* to be the main or most important result of something ○ *What it all boils down to is a lack of communication.*

• **boil over 1** (of a liquid) to rise up in a cooking container and flow over the edge **2** If anger or other feelings boil over, they become too strong to be controlled: *Union members' frustrations boiled over in demonstrations this weekend.*

boiling point *n* [C usually sing] ***chemistry*** the temperature at which a liquid becomes a gas ○ *The boiling point of water is 212°F or 100°C.* ○ Compare FREEZING POINT

boisterous /ˈbɔɪ·stə·rəs/ *adj* noisy and not controlled ○ *The audience burst into boisterous laughter.*

bold BRAVE /boʊld/ *adj* [-er/-est only] **1** brave, or without fear ○ *He is a qualified politician with bold* *ideas.* **2** Bold can also mean not shy, and almost rude: *She was friendly without being bold.* ○ Opposite: TIMID

boldly /ˈboʊl·dli/ *adv* ○ *He dealt boldly with the problem and hoped he was right.*

NOTICEABLE /boʊld/ *adj* [-er/-est only] likely to attract your attention; showy ○ *The costumes were in beautiful, bold colors.*

bologna /bəˈloʊ·ni/, **baloney** *n* [U] a cooked, smoked SAUSAGE (= mixed meat in a tube shape) that is sliced and eaten cold ○ *Lunch was a bologna sandwich and cold soda.*

Bolshevik /ˈboʊl·ʃəˌvɪk, ˈbɔːl-/ *n* [C] ***world history*** a member of the political party introduced by Lenin in Russia in 1917

bolster SUPPORT /ˈboʊl·stər/ *v* [T] to support something, or make something stronger ○ *The UN is sending more troops to bolster the peacekeepers.*

OBJECT ON BED /ˈboʊl·stər/ *n* [C] a long PILLOW (= cloth bag filled with material), usually shaped like a tube

bolt LOCK /boʊlt/ *n* [C] **1** a small metal bar that slides across a door or window to lock it ○ *I fastened the door with a bolt.* **2** A bolt is also a part of a gun that is slid back when getting ready to fire.

bolt /boʊlt/ *v* [T] ○ *Be sure to bolt the door when you go to bed!*

SCREW /boʊlt/ *n* [C] a metal screw without a point, used to fasten things together, often with a NUT (= small piece of metal that attaches to it)

bolt /boʊlt/ *v* [T always + adv/prep] ○ *He sat on a wooden bench bolted to the floor.*

LIGHTNING /boʊlt/ *n* [C] a flash of lightning, esp. followed by thunder ○ *Did a bolt of lightning set fire to the barn?*

MOVE SUDDENLY /boʊlt/ *v* [I/T] to move suddenly and quickly ○ [I] *At the first whiff of smoke, the horse bolted from the barn.* ○ [M] *He bolted down some breakfast.*

ROLL /boʊlt/ *n* [C] a roll of cloth or paper, esp. WALLPAPER

IDIOMS with bolt

• **a bolt from the blue, a bolt out of the blue** something important or unusual that happens suddenly or unexpectedly ○ *The resignation of the chairman came like a bolt from the blue.*

• **bolt upright** vertical and extremely straight ○ *She woke up and sat bolt upright in bed, terrified by her dream.*

bomb WEAPON /bɑm/ *n* [C] a weapon that explodes ○ *Was there any warning before the bomb went off?*

bomb /bɑm/ *v* [T] to explode bombs, or to drop bombs from aircraft ○ *They bombed enemy airfields.*

bomber /ˈbɑm·ər/ *n* [C] **1** a person who makes or explodes bombs **2** A bomber is also an aircraft designed to carry and drop bombs.

FAIL /bɑm/ *v* [I] *infml* to fail completely ○ *A lot of students bombed on that last exam.*

bomb /bɑm/ *n* [C] *infml* ○ *The last play was a bomb.*

bombard /bɑmˈbɑrd, bəm-/ *v* [T] to attack a place with continuous shooting or bombs ○ (*fig.*) *I was bombarded with phone calls and faxes.*

bombardment /bɑmˈbɑrd·mənt, bəm-/ *n* [U]

bombshell /ˈbɑm·ʃel/ *n* [C usually sing] a shocking piece of news ○ *He dropped a bombshell when he announced he would resign.*

bona fide /ˈboʊ·nəˌfɑɪd, ˈbɑn·ə-, -ˌfɑɪd·i/ *adj* [not gradable] real or true; not false ○ *This is my first bona fide job.*

bonanza /bəˈnæn·zə/ *n* [C] something that suddenly produces large profits or great opportunities ○ *The improved economy was a bonanza for local stores.*

bond Ⓐ **CONNECTION** /bɑnd/ *n* [C] a close and lasting relationship between people ○ *The bond between parents and children is usually very strong.*

bond Ⓐ /bɑnd/ *v* [T] ○ *The puppy and his master bonded quickly.*

bonding Ⓐ /ˈbɑn·dɪŋ/ *n* [U] ○ *Much of the bonding between mother and child takes place in those early weeks.*

GLUE /bɑnd/ *v* [I/T] to stick materials together, usually using glue ○ [I] *The pieces will bond in less than a minute.*

DOCUMENT /bɑnd/ *n* [C] an official document that states you will be paid a certain amount of money because you have lent money to a government or company ○ *The county issued $4 million in bonds for road construction.*

bondage /ˈbɑn·dɪdʒ/ *n* [C] the state of one person being owned by another person, as a piece of property ○ *Many enslaved people tried to escape bondage.*

bone /boʊn/ *n* [C] any of the hard pieces that form the SKELETON (= frame) of a human or animal body ○ *She had broken a bone in her foot.* ➤ Picture: **joint**

bony /ˈboʊ·ni/ *adj* very thin, so that bones can be seen, or (of fish) having a lot of bones in it ○ *She had a long, bony face.*

bone /boʊn/ *v* [T] to remove the bones from fish or meat

boneless /ˈboʊn·ləs/, **boned** /boʊnd/ *adj* [not gradable] (of meat or fish) without any bones ○ *boneless breast of chicken*

IDIOM with bone

• **bone of contention** something that two people or groups cannot agree about ○ *Money is a common bone of contention in many marriages.*

PHRASAL VERB with bone

• **bone up** *infml* to study a subject as much as you can in a short period of time ○ *She boned up on her Spanish before going to Mexico.*

bone-chilling *adj* extremely cold ○ *The air at that altitude was bone-chilling.*

bone marrow *n* [U] MARROW ○ *A bone marrow transplant can be risky.*

bonfire /ˈbɑn·fɑɪr/ *n* [C] a large fire that is made outside ○ *We built a bonfire on the beach.*

bongo (drum) /ˈbɑŋ·goʊ (ˌdrʌm)/ *n* [C usually pl] *pl* **bongos, bongoes** one of a pair of small drums that are played with the hands

bonkers /ˈbɑŋ·kərz, ˈbɔːŋ-/ *adj* [not gradable] *slang* very enthusiastic; crazy ○ *Kids really went bonkers over that video game.*

bonnet /ˈbɑn·ət/ *n* [C] a hat for a baby that covers the head and ties under the CHIN, or a woman's hat

bonus /ˈboʊ·nəs/ *n* [C] **1** an extra amount of money given to someone as a reward for work or as encouragement ○ *The salary was $40,000, plus a bonus.* **2** A bonus is also any result that is an unexpected benefit: *After the heart transplant, every day is a bonus for me.*

bony /ˈboʊ·ni/ *adj* ○ See at BONE

boo DISAPPROVE /buː/ *v* [I/T] **boos,** *pres. part.* **booing,** *past* **booed** to call out the word "boo" to express disapproval ○ [T] *They booed him off the stage.*

boo /buː/ *n* [C] *pl* **boos** ○ *Students showed their dislike with a chorus of boos.*

SURPRISE /buː/ *exclamation* used to surprise or frighten another person, and usually said loudly ○ *He snuck up behind me and said, "Boo!"*

boo-boo /ˈbuː·buː/ *n* [C] *pl* **boo-boos** *a child's word* a mistake, or a small cut or injury ○ *I did a boo-boo! I spilled coffee!*

booby prize /ˈbuː·biː ˌprɑɪz/ *n* [C] a prize given as a joke to the person who loses a game or competition

booby trap /ˈbuː·biː ˌtræp/ *n* [C] a hidden weapon that explodes when moved or touched

booby-trap /ˈbuː·biː ˌtræp/ *v* [T] **-pp-** ○ *Don't open the door – it may be booby-trapped.*

boogeyman /ˈbʊg·iː ˌmæn, ˈbuː·giː-/ *n* [C] *pl* **-men** a BOGEY

book TEXT /bʊk/ *n* [C] **1** an object consisting of a number of pages of text or pictures fastened together along one edge and fixed inside two covers ○ *The artist's sketch books filled several shelves.* **2** A book is also a number of similar items fastened together inside a cover: *a book of matches/stamps* ○ See also: BOOKS

bookish /ˈbʊk·ɪʃ/ *adj* enjoying books more than other things ○ *He's pleasant but a shy, bookish type.*

ARRANGE /bʊk/ *v* [I/T] **1** to arrange to have the use of a seat, room, etc. at a particular time in the future ○ [T] *Our travel agent booked us on a flight to Paris.* **2** Someone who books a performer arranges a performance: [T] *They booked the Rolling Stones for two concerts in New York.*

ACCUSE /bʊk/ *v* [T] to officially accuse someone of a crime ○ *Detectives booked him for resisting arrest.*

bookcase /ˈbʊk·keɪs/ *n* [C] a piece of furniture with shelves to hold books

bookend /ˈbʊk·end/ *n* [C] one of a pair of objects used to keep a row of books standing up

bookie /ˈbʊk·i/, **bookmaker** /ˈbʊk ˌmeɪ·kər/ *n* [C] a person whose business is accepting and paying out money risked on a particular result of something, esp. horse races

bookkeeping /ˈbʊk ˌkiː·pɪŋ/ *n* [U] the job or activity of keeping a record of money spent or received by a business or other organization

bookkeeper /ˈbʊk ˌkiː·pər/ *n* [C] ○ *A good bookkeeper does careful work.*

booklet /ˈbʊk·lət/ *n* [C] a small book, usually with a paper cover; a PAMPHLET

bookmark BOOK /ˈbʊk·mɑrk/ *n* [C] anything placed between the pages of a book to show where a person stopped reading

COMPUTER /ˈbʊk·mɑrk/ *n* [C] one of a list of INTERNET addresses that you keep because you visit them often ○ *A bookmark simply serves as a shortcut back to the website.*

bookmark /ˈbʊk·mɑrk/ *v* [T] to save an INTERNET address as a bookmark ○ *Loyal visitors probably already know the URL or have it bookmarked in their Web browsers.*

books /bʊks/ *pl n* written records of money that has been spent or received by a company ○ *The payment was kept* **off the books** (= not put in the records)

bookshelf /ˈbʊk·ʃelf/ *n* [C] a shelf that holds books

bookstore /ˈbʊk·stɔːr, -stoʊr/ *n* [C] a store that sells books

bookworm /ˈbʊk·wɜrm/ *n* [C] *infml* someone who likes to read books

boom PERIOD OF GROWTH /buːm/ *n* [C] ***social studies*** a period of sudden economic growth ○ *Somehow farmers have survived the booms and busts of the past 50 years.*

boom /buːm/ *v* [I] ○ *At that time, Alaska was booming.*

MAKE A DEEP SOUND /buːm/ *v* [I/T] to make a deep, loud sound ○ [I] *A voice boomed through the microphone.*

boom /buːm/ *n* [C] ○ *What you heard was the boom of a rocket.*

POLE /buːm/ *n* [C] **1** a long, movable pole that holds the bottom edge of a sail and is attached to the MAST of a boat **2** In television and movie making, a boom is a long, movable pole that has a MICROPHONE (= device that records sound) or camera on one end.

boom box *n* [C] *slang* a radio and TAPE or CD player that you can carry with you

boomer /ˈbuː·mər/ *n* [C] a BABY BOOMER ○ See at BABY BOOM

boomerang /ˈbuː·məˌræŋ/ *n* [C] a curved stick that, when thrown, comes back toward the person who threw it

boom town *n* [C] a small town that grows quickly as a result of a sudden increase in local economic activity

boon /buːn/ *n* [C] something good or very helpful ○ *Spring rains are a boon to local farmers.*

boondocks /ˈbuːn·dɑks/, **boonies** /ˈbuː·niːz/ *pl n infml* an area far from any city or town, with few people and little to do for entertainment ○ *He edits a little paper in the boondocks.*

boondoggle /ˈbuːn ˌdɑg·əl, -ˌdɔː·gəl/ *n* [C] an expensive program that is a waste of money, esp. one using public money ○ *Voters say they are fed up with such boondoggles.*

boor /bʊr/ *n* [C] a person who behaves rudely
boorish /ˈbʊr·ɪʃ/ *adj* ○ *I'm sick of your boorish behavior.*

boost MAKE BETTER /buːst/ *v* [T] to improve or increase something ○ *We took various steps to try to boost sales.*
boost /buːst/ *n* [C usually sing] ○ *The president's approval rating got a boost following his speech.*
booster /ˈbuː·stər/ *n* [C] **1** *Winning this game was a great morale booster for the team.* **2** A booster is also someone who is an enthusiastic supporter of something.

LIFT /buːst/ *v* [T always + adv/prep] to lift someone or something by pushing from below ○ *She boosted the little boy up to see over the fence.*
boost /buːst/ *n* [C] ○ *I need a boost to get over the wall.*
booster /ˈbuː·stər/ *n* [C] the first stage of a ROCKET (= object sent into space) that pushes it off the ground

boot SHOE /buːt/ *n* [C] a type of shoe that covers the foot and the lower leg ○ *work boots* ○ *cowboy boots*
boot /buːt/ *v* [T] to kick something ○ *She booted the ball down the field.*

MAKE READY /buːt/ *v* [I/T] to cause a computer or a computer program to become ready for use ○ [I] *Before you can do anything, you have to boot up.*

STORAGE SPACE /buːt/ *n* [C] *Br* TRUNK STORAGE SPACE

IDIOM with boot

• **to boot** also or in addition ○ *She gets motion sickness, and she's afraid of flying to boot.*

boot camp *n* [C usually sing] a place where new members of the US military receive their first training

bootee, **bootie** /ˈbuːt̬·i/ *n* [C] a warm, soft sock for a baby

booth /buːθ/ *n* [C] *pl* **booths** **1** a small structure just big enough for one person to use ○ *There was a line of people waiting for the phone booth.* **2** A booth is also a partly enclosed area in a restaurant where people sit on long seats on opposite sides of a table. **3** A booth can also be a small, partly open structure for showing and selling things at a FAIR or market: *If we get separated, let's meet at the information booth.*

bootleg /ˈbuːt·leg/ *adj* [not gradable] made illegally or copied ○ *Bootleg DVDs are sold on the street.*
bootleg /ˈbuːt·leg/ *v* [I/T] **-gg-** ○ [T] *They bootleg software, depriving big companies of income.*
bootlegger /ˈbuːt ˌleg·ər/ *n* [C] someone who sells illegally made goods

booty VALUABLE THINGS /ˈbuːt̬·i/ *n* [U] an amount of money or things of value ○ *His game-show booty amounted to $2.5 million.*

BUTTOCKS /ˈbuːt̬·i/ *n* [C] *slang* the buttocks

booze /buːz/ *n* [U] *infml* alcoholic drink

bop HIT /bɑp/ *v* [T] **-pp-** *infml* to hit something lightly, not hard ○ *The ball bounced up and bopped him on the nose.*
bop /bɑp/ *n* [C] ○ *I got a bop on the head.*

MUSIC /bɑp/, **bebop** /ˈbiː·bɑp/ *n* [U] a type of jazz from the 1940s that has complicated rhythms and is often played fast

border DIVISION /ˈbɔːrd·ər/, **borderline** *n* [C] the line that divides one country from another ○ *The Rio Grande forms part of the US border.*
border /ˈbɔːrd·ər/ *v* [I/T] ○ [T] *Guatemala borders Mexico.* ○ [I] *Wisconsin borders on Illinois.*

EDGE /ˈbɔːrd·ər/ *n* [C] a strip that goes around or along the edge of something, or the edge itself ○ *The card has a pretty design around the border.*
border /ˈbɔːrd·ər/ *v* [T] ○ *The road borders the coast for several miles.*

PHRASAL VERB with border

• **border on** *something* to be almost a certain thing or quality ○ *The team succeeded in a feat considered to border on the impossible.*

borderline /ˈbɔːrd·ər ˌlɑɪn/ *adj* between two very different conditions, with the possibility of being unacceptable ○ *My blood pressure was borderline, and the doctor said I should lose weight.*

bore FAIL TO INTEREST /bɔːr, boʊr/ *v* [T] to make someone lose interest ○ *Am I boring you?*
bore /bɔːr, boʊr/ *n* [C] someone or something that is not interesting ○ *All he talks about is money – he's such a bore.*
bored /bɔːrd, boʊrd/ *adj* ○ *He was getting bored doing the same thing every day.*
boring /ˈbɔːr·ɪŋ, ˈboʊr·ɪŋ/ *adj* ○ *The car ride was really boring.*
boredom /ˈbɔːrd·əm, ˈboʊrd-/ *n* [U] ○ *She varies her workouts to avoid boredom.*

CONFUSABLES

bored or boring?

Bored is used to describe the way that someone feels when something is not interesting.

He didn't enjoy the lesson and he was bored.

~~*He didn't enjoy the lesson and he was boring.*~~

➤

B

Boring is used to describe the uninteresting thing or person that makes you feel **bored**.

The lesson was long and boring.

~~*The lesson was long and bored.*~~

WORD CHOICES **bore**

We often use **bland** instead of boring when describing food.

*This sauce is really **bland**. It doesn't taste of anything.*

If a piece of writing, a performance, or a person is boring, you can say that the person, performance, or writing is **dull**.

*I find her writing a bit **dull**.*

Monotonous is often used about something that you listen to.

*The teacher had a really **monotonous** voice and I almost fell asleep.*

When describing an activity, **tedious** is sometimes used.

*You have to fill in various forms, which is a bit **tedious**.*

If something is boring because it is too long, you can describe it as **drawn-out** or **interminable**.

*He gave a long, **drawn-out** explanation of why he'd changed his mind.*

*Her delay seemed **interminable**.*

You can say that a person who is boring because he or she talks too much is a **bore**.

*He's a real **bore** when he starts talking about trains.*

MAKE A HOLE /bɔːr, bour/ *v* [I/T] to make a hole in something using a tool ○ [I] *Workmen bored through the rock.*

BEAR /bɔːr, bour/ *past simple of* BEAR

WORD FAMILY **bore**

Nouns	bore boredom	*Adjectives*	bored boring
Verbs	bore		

IDIOM with **bore**

•**bored to death**, **bored to tears/bored stiff** *infml* completely bored ○ *I pretended to listen, but I was bored to death.*

born BEGAN TO EXIST /bɔːrn/ *adj, past participle of* BEAR PRODUCE; having come into existence by birth ○ *He was born in 1950.*

NATURAL /bɔːrn/ *adj* [not gradable] having a natural ability or tendency ○ *It was obvious that Rachel was a born leader.* ○ [+ *to* infinitive] *Stephen was born to ride motorcycles.*

born-again *adj* [not gradable] (esp. of Christians) extremely enthusiastic about religion; EVANGELICAL

borne /bɔːrn, bourn/ *past participle of* BEAR

borough /ˈbɜr·oʊ, ˈbʌ·roʊ/ *n* [C] **1** one of the five divisions of New York City or, in some states, a town or part of a town **2** In Alaska, a borough is a political division similar to a COUNTY in other states.

borrow /ˈbɑr·oʊ, ˈbɔːr-/ *v* [I/T] to take something from someone with the intention of giving it back after using it ○ [T] *Could I borrow your bike until next week?* ○ [T] (*fig.*) *We constantly borrow words from other cultures.* ○ Compare LEND

borrower /ˈbɑr·ə·wər, ˈbɔːr-/ *n* [C] ○ *The rate charged to borrowers is 9.7%.*

borrowing /ˈbɑr·ə·wɪŋ, ˈbɔːr-/ *n* [C/U] ○ [U] *Jefferson opposed government borrowing.* ➤ Usage: **lend or borrow?** at LEND

bosom /ˈbʊz·əm/ *n* [C usually sing] **1** a woman's breasts or the front of a person's chest, esp. when thought of as the center of human feelings **2** The bosom of a group is the middle of it: *He felt safe in the bosom of his family.*

bosom buddy *n* [C] a friend that you are very close to

boss /bɔːs, bɑs/ *n* [C] the person who is in charge of an organization or a department and who tells others what to do ○ *I'll ask my boss if I can take the afternoon off.*

bossy /ˈbɔː·si, ˈbɑs·i/ *adj disapproving* ○ *"Move over," she said in a bossy tone.* ➤ Usage: **chief or boss/manager?** at CHIEF PERSON IN CHARGE

PHRASAL VERB with **boss**

•**boss around** *someone* [M] *infml* to tell someone what to do ○ *She waved her friend over as if bossing around a maid.*

botany /ˈbɑt·ən·i/ *n* [U] the scientific study of plants

botanical /bəˈtæn·ɪ·kəl/, **botanic** /bəˈtæn·ɪk/ *adj* [not gradable] ○ *a botanical garden* ○ *botanical specimens*

botanist /ˈbɑt·ən·əst/ *n* [C] a scientist who studies plants

botch /bɑtʃ/ *v* [T] to spoil something by doing it badly ○ *He thinks the police botched the investigation.*

both /boʊθ/ *pronoun, adj* [not gradable] used to refer to two people or things together ○ *Would you like milk or sugar or both in your coffee?* ○ *If both parents work, who will care for the kids?* ○ *Are both of us invited, or just you?* ○ *Keep both hands on the steering wheel.*

bother MAKE AN EFFORT /ˈbɑð·ər/ *v* [I] to make an effort to do something, esp. something that is not convenient ○ *You won't get any credit for doing it, so why bother?* ○ *Don't bother doing the laundry.* ○ [+ *to* infinitive] *He didn't even bother to say goodbye.*

bother /ˈbɑð·ər/ *n* [U] ○ *I'm not sure gardening is worth the bother.*

ANNOY /ˈbɑð·ər/ *v* [I/T] to annoy, worry, or cause problems for someone ○ [T] *The heat was begin-*

ning to bother him, so he sat down. ○ [T] *Does it bother you if your children aren't interested?*
bother /ˈbɑð·ər/ *n* [U] ○ *That dog has never been a bother to anyone.*

bothersome /ˈbɑð·ər·səm/ *adj* causing annoyance or trouble ○ *Bothersome family obligations keep interfering with my plans.*

Botox /ˈboʊ·tɑks/ *n* [U] *trademark* a chemical that doctors may put under people's skin to make them look younger ○ *Julie got Botox injections in her forehead and around her eyes.*

bottle /ˈbɑṭ·əl/ *n* [C] a container for liquids, usually made of glass or plastic, with a narrow neck ○ *a bottle of perfume*
bottle /ˈbɑṭ·əl/ *v* [T] to put liquid into bottles ○ *The soda is bottled in Atlanta.*

PHRASAL VERB with **bottle**

• **bottle up** *something* [M] to refuse to talk about something that angers or worries you ○ *Feelings that had been bottled up for years came flooding out.*

bottleneck /ˈbɑṭ·əlˌnek/ *n* [C] **1** a section of road where traffic moves slowly ○ *Traffic is causing a bottleneck on I-75.* **2** A bottleneck is also any delay: *Bureaucratic bottlenecks delayed the project's start.*

bottom LOWEST PART /ˈbɑṭ·əm/ *n* [C usually sing] **1** the lowest part of something ○ *He stood at the bottom of the stairs and called up to me.* **2** A bottom is the lower part of an item of clothing that consists of two parts: *pajama bottoms* **3** The bottom is also the least important position: *The manager of the hotel started at the bottom 30 years ago.* ○ Opposite: TOP HIGHEST PART
bottomless /ˈbɑṭ·əm·ləs/ *adj* [not gradable] seemingly without a bottom, limit, or end ○ *Could the pond really be bottomless?* ○ *I wish I had a bottomless source of ideas.*

BODY PART /ˈbɑṭ·əm/ *n* [C] the buttocks

PHRASAL VERB with **bottom**

• **bottom out** to reach the lowest point in a changing situation, before any improvement begins ○ *The housing market has bottomed out in this part of the country.*

bottom line FINANCES *n* [C] the total profit or loss of a company at the end of a particular period of time ○ *How will the rise in interest rates affect our bottom line?*
FINAL RESULT *n* [C] the final result or the most important consideration of a situation, activity, or discussion ○ *The bottom line is that they lost the game.*

bough /bɑʊ/ *n* [C] a large branch of a tree

bought /bɔːt/ *past simple and past participle of* BUY

boulder /ˈboʊl·dər/ *n* [C] a large, rounded rock that has been smoothed by the action of the weather or water

boulevard /ˈbʊl·əˌvɑrd, ˈbuː·lə-/, *abbreviation* **blvd** *n* [C] a wide street in a town or city, usually with trees on each side or along the center ○ *Billy opened a pizza place on the boulevard.*

bounce JUMP /bɑʊns/ *v* [I/T] to move up or away after hitting a surface, or to cause something to move this way ○ [I] *The basketball bounced off the rim of the basket.* ○ [T] *She bounced the baby on her knee.* ○ [I] *(fig.) Tom bounced into the room* (= walked in a happy, energetic way).
bounce /bɑʊns/ *n* [C/U] ○ [C] *In tennis you must hit the ball before its second bounce.*
bouncing /ˈbɑʊn·sɪŋ/ *adj* [not gradable] (of babies) happy and healthy ○ *a bouncing baby girl*
bouncy /ˈbɑʊn·si/ *adj* ○ *Hard ground makes balls more bouncy.* ○ *(fig.) He's always bouncy* (= happy and energetic) *in the morning.*
NOT PAY /bɑʊns/ *v* [I/T] *infml* (of a check) to not be paid or accepted by a bank because of a lack of money in the account, or to pay with a check for which there is not enough money in the account ○ [T] *He's bounced checks before, but never on this account.*

IDIOM with **bounce**

• **bounce back** to return to your usual state or activities after having a problem ○ *I bounced back pretty quickly after my operation.*

bouncer /ˈbɑʊn·sər/ *n* [C] *infml* a strong man paid to stand outside a bar or party to stop people from coming in or force them to leave if they cause trouble ○ *a nightclub bouncer*

bound TIE /bɑʊnd/ *past simple and past participle of* BIND TIE
CERTAIN /bɑʊnd/ *adj* [not gradable] certain or extremely likely to happen ○ [+ *to* infinitive] *You're bound to feel nervous about your interview.*
TIED /bɑʊnd/ *adj* [not gradable] tied tightly or fastened ○ *Several of the prisoners had been bound.*
FORCED /bɑʊnd/ *adj* having a moral or legal duty to do something ○ *She is not legally bound to pay the debts, but she has agreed to do it anyway.*
LIMIT /bɑʊnd/ *v* [T] to mark or form the limits of ○ *The town is bounded on one side by a river.*
boundless /ˈbɑʊn·dləs/ *adj* seemingly endless or unlimited ○ *boundless energy*
bounds /bɑʊnz/ *pl n* limits of an activity or behavior ○ *His desire for political power apparently knows no bounds.*
boundary /ˈbɑʊn·dri, -də·ri/ *n* [C] an edge or limit of something ○ *You can camp anywhere inside the boundaries of the park.* ○ *Your work is limited only by the boundaries of your imagination.*
DIRECTION /bɑʊnd/ *adj* [not gradable] traveling in the direction of ○ *She was on a plane bound for Fairbanks.* ○ *(fig.) These two young musicians are bound for success.*
JUMP /bɑʊnd/ *v* [I always + adv/prep] to move quickly with large, jumping movements ○ *A deer bounded across the road.*
bound /bɑʊnd/ *n* [C] ○ *With one bound the dog was over the fence.*

B

bounty **REWARD** /ˈbɑʊnt·i/ *n* [C] a sum of money paid as a reward ○ *City officials offered a bounty for his capture.*

LARGE AMOUNT /ˈbɑʊnt·i/ *n* [C/U] a large amount of something, esp. food ○ [C] *I was amazed by the bounty of our garden.*

bountiful /ˈbɑʊnt·ɪ·fəl/ *adj* (of a person) generous, or (of a thing) large in amount ○ *This field produced a bountiful supply of corn.*

bouquet **FLOWERS** /boʊˈkeɪ, buːˑ/ *n* [C] a group of flowers that have been attractively arranged so that they can be given as a present or carried on a formal occasion

SMELL /boʊˈkeɪ, buː-/ *n* [U] the smell of something, esp. wine ○ *a fruity bouquet*

bourbon /ˈbɜr·bən/ *n* [C/U] a type of WHISKEY (= strong alcoholic drink)

bourgeois /ˈbʊrʒ·wɑ, bʊrʒˈwɑ/ *adj esp. disapproving* belonging to or typical of the MIDDLE CLASS (= the social group between the rich and the poor), esp. in supporting established customs and values or in having a strong interest in money and possessions ○ *She's become very bourgeois since she left college.*

bourgeoisie /ˌbʊrʒˌwɑˈziː/ *n* [U] *esp. disapproving* the social group between the rich and the poor ○ *Hirsch's art is meant to shock the bourgeoisie.*

bout **BRIEF PERIOD** /bɑʊt/ *n* [C] a brief period of illness or involvement in an activity ○ *She had bouts of fever as a child.*

SPORTS /bɑʊt/ *n* [C] a boxing or WRESTLING match

boutique /buːˈtiːk/ *n* [C] a small store that sells fashionable clothes, shoes, jewelry, etc.

bovine /ˈboʊ·vɑɪn/ *adj* connected with cows, or like a cow because of being slow or stupid

bow **BEND** /bɑʊ/ *v* [I/T] to bend the head or body forward as a way of showing respect, expressing thanks, or greeting someone ○ [T] *We knelt and bowed our heads in prayer.*

bow /bɑʊ/ *n* [C] ○ *The troupe's artistic director took a bow with his dancers at the final curtain last night.*

INSTRUMENT /boʊ/ *n* [C] a long, thin piece of wood with many hairs stretched between its ends, used to play musical instruments that have strings ○ *a violin bow*

WEAPON /boʊ/ *n* [C] a weapon for shooting arrows, often used for sport, made of a long, narrow piece of wood bent into a curve by a string that is stretched tightly between its two ends

SHIP PART /bɑʊ/ *n* [C] the front part of a ship ○ Compare STERN **SHIP PART**

KNOT /boʊ/ *n* [C] a knot with two curved parts and two loose ends, which is used as a decoration or to tie shoes

PHRASAL VERBS with bow

• **bow down to** *someone* to obey someone completely ○ *He expects me to bow down to him, but I won't do it.*

• **bow out** to give up something, or to decide not to do something that you were considering doing ○ *He said he was bowing out of the race for senator.*

• **bow to** *something* to accept something unwillingly ○ *The company president finally bowed to pressure and resigned.*

bowel movement *n* [C] the excretion of solid waste from the body

bowels /ˈbɑʊ·əlz, bɑʊlz/, **bowel** /ˈbɑʊ·əl, bɑʊl/ *pl n* **1** a long tube through which food travels while it is being digested after leaving the stomach; INTESTINES **2** *fig.* The bowels of something are the deepest parts of it: *Prisoners were generally confined to the bowels of the ship.*

bowl **DISH** /boʊl/ *n* [C] **1** a round container that is open at the top and is used esp. to hold liquids or other food, or the food it contains ○ *a salad/soup bowl* ○ *She eats a bowl of cereal every morning.* **2** A bowl is also the curved, inside part of something: *a toilet bowl* **3** A bowl is also a large, circular building used esp. for sports, or a special football game played in it after the regular season has ended: *the Rose Bowl*

ROLL /boʊl/ *v* [I/T] to roll a ball along a smooth surface during a game, especially in the game of BOWLING. ○ [I] *It's your turn to bowl.* ○ [T] *She bowled a strike.*

bowling /ˈboʊ·lɪŋ/, **tenpins** *n* [U] a game in which you stand at one end of a long smooth surface and roll a heavy ball along it to try to knock down a group of ten wooden objects arranged in a triangle at the other end

PHRASAL VERB with bowl

• **bowl** *someone* **over** to surprise and please someone greatly ○ *Braxton burst on the scene in 1993 and bowled people over with her beauty and talent.*

bowling alley *n* [C] a building where the sport of BOWLING takes place

bowling ball *n* [C] a heavy ball with three holes for your fingers that is used in the game of BOWLING

bow tie *n* [C] a special type of TIE (= strip of cloth put around a collar) that is tied in the way that you tie a shoe

box **CONTAINER** /bɑks/ *n* [C] **1** a container with stiff sides, shaped like a rectangle, or the contents of such a container ○ *a cardboard/cereal box* ○ *a box of chocolates* (= the container and its contents) **2** A box is also a small space on a form marked by lines in the shape of a square: *If you want to receive electronic updates, put a check in the box.* **3** A box is sometimes a small enclosed place: *the jury box*

box /bɑks/ *v* [T] to put something in a box ○ [M] *Someone from the nursing home must have boxed up his clothes.* ○ [M] *(fig.) My car was boxed in* (= blocked) *by two other cars, and I couldn't get out.*

FIGHT /bɑks/ *v* [I/T] ○ See at BOXING

boxcar /ˈbɑk·skɑr/ *n* [C] a railroad car with sliding doors and a roof, which is used to carry freight

boxer /ˈbɑk·sər/ *n* [C] a type of dog of medium size with short, light brown hair and a flat nose

boxer shorts /ˈbɑk·sər ˈʃɔːrts/ *pl n* loosely fitting men's underwear that covers the area between the waist and the tops of the legs

boxing /ˈbɑk·sɪŋ/ *n* [U] a sport in which two competitors fight by hitting each other with their closed hands
box /bɑks/ *v* [I/T] to fight someone or be active in the sport of boxing ○ [I/T] *I'd like to box him, and there's a chance that we will box again in Germany.*
boxer /ˈbɑk·sər/ *n* [C] ○ *an amateur boxer*

boxing glove *n* [C] either of a pair of large, thick, hand coverings that are worn for protection in the sport of boxing

boxing ring *n* [C] a square area surrounded by ropes where the sport of boxing takes place

box office *n* [C] **1** a place in a theater where tickets are sold **2** Box office is also the financial success or failure of a movie or play measured by ticket sales: *His last few films have been either box-office disappointments or outright flops.*

boy /bɔɪ/ *n* [C] **1** a male child or, more generally, a male of any age ○ *Some boys were playing basketball in the schoolyard.* **2** Boy sometimes means son: *We have two children – a boy and a girl.*
boyhood /ˈbɔɪ·hʊd/ *n* [U] ○ *Much of his boyhood* (= the time when he was a boy) *was spent in Europe.*
boyish /ˈbɔɪ·ɪʃ/ *adj* like a boy ○ *She found his boyish good looks very attractive.*

IDIOM with boy

• **(Oh) boy!** used to express excitement or say something with emphasis ○ *Boy, that was good cake!* ○ *Boy, was I mad!*

boycott /ˈbɔɪ·kɑt/ *v* [T] ***social studies*** to refuse to buy a product or take part in an activity as a way of expressing strong disapproval ○ *The union called on its members to boycott the meeting.*
boycott /ˈbɔɪ·kɑt/ *n* [C] ○ *She organized an economic boycott of the company's products.*

boyfriend /ˈbɔɪ·frend/ *n* [C] a man or boy with whom a person is having a romantic relationship ○ Compare GIRLFRIEND

Boy Scouts *pl n* an organization for boys that encourages them to take part in activities outside and to become responsible and independent
Boy Scout *n* [C]

bozo /ˈboʊ·zoʊ/ *n* [C] *pl* **bozos** *slang* a person who behaves like a fool and does not care about others ○ *Some bozo on a motorcycle almost ran me over just now.*

bra /brɑ/, **brassiere** *n* [C] a piece of women's underwear that supports the breasts

brace PREPARE /breɪs/ *v* [T] to prepare yourself physically or mentally for something unpleasant ○ *The weather forecasters told us to brace ourselves for a heavy storm.*

SUPPORT /breɪs/ *n* [C] something that supports, fastens, or strengthens ○ *He was recently fitted with a brace for his bad back.*
brace /breɪs/ *v* [T] ○ *She braced herself against the dresser.*
braces /ˈbreɪ·səz/ *pl n* **1** a set of wires attached to a person's teeth to move them gradually in order to straighten them **2** *esp. Br* Braces are also SUSPENDERS.

bracelet /ˈbreɪ·slət/ *n* [C] a piece of jewelry that is worn around the wrist or arm ○ *a silver bracelet*

bracket SYMBOL /ˈbræk·ət/ *n* [C usually pl] either of a pair of marks [ ], or the information inside them, used in a piece of writing to show that what is inside these marks should be considered as separate from the main part
bracket /ˈbræk·ət/ *v* [T] to enclose something in brackets ○ *Deleted text is bracketed.*

GROUP /ˈbræk·ət/ *n* [C] a set group with fixed upper and lower limits ○ *Most college students are in the 18 to 22 age bracket.* ○ *Her new job puts her in a higher income/tax bracket.*
bracket /ˈbræk·ət/ *v* [T] to consider something as similar to or connected to something else ○ *The mayor likes to bracket having more cops with the lower crime rate.*

SUPPORT /ˈbræk·ət/ *n* [C] a metal or wood piece, usually L-shaped, whose vertical part is fastened to a wall and whose horizontal part is used to support something, such as a shelf

brackish /ˈbræk·ɪʃ/ *adj* (of water) slightly salty ○ *As a river approaches the sea, its water becomes brackish.*

brag /bræg/ *v* [I] **-gg-** to speak with pride, often with too much pride, about something you have done or something you possess ○ *She was bragging about her golf game.* ○ *The government has been bragging about the good economy.*

braid HAIR /breɪd/ *v* [I/T] to join three or more lengths of hair or other material by putting them over each other in a special pattern ○ [I/T] *My sister taught me how to braid (my hair).*
braid /breɪd/ *n* [C] ○ *Andrea wears her hair in braids.*

CLOTH /breɪd/ *n* [U] a thin strip of cloth or twisted threads used as decoration esp. in uniforms ○ *gold braid*

Braille /breɪl/ *n* [U] a system of printing for blind people in which each letter is represented as a raised pattern that can be read by touching it with the fingers

brain /breɪn/ *n* [C] **1** the organ inside the head that controls thought, memory, feelings, and physical activity ○ *a brain tumor* ○ *brain surgery* ○ *They found fractured ribs, other bone injuries, and brain damage.* **2** *infml* A brain is also a very intelligent person: *We've got the best brains in the country working on this problem.*

B

brainless /ˈbreɪn·ləs/ *adj* stupid or thoughtless ○ *That was a brainless thing to do!*
brains /breɪnz/ *pl n* intelligence ○ *An individual who has brains and foresight can make a lot of money in this business.*
brains /breɪnz/ *n* [U] the most intelligent person in a group or the one who plans what a group will do ○ *He was the brains behind the biggest art theft in recent times.*
brainy /ˈbreɪ·ni/ *adj infml* intelligent ○ *Sarah was beautiful and brainy.*

brainchild /ˈbreɪn·tʃɑɪld/ *n* [U] something originally invented or thought of by someone ○ *The encyclopedia was the brainchild of historian John C. McCormick.*

brain drain *n* [C usually sing] the loss of many highly skilled and educated people from one country to another country

brainstorm SUGGEST IDEAS /ˈbreɪn·stɔːrm/ *v* [I/T] to suggest a lot of ideas for a future activity very quickly before considering some of them more carefully ○ [I] *They brainstormed and mapped plans for dealing with problems like affordable housing and the budget shortfall.*
brainstorming /ˈbreɪn ˌstɔːr·mɪŋ/ *n* [U] ○ *We need to do some brainstorming before we get down to detailed planning.*

NEW IDEA /ˈbreɪn·stɔːrm/ *n* [C] *infml* a sudden, new idea that you are enthusiastic about ○ *They got this brainstorm that they could make a living by buying and selling antiques.*

brainwash /ˈbreɪn·wɑʃ, -wɔːʃ/ *v* [T] to make people believe only what you want them to believe by continually telling them that it is true and preventing any other information from reaching them ○ *Could it be that we're brainwashed to accept these things?*

brake /breɪk/ *n* [C] a device that slows or stops the movement of a vehicle ○ *anti-lock brakes* ○ *He saw a deer crossing the road and hit/slammed on the brakes* (= stopped as quickly as possible).
brake /breɪk/ *v* [I] ○ *When it's icy, you have to brake gently.*

bramble /ˈbræm·bəl/ *n* [C/U] a bush with THORNS (= sharp pointed growths)

bran /bræn/ *n* [U] the outer covering of grain that is separated when making white flour and is valued as a food for its FIBER ○ *We had bran muffins for breakfast.*

branch TREE PART /bræntʃ/ *n* [C] one of the parts of a tree that grows out from the main trunk and has leaves, flowers, or fruit on it ○ *After the storm, the ground was covered with twigs and branches.* ○ (fig.) *This branch of the river* (= lesser part that joins the main flow) *eventually empties into the Atlantic Ocean.*
branch /bræntʃ/ *v* [I] ○ (fig.) *We drove down a narrow track that branched off from the main road* (= started from it and went in a different direction).

PART /bræntʃ/ *n* [C] **1** a part of something larger ○ *Pediatrics is a branch of medicine* (= a subject that is part of a larger subject). **2** A branch is one of the offices or groups that form part of a large business organization: *a local branch of the bank*

PHRASAL VERB with branch

• **branch out** to do something that is related to what you have done in the past but that takes you in a new direction ○ *The clothing manufacturer recently branched out into children's wear.*

brand PRODUCT /brænd/ *n* [C] a type of product made by a particular company ○ *This isn't my usual brand of deodorant.*

JUDGE /brænd/ *v* [T] to consider or refer to someone as being or having done something bad ○ *They branded him as a man without moral convictions.*

MARK /brænd/ *v* [T] to mark the skin of an animal with a particular symbol to show that you own it
brand /brænd/ *n* [C]

brandish /ˈbræn·dɪʃ/ *v* [T] to wave something in the air in a threatening or excited way ○ *He looked silly brandishing one of those Star Wars lightsabers.*

brand name *n* [C] the special name a company gives to its products or services ○ *All the car makers spend heavily to promote their brand names.*
brand-name *adj* [not gradable] ○ *The brand-name airlines* (= those whose names are known to most people) *are slashing their costs to survive and compete with low-cost carriers.*

brand-new /ˈbræn ˈnuː/ *adj* [not gradable] completely new, esp. not used before ○ *It's a brand-new recipe, and I've never tried it before.*

brandy /ˈbræn·di/ *n* [C/U] a strong alcoholic drink, usually made from wine and sometimes flavored with fruit

brash /bræʃ/ *adj* [-er/-est only] **1** having a lot of energy and the confidence to succeed, and not having much respect for others or worrying about their feelings ○ *His lawyer was brash, arrogant, and egocentric, but he usually won his cases.* **2** In fashion, brash can mean energetic and full of new ideas: *a designer known for his brash and innovative style*

brass METAL /bræs/ *n* [U] a bright yellow metal made from COPPER and ZINC ○ *brass lamps* ○ *brass door handles*

MUSICAL INSTRUMENTS /bræs/ *adj* [not gradable] (of a musical instrument) made of a metal tube bent into a particular shape and played by blowing ○ *The trumpet and the trombone are brass instruments.* ○ *He plays in the brass section of the orchestra.*

OFFICERS /bræs/ *n* [U] high-ranking officers in an organization, esp. the military ○ *The Pentagon brass went along with the plan but they were not happy about it.*

brassiere /brəˈzɪr/ *n* [C] BRA

B

brassy /ˈbræs·i/ *adj* having complete confidence in yourself, sometimes in a way that shows a lack of respect ○ *She was a fearless journalist, bold and brassy and never afraid to ask the toughest questions.* ○ *The show's musical numbers are big, brassy* (= loud and showy), *and spectacular.*

brat /bræt/ *n* [C] *infml* a child who behaves badly or one you do not like ○ *My nephew is a little spoiled brat.*

bravado /brəˈvɑd·oʊ/ *n* [U] a show of bravery, esp. when unnecessary and dangerous, to make people admire you

brave /breɪv/ *adj* [*-er/-est* only] showing no fear of dangerous or difficult things ○ *She liked to read stories of brave pioneer women who had crossed the country in covered wagons.* ○ *Of the three organizations criticized, only one was brave enough to face the press.*

brave /breɪv/ *v* [T] ○ *He braved the anger/wrath of his father by quitting law school and becoming an artist.*

bravely /ˈbreɪv·li/ *adv* ○ *"The pain isn't so bad," she said bravely.*

bravery /ˈbreɪ·və·ri/ *n* [U] ○ *They were awarded medals for bravery.*

WORD CHOICES brave

A common alternative to "brave" is the word **courageous**.

*She was a **courageous** woman who never complained about her illness.*

*It was a **courageous** decision to leave and start a new life in Australia.*

If someone is brave because he or she is not afraid of taking risks, you can use the adjectives **daring** or **bold**.

*He made a **daring** escape from his kidnappers.*

*I wasn't **bold** enough to leave my job.*

Someone who is brave because he or she is willing to try things that might be dangerous can be described as **adventurous**.

*She's a very **adventurous** person and enjoys mountain climbing.*

If someone is so brave that people admire what he or she has done, the adjective **heroic** can be used.

*He made a **heroic** attempt to rescue his neighbor from the fire.*

The word **valiant** can be used when someone does something that is brave when there is not much hope of succeeding.

*He made a **valiant** attempt to finish the race but the pain was too much.*

The adjectives **gutsy**, **plucky**, or the phrase **have guts** can be used in informal situations to describe someone who is brave.

*In the movie she plays a **gutsy** mother of six children.*

*She's a **plucky** little girl who refuses to let her disability ruin her life.*

*I didn't **have the guts** to go on my own.*

bravo /ˈbrɑv·oʊ, brɑˈvoʊ/ *exclamation* an expression used to show pleasure and admiration when someone, esp. a performer, has done something well

brawl /brɔːl/ *n* [C] a physical fight involving a group of people, esp. in a public place ○ *A brawl in the cafeteria left the place a mess.*

brawn /brɔːn/ *n* [U] physical strength and big muscles ○ *It is a school where brains are respected much more than brawn.*

brawny /ˈbrɔː·ni/ *adj* ○ *He grabbed me with his brawny arm.*

bray /breɪ/ *v* [I] to make the loud sound that a DONKEY makes

brazen /ˈbreɪ·zən/ *adj* (of something bad) done without trying to hide it ○ *a brazen robbery in the downtown area*

breach BREAK /briːtʃ/ *n* [C] an act of breaking a rule, law, custom, or practice ○ *In a breach of security, unauthorized people were able to board the plane.*

OPENING /briːtʃ/ *n* [C] an opening in a wall or fence or in a line of military defense

breach /briːtʃ/ *v* [T] ○ *The river breached the dams.*

bread /bred/ *n* [C/U] **1** a basic food made from flour, water, and YEAST mixed together and baked ○ [U] *a slice/loaf of bread* **2** *slang* Bread is also money.

breaded /ˈbred·əd/ *adj* [not gradable] (of food) covered with bits of dry bread before being cooked ○ *breaded chicken breasts*

bread and butter *n* [U] the way someone earns the money needed to live ○ *I do a lot of photography, but accounting is my bread and butter.*

bread-and-butter *adj* [not gradable] of the most basic kind and directly relating to most people ○ *Health and education are the sort of bread-and-butter issues that people vote on.*

breadth /bretθ, bredθ/ *n* [U] **1** the distance from one side of an object to the opposite side, esp. when it is shorter than the distance between the object's other two sides ○ *The length of this box is twice its breadth.* **2** Breadth is also the range or areas of knowledge or ability that someone has: *The breadth of his knowledge of history was impressive.*

breadwinner /ˈbred ˌwɪn·ər/ *n* [C] the person in a family who works to provide the money that the family needs to live on ○ *She's always been the breadwinner for her family.*

break DAMAGE /breɪk/ *v* [I/T] *past simp.* **broke**, *past part.* **broken** **1** to separate something suddenly or violently into two or more pieces, or to stop working by being damaged ○ [T] *I broke a glass in the kitchen and have to vacuum it up.* ○ [I] *Our toaster broke, so we have to get a new one.* ○ [M] *The police broke the door down to get into the apartment.* **2** If you break a part of your body, you

B

damage a bone which cracks or separates into pieces: [T] *The top women's downhill skier broke her leg in a freak collision.* **3** If you break a bill of a particular amount of money, you exchange it for smaller bills whose total equals the amount of your bill: [T] *Can you break a $50 bill for me?*

break /breɪk/ *n* [C] **1** *A break in a water main caused a whole section of the city to flood.* **2** A break in a bone is a place where it has cracked or separated into pieces.

breakage /ˈbreɪ·kɪdʒ/ *n* [C/U] **1** the act of damaging something by breaking it **2** Breakage is also the damage caused by breaking something.

WORD CHOICES break

See also: **broken**

An informal word that means the same as "break" is **bust**.

One of the children has ***busted*** *the DVD player.*

If something such as glass breaks into many small pieces, you can use the verbs **shatter** or **smash**.

The baseball hit the window and ***shattered*** *it.*

I dropped the vase and it ***smashed.***

The verb **snap** is used for something that is thin and breaks suddenly into two pieces with a cracking sound.

She bent the ruler and it ***snapped.***

If someone breaks a small piece off the edge of something, the verb **chip** can be used.

I ***chipped*** *the cup when I was putting it away.*

You can use the verb **crack** when something does not separate into pieces but has lines on its surface.

A stone hit the window and ***cracked*** *it.*

When something has very deep lines in it, or breaks into two pieces in a straight line, you can use the verb **split**.

The wood had ***split.***

If parts break off something because it is in bad condition, the phrasal verb **fall apart** can be used.

I've only had these shoes for a week and they're already ***falling apart.***

INTERRUPT /breɪk/ *v* [I/T] *past simp.* **broke,** *past part.* **broken** to interrupt or to stop something for a brief period ○ [I] *Let's continue for another ten minutes and then break for lunch.*

break /breɪk/ *n* [C] **1** an interruption, esp. in a regular activity, or a short period of rest when food or drink is sometimes eaten ○ *a lunch/coffee break* ○ *a break in the heat wave* **2** A break is also a time away from work or school, or a vacation: *I went skiing in the mountains during spring break* (= period in early spring when school classes temporarily stop).

END /breɪk/ *v* [I/T] *past simp.* **broke,** *past part.* **broken** to end or change something, or to stop ○ [I] *Cheryl found the habit of drinking a lot of coffee hard to break.* ○ [T] *She broke the record for the 5000 meters* (= she did better than the record). ○ [T] *They worked hard to break the deadlock in the negotiations.*

SEPARATE /breɪk/ *v* [I/T] *past simp.* **broke,** *past part.* **broken** to escape or separate from something or someone suddenly ○ [I always + adv/prep] *The dog broke free and ran into traffic.* ○ [I always + adv/prep] *The handle on the teapot just broke off.*

NOT OBEY /breɪk/ *v* [T] *past simp.* **broke,** *past part.* **broken** to fail to obey or follow a law, rule, or promise ○ *He didn't know he was breaking the law.* ○ *My daughter got sick and I had to break my appointment.*

MAKE KNOWN /breɪk/ *v* [I/T] *past simp.* **broke,** *past part.* **broken** to become known or cause something to be known, usually to the public ○ [T] *The newspaper reporters who broke the story won the Pulitzer prize.* ○ [I] *People wept when the news broke that the plant was closing for good.*

break /breɪk/ *n* [U] ○ *We set out at the break of day* (= as the sun was rising).

OPPORTUNITY /breɪk/ *n* [C] an opportunity for improving a situation, esp. one that happens unexpectedly ○ *Getting that first job was a lucky break.*

MOVE /breɪk/ *v* [I] (of a wave moving toward land) to suddenly change from a rising curl of water, sometimes showing white, to a layer that spreads out on reaching land

WORD FAMILY break

Nouns	break outbreak	*Adjectives* *Verbs*	broken break

IDIOMS with break

• **break even** to earn enough money to pay for expenses, without any profit ○ *We'd have to sell 2000 copies of the book to break even.*

• **break** *someone's* **heart** to make someone very sad ○ *It breaks my heart to see him so unhappy.*

• **break the ice** to do or say something that makes people who do not know each other feel more comfortable ○ *I tried to break the ice by talking to the people next to me about the weather.*

• **break the news** to tell someone about some important new information ○ *The doctor broke the news to the family that my grandmother had cancer.*

• **break with tradition** to do something different from what is usually done ○ *We decided to break with tradition and have fish for Thanksgiving dinner.*

PHRASAL VERBS with break

• **break away** to end a relationship or connection ○ *The small radical faction broke away from the independence movement.* ○ Related noun: BREAKAWAY

• **break down STOP WORKING** to stop working or not be successful ○ *Our car broke down on the thruway.* ○ Related noun: BREAKDOWN FAILURE ○ Related adjective: BROKEN-DOWN

• **break down BECOME UPSET** to become very upset ○ *The girl broke down and cried when she got a bad grade.* ○ Related noun: BREAKDOWN ANXIETY

B

• **break down** *something* **DIVIDE** [M] to divide something into smaller parts ○ *It's easier to handle the job if you break it down into several specific assignments.* ○ Related noun: BREAKDOWN DIVISION

• **break in** *someone/something* **TRAIN** [M] to train a person to do a new job, to train an animal to behave in an obedient way, or to use something to make it not as new and more comfortable ○ *We will have to break in three new staff members.* ○ *I'm still breaking in this new pair of running shoes.*

• **break in** **ENTER ILLEGALLY** to enter a building illegally, usually by damaging a door or window, esp. for the purpose of stealing something ○ *Thieves broke into our office downtown and stole the computers.* ○ Related noun: BREAK-IN

• **break into** *something* **BEGIN TO DO** to begin suddenly to do something ○ *He broke into a run, and we couldn't catch him.*

• **break into** *something* **USE FORCE** to force your way into something ○ *He's had his apartment broken into twice.*

• **break into** *something* **BE SUCCESSFUL** to begin being successful in a particular type of work or activity ○ *Rising from humble beginnings, he succeeded in Hollywood, broke into politics, and became President.*

• **break off** *something* [M] to end a relationship ○ *The governments broke off diplomatic relations.* ○ *She returned the ring and they broke off their engagement.*

• **break out** *(something)* **BEGIN** to begin, or to begin using or doing something ○ *A fight almost broke out.* ○ *I was afraid I was going to break out crying.*

• **break out** **ESCAPE** to escape from a place or a situation ○ *Two inmates broke out of prison and are still at large.*

• **break out** **SKIN CONDITION** to suddenly begin to have a RASH (= spots on the skin) ○ *Detergents make my hands break out.* ○ *I hate it when I break out in hives.*

• **break through** *something* to force a way through something ○ *High waves broke through the barrier beach.*

• **break up** *(something)* **DIVIDE** [M] to divide something into smaller pieces or separate parts ○ *The company has been totally broken up.* ○ *The ship broke up on the reef.* ○ *We're breaking up our trip by stopping for a few days in Singapore.* ○ Related noun: BREAKUP DIVISION

• **break up** **LOSE CONNECTION** (of a telephone conversation) to become impossible to understand because the connection is not strong enough ○ *He was on the subway when he called and started to break up before I could answer.*

• **break up** **END RELATIONSHIP** [M] to end or cause something to end, esp. a personal or business relationship ○ *The meeting didn't break up until about two a.m.* ○ *Regional phone companies were created when the government broke up the nationwide monopoly.* ○ Related noun: BREAKUP END OF RELATIONSHIP

• **break** *someone* **up** **MAKE LAUGH** *infml* to cause someone to laugh a lot ○ *That show really broke me up.*

• **break with** *something/someone* to act in a way that is different from what happened before or different from other people ○ *The magazine breaks with tradition this week by publishing photographs of its contributors.* ○ *When I came to the Senate, I broke with many in my own party to vote for a balanced budget.*

breakaway /ˈbreɪk·əˌweɪ/ *adj* [not gradable] independent after leaving another group ○ *a breakaway republic/territory* ○ Related verb: BREAK AWAY

breakdown **FAILURE** /ˈbreɪk·dɑʊn/ *n* [C] a mechanical failure, or a failure in a system or a relationship ○ *There was evidently a breakdown in communication leading to the false report.* ○ *Their car trip was a disaster – they had frequent breakdowns and never reached their destination.* ○ Related verb: BREAK DOWN STOP WORKING

DIVISION /ˈbreɪk·dɑʊn/ *n* [C] a division of information into parts that belong together ○ *We need a breakdown of the statistics into age groups.* ○ Related verb: BREAK DOWN DIVIDE

ANXIETY /ˈbreɪk·dɑʊn/ *n* [C] a condition in which you are unable to control thoughts or feelings that prevent you from living and working as you usually do ○ *It's about a middle-aged New York cop who is having a nervous breakdown.* ○ Related verb: BREAK DOWN BECOME UPSET

breakfast /ˈbrek·fəst/ *n* [C/U] a meal eaten in the morning as the first meal of the day ○ [U] *We had scrambled eggs and toast for breakfast.*

break-in *n* [C] the crime of entering a building by damaging a door or window, usually in order to steal ○ *After the break-in, we installed a new security system.* ○ Related verb: BREAK IN ENTER ILLEGALLY

breaking point *n* [C] the stage at which you lose control over yourself or over a situation ○ *We've been working 18 hours a day and we are all at the breaking point.*

breakneck /ˈbreɪk·nek/ *adj* dangerously fast ○ *They were cycling along at breakneck speed.*

breakthrough /ˈbreɪk·θruː/ *n* [C] an important discovery or development that helps to solve a problem ○ *The Polaroid camera was a technological breakthrough.*

breakup **END** /ˈbreɪ·kʌp/ *n* [C] the end of a relationship ○ *The planned breakup of the company will give him a less important role.* ○ Related verb: BREAK UP END RELATIONSHIP

DIVISION /ˈbreɪ·kʌp/ *n* [U] the division of something into smaller parts ○ *The breakup of the oil tanker caused severe damage to animal and plant life.* ○ Related verb: BREAK UP DIVIDE

breast **OF A WOMAN** /brest/ *n* [C] either of the two soft, rounded parts of a woman's chest that can produce milk after she has a baby

OF A BIRD /brest/ *n* [C/U] the front part of a bird's body ○ [U] *Would you prefer breast of chicken?*

B

breast-feed *v* [I/T] (of a mother) to feed a baby with milk from her breasts
breast-feeding *n* [U] ○ *Exclusive breastfeeding for at least six months cuts the baby's chance of developing ear infections in half.*

breaststroke /ˈbres·stroʊk/ *n* [U] a way of swimming in which both arms are moved together forward from your chest under the water and then pulled back toward either side

breath /breθ/ *n* [C/U] the air that you take into and let out of your lungs ○ [C usually sing] *She drew/took a deep breath.* ○ [U] *He seemed a little out of breath* (= to be breathing too fast). ○ [C usually sing] *As he jumped in the pool, he held his breath* (= delayed releasing the air in his lungs).
breathe /briːð/ *v* [I/T] to take air into the lungs and let it out again ○ [I] *He was so choked up with emotion that it was hard to breathe.* ○ [T] *It was great to be outside again and breathe the fresh air.*
breathing /ˈbriː·ðɪŋ/ *n* [U] ○ *Dora was asleep, and I listened to the sound of her deep breathing.*
breather /ˈbriː·ðər/ *n* [C] a brief rest after a period of work ○ *Let's take a breather before we finish loading the truck.*
breathless /ˈbreθ·ləs/ *adj* breathing too fast, and therefore unable to get enough air into your lungs to be comfortable ○ *She was breathless with excitement.*

WORD FAMILY breath

Nouns	breath breather breathing	*Adjectives* *Verbs*	breathless breathe

IDIOMS with breath

• **a breath of fresh air** someone or something that makes a situation feel new, different, and exciting ○ *The last band was a breath of fresh air in an otherwise boring night of music.*
• **breathe easier** to be able to relax esp. after a difficult or dangerous event ○ *The waves were very big, and we all breathed a little easier when we finally sailed back to shore.*
• **breathe life into** to bring new ideas and energy to something ○ *The new chef has breathed life into the failing French restaurant.*

breathtaking /ˈbreθˌteɪ·kɪŋ/ *adj* extremely good, beautiful, or exciting ○ *The violin solo was breathtaking.*
breathtakingly /ˈbreθˌteɪ·kɪŋ·li/ *adv* [not gradable] ○ *breathtakingly beautiful scenery*

breath test *n* [C] a test in which the police ask a driver to blow into a special device to show whether the drive has drunk too much alcohol to drive

breeches, **britches** /ˈbrɪtʃ·əz/ *pl n* pants ○ *She pulled on her riding breeches and got into her boots.*

breed /briːd/ *n* [C] **1** a particular type of animal or plant ○ *the different breeds of dogs* **2** A breed is also a type of person or thing: *Authentic blues singers are a dying breed* (= there are not many of them left).
breed /briːd/ *v* [I/T] *past* **bred 1** to keep animals or plants for the purpose of producing young animals or plants, often for chosen qualities ○ [T] *He bred hogs and cows and sold the meat and dairy products.* **2** When animals breed, they reproduce.
breeding /ˈbriːd·ɪŋ/ *n* [U] *dated* A person who has good breeding has been trained in childhood to be polite and behave correctly.

breeder reactor /ˈbriːd·ər riː ˈæk·tər/ *n* [C] ***physics*** a type of NUCLEAR REACTOR that produces more fuel than it uses

breeding ground *n* [C] a place or condition that produces or causes a lot of something, esp. something bad ○ *Poverty is a breeding ground for crime.*

breeze WIND /briːz/ *n* [C] a light wind ○ *He sat in the sun, enjoying the gentle sea breeze.*
breezy /ˈbriː·zi/ *adj* ○ *It was a sunny, breezy day, just right for sailing.*
WALK /briːz/ *v* [I always + adv/prep] *infml* to walk somewhere quickly and confidently ○ *Twenty minutes into the lecture she just breezed in and took a seat in the front row.*
breezy /ˈbriː·zi/ *adj* [*-er/-est* only] *infml* quick, informal, and confident ○ *She revolutionized fashion reporting with her breezy style.*
SOMETHING EASY /briːz/ *n* [C usually sing] *infml* something that is easy to do ○ *The entrance exam turned out to be a breeze.*
breeze /briːz/ *v* [I always + adv/prep] *infml* to achieve something easily ○ *She breezed to victories in the 100 and 200 meters.* ○ *He breezed through four years of Latin.*

brethren /ˈbreð·rən/ *pl n fml* (used as a form of address to members of an organization or religious group) brothers

brevity /ˈbrev·əţ·i/ *n* [U] **1** the use of few words ○ *The essays were written with admirable brevity.* **2** Brevity can also mean a short time: *the brevity of life*

brew /bruː/ *v* [I/T] **1** (of tea or coffee) to become stronger in taste in the container in which it is made, or to make a hot drink or beer ○ [T] *He's working a new way to brew the perfect cup of coffee.* **2** If something bad is brewing, it is about to start: [I] *I felt that trouble was brewing.*
brew /bruː/ *n* [C] beer or another drink made by brewing
brewery /ˈbruː·ə·ri/ *n* [C] a company that makes beer or a place where beer is made

bribe /brɑɪb/ *n* [C] the act of giving someone money or something else of value, often illegally, to persuade that person to do something you want ○ *Congressmen have been accused of accepting bribes to pass bills favoring particular companies.*
bribe /brɑɪb/ *v* [T] ○ *He was accused of bribing a building inspector.*
bribery /ˈbrɑɪ·bə·ri/ *n* [U] ○ *Charges of bribery and official corruption were made.*

B

bric-a-brac /ˈbrɪk·əˌbræk/ *n* [U] small, decorative objects of various types and of no great value

brick /brɪk/ *n* [C] a rectangular block of hard material used for building walls and houses

brick wall *n* [C usually sing] something that prevents you from doing something ○ *Even the best writers hit a brick wall sometimes and can't make a story work.*

bricklayer /ˈbrɪkˌleɪ·ər/ *n* [C] a person whose job is building walls or buildings using bricks

bride /braɪd/ *n* [C] a woman who is about to get married or just got married ○ *The bride and groom wrote their own wedding vows.*
bridal /ˈbraɪd·əl/ *adj* [not gradable] of a woman about to be married, or of a wedding ○ *a bridal gown*

bridegroom /ˈbraɪd·gruːm, -grʊm/ *n* [C] a GROOM MAN

bridesmaid /ˈbraɪdz·meɪd/ *n* [C] a girl or woman, usually not married, who takes part in a wedding and helps the woman who is getting married

bridge **LARGE STRUCTURE** /brɪdʒ/ *n* [C] a structure that is built over a river, road, or railroad to allow people and vehicles to cross from one side to the other ○ *We drove across the bridge from Brooklyn to Manhattan.*
bridge /brɪdʒ/ *v* [T] **1** *The shopping complex bridges a highway.* **2** If a difference is bridged, it is made smaller: *Swing music bridged the gap between popular and classical music.*

NOSE /brɪdʒ/ *n* [C usually sing] the top part of the nose, between the eyes, or the piece on a pair of glasses that is supported by the top part of the nose ○ *He rubbed the bridge of his nose.*

MUSICAL INSTRUMENT /brɪdʒ/ *n* [C] a small piece of wood on a musical instrument, such as a guitar or VIOLIN, over which strings are stretched

TEETH /brɪdʒ/, **bridgework** /ˈbrɪdʒ·wɜrk/ *n* [C] a piece of material that keeps artificial teeth in place by being fastened to the natural teeth

PART OF A SHIP /brɪdʒ/ *n* [C] the raised part of a ship on which the CAPTAIN and other officers stand and from where they control the movement of the ship

GAME /brɪdʒ/ *n* [U] a card game for four players who play in two pairs and try to win the cards they say they will win

bridle **LEATHER STRAPS** /ˈbraɪd·əl/ *n* [C] a set of leather straps that are put around a horse's head to allow its rider to control it

SHOW ANGER /ˈbraɪd·əl/ *v* [I] to show annoyance or anger ○ *Homeowners bridled at the new regulations.*

brief Ⓐ **SHORT IN TIME** /briːf/ *adj* [-er/-est only] lasting only a short time or containing few words ○ *Rory had a brief career as an actor.*
briefly Ⓐ /ˈbriː·fli/ *adv* for a short time or using few words ○ *We chatted briefly about the weather.*

GIVE INSTRUCTIONS /briːf/ *v* [T] to give someone instructions or information about what to do or say ○ *He is briefing the account executives on the new airline accounts.* ○ Compare DEBRIEF
briefing Ⓐ /ˈbriː·fɪŋ/ *n* [C] information that is given to someone just before the person does something, or a meeting where information is given ○ *He discussed the report at a White House briefing on Tuesday.*

briefcase /ˈbriːf·keɪs/ *n* [C] a usually flat, rectangular container, used esp. for carrying business papers

briefs /briːfs/ *pl n* underwear worn by men and women which covers the area between the waist and the tops of the legs

brigade /brɪˈgeɪd/ *n* [C] one of the groups into which an army is divided, consisting of two or more BATTALIONS, or a group of people who are organized to perform a particular job ○ *A brigade of volunteers campaigned for his election.*

bright **LIGHT** /brɑɪt/ *adj* [-er/-est only] full of light, or shining ○ *the bright lights of downtown*
brighten /ˈbrɑɪt·ən/ *v* [I/T] ○ [I] *The lights dimmed, then brightened.* ○ [M] *Betty painted the room white to brighten it up.*
brights /brɑɪts/ *pl n* a car's HEADLIGHTS (= the powerful lights at the front) when they are on full power
brightly /ˈbrɑɪt·li/ *adv* ○ *a brightly lit room*
brightness /ˈbrɑɪt·nəs/ *n* [U] ○ *The brightness of the summer day made him blink.*

COLOR /brɑɪt/ *adj* [-er/-est only] strong in color ○ *a bright green hat*
brightly /ˈbrɑɪt·li/ *adv* ○ *brightly colored dresses*

INTELLIGENT /brɑɪt/ *adj* [-er/-est only] (of a person) intelligent and quick to learn ○ *He's a bright, well-organized guy.* ○ *She was full of bright ideas.*

HAPPY /brɑɪt/ *adj* full of hope or happiness ○ *He has a bright future ahead of him.*
brighten /ˈbrɑɪt·ən/ *v* [I/T] ○ [T] *Her presence brightens my days.* ○ [I] *Anna's face brightened at the thought of a vacation.*
brightly /ˈbrɑɪt·li/ *adv* ○ *"I'm leaving," Consuela said brightly.*

bright side *n* [C usually sing] the advantages or good characteristics of a situation ○ *On the bright side, the team has nowhere to go but up.*

brilliant **INTELLIGENT** /ˈbrɪl·jənt/ *adj* extremely intelligent or highly skilled ○ *a brilliant plan* ○ *Armstrong was one of the most brilliant musicians in jazz.*
brilliantly /ˈbrɪl·jənt·li/ *adv* ○ *Randy runs his company brilliantly.*
brilliance /ˈbrɪl·jəns/ *n* [U] ○ *Few people want to hear about your child's brilliance.*

SHINING /ˈbrɪl·jənt/ *adj* full of light, shining, or bright in color ○ *The sky was a brilliant blue.*
brilliance /ˈbrɪl·jəns/ *n* [U] ○ *the sun's brilliance*

brim **TOP** /brɪm/ *n* [C] the very top edge of a container ○ *He filled his cup to the brim.*

B

brim /brɪm/ *v* [I] **-mm-** to fill or be full to the top ○ *Her eyes brimmed with tears.* ○ *(fig.) She's brimming with confidence.*

PART OF HAT /brɪm/ *n* [C usually sing] the bottom part of a hat that sticks out ○ *He pulled the brim of his hat down over his eyes.* ○ Compare CROWN **TOP PART**

brine /brɑɪn/ *n* [U] water with salt in it

bring TAKE /brɪŋ/ *v* [T] *past* **brought** to take or carry someone or something to a place or a person, or in the direction of the person speaking ○ *Bring me that book/Bring that book to me.* ○ *I brought my daughter to the office.* ○ [M] *Next time you come, bring your boyfriend along.* ○ [M] *It started raining, so I brought in the laundry.* ○ *This broadcast was brought to you* (= paid for) *by Powdermilk Biscuits.*

> **USAGE**
>
> **bring or take?**
>
> **Bring** means move someone or something toward the speaker or toward the place where you are now.
>
> *Did you bring me any food?*
>
> *I've brought you a birthday present.*
>
> **Take** is used to talk about moving someone or something away from the speaker or the place where you are now.
>
> *Don't forget to take your umbrella with you when you leave.*

CAUSE /brɪŋ/ *v* [T] *past* **brought** to cause, result in, or produce a state ○ *The rain brought some relief from this heat.* ○ *The explosion brought the building crashing to the ground.* ○ *What brings you here?* ○ *Prosecutors brought charges against the program's director.* ○ *Funding cuts brought an end to the project.* ○ *Wicks brought her to the attention of a movie producer.*

FORCE /brɪŋ/ *v* [T] *past* **brought** to make yourself do something that you do not want to do ○ *I couldn't bring myself to disappoint her.*

IDIOMS with bring

• **bring** *someone/something* **into line (with** *someone/something***)** to force someone or something to be similar or of the same standard as someone or something else ○ *Teachers say the raises would bring their salaries into line with other public workers.*

• **bring to light** to cause something to be known ○ *Her research has brought to light new information about Jefferson's early life.*

• **bring to mind** to make you remember something ○ *That music brings to mind our first date.*

• **bring** *something* **to the table** to provide something that will be a benefit ○ *Clarkson was the right person to hire – she brings a lot of experience and some important skills to the table.*

PHRASAL VERBS with bring

• **bring about** *something* [M] to cause something to happen ○ *Harold's working to bring about changes in the industry.*

• **bring** *someone* **around PERSUADE** to persuade someone to have the same opinion as you have ○ *She tried to bring them around to accepting a settlement.*

• **bring** *someone* **around MAKE CONSCIOUS** to make someone become conscious again after being unconscious ○ *Medics tried to bring him around.*

• **bring back** *something* **DO AGAIN** [M] to cause something to come into use or popularity again ○ *He's planning to bring back disco music.*

• **bring back** *something* **THINK OF AGAIN** [M] to cause something to be thought about ○ *That music always brings back happy memories.*

• **bring down** *someone* **MAKE POWERLESS** [M] to cause someone to lose power ○ *An economic crisis could bring down the government.*

• **bring down** *something* **MAKE LESS** [M] to cause something to become less ○ *Drugs can bring your blood pressure down.*

• **bring forth** *something* to cause something to happen or be seen or known ○ *Maddie brought forth a new line of clothes.*

• **bring forward** *something* **MAKE KNOWN** [M] to make something known ○ *Several accusations have been brought forward.*

• **bring forward** *something* **MAKE EARLIER** [M] to change the schedule of something so that it happens earlier ○ *He agreed to bring forward deadlines for reducing phosphates in the lake.*

• **bring in** *something* to earn money ○ *She brings in about $600 a week.*

• **bring off** *something* [M] to succeed in doing something difficult ○ *Terry brought off the presentation without a hitch.*

• **bring on** *something* [M] to cause something to happen, esp. something bad ○ *I think the loud music brought my headache on.*

• **bring out** *something* **PRODUCE A QUALITY** [M] to produce a particular quality ○ *Sometimes a crisis brings out the best in people.* ○ *The right lighting can bring out the beauty in a room.*

• **bring out** *something* **PRODUCE FOR SALE** [M] to produce something for people to buy ○ *The greeting-card company is bringing out a new line of Mother's Day cards.*

• **bring up** *someone* **CARE FOR** [M] to care for a child until it is an adult ○ *An aunt brought him up.* ○ *He was brought up on jazz* (= experienced it a lot as a child).

• **bring up** *something* **TALK** [M] to talk about something ○ *I hate to bring up business at lunch.*

brink /brɪŋk/ *n* [U] the edge of a cliff or other high area, or the point at which something good or bad will happen ○ *The company was on the brink of collapse.*

brinksmanship /ˈbrɪŋk·smən ˌʃɪp/ *n* [U] ***politics & government*** taking a dangerous political situation as far as it will go without failure

briquette, briquet /brɪˈket/ *n* [C] a small block made from coal dust or CHARCOAL, used as fuel in a fire

brisk /brɪsk/ *adj* [-er/-est only] quick, energetic, and active ○ *I took a brisk walk.* ○ *Business has been*

brisk lately. ○ *A brisk* (= cold but pleasant) *wind blew across the field.*
briskly /ˈbrɪs·kli/ *adv* ○ *She moved briskly toward the car.*

bristle /ˈbrɪs·əl/ *n* [C/U] a short, stiff hair ○ [C usually pl] *The old brush had lost most of its bristles.*
bristle /ˈbrɪs·əl/ *v* [I] (of hairs) to stand up because of fear or anger, or (of people) to show anger ○ *The cat's fur bristled.* ○ *She bristles at injustice.*
bristly /ˈbrɪs·li/ *adj* ○ *a bristly chin*

Brit /brɪt/ *adj short form of* BRITISH

britches /ˈbrɪtʃ·əz/ *pl n* BREECHES

British /ˈbrɪt̬·ɪʃ/, *short form* **Brit** *adj* of or coming from the United Kingdom of Great Britain and Northern Ireland
British /ˈbrɪt̬·ɪʃ/ *pl n* people from Great Britain

British English *n* [U] the English language as it spoken and written in England

Briton /ˈbrɪt·ᵊn/ *n* [C] a person from Great Britain

brittle /ˈbrɪt̬·ᵊl/ *adj* delicate and easily broken ○ *As you get older your bones become increasingly brittle.*

bro /broʊ/ *n* [C] *pl* **bros** *abbreviation for* BROTHER

broach /broʊtʃ/ *v* [T] to begin a discussion of something difficult ○ *He hopes they will sponsor the poetry event, but he hasn't broached the subject with them yet.*

broad **WIDE** /brɔːd/ *adj* [*-er/-est* only] very wide ○ *He flashed a broad grin at us.*
broaden /ˈbrɔːd·ᵊn/ *v* [I/T] to become wider, or to cause something to be wider ○ [T] *They are broadening the road to speed up the flow of traffic.*

GENERAL /brɔːd/ *adj* including many types of things; general ○ *The magazine covers a broad range of subjects.* ○ *He explained it in very broad terms.*
broaden /ˈbrɔːd·ᵊn/ *v* [T] to increase the range of something ○ *Going to college will broaden your interests.*
broadly /ˈbrɔːd·li/ *adv* ○ *Broadly speaking, there are five artistic categories within the Western tradition.*

IDIOM with broad

• **in broad daylight** when anyone could see what is happening ○ *We never expected coyotes to come into our yard in broad daylight.*

broadband /ˈbrɔːd·bænd/ *n* [U] a fast INTERNET connection that does not use telephone lines ○ *Starbucks has entered deals that will deliver wireless broadband access in its cafes.*

broadcast /ˈbrɔːd·kæst/ *v past* **broadcast, broadcasted** to send out sound or pictures that are carried over distances using radio waves ○ [T] *The game will be broadcast live on ESPN.* ○ [T] (*fig.*) (*infml*) *Please don't broadcast* (= tell everyone) *that I'm having an operation.*
broadcast /ˈbrɔːd·kæst/ *n* [C] ○ *a television broadcast*
broadcaster /ˈbrɔːd ˌkæs·tər/ *n* [C] a person who presents discussions or information on radio or television, or the owner of a radio or television station
broadcasting /ˈbrɔːd ˌkæs·tɪŋ/ *n* [U] ○ *He's looking for a job in broadcasting.*

broad-minded *adj* willing to accept behavior or beliefs that are different from your own

broadside **ATTACK** /ˈbrɔːd·sɑɪd/ *n* [C] a strong written or spoken attack ○ *Republicans launched another broadside at the president.*

ON THE SIDE /ˈbrɔːd·sɑɪd/ *adv* [not gradable] on or from the side ○ *Her car was struck broadside by a truck.*

Broadway /ˈbrɔːd·weɪ/ *n* [U] a street in the entertainment section of New York City where there are many theaters, or the theater in this area ○ *a Broadway play/musical* ○ *Tyler hopes to be on Broadway one day* (= performing there).

brocade /broʊˈkeɪd/ *n* [U] heavy, decorative cloth with a raised design often of gold or silver threads

broccoli /ˈbrɑk·li/ *n* [U] a vegetable with a thick, green stem and a dense, green top

brochure /broʊˈʃʊr/ *n* [C] a type of small magazine that contains pictures and information on a product or a company ○ *travel brochures*

brogue /broʊg/ *n* [C usually sing] an Irish or Scottish way of speaking English ○ *She spoke with a soft brogue.*

broil /brɔɪl/ *v* [T] to cook something with the heat coming from directly above or below it ○ *Broil the steak for five minutes.*
broiler /ˈbrɔɪ·lər/ *n* [C] **1** a part of a stove in which food can be cooked directly under or over the heat **2** A broiler is also a young chicken.

broke **BREAK** /broʊk/ *past simple of* BREAK

POOR /broʊk/ *adj infml* without money ○ *I can't go to the movies – I'm flat broke.* ○ *Is Social Security going broke* (= changing to a condition in which it has no money)*?*

broken **BREAK** /ˈbroʊ·kən/ *past participle of* BREAK

DAMAGED /ˈbroʊ·kən/ *adj* [not gradable] damaged, or no longer able to work ○ *My camera is broken.*

WORD CHOICES broken

If a piece of equipment is broken (not working properly), you can use adjectives such as **dead**, **defunct**, or, informally, **busted**.

You won't be able to watch the game, the TV's ***busted****.*

The phone's ***dead****; there must be a problem with the line.*

If a piece of equipment or machinery in a public place is broken, you can say that it is **out of order**.

The coffee machine was ***out of order****.* ➤

B

If a piece of equipment has broken, in informal situations you can use the expression **have had it**.

*The kettle's **had it** so you'll have to boil a pan of water.*

INTERRUPTED /ˈbroʊ·kən/ *adj* interrupted or not continuous ○ *a broken line* ○ *He spoke very broken English.*

DISCOURAGED /ˈbroʊ·kən/ *adj* extremely discouraged or sad ○ *After his wife's death, he seemed to be a broken man.* ○ *My mom said my uncle had* **a broken heart** (= was sad because a romance had ended).

ENDED /ˈbroʊ·kən/ *adj* [not gradable] destroyed or ended ○ *He overcame a string of broken dreams to become a success.* ○ *She comes from a broken home* (= the parents no longer live together).

NOT KEPT /ˈbroʊ·kən/ *adj* [not gradable] (of a law, rule, or promise) disobeyed or not kept ○ *a broken promise*

broken-down *adj* in bad condition or not working ○ *a broken-down car* ○ Related verb: BREAK DOWN STOP WORKING

broken-hearted *adj* extremely unhappy about the failure or end of something

broker /ˈbroʊ·kər/ *n* [C] a person who acts for or represents another in the buying and selling of shares in companies or protection against risk, or who arranges for the lending of money ○ *I told my broker to sell the stock.*

broker /ˈbroʊ·kər/ *v* [T] ○ *He brokered a deal to buy the company.*

bromine /ˈbroʊˌmiːn, -maɪn/, *symbol* **Br** ***chemistry*** an element that exists in nature as a poisonous liquid and gives off VAPOR (= gas) that causes uncomfortable physical reactions

bronchitis /brɑŋˈkɑɪţ·əs/ *n* [U] an illness in which the air passages between the WINDPIPE (= tube in the throat) and the lungs become infected and swollen, resulting in coughing and difficulty in breathing

bronco /ˈbrɑŋ·koʊ/ *n* [C] *pl* **broncos** a wild horse of the western US

bronze /brɑnz/ *n* [C/U] hard, bright brown metal made of COPPER and TIN, or a statue made of this metal

bronzed /brɑnzd/ *adj* covered in bronze, or brown esp. from having been in the sun ○ *bronzed baby shoes* ○ *bronzed skin*

bronze medal *n* [C] a disk-shaped prize made of or covered with BRONZE that is given to a person or team that is third in a competition ○ Compare GOLD MEDAL; SILVER MEDAL

brooch /broʊtʃ, bruːtʃ/ *n* [C] a small piece of jewelry with a pin at the back that is fastened to a woman's clothing

brood GROUP /bruːd/ *n* [C] a group of young birds all born at the same time, or *infml* a person's children ○ (*infml*) *I moved in with Annie and her brood.*

THINK /bruːd/ *v* [I] to think silently for a long time about things that make you sad, worried, or angry ○ *He brooded over the insult.*

brooding /ˈbruːd·ɪŋ/ *adj* ○ *Her films have a brooding atmosphere.*

brook STREAM /brʊk/ *n* [C] a small stream ○ *A brook runs past the house.*

ALLOW /brʊk/ *v* [T] to allow or accept something, esp. a difference of opinion or intention ○ *She won't brook any criticism of her work.*

broom /bruːm, brʊm/ *n* [C] a brush with a long handle, used for cleaning the floor ○ *I use that broom to sweep the kitchen floor.*

broomstick /ˈbruːm·stɪk, ˈbrʊm-/ *n* [C] the long handle of a BROOM

broth /brɔːθ/ *n* [U] *pl* **broths** a thin soup, often with vegetables or rice in it, usually made with the liquid in which meat bones have been boiled

brothel /ˈbrɑθ·əl, ˈbrɔː·θəl/ *n* [C] a place where men go and pay to have sex with PROSTITUTES

brother MALE PERSON /ˈbrʌð·ər/ *n* [C] **1** a male who has the same parents as another person ○ *an older/younger brother* **2** A brother is also a member of the same race, church, religious group, or organization: *a fraternity brother* **3** Brother may be used by a man to address another man: *Hey, brother, can you spare a quarter?*

brother-in-law /ˈbrʌð·ə·rənˌlɔː/ *n* [C] *pl* **brothers-in-law** the husband of someone's sister, or the brother of someone's wife or husband, or the husband of the sister of someone's wife or husband

brotherly /ˈbrʌð·ər·li/ *adv* like or characteristic of a brother ○ *brotherly advice*

EXCLAMATION /ˈbrʌð·ər, ˈbrʌˈðɜr/ *exclamation* used to express annoyance or surprise ○ *Oh, brother, are we in a mess now!*

WORD FAMILY brother

Nouns		Adjectives	
	brother		brotherly
	brotherhood		
	brother-in-law		

brotherhood /ˈbrʌð·ərˌhʊd/ *n* [U] **1** a feeling of shared interests and support among men, or more generally, among all humans **2** A brotherhood is also the membership of an organization of men, or the organization itself.

brought /brɔːt/ *past simple and past participle of* BRING

brouhaha /ˈbruːˌhɑːˌhɑː/ *n* [U] a situation that causes upset, anger, or confusion ○ *There was a big brouhaha when the town council decided to close the park.*

brow /brɑʊ/ *n* [C] **1** the FOREHEAD (= the face above the eyes) ○ *He wiped the sweat from his brow.* **2** A brow is also an EYEBROW.

browbeat /ˈbrɑʊ·biːt/ *v* [T] *past simp.* **browbeat**, *past part.* **browbeaten** to ask or demand continually that someone do something ○ *He objected that McDonald was browbeating the witness.*

brown COLOR /braʊn/ *adj, n* [C/U] (of) the color of chocolate or earth ○ *a brown suit*

brown /braʊn/ *v* [T] ○ *First brown the meat and then cook it slowly.*

PERSON /braʊn/ *n* [C] a person with brown skin

brown *adj* [*-er/-est* only]

brownie /ˈbrɑʊ·ni/ *n* [C] a small, square, chocolate cake, often containing nuts

brownie points *pl n humorous* approval for something helpful you have done ○ *I earned some Brownie points for washing the car.*

Brownies /ˈbrɑʊ·niːz/ *pl n* [U] the level of the GIRL SCOUTS for girls 6 to 8 years old

Brownie /ˈbroʊ·ni/ *n* [C] a member of the Brownies

brownstone /ˈbraʊn·stoʊn/ *n* [C] a city house with its front built of a red-brown stone

browse /brɑʊz/ *v* [I/T] to look at or through something to see what is there ○ [I] *I browsed in a bookstore until she showed up.* ○ [T] *You can browse the library's computerized card catalog.*

browser /ˈbrɑʊ·zər/ *n* [C] a special type of computer program that lets you use the INTERNET

bruise /bruːz/ *n* [C] a place on a person's skin that is darker from bleeding under the skin, usually from an injury ○ *My little boy fell off his bike and has a bad bruise on his shoulder.*

bruise /bruːz/ *v* [T] ○ *He crashed into a table and bruised his shin.*

brunch /brʌntʃ/ *n* [C] a meal sometimes eaten in the late morning that combines breakfast and lunch

brunette /bruːˈnet/ *n* [C] a woman or girl with dark hair

brunt IDIOM /brʌnt/

• **the brunt of** *something* the worst problems caused by something ○ *He claimed that the middle class would bear the brunt of the tax increase.*

brush TOOL /brʌʃ/ *n* [C] **1** any of various utensils consisting of hairs or fibers arranged in rows or grouped together, attached to a handle, and used for smoothing the hair, cleaning things, painting, etc. ○ *I need a better brush for my hair.* **2** Brush is often used as a combining form: *hairbrush* ○ *toothbrush* ○ *paintbrush*

brush /brʌʃ/ *v* [T] **1** to remove or improve the appearance of something using your hand or a brush ○ *She brushed a strand of hair from her face.* ○ *She brushed her hair.* **2** To **brush your teeth** is to clean them using a small brush and TOOTHPASTE.

TOUCH /brʌʃ/ *v* [I/T] to touch something lightly ○ [T] *A warm gust of wind brushed my cheek.* ○ [I] *The cat brushed against my leg.*

brush /brʌʃ/ *n* [C usually sing] **1** *The flower's scent is unleashed by the brush of a hand.* **2** A brush with something or someone is a close and usually unpleasant meeting: *The subway system has survived several brushes with bankruptcy.*

BUSHES /brʌʃ/ *n* [U] low, dense bushes that grow on open land ○ *The river banks were covered with brush.*

PHRASAL VERBS with brush

• **brush aside** *something/someone* [M] to refuse to give importance to an opinion or request, or to someone who expresses one ○ *Duke brushed aside suggestions that his campaign was finished.*

• **brush** *yourself* **off** REMOVE DIRT to remove dirt from your clothes with your hands ○ *He rose slowly and brushed himself off.*

• **brush off** *something* CLEAN [M] to clean something or make it neat by rubbing your hand over it ○ *She stood up and brushed off her skirt.*

• **brush off** *someone/something* NOT CONSIDER [M] to refuse to consider what someone says, or to not admit that something may be true or important ○ *The committee chairman brushed her off when she tried to raise the issue.* ○ *Ehrlich brushes off suggestions that he's spending taxpayer dollars for campaign ads.* ○ Related noun: BRUSHOFF

• **brush up on** *something* to improve your knowledge of something already learned but partly forgotten ○ *You'd better brush up on your French before going to Paris.*

brushoff /ˈbrʌʃ·ɔːf/ *n* [U] the act of refusing to listen to or talk to someone ○ *She called to complain but got the brushoff from the store manager.* ○ Related verb: BRUSH OFF

brusque /brʌsk/ *adj* quick and direct in manner or speech, and often not polite ○ *As the president's chief of staff, he offended many with his brusque manner.*

Brussels sprouts /ˌbrʌs·əl ˈsprɑʊts/ *pl n* a green vegetable like very small CABBAGES

brutal /ˈbruːt̬·əl/ *adj* **1** cruel and violent ○ *The attacks on the crew were quite brutal.* **2** *fig.* Brutal can also mean unpleasant or difficult: *The weather was brutal – hot and humid.* **3** Brutal can also mean plain and direct, without worrying about anyone's feelings: *She spoke with brutal honesty about his behavior.*

brutally /ˈbruːt̬·əl·i/ *adv* ○ *He was brutally beaten.* ○ *She's being brutally honest.*

brutality /bruːˈtæl·ət̬·i/ *n* [C/U] an act or behavior that is cruel and violent ○ [U] *The movie's brutality is often hard to watch.*

brutalize /ˈbruːt̬·əlˌɑɪz/ *v* [T] to act cruelly and violently toward someone ○ *As a society we brutalize ourselves when we hurt our own members.*

brute /bruːt/ *n* [C] **1** a person who is offensive and rude, and often violent ○ *Historians have portrayed him as a brute who won only because of superior troop strength.* **2** A brute is also a large, strong animal. **3** If something is done with brute force, it is done with a great amount of force: *They had to use brute force to knock down the door.*

B.S. *n* [C] *abbreviation for* Bachelor of Science (= a first college degree in a science). ○ Compare B.A.

bubble /ˈbʌb·əl/ *n* [C] a ball of air in a liquid or on its surface, or in the air ○ *When water begins to boil, small bubbles form around the edge of the pot.*
bubble /ˈbʌb·əl/ *v* [I] ○ *The water in the pot began to bubble.* ○ (*fig.*) *We were bubbling with excitement as we watched the Olympic flame being lit.*
bubbly /ˈbʌb·li/ *adj* **1** filled with bubbles **2** Bubbly also means very energetic and pleasant: *a bubbly personality*

PHRASAL VERB with **bubble**

• **bubble up** to rise to the surface or become obvious ○ *She laughs, a tinkling musical child's laugh, bubbling up out of her.* ○ *Interesting ideas about education and healthcare are bubbling up all over the country.*

bubble gum *n* [C] CHEWING GUM that you can blow into the shape of a ball

buck MONEY /bʌk/ *n* [C] *infml* a DOLLAR ○ *It cost me ten bucks.*
ANIMAL /bʌk/ *n* [C] a male deer ○ Compare DOE
JUMP /bʌk/ *v* [I] (esp. of a horse) to jump into the air with the head down and the back arched ○ *The horse bucked every time he got in the saddle.*
OPPOSE /bʌk/ *v* [T] to oppose or refuse to go along with something ○ *As a designer, she bucked the trend and succeeded with her own original ideas.*

bucket /ˈbʌk·ət/ *n* [C] a container with an open top and a handle, or the amount such a container will hold ○ *a bucket of water*
buckets /ˈbʌk·əts/ *pl n infml* a great amount; a lot ○ *The rain came down in buckets.*

buckle FASTENER /ˈbʌk·əl/ *n* [C] a fastener for a belt ○ *a silver buckle*
buckle /ˈbʌk·əl/ *v* [I/T] ○ [T] *Please buckle your seat belts.*
BEND /ˈbʌk·əl/ *v* [I/T] **1** to bend or become uneven, often as a result of force, heat, or weakness ○ [I] *After eight hours of hiking, our knees were beginning to buckle.* **2** Someone who buckles or buckles under gives in to something, such as pressure or opposition: [I] *The judge threatened her with jail, but she refused to buckle and would not say where she got the information.*

PHRASAL VERBS with **buckle**

• **buckle down** to start working hard ○ *He'll have to buckle down if he expects to pass the course.*
• **buckle up** to fasten your SEAT BELT (= belt attached to a seat) ○ *We believe in safe driving, buckling up, and observing the speed limit.*

bud /bʌd/ *n* [C] the part of a plant that develops into a flower or leaf
bud /bʌd/ *v* [I] **-dd-** ○ *In early spring the trees begin to bud.*
budding /ˈbʌd·ɪŋ/ *adj* growing or developing ○ *The high school jazz group included a number of budding musicians.*

Buddha /ˈbuːd·ə, ˈbʊd·ə/ *n* [U] a religious leader who lived in India about 2500 years ago, and whose teachings led to the development of Buddhism

Buddhism /ˈbuːdˌɪz·əm, ˈbʊd-/ *n* [U] a religion that originally comes from India and teaches that improvement of the spirit will bring an end to personal confusion and suffering
Buddhist /ˈbuːd·əst, ˈbʊd-/ *n* [C] a follower of Buddhism
Buddhist /ˈbuːd·əst, ˈbʊd-/ *adj* [not gradable] ○ *Buddhist monasteries*

buddy /ˈbʌd·i/ *n* [C] *infml* a close friend ○ *We were great buddies and did many things together.*

budge /bʌdʒ/ *v* [I/T] to move or cause someone or something to move ○ [I] *The demonstrators would not budge from the governor's office.* ○ [T] *We tried to open a window but couldn't budge any of them.*

budget FINANCIAL PLAN /ˈbʌdʒ·ət/ *n* [C] **1** a financial plan that lists expected expenses and income during a particular period ○ *Congress voted more funds for the defense budget.* **2** A balanced budget is a financial plan in which expenses are no greater than income.
budget /ˈbʌdʒ·ət/ *v* [I/T] **1** to plan to spend money for a particular purpose ○ [T] *They budgeted $6000 for property taxes this year.* **2** To budget is also to plan how to use something of which you have a limited supply: [T] *You will have to learn how to budget your time to get all your work done.*
budgetary /ˈbʌdʒ·əˌter·i/ *adj* [not gradable] ○ *In this day and age of budgetary constraints who is going to pay for all of this?*
budget deficit *n* [C] ***politics & government*** The difference between a government's income and how much it spends.
CHEAP /ˈbʌdʒ·ət/ *adj* [not gradable] low in price; cheap ○ *Budget airlines have forced major airlines to lower some of their prices.*

buff MAKE SHINE /bʌf/ *v* [T] to rub a surface with a soft material to make it shine ○ *First you apply the wax to the floor, let it dry, and then buff it.*
PERSON /bʌf/ *n* [C] *infml* a person who is very interested in a subject and knows a lot about it ○ *a history/movie buff*
STRONG /bʌf/ *adj infml* having a strong, healthy body with well-developed muscles ○ *During her stage show, the lithe, buff artist dances through two hours of 26 songs and 9 costume changes.*

buffalo /ˈbʌf·əˌloʊ/ *n* [C] *pl* **buffaloes, buffalo** any of various large animals of the cattle family found in Africa, Asia, and North America ○ *The huge herds of buffalo on the Great Plains of the west were hunted almost to extinction.*

buffer /ˈbʌf·ər/ *n* [C] something that helps protect from harm ○ [C] *Some people buy stocks as a buffer against inflation.*

buffer zone *n* [C] an area of land that separates two other areas and that is designed to prevent fighting or harm coming to something ○ *There is a buffer zone between the wildlife sanctuary and the area where people live.*

buffet MEAL /bəˈfeɪ, buːˈfeɪ/ *n* [C] a meal where people serve themselves food that is arranged on a table ○ *Will it be a buffet or a sit-down meal?*

HIT /ˈbʌf·ət/ *v* [T] to hit something or someone repeatedly and, usually, hard ○ *Many fierce storms had buffeted the coast before, but this one was worse than usual.*

buffoon /bəˈfuːn/ *n* [C] a person who does silly things, sometimes intentionally, that make other people laugh ○ *He was not the buffoon that people said he was.*

bug **INSECT** /bʌg/ *n* [C] **1** an insect ○ *Some tiny white bugs had eaten the leaves of my house plants.* **2** A bug is also a small organism that causes an illness: *The flu bug is going around, and almost everyone is sick.*

buggy /ˈbʌg·i/ *adj* full of annoying bugs ○ *It's too buggy to eat outside this time of year.*

FAULT /bʌg/ *n* [C] a mistake or problem in the way something works ○ *He said they had eliminated all the bugs in the software, and we hoped this was true.*

DEVICE /bʌg/ *n* [C] a small device that is easily hidden, used to record people's conversations without their knowledge

bug /bʌg/ *v* [T] **-gg-** ○ *She suspected that her phone had been bugged.*

ANNOY /bʌg/ *v* [T] **-gg-** *infml* to annoy someone repeatedly ○ *My lawyer is bugging me for stuff I just don't have.*

ENTHUSIASM /bʌg/ *n* [U] *infml* a strong enthusiasm for something ○ *When I was about 17, I was bitten by the acting bug and began to try out for parts.*

bugle /ˈbjuː·gəl/ *n* [C] a small BRASS musical instrument, used esp. in the military, played by blowing into it

build **MAKE** /bɪld/ *v* [I/T] *past* **built** to make a structure or something else by putting materials together in a particular way ○ [T] *Without a plan, you can't build a house.* ○ [T] *Some owls had built a nest in the chimney.* ○ [I] *We decided to build on high ground, above the river.*

builder /ˈbɪl·dər/ *n* [C] ○ *There's a lot of pressure on real estate brokers and home builders to hold down costs.*

DEVELOP /bɪld/ *v* [T] *past* **built** to develop something ○ *They were able to build a family business.* ○ *She was building a reputation as a designer.*

BODY /bɪld/ *n* [C] the particular form of someone's body ○ *He was short, with a muscular build.*

WORD FAMILY build			
Nouns	build builder building	*Verbs*	build rebuild

PHRASAL VERBS with build

• **build** *something* **around** *something* to develop something based on a certain idea or goal ○ *Most people should build their investments around stocks with moderately above-average growth.*

• **build in** *something* [M] to include something when you are making or building a new thing ○ *You must build in some way to cancel this contract if things don't work out.* ○ *We have to be real careful about trying to build that in from the front end.* ○ Related adjective: BUILT-IN

• **build** *something* **into** *something* to include something when something is first created ○ *We have built new safety systems into the software design.*

• **build up** *something* **INCREASE** [M] to cause something to increase or become greater ○ *She does exercises daily to build up her strength.* ○ *We tried to build his confidence up.* ○ Related noun: BUILDUP INCREASE

• **build up** *something* **PRAISE** [M] to praise someone or something, esp. to increase the popularity of that person or thing ○ *The ads built up the show, but it wasn't really that good.* ○ Related noun: BUILDUP PRAISE

building /ˈbɪl·dɪŋ/ *n* [C/U] **1** a structure with walls and a roof, such as a house or factory, to give protection to people, animals, or things ○ [C] *an apartment/office building* ○ [C] *Many buildings were badly damaged or destroyed by the earthquake.* **2** Building is also the activity or business of putting together structures with walls and a roof.

buildup **INCREASE** /ˈbɪl·dʌp/ *n* [C] an increase in number or amount ○ *They're concerned about the buildup of carbon dioxide in the atmosphere.* ○ Related verb: BUILD UP INCREASE

PRAISE /ˈbɪl·dʌp/ *n* [C] praise that is intended to increase popularity ○ *The circus always gets a big buildup when it comes to town.* ○ Related verb: BUILD UP PRAISE

built **BUILD** /bɪlt/ *past simple and past participle of* BUILD

BODY TYPE /bɪlt/ *adj* (of someone's body) having a particular body type, or *slang* being very attractive ○ *He was built like an athlete.*

built-in /ˈbɪlˈtɪn/ *adj* [not gradable] included in something at the time that it is created ○ *Built-in bookcases lined the walls of the library.* ○ *With this software, safeguards are built-in.* ○ Related verb: BUILD IN

bulb **LIGHT** /bʌlb/ *n* [C] a LIGHT BULB ○ *The bulb burned out in the kitchen.*

PLANT /bʌlb/ *n* [C] a ball-like root from which some plants grow ○ *Lilies and tulips grow from bulbs.*

bulge /bʌldʒ/ *v* [I] **1** to stick out or be swollen ○ *The girl's cheek bulged with a wad of gum.* **2** If you say that someone's eyes bulge, you mean that the person's eyes are opened wide, esp. because the person is frightened, surprised, or excited.

bulge /bʌldʒ/ *n* [C] ○ *The bulge in his pocket showed where he kept his wallet.*

bulimia (nervosa) /bjuːˈliː·miː·ə (nərˈvoʊ·sə), -ˈlɪm·iː·ə/ *n* [U] *medical* a condition in which a person eats extremely large amounts of food in a short time and then vomits intentionally ○ *Bulimia is really an eating disorder, and it affects mostly females.* ○ Compare ANOREXIA (NERVOSA)

bulk Ⓐ /bʌlk/ *n* [U] **1** something very large, or a large amount, not divided into smaller parts ○ *Tankers carry bulk shipments of oil.* ○ *We buy a lot of our groceries in bulk* (= in large quantities) *to save* money. **2** The bulk of something is the larger part of it: *He gave the bulk of his paintings to the museum.*

bulky Ⓐ /ˈbʌl·ki/ *adj* ○ *She carried a very bulky package on the bus.*

bull ANIMAL /bʊl/ *n* [C] the male of various animals, such as cattle ○ *Our herd has two bulls and twenty cows.*

NONSENSE /bʊl/ *n* [U] *infml* nonsense or a lie ○ *Don't give me that bull about not getting my message.*

bulldog /ˈbʊl·dɔːg/ *n* [C] a type of dog that looks fierce, with a strong body, short legs, a flat nose, and a large, square face

bulldozer /ˈbʊlˌdoʊ·zər/ *n* [C] a heavy vehicle with a large blade in front used for moving dirt and rocks and making the ground level

bulldoze /ˈbʊl·doʊz/ *v* [T] ○ *Several homes will have to be bulldozed to make room for the highway expansion.*

bullet /ˈbʊl·ət/ *n* [C] a small, metal object that is fired from a gun

bulletin /ˈbʊl·ət·ən, -ə·tən/ *n* [C] a short piece of news on television or radio, or a short report or news item released by an organization ○ *The museum publishes a monthly bulletin about coming events.*

bulletin board *n* [C] a board on a wall for putting up notices

bulletproof /ˈbʊl·ətˌpruːf/ *adj* able to prevent bullets from going through ○ *The limo has bulletproof glass.*

bullfight /ˈbʊl·fɑɪt/ *n* [C] a traditional public entertainment in some countries where a person fights a BULL, sometimes killing it with a sword

bullfighter /ˈbʊlˌfɑɪţ·ər/ *n* [C]

bullhorn /ˈbʊl·hɔːrn/ *n* [C] an electric-powered, cone-shaped device that makes your voice louder when you speak into it

bullion /ˈbʊl·jən/ *n* [U] pure gold or silver formed into bars ○ *A shipment of gold bullion was stolen.*

bullish /ˈbʊl·ɪʃ/ *adj* (of markets and investments) with prices rising, or (of people) expecting good things, esp. of business ○ *She's bullish on high-tech companies.*

bull market /ˈbʊl ˈmɑr·kət/ *n* [U] a period when financial investments are rising in value ○ Compare BEAR MARKET

bullpen /ˈbʊl·pen/ *n* [C] (in baseball) a place near the playing area where PITCHERS can throw the ball to get ready to play in the game

bull's-eye /ˈbʊl·zɑɪ/ *n* [C] the center inside a number of circles that you want to hit when shooting or playing particular games, or the shot or throw that hits this inner circle

bully /ˈbʊl·i/ *v* [T] to threaten to hurt someone, often frightening that person into doing something ○ *He managed to bully her into giving him her car.*

bully /ˈbʊl·i/ *n* [C] ○ *Teachers usually know who the bullies are in a class.*

bum PERSON /bʌm/ *n* [C] *disapproving* **1** a person who gets money by asking other people for it **2** *infml* A bum is also someone who treats other people badly: *Mike called him a bum for throwing gum at a fan.*

bum /bʌm/ *v* [T] **-mm-** to ask someone for esp. money or food with no intention of paying for them ○ *Could I bum a couple of bucks from somebody?*

USELESS /bʌm/ *adj slang* useless or not to be trusted to perform well ○ *He's got a bum knee from playing football.*

bumblebee /ˈbʌm·bəlˌbiː/ *n* [C] a large, hairy bee

bumbling /ˈbʌm·blɪŋ/ *adj* confused, esp. in the way someone moves or speaks ○ *The players look like bumbling idiots on the field.*

bummer /ˈbʌm·ər/ *n* [C] *slang* a situation or event that is unpleasant or disappointing ○ *Waiting all day at the airport is a real bummer.*

bump RAISED AREA /bʌmp/ *n* [C] a raised area on a surface ○ *The mosquito bites left bumps on her face.*

bumpy /ˈbʌm·pi/ *adj* rough or uneven ○ *We drove along bumpy dirt roads for hours.*

HIT /bʌmp/ *v* [I/T] to hit against something or someone, esp. by accident ○ [T] *The child fell and bumped his head.*

PUSH AWAY /bʌmp/ *v* [T] to move someone or something from a place, rank, or job ○ *I knew if they got someone more qualified, I'd be bumped.*

PHRASAL VERBS with bump

• **bump into** *someone* to meet someone unexpectedly ○ *We bumped into Kayla in a shop.*

• **bump off** *someone* [M] *slang* to kill a person ○ *They think someone bumped him off.*

bumper VEHICLE PART /ˈbʌm·pər/ *n* [C] a bar at the front and back of the body of a motor vehicle that keeps it from being damaged when hit

LARGE /ˈbʌm·pər/ *adj* [not gradable] unusually large ○ *Farmers expect a bumper corn crop this year.*

IDIOM with bumper

• **bumper to bumper** with almost no space between one car and the next in a line of cars ○ *The traffic was bumper to bumper all the way home.*

bumper sticker *n* [C] a small sign on a car BUMPER that expresses an opinion or tells a joke

bum rap *n* [C usually sing] *slang* a false or unfair accusation ○ *It's a bum rap to say we didn't try to win.*

bum steer *n* [C usually sing] *slang* bad advice ○ *Someone gave us a bum steer to a hotel that was awful.*

bun **BREAD** /bʌn/ *n* [C] a small, round piece of bread, used for a sandwich, or a small, round, sweet bread ○ *Buy some hamburger buns for supper.*
KNOT /bʌn/ *n* [C] hair arranged into a round knot at the back of the head

bunch /bʌntʃ/ *n* [C] a number of things of the same type fastened or closely grouped together, or any particular group of things or people ○ *We ate a whole bunch of grapes.* ○ *They're a nice bunch of people.* ○ *(infml) I've got a bunch of things to do.*
bunch /bʌntʃ/ *v* [I/T] to pull together or gather into a unit ○ [I] *Beth sat in bed with pillows bunched behind her, reading.*

bundle **GROUP** /ˈbʌn·dəl/ *n* [C] **1** a number of things that are fastened or held together ○ *He carried bundles of newspapers to the garage.* **2** *infml* A bundle is also a large amount of money: *When they sold their house, they made a bundle.*
bundle /ˈbʌn·dəl/ *v* [T] ○ [I/T] *We're supposed to bundle magazines before throwing them away.*
MOVE QUICKLY /ˈbʌn·dəl/ *v* [always + adv/prep] to cause someone to move quickly ○ [I] *We bundled into the car.* ○ [T] *Every morning I bundled the children off to school.*

IDIOM with **bundle**

• **a bundle of nerves** someone who is extremely nervous ○ *Since the robbery, I've been a bundle of nerves.*

PHRASAL VERB with **bundle**

• **bundle up** to wear enough clothing to keep very warm ○ *You'd better bundle up because it's below freezing outside.*

bungalow /ˈbʌŋ·gəˌloʊ/ *n* [C] a small house all on one level

bungle /ˈbʌŋ·gəl/ *v* [T] to do something badly, or spoil something ○ *The police bungled the investigation.*

bunion /ˈbʌn·jən/ *n* [C] a painful swelling on the main joint of the big toe

bunk **BED** /bʌŋk/ *n* [C] either of two beds arranged one above the other ○ *I had the lower bunk, and my older brother had the upper bunk.*
NONSENSE /bʌŋk/ *n* [U] *infml* complete nonsense, or something that is meant to deceive ○ *Most doctors think his theories are bunk.*

bunker /ˈbʌŋ·kər/ *n* [C] an underground shelter used as protection from bombs

bunny (rabbit) /ˈbʌn·i (ˈræb·ət)/ *n* [C] *a child's word* a rabbit

buns /bʌnz/ *pl n slang* the buttocks

buoy **OBJECT IN WATER** /ˈbuː·i, bɔɪ/ *n* [C] an object that floats on the water to show ships where it is safe to go
buoyancy /ˈbɔɪ·ən·si, ˈbuː·jən-/ *n* [U] the ability to float ○ *We tested different materials for buoyancy.*
FEEL HAPPY /ˈbuː·i, bɔɪ/ *v* [T] to encourage or make someone feel better ○ *I was really buoyed by the nice comments on my work.*
buoyant /ˈbɔɪ·ənt, ˈbuː·jənt/ *adj* ○ *It was her wedding day, and she was in a buoyant mood.*

burden /ˈbɜrd·ən/ *n* [C] a duty or responsibility that is hard to bear ○ *I don't want to be a burden on my children.*
burden /ˈbɜrd·ən/ *v* [T] ○ *He was burdened with debts.*

burden of proof *n* [U] *law* the responsibility for proving that something is true

bureau **DEPARTMENT** /ˈbjʊr·oʊ/ *n* [C] a department of government, or a division that performs a particular job ○ *You've got to go to the Bureau of Motor Vehicles to renew your driver's license.*
FURNITURE /ˈbjʊr·oʊ/ *n* [C] a CHEST OF DRAWERS

bureaucracy /bjʊˈrɑk·rə·si/ *n* [C/U] ***politics & government*** **1** the officials, employees, and people who run government departments and offices, or similar officers and employees who manage the details of operating a large business ○ [C] *The city's bureaucracy is almost unmanageable.* **2** *disapproving* Bureaucracy is also official rules that make it difficult to do things: [U] *The president wants to add more bureaucracy to our daily lives.*
bureaucrat /ˈbjʊr·əˌkræt/ *n* [C] a member of a bureaucracy ○ *School administrators, she said, who are the on-the-spot bureaucrats, should make these decisions rather than Washington bureaucrats.*
bureaucratic /ˌbjʊr·əˈkræţ·ɪk/ *adj* ○ *Bureaucratic bungling is the most likely explanation for things going wrong.*

burette /byʊˈret/ *n* [C] a glass tube with measurements marked on it and with a small FAUCET at the bottom, used for adding small amounts of liquid to something

burgeoning /ˈbɜr·dʒə·nɪŋ/ *adj* growing or developing quickly ○ *A burgeoning tourist industry lifted the state's economy.*

burger /ˈbɜr·gər/ *n* [C] *short form of* HAMBURGER

burglar /ˈbɜr·glər/ *n* [C] a person who illegally enters a building by force to steal things
burglarize /ˈbɜr·gləˌrɑɪz/, *infml* **burgle** /ˈbɜr·gəl/ *v* [T] ○ *The doctor's office was burglarized, according to police.*
burglary /ˈbɜr·glə·ri/ *n* [C/U] ○ [C] *He committed more than a dozen burglaries in the last year.*

burial /ˈber·iː·əl/ *n* [C/U] the act of putting a dead body into the ground, or the ceremony performed when this is done ○ [C] *We went back to Minnesota for my uncle's burial.* ○ Related verb: BURY

burial ground *n* [C] an area of land where bodies are buried

burlap /ˈbɜr·læp/ *n* [U] a type of strong, rough cloth, used to make bags and as a covering for something ○ *a burlap bag* ○ *Large plants are wrapped in burlap to protect them from ice.*

burly /ˈbɜr·li/ *adj* (of a person) large and strong ○ *Two burly men pushed the car to the side of the road.*

B

burn BE IN FLAMES /bɜrn/ *v* [I/T] *past* **burned, burnt 1** to produce flames and heat ○ [I] *A fire still burned in the fireplace.* **2** If something burns a fuel, it uses that fuel to produce energy: [I] *Some new fuels burn more efficiently than gasoline.* ○ [M] *Running is a good way to burn off calories.*

burner /ˈbɜr·nər/ *n* [C] anything that produces controlled flames for cooking, or heat for a building

burning /ˈbɜr·nɪŋ/ *adj* [not gradable] **1** hot, or flaming ○ *Fire engines surrounded the burning house.* **2** *fig.* Burning also means of extreme interest or importance: *Building the new school is a burning local issue.* ○ *You have to have a burning desire to win.*

HURT BY FIRE /bɜrn/ *v* [T] *past* **burned, burnt 1** to hurt, damage, or destroy something by fire or extreme heat ○ *She burned her hand on the hot iron.* ○ *People still burn trash although it's illegal.* ○ *The toast was burned to a crisp* (= burned until it was black). **2** *infml* If you are burned by an activity, you are hurt emotionally or financially because of it: *He got burned in an investment and lost a lot of money.*

burn /bɜrn/ *n* [C] ○ *One worker had severe burns on his face and hands.*

WORD FAMILY burn			
Nouns	burn burner	*Adjectives* *Verbs*	burning burn

PHRASAL VERBS with burn

• **burn down** *(something)* [M] to destroy something with fire, or to be destroyed in this way ○ *They weren't injured, but their house burned down.*

• **burn off** *something* [M] **1** to remove something by burning it ○ *Until recently these countries were burning off gas they could not use or sell.* **2** If you burn off pounds or something that you have eaten, you do exercise: *We eat too much and don't burn it off with enough exercise.*

• **burn out** *(something)* **DAMAGE FROM HEAT** [M] to stop working because of damage from heat ○ *When we lost power, many refrigerators and air conditioners burned out.*

• **burn out** *(someone)* **LOSE ENERGY** [M] to cause someone to lose energy and enthusiasm, either from stress or because the person is working too hard ○ *They asked her to slow down because they don't want her to burn out.* ○ Related noun: BURNOUT

• **burn up** *something* **DESTROY** [M] to destroy something with fire ○ *A huge fire burned up the building.*

• **burn up** *someone* **ANGER** [M] to make someone angry ○ *I was really burned up by her comment.*

burnout /ˈbɜr·nɑʊt/ *n* [C/U] the state of having no energy or enthusiasm because of working too hard, or someone who shows the effects of this state ○ [U] *We have found there is much more burnout and sickness among those who don't get help.* ○ [C] *The drummer walked in looking like a rock and roll burnout.* ○ Related verb: BURN OUT LOSE ENERGY

burnt /bɜrnt/ *past simple and past participle of* BURN

burp /bɜrp/ *v* [I/T] **1** to force air from the stomach to come out through the mouth with a noise; BELCH **2** If you burp a baby, you help it to get rid of air in its stomach by gently rubbing or gently hitting its back.

burp /bɜrp/ *n* [C] ○ *The baby gave a contented burp.*

burrito /bəˈriːt̬·oʊ/ *n* [C] *pl* **burritos** a type of food originally from Mexico that is made by folding a TORTILLA (= thin, round piece of bread) and putting esp. meat or beans inside it

burrow /ˈbɜr·oʊ, ˈbʌ·roʊ/ *n* [C] a hole dug in the ground that an animal, such as a rabbit, lives in

burrow /ˈbɜr·oʊ, ˈbʌ·roʊ/ *v* [I always + adv/prep] ○ *Moles burrowed under our lawn.*

bursar /ˈbɜr·sər/ *n* [C] the person in a university or school who is responsible for its finances

burst /bɜrst/ *v* [I/T] *past* **burst 1** to break open or apart suddenly, or to cause something to break open or apart ○ [I] *Fireworks burst across the night sky.* ○ [T] *I thought I might have burst a blood vessel.* **2** *fig.* A person who is bursting is extremely eager or enthusiastic: [I] *I was bursting with excitement.*

burst /bɜrst/ *n* [C] a sudden, brief increase in something, or a short appearance of something ○ *With a burst of speed, the horse won easily.*

IDIOM with burst

• **bursting at the seams** extremely full ○ *When the whole family comes home, the house is bursting at the seams.*

PHRASAL VERB with burst

• **burst in/into** *(somewhere)* to enter a place suddenly or unexpectedly ○ *In the middle of writing class the head of the English department burst in with a note.*

• **burst into** *something* to begin to produce something ○ *I burst into tears.* ○ *The car burst into flames.*

• **burst out** to begin to do something ○ *Everyone burst out laughing.*

bury /ˈber·i/ *v* [T] **1** to put a dead body into the ground ○ *My father is buried in Kentucky.* **2** To bury something is also to put it into the ground: *Squirrels bury nuts and dig them up later to eat them.* **3** To bury something is also to hide it or to make it difficult to find: *She buried her face in her hands.* ○ *The article was buried in the middle of the newspaper.* ○ Related noun: BURIAL

WORD FAMILY bury			
Nouns	burial	*Adjectives*	buried
Verbs	bury		

IDIOM with bury

• **bury the hatchet** to agree to end the disagreement that has divided two people or groups ○ *After years of fighting over who should have gotten Dad's money, my brothers finally buried the hatchet.*

bus VEHICLE /bʌs/ *n* [C] a large motor vehicle with seats for many people ○ *The tour bus was the easiest way to see the area.*
bus /bʌs/ *v* [T] to take people to a place in a bus ○ *The governor bused supporters to the capital for his inauguration.*

SERVE /bʌs/ *v* [T] to move dishes to and from tables in a restaurant as a job ○ *I started out busing tables.*

busboy /ˈbʌs·bɔɪ/ *n* [C] a person who helps in a restaurant, esp. by carrying dishes, passing out bread, and filling water glasses

bush PLANT /bʊʃ/ *n* [C] a low plant with many small branches ○ *The smell of lilac bushes in bloom reminds me of home.* ○ *The meadow was covered with small bushes and grass.*

AREA OF LAND /bʊʃ/ *n* [U] (esp. in Australia and Africa) an area of land covered with bushes and trees that has never been farmed and where few people live ○ *If you live in the bush, a small plane is the best means of transportation.*

bushed /bʊʃt/ *adj infml* very tired ○ *I mowed the lawn this morning, and now I'm bushed.*

bushel /ˈbʊʃ·əl/ *n* [C] a unit of measurement of volume of dry products equal to 32 quarts, or approximately 35.2 liters

bushy /ˈbʊʃ·i/ *adj* (of hair or fur) thick or full ○ *A lot of his face was hidden behind a bushy moustache.*

busily /ˈbɪz·ə·li/ *adv* ○ See at BUSY

business BUYING AND SELLING /ˈbɪz·nəs, -nəz/ *n* [C/U] **1** the activity of buying and selling goods and services, or a particular company that does this, or work in general rather than pleasure ○ [C] *He runs a dry cleaning business.* ○ [U] *I'm in Baltimore on business.* ○ [U] *Our firm does a lot of business with overseas customers.* ○ [U] *She's going into business* (= starting a business) *as a management consultant.* ○ [U] *How's business?* **2** Business is also the degree of success of a company or of your work: [U] *Business has been good.*

A MATTER /ˈbɪz·nəs, -nəz/ *n* [U] a matter or a situation ○ *I have some business to settle with Mr. Redford.* ○ *Preparing your taxes can be a tricky business.*

THINGS YOU DO /ˈbɪz·nəs, -nəz/ *n* [U] the things that you do or the matters that relate only to you ○ *What she does after work is her own business.* ○ *When I asked him what he was doing, he told me it was none of my business* (= it did not involve me).

IDIOMS with **business**

• **business as usual** the state of continuing in the usual way ○ *Today is officially a holiday, but it's business as usual around here.*
• **in business** able to start doing something that you had planned ○ *Once we get the computer installed we'll be in business.*

businesslike /ˈbɪz·nəsˌlɑɪk, -nəz-/ *adj* happening in a way that is practical and effective and is not personal, or typical of business ○ *We hope the meeting can be conducted in a businesslike way, without a lot of emotional statements.*

businessman /ˈbɪz·nəs·mən, -nəz-, -ˌmæn/ *n* [C] *pl* **-men** *male* a man who works in business, esp. one with a job in a company

business people, **businesspeople** /ˈbɪz·nəs ˌpiː·pəl, -nəz-/ *pl n* people of medium and high rank who work in businesses ○ *He told the New York Times that businesspeople are more frightened by trial lawyers than by terrorists.*

businesswoman /ˈbɪz·nəsˌwʊm·ən, -nəz-/ *n* [C] *pl* **-women** *female* a woman who works in business, esp. one with a job in a company

bust BREAK /bʌst/ *v* [I/T] *infml* **1** to burst or break something ○ [I always + adv/prep] *He busted out laughing.* ○ [M] *The cops had to bust the door down.* **2** *slang* A person who is busted is caught doing something wrong, esp. caught by the police and accused of a crime.
bust /bʌst/ *n* [C] *slang* an occasion when people are caught by the police and accused of a crime

STATUE /bʌst/ *n* [C] a statue of the upper part of a person's body ○ *a bust of George Washington*

BREASTS /bʌst/ *n* [C] a woman's breasts, or the measurement around a woman's body at the level of her breasts

bustle /ˈbʌs·əl/ *v* [I] to do things in a hurried and busy way ○ *Thomas bustled around the apartment, getting everything ready.*
bustle /ˈbʌs·əl/ *n* [U] busy activity ○ *the bustle of the downtown business district*

busy /ˈbɪz·i/ *adj* [-er/-est only] **1** (of a person) actively involved in doing something or having a lot of things to do, or (of a time or place) when or where a lot of things are happening ○ *a busy street* ○ *the busy summer months* ○ *I've been so busy lately that I haven't had time to have any social life.* ○ *Getting the house ready for her relatives kept her busy the whole day.* **2** If a telephone is busy, it is being used by someone else: *Her line is still busy.*n
busy /ˈbɪz·i/ *v* [T] ○ *Aimee busied herself with a favorite book.*
busily /ˈbɪz·ə·li/ *adv*

busybody /ˈbɪz·iːˌbɑd·i/ *n* [C] *disapproving* a person who is interested in things that do not involve him or her, esp. other people's private matters

busy signal *n* [C usually sing] a sound that means that the telephone you are calling is being used

but DIFFERENCE /bʌt, bət/ *conjunction* used to express a difference or to introduce an added statement ○ *You can take Route 14 to get there, but it may take you a little longer.* ○ *We enjoyed our vacation a lot, but it was expensive.*
buts /bʌts/ *pl n* an excuse or an argument against something ○ *No buts about it – you're going to school today.*

EXCEPT /bʌt, bət/ *prep* except ○ *Nobody but John was willing to talk to her.* ○ *This car has been nothing but trouble – it's always breaking down!*

butcher /ˈbʊtʃ·ər/ *n* [C] **1** a person whose job is to kill animals for meat or who prepares and sells meat in a store **2** A butcher is also a murderer, esp. of a lot of people.

B

butcher /ˈbʊtʃ·ər/ *v* [T] **1** to kill animals and prepare them to be sold as meat **2** To butcher is also to kill people in a cruel way.

butler /ˈbʌt·lər/ *n* [C] the most important male servant in a house ○ *The British butler was brilliantly played by Anthony Hopkins.*

butt THICK END /bʌt/ *n* [C] the thick end of something, esp. a RIFLE (= type of gun)

CIGARETTE /bʌt/ *n* [C] the part of a cigarette that is left after smoking

BOTTOM /bʌt/ *n* [C] *slang* a person's bottom

HIT /bʌt/ *v* [I/T] to hit the head hard against something, or to have the heads of two people or animals hit against each other ○ [T] (*fig.*) *She often butted heads with school officials in disagreements over her teaching methods.*

PERSON /bʌt/ *n* [C usually sing] a person who is joked about or laughed at ○ *He was fed up with being the butt of their jokes.*

PHRASAL VERBS with butt

• **butt in** *infml* to interrupt ○ *Sorry to butt in on you like this, but there's an important call.*
• **butt out** *slang* to stop being involved in something ○ *This is none of your business, so butt out.*

butte /bjuːt/ *n* [C] a hill that has steep sides and a flat top

butter /ˈbʌt̬·ər/ *n* [U] a pale yellow, fatty solid made from cream that is spread on bread or used in cooking

PHRASAL VERB with butter

• **butter up** *someone* [M] to please someone, esp. by praising that person in order to get him or her to agree to something ○ *A company wishing to influence the government must butter up both parties in the House and the Senate.*

buttercup /ˈbʌt̬·ərˌkʌp/ *n* [C] a small, yellow flower

butterfly /ˈbʌt̬·ərˌflɑɪ/ *n* [C] a type of flying insect with four large, often brightly colored wings

IDIOM with butterfly

• **butterflies in** *your* **stomach** a feeling of being very nervous or frightened about something ○ *I'm meeting her parents tonight, and I have a bad case of butterflies in my stomach.*

buttermilk /ˈbʌt̬·ərˌmɪlk/ *n* [U] the liquid that is left after taking the fat from milk or cream to make butter

butterscotch /ˈbʌt̬·ərˌskɑtʃ/ *n* [C/U] a hard, yellow-brown candy made by boiling butter, brown sugar, and water together, or a flavoring that tastes like this candy

buttock /ˈbʌt̬·ək/ *n* [C usually pl] either of the two soft parts of the body below the back that supports the body when sitting

button CLOTHING FASTENER /ˈbʌt·ᵊn/ *n* [C] **1** a small, usually circular object that is sewn on a shirt, coat, or other piece of clothing, and is used to fasten it **2** A button is also a small, usually circular sign that you can pin on your clothes: *When you pay the admission fee at the museum, they give you a button to wear to show you've paid.*
button /ˈbʌt·ᵊn/ *v* [T] ○ *He buttoned his shirt.*

OBJECT YOU PRESS /ˈbʌt·ᵊn/ *n* [C] a small object that you press to operate a device or a machine ○ *The button on the left starts the tape recorder and the one on the right stops it.*

button-down *adj* [not gradable] (of a shirt) having a collar that has the pointed ends fastened to the shirt by buttons

buttonhole HOLE FOR BUTTON /ˈbʌt·ᵊnˌhoʊl/ *n* [C] a narrow hole that a button is pushed through to fasten a shirt, coat, etc.

MAKE SOMEONE LISTEN /ˈbʌt·ᵊnˌhoʊl/ *v* [T] to stop someone and make the person listen to you

BUTTERFLY

○ *They took out newspaper ads and buttonholed politicians to lobby for the change.*

buttress /ˈbʌ·trəs/ *v* [T] ***art*** to give support to or strengthen something ○ *He looked for things that would buttress the prosecution case and win a conviction.*

buttress /ˈbʌ·trəs/ *n* [C] a structure made of stone or brick that sticks out from and supports a wall of a building

buy PAY FOR /bɑɪ/ *v* [T] *past* **bought** to obtain something by paying money for it ○ *She was saving to buy a car.* ○ *He bought some flowers for his girlfriend.*

buy /bɑɪ/ *n* [C] an occasion in which you pay less for something than what it is worth, and are therefore pleased ○ *The rug turned out to be quite a buy.*

buyer /ˈbɑɪ·ər/ *n* [C] a person who pays money for something, or a person whose job is to decide what goods will be brought into a store for sale ○ *He's still looking for a buyer for his house.*

WORD CHOICES buy

Get is a common word that can be used instead of "buy."

*I need to go to the supermarket and **get** some bread.*

Purchase is a formal word that means the same as "buy."

*Tickets must be **purchased** two weeks in advance.*

If a country buys products from another country, you could use the verb **import**.

*We **import** a large number of cars from Japan.*

The phrasal verb **buy up** can be used when someone buys everything that is available.

*He **bought up** all the land in the area.*

If someone buys something quickly and enthusiastically because it is cheap or exactly what is wanted, you could use **snap up**.

*The tickets for the concert were all **snapped up** within two hours of going on sale.*

Stock up on is often used when people buy large amounts of something so that they have it when they need it.

*People are **stocking up on** supplies in anticipation of the hurricane.*

If you **pick** something **up**, you buy it very cheaply.

*I **picked up** lots of bargains during the sales.*

Invest in could be used when you buy something that you think will be useful even if it is expensive.

*We've decided it's time to **invest in** a new computer.*

If you **splurge on** something, you buy it even though you do not need it.

*I **splurged on** a new outfit for the wedding.*

If you offer to buy something for another person, you could use the verb **treat**.

*I'll **treat** you to a cup of coffee.*

BELIEVE /bɑɪ/ *v* [T] *past* **bought** *infml* to believe that something is true ○ *She'll never buy that story about having to take care of your sick grandmother.*

IDIOM with buy

• **buy time** to do something that allows you to have more time to finish something ○ *He tried to buy time by saying he wasn't feeling well.*

PHRASAL VERBS with buy

• **buy into** *something* **1** to buy a part of a business in order to have some control over it ○ *They bought into a software company.* **2** If you buy into an idea or plan, you give it your support or agree with it: *Parents are expected to buy into the school's philosophy when they enroll their children.*

• **buy off** *someone* [M] to give someone money so that person will help you or let you do something that is not legal ○ *A well-known business executive had bought off government inspectors.*

• **buy out** *someone* [M] to give someone money so that you own the part of a business that previously belonged to that person ○ *She bought out her partner and now she owns the whole company.* ○ Related verb: BUYOUT

• **buy up** *something* [M] to buy large amounts of something, or all that is available ○ *He bought up all the land in the surrounding area.*

buyout /ˈbɑɪ·ɑʊt/ *n* [C] the act of buying all or part of a company from the people who own it ○ *The law firm was active in management buyouts, mergers, and acquisitions.* ○ Related verb: BUY OUT

buzz MAKE SOUND /bʌz/ *v* [I/T] **1** to make a continuous, low sound such as the sound some insects make, or to move quickly while making this sound ○ [I] *Something was buzzing around me as I tried to sleep.* **2** Someone who buzzes you calls you by using a device that makes a low, continuous sound: [T] *All were expected to run, literally, into McLaughlin's office whenever he buzzed them.*

buzz /bʌz/ *n* [C usually sing] **1** *the buzz of conversation* **2** *infml* A buzz is also a telephone call: *I'll give you a buzz early next week.*

buzzer /ˈbʌz·ər/ *n* [C] a device that makes a low, continuous sound

BE FILLED WITH /bʌz/ *v* [I] to be filled with excitement, activity, or sounds ○ *The place was buzzing with excitement.*

buzzard /ˈbʌz·ərd/ *n* [C] a large North American bird that eats the flesh of dead animals; a VULTURE

buzzword /ˈbʌz·wɜrd/ *n* [C] a word or expression that is very often used, esp. in public discussions, because it represents opinions that are popular ○ *"Listening to the people" was the buzz word among politicians.*

by CAUSE /bɑɪ/ *prep* used to show the person or thing that causes something to happen or to exist ○ *The car was driven by a short, bald man.* ○ *I'm reading some short stories by Chekhov.* ○ *I took her umbrella by mistake.*

METHOD /bɑɪ/ *prep* used to show how something is done ○ *They thought about flying to Boston but decided to go by car.* ○ *She did the repair work by herself* (= without help). ○ *Do you want to be paid in cash or by check?* ○ *He learned English by listening to the radio.*

B

ACCORDING TO /bɑɪ/ *prep* according to ○ *By my watch, it's 2 o'clock.* ○ *The students were listed by name.*

NOT LATER THAN /bɑɪ/ *prep* not later than; at or before ○ *She promised to be back by 10 p.m.*

MEASUREMENT /bɑɪ/ *prep* used to show measurements or amounts ○ *Their wages increased by 12%.* ○ *The room measures 15 feet by 20 feet.*

DURING /bɑɪ/ *prep* during ○ *We traveled by night and rested by day.*

NEAR /bɑɪ/ *prep, adv* [not gradable] near, beside, or (in distance or time) past ○ *A small child stood quietly by her side.* ○ *Claire waved as she drove by.* ○ *As time went by, she became more attached to him.*

IDIOMS with by

• **by all means** yes, certainly ○ *"Could I have a glass of water, please?" "By all means – I'll get it for you."*
• **by and large** generally ○ *By and large, the people of this state are not happy with the governor's policies.*
• **by heart** exactly and from your memory ○ *She baked muffins from recipes she knew by heart.*
• **by hook or by crook** using any method possible ○ *We'll get there by hook or by crook.*
• **by the book** exactly according to rules or the law ○ *The lawyers want to make sure we've done everything strictly by the book.*
• **by the same token** because of this same situation or condition ○ *You want to store things, but by the same token, you want to be able to find them again.*

bye /bɑɪ/ *exclamation* short form of GOODBYE

bye-bye /bɑɪ 'bɑɪ/ *exclamation* GOODBYE

bygone /'bɑɪ·gɔːn/ *adj* [not gradable] belonging to or happening in a past time ○ *The empty factories are relics of a bygone era.*

byline /'bɑɪ·lɑɪn/ *n* [C] the writer's name at the top of a newspaper or magazine article

bypass /'bɑɪ·pæs/ *v* [T] to avoid something by going around it ○ *Take the highway that bypasses Richmond to avoid heavy traffic.* ○ (*fig.*) *Posting news on the Internet bypasses traditional news sources such as radio and TV.*

bypass /'bɑɪ·pæs/ *n* [C] a road built around a city to take traffic around the edge of it rather than through it

bypass operation, *short form* **bypass** *n* [C] a medical operation in which the path of a person's blood is changed to improve its flow

byproduct, **by-product** /'bɑɪ ˌprɑd·əkt, -ˌʌkt/ *n* [C] something that is produced as a result of making something else, or something unexpected that happens as a result of something else ○ *The deep depression he fell into was a byproduct of his disease.*

bystander /'bɑɪ ˌstæn·dər/ *n* [C] a person who is standing near and watching something that is happening but is not involved in it ○ *Many innocent bystanders were injured by the explosion.*

byte /bɑɪt/ *n* [C] a unit of computer information, consisting of a group of usually eight BITS (= single units of information)

byword /'bɑɪ·wɜrd/ *n* [C] a name of a person or thing that is closely connected with a particular quality ○ *In Hollywood's golden era, "Betty" was a byword for glamour.*

Byzantine /'bɪz·ənˌtiːn, bə'zæn-, -ˌtɑɪn/ *adj* ***world history*** of or having to do with the ancient city of Byzantium or the Eastern Roman Empire

C c

C LETTER, **c** /siː/ *n* [C] *pl* **C's, Cs, c's, cs** the third letter of the English alphabet

MUSICAL NOTE /siː/ *n* [C/U] *pl* **C's, Cs** ***music*** in Western music, the first note in the SCALE (= series of notes) of C MAJOR, or the a set of notes based on this note

MARK /siː/ *n* [C] *pl* **C's, Cs** a mark given for an exam, a course, or a piece of work which shows that your work is average or acceptable and not particularly good or bad ○ *Rachel got a C on her French exam.*

NUMBER, **c** /siː, 'hʌn·drəd/ *number* the ROMAN NUMERAL for the number 100

TEMPERATURE /siː/ *n abbreviation for* CELSIUS ○ *The temperature today reached 25°C.*

ELECTRICITY /siː/ *n* [C] ***chemistry, physics*** *abbreviation for* COULOMB

cab VEHICLE /kæb/ *n* [C] a TAXI (= car with a driver whom you pay to take you where you want to go)

PART OF VEHICLE /kæb/ *n* [C] the separate part at the front of some vehicles in which the driver sits ○ *the cab of a truck*

cabaret /ˌkæb·ə'reɪ/ *n* [C/U] a restaurant that provides esp. musical entertainment ○ [C] *In Paris, we visited several cabarets.*

cabbage /'kæb·ɪdʒ/ *n* [C/U] a large, round vegetable that is green or red and can be eaten cooked or raw ○ [U] *We had corned beef and cabbage.*

cabdriver /'kæb ˌdrɑɪ·vər/, *infml* **cabbie** /'kæb·i/ *n* [C] a person whose job is driving a TAXI

cabin ROOM /'kæb·ən/ *n* [C] a separate space in an aircraft for passengers or for the people operating it, or a room on a ship equipped with beds for sleeping ○ *They gave us seats in the first-class cabin of the plane.*

HOUSE /'kæb·ən/ *n* [C] a small, simple house ○ *We stayed in a cabin in the mountains for two weeks.*

cabinet FURNITURE /'kæb·ə·nət/ *n* [C] **1** a piece of furniture with shelves or drawers that is used for storing useful things or showing decorative things ○ *a medicine cabinet* **2** A filing cabinet is a set of large drawers in which papers can be stored.

> **USAGE**
>
> **cabinet** or **office**?
>
> **Cabinet** cannot be used to mean a room where people work. In English the word for this is **office**.
>
> *There will be a meeting at 9.00 in my office.*
>
> ~~*There will be a meeting at 9.00 in my cabinet.*~~

GOVERNMENT /'kæb·ə·nət/ *n* [C] ***politics & government*** a small group of people within a government who give advice to the highest leader, such as the president or PRIME MINISTER ○ *In the US, the Secretary of Defense is a member of the president's Cabinet.*

cabin fever *n* [U] a condition in which a person feels unhappy or bored because of spending too much time in the house, esp. in winter

cable WIRE /'keɪ·bəl/ *n* [C/U] (a length of) wire, esp. twisted into thick, strong rope or used to carry electricity ○ [C] *They dug up the road in order to lay phone cables.*

MESSAGE /'keɪ·bəl/ *n* [C] (in the past) a message sent by electric signal
cable /'keɪ·bəl/ *v* [I/T]

cable car *n* [C] a vehicle that is attached to a CABLE which pulls it up steep slopes

cable television *n* [U] a system of sending television pictures and sound along CABLES

cache /kæʃ/ *n* [C] a secret or hidden store of things, or the place where they are kept ○ *Authorities believe the robber was after a hidden cache of $2,500 kept in a box under the counter.*

cachet /kæ 'ʃeɪ/ *n* [U] a quality of someone or something that makes it especially attractive or admirable ○ *the cachet of the Ivy League schools*

cackle /'kæk·əl/ *v* [I] to make the loud sound of a chicken, or (of a person) to laugh or talk in a loud, high voice ○ *The hens cackled in alarm.*
cackle /'kæk·əl/ *n* [C] ○ *He burst into cackles of laughter.*

cactus /'kæk·təs/ *n* [C] *pl* **cacti, cactuses** any of a type of plant that grows in the desert, having thick stems for storing water and usually SPINES (= sharp points)

cadaver /kə'dæv·ər/ *n* [C] *medical* a dead human body, esp. one used by medical students for study

caddie, **caddy** /'kæd·i/ *n* [C] a person who carries the equipment for someone who is playing golf

cadence /'keɪd·ᵊns/ *n* [C] a regular rise and fall of sound, esp. of the human voice ○ *She spoke in the lyrical cadence of her East African accent.*

cadet /kə'det/ *n* [C] a student who is training to be a military or police officer

cadre /'kɑd·ri, 'kæd-, -reɪ/ *n* [C] a small group of trained people who form the basic unit of a military, political, or business organization ○ *I was part of the cadre for a new armored division.*

café, **cafe** /kæ 'feɪ/ *n* [C] a small restaurant where simple meals and drinks are served ○ *We had lunch in a sidewalk café.*

cafeteria /ˌkæf·ə'tɪr·iː·ə/ *n* [C] a restaurant where people choose what they want from the foods and drinks that are offered in a serving area and carry the items to a table after paying for them

caffeine /kæ 'fiːn/ *n* [U] a chemical found in coffee and tea that is a STIMULANT (= something that tends to make you more active)

cage /keɪdʒ/ *n* [C] a structure shaped like a box but with bars or wires as its sides, for keeping pets or for housing animals ○ *The lab was stocked with wire cages for mice.*

cagey /ˈkeɪ·dʒi/ *adj comparative* **cagier**, *superlative* **cagiest** not wanting to say plainly what you think or intend to do ○ *He was pretty cagey about his money.*

C

cajole /kəˈdʒoʊl/ *v* [T] to try to persuade someone to do something by saying things that please the person or make the person feel important ○ *She is constantly cajoling her fellow citizens to adopt modern ideas and methods.*

Cajun /ˈkeɪ·dʒən/ *n* [C] a person belonging to a group of French-speaking people living in southern Louisiana in the US
Cajun /ˈkeɪ·dʒən/ *adj* [not gradable]

cake **FOOD** /keɪk/ *n* [C/U] a sweet food made from flour, eggs, fat, and sugar mixed together and baked ○ [C] *a chocolate cake*
SHAPE /keɪk/ *n* [C] a small, flat object made by pressing together a soft substance ○ *a cake of soap*

caked /keɪkd/ *adj* (of a surface) covered with a thick layer of something ○ *I looked at my fingers, now caked with dirt.*

calamity /kəˈlæm·əṭ·i/ *n* [C] an event that causes much suffering to many people ○ *The factory closings were a calamity for the whole city.*

calcium /ˈkæl·siː·əm/ *n* [U] a chemical element present in teeth, bones, and CHALK (= type of soft, white rock)

calculate /ˈkæl·kjəˌleɪt/ *v* [T] to judge the amount or value of something by using information and esp. numbers ○ [+ question word] *We tried to calculate how fast he was moving when the car crashed.* ○ *I calculated the total cost to be over $9000.* ○ [+ *that* clause] *Lieutenant Chilton calculated that six men had been lost.*
calculation /ˌkæl·kjəˈleɪ·ʃən/ *n* [C/U] ○ [C] *The original calculations ignored weather conditions.*
calculator /ˈkæl·kjəˌleɪṭ·ər/ *n* [C] an electronic device used for doing mathematical processes such as adding, subtracting, dividing, and multiplying numbers

WORD FAMILY calculate			
Nouns	calculation calculator	*Adjectives*	calculated calculating incalculable
Verbs	calculate		

calculated /ˈkæl·kjəˌleɪṭ·əd/ *adj* planned or arranged in order to produce a particular effect ○ *The movie is calculated to appeal to young girls.*
calculating /ˈkæl·kjəˌleɪṭ·ɪŋ/ *adj* using other people or situations as a way to get something you want, esp. in a selfish or secret way ○ *The letter reveals a very calculating young man who had always sought a career in politics.*

calculus /ˈkæl·kjə·ləs/ *n* [U] ***mathematics*** the mathematical study of continually changing values

calendar /ˈkæl·ən·dər/ *n* [C] **1** a printed table showing the arrangement of the days, weeks, and months of the year **2** A calendar is also a list of meetings or things you have to do at particular times: *My calendar is pretty crowded over the next few weeks.* **3** A calendar is also a system for deciding the beginning and end of years, their total length, and the parts into which they are divided: *The Gregorian calendar is used today in most parts of the world.*

calf **ANIMAL** /kæf/ *n* [C] *pl* **calves** a young cow, or the young of various other large mammals, including ELEPHANTS and WHALES
LEG /kæf/ *n* [C] *pl* **calves** the curved part of the back of the human leg below the knee

caliber **QUALITY** /ˈkæl·ə·bər/ *n* [U] the degree of quality or excellence of something or someone ○ *It's not easy to recruit high caliber personnel.*
MEASUREMENT /ˈkæl·ə·bər/ *n* [C] the width of the inside of a pipe, esp. of the long, cylindrical part of a gun, or the width of a bullet ○ *a .22-caliber rifle*

calibrate /ˈkæl·əˌbreɪt/ *v* [T] to make, adjust, or check the SETTING (= the position) of the controls used to make measurements with a tool or measuring device ○ *Our radar was calibrated for 100,000 yards.*

calico /ˈkæl·ɪˌkoʊ/ *n* [U] a cotton cloth with a printed pattern

caliph /ˈkeɪ·ləf, ˈkæl-/ *n* [C] ***world history*** a political and religious leader of Islam in the period following the death of Muhammad

calisthenics /ˌkæl·əsˈθen·ɪks/ *pl n* physical exercises usually done repeatedly to keep your muscles in good condition and improve the way you look or feel ○ *The class began with 20 minutes of calisthenics.*

call **NAME** /kɔːl/ *v* [T] **1** to give someone or something a name, or to know or address someone by a particular name ○ *They can't decide whether to call their new baby Carol or Alice.* ○ *His name is Anthony, but everyone calls him Tony.* **2** To **call someone names** is to use rude or insulting words to describe someone ○ *Politicians waste a lot of time calling each other names and criticizing each other.*
TELEPHONE /kɔːl/ *v* [I/T] **1** to telephone someone ○ [I] *I called last night and left a message.* ○ [T] *Jenny called me and invited us over for the weekend.* **2** If you **call someone collect**, you telephone someone who agrees to pay for the cost of talking to you.
call /kɔːl/ *n* [C] ○ *Did I get any (phone) calls while I was out?* ○ *You have a call from your wife.*
caller /ˈkɔː·lər/ *n* [C] a person who telephones someone else
SAY /kɔːl/ *v* [I/T] **1** to say something in a loud voice, esp. in order to get someone's attention ○ [T] *"Answer 'Here!' when I call your name," the teacher said.* **2** If you **call the roll** you read aloud the names of all the people on a list to make certain that each person is present: *The teacher calls the roll at the beginning of each day.*
call /kɔːl/ *n* [C] a loud sound made by a person or animal ○ *Students tried to imitate the calls of their favorite birds.*

ASK TO COME /kɔːl/ *v* [I/T] to ask someone to come to you ○ [I] *I ran to Jonathan as soon as I heard him call.* ○ [T] *You'd better call an ambulance.* ○ [M] *Susan, would you call in the next patient, please?*

call /kɔːl/ *n* [C] **1** a visit that someone makes, esp. as part of a job ○ *The locksmith is out on a call right now.* **2** People who work in medicine and other important activities are said to be **on call** when they are available to make visits or to speak to someone on the telephone at any time: *Dr. Menendez is on call for the next 24 hours.*

CONSIDER /kɔːl/ *v* [T] to consider someone or something to be something ○ *I wouldn't call him a friend – he's just someone I met.* ○ *The umpire called him safe on a close play.*

call /kɔːl/ *n* [C] a decision ○ *I really don't know what to do – it's your call.*

ASK FOR /kɔːl/ *v* [T] to ask for or demand something, or to decide officially to have a particular event ○ *The mayor called a meeting of local organizations to discuss budget priorities.*

call /kɔːl/ *n* [C/U] a reason or cause ○ [U] *There's no call for you to get so angry – I was just kidding.*

IDIOMS with call

• **call a halt to** *something* to stop an activity or process ○ *The Red Cross had to call a halt to its work because the situation was getting too dangerous.*

• **call it a day** to stop working for the day ○ *You've been studying hard – I think you should call it a day.*

• **call it quits** to agree to stop what you are doing ○ *Let's call it quits for today and get together first thing tomorrow.*

• **call the shots** to be the person who controls or organizes a situation ○ *You're the boss here – you get to call the shots.*

PHRASAL VERBS with call

• **call back** *(someone)* [M] to telephone someone who has telephoned you, often to answer a message the person has left, or to telephone again ○ *He called her three times but she never called the guy back.* ○ *I'll call back later.*

• **call for** *someone* **COME TO GET** to go to a place in order to meet someone and travel together to another place ○ *He'll call for you at seven and bring you to the restaurant.*

• **call for** *something* **SUGGEST STRONGLY** to suggest strongly that something should happen or is necessary ○ *Many minority leaders called for the immediate resignation of the police commissioner.* ○ *Talking that way to your parents just wasn't called for* (= was extreme and not necessary).

• **call forth** *something* *fml* to cause something to exist ○ *His challenge called forth resources in me I didn't know I had.*

• **call in** *someone* **REQUEST** [M] to request that someone come to you ○ *Local police called in the FBI to assist with the investigation.* ○ *Did they call you in and have you demonstrate the software for them?*

• **call in PHONE 1** to telephone the place you work ○ *She hasn't called in with her schedule yet.* **2** If you **call in sick**, you telephone to say that you are unable to work because of illness. **3** You can also call in to a radio or television program or to an organization asking for information from the public: *Call in to this radio station and ask the governor a question.* ○ *People were calling in to report suspicious activity.*

• **call off** *something* [M] **1** to decide that a planned event will not happen ○ *Union leaders called the strike off at the last minute.* **2** To call off a dog is to order it to stop attacking someone or something.

• **call on** *someone* **ASK TO DO 1** to ask someone to do something ○ *She called on Americans to be more tolerant of each other.* **2** To call on someone in a group is to ask that person to speak: *The teacher called on me, and I didn't know the answer.*

• **call on** *someone* **VISIT** to come to see someone; visit ○ *She went to the hospital to call on a sick friend.*

• **call out** *(something)* **SHOUT** [M] to speak loudly ○ *Speak up – call the names out so we can all hear.* ○ *He called out, but she didn't hear him.*

• **call out** *something* **MAKE ACTIVE** [M] to officially order that a military unit become ready for action ○ *The governor called out the National Guard to prepare for the hurricane.*

• **call up** *(someone)* **TELEPHONE** [M] to telephone someone ○ *He used to call me up in the middle of the night.* ○ *I just wanted to call up and say "thanks."*

• **call up** *someone* **ORDER** [M] to order someone to join the armed forces or to start taking part in a military operation ○ *He was called up at the beginning of the war.* ○ Related noun: CALL-UP

calligraphy /kəˈlɪg·rə·fi/ *n* [U] the art of producing beautiful writing, often created with a special pen or brush

call-in *adj* [not gradable] (of broadcasts) allowing members of the public to make their questions and opinions a part of the program ○ *Bell hosts a popular call-in show on a local radio station.*

calling /ˈkɔː·lɪŋ/ *n* [C] *fml* an activity that is a person's most important job, esp. one in which the person has an unusually strong interest and ability ○ *She believes the medical profession should be thought of as a calling.*

callous /ˈkæl·əs/ *adj* without sympathy or feeling for other people ○ *As callous as it may sound, trying to help some students is a waste of time.*

call-up /ˈkɔːl·ʌp/ *n* [C] an order for a group of soldiers to become active in a military operation ○ *December has been one of the heaviest months for call-ups of National Guard members.* ○ Related verb: CALL UP

callus /ˈkæl·əs/ *n* [C] an area of hard, thick skin, esp. on the feet or hands ○ *If you look at my hands, you will see the calluses of a farmer.*

callused, **calloused** /ˈkæl·əst/ *adj* ○ *He stood looking down at the dark, callused palms of his hands.*

calm /kɑm, kɑlm/ *adj* [-er/-est only] **1** peaceful, quiet, or relaxed; without hurried movement, anxiety, or noise ○ *The pilot said we'd have to make an emergency landing, and the flight attendants tried to keep us calm.* **2** If weather is described as calm, it is not windy, and if the sea is described as calm, it is still or has only small waves: *Our ship arrived at the Mississippi delta on a calm, clear night.*

calm /kɑm, kɑlm/ *n* [U] ○ *Amid the calm, there was a sense that something could happen at any moment.*

calm /kɑm, kɑlm/ *v* [I/T] ○ [T] *He tried his best to calm her (down).* ○ [I] *I needed some time to calm down.*

calmly /ˈkɑm·li, ˈkɑlm-/ *adv* ○ *He calmly made both free throws to win the game.*

calmness /ˈkɑm·nəs, ˈkɑlm-/ *n* [U] ○ *The calmness and professionalism of the crew gave us confidence.*

WORD FAMILY calm

Nouns	calm calmness	*Verbs*	calm
		Adverbs	calmly
Adjectives	calm		

WORD CHOICES calm

If someone is calm in a difficult situation, you can use the words **cool** or **unruffled.**

*He was very **cool** about the problem and didn't shout or lose his temper.*

*He seemed remarkably **unruffled** for a man who was about to lose his job.*

The idiom **not lose your head** can also be used when someone stays calm in a difficult situation.

*She **doesn't lose her head** under pressure.*

If someone is very calm and in control of his or her emotions, the word **composed** can be used.

*After being so **composed** throughout this series, the team suddenly became shaky.*

The word **level-headed** can be used for people who are usually calm in difficult situations.

*She's very **level-headed** and unlikely to get upset by what has happened.*

Someone who is usually calm because it is part of his or her nature can be described as **placid.**

*She was a very **placid** baby who hardly ever cried.*

When someone becomes calm again after being angry, you can use the phrasal verb **calm down.**

*Dad was really angry and it was a long time before he **calmed down.***

calorie FOOD /ˈkæl·ə·ri/ *n* [C] a unit used in measuring the amount of energy food provides when eaten and digested ○ *The typical US daily menu contains 3000 calories and should contain 2300.*

HEAT /ˈkæl·ə·ri/ *n* [C] ***science*** a unit equal to the amount of heat needed to increase the temperature of one gram of water by one degree CELSIUS

calorimeter /ˌkæl·əˈrɪm·əṭ·ər/ *n* [C] ***chemistry*** a piece of equipment for measuring the amount of heat produced in a chemical reaction

calves /kævz/ *pl of* CALF

calypso /kəˈlɪp·soʊ/ *n* [C/U] *pl* **calypsos, calypsoes** a type of popular West Indian song whose words are often invented as the song is sung

camaraderie /ˌkɑm·əˈrɑd·ə·ri/ *n* [U] a friendly feeling toward people with whom you share an experience or with whom you work ○ *For me mountain climbing is less about physical effort than about cooperation and camaraderie.*

cambium /ˈkæm·biː·əm/ *n* [U] ***biology*** the layer of growing tissue between the BARK (= outer covering) and the wood of a tree that produces new bark and wood

camcorder /ˈkæmˌkɔːrd·ər/ *n* [C] a type of camera that records and plays images and sound on VIDEOTAPE and is small enough to hold in one hand

came /keɪm/ *past simple of* COME

camel /ˈkæm·əl/ *n* [C] a large animal of desert areas that has a long neck and a back with either one or two HUMPS (= large raised parts)

cameo JEWELRY /ˈkæm·iːˌoʊ/ *n* [C] *pl* **cameos** a piece of usually oval jewelry on which the shape of a head or another shape is represented against a background of a different color

PERFORMANCE /ˈkæm·iːˌoʊ/ *n* [C] *pl* **cameos** a brief but noticeable part, esp. in a movie, television program, or performance in a theater, usually by someone who is famous ○ *The former vice president makes a cameo appearance in the movie.*

camera /ˈkæm·rə/ *n* [C] a device for taking photographs, making films, or recording images on VIDEOTAPE

cameraman /ˈkæm·rəˌmæn/, *female* **camerawoman** /ˈkæm·rəˌwʊm·ən/ *n* [C] *pl* **-men, -women** a man or woman who operates a camera, esp. as a regular job, in making movies or television programs

camisole /ˈkæm·əˌsoʊl/ *n* [C] a piece of women's underwear for the top half of the body with thin straps that go over the shoulders

camomile /ˈkæm·əˌmɑɪl, -ˌmiːl/ *n* CHAMOMILE

camouflage /ˈkæm·əˌflɑʒ, -ˌflɑdʒ/ *n* [U] **1** a condition in which the appearance of someone or something when placed against a background makes the person or thing difficult or impossible to see ○ *The leafhopper is a little green insect that uses camouflage to blend in with the colors of the leaves.* **2** In military use, camouflage is an appearance designed to hide soldiers and equipment on the ground, esp. from being seen by enemy aircraft, by making them look like their surroundings.

camouflage /ˈkæm·əˌflɑʒ, -ˌflɑdʒ/ *v* [T] ○ *(fig.) Her quiet voice camouflages the fierce competitor within her.*

camp TENTS/BUILDINGS /kæmp/ *n* [C/U] **1** a place where people stay in tents or other temporary structures ○ [U] *We set up camp for the night near a stream.* **2** A camp is also a place in the countryside organized for people, esp. children, to visit or live for a while to enjoy nature: [C/U] *We sent our son away to (a) summer camp.* **3** A camp is also a place where people, esp. military people, are trained, where military prisoners are kept, or where people have to live temporarily.

camp /kæmp/ *v* [I] to set up a tent or other temporary structure to give you shelter outside while you sleep or rest ○ *We camped in a valley between the two mountains.* ○ *We used to go camping out west when I was a child.*

camper /ˈkæm·pər/ *n* [C] **1** *In the summer several thousand campers use this park every day.* **2** A camper is also a large vehicle in which you can sleep and eat, sometimes built as one unit with a car and sometimes as a unit that can be separated.

camping /ˈkæm·pɪŋ/ *n* [U] ○ *In 1993, camping was the fifth most popular American vacation activity.*

GROUP /kæmp/ *n* [C] a group of people who share an opinion, esp. a political one ○ *Voters in the governor's camp will believe whatever he says about the state budget.*

PHRASAL VERB with **camp**

• **camp out** to stay and sleep in an outside area for one or more days and nights, usually in a tent ○ *I've done a lot of hiking in that park, but never camped out overnight.*

campaign /kæmˈpeɪn/ *n* [C] a plan consisting of a number of activities directed toward the achievement of an aim ○ *He ran the governor's campaign for reelection.* ○ *"Washington's Crossing" is a history of the military campaign of 1776 and early 1777.*

campaign /kæmˈpeɪn/ *v* [I] to try to achieve something, such as the election of someone to a political office, by taking part in a number of planned activities ○ *She campaigned for a law that would force the town to clean up the lake.*

camper /ˈkæm·pər/ *n* ○ See at CAMP TENTS/BUILDINGS

campfire /ˈkæmp·fɑɪr/ *n* [C] a fire outside that is made and used esp. by people who are staying in tents

campground /ˈkæmp·grɑʊnd/ *n* [C] an area of land that has space for lots of people to put tents or RVS and stay while traveling or on vacation, and that often has bathrooms, a small store, a place for children to play, etc.

camphor /ˈkæm·fər/ *n* [U] a white substance with a strong smell which is used in medicine and to keep MOTHS (= flying insects) away from clothes that are stored

camping /ˈkæm·pɪŋ/ *n* ○ See at CAMP TENTS/BUILDINGS

campsite /ˈkæmp·sɑɪt/ *n* [C] a place in a CAMPGROUND or by itself where you can CAMP ○ *There are still another 50 to 60 campsites available in the park.*

campus /ˈkæm·pəs/ *n* [C/U] the grounds, sometimes including the buildings, of a university, college, or school ○ [C] *Surrounded by lovely trees, the Dartmouth campus is big and beautiful.* ○ [U] *Freshmen at many universities are not allowed to live off campus* (= in houses not on university property).

campy /kæmp·i/ *adj* [*-er/-est* only] (of behavior, appearance, or an activity) amusing because it is obviously intended to be strange or shocking and seems to be ridiculing itself ○ *The movie is a mixed bag of campy humor, wild-eyed fantasy, and high-tech special effects.*

can **CONTAINER** /kæn/ *n* [C] **1** a metal container, esp. a closed, cylindrical container in which food and drink are packaged ○ *a gas/watering can* ○ *The vending machine has soda in cans.* **2** A can is also the amount of food or drink that a can holds: *I had a can of soup for lunch.*

can /kæn/ *v* [T] **-nn-** **1** to preserve food by putting it into a can ○ *They can all kinds of fruit.* **2** *slang* If you get canned, you are dismissed from your job: *No, I'm not on vacation – I got canned last week.*

canned /kænd/ *adj* [not gradable] **1** *We keep a lot of canned food on hand.* **2** *fig.* Canned music is recorded music, esp. played in public places: *Canned music annoys me.*

ABLE /kæn, kən/ *modal verb* **can**, *past simp.* **could** to be able to ○ *She can speak four languages.* ○ *We're doing the best we can, but we won't make our deadline.* ➤ Grammar: **able or can/could?** at ABLE HAVING WHAT IS NEEDED

PERMIT /kæn, kən/ *modal verb* **can**, *past simp.* **could** **1** to be allowed or to have permission ○ *You can park on the street.* ○ *You can do it by yourself.* **2** Can is also used to request something: *Can you help me lift this box?* ○ *Can I have a tissue, please?* ○ **USAGE:** Can is usually used in standard spoken English when asking for permission. It is acceptable in most forms of written English, although in very formal writing, such as official instructions, may is often used instead: *Persons under 14 unaccompanied by an adult may not enter.*

BE POSSIBLE /kæn, kən/ *modal verb past simp.* **could** used to express possibility in the present ○ *You can get stamps at the post office.*

OFFER /kæn, kən/ *modal verb past simp.* **could** used in polite offers of help or by someone who provides service, as in a store ○ *Can I help you with those bags?*

Canadian /kəˈneɪd·iː·ən/ *adj* (a person) of or coming from Canada

Canadian English *n* [U] the English language as it is spoken and written in Canada

canal /kəˈnæl/ *n* [C] a channel of water artificially made for boats to travel through or to carry water from one area to another ○ *Today, the canal is still used by ships.*

canary /kəˈner·i/ *n* [C] a small, yellow bird, popular as a pet in a cage

cancel /ˈkæn·səl/ *v* [I/T] **-l-**, **-ll-** **1** to decide that something arranged in advance will not happen, or to state that you do not wish to receive something ○ [I] *We were supposed to meet for dinner but Elise had to cancel at the last minute.* **2** If a stamp or check is canceled, it is marked to show it has been used: [T] *He collects canceled stamps.*

cancellation /ˌkæn·səˈleɪ·ʃən/ *n* [C/U] ○ [C] *All the tickets were sold, so we waited to see if there were any cancellations.*

WORD CHOICES cancel

Call off is an alternative to "cancel" when talking about events.

*The game has been **called off** because of the weather.*

If something has been canceled, you can say that it is **off**.

*The meeting's **off** because James is ill.*

Scrap can be used when you cancel a plan.

*We've **scrapped** our plans for a trip to France.*

Suspend can be used when something is canceled either temporarily or permanently.

*The ferry service has been **suspended** for the day because of bad weather.*

Postpone can be used when someone cancels something but plans to do it later.

*We've **postponed** the wedding until next year.*

If you cancel something before you have finished it, you could use the words **abandon** or **curtail**.

*They had to **abandon** their attempt to climb the mountain.*

*We **curtailed** our trip when John became ill.*

PHRASAL VERB with cancel

•**cancel out** *something* [M] , **-ll-** to take away the effect of one thing by doing another thing that has the opposite effect ○ *You can't be creative and critical at the same time – one cancels out the other.*

cancer /ˈkæn·sər/ *n* [C/U] a disease in which cells in the body grow without control, or a serious medical condition caused by this disease ○ [U] *He died from cancer of the stomach.* ○ Compare CARCINOMA

cancerous /ˈkæn·sə·rəs/ *adj* ○ *Surgeons removed a cancerous growth from her lung.*

Cancer /ˈkæn·sər/ *n* [C/U] the fourth sign of the ZODIAC, covering the period June 22 to July 22 and represented by a CRAB, or a person born during this period

candid /ˈkæn·dəd/ *adj* truthful and honest ○ *We had a candid discussion about her poor job performance.*

candidate /ˈkæn·dəˌdeɪt, -dəd·ət/ *n* [C] a person who is competing to get a job or elected to a position ○ *There are three candidates running for sheriff.*

candidacy /ˈkæn·dəd·ə·si/ *n* [U] ○ *She announced her candidacy for governor on the weekend.*

candle /ˈkæn·dᵊl/ *n* [C] a piece of wax shaped like a stick with a WICK (= string) in the middle that burns slowly, giving off light

candlestick /ˈkæn·dᵊlˌstɪk/ *n* [C] a tall base for a candle ○ *The silver candlesticks gleamed on the table.*

candor, *Cdn, Br* **candour** /ˈkæn·dər/ *n* [U] the quality of being honest, sincere, and kind in dealing with other people ○ *"We want to help but really don't know how," she said with surprising candor.*

candy /ˈkæn·di/ *n* [C/U] a small piece of sweet food made from sugar with chocolate, fruit, nuts, or flavors added ○ [U] *We dove into the box of chocolate candy as if we were starving.*

candy bar *n* [C] candy shaped like a thin brick ○ *I usually avoid eating candy bars.*

candy cane *n* [C] a piece of flavored hard candy shaped like a CANE (= walking stick)

cane /keɪn/ *n* [C/U] **1** the long, hollow stems of particular plants such as BAMBOO ○ [U] *Chair seats are often woven out of cane.* **2** A cane is also a walking stick with a curved handle, used to help someone walk.

canine /ˈkeɪ·nɑɪn/ *adj* of or like a dog ○ *This vet specializes in canines.*

canister /ˈkæn·ə·stər/ *n* [C] a container with a cover, used for storing foods or objects ○ *I bought brightly colored canisters to hold sugar and flour.*

cannabis /ˈkæn·ə·bəs/ *n* [U] the HEMP plant, whose leaves and flowers are used to make MARIJUANA

cannibal /ˈkæn·ə·bəl/ *n* [C] a person who eats human flesh, or an animal which eats the flesh of its own type of animal

cannon /ˈkæn·ən/ *n* [C] *pl* **cannons, cannon** a large, powerful gun fixed onto a ship or onto a structure on land

cannot /kəˈnɑt, ˈkæn·ɑt/, *contraction* **can't** /kænt, kɑːnt/ *modal verb* can not; to be unable or not allowed to ○ *I cannot imagine what will happen next.*

canny /ˈkæn·i/ *adj* intelligent and careful ○ *He is a canny investor.*

canoe /kəˈnuː/ *n* [C] a small, light, narrow boat, pointed at both ends and moved by a person using a PADDLE (= a stick with a wide, flat end)

canoe /kəˈnuː/ *v* [I always + adv/prep] *pres. part.* **canoeing**, *past* **canoed** ○ *They canoed across the lake.*

canon /ˈkæn·ən/ *n* [C] **1** a principle or law, or a set of these, esp. in a CHRISTIAN church ○ *The canon for lawyers has clear restrictions.* **2** ***music*** the repetition of a musical pattern after it has been sung or played once, although not always in the same OCTAVE or by the same instrument

can opener *n* [C] a device for opening metal cans, esp. cans of food

canopy /ˈkæn·ə·pi/ *n* [C/U] a cover like a roof for shelter or decoration, or the branches and leaves that spread out at the tops of trees in the woods ○ [U] *Many animals live in the forest canopy.*

can't /kænt, kɑːnt/ *contraction of* CANNOT ○ *Speak up! I can't hear you.*

cantaloupe /ˈkænt·ᵊlˌoʊp/ *n* [C] a round MELON (= fruit) with yellow or green skin and sweet, orange flesh ○ *Cantaloupes from Texas are extremely good this year.*

cantankerous /kænˈtæŋ·kə·rəs/ *adj* annoyed and tending to argue and complain ○ *By dinner, we were all tired and cantankerous.*

canteen RESTAURANT /kæn'tiːn/ *n* [C] a small store or restaurant esp. in a factory or school where food and meals are sold

CONTAINER /kæn'tiːn/ *n* [C] a small container for carrying something to drink, esp. water

canter /'kænt·ər/ *v* [I] (of a horse) to move in a way that is like a slow GALLOP

cantor /'kænt·ər/ *n* [C] an official of a Jewish SYNAGOGUE who sings and leads prayers

Canuck /kə'nʌk, -'nʊk/ *n* [C] *infml* someone from Canada, esp. from the part of Canada where French is the most important language

canvas /'kæn·vəs/ *n* [C/U] **1** strong, rough cloth made from cotton or other fibers, used for making tents, sails, strong bags, or work clothes **2** Canvas is also the cloth artists paint on, or a painting itself: [C] *Two valuable canvases hung in the room.*

canvass /'kæn·vəs/ *v* [I/T] to go to each house in an area to find out how many people live there or what their opinions are, or to get support ○ [T] *Candidates canvassed the city's neighborhoods for votes.*

canyon /'kæn·jən/ *n* [C] a deep valley with steep sides and usually a river flowing along the bottom

cap HAT /kæp/ *n* [C] a soft, light hat, esp. one with a curved part sticking out at the front ○ *a painter's cap* ○ *My uncle must have a hundred baseball caps to choose from.*

LIMIT /kæp/ *v* [T] **-pp-** to put a limit on expenses or amounts charged ○ *Our mortgage is capped for five years.*

cap /kæp/ *n* [C] ○ *The state has put a cap on the budget.*

COVER /kæp/ *n* [C] **1** a small lid or cover ○ *a pen cap* ○ *I can't get the cap off this bottle.* **2** A cap is also a CROWN (= cover for a tooth).

cap /kæp/ *v* [T] **-pp-** ○ *From my window, I could see mountains capped with snow.*

EXPLOSIVE /kæp/ *n* [C] a small amount of explosive powder on a paper roll, used esp. in toy guns to make a loud noise

capable Ⓐ /'keɪ·pə·bəl/ *adj* having the skill or ability or strength to do something ○ *She's a very capable lawyer.*

capability Ⓐ /ˌkeɪ·pə'bɪl·ət̬·i/ *n* [C/U] ○ [U] *Automation gives us the capability to do certain jobs quickly and well.*

WORD FAMILY capable			
Nouns	capability	*Adjectives*	capable incapable

capacity Ⓐ AMOUNT /kə'pæs·ət̬·i/ *n* the amount that can be held or produced by something ○ [C] *The stadium has a seating capacity of 50,000.*

ABILITY /kə'pæs·ət̬·i/ *n* [C] the ability to do something in particular ○ *He has an enormous capacity for work.*

POSITION /kə'pæs·ət̬·i/ *n* [C] a particular position or job; a ROLE ○ *She was speaking in her capacity as a judge.*

cape LAND /keɪp/ *n* [C] a very large piece of land that sticks out into the sea ○ *Cape Cod*

COAT /keɪp/ *n* [C] a loose coat without sleeves which is fastened at the neck and hangs from the shoulders

caper ACTIVITY /'keɪ·pər/ *n* [C] **1** an act of stealing or other illegal activity ○ *a bank caper* **2** A caper is also an action that is amusing but wrong: *In this latest caper, Bell was caught using a doctored bat.*

FOOD /'keɪ·pər/ *n* [C usually pl] a small, dark green flower BUD prepared for use as a flavoring for food

capillarity /ˌkæp·ə'ler·ət̬·i/, **capillary action** *n* [U] the force that causes liquid to rise in a tube or other narrow space against the force of GRAVITY

capillary /'kæp·əˌler·i/ *n* [C] ***biology*** the smallest of the tubes that carry blood around the body

capital /'kæp·ət̬·əl ('let̬·ər)/, **capital letter** *n* [C] ***grammar*** a form of a letter used to begin sentences and names of people, places, and organizations ○ *THIS SENTENCE IS PRINTED IN CAPITALS/CAPITAL LETTERS.* ○ Compare SMALL LETTER SIZE

capital /'kæp·ət̬·əl/ *adj* [not gradable] ○ *Do you write "Colin" with a capital "C"?*

capitalize /'kæp·ət̬·əlˌɑɪz/ *v* [T] ○ *The names of streets are always capitalized.* ○ See also: CAPITALIZE ON

capitalization /ˌkæp·ət̬·əl·ə'zeɪ·ʃən/ *n* [U] ○ *Rules of capitalization vary from language to language.*

capital CITY /'kæp·ət̬·əl/ *n* [C] ***politics & government*** a city which is the center of government for a country or other political area

MONEY /'kæp·ət̬·əl/ *n* [U] wealth, esp. money used to produce more wealth through investment or a new business ○ *She invested well, and can live on the interest without touching the capital.*

DEATH /'kæp·ət̬·əl/ *adj* [not gradable] (of a crime) that can be punished by death ○ *a capital offense*

capital gains *pl n* profits made by selling shares of a company or buildings and land

capitalism /'kæp·ət̬·əlˌɪz·əm/ *n* [U] ***politics & government*** an economic system based on private ownership of property and business, with the goal of making the greatest possible profits for the owners ○ Compare COMMUNISM; SOCIALISM

capitalist /'kæp·ət̬·əl·əst/, **capitalistic** /ˌkæp·ət̬·əl'ɪs·tɪk/ *adj* ○ *The US has a capitalist economy.*

capitalist /'kæp·ət̬·əl·əst/ *n* [C] ○ *Anyone can be a capitalist.*

PHRASAL VERB with capitalize

- **capitalize on** *something* to use something to your own advantage ○ *She capitalized on her experience to get a better paying job.* ○ See also: CAPITALIZE at CAPITAL (LETTER)

capital punishment, **death penalty** *n* [U] ***politics & government*** punishment by death for a serious crime

Capitol /'kæp·ət̬·əl/ *n* [C usually sing] the building in which the US Congress meets

Capitol Hill *n* [U] the hill on which the US Capitol stands, or the US legislature which meets there

○ *The president will go to Capitol Hill to meet with lawmakers.*

capitulate /kəˈpɪtʃ·əˌleɪt/ *v* [I] to accept defeat, or to give up or give in ○ *I capitulated and let my daughter go with her friends.*
capitulation /kəˌpɪtʃ·əˈleɪ·ʃən/ *n* [C/U] ○ [C] *This was not a capitulation but an agreement.*

C

cappuccino /ˌkæp·əˈtʃiː·noʊ/ *n* [C/U] *pl* **cappuccinos** strong coffee mixed with hot milk, or a cup of this coffee ○ [U] *Do you prefer espresso or cappuccino?*

capricious /kəˈprɪʃ·əs, -ˈpriː·ʃəs/ *adj* likely to change, or reacting to a sudden desire or new idea ○ *We have had very capricious weather lately.*

Capricorn /ˈkæp·rəˌkɔːrn/ *n* [C/U] the tenth sign of the ZODIAC, covering the period December 22 to January 19 and represented by a goat, or a person born during this period

capsize /ˈkæpˌsɑɪz/ *v* [I/T] to turn over or cause a boat or ship to turn over in the water ○ [I] *A passenger ferry capsized in rough seas Sunday morning.*

capsule **MEDICINE** /ˈkæp·səl, -suːl/ *n* [C] a measured amount of medicine in a very small, rounded, soft container which is swallowed

SPACECRAFT /ˈkæp·səl, -suːl/ *n* [C] the part of an old-fashioned spacecraft where people lived and in which they returned to earth ○ *the Apollo 11 capsule*

captain /ˈkæp·tən/ *n* [C] **1** a naval officer of high rank, above a COMMANDER, or a military officer of middle rank, above a LIEUTENANT **2** A captain is the person in charge of a ship or aircraft. **3** A captain is also an officer in a police or fire department. **4** A captain is also the leader of a sports team.
captain /ˈkæp·tən/ *v* [T] ○ *She captains the women's rowing team.*

caption /ˈkæp·ʃən/ *n* [C] brief text over or under a picture in a book, magazine, or newspaper that describes the picture or explains what the people in it are doing or saying

captivate /ˈkæp·təˌveɪt/ *v* [T] to hold the attention of someone by being extremely interesting, exciting, charming, or attractive ○ *Her singing captivated audiences everywhere.*

captive /ˈkæp·tɪv/ *n* [C] a prisoner, esp. a person held by the enemy during a war
captive /ˈkæp·tɪv/ *adj, adv* ○ *The soldiers were held captive for three months.* ○ *When selling to people in their homes, you've got a captive audience* (= people who cannot leave).
captivity /kæpˈtɪv·ət̬·i/ *n* [U] ○ *Most animals bred in captivity would probably not survive in the wild.*

capture **POSSESS** /ˈkæp·tʃər, -ʃər/ *v* [T] to take someone as a prisoner, or to take something into your possession ○ *These birds were captured in the wild in 1987.*
capture /ˈkæp·tʃər, -ʃər/ *n* [U] ○ *They were shown on TV soon after their capture.*

RECORD /ˈkæp·tʃər, -ʃər/ *v* [T] to record sound or images, or to express a feeling ○ *She captured the incident on video.* ○ *Those songs capture the romantic mood of the movie.*

IDIOM with capture

• **capture** *someone's* **attention**, **capture** *someone's* **imagination** to interest someone ○ *Most of the textbooks we looked at were too dull to capture students' attention.*

car /kɑr/, **automobile** *n* [C] **1** a road vehicle with an engine, usually four wheels, and seating for between one and five people ○ *a car accident* ○ *She goes to work by car.* **2** A car is also one part of a train: *a dining/passenger/freight car*

carafe /kəˈræf, -ˈrɑf/ *n* [C] an open glass container for serving liquids, or the amount it contains

caramel /ˈkɑr·məl; ˈkær·ə·məl, -ˌmel/ *n* [C/U] cooked sugar used to give flavor and a brown color to food, or a chewy candy made from cooked sugar, butter, and milk

carat /ˈkær·ət/ *n* [C] a unit for measuring the weight of jewels ○ *The diamonds had a combined weight of 5.87 carats.* ○ Compare KARAT

caravan /ˈkær·əˌvæn/ *n* [C] a group of people with vehicles or animals who travel together for safety through a dangerous area, esp. across a desert on CAMELS

carbohydrate /ˌkɑr·bəˈhɑɪˌdreɪt/ *n* [C/U] **1** ***biology*** a substance such as sugar or STARCH that provides the body with energy **2** A carbohydrate is also a food that contains a large amount of carbohydrate such as bread, fruits, and vegetables. ○ [C] *Eat your carbohydrates within two hours after your workout.*

carbon /ˈkɑr·bən/ *n* [U] ***biology, chemistry*** a chemical element that is contained in all animals and plants, and that is an important part of other substances such as coal and oil, and exists in its pure form as DIAMONDS and GRAPHITE

carbonated /ˈkɑr·bəˌneɪt̬·əd/ *adj* (of a drink) bubbly because it contains CARBON DIOXIDE ○ *carbonated drinks/water*

carbon copy *n* [C] an exact copy of something ○ *(fig.) The girl is a carbon copy of her mother* (= they are very similar).

carbon cycle *n* [U] ***biology*** the way that CARBON is exchanged between different living organisms on Earth and between living organisms and the environment, for example, when plants take CARBON DIOXIDE from the air, and when animals eat plants

carbon dating, **radiocarbon dating** /ˈreɪd·iːˌoʊˌkɑr·bən ˈdeɪt̬·ɪŋ/ *n* [U] ***science*** a method of calculating the age of extremely old objects by measuring the amount of a particular type of carbon in them

carbon dioxide /dɑɪˈɑk·sɑɪd/ *n* [U] ***biology*** the gas produced when animal or vegetable matter is burned, or when animals breathe out

carbonic acid /kɑrˈbɑn·ɪk ˈæs·əd/ *n* [U] ***chemistry*** a weak acid made of CARBON DIOXIDE (= a gas) mixed with water

C

carboniferous /ˌkɑr·bəˈnɪf·ər·əs/ *adj* [not gradable] ***earth science*** containing or producing carbon

carbon monoxide /məˈnɑk·sɑɪd/ *n* [U] a poisonous gas produced when carbon is partly burned, esp. in car fuel

carburetor /ˈkɑr·bəˌreɪt̬·ər, -bjə-/ *n* [C] the part of an engine that mixes fuel and air, producing the gas that is burned to provide the power needed to operate a vehicle or machine

carcass /ˈkɑr·kəs/ *n* [C] the body of a dead animal ○ *The carcass of a deer lay near the road.*

carcinogen /kɑrˈsɪn·ə·dʒən/ *n* [C] *medical* a substance that can cause CANCER (= a serious illness that causes tissues and cells to grow too quickly)
carcinogenic /ˌkɑr·sə·nəˈdʒen·ɪk/ *adj medical* (of a substance) able or likely to cause CANCER

carcinoma /kɑr·səˈnoʊ·mə/ *n* [C] *medical* a lump of tissue that forms on or inside the body; a TUMOR

card **INFORMATION** /kɑrd/ *n* [C] a small, rectangular piece of stiff paper or plastic with information on it that shows who you are or allows you to do something ○ *a library/membership/business card* ○ *I used my credit/debit/charge card to pay for the groceries.*
card /kɑrd/ *v* [T] *infml* to ask someone to show you a document that shows how old the person is

GAME /kɑrd/, **playing card** *n* [C] one of a set of 52 small, rectangular pieces of stiff paper, each with a number or letter and one of four symbols printed on it, used in games ○ *a deck of cards*
cards /kɑrdz/ *n* [U] any game played with cards, such as POKER or BRIDGE ○ *Let's play cards.*

GREETING /kɑrd/ *n* [C] **1** a rectangular piece of stiff paper, folded in half, usually with a picture on the front and often a message printed inside, sent on a special occasion ○ *a birthday/anniversary/get-well card* **2** A card is also a POSTCARD.

IDIOMS with card

• **in the cards** likely to happen ○ *Marriage isn't in the cards for me right now – I'm focused on my career.* ○ **USAGE:** Used especially in negative sentences.

• **lay** *your* **cards on the table**, **put** *your* **cards on the table** to be honest and not hide what you are thinking or doing ○ *I'm going to lay my cards on the table here, and say that I don't know what to do.*

• **the cards are stacked against** *someone* someone is not likely to succeed, esp. because the person is not being given a fair chance ○ *We tried hard to win, but the cards were stacked against us.*

cardboard /ˈkɑrd·bɔːrd, -boʊrd/ *n* [U] very thick, stiff paper, usually pale brown in color, used esp. for making boxes ○ *She packed the books in a cardboard box.*

cardiac /ˈkɑrd·iːˌæk/ *adj* [not gradable] *medical* of the heart or heart disease ○ *cardiac surgery*

cardiac arrest *n* [U] a condition in which the heart stops beating

cardigan /ˈkɑrd·ɪ·gən/ *n* [C] a SWEATER (= piece of clothing that covers the upper part of the body and the arms) that fastens at the front with buttons and is usually worn over other clothes

cardinal **PRIEST** /ˈkɑrd·ən·əl/ *n* [C] a priest of high rank in the Roman Catholic Church

IMPORTANT /ˈkɑrd·ən·əl/ *adj* of great importance; main ○ *Finding food was a cardinal concern.*

BIRD /ˈkɑrd·ən·əl/ *n* [C] a North American bird, the male of which has bright red feathers and a black face

cardinal (number) /ˈkɑrd·ən·əl (ˈnʌm·bər)/ *n* [C] a number like 1, 2, 3 that represents amount, rather than position in a list ○ Compare ORDINAL (NUMBER)

cardiology /ˌkɑrd·iːˈɑl·ə·dʒi/ *n* [U] *medical* the study and treatment of medical conditions of the heart
cardiologist /ˌkɑrd·iːˈɑl·ə·dʒəst/ *n* [C] *medical* a doctor who specializes in treating medical conditions of the heart

cardiovascular /ˌkɑrd·iː·oʊˈvæs·kjə·lər/ *adj* *medical* of or relating to the heart and the BLOOD VESSELS (= tubes through which the blood flows)

card table *n* [C] a small table with folding legs that is used for playing card games

care **HELP** /ker, kær/ *n* [U] the process of providing for the needs of someone or something ○ *The quality of care at this hospital is very good.* ○ *Trees on city property don't get any care.*

ATTENTION /ker, kær/ *n* [U] serious attention, esp. to the details of a situation or a piece of work ○ *She painted the window frames with great care.*
careful /ˈker·fəl, ˈkær-/ *adj* giving attention to something in order to avoid esp. an accident or problem ○ *Norman is a careful driver.* ○ *Give my suggestion careful consideration.* ○ [+ question word] *He's in a really bad mood so be careful what you say to him.* ○ [+ question word] *Be careful where you put that hot pan.* ○ [+ *to* infinitive] *Be careful to look both ways when you cross the street.*
carefully /ˈker·fə·li, ˈkær-/ *adv* with great attention, esp. to detail or safety ○ *She carefully embroidered the pillow.* ○ *Drive carefully – it's raining.*
careless /ˈker·ləs, ˈkær-/ *adj* not using enough care ○ *Careless drivers cause accidents.* ○ *My son's schoolwork is often careless and sloppy.*
carelessly /ˈker·lə·sli, ˈkær-/ *adv* ○ *She carelessly left her purse on the train.*
carelessness /ˈker·lə·snəs, ˈkær-/ *n* [U] ○ *Carelessness leads to shoddy work.*

WORD CHOICES careful

If someone is careful to avoid risks or danger, you can describe them as **cautious**.

She's a very ***cautious*** *driver.*

The idiom **play it safe** also means "to be careful to avoid risks."

I think I'll ***play it safe*** *and take the earlier train.* ➤

C

If someone does something in a very careful way, paying great attention to detail, you can use adjectives such as **meticulous, methodical,** and **painstaking.**

*This book is the result of years of **meticulous/painstaking** research.*

WORD CHOICES careless

Sloppy is an alternative to the word "careless."

*Spelling mistakes always look **sloppy** in a formal letter.*

The informal adjective **slapdash** can be used when work is careless because it is done too quickly without enough thought.

*His work is always hurried and **slapdash**.*

If someone does something without thinking about the results, the adjective **rash** is often used.

*That was a **rash** decision – you didn't think about the costs involved.*

If someone carelessly says something that could upset someone, you can use the word **thoughtless.**

*The senator made a **thoughtless** remark about the environment.*

Someone who does not properly do something and causes a serious mistake to be made can be described as **negligent.**

*If a doctor is **negligent** in treating a patient, he or she can be sued in court.*

The adjectives **reckless** and **irresponsible** can be used when people are careless and do not think about the dangers of what they are doing.

*He was found guilty of **reckless** driving.*

*Some dog owners are **irresponsible** and do not keep dangerous dogs under control.*

WORRY /ker, kær/ *v* to be interested in something, or to be anxious or upset about something ○ [I] *Don't you care about what happens to the children?* ○ [I] *I really don't care if we go or not* (= It doesn't matter to me). ○ [+ question word] *I don't care how much it costs, just buy it.*

care /ker, kær/ *n* [C/U] ○ [C] *She seemed weighed down by all her cares.*

WANT /ker, kær/ *v* [I] *fml* (used in polite offers and suggestions) to want something ○ [+ *to* infinitive] *Would you care to join us for dinner?*

WORD FAMILY care

Nouns	care carelessness	*Verbs*	care
		Adverbs	carefully carelessly
Adjectives	careful careless		

IDIOM with care

• **(in) care of,** *abbreviation* **c/o** at the address of ○ *You can write me in care of my grandmother.* ○ **USAGE:** Used to give someone a mailing address where you can be contacted when you are staying away from home.

PHRASAL VERBS with care

• **care for** *someone/something* **PROVIDE FOR** to provide for a person or animal's needs and to protect that person or animal ○ *Bob and his sister take turns caring for their elderly mother.*

• **care for** *something/someone* **LIKE** to like something or someone ○ *I don't care for seafood.*

careen /kəˈriːn/ *v* [I] to go forward, esp. quickly, while moving from side to side ○ *The car skidded and careened wildly across several lanes of traffic.*

career JOB /kəˈrɪr/ *n* [C] a job for which you are trained and in which it is possible to advance during your working life, so that you get greater responsibility and earn more money ○ *He's hoping for a career in social work.* ○ *She left college to pursue an acting career.*

career /kəˈrɪr/ *adj* [not gradable] done as a job all your life ○ *a career politician*

SPELLING

career

Many people make mistakes when spelling the word **career**. Note that the correct spelling has "-reer" at the end of the word.

Connors had a long and successful career in the police force.

MOVE /kəˈrɪr/ *v* [I always + adv/prep] (esp. of a vehicle) to move fast and without control ○ *The bus careered down a slope and hit a telephone pole.*

carefree /ˈker·friː, ˈkær-/ *adj* having no worries, problems, or anxieties; happy ○ *Anna has a carefree summer ahead of her.*

careful /ˈker·fəl, ˈkær-/ *adj* ○ See at CARE ATTENTION

carefully /ˈker·fə·li, ˈkær-/ *adv* ○ See at CARE ATTENTION

caregiver /ˈker ˌgɪv·ər, ˈkær-/ *n* [C] someone who provides for the needs of children or of people who are ill or cannot provide for their own needs

careless /ˈker·ləs, ˈkær-/ *adj* ○ See at CARE ATTENTION

carelessly /ˈker·lə·sli, ˈkær-/ *adv* ○ See at CARE ATTENTION

carelessness /ˈker·lə·snəs, ˈkær-/ *n* ○ See at CARE ATTENTION

caress /kəˈres/ *n* [C] a gentle loving touch or kiss ○ *a mother's soft caress*

caress /kəˈres/ *v* [I/T] ○ [T] *I caressed her face.*

caretaker /ˈker ˌteɪ·kər, ˈkær-/ *n* [C] **1** a person employed to take care of a large building or property, doing cleaning, repairs, gardening, or other jobs ○ *The building's caretaker reported the fire.* **2** A caretaker government is one that is in power for a short period of time until a new one is chosen. **3** A caretaker is also a CAREGIVER.

cargo /ˈkɑr·goʊ/ *n* [C/U] *pl* **cargoes, cargos** goods carried by a ship, aircraft, or other vehicle ○ [U] *The department inspects cargo coming into Hawaii.*

Caribbean /ˌkær·əˈbiː·ən, kəˈrɪb·iː·ən/ *adj, n* [U] (relating to) the sea that is east of Central America and north of South America, or the islands in it and the countries that border this sea

Caribbean English *n* [U] the variety of English, influenced strongly by European languages and CREOLE, spoken in many parts of the Caribbean region

caribou /ˈkær·əˌbuː/ *n* [C] *pl* **caribous, caribou** a large deer with long horns with branches that lives in North America

caricature /ˈkær·ɪ·kəˌtʃʊr, -tʃər/ *n* [C/U] a drawing or a written or spoken description that makes part of someone's appearance or character more noticeable than it really is, or the skill of doing this ○ [C] *I saw a wonderful caricature of the president in the newspaper.*

caricature /ˈkær·ɪ·kəˌtʃʊr, -tʃər/ *v* [T] to show or describe a person in a ridiculous way ○ *It's so easy to caricature politicians.*

carjacking /ˈkɑrˌdʒæk·ɪŋ/ *n* [C/U] an act of stealing a car while someone is in it

carnage /ˈkɑr·nɪdʒ/ *n* [U] the violent killing of large numbers of people, esp. in war ○ *The Battle of Gettysburg was a scene of dreadful carnage.*

carnal /ˈkɑrn·əl/ *adj fml* relating to the physical feelings and desires of the body

carnation /kɑrˈneɪ·ʃən/ *n* [C] a small flower that has a sweet smell and is usually white, pink, or red

carnival /ˈkɑr·nə·vəl/ *n* [C/U] **1** a place of outside entertainment where there are machines you can ride on and games that can be played for prizes ○ [C] *There's a carnival in Payson Park this weekend.* **2** A carnival is also a time of public enjoyment and entertainment when people wear unusual clothes, dance, and eat and drink, usually in the streets of a city.

carnivore /ˈkɑr·nəˌvɔːr, -ˌvoʊr/ *n* [C] an animal that eats meat

carnivorous /kɑrˈnɪv·ə·rəs/ *adj* [not gradable] ○ *Lions and tigers are carnivorous.*

carol /ˈkær·əl/ *n* [C] a CHRISTMAS CAROL

carol /ˈkær·əl/ *v* [I] **-l-, -ll-** to sing carols, esp. by going from house to house ○ *We went caroling in the neighborhood.*

carouse /kəˈrɑʊz/ *v* [I] to enjoy yourself with a loud group of people ○ *They were out carousing till dawn.*

carousel **AMUSEMENT** /ˌkær·əˈsel/ *n* [C] a MERRY-GO-ROUND

MOVING STRIP /ˌkær·əˈsel/ *n* [C] a continuous moving strip at an airport, from which passengers pick up their bags at the end of a trip

carp **COMPLAIN** /kɑrp/ *v* [I] to complain about unimportant matters ○ *However much people carp about junk mail, many of them read it.*

FISH /kɑrp/ *n* [C] *pl* **carp, carps** a large, edible fish that lives in lakes and rivers

carpenter /ˈkɑr·pən·tər/ *n* [C] a person whose job is making and repairing wooden objects and structures

carpentry /ˈkɑr·pən·tri/ *n* [U] the skill or trade of a carpenter, or the work done by a carpenter ○ *That staircase is a beautiful piece of carpentry.*

carpet /ˈkɑr·pət/ *n* [C/U] thick, woven material for covering floors, or a piece of this material

carpet /ˈkɑr·pət/ *v* [T] to cover a floor surface with a carpet

carpetbagger, **carpet bagger** /ˈkɑr·pətˌbæg·ər/ *n* [C] ***US history*** a person from the American North who tried to profit in the American South after the Civil War

car pool /ˈkɑr·puːl/ *n* [C] an arrangement in which a group of people take turns driving each other or their children to and from work or school

car-pool /ˈkɑr·puːl/ *v* [I] ○ *It's easier to car-pool, but you can't choose when to leave.*

carport /ˈkɑr·pɔːrt, -poʊrt/ *n* [C] a shelter for cars that has a roof and one or more open sides, and that can be built against the side of a house

carriage **VEHICLE** /ˈkær·ɪdʒ/ *n* [C] **1** a vehicle with four wheels pulled by a horse or horses **2** A carriage is also a BABY CARRIAGE.

POSITION /ˈkær·ɪdʒ/ *n* [U] *fml* the way in which you hold your body when standing or moving around ○ *She had great stage presence and perfect carriage.*

carrot **VEGETABLE** /ˈkær·ət/ *n* [C] a long, pointed, orange root, eaten as vegetable, either raw or cooked

REWARD /ˈkær·ət/ *n* [C] something that is offered to someone in order to encourage that person to do something ○ *If they finished the construction ahead of schedule, they were offered the carrot of a bonus.*

carry **TRANSPORT** /ˈkær·i/ *v* [T] to transport or take from one place to another ○ *The plane carried 116 passengers and a crew of seven.* ○ *Would you like me to carry your bag for you?* ○ *Underground cables carry electricity to all parts of the city.*

carrier /ˈkær·iː·ər/ *n* [C] a person or thing that carries or delivers something ○ *She's got a job as a letter carrier.*

HAVE WITH YOU /ˈkær·i/ *v* [T] to have something with you from one place to another ○ *I carry my wallet in my back pocket.* ○ *I don't carry a lot of cash.*

SPREAD /ˈkær·i/ *v* [T] to take something from one person or thing and give it to another person or thing; to spread ○ *The mosquitoes will be studied to see if they carry the virus.*

carrier /ˈkær·iː·ər/ *n* [C] *medical* a person who can give a disease to other people but may not show any signs of having the disease

HAVE /ˈkær·i/ *v* [T] to have something as a part, quality, or result ○ *All our rental cars carry collision insurance.* ○ *I'm sorry, we don't carry shoes (= we*

do not sell shoes). ○ *His argument carries a lot of conviction* (= is supported by strong belief).

SUPPORT WEIGHT /ˈkær·i/ *v* [T] to support the weight of something ○ *The weight of the roof is carried by steel beams.*

C

KEEP IN OPERATION /ˈkær·i/ *v* [T] to support, keep in operation, or make a success ○ *We cannot afford to carry people who don't do their share of the work.*

WIN /ˈkær·i/ *v* [T] to win the support, agreement, or sympathy of a group of people ○ *Gore is expected to carry* (= get the most votes in) *the midwestern states.*

APPROVE /ˈkær·i/ *v* [T] to win approval or support for something ○ *With 21 votes for, and 8 opposed, the motion is carried.*

COMMUNICATE /ˈkær·i/ *v* [T] to include a particular item of news, information, etc. in something printed, broadcast, or sent over electric wires ○ *Newspapers and radio and TV stations throughout Missouri carried the story.*

REACH /ˈkær·i/ *v* [I] (esp. of sounds) to be able to reach or travel a particular distance ○ *The actors' voices carried all the way to the back of the theater.*

MOVE NUMBER /ˈkær·i/ *v* [T] to put a number into another column when doing addition

MOVE BODY /ˈkær·i/ *v* [T] to move and hold your body in a particular way ○ *You can tell she's a dancer by the way she carries herself.*

IDIOMS with carry

• **carry a tune** to be able to sing the correct musical sounds of a tune ○ *Neither of my brothers can carry a tune, but my sister is a good singer.*

• **carry weight** to be considered serious and important enough to influence other people ○ *The Senator's opinion carries a lot of weight in Congress.*

PHRASAL VERBS with carry

• **carry** *someone* **away** to cause someone to become very excited and to lose control ○ *I got carried away and spent too much money.*

• **carry off** *something* **SUCCEED** [M] to succeed in doing or achieving something, esp. when this is difficult ○ *I wouldn't dare wear anything that outrageous, but Michelle carried it off wonderfully.*

• **carry off** *something* **REMOVE** [M] to remove something ○ *Thieves broke the store window and carried off jewelry worth thousands of dollars.*

• **carry on** *(something)* **CONTINUE** to continue to do or be involved with something ○ *Dianne is carrying on the family tradition by becoming a lawyer.* ○ *You've got to carry on as though nothing happened.*

• **carry on BEHAVE** to behave in an excited or anxious way that is not controlled ○ *The kids have been carrying on all day.*

• **carry out** *something* [M] to perform or complete a job or activity; to fulfill ○ *I was elected to carry out a program, the governor said, and I have every intention of carrying it out.*

• **carry over** *(something)* [M] to move to or to come from a place or time ○ *I try not to let my problems at work carry over into my private life.* ○ *The competitive balance of the regular season has been carried over to the playoffs.*

• **carry** *someone* **through** *something* **HELP** to help someone in a difficult situation ○ *We have only enough money to carry us through the next 3 months.*

• **carry through** *something* **COMPLETE** [M] to bring to a successful end; to complete ○ *We are determined to carry our plans through to completion.*

carry-on *adj* [not gradable] small enough to be carried onto an aircraft with you ○ *All carry-on luggage must be stowed under the seat in front of you or in one of the overhead compartments.*

carryout /ˈkær·iːˌɑʊt/ *n* [C] a TAKEOUT ○ *She ordered a gourmet carryout.*

car seat *n* [C] a seat for a small child that can be attached to a seat in a car

carsick /ˈkɑr·sɪk/ *adj* (of a passenger in a car) feeling like you want to vomit because of the movement of the car

carsickness /ˈkɑr ˌsɪk·nəs/ *n* [U]

cart /kɑrt/ *n* [C] **1** a vehicle with either two or four wheels that is pushed by a person, or pulled by an animal, esp. a horse, and is used for carrying goods **2** A cart is also a SHOPPING CART.

PHRASAL VERB with cart

• **cart away** *something/someone*, **cart off** *something/someone* [M] to take something or someone somewhere, esp. using a lot of effort ○ *We cleaned out the garage and carted tons of stuff away.* ○ *He was carted off to jail.*

cartel /kɑr ˈtel/ *n* [C] a group of similar independent companies or countries who join together to control prices and limit competition

cartilage /ˈkɑrt̬·əl·ɪdʒ/ *n* [U] a strong, elastic type of tissue found in humans in the joints and other places such as the nose, throat, and ears ➤ Picture: **joint**

cartography /kɑr ˈtɑg·rə·fi/ *n* [U] the science or art of making or drawing maps

carton /ˈkɑrt·ən/ *n* [C] a box made from cardboard for storing goods, or a container made from cardboard or plastic in which esp. milk or fruit juice is sold

cartoon DRAWING /kɑr ˈtuːn/ *n* [C] a drawing, esp. in a newspaper or magazine, that tells a joke or makes an amusing political criticism

cartoonist /kɑr ˈtuː·nəst/ *n* [C] ○ *a popular political cartoonist*

MOVIE /kɑr ˈtuːn/, **animated cartoon** *n* [C] a movie made using characters and images that are invented and drawn

cartridge /ˈkɑr·trɪdʒ/ *n* [C] **1** a container that is used in a larger piece of equipment, and which can be replaced with another similar part ○ *a video game cartridge* **2** A cartridge is also a tube containing an explosive substance and often a bullet for use in a gun.

cartwheel /ˈkɑrt·hwiːl, -wiːl/ *n* [C] a fast, skillful movement in which you stretch out your arms and throw yourself sideways and upside down onto one, then both, hands with your legs straight and pointing up, before landing on your feet again

carve /kɑrv/ *v* [I/T] **1** to make something by cutting into esp. wood or stone, or to cut into the surface of stone, wood, etc. ○ [T] *This totem pole is carved from a single tree trunk.* **2** To carve a large piece of cooked meat is to cut thin pieces from it: [I/T] *Would you like me to carve (the turkey)?*

carving /ˈkɑr·vɪŋ/ *n* [C/U] a decorative object made from esp. wood or stone, or the art of making patterns in or objects from these materials

PHRASAL VERBS with **carve**

• **carve out** *something* to create or obtain something that helps you by skillful activities ○ *She carved out a reputation for herself as a high-powered lawyer.*

• **carve up** *something* [M] to divide something into parts ○ *The new owner carved up the company and sold off several divisions.*

cascade /kæsˈkeɪd/ *n* [C] a short, steep WATERFALL (= place where a river falls to a lower level), often one of a series ○ (*fig.*) *A cascade of golden hair fell down her back* (= Her hair seemed to flow down her back).

cascade /kæsˈkeɪd/ *v* [I always + adv/prep] to fall quickly and in large amounts; to flow ○ *The blast shattered windows, sending pieces of glass cascading to the pavement.*

case SITUATION /keɪs/ *n* [C] **1** a particular situation or example of something ○ *We don't normally accept credits from courses taken at another university, but we'll make an exception in your case.* ○ *It was a case of not knowing what to say.* ○ *She said I refused to answer the question, but that is not the case* (= that is not accurate). **2 In case** means if something else should happen: *I think we should leave a little early, in case there's a lot of traffic.* **3 In case of** *something* means if something should happen, esp. something unusual or unexpected ○ *In case of fire, go immediately to the nearest emergency exit.*

PROBLEM /keɪs/ *n* [C] an item or particular matter that is being dealt with as a problem to be solved, or a person considered in this way ○ *Your skin problem may be a mild case of eczema.* ○ *He is a sad case – out of work and with few friends to help him.*

ARGUMENT /keɪs/ *n* [C] **1** arguments, facts, and reasons in support of or against something ○ *He presented the case against cutting the military budget.* **2** *law* In a court of law, a case is a matter to be decided by a judge or JURY (= group of people): *She claimed the city's negligence caused her accident, but she lost the case.*

CONTAINER /keɪs/ *n* [C] a container used for protecting or storing things ○ *an eyeglass case* ○ *a case of seltzer*

GRAMMAR /keɪs/ *n* [C] ***grammar*** the form a noun, pronoun, or adjective takes depending on its relationship to other words in a sentence ○ *The possessive case of a noun is usually formed with the ending -'s.*

case study *n* [C] a detailed examination of a particular process or situation over a period of time ○ *She published a series of case studies on how schools used computers in language learning.*

cash /kæʃ/ *n* [U] money in the form of bills and coins ○ *Are you going to pay by credit card or cash?*

cash /kæʃ/ *v* [T] to get cash in exchange for esp. a check ○ *Can I cash a traveler's check here?*

PHRASAL VERBS with **cash**

• **cash in** *something* [M] to exchange something that represents value for the money it is worth ○ *The fund will have to begin cashing in its Treasury bonds.*

• **cash in on** *something* to use an opportunity to do something to your own advantage, esp. a financial advantage ○ *His hotel is cashing in on the Phoenix area's emergence as a golf mecca.*

• **cash out** *(something)* to accept money in exchange for something that represents value ○ *Many executives cashed out large chunks of stock when the price was near its high.*

cashew /ˈkæʃ·uː, kəˈʃuː/ *n* [C] a small, edible nut

cash flow *n* [U] the rate at which money goes into, or into and out of, a business ○ *As long as that positive cash flow continues, there'll be a need to spend it.*

cashier /kæˈʃɪr/ *n* [C] a person whose job is to receive and pay out money in a store, bank, restaurant, etc.

cash machine *n* [C] an ATM

cashmere /ˈkæʒ·mɪr, ˈkæʃ-/ *n* [U] a type of very soft material that is made from the hair of goats from Kashmir ○ *a fine cashmere sweater*

cash register *n* [C] a machine in a store or other business in which money is stored and that records sales

casing /ˈkeɪ·sɪŋ/ *n* [C] a container or cover that goes around something to hold it together or protect it ○ *A metal casing enclosed the three-inch thick cable.*

casino /kəˈsiː·noʊ/ *n* [C] *pl* **casinos** a building where people play games to win money

cask /kæsk/ *n* [C] a strong, round, wooden container used for storing liquid

casket /ˈkæs·kət/ *n* [C] a COFFIN

casserole /ˈkæs·əˌroʊl/ *n* [C] a dish made by cooking meat, vegetables, or other foods inside a heavy container at low heat, or the heavy, deep container with a lid used in cooking such dishes

cassette /kəˈset/ *n* [C] a flat, rectangular device containing a very long strip of magnetic material that is used to record sound or pictures; an AUDIOCASSETTE or VIDEOCASSETTE ○ *He listens to cassettes, CDs, even vinyl records.* ○ *Insert the cassette and press play.*

cassette player *n* [C] a device used for listening to recorded music that has been replaced mainly by the CD

cast CAUSE TO APPEAR /kæst/ *v* [T] *past* **cast 1** to cause something to appear, as if by throwing something ○ *People complained about the shadows cast by the new skyscraper.* ○ *(fig.) A new scientific study may cast some light on* (= help to explain) *why women live longer than men.* **2** In the sport of fishing, if you cast something, such as a line or a net, you throw it far into the water: *We watched the trout fishermen casting their lines.*

CHOOSE ACTORS /kæst/ *v* [T] *past* **cast** to choose actors to play particular parts in a play, movie, or show, or to choose an actor for a part ○ *They are casting the show in New York right now.* ○ *She's been cast as a young doctor in an upcoming movie.*

cast /kæst/ *n* [C] all the actors in a movie, play, or show

SHAPE /kæst/ *v* [T] *past* **cast** to make an object by pouring liquid, such as melted metal, into a shaped container to become hard ○ *The bronze statue is being cast next week.*

cast /kæst/ *n* [C] an object made in a particular shape by pouring a liquid substance into a container having that shape and letting the liquid harden

COVERING /kæst/ *n* [C] a hard covering used to keep a broken bone in the correct position and protect it until it heals

VOTE /kæst/ *v* [T] *past* **cast** to give a vote ○ *Altogether, 358 votes were cast.*

IDIOM with cast

• **cast doubt on** *someone/something* to cause people to feel uncertainty about something ○ *New evidence has cast doubt on the guilty verdict.*

PHRASAL VERBS with cast

• **cast about**, **cast around** to search in many different places for something that you need ○ *She spent years casting about for a career.*

• **cast off** (of a ship) to leave ○ *The ship was scheduled to cast off at 8 p.m.*

castaway /ˈkæs·təˌweɪ/ *n* [C] a person who has escaped from a ship that has sunk and managed to get to an island or country where there are few or no other people

caste /kæst/ *n* [C/U] ***social studies*** **1** one of the traditional social groups in Hindu society **2** Caste can also refer generally to a social class system in any society: [U] *The founders of the new nation rejected a social system based on caste.*

caster /ˈkæs·tər/ *n* [C] a small wheel, usually one of a set, that is fixed to the bottom, usually of the leg, of a piece of furniture so that it can be moved easily

castigate /ˈkæs·təˌgeɪt/ *v* [T] to criticize someone or something severely ○ *Health inspectors castigated the kitchen staff for not keeping the place clean.*

cast iron *n* [U] a type of iron that is made into shapes by being poured into containers when melted ○ *a cast-iron frying pan*

castle /ˈkæs·əl/ *n* [C] **1** a large building with strong walls, built in the past by a king or other important person for protection against attack **2** A castle is also a ROOK.

castoff /ˈkæs·tɔːf/ *n* [C] something, esp. a piece of clothing, that you no longer want and give away ○ *His family was poor, and he always wore castoffs.*

castrate /ˈkæs·treɪt/ *v* [T] ***biology*** to remove the TESTICLES (= organs that produce sperm) of a male animal

casual **NOT SERIOUS** /ˈkæʒ·ə·wəl/ *adj* not serious or careful in attitude; only partly interested ○ *a casual glance at a magazine* ○ *Even to the casual observer, the forgery was obvious.*

INFORMAL /ˈkæʒ·ə·wəl/ *adj* not formal; relaxed in style or manner ○ *We have a small office and I am very casual and wear slacks and sports shirts and things like that.*

casually /ˈkæʒ·ə·wə·li/ *adv* ○ *We were told to dress casually for the walking tour.*

TEMPORARY /ˈkæʒ·ə·wəl/ *adj* **1** not regular or frequent; temporary or done sometimes ○ *casual laborers* **2** Casual also means slight: *He was only a casual acquaintance – I didn't know him well.*

NOT PLANNED /ˈkæʒ·ə·wəl/ *adj* not intended or planned ○ *a casual remark* ○ *casual conversation*

casualty /ˈkæʒ·wəl·ti, ˈkæʒ·əl·ti/ *n* [C] a person hurt or killed in a war or other destructive event, or something prevented by an event ○ *The number of casualties from Sunday's tsunami continues to rise.* ○ *New team uniforms were a casualty of the budget cuts.*

cat /kæt/ *n* [C] a small, furry animal with four legs and a tail, often kept as a pet, or any of a group of related animals that are wild, and some of which are large and fierce, such as the lion

CAT /kæt/ *n* [U] *abbreviation for* computerized axial tomography (= a way of taking pictures of structures inside the body)

cataclysm /ˈkæt̬·əˌklɪz·əm/ *n* [C] an extremely destructive event or violent change ○ *environmental/natural cataclysms*

cataclysmic /ˌkæt̬·əˈklɪz·mɪk/ *adj*

catalog, **catalogue** /ˈkæt̬·əlˌɔːg, -ˌɑg/ *n* [C] a listing, sometimes with explanations or pictures, of items offered for sale, of items that are available for use, or of objects described for a scientific purpose ○ *The company's spring catalog is filled with pictures of beautifully made clothing for girls.* ○ *Students can search the library's on-line catalog and order books.* ○ *(fig.) I have a whole catalog of things that need to be done.*

catalog, **catalogue** /ˈkæt̬·əlˌɔːg, -ˌɑg/ *v* [T] ○ *Scientists were cataloging the plants of their regions.*

catalyst /ˈkæt̬·əl·əst/ *n* [C] **1** a condition, event, or person that is the cause of an important change **2** ***biology***, ***chemistry*** A catalyst is also a substance that causes or speeds a chemical reaction without itself being changed.

catapult /ˈkæt̬·əˌpʌlt, -ˌpʊlt/ *v* [T always + adv/prep] **1** to become famous or important very suddenly, in the process moving beyond others who had been more famous or important ○ *The album of hit songs catapulted her almost overnight into national stardom.* **2** Something or someone that is catapulted is thrown forward with great force or speed.

cataract **EYE CONDITION** /ˈkæt̬·əˌrækt/ *n* [C] an area of the eye that changes to become unclear, causing a person not to see well, or this condition of the eye

FALLING WATER /ˈkæt̬·əˌrækt/ *n* [C] a place in a river where the water falls to a lower level

catastrophe /kəˈtæs·trə·fi/ *n* [C] a sudden event that causes great suffering or destruction ○ *Losing his job was a financial catastrophe for his family.* ○ *A chemical plant leak could cause an environmental catastrophe.*

catastrophic /ˌkæt̬·əˈstrɑf·ɪk/ *adj* ○ *Continued rain will cause catastrophic flooding.*

catch **TAKE HOLD** /kætʃ, ketʃ/ *v* [I/T] *past* **caught** to take or get hold of a moving object, or to hold and prevent someone from getting away ○ [I] *She tossed him the car keys and yelled, "Catch!"* ○ [T] *He sneaked into the fairgrounds without paying and hoped nobody would catch him.*

catch /kætʃ, ketʃ/ *n* [C/U] **1** the act of taking hold of something that is thrown or comes through the air ○ [C] *The ball was hit well, but the centerfielder made a leaping, one-handed catch to end the game.* **2** Catch is also the activity of throwing and receiving a ball with another person: [U] *My kids are always begging me to play catch.*

catcher /ˈkætʃ·ər, ˈketʃ-/ *n* [C] (in baseball) a player who catches the ball when it is thrown to the player who is hitting for the opposing team

DISCOVER /kætʃ, ketʃ/ *v* [T] *past* **caught** to discover, find, or become aware of something ○ *If the disease is caught in time, most patients get well quickly.* ○ *I hope I catch all the mistakes in my term paper.*

SEE /kætʃ, ketʃ/ *v* [T] *past* **caught** to see or hear something or someone, or to understand ○ *I'm sorry, I didn't quite catch what you said.*

TRAVEL /kætʃ, ketʃ/ *v* [T] *past* **caught** to travel or be able to travel on a train, bus, aircraft, etc. ○ *He always caught the 6:05 train out of Grand Central.*

BECOME INFECTED /kætʃ, ketʃ/ *v* [T] *past* **caught** to get an illness ○ *I caught a cold.*

catching /ˈkætʃ·ɪŋ, ˈketʃ-/ *adj* (of an illness) able to be given to someone else ○ *I've got a rash, but I don't think it's catching.*

PROBLEM /kætʃ, ketʃ/ *n* [C] *infml* a hidden problem or disadvantage ○ *That sales price sounds too good to be true – there must be a catch to it somewhere.*

DEVICE /kætʃ, ketʃ/ *n* [C] a small device with a movable part that is used to fasten something ○ *The catch on the bracelet is broken.*

IDIOMS with **catch**

• **catch** *your* **breath** to wait and rest for a moment when you have been very active, so that you can begin to breathe more slowly ○ *Don't try to talk, just sit down and catch your breath.*

• **catch** *someone's* **eye** to cause someone to notice something or someone ○ *I was looking around the store for a present for my mom, and this book caught my eye.*

• **catch fire** to start burning ○ *When the grass in the yard caught fire, I thought the whole house was going to burn down.*

• **catch** *someone* **off guard**, **catch** *someone* **by surprise** to surprise someone, esp. in a way that makes the person feel confused or uncertain ○ *The news caught her completely off guard – she didn't know what to say.* ○ *The strength of the storm caught many residents by surprise.*

• **catch sight of** *someone/something*, **catch a glimpse of** *someone/something* to see something only for a moment ○ *I caught sight of someone with red hair and knew it was you.*

• **caught up in** *something* **1** so involved in an activity that you do not notice other things ○ *I was so caught up in my school work, that I didn't realize what was happening with my sister.* **2** To be **caught up in something** also means to be involved in an activity that you did not intend to be involved in: *He got caught up in the demonstrations and got arrested.*

• *someone* **wouldn't be caught dead** someone dislikes something very much ○ *I wouldn't be caught dead wearing a dress like that – it's like something my grandmother would wear!*

PHRASAL VERBS with **catch**

• **catch on** **BECOME POPULAR** to become fashionable or popular ○ *Why did the electronic gadget catch on so fast?*

• **catch on** **UNDERSTAND** to understand ○ *We were teasing Jim, but he was slow to catch on that we were joking.*

• **catch up** **REACH ANOTHER** to reach someone or something by moving faster than the other person or thing ○ *She is really fast, and I couldn't catch up with her.* ○ (fig.) *We're a young, growing company, and we're trying to catch up to the competition.* ○ Related noun: CATCH-UP

• **catch up** **TALK** to talk with someone you know in order to exchange news or information ○ *By the time coffee came, R.J. and Angelo had caught up a little bit.*

• **catch up on** *something* to do something that you have not been able to do recently ○ *I have to catch up on my reading.*

catch-22 *n* [C] a situation in which there are only two possibilities, and you cannot do either because each depends on having done the other first

catch-up *n* [U] the activity of trying to do as well as a competitor or of trying to reach a level of achievement ○ *Having started his fund-raising late, he had to* **play catch-up** *if he wanted to get enough money for his political campaign.* ○ Related verb: CATCH UP

catchy /ˈkætʃ·i, ˈketʃ·i/ *adj* (esp. of a tune or song) pleasing and easy to remember ○ *a catchy melody*

catechism /ˈkæt̬·əˌkɪz·əm/ *n* [C] a set of questions and answers used to teach esp. the beliefs of a Christian religion

categorical /ˌkæt̬·əˈgɔːr·ɪ·kəl, -ˈgɑr-/ *adj* without doubt or possibility of not being true; certain ○ *The president issued a categorical denial.*

category Ⓐ /ˈkæt̬·əˌɡɔːr·i, -ˌɡoʊr·i/ *n* [C] a grouping of people or things by type in any systematic arrangement ○ *The light trucks weigh less than 5,000 pounds and are in a category that includes minivans, pickups, and sport utility vehicles.*
categorize Ⓐ /ˈkæt̬·ə·ɡəˌrɑɪz/ *v* [T] ○ *The books are categorized by subject.*
categorization Ⓐ /ˌkæt̬·ə·ɡə·rəˌzeɪˈʃən/ *n* [U]

cater /ˈkeɪt̬·ər/ *v* [I/T] to provide food and drinks for an occasion or event ○ [T] *Who catered your party?*
caterer /ˈkeɪt̬·ə·rər/ *n* [C] ○ *an experienced caterer*

PHRASAL VERB with cater

• **cater to** *someone/something* to provide what someone or something needs or wants ○ *Our magazines cater to professionals such as lawyers and physicians.*

caterpillar /ˈkæt̬·əˌpɪl·ər, ˈkæt̬·ər-/ *n* [C] a small animal with a narrow body and many legs, and which feeds on the leaves of plants and later develops into a BUTTERFLY or MOTH (= flying insect)

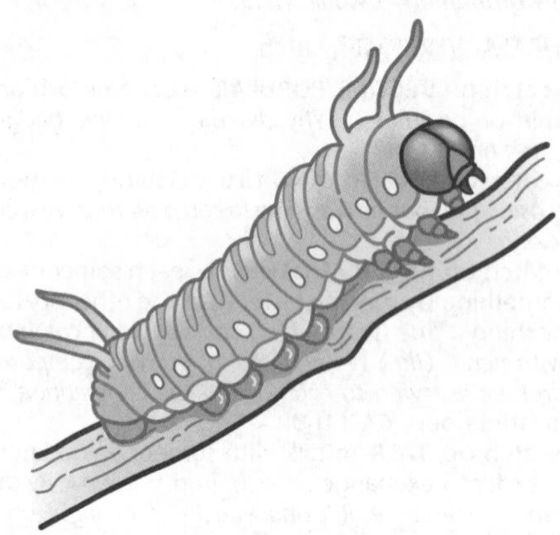

CATERPILLAR

catfish /ˈkæt·fɪʃ/ *n* [C] an edible fish with a flat head and stiff growths like hairs around its mouth, found in rivers and lakes

catharsis /kəˈθɑr·səs/ *n* [C/U] *pl* **catharses** the experience of expressing strong emotions that previously were blocked ○ [C] *It's the director's hope that Germans who see his movie will go through a catharsis similar to his own.*
cathartic /kəˈθɑrt̬·ɪk/ *adj* ○ *a cathartic experience*

cathedral /kəˈθiː·drəl/ *n* [C] a large and important church, esp. one that is the center of a large area

catheter /ˈkæθ·ət̬·ər/ *n* [C] *medical* a thin tube put into the body temporarily to help remove a liquid or to put in medicine

cathode /ˈkæθˌoʊd/ *n* [C] ***chemistry, physics*** one of the ELECTRODES (= object that electricity moves through) in a piece of electrical equipment; the positive electrode in a BATTERY (= device that produces electricity) and the negative electrode in most other electrical devices

cathode ray *n* [C] ***chemistry, physics*** a flow of ELECTRONS sent out by a CATHODE inside a closed container from which the air has been removed or which contains a special gas

cathode ray tube, *abbreviation* **CRT** *n* [C] ***physics*** a tube-shaped part in a television or computer screen, inside which a flow of ELECTRONS (= small pieces of an atom) is produced to create the images or text

Catholic /ˈkæθ·lɪk, -ə·lɪk/ *n, adj* ROMAN CATHOLIC.

Catholicism /kəˈθɑl·əˌsɪz·əm/ *n* [U] ROMAN CATHOLICISM.

catnap /ˈkæt·næp/ *n* [C] a short sleep, esp. during the day

CAT scan /kæt/ *n* [C] a picture of structures inside the body, taken with a special machine

catsup /ˈketʃ·əp, ˈkætʃ·əp/ *n* [U] KETCHUP

cattle /ˈkæt̬·əl/ *pl n* large farm animals kept for their milk or meat; cows and BULLS ○ *beef/dairy cattle*

catty /ˈkæt̬·i/ *adj* (of words, esp. speech) intended to hurt someone; unkind ○ *catty remarks*

catwalk /ˈkæt·wɔːk/ *n* [C] **1** a narrow structure built beside a bridge or building or above a stage, used for walking or performing work **2** A catwalk is also a long, narrow stage used in a fashion show by MODELS (= people employed to show how new clothes look when they are worn).

Caucasian /kɔːˈkeɪ·ʒən/ *n* [C] a white person

caucus /ˈkɔː·kəs/ *n* [C] ***politics & government*** **1** a meeting of the people who run a political party to plan activities and to decide which people the party will support in an election **2** A caucus is also a group of people within a larger organization, esp. Congress, who have similar interests: *the Congressional Black Caucus*

caught /kɔːt/ *past simple and past participle of* CATCH

cauliflower /ˈkɑl·ɪˌflɑʊ·ər, ˈkɔː·lɪ-, -ˌflɑʊr/ *n* [C/U] a firm, round, white vegetable that is eaten cooked or raw

cause REASON /kɔːz/ *n* [C/U] **1** something without which something else would not happen ○ [C] *The investigation will determine the cause of the airplane accident.* ○ [C] *She studied the causes of human behavior.* **2** Cause is also reason for doing or feeling something: [U] *He had just cause to feel disturbed by these events.* ○ [U] *There is no cause for alarm.*
cause /kɔːz/ *v* [T] ○ *The wind and rain caused several accidents.*

WORD CHOICES cause

An alternative to "cause" is the phrasal verb **bring about**.

*Many illnesses are **brought about** by poor diet and lack of exercise.*

When something causes something to happen or exist, you can use the verbs **result in** or **lead to.**

*The fire **resulted in** damage to their house.*

*Reducing speed limits has **led to** fewer deaths on the highways.*

If something causes someone or something to be in a particular state, the verb **make** is often used.

*The heat is **making** me tired.*

The verb **arouse** is sometimes used when something causes a strong feeling or emotion.

*It's a subject which has **aroused** a lot of interest.*

If the feeling it causes is negative, you can use the verb **breed.**

*Favoritism **breeds** resentment.*

The verbs **trigger** or **spark** are sometimes used to talk about something causing something else to happen.

*Some people find that certain foods **trigger** their headaches.*

*Her theories have **sparked** a great deal of debate.*

For talking about the person or thing who causes something to happen, you can use the phrase **responsible for.**

*Last month's bad weather was **responsible for** the crop failure.*

PRINCIPLE /kɔːz/ *n* [C] an idea or principle strongly supported by some people ○ *He devoted himself to charitable causes and gave away millions of dollars.*

causeway /ˈkɔːz·weɪ/ *n* [C] a raised road, esp. across water

caustic /ˈkɔː·stɪk/ *adj* **1** strongly critical ○ *a caustic remark* **2** ***chemistry*** Caustic means able to burn through things.

caution /ˈkɔː·ʃən/ *n* [C] a warning ○ *It's a good time to invest, he said, but a word of caution is in order.*
caution /ˈkɔː·ʃən/ *v* [I/T] to warn someone about a possible problem or danger ○ [T] *They cautioned her not to walk through the park at night.* ○ [I always + adv/prep] *Experts caution against reading too much into the decline of stock market prices.*
cautionary /ˈkɔː·ʃəˌner·i/ *adj* ○ *Some saw the fatal crash as a cautionary tale about the use of cell phones while driving.*

cautious /ˈkɔː·ʃəs/ *adj* not acting quickly in order to avoid risks; careful ○ *Most doctors are cautious about advising you to have surgery.* ○ *Auto companies are taking a cautious approach toward introducing electric cars.*
caution /ˈkɔː·ʃən/ *n* [U] careful attention ○ *Use caution when approaching the railroad crossing.*
cautiously /ˈkɔː·ʃə·sli/ *adv* ○ *She was in the habit of driving cautiously.*

cavalier /ˌkæv·əˈlɪr/ *adj* not serious or caring enough about matters that other people are serious about ○ *a cavalier attitude toward public health concerns*

cavalry /ˈkæv·əl·ri/ *n* [C] an army group which fights from ARMORED vehicles, HELICOPTERS (= type of aircraft) or, esp. in the past, while riding horses

cave /keɪv/ *n* [C] a large hole in the side of a hill, cliff, or mountain, or underground ○ *It was very dark and cold inside the cave.* ➤ Picture: **stalactite; stalagmite**

PHRASAL VERBS with cave

• **cave in FALL IN** (of a structure) to fall in suddenly, esp. because of a lack of support ○ *The building's roof caved in under the weight of the snow.*
• **cave in AGREE TO** to agree to demands that you originally opposed because you have become tired or frightened ○ *She accused the university of caving in to political pressures.*

caveat /ˈkæv·iːˌæt, ˈkɑv·iːˌɑt/ *n* [C] a warning, for example about the use or effectiveness of something ○ *One caveat: Know when passengers must be back on board the plane.*

caveman /ˈkeɪv·mæn/ *n* [C] *pl* **-men** a person who lived in the past, early in human history, when humans made tools from stone and often lived in caves

cavern /ˈkæv·ərn/ *n* [C] a large cave
cavernous /ˈkæv·ər·nəs/ *adj* (of a space) very large ○ *the cavernous Los Angeles Coliseum*

caviar /ˈkæv·iːˌɑr, ˈkɑv-/ *n* [U] the eggs of various large fish, salted and eaten as a DELICACY (= something rare that it good to eat)

cavity /ˈkæv·ət̬·i/ *n* [C] **1** a hole in a surface or a hollow inside something ○ *the abdominal/chest cavity* **2** A cavity is also a hollow place in a tooth caused by decay.

cavort /kəˈvɔːrt/ *v* [I] to dance around, having a noisy good time ○ *A group of teenagers were cavorting in the park.*

cc /siːˈsiː/ *n* [C] *abbreviation for* CUBIC CENTIMETER

CD *n* [C] *abbreviation for* compact disc (= small, plastic disk with a metal surface on which information or sound is recorded) ○ *I bought a new CD player.*

CD-ROM /ˌsiː·diːˈrɑm/ *n* [C] a CD that contains information that can be read on a computer but not changed

C.E. *abbreviation for* **1** Common Era, used for the period of time beginning with the year 1 of the CALENDAR used today in many parts of the world, esp. in Europe and North and South America ○ *The last Roman legions left Britain in 410 C.E.* **2** C.E. is also an *abbreviation for* CHRISTIAN ERA

cease Ⓐ /siːs/ *v* [I/T] to stop an action or condition ○ [T] *Clapp had to cease publication because of lack of money.* ○ [+ to infinitive] *It was hard to accept that one day he would simply cease to exist.*
ceaseless Ⓐ /ˈsiː·sləs/ *adj* [not gradable] continuing without ever stopping ○ *When a baby becomes ill there can be ceaseless crying.*
ceaselessly /ˈsiː·slə·sli/ *adv* [not gradable] ○ *She worked ceaselessly for change.*

ceasefire /ˈsiːs·fɑɪr/ *n* [C] an agreement, esp. between two armies, to stop fighting

cedar /ˈsiːd·ər/ *n* [C/U] a tall, wide, evergreen tree, or its wood, which has a sweet smell ○ [U] *a cedar chest*

C

cede /siːd/ *v* [T] *fml* to give control or possession of something, esp. land to someone else, often unwillingly or because forced to do so ○ *New Orleans was ceded to Spain in 1763.*

ceiling /ˈsiː·lɪŋ/ *n* [C] **1** the upper surface of a room that you see when you look above you ○ *The kitchen ceiling needs painting.* **2** A ceiling is also an upper limit put on something that varies: *There is a 10% ceiling on rent increases.*

celeb /səˈleb/ *n* [C] *short form of* CELEBRITY

celebrate /ˈsel·əˌbreɪt/ *v* [I/T] to recognize an important occasion by taking part in an activity that makes it special ○ [T] *Children's Day has been celebrated in Japan for hundreds of years.*

celebration /ˌsel·əˈbreɪ·ʃən/ *n* [C/U] ○ [C] *a Fourth of July celebration*

WORD FAMILY celebrate			
Nouns	celebration celebrity	*Adjectives*	celebrated
		Verbs	celebrate

celebrated /ˈsel·əˌbreɪt̬·əd/ *adj* famous for some special quality or ability ○ *Kelley was the most celebrated clown of his era.*

celebrity /səˈleb·rət̬·i/, *short form* **celeb** /səˈleb/ *n* [C] someone who is famous, esp. in the entertainment business ○ *Hollywood celebrities turned up at Laguna Beach.*

celery /ˈsel·ə·ri/ *n* [U] a vegetable with long, green stems that can be eaten raw or cooked

celestial /səˈles·tʃəl/ *adj* of or from the sky above us ○ *The moon is a celestial body.*

celibacy /ˈsel·ə·bə·si/ *n* [U] the state of intentionally not being married or having a sexual relationship

celibate /ˈsel·ə·bət/ *adj* [not gradable] ○ *a celibate life*

cell ORGANISM /sel/ *n* [C] ***biology*** the smallest basic unit of a plant or animal ○ Related adjective: CELLULAR

ROOM /sel/ *n* [C] a small room, esp. in a prison

ENERGY /sel/ *n* [C] ***physics*** another name for a BATTERY ELECTRICAL DEVICE

cellar /ˈsel·ər/ *n* [C] a room under the ground floor of a building, esp. a house, that is usually used for storage

-celled /seld/ *suffix* ***biology*** used to form adjectives that describe how many cells an organism has

cello /ˈtʃel·oʊ/ *n* [C/U] *pl* **cellos** a large, wooden musical instrument with four strings which a player rests on the floor, holding it between the legs while sitting, and plays with a BOW (= stick with hairs attached to it), or this type of instrument generally

cellist /ˈtʃel·əst/ *n* [C] ○ *a cellist with the Chicago Symphony*

cellophane /ˈsel·əˌfeɪn/ *n* [U] a thin, transparent material used for covering food and other items

cellular /ˈsel·jə·lər/ *adj* [not gradable] ***biology*** having to do with the cells of an organism

cellular phone /ˈsel·jə·lər ˈfoʊn/, **cell phone** /ˈsel·foʊn/ *n* [C] a telephone that can be used anywhere you go because it operates with radio signals

celluloid /ˈsel·jəˌlɔɪd/ *n* [U] a type of plastic used in the past to make many items, esp. film for movies

cellulose /ˈsel·jəˌloʊs, -ˌloʊz/ *n* [U] the main substance in the cell walls of plants, which is used in making paper, artificial fibers, and plastics

cell wall *n* [C] ***biology*** the hard outer covering that surrounds a plant cell and that consists mainly of CELLULOSE ➤ Picture: **cell**

Celsius /ˈsel·siː·əs/, **centigrade**, *abbreviation* **C** *n* [U] a range of numbers for measuring temperature in which water freezes at 0° and boils at 100° ○ Compare FAHRENHEIT

cement /sɪˈment/ *n* [U] **1** a gray powder that is mixed with water, sand, and other substances, becomes very hard when dry, and is used in making concrete **2** Cement also means concrete: *There weren't any chairs, so she sat on the cement.*

cement /sɪˈment/ *v* [T] **1** to attach firmly, or to cover with cement ○ *The dentist cemented the tooth back in place.* **2** If you cement an agreement or relationship, you make it unlikely to change: *She cemented the sale with a down payment.*

cementation /ˌsiːˌmenˈteɪ·ʃən/ *n* [U] ***earth science*** the process by which solid material that has been dissolved in water sticks together to form rock when the water EVAPORATES (= changes to a gas)

cemetery /ˈsem·əˌter·i/ *n* [C] an area of ground in which dead bodies are buried

censor /ˈsen·sər/ *v* [T] to remove parts of something, such as a book, movie, or letter, that you do

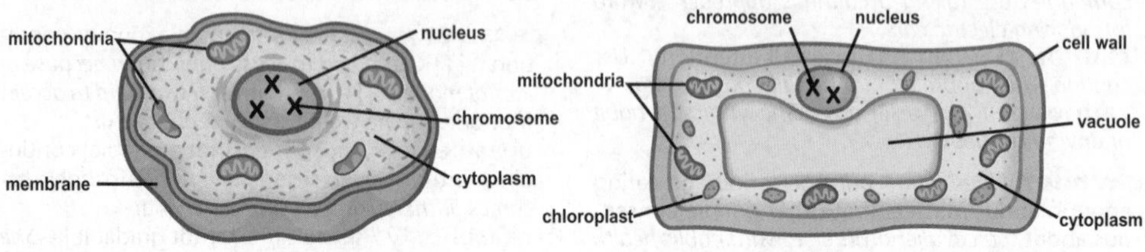

ANIMAL CELL

PLANT CELL

not want someone to see or hear ○ *She opposes efforts to censor the Internet.*
censor /ˈsen·sər/ *n* [C] a person who censors something
censorship /ˈsen·sərˌʃɪp/ *n* [U] the practice of censoring ○ *Artists and critics accused him of censorship.*

censure /ˈsen·tʃər/ *n* [U] strong criticism or disapproval, esp. when it is the official judgment of an organization
censure /ˈsen·tʃər/ *v* [T] ○ *The Senate rarely censures its members.*

census /ˈsen·səs/ *n* [C] ***politics & government*** a count for official purposes, esp. one to count the number of people living in a country and to obtain information such as age, sex, race, etc.

cent /sent/ *n* [C] a unit of money worth 1/100 of a dollar ○ *The newspaper costs 50 cents.*

centennial /senˈten·iː·əl/, **centenary** /senˈten·ə·ri, ˈsent·ənˌer·i/ *n* [C] the day or year that is 100 years after a particular event, esp. an important one; the 100th ANNIVERSARY ○ *The sculpture commemorates Wyoming's centennial.*

center MIDDLE /ˈsent·ər/ *n* [C] **1** the middle point or part ○ *She stood in the center of the stage.* **2** ***politics & government*** In politics, the center is a set of opinions that are not extreme. **3** In some sports, esp. football and BASKETBALL, a center on a team is a player whose position is between other players or in the center.
center /ˈsent·ər/ *v* [T] to put something in the center ○ *The headings should be centered on the page.*

PLACE /ˈsent·ər/ *n* [C] a building or set of buildings having a particular purpose, or a place connected with a particular activity ○ *a shopping center* ○ *the Kennedy Center for the Performing Arts* ○ *New York is a center for the arts.*

WORD FAMILY center

Nouns	center decentralization	*Verbs*	center centralize decentralize
Adjectives	central centrist	*Adverbs*	centrally

IDIOM with center

• **the center of attention** someone who everyone else notices or watches ○ *He likes being the center of attention.*

PHRASAL VERB with center

• **center on** *something*, **center around** *something* to have as the main subject or interest ○ *The discussion centered on how students develop reading comprehension.*

centerpiece /ˈsent·ərˌpiːs/ *n* [C usually sing] the most important part of something ○ *The centerpiece of most environmental studies is conservation.*

centigrade /ˈsen·təˌgreɪd/ *n* [U] CELSIUS.

centimeter /ˈsent·əˌmiːt̬·ər/, *abbreviation* **cm** *n* [C] a unit of measurement of length equal to 0.01 meter or 0.39 inch

centipede /ˈsent·əˌpiːd/ *n* [C] a small animal like a WORM with a long, thin body and many legs

central NEAR THE MIDDLE /ˈsen·trəl/ *adj* in, at, from, or near the center ○ *He grew up in central Illinois.*
centrally /ˈsen·trə·li/ *adv* near the center ○ *We want a hotel that's centrally located.*

IMPORTANT /ˈsen·trəl/ *adj* main or important ○ *American novels often take money as their central concern.*

CONTROLLED /ˈsen·trəl/ *adj* (of something having separate parts) controlled from a single place or by a single organization ○ *A central computer tracks reservations.*
centralize /ˈsen·trəˌlɑɪz/ *v* [T] to bring separate parts together so that they are organized or controlled from one place ○ *The law centralized control over the banking industry.*

central nervous system *n* [C] ***biology*** the main system of nerves in a living thing, consisting of the brain and the SPINAL CORD

centripetal /senˈtrɪp·ət·əl/ *adj* [not gradable] ***physics*** **1** describes a turning object that is moving toward the point around which it is turning **2** **Centripetal force** is the force that pulls an object that is moving in a circle toward the center of the circle. **Centripetal acceleration** is the increase in speed that happens to such an object.

centrist /ˈsen·trəst/ *adj* not extreme in your political opinions ○ *He said all the things that centrist voters seem to want to hear.*

century /ˈsen·tʃə·ri/ *n* [C] **1** a period of 100 years ○ *Her medical career spanned half a century.* **2** A century is also a particular period of 100 years: *the fourth century B.C.* ○ *His music was influential in the 19th and 20th centuries.*

CEO *n* [C] *abbreviation for* CHIEF EXECUTIVE OFFICER

ceramics /səˈræm·ɪks/ *n* [C/U] objects produced by shaping pieces of clay that are then hardened by baking, or the skill of making such objects
ceramic /səˈræm·ɪk/ *adj* [not gradable] ○ *ceramic kitchen tiles*

cereal FOOD /ˈsɪr·iː·əl/ *n* [C/U] a food made from grain that is eaten esp. for breakfast ○ [U] *Do you want cereal or eggs?*

GRASS /ˈsɪr·iː·əl/ *n* [C/U] a type of grass that is grown to produce grain ○ [C] *Wheat, rice, and corn are cereals.*

cerebellum /ˌser·əˈbel·əm/ *n* [C] ***biology*** a large part at the back of the brain that controls the muscles, movement, and balance

cerebral /səˈriː·brəl, ˈser·ə-/ *adj* relating to the brain, esp. the front part of the brain

cerebral palsy *n* [U] a physical condition involving permanent tightening of the muscles that is caused by damage to the brain during or before birth

cerebrum /sə'riː·brəm, 'ser·ə·brəm/ *n* [C] ***biology*** the front part of the brain, which is involved with thought, decision, emotion, and character

ceremony /'ser·ə,moʊ·ni/ *n* [C/U] a set of acts, often traditional or religious, performed at a formal occasion esp. to recognize an important event, or the performing of such acts ○ [C] *a graduation/wedding ceremony* ○ [U] *She was buried without ceremony.*

ceremonial /,ser·ə'moʊ·niː·əl/ *adj* ○ *The queen's role is largely ceremonial.*

certain KNOWING TO BE TRUE /'sɜrt·ən/ *adj* knowing that something is true or will happen and having no cause to feel that it may not be true or may not happen; having no doubt ○ *"I think Emily is going to pick up Judy." "Are you certain?"* ○ *One thing is certain – supporters of the bill are not giving up.* ○ [+ (*that*) clause] *I'm certain (that) he'll be there.* ○ [+ question word] *I'm not certain how much it will cost.* ○ *When you report a robbery, make certain a police report is filled out* (= check that this happens).

certainly /'sɜrt·ən·li/ *adv* **1** *I value his opinion, and I'll certainly miss him.* ○ *I certainly don't spend it watching TV in the evenings.* **2** When said in answer to a question asking for help, certainly means yes: *"Can you give me a hand?" "Certainly."*

PARTICULAR /'sɜrt·ən/ *adj* particular but not named or described ○ *Parents expect their kids to leave home at a certain point.*

certain /'sɜrt·ən/ *pronoun* ○ *Charges were filed against certain of the company's directors.*

LIMITED /'sɜrt·ən/ *adj* [not gradable] some but not exactly stated; limited ○ *She enjoys sports to a certain extent.* ○ *There's a certain amount of exaggeration in all ads.*

WORD FAMILY certain			
Nouns	certainty uncertainty	*Adverbs*	certainly uncertainly
Adjectives	certain uncertain	*Pronouns*	certain

certainty SURE KNOWLEDGE /'sɜrt·ən·ti/ *n* [U] the sure knowledge that something is true ○ *Can you say with absolute certainty that this is the man you saw?*

CERTAIN EVENT /'sɜrt·ən·ti/ *n* [C] something that has no possibility of any other result; something that you know will happen in a particular way ○ *There are few certainties in life.*

certificate /sər'tɪf·ɪ·kət/ *n* [C] an official document that gives information ○ *a birth/death/marriage certificate*

certification /,sɜrt̬·ə·fə'keɪ·ʃən/ *n* [C/U] proof or a document proving that someone is qualified for a particular job, or that something is of good quality ○ [C] *Adult workers are increasingly going back to school for a degree or certification to improve their job opportunities.* ○ [U] *He will seek organic certification of his beef and poultry products.*

certified check *n* [C] a check that a bank has already paid for

certified mail *n* [U] mail for which proof of delivery is obtained

certified public accountant, *abbreviation* **CPA** *n* [C] a person who has completed the training and passed a state exam to become an ACCOUNTANT

certify /'sɜrt̬·ə,fɑɪ/ *v* [T] *fml* to state something officially, esp. that something is true or correct or that someone has been trained to a particular standard ○ *Inspectors must certify that the building is safe.*

certified /'sɜrt̬·ə,fɑɪd/ *adj* [not gradable] having a document that proves you have successfully completed a course of training ○ *a certified teacher* ○ [+ *to* infinitive] *She is certified to practice medicine.*

cervix /'sɜr·vɪks/ *n* [C] *medical* the narrow, lower part of a woman's uterus

cervical /'sɜr·vɪ·kəl/ *adj* [not gradable] *medical* ○ *cervical cancer*

cesarean (section), **caesarean** /sɪ'zær·iː·ən ('sek·ʃən), -'zer-/, *abbreviation* **C-section** *n* [C] *medical* an operation on a woman to allow the birth of her child through a cut made in her ABDOMEN

cessation /ses'eɪ·ʃən/ *n* [C/U] *fml* the ending of a condition or the stopping of an activity ○ [C usually sing] *a cessation of violence*

cesspool /'ses·pɪt/ *n* [C] a large, underground hole or container that is used for collecting and storing human waste and dirty water ○ (*fig.*) *Government there was a cesspool of corruption.*

chafe RUB /tʃeɪf/ *v* [I/T] to make or become damaged or sore by rubbing ○ [T] *That bracelet chafed my wrist.*

BE ANNOYED /tʃeɪf/ *v* [I always + adv/prep] to be or become annoyed or lose patience ○ *Some students chafed at the increased security presence.*

chagrin /ʃə'grɪn/ *n* [U] a feeling of being upset, disappointed, or annoyed, esp. because of a failure or mistake ○ *We grow lots of squash, much to my children's chagrin.*

chagrined /ʃə'grɪnd/ *adj* ○ *She was chagrined to discover her mistake.*

chain CONNECTED RINGS /tʃeɪn/ *n* [C] **1** a length of metal rings that are connected together and used for fastening or supporting, and in machinery ○ *She looped the chain around her bike and locked it to the fence.* **2** A chain is also a length of connected rings worn as jewelry: *Mary wore a silver chain around her neck.*

chain /tʃeɪn/ *v* [T] **1** to tie or connect together with a chain ○ *An old bicycle was chained to a post near the front door.* **2** If you are chained to something, you work for long periods with it: *I had no intention of spending my day chained to the stove.*

RELATED THINGS /tʃeɪn/ *n* [C] a set of connected or related things ○ *a mountain chain* ○ *a chain of supermarkets* ○ *That set in motion a chain of events that changed her life forever.*

chain-link fence *n* [C] a strong metal fence that has the appearance of a series of chains connected together

chain of command *n* [C] the way that people with authority in an organization, esp. in the military, are ranked, from the person with the most authority to the next one below, and so on

chain reaction SERIES OF EVENTS *n* [C] a set of related events in which each event causes the next one ○ *The accident caused a chain reaction in which seven trucks piled up on the bridge.*

NUCLEAR REACTION *n* [C] a series of nuclear reactions in which NEUTRONS (= part of an atom) released by FISSION (= the dividing of an atom) go on to cause more fission

chain saw *n* [C] a cutting tool that is powered by a motor and has a continuous chain with sharp points, used mainly for cutting wood

chair FURNITURE /tʃer, tʃær/ *n* [C] a movable seat that has a part for your back to rest against, usually four legs, and sometimes two side parts for your arms

BE IN CHARGE /tʃer, tʃær/ *v* [T] to be the person in charge of a meeting ○ *Would you chair tomorrow's meeting?*

chair /tʃer, tʃær/ *n* [C] a CHAIRPERSON

chairman /ˈtʃer·mən, ˈtʃær-/ *n* [C] *pl* **-men** a person in charge of a meeting, organization, or department; a CHAIRPERSON ○ **USAGE:** Although chairman can refer to a person of either sex, chairperson or chair is often preferred to avoid giving the idea the person is necessarily male.

chairmanship /ˈtʃer·mən ˌʃɪp, ˈtʃær-/ *n* [C usually sing] the state or period during which a particular person is a CHAIRPERSON ○ *the chairmanship of the Alabama Republican Committee*

chairperson /ˈtʃer ˌpɜr·sən, ˈtʃær-/, **chair** /tʃer, tʃær/ *n* [C] *pl* **chairpeople** a person in charge of a meeting, organization, or department ○ *All the members of the committee take turns acting as chairperson.*

chairwoman /ˈtʃer ˌwʊm·ən, ˈtʃær-/ *n* [C] *pl* **-women** a woman in charge of a meeting, organization, or department; a CHAIRPERSON

chalet /ʃæˈleɪ, ˈʃæl·eɪ/ *n* [C] a small, wooden house found in the mountains and used esp. by people on vacation

chalk /tʃɔːk/ *n* [C/U] a type of soft, white rock, or a similar substance, esp. in the shape of a stick and sometimes colored, used for writing or drawing

PHRASAL VERBS with chalk

• **chalk up** *something* to have or record something good or bad ○ *The team chalked up its first regular-season victory by beating Miami.* ○ *Most of the largest banks in the country chalked up large losses on foreign loans.*

• **chalk** *something* **up to** *something* [M] to consider something as being caused by something else ○ *He was clearly lying, and now he's trying to chalk it up to a poor memory.*

chalkboard /ˈtʃɔːk·bɔːrd, -bourd/, **blackboard** /ˈblæk·bɔːrd, -bourd/ *n* [C] a dark surface on a wall or frame on which you write with CHALK

challenge Ⓐ DIFFICULT JOB /ˈtʃæl·əndʒ/ *n* [C/U] something needing great mental or physical effort in order to be done successfully, or the situation of facing this kind of effort ○ [C] *It's a challenge being in a marriage when both partners have high-pressure jobs.* ○ [C] *No matter how long you write, poetry remains a challenge.* ○ [C] *Germany faces broad challenges in the coming years.*

challenge /ˈtʃæl·əndʒ/ *v* [T] ○ *It's easy enough to crank out college graduates, but a good education should really challenge them.*

challenged Ⓐ /ˈtʃæl·əndʒd/ *adj* having a physical or mental condition that makes ordinary activities more difficult than they are for other people; HANDICAPPED

challenging Ⓐ /ˈtʃæl·ən·dʒɪŋ/ *adj* ○ *For a reporter, covering the White House is a challenging assignment.*

ASK TO COMPETE /ˈtʃæl·əndʒ/ *v* [T] to invite someone to take part in a competition ○ *The other candidates challenged the president to take part in a debate.*

challenge /ˈtʃæl·əndʒ/ *n* [C] something that competes with you or is a threat ○ *The governor barely survived a challenge from an unknown opponent in the primary.*

challenger /ˈtʃæl·ən·dʒər/ *n* [C] someone who tries to win a competition and achieve a position, esp. in politics or sports, against someone who has won it and now has that position ○ *An aide to Buchanan said the conservative challenger for the presidency would hold a press conference tomorrow.*

EXPRESSION OF DOUBT /ˈtʃæl·əndʒ/ *n* [C/U] a questioning or expression of doubt about the truth or purpose of something, or the right of a person to have or do something ○ [U] *Because of the way this research was done, its findings are open to challenge.* ○ [C] *The president is clearly anticipating a new challenge to his authority.*

challenge /ˈtʃæl·əndʒ/ *v* [T] ○ *Advanced computers challenge long-held notions about intelligence and thought.*

WORD FAMILY challenge

Nouns	challenge challenger	*Adjectives*	challenged challenging
Verbs	challenge		

chamber ROOM /ˈtʃeɪm·bər/ *n* [C] a room or space used for a particular purpose ○ *the council chamber*

chambers /ˈtʃeɪm·bərz/ *pl n* a judge's private office, where the judge may have legal discussions with lawyers

LEGISLATURE /ˈtʃeɪm·bər/ *n* [C] a group of people who are part or all of a legislature, or an official place where such a group meets ○ *Most states have two chambers, a senate and a house of representatives, modeled after the US Congress.*

SPACE /ˈtʃeɪm·bər/ *n* [C] an enclosed space ○ *The human heart has two chambers.*

chamber music /ˈtʃeɪm·bər ˌmjuː·zɪk/ *n* [U] music written for a small group of performers

chamber of commerce *n* [C] an organization whose members work together to improve business in their city or local area

chameleon /kə'miːl·jən/ *n* [C] **1** a LIZARD (= type of creature) that changes its skin color to match its surroundings so that it cannot be seen **2** A chameleon is also a person who changes his or her opinions or behavior to please others: *Opponents called him a political chameleon for shifting his position on a range of issues.*

chamomile, **camomile** /'kæm·əˌmɑɪl, -ˌmiːl/ *n* [U] a plant whose white and yellow flowers are used to make tea

champagne /ʃæm'peɪn/ *n* [U] a pale yellow or pink, bubbly wine made in France, or a similar wine from somewhere else ○ *The newlyweds were toasted with champagne.*

champion WINNER /'tʃæm·piː·ən/, *short form* **champ** /'tʃæmp/ *n* [C] someone or something, esp. a person or animal, that has beaten all other competitors in a competition ○ *a tennis champion*
championship /'tʃæm·piː·ənˌʃɪp/ *n* [C] the position of being the best in a particular sport or competition, or the competition that decides who is the best ○ *She has held the championship for the past three years.*

SUPPORT /'tʃæm·piː·ən/ *n* [C] a person who enthusiastically supports, defends, or fights for a belief or principle ○ *a champion of free speech*
champion /'tʃæm·piː·ən/ *v* [T] ○ *He championed protection of the wilderness.*

chance OPPORTUNITY /tʃæns/ *n* [C] an occasion that allows something to be done; an opportunity ○ *If you get a chance, come over and see me.* ○ *You had many chances to back out of the deal, and you didn't do it.* ○ *She'd been a substitute on the team, and she wanted a chance to play every day.*

LIKELIHOOD /tʃæns/ *n* [U] a level of possibility that something will happen; likelihood ○ *I've applied to seven different universities, and there's a good chance I'll get into two of them.*
chances /'tʃæn·səz/ *pl n* ○ *Chances are, they'll be late as usual.* ○ *What are the chances of getting a ticket to the concert tonight?*

RISK /tʃæns/ *n* [C] a possibility that something bad will happen; a risk ○ *There's a chance of injury in almost any sport.* ○ *You don't get anywhere in life without taking chances.*
chance /tʃæns/ *v* [T] to do something although it involves risk ○ *It's a very popular restaurant, and we may not get a table, but let's chance it.*
chancy /'tʃæn·si/ *adj* involving risk ○ *The show's financing was chancy, and that made us all nervous.*

LUCK /tʃæns/ *n* [U] the happening of something in a way that no one could have known, so that it seems to have no cause ○ *Four years ago we met by chance in Paris.* ○ *Do you by any chance know when the last bus leaves tonight?*
chance /tʃæns/ *v* [I] to happen or find something in a way that is not planned or expected ○ *I chanced upon some old love letters in a drawer.*

USAGE

chance or lucky?

Chance is not used when you are talking about good things that happen. In this situation use **lucky**.

We were lucky because the weather was perfect.

~~*We had the chance because the weather was perfect.*~~

chancellor /'tʃæn·sə·lər/ *n* [C] a person in a position of the highest or high rank, esp. in a government or university ○ *Helmut Kohl became the first chancellor of a united Germany in 1990.*

chandelier /ˌʃæn·də'lɪr/ *n* [C] a decorative light that hangs from the ceiling and has several parts like branches for holding LIGHT BULBS or, esp. in the past, candles ○ *A gorgeous crystal chandelier hung in the dining room.*

change BECOME DIFFERENT /tʃeɪndʒ/ *v* [I/T] **1** to make or become different, or to do, use, or get one thing in place of another thing ○ [T] *I've changed jobs twice in the past ten years.* ○ [T] *I changed my hairstyle – do you like it?* ○ [I] *Attitudes about lots of things changed during the 1960s.* ○ [I] *It's surprising how fast kids change during their teen years.* **2** To change over from one thing to something else is to stop doing or using one thing and to start doing or using another: [I] *We just changed from oil heat to gas.*
change /tʃeɪndʒ/ *n* [C/U] **1** [U] *Let me know if you have any change of plans.* **2** **A change** often refers to something unusual or new that is better or more pleasant than what existed before ○ *We decided we needed a change, so we went to Florida for a couple of weeks.* ○ *Why don't we eat on the porch for a change?*
changeable /'tʃeɪn·dʒə·bəl/ *adj* changing often ○ *The weather is very changeable this time of year.*
changed /tʃeɪndʒd/ *adj* [not gradable] (of a person) showing a new and very different behavior or character ○ *After two months in the hospital, he returned home a changed man.*

USAGE

change

When you use **change** as a noun, be careful to use the correct preposition. Use **change in** to describe a change from one situation to a different one.

There has been a change in the attitude of local people over the last few months.

~~*There has been a change on the attitude of local people over the last few months.*~~

Use **change of** when something such as an address or job is being replaced by a different one.

Can you give me your change of address?

Use **change to** in order to describe a change that someone makes so that something is different but not completely different.

We may have to make some changes to the design.

~~*We may have to make some changes in the design.*~~

WORD CHOICES change

The verb **alter** is a common alternative to "change."

*We've had to **alter** our plans.*

If you often change something that you do, you can use the verb **vary**.

*Try to **vary** the children's diet a little.*

If someone changes the purpose or appearance of something, you can use the verb **convert**, or the phrasal verb **turn into**.

*We're going to **convert** the spare bedroom into an office.*

*There are plans to **turn** his latest book **into** a movie.*

If you change something completely and improve it, the verb **transform** is sometimes used.

*The riverside area has been **transformed** into a shopping and sports complex.*

If you change something slightly in order to improve it, you can use the verb **modify**.

*The engine was **modified** to improve its performance.*

If someone changes from doing or using one thing to doing or using another, the verb **switch** is sometimes used.

*We've **switched** over to low-fat milk.*

*Jack has just **switched** jobs.*

CLOTHES/BEDS /tʃeɪndʒ/ *v* [I/T] to remove one set of clothes and put a different set on yourself or someone else, such as a baby, or to remove dirty sheets from a bed and put clean ones on it ○ [I] *I'll just change into* (= put on) *something a little dressier.* ○ [T] *Could you change the baby/the baby's diaper* (= put on a clean one)*?* ○ [T] *I changed the sheets/the bed* (= the sheets on the bed) *in the guest room.*

change /tʃeɪndʒ/ *n* [C] a set of clothes that is additional to the clothes that you are wearing ○ *Bring a change of clothes with you in case we stay overnight.*

MONEY /tʃeɪndʒ/ *v* [T] to get or give money in exchange for money, either because you want it in smaller units, or because you want the same value in foreign money ○ *Can you change a $100 bill for me?* ○ *I had to change some American money into pesetas before I arrived in Spain.*

change /tʃeɪndʒ/ *n* [U] **1** the difference in money, returned to the buyer, between what is paid for something and the lesser amount that it costs ○ *It costs $17 and you gave me $20, so here's your $3 change.* **2** Change also refers to smaller units of money whose total value is equal to that of a larger unit: *I need change for a $50 bill because I want to take a taxi.* ○ *Do you have change for/of a dollar?* **3** Change can refer to coins rather than bills: *Bring a lot of change for using the public telephones.*

TRANSPORT /tʃeɪndʒ/ *v* [I/T] to get off an aircraft, train, bus, etc. and catch another in order to continue a trip ○ [T] *I had to change planes twice to get there.* ○ [I] *Change at Hartford for the train to Springfield.*

change /tʃeɪndʒ/ *n* [C] ○ *You used to have to make a change in Chicago, but now you can fly direct.*

WORD FAMILY change

Nouns	change changeover interchange	*Adjectives*	changeable changed interchangeable unchanged changing
Verbs	change		

IDIOMS with change

• **change hands** to go from one owner to another ○ *The Italian restaurant isn't as good since it changed hands.*

• **change** *your* **mind** to form an opinion or make a decision about something that is not the same as the one you first had ○ *At first I thought she was unfriendly, but I've changed my mind.*

changeover /ˈtʃeɪn ˌdʒoʊ·vər/ *n* [C] a replacement of one system or method by another ○ *The changeover to the new accounting system created a lot of problems.*

channel Ⓐ **DIRECT** /ˈtʃæn·əl/ *v* [T] to direct something into a particular place or situation ○ *A lot of money has been channeled into cancer research.*

channel Ⓐ /ˈtʃæn·əl/ *n* [C] a way of giving, directing, or communicating something ○ *We've established a regular distribution channel for these products.*

PASSAGE /ˈtʃæn·əl/ *n* [C] **1** a passage for water or other liquids to flow along, or a part of a river or other area of water that is deep and wide enough to provide a route for ships to travel along **2** A channel is also a narrow part of the sea between a continent and an island: *the English Channel*

TELEVISION STATION /ˈtʃæn·əl/ *n* [C] a television station ○ *She switched to another channel to watch the news.*

channel-surfing *n* [U] *slang* the practice of changing frequently from one program to another on a television, watching each one for only a short time

chant /tʃænt/ *v* [I/T] to sing a prayer or song to a simple tune, or to repeat or sing a word or phrase continuously ○ [I] *We sat for hours listening to the chanting.*

chant /tʃænt/ *n* [C] ○ *She led the delegates in the chant, "No more taxes."*

Chanukah /ˈhɑn·ə·kə, ˈxɑn-/ *n* [U] HANUKKAH.

chaos /ˈkeɪ·ɑs/ *n* [U] a state of disorder and confusion ○ *Repairs to the major highway this summer will bring chaos to commuters.*

chaotic /keɪˈɑt̬·ɪk/ *adj* ○ *The house is a little chaotic right now – we're in the middle of repainting.*

chapel /ˈtʃæp·əl/ *n* [C] a small church or an enclosed place in a large church for worship by a small group, or a room in a building set apart for worship

C

chaperon, **chaperone** /ˈʃæp·əˌroʊn/ *n* [C] an older person who is present at a social event to encourage correct behavior ○ *Several teachers acted as chaperons for the school dance.*

chaplain /ˈtʃæp·lən/ *n* [C] an official who is responsible for the religious needs of an organization ○ *a military/police chaplain*

chapped /tʃæpt/ *adj* (of skin) sore, rough, and cracked, esp. when caused by cold weather ○ *chapped lips*

chaps /tʃæps, ʃæps/ *pl n* leather clothing worn over pants by COWBOYS when riding a horse

chapter Ⓐ **BOOK PART** /ˈtʃæp·tər/ *n* [C] any of the separate parts into which a book or other piece of text is divided, usually numbered or given a title

PERIOD /ˈtʃæp·tər/ *n* [C] a period that is part of a larger amount of time during which something happens ○ *The Great Depression was a tragic chapter in the history of the nation.*

SOCIETY /ˈtʃæp·tər/ *n* [C] a local division of a larger organization ○ *The local chapter of the League of Women Voters meets at the library.*

Chapter 11 *n* [U] *law* a legal process in the US by which a company, when it owes money that it cannot pay, can stay in business while it organizes itself in a new way and agrees to pay some debts over a period of time

character **QUALITY** /ˈkær·ɪk·tər/ *n* [C/U] **1** the particular combination of things about a person or place, esp. things you cannot see, that make that person or place different from others ○ [C] *The idea was to modernize the house without changing its homey character.* **2** Character is often used in a positive way to mean qualities that are interesting and unusual: [U] *It's a theater with a lot of character.*

characteristic /ˌkær·ɪk·təˈrɪs·tɪk/ *adj* typical of a person or thing ○ *The creamy richness is characteristic of cheese from this region.*

characteristic /ˌkær·ɪk·təˈrɪs·tɪk/ *n* [C] a typical or noticeable feature of someone or something ○ *Curly hair is one of my family characteristics.* ○ *Her distinguishing characteristic is perseverance.*

characteristically /ˌkær·ɪk·təˈrɪs·tɪ·kli/ *adv* ○ *She gave a characteristically brilliant performance.*

characterize /ˈkær·ɪk·təˌrɑɪz/ *v* [T] **1** to have as a typical quality ○ *The current system is characterized by obsolete technology.* **2** To characterize something also means to describe it by stating its main qualities: *She characterized the novel as wordy in places but very funny.*

characterization /ˌkær·ɪk·tə·rəˈzeɪ·ʃən/ *n* [C] ***literature*** a description of the most typical or important characteristics of someone or something ○ *I don't agree with your characterization of my home town as a boring place to live.*

PERSON /ˈkær·ɪk·tər/ *n* [C] **1** ***literature*** a person represented in a movie, play, or story ○ *The story revolves around three main characters.* **2** A character is also a person, esp. with reference to a particular quality that the person has: *There were one or two suspicious-looking characters hanging around.*

characterization /ˌkær·ɪk·tə·rəˈzeɪ·ʃən/ *n* [U] ***literature*** the method by which a writer represents a person using description and speech

MARK /ˈkær·ɪk·tər/ *n* [C] ***grammar*** a letter, number, or other mark or sign used in writing or printing, or the space one of these takes ○ *This computer screen is 66 characters wide.*

WORD FAMILY character			
Nouns	character characteristic characterization	*Adjectives*	characteristic uncharacteristic
		Verbs	characterize
Adverbs	characteristically		

charade /ʃəˈreɪd/ *n* [C] an act or event that is obviously false, although represented as true ○ *From the beginning we knew who would get the job – the interviews were just a charade.*

charades /ʃəˈreɪdz/ *pl n* a team game in which each member tries to communicate to others of his or her team a particular word or phrase while staying silent and using only actions to represent the sounds or meanings

charcoal /ˈtʃɑr·koʊl/ *n* [U] **1** a hard, black substance similar to coal that can be used as fuel or, in the form of sticks, as something to draw with **2** Charcoal gray is a dark gray color: *a charcoal gray suit*

charge **ASK FOR MONEY** /tʃɑrdʒ/ *v* [I/T] to ask for a price for something ○ [T] *I think they charge too much for football tickets.*

charge /tʃɑrdʒ/ *n* [C] ○ *There's no charge for children under six.*

OWE /tʃɑrdʒ/ *v* [T] to buy something and agree to pay for it later ○ *I didn't have any cash, so I charged the food.*

charge /tʃɑrdʒ/ *n* [C] ○ *You have a lot of charges on your bill.*

ACCUSE /tʃɑrdʒ/ *v* [T] to accuse someone of something, esp. to officially accuse someone of a crime ○ *He was charged with resisting arrest.*

charge /tʃɑrdʒ/ *n* [C] ○ *They face civil and criminal charges.*

MOVE FORWARD /tʃɑrdʒ/ *v* [I/T] to move forward quickly, esp. to attack ○ [T] *When the batter was hit with the pitch, he dropped his bat and charged the pitcher.*

CONTROL /tʃɑrdʒ/ *n* [U] responsibility for the control of something or the care of someone ○ *Marilyn agreed to take charge of fundraising.*

charge /tʃɑrdʒ/ *v* [T] ○ *The troopers were charged with guarding the governor.*

STORE ENERGY /tʃɑrdʒ/ *v* [I/T] to put electrical energy into a storage device such as a BATTERY ELECTRICAL DEVICE ○ [I] *It takes several hours for my laptop's batteries to charge.*

charge /tʃɑrdʒ/ *n* [C/U] ***chemistry, physics*** **1** the amount of electricity that an electrical device stores or carries **2** A positive or negative electrical charge is a basic characteristic of matter.

charged /tʃɑrdʒd/ *adj* **1** *They study electrically charged particles.* **2** If an event is charged, people at it are behaving excitedly: *The meeting was emotionally charged.*

INSTRUCT /tʃɑrdʒ/ *v* [T] *law* to instruct (the people deciding a legal case) what the law is in a particular case ○ *The judge charged the jury before deliberations began.*

EXPLOSIVE /tʃɑrdʒ/ *n* [C] the amount of explosive to be fired at one time

IDIOMS with **charge**

• **charged up** excited and full of energy ○ *He was so charged up, he couldn't sleep.*

• **in charge (of *something/someone*)** responsible for something or someone ○ *Who's in charge here?* ○ *The teacher put me in charge of organizing the project.*

charge account *n* [C] an arrangement that allows a customer to buy things and pay for them at a later time

charge card *n* [C] a CREDIT CARD

chariot /ˈtʃær·iː·ət/ *n* [C] a two-wheeled vehicle pulled by a horse, used in ancient times by the military and in racing

charisma /kəˈrɪz·mə/ *n* [U] the ability to attract the attention and admiration of others, and to be seen as a leader ○ *To be a great leader, a person has to have some charisma.*

charismatic /ˌkær·əzˈmæt̬·ɪk/ *adj* ○ *He was the charismatic leader his people had hoped for.*

charitable /ˈtʃær·ət̬·ə·bəl/ *adj* kind and not judging people in a negative way ○ *They are known as a charitable people.*

charitably /ˈtʃær·ət̬·ə·bli/ *adv* ○ *The disagreement was described charitably as a "frank discussion."*

charity /ˈtʃær·ət̬·i/ *n* [C/U] **1** the giving of money, food, or help to those who need it, or an organization that does this ○ [U] *She does a lot of work for charity.* ○ [C] *We donate to a number of charities.* **2** Charity is also the belief that you should help people: [U] *He visits homeless shelters out of charity.*

charitable /ˈtʃær·ət̬·ə·bəl/ *adj* ○ *She was involved in many charitable organizations.*

charlatan /ˈʃɑr·lət·ən, -lə·tən/ *n* [C] a person who pretends to have skills or knowledge that the person does not actually have

charley horse /ˈtʃɑr·liːˌhɔːrs/ *n* [C] *pl* **charley horses** a CRAMP (= a sudden, painful tightening of a muscle), esp. in the leg

charm **ATTRACTION** /tʃɑrm/ *n* [C/U] a special quality of a person or thing that makes the person or thing attractive ○ [C] *I never could resist the charms of the city.*

charm /tʃɑrm/ *v* [T] ○ *Charlie charms everyone.*

charming /ˈtʃɑr·mɪŋ/ *adj* ○ *He was thoughtful and charming.*

LUCKY OBJECT /tʃɑrm/ *n* [C] an object or saying that is believed to bring good luck ○ *Many people carry good luck charms.*

charmed /tʃɑrmd/ *adj*

charred /tʃɑrd/ *adj* burned and made black by fire ○ *The house was just a pile of charred wreckage.*

chart Ⓐ /tʃɑrt/ *n* [C] a way of presenting information, usually by putting it into vertical rows and boxes on a sheet of paper, so it can be easily understood ○ *The chart shows a top-down communication model.* ➤ Picture: **pie chart**

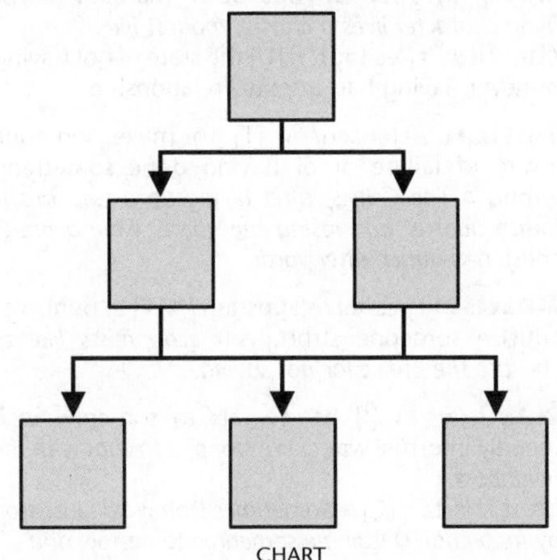

CHART

chart Ⓐ /tʃɑrt/ *v* [T] **1** to record changes in something or the progress of something ○ *The magazine charts current trends in fashion.* **2** Someone who charts a series of actions plans them: *The president plans to chart a new economic policy.*

charter **DOCUMENT** /ˈtʃɑrt̬·ər/ *n* [C] a formal statement, esp. by a government or ruler, of the rights of a group organized for some purpose ○ *The United Nations charter sets forth goals we all admire.*

RENT /ˈtʃɑrt̬·ər/ *v* [T; not gradable] to rent (a vehicle) for a special use ○ *He wanted to charter an airplane.*

charter /ˈtʃɑrt̬·ər/ *n* [C] ○ *Charters with low fares have attracted new airline passengers.*

charter member *n* [C] a member of an organization who helped start the organization or became a member when it began

charter school *n* [C] a school that is paid for with public money but is organized by a private group for a special purpose and admits only students who meet its standards ○ *They formed a charter school for girls who are good at math and science.*

chase **HURRY AFTER** /tʃeɪs/ *v* [I/T] **1** to hurry after in order to catch someone or something ○ [T] *The dog chased squirrels in the park.* **2** To chase something you want is to try very hard to get it: *She is chasing her fourth championship title.* ○ [always + adv/prep] *I was finally able to chase down that address I was looking for.*

chase /tʃeɪs/ *n* [C] ○ *The dog got tired and gave up the chase.*

MAKE LEAVE /tʃeɪs/ *v* [T] to act in a threatening way in order to make a person or animal leave ○ *She's always chasing rabbits out of her garden, but they keep coming back.*

chasm /ˈkæz·əm/ *n* [C] a deep opening in earth or rock ○ *The little bridge over that deep chasm looked very unsafe.*

chassis /ˈtʃæs·i, ˈʃæs·i/ *n* [C] *pl* **chassis** the frame of a vehicle, including the wheels and engine, which supports the upper, covering part

chaste /tʃeɪst/ *adj* without having any sexual activity or involvement outside of marriage ○ *The main character lives a chaste, modest life.*
chastity /ˈtʃæs·tət̬·i/ *n* [U] the state of not having or never having had a sexual relationship

chasten /ˈtʃeɪ·sən/ *v* [T] to make someone aware of failure or of having done something wrong ○ *The Celtics, after giving up a lead in the fourth quarter and losing the game, were a pretty chastened bunch afterwards.*

chastise /tʃæsˈtɑɪz, ˈtʃæs·tɑɪz/ *v* [T] to punish or criticize someone strongly ○ *Economists like to chastise the public for not saving.*

chat /tʃæt/ *v* [I] **-tt-** to talk to someone in a friendly informal way ○ *We stopped to chat with the neighbors.*
chat /tʃæt/ *n* [C] ○ *Sometimes Don would just stop by for a chat.* ○ *Call me sometime tomorrow and we can have a chat.*
chatty /ˈtʃæt̬·i/ *adj* ○ *I sat next to a friendly, chatty woman.*

chateau /ʃæˈtoʊ/ *n* [C] *pl* **chateaus, chateaux** a large house, esp. in France, or a castle in France

chatter /ˈtʃæt̬·ər/ *v* [I] **1** to talk continuously and usually for no serious purpose ○ *The boys and girls kept chattering during the movie.* **2** If your teeth chatter, you are so cold or frightened that you can't stop your upper and lower teeth from hitting against each other. **3** An animal or a machine that chatters makes a sound like fast, continuous talking: *Birds chattered in the trees.* ○ *The printer was chattering away on the desk.*
chatter /ˈtʃæt̬·ər/ *n* [U] ○ *The air was full of the chatter of birds.*

chatterbox /ˈtʃæt̬·ərˌbɑks/ *n* [C] someone who talks continuously ○ *Our three-year-old is a real chatterbox.*

chauffeur /ˈʃoʊ·fər, ʃoʊˈfɜr/ *n* [C] a person employed to drive a private car belonging to someone else
chauffeur /ˈʃoʊ·fər, ʃoʊˈfɜr/ *v* [T] ○ *I was chauffeured around town by my uncle.*

chauvinism /ˈʃoʊ·vəˌnɪz·əm/ *n* [U] the strong and unreasonable belief that your own country, sex, or group is the best or most important ○ *an appeal to national pride and chauvinism*
chauvinist /ˈʃoʊ·və·nəst/ *n* [C]

cheap COST /tʃiːp/ *adj* [*-er/-est* only] **1** costing little money or less than is usual or expected ○ *After World War II, the US had cheap labor, cheap energy, cheap raw materials, cheap housing, cheap food, and cheap transportation.* ○ *Used computers are* **dirt cheap** (= very cheap). **2** If a place that sells goods or services is cheap, it charges low prices: *a cheap department store* **3** Goods that are cheap are low in price but of poor quality: *The cheap rug did not come clean.* **4** *disapproving* Someone who is cheap is unwilling to spend money: *The boss is cheap – he'll never buy a new truck if he can squeeze a few more miles out of the old one.*
cheaply /ˈtʃiː·pli/ *adv* ○ *You can buy paper goods more cheaply if you buy in quantity.*
cheapness /ˈtʃiːp·nəs/ *n* [U] ○ *They chose to build here because of the cheapness and lack of problems the site offered.*

WORD CHOICES cheap

If something is cheap enough for most people to be able to buy, you can say that it is **affordable**, **inexpensive**, or **reasonable**.

*There's very little **affordable** housing around here.*

*They sell **inexpensive** children's clothes.*

*I thought the food was very **reasonable**.*

If something is very cheap, in informal English you can say that it is **dirt cheap**.

*Most of the books they sell are **dirt cheap**.*

The adjective **cut-rate** is sometimes used to describe something that is cheaper than usual.

*We managed to get **cut-rate** tickets the day before the show.*

A piece of equipment that is cheap to use is often described as **economical**.

*I need a car that's reliable and **economical**.*

CHARACTER /tʃiːp/ *adj* [*-er/-est* only] considered to have a low moral character or value ○ *She called him a cheap thug and a liar.*
cheapen /ˈtʃiː·pən/ *v* [T] to make someone or something seem less valuable and less deserving of respect ○ *What the author hates about forgeries is that they cheapen true art.*

cheap shot NEGATIVE REMARK *n* [C] an unfair, negative remark made by someone to achieve an advantage over someone else ○ *Making fun of his name was a cheap shot.*
SPORTS MOVE *n* [C] (in some sports) a sudden, violent, physical move against a player who was not prepared for it

cheapskate /ˈtʃiːp·skeɪt/ *n* [C] someone unwilling to give or spend any money ○ *That cheapskate won't even pay for a postage stamp.*

cheat /tʃiːt/ *v* [I/T] to act in a way that is dishonest, or to make someone believe something that is not true in order to get something for yourself ○ [T] *The insurance companies were found to be cheating consumers.* ○ [T] *They got cheated out of their money.*
cheat /tʃiːt/ *n* [C] ○ *He is a liar and a cheat.*

check EXAMINE /tʃek/ *v* [I/T] to look at or give your attention to something to get information, often to help you decide if something is correct, safe, or suitable ○ [+ *to* infinitive] *Check to see what the weather is like outside.* ○ [T] *I brought the car to the garage to have the brakes checked.* ○ [T] *We checked our records for any information about him.*

○ [I] *We have a claim for lost luggage, and we are checking into it.* ○ [T] *The doctors checked his heart and said it was fine.* ○ [T] *Before you hand in your papers, check your spelling.*

check /tʃek/ *n* [C] ○ *The FBI did a thorough background check on him* (= looked into his past experience and relationships).

STOP /tʃek/ *v* [T] to stop someone from doing or saying something, or to prevent something from increasing or continuing ○ *He started to interrupt but checked himself and said nothing.* ○ *The program is designed to check the spread of malaria.*

check /tʃek/ *n*

MONEY /tʃek/ *n* [C] a printed form, used instead of money, to make payments from your bank account ○ *I've got to cash my pay check.* ○ *She wrote me a check for $120.*

LEAVE /tʃek/ *v* [T] to leave your outer clothing or property temporarily in the care of someone else, usually as a convenience ○ *Let's check our coats before going through the galleries.* ○ *Passengers on this flight will be allowed one carry-on bag, and will have to check any additional bags.*

check /tʃek/ *n* [C] the ticket or small object that you are given and that you use to get back your coat or other personal possessions left in the care of someone else for a short period ○ *I thought I put the coat check in my pocket.*

PATTERN /tʃek/ *n* [C] a pattern made of different colored squares, or one of these squares ○ *The shirt has a pattern of blue and yellow checks.*

checkered /ˈtʃek·ərd/ *adj* having a pattern of different colored squares ○ *a red and white checkered tablecloth*

MARK /tʃek/ *n* [C] a sign (√) that shows that something is correct or done or has been examined ○ *Put a check next to the names of the people who have already paid for their tickets.*

check /tʃek/ *v* [T] ○ *Check the box corresponding to the correct answer to each question.*

REQUEST FOR PAYMENT /tʃek/ *n* [C] a request for payment of money owed to a restaurant, or the piece of paper on which it is written ○ *Waiter, may I have the check, please?*

IDIOM with **check**

• **in check** being controlled within reasonable limits ○ *We've got to find ways of keeping our expenses in check.*

PHRASAL VERBS with **check**

• **check in** to report your arrival, esp. at an airport or hotel, so that you can get the service you are paying for ○ *Be sure to check in at least an hour before your flight.* ○ Related noun: CHECK-IN

• **check off** *something* [M] to mark names or items on a list as correct or as having been dealt with ○ *He checked off their names on the list as they got on the bus.*

• **check out LEAVE** to leave a hotel after paying for your room and services ○ *The Gardners checked out early this morning to catch a plane to Toronto.* ○ Related noun: CHECKOUT

• **check out** *(something)* **PAY FOR** [M] to take the items you have bought, esp. in a large food store, to an area where you pay for them ○ *I had already checked out when I remembered that we were out of milk.* ○ Related noun: CHECKOUT (COUNTER)

• **check out** *something* **EXAMINE** [M] *infml* to examine something or visit a place in order to learn about it ○ *Don't forget you can check us out anytime online.* ○ *You have to check out the nursing home before putting your mother in it.*

• **check out** *(something)* **DECIDE IF TRUE** [M] (of information) to seem to be true because it agrees with other information, or to discover whether information agrees with other information and is therefore likely to be true ○ *Her statement checks out with most of the eyewitness reports.* ○ *The commissioner sent an investigator to check out the rumors.*

• **check out** *something* **GET BOOK** [M] to borrow a book or something else from a LIBRARY (= a place with a collection of books, music, etc.) ○ *We don't think the government should be able to see what citizens check out from public libraries.*

• **check up on** *someone* to find out what someone is doing in order to make certain that the person is behaving correctly or legally ○ *Dad is always checking up on me to make sure I'm doing my homework.*

checkbook /ˈtʃek·bʊk/ *n* [C] a small book of checks on which you write information for making payments or taking money from your bank account

checkers /ˈtʃek·ərz/ *pl n* a game played by two people on a square board, in which each player has twelve circular pieces that are all moved in the same way

check-in *n* [U] the act of recording your arrival at a hotel or at an airport when you are going to travel ○ *The airline also offers online check-in.* ○ Related verb: CHECK IN

checking account *n* [C] a bank account from which you can take money or make payments using a check

checklist /ˈtʃek·lɪst/ *n* [C] a list of things that you must remember to do or consider doing ○ *We went over the checklist of things we had to do before leaving for South Africa.*

checkout /ˈtʃek·ɑʊt/ *n* [U] the act of leaving a hotel and paying your bill ○ *Late checkout should be arranged in advance.* ○ Related verb: CHECK OUT LEAVE

checkout (counter) /ˈtʃek·ɑʊt/ *n* [C] the place in a store where you pay for the things you are buying ○ *She had to wait in line at the checkout.* ○ Related verb: CHECK OUT PAY FOR

checkpoint /ˈtʃek·pɔɪnt/ *n* [C] a place where people or vehicles are stopped and examined by an official

checks and balances *pl n* ***politics & government*** separation of control among several government organizations, such as a JUDICIARY, a LEGISLATURE, and an EXECUTIVE division

checkup /ˈtʃek·ʌp/ *n* [C] a medical examination to test your general state of health ○ *You should have an annual medical checkup.*

cheddar /ˈtʃed·ər/ *n* [U] a hard cheese that is yellow or white in color

C

cheek BODY PART /tʃiːk/ *n* [C] either side of your face below the eyes, where except at the top the skin has no bone behind it and is therefore soft ○ *She welcomed me with a kiss on the cheek.*

RUDE BEHAVIOR /tʃiːk/ *n* [U] rude behavior or lack of respect ○ [+ *to* infinitive] *First he messed up my work and then he had the cheek to accuse me of being disorganized.*

cheekbone /ˈtʃiːk·boʊn/ *n* [C] either of the two bones at the sides of your face just below your eye

cheer /tʃɪr/ *v* [I/T] to give a shout of approval or encouragement for someone ○ [I] *I was one of the people who jumped up and cheered after that speech.*
cheer /tʃɪr/ *n* [C] ○ *He demanded the resignation of the police chief, touching off loud applause and cheers in the audience.*
cheers /tʃɪrz/ *exclamation* a friendly expression spoken before tasting a drink; a TOAST

PHRASAL VERBS with **cheer**

• **cheer** *someone* **on** [M] to express your encouragement and wishes for someone's success ○ *Fans filled every seat available to cheer on the team.*
• **cheer up** *(someone)* [M] to feel encouraged and happier, or to cause someone to feel this way ○ *She plays music to cheer her husband up.* ○ *Cheer up! Things aren't really that bad.*

cheerful /ˈtʃɪr·fəl/ *adj* **1** happy and positive in feeling or attitude ○ *a cheerful face/spirit* ○ *He was a cheerful man with a kind word for everybody.* **2** If a thing or place is cheerful, it is pleasant and friendly and is likely to make you feel positive and happy: *The guest bedroom was bright, airy, and cheerful, overlooking the garden.*
cheerfully /ˈtʃɪr·fə·li/ *adv* ○ *Jonas cheerfully agreed to sleep on the sofa.*
cheery /ˈtʃɪr·i/ *adj* expressing happiness, or making you feel happier ○ *She always gave us a cheery greeting.*
cheerfulness /ˈtʃɪr·fəl·nəs/ *n* [U]

cheerleader /ˈtʃɪrˌliːd·ər/ *n* [C] a young person who leads a crowd at a sports event in shouting encouragement and supporting a team

cheers /tʃɪrz/ *exclamation* ○ See at CHEER

cheese /tʃiːz/ *n* [C/U] a type of solid food made from milk, used with many other foods and eaten plain, esp. with crackers ○ *American/Swiss cheese* ○ [U] *I'd like a pizza with extra cheese, please.*

cheeseburger /ˈtʃiːzˌbɜr·gər/ *n* [C] a HAMBURGER with a slice of melted cheese on it

cheesecake /ˈtʃiːz·keɪk/ *n* [C/U] a cake made from a sweet pastry base covered with a mixture of soft cheese, eggs, sugar, and sometimes fruit ○ [U] *I like strawberry cheesecake.*

cheesy /ˈtʃiː·zi/ *adj* cheap or of low quality ○ *The tourist shops had nothing but cheesy souvenirs.*

cheetah /ˈtʃiːt̬·ə/ *n* [C] a large, wild cat that has yellow-brown fur and black spots and that lives in Africa and south Asia, and is known for its speed

chef /ʃef/ *n* [C] a skilled and trained cook who works in a restaurant, esp. the most important cook

chemical Ⓐ /ˈkem·ɪ·kəl/ *n* [C] any basic substance that is used in or produced by a reaction involving changes to atoms or MOLECULES ○ *His business manufactured farm chemicals.*
chemical Ⓐ /ˈkem·ɪ·kəl/ *adj* ○ *the chemical industry* ○ *a chemical plant producing plastics and rubber*
chemically Ⓐ /ˈkem·ɪ·kli/ *adv* ○ *chemically treated paper*

WORD FAMILY chemical			
Nouns	chemical chemist chemistry	*Adjectives* *Adverbs*	chemical chemically

chemical bond *n* [C] ***chemistry*** an electrical force that holds atoms together to form a MOLECULE (= smallest unit of a substance)

chemical equation *n* [C] ***chemistry*** a statement containing chemical symbols, used to show the changes that happen during a particular chemical reaction

chemical weapon *n* [C] a chemical substance, such as a gas, used as a weapon

chemistry /ˈkem·ə·stri/ *n* [U] ***science*** **1** the basic characteristics of substances and the different ways in which they react or combine with other substances, or the scientific study of such substances and the way they act with other substances ○ *a chemistry department/laboratory* **2** *infml* Chemistry is also the ability of people to have a good relationship: *Building a strong team requires paying attention to team chemistry.*
chemist /ˈkem·əst/ *n* [C] **1** a scientist who works with chemicals or studies their reactions **2** *Br* A chemist or chemist's is a DRUGSTORE.

chemotherapy /ˌkiː·moʊˈθer·ə·pi/ *n* [U] the treatment of diseases, esp. CANCER, using chemicals

cheque /tʃek/ *n* [C] *Cdn, Br* CHECK MONEY

cherish /ˈtʃer·ɪʃ/ *v* [T] to keep hopes, memories, or ideas in your mind because they are important to you and bring you pleasure ○ *We cherish the many memories we have of our dear mother.*
cherished /ˈtʃer·ɪʃt/ *adj* bringing the pleasure of love or caring about someone or something that is important to you ○ *Her most cherished possession is a 1926 letter from F. Scott Fitzgerald.*

cherry /ˈtʃer·i/ *n* [C] a small, round, soft, red or black fruit with a single, hard seed in the middle, or the tree on which the fruit grows

chess /tʃes/ *n* [U] a game played by two people on a square board, in which each player has 16 pieces that can be moved on the board in different ways

chest **BODY PART** /tʃest/ *n* [C] the upper front part of the body of humans and some animals, between the stomach and the neck, enclosing the heart and lungs ○ *He folded his arms across his chest.*

BOX /tʃest/ *n* [C] a large, strong box, usually made of wood, which is used for storing valuable goods or possessions or for moving possessions from one place to another

chesterfield /ˈtʃes·tərˌfiːld/ *n* [C] *Cdn* a SOFA

chestnut /ˈtʃes·nʌt/ *n* [C/U] **1** a large, shiny, red-brown nut, or the tree on which the nuts grow **2** Chestnut is also a deep red-brown color.

chest of drawers, **bureau** /ˈbjʊr·oʊ/ *n* [C] a piece of furniture with drawers in which you keep things such as clothes

chew /tʃuː/ *v* [I/T] to crush food into smaller, softer pieces with the teeth so that it is easier to swallow ○ [I] *The steak was tough and hard to chew.*

chewy /ˈtʃuː·i/ *adj* (of food) needing to be crushed a lot with the teeth before it is swallowed ○ *We enjoyed the fine, chewy, thick-crusted bread.*

PHRASAL VERBS with **chew**

• **chew on** *something* *infml* to think about something ○ *This documentary certainly offers much to chew on.*

• **chew** *someone* **out** [M] to criticize someone angrily ○ *The coach has already chewed out two of his swimmers for arriving late to practice.*

• **chew over** *something* [M] *infml* to think or talk about something, esp. when you need to make a decision ○ *We won't be able to answer right away – we'll need to chew it over.*

• **chew up** *something* [M] to use something quickly ○ *Urban sprawl is chewing up the surrounding farmland.*

chewing gum *n* [U] a soft, usually sweet, sticky substance that you chew to get its flavor, but which you do not swallow

chic /ʃiːk/ *adj* stylish and fashionable ○ *There's an increasing demand for the more chic, higher-quality merchandise.*

chicanery /ʃɪˈkeɪ·nə·ri/ *n* [U] dishonest but attractive talk or behavior that is used to deceive people ○ *The investigation has revealed political chicanery and corruption at the highest levels.*

Chicano /ʃɪˈkɑn·oʊ, tʃɪ-/, *female* **Chicana** /ʃɪˈkɑn·ə, tʃɪ-/ *n* [C] *pl* **Chicanos**, **Chicanas** a person living in the US who was born in Mexico or whose parents came from Mexico

chick /tʃɪk/ *n* [C] a baby bird, esp. a young chicken

chicken **BIRD** /ˈtʃɪk·ən/ *n* [C/U] a type of bird kept on a farm for its eggs or its meat, or the meat of this bird which is cooked and eaten ○ **USAGE:** A male chicken is called a rooster or a cock, and a female chicken is called a hen.

COWARD /ˈtʃɪk·ən/ *n* [C] *infml, disapproving* a person who is too frightened to do something involving a risk

chicken /ˈtʃɪk·ən/ *adj* *infml, disapproving* ○ *Why don't you jump? Are you chicken?*

PHRASAL VERB with **chicken**

• **chicken out** *infml* to decide not to do something because you are too frightened ○ *We were going to go bungee jumping, but Sandra chickened out at the last minute.*

chickenfeed /ˈtʃɪk·ənˌfiːd/ *n* [U] *slang* an amount of money that is so small in comparison with other amounts that it is unimportant and can be ignored ○ *They lost $200,000 on this deal, but that's chickenfeed for a company that big.*

chickenpox /ˈtʃɪk·ənˌpɑks/ *n* [U] an infectious disease that causes a slight fever and red spots on the skin

chicken wire *n* [U] netting made of metal wire, often used as a simple fence to enclose small animals or to keep wild animals out

chickpea /ˈtʃɪk·piː/, **garbanzo (bean)** *n* [C] a hard, pale brown, round seed which can be cooked and eaten ○ *Chickpeas are used to make hummus and falafel.*

chicory /ˈtʃɪk·ə·ri/ *n* [U] a plant with blue flowers, often grown for its edible roots and leaves

chide /tʃɑɪd/ *v* [T] to speak to someone severely because the person has behaved badly ○ *She chided him for his bad manners.*

chief **MOST IMPORTANT** /tʃiːf/ *adj* [not gradable] most important ○ *Their chief objection to the appointment was that she had no judicial experience.*

chiefly /ˈtʃiː·fli/ *adv* ○ *Today John-Philip Sousa is known chiefly for his music played by marching bands all over the US.*

PERSON IN CHARGE /tʃiːf/ *n* [C] the person in charge of a group or organization, or the ruler of a TRIBE (= a group of families) ○ *the chief of police*

chief /tʃiːf/ *adj* [not gradable] highest in position or power ○ *the chief economist/engineer/nurse* ○ *He is chairman and chief executive of the company.*

USAGE

chief or boss/manager?

Chief can only be used to mean "a person in charge of other people" in a few particular senses, such as in the police.

a police chief

Chief can also be used as an adjective in the names of some important jobs.

A new Chief Executive Officer has been appointed this week.

More common words for "a person in charge of other people in a company" are **boss** and **manager**:

I asked my boss/manager if I could have a week off.

~~I asked my chief if I could have a week off.~~

C

chief executive officer, *short form* **chief executive,** *abbreviation* **CEO** *n* [C] the top manager in a company who has the greatest responsibility and makes the most important decisions

chief justice *n* [C] the judge in the highest position in a particular court of law ○ *The Chief Justice of the United States presides over the US Supreme Court.*

chieftain /ˈtʃiːf·tən/ *n* [C] the leader of a TRIBE (= a group of families)

child /tʃɑɪld/ *n* [C] *pl* **children** a person from the time of birth until he or she is an adult, or a son or daughter of any age ○ *Jan has a three-year-old child and two school-age children.* ○ *Now in their 60s, Jerome and Sally have two grown children* (= adult sons or daughters).

childhood /ˈtʃɑɪld·hʊd/ *n* [C/U] the time when a person is a child ○ [C] *She spent most of her childhood on a farm in Texas.*

childish /ˈtʃɑɪl·dɪʃ/ *adj* **1** like or typical of a child, or intended for children ○ *a childish body* ○ *The pictures made the magazine look childish.* **2** When you describe the behavior of an adult or an older child as childish, you mean the person is behaving in a foolish way that is typical of a young child's behavior.

childishness /ˈtʃɑɪl·dɪʃ·nəs/ *n* [U] behavior typical of a child

childless /ˈtʃɑɪl·dləs/ *adj* [not gradable] without children ○ *a childless couple*

childlike /ˈtʃɑɪl·dlɑɪk/ *adj* ○ *childlike enthusiasm/innocence*

childishly /ˈtʃɑɪl·dɪʃ·li/ *adv*

IDIOM with child

• **child's play** something that is very easy to do ○ *For her, computer programming is child's play.*

childbearing /ˈtʃɑɪldˌber·ɪŋ, -ˌbær·ɪŋ/ *n* [C] the process of a woman becoming pregnant and having a child ○ *women of childbearing age*

childbirth /ˈtʃɑɪld·bɜrθ/ *n* [C] the process of giving birth to a baby

child care, **child-care** *n* [U] the job of taking care of children while their parents are at work or are absent for another reason ○ *The child-care providers are closely supervised.*

childproof /ˈtʃɑɪld·pruːf/ *adj* difficult for children to open or use

children /ˈtʃɪl·drən/ *pl of* child

child support *n* [U] money paid by a parent for the living expenses of a child when the parent is no longer living with the child

chili (pepper), **chile** /ˈtʃɪl·i/ *n* [C/U] *pl* **chilies, chiles 1** any of several types of red PEPPER (= type of vegetable) that are used to make foods spicy **2** Chili is also a spicy dish made with beans, chilies, and usually meat.

chill /tʃɪl/ *v* [I/T] to make or become cold but not freeze ○ [I] *Allow the pudding to chill.* ○ [T] *Chill the pudding before serving.*

chill /tʃɪl/ *n* [C] **1** a cold feeling ○ *The sun was bright, but there was a chill in the air.* ○ (*fig.*) *His words sent a chill down her spine* (= made her suddenly very fearful). **2** A chill is also a feeling of cold in your body that makes you shake slightly: *She came home with a headache and chills.*

chilly /ˈtʃɪl·i/ *adj* ○ *a chilly morning* ○ (*fig.*) *Their relationship was decidedly chilly* (= unfriendly) *after the argument.*

chilling /ˈtʃɪl·ɪŋ/ *adj* **1** *a chilling wind* **2** Chilling also means frightening: *The chilling plot of this suspenseful novel moves with amazing quickness.*

IDIOM with chill

• **chilled to the bone** extremely cold ○ *Walking home in the snow, we got chilled to the bone.*

PHRASAL VERB with chill

• **chill out** *slang* to relax instead of worrying or feeling anxious ○ *If anything major happens we're going to find out, so let's chill out and just do what we need to do.*

chime /tʃɑɪm/ *v* [I/T] (of bells) to make a clear ringing sound ○ [I] *The bell in the tower began to chime.*

chime /tʃɑɪm/ *n* [C] a ringing sound

PHRASAL VERB with chime

• **chime in** to speak in a conversation, esp. by interrupting ○ *Everyone at the table began to chime in with their opinions.*

chimney /ˈtʃɪm·ni/ *n* [C] a hollow structure that allows the smoke from a fire inside a building, esp. from a fireplace, to escape to the air outside

chimpanzee /ˌtʃɪmˌpænˈziː/, *short form* **chimp** /tʃɪmp/ *n* [C] an African APE (= animal related to monkeys) with black or brown fur

chin /tʃɪn/ *n* [C] the part of a person's face below the mouth

china /ˈtʃɑɪ·nə/ *n* [U] high quality clay that is shaped and then heated to make it permanently hard, or objects made from this such as cups and plates

Chinatown /ˈtʃɑɪ·nəˌtɑʊn/ *n* [C/U] an area of a city outside China where many Chinese people live and where there are a lot of Chinese restaurants and shops

chink **CRACK** /tʃɪŋk/ *n* [C] a narrow crack or opening ○ *Weeds were growing from a chink in the sidewalk.*

SOUND /tʃɪŋk/ *n* [U] a light ringing sound ○ *the chink of glass against glass*

chinos /ˈtʃiː·noʊz/ *pl n* cotton pants, often of a pale color

chintz /tʃɪns/ *n* [U] cotton cloth, usually printed with patterns of flowers, that has a slightly shiny appearance ○ *chintz curtains*

chintzy /ˈtʃɪn·si/ *adj slang* (of things) cheap and not well made, or (of people) not willing to spend money ○ *He never tipped enough – he was too chintzy.*

chip **PIECE** /tʃɪp/ *n* [C] **1** a small piece of something or a piece that has broken off a larger object ○ *chocolate chips* ○ *wood chips* ○ *Chips of paint from*

the peeling ceiling littered the floor. **2** A chip is also the mark left on an object where a small piece has broken off. **3** A chip is a plastic piece used in some games to represent money or points.
chip /tʃɪp/ *v* [T] **-pp-** ○ *My little boy fell off his bicycle and chipped a tooth.* ○ *This plate is chipped.*

COMPUTER PART /tʃɪp/ *n* [C] a very small piece of SILICON used in a computer and containing electronic systems and devices that can perform particular operations

FOOD /tʃɪp/ *n* [C] a small, flat piece of fried food, esp. a POTATO CHIP or TORTILLA CHIP ○ *a bag of corn chips*

IDIOM with **chip**

• **a chip on** *your* **shoulder** an angry attitude from someone who feels unfairly treated ○ *She's not going to make any friends if she walks around with a chip on her shoulder like that.*

PHRASAL VERB with **chip**

• **chip in** *(something)* to give some money, esp. when several people are giving money to pay for something together ○ *They each chipped in $50 to take their parents out to dinner.*

chipmunk /ˈtʃɪp·mʌŋk/ *n* [C] a small, furry, North American animal with dark strips along its back

chipper /ˈtʃɪp·ər/ *adj* happy and energetic ○ *You seem mighty chipper this morning.*

chips /tʃɪps/ *pl n* **1** POTATO CHIP **2** *Cdn, Br* Chips are FRENCH FRIES.

chiropractor /ˈkɑɪ·rəˌpræk·tər/ *n* [C] a medical person trained to treat pain and injury esp. by pressing the muscles of a person's back to adjust the positions of the bones
chiropractic /ˌkɑɪ·rəˈpræk·tɪk/ *n* [U] the system of treatment used by a chiropractor

chirp /tʃɜrp/ *v* [I] (esp. of a bird) to make a short high sound or sounds

chisel /ˈtʃɪz·əl/ *n* [C] a tool with a long, metal blade that has a sharp edge for cutting esp. wood or stone
chisel /ˈtʃɪz·əl/ *v* [T] to cut with a chisel
chiseled /ˈtʃɪz·əld/ *adj approving* clearly marked with firm lines ○ *a face with finely chiseled features*

chit /tʃɪt/ *n* [C] a note giving information or showing a sum of money that is owed or has been paid ○ *When our flight was delayed, they gave us a chit to get a free meal.*

chitchat, **chit-chat**, /ˈtʃɪt·tʃæt/ *n* [U] informal conversation about unimportant matters

chitin /ˈkɑɪt·ᵊn/ *n* [U] ***biology*** a strong substance in the outer covering of insects and animals such as LOBSTERS, and in the cell walls of some FUNGI

chivalrous /ˈʃɪv·əl·rəs/ *adj* (of men) very polite and kind toward women
chivalry /ˈʃɪv·əl·ri/ *n* [U] very polite behavior, esp. such behavior shown by men toward women

chives /tʃɑɪvz/ *pl n* a plant with long, thin leaves, or the leaves when cut into small pieces and used in cooking to give a flavor similar to onions

chlorine /ˈklɔːr·iːn, ˈkloʊr-/ *n* [U] a poisonous gas, one of the chemical elements, used esp. to make water safe for drinking and swimming
chlorinate /ˈklɔːr·əˌneɪt, ˈkloʊr-/ *v* [T] to add chlorine to water in order to kill organisms that might cause infection

chlorophyll /ˈklɔːr·əˌfɪl, ˈkloʊr-/ *n* [U] ***biology*** the green substance in plants that allows them to use the energy from the sun

chloroplast /ˈklɔːr·əˌplæst, ˈkloʊr-/ *n* [C] ***biology*** one of the parts in a plant cell that contain CHLOROPHYLL and where the energy from the light of the sun is turned into food by PHOTOSYNTHESIS ➤ Picture: **cell**

chock-full /ˈtʃɑkˈfʊl, ˈtʃʌk-/ *adj* [not gradable] very full ○ *The place was chock-full of people.*

chocolate /ˈtʃɑk·lət, ˈtʃɔːk-/ *n* [C/U] a food made from COCOA and often sugar, usually brown and eaten as candy or used in other food such as cakes ○ [U] *chocolate ice cream* ○ [C] *a box of chocolates* (= candies made of chocolate)

choice ACT /tʃɔɪs/ *n* [C/U] an act of choosing; a decision ○ [C] *a difficult/easy choice* ○ [C] *When you're trying to cut the budget deficit, you've got to make tough choices.*

POSSIBILITY /tʃɔɪs/ *n* [C/U] the right to choose, or the possibility of choosing ○ [C] *Well, I still think people have a choice.* ○ [C] *Given a choice, what would you do?* ○ [C] *I asked if I could have a choice which science course to take.* ○ [U] *We have no choice but to drive to the airport* (= That is the only thing we can do).

VARIETY /tʃɔɪs/ *n* [C] a range of different things you can choose ○ [C] *A wide choice of colors is available in this size.*

PERSON/THING /tʃɔɪs/ *n* [C] a person or thing that has been chosen or that can be chosen ○ *She would be my first choice for the job.*

EXCELLENT /tʃɔɪs/ *adj* [*-er/-est* only] of high quality ○ *a choice cut of meat*

choir /kwɑɪr/ *n* [C] a group of people who sing together, esp. for a church or school

choke STOP BREATHING /tʃoʊk/ *v* [I/T] **1** to be unable to breathe because the air passage inside the throat is blocked, or to cause someone to be unable to breathe ○ [I] *He was eating a piece of steak when he began to choke and turn red.* ○ [T] *(fig.) The narrow streets were choked* (= blocked) *with traffic.* **2** To choke someone is to press very hard on that person's neck with your hands.

FAIL /tʃoʊk/ *v* [I] *infml* to be unable to do something, esp. win a competition, because you are aware of its importance and worried about not doing well ○ *He always ran well in practice, but at major meets he usually choked and finished last.*

PHRASAL VERBS with **choke**

• **choke off** *something* to stop the movement or progress of something ○ *He told his staff to stop discussing the scandal in the hope of choking off damaging publicity.*

C

• **choke** *(someone)* **up** [M] to show strong emotion while speaking,or to cause someone to do this ○ *Jon admits to choking up a little during his emotional proposal.* ○ *Just thinking about it chokes me up.*

choker /ˈtʃoʊ·kər/ *n* [C] a piece of jewelry that fits very closely around the neck ○ *a pearl choker*

cholera /ˈkɑl·ə·rə/ *n* [U] a serious infection of the bowels caused by bacteria esp. in water, causing severe DIARRHEA and sometimes death

cholesterol /kəˈles·təˌrɔːl/ *n* [U] a fatty substance that is found in the body tissue and blood of all animals, and which is thought to be part of the cause of heart disease if there is too much of it

chomp /tʃɑmp, tʃɔːmp/, **champ** *v* [I/T] to bite on something and make a chewing movement with your teeth ○ [I] *He chomped on his potato chips.*

choose /tʃuːz/ *v* [I/T] *past simp.* **chose,** *past part.* **chosen** to think about which one of several things is the one you want, and take the action to get it ○ [T] *Parents can choose the schools that they want their kids to go to.* ○ [I] *I can't choose – I like both lamps.* ○ [+ *to* infinitive] *On this issue, Congress chose to fight the president.* ○ [I] *There was not much to choose between them* (= They are similar). ○ [+ question word] *You can choose what you like and we'll send it to you.*

choosy /ˈtʃuː·zi/ *adj* difficult to please because of being very exact about what you like ○ *He's choosy about where he buys fresh fruit and vegetables.*

WORD CHOICES choose

The verbs **pick** and **select** are often used when someone chooses someone or something after thinking carefully.

He's been ***picked*** *for the school football team.*

We've ***selected*** *three candidates.*

In more informal situations **go for, opt for,** or **decide on** are sometimes used.

I've ***decided on*** *blue walls for the bathroom.*

I think I'll ***go for*** *the chocolate cake.*

Mike's ***opted for*** *early retirement.*

The verbs **opt** and **decide** can also be used when someone chooses to do something.

Most people ***opt*** *to have the operation.*

I've ***decided*** *to take the job.*

chop CUT /tʃɑp/ *v* [T] **-pp- 1** to cut something into pieces with a sharp tool, such as an AX ○ *Cal went out to chop some wood for the fireplace.* **2** To chop something off is to separate it from what it was part of by cutting: *Chop the ends off the carrots.* **3** If you chop up something, you cut it into small pieces: *She chopped up some celery for the salad.*

MEAT /tʃɑp/ *n* [C] a small piece of meat with a bone still in it ○ *a lamb/pork/veal chop*

chopper /ˈtʃɑp·ər/ *n* [C] a HELICOPTER

choppy /ˈtʃɑp·i/ *adj* (of the sea or other area of water) with lots of small waves caused by a strong wind

chopstick /ˈtʃɑp·stɪk/ *n* [C usually pl] either of a pair of thin, narrow sticks used for eating food

choral /ˈkɔːr·əl, koʊr-/ *adj* ○ See at CHORUS SINGING GROUP

chord NOTES /kɔːrd/ *n* [C] ***music*** three or more musical notes played at the same time

LINE /kɔːrd/ ***mathematics*** a line SEGMENT (= part) whose end points are points on a circle ➤ Picture: **circle**

chore /tʃɔːr, tʃoʊr/ *n* [C] **1** a job or piece of work that needs to be done regularly ○ *By the time he'd finished all the household chores it was mid-afternoon.* **2** A chore is also something that is difficult and unpleasant: *It was a real chore trying to give our dog a bath.*

choreography /ˌkɔːr·iːˈɑg·rə·fi, ˌkoʊr-/ *n* [U] the movements used by dancers esp. in performing BALLET, or the art of planning such movements

choreographer /ˌkɔːr·iːˈɑg·rə·fər, ˌkoʊr-/ *n* [C]

chortle /ˈtʃɔːrt̬·əl/ *v* [I] to laugh with pleasure and satisfaction

chorus SONG PART /ˈkɔːr·əs, ˈkoʊr-/ *n* [C] a part of a song that is repeated, usually after each VERSE (= the set of lines that are new in each part of the song) ○ *I'll sing the verses but I'd like all of you to join in the chorus.*

SINGING GROUP /ˈkɔːr·əs, ˈkoʊr-/ *n* [C] **1** a group of people who are trained to sing together ○ *He sings in a men's chorus.* **2** A chorus is also a musical part intended to be sung by a chorus or a CHOIR.

choral /ˈkɔːr·əl, ˈkoʊr-/ *adj* relating to music intended to be sung by a chorus or a CHOIR ○ *choral music*

THEATER GROUP /ˈkɔːr·əs, ˈkoʊr-/ *n* [C] a group of performers who, as a team, have a supporting position singing or dancing in a show ○ *She was a member of the chorus before she took over the lead role.*

IDIOM with chorus

• **a chorus of** *something* an opinion given by a large group of people at the same time, or a large group of people giving their opinion ○ *The publication of the book was greeted with a chorus of acclaim.* ○ *A chorus of western economists has expressed their unhappiness with the policy.*

chose /tʃoʊz/ *past simple of* CHOOSE

chosen /ˈtʃoʊ·zən/ *past participle of* CHOOSE

chow /tʃɑʊ/ *n* [U] *slang* food, esp. when prepared for a meal

chowder /ˈtʃɑʊd·ər/ *n* [U] a type of thick soup made with milk, vegetables, and often fish or other sea creatures ○ *clam/corn chowder*

Christ /krɑɪst/ *n* [U] JESUS (CHRIST).

christen /ˈkrɪs·ən/ *v* [T] **1** to call a person, esp. a baby, a Christian through the ceremony of BAPTISM and by naming the person ○ *The parents christened their second child Maria.* **2** If a ship is christened, it is officially given its name: *The First Lady christened the ship, "USS Arizona."* **3** If you

christen something new, you use it for the first time: *I'm going to christen my new golf clubs this week.*
christening /ˈkrɪs·ə·nɪŋ/ *n* [C] ○ *We celebrated the christening of my boss's new baby in grand style.*

Christian /ˈkrɪs·tʃən, ˈkrɪʃ-/ *n* [C] a person who follows or belongs to a religion based on the worship of one God and the teachings of JESUS CHRIST as described in the BIBLE ○ *The Roman Catholic Church is the largest of the Christian churches.*
Christian /ˈkrɪs·tʃən, ˈkrɪʃ-/ *adj* [not gradable] **1** following or belonging to the Christian religion **2** If you describe a person or a person's actions as Christian, you mean that he or she acts according to Christian principles of goodness and kindness toward others: *It wasn't very Christian of you to make him walk home in this rain.*
Christianity /ˌkrɪs·tʃiː ˈæn·əṭ·i, ˌkrɪʃ-/ *n* [U] the Christian faith, a religion based on the belief in one God and on the teachings of JESUS CHRIST, as set forth in the BIBLE

Christian era, *abbreviation* **C.E.** *n* [U] the period of time from the year when Jesus Christ was born to the present

Christian name *n* [C] a name someone is given at BAPTISM (= a ceremony at which a person is named as a Christian)

Christian Science *n* [C] a Christian religion whose members believe illness can be cured by belief and a true understanding of the teachings of Jesus Christ, and by following those teachings

Christmas /ˈkrɪs·məs/ *n* [C/U] December 25th, a day celebrated each year to honor the birth of Jesus, or the period of time just before and after December 25th ○ [U] *People usually visit their families at Christmas.* ○ [C] *I hope you have a very Merry Christmas!*

Christmas card *n* [C] a decorated card expressing good wishes and sent to someone at Christmas

Christmas carol *n* [C] a song about Christmas or winter, sung at Christmas

Christmas Day *n* [C] December 25th

Christmas Eve *n* [C] December 24th, the day before Christmas.

Christmastime /ˈkrɪs·məsˌtɑɪm/ *n* [U] the Christmas season, or the period from about December 24th to January 1st or January 6th

Christmas tree *n* [C] an evergreen tree that is decorated during the Christmas season and placed where people can enjoy looking at it, either inside or outside a building

chromatic aberration /kroʊˈmæṭ·ɪk ˌæb·əˈreɪ·ʃən/ *n* [U] ***physics*** a failure of colors to be seen correctly through a LENS (= curved piece of glass), caused by the lens not being perfect

chromatography /ˌkroʊ·məˈtɑg·rə·fi/ *n* [U] ***chemistry***, ***biology*** a method of finding what separate substances a mixture contains by making it flow, as a liquid or gas, through a material such as paper, which different substances will flow through at different speeds

chrome /kroʊm/ *n* [U] CHROMIUM ○ *The car has bright chrome trim.*

chromium /ˈkroʊ·miː·əm/ *n* [U] a hard, blue-gray, element used in combination with metals or put on a material to form a shiny covering

chromosome /ˈkroʊ·məˌzoʊm, -ˌsoʊm/ *n* [C] ***biology*** any of the structures shaped like rods that are found in living cells and contain the GENES (= chemical patterns) which control what an animal or plant is like ➤ Picture: **cell**
chromosomal /ˌkroʊ·məˈzoʊ·məl, -ˈsoʊ·məl/ *adj* [not gradable] relating to chromosomes

chronic /ˈkrɑn·ɪk/ *adj* (esp. of a disease or something bad) continuing for a long time ○ *Mr. George is resigning because of chronic heart disease.* ○ *There is a chronic shortage of teachers.*
chronically /ˈkrɑn·ɪ·kli/ *adv* ○ *The hospital provides care to chronically ill patients for as long as they need it.*

Chronic Fatigue Syndrome *n* [U] a group of illnesses that causes people to be extremely tired

chronicle /ˈkrɑn·ɪ·kəl/ *n* [C] a record of events in the order in which they happened ○ *This book is the most eloquent chronicle of an empire's downfall that I have seen.* ○ (*infml*) *The diary, although a personal story, is really a chronicle of an important period of history.*
chronicle /ˈkrɑn·ɪ·kəl/ *v* [T] to make a record or tell the history of something ○ *His one-man show chronicles the life of Mark Twain.*

chronology /krəˈnɑl·ə·dʒi/ *n* [C] a list or explanation of events in the order in which they happened ○ *He gave a detailed chronology of the events of the past three days.*
chronological /ˌkrɑn·əˈlɑdʒ·ɪ·kəl/ *adj* ○ *Give me the dates in chronological order.*
chronologically /ˌkrɑn·əˈlɑdʒ·ɪ·kli/ *adv* ○ *Please name the presidents chronologically.*

chrysalis /ˈkrɪs·ə·ləs/ *n* [C] an insect at the stage of development when it is like a WORM protected by a hard cover, before it becomes a MOTH or BUTTERFLY

chrysanthemum /krəˈsæn·θə·məm/, *short form* **mum** *n* [C] any of several types of garden plants that flower in the fall, including some that produce many small flowers and others that have very large, brightly colored flowers

chubby /ˈtʃʌb·i/ *adj* (esp. of children) rounded in a pleasant and attractive way ○ *The perfect baby has, we are told, chubby little fingers and toes, chubby legs, and chubby cheeks.*

chuck **THROW** /tʃʌk/ *v* [T] to throw something without giving it your attention ○ *Chuck me the keys.*
END /tʃʌk/ *v* [T] *infml* to end, give up, or leave something ○ *Last summer, he chucked his ten-year career*

as a stockbroker. ○ *How can you chuck an old friendship like that?*

chuckle /ˈtʃʌk·əl/ *v* [I] to laugh quietly ○ *She was chuckling as she read the letter.*
chuckle /ˈtʃʌk·əl/ *n* [C] ○ *I always get a chuckle out of the Doonesbury comic strip.*

C

chug MAKE SOUND /tʃʌg/ *v* [I always + adv/prep] **-gg- 1** to make the sound of an engine or motor, or to move making this sound ○ *The train chugged up the hill.* **2** To chug also means to move steadily, like a little train: *Yeah, my life is chugging right along, thanks.*
chug /tʃʌg/ *n* [C] ○ *We heard the chug of the boat's engine in the distance.*

DRINK /tʃʌg/, **chug-a-lug** /ˈtʃʌg·əˌlʌg/ *v* **-gg-** *slang* to swallow a drink completely without stopping to breathe ○ [T] *He was so thirsty he chugged three glasses of water.*

chum /tʃʌm/ *n* [C] *infml* a friend ○ *Some of our college chums are a little wild.*
chummy /ˈtʃʌm·i/ *adj infml* ○ *She tells the two of them to look chummy for the picture.*

chump /tʃʌmp/ *n* [C] *infml* a foolish or stupid person ○ *What a chump he was to quit his job.*

chunk /tʃʌŋk/ *n* [C] **1** a thick piece or lump ○ *A large chunk of plaster crashed down from the ceiling.* **2** *infml* A chunk is a large part of something: *Her books must be read in chunks to follow the plot.*
chunky /ˈtʃʌŋ·ki/ *adj* **1** *She wears chunky earrings and rings and a baggy sweater.* **2** Chunky foods have pieces or lumps mixed into a smooth base: *I love chunky peanut butter!* **3** A person who is chunky is strong and built solidly: *She's a chunky woman with a powerful personality.*

church BUILDING /tʃɜrtʃ/ *n* [C] a building for Christian religious activities ○ *We came to a church and went inside to sit and enjoy the quiet.*

ORGANIZATION /tʃɜrtʃ/ *n* [C/U] **1** a Christian religious organization ○ [U] *He went on a trip with some of his friends from church.* **2** Church is also a group of people meeting for a religious gathering: [U] *I'll see you after church.* **3** A church is also one of the larger divisions within Christianity: [C] *The Episcopal and Roman Catholic churches have many similarities.* **4** Church can also mean organized religion generally: [U] *The separation of church and state is an important feature of the US Constitution.*

churchgoer /ˌtʃɜrtʃˌgoʊ·ər/ *n* [C] someone who goes to church regularly

Church of Jesus Christ of Latter-day Saints *n* [U] the church to which MORMONS belong

churchyard /ˌtʃɜrtʃ·jɑrd/ *n* [C] an area around a church, often where people are buried

churlish /ˈtʃɜr·lɪʃ/ *adj* rude, unfriendly, and unpleasant ○ [+ *to* infinitive] *They invited me to dinner and I thought it would be churlish to refuse.*
churlishly /ˈtʃɜr·lɪʃ·li/ *adv* ○ *I churlishly told him to go bother someone else.*

churn /tʃɜrn/ *v* [I/T] **1** to move violently ○ [I] *The water was churning and the boat was rocking.* ○ [M] *The fish churned up the water when we threw them some food.* ○ [T] *(fig.) Seeing the car ahead flip over churned his stomach.* **2** To churn butter means to beat cream into butter using a special container.
churn /tʃɜrn/ *n* [C] a container in which cream is made into butter

PHRASAL VERB with churn

• **churn out** *something* [M] to produce something automatically, without much thought, and in large amounts ○ *Hollywood studios have been churning out some very bad movies over the past several years.*

chute SLIDE /ʃuːt/ *n* [C] a narrow, steep slide for objects or people to go down ○ *The garbage chute empties into a big bin.* ○ *We had to use the emergency chute to get out of the plane.*

CLOTH DEVICE /ʃuːt/ *n* [C] *short form of* PARACHUTE

chutney /ˈtʃʌt·ni/ *n* [C/U] a sauce containing small pieces of fruit, spices, sugar, and vinegar, eaten with cold meats and other foods to add flavor ○ [C] *Mango chutney is absolutely my favorite.*

chutzpah /ˈhʊt·spə, ˈxʊt-/ *n* [U] behavior that is extremely confident and often rude, with no respect for the opinions or abilities of anyone else ○ *The movie was made with a little money and a lot of chutzpah.* ○ *I wonder who had the chutzpah to disagree with him?*

CIA *n* [U] *abbreviation for* Central Intelligence Agency (= the US government organization that collects information about other countries and decides the importance of that information)

ciao /tʃɑʊ/ *exclamation infml* hello or goodbye ○ *He greeted me with his usual all-purpose "Ciao, baby!"*

cicada /səˈkeɪd·ə, -ˈkɑd·ə/ *n* [C] *pl* **cicadas** a large insect with transparent wings which it rubs together to produce a high, continuous sound esp. when the weather is hot ○ *Cicadas buzzing in the maple trees is the sound of hot summer.*

cider /ˈsɑɪd·ər/ *n* [U] apple juice made from crushed apples, used as a drink or to make vinegar

cigar /sɪˈgɑr/ *n* [C] a tight roll of dried tobacco leaves used for smoking ○ *Cuban cigars*

cigarette /ˌsɪg·əˈret/ *n* [C] a small tube of thin paper filled with pieces of cut tobacco that is used for smoking ○ *Cigarette smoking is a major cause of heart disease.*

cinch SOMETHING EASY /sɪntʃ/ *n* [C] *infml* something that is very easy or certain to be done or happen ○ *Training a puppy is a cinch if you bribe him with treats.*

STRAP /sɪntʃ/ *n* [C] a strap that goes around esp. a horse to hold the SADDLE (= the seat put on an animal for a rider) in place
cinch /sɪntʃ/ *v* [T] ○ *My guide cinched the llama's saddle tight enough to stay in place.*

Cinco de Mayo /ˌsɪŋ·koʊ·ðeɪˈmɑɪ·oʊ, -də-/ *n* [C/U] May 5th, a Mexican holiday celebrating a victory by Mexican fighters over a French army in 1862 ○ [U] *Cinco de Mayo events this year include cookouts, parades, and dances.*

cinder /ˈsɪn·dər/ *n* [C] a small piece of partly burned coal or wood ○ *Get rid of the cinders before you build a new fire.*

cinder block *n* [C] a hollow block made of concrete mixed with CINDERS that is used esp. in building walls

Cinderella /ˌsɪn·dəˈrel·ə/ *n* [C] someone or something suddenly successful but previously unknown or given little attention, from a traditional story ○ *All four Cinderella teams lost in the semifinals, leaving no true underdogs.*

cinema /ˈsɪn·ə·mə/ *n* [C/U] **1** movies, or the art or business of making movies ○ [U] *Her lectures on the cinema were very interesting.* **2** *esp. Cdn, Br* A cinema is also a movie theater: [C] *We'd already been to the local cinema twice that week.*
cinematic /ˌsɪn·əˈmæt̬·ɪk/ *adj* ○ *The cinematic effects in this film are utterly remarkable.*

cinematography /ˌsɪn·ə·məˈtɑg·rə·fi/ *n* [U] the art and methods of using cameras in making a movie ○ *The cinematography is what makes this film as wonderful as it really is.*

cinnamon /ˈsɪn·ə·mən/ *n* [U] **1** a spice, made from the BARK (= outer covering) of a tropical tree, usually available in the form of powder or a rolled piece of bark ○ *The smell of cinnamon makes me hungry for cookies.* **2** Cinnamon is also a red-brown color: *The dress is available in cinnamon and green.*

cinnamon roll, cinnamon bun *n* [C] a round, sweet bread flavored with CINNAMON ○ *Robert had stuffed half a cinnamon bun in his mouth and couldn't say a word.*

cipher SECRET WRITING /ˈsɑɪ·fər/ *n* [C] a system of writing that most people cannot understand, so that the message is secret; a CODE ○ *We spent a lot of time figuring out the enemy's cipher.*

NOTHING /ˈsɑɪ·fər/ *n* [C] a zero, or a person or thing that has no value or importance ○ *In the hands of a lesser actor, the role could have easily been a cipher.*

circa /ˈsɜr·kə, ˈkɪr·kɑ/, *abbreviation* **c**, *abbreviation* **ca** *prep fml* (used before a year) about or approximately ○ *The Greek philosopher Socrates was born circa 470 BC.*

circle SHAPE /ˈsɜr·kəl/ *n* [C] ***geometry*** a continuous curved line which is always the same distance away from a fixed central point, or the area enclosed by such a line ○ *Colored paper was cut into circles, squares, and triangles.* ○ *A circle of chairs had been arranged in the center of the room.*
circle /ˈsɜr·kəl/ *v* [I/T] **1** [I] *A hawk circled high overhead, looking for food.* ○ [T] *I circled the block to find a parking space.* **2** *fig.* If you circle around a subject, you talk about things related to it, often to avoid talking about the subject itself: [I] *He circled around the idea of paying authors more for their books.*

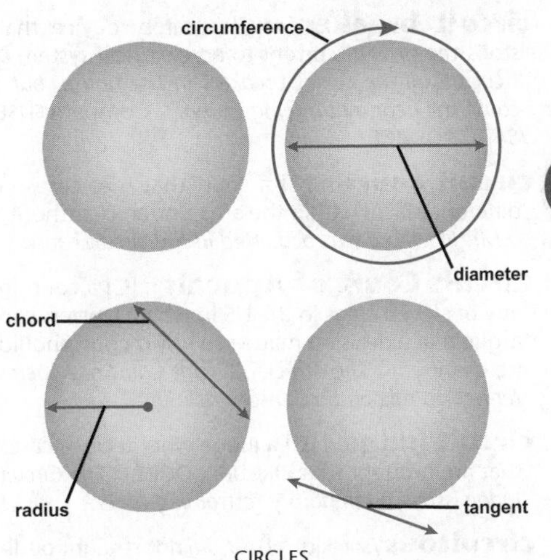

CIRCLES

GROUP /ˈsɜr·kəl/ *n* [C] a group of people who are connected by family, work, or society, or who share an interest ○ *There's a small circle of people who sell and exhibit their work at the same shows.* ○ *The mayor's inner circle met with him throughout the crisis to give advice.*

WORD FAMILY circle			
Nouns	circle circular circulation semicircle	*Adjectives* *Verbs*	circular semicircular circle circulate

IDIOM with circle

• **go (around) in circles**, to do a lot or seem very busy without achieving anything ○ *We just keep going around in circles, talking without deciding anything.*

circuit CLOSED SYSTEM /ˈsɜr·kət/ *n* [C] **1** ***physics*** a closed system esp. of wires through which electricity can flow ○ *Big electronic circuits can carry huge amounts of data.* **2** A circuit is also a system that allows people to communicate with each other: *Holiday phone calls always overload the circuits.*
circuitry /ˈsɜr·kə·tri/ *n* [U] ○ *The circuitry in this computer is protected from power surges.*

CIRCLE /ˈsɜr·kət/ *n* [C] **1** something shaped like a circle, esp. a route, path, or sports track that starts and ends in the same place ○ *She has ridden on tough racing circuits such as the New York and Florida tracks.* **2** A circuit can be a path or route in the shape of a circle: *Fish swam continuously, making the endless circuit of the tank.*

SERIES /ˈsɜr·kət/ *n* [C] a regular series of events that happen in different places ○ *She has won a number of tournaments on this year's tennis circuit.*

LEGAL AREA /ˈsɜr·kət/ *n* [C] an area under the authority of a particular court

circuit board *n* [C] a small board on which electrical CIRCUITS are attached or printed

circuit breaker *n* [C] a safety device that stops the flow of current to an electrical system ○ *I cut off all the circuit breakers in the house, but I could still hear a humming sound.* ○ Compare FUSE SAFETY DEVICE

C

circuit court *n* [C] a court that tries cases in different places within the area under its authority ○ *Mr. Blackford was acquitted in the circuit court.*

Circuit Court of Appeals *n* [C] a court in any of eleven areas in the US in which lawyers can argue that a decision made in a lower court should be changed ○ *The 4th U.S. Circuit Court of Appeals refused to rule on that case.*

circuit judge *n* [C] a judge who decides cases that are brought to a CIRCUIT COURT ○ *The Circuit Judge issued a temporary restraining order.*

circuitous /sərˈkjuː·ət̬·əs/ *adj* not straight or direct; ROUNDABOUT ○ *We took a circuitous route home.*

circuitously /sərˈkjuː·ət̬·ə·sli/ *adv* ○ *The train tracks wound circuitously through the canyons.*

circular **ROUND** /ˈsɜr·kjə·lər/ *adj* **1** in the shape of a circle; round ○ *One man built a circular barn for his cows.* ○ *The circular area is used for parking.* **2** A circular argument or discussion is one which keeps returning to the same points and does not advance to any new points or to agreement.

PRINTED PAPER /ˈsɜr·kjə·lər/ *n* [C] a letter or notice given to a large number of people ○ *The discount chain advertises sales with circulars.*

circulate /ˈsɜr·kjəˌleɪt/ *v* **1** to move around or through ○ [T] *circulate a letter/memo/proposal* ○ [I] *Hot water circulates through the pipes.* **2** ***biology*** Blood circulates inside the body by moving from the heart through the ARTERIES and back to the heart through the VEINS.

circulation /ˌsɜr·kjəˈlei·ʃən/ *n* [C/U] **1** ***biology*** the movement of blood inside the body **2** Circulation is also the movement of air or water in a space or system: [U] *The fans in the air circulation system make a lot of noise.* **3** A magazine or newspaper's circulation is the number of people who read it: [C] *The Chronicle has a daily circulation of 505,000.* **4** If something is in circulation, it is available: [U] *Are the new dollar coins in circulation yet?* **5** If something is out of circulation, it is not available: [U] *The company takes its movies out of circulation, then shows them again.* ○ [U] (*fig.*) (*infml*) *She's been out of circulation since her accident.*

circulatory /ˈsɜr·kjə·ləˌtɔːr·i, -ˌtoʊr·i/ *adj* [not gradable] ***biology*** relating to the system that moves blood through the body and that includes the heart, ARTERIES, and VEINS

circumcise /ˈsɜr·kəmˌsaɪz/ *v* [T] to cut off the FORESKIN

circumcision /ˌsɜr·kəmˈsɪʒ·ən/ *n* [C/U]

circumference /sərˈkʌm·fə·rəns/ *n* [C/U] **1** ***geometry*** the distance around a circle ○ [U] *Draw a circle 5 inches in circumference.* **2** A circumference is also the distance around the widest part of a round object, or a line enclosing a circular space. **3** The circumference of an area of any size or shape is its complete outside edge: [C] *We walked the circumference of the field so we wouldn't interrupt the game.* ➤ Picture: **circle**

circumnavigate /ˌsɜr·kəmˈnæv·əˌgeɪt/ *v* [T] to travel all the way around something, esp. the earth

circumstance Ⓐ /ˈsɜr·kəmˌstæns/ *n* [C/U] an event or condition connected with what is happening or has happened ○ [C] *The circumstances of the theft of the painting were not known.* ○ [C] *The circumstances surrounding his disappearance are under investigation.* ○ *He said that under no circumstances was he returning to Phoenix.*

circumstantial /ˌsɜr·kəmˈstæn·tʃəl/ *adj* relating to the circumstances in which something happened, but not to the thing itself ○ *The report said most of the data was circumstantial, so no conclusions could be drawn from it.* ○ *The judge reminded the jury that circumstantial evidence is information that may be important but is not proof of guilt.*

circumvent /ˌsɜr·kəmˈvent/ *v* [T] to avoid something by going around it ○ *Young people still want to circumvent their parents' control.*

circus /ˈsɜr·kəs/ *n* [C] **1** a group of traveling entertainers including ACROBATS, CLOWNS, and trained animals, or a performance by such a group, often in a tent ○ *He quit school in the eighth grade to join the circus.* ○ *We saw the circus set up in a tent in the middle of the city.* **2** A circus is also something noisy and confused: *The media circus covering the trial took over the courthouse steps.*

cirrhosis /səˈroʊ·səs/ *n* [U] *medical* a serious disease of the LIVER (= an organ in the body) that can result in death

cistern /ˈsɪs·tərn/ *n* [C] a large container for storing water, esp. one kept on the roof of a large building to catch rain

cite Ⓐ **MENTION** /sɑɪt/ *v* [T] **1** to mention something as proof for a theory or as a reason why something has happened, or to speak or write words taken from a written work ○ *He cited a study of the devices as proof that the company knew they were dangerous.* ○ *Scientists cite this experiment as their main support for this theory.* **2** To cite someone else's words when speaking or writing is to use them: *If you cite too many writers, readers will wonder if you have any ideas of your own.* **3** In law, a person or organization which is cited is named in a legal action: *The mine operator was cited with 33 violations of federal safety standards.*

citation Ⓐ /sɑɪˈteɪ·ʃən/ *n* [C/U] **1** [U] *Citation of her mother's wisdom did not change her ways.* ○ [C] *She checked all the citations from other writers I used in my book.* **2** *law* A citation is an official notice from a court of law: [C] *The court could issue a citation against her for disclosing information.* ○ [C] *County police say that no citations have been issued since the law went into effect.*

PRAISE /sɑɪt/ *v* [T] to praise someone publicly for something the person has done ○ *He was cited for bravery.*

citation /sɑɪˈteɪ·ʃən/ *n* [C] ○ *Cory received a citation from the mayor for her achievements.*

citizen /ˈsɪt̬·ə·zən/ *n* [C] **1** ***politics & government*** a person who was born in a particular country and has certain rights or has been given certain rights because of having lived there ○ *Nabokov was a Russian, then had British citizenship, and then became an American citizen.* ○ *A large part of our job is to educate citizens about their rights.* ○ *Old people have been treated like second-class citizens.* **2** A citizen is also a person who lives in a particular place: *My sister is now a New Hampshire citizen.*

citizenry /ˈsɪt̬·ə·zən·ri/ *n* [U] the group of people who live in a particular country or place ○ *An angry citizenry organized resistance to the harsh new laws.*

citizenship /ˈsɪt̬·ə·zən ˌʃɪp/ *n* [U] **1** ***politics & government*** the state of having the rights of a person born in a particular country ○ *He was granted Canadian citizenship last year.* ○ *Harold holds dual citizenship in New Zealand and the US.* **2** Citizenship is also carrying out the duties and responsibilities of a member of a particular society: *Good citizenship requires that you do all the things a citizen is supposed to do, such as pay taxes, serve on juries, and vote.*

citrus /ˈsɪ·trəs/ *n* [C] *pl* **citrus, citruses** any of a group of plants that produce juicy fruits with a slightly sour taste ○ *Oranges, lemons, limes, and grapefruit are types of citrus fruit.*

city /ˈsɪt̬·i/ *n* [C] a place where many people live, with many houses, stores, businesses, etc., and which is bigger than a town ○ *Canadians have built big, pleasant, and livable cities.* ○ *When their team won the World Series, the whole city celebrated.* ○ *Wellington is the capital city of New Zealand.*

city council *n* [C] the legislature of a city

city hall *n* [C] **1** a building that is used by the government of a city, and that usually contains the city offices ○ *Protesters hurled eggs during a ceremony in front of city hall.* **2** City hall is also the government of a city: *If city hall hadn't stopped him, he would have erected the statue in his front yard.*

city-state /ˈsɪt̬·iː ˌsteɪt, -ˈsteɪt/ *n* [C] ***politics & government*** a city and its surrounding territory that together make an independent state

citywide /ˈsɪt̬·iː ˌwɑɪd/ *adj, adv* [not gradable] including all of a city and everyone who lives there ○ *In a series of hearings held citywide, residents complained more about the schools than about crime.*

civic /ˈsɪv·ɪk/ *adj* [not gradable] ***social studies*** of a town or city or the people who live in it ○ *A group of prominent civic leaders have been among the school system's harshest critics.*

civics /ˈsɪv·ɪks/ *n* [U] ***social studies*** the study of the rights and duties of citizens

civic /ˈsɪv·ɪk/ *adj* [not gradable] ○ *Civic responsibility includes voting and serving on juries.*

civil Ⓐ **ORDINARY** /ˈsɪv·əl/ *adj* **1** of or relating to the ordinary people of a country, rather than members of religious organizations or the military ○ *These helicopters are for rescue and other civil use.* ○ *We were married in a civil ceremony.* **2** ***politics & government*** Civil also refers to the legal system governing personal and business matters: *civil court* ○ Compare CRIMINAL

civilian /səˈvɪl·jən/ *n* [C] ***politics & government*** a person who is not a member of the police, the armed forces, or a fire department ○ *The senator is not the only civilian who would like to ride in a space shuttle.*

civilian /səˈvɪl·jən/ *adj* [not gradable] ○ *the civilian population* ○ *civilian workers/employees*

POLITE /ˈsɪv·əl/ *adj* polite and formal ○ *We were civil to each other, but we were both still angry.*

civility /səˈvɪl·ət̬·i/ *n* [U] ○ *I learned how much smoother the day goes when people act with civility* (= behave in a polite way).

civil disobedience *n* [C/U] ***politics & government*** the refusal of citizens to obey certain laws or pay taxes as a peaceful way to express disapproval of those laws or taxes ○ [U] *Campaigns of civil disobedience forced an end to segregation.*

civil engineering *n* [U] the planning and building of public roads, bridges, and buildings

civil engineer *n* [C]

civilization /ˌsɪv·ə·ləˈzeɪ·ʃən, -lɑɪ-/ *n* [C/U] a highly developed culture, including its social organization, government, laws, and arts, or the culture of a social group or country at a particular time ○ [U] *Widespread use of the Internet may change modern civilization.* ○ [C] *The Inca civilization flourished for a long time.*

civilize /ˈsɪv·əˌlɑɪz/ *v* [T] to educate people or a society to develop it further ○ *Dedicated teachers labored under difficult conditions to civilize frontier society.*

civilized /ˈsɪv·əˌlɑɪzd/ *adj* **1** having a well-developed way of life and social systems ○ *"A civilized society allows for tolerance," he said.* **2** Civilized also means pleasant, comfortable, well-educated, or orderly: *civilized behavior* ○ *a civilized vacation*

civil liberty *n* [C/U] ***politics & government*** the right of people to basic freedoms and to live without the government becoming involved in private matters ○ *The right of free speech is one of our most important civil liberties.*

civil rights *pl n* ***politics & government*** the rights of each person in a society, including equality under the law and in employment and the right to vote ○ *In the 1960s, civil rights were extended by law to include all Americans.*

civil servant *n* [C] a person who works for local, state, or esp. the federal government

civil service *n* [C] ***politics & government*** all government departments that are not part of the military

civil war *n* [C] a war fought between groups of people living in the same country

clack /klæk/ *n* [C usually sing] a short sound made when two hard objects hit
clack /klæk/ *v* [I] ○ *Her shoes clacked on the tile floor.*

clad /klæd/ *adj* [not gradable] ***literature*** (of people) dressed, or (of things) covered ○ *A stranger appeared, clad in white.*

claim **SAY** /kleɪm/ *v* [T] to state that something is true or is a fact ○ [+ (*that*) clause] *Ervin claims (that) he is bankrupt.*
claim /kleɪm/ *n* [C] ○ *They say it works, but there is no evidence to support those claims.*

REQUEST /kleɪm/ *v* [T] **1** to demand something of value because you believe it belongs to you or you have a right to it ○ *If no one claims the money, I can keep it.* **2** If a storm, crime, or other violence claims someone's life, the person was killed suddenly as a result of that event: *The earthquake claimed hundreds of lives.*
claim /kleɪm/ *n* [C] **1** a written request to an organization to pay you a sum of money which you believe it owes you ○ *After the storm, dozens of claims were filed to collect crop insurance.* **2** A claim is also a statement saying that you have a right to something: *They asserted their claim to citizenship.*

IDIOM with claim

• **claim to fame** a reason why someone or something is famous ○ *This little town's claim to fame is that a president was born here.*

clam /klæm/ *n* [C] a type of sea creature with a hard shell in two parts, or its soft body that can be eaten raw or cooked

PHRASAL VERB with clam

• **clam up** *infml* to refuse to talk or answer ○ *He just clammed up when I walked in.*

clamber /ˈklæm·bər, -ər/ *v* [I always + adv/prep] to climb somewhere with difficulty, often needing to use both hands and feet ○ *The baby clambered up the stairs.*

clammy /ˈklæm·i/ *adj* slightly wet and cool, in an unpleasant way ○ *Her forehead was hot, but her hands were clammy.*

clamor, *Cdn, Br* **clamour** /ˈklæm·ər/ *v* [I] to make a loud complaint or demand ○ *The audience clamored for an encore.*
clamor, *Cdn, Br* **clamour** /ˈklæm·ər/ *n* [U] **1** *The clamor for freedom in recent years has been strong.* **2** Clamor is also loud noise, esp. made by people's voices: *The clamor of their voices rose.*

clamp /klæmp/ *n* [C] a device used to hold something tightly ○ *A small clamp at the bottom edge holds it in place.*
clamp /klæmp/ *v* [T always + adv/prep] **1** to use a device to hold something tightly ○ [M] *Clamp the pieces together while the glue dries.* **2** If you clamp something, you hold it firmly so that it does not move: *He abruptly clamped his jaw shut.*

PHRASAL VERB with clamp

• **clamp down on** *something/someone* to stop or limit an activity or the people doing it, esp. a bad or illegal activity ○ *Stores use electronic devices to clamp down on theft.*

clan /klæn/ *n* [C] *infml* a family, esp. a large group of people who are related ○ *Is the whole clan gathering at your house for Thanksgiving?*

clandestine /klænˈdes·tən/ *adj* planned or done in secret ○ *a clandestine meeting*
clandestinely /klænˈdes·tən·li/ *adv* ○ *The virus clandestinely burrowed its way into computers across the globe.*

clang /klæŋ/ *v* [I/T] to make a loud, ringing sound like metal being hit, or to cause something to make such a sound ○ [I] *There was none of the hissing and clanging one expects in factories.*
clang /klæŋ/ *n* [C usually sing] ○ *The door rolled shut with a clang.*

clank /klæŋk/ *v* [I/T] to make a short, loud sound like that of metal objects hitting each other, or to cause something to make such a sound ○ [I] *Ray's van clanked down the driveway.*
clank /klæŋk/ *n* [C usually sing] ○ *the clank of silverware on plates*

clap **PUT HANDS TOGETHER** /klæp/ *v* [I/T] **-pp- 1** to make a short, loud noise by hitting your hands together ○ [T] *She clapped her hands to call the dog in.* **2** People will clap at the end of a speech or a performance to show that they are pleased: [I] *Everyone was clapping and cheering.*
clap /klæp/ *n* [C] **1** *There were a few claps, and then embarrassing silence.* **2** A clap of thunder is the sudden, loud noise of thunder.

HIT LIGHTLY /klæp/ *v* [T always + adv/prep] **-pp-** to hit someone lightly on the shoulder or back in a friendly way to express pleasure ○ *The governor clapped him on the back and congratulated him.*

clapboard /ˈklæb·ərd; ˈklæp·bɔːrd, -bourd/ *n* [U] a narrow board used to cover the outside walls of a building by laying one board over part of the one already attached below it

clapper /ˈklæp·ər/ *n* [C] a piece of metal hanging inside a bell which makes the bell ring by hitting its sides

clarify Ⓐ /ˈklær·əˌfɑɪ/ *v* [T] to make something clearer or easier to understand ○ *I hope this analysis will clarify the debate.* ○ *Talking it through with you has helped me to clarify my own thinking about the problem.*
clarification Ⓐ /ˌklær·ə·fəˈkeɪ·ʃən/ *n* [C/U] ○ [U] *Two of your points deserve further clarification.*

clarinet /ˌklær·əˈnet/ *n* [C/U] a tube-shaped musical instrument that is played by blowing through a single REED (= thin piece of wood) and pressing keys on its front to produce notes, or this type of instrument generally; a WOODWIND
clarinetist, **clarinettist** /ˌklær·əˈnet̬·əst/ *n* [C] ○ *He's a respected jazz clarinetist.*

clarity /ˈklær·ət̬·i/ *n* [U] the quality of being clear and easy to understand, see, or hear ○ *He conveys information with great clarity.* ○ *The story is filmed with razor-sharp clarity.* ○ *The sound was loud, but it lacked clarity.*

clash FIGHT /klæʃ/ *v* [I] to fight or disagree ○ *The president and Congress clashed again over the budget.*
clash /klæʃ/ *n* [C] ○ *a clash of interests/personalities* ○ *clashes between demonstrators and police*
NOT MATCH /klæʃ/ *v* [I] (of colors or styles) to look ugly or wrong together ○ *I do not think that red clashes with orange.*
SOUND /klæʃ/ *n* [C] a loud sound like that made when metal objects hit
clash /klæʃ/ *v* [I/T] ○ [I] *From the kitchen you could hear dishes clashing as they were stacked.*

clasp /klæsp/ *v* [T] to hold someone or something firmly in your hands or arms ○ *He clasped the vase, afraid he would drop it.*
clasp /klæsp/ *n* [C] **1** *She had a firm clasp on her daughter's hand.* **2** A clasp is a small metal device used to fasten a belt, a bag, or a piece of jewelry.

class TEACHING GROUP /klæs/ *n* [C] **1** a group of students who are taught together at school, or a short period in which a particular subject is taught ○ *She got in trouble for talking in class.* **2** The class of a particular year is the group of students who will complete their studies that year: *The class of 2003 is very large.*

USAGE
class or classroom?
Class cannot be used to mean the room where a lesson happens. For this meaning you must use **classroom**.
Every classroom in the entire school has a new whiteboard.
~~*Every class in the entire school has a new whiteboard.*~~

ECONOMIC GROUP /klæs/ *n* [C/U] a group of people within a society who have the same economic and social position ○ [U] *Most of us think of ourselves as middle class.*
BIOLOGY /klæs/ *n* [C] ***biology*** a group of plants or animals with similar biological structure
RANK /klæs/ *n* [C] the ranking of goods and services or people's skills according to what they provide or how good they are ○ *Whenever I fly, I go business class.* ○ *She's a first-class teacher.*
class /klæs/ *v* [T] to rank ○ *I would class her with the best American violinists.*
STYLE /klæs/ *n* [U] the quality of being stylish or fashionable ○ *She dresses with a lot of class.*
classy /ˈklæs·i/ *adj* ○ *He drives a very classy car.*

IDIOM with **class**
• **in a class by *your/itself*** excellent, or the best of its kind ○ *Her singing is in a class by itself.*

class action *n* [C/U] *law* legal action for the benefit of a large group of people claiming to have suffered similar harm

classic Ⓐ STANDARD /ˈklæs·ɪk/ *adj* being of a high standard against which others of the same type are judged ○ *classic literature* ○ *John Steinbeck's classic American novel, "The Grapes of Wrath"*
classic /ˈklæs·ɪk/ *n* [C] a well-known piece of writing, musical recording, or film which is of high quality and lasting value ○ *Chaplin's films are regarded as American classics.*
TRADITIONAL /ˈklæs·ɪk/ *adj* traditional in design or style ○ *She wore a classic blue suit and a straw hat.*
TYPICAL /ˈklæs·ɪk/ *adj* having all the characteristics or qualities that are typical of something ○ *The building is a classic example of poor design.*

classical Ⓐ ANCIENT /ˈklæs·ɪ·kəl/ *adj* ***world history*** belonging to or relating to the culture of ancient Rome and Greece ○ *classical architecture/languages* ○ Related noun: CLASSICS
TRADITIONAL /ˈklæs·ɪ·kəl/ *adj* traditional in style or form, or using methods developed over a long period of time ○ *classical ballet*

classical music *n* [C] a form of music developed from a European tradition mainly in the 18th and 19th centuries ○ *My wife likes classical music but I prefer jazz.*

classics Ⓐ /ˈklæs·ɪks/ *pl n* the study of ancient Greek and Roman culture, esp. their languages and literature ○ Related adjective: CLASSICAL ANCIENT

classified /ˈklæs·əˌfɑɪd/ *adj* (of information) officially secret ○ *These documents contain classified material.*

classified (ad) /ˈklæs·əˌfɑɪd (ˈæd)/, **want ad** *n* [C] a small advertisement in a newspaper or magazine offering or requesting a job, furniture, cars, houses, etc.

classify /ˈklæs·əˌfɑɪ/ *v* [T] **1** to divide things into groups according to type ○ *We classify our books by subject.* **2** ***biology*** Classify also means to divide organisms into groups according to particular characteristics.
classification /ˌklæs·ə·fəˈkeɪ·ʃən/ *n* [C/U] **1** the division of things into groups by type ○ [U] *The new pay classification takes effect next week.* ○ [C] *Hotels are listed in four classifications from economy to deluxe.* **2** ***biology*** Classification is also the division of organisms into groups according to particular characteristics.

classmate /ˈklæs·meɪt/ *n* [C] someone who is in the same class as you in school ○ *Trish is taller than most of her classmates.*

classroom /ˈklæs·ruːm, -rʊm/ *n* [C] a room where groups of students are taught ➤ Usage: **class or classroom?** at CLASS TEACHING GROUP

classwork /ˈklæs·wɜrk/ *n* [C] work that you do in a school class

clastic /ˈklæs·tɪk/ *adj* [not gradable] ***earth science*** describes a type of rock consisting of broken pieces of other rock

clatter /ˈklæt̬·ər/ *v* [I/T] to make loud noises, or to hit hard objects against each other ○ [T] *Don't clatter the pots and pans – you'll wake the baby up.*
clatter /ˈklæt̬·ər/ *n* [U] ○ *She could hear the clatter of horses' hooves trotting down the road.*

clause Ⓐ GRAMMAR /klɔːz/ *n* [C] ***grammar*** a group of words that includes a subject and a verb to form a simple sentence or only part of a sentence ○ *"If I go to town" is a clause, but not a sentence.*

LEGAL STATEMENT /klɔːz/ *n* [C] *law* a part of a written legal document ○ *He had a clause in his movie contract that let him work in the theater.*

C

claustrophobia /ˌklɔː·strəˈfoʊ·biː·ə/ *n* [U] an extreme fear of being in an enclosed or crowded space

claustrophobic /ˌklɔː·strəˈfoʊ·bɪk/ *adj* ○ *I feel claustrophobic in an elevator.*

claw /klɔː/ *n* [C] **1** one of the sharp, curved nails at the end of each of the toes of some animals and birds ○ *Our cat likes to sharpen her claws on the legs of the dining table.* **2** A claw is also the curved, movable part at the end of the leg of some insects and sea animals, such as CRABS and LOBSTERS: *Watch out – the lobster's claws pinch.*

claw /klɔː/ *v* [I/T] **1** to cut esp. flesh with claws ○ [T] *Nora's cat attacked him and began clawing his back.* **2** Someone who claws his or her way somewhere uses a lot of effort to achieve something: [I] *The team trailed, 24-13, after one quarter but clawed to 26-18 by halftime.*

clay /kleɪ/ *n* [U] thick, heavy earth that is soft when wet, and hard when dry or baked ○ *Clay is used for making bricks and pots.*

clean **NOT DIRTY** /kliːn/ *adj* [*-er/-est* only] **1** free of dirt or other unwanted parts or pieces ○ *Make sure you wear a clean shirt.* ○ *Hospital rooms have to be kept clean.* **2** Clean also means free from harmful substances, or pure: *clean air/water*

clean /kliːn/ *v* [I/T] to remove dirt or unwanted parts or pieces from something ○ [T] *Saturday morning is our time to clean the house.* ○ [T] *You should clean a wound immediately to avoid infection.*

cleaner /ˈkliː·nər/ *n* [C] **1** a business that cleans clothes by using chemicals **2** A cleaner is also a person whose job is cleaning: *a window cleaner* **3** A cleaner is also a product that removes dirt: *a household cleaner*

cleanliness /ˈklen·liː·nəs/ *n* [U] the habit or state of keeping yourself or your environment free from dirt ○ *Her job involved checking the cleanliness of restaurants.*

WORD CHOICES clean

To emphasize that something is very clean, you could use the adjectives **immaculate** or **spotless**.

The whole house was ***immaculate****.*

He was wearing a ***spotless*** *white shirt.*

An informal phrase you can use for a place that is clean and neat is **spick-and-span**.

Their house is always ***spick-and-span****.*

If air or water is clean and has no harmful substances in it, the word **pure** can be used.

I love the ***pure*** *mountain air.*

If an object is clean and has no bacteria on it, you can use the adjective **sterile**.

All equipment used in medical operations must be ***sterile****.*

HONEST /kliːn/ *adj* [*-er/-est* only] **1** honest or fair; not breaking rules or laws ○ *"Let's make it a clean fight," said the referee.* ○ *Before his conviction for fraud, he had a clean record* (= he had not been involved in crime previously). ○ (*slang*) *They searched him, but he was clean* (= he was not carrying anything illegal or not allowed). **2** Clean also means morally acceptable and not giving offense: *clean living* ○ *a clean joke*

COMPLETE /kliːn/ *adj* [*-er/-est* only] complete ○ *It's better for both of us if we make a clean break and stop seeing each other.*

clean /kliːn/ *adv* [not gradable] *infml* ○ *The bullet went clean through his shoulder and out the other side.*

NOT USED /kliːn/ *adj* [*-er/-est* only] new and not used ○ *a clean sheet of paper*

WORD FAMILY clean

Nouns	cleaner	*Adjectives*	clean
	cleanliness		unclean
	cleanser	*Verbs*	clean
Adverbs	clean		cleanse

IDIOMS with clean

• **a clean slate** a state in which you are starting an activity or process again, not considering what has happened in the past at all ○ *The previous negotiations did not go anywhere, and we intend to start them again next week with a clean slate.*

• **clean up** *your* **act** to change the way you behave, so that you stop doing bad or dishonest things ○ *You're going to have to clean up your act if you want to get into a good college.*

PHRASAL VERBS with clean

• **clean out** *something* **MAKE NEAT** [M] to remove dirt from something or make something neat ○ *I wish I could find the time to clean out these closets.* ○ *You can use old paint cans, but be sure to clean them out first.*

• **clean out** *someone* **TAKE MONEY** [M] *infml* to take or steal all the money or goods of someone ○ *Buying our new house just about cleaned us out.*

• **clean up** *something* **MAKE NEAT** [M] to remove dirt from something or make something neat ○ *We need to do something to clean up this mess and then get out of there.* ○ *I have to clean things up before the guests arrive.*

• **clean up** *something* **REMOVE EVILS** [M] to remove illegal or dishonest activity from a place ○ *We need a mayor who is tough enough to clean up this town.*

clean-cut *adj* neat and attractive in appearance and style of clothing ○ *Whitmore fits the profile of a conservative, clean-cut, competent guy.*

cleanse /klenz/ *v* [T] to remove all the dirt or harmful substances from something ○ *Thoroughly cleanse the wound and the area around it.*

cleanser /ˈklen·zər/ *n* [C/U] a substance used for cleaning ○ [C] *kitchen cleansers*

clean-shaven *adj* (of a man) having no BEARD or MUSTACHE on his face

cleanup /ˈkliː·nʌp/ *n* [U] the process of removing a dirty or dangerous substance, esp. when it has been left in the environment as a result of an accident ○ *The cleanup after the oil spill cost over $10,000,000.*

clear UNDERSTANDABLE /klɪr/ *adj* [*-er/-est* only] easy to understand, or easy to see or hear ○ *I left clear instructions that no one was to come in my office.* ○ *He spoke in a clear voice.* ○ *It wasn't clear what he meant.*

clearly /ˈklɪr·li/ *adv* ○ *I think this report clearly shows why we have to act now.*

CERTAIN /klɪr/ *adj* [*-er/-est* only] certain or obvious; not in any doubt ○ [+ *that* clause] *It's clear now that it was a mistake to have raised prices last spring.* ○ [+ question word] *It isn't clear how long the strike will continue.*

clearly /ˈklɪr·li/ *adv* certainly; obviously; without a doubt ○ *The accident was clearly the truck driver's fault.*

NOT CONFUSED /klɪr/ *adj* [*-er/-est* only] free from confusion; able to think quickly and well ○ *Mary is good at making decisions because she's a very clear thinker.*

BE NOT GUILTY /klɪr/ *v* [T] to show someone to be not guilty ○ *He was cleared of all charges, and the judge said he was free to go.*

clear /klɪr/ *adj* [*-er/-est* only] free from guilt ○ *My conscience is clear – I did what I could to help her.*

GET RID OF /klɪr/ *v* [T] to remove or get rid of something or remove something blocking the way, or to move people away from a place ○ *It took several hours to clear the road after the accident.* ○ *Please clear the aisle and take your seats.* ○ [M] *Just let me clear the dishes off the table and put them in the sink.*

clear /klɪr/ *adj* [*-er/-est* only] not blocked or filled; open or available ○ *We have a clear view of the ocean from our hotel window.* ○ *The only time the doctor has clear today is 3:30 – can you make it then?*

clearance /ˈklɪr·əns/ *n* [U] If goods are reduced for clearance, they are offered for sale at a lower than usual price so that people will buy them and there will be space for new goods: *a clearance sale* ○ See also: CLEARANCE at CLEAR NOT TOUCH; CLEARANCE at CLEAR GIVE PERMISSION

clearing /ˈklɪr·ɪŋ/ *n* [C] an area in a woods or forest from which trees and bushes have been removed

SEEING THROUGH /klɪr/ *adj* [*-er/-est* only] **1** easy to see through; not cloudy or foggy ○ *clear water* ○ *a clear day* ○ (fig.) *I have clear memories of* (= I can remember well) *visiting my grandfather's farm when I was a child.* **2** If a person's skin is clear, it has no marks or spots on it: *a clear complexion*

clear /klɪr/ *v* [I] ○ *The children stirred the mud at the bottom of the pond, then watched the water slowly clear.*

NOT TOUCH /klɪr/ *v* [I/T] to pass near something without touching it ○ [I] *With the high-jump bar at 6 feet 2 inches, she cleared easily.*

clear /klɪr/ *adv* [not gradable] ○ *Stand clear of the doors, please.* ○ (fig.) *His parents warned him to keep/stay clear of* (= avoid) *trouble.*

clearance /ˈklɪr·əns/ *n* [U] the amount of space available for an object to pass through an opening without touching anything, or for two objects to pass each other without touching ○ *The sign on the overpass says that its clearance is 12 feet, and our truck is 10 feet high, so we should have 2 feet of clearance when we go under it.* ○ See also: CLEARANCE at CLEAR GET RID OF; CLEARANCE at CLEAR GIVE PERMISSION

GIVE PERMISSION /klɪr/ *v* [T] to give official permission for something, or to satisfy the official conditions of something ○ *Our plane has been cleared for takeoff, so will the flight attendants please be seated.* ○ *I'm still waiting for my paycheck to clear* (= be officially approved and processed) *so I can pay my bills.*

clearance /ˈklɪr·əns/ *n* [U] ○ *The pilot announced we had received clearance for take off.* ○ See also: CLEARANCE at CLEAR GET RID OF; CLEARANCE at CLEAR NOT TOUCH

WORD FAMILY clear

Nouns	clearance clearing clarity	*Verbs*	clear
		Adverbs	clear clearly unclearly
Adjectives	clear clear-cut unclear		

IDIOMS with clear

• **(as) clear as mud** *humorous* very difficult to understand ○ *The computer manual was as clear as mud, so we stopped reading it.*

• **clear the air** to get rid of bad feelings between two people or groups ○ *We had a big argument, but I guess it helped clear the air between us.*

• **clear the way (for** *someone/something***)** to make it easier for someone or possible for something to happen ○ *The owners closed the store to clear the way for a new restaurant.*

• **clear** *your* **throat** to give a small cough to remove anything that makes speaking difficult ○ *She cleared her throat and began to read the poem.*

• **in the clear** not guilty of a crime, or not involved in doing something bad ○ *His lawyers say that Wilson is in the clear.*

PHRASAL VERBS with clear

• **clear out** to leave a building or other place, esp. without much warning ○ *Her landlord gave her a week to clear out of her apartment.*

• **clear up** *something* REMOVE DOUBT [M] to remove doubts, confusion, or wrong ideas ○ *I want to clear up any misconceptions you might still have.*

• **clear up** GET BETTER (of an illness or bad weather) to go away, changing into a better condition ○ *If my cold doesn't clear up, it will ruin my vacation.* ○ *Let's hope the weather clears up.*

clear-cut *adj* not having any characteristics that would cause doubt or uncertainty ○ *It was a clear-cut case of fraud.*

clearheaded /ˌklɪr ˈhed·ɪd/ *adj* able to think clearly ○ *He says that his work keeps him alert and clearheaded.*

cleat /kliːt/ *n* [C usually pl] one of the small, hard pieces on the bottom of special shoes worn in some sports because they catch in the ground and keep you from falling

cleavage /ˈkliː·vɪdʒ/ *n* [U] ***earth science*** the tendency of a MINERAL (= hard substance obtained from the earth) to break in a particular way because of its structure

cleave /kliːv/ *v* [I/T] *past* **cleaved, cleft, clove,** *past part.* **cleaved, cleft, cloven,** *pres. part.* **cleaving** to cut or break into two or more parts ○ [I] *The volcano cleaved nearly in half after its last eruption.*

cleaver /ˈkliː·vər/ *n* [C] a knife with a large, square blade, used esp. for cutting meat

clef /klef/ *n* [C] a sign put at the beginning of a line of music to show how high or low the notes are

cleft /kleft/ *n* [C] an opening or crack, esp. in a rock or the ground
cleft /kleft/ *adj* ○ *He was strikingly handsome, with dark, wavy hair, a cleft chin* (= with a deep vertical line)*, and penetrating blue eyes.*

cleft palate *n* [C] a condition in which a person is born with an opening in the roof of the mouth

clemency /ˈklem·ən·si/ *n* [U] an act of mercy by a person in authority toward someone who has committed a crime, esp. by reducing a punishment ○ *The governor refused to grant him clemency, and he was executed at 9 a.m. yesterday.*

clench /klentʃ/ *v* [T] to hold something tightly, or press together your lips or your hands in anger or determination ○ *He clenched his fist and waved it at the crowd.*

clergy /ˈklɜr·dʒi/ *pl n* the religious leaders whose job is serving the needs of their religion and its members; priests, ministers, rabbis, etc.

clergyman /ˈklɜr·dʒiː·mən/, *female* **clergywoman** /ˈklɜr·dʒiːˌwʊm·ən/ *n* [C] *pl* **clergymen,** *pl* **clergywomen** a member of the clergy

cleric /ˈkler·ɪk/ *n* [C] a religious leader; a member of the CLERGY ○ *The committee was composed of Jewish, Catholic, Protestant, and Muslim clerics.*

clerical /ˈkler·ɪ·kəl/ *adj* relating to the type of work usually done in an office, or to the work of a CLERK

clerk /klɜrk/ *n* [C] **1** a person who works in an office, dealing with records or performing general office duties **2** A clerk is also a person who deals with customers in a store or hotel: *The sales clerk helped me find a sweater in my size.*

clever /ˈklev·ər/ *adj* having or showing a quick intelligence in doing something or in persuading people to do something ○ *It was certainly a clever ad and got a lot of attention.*
cleverly /ˈklev·ər·li/ *adv* ○ *Did you notice how she cleverly avoided answering most of my questions?*

cliché /kliːˈʃeɪ/ *n* [C] ***writing*** an idea or expression that has been used too often and is often considered a sign of bad writing or old-fashioned thinking ○ *The story is shamelessly corny, and grownups will groan at its clichés.*

click SOUND /klɪk/ *n* [C] a short sound made when when one object hits or is fastened to another ○ *You'll know your seat belt is fastened properly when you hear a click.*
click /klɪk/ *v* [I/T] ○ [I] *As the door clicked shut behind her, she realized she'd forgotten her key.*

BECOME FRIENDLY /klɪk/ *v* [I] *infml* to become friendly or be successful ○ *Liz and I really clicked, from the first time we met.* ○ *The show never really clicked.*

BECOME CLEAR /klɪk/ *v* [I] *infml* to be understood or become clear suddenly ○ *Something clicked, and I remembered where I'd seen her before.*

client /ˈklɑɪ·ənt/ *n* [C] a person who receives services, esp. from a lawyer or other person who gives advice ○ *He's a sports agent and has a lot of basketball players as clients.*

clientele /ˌklɑɪ·ənˈtel, ˌkliː-/ *n* [C] all the customers of a business when they are considered as a group

cliff /klɪf/ *n* [C] a high area of rock with a steep side, often on a coast

cliffhanger /ˈklɪfˌhæŋ·ər/ *n* [C] a story or situation, often dangerous or of great importance, where two opposite results are possible and you do not know what the result will be until the last moment ○ *The polls are too close to call, and it looks like this election is going to be a real cliffhanger.*

climactic /klɑɪˈmæk·tɪk/ *adj* being the most important or exciting point in a story or situation ○ *She was marvelous in the climactic sleepwalking scene in Macbeth.* ○ Related noun: CLIMAX

climate WEATHER /ˈklɑɪ·mət/ *n* [C/U] ***earth science*** the general weather conditions usually found in a particular place ○ [C] *My parents like the warm, dry climate of Arizona.*
climatic /klɑɪˈmæṭ·ɪk, klə-/ *adj* [not gradable] ***earth science*** relating to or causing weather conditions

ATTITUDE /ˈklɑɪ·mət/ *n* [C] a general attitude, opinion, or feeling ○ *There's never been a climate of trust between labor and management in this industry.*

climatology /ˌklɑɪ·məˈtɑl·ə·dʒi/ *n* [U] ***earth science*** the study of weather conditions as they exist over a long period of time
climatological /ˌklɑɪ·mət·əlˈɑdʒ·ɪ·kəl/ *adj* [not gradable] ***earth science*** relating to the study of weather conditions

climax /ˈklɑɪ·mæks/ *n* [C] ***literature*** the most important or exciting part in the development of a story or situation, which usually happens near the end ○ *The novel built to a shattering climax, leaving me breathless.* ○ Related adjective: CLIMACTIC
climax /ˈklɑɪ·mæks/ *v* [I] to reach the greatest point or level of activity ○ *A late season hurricane on October 17–18 climaxed the very active hurricane season of 1950.*

climb **RISE** /klaɪm/ *v* [I/T] **1** to go up, or go up something or to the top of something ○ [I] *We climbed to the top of the hill, where we had a great view.* ○ [T] *She climbed the stairs to the third floor.* ○ [I] *The plane is still climbing and will level off at 33,000 feet.* ○ [I] *(fig.) As he climbed the corporate ladder* (= moved into better and better positions in business), *his salary increased dramatically.* **2** To climb is also to increase: [I] *The cost of goods is climbing.*

climb /klaɪm/ *n* [C] an act of going up ○ *It was a long, difficult climb to the top of the hill.*

climber /ˈklaɪ·mər/ *n* [C] a person who climbs mountains as a sport

MOVE /klaɪm/ *v* [I always + adv/prep] to move in a way that uses your arms and legs and often involves careful control over your body ○ *He climbed down from the ladder to get some more paint.*

clinch /klɪntʃ/ *v* [T] to succeed in making an agreement certain, esp. after a long period of discussion ○ *The deal was clinched when they agreed to share the shipping costs.*

clincher /ˈklɪn·tʃər/ *n* [C] *infml* a final item to be considered that makes a decision firm after you have been tending toward it, or anything that finally decides a matter ○ *The minivan was big enough for eight people and when we heard the price – that was the clincher!*

cling /klɪŋ/ *v* [I] *past* **clung** to hold tightly or to stick; to refuse to stop holding ○ *They clung together in terror.* ○ *We were soaking wet and our clothes clung to us.* ○ *(fig.) Farmers and herders cling to the valleys* (= stay in the valleys) *where the soil is less sandy.*

clinic **BUILDING** /ˈklɪn·ɪk/ *n* [C] a building or part of a hospital where people go for medical care or advice ○ *Prenatal clinics provide care for pregnant women.*

INSTRUCTION /ˈklɪn·ɪk/ *n* [C] instruction to a group of people in a particular subject, activity, or sport ○ *a summer baseball clinic for boys*

clinical /ˈklɪn·ɪ·kəl/ *adj* [not gradable] **1** (of medical work or teaching) relating to examining and treating someone who is ill ○ *Clinical tests have so far failed to show the cause of her illness.* **2** Clinical also means considering a situation without showing or feeling any emotion: *Mac's air of clinical disinterest did not always sit well with his associates.*

clink /klɪŋk/ *v* [I/T] to make a short, ringing sound like that of pieces of glass or metal knocking together

clink /klɪŋk/ *n* [C/U] ○ [U] *the clink of coins*

clip **FASTENER** /klɪp/ *n* [C] a usually metal or plastic object used for fastening things together or holding them in position ○ *Her long hair was held back with a hair clip.* ➤ Picture: **microscope**

clip /klɪp/ *v* [always + adv/prep] **-pp-** to fasten with a clip ○ [T] *He had a beeper clipped to his belt.*

CUT /klɪp/ *v* [T] **-pp-** to cut a piece from something larger or whole ○ *She clipped the coupons out of the newspaper.* ○ *He had his beard clipped.*

clip /klɪp/ *n* [C] **1** a small piece of something **2** A clip is a short part of a film or VIDEO shown alone: *a news clip*

clippers /ˈklɪp·ərz/ *pl n* any of various tools used for clipping esp. nails, hair, wire, or plants

SPEED /klɪp/ *n* [U] *infml* a rate of speed ○ *I drove home at a good clip.*

GUN PART /klɪp/ *n* [C] a container holding bullets and that is put into a gun

clipboard /ˈklɪp·bɔːrd, -bourd/ *n* [C] a board with a piece of metal at the top that holds sheets of paper in position and provides a surface for writing on

clip-on *adj* [not gradable] attaching with a CLIP ○ *clip-on earrings*

clique /kliːk, klɪk/ *n* [C] a small group of people who spend time together and do not want other people to join the group

clitoris /ˈklɪţ·ə·rəs/ *n* [C] a small organ above the VAGINA

cloak **PIECE OF CLOTHING** /klouk/ *n* [C] a loose outer piece of clothing without sleeves that fastens at the neck and hangs from the shoulders

HIDE /klouk/ *v* [T] to cover or hide something ○ *The deal was cloaked in secrecy.*

cloak /klouk/ *n* [C usually sing]

cloak-and-dagger *adj* [not gradable] involving mystery and secrecy ○ *a cloak-and-dagger spy mission*

cloakroom /ˈklouk·ruːm, -rum/ *n* [C] a room in a public building where coats, bags, and hats can be left while their owners are in the building

clobber **HIT** /ˈklab·ər/ *v* [T] *infml* to hit hard ○ *He got clobbered by a piece of falling rock.* ○ *(fig.) A severe storm clobbered the region.*

DEFEAT /ˈklab·ər/ *v* [T] to defeat completely ○ *The party has been clobbered by a string of humiliating political losses.*

clock /klak/ *n* [C] a device for measuring and showing time, often placed on a surface or attached to a wall ○ *an alarm clock* ○ *The clock is about ten minutes fast/slow* (= it shows a later/earlier time than it should). ○ *Cleveland tied the game with five seconds on the clock* (= still available).

clock /klak/ *v* [T] to use an amount of time, esp. as measured by a clock ○ *She clocked the fastest time in practice runs for the women's downhill skiing event.*

clockwise /ˈklak·waɪz/ *adj, adv* [not gradable] (moving around) in the same direction as the pointers of a clock or watch ○ Compare COUNTERCLOCKWISE

clock radio *n* [C] a radio that shows the time and can be set so the radio automatically begins to play at a time you choose

clockwork /ˈklak·wɜrk/ *n* [U] **1** machinery with springs and wheels that makes older types of clocks, toys, and other devices work **2** Something that is **like clockwork** runs easily, automatically, and always in the same way: *The Cardinals have been winning like clockwork for most of the season.*

clod LUMP /klɑd/ *n* [C] a lump of dirt

PERSON /klɑd/ *n* [C] *infml* a stupid or awkward person

clog BLOCK /klɑg, klɔːg/ *v* [I/T] **-gg-** to become blocked or filled so that movement or activity is slowed or stopped, or to cause this to happen ○ [T] *During rush hour, downtown streets are clogged with commuters.* ○ [M] *Too much cholesterol clogs up your arteries.*

SHOE /klɑg, klɔːg/ *n* [C] a shoe with a thick, often wooden bottom and a top that covers the front of the foot, but not the heel

cloister /ˈklɔɪ·stər/ *n* [C] a covered passage around esp. a square open space within a religious building, or the space such a passage goes around

clone /kloʊn/ *n* [C] ***biology*** a cell or organism that has the exact same chemical patterns in its cells as the original from which it was artificially produced

clone /kloʊn/ *v* [T] to produce a clone

cloning /ˈkloʊ·nɪŋ/ *n* [U] the process of producing a clone

close NEAR /kloʊs/ *adj, adv* [*-er/-est* only] near in position, time, or condition ○ *The store was close by, so they decided to walk.* ○ *It's close to 7 o'clock – we'd better leave now.* ○ *The child moved closer to his mother.* ○ *She was very close to death for awhile.*

closely /ˈkloʊ·sli/ *adv* ○ *We had to huddle more closely together.*

CONNECTED /kloʊs/ *adj* [*-er/-est* only] connected or involved in strong relationship with someone ○ *Charmaine is my closest friend.* ○ *Joyce and I used to be close, but now we seldom see each other.*

closely /ˈkloʊ·sli/ *adv* [not gradable] ○ *We worked together closely for years.* ○ *The city and the air force base have been closely linked since 1943.*

SIMILAR /kloʊs/ *adj* [*-er/-est* only] **1** similar; of the same type ○ *Your computer is pretty close to the one I have.* **2** If a game or competition is close, both sides have almost the same score.

CAREFUL /kloʊs/ *adj* [*-er/-est* only] giving your full attention to something so that you notice its details ○ *I wasn't the one driving, so I wasn't paying close attention to the route we took.*

closely /ˈkloʊ·sli/ *adv* [not gradable] ○ *We watched her closely to make sure her fever did not go up again.* ○ *Economists closely follow auto sales.*

WARM /kloʊs/ *adj* [not gradable] very warm, with no movement of air ○ *It was uncomfortably close in the gym.*

MAKE NOT OPEN /kloʊz/ *v* [I/T] to change from being open to not being open, or to cause this to happen ○ [T] *Come in and close the door.* ○ [T] *Because of an accident, police closed* (= blocked) *two lanes of the expressway.* ○ [T] *Grace closed her eyes to think.*

closed /kloʊzd/ *adj* [not gradable] If a society or economy is closed, it does not allow free exchanges or trade with other societies or countries.

➤ Confusables: **open and close** at OPEN READY FOR USE

END/STOP /kloʊz/ *v* [I/T] **1** to end or stop operating, or to cause this to happen ○ [T] *Authorities closed the aging nuclear plant.* ○ [I] *After a run of three months, the show closes on Saturday.* **2** (esp. of a business) To close is also to temporarily stop being available to customers: [I] *The store closes at 9 tonight.*

close /kloʊz/ *n* [C usually sing] ○ *The ski season has come to a close.*

closed /kloʊzd/ *adj* [not gradable] temporarily not open for business ○ *The library is closed on Tuesday.*

COMPLETE /kloʊz/ *v* [I/T] to make a financial or business arrangement complete ○ [T] *The manufacturer is closing a deal to sell its boating division.*

closing /ˈkloʊ·zɪŋ/ *n* [C] ○ *The closing for the house was set for April.*

WORD FAMILY close			
Nouns	closeness	*Adverbs*	close closely
Adjectives	close		

IDIOM with close

• **close call**, **close shave** something bad that almost happened ○ *We almost got hit by another car driving over here – it was really a close call.*

PHRASAL VERBS with close

• **close down** *(something)* [M] to end the operation of something, or (esp. a place of business) to stop operating ○ *He said he would close down before he would force all hands to join the union.*

• **close in** to move toward someone or something gradually and from all directions ○ *It felt as though the walls of the room were closing in on her.*

• **close off** *something* [M] to stop people or vehicles from going to a place ○ *They closed Pennsylvania Avenue off to vehicles.*

• **close out** *something* [M] to complete something by doing the last thing that is needed or possible ○ *They closed out 2003 by winning three of their final five games.*

closed /kloʊzd/ *adj* ○ See at CLOSE MAKE NOT OPEN; CLOSE END/STOP

closed-circuit *adj* [not gradable] involving a television system with cameras that operate within or around a building as a way to prevent stealing or other illegal activities

closed shop *n* [C] a place of work where you have to belong to a particular LABOR UNION (= organization of workers)

close-knit *adj* involving groups of people in which everyone supports each other

closet /ˈklɑz·ət/ *n* [C] a small room or space in a wall where you can store things such as clothes, sheets, etc., often having a door so that it can be closed ○ *a clothes/linen closet*

closet /ˈklɑz·ət/ *adj* kept secret from others ○ *a closet liberal*

closet /ˈklɑz·ət/ *v* [T always + adv/prep] to arrange to meet privately with someone where you will not be interrupted ○ *The president and his advisers closeted themselves with the congressional leadership.*

closeup /ˈkloʊ·sʌp/ *n* [C] an image taken from very near so that the subject appears large

closure STOP OPERATING /ˈkloʊ·ʒər/ *n* [C] the act of stopping operations of a business, school, hospital, etc. ○ *A storm forced the closure of many schools and businesses.*

SATISFACTION /ˈkloʊ·ʒər/ *n* [U] the feeling or act of bringing something bad to an end ○ *a sense of closure* ○ *Yesterday's vote will bring closure to a painful chapter in history.*

clot /klɑt/ *n* [C] a lump, esp. a lump of thick blood ○ *Heart attacks occur when a blood clot blocks vessels to the heart.*
clot /klɑt/ *v* [I/T] to become thicker and more solid, or to cause a liquid to do this ○ [T] *My hair was all clotted with dust and mud.*

cloth /klɔːθ/ *n* [C/U] material made by weaving cotton, wool, or other fibers, or a piece of such material ○ [U] *cloth diapers* ○ [U] *cloth napkins* ○ [U] *a cloth coat* ○ [C] *He used a damp cloth to clean the windshield.*

clothe /kloʊð/ *v* [T] to provide or cover someone with things to wear ○ *They have eight kids to feed and clothe.*

WORD FAMILY clothe			
Nouns	clothes clothing	*Verbs*	clothe

clothes /kloʊðz, kloʊz/ *pl n* things you wear to cover your body and keep you warm, to be comfortable, or for the way they make you look ○ *I've got all these clothes that I never wear.*

clothesline /ˈkloʊz·lɑɪn, ˈkloʊðz-/ *n* [C] a length of rope from which wet clothes are hung, usually outside, to dry

clothespin /ˈkloʊz·pɪn, ˈkloʊðz-/ *n* [C] a small plastic or wooden object that is used to fasten clothes to a CLOTHESLINE while they dry

clothing /ˈkloʊ·ðɪŋ/ *n* [U] things you wear to cover your body; clothes ○ *The boys must wear heavy clothing in winter.*

cloud /klɑʊd/ *n* [C/U] **1** a white or gray mass of very small drops of water or ice that float in the sky ○ [C] *Those dark clouds look like we're going to get some rain.* **2** A cloud is also a mass of something, such as dust or smoke, that moves together: *The distant cloud of dust in the valley announced the approach of a car.* **3** A cloud is also something which causes sadness or fear: [C] *After the diagnosis of cancer, she lived under a cloud.*
cloud /klɑʊd/ *v* [T] **1** [T] *Smoke clouded the sky.* **2** If something clouds a situation or feeling, it makes it less clear: *The fact that Jack was an old friend clouded her judgment.*
cloudless /ˈklɑʊd·ləs/ *adj* [not gradable] (of the sky) without clouds
cloudy /ˈklɑʊd·i/ *adj* full of clouds ○ *a cloudy day*

PHRASAL VERB with cloud

• **cloud over/up** to become filled with clouds ○ *The sky clouded over, and you could hear thunder in the distance.* ○ *It looks like it's clouding up* (= the sky is becoming filled with clouds).

cloudburst /ˈklɑʊd·bɜrst/ *n* [C] a heavy fall of rain that begins and ends suddenly

clout POWER /klɑʊt/ *n* [U] power and influence over other people or events ○ *The small firms banded together so they would have more clout in Washington.*

HIT /klɑʊt/ *v* [T] *infml* to hit someone heavily with the hand or an object

clove PLANT PART /kloʊv/ *n* [C] a section of the ball-like root of a GARLIC plant

SPICE /kloʊv/ *n* [C/U] a spice that is the dried flower of a tree

clover /ˈkloʊ·vər/ *n* [C/U] a small plant with three round, green leaves that are joined together

cloverleaf /ˈkloʊ·vər ˌliːf/ *n* [C] *pl* **cloverleafs, cloverleaves** a connection between two roads consisting of four smaller, curved roads which allows vehicles to move from one road to the other without crossing the flow of traffic

clown /klɑʊn/ *n* [C] **1** an entertainer who wears silly clothes and makes people laugh by performing tricks without speech **2** *infml* A clown is also someone who behaves in a foolish or stupid way: *The people running this school are a bunch of clowns.*
clown /klɑʊn/ *v* [I] to act silly ○ *Stop clowning around and get serious!*

club GROUP /klʌb/ *n* [C] **1** an organization of people with a common purpose or interest who meet regularly and share activities ○ *My book club meets the first Tuesday of every month to discuss a new book we've all read.* **2** A club is also a team: *a major league baseball club*

GOLF STICK /klʌb/ *n* [C] a long, thin stick with a wide part at the bottom, used to hit the ball in the game of golf

WEAPON /klʌb/ *n* [C] a heavy stick used as a weapon
club /klʌb/ *v* [T] **-bb-**

clubs /klʌbz/ *pl n* one of the four SUITS (= groups) of playing cards, the symbol for which is a black sign with three circular parts and a stem

club soda /klʌb ˈsoʊd·ə/ *n* [C/U] bubbly water that is sometimes mixed with other drinks

cluck /klʌk/ *v* [I/T] to make a sound like a chicken

clue /kluː/ *n* [C] information that helps you to find the answer to a problem, question, or mystery ○ *For five months, Russell remained a fugitive, leaving no clues as to his whereabouts.*

PHRASAL VERB with clue

• **clue** *someone* **in** *infml* to give someone information that is necessary or new ○ *He should clue everyone in on his plans and explain how they might be carried out.*

clump GROUP /klʌmp/ *n* [C] a group, esp. of plants ○ *Small clumps of hardy grass had sprung up between the rocks.*
clump /klʌmp/ *v* [I/T] to gather in a group, or to cause this to happen ○ [T] *In our office, the desks are clumped together with partitions around them.*

WALK /klʌmp/ *v* [I always + adv/prep] to walk in a noisy way with heavy steps ○ *He clumped up the steps.*

clumsy /ˈklʌm·zi/ *adj* **1** awkward in movement or manner ○ *I'm so clumsy – I keep dropping things.* **2** Clumsy also means done in an awkward or embarrassing way: *He subsequently wrote a letter to the magazine in an admittedly clumsy try at explaining his viewpoint.* **3** Something that is clumsy is too big or complicated to be dealt with easily: *She would be at the mercy of a clumsy bureaucracy.*

clung /klʌŋ/ *past simple and past participle of* CLING

clunk /klʌŋk/ *v* [T] to make the sound of heavy objects hitting together, or to cause this sound to be made ○ *She emptied the change out of her purse and clunked it into her piggy bank.*
clunk /klʌŋk/ *n* [C] ○ *We heard a loud clunk as the ferry hit the side of the dock.*

cluster /ˈklʌs·tər/ *v* [I] to form or gather together ○ *All his grandchildren clustered around him.*
cluster /ˈklʌs·tər/ *n* [C] a group of similar things growing or held together, or a group of people or things that are close together ○ *dense clusters of delicate pink blossoms* ○ *This section of town has a large cluster of fast-food restaurants.*

clutch HOLD /klʌtʃ/ *v* [I/T] to hold or try to hold something tightly, often because of a state of fear or anxiety ○ [T] *The preschooler clutched his mother tightly.*
clutches /ˈklʌtʃ·əz/ *pl n* **1** a hold on someone or something ○ *The family dog saved their daughter from the icy clutches of the river.* **2** Clutches can also mean control or power over someone, esp. harmful control or power: *They are not beyond the clutches of the courts.*

VEHICLE PART /klʌtʃ/ *n* [C usually sing] a device in a car or other vehicle that you press with your foot in order to change GEARS (= set of wheels that control power)

GROUP /klʌtʃ/ *n* [C] **1** a group of eggs or young animals hatched from eggs ○ *several clutches of the infant sea turtles* **2** A clutch is also a group of people, animals, or things: *The herders tend to small clutches of cattle and llamas.*

BAG /klʌtʃ/ *n* [C] a small bag with no handle or strap, used esp. by women for carrying small personal items

PERFORMING WELL /klʌtʃ/ *adj* able to do something when it is especially needed ○ *Moose, always reliable under pressure, was a tremendous clutch hitter.*
clutch /klʌtʃ/ *n* [U] ○ *Rhoda always comes through in the clutch* (= You can depend on her to do what is needed).

clutter /ˈklʌt̬·ər/ *n* [U] a condition of disorder, or a lot of objects that are in a state of disorder ○ *The basement work area is filled with creative clutter.*
clutter /ˈklʌt̬·ər/ *v* [T] ○ *The family room was cluttered with toys.*

cm *n* [C] *pl* **cm** *abbreviation for* CENTIMETER

c'mon /kəˈmɔːn, -ˈmɑn/ *contraction of* COME ON **HURRY** ○ *C'mon in, the door's open.* ○ **USAGE:** spelled the way it is often spoken

Co. /ˈkʌm·pə·ni, koʊ/ *n* [U] *abbreviation for* COMPANY **BUSINESS** ○ *Doubleday & Co., publishers*

co- /koʊ/ *prefix* together; with ○ *co-author* ○ *co-founder* ○ *They were named co-winners of the player of the week award.*

c/o *abbreviation for* care of ○ *You can write me c/o Roberta Moody, at 12 Townsend Place, Newark, New Jersey.* ○ **USAGE:** Used in written addresses.

coach TEACHER /koʊtʃ/ *n* [C] **1** (esp. in sports) a person who is responsible for managing and training a person or a team ○ *a basketball coach* **2** A coach is also an expert who trains someone learning or improving a skill, esp. one related to performing: *an acting coach*
coach /koʊtʃ/ *v* [I/T] ○ [I/T] *He coached the Giants until 1997.*

PART OF VEHICLE /koʊtʃ/ *n* [C/U] **1** the less expensive sections of an aircraft that most people sit in ○ [U] *We were in coach on the flight to Seattle.* **2** A coach is also one of the separate parts of a train. **3** A coach is also a kind of old-fashioned vehicle pulled by one or more horses. **4** *Br* A coach is a BUS.

coagulate /koʊˈæg·jəˌleɪt/ *v* [I/T] (of a liquid) to become or cause to become thicker so that it will not flow ○ [I] *When making cheese, enzymes are added to make the milk coagulate.*

coal /koʊl/ *n* [C/U] a hard, black substance that is dug from the earth in lumps and used as a fuel, or a single piece of this substance ○ [U] *Some of those schools still use coal for their heating.*

coalesce /ˌkoʊ·əˈles/ *v* [I/T] to combine into a single group or thing ○ [I] *The theory is that galaxies coalesced from smaller groupings of stars.*

coalition /ˌkoʊ·əˈlɪʃ·ən/ *n* [C] ***politics & government*** a group formed of different organizations or people who agree to act together, usually temporarily, to achieve something ○ *a governing coalition* ○ *the National Coalition on Black Voter Participation*

coal mine *n* [C] a deep hole or connected long narrow openings under the ground from which coal is removed

coarse ROUGH /kɔːrs, koʊrs/ *adj* [*-er/-est* only] rough and not smooth or soft ○ *coarse hair* ○ *coarse linen shirts*
coarsely /ˈkɔːr·sli, ˈkoʊr-/ *adv* ○ *Our recipe calls for coarsely chopped pistachios.*

RUDE /kɔːrs, koʊrs/ *adj* [*-er/-est* only] rude or offensive in manner or speech ○ *Now and then coarse laughter broke out.*
coarseness /ˈkɔːr·snəs, ˈkoʊr-/ *n* [U] ○ *He was shocked by the coarseness of his guest.*

coast LAND /koʊst/ *n* [C] the land next to or close to the sea ○ *We lived on the southeast coast of Florida.*
coastal /ˈkoʊ·stəl/ *adj* [not gradable] near the coast ○ *coastal waters* ○ *coastal communities*

C

MOVE EASILY /koʊst/ *v* [I] **1** (of a vehicle) to continue moving from its own forward force, without the addition of any power ○ *He coasted to a stop.* **2** To coast is also to advance without effort: *She coasted through her senior year of high school.*

IDIOMS with coast

• **coast to coast 1** everywhere or all across a country, esp. the U.S. ○ *The country is experiencing a heatwave, coast to coast.* **2** To go **coast to coast** means to travel from one side of a country with coasts on each side, to the other side: *We drove coast to coast in my parents' minivan.*

• **the coast is clear** someone can safely do something without being seen or noticed ○ *My brother went to see if the coast was clear, and we snuck out of our bedroom.*

coaster /ˈkoʊ·stər/ *n* [C] a small, flat piece of material, often decorative, that you put a glass or cup on in order to protect the surface of furniture

Coast Guard *n* [U] a part of the US military forces that is responsible for guarding the land next to the sea, seeing that boats and ships follow US laws, and helping people in emergencies

coastline /ˈkoʊst·lɑɪn/ *n* [C/U] the shape of the land next to the sea, esp. when seen from the air or as shown on a map

coat CLOTHING /koʊt/ *n* [C] **1** any of various types of outer clothing that are worn over other clothes, usually open in the front, and are often used for warmth ○ *She put on her heavy winter coat.* **2** When you say a man is wearing a coat and tie, the coat is a jacket or part of a SUIT. **3** Coat is often used as a combining form: *a raincoat*

ANIMAL /koʊt/ *n* [C] the natural hair, wool, or fur of an animal ○ *The dog's coat is shiny and clean.*

LAYER /koʊt/ *n* [C] a layer of a substance ○ *There were about six coats of paint over the brick.*

coat /koʊt/ *v* [T] ○ *Everything was coated with a fine layer of dust.*

coating /ˈkoʊţ·ɪŋ/ *n* [C] a COAT LAYER ○ *Use a baking pan with a nonstick coating.*

coat hanger *n* [C] a HANGER

coax /koʊks/ *v* [T] to try to persuade someone to do something by gently asking or patiently encouraging the person ○ *He'll talk if you coax him.*

cobalt /ˈkoʊˌbɔːlt/ *n* [U] ***chemistry*** a hard, gray chemical element that is a metal and is used in making paint and ALLOYS (= mixtures of metals)

cobbled /ˈkɑb·əld/ *adj* [not gradable] surfaced with a layer of stones ○ *cobbled streets*

cobra /ˈkoʊ·brə/ *n* [C] a poisonous snake from Africa or southern Asia that can make itself look bigger by spreading the skin at the back of its head

cobweb /ˈkɑb·web/ *n* [C usually pl] a structure of thin, sticky threads made by a SPIDER (= small creature with eight legs), esp. when the threads are covered with dust ○ *Cobwebs hung down from the rafters.*

cock BIRD /kɑk/ *n* [C] a ROOSTER (= an adult male chicken)

TURN /kɑk/ *v* [T] to turn a part of the body in a particular direction ○ *He cocked his head to one side.*

PREPARE GUN /kɑk/ *v* [T] to prepare a gun so that it is ready for firing

cock-a-doodle-do /ˌkɑk·əˌduːd·əlˈduː/ *exclamation a child's word* the sound made by a ROOSTER (= type of bird)

cockamamie /ˌkɑk·əˈmeɪ·mi/ *adj slang* ridiculous or crazy ○ *He had some cockamamie idea for turning hay into food for people.*

cockeyed SLOPING /ˈkɑkˈɑɪd/ *adj, adv* not level but set at an angle ○ *That picture looks cockeyed – it tilts to the left.*

RIDICULOUS /ˈkɑkˈɑɪd/ *adj* completely unreasonable; ridiculous ○ *The movie is based on a cockeyed premise.*

cockpit /ˈkɑk·pɪt/ *n* [C] the enclosed space where the PILOT sits in an aircraft, or where the driver sits in a racing car

cockroach /ˈkɑk·roʊtʃ/, *short form* **roach** *n* [C] a flat brown or black insect sometimes found in a house

cocksure /ˈkɑkˈʃʊr, *Southern often* -ˈʃoʊr/ *adj* [not gradable] *disapproving* too confident ○ *a strong, cocksure young man*

cocktail DRINK /ˈkɑk·teɪl/ *n* [C] **1** a drink made by mixing two or more drinks together ○ *Would you like a cocktail?* **2** A cocktail is also a mixture of different things: *The cocktail of drugs to treat TB is taken for six to nine months.*

FOOD /ˈkɑk·teɪl/ *n* [C/U] a small dish of particular foods sometimes eaten at the beginning of a meal ○ [C] *I'd like the shrimp cocktail, please.*

cocktail dress *n* [C] a stylish dress suitable for an evening party

cocktail party *n* [C] a party, usually in the early evening, at which drinks are served

cocky /ˈkɑk·i/ *adj* too confident ○ *Hugh is knowledgeable but not cocky.*

cocoa /ˈkoʊ·koʊ/ *n* [U] **1** a dark brown powder made from the crushed beans of a tree, used to make chocolate and give the taste of chocolate to food and drink **2** Cocoa is also a drink made from cocoa powder that is sweetened and mixed with hot water or milk.

coconut /ˈkoʊ·kəˌnʌt/ *n* [C/U] a large fruit with a hard, brown shell and firm, white, edible flesh, or the white flesh of this fruit, sometimes used in cooking

cocoon /kəˈkuːn/ *n* [C] **1** the silky covering that encloses and protects CATERPILLARS (= a type of insect) during a stage in their lives before they develop into adults **2** *fig.* A cocoon is also a safe, quiet place: *the warm, safe cocoon of childhood*

cod /kɑd/ *n* [C/U] *pl* **cod** a large sea fish that can be eaten

C

C.O.D. *adv* [not gradable] *abbreviation for* cash/collect on delivery (= payment will be made when goods are delivered) ○ *Can I have that shipped C.O.D.?*

coddle /ˈkɑd·əl/ *v* [T] to protect and treat someone or something with great care ○ *The coach does not coddle his players.*

code Ⓐ **SPECIAL LANGUAGE** /koʊd/ *n* [C/U] a system for representing information with signs or symbols that are not ordinary language, or the signs or symbols themselves ○ [U] *Andrew writes computer code.* ○ [C] *Callers punch in four-digit access codes for various topics.*

code Ⓐ /koʊd/ *v* [T] ○ *Many areas of the brain code and store information.*

coded Ⓐ /ˈkoʊd·əd/ *adj* [not gradable] ○ *Electronically coded cards are issued to food-stamp recipients.*

PATTERN /koʊd/ *n* [C] ***biology*** GENETIC CODE

RULES /koʊd/ *n* [C] rules for the way people should behave, or a set of written rules or laws that tell people what to do ○ *Faculty members are expected to follow the school's honor code.* ○ *Is there a dress code where you work?* ○ *Fire codes prohibit locking classroom doors.*

codeine /ˈkoʊ·diːn/ *n* [U] a drug which is used in medicine to block pain

code word *n* [C] a word or sign with a special meaning, or a word used to keep something secret ○ *"Long," "very thorough," and "frank" are all diplomatic code words for continuing disagreement.*

codify /ˈkɑd·əˌfɑɪ, ˈkoʊd-/ *v* [T] ***politics & government*** to organize and write a law or system of laws

codon /ˈkoʊˌdɑn/ *n* [C] ***biology*** a group of three chemical substances in DNA that contains the information for one of the AMINO ACIDS, which are necessary for making PROTEIN (= substance necessary for the body to grow)

coed /ˈkoʊ·ed/ *adj* [not gradable] for male and female students together ○ *a coed private school*

coed /ˈkoʊ·ed/ *n* [C] *dated* a female student in a college or university that has both male and female students

coefficient /ˌkoʊ·ɪˈfɪʃ·ənt/ *n* [C] **1** ***mathematics*** a number or symbol that is written in front of and multiplies another number or symbol **2** ***chemistry*** A coefficient is also a number that is used to measure the characteristics of a substance. **3** ***physics*** The **coefficient of friction** is a measure of how easily one object slides across the surface of another, calculated by the force that is being used and the amount of FRICTION.

coenzyme /koʊˈenˌzɑɪm/ *n* [C] ***biology*** a substance, often containing a VITAMIN (= substance necessary for growth and good health), that improves the chemical activity of an ENZYME

coerce /koʊˈɜrs/ *v* [T] to persuade someone forcefully to do something that he or she may not want to do ○ *I don't think anybody should be coerced into leaving.*

coercion /koʊˈɜr·ʒən/ *n* [U] ○ *They used threats and coercion to keep the others in line.*

coercive /koʊˈɜr·sɪv/ *adj* ○ *coercive threats/governments*

coexist /ˌkoʊ·ɪɡˈzɪst/ *v* [I] to live or exist together, esp. in peace, at the same time or in the same place ○ *The two communities coexist peacefully.*

coexistence /ˌkoʊ·ɪɡˈzɪs·təns/ *n* [U] ○ *Peaceful coexistence is our only real hope.*

coffee /ˈkɔː·fi, ˈkɑf·i/ *n* [C/U] a dark brown, slightly bitter drink that is usually served hot, esp. in the morning and at the end of meals, or the beans from which this drink is made ○ [U] *Would you like some more coffee?*

coffee break *n* [C] a short rest from work in the morning or afternoon

coffeehouse /ˈkɔː·fiːˌhɑʊs/ *n* [C] a small, informal restaurant where people can buy drinks and small meals and where there is sometimes entertainment

coffeemaker /ˈkɔː·fiːˌmeɪ·kər/ *n* [C] a machine that makes coffee

coffee pot *n* [C] a container for making or serving coffee

coffee shop *n* [C] an informal restaurant where drinks and simple meals are served

coffee table *n* [C] a low table usually placed in front of a SOFA (= long, soft seat) on which to set drinks, magazines, and other small objects

coffers /ˈkɔː·fərz, ˈkɑf·ərz/ *pl n* the financial accounts of a government or an organization ○ *Tourism brought $200 million into local government coffers.*

coffin /ˈkɔː·fən, ˈkɑf·ən/ *n* [C] a long box used to bury or CREMATE (= burn) a dead person

cog /kɑɡ/ *n* [C] a part shaped like a tooth around the edge of a wheel in a machine that fits between those on a similar wheel, causing both wheels to move

cogent /ˈkoʊ·dʒənt/ *adj* persuasive and well expressed ○ *He makes a cogent argument for improving early childhood education.* ○ **USAGE:** said about an argument or opinion

cogency /ˈkoʊ·dʒən·si/ *n* [U] *fml* ○ *Her writing combines fluency with cogency.*

cognac /ˈkoʊn·jæk, ˈkɔːn-/ *n* [C/U] high quality BRANDY (= strong alcoholic drink) from western France, or a glass of this

cognitive /kɑɡ·nət·ɪv, -nə·tɪv/ *adj* relating to or involving the processes of thinking and reasoning ○ *Studies show a connection between aerobic exercise and cognitive ability.*

coherent Ⓐ /koʊˈhɪr·ənt/ *adj* **1** ***writing*** having its parts related in an organized and reasonable way ○ *The president has not presented a coherent plan for dealing with it.* **2** Coherent also means expressing yourself clearly: *I should warn you, she's not always coherent.*

coherence Ⓐ /koʊˈhɪr·əns/ *n* [U] ***literature*** a clear relationship between parts, esp. in a work of literature or art: *Is there a larger vision, a coherence behind any of this?*

coherently Ⓐ /koʊˈhɪr·ənt·li/ *adv*

cohesion /koʊˈhiː·ʒən/ *n* [U] (of objects) the state of sticking together, or (of people) being in close agreement and working well together ○ *The team just seems to lack cohesion.*

cohesive /koʊˈhiː·sɪv, -zɪv/ *adj* ○ *We were not a very cohesive family.*

coil /kɔɪl/ *n* [C] **1** a length of rope or wire curled to form a series of circles, one above the other ○ *Rob raised the heavy coil of rope to his shoulder.* **2** A coil is also anything having the shape of a series of circles, one above the other: *A coil of smoke rose from the chimney.*

coil /kɔɪl/ *v* [I/T] ○ [T] *She coiled my hair, clipping curls with bobby pins.*

coin MONEY /kɔɪn/ *n* [C] a small, flat, round piece of metal used as money, with a number showing its value and often a decorative picture ○ *Let's flip a coin to see who goes first.* ○ *He fished about in his pockets, taking out a handful of coins.*

INVENT /kɔɪn/ *v* [T] to invent or be the first to use a new word or expression ○ *Kraft coined the term "middle America" in the 1960s.*

coinage /ˈkɔɪ·nɪdʒ/ *n* [U] ***politics & government*** **1** money made of coins **2** Coinage is also a system or type of money used in a country.

coincide Ⓐ /ˌkoʊ·ənˈsɑɪd/ *v* [I] to come together in position or happen at or near the same time ○ *Power failures coincided with the hottest weather.*

coincidence Ⓐ /koʊˈɪn·səd·ᵊns, -səˌdens/ *n* [C/U] an occasion when two or more things happen at the same time, esp. in a way that is unexpected or unlikely, or the unlikely fact of such things happening at the same time ○ [C] *Was our meeting here a coincidence?* ○ [U] *By coincidence, both teams happen to be coached by men.*

coincidental Ⓐ /koʊˌɪn·səˈdent·ᵊl/ *adj* [not gradable] ○ *Resemblances between their stories are purely coincidental.*

coincidentally /koʊˌɪn·səˈdent·ᵊl·i/ *adv* [not gradable] ○ *Mo shut his eyes and swung, the ball and the bat coincidentally arriving at the same place at the same time.*

coke /koʊk/ *n* [U] a solid substance obtained from coal and used as a fuel

Coke /koʊk/ *n* [C/U] *trademark* COCA-COLA.

cola /ˈkoʊ·lə/ *n* [C/U] a sweet, bubbly, brown drink that does not contain alcohol

colander /ˈkɑl·ən·dər, ˈkʌl-/ *n* [C] a bowl with many holes in it, used for washing food or for removing water from food that has been cooked

cold LOW TEMPERATURE /koʊld/ *adj* [-*er*/-*est* only] having a low temperature, esp. when compared to the temperature of the human body, and not hot or warm ○ *cold weather* ○ *I forgot my gloves and my hands are getting cold.*

cold /koʊld/ *n* [U] The cold is cold temperature or cold weather: *Don't stand out there in the cold – come in here and get warm.*

WORD CHOICES cold

If the weather outside or the temperature inside is very cold, you can use the adjectives **bitter** or **freezing**.

Wrap up warmly – it's ***bitter*** *outside!*

It's absolutely ***freezing*** *in here!*

If the weather, especially the wind, is so cold that it is unpleasant to be in, the adjectives **biting** and **icy** are sometimes used.

A ***biting/icy*** *wind blew in her face as she opened the door.*

The adjective **chilly** is often used to describe weather or temperatures that feel slightly cold and unpleasant.

It's a bit ***chilly*** *in here – can you turn up the heat?*

If the temperature feels cold but pleasant, you can say that it is **cool**.

That's a nice ***cool*** *breeze.*

Cold weather in fall or winter that is dry and pleasant is sometimes described as **crisp**.

We walked through the forest on a ***crisp*** *autumn day.*

UNFRIENDLY /koʊld/ *adj* [-*er*/-*est* only] not showing or influenced by affection, kindness, or feeling; not friendly ○ *a cold greeting/reception*

coldly /ˈkoʊl·dli/ *adv* ○ *"Please don't come here again," he said coldly.*

ILLNESS /koʊld/ *n* [C] a common infection, esp. in the nose and throat, which often causes you to sneeze and cough, to feel tired, and sometimes to have pain in the muscles ○ *I'm afraid I'm catching a cold.*

IDIOMS with cold

- **cold turkey** suddenly and completely ○ *She decided to give up coffee and quit cold turkey.* ○ **USAGE:** Used to talk about stopping a habit, esp. one that you are dependent on.
- **get cold feet, have cold feet** to feel too frightened to do something that you had planned to do ○ *I was going to try bungee jumping, but I got cold feet.*
- **in cold blood** intentionally and without emotion ○ *killed in cold blood*

cold-blooded VARYING TEMPERATURE *adj* having a body temperature that varies with the environment ○ Compare WARM-BLOODED

LACKING SYMPATHY *adj* lacking the sympathy and kindness that all people should show

cold cuts *pl n* thin, flat slices of cold meat

cold-hearted *adj* having or showing a lack of care for others ○ *She said that the city's decision to close the homeless shelter was cold-hearted.*

cold snap *n* [C] a short period of very cold weather

cold sore *n* [C] a painful, red swelling on the lips or nose which is caused by a viral infection

C

cold war *n* [C] **1** ***politics & government*** a continuing and dangerous unfriendly situation existing between countries that is expressed in political ways, often including threats of war **2** ***world history*** The Cold War was a period of political difficulty involving the US and the USSR between 1945 and 1991.

coleslaw /ˈkoʊl·slɔː/ *n* [U] raw vegetables, esp. CABBAGE leaves, cut in thin strips and covered in a thick, creamy sauce and eaten cold

colic /ˈkɑl·ɪk/ *n* [U] a severe but not continuous pain in the bottom part of the stomach or bowels, esp. of babies

collaborate **WORK WITH** /kəˈlæb·əˌreɪt/ *v* [I] to work together or with someone else for a special purpose ○ *Rodgers and Hammerstein collaborated on a number of successful musicals for the Broadway stage.*

collaborative /kəˈlæb·əˌreɪt̬·ɪv, -ˈlæb·rət̬·ɪv/ *adj* ○ *Several speakers talked of the collaborative effort put forth by business leaders, politicians and community members.*

collaboration /kəˌlæb·əˈreɪ·ʃən/ *n* [C/U]

SUPPORT AN ENEMY /kəˈlæb·əˌreɪt/ *v* [I] to help an enemy of your own country, esp. one which has taken control of your country ○ *The Soviet government accused them of collaborating with Nazis in World War II.*

collage /kəˈlɑʒ, kɔː-/ *n* [C/U] ***art*** a picture that includes various materials or objects glued to a surface, or the art of making such a picture

collapse Ⓐ **FALL** /kəˈlæps/ *v* [I/T] to fall down suddenly, or to cause to fall down ○ [I] *A piece of the wall collapsed on top of him.*

collapse Ⓐ /kəˈlæps/ *n* [U] ○ *Toward the end of the race he was near collapse.*

FAIL /kəˈlæps/ *v* [I] to be unable to continue or to stay in operation; fail ○ *Talks between management and unions collapsed today.*

collapse Ⓐ /kəˈlæps/ *n* [C/U] ○ [U] *the collapse of the Soviet empire*

collapsible Ⓐ /kəˈlæp·sɪ·blˌ/ *adj* [not gradable] designed to be folded into a smaller shape or size for easy storage

collar **NECK** /ˈkɑl·ər/ *n* [C] **1** the part of a piece of clothing that goes around the neck **2** A collar is also a narrow piece made of leather or other strong material that is put around the neck of an animal, esp. a dog or cat kept as a pet.

CATCH /ˈkɑl·ər/ *v* [T] *infml* to catch and hold someone so that the person can't escape ○ (*fig.*) *We decided to skip the meeting but she collared us in the hotel lobby.*

collarbone /ˈkɑl·ərˌboʊn/ *n* [C] a bone between the shoulder and the base of the neck on each side of the body

collate /kəˈleɪt, ˈkɑl·eɪt, ˈkoʊ·leɪt/ *v* [I/T] to collect and arrange in correct order the sheets of a document ○ [T] *Will the new photocopier collate the pages?*

collateral /kəˈlæt̬·ə·rəl/ *n* [U] valuable property owned by someone who wants to borrow money, which the person agrees will become the property of the LENDER (= person or business that lends money) if the debt is not paid back ○ *She put up her house as collateral for the loan.*

colleague Ⓐ /ˈkɑl·iːg/ *n* [C] one of a group of people who work together ○ *He always got along well with his colleagues in the university.*

collect **GATHER** /kəˈlekt/ *v* [I/T] **1** to come or bring together from a variety of places or over a period of time ○ [I] *A crowd of people soon collected at the scene of the accident.* ○ [T] *Information about employment is collected from every state.* **2** People sometimes collect one particular type of object as a hobby: [T] *I've got three kids who collect football cards.*

collection /kəˈlek·ʃən/ *n* [C] ○ *We're taking (up) a collection for his retirement gift* (= getting money from people who want to give it).

collector /kəˈlek·tər/ *n* [C] someone who collects certain things as a job or as a hobby ○ *An avid art collector, he owned at least a dozen Picassos.*

collectible /kəˈlek·tə·bəl/ *n* [C] an item that some people want to collect as a hobby

RECEIVE /kəˈlekt/ *v* [I/T] to receive money that you are owed or have earned ○ [T] *You can begin to collect benefits under Social Security at age 62.*

TELEPHONE /kəˈlekt/ *adj, adv* [not gradable] (of a telephone call or the act of calling) done in a way that will be paid by the person receiving it ○ *a collect call* ○ *You can call me collect.*

WORD FAMILY collect			
Nouns	collection collector collectible	*Adjectives*	collected collective
		Adverbs	collectively
Verbs	collect		

collective /kəˈlek·tɪv/ *adj* of or shared by every member of a group of people ○ *It was a collective decision/effort.*

collectively /kəˈlek·tɪv·li/ *adv* ○ *The industry is willing to work collectively to find a solution.*

collectivism /kəˈlek·təˌvɪz·əm/ *n* [U] ***politics & government*** a political system in which a country's land and industry are owned and managed by a government or by all of its citizens together

collectivization /kəˌlek·tə·vəˈzeɪ·ʃən/ *n* [U] ***politics & government*** the organization of all of a country's production and industry into government ownership and management.

collective bargaining *n* [U] ***social studies*** a system in which employees deal with their employers as a group and try to agree on matters such as pay and working conditions

collective security *n* [U] ***politics & government*** an agreement among a group of nations to act on behalf of each other.

college /ˈkɑl·ɪdʒ/ *n* [C] **1** a place of higher education usually for people who have finished twelve years of schooling and where they can obtain more advanced knowledge and get a degree to recognize this **2** A college is also one of the separate parts into which some universities are divided:

She graduated from the university's College of Business Management.

collegiate /kəˈliː·dʒət/ *adj* of or belonging to a college or its students ○ *collegiate activities/sports*

collide /kəˈlɑɪd/ *v* [I always + adv/prep] (esp. of moving objects) to hit something violently ○ *He went off the road to avoid colliding with another car.*

collision /kəˈlɪʒ·ən/ *n* [C] the violent coming together of two or more moving objects, such as vehicles ○ *The collision involved a pickup truck and a car.*

IDIOM with collision

• **on a collision course** having very different aims or opinions and therefore likely to strongly disagree or fight ○ *The governor put himself on a collision course with state lawmakers over energy policy.*

collie /ˈkɑl·i/ *n* [C] any of several types of dogs with long hair, originally bred for controlling sheep

collinear /kəˈlɪn·iː·ər/ *adj* ***geometry*** of points, on a single straight line ○ **USAGE:** Usually said about three or more points

colloquial /kəˈloʊ·kwiː·əl/ *adj* (of words and expressions) informal and conversational, and more suitable for use in speech than in writing

collusion /kəˈluː·ʒən/ *n* [U] agreement, esp. in secret for an illegal or dishonest reason ○ *The companies were accused of acting in collusion to fix prices.*

cologne /kəˈloʊn/ *n* [U] a type of PERFUME (= liquid having a pleasant smell that is put on the body)

colon **MARK** /ˈkoʊ·lən/ *n* [C] a mark (:) used in writing esp. to introduce a list of things or a sentence or phrase taken from somewhere else

BODY PART /ˈkoʊ·lən/ *n* [C] the lower and larger part of the bowels through which food travels while it is being digested

colonel /ˈkɜrn·əl/ *n* [C] a military officer of high rank, above a MAJOR

colonnade /ˌkɑl·əˈneɪd/ *n* [C] a row of columns separated from each other by an equal distance

colony /ˈkɑl·ə·ni/ *n* [C] **1** ***politics & government*** a country or area controlled politically by a more powerful country **2** A colony is also a group of people with a shared interest or job who live together: *an artists' colony* **3** A colony is also a group of animals, insects, or plants of the same type that live together: *an ant colony*

colonial /kəˈloʊ·niː·əl/ *adj* ***politics & government*** involving a period of political control by a more powerful country.

colonialism /kəˈloʊ·niː·əˌlɪz·əm/ *n* [U] ***politics & government*** a policy or system in which a country controls another country or area.

colonist /ˈkɑl·ə·nəst/ *n* [C] ***politics & government*** a person living in a country or area controlled politically by a more powerful country ○ *He arrived in Maryland with the first American colonists in 1634.*

colonize /ˈkɑl·əˌnɑɪz/ *v* [T] ○ *Peru was colonized by the Spanish in the 16th century.*

color **APPEARANCE**, *Cdn, Br* **colour** /ˈkʌl·ər/ *n* [C/U] **1** the appearance that something has as a result of reflecting light ○ [C] *The dress comes in blue, green, red, and other colors.* ○ [U] *Some of the pictures in the book are in color, and some are in black and white.* **2** ***art*** A color is also a substance, such as a paint or DYE, which you add to something to make it have the appearance of a particular color.

color, *Cdn, Br* **colour** /ˈkʌl·ər/ *adj* [not gradable] showing things in all their colors, not just black and white ○ *color photos* ○ *a color TV*

color, *Cdn, Br* **colour** /ˈkʌl·ər/ *v* [I/T] **1** to change the color of something by using paint or a DYE ○ [I always + adv/prep] *He gives the boy books to read, and he buys him paints to color with.* **2** *fig.* If something or someone colors your thoughts or opinions, it influences them, often in a negative way: [T] *The report is colored by the fiscal crises of the last four years.*

colored, *Cdn, Br* **coloured** /ˈkʌl·ərd/ *adj* ○ *I saw an unusual, beautifully colored fish.*

colorful, *Cdn, Br* **colourful** /ˈkʌl·ər·fəl/ *adj* having a bright color or a lot of different colors ○ *a colorful blue and yellow dress* ○ See also: COLORFUL

coloring, *Cdn, Br* **colouring** /ˈkʌl·ə·rɪŋ/ *n* [C] a substance added to food or drink to change its color artificially ○ *The label says that no preservatives or artificial colorings were added to this cake.*

colorless, *Cdn, Br* **colourless** /ˈkʌl·ər·ləs/ *adj* [not gradable] containing no color ○ *Carbon monoxide is a colorless, odorless, poisonous gas.* ○ See also: COLORLESS

SKIN, *Cdn, Br* **colour** /ˈkʌl·ər/ *n* [U] **1** the natural color of a person's skin, esp. when considered in terms of race **2** Many people with dark skin describe themselves as **people of color**: *We need to protect the rights of people of color.* **3** Color can mean a healthy appearance of the skin: *She'd been ill for a while, but when I saw her last Friday, she had good color.*

colored, *Cdn, Br* **coloured** /ˈkʌl·ərd/ *adj* [not gradable] *dated* having dark skin ○ **USAGE:** In the US, colored was used esp. of people whose family originally came from Africa. This word is now offensive.

coloring, *Cdn, Br* **colouring** /ˈkʌl·ə·rɪŋ/ *n* [U] the combined effect of the colors of a person's skin and hair ○ *He claimed that when people don't get enough protein in their food, their coloring isn't so good.*

WORD FAMILY color			
Nouns	color colors coloring discoloration	*Adjectives*	colored colorful colorless
		Verbs	color discolor

colorblind **NOT SEEING COLORS**, **color-blind**, *Cdn, Br* **colour-blind** /ˈkʌl·ərˌblɑɪnd/ *adj* unable to tell the difference between certain colors, esp. green and blue

NOT CONSIDERING RACE, **color-blind**, *Cdn, Br* **colour-blind** /ˈkʌl·ərˌblɑɪnd/ *adj* not considering race when making decisions ○ *Children's theaters have pioneered color-blind casting and plays aimed at an ethnically and racially diverse audience.*

colorful, *Cdn, Br* **colourful** /ˈkʌl·ər·fəl/ *adj* having a lot of variety and therefore interesting ○ *colorful language* ○ *He had a colorful past and could tell some amusing stories.* ○ See also: COLORFUL at COLOR APPEARANCE

C

colorless, *Cdn, Br* **colourless** /ˈkʌl·ər·ləs/ *adj* having no unusual qualities and therefore not interesting ○ *He plays the part of a shy, colorless, average man.* ○ See also: COLORLESS at COLOR APPEARANCE

colors, *Cdn, Br* **colours** /ˈkʌl·ərz/ *pl n* the official flag of a country, ship, or military group

colossus /kəˈlɑs·əs/ *n* [C] *pl* **colossi** a very large statue, or *fig.* someone or something that is very great in size or importance ○ *a marble colossus from the sixth century B.C.* ○ *(fig.) He talked about the emerging colossus of the Internet.*

colossal /kəˈlɑs·əl/ *adj* [not gradable] (esp. of something bad) very great ○ *The whole business has been a colossal failure/mistake.* ○ *It was a colossal waste of time.*

colt /koʊlt/ *n* [C] a young, male horse ○ Compare FILLY

column BUILDING /ˈkɑl·əm/ *n* [C] **1** a tall, vertical post used as a support for the roof of a building or for decoration **2** A column is also anything or any set of things having a long, narrow shape: *a column of soldiers* ○ *a column of smoke*

PRINTING /ˈkɑl·əm/ *n* [C] **1** one of several vertical blocks of print into which a page of a newspaper or magazine is divided ○ *The article filled two columns.* **2** A column is also a piece of writing in a newspaper or magazine that is written by the same person and appears regularly, usually on a particular subject: *a column on sports* **3** A column is also any vertical block of words or numbers: *a column of figures*

columnist /ˈkɑl·əm·nəst/ *n* [C] someone who writes a regular article for a newspaper or magazine

.com /dɑtˈkɑm/ *n* [U] used at the end of some INTERNET addresses belonging to businesses

coma /ˈkoʊ·mə/ *n* [C] a state of being unconscious, in which a person cannot be waked, usually caused by illness or injury ○ *He had a high fever and fell into a coma.*

comatose /ˈkoʊ·məˌtoʊs, ˈkɑm·ə-/ *adj medical* (of a person) unconscious and not able to wake up, usually because of illness or injury ○ *The traffic accident left him comatose with massive brain damage.*

comb HAIR TOOL /koʊm/ *n* [C] a strip of plastic, wood, or metal with a row of long, narrow parts along one side, which is used to arrange or hold the hair ○ *Combs have been used from ancient times by women to hold and fix their hair.*

comb /koʊm/ *v* [T] ○ *She combed her hair and put on some lipstick.*

SEARCH /koʊm/ *v* [T] to search a place or an area very carefully ○ *The police combed the surrounding woods for evidence.*

combat /ˈkɑm·bæt/ *n* [U] **1** fighting during a time of war ○ *a combat jacket/zone/casualty* ○ *No one knew how many troops had died in combat.* **2** Combat is also a fight between two people or things: *The film explores the combat between good and evil.*

combat /kəmˈbæt, ˈkɑm·bæt/ *v* [T] to try to stop something unpleasant or harmful from happening or increasing ○ *We must try to combat poverty and illiteracy.*

combatant /kəmˈbæt·ᵊnt, ˈkɑm·bət̬·ənt/ *n* [C] a person who fights in a war

combative /kəmˈbæt̬·ɪv/ *adj* ○ *When you are in a combative mood, you are not pleasant company.*

combine /kəmˈbɑɪn/ *v* [I/T] **1** to unite or to join together to make a single thing or group ○ [T] *None of us has much money so let's combine what we've got.* ○ [+ *to* infinitive] *When hydrogen and oxygen molecules combine to form water, heat and electricity are produced.* **2** If you combine two activities, you do both at the same time: [T] *She manages to successfully combine motherhood and a career.*

combine /ˈkɑm·bɑɪn/ *n* [C] a group of people or organizations acting together ○ *Over the years they established a large media combine.*

combination /ˌkɑm·bəˈneɪ·ʃən/ *n* [C/U] a mixture obtained when two or more things are combined ○ [C] *Green is a combination of blue and yellow.* ○ [C] *A combination of tiredness and boredom made me doze off in class.* ○ *We'll be working in combination with* (= together with) *two other departments on this project.*

WORD FAMILY **combine**	
Nouns combination combine combo	*Verbs* combine

combining form *n* [C] ***grammar*** a word part to which prefixes and word endings or other combining forms can be added to make a word, as "bio-," "-graphy," and "-logy" combine to make "biology" and "biography"

combo /ˈkɑm·boʊ/ *n* [C] *pl* **combos** a small group of musicians who play together, esp. jazz musicians

combustion /kəmˈbʌs·tʃən/ *n* [U] the process of burning ○ *Fuel combustion produces energy to run machines.*

combustible /kəmˈbʌs·tə·bəl/ *adj* ○ *Gasoline is a highly combustible substance.*

come APPROACH /kʌm/ *v* [I] *past simp.* **came,** *past part.* **come** to move or travel toward the speaker or with the speaker ○ *Will you come here, please?* ○ *Did you come here by car?* ○ *Come on in! The water's great.* ○ *Are you coming over to my house tonight?* ○ *Is he coming to the movies with us?* ○ *The man is coming to fix the dryer this afternoon.* ○ *He came rushing over when I fell.*

coming /ˈkʌm·ɪŋ/ *adj* ○ *We look forward to even greater success in the coming year.*

MOVE TO LISTENER /kʌm/ *v* [I] *past simp.* **came,** *past part.* **come** to move or travel in the direction of the person being spoken to ○ *I thought I'd come and see your new house.* ○ *I've come to read the gas meter.*

ARRIVE /kʌm/ *v* [I] *past simp.* **came**, *past part.* **come** **1** to get to a particular place ○ *Has the mail come yet?* ○ *Spring came early this year – look at all the flowers!* **2** When something comes in it is received: *Reports are just coming in of the fire.*

BE FROM /kʌm/ *v* [I always + adv/prep] *past simp.* **came**, *past part.* **come** to be or start from a particular place ○ *She comes from Italy.* ○ *Does that quotation come from Shakespeare?*

EXIST /kʌm/ *v* [I always + adv/prep] *past simp.* **came**, *past part.* **come** to exist or be available ○ *The dress comes in three sizes – small, medium, and large.* ○ *This cuddly doll comes with her own blanket and bottle.*

HAPPEN /kʌm/ *v* [I] *past simp.* **came**, *past part.* **come** to happen ○ *Your birthday only comes around once a year.* ○ [+ to infinitive] *How did you two come to be friends?* ○ *The earthquake's aftereffects came without warning.*

ORDER /kʌm/ *v* [I always + adv/prep] *past simp.* **came**, *past part.* **come** **1** to be in a particular relation to others in an order ○ *April comes before May.* ○ *In your cookbook you'll see that pies come under the heading "Desserts."* **2** If something comes under an official organization, that organization is responsible for it: *Snow removal comes under the highway department.*

CHANGE /kʌm/ *v past simp.* **came**, *past part.* **come** to change or be in a different position or condition ○ [I always + adv/prep] *The stitching on my briefcase is coming apart.* ○ [L] *A wire had come loose at the back.* ○ [I always + adv/prep] *He pulled the knob and it came off in his hand.* ○ [+ to infinitive] *I couldn't stand him at first, but I've come to like him.*

IDIOMS with **come**

• **come before** to be more important than something ○ *His job always came before his family.*

• **come forward** to offer to give help ○ *Nobody has come forward yet with information about the accident.*

• **come in handy** to be useful ○ *This money will come in handy when we go on vacation.*

• **come of age** to reach the age when you are legally an adult ○ *My parents came of age during the 1960s.*

• **come off it** *infml* used to tell someone that you think what the person is saying is silly or stupid ○ *Come off it, Pete – you know that's not true!*

• **come on strong** to act in a forceful way ○ *The team came on strong in the second half and won.*

• **come out of** *your* **shell** to become more comfortable and friendly with people ○ *It took Dan a few weeks to come out of his shell, but he's doing well now.*

• **come to a head** reach a point where some strong action has to be taken ○ *The situation finally came to a head when she failed to show up at school.*

• **come to an end** to stop or end ○ *I'm enjoying my English class, but it's about to come to an end.*

• **come to light** to become known ○ *Fresh evidence has recently come to light.*

• **come to rest** to stop moving ○ *The car hit the curb and came to rest in a ditch.*

• **come to** *someone's* **rescue** to help someone out of a bad situation ○ *I was about to drop a huge tray of dishes when Brad came to my rescue.*

• **come to** *your* **senses** to begin to use good judgment ○ *It's time she came to her senses and got a job.*

• **come to terms with** *something* to learn to understand and accept something ○ *He made little effort to come to terms with his critics.*

• **come true** to happen in the way you had hoped ○ *I'd always dreamed of owning my own home, and now my dream has come true.*

• *something* **comes to** *your* **attention** *fml* you see or learn about something ○ *The matter first came to my attention when I was working at the college.* ○ *It has come to my attention that several people have been arriving late for work.*

• **have come a long way** to have improved greatly ○ *In the past 20 years, information technology has come a long way.*

PHRASAL VERBS with **come**

• **come across** *something/someone* **FIND** to find something or someone by chance ○ *He came across some old love letters.*

• **come across SEEM** to give other people a certain feeling or opinion ○ *He comes across as a bit of a bore.* ○ *We don't mean to be vague, but I know that's how it comes across.*

• **come along** to advance or improve ○ *How's your English coming along?*

• **come apart SEPARATE** to separate into pieces ○ *The windows come apart for easy cleaning.*

• **come apart FAIL** to be unsuccessful, or fail to produce the intended results ○ *The global economy is showing signs of coming apart.* ○ *His public life began to come apart early in 1987.*

• **come around CHANGE YOUR MIND** to change your opinion of something ○ *He'll come around to my point of view eventually.*

• **come around BECOME CONSCIOUS** to become conscious again after an accident or medical operation ○ *She hasn't come around yet.*

• **come at** *someone* to move quickly toward someone to attack that person ○ *He suddenly came at me.*

• **come away (with** *something)* to leave a place or situation with the stated feeling, idea, condition, etc. ○ *I recently spent about 90 minutes shopping on the Internet, and I came away empty-handed.* ○ *Some 39 percent said they came away with a more favorable view of the candidate.*

• **come back RETURN** to return ○ *Come back and see us again sometime.* ○ Related noun: COMEBACK

• **come back REMEMBER** to remember something you had previously forgotten ○ *As soon as she entered the school, childhood memories came rushing back.*

• **come between** *someone* to cause problems between two people or interrupt two people ○ *Don't let one little quarrel come between you!*

C

• **come by** *something* to obtain something ○ *A good boss is not so easy to come by.* ○ *It's unclear how he came by his wealth.*
• **come down** to become lower in position or value ○ *I am not going to buy any more coffee until the price comes down.* ○ Related noun: COMEDOWN
• **come down on** *someone* to punish someone or treat someone severely ○ *They're coming down heavily on people for not paying their taxes.*
• **come down to** *something* to have a particular thing as the most important matter ○ *It all comes down to money in the end.*
• **come down with** *something* to catch or show signs of an illness ○ *I feel like I'm coming down with a cold.*
• **come in** (of the ocean TIDE) to be rising to a higher level ○ *By the time we got to the beach the tide had come in.* ○ Compare GO OUT FLOW AWAY
• **come in for** *something* to receive blame or criticism ○ *The mayor came in for a lot of criticism of his remarks.*
• **come into** *something* **1** to enter a place or a new position or state ○ *The new safety regulations come into effect at the beginning of the month.* ○ *As we drove over the hill, the ocean came into view.* **2** Someone who comes into money or property receives it as a result of the death of a relative: *I came into a little money and bought a house.*
• **come off** **SUCCEED** to happen as planned or to succeed ○ *I thought the party came off really well.*
• **come off** **END UP** to end up in a particular position ○ *The team played hard and came off with a victory.*
• **come off** **COMPLETE** to be finished with or removed from something ○ *Marcia comes off maternity leave in March.*
• **come on** **HURRY**, *not standard* **c'mon** used for telling someone to move or act quickly or more quickly ○ *Come on – we're going to be late if you don't hurry!*
• **come on** **LACK BELIEF** *not standard* **c'mon** used for telling someone you do not believe what the person is saying or you think the person is not being serious ○ *Oh, come on. You have no evidence whatsoever.*
• **come on** **START TO DEVELOP** to start to develop gradually, as an illness or a mood ○ *He felt one of his headaches coming on.*
• **come on** *something* **FIND** COME UPON
• **come out** **BECOME KNOWN** **1** to become known or be made public ○ *When the facts came out, there was public outrage.* **2** A person who comes out tells something personal that has been kept secret. **3** When a book, magazine, or newspaper comes out, it begins to be sold to the public: *Her latest book is coming out in July.*
• **come out** **APPEAR** to move into full view ○ *Later in the afternoon, it stopped raining and the sun came out.*
• **come out** **GIVE OPINION** to express an opinion in public ○ *The candidate came out in favor of lower taxes.*
• **come out** **FINISH** to be in a particular condition when finished ○ *Your painting came out really well.*
• **come out** **MAKE A PICTURE** to produce a picture on film ○ *My camera broke and none of the skiing photographs came out.*
• **come out with** *something* to say something unexpectedly or suddenly ○ *You come out with some strange comments sometimes!*
• **come over** **VISIT** to visit someone's home ○ *Ron came over for dinner the other night.*
• **come over** *someone* **INFLUENCE** to influence someone suddenly to behave in a particular way ○ *I'm sorry! That was a stupid thing to say – I don't know what came over me.*
• **come through** **SUCCEED** to succeed in a difficult situation ○ *He's a great leader who always comes through under pressure.* ○ *Investors had faith we would come through for them in the long run.*
• **come through** *something* **DEAL WITH DIFFICULTY** to continue to live after an accident or a difficult or dangerous situation ○ *It was a miracle that he came through that car crash alive.*
• **come to** *something* **REACH** to reach a particular point ○ *His hair comes down to his shoulders.* ○ *We haven't come to a decision on the matter yet.*
• **come to** **BECOME CONSCIOUS** to become conscious again after an injury or medical operation ○ *She sat by the child's bedside until he came to.*
• **come together** to start working successfully with each other ○ *I remember how the community came together and were so supportive of each other.*
• **come under** *something* **CONTROL** to be judged or controlled by a law, rule, or authority ○ *Much of the Aegean came under the rule of the Ptolemies, along with Egypt.*
• **come under** *something* **EXPERIENCE** to start to experience something unpleasant ○ *But the plan quickly came under criticism from the opposing political party.*
• **come up** **BE MENTIONED** to be mentioned or talked about in conversation ○ *What points came up at the meeting?*
• **come up** **HAPPEN** to happen, usually unexpectedly ○ *I've got to go – something's just come up at home and I'm needed there.*
• **come up with** *something* to suggest or think of an idea or plan ○ *He came up with a great idea for the ad campaign.*
• **come upon** *someone/something*, **come on** to find or meet someone or something, esp. unexpectedly ○ *She came upon an odd little man in the forest.*

comeback /ˈkʌm·bæk/ *n* [C] a return to an earlier and better position or condition ○ *The band was popular in the late '70s, and had a comeback in the early '90s.* ○ Related verb: COME BACK

comedown /ˈkʌm·dɑʊn/ *n* [U] a reduction in position, value, or enjoyment ○ *I liked most of the book, but the ending was a real comedown.* ○ Related verb: COME DOWN

comedy /ˈkɑm·əd·i/ *n* [C/U] **1** a movie, play, or book that is intentionally amusing either in its characters or its action ○ [C] *A lot of Shakespeare's plays are comedies.* **2** Comedy is also the amusing part of a situation: [U] *When John forgot his lines in the middle of the speech it provided some good comedy.*

comedian /kəˈmiːd·iː·ən/, **comic** /ˈkɑm·ɪk/, *female* **comedienne** /kəˌmiːd·iːˈen/ *n* [C] a person whose job is to make people laugh by telling jokes and amusing stories or by copying the behavior or speech of famous people ○ *a stand-up comedian*

come-on *n* [C] *infml* something that is intended to attract a customer to a product ○ *Offering cash back on a purchase is one of the oldest come-ons in the world.*

comet /ˈkɑm·ət/ *n* [C] ***earth science*** a body of rock and ice that travels around the sun and that, as it nears the sun, develops a long tail of small pieces that can be seen

comeuppance /kʌmˈʌp·əns/ *n* [U] a punishment or some bad luck that is considered to be fair and deserved punishment for something bad that someone has done ○ *She'll get her comeuppance, don't worry.*

comfort /ˈkʌm·fərt/ *n* [C/U] the pleasant and satisfying feeling of being physically or mentally free from pain and suffering, or something that provides this feeling ○ [C] *He's a great comfort to his mother.* ○ [U] *I have to take an exam, too, if it's any comfort to you.*
comfort /ˈkʌm·fərt/ *v* [T] ○ *I tried to comfort him, but it was no use.*

WORD FAMILY comfort

Nouns	comfort comforter discomfort	*Adjectives*	comfortable uncomfortable
Verbs	comfort	*Adverbs*	comfortably uncomfortably

comfortable /ˈkʌm·fərt̬·ə·bəl, ˈkʌmf·tər·bəl/, *infml* **comfy** /ˈkʌm·fi/ *adj* **1** producing a relaxing feeling of physical comfort esp. because of shape or materials ○ *a comfortable bed/car/dress* ○ *Are you comfortable or is it too hot?* **2** Comfortable also means relaxed: *I'm not comfortable speaking in front of an audience.* **3** Comfortable also means having enough money for a good standard of living: *They're not rich but I think they're quite comfortable.* **4** In a competition, if you have a comfortable lead over the other competitors you are winning easily.
comfortably /ˈkʌm·fərt̬·ə·bli, ˈkʌmf·tər·bli/ *adv* ○ *They were comfortably settled in on the sofa.* ○ *After three periods, the Knicks comfortably led the Pacers.*

comforter /ˈkʌm·fərt̬·ər/ *n* [C] a thick cover for a bed filled with feathers or other material for extra warmth

comic AMUSING /ˈkɑm·ɪk/ *adj* making you want to laugh; amusing ○ *a comic actor/performance/writer*
comical /ˈkɑm·ɪ·kəl/ *adj* ○ *Tell me the truth – do I look comical* (= strange or foolish) *in this hat?*

MAGAZINE /ˈkɑm·ɪk/, **comic book** /ˈkɑm·ɪkˌbʊk/ *n* [C] a magazine, esp. for children, that contains a set of stories told in pictures with a small amount of writing

PERSON /ˈkɑm·ɪk/ *n* [C] a COMEDIAN

comic strip *n* [C] a short series of amusing drawings with a small amount of writing that is usually published in a newspaper

comings and goings /ˈkʌm·ɪŋ·zən ˈgoʊ·ɪŋz/ *pl n* movement or activity ○ *With so many comings and goings in this office I just can't seem to concentrate.*

comma /ˈkɑm·ə/ *n* [C] a mark (,) used in writing to separate parts of a sentence showing a slight pause, or to separate the various single items in a list

command ORDER /kəˈmænd/ *v* [T] to give someone an order or orders with authority ○ *The police commanded the driver to stop the car.*
command /kəˈmænd/ *n* [C/U] **1** an order, or the authority to give orders ○ [C] *"When I give the command, fall in!" the officer shouted.* ○ [U] *General MacArthur took command of* (= took military control over) *United Nations forces in South Korea.* **2** In computing, a command is an instruction to a computer to perform a specific action.
commanding /kəˈmæn·dɪŋ/ *adj* **1** having a position of authority or control ○ *Her commanding officer said her performance was excellent.* **2** A commanding voice or manner is one that seems to have authority and therefore gets your attention.

command KNOWLEDGE /kəˈmænd/ *n* [U] a good knowledge of something and the ability to use it ○ *The study of physics requires a command of mathematics.*

RECEIVE /kəˈmænd/ *v* [T] to deserve and receive because of special qualities or actions ○ *She commands one of the highest salaries in Hollywood.*

commandant /ˈkɑm·ənˌdænt, -ˌdɑnt/ *n* [C] an officer who is in charge of a military unit or school ○ *the commandant of West Point*

commandeer /ˌkɑm·ənˈdɪr/ *v* [T] to take possession or control of private property, esp. by force ○ *Some visitors commandeered outdoor tables on the balcony.*

commander /kəˈmæn·dər/ *n* [C] a naval officer of middle rank, above LIEUTENANT

commander in chief *n* [C] a military leader who is in charge of all the armed forces of a country or of all the forces fighting in a particular area or operation ○ *The president of the United States is also commander in chief.*

Commandment /kəˈmænd·mənt/ *n* [C] any of the ten important rules of behavior that the Bible says were given by God to Moses

commando /kəˈmæn·doʊ/ *n* [C] *pl* **commandos** a small group of soldiers trained to make quick and often dangerous attacks inside enemy areas, or a member of such a group ○ *a team of commandos*

commemorate /kəˈmem·əˌreɪt/ *v* [T] to show honor to the memory of an important person or event in a special way ○ *The ceremonies commemorated the 20th anniversary of the founding of the school.*
commemorative /kəˈmem·ə·rət̬·ɪv/ *adj* ○ *The Elvis Presley commemorative stamp was eagerly bought by collectors.*

C

commence Ⓐ /kə'mens/ *v* [I/T] to begin something ○ [T] *He commenced speaking before all the guests had arrived.*
commencement Ⓐ /kə'men·smənt/ *n* [C/U] **1** *fml* the beginning of something ○ *the Senate's commencement of closed-door deliberations* **2** A commencement is also a ceremony at which students formally receive their DIPLOMAS (= documents to show they have successfully completed their studies).

commend /kə'mend/ *v* [T] to formally praise or mention with approval someone or something ○ *Lamos should be commended for creating important opportunities for minority actors.*
commendable /kə'men·də·bəl/ *adj* ○ *The reporter did a commendable job under difficult circumstances.*
commendation /ˌkɑm·ən'deɪ·ʃən/ *n* [C/U] A commendation is a formal statement of praise for someone who has done something admirable.

commensurate /kə'men·sə·rət/ *adj* suitable in amount or quality compared to something else; matching in degree ○ *The agency's workload has increased without any commensurate increase in staff.*

comment Ⓐ /'kɑm·ent/ *v* [I] to express an opinion ○ *The lawyer won't comment publicly on the case.*
comment Ⓐ /'kɑm·ent/ *n* [C/U] an opinion or remark ○ [C] *One of his comments had to do with the state taxes.* ○ [U] *The reporter couldn't reach any government officials for comment* (= to ask for their opinions).

commentary Ⓐ /'kɑm·ənˌter·i/ *n* [C/U] a series of remarks describing an event, esp. on radio or television, or a set of written notes explaining or expressing an opinion on a text or subject ○ [C] *the television commentary on the Olympic Games*

commentator Ⓐ /'kɑm·ənˌteɪt̬·ər/ *n* [C] a person on radio or television who describes and discusses news events, sports, books, or other subjects

commerce /'kɑm·ɜrs/ *n* [U] ***social studies*** the buying and selling of goods and services, esp. in large amounts ○ *Congress has the power to regulate commerce between the states.*
commercial /kə'mɜr·ʃəl/ *adj* intended to make money, or relating to a business intended to make money ○ *The movie was a commercial success* (= it made money), *but the critics hated it.*
commercialism /kə'mɜr·ʃəˌlɪz·əm/ *n* [U] the methods used to advertise and sell goods and services, esp. (disapproving) such methods used only and obviously for profit
commercialize /kə'mɜr·ʃəˌlɑɪz/ *v* [T] ○ *Many universities are trying to commercialize their research* (= make use of it for profit).
commercially /kə'mɜr·ʃə·li/ *adv*
commercialization /kəˌmɜr·ʃə·lə'zeɪ·ʃən/ *n* [U]

commercial /kə'mɜr·ʃəl/ *n* [C] a paid advertisement on radio or television ○ *We all ran to get something to eat during the commercials.*

commie /'kɑm·i/ *n* [C] *dated, slang, short form of* COMMUNIST

commiserate /kə'mɪz·əˌreɪt/ *v* [I] to feel or express sympathy for someone's suffering or unhappiness ○ *She called to commiserate over his loss.*
commiseration /kəˌmɪz·ə'reɪ·ʃən/ *n* [U]

commission Ⓐ **GROUP** /kə'mɪʃ·ən/ *n* [C] a group of people who have been formally chosen and given the authority to get information about a problem or to perform other special duties ○ *Congress appointed a commission to study immigration policy.*

WORK REQUEST /kə'mɪʃ·ən/ *n* [C] a formal request to do a special piece of work for payment ○ *She received a commission to paint the governor's portrait.*
commission Ⓐ /kə'mɪʃ·ən/ *v* [T] to choose someone to do a piece of work, or to have a piece of work done ○ *The newspaper commissioned a series of articles on the fashion industry.*

MILITARY /kə'mɪʃ·ən/ *n* [C] the official authority to be an officer in the armed forces ○ *She received her commission as a lieutenant in the US Army.*
commission /kə'mɪʃ·ən/ *v* [T] ○ *He was commissioned a captain in the navy last June.*

CRIME /kə'mɪʃ·ən/ *n* [U] the act of doing something that is illegal or considered wrong ○ *the commission of a crime*

PAYMENT /kə'mɪʃ·ən/ *n* [C/U] a system of payment based on a percentage of the value of sales or other business done, or a payment to someone working under such a system ○ [C] *As a real estate agent, her commission is between 4% and 6% on every sale.*

commissioner Ⓐ /kə'mɪʃ·ə·nər/ *n* [C] an official in charge of a government department or other organization ○ *the police commissioner*

commit Ⓐ **PROMISE** /kə'mɪt/ *v* [I/T] **-tt- 1** to promise to give yourself, your money, your time, etc. to support something ○ [I/T] *They wouldn't commit (to giving) enough time or money to the project.* **2** If you do not commit yourself about something, you refuse to express an opinion about it: [T] *Neither candidate would commit himself on the issue of tax reform.*
commitment Ⓐ /kə'mɪt·mənt/ *n* [C/U] ○ [C] *Try the product for two weeks with no commitment to buy.*

PUT /kə'mɪt/ *v* [T] to actively put information in your memory or write it down ○ *These rules must be committed to memory.* ○ *I wouldn't want to commit these comments to paper.*

CRIME /kə'mɪt/ *v* [T] **-tt-** to do something illegal or considered wrong ○ *He committed a crime in providing the information to a reporter.*

SEND FOR TREATMENT /kə'mɪt/ *v* [T] **-tt-** *fml* to cause someone to stay in a mental hospital or treatment center ○ *He was once committed to a state mental hospital.*

WORD FAMILY commit			
Nouns	commitment	*Verbs*	commit
Adjectives	noncommittal		

committee /kə'mɪt̬·i/ *n* [C] a group of people chosen from a larger group to act on or consider matters of a particular kind ○ *She sits on the city's finance committee.*

commodity Ⓐ /kə'mɑd·əţ·i/ *n* [C] ***social studies*** anything that can be bought and sold ○ *The goal is to raise the productivity of basic food commodities such as grains.*

common USUAL /'kɑm·ən/ *adj* found frequently in many places or among many people ○ *Money worries are a common problem for people raising children.*

commonly /'kɑm·ən·li/ *adv* ○ *"The" is the most commonly used word in English.*

SHARED /'kɑm·ən/ *adj* [not gradable] belonging to or shared by two or more people or things ○ *Guilt and forgiveness are themes common to all of her works.*

LAND /'kɑm·ən/ *n* [C] an area of grassy land that is open for everyone to use, usually near the center of a town or city ○ *The Boston Common is the oldest park in the US.*

IDIOMS with common

• **common denominator** a fact or quality that is shared by two or more people or groups ○ *Trade is a major common denominator between the two countries.*

• **common ground** an area of shared interests or opinions held by two or more people or groups ○ *When I found out he was also going to Alaska, we were on common ground.*

• **common knowledge** something that is known to many people but often not made known officially ○ *It was common knowledge that several doctors at that hospital were incompetent.*

• **have** *something* **in common** to share the same interests or have similar characteristics ○ *I didn't think Larry and Patricia had anything in common, but they talked all evening.*

Common Era, *abbreviation* **C.E.** *n* [U] used for the period of time beginning with the year 1 in the CALENDAR used in many parts of the world, esp. in Europe and North and South America; CHRISTIAN ERA

common cold *n* [C] a slight infectious disease that causes a cough and sore throat and makes breathing through the nose difficult

common law *n* [C/U] ***politics & government*** a legal system that has developed over a period of time from customs and court decisions

common noun *n* [C/U] (in grammar) a name for any group of people, places, or things that are of the same type ○ *The words "teacher," "river," and "table" are common nouns.* ○ Compare PROPER NOUN

commonplace /'kɑm·ən,pleɪs/ *adj* happening or seen frequently and so not considered special or unusual ○ *Public financing for sports stadiums has become commonplace.*

Commons /'kɑm·ənz/ *n* [U] *Cdn, infml* the HOUSE OF COMMONS

common sense *n* [U] the ability to use good judgment in making decisions and to live in a reasonable and safe way

commonwealth /'kɑm·ən,welθ/ *n* [C] ***politics & government*** **1** a country or state that is governed by its people or their elected representatives **2** A commonwealth is an organized group of independent self-governing countries. **3** A commonwealth is also a US state. **4** A commonwealth is also a self-governing place associated with the US, such as Puerto Rico.

commotion /kə'moʊ·ʃən/ *n* [C/U] a sudden, brief period of noise, confusion, or excited movement ○ [C] *There was a commotion outside the embassy.*

communal /kə'mjuːn·əl, 'kɑm·jən·əl/ *adj* belonging to or used by all members of a group ○ *The neighborhood council organized voluntary communal patrols.*

commune /'kɑm·juːn/ *n* [C] **1** ***politics & government*** the smallest unit of local government in some countries **2** A commune is also a group of people who live and work together and share responsibilities.

communicate Ⓐ /kə'mjuː·nə,keɪt/ *v* [I/T] **1** to give messages or information to others through speech, writing, body movements, or signals ○ [T] *She said we should communicate our requests in writing rather than over the telephone.* **2** If two people communicate with each other, they are able to understand each other and have a satisfactory relationship: [I] *The play deals with the inability of people to communicate with the people they love.*

communicable Ⓐ /kə'mjuː·nɪ·kə·bəl/ *adj* able to be given to others ○ *a communicable disease*

communication Ⓐ /kə,mjuː·nə'keɪ·ʃən/ *n* [C/U] **1** the process by which messages or information is sent from one place or person to another, or the message itself ○ [U] *E-mail is an increasingly important means of business communication.* **2** Communication is also the exchange of information and the expression of feeling that can result in understanding: [U] *There was very little communication between the two brothers.*

communications Ⓐ /kə,mjuː·nə'keɪ·ʃənz/ *pl n* **1** the various systems used for sending esp. electronic information, such as radio, television, telephone, and computer networks ○ *They have made heavy investments in the communications industry.* **2** Communications are also the exchanges of information and expressions of feeling that can result in understanding: *A breakdown in communications between labor and management led to the strike.*

communicative Ⓐ /kə'mjuː·nɪ·kəţ·ɪv, -,keɪţ·ɪv/ *adj* willing to talk to people and give them information

communicatively Ⓐ /kə'mjuː·nɪ·kəţ·ɪv·li, -,keɪţ·ɪv-/ *adv*

WORD FAMILY communicate

Nouns	communication communications	*Adjectives* *Verbs*	communicable communicate

communion /kə'mjuːn·jən/ *n* [U] *fml* the condition of sharing thoughts and feelings

C

Communion a Christian ceremony in which bread and wine or juice are eaten in memory of Christ

communism /ˈkɑm·jəˌnɪz·əm/ *n* [U] ***politics & government*** an economic system based on public ownership of property and control of the methods of production, and in which no person profits from the work of others ○ Compare CAPITALISM; SOCIALISM

communist /ˈkɑm·jə·nəst/ *adj* [not gradable] ○ *the Communist party*

communist /ˈkəm·jə·nəst/ *n* [C] a person who believes in or belongs to a party that supports communism

community Ⓐ /kəˈmjuː·nəṭ·i/ *n* [C/U] **1** all the people who live in a particular area, or a group of people who are considered as a unit because of their shared interests or background ○ [C] *the scientific community* ○ [C] *Bus fares were raised despite the protests of the community.* ○ [U] *There's a real sense of community* (= caring and friendly feeling) *in this neighborhood.* **2** ***biology*** A community is also all the various living things that live in a particular area. **3** The community is sometimes used to mean society in general: [U] *She believed that the greatest goal in life was to serve the community.*

community college, *dated* **junior college** *n* [C] a local two-year college at which students can learn a skill or prepare to enter a university

community service *n* [U] work that people do without payment to help other people, and which people may sometimes be ordered to do as punishment for crimes that are not too serious ○ *The judge ordered him to pay a fine and perform 100 hours of community service.*

commutative /kəˈmjuː·təˌtɪv/ *adj* ***mathematics*** of a calculation, giving the same result whatever order the values are in ○ Compare DISTRIBUTIVE

commute **TRAVEL** /kəˈmjuːt/ *v* [I] to travel regularly a distance between work and home ○ *She commutes to the city by car every day.*

commute /kəˈmjuːt/ *n* [C] ○ *The commute is not too bad – just over an hour.*

commuter /kəˈmjuːṭ·ər/ *n* [C] ○ *The 5:30 train is always packed with commuters.*

CHANGE /kəˈmjuːt/ *v* [T] to change a punishment into another that is less severe ○ *The governor commuted the sentence and released the prisoner.*

compact **CLOSE TOGETHER** /kəmˈpækt, kɑm-; ˈkɑm·pækt/ *adj* closely or neatly put together ○ *The newer cameras have a flatter, more compact design.*

compact /kəmˈpækt, kɑm-; ˈkɑm·pækt/ *v* [T] to press something tightly and solidly together ○ *The morning traffic had compacted the snow until it was a sheet of ice.*

compactor /kəmˈpæk·tər, ˈkɑmˌpæk-/ *n* [C] a device that crushes garbage into a smaller and denser form

AGREEMENT /ˈkɑm·pækt/ *n* [C] an agreement between two or more people, organizations, or countries ○ *The parties to the settlement made a compact not to reveal any details.*

CAR /ˈkɑm·pækt/ *n* [C] a small car ○ *Compacts are easier to park than full-size cars and save on gas.*

CASE /ˈkɑm·pækt/ *n* [C] a small, flat case that usually contains face powder and a mirror

compact disc *n* [C] a CD

compaction /kəmˈpæk·ʃən/ *n* [U] ***earth science*** the process by which the pressure on buried solid material causes the material to stick together and change to rock

companion /kəmˈpæn·jən/ *n* [C] someone or something you spend a lot of time with or travel with, or a friend who lives with you ○ *a pleasant traveling companion* ○ *He shared his cabin with his wife and constant companion of 62 years.*

companionable /kəmˈpæn·jə·nə·bəl/ *adj* friendly and pleasant to be with

companionship /kəmˈpæn·jənˌʃɪp/ *n* [U] the enjoyment of being with someone ○ *Besides sharing the cost of my apartment, he provides companionship.*

company **BUSINESS** /ˈkʌm·pə·ni/ *n* [C] an organization that produces or sells goods or services in order to make a profit ○ *He owns part of a company that manufactures software for personal computers.* ➤ Usage: **society or company?** at SOCIETY ORGANIZATION

OTHER PEOPLE /ˈkʌm·pə·ni/ *n* [U] the state of having someone with you, or the person or people who are with you ○ *It was a long trip and I was grateful for his company.* ○ *I traveled to Chicago in the company of two teachers* (= with them). ○ *We're having company* (= guests) *for dinner tonight.*

GROUP /ˈkʌm·pə·ni/ *n* [C] **1** a group of people who work or perform together ○ *She's spending the summer as part of a touring theatrical company.* **2** A company is also a military unit consisting of a large group of soldiers, usually with a CAPTAIN in charge of them.

comparative /kəmˈpær·əṭ·ɪv/ *n* [C] ***grammar*** the form of an adjective or adverb that shows the thing or action described has more of the quality than some others of the same type ○ *"Faster" is the comparative of "fast."* ○ *"Better" is the comparative of "good."* ○ Compare SUPERLATIVE GRAMMAR

comparative /kəmˈpær·əṭ·ɪv/ *adj* [not gradable]

compare **EXAMINE DIFFERENCES** /kəmˈper, -ˈpær/ *v* [T] to examine or look for the differences between persons or things ○ *This store's prices are high compared to what some other stores charge.*

comparative /kəmˈpær·əṭ·ɪv/ *adj* [not gradable] considering the differences between one thing and another ○ *The research examined the comparative effectiveness of the two medical treatments.*

comparatively /kəmˈpær·əṭ·ɪv·li/ *adv* ○ *The job was comparatively well paid, as factory jobs go.*

CONSIDER SIMILARITIES /kəmˈper, -ˈpær/ *v* [I/T] to consider or suggest that something is similar or equal to something else ○ [I] *Instant coffee doesn't* *compare with freshly ground coffee* (= fresh coffee is much better).

comparable /ˈkɑm·pə·rə·bəl/ *adj* ○ *The candidates have comparable* (= similar) *educational backgrounds.*

WORD FAMILY compare			
Nouns	comparison comparative	*Adjectives*	comparative comparable incomparable
Verbs	compare	*Adverbs*	comparatively

IDIOM with compare

• **compare notes** to exchange information and opinions ○ *We met at the coffee shop to compare notes on the new professor.*

comparison DIFFERENCE /kəmˈpær·ə·sən/ *n* [C/U] an examination of the differences between persons or things ○ [U] *We kept a copy of an earlier letter for comparison.* ○ [U] *Though over six feet tall, he was small by comparison with* (= compared to) *his teammates on the basketball team.*

SIMILARITY /kəmˈpær·ə·sən/ *n* [C/U] the act of showing that something is similar or equal to something else ○ [C] *She drew a comparison* (= showed the similarities) *between the Roosevelt and Kennedy administrations.*

compartment /kəmˈpɑrt·mənt/ *n* [C] any of the enclosed parts into which a space, a vehicle, or an object used for storing things is divided ○ *She folded her coat and put it in the overhead luggage compartment.*

compass DIRECTION /ˈkʌm·pəs/ *n* [C] a device for finding direction with a thin pointed metal part that turns to always point north

COMPASS

DRAWING /ˈkʌm·pəs/, **compasses** /ˈkʌm·pə·səz/ *n* [C] a device in the shape of an upside down V whose two pointed, movable parts can be used to draw circles or measure distances on maps

compassion /kəmˈpæʃ·ən/ *n* [U] a strong feeling of sympathy and sadness for other people's suffering or bad luck and a desire to help

compassionate /kəmˈpæʃ·ə·nət/ *adj* ○ *a compassionate man*

compatible Ⓐ /kəmˈpæt̬·ə·bəl/ *adj* **1** able to exist or work with something else, or (of a person) able to live or work with someone else ○ *The computer software isn't compatible with your operating system.* ○ *Levine said he is lucky he and his roommate are compatible.* **2** Compatible also means being suitable or right for: *Their blood types are not compatible, so we cannot use his blood.*

compatibility Ⓐ /kəmˌpæt̬·əˈbɪl·ət̬·i/ *n* [C/U]

compatriot /kəmˈpeɪ·triː·ət/ *n* [C] **1** a person who comes from your own country ○ *This writer and several of her Russian compatriots now live in New York.* **2** A compatriot is also a friend or someone you work with: *After work, I went to dinner with some of my office compatriots.*

compel /kəmˈpel/ *v* [T] **-ll-** to force someone to do something ○ *At school, we were compelled to wear uniforms, which I hated.*

compelling /kəmˈpel·ɪŋ/ *adj* **1** forceful and persuasive ○ *a compelling argument* **2** A performance, painting, or other work of art is compelling when it has unusual power to hold your attention: *His account of his life is one of the most compelling autobiographies I've read.*

compendium /kəmˈpen·diː·əm/ *n* [C] *pl* **compendiums, compendia** a short but complete account of a particular subject, esp. in the form of a book ○ *She put together a compendium of early American furniture.*

compensate Ⓐ PAY MONEY /ˈkɑm·pənˌseɪt/ *v* [T] to pay someone money in exchange for work done, for something lost or damaged, or for some inconvenience ○ *Our company tries to keep salaries low, and they compensate employees more with bonuses.*

compensation Ⓐ /ˌkɑm·pənˈseɪ·ʃən, -ˌpen-/ *n* [U] ○ *The chief executive's compensation package was worth $350,000.* ○ *He applied for unemployment compensation* (= money paid to you by a government, usually temporarily, when you do not have a job).

compensatory /kəmˈpen·səˌtɔːr·i, -toʊr·i/ *adj*

EXCHANGE /ˈkɑm·pənˌseɪt/ *v* [I] to take the place of something useful or needed with something else of similar value ○ *When you have a disability, you learn to compensate by doing other things well.*

compete /kəmˈpiːt/ *v* [I] **1** to do an activity with others and try to do better than they do ○ *Two TV stations are competing for the top spot in the state of Iowa.* **2** To compete is also to be part of a sports activity in which you are trying to win: *He will compete in track this spring and play football next fall.*

WORD FAMILY compete			
Nouns	competition competitor competitiveness	*Adjectives*	competitive
		Verbs	compete
		Adverbs	competitively

competent /ˈkɑm·pət̬·ənt/ *adj* **1** having the skills or knowledge to do something well enough to meet a basic standard ○ [+ *to* infinitive] *All we want is someone competent to manage the staff.* **2** *law* having enough mental ability for a particular

purpose: [+ to infinitive] *The judge decided that he was competent to stand trial.*
competence /ˈkɑm·pət̬·əns/ *n* [U] ○ *He reached a reasonable level of competence in English.*

C

competition /ˌkɑm·pəˈtɪʃ·ən/ *n* [C/U] **1** an activity done by a number of people or organizations, each of which is trying to do better than all of the others ○ [U] *Competition for the job was fierce.* ○ [U] *Traditional booksellers face stiff competition from companies selling via the Internet.* **2** The competition is the people or organizations you are trying to do better than: [U] *In this business, we always have to be aware of the competition.* **3** Competition is also the activity of a sport in which each of the people or teams is trying to win, or a particular event at which this activity happens: [U] *Few of the players on the team were experienced in international competition.* ○ [C] *The figure-skating competition will be held in the main arena.* **4** ***biology*** Competition is also a situation in which the various organisms living in the same area try to compete for a limited supply of food, water, space, etc.
competitiveness /kəmˈpet̬·ət̬·ɪv·nəs, -ə·tɪv·nəs/ *n* [U] ○ *The President sees education as a way to improve competitiveness* (= the ability of people to compete successfully).
competitor /kəmˈpet̬·ət̬·ər/ *n* [C] ○ *He's a tough competitor and will probably do well in business.*
competitive /kəmˈpet̬·ət̬·ɪv, -ə·tɪv/ *adj* **1** *a competitive person* ○ *We will be facing weaker teams, which should give us a competitive advantage/edge.* **2** Competitive also means able to compete at the same level: *If we have to lower our prices to remain competitive, we will.*

compile Ⓐ /kəmˈpɑɪl/ *v* [T] to collect information from a variety of places and arrange it in a book, report, or list ○ *We're compiling some facts and figures for an article on the Russian economy.*
compilation Ⓐ /ˌkɑm·pəˈleɪ·ʃən/ *n* [C/U] **1** [U] *The compilation of all his speeches took several months.* **2** A compilation is also a book, report, etc., that is a collection of separate things: [C] *a compilation of modern poetry*

complacency /kəmˈpleɪ·sən·si/ *n* [U] *esp. disapproving* a feeling of calm satisfaction with your own abilities or situation that prevents you from trying harder ○ *We're finally making a profit, but there is no reason for complacency.*
complacent /kəmˈpleɪ·sənt/ *adj esp. disapproving* ○ *a complacent attitude*

complain /kəmˈpleɪn/ *v* [I] **1** to say that something is wrong or not good enough ○ *Bill and Nancy are always complaining about their neighbor, whose dog frightens their kids.* ○ [+ that clause] *She complained that she had too much work to do.* **2** If you complain of a physical condition, you describe something that hurts or makes you feel ill: *She complained of aching knees from her arthritis.*
complaint /kəmˈpleɪnt/ *n* [C/U] **1** a statement that something is wrong or not good enough, the act of complaining, or the thing you are complaining about ○ [U] *a letter of complaint* ○ [C] *Her only complaint is that she sometimes didn't get enough heat in her apartment.* **2** *law* A complaint is also a formal statement to a government authority that you have a legal cause to complain about the way you have been treated: [C] *He filed a complaint with the commission, charging discrimination based on his disability.*

USAGE

complain

Do not use prepositions like **for** or **on** after the verb **complain**. The correct preposition is **about**.

I am writing to complain about the trip I took last month.

~~*I am writing to complain for the trip I took last month.*~~

WORD CHOICES complain

The verbs **grumble** and **whine** are sometimes used when someone is complaining about things which are not important.

*She's always **grumbling** about something.*

*I hope you don't think I'm just **whining**.*

If someone, especially a child, complains in an annoying way, **whine** is often used.

*Stop **whining**, Tom – it's not that bad!*

The expression **make a fuss** is sometimes used in informal contexts, especially when someone is complaining that something has not happened in the way he or she wanted.

*If the food doesn't come soon, I'm going to **make a fuss**.*

If you complain formally to someone in authority, you can use the phrase **file a complaint**.

*I've **filed a complaint** with the police about the noise.*

complement Ⓐ /ˈkɑm·pləˌment/ *v* [T] to help make something or someone more complete or effective ○ *She used photographs to complement the text of the news story.*
complement Ⓐ /ˈkɑm·plə·mənt/ *n* [C] **1** *He sees rail travel as a complement to road travel, not as a replacement.* **2** A complement is a number of people or things that makes something complete: *We had a full complement of reporters and photographers along.* **3** ***grammar*** A complement is part of a word or phrase that completes the PREDICATE (= the part of a sentence that gives information about the subject), as "nothing" in "They told him nothing."
complementary Ⓐ /ˌkɑm·pləˈment·ə·ri, -ˈmen·tri/ *adj* ○ *This ancient Chinese therapy is part of the complementary treatment program for pain.*

complementary angles *pl n **geometry*** two angles that together add up to 90° ➤ Picture: **angle**

complete WHOLE /kəmˈpliːt/ *adj* containing all the parts or pieces; whole ○ *a complete set of dishes* ○ *the complete works of Dickens* ○ *We wanted a complete record of what everyone said.*

complete /kəmˈpliːt/ *v* [T] ○ *She needed one more course to complete the requirements for a teaching degree.*

FINISH /kəmˈpliːt/ *v* [T] to finish doing something ○ *John has completed 15 marathons.* ○ *She completed three years of college, and then took a year off.*

complete /kəmˈpliːt/ *adj* ○ *The painting is nearly complete.*

completion /kəmˈpliː·ʃən/ *n* [U] ○ *He was the architect who supervised the completion of the hotel.*

VERY GREAT /kəmˈpliːt/ *adj* very great, without limit, or to the largest degree possible ○ *The trip began in complete confusion.* ○ *She gave me a look of complete indifference.* ○ *Toby and Alfredo are complete opposites.*

completely /kəmˈpliːt·li/ *adv* ○ *To be completely honest, I was too scared to say anything.*

WORD FAMILY complete

Nouns	completion incomplete	*Adjectives*	complete incomplete
Verbs	complete	*Adverbs*	completely

complex Ⓐ **HAVING MANY PARTS** /kəmˈpleks, ˈkɑm·pleks/ *adj* having many parts related to each other in ways that may be difficult to understand ○ *a complex surgical procedure* ○ *The question of who is legally responsible is a complex issue.*

complexity Ⓐ /kəmˈplek·sət̬·i/ *n* [C/U] ○ [U] *You must understand the variety and complexity of tasks assigned to the police.*

BUILDING /ˈkɑm·pleks/ *n* [C] a group of buildings that are related, or a large building having different parts ○ *an apartment complex for elderly people*

ATTITUDES /ˈkɑm·pleks/ *n* [C] a group of attitudes and feelings that influence a person's behavior, often in a negative way ○ *an inferiority complex*

complex fraction *n* [C] ***mathematics*** a FRACTION (= division of a number) in which either the NUMERATOR (= number above the line) or the DENOMINATOR (= number below the line) is itself a fraction

complexion /kəmˈplek·ʃən/ *n* [C] the color or appearance of the skin of a person's face ○ *a dark/light complexion*

complex number *n* [C] ***mathematics*** a value that contains both a REAL NUMBER and an IMAGINARY NUMBER

compliance /kəmˈplɑɪ·əns/ *n* [U] ○ See at COMPLY

complicate /ˈkɑm·pləˌkeɪt/ *v* [T] to make something more difficult to deal with or do ○ *The rescue operation was complicated by bad weather.* ○ *His recovery was complicated by his generally poor condition.*

complicated /ˈkɑm·pləˌkeɪt̬·əd/ *adj* having many parts that are organized in a way that may be difficult to understand ○ *a complicated machine/process* ○ *He gave me directions, but they were so complicated I got lost.*

complication /ˌkɑm·pləˈkeɪ·ʃən/ *n* [C] **1** something that makes a situation more difficult ○ *This complication had not been foreseen.* **2** *medical* A complication is a problem that develops from an existing illness, making treatment more difficult: *He died from complications of diabetes.*

WORD FAMILY complicate

Nouns	complication	*Verbs*	complicate
Adjectives	complicated		

complicity /kəmˈplɪs·ət̬·i/ *n* [U] *fml* involvement with others in a crime or in another activity that is wrong

compliment /ˈkɑm·plə·mənt/ *n* [C] a remark or action that expresses approval, admiration, or respect ○ *She paid him a high compliment by saying she read all his books.* ○ *He was surprised by her remark, but decided to take it as a compliment.*

compliment /ˈkɑm·pləˌment/ *v* [T] ○ *I complimented Robert on his great cooking.*

complimentary /ˌkɑm·pləˈment·ə·ri/ *adj* **1** *Everybody was complimentary about the hotel service.* **2** If something is complimentary, it is given to you without charge: *As theater employees, we get complimentary tickets.*

comply /kəmˈplɑɪ/ *v* [I] *fml* to obey an order, rule, or request ○ *Comosa says he will comply with the judge's ruling.*

compliance /kəmˈplɑɪ·əns/ *n* [U] *fml* ○ *The company said that it had always acted in compliance with environmental laws.*

component Ⓐ /kəmˈpoʊ·nənt/ *n* [C] **1** one of the parts of a system, process, or machine ○ *Fair pay for child-care providers is a vital component of welfare reform.* **2** ***physics*** A component of a VECTOR is one of the things that the vector represents, such as force or speed.

compose **CREATE** /kəmˈpoʊz/ *v* [T] to produce or create music, poems, or a piece of writing ○ *The opera was composed in 1931 but wasn't performed until 1940.*

composer /kəmˈpoʊ·zər/ *n* [C] a person who writes music

FORM /kəmˈpoʊz/ *v* [T] to form or make up something ○ *The metropolitan area is composed of New York City and parts of New Jersey and Connecticut.*

COMMON LEARNER ERROR

compose or dial?

Compose cannot be used when you are talking about pressing the buttons on a telephone when you make a call. The correct verb to use is **dial**.

If you're phoning from Geneva, you'll have to dial the code 021.

~~*If you're phoning from Geneva, you'll have to compose the code 021.*~~

composite /kɑmˈpɑz·ət, kəm-/ *adj* made of various parts or substances ○ *a composite material* ○ *a composite sketch of a man wanted for questioning*

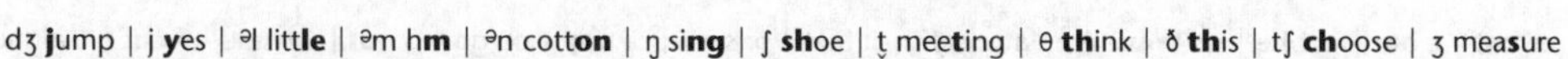

C

composite number *n* [C] ***mathematics*** a POSITIVE number (= larger than zero) that can be divided by positive numbers other than 1 and itself

composition **WRITING** /ˌkɑm·pəˈzɪʃ·ən/ *n* [C/U] ***art, literature, music*** something that a person has created or written, esp. a text, a work of art, or a piece of music, or the act of creating or writing something ○ [C] *a composition for piano and flute* ○ [C] *In school we had to write a composition* (= short piece of writing) *on our favorite TV programs.*

MIXTURE /ˌkɑm·pəˈzɪʃ·ən/ *n* [U] the mixture of things or people that are combined to form something ○ *the composition of the atmosphere* ○ *The composition of the city's population has changed dramatically in the past 20 years.*

compost /ˈkɑm·poʊst/ *n* [U] decaying material of plants, unwanted food, etc., added to dirt to improve the growth of new plants

composure /kəmˈpoʊ·ʒər/ *n* [U] the quality of being calm and not emotional ○ *You may feel nervous but don't lose your composure in front of the camera.*

compound Ⓐ **COMBINATION** /ˈkɑm·pɑʊnd/ *n* [C] **1** a mixture of two or more different parts or elements ○ *His jokes have been described as a compound of fears, anxieties, and insecurities.* **2** ***chemistry*** A compound is a chemical substance that combines two or more elements. **3** ***grammar*** A compound is a word consisting of two or more words: *"Black eye" and "teaspoon" are compounds.*

WORSEN /kɑmˈpɑʊnd, ˈkɑm·pɑʊnd/ *v* [T] to make something worse by increasing or adding to it ○ *Lack of rain compounded the problems farmers are having.*

AREA /ˈkɑm·pɑʊnd/ *n* [C] a fenced or enclosed area that contains buildings ○ *We left the compound early to find and photograph wild animals.*

compound sentence *n* [C] ***grammar*** a sentence made from two independent sentences joined by "and," "or," or "but," as in "Mary read and Tom slept."

comprehend /ˌkɑm·prəˈhend/ *v* [T] to understand something completely ○ *If you don't comprehend something, don't be afraid to seem dumb, just speak out.*

comprehensible /ˌkɑm·prəˈhen·sə·bəl/ *adj* ○ *The directions were written in clear, comprehensible English.*

comprehension /ˌkɑm·prəˈhen·tʃən/ *n* [U] the ability to understand something completely ○ *a reading comprehension test* ○ *In dealing with molecules, numbers quickly grow beyond comprehension.*

comprehensive Ⓐ /ˌkɑm·prəˈhen·sɪv/ *adj* including everything that is necessary; complete ○ *They put forward comprehensive legislation to revise the rules for financing political campaigns.*

comprehensively Ⓐ /ˌkɑm·prəˈhen·sɪv·li/ *adv*

compress **PRESS** /kəmˈpres/ *v* [T] **1** to press something into a smaller space ○ *Snow in the crater compresses into a fastest-growing glacier.* ○ *Firmly compress the dirt in the pot to hold the plant upright.* **2** To compress also means to shorten something so that it takes less time: *Four years of normal mortgage business is being compressed into two months.*

compression /kəmˈpreʃ·ən/ *n* [U] ○ *data compression*

CLOTH /ˈkɑm·pres/ *n* [C] a thick, soft piece of cloth that is pressed to a part of a person's body esp. to help a healing process ○ *Apply warm compresses to the infected area.*

comprise Ⓐ /kəmˈprɑɪz/ *v* [L] to consist of or to be made up of ○ *The Pacific Rim comprises countries bordering the Pacific, including the US, Canada, Japan, China, and the Koreas.* ○ *The ninth district is comprised of* (= consists of) *15 cities and towns, including Boston.*

compromise **AGREEMENT** /ˈkɑm·prəˌmɑɪz/ *n* [C] an agreement between two sides who have different opinions, in which each side gives up something it had wanted ○ *Under the compromise, car manufacturers must use cleaner fuel but have more time to do it.*

compromise /ˈkɑm·prəˌmɑɪz/ *v* [I] ○ *Republicans were refusing to compromise on health-care legislation.*

LOWER STANDARDS /ˈkɑm·prəˌmɑɪz/ *v* [T] to lower or weaken standards ○ *His opponents charged that the deal would compromise conservative principles.*

compromising /ˈkɑm·prəˌmɑɪ·zɪŋ/ *adj* tending to lower respect for someone; embarrassing ○ *compromising documents*

comp time /ˈkɑmp·tɑɪm/ *n* [U] extra time put in by a worker that can be exchanged for an equal amount of time to be used as vacation days, with no loss in pay

comptroller /kənˈtroʊ·lər, ˈkɑmˌtroʊ-/ *n* [C] a CONTROLLER

compulsion /kəmˈpʌl·ʃən/ *n* [U] a force that makes you do something ○ *Management felt no compulsion to provide housing for families.*

compulsive /kəmˈpʌl·sɪv/ *adj* having a very strong desire to do something repeatedly ○ *We're really not compulsive shoppers, you know.*

compulsion /kəmˈpʌl·ʃən/ *n* [C] ○ *an arsonist's compulsion to set fires*

compulsively /kəmˈpʌl·sɪv·li/ *adv* ○ *He is compulsively neat.*

compulsory /kəmˈpʌl·sə·ri/ *adj* (of something) that must be done; necessary by law or a rule ○ *Education is compulsory for children between the ages of 5 and 16.*

compunction /kəmˈpʌŋ·ʃən/ *n* [U] a feeling of guilt or anxiety about something you have done or might do ○ *I would have no compunction about quitting.*

compute Ⓐ /kəmˈpjuːt/ *v* [T] ***mathematics*** to calculate something using mathematics or a CALCULATOR (= a device for doing mathematical processes)

computable Ⓐ /kəmˈpjuː·ţə·bəl/ *adj*

computation Ⓐ /ˌkɑm·pjəˈteɪ·ʃən/ *n* [C/U] ***mathematics*** calculation ○ [U] *the computation of the square root of pi*

computational Ⓐ /ˌkɑm·pjəˈteɪ·ʃən·əl/ *adj mathematics*
computationally /ˌkɑm·pjəˈteɪ·ʃən·əl·i/ *adv mathematics*

computer Ⓐ /kəmˈpjuːt̬·ər/ *n* [C] an electronic device that can store large amounts of information and be given sets of instructions to organize and change it very quickly ○ *a desktop/personal computer* ○ *a computer program* ○ *computer hardware/software*
computerize /kəmˈpjuːt̬·əˌrɑɪz/ *v* [T] to use computers to operate or store something ○ *Our law firm is in the process of computerizing our old files.*
computerization /kəmˌpjuːt̬·ə·rəˈzeɪ·ʃən/ *n* [U]

WORD FAMILY computer			
Nouns	computer computerization	*Verbs*	computerize

computing Ⓐ /kəmˈpjuːt̬·ɪŋ/ *n* [U] the use of computers ○ *companies that promote computing in higher education*

comrade /ˈkɑm·ræd/ *n* [C] a friend or trusted companion, esp. one with whom you have been involved in difficult or dangerous activities, or another soldier in a soldier's group ○ *After 20 years he reunited with comrades from his army unit.*

con /kɑn/ *v* [T] **-nn-** *infml* to deceive someone by using a trick, or to cheat someone of money ○ *I know when I'm being conned.*
con /kɑn/ *n* [C] something done to trick or deceive someone ○ *a con game/job* ○ *It was a con, and he fooled us all.*

concave /kɑnˈkeɪv, kɑŋ-/ *adj* curved inward ○ *a concave lens* ○ Compare CONVEX ➤ Picture: **lens**

conceal /kənˈsiːl/ *v* [T] to prevent something from being seen or known about; to hide something ○ *He made no attempt to conceal his satisfaction.*

concede /kənˈsiːd/ *v* **1** to admit that something is true, or to allow something ○ [+ (*that*) clause] *Officials concede (that) the plan isn't the best one.* **2** If you concede in a competition, you admit that you have lost: [I/T] *She conceded (the election) yesterday.*

conceit /kənˈsiːt/ *n* [U] the habit or attitude of thinking yourself better than others, even when there is no reason to think so
conceited /kənˈsiːt̬·əd/ *adj* ○ *He's a great musician, and not conceited at all.*

conceive Ⓐ **IMAGINE** /kənˈsiːv/ *v* to bring a thought or idea into being; imagine ○ [I always + adv/prep] *When they talk about billions of dollars, I can't even conceive of that much money.* ○ [+ question word] *It's hard to conceive what the world will be like a hundred years from now.*
conceivable Ⓐ /kənˈsiː·və·bəl/ *adj* possible to imagine or think of ○ *Books on every conceivable subject lined one wall.* ○ [+ (*that*) clause] *It's conceivable (that) none of the proposals will be accepted.*
conceivably Ⓐ /kənˈsiː·və·bli/ *adv* [not gradable] ○ *We could conceivably finish ahead of schedule.*

BECOME PREGNANT /kənˈsiːv/ *v* [I/T] *fml* to become pregnant, or to cause a baby to begin to form

concentrate Ⓐ **GIVE ATTENTION** /ˈkɑn·sənˌtreɪt/ *v* [I/T] to direct a lot of attention and thought to an activity or subject, or to direct effort toward achieving a result ○ [I always + adv/prep] *In her later years, she concentrated on her writing and teaching.* ○ [T] *The police are concentrating their search in the area where the child was last seen.*
concentration Ⓐ /ˌkɑn·sənˈtreɪ·ʃən/ *n* [U] ○ *He had a look of intense concentration on his face.*

COME TOGETHER /ˈkɑn·sənˌtreɪt/ *v* [I/T] to bring or come together in a large number or amount in one particular area ○ [T] *Most of the country's population is concentrated in the cities.*
concentration /ˌkɑn·sənˈtreɪ·ʃən/ *n* a large amount of something in the same place ○ [C] *There's a heavy concentration of poor and elderly in the district.*

SUBSTANCE /ˈkɑn·sənˌtreɪt/ *v* [T] ***chemistry*** to make a substance stronger or purer by removing water or other substances
concentrate *n* [C/U] a substance from which water or other substances have been removed
concentration *n* [U] the amount of a substance that is mixed with water or another substance

WORD FAMILY concentrate			
Nouns	concentration	*Verbs*	concentrate
Adjectives	concentrated		

concentration camp *n* [C] a prison where, esp. during a war, people who are considered enemies are forced to stay

concentric /kənˈsen·trɪk/ *adj* (of circles and rings) being one inside another and having the same center

concept Ⓐ /ˈkɑn·sept/ *n* [C] a principle or idea ○ *He introduced the concept of selling books via the Internet.*
conceptual Ⓐ /kənˈsep·tʃə·wəl/ *adj* ○ *Legislators say they have reached conceptual agreements* (= agreements in the form of ideas only) *on several budget issues.*
conceptually Ⓐ /kənˈsep·tʃə·wə·li/ *adv*

conception Ⓐ **IDEA** /kənˈsep·ʃən/ *n* [C/U] an idea or a particular way you understand or think about something, or a basic understanding of a situation or principle ○ [U] *Most children have no conception of time.*

BABY /kənˈsep·ʃən/ *n* [U] the process in which a baby starts to form in the uterus from the coming together of a sperm and an egg

conceptualize Ⓐ /kənˈsep·tʃə·wəˌlɑɪz/ *v* [I/T] to form an idea or theory in your mind ○ [T] *How do Americans conceptualize the global climate system?*
conceptualization Ⓐ /kənˌsep·tʃə·wə·ləˈzeɪ·ʃən/ *n* [C/U]

C

C

concern **WORRY** /kən'sɜrn/ *v* [T] to trouble someone with feelings of anxiety; worry ○ *The loss didn't bother him, but his team's confidence concerns him.*
concern /kən'sɜrn/ *n* [C/U] a worried feeling, or a state of anxiety ○ [C] *Parents expressed a lot of concerns about the changes in school policies.*
concerned /kən'sɜrnd/ *adj* ○ *Sarah is very concerned about your safety.*
INVOLVE /kən'sɜrn/ *v* [T] **1** to involve someone or something; have to do with ○ *This is an issue that should concern everyone.* **2** If a story concerns a particular subject, it tells a story about that subject: *The novel concerns the daily life of a family living in a trailer.*
concern /kən'sɜrn/ *n* [U] a matter of importance esp. because it involves you ○ *Issues of good and evil are not our primary concern here.* ○ *What you do is no concern of mine* (= I do not care).
concerned /kən'sɜrnd/ *adj* [not gradable] involved or involving ○ *They say that free trade will benefit all concerned.* ○ *Her job is only concerned with costs and fees.*
concerning /kən'sɜr·nɪŋ/ *prep* about ○ *If you have any information concerning the incident, please contact the police.*
BUSINESS /kən'sɜrn/ *n* [C] *fml* a company ○ *He heads a large concern in the midwest.*

WORD FAMILY concern			
Nouns	concern	*Verbs*	concern
Adjectives	concerned unconcerned	*Prepositions*	concerning

concert /'kɑn·sərt, -sɜrt/ *n* [C] a performance of music by one or more musicians

concerted /kən'sɜrt̬·əd/ *adj* (of an attempt to do something) determined and serious, or done together with others ○ *I really made a concerted effort to get involved in community affairs.*

concerto /kən'tʃert̬·oʊ/ *n* [C] *pl* **concertos** ***music*** a piece of music usually written for one instrument and an ORCHESTRA (= a large combined group of musicians) ○ *a violin/piano concerto*

concession **SOMETHING GIVEN UP** /kən'seʃ·ən/ *n* [C/U] **1** something allowed or given up, often in order to end a disagreement, or the act of allowing or giving up something ○ [C] *Both sides involved in the talks made concessions.* **2** Concession can also be the act of admitting defeat: [U] *a concession speech*
SALES PLACE /kən'seʃ·ən/ *n* [C] permission to sell something, esp. in part of a store owned by someone else, or a business that sells something ○ *A lot of movie theater profits come from their candy concessions.*

conciliatory /kən'sɪl·iː·əˌtɔːr·i, -ˌtoʊr·i/ *adj* intended to show that you care about the feelings or opinions of someone who is angry or upset with you ○ *Fitzwater struck a conciliatory tone, saying he didn't think anybody was to blame.*
conciliation /kənˌsɪl·iː'eɪ·ʃən/ *n* [U] ○ *Conciliation, not confrontation, is the key to ending the conflict.*

concise /kən'sɑɪs/ *adj* expressing what needs to be said without unnecessary words; short and clear ○ *She wrote up a concise summary of the day's events.*

conclude Ⓐ **END** /kən'kluːd/ *v* [I/T] **1** to cause something to end, or to end ○ [T] *She concluded her remarks by thanking her supporters.* ○ [I] *I'd like to conclude with a song by Tim Buckley.* **2** If you conclude a business deal or official agreement, you agree on it: [T] *Everyone was intent on concluding the agreement.*
conclusion Ⓐ /kən'kluː·ʒən/ *n* [C] the last part of something ○ *The novel's conclusion is disappointing.*
JUDGE /kən'kluːd/ *v* [T] to judge after some consideration ○ [+ *that* clause] *We concluded that we could not afford to buy a new car.* ○ *The judges concluded the same thing I did.*
conclusion Ⓐ /kən'kluː·ʒən/ *n* [C] a decision made after a lot of consideration ○ *Dr. Gille couldn't reach any conclusions based on the symptoms I described.* ○ [+ *that* clause] *We came to the conclusion that someone was not telling the truth.*

WORD FAMILY conclude			
Nouns	conclusion	*Adjectives*	concluding conclusive inconclusive
d*Verbs*	conclude		
Adverbs	conclusively		

IDIOM with conclude

• **in conclusion** *fml* finally ○ *In conclusion, I'd like to express my thanks to everyone who participated in this project.* ○ **USAGE:** Used by a speaker or writer to begin a final statement.

conclusive Ⓐ /kən'kluː·sɪv, -zɪv/ *adj* (of facts, proof, or arguments) ending any doubt or uncertainty about a situation ○ *There's no conclusive evidence that power lines are a health risk.*
conclusively Ⓐ /kən'kluː·sɪv·li/ *adv* without any doubt ○ *Polls conclusively show public support for the bill.*

concoct /kən'kɑkt/ *v* [T] **1** to invent a story or excuse, esp. to deceive others ○ *He concocted the story because he did not want to do his chores.* **2** To concoct is also to make something new from different things: *He concocted a tasty stew from the leftovers.*
concoction /kən'kɑk·ʃən/ *n* [C] something put together from several different things ○ *She drinks this herbal concoction.*

concourse /'kɑn·kɔːrs, 'kɑŋ-, -koʊrs/ *n* [C] a large space or room in a public building such as an airport or train station, which people gather in or pass through

concrete **HARD MATERIAL** /'kɑn·kriːt, kɑn'kriːt/ *n* [U] a very hard building material made by mixing together CEMENT (= powdered substance), sand, small stones, and water ○ *concrete steps*
CERTAIN /'kɑn·kriːt, kɑn'kriːt/ *adj* **1** based on sure facts or existing things rather than guesses or theories ○ *Police have no concrete evidence linking him to the crime.* ○ *We have not yet received a concrete proposal.* **2** ***English*** If a statement, argument, or

discussion is concrete, it is based on actual things and particular examples. ○ Compare ABSTRACT

concur /kən ˈkɜr/ *v* [I] **-rr-** *fml* to agree or have the same opinion as someone else ○ *He said the mayor should not be reelected, and the voters concurred.*

concurrent Ⓐ /kən ˈkɜr·ənt, -ˈkʌ·rənt/ *adj* **1** happening at the same time ○ *He's serving two concurrent 10-year sentences.* **2** ***physics*** A concurrent force is one of two or more forces that are in effect at the same time.

concurrently Ⓐ /kən ˈkɜr·ənt·li, -ˈkʌ·rənt-/ *adv* ○ *He dealt with several issues concurrently.*

concussion /kən ˈkʌʃ·ən/ *n* [U] a usually temporary injury to the brain caused by a fall or hit on the head or by violent shaking

condemn **CRITICIZE** /kən ˈdem/ *v* [T] to criticize something or someone strongly, usually for moral reasons ○ *The movie was condemned for glorifying violence.*

condemnation /ˌkɑn·dəm ˈneɪ·ʃən, -ˌdem-/ *n* [U] ○ *The statement brought swift condemnation from world leaders.*

PUNISH /kən ˈdem/ *v* [T] to severely punish someone who has committed a crime, or to force (someone) to suffer ○ *Those who remember the past are not condemned to repeat it.* ○ *Illness condemned her to spend her remaining days in a home.*

CALL NOT SAFE /kən ˈdem/ *v* [T] to decide officially that a building is not safe for people to use

condensation /ˌkɑn·dən ˈseɪ·ʃən, ˌkɑn ˌden-/ *n* [U] **1** ***chemistry*** the change of a gas to its liquid or solid form **2** ***earth science*** Condensation is also the process by which water VAPOR in the ATMOSPHERE (= air surrounding the earth) cools and changes into liquid water.

condense **MAKE SHORTER** /kən ˈdens/ *v* [T] to make a text shorter by using fewer words to express the same idea ○ *Condense the report to a single page.*

MAKE WATER APPEAR /kən ˈdens/ *v* [I/T] to make water in the air appear on a surface ○ [I] *Humidity condensed on the bathroom walls.*

condensation /ˌkɑn·dən ˈseɪ·ʃən, -ˌden-/ *n* [U] the drops of water that appear on cold surfaces such as windows as a result of hot air or steam becoming cool

condensed /kən ˈdenst/ *adj* with water removed ○ *condensed soup*

condensed milk *n* [U] thick, sweet milk from which water has been removed and to which sugar has been added

condescend /ˌkɑn·dɪ ˈsend/ *v* [I] to behave in a way which shows that you consider yourself to be better or more intelligent than other people ○ *He treats his players fairly and never condescends to them.*

condescending /ˌkɑn·dɪ ˈsen·dɪŋ/ *adj* showing that you consider yourself better or more intelligent ○ *His condescending attitude offended his teammates.*

condescension /ˌkɑn·dɪ ˈsen·tʃən/ *n* [U] ○ *Some directors treat actors with condescension.*

condiment /ˈkɑn·də·mənt/ *n* [C] a substance such as a spice that you add to food to improve its taste

condition **STATE** /kən ˈdɪʃ·ən/ *n* **1** the particular state that something or someone is in ○ [U] *We spent a lot of money to get the house in good condition.* ○ [U] *She was hospitalized in fair condition after the accident.* ○ [+ to infinitive] *He's in no condition to drive* (= He should not drive). **2** A condition can also be a state of not operating correctly: [C] *a heart condition*

conditions /kən ˈdɪʃ·ənz/ *pl n* all the particular things that influence someone's living or working environment ○ *Working conditions here are primitive.* ○ *Riis devoted his life to improving conditions in urban slums.*

> **USAGE**
>
> **condition or health?**
>
> **Condition** is not usually used to describe someone's general health or fitness. The correct words to use are **health** or **fitness**.
>
> *After a few weeks at the gym you should notice improvements in health and fitness.*
>
> ~~*After a few weeks at the gym you should notice improvements in condition.*~~

AGREED LIMITATION /kən ˈdɪʃ·ən/ *n* [C] something that must exist before something else can happen ○ *Certain conditions must be met before the aid will be provided.* ○ *He spoke on condition that he not be identified.*

conditional /kən ˈdɪʃ·ən·əl/ *adj* ○ *The sales is conditional on approval from government regulators.*

WORD FAMILY condition

Nouns	condition precondition conditioner	*Adjectives*	conditional unconditional
		Adverbs	conditionally
Verbs	condition		

conditional /kən ˈdɪʃ·ən·əl/ *adj* [not gradable] ***grammar*** **1** relating to a sentence, often starting with "if" or "unless," in which one half expresses something which depends on the other half **2** ***mathematics*** A **conditional statement** describes that if one state exists, then another one also exists.

conditioner /kən ˈdɪʃ·ə·nər/ *n* [U] a thick liquid that people put on their hair after washing it to improve its appearance

condolence /kən ˈdoʊ·ləns/ *n* [C/U] an expression of sympathy esp. for the family of a person who has recently died, or the sympathy expressed ○ [U] *a letter of condolence* ○ [C] *The mayor offered his condolences.*

condom /ˈkɑn·dəm/ *n* [C] a thin, rubber covering that a man can wear on his PENIS (= sex organ) during sex to prevent pregnancy or protect against disease

condominium /ˌkɑn·də ˈmɪn·iː·əm/, *short form* **condo** /ˈkɑn·doʊ/ *n* [C] an apartment in a building in which each apartment is owned separately by the people living in it, or a building having such apartments

condone /kən ˈdoʊn/ *v* [T] *disapproving* to ignore or accept behavior that some people consider wrong ○ *I don't condone such rude behavior.*

C

conducive /kən ˈduː·sɪv/ *adj* providing the right conditions for something to happen or exist ○ *Our mild climate is conducive to outdoor entertaining.*

conduct Ⓐ **DIRECT** /kən ˈdʌkt/ *v* [T] **1** to organize and direct a particular activity ○ *The experiments were conducted by leading scientists.* **2** *fml* To conduct people to a place is to walk there with them: *The usher conducted us to our seats.*

MUSIC /kən ˈdʌkt/ *v* [I/T] to direct the performance of musicians or a piece of music ○ [T] *The orchestra was conducted by Thomas.*

conductor /kən ˈdʌk·tər/ *n* [C] ○ *He's the conductor of the Toronto Symphony.*

BEHAVE /kən ˈdʌkt/ *v* [T] to cause yourself to behave in a particular or controlled manner ○ *I won't tell them how to conduct their lives.*

conduct /ˈkɑn·dʌkt/ *n* [U] behavior ○ *His conduct at the meeting was inappropriate.*

ALLOW THROUGH /kən ˈdʌkt/ *v* [T] ***physics, chemistry*** to allow electricity or heat to flow through

conduction /kən ˈdʌk·ʃən/ *n* [U] ***physics, chemistry*** the flow of electricity or heat through a substance

conductive /kən ˈdʌk·tɪv/ *adj* ***physics, chemistry*** describes a substance that conducts electricity or heat

conductivity /ˌkɑn·dʌk ˈtɪv·ət̬·i, kən-/ *n* [U] ***physics, chemistry*** the power to conduct electricity or heat

conductor /kən ˈdʌk·tər/ *n* [C] ***physics, chemistry*** a substance that conducts electricity or heat

conductor /kən ˈdʌk·tər/ *n* [C] a person who is in charge on a train or other public vehicle and also sells or checks tickets

cone /koʊn/ *n* [C] ***geometry*** **1** a solid shape with a round base that narrows to a point at the top ➤ Picture: **solid** **2** A cone is also any object shaped like a cone, some of which are hollow and open at the end: *ice cream in a waffle cone* **3** A cone is also an ICE-CREAM CONE. **4** A cone is also the hard, oval fruit of an evergreen tree.

conical /ˈkɑn·ɪ·kəl/, **conic** *adj* ***geometry*** shaped like a cone

Confederacy /kən ˈfed·ə·rə·si/ *n* [C/U] **1** ***US history*** the eleven southern states that left the US and fought against the north in the US Civil War. **2** A confederacy is also a CONFEDERATION.

Confederate /kən ˈfed·ə·rət/ *adj* ○ *Confederate soldiers*

confederate /kən ˈfed·ə·rət/ *n* [C] a soldier or supporter of the Confederacy

Confederate States *pl n* ***US history*** the CONFEDERACY

confederation /kən ˌfed·ə ˈreɪ·ʃən/, **confederacy** /kən ˈfed·ə·rə·si/ *n* [C/U] ***politics & government*** **1** a group of countries, organizations, or people who have joined together for economic or political reasons ○ [C] *a union confederation* **2** *Cdn* Confederation is the joining of regions that had been British to create the independent country of Canada.

confer Ⓐ **TALK** /kən ˈfɜr/ *v* [I] **-rr-** to talk together and exchange ideas, often with the intention of reaching a decision about something ○ *I need to confer with my lawyer.*

GIVE /kən ˈfɜr/ *v* [T] **-rr-** to give an honor, official title, or ability to someone ○ *The US Constitution confers certain powers on the president.*

conference Ⓐ /ˈkɑn·fə·rəns/ *n* [C/U] a large, formal meeting at which there are groups of talks on a particular subject, or a small, private meeting for discussion of a particular matter ○ [C] *She spoke at a conference in Geneva.*

confess /kən ˈfes/ *v* [I/T] **1** to admit that you have done something wrong, or to admit unwillingly that something is true ○ [T] *I've got something to confess – I ate the pie.* ○ [I] *He confessed to the crime.* **2** In some Christian religions, esp. the Roman Catholic Church, to confess is to tell God or a priest what you have done wrong so God will forgive you.

confession /kən ˈfeʃ·ən/ *n* [C/U] **1** [C] *He made a confession to the police.* ○ [C] *I've got a confession – I lost the book you lent me.* **2** Confession is the activity of telling God or a priest what you have done wrong so God will forgive you.

confetti /kən ˈfet̬·i/ *n* [U] small bits of colored paper that you throw when celebrating ○ *At midnight, we all cheered and threw confetti.*

confidant /ˈkɑn·fə ˌdænt, -ˌdɑnt/ *n* [C] a person with whom you can share your feelings and secrets ○ *Her brother is her closest confidant.*

confide /kən ˈfɑɪd/ *v* to tell something secret or personal to someone whom you trust not to tell anyone else ○ [I] *As sisters, they have always confided in each other.* ○ [+ *that* clause] *She confided that most of her clients were actors.*

WORD FAMILY confide

Nouns	confidence confidentiality	*Adjectives*	confident confidential
Verbs	confide	*Adverbs*	confidently

confidence **SURE FEELING** /ˈkɑn·fəd·əns, -fə ˌdens/ *n* [U] a feeling of having little doubt about yourself and your abilities, or a feeling of trust in someone or something ○ *He has a sense of confidence, even arrogance, about what he does.* ○ *Consumers' confidence in the economy is strong.* ○ *Her colleagues lost confidence in her.*

confident /ˈkɑn·fəd·ənt, -fə ˌdent/ *adj* ○ *a confident smile* ○ *I'm confident we'll succeed.*

confidently /ˈkɑn·fəd·ənt·li, -fəˌdent·li/ *adv* ○ *North confidently predicted victory.*

> **WORD CHOICES confidence**
>
> **Self-assured** and **self-confident** are words that mean the same as "confident."
>
> *The interview showed her as a very* ***self-assured*** *woman.*
>
> **Assertive** can be used to describe people who are confident because they are not frightened to say what they want or believe.
>
> *You'll have to be more* ***assertive*** *if you want to be promoted.*
>
> **Bold** can be used when someone is very confident, especially in a way that shows a lack of respect.
>
> *He was a* ***bold*** *and defiant little boy.*
>
> The phrase **be sure of yourself** can be used when someone is very confident or too confident.
>
> *He seems very* ***sure of himself.***
>
> If someone is confident in an unpleasant or rude way, you could use the adjective **cocky** in informal English or **brash**.
>
> *He's a* ***cocky*** *young man.*

SECRET /ˈkɑn·fəd·əns, -fəˌdens/ *n* [C/U] a secret, or a feeling of trust that a secret will be kept ○ [C] *They exchanged confidences like old friends.* ○ [U] *I'm telling you this in confidence.*

confidential /ˌkɑn·fəˈden·tʃəl/ *adj* ○ *confidential reports/memos* ○ *All applications are strictly confidential.*

confidentiality /ˌkɑn·fəˌden·tʃiːˈæl·əţ·i/ *n* [U] ○ *Tests will be handled with absolute confidentiality.*

configuration /kənˌfɪg·jəˈreɪ·ʃən/ *n* [C] the particular arrangement of the parts of something or of a group of things ○ *The two-lane configuration of the road leads to congestion.*

confine Ⓐ /kənˈfɑɪn/ *v* [T] **1** to keep someone or something within limits ○ *The animals were confined in a large pen.* ○ *Harris does not confine her stage work to Broadway.* **2** If something is confined to a particular group of people, it exists only among them: *Cancer is not confined to old people.*

confined Ⓐ /kənˈfɑɪnd/ *adj* ○ *You can't keep kids in a confined space for long.*

confinement /kənˈfɑɪn·mənt/ *n* [U] ○ *He was tired of the constant confinement of his office.*

confines Ⓐ /ˈkɑn·fɑɪnz, kənˈfɑɪnz/ *pl n* the limits or borders of something ○ *He feels safe within the confines of his home.*

confirm Ⓐ **MAKE PLANS** /kənˈfɜrm/ *v* [T] to make an arrangement, plan, or meeting certain or fixed ○ *The hotel has confirmed our reservation.* ○ [+ *that* clause] *Seventy people have confirmed that they will attend the conference.*

confirmation Ⓐ /ˌkɑn·fərˈmeɪ·ʃən/ *n* [C/U] ○ [U] *He'd heard rumors of the sale, but had no confirmation of it yet.*

APPROVE /kənˈfɜrm/ *v* [T] to approve someone or something officially by formal agreement ○ *His appointment has not been confirmed by the Senate.*

confirmation /ˌkɑn·fərˈmeɪ·ʃən/ *n* [U] ○ *confirmation hearings*

PROVE TRUE /kənˈfɜrm/ *v* [T] to prove or state the truth of something that was previously not completely certain ○ [+ *that* clause] *Health officials confirmed that there's a flu epidemic underway.*

confirmation /ˌkɑn·fərˈmeɪ·ʃən/ *n* [U] a statement or proof that something is true ○ *We will be sending you confirmation of your registration.*

RELIGION /kənˈfɜrm/ *v* [T] in some Christian religions, to formally accept as a member

confirmation /ˌkɑn·fərˈmeɪ·ʃən/ *n* [C/U] **1** a formal Christian ceremony to accept someone as a member **2** Confirmation is also a formal Jewish ceremony to show that a young person has completed religious studies.

WORD FAMILY confirm

Nouns	confirmation	*Adjectives*	confirmed unconfirmed
Verbs	confirm		

confirmed Ⓐ /kənˈfɜrmd/ *adj* firmly fixed in a particular habit or way of life and unlikely to change ○ *a confirmed bachelor*

confiscate /ˈkɑn·fəˌskeɪt/ *v* [T] to officially take private property away from someone, usually by legal authority ○ *Customs agents confiscated her bags.*

confiscation /ˌkɑn·fəˈskeɪ·ʃən/ *n* [C/U] ○ [U] *The law allows for confiscation of vehicles used in crimes.*

conflict Ⓐ **DISAGREEMENT** /ˈkɑn·flɪkt/ *n* [C/U] **1** an active disagreement, as between opposing opinions or needs ○ [C] *Conflicts between parents and children become more frequent when the children become teenagers.* ○ [U] *This technology may be in conflict copyright law.* **2** A conflict is also fighting between two or more countries or groups of people: [U] *Negotiations with both sides have not yet led to a resolution of the conflict.*

conflict Ⓐ /kənˈflɪkt/ *v* [I] ○ *We received reports that conflict with each other.*

conflicting Ⓐ /kənˈflɪk·tɪŋ/ *adj* ○ *There are many conflicting cancer studies.*

STRUGGLE /ˈkɑn·flɪkt/ *n* [U] ***literature*** **1** the forces that oppose each other to create the plot in a story, book, or film **2** **External conflict** is a struggle between characters or between characters and nature or society. **3** Characters' struggles to change or understand themselves is **internal conflict**.

conflict of interest *n* [C] a situation in which someone's private interests are opposed to that person's responsibilities to other people ○ *Council members should avoid any potential conflict of interest.*

conform Ⓐ /kənˈfɔːrm/ *v* [I] to behave according to a group's usual standards and expectations, or to operate according to a rule ○ *The contract requires that managers conform to high standards of personal conduct.* ○ *Wood-burning stoves must conform to the fire code.*

conformity Ⓐ /kən ˈfɔːr·məṭ·i/ *n* [U] ○ *He felt suffocated by the conformity of suburban life.*
conformist Ⓐ /kən ˈfɔːr·məst/ *n* [C] someone who behaves or thinks like the other people in a group and doesn't do anything unusual

confound /kən ˈfɑʊnd, kɑn-/ *v* [T] to confuse someone by being difficult to explain or deal with ○ *She likes to confound others' expectations about her.*

confront /kən ˈfrʌnt/ *v* [T] **1** to deal with a difficult problem, situation, or person ○ *He forced the country to confront the issue of deforestation.* ○ *When I took office, I was confronted with new guidelines.* ○ *Becca will have to confront some frightening truths about this disease.* **2** To confront someone is to meet with a person with whom you disagree or whom you will accuse of something: *I had to confront him about the damage to the car.*
confrontation /ˌkɑn·frən ˈteɪ·ʃən/ *n* [C/U] an argument or fight ○ [C] *I had a confrontation this morning with my boss.*
confrontational /ˌkɑn·frən ˈteɪ·ʃən·əl/ *adj* ○ *His confrontational style often angers people.*

confuse /kən ˈfjuːz/ *v* [T] **1** to cause someone to feel uncertain or unclear, or to make something difficult to understand ○ *You're confusing me – please repeat the directions more slowly.* **2** Someone who confuses one thing with another thinks the first thing is the second: *You're confusing me with my sister – she's the one who moved to Colorado.*
confused /kən ˈfjuːzd/ *adj* ○ *Her confused reaction is understandable.*
confusing /kən ˈfjuː·zɪŋ/ *adj* ○ *The directions were confusing, and I got lost.*
confusion /kən ˈfjuː·ʒən/ *n* [C/U] a lack of understanding, or a state of disorder ○ [C] *She writes about the confusions of her life.* ○ [U] *In the confusion, I lost my wallet.*
confusable /kən ˈfjuː·zə·bəl/ *adj, n* [C]

WORD FAMILY confuse

Nouns	confusion	*Adjectives*	confused
Verbs	confuse		confusing

congeal /kən ˈdʒiːl/ *v* [I] to change from a liquid or soft state to a thick or solid state ○ *The grease in the frying pan congealed as it cooled.*

congenial /kən ˈdʒiːn·jəl/ *adj* pleasant and friendly; producing a feeling of comfort or satisfaction ○ *We spent a relaxed evening with congenial friends.*

congenital /kən ˈdʒen·əṭ·əl/ *adj* [not gradable] existing at or from birth ○ *a congenital defect*

congested /kən ˈdʒes·təd/ *adj* **1** too crowded or blocked ○ *Congested roads are normal on holiday weekends.* **2** Someone who is congested has a blocked nose and cannot breathe through it, usually because of a cold.
congestion /kən ˈdʒes·tʃən/ *n* [U] ○ *The restaurant would increase traffic congestion and noise.*

conglomerate /kən ˈglɑm·ə·rət/ *n* [C] a very large company consisting of several smaller companies or divisions that supply varied products or services

conglomeration /kən ˌglɑm·ə ˈreɪ·ʃən/ *n* [C] a large group or mass of different things gathered together ○ *The dish is a wonderful conglomeration of sausage, chicken, seafood, and rice.*

congratulate /kən ˈgrætʃ·əˌleɪt, -ˈgrædʒ-/ *v* [T] to praise someone by expressing pleasure at that person's success or happiness ○ *I congratulated Jill on winning the award.*
congratulations /kən ˌgrætʃ·ə ˈleɪ·ʃənz, -ˌgrædʒ-/ *exclamation, pl n* ○ *"I passed my driving test." "Congratulations!"* ○ *Give him my congratulations when you see him.*

congregate /ˈkɑŋ·grəˌgeɪt/ *v* [I] to gather together into a large group ○ *A crowd congregated around City Hall.*

congregation /ˌkɑŋ·grə ˈgeɪ·ʃən/ *n* [C] a group of people gathered together for religious worship ○ *a congregation of 300 members*

congress /ˈkɑŋ·grəs/ *n* [C] a formal meeting of representatives from countries or organizations at which ideas are discussed and information is exchanged ○ *the fourth congress of the European Association for Lexicography*

Congress /ˈkɑŋ·grəs/ *n* [U] ***politics & government*** the elected group of people in the US who are responsible for making the law, consisting of the Senate and the House of Representatives ○ *Congress has rejected the president's plan.*
congressional /kən ˈgreʃ·ən·əl/ *adj* [not gradable] ○ *a congressional committee*

congressman /ˈkɑŋ·grəs·mən/ *n* [C] *pl* **-men** a member of the US House of Representatives; a REPRESENTATIVE

congresswoman /ˈkɑŋ·grəsˌwʊm·ən/ *n* [C] *pl* **-women** a female member of the US House of Representatives; a REPRESENTATIVE

congruent /kən ˈgruː·ənt, ˈkɑŋˌgruː·ənt/, *symbol* ≅ *adj* ***geometry*** **1** having the same size and shape, or matching in size and shape ○ *congruent figures* **2** ***geometry*** **Congruent angles** are angles that have the same degree measurement. **3** ***geometry*** **Congruent circles** are circles that have the same RADIUS (= measurement from the center to the edge). **4** ***geometry*** **Congruent polygons** are POLYGONS (= flat shapes with three or more sides) in which the matching sides are the same length and the angles have the same degree measurements. **5** ***geometry*** **Congruent segments** are SEGMENTS (= parts of a line) that are the same length. **6** ***geometry*** **Congruent triangles** are triangles that match one of these conditions: all three sides have the same length; two sides and the included angle are the same; two angles and the included side are the same; or two angles and the side opposite one of them are the same as those parts of the other triangle. ➤ Picture: **angle; geometry; triangle**
congruence /kən ˈgruː·əns, ˈkɑŋˌgruː·əns/ *n* [U] ***geometry***

conical /ˈkɑn·ɪ·kəl/ *adj* ○ See at CONE

conifer /ˈkɑn·ə·fər/ *n* [C] any of various types of mostly evergreen trees that produce a CONE

conjecture /kənˈdʒek·tʃər, -ʃər/ *n* [C/U] an opinion or judgment that is not based on proof; a guess ○ [U] *What lay behind the decision is open to conjecture.*

conjecture /kənˈdʒek·tʃər, -ʃər/ *v* [I/T] ○ [+ *that* clause] *Some employees conjecture that it was a money-saving move.*

conjugal /ˈkɑn·dʒə·gəl, kənˈdʒuː-/ *adj* [not gradable] *fml* connected with the relationship between married people

conjugate /ˈkɑn·dʒəˌgeɪt/ *v* [I/T] ***grammar*** to list the forms of a verb in a particular order

conjugation /ˌkɑn·dʒəˈgeɪ·ʃən/ *n* [C] ***grammar*** the complete set of grammatical forms of a verb ○ *the conjugation of the French verb "avoir"*

conjunction CONNECTING WORD /kənˈdʒʌŋ·ʃən/ *n* [C] ***grammar*** a word such as "and," "but," "because," or "although" that connects words, phrases, and clauses in a sentence

COMBINATION /kənˈdʒʌŋ·ʃən/ *n* [C/U] a combination of events or conditions ○ [U] *Physicists are working in conjunction with engineers on the project.*

conjure /ˈkɑn·dʒər/ *v* [T] to make something appear by magic or as if by magic ○ [T] *His words conjured images of far-away action.*

conk /kɑŋk, kɔːŋk/ *v* [T] *infml* to hit someone on the head ○ *A book fell from the shelf and conked him on the head.*

PHRASAL VERB with **conk**

• **conk out** *infml* (of a machine or engine) to stop working or fail suddenly, or (of a person) to go to sleep ○ *My radio conked out again.*

con man, **con artist** *n* [C] a person who uses tricks to cheat people, esp. to get their money or possessions

connect JOIN /kəˈnekt/ *v* [I/T] to join together two things, or to be joined together ○ [I] *The printer connects to the computer.* ○ [T] *A ferry connects the island to the mainland.* ○ [T] *Is your electricity connected yet* (= has your home been joined to the supply)*?*

connected /kəˈnek·təd/ *adj* [not gradable] ○ *the connected parts of a machine*

connecting /kəˈnek·tɪŋ/ *adj* [not gradable] ○ *They turned down a connecting road.*

connection /kəˈnek·ʃən/ *n* [C] ○ [C] *a sewer connection*

RELATE /kəˈnekt/ *v* [T] to consider a person or thing as related in some way to something else ○ [T] *I connect Roberta Peters with the theater rather than movies.* ○ [I] *He's always found a way to connect with his audience.*

connected /kəˈnek·təd/ *adj* [not gradable] **1** *some loosely connected stories* **2** If you are connected, you know important people: *He's a politically connected lawyer.*

connection /kəˈnek·ʃən/ *n* [C] ○ *Science has not shown a connection between drinking raw milk and disease prevention.* ○ *Two men have been arrested* **in connection with** *the theft* (= in some relation to it). ○ *He got the job through connections* (= people who helped him).

TELEPHONE /kəˈnekt/ *v* [T] to make it possible for someone to communicate by telephone ○ *Operator, please connect me with room 1125.*

TRANSPORT /kəˈnekt/ *v* [I] (of aircraft, trains, etc.) to arrive before a second vehicle leaves on which passengers can continue their trip ○ *The flight to Chicago connects with a flight to New York.*

connection /kəˈnek·ʃən/ *n* [C] ○ *We were delayed and missed our connection.*

WORD FAMILY connect			
Nouns	connection disconnect	*Verbs*	connect disconnect
Adjectives	connected connecting		

conniving /kəˈnɑɪ·vɪŋ/ *adj* planning secretly, esp. in doing something wrong ○ *a cold, conniving man*

connoisseur /ˌkɑn·əˈsɜr, -ˈsʊr/ *n* [C] a person who has expert knowledge of something, esp. an art, food, or drink, and is qualified to judge and appreciate its quality ○ *The mushrooms had the chewy, savory flavor preferred by connoisseurs.*

connotation /ˌkɑn·əˈteɪ·ʃən/ *n* [C] ***grammar*** a feeling or idea that is suggested by a word in addition to its basic meaning, or something suggested by an object or situation ○ *"Resolute" means stubborn, but with a more positive connotation.*

conquer /ˈkɑŋ·kər/ *v* [T] **1** to defeat an enemy, or to take control or possession of a foreign land ○ *I felt like I had conquered the world.* **2** If you conquer a disease or condition, you succeed in dealing with or fighting against it: *Students have to conquer their initial shyness.*

conqueror /ˈkɑŋ·kə·rər/ *n* [C] ○ *the conqueror Genghis Khan*

conquest /ˈkɑn·kwest, ˈkɑŋ-/ *n* [C/U] ○ [C] *Several generations turned their attention towards the conquest of the Mediterranean region.*

conquistador /kənˈkiː·stəˌdɔːr, kɑnˈkɪs·tə-/ *n* [C] ***world history*** a soldier during the 16th and 17th centuries who defeated people in the Americas and took their land for Spain

conscience /ˈkɑn·tʃəns/ *n* [C/U] the feeling that you know and should do what is right and should avoid doing what is wrong, and that makes you feel guilty when you have done something you know is wrong ○ [C] *I have a guilty conscience for spending so little time with my kids.*

conscientious /ˌkɑn·tʃiːˈen·tʃəs/ *adj* feeling a moral responsibility to do your work carefully and to be fair to others ○ *She was a conscientious worker, and I'll miss her.*

conscious AWAKE /ˈkɑn·tʃəs/ *adj* awake, aware of what is happening around you, and able to think ○ *She's out of surgery but not fully conscious yet.* ○ Opposite: UNCONSCIOUS

consciousness /ˈkɑn·tʃə·snəs/ *n* [U] ○ *He lost consciousness on the way to the hospital, and regained consciousness the next day.*

NOTICING /ˈkɑn·tʃəs/ *adj* noticing the existence of something ○ *People have become much more conscious of the need to exercise regularly.*

INTENTIONAL /ˈkɑn·tʃəs/ *adj* determined and intentional ○ *Was it a conscious decision to break up the group, or did it just happen?*

consciously /ˈkɑn·tʃə·sli/ *adv* ○ *I've never done anything consciously to offend anyone.*

AWARE /ˈkɑn·tʃəs/ *adj* being especially aware of or worried about something ○ *Consumers aren't as conscious of prices as they were last year.*

consciousness /ˈkɑn·tʃə·snəs/ *n* [U] ○ *There's definitely a consciousness of the employment market among the students.*

WORD FAMILY conscious			
Nouns	consciousness subconscious unconscious	*Adverbs*	consciously subconsciously unconsciously
Adjectives	conscious subconscious unconscious		

consciousness-raising *n* [U] the effort to increase people's awareness of social and political matters

conscript /kənˈskrɪpt/ *v* [T] to force someone to work as a member of a group ○ *Soldiers conscripted factory workers to build a wall around the city.*

conscript /ˈkɑn·skript/ *n* [C] ○ *We were volunteers, not conscripts.*

conscription /kənˈskrɪp·ʃən/ *n* [U] ○ *He emigrated from Germany in the 1850s to avoid conscription into the army.*

consecrate /ˈkɑn·səˌkreɪt/ *v* [T] to officially make something holy and suitable to be used for religious ceremonies ○ *The church was completed and consecrated in the 1890s.*

consecrated /ˈkɑn·səˌkreɪt̬·əd/ *adj* [not gradable] ○ *consecrated ground*

consecutive /kənˈsek·jət̬·ɪv/ *adj* following one after another without an interruption ○ *We've had five consecutive days of rain.*

consecutively /kənˈsek·jət̬·ɪv·li/ *adv*

consensual /kənˈsen·tʃə·wəl/ *adj* agreed to by everyone involved ○ *Unions and management typically reach consensual agreements before a judge has to rule.*

consensus Ⓐ /kənˈsen·səs/ *n* [U] a generally accepted opinion; wide agreement ○ *They're trying to build a consensus on the need to improve the city's schools.*

consent Ⓐ /kənˈsent/ *n* [U] permission or agreement obtained from someone or something having authority or power ○ *I asked to leave the room, and the teacher gave his consent.*

consent Ⓐ /kənˈsent/ *v* [I] to give permission ○ [+ *to* infinitive] *The director consented to change the ending of the movie.*

consequence Ⓐ **RESULT** /ˈkɑn·sə·kwəns, -ˌkwens/ *n* [C usually pl] a result of an action or situation, esp. (in the plural) a bad result ○ *For someone who is old and weak, the consequences of a broken hip can be serious.*

consequent Ⓐ /ˈkɑn·sə·kwənt, -ˌkwent/ *adj* [not gradable] resulting ○ *Stock values declined, with consequent financial losses.*

consequently Ⓐ /ˈkɑn·sə·kwənt·li, -ˌkwent·li/ *adv* [not gradable] as a result; therefore ○ *I was very worried, and consequently I couldn't concentrate.*

IMPORTANCE /ˈkɑn·sə·kwəns, -ˌkwens/ *n* [U] the condition of having a lasting effect; importance ○ *Last summer there were 15 hurricanes, but only one was of any consequence.*

WORD FAMILY consequence			
Nouns	consequence	*Adjectives*	consequent inconsequential
Adverbs	consequently		

conservatism /kənˈsɜr·vəˌtɪz·əm/ *n* [U] a tendency to preserve traditional values and oppose change, esp. in politics

conservative **SOCIAL** /kənˈsɜr·vət̬·ɪv/ *adj* **1** tending to emphasize the importance of preserving traditional cultural and religious values, and to oppose change, esp. sudden change **2** If you are conservative in your appearance, you wear clothes in traditional colors and styles: *He wore a conservative business suit for his interview.*

conservatively /kənˈsɜr·vət̬·ɪv·li/ *adv* ○ *She was conservatively dressed in a gray suit.*

POLITICS /kənˈsɜr·vət̬·ɪv/ *adj* ***politics & government*** tending to emphasize the importance of personal responsibility and traditional values and to oppose depending on government for social services ○ *conservative Republicans* ○ Compare LIBERAL POLITICS

conservative /kənˈsɜr·vət̬·ɪv/ *n* [C] ○ *The Congressional committee had an equal number of conservatives and liberals.*

LOW /kənˈsɜr·vət̬·ɪv/ *adj* (of guesses and calculations) likely to be less than the real amount ○ *Even by conservative estimates, the company will lose $2,000,000 this year.*

conserve /kənˈsɜrv/ *v* [T] to keep and protect from waste, loss, or damage; preserve ○ *In order to conserve fuel, they put in extra insulation.*

conservation /ˌkɑn·sərˈveɪ·ʃən/ *n* [U] **1** Conservation is a plan for avoiding the unnecessary use of natural materials such as wood, water, or fuel: *The university is saving $300,000 per year by its energy conservation efforts.* **2** Conservation is also the protection of plants, animals, and natural areas, esp. from the damaging effects of human activity: *wildlife conservation*

conservationist /ˌkɑn·sərˈveɪ·ʃə·nəst/ *n* [C] a person who believes in or works for the protection of plants, animals, and natural areas, esp. from the damaging effects of human activity

consider **THINK ABOUT** /kənˈsɪd·ər/ *v* [T] to think about a particular subject or thing or about doing something or about whether to do something ○ *Consider Clara Barton, who founded the*

American Red Cross. ○ *We considered moving to California, but decided not to.* ○ [+ question word] *We have to consider what to do next.*

consideration /kən ˌsɪd·əˈreɪ·ʃən/ *n* [C/U] ○ [C] *Financial considerations were a factor in the decision.* ○ [U] *You should take his youth into consideration before you punish him.*

considering /kənˈsɪd·ə·rɪŋ/ *prep, conjunction, adv* [not gradable] used to mention a condition or fact that has an influence, esp. a disadvantageous one, on something else that you want to mention ○ *Considering the weather, they were lucky to get here at all.*

CARE ABOUT /kənˈsɪd·ər/ *v* [T] to care about or respect ○ *Before raising the admission prices, consider the fans.*

considerate /kənˈsɪd·ə·rət/ *adj* ○ *He is always a kind and considerate host.*

consideration /kən ˌsɪd·əˈreɪ·ʃən/ *n* [U] ○ *He showed very little consideration for anyone but himself.*

HAVE AN OPINION /kənˈsɪd·ər/ *v* [T] to believe to be; to think of as ○ *What some people would consider a personal attack, Andy considers a friendly discussion.*

WORD FAMILY consider			
Nouns	consideration	*Adjectives*	considerable considerate inconsiderate
Verbs	consider reconsider		
Adverbs	considerably considering	*Prepositions*	considering
		Conjunctions	considering

considerable /kənˈsɪd·ə·rə·bəl/ *adj* very large or much ○ *He exhibited considerable skill in driving through the snowstorm.*

considerably /kənˈsɪd·ə·rə·bli/ *adv* ○ *Technology has advanced considerably since then.*

consign /kənˈsɑɪn/ *v* [T] to give or send, or to put someone in an unpleasant place or situation ○ *She refused to consign her children to a life of poverty.*

consignment /kənˈsɑɪn·mənt/ *n* [C/U] **1** the act of sending goods to a business that ordered them ○ [C] *The last consignment of dresses was shipped yesterday.* **2** If goods are on consignment, the person or company that has them pays for them only after selling them.

consist of *something* /kənˈsɪst·əv, -ʌv, -ɑv/ *phrasal verb* to be something that is made or formed of various specific things ○ *The crowd consisted mostly of college kids and office workers.* ○ *Her responsibilities consist of answering the phone and greeting visitors.*

consistency /kənˈsɪs·tən·si/ *n* [C/U] the quality expressing how thick or firm a mixture is, esp. a liquid ○ [C] *It had a consistency like that of thick glue.*

consistent NOT VARYING /kənˈsɪs·tənt/ *adj* always happening or behaving in a similar way ○ *The president has been remarkably consistent on economic issues.*

consistency /kənˈsɪs·tən·si/ *n* [U] ○ *The team's success will depend on the consistency of its pitching.*

consistently /kənˈsɪs·tənt·li/ *adv* ○ *His movies are consistently thought-provoking.*

AGREEING /kənˈsɪs·tənt/ *adj* agreeing with something said or done previously ○ *The witness's story is consistent with the police report.*

consolation prize *n* [C] a small prize given to someone who has taken part in a competition but has not won

console COMFORT /kənˈsoʊl/ *v* [T] to give comfort and sympathy to someone who is sad or disappointed ○ *The boys consoled one another after their team's first defeat.*

consolation /ˌkɑn·səˈleɪ·ʃən/ *n* [C/U] ○ [C] *The main consolation for me was that I wouldn't have to leave Boston.*

CONTROLS /ˈkɑn·soʊl/ *n* [C] **1** a special area containing a set of controls for electric equipment, esp. on an aircraft or boat ○ *The jet's console contains dozens of dials, meters, and switches.* **2** A console is also a cabinet that sits on the floor and contains an electrical unit such as a television.

consolidate /kənˈsɑl·əˌdeɪt/ *v* [I/T] **1** to bring together or unite things that were separate ○ [I] *Our offices had been spread among three buildings, and then we consolidated into one new high-rise.* **2** To consolidate is also to make stronger by some action or event: [T] *The governor consolidated his power, getting his allies into key state jobs.*

consolidated /kənˈsɑl·əˌdeɪt̬·əd/ *adj* [not gradable]

consolidation /kən ˌsɑl·əˈdeɪ·ʃən/ *n* [U]

consommé /ˈkɑn·səˌmeɪ/ *n* [U] a thin soup, usually made from juices of boiled meat

consonant /ˈkɑn·sə·nənt/ *n* [C] ***grammar*** **1** a speech sound produced by human beings when the breath that flows out through the mouth is blocked by the teeth, tongue, or lips **2** A consonant is also a letter that represents a sound produced in this way: *Except for the vowels in English – a, e, i, o, u, and sometimes y – all the letters are consonants.* ○ Compare VOWEL

consort /kənˈsɔːrt, ˈkɑn·sɔːrt/ *v* [I] *usually disapproving* to spend time in the company of particular people ○ *She warned him against consorting with suspicious characters.*

consortium /kənˈsɔːr·ʃiː·əm/ *n* [C] a group of companies or people with the same goal who are working together to achieve that goal

conspicuous /kənˈspɪk·jə·wəs/ *adj* easily noticed; obvious ○ *He was conspicuous as usual with a big yellow bow tie.*

conspire /kənˈspɑɪr/ *v* [I] **1** to plan secretly with other people to do something bad, illegal, or against someone's wishes ○ [+ *to* infinitive] *Moore conspired with Graham to rob the bank.* **2** To conspire can also mean to make something happen that is difficult to do: [+ *to* infinitive] *They somehow conspired to keep the theater alive when all government funding ended.*

conspiracy /kənˈspɪr·ə·si/ *n* [C/U] ○ [U] *I think there was a conspiracy to keep me off the committee.*

conspirator /kən ˈspɪr·ət̬·ər/ *n* [C] a person who plans secretly with other people to do something bad, illegal, or against someone's wishes

constable /ˈkɑn·stə·bəl/ *n* [C] (in the US) an official in a town or village having some of the responsibilities of a police officer

C

constant CONTINUOUS /ˈkɑn·stənt/ *adj* **1** nearly continuous or very frequent ○ *We had a constant stream of visitors.* **2** Constant also means not changing, or staying the same: *Even in this age of high technology, the popularity of hunting and fishing remains constant.*

constantly /ˈkɑn·stənt·li/ *adv* [not gradable] ○ *They worry constantly about their weight.*

QUANTITY /ˈkɑn·stənt/ *n* [C] ***mathematics*** a number or value that does not change

constellation /ˌkɑn·stəˈleɪ·ʃən/ *n* [C] a group of stars in the sky that appear to form a pattern and that have a name

consternation /ˌkɑn·stərˈneɪ·ʃən/ *n* [U] a feeling of strong annoyance and anger, usually because of something bad that you cannot change or that is completely unexpected ○ *The power failure caused consternation among local officials.*

constipated /ˈkɑn·stəˌpeɪt̬·əd/ *adj* unable to excrete the contents of the bowels often enough or in large enough amounts

constipation /ˌkɑn·stəˈpeɪ·ʃən/ *n* [U] ○ *A diet that is high in fiber may relieve constipation.*

constituency Ⓐ /kənˈstɪtʃ·ə·wən·si/ *n* [C] ***politics & government*** the people in a particular area of a country who are represented by an elected official, or the area ○ *Republican constituencies are mainly in suburban areas.*

constituent Ⓐ /kənˈstɪtʃ·ə·wənt/ *n* [C usually pl] ***politics & government*** a person represented by an elected official ○ *The senator mails a newsletter to his constituents every two months.*

constitute Ⓐ BE CONSIDERED AS /ˈkɑn·stəˌtuːt/ *v* [L] to be or be considered as ○ *The president said that these policies constitute a threat to the United States.*

EQUAL /ˈkɑn·stəˌtuːt/ *v* [L] to form or make (something); equal ○ *Asians constitute seven percent of the population in this county.*

constituent /kənˈstɪtʃ·ə·wənt/ *n* [C] one of the parts that a substance or mixture is made of ○ *Oxygen is a constituent of air.*

constitution Ⓐ LAWS /ˌkɑn·stəˈtuː·ʃən/ *n* [C] ***politics & government*** **1** the set of political principles by which a place or organization is governed, or the written document that records it ○ *The first ten amendments to the Constitution of the United States are called the Bill of Rights.* **2** ***US history*** The Constitution of the United States is a document that establishes the basic rules and laws of the American government.

constitutional Ⓐ /ˌkɑn·stəˈtjuː·ʃən·əl/ *adj* [not gradable] ***politics & government*** relating to or following the rules of the US Constitution ○ *Freedom of speech is a constitutional guarantee in the United States.*

constitutionally Ⓐ /ˌkɑn·stəˈtuː·ʃən·əl·i/ *adv* [not gradable] ***politics & government*** according to the rules in a constitution ○ *constitutionally protected rights*

constitutionality /ˌkɑn·stəˌtuː·ʃəˈnæl·ət̬·i/ *n* [U] ***politics & government*** (esp. of a law) legality based on agreement with a constitution ○ *The Supreme Court upheld the constitutionality of that law.*

HEALTH /ˌkɑn·stəˈtuː·ʃən/ *n* [C usually sing] a person's physical condition, esp. as shown by strength and staying well ○ *a weak constitution*

constitutional monarchy, limited monarchy *n* [C] ***politics & government*** a system of government in which a king or queen is head of state, but laws are made and put into effect by a legislature, or a country that has this system of government

constrain Ⓐ /kənˈstreɪn/ *v* [T] to limit someone's freedom, or to limit the way something develops or grows ○ *Rising energy costs are constraining consumer and business spending.*

constraint Ⓐ /kənˈstreɪnt/ *n* [C] something that limits the range of a person's actions or freedom ○ *In Egypt, the biggest constraint on new agricultural production is water.*

constrained /kənˈstreɪnd/ *adj* forced to act or behave in a particular way ○ *Our opportunities are constrained by lack of money.*

constrict /kənˈstrɪkt/ *v* [I/T] to make or become tighter and narrower ○ [T] *Bright sunlight constricts the pupil of the eye.*

constriction /kənˈstrɪk·ʃən/ *n* [C]

construct Ⓐ /kənˈstrʌkt/ *v* [T] **1** to build something made of many parts ○ *They approved funds to construct a new ferry terminal.* **2** To construct is also to put together different parts to form something new: *to construct a sentence* ○ *to construct a new economic theory*

construction Ⓐ /kənˈstrʌk·ʃən/ *n* [U] the act or result of putting different things together ○ *A new hotel is now under construction* (= being built).

constructive Ⓐ /kənˈstrʌk·tɪv/ *adj* intended to help someone or improve understanding ○ *She was my most constructive critic.*

constructive interference *n* [C] ***physics*** the INTERFERENCE produced when two or more energy WAVES that are in PHASE (= in the same stages of the repeating pattern) combine to create a stronger wave ○ Compare DESTRUCTIVE INTERFERENCE

construe /kənˈstruː/ *v* [T] to understand the meaning of something in a particular way ○ *That comment could be construed in either of two ways.*

construction /kənˈstrʌk·ʃən/ *n* [C] *fml* ○ *The construction you are putting on my client's statement is unfair.*

consul /ˈkɑn·səl/ *n* [C] a government official who lives in a foreign city in order to take care of the people from the official's own country who are traveling or living there and to protect the trade interests of that government

consulate /ˈkɑn·sə·lət/ *n* [C] the offices or building used by a consul

consult Ⓐ /kən ˈsʌlt/ *v* [T] **1** to get information or advice from a person, esp. an expert, or to look at written material in order to get information ○ [T] *If you don't know the meaning of a word, consult a dictionary.* **2** To consult is also to inform someone about a situation, often in order to get approval for an action you plan to take: [T] *The committee will consult people in the neighborhood before making a recommendation.*

consultant Ⓐ /kən ˈsʌlt·ənt/ *n* [C] a person who is a specialist in a particular subject and whose job is to give advice and information to businesses, government organizations, etc. ○ *The former general now serves as a consultant to the Pentagon.*

consultation Ⓐ /ˌkɑn·səl ˈteɪ·ʃən/ *n* [C/U] **1** the act of exchanging information and opinions about something in order to reach a better understanding of it or to make a decision, or a meeting for this purpose ○ [U] *We hope to work in consultation with Congress on how the law should be interpreted.* **2** A consultation is also a meeting with a doctor who is specially trained to give advice to you or other doctors about an illness or its treatment: [C] *The consultation with the pathologist convinced me to have surgery right away.*

consultative Ⓐ /kən ˈsʌl·ṭəṭ·ɪv, ˈkɑn·səl ˌteɪṭ·ɪv/ *adj*

consume Ⓐ /kən ˈsuːm/ *v* [T] **1** to use fuel, energy, or time, esp. in large amounts ○ *Weekend shopping chores consumed much of her time.* **2** To consume is also to eat or drink: *They consume a lot of candy.* **3** If a fire consumes something, it destroys it completely: *Fire had consumed the whole building.* **4** Someone can be said to be consumed by/with a feeling if that feeling is extremely strong: *We were consumed with joy and relief, as well as profound gratitude.*

consumer Ⓐ /kən ˈsuː·mər/ *n* [C] ***social studies*** someone who buys goods or services for personal use ○ *consumer goods/spending* ○ *American consumers are becoming informed about the safety of products made for children.*

consumerism *n* [U] ***social studies*** protection of consumers against harmful products or business methods

consummate /ˈkɑn·sə·mət, kən ˈsʌm·ət/ *adj* perfect; complete in every way ○ *consummate skill*

consummate /ˈkɑn·səˌmeɪt/ *v* [T] **1** to complete ○ *The deal was consummated with a handshake.* **2** To consummate a marriage is to make it complete by having sex.

consumption Ⓐ /kən ˈsʌm·ʃən/ *n* [U] **1** an amount of something that is used, or the process of using something, esp. so that there is less of it ○ *Consumption of electricity is always higher during the summer months because of air-conditioning.* **2** ***social studies*** Consumption is the using of goods and services in an economy, or the amount of goods and services used.

contact COMMUNICATION /ˈkɑn·tækt/ *n* [U] communication with someone, or with a group or organization ○ *Have you kept in contact with your friends from college?* ○ *The pilot was always in contact with an air traffic controller.*

contact /ˈkɑn·tækt/ *v* [T] ○ *I tried to contact him at his office but he was out to lunch.*

> **USAGE**
>
> **contact**
>
> Remember to use the preposition **with** when you use the phrases **make/be in/keep in/lose contact with** *someone.*
>
> *When you live abroad it's important not to lose contact with friends and family at home.*
>
> ~~*When you live abroad it's important not to lose contact to friends and family at home.*~~

TOUCH /ˈkɑn·tækt/ *n* [U] the touching of two objects or surfaces ○ *Don't let that glue come into contact with your skin.*

HELPFUL PERSON /ˈkɑn·tækt/ *n* [C] **1** a person whom you know and who may be able to help you in a useful way, esp. by influencing other people or by sharing knowledge with you ○ *He tried to use his contacts to get a better job in advertising.* **2** A contact is also a person you meet: *My face-to-face contacts outside of the office had been mostly hotel clerks, policemen, and waitresses.*

contact lens *n* [C] a small, round, curved piece of transparent material, esp. plastic, that fits on the surface of an eye to improve sight ○ *I need new contact lenses.*

contagious /kən ˈteɪ·dʒəs/ *adj* **1** (of a disease) able to be caught by touching someone with the disease or something the person has touched or worn, or (of a person) having this type of disease ○ *a highly contagious strain of flu* **2** *fig.* Contagious also means moving easily from one person to another: *The mood was contagious, and soon everyone was laughing.*

contain HAVE INSIDE /kən ˈteɪn/ *v* [T] (of an object or area) to have an amount of something inside or within it ○ *How much liquid does this bottle contain?* ○ *Each large crate contains 12 boxes.*

container /kən ˈteɪ·nər/ *n* [C] a hollow object, such as a box or a bottle, which can be used for holding something esp. for the purposes of carrying or storing ○ *plastic milk containers*

> **USAGE**
>
> **contain or include?**
>
> Use **contain** to talk about objects that have something else inside them.
>
> *This folder contains important letters.*
>
> *This soup contains garlic and onions.*
>
> Use **include** to say that something or someone is a part of something else but that there are other parts as well.
>
> *The team includes two new players.*
>
> *The price of the ticket includes insurance and tax.*

INCLUDE /kən ˈteɪn/ *v* [T] to have as a part, or be equal to; include ○ *The information contained on forms would be kept strictly confidential.* ○ *Each food serving contains 95 calories.* ○ *You could retrieve all files that contained certain key words.*

CONTROL /kənˈteɪn/ *v* [T] to keep within limits; not to allow to spread ○ *Medical teams were scrambling to contain the illness that has already killed thousands in Latin America.*

containment /kənˈteɪn·mənt/ *n* [U] ○ *I think there are some solid things that can be done in terms of cost containment* (= limiting the cost). ○ See also: CONTAINMENT

containment /kənˈteɪn·mənt/ *n* [U] **1** the control or limitation of something ○ *I think there are some solid things that can be done in terms of cost containment* (= limiting the cost). ○ See also: CONTAINMENT at **2** ***politics & government*** Containment was also a policy of the United States and other countries to prevent an increase in Soviet influence after World War II.

contaminant /kənˈtæm·ə·nənt/ *n* [C] a substance that pollutes, spoils, or poisons something ○ *High levels of contaminants have been found in the groundwater, causing concerns about possible health risks to nearby neighborhoods.*

contaminate /kənˈtæm·əˌneɪt/ *v* [T] to make something less pure or make it poisonous ○ *The disease can be caused by a variety of viruses, bacteria, and other small organisms that contaminate food or water.*

contaminated /kənˈtæm·əˌneɪt̬·əd/ *adj* ○ *contaminated water*

contamination /kənˌtæm·əˈneɪ·ʃən/ *n* [U]

contemplate /ˈkɑnt·əmˌpleɪt/ *v* [I/T] to spend time considering a possible future action, or to consider one particular thing for a long time in a serious way ○ [T] *The owner of the team contemplated moving his football club to another city.* ○ [T] *Sharon is contemplating going to graduate school.*

contemplation /ˌkɑnt·əmˈpleɪ·ʃən/ *n* [U]

contemporary Ⓐ **EXISTING NOW** /kənˈtem·pəˌrer·i/ *adj* existing or happening now ○ *contemporary literature/music*

contemporary Ⓐ /kənˈtem·pəˌrer·i/ *n* [C] a person who is the same age as you ○ *The language you use with your contemporaries may not be appropriate in the classroom.*

OF THE SAME PERIOD /kənˈtem·pəˌrer·i/ *adj* belonging to the same or a stated period in the past ○ *She's been reading contemporary accounts of New York from the early 1900s.*

contemporary Ⓐ /kənˈtem·pəˌrer·i/ *n* [C] someone living during the same period as another ○ *Franklin and Jefferson were contemporaries.*

contempt /kənˈtemt/ *n* [U] a strong feeling of lack of respect for someone or something ○ *They were bullies, and they showed contempt for everyone and everything.*

contemptible /kənˈtem·tə·bəl/ *adj* deserving blame ○ *His behavior was contemptible.*

contemptuous /kənˈtem·tʃə·wəs/ *adj* expressing or feeling a lack of respect ○ *As one of the senior members of the Senate, he was openly contemptuous of its junior members.*

contemptuously /kənˈtem·tʃə·wə·sli/ *adv* ○ *He spoke contemptuously of his former boss.*

contend **COMPETE** /kənˈtend/ *v* [I] to compete in order to win something or to achieve a position of leadership ○ *The top tennis players in the world are contending for this title.*

contender /kənˈten·dər/ *n* [C] ○ *He is a top contender for Senate majority leader.*

contention /kənˈten·tʃən/ *n* [U] ○ *The big names slowly dropped out of contention at the tournament.* ○ See also: CONTENTION DISAGREEMENT; CONTENTION OPINION

CLAIM /kənˈtend/ *v* to state as the truth; claim ○ [+ *that* clause] *I contend that a novel should tell a story and tell it well.*

PHRASAL VERB with **contend**

• **contend with** *something/someone* to try to deal with a difficult situation or person ○ *At the age of nine he had to contend with the death of both parents.*

content **HAPPY** /kənˈtent/ *adj* pleased with your situation and not needing or desiring it to be better ○ *Skating this year with a sprained ankle, he said he was content just to make the Olympic team.*

content /kənˈtent/ *v* [T] to make yourself accept something as satisfactory, although it could be better ○ *We had to content ourselves with watching the sea lions from the shore.*

contented /kənˈtent·əd/ *adj* ○ *Our dog leads a happy and contented life.*

contentment /kənˈtent·mənt/, **content** *n* [U] ○ *Her greatest happiness and contentment was found in being a devoted wife, mother, and grandmother.*

SUBJECT /ˈkɑn·tent/ *n* [U] **1** the subject or ideas contained in something written, said, created, or represented ○ *academic/educational content* ○ *It's easy to update the content of the Web site.* **2** ***art*** Content is also the things represented or suggested in something written or created as art, or the ideas it communicates.

contents /ˈkɑn·tents/ *pl n* ○ *He went on to cite the contents of that report.*

AMOUNT /ˈkɑn·tent/ *n* [U] the amount of a particular substance contained in something ○ *This type of milk has a lower fat content.*

contention **DISAGREEMENT** /kənˈten·tʃən/ *n* [U] disagreement resulting from opposing arguments ○ *Their refusal to sign the treaty remains a source of contention between the two countries.* ○ See also: CONTENTION at CONTEND COMPETE

contentious /kənˈten·tʃəs/ *adj* causing or likely to cause disagreement ○ *a contentious subject*

OPINION /kənˈten·tʃən/ *n* [C] an opinion expressed in an argument ○ [+ *that* clause] *It's her contention that exercise is almost as important as diet if you want to lose weight.* ○ See also: CONTENTION at CONTEND COMPETE

contents /ˈkɑn·tents/ *pl n* everything that is contained within something ○ *They ran through the apartment, pulling out the drawers of the bureaus, tumbling the contents on the floor.*

contest /ˈkɑn·test/ *n* [C] a competition to do better than other people, esp. to win a prize or achieve a position of leadership or power ○ *In the last election, he survived a close contest against a political newcomer.*

contest /kən'test/ *v* [T] **1** to oppose esp. in argument ○ *The campaign's organizers hotly contest much of the criticism that has been leveled at them.* **2** To contest is also to claim that a particular action is not fair or is not legal: *The lawyers may decide to contest the fine.*
contestant /kən'tes·tənt/ *n* [C] ○ *She was once a contestant on a television quiz show.*

context Ⓐ RELATED EVENTS /'kɑn·tekst/ *n* [C] the influences and events related to a particular event or situation ○ *a historical/literary context* ○ *He is willing to look for solutions in the context of changes to the health-care system.*
contextual Ⓐ /kən'teks·tʃə·wəl, kɑn-/ *adj*
contextualize Ⓐ /kən'teks·tʃə·wə,lɑɪz, kɑn-/ *v* [T] ○ *That information would help me to contextualize my kid's performance.*

SURROUNDING WORDS /'kɑn·tekst/ *n* [C] ***English*** the text or speech that comes immediately before and after a particular phrase or piece of text and that influence how it is used and what it means
contextual Ⓐ /kən'teks·tʃə·wəl, kɑn-/ *adj*
contextualize Ⓐ /kən'teks·tʃə·wə,lɑɪz, kɑn-/ *v* [T]

continent /'kɑnt·ən·ənt/ *n* [C] one of the seven large land masses on the earth's surface, surrounded or mainly surrounded by sea ○ *Asia and Africa are the two biggest continents.*
continental /,kɑnt·ən'ent·əl/ *adj* [not gradable]

Continental Congress *n **US history*** one of several ASSEMBLIES in the 1700s of representatives from each of the American COLONIES in which they organized against the British

continental drift *n* [U] ***earth science*** the theory that the continents were once one large area of land that broke apart and are now slowly moving away from each other ➤ Picture: **tectonic plate**

continental breakfast /,kɑnt·ən'ent·əl 'brek·fəst/ *n* [C] a simple breakfast that consists of coffee, bread or pastries, and a fruit juice

contingent GROUP /kən'tɪn·dʒənt/ *n* [C] a group of people representing an organization or country, or a part of a military force ○ *The conservative contingent walked out of the convention when their plan was rejected.*

DEPENDING /kən'tɪn·dʒənt/ *adj* depending on or influenced by something else ○ *Buying the new house was contingent on selling the old one.*
contingency /kən'tɪn·dʒən·si/ *n* [C] something that might possibly happen in the future, usually causing problems or making further plans and arrangements necessary ○ *We must prepare for all possible contingencies.*

continue /kən'tɪn·juː/ *v* [I/T] **1** to keep happening or to keep doing something without stopping ○ [+ *to* infinitive] *If it continues to rain, we may have to cancel the outdoor concert.* ○ [+ *to* infinitive] *I will continue to say what I believe.* ○ *They continued hoping there would be additional survivors.* **2** You can also continue to do something or continue doing something if you start to do it again after a pause: [T] *After a break for lunch, they continued their discussions.*
continual /kən'tɪn·jə·wəl/ *adj* [not gradable] happening often; repeating ○ *There was a continual string of formal parties, dances, and receptions.*
continually /kən'tɪn·jə·wə·li/ *adv* ○ *I think that we could get by without continually raising taxes.*
continuous /kən'tɪn·jə·wəs/ *adj* [not gradable] without a pause or break ○ *a continuous line of traffic*
continuously /kən'tɪn·jə·wə·sli/ *adv* [not gradable] ○ *He spoke continuously for more than two hours.*
continuation /kən,tɪn·jə'weɪ·ʃən/ *n* [C/U] something that is connected to something else, or the state of being continued ○ [C] *It's really just a continuation of the same street but called by a different name.*
continuity /,kɑnt·ən'uː·əţ·i/ *n* [U] the state of continuing over time, esp. without change or interruption ○ *He argued that the country needed to maintain some continuity in foreign policy.*

WORD FAMILY continue			
Nouns	continuation continuity	*Verbs*	continue discontinue
Adjectives	continual continuous	*Adverbs*	continually continuously

contorted /kən'tɔːrţ·əd/ *adj* twisted or bent in a way that does not seem natural ○ *His face was contorted in anger.*

contour /'kɑn·tʊr/ *n* [C] the shape of a mass of land or other object, esp. of its surface, or the shape formed by its outer edge ○ *the distinctive contour of Florida's coast*

contour line *n* [C] ***earth science*** a line on a map connecting points that have the same height above the surface of the earth

contraband /'kɑn·trə,bænd/ *n* [U] goods that are secretly or illegally brought into or taken out of a country
contraband /'kɑn·trə,bænd/ *adj* [not gradable] ○ *contraband chemicals/goods*

contraception /,kɑn·trə'sep·ʃən/ *n* [U] methods used to prevent pregnancy
contraceptive /,kɑn·trə'sep·tɪv/ *n* [C] a product, device, or pill that prevents pregnancy
contraceptive /,kɑn·trə'sep·tɪv/ *adj* [not gradable]

contract AGREEMENT /'kɑn·trækt/ *n* [C] a legal document that states and explains a formal agreement between two different people or groups, or the agreement itself ○ *She already has a contract for her next book with a publisher.*
contract /'kɑn·trækt, kən'trækt/ *v* [T] **1** *The company had been contracted to build shelters for the homeless.* **2** To contract out a job is to formally arrange for other people to do it: [M] *The university contracts out the cleaning to a private company.*
contractual /kən'træk·tʃə·wəl/ *adj* [not gradable] ○ *I have no other contractual obligations.*

SHORTEN /kən'trækt/ *v* [I/T] to make or become shorter or narrower, or smaller ○ [I] *When wet fibers dry, they contract.*

contraction /kən'træk·ʃən/ *n* [C/U] **1** a reduction in size or amount ○ [C] *an economic contraction* ○ [U] *Heat differences cause rapid expansion and contraction of the gas.* **2** A contraction is a shortening of a muscle intentionally, or a sudden, unexpected, and often painful shortening of a muscle: [C] *voluntary/involuntary contractions* ○ [U] *Contraction of the muscle raises your arm.* ○ [C] *Researchers think olive oil may slow stomach contractions.* **3** *grammar* A contraction is also a shortened form of a word or combination of words: [C] *"Can't" is a contraction of "cannot."*

BECOME ILL /kən'trækt/ *v* [T] to catch or become ill with a disease ○ *She contracted pneumonia and was hospitalized.*

contractor Ⓐ /'kɑn,træk·tər/ *n* [C] a person or company that arranges to supply materials or workers, esp. for building

contradict Ⓐ /,kɑn·trə'dɪkt/ *v* [T] (of people) to state the opposite of what someone has said, or of one fact or statement to be so different from another fact or statement that one of them must be wrong ○ *Her testimony contradicted the policeman's testimony, and the jury had to decide who was telling the truth.*

contradiction Ⓐ /,kɑn·trə'dɪk·ʃən/ *n* [C/U] ○ [C] *(fig.) His life was full of contradictions* (= things that are not likely to appear together).

contradictory Ⓐ /,kɑn·trə'dɪk·tə·ri/ *adj* ○ *We received contradictory accounts about the success of the military campaign.*

contralto /kən'træl·toʊ/ *n* [C] *pl* **contraltos** a woman's singing voice in the lowest range, or a woman with this range

contraption /kən'træp·ʃən/ *n* [C] an awkward or old-fashioned looking device or machine

contrary Ⓐ **OPPOSITE** /'kɑn,trer·i/ *n* [U] a fact or opinion that is the opposite of one already stated ○ *We expected the play to be a bore, but the contrary was true.*

contrary Ⓐ /'kɑn,trer·i/ *adj* ○ *Most people supported the proposal, but Liz expressed a contrary opinion.*

UNREASONABLE /kən'trer·i, 'kɑn,trer·i/ *adj* (of a person) intentionally wanting to disagree with and annoy other people ○ *I'm in a contrary mood – I don't feel like practicing today.*

IDIOM with contrary

• **on the contrary, to the contrary** *fml* actually the opposite is true ○ *The crime problem has not disappeared. On the contrary, it seems to be becoming worse again.* ○ *Experts predicted the economy would collapse, but, to the contrary, it continues to do extremely well.*

contrast Ⓐ /'kɑn,træst/ *n* [C/U] **1** an easily noticed or understood difference between two or more things ○ [U] *She is quite petite, in contrast with her tall sister.* ○ [C] *Contrasts between Manhattan's rich and poor astonished him.* **2** *art* In art and photographs, contrast is the difference between dark and light colors or dark and light areas.

contrast Ⓐ /kən'træst, 'kɑn,træst/ *v* [I/T] to compare someone or something with another or others, or to show the differences between two or more things ○ [T] *She contrasted Hamilton's Federalist ideas with the Anti-Federalist views of Thomas Jefferson.* ○ [I] *His aggressive style contrasts sharply with that of his low-key predecessor.*

contrasting Ⓐ /kən'træs·tɪŋ, 'kɑn,træs·tɪŋ/ *adj* very different ○ *The sudden changes at the political top have spawned two contrasting interpretations.*

contribute Ⓐ /kən'trɪb·juːt, -jət/ *v* [I/T] **1** to help by providing money or support, esp. when other people or conditions are also helping ○ [I] *Tourism contributes substantially to the local economy.* **2** If you contribute something you wrote or created, you allow it to be published or shown with pieces by other people: [T] *She soon began to contribute articles to newspapers and magazines.*

contributor Ⓐ /kən'trɪb·jəṭ·ər/ *n* [C] a person who helps by giving money, or someone whose writing or art is published or shown with pieces by other people ○ *a campaign contributor* ○ *He became a regular contributor to The New Yorker.*

contribution Ⓐ /,kɑn·trə'bjuː·ʃən/ *n* [C/U] money, support, or other help ○ [C] *He made a substantial contribution to the building fund.*

WORD FAMILY contribute

Nouns		Verbs	
	contribution		contribute
	contributor		

contrite /'kɑn·trɑɪt, kən'trɑɪt/ *adj* feeling regret and guilt for something bad that you have done ○ *She seemed genuinely contrite when she apologized.*

contrition /kən'trɪʃ·ən/ *n* [U] ○ *Some of the worst offenders expressed contrition.*

contrive /kən'trɑɪv/ *v* [I/T] to arrange for something to happen or be done by being smart or deceiving others ○ [I] *He somehow contrived to get tickets for the concert.* ○ [T] *The two of them are contriving a plan.*

contrived /kən'trɑɪvd/ *adj* too obviously designed to produce a particular result, and therefore not seeming to happen naturally ○ *The movie's plot was much too contrived.*

control /kən'troʊl/ *n* [C/U] **1** the ability or power to decide or strongly influence the particular way in which something will happen or someone will behave, or the condition of having such ability or power ○ [U] *The first few months he was running the company, Randy didn't really feel in control.* ○ [U] *The man lost control of his car and crashed into a tree.* ○ [U] *The fire was out of control for nearly two hours before firefighters were able to get it under control.* **2** A control is a rule or law that sets a limit on something: [C] *She argued for tightening controls on air pollution.*

control /kən'troʊl/ *v* [T] **-ll-** ○ *It's hard to control your temper when you're two years old.* ○ *The temperature is controlled by a thermostat.*

controller, comptroller /kən'troʊ·lər/ *n* [C] a person in a business organization or government who is responsible for managing its finances ○ *Perkins was promoted to corporate controller.*

controls /kən'troulz/ *pl n* devices that are used to operate a machine, vehicle, or aircraft ○ *He was at the controls when the airplane crashed.*

WORD FAMILY control			
Nouns	control controls controller	*Adjectives*	uncontrollable
		Verbs	control
		Adverbs	uncontrollably

control tower *n* [C] a tall building in an airport from which air traffic is watched and directed

controversy Ⓐ /'kɑn·trəˌvɜr·si/ *n* [C/U] a disagreement, often a public one, that involves different ideas or opinions about something ○ [C] *Publication of the article unleashed a scientific controversy that raged for years.* ○ [U] *The president's decisions stirred up a lot controversy.*

controversial Ⓐ /ˌkɑn·trə'vɜr·ʃəl, -'vɜr·siː·əl/ *adj* causing or likely to cause disagreement ○ *a controversial theory/movie*

controversially Ⓐ /ˌkɑn·trə'vɜr·ʃə·li, -'vɜr·siː·ə·li/ *adv*

conundrum /kə'nʌn·drəm/ *n* [C] a problem that is difficult to deal with ○ *The best shows pose moral conundrums that are hard to solve.*

convalesce /ˌkɑn·və'les/ *v* [I] **1** to rest in order to get better after an illness or operation ○ *Dad's out of the hospital and convalescing at home.* **2** A convalescent home is a place where people go when they need medical care but do not need to be in a hospital.

convalescence /ˌkɑn·və'les·əns/ *n* [C/U] the process or period of resting in order to get better after an illness or operation

convalescent /ˌkɑn·və'les·ənt/ *adj* [not gradable]

convection /ken'vek·ʃən/ *n* [U] *science* the flow of heat through a gas or a liquid as the hotter part rises and the cooler part falls

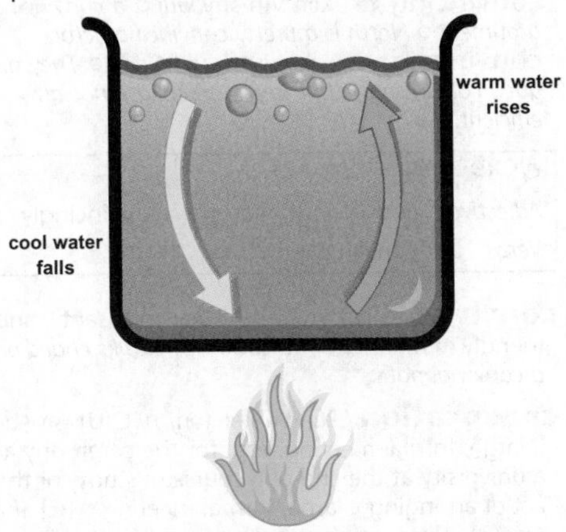

CONVECTION

convection cell *n* [C] *earth science* the circular pattern of a gas, such as air, or a liquid, such as MAGMA (= melted rock under the surface of the earth) rising and falling as it becomes hotter and cooler

convene Ⓐ /kən'viːn/ *v* [I/T] to meet formally as a group, or to arrange a meeting of people or groups for a serious purpose ○ [I] *Peace talks will convene next month.*

convenience store *n* [C] a small store, often open for long hours, that sells popular foods and other products

convenient /kən'viːn·jənt/ *adj* **1** suitable for your purposes and causing no difficulty for your schedule or plans ○ *Would 3 o'clock be a convenient time to meet?* ○ *I shop here because it's convenient.* **2** Convenient can also mean helpful to you but not completely honest: *Both men suffered convenient lapses of memory while testifying.*

conveniently /kən'viːn·jənt·li/ *adv* ○ *Our house is conveniently located near the station.*

convenience /kən'viːn·jəns/ *n* [C/U] **1** [U] *I enjoy the convenience of having my groceries delivered.* ○ [U] *Repairs were scheduled at the customer's convenience.* **2** A convenience is also anything that is easy to use and makes life comfortable: [C] *modern conveniences like a microwave oven*

SPELLING

convenient

Many people make mistakes when spelling this word. One way to remember the correct spelling is that the "e" of the second syllable is pronounced with a "long e" sound as in the word **me**.

Well, 6 a.m. is not convenient for me.

WORD FAMILY convenient			
Nouns	convenience inconvenience	*Adjectives*	convenient inconvenient
Verbs	inconvenience	*Adverbs*	conveniently

convent /'kɑn·vent, -vənt/ *n* [C] a building or group of buildings in which NUNS (= religious women) live or worship ○ Compare MONASTERY

convention Ⓐ **CUSTOM** /kən'ven·tʃən/ *n* [C/U] **1** a way of doing something or appearing that is considered usual and correct ○ [C] *literary conventions* ○ [U] *He flouted convention by wearing sneakers with his tuxedo.* **2** *grammar* The accepted rules and practice of spelling, writing, and punctuation are conventions.

conventional Ⓐ /kən'ven·tʃən·əl/ *adj* **1** following the usual practices of the past ○ *We were raised in a conventional, middle-class family.* ○ *It's a conventional hot-water heater* (= of the usual type). **2** Conventional weapons are not nuclear.

conventionally Ⓐ /kən'ven·tʃən·əl·i/ *adv* ○ *He was conventionally dressed in suit and tie.*

MEETING /kən'ven·tʃən/ *n* [C] **1** a large meeting of a group of people who are involved in the same type of work or who have similar interests ○ *the Dairy Association's annual convention* ○ *a convention of travel agents* ○ *a Star Trek convention* **2** *politics & government* A political convention is a meeting of a political party, esp. to choose someone to represent it in an election for a public office: *the Democratic/Republican national convention*

AGREEMENT /kən'ven·tʃən/ *n* [C] ***politics & government, world history*** a formal agreement between countries ○ *the Geneva Conventions* ○ *the United Nations Conventions on the Law of the Sea*

convention center *n* [C] a building or group of buildings where large groups of people gather for meetings or events

converge /kən'vɜrdʒ/ *v* [I] to move toward the same point and come closer together or meet ○ *Six fire trucks converged on the burning factory.*

convergence /kən'vɜr·dʒəns/ *n* [C/U] ○ [C] *There's a convergence of interests among the US, Canada, and Latin America.*

convergent /kən'vɜr·dʒənt/ *adj* [not gradable] coming closer together or meeting

converging lens /kən'vɜrdʒ·ɪŋ 'lenz/ *n* [C] ***physics*** a LENS (= curved piece of glass) that bends light so that it can produce an image

conversant /kən'vɜr·sənt/ *adj* familiar with, having experience of, or knowing ○ *She's conversant with US foreign policy.* ○ *John's conversant in Mandarin* (= can use it in conversation.)

conversation /ˌkɑn·vər'seɪ·ʃən/ *n* [C/U] **1** an informal, usually private, talk in which two or more people exchange thoughts, feelings, or ideas, or in which news or information is given or discussed ○ [C] *We had a brief conversation Friday.* ○ [U] *The topic of conversation was college plans.* **2** If you make conversation, you cause someone to talk to you, esp. about unimportant matters.

conversational /ˌkɑn·vər'seɪ·ʃən·əl/ *adj* ○ *He rarely speaks in a normal conversational tone.*

conversation piece *n* [C] an unusual object that causes people to start talking

converse Ⓐ **OPPOSITE** /'kɑnˌvɜrs/ *n* [U] the opposite ○ *However, the converse of this theory may also be true.*

converse Ⓐ /kən'vɜrs, 'kɑnˌvɜrs/ *adj* [not gradable] ○ *Why can't Keyes make the converse argument about the GOP?*

conversely Ⓐ /kən'vɜr·sli, 'kɑnˌvɜr·sli/ *adv*

TALK /kən'vɜrs/ *v* [I] to talk with someone ○ *She likes to converse with people from all walks of life.*

conversely /kən'vɜr·sli, 'kɑnˌvɜr·sli/ *adv* [not gradable] from a different and opposite way of looking at this ○ *He was regarded either as too imitative to be considered original or, conversely, as being overly original.*

convert Ⓐ /kən'vɜrt/ *v* [I/T] **1** to change the character, appearance, or operation of something ○ [T] *We converted our oil furnace to gas to save money.* **2** Someone who is converted to something is persuaded to accept new preferences or beliefs: [I] *Most of the families in the community are recent converts.* ○ [T] *My kids are trying to convert me to country music.*

convert /'kɑn·vɜrt/ *n* [C] someone who accepts a new religion or belief ○ *The candidate won millions of converts to his tax proposal.* ○ *Jim called himself a new convert to the Republican Party.*

conversion Ⓐ /kən'vɜr·ʒən/ *n* [C/U] ○ [U] *Conversion to the metric system has been underway in this country for decades.*

convertible Ⓐ /kən'vɜrt̬·ə·bəl/ *n* [C] **1** a car whose top can be folded back or removed so that there is no roof **2** A convertible is also a SOFA (= long, soft seat) that can be folded out to make a bed.

convex /kɑn'veks, kən-; 'kɑn·veks/ *adj* curved or swelling out ○ *a convex lens* ○ Compare CONCAVE ➤ Picture: **lens**

convey COMMUNICATE /kən'veɪ/ *v* [T] to express feelings, thoughts, or information to other people ○ *He always conveyed a sense of genuine interest in his students.*

TRANSPORT /kən'veɪ/ *v* [T] to take or carry someone or something to a particular place ○ *Water flows into the channels and those channels convey it to the fields.*

conveyer belt /kən'veɪ·ər 'belt/ *n* [C] a continuous moving strip or surface that is used to transport objects from one place to another

convict /kən'vɪkt/ *v* [I/T] to decide officially in a court of law that someone is guilty of a particular crime ○ [T] *There might not have been enough evidence to convict him.* ○ Opposite: ACQUIT **DECIDE NOT GUILTY**

convict /'kɑn·vɪkt/ *n* [C] someone who has been judged guilty of a crime and is in prison as a result

conviction /kən'vɪk·ʃən/ *n* [C/U] ○ [C] *His criminal record includes convictions for robberies in several states.*

conviction /kən'vɪk·ʃən/ *n* [C/U] a strong belief that is not likely to change, or the strong feeling that your beliefs are right ○ [C] *He has no ability to communicate his convictions.* ○ [U] *His followers believed with varying degrees of conviction.*

convince Ⓐ /kən'vɪns/ *v* [T] to cause someone to believe something or to do something ○ *We tried to convince my grandfather to live with us.* ○ [+ (*that*) clause] *I'm convinced (that) she's lying.*

convincing Ⓐ /kən'vɪn·sɪŋ/ *adj* ○ *a convincing argument* ○ *North is a pretty convincing actor.*

convincingly Ⓐ /kən'vɪn·sɪŋ·li/ *adv* ○ *They argued convincingly that free markets are not always efficient.*

WORD FAMILY convince			
Adjectives	convincing	*Adverbs*	convincingly
Verbs	convince		

convivial /kən'vɪv·iː·əl/ *adj* pleasant and friendly in manner or attitude ○ *The talks ended on a convivial note.*

convocation /ˌkɑn·və'keɪ·ʃən/ *n* [C/U] *esp. Cdn* a large, formal meeting, esp. for the ceremony at a university at the end of a course of study, or the act of arranging a large, formal meeting ○ [C] *She was awarded an honorary degree at the spring convocation.*

convoluted /'kɑn·vəˌluːt̬·əd/ *adj* (esp. of expression in speech or writing) having a complicated structure and therefore difficult to understand ○ *a convoluted story/speech/plot*

convoy /ˈkɑn·vɔɪ/ *n* [C] a group of ships or vehicles that travel together, esp. for protection ○ *a convoy of supply ships*

convulse /kənˈvʌls/ *v* [I/T] to shake violently, or to cause someone to shake without control ○ [I] *The audience convulsed with laughter.*
convulsion /kənˈvʌl·ʃən/ *n* [C usually pl] a shaking movement of the body that cannot be controlled, often caused by illness ○ *The syndrome brought on convulsions.*
convulsive /kənˈvʌl·sɪv/ *adj* ○ *convulsive laughter/sobs*

coo /kuː/ *v* [I] **coos**, *pres. part.* **cooing**, *past* **cooed** (esp. of some birds, such as PIGEONS) to make a low, soft call, or (of people) to speak in a soft, gentle way ○ *My baby gazed back at me and cooed.*

cook /kʊk/ *v* [I/T] to prepare food by heating it in a particular way, or (of food) to be prepared in this way ○ [T] *I'll cook the steaks on the grill.* ○ [I] *Who's cooking tonight, you or me?* ○ [I] *The potatoes are cooking.*
cook /kʊk/ *n* [C] ○ *He's an excellent cook.*
cooking /ˈkʊk·ɪŋ/ *n* [U] **1** the skill or activity of preparing and heating food to be eaten ○ *My mother always hated cooking.* **2** Cooking can also refer to a particular style of preparing food: *Southern/Italian cooking*

WORD FAMILY cook	
Nouns cook, cooking	*Verbs* cook

PHRASAL VERBS with cook

• **cook up** *something* **PREPARE FOOD** [M] to cook food, esp. for others ○ *I know this place where they cook up a nice steak.*
• **cook up** *something* **INVENT SOMETHING** [M] *infml* to invent something using your imagination and sometimes dishonestly ○ *I'd like to find out who cooked up this scheme.*

cookbook /ˈkʊk·bʊk/ *n* [C] a book containing detailed information on how to prepare and cook different foods

cookie **FOOD** /ˈkʊk·i/ *n* [C] a sweet, usually round, flat cake ○ *She served chocolate chip/oatmeal/peanut butter cookies for dessert.*
PERSON /ˈkʊk·i/ *n* [C] *slang* a person ○ *She's one tough cookie.*

cookout /ˈkʊk·ɑʊt/ *n* [C] a meal cooked and eaten outside, often with a group of people

cool **COLD** /kuːl/ *adj* [-er/-est only] slightly cold; of a low temperature ○ *a cool evening/breeze* ○ *Cereals should be stored in a cool, dry place.*
cool /kuːl/ *v* [I/T] to lose heat or cause someone or something to lose heat ○ [I] *Remove the pie from the oven and let it cool for 30 minutes.* ○ [I/T] *He jumped into the pool to cool (himself) off.*
cool /kuːl/ *n* [U] ○ *He loved the cool* (= slight coldness) *of the early morning.*
cooler /ˈkuː·lər/ *n* [C] a container used for keeping food and drinks cold ○ *a cooler full of water*
coolness /ˈkuːl·nəs/ *n* [U] ○ *There's a slight coolness in the air.*
UNFRIENDLY /kuːl/ *adj* [-er/-est only] unfriendly or not showing affection or interest in something or someone ○ *"Well, that's just too bad," Bill replied in a cool tone.*
coolly /ˈkuːl·li/ *adv* ○ *She responded coolly to his suggestion of dinner and a movie.*
coolness /ˈkuːl·nəs/ *n* [U] ○ *Grace had felt some coolness between them.*
CALM /kuːl/ *adj* [-er/-est only] calm and not anxious or frightened ○ *What's needed now is calm, cool thinking.* ○ *He made a cool assessment of the situation.*
cool /kuːl/ *n* [U] *infml* the ability to stay calm and not get upset or angry ○ *He's gone swimming with sharks without losing his cool.*
coolness /ˈkʊl·nəs/ *n* [U] ○ *She's known for her coolness under pressure on the tennis court.*
cool /kuːl/ *v* [I/T] to (cause to) become calm or weaker in feeling ○ [I] *We need to allow time for tempers to cool.* ○ [T] *I wish Casey would cool his enthusiasm for video games.*
GOOD /kuːl/ *adj* [-er/-est only] *infml* **1** excellent; very good ○ *It's way cool to see you again!* **2** Cool is also used to show agreement with or acceptance of what someone says: *"He wants to come with us." "Cool."*
COLORS /kuːl/ *adj* ***art*** (of colors) not very bright or dark, and esp. containing green, blue, or gray

WORD FAMILY cool	
Nouns cool, cooler, coolness	*Adjectives* cool
	Verbs cool
	Adverbs coolly

IDIOM with cool

• **cool it** *slang* to become calmer ○ *The two of you need to cool it, or I'll call the cops.* ○ **USAGE:** Used to tell someone to do this.

PHRASAL VERBS with cool

• **cool down** **EXERCISE** to continue to exercise gently to prevent injury after you have done more difficult exercises ○ *After you've cooled down from a hard run, you should refuel as soon as you can.*
• **cool** *(someone)* **down/off** **CONTROL ANGER** [M] to stop feeling angry, or cause someone to stop feeling angry ○ *She hoped that keeping the boys apart for a few hours might cool them down.*

coop /kuːp, kʊp/ *n* [C] a cage where small animals and birds are kept ○ *a chicken coop*

co-op /ˈkoʊ·ɑp/ *n* [C] *short form of* COOPERATIVE

cooped up /ˈkuːpˈtʌp, ˈkʊp-/ *adj* kept inside, or kept in a place that is too small ○ *I hate being cooped up in the house all day long.*

cooperate Ⓐ /koʊˈɑp·əˌreɪt/ *v* [I] to act or work together for a shared purpose, or to help willingly when asked ○ *The company promised to cooperate fully with the law-enforcement authorities.* ○ *He refused to cooperate.*
cooperation Ⓐ /koʊˌɑp·əˈreɪ·ʃən/ *n* [U] ○ *Without the cooperation of local residents, this movie could not have been made.*

cooperative Ⓐ /koʊˈɑp·ə·rət̬·ɪv/ *adj* ○ *It was a cooperative effort.*
cooperatively Ⓐ /koʊˈɑp·ə·rət̬·ɪv·li/ *adv*

cooperative Ⓐ /koʊˈɑp·ə·rət̬·ɪv/, *short form* **co-op** *n* [C] **1** a company owned and managed by the people who work in it ○ *a farmers' cooperative* **2** A cooperative is also an apartment building in which ownership is shared by all the people living in it.
cooperative Ⓐ /koʊˈɑp·ə·rət̬·ɪv/ *adj* [not gradable] ○ *farm cooperative organizations* ○ *a cooperative day care center*

co-opt /koʊˈɑpt, ˈkoʊ·ɑpt/ *v* [T] **1** to persuade someone who criticizes or disagrees with you to join your group so that the person can no longer oppose you ○ *The president co-opted journalists by inviting them to private dinners in the White House.* **2** To co-opt is also to claim something as your own when it was really created by others: *Republicans said the Democrats had co-opted their plan for tax reform.*

coordinate Ⓐ **BRING TOGETHER** /koʊˈɔːrd·ᵊn ˌeɪt/ *v* [T] to make various, separate things work together ○ *Voluntary organizations will need to coordinate their efforts to help the homeless.* ○ *Patients learn how to coordinate movements of their arms and legs.*
coordination Ⓐ /koʊˌɔːrd·ᵊnˈeɪ·ʃən/ *n* [U] **1** the activity of organizing separate things so that they work together ○ *We need better coordination between state and local authorities.* **2** Coordination is also the ability to make all the parts of your body work together ○ *Your child's improved hand-eye coordination will enable him to make a tower out of at least two blocks.*
coordinated Ⓐ /koʊˈɔːrd·ᵊnˌeɪt̬·əd/ *adj* able to move in a very easy and controlled way, especially when playing sports or dancing
coordinator Ⓐ /koʊˈɔːrd·ᵊnˌeɪt̬·ər/ *n* [C] ○ *Mrs. Steed is the Atlanta area coordinator for an international diabetes study.*

NUMBER /koʊˈɔːrd·ᵊn·ət/ *n* [C] ***mathematics*** a number along one AXIS (= line) of a COORDINATE PLANE (= region formed by two number lines)

coordinate plane *n* [C] ***mathematics*** a region formed by a horizontal number line and a vertical number line that meet at their zero points

cop /kɑp/ *n* [C] *infml* a police officer

cope /koʊp/ *v* [I] to deal with problems or difficulties, esp. with a degree of success ○ *Inside homes, many residents coped with broken glass and collapsed walls and chimneys.* ○ *Victims cope with feelings of anxiety, pain, anger, and fear.*

copier /kɑp·iː·ər/ *n* [C] a machine to make copies of pages with printing, writing, or drawing on them; a PHOTOCOPIER

copilot /ˈkoʊˌpɑɪ·lət/, **co-pilot** *n* [C] a second PILOT (= person who flies an aircraft) in an aircraft, who helps the pilot who is in charge

copious /ˈkoʊ·piː·əs/ *adj* [not gradable] in large amounts; more than enough ○ *She took copious notes, filling page after page.*

cop-out /ˈkɑp·ɑʊt/, **cop out** *n* [C] *slang* a way or an excuse to avoid responsibility or to avoid doing something ○ *A plea of temporary insanity is a cop-out and should not be allowed, he said.*

copper **METAL** /ˈkɑp·ər/ *n* [U] a soft, red-brown metal, used mostly in electrical equipment and for making wire and coins

COLOR /ˈkɑp·ər/ *adj, n* [U] (of) a bright red-brown color

copter /ˈkɑp·tər/ *n* [C] *short form of* HELICOPTER

copulate /ˈkɑp·jəˌleɪt/ *v* [I] to have sex
copulation /ˌkɑp·jəˈleɪ·ʃən/ *n* [U]

copy **PRODUCE** /ˈkɑp·i/ *v* [T] to produce something that is exactly like another thing, or to do something meant to be like someone or something else ○ *The design was copied from a 19th-century wallpaper.* ○ *He copied the file onto a diskette.*
copy /ˈkɑp·i/ *n* [C] **1** *I always keep copies of letters I have written.* ○ *Please make two copies of this.* **2** A copy is also a single unit of something produced in large numbers, usually for sale: *I had a copy of her latest CD somewhere.* ○ *We ordered ten copies of the book.*

TEXT /ˈkɑp·i/ *n* [U] text that is to be printed, or text that is used to sell a product ○ *She writes advertising copy.*

copycat /ˈkɑp·iːˌkæt/ *adj* [not gradable] done to copy someone or something

copyright /ˈkɑp·iːˌrɑɪt/, *n* [C/U] the legal right to control all use of an original work, such as a book, play, movie, or piece of music, for a particular period of time

coral /ˈkɔːr·əl, ˈkɑr-/ *n* [U] a hard substance formed in the sea from masses of shells of very small sea animals, usually orange or red in color

cord **THIN ROPE** /kɔːrd/ *n* [C] a length of twisted threads or fibers ○ *She pulled the cord of the Venetian blinds to raise them and let in the sun.*

WIRE /kɔːrd/ *n* [C] a length of covered wire that connects electrical equipment to an electrical supply or to other equipment ○ *an electric cord* ○ *a telephone cord*
cordless /ˈkɔːrd·ləs/ *adj* (of a device) operated without a wire connected to an electrical supply by using electricity produced by a BATTERY ○ *a cordless phone*

cordial /ˈkɔːr·dʒəl/ *adj* friendly or pleasant ○ *a cordial greeting/smile* ○ *cordial relations*

cordon /ˈkɔːrd·ᵊn/ *n* [C] a line of police, soldiers, vehicles, etc., positioned around an area to guard it or to close it off

PHRASAL VERB with cordon

• **cordon off** *something* [M] to close an area to people and vehicles ○ *The building was cordoned off and only employees with building IDs could enter.*

corduroy /ˈkɔːrd·əˌrɔɪ/ *n* [U] a thick, cotton material woven with raised parallel lines on the outside, used esp. for jackets and pants

core Ⓐ CENTER /kɔːr, koʊr/ *n* [C] **1** the center or most important part of something ○ *Farmers formed the core of traditional party support.* ○ *Safety concerns are at the core of the new federal policies.* **2** *earth science* The core of the earth is its center, made up of a liquid inner core and a solid outer core. ➤ Picture: **earth**

core Ⓐ /koʊr/ *adj* [not gradable] central; basic ○ *We want to appeal to our core supporters without turning off undecided voters.* ○ *The notion of love is one of the core values of our civilization.* ○ *We have to concentrate on the core business, management said.*

FRUIT /koʊr/ *n* [C] the hard, central part of some fruits, such as apples, which contains the seeds

core Ⓐ /kɔːr, koʊr/ *v* [T] to remove the core of fruit

Coriolis effect /kɔːr·iː ˈoʊ·ləs ɪˌfekt/ *n* [U] *earth science* the effect of the earth's turning on the direction of the wind, which is to the right in the Northern Hemisphere and to the left in the Southern Hemisphere

cork /kɔːrk/ *n* [C/U] a light material obtained from the BARK (= outer layer) of a tree, or a small, soft cylinder of this material that is pushed into the top of a bottle to close it ○ [C] *The waiter took the cork out of the bottle.*

corkscrew /ˈkɔːrk·skruː/ *n* [C] a device for pulling a CORK out of a bottle

corn FOOD /kɔːrn/ *n* [U] a tall plant grown for its whole yellow or white seeds which are eaten cooked, made into flour, or fed to animals ○ *Let's pick up a half dozen ears of corn for supper.*

SKIN /kɔːrn/ *n* [C] a small, often painful area of hard skin that forms on the foot, esp. on the toes

corn bread, **cornbread** /ˈkɔːrn·bred/ *n* [U] sweet bread made from CORNMEAL

cornea /kɔːrˈniː·ə/ *n* [C] the transparent covering of the eye that protects the front of it

corned beef /kɔːrndˈbiːf/ *n* [U] BEEF (= meat from cattle) that has been preserved in salted water and spices

corner /ˈkɔːr·nər/ *n* [C] **1** the point or angle formed when two lines or surfaces meet ○ *the corner of a table* ○ *We could put that chair in the far corner of the room.* **2** A corner is also a place where two streets meet: *I'll meet you at the corner of Pine and Market at 7:30.* **3** A corner can also be a part or area of a place: *They lived in a remote corner of Wyoming.*

corner /ˈkɔːr·nər/ *v* [I/T] to force a person or animal into a place or situation from which there is no escape ○ [T] *After a chase, the police cornered him in a hallway.*

IDIOM with corner

• **corner the market** to control the available supply of a type of product or the ability to sell it ○ *The company quickly cornered the market on desktop software products.*

cornerstone STONE IN BUILDING /ˈkɔːr·nər ˌstoʊn/ *n* [C] a large stone near the base of a building where two walls meet, often giving information about the building and sometimes put in position with a ceremony ○ *A large group of officials attended a cornerstone laying at that new plant.*

MOST IMPORTANT PART /ˈkɔːr·nər ˌstoʊn/ *n* [C] something of great importance on which everything else depends ○ *Funds for the school system were the cornerstone of his budget proposal.* ○ *All the parties to the dispute agree that ready access to the law is a cornerstone of democracy.*

cornfield /ˈkɔːrn·fiːld/ *n* [C] a field used for growing corn

corn flakes *pl n* a breakfast food of small, dry pieces of crushed corn, often served with milk and sugar

cornice /ˈkɔːr·nəs/ *n* [C] a decorative border of wood or stone at the edge of the ceiling of a room or under the roof of a building

cornmeal /ˈkɔːrn·miːl/ *n* [U] yellow or white flour made from corn

corn on the cob *n* [U] the tube shaped part of corn with its sweet yellow or white KERNELS (= seeds) left on it, served as a cooked vegetable

cornrow /ˈkɔːrn·roʊ/ *n* [C] one of a number of strips of hair that have been twisted close to the head in thin rows

cornstarch /ˈkɔːrn·stɑrtʃ/ *n* [U] a flour made from corn, used in cooking for making liquids thicker

corn syrup *n* [U] a sweet, thick liquid made from corn, used in making food ○ *Maple syrup is often mixed with corn syrup to make commercial sweeteners.*

corny /ˈkɔːr·ni/ *adj infml* emotional and obvious from having been used too often ○ *It sounds corny, but when I get to the beach I feel like a kid again.*

coronary /ˈkɔːr·əˌner·i, ˈkɑr-/ *adj* [not gradable] *medical* relating to the BLOOD VESSELS (= tubes carrying blood) around the heart, or to the heart and diseases of the heart ○ *coronary artery/heart disease* ○ *the hospital coronary care unit*

coronary /ˈkɔːr·əˌner·i, ˈkɑr-/ *n* [C] a HEART ATTACK

coronation /ˌkɔːr·əˈneɪ·ʃən, ˌkɑr-/ *n* [C] a ceremony at which a person is made king or queen

coroner /ˈkɔːr·ə·nər, ˈkɑr-/ *n* [C] an official who examines the causes of a person's death, esp. if it was violent or unexpected

corporal /ˈkɔːr·prəl, -pə·rəl/ *n* [C] a person in the military of low rank, below a SERGEANT

corporal punishment /ˈkɔːr·prəlˈpʌn·ɪʃ·mənt, -pə·rəl-/ *n* [C] physical punishment, esp. by hitting with the hand or with a stick

corporation Ⓐ /ˌkɔːr·pəˈreɪ·ʃən/, *abbreviation* **Corp.** *n* [C] an organization, esp. a business, that has a legally separate existence from the people who run it ○ *multinational corporations* ○ *She was elected to the board of directors of the corporation.*

C

corporate Ⓐ /ˈkɔːr·pə·rət/ *adj* ○ *corporate finance/law*

corps /kɔːr, kour/ *n* [C] *pl* **corps 1** a group of people who work together in a particular activity ○ *The diplomatic corps in Washington includes representatives of most of the countries in the world.* **2** A corps is also a military unit or a special part of a country's military forces: *the Marine Corps*

corpse /kɔːrps/ *n* [C] a dead body, esp. of a human

corpulent /ˈkɔːr·pjə·lənt/ *adj fml* fat ○ *a corpulent man*

corpus /ˈkɔːr·pəs/ *n* [C] *pl* **corpora** a collection of written and spoken language used in the study of language and in writing dictionaries

corpuscle /ˈkɔːr ˌpʌs·əl/ *n* [C] any of the red or white cells in the blood

corral /kəˈræl/ *n* [C] an area surrounded by a fence for keeping horses or cattle

corral /kəˈræl/ *v* [T] **-ll-** ○ *A couple of cowboys corralled the horses.* ○ *(fig.) The party has to learn how to corral younger voters if it wants to win the next election.*

correct /kəˈrekt/ *adj* in agreement with the true facts or with a generally accepted standard ○ *It's your responsibility to see that your tax return is correct.* ○ *Do you have the correct time?* ○ *"Did you testify that you recognized this man?" "That's correct."*

correct /kəˈrekt/ *v* [T] to show or fix what is wrong; make right ○ *He knew she was mistaken but made no effort to correct her.* ○ *It is the policy of this newspaper to correct errors of fact that appear in its news columns.* ○ *Doctors can now use laser surgery to correct certain eye problems.*

correctly /kəˈrek·tli/ *adv* ○ *Have I pronounced your name correctly?*

correction /kəˈrek·ʃən/ *n* [C/U] a change to make something right or correct, or the act of making such changes ○ [C] *I made a number of corrections to the manuscript.* ○ [U] *Several errors in this report need correction.*

corrective /kəˈrek·tɪv/ *adj fml* intended to improve something or make it right ○ *Corrective measures must be taken at once.*

correctness /kəˈrekt·nəs/ *n* [U]

USAGE

correct or right?

Correct means "accurate" or "without mistakes."

All the details were correct.

Right is another word for **correct**. It also means "suitable" or "morally acceptable."

She was careful to choose the right word.

You have to do what you think is right.

Remember that **correct** does not mean "good."

The hotel was cheap but good.

~~The hotel was cheap but correct.~~

WORD FAMILY correct

Nouns	correction correctness corrections	*Adjectives*	correct incorrect corrective
Adverbs	correctly incorrectly	*Verbs*	correct

WORD CHOICES correct

Instead of "correct," the word **right** is often used.

*All his answers were **right**.*

If something is correct because there are no mistakes, you can use the adjective **accurate**.

*Her novel is an **accurate** reflection of life in Spain.*

The adjectives **exact** and **precise** can be used when something is exactly correct in every small detail.

*"I still owe you $7.00, don't I?" "Actually, it's $7.30 to be **exact**."*

*We still don't know the **precise** details of what happened.*

corrections /kəˈrek·ʃənz/ *pl n* the government system responsible for people who have committed crimes ○ *corrections officers* ○ *the department of corrections*

correlation /ˌkɔːr·əˈleɪ·ʃən, ˌkɑr-/ *n* [C] a connection between two or more things ○ *There is a proven correlation between educational level and income.*

correlate /ˈkɔːr·əˌleɪt, ˈkɑr-/ *v* [I/T] ○ [T] *The study found that weather conditions were not correlated with joint pain.*

correspond Ⓐ **BE SIMILAR** /ˌkɔːr·əˈspɑnd, ˌkɑr-/ *v* [I] to be similar or the same in some way ○ *Her version of that meeting does not correspond with what I remember* (= I remember it differently).

corresponding Ⓐ /ˌkɔːr·əˈspɑn·dɪŋ, ˌkɑr-/ *adj* [not gradable] ○ *Income was up compared to the corresponding* (= similar) *period last year.*

correspondingly Ⓐ /ˌkɔːr·əˈspɑn·dɪŋ·li, ˌkɑr-/ *adv*

WRITE /ˌkɔːr·əˈspɑnd, ˌkɑr-/ *v* [I] to exchange letters ○ *I corresponded with him when he was at school.* ○ *We correspond by e-mail.*

correspondence Ⓐ /ˌkɔːr·əˈspɑn·dəns, ˌkɑr-/ *n* [U] letters written from one person to another, or the activity of writing and receiving letters ○ *She was behind in her correspondence, and had at least six letters to write.*

correspondent /ˌkɔːr·əˈspɑn·dənt, ˌkɑr-/ *n* [C] ○ *Willa was not a good correspondent, and often didn't write for months.*

correspondent /ˌkɔːr·əˈspɑn·dənt, ˌkɑr-/ *n* [C] a person employed by a newspaper, magazine, television station, etc., to report news on a particular subject or from a place that is far away ○ *He works as a correspondent in Moscow.*

corresponding angles *pl n* ***geometry*** two equal angles on the same side of a line that crosses two parallel lines and on the same side of each parallel line ➤ Picture: **angle**

corresponding sides *pl n geometry* sides of two or more POLYGONS (= flat shapes) that are matched so they can be compared

corridor PASSAGE /ˈkɔːr·əd·ər, ˈkɑr-, -əˌdɔːr/ *n* [C] a long passage in a building, ship, or train, esp. with rooms on one or both side ○ *The bathroom is at the end of the corridor.*

REGION /ˈkɔːr·əd·ər, ˈkɑr-, -əˌdɔːr/ *n* [C] a long, narrow region between two or more large cities, or an area along a busy road ○ *the Boston to Washington corridor* ○ *the Route 28 corridor*

corroborate /kəˈrɑb·əˌreɪt/ *v* [T] to add information in support of an idea, opinion, or statement ○ *Recent research seems to corroborate the theory.*

corroboration /kəˌrɑb·əˈreɪ·ʃən/ *n* [U] ○ *She accused him without corroboration of any kind.*

corrode /kəˈroʊd/ *v* [I/T] to destroy or be destroyed, esp. by acid or RUST, usually over a long period of time ○ [T] *Rain water corroded the metal pipes.*

corrosion /kəˈroʊ·ʒən/ *n* [U] ○ *These alloys protect against corrosion.*

corrosive /kəˈroʊ·sɪv, -zɪv/ *adj* ○ *highly corrosive acid*

corrugated /ˈkɔːr·əˌgeɪt̬·əd, ˈkɑr-/ *adj* [not gradable] (esp. of sheets of iron and cardboard) having parallel rows of folds that look like a series of waves when seen from the edge ○ *corrugated tin/cardboard*

corrupt /kəˈrʌpt/ *adj* **1** dishonest and willing to use your position or power to your own advantage, esp. for money ○ *It's been called the most politically corrupt city in the nation.* **2** Corrupt also means bad: *Your philosophy is corrupt.*

corrupt /kəˈrʌpt/ *v* [T] **1** *Power corrupts, and absolute power corrupts absolutely.* ○ *Don't let your friends corrupt you* (= have a bad moral influence on you). **2** If information in a computer is corrupted, it is damaged and can no longer be used.

corruption /kəˈrʌp·ʃən/ *n* [U] ○ *political corruption*

corsage /kɔːrˈsɑʒ, -ˈsɑdʒ/ *n* [C] a small group of flowers that a woman pins to her clothes near her chest or wears on her wrist, usually for a special occasion

corset /ˈkɔːr·sət/ *n* [C] a tight piece of underwear made from elastic material, worn in the past on the middle part of a woman's body to make her waist appear smaller

cortege /kɔːˈteʒ/ *n* [C] a slowly moving line of people or cars at a funeral

cortisone /ˈkɔːrt̬·əˌzoʊn, -ˌsoʊn/ *n* [U] a HORMONE (= chemical produced by some organs of the body) that is used medically, esp. for treating painful joints and skin problems

cosecant /koʊˈsiːˌkænt, -kənt/ *n* [C] ***trigonometry*** a FUNCTION (= mathematical relation) of an angle that is the RECIPROCAL (= number) of SINE

cosine /ˈkoʊ·sɑɪn/, *abbreviation* **cos** *n* [C] ***trigonometry*** in a triangle that has one angle of 90°, the RATIO (= relationship) of the length of the side next to an angle less than 90°, divided by the length of the HYPOTENUSE (= the side opposite the 90° angle)

cosmetic /kɑzˈmet̬·ɪk/ *adj* (esp. of changes and improvements) intended to improve the appearance of something without changing its basic structure; SUPERFICIAL ○ *Whether the change is more cosmetic than concrete is a matter of opinion.*

cosmetics /kɑzˈmet̬·ɪks/ *pl n* substances put on the face or body that are intended to improve its appearance or quality ○ *Some women spend a fortune on cosmetics.*

cosmetic surgery *n* [C/U] any medical operation that is intended to improve someone's appearance rather than someone's health

cosmonaut /ˈkɑz·məˌnɔːt, -ˌnɑt/ *n* [C] a Soviet or Russian ASTRONAUT (= a person trained to go into space)

cosmopolitan /ˌkɑz·məˈpɑl·ət·ən/ *adj* containing people and things from many different parts of the world, or having experience of many different places and things ○ *a cosmopolitan city* ○ *Gwen's a very cosmopolitan young woman.*

cosmos /ˈkɑz·məs, -moʊs/ *n* [U] the universe considered as a system with an order and pattern

cosmic /ˈkɑz·mɪk/ *adj* **1** of or relating to the cosmos rather than to the earth alone ○ *cosmic dust/rays* **2** *infml* Cosmic also means very great: *a disaster of cosmic proportions*

cost MONEY /kɔːst/ *n* [C/U] **1** the amount of money needed to buy, do, or make something, or an amount spent for something ○ [C] *Education costs continue to rise.* ○ [U] *Most computers come with software included at no extra cost.* ○ [U] *The area has both high-cost and low-cost housing.* **2** *law* Costs is the money given to a person who wins a legal case to pay for the cost of taking the matter to a law court.

cost /kɔːst/ *v* [T] *past* **cost** ○ *The trip will cost (you) $1000.* ○ *It costs a lot to buy a house these days.*

costly /ˈkɔːs·tli/ *adj* expensive ○ *This procedure can be very costly.*

SOMETHING GIVEN /kɔːst/ *n* [U] that which is given, needed, or lost in order to obtain something ○ *The fire cost 14 people their lives.*

cost /kɔːst/ *v* [T] *past* **cost** ○ *If you give him a chance to hit the ball, it could cost you the ballgame.*

costly /ˈkɔːs·tli/ *adj* ○ *Her costly mistake allowed the opponents to score.*

IDIOMS with cost

- **at any cost, at all costs** no matter what dangers or difficulties are involved ○ *We realized we had to fight the lawsuit at any cost.*
- **at cost** without a profit ○ *We bought the furniture at cost from a friend who works in the furniture business.*
- **cost (*someone*) an arm and a leg** to be very expensive ○ *The repair work cost an arm and a leg.*

costar /ˈkoʊ·stɑr/ *n* [C] a famous actor appearing with one or more other famous actors in a film or a play

costar /ˈkoʊ·stɑr, ˈkoʊˈstɑr/ *v* [I/T] **-rr-** ○ [I] *Bergman and Bogart costarred in "Casablanca."*

C

cost-effective *adj* providing good value for the amount paid ○ *It's not cost-effective to heat the whole building if only three people are working here.*

cost of living *n* [U] the amount of money that a person needs to buy food, housing, and other basic things ○ *The cost of living is lower in the Midwest.*

costume /ˈkɑs·tuːm, -tʃuːm/ *n* [C/U] **1** a set of clothes worn in order to look like someone else, esp. for a party or as part of an entertainment ○ [C] *a clown costume* **2** A costume is also the set of clothes typical of a particular country or period of history: [U] *The dancers dressed in national costume.*

costume jewelry *n* [C/U] jewelry that is not expensive or is made from artificial jewels

cot /kɑt/ *n* [C] a narrow bed made of strong material attached to a frame, esp. one that can be folded and easily carried

cotangent /koʊˈtæn·dʒənt/ *n* [C] ***trigonometry*** a FUNCTION (= mathematical relation) of an angle that is the RECIPROCAL (= number) of TANGENT

cottage /ˈkɑt̬·ɪdʒ/ *n* [C] a small house, usually away from a city or town

cottage cheese /ˌkɑt̬·ɪdʒˈtʃiːz/ *n* [U] soft, white cheese made from sour milk

cotton /ˈkɑt·ᵊn/ *n* [U] thread or cloth made from the fiber surrounding the seeds of a tall plant, or these fibers themselves ○ *a cotton shirt/dress*

cotton ball a small ball of cotton fibers used esp. for cleaning the skin

cotton candy *n* [U] a large, soft ball of sugar that has been spun in a special machine to form long fibers which are collected on a stick

cottonwood /ˈkɑt·ᵊnˌwʊd/ *n* [C] a type of POPLAR tree that grows in North America and produces seeds with soft, white fibers that look like cotton

cotyledon /ˌkɑk·əlˈiːd·ᵊn/ *n* [C] ***biology*** a type of leaf that is part of the developing plant inside a seed and that either stores food or grows from the seed to produce food

couch **SEAT** /kɑʊtʃ/ *n* [C] a piece of furniture with a back and usually arms, that two or more people can sit on at once; a SOFA

EXPRESS /kɑʊtʃ/ *v* [T] to express something in a particular way, esp. in order not to upset or anger the person addressed ○ *They want to couch their response in diplomatic, not threatening, terms.*

couch potato *n* [C] *infml* a person who sits and watches a lot of television and does not have an active life

cougar /ˈkuː·gər/, **mountain lion, puma, panther** *n* [C] a large, brown, wild cat found in North and South America

cough /kɔːf/ *v* [I] to force air out of your lungs through your throat with a short, loud sound ○ *The smoke from the bonfire made me cough.* ○ *(fig.) The car engine coughed a few times, but wouldn't start.*

cough /kɔːf/ *n* [C] ○ *a dry cough* ○ *There are lots of coughs and colds going around this winter.*

PHRASAL VERBS with cough

• **cough up** *something* **FORCE OUT LIQUID** [M] to force liquid out of your lungs ○ *She coughed up a lot of phlegm.*

• **cough up** *something* **PAY** [M] *infml* to produce or give something unwillingly, esp. money ○ *I had to cough up $85 for a parking fine.*

cough drop *n* [C] a hard piece of candy that you suck so that you will cough less

cough syrup *n* [U] a liquid that you take to help stop coughing

could **CAN** /kʊd, kəd/ *past simple of* CAN ○ *You said we could watch television when we finished our homework.* ○ *When I was younger I could stay up all night and then go to work.*

ASK PERMISSION /kʊd, kəd/ *modal verb* **could** used as a more polite form of can when asking for permission ○ *Could I speak to Mr. Harley, please?*

REQUEST /kʊd, kəd/ *modal verb* **could** used as a more polite form of can when making a request ○ *Could you lend me $5?*

BE POSSIBLE /kʊd, kəd/ *modal verb* used to express possibility, esp. slight or uncertain possibility ○ *A lot of these problems could be prevented.* ○ *It could be days before we hear from her.* ○ *I could have been an actor.*

SUGGEST /kʊd, kəd/ *modal verb* **could** used for making a suggestion ○ *We could go to the movies.*

SHOULD /kʊd, kəd/ *modal verb* **could** used for saying what you think someone else should do ○ *You could try to look a little more enthusiastic.*

IDIOMS with could

• **could care less** not care at all ○ *Most fans could care less about how players behave off the field.*

• **could have died** *infml* felt very embarrassed ○ *I could have died when my friends saw me shopping for clothes with my mom.*

• **could use, could do with** to need or want something ○ *I could use some help over here!* ○ *You could do with a haircut.*

couldn't /ˈkʊd·ᵊnt/ *contraction of* could not ○ *Couldn't you leave on Saturday instead?*

IDIOMS with couldn't

• **couldn't agree more** to strongly agree ○ *Bob says it's the government's fault, and I couldn't agree more.*

• **couldn't care less** to not care at all ○ *I couldn't care less if he doesn't want to talk to me.*

could've /ˈkʊd·əv, kəd·əv/ *contraction of* could have ○ *It could've been anybody.*

coulomb /ˈkuːˌlɑm, -ˌloʊm/, *abbreviation* **C** *n* [C] ***chemistry, physics*** a unit of measurement for electric CHARGE, representing the charge carried by one AMPERE (= unit of electric current) in one second

council /ˈkɑʊn·səl/ *n* [C] a group of people elected or chosen to make decisions or give advice on a particular subject, to represent a particular group of people, or to run a particular organization ○ *the UN Security Council* ○ *The council is being pressured to approve the plan.*
councilor, **councillor** /ˈkɑʊn·sə·lər/ *n* [C] an elected member of a local government

councilman /ˈkoʊn·səl·mən/ *n* [C] *pl* **-men** a man who is an elected member of a local government

councilwoman /ˈkoʊn·səl ˌwʊm·ən/ *n* [C] *pl* **-women** a woman who is an elected member of a local government

counsel /ˈkɑʊn·səl/ *v* [T] **-l-**, **-ll-** to give advice, esp. on social or personal problems ○ *He was counseling athletes not to take steroids.*
counsel /ˈkɑʊn·səl/ *n* [U] *fml* **1** *The president sought counsel from his advisers.* **2** *law* Counsel is one or more of the lawyers taking part in a case or legally representing a person or organization: *Maloney skipped the meeting on the advice of counsel.*
counselor, **counsellor** /ˈkɑʊn·sə·lər/ *n* [C] **1** a person whose job is to provide advice, help, or encouragement ○ *a marriage/guidance counselor* ○ *a camp counselor* **2** *law* Counselor is used to address a lawyer: *Good afternoon, counselor.* ➤ Usage: **lawyer, counsel, or attorney?** at LAWYER

count CALCULATE /kɑʊnt/ *v* [I/T] to say the names of numbers one after the other in order, or to calculate the number of units in a group ○ [I] *By the time I count to three, you'd better be in bed.* ○ [T] *The teachers counted the students as they boarded the bus.* ○ [T] *There'll be eight for dinner, counting* (= including) *us.* ○ [+ question word] *Can you count how many pencils are left?*
count /kɑʊnt/ *n* [C/U] a calculation, esp. a scientific one, of the number of units in a group ○ *a low blood count* ○ [C] *We need a count of the number of e-mail inquiries.*
CONSIDER /kɑʊnt/ *v* [I/T] to consider or be considered as ○ [T] *He counts Lucy as one of his closest friends.* ○ [I] *Does homework count toward my grade?*
VALUE /kɑʊnt/ *v* [I] to have value or importance ○ *I've always believed that happiness counts more than money.*
CRIME /kɑʊnt/ *n* [C] *law* a separate item included in a criminal accusation against someone ○ *She was found guilty on two counts of fraud.*
OPINION /kɑʊnt/ *n* [C usually pl] a statement of belief in a discussion or argument ○ *I think you're wrong on all counts.*

WORD FAMILY count

Nouns	count recount	*Adjectives*	countable uncountable countless
Verbs	count recount		

IDIOMS with count

• **don't count your chickens before they hatch** you should not make plans that depend on something good happening before you know that it has actually happened ○ *She wanted to buy a dress in case someone asked her to the dance, but I told her not to count her chickens before they hatched.*
• **on the count of** *something* after counting to a particular number ○ *On the count of three, run.*

PHRASAL VERBS with count

• **count** *(something)* **against** *someone/something* to have a negative effect on someone or something ○ *Parking tickets don't count against your driving record.*
• **count down** to count backwards to zero ○ *She counts down the top 10 music videos every week.* ○ Related noun: COUNTDOWN
• **count** *someone* **in** *infml* to include someone in an activity or plan ○ *"We're going to the ballgame – want to come?" "Sure, count me in."*
• **count on** *someone/something* to depend on someone or expect something ○ *You can always count on Michael in a crisis.* ○ *She didn't count on rain, and didn't bring an umbrella.*
• **count out** *something* SEPARATE ITEMS to count each item in a group one at a time ○ *She pulled out her wallet and slowly counted out what money she had.*
• **count** *someone* **out** OMIT *infml* to not include someone in an activity ○ *"Who's coming swimming?" "Count me out – it's too cold."*

countable noun /ˈkɑʊnt·ə·bəl/ *n* [C] ***grammar*** a noun that has both a singular and a plural form and names something that can be counted because there can be one or more of it ○ *"Book" and "decision" are both countable nouns.* ○ **USAGE:** Countable nouns are marked [C] in this dictionary. ○ Compare UNCOUNTABLE NOUN

countdown /ˈkɑʊnt·dɑʊn/ *n* [C] an act of counting backwards to zero, esp. before sending a spacecraft into space or before the start of an important event ○ *The countdown to Tuesday's primary elections has begun.* ○ Related verb: COUNT DOWN

countenance FACE /ˈkɑʊnt·ᵊn·əns/ *n* [C/U] ***literature*** the appearance or expression of someone's face ○ [C] *Her countenance masked her feelings.*
APPROVE OF /ˈkɑʊnt·ᵊn·əns/ *v* [T] to find an activity acceptable; to approve of or give support to something ○ *This school will not countenance lateness.*

counter SURFACE /ˈkɑʊnt·ər/ *n* [C] **1** a long, flat, narrow surface in a store, bank, restaurant, etc., at which people are served ○ *He sat down at the counter of the diner and ordered a cup of coffee.* **2** A counter is also a flat surface in a kitchen on which food can be prepared.
OPPOSE /ˈkɑʊnt·ər/ *v* [I/T] to react to something with an opposing opinion or action; to defend yourself against something ○ [T] *To counter the inaccuracies in the movie, researchers used computer models to project climate changes.*
counter /ˈkɑʊnt·ər/ *adv* [not gradable] ○ *David's decision to drop out of school to write plays ran counter to* (= was directly opposite to) *his parent's expectations.*

counteract /ˌkɑʊnt·əˈrækt/ *v* [T] to reduce or remove the effect of something by producing an opposite effect ○ *The tax must be adjusted upward to counteract inflation.*

counterattack /ˈkɑʊnt·ə·rəˌtæk/ *n* [C] an attack intended to stop or oppose an attack by an enemy or competitor
counterattack /ˈkɑʊnt·ə·rəˌtæk/ *v* [I] ○ *Faced with a lawsuit for negligence, he counterattacked by filing charges against his accusers.*

counterclockwise /ˌkɑʊnt·ərˈklɑkˌwɑɪz/ *adj, adv* [not gradable] (moving around) in a direction opposite to that of the HANDS (= long narrow parts that move) of a clock or watch ○ Compare CLOCKWISE at CLOCK

counterfeit /ˈkɑʊnt·ərˌfɪt/ *adj* [not gradable] copied exactly in order to make someone believe that the copy is the original ○ *A lot of brand-name merchandise sold on the streets is counterfeit.*
counterfeit /ˈkɑʊnt·ərˌfɪt/ *n* [C] ○ *The bank said this $100 bill was a counterfeit.*
counterfeit /ˈkɑʊnt·ərˌfɪt/ *v* [T] ○ *They were accused of counterfeiting credit cards and selling them.*

counterpart /ˈkɑʊnt·ərˌpɑrt/ *n* [C] a person or thing that has the same position or purpose as another person or thing in a different place or organization ○ *The president will meet with his Brazilian counterpart tomorrow.*

counterproductive /ˌkɑʊnt·ər·prəˈdʌk·tɪv/ *adj* having an effect that is the opposite of what you intend or desire ○ *As a way to improve traffic, widening roads can be counterproductive, as it may just encourage more people to drive.*

counterterrorism, **counter-terrorism** /ˌkɑʊnt·ərˈter·əˌrɪz·əm/ *n* [U] action intended to prevent violence for political purposes ○ *The city has less than 10 officers assigned to counter-terrorism.* ○ *Counterterrorism experts concede that the threat is real.*

countless /ˈkɑʊnt·ləs/ *adj* [not gradable] very many; too many to be counted ○ *Countless times when I needed someone to talk to, she would listen.*

country POLITICAL UNIT /ˈkʌn·tri/ *n* [C] an area of land that forms an independent political unit with its own government; a nation considered esp. as a place ○ *Cuba is my native country, but I now live in Florida.*

> **USAGE**
>
> **country, land, nation, or state?**
>
> **Country** is the most general of these words. It usually means an area of land with its own government and people.
>
> *China, Japan, and other countries in Asia*
>
> **Nation** is used to talk about a country, especially when you mean the people or the culture of that country.
>
> *The whole nation celebrated the 100th anniversary of independence.*
>
> **State** is used to talk about a country as a political or official area. The US and some other countries are divided into political units that are also called **states**.
>
> *Belgium became an independent state in 1830.*
>
> *Mexico is divided into 31 states.*
>
> *the state of Florida*
>
> **Land** means an area of ground, especially when used for farming or building. It can also be used to mean a country, but this is a literary usage.
>
> *We bought some land to build a house on.*
>
> *He told stories of distant lands.*

NATURAL LAND /ˈkʌn·tri/ *n* [U] land that is not in towns, cities, or industrial areas and is either used for farming or left in its natural condition ○ *I'm spending next weekend in the country with a friend.*

country and western, *short form* **country** *abbreviation* **C&W** *n* [C] a style of popular music based on traditional music of the western and southern US

country club *n* [C] a private social and sports organization in the countryside, open only to its members and their guests

countryman /ˈkʌn·triː·mən/, *female* **countrywoman** /ˈkʌn·triːˌwʊm·ən/ *n* [C] *pl* **countrymen, countrywomen** a person from your own country

countryside /ˈkʌn·triːˌsɑɪd/ *n* [U] land not in towns, cities, or industrial areas which is either used for farming or left in its natural condition ○ *Much of Connecticut's countryside is dotted with large estates and horse farms.* ➤ Usage: **nature, the environment, or the countryside?** at NATURE LIFE

county /ˈkɑʊnt·i/ *n* [C] the largest political division of most states in the US ○ *Texas is divided into 254 counties.*

coup /kuː/ *n* [C] *pl* **coups** an unexpectedly successful achievement ○ *It was quite a coup for her to get an interview with the First Lady.*

coup d'état /ˌkuːˌdeɪˈtɑ/, *short form* **coup** *n* [C] *pl* **coups d'état** sudden defeat of a government through illegal force by a small group, often a military one

couple Ⓐ SOME /ˈkʌp·əl/ *n* [U] two or a few things that are similar or the same, or two or a few people who are in some way connected ○ *I'm packing a couple of sweaters in case it gets cold.*
TWO PEOPLE /ˈkʌp·əl/ *n* [C] two people who are married or who spend a lot of time together esp. in a romantic relationship ○ *We're having two couples over for dinner.*

PHRASAL VERB with couple

• **couple** *something* **with** *something* Ⓐ to consider one thing along with or in addition to something else ○ *The new city tax, coupled with Social Security deductions, will take a huge bite out of everybody's paycheck.*

couplet /ˈkʌp·lət/ *n* [C] ***literature*** a pair of lines in a poem, esp. when connected by rhythm, RHYME (= words that end with the same sound), or meaning

coupon /ˈkuː·pɑn, ˈkjuː-/ *n* [C] a piece of paper that you can use to buy a product or service at a reduced price or to get it free, or to get information ○ *Send in this coupon with your name and address for a free travel brochure.* ○ *You can collect points from the soda bottles and use them to get discount coupons.*

courage /ˈkɜr·ɪdʒ, ˈkʌ·rɪdʒ/ *n* [U] the ability to control fear and to be willing to deal with something that is dangerous, difficult, or unpleasant ○ *He lacked the courage to tax the American people to pay for his Great Society programs.* ○ *It took me several months to get up the courage to ask her to lunch.*
courageous /kəˈreɪ·dʒəs/ *adj* ○ *She showed herself to be a courageous journalist.*

courier /ˈkʊr·iː·ər, ˈkɜr·iː-, ˈkʌ·riː-/ *n* [C] a person who carries messages or documents for someone else

course DIRECTION /kɔːrs, koʊrs/ *n* [C] the particular path something such as an aircraft or ship takes as it moves, or the path along which a river flows ○ *A southern course will take our flight over Texas.* ○ *The ship was blown* **off course** (= away from its course) *in the storm.*

DEVELOPMENT /kɔːrs, koʊrs/ *n* [C] the often gradual development of something, or the way something happens, or a way of doing something ○ *He always chats with waiters and waitresses and becomes their best friends during the course of dinner.*

CLASSES /kɔːrs, koʊrs/ *n* [C] a set of classes in a subject at a school or university ○ *He taught a course in film history at Harvard University.*

SPORTS AREA /kɔːrs, koʊrs/ *n* [C] an area used for a sports event ○ *a golf course*

MEAL /kɔːrs, koʊrs/ *n* [C] a part of a meal served separately from the other parts ○ *the meat course*

IDIOMS with course

• **of course** yes, certainly ○ *"May I use your telephone?" "Of course, go right ahead."*
• **of course not** definitely no or definitely not ○ *"The pie is delicious! Do you mind if I have a second helping?" "Of course not, I'm glad you like it."*

court LAW /kɔːrt, koʊrt/ *n* [C/U] **1** the place where trials and other legal cases happen ○ [U] *He is bringing charges against us and said, "I'll see you in court."* ○ [U] *The newspaper agreed to settle the case out of court* (= agreed to a deal that avoided a trial). **2** The court is the judge or judges who are in charge of the way a legal case happens and sometimes make decisions about it.

SPORTS /kɔːrt, koʊrt/ *n* [C] a rectangular area used as the playing area in some sports ○ *a racquetball/tennis court*

PLEASE /kɔːrt, koʊrt/ *v* [T] to try to please someone in the hope of receiving that person's support, approval, or affection, or to try to get something that benefits you ○ *Both candidates had been courting independent voters, who are likely to decide the election.*
courtship /ˈkɔːrt·ʃɪp, ˈkoʊrt-/ *n* [C/U] *dated* the period in which two people have a romantic relationship that often leads to marriage ○ [C] *They were married in 1923 after a long courtship.*

RISK /kɔːrt, koʊrt/ *v* [T] to increase the risk of something bad happening ○ *If you hire people who are not very sharp or creative, you're courting disaster.*

courteous /ˈkɜrt̬·iː·əs/ *adj* polite and showing respect ○ *The ticket clerk was courteous and helpful.*

courtesy /ˈkɜrt̬·ə·si/ *n* [C/U] polite behavior, or a polite action ○ [U] *They should teach drivers to show pedestrians some courtesy.*

IDIOM with courtesy

• **courtesy of** *someone* from someone as a gift ○ *We got these gift certificates for nothing, courtesy of two local businesses.* ○ USAGE: Used to say who gave you something that you would usually have to pay for.

courthouse /ˈkɔːrt·hɑʊs, ˈkoʊrt-/ *n* [C] a building that contains rooms where trials and other legal cases happen ○ *a county courthouse*

court-martial /ˈkɔːrt ˌmɑr·ʃəl, ˈkoʊrt-/ *n* [C] *pl* **courts-martial, court-martials** a military court, or a trial in a military court, that judges members of the armed forces
court-martial /ˈkɔːrt ˌmɑr·ʃəl, ˈkoʊrt-/ *v* [T] ○ *He was court-martialed for leaving his post without permission.*

courtroom /ˈkɔːrt·ruːm, ˈkoʊrt-, -rʊm/ *n* [C] a usually large room where trials and other legal cases happen

courtyard /ˈkɔːrt·jɑrd, ˈkoʊrt-/ *n* [C] an area of flat ground outside and partly or completely surrounded by one or more buildings ○ *Entrance to the apartment building is through a central courtyard.*

cousin /ˈkʌz·ən/ *n* [C] a child of a person's aunt or uncle

covalent bond /koʊˈveɪ·lənt ˈbɑnd/ *n* [C] a CHEMICAL BOND in which two atoms share one or more pairs of ELECTRONS, which hold them together

cove /koʊv/ *n* [C] a curved part of a coast that partly encloses an area of water; a small BAY

covenant /ˈkʌv·ə·nənt/ *n* [C] a formal agreement between countries, organizations, or people

cover PLACE OVER /ˈkʌv·ər/ *v* [T] **1** to put or spread something over something, or to lie on the surface of something ○ *Once the rice comes to a boil, turn down the flame and cover the pot.* ○ *She covered the child with a blanket.* **2** If something covers an area of a particular size, it is equal to an area of that size: *Grand Canyon National Park covers over a million acres.*
cover /ˈkʌv·ər/ *n* [C] **1** something that is placed over something, often for protection, or that lies over something else to form a layer ○ *I keep my computer printer under a plastic cover.* **2** The cover of a book or magazine is the stiff, outside part of it, usually made of thick paper or cardboard. **3** A cover is also a layer of a material used to keep a person in bed warm: [pl] *On cold days, she pulled the covers up to her chin.*

TRAVEL /ˈkʌv·ər/ *v* [T] to travel a particular distance ○ *We covered 600 miles in the last two days.* ○ *(fig.) Her lecture covered a lot of ground, from Renaissance art to modern art.*

INCLUDE /ˈkʌv·ər/ *v* [T] to deal with or include someone or something ○ *The travel guide covers all the museums and historic places.*

REPORT /ˈkʌv·ər/ *v* [T] to report or write about a particular subject for a newspaper, magazine, television, or radio ○ *Harold covers sports for the Times, and Joan covers real-estate developments.*

coverage /ˈkʌv·ə·rɪdʒ/ *n* [U] ○ *The TV station is trying to improve its coverage of local news.*

BE ENOUGH /ˈkʌv·ər/ *v* [T] to be enough money to pay for ○ *Will $150 cover your expenses?*

PROTECT /ˈkʌv·ər/ *v* [T] to protect someone or something from financial loss, damage, accident, or having something stolen; to INSURE ○ *Our car insurance covers us up to $250,000 for personal injury.*

coverage /ˈkʌv·ə·rɪdʒ/ *n* [U] ○ *I've got $50,000 worth of coverage for the contents of my house.*

SHELTER /ˈkʌv·ər/ *n* [U] shelter or protection, esp. in a dangerous situation ○ *Folks heard the storm was coming and took cover.*

DO SOMEONE'S JOB /ˈkʌv·ər/ *v* [I always + adv/prep] to do someone else's job or duty when that person is absent ○ [T] *Could you cover the phones while I'm away from the office?*

WORD FAMILY cover			
Nouns	cover coverage	*Verbs*	cover uncover
Adjectives	undercover		

IDIOMS with cover

• **cover (all) the bases** to do everything necessary to be sure that something is successful ○ *I think I've covered all the bases – I called everyone, ordered the food, and bought some decorations.*

• **(from) cover to cover** read all the way through from the beginning to the end ○ *I read that book from cover to cover in one day.*

• **cover *your* tracks** to do things that hide your activities from other people, so that they cannot find out what you have been doing ○ *He transferred money illegally into his own account, and then tried to cover his tracks by destroying the computer records.*

PHRASAL VERBS with cover

• **cover for** *someone/something* to provide an excuse for someone, or an explanation for something that has gone wrong ○ *She would cover for her brothers when they came in late.*

• **cover up** *(something)* [M] to keep something unpleasant or illegal secret or hidden ○ *He accused the police of covering up for each other.* ○ *They're trying to cover up the truth.* ○ Related noun: COVERUP

coveralls /ˈkʌv·əˌrɔːlz/ *pl n* a type of clothing made in one piece that cover and protect most of the body and are worn for doing dirty work

cover charge *n* [C] a charge added to the amount that a customer pays for food and drink in a restaurant or NIGHTCLUB to pay for service or entertainment

covered wagon *n* [C] a large vehicle with four wheels and a high, covered frame which is pulled by horses or other animals, used in the past to transport people and goods to the western part of the US

cover story *n* [C] a report or article connected with the picture on the front of a magazine

covert /ˈkoʊ·vərt, koʊˈvɜrt/ *adj* hidden or secret ○ *covert military operations* ○ Opposite: OVERT

coverup /ˈkʌv·əˌrʌp/ *n* [C] an attempt to prevent the public from discovering information about a serious crime or mistake ○ *I'm convinced there was an intentional coverup, that officials haven't told all they know about what happened.* ○ Related verb: COVER UP

coveted /ˈkʌv·ət̬·əd/ *adj* strongly desired by many ○ *The Caldecott Medal is a coveted children's book award.*

cow ANIMAL /kɑʊ/ *n* [C] **1** the adult female of cattle that is kept on a farm to produce milk or meat **2** A cow is also any of other large female, adult mammals, such as ELEPHANTS or WHALES.

FRIGHTEN /kɑʊ/ *v* [T] to frighten or control someone by using threats or violence ○ *The dictator has succeeded in cowing his public opponents into near silence.*

coward /ˈkɑʊ·ərd/ *n* [C] *disapproving* person who is not brave, is easily frightened, or tries to avoid danger or difficulties ○ *A coward is someone who sends you a nasty letter without signing it.*

cowardly /ˈkɑʊ·ərd·li/ *adj* [not gradable] *disapproving* ○ *a cowardly act*

cowardice /ˈkɑʊ·ərd·əs/ *n* [U] *disapproving* the condition of lacking bravery, being easily frightened, or being eager to avoid danger

cowboy /ˈkɑʊ·bɔɪ/, *female* **cowgirl** /ˈkɑʊ·gɜrl/ *n* [C] a person employed to take care of cattle, who usually rides a horse

cowboy hat *n* [C] a hat with a wide, curved BRIM (= bottom part)

cower /ˈkɑʊ·ər, kɑʊr/ *v* [I] to bend down or move backward with your head down because you are frightened ○ *The dog cowered in the corner, realizing she'd done something wrong.*

co-worker, **coworker** /ˈkoʊˌwɜr·kər/ *n* [C] a person working with another worker, esp. as a partner or one who helps

coy /kɔɪ/ *adj* [-er/-est only] acting shy, uncertain, or unwilling to say much, often in order to increase interest in something by keeping back information about it ○ *McIntyre is coy about his future in football.*

coyly /ˈkɔɪ·li/ *adv* [not gradable] ○ *She smiled coyly.*

coyote /kɑɪˈoʊţ·i, ˈkɑɪ·oʊt/ *n* [C] a wild animal related to dogs that lives in parts of North America, esp. in the west

cozy /ˈkoʊ·zi/ *adj* comfortable, pleasant, and inviting, esp. (of a room or building) because small and warm

PHRASAL VERB with cozy

• **cozy up (to** *someone***)** to be very friendly to someone with the hope of getting an advantage ○ *Opponents say he has a record of cozying up to polluters and accepting their campaign donations.*

CPA *n* [C] *abbreviation for* CERTIFIED PUBLIC ACCOUNTANT

CPR *n* [U] *abbreviation for* cardiopulmonary resuscitation (= medical actions performed in an emergency to make the heart and lungs begin to work again)

crab /kræb/ *n* [C/U] a sea animal that has five pairs of legs and a round, flat body covered by a shell, or its flesh eaten as food

crack DAMAGE /kræk/ *v* [I/T] to damage something by causing thin lines or spaces to appear on its surface; break slightly ○ [I] *The concrete on the front of the building had begun to crack.* ○ [T] *The X-ray showed that she had cracked a bone in her foot.*

crack /kræk/ *n* [C] **1** a thin line or space in the surface of something, usually a sign of damage ○ *A series of cracks developed in the road surface.* **2** A crack is also a narrow space: *She opened the door a crack.*

cracked /krækt/ *adj* ○ *cracked bathroom tiles*

HIT SOMETHING /kræk/ *v* [T always + adv/prep] to hit something hard ○ *He fell backward, his head cracking against a tree.*

OPEN /kræk/ *v* [T] **1** to break something open, esp. in order to reach or use what is inside ○ *He cracked three eggs into a mixing bowl.* **2** If you crack a CODE (= message in symbols), you discover what it means.

MAKE A NOISE /kræk/ *v* [I/T] to make a sudden, sharp noise or to cause something to make such a noise ○ [I] *All around us the lightning was cracking.*

crack /kræk/ *n* [C] ○ *Then we heard the crack of Jones's bat as he hit a three-run homer.*

LOSE CONTROL /kræk/ *v* [I] to weaken and become less able to think in a reasonable way, esp. because of anxiety or fear ○ *In spite of intense questioning for over eight hours, she never cracked.*

ATTEMPT /kræk/ *n* [C] an attempt; a try ○ *I've never tried to cook this before, but I thought I'd have a crack at it.*

SKILLFUL /kræk/ *adj* [not gradable] skillful; expert ○ *The man's a crack technician.*

JOKE /kræk/ *v* [T] to make a joke or amusing remark ○ *Jerry's always cracking jokes.*

crack /kræk/ *n* [C] a joking remark that is critical of someone or slightly insulting ○ *She's always making cracks about how much I eat.*

IDIOMS with crack

• **crack a joke** to tell a joke ○ *I cracked a few jokes to try to cheer everyone up.*

• **crack a smile** to smile slightly ○ *The coach cracked a smile, but didn't say anything.*

• **crack the whip** to act with authority to make someone work harder ○ *I'm going to have to crack the whip to get these kids to study more before finals.*

• **not all it's cracked up to be, not everything/what it's cracked up to be** to not be as good as people have said ○ *This software isn't all it's cracked up to be.*

PHRASAL VERBS with crack

• **crack down** to take strong action to stop something ○ *The law limits engine idling to four minutes, but there aren't enough police officers to crack down on the problem.* ○ Related noun: CRACKDOWN

• **crack up** *(someone)* [M] *slang* to laugh with great enthusiasm, or to cause someone to laugh in this way ○ *The stories they told cracked me up.*

crackdown /ˈkræk·dɑʊn/ *n* [C] an action by an authority to stop something ○ *The government is calling for a crackdown on drivers who speed through red lights.* ○ Related verb: CRACK DOWN

cracker /ˈkræk·ər/ *n* [C] a hard, dry, thin piece of baked bread

cracking /ˈkræk·ɪŋ/ *n* [U] ***chemistry*** a process in which large molecules of a HYDROCARBON are broken down into smaller molecules

crackle /ˈkræk·əl/ *v* [I] to make a set of short, sharp sounds ○ *The fire spread to an evergreen tree, which crackled with flames.*

crackle /ˈkræk·əl/ *n* [C] ○ *the crackle of a radio broadcast*

crack of dawn *n* [U] the early part of the morning when the sun first appears

crackpot /ˈkræk·pɑt/ *n* [C] *infml* a crazy or strange person ○ *They obviously think we're a bunch of crackpots.*

cradle BED /ˈkreɪd·ᵊl/ *n* [C] a small bed for a baby, esp. one with raised sides that can be pushed gently so that it moves from side to side

SUPPORT /ˈkreɪd·ᵊl/ *v* [T] to hold someone or something gently ○ *Joe cradled his cup of coffee and began to speak.*

IDIOM with cradle

• **the cradle of** *something* the place or society where something began ○ *Philadelphia is known as the cradle of American democracy.*

craft SKILL /kræft/ *n* [C/U] skill in knowing how to do or make something, or a job or activity needing such skill ○ [U] *He talked about the craft of writing popular fiction.* ○ [C] *I love to do all kinds of crafts and sewing.*

craft /kræft/ *v* [T] ○ *The speech was well crafted* (= made with skill).

TRANSPORT /kræft/ *n* [C] *pl* **craft** a boat, aircraft, or spacecraft

C

craftsman /ˈkræf·smən/, *female* **craftswoman** /ˈkræfˌswʊm·ən/ *n* [C] *pl* **craftsmen, craftswomen** a person who is skilled in doing or making something

craftsmanship /ˈkræf·smənˌʃɪp/ *n* [U] skill at making things, or the skill with which something was made or done ○ *The craftsmanship of the Tiffany lamp was superb.*

crafty /ˈkræf·ti/ *adj* skillful in argument but likely to be dishonest ○ *a crafty lawyer*

craggy /ˈkræg·i/ *adj* rough and having many rocks ○ *a craggy shoreline* ○ (*fig.*) *His craggy* (= attractively rough) *features seemed at last to relax.*

cram FORCE /kræm/ *v* [T always + adv/prep] **-mm-** to force something into a small space, or to fill an area with people ○ *Six children were crammed into the back of the car.*

LEARN QUICKLY /kræm/ *v* [I] **-mm-** to try to learn a lot very quickly before an exam ○ *She's cramming for her history exam.*

cramp /kræmp/ *n* [C] a sudden, painful tightening of a muscle ○ *stomach cramps* ○ *a foot cramp*

cramped /kræmt/ *adj* [not gradable] limited in the freedom to move because there is not enough space ○ *He managed to get a bed in a cramped student apartment.*

cranberry /ˈkrænˌber·i, -bə·ri/ *n* [C] a small, round red fruit with a sour taste, used esp. to make juice and sauce

crane MACHINE /kreɪn/ *n* [C] a large machine with a long, movable part to which is fixed CABLES (= strong wires) for lifting and moving heavy objects

BIRD /kreɪn/ *n* [C] a large water bird with long, thin legs and a long neck

STRETCH /kreɪn/ *v* [I/T] to stretch in order to look at something ○ [I/T] *We were all craning (our necks) to get a glimpse of the movie star.*

crank PERSON /kræŋk/ *n* [C] a person who has strange ideas and behaves in strange ways ○ *He just seemed like a harmless crank to me.*

HANDLE /kræŋk/ *n* [C] a handle or bar on a machine that you can turn to make another part turn

PHRASAL VERBS with crank

- **crank out** *something* [M] *infml* to produce something in large amounts, like a machine does ○ *She cranks out two new books a year.*
- **crank up** *something* [M] *infml* to increase something, esp. the sound of a radio, television, or STEREO ○ *The kids cranked up the volume on the stereo.* ○ *The pressure to succeed in school has been cranked up a notch.*

cranky /ˈkræŋ·ki/ *adj* easily annoyed and angry

crap /kræp/ *n* [U] *infml* something that is bad or worthless; nonsense ○ *She thinks that most of what's on television now is crap.*

crappy /ˈkræp·i/ *adj* [-er/-est only] *infml* sick ○ *He said he was feeling really crappy.*

crash ACCIDENT /kræʃ/ *n* [C] a serious accident in which one or more cars, trucks, or other vehicles hit something, or in which an aircraft hits the ground or another aircraft ○ *She was killed in an airplane crash in 1983.*

crash /kræʃ/ *v* [I/T] ○ [I] *The plane crashed into the mountainside, killing all aboard.*

NOISE /kræʃ/ *n* [C] a loud noise that sounds as if it is caused by something violently breaking apart or hitting something else ○ *There was a loud crash, and we rushed over to see what had fallen.*

crash /kræʃ/ *v* [always + adv/prep] **1** to fall or hit something in a noisy or violent way ○ [I] *All the dishes the waitress was carrying crashed to the floor.* **2** To crash is also to move in a noisy or violent way: [I] *A big black bear came crashing through the underbrush.*

FAILURE /kræʃ/ *n* [C] a sudden loss of value of investments, or a failure of a business

crash /kræʃ/ *v* [I] **1** *When the market crashed, everyone lost money.* **2** If a computer crashes, it suddenly stops operating.

NOT INVITED /kræʃ/ *v* [T] *infml* to go to a party or other event without an invitation ○ *Some guys tried to crash the party but they weren't allowed in.*

SLEEP /kræʃ/ *v* [I] *slang* to sleep, or to stay at a place to sleep temporarily ○ *I was so tired after work, I crashed on the sofa.*

QUICK /kræʃ/ *adj infml* **1** involving great effort to achieve a lot quickly **2** A crash diet is a way of losing body weight quickly by eating very little.

crash course *n* [C] **1** a short period of instruction in which much is learned about a subject **2** A crash course is also an experience that is difficult or unexpected but provides new and useful information: *To prepare for his role in the movie, he took a crash course in doing farm chores like plowing fields and shearing sheep.*

crass /kræs/ *adj* [-er/-est only] offensive in manner or style ○ *I don't know anyone who would speak in such a crass manner.*

crate /kreɪt/ *n* [C] a large wooden box, used esp. for packing, storing, or sending things ○ *The wooden shipping crates were unloaded at the dock.*

crater /ˈkreɪt̬·ər/ *n* [C] **1** ***earth science*** a large hole in the top of a VOLCANO (= mountain made from liquid rock) **2** A crater is also a large hole made by something hitting the ground with force: *The meteorite left a crater six feet deep.*

crave /kreɪv/ *v* [T] to desire something strongly ○ *The neglected kids just crave attention.*

craving /ˈkreɪ·vɪŋ/ *n* [C] a strong or uncontrollable desire ○ *We had a craving for zucchini bread.*

crawfish /ˈkrɔː·fɪʃ/, **crayfish** /ˈkreɪ·fɪʃ/ *n* [C/U] a small animal similar to a LOBSTER, that lives in rivers and streams, or its flesh eaten as food

crawl MOVE /krɔːl/ *v* [I] to move slowly with the body stretched out along the ground or (of a human) on hands and knees ○ *a caterpillar crawling in the grass* ○ *The child crawled across the floor.* ○ (*fig.*) *The train crawled slowly through the night.*

crawl /krɔːl/ *n* [C usually sing] ○ *Traffic slowed to a crawl* (= a very slow speed).

SWIMMING /krɔːl/ *n* [U] a way of swimming fast by lying with your chest down, kicking your legs, and raising first one arm then the other out of the water to move yourself forward

IDIOM with crawl

• **crawling with** *something* covered with or full of something ○ *The jungle was crawling with insects.* ○ *The Internet is crawling with sports fans.*

crawl space *n* [C] a space in a part of a house, esp. under the bottom floor, that is not high enough for a person to stand in

crayon /ˈkreɪ·ən, -ˌɑn/ *n* [C] a small stick of colored wax used for drawing or writing ○ *a box of crayons*

craze /kreɪz/ *n* [C usually sing] an activity, style, or fashion that is very popular, usually for a short time ○ *Cycling shorts were the craze that year.*

crazed /kreɪzd/ *adj* [not gradable] behaving wildly ○ *His baseball glove is among the objects crazed collectors want to buy.*

crazy /ˈkreɪ·zi/ *adj* **1** very strange or foolish ○ *She's the craziest person I've ever met.* ○ [+ to infinitive] *You're crazy to rent the place without seeing it first.* **2** Crazy can mean mentally ill. **3** Crazy can also mean behaving in a strange way esp. because of stress, as if you are mentally ill: *The constant whine of the machine nearly drove* (= made) *me crazy.* ○ *I think she'll go* (= become) *crazy if she doesn't take a vacation soon.*
crazy /ˈkreɪ·zi/ *n* [C usually pl] *infml* a person who acts in a strange or threatening way, esp. one who is mentally ill ○ *Are we talking about a bunch of crazies or about a legitimate military force?*
crazily /ˈkreɪ·zə·li/ *adv* [not gradable]
craziness /ˈkreɪ·ziː·nəs/ *n* [U]

IDIOM with crazy

• **crazy about** *someone/something* to like someone or something very much ○ *I was crazy about baseball when I was seven.* ○ *He's crazy about my sister.*

creak /kriːk/ *v* [I] to make a high noise, usually caused by a stiff material such as wood or metal that is made to move slightly ○ *The old floorboards creaked when I walked across the floor.* ○ *He heard a prison cell door creak open and slam shut.*
creak /kriːk/ *n* [C]
creaky /ˈkriː·ki/ *adj* ○ *a creaky elevator*

cream LIQUID /kriːm/ *n* [U] **1** the thick, yellow-white liquid that forms on the top of milk ○ *Do you take cream in your coffee?* **2** Cream is also a pale yellow-white color. **3** Cream also refers to any of various foods that contain cream or that are smooth like cream: *cream of chicken soup* ○ *chocolate cream pie*
creamy /ˈkriː·mi/ *adj* thick and smooth, like cream

THICK SUBSTANCE /kriːm/ *n* [U] a thick, smooth substance that you put on your skin to keep it soft or to treat it medically ○ *a facial cream*

IDIOM with cream

• **the cream of the crop** the best of a group of similar things or people ○ *The medical school's graduates are considered to be the cream of the crop and can get jobs wherever they want to.*

cream cheese *n* [U] a type of soft, white cheese

crease /kriːs/ *n* [C] a line or mark made on material by folding or pressing it, or a line in a person's skin, esp. in the face ○ *There were tiny creases in her eye shadow.*
crease /kriːs/ *v* [I/T] ○ [T] *A frown creased Mr. Cuna's boyish face.*

create Ⓐ /kriːˈeɪt/ *v* [T] to cause something to exist, or to make something new or imaginative ○ *He created some of the most magnificent works of art ever made.* ○ *The new hotel is expected to create 200 jobs.*
creation Ⓐ /kriːˈeɪ·ʃən/ *n* [C/U] **1** [U] *Huge amounts of money went into the creation of a new highway.* **2** In the Bible, (the) Creation is the making of the world by God. **3** A creation is something that is made: [C] *The fashion magazine had photos of the latest Paris creations.*
creator Ⓐ /kriːˈeɪṭ·ər/ *n* [C] **1** a person who creates something **2** God is sometimes called the Creator.

WORD FAMILY create			
Nouns	creation creativity creator	*Adjectives* *Verbs* *Adverbs*	creative create creatively

creative Ⓐ /kriːˈeɪṭ·ɪv/ *adj* [not gradable] producing or using original and unusual ideas ○ *a creative designer/person* ○ *creative talents*
creativity Ⓐ /ˌkriː·eɪˈtɪv·əṭ·i, ˌkriː·ə-/ *n* [U] the ability to produce original and unusual ideas, or to make something new or imaginative
creatively Ⓐ /kriːˈeɪṭ·ɪv·li/ *adv* [not gradable]

creature /ˈkriː·tʃər/ *n* [C] **1** any living thing, esp. an animal **2** A creature can be a person when an opinion is being expressed about them: *It seems clear to me that people are creatures of emotion.*

IDIOM with creature

• **creature of habit** someone who always wants to do the same things in the same way ○ *I'm a creature of habit – I don't really like trying new foods.*

creature comfort *n* [C usually pl] any of the things that make life pleasant, such as warmth, good food, and a comfortable home

creche /kreʃ/ *n* [C] a model of the people and animals present at the birth of Jesus, used as a decoration at Christmas

credence /ˈkriːd·ᵊns/ *n* [U] *fml* acceptance, support, or belief that something is true ○ *I've heard rumors over the years, but I never gave them any credence whatsoever.*

credentials /krɪˈden·tʃəlz/ *pl n* documents that state the abilities and experience of a person and show that the person is qualified for a particular job or activity ○ *I got my teaching credentials from San Jose State.*

credible /ˈkred·ə·bəl/ *adj* able to be believed or trusted ○ *Investigators found no credible evidence of a crime.*

credibly /ˈkred·ə·bli/ *adv* ○ *The show credibly deals with topical issues.*

credibility /ˌkred·əˈbɪl·ət̬·i/ *n* [U] ○ *Once his lies were revealed, he lost all credibility as a leader.*

WORD FAMILY credible			
Nouns	credibility	*Adjectives*	incredible
Adverbs	incredibly		credible
			incredulous

credit Ⓐ **PAYMENT LATER** /ˈkred·ət/ *n* [U] a method of buying goods or services that allows you to pay for them in the future ○ *We bought our sofa on credit.* ○ *The bank offers small businesses credit.*

creditor Ⓐ /ˈkred·ət̬·ər/ *n* [C] a country, organization, or person to whom money is owed ○ *He's trying to earn enough to pay off his creditors.* ○ Compare DEBTOR at DEBT

PRAISE /ˈkred·ət/ *n* [C/U] praise or approval, esp. to recognize achievement ○ [U] *You have to give him credit for being so honest.* ○ [U] *How can he take credit for work he didn't do?*

MONEY AVAILABLE /ˈkred·ət/ *n* [C/U] **1** an amount of money available to you because you paid for something earlier, or a record of this money ○ [C] *We returned the clothes and got a store credit.* **2** A credit is also an amount of money you do not have to pay: [C] *a tax credit* ○ Opposite: DEBIT

credit /ˈkred·ət/ *v* [T] ○ *I'll be glad to credit your account for the items you returned.*

BELIEVE /ˈkred·ət/ *v* [T] to believe or trust something that may not be true ○ *If you can credit what the doctor says, the illness isn't serious.*

creditable /ˈkred·ət̬·ə·bəl/ *adj* ○ *She gave a creditable performance of a woman in love.*

COURSE UNIT /ˈkred·ət/ *n* [C] a unit of measurement of the value contributed by an educational course to a college degree ○ *Comparative religion is a three-credit course.*

IDIOMS with credit

• **a credit to** *someone/something* to be so good or successful that the people or things that made you successful should be mentioned ○ *Thomas is a credit to our school system.*

• **to** *someone's* **credit** deserving praise and respect ○ *It is to his credit that he's willing to admit he has a problem.*

PHRASAL VERB with credit

• **credit** *someone* **with** *something* to consider someone as having good qualities or good achievements ○ *I credited him with more sense than he showed.*

credit card *n* [C] a small plastic card that you can use to buy something and pay for it in the future

credit rating *n* [C] a judgment of whether a person or organization is likely to pay for things that are bought using CREDIT ○ *Late payments give you a bad credit rating.*

credits /ˈkred·əts/ *pl n* the list of the names of people and organizations who helped to make a movie or television program which is shown at the beginning or the end of it

credit union *n* [C] an organization that lends money to its members at low rates of INTEREST (= extra money)

credo /ˈkriː·doʊ, ˈkreɪd-/ *n* [C] *pl* **credos** a statement of basic belief ○ *His credo is "Less is more."*

creed /kriːd/ *n* [C/U] a formal statement or system of esp. religious beliefs ○ [U] *The law forbids discrimination because of race, color, or creed.*

creek /kriːk, *esp. Northern and Western* krɪk/ *n* [C] a small river or stream

creep MOVE CAREFULLY /kriːp/ *v* [I always + adv/prep] *past* **crept** to move quietly and carefully, usually in order to avoid being noticed ○ *I crept around the corner, hoping my brother wouldn't see me.*

MOVE SLOWLY /kriːp/ *v* [I always + adv/prep] *past* **crept** to move very slowly ○ *We were creeping along in rush-hour traffic.*

PERSON /kriːp/ *n* [C] *slang* a person you think is unpleasant and to be avoided ○ *That guy upstairs is such a creep.*

PHRASAL VERB with creep

• **creep up on** *someone* **1** to approach someone quietly, so that the person is suddenly surprised ○ *Did you have to creep up on me like that?* **2** If an event, day, or condition creeps up on you, you are surprised by its arrival, esp. because it has come gradually ○ *Budget time is creeping up on us and if we don't put in a proposal we're not going to get the money that we want next year.*

creeps /kriːps/ *pl n infml* a feeling of fear and disgust ○ *You give me the creeps.*

creepy /ˈkriː·pi/ *adj infml* strange and slightly frightening ○ *a creepy old house*

cremate /ˈkriː·meɪt, krɪˈmeɪt/ *v* [T] to burn a dead person's body

cremation /krɪˈmeɪ·ʃən/ *n* [C/U] ○ [U] *The body was sent for cremation.*

crematorium /ˌkriː·məˈtɔːr·iː·əm, ˌkrem·ə-, -ˈtoʊr-/ *n* [C] *pl* **crematoriums, crematoria** a building where dead people's bodies are burnt

Creole LANGUAGE /ˈkriː·oʊl/ *n* [C] any of several languages developed in some Caribbean islands that combine African languages and Indian languages with French or Spanish ○ *Creole is one of the official languages of Haiti.*

PERSON /ˈkriː·oʊl/ *n* [C] a white person who is related to the original group of Spanish or French people who came to the Caribbean or Louisiana, or a person of color from some Caribbean islands who is of mixed African and European origin and who speaks esp. French Creole

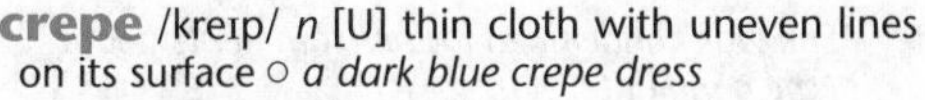

crepe /kreɪp/ *n* [U] thin cloth with uneven lines on its surface ○ *a dark blue crepe dress*

crepe paper *n* [U] thin, usually brightly colored, paper that is not smooth and that is used esp. for decoration

crept /krept/ *past simple and past participle of* CREEP

crescendo /krəˈʃen·doʊ/ *n* [C usually sing] *pl* **crescendos** a gradual increase in loudness, or the moment when a noise or piece of music is at its loudest

crescent /ˈkres·ənt/ *n* [C] **1** a curved shape that has two narrow pointed ends **2** A crescent moon is the moon when more than half the side you can see is dark.

crest /krest/ *n* [C] the top or highest part of something such as a wave or a hill ○ *We climbed to the crest of the hill.*

crest /krest/ *v* [I] ○ *The flood waters crested Thursday* (= reached their highest level).

crevice /ˈkrev·əs/ *n* [C] a deep crack or opening in a surface, esp. in rock ○ *He slipped on the mountain and landed in a crevice.*

crew /kruː/ *n* [C/U] all the people who work together, esp. to operate a ship or aircraft, or all the people of lower rank ○ [U] *The captain and crew would like to welcome you on board.* ○ [C] *Jack worked on a road-repair crew.*

crew cut /ˈkruː·kʌt/ *n* [C] a hairstyle for men and boys in which the hair is cut very short

crewneck /ˈkruː·nek/ *adj* (of clothing, esp. a SWEATER) having a round, flat, closely fitting opening for the neck

crib /krɪb/ *n* [C] a baby's bed with high sides and usually bars that prevent the baby from falling out

crib death *n* [C/U] a baby's death during sleep that cannot be explained by any known illness

crick /krɪk/ *n* [C] a painful, usually sudden stiffness in the muscles of the neck or back ○ *I got a crick in my neck from painting the ceiling.*

cricket **INSECT** /ˈkrɪk·ət/ *n* [C] a brown jumping insect that makes a loud, high, often repeated noise that you hear esp. at night

GAME /ˈkrɪk·ət/ *n* [U] a team sport popular in England and some other countries, played with a small, hard ball and a BAT (= wooden stick)

cried /krɑɪd/ *past simple and past participle of* CRY

cries /krɑɪz/ *third person singular of* CRY

crime /krɑɪm/ *n* [C/U] **1** an action or activity that is against the law, or illegal activity generally ○ [U] *Violent crime has been reduced.* ○ [C] *It's a crime to yell "fire" in a crowded theater if there isn't one.* ○ [C] *If you commit a crime, you will be punished.* **2** People say something is a crime if it is wrong: [C usually sing] *It's a crime that people go to bed hungry in this country.* ○ Related adjective: CRIMINAL

WORD FAMILY crime

Nouns	crime criminal	*Adjectives*	criminal incriminating
Verbs	incriminate	*Adverbs*	criminally

criminal /ˈkrɪm·ən·əl/ *adj* involving or having the character of a crime ○ *She may face criminal charges for lying to a grand jury.* ○ *He had an extensive criminal record* (= an official record of having committed many crimes). ○ *The way she blames other people for her own mistakes is criminal* (= wrong).

criminal /ˈkrɪm·ən·əl/ *n* [C] a person who has committed a crime or been found guilty of committing a crime

criminally /ˈkrɪm·ən·əl·i/ *adv* [not gradable] ○ *Parents can be held criminally responsible for their children's actions.*

crimp **PRESS** /krɪmp/ *v* [T] to press something into small folds or curves ○ *She had her hair crimped.*

crimson /ˈkrɪm·zən/ *adj, n* [U] (of) a deep red, slightly purple color ○ *His face was crimson with anger.*

cringe /krɪndʒ/ *v* [I] **1** to feel embarrassed and ashamed about something ○ *I cringed when I realized what I'd said.* **2** To cringe is also to pull back in fear from someone or something that seems powerful and dangerous: *He cringes every time he hears the dentist's drill.*

crinkle /ˈkrɪŋ·kəl/ *v* [I/T] to have or cause to have many little lines and folds ○ [I] *The paper was old and crinkled.*

crinkle /ˈkrɪŋ·kəl/ *n* [C] ○ *The machine won't take your bills unless you smooth out the crinkles.*

crinkly /ˈkrɪŋ·kə·li, -kli/ *adj* ○ *I love those crinkly French fries.*

cripple **DAMAGE** /ˈkrɪp·əl/ *v* [T] to make something much less effective; damage ○ *Economic sanctions have crippled the country's economy.*

crippling /ˈkrɪp·lɪŋ/ *adj* ○ *The city faces crippling cuts in services.*

INJURE /ˈkrɪp·əl/ *v* [T] to cause someone to be unable to move or walk in the usual way because of an injury or illness ○ *The accident crippled him.*

crippling /ˈkrɪp·lɪŋ, -ə·lɪŋ/ *adj* ○ *a crippling injury* ○ *crippling pain*

crisis /ˈkrɑɪ·səs/ *n* [C/U] *pl* **crises** an extremely dangerous or difficult situation ○ [C] *an economic crisis* ○ [U] *People react in times of crisis, but ignore us the rest of the time.*

crisp **HARD** /krɪsp/ *adj* (of food) hard enough to be broken easily instead of bent ○ *crisp bacon* ○ *crisp rolls*

crispy /ˈkrɪs·pi/ *adj approving* ○ *hot, crispy noodles*

FRESH /krɪsp/ *adj* fresh and clean ○ *I like to sleep on crisp cotton sheets.* ○ *The teller handed me a crisp hundred-dollar bill.*

COOL /krɪsp/ *adj* (of air) cool, clear, and likely to make you feel awake and active ○ *Crisp breezes*

C

bring out boats of every size. ○ *It was a crisp, midwinter morning in Massachusetts.*

DIRECT /krɪsp/ *adj* (of speech or writing) quick and direct ○ *I prefer Channel 1's crisp presentation of the news.*

crisply /ˈkrɪs·pli/ *adv* ○ *a crisply written book*

FRIED POTATO /krɪsp/ *n* [C usually pl] *Br* POTATO CHIP

crisscross /ˈkrɪs·krɔːs/ *v* [I/T] to move or exist in a pattern of crossing lines ○ [T] *From the air, we saw highways crisscrossing the farmland below.*

criterion Ⓐ /krɑɪˈtɪr·iː·ən/, *not standard* **criteria** /krɑɪˈtɪr·iː·ə/ *n* [C] *pl* **criteria** a condition or fact used as a standard by which something can be judged or considered ○ *Eight criteria will be used to select new stadium sites.* ○ *(not standard) Is height a criteria for hiring police officers?* ○ **USAGE**: The use of criteria as a singular noun is common, esp. in speech.

critic **JUDGE OF ENTERTAINMENT** /ˈkrɪt̬·ɪk/ *n* [C] a person whose job is to give an opinion about books, movies, and music and theater performances ○ *The critics hated it, but it was popular at the box office.*

critical /ˈkrɪt̬·ɪ·kəl/ *adj* ○ *The movie was a financial and critical success.*

critically /ˈkrɪt̬·ɪ·kli/ *adv* ○ *a critically acclaimed novel*

DISAPPROVING PERSON /ˈkrɪt̬·ɪk/ *n* [C] a person who expresses disagreement with something or disapproval of someone ○ *He has been one of the most outspoken critics of this administration.*

critical /ˈkrɪt̬·ɪ·kəl/ *adj* expressing an opinion about something or someone, esp. a negative opinion ○ *My mother is always so critical of the way I dress!*

critically /ˈkrɪt̬·ɪ·kli/ *adv* ○ *Industry spokesmen reacted critically to the report.*

criticism /ˈkrɪt̬·əˌsɪz·əm/ *n* [C/U] **1** an opinion given about something or someone, esp. a negative opinion, or the activity of making such judgments ○ [C] *It was meant as a suggestion, not a criticism.* ○ [U] *He was singled out for strong criticism.* **2** Criticism is also a careful discussion of something in order to judge its quality or explain its meaning: [U] *art criticism*

criticize /ˈkrɪt̬·əˌsɑɪz/ *v* [I/T] to express disagreement with or disapproval of something or someone ○ [I/T] *It's a lot easier to criticize (a plan) than to offer useful suggestions.*

WORD FAMILY critic

Nouns	critic criticism	*Verbs*	criticize
Adjectives	critical	*Adverbs*	critically

WORD CHOICES critic

Attack, **condemn**, and **denounce** can all be used when someone criticizes someone or something severely.

*She wrote an article **attacking** the judge and the way the trial had been conducted.*

*She was **condemned** for her comments about the candidate.*

*The government's economic policy has been **denounced** on all sides.*

If someone is criticized strongly and publicly, you could also use or the phrase **come under fire**.

*The government program has **come under fire** for mismanaging the money Congress gave it.*

A formal word which means the same as "criticize" is **censure**.

*The trial judge was **censured** for incompetence.*

Blast and **pan** are both informal ways of saying "criticize."

*The senator **blasted** the President's record on taxes, foreign policy, and the economy.*

*Her latest movie has been **panned** by critics.*

If a person criticizes someone in a very unpleasant way, you could use the informal verb **badmouth**.

*The coach was suspended for **bad-mouthing** a referee.*

If you think someone is criticizing something unfairly, you could use the phrase **find fault with**.

*He's always **finding fault with** my work.*

If you think someone is criticizing a person or thing unfairly, you could use the verbs **knock** or **run down**.

*Don't **knock** him. He's trying his best.*

*Stop **running him down**.*

critical **IMPORTANT** /ˈkrɪt̬·ɪ·kəl/ *adj* of the greatest importance ○ *critical industries* ○ *What happens in the next 48 hours is critical.*

critically /ˈkrɪt̬·ɪ·kli/ *adv*

VERY BAD /ˈkrɪt̬·ɪ·kəl/ *adj* very bad or dangerous ○ *He was admitted to Metropolitan Hospital in critical condition.*

critically /ˈkrɪt̬·ɪ·kli/ *adv* ○ *She was critically injured in the crash.*

critical temperature *n* [U] ***chemistry*** the highest temperature at which a gas can be changed into a liquid

critique /krəˈtiːk/ *n* [C] a report that discusses a situation or the writings or ideas of someone and offers a judgment about them ○ *She produced a detailed, page-by-page critique of the book.*

critter /ˈkrɪt̬·ər/ *n* [C] *infml* a creature ○ *That dog's a mean old critter.*

croak **MAKE SOUND** /kroʊk/ *v* [I/T] (of animals) to make deep sounds such as a FROG makes, or as a person might make because of a very dry throat ○ [I] *Frogs croaked in the swamp.* ○ [T] *He croaked a greeting, and we realized he could hardly talk.*

croak /kroʊk/ *n* [C]

DIE /kroʊk/ *v* [I] *slang* to die

crochet /kroʊˈʃeɪ/ *v* [I/T] to make cloth or clothing by connecting wool or other thread into joined rows using a single needle with a hook ○ [T] *My mother crocheted a blanket for the baby.*

crock CONTAINER /krɑk/ *n* [C] a container made of baked clay ○ *Dad kept sauerkraut in a twenty-gallon crock.*

NONSENSE /krɑk/ *n* [U] *slang* something that is completely false or ridiculous; nonsense ○ *They claimed they wrote that song? What a crock!*

crockery /ˈkrɑk·ə·ri/ *n* [U] cups, plates, bowls, etc., made of baked clay ○ *The store sells gift items such as crockery and soaps.*

crocodile /ˈkrɑk·əˌdɑɪl/ *n* [C] a large, hard-skinned REPTILE (= type of animal) with a longer and narrower nose than that of an ALLIGATOR which lives in and near rivers and lakes in hot, wet places

crocus /ˈkroʊ·kəs/ *n* [C] a small yellow, white, or purple spring flower

croissant /krəˈsɑnt, kwɑˈsɑ̃/ *n* [C] a piece of light bread having a curved shape with two narrow pointed ends ○ *Pick up some croissants for breakfast tomorrow.*

crony /ˈkroʊ·ni/ *n* [C] *often disapproving* a close friend or companion, esp. someone who may not be honest ○ *I'd like to see the president and his cronies booted out of office.*

crook BAD PERSON /krʊk/ *n* [C] a person who is dishonest, esp. someone who cheats or steals ○ *She thinks all politicians are crooks.*

crooked /ˈkrʊk·əd/ *adj* ○ *Their efforts centered on crooked deals in which officials took bribes.*

BENT PART /krʊk/ *n* [C usually sing] a bent part of something, esp. the inner part ○ *Kids should learn to sneeze and cough into the crooks of their elbows.*

crooked /ˈkrʊk·əd/ *adj* not straight or not even; twisted, bent, or uneven ○ *That dog's tail is crooked.* ○ *Your glasses are on crooked.*

croon /kruːn/ *v* [I/T] to sing or talk in a low, gentle, musical voice ○ [I] *He held his baby in his arms and crooned softly to her.*

crop PLANT /krɑp/ *n* [C] **1** a plant such as a grain, vegetable, or fruit grown in large amounts on a farm, or the total amount gathered of such a plant ○ *Apple growers celebrated their biggest crop ever last year.* **2** A crop is also any group of similar things or people: *We've got a new crop of students coming in every year.*

CUT /krɑp/ *v* [T] **-pp-** to cut something to make it shorter ○ *The brothers both had their hair cropped.*

PHRASAL VERB with **crop**

• **crop up** to happen or appear unexpectedly ○ *Her name keeps cropping up in their conversations.*

croquet /kroʊˈkeɪ/ *n* [U] a game in which players use MALLETS (= long wooden hammers) to hit wooden balls through small metal arches sunk in the grass

cross GO ACROSS /krɔːs/ *v* [I/T] to go from one side of something to the other ○ [T] *Look both ways before you cross the street.*

crossing /ˈkrɔː·sɪŋ/ *n* [C] a marked place where a road can be crossed safely; CROSSWALK ○ *a pedestrian crossing*

LIE ACROSS /krɔːs/ *v* [I/T] to put one thing across another, or to lie this way ○ [T] *Weaver Street crosses the Post Road.*

crossing /ˈkrɔː·sɪŋ/ *n* [C] a place where a road and a railroad cross

MARK /krɔːs/ *n* [C] **1** a mark or object in the shape of two lines across each other, usually ✗ or X ○ *He marked off their names with penciled crosses.* **2** A cross with a longer vertical line and a shorter horizontal line is the sign of Christianity.

cross /krɔːs/ *v* [T] When Christians cross themselves, they move their hand over their body in the shape of a cross.

ANNOYED /krɔːs/ *adj* annoyed or angry ○ *Don't be cross, I was just joking.*

OPPOSE /krɔːs/ *v* [T] to oppose someone by disagreeing or by not doing or saying what the person wants ○ *I wouldn't cross him if I were you.*

MIXTURE /krɔːs/ *n* [C] a mixture of two different things which have been combined to produce something new ○ *He's a cross between Clint Eastwood and Cary Grant.*

IDIOMS with **cross**

• **cross** *your* **fingers** to put one finger over another because you hope that something will happen as you want it to happen ○ *I'll just cross my fingers and hope for the best.*

• **cross the line**, **cross a line** to do something that is beyond what is consdered right, kind, or wise ○ *He crossed the line when he insulted my family.*

• **it crosses** *your* **mind (that)**, **the thought crosses** *your* **mind (that)** you think of something ○ *It crossed my mind yesterday that you might want to come with us.*

PHRASAL VERBS with **cross**

• **cross** *someone/something* **off** *(something)* [M] to remove someone or something, such as a name (from a list) by drawing a line through it ○ *Cross off each item as I put it on the shelf.*

• **cross out** *something* [M] to draw a line through writing ○ *Cross out the mistakes.*

• **cross over** to start to belong to or support a different group ○ *Now here's where the show has crossed over into science-fiction.* ○ Related noun: CROSSOVER

cross-country INVOLVING DISTANCES *adj* [not gradable] (of sports) involving movement over some distance through natural areas ○ *cross-country skiing/running*

ACROSS A COUNTRY *adj* [not gradable] across the length or width of a country ○ *After college we bought a camper and traveled cross-country for two months.*

cross-examine /ˌkrɔː·sɪɡˈzæm·ən/ *v* [T] to ask detailed questions of someone, esp. during a trial, in order to discover if the person has been telling the truth ○ *Defense attorneys cross-examined the witness.*

cross-examination /ˌkrɔː·sɪɡ ˌzæm·əˈneɪ·ʃən/ *n* [C/U] ○ [U] *Under cross-examination, she admitted she'd lied.*

C

cross-eyed *adj* having each eye looking toward the middle of the face

crossfire /ˈkrɔːs·fɑɪr/ *n* [U] the act of firing guns from two or more places at the same time, so that the paths of the bullets cross ○ *Some civilians were caught in the crossfire.*

cross-legged *adv* [not gradable] in a position with both legs bent, one resting under the other ○ *She sits cross-legged with her feet buried in the sand.*

crossover /ˈkrɔːˌsoʊ·vər/ *n* [U] a change from one form to another, or a mixture of different types ○ *There's been a lot of crossover from comic books to movies.* ○ *His crossover music blends Western and ethnic styles.* ○ Related verb: CROSS OVER

cross-pollination *n* [U] ***biology*** the process by which POLLEN (= powder produced by the male part of a flower) is carried from one flower to another by wind, insects, etc.

cross-purposes /ˈkrɔːˈspɜr·pə·səz/ *pl n* If two people or groups are **at cross-purposes** they do not understand each other because they have different intentions ○ *They're talking at cross-purposes without realizing it.*

cross-reference /ˈkrɔːsˈref·rəns/ *n* [C] (in books) an instruction to look somewhere else in the same book for related information

crossroads /ˈkrɔːs·roʊdz/ *n* [C] *pl* **crossroads** a place where two roads meet and cross each other ○ (fig.) *With funding coming up for review, the program is at a crossroads* (= has reached an important but uncertain stage).

cross-section **INSIDE VIEW** /ˈkrɔːsˌsek·ʃən/ *n* [C] a part of something cut from the rest of it, usually cut from side to side, in order to see its inside structure, or a drawing of this ○ *a cross-section of a human heart*

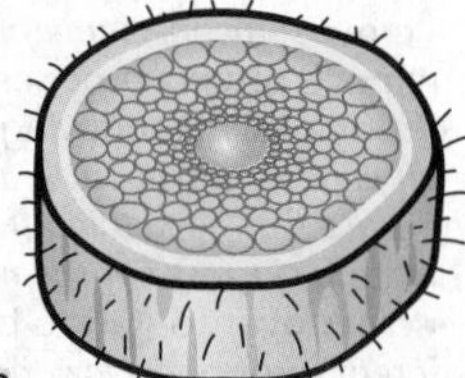

CROSS SECTION

REPRESENTATIVE GROUP /ˈkrɔːsˌsek·ʃən/ *n* [C] part of a group which is representative of all the different types within the total group ○ *A jury should represent a reasonable cross-section of the community.*

crosswalk /ˈkrɔː·swɔːk/ *n* [C] a marked place in a street where traffic must stop to allow people to walk across

crossword puzzle /ˈkrɔːˌswɜrd ˌpʌz·əl/ *n* [C] a word game in which you have to guess the answers to CLUES and write the words into numbered squares that go across and down

crotch /krɑtʃ/ *n* [C] the part of your body where your legs join at the top, or the part of pants or underwear which covers this area

crotchety /ˈkrɑtʃ·ət̬·i/ *adj* easily annoyed or angered ○ *After ten hours in the car, we were all getting crotchety.*

crouch /krɑʊtʃ/ *v* [I] to bend your knees and lower yourself so that you are close to the ground and leaning forward slightly ○ *She crouched down behind a bush to hide.*

crouch /krɑʊtʃ/ *n* [C usually sing] ○ *The goalie waited in a crouch.*

crow **BIRD** /kroʊ/ *n* [C] a large, black bird with a loud cry

CRY /kroʊ/ *v* [I] *past* **crowed** **1** (of a male chicken) to make a loud cry ○ *A rooster crowed repeatedly.* **2** Someone who crows expresses a lot of happiness or pride: *"I told you so," my little brother crowed.*

crowbar /ˈkroʊ·bɑr/ *n* [C] a heavy, iron bar with a bent end that is used to lift heavy objects off the ground or to force things open

crowd /krɑʊd/ *n* [C] **1** a large group of people who have gathered together ○ *A crowd formed outside the club.* ○ *Crowds of people watched the fireworks.* **2** *infml* A crowd is also a group of friends: *I don't know many people in Edsel's crowd.* **3** A crowd is also a group of people with similar interests: *the art/theater crowd*

crowd /krɑʊd/ *v* [I/T] **1** (of people) to fill a place ○ [T] *Street vendors crowded the sidewalks.* ○ [I] *As soon as he appeared, reporters crowded around him.* **2** If you crowd someone, you make the person uncomfortable by standing too close: [T] *Don't crowd me!* **3** If people crowd into a place, they fill it completely: [I] *Commuters crowded into the train.*

crowded /ˈkrɑʊd·əd/ *adj* full of people ○ *It's a popular and often crowded place.*

WORD FAMILY crowd			
Nouns	crowd overcrowding	*Adjectives*	crowded overcrowded
Verbs	crowd		

PHRASAL VERB with crowd

• **crowd out** *someone/something* [M] to make it impossible for someone or something to succeed because of great numbers or strength ○ *Invasive foreign plants crowd out native species and harm wildlife.*

crown **HEAD COVERING** /krɑʊn/ *n* [C] **1** a circular decoration for the head, usually made of gold and jewels, worn by a king or queen at official ceremonies **2** In a sports competition, a crown is a prize or position which you get for beating all the other competitors: *They won six NBA crowns in seven years.*

crown /krɑʊn/ *v* [T] ○ *Queen Elizabeth II was crowned in 1953* (= made queen).

TOP PART /krɑʊn/ *n* [C] **1** the top part of something, esp. a person's head ○ *Her hair stuck straight* *up from her crown.* **2** The crown of a hat is the part that covers the top of your head. ○ Compare BRIM PART OF HAT

crown /krɑʊn/ *v* [T] to be on or around the top of something ○ *mountains crowned with snowy caps*

BE BEST /krɑʊn/ *v* [T] to be the best or most successful part of an activity or life ○ *He hoped that health-care was the achievement that would crown his administration.*

crowning /ˈkrɑʊ·nɪŋ/ *adj* [not gradable] ○ *Building the team into a winner was the crowning achievement of Rory's coaching career.*

TOOTH /krɑʊn/ *n* [C] an artificial piece used to cover the top and sides of a tooth, esp. if it is damaged ○ *a gold crown*

crown /krɑʊn/ *v* [T] ○ *She had her two front teeth crowned.*

Crown attorney *n* [C] *Cdn* a lawyer who represents the government in court trials

Crown corporation *n* [C] *Cdn* a company that is owned by the Canadian government

Crown prosecutor *n* [C] *Cdn* a CROWN ATTORNEY

crow's feet *pl n* the narrow lines at the outer edge of a person's eyes

crucial Ⓐ /ˈkruː·ʃəl/ *adj* (of a decision or event) extremely important because many other things depend on it ○ *The behavior of the oceans is a crucial aspect of global warming.*

crucially Ⓐ /ˈkruː·ʃə·li/ *adv* ○ *The band wants to win over fans and, more crucially, radio programmers.*

crucible /ˈkruː·sə·bəl/ *n* [C] a container for melting metals

crucifix /ˈkruː·səˌfɪks/ *n* [C] a model or picture representing Jesus on a cross

crucifixion /ˌkruː·səˈfɪk·ʃən/ *n* [C/U] the act of killing someone by fixing that person to a cross and leaving him or her to die, or the death of Jesus on a cross

crucify /ˈkruː·səˌfɑɪ/ *v* [T] **1** to kill someone by tying or nailing the person to a cross **2** To crucify is also to criticize someone or something severely: *The media have a tendency to crucify organizations that try to do things differently.*

crud /krʌd/ *n* [U] *slang* any offensive substance ○ *You couldn't see a thing with all the crud in the air.*

cruddy /ˈkrʌd·i/ *adj slang* ○ *a cruddy book*

crude SIMPLE /kruːd/ *adj* [-*er*/-*est* only] simple and not skillfully done or made ○ *He made a crude table out of an old crate.*

crudely /ˈkruːd·li/ *adv* ○ *Crudely painted signs threatened trespassers.*

RUDE /kruːd/ *adj* [-*er*/-*est* only] rude and offensive ○ *a crude joke/remark* ○ *crude barbaric men*

crudely /ˈkruːd·li/ *adv* ○ *He spoke plainly, sometimes crudely.*

crude oil *n* [U] oil from underground that has not yet been made into other products

cruel /ˈkruː·əl/ *adj* extremely unkind and intentionally causing pain ○ *Her classmates made some cruel remarks.* ○ *Is the death penalty cruel and unusual punishment?* ○ *I think it's cruel to put a dog in a cage.*

cruelly /ˈkruː·ə·li/ *adv* ○ *She treated him cruelly before the divorce.*

cruelty /ˈkruː·əl·ti/ *n* [C/U] ○ [U] *The foundation works to end cruelty to animals.* ○ [U] *Deliberate cruelty will not be tolerated.*

WORD FAMILY cruel

Nouns	cruelty	*Adverbs*	cruelly
Adjectives	cruel		

WORD CHOICES cruel

If something is extremely cruel and unpleasant, you could describe it as **barbaric** or **inhumane**.

The world must condemn their actions as ***barbaric****.*

We are trying to end the most ***inhumane*** *forms of punishment.*

Callous, cold-blooded, or **ruthless** can be used when someone is very cruel and would hurt someone and not care if the person suffers.

He had a ***callous*** *disregard for the feelings of others.*

The budget is based on a ***cold-blooded*** *analysis of the markets.*

He was a ***ruthless*** *dictator.*

Heartless can be used about people who are cruel because they do not care about other people.

He has been described as a ***heartless*** *boss by several employees.*

If something is cruel because it is intended to upset or harm someone, the word **malicious** is often used.

People were spreading ***malicious*** *rumors about him.*

You could use **sadistic** if someone is cruel to other people and seems to enjoy it.

He was described as cold, mean, vicious, and ***sadistic****.*

If someone is slightly cruel to someone, you could use the words **nasty** or **mean** to describe them.

Don't be so ***nasty*** *to him!*

Don't listen to him. He's just being ***mean****.*

cruise /kruːz/ *v* [I] **1** to travel at a continuous speed ○ *The plane is cruising at 240 knots.* **2** If you cruise in a car, you drive for pleasure: *We went cruising around downtown on Friday night.* **3** Cruise can also mean to travel on large ships for pleasure.

cruise /kruːz/ *n* [C] a trip on a large ship for pleasure ○ *a Caribbean cruise*

cruiser /ˈkruː·zər/ *n* [C] a type of boat with an engine, usually used for pleasure

crumb /krʌm/ *n* [C] a very small piece of bread or cake ○ *The floor was covered with crumbs after breakfast.*

C

crumble /ˈkrʌm·bəl/ *v* [I/T] to break into small pieces ○ [I] *That old wall is starting to crumble.*

crummy /ˈkrʌm·i/ *adj slang* of very bad quality ○ *crummy weather* ○ *a crummy job* ○ *a crummy movie*

crumple /ˈkrʌm·pəl/ *v* [I/T] **1** to become full of irregular folds ○ [M] *Stephanie crumpled up the letter and threw it away.* **2** Someone or something that crumples falls suddenly: [I] *The top of the mast was starting to crumple.*

crunch MAKE NOISE /krʌntʃ/ *v* [I/T] to crush hard food loudly between the teeth, or to make a sound as if something is being crushed or broken ○ [I] *She was crunching noisily on an apple.* ○ [I] *The gravel crunched underfoot as we walked up the path.*
crunch /krʌntʃ/ *n* [C usually sing] ○ *We heard a loud crunch as the car hit the wall.*
crunchy /ˈkrʌn·tʃi/ *adj* (of food) firm and making a loud noise when it is eaten ○ *crunchy toast*

DIFFICULTY /krʌntʃ/ *n* [U] *slang* a difficult situation which forces you to make a decision or act ○ *a financial crunch*

CALCULATE /krʌntʃ/ *v* [T] to calculate numbers or process information ○ *The project seems worthwhile, but you have to crunch the numbers to see if it's affordable.*

crunch time *n* [U] a point at which something difficult must be done ○ *He plays fine without pressure, but can he produce at crunch time?*

crusade /kruːˈseɪd/ *n* [C] **1** a long and determined attempt to achieve something you strongly believe in ○ *She's involved in the crusade for racial equality.* **2** ***world history*** **The Crusades** were a series of wars in the 11th, 12th, and 13th centuries fought between Christians from Europe and Muslims in the region around the eastern Mediterranean Sea.
crusade /kruːˈseɪd/ *v* [I] ○ *He crusaded tirelessly for civil rights.*
crusader /kruːˈseɪd·ər/ *n* [C] ○ *a crusader for social justice*

crush PRESS /krʌʃ/ *v* [T] to press something very hard so that it is broken or its shape is destroyed ○ *The package got crushed in the mail.* ○ *Her car was crushed by a falling tree.*
crush /krʌʃ/ *n* [U] a crowd of people ○ *I can't stand the crush of holiday shoppers at the mall.*

SHOCK /krʌʃ/ *v* [T] to upset or shock someone badly ○ *I was crushed because I didn't complete the race.*

DESTROY /krʌʃ/ *v* [T] to defeat someone completely ○ *They'll stop at nothing to crush the opposition.*

ATTRACTION /krʌʃ/ *n* [C] *infml* a strong but temporary attraction for someone

crust BREAD /krʌst/ *n* [C/U] a hard, outer covering, esp. on a loaf of bread or a pastry
crusty /ˈkrʌs·ti/ *adj* ○ *fresh, crusty bread*

crust EARTH /krʌst/ *n* [C] the outer layer of the earth ➤ Picture: **earth**
crustal /ˈkrʌs·təl/ *adj* [not gradable] ○ *crustal displacement*

crustacean /krʌsˈteɪ·ʃən/ *n* [C] any of various types of animals that live in water and have a hard outer shell and many legs ○ *Crabs, lobsters, and shrimps are crustaceans.*

crusty /ˈkrʌs·ti/ *adj* unhappy and easily annoyed ○ *He's a crusty, old bachelor who lives alone.*

crutch /krʌtʃ/ *n* [C] a stick with a piece that fits under or around the arm which someone who is having difficulty walking leans on for support ○ *Marty was on crutches for six weeks when he broke his leg.*

crux /krʌks/ *n* [U] the most important problem, question, or part ○ *The crux of the matter is that most people just don't vote.*

cry PRODUCE TEARS /krɑɪ/ *v* [I/T] to produce tears as the result of a strong emotion, such as unhappiness or pain ○ [I] *I heard someone crying in the next room.*
cry /krɑɪ/ *n* [U] ○ *"Go on, have a good cry," he said.*

SHOUT /krɑɪ/ *v* [I/T] to call out or speak loudly ○ [T] *"Help me!" he cried.* ○ [I] *She cried out in pain as she fell.*
cry /krɑɪ/ *n* [C] **1** *They were wakened by cries of "Fire!"* **2** A cry is also the noise that a bird or animal makes: *the cries of an eagle*

USAGE

cry, scream, or shout?

When **cry** is used to mean "to call out loudly," it is usually only used with speech.

"Get me out of here!" she cried.

The most common words used to mean "to call out loudly" are **scream** or **shout**. **Scream** is usually something you do when you are frightened or being attacked and is often just sounds not words.

As he grabbed her arm, she screamed and tried to get away.

~~*As he grabbed her arm, she cried and tried to get away.*~~

Shout is a more general word for "to call out loudly."

Alex shouted something to me across the street.

~~*Alex cried something to me across the street.*~~

WORD FAMILY cry

Nouns	cry outcry	*Adjectives*	crying
		Verbs	cry

IDIOMS with cry

• **cry over spilled milk** to express regret about something that has already happened or cannot be changed ○ *Yes, we made a mistake, but there's no point in crying over spilled milk.*

• **cry wolf** to ask for help when you do not need it, which may prevent people from helping you when you do need it ○ *The administration has cried wolf so many times, it's difficult to know if there's a problem or not.*

crybaby /ˈkrɑɪˌbeɪ·bi/ *n* [C] *infml, disapproving* someone who cries or complains a lot without good reason

crying /ˈkrɑɪ·ɪŋ/ *adj* [not gradable] very serious and needing urgent attention ○ *There's a crying need for better schools.*

IDIOM with crying

• **a crying shame** a great misfortune ○ *It's a crying shame that new mothers have to go back to work after six weeks.*

crypt /krɪpt/ *n* [C] a room or rooms under the floor of a church where people are sometimes buried

cryptic /ˈkrɪp·tɪk/ *adj* mysterious and difficult to understand ○ *a cryptic message/remark*

crystal **ROCK** /ˈkrɪs·tᵊl/ *n* [C/U] transparent rock that looks like ice, or a piece of it

GLASS /ˈkrɪs·tᵊl/ *n* [C/U] **1** transparent glass of high quality, usually with its surface cut into patterns that reflect light **2** A crystal is a transparent glass or plastic cover for a watch or clock.

REGULAR SHAPE /ˈkrɪs·tᵊl/ *n* [C] ***science*** the solid state of many simple substances, which have a regular shape and surfaces arranged in similar patterns

crystallize /ˈkrɪs·tᵊlˌɑɪz/ *v* [I/T] (of a substance) to turn into a crystal or crystals

crystallization /ˌkrɪs·tᵊl·əˈzeɪ·ʃən, -ˌɑɪˈzeɪ·ʃən/ *n* [U]

crystal ball *n* [C] (in stories) a transparent ball of CRYSTAL or glass that produces images of future events by magic

crystal clear *adj* [not gradable] very clear or very obvious ○ *The townspeople have made it crystal clear that they don't want the new highway built.*

crystalline /ˈkrɪs·tə·lən, -ˌlɑɪn, -ˌliːn/ *adj* [not gradable] ***science*** having the regular structure of a CRYSTAL

C-section /ˈsiːˌsek·ʃən/ *n* [C] *medical, abbreviation for* CESAREAN (SECTION)

cub /kʌb/ *n* [C] the young of particular wild animals, such as bears and lions

cubbyhole /ˈkʌb·iːˌhoʊl/ *n* [C] a very small room or space

cube **SHAPE** /kjuːb/ *n* [C] ***geometry*** a solid object with six square sides of equal size ➤ Picture: **solid**

NUMBER /kjuːb/ *n* [C] ***mathematics*** the number made by multiplying a number twice by itself ○ *The cube of 2 (= 2 x 2 x 2) is 8.*

cubic /ˈkjuː·bɪk/ *adj* [not gradable] ***mathematics*** used in units of volume to show when the length of something has been multiplied by its width and height ○ *A cubic centimeter is a centimeter high, a centimeter long, and a centimeter wide.*

cubic centimeter, *abbreviation* **cc** *n* [C] a measurement equal to the volume of a CUBE (= solid object with six equal sides) measuring one centimeter on each edge

cubicle /ˈkjuː·bɪ·kəl/ *n* [C] a small room, often only large enough for one person, within a larger room or area ○ *a work cubicle*

Cub Scouts *pl n* an organization modeled after the BOY SCOUTS but for younger boys 7 to 10 years old

Cub Scout *n* [C]

cucumber /ˈkjuːˌkʌm·bər/, *short form* **cuke** *n* [C] a long, thin vegetable that has a dark green outer skin and is pale green inside ○ *Cucumbers are usually sliced and eaten raw in salads.*

cuddle /ˈkʌd·ᵊl/ *v* [I/T] **1** to put your arms around someone and hold him or her in a loving way, or of two people, to hold each other close for affection or comfort ○ [T] *She cuddled the baby in her arms.* **2** To cuddle up is to sit or lie close to someone or something: [I] *I like to cuddle up in front of the fireplace with a good book.*

cuddle /ˈkʌd·ᵊl/ *n* [C] ○ *I need a cuddle.*

cuddly /ˈkʌd·ᵊl·i/ *adj* of the kind that you want to put your arms around ○ *a cuddly teddy bear*

cue **SIGNAL** /kjuː/ *n* [C] a signal for someone to do or say something, esp. in a play or movie ○ *She waited for her cue – the ring of the telephone – to come on stage.* ○ *Being passed over for promotion twice was his cue to start looking for another job.*

STICK /kjuː/ *n* [C] in the game of POOL, a long, round, wooden stick held at one end and used to hit a white ball and move it against another or other balls to roll them into holes around the edge of a table covered with cloth

IDIOM with cue

• **(right) on cue** as if planned to happen exactly at that moment ○ *We were just about to say "I do" when, right on cue, my little cousin started crying.*

cue ball *n* [C] the white ball that a player hits with the CUE in order to move other balls

cuff **MATERIAL** /kʌf/ *n* [C] (in a shirt) the thicker material at the end of a sleeve around the wrist, or (in a pair of pants) the turned-up part at the bottom of a leg

HIT /kʌf/ *v* [T] to hit someone with your hand ○ *The boys cuffed Zackie on the shoulder.*

FASTEN /kʌf/ *v* [T] *short form of* HANDCUFF

cuff link *n* [C] one of a pair of fasteners used instead of a button to hold together the CUFFS of the sleeve of a shirt

cuffs /kʌfs/ *pl n short form of* HANDCUFFS

cuisine /kwɪˈziːn, kwiː-/ *n* [U] a style of cooking ○ *Southern/Japanese/Mexican cuisine* ➤ Learner error: **kitchen or cuisine?** at KITCHEN

cuke /kjuːk/ *n* [C] *short form of a* CUCUMBER

cul-de-sac /ˈkʌl·dəˌsæk, ˈkʊl-/ *n* [C] a street that is closed at one end

culinary /ˈkʌl·əˌner·i, ˈkjuː·lə-/ *adj* [not gradable] connected with cooking, esp. as a developed skill or art ○ *a culinary school*

cull /kʌl/ *v* [T] **1** to collect parts or pieces of something to use for another purpose ○ *She went to strange lands to cull recipes for her book.* **2** If you cull animals or plants, you kill or remove them: *to cull growing herds before they run out of food* ○ *culling dead timber*

culminate /ˈkʌl·məˌneɪt/ *v* [I/T] to have as a result or be the final result of a process ○ [I] *Secret negotiations culminated in the historic peace accord.* ○ [T] *The discovery culminated many years of research.*
culmination /ˌkʌl·məˈneɪ·ʃən/ *n* [U]

culottes /ˈkuː·lɑts, ˈkjuː-/ *pl n* women's pants that end at the knee or just below, and that look like a skirt

culpable /ˈkʌl·pə·bəl/ *adj fml* deserving to be blamed or considered responsible for something bad ○ *The landowner could be proved culpable for starting the fire.*
culpability /ˌkʌl·pəˈbɪl·ət̬·i/ *n* [U]

culprit /ˈkʌl·prət/ *n* [C] **1** someone who has committed a crime or done something wrong **2** A culprit is also anything that causes harm or trouble: *The culprit was identified as a microorganism that contaminated mayonnaise.*

cult /kʌlt/ *n* [C] **1** a system of religious belief, esp. one not recognized as an established religion, or the people who worship according to such a system of belief **2** A cult is also something that is very popular with some people, or a particular set of beliefs or behavior: *a cult movie* ○ *the cult of celebrity*

cultivate GROW /ˈkʌl·təˌveɪt/ *v* [T] to prepare land and grow crops on it, or to grow a particular crop ○ *He cultivated soybeans on most of the land.*
cultivation /ˌkʌl·təˈveɪ·ʃən/ *n* [U] ○ *Simple changes in rice cultivation can reduce methane emissions.*

DEVELOP /ˈkʌl·təˌveɪt/ *v* [T] **1** to create a new condition by directed effort ○ *We're trying to help these kids cultivate an interest in science.* **2** To cultivate is also to try to become friendly with someone because that person may be able to help you: *to cultivate friendships*
cultivated /ˈkʌl·təˌveɪt̬·əd/ *adj* well educated ○ *a cultivated accent*

culture Ⓐ WAY OF LIFE /ˈkʌl·tʃər/ *n* [C/U] ***social studies*** the way of life of a particular people, esp. as shown in their ordinary behavior and habits, their attitudes toward each other, and their moral and religious beliefs ○ [U] *He studied the culture of the Sioux Indians.*
cultural Ⓐ /ˈkʌl·tʃə·rəl/ *adj* relating to the way of life of a country or a group of people ○ *The country has a rich cultural heritage.*
culturally Ⓐ /ˈkʌl·tʃə·rə·li/ *adv*

ARTS /ˈkʌl·tʃər/ *n* [U] the arts of describing, showing, or performing that represent the traditions or the way of life of a particular people or group; literature, art, music, dance, theater, etc.
cultural /ˈkʌl·tʃə·rəl/ *adj* ○ *the great cultural centers of Europe*
cultured /ˈkʌl·tʃərd/ *adj* educated in and familiar with literature, art, music, etc.

ARTIFICIAL GROWTH /ˈkʌl·tʃər/ *n* [C] ***biology*** the growing of a group of MICROORGANISMS (= very small organisms) or other cells in an artificial environment for scientific purposes, or a group of organisms so grown
culture /ˈkʌl·tʃər/ *v* [T] ***biology*** to grow cells, bacteria, or similar things for scientific purposes

WORD FAMILY culture			
Nouns	culture subculture	*Adjectives*	cultural cultured
Adverbs	culturally		

culture shock *n* [U] a feeling of confusion that results from suddenly experiencing a culture with customs that are not familiar to you

-cum- /kʊm, kʌm/ *prep* used to join two nouns, showing that a person or thing does two things or has two purposes; combined with ○ *She appointed the actor-cum-diplomat to the post.*

cumbersome /ˈkʌm·bər·səm/ *adj* difficult to do or manage and taking a lot of time and effort ○ *Critics say that the process for amending the Constitution is cumbersome, but others defend it.*

cumulative /ˈkjuː·mjə·lət̬·ɪv/ *adj* increasing as each new amount is added or as each new fact or condition is considered ○ *No single development is causing the company's financial trouble – it's the cumulative effect of years of weak leadership.*
cumulatively /ˈkjuː·mjə·lət̬·ɪv·li/ *adv*

cumulonimbus /ˌkjuː·mjəˌloʊˈnɪm·bəs/ *n* [U] ***earth science*** a large, tall type of cloud that is often dark and brings heavy rain

cuneiform /kjʊˈniː·əˌfɔːrm, ˈkjuː·niː·ə-/ *n* [C] ***social studies*** an ancient Mesopotamian and Persian form of writing in which thin wooden sticks with triangular ends are pressed into wet clay.

cunning /ˈkʌn·ɪŋ/ *adj* skillful in planning and ready to deceive people in order to get what you want ○ *a cunning scheme*
cunning /ˈkʌn·ɪŋ/ *n* [U] ○ *They made their way safely back through enemy territory by stealth and cunning.*

cup /kʌp/ *n* [C] **1** a small, round container, usually with a handle, used esp. for hot drinks such as coffee and tea ○ *Would you like a cup of coffee?* **2** A cup is also a unit of measure equal to half a PINT and often used in cooking: *a cup of flour*
cup /kʌp/ *v* [T] **-pp-** to press your hands together to form a ball-like shape with an opening at the top between your thumbs, or to hold something gently with a hand or between both hands ○ *He cupped his hands and dipped them in the water to get a drink.* ○ *She cupped her baby's face in her hands and kissed him.*
cupful /ˈkʌp·fʊl/ *n* [C] the amount held by a cup

cupboard /ˈkʌb·ərd/ *n* [C] a piece of furniture or a small part of a room with a door behind which there is space for storing things, usually on shelves ○ *kitchen cupboards*

cupcake /ˈkʌp·keɪk/ *n* [C] a small, round cake, usually for one person

cupid /ˈkjuː·pəd/ *n* [C] a statue or painting representing the Roman god of love, shown as a naked baby boy with wings

curable /ˈkjʊr·ə·bəl/ *adj* ○ See at CURE MAKE WELL

curator /ˈkyʊrˌeɪt̬·ər, kjʊˈreɪt̬-/ *n* [C] a person in charge of a department of a MUSEUM or other place where objects of art, science, or from the past are collected, or a person who organizes and arranges a showing of art or other objects of interest

curb EDGE /kɜrb/ *n* [C] a raised edge along the side of a street, often forming part of a path for people to walk on ○ *She stood on the curb and waited until the light turned green to cross the street.*

CONTROL /kɜrb/ *v* [T] to control the growth or expression of something ○ *You've got to learn to curb your temper.*

curbside /ˈkɜrb·sɑɪd/ *adj* [not gradable] at or nearer to the CURB ○ *A uniformed driver had the rear curbside door open for her.* ○ *curbside recycling*

curd /kɜrd/ *n* [U] the solid substance that is left when the liquid is removed from milk

curdle /ˈkɜrd·əl/ *v* [I] to change into CURD, or to become sour

cure MAKE WELL /kjʊr/ *v* [T] to make someone healthy again, or to cause an illness to go away ○ *She was cured of her migraine headaches when she changed her diet.* ○ (fig.) *He worked to promote programs to cure America's social and economic ills.*

cure /kjʊr/ *n* [C] the process of making a person healthy again, esp. by giving treatment, or a treatment that causes a disease to go away ○ *the effort to find a cure for cancer*

curable /ˈkjʊr·ə·bəl/ *adj* (of a disease) able to be treated in such a way that it will go away and the person who had it can become well again

PRESERVE /kjʊr/ *v* [T] to treat plant or animal products by drying, smoking, salting, etc., to preserve it from decay ○ *Sodium nitrite is used to cure meat.*

WORD FAMILY cure			
Nouns	cure	*Adjectives*	curable incurable
Verbs	cure		

cure-all *n* [C] something that cures any illness or solves any problem ○ *There's a danger in believing that the drug is a cure-all.*

curfew /ˈkɜr·fjuː/ *n* [C] a rule that some or all people must stay off the streets during particular hours, used esp. to maintain peace during a period of violence ○ *to impose/lift a curfew*

curio /ˈkjʊr·iːˌoʊ/ *n* [C] *pl* **curios** a small and unusual object considered to be of special interest or value ○ *a curio shop*

curiosity INTEREST /ˌkjʊr·iːˈɑs·ət̬·i/ *n* [U] an eager desire to know or learn about something ○ *Just out of curiosity I decided to go through the files.*

STRANGE OBJECT /ˌkjʊr·iːˈɑs·ət̬·i/ *n* [C] something that is interesting because it is rare and unusual ○ *The museum had a collection of mummies and Egyptian curiosities.*

curious INTERESTED /ˈkjʊr·iː·əs/ *adj* interested in learning about people or things around you ○ [+ *to* infinitive] *I'm curious to see what's going to happen on the political scene.*

UNUSUAL /ˈkjʊr·iː·əs/ *adj* unusual and therefore worth noticing ○ *A curious figure in a red cape and black boots darted into the building.*

curiously /ˈkjʊr·iː·ə·sli/ *adv* strangely ○ *Curiously enough, they never explained why they arrived an hour early.*

curl /kɜrl/ *n* [C/U] a piece of hair having a curving shape, like part of a circle, or something else having a circular shape ○ [C] *He loved that dark curl at the back of her neck.* ○ [C] *We watched the curls of smoke rise from his pipe.*

curl /kɜrl/ *v* [I/T] to form or cause something to form a curving or twisted shape ○ [T] *If I don't curl my hair, it looks too stringy.*

curler /ˈkɜr·lər/ *n* [C] one of a number of small tubes that are put in a person's hair to make it curl

curly /ˈkɜr·li/ *adj* ○ *curly hair*

curliness /ˈkɜr·liː·nəs/ *n* [U]

PHRASAL VERB with curl

• **curl up** to lie in a comfortable curved position ○ *The cat was curled up on the couch, sleeping happily.*

curling /ˈkɜr·lɪŋ/ *n* [U] a game played on ice esp. in Scotland and Canada, in which special flat, round stones are slid toward a mark

curler /ˈkɜr·lər/ *n* [C] ○ *On Thursday night the rink was taken over by the women curlers.*

currant /ˈkɜr·ənt, ˈkʌ·rənt/ *n* [C] **1** a sour BERRY (= small, round fruit) that grows on bushes, or the plant on which it grows ○ *red currant jelly* **2** A currant is also a small RAISIN (= dried fruit) used esp. in baking.

currency Ⓐ MONEY /ˈkɜr·ən·si, ˈkʌ·rən-/ *n* [C/U] the money in use in a particular country ○ [C] *The US dollar fell yesterday against most foreign currencies.*

ACCEPTANCE /ˈkɜr·ən·si, ˈkʌ·rən-/ *n* [U] *fml* the state of being commonly known or accepted, or of being used in many places ○ *The idea that computer use enhances students' motivation has gained currency in recent years.*

current HAPPENING NOW /ˈkɜr·ənt, ˈkʌ·rənt/ *adj* of the present time or most recent ○ *Under current state law, students can drop out of school legally at age 17.*

currently /ˈkɜr·ənt·li, ˈkʌ·rənt-/ *adv* [not gradable] at the present time; now ○ *He currently is directing TV sitcoms.* ➤ Usage: **actual or current?** at ACTUAL

MOVEMENT /ˈkɜr·ənt, ˈkʌ·rənt/ *n* [C] **1** a movement of water or air ○ *The boat drifted with the current until it was miles from shore.* **2** ***physics*** Electric current is the passage of electricity through a wire.

curriculum /kə'rɪk·jə·ləm/ *n* [C] *pl* **curricula, curriculums** all the courses given in a school, college, etc., or a particular course of study in one subject

C

curry /'kɜr·i, 'kʌ·ri/ *n* [C/U] a dish, originally from India, consisting usually of meat or vegetables cooked in a spicy sauce ○ [U] *Lamb curry is this restaurant's specialty.*

curse SWEAR /kɜrs/ *v* [I/T] to say rude or offensive words about something or someone because you are angry ○ [I] *I cursed at the behavior of these people.*
curse /kɜrs/ *n* [C] ○ *Shouts and curses could be heard down the hall.*
WISH EVIL /kɜrs/ *v* [T] to wish for something evil or unpleasant to happen to someone or something, as by asking a magical power
curse /kɜrs/ *n* [C] ○ *In the story, a curse was put on the prince, turning him into a frog.*

cursor /'kɜr·sər/ *n* [C] a movable symbol on a computer screen that shows the point where you can change a text or image ○ *You can move the cursor by using the mouse.*

cursory /'kɜr·sə·ri/ *adj* done quickly with little attention to detail ○ *He gave the picture a cursory glance.*

curt /kɜrt/ *adj* (of a person's manner or speech) rude as a result of being very quick or brief ○ *He sent a curt, one-sentence letter of resignation to the mayor.*
curtly /'kɜrt·li/ *adv* ○ *She nodded to him curtly and kept talking to someone else.*

curtail /kər'teɪl/ *v* [T] to reduce or limit something, or to stop something before it is finished ○ *He had to curtail his speech when time ran out.*
curtailment /kər'teɪl·mənt/ *n* [U]

curtain /'kɜrt·ᵊn/ *n* [C] **1** a piece of cloth or other material that hangs across a window or space to decorate a room or to make it dark or private ○ *In the restaurant, arches covered with beaded curtains divide the room.* **2** In a theater, the curtain is a large, movable sheet of heavy material that separates the stage from the area where people are sitting. **3** The curtain is also the time at which a performance begins: *The curtain is at 8 o'clock.*

curtain rod *n* [C] a pole from which a curtain hangs

curvaceous /kər'veɪ·ʃəs/ *adj* having noticeable curves

curvature /'kɜr·və·tʃər, -ˌtʃʊr/ *n* [U] the state of being curved or bent, or the way in which something curves ○ *the curvature of the earth*

curve /kɜrv/ *v* [I/T] to form or move in the direction of a line that turns continuously and has no straight parts, or to cause something to do this ○ [I] *The road curves around the cemetery.*
curve /kɜrv/ *n* [C] ○ *a curve in a road*
curvy /'kɜr·vi/ *adj* having a shape with a lot of curves ○ *a curvy road*

curvilinear /ˌkɜr·və'lɪn·iː·ər/ *adj* ***art*** containing or consisting of curved lines

cushion /'kʊʃ·ən/ *n* [C] a large, usually square bag filled with soft material, used as a movable part of a chair or SOFA, for sitting on or resting your back against, or a similar but smaller bag used to make yourself more comfortable while sitting ○ *She sank back against the sofa cushions.*
cushion /'kʊʃ·ən/ *v* [T] ○ *The soft grass cushioned his fall* (= made it hurt less).

cushy /'kʊʃ·i/ *adj infml* very easy ○ *a cushy job*

cuss /kʌs/ *v* [I] *infml* to CURSE SWEAR

custard /'kʌs·tərd/ *n* [U] a soft, usually sweet food made from a mixture of eggs, milk, flavoring, and sugar

custodian /kʌs'toʊd·iː·ən/ *n* [C] a person or organization that has responsibility for protecting, caring for, or maintaining something or someone ○ *The library is a traditional custodian of information.* ○ *The school's crisis team includes teachers, custodians, and the principal.*
custodial /kʌs'toʊd·iː·əl/ *adj* [not gradable] ○ *custodial care* ○ *a custodial staff*

custody CARE /'kʌs·təd·i/ *n* [U] the right or duty to care for someone or something, as for a child whose parents have separated or died ○ *The court awarded custody of the child to the mother.*
KEPT BY POLICE /'kʌs·təd·i/ *n* [U] the state of being kept by the police, usually while waiting to go to court for trial ○ *The police have taken the suspect into custody.*

custom TRADITION /'kʌs·təm/ *n* [C/U] a way of behaving or a belief that has been established for a long time among a group of people ○ [C] *It was a time-honored custom of the club that blue chairs were reserved for senior members only.* ○ [C] *She's studying the language and customs of the Hopi Indians.*
customary /'kʌs·təˌmer·i/ *adj* ○ *We thought tipping wasn't customary in Japan.*
USUAL ACTIVITY /'kʌs·təm/ *n* [C] something you usually do ○ *He left the house at nine exactly, as was his custom.*
customary /'kʌs·təˌmer·i/ *adj* usual ○ *She's not her customary cheerful self today.* ○ *The students sat in their customary classroom seats.*
customarily /ˌkʌs·tə'mer·ə·li/ *adv* [not gradable] usually ○ *People who receive gifts do not customarily ask what they cost.*
MADE ONCE /'kʌs·təm/ *adj* [not gradable] made for a particular person to buy ○ *custom drapes/woodworking*
customize /'kʌs·təˌmɑɪz/ *v* [T] ○ *We will customize existing software to meet our clients' needs.*

WORD FAMILY custom

Nouns	custom customer customs	*Adjectives*	customary custom-made accustomed
Verbs	accustom customize	*Adverbs*	customarily

customer /ˈkʌs·tə·mər/ *n* [C] a person who buys goods or a service ○ *We try to give all our customers good service.*

custom-made *adj* [not gradable] made for one particular person or purpose

customs /ˈkʌs·təmz/ *pl n* money paid to the government when you take particular goods from one country to another
customs /ˈkʌs·təmz/ *n* [U] the place at a port, airport, or border where travelers' bags are examined for illegal or taxable goods ○ *customs officials* ○ *It took us ages to get through customs when we got back from Italy.*

cut DIVIDE /kʌt/ *v* [I/T] *pres. part.* **cutting**, *past* **cut** **1** to use a sharp tool such as a knife to break the surface of something, or to divide or make something smaller ○ [T] *Cut the apple in half.* ○ [T] *She wanted to have her hair cut* (= made shorter). ○ [M] *We had to cut two trees down* (= remove them) *to make room for the swimming pool.* ○ [M] *The children cut the pictures out* (= removed them by cutting) *and stuck them in their scrapbooks.* **2** A person who is cut is injured by something sharp that breaks the skin and causes bleeding: [T] *I stepped on a piece of glass and cut my foot.*
cut /kʌt/ *n* [C] **1** something made by cutting ○ *She went to the butcher's to get a good cut of meat.* **2** A cut is an injury to the skin made by a sharp object: *She had a nasty cut on her hand.* **3** A cut is also the particular way clothing looks: *the cut of a suit* **4** *infml* A cut is also a share: *I was part-owner of the business, and when my sister sold it, I said I wanted my cut.*
cut /kʌt/ *adj* [not gradable] ○ *These cut flowers will last three days in fresh water.*
cutting /ˈkʌt̬·ɪŋ/ *n* [C] a piece cut from a plant and used to grow a new plant ○ See also: CUTTING

WORD CHOICES cut

The verb **chop** means "to cut something into pieces."
*He was **chopping** vegetables to make a stew.*
When you cut something into thin, flat pieces, you can use the word **slice**.
***Slice** the mushrooms and fry them in butter.*
The verb **snip** means "to cut something with scissors, usually with small quick cuts."
*She **snipped** the corner off the soup packet.*
If you make a long straight cut in something, the verb **slit** could be used.
*He **slit** open the envelope with a knife.*
If someone cuts stone or wood, the verb **carve** is often used.
*He **carved** her name on a tree.*
Carve can also be used when someone cuts slices off a large piece of meat.
*Would you like me to **carve** the chicken?*
If you cut a small amount of something in order to make it neater, you could use the verb **trim**.
*I'm going to get my hair **trimmed**.*
The verbs **slash** or **hack** can be used when someone cuts something in a rough or violent way,
*The museum was broken into and several paintings were **slashed**.*
*He **hacked** the wood with an axe.*

REDUCE /kʌt/ *v* [T] *pres. part.* **cutting**, *past* **cut** to make less in size, amount, length, etc. ○ *We've got to cut costs.* ○ *The original movie was almost four hours long, but it was later cut to two hours.*
cut /kʌt/ *n* [C] ○ *Many workers had to take a cut in pay.* ○ *For the TV version, they made several cuts in the movie.*

MISS /kʌt/ *v* [T] *pres. part.* **cutting**, *past* **cut** to stay away from a class, talk, performance, etc., you have a duty to go to ○ *He was cutting classes and getting failing grades.*

STOP /kʌt/ *v* [I/T] *pres. part.* **cutting**, *past* **cut** to stop or interrupt something, or to stop working suddenly or cause this to happen ○ [I always + adv/prep] *Since his illness he's cut out eating sweets altogether.* ○ [T] *Because of failing grades, he was cut* (= released) *from the team.* ○ [I] *"Cut!* (= Stop filming!)*" shouted the director.*

GROW TEETH /kʌt/ *v* [T] *pres. part.* **cutting**, *past* **cut** to grow a new tooth ○ *The baby was cranky last night because she's cutting a tooth.*

CROSS /kʌt/ *v* [I always + adv/prep] *pres. part.* **cutting**, *past* **cut** to go through or across a place, esp. in order to get somewhere quickly ○ *To get to school I cut through the field.*

CARDS /kʌt/ *v* [I/T] *pres. part.* **cutting**, *past* **cut** to divide a pile of cards into two parts ○ [I/T] *Who's going to cut (the cards)?*

RECORD /kʌt/ *v* [T] *pres. part.* **cutting**, *past* **cut** to make a recording of music or speech on a record ○ *When did Elvis cut his first record?*

WORD FAMILY cut

Nouns	cut cutting	*Verbs*	cut undercut
Adjectives	cut cutting		

IDIOMS with cut

• **cut both ways** to have both advantages and disadvantages ○ *The promotion cuts both ways because though I'll make more money, I'll have to be away from my family more often.*
• **cut corners** to do something in the easiest, cheapest, or fastest way ○ *I don't like to cut corners when I have company for dinner.*
• **Cut it out!** *infml* stop doing that ○ *Cut it out, you two – I'm tired of listening to you argue!*
• **cut off** *your* **nose to spite** *your* **face** to cause problems for yourself by trying to punish someone else ○ *If you stay home because your ex-boyfriend is at the party, aren't you cutting off your nose to spite your face?*
• **cut** *someone* **some slack** *infml* to give someone additional freedom ○ *Because it was the last day of class, the teachers cut us some slack.*
• **not cut it**, **not cut the mustard** to not be able to deal with problems or difficulties satisfactorily ○ *We were playing against a more experienced team, and we just couldn't cut it.*

C

PHRASAL VERBS with cut

• **cut across** *something* to include several things that usually are separated from each other ○ *Iron deficiency in women cuts across all socioeconomic levels.*
• **cut back** *(something)* [M] to reduce or stop ○ *He was advised to cut back on sugary sodas.* ○ *Cancel the service, or cut it back to "basic."* ○ Related noun: CUTBACK
• **cut down** *(something)* [M] to reduce something in amount, size, or number of times repeated ○ *I've decided to cut down on snacks.* ○ *Seat belts have cut down the number of injuries in car accidents.*
• **cut in** **INTERRUPT** to interrupt someone who is talking ○ *I was talking to Jeff when Amy cut in.*
• **cut** *someone* **in** **INCLUDE** to include someone in a plan, activity, or process ○ *Next time you get free concert tickets, cut me in.*
• **cut off** *something/someone* **STOP** [M] to stop or interrupt something suddenly, or to stop someone from speaking ○ *We were cut off in the middle of our phone conversation.* ○ Related noun: CUTOFF LIMIT
• **cut off** *someone/something* **DRIVE** [M] (of a driver or vehicle) to move suddenly in front of another driver or vehicle, leaving too little space ○ *He claimed that a truck had cut him off just before the accident.*
• **cut** *someone* **out** [M] to keep someone from taking part in a plan, activity, or process ○ *Some critics say the proposed amendment is effectively cutting others out of the planning process.* • **cut out for** *something* to be the right type of person for a particular job or activity ○ *He's just not cut out for politics.*
• **cut** *something* **short** [M] to stop something suddenly before it is completed ○ *We cut short our vacation when we learned of my mother's illness.*
• **cut through** *something* to understand something that is not easy to understand ○ *She can cut through the confusing statistics and get at the important facts.*

cut-and-dried, **cut-and-dry** *adj* clear and simple and removing any further uncertainty or difficulty ○ *Unfortunately, there is no cut-and-dried answer to the problem of immigration.*

cutback /ˈkʌt·bæk/ *n* [C] a reduction, esp. one made to save money ○ *Cutbacks in public spending are expected in the next budget.* ○ Related verb: CUT BACK

cute **CHARMING** /kjuːt/ *adj* [*-er/-est* only] **1** (esp. of something or someone small or young) charming and attractive ○ *She was a really cute baby.* **2** Something described as cute is attractive and pleasant: *She had a cute apartment with a little garden.*

DECEIVING /kjuːt/ *adj* [*-er/-est* only] *disapproving* too carefully designed to get approval or appear attractive, and therefore seeming dishonest ○ [+ *to* infinitive] *He thinks it's cute to misbehave, but it's not.*

cutesy /ˈkjuːt·si/ *adj* [*-er/-est* only] *disapproving* artificially attractive and charming, esp. in a way suitable for a child ○ *The house is full of cutesy pictures of kittens.*

cuticle /ˈkjuːt̬·ɪ·kəl/ *n* [C] **1** the thin skin at the base of the nails on the fingers and toes **2** ***biology*** Cuticle is also the outer layer of a plant, which protects it.

cutlery /ˈkʌt·lə·ri/ *n* [U] knives, forks, and spoons used for eating food; SILVERWARE

cutlet /ˈkʌt·lət/ *n* [C] a small slice of meat, esp. from the RIBS, that is usually fried ○ *veal cutlets*

cutoff **LIMIT** /ˈkʌt̬·ɔːf/ *n* [C] a fixed point or limit at which something is stopped ○ *The cutoff for blood donations is usually age 65.* ○ Related verb: CUT OFF STOP

ROAD /ˈkʌt̬·ɔːf/ *n* [C] a road that leaves another and provides a shorter route ○ *We took the cutoff and saved 20 minutes on the trip home.*

cutoffs /ˈkʌt̬·ɔːfs/, **cutoff jeans** /ˌkʌt̬ˌɔːfˈdʒiːnz/ *pl n* a pair of JEANS with the legs removed at or above the knee

cutout /ˈkʌt̬·ɑʊt/ *n* [C] a shape cut out, or to be cut out, from something ○ *This children's book has animal cutouts.*

cut-rate /ˌkʌtˌreɪt/ *adj* [not gradable] available at a lower price than usual ○ *cut-rate merchandise*

cutthroat /ˈkʌt·θroʊt/ *adj* showing no care or consideration for the harm done to others with whom you are in competition ○ *He was unhappy working in the cutthroat world of advertising.*

cutting /ˈkʌt̬·ɪŋ/ *adj* said or done to hurt someone's feelings ○ *She made a cutting remark about his table manners.* ○ See also: CUTTING at CUT DIVIDE

cutting edge *n* [U] the most recent stage in the development of something ○ *His research is at the cutting edge of new therapies for cancer.*

CV /siː ˈviː/ *n* [C] a written description of your education, achievements, and previous employment, used esp. to show someone who may employ you in a new job, or to qualify for an honor

cyanide /ˈsɑɪ·əˌnɑɪd/ *n* [U] an extremely powerful poison

cyber- /ˈsɑɪ·bər/ *prefix* computer ○ *cybercrime*

cyberspace /ˈsɑɪ·bərˌspeɪs/ *n* [U] an electronic system that allows computer users around the world to communicate with each other or to access information for any purpose ○ *A group of knitters has banded together in cyberspace to offer free patterns.*

cycle Ⓐ **SERIES** /ˈsɑɪ·kəl/ *n* [C] a complete set of events that repeat themselves regularly in the same order, or a regularly repeated period of time ○ *Some economists predict the business cycle will turn downward.*

cyclical Ⓐ /ˈsɑɪ·klɪ·kəl, ˈsɪk·lə-/, **cyclic** /ˈsɑɪ·klɪk, ˈsɪk·lɪk/ *adj* ○ *Changes in the economy often follow a cyclical pattern.*

BICYCLE /ˈsɑɪ·kəl/ *n* [C] *short form of* BICYCLE

cycle Ⓐ /ˈsɑɪ·kəl/ *v* [I] ○ *We cycled around campus in the afternoon.*

cyclist /ˈsɑɪ·kləst/ *n* [C] a person who rides a bicycle ○ *There's a special lane for cyclists.*

cyclone /ˈsɑɪ·kloʊn/ *n* [C] a violent and often destructive storm in which the wind moves very fast in a circular direction

cylinder SHAPE /ˈsɪl·ən·dər/ *n* [C] ***geometry*** a solid that has long straight sides and circular ends of equal size, or a hollow object shaped like this and often used as a container ○ *Inside a roll of paper towels there's a cardboard cylinder.* ➤ Picture: **solid**

cylindrical /səˈlɪn·drɪ·kəl/ *adj* ***geometry*** ○ *cylindrical structures*

ENGINE PART /ˈsɪl·ən·dər/ *n* [C] the tube-shaped part of an engine inside of which the PISTON (= part that causes the fuel to produce power) moves up and down ○ *The engine isn't firing on all its cylinders.*

cymbal /ˈsɪm·bəl/ *n* [C usually pl] a flat, round musical instrument made of BRASS (= metal) that is hit with a stick or struck against another such instrument to make a loud noise

cynical /ˈsɪn·ɪ·kəl/ *adj* not trusting or respecting the goodness of other people and their actions, but believing that people are interested only in themselves ○ *Listening to politicians for too long can make you cynical.* ○ *She's become cynical about men.*

cynic /ˈsɪn·ɪk/ *n* [C] a person who believes that other people are interested only in themselves and therefore doubts that they can be good

cynicism /ˈsɪn·əˌsɪz·əm/ *n* [U] ○ *He's often been accused of cynicism, but he says he's just realistic.*

cyst /sɪst/ *n* [C] a round growth under the skin or deeper in the body, containing liquid or tissue

cyton /ˈsɑɪˌtɑn/ *n* [C] ***biology*** the central part of a NEURON (= cell that sends and receives messages within the brain and nerves)

cytoplasm /ˈsɑɪt̬·əˌplæz·əm/ *n* [U] ***biology*** the substance inside a cell which surrounds the cell's NUCLEUS (= central part) ➤ Picture: **cell**

czar /zɑr, tsɑr/ *n* [C] **1** ***world history*** (before 1917) the Russian ruler **2** *infml* A czar is also a person who has a lot of power in a particular activity: *The nation's anti-corruption czar says much of the cash has disappeared.*

D d

D

D LETTER, **d** /diː/ *n* [C] *pl* **D's, Ds, d's, ds** the fourth letter of the English alphabet

MUSICAL NOTE /diː/ *n* [C/U] *pl* **D's, Ds** *music* in Western music, the second note in the SCALE (= series of notes) that begins on the note C, or a set of notes based on this note

MARK /diː/ *n* [C] *pl* **D's, Ds** a mark given for an exam, a course, or a piece of work which shows that your work is thought of as below average and that it needs improvement ○ *I can't believe I got a D in history last semester.*

NUMBER, **d** /diː, fɑɪv ˈhʌn·drəd/ *number* the ROMAN NUMERAL for the number 500

D.A. *n* [C] *abbreviation for* DISTRICT ATTORNEY

dab /dæb/ *v* [I/T] **-bb- 1** to touch something lightly and quickly, usually repeatedly ○ [I] *He dabbed at his eyes with a tissue.* **2** If you dab something on a surface, you put a small amount of something on it: [T] *She dabbed a little perfume on her wrists.*

dab /dæb/ *n* [C] a small amount of a substance ○ *a dab of lipstick*

dabble /ˈdæb·əl/ *v* [I] to take a slight and not very serious interest in a subject or try a particular activity for a short period ○ *I don't paint much, I just dabble.*

dachshund /ˈdɑks·hʊnt, -hʊnd; ˈdɑk·sənd/ *n* [C] a type of dog that is small and has a long body and short legs

dad /dæd/ *n* [C] *infml* a father ○ *Can you give me $20, Dad?* ○ *My dad's a fireman.*

daddy /ˈdæd·i/ *n* [C] *a child's word* a father ○ *Why don't you have any hair on your head, Daddy?* ○ *Mommy and Daddy are taking me to the circus.*

daddy longlegs /ˌdæd·iːˈlɔːŋˌlegz/ *n* [C] *pl* **daddy longlegs** *infml* a small creature with eight legs that looks like a SPIDER

daffodil /ˈdæf·əˌdɪl/ *n* [C] a yellow, bell-shaped flower with a long stem, commonly seen in the spring

dagger /ˈdæg·ər/ *n* [C] a short, pointed knife that is sharp on both sides, used esp. in the past as a weapon

daily /ˈdeɪ·li/ *adj, adv* [not gradable] happening on or relating to every day, or every working day ○ *Take the pills twice daily.* ○ *Exercise is part of my daily routine.*

daily /ˈdeɪ·li/ *n* [C] a newspaper published every day of the week or every day except the weekend

dainty /ˈdeɪnt·i/ *adj* small and attractive in a delicate way ○ *a dainty wrist/hand* ○ *dainty flowers*

dairy /ˈder·i, dær·i/ *n* [C/U] a place on a farm where milk and cream are kept and cheese and butter are made, a company that supplies milk and products made from milk, or milk and products made from milk ○ [U] *She eats no meat and very little dairy.* ○ [U] *I'll only buy nonfat dairy products.*

daisy /ˈdeɪ·zi/ *n* [C] a type of flower with a round, yellow center and a lot of thin, white petals

dally /ˈdæl·i/ *v* [I] to waste time or do something slowly ○ *She dallied over her morning coffee.*

dam /dæm/ *n* [C] a wall built across a river to stop the flow and collect the water, esp. to make a RESERVOIR (= an artificial lake) that provides water for an area or can be used to make electricity

dam /dæm/ *v* [T] **-mm-** to build a dam across a river in order to store the water ○ [M] *Fish are affected when a river is dammed up.*

damage /ˈdæm·ɪdʒ/ *v* [T] to harm or spoil something ○ *Many buildings were badly damaged by the earthquake.* ○ *News reports damaged the senator's reputation.*

damage /ˈdæm·ɪdʒ/ *n* [U] ○ *The fire did serious damage to the buildings.* ○ *He suffered brain damage in the accident.*

WORD FAMILY damage			
Nouns	damage damages	*Verbs*	damage

damage control *n* [C] the process of limiting the damaging effects of an action or mistake ○ *You can't live on junk food and then attempt dietary damage control with handfuls of vitamins.*

damages /ˈdæm·ɪ·dʒɪz/ *pl n law* money that is paid to someone by a person or organization who was responsible for causing some injury or loss ○ *They were awarded $500,000 in damages.*

dame /deɪm/ *n* [C] *dated, slang* a woman ○ *a fast-talking dame*

damn EXPRESSION /dæm/, **damn it** /ˈdæm·ət, -ɪt/, **dammit** /ˈdæm·ət, -ɪt/ *exclamation infml* an expression of anger or annoyance ○ *Damn! I spilled coffee on my blouse.* ○ **USAGE:** This word may be considered offensive by some people.

damn /dæm/ *n* [U] *infml* the least amount ○ *This old car isn't worth a damn.*

damn /dæm/, **damned** /dæmd/ *adj* [not gradable] *infml* ○ *a damn shame*

SURPRISE /dæm/ *exclamation infml* used to express surprise ○ *Damn, I guess they decided to buy that house.*

damnedest /ˈdæm·dəst/ *adj* [not gradable] *infml* ○ *Well, that's the damnedest thing I ever heard!*

VERY /dæm/ *adj, adv* [not gradable] *infml* very; great ○ *You're a damn fool to try and drive that old car cross-country.*

damnedest /ˈdæm·dəst/ *n infml*

BLAME /dæm/ *v* [T] to blame or strongly criticize ○ *The novel was damned by the critics for being too political.*

damning /ˈdæm·ɪŋ/ *adj* very critical, or showing clearly that someone is wrong or guilty ○ *a damning report/finding*

PUNISH /dæm/ *v* [T] to force someone to stay in hell and be punished forever
damned /dæmd/ *pl n* the people who have been sent to hell after their deaths

IDIOMS with damn

• **damned if** *you* **do and damned if** *you* **don't** criticized whatever you decide to do ○ *Well, this is one of these things where you're damned if you do and damned if you don't.*
• **do** *your* **damnedest, try** *your* **damnedest** to try very hard ○ *We're going to do our damnedest to get the agency to respond.*

damp /dæmp/ *adj* [-er/-est only] slightly wet, esp. in a way that is not pleasant or comfortable ○ *damp socks* ○ *a cold, damp day*
dampen /ˈdæm·pən/ *v* [T] **1** *Rain dampened the tent, but it dried in the sun.* **2** If something dampens feelings, esp. of excitement or enjoyment, it makes them less strong: *I think the accident dampened his enthusiasm for baseball.*
dampness /ˈdæmp·nəs/ *n* [U] ○ *The dampness bothers my arthritis.*

damsel /ˈdæm·zəl/ *n* [C] *dated* ***literature*** a young woman who is not married ○ *The heroine in this movie isn't like some damsel in distress* (= woman needing a man's help) *waiting to be saved.*

dance /dæns/ *v* [I/T] **1** to move the body and feet in rhythm to music ○ [I] *Who was she dancing with at the party?* ○ [T] *They danced a waltz.* **2** If something dances, it moves quickly and easily: [I] *Sunlight danced on the water.*
dance /dæns/ *n* [C/U] **1** an act of dancing, or a particular set of movements ○ [C] *"May I have this dance?" he asked.* ○ [C] *The next dance will be a waltz.* ○ [U] *Do you take dance lessons?* **2** A dance is also a social occasion at which people dance: [C] *the eighth-grade dance*
dancer /ˈdæn·sər/ *n* [C] ○ *He's a dancer with the New York City Ballet.*

dandelion /ˈdæn·dəlˌɑɪ·ən/ *n* [C] a small, bright yellow flower that grows wild and makes light, white seeds that are easily blown

dandruff /ˈdæn·drəf/ *n* [U] small, white bits of dead skin that sometimes gather in the hair or fall on the clothes, esp. on the shoulders

dandy /ˈdæn·di/ *adj infml* very good ○ *I'm doing just dandy, thanks.*

danger /ˈdeɪn·dʒər/ *n* [C/U] **1** the possibility of harm or death, or of something unpleasant happening ○ [C] *I quickly understood the dangers of rock climbing.* ○ [U] *I felt my life was in danger.* ○ [U] *They're in danger of losing the playoffs.* **2** A danger is also a harmful influence: [C] *the dangers of air pollution*
dangerous /ˈdeɪn·dʒə·rəs/ *adj* ○ *dangerous chemicals/bacteria* ○ *Whooping cough is most dangerous for infants.*
dangerously /ˈdeɪn·dʒə·rə·sli/ *adv* ○ *dangerously high winds*

WORD FAMILY danger

Nouns	danger	*Verbs*	endanger
Adjectives	endangered dangerous	*Adverbs*	dangerously

WORD CHOICES dangerous

If something is extremely dangerous, you can use the adjectives **hazardous, perilous** or **treacherous.**

Ice had made the roads ***treacherous.***

Heavy rain is causing ***hazardous*** *driving conditions.*

A ***perilous*** *journey through the mountains was their only escape route.*

Substances which are dangerous are often described as **harmful** or **hazardous.**

Please be aware that these chemicals are ***harmful/hazardous*** *to human health.*

If something is so dangerous that it is likely to kill someone, you can describe it as **lethal.**

These medications can be ***lethal*** *if they get into the wrong hands.*

If something is dangerous because something bad might happen, you can say that it is **risky.**

Surgery at his age would be too ***risky.***

dangle /ˈdæŋ·gəl/ *v* [I/T] to hang loosely, or to cause something to hang ○ [I] *A loose wire was dangling from the wall.* ○ [T] *He dangled the puppet in front her.*

Danish (pastry) /ˈdeɪ·nɪʃ (ˈpeɪ·stri)/ *n* [C/U] a type of sweet pastry for one person, often filled with fruit or cheese

dank /dæŋk/ *adj* [-er/-est only] (esp. of buildings and air) wet, cold, and unpleasant ○ *For years they lived in a dank, dark basement apartment.*

dapper /ˈdæp·ər/ *adj* (of a man) looking stylish and neat

dare BE BRAVE /der, dær/ *v* **dares, dare** to be brave enough to do something difficult or dangerous or that you should not do ○ [T] *She wouldn't dare go out alone there at night.* ○ [I] *He wanted to touch it, but he didn't dare.* ○ [+ to infinitive] *I can't believe you dare to talk to me this way!*
daring /ˈder·ɪŋ, ˈdær-/ *adj* showing bravery and willingness to risk danger or criticism ○ *a daring, experimental performance* ○ *Specially trained troops carried out a daring rescue operation.*

ASK /der, dær/ *v* [T] to ask someone to do something that involves risk ○ *I dare you to ask him to dance.*
dare /der, dær/ *n* [C] ○ *He jumped into the river on a dare.*

WORD FAMILY dare

Nouns	dare daredevil	*Adjectives* *Verbs*	daring dare

daredevil /ˈderˌdev·əl, ˈdær-/ *n* [C] a person who does dangerous things and takes risks

dark WITHOUT LIGHT /dɑrk/ *adj* [-er/-est only] **1** with little or no light, or having little brightness ○ *It was too dark to see much of anything.* ○ *What time does it get dark in the summer?* **2** Dark colors have less white in them: *a dark blue dress* ○ *dark hair/eyes*

D

dark /dɑrk/ *n* [U] the absence of light ○ *Does eating carrots really help you to see in the dark?* ○ *She arrived home well before/after dark* (= before/after the sun had gone down).

darken /ˈdɑr·kən/ *v* [I/T] ○ [I] *The sky darkened as thick smoke billowed from the refinery.* ○ [T] *She pulled down the shades to darken the room.*

darkness /ˈdɑrk·nəs/ *n* [U] ○ *The city was plunged into darkness by the power blackout.*

SAD /dɑrk/ *adj* [-er/-est only] unhappy or sad; GLOOMY ○ *The report contains dark predictions about the future.*

EVIL /dɑrk/ *adj* [-er/-est only] evil or threatening ○ *He gave me a dark look when I criticized his work.*

WORD FAMILY **dark**			
Nouns	dark darkness	Adjectives Verbs	dark darken

IDIOM with **dark**

• **in the dark** not informed about things that might be useful to know ○ *Our boss tends to keep us in the dark most of the time.* ○ *"Do you know anything?" "No, I'm completely in the dark, like everyone else."*

dark glasses *pl n* SUNGLASSES

dark horse /ˈdɑrk ˈhɔːrs/ *n* [C] *infml* a person who is not expected to succeed in or unexpectedly wins an election, race, or other competition ○ *a dark horse in the primaries*

darling /ˈdɑr·lɪŋ/ *n* [C] used to show affection when speaking to someone ○ *Hello, darling.*

darling /ˈdɑr·lɪŋ/ *adj* [not gradable] much loved ○ *Here's a picture of my darling child.*

darn REPAIR /dɑrn/, *v* [T] to repair a hole or a piece of clothing with long stitches across the hole and other stitches woven across them ○ *to darn socks*

EXPRESSION /dɑrn/, **darn it** /ˈdɑr·nət, -nɪt/ *exclamation infml* used to express annoyance or surprise ○ *Darn it! I missed my bus.*

darn /dɑrn/, **darned** /dɑrnd/ *adj, adv* [not gradable] *infml* **1** *Where's my darn notebook?* **2** Darn can also mean extremely: *I'm too darn tired to go out tonight.*

dart MOVE QUICKLY /dɑrt/ *v* [I always + adv/prep] to (cause to) move quickly or suddenly ○ *She darted out from between two parked cars.*

POINTED OBJECT /dɑrt/ *n* [C] a small object with a thin pointed end that is thrown or shot ○ *tranquilizer dart*

darts /dɑrts/ *n* [U] a game in which darts are thrown at a circular board, scoring the number of points marked on the board

FOLD /dɑrt/ *n* [C] a fold sewn into a piece of clothing to make it fit better

dash MOVE QUICKLY /dæʃ/ *v* [I] to move quickly ○ *She dashed to the store for some juice.* ○ *Mary's always dashing from one meeting to another.*

dash /dæʃ/ *n* [C usually sing] **1** *We made a dash for the plane.* **2** A dash is also a race over a short distance: *a 50-yard dash*

HIT /dæʃ/ *v* [I/T] to hit with great force, esp. causing damage ○ [I] *Waves dashed against the cliffs.* ○ [T] *(fig.) Hopes of an economic recovery have been dashed* (= destroyed) *by the latest unemployment statistics.*

SMALL AMOUNT /dæʃ/ *n* [C] a small amount of something added to or mixed with something else ○ *Add a dash of salt to the mixture.*

LINE /dæʃ/ *n* [C] a short, horizontal mark (–) used to separate parts of sentences

dashboard /ˈdæʃ·bɔːrd, -bourd/, *short form* **dash** *n* [C] the part of a car that contains some of the controls used for driving and the devices for measuring esp. speed and distance

dashing /ˈdæʃ·ɪŋ/ *adj dated* attractive and stylish because of being energetic, exciting, and confident ○ *a dashing young man*

data Ⓐ /ˈdeɪt̬·ə, ˈdæt̬·ə, ˈdɑt̬·ə/ *n* [U] ***mathematics, science*** information collected for use ○ *They had data on health, education, and economic development.* ○ USAGE: Although originally a plural (the rarely used singular is **datum**) and used with a plural verb, data is now often used as an uncount noun with a singular verb.

database /ˈdeɪt̬·əˌbeɪs, ˈdæt̬·ə-, ˈdɑt̬·ə-/ *n* [C] a large amount of information stored in a computer system in such a way that it can be easily looked at or changed

data processing *n* [U] the use of computers to store, organize, and perform calculations on information

date DAY /deɪt/ *n* [C] a numbered day in a month, often given with the name of the month or with the month and the year ○ *Today's date is June 24, 1998.* ○ *We agreed to meet again at a later date.* ○ *Please fill in your date of birth on the application form.* ○ *I've made a date* (= agreed to a date and time) *to see her about the house.*

date /deɪt/ *v* [I/T] ○ [T] *The last letter I received from the insurance company was dated August 30, 1999.* ○ [I] *This signature dates from* (= originated at the time of) *the 1800s.*

MEETING /deɪt/ *n* [C] **1** a social meeting planned in advance ○ *We made a date to meet Evelyn and Josie at noon tomorrow for lunch.* **2** A date is a person you are planning to meet socially and in whom you might have a romantic interest: *Who is your date for the prom?*

date /deɪt/ *v* [I/T] ○ [I] *They dated for five years before they got married.*

FRUIT /deɪt/ *n* [C] the sweet, brown fruit of various types of PALM tree

WORD FAMILY date			
Nouns	date	*Verbs*	date
Adjectives	dated outdated		predate

IDIOM with date

• **to date** up to now ○ *I wrote to you two months ago, but I have not received any response to date.*

dated /ˈdeɪt̬·əd/ *adj* showing the facts or style of the past rather than of the present ○ *This information is dated.*

dative /ˈdeɪt̬·ɪv/ *adj* [not gradable] ***grammar*** having or relating to the CASE (= form) of a noun, pronoun, or adjective used to show that a word is the INDIRECT OBJECT of a verb that has two objects

daub /dɔːb, dɑb/ *v* [T always + adv/prep] to spread a thick liquid on or in something ○ *The children daubed finger paint on large sheets of paper.*

daughter /ˈdɔːt̬·ər/ *n* [C] a female child in relation to her parents ○ *We have a son and a daughter.*

daughter-in-law /ˈdɔːt̬·ə·rən ˌlɔː/ *n* [C] *pl* **daughters-in-law** the wife of a person's son

daunt /dɔːnt, dɑnt/ *v* [T] to make someone feel slightly frightened or worried about his or her ability to achieve something; to discourage ○ *She's not at all daunted by criticism.*

daunting /ˈdɔːnt·ɪŋ, ˈdɑnt-/ *adj* ○ *Reforming the welfare system is a daunting task.*

dawdle /ˈdɔːd·əl/ *v* [I] to do something very slowly, as if you do not want to finish it ○ *She told her daughter to quit dawdling and get dressed or she'd be late for school.*

dawn /dɔːn, dɑn/ *n* the period in the day when light from the sun begins to appear in the sky ○ [U] (*fig.*) *Computers mark the dawn of a new age.*

dawn /dɔːn, dɑn/ *v* [I] ○ *Winston left his house as the day was dawning.*

PHRASAL VERB with dawn

• **dawn on** *someone* to become known or obvious to someone, often suddenly ○ *It finally dawned on him that she'd been joking.*

day TIME /deɪ/ *n* [C] **1** a period of 24 hours, esp. from 12 o'clock one night to 12 o'clock the next night, or the part of this period after the sun rises but before it goes down, when there is light ○ *My husband picks up our son every day after school.* ○ *In summer the days are longer and we have cookouts in the backyard.* ○ *We leave on vacation the day after tomorrow.* **2** A day is also the part of a period of 24 hours that you spend at work: *He's been working 12-hour days this week.* **3** Days can mean a long period of time: *In those days* (= that period in history), *people had large families.*

USAGE

day

Be careful to use the correct preposition with the word **day**. You usually need to use the preposition **on**.

On the second day of our holiday we went to the beach.

~~*In the second day of our holiday we went to the beach.*~~

WORD FAMILY day			
Nouns	day	*Adverbs*	daily
Adjectives	daily		

IDIOMS with day

• **day after day** repeatedly for many days ○ *The same problems keep coming up day after day.*

• **day and night** all the time ○ *The noise is awful – you can hear the traffic day and night.*

• **day by day** gradually over many days ○ *Day by day my father grew stronger.*

• **day in, day out**, **day in and day out** every day ○ *I do the same things day in, day out.* ○ **USAGE**: Used to say that a repeated event or task is boring.

daybreak /ˈdeɪ·breɪk/ *n* [U] DAWN

day care, **daycare** /ˈdeɪ·ker, -kær/ *n* [U] care provided during the day for young children, esp. in order to allow their parents to work

day-care center, **daycare center** /ˈdeɪ·ker ˌsent·ər, -kær-/ *n* [C] a place where parents pay to leave their children while the parents work ○ *She ran a day-care center for working mothers.*

daydream /ˈdeɪ·driːm/ *n* [C] a set of pleasant thoughts about something that you would like to do or achieve, but which is not likely ○ *I had a daydream that I'd win the road race.*

daydream /ˈdeɪ·driːm/ *v* [I] ○ *She would daydream in class about horseback riding and other things she'd rather be doing.*

daylight /ˈdeɪ·lɑɪt/ *n* [U] natural light from the sun, or the period during a day when there is light ○ *She had little free time during the daylight hours.*

daylight saving time *n* [U] the time set usually one hour later in summer so that there is a longer period of light in the evening ○ Compare STANDARD TIME

Day of Atonement *n* [C] YOM KIPPUR

daytime /ˈdeɪ·tɑɪm/ *n* [U] the period of each day when the sun is up and there is light

day-to-day *adj* ordinary and regular ○ *Your day-to-day responsibilities will include sorting the mail and making appointments.*

day trip *n* [C] a visit to a place in which you return home or to your hotel on the same day

day-tripper *n* [C] ○ *A lot of the people on the beach are day-trippers.*

dazed /deɪzd/ *adj* confused or unable to think clearly, esp. as a result of an injury or from shock

○ *The driver in the accident appeared dazed but not badly hurt.*

daze /deɪz/ *n* [U] ○ *She was so happy she was in a daze.*

dazzle /ˈdæz·əl/ *v* [T] **1** to cause someone to feel strong admiration of something or someone ○ *He was dazzled by Rome's architectural treasures.* **2** A person or animal who is dazzled by a light cannot see because the light is too bright to look at.

dazzling /ˈdæz·ə·lɪŋ/ *adj* causing or likely to cause strong admiration ○ *A dazzling smile flashed across his face.*

D

DDT /ˌdiːd ˌiː ˈtiː/ *n* [U] a poisonous chemical used in the past for killing insects

deacon /ˈdiː·kən/ *n* [C] (in some church groups) a church official of lower rank than a priest, or a church member who helps a minister

dead NOT LIVING /ded/ *adj* [not gradable] **1** no longer living ○ *dead leaves* ○ *Local residents found the whale dead on the beach.* **2** If a piece of machinery or equipment is dead, it is no longer working: *a dead battery* ○ *The phone suddenly went dead.* **3** *infml* If you describe a place as dead, you mean there is not much activity there that interests you: *I love my hometown, but as a teenager I always found it dead.* ○ Related noun: DEATH

dead /ded/ *pl n* people who are no longer living ○ *She did not know any of the names listed among the dead.*

deaden /ˈded·ᵊn/ *v* [T] to reduce the severity or effect of something ○ *He asked for some stronger medication to deaden the pain.*

deadly /ˈded·li/ *adj* dangerous and able to kill ○ *a deadly poison* ➤ Usage: **died or dead?** at DIE

COMPLETE /ded/ *adj* [not gradable] complete or exact ○ *The conductor waited for dead silence before lifting his baton.* ○ *He aimed for the dead center of the target.*

dead /ded/ *adv* [not gradable] completely or extremely ○ *After a hard day's work, I was dead tired.*

dead /ded/ *n* [U] the deepest or most extreme part of something

deadly /ˈded·li/ *adj, adv* ○ *She was deadly* (= extremely accurate) *with a bow and arrow.* ○ *The movie was deadly* (= very) *dull.*

WORD FAMILY dead			
Nouns	dead death	*Adjectives*	dead deadly deathly
Adverbs	deadly deathly	*Verbs*	deaden

IDIOMS with dead

• **(as) dead as a doornail** completely dead ○ *The fox in the road was as dead as a doornail.*

• **dead of night** the middle of the night, when it is very dark ○ *I lay in my tent in the dead of night, listening to the noises in the woods.*

• **dead of winter** the middle of winter, when it is very cold ○ *It was the dead of winter and the ground was covered in deep snow.*

• **dead set against** *something* completely opposed to something ○ *She wanted to move to Los Angeles but both her parents were dead set against it.*

deadbeat /ˈded·biːt/ *n* [C] someone who owes money and does not pay it, or someone who avoids doing work

dead end *n* [C] a road or path that has no way out at one end ○ *(fig.) Negotiators have reached a dead end* (= have not been successful and cannot go further) *in their attempts to find a peaceful solution.*

dead heat *n* [C] a race in which two or more competitors finish at exactly the same time ○ *The two horses finished in a dead heat.* ○ *(fig.) Opinion pollsters call the Congressional race a dead heat, saying it is too close to call.*

dead language *n* [C] a language that is no longer used for ordinary communication ○ *Latin is a dead language.*

deadline /ˈded·lɑɪn/ *n* [C] a time or day by which something must be done ○ *The deadline for filing income taxes is April 15th.*

deadlock /ˈded·lɑk/ *n* [C/U] a state or situation in which agreement in an argument cannot be reached because neither side will change its demands or accept the demands of the other side ○ [U] *The long deadlock over clean air legislation has been broken.*

deadlocked /ˈded·lɑkt/ *adj* unable to make any progress toward reaching agreement ○ *A second trial, in 1982, ended in a mistrial with a deadlocked jury.*

deadpan /ˈded·pæn/ *adj, adv* looking or seeming serious when you are not, or without an emotion ○ *As an overweight neighbor who drops in periodically, Karen Vaccaro offers a funny deadpan performance.*

dead wood *n* [U] people, esp. employees, who are no longer useful ○ *When she took over the agency, she streamlined the operation by getting rid of a lot of dead wood.*

deaf /def/ *adj* unable to hear ○ *She's becoming increasingly deaf.*

deafening /ˈdef·ə·nɪŋ/ *adj* (of a sound) extremely loud ○ *a deafening explosion* ○ *deafening applause*

deal AGREEMENT /diːl/ *n* [C] an agreement or arrangement, esp. in business ○ *They bargained with each other but finally agreed to a deal.* ○ *She got a really good deal* (= paid a low price) *on her new car.*

deal /diːl/ *v* [I/T] *past* **dealt** to do business with or be involved with someone or something ○ [I] *We only deal with companies that have a good credit record.* ○ [I] *They mainly deal in* (= buy and sell) *mutual funds.*

dealer /ˈdiː·lər/ *n* [C] ○ *an antiques dealer* ○ *a used-car dealer*

dealership /ˈdiː·lərˌʃɪp/ *n* [C] a business that has the right to sell a company's products in a particular area using the company's name ○ *a Toyota dealership*

dealings /ˈdiː·lɪŋz/ *pl n* activities or relations involving other people, esp. in business ○ *He was accused of being involved in shady financial dealings.*

GIVE OUT /diːl/ *v* [I/T] *past* **dealt** to give or give out something, esp. playing cards ○ [I/T] *Whose turn is it to deal (the cards)?* ○ [T] *(fig.) Tonight's defeat dealt a blow to* (= damaged) *her hopes of making it to the finals.*

deal /diːl/ *n* [C] a turn to give out playing cards ○ *It's your deal.*

AMOUNT /diːl/ *n* [U] a large amount or very much ○ *She used to talk a great deal about her childhood in Indiana.*

WORD FAMILY deal			
Nouns	deal dealer dealings dealership	*Verbs*	deal

PHRASAL VERBS with deal

• **deal with** *someone/something* **MANAGE** to develop a way to manage or relate to someone or something ○ *We have to deal with problems as they arise.* ○ *She had a marvelous ability to deal with people.*

• **deal with** *something* **BE ABOUT** to be about or be on the subject of something ○ *She likes novels that deal with serious moral issues.* ○ *The lecture dealt with his trip to South Africa.*

deamination /ˌdiːˌæm·əˈneɪ·ʃən/ *n* [U] ***biology, chemistry*** the process by which one or more of the groups of atoms containing NITROGEN (= a gas that is a chemical element) are removed from a MOLECULE (= smallest unit of a substance)

dean /diːn/ *n* [C] a high-ranking official in a college or university responsible for a department, teachers, students, etc. ○ *Langer is the dean of the law school.*

dear **LOVED** /dɪr/ *adj* [-er/-est only] **1** loved or greatly liked ○ *She's a dear friend.* **2** Dear is used at the beginning of a letter to greet the person you are writing to: *Dear Kerrie/Mom and Dad/Ms. Smith/Sir* **3** Dearest can be used in a letter to greet someone you love: *Dearest Ben, I think of you every day.*

dear /dɪr/ *n* [C] **1** *Annie's such a dear.* **2** Dear is used to address someone in a friendly way, esp. someone you love or a child: *Have something to eat, dear.*

EXPRESSION /dɪr/ *exclamation infml* used to express annoyance, disappointment, unhappiness, or surprise ○ *Oh dear! I've lost my keys again.*

dearly /ˈdɪr·li/ *adv* very much ○ *We would dearly love to move to the country.* ○ *You'll pay dearly for breaking the law in this town.*

dearth /dɜrθ/ *n* [U] an amount of something that is too small: a lack ○ *The region is suffering from a dearth of medical specialists.*

death /deθ/ *n* [C/U] the end of life ○ [C] *a sudden/natural death* ○ [U] *I hope she finds the peace in death she never found in life.* ○ [U] *Fire ants stung a woman to death* (= caused her to die). ○ Related adjective: DEAD **NOT LIVING**

deathly /ˈdeθ·li/ *adj, adv* seeming like death ○ *Madeline looked deathly pale.* ○ *The crowd was deathly silent.*

IDIOMS with death

• **on** *someone's* **deathbed** just before someone's death ○ *He told her he loved her on his deathbed.*

• **to death** a lot ○ *The movie scared the kids to death.*

death knell *n* [C] a warning of the end of something ○ *Defeat of this bill sounds a death knell for consumer protection*

D

death penalty *n* [C] the legal punishment of particular crimes by death

death row *n* [C] the place in a prison where prisoners wait to be killed as punishment

death toll *n* [C] the number of people who died as a result of an event ○ *The day after the earthquake the death toll had risen to 90.*

deathtrap /ˈdeθˌtræp/ *n* [C] something that is very dangerous and could cause death ○ *With no fire exits, the hall was a deathtrap.*

debacle /dɪˈbɑk·əl, diː-, -ˈbæk-/ *n* [C] an event or situation that is a complete failure ○ *The candidate's behavior during the debate turned what could have been a victory into a political debacle.*

debase /dɪˈbeɪs/ *v* [T] to reduce in quality or value ○ *Television is often blamed for debasing American politics.*

debatable Ⓐ /dɪˈbeɪt̬·ə·bəl/ *adj* not clear, not certain, or not fixed; possibly not true ○ *It's debatable whether he could get a fair trial here.*

debate Ⓐ /dɪˈbeɪt/ *n* [C/U] ***English*** a discussion, esp. one in which several people with different opinions about something discuss them seriously, or the process of discussing something ○ [U] *Education is always a topic of interest and public debate.*

debate /dɪˈbeɪt/ *v* [I/T] ○ [I] *Congress debated for several hours without reaching a vote.*

debilitating /dɪˈbɪl·əˌteɪt̬·ɪŋ/ *adj* causing weakness ○ *Strokes are a common debilitating condition of old age.*

debit /ˈdeb·ət/ *n* [C/U] money taken out of a financial account, or a record of money taken ○ Opposite: CREDIT **MONEY AVAILABLE**

debit /ˈdeb·ət/ *v* [T] ○ *We have debited your account $30.*

debit card *n* [C] a small plastic card used to make a payment by taking the amount of the payment automatically from your bank account ○ *The supermarket takes debit cards, credit cards, cash, and checks.*

debrief /diːˈbriːf/ *v* [T] to question someone in detail to get useful information about something that person has done for you ○ *After every flight, engineers thoroughly debrief the test pilot.* ○ Compare BRIEF **GIVE INSTRUCTIONS**

debris /dəˈbriː, deɪ-/ *n* [U] broken or torn pieces left from the destruction of something larger ○ *After the tornado, debris from damaged trees and houses littered the town.*

debt /det/ *n* [C] **1** something owed, esp. money ○ *He managed to pay off his debts in two years.* **2** If you are in debt, you owe money: *We seem to be perpetually in debt.* **3** If you go into debt, you borrow money. ○ See also: INDEBTED GRATEFUL; INDEBTED OWING

debtor /ˈdet̬·ər/ *n* [C] a country, organization, or person who owes money ○ *Student loans force students to graduate as debtors.* ○ Compare CREDITOR at CREDIT PAYMENT LATER

D

IDIOM with debt

• **in** *someone's* **debt** grateful for something someone did for you ○ *I'm in Senator Obama's debt for getting my husband a visa.*

debug /diːˈbʌg/ *v* [T] **-gg-** to remove BUGS (= mistakes) from a computer program ○ *He spent weeks debugging the program.*

debunk /diːˈbʌŋk/ *v* [T] to show that something is not true ○ *Every week some long-held medical theory is debunked.*

debut /ˈdeɪ·bjuː, deɪˈbjuː/ *n* [C usually sing] a first public appearance or activity ○ *Cassavetes made his film debut in "Taxi" in 1953.*

debut /ˈdeɪ·bjuː, deɪˈbjuː/ *v* [I/T] ○ [T] *I'll be debuting this song next Saturday night.*

Dec. *n* [U] *abbreviation for* DECEMBER.

decade Ⓐ /ˈdek·eɪd, deˈkeɪd/ *n* [C] **1** a period of ten years ○ *The economy is growing at its fastest rate this decade.* **2** Decades means a long time: *They're enjoying new popularity after decades of neglect.*

decadence /ˈdek·əd·ᵊns/ *n* [U] a state of low standards in a society; social decay

decadent /ˈdek·əd·ᵊnt/ *adj* ○ *The US was widely condemned as a decadent society.*

decaf /ˈdiː·kæf/ *n* [C usually sing] coffee that has had CAFFEINE (= a chemical substance) removed ○ *Do you have any decaf?*

decaffeinated /diːˈkæf·əˌneit̬·əd/, *short form* **decaf** /ˈdiː·kæf/ *adj* [not gradable] having had CAFFEINE removed ○ *decaffeinated coffee/tea/cola*

decal /ˈdiː·kæl, dɪˈkæl/ *n* [C] a picture or design on special paper, which can be put onto another surface, such as metal or glass

decanter /dɪˈkænt·ər/ *n* [C] an attractive glass bottle used for storing and serving liquids

decapitate /dɪˈkæp·əˌteɪt/ *v* [T] to cut off the head of a person or animal

decathlon /dɪˈkæθˌlɑn/ *n* [C] a competition in which male ATHLETES compete in ten sporting events over two days ○ Compare HEPTATHLON

decay DAMAGE /dɪˈkeɪ/ *n* [U] damage, or a state that becomes gradually worse ○ *The dentist says I have a lot of tooth decay.* ○ *There's still too much crime, poverty, and decay in the neighborhood.* ○ *Your attitude just contributes to the growing social decay.*

decay /dɪˈkeɪ/ *v* [I/T] ○ [I] *City services are rapidly decaying.*

decaying /dɪˈkeɪ·ɪŋ/ *adj* [not gradable] ○ *Empty lots stand next to abandoned, decaying buildings.*

PROCESS /dɪˈkeɪ/ *n* [U] ***physics*** the process by which a RADIOACTIVE substance breaks down and sends out harmful RADIATION

decay /dɪˈkeɪ/ *v* [I]

deceased /dɪˈsiːst/ *adj* [not gradable] dead ○ *The paintings are by his deceased brother, Dan.*

deceased /dɪˈsiːst/ *n* [C] someone who has recently died ○ *There will be no service, at the deceased's request.*

deceit /dɪˈsiːt/ *n* [U] speech or behavior that keeps the truth hidden ○ *All we hear from them are lies and deceit.*

deceitful /dɪˈsiːt·fəl/ *adj* ○ *She just assumes that elected leaders are cynical and deceitful.*

deceive /dɪˈsiːv/ *v* [T] **1** to persuade someone that something false is the truth; trick or fool ○ *Some parents try to deceive school officials and enroll their children in other districts.* **2** If you deceive yourself, you pretend something is true: *We should not deceive ourselves into thinking this will be the end of it.* ○ See also: DECEPTION

WORD FAMILY deceive

Nouns	deceit deception	*Adjectives*	deceitful deceptive
Verbs	deceive	*Adverbs*	deceptively

December /dɪˈsem·bər/, *abbreviation* **Dec.** *n* [C/U] the twelfth and last month of the year, after November and before January

decent /ˈdiː·sənt/ *adj* **1** acceptable, satisfactory, or reasonable ○ *We get good benefits, and the pay is decent.* ○ *It costs $100 to buy a decent sleeping bag.* **2** Decent also means good or kind: *They're just decent, ordinary people.* **3** *infml* Decent also means wearing socially acceptable clothing: *When the players were showered and decent, the reporters were allowed in.*

decently /ˈdiː·sənt·li/ *adv* ○ *Their employer treats them decently.*

decency /ˈdiː·sən·si/ *n* [U] ○ [+ *to* infinitive] *She didn't even have the decency to apologize.*

decentralize /diːˈsen·trəˌlɑɪz/ *v* [T] to move the operations of a business or other organization from a single, central place to several smaller ones ○ *The company uses an unusual decentralized distribution system.*

decentralization /ˌdiːˌsen·trə·ləˈzeɪ·ʃən/ *n* [U] ○ *Many local people favor decentralization of the schools.*

deception /dɪˈsep·ʃən/ *n* [C/U] a statement or action that hides the truth, or the act of hiding the truth ○ [U] *Most advertising involves at least some deception.* ○ Related verb: DECEIVE

deceptive /dɪˈsep·tɪv/ *adj* ○ *Appearances can be very deceptive.*

deceptively /dɪˈsep·tɪv·li/ *adv* ○ *He makes it sound deceptively simple.*

decibel /ˈdes·əˌbel, -bəl/ *n* [C] a unit for measuring the loudness of sound

decide /dɪˈsɑɪd/ *v* **1** to choose between one possibility or another ○ [T] *I decided I would try it.* ○ [+ to infinitive] *In the end, we decided to go to the theater.* ○ [+ question word] *We're trying to decide how to proceed.* ○ [+ (that) clause] *He decided (that) it was his business.* **2** If something decides a result in a competition, it causes that result: [T] *A mistake by our team decided the game against us.* **3** A deciding factor is something so important that it forces a particular decision: *The deciding factor in choosing this school was that it was far from home.*

WORD FAMILY decide

Nouns	decision indecision	*Adjectives*	decided undecided decisive indecisive
Verbs	decide		
Adverbs	decidedly decisively		

WORD CHOICES decide

If someone is deciding a time or an amount, especially an exact date or price, the verbs **fix** and **set** are often used.

*The price has been **set/fixed** at $10.*

*Have you **set/fixed** a date for the wedding?*

If someone makes a final and certain decision about a plan, date, etc., the verb **finalize** is sometimes used.

*We've chosen a venue for the wedding, but we haven't **finalized** the details yet.*

The verb **settle** and the phrasal verb **settle on/upon** are also often used when someone is making a final decision.

*Have you **settled on** a place to live yet?*

*OK then, we're going to Spain. That's **settled**.*

To **resolve** to do something, is to decide definitely that you will do it.

*Emma weighed herself and **resolved** to lose some weight.*

The expression **make up your mind** is often used to mean "to decide."

*I like them both – I just can't **make up my mind** which one to pick.*

*Have you **made up your mind** whether you're going?*

If someone is unable to decide between two choices, in informal situations you can use the expression **be torn between** something **and** something else.

*I'm **torn between** the fish **and** the beef.*

decided /dɪˈsɑɪd·əd/ *adj* clear; certain ○ *There's been a decided improvement in subway service.*

decidedly /dɪˈsɑɪd·əd·li/ *adv* ○ *He was decidedly careful about what he told me.*

deciduous /dɪˈsɪdʒ·ə·wəs/ *adj* [not gradable] ***biology*** (of a tree) losing its leaves in the fall ○ Compare EVERGREEN

decimal /ˈdes·ə·məl/ *adj* [not gradable] of a system of counting or money based on the number ten

decimal /ˈdes·ə·məl/ *n* [C] ○ *Three-fifths expressed as a decimal is 0.6.*

decimal point *n* [C] a mark used in numbers to separate whole numbers from parts of numbers ○ *To divide by ten, move the decimal point one place to the left.*

decimate /ˈdes·əˌmeɪt/ *v* [T] to destroy large numbers of people, animals, or other creatures, or to harm something severely ○ *Overfishing has decimated the cod population.* ○ *We decimated public transportation in the 1950s and '60s.*

decipher /dɪˈsɑɪ·fər/ *v* [T] to discover the meaning of something hard to understand or which contains a hidden message ○ *I have a hard time deciphering my phone bill.*

decision /dɪˈsɪʒ·ən/ *n* [C] something you choose; a choice ○ *The board will make its decision shortly.* ○ [+ to infinitive] *Their decision not to attend the party puzzled everyone.*

decisive /dɪˈsɑɪ·sɪv/ *adj* **1** making choices quickly and surely, without having any doubts ○ *In an emergency, decisive action is called for.* **2** Decisive also means without doubt or question, and of the greatest importance: *DNA test results were decisive in proving his innocence.*

decisively /dɪˈsɑɪ·sɪv·li/ *adv* ○ *We had to act quickly and decisively to put out the fire.*

decision-making *n* [U] the process of making choices, esp. important choices ○ *She plays no part in the daily decision-making.* ○ *The bank gave decision-making authority to individual businesses, allowing them to better cater to their customers.*

deck FLOOR /dek/ *n* [C] **1** a wooden floor outside a house, usually with RAILINGS (= a low fence) and without a roof ○ *In summer, we always eat out on the deck – except when it rains.* **2** A ship's deck is a floor laid between the sides of the ship: *Waves washed over the deck.*

SET OF CARDS /dek/, **pack** *n* [C] a set of cards used for playing card games

HIT /dek/ *v* [T] *slang* to hit somone and cause that person to fall ○ *A key player was decked three times during yesterday's basketball game.*

PHRASAL VERB with deck

• **deck out** *someone/something* [M] to dress someone in special clothes, or decorate something for a special occasion ○ *Stanton was decked out in cowboy boots and a work shirt.*

Declaration of Independence *n* [C usually sing] ***US history*** a document claiming freedom for the United States from political control by Britain on July 4, 1776

declarative sentence /dɪˈklær·ət̬·ɪv ˈsent·əns/ *n* [C] ***grammar*** a sentence that makes a statement or states a fact

declare /dɪˈkler, -ˈklær/ *v* [T] to announce or express something clearly and publicly, esp. officially ○ *The courts declared the policy unconstitutional.* ○

A state of emergency has been declared because of severe flooding. ○ *People use their license plates to declare their team loyalty.* ○ [+ *that* clause] *I declare that is the best chocolate cake I've ever eaten!*
declaration /ˌdek·ləˈreɪ·ʃən/ *n* [C] an official, public, usually written statement ○ *a customs declaration* ○ *a declaration of principles* ○ *the American Declaration of Independence*

D

decline Ⓐ **GO DOWN** /dɪˈklɑɪn/ *v* [I] to go down in amount or quality; lessen or weaken ○ *His interest in the project declined after his wife died.* ○ *Her health declined quickly.*
decline /dɪˈklɑɪn/ *n* [C/U] ○ [C usually sing] *Unemployment increased this month after a modest decline.* ○ [U] *Civilization is in decline.*

REFUSE /dɪˈklɑɪn/ *v* [I/T] to refuse something ○ [T] *She declined their job offer.*

decode /diːˈkoʊd/ *v* [T] to discover the meaning of information given in a secret or complicated way ○ *Scientists are decoding the genetic sequences in DNA.*

decolonization /ˌdiːˌkɑl·ə·nəˈzeɪ·ʃən/ *n* [U] **1** ***politics & government*** the release of one country or territory from political control by another country **2** ***world history*** Decolonization was also the political independence received by European COLONIES (= a country or area controlled politically by a more powerful country) in Africa and Asia after World War II.

decompose /ˌdiː·kəmˈpoʊz/ *v* [I/T] **1** to destroy something by breaking it into smaller parts ○ [I] *Certain kinds of plastic decompose quickly.* **2** ***biology*** If dead plant or animal material decomposes, it decays. **3** ***chemistry*** If a substance decomposes it separates into its parts.
decomposition /ˌdiːˌkɑm·pəˈzɪʃ·ən/ *n* [U]

decomposer /ˌdiː·kəmˈpoʊ·zər/ *n* [C] ***biology*** an organism such as some types of bacteria or FUNGI that feeds on dead plant and animal material and causes it to decay

decongestant /ˌdiː·kənˈdʒes·tənt/ *n* [C] a medicine that helps you to breathe more easily, esp. when you have a COLD **ILLNESS**

decor /deɪˈkɔːr, dɪ-; ˈdek·ɔːr/ *n* [C/U] the choice of color, style of furniture, and arrangement of objects in a room ○ [C] *Actually, the ironing board is part of my decor.*

decorate **MAKE ATTRACTIVE** /ˈdek·əˌreɪt/ *v* [T] to add something to an object or place, esp. to make it more attractive ○ *They decorated the table with flowers and candles.*
decoration /ˌdek·əˈreɪ·ʃən/ *n* [C/U] ○ [C] *The molding has a floral decoration carved into it.* ○ [U] *Some women wear barrettes as decoration.*
decorative /ˈdek·ə·rət̬·ɪv/ *adj* attractive ○ *decorative patterns/accessories*
decorator /ˈdek·əˌreɪt̬·ər/ *n* [C] an INTERIOR DECORATOR

WORD CHOICES decorate

The verbs **refurbish, renovate,** and **revamp** are common alternatives to "decorate" when you are talking about improving the appearance of a room or building.

*The University library is currently being **refurbished**.*

*They were in the process of **renovating** an old barn.*

*The restaurant has recently been **revamped**.*

Another alternative used in more informal situations is the phrasal verb **do over**.

*He's bought an old cottage and is gradually **doing** it **over**.*

HONOR /ˈdek·əˌreɪt/ *v* [T] to reward or honor a person by giving him or her a MEDAL, BADGE, etc. ○ *All four firefighters were decorated for bravery.*
decoration /ˌdek·əˈreɪ·ʃən/ *n* [C] ○ *He received the country's highest decoration for bravery.*

WORD FAMILY decorate

Nouns	decoration decorator	*Adjectives*	decorative
		Verbs	decorate

decorum /dɪˈkɔːr·əm, -ˈkoʊr·əm/ *n* [U] *fml* behavior that is socially correct, calm, and polite ○ *The witness endured the lawyer's badgering with remarkable decorum.*

decoy /ˈdiː·kɔɪ, dɪˈkɔɪ/ *n* [C] something used to trick or confuse a person or animal ○ *He carves duck decoys for hunters.*

decrease /dɪˈkriːs, ˈdiː·kriːs/ *v* [I/T] to become smaller or make something less ○ [I] *Car sales decreased sharply this year.* ○ Opposite: INCREASE
decrease /ˈdiː·kriːs, dɪˈkriːs/ *n* [C] ○ *I haven't noticed any decrease in ticket sales.*

WORD CHOICES decrease

The verbs **lessen, lower,** and **reduce,** and the phrasal verb **bring down** are often used when someone decreases an amount or level.

*They've just **lowered** the age at which you can join.*

*Exercise **reduces** the chance of heart disease.*

*They are **bringing down** their prices.*

Drop, fall, go down, and **come down** are often used when a level or amount decreases.

*Unemployment has **dropped/fallen** from 8% to 6% in the last year.*

*Prices always **come/go down** in January.*

If a level or amount decreases very quickly, the verbs **plummet** and **plunge** are sometimes used.

*Temperatures last night **plummeted/plunged** below zero.*

If a level or amount decreases gradually, the verbs **dwindle** and **decline** are sometimes used.

*The number of students in the school has **dwindled** to around 200.*

*The number of members has **declined** by 25% over the last 30 years.*

If the size of something decreases, the verb **shrink** is sometimes used. The verb **contract** is used in technical contexts.

*Forests have **shrunk** to almost half the size they were 20 years ago.*
*As the metal cools, it **contracts**.*

decree /dɪˈkriː/ *n* [C] an order or statement of an official decision ○ *He refused to carry out the board's decree.*
decree /dɪˈkriː/ *v* [T] ○ [+ *that* clause] *The Olympic charter decrees that the Games be opened by a head of state.*

decrepit /dɪˈkrep·ət/ *adj* weak and in poor condition, esp. from age or long use ○ *The town had two decrepit fire trucks that were constantly breaking down.*

decriminalize /diːˈkrɪm·ə·nəˌlɑɪz/ *v* [T] to make a particular act no longer illegal by changing a law
decriminalization /ˌdiːˌkrɪm·ən·əl·əˈzeɪ·ʃən/ *n* [U] ○ *decriminalization of minor offenses*

decry /dɪˈkrɑɪ/ *v* [T] to publicly criticize something as being undesirable or harmful ○ *Mitchell decried the high rate of unemployment in the state.*

dedicate /ˈded·əˌkeɪt/ *v* [T] **1** to give completely your energy, time, etc. to something ○ *He dedicated his life to helping the poor.* **2** If you dedicate a book, play, performance, etc., to someone or something, you say publicly that it is in that person or thing's honor: *This book is dedicated to my children, Claire and Tom.*
dedicated /ˈded·əˌkeɪt̬·əd/ *adj* believing that an activity or idea is important and giving a lot of energy and time to it ○ *The Boy Scouts organization is dedicated to helping boys become moral and productive adults.*
dedication /ˌded·əˈkeɪ·ʃən/ *n* [C/U] **1** the activity of giving a lot of your energy and time to something you think is important ○ [U] *dedication to worthy causes* **2** A dedication is also a ceremony in which something is formally opened or made available to the public: [U] *The mayor made a speech at the dedication ceremony for the new school.*

deduce Ⓐ /dɪˈduːs/ *v* [T] to reach an answer by thinking about a general truth and its relationship to a specific situation ○ [+ question word] *In an attempt to deduce what happened to the jet, investigators are looking at other similar planes.*
deduction Ⓐ /dɪˈdʌk·ʃən/ *n* [C/U] the process of learning something by considering a general set of facts and thinking about how something specific relates to them ○ [C] *Sherlock Holmes was famous for making clever deductions.*

deduct /dɪˈdʌkt/ *v* [T] **1** to take away an amount or part from a total ○ *The company deducts $31.93 each week from my salary for health insurance.* **2** To deduct is also not to have to pay taxes on an amount that you have earned: *Homeowners can deduct the interest they pay on their mortgages.*
deductible /dɪˈdʌk·tə·bəl/ *adj* [not gradable] A deductible expense is a cost that you can subtract from the earnings on which you have to pay income tax: *Mortgage interest is deductible.*
deductible /dɪˈdʌk·tə·bəl/ *n* [C] an amount of money that you are responsible for paying before your INSURANCE (= protection against loss) will pay you for an expense ○ *Judy's car insurance policy had a $500 deductible.*
deduction /dɪˈdʌk·ʃən/ *n* [C/U] an amount or part taken away from a total, esp. an expense that you do not have to pay taxes on, or the process of taking away an amount or part ○ [C] *New tax regulations would cut the deduction for business lunches.*

deed ACTION /diːd/ *n* [C/U] an intentional act, esp. a very bad or very good one ○ [C] *Whatever his motives, the deed did save a hundred thousand lives.*
DOCUMENT /diːd/ *n* [C] *law* a legal document that is an official record and proof of ownership of property ○ *According to the deed, she owns the land from here to the river.*

deem /diːm/ *v* [T] to consider or judge ○ *The president asked Congress for authority to take whatever steps he deemed necessary, including the use of force.*

deep DOWN /diːp/ *adj, adv* [*-er/-est* only] going or being a long way down from the top or surface, or being at a particular distance down from the top ○ *She had a deep cut on her left arm.* ○ *During the flood, the water in the basement was knee-deep* (= it would reach the knees of an average adult). ○ Related noun: DEPTH DISTANCE DOWN
FRONT TO BACK /diːp/ *adj* having a (sometimes stated) distance from front to back ○ *I want the bookcase shelves to be 12 inches deep.* ○ *The crowd along the parade route was six deep* (= in six rows). ○ Related noun: DEPTH DISTANCE BACKWARD
STRONGLY FELT /diːp/ *adj* strongly felt or experienced, or having a strong and lasting effect ○ *Our deep love for each other will last forever.* ○ *He awoke from a deep sleep.* ○ *Joseph, deep in thought* (= thinking so much that he is not aware of others), *didn't hear Erin enter the room.*
deepen /ˈdiː·pən/ *v* [I/T] ○ [I] *Over the years, her love for him deepened.*
deeply /ˈdiː·pli/ *adv* ○ *Everyone was deeply impressed by his performance.*
COMPLICATED /diːp/ *adj* [*-er/-est* only] difficult to understand; complicated ○ *His book on how the brain works is too deep for me.*
LOW SOUND /diːp/ *adj* [*-er/-est* only] (of a sound) low ○ *He was a large man with a deep voice.*
DARK /diːp/ *adj* [*-er/-est* only] (of a color) strong and dark ○ *The sky is a deep blue.*

WORD FAMILY deep

Nouns	depth	*Verbs*	deepen
Adjectives	deep	*Adverbs*	deeply

IDIOMS with deep

• **deep down** in the part of your mind where your strongest and often most secret feelings are ○ *You* *say you forgive him, but deep down, aren't you still angry?*

• **have deep pockets** to have deep pockets ○ *The politicians with the deepest pockets usually win the election.*

• **in deep (trouble)** in serious trouble ○ *You will be in deep trouble with Dad if you don't tell him the truth now.*

D

deep-fry *v* [I/T] to fry food in a lot of oil ○ *deep-fried chicken*

Deep South *n* [U] the part of the US that is in the farthest south and east, including South Carolina, Georgia, Alabama, Mississippi, and Louisiana, but usually not including Florida

deer /dɪr/ *n* [C] *pl* **deer** a large animal, the males of which have wide horns that stick out like branches, that lives in forests and eats grass and leaves

deface /dɪˈfeɪs/ *v* [T] to intentionally spoil the appearance of something by writing on or marking it ○ *They used spray paint to deface the sign.*

de facto /dɪˈfæk·toʊ, deɪ-/ *adj, adv* [not gradable] existing in fact, although not necessarily intended or legal ○ *He has made the candidates for city council de facto school committee members.*

defame /dɪˈfeɪm/ *v* [T] to damage someone's or something's reputation by saying or writing bad things that are not true ○ *He was behind the propaganda campaign to defame his political opponent.*

defamation /ˌdef·əˈmeɪ·ʃən/ *n* [U]

default FAIL TO PAY /dɪˈfɔːlt/ *v* [I] to fail to do something, such as pay a debt, that you legally have to do ○ *The company defaulted on a $133 million loan.*

default /dɪˈfɔːlt, ˈdiː·fɔːlt/ *n* [C/U] **1** [C] *Defaults rose to 4 percent of all the bank's loans.* **2** In sports, to win or lose by default is to win or lose because one side did not compete: [U] *Humphrey never showed up, so Wilson won by default.*

STANDARD SETTING /ˈdiː·fɔːlt, dɪˈfɔːlt/ *n* [U] a standard setting esp. of computer SOFTWARE, such as of type size or style ○ *The default color of text on the screen is black.*

defeat /dɪˈfiːt/ *v* [T] to oppose and cause someone to lose in a competition or war so that you can win ○ *Bill Clinton defeated George Bush for the presidency in 1992.*

defeat /dɪˈfiːt/ *n* [C/U] **1** success in competition with an opponent, causing the opponent to lose so that you can win ○ [U] *In the American Civil War, the North's defeat of the South involved tremendous loss of life on both sides.* **2** A defeat is also the action or fact of losing a competition or war: [C] *This was the team's fifth straight defeat.*

WORD FAMILY defeat			
Nouns	defeat	Adjectives	undefeated
	defeatism		defeatist
	defeatist	Verbs	defeat

defeatism /dɪˈfiːt̬ˌɪz·əm/ *n* [U] a way of thinking or behaving that shows that you expect to fail ○ *He criticized his party for defeatism.*

defeatist /dɪˈfiːt̬·əst/ *adj* ○ *You'll never get anywhere with a defeatist attitude.*

defecate /ˈdef·əˌkeɪt/ *v* [I] to excrete the contents of the bowels

defect SOMETHING WRONG /ˈdiː·fekt, dɪˈfekt/ *n* [C] something that is lacking or that is not exactly right in someone or something ○ *The cars have a defect in the electrical system that may cause them to stall.*

defective /dɪˈfek·tɪv/ *adj* ○ *I replaced the defective light switch.*

LEAVE /dɪˈfekt/ *v* [I] to leave a country or a group you belong to, esp. in order to join an opposing one ○ *Some of the mayor's long-time supporters have defected to other candidates.*

defection /dɪˈfek·ʃən/ *n* [C/U] ○ [C] *There have been defections to the US by several Cuban baseball players.*

defector /dɪˈfek·tər/ *n* [C] a person who leaves his or her own country or group to join an opposing one

defend PROTECT /dɪˈfend/ *v* [T] **1** to protect someone or something from attack or harm ○ *Communities will fight to defend themselves.* ○ *How can people best defend themselves against disease?* **2** To defend is also to argue in support of something, esp. when it has been criticized: *She defended her husband against the accusations.*

defendant /dɪˈfen·dənt/ *n* [C] *law* a person in a court of law who is accused of having done something wrong ○ *The prosecutor must prove beyond a reasonable doubt that the defendant is guilty.* ○ Compare PLAINTIFF

defender /dɪˈfen·dər/ *n* [C] a person who supports someone or something, esp. when attacked or criticized ○ *She is a defender of women's rights.*

defensible /dɪˈfen·sə·bəl/ *adj* Something that is defensible can be supported, esp. when criticized: *He's presenting a plan that is morally defensible and politically realistic.*

SPORTS /dɪˈfend/ *v* [I/T] (in sports) to try to prevent the opposition from scoring points in a competition, or to guard a goal or other position ○ [I] *Jones is a difficult player to defend against.*

defender /dɪˈfen·dər/ *n* [C] ○ *Murray dribbled past a defender and fired the ball right into the basket.*

WORD FAMILY defend			
Nouns	defense	Adjectives	defenseless
	defendant		defensible
	defender		indefensible
	defensive		defensive
	defenselessness	Adverbs	defensively
Verbs	defend		

defense PROTECTION /dɪˈfens/ *n* [C/U] **1** the ability to protect against attack or harm, or something used to protect against attack or harm ○ [C] *The vaccine strengthens the body's defenses against* *infection.* **2** A defense is also an argument in support of something, esp. when it has been criticized: [U] *Her defense consisted of denying that she knew anything about the missing check.* **3** *law* The defense is the person or people in a court who have been accused of doing something wrong, and their lawyer: [U] *The defense rests* (= This side has finished giving its argument).

defensive /dɪ ˈfen·sɪv/ *adj* **1** intended to protect against attack or harm ○ *a defensive strategy* ○ *It's too late to sign up for the defensive driving class.* **2** If someone is defensive, the person feels criticized and quickly tries to explain: *Don't be defensive – I'm just asking why you didn't vote.*

defenseless /dɪ ˈfen·sləs/ *adj* having no way to protect yourself from attack or harm ○ *Youngsters are often the most defenseless against mosquitoes.*

defenselessness /dɪ ˈfen·slə·snəs/ *n* [U]

defensive /dɪ ˈfen·sɪv/ *n* [U]

SPORTS /dɪ ˈfens, ˈdiː·fens/ *n* [U] (in sports) the ability to prevent the opposition from scoring points in a competition, or, esp. in football, the team without the ball that is trying to prevent its opposition from scoring points ○ *The team has pretty good scoring ability, but it's weak on defense.* ○ Compare OFFENSE SCORING ABILITY

defensive /dɪ ˈfen·sɪv/ *adj* ○ *The team's defensive strategy was effective.*

defensively /dɪ ˈfen·sɪv·li/ *adv*

IDIOM with **defense**

• **on the defensive** protecting yourself from criticism instead of attacking or criticizing others ○ *The speech produced a firestorm of protest, putting him on the defensive.*

defense mechanism *n* [C] an automatic way of behaving or thinking by which you protect yourself from something, especially from feeling unpleasant emotions ○ *Arrogance is often a defense mechanism.*

defense spending *n* [U] ***politics & government*** money spent by a government to provide its military with weapons, equipment, and soldiers

defer /dɪ ˈfɜr/ *v* [T] **-rr-** to delay something until a later time; to POSTPONE ○ *You can order the furniture now and defer payment until September.*

deferment /dɪ ˈfɜr·mənt/ *n* [C/U] (a) temporary delay in taking someone into the military forces ○ [C] *They got draft deferments as graduate students.*

PHRASAL VERB with **defer**

• **defer to** *someone* to let another person decide, or to accept another person's opinion, usually because you respect the knowledge or experience of that person ○ *I deferred to Brian on the question of what to serve at the party.*

deference /ˈdef·ə·rəns/ *n* [U] respect shown for another person esp. because of that person's experience, knowledge, age, or power ○ *In deference to nature lovers, the town refused to grant a permit to builders who would have filled in a swamp used by many birds.*

deferential /ˌdef·əˈren·tʃəl/ *adj* ○ *A smart lawyer is always deferential to a judge.*

defiance /dɪ ˈfɑɪ·əns/ *n* ○ See at DEFY

defiant /dɪ ˈfɑɪ·ənt/ *adj* ○ See at DEFY

defiantly /dɪ ˈfɑɪ·ənt·li/ *adv* ○ See at DEFY

deficiency /dɪ ˈfɪʃ·ən·si/ *n* [C/U] the lack of something that is needed in order to meet a particular standard or level of quality, or the thing that is lacking ○ [U] *Many women suffer from iron deficiency.*

deficient /dɪ ˈfɪʃ·ənt/ *adj* ○ *A diet that is deficient* (= lacking) *in protein is harmful to children.*

deficit /ˈdef·ə·sət/ *n* [C] the amount by which money spent is more than money received ○ *The theater has been operating at a deficit of over $150,000 a year.*

defied /dɪ ˈfɑɪd/ *past simple and past participle of* DEFY

defile /dɪ ˈfɑɪl/ *v* [T] to spoil the goodness or beauty of something ○ *Cans, paper bags, and other trash defiled the landscape.*

define Ⓐ **EXPLAIN** /dɪ ˈfɑɪn/ *v* [T] ***English*** to describe the meaning of something, esp. a word, or to explain something more clearly so that it can be understood ○ *How would you define "jaded"?*

definable Ⓐ /dɪ ˈfɑɪ·nə·bəl/ *adj*

SHOW /dɪ ˈfɑɪn/ *v* [T] to show clearly the edge or shape of something ○ *The dark figures are sharply defined on the white background.*

WORD FAMILY **define**			
Nouns	definition	*Verbs*	define
Adjectives	definite indefinite definitive	*Adverbs*	definitely indefinitely

definite Ⓐ /ˈdef·ə·nət/ *adj* fixed, certain, or clear ○ *We haven't picked a definite date, but it will probably be in June.*

definitely Ⓐ /ˈdef·ə·nət·li/ *adv* without any doubt; certainly ○ *I don't like that place – I'm definitely not going back there.* ○ *"Are you really going to quit your job?" "Definitely!"* ○ **USAGE:** Definitely is often used for emphasis, esp. in speech.

definite article *n* [C] ***grammar*** the word "the" in English, or the words in other languages that have a similar use ○ Compare INDEFINITE ARTICLE

definition Ⓐ **EXPLANATION** /ˌdef·əˈnɪʃ·ən/ *n* [C] ***English*** a statement that explains the meaning of a word or phrase ○ *What is the definition of "mood"?*

SEEING CLEARLY /ˌdef·əˈnɪʃ·ən/ *n* [U] the degree to which something can be clearly seen or heard ○ *The tape recorded conversation lacked definition – there was too much background noise.*

IDIOM with **definition**

• **by definition** because of the nature of someone or something ○ *Circus performers are, by definition, risk takers.*

definitive Ⓐ /dɪ ˈfɪn·ət̬·ɪv/ *adj* firm, final, and complete; not to be questioned or changed ○

D

There is no definitive scientific evidence that coffee is harmful.

deflate /dɪˈfleɪt/ *v* [I/T] **1** to allow air or gas to escape from within a container ○ [T] *When the roads are icy, you may have to deflate your tires a bit.* **2** *fig.* Someone or something that is deflated suddenly feels or is considered less important: [T] *The allegations deflate the respect people have for the presidency.*

D

deflect /dɪˈflekt/ *v* [T] to cause something to change direction, or to suddenly go in a different direction ○ *The ionosphere deflects radio waves.* ○ (*fig.*) *The mayor deflected* (= did not answer directly) *questions about his political plans.*
deflection /dɪˈflek·ʃən/ *n* [U]

deform /dɪˈfɔːrm/ *v* [I/T] to change the shape or structure, esp. by using great pressure ○ *Heat generated by intense pressure deforms the rock.*
deformed /dɪˈfɔːrmd/ *adj* spoiled by not having a usual or regular shape or structure ○ *The shale in this area is deformed and folding of the rock can be seen.* ○ *The child was born with a deformed heart.*
deformity /dɪˈfɔːr·mət̬·i/ *n* [C/U] ○ [C] *She was born with a deformity of the spine.*

defraud /dɪˈfrɔːd/ *v* [T] to take or keep something illegally from someone by deceiving the person ○ *She is charged with defrauding the Internal Revenue Service.*

defrost /dɪˈfrɔːst/ *v* [I/T] to become or cause something to become free of ice or no longer frozen ○ [I] *Take some meat out of the freezer to defrost for supper.*

deft /deft/ *adj* [-er/-est only] skillful, effective, and quick ○ *He cut some logs up for firewood with a few deft strokes of his ax.*
deftly /ˈdef·tli/ *adv* ○ *She deftly answered the tough questions.*

defunct /dɪˈfʌŋkt/ *adj* [not gradable] no longer existing ○ *He was a reporter for the defunct New York Herald newspaper.*

defuse /dɪˈfjuːz/ *v* [T] **1** to make a difficult or dangerous situation calmer ○ *The two groups are trying to defuse tensions in the town council over the budget.* **2** If you defuse a bomb, you prevent it from exploding.

defy /dɪˈfɑɪ/ *v* [T] to refuse to obey or to do something in the usual or expected way ○ *They defied an evacuation order and stayed in town during the hurricane.* ○ *He defied the odds* (= did what no one expected) *and won the race for mayor.*
defiance /dɪˈfɑɪ·əns/ *n* [U] proud and determined opposition against authority or against someone more powerful than you are ○ *They are continuing to publish their newspaper, in defiance of government attempts to close it down.*
defiant /dɪˈfɑɪ·ənt/ *adj* ○ *She is defiant, angry, and tough.*
defiantly /dɪˈfɑɪ·ənt·li/ *adv* ○ *When I said she might fail, she replied defiantly, "No, I won't!"*

degenerate /dɪˈdʒen·əˌreɪt/ *v* [I] to become worse ○ *Standards of courtesy have degenerated since I was a girl.*
degenerate /dɪˈdʒen·ə·rət/ *adj* bad or worse in quality or character, or (of a person) morally bad ○ *He was a lazy, degenerate young man.*
degeneration /dɪˌdʒen·əˈreɪ·ʃən, ˌdiː-/ *n* [U] the process of becoming worse ○ *X-rays showed some degeneration of bone.*

degradable /dɪˈgreɪd·ə·bəl/ *adj* short form of BIODEGRADABLE

degradation /ˌdeg·rəˈdeɪ·ʃən/ *n* [U] the process by which something is made worse, esp. the quality of land ○ *One of the effects of environmental degradation is the absence of fish in that river.*

degrade REDUCE /dɪˈgreɪd/ *v* [T] **1** to reduce the quality of something ○ *degrading water/air quality* ○ *degraded sound quality* ○ *The state is funding projects to restore degraded wetlands.* **2** ***chemistry, physics*** A substance that degrades changes to chemical structures that are more simple.

LESSEN WORTH /dɪˈgreɪd/ *v* [T] to cause someone to seem to be worth less and lose the respect of others ○ *His depiction in the movie degrades him.*
degrading /dɪˈgreɪd·ɪŋ/ *adj* making you feel ashamed and worthless as a person ○ *a degrading job*

degree AMOUNT /dɪˈgriː/ *n* [C/U] an amount or level of something ○ [C] *This job demands a high degree of skill.* ○ [C] *The house had also been damaged, but to a lesser degree.*

TEMPERATURE UNIT /dɪˈgriː/, *symbol* ° *n* [C] a unit of measurement of temperature, often shown by the symbol ° written after a number ○ *The temperature is expected to climb to 90° tomorrow.*

ANGLE MEASUREMENT /dɪˈgriː/, *symbol* ° *n* [C] ***geometry*** a unit of measurement of angles, often shown by the symbol ° written after a number

NUMBER /dɪˈgriː/ *n* [C] ***algebra*** **1** an EXPONENT NUMBER (= number that shows how many times another number is to be multiplied by itself) **2** A **degree of a monomial** is the total of the EXPONENTS in a mathematical statement. **3** A **degree of a polynomial** is the largest of the EXPONENTS in a mathematical statement.

ACHIEVEMENT /dɪˈgriː/ *n* [C] the level of achievement recognized for a student who has completed a course of study at a college or university ○ *She earned a bachelor's degree in history from Yale.*

dehydrate /ˌdiːˌhɑɪˈdreɪt/ *v* [I/T] to lose water, or to cause something to lose water ○ [T] *The vegetables were dehydrated and frozen.*
dehydration /ˌdiːˌhɑɪˈdreɪ·ʃən/ *n* [U] ○ *In hot, dry weather you need to drink lots of water to avoid dehydration.*

deign /deɪn/ *v* [+ *to* infinitive] to agree to do something although you consider yourself too important to have to do it ○ *Mr. Clinton did not deign to reply.*

deity /ˈdiː·ət̬·i, ˈdeɪ-/ *n* [C] **1** a god ○ *Zeus was an ancient Greek deity.* **2** The Deity is God.

déjà vu /ˌdeɪˌʒɑˈvuː/ *n* [U] the strange feeling that in some way you have already experienced what is happening now

dejected /dɪˈdʒek·təd/ *adj* unhappy, disappointed, or lacking hope ○ *William felt dejected because he had sprained his ankle and had to sit out the game.*

dejection /dɪˈdʒek·ʃən/ *n* [U]

delay /dɪˈleɪ/ *v* [I/T] to cause to be late or to cause to happen at a later time, or to wait before acting ○ [T] *He wants to delay the meeting until Wednesday.* ○ [T] *The space launch was delayed because of bad weather.* ○ [I] *Don't delay in ordering tickets to the show.*

delay /dɪˈleɪ/ *n* [C/U] a period when something that might happen does not happen or does not happen quickly enough, or the failure to act quickly ○ [U] *You need to call back without delay.* ○ [C] *The holiday traffic is likely to cause long delays.* ○ [C] *Any further delay would threaten the entire project.*

delectable /dɪˈlek·tə·bəl/ *adj* giving great pleasure ○ *a delectable cake*

delegate CHOSEN PERSON /ˈdel·ə·gət/ *n* [C] a person chosen or elected by a group to represent them, esp. at a meeting ○ *Each state chooses delegates to the national convention.*

delegate /ˈdel·əˌgeɪt/ *v* [T] ○ *Four teachers were delegated to represent the school at the conference.*

delegation /ˌdel·əˈgeɪ·ʃən/ *n* [C] a set of people chosen or elected to represent a larger group

GIVE /ˈdel·əˌgeɪt/ *v* [I/T] to give a job or responsibility to someone in a lower position instead of doing it yourself ○ [T] *Personnel matters made him uncomfortable, and he increasingly delegated them to others.*

delete /dɪˈliːt/ *v* [I/T] to remove (part or all of) a written or electronic text ○ [T] *She accidentally deleted one of her computer files.* ○ [T] *The editor deleted the last three paragraphs.*

deletion /dɪˈliː·ʃən/ *n* [C/U] **1** a part removed from a written or electronic text, or the act of removing such a part ○ [C] *You will have to make some deletions to cut the article to 3000 words.* **2** ***biology*** A deletion is also the loss of part of a CHROMOSOME (= structure containing the information that controls what plants and animals are like), or the chromosome that results from such a loss.

deli /ˈdel·i/ *n* [C] *pl* **delis** *short form of* DELICATESSEN

deliberate INTENTIONAL /dɪˈlɪb·ə·rət/ *adj* **1** (of an action or a decision) intentional or planned, often with the result of being harmful to someone ○ *a deliberate insult* ○ *He accused her of writing deliberate untruths.* **2** Someone who moves, acts, or thinks in a deliberate way moves, acts, or thinks slowly and usually carefully.

deliberately /dɪˈlɪb·ə·rət·li/ *adv* ○ *He did it deliberately to annoy me.*

CONSIDER /dɪˈlɪb·əˌreɪt/ *v* [I/T] to think or talk seriously and carefully about something ○ [I] *The jury deliberated for two days before reaching a verdict.*

deliberation /dɪˌlɪb·əˈreɪ·ʃən/ *n* [C/U] ○ [U] *After much deliberation, she decided to accept their offer.*

delicacy /ˈdel·ɪ·kə·si/ *n* [C] something esp. rare or expensive that is good to eat ○ *a dinner of Vietnamese delicacies*

delicate EASILY DAMAGED /ˈdel·ɪ·kət/ *adj* **1** needing careful treatment, esp. because easily damaged ○ *a delicate flower* ○ *delicate jewelry* **2** Delicate also means needing to be dealt with carefully in order to avoid causing trouble or offense: *The negotiations have reached a delicate stage.* ○ *It's a delicate operation, and you want an experienced surgeon to do it.*

delicately /ˈdel·ɪ·kət·li/ *adv* ○ *Please handle the china delicately.*

delicacy /ˈdel·ɪ·kə·si/ *n* [U] ○ *We need to discuss a matter of some delicacy* (= needing to be handled carefully in order not to cause trouble or offense).

PLEASANT /ˈdel·ɪ·kət/ *adj* pleasant but not easily noticed or strong ○ *a delicate flavor* ○ *We chose a delicate floral pattern for our bedroom curtains.*

delicatessen /ˌdel·ɪ·kəˈtes·ən/, *short form* **deli** *n* [C] a store that sells foods such as cheeses, types of cold meat, salads, and often cooked foods

delicious /dɪˈlɪʃ·əs/ *adj* very pleasant, esp. to taste or smell ○ *Judy's fried chicken is delicious.*

delight /dɪˈlɑɪt/ *n* [C/U] great pleasure, satisfaction, or happiness, or something or someone that gives this ○ [C] *My sister's little boy is a real delight.* ○ [U] *His music teacher expressed delight with his performance.*

delight /dɪˈlɑɪt/ *v* [T] ○ *The songs of countrypeople and of sailors delight me.* ○ *Peter's success at college delighted his family.*

delighted /dɪˈlɑɪt·əd/ *adj* ○ *a delighted expression* ○ [+ to infinitive] *I'm delighted to meet you.*

delightful /dɪˈlɑɪt·fəl/ *adj* full of pleasure ○ *We spent a delightful weekend in Maine.*

PHRASAL VERB with **delight**

• **delight in** *something* to enjoy something, esp. doing something annoying to someone else ○ *My brother always delights in telling me when I make a mistake.*

delineate SHOW BORDER /dɪˈlɪn·iːˌeɪt/ *v* [T] to mark the border of something ○ *The boundary of the park is delineated by a row of trees.*

DESCRIBE /dɪˈlɪn·iːˌeɪt/ *v* [T] to describe something completely, including details ○ *The constitution carefully delineates the duties of the treasurer's office.*

delinquency /dɪˈlɪŋ·kwən·si/ *n* [U] illegal or unacceptable behavior ○ *efforts to combat juvenile delinquency*

delinquent /dɪˈlɪŋ·kwənt/ *adj fml* late in paying money owed ○ *She was delinquent in paying her taxes.*

delirious /dɪˈlɪr·iː·əs/ *adj* **1** thinking or speaking in a way that is not reasonable because of mental confusion ○ *He grew feverish and then delirious.* **2** Delirious also means extremely happy: *delirious with joy*

deliver TAKE TO /dɪˈlɪv·ər/ *v* [I/T] to take goods, letters, or packages to people's houses or places of work ○ [T] *We had the pizza delivered.* ○ [T] *We call* *our pharmacy with the doctor's prescription and ask them to deliver it.* ○ [I] *We deliver anywhere in the city.*

delivery /dɪˈlɪv·ə·ri/ *n* [C/U] ○ [C] *The company gets two deliveries a day.* ○ [U] *You can pay for the rug on delivery* (= when it is received).

GIVE /dɪˈlɪv·ər/ *v* [T] to give or produce a speech or result ○ *The president is scheduled to deliver a speech on foreign policy.* ○ *The jury delivered a verdict of not guilty.*

delivery /dɪˈlɪv·ə·ri/ *n* [U] the manner in which someone speaks, esp. in public ○ *His dialogue was offbeat, his delivery fast.*

GIVE BIRTH /dɪˈlɪv·ər/ *v* [T] to give birth to a baby, or to help someone do this ○ *Dr. Adams delivered all three of my children.*

delivery /dɪˈlɪv·ə·ri/ *n* [C] the act or process of birth

PRODUCE /dɪˈlɪv·ər/ *v* [I/T] to achieve or produce something promised or expected ○ [I] *You pay your dues, and you expect the union to deliver.*

delta /ˈdel·tə/ *n* [C] an area of low, flat land, sometimes shaped approximately like a triangle, where a river divides into several smaller rivers before flowing into the sea ○ *the Mississippi delta*

delude /dɪˈluːd/ *v* [T] to fool yourself into believing something is true because you want it to be true, when it is actually not true ○ *He's deluding himself if he thinks he's going to get that promotion.*

deluge LARGE AMOUNT /ˈdel·juːdʒ, -juːʒ/ *n* [C usually sing] a very large volume of something, more than can be managed ○ *The newspaper received a deluge of complaints about the article.*

deluge /ˈdel·juːdʒ, -juːʒ/ *v* [T] ○ *The senator's office was deluged with calls asking for clarification.*

RAIN /ˈdel·juːdʒ, -juːʒ/ *n* [C] a very large amount of rain or water

delusion /dɪˈluː·ʒən/ *n* [C] something a person believes and wants to be true, when it is actually not true ○ [C] *We have no delusions that these kids are going to play pro basketball, but they are having fun.*

deluxe /dɪˈlʌks/ *adj* [not gradable] of very high quality ○ *a deluxe hotel*

delve into *something* /ˈdelv ˈɪn·tuː, -ˈɪn·tə/ *phrasal verb* to search in order to find a thing or information ○ *She said she was tired of journalists delving into her private life.*

demagogue /ˈdem·əˌɡɑɡ/ *n* [C] *disapproving* a person, esp. a political leader, who wins support by exciting people's emotions rather than giving them reasons

demand /dɪˈmænd/ *v* **1** to ask for forcefully, in a way that shows that refusal is not expected and will not be accepted ○ [T] *The library demanded $5 for each book returned late.* ○ [+ to infinitive] *I demand to see the person in charge.* **2** To demand is also to need something: [T] *The twins demand a lot of attention.*

demand /dɪˈmænd/ *n* [C/U] **1** something asked for forcefully, or something that you accept as necessary ○ [C] *The union's major demand was for improved benefits.* ○ [C] *The demands of nursing are too great for a lot of people.* **2** Demand is also need: [C] *We can't meet the demand for tickets to the game.* ○ [U] *Good teachers are always in demand* (= needed). **3** Demand is also the desire to buy goods: *There was weak demand for imported goods last month.*

demanding /dɪˈmæn·dɪŋ/ *adj* someone or something that needs a lot of attention, effort, or time ○ *I'm trying to learn English, and I find it very demanding.*

USAGE

demand or ask?

Demand is stronger than the word **ask** and it sounds as if you are forcing someone to do something.

I demand to speak to the manager.
He asked the teacher to repeat the question.
~~*He demanded the teacher to repeat the question.*~~

WORD FAMILY demand			
Nouns	demand	*Verbs*	demand
Adjectives	demanding		

demean /dɪˈmiːn/ *v* [T] to cause to become less respected ○ *I wouldn't demean myself by asking my father for money.*

demeaning /dɪˈmiː·nɪŋ/ *adj* ○ *It was demeaning to be asked to leave because I was dressed informally.*

demeanor, *Cdn, Br* **demeanour** /dɪˈmiː·nər/ *n* [U] a way of looking and behaving ○ *The boss has a calm, reassuring demeanor.*

demented /dɪˈment·əd/ *adj* mentally ill

dementia /dɪˈmen·tʃə/ *n* [U] a disease or condition that exists esp. among older people, and that results in the gradual loss of mental abilities, such as the ability to think, reason, and remember things

demilitarize /diːˈmɪl·ə·təˌrɑɪz/ *v* [T] ***politics & government*** to remove all soldiers and weapons from a place so that war cannot happen there

demise /dɪˈmɑɪz/ *n* [U] **1** the end of the operation or existence of something ○ *Huge corporate farms have led to the demise of many small, family-owned farms.* **2** *fml* (of a person) Demise means death.

demo /ˈdem·oʊ/ *n* [C] *pl* **demos** *short form of* DEMONSTRATION ○ *I saw several interesting demos at the trade show last week.*

demobilize /diːˈmoʊ·bəˌlɑɪz/, *short form* **demob** /diːˈmɑb/ *v* [I/T] ***politics & government*** **1** to remove a soldier or soldiers from military service **2** To demobilize can also mean to stop all military operations at the end of a war.

democracy /dɪˈmɑk·rə·si/ *n* [C/U] ***politics & government*** **1** the belief in freedom and equality between people, or a system of government based on this belief, in which power is either held by elected representatives or directly by the people themselves **2** A democracy is a country in which power is held by elected representatives.

democratic /ˈdem·əˌkræt̬·ɪk/ *adj* **1** (of a nation) using the principles of democracy in elections and government **2** A person or a group that is democratic believes in, encourages, or supports democracy in people, groups, or nations.

WORD FAMILY democracy			
Nouns	democracy democrat	*Adjectives*	democratic

democrat /ˈdem·əˌkræt/ *n* [C] ***politics & government*** a person who supports or believes in government by the people or their representatives

democratic /ˌdem·əˈkræt̬·ɪk/ *adj* ***politics & government*** ○ *That country has never had a democratic election* (= an election in which all adults can vote).

Democratic Party *n* [U] one of the two main political parties in the US

demographic /ˌdem·əˈgræf·ɪk, ˌdiː·mə-/ *adj* [not gradable] ***social studies*** relating to human POPULATIONS and the information collected about them, such as their size, growth, ages, and education ○ *More than any other demographic group, it is the educated young adult who has been the industry's favorite customer.*

demographics /ˌdem·əˈgræf·ɪks, ˌdiː·mə-/ *pl n* ***social studies*** ○ *Southern California's demographics make it a particularly good used-car market.*

demolish /dɪˈmɑl·ɪʃ/ *v* [T] to completely destroy buildings or other structures ○ *Most of the town was demolished by the tornado.* ○ *They demolished the old school to build a new one.*

demolition /ˌdem·əˈlɪʃ·ən/ *n* [C/U] the act of destroying something, such as a building or other structure ○ [C] *They tried unsuccessfully to stop the demolition of the old hotel.*

demon /ˈdiː·mən/ *n* [C] an evil spirit

demonize /ˈdiː·məˌnɑɪz/ *v* [T] to try to make someone or a group of people seem completely evil ○ *The mayor demonizes anyone who disagrees with him.*

demonstrate Ⓐ **SHOW HOW** /ˈdem·ənˌstreɪt/ *v* [T] to show how to do something; explain ○ [+ question word] *He demonstrated how to use the new software.* ○ *The surgeon demonstrated the use of lasers for certain operations.*

demonstration Ⓐ /ˌdem·ənˈstreɪ·ʃən/, *short form* **demo** *n* [C/U] ○ [C] *Let me give you a demonstration of how the camera works.*

demonstrable Ⓐ /dɪˈmɑn·strə·bəl/ *adj* ○ *Governments must make demonstrable progress toward this goal by 2010.*

demonstrably Ⓐ /dɪˈmɑn·strə·bli/ *adv*

PROVE /ˈdem·ənˌstreɪt/ *v* [T] to show that something is true; prove ○ [+ *that* clause] *Research demonstrates that babies can recognize their mother's voice very soon after birth.* ○ *She was eager to demonstrate her skill at chess.*

demonstrable Ⓐ /dɪˈmɑn·strə·bəl/ *adj* ○ *Mr. Ambrose, to be credible, needed some demonstrable facts.*

demonstrably Ⓐ /dɪˈmɑn·strə·bli/ *adv*

EXPRESS /ˈdem·ənˌstreɪt/ *v* [T] to express or show that you have a feeling, quality, or ability ○ *His answer demonstrated a complete lack of understanding of the question.*

demonstration Ⓐ /ˌdem·ənˈstreɪ·ʃən/ *n* [C/U] ○ [C] *a demonstration of friendship*

demonstrative Ⓐ /dɪˈmɑn·strət̬·ɪv/ *adj* behaving in a way that clearly shows your feelings ○ *She was always a demonstrative child.*

demonstratively Ⓐ /dɪˈmɑn·strət̬·ɪv·li/ *adv*

MARCH /ˈdem·ənˌstreɪt/ *v* [I] (of a group of people) to make a public expression of complaint about a problem or support for something, esp. by marching or meeting

demonstration /ˌdem·ənˈstreɪ·ʃən/ *n* [C] ○ *Students staged a protest demonstration in the school gym.*

demonstrator /ˈdem·ənˌstreɪt̬·ər/ *n* [C] ○ *Several demonstrators were arrested when they sat down in the middle of Broadway.*

WORD FAMILY demonstrate			
Nouns	demonstration demonstrator	*Adjectives* *Verbs*	demonstrative demonstrate

demonstrative /dɪˈmɑn·strət̬·ɪv/ *adj* ***grammar*** showing which person or thing is being referred to ○ *a demonstrative adjective* ○ *In "This is my brother," "this" is a demonstrative pronoun.*

demoralize /dɪˈmɔːr·əˌlɑɪz, diː-, -ˈmɑr-/ *v* [T] to weaken the confidence of someone ○ *The team was tired and thoroughly demoralized.*

demote /dɪˈmoʊt/ *v* [T] to lower someone in rank or position ○ *The department is planning to demote some managers as a cost-saving measure.* ○ Opposite: PROMOTE ADVANCE

demotion /dɪˈmoʊ·ʃən/ *n* [C/U] ○ [U] *He faces possible demotion.*

demur /dɪˈmɜr/ *v* [I] **-rr-** to express disagreement or refusal to do something ○ *Jack urged me to go, but I demurred.*

demure /dɪˈmjʊr/ *adj* (esp. of women and girls) quiet and well behaved ○ *Two demure little girls sat near their mother.*

den /den/ *n* [C] **1** a room in a home that is used esp. for reading and watching television ○ *We have a computer in the den.* **2** A den is also the home of some types of wild animals.

dendrite /ˈden·drɑɪt/ *n* [C] ***biology*** the short parts like threads at the edge of a nerve cell that carry messages to the cell

denial /dɪˈnɑɪ·əl/ *n* See at DENY

WORD FAMILY denial			
Nouns	denial	*Verbs*	deny
Adjectives	undeniable	*Adverbs*	undeniably

denigrate /ˈden·əˌɡreɪt/ *v* [T] to say that someone or something is not good or important

denim /ˈden·əm/ *n* [U] a thick, strong, cotton cloth, often blue

denitrify /diːˈnɑɪ·trəˌfɑɪ/ *v* [T] ***biology*** **1** to remove NITROGEN (= one of the gases that surrounds the earth) or chemicals containing nitrogen, for example, from the SOIL (= material on the surface of the ground), and so release it into the air **2 Denitrifying bacteria** are bacteria that help to release nitrogen into the air by reducing the amount in chemicals that contain it.

D

denomination RELIGIOUS GROUP /dɪˌnɑm·əˈneɪ·ʃən/ *n* [C] a religious group whose beliefs differ in some ways from other groups in the same religion ○ *The petition was signed by clergy from over 20 Protestant denominations.*

denominational /dɪˌnɑm·əˈneɪ·ʃən·əl/ *adj* [not gradable] ○ *He avoids denominational rivalries.*

VALUE /dɪˌnɑm·əˈneɪ·ʃən/ *n* [C] a unit of value, esp. of money ○ *The machines take coins of any denomination.*

denominator /dɪˈnɑm·əˌneɪt̬·ər/ *n* [C] ***mathematics*** in a FRACTION (= part of a whole number), the number written below the line, showing how many parts the whole contains ○ Compare NUMERATOR

denote /dɪˈnoʊt/ *v* [T] to represent or mean something ○ *His angry tone denoted extreme displeasure.*

denouement /ˌdeɪ·nuːˈmɑ̃/ *n* [C] ***literature*** the final part of a work of literature, after the CLIMAX (= the most important or exciting part)

denounce /dɪˈnɑʊns/ *v* [T] to criticize someone or something strongly and publicly ○ *The teachers denounced the contract offer as inadequate.*

dense THICK /dens/ *adj* [*-er/-est* only] **1** close together and difficult to go or see through; thick ○ *dense fog* ○ *I had trouble getting through the dense crowd.* **2** Dense can also mean stupid: *There are some really dense people in our class.*

densely /ˈden·sli/ *adv* ○ *a densely packed room*

density /ˈden·sət̬·i/, **denseness** /ˈden·snəs/ *n* [C/U] ○ [U] *The density of the smoke made it difficult to breathe.*

CONTAINING MATTER /dens/ *adj* [*-er/-est* only] ***science*** (of a substance) containing a lot of matter in a small space ○ *Plutonium is very dense.*

density /ˈden·sət̬·i/ *n* [C/U] ***physics*** the relationship between the mass of a substance and its size ○ [C] *Lead has a high density.*

dent /dent/ *n* [C] a small, hollow mark in the surface of something caused by pressure or being hit ○ *She ran into my car and put a dent in it.*

dent /dent/ *v* [T] ○ *I dented the table with my hammer.*

IDIOM with dent

• **make a dent in** *something*, **put a dent in** *something* to reduce an amount of something, esp. money or work ○ *Buying a new car put a big dent in our savings.* ○ *I haven't even made a dent in that huge stack of papers I have to read.*

dental /ˈdent·əl/ *adj* [not gradable] relating to the teeth ○ *dental health*

dental floss *n* [U] a type of thread that is used for cleaning between the teeth

dentist /ˈdent·əst/ *n* [C] a person whose job is treating people's teeth

dentistry /ˈdent·ə·stri/ *n* [U] the work or science of treating people's teeth ○ *Where did Dr. Yee study dentistry?*

dentures /ˈden·tʃərz/ *pl n* artificial teeth worn by people who do not have their own teeth ○ *a set of dentures*

denunciation /dɪˌnʌn·siːˈeɪ·ʃən/ *n* [C/U] a strong, public criticism ○ [C] *He gave a ringing denunciation of fascism.*

deny Ⓐ CLAIM TO BE NOT TRUE /dɪˈnɑɪ/ *v* [T] to say that something is not true ○ *The governor denied reports that he will resign.* ○ [+ *that* clause] *She has denied that she plans to run for mayor.*

denial Ⓐ /dɪˈnɑɪ·əl/ *n* [C] ○ *His statement is not a denial.*

deniable Ⓐ /dɪˈnɑɪ·ə·bəl/ *adj*

REFUSE /dɪˈnɑɪ/ *v* [T] to refuse to permit or allow someone to do something ○ *She denied herself the things that would make her happy.*

denial Ⓐ /dɪˈnɑɪ·əl/ *n* [U] ○ *Planning staff recommended denial of the project.* ○ See also: SELF-DENIAL

NOT ADMIT /dɪˈnɑɪ/ *v* [T] to fail to admit that you have knowledge, responsibility, or feelings ○ *He denied knowing about the plan.*

denial Ⓐ /dɪˈnɑɪ·əl/ *n* [C] ○ *He claims he's not sick, but I think he's just in denial.*

deodorant /diːˈoʊd·ə·rənt/ *n* [C/U] a substance that is used to prevent or hide unpleasant smells, esp. those of the body ○ [C/U] *Someone should tell him to use (a) deodorant.*

deoxyribonucleic acid /diːˌɑk·siːˌrɑɪ·boʊ·nuːˌkliː·ɪkˈæs·əd, -ˌkleɪ·ɪk/ *n* [U] ***biology*** DNA.

depart /dɪˈpɑrt/ *v* [I] **1** to go away from a place, esp. on a trip ○ *The last flight to Cleveland departs at 8 p.m.* ○ *He shook hands and then departed.* **2** If you depart from your usual or intended activity or behavior, you do something different: *On the last show, they departed from their usual format.*

department /dɪˈpɑrt·mənt/, *abbreviation* **dept.** *n* [C] any of the divisions or parts of esp. a school, business, or government ○ *Chavez is the head of the geography department.* ○ *The shoe department is on the fifth floor.* ○ *She lives in Washington and works for the Department of Defense.* ○ *(fig.)* *(infml)* *I thought buying the tickets was your department* (= area of responsibility).

departmental /dɪˌpɑrtˈment·əl, ˌdiː-/ *adj* [not gradable] ○ *a departmental meeting*

department store *n* [C] a large store divided into several different areas, each of which sells different types of things

departure /dɪˈpɑr·tʃər/ *n* [C/U] **1** the act of leaving a place, job, etc., or an occasion when this happens ○ [U] *Departure is scheduled for 2 p.m.* ○ [C] *Our departure was delayed because of bad weather.* **2** A departure from usual behavior is a change in the way you do something: [C] *His departure from his usual optimism startled his staff.*

depend /dɪˈpend/ *v* [I] to be influenced or determined by something else ○ *All of this* **depends on** *how the test is constructed.* ○ *"Do you eat out at lunchtime?" "Well,* **it depends***. I usually bring lunch, but sometimes I go out."*

> USAGE
> **depend**
> Remember that the correct preposition after **depend** is **on** when a noun follows.
> *I might go sailing on Friday, it depends on the weather.*
> ~~*I might go sailing on Friday, it depends from the weather.*~~

WORD FAMILY depend

Nouns	dependent dependence independence dependency	*Adjectives*	dependable dependent independent
		Adverbs	independently
Verbs	depend		

PHRASAL VERBS with depend

• **depend on/upon** *someone/something* **NEED SUPPORT** to need the support of someone or something ○ *Children depend on their parents.* ○ *The country depends heavily upon foreign aid.*

• **depend on/upon** *someone/something* **HAVE TRUST** to have confidence in someone or something; trust ○ *You can always depend on Michael in a crisis.*

dependable /dɪˈpen·də·bəl/ *adj* deserving of trust or confidence ○ *I need a dependable babysitter.*

dependence /dɪˈpen·dəns/, **dependency** /dɪˈpen·dən·si/ *n* [U] a state of needing something or someone, esp. in order to continue existing or operating ○ *The company is reducing its dependence on foreign markets.*

dependent /dɪˈpen·dənt/ *adj* needing the support of something or someone in order to continue existing or operating ○ *She has three dependent children.* ○ *West Virginia's economy is highly dependent on the mining industry.* ○ *Grapes need a long, slow ripening period, and that is dependent on temperature.*

dependent /dɪˈpen·dənt/ *n* [C] a person who is financially supported by another person ○ *Jack and Marion have four dependents.*

dependent clause *n* [C] ***grammar*** a clause in a sentence that cannot form a separate sentence but can be joined to a main clause to form a sentence

dependent variable *n* [C] ***algebra*** a number or amount whose value depends on the value of another VARIABLE (= number) in the same mathematical statement

depict /dɪˈpɪkt/ *v* [T] to represent or show something in a picture, story, movie, etc.; PORTRAY ○ *The movie depicts his father as a tyrant.*

depiction /dɪˈpɪk·ʃən/ *n* [C/U] ○ [C] *It's a wonderful depiction of a female friendship.*

deplete /dɪˈpliːt/ *v* [T] to reduce something in size or amount, esp. supplies, energy, or money ○ *Acid rain depletes the region's fish stocks.*

depletion /dɪˈpliː·ʃən/ *n* [C/U] ○ [U] *The depletion of our savings is starting to worry me.*

deplore /dɪˈplɔːr, -ˈploʊr/ *v* [T] to say or think that something is very bad; CONDEMN CRITICIZE ○ *The editors deplore the lack of attention given to climate change.*

deplorable /dɪˈplɔːr·ə·bəl, -ˈploʊr-/ *adj* very bad ○ *The children were raised in deplorable conditions.*

deploy /dɪˈplɔɪ/ *v* [I/T] **1** to put something into use ○ [I] *When airbags deploy, they save lives.* ○ [T] *Automobiles deploy air bags in crashes of 8 to 12 miles per hour.* **2** To deploy is also to move weapons or military forces to where they will be used when they are needed: [T] *The UN is deploying observers.*

deployment /dɪˈplɔɪ·mənt/ *n* [U] ○ *the deployment of missiles/troops*

deport /dɪˈpɔːrt, -ˈpoʊrt/ *v* [T] to force a person to leave a country ○ *The government hopes to deport the criminals.*

deportation /ˌdiːˌpɔːrˈteɪ·ʃən, -ˌpoʊr-/ *n* [C/U] ○ [U] *They await deportation.*

depose /dɪˈpoʊz, diː-/ *v* [T] to remove someone from a position of authority ○ *The exiled president was deposed during a military coup last year.*

deposit **MONEY** /dɪˈpɑz·ət/ *n* [C] **1** an amount of money paid into an account ○ *She made a large deposit last Thursday.* **2** A deposit is also a sum of money that is given in advance as part of a total payment for something: *Will you get your deposit back if you cancel the trip?* **3** A deposit is also an additional sum of money that you pay when you rent something to make sure you return the item or to pay for repairs: *The apartment rents for $1200 a month, and we want one month's rent for a deposit.* **4** A deposit is also an amount paid in addition to the cost of something to make sure you bring its container back when you have used it: *a bottle deposit*

deposit /dɪˈpɑz·ət/ *v* [T] to put money in a bank ○ *I deposited $500 in my savings account last week.*

depositor /dɪˈpɑz·ət̬·ər/ *n* [C] a person who keeps money at a bank ○ *Depositors will be informed of any change in interest rates.*

LAYER /dɪˈpɑz·ət/ *n* [C] a layer of a substance ○ *The flood left a thick deposit of mud on the floor.* ○ *The region has lots of gas and coal deposits.*

LEAVE /dɪˈpɑz·ət/ *v* [T always + adv/prep] to leave something somewhere ○ *The cat deposited a dead mouse at my door.*

deposition **STATEMENT** /ˌdep·əˈzɪʃ·ən, ˌdiː·pə-/ *n* [C] *law* a formal written statement by a WITNESS in a legal matter

CHANGE /ˌdep·əˈzɪʃ·ən, ˌdiː·pə-/ *n* [U] ***chemistry*** a process in which a gas changes to a solid without first becoming a liquid

SUBSTANCE /ˌdep·əˈzɪʃ·ən/ *n* [C/U] ***earth science*** the process by which solid materials, such as earth and rock, are added to gradually by the action of wind or water, or the structure resulting from this process

D

depot /ˈdep·oʊ, ˈdiː·poʊ/ *n* [C] **1** a building where supplies or vehicles are kept ○ *a fuel depot* **2** A depot is also a building that buses and trains leave from.

depreciate /dɪˈpriː·ʃiːˌeɪt, -ˈprɪʃ·iː-/ *v* [T] to cause something to lose value, esp. over time ○ *Malawi's currency was rapidly depreciating.*

depreciation /dɪˌpriː·ʃiːˈeɪ·ʃən, -ˌprɪʃ·iː-/ *n* [U] ○ *The dollar's depreciation will lead to higher inflation and interest rates, hurting the economy.*

depress Ⓐ **CAUSE UNHAPPINESS** /dɪˈpres/ *v* [T] to cause a person to feel unhappy and without hope ○ *Bad weather depresses a lot of people.* ○ *It depresses me to think about it.*

depressant /dɪˈpres·ənt/ *n* [C] a substance that causes you to feel sad or calm

depressed Ⓐ /dɪˈprest/ *adj* ○ *He's depressed about his losing his job.*

depressing Ⓐ /dɪˈpres·ɪŋ/ *adj* ○ *Life is depressing enough, I don't need depressing movies.*

depressingly /dɪˈpres·ɪŋ·li/ *adv* ○ *My score was depressingly low.*

depression Ⓐ /dɪˈpreʃ·ən/ *n* [U] a feeling of sadness, or *medical* a type of mental illness that causes long periods of unhappiness ○ *I'm just beginning to get over the depression from losing my job.* ○ *(medical) Tiredness, loss of appetite, and sleeping problems are symptoms of depression.* ○ See also: DEPRESSION at DEPRESS REDUCE; DEPRESSION at DEPRESS PRESS DOWN

REDUCE /dɪˈpres/ *v* [T] to reduce the value of something, esp. money, or to reduce the amount of activity in something such as a business operation ○ *A surplus of corn depressed grain prices.*

depressed Ⓐ /dɪˈprest/ *adj* ○ *This is an economically depressed area.*

depression Ⓐ /dɪˈpreʃ·ən/ *n* [C] ***world history*** a period in which there is very little business activity and little employment ○ *My parents lived through the Great Depression of the 1930s.* ○ See also: DEPRESSION at DEPRESS CAUSE UNHAPPINESS; DEPRESSION at DEPRESS PRESS DOWN

PRESS DOWN /dɪˈpres/ *v* [T] to press down on something ○ *His finger depressed the stop button.*

depression Ⓐ /dɪˈpreʃ·ən/ *n* [C] a part in a surface that is slightly lower than the rest ○ *There was a depression in the sand where he'd been lying.* ○ See also: DEPRESSION at DEPRESS CAUSE UNHAPPINESS; DEPRESSION at DEPRESS REDUCE

deprivation /ˌdep·rəˈveɪ·ʃən/ *n* [C/U] an absence or too little of something important ○ [C] *There were food shortages and other deprivations during the war.*

deprive *someone* **of** *something* /dɪˈpraɪv·əv/ *phrasal verb* to take something, esp. something necessary or pleasant away from someone ○ *He was deprived of food for three days.*

deprived /dɪˈprɑɪvd/ *adj* lacking something that is needed to live the way most people live ○ *He took pictures in deprived areas of the city.*

dept. *n abbreviation for* DEPARTMENT

depth **DISTANCE DOWN** /depθ/ *n* [C/U] the distance down from the top surface of something to the bottom ○ [C] *They were scuba diving at a depth of 22 meters.* ○ [U] *The numbers on the left show the depth in inches.* ○ Related adjective: DEEP DOWN

DISTANCE BACKWARD /depθ/ *n* [C/U] the distance from the front to the back of something ○ [U] *Bookshelves should be at least nine inches in depth.* ○ Related adjective: DEEP FRONT TO BACK

STRENGTH /depθ/ *n* [C/U] the strength, quality, or degree of being complete ○ [U] *It's hard to get a handle on the depth of her knowledge.* ○ See also: DEEP STRONGLY FELT

SERIOUSNESS /depθ/ *n* [C/U] **1** the ability to think seriously about something ○ [U] *Don't look for depth in this show.* **2** Something done **in depth** is done carefully and in great detail: *I interviewed her in depth.* ○ *an in-depth report* ○ See also: DEEP COMPLICATED

IDIOM with depth

• **in the depths of** *something* **1** in the middle of a difficult or unpleasant time or situation ○ *At the time, America was in the depths of the Depression.* **2** If you are **in the depths of** a negative feeling, you feel it very strongly: *He was in the depths of despair about losing his job.*

deputy /ˈdep·jət̬·i/ *n* [C] a person who is given the power to act instead of, or to help do the work of, another person ○ *a deputy chairman* ○ *the deputy editor* ○ *a sheriff's deputy*

derail /dɪˈreɪl, diː-/ *v* [T] to cause a train to run off the tracks ○ *(fig.) Renewed fighting threatens to derail the peace talks* (= stop them from continuing).

deranged /dɪˈreɪndʒd/ *adj* behaving in a way that is dangerous or not controlled because of mental illness ○ *a deranged patient*

derby /ˈdɜr·bi/ *n* [C] a man's hat that has a round, hard top and is usually black

deregulate Ⓐ /diːˈreg·jəˌleɪt/ *v* [T] to remove government controls or rules from a business or other activity

deregulation Ⓐ /ˌdiː·reg·jʊˈleɪ·ʃᵊn/ *n* [U] ○ *The president's advisors recommend further banking-industry deregulation.*

derelict **IN BAD CONDITION** /ˈder·əˌlɪkt/ *adj* (of buildings or equipment) not cared for and in bad condition

PERSON /ˈder·əˌlɪkt/ *n* [C] a person with no home, job, or money who often lives on the streets

deride /dɪˈrɑɪd/ *v* [T] to show that you think someone or something is ridiculous or of no value ○ *His blustery style is derided by many political pros.*

derision /dɪˈrɪʒ·ən/ *n* [U] ○ *Talk of tougher laws was met with derision.*

derisive /dɪˈrɑɪ·sɪv, -zɪv/, **derisory** /dɪˈrɑɪ·sə·ri, -zə·ri/ *adj* ○ *derisive laughter*

derivation Ⓐ /ˌder·əˈveɪ·ʃən/ *n* [U] the origin from which something developed ○ *Does anyone know the derivation of the word "OK"?*

derivative Ⓐ /dɪˈrɪv·ət̬·ɪv/ *adj* having qualities taken from something else ○ *Too much of the music feels derivative.*

derivative Ⓐ /dɪˈrɪv·ət̬·ɪv/ *n* [C] **1** something made from something else ○ *Retinol is a derivative of vitamin A.* **2** ***grammar*** A derivative is also a word that is made from another word.

derive Ⓐ /dɪˈrɑɪv/ *v* [T always + adv/prep] to get or obtain something ○ *The institute derives all its money from foreign investments.*

PHRASAL VERB with derive

• **derive from** *something* to come from something ○ *The story derives from a very common folktale.*

dermatitis /ˌdɜr·məˈtɑɪt̬·əs/ *n* [U] *medical* a red and painful condition of the skin

derogatory /dɪˈrɑg·əˌtɔːr·i, -ˌtoʊr·i/ *adj* expressing criticism or insult ○ *She was upset by derogatory comments made about her clothes.*

derrick /ˈder·ɪk/ *n* [C] a type of CRANE (= machine with a part like a long arm) used for moving heavy things esp. on ships, or a tall structure above a WELL (= hole in the ground) from which oil is taken

descend /dɪˈsend/ *v* [I/T] to go down or come down something ○ [I] *The path descends to the valley below.* ○ [T] *Jane descended the stairs slowly in her wedding gown.*

descent /dɪˈsent/ *n* [C] a way down, such as a path, or an act of coming down ○ *A steep descent from the peak brings you to a meadow.* ○ *The plane is making its final descent into the airport.*

PHRASAL VERBS with descend

• **descend from** *someone/something* **1** to have a particular person, group, or type of people in your family background ○ *He is descended from a long line of farmers.* **2** If one thing descends from or is descended from another, the later thing develops from the earlier thing: *Romance languages are directly descended from Latin.*

• **descend on/upon** *someone/somewhere* to visit someone or arrive somewhere suddenly, without warning or without being invited ○ *Tourists descend on Prince Edward Island every summer.* ○ (*fig.*) *Homesickness descended upon him.*

descendant /dɪˈsen·dənt/ *n* [C] a person related to someone from an earlier GENERATION (= all the people of about the same age within a particular family) ○ *The Pennsylvania Dutch are descendants of early German immigrants.*

descent FAMILY BACKGROUND /dɪˈsent/ *n* [U] the origin of people in your family background ○ *Their mother is of Irish descent* (= family origin).

ARRIVAL /dɪˈsent/ *n* [C usually sing] the arrival of something or someone, esp. when it is unpleasant or unwanted ○ *The descent of dozens of motorcycles terrified local residents.*

describe /dɪˈskrɑɪb/ *v* [T] to give a written or spoken report of how something is done or of what someone or something is like ○ *The scientists described their findings and research methods.* ○ *They want us to prepare a report describing the area.* ○ [+ question word] *Just describe what happened.* ○ *The Democrats describe their rivals as the party of the rich.*

WORD FAMILY describe			
Nouns	description	*Adjectives*	indescribable
Verbs	describe		nondescript
			descriptive

description /dɪˈskrɪp·ʃən/ *n* [C/U] ***literature*** a statement or a piece of writing that tells what something or someone is like ○ [C] *Your description of Della was hilarious.* ○ [U] *Boats of every description* (= of all types) *entered the harbor.* ○ [U] *The beauty of the Rockies is beyond description* (= is impossible to describe).

descriptive /dɪˈskrɪp·tɪv/ *adj* ○ *His poetry skillfully incorporates descriptive details.*

desecrate /ˈdes·əˌkreɪt/ *v* [T] to damage or show a lack of respect toward something holy or respected ○ *Vandals desecrated the monument.*

desecration /ˌdes·əˈkreɪ·ʃən/ *n* [U] ○ *the desecration of a cemetery/shrine/house of worship*

desegregate /diːˈseg·rəˌgeɪt/ *v* [T] ***US history*** to end SEGREGATION (= separation of races) in schools, housing, organizations, etc. ○ *President Truman desegregated the American armed forces in 1948.*

desegregation /ˌdiːˌseg·rəˈgeɪ·ʃən/ *n* [U] ○ *King's campaign was aimed at the desegregation of all public services, including schools, restaurants, and transportation.*

desert LEAVE BEHIND /dɪˈzɜrt/ *v* [T] **1** to leave someone or something without help or in a difficult situation ○ *Local people deserted the city as hordes of tourists arrived.* **2** If you desert the armed forces, you leave without permission and with no intention of returning: *He denied that he had deserted his post.*

deserted /dɪˈzɜrt̬·əd/ *adj* having no people or things in it; empty ○ *These resort towns are largely deserted in winter.* ○ *We parked in a deserted lot near the river.*

deserter /dɪˈzɜrt̬·ər/ *n* [C] a person who leaves the armed forces without permission and with no intention of returning

desertion /dɪˈzɜr·ʃən/ *n* [U] ○ *the act of leaving without permission, or without planning to return* ○ *the act of leaving someone in a difficult situation or without help*

SANDY AREA /ˈdez·ərt/ *n* [C/U] a large, dry area where there is very little rain and few plants ○ [U]

When you live in the desert, water is your most vital resource.

deserve /dɪˈzɜrv/ *v* to have earned something or be given something because of your actions or qualities ○ [T] *These charities deserve your support.* ○ [+ *to* infinitive] *The American people deserve to know what went wrong.* ○ [T] *I hope those crooks get what they deserve* (= receive a punishment that suits their crime).

D

design Ⓐ **PLAN** /dɪˈzɑɪn/ *v* [I/T] to make or draw plans for something ○ [T] *A famous engineer designed the new bridge.* ○ [I] *She designs for a dress manufacturer.*

design Ⓐ /dɪˈzɑɪn/ *n* [C/U] **1** a plan or drawing ○ [C] *Have you seen the designs for the new lobby?* **2** Design is the skill of making plans or drawings for something: [U] *She's an expert in software design.* **3** ***art*** Design is also the way in which something is arranged or shaped: [U] *I like the design of this microwave oven.* **4** ***art*** A design is also a pattern used to decorate something: *a geometric design*

designer Ⓐ /dɪˈzɑɪ·nər/ *n* [C] a person who imagines how something could be made and draws or creates plans for it ○ *a fashion/graphic designer*

INTEND /dɪˈzɑɪn/ *v* [T] to intend a result ○ *These measures are designed to reduce pollution.*

design Ⓐ /dɪˈzɑɪn/ *n* [U] purpose or intention ○ *The details of the case are unclear, and this is* **by design** (= intentional). ○ See also: DESIGNS

designate /ˈdez·ɪɡˌneɪt/ *v* [T] to choose someone or something for a special job or purpose, or to state that something has a particular character or purpose ○ *The chairman designated his daughter as his successor.* ○ *North-south streets are designated by numbers.*

designated /ˈdez·ɪɡˌneɪt̬·əd/ *adj* [not gradable] ○ *a designated waiting area* ○ Compare ELECT

designation /ˌdez·ɪɡˈneɪ·ʃən/ *n* [C/U] ○ [C] *Associate professor is her official designation* (= title).

designated driver *n* [C] someone in a group who will avoid drinks containing alcohol and is then able to drive the others to and from a social event

designer /dɪˈzɑɪ·nər/ *n* ○ See at DESIGN **PLAN**

designs /dɪˈzɑɪnz/ *pl n* plans to get something or someone for yourself, esp. secret or dishonest plans ○ *Troop movements suggest the country has designs on its neighbor.*

desire /dɪˈzɑɪr/ *n* [C/U] a strong feeling of wanting something, or something you want ○ [U] *He claims to have no desire for wealth.* ○ [C] *She expressed a desire to speak with her attorney.* ○ [C] *Teenagers often have a burning desire to look older.* ○ [C] *My desires in life are few.*

desire /dɪˈzɑɪr/ *v* [T] to want something strongly ○ *They don't really seem to desire change.*

desired /dɪˈzɑɪrd/ *adj* wanted ○ *He dressed carefully, hoping to achieve the desired effect.*

desirable /dɪˈzɑɪ·rə·bəl/ *adj* worth wanting or having ○ *Good pay and interesting work make this a very desirable job.* ○ *The new store is in a highly desirable location.*

desirability /dɪˌzɑɪ·rəˈbɪl·ət̬·i/ *n* [U] ○ *Taxes can limit the desirability of home ownership.*

desist /dɪˈzɪst, -ˈsɪst/ *v* [I] *fml* to stop doing something ○ *She was ordered to desist from playing music after 11 p.m.*

desk **TABLE** /desk/ *n* [C] a type of table for working at, usually one with drawers ○ *Tommy sits at the desk in front of me in English.*

SERVICE AREA /desk/ *n* [C] a place where you can get information or service, esp. in a hotel, airport, or large store ○ *The woman at the front desk was very helpful.*

desktop **FOR USE IN ONE PLACE** /ˈdesk·tɑp/ *adj* [not gradable] designed to be used on or at a DESK, and not carried around ○ *a desktop computer*

WORK AREA /ˈdesk·tɑp/ *n* [C] the screen area of a personal computer when no programs are being used, or the top of a DESK ○ *A shortcut to the program will be created on your desktop.*

desktop publishing *n* [U] the process of producing printed material by using a small computer and a printer

desolate **EMPTY** /ˈdes·ə·lət/ *adj* (of a place) having no living things; empty ○ *a desolate landscape*

desolation /ˌdes·əˈleɪ·ʃən/ *n* [U] ○ *It was difficult to describe the emptiness, the desolation of the area.*

SAD /ˈdes·ə·lət/ *adj* (of a person) extremely sad and feeling alone ○ *When her son left for a year abroad, she felt desolate.*

despair /dɪˈsper, -ˈspær/ *n* [U] a feeling of being without hope or of not being able to improve a situation ○ *A few sad moments doesn't imply feelings of despair.* ○ *She flung up her arms in despair and wailed.*

despair /dɪˈsper, -ˈspær/ *v* [I] to lose hope or be without hope ○ *Don't despair – things will improve.* ○ *He began to despair of ever finding a job.*

desperate **RISKY** /ˈdes·pə·rət/ *adj* **1** showing a willingness to take any risk in order to change a bad or dangerous situation ○ *The ads are a desperate attempt to win last-minute votes.* **2** A desperate person is willing to take any measures and may be dangerous: *desperate criminals*

desperation /ˌdes·pəˈreɪ·ʃən/ *n* [U] the feeling of being in such a bad situation that you will take any risk to change it ○ *In desperation, they jumped out of the window to escape the fire.*

SERIOUS /ˈdes·pə·rət/ *adj* very serious or dangerous ○ *There's a desperate shortage of medical supplies in the area.* ○ *The earthquake survivors are in desperate need of help.*

desperately /ˈdes·pə·rət·li/ *adv* extremely or very much ○ *For years they had desperately wanted a child.*

IN NEED /ˈdes·pə·rət/ *adj* having a very great need ○ *She was desperate for news of her family.* ○ *I'm desperate for some coffee.*

despise /dɪˈspɑɪz/ *v* [T] to feel a strong dislike for someone or something that you think is bad or worthless ○ *He adored his daughter, but despised his son.*
despicable /dɪˈspɪk·ə·bəl, ˈdes·pɪk-/ *adj* deserving to be hated or strongly criticized ○ *It was a despicable effort to blackmail voters.*

despite Ⓐ /dɪˈspɑɪt/ *prep* without being influenced or prevented by ○ *The game continued despite the rain.* ○ *Despite her illness, she came to work.*

despondent /dɪˈspɑn·dənt/ *adj* unhappy and discouraged because you feel you are in a situation that is unlikely to improve ○ *He grew increasingly despondent when his paintings failed to sell.*

despot /ˈdes·pət, -ˌpɑt/ *n* [C] a ruler who has unlimited power and often uses it unfairly and cruelly
despotic /desˈpɑt̬·ɪk, dɪs-/ *adj* ○ *a despotic regime*

dessert /dɪˈzɜrt/ *n* [C/U] sweet food eaten at the end of a meal ○ [U] *He had apple pie with ice cream for dessert.*

destination /ˌdes·təˈneɪ·ʃən/ *n* [C] the place where someone is going or where something is being sent or taken ○ *The Virgin Islands are a popular tourist destination.*

destined /ˈdes·tənd/ *adj* **1** intended for or being sent to a particular place ○ *The mail was destined for addresses throughout the Northeast.* **2** To be destined can mean to happen in a particular way that seems to have been decided in advance: [+ *to* infinitive] *He was destined to die before he could complete the poem.*

destiny /ˈdes·tə·ni/ *n* [C/U] **1** the particular state of a person or thing in the future, considered as resulting from earlier events ○ [C] *We all want to determine our own destinies.* **2** Destiny is the force that some people think controls what happens in the future, and which cannot be influenced by people.

destitute /ˈdes·təˌtuːt/ *adj* without money, possessions, or any of the things needed to live ○ *These groups gathered clothing, schoolbooks, and medical supplies for the destitute flood victims.*

destroy /dɪˈstrɔɪ/ *v* [T] to damage something, esp. in a violent way, so that it can no longer be used or no longer exists ○ *You can use a shredder to destroy old bank statements.* ○ *Losing his job seemed to completely destroy his confidence.*
destroyer /dɪˈstrɔɪ·ər/ *n* [C] a small, fast, military ship that carries weapons

WORD FAMILY destroy			
Nouns	destroyer destruction	*Adjectives*	indestructible destructive
Verbs	destroy		

destruction /dɪˈstrʌk·ʃən/ *n* [U] the action of destroying something, or the state of being destroyed ○ *Unusually high winds left widespread destruction over the area.*

destructive /dɪˈstrʌk·tɪv/ *adj* ○ *The child needs help to control his destructive behavior.*

destructive interference *n* [C] ***physics*** the INTERFERENCE produced when two or more WAVES ENERGY FORM are not in PHASE and create a wave that is weaker then either of them ○ Compare CONSTRUCTIVE INTERFERENCE

detach /dɪˈtætʃ/ *v* [T] to separate or remove something from something else that it is connected to ○ *Detach the lower half of the form and return it to the above address.*
detached /dɪˈtætʃt/ *adj* ○ *Their new house has a detached garage.*
detachment /dɪˈtætʃ·mənt/ *n* [C] a group of soldiers who are separated from the main group in order to perform a particular duty ○ *a detachment of paratroopers*

detached /dɪˈtætʃt/ *adj* (of a person) not emotionally involved in a situation ○ *As a writer, he took the role of a detached observer of life.*

detail INFORMATION /dɪˈteɪl, ˈdiː·teɪl/ *n* [C/U] a particular fact or item of information, often noticed only after giving something your close attention, or such facts or items considered as a group ○ [C] *We have a report of a serious accident on Route 23, but so far no details.* ○ [U] *She showed a businesslike attention to detail.* ○ [U] *I can't go into much detail, but I've been having some health problems recently.* ○ *We know roughly what he wants to do, but we haven't discussed his plans in detail* (= considering all the particular facts).
detail /dɪˈteɪl, ˈdiː·teɪl/ *v* [T] to give exact and complete information about something ○ *The committee members issued a brief statement detailing their plans.*
detailed /dɪˈteɪld, ˈdiː·teɪld/ *adj* ○ *a detailed account/description*

GROUP /dɪˈteɪl, ˈdiː·teɪl/ *n* [C] a small group, esp. of soldiers or police, ordered to perform a particular duty ○ *A detail of five police officers accompanied the diplomat to his hotel.*

detain /dɪˈteɪn/ *v* [T] **1** to force someone officially to stay in a place ○ *A suspect is being detained by the police for further questioning.* **2** To detain someone is also to delay that person for a short period of time: *We were detained in traffic and arrived at the theater a little late.* ○ Related noun: DETENTION
detainee /dɪˌteɪˈniː/ *n* [C] someone kept in prison, esp. for political reasons ○ *Less than half the detainees with lawyers have been given a trial date.*

detect Ⓐ /dɪˈtekt/ *v* [T] to notice something that is partly hidden or not clear or to discover something, esp. using a special method ○ *Some sounds cannot be detected by the human ear.* ○ *X-ray procedures can detect a tumor when it is still small.*
detectable Ⓐ /dɪˈtek·tə·bəl/ *adj* ○ *There has been no detectable change in the patient's condition.*
detection Ⓐ /dɪˈtek·ʃən/ *n* [U] ○ *These tests can result in the early detection of disease.*

detector Ⓐ /dɪˈtek·tər/ *n* [C] ○ *Motion detectors help monitor elderly residents who live alone.*

detective Ⓐ /dɪˈtek·tɪv/ *n* [C] a police officer whose job is to discover information about crimes and find out who is responsible for them

détente, **detente** /deɪˈtɑnt/ *n* [U] ***politics & government*** an improvement in the relationship between two countries that in the past were not friendly and did not trust each other

D

detention /dɪˈten·tʃən/ *n* [C/U] **1** the act or condition of being officially forced to stay in a place ○ [U] *He claimed that his detention by the authorities was unlawful.* **2** Detention is also a punishment in which a student must remain in school for a short time after classes have ended for the day. ○ Related verb: DETAIN

deter /dɪˈtɜr/ *v* [T] **-rr-** to prevent or discourage someone from doing something ○ *High prices are deterring a lot of young couples from buying houses.*
deterrent /dɪˈtɜr·ənt, -ˈter-/ *n* [C] ○ *The company says this alarm is an effective deterrent against theft.*

detergent /dɪˈtɜr·dʒənt/ *n* [C/U] a chemical substance in the form of a powder or a liquid for removing dirt esp. from clothes or dishes

deteriorate /dɪˈtɪr·iː·əˌreɪt/ *v* [I] to become worse ○ *She went into the hospital when her condition began to deteriorate.*
deterioration /dɪˌtɪr·iː·əˈreɪ·ʃən/ *n* [U] ○ *a deterioration in relations between the two countries*

determine DECIDE /dɪˈtɜr·mən/ *v* to control or influence directly; to decide ○ [T] *We should be allowed to determine our own future.* ○ [T] *Eye color is genetically determined.* ○ [+ to infinitive] *He determined to find out the real reason.*
DISCOVER /dɪˈtɜr·mən/ *v* [T] to find out or make certain facts or information ○ *The police never actually determined the cause of death.* ○ [+ question word] *I can't determine why your phone isn't working.* ○ [+ *that* clause] *The investigation determined that the death was accidental.*

WORD FAMILY determine			
Nouns	determination determiner	*Adjectives*	determined indeterminate
Verbs	determine		

determined /dɪˈtɜr·mənd/ *adj* showing the strong desire to follow a particular plan of action even if it is difficult ○ *a very determined young man* ○ *She had a determined look on her face.* ○ [+ to infinitive] *I'm determined to finish this book today.*
determination /dɪˌtɜr·məˈneɪ·ʃən/ *n* [U] ○ [+ to infinitive] *She has a lot of determination to succeed.*

determiner /dɪˈtɜr·mə·nər/ *n* [C] ***grammar*** a word that is used before a noun to show which particular example of the noun you are referring to ○ *In the phrase "my history book" the word "my" is a determiner.*

deterrent /dɪˈtɜr·ənt, -ˈter-/ *n* ○ See at DETER

detest /dɪˈtest/ *v* [T] to hate; dislike extremely ○ *She detested traveling in hot weather.*

detonate /ˈdet·ənˌeɪt/ *v* [I/T] to explode, or to cause a bomb to explode ○ [T] *A remote control device was used to detonate the bomb.*
detonator /ˈdet·ənˌeɪt̬·ər/ *n* [C] a device used to cause an explosive to detonate

detour /ˈdiː·tʊr/ *n* [C] a way of getting to a place that is indirect and longer than the usual way, and which is taken in order to avoid a particular problem or to do something special ○ *You're advised to take a detour to avoid the road construction.* ○ *We made a little detour to drop Sarah off on the way home.*
detour /ˈdiː·tʊr/ *v* [I] ○ *We had to detour around the flooded road.*

detoxify /diːˈtɑk·sə-, faɪ/ *v* [I/T] ***chemistry*** to make a TOXIC (= poisonous) substance harmless, or to remove a harmful or toxic chemical from another substance ○ *The liver's tasks include detoxifying the blood.*
detoxification /diːˌtɑk·sə·fəˈkeɪ·ʃən/, *n* [U] the process of removing harmful or toxic chemicals

detract from *something* /dɪˈtrækt·frəm/ *phrasal verb* to make something seem less valuable or less deserving of admiration ○ *These small faults, however, do not detract from the overall quality of the book.*

detractor /dɪˈtræk·tər/ *n* [C usually pl] a person who criticizes something or someone, often unfairly ○ *He is much more popular with his teammates than his detractors would have you believe.*

detriment /ˈde·trə·mənt/ *n* [U] harm or damage ○ *She was very involved with sports at college, to the detriment of her studies.*
detrimental /ˌde·trəˈment·əl/ *adj* ○ *chemicals that have a detrimental effect on the environment*

deuterium /duːˈtɪr·iː·əm/ *n* [U] ***chemistry*** a type of HYDROGEN (= gas) that is twice as heavy as the usual form of hydrogen

devastate /ˈdev·əˌsteɪt/ *v* [T] to cause great damage or suffering to something or someone, or to violently destroy a place ○ *Waves of corporate downsizing have devastated employee morale.* ○ *I was so devastated I was crying constantly.* ○ *The town was devastated by a hurricane in 1928.*
devastating /ˈdev·əˌsteɪt̬·ɪŋ/ *adj* ○ *devastating criticisms* ○ *It will have a devastating impact on the economy.*
devastation /ˌdev·əˈsteɪ·ʃən/ *n* [U] ○ *The tornado has already left a trail of devastation through four states from Nebraska to Missouri.*

develop GROW /dɪˈvel·əp/ *v* [I/T] to grow or cause to grow or change into a more advanced form ○ [T] *This exercise will help develop the shoulder and back muscles* (= It will make them stronger). ○ [I] *If Kareem keeps working hard, he could develop* *into a first-class athlete.* ○ [I] *The tourist industry is continuing to develop in the lake region.* ○ [T] *Your essay is good, but you need to develop your ideas more fully* (= give more details).

developed /dɪ ˈvel·əpt/ *adj* **1** *Sharks have a highly developed sense of smell.* **2** ***politics & government*** Developed countries have a lot of industry and wealth.

developing /dɪ ˈvel·ə·pɪŋ/ *adj* [not gradable] **1** *a developing fetus* **2** ***politics & government*** Developing countries have less advanced industries and little wealth but have the ability to become more advanced.

development /dɪ ˈvel·əp·mənt/ *n* [C/U] **1** [U] *A good diet and lots of exercise are essential for a child's healthy growth and development.* ○ [U] *I took a history course that dealt with the development of popular culture.* **2** ***literature*** In a literary work, development is the movement from one event to another or the changes in the characters' understanding. **3** A development is a recent important event that is the latest in a series of related events: [C] *There is a new development in the plans to reorganize the fire department.* **4** ***politics & government*** Development is also the organized increase of a country's industry and wealth.

developmental /dɪ ˌvel·əp ˈment·əl/ *adj* ○ *The program offers adventures for people with developmental disabilities* (= physical or mental conditions that prevent someone from growing and developing in a way that is considered usual).

START /dɪ ˈvel·əp/ *v* [I/T] **1** to bring or come into existence ○ [I] *Large cracks are developing in the wall of the house.* ○ [T] *George has developed an interest in archaeology.* **2** If you develop an illness, you catch it or start to suffer from it: [T] *She developed a skin rash.* **3** If an area of land is developed, it is built on, usually by a company that hopes to make a profit in this way: [T] *We have plans to develop the site.*

developer /dɪ ˈvel·ə·pər/ *n* [C] a person or company that makes money by buying land and building new houses, stores, or offices on it ○ *real estate developers*

development /dɪ ˈvel·əp·mənt/ *n* [C/U] **1** [U] *We were waiting for the development of new plans for the city's convention center.* ○ [U] *I'm in charge of product development* (= the creation and design of new products) *for the company.* ○ [C] *Cotton fields were replaced by housing developments* (= groups of similar houses built at the same time) *as the city experienced rapid growth.* **2** Development is also the building of houses, stores, or offices, esp. by a company to make a profit, on an area of land where there were none before.

PROCESS FILM /dɪ ˈvel·əp/ *v* [I/T] to put film in chemicals until an image appears

WORD FAMILY develop

Nouns	developer development redevelopment	*Adjectives*	developed developing developmental undeveloped
Verbs	develop		

deviant /ˈdiː·viː·ənt/ *adj* differing from the accepted standard

deviance /ˈdiː·viː·əns/ *n* [U]

deviate Ⓐ /ˈdiː·viː ˌeɪt/ *v* [I] to change from the usual way, or to go in a different direction ○ *He never deviated from his strict vegetarian diet.* ○ *We need to know when the bus deviates from its scheduled route.*

deviation Ⓐ /ˌdiː·viː ˈeɪ·ʃən/ *n* [C/U] ○ [U] *Any deviation from the party line is seen as betrayal.*

device Ⓐ **OBJECT** /dɪ ˈvɑɪs/ *n* [C] an object or machine that has been invented to fulfill a particular purpose ○ *a handheld device* ○ *a safety device* ○ *electronic/mechanical devices* ○ *He invented a device for measuring very small distances exactly.*

METHOD /dɪ ˈvɑɪs/ *n* [C] a method that is used to produce a desired effect ○ *His temper tantrums were just a device for attracting attention.*

devil /ˈdev·əl/ *n* [C] **1** an evil being, often represented in human form but with a tail and horns **2** **The Devil**, in Christianity, Islam, and Judaism, is the most powerful evil spirit. **3** The devil can be used to give emphasis to a question: *What the devil are you doing?*

devilish /ˈdev·ə·lɪʃ/ *adj* **1** slightly bad, but sometimes in an amusing way ○ *a devilish grin* **2** Devilish can also mean extremely difficult: *a devilish problem*

devil's advocate *n* [C] someone who supports an opposite argument or one that is not popular in order to make people think seriously

devious /ˈdiː·viː·əs/ *adj* **1** using indirect ways to get what you want, esp. without showing your real purpose ○ *devious methods* **2** Devious also means indirect: *They went by a devious route.*

devise /dɪ ˈvɑɪz/ *v* [T] to invent something, esp. with intelligence or imagination ○ *He devised a new way to treat mental depression.* ○ *The committee is devising an agenda for the upcoming political convention.*

devoid /dɪ ˈvɔɪd/ *adj* [not gradable] Someone or something is **devoid of** something it is completely lacking: *He seems to be devoid of any feeling for his parents.*

devote *something/yourself* **to** *something/someone* Ⓐ /dɪ ˈvoʊt·tə, -ˌtʊ, -ˌtuː/ *phrasal verb* to give your time or effort completely to something you believe in or to a person, or to use a particular amount of time or energy doing something ○ *He devoted his life to serving his family, friends, and neighbors.* ○ *Over half his speech was devoted to the issue of saving Social Security.*

devoted Ⓐ /dɪ ˈvoʊt̬·əd/ *adj* extremely loving and loyal ○ *a devoted fan/husband/mother*

devotedly Ⓐ /dɪ ˈvoʊt̬·əd·li/ *adv*

devotee /ˌdev·ə ˈtiː, -ˈteɪ; dɪ ˌvoʊ ˈtiː/ *n* [C] a person who strongly admires a particular person or is extremely interested in a subject ○ *Devotees of jazz won't want to miss this!*

D

devotion Ⓐ **SUPPORT** /dɪ ˈvoʊ·ʃən/ *n* [U] support and affection ○ *He is a teacher who inspires respect and devotion from his students.*

WORSHIP /dɪ ˈvoʊ·ʃən/ *n* [C/U] religious worship or belief, or prayer and other acts of religious worship ○ [U] *a life of religious devotion* ○ [C] *devotions to the saints*

D

devour /dɪ ˈvɑʊr/ *v* [T] to eat eagerly and in large amounts, so that nothing is left ○ *He devoured the entire plate of spaghetti.* ○ (*fig.*) *She devoured* (= read eagerly and quickly) *the novels of Jane Austen.*

devout /dɪ ˈvɑʊt/ *adj* believing strongly in a religion and obeying all the rules or principles of that religion ○ *a devout Christian/Jew/Muslim*

devoutly /dɪ ˈvɑʊt·li/ *adv* ○ *a devoutly religious family*

dew /duː, djuː/ *n* [U] small drops of water that form on the ground and other surfaces outside esp. during the night

dewpoint /ˈduː·pɔɪnt/ *n* [C] ***earth science*** the temperature at which air can no longer hold all the water in it, and the water starts to form drops on surfaces

dexterity /dekˈster·ət̬·i/ *n* [U] the ability to use the hands skillfully in doing something ○ *Playing with blocks improves a child's manual dexterity.*

diabetes /ˌdɑɪ·əˈbiːt̬·iːz, -əs/ *n* [U] a disease in which the body cannot control the amount of sugar in the blood

diabetic /ˌdɑɪ·əˈbet̬·ɪk/ *adj* ○ *a diabetic patient*

diabetic /ˌdɑɪ·əˈbet̬·ɪk/ *n* [C] a person who has diabetes

diabolical /ˌdɑɪ·əˈbɑl·ɪ·kəl/ *adj* very evil but often intelligent ○ *a diabolical genius*

diagnose /ˈdɑɪ·ɪɡˌnoʊs, -ˌnoʊz/ *v* [T] to recognize and name the exact character of a disease or other problem by making an examination ○ *He was diagnosed with cancer that year.* ○ *It was not easy to diagnose what was wrong with the business.*

diagnosis /ˌdɑɪ·ɪɡˈnoʊ·səs/ *n* [C/U] *pl* **diagnoses** the making of a judgment about the exact character of a disease or other problem, esp. after an examination, or such a judgment ○ [U] *Respiratory therapy involves the diagnosis and treatment of breathing disorders.*

diagnostic /ˌdɑɪ·ɪɡˈnɑs·tɪk/ *adj* ○ *The hospital is doing some diagnostic tests to see if they can figure out why she's running a fever.*

diagonal /dɑɪˈæɡ·ən·əl/ *adj* ***geometry*** (of a line) straight and sloping, so that it is neither horizontal nor vertical ○ *A diagonal line in a circle is often used as a symbol to show that certain behavior is forbidden.*

diagram /ˈdɑɪ·əˌɡræm/ *n* [C] a simple plan drawn to represent something, such as a machine, usually to explain how it works or how it is put together ○ *The teacher drew a diagram showing how blood flows through the heart.* ➤ Picture: **Venn diagram**

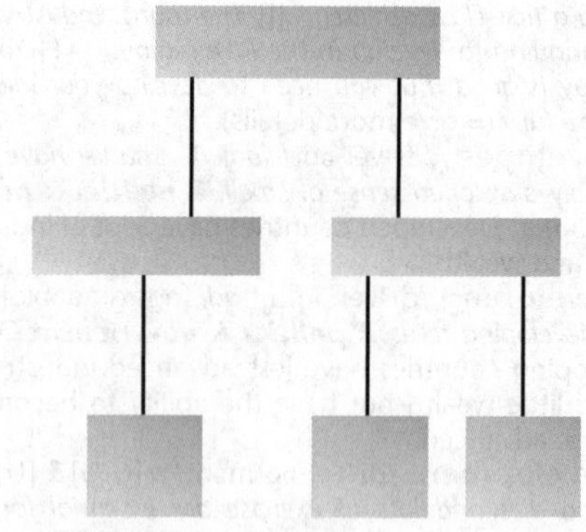

DIAGRAM

dial TELEPHONE /dɑɪl/ *v* [I/T] to make a telephone call by pressing the buttons or turning the disk on a telephone to be connected to a particular number ○ [T] *What number did you dial?* ➤ Learner error: **compose or dial?** at COMPOSE FORM

MEASURING DEVICE /ˈdɑɪl/ *n* [C] **1** the part of a machine or device that shows a measurement, such as of speed or time, often a numbered circle with a moving POINTER (= long narrow part with a point) **2** A dial is also a part of an instrument that you can turn or move to control it: *Turn the dial of the radio and get some music.*

dialect /ˈdɑɪ·əˌlekt/ *n* [C/U] ***grammar*** a form of a language that is spoken in a particular part of a country or by a particular group of people and that contains some words, grammar, or PRONUNCIATIONS (= the ways in which words are said) that are different from the forms used in other parts or by other groups

dialogue CONVERSATION, **dialog** /ˈdɑɪ·əˌlɔːɡ, -ˌlɑɡ/ *n* [C/U] ***literature*** conversation between the characters in a story, such as in a book or movie ○ [U] *Oscar Wilde's plays are famous for their witty dialogue.*

EXCHANGE OF OPINION, **dialog** /ˈdɑɪ·əˌlɔːɡ, -ˌlɑɡ/ *n* [C/U] a serious exchange of opinion, esp. among people or groups that disagree ○ [C] *We have held a number of meetings, and the dialogue is ongoing.*

dial tone *n* [C] the continuous sound you hear when you pick up the telephone, letting you know that you can call a number

diameter /dɑɪˈæm·ət̬·ər/ *n* [C/U] ***geometry*** the distance from one side to the opposite side of a circle, measured by a line passing through the center of the circle ○ [C] *We need a pipe with a diameter of about six inches.* ➤ Picture: **circle**

diametrically /ˌdɑɪ·əˈme·trɪ·kli/ *adv* completely ○ *Father and son had diametrically opposed views on politics.*

diamond STONE /ˈdɑɪ·mənd, -ə·mənd/ *n* [C/U] an extremely hard, valuable stone prized as a jewel and having many uses in industry ○ [U] *a diamond engagement ring*

SHAPE /ˈdɑɪ·mənd, -ə·mənd/ *n* [C] ***geometry*** a shape with four straight sides that meet to form two wide and two narrow angles, or a square placed with a corner at the bottom ➤ Picture: **geometry**

diamonds /ˈdɑɪ·məndz, -ə·məndz/ *pl n* one of the four SUITS (= groups) of playing cards, the symbol for which is a DIAMOND shape

diaper /ˈdɑɪ·pər, ˈdɑɪ·ə·pər/ *n* [C] a thick, soft, cloth or plastic-covered paper that can be placed between the legs and fastened around the waist, used for a baby who has not yet learned to use a toilet ○ *disposable diapers*

diaphragm /ˈdɑɪ·əˌfræm/ *n* [C] a thin piece of material that is stretched across an opening, esp. the muscle that separates the chest from the lower part of the body containing the stomach and bowels

diarrhea /ˌdɑɪ·əˈriː·ə/ *n* [U] an illness in which a person's solid waste is too watery and is excreted too frequently

diary /ˈdɑɪ·ə·ri, ˈdɑɪ·ri/ *n* [C] **1** a person's private record of events, thoughts, feelings, etc., that are written down every day, or a book where such things are recorded **2** A diary is also a book in which you keep a personal record of the people you are planning to see or the things you are planning to do: *Let me check the doctor's diary and see if she can see you then.*

diaspora, Diaspora /dɑɪˈæs·pə·rə/ *n* [C/U] ***politics & government*** **1** the scattering of people from their original country to other places **2** ***world history*** Diaspora is the forced movement of Jews from Israel. **3** ***world history*** The Diaspora is also the Jews who live outside of Israel.

diastole /dɑɪˈæs·tə·li/ *n* [C] ***biology*** the part of a heart's action during which it fills with blood

diatomic /ˌdɑɪ·əˈtɑm·ɪk/ *adj* [not gradable] ***chemistry*** describes a MOLECULE that has two atoms of the same kind

diatonic scale /ˌdɑɪ·əˈtɑn·ɪk ˈskeɪl/ *n* [C] ***music*** a musical SCALE that is either MAJOR or MINOR

dice GAME /dɑɪs/ *pl n* two small CUBES (= square, box-shaped solids) that are the same, each with a different number of spots on each of its six sides, used in games

CUT /dɑɪs/ *v* [T] to cut food into small squares ○ *Peel and dice the carrots.*

dicey /ˈdɑɪ·si/ *adj comparative* **dicier**, *superlative* **diciest** *infml* not certain or safe; RISKY ○ *Things are going to be a bit dicey until we know whether the budget was approved.*

dichotomy /dɑɪˈkɑt̬·ə·mi/ *n* [C] *fml* the division of two things that are completely different ○ *I try to examine the dichotomy between what people think they are and what they do.*

dicker /ˈdɪk·ər/ *v* [I] to argue with someone, esp. about the price of goods ○ *She dickered with the driver for several minutes over the fare.*

dictate GIVE ORDERS /ˈdɪk·teɪt, dɪkˈteɪt/ *v* [T] **1** to give orders, or state something with total authority ○ [+ question word] *Tennis club rules dictate what kind of footwear may be worn on the courts.* **2** To dictate also means to make necessary: *The characteristics of the land dictate much of what can be built.*

SPEAK /ˈdɪk·teɪt, dɪkˈteɪt/ *v* [I/T] to say something aloud for another person or for a machine to record, so that your words can be prepared in writing for use in business or a legal case ○ [T] *She spent the morning dictating letters.*

dictation /dɪkˈteɪ·ʃən/ *n* [U] **1** *Can we get someone from the agency who takes dictation?* **2** Dictation is also the reading aloud of a piece of writing in a language being learned in order to test the ability of students to hear and write the language correctly: *a dictation exercise*

dictator /ˈdɪkˌteɪt̬·ər, dɪkˈteɪt̬-/ *n* [C] ***politics & government*** someone who rules a country with complete power, has complete control over the armed forces, and destroys any political opposition

dictatorial /ˌdɪk·təˈtɔːr·iː·əl, -ˈtoʊr-/ *adj* ***politics & government*** ○ *dictatorial powers*

dictatorship /dɪkˈteɪt̬·ərˌʃɪp/ *n* [C/U] ***politics & government*** a country ruled by a dictator, or the condition of being so ruled ○ [U] *A flood of refugees fled the brutal dictatorship then existing that country.*

diction /ˈdɪk·ʃən/ *n* [U] the manner in which words are pronounced

dictionary /ˈdɪk·ʃəˌner·i/ *n* [C] a book that lists words with their meanings given in the same or in another language, and often includes other information

did /dɪd/ *past simple of* DO

didactic /dɑɪˈdæk·tɪk/ *adj fml* intended to teach, or to improve morals by teaching ○ *Children's books possess a practical, didactic purpose – to instill a love for reading.*

didn't /ˈdɪd·ᵊnt/ *contraction of* did not ○ *We didn't arrive until after midnight.*

die /dɑɪ/ *v* [I] *pres. part.* **dying**, *past* **died** **1** to stop living ○ *He died of a heart attack.* ○ *She died in her sleep at the age of 94.* ○ *(fig.) The engine just died* (= stopped working). **2** If you say that you could have/nearly died of a particular feeling, you mean that you felt the feeling very strongly: *I was so embarrassed, I could have died.* **3** To **be dying** to do something, or for something, is to be eager to do or to have it: *I'm dying to hear the news.* ○ *I'm dying for a cup of coffee.*

USAGE

died or **dead**?

Do not confuse the verb and adjective. **Died** is the simple past and past participle of the verb **die**.

Her father died last year.

Dead is an adjective that means "not alive."

Her father is dead.

~~*Her father is died.*~~

D

WORD CHOICES die

The phrasal verbs **pass away** or **pass on** are sometimes used to avoid saying "die" in case it upsets someone.

*He **passed away** peacefully in the hospital.*

If people die as the result of an accident or violence, you can say that they **were killed** or **lost their lives.**

*His sister **was killed** in a car accident.*

*Many people **lost their lives** in the war.*

Someone who dies very suddenly while doing something is sometimes said to have **dropped dead.**

*He **dropped dead** on the tennis court at the age of 42.*

You can use the verb **lose** to say that a person in someone's family has died.

*She **lost** her husband last year.*

In informal situations and if you are trying to be humorous, you can use the phrase **kick the bucket.**

*When I **kick the bucket**, you can do what you want.*

PHRASAL VERBS with die

• **die down** to become reduced in strength ○ *A storm is expected tonight, but the wind and rain should die down by morning.*

• **die off** (of the members of a group) to stop living, one by one, until there are none left ○ *The veterans of World War II are now old and gradually dying off.*

• **die out** to become less common and finally stop existing ○ *Dinosaurs died out millions of years ago.*

diehard /ˈdɑɪ·hɑrd/ *adj* [not gradable] unwilling to change or give up your ideas or ways of behaving, even when there are good reasons to do so ○ *a diehard conservative*

diesel /ˈdiː·zəl/ *n* [U] **1** a type of heavy oil used as a fuel **2** A diesel is also any vehicle that has an engine using this type of oil as fuel.

diet /ˈdɑɪ·ət/ *n* [C/U] **1** the food and drink usually taken by a person or group ○ [C] *A healthy diet includes fresh vegetables.* ○ [C] (*fig.*) *Gifted students given a steady diet of grade-level curriculum learn they don't need to work hard.* **2** A diet is also the particular food and drink you are limited to when you cannot eat or drink whatever you want to: [C] *a low-salt diet* ○ [C] *I'm going on a diet because I've got to lose some weight.*

diet /ˈdɑɪ·ət/ *v* [I] to limit the food that you take, esp. in order to lose weight ○ *He began dieting a month ago and says he has lost ten pounds already.*

diet /ˈdɑɪ·ət/ *adj* [not gradable] (of food or drink) containing much less sugar than usual and often sweetened artificially, or containing less fat than usual ○ *diet soda*

dietary /ˈdɑɪ·əˌter·i/ *adj* ○ *Health experts say dietary changes have to start with children, who can be taught to appreciate a healthy diet.*

dieter /ˈdɑɪ·əţ·ər/ *n* [C] ○ *Studies show there may be as many as 30 million American dieters at any one moment.*

differ /ˈdɪf·ər/ *v* [I] **1** to be not like something else; to be different ○ *American English and British English obviously differ in pronunciation.* **2** To differ is also to disagree: *We may differ on what the numbers are, but there is general agreement that we have to do something to cut costs.*

WORD FAMILY differ

Nouns	difference indifference differential	*Adjectives*	different indifferent differential
Verbs	differ differentiate	*Adverbs*	differently

different /ˈdɪf·rənt, -ə·rənt/ *adj* not the same ○ *Monet and other Impressionists painted the same scene at different times of day to discover how the colors change in the different light.* ○ *The weather down here is a lot different than it is at home.* ○ *Emily is entirely different from her sister.*

difference /ˈdɪf·rəns, -ə·rəns/ *n* [C/U] the way in which two things being compared are not the same, or the fact of not being the same ○ [C] *We try to teach the kids the difference between right and wrong.* ○ [C] *We'd like better seats, but if the difference in price is too much, we'll keep what we have.*

differently /ˈdɪf·rənt·li, -ə·rənt·li/ *adv* ○ *I would have done things differently if I had the chance to do them over again.*

USAGE

difference

Be careful to use the correct preposition. You talk about the **difference between** two things when you are comparing them.

What's the difference between a cup and a mug?

You talk about the **difference in** something or someone when you want to say how something or someone has changed.

Have you noticed a difference in him since last year?

WORD CHOICES different

See also: **unusual**

If something is different from what people normally expect, you can say that it is **unusual.**

*Carina – that's quite an **unusual** name.*

The adjective **alternative** is often used to describe something which is different from something else but can be used instead of it.

*The hotel's being renovated, so we're looking for an **alternative** venue.*

If something is very different and separate from other things, you can describe it as **distinct** or **distinctive.**

*She's got really **distinctive** handwriting.*

*The word has three **distinct** meanings.*

The preposition **unlike** is often used to compare people or things that are very different from each other.

*Dan's actually quite nice, **unlike** his father.*

*The furniture was **unlike** anything she had ever seen.*

IDIOMS with different

• **difference of opinion** a disagreement ○ *There was a difference of opinion about the best way to run the business, and as a result I left the company.*
• **have** *your* **differences** to disagree with someone on one or more matters ○ *We've had our differences, but we've learned how to work together very well.*

differential /ˌdɪf·əˈren·tʃəl/ *n* [C] the difference between two amounts ○ *There's anywhere from a $1000 to $2400 price differential between the vehicles.*
differential /ˌdɪf·əˈren·tʃəl/ *adj* ○ *The contract includes a 35-cent per hour increase in night shift differential pay.*

differentiate Ⓐ /ˌdɪf·əˈren·tʃiːˌeɪt/ *v* [I/T] to show or find the difference between one thing and another, or between things that are compared ○ [T] *What differentiates wheat from other crops is that it is almost exclusively used as a food product.* ○ [I always + adv/prep] *The axons are like phone wires that carry the signals that allow the brain to differentiate between various smells.*
differentiation Ⓐ /ˌdɪf·əˌren·tʃiːˈeɪ·ʃən/ *n* [C/U]

differentiation GROWING CELL /ˌdɪf·əˌren·tʃiːˈeɪ·ʃən/ *n* [U] ***biology*** the process by which cells in an EMBRYO (= growing organism in the uterus, egg, or seed) become different types of cells and organs

ROCKS /ˌdɪf·əˌren·tʃiːˈeɪ·ʃən/ *n* [U] ***earth science*** the process by which different kinds of rock are created from MAGMA (= melted rock) as it cools because of various chemical and physical forces

difficult /ˈdɪf·ə·kəlt, -ˌkʌlt/ *adj* **1** not easy or simple; hard to do or to understand ○ *It's a difficult choice, but I've got to decide which job is better.* **2** Difficult also means having problems: *He's in a difficult situation and could go bankrupt.* **3** A person who is difficult is not easy to deal with: *I loved him, but he could be difficult at times.*
difficulty /ˈdɪf·ə·kəl·ti, -ˌkʌl·ti/ *n* [C/U] **1** the fact of not being easy, or of being hard to do or understand ○ [U] *He has some difficulty hearing people when they speak softly.* **2** A difficulty is also a problem: [C usually pl] *In 1986 he experienced financial difficulties and was forced to sell his business.*

USAGE

difficulty

You can say you **have difficulty** *doing something* or **have difficulty in** *doing something.*

She has difficulty walking.

She has difficulty in walking.

~~*She has difficulty to walk.*~~

WORD CHOICES difficult

Hard is very often used instead of "difficult" and means exactly the same.

*The exam was really **hard**.*

*It must be **hard** to study with all this noise.*

If something is difficult to understand or do because it has a lot of different parts or stages, you can say that it is **complicated** or **complex**.

*The instructions were so **complicated** I just couldn't follow them.*

*Designing a house is a **complex** process.*

Tricky describes something difficult that needs skill or needs you to be very careful.

*It's quite **tricky** getting the puzzle pieces to fit together.*

*It's a **tricky** situation – I don't want to upset anyone.*

Awkward describes something that is difficult to deal with and could cause problems.

*Luckily, she didn't ask any **awkward** questions.*

Demanding means "needing a lot of your time, attention, or effort."

*She has a very **demanding** job.*

*Like most young children, he's very **demanding**.*

A situation or piece of work that is **challenging** is difficult and needs all your skills and determination.

*This has been a **challenging** time for us all.*

*I found the class very **challenging**.*

You say **easier said than done** about something that is impossible or very difficult to do.

*I know I should stop smoking but it's **easier said than done**.*

diffract /dɪˈfrækt/ *v* [T] ***physics*** to break up light or sound waves by making them go through a narrow space or across an edge
diffraction /dɪˈfræk·ʃən/ *n* [U] ***physics***

diffuse /dɪˈfjuːz/ *v* [I/T] **1** to spread or cause something to spread in many directions ○ [T] *Television is a powerful means of diffusing knowledge.* **2** To diffuse is also to make something less noticeable or weaker: [T] *The guide tried to diffuse the tension with his grin.*
diffuse /dɪˈfjuːs/ *adj* not dense but spread out over a large area or space ○ *The smoke may have been too diffuse to detect.*

diffuse reflection /dɪˈfjuːs rɪˈflek·ʃən/ *n* [U] ***physics*** the effect that is created when light is reflected at many different angles and there is no clear image

diffusion /dɪˈfjuː·ʒən/ *n* [U] **1** ***science*** (of gases and liquids) the process of spreading into a surrounding substance **2** ***biology*** Diffusion is also the method by which substances pass in and out of cells through their MEMBRANE (= outside covering). **3** ***physics*** Diffusion is also the way light spreads when it is reflected from a rough surface or passed through a TRANSLUCENT substance (= substance that allows only some light to pass through).

D

dig **MOVE EARTH** /dɪɡ/ *v pres. part.* **digging,** *past* **dug** to move and break up earth using a tool, a machine, or your hands, or to make a hole, channel, etc. by moving and breaking up earth ○ [I] *Friends came with rakes and shovels ready to dig into the earth.* ○ [M] *I was planning to go out and dig up some hibiscus plants.* ○ [T] *Most people out in the country have to dig their own wells.*

dig /dɪɡ/ *n* [C] the activity of removing earth to find objects of interest to history or science

PRESS /dɪɡ/ *v* [T] *pres. part.* **digging,** *past* **dug** to press or push strongly ○ *He dug his hand into his pocket, searching for a quarter.*

REMARK /dɪɡ/ *n* [C] a criticism, esp. a remark about someone that does not seem intentional but actually is ○ *His reference to how busy we were was a dig at us for forgetting to greet him properly.*

IDIOM with **dig**

• **dig a hole for** *yourself* to take an action that is going to cause a lot of trouble for you ○ *He keeps borrowing more money, and I think he's beginning to dig a hole for himself.*

PHRASAL VERBS with **dig**

• **dig in** *infml* to start eating, esp. eagerly ○ *The food's getting cold – dig in!*

• **dig out** *something* [M] to search and find something that has been put away for a long time ○ *There are always people who dig out their old uniforms and put them on for a parade.*

• **dig up** *something* [M] to discover information about someone, esp. damaging information ○ *The firm hired a private detective to dig up information on the former supervisor.*

digest **EAT** /dɪˈdʒest, dɑɪ-/ *v* [I/T] ***biology*** (of the body of a living creature) to chemically change food into smaller forms that the body can absorb and use

digestion /dɪˈdʒes·tʃən, dɑɪ-/ *n* [C/U] the ability of the body to change food chemically so that it can be used

digestive /dɪˈdʒes·tɪv, dɑɪ-/ *adj* relating to the body's process of changing food chemically into a form that it can use

UNDERSTAND /dɪˈdʒest, dɑɪ-/ *v* [T] to take information into your mind in a way that gives you the ability to use it ○ *He could digest an enormous amount of information with amazing speed.*

digest /ˈdɑɪ·dʒest/ *n* [C] a short written report containing the most important parts of a longer piece, or a short written report of recent news ○ *The Sunday newspaper includes a digest of last week's major stories.*

digit **NUMBER** /ˈdɪdʒ·ət/ *n* [C] ***mathematics*** any one of the numbers 0 through 9 ○ *6735 is a four-digit number.*

digital /ˈdɪdʒ·ət̬·əl/ *adj* [not gradable] **1** recording or showing information in the form of numbers, esp. 0 and 1 ○ *The old movie was re-released with digital sound.* **2** A digital watch or clock shows the time with numbers that change as the time changes.

digitize /ˈdɪdʒ·əˌtɑɪz/ *v* [T] to put information into the form of a series of the numbers 0 and 1, usually so that it can be processed electronically ○ *to digitize sound*

FINGER /ˈdɪdʒ·ət/ *n* [C] one of the fingers or toes

dignified /ˈdɪɡ·nəˌfɑɪd/ *adj* serious and graceful in manner or style in a way that deserves respect ○ *a quiet, dignified person*

dignitary /ˈdɪɡ·nəˌter·i/ *n* [C] a person who has an important position in a society ○ *His responsibilities included welcoming visiting dignitaries from foreign countries.*

dignity /ˈdɪɡ·nət̬·i/ *n* [U] the quality of a person that makes him or her deserving of respect, sometimes shown in behavior or appearance ○ *Laws of privacy are designed to protect the dignity of individuals.*

digress /dɑɪˈɡres/ *v* [I] *fml* (in speech or writing) to move away from the main subject and discuss something else ○ *He digressed from his subject in order to criticize the accuracy of a newspaper story.*

digression /dɑɪˈɡreʃ·ən, dɪ-/ *n* [C] ○ *His speech was full of digressions about his time in the army.*

dike **ROCK LAYER** /dɑɪk/ *n* [C] ***earth science*** a layer of newer rock that is created when melted rock flows into spaces in older rock and then hardens

WALL /dɑɪk/ *n* [C] a long wall that prevents water, esp. from the sea, from flooding a place

dilapidated /dəˈlæp·əˌdeɪt̬·əd/ *adj* (esp. of a structure) in bad condition and needing repair ○ *We still use the dilapidated barn for storing tools.*

dilate /dɑɪˈleɪt, ˈdɑɪ·leɪt/ *v* [I/T] *esp. medical* to become or make something, esp. an opening, wider or more open ○ [T] *The doctor put drops in my eyes to dilate the pupils.*

dilation /dɑɪˈleɪ·ʃən/ *n* [U] *esp. medical*

dilation /dɑɪˈleɪ·ʃən/ *n* [C] ***geometry*** a change in the shape of a FIGURE SHAPE in which is it made larger or smaller according to a SCALE (= relationship of sizes)

dilemma /dəˈlem·ə, dɑɪ-/ *n* [C] a situation in which a choice has to be made between possibilities that will all have results you do not want ○ *The dilemma was over how to protect a charming little island and at the same time allow economic development on it.*

dilettante /ˈdɪl·əˌtɑnt, -ˌtænt/ *n* [C] *usually disapproving* a person who is or seems to be interested in a subject, but who is not involved with it in a serious and determined way ○ *To serious artists, he was merely a dilettante.*

diligent /ˈdɪl·ə·dʒənt/ *adj* careful and serious in your work, or done in a careful and determined way ○ *a diligent worker* ○ *They made diligent efforts to carry out their programs.*

diligence /ˈdɪl·ə·dʒəns/ *n* [U]

dill /dɪl/ *n* [U] an herb whose seeds and leaves are used to flavor foods in cooking

dilute /daɪˈluːt, də-/ *v* [T] **1** to make a liquid weaker by mixing it with water or another liquid ○ *Dilute the bleach in water before adding it to the wash.* **2** ***chemistry*** If you dilute a substance you make it weaker or less pure by mixing it with another substance.
dilute /daɪˈluːt, də-/ *adj* ***chemistry*** made weaker or less pure by the addition of another substance
diluted /daɪˈluːt̬·əd, də-/ *adj* ○ *He disinfected the tub with a solution of diluted bleach.*

dim /dɪm/ *adj* [*-er/-est* only] **-mm- 1** not bright; not giving or having much light ○ *A dim bulb provides the only light in the hall.* **2** Something that is dim is also not clear in your mind or memory or not likely to happen: *I had only a dim memory of a tall, slender man.*
dim /dɪm/ *v* [I/T] **-mm-** to become or make something less bright ○ [I] *In the middle of the storm, the lights suddenly dimmed.*
dimly /ˈdɪm·li/ *adv* ○ *a dimly lit hallway*

dime /dɑɪm/ *n* [C] in the US and Canada, a coin worth ten cents

IDIOM with **dime**

• **a dime a dozen** common and not special ○ *Plastic toys like this are a dime a dozen.*

dimension Ⓐ **MEASUREMENT** /dəˈmen·tʃən/ *n* [C] a measurement of something in a particular direction, esp. its height, length, or width ○ *The dimensions of the room are 26 feet by 15 feet.*
-dimensional Ⓐ /dəˈmen·ʃən·əl/ *suffix* ○ *a three-dimensional* (= having three measurements in different directions) *figure*

QUALITY /dəˈmen·tʃən/ *n* [C] a part or quality of a thing or situation that has an effect on the way you think about it ○ *The new script gave the story a psychological dimension.*
-dimensional Ⓐ /dəˈmen·ʃən·əl/ *suffix* ○ *a multi-dimensional problem.*

diminish Ⓐ /dəˈmɪn·ɪʃ/ *v* [I/T] to reduce or be reduced in size or importance ○ [I] *The threat of inflation is diminishing.* ○ [T] *A single-payer system would diminish the bureaucratic cost of health care.*
diminution Ⓐ /ˌdɪm·əˈnuː·ʃən, -ənˈjuː·ʃən/ *n* [C/U]

diminutive /dəˈmɪn·jət̬·ɪv/ *adj* small ○ *My grandmother was a diminutive woman, less than 5 feet tall.*

dimly /ˈdɪm·li/ *adv* ○ See at DIM

dimple /ˈdɪm·pəl/ *n* [C] a small hollow place, esp. in a person's face and usually considered attractive ○ *He has a dimple in his chin.*
dimpled /ˈdɪm·pəld/ *adj* ○ *dimpled cheeks*

din /dɪn/ *n* [U] a loud and unpleasant noise or mixture of noises, esp. one that continues for some time ○ *The teacher had to yell to be heard over the din.*

dine /dɑɪn/ *v* [I] to eat, esp. the main meal of the day, usually in the evening ○ *He dined alone that night.* ○ *This evening we'll be dining out* (= having an evening meal away from home).

diner /ˈdɑɪ·nər/ *n* [C] **1** someone who eats a meal, esp. in a restaurant ○ *He comes in very early – he's an early diner.* **2** A diner is a cheap, informal restaurant that traditionally is long and narrow and looks like part of a train, in which people sit at a COUNTER (= long table) and also in BOOTHS (= partly enclosed areas on either side of a table).

ding-dong /ˈdɪŋ·dɔːŋ, -dɑŋ/ *n* [U] the sound made by a bell

dinghy /ˈdɪŋ·i, -gi/ *n* [C] a small, open boat powered by ROWING (= using long poles with flat ends to push through the water), a motor, or sails, used for pleasure or for moving people to or from a ship

dingy /ˈdɪn·dʒi/ *adj* (of a place or material) dark and unattractive esp. because of being dirty or not cared for ○ *The stores seemed old and dingy, their lights too dim and their ceilings too low.*

dining hall *n* [C] a large room or building where many people can eat at the same time

dining room *n* [C] a room in which meals are eaten

dinky /ˈdɪŋ·ki/ *adj* [*-er/-est* only] *infml* very small or slight ○ *She had a dinky little apartment.*

dinner /ˈdɪn·ər/ *n* [C/U] **1** the main meal of the day, whether eaten in the evening or in the middle part of the day ○ [U] *The restaurant is open for dinner from 5 p.m. to 10 p.m.* ○ [U] *What's for dinner* (= What food are we having for our main meal)*?* ○ [U] *Conversation around the dinner table was always lively.* **2** A dinner is also a formal social occasion in the evening at which a meal is served: [C] *There will be a black-tie dinner and fund-raiser for Jubilee Housing on April 18th at the Mayflower Hotel.*

dinner party *n* [C] a social event where a number of people are invited by someone to eat a meal together, usually in the person's home

dinnertime /ˈdɪn·ərˌtɑɪm/ *n* [U] the time at which the main meal of the day is eaten

dinosaur /ˈdɑɪ·nəˌsɔːr/ *n* [C] **1** a REPTILE (= cold-blooded animal), some types of which were extremely large, that stopped existing a very long time ago **2** A dinosaur is also something that is old and that has not been able to change when conditions have changed and is therefore no longer useful: *The old car was a gas-guzzling dinosaur and we had to get rid of it.*

dint /dɪnt/ *n* If something is done **by dint of** something else, it is done as a result of that thing: *She achieved her success by dint of hard work.*

diocese /ˈdɑɪ·ə·səs, -ˌsiːz, -ˌsiːs/ *n* [C] (in the Roman Catholic Church) the area that is under the control of a BISHOP (= priest of high rank)
diocesan /dɑɪˈɑs·ə·sən, -zən/ *adj* [not gradable]

dip **PUT INTO LIQUID** /dɪp/ *v* [T] **-pp-** to put something briefly into a liquid ○ *He dipped his doughnut in the coffee.*
dip /dɪp/ *n* [C] **1** A dip is a thick sauce you can put crackers, raw vegetables, etc., into before eating

them. **2** A dip is also a quick swim: *He took a dip in the pool.*

DROP /dɪp/ *v* [I] **-pp-** to go down to a lower level; become less or lower ○ *Beans and lettuce may suffer if temperatures dip below freezing.* ○ *Stock market prices dipped slightly, losing four points.*

dip /dɪp/ *n* [C usually sing] ○ *After the yellow house, there's a dip in the road.*

D

PHRASAL VERB with dip

• **dip into** *something* to spend some of your money ○ *We had to dip into our savings to pay for the repairs.*

dipeptide /dɑɪ'pep·tɑɪd/ *n* [C] ***biology*** a chemical substance formed of two connected AMINO ACIDS (= chemical substance in all plants and animals)

diphtheria /dɪf'θɪr·iː·ə, dɪp-/ *n* [U] a serious infectious disease that causes fever and difficulty in breathing and swallowing

diploid /'dɪp·lɔɪd/ *adj* [not gradable] ***biology*** having two sets of CHROMOSOMES (= structures containing the chemical patterns controlling what a plant or animal is like), one set from each parent

diploma /də'ploʊ·mə/ *n* [C] a document given by a school, college, or university to show that you have successfully completed a course of study ○ *It's hard to find a good job if you don't have a high school diploma.*

diplomat /'dɪp·lə,mæt/ *n* [C] ***politics & government*** a person who officially represents a country's interests in a foreign country ○ *She is a skilled diplomat and an expert negotiator.*

diplomatic /,dɪp·lə'mæṭ·ɪk/ *adj* ***politics & government*** **1** *He began the diplomatic discussions that resulted in the establishment of NATO.* **2** If you say that someone is diplomatic, you mean that the person is able to control a difficult situation without upsetting anyone: *Lawyers should be diplomatic in dealing with a judge.*

diplomacy /də'ploʊ·mə·si/ *n* [U] **1** ***politics & government*** the management of relationships between countries ○ *Quiet diplomacy is sometimes better than public threats.* **2** Diplomacy is also the ability to control a difficult situation without upsetting anyone: *It took all her diplomacy to persuade him not to resign.*

dipstick /'dɪp·stɪk/ *n* [C] a long, thin stick for measuring the amount of liquid in a container, esp. the oil in a car engine

dire /dɑɪr/ *adj* very serious or extreme ○ *Cheating will bring dire consequences.*

IDIOM with dire

• **in dire straits** in a very bad situation that is difficult to fix ○ *These kids are in dire straits, and the schools are doing nothing to help them!*

direct **STRAIGHT** /də'rekt, dɑɪ-/ *adj* **1** going in a straight line toward somewhere or someone without stopping or changing direction and without anything coming in between ○ *Is there a direct flight to Madison, or do we have to change planes in Chicago?* ○ *This plant should be kept out of direct sunlight.* **2** Direct also means without anyone or anything else being involved: *She fired the principal and took direct control of the school.* **3** Direct also means very honest in saying what you mean: *Her manner was businesslike and direct.*

direct /də'rekt, dɑɪ-/ *adv* ○ *Can I dial this number direct* (= without anything or anyone else being involved) *or do I have to go through the operator?*

directly /d+ə'rek·tli, dɑɪ-/ *adv* without anything coming in between ○ *He went directly home* (= without stopping anywhere first).

directness /də'rekt·nəs, dɑɪ-/ *n* [U] a very honest way of saying what you mean

AIM /də'rekt, dɑɪ-/ *v* [T always + adv/prep] **1** to aim something in a particular direction or at particular people ○ *His criticism was directed at everybody who disagreed with him.* **2** To direct is also to show someone the particular way to get somewhere: *Can you direct me to the nearest bus stop?*

CONTROL /də'rekt, dɑɪ-/ *v* [I/T] **1** to control or be in charge of an activity, organization, etc. ○ [T] *General Eisenhower directed the allied forces in World War II.* **2** When someone directs a movie, play, etc., that person tells the actors how to play their parts.

direction /də'rek·ʃən, dɑɪ-/ *n* [U] the condition of being in charge or in control ○ *Under her direction, the agency doubled in size.*

director /də'rek·tər, dɑɪ-/ *n* [C] **1** a person in charge of an organization or of a particular part of a company's business ○ *a marketing director* **2** A director is also a person who tells actors in a movie or play how to play their parts.

ORDER /də'rekt, dɑɪ-/ *v* [T] *fml* to give an order or instruction to someone ○ *The judge directed the defendant to be quiet.*

directive /də'rek·tɪv, dɑɪ-/ *n* [C] ○ *A federal directive forbids fund-raising in government offices.*

WORD FAMILY direct			
Nouns	directness direction directions director directive directory	*Adjectives*	direct indirect
		Verbs	direct
		Adverbs	direct directly indirectly

direct current *n* [U] ***physics*** electric current that moves only in one direction, like the electricity that comes from a BATTERY ELECTRICAL DEVICE

direct election *n* [C] ***politics & government*** an election in which citizens vote for themselves instead of representatives voting for them

direction /də'rek·ʃən, dɑɪ-/ *n* [C] the position toward which someone or something moves or faces ○ *Cars were facing every direction after slamming into each other on the icy road.* ○ *I glanced in her direction* (= toward her). ○ *You're headed in the direction of* (= toward) *Toronto.*

directions /də'rek·ʃənz, dɑɪ-/ *pl n* ○ *We're lost – let's stop and ask (for) directions* (= to be told how to find the place we are looking for).

directly /də'rek·tli, dɑɪ-/ *adv* [not gradable] very soon or immediately ○ *Dr. Schwartz will be with you directly.*

direct object *n* [C] (in grammar) the word or phrase naming who or what receives the action of the verb ○ *In the sentence "I saw Mary," "Mary" is the direct object.* ○ Compare INDIRECT OBJECT ○ See also: OBJECT GRAMMAR

directory /də'rek·tə·ri, dɑɪ-/ *n* [C] a list of telephone numbers, names, addresses, or other information ○ *I found your address in the directory of university graduates.*

dirt EARTH /dɜrt/ *n* [U] **1** earth or a substance like it that has gotten on the surface of something such as your skin ○ *I sat on the ground and got dirt on my pants.* **2** Dirt is also loose earth on the ground: *After the rain, the woods smelled of wet dirt and greenery.* **3** Dirt is also the earth considered as a surface: *The basement has a dirt floor.*

dirty /'dɜrţ·i/ *adj* [-er/-est only] having esp. dirt on the surface of something ○ *He left his dirty towels on the bathroom floor.*

dirty /'dɜrţ·i/ *v* [T] to allow something to get dirt on it ○ *Don't sit on the ground – you'll dirty your new suit.*

WORD CHOICES dirt

If something is extremely dirty, you can say it is **filthy**.

*Wash your hands before supper – they're **filthy**!*

If something or someone looks dirty and untidy, you can say that the person or thing is **scruffy** or **messy**.

*He's the typical **scruffy** student.*

*Ben's bedroom is always really **messy**.*

If something is covered in dirt and needs washing, the adjectives **grimy** and **grubby** are often used.

*Don't wipe your **grimy** hands on that clean towel!*

*He was wearing an old pair of jeans and a **grubby** T-shirt.*

The adjective **soiled** is a rather formal way of describing something, especially something made of cloth, that is dirty.

***Soiled** tablecloths should be soaked in detergent.*

If a place is extremely dirty and unpleasant, the adjective **squalid** is sometimes used.

*He lived in a **squalid** dormitory.*

INFORMATION /dɜrt/ *n* [U] personal information about something wrong that someone has done ○ *They are more interested in looking for dirt than in reporting fairly about him.*

dirty /'dɜrţ·i/ *adj* [-er/-est only] **1** unfair or dishonest ○ *That was a dirty trick – telling me you were out of town when you were right here all the time!* **2** Dirty is also used to emphasize how strongly you feel that something is wrong or bad: *That's a dirty lie!*

dirt bike *n* [C] a bicycle with wide tires for traveling over rough ground

dirty work *n* [C usually sing] an unpleasant or dishonest job, esp. something that other people do not want to do ○ *My boss gives me all his dirty work to do, so he doesn't get blamed when things go wrong.*

dis /dɪs/ *v* [T] **-ss-** *slang* to say or do something that shows a lack of respect for someone and is often intended to insult

disable /dɪs'eɪ·bəl/ *v* [T] to make something or someone unable to act in the correct or usual way ○ *Thieves disabled the museum's alarm system.*

disabled /dɪs'eɪ·bəld/ *adj* lacking one or more of the physical or mental abilities that most people have ○ *a disabled war veteran* ○ *US law requires that all public buildings be accessible to the disabled.* ○ *They opened a group home for mentally disabled adults.*

disability /ˌdɪs·ə'bɪl·əţ·i/ *n* [C/U] a physical or mental condition that makes someone unable to act in a way that is considered usual for most people ○ [C] *The law bars discrimination against those with disabilities.* ○ [U] *The regulations apply to people unable to work because of disability.*

disaccharide /dɑɪ'sæk·əˌrɑɪd/ *n* [C] ***biology*** a type of sugar that is formed of two simple sugar MOLECULES (= smallest unit of a substance)

disadvantage /ˌdɪs·əd'vænt·ɪdʒ/ *n* [C] **1** something that makes a successful result less likely, esp. less likely for you than it is for others ○ *There are disadvantages to living in a rural area.* **2** If you are **at a disadvantage**, you are in a situation in which you are less likely to succeed than others: *She felt that being so young put her at a disadvantage for the executive position.*

disadvantaged /ˌdɪs·əd'vænt·ɪdʒd/ *adj* (of people) not having the benefits, such as enough money and a healthy social situation, that others have, and therefore having less opportunity to be successful ○ *Head Start is an educational program for disadvantaged preschool children.*

disaffected /ˌdɪs·ə'fek·təd/ *adj* feeling unhappy about and separate from an organization or idea that you once supported ○ *Charges of incompetence were made by disaffected members of the club.*

disagree /ˌdɪs·ə'griː/ *v* [I] to have a different opinion or be unable to agree ○ *I disagree with you about that.* ○ *Most scientists agree there is a risk, but disagree over the exact amount of risk.*

disagreement /ˌdɪs·ə'griː·mənt/ *n* [C/U] a situation in which people have different opinions, or an inability to agree ○ [C] *The candidates had few disagreements about the major issues.*

WORD FAMILY disagree

Nouns	disagreement	*Verbs*	disagree
Adjectives	disagreeable		

D

PHRASAL VERB with disagree

• **disagree with** *someone* to cause someone to feel ill ○ *I must have eaten something that disagreed with me.*

disagreeable /ˌdɪs·əˈgriː·ə·bəl/ *adj* unpleasant; unattractive ○ *The drinking water had a disagreeable oily taste.*

D

disappear /ˌdɪs·əˈpɪr/ *v* [I] (of a person or thing) to go to a place or into a condition where the person or thing cannot be seen ○ *She disappeared into the house.* ○ *He disappeared for a few hours* (= went somewhere unknown). ○ *They watched the plane until it disappeared* (= could no longer be seen).

disappearance /ˌdɪs·əˈpɪr·əns/ *n* [U] ○ *The district attorney is looking into the disappearance of the money.* ○ *Her disappearance remains unexplained.*

WORD CHOICES disappear

Go away is an alternative to "disappear."

*It was weeks before the bruises **went away**.*

Vanish or the phrase **vanish into thin air** can be used when someone or something disappears, especially in a sudden and surprising way.

*Dinosaurs **vanished** from the Earth 65 million years ago.*

If people or things disappear and no one knows where they are, you can say that they **go missing**.

*The computer files containing nuclear secrets **went missing** for a short time.*

If something disappears slowly, you can say it **fades away**.

*As the years passed, the memories **faded away**.*

disappoint /ˌdɪs·əˈpɔɪnt/ *v* [T] to fail to satisfy someone's hopes or expectations ○ *I hate to disappoint you, but we don't have the book you wanted.*

disappointed /ˌdɪs·əˈpɔɪnt·əd/ *adj* unhappy or discouraged because your hopes or expectations about something or someone were not satisfied ○ *Obviously, we were disappointed in the jury's verdict.* ○ *I'm disappointed by the way our team played today.* ○ [+ to infinitive] *We were extremely disappointed to receive this information.*

disappointing /ˌdɪs·əˈpɔɪnt·ɪŋ/ *adj* not as good as you had hoped or expected; not satisfactory ○ *The team has had two disappointing seasons.* ○ *Kerrigan finished the race a disappointing fifth.*

disappointment /ˌdɪs·əˈpɔɪnt·mənt/ *n* [C/U] the unhappiness or discouragement that results when your hopes or expectations have not been satisfied, or someone or something that is not as good as you had hoped or expected ○ [U] *Her disappointment showed on her face.* ○ [C] *After two losing seasons, we felt he was a disappointment as a coach.*

SPELLING

disappoint

Many people make mistakes when spelling this word. The correct spelling has one "s" and two "p's."

I was so disappointed.

The film was pretty disappointing.

WORD FAMILY disappoint

Nouns	disappointment	*Adjectives*	disappointed
Verbs	disappoint		disappointing

WORD CHOICES disappoint

If someone feels very disappointed about something that has happened, you can use the adjective **disheartened**.

*He was very **disheartened** by the results of the test.*

A person who does not do what he or she agreed to do can be said to have **let *someone* down**.

*John had promised to go but he **let** me **down** at the last minute.*

A situation that makes someone feel disappointed is often described as a **letdown**.

*After finally winning the playoffs, the loss of the championship game was a real **letdown**.*

An **anticlimactic** experience is a disappointing experience, often one that you thought would be exciting before it happened or one that comes after a more exciting experience.

*After so much preparation, the party itself was a little **anticlimactic**.*

disapprove /ˌdɪs·əˈpruːv/ *v* [I] to think that something is wrong, or to have a bad opinion about someone ○ *Some people disapproved of the School Board's decision to have students wear uniforms.* ○ *They disapproved of his conduct.*

disapproval /ˌdɪs·əˈpruː·vəl/ *n* [U] the expression or feeling that something done or said is wrong ○ *The boy sensed his mother's disapproval.* ○ *He decided to marry her, to the great disapproval of his father.*

disarm REMOVE WEAPONS /dɪsˈɑrm/ *v* [I/T] to take weapons away from someone, or give up weapons ○ [T] *Store security guards disarmed him and held him for the police.* ○ [I] *The revolutionary group refused to disarm.* ○ [T] *Bomb experts disarmed the device* (= made it unable to explode).

disarmament /dɪsˈɑr·mə·mənt/ *n* [U] ***politics & government*** a reduction in or limitation of the number of weapons in the armed forces of a country ○ *nuclear disarmament* ○ *disarmament talks*

CHARM /dɪsˈɑrm/ *v* [T] to make someone begin to like you, esp. unexpectedly ○ *He was disarmed by the older man's wit and intelligence.*

disarming /dɪsˈɑr·mɪŋ/ *adj* approving ○ *He had a disarming reason for arriving late – he was reading to his children.*

disarray /ˌdɪs·əˈreɪ/ *n* [U] a messy or confused condition, showing a lack of organization ○ *Many party members believe the campaign is in disarray.* ○ *The apartment was in complete disarray.*

disaster /dɪˈzæs·tər, -ˈsæs·tər/ *n* [C/U] **1** an event causing great harm, damage, or suffering ○ [C/U] *financial disaster* ○ [U] *disaster aid/relief* ○ [C] *Over 100 people died in the disaster.* ○ [C] *The hurricane may be the costliest natural disaster in US history.* **2** *fig.* A disaster is also a complete failure: [C] *Our last dinner party was an absolute disaster.*
disastrous /dɪˈzæs·trəs, -ˈsæs·trəs/ *adj* **1** *It was a disastrous mistake which he lived to regret.* ○ *In 1837, there was a disastrous smallpox epidemic.* **2** *fig.* Something that is disastrous is a complete failure: *His attempt to play the piano disastrous.*

WORD FAMILY disaster	
Nouns disaster	*Adjectives* disastrous

disavow /ˌdɪs·əˈvɑʊ/ *v* [T] to say that you know nothing about or have no responsibility for something ○ *He disavowed his earlier confession to the police.*

disband /dɪsˈbænd/ *v* [I/T] (of a group) to stop existing, or to cause a group to stop existing ○ [T] *The managers planned to disband the team.*

disbelief /ˌdɪs·bəˈliːf/ *n* [U] the refusal to believe that something is true ○ *He shook his head in disbelief when I told him about the crash.*

disc /dɪsk/ *n* [C] **1** a DISK **2** Disc is also another name for a musical record or a CD: *This recording is available on disc and on tape.*

discard /dɪsˈkɑrd/ *v* [T] to throw away or get rid of something because you no longer want it ○ *Cut the melon in half and discard the seeds.* ○ *He makes toys from things people discard.*

discern /dɪsˈɜrn, dɪz-/ *v* [T] to be able to see, recognize, understand, or decide something ○ *He could discern the note of urgency in their voices.* ○ *The exhibit is arranged in no important order that the viewer can discern.*
discernible /dɪsˈɜr·nə·bəl, dɪz-/ *adj* able to be seen, recognized, or understood ○ *If there was meat in the soup, it was not discernible.*
discerning /dɪsˈɜr·nɪŋ, dɪz-/ *adj approving* able to make or usually making careful judgments about the quality of similar things ○ *Marion is a discerning judge of good design.*

discharge ALLOW TO LEAVE /dɪsˈtʃɑrdʒ, ˈdɪs·tʃɑrdʒ/ *v* [T] **1** to allow someone to leave ○ *Allen was discharged from the hospital yesterday.* **2** Someone who is discharged from a job is asked to leave it.
discharge /ˈdɪs·tʃɑrdʒ/ *n* [C/U] ○ [C] *McCarthy held the rank of captain at the time of his discharge from the army.*
SEND OUT /dɪsˈtʃɑrdʒ, ˈdɪs·tʃɑrdʒ/ *v* [I/T] to send out a substance, esp. waste matter ○ [I] *The soapy water from the washing machine will discharge directly into the waste line.*
discharge /ˈdɪs·tʃɑrdʒ/ *n* [C/U] **1** [C] *an oily discharge* **2** A discharge is also liquid matter that comes from a part of the body.
SHOOT /dɪsˈtʃɑrdʒ, ˈdɪs·tʃɑrdʒ/ *v* [I/T] to shoot a gun ○ [I] *A gun accidentally discharged.*
PERFORM /dɪsˈtʃɑrdʒ, ˈdɪs·tʃɑrdʒ/ *v* [T] *fml* to perform a duty, esp. an official one ○ *He continued to discharge his duties as administrator of the fund.*

disciple /dɪˈsɑɪ·pəl/ *n* [C] **1** a person who believes in the ideas of a leader, esp. a religious or political one, and tries to live according to those ideas ○ *Jesse Jackson was a disciple of Martin Luther King, Jr.* **2** The Disciples were the twelve men who followed Jesus during his life.

D

discipline TRAINING /ˈdɪs·ə·plən, -ˌplɪn/ *n* [U] **1** training that produces obedience or self-control, often in the form of rules and punishments if these are broken, or the obedience or self-control produced by this training ○ *military discipline* **2** Discipline is also the ability to control a mental activity: *Learning a foreign language requires discipline.*
discipline /ˈdɪs·ə·plən, -ˌplɪn/ *v* [T] ○ *He was disciplined* (= punished) *for his bad conduct.*
disciplinary /ˈdɪs·ə·pləˌner·i/ *adj* [not gradable] ○ *Some disciplinary action was obviously called for.*
SUBJECT /ˈdɪs·ə·plən, -ˌplɪn/ *n* [C] a particular area of study, esp. a subject studied at a college or university ○ *an academic discipline*

WORD FAMILY discipline			
Nouns	discipline	*Verbs*	discipline
Adjectives	disciplinary		

disc jockey, *abbreviation* **DJ** *n* [C] someone who plays recorded music on the radio or at a dance, party, or other event

disclaim /dɪˈskleɪm/ *v* [T] to say you are not responsible for or do not know anything about something ○ *The officers disclaimed any knowledge of the incident.*
disclaimer /dɪˈskleɪ·mər/ *n* [C] *fml* a statement that you are not responsible for something ○ *The disclaimer reminded viewers that the movie is a drama, not a documentary.*

disclose /dɪˈskloʊz/ *v* [T] to give information to the public that was not previously known ○ *Terms of the agreement were not disclosed.*
disclosure /dɪˈskloʊ·ʒər/ *n* [C/U] ○ [U] *Full financial disclosure is required.* ○ [C] *Some of the disclosures in the final report were very surprising.*

disco /ˈdɪs·koʊ/ *n* [C] *pl* **discos** a place where people dance to recorded music for entertainment ○ *disco dancing*

discolor, *Cdn, Br* **discolour** /dɪsˈkʌl·ər/ *v* [I/T] to cause a substance or material to change from its original color when you do not want it to ○ [T] *Direct sunlight will discolor this fabric.*
discoloration /dɪsˌkʌl·əˈreɪ·ʃən/ *n* [C/U]

discomfort /dɪsˈkʌm·fərt/ *n* [C/U] **1** the feeling of not being comfortable, either from a physical cause or from a situation, or something that causes this feeling ○ [U] *It's clear that both parties* *have some degree of discomfort with the idea.* ○ [U] *She laughed at his discomfort* (= embarrassment). **2** Discomfort is also pain, usually not severe: [U] *I could move my arm, but I had a lot of discomfort.*

disconcert /ˌdɪs·kənˈsɜrt/ *v* [T] to make someone feel suddenly uncertain or worried ○ *He was disconcerted by all the attention he was getting.*

disconcerting /ˌdɪs·kənˈsɜrt̬·ɪŋ/ *adj* ○ *So this deliberate lack of interest in noticing us was most disconcerting.*

D

disconnect /ˌdɪs·kəˈnekt/ *v* [T] **1** to break a connection that carries a substance or electricity, or to break such a connection used by someone or something ○ *He disconnected a gas line.* ○ *Carefully tip the grill on its back and disconnect the burner from the gas valves.* ○ *Our phone was disconnected* (= turned off by the telephone company). **2** If you are disconnected while speaking on the telephone, the telephone connection is suddenly stopped and you can no longer continue your conversation.

disconnect /ˌdɪs·kəˈnekt/ *n* [C] *infml* a lack of connection; a failure of two things to relate ○ *There's a disconnect between the public and the media.*

discontent /ˌdɪs·kənˈtent/ *n* [U] a feeling of not being satisfied with your situation or with the way you are being treated ○ *Mexican-American leaders expressed discontent with the administration.*

discontented /ˌdɪs·kənˈtent·əd/ *adj* ○ *Discontented with her job, Cassandra often talked of leaving.*

discontinue /ˌdɪs·kənˈtɪn·juː/ *v* [T] to stop doing, using, or operating something ○ *Discontinue the medication if you have cramps.* ○ *The airline announced that weekday flights to Kansas City would be discontinued.*

discord /ˈdɪs·kɔːrd/ *n* [U] a lack of agreement or feeling of trust between people ○ *The plan to build the highway created discord in our community.*

discount REDUCTION /ˈdɪs·kɑʊnt/ *n* [C] a reduction in the usual price for something ○ *Students receive a 10 percent discount.* ○ *He gets a senior citizen discount at the theater.*

discount /dɪsˈkɑʊnt, ˈdɪs·kɑʊnt/ *v* [T] ○ *The airline has discounted domestic fares.*

NOT CONSIDER /dɪsˈkɑʊnt, ˈdɪs·kɑʊnt/ *v* [T] to decide that something or someone is not worth consideration or attention ○ *He discounted fears about computer programming problems involving the year 2000 as exaggerated.*

discount store *n* [C] a store that sells products at cheap prices

discourage MAKE LESS CONFIDENT /dɪsˈkɜr·ɪdʒ, -ˈkʌ·rɪdʒ/ *v* [T] to cause someone to feel less confident or less hopeful ○ *She sometimes got discouraged about her social life, which was going nowhere, she felt.*

discouraging /dɪsˈkɜr·ə·dʒɪŋ, -ˈkʌ·rə-/ *adj* ○ *It's discouraging to feel that opportunities have passed you by.*

discouragement /dɪsˈkɜr·ɪdʒ·mənt, -ˈkʌ·rɪdʒ-/ *n* [U] ○ *He had known discouragement and failure, but in the end he persevered and wound up with a successful business.*

PREVENT /dɪsˈkɜr·ɪdʒ, -ˈkʌ·rɪdʒ/ *v* [T] to try to prevent something from happening or someone from doing something, or to have the effect of making something less likely ○ *We tried to discourage him from spending so much money.* ○ *Higher taxes could discourage business investment.* ○ *The tough competition discourages many athletes from making a serious attempt to make the Olympic team.*

discourse /ˈdɪs·kɔːrs, -kours/ *n* [C/U] ***literature*** spoken or written discussion ○ [U] *political discourse* ○ [C] *The play is a wonderful discourse on love.*

discourteous /dɪsˈkɜrt̬·iː·əs/ *adj* not caring enough about other people's feelings; not polite ○ *I felt it was discourteous of him to leave immediately after his talk.*

discourtesy /dɪsˈkɜrt̬·ə·si/ *n* [C/U] ○ [C] *She was never guilty of the slightest discourtesy.*

discover /dɪˈskʌv·ər/ *v* [T] **1** to find something for the first time, or something that had not been known before ○ [+ (*that*) clause] *Doctors later discovered (that) he had a cut on his left ankle.* ○ [+ question word] *We reviewed enrollment figures to discover exactly when and why the student population declined.* ○ *Researchers hope to discover new treatments that may help people suffering from migraine headaches.* **2** To discover is also to realize or learn: [+ *that* clause] *When you go on a trip, you always discover that you forgot a few things.*

discoverer /dɪˈskʌv·ə·rər/ *n* [C] ○ *The Canadians Frederick Banting and Charles Best were the discoverers of insulin.*

discovery /dɪˈskʌv·ə·ri/ *n* [C/U] **1** the act of finding something that had not been known before ○ [C] *Many scientific discoveries have been made by accident.* ○ [U] *The discovery of gold in California opened up the west.* **2** A discovery is also something that you did not know about before: [C] *It was quite a discovery when I came upon this beautiful mountain stream.*

WORD FAMILY discover			
Nouns	discoverer discovery	Verbs	discover

discredit /dɪsˈkred·ət/ *v* [T] to give people reason to stop believing someone or to doubt the truth of something ○ *The old Soviet economic model has been thoroughly discredited.* ○ *It's the job of the defense to discredit prosecution witnesses.*

discredit /dɪsˈkred·ət/ *n* [U] *fml* ○ *He's brought discredit on himself.*

discreet /dɪˈskriːt/ *adj* careful not to cause embarrassment or attract a lot of attention ○ *She hung the laundry on a line in a discreet corner of the yard.* ○ *There was a discreet knock on the door.*

discreetly /dɪˈskriːt·li/ *adv* ○ *Some of Nelle's acquaintances discreetly suggested she get a divorce.*

discrepancy /dɪˈskrep·ən·si/ *n* [C] an unexpected difference, esp. in two amounts or two sets of facts or conditions, which suggests that something is wrong and has to be explained ○ *There were troubling discrepancies between his public and private opinions on how to balance the budget.*

discrete /dɪˈskriːt/ *adj* having an independent existence or form apart from other similar things; separate ○ *This area has four discrete neighborhoods centered around a school.*

discretion Ⓐ /dɪˈskreʃ·ən/ *n* [U] choice, or the right to make a choice, based on judgment ○ *Troopers have discretion in deciding whom to stop for speeding.* ○ *Whether or not to hold the meeting is at the discretion of the president* (= a decision to be made by the president).

discretionary Ⓐ /dɪˈskreʃ·əˌner·i/ *adj* available to someone by choice, without having to get permission or authority ○ *Once your kids have discretionary money of their own, they can pay for their own DVDs.*

discriminate Ⓐ **TREAT WORSE** /dɪˈskrɪm·əˌneɪt/ *v* [I] to treat a person or particular group of people differently and esp. unfairly, in a way that is worse than the way people are usually treated ○ *It is illegal to discriminate on the basis of race, sex, national origin, or age.* ○ *They argued that whites in the area in the 1800s discriminated against the Lakota.*

discrimination Ⓐ /dɪˌskrɪm·əˈneɪ·ʃən/ *n* [U] **1** *Some immigrants were victims of discrimination.* ○ *The law made racial discrimination in employment a serious crime.* ○ *She claims she is a victim of age discrimination.* **2** ***politics & government*** Discrimination is also PREJUDICE against people and a refusal to give them their RIGHTS.

discriminatory /dɪˈskrɪm·ə·nəˌtɔːr·i, -ˌtoʊr·i/ *adj* ○ *discriminatory practices*

SEE A DIFFERENCE /dɪˈskrɪm·əˌneɪt/ *v* [I/T] to be able to see the difference between two things or types of things ○ [I] *We need to discriminate between stopgap methods and long-term solutions.*

discriminating Ⓐ /dɪˈskrɪm·əˌneɪt̬·ɪŋ/ *adj* able to judge the quality of something based on its difference from other, similar things ○ *a discriminating music lover* ○ *discriminating buyers/shoppers*

discrimination Ⓐ /dɪˌskrɪm·əˈneɪ·ʃən/ *n* [U] ○ *He showed discrimination in his reading habits.*

discus /ˈdɪs·kəs/ *n* [C] a round object shaped like a plate that is thrown in sports competitions, or the sport in which this object is thrown

discuss /dɪˈskʌs/ *v* [T] to talk about something to other people, often exchanging ideas or opinions ○ *We have been discussing the possibility of working together.* ○ [+ question word] *This booklet discusses how to invest money wisely.*

discussion /dɪˈskʌʃ·ən/ *n* [C/U] ○ [U] *The matter is still under discussion* (= being considered). ○ [C] *The council had discussions on issues such as housing and living conditions.*

disdain /dɪsˈdeɪn/ *n* [U] dislike of someone or something that you feel does not deserve your interest or respect ○ *The mayor's disdain for his opponents was well known.*

disdain /dɪsˈdeɪn/ *v* [T] ○ *He disdains the flashy trappings of many Dixieland bands, the striped shirts and straw hats and such.*

disease /dɪˈziːz/ *n* [C/U] a condition of a person, animal, or plant in which its body or structure is harmed because an organ or part is unable to work as it usually does; an illness ○ [C] *Mumps is an infectious disease.* ○ [U] *He suffers from heart disease.* ○ [U] *Hundreds of thousands of trees died from Dutch elm disease.*

disembark /ˌdɪs·əmˈbɑrk/ *v* [I] to leave a ship, aircraft, etc., after a trip ○ *They disembarked in Seattle.*

disembodied /ˌdɪs·əmˈbɑd·iːd/ *adj* [not gradable] existing without a body ○ *A disembodied voice crackled from the radio.*

disenchanted /ˌdɪs·ənˈtʃænt·əd/ *adj* no longer believing in the value of something, esp. after having learned of the faults that it has ○ *I have become disenchanted with politics.*

disenfranchise /ˌdɪs·ənˈfræn·tʃɑɪz/ *v* [T] ***politics & government*** to take away a person's RIGHT to vote

disengage /ˌdɪs·ənˈgeɪdʒ/ *v* [I/T] to become separate or not connected, or to cause this to happen ○ [I] *The US should not disengage from Europe, she said.*

disentangle /ˌdɪs·ənˈtæŋ·gəl/ *v* [T] to separate things that have become joined or confused ○ *It's hard to disentangle the truth from all her lies.*

disfigure /dɪsˈfɪg·jər/ *v* [T] to spoil completely the appearance of someone or something ○ *She was horribly disfigured by burns.*

disgrace /dɪsˈgreɪs/ *n* [U] embarrassment and the loss of other people's respect, or behavior that causes this ○ *He resigned in disgrace.* ○ *He's a disgrace to his family.*

disgraceful /dɪsˈgreɪs·fəl/ *adj* ○ *The lies my opponent is telling about me are disgraceful.*

disgruntled /dɪsˈgrʌnt·əld/ *adj* unhappy, annoyed, and disappointed about something ○ *a disgruntled employee*

disguise /dɪsˈgɑɪz/ *v* [T] **1** to give a new appearance to a person or thing, esp. in order to hide its true form ○ *His mask doesn't disguise his identity.* ○ *I think mom could disguise her voice better than you could disguise yours.* **2** To disguise an opinion, feeling, etc., is to hide it: *I couldn't disguise my unhappiness at this decision.*

disguise /dɪsˈgɑɪz/ *n* [C/U] ○ [U] *In Shakespeare's plays, many characters appear in disguise.*

disgust /dɪsˈgʌst/ *n* [U] a strong feeling of disapproval or dislike, or a feeling of becoming ill caused by something unpleasant ○ *She resigned from the committee in disgust at their inefficiency.* ○ *Something in the kitchen smelled so bad that we all left in disgust.*

disgust /dɪsˈgʌst/ *v* [T] ○ *I'm disgusted by how dirty this oven is.*
disgusted /dɪsˈgʌs·təd·li/ *adj* ○ *He gave her a disgusted look.*
disgusting /dɪsˈgʌs·tɪŋ/ *adj* ○ *When you burn garbage, you've got some pretty disgusting stuff going up in the atmosphere.*

D

dish CONTAINER /dɪʃ/ *n* [C] **1** a round, flat container with a raised edge, used for serving or holding food **2** The dishes are all the plates, glasses, knives, forks, etc., that have been used during a meal: *Who's going to do the dishes* (= clean the plates, glasses, etc.)*?*

FOOD /dɪʃ/ *n* [C] a particular type of food or food prepared in a particular way as part of a meal ○ *This restaurant serves both Cuban and Chinese dishes.*

IDIOM with **dish**

• *someone* **can dish it out but** *he or she* **can't take it** someone easily criticizes other people but does not like it when other people criticize him or her ○ *He's mad at me for teasing him – he can dish it out, but he can't take it!*

PHRASAL VERBS with **dish**

• **dish out** *something* [M] *infml* to give something, or to tell something such as information or your opinions ○ *NBC dished out more than $790 million to broadcast the Athens Games to U.S. audiences.* ○ *The players won't accept the bullying the coach dishes out.* ○ *His collaborators are dishing out misinformation.*

• **dish up/out** *something* [M] *infml* to put food onto dishes; or to provide a meal ○ *The crew dished up fish sandwiches to the hungry workers.* ○ *The candidates were at the fair to shake hands, dish out baked beans, and kiss babies.*

disheartening /dɪsˈhɑrt·ᵊn/ *adj* causing a person to lose confidence, hope, and energy; discouraging ○ *The new injury, after he had come back from the last, was disheartening.*

disheveled /dɪˈʃev·əld/ *adj* (of people or their appearance) not neat; messy ○ *disheveled hair/clothes*

dishonest /dɪsˈɑn·əst/ *adj* not honest ○ *He's been dishonest with us, and I'll never trust him again.*
dishonesty /dɪsˈɑn·ə·sti/ *n* [U]

WORD CHOICES **dishonest**

In informal situations, you can use the adjective **crooked** instead of "dishonest."

crooked salesmen

Unscrupulous can be used when someone is dishonest or unfair in order to get what he or she wants.

This list will help you avoid ***unscrupulous*** *financial advisers.*

If you want to say that someone is dishonest in his or her job and tries to get money or use power wrongly, you can use the adjective **corrupt**.

There are always a few ***corrupt*** *government officials who will accept bribes.*

Someone who is hiding the truth can be described as **deceitful**.

He was being ***deceitful*** *by not telling his parents that he was going to see a movie.*

The adjective **devious** means that a person or plan is slightly dishonest, often in a way that is complicated but clever and successful.

You often have to be a bit ***devious*** *if you're going to succeed in business.*

Fraudulent is often used when someone is being deliberately dishonest to try and get money.

fraudulent *insurance claims*

dishonor, *Cdn, Br* **dishonour** /dɪsˈɑn·ər/ *n* [U] a feeling of embarrassment and loss of people's respect, or something that causes this ○ *It is no dishonor to lose to a champion.*
dishonorable, *Cdn, Br* **dishonourable** /dɪsˈɑn·ə·rə·bəl/ *adj* ○ *He served two years in an army prison and received a dishonorable discharge.*

dishtowel /ˈdɪʃˌtɑʊ·əl, -tɑʊl/ *n* [C] a cloth used for drying dishes

dishwasher /ˈdɪʃˌwɑʃ·ər, -wɔː·ʃər/ *n* [C] a machine for washing dishes

disillusion /ˌdɪs·əˈluː·ʒən/ *v* [T] to disappoint someone by making the person realize the unpleasant truth about something or someone thought to be good ○ *He's become disillusioned with his job and the company.*
disillusioned /ˌdɪs·əˈluː·ʒənd/ *adj* ○ *He died a disillusioned man.*
disillusionment /ˌdɪs·əˈluː·ʒən·mənt/ *n* [U]

disinfect /ˌdɪs·ənˈfekt/ *v* [T] to clean by using chemicals to kill bacteria that cause disease
disinfectant /ˌdɪs·ənˈfek·tənt/ *n* [C/U] a substance that contains chemicals that kill bacteria and is used esp. for cleaning surfaces in bathrooms and kitchens

disingenuous /ˌdɪs·ənˈdʒen·jə·wəs/ *adj* (of people or their behavior) slightly dishonest; not speaking the complete truth ○ *a disingenuous compliment*

disintegrate /dəˈsɪnt·əˌgreɪt/ *v* [I] to become weaker or be destroyed by breaking into small pieces ○ *The spacecraft disintegrated as it entered the earth's atmosphere.*
disintegration /dəˌsɪnt·əˈgreɪ·ʃən/ *n* [U]

disinterest /dɪsˈɪn·trəst, -ˈɪnt·ə·rəst/ *n* [U] lack of interest ○ *He gave an impression of calm disinterest in the world about him.*
disinterested /dɪsˈɪn·trə·stəd, -ˈɪnt·əˌres·təd/ *adj* ○ *Unlike most boys his age, he was totally disinterested in cars or girls.*

disinterested /dɪsˈɪn·trə·stəd, -ˈɪnt·əˌres·təd/ *adj* having no personal involvement or receiving no personal advantage, and therefore free to act fairly ○ *disinterested advice* ○ *a disinterested observer*

disjointed /dɪsˈdʒɔɪnt·əd/ *adj* (esp. of words or ideas) not well connected or well ordered, and therefore often confusing ○ *She gave a disjointed account of getting lost in the woods.*

disk, **disc** /dɪsk/ *n* [C] **1** a flat, circular object ○ *The dog's name is on a metal disk attached to its collar.* **2** A disk is also a small piece of CARTILAGE (= strong, elastic body tissue) between the bones of a person's back. **3** A disk is also a flat, circular device that has a magnetic covering and is used for storing computer information: *a hard disk* ○ See also: DISC

disk drive *n* [C] a piece of equipment that reads from and allows you to store information on computer disks

diskette /dɪsˈket/ *n* [C] a flat, circular device that has a magnetic covering, used to copy computer information and store it separately from a computer

dislike /dɪsˈlɑɪk/ *v* [T] to not like; to find someone or something unpleasant, difficult, etc. ○ *I dislike the idea of leaving him home alone all evening.*
dislike /dɪsˈlɑɪk/ *n* [C/U] ○ [C] *a dislike of flying*

dislocate /dɪsˈloʊˌkeɪt/ *v* [T] to force a bone suddenly out of its correct position ○ *He dislocated his elbow in the crash.*

dislodge /dɪsˈlɑdʒ/ *v* [T] to force someone or something from a place or position ○ *Heavy rains have dislodged big slabs of sidewalk in front of the school.* ○ *It took a professional trapper to dislodge a family of racoons from my cottage.*

disloyal /dɪsˈlɔɪ·əl/ *adj* not loyal; acting to hurt someone you are expected to support ○ *His sisters thought that his autobiography was disloyal to the family.*

dismal /ˈdɪz·məl/ *adj* dark and sad, without hope, or very bad ○ *The trip was a dismal failure.*

dismantle /dɪsˈmænt·əl/ *v* [T] to take a machine or something complicated apart, usually to make it unable to work ○ *The government voted to dismantle its nuclear warheads.* ○ *They worried that dismantling the welfare state would increase poverty.*

dismay /dɪˈsmeɪ/ *n* [U] a feeling of shock and unhappiness ○ *She discovered, to her dismay, that she had locked her keys inside her car.*
dismay /dɪˈsmeɪ/ *v* [T] ○ *They enjoyed the meal but were dismayed by how much it cost.*

dismember /dɪˈsmem·bər/ *v* [T] to cut a body, esp. of an animal, into pieces

dismiss NOT CONSIDER /dɪˈsmɪs/ *v* [T] to decide that something or someone is not important and not worth considering ○ *Let's not dismiss the idea without discussing it.*
dismissal /dɪˈsmɪs·əl/ *n* [C/U] ○ *The lawyer is seeking a dismissal of the charges against his client.*
dismissive /dɪˈsmɪs·ɪv/ *adj* ○ *a dismissive, angry look*
SEND AWAY /dɪˈsmɪs/ *v* [T] **1** to formally ask or order someone to leave ○ *The teacher dismissed the class early.* **2** Someone who is dismissed from a job is officially told not to work at that job any longer.

dismount /dɪˈsmɑʊnt/ *v* [I] to get off a horse or a bicycle

disobedient /ˌdɪs·əˈbiːd·iː·ənt/ *adj* not doing what you are told to do ○ *a disobedient child*
disobedience /ˌdɪs·əˈbiːd·iː·əns/ *n* [U]

disobey /ˌdɪs·əˈbeɪ/ *v* [I/T] to intentionally fail to do what you are told or expected to do; not obey ○ [T] *Half of the city's drivers tend to disobey rules and behave poorly.*

disorder CONFUSION /dɪsˈɔːrd·ər/ *n* [U] a state in which objects or conditions are in no particular order; lack of system or planned organization ○ *The room was in such disorder that she couldn't find anything.*
disorderly /dɪsˈɔːrd·ər·li/ *adj*
ILLNESS /dɪsˈɔːrd·ər/ *n* [C/U] an illness of the mind or body ○ [C] *a mental/physical disorder* ○ [C] *She suffers from an eating disorder.*
SITUATION /dɪsˈɔːrd·ər/ *n* [U] a situation in which some people behave in a way that threatens the safety of other people or the peace of a neighborhood ○ *public disorder*
disorderly /dɪsˈɔːrd·ər·li/ *adj* ○ *a disorderly crowd* ○ *He was charged with disorderly conduct.*

disorganized /dɪsˈɔːr·gəˌnɑɪzd/ *adj* badly planned and lacking order ○ *According to one officer, things are so disorganized that no one knows who is where.*
disorganization /dɪsˌɔːr·gə·nəˈzeɪ·ʃən/ *n* [U]

disorient /dɪsˈɔːr·iːˌent/ *v* [T] to make people confused about where they are and where they are going ○ *It's easy to get disoriented because all the streets look alike.*

disown /dɪsˈoʊn/ *v* [T] to state that you no longer have any connection with someone that you used to be closely connected with

disparage /dɪˈspær·ɪdʒ/ *v* [T] to criticize someone or something in a way that shows a lack of respect ○ *He disparages his business competitors, saying they are all a bunch of amateurs compared to him.*
disparaging /dɪˈspær·ə·dʒɪŋ/ *adj* ○ *My distress has not stopped him from making other disparaging remarks.*
disparagingly /dɪˈspær·ə·dʒɪŋ·li/ *adv* ○ *He spoke disparagingly of his political opponent.*

disparate /ˈdɪs·pə·rət, dɪˈspær·ət/ *adj* different in every way ○ *German newspapers have carried reports of sightings in such disparate places as Switzerland, Iran, and Paraguay.*

disparity /dɪˈspær·əṭ·i/ *n* [C/U] a lack of equality and similarity, esp. in a way that is not fair ○ [C] *He will oppose a gross disparity in salary increases between teachers and other state employees.*

dispassionate /dɪˈspæʃ·ə·nət/ *adj* able to think clearly or make good decisions because not influenced by emotions ○ *The book is intended to*

provide a more dispassionate understanding of recent history.
dispassionately /dɪˈspæʃ·ə·nət·li/ *adv*

dispatch /dɪˈspætʃ/ *v* [T] to send someone or something to a place for a particular purpose ○ *Within seconds the university police can identify the exact origin of the alarm and dispatch officers to investigate.*
dispatch /dɪˈspætʃ/ *n* [C/U] **1** If something is done with dispatch, it is done quickly. **2** A dispatch is a report sent to you from another place: [U] *In her latest dispatch, our correspondent reports on new negotiations.* ○ [C] *a military dispatch*

D

dispel /dɪˈspel/ *v* [T] **-ll-** to remove fears, doubts, or false ideas, usually by proving them wrong or unnecessary ○ *We need to dispel the myths and establish real facts.*

dispensary /dɪˈspen·sə·ri/ *n* [C] a place where medicines are prepared and given out, often in a hospital or a school

dispense /dɪˈspens/ *v* [T] to give out or provide an item or substance ○ *Is there a tourism agency that dispenses city maps?* ○ *This gasoline pump is capable of dispensing eight blends of gasoline.*
dispenser /dɪˈspen·sər/ *n* [C] A dispenser is a machine from which you can get an item, usually by putting coins in it.

PHRASAL VERB with dispense

• **dispense with** *something* to get rid of or do without something ○ *Let's dispense with the formalities and get right down to business.*

disperse /dɪˈspɜrs/ *v* [I/T] to scatter or move away over a large area, or to cause this to happen ○ [I] *It took several hours for the crowd to disperse.*
dispersal /dɪˈspɜr·səl/ *n* [U]

dispersion /dɪˈspɜr·ʒən/ *n* [C] ***chemistry*** a mixture in which very small pieces of one substance are scattered within another substance
/dɪˈspɜr·ʒən/ *n* [U] ***physics*** the separation of light into different colors

dispirited /dɪˈspɪr·əṭ·əd/ *adj* not feeling hopeful about a situation or problem ○ *The poor are dispirited.*

displace Ⓐ /dɪˈspleɪs/ *v* [T] to force something or someone out of its usual or original place ○ *A major government offensive against rebel groups threatens to displace large numbers of people.*
displacement Ⓐ /dɪˈspleɪ·smənt/ *n* [U] **1** when people are forced to leave the place where they normally live **2** ***physics*** Displacement is also the weight of liquid that is forced out of position by an object that is floating on or in it.

display Ⓐ **SHOW** /dɪˈspleɪ/ *v* [T] to show something or a collection of things in an organized way for people to see ○ *The museum displays the tools and clothes of native Indians.*
display /dɪˈspleɪ/ *n* [C/U] ○ [U] *Paintings and carvings of birds and animals will be on display in the main ballroom of the hotel.*

BECOME KNOWN /dɪˈspleɪ/ *v* [T] to let something become known by what you say or do, or how you look ○ *He doesn't display much emotion.*
display /dɪˈspleɪ/ *n* [C] ○ *It was an impressive display of unity and goodwill among South Africa's diverse legislators.*

displease /dɪsˈpliːz/ *v* [T] to cause someone to be annoyed ○ *The city council said it was displeased with the way the mayor had allocated parking spaces.*
displeasure /dɪsˈpleʒ·ər/ *n* [U] ○ *They refused to work overtime, much to the displeasure of their boss.*

disposable Ⓐ /dɪˈspoʊ·zə·bəl/ *adj* intended to be thrown away after use ○ *disposable cups*

disposal Ⓐ /dɪˈspoʊ·zəl/ *n* [U] the act of getting rid of something ○ *the disposal of toxic wastes*

dispose Ⓐ /dɪˈspoʊz/ *v* [T] to make someone feel a particular, and often bad, way toward someone else, or to influence someone in a particular way ○ *Her sense of humor disposed me to like her.*
disposed Ⓐ /dɪˈspoʊzd/ *adj* **1** *We were always well disposed toward my uncle* (= We liked him). **2** To be disposed to do something is to feel that you may want to do it: [+ *to* infinitive] *I didn't feel disposed to help her.*
disposal Ⓐ /dɪˈspoʊ·zəl/ *n* [U]

IDIOM with dispose

• **at** *your* **disposal** able to be used by you; able to help you ○ *I don't have a car at my disposal.*

PHRASAL VERB with dispose

• **dispose of** *something* to get rid of something; throw out or destroy ○ *Every month he must dispose of the oil his restaurant uses to fry potatoes.* ○ *The House will take up other issues once the tax bill is disposed of* (= dealt with and completed).

disposition /ˌdɪs·pəˈzɪʃ·ən/ *n* [C] a person's usual way of feeling or behaving; the tendency of a person to be happy, friendly, anxious, etc. ○ *a cheerful disposition*

dispossess /ˌdɪs·pəˈzes/ *v* [T] to force someone to give up the possession of a house, land, or other property ○ *Many people were dispossessed of their homes during the war.*

disproportionate Ⓐ /ˌdɪs·prəˈpɔːr·ʃə·nət/ *adj* too great or too small when compared to something else ○ *The sheer size of the company gave it disproportionate influence in dealing with the Pentagon and Congress.*
disproportionately Ⓐ /ˌdɪs·prəˈpɔːr·ʃə·nət·li/ *adv* ○ *Unemployment in Iowa is disproportionately high.*

disprove /dɪˈspruːv/ *v* [T] to prove that an idea, statement, etc. is not true ○ *Given the thoroughness of the author's research, the burden rests on critics to disprove the facts he presents.*

dispute /dɪˈspjuːt/ *n* [C/U] an argument or disagreement ○ [C] *Management and the union are trying to resolve the dispute over working conditions.* ○ *Her skill is not* **in dispute** (= there is no disagreement about her skill), *but she doesn't produce enough work.*

dispute /dɪˈspjuːt/ *v* [I/T] ○ [+ *that* clause] *I don't dispute that his films are entertaining, but they don't have much depth.*

disqualify /dɪsˈkwɑl·əˌfɑɪ/ *v* [T] to take away from someone the ability to do or play a part in something because that person is unsuitable or has done something wrong ○ *He was disqualified from competing in the games.*

disqualification /dɪsˌkwɑl·ə·fəˈkeɪ·ʃən/ *n* [C/U]

disquieting /dɪsˈkwɑɪ·ət̬·ɪŋ/ *adj* causing anxiety; worrying ○ *The sheer size of their armed forces is a disquieting factor for neighboring countries.*

disregard /ˌdɪs·rɪˈgɑrd/ *n* [U] lack of consideration or respect ○ *The writer has shown a reckless disregard for the truth.*

disregard /ˌdɪs·rɪˈgɑrd/ *v* [T] to not allow something to influence you; ignore ○ *The jury was told to disregard the comments made by the witness.*

disrepair /ˌdɪs·rɪˈper/ *n* [U] the state of being broken or old and needing to be repaired ○ *The building had fallen into disrepair over the years.*

disreputable /dɪsˈrep·jət̬·ə·bəl/ *adj* having a bad reputation; not approved of ○ *The information came from disreputable sources.*

disrepute /ˌdɪs·rɪˈpjuːt/ *n* [U] *fml* the state of not being respected or trusted ○ *The judge's behavior, he said, had brought the law profession into disrepute.*

disrespect /ˌdɪs·rɪˈspekt/ *n* [U] lack of respect ○ *She apologized for not responding to the letter and said she had meant no disrespect.*

disrespectful /ˌdɪs·rɪˈspekt·fəl/ *adj* ○ *It is disrespectful to mourners at the funeral to have unruly children running around.*

disrespectfully /ˌdɪs·rɪˈspekt·fə·li/ *adv*

disrupt /dɪsˈrʌpt/ *v* [T] to prevent something, esp. a system, process, or event, from continuing as usual or as expected ○ *A heavy fall of snow disrupted traffic during the rush hour.*

disruption /dɪsˈrʌp·ʃən/ *n* [C/U] ○ [C] *Strikes threaten more disruptions for the tourist industry.*

disruptive /dɪsˈrʌp·tɪv/ *adj* tending to damage the orderly control of a situation ○ *disruptive social changes* ○ *The teacher said disruptive behavior would not be tolerated.*

dissatisfied /dɪsˈsæt̬·əsˌfɑɪd/ *adj* not pleased with something; feeling that something is not as good as it should be ○ *She was dissatisfied with her job and decided to look for a new one.*

dissatisfaction /dɪsˌsæt̬·əsˈfæk·ʃən/ *n* [U] ○ *Many of the opinion surveys show deep dissatisfaction with Congress as an institution.*

dissect /dɪˈsekt, dɑɪ-/ *v* [T] **1** to cut apart the body of an animal or plant in order to study its structure ○ *We had to dissect a frog in our biology class.* **2** To dissect is also to examine something in detail: *The more experts dissect his tax revision plan, the more inconsistencies turn up.*

disseminate /dɪˈsem·əˌneɪt/ *v* [T] to spread or give out news, information, ideas, etc. to many people ○ *The purpose of a university press is to disseminate knowledge by publishing books and journals.*

dissemination /dɪˌsem·əˈneɪ·ʃən/ *n* [U] ○ *the rapid dissemination of new technology*

dissension /dɪˈsen·tʃən/ *n* [U] strong disagreement, esp. within an organization ○ *There was a good deal of dissension within women's rights organizations about setting political goals.*

dissent /dɪˈsent/ *n* [U] **1** strong difference of opinion; disagreement esp. about official decisions ○ *There was very little room for dissent or different points of view.* **2** *law* A dissent is also a legal opinion by a judge in a court that differs from the opinion of most of the other judges of the court.

dissent /dɪˈsent/ *v* [I] *law* (of a judge) to offer a legal opinion in a court that differs from the opinion of most of the other judges of the court ○ *A staunch conservative, he frequently dissented from the court's majority opinion.*

dissertation /ˌdɪs·ərˈteɪ·ʃən/ *n* [C] a long piece of writing on a particular subject, esp. one that is done for a PH.D. (= high university degree)

disservice /dɪsˈsɜr·vəs/ *n* [U] an unfair or harmful action ○ *Calling him a liar does him a great disservice.*

dissident /ˈdɪs·əd·ənt/ *n* [C] ***politics & government*** a person who strongly disagrees with and publicly criticizes a government or the official rulings of a group or organization ○ *Union dissidents have challenged the leadership of the current president.*

dissident /ˈdɪs·əd·ənt/ *adj* [not gradable] ○ *dissident views*

dissimilar Ⓐ /dɪsˈsɪm·ə·lər/ *adj* not similar; different ○ *Her diagnosis was not dissimilar* (= was similar) *to that of the previous doctor.*

dissipate /ˈdɪs·əˌpeɪt/ *v* [I/T] to disappear gradually, or to cause something to disappear gradually ○ [T] *It took months of effort to dissipate the oil spill in the North Sea.*

dissipation /ˌdɪs·əˈpeɪ·ʃən/ *n* [U]

dissolute /ˈdɪs·əˌluːt/ *adj* showing a lack of good character and morals; immoral ○ *a dissolute life*

dissolution /ˌdɪs·əˈluː·ʃən/ *n* [U] the ending of esp. an official organization or a legal arrangement ○ *the dissolution of the Spanish Empire*

dissolve **BE ABSORBED** /dɪˈzɑlv, -ˈzɔːlv/ *v* [I/T] to be absorbed or to cause a solid to be absorbed by a liquid, or of a liquid to absorb a solid ○ [T] *Dissolve two teaspoons of yeast in warm water.*

END /dɪˈzɑlv, -ˈzɔːlv/ *v* [I/T] to end an official organization or a legal arrangement ○ [T] *They decided to dissolve the partnership.*

PHRASAL VERB with **dissolve**

• **dissolve into** *something* to change from one condition to another, esp. as a result of a loss of control

○ *The little girl dissolved into tears after her drawing was torn up.* ○ *She knew if she looked at her friend that she'd dissolve into laughter* (= lose control of her emotions and begin laughing).

dissuade /dɪ'sweɪd/ *v* [T] to persuade someone not to do something ○ *The group hopes to dissuade Congress from cutting funds for health programs.*

D

distance /'dɪs·təns/ *n* [C/U] **1** the amount of space between two places or things ○ [C] *The distance from San Francisco to Los Angeles is about 400 miles.* **2 At/From a distance** means if you are not too near: *From a distance, he looks a little like his mother.* **3 In the distance** means at or from a point far away: *We could see the mountains in the distance.*

distance /'dɪs·təns/ *v* [T] If you distance yourself from something, you try to become less involved or connected with it: *The candidate distanced himself from the extremists in the party.*

distant /'dɪs·tənt/ *adj* **1** far away in space or time ○ *She dreamed of traveling to distant lands.* ○ *We could hear the sound of distant thunder.* **2** Someone whose manner is distant does not show much emotion and is not friendly.

WORD FAMILY distance			
Nouns	distance	*Verbs*	distance
Adjectives	distant		

distaste /dɪs'teɪst/ *n* [U] a dislike of something because you consider it unpleasant or unacceptable ○ *She has a distaste for hot, humid weather.*

distasteful /dɪs'teɪst·fəl/ *adj* ○ *Cutting a player from a team is a distasteful task for any coach.*

distill /dɪ'stɪl/ *v* [T] **1** ***chemistry*** to heat a liquid until it changes to a gas and then make it liquid again by cooling **2** To distill something said or written is to reduce it but keep the most important part: *She distilled the report into a paragraph.*

distillery /dɪ'stɪl·ə·ri/ *n* [C] a factory where strong alcoholic drinks are produced by the process of distilling

distillation /ˌdɪs·tə'leɪ·ʃən/ *n* [C/U] ***chemistry*** the process of heating a liquid until it becomes a gas, then making it liquid again by cooling

distinct Ⓐ **DIFFERENT** /dɪ'stɪŋt/ *adj* clearly separate and different ○ *The two languages are quite distinct from each other.* ○ *The dogs are of distinct breeds.*

distinctive Ⓐ /dɪ'stɪŋ·tɪv/ *adj* marking something as clearly different from others ○ *a distinctive flavor/writing style*

distinction Ⓐ /dɪ'stɪŋ·ʃən/ *n* [C/U] ○ [C] *The comment drew/made a false distinction between domestic and foreign affairs, which are really closely related.* ○ [U] *Martin Luther King, Jr. clearly understood and accepted the distinction between preaching and scholarly criticism.*

distinctively Ⓐ /dɪ'stɪŋ·tɪv·li/ *adv*

NOTICEABLE /dɪ'stɪŋt/ *adj* not to be ignored; real and present ○ *There's a distinct possibility of rain today.* ○ *There were distinct advantages to the first job offer.*

distinctly Ⓐ /dɪ'stɪŋ·tli/ *adv* ○ *I distinctly* (= clearly) *remember asking Ralph not to tell anyone about it.*

distinction Ⓐ **QUALITY** /dɪ'stɪŋ·ʃən/ *n* [U] the quality of being excellent or special in some way ○ *He was a scientist of great distinction.*

HONOR /dɪ'stɪŋ·ʃən/ *n* [C] honor obtained or given because of excellence ○ *Winning a Guggenheim fellowship carries great distinction.*

distinguish SEPARATE /dɪ'stɪŋ·gwɪʃ, -wɪʃ/ *v* [I/T] to recognize or understand the difference between two things, or to provide a quality that makes someone or something different or special ○ [I always + adv/prep] *It's important to distinguish between scientific fact and fiction.* ○ [T] *Samuel F. B. Morse distinguished himself both as an inventor and as a painter.*

distinguished /dɪ'stɪŋ·gwɪʃt, -wɪʃt/ *adj* **1** (of a person or a body of work) respected and admired for excellence ○ *He had a long and distinguished career as a diplomat.* **2** A person, esp. an older person, might be described as being distinguished in appearance if the person looks important and respected.

SEE/HEAR /dɪs'tɪŋ·gwɪʃ, -wɪʃ/ *v* [T] to see, hear, or experience something, esp. with difficulty ○ *In the dark, I could barely distinguish the shape of a person.*

distort Ⓐ /dɪ'stɔːrt/ *v* [T] to change something from its natural or usual shape or condition ○ *Agony distorted his face.* ○ *There are those who would distort the facts to serve their own political ends.*

distorted Ⓐ /dɪ'stɔːrt̬·əd/ *adj* ○ *The article presents a distorted view of life in small-town America.*

distortion Ⓐ /dɪ'stɔːr·ʃən/ *n* [C/U] ○ [C] *Dole charged his opponent with making deliberate distortions of his record.*

distract /dɪ'strækt/ *v* [T] to take someone's attention away from what the person is doing or should be doing ○ *She liked to work with the radio playing and said it did not distract her.*

distraction /dɪ'stræk·ʃən/ *n* [C/U] ○ [U] *It's impossible to work with all this distraction.*

distraught /dɪ'strɔːt/ *adj* extremely anxious and upset ○ *We were all distraught over the loss of our homes in the flood.*

distress /dɪ'stres/ *n* [U] great mental or physical suffering, such as extreme anxiety, sadness, or pain, or the state of being in danger or urgent need ○ *emotional/financial distress* ○ *Four men were rescued from a fishing boat in distress off the coast.*

distress /dɪ'stres/ *v* [T] ○ *Rice appeared distressed about the argument, and could not talk about it.*

distressing /dɪ'stres·ɪŋ/ *adj* ○ [+ *that* clause] *It is distressing that so little progress has been made after all this time.*

distribute Ⓐ /dɪ'strɪb·jət/ *v* [T] to divide something among several or many people, or to spread or scatter something over an area ○ *Food and clothing are being distributed among/to the flood victims.* ○ *Shopping malls are widely distributed across the country.*

distribution Ⓐ /ˌdɪs·trə'bju:·ʃən/ *n* [U] **1** *The bill would prohibit the sale and distribution of firearms.* **2** Distribution is also the position or arrangement of something in space or time, or among a group of people ○ *a very substantial upward distribution of wealth in society*

distributor Ⓐ /dɪ'strɪb·jəţ·ər/ *n* [C] **1** a person or company that supplies goods to the businesses that sell them **2** A distributor in an engine is a device that sends electricity to each of the SPARK PLUGS (= devices that cause the engine to start).

distributive /dɪ'strɪb·jəţ·ɪv/ *adj* [not gradable] **1** ***mathematics*** (of a mathematical operation) giving the same result whether parts are acted on in combination or separately ○ Compare COMMUTATIVE **2** ***grammar*** (of an adjective) showing that the members of a group are to be treated separately, rather than as a group ○ *'Each' and 'every' are distributive adjectives.*

district /'dɪs·trɪkt/ *n* [C] an area of a country, state, or city that has been given fixed borders for official purposes, or one having a particular feature that makes it different from surrounding areas ○ *The theater district in New York is in midtown Manhattan.*

district attorney, *abbreviation* **D.A.** *n* [C] a lawyer who represents the government of a region in court trials, and who decides which cases the government will take to court

distrust /dɪs'trʌst/ *n* [U] lack of trust or confidence ○ *Many Americans have a deep distrust of advertising.*

distrust /dɪs'trʌst/ *v* [T] ○ *According to this history book, John Adams, the second US president, hated and distrusted Britain.*

distrustful /dɪs'trʌst·fəl/ *adj*

disturb **INTERRUPT** /dɪ'stɜrb/ *v* [T] to cause someone to stop what the person is doing, or to interrupt an activity ○ *Please don't disturb Jimmy – he's trying to do his homework.*

disturbance /dɪ'stɜr·bəns/ *n* [U] ○ *I hope I can work today without disturbance.*

WORRY /dɪ'stɜrb/ *v* [T] to cause someone to feel troubled or upset ○ *This year's election campaign has disturbed a lot of voters who don't like either candidate.*

disturbing /dɪ'stɜr·bɪŋ/ *adj* ○ [+ *to* infinitive] *It's deeply disturbing to see intelligent and educated people make fun of us.*

MOVE /dɪ'stɜrb/ *v* [T] to move or change something from its usual position or arrangement ○ *Be careful not to disturb anything.*

WORD FAMILY disturb			
Nouns	disturbance	*Adjectives*	disturbed
Verbs	disturb		disturbing

disturbance /dɪ'stɜr·bəns/ *n* [C] **1** something that interrupts you, esp. something loud or causing trouble ○ *You must take care of yourself and avoid upsetting disturbances.* **2** ***earth science*** A disturbance is also something that affects usual wind conditions: *The disturbance became a typhoon in the Philippine Sea and headed due west.*

disturbed /dɪ'stɜrbd/ *adj* so mentally confused or ill that special treatment is necessary ○ *He wrote a book on the treatment of emotionally disturbed children.*

ditch **CHANNEL** /dɪtʃ/ *n* [C] a long, narrow, open channel dug in the ground, usually at the side of a road or field, used esp. for supplying or removing water

GET RID OF /dɪtʃ/ *v* [T] *infml* to get rid of or not continue with something or someone that is no longer wanted ○ *The thief ditched Maxine's purse in a trash can but kept the money.* ○ *It's time to ditch this old, torn sweater.*

dither /'dɪð·ər/ *v* [I] to be anxious about something and not be able to decide what to do about it ○ *Both sides in the dispute continue to dither over who should make the first move.*

ditto /'dɪţ·oʊ/ *adv* [not gradable] *infml* as said before; similarly ○ *It rained Saturday and it rained Sunday. Ditto Monday.*

ditty /'dɪţ·i/ *n* [C] a short, simple song

dive **MOVE DOWN** /dɑɪv/ *v* [I] *past simp.* **dived, dove,** *past part.* **dived** to jump head first into water, esp. with your arms held straight above your head, or to move down quickly through water or the air ○ *Mark dove off the cliff into the ocean.* ○ *Dolphins can dive to great depths.* ○ [+ *to* infinitive] *The plane dived to avoid enemy aircraft fire.*

dive /dɑɪv/ *n* [C] ○ (*fig.*) *The firm's profits took a dive* (= fell by a large amount) *last quarter.*

diver /'dɑɪ·vər/ *n* [C] a person who dives into water

diving /'dɑɪ·vɪŋ/ *n* [U] ○ *deep-sea diving*

MOVE QUICKLY /dɑɪv/ *v* [I always + adv/prep] *past simp.* **dived, dove,** *past part.* **dived** to jump or move quickly into or at something ○ *When the football came loose, he dove at the ball and grabbed it.* ○ *They dived for cover when it suddenly began to rain.*

dive /dɑɪv/ *n* [U] ○ *White's 1-yard dive with seconds left won the football game.*

PLACE /dɑɪv/ *n* [C] *infml* a cheap, unattractive bar or place for entertainment

diverge /dɪ'vɜrdʒ, dɑɪ-/ *v* [I] to go in different directions from the same point, or to become different ○ *The tone of the final report isn't likely to diverge much from the earlier report.*

diverse Ⓐ /dɪ'vɜrs, dɑɪ-; 'dɑɪ·vɜrs/ *adj* varied or different ○ *Lowell, Massachusetts, is noted for its diverse ethnic communities, among them French-Canadians, English, Irish, Greeks, Poles, and Cambodians.*

diversity Ⓐ /dɪ'vɜr·səţ·i, dɑɪ-/ *n* [U] **1** the condition or fact of being different or varied; variety ○ *genetic/biological diversity* ○ *a wide diversity of opinion/ideas* **2** ***social studies*** Diversity is also the mixture of races and religions that make up a group of people.

diversely Ⓐ /dɪˈvɜr·sli, dɑɪ-; ˈdɑɪ·vɜr·sli/ *adv*

diversify Ⓐ /dɪˈvɜr·səˌfɑɪ, dɑɪ-/ *v* [I/T] to become varied or different, or to make something varied or different ○ [T] *People are advised to diversify their investments in the stock market to reduce risk.*

diversification Ⓐ /dɪˌvɜr·sə·fəˈkeɪ·ʃən, dɑɪ-/ *n* [U]

diversified Ⓐ /dɪˈvɜr·səˌfɑɪd, dɑɪ-/ *adj* ○ *diversified financial services companies*

divert CHANGE DIRECTION /dɪˈvɜrt, dɑɪ-/ *v* [T] **1** to cause something or someone to turn in a different direction ○ *Our flight was diverted from San Francisco to Oakland because of the fog.* **2** To divert something or someone is also to cause the thing or person to be used for a different purpose: *The administration had to divert funds from the defense budget to pay for the emergency relief effort.*

diversion /dɪˈvɜr·ʒən, dɑɪ-/ *n* [C/U] ○ [U] *A snowstorm closed the airport, and the diversion of air traffic was therefore necessary.*

TAKE ATTENTION AWAY /dɪˈvɜrt, dɑɪ-/ *v* [T] **1** to take attention away from something ○ *Military action now could divert attention from imminent votes in Congress on health-care legislation.* **2** *fml* To divert can also mean to amuse: *The dog kept the children diverted for a while.*

diversion /dɪˈvɜr·ʒən, dɑɪ-/ *n* [C] an action that takes attention away from something, esp. one that gives pleasure or enjoyment ○ *This lawyer-bachelor devoted his life to the Senate, his only real diversion being baseball.*

divest /dɑɪˈvest, dɪ-/ *v* [T] **1** to get rid of an investment, part of a business, etc. by selling ○ *He had encouraged the state to divest such holdings.* **2** If you divest yourself of a property, you get rid of it, usually by selling: *The company has divested itself of some of its money-losing operations.*

divide SEPARATE /dɪˈvɑɪd/ *v* [I/T] **1** to separate into parts or groups, or to cause something to separate in such a way ○ [T] *Divide the cake into six equal parts.* ○ [I] *The votes divided equally for and against the proposal.* **2** If something divides two areas, it marks the edge or limit of both of them: [T] *A narrow driveway divides our house from the one next door.* **3** To divide a group of people is to cause them to disagree: [T] *The issue of tax reform continues to divide the country.*

divide /dɪˈvɑɪd/ *n* [C] a separation ○ *The river forms a divide between mountains and coastal plains.* ○ *It's on taxes that the divide between the two candidates is widest.*

division /dɪˈvɪʒ·ən/ *n* [C/U] **1** the separation of something into parts or groups, or one of the parts or groups that has been separated ○ [U] *The division of responsibilities among the officers of the company was spelled out in detail.* **2** A division is a unit of an organization: [C] *An army division is commanded by a major general.* ○ [C] *He works for the company's research division.* ○ [C] *The game for the Eastern Division championship of the National Football League is scheduled for tomorrow.*

divisive /dɪˈvɑɪ·sɪv, -ˈvɪs·ɪv/ *adj disapproving* tending to cause disagreements that separate people into opposing groups ○ *The campaign for the mayor's office was racially divisive.*

CALCULATE /dɪˈvɑɪd/ *v* [I/T] ***mathematics*** to calculate the number of times one number is contained in another ○ [T] *10 divided by 5 is/equals 2.* ○ [T] *What do you get if you divide 6 into 18?* ○ Compare MULTIPLY CALCULATE; SUBTRACT

division /dɪˈvɪʒ·ən/ *n* [U] ***mathematics*** the process of finding the number of times one number is contained within another

WORD FAMILY divide			
Nouns	division subdivision dividend	*Adjectives*	divided undivided divisible divisive
Verbs	divide subdivide		

divided highway *n* [C] a main road that has an area in the middle that separates traffic moving in opposite directions

dividend /ˈdɪv·əˌdend, -əd·ənd/ *n* [C] a payment by a company of a part of its profit to the people who own SHARES (= units of ownership) in the company

divine GODLIKE /dɪˈvɑɪn/ *adj* [not gradable] connected with or like God or a god ○ *divine love*

divinity /dɪˈvɪn·ət̬·i/ *n* [U] **1** the state of being a god ○ *Christians believe in the divinity of Jesus Christ.* **2** Divinity is the study of religion: *She has a Doctorate in Divinity from Georgetown University.*

divinely /dɪˈvɑɪn·li/ *adv* [not gradable] ○ *divinely inspired truth*

VERY GOOD /dɪˈvɑɪn/ *adj infml* extremely good or pleasing ○ *The dessert was simply divine.*

divinely /dɪˈvɑɪn·li/ *adv infml* ○ *She sings divinely.*

GUESS /dɪˈvɑɪn/ *v* [T] to guess something, or to discover something without being told about it ○ [+ *that* clause] *I divined from his grim expression that the news was bad.*

divine right *n* [U] ***politics & government*** a belief that a king or queen represents, and has been given power by, God

diving /ˈdɑɪ·vɪŋ/ *n* [U] ○ See at DIVE MOVE DOWN

diving board *n* [C] a board that sticks out over water so that people can DIVE into it

divisible /dɪˈvɪz·ə·bəl/ *adj* ***mathematics*** able to be divided

divisibility /dɪˌvɪz·əˈbɪl·ət̬·i/ *adv* ***mathematics***

division /dɪˈvɪʒ·ən/ *n* ○ See at DIVIDE SEPARATE; DIVIDE CALCULATE

division sign *n* [C] ***mathematics*** the symbol ÷ or the symbol / used between two numbers to show that the first number should be divided by the second

divisive /dɪˈvɑɪ·sɪv, -ˈvɪs·ɪv/ *adj* ○ See at DIVIDE SEPARATE

divorce /dɪˈvɔːrs, -ˈvoʊrs/ *v* [I/T] to cause a marriage to a husband or wife to end by an official or legal process, or to have a marriage ended in this way ○ [T] *Ford divorced his wife, Anne, in 1964, and married Cristina a year later.* ○ [T] *They didn't get divorced* (= end their marriage legally) *until 2007.*

divorce /dɪˈvɔːrs, -ˈvoʊrs/ *n* [C/U] ○ [C] *Both of them agreed to the divorce.*

divorcé /dɪˌvɔːrˈseɪ, -ˌvoʊr-, -ˈsiː/ *n* [C] a man whose marriage officially ended while his wife was still alive

divorcee, divorcée /dɪˌvɔːrˈseɪ, -ˌvoʊr-, -ˈsiː/ *n* [C] a woman whose marriage officially ended while her husband was still alive

WORD FAMILY divorce

Nouns	*Verbs*
divorce divorcé divorcee	divorce

PHRASAL VERB with divorce

• **divorce** *something* **from** *something* to separate something from something else ○ *I don't see how you can divorce politics from tax policy.*

divulge /dɪˈvʌldʒ, daɪ-/ *v* [T] to make something secret known ○ *Someone divulged their plans to their competitors.* ○ *He did not divulge details of his plan.*

divvy up *something* /ˈdɪv·iː ˈʌp/ *phrasal verb* [M] *infml* to divide something into parts or shares ○ *They finally decided how to divvy up the money.*

Dixie /ˈdɪk·si/ [U] the southern states of the US that fought against the northern states during the Civil War

Dixieland (jazz) /ˈdɪk·siː ˌlænd (ˈdʒæz)/ *n* [U] a style of traditional jazz with a two-beat rhythm, which began in New Orleans in the 1920s

dizzy /ˈdɪz·i/ *adj* having or causing a feeling of spinning around and being unable to balance ○ *She felt dizzy and needed to sit down.* ○ (*fig.*) *In the computer industry, change comes at a dizzy pace* (= very fast).

dizziness /ˈdɪz·iː·nəs/ *n* [U]

DJ /ˈdiː·dʒeɪ/ *n* [C] *abbreviation for* DISC JOCKEY

DNA *n* [U] ***biology*** *abbreviation for* deoxyribonucleic acid (= the chemical at the center of the cells of living things that controls the structure and purpose of each cell and carries GENETIC information during reproduction)

DNA fingerprint *n* [C] the particular way in which GENETIC information is contained in the cells of a person and which is different in every person

do **FOR QUESTIONS/NEGATIVES** /duː/ *auxiliary verb* **does**, *past simp.* **did**, *past part.* **done** used with another verb to form questions and negative sentences ○ *Where do you work?* ○ *Why don't we have lunch together on Friday?* ○ *"Didn't you know Sophie was coming?" "Of course I did."* ○ *Don't talk about that.* ○ **USAGE:** The negative contractions are doesn't, didn't, and don't.

FOR EMPHASIS /duː/ *auxiliary verb* **does**, *past simp.* **did** used to give extra force to the main verb ○ *Do be careful.* ○ *I did say she was a liar, but I was wrong.* ○ *"Can I buy stamps here?" "Well, we do sell them, but we're out of them right now."*

TO AVOID REPEATING /duː/ *auxiliary verb* **does**, *past simp.* **did**, *past part.* **done 1** used to avoid repeating a verb or verb phrase ○ *"I don't like either candidate." "Neither do I."* ○ *He said he'd leave the car in the garage, but he didn't.* ○ *"May I join you?" "Please do!"* ○ *"Did you leave the door open?" "Yes, I did."* **2** Do can also replace the main verb in questions that are added to the end of a sentence: *You met him at a conference, didn't you?*

CAUSE TO HAPPEN /duː/ *v* [T] **does**, *past simp.* **did**, *past part.* **done 1** to cause something to happen or be the cause of something happening; perform or have a part in an activity ○ *Inviting the whole family was a really nice thing to do.* ○ *What are you doing over the weekend?* ○ *I've got to stay home and do my homework.* ○ *The theater club is doing "South Pacific" this year.* ○ *I'm sorry, there's nothing more to be done* (= nothing else will help). ○ *It isn't important whether you win or lose – just do your best.* ○ *It's been a pleasure doing business with you* (= dealing with you). ○ *The company is counting on each of you to do your part/share.* ○ *Would you do me a favor* (= help me) *and get some bread while you're out?* ○ *A little fresh air will do you some good* (= make you feel better). ○ *What are these toys doing here* (= Why are they here)*?* ○ *I've been trying to do* (= solve) *this puzzle for hours.* ○ *What can I do for you* (= How can I help you)*?* ○ *What have you done with my coat* (= Where have you put it)*?* ○ *Since she retired, she doesn't know what to do with herself* (= how to keep herself busy). **2** To do can mean to work at as a regular job: *"What do you do?" "I teach high school math."* **3** If you ask or say how someone is doing, you are asking or saying how the person is feeling or what the person's condition is: *How are you folks doing today?* ○ *Both the mother and her new baby are doing fine.* ○ *We've had some difficult times, but we're doing all right now.* **4** If you say what's doing or what's doing at a particular place, you are asking what is happening there: *What's doing at the office?*

doable /ˈduː·ə·bəl/ *adj* [not gradable] able to be achieved or performed ○ *The bank officer said that our loan was doable.*

doing /ˈduː·ɪŋ/ *n* [U] ○ *It was none of my doing* (= My actions were not the cause of this).

USAGE

do or make?

Do usually means to perform an activity or job.

I should do my homework.

~~*I should make my homework.*~~

Make usually means to create or produce something.

Did you make the dress yourself ?

~~*Did you do the dress yourself?*~~

ARRANGE /duː/ *v* [T] **does**, *past simp.* **did**, *past part.* **done** to shape, arrange, or fix something in an attractive way ○ *Who does your hair?*

TRAVEL /duː/ *v* [T] **does,** *past simp.* **did,** *past part.* **done** to travel at a stated speed or over a particular distance ○ *We were only doing 70 miles per hour.* ○ *We did 400 miles yesterday.*

BE ACCEPTABLE /duː/ *v* [I] **does,** *past simp.* **did,** *past part.* **done** to be acceptable, suitable, or enough ○ *"Will this room do?" "Yes, it'll be fine."* ○ *This kind of behavior just won't do.*

D

WORD FAMILY do

Nouns	doing	*Adjectives*	doable
Verbs	do		done
	outdo		overdone
	overdo		undone
	undo		

IDIOMS with do

• **do credit to** *someone,* **do** *someone* **credit** to bring praise and respect to someone ○ *The teacher's fairness to all her students does her credit.*

• **do justice to** *someone/something,* **do** *someone/something* **justice** to be accurate or fair by representing someone or something as that person or thing truly is ○ *Just calling the movie "fun" doesn't do it justice* (= it is better than just "fun"). ○ *This is the only picture I have that does full justice to her beauty* (= shows her to be as beautiful as she is).

• **do more harm than good** to be damaging rather than helpful ○ *Modernizing historic buildings often does more harm than good.*

• **do the trick, do the job** *infml* to achieve the desired result ○ *I need something to put these papers in – this folder should do the trick.*

• **do wonders for** *something/someone* to cause improvements or have a very good effect ○ [C] *That new guy is great – he's done wonders for the company.* ○ Compare WORK WONDERS at WORK IDIOMS

• **dos and don'ts** rules about how people should and should not behave ○ *Where I work, the old dos and don'ts about how to dress don't really matter.*

PHRASAL VERBS with do

• **do away with** *something* to get rid of or destroy something ○ *The governor is proposing to do away with the state transportation department.*

• **do** *someone* **in TIRE** *infml* to tire someone ○ *That five-mile hike did me in.*

• **do** *someone* **in CAUSE TO FAIL** [M] *infml* to be the cause of someone's failure ○ *A couple of key losses did the team in.*

• **do** *someone* **out of** *something* *infml* to cheat someone by preventing that person from obtaining or keeping something of value ○ *Con men did him out of over $10,000 of his hard-earned money.*

• **do over** *something* [M] to decorate a room or part of a house in a new way ○ *We plan to do over the kitchen next year.*

• **do without** *something/someone* to manage, work, or perform successfully without having someone or something present ○ *The country cannot do without foreign investment.* ○ *There are a great number of things that he can easily do without.*

doable /ˈduː·ə·bəl/ *adj* [not gradable] ○ See at DO CAUSE TO HAPPEN

doc /dɑk/ *n* [C] *infml* a DOCTOR MEDICINE

docile /ˈdɑs·əl, -ˌɑɪl/ *adj* calm in manner and easy to control ○ *They have a big dog, but he's real friendly and docile.*

dock **STRUCTURE** /dɑk/ *n* [C] **1** a structure built out over water in a port along which ships can land to load and unload, or the enclosed area of water between two such structures **2** A dock is also a flat, raised area attached to a building and used for loading and unloading trucks.

dock /dɑk/ *v* [I/T] ○ [I] *The ship docked in Japan, and he took another to Korea.*

REMOVE /dɑk/ *v* [T] to take away a part of someone's pay ○ *I've used up my sick days, and if I take another day off they'll dock me a day's pay.*

docket /ˈdɑk·ət/ *n* [C] *law* a list of cases to be dealt with in a law court

doctor **MEDICINE** /ˈdɑk·tər/, *abbreviation* **Dr.** *n* [C] a person with a medical degree whose job is to treat people who are ill or injured ○ *This health plan lets you choose your own doctor.*

EDUCATION /ˈdɑk·tər/, *abbreviation* **Dr.** *n* [C] a person who has one of the highest-ranking degrees given by a university

doctoral /ˈdɑk·tə·rəl/ *adj* ○ *She's a doctoral student in geology.*

doctorate /ˈdɑk·tə·rət/ *n* [C] ○ *He earned a doctorate* (= the highest-ranking degree) *at the University of Chicago.*

CHANGE /ˈdɑk·tər/ *v* [T] to change something in order to deceive people ○ *He claimed the photo had been doctored.*

doctor's degree *n* [C] one of the highest-ranking degrees given by a university

doctrine /ˈdɑk·trən/ *n* [C/U] a belief, theory, or set of beliefs, esp. political or religious, taught and accepted by a particular group ○ [U] *church doctrine*

docudrama /ˈdɑk·jəˌdrɑm·ə, -ˌdræm·ə/ *n* [C/U] a television program whose story is based on an event or situation that really happened, although it is not accurate in every detail

document Ⓐ /ˈdɑk·jə·mənt/ *n* [C] **1** a paper or set of papers with written or printed information, esp. of an official type ○ *Do you have all your documents in order to apply for a passport?* **2** A document is also a file on a computer in which text is stored.

document Ⓐ /ˈdɑk·jəˌment/ *v* [T] to record information about something by writing about it or taking photographs of it ○ *The study documents various aspects of Indian life in this period.*

documentary Ⓐ /ˌdɑk·jəˈment·ə·ri/ *adj* [not gradable] ○ *documentary evidence*

documentation Ⓐ /ˌdɑk·jə·menˈteɪ·ʃən/ *n* [U] **1** official papers, or written material that provides proof of something **2** ***writing*** Documentation is also the process of providing proof for the things you write about and naming the texts that you use.

documentary /ˌdɑk·jəˈment·ə·ri/ *n* [C] a film or television or radio program that gives information about a subject and is based on facts ○ *a documentary on animal communication*

dodecahedron /doʊˌdek·əˈhiː·drən/ *n* [C] *pl* **dodecahedrons, dodecahedra** *geometry* a solid shape that has twelve flat surfaces of equal size, each with five sides ➤ Picture: **solid**

dodge /dɑdʒ/ *v* [I/T] **1** to avoid being hit by something by moving quickly to one side ○ (*fig.*) *We have dodged a bullet a lot of times in the last three or four years.* **2** To dodge something unpleasant is to avoid it: [T] *Few men still talk about how they dodged the draft.*

dodge /dɑdʒ/ *n* [C] a trick to deceive someone or to avoid doing something that you do not want to do ○ *She sells antiques as a tax dodge.*

doe /doʊ/ *n* [C] a female deer ○ Compare BUCK ANIMAL

does /dʌz, dəz/ *present simple of* DO, used with he/she/it

doesn't /ˈdʌz·ənt/ *contraction of* does not ○ *Doesn't she look lovely in her wedding gown?*

dog ANIMAL /dɔːg/ *n* [C] an animal with four legs, commonly kept as a pet, and sometimes used to guard things

PERSON /dɔːg/ *n* [C] *slang* a person of a stated type ○ *You won $1000? You lucky dog!*

FOLLOW /dɔːg/ *v* [T] **-gg-** to follow someone closely and continually ○ *The scandal seems likely to dog him for months to come.*

dog biscuit *n* [C] a hard, baked cracker, often flavored with meat, for dogs to eat

dog-eared /ˈdɔː·gɪrd/ *adj* (of a book or paper) with part of the pages folded down as the result of a lot of use

dogfight /ˈdɔːg·fɑɪt/ *n* [C] a fight between two military aircraft, or any fierce fight ○ *They are a tough team, and we knew we were in for a real dogfight.*

dogged /ˈdɔː·gəd/ *adj* determined to do something, even if it is very difficult ○ *John Regan credited the capture to dogged persistence by police.*

doggedly /ˈdɔː·gəd·li/ *adv* ○ *Gove spent much of the last decade of his life doggedly defending his principles.*

doggie /ˈdɔː·gi/ *n* [C] *a child's word* a dog

doggone /ˈdɔː·gɔːn, ˈdɑg·ɑn/ *exclamation infml* used to express annoyance ○ *Doggone it, where's that letter?*

doggy bag /ˈdɔː·giː ˌbæg/ *n* [C] a container that a restaurant provides so you can take home any food you have not finished

doghouse /ˈdɔːg ˌhɑʊs/ *n* [C] a small shelter outside of a house for a dog to sleep in

IDIOM with doghouse

• **in the doghouse** in a situation in which someone is angry at you for something you did or did not do ○ *If I don't do something for Mother's Day, I'll really be in the doghouse.*

dogma /ˈdɔːg·mə, ˈdɑg-/ *n* [C/U] a fixed belief or set of beliefs that people are expected to accept without any doubts ○ [U] *liberal/conservative dogma*

dogmatic /dɔːgˈmæt̬·ɪk, dɑg-/ *adj* (of a person or a group) strongly expressing your beliefs as if they were facts ○ *He has written a stimulating but dogmatic book.*

dog tag /ˈdɔːg·tæg/ *n* [C] *pl* **dog tags** a small piece of metal worn around the neck by soldiers, on which the soldier's name, official number, and other information is given

dogwood /ˈdɔː·gwʊd/ *n* [C/U] a bush or tree that has white or pink flowers in the spring and grows wild or in a garden

doing /ˈduː·ɪŋ/ *n* [U] ○ See at DO CAUSE TO HAPPEN

doldrums /ˈdoʊl·drəmz, ˈdɔːl-, ˈdɑl-/ *pl n* a state of lack of activity or lack of success ○ *Business leaders predict a hard year ahead with the economy in the doldrums.*

dole out *something* /ˈdoʊl ˈɑʊt/ *phrasal verb* [M] to give money, food, or something else that can be divided to several people ○ *I can't keep doling out money to you kids.*

doleful /ˈdoʊl·fəl/ *adj* very sad ○ *a doleful expression/look*

doll /dɑl, dɔːl/ *n* [C] **1** a child's toy in the shape of a person, esp. a baby or child **2** *infml* You can call someone a doll to show that you like the person or think the person is attractive or pleasant: *She's a doll, she's a love, she really is.*

dollar /ˈdɑl·ər/ *n* [C] a unit of money, used in the US, Canada, Australia, New Zealand, and other countries, that is worth 100 cents ○ *Could you lend me ten dollars?*

dollar sign *n* [C] the symbol $, which is put in front of amounts of money in dollars

dollop /ˈdɑl·əp/ *n* [C] a small amount of a substance ○ *a dollop of whipped cream*

dolly /ˈdɑl·i, ˈdɔː·li/ *n* [C] *a child's word* a DOLL

dolphin /ˈdɑl·fən, ˈdɔːl-/ *n* [C] a sea mammal that looks like a large fish with a pointed mouth

domain Ⓐ INTEREST /doʊˈmeɪn, də-/ *n* [C] an area of interest or an area over which a person has control ○ *the domain of polymer science* ○ *public and private domains*

GROUP OF VALUES /doʊˈmeɪn/ *n* [C] *mathematics* a group of all the possible replacements for a VARIABLE (= letter or symbol that represents any set of values)

dome /doʊm/ *n* [C] a rounded roof on a building ○ *The dome of city hall could be seen in the distance.*

domestic Ⓐ HOME /dəˈmes·tɪk/ *adj* relating to the home, house, or family ○ *I've never been fond of domestic chores like cooking and cleaning.*

domestic /dəˈmes·tɪk/ *n* [C] *dated* someone paid to help with work that needs to be done in a house, such as cleaning and washing clothes
domesticity /ˌdoʊˌmesˈtɪs·ət̬·i, -məs-/ *n* [U] the state of being at home a lot with your family ○ *Since they had their baby, they've settled happily into domesticity.*
domestically Ⓐ /dəˈmes·tɪ·kli/ *adv*

D

COUNTRY /dəˈmes·tɪk/ *adj* ***politics & government*** relating to a person's own country ○ *The president's domestic policy has been more successful than his foreign policy.*
domestically Ⓐ /dəˈmes·tɪ·kli/ *adv* ○ *The movie took in $77.9 million domestically, but only made $9.1 million overseas.*

domesticate Ⓐ /dəˈmes·tɪˌkeɪt/ *v* [T] to bring animals or plants under human control so that humans may use them as food, for power, or as friends
domesticated Ⓐ /dəˈmes·təˌkeɪt̬·əd/ *adj* [not gradable] brought under human control ○ *the wild ancestors of our domesticated chickens* ○ **USAGE:** Used to describe an animal or plant.

domicile /ˈdɑm·əˌsɑɪl, ˈdoʊ·mə-/ *n* [C] *law* the place where a person lives ○ *Any change of domicile should be reported to the proper authorities.*

dominant Ⓐ /ˈdɑm·ə·nənt/ *adj* more important, strong, or noticeable than anything else of the same type ○ *a dominant personality* ○ *For years the Democrats were the dominant party in Congress.*
dominance Ⓐ /ˈdɑm·ə·nəns/ *n* [U] ○ *military dominance*

dominate Ⓐ /ˈdɑm·əˌneɪt/ *v* [I/T] to have control over a place or a person, or to be the most important person or thing ○ [T] *It was the story that dominated the headlines this week.* ○ [T] *The Rams dominated the football game in handing the Eagles their second loss.*
domination Ⓐ /ˌdɑm·əˈneɪ·ʃən/ *n* [U] the state of having control over people or a situation ○ *Her domination of the tennis world is undisputed.*

domineering /ˌdɑm·əˈnɪr·ɪŋ/ *adj* having a strong tendency to try to control other people without taking their feelings into consideration ○ *a domineering personality*

dominion /dəˈmɪn·jən/ *n* [C/U] control over a country or people, or the land that belongs to a ruler ○ [U] *The collapse of Spain's empire prepared the way for Britain's dominion over the seas.*

domino /ˈdɑm·əˌnoʊ/ *n* [C] *pl* **dominoes** one of a set of small rectangular pieces of wood or plastic marked with a particular number of spots on each half of one surface, used in playing a game
dominoes /ˈdɑm·əˌnoʊz/ *n* [U] a game in which you try to match the spots of a domino put down by another player

domino theory *n* [C usually sing] ***politics & government*** a belief in the 1950s and 1960s that if one country became COMMUNIST, other close countries would more easily also become Communist

donate /ˈdoʊ·neɪt, doʊˈneɪt/ *v* [I/T] to give something, esp. to an organization, without wanting anything in exchange ○ [T] *Over $12 million was donated to the building fund.* ○ [T] *Some businesses have agreed to donate computers to schools.*
donation /doʊˈneɪ·ʃən/ *n* [C/U] ○ [C] *Donations of food and clothing are gratefully accepted.*

done /dʌn/ *past participle of* **1** DO **2** You can say "done" to show that you agree to something: *"I'll give you $25 for the chair." "Done!"*

done for /ˈdʌn·fɔːr/ *adj* [not gradable] about to die or suffer greatly because of a serious difficulty or danger ○ *We thought we were done for when we smelled smoke and the lights went out.*

donkey /ˈdɑŋ·ki, ˈdʌŋ-, ˈdɔːŋ-/ *n* [C] a gray or brown animal like a small horse with long ears

donor /ˈdoʊ·nər/ *n* [C] **1** a person who gives money or something else of value to an organization ○ *A large gift from an anonymous donor will allow us to continue our work.* **2** A donor is also someone who gives blood or who agrees to give an organ or body part to help someone else.

don't /doʊnt/ *contraction of* do not ○ *Please don't make any noise while they are recording.*

IDIOMS with don't

• **don't ask me** *infml* I do not know ○ *"Who left this mess in the kitchen?" "Don't ask me."* ○ *He doesn't want to come with us to the game – don't ask me why.*
• **don't (even) go there, you/we don't want to go there** *infml* do not even talk or think about that subject ○ *"We could just lend her the money." "No, don't even go there – we're not lending her anything."*
• **don't you dare!** *infml* I will be very angry at you if you do ○ *"I'm going to tell Billy what you said about him." "Don't you dare!"*

donut /ˈdoʊ·nʌt, -nət/ *n* [C] a DOUGHNUT

doodad /ˈduː·dæd/, **doohickey** /ˈduːˌhɪk·i/ *n* [C] *infml* any small device or object whose name you cannot remember or do not know

doodle /ˈduːd·əl/ *n* [C] a drawing or pattern that you make while thinking about something else or when you are bored
doodle /ˈduːd·əl/ *v* [I]

doom /duːm/ *n* [U] death, destruction, or any very bad situation that cannot be avoided ○ *A sense of doom hung over the entire country.*
doom /duːm/ *v* [T] to be the certain cause of someone or something having a bad end, esp. to die or to fail ○ *The effort is doomed to failure.* ○ *He was doomed to be a one-term president like Jimmy Carter.*

doomsday /ˈduːmz·deɪ/ *n* [U] **1** the end of the world **2** Doomsday is also JUDGMENT DAY.

door /dɔːr, doʊr/ *n* [C] **1** a flat, usually rectangular, object that is fixed at one edge and is used to close the entrance to something such as a room, building, or vehicle, or the entrance itself ○ *the front/back door* ○ *We'd like to rent a four-door car.* ○ *I'll meet you at the main door of the library.* ○ *Would you open/close/shut the door, please?* ○ *The door to his bedroom was locked from the inside.* ○ *Mom, there's someone at the door* (= outside the front door). **2** Door is also used to refer to a house or other building: *Sam lives just a few doors away/up/down from us.* ○ *They live next door to us* (= in the house beside ours).

doorman /ˈdɔːr·mən, ˈdoʊr-, -ˌmæn/ *n* [C] *pl* **-men** a person whose job is to stand by the door of a hotel or public building and let people in or out, open their car doors, etc.

IDIOM with **door**

•**door to door 1** from the beginning of a trip to the end ○ *The trip takes an hour door to door.* **2** If you go **door to door** you stop at or go to every house: *Harris went door to door during the campaign, visiting with voters.*

doorbell /ˈdɔːr·bel, ˈdoʊr-/ *n* [C] an electrical device with a button near the outside door of a house or apartment that makes a noise when pressed, to let the people inside know someone is there ○ *He rang the doorbell twice.*

doorknob /ˈdɔːr·nɑb, ˈdoʊr-/ *n* [C] a round handle that you turn to open a door

doormat /ˈdɔːr·mæt, ˈdoʊr-/ *n* [C] a piece of usually rough material outside a door to a house or apartment where people can clean their shoes before entering

doorstep /ˈdɔːr·step, ˈdoʊr-/ *n* [C] a step outside the door to a building ○ (*fig.*) *We need to be more proactive and seek out dangers before they're* **on our doorstep** (= too near to be ignored).

doorway /ˈdɔːr·weɪ, ˈdoʊr-/ *n* [C] the space for a door through which you go into and out of a room or building

dope DRUG /doʊp/ *n* [U] *infml* any illegal drug

doping /ˈdoʊ·pɪŋ/ *n* [U] the use of illegal drugs to improve the performance of a person or an animal in a sports competition

PERSON /doʊp/ *n* [C] *infml* a stupid or foolish person ○ *You shouldn't have told him, you dope!*

INFORMATION /doʊp/ *n* [U] *slang* information known by only a few people ○ *A new column of inside dope about the film industry begins next month.*

Doppler effect /ˈdɑp·lər ɪˌfekt/ *n* [U] ***physics*** a change that someone experiences in the FREQUENCY of WAVES, for example, of sound or light, when the distance between that person and the origin of the waves changes

dork /ˈdɔːrk/ *n* [C] *slang* a stupid, awkward person ○ *I felt like a real dork when I realized my mistake.*

dormant /ˈdɔːr·mənt/ *adj* (of things) not active or growing, but having the ability to be active at a later time ○ *a dormant volcano* ○ *Most roses being sold now are dormant, and without any soil around their roots.*

dormer (window) /ˈdɔːr·mər (ˈwɪn·doʊ)/ *n* [C] a small, roofed structure on a sloping roof with a vertical window built into it

dormitory /ˈdɔːr·məˌtɔːr·i, -ˌtoʊr·i/, *short form* **dorm** /dɔːrm/ *n* [C] a large room or building containing many beds, esp. in a college or BOARDING SCHOOL

D

dose /doʊs/ *n* [C] **1** a measured amount of a drug ○ *She was given large doses of a powerful antibiotic.* **2** A dose is also an amount of something: *Stories of dramatic cancer cures should be taken with a healthy dose of skepticism.*

dosage /ˈdoʊ·sɪdʒ/ *n* [C] a measured amount of a medicine ○ *He needed a high dosage to do any good.*

dot /dɑt/ *n* [C] **1** a very small, round mark ○ *The ducks were black dots in the distance.* **2** Dot (*symbol.*) is also used in an INTERNET address to separate its parts: *Go to w w w dot cambridge dot org.*

dot /dɑt/ *v* [T] **-tt-** When an area is dotted with things, it has many of them in different places: *Minnesota is dotted with lakes, especially in the north.*

IDIOM with **dot**

•**dot the i's and cross the t's** finish the details ○ *The proposal's almost complete – all we have to do now is dot the i's and cross the t's.*

dote on *someone* /doʊt̬·ɔn, -ɑn/ *phrasal verb* to love someone very much, sometimes too much ○ *They dote on their grandchild.*

dotted line *n* [C] the place on a contract or other agreement where you sign your name ○ *Lawmakers want to ensure these changes are good for Virginia before they sign on the dotted line.*

double TWICE /ˈdʌb·əl/ *adj, adv* [not gradable] **1** twice the size, amount, price, etc., or consisting of two similar things together ○ *The cost of going to the movies is almost double what it was a few years ago.* ○ *Fold the blanket double* (= so that it is in two layers) *and then you won't be cold.* ○ Compare SINGLE ONE **2** A double bed is a bed for two people. **3** If you are seeing double, you are seeing two of everything.

double /ˈdʌb·əl/ *v* [I/T] **1** [I] *Company profits have doubled in the last year.* ○ [T] *For four people, just double the recipe* (= make twice as much). **2** If something or someone doubles as something or someone else, that person or thing has a second use or job: [I] *The kitchen table doubles as my desk.*

doubles /ˈdʌb·əlz/ *pl n* (esp. in tennis) a game played with two players on each side

doubly /ˈdʌb·li/ *adv* [not gradable] twice the amount or degree ○ *He is doubly talented, as a composer and as a pianist.*

PERSON /ˈdʌb·əl/ *n* [C usually sing] a person who looks the same as someone else ○ *She is a double for Mary Tyler Moore.*

PHRASAL VERBS with **double**

•**double over** to suddenly bend forward and down, usually because of pain or laughter ○ *A sudden, sharp pain made him double over.*

• **double up** to share something, esp. a room, with someone else ○ *The two boys will have to double up in the front bedroom.*

double negative *n* [C] the use of two negative words together in a statement that has a negative meaning, as in "I didn't do nothing."

D

double bass /ˌdʌb·əl ˈbeɪs/, *infml* **bass fiddle** *n* [C/U] a very large, wooden musical instrument with four strings that a player holds up while standing and plays with a BOW (= stick with hairs attached to it), or this type of instrument generally

double bed *n* [C] a bed big enough for two people to sleep in, but smaller than QUEEN-SIZED

double-breasted *adj* [not gradable] (of a jacket) having two sets of buttons and two wide parts at the front ○ *a double-breasted suit*

double-check *v* [I/T] to make certain that something is correct or safe, usually by examining it again ○ *I always double-check to make sure I locked the door.*

double chin *n* [C] a fold of skin under the face along the front of the neck, caused by a layer of fat

double-cross *v* [T] to cheat or be dishonest to someone who trusted you

double-edged *adj* [not gradable] having two possible and different meanings or effects ○ *Climate changes are potentially double-edged in their consequences.* ○ *Wealth and fame can be a* **double-edged sword** (= a situation with both positive and negative effects).

double feature *n* [C] a movie event in which two different movies are shown one after the other

double figures *pl n* an amount more than 10 but less than 100 ○ *Six players scored in double figures.*

double helix *n* [U] *science* the shape like two curving lines twisted together that is made by two STRANDS (= strings) of DNA (= the chemical that controls each cell)

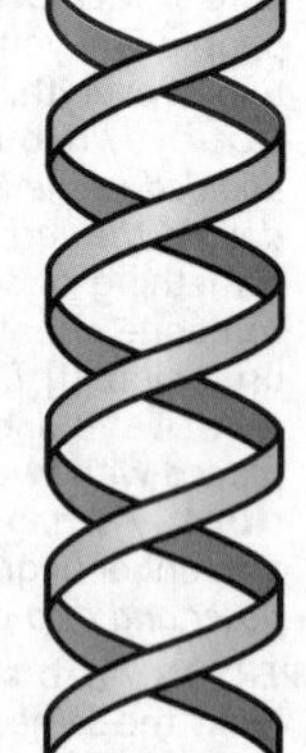
DOUBLE HELIX

double-park *v* [I/T] to leave your car in the street along the side of a car that is already parked, so that your car is blocking other cars

double room *n* [C] a room in a hotel for two people

double-spaced *adj* [not gradable] (of printed text) having an empty line between each printed line

double standard *n* [C] the habit of treating one group differently than another when both groups should be treated the same

double take *n* [C] a delayed surprised reaction at seeing someone or something ○ *With her hair cut short and dyed red, I did a double take at first.*

double-talk *n* [U] *disapproving* talk that has no real meaning or that is intended to confuse

double whammy *n* [C] a situation that includes two disadvantages or difficulties ○ *Consumers were hit by the double whammy of rising interest rates and gasoline prices.*

doubt /dɑʊt/ *n* [C/U] a feeling of not knowing what to believe or what to do, or the condition of being uncertain ○ [C] *If you have any doubt about her ability, don't hire her.* ○ [+ *that* clause] *There's no doubt that the show will be successful.* ○ [U] *The future of the entire project is in some doubt.* ○ [C] *She is without a doubt* (= certainly) *one of the best students I've ever had.*

doubt /dɑʊt/ *v* [T] to be uncertain about something or someone, or to have difficulty believing something ○ [T] *He may come back tomorrow with the money, but I doubt it.*

doubtful /ˈdɑʊt·fəl/ *adj* uncertain or unlikely ○ [+ (*that*) clause] *It was doubtful (that) the money would ever be found.* ○ *She gave me a long, doubtful look* (= look full of doubt) *and told me to wait.*

doubtless /ˈdɑʊt·ləs/ *adv* [not gradable] very probably ○ *He will doubtless be cast in the lead role of this movie comedy.*

WORD FAMILY doubt

Nouns	doubt	*Verbs*	doubt
Adjectives	doubtful doubtless	*Adverbs*	undoubtedly

dough FLOUR /doʊ/ *n* [U] flour mixed with water and other food substances so that it is ready for baking esp. into bread or pastry

MONEY /doʊ/ *n* [U] *dated, slang* money

doughnut, **donut** /ˈdoʊ·nʌt, -nət/ *n* [C] a small, circular cake, fried in hot fat, sometimes with a hole in the middle

dour /dɑʊr, dʊr/ *adj* [*-er/-est* only] (of a person's appearance or manner) very serious and sad, and likely to judge people severely ○ *a dour look*

douse /dɑʊs, dɑʊz/ *v* [T] **1** to throw water or another liquid on someone or something ○ *To get rid of weeds, I douse them with plain white vinegar.* ○ (*fig.*) *The room was doused in light* **2** To douse something is also to end it, esp. to stop a fire by putting water on it; EXTINGUISH: *Efforts to douse the flames were hampered by high winds* ○ *Douse the lights* (= turn off the lights).

dove BIRD /dʌv/ *n* [C] a bird with short legs, a large body, and a small head, often used as a symbol of peace

MOVE DOWN /doʊv/ *past simple of* DIVE

dovetail /ˈdʌv·teɪl/ *v* [I/T] to fit together well, or to cause something to fit together well with something else ○ [I] *Our plans dovetailed, and we were able to meet that evening.*

dowdy /ˈdɑʊd·i/ *adj* (esp. of clothes or the person wearing them) unattractive and not stylish, often because of being old-fashioned

down IN A LOWER POSITION /dɑʊn/ *prep, adv* [not gradable] **1** in or toward a low or lower position, from a higher one ○ *There's a bathroom down the stairs and to the right.* ○ *He poured the rest of the coffee down the drain.* ○ *The cat jumped down from the chair.* ○ *Please sit down* (= stop standing and come to a sitting position). ○ *If you feel ill, why don't you lie down* (= stop standing and come to a lying position) *for a while?* **2** Down also means to the ground, esp. as a result of an action that causes something to fall: *We're going to have to cut down this tree.* **3** Down also means firmly, in a fixed position, esp. as a result of an action: *Workers in the convention center taped down the edges of the carpets.* ○ *(fig.) We hope to nail down the agreement at tomorrow's meeting.*

down /dɑʊn/ *v* [T] to eat or drink something quickly ○ *She quickly downed her tea and left to catch the bus.*

AT A LOWER LEVEL /dɑʊn/ *adj, adv* [not gradable] **1** in or toward a lower place or level, a smaller amount, or a simpler state ○ *Unemployment went down last month, dropping to under 6%.* ○ *Lots of stores are having sales, and prices are coming down.* ○ *He was down to his last $5* (= that was all he had left). **2** Down is used with a lot of verbs to show that something is becoming smaller, weaker, slower, or less: *The fire burned down.* ○ *She's slimmed down a lot in the past few months.* ○ *Would you please turn down the music – it's too loud.*

FAR AWAY /dɑʊn/ *adv* [not gradable] used, esp. with prepositions, to emphasize that a place is far from the speaker or in or toward the south ○ *I'll meet you down at the health club after work.* ○ *My parents moved down to Florida after they retired.*

ALONG /dɑʊn/ *prep* along ○ *Her office is down the hall on the right.*

IN WRITING /dɑʊn/ *adv* [not gradable] in writing or on paper ○ *He agreed to the deal, but until we get it down on paper, we don't have a legal contract.*

UNHAPPY /dɑʊn/ *adj* unhappy ○ *I'm feeling a little down, I guess because most people have gone home for the holidays and I'm still here.*

downer /ˈdɑʊ·nər/ *n* [C] *infml* an event or experience that makes you unhappy and lacking in hope, confidence, or energy ○ *Your car's been stolen? That's a real downer!*

WORSE /dɑʊn/ *adj, adv* [not gradable] into a worse position or state ○ *Michigan, down (by)* (= losing by) *ten points at the half, came back to win the football game.*

WHEN BUYING /dɑʊn/ *adv* [not gradable] at the time of buying ○ *She paid $100 down and the rest in installments.*

NOT IN OPERATION /dɑʊn/ *adj* [not gradable] (of a system or machine, esp. a computer) not in operation or not working, usually only for a limited period of time ○ *The network will be down until noon today.*

HAIR /dɑʊn/ *n* [U] small, soft feathers or hair, esp. those of a young bird

IDIOMS with down

• **down in the dumps** unhappy ○ *She's down in the dumps because all her friends are out of town.*

• **down on** *someone/something* feeling angry or disappointed with someone or something ○ *Dad's down on me since I scraped the car backing out of the garage.*

• **down the drain, down the toilet** wasted or lost ○ *I can't believe it's broken already – well, there's seventy bucks down the drain.*

• **down the road, down the line** in the future ○ *Lots of things will have changed a few years down the road*

• **down to the wire** having a result that is not known until the end ○ *I think the election will go right down to the wire.*

• **shove** *something* **down** *someone's* **throat, ram/cram** *something* **down** *someone's* **throat** to force someone to accept something unpleasant ○ *I'm tired of Dave shoving his opinions down our throats.*

down-at-the-heels *adj* not dressed well or in bad condition, because of a lack of money ○ *The city has a down-at-the-heels look.*

downcast /ˈdɑʊn·kæst/ *adj* **1** looking down, usually because of being shy or sad **2** A person who is downcast is sad or upset.

downfall /ˈdɑʊn·fɔːl/ *n* [C] something that causes the destruction of a person, organization, or government and that causes a loss of power, money, or health ○ *In the end, ambition was his downfall.*

downgrade /ˈdɑʊn·greɪd/ *v* [T] to reduce someone or something to a lower rank or position; to make less important or less valued ○ *They threatened to downgrade my credit rating if I don't pay the bill immediately.*

downhearted /ˈdɑʊn ˈhɑrt̬·əd/ *adj* unhappy, esp. because of failure or because you are disappointed

downhill /ˈdɑʊn ˈhɪl/ *adj, adv* **1** toward or going toward the bottom of something or to a lower place ○ *a steep downhill path* ○ *She let the bike coast downhill.* **2** If something goes downhill it becomes worse or worth less money: *The automobile industry started to go downhill.*

download /ˈdɑʊn·loʊd/ *v* [T] to copy programs or information to a computer, usually over the INTERNET

down payment *n* [C] an amount of money that is part of the total cost, paid at the time when you buy something

downplay /ˈdɑʊn·pleɪ/ *v* [T] to make something seem less important or not as bad as it really is ○ *The mayor is trying to downplay the crisis.*

downpour /ˈdɑʊn·pɔːr, -poʊr/ *n* [C] a lot of rain falling in a short time

downright /ˈdɑʊn·rɑɪt/ *adv* [not gradable] actually or completely ○ *Their working conditions were downright unhealthy.*

downside /ˈdɑʊn·sɑɪd/ *n* [U] the negative part of a situation ○ *It's a great plan – the downside is* *that it's going to cost a lot of money.* ○ Compare UPSIDE

downsize /ˈdɑʊn·sɑɪz/ *v* [I] (of a company) to reduce the number of employees, usually as part of a larger change in the structure of an organization ○ *The company was forced to downsize in order to remain competitive.*

downstairs /ˈdɑʊn ˈsterz, -ˈstærz/ *adj, adv* [not gradable] on or to a lower floor of a building, esp. the ground floor, or down the stairs ○ *a downstairs bathroom* ○ *I hear someone downstairs.*

downstream /ˈdɑʊn ˈstriːm/ *adj, adv* [not gradable] in the same direction as the current of a river is flowing ○ *The boat landing is about half a mile downstream from here.* ○ Compare UPSTREAM

downtime /ˈdɑʊn·tɑɪm/ *n* [C] **1** the time during which a machine, esp. a computer, is not working or is not able to be used **2** Downtime for a person is a time when the person can relax: *I have three kids, so downtime is scarce.*

down-to-earth *adj* practical and direct in dealing with people ○ *The players like the coach because he's down-to-earth and honest with them.*

downtown /ˈdɑʊn ˈtɑʊn/ *adj, adv* [not gradable] in or to the business or central part of a city ○ *downtown Los Angeles*
downtown /ˈdɑʊn ˈtɑʊn/ *n* [U] ○ *The hotel is situated two miles north of downtown.*

downtrodden /ˈdɑʊn ˈtrɑd·ən/ *adj* not provided with opportunities because of having been treated unfairly by someone in authority

downturn /ˈdɑʊn·tɜrn/ *n* [C] a reduction in the amount or success of something ○ *a downturn in car sales*

downward /ˈdɑʊn·wərd/, **downwards** /ˈdɑʊn·wərdz/ *adv* [not gradable] toward a lower position, level, or amount ○ *The road slopes gently downward for a mile or two.*
downward /ˈdɑʊn·wərd/ *adj* [not gradable] ○ *The trend has been downward ever since, with donations falling to $143,000 last year.*

downwind /ˈdɑʊn ˈwɪnd/ *adj, adv* in the direction in which the wind is blowing ○ *We were downwind of the garbage dump and the smell was awful.* ○ Opposite: UPWIND

dowry /ˈdɑʊr·i/ *n* [C] in some societies, an amount of money or property that a woman's parents give to the man she marries

doze /doʊz/ *v* [I] **1** to have a short period of sleep, esp. during the day ○ *My cat was dozing in front of the fireplace.* **2** If you doze off, you start to sleep, esp. during the day: *I must have dozed off, because I don't remember what happened next.*

dozen /ˈdʌz·ən/ *n* [C] a group or collection of twelve ○ *a dozen eggs* ○ *I brought home a half dozen/half a dozen (= six) eggs.*

Dr. /ˈdɑk·tər/ *n pl* **Drs.** *abbreviation for* DOCTOR MEDICINE or DOCTOR EDUCATION

drab /dræb/ *adj* [*-er/-est* only] **-bb-** plain and not interesting, or not bright in appearance ○ *He found London disagreeable, with its thick fog, cold drizzle, and drab food.*

draconian /drəˈkoʊ·niː·ən/ *adj* (esp. of a rule, law, or punishment) extremely severe ○ *The governor proposed draconian cuts in state aid to education.*

draft Ⓐ PLAN /dræft/ *n* [C] ***writing, art*** a piece of writing or drawing that is done early in the development of a work to help prepare it in its final form ○ *The architects gave us their first draft of the design.*
draft Ⓐ /dræft/ *v* [T] to write something, esp. at an early stage before it is in final form ○ *She drafted a letter to her lawyer.*

CHOOSING PEOPLE /dræft/ *n* [U] the process by which people are ordered by law to become members of the armed forces, or the process by which players are chosen to play for PROFESSIONAL (= paid) sports teams
draft /dræft/ *v* [T] **1** to order a person to become a member of the armed forces **2** In sports, to draft is to choose someone, esp. someone in a college or university to become available as a player for a team that pays its players: *The Cleveland Cavaliers drafted him in the first round.*
draftee /dræf ˈtiː/ *n* [C] a person who has been ordered by law to become a member of the armed forces

COLD AIR /dræft/ *n* [C] a current of cold air inside a room ○ *She felt a cold draft every time the door was opened.*
drafty /ˈdræf·ti/ *adj* full of currents of cold air

BANKING /dræft/ *n* [C] a written order for money to be paid by a bank ○ *a bank draft*

drag PULL /dræg/ *v* [I/T] **-gg- 1** to move something heavy by pulling it along the ground ○ [T] *If the box is too heavy to lift, just drag it over here.* **2** *fig.* To drag someone away/out is to persuade someone to leave or do something when the person does not want to do it: [T] *I hate to drag you away from the party, but we really have to go.* **3** If you drag out an event, you cause it to continue for longer than is necessary or convenient: [M] *They should make a decision now instead of dragging out the discussion.* **4** If an event drags, it seems to happen very slowly: [I] *The play dragged in the second act.*
drag /dræg/ *n* [C] something or someone that slows progress or development, or that makes success less likely ○ *Keeping a large staff is a drag on our income.*

BORING EVENT /dræg/ *n* [U] *infml* someone or something that is unpleasant and boring ○ *Waiting in a doctor's office is such a drag!*

CLOTHES /dræg/ *n* [U] *slang* women's clothes worn by a man

IDIOM with **drag**

• **drag** *your* **feet** to do something slowly or not start it because you do not want to do it ○ *He* *knows he should see a doctor, but he's dragging his feet.*

dragon /ˈdræg·ən/ *n* [C] a large, fierce, imaginary animal, usually represented with wings, a long tail, and fire coming out of its mouth

dragonfly /ˈdræg·ən ˌflɑɪ/ *n* [C] a flying insect with a long, thin body and two pairs of transparent wings

drag race /ˈdræg·reɪs/ *n* [C] a race between cars over a flat, straight road from a start at which both cars are not moving

drain /dreɪn/ *v* [I/T] **1** to allow or cause liquid to flow away from something ○ [I] *Wash the lettuce in the sink and let it drain.* ○ [T] *Drain the lettuce and then pat it dry with paper towels.* **2** If something drains you, it makes you very tired: [T] *It drains you to work with a class of 20 four-year-olds, let me tell you.*

drain /dreɪn/ *n* [C] **1** a pipe or channel that carries away waste water or other liquids ○ *She spilled some sugar in the sink and washed it down the drain.* **2** Something that is a drain on you takes away a lot of your energy and makes you tired: *Taking care of his sick mother was quite a drain on him.* **3** If something is a drain on your money or something else, it uses a lot of it or makes it weaker: *Having two mortgages was a tremendous drain on their resources.*

draining /ˈdreɪ·nɪŋ/ *adj* causing you to lose most of your energy; very tiring ○ *He found the funeral service emotionally draining.*

drainage /ˈdreɪ·nɪdʒ/ *n* [U] the process by which water or other liquids flow away into pipes or into the ground ○ *The swamp has poor drainage throughout.*

drama Ⓐ **THEATER** /ˈdrɑm·ə, ˈdræm·ə/ *n* [C/U] a play, esp. a serious one, written to be performed by actors, the writing of plays, or the art of showing plays ○ [C] *She's been in several television dramas.* ○ [U] *Arthur Miller, a master of drama, wrote "Death of a Salesman."*

dramatic Ⓐ /drəˈmæţ·ɪk/ *adj* ○ *He's as good in comedies as he is in dramatic roles.*

dramatist Ⓐ /ˈdrɑm·əţ·əst, ˈdræm-/ *n* [C] a writer of plays, esp. serious ones

dramatize Ⓐ /ˈdrɑm·əˌtɑɪz, ˈdræm-/ *v* [T] to change a piece of writing into a play to be performed ○ *He was hired by a movie production company to dramatize the novel.*

dramatization Ⓐ /ˌdrɑm·əţ·əˈzeɪ·ʃən/ *n* [C/U] ○ [U] *tense and moving dramatization* ○ [C] *The dramatization was faithful to the facts.*

EXCITEMENT /ˈdrɑm·ə, ˈdræm·ə/ *n* [U] excitement and strong interest produced by an unexpected or surprising event or situation ○ *Watching on television was not the same as experiencing the drama of the event in person.*

dramatic Ⓐ /drəˈmæţ·ɪk/ *adj* **1** (of an event or situation) producing excitement and strong interest because unexpected, surprising, or dangerous ○ *In a dramatic rescue, 10 crewmen were lifted to a helicopter just minutes before their ship sank.* **2** Dramatic also means sudden and showing a big change: *There has been a dramatic reduction in crime in New York City.*

dramatize Ⓐ /ˈdrɑm·əˌtɑɪz, ˈdræm-/ *v* [T] to make something seem more exciting or surprising than it is ○ *The event was staged to dramatize the shortage of skilled carpenters.*

dramatically Ⓐ /drəˈmæţ·ɪ·kli/ *adv*

dramatic monologue *n* [C] ***literature*** a poem written as if someone is speaking to an unseen listener about important events or thoughts

drank /dræŋk/ *past simple of* DRINK

drape /dreɪp/ *v* [T] to hang or cover with something loosely and often in a decorative way ○ *She draped a warm scarf around her shoulders.*

drapes /dreɪps/, **draperies** /ˈdreɪ·pə·riːz, -priːz/ *pl n* curtains of thick cloth ○ *I've ordered new drapes for the living room.*

drastic /ˈdræs·tɪk/ *adj* (of a change) severe and sudden; extreme ○ *In the desert there's a drastic change in temperature from day to night.*

drastically /ˈdræs·tɪ·kli/ *adv* ○ *Our lives changed drastically when dad died and we had to move.*

draught /dræft, drɑːft/ *n* [C] *Br* DRAFT

draw **PICTURE** /drɔː/ *v* [I/T] *past simp.* **drew**, *past part.* **drawn** to make a picture of something or someone with a pencil, pen, etc. ○ [T] *The child drew a picture of a dog.*

drawing /ˈdrɔː·ɪŋ/ *n* [C/U] the art or process of making pictures with a pencil, pen, etc., or a picture made in this way ○ [C] *a beautiful drawing of flowers* ○ [U] *I plan to take a course in drawing next semester.*

MOVE /drɔː/ *v* [I always + adv/prep] *past simp.* **drew**, *past part.* **drawn** to move in a particular direction ○ *As we drew near, a dog started to bark.*

PULL/PULL IN /drɔː/ *v* [I/T] *past simp.* **drew**, *past part.* **drawn** **1** to pull or direct something or someone in a particular direction, or attract someone toward a particular place ○ [T] *The Grand Canyon draws millions of tourists each year.* ○ [T] *I would like to thank Professor Reynolds for drawing my attention to this article.* **2** To draw is also to pull together or close something covering a window, so that no one can see you: [T] *She drew the blinds and sat down to read.* **3** To draw is also to suck in: [I] *He sharply drew his breath.*

draw /drɔː/ *n* [C] *infml* someone or something that attracts a lot of interest, esp. of paying customers ○ *Every team needs a superstar who will be a big draw.*

TAKE OUT /drɔː/ *v* [T] *past simp.* **drew**, *past part.* **drawn** to remove something ○ *It was my turn to draw a card.*

DECIDE ON /drɔː/ *v* [T] *past simp.* **drew**, *past part.* **drawn** to decide on something as a result of thinking about it ○ *We can draw some conclusions about the causes of this disease.*

CAUSE /drɔː/ *v* [T] *past simp.* **drew**, *past part.* **drawn** to cause a reaction from someone ○ *The criticism drew an angry response from the mayor.*

D

EQUAL /drɔː/ *n* [C] (in sports and games) a situation in which each side or team has equal points or is in an equal position and neither side wins ○ *The hockey game ended in a draw, 2 to 2.*

IDIOMS with draw

• **draw a blank** to fail to remember something ○ *He said we'd met before, but I just drew a blank* (= I did not remember him).

D

• **draw the line** to put a limit on what you will do or allow to happen, esp. because you feel something is wrong ○ *I'll do whatever my company asks me to, but I draw the line when someone asks me to lie for them.*

PHRASAL VERBS with draw

• **draw out** *something* **LENGTHEN** [M] to cause something to last longer than is usual or necessary ○ *The trial was drawn out because of the need to translate everything.* ○ Related adjective: DRAWN-OUT

• **draw out** *someone* **ENCOURAGE** [M] to encourage or persuade someone to express his or her thoughts and feelings ○ *She was good at drawing out young people and getting them to talk about their fears and hopes.*

• **draw up** *something* **PREPARE** [M] to prepare something in writing, esp. plans or a formal document ○ *The lawyers drew up a contract over the weekend.*

• **draw** *yourself* **up STRAIGHTEN** to make yourself stand straight with the shoulders back ○ *She drew herself up like the Statue of Liberty and lifted an arm over her head.*

drawback /ˈdrɔː·bæk/ *n* [C] a disadvantage or problem; the negative part of a situation ○ *One of the drawbacks of working for a big company is that you have to follow a lot of rules.*

drawer /drɔːr, ˈdrɔː·ər/ *n* [C] a wide but not very deep container, open at the top, that is part of a piece of furniture and that a person can pull partly out from its front to put things in and then push back to make it even with the front of the furniture ○ *I keep my socks in the bottom drawer of my dresser.*

drawl /drɔːl/ *n* [C] a way of speaking esp. in the southern US in which some vowel sounds are made longer and which therefore seems slower than usual ○ *He had bright blue eyes and a beautiful southern drawl.*

drawn DRAW /drɔːn/ *past participle of* DRAW

TIRED /drɔːn/ *adj* (usually of the face) appearing tired and anxious or worried ○ *He's not as sick as he was, but he still looks thin and drawn.*

drawn-out *adj* lasting longer than is usual or necessary ○ *We had another drawn-out discussion after the meeting ended.* ○ Related verb: DRAW OUT LENGTHEN

dread /dred/ *n* [U] extreme fear or anxiety about something that is going to happen or might happen ○ *a dread of drowning*

dread /dred/ *v* [T] ○ *We dreaded hearing the results of the blood tests.*

dreadful /ˈdred·fəl/ *adj* very bad ○ *I realized I had committed a dreadful mistake.*

dreadfully /ˈdred·fə·li/ *adv*

dreadlocks /ˈdred·lɑks/ *pl n* a hairstyle in which long, tightly twisted lengths of hair hang down

dream SLEEP /driːm/ *n* [C] the activities, images, and feelings experienced by the mind during sleep ○ *In the dream I had last night, someone was chasing me, but I didn't know who it was.*

dream /driːm/ *v past* **dreamed, dreamt** ○ [I] *What did you dream about last night?* ○ [+ that clause] *I dreamed that I was in a boat on a big lake, and I was trying to get back to land.*

dreamily /ˈdriː·mə·li/ *adv* in a way that suggests you are imagining something pleasant and not giving much attention to what is happening around you ○ *When I mentioned Dave, Amanda smiled dreamily.*

dreamlike /ˈdriːm·lɑɪk/ *adj* ○ *There was a strange, dreamlike* (= as if imagined while sleeping) *quality to the crash, which seemed to happen in slow motion.*

dreamy /ˈdriː·mi/ *adj* imagining something pleasant and not giving much attention to what is happening around you, or likely to behave this way often ○ *The music put me into a dreamy mood and for a moment I forgot where I was.*

HOPE /driːm/ *n* [C] **1** an event or condition that you hope for very much, although it is not likely to happen ○ *It was his dream to be a dancer.* **2** Dream is sometimes used before a noun when you want to say that something is almost perfect: *If there were one more bedroom, it would be my dream house.*

dream /driːm/ *v* [I] *past* **dreamed, dreamt** to desire something very much and hope that it happens ○ *Ever since that defeat, he had dreamed of revenge.*

WORD FAMILY dream

Nouns	dream	*Adjectives*	dream dreamlike dreamy
Verbs	dream		
Adverbs	dreamily		

IDIOMS with dream

• **dream come true** something you have wanted very much for a long time that has now happened ○ *For her, making the Olympic team was a dream come true.*

• *someone* **would not dream of** *doing something* someone would never do something, esp. because it would be wrong to do it ○ *When I was your age, my parents wouldn't have dreamed of letting me stay out until 10:00 at night.*

PHRASAL VERB with dream

• **dream up** *something* [M] to invent something new by using a lot of imagination ○ *The Gerbils is an odd name for a baseball team – who dreamed it up?*

dreary /ˈdrɪr·i/ *adj* unattractive and having nothing of any interest, and therefore likely to make you sad ○ *It was a gray, dreary day, with periods of rain.*

dredge /dredʒ/ *v* [T] to pull up a lot of sand or other things from the bottom of an area of water ○ *The harbor is being dredged.*

PHRASAL VERB with **dredge**

• **dredge up** *something* [M] to mention something bad that happened in the past, so that people become aware of it again ○ *Survivors of the disaster are still dredging up new fragments of their ordeal.*

dregs /dregz/ *pl n* **1** small, solid pieces that sink to the bottom of a liquid ○ *coffee dregs* **2** The dregs is the part of something that is considered unimportant and unwanted: *the dregs of society*

drench /drentʃ/ *v* [T] to make someone or something extremely wet ○ *The rain drenched my clothes.*

dress PIECE OF CLOTHING /dres/ *n* [C] a piece of clothing for a woman that covers the top of the body and part or all of the legs ○ *Cindy wore a black dress to the party.*

PUT ON CLOTHES /dres/ *v* [I/T] **1** to put clothes on yourself or someone else, esp. a child ○ [T] *She dresses the kids for school every day.* **2** To dress is also to wear clothes of a particular type: [I] *He always dresses neatly.*

dress /dres/ *n* [U] clothes of a particular type or style

dressed /drest/ *adj* wearing clothes, or wearing all your usual clothes ○ *I'm getting dressed – I'll be ready in a minute.*

dressy /ˈdres·i/ *adj* (of clothing) suitable for formal occasions ○ *I have some dressy shoes that I can wear to the wedding.*

SALAD /dres/ *v* [T] to add a liquid mixture, such as oil and vinegar, to a salad for additional flavor

dressing /ˈdres·ɪŋ/ *n* [C/U] SALAD DRESSING

INJURY /dres/ *v* [T] to treat an injury by cleaning it and putting medicine or a covering on it ○ *A doctor in the emergency room dressed the wound.*

dressing /ˈdres·ɪŋ/ *n* [C] a covering put on an injury, esp. when there has been bleeding through the skin ○ *You have to change the dressing every day.*

WORD FAMILY **dress**			
Nouns	dress dresser dressing	*Adjectives*	dressed undressed dressy
Verbs	dress undress		

PHRASAL VERBS with **dress**

• **dress up** WEAR FORMAL CLOTHES to wear more formal clothes than you usually wear ○ *You don't need to dress up for the party.*

• **dress up** CHANGE APPEARANCE to change your appearance by wearing special or unusual clothes ○ *The kids were all dressed up for the costume party.*

• **dress up** *(something)* IMPROVE [M] to make something look better than it usually would ○ *Satin and gold dress up a basic pair of jeans.* ○ *His record is a string of failures dressed up as victories.*

dress code *n* [C] a set of rules about clothing and appearance in a school or place of work ○ *The school's dress code does not permit anyone to wear jeans.*

dresser /ˈdres·ər/ *n* [C] a piece of furniture with drawers, usually with a mirror on top, used esp. for keeping clothes in ○ *I keep my socks in the bottom drawer of the dresser.*

dressing room *n* [C] a room, esp. in a theater, where a person can dress and get ready for a performance

dressy /ˈdres·i/ *adj* ○ See at DRESS PUT ON CLOTHES

drew /druː/ *past simple of* DRAW

dribble MOVE SLOWLY /ˈdrɪb·əl/ *v* [I] **1** to move or happen slowly in small amounts or a few at a time ○ *Customers dribbled in and out all day.* **2** When a liquid dribbles, it escapes slowly in small drops: *Juice dribbled down the baby's chin.*

dribble /ˈdrɪb·əl/ *n* [C] ○ *Water leaked from the tank in dribbles.*

MOVE BALL /ˈdrɪb·əl/ *v* [I/T] in BASKETBALL, to move a ball by using your hand to bounce it against the ground, or in SOCCER by kicking it repeatedly

dribble /ˈdrɪb·əl/ *n* [C] ○ *He took one dribble and then passed the ball.*

dribs IDIOM /ˈdrɪbz/

• **in dribs and drabs** in small amounts, or a few at a time ○ *The audience arrived in dribs and drabs.*

dried /drɑɪd/ *past simple and past participle of* **dry**, see at DRY NOT WET

drier /ˈdrɑɪ·ər/ *adj comparative of* DRY ○ See also: DRYER at DRY NOT WET

dries /drɑɪz/ *present simple of* DRY

drift MOVE /drɪft/ *v* [I] **1** to move slowly, esp. as a result of outside forces, with no control over direction ○ *He stopped rowing and let the boat drift.* **2** Someone or something that drifts changes in a gradual way that seems to be controlled by outside forces: *I finally drifted off to sleep.*

drift /drɪft/ *n* [C] **1** a gradual change that seems to be controlled by outside forces ○ *Many people experience a drift toward more conservative politics as they get older.* **2** A drift is also a pile of something that is made larger by the force of the wind: *The state police closed the highway because of deep snow drifts.*

drifter /ˈdrɪf·tər/ *n* [C] *disapproving* a person who moves from one place to another or from one job to another without any real purpose

MEANING /drɪft/ *n* [U] the general meaning or message of something said or written ○ *After a minute I caught his drift and grinned back.*

driftwood /ˈdrɪf·twʊd/ *n* [U] wood floating in the sea or left on a beach by the action of the waves

drill CUT A HOLE /drɪl/ *v* [I/T] to cut or dig a hole into something ○ [T] *First, drill a small hole in the board.*

drill /drɪl/ *n* [C] a tool or machine that cuts or digs into something to make holes

REPEATED ACTIVITY /drɪl/ *n* [C/U] practice involving repetition of an activity in order to improve a skill, or a particular occasion for such practice ○ [C] *For homework, complete the drill on irregular verbs on pages 30 through 35.*

drill /drɪl/ *v* [T] ○ *The teacher drills them in arithmetic every day.*

PHRASAL VERB with drill

• **drill** *something* **into** *someone* to tell something to someone again and again until the person knows it ○ *This attention to detail is drilled into the top managers.*

drily /ˈdrɑɪ·li/ *adv* DRYLY ○ See at DRY AMUSING

drink TAKE LIQUID /drɪŋk/ *v* [I/T] *past simp.* **drank**, *past part.* **drunk** to take in and swallow an amount of liquid through the mouth ○ [T] *She drinks a glass of orange juice every morning.*

drink /drɪŋk/ *n* [C/U] ○ [C] *May I have a drink of water?*

drinker /ˈdrɪŋ·kər/ *n* [C] a person who drinks (a stated type of liquid) ○ *a coffee drinker*

drinking /ˈdrɪŋ·kɪŋ/ *n* [U]

WORD CHOICES drink

The verb **have** is often used instead of "drink."

I'll just ***have*** *a cup of coffee before we go out.*

If someone drinks something taking only a small amount at a time, the verb **sip** is often used.

She ***sipped*** *the tea carefully because it was hot.*

The verb **swig** is often used when someone takes a large amount into their mouth.

He was ***swigging*** *soda from the bottle.*

When someone drinks something very quickly, you can use the verb **gulp down**.

She ***gulped down*** *the rest of her coffee and then left.*

The verb **slurp** can be used when someone drinks in a noisy way.

The children were eating pizza and ***slurping*** *lemonade.*

ALCOHOL /drɪŋk/ *n* [C] a liquid containing alcohol

drink /drɪŋk/ *v* [I] *past simp.* **drank**, *past part.* **drunk** to take in an alcoholic liquid

drinker /ˈdrɪŋ·kər/ *n* [C] a person who drinks liquids that contain alcohol, esp. regularly

WORD FAMILY drink

Nouns	drink drinker drinking drunk drunkenness	Adjectives Verbs	drunk drunken drink

PHRASAL VERB with drink

• **drink to** *something/someone* (of two or more people) to hold your glasses up, often touch them together, and then drink from them to express your respect or good wishes for something or someone ○ *Let's drink to Jessica and wish her well in her new job.*

drinking fountain *n* [C] a device, usually in a public place, that can send up a flow of water for drinking

drinking water *n* [U] water that is clean enough to drink

drip /drɪp/ *v* [I/T] **-pp-** to fall in drops, or let liquid fall in drops ○ [I] *The sweat dripped down his nose and cheeks.*

drip /drɪp/ *n* [C/U] ○ [U] *He heard the drip of a leaky faucet.*

dripping /ˈdrɪp·ɪŋ/ *adj* [not gradable] ○ *She arrived in a rainstorm, dripping wet* (= with her clothes completely wet).

drip-dry *adj* [not gradable] (of clothing) not needing IRONING (= using a device that presses it to make it flat) ○ *a drip-dry shirt*

drive USE VEHICLE /drɑɪv/ *v* [I/T] *past simp.* **drove**, *past part.* **driven** to travel in a motor vehicle, esp. as the person who operates it ○ [T] *We drove 40 miles to visit my aunt.* ○ [I] *She drove through Pennsylvania to Ohio.* ○ [I] *She never learned how to drive* (= operate a car). ○ [T] *I'll drive you to the station* (= take you there in my car).

drive /drɑɪv/ *n* [C] **1** *We have a 200-mile drive ahead of us.* **2** A drive is also a road for cars and is sometimes used as part of a name: *Riverside Drive*

driver /ˈdrɑɪ·vər/ *n* [C] ○ *a bus driver*

USAGE

drive or ride?

If you operate a car, truck, bus, or train, you **drive** it.

She drives a blue SUV.

If you operate a bicycle, motorcycle, or horse, you **ride** it.

My brother is learning to ride a bicycle.

~~*My brother is learning to drive a bicycle.*~~

FORCE /drɑɪv/ *v* [T] *past simp.* **drove**, *past part.* **driven** to force someone or something to go somewhere or do something ○ *He drove a nail into the wall.* ○ *He was driven* (= His actions were caused) *by greed.*

drive /drɑɪv/ *n* [C/U] strong determination to do or achieve something ○ [U] *Intelligence isn't enough – you've got to have the drive to succeed.*

driving /ˈdrɑɪ·vɪŋ/ *adj* [not gradable] **1** happening with great power or force ○ *They arrived in a driving rainstorm.* **2** A **driving force** is the person or thing that is most important in making something happen: *He was the driving force behind the new ballet company.*

PROVIDE POWER /drɑɪv/ *v* [T] *past simp.* **drove**, *past part.* **driven** to provide the power to make a machine operate ○ *The water pump is driven by a windmill.*

PLANNED EFFORT /drɑɪv/ *n* [C] a planned, usually long-lasting, effort to achieve something ○ *The university sponsored a blood drive* (= effort to collect blood) *for the Red Cross.*

WORD FAMILY drive			
Nouns	drive driver driving drive-in driveway	*Adjectives* *Verbs*	driving drive-by drive

IDIOMS with **drive**

• **drive a hard bargain** to strongly defend a position that is very much to your advantage when reaching an agreement ○ *He drives a hard bargain, but we finally made a deal.*

• **drive** *someone* **crazy**, **drive** *someone* **nuts/up the wall** *infml* to make someone upset or annoyed ○ *We love our two-year-old, but sometimes she drives us crazy.* ○ *Be quiet! You're driving me up the wall!*

PHRASAL VERB with **drive**

• **drive at** *something* to try to explain or say something ○ *I can't understand what she's driving at.*

drive-by *adj* [not gradable] happening or done while passing by in a vehicle

drive-in *n* [C] a business or part of a business that you can use or visit while staying in your car ○ *a drive-in restaurant* ○ *I deposited my check at the bank's drive-in window.*

drivel /ˈdrɪv·əl/ *n* [U] something written or said that is completely worthless; nonsense ○ *The papers are filled with drivel about movie stars.*

driver's license *n* [C] a document that allows you to drive a car or other motor vehicle legally ○ *I got my driver's license when I was 16.*

driveway /ˈdrɑɪv·weɪ/ *n* [C] a short private road that leads from a street to a person's house or GARAGE (= building where a car is kept)

drizzle /ˈdrɪz·əl/ *n* [U] a slight rain ○ *We had fog and drizzle earlier, but now it's sunny.*

drizzle /ˈdrɪz·əl/ *v* [I] ○ *It's been drizzling on and off all day.*

droll /droʊl/ *adj* [*-er/-est* only] amusing in an unusual way ○ *I always loved his droll sense of humor.*

drone /droʊn/ *n* [U] a low, continuous noise ○ *I could hear the drone of an airplane.*

drone /droʊn/ *v* [I] **1** *The radio droned in the background while we talked.* **2** To drone on is to talk in a low voice that does not change and is considered boring.

drool /druːl/ *v* [I] **1** to have some SALIVA (= natural, watery liquid) come out of the mouth ○ *The baby drools and laughs, and it makes me happy.* **2** *infml* To drool is also to show great interest and pleasure: *Some businesspeople would drool at the thought of such low taxes.*

droop /druːp/ *v* [I] to bend or hang down ○ *The old woman sighed and pushed back a drooping strand of iron-gray hair.*

drop **FALL** /drɑp/ *v* [I/T] **-pp-** to fall intentionally or unintentionally, or to let something fall ○ [T] *She dropped her keys on a table beside the door.* ○ [I] *The book dropped to the floor.* ○ [I] (*fig.*) *I was so exhausted that I was ready to drop* (= to fall down).

drop /drɑp/ *n* [C]

LOWER /drɑp/ *v* [I/T] **-pp-** to move or change to a lower level, or to make something lower or less ○ [I] *The temperature dropped nearly 50 degrees in 24 hours.* ○ [T] *We are going to have to drop our prices.*

drop /drɑp/ *n* [U] ○ *It's a drop* (= distance down) *of over 150 feet from the top of the Niagara Falls.*

STOP /drɑp/ *v* [T] **-pp-** to stop something you were doing or planning to do ○ *After winning a pay raise, the union dropped its other demands.* ○ *He was dropped from* (= taken off) *the team because of his grades.*

SMALL AMOUNT /drɑp/ *n* [C] a very small amount of a liquid ○ *I just felt a drop of rain.*

dropper /ˈdrɑp·ər/ *n* [C] a small tube with a rubber container at one end which is pressed and released to draw a liquid into the tube, and which can then be lightly pressed to release very small amounts of the liquid

IDIOMS with **drop**

• **a drop in the bucket** something small and unimportant, esp. when compared with something else ○ *We were paid about $50,000, but that was a drop in the bucket compared to what some other companies got.*

• **at the drop of a hat** easily, with little encouragement ○ *I hate to speak in public, but she'll get up on stage at the drop of a hat.*

• **drop a hint** to suggest something without saying it directly ○ *He dropped a few hints about some gifts he'd like to get.*

• **drop dead** **1** to die suddenly and unexpectedly **2** *infml* If you tell someone to **drop dead**, you are saying that you are very angry with that person.

• **drop everything** to immediately stop what you were doing in order to do something else ○ *We realized we were late and had to drop everything and rush out the door.*

• **drop the ball** to fail to keep working to reach a goal ○ *Public schools have dropped the ball when it comes to teaching kids about art and music.*

PHRASAL VERBS with **drop**

• **drop by** *(somewhere)* to come to see someone, sometimes at a stated place, usually briefly and without a specific invitation ○ *He dropped by the woman's house to ask for money.* ○ *The publisher told the writers they should drop by if they ever wanted a newspaper job.*

• **drop in** to come for a visit, esp. without having received an invitation for a specific time ○ *Drop in whenever you're in the neighborhood.*

• **drop off** **BEGIN TO SLEEP** to begin to sleep ○ *I must have dropped off during the show, because I don't remember how it ended.*

• **drop off** *something/someone* **LEAVE** [M] to take someone or something, esp. by car, to a particular place ○ *I'm about to leave – can I drop you off somewhere on my way home?*

• **drop out** to stop going to school before finishing the course of instruction ○ *He dropped out of school when he was 16.* ○ Related noun: DROPOUT

droplet /ˈdrɑp·lət/ *n* [C] a very small drop of a liquid

dropout /ˈdrɑp·ɑʊt/ *n* [C] a student who leaves school before finishing the course of instruction ○ *As a high school dropout he'll never get a decent job.* ○ Related verb: DROP OUT

droppings /ˈdrɑp·ɪŋz/ *pl n* excrement produced by animals or birds ○ *We found mouse droppings in the garage.*

drought /drɑʊt/ *n* [C/U] a long period when there is little or no rain

drove /droʊv/ *past simple of* DRIVE

droves /droʊvz/ *pl n* large numbers ○ *Local reporters arrived in droves.*

drown /drɑʊn/ *v* [I/T] **1** to die by being under water and unable to breathe, or to kill someone by causing this to happen ○ [I] *He drowned in a boating accident.* **2** to have or experience too much of something: [always + adv/prep] *drowning in debt/sorrow*

PHRASAL VERB with **drown**

• **drown out** *something* [M] (of a sound) to be loud enough to block the sound of something else ○ *The sound of the telephone was drowned out by the vacuum cleaner.*

drowsy /ˈdrɑʊ·zi/ *adj* feeling sleepy esp. when it is not the usual time to sleep ○ *The room is so warm it's making me drowsy.*

drowsiness /ˈdrɑʊ·ziː·nəs/ *n* [U]

drubbing /ˈdrʌb·ɪŋ/ *n* [C usually sing] a beating or bad defeat, esp. in a sports competition

drudgery /ˈdrʌdʒ·ə·ri/ *n* [U] hard, boring work ○ *Cleaning the oven is sheer drudgery.*

drug **MEDICINE** /drʌg/ *n* [C] any chemical that is used as a medicine ○ *over-the-counter/prescription drugs*

drug /drʌg/ *v* [T] **-gg-** to give a person or animal a chemical that causes a loss of feeling or the condition of being unconscious ○ *He couldn't talk to us because he had been drugged.*

druggist /ˈdrʌg·əst/ *n* [C] a PHARMACIST

ILLEGAL SUBSTANCE /drʌg/ *n* [C/U] a chemical or other substance that is illegally used, sometimes to improve performance in an activity or because a person cannot stop using it

drugstore /ˈdrʌg·stɔːr, -stoʊr/ *n* [C] a store that sells medicines and usually other goods, esp. products relating to cleaning and caring for the body

drum **INSTRUMENT** /drʌm/ *n* [C] a musical instrument, usually with a skin stretched over the end of a hollow tube or bowl, played by hitting with the hand or a stick

drum /drʌm/ *v* [I] **-mm-** to make a rhythmic sound by hitting repeatedly ○ *The rain drummed on the tin roof.*

drummer /ˈdrʌm·ər/ *n* [C] a musician who plays a drum

CONTAINER /drʌm/ *n* [C] a large, cylindrical container usually used for storing liquids ○ *an oil drum*

PHRASAL VERBS with **drum**

• **drum** *something* **into** *someone* to teach something to someone by frequent repeating ○ *The teacher drummed the names of the state capitals into our heads.*

• **drum** *someone* **out of** *something* to remove someone from a job, group, etc. because of something bad the person has done ○ *The chairman was drummed out of office.*

• **drum up** *something* [M] to encourage the development of something ○ *I'm making calls to drum up some business.*

drumstick **FOR DRUM** /ˈdrʌm·stɪk/ *n* [C] a stick for beating a drum

BIRD MEAT /ˈdrʌm·stɪk/ *n* [C] the lower part of the leg of a TURKEY (= large bird) or chicken eaten as food ○ *turkey drumsticks*

drunk **LIQUID** /drʌŋk/ *past participle of* DRINK

TOO MUCH ALCOHOL /drʌŋk/ *adj* unable to behave correctly or as usual because of drinking too much alcohol

drunk /drʌŋk/ *n* [C] a person who regularly drinks too much alcohol

drunken /ˈdrʌŋ·kən/ *adj* under the influence of alcohol, or a situation in which a lot of alcohol has been drunk

drunkenness /ˈdrʌŋ·kən·nəs/ *n* [U]

drunk driving *n* [U] the act of driving a motor vehicle after drinking too much alcohol

dry **NOT WET** /drɑɪ/ *adj* [-er/-est only] **1** without water or liquid in, on, or around something ○ *Are the clothes dry yet?* **2** If hair or skin is dry, it lacks natural oils: *Do you have a shampoo for dry hair?* **3** If the weather is dry, there is very little water in the air and no chance of rain.

dry /drɑɪ/ *v* [I/T] **dries**, *pres. part.* **drying**, *past* **dried** ○ [I] *I can't go out until my hair dries.* ○ [T] *The woman dried her hands on a towel and returned to the table.* ○ [I] *If you don't keep food covered, it dries out.*

dryer, **drier** /ˈdrɑɪ·ər/ *n* [C] a machine that makes wet things dry ○ *a hair/clothes dryer*

dryness /ˈdrɑɪ·nəs/ *n* [U]

NO ALCOHOL /drɑɪ/ *adj* [not gradable] (of a place) not permitting alcoholic drinks to be sold

NOT INTERESTING /drɑɪ/ *adj* [-er/-est only] not interesting or exciting ○ *The book is packed with information but it is a little dry.*

AMUSING /drɑɪ/ *adj* [-er/-est only] amusing in a way that is not obvious ○ *a dry wit*

dryly, **drily** /ˈdrɑɪ·li/ *adv* ○ *Thanks for the warning, Tachi said dryly.*

dry-clean *v* [I/T] to clean clothes with chemicals, not water
dry-cleaning *adj* [not gradable] ○ *There are about 150,000 dry-cleaning machines in the world.*

dry cleaner, **dry cleaners** *n* [C] a store where clothes are cleaned with chemicals

dry cleaning *n* [U] clothes that you take to or pick up from a DRY CLEANER

dry run /ˈdrɑɪˈrʌn/ *n* [C] an occasion in which you practice a particular activity or performance in preparation for the real event ○ *We had a dry run of the inauguration ceremony yesterday.*

DSL *n* [U] *abbreviation for* digital subscriber line (= a system for sending and receiving information at high speeds over ordinary telephone lines) ○ *In some respects, DSL is superior to cable for Internet access.*

dual /ˈduː·əl/ *adj* [not gradable] **1** having two parts, or combining two things ○ *This room serves a dual purpose – it's both a study and a guest room.* **2** Someone with dual citizenship is a citizen of two countries at the same time.

dub **NAME** /dʌb/ *v* [T] **-bb-** to give something or someone a particular name, esp. describing what you think of that person or thing ○ *At age 21 Ella Fitzgerald was dubbed "The First Lady of Swing."*

CHANGE /dʌb/ *v* [T] **-bb-** to use different voices, sounds, or images in a movie, television program, recording, etc., to replace others made originally or as added parts ○ *She is no singer, and her rock 'n' roll numbers were dubbed.* ○ *The scenery is dubbed into the CD-ROM movie using computer-graphics software.*

dubious /ˈduː·biː·əs/ *adj* **1** probably not true or not completely true; doubtful ○ *The team had the dubious distinction of ranking 31st in the league.* **2** Dubious can also mean not to be trusted, or not completely moral: *a dubious character*

duchess /ˈdʌtʃ·əs/ *n* [C] (in some countries) the title of a woman who has a very high social rank, or who is the wife of a DUKE, or the person of that rank

duck **BIRD** /dʌk/ *n* [C/U] a bird that lives by water and has short legs with WEBBED feet (= feet with toes joined by skin), or the meat of this bird

MOVE /dʌk/ *v* [I/T] **1** to move your head or the top part of your body quickly down, esp. to avoid being hit ○ [T] *Duck your head or you'll bang it on the door frame.* ○ [I] *She ducked below the surface of the rippling water.* **2** To duck is also to move quickly to a place, esp. in order not to be seen: [I] *When he saw them coming, he ducked into a store.* **3** To duck a subject or question is to avoid it: [T] *He accused the president of ducking the issue of campaign finance reform.*

duct /dʌkt/ *n* [C] **1** a tube or pipe in a building that carries liquid or air or protects wires ○ *Air conditioning requires ventilating ducts.* **2** A duct is also a narrow tube in the body that carries a liquid: *tear ducts*

ductility /dʌkˈtɪl·əţ·i/ *n* [U] ***chemistry*** the ability of a substance such as a metal to be stretched or shaped without breaking

dud /dʌd/ *n* [C] something that is not successful or is of little value ○ *The movie turned out to be a dud.*

dude /duːd/ *n* [C] *slang* any man, or one who comes from a city and dresses in a stylish way

dude ranch *n* [C] a place to go for a vacation where activities such as riding horses are offered

due **OWED** /duː/ *adj* [not gradable] owed as a debt or as a right ○ *I'm due a refund for the sweater I returned.* ○ *Our thanks are due to everyone who gave so generously.* ○ *The rent is now due* (= should be paid).
dues /duːz/ *pl n* the official payments you make to an organization that you belong to ○ *Members of the club pay $50 in annual dues.*

EXPECTED /duː/ *adj* [not gradable] expected (to happen, arrive, etc.) at a particular time ○ *What time is the next train due?* ○ [+ to infinitive] *The meeting is now due to take place next week.*

RESULTING /duː/ *adj* **Due to** can mean because of: *Due to computer problems, the checks will be late.* ○ *The flight was canceled due to bad weather.*

USUAL/CORRECT /duː/ *adj* [not gradable] according to the usual custom or the correct process ○ *Phillips took due note of the key statistics.* ○ *In due course the business became a real money maker.*
duly /ˈduː·li/ *adv* [not gradable] ○ *duly elected officials* ○ *Duly signed by the president, the bill will become law.*

STRAIGHT /duː/ *adv* [not gradable] (of north, south, east, or west) exactly, straight ○ *They headed due north.*

WORD FAMILY due

Nouns	dues	*Adverbs*	due duly unduly
Adjectives	due undue		

duel /ˈduː·əl/ *n* [C] a formal fight, using guns or SWORDS (= weapons with long, sharp blades), arranged esp. in the past between two people to decide an argument

due process, *short form of* **due process of law** *n* [C usually sing] ***politics & government*** a citizen's fair treatment within the rules of a government's legal system

duet /duːˈet/ *n* [C] two people who sing or play musical instruments together, or a piece of music written for two people ○ Compare QUARTET; QUINTET; TRIO

duffel bag, **duffle bag** /ˈdʌf·əlˌbæg/ *n* [C] a strong bag with a round bottom, often with a string or strap at the top that is used to close it and to carry it

dug /dʌg/ *past simple and past participle of* DIG

dugout /ˈdʌg·ɑʊt/ *n* [C] a shelter where baseball players sit when they are not on the field

duh /dʌ/ *exclamation slang* used to express your belief that what was said was extremely obvious ○ *"A lot of people care about money." "Well, duh."*

DUI /ˌdiː ˌjuː ˈɑɪ/ *n* [U] *law, abbreviation for* driving under the influence (= driving while affected by more than the legal amount of alcohol)

du jour /dəˈʒʊr/ *adj* [only after n] (of food in a restaurant) the particular type available today ○ *The soup du jour is tomato rice.*

D

duke /duːk/ *n* [C] (in some countries) a title of a man who has a very high social rank or who is the ruler of a small, independent country, or the person himself

dull **BORING** /dʌl/ *adj* [*-er/-est* only] not interesting or exciting; boring ○ *Many of the courtroom events were dull and routine.* ○ *The lecture was dry, dull, and full of statistics.*

NOT BRIGHT /dʌl/ *adj* [*-er/-est* only] not clear, bright, or shiny ○ *The day started off dull and overcast with a threat of showers.*

NOT SHARP /dʌl/ *adj* [*-er/-est* only] (esp. of sound or pain) not sharp or clear ○ *a dull knife* ○ *I heard a dull thud from the kitchen.* ○ *She felt a dull ache at the back of her head.*

dull /dʌl/ *v* [T] ○ *Lack of sleep will dull your reflexes.*

duly /ˈduː·li/ *adv* [not gradable] ○ See at DUE USUAL/CORRECT

dumb **STUPID** /dʌm/ *adj* [*-er/-est* only] *infml* stupid ○ *Don't say anything – just act/play dumb* (= pretend to be stupid or not to know something).

SILENT /dʌm/ *adj* [not gradable] permanently or temporarily unable to speak

dumbbell /ˈdʌm·bel/ *n* [C] a short metal bar with a weight on each end that you lift up and down to strengthen your arms and shoulders

dumbfounded /ˈdʌm ˌfɑʊn·dəd, dʌm ˈfɑʊn-/ *adj* [not gradable] so shocked and surprised that you cannot speak ○ *Ray is dumbfounded at the questions.*

dummy **MODEL** /ˈdʌm·i/ *n* [C] a large model of a human ○ *They use crash-test dummies in order to improve safety equipment in cars.*

NOT REAL /ˈdʌm·i/ *adj* [not gradable] not real but having a similar appearance to something else ○ *They set up a dummy corporation to try to hide their identities.*

STUPID PERSON /ˈdʌm·i/ *n* [C] a stupid or silly person ○ *Taxpayers are not dummies, and they are going to know how politicians are trying to fool them.*

dump /dʌmp/ *v* [T] to put down or drop something heavy without caring where it goes, or to get rid of something or someone no longer wanted ○ *The ship was accused of dumping garbage overboard.* ○ *She missed too many rehearsals and was dumped from the cast.*

dump /dʌmp/, **garbage dump** *n* [C] **1** a place where people are allowed to leave their garbage ○ *You have to bring household garbage to the town dump.* **2** *infml* A dump is also any place that is messy or that you do not like because it is of low quality: *Why are you staying in this dump?*

dumpling /ˈdʌm·plɪŋ/ *n* [C] a small ball of DOUGH (= flour and water mixed together) cooked and eaten with soup or meat, or a filling of fruit, meat, or vegetables covered with dough and steamed, baked, or fried

dumps **IDIOM** /dʌmps/

• **in the dumps** not successful ○ *The team has been in the dumps all season.*

Dumpster /ˈdʌm·stər/ *n* [C] *trademark* a large, metal container into which people put garbage or building waste, and which is brought to and taken away from a place by a special truck when requested

dump truck *n* [C] a truck with an open container at the back that can be raised at an angle so that its load falls out

dumpy /ˈdʌm·pi/ *adj* short and fat ○ *Does this dress make me look dumpy?*

dune /duːn/, **sand dune** *n* [C] a hill of sand beside a beach or in a desert

dung /dʌŋ/ *n* [U] solid excrement from animals, esp. cattle and horses; MANURE

dungarees /ˌdʌŋ·gəˈriːz/ *pl n* pants or work clothes made of DENIM (= strong cotton cloth)

dungeon /ˈdʌn·dʒən/ *n* [C] an underground prison

dunk /dʌŋk/ *v* [T] **1** to put a cookie, bread, pastry, etc. into a liquid such as coffee or soup for a short time before eating it ○ *She dunked her doughnut in her coffee.* **2** If you dunk a person, you push the person under water: *The kids in the pool kept dunking one another.* **3** If you dunk a BASKETBALL, you score by jumping high enough to throw the ball down through the goal.

dunno /dəˈnoʊ/ *exclamation not standard* (spelled the way it is sometimes spoken) I don't know ○ *"Where are we exactly?" "Dunno."*

duo /ˈduː·oʊ/ *n* [C] *pl* **duos** a pair, esp. of musicians or other performers

dupe /duːp/ *v* [T] to cheat someone by telling lies or by deceiving the person ○ *They duped me into giving them money by saying it would go to charity.*

dupe /duːp/ *n* [C] someone who has been tricked ○ *an innocent dupe*

duplex /ˈduː·pleks/ *n* [C] a house having two separate apartments, each with its own entrance

duplex apartment *n* [C] an apartment on two floors of a building

duplicate /ˈduː·plɪ ˌkeɪt/ *v* [T] to make an exact copy of something ○ *Businesses should make sure important records and files are duplicated and stored in another location.*

duplicate /ˈduː·plɪ·kət/ *adj* [not gradable] ○ *a duplicate key*

duplicate /ˈduː·plɪ·kət/ *n* [C] **1** *I lost the original form so they sent me a duplicate.* **2** If a form is **in duplicate**, an exact copy has been made of it: *The application has to be completed in duplicate.*

duplication /ˌduː·plɪˈkeɪ·ʃən/ *n* [U]

durable /ˈdʊr·ə·bəl/ *adj* able to last a long time without being damaged
durability /ˌdʊr·əˈbɪl·ət̬·i/ *n* [U] ○ *The fabric is the perfect blend for comfort, breathability and durability.*

durable goods *pl n* items like cars and home APPLIANCES (= large pieces of equipment for the home) that are intended to last several years

duration Ⓐ /dʊˈreɪ·ʃən/ *n* [U] the length of time that something lasts ○ *He planned a stay of two years' duration.*

duress /dʊˈres/ *n* [U] threats used to force a person to do something ○ *He signed the contract under duress.*

during THROUGH /ˈdʊr·ɪŋ/ *prep* from the beginning to the end of (a particular period) ○ *They work during the night and sleep by day.*

> **USAGE**
> **during or for?**
> Use **during** to talk about a period of time when something happens.
> *I'm at work during the day, so it's better to call in the evening.*
> *Please don't take photos during the performance.*
> Use **for** to say how long something happens or continues.
> *I've been in Chicago for six months now.*
> *We waited for an hour and then left.*
> ~~*We waited during an hour and then left.*~~

AT SOME POINT IN /ˈdʊr·ɪŋ/ *prep* at some time between the beginning and the end of (a period) ○ *We hope to spend some weekends in the country during the summer.*

dusk /dʌsk/ *n* [U] the time just before night when the day is losing its light but it is not yet dark

dust /dʌst/ *n* [U] dry dirt in the form of powder that covers surfaces inside a building, or very small dry pieces of earth, sand, or other substances ○ *The furniture was covered with dust.*
dust /dʌst/ *v* [I/T] to remove dry dirt in the form of powder from a surface ○ [I/T] *I was dusting (her desk) when I noticed the piece of paper.*
dusty /ˈdʌs·ti/ *adj* ○ *Piles of dusty books lay on the floor.*

PHRASAL VERB with **dust**

• **dust off** *something* [M] to prepare something for use after it has not been used for a long time ○ *Winter is coming, so dust off your skis.*

dust jacket *n* [C] a sheet of stiff paper, often in color, wrapped around the cover of a book to protect and advertise it

duty RESPONSIBILITY /ˈduːt̬·i/ *n* [C/U] **1** something that you have to do because it is part of your job, or something that you feel is the right thing to do ○ [U] *Joe is still on jury duty.* ○ [C] *Nobody likes it, but we have a duty to pay taxes.* ○ [C] *One of her duties was to see that all the merchandise was locked away.* **2** To be **on duty** is to be actively working on your job: *The two policemen on duty that night were officers Marks and Tobin.*
dutiful /ˈduːt̬·ɪ·fəl/ *adj* (of a person) obedient or (of an action) done because it is necessary or expected ○ *a dutiful child*

TAX /ˈduːt̬·i/ *n* [C/U] a tax paid to the government, esp. on things that you bring into a country

duty-free *adj* [not gradable] sold without any tax added, esp. at airports

DVD *n* [C] *abbreviation for* digital video disk or digital versatile disk (= a disk that can store large amounts of sound, movies, games, and information)

dwarf SMALL PERSON /dwɔːrf/ *n* [C] a person who is much smaller than the usual size, or (in stories for children) a creature like a little man, esp. one having magical powers
dwarf /dwɔːrf/ *v* [T] to make something seem small by comparison ○ *This year's budget dwarfs all previous ones.*

STAR /dwɔːrf/ *n* [C] ***earth science*** any of a group of stars that, compared to other stars, are not very large or bright, including the sun

dweeb /dwiːb/ *n* [C] *slang* a person who is physically and socially awkward and lacks confidence

dwell /dwel/ *v* [I always + adv/prep] *past* **dwelt**, **dwelled** *fml* to live in a place or in a particular way ○ *She dwelt in South Africa for ten years.*
dweller /ˈdwel·ər/ *n* [C] a person who lives in a particular type of place ○ *city dwellers*
dwelling /ˈdwel·ɪŋ/ *n* [C] *fml* a place where people live ○ *The house was a modest one-story dwelling.*

PHRASAL VERB with **dwell**

• **dwell on** *something* to think or talk about something a lot of the time ○ *"Let's not dwell on the past," she said.*

DWI *n* [U] *law, abbreviation for* driving while intoxicated (= driving while affected by more than the legal amount of alcohol)

dwindle /ˈdwɪn·dᵊl/ *v* [I] to become less in number or smaller ○ *The community had dwindled to a tenth of its former size.*

dye /daɪ/ *v* [T] *pres. part.* **dyeing**, *past* **dyed** to change the color of something using a special liquid ○ *He dyed his hair black.*
dye /daɪ/ *n* [C/U] a liquid substance for changing the color of things ○ [U] *She dipped the material into the dye.*

dyed-in-the-wool *adj* having opinions that are very strong and do not change ○ *My parents are dyed-in-the-wool liberals.*

dying /ˈdaɪ·ɪŋ/ *present participle of* DIE

dynamic Ⓐ /daɪˈnæm·ɪk/ *adj* having a lot of ideas and enthusiasm; energetic and forceful ○ *a dynamic person*
dynamically Ⓐ /daɪˈnæm·ɪ·kli/ *adv*
dynamism /ˈdaɪ·nəˌmɪz·əm/ *n* [U]

dynamics Ⓐ /daɪˈnæm·ɪks/ *pl n* **1** forces that produce movement or change ○ *The fight for the leadership revealed a lot about the group's dynamics.* **2** ***physics*** Dynamics is also the scientific study of the forces that produce movement. **3** ***music*** Dynamics are how loud or soft music is sung or played, or the words and signs that show this.

D

dynamite /ˈdaɪ·nəˌmɑɪt/ *n* [U] **1** a type of explosive ○ *a stick of dynamite* **2** A subject can be called dynamite if it could have a sudden and important influence on the way many people think or feel: *The Social Security issue is political dynamite.*
dynamite /ˈdaɪ·nəˌmɑɪt/ *v* [T] to use dynamite to destroy or break apart something in an explosion ○ *A work crew dynamited the concrete pillars.*

dynamo /ˈdaɪ·nəˌmoʊ/ *n* [C] *pl* **dynamos** a device that changes energy of movement into electrical energy ○ *(fig.) She's a real dynamo* (= energetic force).

dynasty /ˈdaɪ·nə·sti, -ˌnæs·ti/ *n* [C] ***politics & government*** a series of rulers or leaders who are all from the same family, or a period when a country is ruled by them

dysentery /ˈdɪs·ənˌter·i/ *n* [U] an infectious disease of the bowels that causes the contents to be excreted more often and in a more liquid form than usual

dysfunction /dɪsˈfʌŋk·ʃən/ *n* [U] failure to operate or work well ○ *Lab tests indicate he has some liver dysfunction.*
dysfunctional /dɪsˈfʌŋk·ʃən·əl/ *adj* ○ *a dysfunctional family*

dyslexia /dɪsˈlek·siː·ə/ *n* [U] *medical* a difficulty with reading and writing often including a person's inability to see the difference between some letter shapes
dyslexic /dɪsˈlek·sɪk/ *adj medical*

E e

E LETTER, e /iː/ *n* [C] *pl* **E's, Es, e's, es** the fifth letter of the English alphabet

E. EAST *adj, n* [U] *abbreviation for* EAST or EASTERN

MUSICAL NOTE /iː/ *n* [C/U] *pl* **E's, Es** ***music*** in Western music, the third note in the SCALE (= series of notes) that begins on the note C, or a set of notes based on this note

e- /iː/ *prefix abbreviation for* ELECTRONIC ○ *e-commerce* ○ *e-mail*

each /iːtʃ/ *adv* [not gradable] every thing, person, etc., in a group of two or more, considered separately ○ *There are five leaflets – please take one of each.* ○ *Each of the brothers has a different personality.* ○ *It's 500 miles each way.* ○ *The bill comes to $80, so that's $20 each.*

each other /iː ˈtʃʌð·ər/, **one another** *pronoun* (not used as the subject of a sentence) the other person, or any or all the other people in a group ○ *The couple kept looking at each other and smiling.* ○ *They're always wearing each other's clothes.*

eager /ˈiː·gər/ *adj* [not gradable] having or showing desire or interest ○ *Lots of eager volunteers responded to the appeal for help.*

eagerly /ˈiː·gər·li/ *adv* [not gradable]

eagerness /ˈiː·gər·nəs/ *n* [U]

WORD CHOICES eager

Avid can be used about someone who is extremely eager or interested.

*He took an **avid** interest in the project.*

*an **avid** football fan*

If someone is eager to be involved in something, you could describe that person as **enthusiastic**.

*He was very **enthusiastic** about the idea of moving to Spain.*

The phrases **be dying to do *something*** or **be dying for *something*** mean "to be extremely eager to do or have something."

*I'm **dying to** hear your news.*

*I'm **dying for** a glass of water.*

Someone who is **raring** to do something is very eager to start something.

*I've bought all the paint and I'm **raring** to get started on the decorating.*

Someone who accepts something in a very eager way can be said to **jump at** it.

*She **jumped at** the chance of a trip to Paris.*

eagle /ˈiː·gəl/ *n* [C] a large, strong bird with a curved beak that eats meat and has good sight

ear BODY PART /ɪr/ *n* [C] either of the two organs in the head by which people or animals hear sounds, or the part of this organ that is outside the head

PLANT PART /ɪr/ *n* [C] the top part of a grain plant, such as wheat, which contains the seeds ○ *an ear of corn*

IDIOM with ear

• **an ear for *something*** good at hearing, repeating, or understanding music or languages ○ *He realized he had an ear for languages, and decided to study abroad.*

earache /ˈɪr·eɪk/ *n* [C] a pain inside your ear

eardrum /ˈɪr·drʌm/ *n* [C] a thin piece of tissue inside the ear that allows you to hear

earful /ˈɪr·fʊl/ *n* [U] angry, complaining speech ○ *I'd better not be late for practice or the coach will give me an earful.*

earlobe /ˈɪr·loʊb/ *n* [C] the soft, round part at the bottom of the ear

early /ˈɜr·li/ *adj, adv* [*-er/-est* only] near the beginning of (a period of time), or before the usual, expected, or planned time ○ *I got up early this morning to walk the dog.* ○ *Sheena's in her early thirties.* ○ *She arrived early for the interview.* ○ *If you finish early* (= before the end of the allowed time) *you can go home.* ○ *Detroit has been an automotive center since the early days/years* (= the beginning time) *of car manufacturing.* ○ *Here's a dish I prepared earlier* (= I made a short time ago). ○ *It was a great race for Needles, who took the lead* **early on** (= soon after the start). ○ Compare LATE NEAR THE END; LATE AFTER

IDIOM with early

• **the early bird gets the worm, the early bird catches the worm** the person who arrives first is the one who is successful ○ *We'll want to be at the theater early for the best seats – the early bird gets the worm!*

early bird *n* [C] a person who gets up or arrives early

earmark /ˈɪr·mɑrk/ *v* [T] to intend something for a particular purpose ○ *Ten thousand dollars of this year's budget is earmarked for the renovation of the building.*

earmuffs /ˈɪr·mʌfs/ *pl n* a pair of warm pieces of material that cover the ears and that are connected by a curved strip that goes over the head

earn /ɜrn/ *v* [T] to receive money as payment for work that you do, or to get something that you deserve because of your abilities or actions ○ [T] *This month's raise means that I'll be earning $45,000 a year.* ○ [T] *After all the work I've done, I've earned a vacation.*

earner /ˈɜr·nər/ *n* [C] someone or something that earns money ○ *tax credit programs for low-wage earners*

earnings /ˈɜr·nɪŋz/ *pl n* the amount of money that you are paid for the work you do, or the profit that a company makes

WORD FAMILY earn

Nouns	earner earnings	Verbs	earn

earnest /ˈɜr·nəst/ *adj* [not gradable] **1** sincere and serious ○ *She made an earnest attempt to convert me to her point of view.* **2** If something is done **in earnest**, it is done seriously. ○ *Work on the building began, in earnest, in late spring.*
earnestly /ˈɜr·nəs·tli/ *adv* [not gradable]
earnestness /ˈɜr·nəst·nəs/ *n* [U]

earphones /ˈɪr·foʊnz/ *pl n* an electrical device that fits over your ears, allowing you to listen to a radio or STEREO

E

earring /ˈɪr·rɪŋ/ *n* [C] a piece of jewelry, usually one of a pair, worn in a hole in the ear or fixed to the ear by a fastener

earshot /ˈɪr·ʃɑt/ *n* [U] the range of distance within which you can be heard or hear what someone is saying ○ *I hope the boss was well out of earshot when you made that nasty remark.*

ear-splitting *adj* extremely loud

earth **PLANET** /ɜrθ/ *n* [U] the planet third in order of distance from the sun, after Venus and before Mars; the world on which we live ○ *Earth looks incredibly beautiful from space.* ○ *His trainer called him the greatest boxer on earth* (= in the world). ➤ Picture: **solar system**
earthly /ˈɜrθ·li/ *adj* [not gradable] happening in or related to the physical world or real life ○ *All my earthly possessions are in that moving van.*
SUBSTANCE /ɜrθ/ *n* [U] the loose substance of which a large part of the surface of the ground is made, and in which plants can grow; the land surface of the earth rather than the sky or sea ○ *The plowed earth looked dark and fertile.*
earthy /ˈɜr·θi/ *adj* of or relating to earth ○ *The cabin has an earthy smell.*

WORD FAMILY earth			
Nouns	earth	*Adjectives*	earthy
Verbs	unearth		earthly
			unearthly

IDIOM with earth

• **on earth** *infml* in any conditions; of all possible things ○ *How on earth did this happen?* ○ *What on earth is that awful noise?* ○ Compare IN THE WORLD at WORLD **IDIOMS** ○ **USAGE:** Used after the question words how, what, when, where, who, and why to emphasize that you are very suprised or annoyed.

earthly /ˈɜrθ·li/ *adj* [not gradable] (used in questions or negatives) possible ○ *What earthly reason can she have for being so rude?*

earthquake /ˈɜrθ·kweɪk/ *n* [C] ***earth science*** a sudden, violent movement of the earth's surface, often causing damage and sometimes deaths

earthshaking /ˈɜrθ,ʃæt̬·ə·rɪŋ/, **earth-shattering** *adj* extremely important or great in effect ○ *Earthshaking reforms are unlikely in the near future.*

earthworm /ˈɜrθ·wɜrm/ *n* [C] a common type of WORM (= small animal with a long, narrow, soft body), that moves through the earth

earthy /ˈɜr·θi/ *adj* enjoying and being honest or clear about things connected to life, such as the body and emotions ○ *Some readers may not like his earthy humor.*

ease **LESSEN** /iːz/ *v* [I/T] to make or become less severe, difficult, unpleasant, or painful ○ [T] *These pills should ease the pain.*
MOVE /iːz/ *v* [I/T] to move something slowly and carefully in a particular direction or into a particular position ○ [I] *I eased through the crowd to the stage.*
EASY EFFORT /iːz/ *n* [U] **1** freedom from difficulty, effort, or pain ○ *She won the match with ease* (= without difficulty). ○ *He felt completely* **at ease** (= relaxed and comfortable) *with them.* **2** Soldiers who are **at ease** stand in a slightly relaxed position with their feet apart and their hands behind their back.

WORD FAMILY ease			
Nouns	ease	*Verbs*	ease
	unease	*Adverbs*	easily
Adjectives	easy		uneasily
	uneasy		easy

PHRASAL VERBS with ease

• **ease up STOP** to gradually stop or become less ○ *At last the rain began to ease up.*
• **ease up TREAT BETTER** to treat someone less severely ○ *If his father doesn't ease up on him, he's going to leave home.*

easel /ˈiː·zəl/ *n* [C] a frame, usually with three legs, that holds a picture, esp. one that an artist is painting or drawing

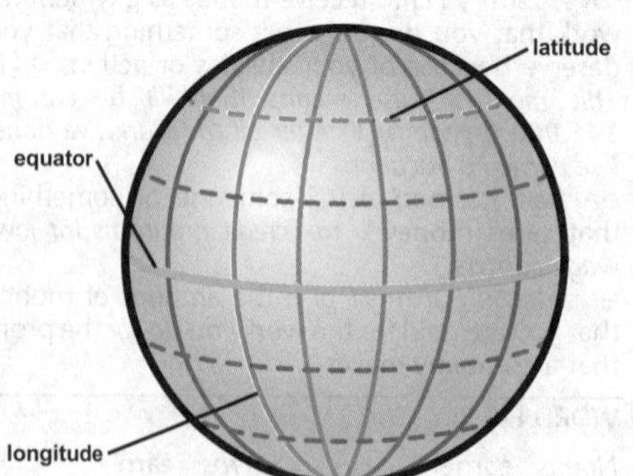

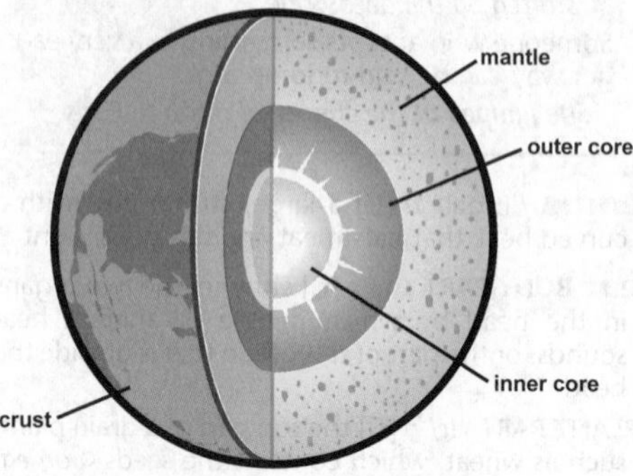

EARTH

easily /ˈiː·zə·li/ *adv* [not gradable] ○ See at EASY NOT DIFFICULT

east /iːst/, *abbreviation* **E.** *n* [U] **1** the direction where the sun rises in the morning that is opposite west, or the part of an area or country that is in this direction ○ *The points of the compass are north, south, east, and west.* ○ *Most of the state's heavy industry is in the east.* **2 The East** is Asia, esp. its eastern and southern parts: *She spent her childhood in the East, mostly in China and Japan.* **3** In the US, **the East** is the part of the country east of the Mississippi River.

east /iːst/, *abbreviation* **E.** *adj, adv* [not gradable] ○ *the east bank* ○ *Texas is east of New Mexico.*

easterly /ˈiː·stər·li/ *adj* toward or near the east ○ *an easterly direction*

eastern /ˈiː·stərn/, *abbreviation* **E.** *adj* [not gradable] ○ *Milwaukee is in the eastern part of Wisconsin.*

easterner /ˈiː·stər·nər, -stə·nər/ *n* [C] a person from the eastern part of a country, or (in the US) a person from the part of the country east of the Mississippi River

eastward /ˈiːs·twərd/ *adj* [not gradable] toward the east ○ *the eastward trail*

eastward /ˈiːs·twərd/, **eastwards** /ˈiːs·twərdz/ *adv* [not gradable] toward the east ○ *The storm moved eastward toward Florida.*

WORD FAMILY east

Nouns		Adjectives	
	east		east
	easterner		easterly
Adverbs	east		eastern
	eastward		eastward

East coast *n* [U] (in the US) the area near the Atlantic Ocean, from Maine to Florida

Easter /ˈiː·stər/ *n* [C usually sing] a Christian religious holiday that celebrates Jesus Christ's return to life

Easter egg *n* [C] an egg with a painted or decorated shell

easy NOT DIFFICULT /ˈiː·zi/ *adj, adv* needing little effort; not difficult ○ *She looked through the test trying to find an easy question.* ○ *Would a 10 a.m. appointment be easier for you?* ○ [+ to infinitive] *She is very easy to talk to.* ○ *Let's run the last two miles at an easy* (= not fast) *pace.*

easily /ˈiː·zə·li/ *adv* ○ *Ever since his surgery he tires very easily* (= more quickly than usual).

WORD CHOICES easy

If something is easy to do or understand, we often use the adjectives **simple** or **straightforward**.

*The recipe is so **simple** – you just mix all the ingredients together.*

*It seems like a fairly **straightforward** assignment.*

If a machine or system is easy to use, we often describe it as **user-friendly**.

*This latest version of the software is much more **user-friendly**.*

In informal situations there are also some fixed expressions you can use to say that something is very easy to do, for example:

*My last exam was **a piece of cake**.*

*Once we reached the main road the trip was **clear sailing**.*

In informal situations, you can use the word **cushy** if you think that someone's job or situation is too easy and you do not approve.

*He has a very **cushy** job in an office.*

COMFORTABLE /ˈiː·zi/ *adj, adv* [*-er/-est* only] free from worry, pain, or trouble; comfortable or calm ○ *With three children to support, her life has been far from easy.* ○ *I don't feel easy about leaving him alone in the house all day.*

IDIOMS with easy

• **easier said than done** easy to suggest, but much more difficult to make happen ○ *"Why don't you just ask your dad to give you the money?" "That's easier said than done."*

• **(as) easy as pie** very easy ○ *For Judy, getting a pilot's license was easy as pie – she seemed to have a natural talent for it.*

• **easy does it** do it slowly and carefully ○ *"Can I put it down now?" "Yes, but it's fragile so easy does it."*

• **the easy way out** the easiest but not the best way of doing something, esp. a way that does not involve much effort ○ *If you take the easy way out and only do things you know you're good at, you'll never learn anything.*

easy chair *n* [C] a big, soft, comfortable chair with arms

easygoing, **easy-going** /ˈiː·ziː ˈɡoʊ·ɪŋ/ *adj* able to stay calm about things that anger or worry most people

easy listening *n* [U] quiet music that does not need much of your attention

easy money *n* [U] *infml* money that you get with little effort ○ *Schools facing tight budgets see corporate sponsorship as easy money.*

eat HAVE FOOD /iːt/ *v* [I/T] *past simp.* **ate**, *past part.* **eaten** to put food into the mouth, chew it, and swallow it ○ [T] *He ate a hamburger for lunch.* ○ [I] *When I've got a cold, I don't feel like eating.* ○ [I] *We usually eat* (= have a meal) *at about 7 p.m.* ○ [I] *Let's eat in/out* (= have a meal at home/at a restaurant) *tonight.*

WORD CHOICES eat

Have is very often used instead of "eat."

*I'll just **have** one more piece of chocolate cake.*

A more formal alternative is the verb **consume**.

*He **consumes** vast quantities of bread with every meal.*

If someone eats something quickly because that person is very hungry, the verb **devour** is sometimes used. ➤

*The children **devoured** a whole box of cookies.*

Bolt down, **gobble up**, and **wolf down** are also used to describe the action of eating something very quickly.

*He **gobbled up** his food before anyone else had started.*

*I gave her a plate of pasta and she **wolfed** it **down**.*

The verb **scarf** can be used in informal situations when someone eats a lot of something very quickly.

*Who **scarfed** all the cake?*

The verb **snack** means "to eat a little food between main meals."

*I've been **snacking** on potato chips all afternoon.*

To **eat out** is to eat in a restaurant.

*I thought we could **eat out** tonight.*

The phrasal verb **pick at** is sometimes used when someone eats only a little of something.

*He didn't feel hungry, and sat at the table **picking at** his food.*

The informal phrases **stuff yourself** and **stuff your face** mean "to eat a lot."

*He'd been **stuffing himself** with snacks all afternoon and didn't want any dinner.*

*I've been **stuffing my face** all morning.*

DAMAGE /iːt/ *v* [I/T] *past simp.* **ate**, *past part.* **eaten** to damage or destroy something ○ [I always + adv/prep] *Running water had gradually eaten into the rock, forming a channel.*

IDIOMS with eat

• **eat like a bird** to only be able to eat small amounts of food ○ *You eat like a bird – I don't know how you stay healthy.*
• **eat like a horse** to be able to eat a lot of food ○ *My brother eats like a horse.*
• **eat** *your* **words** to be forced to admit that you were wrong about something ○ *I said he'd never win, but I had to eat my words.*

PHRASAL VERBS with eat

• **eat away at** *something* to slowly damage or destroy something ○ *Waves had eaten away at the sand dunes.*
• **eat up** *something* to use something so that little or nothing is left ○ *Legal costs ate up most of her savings.*

eating disorder *n* [C] *medical* an illness involving the amount of food a person eats, such as BULIMIA (NERVOSA) or ANOREXIA (NERVOSA)

eaves /iːvz/ *pl n* the edge of a roof that sticks out over the walls

eavesdrop /ˈiːvz·drɑp/ *v* [I] **-pp-** to listen secretly to someone's private conversation

ebb /eb/ *v* [I] (of the sea or its TIDE) to move away from the coast and fall to a lower level, or, more generally, (of something) to become less or disappear ○ *He could feel his strength ebbing (away).*
ebb /eb/ *n* [U]

IDIOM with ebb

• **ebb and flow** a frequently changing situation ○ *The ebb and flow of politics in Washington goes on as usual.*

ebony /ˈeb·ə·ni/ *n* [U] a very hard, dark-colored wood, used esp. for making furniture

ebullient /ɪˈbʊl·jənt, ɪˈbʌl-/ *adj* excited and enthusiastic ○ *He was openly ebullient after the election.*

eccentric /ɪkˈsen·trɪk, ek-/ *adj* strange or unusual, sometimes in an amusing way ○ *eccentric behavior*
eccentric /ɪkˈsen·trɪk, ek-/ *n* [C] ○ *She was an elderly eccentric who lived with 25 cats.*
eccentricity /ˌek ˌsenˈtrɪs·ət̬·i/ *n* [C/U] ○ [U] *Although his reputation for eccentricity was well deserved, it was not true that he had asked to be buried in his car.*

ecclesiastical /ɪˌkliː·ziːˈæs·tɪ·kəl/, **ecclesiastic** /ɪˌkliː·ziːˈæs·tɪk/ *adj* [not gradable] belonging to or connected with the Christian religion ○ *ecclesiastical history*

echo **SOUND** /ˈek·oʊ/ *n* [C] *pl* **echoes** a sound that is heard again after it has been reflected off a surface such as a wall or a cliff ○ *The cave was filled with the echoes of our voices.*
echo /ˈek·oʊ/ *v* [I] **echoes**, *pres. part.* **echoing**, *past* **echoed** ○ *The sound of footsteps echoed through the hall.*

REPEAT /ˈek·oʊ/ *v* [T] **echoes**, *pres. part.* **echoing**, *past* **echoed** to express or think what someone else has said or thought ○ *Brownell's comments echoed the opinion of the majority of the commission members.*
echo /ˈek·oʊ/ *n* [C] *pl* **echoes** ○ *The son's behavior is a clear echo of his father's.*

eclectic /ɪˈklek·tɪk, ekˈlek-/ *adj* consisting of different types, methods, styles, etc. ○ *It was an eclectic mix of our ethnic foods and traditional Thanksgiving food.*

eclipse **SUN/MOON** /ɪˈklɪps/ *n* [C] ***earth science*** **1** a period of time when the light from an object in the sky cannot be seen because another object has come between you and it **2** In a **solar eclipse**, the moon travels in between the earth and the sun. **3** In a **lunar eclipse**, the earth travels in between the moon and the sun.

BLOCK /ɪˈklɪps/ *v* [T] to become much more important and noticeable than something ○ *The state of the economy has eclipsed all other issues during the election campaign.*

E. coli, **E coli** /ˈiː ˈkoʊ·lɑɪ/ *n* [U] ***biology*** a type of bacteria that lives in the INTESTINES of humans and other animals and that sometimes causes severe illness

ecology /ɪˈkɑl·ə·dʒi/ *n* [U] the relationship of living things to their environment and to each other, or the scientific study of this ○ *The oil spill caused great damage to the fragile ecology of the coastline.*

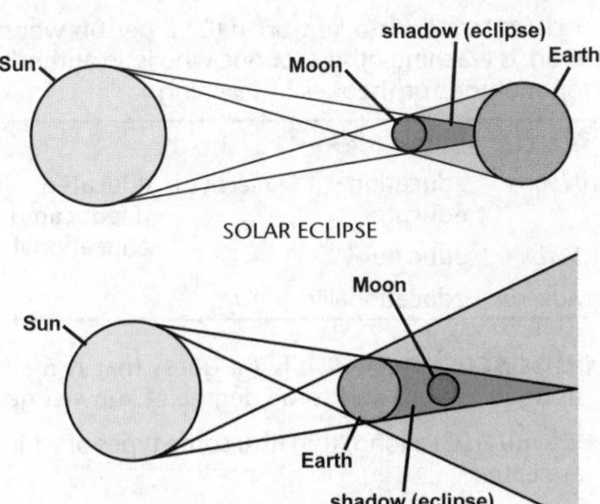

ecologist /ɪˈkɑl·ə·dʒəst/ *n* [C] a person who studies the relationship between living things and their environment
ecological /ˌiː·kəˈlɑdʒ·ɪ·kəl, ˌek·ə-/ *adj*

economy Ⓐ **SYSTEM** /ɪˈkɑn·ə·mi/ *n* [C] ***social studies*** the system of trade and industry by which the wealth of a country or region is made and used ○ *Tourism contributes millions of dollars to the region's economy.*
economic Ⓐ /ˌiː·kəˈnɑm·ɪk, ˌek·ə-/ *adj* ○ *economic growth/policies*
economics Ⓐ /ˌiː·kəˈnɑm·ɪks, ˌek·ə-/ *n* [U] ***social studies*** the scientific study of the system by which a country's wealth is made and used
economist Ⓐ /ɪˈkɑn·ə·məst/ *n* [C] a person who studies or has a special knowledge of economics
economically Ⓐ /ˌiː·kəˈnɑm·ɪ·kli, ˌek·ə-/ *adv* [not gradable]

USAGE

economic, economical or **financial?**

Economic describes something that is connected to the economy of a country.

economic growth/policy/advisors

~~*economical growth/policy/advisors*~~

Economical describes something that saves you money, especially by using less of something than normal.

New cars tend to be more economical because their engines use less gas.

Financial relates to a supply of money and can be used in connection with individuals.

She's a single mother who doesn't receive any financial support from the child's father.

~~*She's a single mother who doesn't receive any economical support from the child's father.*~~

SAVING MONEY /ɪˈkɑn·ə·mi/ *n* [U] the careful use and management of money or of time, energy, words, etc. ○ *For the purpose of economy, you may prefer to use a cheaper cut of meat in this recipe.*
economical Ⓐ /ˌiː·kəˈnɑm·ɪ·kəl, ˌek·ə-/ *adj* ○ *With rents so high, it wasn't economical to continue to live in the city.*
economize /ɪˈkɑn·əˌmɑɪz/ *v* [I] to intentionally reduce what you are spending or using ○ *You could economize on food by not eating in restaurants all the time.*

WORD FAMILY economy			
Nouns	economics economist economy	*Adjectives*	economic economical
		Adverbs	economically
Verbs	economize		

economy class *n* [U] the part of an aircraft with the cheapest seats

economy-sized, **economy-size** *adj* [not gradable] (of containers) large and cheap when compared with the price for a smaller container

ecosystem /ˈiː·koʊˌsɪs·təm, ˈek·oʊ-/ *n* [C] ***earth science*** all the plants, animals, and people living in an area considered together with their environment as a system of relationships ○ *They are working to preserve the delicately balanced ecosystem of these wetlands.*

ecstasy /ˈek·stə·si/ *n* [U] a state of extreme happiness or pleasure ○ *We shared a moment of ecstasy as the chocolate melted on our tongues.*
ecstatic /ɪkˈstæt̬·ɪk/ *adj* very happy and excited ○ *The new president was greeted by an ecstatic crowd.*

ectoderm /ˈek·təˌdɜrm/ *n* [C] ***biology*** the cells in the EMBRYO (= growing organism before it is born) of a human or animal that develop into skin, hair, and the nervous system

ecumenical /ˌek·jəˈmen·ɪ·kəl/ *adj* tending to support and encourage unity among different religions ○ *an ecumenical movement*

eczema /ˈek·sə·mə, ˈeg·zə-, ɪgˈziː-/ *n* [U] a skin condition in which areas of the skin become red, rough, and sore

eddy /ˈed·i/ *v* [I] (of water, wind, smoke, etc.) to move fast in a circle ○ *The water eddied ceaselessly in the wake of the boat.*
eddy /ˈed·i/ *n* [C]

edge **OUTER POINT** /edʒ/ *n* [C] the outer or farthest point of something ○ *the edge of a cliff/table* ○ *They walked down to the water's edge.* ○ *(fig.) Hitchcock's films often kept moviegoers at the edge of their seats* (= kept them eagerly interested).
LIMIT /edʒ/ *n* [C usually sing] a point beyond which something unpleasant or very noticeable is likely to happen ○ *It was reported that the company is on the edge of collapse.* ○ *The loss of his job almost pushed him over the edge.*
BLADE /edʒ/ *n* [C] the side of a blade that cuts, or any sharp part of an object ○ *Careful with that open can – it's got a very sharp edge.*
MOVE /edʒ/ *v* [always + adv/prep] to move slowly with gradual movements or in gradual stages ○ [T] *A long line of traffic edged its way forward.* ○ [I] *Inflation has begun to edge up during the last six months.*
ADVANTAGE /edʒ/ *n* [U] an advantage ○ *Because of her experience she has the edge over the other applicants.*

NERVOUS CONDITION /edʒ/ *n* [U] If you are **on edge**, you are nervous and not relaxed ○ *Carly seemed on edge while her family was away.*

edgy /ˈedʒ·i/ *adj* nervous or easily upset ○ *He paced the hallway looking edgy and impatient.*

edible /ˈed·ə·bəl/ *adj* suitable or safe for eating ○ *Only the leaves of the plant are edible.*

edict /ˈiːd·ɪkt/ *n* [C] *law* a public order given by an authority ○ *a court edict*

E

edifice /ˈed·ə·fəs/ *n* [C] *fml* a large building ○ *The state capitol is an imposing edifice topped by a large dome.*

edit Ⓐ /ˈed·ət/ *v* [T] **1** to prepare text or film for printing or viewing by correcting mistakes, deciding what will be removed, etc., or to be in charge of what is reported in a newspaper, magazine, etc. ○ *He edits the local newspaper.* **2** If you edit something out, you remove it before it is broadcast or printed: [M] *Some of the best jazz performances were recorded in the 1930s, before musicians had the luxury of editing out mistakes.*

edit Ⓐ /ˈed·ət/ *n* [C] ***writing*** the activity of editing a text or film ○ *Lee completed the final edit for her latest film.*

editor Ⓐ /ˈed·ət̬·ər/ *n* [C] a person who corrects and make changes to texts or films before they are printed or shown, or a person who is in charge of a newspaper, magazine, etc., and is responsible for all of its reports ○ *a textbook/film editor*

editorial Ⓐ /ˌed·əˈtɔːr·iː·əl, -ˈtoʊr-/ *adj* ○ *an editorial staff* ○ *He insisted that it was an editorial decision to cut the story.*

editorial Ⓐ /ˌed·əˈtɔːr·iː·əl, -ˈtoʊr-/ *n* [C] a statement in a newspaper or magazine, or on radio or television, that expresses the opinion of the editors or owners on a subject of particular interest ○ *an editorial on the new tax proposal*

edition Ⓐ /ɪˈdɪʃ·ən/ *n* [C] ***writing*** a particular form in which a book, magazine, or newspaper is published, or the total number of copies of a book, magazine, or newspaper that are published at the same time ○ *a regional edition of a newspaper* ○ *The book comes in both paperback and hardback editions.*

edu /ˌiːˌdiːˈjuː, ˈed·juː/ *n* [U] used at the end of US INTERNET addresses to show that the address belongs to a university ○ *info@harvard.edu*

educate /ˈedʒ·əˌkeɪt/ *v* [T] to teach someone, esp. in the formal system of schools ○ *His application form says he was educated in Germany.* ○ *It's every citizen's responsibility to be educated about his or her rights.*

educated /ˈedʒ·əˌkeɪt̬·əd/ *adj* ○ *a highly educated man*

education /ˌedʒ·əˈkeɪ·ʃən/ *n* [U] **1** *a high school/college education* **2** Education is also the study of methods and theories of teaching: *She has a master's degree in early childhood education.*

educational /ˌedʒ·əˈkeɪ·ʃən·əl/ *adj* ○ *Traveling abroad will be an educational experience for her* (= an experience from which she can learn).

educator /ˈedʒ·əˌkeɪt̬·ər/ *n* [C] a person whose work is teaching others, or one who is an authority on methods or theories of teaching

WORD FAMILY educate

Nouns	education educator	*Adjectives*	educated uneducated educational
Verbs	educate		
Adverbs	educationally		

educated guess *n* [C] a guess that is made using judgment and some degree of knowledge

eel /iːl/ *n* [C] a long, thin fish, some types of which are eaten

eerie /ˈɪr·i/ *adj* strange in a frightening and mysterious way ○ *Dust lay thick on the furniture, and cobwebs formed eerie patterns in the shadowy corners.*

effect **RESULT** /ɪˈfekt/ *n* [C/U] the result of a particular influence; something that happens because of something else ○ [C] *The medicine had the effect of making me sleepy.* ○ [C] *Cold water slows hurricane growth, but warm water has the opposite effect.* ○ [U] *The new management actually has not had much effect on us.* ➤ Confusables: **affect or effect?** at AFFECT INFLUENCE

effective /ɪˈfek·tɪv/ *adj* producing the intended results, or (of a person) skilled or able to do something well ○ *an effective policy/strategy* ○ *We've found that giving away samples of our product is the most effective way to promote it.* ○ *She's an effective administrator and knows how to get things done.*

effectively /ɪˈfek·tɪv·li/ *adv* **1** *Though barely winning election, he governed effectively and was reelected.* **2** Effectively also means having as a certain result in reality, though not in theory: *If she loses this match, she's effectively eliminated from the tournament.*

effectiveness /ɪˈfek·tɪv·nəs/ *n* [U] ○ *The drug's effectiveness is doubtful.*

USE /ɪˈfekt/ *n* [U] (esp. of rules or laws) official or legal use ○ *Winter parking rules are in effect* (= must be obeyed). ○ *All salary increases will take effect* (= begin) *in January.*

effective /ɪˈfek·tɪv/ *adj* ○ *The law becomes effective next month.*

ACHIEVE /ɪˈfekt/ *v* [T] to achieve something and cause it to happen ○ *It will take years to effect meaningful changes in the educational system.*

WORD FAMILY effect

Nouns	effect effectiveness	*Adjectives*	effective effectual ineffective ineffectual
Verbs	effect		
Adverbs	effectively ineffectively		

effectual /ɪˈfek·tʃə·wəl/ *adj fml* successful in producing the intended results ○ *Unfortunately, efforts to stop the fighting have not been effectual.*

efficacy /ˈef·ɪ·kə·si/ *n* [U] the quality of being effective; effectiveness ○ *The drug's efficacy has been questioned by consumer advocates.*

efficient /ɪˈfɪʃ·ənt/ *adj* working or operating in a way that gets the results you want without any waste ○ *an efficient organization* ○ *They are developing a more fuel-efficient car to save gas.*

efficiently /ɪˈfɪʃ·ənt·li/ *adv* ○ *She manages the business efficiently.*

efficiency /ɪˈfɪʃ·ən·si/ *n* [C/U] the condition or fact of producing the results you want without waste, or a particular way in which this is done ○ [U] *The use of high-speed machinery improved the efficiency of the factory.* ○ [C usually pl] *They reduced costs through production efficiencies.*

effigy /ˈef·ə·dʒi/ *n* [C] a model of a person

effluent /ˈef ˌluː·ənt/ *n* [C/U] liquid waste that is sent out from factories or other places, often into the sea or rivers ○ [C] *Industrial effluents and sewage remain problems.*

effort /ˈef·ərt/ *n* [C/U] physical or mental activity needed to achieve something, or an attempt to do something ○ [C] *They met again in an effort to end the strike and get people back to work.* ○ [U] *It took years to write the book, but it was worth the effort.* ○ [U] *He established the Help Committee to coordinate the relief effort.* ○ [C] *Efforts to reach the senator for comment were not successful.*

effortless /ˈef·ərt·ləs/ *adj* (of an action or activity) done so well that it seems not to need much mental or physical activity ○ *Her dancing looks effortless.*

effortlessly /ˈef·ərt·lə·sli/ *adv*

WORD FAMILY effort			
Nouns	effort	*Adjectives*	effortless
Adverbs	effortlessly		

effusion /ɪˈfjuː·ʒən/ *n* [C] ***chemistry*** a flow of a gas through a small hole in a container

effusive /ɪˈfjuː·sɪv, -zɪv/ *adj* strongly expressed, or expressed with a lot of emotion ○ *Carville delivered his message to reporters in his typical effusive, arm-waving style.*

EFL *n* [U] *abbreviation for* ENGLISH AS A FOREIGN LANGUAGE.

e.g. *abbreviation for* exempli gratia (= Latin for "for example") ○ *Eat foods containing a lot of fiber, e.g., fruits, vegetables, and whole grains.* ○ **USAGE:** In spoken English, people usually say "for example" or "such as" instead of "e.g."

egalitarian /ɪˌɡæl·əˈter·iː·ən/ *adj* based on the idea that people are equally important and should have the same rights and opportunities ○ *an egalitarian society*

egg **REPRODUCTION** /eɡ, eɪɡ/ *n* [C] ***biology*** **1** an oval, rounded object with a hard shell produced by female birds and particular female REPTILES, from which a baby animal is born when it is developed **2** An egg is also a cell produced by a woman or female animal from which a baby might develop if it combines with sperm from a male.

FOOD /eɡ, eɪɡ/ *n* [C] the oval or rounded object with a hard shell that is produced by chickens, collected before a baby bird can develop within it, and used as food ○ *The recipe calls for four eggs and a pint of milk.* ○ *I'd like two scrambled eggs with bacon, please.*

IDIOM with egg

• **have egg on** *your* **face** to be very embarrassed because of something you said or did ○ *He told everyone the deal was happening, and if it falls through now he'll have egg on his face.*

PHRASAL VERB with egg

• **egg on** *someone* [M] to encourage someone to do something, esp. something unwise or bad ○ *Egged on by his top aides, he was determined to win.*

eggplant /ˈeɡ·plænt, ˈeɪɡ-/ *n* [C/U] an oval vegetable with a shiny, dark purple skin

eggshell /ˈeɡ·ʃel/ *n* [U] the hard outside covering of an egg

egg white *n* [U] the transparent part of an egg that becomes white when it is cooked

ego /ˈiː·ɡoʊ/ *n* [C] *pl* **egos** the idea or opinion that you have of yourself, esp. the level of your ability and intelligence, and your importance as a person ○ *That man has an enormous ego.* ○ *Getting that job should give her ego a boost* (= give her confidence).

egotism /ˈiː·ɡəˌtɪz·əm/ *n* [U] the tendency to think only about yourself and consider yourself better and more important than other people

egotist /ˈiː·ɡə·təst/ *n* [C] ○ *My brother is such an egotist.*

egotistical /ˌiː·ɡəˈtɪs·tɪ·kəl/ *adj*

egregious /ɪˈɡriː·dʒəs/ *adj* (of something bad) extreme; beyond any reasonable degree ○ *egregious errors of fact* ○ *an egregious example of misrepresentation*

eh /eɪ, e/ *exclamation Cdn, infml* used as a pause in conversation ○ *So I'm speeding down the Trans-Canada, eh, and I look in my mirror and see this Mountie, eh.*

eight /eɪt/ *number* 8 ○ *Eight people are coming to dinner.*

eighth /eɪtθ, eɪθ/ *adj, adv, n* [C] **1** *He finished eighth in the race.* ○ [C] *Clarice was born on the eighth of August.* **2** An eighth is one of eight equal parts of something.

eighteen /eɪˈtiːn/ *number* 18 ○ *There are eighteen glasses in the cabinet.* ○ *an eighteen-hole golf course*

eighteenth /eɪˈtiːnθ/ *adj, adv, n* [C] **1** *He ranks eighteenth in the world.* ○ [C] *Ann-Marie's birthday is the eighteenth of October.* **2** An eighteenth is one of eighteen equal parts of something.

eighth note *n* [C] ***music*** a note that is typically equal to half the length of a QUARTER NOTE ➤ Picture: **notation**

eighty /ˈeɪt̬·i/ *number* 80 ○ *I bought a package of eighty plastic cups.* ○ *an eighty-piece puzzle*

eighties, **80s**, **80's** /ˈeɪt̬·iːz/ *pl n* the numbers 80 through 89 ○ *The temperature is expected to be in*

E

the eighties (= between 80° and 89°) *tomorrow.* ○ *Ronald Reagan was president in the eighties* (= between 1980 and 1989). ○ *My grandmother is in her eighties* (= between 80 and 89 years old).

eightieth /ˈeɪt̬·iː·əθ/ *adj, adv, n* [C] **1** *They finished eightieth out of a hundred.* **2** An eightieth is one of eighty equal parts of something.

either ALSO /ˈiː·ðər, ˈɑɪ-/ *adv* [not gradable] used in negatives instead of also or too ○ *The restaurant has good food, and it's not expensive either.*

E

CHOICE /ˈiː·ðər, ˈɑɪ-/ *adj, pronoun, conjunction* **1** one or the other of two ○ *Either person would be fine for the job.* ○ *You can go by train or bus – either way it'll take an hour.* ○ *I left it either at home or in the car.* **2** You can also use either to mean both: *Friends sat on either side of me on the plane.*

ejaculate SPERM /ɪˈdʒæk·jəˌleɪt/ *v* [I] ***biology*** (of a man or male animal) to push out a liquid containing sperm from the PENIS

ejaculation /ɪˌdʒæk·jəˈleɪ·ʃən/ *n* [C/U] ***biology***

SAY /ɪˈdʒæk·jəˌleɪt/ *v* [T] to shout or say something suddenly, sometimes unexpectedly

eject /ɪˈdʒekt/ *v* [T] **1** to force someone to leave a particular place, or to send out something quickly and often with force ○ *It was difficult to eject squatters from the abandoned building.* **2** A player who is ejected during a game is told to leave the playing area by the REFEREE because the player has done something wrong: *Very seldom do you see any player get ejected from a playoff game in football and baseball.*

eke out *something* /ˈiːˌkɑʊt/ *phrasal verb* to obtain or win something only with difficulty or great effort ○ *The company expects to eke out a small profit this year.*

elaborate DETAILED /ɪˈlæb·ə·rət/ *adj* containing a lot of connected parts or many complicated details ○ *an elaborate ceremony* ○ *an elaborate fireworks display* ○ *They had created elaborate computer programs to run the system.*

elaborately /ɪˈlæb·ə·rət·li/ *adv* ○ *an elaborately decorated dining room*

EXPLAIN /ɪˈlæb·əˌreɪt/ *v* [I] to add more information or explain something that you have said ○ *He refused to elaborate on why he had resigned.*

elapse /ɪˈlæps/ *v* [I] (of time) to go past ○ *Four years had elapsed since she last saw him.*

elastic /ɪˈlæs·tɪk/ *adj* **1** (of a material) able to stretch and be returned to its original shape or size ○ *She bunched her ponytail and slipped on an elastic hair band.* **2** If something that is not a physical object is elastic, it is able or likely to be changed: *Our plans are still very elastic.*

elastic potential energy *n* [U] ***physics*** the energy that is stored in a SPRING when the spring is either stretched or pressed together

elated /ɪˈleɪt̬·əd/ *adj* extremely happy and excited, often because something has happened or been achieved ○ *He was elated by the news that he had won a full scholarship.*

elbow /ˈel·boʊ/ *n* [C] the bony point at which the arm bends, or the part of a piece of clothing which covers this area ○ *His shirt sleeve was torn at the elbow.*

elbow /ˈel·boʊ/ *v* [T] to push with an elbow, or to push rudely, esp. to get past someone ○ *He elbowed his way through the crowd.*

elbow grease *n* [U] a lot of effort that you put into doing something

elbow room *n* [U] space in which to move around ○ *With five people in my little car, there won't be enough elbow room.*

elder /ˈel·dər/ *n* [C] **1** an older person, esp. one who deserves respect ○ *You should listen to your elders.* **2** An elder is also an official in particular religious groups.

elder /ˈel·dər/ *adj* [not gradable] (of a family member) older ○ *an elder brother/sister*

elderly /ˈel·dər·li/ *adj* ○ *William is nearly 50, and his parents are elderly.* ○ Compare OLD EXISTING A LONG TIME

elderly /ˈel·dər·li/ *pl n* old people considered as a group ○ *The city is building new housing for the elderly.* ➤ Usage: **old or elderly?** at OLD EXISTING A LONG TIME

> **USAGE**
>
> **elder/eldest or older/oldest?**
>
> **Elder** and **eldest** are comparative and superlative forms of the adjective **old**, but they are only used before nouns, usually when comparing members of a family.
>
> *My elder sister is a teacher.*
>
> The forms **older** and **oldest** can be used the same way, but they are also used in other contexts.
>
> *My older sister is getting married.*
>
> *My sister is three years older than me.*
>
> ~~*My sister is three years elder than me.*~~
>
> *The oldest house in town was built in 1805.*

elder statesman *n* [C] an older person who is respected and asked for advice because of his or her past experience ○ *He is one of basketball's elder statesmen.*

eldest /ˈel·dəst/ *adj* [not gradable] oldest (of three or more people, esp. within a family) ○ *He's my eldest brother.*

elect /ɪˈlekt/ *v* to decide on or choose, esp. to choose a person for a particular job by voting ○ [T] *We elect representatives every two years.* ○ [T] *She was elected to the board of directors.* ○ [+ *to* infinitive] *He was invited to join them at the concert, but he elected to stay home and watch the ballgame.*

elect /ɪˈlekt/ *adj* [only after n] [not gradable] (of a person) who has won a vote but not yet taken office ○ *the president-elect*

election /ɪˈlek·ʃən/ *n* [C/U] ***politics & government*** the act or occasion of being chosen for a particular job, esp. by voting ○ [C] *congressional/*

presidential elections ○ [U] *His election to the Senate was all but assured.* ○ [U] *Election Day is the first Tuesday in November.*
elective /ɪˈlek·tɪv/ *adj* [not gradable] **1** chosen or decided by voting ○ *an elective office* **2** Elective also means chosen but not necessary: *elective surgery*
electoral /ɪˈlek·tə·rəl/ *adj* [not gradable] ○ *The committee endorses electoral reforms for fairer elections.*
electorate /ɪˈlek·tə·rət/ *n* [C] the people who are allowed to vote

WORD FAMILY elect			
Nouns	election reelection electorate	*Adjectives*	elect elective electoral
Verbs	elect reelect		

electoral college *n* [U] ***politics & government*** a group of people whose votes are determined by how the people vote in each state, and who officially elect the president and VICE PRESIDENT in the US

electric /ɪˈlek·trɪk/ *adj* **1** powered by electricity ○ *electric power* ○ *an electric light/motor* **2** Something might be described as electric if it is very exciting: *The aerial acrobats at the circus gave an electric performance.*
electrical /ɪˈlek·trɪ·kəl/ *adj* [not gradable] ***physics*** using electricity for power, involved in the production or movement of electricity, or related in some way to electricity ○ *electrical equipment*
electrically /ɪˈlek·trɪ·kli/ *adv* [not gradable] ○ *electrically powered*
electrician /ɪˌlekˈtrɪʃ·ən/ *n* [C] a person who puts in and maintains wires which carry electricity into a building
electrify /ɪˈlek·trəˌfɑɪ/ *v* [T] **1** to equip with electricity ○ *They recently electrified this part of the railway line.* **2** If you electrify a group of people, you do something that makes them very excited: *Her performance electrified the audience.*

WORD FAMILY electric			
Nouns	electrician electricity	*Adjectives*	electric electrical
Verbs	electrify	*Adverbs*	electrically

electric chair *n* [C] a special chair used to kill a criminal with electricity

electric fence *n* [C] a fence with a low electric current to keep dogs or other animals from going outside it

electric field *n* [C] ***physics*** the area surrounding an object with an electrical CHARGE where positive and negative PARTICLES are reacting with each other. **Electric field intensity** is the strength of electrical energy at a given point in the electric field.

electricity /ɪˌlekˈtrɪs·əţ·i/ *n* [U] a form of energy that provides power to motors and devices that create light or heat ○ *They lived on an island with no electricity and no running water.*

electrochemical /ɪˌlek·troʊˈkem·ɪ·kəl/ *adj* [not gradable] ***chemistry, physics*** relating to the production of chemical changes using electricity, and the electricity produced by chemical changes

electrocute /ɪˈlek·trəˌkjuːt/ *v* [T] to send electricity through someone's body, causing death
electrocution /ɪˌlek·trəˈkjuː·ʃən/ *n* [C/U]

electrode /ɪˈlekˌtroʊd/ *n* [C] ***science*** the point at which an electric current enters or leaves something, for example, a BATTERY

electrolysis /ɪ·lekˈtrɑl·ə·səs/ *n* [U] ***chemistry*** the use of an electric current to cause chemical change in a liquid

electrolyte /ɪˈlek·trəˌlɑɪt/ *n* [C] ***chemistry*** a liquid that electricity can go through or that breaks into its parts when electricity goes through it
electrolytic /ɪˌlek·trəˈlɪţ·ɪk/ *adj* [not gradable]

electromagnetic /ɪˌlek·troʊ·mægˈneţ·ɪk/ *adj* [not gradable] **1** ***physics*** relating to or caused by MAGNETISM (= the power of an object to attract other objects to it) that is produced by electricity **2** ***physics*** Electromagnetic also means relating to the science that deals with the relationship between electricity and magnetism. **3** ***physics, chemistry*** **Electromagnetic force** is the form of energy that causes all reactions between PARTICLES (= extremely small pieces) of matter, which have either positive or negative electrical characteristics.

electromotive /ɪˌlek·troʊˈmoʊţ·ɪv/ *adj* ***physics*** producing a flow of electricity

electron /ɪˈlekˌtrɑn/ *n* [C] ***physics, chemistry*** the part of an atom with a negative electrical CHARGE, which moves around the atom's NUCLEUS (= central part) ○ Compare NEUTRON; PROTON ➤ Picture: **atom**

electronegativity /ɪˌlek·troʊˌneg·əˈtɪv·əţ·i/ *n* [U] ***chemistry*** the ability of an atom to attract ELECTRONS in a CHEMICAL BOND

electronic /ɪˌlekˈtrɑn·ɪk/ *adj* [not gradable] involving a system of operation that involves the control of a flow of ELECTRONS esp. in various devices including computers ○ *electronic components/equipment* ○ *electronic banking* ○ *The huge electronic scoreboard showed a replay of the last goal.*
electronics /ɪˌlekˈtrɑn·ɪks/ *n* [U] ○ *a degree in electronics* ○ *the electronics industry*
electronically /ɪˌlekˈtrɑn·ɪ·kli/ *adv* [not gradable]

WORD FAMILY electronic			
Nouns	electronics	*Adverbs*	electronically
Adjectives	electronic		

electrostatic /ɪˌlek·troʊˈstæţ·ɪk/ *adj* ***physics*** involving or producing STATIC ELECTRICITY (= electricity that is stored on surfaces)

elegant /ˈel·ɪ·gənt/ *adj* graceful and attractive in appearance or behavior ○ *We met a young businesswoman, elegant in a black suit.*
elegantly /ˈel·ɪ·gənt·li/ *adv* ○ *elegantly dressed*
elegance /ˈel·ɪ·gəns/ *n* [U] ○ *He was known for his elegance and wit.*

elegy /ˈel·ə·dʒi/ *n* [C] ***literature*** a sad poem or song, esp. remembering someone who has died or something in the past

E

element Ⓐ **PART** /ˈel·ə·mənt/ *n* [C] one of the parts of something that makes it work, or a quality that makes someone or something effective ○ *the heating element of a toaster* ○ *Having a second income is an important element for most home buyers.* ○ *They had all the elements of a great team.*
AMOUNT /ˈel·ə·mənt/ *n* [C] a small amount or degree ○ *There was an element of truth in what she said, but it was an exaggeration.*
SUBSTANCE /ˈel·ə·mənt/ *n* [C] ***chemistry, physics*** a substance that cannot be reduced to smaller chemical parts and that has an atom different from that of any other substance
elementary /ˌel·əˈmen·tri, -ˈment·ə·ri/ *adj* [not gradable] ***chemistry, physics*** relating to the chemical elements ○ *The elementary charge* (= the electrical charge in the nuclear material of an element) *is one of the constants that characterizes the basic particles of matter.*

IDIOM with element

• **in** *your* **element** in a situation you know well and enjoy ○ *Gerard stood up to sing in front of his classmates, and you could see he was in his element.*

elemental /ˌel·əˈment·əl/ *adj* basic or simple but strongly felt ○ *elemental needs/desires*

elementary /ˌel·əˈmen·tri, -ˈment·ə·ri/ *adj* simple or easy; basic ○ *I'm taking a course in elementary Russian.*

elementary school, grade school, primary school, *dated* **grammar school** *n* [C] a school that provides the first part of a child's education, usually for children between five and eleven years old

elements /ˈel·ə·mənts/ *pl n* weather conditions, esp. bad ones ○ *We decided to brave the elements and take a walk.*

elephant ANIMAL /ˈel·ə·fənt/ *n* [C] a very large, gray animal that has a TRUNK (= long nose) with which it can pick things up

IDIOM with elephant

• **the elephant in the room** an obvious problem that no one wants to discuss ○ *I don't want to ask the question, but it is the big elephant in the room.*

elevate IMPROVE POSITION /ˈel·əˌveɪt/ *v* [T] to give someone a higher or more important position ○ *He was elevated to the chairmanship of the House Armed Services Committee.* ○ *They hoped to elevate the position of women in society.*
RAISE /ˈel·əˌveɪt/ *v* [T] to raise or lift up ○ *She wore high heels that elevated her a few inches above 5 feet.*

elevation /ˌel·əˈveɪ·ʃən/ *n* [C/U] height above the surface of the earth, or an area that is higher than the surrounding land ○ [C] *At higher elevations, the air is colder.*

elevator /ˈel·əˌveɪt·ər/ *n* [C] a piece of equipment, usually in the form of a small room, that carries people or goods straight up and down in tall buildings

eleven /ɪˈlev·ən/ *number* 11 ○ *The child is eleven.* ○ *an eleven-story building*
eleventh /ɪˈlev·ənθ/ *adj, adv, n* [C] **1** *We were seated in the eleventh row.* ○ *Today is the eleventh of June.* **2** An eleventh is one of eleven equal parts of something.

elf /elf/ *n* [C] *pl* **elves** a small, imaginary person, usually shown in pictures dressed in green with pointed ears and a tall hat, and often described in stories as playing tricks and having magical powers

elicit /ɪˈlɪs·ət/ *v* [T] to obtain something, esp. information or a reaction ○ *The program has also elicited both positive and negative responses.*

eligible /ˈel·ə·dʒə·bəl/ *adj* **1** having the necessary qualities or fulfilling the necessary conditions ○ *an eligible voter* ○ *You have to be employed six months to be eligible for medical benefits.* **2** If you refer to a man or a woman as eligible, you mean the man or woman is not married and is desirable as a marriage partner: *The magazine listed 50 of the world's most eligible bachelors.*
eligibility /ˌel·ə·dʒəˈbɪl·əṭ·i/ *n* [U]

eliminate Ⓐ /ɪˈlɪm·əˌneɪt/ *v* [T] to remove or take away something ○ *You can never totally eliminate the possibility of human error.*
elimination Ⓐ /ɪˌlɪm·əˈneɪ·ʃən/ *n* [U] ○ *Arts programs face elimination in some school systems.*

elite /eɪˈliːt, ɪ-/ *n* [C] those people or organizations that are considered the best or most powerful compared to others of a similar type
elite /eɪˈliːt, ɪ-/ *adj* ○ *elite female athletes*
elitist /eɪˈliːṭ·əst, ɪ-/ *adj often disapproving* characteristic of the elite, and esp. not caring about the interests or values of ordinary people ○ *He denounced the plan as impracticable and elitist.*

elk /elk/ *n* [C] a type of large deer with large, flat horns

ellipse /ɪˈlɪps/ *n* [C] ***geometry*** a curve in the shape of an oval

elliptical /ɪˈlɪp·tɪ·kəl/ *adj* ***geometry*** shaped like an ELLIPSE

elm /elm/ *n* [C/U] a large tree valued for the shade it provides, or the hard wood from this tree

El Niño /elˈniːn·joʊ/ *n* [C] ***earth science*** a period during which a warm water current develops in the Pacific Ocean near South America and causes changes to the weather in many parts of the world

elongated /iːˈlɔŋˌgeɪṭ·əd, ɪ-/ *adj* longer and thinner than usual, as if stretched ○ *Giacometti's elongated sculptures of young women*

elope /ɪˈloʊp/ *v* [I] to leave home secretly to get married

elopement /ɪˈloʊp·mənt/ *n* [C]

eloquent /ˈel·ə·kwənt/ *adj* **1** using language to express ideas or opinions clearly and well, so that they have a strong effect on others ○ *When required, he could be an eloquent speaker, but preferred talking to small groups.* **2** Eloquent also means giving a clear, strong message: *The pictures of destruction served as an eloquent reminder of the hurricane's power.*
eloquence /ˈel·ə·kwəns/ *n* [U] ○ *I was impressed by her eloquence.*
eloquently /ˈel·ə·kwənt·li/ *adv*

else /els/ *adv* [not gradable] (after words beginning with any-, every-, no-, and some-, or after how, what, where, who, and why, but not which) other, another, different, additional ○ *If it doesn't work, try something else* (= something different/another way or thing). ○ *Let's go before anyone else* (= another/an additional person) *arrives.* ○ *The book isn't here – where else* (= In what other place) *should I look?*

elsewhere /ˈels·hwer, -wer, -hwær, -wær/ *adv* [not gradable] (at, in, from, or to) another place or other places; anywhere or somewhere else ○ *It's hot and sunny on the coast but not elsewhere.*

elucidate /ɪˈluː·səˌdeɪt/ *v* [I/T] *fml* to explain or make clear ○ [T] *I hope my book will elucidate the complex issues we face.*

elude /ɪˈluːd/ *v* [T] **1** to avoid someone or something ○ *The bear that had eluded capture for so long was caught at last.* **2** If something eludes you, you do not succeed in achieving it: *It was simply her misfortune that an Olympic medal eluded her in 1988.*
elusive /ɪˈluː·sɪv, -zɪv/ *adj* ○ *elusive memories*

elves /elvz/ *pl of* ELF

emaciated /ɪˈmeɪ·ʃiːˌeɪt̬·əd/ *adj* (esp. of people and animals) very thin and weak, usually because of illness or not eating enough

e-mail /ˈiː·meɪl/, **email** *n* [C/U] a message sent from one person to another by computer ○ [U] *I save all my e-mail.* ○ [C] *She sent an e-mail to her children with the subject line, "Sad day."*
e-mail, **email** /ˈiː·meɪl/ *v* [T] to send something or write to someone using e-mail ○ *She had emailed us about a league workshop on Wednesday.* ○ *Late last week, the hospital e-mailed a statement declining to comment on the patient's case.*

emanate /ˈem·əˌneɪt/ *v* [I/T] to come from or out of ○ [I always + adv/prep] *Angry voices emanated from the next room.*

emancipate /ɪˈmæn·səˌpeɪt/ *v* [T] to free a person from another person's control
emancipated /ɪˈmæn·səˌpeɪt̬·əd/ *adj* free from another person's control, or free from social or political limitations: *an emancipated woman* ○ *emancipated slaves*
emancipation /ɪˌmæn·səˈpeɪ·ʃən/ *n* [U] **1** *emancipation from slavery* **2** ***US history*** The Emancipation Proclamation, made by President Abraham Lincoln in 1863, freed SLAVES in the southern American states during the US Civil War.

embankment /ɪmˈbæŋk·mənt/ *n* [C] an artificial slope made of earth or stones ○ *a river embankment*

embargo /ɪmˈbɑr·goʊ/ *n* [C] *pl* **embargoes** ***politics & government*** a government order to temporarily stop trading certain goods or with certain countries ○ *They put an embargo on imports of steel.*

embark /ɪmˈbɑrk/ *v* [I] to go on to a ship or an aircraft ○ *We embarked at Miami for our Caribbean cruise.*

PHRASAL VERB with embark

• **embark on/upon** *something* to start something big or important ○ *We've embarked on an exciting new project.*

embarrass /ɪmˈbær·əs/ *v* [T] to cause someone to feel anxious, ashamed, or uncomfortable ○ *He knew that letter would embarrass him and later he tried to get rid of it.*
embarrassed /ɪmˈbær·əst/ *adj* ○ *They sat in embarrassed silence.*
embarrassing /ɪmˈbær·ə·sɪŋ/ *adj* ○ [+ *to* infinitive] *It's embarrassing to be caught telling a lie.*
embarrassingly /ɪmˈbær·ə·sɪŋ·li/ *adv* ○ *an embarrassingly poor performance*
embarrassment /ɪmˈbær·ə·smənt/ *n* [C/U] ○ [U] *She forgot her lines and blushed with embarrassment.*

SPELLING

embarrass

Many people make mistakes when spelling this word. The correct spelling has two "r's" and two "s's."

Oh, her jokes are so embarrassing!

COMMON LEARNER ERROR

embarrassing or annoying?

Someone or something that is **embarrassing** makes you feel uncomfortable and ashamed in front of other people.

It's so embarrassing when your child starts yelling in public.

Something or someone that is **annoying** makes you feel slightly angry.

There's nothing more annoying than missing a good film on TV.

~~There's nothing more embarrassing than missing a good film on TV.~~

WORD FAMILY embarrass

Nouns	embarrassment	*Verbs*	embarrass
Adjectives	embarrassed embarrassing	*Adverbs*	embarrassingly

embassy /ˈem·bə·si/ *n* [C] the group of people who officially represent their country in a foreign country, or the building they work in ○ *I'll be working at the American embassy in Paris.*

embattled /ɪmˈbæt̬·əld/ *adj* having a lot of problems or difficulties ○ *The embattled leaders are trying to hold on to their positions.*

embedded /ɪm ˈbed·əd/ *adj* existing or firmly attached within something or under a surface ○ *A threat is embedded in the language of the statement.*

embellish /ɪm ˈbel·ɪʃ/ *v* [T] **1** to make something more beautiful or interesting by additions or details ○ *Many early building entrances were richly embellished.* **2** If you embellish a story or statement, you add details that are not completely true in order to make it more interesting: *He couldn't resist embellishing his account of the African safari.*

E

ember /ˈem·bərz/ *n* [C usually pl] a small piece of wood or coal that is burning without a flame ○ *glowing embers*

embezzle /ɪm ˈbez·əl/ *v* [T] to secretly and illegally take money that is in your care or that belongs to an organization or business you work for
embezzlement /ɪm ˈbez·əl·mənt/ *n* [U] ○ *They were arrested for the embezzlement of company funds.*

embitter /ɪm ˈbɪt̬·ər/ *v* [T] to make someone feel angry and unhappy for a long time ○ *In his later years, he was embittered by the loss of his money and fame.*

emblazoned /ɪm ˈbleɪ·zənd/ *adj* [not gradable] marked or shown in order to be very noticeable ○ *The slogan was emblazoned in red paint.*

emblem /ˈem·bləm/ *n* [C] an object that is used to represent a particular person, group, or idea, or a picture of the object ○ *A dove is often used as an emblem of peace.*

embody /ɪm ˈbɑd·i/ *v* [T] to have and show particular qualities or ideas; represent ○ *Arthur Ashe embodied the ideals of good sportsmanship.*
embodiment /ɪm ˈbɑd·iː·mənt/ *n* [U] ○ *This cruise ship is the embodiment of luxury.*

embolden /ɪm ˈboʊl·dən/ *v* [T] to make someone brave or willing to take more risks ○ *Emboldened by her earlier success, Lynn's recent work has been even more imaginative.*

embrace **HOLD** /ɪm ˈbreɪs/ *v* [I/T] to hold someone close to you with your arms to express affection, love, or sympathy, or when greeting or leaving someone ○ [I/T] *They embraced (each other) before saying good-bye.*
embrace /ɪm ˈbreɪs/ *n* [C] ○ *They greeted each other with a warm embrace.*

ACCEPT /ɪm ˈbreɪs/ *v* [T] to accept something with great interest or enthusiasm ○ *He has wholeheartedly embraced life in south Louisiana.*

embroider **DECORATE** /ɪm ˈbrɔɪd·ər/ *v* [I/T] to decorate cloth or clothing with patterns or pictures sewn directly onto the material, or to create a pattern or picture in such a way
embroidery /ɪm ˈbrɔɪd·ə·ri/ *n* [C/U]

ADD /ɪm ˈbrɔɪd·ər/ *v* [T] to make a story more entertaining by adding imaginary details to it ○ *Caroline sometimes embroiders the facts, so don't believe every word she says.*

embroil /ɪm ˈbrɔɪl/ *v* [T] to cause someone or something to become involved in an argument or a difficult situation ○ *The UN was reluctant to get its forces embroiled in another war.*

embryo /ˈem·briː ˌoʊ/ *n* [C] *pl* **embryos** ***biology*** a human being or animal in an early stage of development, either in its mother's uterus or in an egg, or a plant that is developing in a seed

embryonic /ˌem·briː ˈɑn·ɪk/ *adj* [not gradable] **1** ***biology*** of or relating to an EMBRYO **2** *fig.* If a plan or process is an embryonic stage, it is in a very early stage of development: *The region's embryonic tourist industry would be damaged by this development.*

emcee /ˈem ˈsiː/ *n* [C] MASTER OF CEREMONIES

emerald /ˈem·ə·rəld/ *n* [C/U] a bright green, transparent, precious stone often used in jewelry

emerge Ⓐ **APPEAR** /ɪ ˈmɜrdʒ/ *v* [I] to appear by coming out of something or out from behind something ○ *The runway lights flashed on, and the first models emerged from behind the stage set.* ○ (*fig.*) *The president emerged unscathed from the scandal* (= He came out of it with no damage to his reputation). ○ (*fig.*) *We debated which of the candidate will emerge* (= result) *as the winner.*
emergence Ⓐ /ɪ ˈmɜr·dʒəns/ *n* [U] ○ *The agreement set the stage for the company's emergence from bankruptcy.*

DEVELOP /ɪ ˈmɜrdʒ/ *v* [I] to become known or develop as a result of something ○ *New business opportunities will emerge with advances in technology.*
emergence Ⓐ /ɪ ˈmɜr·dʒəns/ *n* [U] ○ *The emergence of a pandemic flu virus is not only inevitable, but overdue.*
emerging Ⓐ /ɪ ˈmɜr·dʒɪŋ/ *adj* [not gradable] growing and developing, esp. in business investment ○ *US government and business must become partners in breaking into these emerging markets.*
emergent Ⓐ /ɪ ˈmɜr·dʒənt/ *adj* [not gradable] starting to exist or to become known ○ *We have the flexibility to adjust our rates to meet emergent customer needs.*

emergency /ɪ ˈmɜr·dʒən·si/ *n* [C] a dangerous or serious situation, such as an accident, that happens suddenly or unexpectedly and needs immediate action ○ *In an emergency, dial 911 for an ambulance.*

emergency room *n* [C] the part of a hospital where people who are hurt in accidents or suddenly become ill are taken for treatment

emeritus /ɪ ˈmer·ət̬·əs/ *adj* [not gradable] previously in the stated job or position ○ *Murphy is professor emeritus of international relations at Wellesley College.*

emery board /ˈem·ə·ri ˌbɔːrd, -ˌboʊrd/ *n* [C] a narrow piece of cardboard with a rough surface, for smoothing and shaping the ends of your finger nails

emigrate /ˈem·əˌgreɪt/ *v* [I] ***social studies*** to leave a country permanently and go to live in another one ○ *Millions of Germans emigrated from Europe in the nineteenth century.* ○ Compare IMMIGRATE at IMMIGRANT
emigrant /ˈem·ɪ·grənt/ *n* [C] ***social studies*** a person who leaves a country permanently to live in another one ○ Compare IMMIGRANT

emigration /ˌem·əˈɡreɪ·ʃən/ *n* [C/U] ***social studies***

eminent FAMOUS /ˈem·ə·nənt/ *adj* famous and important ○ *The commission consisted of fifteen eminent political figures.*
eminence /ˈem·ə·nəns/ *n* [U]

NOTICEABLE /ˈem·ə·nənt/ *adj* noticeable or worth remarking on, or very great ○ *This shows eminent good sense.*
eminently /ˈem·ə·nənt·li/ *adv* [not gradable] very, or very well ○ *She's eminently qualified to handle the job.* ○ *The story is eminently worth reading.*

emissary /ˈem·əˌser·i/ *n* [C] a person sent by one government or political leader to another to deliver messages or to take part in discussions

emit /iːˈmɪt, ɪ-/ *v* [T] **-tt-** to send out light, sound, or a smell, or a gas or other substance ○ *The alarm emits a high-pitched sound if anyone tries to break in.*
emission /iːˈmɪʃ·ən, ɪ-/ *n* [C/U] ○ [C] *The regulations require a reduction in harmful emissions.*

Emmy /ˈem·i/ *n* [C] *trademark* one of a set of American prizes given each year to actors and other people involved in making television programs

emotion /ɪˈmoʊ·ʃən/ *n* [C/U] (a) strong feeling, such as of love, anger, fear, etc. ○ [C] *He's driven by his emotions, not by careful thought.*
emotional /ɪˈmoʊ·ʃən·əl/ *adj* connected with or showing feelings ○ *The mayor made an emotional appeal for aid following the tornado.*
emotionally /ɪˈmoʊ·ʃən·əl·i/ *adv* ○ *The coach appeared emotionally drained after yesterday's loss.*

WORD FAMILY emotion			
Nouns	emotion	*Adverbs*	emotionally
Adjectives	emotional		

empathy /ˈem·pə·θi/ *n* [U] the ability to share someone else's feelings or experiences by imagining what it would be like to be in that person's situation ○ *He loves children and has a certain empathy with them.*

emperor /ˈem·pə·rər/ *n* [C] a male ruler of an EMPIRE

emphasis Ⓐ /ˈem·fə·səs/ *n* [C/U] *pl* **emphases** special attention given to something because it is important or because you want it to be noticed, or an example of this ○ [U] *She paused for emphasis.* ○ [U] *In schools, the emphasis on programming has declined in recent years.*

WORD FAMILY emphasis			
Nouns	emphasis	*Verbs*	emphasize
Adjectives	emphatic	*Adverbs*	emphatically

emphasize Ⓐ /ˈem·fəˌsɑɪz/ *v* [T] to state or show that something is especially important or deserves special attention ○ *She emphasized the importance of good nutrition.*

emphatic Ⓐ /emˈfæt̬·ɪk, ɪm-/ *adj* strong and determined in speech or action, so that what is said or done gets attention ○ *Godard is emphatic about his preference.*
emphatically Ⓐ /emˈfæt̬·ɪ·kli, ɪm-/ *adv* ○ *He emphatically denied the rumors.*

emphysema /ˌem·fəˈziː·mə, -ˈsiː-/ *n* [U] *medical* a condition in which some parts within the lungs become stretched, causing breathing difficulties

empire /ˈem·pɑɪr/ *n* [C] ***politics & government*** a group of countries ruled by a single person, government, or country ○ *the British/Soviet Empire*

empirical Ⓐ /ɪmˈpɪr·ɪ·kəl, em-/ *adj* based on what is experienced or seen rather than on theory ○ *We have no empirical evidence that the industry is in trouble.*
empiricism Ⓐ /ɪmˈpɪr·əˌsɪz·əm, em-/ *n* [U] ***science*** the belief in using empirical methods
empirically Ⓐ /ɪmˈpɪr·ɪ·kli, em-/ *adv*

employ WORK /ɪmˈplɔɪ/ *v* [T] to pay someone to work or do a job for you ○ *The factory employs 87 workers.*
employee /ɪmˌplɔɪˈiː, em-/ *n* [C] a person who is paid to work for someone else ○ *Some of their employees do not have insurance.*
employer /ɪmˈplɔɪ·ər/ *n* [C] a person, company, or organization that pays people to work for them ○ *The Air Force is the largest employer in this area.*
employment /ɪmˈplɔɪ·mənt/ *n* [U] work, esp. for someone else, for which you are paid, or a period of work ○ *After leaving Pearson, it took Friedman months to find new employment.*
employ /ɪmˈplɔɪ/ *n* [U] *fml* ➤ Usage: **staff or employee?** at STAFF PEOPLE

USE /ɪmˈplɔɪ/ *v* [T] to use something for a particular purpose ○ *Jacobs employs this phrase repeatedly.*
employment /ɪmˈplɔɪ·mənt/ *n* [U] the use of something for a particular purpose ○ *She studied advertisers' employment of images in food ads.*

WORD FAMILY employ			
Nouns	employ employee employer employment unemployed unemployment	*Adjectives* *Verbs*	unemployed employ

IDIOM with employ

• **in** *someone's* **employ, in the employ of** *someone* working for someone ○ *Mr. Neil is currently in our employ.*

employment agency *n* [C] a business that finds jobs for people and finds people who suit particular jobs

empower /ɪmˈpɑʊ·ər, -ˈpɑʊr/ *v* [T] **1** to encourage and support the ability to do something ○ *We want to empower individuals to get the skills they need.* **2** To empower is also to give legal authority for something ○ *The state constitution does not empower counties to create housing authorities.*
empowerment /ɪmˈpɑʊ·ər·mənt, -ˈpɑʊr-/ *n* [U] ○ *Company programs encourage worker empowerment.*

empty /ˈem·ti/ *adj* **1** having nothing inside ○ *He set the empty glass down.* **2** If a place is empty, no one is using it or is present: *It was past midnight, and the streets were empty.* **3** Empty also means without any meaning or purpose: *We need jobs, not empty promises.*

empty /ˈem·ti/ *v* [I/T] to take out everything from inside something, or to lose what is inside so that nothing is left ○ [T] *She emptied her husband's mug in the sink.* ○ [I] *Once the movie ended, the theater emptied quickly.* ○ [I] *The Tombigbee River empties into Mobile Bay* (= its water flows there).

empty /ˈem·ti/ *n* [C usually pl] a container with nothing in it, esp. one whose contents have been used ○ *Bring the empties to the recycling center.*

emptiness /ˈem·tiː·nəs/ *n* [U] ○ *She loves the emptiness of the desert.* ○ *He tried to ignore the feeling of emptiness* (= lack of meaning or purpose).

WORD CHOICES empty

If a place is empty because there are no people in it, you can describe it as **deserted.**

*It was 3 o'clock in the morning and the streets were **deserted**.*

Desolate can be used about places that are empty and unattractive.

*The house stood in a bleak and **desolate** landscape.*

If a place or building is empty because no people live there, you could use the word **uninhabited.**

*The island is **uninhabited**.*

If a room or building is empty because it has no furniture in it, you could describe it as **bare** or **unfurnished**.

*The room was completely **bare**.*

*The house was **unfurnished**.*

Vacant is a word you can use to describe something that is empty and available to be used.

*The hospital has no **vacant** beds.*

Blank can be used about empty places on a piece of paper.

*Sign your name in the **blank** space at the bottom of the form.*

IDIOM with empty

• **on an empty stomach** when you have not eaten anything ○ *Never take this medicine on an empty stomach.*

empty-handed *adj* [not gradable] not having anything to bring or to take away ○ *The two would-be robbers fled empty-handed.*

emulate /ˈem·jəˌleɪt/ *v* [T] to copy someone's behavior or try to be like someone else because you admire or respect that person ○ *Officials are looking to emulate successful ideas from other cities.* ○ *He just wants to emulate his dad.*

enable Ⓐ /ɪˈneɪ·bəl/ *v* [T] to make someone or something able to do something by providing whatever is necessary to achieve that aim ○ *Saving enough money now will enable you to retire comfortably.*

enact /ɪˈnækt/ *v* [T] to make a law, or to make an idea into a law ○ *For the second year, national lawmakers failed to enact environmental legislation.*

enactment /ɪˈnækt·mənt/ *n* [U] the making of a law, or a particular act of making a law ○ *Supporters were pleased with the enactment of the bill.*

enamel /ɪˈnæm·əl/ *n* [C/U] **1** a substance made from glass that is used to decorate or protect clay, metal, and glass objects, or an object covered with this substance ○ [U] *The enamel on the sink was chipped.* **2** Enamel is also a type of paint that forms a shiny surface when dry: [C] *I used a blue enamel for the trim.* **3** Enamel is also the hard, white, shiny substance that forms the covering of a tooth.

enamored /ɪˈnæm·ərd/ *adj* liking a lot ○ *Not everyone is enamored of steak.*

encase /ɪnˈkeɪs, en-/ *v* [T] to cover or enclose something completely ○ *The medal was encased in clear plastic.*

enchant PLEASE /ɪnˈtʃænt/ *v* [T] to charm or please someone a lot ○ *He was enchanted by stories of the Old West.*

enchanting /ɪnˈtʃænt·ɪŋ/ *adj* ○ *Belgium is an enchanting country.*

USE MAGIC /ɪnˈtʃænt/ *v* [T] (in stories) to put someone completely under your control by using magic

enchanted /ɪnˈtʃænt·əd/ *adj* ○ *The princess lives in an enchanted castle.*

enchilada /ˌen·tʃəˈlɑd·ə/ *n* [C] a food consisting of a TORTILLA (= type of flat, round bread) wrapped around meat, beans, or cheese, and covered with a sauce that is usually spicy

encircle /ɪnˈsɜr·kəl/ *v* [T] to surround or form a circle around something ○ *A parking lot encircles the mall.*

enclave /ˈen·kleɪv, ˈɑn-/ *n* [C] an area that is different from the larger area or country surrounding it, or a group of people who are different from the people living in the surrounding area ○ *Yorkville was an enclave of German immigrants.*

enclose SURROUND /ɪnˈkloʊz/ *v* [T] to surround ○ *The garden is enclosed by four walls.*

enclosed /ɪnˈkloʊzd/ *adj* (of a place) surrounded by a wall and often covered ○ *It's the largest fully-enclosed shopping center in the world.*

SEND /ɪnˈkloʊz/ *v* [T] to send something in the same envelope or package as something else ○ *Please enclose a stamped, self-addressed envelope.*

enclosure SEPARATE AREA /ɪnˈkloʊ·ʒər/ *n* [C] an area surrounded by a fence or other structure in order to be kept separate from other areas ○ *The dogs are in a fenced enclosure in the backyard.*

LETTER /ɪnˈkloʊ·ʒər/ *n* [C] something extra that is sent in a letter or package with the main message ○ *You will find two enclosures with this letter – a check and a photograph.*

encompass /ɪnˈkʌm·pəs/ *v* [T] to include several different things ○ *The plan encompasses repaving the street and planting 40 new trees.*

encore /ˈɑn·kɔːr, -kour/ *exclamation, n* [C] the performance of an additional song or piece of music after a show has formally ended, or the word people sometimes call out while clapping to request this performance ○ *The audience demanded encore after encore.*

encounter Ⓐ /ɪnˈkɑʊnt·ər/ *v* [T] to meet someone unexpectedly, or to experience, esp. something unpleasant ○ *In the kitchen I encountered a woman I had never seen before.* ○ *He was shocked by the hostility he encountered.*
encounter /ɪnˈkɑʊnt·ər/ *n* [C] ○ *My first encounter with death was when Abraham died.*

encourage /ɪnˈkɜr·ɪdʒ, -ˈkʌ·rɪdʒ/ *v* [T] **1** to help someone to feel confident and able to do something, or to give advice to someone to do something ○ *Our parents always encouraged us to ask questions.* **2** If something encourages an activity, it supports it or makes it more likely: *The city needs to encourage job creation.*
encouraging /ɪnˈkɜr·ə·dʒɪŋ, -ˈkʌ·rə-/ *adj* ○ *Early results of the experiment were extremely encouraging.*
encouragement /ɪnˈkɜr·ɪdʒ·mənt, -ˈkʌ·rɪdʒ-/ *n* [U] ○ *My parents gave me encouragement and support.*

WORD FAMILY encourage

Nouns	encouragement discouragement	*Adjectives*	encouraging discouraging
Verbs	encourage discourage		

encroach /ɪnˈkroʊtʃ/ *v* [I] to take control or possession of something in a gradual way and often without being noticed ○ *Farmers encroached on forest land to grow crops.* ○ *These devices are encroaching on people's privacy.*
encroachment /ɪnˈkroʊtʃ·mənt/ *n* [C/U] ○ [C] *Human encroachment threatens the birds' nesting sites.*

encrusted /ɪnˈkrʌs·təd/ *adj* covered with a hard layer or something, or with something decorative ○ *All our belongings were encrusted with mud.*

encrypt /ɪnˈkrɪpt, en-/ *v* [T] to put information into a special form so that most people cannot read it ○ *Protected websites will tell you that the transfer is encrypted, and your browser will usually display a symbol confirming this.*
encryption /ɪnˈkrɪp·ʃən, en-/ *n* [U] ○ *Never give out a credit number online unless the site has encryption software.*

encumbered /ɪnˈkʌm·bərd/ *adj* prevented from making quick progress by having to carry heavy objects or deal with important duties and responsibilities ○ *She was encumbered by concern over her husband's health.*

encyclopedia, **encyclopaedia** /ɪnˌsɑɪ·kləˈpiːd·iː·ə/ *n* [C] a large collection of information about one or many subjects, often arranged alphabetically in articles in a book or set of books, or available through a computer

encyclopedic, **encyclopaedic** /ɪnˌsɑɪ·kləˈpiːd·ɪk/ *adj* covering a large range of knowledge, often in great detail ○ *He has boundless energy and an encyclopedic memory.*

end LAST PART /end/ *n* [C] **1** the last or farthest part of something or of a period of time, beyond which it does not exist ○ *She tied one end of the rope to a tree.* ○ *The punctuation at the end of this sentence is a period.* ○ *Did you stay to the end of the movie?* ○ *Steve can swim to the far end of the lake and back.* **2** To be **at an end** is to be finished: *His career was at an end.* **3** If things are **end to end**, they are all facing in the same direction, with the back end of each against the front end of the next one: *The new cars were lined up end to end.*
end /end/ *v* [I/T] ○ [T] *She ended her speech on an optimistic note.* ○ [I] *Our arguments always end in tears.*
ending /ˈen·dɪŋ/ *n* [C] **1** the last part of a process, esp. the way in which something stops existing ○ *The movie's ending is so romantic!* **2** ***grammar*** An ending is a part added to a word that changes its meaning: *To make "dog" plural, you add the ending "-s."*
endless /ˈen·dləs/ *adj* [not gradable] If something is endless, it never finishes or seems never to finish because it continues for so long: *When I was a child, the summers seemed endless.*
endlessly /ˈen·dlə·sli/ *adv* [not gradable] ○ *Education policy is endlessly debated.*

PART /end/ *n* [C] a specific part or division of an activity ○ *She takes care of the financial end of the business and I handle the marketing end.*

INTENTION /end/ *n* [C] something that your actions or efforts are intended to achieve; an aim ○ *To accomplish that end, you will have to work hard and be lucky, too.*

FOOTBALL PLAYER /end/ *n* [C] (in football) one of two players who begin play farthest from the ball ○ *a defensive end*

WORD FAMILY end

Nouns	end ending	*Adjectives*	unending endless
Verbs	end	*Adverbs*	endlessly

IDIOMS with end

• **at the end of** ***your*** **rope, at the end of** ***your*** **tether** to have no more patience or strength ○ *I'm at the end of my rope with these kids!*
• **in the end** after considering everything ○ *In the end, she chose to go to Oberlin College.*
• **not the end of the world** not the worst thing that could happen ○ *We're hoping to win, but if we finish second it won't be the end of the world.*
• **on end** continuously ○ *She practices the violin for hours on end.* ○ Compare AT A STRETCH at STRETCH IDIOMS

PHRASAL VERB with end

• **end up** to reach a particular place or achieve a situation after other activities ○ *After two weeks of traveling around Europe, we ended up in Paris.* ○ *The deals were popular at the time, but many ended up losing money.*

endanger /ɪn ˈdeɪn·dʒər/ *v* [T] to put someone or something in a situation in which it is likely to be harmed, damaged, or destroyed ○ *Revealing that information might endanger our national security.*
endangered /ɪn ˈdeɪn·dʒərd/ *adj*

endangered species *n* [C] a type of animal or plant that might stop existing because there are only a few of that type alive

E

endear *someone* **to** *someone* /ɪn ˈdɪr·tə, -tʊ, -ˌtuː/ *phrasal verb* to cause someone to be liked by another person ○ *His fiery temper did not endear him to his coworkers.*

endearing /ɪn ˈdɪr·ɪŋ/ *adj* easily able to make people like you ○ *Pickwick is endearing, as so many fools are.*

endeavor, *Cdn, Br* **endeavour** /ɪn ˈdev·ər/ *n* [C/U] an effort or attempt to do something ○ [C] *Writing is a very different endeavor than teaching.*
endeavor, *Cdn, Br* **endeavour** /ɪn ˈdev·ər/ *v* [+ *to* infinitive] *fml* to try to do something ○ *I endeavored to explain the legal consequences of his action.*

endemic /en ˈdem·ɪk, ɪn-/ *adj* (esp. of a disease or social condition) found particularly in a specific area or group ○ *Some of these problems are endemic to big US cities.*

endive /ˈen·dɑɪv, ˈɑn·diːv/ *n* [U] a plant with long, narrow leaves that curl at the edges and that is eaten in salads

endless /ˈen·dləs/ *adj* ○ See at END LAST PART

endocrine /ˈen·də·krɪn, -ˌkriːn/ *adj* [not gradable] ***biology*** of or relating to any of the organs of the body that make HORMONES (= chemicals which make the body grow and develop) and put them into the blood, or the hormones that they make

endonuclease /ˌen·doʊ ˈnuː·kliːˌeɪs, -eɪz/ *n* [C] ***biology*** a chemical substance produced in the body that breaks connections in DNA (= chemical that controls the structure and purpose of cells)

endoplasmic reticulum /ˌen·doʊ ˈplæz·mɪk rə ˈtɪk·jə·ləm/ *n* [C] a network of tubes within a cell that transports substances inside the cell and is needed for the production of PROTEINS (= chemicals that are a necessary part of cells of living things)

endorse SUPPORT /ɪn ˈdɔːrs/ *v* [T] **1** to make a public statement of your approval or support for something or someone ○ *We're not endorsing tax increases.* ○ *My wife has publicly endorsed Lunny for city council.* **2** If someone endorses a product, a statement saying the person likes or uses the product is used in advertising the product.
endorsement /ɪn ˈdɔːr·smənt/ *n* [C/U] **1** [U] *Both candidates have been seeking the union's endorsement.* **2** An endorsement is also a public statement, esp. by someone who is famous, that the person uses or likes a particular product: [C] *Some athletes get contracts for product endorsements worth millions of dollars.*

SIGN /ɪn ˈdɔːrs/ *v* [T] to write your name on a check ○ *He endorsed the check and deposited it in his account.*
endorsement /ɪn ˈdɔːr·smənt/ *n* [C] ○ *The bank won't take checks that have no endorsements.*

endothermic reaction /ˌen·doʊ ˈθɜr·mɪk riː ˈæk·ʃən/ *n* [C] ***chemistry*** a chemical reaction that needs heat to happen

endow /ɪn ˈdɑʊ/ *v* [T] **1** to give money that will provide an income for a college or university, hospital, or other organization ○ *In 1937 Mellon endowed the National Gallery of Art.* **2** If someone or something is **endowed with** a particular quality or feature, the person or thing naturally has that quality or feature: *People think Jefferson was endowed with great wisdom.*
endowment /ɪn ˈdɑʊ·mənt/ *n* [C] ○ *We are trying to set up an endowment to support the library.*

endpoint /ˈend ˌpɔɪnt/ *n* [C] ***geometry*** a point at which a line SEGMENT ends

end product *n* [C] the thing that is produced by an industrial process or an activity ○ *Greed and selfishness are the end products of a system that always puts the individual first.* ○ Compare BY-PRODUCT

end result *n* [C] what finally happens from a series of events ○ *I followed the recipe, but the end result was disappointing.*

endure /ɪn ˈdʊr/ *v* [I/T] to experience and bear something difficult, painful, or unpleasant ○ [T] *We had to endure a nine-hour delay at the airport.* ○ *Sinatra's popularity endured for decades.*
endurance /ɪn ˈdʊr·əns/ *n* [U] the ability to continue doing something for a long time ○ *He began visiting the gym to build up his strength and endurance.*
enduring /ɪn ˈdʊr·ɪŋ/ *adj* continuing for a long time; lasting ○ *He believed in the enduring power of love.*

end zone *n* [C] (in football) the area at the end of the field where a player with the ball can score a goal

enemy /ˈen·ə·mi/ *n* [C] **1** a person who hates or opposes another person and tries to harm that person ○ *Some enemies are spreading nasty gossip about her.* ○ *He views the press as the enemy.* **2** The enemy is a country or the armed forces or people of a country that is at war with your own country: *He was charged with espionage and aiding the enemy.*

energetic Ⓐ /ˌen·ər ˈdʒet̬·ɪk/ *adj* very active physically and mentally ○ *The president was an energetic campaigner.*
energetically Ⓐ /ˌen·ər ˈdʒet̬·ɪ·kli/ *adv* ○ *She energetically promotes women's sports.*

energy Ⓐ STRENGTH /ˈen·ər·dʒi/ *n* **1** the power and ability to be physically and mentally active ○ [U] *They spent a lot of time and energy on the grant proposal.* ○ [U] *He wrote with a great burst of energy.* **2** Your energies are the total amount of your physical and mental strength to do something: [pl] *All* *my energies were directed toward establishing an academic career.*

energize /ˈen·ərˌdʒɑɪz/ *v* [T] to make something more active ○ *The candidate is trying to energize voters.*

POWER /ˈen·ər·dʒi/ *n* [C/U] ***physics*** power to do work that produces light, heat, or motion, or the fuel or electricity used for power ○ *Certain materials acquired the ability to carry an electric charge with no loss of energy.* ○ *The cost of energy rose last month.*

WORD FAMILY energy			
Nouns	energy	*Verbs*	energize
Adjectives	energetic	*Adverbs*	energetically

enervating /ˈen·ərˌveɪt̬·ɪŋ/ *adj* causing you to feel weak and lacking in energy ○ *We found it enervating to work in the humid jungle heat.*

enforce Ⓐ /ɪnˈfɔːrs, -ˈfoʊrs/ *v* [T] to cause a law or rule to be obeyed ○ *We need to enforce the traffic laws.*

enforcement Ⓐ /ɪnˈfɔːr·smənt, -ˈfoʊr-/ *n* [U] ○ *law enforcement*

enfranchise /ɪnˈfrænˌtʃɑɪz/ *v* [T] ***politics & government*** to give a person or group of people the right to vote in elections

enfranchisement /ɪnˈfrænˌtʃɑɪz·mənt/ *n* [U]

engage **INTEREST** /ɪnˈgeɪdʒ/ *v* [T] to cause someone to become interested or involved in an activity, or to attract someone's interest ○ *He wrote about things that engaged him.*

FIT TOGETHER /ɪnˈgeɪdʒ/ *v* [I/T] to fit one part of a machine into another so they move together, or cause something to fit into and move together ○ [I] *The gears won't engage.* ○ [T] *You need to engage second gear.*

BEGIN FIGHTING /ɪnˈgeɪdʒ/ *v* [T] to attack or begin to fight an enemy in a military operation ○ *The marines engaged the enemy.*

engagement /ɪnˈgeɪdʒ·mənt/ *n* [C] ○ *a military engagement* ○ See also: ENGAGEMENT; ENGAGEMENT at ENGAGED

EMPLOY /ɪnˈgeɪdʒ/ *v* [T] to arrange to employ someone; HIRE ○ *She decided to engage a personal assistant.* ○ *Her family engaged a tutor to teach her French.*

PHRASAL VERB with engage

• **engage in** *something* to take part in or do something ○ *Most students engage in extracurricular activities after school and on weekends.* ○ *The men were engaged in a heated dispute.*

engaged /ɪnˈgeɪdʒd/ *adj* [not gradable] publicly promising that you intend to marry someone ○ *They decided to get engaged.*

engagement /ɪnˈgeɪdʒ·mənt/ *n* [C] ○ *They announced their engagement.* ○ See also: ENGAGEMENT; ENGAGEMENT at ENGAGE BEGIN FIGHTING

engagement /ɪnˈgeɪdʒ·mənt/ *n* [C] an arrangement to do something or meet someone at a particular time and place ○ *We have a dinner engagement Thursday.* ○ *The Dance Theatre of Harlem began a two-week engagement at the Kennedy Center.* ○ *The governor has numerous speaking engagements* (= arrangements to give formal speeches) *next month.* ○ See also: ENGAGEMENT at ENGAGE BEGIN FIGHTING; ENGAGEMENT at ENGAGED

engagement ring *n* [C] a ring given by a man to a woman as a formal sign that they have decided to get married

engaging /ɪnˈgeɪ·dʒɪŋ/ *adj* tending to please; attractive ○ *He has an engaging manner.*

engender /ɪnˈdʒen·dər/ *v* [T] to cause something to come into existence ○ *Your book has engendered much controversy.*

engine /ˈen·dʒən/ *n* [C] **1** a machine that uses the energy from fuel or steam to produce movement ○ *The car has a four-cylinder engine.* ○ (fig.) *The health-care industry has been an engine of growth.* ○ *The plane was forced to land because of engine problems.* **2** An engine (also **locomotive**) is a separate part of a train that pulls the other parts of the train.

engineer **PERSON** /ˌen·dʒəˈnɪr/ *n* [C] **1** a person specially trained to design and build machines, structures, and other things, including bridges, roads, vehicles, and buildings ○ *He is an engineer at a large electronics company.* **2** An engineer is also a person whose job is to drive railroad trains.

engineer /ˌen·dʒəˈnɪr/ *v* [T] to plan, design, or build according to scientific principles ○ *The bridge is engineered to withstand an earthquake.*

engineering /ˌen·dʒəˈnɪr·ɪŋ/ *n* [U] the study of using scientific principles to design and build machines, structures, and other things, including bridges, roads, vehicles, and buildings ○ *civil/electrical/mechanical engineering* ○ *an engineering firm/degree*

PLAN SKILLFULLY /ˌen·dʒəˈnɪr/ *v* [T] to plan or do something in a skillful way ○ *The administration engineered a compromise.*

English /ˈɪŋ·glɪʃ, -lɪʃ/ *n* [U] [not gradable] **1** the language of the United Kingdom and the United States, used also in many other parts of the world ○ *American/British/Canadian/Australian English* **2** ***English*** English is also a subject in school where you study the English language, literature, and writing.

English as a foreign language, *abbreviation* **EFL** *n* [U] English as taught to people whose main language is not English and who live in a country where English is not the official or main language.

English as a second language, *abbreviation* **ESL** *n* [U] English as taught to people whose main language is not English and who live in a country where English is an official or main language.

English muffin /ˌɪŋ·glɪʃˈmʌf·ən, -lɪʃ-/ *n* [C] a type of small, flat, round bread that is usually heated before being eaten

engrave /ɪn ˈgreɪv/ *v* [T] **1** to cut a picture or design, or letters into the surface of a hard substance such as metal, wood, or stone ○ *The 2000-year-old ivories are intricately carved and engraved with scenes of palace life.* **2** If something is engraved in your memory, mind, or heart, it is something you will never forget.

engraving /ɪn ˈgreɪ·vɪŋ/ *n* [C/U] a picture or design printed on paper from a hard, usually metal, surface in which cuts have been made, or this process ○ [C] *The museum owns many fine 18th-century engravings.* ○ [U] *The book describes the art of engraving.*

E

engrossed /ɪn ˈgroʊst/ *adj* giving all your attention to something ○ *We were engrossed in conversation.*

engrossing /ɪŋ ˈgroʊ·sɪŋ/ *adj* taking all your attention; very interesting ○ *She had written an engrossing and moving story.*

engulf /ɪn ˈgʌlf/ *v* [T] to surround and cover completely ○ *Floodwaters engulfed midwestern farmlands.*

enhance Ⓐ /ɪn ˈhæns/ *v* [T] to improve the quality, amount, or strength of something ○ *The marinade enhances the flavor of the fish.* ○ *The county took steps to enhance water quality.*

enhancement Ⓐ /ɪn ˈhæn·smənt/ *n* [C/U] ○ [C] *The new system is a major enhancement in security.* ○ [U] *Enhancement of local transportation is a priority.*

enigma /ɪ ˈnɪg·mə/ *n* [C] someone or something that is mysterious and impossible to understand ○ *He is an enigma to most people.*

enigmatic /ˌen·ɪg ˈmæṭ·ɪk/ *adj* ○ *an enigmatic smile*

enjoin /ɪn ˈdʒɔɪn/ *v* [T] **1** to legally forbid or stop something by order of a court ○ *The prosecutor's office hopes the court will enjoin the city from enforcing the law.* **2** Enjoin also means to order or strongly encourage someone to do something: *Lawyers are enjoined to follow high ethical principals.*

enjoy LIKE TO DO /ɪn ˈdʒɔɪ/ *v* [T] **1** to feel happy because of doing or experiencing something ○ *We enjoyed the scenery.* ○ *I enjoyed your book very much.* ○ *Enjoy your weekend.* ○ *She liked her job because she enjoyed meeting people.* **2** To enjoy yourself is to feel happy because of a situation or an event in which you took part: *I really enjoyed myself last night.*

enjoyable /ɪn ˈdʒɔɪ·ə·bəl/ *adj* making you feel happy ○ *The kids had an enjoyable time at the movies.*

enjoyment /ɪn ˈdʒɔɪ·mənt/ *n* [U] ○ *He gets a lot of enjoyment from listening to music.*

GRAMMAR

enjoy

When **enjoy** is followed by a verb, the verb must be in the **-ing** form.

My parents enjoy walking in the mountains.

~~*My parents enjoy to walk in the mountains.*~~

WORD CHOICES enjoy

A more formal way of saying "enjoy" is **relish**.

Jonathan always ***relishes*** *a challenge.*

When someone enjoys a situation or activity very much, you can use the phrasal verbs **lap up** or **revel in**.

He ***lapped up*** *all the attention they gave him.*

She ***reveled in*** *her role as team manager.*

If someone enjoys doing something that other people think is unpleasant, the phrasal verb **delight in** is sometimes used.

She seems to ***delight in*** *making other people look stupid.*

The verb **savor** is sometimes used when someone enjoys something slowly so that he or she can appreciate it as much as possible.

It was the first chocolate he'd had for over a year, so he ***savored*** *every mouthful.*

When people enjoy themselves very much, in informal situations you can say that they are having a **ball** or a **whale of a** time.

We had a ***ball*** *in Miami.*

I had ***a whale of a*** *time on the class trip.*

BENEFIT /ɪn ˈdʒɔɪ/ *v* [T] to have the benefit of something ○ *The schools here enjoy strong community support.* ○ *She enjoyed good health well into her 90s.*

enjoyment /ɪn ˈjɔɪ·mənt/ *n* [U] benefit; use ○ *Public parks are for the enjoyment of all the people.*

WORD FAMILY enjoy

Nouns	enjoyment	*Verbs*	enjoy
Adjectives	enjoyable	*Adverbs*	enjoyably

enlarge /ɪn ˈlɑrdʒ/ *v* [T] **1** to become larger, or to cause something to become larger ○ *The city council voted to enlarge the park.* **2** If you enlarge a photograph, you print a bigger copy of it.

enlarged /ɪn ˈlɑrdʒd/ *adj* [not gradable] ○ *He suffers from an enlarged heart.*

enlargement /ɪn ˈlɑrdʒ·mənt/ *n* [C/U] ○ [C] *My mother had an enlargement of the photograph framed.* ○ [U] *The new budget would have resulted in enlargement of the deficit.*

PHRASAL VERB with enlarge

• **enlarge on/upon** [T] to speak or write about something in detail or in more detail ○ *I was asked to enlarge upon my theory.*

enlighten /ɪn ˈlɑɪt·ən/ *v* [I/T] to cause someone to understand something by explaining it or by bringing new information or facts to that person's attention ○ [I] *The show is meant to both enlighten and entertain.* ○ [T] *We hope the pamphlet will enlighten voters about the issues.*

enlightened /ɪn ˈlɑɪt·ənd/ *adj* **1** showing understanding and wisdom in dealing with others ○ *This company is an enlightened and reasonable employer.* **2** Enlightened also means open to new ideas and facts based on reason and science rather than following old, false beliefs: *Every enlightened person rejects racism in all its forms.*

enlightening /ɪn ˈlɑɪt·ᵊn·ɪŋ/ *adj* ○ *The discussion was enlightening.*

enlightenment /ɪn ˈlɑɪt·ᵊn·mənt/ *n* [U] **1** *Meditation helps me achieve enlightenment and serenity.* **2** ***world history*** The Enlightenment was the period in the 18th century in Europe when particular thinkers began to emphasize the importance of science and reason rather than religion and tradition.

enlist **JOIN** /ɪn ˈlɪst/ *v* [I] **1** to join (an organization, esp. the armed forces) ○ *He enlisted in the air force.* **2** An enlisted man/woman is a person in the armed forces who is not an officer.

ASK FOR HELP /ɪn ˈlɪst/ *v* [T] to ask someone for help or support, or to ask for and obtain help and support ○ *The program enlists businesses in hiring inner city kids.*

enliven /ɪn ˈlɑɪ·vən/ *v* [T] to make more interesting or active ○ *Entertainment enlivened the meeting.*

enmity /ˈen·mət̬·i/ *n* [U] strong dislike or hate

enormity Ⓐ **LARGENESS** /ɪˈnɔːr·mət̬·i/ *n* [U] great size or amount ○ *The enormity of the wilderness awed us.*

TERRIBLE QUALITY /ɪˈnɔːr·mət̬·i/ *n* [C/U] a terrible or immoral act, or how terrible or immoral something is ○ [U] *Shock over the enormity of the crime has subsided.* ○ [C] *Goya's etchings depict in shocking detail the enormities of war.*

enormous Ⓐ /ɪˈnɔːr·məs/ *adj* extremely large or great ○ *He ate an enormous helping of pasta.* ○ *The wealthy will get enormous tax cuts under the proposal.*

enormously Ⓐ /ɪˈnɔːr·mə·sli/ *adv* very or very much ○ *She was enormously rich.*

WORD FAMILY enormous

Nouns	enormity	*Adverbs*	enormously
Adjectives	enormous		

enough /ɪˈnʌf/ *adj, adv, pronoun* **1** as much as is necessary; in the amount or to the degree needed ○ *Do we have enough lettuce for a salad?* ○ *He had just enough time to make his train.* ○ [+ *to* infinitive] *Have you had enough to eat?* ○ [+ *to* infinitive] *I think she's well enough now to make the trip.* ○ *You'll find out when we're leaving soon enough.* **2** Enough can also mean as much or more than is wanted: *I think we've heard enough.* ○ [+ *to* infinitive] *I have enough to do without taking on any more work.*

IDIOMS with enough

• **enough is enough** this must stop ○ *The play was dull and I decided enough is enough and left early.*

• **strangely enough, funnily/oddly enough** *infml* even though it sounds unusual or strange ○ *You mentioned Chris Martin – well funnily enough I saw him yesterday after all these years!*

enrage /ɪnˈreɪdʒ/ *v* [T] to cause someone to become very angry ○ *School curriculum changes enraged a number of parents.* ○ *Enraged readers boycotted the newspaper.*

enrich /ɪn ˈrɪtʃ/ *v* [T] **1** to improve the quality of something by adding something else ○ *The heritage of Africa has greatly enriched American life.* ○ *Uranium is enriched for use in nuclear reactors.* **2** To enrich is also to make richer: *The rock music of the 1960s enriched the big recording companies.*

enrichment /ɪn ˈrɪtʃ·mənt/ *n* [U] ○ *a course offering language enrichment*

enroll /ɪn ˈroʊl/ *v* [I/T] to put yourself or someone else on an official list for an activity or for membership in a group, or to accept someone in such a list ○ [T] *We have enrolled eighty children in this day-care program.* ○ [I] *He enrolled at Penn State University.* ○ [+ *to* infinitive] *She enrolled in English.*

enrollment /ɪn ˈroʊl·mənt/ *n* [C] ○ [C] *Enrollments at medical schools are down this year.* ○ *Enrollment figures for next year are now available.*

en route /ɑn ˈruːt, en-, ɑ̃-/ *adv* [not gradable] on the way to or from somewhere ○ *The ambulance is en route to the hospital.* ○ *En route from New York to Boston, the bus crashed into a stalled car.*

ensconce /ɪn ˈskɑns/ *v* [T always + adv/prep] to put in a place or comfortable position as if to stay there ○ *She is fully ensconced in the Senate.* ○ *He was ensconced in a large armchair in his warm living room.*

ensemble /ɑn ˈsɑm·bəl, ɑ̃-/ *n* [C] a group of people who perform music together, or a collection of things intended to be used together ○ *a woodwind ensemble* ○ *I admired her ensemble of coat, hat, and shoes.*

enshrine /ɪn ˈʃrɑɪn/ *v* [T always + adv/prep] to contain or keep in a place that is highly admired and respected ○ *Only eight second basemen are enshrined in the baseball Hall of Fame.* ○ *This principle is enshrined in the Constitution.*

ensign **FLAG** /ˈen·sən/ *n* [C] a flag on a ship showing the country the ship belongs to

OFFICER /ˈen·sən/ *n* [C] a naval officer of the lowest rank

enslave /ɪn ˈsleɪv/ *v* [T] to control someone by keeping the person in a bad or difficult situation where the person is not free, or to make a SLAVE (= person legally owned) of someone

ensue /ɪn ˈsuː/ *v* [I] to happen after something else, esp. as a result of it ○ *Chaos ensued when 60 charter schools run by one company were all suddenly closed.* ○ *After his outburst, a long silence ensued.*

ensuing /ɪn ˈsuː·ɪŋ/ *adj* [not gradable] happening after or following something else ○ *In the ensuing decades he specialized in neurology.* ○ *Ensuing tests disclosed an irregular heartbeat.*

ensure Ⓐ /ɪn ˈʃʊr/ *v* [T] INSURE **MAKE CERTAIN**

entail /ɪn ˈteɪl/ *v* [T] to involve or make something necessary ○ *Any investment entails risk.*

entangle /ɪn ˈtæŋ·gəl/ *v* [T] to trap something within something else from which it is difficult to escape ○ *A seal became entangled in the fishing net.* ○ (*fig.*) *The movie explores the entangled* (= mixed together in many ways) *lives of the five characters.*

entanglement /ɪn'tæŋ·gəl·mənt/ *n* [C] **1** the condition of being wrapped and twisted together in a mass ○ *entanglements of cables and wires* **2** An entanglement is a situation or relationship that you are involved in and that is difficult to escape from: *a legal entanglement*

enter GO IN /'ent·ər/ *v* [I/T] **1** to come or go into a place ○ [T] *The orchestra entered the hall.* ○ [T] *He entered a shelter for the homeless.* ○ [I] *Half of the museum's visitors are children who enter for free.* **2** To enter is also to be admitted to or become a member of an organization: [I] *He entered the army at the age of 18.*

E

USAGE

enter

When it means to come or go into a place, the verb **enter** is not followed by a preposition.

I entered the classroom.

~~*I entered in the classroom.*~~

Be careful not to use **enter** when you are talking about getting into a vehicle.

She got into the car.

~~*She entered the car.*~~

BEGIN /'ent·ər/ *v* [I/T] to begin or become involved in something ○ [T] *The president maintained we were about to enter a period of unprecedented economic growth.* ○ [I] *She entered into an exclusive contract with an international sports shoe company.*

RECORD /'ent·ər/ *v* [T] **1** to make a record of something; list ○ *Did you enter your names in the guest book?* ○ *Use this computer to enter the data.* ○ *He was entered* (= listed officially as taking part) *in the shot put and discus events.* **2** *law* To enter is to make something, such as a statement or a piece of EVIDENCE, a part of the official record: *He entered a plea of not guilty.*

WORD FAMILY enter

Nouns	entrance entrant entry	*Verbs*	enter

enterprise /'ent·ər,prɑɪz/ *n* [C/U] **1** an organization, esp. a business, or a difficult and important plan, esp. one that will earn money ○ [U] *private enterprise* ○ [C] *The road is bordered by shopping centers, restaurants, retail outlets, and other commercial enterprises.* **2** Enterprise is also the willingness and energy to do something new that takes a lot of effort: [U] *They've showed a great deal of enterprise in setting up this project.*

enterprising /'ent·ər,prɑɪ·zɪŋ/ *adj* (of a person) good at thinking of and doing new and difficult things, esp. those that will make money ○ *The business was started by a couple of enterprising women.*

entertain AMUSE /,ent·ər'teɪn/ *v* [I/T] to keep a person or a group of people interested or amused ○ [I] *Children's games and books seek to teach and entertain at the same time.* ○ [T] *Kerry and Bill entertained listeners of their radio show with tales of their adventures on an ocean cruise.*

entertainer /,ent·ər'teɪ·nər/ *n* [C] someone who sings, dances, tells jokes, etc., as a job

entertaining /,ent·ər'teɪ·nɪŋ/ *adj* amusing and enjoyable ○ *an entertaining movie*

entertainment /,ent·ər'teɪn·mənt/ *n* [C/U] public shows, performances, or other ways of enjoying yourself ○ [C] *popular/family entertainment* ○ *the entertainment industry* ○ [U] *We've set a budget for household expenses, clothing, and entertainment.*

INVITE /,ent·ər'teɪn/ *v* [I/T] to invite one or more people to your house and give food and drink to them ○ [T] *She was a good cook and liked to entertain her friends with new dishes.* ○ [I] *We didn't entertain much over the holidays this year.*

THINK ABOUT /,ent·ər'teɪn/ *v* [T] to hold in your mind or to be willing to consider or accept ○ *He entertained some doubts about how truthful the government was.*

WORD FAMILY entertain

Nouns	entertainer entertainment	*Verbs*	entertain
		Adverbs	entertainingly
Adjectives	entertaining		

enthrall /ɪn'θrɔːl/ *v* [T] to keep someone completely interested ○ *I was always enthralled by the rotary engine, and thought it was a neat idea.*

enthralling /ɪn'θrɔː·lɪŋ/ *adj* ○ *Her performance was enthralling.*

enthuse /ɪn'θuːz/ *v* [I] to express excitement or interest ○ *You don't sound too enthused about the party tonight.*

enthusiasm /ɪn'θuː·ziː,æz·əm/ *n* [C/U] a feeling of energetic interest in a particular subject or activity and a desire to be involved in it, or a subject that produces such a feeling ○ [U] *I find that I'm losing my enthusiasm for the game.* ○ [C] *Parents need to share their enthusiasms with their children.*

enthusiast /ɪn'θuː·ziː,æst, -əst/ *n* [C] someone who is very interested in and involved with a particular subject or activity ○ *a computer-games enthusiast*

enthusiastic /ɪn,θuː·ziː'æs·tɪk/ *adj* ○ *You don't seem very enthusiastic about the movie.*

enthusiastically /ɪn,θuː·ziː'æs·tɪ·kli/ *adv* ○ *She was welcomed enthusiastically by the crowd.*

WORD FAMILY enthusiasm

Nouns	enthusiasm enthusiast	*Verbs*	enthuse
		Adverbs	enthusiastically
Adjectives	enthusiastic unenthusiastic		unenthusiastically

entice /ɪn'tɑɪs/ *v* [T] to attract someone to a particular place or activity by offering something pleasant or advantageous ○ *People are enticed away from government jobs by higher salaries.*

entire /ɪn'tɑɪr/ *adj* [not gradable] whole or complete, with nothing lacking, or continuous, without interruption ○ *He read the entire book on the flight to Buenos Aires.* ○ *Her entire family gathered for their annual reunion.* ○ *I spent an entire month writing that report.*

entirely /ɪn'tɑɪr·li/ *adv* [not gradable] ○ *I admit it was entirely my fault.*

entirety /ɪnˈtɑɪ·rəţ·i, -ˈtɑɪrţ·i/ *n* [U] Something **in its entirety** means all of something from beginning to end ○ *I never read the contract in its entirety, just parts of it.*

entitle ALLOW /ɪnˈtɑɪţ·əl/ *v* [T] to give someone the right to do or have something ○ *He's entitled to his opinion even if you don't agree with him.* ○ *Being over 65 entitles you to a discount at the movies.*

entitlement /ɪnˈtɑɪţ·əl·mənt/ *n* [C/U] something, often a benefit from the government, that you have the right to have ○ [U] *Social Security and Medicare are popular entitlement programs in the US.*

GIVE TITLE /ɪnˈtɑɪţ·əl/ *v* [T] to give a title to a book, movie, etc. ○ *Her latest novel, entitled "The Forgotten Child," is arriving in bookstores this week.*

entity Ⓐ /ˈent·əţ·i/ *n* [C] something that exists apart from other things, having its own independent existence ○ *Although the two buildings are in separate locations, the museum they are part of is a single entity.*

entourage /ˌɑn·tʊˈrɑʒ/ *n* [C] the group of people who travel with and work for an important or famous person ○ *Her usual entourage includes musicians, backup singers, and technicians.*

entrance WAY IN /ˈen·trəns/ *n* [C/U] **1** a door, gate, etc., by which you can enter a building or place ○ [C] *There are two entrances – one at the front and one at the back of the building.* **2** Entrance is also the right to be admitted to a place or to an organization: [U] *Entrance to the museum is free on Sundays.* ○ [U] *He took the entrance exam to law school yesterday.*

INTEREST /ɪnˈtræns/ *v* [T] to hold the complete interest and attention of someone ○ *We were entranced by mourners singing in glorious harmony, accompanied by guitar music.*

entrant /ˈen·trənt/ *n* [C] a person who takes part in a competition, or a new member of a school or organization ○ *All entrants in the race should go to the starting line now.*

entrap /ɪnˈtræp/ *v* [T] **-pp-** to deceive someone into doing something wrong so that the person will be caught

entrapment /ɪnˈtræp·mənt/ *n* [U] ○ *He claimed he was the victim of FBI entrapment.*

entrée /ˈɑn·treɪ/ *n* [C] the main dish of a meal

entrenched /ɪnˈtrentʃt/ *adj esp. disapproving* established firmly so that it cannot be changed ○ *An entrenched bureaucracy stalled Gorbachev's efforts to modernize Soviet society.*

entrepreneur /ˌɑn·trə·prəˈnɜr, -ˈnʊr/ *n* [C] a person who attempts to make a profit by starting a company or by operating alone in the business world, esp. when it involves taking risks ○ *He's an entrepreneur who made his money in computer software.*

entrepreneurial /ˌɑn·trə·prəˈnɜr·iː·əl, -ˈnʊr-/ *adj*

entropy /ˈen·trə·pi/, *symbol* S *n* [U] ***physics, chemistry*** a measure of the amount of heat ENERGY that is not available to do work

entrust /ɪnˈtrʌst/ *v* [T always + adv/prep] to make someone responsible for someone or something ○ *We entrusted our dog to a neighbor when we went away on a trip.*

entry WAY IN /ˈen·tri/ *n* [C/U] the act or manner of entering a place or of entering into an organization or relationship with others ○ [U] *America's entry into the war was delayed.* ○ [U] *Entry to the basement is through a back stairway.* ○ [U] *Police gained entry by breaking a window.*

COMPETITION /ˈen·tri/ *n* [C] a person or thing that is part of a competition ○ *There were five entries for best picture of the year.*

RECORD /ˈen·tri/ *n* [C] a single written item in a list or collection of records ○ *an entry in a diary*

DICTIONARY /ˈen·tri/ *n* [C] ***English*** a word listed in a dictionary and the information about it, or a subject in an ENCYCLOPEDIA

entryway /ˈen·triːˌweɪ/ *n* [C] an enclosed area through which you enter a building or a set of rooms within a building

entwine /ɪnˈtwɑɪn/ *v* [T] to twist together or around something ○ *The old-fashioned porch was entwined with many creeping plants.* ○ (fig.) *In the old days, moviemaking was entwined with political and social life.*

enumerate /ɪˈnuː·məˌreɪt/ *v* [T] to name things separately, one by one ○ *The salesman enumerated the features of the car.*

enunciate /ɪˈnʌn·siːˌeɪt/ *v* [I/T] *fml* **1** to state something clearly and often officially ○ [T] *The administration enunciated a new policy on security issues.* **2** To enunciate is also to pronounce words: [T] *He enunciated his words carefully.*

envelop /ɪnˈvel·əp/ *v* [T] to cover or surround something completely ○ *The entire area was enveloped in fog.*

envelope /ˈen·vəˌloʊp, ˈɑn-/ *n* [C] a usually rectangular paper container for a letter ○ *Don't forget to put a stamp on the envelope.*

enviable /ˈen·viː·ə·bəl/ *adj* ○ See at ENVY

envious /ˈen·viː·əs/ *adj* ○ See at ENVY

environment Ⓐ NATURE /ɪnˈvɑɪ·rən·mənt, -ˈvɑɪrn-/ *n* [U] ***earth science*** the air, water, and land in or on which people, animals, and plants live ○ *We're trying to protect the environment from pollution.*

environmental Ⓐ /ɪnˌvɑɪ·rənˈment·əl, -ˌvɑɪrn-/ *adj* [not gradable] ***earth science*** ○ *We're here to discuss environmental issues.*

environmentalist Ⓐ /ɪnˌvɑɪ·rənˈment·əl·əst, -ˌvɑɪrn-/ *n* [C] ***earth science*** a person who has a specially strong interest in or knowledge of the natural environment, and who wants to preserve it and prevent damage to it ○ *Environmentalists are working to improve the quality of our lakes and rivers.*

environmentally Ⓐ /ɪnˌvɑɪ·rənˈment·əl·i, -ˌvɑɪrn-/ *adv* [not gradable] ***earth science*** ➤ Usage: **nature, the environment, or the countryside?** at NATURE LIFE

E

SURROUNDINGS /ɪnˈvɑɪ·rən·mənt, -ˈvɑɪrn-/ *n* [C] the conditions that you live or work in and the way that they influence how you feel or how effectively you can work ○ *a good business environment* ○ *For preschoolers, the most stimulating environments are bright, airy, and offer daily outdoor activities.*

WORD FAMILY environment	
Nouns environment environmentalist	*Adjectives* environmental *Adverbs* environmentally

E

environs /ɪnˈvɑɪ·rənz, -ˈvɑɪ·ərnz/ *pl n* the area surrounding a place, esp. a town

envision /ɪnˈvɪʒ·ən/, **envisage** /ɪnˈvɪz·ɪdʒ/ *v* [T] to imagine or expect that something is a likely or desirable possibility in the future ○ *He envisioned a partnership between business and government.* ○ *The company envisions adding at least five stores next year.*

envoy /ˈen·vɔɪ, ˈɑn-/ *n* [C] someone who is sent as a representative from one government or organization to another

envy /ˈen·vi/ *v* [T] to wish that you had a quality or possession that another person has ○ *I envy people so much who feel carefree.*
envy /ˈen·vi/ *n* [U] ○ *His new car is the envy of* (= liked and wanted by) *all his friends.*
enviable /ˈen·viː·ə·bəl/ *adj* (esp. of a quality or advantage) causing you to wish that you also possessed it; desirable ○ *She has an enviable ability to work under pressure.*
envious /ˈen·viː·əs/ *adj* wanting something another person has ○ *I'm envious of people that have those big boats.*

enzyme /ˈen·zɑɪm/ *n* [C] ***biology*** any of a group of chemical substances that are produced by living cells and which cause particular chemical reactions to happen

ephemeral /ɪˈfem·ə·rəl/ *adj* lasting for only a short time ○ *ephemeral fame*

epic /ˈep·ɪk/ *n* [C] **1** a book or movie that is long and contains a lot of action, usually about a subject from the past **2** ***literature*** An epic is also a long poem about events in the past, often involving gods or kings and queens: *The Iliad is the most famous Greek epic.*
epic /ˈep·ɪk/ *adj* happening over a long period and including a lot of difficulties ○ *an epic struggle to achieve equality for African Americans*

epicenter /ˈep·ɪˌsent·ər/ *n* [C] ***earth science*** **1** the point on the earth's surface directly above the origin of an EARTHQUAKE ○ *The Great Nicobar islands lie at the closest point to the epicenter of the earthquake.* **2** An epicenter is also the place that has the highest level of an activity: *The U.S. cannot simply assume that it will remain the epicenter of scientific research and technological innovation.*

epidemic /ˌep·əˈdem·ɪk/ *n* [C] the appearance of a particular disease in a very large number of people during the same period of time ○ *a flu epidemic*

epidermis /ˌep·əˈdɜr·məs/ *n* [C/U] ***biology*** the thin outer layer of the skin

epiglottis /ˌep·əˈglɑt̬·əs/ *n* [C] ***biology*** a flat part at the back of the tongue, which closes when you swallow to stop food from entering the tube that air goes down

epigram /ˈep·əˌgræm/ *n* [C] a short saying or poem that expresses an idea in an amusing way

epilepsy /ˈep·əˌlep·si/ *n* [U] a disease of the brain that may cause a person to become unconscious and fall, and to lose control of his or her movements for a short time
epileptic /ˌep·əˈlep·tɪk/ *adj* [not gradable]

epilogue /ˈep·əˌlɑg, -ˌlɔːg/ *n* [C] ***literature*** a speech or piece of text added to the end of a play or book, often giving a short statement about what happens to the characters after the play or book finishes

Episcopal /ɪˈpɪs·kə·pəl/ *adj* [not gradable] of a Christian religious group that is one of the Protestant churches ○ *an Episcopal church/minister*
Episcopalian /ɪˌpɪs·kəˈpeɪl·jən/ *n* [C] ○ *George is an Episcopalian.*
Episcopalian /ɪˌpɪs·kəˈpeɪl·jən/ *adj* [not gradable]

episode /ˈep·əˌsoʊd/ *n* [C] **1** a single event or group of related events ○ *That was an episode in my life that I'd like to forget.* **2** ***literature*** An episode is a series of actions or events that take place at one time in a work of literature. **3** An episode is also one of the parts of a television or radio program that is given as a series over a period of time.

epitaph /ˈep·əˌtæf/ *n* [C] a short piece of writing or a poem about a dead person, esp. one written on a TOMBSTONE (= the stone over the place where someone is buried)

epithet /ˈep·əˌθet/ *n* [C] a word or phrase to describe someone, often as an insult ○ *a racial epithet* ○ *His stubbornness earned him the epithet "Senator No."*

epitome /ɪˈpɪt̬·ə·mi/ *n* [U] the typical or highest example of a stated quality, as shown by a particular person or thing ○ *He was the epitome of the fashionable gentleman.*
epitomize /ɪˈpɪt̬·əˌmɑɪz/ *v* [T] ○ *His recordings came to epitomize American popular singing at its finest.*

epoch /ˈep·ək, -ˌɑk/ *n* [C] *pl* **epochs** a long period of time, esp. one in which there are new advances and great change

equal **SAME IN AMOUNT** /ˈiː·kwəl/, *symbol* = *adj* ***mathematics*** the same in amount, number, or size ○ *One quart is equal to four cups.* ○ *Divide the class into equal groups.*
equal /ˈiː·kwəl/, *symbol* = *v* ***mathematics*** ○ [L] *10 + 10 = 20* ○ [T] *We hope to equal the amount of money we raised last year.*
equally /ˈiː·kwə·li/ *adj* ○ *The money was shared equally among the three sisters.*

DESERVING THE SAME /ˈiː·kwəl/ *adj* the same in importance and (of people) deserving the same treatment ○ *equal rights* ○ *We want a society that promotes equal opportunity for all of its citizens.*

equal /ˈiː·kwəl/ *n* [C] ○ *In this country, we're all equals with the same rights.* ○ *As an all-around athlete he has no equal* (= no one else is as good).

equality /ɪˈkwɑl·ət̬·i/ *n* [U] the right of different groups of people to receive the same treatment ○ *racial equality*

equal protection *n* [U] ***US history*** a principle included in the 14th AMENDMENT that says all people are to be treated equally by the law

equal sign, equals sign *n* [C] ***mathematics*** the symbol = used between two written things to show that they are the same, esp. between the parts of a mathematical EQUATION

equanimity /ˌek·wəˈnɪm·ət̬·i, ˌiː·kwə-/ *n* [U] the state of being calm and in control of your emotions, esp. in a difficult situation ○ *In spite of her financial troubles, she faced the future with equanimity.*

equate Ⓐ /ɪˈkweɪt/ *v* [T always + adv/prep] to consider as the same, or to connect in your mind ○ *People sometimes equate money with happiness.*

equation Ⓐ /ɪˈkweɪ·ʒən/ *n* [C] ***mathematics*** a mathematical statement that two amounts, or two symbols or groups of symbols representing an amount, are equal ○ *In the equation 3x - 3 = 15, x equals 6.*

equator /ɪˈkweɪt̬·ər/ *n* [U] ***earth science*** an imaginary line around the earth or another planet at an equal distance from the North Pole and the South Pole ➤ Picture: **earth**

equatorial /ˌek·wəˈtɔːr·iː·əl, ˌiː·kwə-/ *adj* ***earth science*** near the earth's or another planet's equator, or typical of areas at and near the equator ○ *the equatorial Pacific*

equestrian /ɪˈkwes·triː·ən/ *adj* [not gradable] **1** connected with the riding of horses **2** An equestrian statue is a statue of a person on a horse.

equidistant /ˌiː·kwəˈdɪs·tənt/ *adj* ***mathematics*** equally distant

equilateral triangle /ˌiː·kwəˈlæt̬·ə·rəl ˈtrɑɪˌæŋ·gəl, ˌek·wə-/ *n* [C] ***geometry*** a triangle that has all sides the same length ➤ Picture: **triangle**

equilibrant /ˌek·wəˈlɪb·rənt, ɪˈkwɪl·ə·brənt/ *n* [C] ***physics*** a force that is able to balance a system of forces

equilibrium /ˌiː·kwəˈlɪb·riː·əm, ˌek·wə-/ *n* [U] **1** a state of balance ○ *He devised a mathematical method to prove the existence of equilibrium among prices, production, and consumer demand.* **2** ***biology*** Equilibrium is also the state of balance maintained by the various organisms that live in a particular environment. **3** ***physics*** Equilibrium also means a state of balance between opposing forces. **4** Equilibrium is also a state of mental calm.

equinox /ˈiː·kwəˌnɑks, ˈek·wə-/ *n* [C] either of the two times during the year when the sun crosses the equator and day and night are of equal length, about March 21st and September 23rd ○ Compare SOLSTICE

equip Ⓐ **PROVIDE** /ɪˈkwɪp/ *v* [T] **-pp-** to provide someone or something with objects that are needed for a particular activity or purpose ○ *All of our classrooms are equipped with computers.*

equipment Ⓐ /ɪˈkwɪp·mənt/ *n* [U] the set of tools, clothing, etc., needed for a particular activity or purpose ○ *computer/electrical/farm equipment*

> **GRAMMAR**
>
> **equipment**
>
> Remember **equipment** is uncountable and cannot be plural.
>
> *Have you packed all the camping equipment?*
>
> ~~*Have you packed all the camping equipments?*~~

PREPARE /ɪˈkwɪp/ *v* [T] **-pp-** to prepare someone or something with whatever is needed to deal with a particular situation ○ *The convention center is equipped to handle 20,000 people daily.* ○ *I am not really equipped to discuss international affairs.*

equitable /ˈek·wət̬·ə·bəl/ *adj* treating everyone equally; fair ○ *She charged that women are being denied equitable pay.*

equity /ˈek·wət̬·i/ *n* [U] equal treatment; fairness

equity /ˈek·wət̬·i/ *n* [C/U] **1** the money value of a property or business after debts have been subtracted ○ [U] *How much equity do you have in your home?* **2** An equity is also one of the equal parts, or shares, into which the value of a company is divided.

equivalent Ⓐ /ɪˈkwɪv·ə·lənt/ *adj* **1** equal to or having the same effect as something else ○ *A mile is equivalent to about 1.6 kilometers.* **2** ***mathematics*** **Equivalent equations** are two EQUATIONS (= mathematical statements) that have the same solutions.

equivalent /ɪˈkwɪv·ə·lənt/ *n* [C] ○ *A day on the planet Mercury is the equivalent of 176 days on Earth.*

equivocal /ɪˈkwɪv·ə·kəl/ *adj* (of statements) unclear and seeming to have two opposing meanings, or (of actions or ways of behaving) confusing and able to be understood in two different ways ○ *She gave an equivocal response.*

ER *n* [C] *abbreviation for* EMERGENCY ROOM (= the place in a hospital for people who need immediate medical care) ○ *You should go to the ER if you have chest pains.*

era /ˈɪr·ə, ˈer·ə, ˈiː·rə/ *n* [C] a period of time known for particular events or developments ○ *She was one of the more remarkable women of her era.*

eradicate /ɪˈræd·əˌkeɪt/ *v* [T] to get rid of or destroy something completely ○ *A new vaccine eradicated polio.*

erase **DESTROY** /ɪˈreɪs/ *v* [T] to destroy or remove something completely ○ *A subdirectory filled with precious data can be erased if you are not careful.*

RUB AWAY /ɪˈreɪs/ *v* [T] to remove something written or a mark by rubbing ○ *I kept changing my mind and erasing my answers on the test.*

eraser /ɪ'reɪ·sər/ *n* [C] a small piece of rubber that can be used to remove marks, esp. pencil marks on paper

erect BUILD /ɪ'rekt/ *v* [T] to build a building or other structure ○ *They decided to erect a bridge across the Niagara Gorge.*
VERTICAL /ɪ'rekt/ *adj* in a straight vertical position ○ *erect posture*
erect /ɪ'rekt/ *v* [T] to put up or raise to a vertical position ○ *They're erecting a big circus tent.*

E

erode Ⓐ /ɪ'roʊd/ *v* [I/T] **1** to weaken or damage something by taking away parts of it gradually, or to become weaker in this way ○ [T] *Budget cuts could further erode the benefit package provided for by the contract.* **2** ***earth science*** If a natural feature or physical object erodes, it is damaged by the effect of weather.
erosion Ⓐ /ɪ'roʊ·ʒən/ *n* [U] **1** the weakening or damage done to something by a series of gradual losses of parts of it ○ *an erosion of academic standards* **2** ***earth science*** Erosion of a natural feature or physical object is damage caused by the effect of weather: *soil erosion*
erosional /ɪ'roʊ·ʒən·əl/ *adj* ***earth science***

erotic /ɪ'rɑt̬·ɪk/ *adj* causing or related to sexual feelings

err /er, ɜr/ *v* [I] to make a mistake ○ *It's preferable to err on the side of caution* (= to be too careful) *rather than risk disaster.*

errand /'er·ənd/ *n* [C] a short trip you make to do something, such as buying or delivering things in the neighborhood ○ *He would clean, do errands, and babysit for their 7-year-old daughter.* ○ *I've got to* **run** *a few* **errands** (= do errands) *and then stop by my mother's.*

errant /'er·ənt/ *adj* [not gradable] **1** going in a wrong direction ○ *An errant throw cost them the game.* **2** not correctly done or not behaving well ○ *Teachers dislike errant spellings and misused words.*

erratic /ɪ'ræt̬·ɪk/ *adj* changing suddenly and unexpectedly ○ *an erratic schedule*

erroneous Ⓐ /ɪ'roʊ·niː·əs/ *adj* based on false information and therefore wrong; false ○ *an erroneous assumption*
erroneously Ⓐ /ɪ'roʊ·niː·ə·sli/ *adv*

error Ⓐ /'er·ər/ *n* [C/U] a mistake, esp. in a way that can be discovered as wrong, or the making of such mistakes ○ [C] *a spelling/mathematical error* ○ [U] *Investigators said the train crash was caused by human error rather than mechanical failure.* ➤ Usage: **fault or mistake/error?** at FAULT SOMETHING WRONG

erudite /'er·jə,dɑɪt/ *adj fml* having or showing a lot of knowledge, esp. from reading and studying ○ *She is a scholarly and erudite person.*

erupt /ɪ'rʌpt/ *v* [I] **1** to burst out suddenly or explode ○ *The crowd erupted in cheers.* ○ *The building erupted in flames when the plane struck it.* **2** ***earth science*** If a VOLCANO (= type of mountain) erupts, it begins to throw out hot rocks and burning substances.
eruption /ɪ'rʌp·ʃən/ *n* [C] ***earth science***

escalate /'es·kə,leɪt/ *v* [I/T] to make or become greater or more serious ○ [T] *Sending in more troops would escalate the war.* ○ [I] *Our costs escalated considerably over the next few years.*
escalating /'es·kə,leɪt̬·ɪŋ/ *adj* [not gradable] ○ *escalating tensions/prices*
escalation /,es·kə'leɪ·ʃən/ *n* [C/U] the process of becoming greater or more serious, or a particular situation when this happens ○ [U] *the escalation of costs* ○ [C] *military escalation*

escalator /'es·kə,leɪt̬·ər/ *n* [C] a set of stairs that moves by electric power and on which people can stand to be taken up and down from one level to another, usually within a building

escapade /'es·kə,peɪd/ *n* [C usually pl] an act or situation that is exciting because it shows behavior that is not controlled as it usually is ○ *Their escapades sound as if they could be ripped from the pages of "Tom Sawyer" and "Huckleberry Finn."*

escape /ɪ'skeɪp/ *v* [I/T] to become free or get free from, or to avoid something ○ [I] *to escape from prison/a burning house* ○ [T] *The book's faults have not escaped the notice of* (= not been avoided being noticed by) *critics.*
escape /ɪ'skeɪp/ *n* [C/U] **1** the act or possibility of becoming free or getting away from a place where you are kept esp. by force, or of avoiding a dangerous situation ○ [C] *The blast knocked me down – it was a narrow escape* (= I was almost hurt badly). **2** An escape is also an unintentional loss: [C] *an escape of radioactive fuel*

WORD FAMILY escape			
Nouns	escape escapism	*Verbs*	escape
		Adverbs	inescapably
Adjectives	inescapable		

escapism /ɪ'skeɪ,pɪz·əm/ *n* [U] the activity of avoiding reality by imagining exciting but impossible activities

escarpment /ɪ'skɑrp·mənt/ *n* [C] ***earth science*** a long, high area of continuous rock that has one steep side

eschew /ɪs'tʃuː/ *v* [T] *fml* to avoid something intentionally, or to give up something ○ *The leaders of the organization eschewed the term "union," preferring "guild."*

escort /ɪs'kɔːrt, es-/ *v* [T] to go with someone or something as a companion or guard ○ *He escorted her to her car in the parking lot because it was after dark.*
escort /'es·kɔːrt/ *n* [C] a companion or guard for someone or something ○ *Anytime a clerk transfers money, he is provided with an armed escort.*

Eskimo /'es·kə,moʊ/, **Inuit** *n* [C] *pl* **Eskimos** a member of a group of people who live in the cold northern areas of North America, Russia, and Greenland ○ **USAGE:** This word is considered offensive by some people. In Canada and Greenland, the preferred name is Inuit.

ESL *n* [U] *abbreviation for* ENGLISH AS A SECOND LANGUAGE ○ *Luisa teaches ESL in California.*

esophagus /ɪˈsɑf·ə·gəs/ *n* [C] ***biology*** the tube in the body that carries food from the mouth to the stomach

esoteric /ˌes·əˈter·ɪk/ *adj* intended for or understood by only a few people who have special knowledge ○ *Literary readings can sometimes seem esoteric, but we are trying to make them more attractive to more people.*

esp. *adv abbreviation for* ESPECIALLY

especially /ɪˈspeʃ·li, -ə·li/ *adv* (used to emphasize the importance of one thing among others of its type or to point to one thing among others) very; particularly ○ *He was especially fond of his youngest brother.* ○ *She campaigned throughout the US, but especially in the northeast.* ➤ Confusables: **specially or especially?** at SPECIAL PARTICULAR

espionage /ˈes·piː·əˌnɑʒ, *Cdn often* -ˌnæʒ/ *n* [U] the discovering of a country's or business organization's secrets by using SPIES (= people who secretly gather information within a country or organization) ○ *industrial espionage*

espouse /ɪsˈpɑʊz/ *v* [T] *fml* to support an activity or opinion ○ *He espoused conservative political views.*

espresso /esˈpres·oʊ, ɪkˈspres-/ *n* [C/U] *pl* **espressos** coffee made by forcing steam through crushed coffee beans and served without milk, or a small cup filled with this coffee

esprit de corps /esˌpriːd·əˈkɔːr, -ˈkoʊr/ *n* [U] the proud and comfortable feeling that you are a member of a group whose purpose you believe in ○ *People who live on houseboats have a certain esprit de corps.*

essay /ˈes·eɪ/ *n* [C] **1** ***literature*** a short piece of writing on a particular subject, often expressing personal views **2** In a school test, an essay is a written answer that includes information and discussion, usually to test how well the student understands the subject.

essence IMPORTANCE /ˈes·əns/ *n* [U] **1** the basic meaning or importance of something ○ *The essence of punk was a revolt against both the sound and the system of popular music.* **2 In essence** means that what follows is a brief statement of the basic meaning of something: *In essence, she's saying that she may quit her job.*

SMELL/TASTE /ˈes·əns/ *n* [C] a chemical substance obtained from plants that has a strong smell or taste and can be used to flavor foods or provide a pleasant smell, such as in PERFUMES

WORD FAMILY essence			
Nouns	essence essentials	*Adjectives* *Adverbs*	essential essentially

essential /ɪˈsen·tʃəl/ *adj* **1** extremely important or necessary ○ *A knowledge of Spanish is essential for this job.* **2** Essential also means basic to the nature of someone or something: *There is an essential difference between the two sisters in their approach to life.*

essential /ɪˈsen·tʃəl/ *n* [C usually pl] **1** the basic things you need to live ○ *The study estimated the cost of essentials for a family of four – its food, shelter, and clothing needs.* **2** Essentials are also the basic or most important part of something: *the essentials of chemistry*

essentially /ɪˈsen·tʃə·li/ *adv* [not gradable] ○ *Essentially she's saying that she is not interested in seeing you again.*

establish Ⓐ **START** /ɪˈstæb·lɪʃ/ *v* [T] to start something that will last for a long time, or to create or set something in a particular way ○ *He helped to establish the University of California at Berkeley.* ○ *Once we establish the price, we can begin to market the product.*

establishment Ⓐ /ɪˈstæb·lɪʃ·mənt/ *n* [U] ○ *She called for the establishment of nationwide academic standards.*

ACCEPT /ɪˈstæb·lɪʃ/ *v* [T] to cause someone or something to be accepted generally ○ *She's established herself as a leading authority on urban problems.*

established Ⓐ /ɪˈstæb·lɪʃt/ *adj* generally accepted or familiar, esp. because of having a long history ○ *an established procedure*

PROVE /ɪˈstæb·lɪʃ/ *v* [T] to prove something or show the state of something, esp. by collecting facts or information about it ○ *The coroner has not yet established the cause of death.* ○ [+ question word] *We're trying to establish what happened here.*

establishment Ⓐ /ɪˈstæb·lɪʃ·mənt/ *n* [C] **1** the people who have most of the power within government or society or in a particular business or activity ○ *the diplomatic/educational/literary establishment* **2** An establishment is a particular place of business: ○ *Visitors come to shop in the fashionable new establishments downtown.*

estate Ⓐ /ɪˈsteɪt/ *n* [C] **1** a large, privately owned area of land in the country, often with a large house **2** *law* A person's estate is everything the person owns when he or she dies. **3** *Br* An estate is a group of houses or factories built in a planned way.

estate agent *n* [C] *Br* a REAL ESTATE AGENT.

Estates-General, **States General** *n* [U] ***world history*** the legislative ASSEMBLY in France until 1789, made up of CLERGY, the NOBILITY, and ordinary people

esteem /ɪˈstiːm/ *n* [U] respect for or a high opinion of someone ○ *We held them in high/low esteem* (= We respected them a lot/very little).

esteemed /ɪˈstiːm/ *adj fml* highly respected ○ *It is my honor to introduce our esteemed senator.*

ester /ˈes·tər/ *n* [C] ***chemistry*** any of several substances produced by a reaction between an acid and an alcohol

esterification /eˌster·ə·fəˈkeɪ·ʃən/ *n* [U] ***chemistry*** the process of changing a substance into an ESTER

E

esthetic /es'θet̬·ɪk, ɪs-/ *adj* AESTHETIC

estimable /'es·tə·mə·bəl/ *adj* [not gradable] *fml* considered with respect ○ *She ran an estimable if obscure publishing house for nearly fifty years.*

estimate Ⓐ /'es·tə·mət/ *n* [C] **1** a judgment or calculation of approximately how large or how great something is ○ *I can only make a rough estimate* (= an amount that is not exact) *of how many people will attend.* **2** An estimate is also a statement of the likely cost of building something or doing some other work.

estimate Ⓐ /'es·tə,meɪt/ *v* [T] ○ *We estimated his wealth at $500 million.* ○ [+ (*that*) clause] *Doctors estimate (that) he has a 70 percent chance of recovering.*

estimation Ⓐ /,es·tə'meɪ·ʃən/ *n* [U] judgment; opinion ○ *The first novel was successful, whereas the second, in my estimation, was not.*

WORD FAMILY estimate			
Nouns	estimate	Verbs	estimate
	estimation		overestimate
			underestimate

estranged /ɪ'streɪndʒd/ *adj* [not gradable] lacking interest in and no longer close or friendly with someone, esp. a family member or friend

estrogen /'es·trə·dʒən/ *n* [U] ***biology*** a female HORMONE (= chemical substance produced in the body) that is important in sexual development and that causes changes in the uterus

estuary /'es·tʃə,wer·i/ *n* [C] the part of a river or other area of water where it joins the sea, and where fresh water and salt water are mixed

et al. /et̬'æl/ *adv abbreviation for* et alii (= and other people) ○ *The method is described in an article by Feynman et al.* ○ **USAGE:** Used, esp. in writing, after one or more names.

etc. /et,set̬·ə·rə, ɪt-, -'se·trə/ *adv abbreviation for* et cetera (= and other similar things) ○ *The children use computers in many instructional areas, including math, science, language study, etc.* ○ **USAGE:** Used after a list.

etch /etʃ/ *v* [T] to cut a pattern, picture, etc., in a surface ○ *Rory ordered a baseball bat with his own name etched in the wood.* ○ (*fig.*) *The building had become etched in clear detail in her mind.*

etching /'etʃ·ɪŋ/ *n* [C] a picture produced by printing from a metal plate that has been prepared with acid

eternal /ɪ'tɜrn·əl, iː-/ *adj* [not gradable] lasting forever, or seeming to be without end ○ *They swore eternal loyalty to each other.*

eternally /ɪ'tɜrn·əl·i, iː-/ *adv* [not gradable] ○ *I'd be eternally grateful if you'd handle it.*

eternity /ɪ'tɜr·nət̬·i, iː-/ *n* [U] time that never ends ○ *At her age, even a few months can seem like an eternity.*

ethane /'eθ·eɪn/ *n* [U] ***chemistry*** a gas with no smell or color, which burns easily and is found in NATURAL GAS and PETROLEUM

ethanol /'eθ·ə,nɔːl, -,noʊl/, **ethyl alcohol** *n* [U] ***chemistry*** a colorless alcohol made from grain and sugar that is VOLATILE (= easily changes to a gas) and burns easily, and is used in medicines and other substances and in alcoholic drinks

ethene /'eθ·iːn/ *n* [U] ***chemistry*** ETHYLENE

ether /'iː·θər/ *n* [U] ***chemistry*** a colorless liquid used, esp. in the past, to put people to sleep before an operation

ethereal /ɪ'θɪr·iː·əl/ *adj* extremely light and delicate, as if not of this world ○ *ethereal music* ○ *an ethereal beauty*

ethic Ⓐ /'eθ·ɪk/ *n* [C usually pl] a system of accepted beliefs that control behavior, esp. such a system based on morals ○ *Our school promotes an ethic of service to the community.*

ethical Ⓐ /'eθ·ɪ·kəl/ *adj* ○ *No ethical physician would prescribe that drug.*

ethically Ⓐ /'eθ·ɪ·kli/ *adv* ○ *Laughing at your clients is ethically wrong.*

ethics Ⓐ /'eθ·ɪks/ *n* [U] the study of what is morally right and wrong, or a set of beliefs about what is morally right and wrong ○ *They're completely lacking in ethics.*

ethnic Ⓐ /'eθ·nɪk/ *adj* relating to or characteristic of a large group of people who have the same national, racial, or cultural origins, and who usually speak the same language ○ *an ethnic neighborhood* ○ *She loves ethnic foods, especially Ethiopian and Japanese.*

ethnically /'eθ·nɪ·kli/ *adv* ○ *an ethnically diverse community*

ethnicity Ⓐ /eθ'nɪs·ət̬·i/ *n* [C/U] ○ [U] *They place no importance on ethnicity.*

ethnic cleansing *n* [U] ***world history*** the organized, often violent attempt by one cultural or racial group to remove from a country or area all members of a different group

ethnocentric /,eθ·noʊ'sen·trɪk/ *adj* ***social studies*** preferring a particular race or culture to all others

ethnocentrism /,eθ·noʊ'sen·trɪz·əm/ *n* [U] belief that a particular race or culture is better than others

ethos /'iː·θɑs/ *n* [U] the set of moral beliefs, attitudes, habits, etc., that are characteristic of a person or group ○ *Violence is part of their ethos.*

ethylene /'eθ·ə,liːn/, **ethene** /'eθ·iːn/ *n* [U] ***chemistry*** a colorless gas with a slightly sweet smell that burns easily and is often used in industry

etiquette /'et̬·ə·kət/ *n* [U] the set of rules or customs that control accepted behavior in particular social groups or social situations

etymology /,et̬·ə'mɑl·ə·dʒi/ *n* [C/U] ***English*** the origin and history of a word or words, or the study of word origins

EU *n* [U] *abbreviation for* EUROPEAN UNION

Eucharist /'juː·kə·rəst/ *n* [U] the Christian ceremony based on Jesus's last meal with those who followed him, or the bread and wine used in this ceremony

eukaryotic /ˌjuː ˌkær·iː ˈɑt̬·ɪk/ *adj* [not gradable] ***biology*** (of a cell) containing a NUCLEUS and other structures, each with its own purpose

eulogy /ˈjuː·lə·dʒi/ *n* [C/U] a speech or piece of writing containing great praise, esp. for someone who has recently died ○ [C] *He delivered the eulogy at his father's funeral.*

eunuch /ˈjuː·nək, -nɪk/ *n* [C] *pl* **eunuchs** a man who has been CASTRATED (= had the sex organs that produce sperm removed)

euphemism /ˈjuː·fəˌmɪz·əm/ *n* [C/U] the use of a word or phrase to avoid saying another word or phrase that may be unpleasant or offensive, or the word or phrase used ○ [C] *The phrase "left to pursue other interests" is a euphemism for "fired."*
euphemistic /ˌjuː·fəˈmɪs·tɪk/ *adj* ○ *euphemistic words for "dead"*

euphoria /jʊˈfɔːr·iː·ə, -ˈfoʊr-/ *n* [U] a feeling of extreme happiness or confidence ○ *We were caught up in the euphoria of the moment.*
euphoric /jʊˈfɔːr·ɪk, -ˈfɑr-/ *adj* ○ *a euphoric expression* ○ *a euphoric mood*

euro /ˈjʊr·oʊ/ *n* [C] *pl* **euros** the basic unit of money of the European Union

European /ˌjʊr·əˈpiː·ən/ *adj, n* [C] (a person) of or coming from Europe

European Union, *abbreviation* **EU** *n* [U] a group of European countries that act together in political and economic matters

euthanasia /ˌjuː·θəˈneɪ·ʒə/ *n* [U] the killing of someone who is very ill to end the person's suffering

evacuate /ɪˈvæk·jəˌweɪt/ *v* [I/T] **1** to remove people from a dangerous place ○ [T] *Residents were ordered to evacuate the area before the hurricane made landfall.* **2** ***science*** Evacuate means to remove something, esp. a gas or liquid, from a container.
evacuation /ɪˌvæk·jəˈweɪ·ʃən/ *n* [C/U] ○ [U] *A chemical spill prompted the evacuation of area residents.*

evade /ɪˈveɪd/ *v* [T] to avoid something unpleasant or unwanted, or to manage not to do (something that should be done) ○ *She's trying to evade my questions.* ○ *He was convicted of evading taxes.*
evasion /ɪˈveɪ·ʒən/ *n* [C/U] ○ [U] *tax evasion* ○ [C] *a political speech full of evasions*
evasive /ɪˈveɪ·sɪv, -zɪv/ *adj* ○ *Are you being deliberately evasive?* ○ *The pilot had to take evasive action to avoid the other plane.*

evaluate Ⓐ /ɪˈvæl·jəˌweɪt/ *v* [T] to judge or calculate the quality, importance, amount, or value of something ○ *Doctors evaluate the patient's condition.* ○ [+ question word] *Have they evaluated what their next step is?*
evaluation Ⓐ /ɪˌvæl·jəˈweɪ·ʃən/ *n* [C/U] ○ [C] *Student evaluations of the class will be collected next week.*

evangelical /ˌiː ˌvænˈdʒel·ɪ·kəl, ˌev·ən-/ *adj* [not gradable] according to the teachings of the Christian religion and GOSPELS, or relating to Christian groups that believe in the importance of the Bible, acceptance of God, and SALVATION
evangelical /ˌiː ˌvænˈdʒel·ɪ·kəl, ˌev·ən-/ *n* [C] ○ *a member of an evangelical group*

evangelist /ɪˈvæn·dʒə·ləst/ *n* [C] a person who speaks in public and tries to persuade people to become Christians, esp. in the past by traveling and holding religious meetings
evangelism /ɪˈvæn·dʒəˌlɪz·əm/ *n* [U]
evangelistic /ɪˌvæn·dʒəˈlɪs·tɪk/ *adj*

evaporate /ɪˈvæp·əˌreɪt/ *v* [I/T] **1** ***chemistry, biology, earth science*** to cause a liquid to change to a gas, esp. by heating ○ *Some water evaporates to form clouds.* **2** **3** If something such as a feeling or problem evaporates, it suddenly disappears. ○ [I] *The issue of global warming is not just going to evaporate.*
evaporation /ɪˌvæp·əˈreɪ·ʃən/ *n* [U] ***chemistry, biology*** the process of changing from a liquid to a gas, or a change from a liquid to a gas

evapotranspiration /ɪˈvæp·oʊˌtran·spəˈreɪ·ʃən/ *n* [U] ***earth science*** the process in which water moves from the earth to the air from EVAPORATION (= water changing to a gas) and from TRANSPIRATION (= water lost from plants)

evasion /ɪˈveɪ·ʒən/ *n* [C/U] ○ See at EVADE

evasive /ɪˈveɪ·sɪv, -zɪv/ *adj* ○ See at EVADE

eve /iːv/ *n* [U] the evening or day before a holiday, or the period immediately before an important event ○ *New Year's Eve* ○ *the eve of the election*

even **EQUAL** /ˈiː·vən/ *adj* equal or equally balanced ○ *The class has a pretty even mix of boys and girls.* ○ *I bought the tickets, so if you pay for dinner we'll be even* (= you will not owe me any money).
evenly /ˈiː·vən·li/ *adv* ○ *Divide the mixture evenly between the two pans.*
even /ˈiː·vən/ *v* [I/T] to make equal ○ [T] *Tonight's win evens their record at 6-6.* ○ [M] *They won the next night to even up the score.* ○ [M] *Taking me to the movies isn't going to even things out.*

CONTINUOUS /ˈiː·vən/ *adj* continuous or regular ○ *We walked at an even pace.*
evenly /ˈiː·vən·li/ *adv* **1** *She breathed evenly.* **2** To say something evenly is to speak without showing emotion: *"You have no right to do that," he said evenly.*

FLAT /ˈiː·vən/ *adj* flat and smooth, or on the same level ○ *The snow was even with the kitchen doorstep.*

NUMBER /ˈiː·vən/ *adj* [not gradable] (of numbers) able to be exactly divided by two ○ *The result should be an even number.* ○ Compare ODD NUMBER

EMPHASIS /ˈiː·vən/ *adv* [not gradable] used to emphasize a comparison or the unexpected or extreme characteristic of something ○ *Even smart people can make mistakes.* ○ *She never cried – not even when she was badly hurt.* ○ *Even with a good education, you need some common sense to get ahead.* ○ *The new service is one of the most useful and popular on the Web. Even better, it's free to use.*

MORE EXACTLY /ˈiː·vən/ *adv* [not gradable] used when you want to be more exact or detailed about something you have just said ○ *I'd like to get a place in the Rocky Mountains, maybe Colorado or Montana – Idaho even.*

IDIOMS with even

• **even if** whether or not ○ *Even if you apologize, she still may not forgive you.*
• **even so** although it is true ○ *The phone system has improved, but even so, there are still very few houses with phones.*
• **even though** despite the fact that ○ *Even though he never completed college, he runs a successful software company.*

even-handed *adj* fair to everyone involved ○ *even-handed coverage of a volatile issue*

evening /ˈiːv·nɪŋ/ *n* [C/U] the part of the day between the afternoon and the night ○ [C] *We always go to the movies on Friday evenings.*

evening dress, **evening gown** *n* [C] a dress worn to formal evening parties and events

event /ɪˈvent/ *n* [C] **1** anything that happens, esp. something important or unusual ○ *sporting events* ○ *a charity/fundraising event* ○ *political/world events* ○ *She later gave me her version of events.* **2** ***mathematics*** An event is also one particular group of OUTCOMES (= results) among all possible outcomes when experimenting with PROBABILITY (= the likelihood of something happening). **3** An event is also one of a set of races or competitions: *the women's 200-meter event*

eventful /ɪˈvent·fəl/ *adj* full of important or interesting happenings ○ *She led a long and eventful life.*

WORD FAMILY event

Nouns	event	Adjectives	eventful
Adverbs	eventfully		uneventful
	eventually		eventual

IDIOMS with event

• **in any event** whatever happens ○ *I hope to see her this afternoon, but in any event I'm leaving town tomorrow.*
• **in the event of** *something*, **in the event that** *something* **happens** if something should happen ○ *In the event of an actual emergency, you will be told what to do.* ○ *In the event that the performance is canceled, you can get your money back.*

eventual Ⓐ /ɪˈven·tʃə·wəl/ *adj* [not gradable] happening at a later time or as a result at the end ○ *The eventual cost of the new facility has not been revealed.*

eventually Ⓐ /ɪˈventʃ·wə·li/ *adv* [not gradable] ○ *You learn a lot in school, but eventually you forget most of it.*

COMMON LEARNER ERROR

eventual/eventually

These words have only a single meaning: "happening at a later time or as a result at the end."

Be careful not to use **eventually** like "finally" at the end of a list of points in an argument.

Firstly...Secondly...Thirdly...Finally.

~~*Firstly...Secondly...Thirdly...Eventually.*~~

Eventually also cannot be used to mean "possible" or "possibly."

It would be great if the kids could see and, if possible, touch the animals.

~~*It would be great if the kids could see and, eventually, touch the animals.*~~

Eventually also cannot be used to mean "in fact."

He confessed that in fact he had never sent the letter.

~~*He confessed that he eventually had never sent the letter.*~~

eventuality Ⓐ /ɪˌven·tʃəˈwæl·ət̬·i/ *n* [C] a possible happening or result ○ *I thought I could cope with any eventuality.*

ever AT ANY TIME /ˈev·ər/ *adv* [not gradable] at any time ○ *Nothing ever happens here.* ○ *Have you ever been to Europe?* ○ *I thought she was famous, but none of my friends have ever heard of her.* ○ *We are spending more money than ever.* ○ *He hardly ever washes the dishes* (= almost never).

ALWAYS /ˈev·ər/ *adv* [not gradable] always, or continuously ○ *Her record grows ever more impressive over the years.* ○ *There's an ever-increasing demand for new styles.* ○ *I have taught school ever since my children were little.*

EMPHASIS /ˈev·ər/ *adv* [not gradable] used to emphasize an adjective ○ *I saw John Coltrane's last concert ever.* ○ *Was she ever angry* (= She was very angry)*!*

evergreen /ˈev·ərˌgriːn/ *adj* [not gradable] (of a plant, bush, or tree) having leaves for the whole year ○ Compare DECIDUOUS

evergreen /ˈev·ərˌgriːn/ *n* [C] ○ *Spruces, pines, and ivy are evergreens.*

everlasting /ˌev·ərˈlæs·tɪŋ/ *adj* [not gradable] lasting forever, or continuing for a long time ○ *To his everlasting credit, he's the only one who said it was wrong.*

every ALL /ˈev·ri/ *adj* used when referring to all the members of a group of three or more considered separately ○ *Every employee will receive a bonus this year.* ○ *They're open every day.* ○ *Make sure you eat every bit of dinner.* ○ *Tour guides tend to travelers' every need* (= all their needs).

SPELLING

every

When **every-** is used as a combining form, such as with **body**, **one**, **thing**, or **where**, you write the words together as one word.

Everybody needs to bring something to eat.

Can everyone see the blackboard?

Have you got everything you need?

~~*Have you got every thing you need?*~~

I've looked everywhere for it.
~~*I've looked every where for it.*~~

In other situations, where **every** is used as an adjective, a space is used between it and the follow noun.

You have to take your membership card every time you go.
Do you go jogging every morning?

REPEATED /ˈev·ri/ *adj* used to show that something is repeated regularly ○ *Computers perform millions of calculations every second.* ○ *In many places, malnutrition affects every third child* (= one child in three).

GREATEST /ˈev·ri/ *adj* the greatest possible ○ *Every effort is being made to fix it.* ○ *She has every right to be proud of herself.*

IDIOMS with every

• **every inch of** *something* all of something ○ *Cassandra knows every inch of Boston.*

• **every nook and cranny** every part of a place ○ *Books were stuffed into every nook and cranny of his office.*

• **every now and then**, **every now and again** sometimes, but not regularly ○ *We still get together for lunch every now and then.*

• **every once in a while**, **every so often** sometimes, but not regularly ○ *You meet some really interesting people every once in a while.*

• **every other** *something* not each one in a series, but every two ○ *The conference used to be held every year, but now it takes place every other year.* ○ *We get together every other Saturday for lunch.*

• **every single**, **every last** each ○ *I don't need to know every single detail of his life.* ○ **USAGE:** Used for emphasis.

everybody /ˈev·riː ˌbɑd·i, -ˌbʌd·i/ *pronoun* EVERYONE

everyday /ˈev·riː ˌdeɪ/ *adj* ordinary, typical, or usual ○ *The movie is about the everyday lives of working mothers.*

everyone /ˈev·riː·wən/, **everybody** /ˈev·riː ˌbɑd·i, -ˌbʌd·i/ *pronoun* every person ○ *You have to wait your turn like everyone else.* ○ *Goodbye, everybody – I'll see you next week.* ➤ Usage: **every** at EVERY ALL

everything /ˈev·riː ˌθɪŋ/ *pronoun* all things ○ *They lost everything in the fire.* ○ *In spite of everything, I still love him.* ○ *The price of gasoline affects everything else.* ○ *"Is everything all right?" "Everything is fine."* ○ *Money isn't everything* (= it is not the only important thing). ○ *Her children are everything to her* (= the most important part of her life). ○ *They're very busy with their new house and everything* (= all the things connected with it). ➤ Usage: **every** at EVERY ALL

IDIOM with everything

• **everything but the kitchen sink** almost all that you can imagine of something ○ *Here's a website that has everything but the kitchen sink.*

everywhere /ˈev·riː ˌhwer, -ˌwer, -ˌhwær, -ˌwær/, *infml* **everyplace** /ˈev·riː ˌpleɪs/ *adv* [not gradable] in or to every place or part ○ *There were stacks of newspapers everywhere in the apartment.* ○ *We've got relatives in Florida, New Jersey, just about everywhere.* ➤ Usage: **every** at EVERY ALL

evict /ɪˈvɪkt/ *v* [T] to force someone to leave a place ○ *Long-time residents are being evicted from the buildings.*

eviction /ɪˈvɪk·ʃən/ *n* [C/U] ○ [U] *He's been threatened with eviction for not paying his rent.*

E

evidence Ⓐ /ˈev·əd·ənsy/ *n* [U] anything that helps to prove that something is or is not true ○ *These figures are being given as evidence of economic growth.* ○ *The FBI has found no evidence of a crime.* ○ *The weight of the evidence is against him.* ○ *Juries examine the evidence and decide on the basis of the facts.*

evident Ⓐ /ˈev·əd·ənt/ *adj* easily seen or understood; obvious ○ *It quickly became evident that someone had broken in.* ○ *Twain's interest in Adam is evident in all his work.* ○ See also: SELF-EVIDENT

evidently Ⓐ /ˈev·əd·ənt·li/ *adv* ○ *I thought she'd want to see me. Evidently, she doesn't.*

USAGE

evident or obvious?

Evident is more formal than **obvious** and it usually refers to something that can be seen.

The effects of the drought were evident everywhere we looked.

Obvious suggests that something is easy to see, discover, or understand.

The advantages of living close to where you work are obvious.
~~*The advantages of living close to where you work are evident.*~~

evil /ˈiː·vəl/ *n* [C/U] the condition of being immoral, cruel, or bad, or an act of this type ○ [U] *a contest between good and evil*

evil /ˈiː·vəl/ *adj* ○ *an evil ruler*

evoke /ɪˈvoʊk/ *v* [T] to cause something to be remembered or expressed ○ *The smell of chalk always evokes memories of my school days.*

evocative /ɪˈvɑk·ət̬·ɪv/ *adj* ○ *The new fashions were evocative of the 1920s.*

evolution Ⓐ /ˌev·əˈluː·ʃən, ˌiː·və-/ *n* [U] **1** a gradual process of change and development **2** ***biology*** Evolution is the process by which the physical characteristics of types of creatures change over time, new types of creatures develop, and others disappear.

evolutionary Ⓐ /ˌev·əˈluː·ʃəˌner·i, ˌiː·və-/ *adj* ***biology*** relating to or resulting from the process of evolution

evolutionist Ⓐ /ˌev·əˈluː·ʃə·nəst, ˌiː·və-/ *n* [C] ***science*** someone who believes in or supports the theory of evolution

evolve Ⓐ /ɪˈvɔːlv, -ˈvɑlv/ *v* [I] **1** to change or develop gradually ○ *These countries are evolving to-*

ward more democratic societies. **2** ***biology*** If a creature evolves, it changes over time by the process of EVOLUTION.

ex- /eks/ *prefix* used to show that someone is no longer in the situation or condition the person had been in; FORMER **EARLIER** ○ *The governor of Minnesota is an ex-wrestler.*
ex /eks/ *n* [C] *pl* **exes** *infml* someone you are no longer married to

exacerbate /ɪɡˈzæs·ərˌbeɪt/ *v* [T] to make something that is already bad worse ○ *Her allergy was exacerbated by the dust.*

exact **CORRECT** /ɪɡˈzækt/ *adj* **1** in perfect detail; complete and correct ○ *The exact distance is 3.4 miles.* ○ *Do you have the exact time?* ○ *"Is it 12 o'clock yet?" "It's 12:03 to be exact."* **2** Exact is sometimes used to increase emphasis on the following word: *She's going through the exact same things I went through.*
exactly /ɪɡˈzæk·tli/ *adv* **1** *We've come exactly 41 miles.* ○ *Make sure you measure the window exactly, otherwise the shade won't fit.* **2** Exactly is sometimes used to increase emphasis: *The businessmen who work in banking, she thought, all look exactly the same.* ○ *You're exactly right.*

OBTAIN /ɪɡˈzækt/ *v* [T] *fml* to demand and obtain something, sometimes using threats or force ○ *to exact revenge*
exacting /ɪɡˈzæk·tɪŋ/ *adj* demanding a lot of effort, care, or attention ○ *All our aircraft meet exacting safety standards.*

exaggerate /ɪɡˈzædʒ·əˌreɪt/ *v* [I/T] to make something seem larger, more important, better, or worse than it really is ○ [T] *The media exaggerate the risks and benefits of research findings.* ○ [I] *I don't want to exaggerate, but it was a dangerous situation.*
exaggeration /ɪɡˌzædʒ·əˈreɪ·ʃən/ *n* [C/U] ○ [U] *It is no exaggeration to say that she saved my life.*

exalt /ɪɡˈzɔːlt/ *v* [T] *fml* to praise someone a lot, or to raise someone to a higher rank or more powerful position
exalted /ɪɡˈzɔːl·təd/ *adj* ○ *He felt an exalted sense of power now that he was in line to run the company.*

exaltation /ˌeɡˌzɔːlˈteɪ·ʃən, ˌekˌsɔːl-/ *n* [U] **1** the act of raising someone or something to a more important position ○ *the exaltation of art* **2** Exaltation is a feeling of great happiness.

exam /ɪɡˈzæm/, **examination** /ɪɡˌzæm·əˈneɪ·ʃən/ *n* [C] a test of a student's knowledge or skill in a particular subject ○ *The final exams are scheduled for next week.*

> **USAGE**
> **exam**
> To **take an exam** means to do an official test.
> *We have to take an exam at the end of the course.*
> ~~*We have to write an exam at the end of the course.*~~

examine /ɪɡˈzæm·ən/ *v* [T] to look at or consider a person or thing carefully in order to discover something about the person or thing ○ *Investigators examined the wreckage for clues about the cause of the explosion.*
examination /ɪɡˌzæm·əˈneɪ·ʃən/, *short form* **exam** *n* [C/U] the act or process of carefully looking at someone or something to learn about its condition or to discover facts ○ [C] *You have to have a physical examination/exam in order to get life insurance.* ○ [U] *The evidence is still under examination* (= being examined).

WORD FAMILY examine			
Nouns	exam examination cross-examination	*Verbs*	examine cross-examine

example **TYPICAL CASE** /ɪɡˈzæm·pəl/ *n* [C] something that is typical of the group that it is a member of or that can be used to represent it ○ *Let me give you an example of what I mean.* ○ *For example* (= as a particular case showing a more general situation), *some states allow one adult to care for as many as 12 infants.*

BEHAVIOR /ɪɡˈzæm·pəl/ *n* [C] a person or a person's behavior when considered as suitable to copy ○ *We want our teachers to set a good example.* ○ *They followed the example of their father, who also played basketball in college.*

PUNISHMENT /ɪɡˈzæm·pəl/ *n* [C] (a person who receives) a punishment that is intended to warn others against doing the thing that is being punished ○ *The judge made an example of him and sentenced him to prison.*

exasperate /ɪɡˈzæs·pəˌreɪt/ *v* [T] to cause anger or extreme annoyance in someone ○ *His assistant's carelessness is exasperating him.*

excavate /ˈek·skəˌveɪt/ *v* [I/T] **1** to dig a hole or channel in the ground, or to make a hole or channel by removing earth ○ [I] *We'll be excavating here for the foundation of the building.* **2** To excavate is also to remove earth from a place in order to find old objects buried there: [T] *Archaeologists are excavating a site near the cathedral.*
excavation /ˌek·skəˈveɪ·ʃən/ *n* [C/U] ○ [C] *an excavation 40 feet deep*

exceed Ⓐ /ɪkˈsiːd/ *v* [T] to be greater than a number or amount, or to go beyond a permitted limit ○ *He was exceeding the speed limit by 15 miles an hour.*

exceedingly /ɪkˈsiːd·ɪŋ·li/ *adv* to a very great degree; extremely ○ *He is exceedingly rich.*

excel /ɪkˈsel/ *v* [I/T] **-ll-** to do something very well or be highly skilled, and be better than most others ○ [I] *They all performed well, but the lead dancer really excelled.*

WORD FAMILY excel			
Nouns	excellence	*Verbs*	excel
Adjectives	excellent	*Adverbs*	excellently

excellent /'ek·sə·lənt/ *adj* extremely good ○ *The car is in excellent condition.*
excellence /'ek·sə·ləns/ *n* [U] ○ *The school is known for its excellence.*

except /ɪk'sept/ *prep, conjunction* **1** not including; but not ○ *It's cool and quiet everywhere except (for) the kitchen.* ○ *Everyone is here except Peter.* **2** Except also means with this difference or in this case only: *The twins look exactly alike except (that) one is slightly taller.* ○ *The deserted town is silent, except when wind rustles the weeds or bangs a door.*
except /ɪk'sept/ *v* [T] to not include something or someone ○ *When I say I didn't like the Midwest, I except Chicago.*
excepting /ɪk'sep·tɪŋ/ *prep, conjunction* ○ *Excepting the two people who left early, I think everyone enjoyed the tour.*
exception /ɪk'sep·ʃən/ *n* [C/U] something that is not included, or the action of not including something ○ [C] *We don't usually accept late applications, but since you were so sick I'll make an exception* (= do something different from what is usual). ○ [C] *Teen movies usually aren't very good, but this one is an exception to the rule.* ○ [U] *Every apple in the box, without exception, was rotten.*

exceptional /ɪk'sep·ʃən·əl/ *adj* **1** not like most others of the same type; unusual ○ *This is an exceptional contract, guaranteeing no layoffs.* **2** Exceptional also means unusually good: *Davis has done an exceptional job of reporting.*
exceptionally /ɪk'sep·ʃən·əl·i/ *adv* ○ *The drawing had exceptionally fine detail.*

excerpt /'ek·sɜrpt, 'eg·zɜrpt/ *n* [C] ***writing*** a short part taken from a speech, book, etc.
excerpt /ek'sɜrpt, eg'zɜrpt/ *v* [T] ○ *This article is excerpted from the full report.*

excess /ɪk'ses, 'ek·ses/ *n* [U] an amount that is more than acceptable, expected, or reasonable ○ *They both eat to excess* (= a lot more than they need). ○ *The company's losses are in excess of* (= more than) *$5 million.*
excess /ɪk'ses, 'ek·ses/ *adj* [not gradable] more than is necessary; too much ○ *excess baggage*
excesses /ɪk'ses·əz, 'ekˌses·əz/ *pl n* actions beyond the limit of what is acceptable ○ *These villages are unspoiled by tourists and the excesses of modern life.* ○ *The prosecutor's thirst for publicity led to troubling excesses.*
excessive /ɪk'ses·ɪv/ *adj* ○ *We felt the charges were excessive.*

exchange /ɪks'tʃeɪndʒ/ *v* [T] to change something for something else of a similar value or type ○ *This shirt is too small – can I exchange it for one in a larger size?* ○ *Before we left the meeting, she and I exchanged phone numbers* (= I told her mine and she told me hers).
exchange /ɪks'tʃeɪndʒ/ *n* [C/U] ○ [C] *an exchange of ideas* ○ [C] *an exchange of prisoners*

exchange rate *n* [C] the rate at which the money of one country can be changed for the money of another country

excise TAX /'ek·saɪz/ *n* [U] a tax on some types of goods produced and used within a single country

REMOVE /ɪk'saɪz/ *v* [T] *medical* to remove by cutting ○ *The surgeon excised a small tumor from my leg.*

excite MAKE HAPPY /ɪk'saɪt/ *v* [T] to make someone have strong feelings, esp. of happiness and enthusiasm ○ *In some science fiction movies, the music and special effects can really excite audiences.*
excited /ɪk'saɪt̬·əd/ *adj* ○ *She was excited about the trip because she was going to learn to ski.*
excitedly /ɪk'saɪt̬·əd·li/ *adv* ○ *She ran excitedly outside to greet her cousins.*
exciting /ɪk'saɪt̬·ɪŋ/ *adj* ○ *It was an exciting role to play, and I was thrilled to get the part.*
excitement /ɪk'saɪt·mənt/ *n* [U] ○ *Robin's heart was pounding with excitement.*

WORD CHOICES excite

If something is so exciting that it holds your attention completely, you can say that it is **gripping** or **riveting**.

The book was ***gripping*** *– I couldn't put it down.*

I found the movie absolutely ***riveting****.*

Sports and outdoor activities which are exciting are often described as **exhilarating**.

I find skiing absolutely ***exhilarating****.*

The adjective **action-packed** is often used to describe a story or period of time that is full of exciting events.

We had an ***action-packed*** *week of vacation.*

The movie is described as "an ***action-packed*** *thriller."*

If something is very exciting, especially because you are not sure what will happen, you can describe it as **thrilling**.

It was a ***thrilling*** *game in which both teams played well.*

An exciting atmosphere is sometimes described as **electric**.

The atmosphere backstage was ***electric****.*

Vibrant is often used to describe places which are exciting.

This is one of the country's most ***vibrant*** *cities.*

CAUSE TO REACT /ɪk'saɪt/ *v* [T] *fml* **1** to cause (a particular reaction) in someone ○ *The strange noises excited my curiosity.* **2** ***physics*** To excite an atom is to raise it to a state higher than its lowest energy state.
excitable /ɪk'saɪt̬·ə·bəl/ *adj* (of a person or an animal) tending to react quickly and strongly to things ○ *The dog is excitable, so don't come too close.*

WORD FAMILY excite

Nouns	excitement	*Adjectives*	excitable
Verbs	excite		excited
Adverbs	excitedly		exciting
	excitingly		unexciting

exclaim /ɪk'skleɪm/ *v* to say or shout something suddenly because of surprise, fear, pleasure, etc. ○ [I] *She exclaimed with delight when she saw the baby.*

exclamation /ˌek·skləˈmeɪ·ʃən/ *n* [C] a sudden expression of pleasure, surprise, agreement, etc. ○ *exclamations of delight*

exclamation /ˌek·skləˈmeɪ·ʃən/ *n* [C] ***grammar*** a word that expresses sudden pain, surprise, anger, excitement, happiness, or other emotion ○ *"Ouch," "hey," and "wow" are exclamations.*

exclamation point, **exclamation mark** *n* [C] the mark (!) used in writing immediately after an expression to show that it is sudden or surprising, or that it is a greeting or an order

E

exclamatory sentence /ɪkˈsklæm·əˌtɔːr·i ˈsent·ᵊns, -ˌtoʊr·i/ *n* [C] ***grammar*** a sentence containing an exclamation or strong emphasis ○ *"Oh, no!" and "What a large dog!" are exclamatory sentences.*

exclude Ⓐ /ɪkˈskluːd/ *v* [T] to keep out or omit (something or someone) ○ *The advertised price excludes the sales tax.*

excluding Ⓐ /ɪkˈskluːd·ɪŋ/ *prep* not including; apart from ○ *The aircraft carries 250 people, excluding the crew.*

exclusion Ⓐ /ɪkˈskluː·ʒən/ *n* [C/U] ○ [U] *Her exclusion from the invitation list was a mistake.*

exclusive Ⓐ /ɪkˈskluː·sɪv, -zɪv/ *adj* **1** limited to only one person or group of people ○ *The pool is for the exclusive use of residents of Springfield.* **2** A place that is exclusive provides goods and services for a limited number of people, esp. those who are wealthy: *an exclusive club*

exclusively Ⓐ /ɪkˈskluː·sɪv·li, -zɪv·li/ *adv* limited to a specific thing or group ○ *Our employment agency deals exclusively with the advertising industry.*

excommunicate /ˌek·skəˈmjuː·nəˌkeɪt/ *v* [T] (of the Christian Church, esp. the Roman Catholic Church) to refuse to allow someone to be a member of the church

excrement /ˈek·skrə·mənt/ *n* [U] waste material that leaves the body through the bowels

excrete /ɪkˈskriːt/ *v* [I/T] ***biology*** to get rid of waste from the cells or from the body

excretion /ɪkˈskriː·ʃən/ *n* [C/U]

excretory /ˈek·skrəˌtɔːr·i, -ˌtoʊr·i/ *adj* [not gradable]

excruciating /ɪkˈskruː·ʃiːˌeɪt̬·ɪŋ/ *adj* (of pain) extremely strong ○ *an excruciating headache*

excursion /ɪkˈskɜr·ʒən/ *n* [C] a short trip usually made for pleasure, often by a group of people ○ *My class is going on an excursion to Niagara Falls.*

excuse FORGIVE /ɪkˈskjuːz/ *v* [T] **1** to forgive someone ○ *Please excuse me for being so late – there was a lot of traffic.* ○ *It was hard to excuse him for treating me so badly.* **2** To **excuse** someone **from** an activity is to give that person permission to stop doing it or not do it: *I was excused from jury duty because I had to take care of my sick mother.*

excusable /ɪkˈskjuː·zə·bəl/ *adj* ○ *Considering her difficult childhood, her behavior is excusable.*

EXPLANATION /ɪkˈskjuːs/ *n* [C] the explanation given for bad behavior, absence, etc. ○ *You're always making excuses for not helping with the housework.*

WORD FAMILY excuse			
Nouns	excuse	*Verbs*	excuse
Adjectives	excusable inexcusable	*Adverbs*	inexcusably

IDIOM with excuse

• **excuse me 1** I am sorry to interrupt you ○ *Excuse me, where is the bathroom?* **2 Excuse me** is also used to say you are sorry for having done something, esp. unintentionally, that might be annoying to other people. **3** You might also use **excuse me** as a question when you want someone to repeat something that person has said because you could not hear it: *"Excuse me? I didn't get that last part."*

execute DO /ˈek·səˌkjuːt/ *v* [T] to do or perform something planned ○ *Now that we have approval, we can go ahead and execute the plan.*

execution /ˌek·səˈkjuː·ʃən/ *n* [U] ○ *The guitarist's execution of the ballad was superb.*

executor /ɪgˈzek·jət̬·ər/ *n* [C] *law* a person who deals with the wishes expressed in a WILL (= formal statement of what will happen to a dead person's money and property)

KILL /ˈek·səˌkjuːt/ *v* [T] to kill someone as a legal punishment

execution /ˌek·səˈkjuː·ʃən/ *n* [C/U]

executive /ɪgˈzek·jət̬·ɪv/, *infml* **exec** /ɪgˈzek/ *n* [C/U] **1** someone in a high position, esp. in business, who makes decisions and acts according to them ○ [C] *a chief executive* **2** ***US history*** The executive BRANCH of the US government, including the president, the CABINET, and several departments, manages the duties of government and its laws.

executive /ɪgˈzek·jət̬·ɪv/ *adj* ○ *In the US, the president is the head of the executive branch of government.*

executive privilege *n* [U] ***politics & government*** the principle that a president or other important EXECUTIVE official should not have to tell protected information to others

exemplary /ɪgˈzem·plə·ri/ *adj* extremely good of its type, so that it might serve as a model for others ○ *He saw action in the Marines, and his performance was exemplary.*

exemplify /ɪgˈzem·pləˌfɑɪ/ *v* [T] to be a typical example of something ○ *American fashion is exemplified by jeans and T-shirts.*

exempt /ɪgˈzempt/ *adj* [not gradable] not having to obey a rule or to do something that is usually necessary ○ *Nonprofit organizations are exempt from taxes.*

exempt /ɪgˈzemt/ *v* [T] ○ *The governor plans to exempt small businesses from the tax increase.*

exemption /ɪgˈzem·ʃən/ *n* [C/U] **1** [U] *He was granted exemption from military service during World War II.* **2** An exemption is a particular amount of money that is not taxed: [C] *a tax exemption*

exercise **HEALTHY ACTIVITY** /ˈek·sərˌsɑɪz/ *n* [C/U] (a) physical action performed to make or keep your body healthy ○ [U] *You should get some exercise even when you're pregnant.* ○ [C] *I do five different exercises every morning to limber up.*
exercise /ˈek·sərˌsɑɪz/ *v* [I/T] ○ [I] *She goes to the gym to exercise every evening.*

PRACTICE /ˈek·sərˌsɑɪz/ *n* [C] **1** an action or actions intended to improve something or make something happen ○ *The military exercises will involve several thousand soldiers.* ○ *The whole thing was an exercise in futility* (= actions that were useless). **2** An exercise can be written work that you do to practice something you are learning: *The book has exercises at the end of every chapter.*

USE /ˈek·sərˌsɑɪz/ *v* [T] *fml* to use something ○ *Always exercise caution when handling poisonous substances.*
exercise /ˈek·sərˌsɑɪz/ *n* [U] ○ *The exercise of restraint in this situation may be difficult.*

exert **USE** /ɪɡˈzɜrt/ *v* [T] to use power or the ability to make something happen ○ *To cut costs, health-insurance plans are exerting tighter control over paying for medical care.*

MAKE AN EFFORT /ɪɡˈzɜrt/ *v* [T] to cause yourself to make an effort ○ *She will have to exert herself a lot more if she wants to succeed in this business.*
exertion /ɪɡˈzɜr·ʃən/ *n* [C/U] ○ [U] *Physical exertion isn't always a good thing in a hot climate.*

exhale /eksˈheɪl/ *v* [I/T] to breathe out air ○ [I] *She held her breath for a moment and then exhaled.*

exhaust **TIRE** /ɪɡˈzɔːst/ *v* [T] to make a person or an animal extremely tired ○ *The long hike up the mountain exhausted us all.*
exhausting /ɪɡˈzɔː·stɪŋ/ *adj* [not gradable] ○ *The pace of twelve-hour days, seven days a week proved exhausting.*
exhaustion /ɪɡˈzɔːs·tʃən/ *n* [U] ○ *Murayama was sidelined shortly after his arrival by what aides said was exhaustion.*

USE /ɪɡˈzɔːst/ *v* [T] to use something completely ○ *After a whole day with the kids, her patience was nearly exhausted.*
exhaustive /ɪɡˈzɔː·stɪv/ *adj* detailed and complete ○ *an exhaustive study of the tax law*
exhaustively /ɪɡˈzɔː·stɪv·li/ *adv*

GAS /ɪɡˈzɔːst/ *n* [C/U] the waste gas from an engine, esp. a from a car, or the pipe this gas flows through

exhibit Ⓐ **SHOW AN OBJECT** /ɪɡˈzɪb·ət/ *v* [I/T] to show something in public for competition, sale, or amusement ○ [T] *The gallery is exhibiting his paintings and watercolors.*
exhibit Ⓐ /ɪɡˈzɪb·ət/ *n* [C] **1** *The museum's exhibits range from Iron Age pottery to Eskimo clothing.* **2** *law* An exhibit is an item used as EVIDENCE (= proof) in a trial.
exhibition Ⓐ /ˌek·səˈbɪʃ·ən/ *n* [C/U] a collection of things shown publicly ○ [C] *an exhibition of model airplanes*
exhibitionism /ˌek·səˈbɪʃ·əˌnɪz·əm/ *n* [U] a tendency to behave in a way intended to attract attention
exhibitionist /ˌek·səˈbɪʃ·ə·nəst/ *n* [C]

SHOW A QUALITY /ɪɡˈzɪb·ət/ *v* [T] to show something, esp. a quality, by your behavior ○ *He exhibited poor judgment.*

exhilarating /ɪɡˈzɪl·əˌreɪţ·ɪŋ/ *adj* [not gradable] causing you to feel excited and happy ○ *An exhilarating sense of new beginnings swept through him.*

exhort /ɪɡˈzɔːrt/ *v* [T] *fml* to strongly encourage or persuade someone to do something ○ *She exhorted all of us to do our very best.*

exhume /ɪɡˈzuːm, ɪksˈjuːm/ *v* [T] to remove a dead body from the ground after it has been buried

exile /ˈeg·zɑɪl, ˈek·sɑɪl/ *v* [T] to send or keep someone away from his or her own country or home, esp. for political reasons
exile /ˈeg·zɑɪl, ˈek·sɑɪl/ *n* [C/U] the condition being exiled, or a person who is exiled ○ [C] *Many Cuban exiles live in Florida.*

exist **TO BE** /ɪɡˈzɪst/ *v* [I] to be; have the ability to be known, recognized, or understood ○ *Can the mind exist independently of the body?* ○ *Programs like Medicaid for the poor did not exist at that time.*
existence /ɪɡˈzɪs·təns/ *n* [U] ○ *During the first few years of its existence, the theater had no permanent home.*

BE PRESENT /ɪɡˈzɪst/ *v* [I] to be present or be a condition ○ *Your local agency can tell you if a similar program exists in your community.*
existence /ɪɡˈzɪz·təns/ *n* [U] ○ *the existence of poverty*
existing /ɪɡˈzɪs·tɪŋ/ *adj* [not gradable] ○ *Under existing conditions, many children are not getting an adequate education.*

LIVE /ɪɡˈzɪst/ *v* [I] to be able to live ○ *No one can be expected to exist on such a low salary.*
existence /ɪɡˈzɪs·təns/ *n* [C usually sing] a way of living, esp. a difficult one ○ *I lead a rather isolated existence here in Washington.*

WORD FAMILY exist			
Nouns	existence coexistence	*Adjectives*	existing
		Verbs	exist coexist

exit /ˈek·sət, ˈeg·zət/ *n* [C] **1** the door through which you might leave a room, building, or large vehicle, or a place on a main road where a vehicle can leave it by taking a smaller road ○ *In case of fire, use the emergency exit next to the elevator.* ○ *Stay on the freeway until you get to the Ventura exit.* **2** An exit is also the act of leaving a place, esp. a public place such as the stage of a theater: *She made her exit to rapturous applause.*
exit /ˈek·sət, ˈeg·zət/ *v* [I/T] **1** [I/T] *Please exit (the theater) by the side doors.* **2** If you exit a computer or computer program, you stop using it.

exodus /ˈek·səd·əs, ˈeg·zəd-/ *n* [C usually sing] the movement of a lot of people from a place at the same time ○ *The hurricane warning caused a mass exodus.*

exogenous /ek'sɑdʒ·ə·nəs/ *adj* [not gradable] ***biology*** coming from or produced outside an organism or cell

exonerate /ɪɡ'zɑn·ə,reɪt/ *v* [T] to show or state that someone or something is not to be blamed for something bad that happened ○ *The police officer was exonerated by a grand jury, but the protests continued.*
exoneration /ɪɡ,zɑn·ə'reɪ·ʃən/ *n* [U]

E

exorbitant /ɪɡ'zɔːr·bət̬·ənt/ *adj* [not gradable] (of prices and demands) much too large ○ *The hotel charges were exorbitant.*

exorcise /'ek,sɔːr,sɑɪz, 'ek·sər-/ *v* [T] to get rid of someone or something evil
exorcist /'ek,sɔːr·səst, 'ek·sər-/ *n* [C]

exoskeleton /,ek·soʊ'skel·ət·ən/ *n* [C] ***biology*** a hard outer layer that covers and protects the body of some animals such as insects

exothermic /,ek·soʊ'θɜr·mɪk/ *adj* [not gradable] ***chemistry*** describes a chemical reaction that produces heat
exothermically /,ek·soʊ'θɜr·mɪ·kli/ *adv* [not gradable]

exothermic /,ek·soʊ'θɜr·mɪk/ *adj* ***earth science*** involving the release or loss of heat ○ *magnesium starts an exothermic reaction in water.*

exothermic reaction *n* [C] ***chemistry*** a chemical reaction that produces heat

exotic /ɪɡ'zɑt̬·ɪk/ *adj* [not gradable] unusual and specially interesting because of coming from a country that is far away ○ *exotic pets like snakes and tropical birds*

expand Ⓐ /ɪk'spænd/ *v* [I/T] to increase something in size, number, or importance ○ [I] *The air in the balloon expands when heated.* ○ [T] *They expanded their number of stores significantly in the 1990s.*
expansion Ⓐ /ɪk'spæn·tʃən/ *n* [U] ○ *Expansion into new areas of research might be possible.*
expansionism Ⓐ /ɪk'spæn·tʃə,nɪz·əm/ *n* [U] ***world history*** increasing the amount of land ruled by a country, or the business performed by a company ○ *As a consequence of expansionism by some European countries, many ancient cultures have suffered.*

PHRASAL VERB with expand

• **expand on/upon** *something* [T] to give more details about something said or written ○ *He studied with Sigmund Freud and expanded upon many of his theories.*

expanse /ɪk'spæns/ *n* [C] a very wide space or area ○ *the vast expanse of Russia*
expansive Ⓐ /ɪk'spæn·sɪv/ *adj* wide in area ○ *The seals form small groups on the expansive beaches where they breed.*

expansionism /ɪk'spæn·tʃə,nɪz·əm/ *n* [U] ***politics & government*** the act or habit of one country taking land from others

expansive /ɪk'spæn·sɪv/ *adj* [not gradable] friendly, generous and willing to talk

expatriate /ek'speɪ·triː·ət/ *n* [C] someone who does not live in his or her own country

expect /ɪk'spekt/ *v* **1** to think or believe that something will happen, or that someone will arrive ○ [T] *We are expecting about 100 people for the lecture.* ○ [T] *His plane is expected to land at about 7:30 this evening.* ○ [+ to infinitive] *We expected to see her here, but I guess she decided not to come.* **2** To expect is also to ask for something to happen because you think you have a right to ask for it: [T] *The boss wants me to work this weekend – that's expecting a lot!* **3** If you say that a woman **is expecting**, you mean that she is pregnant.
expectancy /ɪk'spek·tən·si/ *n* [U] ○ *There was an air of expectancy as the chairman rose to speak.*
expectant /ɪk'spek·tənt/ *adj* [not gradable] An expectant mother/father/parent is someone whose child has not yet been born.
expectantly /ɪk'spek·tənt·li/ *adv* [not gradable] ○ *She looked up at him expectantly.*
expectation /,ek·spek'teɪ·ʃən/ *n* [C/U] the feeling or belief that something will or should happen ○ [U] *Considering his grades, there is little expectation of his getting into medical school.* ○ [C usually pl] *Last year's predictions fell a bit short of expectations.* ➤ Usage: **attend or wait/expect?** at ATTEND; **wait or expect?** at WAIT

WORD FAMILY expect

Nouns	expectancy expectation	*Verbs*	expect
		Adverbs	expectantly unexpectedly
Adjectives	expectant unexpected		

expedient /ɪk'spiːd·iː·ənt/ *adj* [not gradable] helpful or useful in a particular situation, and without considering any moral question that might influence your decision ○ *We thought it expedient not to pay the builder until he finished the work.*
expediency /ɪk'spiːd·iː·ən·si/, **expedience** /ɪk'spiːd·iː·əns/ *n* [U] ○ *political expediency*

expedite /'ek·spə,dɑɪt/ *v* [T] to cause something to be done or progress more quickly ○ *We've got to expedite this order because they need it by tomorrow.*

expedition /,ek·spə'dɪʃ·ən/ *n* [C] a long, organized trip for a particular purpose, or the people, vehicles, or ships making such a trip ○ *a military expedition*

expel /ɪk'spel/ *v* [T] **-ll-** to force someone to leave a country, organization, or school ○ *He was expelled from school for his continued bad behavior.* ○ Related noun: EXPULSION

expend /ɪk'spend/ *v* [T] to use or spend something, esp. time, effort, or money ○ *They expend all their energy fixing up their house.*

expendable /ɪk'spen·də·bəl/ *adj* [not gradable] not worth keeping or no longer useful ○ *He was considered expendable and dropped from the team.*

expenditure /ɪk'spen·də·tʃər/ *n* [C/U] an amount of money, time, or effort that is spent ○ [C] *a large expenditure of funds*

expense /ɪkˈspens/ *n* [C/U] an amount of money needed or used to do or buy something; cost ○ [C] *We have to start cutting down on our expenses.* ○ [U] *The house was redecorated at great expense.*

expensive /ɪkˈspen·sɪv/ *adj* [not gradable] costing a lot of money ○ *Housing in this part of the country is very expensive.*

expensively /ɪkˈspen·sɪv·li/ *adv* [not gradable] ○ *She was expensively dressed.*

WORD FAMILY expense

Nouns	expenditure expense expenses	*Adjectives*	expensive inexpensive
Verbs	expend	*Adverbs*	expensively inexpensively

WORD CHOICES expense

The adjectives **costly** and **pricey** (*informal*) mean the same as "expensive."

*Consulting a lawyer can be a **costly** business.*

*I liked the shirt but I didn't buy it because it was a bit **pricey**.*

To talk about a place that is very expensive, you can use the adjective **exclusive** or in informal English, **fancy** or **posh**.

*They have an apartment in an **exclusive** part of town.*

*We stayed in a **fancy** hotel on the beach.*

*He took me to a **posh** restaurant.*

In informal situations, the expression **cost a fortune** or, more informally, the idiom **cost an arm and a leg** can be used to say that something is very expensive.

*That coat must have **cost a fortune**.*

*I'd love to buy a Rolls Royce but they **cost an arm and a leg**.*

If the price of something is more expensive than it should be, you can use the word **exorbitant** or in more informal situations, you could describe something as **steep** or a **rip-off**.

*Customers are charged **exorbitant** prices for drinks.*

*Isn't $5 for a cup of coffee a little **steep**?*

*You paid $300 for that shirt? That's a complete **rip-off**!*

IDIOMS with expense

• **at the expense of** *someone*, **at** *someone's* **expense** in a way that embarrasses or harms someone ○ *They all had a good laugh at her expense.*

• **at the expense of** *something* resulting in the loss of something ○ *Do we really want to speed the process up at the expense of safety?*

expense account *n* [C] an amount of money that employees can spend to travel or buy things related to their jobs and which their employers will pay for

experience /ɪkˈspɪr·iː·əns/ *n* [C/U] (the process of getting) knowledge or skill that is obtained from doing, seeing, or feeling things, or something that happens which has an effect on you ○ [U] *Do you have any experience working with children?* ○ [U] *I know from experience that it can get quite cold in Maine this time of year.*

experience /ɪkˈspɪr·iː·əns/ *v* [T] ○ *The community has experienced rapid residential growth.* ○ *She began to experience* (= to feel) *sharp pains in her elbow.*

experienced /ɪkˈspɪr·iː·ənst/ *adj* [not gradable] having the skill and knowledge to do something, esp. because of having done it for a long time ○ *Martin is an experienced sailor.*

WORD FAMILY experience

Nouns	experience inexperience	*Adjectives*	experienced inexperienced
Verbs	experience		

experiment /ɪkˈsper·ə·mənt, -ˈspɪr-/ *n* [C/U] ***science*** a test done in order to learn something or to discover whether something works or is true ○ [C] *His experiments were designed to find better methods of using heat energy.*

experiment /ɪkˈsper·əˌment, -ˈspɪr-/ *v* [I] to test or to try a new way of doing something ○ *The school is experimenting with new teaching methods.*

experimental /ɪkˌsper·əˈment·əl, -ˌspɪr-/ *adj* [not gradable] using or based on new ideas

experimentation /ɪkˌsper·ə·mənˈteɪ·ʃən, -ˌspɪr-/ *n* [U]

WORD FAMILY experiment

Nouns	experiment experimentation	*Verbs*	experiment
		Adverbs	experimentally
Adjectives	experimental		

expert Ⓐ /ˈek·spɜrt/ *n* [C] a person having a high level of knowledge or skill in a particular subject ○ *He is the administration's foreign-policy expert for eastern Europe.*

expert Ⓐ /ˈek·spɜrt, ɪkˈspɜrt/ *adj* [not gradable] ○ *She's an expert swimmer.*

expertly Ⓐ /ˈekˌspɜrt·li, ɪkˈspɜrt·li/ *adv* [not gradable]

WORD FAMILY expert

Nouns	expert expertise	*Adjectives*	expert
		Adverbs	expertly

expertise Ⓐ /ˌek·spərˈtiːz, -ˈtiːs/ *n* [U] a high level of skill or knowledge ○ *She was widely known for her expertise as a trial lawyer.*

expiration date *n* [C] the last day on which a product or service can be used ○ *What is the expiration date of your credit card?*

expire END /ɪkˈspaɪr/ *v* [I] (of something that lasts for a fixed length of time) to end or stop being in use ○ *My passport will expire next year.*

expiration /ˌek·spəˈreɪ·ʃən/ *n* [U] the end of a period of time during which an agreement or official document can be used ○ *He stayed on past the expiration of his tourist visa.*

DIE /ɪkˈspaɪr/ *v* [I] *fml* to die

explain /ɪk'spleɪn/ *v* [I/T] **1** to make something clear or easy to understand by describing or giving information about it ○ [I] *If there's anything you don't understand, I'll be happy to explain.* ○ [T] *The teacher explained the procedure to the students.* ○ [+ question word] *Bill explained how the program works.* **2** To explain is also to give a reason for doing something: [+ question word] *He couldn't explain why he did it.*

explanation /ˌek·splə'neɪ·ʃən/ *n* [C/U] **1** [C] *She gave a detailed explanation of the administration's health-care proposal.* **2** An explanation is also a reason or an excuse for doing something: [C] *He had no explanation for his absence the day before.*

explanatory /ɪk'splæn·əˌtɔːr·i, -ˌtoʊr·i/ *adj* [not gradable] helping to make something clear or understandable ○ *an explanatory note*

WORD FAMILY explain

Nouns	explanation	Adjectives	unexplained
Verbs	explain		explanatory
Adverbs	inexplicably		explicable
			inexplicable

WORD CHOICES explain

If someone is explaining something in order to make it easier for someone else to understand, you can use the verb **clarify**.

*Let me just **clarify** what I mean here.*

The verb **define** is sometimes used when explaining exactly what something means.

*Your responsibilities are clearly **defined** in the contract.*

If something is being explained clearly in writing, the phrasal verb **set out** is sometimes used.

*Your contract will **set out** the terms of your employment.*

If something is being explained in great detail, the phrasal verb **spell out** is often used.

*They sent me a letter **spelling out** the details of the agreement.*

PHRASAL VERB with explain

• **explain away** *something* [M] to try to escape being blamed for something bad, usually by making it seem unimportant ○ *He tried to explain the error away by saying it was a simple typing mistake.*

expletive /'ek·splət̬·ɪv/ *n* [C] a rude or offensive word used to express anger, pain, annoyance, etc.

explicit Ⓐ /ɪk'splɪs·ət/ *adj* [not gradable] **1** communicated directly in a clear and exact way ○ *I gave them explicit directions on how to get here.* **2** Explicit also means showing full details, without anything hidden or suggested. ○ Compare IMPLICIT SUGGESTED

explicitly Ⓐ /ɪk'splɪs·ət·li/ *adv* [not gradable]

explode BURST /ɪk'sploʊd/ *v* [I/T] to burst violently and usually with a loud noise, or to cause this to happen ○ [I] *A bomb exploded nearby.* ○ [C] *Black holes are left behind by exploding stars called supernovas.* ○ [I] *(fig.) Yoga has exploded in popularity as a way to achieve physical and mental health.* ○ Related noun: EXPLOSION BURST

SHOW EMOTION /ɪk'sploʊd/ *v* [I] to show sudden violent emotion, esp. anger ○ *He exploded in anger when told his luggage had been lost.*

INCREASE /ɪk'sploʊd/ *v* [I] to increase very quickly ○ *The population is exploding in that part of the world.* ○ Related noun: EXPLOSION INCREASE

PROVE FALSE /ɪk'sploʊd/ *v* [T] to prove to be false or wrong ○ *She hopes that this book will explode myths about poverty and intelligence.*

WORD FAMILY explode

Nouns	explosion	Verbs	explode
	explosive	Adverbs	explosively
Adjectives	explosive		

exploit Ⓐ USE UNFAIRLY /ɪk'splɔɪt, 'ek·splɔɪt/ *v* [T] to use someone unfairly for your own advantage ○ *Factories here are coming under criticism for exploiting workers.*

exploitation Ⓐ /ˌekˌsplɔɪ'teɪ·ʃən/ *n* [U] **1** *She favors legislation to curb the exploitation of child labor.* **2** ***politics & government*** Exploitation of COLONIES leaves them at a disadvantage and makes the COLONIZING nations more wealthy and powerful.

USE WELL /ɪk'splɔɪt, 'ekˌsplɔɪt/ *v* [T] to use something for your own benefit ○ *The two companies joined forces to exploit the potential of the Internet.*

ACT /'ek·splɔɪt, ɪk'splɔɪt/ *n* [C] a brave, interesting, or unusual act ○ *daredevil exploits* ○ *He is not content to limit himself to his exploits on the basketball court.*

explore TRAVEL /ɪk'splɔːr, -'sploʊr/ *v* [I/T] to travel to a new place to learn about it or become familiar with it ○ [T] *They set out to explore the city.*

exploration /ˌek·splə'reɪ·ʃən, ˌekˌsplɔː-/ *n* [C/U] ○ [U] *oil/gas exploration* ○ [U] *space exploration*

explorer /ɪk'splɔːr·ər, ɪk'sploʊr·ər/ *n* [C] ○ *French explorers traded with the Indians in many parts of North America.*

DISCOVER /ɪk'splɔːr, -'sploʊr/ *v* [T] to try to discover; learn about ○ *We have to explore new ways to market our products.* ○ *Many scholars have explored this issue.*

exploratory /ek'splɔːr·əˌtɔːr·i, ek'sploʊr·əˌtoʊr·i/ *adj* [not gradable] intended to learn more about something ○ *After the illness had dragged on for too long, Jake decided that an exploratory operation was necessary.*

WORD FAMILY explore

Nouns	exploration	Adjectives	exploratory
	explorer	Verbs	explore

explosion BURST /ɪk'sploʊ·ʒən/ *n* [C/U] a violent burst, often with a loud noise ○ [C] *The fire was caused by a gas explosion.* ○ [U] *The explosion of the space shuttle shocked the nation.* ○ Related verb: EXPLODE BURST

explosive /ɪk'sploʊ·sɪv, -zɪv/ *n* [C] a substance that can be made to burst violently ○ *Explosives are sometimes used to blast away rock in construction.* ○ *Dynamite is a powerful explosive.*

explosive /ɪk'sploʊ·sɪv, -zɪv/ *adj* **1** *an explosive device* ○ *Certain gases are highly explosive.* ○ *(fig.) It was a politically explosive issue.* **2** Explosive also means difficult to control and likely to be violent: *She has an explosive temper.*

INCREASE /ɪk'sploʊ·ʒən/ *n* [C] a quick and big increase ○ *Auto dealers report an explosion of interest in family-style vans.* ○ Related verb: EXPLODE INCREASE

explosive /ɪk'sploʊ·sɪv, -zɪv/ *adj* ○ *There has been an explosive increase in the number households owning a computer.*

expo /'ek·spoʊ/ *n* [C] *short form of* EXPOSITION SHOW

exponent **PERSON** /ɪk'spoʊ·nənt, 'ek,spoʊ-/ *n* [C] someone who supports an idea, plan, or position ○ *He was the leading exponent of the behavioral approach to psychology.*

NUMBER /ɪk'spoʊ·nənt/ *n* [C] ***mathematics*** a number or sign that shows how many times another number is to be multiplied by itself

exponential *adj* ***mathematics*** An **exponential equation** is an EQUATION (= mathematical statement) in which the VARIABLE (= letter or symbol) appears in an exponent.

export Ⓐ /ek'spɔːrt, -'spoʊrt/ *v* [I/T] to send goods to another country for sale or use ○ [T] *Chile exports a large amount of copper to Japan.* ○ Compare IMPORT BRING IN

export Ⓐ /'ek·spɔːrt, -spoʊrt/ *n* [C/U] **1** something sold and taken out of a country and into another ○ [C] *Coffee is one of Brazil's main exports.* **2** Export is also the business of sending goods to another country in order to sell them there.

exporter Ⓐ /ek'spɔːrt̬·ər, ek'spoʊrt̬·ər/ *n* [C] ○ *Japan is a major exporter of cars.*

expose Ⓐ **BE SEEN** /ɪk'spoʊz/ *v* [T] to make something covered or hidden able to be seen ○ *The plaster was removed to expose the original brick wall.*

exposed Ⓐ /ɪk'spoʊzd/ *adj* ○ *He left some exposed wires that should be covered up.*

SHOW THE TRUTH /ɪk'spoʊz/ *v* [T] to publicly show that someone or something is bad or dishonest ○ *He was exposed as a fraud and a liar.*

BE HARMED /ɪk'spoʊz/ *v* [T] to create a situation or a condition that makes someone likely to be harmed ○ *His behavior on the Senate floor exposed him to ridicule.* ○ *Be sure your child wears sunscreen whenever she's exposed to the sun.*

GIVE OPPORTUNITY /ɪk'spoʊz/ *v* [T] to create conditions that allow someone to have the opportunity to learn or experience new things ○ *Kate was exposed to new ideas when she went to college.*

exposé /,ek·spoʊ'zeɪ, -spə-/ *n* [C] a public report about a situation that is shocking or that has been kept secret

exposition **EXPLANATION** /,ek·spə'zɪʃ·ən/ *n* [C] *fml* **1** a statement that explains something clearly **2** ***literature*** Exposition in a written work is the passages which explain where events take place, what happened before the story begins, and the background of the characters.

expository /ɪk'spɑz·ə,tɔːr·i, -,toʊr·i/ *adj* [not gradable] explaining or describing an event or situation ○ *expository writing*

SHOW /,ek·spə'zɪʃ·ən/, *short form* **expo** *n* [C] a big public event in which the goods of many different companies or organizations are shown ○ *the San Francisco exposition*

exposure Ⓐ **HARMFUL CONDITION** /ɪk'spoʊ·ʒər/ *n* [U] **1** a situation or condition that makes someone likely to be harmed, esp. because the person has not been protected from something dangerous ○ *A federal court jury found the workers had been harmed by prolonged exposure to asbestos fibers.* ○ *Avoid prolonged exposure to sunlight.* **2** Exposure is also a serious medical condition that is caused by being outside without protection from the weather.

OPPORTUNITY /ɪk'spoʊ·ʒər/ *n* [U] the conditions that make available an opportunity to learn or experience new things ○ *Additional exposure to the Japanese language was provided at meals.* ○ *Students deserve exposure to creative teachers.*

PUBLIC ATTENTION /ɪk'spoʊ·ʒər/ *n* [U] the attention given to someone or something by television, newspapers, magazines, etc. ○ *More races means more exposure for the team.* ○ *He gained wide exposure in both the print and sound media.*

MAKE PUBLIC /ɪk'spoʊ·ʒər/ *n* [U] the act of stating facts publicly that show that someone is dishonest or dangerous ○ *Party officials have succeeded in keeping a lid on exposure of the senator's misdeeds.*

DIRECTION /ɪk'spoʊ·ʒər/ *n* [C usually sing] the condition of facing in (a stated direction) ○ [C] *Our dining room has a southern exposure, so we get plenty of sun.*

PHOTOGRAPH /ɪk'spoʊ·ʒər/ *n* [C] one of the positions in a strip of film that can produce a photograph ○ *Get a roll of film with 36 exposures.*

express **SHOW** /ɪk'spres/ *v* [T] to show a feeling or idea by what you say or do or by how you look ○ *She's expressed interest in doing some camping.* ○ *Several victims expressed disappointment at the small amount of money they were offered.* ○ *He wrote to express his sympathy after the death of her mother.* ○ *The program tries to get students to express themselves verbally.*

expression /ɪk'spreʃ·ən/ *n* [C/U] the act of showing a feeling or idea, or a feeling or idea that is shown ○ [C] *She had such a sad expression on her face that I wondered what was wrong.* ○ [U] *Freedom of expression is a cherished right in democracies.* ○ See also: EXPRESSION

expressionless /ɪk'spreʃ·ən·ləs/ *adj* showing no emotion ○ *His face was expressionless as the verdict was announced.*

expressive /ɪk'spres·ɪv/ *adj* showing your feelings in your voice, behavior, or appearance ○ *His singing was beautiful and expressive.*

FAST /ɪk'spres/ *adj* [not gradable] (esp. of transportation or a service) fast, or direct ○ *The express train makes very few stops.*

express /ɪk'spres/ *n* [C] a train or bus that does not stop at many places on its route and therefore is faster in getting people to where they want to go ○ *Change here to get the express.* ○ Compare LOCAL VEHICLE

CLEAR /ɪk'spres/ *adj* clearly and intentionally stated ○ *It was her express wish that art collection be given to the university's museum.*

expressly /ɪk'spres·li/ *adv* ○ *He wrote the play expressly for her.*

WORD FAMILY express			
Nouns	expression	*Verbs*	express
Adjectives	expressive expressionless	*Adverbs*	expressively

E

expression /ɪk'spreʃ·ən/ *n* [C] **1** a word or group of words having a particular meaning or used in a particular way ○ *That was an expression he hadn't heard before, and wondered what it meant.* **2** ***mathematics*** An expression is also a mathematical statement that includes numbers, symbols, or both. ○ See also: EXPRESSION at EXPRESS **SHOW**

expressway /ɪk'spres,weɪ/ *n* [C] a wide road built for fast-moving traffic, with a limited number of places where drivers can enter and leave it

expropriate /ek'sproʊ·priː,eɪt/ *v* [T] to take and keep money or property belonging to someone else

expulsion /ɪk'spʌl·ʃən/ *n* [C] the act of forcing someone, or of being forced, to leave somewhere ○ *The government ordered the expulsion of foreign journalists.* ○ Related verb: EXPEL

exquisite /ɪk'skwɪz·ət, 'ek·skwɪz·ət/ *adj* especially beautiful or admirable ○ *exquisite Chinese embroideries* ○ *the most exquisite French cuisine*

exquisitely /ɪk'skwɪz·ət·li, 'ek·skwɪz-/ *adv* [not gradable] ○ *Their house is exquisitely furnished.*

ext. *n* [C] *abbreviation for* EXTENSION

extant /'ek·stənt, ek'stænt/ *adj* still existing ○ *Phyllis Wheatley is the author of the earliest extant volume of poetry by an African American.*

extemporaneous /ek,stem·pə'reɪ·niː·əs/ *adj* done or said without preparation ○ *He made some extemporaneous remarks before the award ceremony.*

extend **REACH** /ɪk'stend/ *v* [I/T] to reach, continue, or stretch ○ [I] *Farmland extends for miles in every direction.* ○ [I] *The meeting extended into the late hours of the night.* ○ [T] *He extended his hand to greet me.*

extended /ɪk'sten·dəd/ *adj* ○ *There will be extended election day coverage on the evening news.* ○ *They're taking an extended* (= long) *vacation.*

extensive /ɪk'sten·sɪv/ *adj* **1** covering a large area; having or being a large amount ○ *Extensive roadway repairs are causing traffic problems.* **2** Extensive also means wide in range and including much detailed information: *Her knowledge of music is extensive.* ○ *Foster did extensive research on electromagnetic fields.*

extensively /ɪk'sten·sɪv·li/ *adv* ○ *The house was extensively rebuilt.*

INCREASE /ɪk'stend/ *v* [T] **1** to add to something in order to make it longer; increase ○ *The store has recently extended its hours.* ○ *I might have extended this essay to include more information.* **2** To extend something is also to increase its range so that it includes more: *The proposed law would extend health insurance to all children.*

extension /ɪk'sten·tʃən/ *n* [C/U] an amount by which something is increased, or something added to something else ○ *a contract extension* ○ *I applied for an extension to my visa.* ○ [C] *We're building an extension on our house to enlarge the kitchen.*

OFFER /ɪk'stend/ *v* [T] to offer or give ○ *I would like to extend my thanks to everybody for making this evening a success.* ○ *We'd like to extend our condolences to the family.*

extended family *n* [C] a family that includes GRANDPARENTS, aunts, uncles, and others in addition to parents and children ○ Compare NUCLEAR FAMILY

extension /ɪk'sten·tʃən/, *abbreviation* **ext.** *n* [C] **1** any of two or more telephones in the same house that share the same number ○ *We have an extension in our bedroom.* **2** An extension is also any of the telephones connected to a central system, esp. in a business.

extension cord *n* [C] a wire that can be connected to the wire of an electrical device to make it longer

extensor /ɪk'sten·sər/ *n* [C] ***biology*** a muscle that allows you to make part of your body straight ○ Compare FLEXOR

extent **AREA** /ɪk'stent/ *n* [U] the area, length, or size of something ○ *Approaching the airport, you could see the full extent of the island.*

DEGREE /ɪk'stent/ *n* [U] the degree or limit of something; how great or severe something is ○ *To some extent it was my fault, though I didn't mean any harm.* ○ *We didn't know the extent of his injuries.* ○ *It makes sense to a certain extent to write down everything.*

extenuating /ɪk'sten·jə,weɪt̬·ɪŋ/ *adj* acting to excuse something bad or causing something bad to be judged less seriously ○ *There were extenuating circumstances.*

exterior /ek'stɪr·iː·ər/ *adj* [not gradable] outer; on or from the outside ○ *The exterior walls of the house are painted pink.* ○ Compare INTERIOR

exterior /ek'stɪr·iː·ər/ *n* [C] ○ *The exterior of the house needs painting.*

exterminate /ɪk'stɜr·mə,neɪt/ *v* [T] to kill all the animals or people in a particular place or of a particular type

extermination /ɪk,stɜr·mə'neɪ·ʃən/ *n* [U] ○ *International measures have been taken to prevent the extermination of whales.*

exterminator /ɪk'stɜr·mə,neɪt̬·ər/ *n* [C] a person whose job it is to kill unwanted insects or animals

external Ⓐ /ek'stɜrn·ᵊl/ *adj* [not gradable] existing, intended for, or happening outside a person, organization, place, country, etc. ○ *This skin cream is for external use only.* ○ *She handles the company's external relations.* ○ *His paintings show external influences* (= influences coming from other people). ○ Compare INTERNAL

externalize Ⓐ /ek'stɜrn·əl ˌɑɪz/ *v* [I/T] *fml* to express difficult thoughts or feelings openly

externally Ⓐ /ek'stɜrn·əl·i/ *adv* [not gradable]

extinct /ɪk'stɪŋt/ *adj* [not gradable] **1** no longer existing ○ *There is concern that the giant panda will soon become extinct.* **2** An extinct VOLCANO (= mountain made from burned materials) is one that is no longer active.

extinction /ɪk'stɪŋ·ʃən/ *n* [U] ○ *Many species of plants and animals are threatened with extinction.*

extinguish /ɪk'stɪŋ·gwɪʃ, -wɪʃ/ *v* [T] to stop a fire or light from burning ○ *It took the firefighters four hours to extinguish the flames.*

extol /ɪk'stoʊl/ *v* [T] **-ll-** to praise highly ○ *He often extols the virtues of his students.*

extort /ɪk'stɔːrt/ *v* [T] to obtain by force or threat ○ *The gang is accused of extorting money from local store owners.*

extortion /ɪk'stɔːr·ʃən/ *n* [U] ○ *He was found guilty of extortion.*

extra /'ek·strə/ *adj, adv* [not gradable] added, additional, or more than expected ○ *Some students needed extra help.* ○ *He's been working an extra two hours a day.* ○ *I bought some extra batteries.*

extra /'ek·strə/ *n* [C] **1** *We didn't get any extras on our new car except for the CD player.* **2** An extra is also a person in a movie who does not have a speaking part and is usually in the background or in a crowd.

extracellular /ˌek·strə'sel·jə·lər/ *adj* [not gradable] ***biology*** being or happening outside a cell

extract Ⓐ **REMOVE** /ɪk'strækt/ *v* [T] to remove or take out something ○ *The dentist had to extract one of Miguel's teeth.*

extract Ⓐ /'ek·strækt/ *n* [C/U] a substance removed from another substance, often a food, and containing a basic quality or flavor ○ [U] *vanilla extract*

extraction Ⓐ /ɪk'stræk·ʃən/ *n* [C/U] **1** [C] *a tooth extraction* **2** If you say that a person is of a particular extraction, you mean that the person originally came from the stated nation or country: [U] *She is of Korean extraction.*

TEXT /'ek·strækt/ *n* [C] ***writing*** a small part of a book or other writing that is published separately ○ *The newspaper printed extracts from the court documents.*

extracurricular /ˌek·strə·kə'rɪk·jə·lər/ *adj* [not gradable] (of activities or subjects) not part of the usual school or college course ○ *Popular extracurricular activities include pottery, chess, choir, tennis, and swimming.*

extradition /ˌek·strə'dɪʃ·ən/ *n* [U] the return of someone accused of a crime to the country where the crime was committed ○ *They have applied for his extradition to the United States.*

extradite /'ek·strəˌdɑɪt/ *v* [T] ○ *One of the defendants fled to Egypt, which extradited him to the US.*

extraneous /ek'streɪ·niː·əs/ *adj* not directly connected or related to a matter being considered ○ *We must not be distracted by extraneous issues, she said.*

extraordinary /ɪk'strɔːrd·ən ˌer·i, ˌek·strə 'ɔːrd-/ *adj* very unusual and special; different in type or greater in degree than the usual or ordinary ○ *Being chairman gave him an extraordinary sense of power.* ○ *She was an extraordinary woman, and no one will ever forget her.*

extraordinarily /ɪkˌstrɔːrd·ən'er·ə·li, ˌek·strə ˌɔːrd-/ *adv*

extraterrestrial /ˌek·strə·tə'res·triː·əl/ *adj* [not gradable] (coming from) outside the planet earth ○ *extraterrestrial objects like meteorites and asteroids*

extraterritoriality /ˌek·strəˌter·əˌtɔːr·iː'æl·əţ·i, -ˌtoʊr-/ *n* [U] ***politics & government*** the RIGHT of foreign citizens to be TRIED by the laws of the country they are from, not the laws of the country where they live

extravagant **EXPENSIVE** /ɪk'stræv·ə·gənt/ *adj* more expensive than is necessary or reasonable, or having the characteristics of being expensive ○ *Company executives enjoyed an extravagant lifestyle.* ○ *Top athletes are showered with extravagant gifts.*

extravagance /ɪk'stræv·ə·gəns/ *n* [C/U] ○ [C] *In those days, a second car seemed like a needless extravagance.*

extravagantly /ɪk'stræv·ə·gənt·li/ *adv*

UNREASONABLE /ɪk'stræv·ə·gənt/ *adj* beyond any reasonable expectation ○ *Parents who have extravagant hopes for their children are bound to be disappointed.*

extreme **GREAT** /ɪk'striːm/ *adj* very great; beyond what is usual or what might be expected ○ *Use extreme caution, as the steps are very slippery.* ○ *The extreme cold kept most people indoors.*

extreme /ɪk'striːm/ *n* [C] ○ *The security staff went to extremes to insure the safety of the world leaders.*

extremely /ɪk'striːm·li/ *adv* ○ *She was extremely intelligent.*

FURTHEST /ɪk'striːm/ *adj* **1** at the furthest point; to the greatest degree ○ *At the extreme end of the lake there is a hunting lodge.* **2** Extreme opinions, ideas, etc., are beyond the usual range of variety and would seem unreasonable to most people.

extremism /ɪk'striːˌmɪz·əm/ *n* [U] ○ *political extremism*

extremist /ɪk'striː·məst/ *n* [C] someone who has an opinion or ideas that seem unreasonable to most people

MATH /ɪk'striːm/ *n* [C] ***mathematics*** the first or fourth TERMS (= numbers or symbols) of a PROPORTION (= a mathematical statement with a comparison of two numbers calculated by division on

E

each side) ○ *In the proportion a/b=t/z the terms a and z are the extremes.*

WORD FAMILY extreme

Nouns		Adjectives	
	extreme		extreme
	extremism		extremist
	extremist	Adverbs	extremely

extremities /ɪk'strem·ət̬·iːz/ *pl n* the hands and feet

E

extricate /'ek·strəˌkeɪt/ *v* [T] to remove, release, or free someone or something from a difficult condition or situation ○ *They need education and other economic opportunities in order to extricate themselves from poverty.* ○ *The president outlined a plan to extricate the troops if the situation worsened.*

exuberant /ɪg'zuː·bə·rənt/ *adj* (esp. of people and their behavior) very energetic, and showing the happiness of being alive ○ *He is an exuberant dancer.*

exuberance /ɪg'zuː·bə·rəns/ *n* [U] ○ *His exuberance is contagious.*

exude /ɪg'zuːd/ *v* [T] **1** to have a lot of a particular quality or feeling ○ *Sal exudes confidence.* **2** To exude is also to produce from the inside and spread out slowly: *Some trees exude a sap that repels insect parasites.*

exult /ɪg'zʌlt/ *v* [I] to express great pleasure or happiness, esp. at your success or at someone else's failure ○ *He exulted in the publicity he received.*

exultant /ɪg'zʌlt·ᵊnt/ *adj* ○ *He was exultant at the news of his team's victory.*

exultation /ˌeg·zəl'teɪ·ʃən/ *n* [U]

exurb /'ek·sɜrb, 'eg·zɜrb/ *n* [C] a region beyond the SUBURBS (= areas built around cities), which is not highly developed and where rich people often live

exurban /ek'sɜr·bən, eg'zɜr-/ *adj* ○ *an exurban community*

eye /ɑɪ/ *n* [C] **1** one of the pair of organs of seeing in the faces of humans and animals ○ *She has green eyes.* ➤ Picture: **butterfly 2** The eye of a needle is the hole through which you put the thread.

eye /ɑɪ/ *v* [T] *pres. part.* **eyeing,** *past* **eyed** ○ *She eyed the other passengers* (= looked closely at them).

IDIOMS with eye

• **an eye for an eye** the idea that a person who causes another person to suffer should suffer in an equal amount ○ *I don't believe in that kind of eye for an eye justice.*

• **cannot take** *your* **eyes off** *someone/something* to not be able to stop looking at someone or something ○ *You can't take your eyes off that guy when he's talking.*

eyeball /'ɑɪˌbɔːl/ *n* [C] the whole eye, including the part that cannot usually be seen

eyebrow /'ɑɪ·brɑʊ/ *n* [C] the line of short hairs that humans have above each eye

eye contact *n* [U] the act of looking directly in the eyes of another person as the other person looks at you

eyeglasses /'ɑɪˌglæs·əz/ *pl n* GLASSES ○ See at GLASS

eyelash /'ɑɪ·læʃ/ *n* [C] one of the short hairs that grow along the edges of your EYELID

eyelid /'ɑɪ·lɪd/ *n* [C] either of the two pieces of skin that you can close over each eye

eye-opener *n* [C] *infml* something that is surprising and that teaches you something new

eye shadow *n* [U] a colored cream or powder that is put around the eyes to make them look larger or more attractive

eyesight /'ɑɪ·sɑɪt/ *n* [U] the ability to see ○ *Her eyesight is not as good as it used to be.*

eyesore /'ɑɪ·sɔːr, -soʊr/ *n* [C] an unpleasant or ugly sight in a public place ○ *These billboards by the side of the road are an eyesore.*

eyewitness /'ɑɪ'wɪt·nəs/ *n* [C] a person who saw something happen, for example a crime or an accident ○ *Police were looking for eyewitnesses.*

F f

F LETTER, **f** /ef/ *n* [C] *pl* **F's, Fs, f's, fs** the sixth letter of the English alphabet

MUSICAL NOTE /ef/ *n* [C/U] *pl* **F's, Fs** ***music*** in Western music, the fourth note in the SCALE (= series of notes) that begins on the note C, or a set of notes based on this note

MARK /ef/ *n* [C] *pl* **F's, Fs** a mark given for an exam, a course, or a piece of work which shows that your work has failed to meet the lowest acceptable standard ○ *I'm giving you an F if your paper isn't in by Thursday.*

TEMPERATURE *n* [U] *abbreviation for* FAHRENHEIT ○ *Yesterday the temperature was 90°F.*

fable /ˈfeɪ·bəl/ *n* [C] ***literature*** a short story that tells a moral truth, often using animals as characters ○ *Latisha loves the fable about the grasshopper and the ant.*

fabled /ˈfeɪ·bəld/ *adj* famous, esp. because of having been frequently written about ○ *Atlantis, Plato's fabled lost continent under the sea*

fabric CLOTH /ˈfæb·rɪk/ *n* [C/U] cloth or woven material, or a type of this material ○ [U] *cotton fabric* ○ [C] *Wash delicate fabrics by hand.*

STRUCTURE /ˈfæb·rɪk/ *n* [U] the structure of something; the parts of something that hold it together and make it what it is ○ *Extreme social activism might rip apart the social fabric.*

fabricate /ˈfæb·rəˌkeɪt/ *v* [T] to invent or produce something in order to deceive ○ *She fabricated charges that her boss was stealing money.*

fabrication /ˌfæb·rəˈkeɪ·ʃən/ *n* [C] ○ *That story is a complete fabrication.*

fabulous GOOD /ˈfæb·jə·ləs/ *adj infml* very good; wonderful ○ *This is a fabulous place!*

fabulously /ˈfæb·jə·lə·sli/ *adv* ○ *She dressed him fabulously.*

LARGE /ˈfæb·jə·ləs/ *adj* great in size or amount ○ *fabulous profits*

fabulously /ˈfæb·jə·lə·sli/ *adv* ○ *They were fabulously successful.*

façade, **facade** /fəˈsɑd/ *n* [C] **1** the front of a building ○ *The façade is made of limestone.* **2** A person's façade is the image that person presents to others: *Behind her façade of gentleness was a tough competitor.*

face HEAD /feɪs/ *n* [C] the front of the head including the eyes, nose, and mouth ○ *Cal hid his face in his hands.*

facial /ˈfeɪ·ʃəl/ *adj* [not gradable] ○ *Casey suffered a facial cut in the accident.*

facial /ˈfeɪ·ʃəl/ *n* [C] a beauty treatment that cleans and improves the skin of the face with creams, gentle rubbing, etc.

faceless /ˈfeɪ·sləs/ *adj* [not gradable] lacking any particular character; difficult to describe or deal with ○ *faceless bureaucracy*

FRONT /feɪs/ *n* [C] **1** the front or surface of an object ○ *We climbed the north face of Mount Washington.* **2** The face of a clock or a watch is the surface that has the numbers or marks on it that show what time it is.

DEAL WITH /feɪs/ *v* [T] to deal with a difficult situation ○ *They are faced with major financial problems.* ○ *I can't face climbing those stairs again.*

BE POSITIONED /feɪs/ *v* [I/T] to have the front of something positioned toward, or to turn toward something or someone ○ [I always + adv/prep] *The balcony faces south.* ○ [T] *Please face the front of the room.*

IDIOMS with face

• **at face value** for what something appears to be ○ *I took the offer at face value because I didn't think they would try to trick me.*

• **face the music** to accept responsibility for something you have done ○ *If she lied to me, then she'll just have to face the music.*

• **face-to-face (with** *someone***)** looking at another person ○ *We sat face-to-face.*

• **face-to-face (with** *something***)** having to deal with something unpleasant ○ *He's suddenly come face-to-face with his own weakness.*

• **in** *your* **face** *slang* rudely annoying someone ○ *One of the managers is always in my face.*

• **in the face of** *something* **1** despite ○ *She left home in the face of strong opposition from her parents.* **2** Also, **in the face of** can mean being threatened with something: *In the face of several lawsuits, the company took the product off the market.*

• **on the face of it** when first considered ○ *The story seems simple on the face of it, but it's really pretty complicated.*

• **to** *someone's* **face** directly to you, without trying to hide anything or be kind ○ *I know he's lying, and I'll tell him so to his face.*

PHRASAL VERB with face

• **face down** *someone/something* [M] to defeat someone or something that is opposing you by being brave and strong ○ *He admired the President's ability to face down critics.* ○ *She faced down a mid-career crisis and emerged with a high position with one of the industry leaders.*

face-lift OPERATION, **facelift** /ˈfeɪs·lɪft/ *n* [C] a medical operation that tightens loose skin to make the face look younger

IMPROVEMENT, **facelift** /ˈfeɪs·lɪft/ *n* [C] an improvement made to something to make it more modern or to change its appearance ○ *The bank is planning to give its 1930 building a complete facelift.*

facet /ˈfæs·ət/ *n* [C] one of the parts or features of something ○ *There's always one facet of my golf game that isn't working.*

facetious /fəˈsiː·ʃəs/ *adj* not seriously meaning what you say, usually in an attempt to be humor-

F

ous or to trick someone ○ *I make so much money that we never have to worry – I'm being facetious.*
facetiously /fə'siː·ʃə·sli/ *adv* ○ *"We could spend all our income on health care," she said facetiously.*

face value *n* [C usually sing] the value or price shown, for example on a stamp, a coin, or a bill ○ See also: AT FACE VALUE at FACE IDIOMS

facile /'fæs·əl/ *adj* easy or too easy; not needing effort ○ *He does not permit himself facile answers.*

facilitate Ⓐ /fə'sɪl·əˌteɪt/ *v* [T] to make something possible or easier ○ *To facilitate learning, each class is no larger than 30 students.*
facilitation Ⓐ /fəˌsɪl·ə'teɪ·ʃən/ *n* [U] ○ *Somerville was charged with conspiracy and criminal facilitation.*
facilitator Ⓐ /fə'sɪl·əˌteɪṭ·ər/ *n* [C] someone who helps to make something happen, or who makes it easier ○ *I see my role as that of a facilitator, enabling other people to work in the way that suits them best.*

facility Ⓐ **ABILITY** /fə'sɪl·əṭ·i/ *n* [U] an ability or skill at doing something ○ *His facility for memorizing dates was astonishing.*
PLACE /fə'sɪl·əṭ·i/ *n* [C] something such as a place, building, or equipment used for a particular purpose or activity ○ *The new sports facility has a swimming pool.*

facsimile /fæk'sɪm·ə·li/ *n* [C] **1** an exact copy, esp. of a document **2** A facsimile is also a FAX.

fact **SOMETHING KNOWN** /fækt/ *n* [C] something known to have happened or to exist ○ *No one disputes the fact that the accident could have been avoided.*

WORD FAMILY fact			
Nouns	fact	*Adverbs*	factually
Adjectives	factual		

IDIOMS with fact

•**fact of life** something unpleasant that cannot be avoided ○ *Driving to work on overcrowded highways is a fact of life for millions of commuters.*
•**facts of life** the details about sex and sexual reproduction
•**in fact** actually ○ *He was in fact near death by the time they reached him.* ○ Compare AS A MATTER OF FACT at AS IDIOMS

faction /'fæk·ʃən/ *n* [C] a group within a larger group, esp. one with slightly different ideas than the main group ○ *The president's advisors represent every faction of his party.*

factor Ⓐ **SITUATION** /'fæk·tər/ *n* [C] a fact or situation that influences a result ○ *Economic factors had a lot to do with their decision to sell the company.*
NUMBER /'fæk·tər/ ***algebra*** **1** a number or VARIABLE (= letter or symbol) that is being multiplied in a PRODUCT (= result of multiplying) ○ *In* 6×3=18, *6 and 3 are factors of the product* 18. **2** A factor of a product is a number that the product can be divided by exactly.
factoring /'fæk·tər·ɪŋ/ *n* [U] ***algebra*** **1** the process by which a number or VARIABLE is written as a PRODUCT of two or more TERMS (= numbers or symbols) **2 Factoring completely** is the process of factoring a number until no other factors can be found.

PHRASAL VERB with factor

•**factor in** *something* [M] to consider information, esp. as something that might influence a result ○ *It's going to feel like 110° there when you factor in the humidity.*

factory /'fæk·tə·ri, 'fæk·tri/ *n* [C] a building or buildings where people use machines to produce goods ○ *She worked in a factory that produced air conditioners.*

factual /'fæk·tʃə·wəl/ *adj* based on facts ○ *a factual account*
factually /'fæk·tʃə·wə·li/ *adv* ○ *The newspaper account was factually incorrect.*

faculty **COLLEGE TEACHERS** /'fæk·əl·ti/ *n* [C] the people who teach in a college or university, or in a department of a college or university
ABILITY /'fæk·əl·ti/ *n* [C] any natural ability, such as hearing, seeing, or thinking ○ *Even though she is 102, she still has all of her faculties.*

fad /fæd/ *n* [C] a style or activity that suddenly becomes popular but which usually does not stay popular for very long ○ *He thought computers would be just a fad.*

fade /feɪd/ *v* [I] **1** to lose color, brightness, or strength gradually ○ *If you hang your clothes out in the bright sun, they will fade.* **2** If something fades away/out, it becomes less clear and then disappears: *The voice on the radio faded out.*

Fahrenheit /'fær·ənˌhɑɪt/, *abbreviation* **F** *n* [U] a range of numbers for measuring temperature in which water freezes at 32° and boils at 212° ○ *The Fahrenheit scale is still used throughout the US.* ○ Compare CELSIUS

fail **NOT SUCCEED** /feɪl/ *v* [I] **1** to not be able to do what you are trying to achieve or are expected to do ○ [+ *to* infinitive] *She applied to Harvard University but failed to get accepted.* **2** If you fail to see/understand what something is, you do not agree with someone's description of a situation: [+ *to* infinitive] *I fail to see what the problem is* (= I don't think there is a problem).
failed /feɪld/ *adj* unsuccessful ○ *Since his failed attempt in college, John has always wanted to write a novel.*
NOT PASS /feɪl/ *v* [I/T] to be unsuccessful, or to judge that someone has been unsuccessful in a test or examination ○ [I/T] *A lot of people fail (their driving test) the first time.* ○ [T] *She said she would fail any student who misses two exams.*
NOT DO /feɪl/ *v* [I/T] **1** to not do something that should be done ○ [+ *to* infinitive] *He promised to help, but failed to send a check.* ○ [+ *to* infinitive] *She never fails to meet a deadline.* **2** To fail is also

to not help someone when expected to: [T] *He failed her when she most needed him.*

STOP /feɪl/ *v* [I] **1** to become weaker or stop working completely ○ *The bus driver said the brakes failed.* **2** If a business fails, it is unable to continue because of money problems.

failing /ˈfeɪ·lɪŋ/ *adj* [not gradable] ○ *He is in failing health and seldom goes outside any more.*

WORD FAMILY fail			
Nouns	failure	*Adjectives*	failed
Verbs	fail		failing
Adverbs	unfailingly		unfailing

failing **WEAKNESS** /ˈfeɪ·lɪŋ/ *n* [C] a fault or weakness ○ *His one big failing is that he can't say he's sorry.*

WITHOUT /ˈfeɪ·lɪŋ/ *prep* used to show what will happen if something is not possible or available ○ *She will very likely be the next president of the company, or failing that, the marketing director.*

fail-safe *adj* designed so that if one part of a device does not work, the whole thing stops working to avoid a dangerous situation

failure **LACK OF SUCCESS** /ˈfeɪl·jər/ *n* [C/U] a lack of success in doing something ○ [U] *Their attempt to sail across the Atlantic Ocean ended in failure.* ○ [C] *He was a failure as a businessman.*

SOMETHING NOT DONE /ˈfeɪl·jər/ *n* [U] the fact of not doing something you should have done ○ [+ *to infinitive*] *His failure to return her phone call told her that something was wrong.*

SOMETHING NOT WORKING /ˈfeɪl·jər/ *n* [C/U] the fact of something not working as it should ○ [U] *He died of heart failure.* ○ [C] *The new computer system was a complete failure* (= It did not work).

faint **LOSE CONSCIOUSNESS** /feɪnt/ *v* [I] to become unconscious unexpectedly for a short time ○ *I nearly fainted from the heat.*

faint /feɪnt/ *adj* [*-er/-est* only] very weak and nearly becoming unconscious ○ *He felt faint from hunger.*

SLIGHT /feɪnt/ *adj* [*-er/-est* only] not strong or clear; slight ○ *He walked along, guided only by the faint light of the moon.*

faintly /ˈfeɪnt·li/ *adv* ○ *The hospital room smelled faintly of disinfectant.*

fair **RIGHT** /fer, fær/ *adj* [*-er/-est* only] **1** treating someone in a way that is right or reasonable, or treating people equally and not allowing personal opinions to influence your judgment ○ *All he asks is a fair chance to prove his innocence.* ○ *I'm willing to do my fair share of the work* (= equal part). **2** If a game or competition is fair, it is done according to the rules: *It was a fair fight.* **3** In some sports, esp. baseball, fair means within the playing field: *The umpire ruled it a fair ball.* ○ Opposite: FOUL SPORTS

fairly /ˈfer·li, ˈfær-/ *adv* ○ *It's the responsibility of a judge to treat both sides fairly.*

fairness /ˈfer·nəs, ˈfær-/ *n* [U] ○ *In all fairness, she deserves the award.*

WORD CHOICES fair

Right or **just** can be used when something is considered fair and morally acceptable by most people.

I don't believe they should have put him in prison. It isn't ***right****.*

It wasn't a ***just*** *punishment in my view.*

Even-handed or **balanced** can be used when something is fair because it does not favor one person more than another.

The article contained very ***even-handed*** *reporting.*

The report gives a ***balanced*** *view of what happened.*

If something is fair because everyone has the same opportunities and treatment, you could use the word **egalitarian** in formal English.

We are working towards an ***egalitarian*** *society.*

Equitable can also be used in formal English when a system is fair because everyone is treated in the same way.

This is not an ***equitable*** *tax system.*

When something is fair because a person is not influenced by their own opinions or trying to gain an advantage, you could use the words **unbiased** or **impartial**.

The magazine provides ***unbiased*** *information on the products available.*

I want some ***impartial*** *advice.*

If someone plays a game in a very fair way, you could describe them as **sportsmanlike**.

That was very ***sportsmanlike*** *of you.*

AVERAGE /fer, fær/ *adj* [not gradable] neither very good nor very bad ○ *He's good in physics but only fair in math.*

LARGE /fer, fær/ *adj* [not gradable] large or great in comparison ○ *We still had a fair amount of foreign money when we returned.*

fairly /ˈfer·li, ˈfær-/ *adv* [not gradable] more than a little; to some degree ○ *I know him fairly well.* ○ *I saw her fairly recently* (= not very long ago).

CORRECT /fer, fær/ *adj* [not gradable] likely to be correct; accurate ○ *The architect's drawing will give you a pretty fair idea of what the completed house will look like.*

WEATHER /fer, fær/ *adj* [*-er/-est* only] (of weather) pleasant and dry

PUBLIC EVENT /fer, fær/ *n* [C] **1** a public event, usually held outside, where goods and sometimes farm animals are shown and sold and where there is often food and entertainment **2** A **county/state fair** is one where farm animals and products from that region are shown to compete for prizes and there is food and entertainment. **3** A **street fair** is one where a city street is closed to cars so that goods and food can be sold to people walking through it. **4** A fair is also a show at which people who work in a particular industry meet to sell and advertise their products: *a book/antiques/toy fair*

PALE /fer, fær/ *adj* [-*er*/-*est* only] (of skin) pale, or (of hair) light in color ○ *If you have fair skin, you'll get a sunburn easily.*

WORD FAMILY fair			
Nouns	fairness unfairness	*Adverbs*	fairly unfairly
Adjectives	fair unfair		

IDIOM with fair

• **fair and square** honestly and according to the rules ○ *She won the election fair and square.*

fair game *n* [U] someone or something considered reasonable to criticize ○ *Anyone running for the presidency is fair game.*

fairgrounds /ˈfer·graʊnz/ *pl n* a large outside area used for public events

fair-minded *adj* willing to treat everyone equally

fair play *n* [U] equal and honest treatment of others, esp. in following accepted rules

fair-weather friend *n* [C] someone who can be depended on only when everything is going well

fairy /ˈfer·i, ˈfær·i/ *n* [C] an imaginary creature with magical powers who looks like a small person with wings

fairy tale *n* [C] ***literature*** a traditional story, usually written for children, which often involves imaginary creatures and magic

faith TRUST /feɪθ/ *n* [U] a high degree of trust or confidence in something or someone ○ [+ *that* clause] *I have faith that she will do the right thing.*

faithful /ˈfeɪθ·fəl/ *adj* **1** trusted; loyal ○ *She has been a faithful employee for 30 years.* **2** If something, such as a copy or recording, is faithful, it is exactly like or very similar to the original: *The painting was a faithful reproduction of the original.* **3** If you are faithful to someone or something, you remain loyal and keep the promises you made: *You've been faithful to your family.*

faithfully /ˈfeɪθ·fə·li/ *adv* ○ *I always faithfully* (= carefully) *follow the instructions of my doctor when taking medicine.*

RELIGION /feɪθ/ *n* [C/U] a particular religion, or belief in God ○ [C] *the Christian/Jewish/Muslim faith* ○ [C] *We welcome people of all faiths.* ○ [U] *Put your faith in God.*

WORD FAMILY faith			
Nouns	faith	*Adverbs*	faithfully unfaithfully
Adjectives	faithful unfaithful		

fake COPY /feɪk/ *n* [C] something that is intended to look like and be mistaken for something else, esp. a copy made in order to deceive ○ *She discovered that the documents were fakes.*

fake /feɪk/ *adj* intended to look like something else, esp. in order to deceive ○ *He was caught with a fake passport.* ○ *"Is that a real fur coat?" "No, it's fake."*

fake /feɪk/ *v* [T] ○ *She faked her mother's signature on the permission form.*

PRETEND /feɪk/ *v* [I/T] to pretend ○ [I] *He isn't really crying, he's just faking.*

falcon /ˈfæl·kən, ˈfɔːl-/ *n* [C] a bird with pointed wings and a long tail that hunts and kills other birds and small animals

fall ACCIDENT /fɔːl/ *v* [I] *past simp.* **fell**, *past part.* **fallen** (of people and animals) to move unintentionally or unexpectedly onto or toward the ground from a higher place ○ *He fell and hurt his arm.* ○ *Don't fall over, honey!* ○ *I fell down the stairs.* ○ *She fell off the top of the ladder.* ○ *Kathy tripped and fell (flat) on her face* (= fell facing the ground).

fall /fɔːl/ *n* [C usually sing] ○ *She injured herself in a fall.*

COMMON LEARNER ERROR

fall or feel?

The past forms of the verbs **fall** and **feel** are often confused. The past tense of **fall** is **fell**.

He fell off the roof and broke his leg.

The past tense of **feel** is **felt**.

I felt very nervous.

WORD CHOICES fall

Drop can sometimes be used instead of "fall."

*Several apples **dropped** from the tree.*

Collapse can be used when someone or something falls down suddenly because of pressure or weakness.

*Several buildings **collapsed** in the earthquake.*

*He had a heart attack and **collapsed**.*

If someone falls to the ground suddenly, you could use the verb **crumple**.

*He fainted and **crumpled** into a heap on the floor.*

Tumble means "to fall quickly without control."

*A huge rock **tumbled** down the mountain.*

Plunge or **plummet** are verbs that are used when someone or something falls suddenly and a long way down or forward.

*The car went out of control and **plunged**/**plummeted** over the cliff.*

If you fall or almost fall because you step awkwardly while walking or running, the verb **stumble** could be used.

*The waiter **stumbled** and dumped the food in my lap.*

Trip could be used if you fall or almost fall after knocking your foot against something while you are walking or running.

*She **tripped** over a crack in the sidewalk and broke her wrist.*

MOVE DOWN /fɔːl/ *v* [I] *past simp.* **fell**, *past part.* **fallen** to move down toward or drop to a lower position ○ *They expect three inches of snow to fall tonight.* ○ *Tears rolled down her cheeks and fell into her lap.* ○ *Plaster was falling off the walls.*

falls /fɔːlz/ *pl n* a WATERFALL

SEASON /fɔːl/, **autumn** *n* [C/U] the season of the year between summer and winter, lasting from September to December north of the equator and from March to June south of the equator, when fruits and crops finish growing and the leaves fall off the trees ○ [U] *Fall is my favorite time of year.* ○ [U] *She wants to take a vacation before fall classes start.*

BECOME LESS /fɔːl/ *v* [I] *past simp.* **fell**, *past part.* **fallen** to become less or lower in size, amount, or strength ○ *Stock prices fell sharply in late March and early April.* ○ *Her blood sugar levels fell below normal.*

fall /fɔːl/ *n* [C usually sing] ○ *a fall in temperature*

CHANGE STATE /fɔːl/ *v* [L] *past simp.* **fell**, *past part.* **fallen** used to show a change from one state to another ○ *He fell asleep reading the newspaper.*

BE DEFEATED /fɔːl/ *v* [I] *past simp.* **fell**, *past part.* **fallen** **1** to be defeated or fail ○ *The city fell to the enemy.* **2** If soldiers fall, they die: *The statue honors soldiers who fell in battle.*

fall /fɔːl/ *n* [C usually sing] ○ *the fall of the Roman Empire*

HAPPEN /fɔːl/ *v* [I] *past simp.* **fell**, *past part.* **fallen** to happen at a particular time ○ *My birthday falls on a Friday this year.* ○ *By the time we got home, night had fallen* (= begun).

BELONG TO /fɔːl/ *v* [I always + adv/prep] *past simp.* **fell**, *past part.* **fallen** to belong to a particular group, or to be part of a particular subject ○ *Archaeology falls under the general subject of natural history.*

HANG DOWN /fɔːl/ *v* [I always + adv/prep] *past simp.* **fell**, *past part.* **fallen** (of hair or cloth) to hang down loosely ○ *Her long, dark hair fell to her waist.*

IDIOMS with fall

• **fall by the wayside** to no longer be active or successful ○ *I've seen a lot of bands split up and fall by the wayside.*

• **fall flat** to not be funny or entertaining ○ *Some of the jokes were pretty funny, others fell flat.*

• **fall into line (with** *someone/something***)** to begin to have a similar standard or to do something in a similar way to someone or something ○ *House prices in this area have fallen into line with the national average.*

• **fall into place** to become well organized in a way that makes success likely ○ *After a lot of work over the past few years, my career goals are beginning to fall into place.*

• **fall into the trap of** *doing something* to make a bad decision ○ *Don't fall into the trap of buying a house that is more expensive than you can afford.*

• **fall into the wrong hands** to be found and taken by someone who is not the owner ○ *I wouldn't want my machine to fall into the wrong hands.*

• **fall short** to not reach a desired amount or standard ○ *They needed 60 votes to pass the bill, but they fell short by 12 votes.*

• **fall victim to** *something* to fail or suffer because of something ○ *The movie industry fell victim to its own success.*

PHRASAL VERBS with fall

• **fall apart** **BREAK** to break into separate pieces ○ *Our furniture is falling apart.*

• **fall apart** **FAIL** to fail completely and be unable to continue in the usual way ○ *The deal fell apart because of a lack of money.* ○ *When his wife died, he fell apart* (= was unable to continue with life in the usual way).

• **fall back on** *something* to use something for help because no other choice is available ○ *The organization has no income and no reserves to fall back on.*

• **fall behind** *(something)* to fail to do something fast enough or on time ○ *We fell behind schedule.* ○ *He fell behind in his work.*

• **fall for** *someone* **LOVE** *infml* to be attracted to someone and start to love that person ○ *Mike has fallen for Heather.*

• **fall for** *something* **BE TRICKED** *infml* to be deceived by something, esp. a lie ○ *I said I was an art collector, and they fell for it.*

• **fall into** *something* to suddenly be in a condition, esp. a bad one ○ *She fell into a coma.*

• **fall off** to become less in number, amount, or quality ○ *Production fell off last month.*

• **fall out** **BREAK OFF** (of objects) to drop from a place where they were attached ○ *A few pages fell out of the book.*

• **fall out** **END RELATIONSHIP** to have an argument or disagreement that ends a relationship ○ *The two fell out over coaching tactics a long time ago.*

• **fall through** to fail to happen ○ *The sale of the house fell through.*

fallacy /ˈfæl·ə·si/ *n* [C] a false belief ○ [+ *that* clause] *It is a common fallacy that only men are good at math.*

fallacious /fəˈleɪ·ʃəs/ *adj* [not gradable] ○ *a fallacious argument*

fall guy /ˈfɔːlˈgɑɪ/ *n* [C] *infml* a person who is blamed for something bad when others who were also responsible are not blamed ○ *The cops made him the fall guy, even after they knew he was innocent.*

fallible /ˈfæl·ə·bəl/ *adj* (of a person) able to fail or likely to make mistakes, or (of an object or system) likely not to work satisfactorily ○ *Human beings are fallible.*

fallibility /ˌfæl·əˈbɪl·ət̬·i/ *n* [U] ○ *Women are urged to take the test, despite its fallibility.*

falling star *n* [C] *infml* a METEOR

fallout **EFFECT** /ˈfɔː·lɑʊt/ *n* [U] the unpleasant results or effects of an action or event ○ *He blamed the political fallout from the scandal on the Republicans.*

DUST /ˈfɔː·lɑʊt/ *n* [U] the RADIOACTIVE dust in the air after a nuclear device explodes

false **NOT REAL** /fɔːls/ *adj* [not gradable] (of things) not real, but made to look real, or (of information) not true but made to seem true in order to deceive ○ *Haban used false identification to*

F

enter France. ○ *The company presented clients with documents containing false information.*

falsify /ˈfɔːl·səˌfɑɪ/ *v* [T] ○ *She falsified the accounting records.*

NOT CORRECT /fɔːls/ *adj* [not gradable] not correct or true ○ *"Three plus three is seven. True or false?" "False."* ○ **USAGE:** said about information or an idea

falsehood /ˈfɔːls·hʊd/ *n* [C/U] something that is not true; a lie

falsely /ˈfɔːl·sli/ *adv* [not gradable] ○ *She was falsely accused of shoplifting.*

falsity /ˈfɔːl·sət̬·i/, **falseness** /ˈfɔːl·snəs/ *n* [U] *fml* ○ *We're trying to determine the truth or falsity of your previous statement.*

F

NOT SINCERE /fɔːls/ *adj* [not gradable] (of people or their manner) dishonest or not sincere ○ *"I think of myself as great," said Tyler, abandoning false modesty.*

false alarm *n* [C] a warning or a signal of danger that is given but is unnecessary

false start **SITUATION** *n* [C] a situation in a race when a competitor starts before the signal has been given

ATTEMPT *n* [C] an attempt to do something you are not ready or able to do ○ *She began writing fiction, and after several false starts she wrote "Gone With the Wind."*

false teeth *pl n* artificial teeth used to fill the spaces in a person's mouth where teeth once were

falsetto /fɔːlˈset̬·oʊ/ *n* [C/U] *pl* **falsettos** (esp. of a man) a method of singing in a voice much higher than usual

falsetto /fɔːlˈset̬·oʊ/ *adj, adv* ○ *He sings a weird falsetto version of "Barbara Ann."*

falter /ˈfɔːl·tər/ *v* [I] **1** to lose strength or purpose and pause or stop ○ *His career began to falter.* **2** To falter is also to move or speak without confidence or with pauses.

faltering /ˈfɔːl·tə·rɪŋ/ *adj* ○ *faltering speech*

fame /feɪm/ *n* [U] the state of being known for having or doing something important ○ *She came to the city seeking fortune and fame.* ○ Related adjective: FAMOUS

famed /feɪmd/ *adj* known about by many people; famous ○ *The famed transatlantic liner Queen Mary is moored here as a tourist attraction.*

WORD FAMILY fame

Nouns	fame infamy	*Adjectives*	famed famous infamous
Adverbs	famously infamously		

familiar **KNOWN** /fəˈmɪl·jər/ *adj* easy to recognize because previously experienced ○ *familiar sights* ○ *a familiar face* ○ *I'm not familiar with current research in the field.*

familiarity /fəˌmɪl·ˈjær·ət̬·i/ *n* [U] ○ *Harry's familiarity with the city makes him a good tour guide.*

familiarize /fəˈmɪl·jəˌrɑɪz/ *v* [T] ○ *Teachers needed to familiarize themselves with the new software.*

INFORMAL /fəˈmɪl·jər/ *adj* informal or friendly, esp. more than is expected ○ *Her familiar tone makes her writing more effective.*

familiarly /fəˈmɪl·jər·li/ *adv* ○ *Greenwich Village is familiarly known as "the Village."*

WORD FAMILY familiar

Nouns	familiarity family	*Adjectives*	familiar unfamiliar
Verbs	familiarize	*Adverbs*	familiarly

family **PARENTS AND CHILDREN** /ˈfæm·ə·li, ˈfæm·li/ *n* [C/U] a social group of parents, children, and sometimes GRANDPARENTS, uncles, aunts, and others who are related ○ [C] *Her family moved here when she was eleven.* ○ [U] *Many people cope with the demands of both career and family.* ○ [C] *She wants to get married and have a family* (= have children).

BIOLOGICAL TYPE /ˈfæm·ə·li, ˈfæm·li/ *n* [C] ***biology*** a large group of related types of animals or plants ○ *The lion is a member of the cat family.*

family name *n* your LAST NAME

family planning *n* [U] the process of controlling how many children you have and when you have them

family room *n* [C] a room in a family's home that is used for relaxing, esp. for watching television

family tree *n* [C] a drawing that shows all the members of a family, usually over a long period of time, and how they are related to each other

famine /ˈfæm·ən/ *n* [C/U] an extreme lack of food in a region, causing suffering and death ○ [U] *Widespread famine was reported in the region.*

famished /ˈfæm·ɪʃt/ *adj infml* very hungry ○ *I'm famished! When do we eat?*

famous /ˈfeɪ·məs/ *adj* known by very many or most people ○ *a famous actor/singer* ○ *Marie Curie is famous for discovering radium.* ○ Related noun: FAME

WORD CHOICES famous

Well known or **renowned** are common alternatives to "famous."

*The area is **renowned** for its beauty.*

*She's a **well-known** local artist.*

If someone or something is famous everywhere, you can say **world-famous**.

*a **world-famous** hotel*

If someone or something is famous for some special quality or ability, you could use the word **celebrated**.

*He's a **celebrated** writer of children's stories.*

Legendary means "very famous and admired or spoken about."

*He once met the **legendary** singer, Eartha Kitt.*

Someone who is famous in the entertainment business can be described as a **celebrity** or a **star**.

*Many **celebrities** had been invited to the movie's premiere.*

***Stars** from the sports world attended the dinner.*

High-profile and **prominent** can be used when someone is famous because of their importance.

*He's a **prominent** member of the Saudi royal family.*

***high-profile** politicians*

If someone is famous in a particular job or area of study, you could use **eminent** to describe them.

*Darwin and other **eminent** scientists*

Infamous and **notorious** are usually used when someone is famous for something bad.

*He is one of history's most **notorious/infamous** criminals.*

famously /ˈfeɪ·mə·sli/ *adv* very well ○ *Maria and her roommate get along famously.*

fan DEVICE /fæn/ *n* [C] a device to provide a flow of air, either an object that you wave in front of you or a device with blades that are turned by a motor ○ *a window fan*
fan /fæn/ *v* [T] **-nn-** ○ *It was very hot in the car, so I fanned myself with the road map.*

ADMIRER /fæn/ *n* [C] a person who is very much interested in and spends a lot of time watching or reading about esp. an entertainer or sports team ○ *a baseball fan*

PHRASAL VERB with fan

• **fan out** to spread out over a wide area ○ *The police fanned out over the west side of the park.*

fanatic /fəˈnæt̬·ɪk/ *n* [C] a person whose strong admiration for something is extreme and unreasonable ○ *a fitness/exercise fanatic*
fanatical /fəˈnæt̬·ɪ·kəl/ *adj* ○ *Her devotion to her pets was fanatical.*

fancy DECORATIVE /ˈfæn·si/ *adj* [-*er*/-*est* only] decorative or complicated, or (of restaurants, stores, or hotels) expensive ○ *I wanted a simple black dress, nothing fancy.* ○ *a fancy hotel*

IMAGINE /ˈfæn·si/ *v* [T] to imagine or think that something is so ○ *When she was young she fancied herself a rebel.*
fanciful /ˈfæn·sə·fəl/ *adj* ○ *fanciful ideas/notions*

LIKE /ˈfæn·si/ *v* [T] to like or wish for ○ *There are two things he fancies – fast cars and thunderous music.*
fancy /ˈfæn·si/ *n* [U]

IDIOM with fancy

• **strike** *your* **fancy**, **catch/tickle** *your* **fancy** to seem interesting or pleasing to someone ○ *She has enough money to buy anything that strikes her fancy.*

fanfare /ˈfæn·fer, -fær/ *n* [U] showy activity meant to draw attention to something ○ *Earth Day was observed without a great deal of fanfare this week.*

fang /fæŋ/ *n* [C] a long, sharp tooth that animals such as snakes and dogs have ➤ Picture: **spider**

fanny /ˈfæn·i/ *n* [C] *infml* a person's buttocks

fanny pack *n* [C] a small bag that has a belt you fasten around your waist, and that is used for carrying small objects or money

fantasize /ˈfænt·əˌsɑɪz/ *v* ○ See at FANTASY

fantastic GOOD /fænˈtæs·tɪk/ *adj* very good ○ *You look fantastic in that outfit.*

NOT REAL /fænˈtæs·tɪk/ *adj* strange and imaginary ○ *He drew fantastic animals with two heads and large wings.*

LARGE /fænˈtæs·tɪk/ *adj* (of an amount) very large ○ *a fantastic sum of money*

fantasy /ˈfænt·ə·si, -zi/ *n* [C/U] **1** a pleasant but unlikely situation that you enjoy thinking about, or the activity of thinking in this way ○ [C] *Writing songs was just a fantasy of mine.* ○ [U] *She retreated from life into a world of fantasy.* **2** ***literature*** Fantasy is imaginative literature, often set in strange places with unusual characters and the use of magic.
fantasize /ˈfænt·əˌsɑɪz/ *v* [I] ○ *He fantasized about winning the Nobel Prize.*

far DISTANCE /fɑr/ *adv comparative* **farther**, **further**, *superlative* **farthest**, **furthest** at, to, or from a great distance in space or time ○ *One day, perhaps far in the future, you'll regret what you've done.* ○ *How far is it from Los Angeles to San Francisco?* ○ *She doesn't live far from here.*
far /fɑr/ *adj comparative* **farther**, **further**, *superlative* **farthest**, **furthest** **1** *the far* (= most distant) *side of the park* ○ *Even the closest stores are pretty far.* **2** The **far left** is the political position that is most LIBERAL, and the **far right** is the political position that is most CONSERVATIVE.

USAGE

far

Be careful with the word **far** when describing distances. You can use it in questions or when describing an approximate distance.

How far is Omaha from Des Moines?

It isn't far from my apartment to the school.

You should not use **far** when giving the exact distance between two places. You just need to give the distance and the preposition **from**.

I live in a small village 30 miles from Denver.

~~I live in a small village 30 miles far from Denver.~~

AMOUNT /fɑr/ *adv* [not gradable] much ○ *Her new school is far better than the old one.*

IDIOMS with far

• **as far as** *someone* **is concerned**, **so far as** *someone* **is concerned** according to what someone thinks or feels ○ *There's no reason to wait, as far as I'm concerned.* ○ *So far as those big companies are concerned, we're just another little company that they can step on.*

• **as far as** *someone* **knows**, **as far as** *someone* **can tell** based on what someone knows ○ *As far as I*

know, he isn't coming until tomorrow. ○ *As far as the doctors can tell, she didn't have a stroke.*
• **by far** by a great amount ○ *She is by far the best student in the class.*
• **far from** not at all ○ *We were far from disappointed when they told us they couldn't come to visit.*
• **far from it** almost the opposite is true ○ *Jim, selfish? Far from it – he's probably one of the kindest people I know.*

faraway /ˈfɑr·əˌweɪ/ *adj* lying at a great distance away ○ *The story told of strange customs in faraway lands.*

F

faraway look *n* [C] an expression that makes you appear to be thinking about something completely different from what is going on around you

farce **PLAY** /fɑrs/ *n* [C/U] a humorous play in which the characters become involved in unlikely situations, or the humor in this type of play
SITUATION /fɑrs/ *n* [C] a ridiculous situation or event, or something considered a waste of time ○ *The meeting turned out to be a farce since no one had prepared anything.*

fare **PAYMENT** /fer, fær/ *n* [C] the money that you pay for traveling on a vehicle such as a bus or train ○ *We shared a taxi and split the fare.*
PROGRESS /fer, fær/ *v* [I always + adv/prep] to progress or to be in a particular condition ○ *Middle-income families will fare better/worse under the new tax laws.*
FOOD /fer, fær/ *n* [U] *fml* (in a restaurant) the type of food that is served ○ *Middle Eastern fare*

Far East *n* [U] ***world history*** the countries on the Pacific coast of Asia

farewell /ferˈwel, fær-/ *exclamation, n* [C] goodbye ○ *We said our farewells to our dear friends.*
farewell /ferˈwel, fær-/ *adj* [not gradable] done at the time someone is leaving a place or job ○ *a farewell speech* ○ *We gave Latoya a farewell party on her last day.*

far-fetched /ˈfɑrˈfetʃt/ *adj* difficult to believe and unlikely to be true ○ *Her story about being chased away from school by wolves seems pretty far-fetched.*

farm /fɑrm/ *n* [C] **1** an area of land, esp. together with a house and other buildings, used for growing crops or keeping animals **2** A farm can also be a place where a specific type of animal is raised in large numbers to be sold: *a cattle/mink farm*
farm /fɑrm/ *v* [I/T] ○ [I/T] *Their family has farmed (this land) for three generations.*
farmer /ˈfɑr·mər/ *n* [C] a person who owns or takes care of a farm
farming /ˈfɑr·mɪŋ/ *n* [U]

PHRASAL VERB with farm

• **farm out** *something* [M] to give work to other people to do ○ *Magazines often farm out articles to freelance journalists.*

farmhand /ˈfɑrm·hænd/ *n* [C] a person who is paid to work on a farm

farmhouse /ˈfɑrm·hɑʊs/ *n* [C] the house on a farm where people live, or this style of house ○ *Washington used the farmhouse as his headquarters before and after the battle.*

farmland /ˈfɑrm·lænd/ *n* [C usually sing] land that is used for farming ○ *In the past 18 years, the average price of Iowa farmland has increased 234 percent.*

far-off *adj* happening a long way from the present, either in the past or the future, or at a great distance away

far-out *adj infml* strange and unusual ○ *They had some far-out ideas.*

far-reaching *adj* likely to influence many people or things ○ *The effects of the riots will be far-reaching.*

farsighted **ABLE TO SEE** /ˈfɑrˌsɑɪt̬·əd/ *adj* able to see clearly only objects that are not close ○ Compare NEARSIGHTED
WISE /ˈfɑrˌsɑɪt̬·əd/ *adj* able to make wise judgments about the results far in the future of an action you take now ○ *a farsighted proposal*

farther /ˈfɑr·ðər/ *adv* to a greater distance; *comparative of* FAR **DISTANCE** ○ *How much farther is it to the airport?* ○ *Now that they live farther away we don't see them so often.*
farther /ˈfɑr·ðər/ *adj* ○ *Birds from farther north appeared in the fall.* ➤ Confusables: **further or farther?** at FURTHER **GREATER DISTANCE**

farthest /ˈfɑr·ðəst/ *adv superlative of* FAR **DISTANCE** ○ *What's the farthest you've ever run in your life?* ○ **USAGE:** See the usage note at FURTHEST **DISTANCE**.
farthest /ˈfɑr·ðəst/ *adj* ○ *The farthest landmark visible is about twenty miles away.*

fascinate /ˈfæs·əˌneɪt/ *v* [T] to have someone's complete interest and attention ○ *Anything to do with airplanes and flying fascinates him.* ○ *The children were fascinated by the story.*
fascinating /ˈfæs·əˌneɪt̬·ɪŋ/ *adj* ○ *The movie has a fascinating plot.*
fascination /ˌfæs·əˈneɪ·ʃən/ *n* [U] ○ *Her fascination with modern art began when she saw the Picasso show.*

fascism /ˈfæʃˌɪz·əm/ *n* [U] ***politics & government*** a political system based on a very powerful leader, state control of social and economic life, and extreme pride in country and race, with no expression of political disagreement allowed
fascist /ˈfæʃ·əst/ *adj* [not gradable] ○ *fascist groups*
fascist /ˈfæʃ·əst/ *n* [C] ○ *He left Germany when the fascists took over.*

fashion **CUSTOM** /ˈfæʃ·ən/ *n* [U] a custom, look, or way of doing things that is considered acceptable ○ *Long skirts are back in fashion this season.* ○ *Formal dinner parties seem to be out of fashion.*
fashionable /ˈfæʃ·ə·nə·bəl/ *adj* popular at a particular time ○ [+ to infinitive] *fashionable restaurants/clothing*
fashionably /ˈfæʃ·ə·nə·bli/ *adv* ○ *We were fashionably late.*

WORD CHOICES fashion

If something is fashionable, in informal English you can say that it is **in**.

Short jackets are ***in*** *this season.*

Cool, **hip**, and **trendy** are all informal words that mean "fashionable."

He was wearing a pair of ***cool*** *sunglasses.*

trendy *clothes*

A slang word for things which are fashionable in an unusual and noticeable way is **funky**.

You will look and feel great in these ***funky*** *shoes.*

Chic can be used about things that are very stylish and fashionable.

a ***chic*** *restaurant*

You can use the phrase **the latest thing** for something that is new and fashionable.

This doll is ***the latest thing*** *for young girls.*

If something is always fashionable because it has a simple style, you could describe it as **classic**.

She was wearing a ***classic*** *black suit.*

CLOTHING /ˈfæʃ·ən/ *n* [C/U] clothing that is considered stylish ○ [U] *She has a flair for fashion.* ○ [C] *He plays golf and dresses in the latest fashions.*

fashionable /ˈfæʃ·ə·nə·bəl/ *adj* ○ *She didn't just go out out and buy a whole lot of fashionable clothes.*

fashionably /ˈfæʃ·ə·nə·bli/ *adv* ○ *fashionably dressed women*

MANNER /ˈfæʃ·ən/ *n* [U] a way of doing things ○ *The sale of the property has to be conducted in a systematic fashion.*

MAKE /ˈfæʃ·ən/ *v* [T] to create something, using the hands or the imagination ○ *She fashioned an elaborate sculpture out of newspapers and glue.*

WORD FAMILY fashion

Nouns	fashion	*Verbs*	fashion
Adjectives	fashionable unfashionable	*Adverbs*	fashionably unfashionably

fast **QUICK** /fæst/ *adj* [-*er*/-*est* only] **1** moving or happening quickly or able to move or happen quickly ○ *a fast car* ○ *The fastest way to get there is by plane.* **2** If your watch or clock is fast, it shows a time later than the real time.

fast /fæst/ *adv* [-*er*/-*est* only] ○ *The accident was caused by people driving too fast in bad conditions.* ○ *This type of wilderness area is disappearing fast.*

WORD CHOICES fast

If you want to use "fast" as an adjective, a very common alternative is **quick**.

I tried to catch him, but he was too ***quick*** *for me.*

If something is done fast, without waiting, you can use the adjectives **prompt**, **speedy**, or **swift**.

A ***prompt*** *reply would be very much appreciated.*

He made a ***speedy*** *recovery.*

His comments caused a ***swift*** *response.*

If something is done too fast, without thinking carefully, the adjectives **hasty** and **hurried** are often used.

I don't want to make a ***hasty*** *decision.*

We left early after a ***hurried*** *breakfast.*

A fast walk is often described as **brisk**.

We took a ***brisk*** *walk through the park.*

The adjective **rapid** is often used to describe fast growth or change.

The 1990's were a period of ***rapid*** *change/growth.*

If you want to use "fast" as an adverb, a very common alternative is **quickly**.

The problem needs to be solved as ***quickly*** *as possible.*

If someone does something very fast, in informal situations you can use the expression **in a flash**.

I'll be back ***in a flash.***

ATTACHED /fæst/ *adj, adv* [not gradable] connected or attached in a way that is not easily unfastened ○ *Tie the boat fast to the pier.*

NOT EAT /fæst/ *v* [I] to have a period of time when you eat no food ○ *We will be fasting until sundown tomorrow.*

fast /fæst/ *n* [C] ○ *They organized a fast to draw attention to the issue of hunger.*

IDIOM with fast

• **in the fast lane** in a way that is exciting and slightly dangerous ○ *He lived life in the fast lane when he was young.*

fastball /ˈfæst·bɔːl/ *n* [C] a PITCH in baseball that is thrown at the highest speed

fasten /ˈfæs·ən/ *v* [I/T] to make or become firmly attached or closed ○ [I] *This skirt fastens at the back.* ○ [T] *Fasten your seatbelt.*

fastener /ˈfæs·ə·nər/ *n* [C] a button or other device for joining together the separate parts of something, esp. clothes

WORD FAMILY fasten

Nouns	fastener	*Verbs*	fasten unfasten

fast food *n* [U] cheap, often hot food that is prepared and served quickly in a restaurant

fastidious /fæsˈtɪd·iː·əs/ *adj* having high standards and giving a lot of attention to details ○ *The restaurant offers elaborate food and fastidious service at high prices.*

fast track *n* [C usually sing] the quickest, but usually most competitive, route to success or improvement

fat **FLESHY** /fæt/ *adj* [-*er*/-*est* only] -**tt**- **1** having a lot of flesh on the body ○ *Her weight's normal but she insists she's fat.* **2** Fat can also mean thick or big: *a fat telephone book*

fattening /ˈfæt·ᵊn·ɪŋ/ *adj* (of food) containing a lot of fat, sugar, etc., that would make you fatter if you ate a lot of it ○ *I love desserts, but they're so fattening.*

WORD CHOICES fat

Overweight is another way of saying "fat."
*He used to be **overweight**.*
If someone is extremely fat in a way that is bad for their health, you could use the word **obese**.
*More and more children are becoming **obese**.*
Plump is a polite way of saying that someone is fat.
*He's gotten rather **plump** since I last saw him.*
Chubby is often used about children who are fat in a pleasant and attractive way.
*Look at the baby's **chubby** little legs.*
Corpulent is a formal word that means "fat."
*He was **corpulent** and red-faced.*
If an older man is fat, you could describe him as **portly**.
*Dino was a **portly** man with a bushy moustache.*

SUBSTANCE /fæt/ *n* [C/U] **1** ***biology*** the substance under the skin of humans and animals that stores energy and keeps them warm **2** Fat is also a solid or liquid substance obtained from animals or plants and used esp. in cooking.
fatty /ˈfæt̬·i/ *adj* containing too much fat ○ *fatty meat*

WEALTHY /fæt/ *adj* [-*er*/-*est* only] **-tt-** *infml* having or worth a lot of money ○ *a fat profit*

WORD FAMILY fat

Nouns	fat	*Adjectives*	fat
Verbs	fatten		fattening
			fatty

IDIOM with fat

• **fat chance** *infml* there is no chance of that happening ○ *"Maybe they'll invite you to go with them." "Fat chance!"*

fatal /ˈfeɪt̬·ᵊl/ *adj* [not gradable] **1** (of illness, accidents, etc.) causing death ○ *a fatal heart attack* **2** Fatal can also mean severe enough to produce a very bad result: *a fatal mistake/flaw*
fatally /ˈfeɪt̬·ᵊl·i/ *adv* [not gradable] ○ *Several people were injured, two fatally.*
fatality /feɪˈtæl·ət̬·i/ *n* [C] ○ *The first fatalities (= deaths) of the war have been civilians.*

fatalism /ˈfeɪt̬·ᵊlˌɪz·əm/ *n* [U] the belief that people cannot change the way events will happen and that esp. bad events cannot be avoided
fatalistic /ˌfeɪt̬·ᵊlˈɪs·tɪk/ *adj*

fat cat *n* [C] *slang* someone who is rich and has a lot of influence, esp. in politics or business

fate /feɪt/ *n* [C usually sing] **1** something that happens to a person or thing, esp. something final or negative, such as death or defeat ○ *The fate of numerous smaller buildings is under debate.* ○ *Attendance has not picked up, and the fate of the show is still in doubt.* **2** Fate is also a power that is considered to cause and control all events, so that people cannot change or control the way things will happen: *When we met again by chance, she said, "It must be fate."*
fateful /ˈfeɪt·fəl/ *adj* an event or period of time that is very important because of its often negative effect on the future ○ *In 1971, President Richard Nixon made a fateful decision to install tape recorders in the White House.*

IDIOM with fate

• **a fate worse than death** something you do not want to experience because it is so unpleasant or embarrassing ○ *Being seen with my parents at the beach would have been a fate worse than death.*

fat-free *adj* containing no fats

father /ˈfɑð·ər/ *n* [C] **1** a male parent ○ *My father retired seven years ago.* **2** If you describe a man as **the father of** something, you mean that he began it, or first made it important: *Freud was the father of psychoanalysis.*
Father The title Father is used by Christian priests.
father /ˈfɑð·ər/ *v* [T] to become a father by causing a woman to produce a child ○ *to father twins*
fatherhood /ˈfɑð·ərˌhʊd/ *n* [U] ○ *Fatherhood is a lifelong responsibility.*
father-in-law /ˈfɑð·ə·rənˌlɔː/ *n* [C] *pl* **fathers-in-law** the father of someone's husband or wife
fatherly /ˈfɑð·ər·li/ *adj* typical of a kind or caring father

father figure *n* [C] a man who treats you as a father would, for example by giving advice, help, or support

fathom **MEASUREMENT** /ˈfæð·əm/ *n* [C] a unit of measurement of the depth of water equal to 6 feet or 1.8 meters

UNDERSTAND /ˈfæð·əm/ *v* [T] to discover the meaning of something ○ *I just couldn't fathom what he was talking about.*

fatigue /fəˈtiːg/ *n* [U] the condition of being extremely tired ○ *The doctor said he was suffering from fatigue and work-related stress.*

fatigues /fəˈtiːgz/ *pl n* the brownish green uniform worn esp. by soldiers when working or fighting ○ *combat fatigues*

fattening /ˈfæt·ᵊn·ɪŋ/ *adj* ○ See at FAT **FLESHY**

fatty /ˈfæt̬·i/ *adj* ○ See at FAT **SUBSTANCE**

fatty acid *n* [C] ***biology, chemistry*** any of a large group of acids, especially those found in fats and oils

fatuous /ˈfætʃ·ə·wəs/ *adj* foolish or done without thinking ○ *a fatuous remark*

faucet /ˈfɔː·sət, ˈfɑs·ət/, **tap** *n* [C] a device that controls the flow of liquid, esp. water, out of a pipe ○ *We have a leaky faucet in the bathroom sink.*

fault SOMETHING WRONG /fɔːlt/ *n* [C] a quality in a person that shows that the person is not perfect, or a condition of something that shows that it is not working perfectly ○ *He loves me in spite of my faults.* ○ *Some people find fault in everything they see.*
faultless /ˈfɔːlt·ləs/ *adj* [not gradable] perfect ○ *He gave a faultless performance at the piano recital.*
faulty /ˈfɔːl·ti/ *adj* [-er/-est only] not working correctly, or not correct ○ *faulty brakes* ○ *His arguments were based on faulty reasoning.*

USAGE

fault or mistake/error?

Use **fault** when explaining who is responsible for something bad.

It's my fault that the car was stolen. I left the window open.

~~*It's my mistake the car was stolen. I left the window open.*~~

Use **mistake** or **error** for talking about something you did or thought that was wrong. **Error** is slightly more formal than **mistake**.

I still make lots of mistakes in my essays.

We lost a week's work due to a computer error.

~~*I still make lots of faults in my essays.*~~

RESPONSIBILITY /fɔːlt/ *n* [U] responsibility for a mistake or for having done something wrong ○ *I screwed up, so it was my fault we didn't finish on time.* ○ *The driver was* **at fault** (= responsible) *for the accident – he was going too fast.*
fault /fɔːlt/ *v* [T] to blame someone ○ *Professional athletes cannot be faulted for making millions of dollars when they attract the fans that make the sport popular.*

CRACK /fɔːlt/ *n* [C] ***earth science*** a crack in the earth's surface where the rock is divided into two parts that can move against each other in an EARTHQUAKE (= a sudden, violent movement of the earth's surface)

WORD FAMILY fault

Nouns	fault	Verbs	fault
Adjectives	faultless faulty	Adverbs	faultlessly

IDIOM with fault

• **to a fault** more than is necessary ○ *Keri is generous to a fault.*

fauna /ˈfɔː·nə/ *n* [U] ***biology*** all the animals of a particular area or period of time ○ Compare FLORA

faux pas /ˈfoʊ·pɑ/ *n* [C] *pl* **faux pas** a remark or action in a social situation that is a mistake and causes embarrassment or offense ○ *She made the faux pas of referring to Wales as "part of England."*

favor SUPPORT, *Cdn, Br* **favour** /ˈfeɪ·vər/ *n* [U] approval or support of someone or something ○ *In applying for this job, Tiffany has a lot* **in** *her* **favor** (= to her advantage). ○ *The city council voted* **in favor of** (= in support of) *the proposed housing development.*
favor, *Cdn, Br* **favour** /ˈfeɪ·vər/ *v* [T] ○ *Democrats favored a temporary increase in the state sales tax.*
favorable, *Cdn, Br* **favourable** /ˈfeɪ·və·rə·bəl/ *adj* positive or pleasing ○ *The movie received generally favorable reviews.*
favorably, *Cdn, Br* **favourably** /ˈfeɪ·və·rə·bli/ *adv* ○ *Consumers responded favorably to the new product.*

HELPFUL ACT, *Cdn, Br* **favour** /ˈfeɪ·vər/ *n* [C] something you do to help someone, often after being asked to ○ *Will you do me a favor and turn the oven on at four o'clock?*

PRESENT, *Cdn, Br* **favour** /ˈfeɪ·vər/ *n* [C] a small present given to guests at a party ○ *party favors*

favorite, *Cdn, Br* **favourite** /ˈfeɪ·və·rət, ˈfeɪv·rət/ *adj* best liked or most enjoyed ○ *This is one of my favorite restaurants.*
favorite, *Cdn, Br* **favourite** /ˈfeɪ·və·rət, ˈfeɪv·rət/ *n* [C] **1** *Those gold earrings are my favorites.* **2** A favorite is also a competitor likely to win: *The Chicago Bears are 10-point favorites over the Rams in the Super Bowl.*
favoritism, *Cdn, Br* **favouritism** /ˈfeɪ·və·rəˌtɪz·əm, ˈfeɪv·rə-/ *n* [U] unfair support shown to one person or group, esp. by someone in authority ○ *The teacher was careful not to show favoritism to any one student.*

fawn DEER /fɔːn/ *n* [C] a young deer

PRAISE /fɔːn/ *v* [I] to give someone a lot of attention and praise in order to get that person's approval ○ *Big movie stars are fawned over by the waiters at the restaurant.*

fax /fæks/ *n* [C] **1** a document that is sent by electronic image through a telephone line ○ *I'll send you a fax of the proposal.* **2** A fax (also **fax machine**) is also the machine that sends or receives such an image.
fax /fæks/ *v* [T] ○ *I faxed the changes to my publisher.*

faze /feɪz/ *v* [T] to upset or confuse someone ○ *Speaking in public does not faze her.*

FBI /ˌefˌbiːˈɑɪ/ *n* [U] *abbreviation for* Federal Bureau of Investigation (= the government department that examines certain crimes against federal law).

fear /fɪr/ *n* [C/U] a strong emotion caused by great worry about something dangerous, painful, or unknown that is happening or might happen ○ [U] *Even when the boat was rocked by waves, the boy showed no fear.* ○ [C] *The low sales continued, confirming our worst fears.* ○ [U] *She stood very still* **for fear of** (= because she was worried about) *being noticed.*
fear /fɪr/ *v* **1** [I] *The cab driver was going so fast, I feared for our safety.* **2** To fear is also to be worried or upset: [+ *that* clause] *They fear that Congress may not allocate the money needed.*
fearful /ˈfɪr·fəl/ *adj* ○ *a fearful expression/reaction* ○ *fearful dangers* ○ *He was fearful of driving on the icy streets.*

fearless /ˈfɪr·ləs/ *adj* ○ *He was a tough, fearless soldier.*

WORD FAMILY fear			
Nouns	fear	*Verbs*	fear
Adjectives	fearful fearless	*Adverbs*	fearfully fearlessly

WORD CHOICES fear

See also: **frightened**

Extreme fear can be described as **terror**.

*She fled from the attacker in **terror**.*

Extreme fear about something which might happen can be described as **dread**.

*The thought of giving a speech filled me with **dread**.*

Alarm is often used when someone experiences sudden fear and worry that something dangerous might happen.

*I don't want to cause you any **alarm**, but there's a rattlesnake in the path ahead of you.*

Fright can be used when you have a sudden feeling of fear.

*The family ran from their home in **fright** when the earthquake struck.*

If fear is sudden and stops people from thinking and behaving normally, you could use the word **panic**.

***Panic** spread through the crowd when someone shouted "Fire!"*

A **phobia** is an extreme fear of a particular thing or situation.

*I've got a **phobia** of worms.*

IDIOM with fear

• **fear the worst** to feel certain that the worst possible thing has happened or is likely to happen ○ *When the doctor finally called, she feared the worst.*

feasible /ˈfiː·zə·bəl/ *adj* [not gradable] possible, reasonable, or likely ○ *It's no longer feasible to fund this research.*

feast /fiːst/ *n* [C] **1** a large, special meal, often for many people, to celebrate someone or something ○ *a wedding feast* **2** A feast is also a large meal: *We had a feast of fresh seafood.*

feast /fiːst/ *v* [I always + adv/prep] ○ *The two of us feasted on smoked salmon.*

feat /fiːt/ *n* [C] an act that shows skill, strength, or bravery ○ *a feat of unusual strength* ○ *Getting the house painted was quite a feat.*

feather /ˈfeð·ər/ *n* [C] one of the long, light objects that cover a bird's body, having soft fibers along each side of a thin, stiff, central stem

feather /ˈfeð·ər/ *v*

IDIOMS with feather

• **feather in** *your* **cap** an achievement to be proud of ○ *The award was another feather in his cap.*

• **feather** *your* **(own) nest** to make yourself rich, esp. by taking unfair advantage of others ○ *He used the classified information to feather his own nest.*

feature Ⓐ **CHARACTERISTIC** /ˈfiː·tʃər/ *n* [C] a noticeable or important characteristic or part ○ *This car has excellent safety features.* ○ *She has fine, delicate features* (= parts of the face).

feature Ⓐ /ˈfiː·tʃər/ *v* [T] to show or advertise someone or something as the most important or most obvious part ○ *Tonight's program features some outstanding performers.*

NEWSPAPER/TELEVISION /ˈfiː·tʃər/ *n* [C] **1** (in newspapers and magazines or on television) a special or important article or program, esp. one that gives details about something that is not part of the main news ○ *They're running a three-part feature on the city's child welfare agency.* **2** A feature is also the main movie shown in a movie program.

February /ˈfeb·jəˌwer·i, ˈfeb·rə-/, *abbreviation* **Feb.** *n* [C/U] the second month of the year, after January and before March

feces /ˈfiː·siːz/ *pl n fml* solid waste excreted from the body of a human or animal through the bowels

fed /fed/ *past simple and past participle of* FEED

federal Ⓐ /ˈfed·ə·rəl/ *adj* [not gradable] ***politics & government*** of or connected with the central government of some countries ○ *the federal government* ○ *Federal law regulates trade with other countries.*

federalism /ˈfed·ə·rəˌlɪz·əm/ *n* [U] a system of government in which states unite and give up some of their powers to a central authority

federalist /ˈfed·ə·rə·ləst/ *n* [C] **1** someone who believes that a federation is a good system of government, or *Cdn* someone who believes Quebec should remain part of Canada **2** ***US history*** The Federalists supported the US Constitution from 1787 to 1788 and wanted a powerful central government.

federally /ˈfed·ə·rə·li, ˈfed·rə·li/ *adv* ○ *a federally funded agency that provides free legal services to the poor*

federation Ⓐ /ˌfed·əˈreɪ·ʃən/ *n* [C] a group of organizations, states, etc., that have united to form a larger organization or government ○ *Canada is a federation of provinces and territories.*

/fedz/ *pl n infml* federal officers or officials ○ *The feds worked with local police on the case.*

fed up /ˈfedˈʌp/ *adj infml* annoyed or disgusted by something that you have experienced for too long ○ *I'm just fed up with his excuses for not getting his work done.*

fee Ⓐ /fiː/ *n* [C] an amount of money charged for a service or for the use of something ○ *an admission fee* ○ *The doctor's usual fee is $125.*

feeble /ˈfiː·bəl/ *adj* weak ○ *a feeble joke* ○ *He's pretty feeble, and has to use a cane to get around.*

feebleminded /ˌfiː·bəlˈmaɪn·dəd/ *adj dated* unable to think carefully ○ *These regulations will protect the foolish and feeble-minded.*

feed GIVE FOOD /fiːd/ *v* [I/T] *past* **fed 1** to give food to a person or animal, or of an animal to eat ○ [T] *We fed the kids some leftovers.* ○ [I] *The cows were feeding in the pasture.* **2** If you feed a plant, you give it substances that help it grow.
feed /fiːd/ *n* [U] food for animals, esp. animals that are not kept as pets ○ *chicken feed*
feeding /ˈfiːd·ɪŋ/ *n* [C] a baby's or animal's meal ○ *She has a midnight feeding, then sleeps until morning.*
SUPPLY /fiːd/ *v* [T] *past* **fed 1** to supply something, esp. regularly or continuously ○ *We had to keep feeding quarters into the parking meter.* **2** If someone feeds you information, that person tells you things that may not be completely true: *They fed him a line about how important this work is to our country.*

feedback /ˈfiːd·bæk/ *n* [U] reaction to a process or activity, or the information obtained from such a reaction ○ *positive/negative feedback* ○ *We're hoping to get feedback on how well the program is working.*

feeding frenzy HUNTING *n* a condition of great excitement and confusion when an animal hunts and eats another animal
COMPETITION *n* [C] a fierce competition between people who all want the same thing ○ *The judge in this case wants to avoid a media feeding frenzy.*

feel EXPERIENCE /fiːl/ *v past* **felt** to experience or be aware of something emotional or physical ○ [L] *"How are you feeling?" "Oh, I don't feel very good."* ○ [L] *She said she didn't want anyone to feel sorry for her.* ○ [L] *I feel comfortable with you, Nick.* ○ [L] *He felt compelled to report the incident.* ○ [T] *When the anesthesia wore off, I felt a lot of pain.*
feeling /ˈfiː·lɪŋ/ *n* [C/U] **1** a physical or emotional experience or awareness ○ [U] *My toes were so cold that I lost all feeling in them.* ○ [C] *I have a feeling that I'm not welcome.* **2** Your feelings are your awareness of the way you should be treated, esp. when you are treated rudely: [pl] *He doesn't mean to hurt your feelings.* ➤ Confusables: **fall or feel?** at FALL ACCIDENT ➤ Usage: **sentiments or feelings?** at SENTIMENT GENERAL FEELING

WORD CHOICES feel

A very common alternative to the noun "feeling" is **emotion.**

*He finds it hard to express his **emotions**.*

The nouns **pang** or **stab** are sometimes used to describe a sudden, strong, bad feeling.

*Amelia felt a sharp **pang** of jealousy when she saw her sister's new house.*

*He felt a **stab** of regret for having behaved so badly toward his friend.*

A small amount of a sad feeling is often described as a **tinge.**

*It was with a **tinge** of sadness that she finally said goodbye.*

TOUCH /fiːl/ *v* [I/T] *past* **felt** to touch, esp. with the fingers, in order to examine something ○ [T] *Feel the softness of the baby's skin.* ○ [I] *She felt around* (= searched with her hands) *for the light switch.*
feel /fiːl/ *n* [U] ○ *I love the feel of silk against my skin.*
feeler /ˈfiː·lər/ *n* [C usually pl] one of the two long parts on an insect's head that it uses to touch things
HAVE OPINION /fiːl/ *v* [T] *past* **felt** to have as an opinion or belief ○ [+ (*that*) clause] *I feel (that) I should be doing more to help her.*
feeling /ˈfiː·lɪŋ/ *n* [C] ○ *My feeling is that we should wait until they come back.* ○ *He has strong feelings about environmental issues.*
UNDERSTANDING /fiːl/, **feeling** /ˈfiː·lɪŋ/ *n* [U] an understanding or natural ability ○ *Marcia has a good feel for this kind of work.*

WORD FAMILY feel

Nouns	feel feeler feeling feelings	*Adjectives* *Verbs*	unfeeling feel

IDIOMS with feel

•**feel bad** to believe you have done something wrong and blame yourself ○ *I feel bad about not inviting him to the party.*
•**feel free (to do** *something*) to know that you have permission to do something ○ *Feel free to help yourself to more coffee.*
•**feel good** to have satisfaction or pleasure about something ○ *It feels good to be done with finals.*
•**feel** *something* **in** *your* **bones** to believe something very strongly ○ *I just know you'll do well in college, I can feel it in my bones.*
•**feel like (doing)** *something* ***infml*** to want to have or do something ○ *I feel like going to get ice cream – want to come?*
•**feel** *your* **way** to do something slowly and carefully ○ *I've only been doing the job for two months, so I'm still feeling my way.*

PHRASAL VERBS with feel

•**feel for** *someone* to experience sympathy for someone ○ *I know she's unhappy, and I feel for her.*
•**feel like** *something* **SEEM** to seem to be something, or (esp. of weather) to seem likely to do something ○ *I felt like a fool when I couldn't remember her name.* ○ *She said she didn't feel like herself today.* ○ *It feels like rain.*
• **DESIRE** to have a desire to do or have something ○ *He was so rude, I felt like leaving immediately.* ○ *I feel like Chinese food.*
•**feel** *someone/something* **out** [M] to try to get information from someone or from a situation without asking direct questions ○ *Why don't you feel them out to see if they'll invite me over too?* ○ *I think they are trying to feel out what the new relationship should be.*
•**feel up to** *something* [T] to have the energy to do something ○ *I don't feel up to going out tonight.*

feet /fiːt/ *pl of* FOOT

feign /feɪn/ *v* [T] to pretend to have a feeling or condition ○ *He feigned sickness so he wouldn't have to go to school.*

feint /feɪnt/ *n* [C] an action or movement intended to take attention away from something else ○ *We had been kept unsure of his plans by feints.*
feint /feɪnt/ *v* [I/T] ○ [I] *He feinted to the left, then turned right.*

feisty /ˈfɑɪ·sti/ *adj approving* active, forceful, and determined ○ *She's a feisty kid who is not afraid to challenge authority.*

feline /ˈfiː·lɑɪn/ *adj* [not gradable] of or like an animal of the cat family

fell **FALL** /fel/ *past simple of* FALL

F

CUT DOWN /fel/ *v* [T] to cut down a tree ○ *He decided the diseased trees had to be felled.* ○ *(fig.) He was felled* (= killed) *by a heart attack.*

fella /ˈfel·ə/ *n* [C] *not standard* (spelled the way it is often spoken) FELLOW MAN ○ *Where did you meet this fella?*

fellow **MAN** /ˈfel·oʊ, -ə/ *n* [C] a man ○ *He was a big fellow with broad shoulders.*

SHARED /ˈfel·oʊ, -ə/ *adj* [not gradable] used of people or a person with whom you share something, esp. the same kind of job, interest, or experience ○ *She introduced me to a few of her fellow students.*
fellowship /ˈfel·əˌʃɪp/ *n* [C/U] **1** people with the same purpose, experience, or interest, or a formal organization of these people ○ [C] *the Artists' Fellowship* **2** Fellowship is also a friendly feeling that exists between people who have a shared interest or who do something as a group: [U] *I like the game, and I enjoy the fellowship of the guys on the team.*

MEMBER /ˈfel·oʊ, -ə/ *n* [C] a member of some groups that you must have special training to join ○ *Dr. Rodriguez is a Fellow of the American College of Physicians.*

fellowship /ˈfel·əˌʃɪp/ *n* [C] money for teaching or study given to a student studying for an advanced degree, or a position at a university paid for in this way ○ *She applied for a fellowship to continue her studies.*
fellow /ˈfel·oʊ, -ə/ *n* [C] a teacher or student who has a fellowship at a university ○ *He was a fellow at Harvard.*

felony /ˈfel·ə·ni/ *n* [C] *law* a serious crime that can be punished by more than one year in prison ○ *Robbery is a felony.*
felon /ˈfel·ən/ *n* [C] *law* a person who is guilty of a serious crime ○ *a convicted felon*

felsic /ˈfel·sɪk, -zɪk/ *adj* [not gradable] ***earth science*** describes rocks containing more light-colored substances and ALUMINUM than other rocks ○ Compare MAFIC

felt **FEEL** /felt/ *past simple and past participle of* FEEL

CLOTH /felt/ *n* [U] a thick cloth made from a pressed mass of wool, hair, or fur ○ *a felt hat*

felt-tip pen *n* [C] a pen that has a point made of fibers

female /ˈfiː·meɪl/ *adj* [not gradable] **1** of the sex that can produce eggs and give birth to young ○ *There are now more opportunities for female* (= women) *athletes in universities.* **2** In plants and flowers, female refers to a plant which produces flowers that will later develop into fruit. ○ Compare MALE
female /ˈfiː·meɪl/ *n* [C] ○ *The number of females competing in college sports has increased.*

feminine **FEMALE** /ˈfem·ə·nən/ *adj* having qualities traditionally considered to be suitable for a woman ○ *Even with the tailored look of a suit, sometimes I like to have something that's just a little feminine.* ○ Compare MASCULINE MALE
femininity /ˌfem·əˈnɪn·ət̬·i/ *n* [U] ○ *Long hair has traditionally been regarded as a sign of femininity.*

GRAMMAR /ˈfem·ə·nən/, *abbreviation* **fem.** *adj* [not gradable] ***grammar*** being a noun or pronoun of a type that refers to females, or in some other languages, being a noun of a type that refers to things considered as female

feminism /ˈfem·əˌnɪz·əm/ *n* [U] ***world history*** an organized effort to give women the same economic, social, and political rights as men
feminist /ˈfem·ə·nəst/ *n* [C] ○ *In the 19th century, feminists argued that women should be allowed to vote.*

fence **STRUCTURE** /fens/ *n* [C] a structure of wood or wire forming a wall around a house or a piece of land, often to keep people or animals from coming in or going out ○ *He put up a fence to keep his dog in the backyard.*
fence /fens/ *v* [T] ○ *The area is fenced on three sides but not along the highway.*

SPORT /fens/ *v* [I] to take part in the sport of attacking and defending with a weapon having a long blade
fencing /ˈfen·sɪŋ/ *n* [U] the sport of attacking and defending with a weapon having a long blade

CRIMINAL /fens/ *n* [C] a person who buys and sells stolen goods

IDIOM with fence

• **on the fence** not able to decide something ○ *Many consumers are still on the fence, waiting for a less expensive computer to come along.* ○ *Todd's still sitting on the fence, trying to decide which school he wants to go to.*

PHRASAL VERBS with fence

• **fence** *something* **in** [M] to protect an area by putting a fence around it ○ *Much of the land has been fenced in and is patrolled by guards.*
• **fence** *something* **off** [M] to prevent access to an area by putting a fence around it ○ *They're fencing off the construction site.*

fend for *yourself* /ˈfend·fər/ *phrasal verb* to take care of and provide for yourself, without depending on anyone else ○ *The strike left a million commuters to fend for themselves in getting to work.*

fend off *someone/something* /ˈfendˈɔːf/ *phrasal verb* [M] to defend yourself successfully against an attack, criticism, or some other unwanted thing ○ *He's an international celebrity with* *a staff to help fend off reporters.* ○ *The Social Democrat government fended off a challenge by the opposition to win re-election.*

fender /ˈfen·dər/ *n* [C] the part of a car or other vehicle that covers and protects the wheels

ferment CHANGE CHEMICALLY /fərˈment/ *v* [I/T] ***biology, chemistry*** to change chemically through the action of living substances, such as YEAST or bacteria, or to use a substance to produce a chemical change

fermentation /ˌfɜr·menˈteɪ·ʃən/ *n* [U] Alcoholic fermentation is a type of ANAEROBIC RESPIRATION (= a chemical change without the use of oxygen) in which sugar is changed into alcohol and CARBON DIOXIDE (= a gas).

CONFUSION /ˈfɜr·ment/ *n* [U] a state of confusion or excited expectation, esp. because of suddenly changing conditions ○ *He was a central figure in the intellectual ferment of his time.*

fern /fɜrn/ *n* [C] a green plant with long stems, wide, thin leaves, and no flowers

ferocious /fəˈroʊ·ʃəs/ *adj* fierce and violent ○ *ferocious wild dogs*

ferret /ˈfer·ət/ *n* [C] a type of WEASEL (= small animal with a long, thin body) that usually has black feet and black fur around its eyes

PHRASAL VERB with ferret

•**ferret out** *something/someone* [M] to discover someone or something, esp. information, after searching ○ *Officials are attempting to ferret out abuses in the welfare program.* ○ *If there are others who are responsible it might be worth an attempt to ferret them out.*

Ferris wheel /ˈfer·əs ˌhwiːl, -ˌwiːl/ *n* [C] a structure in an AMUSEMENT PARK consisting of a large wheel that turns slowly and has seats attached to its outer edge

ferromagnetic /ˌfer·oʊ·mægˈneţ·ɪk/ *adj* ***physics*** having the same kind of MAGNETISM (= power to attract other objects) that iron has

ferry /ˈfer·i/ *n* [C] a boat or ship for taking passengers and often vehicles across an area of water, esp. as a regular service ○ *There's no bridge around here, but you can take a ferry across the river.*

ferry /ˈfer·i/ *v* [T always + adv/prep] to transport someone or something repeatedly or regularly ○ *As parents, we seem to spend most of our time ferrying the kids to and from their friends' homes.*

fertile GROWING PLANTS /ˈfɜrt·əl/ *adj* (of land) able to produce a large number of high-quality crops ○ *fertile soil*

fertilize /ˈfɜrt·əlˌɑɪz/ *v* [T] to spread a natural or chemical substance on land in order to make plants grow well ○ *You have to fertilize your garden.*

fertilizer /ˈfɜrt·əlˌɑɪ·zər/ *n* [C/U] a natural or chemical substance that is spread on land in order to make plants grow well

ABLE TO PRODUCE /ˈfɜrt·əl/ *adj* **1** ***biology*** (of people or animals) able to produce young **2** *fig.* Someone who has a fertile imagination has an active mind and is able to produce a lot of new and original ideas.

fertility /fərˈtɪl·əţ·i/ *n* [U] ***biology*** the ability to produce young

fertilize /ˈfɜrt·əlˌɑɪz/ *v* [T] ***biology*** (in plants and animals) to join male and female sexual cells so that young begin to develop

fertilization /ˌfɜrt·əl·əˈzeɪ·ʃən/ *n* [U] ***biology*** the process of joining male and female sexual cells to produce young

Fertile Crescent *n* [C usually sing] ***world history*** a large, curved piece of land in the Middle East between the Tigris and Euphrates Rivers, important to the growth of human CIVILIZATION

fervent /ˈfɜr·vənt/ *adj* showing strong and sincere feelings or beliefs ○ *She was a fervent supporter of art and culture.*

fervently /ˈfɜr·vənt·li/ *adv* ○ *I fervently hope he's right.*

fervor, *Cdn, Br* **fervour** /ˈfɜr·vər/ *n* [U] strong, sincere feelings ○ *The country was swept by patriotic fervor.*

fess up /ˈfesˈʌp/ *phrasal verb infml* to tell the truth or say that you are responsible; CONFESS ○ *How can we force the president to fess up and accept responsibility for his behavior?*

fester /ˈfes·tər/ *v* [I] **1** (of an injury such as a cut) to become infected and form PUS (= thick yellow liquid) **2** *fig.* If a bad situation such as an argument festers, it becomes worse because it is being ignored: *It was better that she expressed her anger rather than let it fester inside her.*

festival /ˈfes·tə·vəl/, *infml* **fest** /fest/ *n* [C] an organized set of special events, such as musical performances or plays, usually happening in one place, or a special day or period, usually in memory of a religious event, with its own social activities, food, or ceremonies ○ *a film/food/music festival* ○ *the festival of Eid al-Adha/Hanukkah/Diwali* ○ *a solstice festival*

festive /ˈfes·tɪv/ *adj* typical of a holiday when people are in a good humor and expect to have a good time ○ *festive colored lights*

festivities /fesˈtɪv·əţ·iz/ *pl n* Festivities are the parties, meals, and other social activities with which people celebrate a special occasion.

festoon /fesˈtuːn/ *v* [T] to decorate a place or thing with strips of cloth or chains of paper, lights, flowers, etc. ○ *a straw hat festooned with paper flowers*

fetal /ˈfiːţ·əl/ *adj* ○ See at FETUS

fetal position *n* [C usually sing] a position in which you lie on your side with your knees bent and raised against your chest and your arms around your legs

fetch GET /fetʃ/ *v* [I/T] to go get something or someone and bring the thing or person back ○ [I] *She's been teaching the dog to fetch* (= get a stick or ball that is thrown and bring it back).

SELL /fetʃ/ *v* [T] to be sold for a price ○ *The collection of paintings fetched over a million dollars.*

fetching /ˈfetʃ·ɪŋ/ *adj* pleasant or attractive ○ *a fetching jacket/smile/hairstyle* ○ *A new interstate just to the west has made the town more fetching.*

fete /feɪt, fet/ *n* [C] a special celebration, often for a particular purpose, or to honor someone ○ *The annual fete to raise money for cancer research netted more than $90,000.*
fete /feɪt, fet/ *v* [T] ○ *The magazine's founding editor was feted with a dinner on her 80th birthday.*

F

fetish **INTEREST** /ˈfet̬·ɪʃ/ *n* [C] an activity or object that someone is interested in to an extreme degree and that the person gives an unreasonable amount of time or thought to ○ *He had a fetish about clothes.*

OBJECT /ˈfet̬·ɪʃ/ *n* [C] an object believed to have special power to protect

fetters /ˈfet̬·ərz/ *pl n* (esp. in the past) chains that were used to tie prisoners to a place by the legs

fetus /ˈfiːt̬·əs/ *n* [C] a human being or animal as it is developing in the uterus before birth, after the organs have started to form
fetal /ˈfiːt̬·əl/ *adj* [not gradable] ○ *The electronic device monitored the fetal heart rate.*

feud /fjuːd/ *n* [C] an angry and sometimes violent argument that has continued for a long time between two people, families, or groups ○ *a feud between two influential families* ○ *(fig.) The mayor has a longstanding feud with the media.*
feud /fjuːd/ *v* [I] ○ *The two brothers have been feuding for years.*

feudalism /ˈfjuːd·əlˌɪz·əm/ *n* [U] ***world history*** the social system that developed in western Europe in the eighth and ninth centuries in which people served a man of high rank by working and fighting for him and in exchange were supported and given land and protection
feudal /ˈfjuːd·əl/ *adj* [not gradable] ○ *the feudal system*

fever **BODY TEMPERATURE** /ˈfiː·vər/ *n* [C/U] a condition in which the body's temperature is higher than usual, esp. as a sign of illness ○ [C] *The child has a rash and a high fever.*
feverish /ˈfiː·və·rɪʃ/ *adj* ○ *I'm feeling a little feverish – I hope it's not the flu.*

EXCITEMENT /ˈfiː·vər/ *n* [U] a state of great excitement or enthusiasm ○ *Texas was in the grip of football fever.*
feverish /ˈfiː·və·rɪʃ/ *adj* quickly or with great excitement ○ *They worked from dark to dawn at a feverish pace.*
feverishly /ˈfiː·və·rɪʃ·li/ *adv* ○ *Doctors and nurses worked feverishly to save his life.*

few /fjuː/ *adj, pronoun, n* **1** a small number, not many, or not enough (of something) ○ *He is one of the few (people) I can trust to keep a secret.* **2** A few means a small number of: *I'm going to the supermarket to get a few things.* ○ *We've been having a few problems with the new computer.* ○ *"How many tomatoes do we need?" "Just a few."* ➤ Confusables: **less or fewer?** at LESS SMALLER AMOUNT

IDIOM with few

• **few and far between** not very many or not appearing very frequently ○ *Sunny, warm weekends have been few and far between this summer.*

fiancé, *female* **fiancée** /ˌfiː ˌɑn ˈseɪ, fiː ˈɑn ˌseɪ/ *n* [C] a person who has formally promised to marry another ○ *I'd like you to meet Irene, my fiancée.*

fiasco /fiː ˈæs·koʊ/ *n* [C] *pl* **fiascoes, fiascos** a complete failure ○ *The entire political campaign was a fiasco, and at the end he drew only 30% of the votes.*

fiat /ˈfiː·æt, -ɑt, -ət/ *n* [U] *fml* the giving of orders by someone who has complete authority ○ *The general ruled by fiat for eight years after seizing power.*

fib /fɪb/ *n* [C] *infml* an unimportant lie ○ *Have you been telling fibs about me?*
fib /fɪb/ *v* [I] **-bb-** *infml* ○ *George was fibbing some to make things seem more exciting.*

fiber **MATERIAL** /ˈfɑɪ·bər/ *n* [C/U] **1** any of the thin parts like thread that form plant or artificial material, esp. those that can be made into cloth, or a mass of such parts twisted together ○ [C] *Police detectives found cloth fibers at the crime scene that matched those from the coat the suspect was wearing.* **2** Fiber can also refer to thin, strong structures that connect the body: [U] *muscle fiber*

CHARACTER /ˈfɑɪ·bər/ *n* [U] the quality of a person's character, esp. its moral strength ○ *He lacked the moral fiber to be president.*

FOOD /ˈfɑɪ·bər/ *n* [U] the part of foods eaten that is not digested but that passes through the body and is excreted as waste ○ *Doctors recommend a diet of fruits, vegetables, and grains that are high in fiber.*

fiberglass /ˈfɑɪ·bər ˌglæs/ *n* [U] a material made from small threads of glass twisted together, used within the walls of houses to keep out cold and pressed into hard plastic for use in boats and other structures

fiber optics *pl n* ***science*** glass or plastic fibers used to send light that contains information or images around curves
fiber-optic *adj* ○ *Fiber-optic devices are used in medicine to examine internal organs.* ○ *The cable TV company is laying miles of fiber-optic cables.*

fickle /ˈfɪk·əl/ *adj* **1** likely to change your opinion or your feelings suddenly and without a good reason ○ *He criticized the fickle behavior of football fans who cheer you one week and boo you the next.* **2** The weather is described as fickle if it tends to change suddenly: *Fickle winds made sailing conditions difficult.*
fickleness /ˈfɪk·əl·nəs/ *n* [U]

fiction /ˈfɪk·ʃən/ *n* [C/U] ***literature*** the type of book or story that is written about imaginary characters and events and does not describe real people or deal with facts, or a false report or statement that you pretend is true ○ [U] *She wrote detective fiction and made a good living at it.* ○ [C usually sing] *It was a fiction, though widely believed, that he had once been rich.* ○ Compare NONFICTION

fictional /ˈfɪk·ʃən·əl/ *adj* [not gradable] ○ *The characters in the movie are purely fictional.*

fictionalized /ˈfɪk·ʃən·əlˌɑɪzd/ *adj* [not gradable] based on a real event or character but with imaginary details added or some facts changed ○ *This is the fictionalized story of the American painter James McNeill Whistler.*

WORD FAMILY fiction			
Nouns	fiction nonfiction	*Adjectives*	fictional fictionalized

fictitious /fɪkˈtɪʃ·əs/ *adj* [not gradable] invented and not true or existing; false ○ *He registered at the hotel under a fictitious name.*

fiddle MOVE THINGS /ˈfɪd·əl/ *v* [I always + adv/prep] to move things around or touch things without a particular purpose ○ *He stood there fiddling with his keys.*

INSTRUMENT /ˈfɪd·əl/ *n* [C] a VIOLIN

fiddler /ˈfɪd·lər, ˈfɪd·əl·ər/ *n* [C] a person who plays the VIOLIN (= small, stringed instrument), esp. in music popular in rural areas

PHRASAL VERB with fiddle

• **fiddle around** to take part in activity that doesn't achieve anything, esp. when this annoys someone ○ *The legislature has fiddled around while our schools are falling apart.* ○ *I wish they'd quit fiddling around with the tax law* (= changing it without improving it).

fidelity BEING LOYAL /fəˈdel·ət̬·i/ *n* [U] the state of remaining loyal to someone and keeping the promises you made to that person

ACCURACY /fəˈdel·ət̬·i/ *n* [U] the degree to which a copy of something shows the true character of the original ○ *The fidelity of the tape recording was so poor that you could not understand much of what was said.*

fidget /ˈfɪdʒ·ət/ *v* [I] to make continuous small movements because you are uncomfortable or bored ○ *Children can't sit still for long without fidgeting.*

field LAND /fiːld/ *n* [C] **1** an area of land with grass or crops growing on it ○ *We drove past fields of wheat.* **2** A field can also be a large area covered by something or having something under its surface: *an oil field* **3 The field** is a place where practical work is being done: *He was a working reporter in the field, not some anchorman in a studio.*

AREA OF FORCE /fiːld/ *n* [C] ***physics*** an area in which a particular force has some effect ○ *the magnetic field that surrounds the earth*

SPORTS /fiːld/ *n* [C] a grassy area used for playing sports ○ *He ran laps around the football field after school.*

field /fiːld/ *v* [I/T] **1** (in baseball) to catch or pick up the ball after it has been hit in order to prevent the other team from scoring ○ [T] *He fielded the ball cleanly and threw to first base.* **2** To field also means to have a person or a team play a sport: [T] *The university fields teams in 14 sports.*

fielder /ˈfiː·l·dər/ *n* [C] (in baseball) a person playing defense who tries to catch or pick up the ball after it has been hit

COMPETITORS /fiːld/ *n* [C/U] all the competitors taking part in a race or activity, or all the competitors other than the leader ○ [C] *The cross-country race started with a field of 85 competitors.*

AREA OF INTEREST /fiːld/ *n* [C] an area of activity or interest ○ *She is an expert in the field of economics.*

ANSWER /fiːld/ *v* [T] to answer questions, esp. difficult or unexpected ones ○ *Be prepared to field some tough questions from the senators after your presentation.*

IDIOM with field

• **have a field day** to gain advantage or success from a situation, esp. one that is bad for someone else ○ *When the press found out about the stolen money, they had a field day.*

field day *n* [C] a special day of organized sports or other outside activities for students

field event *n* [C] a competition that involves throwing objects such as a JAVELIN or jumping, but not running in races ○ Compare TRACK EVENT

field glasses *pl n* BINOCULARS

field goal *n* [C] a play in football worth three points made by kicking the ball between the other team's GOALPOSTS

field hockey *n* [U] a game in which two teams of 11 players each try to score points by using special sticks to hit a small ball into a net at either end of the field

field house *n* [C] a building esp. in a university where sports events can be held inside and where there is equipment that can be used in exercising ○ *Drake University's field house seats 12,500 people.*

field lines *pl n* ***physics*** a series of lines that represent the strength and direction of a FIELD AREA OF FORCE

field trip *n* [C] a visit made by students to study something away from their school ○ *Mrs. Rhines took her class on a field trip to the zoo.*

fieldwork /ˈfiːld·wɜrk/ *n* [U] the testing of scientific theories in real situations ○ *Marjory did a lot of her fieldwork in the rain forests of Brazil.*

fiend /fiːnd/ *n* [C] *usually humorous* **1** an evil or cruel person or spirit ○ *Who was the fiend who designed such ugly clothes?* **2** A fiend can also be a person who likes something in an extreme way: *a chocolate fiend*

fiendish /ˈfiːn·dɪʃ/ *adj usually humorous* cruel or evil ○ *He took fiendish delight in making them wait.*

fiendishly /ˈfiːn·dɪʃ·li/ *adv* extremely ○ *The murder mystery had a fiendishly clever plot.*

fierce /fɪrs/ *adj* **1** violent and forceful ○ *fierce thunderstorms* ○ *The city had been under fierce at-*

tack. **2** Fierce can also mean severe or extremely strong: *She's a fierce critic of US policies.* ○ *He was a fierce competitor.*

fiercely /ˈfɪr·sli/ *adv* ○ *He's fiercely* (= very strongly) *committed to excellence in education.*

fiery FLAMING /ˈfɑɪ·ri/ *adj* flaming or extremely bright, hot, or of a red color like fire ○ *a fiery explosion* ○ *the fiery rays of the sun* ○ (*fig.*) *fiery* (= spicy hot) *chili*

EMOTIONAL /ˈfɑɪ·ri/ *adj* emotional or easily made angry ○ *He's known for his fiery temper.*

F

fiesta /fiːˈes·tə/ *n* [C] a public celebration, esp. on a religious holiday, in Spain or South America

fifteen /fɪfˈtiːn/ *number* 15 ○ *My brother is fifteen.* ○ *a fifteen-story building*

fifteenth /fɪfˈtiːnθ/ *adj, adv, n* [C] **1** *Our team is ranked fifteenth in the country.* ○ [C] *Her birthday is on the fifteenth of May.* **2** A fifteenth is one of fifteen equal parts of something.

fifth /fɪfθ, fɪθ/ *adj, adv, n* [C] **1** (a person or thing) coming immediately after the fourth and before all others ○ *Leo was fifth in the race.* ○ [C] *Tomorrow is the fifth of September.* **2** A fifth is one of five equal parts of something. ○ Related Number: FIVE

fifty /ˈfɪf·ti/ *number* 50 ○ *My father is fifty.* ○ *a fifty-minute ride*

fifties, **50s**, **50's** /ˈfɪf·tiz/ *pl n* **1** the numbers 50 through 59 ○ *The temperature has been in the fifties* (= between 50° and 59°). ○ *My dad is in his fifties* (= between 50 and 59 years old). **2** The fifties are the years between 1950 and 1959.

fiftieth /ˈfɪf·tiː·əθ/ *adj, adv, n* [C] **1** *a fiftieth wedding anniversary* **2** A fiftieth is one of fifty equal parts of something.

fifty-fifty *adj, adv* (into) equal halves ○ *They divided the work fifty-fifty.*

IDIOM with fifty-fifty

• **a fifty-fifty chance** a result is equally likely to happen or not happen ○ *There's only a fifty-fifty chance that she'll survive the operation.*

fig /fɪg/ *n* [C] a tree that grows in warm places, or its soft, sweet edible fruit

fig. *n abbreviation for* FIGURE PICTURE or FIGURATIVE ○ USAGE: Used esp. in writing.

fight /fɑɪt/ *v* [I/T] *past* **fought 1** to argue with or use force against another person or a group of people, or to oppose something ○ [T] *Rebels have been fighting fierce battles with government forces.* ○ [I] *They're fighting against some powerful organizations.* ○ [I] *She's willing to fight for a more just society.* ○ [I] *Those two little kids were fighting over a toy.* ○ [T] *Gordon has been fighting an uphill battle to attract investors.* **2** Two people who fight may be boxing: [T] *Lewis will fight Akinwande for the heavyweight title.*

fight /fɑɪt/ *n* [C] ○ *Isabelle is looking for a fight.* ○ *A patient's attitude is important in the fight against the disease.* ○ *Have you got tickets for the fight* (= a competition between two boxers)?

fighter /ˈfɑɪt̬·ər/ *n* [C] **1** someone who is willing to argue for and put effort into what he or she believes ○ *She proved herself to be a real fighter.* ○ *Ali was the greatest fighter* (= boxer) *of all time.* **2** A fighter is also a small, fast military aircraft.

fighting /ˈfɑɪt̬·ɪŋ/ *n* [U] ○ *The fighting lasted a long time.*

WORD CHOICES fight

A noisy, rough fight between people in a public place can be described as a **brawl**.

*He was injured in a **brawl** outside the stadium.*

If a short fight starts suddenly, you can use the word **scuffle**.

*There were a few **scuffles** between fans after the soccer game.*

A fight between large groups of people can be described as a **clash**.

*Five people were injured in **clashes** between strikers and owners.*

If someone fights against a person who is attacking them, you can describe it as a **struggle**.

*He managed to escape after a **struggle**.*

The word **battle** is often used for a fight between armies.

*Many soldiers were killed in the **battle**.*

IDIOM with fight

• **fight it out** to argue until a decision is reached between two people or groups ○ *Let them fight it out.*

PHRASAL VERBS with fight

• **fight back** DEFEND to defend yourself against attack or criticism ○ *You've seen him fight back every time he's been unfairly attacked.*

• **fight** *something* **back** NOT SHOW [M] to try hard not to show a strong emotion ○ *She fought back the tears as she watched her brother go.*

• **fight** *something* **off** [M] to free yourself from an illness or a desire to do something you should not do ○ *I was trying to fight off the urge to sneak into the kitchen for something to eat.* ○ *Her body couldn't fight the infection off.*

fighting chance *n* [C usually sing] a small but real possibility of success ○ *Doctors gave him a fighting chance to make a complete recovery.*

figment IDIOM /ˈfɪg·mənt/

• **a figment of** *your* **imagination** something imagined or created by your mind ○ *The dinosaurs he said he saw were figments of his imagination.*

figurative /ˈfɪg·jə·rət̬·ɪv/, *abbreviation* **fig.** *adj* [not gradable] **1** ***English*** (of words and phrases) used not with their basic meaning but to suggest part of that meaning ○ *literal and figurative meanings* **2** ***art*** Figurative art is based on the shapes of real objects.

figuratively /ˈfɪg·jə·rət̬·ɪv·li/ *adv* ○ *Figuratively speaking, negotiators succeeded in building a bridge over a wide river in reaching this agreement.*

figure **NUMBER** /ˈfɪg·jər/ *n* [C] a number or an amount ○ *The collection was valued at $20 million, a figure that might cover the cost of having artists recreate the drawings.*

> **USAGE**
> **figure** or **figures**?
> When referring to a set of numbers always use the plural form.
> *This report shows the company's sales figures for Asia.*
> ~~*This report shows the company's sales figure for Asia.*~~

SHAPE /ˈfɪg·jər/ *n* [C] a shape or form ○ *geometric/abstract figures*

BODY /ˈfɪg·jər/ *n* [C] the shape of a person's body, or a body seen not clearly or from a distance ○ *I could see two figures crossing the field in the distance.*

PERSON /ˈfɪg·jər/ *n* [C] A particular type of figure is a person with that characteristic: *Our consultants are prominent figures in their field.*

PICTURE /ˈfɪg·jər/, *abbreviation* **fig.** *n* [C] a picture or drawing, often numbered, in a book or document ○ *Figure 10.3 shows the maximum length of the bridges.*

EXPECT /ˈfɪg·jər/ *v* [I/T] **1** to expect, believe, decide, or think that something will happen or that certain conditions will exist ○ [+ (*that*) clause] *They figured (that) about twenty people would be there.* ○ [I] *You can't figure on going out and being back in two hours.* **2** *fig.* If something figures, you are unhappy about it but you expected it: [I] *"He'll be late for dinner." "That figures!"*

IDIOM with figure

• **a figure of speech** an expression that uses words to mean something different than what they usually mean ○ *You usually use the figure of speech "break a leg" to wish actors good luck.*

PHRASAL VERB with figure

• **figure out** *someone/something* [M] to understand someone or something, or to find the answer to something by thinking ○ *I've never been able to figure her out.* ○ *Can you figure out how to open this?*

figure eight *n* [C] the shape made when drawing an 8 ○ *She skated a perfect figure eight.*

figurehead /ˈfɪg·jərˌhed/ *n* [C] someone who has the position of a leader but who has no real power ○ *The company chairman is basically a figurehead.*

figure skating *n* [U] a type of ICE SKATING involving patterns, jumps, and dance steps
figure skater *n* [C] ○ *Thirty-five figure skaters will compete in the national competition.*

filament **WIRE** /ˈfɪl·ə·mənt/ *n* [C] a thin thread or wire, esp. the wire inside a LIGHT BULB

STEM /ˈfɪl·ə·mənt/ *n* [C] ***biology*** the long thin stem that carries the part of a flower that produces pollen

filch /fɪltʃ/ *v* [T] *infml* to steal something of little value ○ *OK – who filched my pencils?*

file Ⓐ **COLLECTION** /fɑɪl/ *n* [C/U] **1** a folded piece of stiff paper used to store papers, letters, or other documents in an ordered way, esp. in an office, or a box or container in which documents are stored ○ [C] *You'll find it in the files under C.* ○ [U] *We keep your records on file for five years.* **2** A file in a computer is a collection of information stored as one unit with one name: [C] *I'm going to copy/save this file.*
file Ⓐ /fɑɪl/ *v* [T] **1** *We file the reports by zip code.* ○ *to file criminal charges* **2** To file something can mean to make an official record of it, or to begin a legal process: *to file an insurance claim*
filing /ˈfɑɪ·lɪŋ/ *n* [U] ○ *Her job involves filing and answering phones.*

LINE /fɑɪl/ *n* [C/U] a line of people or animals, one behind another ○ [U] *They walked (in) single file.*
file /fɑɪl/ *v* [I always + adv/prep] ○ *The bride's family filed in.*

TOOL /fɑɪl/ *n* [C] a usually flat tool with rough surfaces for rubbing objects to make them smooth or to change their shape
file /fɑɪl/ *v* [I/T] ○ [T] *She carefully filed her nails before applying nail polish.*

file cabinet *n* [C] a piece of office furniture in which files can be stored

filet /fɪˈleɪ, ˈfɪl·eɪ/ *n, v* FILLET

filet mignon *n* [U] a very high-quality piece of meat

filibuster /ˈfɪl·əˌbʌs·tər/ *n* [C] ***politics & government*** (in a legislature) a way of preventing a law from being passed by using the rules or making long speeches to delay voting on it
filibuster /ˈfɪl·əˌbʌs·tər/ *v* [I/T] ○ [I] *The senator threatened to filibuster if jobs in his state were not protected.*

filigree /ˈfɪl·əˌgriː/ *n* [U] thin gold or silver wire shaped into delicate patterns and used esp. in jewelry

filing cabinet *n* [C] a FILE CABINET

fill /fɪl/ *v* [I/T] **1** to make or become fuller or full; to use empty space ○ [T] *I filled the bucket.* ○ [I] *After all that rain, the reservoirs are finally filling.* ○ [T] *The dentist says I need to have four teeth filled* (= treated to replace decayed material). **2** If a product or service fills a need, it gives people something they want. **3** To fill a job or position is to employ someone to do that job: [T] *I'm sorry, the position has already been filled.*
fill /fɪl/ *n* [U] an amount that is enough ○ *to eat/drink your fill*
filling /ˈfɪl·ɪŋ/ *n* [C/U] **1** a material put inside of something ○ [U] *What sort of filling do these pillows have?* **2** A filling is also a substance put into the space in a tooth where decayed material has been removed.
filling /ˈfɪl·ɪŋ/ *adj* ○ *This chocolate cake is very filling* (= a small amount makes me feel full).

WORD FAMILY fill

Nouns	fill refill filling	*Adjectives*	filling
		Verbs	fill refill

IDIOMS with fill

• **fill** *someone's* **shoes** to do someone's job or accept someone's responsibilities ○ *The senator will step down this year, but two well-known Republicans are ready to fill his shoes.*

• **get** *your* **fill of** *something*, **have** *your* **fill of** *something* to have or experience as much as you want of something ○ *I go to my mother's house every week to get my fill of her home cooking.*

PHRASAL VERBS with fill

• **fill in** *someone* **GIVE INFORMATION** [M] to informally tell someone information that is wanted or needed ○ *We filled her in on all the latest gossip.*

• **fill in REPLACE** to do someone else's job temporarily ○ *The gym teacher was sick today, so a substitute filled in for her.*

• **fill in/out** *something* [M] to give written information, esp. by completing a form ○ *Please fill in the application and sign it.* ○ *I got the membership form and filled it out.*

• **fill out** to become larger ○ *When John is older and fills out some, he'll be an outstanding athlete.*

• **fill up** *something* [M] to make something completely full ○ *I want to fill up the gas tank.* ○ *That sandwich filled me up.*

• **fill** *(someone/something)* **with** *something* to cause a person, place, or period of time to have a lot of something ○ *His childhood was filled with happiness.* ○ *The kitchen is filled with the smell of fresh coffee.*

fillet, **filet** /fɪˈleɪ, ˈfɪl·eɪ/ *n* [C/U] a piece of meat or fish without bones

fillet, **filet** /fiˈleɪ, ˈfɪl·eɪ/ *v* [T] to cut the flesh away from the bones of a fish ○ *The customer wanted her fish filleted.*

filling station *n* [C] a GAS STATION

filly /ˈfɪl·i/ *n* [C] a young, female horse ○ Compare COLT

film PICTURE /fɪlm/ *v* [I/T] to make pictures of something in making a movie, or to make a movie ○ [T] *Her last movie was filmed in Spain.*

film /fɪlm/ *n* [C] a movie

MATERIAL /fɪlm/ *n* [U] (a length of) dark, thin material like plastic on which you can record images as photographs or as moving pictures ○ *a roll of film* ○ *I didn't get my film developed yet.*

LAYER /fɪlm/ *n* [C] a thin layer of something on something else ○ *A film of oil glistened on the surface of the water.*

filmmaker /ˈfɪlm ˌmeɪ·kər/ *n* [C] someone who controls the making of a movie, usually its DIRECTOR

film noir *n* [U] NOIR

filter /ˈfɪl·tər/ *n* [C] a piece of equipment or a device for removing solids from liquids or gases, or for limiting the particular type of light, sound, or electricity going through it ○ *an oil filter* ○ *a coffee filter* ➤ Picture: **filtration**

filter /ˈfɪl·tər/ *v* [I/T] **1** [T] *Clams filter water to extract food.* ○ [M] *Devices in the chimneys filter out particles from smoke.* **2** If something filters down, in, out, or through, it appears or happens gradually or to a limited degree: [I always + adv/prep] *Reports of the accident began to filter in.* ○ [I always + adv/prep] *Sunlight filtered through the branches.*

filthy /ˈfɪl·θi/ *adj* extremely dirty ○ *Trucks poured out clouds of filthy, black smoke.*

filth /fɪlθ/ *n* [U] *There were beggars in the streets and filth everywhere.*

filthiness /ˈfɪl·θiː·nəs/ *n* [U]

IDIOM with filthy

• **filthy rich** extremely rich ○ *His parents are filthy rich, so he gets everything he wants.*

filtrate /ˈfɪl·treɪt/ *n* [C] ***biology***, ***chemistry*** a liquid, gas or other substance that has passed through a FILTER (= piece of equipment that removes substances that are not wanted)

filtration /fɪlˈtreɪ·ʃən/ *n* [U] the act of passing a liquid or gas through a filter

filtration /fɪlˈtreɪ·ʃən/ *n* [C] ***science*** the process of using a filter to remove solids from liquids or gasses

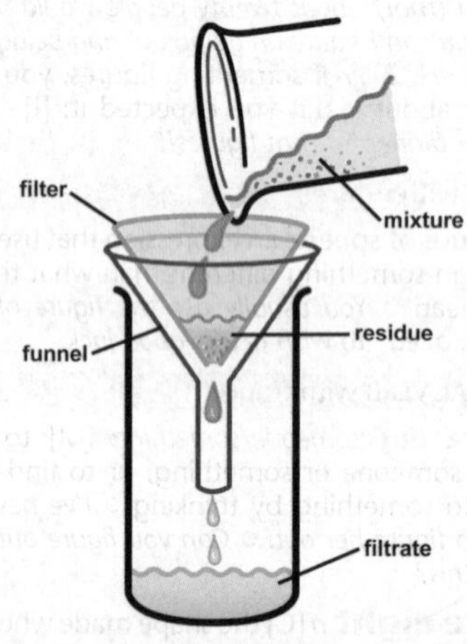

FILTRATION

fin /fɪn/ *n* [C] a thin, wing-shaped part of a fish that helps it to swim, or a wing-shaped part of a ship, aircraft, or car

finagle /fəˈneɪ·gəl/ *v* [I/T] to get something by using an indirect method ○ [T] *How can I finagle a place on the guest list for the big party?*

final Ⓐ **LAST** /ˈfɑɪn·əl/ *adj* [not gradable] last ○ *The other team scored twice in the final minute.* ○ *The recommendation will be sent to the City Council for final approval.* ○ (infml) *I'm not coming and that's final* (= I do not want to discuss it any longer).

final (exam) /ˈfɑɪn·əl (igˈzæm)/ *n* [C] a test taken on a subject at the end of a school year or course ○ *a math final* ○ *Spring brought final exams and the end of the year.*

finality Ⓐ /fɑɪˈnæl·ət̬·i, fə-/ *n* [U] ○ *The finality of death is sometimes hard to accept.*

finalize Ⓐ /ˈfɑɪn·əlˌɑɪz/ *v* [T] ○ *Details of the deal are being finalized.*

finally Ⓐ /ˈfɑɪn·əl·i, ˈfɑɪn·li/ *adv* [not gradable] at the end, or after some delay ○ *Finally, I just said, "I don't care."* ○ *We finally got home at midnight.*

COMPETITION /ˈfɑɪn·əl/ *n* [C usually pl] the last in a series of games, races, or competitions ○ *The women's basketball finals will be on Sunday.*

finalist /ˈfɑɪn·əl·əst/ *n* [C] ○ *a finalist for the award*

WORD FAMILY final

Nouns	final finality finalist finale semifinal	*Adjectives* *Verbs* *Adverbs*	final finalize finally

finale /fəˈnæl·i, -ˈnɑl·i/ *n* [C usually sing] the last part of something, esp. a musical or theater performance ○ *a grand finale*

finance Ⓐ /fəˈnæns, ˈfɑɪ·næns/ *n* the management of money, or the money belonging to a person, group, or organization ○ [U] *corporate/personal finance* ○ [pl] *the city's finances*

finance Ⓐ /fəˈnæns, ˈfɑɪ·næns/ *v* [T] ○ *How will you finance a new house* (= provide the money to obtain it)*?*

financing Ⓐ /fəˈnæn·sɪŋ, ˈfɑɪˌnæn-/ *n* [U] the money needed to do a particular thing, or the way of getting the money ○ *BP will provide 65 percent of the financing for the project.*

financial Ⓐ /fəˈnæn·tʃəl, fɑɪ-/ *adj* [not gradable] ○ *financial problems*

financially Ⓐ /fəˈnæn·tʃə·li, fɑɪ-/ *adv* [not gradable] ○ *We're in fairly good shape financially.*
➤ Usage: **Economic, economical, or financial?** at ECONOMY SYSTEM

financier Ⓐ /ˌfɪn·ənˈsɪr, ˌfɑɪˌnæn-/ *n* [C] someone who controls a large amount of money and can give or lend it to people or organizations

finch /fɪntʃ/ *n* [C] a small singing bird with a short, wide, pointed beak

find DISCOVER /fɑɪnd/ *v* [T] *past* **found 1** to see where a thing or person is, either unexpectedly or by searching; discover ○ *I found a ten-dollar bill in my pocket.* ○ *I hope I can find a place to live near work.* ○ *Many plant and animal species are found* (= exist) *only in the rain forests.* **2** Someone who finds information begins to understand something: [+ *that* clause] *The study found that men who took an aspirin a day have fewer heart attacks.* ○ *Some insects have been found to live several years without water.* **3** If you find a quality within yourself, you suddenly develop it or learn that you have it: *She found the courage to leave the town where she was born.* **4** To find someone means to meet someone you can have a close, loving relationship with: *Ellen found Sascha, married him, and soon after they had twins.*

find /fɑɪnd/ *n* [C] a good or valuable thing or a special person that has been discovered ○ *She's a real find – singers like her don't grow on trees.*

finding /ˈfɑɪn·dɪŋ/ *n* [C usually pl] information that has been discovered esp. by detailed study

WORD CHOICES find

A very common alternative to "find" is the verb **discover.**

The missing wallet was ***discovered*** *under the chair.*

I finally ***discovered*** *the letters in a drawer.*

If someone finds the exact position of someone or something, in formal situations the verb **locate** is sometimes used.

Police are still trying to ***locate*** *the suspect.*

If someone finds something that has been secret or hidden, then the verbs **uncover** or **unearth** are sometimes used.

Reporters ***uncovered/unearthed*** *evidence of corruption.*

The phrasal verbs **come across** and **stumble across/on** are used when someone finds something by chance.

I ***stumbled upon*** *these photographs when I was cleaning out my desk.*

We ***came across*** *a lovely little restaurant in the village.*

If someone finds something or someone after looking carefully in different places, you can use the verb **trace** or the phrasal verb **track down.**

Police have so far failed to ***trace/track down*** *the missing woman.*

JUDGE /fɑɪnd/ *v* [I/T] *past* **found** *law* to make a judgment in a law court ○ [T] *to be found guilty/innocent*

IDIOMS with find

• **find** *your* **self** *somewhere* to learn you have arrived somewhere ○ *We fell asleep in the back of the car and woke up to find ourselves in Atlanta.*

• **find (the) time** have enough time ○ *I wish I could find the time to do more reading.*

PHRASAL VERB with find

• **find out** *(something)* [M] to obtain knowledge of something, or to obtain knowledge of someone's activities, esp. dishonest ones ○ *How did you find out about the party?* ○ *I just found out that he was cheating on the test.* ○ *He wondered whether his boss was involved, but he saw no way of finding that out.*
➤ Usage: **know or find out?** at KNOW HAVE INFORMATION

fine SATISFACTORY /fɑɪn/ *adj, adv* [not gradable] very good or very well; satisfactory or satisfactorily ○ *I was sick last night, but I feel fine this morning.* ○ *The apartments are very small, which is fine if you're single.* ○ *The car was working fine yesterday.* ○ *"Is something wrong?" "No, everything's just fine, thanks."*

EXCELLENT /fɑɪn/ *adj* [-er/-est only] **1** of excellent quality or much better than average ○ *Although still* *young, he is already a fine musician.* ○ *We had lunch in one of the city's finest restaurants.* **2** Fine is sometimes used with an opposite meaning to show that you are annoyed: *That's a fine thing to say after all I've done for you.*

THIN /fɑɪn/ *adj* [*-er/-est* only] very thin or in very small grains or drops ○ *fine blond hair* ○ *The paint comes out of the can in a fine spray.* ○ *She has her mother's fine* (= delicate and beautiful) *features.*

finely /ˈfɑɪn·li/, **fine** /fɑɪn/ *adv* ○ *finely ground coffee*

PUNISHMENT /fɑɪn/ *n* [C] an amount of money that has to be paid as a punishment for not obeying a rule or law ○ *If found guilty, he faces six months in jail and a heavy fine.*

fine /fɑɪn/ *v* [T] ○ *They fined him $125 for driving through a red light.*

fine art *n* [U] a type of art that is admired for its beauty, for example painting, SCULPTURE, music, and dance

fine print *n* [U] important information printed in small letters in an agreement or document ○ *Make sure you examine the fine print before you sign the contract.*

finery /ˈfɑɪ·nə·ri/ *n* [U] decorative and expensive clothing and jewelry worn on a special occasion ○ *The stars arrived for the Oscars dressed in all their finery.*

finesse /fəˈnes/ *n* [U] great skill or style ○ *She has handled these difficult negotiations with real finesse.*

fine-tune *v* [T] to make small changes in (something) in order to make it work as well as possible

finger /ˈfɪŋ·gər/ *n* [C] **1** any of the long, thin parts of the hand that bend and hold things, esp. one other than the thumb ○ *I cut my finger when I was chopping onions.* **2** A finger is also a part of a GLOVE (= piece of clothing for the hand) that covers a finger.

finger /ˈfɪŋ·gər/ *v* [T] **1** to touch or feel something with the fingers ○ *He fingered his watch nervously as he waited for the exam to begin.* **2** *slang* If you finger someone, you tell the police that the person is guilty of a crime.

IDIOM with finger

• **at** *your* **fingertips** convenient and easy to find ○ *She had all the facts at her fingertips.*

fingernail /ˈfɪŋ·gərˌneɪl/ *n* [C] the hard, smooth covering that protects the upper part of the end of a finger

finger-pointing *n* [C usually sing] the action of blaming particular people ○ *The Republicans won, and the finger-pointing among the Democrats began.*

fingerprint /ˈfɪŋ·gərˌprɪnt/, *short form* **print** *n* [C] the mark left by the pattern of curved lines on the end of a finger or thumb

fingerprint /ˈfɪŋ·gərˌprɪnt/ *v* [T] ○ *The police fingerprinted the suspects.*

fingertip /ˈfɪŋ·gərˌtɪp/ *n* [C] the end of a finger

finicky /ˈfɪn·ɪ·ki/ *adj* giving too much attention to small details; hard to please ○ *a finicky dresser* ○ *a finicky eater*

finish /ˈfɪn·ɪʃ/ *v* [I/T] **1** to come to an end ○ [I] *The meeting should finish at four o'clock.* ○ [T] *If you'll let me finish my sentence, I'll explain it to you.* **2** To finish can also mean to complete something: [I] *She didn't win but she did finish second.* ○ [T] *Have you finished that magazine?* **3** To finish can also mean to use completely: [T] *We may as well finish the rest of this pasta.*

finish /ˈfɪn·ɪʃ/ *n* [C] **1** *Both candidates are predicting a close finish in this election.* **2** A finish is the appearance of the surface of something or the last covering, as of paint, put onto it: *a glossy finish*

finished /ˈfɪn·ɪʃt/ *adj* [not gradable] ○ *Raw materials make up only a small part of the cost of the finished* (= completed) *product.* ○ *As a result of this latest scandal, the senator's career is finished* (= brought to an end).

finisher /ˈfɪn·ɪ·ʃər/ *n* [C usually pl] ○ *She was one of the top ten finishers in the race.*

WORD FAMILY finish

Nouns	finish finisher	*Adjectives*	finished unfinished
Verbs	finish		

WORD CHOICES finish

The verb **end** is a common alternative to "finish" when it means "stop."

What time does the concert ***end****?*

When someone finishes doing or making something, the verb **complete** is sometimes used.

Have you ***completed*** *all the questions?*

The project took five years to ***complete****.*

The verb **conclude** is used when someone finishes a speech, meeting, or piece of writing by doing something.

She ***concluded*** *her speech by thanking everyone who had helped her.*

If someone finishes something quickly and easily, especially food or a piece of work, in informal situations you can use the phrasal verb **polish off**.

He's just ***polished off*** *two huge bowls of pasta.*

The phrasal verb **wind up** is sometimes used when an activity is gradually finishing.

It's time to ***wind up*** *the game now.*

PHRASAL VERBS with finish

• **finish** *someone/something* **off DESTROY** [M] to destroy or completely defeat someone or something ○ *Lack of water finished off the agricultural communities in the valley.* ○ *He says he refuses to let the disease finish him off.*

• **finish off** *something* **COMPLETE** [M] to complete or use all of something ○ *I started the project and someone else finished it off.* ○ *They helped finish off his birthday cake.*

•**finish up** *something* [M] to complete something ○ *She started the job, had lunch, and then came back to finish it up.* ○ *They were finishing up breakfast.*

finish line *n* [C] the line at the end of a race

finite Ⓐ /ˈfɑɪ·nɑɪt/ *adj* having a limit or end ○ *We have only a finite amount of time to complete this project.*

fink on *someone* /ˈfɪŋ·kɑn, -kɔːn/ *phrasal verb slang* to tell secret and damaging information about someone ○ *Someone finked on him to the cops.*

fink out /ˈfɪŋˈkɑʊt/ *phrasal verb slang* to fail to do something, esp. something promised ○ *We'd planned to go camping but at the last minute Ron finked out.*

fir (tree) /fɜr (triː)/ *n* [C] any of several types of evergreen trees that have very thin leaves and are grown esp. for their wood or for use as CHRISTMAS TREES

fire FLAMES /fɑɪr/ *n* [C/U] **1** the state of burning, or a burning mass of material ○ [U] *The factory had to be closed because the risk of fire was too great.* ○ [C] *There have been a lot of forest fires because of the drought.* ○ [C] *The library was badly damaged in the fire.* ○ [U] *The theater was destroyed by fire.* ○ [C] *Over a hundred volunteers were needed to put out the fire* (= stop it). **2** A fire is also a small controlled mass of burning material that is used for heating or cooking: [C] *Light a fire in the fireplace.* **3** If something is **on fire**, it is burning, esp. when it is not meant to be. ○ *By the time the firefighters arrived, the whole house was on fire.*

SHOOT /fɑɪr/ *v* [I/T] to shoot bullets or other explosives from a weapon ○ [T] *He fired his gun into the air.* ○ [I] *The soldiers began firing.* ○ [T] (*fig.*) *The journalists kept firing questions at the president* (= asking him questions quickly one after the other). ○ [I] (*fig.*) *"I'd like to ask you some personal questions." "Fire away* (= You can start immediately)*!"*

fire /fɑɪr/ *n* [U] ○ *The troops were ordered to cease fire* (= stop shooting). ○ *The soldiers opened fire* (= started shooting).

LOSE JOB /fɑɪr/ *v* [T] to order someone to give up his or her job ○ *She was fired for stealing from her employer.*

EXCITE /fɑɪr/ *v* [T] to cause a strong emotion in someone ○ *She's all fired up* (= excited) *about going to college.*

fire /fɑɪr/ *n* [U] strong emotion ○ *The fire in her speech inspired everyone to carry on in spite of recent setbacks.*

IDIOMS with fire

•**fire in** *your* **belly** a strong determination to succeed ○ *Neither of the candidates has a fire in his belly, so it's hard to get excited about them.*

•**on the firing line, in the firing line** in a situation that attracts criticism ○ *The judge found himself in the firing line after his remarks about women staying home with their children.*

PHRASAL VERB with fire

•**fire off** *something* [M] to write something quickly, esp. when you are angry ○ *He fired off an e-mail to one of his aides.*

fire alarm *n* [C] a device that makes a loud continuous noise to warn people to leave a burning building

firearm /ˈfɑɪr·ɑrm/ *n* [C] a gun that can be carried easily ○ *Pistols and revolvers are firearms.*

fireball /n/ *n* [C] a great mass of fire high in the air, esp. one caused by a powerful explosion

firebomb /ˈfɑɪr·bɑm/ *n* [C] a bomb that causes a lot of destruction by spreading fire

firebomb /ˈfɑɪr·bɑm/ *v* [T] ○ *to destroy something using a bomb that causes fire*

firecracker /ˈfɑɪr ˌkræk·ər/ *n* [C] a small, usually paper or cardboard container filled with an explosive that makes a loud noise

fire department *n* [C] an organization in charge of preventing or putting out fires, esp. one working for a local government

fire drill *n* [C] an occasion when people practice what they must do to leave a burning building safely

fire engine *n* [C] a large vehicle that carries specially trained people and their equipment to fight a fire

fire escape *n* [C] a set of metal stairs on the outside of a building that allows people to leave a burning building

fire extinguisher *n* [C] a container filled with water or special chemicals that you spray on a fire to stop it from burning

firefighter /ˈfɑɪr ˌfɑɪt̬·ər/, **fireman** /ˈfɑɪr·mən/ *n* [C] *pl* **-men** someone whose job is to stop fires and to save people and property from being harmed

firefly /ˈfɑɪr·flɑɪ/, **lightning bug** *n* [C] a small insect that produces flashes of light when it flies at night

firehouse /ˈfɑɪr·hɑʊs/ *n* [C] a FIRE STATION

fire hydrant *n* [C] a vertical pipe in the street from which FIREFIGHTERS get water to stop a fire

fireplace /ˈfɑɪr·pleɪs/ *n* [C] a space in the wall of a room for a fire to burn in, or the decorated part that surrounds this space ○ *We usually stack some wood next to the fireplace.*

firepower /ˈfɑɪr ˌpɑʊ·ər/ *n* [U] **1** the ability to destroy things using weapons ○ *The small force cound not withstand the enemy's superior firepower.* **2** Firepower is also the things, such as money or skill, that you need to produce results: *The campaigns are focusing their financial firepower on Florida.*

fireproof /ˈfɑɪr·pruːf/ *adj* impossible or difficult to burn in a fire

fire sale *n* [C] a sale of goods at low prices because they have been slightly damaged in a fire

fireside /ˈfɑɪr·sɑɪd/ *n* [C] an area in a room near a FIREPLACE ○ *She liked to curl up by the fireside with a good book.*

fire station *n* [C] a building where equipment used to stop fires is kept and where FIREFIGHTERS are based

firestorm /ˈfɑɪr·stɔːrm/ *n* [C] a sudden, and sometimes violent reaction ○ *The senator's remarks caused a firestorm of protest.*

F

firetrap /ˈfɑɪr·træp/ *n* [C] a building that would burn easily if a fire started and would be difficult to escape from

fire truck *n* [C] a FIRE ENGINE

firewood /ˈfɑɪr·wʊd/ *n* [U] wood used as fuel for a fire

fireworks /ˈfɑɪr·wɜrks/ *pl n* **1** small containers filled with explosive chemicals that make a loud noise when they explode and sometimes produce bright, colored patterns **2** Fireworks can also mean the pattern of colorful explosions in the air planned as a show: *What time do the fireworks start?*

firing squad *n* [C] a group of soldiers whose job is to shoot and kill someone as a punishment

firm **FIXED** /fɜrm/ *adj, adv* [*-er/-est* only] set in place and unable or unlikely to move, come loose, or fall over ○ *The rocks were wet, and we couldn't get a firm footing.* ○ *(fig.) Sometimes it takes more courage to admit you're wrong than to stand firm* (= continue to defend an opinion). ○ *(fig.) The dean is holding firm and refusing to give in to student demands.*

firmly /ˈfɜrm·li/ *adv* ○ *Fasten your seatbelt firmly.*

HARD /fɜrm/ *adj* [*-er/-est* only] not soft when pressed; solid or strong ○ *a firm mattress* ○ *a firm body* ○ *(fig.) No one seems to have a firm grip on* (= be in control of) *the situation at the moment.*

firmly /ˈfɜrm·li/ *adv* ○ *He shook my hand firmly.*

firmness /ˈfɜrm·nəs/ *n* [U]

CERTAIN /fɜrm/ *adj* [*-er/-est* only] **1** certain or fixed in a belief, opinion, etc., and unlikely to change, or so certain as to be beyond doubt or question ○ *a firm believer in the Constitution* ○ *They made a firm commitment to complete the job this week.* ○ *The decision is firm – there will be a strike.* **2** Firm can also mean showing control and making sure you will be obeyed: *A new teacher has to be firm with her students.*

firmly /ˈfɜrm·li/ *adv* ○ *The mayor is firmly committed to reducing crime in the city.*

firmness /ˈfɜrm·nəs/ *n* [U]

BUSINESS /fɜrm/ *n* [C] a company or business ○ *a law firm*

WORD FAMILY firm

Nouns	firmness infirmity	*Adjectives*	firm infirm
Adverbs	firmly		

first /fɜrst/ *adj, adv, n* [C] **1** (a person or thing) coming before all others in order, time, amount, quality, or importance ○ *Would you like to go first?* ○ [C] *We leave on the first of August.* ○ **At first** (= In the beginning) *I thought he was joking, but then I realized he meant it.* **2** First also means FIRST BASE. ○ Related Number: ONE

IDIOMS with first

• **at first glance, at first blush** when first considering something, before having a chance to look at it carefully ○ *At first glance the deal looked wonderful, but after reading the fine print he wasn't so sure.*

• **first (of all), first off** before anything else ○ *First of all, I'd like to ask you a few questions.*

• **first and foremost** more than anything else ○ *In spite of her recent success as a novelist, she remains first and foremost a poet.*

• **first come, first served** only the first people to arrive or ask for something will receive it ○ *Free tickets will be given out on a first come, first served basis.*

• **first thing** early in the morning ○ *He said he'd call back first thing tomorrow.*

• **first things first** more important things should be done or considered before other things ○ *First things first – was anyone hurt?* ○ **USAGE:** Used to tell someone what you intend to do first or what you think is most important.

• **in the first place** in the beginning ○ *We should never have agreed to let him borrow the money in the first place.*

• **on a first-name basis** knowing someone well enough that you call each other by your first names ○ *I've met her, but I'm not on a first-name basis with her.*

first aid *n* [U] emergency medical treatment given to someone who is injured or ill

first base **PLACE** *n* [U] the first place a baseball player has to touch in order to score, or the position near this place played by a member of the team in the field

STAGE *n* [U] the first successful stage in a series of actions you take to achieve a goal ○ His proposal didn't get to first base with the committee.

first-class **QUALITY** *adj* of the highest quality or standard ○ *a first-class education*

first class *n* [U] ○ *I upgraded my plane ticket to first class from tourist class.*

MAIL *adj* of or having to do with the standard way of mailing letters and cards ○ *The price of a first-class stamp has gone up again.*

first cousin *n* [C] a COUSIN

first floor *n* [U] the GROUND FLOOR

firsthand /ˈfɜrstˈhænd/ *adj, adv* obtained personally, or directly from someone who is personally involved in something ○ *He has firsthand experience of what war is like.*

First Lady *n* [C] the wife of the US president or of a governor or other public official

first language *n* [C] the language you learn from your parents as you are growing up

first name *n* [C] your personal name, which comes before your other names ○ *"James" and "Sarah" are first names.* ○ Compare LAST NAME; MIDDLE NAME

First Nation *n* [C] *esp. Cdn* one of the groups of people whose ANCESTORS lived in North America before the arrival of Europeans

first person *n* [U] **1** ***grammar*** the form of pronouns and verbs people use when speaking or writing about themselves ○ *"I," "me," and "my" are first person singular pronouns, and "we," "us," and "our" are first person plural pronouns.* ○ Compare SECOND PERSON; THIRD PERSON **2** ***literature*** The first person is a style of writing in which a story is told in the voice of one of the characters: ○ *Autobiographies are written in the first person.*

first quarter *n* [C] a HALF MOON

first-rate *adj* extremely good ○ *a first-rate performance*

fiscal /ˈfɪs·kəl/ *adj* [not gradable] relating to public money or other financial matters ○ *a sound fiscal policy*

fiscal year *n* [C] a period of twelve months (not always January 1st to December 31st) for which a government or business plans its management of money

fish ANIMAL /fɪʃ/ *n* [C/U] *pl* **fish, fishes** an animal without legs that lives in water, has a soft outer body, uses its tail and FINS to help it swim, and takes in oxygen from the water ○ [C] *How many fish live in the pond?* ○ [U] *We had fish for dinner.*

fish /fɪʃ/ *v* [I] to try to catch fish ○ *We were fishing for tuna.*

fishing /ˈfɪʃ·ɪŋ/ *n* [U] ○ *I'd like to do a little fishing this weekend.*

> **USAGE**
> **fish or fishes?**
> **Fish** is the usual plural.
> *I caught six fish in the river.*
> ~~*I caught six fishes in the river.*~~
> **Fishes** is sometimes used to talk about different types of fish.
> *In the Pacific there are exotic fishes that you never see in aquariums.*

SEARCH /fɪʃ/ *v* [I always + adv/prep] to to try to get something ○ *Chimpanzees use grass to fish around in termite nests.* ○ *We're trying to fish for some answers.*

WORD FAMILY fish

Nouns	fish fishing	*Verbs*	fish
		Adverbs	fishily
Adjectives	fishy		

IDIOMS with fish

• **a fish out of water** someone who is uncomfortable in a specific situation ○ *I felt like a fish out of water at my new school.*

• **fish for compliments** to try to get people to say good things about you ○ *I'm not trying to fish for compliments, but do you like my new haircut?*

PHRASAL VERB with fish

• **fish** *something* **out** [M] to remove something from somewhere or make something appear, esp. after searching ○ *He fished a tissue out of his pocket.* ○ *The magician reached into his bag and fished out a couple of balloons for the kids.*

fishbowl /ˈfɪʃ·boʊl/ *n* [C] a round glass container for fish that you keep as pets

fisherman /ˈfɪʃ·ər·mən/, *n* [C] *pl* **-men** someone who catches fish, either as a job or as a sport ○ *Maine fishermen are finding it difficult to make a living.*

fishery /ˈfɪʃ·ə·ri/ *n* [C/U] **1** a place where fish are grown for food, or where they are caught ○ *Officials are concerned about how best to protect the fisheries and water quality in the river.* **2** Fishery is also the activity of growing fish for food, or catching fish to sell: *Federal fishery regulators this week set the 2005 catch limit at nearly 3.3 billion pounds.*

fishing pole, fishing rod *n* [C] a long rod that has a strong string attached to it with a hook at the end, used for catching fish

fishnet /ˈfɪʃ·net/ *n* [U] a type of material that is woven of threads and is similar to a net

fishy /ˈfɪʃ·i/ *adj infml* seeming dishonest or false ○ *There's something fishy going on.*

fission /ˈfɪʃ·ən, ˈfɪʒ-/ *n* [U] **1** ***physics*** the dividing of the NUCLEUS of an atom, producing energy **2** ***biology*** Fission is also the division of a living cell during reproduction in some very small organisms

fissure /ˈfɪʃ·ər/ *n* [C] a deep crack, esp. one in rock or ice or in the ground

fist /fɪst/ *n* [C] a hand with the fingers turned in tightly and the thumb held against them ○ *She clenched her fist.*

fistful /ˈfɪst·fʊl/ *n* [C] ○ *Anna had a fistful of candy.*

fistfight /ˈfɪst·fɑɪt/ *n* [C] a fight in which people hit each other using their tightly closed hands ○ *The boys got into a fistfight.*

fit CORRECT SIZE /fɪt/ *v* [I/T] *pres. part.* **fitting,** *past* **fitted, fit** to be the right size or shape for someone or something ○ [T] *The jacket fits you perfectly.* ○ [I] *The refrigerator won't fit in our kitchen.*

fit /fɪt/ *n* [U] ○ *These shoes are a perfect/terrible fit.*

fitted /ˈfɪt·ɪd/ *adj* ○ *He bought a fitted suit* (= made to his exact size).

fitting /ˈfɪţ·ɪŋ/ *n* [C] an occasion when you try on clothing being made or adjusted ○ *a fitting for a wedding gown*

> **USAGE**
> **fit or suit?**
> Remember that the verb **fit** means to be the right shape or size.
> *This jacket doesn't fit me – it's too tight.* ➤

Use **suit** when you want to say that something is right for someone or makes them look more attractive.

You should wear more red – it suits you.
Life in the big city didn't suit him.
~~*Life in the big city didn't fit him.*~~

SUIT /fɪt/ *v* [T] *pres. part.* **fitting,** *past* **fitted, fit** to be suitable for someone or something ○ *The job fits him well.*
fit /fɪt/ *adj* [-er/-est only] **-tt-** ○ *She's not fit to be treasurer.*
fitness /ˈfɪt·nəs/ *n* [U] ○ *No one questioned her fitness for the job.*
fitting /ˈfɪt̬·ɪŋ/ *adj* ○ *a fitting tribute*

HEALTHY /fɪt/ *adj* [-er/-est only] **-tt-** in good health, esp. as a result of exercise; strong ○ *You look fit.*
fitness /ˈfɪt·nəs/ *n* [U] ○ *physical fitness*

BRIEF PERIOD /fɪt/ *n* [C] a sudden, brief period when something happens that is beyond your control ○ *a coughing/sneezing fit* ○ *Epilepsy can cause severe fits* (= sudden muscle movements that you cannot control).
fitful /ˈfɪt·fəl/ *adj* going off and on irregularly ○ *Her breathing is fitful.*
fitfully /ˈfɪt·fə·li/ *adv* ○ *She slept fitfully.*

EMOTIONAL EXPERIENCE /fɪt/ *n* [C] **1** an experience of a strong emotion or reaction ○ *a fit of laughter/jealousy* **2** A fit can be a feeling or expression of great anger: *Your mother will have/throw a fit when she sees this mess.*

WORD FAMILY fit

Nouns	fit fitness fitting	*Adjectives*	fit fitted fitting
Verbs	fit	*Adverbs*	fittingly

IDIOMS with fit

• **fit like a glove** to be the perfect size and shape for someone ○ *I love these pants because they fit like a glove and they're so comfortable.*
• **fit the bill** to be suitable ○ *"I'm looking for a fun novel to read on the plane." "This one should fit the bill."*
• **fit to be tied** extremely angry ○ *He was fit to be tied when she showed up an hour late.*
• **fits and starts** periods of activity mixed with periods when nothing happens ○ *The reform process has proceeded in fits and starts.*
• **have a fit, throw a fit** to become very angry ○ *My mother threw a fit when she saw the mess we made.*

PHRASAL VERBS with fit

• **fit in BE ACCEPTED** to belong with other things, or to be accepted by other people in a group ○ *This chair doesn't fit in with our furniture.* ○ *She fit in well at school.*
• **fit in** *something/someone* **FIND TIME** [M] to find time to do something or to deal with someone ○ *The doctor can fit you in at three o'clock.*

five /fɑɪv/ *number* **1** 5 ○ *We work five days a week.* ○ *a five-room apartment* **2** Five can also mean five o'clock. ○ Related Number: FIFTH

fix REPAIR /fɪks/ *v* [T] to repair or adjust something ○ *I'll fix that broken chair today.*

ARRANGE /fɪks/ *v* [T] **1** to arrange or put in place ○ *I need to fix my hair.* **2** To fix something such as a race or game or an election is to illegally arrange who will win.

CHOOSE /fɪks/ *v* [T] to choose a time or place to do something ○ *Let's fix a date for our next meeting.*

ATTACH /fɪks/ *v* [T] to attach in order to keep in one place ○ *Fix the shelf to the wall with screws.* ○ *I tried to fix the directions in my mind.*

BAD SITUATION /fɪks/ *n* [C usually sing] a situation causing trouble or problems ○ *He's in a fix and needs our help.*

PUNISH /fɪks/ *v* [T] to hurt or punish someone ○ *I'll fix you if you come around here taking vegetables from my garden again!*

PREPARE FOOD /fɪks/ *v* [T] to cook or prepare food or drink ○ *Will you fix dinner?*

STOP REPRODUCTION /fɪks/ *v* [T] to remove an organ an animal needs to reproduce ○ *We had our cat fixed.*

WORD FAMILY fix

Nouns	fix fixation fixture	*Adjectives*	fixed fixated transfixed unfixed
Verbs	fix	*Adverbs*	fixedly

PHRASAL VERBS with fix

• **fix up** *someone* **PROVIDE** [M] to provide something that someone needs ○ *Before he left town Pat saw to it that I was fixed up with a job.*
• **fix up** *something* **IMPROVE** [M] to repair, decorate, or change something so that it is ready for use ○ *He recently finished fixing up the 1920s-era bungalow he bought in 1992.*

fixated /ˈfɪk·seɪ·tɪd/ *adj* thinking hard about something all the time ○ *I am fixated on making tomorrow better.*
fixation /fɪkˈseɪ·ʃən/ *n* [C] ○ *Jen has a fixation on food.*

fixed /fɪkst/ *adj* [not gradable] not changing ○ *a fixed stare* ○ *a fixed address*
fixedly /ˈfɪk·səd·li/ *adv* [not gradable] ○ *She stared fixedly at the screen.*

fixture /ˈfɪks·tʃər/ *n* [C] a piece of equipment that stays attached to a house or other building ○ *a light fixture* ○ *bathroom fixtures* ○ *(fig.) He became a fixture* (= a regular feature) *on television in the 1980s.*

fizz /fɪz/ *v* [I] (of a liquid) to produce gas bubbles ○ *The soda fizzed as she poured it.*
fizz /fɪz/ *n* [U] ○ *This soda has lost its fizz.*

fizzle /ˈfɪz·əl/ *v* [I] to finish slowly in a way that is disappointing or has become less interesting ○ *I like the way the movie starts but then it fizzles out.*

flab /flæb/ *n* [U] soft, loose flesh on the body of a person or an animal ○ *I'm trying to burn off excess flab.*
flabby /ˈflæb·i/ *adj* ○ *Carol scratched at her flabby upper arm.*

flabbergasted /ˈflæb·ərˌgæs·tɪd/ *adj* shocked by the unexpected ○ *I was absolutely flabbergasted at what she was paid.*

flaccid /ˈflæs·əd, ˈflæk·səd/ *adj* soft and weak; not firm ○ *flaccid skin* ○ *a politician's flaccid remarks*

flack /flæk/ *n* [U] FLAK

flag SYMBOL /flæg/ *n* [C] a piece of cloth with a special color and pattern, used as a symbol esp. to represent a particular country or group ○ *the American flag* ○ *The man waved a red warning flag.*

MARK /flæg/ *v* [T] **-gg-** to mark something so it can be found easily among other similar things ○ *She asked me to flag the names that appear on both lists.*

BECOME TIRED /flæg/ *v* [I] **-gg-** to become tired or less strong ○ *My interest in the story flagged.*

PHRASAL VERB with flag

• **flag down** *something/someone* [M] to signal that a vehicle or person should stop by waving ○ *A police officer flagged us down.*

flagellum /fləˈdʒel·əm/ *n* [C] *pl* **flagella, flagellums** ***biology*** a long thin part similar to a tail, which is used for movement by some cells, bacteria, and other very small organisms

flagpole /ˈflæg·poʊl/ *n* [C] a tall pole to which a flag can be attached

flagrant /ˈfleɪ·grənt/ *adj* shocking because of being so bad and so obvious ○ *a flagrant violation of the rules*
flagrantly /ˈfleɪ·grənt·li/ *adv* ○ *He flagrantly broke the law.*

flagship SHIP /ˈflæg·ʃɪp/ *n* [C] the ship among a group of ships on which the most important officer sails

BEST ONE /ˈflæg·ʃɪp/ *n* [C usually sing] the best or most important thing among a group ○ *The retail chain has its flagship in New York and branches in 19 states.*

flagstone /ˈflæg·stoʊn/, **flag** /flæg/ *n* [C] a flat piece of stone used esp. outside a building to make floors, stairs, and paths

flail /fleɪl/ *v* [I/T] to wave something, esp. arms or legs, energetically but with little or no control ○ [I] *His hands flailed wildly.*

flair /fler, flær/ *n* [U] the ability to do something well ○ *Alan has a flair for public speaking.*

flak /flæk/, **flack** *n* [U] *infml* strong criticism or opposition ○ *She caught some flak from her parents.*

flake THIN PIECE /fleɪk/ *n* [C] a small, thin piece, esp. of a layer on a surface ○ *Flakes of paint fell from the ceiling.*
flake /fleɪk/ *v* [I] ○ *Plaster is flaking off the walls.*

PERSON /fleɪk/ *n* [C] *infml* a person who does not seem to pay attention and is sometimes silly ○ *That guy is a real flake.*

flamboyant /flæmˈbɔɪ·ənt/ *adj* intended to be noticed, esp. by being brightly colored ○ *a flamboyant gesture* ○ *flamboyant clothes*

flame LIGHT /fleɪm/ *n* [C/U] the hot light of a fire ○ [U] *The logs in the fireplace burst into flame.* ○ *The house was* **in flames** (= burning).
flame /fleɪm/ *v* [I] ○ *The fire suddenly flamed (up).*

ANGER /fleɪm/ *v* [I/T] **1** to show anger by turning red ○ [I] *His face flamed and he started stammering.* **2** If you flame someone you disagree with, you send insulting electronic messages about that person over the INTERNET: [T] *He was flamed by several other men in the chat room.*

flamingo /fləˈmɪŋ·goʊ/ *n* [C] *pl* **flamingos, flamingoes** a bird with pink feathers, a long neck, and long, thin legs, and which lives near the water in warm places

flammable /ˈflæm·ə·bəl/, **inflammable** /ɪnˈflæm·ə·bəl/ *adj* able to catch fire easily ○ *This solvent is flammable.* ○ Opposite: NONFLAMMABLE

flank /flæŋk/ *v* [T] to be at the side of someone or something ○ *Secret Service agents flanked the president's car.*
flank /flæŋk/ *n* [C] **1** *Troops attacked the enemy's left flank.* **2** A person's or animal's flanks are the sides of its body between the RIBS and the hips.

flannel /ˈflæn·əl/ *n* [U] a soft cloth usually made from cotton or wool ○ *flannel pajamas* ○ *a flannel shirt*

flap WAVE /flæp/ *v* [I/T] **-pp-** (of a bird's wings) to wave up and down while flying, or (of objects that cannot fly) to move quickly from side to side or up and down ○ [T] *A small bird flapped its wings.* ○ [I] *Flags flapped in the breeze.*
flap /flæp/ *n* [C] ○ *The bird flew into the air with a flap of its wings.*

PIECE /flæp/ *n* [C] a piece of cloth or other material attached along one edge to something else ○ *a pocket/tent flap*

EMOTIONAL STATE /flæp/ *n* [C] a state of excitement or worry ○ *She caused a big flap when she told her husband about her parents' visit.*

flapjack /ˈflæp·dʒæk/ *n* [C] a PANCAKE

flare BURN /fler, flær/ *v* [I] to burn brightly either for a short time or on and off ○ *The candle flared then went out.*
flare /fler, flær/ *n* [C] something that produces a flame or bright light and is usually used as a signal, or the flame or light itself ○ *The boat is equipped with flares.* ○ *Did you see that flare?*

BECOME WIDER /fler, flær/ *v* [I/T] to become wider, or to make something wider ○ [I] *These trousers flare slightly at the ankle.*

HAPPEN SUDDENLY /fler, flær/ *v* [I] to happen in a sudden and often violent way ○ *The dispute threatens to flare into a lawsuit.* ○ *The argument quieted down then flared up again.*

flare-up /ˈfler·ʌp, ˈflær-/ *n* [C] a sudden increase in or occasion of something such as an illness, violence, or an expression of emotion ○ *a flareup of arthritis* ○ *There were flare-ups of anger during the long meetings.*

flash SHINE /flæʃ/ *v* [I/T] to shine suddenly and usually brightly, but only for a short time ○ [T] *Stop flashing that light in my eyes.*
flash /flæʃ/ *n* [C] ○ *A flash of lightning lit the sky.*
HAPPEN QUICKLY /flæʃ/ *v* [I always + adv/prep] to move or happen quickly ○ *A fire engine flashed by.*
flash /flæʃ/ *n* [C]
SHOW /flæʃ/ *v* [I/T] to show something quickly or for a short time ○ [T] *The officer flashed her badge.* ○ [I] *A smile flashed across her face.*
PHOTOGRAPHY /flæʃ/ *n* [C] a device used to produce a bright light for a brief time when taking a photograph

IDIOMS with flash

• **a flash in the pan** something that is interesting for only a short time ○ *The band was just a flash in the plan with one hit in 2003.*
• **in a flash** suddenly ○ *The answer came to her in a flash.*

flashback /ˈflæʃ·bæk/ *n* [C] ***literature*** a memory, or a short part of a movie, story, or play describing past events ○ *This party is like a '70s flashback.*

flash card /ˈflæʃ·kard/ *n* [C] a small piece of stiff paper with a word, picture, or question on it that is to teach something ○ *She is learning math with flash cards.*

flash flood *n* [C] a sudden, severe flood, usually caused by a heavy rain that falls over a short period of time

flashlight /ˈflæʃ·lɑɪt/ *n* [C] a small electric light you can carry in your hand

flashy /ˈflæʃ·i/ *adj* [-*er*/-*est* only] expensive or stylish, or brightly colored ○ *He wears flashy clothes.*

flask /flæsk/ *n* [C] a small container, usually with a wide base and a narrow neck ○ *a flask of water*

FLASK

flat LEVEL /flæt/ *adj* [-*er*/-*est* only] -**tt**- **1** level and smooth; having little or no height and not raised or round ○ *A desk provides a flat surface to work on.* ○ *Campers look for flat ground to put up their tents.* **2** A drink that is flat has stopped bubbling: *If you don't put the top back on the soda bottle, it will go flat.* **3** If a tire is flat, the air has gone out of it so that it does not give the support it should: *One of my tires is flat and I'll have to change it.*
flat /flæt/ *n* [C] **1** something flat, esp. a tire that has lost its air, so that it does not give the support that it should ○ *We pulled off to the side of the road to change a flat.* **2** The flat of the hand is the inside, level part of the hand with the fingers straight: *He swatted the table with the flat of his hand.*
flat /flæt/ *adv* [-*er*/-*est* only] -**tt**- ○ *He hurt his back and could only sleep lying flat on his back* (= with his back down, against the surface on which he was lying).
flatten /ˈflæt·ᵊn/ *v* [I/T] to make or become flat ○ [I] *In the road race, you go over a few steep hills but then the course flattens out.*
COMPLETE /flæt/ *adj* [not gradable] complete and certain ○ *His request for time off from work was met with a flat refusal.*
flat /flæt/ *adv* [not gradable] ○ *When he asked for a raise, the boss turned him down flat.* ○ *I'm flat broke* (= I have no money).
flatly /ˈflæt·li/ *adv* [not gradable] ○ *He flatly denied that he saw what had happened.*
NOT CHANGING /flæt/ *adj* [not gradable] (esp. of an amount of money) not changing or varying ○ *We charge a flat rate of $25 per hour.* ○ *Sales are flat* (= low and not changing) *during this time of year.*
flat /flæt/ *adv* [only after n] [not gradable] exactly ○ *We managed to get to the station in five minutes flat.*
MUSIC /flæt/ *adj, adv* [-*er*/-*est* only] -**tt**- ***music*** lower in PITCH than a particular or the correct note ○ Compare SHARP MUSIC ➤ Picture: **notation**
flat *n* [C] ***music*** a mark in written music showing that a note should be played a HALF STEP lower
APARTMENT /flæt/ *n* [C] *esp. Br* an APARTMENT ○ *They have a house in the country and a flat in London.*

WORD FAMILY flat			
Nouns	flat	*Verbs*	flatten
Adjectives	flat	*Adverbs*	flat flatly

IDIOMS with flat

• **(as) flat as a pancake** very level ○ *In some parts of the West, the land is as flat as a pancake.*
• **flat out** as fast as possible ○ *I ran flat out and won the race by inches.*

flat feet *pl n* feet with the whole bottom part of each foot level and touching the ground

flat-footed *adj* having feet with a bottom part that is not curved up in an arch, as is usual, but is level so that it touches the ground

flats LAND /flæts/ *pl n* land that has no hills or mountains ○ *Far in the distance, out on the sage flats, an ore train labored northward toward the mill.*
SHOES /flæts/ *pl n* women's shoes that are flat on the bottom ○ *Ballet flats are one of the hottest trends in Hollywood right now.*

flat tax *n* [C] ***social studies*** a tax rate that is the same for everyone, whether the person's income is high or low

flatter /ˈflæt̬·ər/ *v* [T] to make someone feel important or attractive, or to praise someone in order to please him or her ○ *They were flattered by the invitation from the mayor.*

flattering /ˈflæt̬·ə·rɪŋ/ *adj* ○ *That suit is flattering on you* (= makes you look attractive).
flattery /ˈflæt̬·ə·ri/ *n* [U] ○ *Saying I was the best ever was too obvious an attempt at flattery.*

flatulence /ˈflætʃ·ə·ləns/ *n* [U] *fml* the uncomfortable condition of having gas in the stomach and bowels

flatware /ˈflæt·wer, -wær/ *n* [U] objects used for eating and serving food, esp. utensils; SILVERWARE

flaunt /flɔːnt, flant/ *v* [T] to intentionally make obvious something you have in order to be admired ○ *You go to the mall and you see fourteen-year-old kids flaunting money their parents give them.*

flavor, *Cdn, Br* **flavour** /ˈfleɪ·vər/ *n* [C/U] the particular way a substance, esp. food or drink, is recognized from its taste and smell ○ [C] *We sell 32 different flavors of ice cream.* ○ [U] *This soup doesn't have much flavor.* ○ [U] (*fig.*) *This brief description should give you a flavor of what the book is like* (= show you the character of the book).
flavor, *Cdn, Br* **flavour** /ˈfleɪ·vər/ *v* [T] ○ *Use some garlic to flavor the stew.*
flavorful, *Cdn, Br* **flavourful** /ˈfleɪ·vər·fəl/ *adj* having a lot of flavor ○ *A veal chop was flavorful but too fatty.*
flavoring, *Cdn, Br* **flavouring** /ˈfleɪ·və·rɪŋ/ *n* [C/U] a substance added to improve or change the taste of something ○ [U] *A little vanilla flavoring improves the taste of the dessert.*

flaw /flɔː/ *n* [C] a fault or weakness, esp. one that happens while something is being planned or made and that makes it not perfect ○ *A flaw in the steering mechanism led to a recall of 200,000 cars.*
flawless /ˈflɔː·ləs/ *adj* [not gradable] containing no faults or mistakes; perfect ○ *The countdown was flawless, and the space missile went off exactly on schedule.*

flea /fliː/ *n* [C] a very small jumping insect without wings that feeds on the blood of animals and people

flea market /ˈfliː ˌmar·kət/ *n* [C] a place, usually outside, where people sell esp. old or used items at cheap prices ○ *There's a flea market every Saturday in the school parking lot.*

fleck /flek/ *n* [C] a small mark, esp. of a different color ○ *I got a few flecks of paint on the window when I was painting the frames.*
fleck /flek/ *v* [T] ○ *Her hair is flecked with gray.*

fled /fled/ *past simple and past participle of* FLEE

fledgling /ˈfledʒ·lɪŋ/ *adj* [not gradable] new and not experienced ○ *Still in his teens, he pursued his fledgling career in journalism.*

flee /fliː/ *v* [I/T] *past* **fled** to escape by running away, esp. because of danger or fear ○ [I] *An FBI spokesman said Stewart fled before police arrived.*

fleece SHEEP /fliːs/ *n* [C/U] the wool of a sheep, or a soft, artificial material that looks like wool ○ [C] *Polyester fleeces are especially popular to provide warmth in coats.*

CHEAT /fliːs/ *v* [T] to charge too much money or cheat someone ○ *He was fleecing investors by setting up bogus companies and then manipulating the price of their stocks.*

fleet SHIPS /fliːt/ *n* [C] all the ships in the navy of a country, or a number of ships operating as a unit within a navy

VEHICLES /fliːt/ *n* [C] a number of aircraft, buses, cars, or other vehicles under the control of one company or organization ○ *He owns a fleet of taxis.*

fleeting /ˈfliːt̬·ɪŋ/ *adj* brief or quick ○ *He had a fleeting moment of panic but quickly recovered.*

flesh /fleʃ/ *n* [U] **1** the soft part of the body of a person or animal covering the bones and organs ○ *The roast duck has robust flavor and tender flesh.* **2** The flesh of a fruit or vegetable is the soft, inner part: *Peel the tomatoes and use only the flesh.*
fleshy /ˈfleʃ·i/ *adj* having a lot of flesh ○ *He extended a broad, fleshy hand before him.*

IDIOM with flesh

• **in the flesh** physically in front of you ○ *I've seen her perform on television, but never in the flesh.*

PHRASAL VERB with flesh

• **flesh out** *something* [M] to add more detail when describing or explaining something ○ *Emily should have included these pieces of information to flesh out her argument.*

flesh and blood PEOPLE *n* [U] people ○ *This decision is not about legal theory, it's about flesh and blood, about boys and girls who deserve a decent education.* ○ USAGE: Used to emphasize the qualities all people have.

FAMILY *n* [U] someone from your family ○ *I was surprised at how much I cared for this girl who wasn't even my flesh and blood.*

flesh-colored *adj* approximately the color of white people's skin ○ *flesh-colored tights*

flesh wound *n* [C] an injury only to the flesh and not to the bones or inner organs ○ *Fortunately it was only a flesh wound, and he was expected to recover completely.*

flew /fluː/ *past simple of* FLY

flex /fleks/ *v* [T] to bend a part of the body, esp. an arm or leg, or to tighten a muscle ○ *Keep your knees flexed at all times.*

IDIOM with flex

• **flex** *your* **muscle, flex your muscles** to show your power or strength ○ *Conservatives were beginning to flex their muscles in Utah.*

flexible Ⓐ CHANGEABLE /ˈflek·sə·bəl/ *adj* able to change or be changed easily according to the situation ○ *I'm fortunate because my job has flexible hours, and I can come and go pretty much as I want.*
flexibility Ⓐ /ˌflek·səˈbɪl·ət̬·i/ *n* [U] ○ *The new law gives auto makers more flexibility in meeting lower pollution targets.*

ABLE TO BEND /ˈflek·sə·bəl/ *adj* able to bend or be bent easily without breaking ○ *The wire has to be flexible enough to go around corners of the room.*

F

flexor /ˈflek·sər/ *n* [C] ***biology*** a muscle that allows you to bend part of your body ○ Compare EXTENSOR

flextime /ˈflek·stɑɪm/ *n* [U] a system of working in which employees can vary the time they start and finish work as long as they work the agreed number of hours

flick MOVE /flɪk/ *v* [I/T] to make a short, sudden movement that causes something to move ○ [T] *Brina flicked her hair over her shoulder.* ○ [M] *He flicked the light switch on/off.* ○ [I always + adv/prep] *She flicked through the pages of a magazine* (= turned them quickly).
flick /flɪk/ *n* [C] ○ *With a flick of the wrist, he tossed me the Frisbee.*
MOVIE /flɪk/ *n* [C] *infml* a movie ○ *Do you want to go to a flick tonight?*

flicker /ˈflɪk·ər/ *v* [I] to burn, shine, or move like a flame in quickly changing forms of light and dark ○ *Candles flickered on all the tables in the restaurant.* ○ *A smile flickered across her face.*
flicker /ˈflɪk·ər/ *n* [C] any slight and quick expression ○ *The planes searched the ground for a flicker of movement among the wreckage.*

flier PAPER, **flyer** /ˈflɑɪ·ər/ *n* [C] a piece of paper containing an advertisement or information, usually given out to people walking by ○ *They handed out fliers asking you to vote for Jane Schumacker.* ○ See also: FLYER at FLY TRAVEL THROUGH AIR
PERSON /ˈflɑɪ·ər/ *n* [C] a FLYER

flight FLYING /flɑɪt/ *n* [C/U] **1** an aircraft trip, or the occasion of being a passenger in an aircraft ○ [C] *We'll be arriving home on Tuesday on flight 147.* ○ [C] *All flights out of Midway have been canceled because of bad weather.* ○ [C] *We had a smooth flight all the way.* **2** Flight is also the act or process of flying: [C] *We watched a flight of geese* (= a group flying together). ○ [U] *Some people think that too much money is spent on space flight.*
ESCAPE /flɑɪt/ *n* [U] escape from a particular situation, or the act of leaving ○ *their flight from poverty* ○ *The flight of manufacturers to the South stripped Massachusetts of its factories.*
STAIRS /flɑɪt/ *n* [C] a set of stairs connecting one floor and the next in a building or other structure ○ *We had to climb three flights of stairs.*

flight attendant *n* [C] a person in an aircraft whose job is to serve passengers and to make sure they obey safety rules

flight recorder, **flight data recorder** *n* [C] a small machine that records information about an aircraft during its flight, and which is used to discover the cause of an accident

flighty /ˈflɑɪţ·i/ *adj* not able to keep your attention or interest on one thing for long ○ *She played the part of a flighty, unsuccessful writer.*

flimsy /ˈflɪm·zi/ *adj* **1** (of material) very thin, or (of a structure or object) badly made and weak, and therefore easily broken or destroyed ○ *a flimsy dress* ○ *a flimsy building* **2** Flimsy also means weak and not persuasive: *They convicted the defendant on very flimsy evidence.*

flinch /flɪntʃ/ *v* [I] to make a sudden small movement because of pain or fear ○ *Now I'm going to move the eyepiece right up against your eye for a second – try not to flinch.*

fling THROW /flɪŋ/ *v* [T] *past* **flung** to throw or move something suddenly and with force ○ *I rushed right up to him and flung my arms around his neck and hugged him.* ○ *She flung open the door and greeted us warmly.*
PERIOD /flɪŋ/ *n* [C usually sing] *infml* a short period of doing enjoyable things that you usually do not do

flint /flɪnt/ *n* [C/U] a very hard gray or black stone

flip /flɪp/ *v* [I/T] **-pp-** to cause something to turn over quickly one or more times, or to cause something to move by making a short, quick motion ○ [I/T] *I flipped (through) the pages of the dictionary to look up a word.* ○ [T] *You just flip a switch to turn on the computer.* ○ [T] *At the beginning of a football game, the referee flips a coin* (= throws it into the air so that it spins in falling) *to see which team gets the ball first.*
flip /flɪp/ *n* [C] **1** *They settled the issue by a flip of the coin.* **2** A flip is also a jump in which you swing your legs over your head as your whole body turns around, so that you come down on your feet in the position you started from.

PHRASAL VERB with flip

• **flip out** *slang* to become extremely angry or to lose control of yourself from surprise or shock ○ *I nearly flipped out when she told me she and David were getting married.*

flip-flop *n* [C] a sudden and complete change of plans or opinion ○ *They did a complete flip-flop by deciding to have a large wedding rather than getting married secretly.*

flippant /ˈflɪp·ənt/, *infml* **flip** /flɪp/ *adj* showing or having a rude attitude of not being serious esp. by trying to be amusing when most people expect you to be serious ○ *We had lost thousands of dollars, so we did not appreciate his flippant remark about "better luck next time."*

flipper /ˈflɪp·ər/ *n* [C] **1** a part similar to an arm used for swimming by any of various sea animals, such as SEALS and PENGUINS **2** A flipper is also a long, wide rubber shoe used for swimming.

flip side *n* [U] an opposite or unattractive result of a popular or attractive action ○ *More homelessness is the flip side of getting people off welfare.*

flirt /flɜrt/ *v* [I] to behave as if you are interested in someone, in a not serious way ○ *They were flirting with each other at the party.* ○ (fig.) *If he gets deeper into debt, he's flirting with disaster* (= he is risking very bad trouble).
flirt /flɜrt/ *n* [C] ○ *He's a shameless flirt.*
flirtation /flərˈteɪ·ʃən/ *n* [C] a short period of interest in something ○ *He thought about running for Congress, but his flirtation with* (= period of interest in) *a House run was short-lived.*

flirtatious /flərˈteɪ·ʃəs/ *adj* ○ *She had a lively, outgoing manner and was a bit flirtatious at times.*

PHRASAL VERB with flirt

• **flirt with** *something* to consider an idea or action briefly without being serious about it ○ *At one time he flirted with the idea of running for president, but nothing came of it.*

flit /flɪt/ *v* [I always + adv/prep] **-tt-** to fly or move quickly and lightly ○ *Bees flitted from flower to flower in the garden.*

float **MOVE ON LIQUID** /floʊt/ *v* [I/T] **1** to stay or move easily on or over the surface of a liquid, or to cause something to move in this way ○ [I] *An empty bottle will float on water.* ○ [I] *I'd float around for hours, just fishing.* ○ [T] *Fill the cups with hot coffee and float heavy cream on top.* ○ [I] *We spent a lazy afternoon floating down the river.* ○ [I] *(fig.) She removes the pins and her hair floats* (= moves gracefully) *down around her.* ○ [I] *(fig.) Reports have been floating around* (= heard from various people) *that the company might be for sale.* **2** Float also means to move easily through air: [I] *Fluffy white clouds were floating across the sky.*

float /floʊt/ *n* [C] a piece of light material that stays on the surface of water ○ *the float in a toilet tank*

MONEY /floʊt/ *v* [T] to sell BONDS (= official papers given to people who lend money to a government or company) ○ *Cities float bond issues that are payable from property taxes.*

VEHICLE /floʊt/ *n* [C] a large vehicle that is decorated and used in PARADES (= public celebrations in which people march, walk, and ride along a planned route) ○ *Marching bands and elaborate floats will be featured in the parade.*

DRINK /floʊt/ *n* [C] a sweet drink with ice cream floating in it ○ *a root beer float*

flock /flɑk/ *n* [C] **1** a group of sheep, goats, or birds, or a group of people ○ *a flock of ducks* ○ *a flock of reporters* **2** A flock is also the people who are members of a church.

flock /flɑk/ *v* [I] to move or gather together in large numbers ○ *Tourists flock to the village.* ○ [+ to infinitive] *Crowds of people flocked to see the Picasso exhibition.*

flog /flɑg, flɔːg/ *v* [T] **-gg-** (esp. in the past) to beat very hard with a stick or a WHIP as a punishment

flood **COVER WITH WATER** /flʌd/ *v* [I/T] to fill or become covered with water or to cause this to happen to something ○ [T] *A burst pipe flooded the bathroom.* ○ [I] *The basements of many downtown buildings would flood whenever it rained.*

flood /flʌd/ *n* [C] a large amount of water covering an area that is usually dry ○ *Kingston was heavily damaged by a flood.*

flooding /ˈflʌd·ɪŋ/ *n* [U] ○ *Rain caused flooding that washed out bridges and covered roads.*

FILL /flʌd/ *v* [I/T] **1** to fill or be filled with a large amount or too much of something ○ [I always + adv/prep] *Sunlight floods in through a skylight in the ceiling.* ○ [I always + adv/prep] *In the 1960s, Cuban immigrants began to flood into Florida.* ○ [T] *We don't want them to flood the market with cheap imports.* **2** If you flood an engine, you fill it with so much fuel that it will not start.

flood /flʌd/ *n* [C] ○ *Planners are hoping for a flood of visitors when the center opens.* ○ *He was filled with a flood of new emotions.*

floodlight /ˈflʌd·lɑɪt/ *n* [C] a large, powerful electric light used for lighting outside areas, such as sports fields or buildings ○ *Tonight's game will be played under floodlights.*

floodlit /ˈflʌd·lɪt/ *adj* lit by FLOODLIGHTS ○ *The couple was standing in a floodlit aisle.*

floodplain /ˈflʌd·pleɪn/ *n* [C] ***earth science*** an area of low, flat land near a river that often floods when the level of the river rises and flows over its sides

floor **SURFACE** /flɔːr, floʊr/ *n* [C] the flat surface that you walk on when you are inside a building ○ *a tile floor* ○ *hardwood floors* ○ *The children sat on the floor.*

LEVEL OF BUILDING /flɔːr, floʊr/ *n* [C] a level of a building; a STORY LEVEL ○ *They rented office space on the second floor.* ○ **USAGE:** In the US, the first floor of a building is usually at ground level.

> **USAGE**
>
> **floor**
>
> Remember to use the preposition **on** when you are referring to the location of something in a building.
>
> *Their office is on the 12th floor.*
>
> ~~*Their office is in the 12th floor.*~~

BOTTOM /flɔːr, floʊr/ *n* [C usually sing] the bottom surface of the sea, a forest, a valley, etc. ○ *Submarines were exploring the ocean floor for signs of the wreck.*

OPEN SPACE /flɔːr, floʊr/ *n* [C usually sing] a public space for having formal discussions ○ *The proposition was discussed on the Senate floor.* ○ *The chairman said that he would now take questions from the floor* (= from the ordinary people at the meeting).

SURPRISE /flɔːr, floʊr/ *v* [T] to surprise or shock someone ○ *She was completely floored when she heard that he was leaving the country.*

GO FAST /flɔːr, floʊr/ *v* [T] to drive a car as fast as it will go ○ *His buddy started the car and floored it.*

floorboard **WOOD** /ˈflɔːr·bɔːrd, ˈfloʊr·boʊrd/ *n* [C] a long straight piece of wood used in a floor ○ *The floorboards creaked as we tiptoed across the room.*

FLOOR /ˈflɔːr·bɔːrd, ˈfloʊr·boʊrd/ *n* [C] a floor in a car

floor lamp *n* [C] an electric light supported by a tall pole with a base on the floor

floor plan *n* [C] a drawing that shows the shape, size, and arrangement of rooms in a building as viewed from above

F

flop **FALL** /flɑp/ *v* [I always + adv/prep] **-pp-** to fall or drop heavily ○ *A newborn baby's head flops backward if you don't support it.*
flop /flɑp/ *n* [U] ○ *He fell with a flop* (= he dropped heavily) *on the bed.*

FAILURE /flɑp/ *n* [C usually sing] *infml* a failure ○ *The movie was a complete flop.*
flop /flɑp/ *v* [I] **-pp-** ○ *Her first book flopped, but her second became a bestseller.*

flophouse /ˈflɑp·hɑʊs/ *n* [C] *pl* **flophouses** a cheap, usually dirty, hotel ○ *That area of Manhattan used to be full of flophouses.*

F

floppy /ˈflɑp·i/ *adj* soft and easily bent; not able to maintain a firm shape or position ○ *a floppy hat* ○ *a dog with big, floppy ears*

floppy disk *n* [C] a small soft piece of plastic that is protected by a hard cover and is used to store computer information

flora /ˈflɔːr·ə, ˈfloʊr·ə/ *n* [U] ***biology*** all the plants of a particular area or period of time ○ Compare FAUNA

floral /ˈflɔːr·əl, ˈfloʊr·əl/ *adj* made of flowers, or decorated with images of flowers ○ *a floral display* ○ *floral curtains/wallpaper*

florid **RED** /ˈflɔːr·əd, ˈflɑr·əd/ *adj fml* too red, esp. in a way that is unhealthy ○ *a florid complexion* ○ **USAGE:** said about a person's face

DECORATED /ˈflɔːr·əd, ˈflɑr·əd/ *adj* with too much decoration or detail ○ *a florid architectural style* ○ *florid prose/speech*

florist /ˈflɔːr·əst, ˈflɑr-/ *n* [C] a person who sells cut flowers and plants for inside the house

floss /flɑs, flɔːs/ *v* [T] to clean between your teeth using DENTAL FLOSS (= thin thread made especially for this purpose)
floss /flɑs, flɔːs/ *n* [C/U] DENTAL FLOSS

flotilla /floʊˈtɪl·ə/ *n* [C] a large group of boats or small ships, esp. military ships

flounce /flɑʊns/ *v* [I always + adv/prep] to walk quickly with large, noticeable movements, esp. to attract attention or show that you are angry ○ *"Don't expect any help from me!" she said, as she flounced out of the room.*

flounder **MOVE AWKWARDLY** /ˈflɑʊn·dər/ *v* [I] to move awkwardly or to be in an awkward or difficult situation ○ *She floundered around in the water.* ○ *He lost the next page of his speech and floundered for a few seconds.* ○ *His business was flourishing, but his marriage was floundering.*

FISH /ˈflɑʊn·dər/ *n* [C] *pl* **flounder** a flat fish that is used as food

flour /flɑʊr/ *n* [U] powder made from grain, esp. wheat, used for making bread, cakes, pasta, pastry, etc. ○ *wheat/rye flour* ○ *three cups of flour*
flour /flɑʊr/ *v* [T] to put a thin layer of flour on something ○ *Flour the board, then roll out the dough.*

flourish **SUCCEED** /ˈflɜr·ɪʃ/ *v* [I] to grow or develop successfully ○ *Parts of the city continue to flourish.* ○ *This is the perfect environment for our company to flourish and expand in.*

WAVE /ˈflɜr·ɪʃ/ *v* [T] to move something in your hand in order to make people look at it ○ *She ran up to her father, flourishing her diploma.*
flourish /ˈflɜr·ɪʃ/ *n* [C] ○ *I pulled into the driveway with a flourish* (= a noticeable movement).

flout /flɑʊt/ *v* [T] to intentionally disobey a rule or law, or to intentionally avoid behavior that is usual or expected ○ *They think they can flout the law and get away with it.* ○ *He conducted business in his pajamas to flout convention.*

flow /floʊ/ *v* [I] **1** (esp. of liquids, gases, or electricity) to move in one direction, esp. continuously and easily ○ *Air flows over an aircraft's wing faster than it flows under it.* ○ *Lava from the volcano was flowing down the hillside.* ○ *An electrical current flows from positive to negative.* ○ *Many rivers flow into the Pacific Ocean.* ○ *With fewer cars on the roads, traffic is flowing* (= moving forward) *more smoothly than usual.* ○ (*fig.*) *My thoughts flow more easily* (= I can think more easily) *if I work on a word processor.* **2** Something can be said to flow if it hangs down loosely and attractively: *Her long, red hair flowed down over shoulders.*
flow /floʊ/ *n* [C usually sing] **1** movement of a liquid ○ *This drug increases the flow of blood to the heart.* ○ (*fig.*) *Music interrupted the flow of the conversation* (= the regular exchange between speakers). **2** ***earth science*** A flow is also large mass of material, such as LAVA (= melted rock from a volcano), that is flowing or has flowed in the past.

flower /ˈflɑʊ·ər, flɑʊr/ *n* [C] ***biology*** the part of a plant that produces seeds, is often brightly colored, and sometimes has a pleasant smell, or a plant that produces this part ○ Related adjective: FLORAL
flower /ˈflɑʊ·ər, flɑʊr/ *v* [I] ○ *Our shrubs flower* (= produce flowers) *in late summer.*
flowered /ˈflɑʊ·ərd, flɑʊrd/ *adj* decorated with pictures of flowers ○ *flowered curtains* ○ *a flowered dress*
flowery /ˈflɑʊ·ə·ri, ˈflɑʊr·i/ *adj* **1** covered with pictures of flowers ○ *a flowery blouse* **2** *disapproving* If a speech or writing style is flowery, it uses too many complicated or unusual words or phrases.

WORD FAMILY flower			
Nouns	flower	*Adjectives*	flowered flowery
Verbs	flower		

flowerbed /ˈflɑʊ·ərˌbed, ˈflɑʊr-/ *n* [C] an area of ground where flowers are planted

flowerpot /ˈflɑʊ·ərˌpɑt, ˈflɑʊr-/ *n* [C] a container in which to grow a plant

flown /floʊn/ *past participle of* FLY

fl. oz. *abbreviation for* FLUID OUNCE

flu /fluː/, *esp. fml* **influenza** /ˌɪn·fluːˈen·zə/ *n* [U] an infectious illness like a very bad cold that also causes a fever ○ *Robby has a bad case of the flu.*

flub /flʌb/ *v* [I/T] **-bb-** *infml* to fail or make a mistake, esp. when performing ○ [I] *He really flubbed* *badly by not catching the ball.* ○ [T] *Sheila flubbed her lines in the second act.*

fluctuate Ⓐ /ˈflʌk·tʃəˌweɪt/ *v* [I] to change or vary frequently between one level or thing and another ○ *Vegetable prices fluctuate according to the season.* ○ *I fluctuate between feeling really happy and utterly miserable.*
fluctuation Ⓐ /ˌflʌk·tʃəˈweɪ·ʃən/ *n* [C/U] ○ [C] *fluctuations in temperature* ○ [U] *A certain amount of fluctuation in quality is unavoidable.*

flue /fluː/ *n* [C] a pipe that leads from a fire, STOVE, or heating device to the outside of a building, taking smoke, gases, or hot air away

fluent /ˈfluː·ənt/ *adj* (of a person) able to speak a language easily and well, or (of a language) spoken easily and without many pauses ○ *She was fluent in French by the time she was five.* ○ *He speaks fluent Chinese.*
fluently /ˈfluː·ənt·li/ *adv* ○ *I'd like to speak English fluently.*
fluency /ˈfluː·ən·si/ *n* [U] ○ *This job requires fluency in two or more African languages.*

fluff SOFT MASS /flʌf/ *n* [U] a soft mass of fibers, feathers, or hair ○ *cotton fluff* ○ *The cat, a ball of white fluff, darted into the house and started to lick its fur.* ○ *We'd lie on our backs and blow the dandelion fluff into the neighbor's yard.*
fluff /flʌf/, **fluff out/up** *something v* [T] to shake a mass of fibers, feathers, or hair so the mass appears larger ○ *Make the beds and don't forget to fluff the pillows.* ○ *She fluffed out her hair.*
fluffy /ˈflʌf·i/ *adj* light and full of air, or soft and furry ○ *a fluffy mohair sweater* ○ *Beat the eggs and sugar together until they are light and fluffy.*
USELESS INFORMATION /flʌf/ *n* [U] useless or unimportant information ○ *Don't expect all fluff – like most good satire, this contains some moments of truth.*

fluid /ˈfluː·əd/ *n* [C/U] **1** a substance that flows and is not solid ○ [U] *The doctor drained some fluid from her lungs.* **2** *medical* Fluids are liquids that you drink: [C] *Dr. Tay says I need rest and lots of fluids.*
fluid /ˈfluː·əd/ *adj* having a flowing or changing quality ○ *a dancer's fluid movements* ○ *The situation remains fluid – we offered her the job, but she hasn't responded yet.*

fluid ounce, *abbreviation* **fl. oz.** *n* [C] a measurement of liquid equal to .03 liter

fluke /fluːk/ *n* [C usually sing] something, usually a good thing, that has happened as result of chance instead of skill or planning ○ *He's trying to prove that his last victory wasn't a fluke.*

flung /flʌŋ/ *past simple and past participle of* FLING THROW

flunk /flʌŋk/ *v* [I/T] *infml* to fail an exam or course of study ○ [T] *I almost flunked chemistry.*

PHRASAL VERB with **flunk**

• **flunk out** to be forced to leave school because you have not done well enough in your courses ○ *She flunked out of high school.* ○ *If you don't study harder, you're going to flunk out.*

flunky /ˈflʌŋ·ki/ *n* [C] a person who does unimportant work or who has few or no important responsibilities and shows too much respect toward his or her employer ○ *He could snap his fingers and get his flunky to do it.*

fluorescent /ˌflʊrˈes·ənt, ˌflɔːr-, ˌfloʊr-/ *adj* (of a substance) giving off a very bright light when electricity or other waves go through it ○ *The map was marked with a thin, fluorescent-green line.*

fluorescent light *n* [C] a very bright, usually tube-shaped electric light used esp. in offices

fluoride /ˈflʊr·ɑɪd, ˈflɔːr-, ˈfloʊr-/ *n* [U] a chemical substance sometimes added to water or TOOTHPASTE (= substance for cleaning teeth) in order to help keep teeth healthy

flurry /ˈflɜr·i/ *n* [C] **1** a sudden light fall of snow, blown in different directions by the wind ○ *Heavy snow will be tapering off to flurries in the morning.* **2** A flurry is also a lot of sudden activity: *There was a flurry of excitement as the president walked in.*

flush BECOME RED /flʌʃ/ *v* [I] (of a person) to become red in the face ○ *The force of the adrenaline-filled blood rushing through your body causes you to flush.*
flush /flʌʃ/ *n* [C usually sing] ○ *a flush of embarrassment*
flushed /flʌʃt/ *adj* ○ *Her cheeks were flushed and she was breathing hard.*
LEVEL /flʌʃ/ *adj, adv* on the same level so that no part is higher or lower or sticks out more than another ○ *The sprinklers are mounted flush with the ceiling.*
RICH /flʌʃ/ *adj infml* having a lot of money ○ *The organization is not as flush as it once was.*
CARD GAMES /flʌʃ/ *n* [C] a number of playing cards held by one player that are all from the same SUIT (= type)
EMPTY /flʌʃ/ *v* [I/T] to operate a toilet after it has been used by pressing a handle or button, or (of a toilet) to operate in this way ○ [T] *Flush the toilet before you clean it.* ○ [I] *I can't get the toilet to flush.*
flush /flʌʃ/ *n* [C] ○ *The toilet tank empties during a flush.*

PHRASAL VERBS with **flush**

• **flush (out)** *something* [M] to clean something by forcing a large amount of water on or through it ○ *Rinse the fabric in cool water to flush out the paint.*
• **flush out** *someone/something* [M] to force a person or animal to leave a hiding place ○ *He had to climb down the side of the tunnel to flush out the birds.*

fluster /ˈflʌs·tər/ *v* [T] to make someone nervous or upset, esp. when the person is trying to do something ○ *Don't let that new tax form fluster you – it's not as bad as it looks.*
flustered /ˈflʌs·tərd/ *adj* ○ *If I look flustered it's because I'm trying to do 20 things at once.*

flute /fluːt/ *n* [C/U] a tube-shaped musical instrument with a row of holes along its side that are

F

covered by the fingers to vary the notes and played by blowing into a hole near one end, or this type of instrument generally

flutist /ˈfluːt̬·əst/ *n* [C] a flute player

flutter /ˈflʌt̬·ər/ *v* [I/T] **1** to move in quick irregular motions, or to cause something to move this way ○ [I] *The flags fluttered in the breeze.* **2** If your heart flutters, it beats faster than usual, often from excitement.

flutter /ˈflʌt̬·ər/ *n* [C usually sing] ○ *There was a flutter of wings overhead.*

F

flux /flʌks/ *n* [U] continuous change ○ *Everything is in a state of flux.*

fly TRAVEL THROUGH AIR /flɑɪ/ *v* [I/T] *past simp.* **flew**, *past part.* **flown** (of creatures, objects, or aircraft) to move through the air, or (of people) to travel by aircraft ○ [I] *The building just exploded, and glass flew through the air.* ○ [I] *We enjoy watching the birds fly over the water.* ○ [I] *Are you planning to fly or drive to Toronto?* ○ [I] *Some of our pilots have been flying* (= operating an aircraft) *for 20 years.* ○ [I/T] *What airline are you flying (on)* (= traveling on as a passenger)*?*

fly /flɑɪ/, **fly ball** /ˈflɑɪ ˈbɔːl/ *n* [C] in baseball, a ball that has been hit high into the air ○ *He caught the fly in deep center field.*

flyer, **flier** /ˈflɑɪ·ər/ *n* [C] a person who operates an aircraft or travels on one as a passenger

MOVE QUICKLY /flɑɪ/ *v* [I] *past simp.* **flew**, *past part.* **flown** to move or go quickly or suddenly ○ *Theo was startled when the door flew open.* ○ *Saying she was late, Cathy flew by me and ran outside.* ○ *The summer seems to have flown by* (= passed quickly).

INSECT /flɑɪ/ *n* [C] a small insect with two wings

PANTS /flɑɪ/ *n* [C usually sing] the covered opening at the front of a pair of pants

WAVE /flɑɪ/ *v* [I/T] *past simp.* **flew**, *past part.* **flown** to move around in the air while being held at one end, or to cause something attached at one end to be moved ○ [I] *Flags flew from the front of every house.*

IDIOMS with fly

• **fly by the seat of** *your* **pants** to do something difficult without the necessary skill or experience ○ *I had no idea how to do it – I was just flying by the seat of my pants.*

• **fly in the ointment** something that spoils a situation that could have been pleasant ○ *The party was great – the only fly in the ointment was that my grumpy uncle was there.*

• **fly off the handle**, **fly into a rage** to suddenly become very angry ○ *You have to be very careful because he flies off the handle very easily.*

fly-by-night /ˈflɑɪ·bɑɪ ˌnɑɪt/ *adj* [not gradable] *disapproving* (esp. of a business) not able to be trusted, and likely to stop operating without any notice ○ *a fly-by-night operation*

flyer /ˈflɑɪ·ər/ *n* [C] a FLIER PAPER ○ See also: FLYER at FLY TRAVEL THROUGH AIR

flying saucer *n* [C] a UFO that has the shape of a disk

FM /ˈefˌem/ *n* [U] *abbreviation for* frequency modulation (= one of two main types of radio waves used to broadcast in the US) ○ Compare AM RADIO

foal /foʊl/ *n* [C] a young horse

foam /foʊm/ *n* [U] **1** a mass of small, usually white, bubbles formed on the surface of a liquid ○ *The waves were high and capped with foam.* **2** Foam is also a type of light material made by adding gas bubbles to a liquid, then letting it cool, used esp. in packaging.

foam /foʊm/ *v* [I] ○ *The suds in the sink foamed up when she added hot water.*

foam rubber *n* [U] a soft rubber that contains very small bubbles of air ○ *The cushions are filled with foam rubber.*

fob off *something/someone* /fɑːb ɔːf/ *phrasal verb* [M] to persuade someone to accept someone or something you want to get rid of ○ *Politics can be a way to fob off theoretical solutions on people demanding practical ones.*

focal point /ˈfoʊ·kəl ˌpɔɪnt/ *n* [C] **1** a FOCUS MAIN OBJECT or FOCUS POSITION. **2** ***art*** A focal point is the feature of a work of art that is the most interesting or important or the most strongly emphasized.

focus Ⓐ MAIN OBJECT /ˈfoʊ·kəs/, **focal point** /ˈfoʊ·kəl ˌpɔɪnt/ *n* [C] *pl* **focuses**, **foci** the main object or interest, or the attention given something ○ *The focus of attention has shifted from the economy to improving the public schools.* ○ *State officials urge continued focus on mosquito control.*

focus /ˈfoʊ·kəs/ *v* [I/T] to direct attention toward something or someone ○ [I] *Tonight's program focuses on homelessness.*

POSITION /ˈfoʊ·kəs/ *n* [C/U] *pl* **focuses**, **foci** **1** ***physics*** the exact place or position where beams of light, heat, or sound meet after moving toward each other; FOCAL POINT ➤ Picture: **lens** **2** ***earth science*** A focus is also the exact position inside the earth where an EARTHQUAKE begins. **3** A photograph or an image seen through a device with a LENS, such as a MICROSCOPE, TELESCOPE, or camera that is **in focus** is clear and one that is **out of focus** is not clear.

focus /ˈfoʊ·kəs/ *v* [I/T] to adjust something in order to see more clearly ○ [T] *I focused the binoculars on the bird on a branch of the tree.*

fodder /ˈfɑd·ər/ *n* [U] food given to cows, horses, and other farm animals ○ *(fig.) The charges of scandal in the White House are fodder for* (= have encouraged) *late-evening jokes on television.*

foe /foʊ/ *n* [C] an enemy, or a competitor ○ *Foes of the plan were there to voice their concerns.*

fog /fɔːg, fɑg/ *n* [C/U] a mass of cloud consisting of small drops of water near the surface of the earth ○ [U] *Heavy fog made driving conditions dangerous.*

foggy /ˈfɔː·gi, ˈfɑg·i/ *adj* ○ *a cold, foggy day*

fog /fɔːg, fɑg/ *v* [I/T] **-gg-**

PHRASAL VERB with fog

• **fog up** *(something)* [M] to cover a surface such as glass or a mirror with small drops of water and make it difficult to see through or reflect an image ○ *My windshield kept fogging up, and it was hard to see the road.* ○ *The steam fogged my glasses up.*

fogbound, **fog-bound** /ˈfɔːɡ·bɑʊnd, ˈfɑɡ-/ *adj* [not gradable] unable to operate as usual because of fog ○ *Their flight was canceled because the airport was fogbound.*

foghorn /ˈfɔːɡ·hɔːrn, ˈfɑɡ-/ *n* [C] a loud HORN that a ship uses in a fog to warn other ships of its position

foible /ˈfɔɪ·bəl/ *n* [C usually pl] a small fault or foolish habit ○ *We all have our little foibles.*

foil **METAL SHEET** /fɔɪl/ *n* [U] a very thin sheet of metal, used esp. for wrapping food ○ *aluminum foil*

PREVENT /fɔɪl/ *v* [T] to prevent someone or something from being successful ○ *An attempted coup against the country's military ruler was foiled yesterday.*

COMPARISON /fɔɪl/ *n* [C] someone or something that makes another's good or bad qualities all the more noticeable ○ *The older, cynical character in the play is the perfect foil for the innocent William.*

BLADE /fɔɪl/ *n* [C] a thin, light weapon with a long blade used in the sport of FENCING

FOIL /fɔɪl/ *n* [U] ***mathematics*** *abbreviation for* first, outer, inner, last, the rule for multiplying two BINOMIALS (= statements that have two numbers or symbols each)

foist *something* **on/upon** *someone* /ˈfɔɪst·ɔːn, -ɑn, -əˌpɑn/, **foist off** *something* **on** *someone* /fɔɪstˈɔːf·ɔːn, -ɑn/ *phrasal verb* to force someone to have or experience something unwanted or undesirable ○ *She charged that junk food is being foisted on children by TV commercials.*

fold **BEND** /foʊld/ *v* [I/T] **1** to bend something such as paper or cloth so that one part of it lies on the other part, or to be able bend in this way ○ [T] *He took his clothes out of the dryer and carefully folded them.* ○ [M] *She folded up the map and put it back in her bag.* ○ [I] *The tray table folds up so that it fits in a closet.* **2** If you fold your hands or arms, you bring them together and cross them: [T] *He folded his arms across his chest.*

folding /ˈfoʊl·dɪŋ/ *adj* designed to be folded into a smaller size for storage or carrying ○ *We helped the janitor put away the folding chairs.*

fold /foʊld/ *n* [C] ○ *If you just make folds along the dotted lines, you can seal it and mail it as an envelope.*

FAIL /foʊld/ *v* [I] (of a business) to close because of failure ○ *Many small businesses fold within the first year.*

SHARED BELIEFS /foʊld/ *n* [C/U] **1** the safety or comfort of belonging to a group that shares the same beliefs ○ [U] *The Democrats attracted many immigrants to the fold.* **2** A fold is a fenced area on a farm where sheep are kept during the night.

WORD FAMILY fold

Nouns	fold folder	*Verbs*	fold unfold
Adjectives	folding		

PHRASAL VERB with fold

• **fold in** *something* [M] to mix a food substance into another by turning it gently with a spoon ○ *Fold in the flour and add two eggs.*

-fold /ˌfoʊld/ *suffix* having the stated number of parts, or multiplied by the stated number ○ *There has been more than a 30-fold increase in Internet users in the past two years.*

folder /ˈfoʊl·dər/ *n* [C] a folded piece of thin cardboard for holding loose papers

foliage /ˈfoʊ·liː·ɪdʒ/ *n* [U] the leaves of a plant or tree ○ *Dense foliage blocked the path.*

foliated /ˈfoʊ·liːˌeɪt·əd/ *adj* ***earth science*** describes rocks consisting of thin layers that can be separated

foliation /ˌfoʊ·liːˈeɪ·ʃən/ *n* [U] ***earth science***

folk /foʊk/ *adj* [not gradable] traditional to or typical of the people of a particular group or country ○ *folk art/dance*

folklore /ˈfoʊk·lɔːr, -loʊr/ *n* [U] the traditional stories, beliefs, and customs of a group of people

folk music *n* [U] the traditional music of a particular region or group of people

folks /foʊks/, **folk** /foʊk/ *pl n* **1** people, esp. those of a particular group or type ○ *Some folks have been waiting over an hour to buy tickets.* **2** Your folks are your parents: *I'm going home over Thanksgiving to see my folks.* **3** You can say folks if you want to speak in a friendly way to people you do not know: *Well, folks, thanks for watching Channel 4 news – that's about it for this evening.*

folk singer *n* [C] someone who specializes in singing folk songs

folk song *n* [C] a traditional song of a particular region or group of people

folksy /ˈfoʊk·si/ *adj* [-er/-est only] very friendly and informal in style ○ *His folksy personality sets the tone for the show.*

folktale /ˈfoʊk·teɪl/ *n* [C] ***literature*** a traditional story that people of a particular region or group repeat among themselves

follicle /ˈfɑl·ɪ·kəl/ *n* [C] ***biology*** **1** any of the very small holes in the skin that a hair grows from **2** A follicle is also a structure like a small bag in a woman's OVARY (= organ that produces eggs) in which an egg develops.

follow **MOVE AFTER** /ˈfɑl·oʊ/ *v* [I/T] **1** to move along after someone or something, or to move along a route or path ○ [T] *The dog followed us home.* ○ [I] *He drove ahead and we followed in our own car.* ○ [T] *Follow this road for the next two miles.* **2** To follow someone is also to move along after a person in order to watch where that person is going: [T] *She had the feeling she was being followed.*

WORD CHOICES follow

The verbs **chase** or **pursue** can be used when someone follows and tries to catch someone else.

*He was running and the dog was **chasing** him.*

*The robber was **pursued** by several members of the public.*

If someone is following someone else in order to watch that person and find out where he or she goes, the verbs **tail** or **shadow** can be used.

*The car was **tailed** by police for several hours.*

*The police think the robbers **shadowed** their victims for days before the crime.*

If someone is following another person very closely to try to catch that person, you can use the idiom **in hot pursuit**.

*She ran down the steps with a group of journalists **in hot pursuit**.*

F

HAPPEN AFTER /ˈfɑl·oʊ/ *v* [I/T] to happen after something else in order or time ○ [I] *We were not prepared for what followed.* ○ [T] *A reception will follow the meeting, so please stay.*

following /ˈfɑl·ə·wɪŋ/ *adj* [not gradable] ○ *I'm busy on Thursday, but I'm free the following day.* ○ *The following items were found – a ring, a wallet, and a watch.*

following /ˈfɑl·ə·wɪŋ/ *pl n* ○ *Will the following please stand – Neal, Crisonino, Druback, Thompson.*

following /ˈfɑl·ə·wɪŋ/ *prep* ○ *Following the ballgame, there will be a fireworks display.*

OBEY /ˈfɑl·oʊ/ *v* [T] to obey someone, or to act according to something ○ *Follow the instructions in taking the medicine.* ○ *I decided to follow her advice.* ○ *If you follow the signs, you will have no trouble finding the airport.*

follower /ˈfɑl·ə·wər/ *n* [C] someone who obeys or supports another person or that person's ideas ○ *The newly elected governor appeared overcome with emotion as he thanked his followers.*

following /ˈfɑl·ə·wɪŋ/ *n* [C] ○ *The candidate has a large following among young people.*

UNDERSTAND /ˈfɑl·oʊ/ *v* [T] to understand ○ *He spoke so rapidly we could hardly follow what he said.*

INTERESTED IN /ˈfɑl·oʊ/ *v* [T] to be actively interested in something, or to give your attention to something ○ *Do you follow football?* ○ *We've followed her political career for many years.*

follower /ˈfɑl·ə·wər/ *n* [C]

BE RESULT /ˈfɑl·oʊ/ *v* [I] to happen as a result, or to be a likely result ○ [+ *that* clause] *Fuel prices for transporting goods have increased, so it would follow that those prices are getting passed on to customers.*

WORD FAMILY follow

Nouns	follower following	*Adjectives*	following
		Verbs	follow

IDIOMS with follow

•**follow in** *someone's* **footsteps** to do the same thing as someone else, esp. someone in your family, previously did ○ *She followed in her mother's footsteps and started her own business.*

•**follow** *your* **nose** to move forward ○ *There's a gas station up ahead about a mile, so just follow your nose.*

•**follow suit** to do the same thing ○ *When one airline reduces its ticket prices, the rest usually follow suit.*

PHRASAL VERBS with follow

•**follow through 1** to continue something until it is completed ○ *The city has raised the money for more teachers – now it has to follow through and hire them.* **2** In sports, to follow through is to continue a swinging motion of the arms or legs when making a play: *You can't drive the golf ball unless you follow through after hitting it.* ○ Related noun: FOLLOW-THROUGH

•**follow** *something* **up**, **follow up on** *something* [M] to discover more about something or to take further action connected with it ○ *As a news reporter, when something important happens, I have to follow it up.* ○ *Brocchini failed to follow up on leads pointing to any other suspects.* ○ Related noun: FOLLOW-UP

follow-through *n* [C/U] **1** the action of completing something ○ [U] *They made a good start at improving prison conditions, but unless there's follow-through, the reforms won't last.* **2** In sports, a follow-through is the action of continuing a swinging motion of the arms or legs when making a play: [C usually sing] *My tennis instructor says I need to have a better follow-through on my backhand.* ○ Related verb: FOLLOW THROUGH

follow-up *n* [C] something done after an earlier event that is connected with it ○ *I've got to go in for a follow-up to the dentist next week.*

follow-up *adj* [not gradable] ○ *a follow-up visit* ○ *Reporters can have one follow-up question.* ○ Related verb: FOLLOW UP

folly /ˈfɑl·i/ *n* [C/U] the condition of being foolish, or a foolish action or belief ○ [+ *to* infinitive] *It would be folly to attempt a trip in this snowstorm.*

foment /foʊˈment/ *v* [T] *fml* to cause something bad or illegal to develop ○ *to foment revolution*

fond /fɑnd/ *adj* [*-er/-est* only] having feelings of affection for someone or something, or having a liking for an activity ○ *I'm really fond of my aunt and enjoy seeing her.* ○ *She had fond memories of her childhood.* ○ *Charles is fond of driving, so I'm happy just to be a passenger.*

fondly /ˈfɑn·dli/ *adv* ○ *He smiled fondly at his wife.*

fondness /ˈfɑnd·nəs/ *n* [U] ○ *Ruth has a real fondness* (= liking) *for old houses.*

fondle /ˈfɑn·dəl/ *v* [T] to touch in a gentle and loving way ○ *He fondled the baby's feet.*

font LETTERS /fɑnt/ *n* [C] a set of printed letters, numbers, and other symbols of the same style ○ *The printer can produce a variety of fonts in virtually any type size.*

CONTAINER /fɑnt/ *n* [C] a container for the water used in BAPTISM (= religious ceremony)

food /fuːd/ *n* [C/U] **1** something that can be taken in by an animal and used to keep it alive and allow it to grow or develop, or such things considered as a whole ○ [U] *baby/cat food* ○ [C] *There were a lot of frozen foods in the refrigerator.* **2** Sometimes food means only the solid material eaten by animals, and not liquids: [U] *He has had no food or drink for 24 hours.*

IDIOM with food

•**food for thought** something worth thinking seriously about ○ *Thank you for your suggestion – it gave us a lot of food for thought.*

food chain *n* [U] ***biology*** a series of living things in which each group eats organisms from the group lower than itself in the series

food poisoning *n* [U] an illness caused by eating food that contains harmful bacteria

food processor *n* [C] a piece of electric equipment used for cutting, slicing, or mixing food quickly

food stamp *n* [C usually pl] a specially printed piece of paper worth a specific dollar amount which the US government provides to poor people for buying food

foodstuff /ˈfuːd·stʌf/ *n* [C usually pl] any substance used as food

fool /fuːl/ *n* [C] a person who behaves in a silly way, or someone who lacks judgment ○ *Crazy I may be, but I try not to be a fool.* ○ *I know I'm making a fool of myself, but I can't help it.* ○ *They were dressed up like a bunch of fools.*

fool /fuːl/ *v* [I/T] ○ [T] *She tries to fool* (= deceive) *people about her age by wearing heavy makeup and coloring her hair.* ○ [I] *You don't owe me a penny, I was only fooling* (= joking).

fool /fuːl/ *adj* [not gradable] *not standard* ○ *I made a damn fool* (= stupid) *mistake, but I'll never do it again.*

foolish /ˈfuː·lɪʃ/ *adj* stupid or unwise ○ *She was afraid that she would look foolish if she refused to go along with her friends.* ○ *It would be foolish of us to assume that everything will work out fine.*

foolishly /ˈfuː·lɪʃ·li/ *adv* ○ *I would just like to know that my taxes are not being foolishly spent.*

foolishness /ˈfuː·lɪʃ·nəs/ *n* [U] ○ *My father was not one to tolerate foolishness.*

WORD CHOICES fool

Some common alternatives to "foolish" are **stupid** or **silly**.

*She was really **stupid** to quit her job like that.*

*It was **silly** of you to go out in the sun without a hat.*

If something or someone is so foolish that that thing or person is funny or strange, you can use the words **absurd, ridiculous**, or **ludicrous**.

*What an **absurd** thing to say!*

*Do I look **ridiculous** in this hat?*

*I think giving young children such expensive jewelry is a **ludicrous** idea.*

You can describe a foolish person as a **fool** or an **idiot**.

*You were a **fool** not to take that job.*

*Some **idiot** put a lit match in the wastepaper basket.*

In informal situations, if you think people have been foolish, you can say that they are **out of their minds.**

*You must be **out of your mind** spending so much money on a car.*

PHRASAL VERBS with fool

•**fool around** **BE SILLY/DANGEROUS** to behave in a silly or dangerous way ○ *The kids were fooling around in the pool.* ○ *Stop fooling around with your dad's tools.*

•**fool around** **CHANGE SOMETHING** to change something a little, esp. in order to try to make it better ○ *Sometimes when you start fooling around with a recipe, all sorts of unexpected things happen.*

•**fool with** *something* to use or work with something difficult or dangerous ○ *I just don't like to fool with these computers.*

foolhardy /ˈfuːlˌhɑrd·i/ *adj* [*-er/-est* only] taking unnecessary or foolish risks ○ *He made a foolhardy attempt to climb the tree to recover his kite.*

foolproof /ˈfuːl·pruːf/ *adj* [not gradable] (of a plan, method, or machine) designed to be easily done or operated without possibility of mistake or failure ○ *It's not a foolproof system and it never will be.*

foot **BODY PART** /fʊt/ *n* [C] *pl* **feet** the part of the body at the bottom of the leg on which a person or animal stands ○ *I've got a blister on my left foot.* ○ *He got to/jumped to/rose to his feet* (= stood up) *to get a better look at the parade passing by.* ○ *I've been* **on** *my* **feet** (= standing) *all day serving customers.* ○ *The driver of the stolen car fled the scene* **on foot** (= walking).

MEASUREMENT /fʊt/, *abbreviation* **ft.**, *symbol* **′** *n* [C] *pl* **foot**, **feet** a unit of measurement of length equal to 12 inches or 0.3048 meters

BOTTOM /fʊt/ *n* [U] the bottom or end of a space or object ○ *She dreamed she saw someone standing at the foot of her bed.*

IDIOMS with foot

•**foot the bill** to pay for something, esp. something expensive ○ *His parents can't afford to foot the bill for his college education.*

•**(back) on** *your* **feet** healthy again ○ *The doctor said he'd be back on his feet again soon.*

footage /ˈfʊt̬·ɪdʒ/ *n* [U] film or VIDEOTAPE that shows a single event or place ○ *Footage showing entire city blocks in flames flickered nightly on TV.*

football /ˈfʊt·bɔːl/ *n* [C/U] **1** (the oval ball used in) a game played by two teams in which each team tries to kick, run with, or throw the ball across the opposing team's goal line to score points. American and Canadian football differ in the number of players, the size of the field, and some rules

F

of play. ○ [C] *Mom bought me a football.* ○ [U] *Let's play football after lunch.* **2** Football also means SOCCER in most of the world.

footbridge /ˈfʊt·brɪdʒ/ *n* [C] a bridge for people to walk across

foothill /ˈfʊt·hɪl/ *n* [C usually pl] a low hill at the base of a mountain or group of mountains

foothold **SAFE PLACE** /ˈfʊt·hoʊld/ *n* [C] a place where you can safely put your feet, esp. when climbing ○ *She searched desperately for a foothold in the steep rock.*

SITUATION /ˈfʊt·hoʊld/ *n* [C] a situation in which someone has obtained the power or influence needed to get what is wanted ○ *In buying their business, the company gains a major foothold in a market it considers critical to the future of the industry.*

footing **FEET** /ˈfʊt̬·ɪŋ/ *n* [U] a firm position of the feet ○ *He lost his footing and tumbled into the water.*

CONDITION /ˈfʊt̬·ɪŋ/ *n* [U] a position or condition on which something exists ○ *Both sides need to begin negotiations on equal footing.*

footlights /ˈfʊt·lɑɪts/ *pl n* the lights that are in a row along the floor at the front of a STAGE in a theater

footlocker /ˈfʊtˌlɑk·ər/ *n* [C] a large, rectangular container used to hold clothing and personal possessions

footloose /ˈfʊt·luːs/ *adj* free to do what pleases you or go where you like ○ *He's able to go from footloose farm boy in the morning to concerned businessman in the afternoon.*

footnote /ˈfʊt·noʊt/ *n* [C] a note at the bottom of a page that gives extra information about something in the text on that page

footpath /ˈfʊt·pæθ/ *n* [C] a path for walking

footprint **FOOT MARK** /ˈfʊt·prɪnt/ *n* [C] a mark left on a surface by a foot ○ *There was not a single footprint in the sand.*

AREA /ˈfʊt·prɪnt/ *n* [C] the shape on the ground that is covered by something such as a building

footstep /ˈfʊt·step/ *n* [C] the movement or sound of each step a person takes when walking ○ *We never saw anyone in the building, but sometimes we heard footsteps down the hall.*

footstool /ˈfʊt·stuːl/ *n* [C] a low piece of furniture on which you can rest your feet while sitting

footwear /ˈfʊt·wer, -wær/ *n* [U] shoes, boots, or other outer coverings for the feet

footwork /ˈfʊt·wɜrk/ *n* [U] the way someone uses the feet in sports and dancing, esp. when it is skillful ○ *He was one of the all-time great boxers with his quick jab and dazzling footwork.*

for **TO BE GIVEN** /fɔːr, fər/ *prep* intended to be given to ○ *There's a phone message for you on your desk.* ○ *There will be a prize for the best costume at the party.*

PURPOSE /fɔːr, fər/ *prep* having the purpose of ○ *What do you imagine he uses this old thing for?* ○ *Why don't you take an aspirin for your headache* (= to stop it)*?*

BECAUSE OF /fɔːr, fər/ *prep* because of; as a result of (doing something) ○ *She was stopped for speeding.* ○ *The things we do for love!* ○ *For some reason, she isn't interested in going out at all tonight.* ○ *Certain Chicago restaurants are famous for their deep-dish pizza.*

INSTEAD OF /fɔːr, fər/ *prep* instead of; to help ○ *Let me carry those groceries to the car for you.*

TIME/DISTANCE /fɔːr, fər/ *prep* showing amount of time or distance ○ *We drove for miles.* ○ *She's out of town for a few days on business.* ➤ Usage: **during or for?** at DURING **THROUGH**

OCCASION /fɔːr, fər/ *prep* on the occasion of or at the time of ○ *What are you getting Mom and Dad for their anniversary?* ○ *We're planning a party for Stephen's birthday.* ○ *The neighbors invited us for dinner* (= to eat with them). ○ *What's for lunch* (= what will we eat)*?*

CONSIDERING /fɔːr, fər/ *prep* considering (something or someone with reference to things or people as they usually are) ○ *This winter has been mild for Canada.* ○ *I think Kristy is very mature for her age.*

SUPPORT /fɔːr, fər/ *prep* in support of or agreement with ○ *I voted for her in the last election.* ○ *We thought about moving, and I was all for it, but my wife didn't want to.*

IN RELATION TO /fɔːr, fər/ *prep* in relation to (someone or something) ○ *Her feelings for him were obvious.* ○ *That jacket is a bit big for you.*

PAYMENT /fɔːr, fər/ *prep* (getting) in exchange ○ *If I take the car in, it'll be $45 for a tuneup.*

REPRESENTING /fɔːr, fər/ *prep* representing (an organization or country) ○ *Michael works for a Washington-based foundation.* ○ *She carried the flag for the US at the opening ceremonies.*

TOWARD /fɔːr, fər/ *prep* toward; in the direction of ○ *Just follow signs for the airport once you're on the highway.*

MEANING /fɔːr, fər/ *prep* meaning; representing ○ *What's another word for "happy"?*

TO GET /fɔːr, fər/ *prep* in order to get or have ○ *I had to wait half an hour for the bus.* ○ *Call the phone number below for more information.*

DUTY /fɔːr, fər/ *prep* the duty or responsibility of ○ *It's not for her to say whether I should cut my hair.*

BECAUSE /fɔːr, fər/ *conjunction* because; as ○ *She told the truth, for she had nothing to lose.*

USAGE

for or because?

For is mostly used to mean "because" or "as a result of" in very old-fashioned, especially literary English.

Forgive them O Lord, for they know not what they do.

The usual word today is **because**.

Erik ate nothing because he was feeling sick.

~~*Erik ate nothing for he was feeling sick.*~~

IDIOMS with for

- **for a price** for a lot of money ○ *You can buy anything you want there – for a price.* ○ Compare AT A PRICE at PRICE IDIOM
- **for a song** *infml* very cheaply ○ *She bought that antique chest for a song.*
- **for crying out loud** *infml* I am annoyed or surprised by this ○ *Oh, for crying out loud, would you stop leaving your magazines all over the house!*
- **for dear life** as if you fear you will die ○ *Once the rollercoaster got going, we were hanging on for dear life.*
- **for effect** said or done to get a particular reaction from someone ○ *He sounds mean, but he's not – he just says those things for effect.*
- **for good** permanently ○ *She says she's leaving him for good.*
- **for goodness' sake, for Pete's/heaven's/pity's sake** I am surprised or annoyed by this ○ *For goodness' sake, don't tell anyone else about this!*
- **for keeps** to have forever ○ *You can have that book for keeps.*
- **for old times' sake** done as a reminder of the good times you had in the past ○ *Let me buy you lunch, for old times' sake.*
- **for one thing** one reason is ○ *Celluloid film wasn't perfect – for one thing, it was flammable.*
- **for real** *infml* actual, true, or real ○ *Is this letter a joke or is it for real?* ○ *"I'm not talking to him anymore." "For real? (= Is that really true?)"*
- **for short** using a short form ○ *Her name's Alexandra, or Alex for short.*
- **for starters** *infml* as a beginning, with more to follow ○ *You have to put down a $500 deposit, and that's just for starters.*
- **for sure, for certain** *infml* definitely, without a doubt ○ *I saw him and knew for sure that he had come to see me.*
- **for the asking** easily available ○ *There are a lot of organizations that have scholarship money for the asking.*
- **for the better** improving a situation ○ *The new teacher made a lot of changes, mostly for the better.*
- **for the heck of it** *infml* without any purpose except for fun ○ *I drove my van across country just for the heck of it.*
- **for the time being, for now/for the moment** at this time ○ *The union voted not to strike for the time being.* ○ *The situation seems to be peaceful, for now at least.* ○ **USAGE:** Used to say that although one set of conditions exists now, the situation could change.
- **for the worse** making a situation worse ○ *The doctor says her condition has changed for the worse.*
- **for what it's worth** *infml* used to show that you know someone may not care, but you are going to say something anyway ○ *Nonetheless, I'd like to give my opinion, for what it's worth.*
- **not** *(do something)* **for anything (in the world)** *infml* to not do something under any conditions ○ *It was a fantastic party – I wouldn't have missed it for anything.*

forage /ˈfɔːr·ɪdʒ, ˈfɑr-/ *v* [I/T] to go searching, esp. for food ○ [I] *Wild dogs roam the streets, foraging for food.*

foray /ˈfɔːr·eɪ, ˈfoʊr-/ *n* [C] **1** a brief attempt at or involvement in an activity outside a person's or organization's usual range of activities ○ *The opera company has made curious forays into contemporary music in recent seasons.* **2** A foray is also a sudden and quick attack by a group of soldiers on an enemy area.

forbid /fərˈbɪd, fɔːr-/ *v* [T] *pres. part.* **forbidding,** *past simp.* **forbade, forbid,** *past part.* **forbidden** to not allow something, or to order someone not to do something ○ *You can't forbid me to go.*

forbidden /fərˈbɪd·ᵊn, fɔːr-/ *adj* not permitted, esp. by rule or law ○ *Automobiles are forbidden on the island.* ○ *He was strictly forbidden to talk with them.*

WORD CHOICES forbid

A common alternative to "forbid" is the phrase **not allow** or **not let.**

*My parents do**n't let** me stay out late.*

The verbs **ban, prohibit,** or **outlaw** can be used to talk about officially forbidding something using a rule or law.

*The government has **banned** the sale of lead-based paint.*

*Vehicles are **prohibited** from parking on the grass.*

*The new law **outlaws** smoking in public places.*

If someone uses official authority to forbid something, the verb **veto** can be used.

*The President **vetoed** the law after it was passed by a narrow margin in the Senate.*

If you forbid someone from taking part in an activity, especially because that person has done something wrong, you can use the verbs **disqualify** or **bar.**

*She was **disqualified** from the competition for cheating.*

*The incident led to him being **barred** from playing for the rest of the season.*

IDIOM with forbid

- **God forbid, heaven forbid** I hope this does not happen ○ *If there was a fire, God forbid, we'd be able to respond to the disaster.*

forbidding /fərˈbɪd·ɪŋ, fɔːr-/ *adj* appearing unfriendly, threatening, or difficult ○ *The mountains looked dark and forbidding.*

force PHYSICAL POWER /fɔːrs, foʊrs/ *n* [C/U] **1** physical, often violent, strength or power ○ [U] *The force of the wind knocked down many trees during the hurricane.* ○ [U] *She had to use force to get the old window open.* **2** ***physics*** A force is a power that causes an object to move or that changes movement. ➤ Picture: **lever**

force /fɔːrs, foʊrs/ *v* [T] **1** *If the piece won't fit in the hole, don't force it.* ○ *He forced his way through the crowd to reach the exit.* **2** To force a lock, door, window, etc., is to break it in order to get in: *I forgot my house key, so I had to force a window.*

forced /fɔːrst, fourst/ *adj* [not gradable] ○ *There were no obvious signs of forced entry into the house.*
forcible /ˈfɔːr·sə·bəl, ˈfour-/ *adj* ○ *The youths had been arrested for forcible entry and burglary.*
forcibly /ˈfɔːr·sə·bli, ˈfour-/ *adv* ○ *The Ponca Indians were forcibly removed from their lands in 1877.*

INFLUENCE /fɔːrs, fours/ *n* [C/U] strong influence and energy, or a person with strong influence and energy ○ [U] *The sheer force of her words kept the audience glued to their seats.* ○ [C] *He was a powerful force in national politics for 30 years.*
forceful /ˈfɔːrs·fəl, ˈfours-/ *adj approving* ○ *He developed a forceful, emotional preaching style.*
forcefully /ˈfɔːrs·fə·li, ˈfours-/ *adv approving* ○ *He argues his case forcefully.*

F

MAKE DO UNWILLINGLY /fɔːrs, fours/ *v* [T] to make someone do something, or make something happen, esp. by threatening or not offering the possibility of choice ○ *I hate string beans, so I had to force myself to eat them.* ○ [+ to infinitive] *Anderson was forced to leave the game with a bruised knee.* ○ *I didn't actually want any more dessert, but Julia forced it on me.* ○ *If callers have information about the crime and would like to give their names that is fine, but we're not going to force the issue* (= make them give their names).
forced /fɔːrst, fourst/ *adj* [not gradable] **1** *The plane made a forced landing in Denver* (= it was unexpected but necessary). **2** Forced laughter or a forced smile is produced with effort and not sincerely felt.
forcible /ˈfɔːr·sə·bəl, ˈfour-/ *adj* ○ *The editorial board of the newspaper called for her forcible retirement from public life.*
force /fɔːrs, fours/ *n* [C/U]

MILITARY /fɔːrs, fours/ *n* [C] **1** an organized and trained military group ○ *the armed forces* ○ *the Air Force* ○ *UN forces continue to provide relief in the war-torn region.* **2** Force is also military strength.

GROUP /fɔːrs, fours/ *n* [C] **1** a group of people who do the same job ○ *a sales force* ○ *the police force* **2** If a person or group joins or combines forces with another person or group, they agree to work together.

WORD FAMILY force

Nouns	force	Verbs	force
Adjectives	forced	Adverbs	forcefully
	forceful		forcibly
	forcible		

IDIOMS with force

• **a force to be reckoned with** an organization or a person with a lot of power and influence ○ *The senator was still a force to be reckoned with, in spite of his age.*
• **by force of habit** because it is a habit ○ *By force of habit I always hung the house keys on a hook next to the front door.*
• **in force 1** in large numbers ○ *Volunteers turned out in force to plant pines, crab-apple trees, and lilac bushes.* **2** If laws, rules, or systems are **in force**, they exist and are being used: *New regulations limiting fishing on this river are now in force.*

force-feed FEED *v* [T] *past* **-fed** to force (a person or animal) to eat and drink, often by sending food to the stomach through a tube in the mouth
TEACH *v* [T] *past* **-fed** to force (someone) to learn something or accept an opinion or belief ○ *Children should not be force-fed this nonsense in school.*

forceps /ˈfɔːr·səps, -seps/ *pl n* a medical instrument used for holding things firmly

ford /fɔːrd, fourd/ *n* [C] a place in a river where the water is not deep, making it possible to get across
ford /fɔːrd, fourd/ *v* [T] ○ *The horses forded the river without any problems.*

fore /fɔːr, four/ *n* **1** a noticeable or public position: *The presidential campaign has brought the issue of big political contributions* **to the fore**. **2** The fore is also the front, or a position at the front
fore /fɔːr, four/ *adj, adv* [not gradable] in or toward the front part of something, esp. a boat

forearm /ˈfɔːr·ɑrm, ˈfour-/ *n* [C] the lower part of the arm, between the wrist and the ELBOW

forebear, **forbear** /ˈfɔːr·ber, ˈfour-, -bær/ *n* [C usually pl] an ANCESTOR

foreboding /fɔːrˈboud·ɪŋ, four-/ *n* [U] the feeling that something bad is going to happen ○ *The gloomy weather gave me a sense of foreboding.*

forecast /ˈfɔːr·kæst, ˈfour-/ *n* [C] a statement of what is likely to happen in the future ○ *The forecast is heavy rain for tomorrow.*
forecast /ˈfɔːr·kæst, ˈfour-/ *v* [T] *past* **forecast, forecasted** ○ *The government is forecasting that unemployment will continue to fall.*
forecaster /ˈfɔːrˌkæs·tər, ˈfour-/ *n* [C] ○ *a weather forecaster*

foreclose /fɔːrˈklouz, four-/ *v* [I] (esp. of banks) to take control of the property of owners because they did not pay back the bank's money borrowed to pay for it

forefathers /ˈfɔːrˌfɑð·ərz, ˈfour-/ *pl n* members of a family, national, or religious group who lived in the past ○ *Mario is spending the summer in Italy, the land of his forefathers.*

forefinger /ˈfɔːrˌfɪŋ·gər, ˈfour-/ *n* [C] the finger next to the thumb; INDEX FINGER ○ *He held a tiny seed between his thumb and forefinger.*

forefront /ˈfɔːr·frʌnt, ˈfour-/ *n* [U] the most important or leading position ○ *She was in the forefront on many social issues of her day.*

forego /fɔːrˈgou, four-/ *v* [T] ○ See at FORGO

foregone conclusion /ˌfɔːrˌgɔːn·kən ˈkluː·ʒən, ˌfour-, -ˌgɑn-/ *n* [C] a result that is obvious before it happens ○ *Democrats so outnumber Republicans here that if you are nominated as a Democrat, it's a foregone conclusion you will be elected.*

foreground /ˈfɔːr·graʊnd, ˈfour-/ *n* [C] ***art*** the things in a picture that seem nearest to you ○ *The children are in the foreground in front of our house.* ○ Compare BACKGROUND THINGS BEHIND

forehand /ˈfɔːr·hænd, ˈfoʊr-/ *n* [C] (in sports such as tennis) a way of hitting the ball in which the inside part of the hand that is holding the RACKET (= piece of equipment) faces the direction of movement of the ball, or the player's ability to perform this hit ○ Compare BACKHAND

forehead /ˈfɑr·əd, ˈfɔːr-; ˈfɔːr·hed, ˈfoʊr-/ *n* [C] the flat part of the face, above the eyes and below the hair

foreign /ˈfɔːr·ən, ˈfɑr-/ *adj* [not gradable] belonging or connected to a country that is not your own or is not the one you are in ○ *a foreign country* ○ *a foreign language*

foreigner /ˈfɔːr·ə·nər, ˈfɑr-/ *n* [C] a person who comes from another country ➤ Usage: **strange or foreign?** at STRANGE NOT FAMILIAR

SPELLING

foreign

Many people make mistakes when spelling this word. The correct spelling of the last syllable is "eign."

*The past is a for**eign** country.*

foreign policy *n* [C] ***politics & government*** a country's ways of dealing with other countries

foreman /ˈfɔːr·mən, ˈfoʊr-/ *n* [C] *pl* **-men 1** a skilled person who is in charge of a group of workers ○ *After four years on the job, he was promoted to foreman.* **2** *law* In a court of law, the foreman on the JURY is the person who is in charge of and speaks for the jury.

foremost /ˈfɔːr·moʊst, ˈfoʊr-/ *adj* [not gradable] best known or most important ○ *He was one of the foremost actors of his day.*

forensic /fəˈren·sɪk, -zɪk/ *adj* [not gradable] using the methods of science to provide information about a crime ○ *forensic medicine*

forerunner /ˈfɔːrˌrʌn·ər, ˈfoʊr-/ *n* [C] an early, often less advanced model of something ○ *His machine was a forerunner of the modern computer.*

foresee /fɔːrˈsiː, foʊr-/ *v* [T] *past simp.* **foresaw**, *past part.* **foreseen** to realize or understand something in advance or before it happens ○ *He foresaw the need for cars that would be less polluting.*

foreseeable /fɔːrˈsiː·ə·bəl, foʊr-, fər-/ *adj* [not gradable] able to be understood in advance ○ *Unfortunately, he was likely to remain in power for the foreseeable future* (= for a long time, beyond which no one could say what would happen).

foreshadow /fɔːrˈʃæd·oʊ, foʊr-/ *v* [T] (of a past event) to suggest the happening of a future event ○ *Low unemployment may foreshadow wage and price increases.*

foreshadowing /fɔːrˈʃæd·oʊ·ɪŋ, foʊr-/ *n* [U] ***literature*** the use of details, description, and mood that will take on more meaning later in a written work

foresight /ˈfɔːr·sɑɪt, ˈfoʊr-/ *n* [U] the ability to judge correctly what is going to happen ○ [+ *to* infinitive] *She had the foresight to sell her house just before prices came down.*

foreskin /ˈfɔːr·skɪn, ˈfoʊr-/ *n* [C] the loose skin that covers the end of the PENIS (= male sex organ)

forest /ˈfɔːr·əst, ˈfɑr-/ *n* [C/U] a large area full of trees, usually wild ○ [U] *We camped out in a clearing in the forest.*

forestry /ˈfɔːr·ə·stri, ˈfɑr-/ *n* [U] the science of caring for forests ○ *He studied forestry at Colorado State University.*

WORD FAMILY forest

Nouns	forest
	forestry

forestall /fɔːrˈstɔːl, foʊr-/ *v* [T] to prevent something from happening by acting first ○ *Many doctors prescribe aspirin to forestall second heart attacks.*

foretaste /ˈfɔːr·teɪst, ˈfoʊr-/ *n* [C] an experience that lets you know in advance what something will be like ○ *Her job as an intern during the summer gave her a foretaste of the world of work.*

forever /fəˈrev·ər, fɔː-; *esp. Southern* fəˈev·ər/ *adv* [not gradable] **1** for all time, without end ○ *Nobody lives forever.* **2** Forever can also mean always or frequently: *She was forever late for appointments.* ○ *He was forever saying that he'd pay me back, but he never did.*

forewoman /ˈfɔːrˌwʊm·ən, ˈfoʊr-/ *n* [C] *pl* **-women 1** a skilled woman who is in charge of a group of workers **2** *law* In a court of law, the forewoman on the JURY is a woman who is in charge of and speaks for the jury. ○ *The jury forewoman slowly read each of the not-guilty verdicts.*

foreword /ˈfɔːr·wərd, ˈfoʊr-/ *n* [C] ***writing*** an introduction to a book, sometimes by someone who is not the person who wrote the book

forfeit /ˈfɔːr·fət, -fɪt/ *v* [T] to give up or lose something because you cannot do something that the rules or the law says you must do ○ *She had to forfeit the tennis match after she fell and hurt her wrist.*

forfeit /ˈfɔːr·fət, -fɪt/ *n* [C/U] ○ [C] *Throwing objects on the field, the umpire said, would result in the forfeit of the game by the home team.*

forgave /fərˈgeɪv, fɔːr-/ *past simple of* FORGIVE

forge COPY ILLEGALLY /fɔːrdʒ, foʊrdʒ/ *v* [T] to make an illegal copy of something in order to deceive ○ *He was accused of forging his father's signature on the check.*

forger /ˈfɔːr·dʒər, ˈfoʊr-/ *n* [C] ○ *He was the forger of a painting sold as a Rembrandt.*

forgery /ˈfɔːr·dʒə·ri, ˈfoʊr-/ *n* [C/U] ○ [C] *These twenty-dollar bills are forgeries.* ○ [U] *He was convicted of forgery.*

MAKE /fɔːrdʒ, foʊrdʒ/ *v* [T] to make or produce, esp. with difficulty ○ *Baker had worked for months to forge a peace plan that both sides could accept.*

MOVE /fɔːrdʒ, foʊrdʒ/ *v* [I always + adv/prep] to move forward in a determined way although pro-

F

gress is difficult ○ *She forged ahead with her plans to stage a protest in Washington.*

WORK AREA /fɔːrdʒ, fourdʒ/ *n* [C] a working area with a fire for heating metal until it is soft enough to be beaten into different shapes ○ *a blacksmith's forge*

forget /fərˈget, fɔːr-/ *v* [I/T] *pres. part.* **forgetting**, *past simp.* **forgot**, *past part.* **forgotten**, **forgot** **1** to be unable to remember; fail to remember ○ [T] *You'd better not forget your mother's birthday.* ○ [+ (*that*) clause] *She forgot (that) she had a dental appointment.* ○ [+ *to* infinitive] *Don't forget to lock the car.* **2** To forget (about) is to stop thinking about someone or something, or to stop thinking about doing something: [T] *I wish I could forget him but I can't.* ○ [I] *I'm afraid we'll have to forget about going to the beach – it's raining.*

forgetful /fərˈget·fəl, fɔːr-/ *adj* likely to forget things ○ *She worries because her father is getting forgetful.*

WORD FAMILY forget

Adjectives	forgetful unforgettable	Verbs Adverbs	forget forgetfully

WORD CHOICES forget

The expression **slip someone's mind** is often used informally when someone forgets to do something.

I meant to tell you that he'd phoned, but it completely ***slipped my mind.***

If a word is **on the tip of your tongue**, you have forgotten it but think that you will very soon remember it.

Oh, what was that movie called? It's ***on the tip of my tongue.***

If something such as a name **escapes** you, you cannot remember it.

The name of her book ***escapes*** *me at the moment.*

If someone suddenly forgets something, you can say their **mind goes blank.**

I tried to remember her name but my ***mind went blank.***

IDIOM with forget

• **forget (about) it** *infml* used to say that something that happened was not important or not something to worry about: *"I'm sorry I was late." "Forget it."*

forget-me-not /fərˈget·miː ˌnɑt, fɔːr-/ *n* [C] a plant having small blue flowers

forgive /fərˈgɪv, fɔːr-/ *v* [T] *past simp.* **forgave**, *past part.* **forgiven** to stop being angry with someone who has done something wrong ○ *She apologized and he forgave her.* ○ *I can't forgive someone who has treated me so badly.*

forgiveness /fərˈgɪv·nəs, fɔːr-/ *n* [U] ○ *To my family and friends, I beg your forgiveness for the lies I've told.*

WORD FAMILY forgive

Nouns	forgiveness	Verbs	forgive

forgo, **forego** /fɔːrˈgou, four-/ *v* [T] **forgoes**, *pres. part.* **forgoing**, *past simp.* **forwent**, *past part.* **forgone** to give up or do without ○ *She decided to forgo flowers at the funeral and asked people to send money to a charity instead.*

fork **TOOL** /fɔːrk/ *n* [C] a common tool used in eating that usually has three or four stiff metal points attached to a handle ○ *The knives and forks go in the middle drawer.*

DIVISION /fɔːrk/ *n* [C] the place where a single thing divides into two or more parts, or one of the parts ○ *a fork in the road*

fork /fɔːrk/ *v* [I] ○ *You'll come to our house just before the road forks.*

PHRASAL VERB with fork

• **fork over** *something* [M] *infml* to give away something, esp. on demand ○ *He had to fork over $125 for the traffic ticket.*

forklift /ˈfɔːˌklɪft/ *n* [C] a vehicle with two bars in the front for moving and lifting heavy goods

forlorn /fɔːrˈlɔːrn, fər-/ *adj* looking or feeling alone and sad because you need help but do not expect to get it ○ *As I left little Bobby on his first day of school, he gave me such a forlorn look.*

form **COME TOGETHER** /fɔːrm/ *v* [I/T] to come together and make a particular order or shape ○ [+ *to* infinitive] *A crowd formed to watch the fire.* ○ [T] *Please form a single line.* ○ [T] *The geese flying overhead formed a V-shaped pattern.*

form /fɔːrm/ *n* [C] the shape or appearance of something ○ *The stadium was in the form of a circle.*

formation /fɔːrˈmeɪ·ʃən/ *n* [C/U] **1** the process by which something comes into existence or begins to have a particular order or shape ○ [U] *They called for the formation of a committee to investigate corruption.* **2** A formation is the particular form that something has taken, or the things or people having this form: [C] *unusual cloud formations* ○ [U] *The soldiers marched in formation* (= in an orderly arrangement).

formative /ˈfɔːr·mət̬·ɪv/ *adj* [not gradable] developing and not yet completely formed ○ *the formative years of adolescence*

BEGIN HAVING /fɔːrm/ *v* [T] to begin to have ○ *I formed the opinion that I was not really welcome there any more.*

BEGIN /fɔːrm/ *v* [T] to begin something, esp. organizing people or things ○ *We formed a community group to help people who are sick or disabled.* ○ *They formed a new publishing company.*

TYPE /fɔːrm/ *n* [C] a type or kind of something, or the particular way in which something exists ○ *I was always more interested in poetry than in other forms of literature.* ○ *She has a mild form of the flu and should be OK in a few days.* ○ *The medicine comes in the form of a liquid or pills.*

DOCUMENT /fɔːrm/ *n* [C] something, usually paper, that has spaces marked where you fill in information ○ *Fill out an application form and we will let you know if a job opens up.*

ART/MUSIC /fɔːrm/ *n* [C] **1** ***literature*** the organization, shape, and structure of a written work **2** ***art, music*** Form in a work of art or piece of music is the design or arrangement of it that it shares with other works of the same type

BEHAVIOR /fɔːrm/ *n* [U] the way in which someone does something ○ *He was in great form and won the golf tournament by 7 strokes.*

WORD FAMILY form			
Nouns	form formation reformation transformation reformer transformer	*Adjectives*	reformed formative
		Verbs	form reform transform

formal /ˈfɔːr·məl/ *adj* **1** using an agreed and often official or traditional way of doing things ○ *There are formal procedures for applying to become a US citizen.* **2** If a social occasion is formal, you wear traditional or very good clothes: *It was a formal affair, and men were supposed to wear dark suits or tuxedos.* **3** Formal language is the language used esp. in writing in situations that are official and which is often more difficult than the language used in ordinary conversation. **4** Formal education/training is the learning of a subject or skill from courses in a school: *His formal education ended at the sixth grade, but he became a millionaire at the age of thirty.*

formal /ˈfɔːr·məl/ *n* [C] a dance at which women wear fashionable, expensive dresses and men wear TUXEDOS or similar clothes

formally /ˈfɔːr·mə·li/ *adv* ○ *You will receive a letter formally confirming* (= officially stating) *your appointment as professor of English.*

formalize /ˈfɔːr·məˌlɑɪz/ *v* [T] to make something official ○ *The trade agreement was formalized with Congress's approval of the bill.*

formality /fɔːrˈmæl·ət̬·i/ *n* **1** something done because it follows the usual or accepted way of doing things, although it may not be important ○ [C] *There were only a few legal formalities to be finished, and he would be free to leave the country.* ○ [C] *It was just a mere formality.* **2** Formality is also formal behavior or appearance. ➤ Confusables: **typical or formal?** at TYPE CHARACTERISTICS

WORD FAMILY formal			
Nouns	formal formality informality	*Adjectives*	formal informal
		Adverbs	formally informally
Verbs	formalize		

format Ⓐ /ˈfɔːr·mæt/ *n* [C] the way in which something is shown or arranged ○ *The two candidates could not agree on the format of the TV debate.*

format /ˈfɔːr·mæt/ *v* [T] **-tt-** If you format a text or a disk on a computer, you organize it according to chosen patterns.

formation /fɔːrˈmeɪ·ʃən/ *n* [C/U] ***earth science*** a large area of rock that has characteristics different from the land surrounding it

former **EARLIER** /ˈfɔːr·mər/ *adj* [not gradable] of an earlier time, but not now ○ *The former president lives on his ranch.*

formerly /ˈfɔːr·mər·li/ *adv* [not gradable] before the present time or in the past ○ *Formerly, he had gone regularly to Europe, but now he seldom traveled.*

FIRST /ˈfɔːr·mər/ *n* [U] the first of two people, things, or groups previously mentioned ○ *Of the two suggestions, I prefer the former.* ○ Compare LATTER SECOND

formidable /ˈfɔːr·məd·ə·bəl, fɔːrˈmɪd-, fərˈmɪd-/ *adj* strong and powerful, and therefore difficult to deal with if opposed to you ○ *There were formidable obstacles to reaching an early settlement of the dispute.*

formula Ⓐ /ˈfɔːr·mjə·lə/ *n* [C/U] **1** the exact chemical parts that a mixture consists of ○ [C] *The company announced that it was changing its soft-drink formula to make it sweeter.* **2** Formula is a liquid food mixture that is fed to babies instead of mother's milk. **3** A formula is also any plan or method for doing something well: [C usually sing] *The formula for success in business, he said, is a willingness to take risks.* **4** ***mathematics*** A formula is an EQUATION (= set of numbers and letters representing two equal amounts) that shows how one amount depends on one or more other amounts.

formulation Ⓐ /ˌfɔːr·mjəˈleɪ·ʃən/ *n* [C/U] **1** the activity of creating or preparing something ○ *His main achievement was the formulation of compounds needed to sustain cells in test tubes.* **2** A formulation is also a particular combination of ideas, words, or substances: *The preservative has been phased out of most flu formulations because of side effects.*

formulate Ⓐ /ˈfɔːr·mjəˌleɪt/ *v* [T] to create something, esp. by putting together different parts ○ *The Administration said it was formulating a new policy for the Middle East.* ○ *New drugs are being formulated to combat AIDS.*

forsake /fərˈseɪk, fɔːr-/ *v* [T] *past simp.* **forsook**, *past part.* **forsaken** *fml* to leave forever or to give up completely ○ *I thought she might forsake ballet in favor of Irish dancing.*

fort /fɔːrt, fourt/ *n* [C] a building or group of buildings contained in an area enclosed by a strong wall and designed to be used by soldiers in defending against attack

forte /ˈfɔːr·teɪ, fɔːrt, fourt/ *n* [C usually sing] something that a person can do well; a strong ability ○ *Singing is definitely her forte.*

forth /fɔːrθ, fourθ/ *adv* [not gradable] out so that it can be seen or heard ○ *A round of applause burst forth.*

forthcoming Ⓐ **SOON** /fɔːrθˈkʌm·ɪŋ, fourθ-/ *adj* [not gradable] happening soon ○ *the forthcoming conference*

WILLING /fɔːrθˈkʌm·ɪŋ, foʊrθ-/ *adj* willing to give information or to talk; friendly and helpful ○ *He has not been forthcoming about the details of his contract.*

SUPPLIED /fɔːrθˈkʌm·ɪŋ, foʊrθ-/ *adj* [not gradable] supplied or offered when wanted ○ *No explanation for his absence was forthcoming.*

forthright /ˈfɔːr·θrɑɪt, ˈfoʊr-/ *adj* honest or direct in expressing one's thoughts or feelings ○ *forthright comments* ○ *She's pretty forthright about her opinions.*

fortieth /ˈfɔːrt̬·iː·əθ/ *adj, adv, n* ○ See at FORTY

fortify /ˈfɔːrt̬·əˌfɑɪ/ *v* [T] to strengthen something, esp. in order to protect it ○ *Property owners have to fortify their oceanfront homes against weather damage.* ○ *These reforms are aimed at fortifying the political system.*

fortified /ˈfɔːrt̬·əˌfɑɪd/ *adj* **1** *Children should not eat highly fortified cereals* (= ones with added healthful substances). **2** A fortified town has strong walls that can be defended against enemies.

fortification /ˌfɔːrt̬·ə·fəˈkeɪ·ʃən/ *n* ○ [U] *I had a cup of tea as fortification for the afternoon's work.* ○ [pl] *Those towers were part of the city's fortifications* (= buildings, walls, etc., built as protection).

fortitude /ˈfɔːrt̬·əˌtuːd/ *n* [U] bravery when dealing with pain or difficulty, esp. over a long period ○ *Throughout his illness, he showed great fortitude.*

fortnight /ˈfɔːrt·nɑɪt, ˈfoʊrt-/ *n* [C usually sing] *Br* a period of two weeks

fortress /ˈfɔːr·trəs/ *n* [C] a large, strong building or group of buildings that can be defended from attack

fortuitous /fɔːrˈtuː·ət̬·əs/ *adj* (esp. of something to your advantage) happening by chance ○ *We made a fortuitous escape.* ○ *The discovery of the files was fortuitous.*

fortuitously /fɔːrˈtuː·ət̬·ə·sli/ *adv* ○ *They had fortuitously been out of the house when the fire started.*

fortunate /ˈfɔːr·tʃə·nət/ *adj* receiving or bringing a good thing that was uncertain or unexpected ○ *a fortunate choice* ○ [+ to infinitive] *You're fortunate to have found such a pleasant house.* ○ [+ *that* clause] *It was fortunate that you left in time.*

fortunately /ˈfɔːr·tʃə·nət·li/ *adv* [not gradable] ○ *Fortunately we were already home when it started to snow.*

fortune **WEALTH** /ˈfɔːr·tʃən/ *n* [C] a very large amount of money or property ○ *They made a fortune in real estate.* ○ *This dress cost a (small) fortune* (= a lot of money).

CHANCE /ˈfɔːr·tʃən/ *n* [C/U] **1** the set of good or bad events that happen to you and have an effect on your life ○ [U] *He had the good fortune to be awarded a scholarship.* **2** If someone tells your fortune, that person tries to discover what will happen to you in the future, for example by looking at the lines on your hands or by using a special set of cards.

WORD FAMILY fortune

Nouns	fortune	*Adverbs*	fortunately
			unfortunately
Adjectives	fortunate		
	unfortunate		

fortune cookie *n* [C] a cookie containing a message, usually about your future, that you get at Chinese restaurants in the US

fortune teller *n* [C] a person who tells you what that person thinks will happen to you in the future

forty /ˈfɔːrt̬·i/ *number* 40 ○ *Forty children have signed up for the trip.* ○ *a forty-gallon tank*

forties, **40s**, **40's** /ˈfɔːrt̬·iz/ *pl n* the numbers 40 through 49 ○ *The temperature will be in the forties* (= between 40° and 49°) *today.* ○ *Our house was built in the forties* (= between 1940 and 1949). ○ *They are both in their forties* (= between 40 and 49 years old).

fortieth /ˈfɔːrt̬·iː·əθ/ *adj, adv, n* [C] **1** *He married in his fortieth year.* **2** A fortieth is one of forty equal parts of something.

forum /ˈfɔːr·əm, ˈfoʊr-/ *n* [C] an occasion or a place for talking about a matter of public interest ○ *The university sponsored a forum on affirmative action.*

forward **LEADING** /ˈfɔːr·wərd/ *adj* [not gradable] directed toward the front or in the direction you are facing, or directed toward the future ○ *a forward motion* ○ *the forward part of an airplane*

forward /ˈfɔːr·wərd/, **forwards** /ˈfɔːr·wərdz/ *adv* [not gradable] toward the front, toward the direction in which you are facing, or toward a future time or better condition ○ *I leaned forward and glared at her.* ○ *The project moved forward slowly.* ○ *Set your clocks forward one hour to daylight saving time.* ○ *(fig.) Because of the story in the paper, a witness came forward* (= spoke to authorities). ○ Compare BACKWARD TOWARD THE BACK

TOO CONFIDENT /ˈfɔːr·wərd/ *adj* too noticeable or confident; rude ○ *It was awfully forward of him to invite himself over for dinner.*

SEND /ˈfɔːr·wərd/ *v* [T] **1** to send E-MAIL to someone else or to a different address after you have received it ○ *I'll forward that e-mail to you.* **2** To forward something that you have received means to send it to a different place: *The post office will forward my mail while I'm away.*

SPORTS /ˈfɔːr·wərd/ *n* [C] a player whose position is nearer the opposing team's goal in team sports such as BASKETBALL, SOCCER, and HOCKEY

forwarding address *n* [C] the address where you want your mail sent after you have left the place where it was originally sent

forward-looking, **forward-thinking** *adj* planning for the future, esp. in a new or creative way

forwent /fɔːr ˈwent, four-/ *past simple of* FORGO

fossil /ˈfɑs·əl/ *n* [C] ***biology, earth science*** part of a plant or animal, or its shape, that has been preserved in rock or earth for a very long period

fossilize /ˈfɑs·əˌlɑɪz/ *v* [I] ***earth science*** to become a fossil

fossil fuel *n* [C] a fuel such as gas, coal, and oil that has been produced in the earth from plants and animals

fossil record *n* [C/U] ***earth science*** **1** the FOSSILs in a particular group of rocks that give information about how and when those rocks formed **2** The fossil record is also the set of all fossils together that can be used to tell the history of the earth.

foster TAKE CARE OF /ˈfɔːs·tər, ˈfɑs-/ *v* [T] to take care of a child as if it were your own, usually for a limited time, without being the child's legal parent ○ Compare ADOPT TAKE CHILD

foster /ˈfɔːs·tər, ˈfɑs-/ *adj* [not gradable] ○ *A social service agency placed the child with a foster family.*

ENCOURAGE /ˈfɔːs·tər, ˈfɑs-/ *v* [T] to encourage the development or growth of ideas or feelings ○ *I try to foster an appreciation for classical music in my students.*

Foucault pendulum /fuː ˈkoʊ ˈpen·dʒə·ləm/ *n* [C] ***earth science*** a PENDULUM (= weight on a long rod) that can be used to show that the earth spins around

fought /fɔːt/ *past simple and past participle of* FIGHT

foul UNPLEASANT /fɑʊl/ *adj* [-er/-est only] extremely unpleasant ○ *a foul odor* ○ *a foul mood* ○ *They were using foul language* (= rude or offensive language).

SPORTS /fɑʊl/ *n* [C] **1** (esp. in BASKETBALL) an act that is against the rules of a sport, sometimes causing injury to another player, or a punishment given to a player for breaking the rules ○ *an intentional foul* ○ *a flagrant foul* **2** In baseball, foul also means FOUL BALL.

foul /fɑʊl/ *v* [I/T] ○ [I] *Sahlstrom was fouled after the shot.*

MAKE DIRTY /fɑʊl/ *v* [T] to pollute something or make it dirty ○ *The oil slick fouled the California coastline.*

PHRASAL VERB with foul

• **foul up** *(something)* [M] *infml* to spoil or damage something, esp. by making a mistake or doing something stupid ○ *I think antipollution devices really foul up a lot of engines.* ○ *If you foul up, tell the president and correct it fast.* ○ Related noun: FOUL-UP

foul ball *n* [C] in baseball, a ball hit outside the playing field on either side

foul play *n* [U] a criminal, usually violent, act, esp. murder

foul shot *n* [C] in BASKETBALL, a FREE THROW

foul-up *n* [C] *infml* a big or stupid mistake that upsets people ○ *I do not allow any foul-ups in this company.* ○ Related verb: FOUL UP

found Ⓐ FIND /fɑʊnd/ *past simple and past participle of* FIND

BEGIN /fɑʊnd/ *v* [T] to bring something into existence ○ *She donated money to help found a wildlife refuge.* ○ *New Orleans was founded by the French in 1718.*

foundation Ⓐ /fɑʊn ˈdeɪ·ʃən/ *n* [U] ○ *The foundation of the children's home was made possible by a generous contributor.*

founder Ⓐ /ˈfɑʊn·dər/ *n* [C] ○ *She is the founder and managing director of the company.* ○ See also: FOUNDER

BASE /fɑʊnd/ *v* [T always + adv/prep] to base a belief, claim, idea, etc. on something ○ *This case was founded on insufficient evidence.*

foundation /fɑʊn ˈdeɪ·ʃən/ *n* [U] ○ *These charges are completely without foundation* (= false).

foundation Ⓐ BASE /fɑʊn ˈdeɪ·ʃən/ *n* [C] the base that is built below the surface of the ground to support a building ○ *a concrete foundation* ○ *(fig.) The two leaders have laid the foundations of a new era of cooperation between their countries.*

ORGANIZATION /foʊn ˈdeɪ·ʃən/ *n* [C] an organization that has been established to provide financial support for activities and groups that are useful or helpful ○ *the Ford Foundation*

founder /ˈfɑʊn·dər/ *v* [I] to fill with water and sink, or *fig.* to fail ○ *The ship foundered in a heavy storm.* ○ *(fig.) Plans for a new airport have foundered because of budget cuts.* ○ See also: FOUNDER at FOUND BEGIN

founding father *n* [C] ***world history*** a FOUNDER of a country, organization, or idea ○ *The Founding Fathers of the United States were the men who wrote and approved the US Constitution in 1787.*

foundry /ˈfɑʊn·dri/ *n* [C] a factory where metal is melted and poured into specially shaped containers to produce machine parts

fountain /ˈfɑʊnt·ᵊn/ *n* [C] a stream of water that is forced up into the air through a small hole, esp. for decorative effect, or the structure from which this flows ○ *the fountain in Central Park*

four /fɔːr, foʊr/ *number* **1** 4 ○ *A square has four sides.* ○ *a four-part television series* **2** Four can also mean four o'clock.

fourth /fɔːrθ, foʊrθ/ *adj, adv, n* [C] **1** *Mark finished fourth in the race.* ○ [C] *My birthday is on the fourth of December.* **2** A fourth is one of four equal parts of something.

four-leaf clover *n* [C] a CLOVER plant that has four leaves, instead of the usual three, and that some people think brings good luck

four-letter word *n* [C] a short, rude or offensive word

F

fourteen /fɔːrtˈtiːn, fourt-/ *number* 14 ○ *Fourteen people will be coming to dinner.* ○ *a fourteen-week program*
fourteenth /fɔːrtˈtiːnθ, fourt-/ *adj, adv, n* [C] **1** *the fourteenth edition of the book* ○ [C] *Could we arrange a meeting for the fourteenth of April?* **2** A fourteenth is one of fourteen equal parts of something.

Fourth of July *n* [C usually sing] the national holiday in the US that celebrates its independence from Great Britain in 1776 ○ *The Fourth of July is traditionally celebrated with fireworks.*

F

four-wheel drive *n* [U] a system by which the engine of a vehicle supplies power to all four wheels, so that it can travel easily over rough ground

fowl /fɑʊl/ *n* [C/U] *pl* **fowl, fowls** a bird of a type that is used to produce meat or eggs ○ [U] *I now eat more fish and fowl and less red meat.*

fox /fɑks/ *n* [C/U] a wild mammal belonging to the dog family which has a pointed face and ears, a wide furry tail, and often red-brown fur, or the fur of this animal ○ [C] *A fox who had smelled the chickens came out of the woods into the yard.*
foxy /ˈfɑk·si/ *adj* ○ *The company's foxy* (= quick and intelligent) *chairman outmaneuvered his competitors.*

foxhole /ˈfɑks·hoʊl/ *n* [C] a hole dug in the ground and used by soldiers as a shelter from enemy attack

foyer /ˈfɔɪ·ər, ˈfɔɪ·eɪ/ *n* [C] **1** a large, open area just inside the entrance of a public building such as a theater or hotel; LOBBY **2** A foyer is also the room in a house or apartment that leads from the front door to other rooms.

fracas /ˈfreɪ·kəs, ˈfræk·əs/ *n* [C] a noisy argument or fight ○ *The players got into a scuffle, both benches cleared, and some fans joined the fracas.*

fraction /ˈfræk·ʃən/ *n* [C] **1** ***mathematics*** a number that results from dividing one WHOLE NUMBER (= a number with no part of a number after it) by another ○ *1/4 and 0.25 are different ways of representing the same fraction.* **2** A fraction is also a very small part or amount of something: *Counterfeits are sold at a fraction of the cost of the genuine articles.* ○ *Juries often hear only a fraction of the story.*
fractional *adj* ***mathematics***

fractional distillation /ˈfræk·ʃən·əl ˌdɪs·təˈleɪ·ʃən/ *n* [U] ***chemistry*** the process of separating parts of a liquid by heating it gradually so that different parts become gas, rise up, then turn back into liquid that can be collected as they cool

fractious /ˈfræk·ʃəs/ *adj* tending to argue, fight, or complain, and hard to control ○ *fractious relationships* ○ *the fractious nature of politics*

fracture /ˈfræk·tʃər/ *v* [I/T] to crack or break something, esp. a bone ○ [T] *She fractured her skull in the accident.* ○ [I] *This mineral fractures along straight lines.*

fracture /ˈfræk·tʃər/ *n* [C/U] **1** *He had a hairline fracture of the toe* (= a thin crack in the bone). **2** ***earth science*** Fracture is also the way that a particular kind of rock usually breaks, or the shape of broken pieces.

fragile /ˈfrædʒ·əl, -ɑɪl/ *adj* easily damaged, broken, or harmed ○ *a fragile piece of metal* ○ *Their argument showed us how fragile the teammate relationship can be.* ○ *I feel fragile, as if a breath of wind could knock me over.*
fragility /frəˈdʒɪl·ət̬·i/ *n* [U] ○ *She was a strong woman, with no hint of fragility about her.*

fragment /ˈfræg·mənt/ *n* [C] a small piece or part, esp. one that is broken off of something ○ *a bone fragment* ○ *a fragment of Indian pottery* ○ *She read a fragment of the story.*
fragmented /ˈfrægˌment·əd/ *adj* separated into or consisting of several parts ○ *a fragmented narrative* ○ *a country fragmented by social strife*
fragmentary /ˈfræg·mənˌter·i/ *adj* existing only in small parts and not complete ○ *Tom talks in images that are fast and fragmentary.* ○ *The surviving evidence is fragmentary.*

fragrance /ˈfreɪ·grəns/ *n* [C] a sweet or pleasant smell ○ *The shampoo has a light fragrance of herb and plant extracts.*
fragrant /ˈfreɪ·grənt/ *adj* ○ *the fragrant bouquet of roses*

frail /freɪl/ *adj* [-er/-est only] physically weak, or easily damaged, broken, or harmed ○ *He's always in frail health.* ○ *The shirt is old and frail, and the threads look ready to part.*
frailty /ˈfreɪl·ti/ *n* [C/U] **1** [U] *Despite his frailty, he continued to travel.* **2** Frailty also means moral weakness: [C] *human frailties such as selfishness and greed*

frame BORDER /freɪm/ *n* [C] a border that encloses and supports a picture, mirror, etc. ○ *She put his picture in a silver frame.*
frame /freɪm/ *v* [T] to fix a border around a picture, photograph, etc., often with glass in front of it ○ *We had our wedding pictures framed.* ○ (*fig.*) *Her small face was framed by the open door.*

STRUCTURE /freɪm/ *n* [C] a structure that holds the parts of an object in position and gives them support ○ *The houses have wood frames built on concrete slabs.*
frames /freɪmz/ *pl n* the part of a pair of eyeglasses that holds the LENSES (= parts that you see through) in position

BODY /freɪm/ *n* [C] a person's body when referring to its size or structure ○ *He eased his lean frame into a chair.*

EXPRESS /freɪm/ *v* [T] to carefully plan or organize ideas, suggestions, methods, etc., in a particular way ○ *Their conclusions are framed in such a way that if one piece of evidence were shown to be false, the argument would be suspect.*
frame /freɪm/ *n*

MAKE GUILTY /freɪm/ *v* [T] *infml* to make a person seem to be guilty of a crime by providing false information ○ *It looked like somebody was trying to frame him.*

IDIOM with frame

• **frame of mind** someone's mood or the particular way someone thinks or feels about something ○ *That music puts me in a romantic frame of mind.*

frame of reference *n* [C] *pl* **frames of reference** **1** a set of ideas or facts that a person accepts and that influences the person's behavior, opinions, or decisions ○ *The report provided a common frame of reference for discussing public policy.* **2** ***physics*** A frame of reference is also a system of lines and clocks that you can use to measure the position and motion of a set of objects and events in relation to each other.

framework STRUCTURE /ˈfreɪm·wɜrk/ *n* [C] a structure around or over which something is built ○ *the steel framework of a bridge*

ORGANIZATION /ˈfreɪm·wɜrk/ *n* [C] the ideas, information, and principles that form the structure of an organization or plan ○ *They're operating within the framework of a military bureaucracy.* ○ *The agreement outlines a framework and schedule for resolving the issues.*

franchise BUSINESS /ˈfræn·tʃɑɪz/ *n* [C] a right to sell a company's products in a particular area using the company's name

VOTE /ˈfræn·tʃɑɪz/ *n* [U] ***politics & government*** the right to vote ○ *Women in the US won the franchise in 1920.*

frank /fræŋk/ *adj* honest, sincere, and truthful, even if there is a risk of causing bad feelings ○ *To be perfectly frank, I don't think you are as well qualified as some of the other candidates.*

frankly /ˈfræŋ·kli/ *adv* ○ *She spoke frankly about her troubled marriage.* ○ *Frankly, I'm worried.*

frankness /ˈfræŋk·nəs/ *n* [U] ○ *We appreciate your frankness.*

frankfurter /ˈfræŋk ˌfɜrt̬·ər/, *short form* **frank** /ˈfræŋk/ *n* [C] a long, tube-shaped, cooked SAUSAGE (= meat), usually eaten in a long ROLL (= loaf of bread); HOT DOG ○ *I'll have a frankfurter with mustard and sauerkraut.*

frantic HURRIED /ˈfrænt·ɪk/ *adj* done in a very great hurry and often in a state of excitement or confusion ○ *Rescuers made frantic efforts to dig out people buried by the mudslide.*

frantically /ˈfrænt·ɪ·kli/ *adv* ○ *Inside, decorators worked frantically to solve last-minute problems.*

EMOTIONAL /ˈfrænt·ɪk/ *adj* extremely upset, esp. because of anxiety or fear ○ *When his wife arrived at the hospital she was frantic with worry.*

frantically /ˈfrænt·ɪ·kli/ *adv* ○ *With his heart pounding, Maurin frantically hollered through his two-way radio to a co-worker inside the building.*

fraternal /frəˈtɜrn·əl/ *adj* relating to brothers, or friendly like brothers ○ *He's a member of a fraternal order/organization* (= organized group of men).

fraternal twin *n* [C usually pl] either of two people born to the same mother at the same time who came from different eggs, may be of different sexes, and do not always look similar ○ Compare IDENTICAL TWIN

fraternity /frəˈtɜr·nət̬·i/, *infml* **frat** /fræt/ *n* [C] **1** a social organization for male students at a college or university **2** A fraternity is also a group of people who have the same job or interest: *the coaching fraternity* ○ Compare SORORITY

fraternize /ˈfræt̬·ərˌnɑɪz/ *v* [I] to meet socially with someone who belongs to a different or opposing group ○ *The soldiers were told not to fraternize with any of the local people.*

fraud CRIME /frɔːd/ *n* [U] the crime of obtaining money or property by deceiving people ○ *Convicted of tax fraud, he was sentenced to two years in prison.*

fraudulent /ˈfrɔː·dʒə·lənt/ *adj* ○ *There's been a rise in fraudulent insurance claims.*

FALSE /frɔːd/ *n* [C] a person or thing that is not what it claims or pretends to be ○ *He says he's been everywhere and done everything, but I think he's a fraud.*

fraudulent /ˈfrɔː·dʒə·lənt/ *adj* ○ *fraudulent advertising*

fraught /frɔːt/ *adj* full of (unpleasant things such as problems or dangers) ○ *Writing about science at a popular level is a task fraught with difficulty.*

fray LOOSEN /freɪ/ *v* [I/T] to become or to cause the threads in cloth or rope to become slightly separated and loose at the edge or end ○ [I] *All his shirts are fraying at the collar.* ○ [I] (*fig.*) *My nerves are getting frayed* (= I am becoming nervous) *from the constant noise around here.*

FIGHT /freɪ/ *n* [U] **1** a fight or argument, esp. one in which several people take part **2** A fray is also a situation in which people or organizations compete forcefully: *A third buyer has entered the fray.*

frazzled /ˈfræz·əld/ *adj* tired and nervous or anxious, often because of having to deal with too many things at the same time ○ *She was a bit frazzled from all the media attention.*

freak UNUSUAL /friːk/, **freakish** /ˈfriː·kɪʃ/ *adj* [not gradable] extremely unusual or unlikely ○ *She died in a freak automobile accident.* ○ *A freak midsummer hailstorm caught us all by surprise.*

freak /friːk/ *n* [C] someone or something that is strange or unusual and not like others of its type ○ *In my school, everyone thought you were some kind of freak if you didn't like sports.*

ENTHUSIAST /friːk/ *n* [C] *infml* a person who is enthusiastic about the stated thing ○ *My eight-year-old grandson is a real sports freak.* ○ *This guy is a control freak* (= wants to control everything).

PHRASAL VERB with freak

• **freak** *(someone)* **out** [M] *slang* to be very excited or emotional, or to cause someone be this way ○ *Here in Texas they freak out when there's snow on* *the ground.* ○ *The bankruptcy scare that freaked out investors didn't bother the company's new chairman.* ○ *Her latest album just freaked me out.*

freckle /ˈfrek·əl/ *n* [C] a small brown spot on the skin, esp. on a light-skinned person ○ *The brothers were in their early teens, and both had reddish hair and freckles.*
freckled /ˈfrek·əld/ *adj* ○ *a freckled nose*

free **NOT LIMITED** /friː/ *adj, adv* [*-er/-est* only] not limited or controlled ○ [+ *to* infinitive] *You are free to come and go as you please.* ○ [+ *to* infinitive] *Please feel free to ask questions.* ○ *Free elections will be held in two months.*
free /friː/ *v* [T] ○ [+ *to* infinitive] *The inheritance freed him to travel.*
freely /ˈfriː·li/ *adv* ○ *The animals are allowed to roam freely instead of being kept in cages.* ○ *Everyone is encouraged to speak freely* (= talk honestly).

NOT IN PRISON /friː/ *adj, adv* not or no longer a prisoner or an enslaved person ○ *She left the court a free woman.* ○ *In the 1700s, Mamaroneck was home to a free black community.*
free /friː/ *v* [T]

NO CHARGE /friː/ *adj, adv* [not gradable] costing nothing; not needing to be paid for ○ *When you buy a dinner for over $10, you get a soda free.* ○ *We will install your washing machine* **free of charge** (= without cost).
-free /friː/ *suffix* ○ *tax-free* ○ *toll-free* ○ *The superintendent lives here rent-free.*

NOT BUSY /friː/ *adj* [not gradable] not doing anything planned or important, or not being used ○ *We have plans for Friday night but we're free the rest of the weekend.* ○ *I do a lot of reading in my free time.*

NOT HELD /friː/ *adj, adv* [*-er/-est* only] not held in a fixed position or not joined to anything ○ *He grabbed the free end of the rope.* ○ *Mechanics checked the plane to see if any of the bolts had worked themselves free.*
free /friː/ *v* [T] ○ *They worked to free the man trapped in the wreckage of his car.*
freely /ˈfriː·li/ *adv* ○ *The steering wheel should move freely.*

WITHOUT /friː/ *adj* [*-er/-est* only] not having something that is unwanted or unpleasant ○ *After many months of treatment, she was declared free of disease.*
free /friː/ *v* [T always + adv/prep] to release ○ *He longed to be freed of all his obligations.*

WORD FAMILY free			
Nouns	freebie freedom	*Verbs*	free
		Adverbs	free freely
Adjectives	free		

IDIOMS with free

• **free and clear** without debt or legal claims ○ *They paid off the mortgage and own their house free and clear.*
• **free lunch** something you get free that you usually have to work or pay for ○ *There's no such thing as a free lunch.* ○ *It may seem like a free lunch, but your tax dollars are still paying for it.*
• **free ride** the acceptance of your plans or ideas without having anyone question or criticize them ○ *No one has seriously examined the president's trade policy – he's gotten a free ride so far.*

PHRASAL VERB with free

• **free up** to make something available to be used ○ *I need to free up some time this weekend to finish the report.*

freebie /ˈfriː·bi/ *n* [C] *infml* something that is usually sold but that is given to you without your having to pay for it ○ *They're giving out freebies of a new diet drink.*

freedman /ˈfriːd·mən, -mæn/ *n* [C] *pl* **freedmen** ***US history*** an EMANCIPATED SLAVE

freedom /ˈfriːd·əm/ *n* [C/U] **1** the condition or right of being able or allowed to do whatever you want to, without being controlled or limited ○ *freedom of speech* ○ *If children aren't allowed some freedom, they won't learn to be independent.* ○ [U] *We were promised freedom from persecution.* **2** Freedom is also the state of not being in prison or in the condition of SLAVERY (= condition of being legally owned by someone else). **3** ***US history*** Freedoms are RIGHTS given by the CONSTITUTION LAWS and the BILL OF RIGHTS, such as the freedom of speech (= the right to say and write what you believe or think, with some limitations) and freedom of religion (= the right to worship or to take part in a religion).

Freedom Rider *n* [C] ***US history*** a person who challenged SEGREGATION laws in the southern US states during the 1960s

free enterprise *n* [U] ***social studies*** an economic system in which private businesses compete with each other to sell goods and services in order to make a profit

free fall **FALL** *n* [U] ***physics*** a fast fall from a great height under the influence of GRAVITY (= the natural force that attracts things toward the earth) without any other force acting to reduce speed ○ *The parachutists are briefly in free fall before opening their parachutes.*

LOSS *n* [U] a sudden, fast loss, for example in price, popularity, or value ○ *The government had to act to keep the dollar from going into free fall against other currencies.*

free-for-all *n* [C] an argument or fight in which many people take part

free hand *n* [U] the authority to do whatever you think is necessary ○ *The company has given me a free hand to negotiate a deal with the Japanese.*

freehand /ˈfriː·hænd/ *adj, adv* [not gradable] (of a design or picture) drawn while holding a pen, pencil, etc., without the help of any special equipment ○ *She made a freehand sketch of the layout of the apartment.*

freelance /ˈfriː·læns/ *adj, adv* [not gradable] working independently usually for various organizations rather than as an employee of a particular one ○ *a freelance musician/photographer/writer*
freelance /ˈfriː·læns/ *v* [I] ○ *She freelanced for years while her children were in school.*
freelancer /ˈfriːˌlæn·sər/, **freelance** /ˈfriː·læns/ *n* [C]

freeloader /ˈfriːˌloʊd·ər/ *n* [C] *disapproving* a person who has the advantage of something given, such as money, food, or a place to stay, without offering anything in exchange

freely /ˈfriː·li/ *adv* ○ See at FREE NOT LIMITED; FREE NOT HELD

free market *n* [C] ***social studies*** an economic system with only a small amount of government control, in which prices and earnings are decided by the level of demand for, and production of, goods and services ○ *a free-market economy*

free rein *n* [U] freedom to act and make decisions without first getting permission ○ *The young filmmakers were given free rein to experiment with new themes and techniques*

free speech *n* [U] the right to express your opinions publicly

freestanding /ˈfriːˌstæn·dɪŋ/ *adj* standing alone without needing to be attached to anything ○ *a freestanding sculpture*

freestyle /ˈfriː·stɑɪl/ *n* [U] a sports competition, esp. a swimming race, in which each competitor can choose to use any style or method, or a style of swimming in which you lie on your front and move first one arm then the other over your head, while kicking your legs

free throw *n* [C] (in BASKETBALL) an opportunity or attempt to score one or more points without opposition because of a FOUL committed by a member of the other team

free trade *n* [U] ***social studies*** the buying and selling of goods, without limits on the amount of goods that one country can sell to another, and without special taxes on the goods bought from a foreign country ○ *a free-trade agreement*

free verse *n* [U] ***literature*** a style of writing poems without regular rhythm or RHYME (= two or more words ending with the same sound)

freeway /ˈfriː·weɪ/ *n* [C] a wide road for fast moving traffic traveling long distances, with a limited number of places at which drivers can enter and leave it ○ *the Santa Monica freeway in California*

freewheeling /ˈfriˈhwiːl·ɪŋ, -ˈwiːl-/ *adj* [not gradable] willing to experiment and take risks by going beyond the usual rules or accepted ways of doing things ○ *There is an independence and freewheeling spirit in Alaska.*

free will *n* [U] the ability to act and make choices independent of any outside influence ○ *She signed the confession of her own free will.*

freeze /friːz/ *v* [I/T] *past simp.* **froze**, *past part.* **frozen 1** to become cold enough to become solid ○ [I] *The rainwater froze overnight, leaving the roads icy.* **2** If you freeze food, you preserve it by storing it at a very low temperature. **3** Someone such as a police officer who says freeze is ordering you not to move except as the person tells you: [I] *Freeze! Keep your hands up!* **4** To freeze something such as pay or prices is to fix them at a particular level and not allow any increases: [T] *The company has frozen salaries.* **5** To freeze money or property is to officially and legally prevent it from being used or moved: [T] *The government froze his assets.*
freeze /friːz/ *n* [C] **1** a period when the air temperature is low enough so that water will freeze ○ *The first freeze didn't come until mid-December.* **2** A freeze is a temporary stopping of something: *The company has imposed a wage/hiring freeze.*
freezing /ˈfriː·zɪŋ/ *adj* [not gradable] **1** *We can expect freezing temperatures all week.* **2** *fig.* Freezing also means very cold: *It's freezing in here – turn off the air conditioner!*
freezer /ˈfriː·zər/ *n* [C] an electrically powered container or part of a REFRIGERATOR that freezes foods so that they can be preserved safely for a long time ○ *Put the steaks in the freezer.*

WORD FAMILY freeze

Nouns	freeze freezer	*Adjectives*	freezing frozen
Verbs	freeze		

PHRASAL VERBS with freeze

• **freeze out** *someone* [M] *infml* to intentionally prevent someone from being involved in an activity ○ *They tried to freeze me out of the bonus money.*
• **freeze over** to become covered with ice ○ *By January, the lake had started to freeze over.*

freeze-dry *v* [T] **-dries**, *pres. part.* **-drying**, *past* **-dried** to preserve something, esp. food, by freezing and then drying it ○ *freeze-dried instant coffee*

freezing /ˈfriː·zɪŋ/ *n* [U] ***chemistry*** the change or process of changing from a liquid to a solid substance ○ Compare MELTING

freezing point *n* [C] ***chemistry***, ***earth science*** the temperature at which a liquid becomes solid ○ Compare BOILING POINT

freight /freɪt/ *n* [U] **1** goods that are transported from one place to another by ship, aircraft, train, or truck ○ *Most planes carry both freight and passengers.* **2** A freight train is a train that carries only goods.
freighter /ˈfreɪt̬·ər/ *n* [C] a large ship or aircraft for carrying goods

French bread /ˈfrentʃ·bred/ *n* [U] a type of usually white bread in the form of a long, thin loaf with a hard CRUST (= outer layer)

French Canadian /ˈfrentʃ·kəˈneɪd·iː·ən/ *n* [C] a person of or coming from the part of Canada where French is the most important language
French Canadian /ˈfrentʃ·kəˈneɪd·iː·ən/ *adj* [not gradable]

French fries /ˈfrentʃ·frɑɪz/, **fries** /ˈfrɑɪz/, **French-fried potatoes** /ˈfrentʃˌfrɑɪd·pəˈteɪţ·əz, -oʊz/ *pl n* long, thin pieces of potato that are fried and eaten hot ○ *I'd like a hamburger and French fries.*

French horn /ˈfrentʃˈhɔːrn/ *n* [C/U] a BRASS musical instrument shaped in a circle, with keys that are pressed to vary the notes and played by blowing into it, or this type of instrument generally; a HORN

French toast /ˈfrentʃˈtoʊst/ *n* [U] bread that has been put in a mixture of egg and milk and then fried, and which is usually eaten at breakfast

F

frenetic /frəˈneţ·ɪk/ *adj* involving a lot of movement or activity; extremely active, excited, or uncontrollable ○ *Americans like fast cars, fast-food restaurants, and a frenetic pace of life.*

frenzy /ˈfren·zi/ *n* [C/U] excited, uncontrollable, and sometimes violent behavior or emotion ○ [C usually sing] *Duncan's game-winning shot sent the crowd into a frenzy.* ○ [C usually sing] *The Saturday night sale can best be described as a buying frenzy.*
frenzied /ˈfren·ziːd/ *adj* ○ *a frenzied crowd*

frequency /ˈfriː·kwən·si/ *n* [C] ***physics*** the number of times that a WAVE ENERGY FORM is produced within a particular period, esp. within one second ○ *Dogs can hear very high frequencies.*

frequent COMMON /ˈfriː·kwənt/ *adj* happening often; common ○ *She makes frequent trips home to Beijing.*
frequently /ˈfriː·kwənt·li/ *adv* ○ *I frequently disagree with him.* ○ *I moved much more frequently than I wanted to.*
frequency /ˈfriː·kwən·si/ *n* [U] the number of times something is repeated, or the fact of something happening often ○ *Houses are sold here with greater frequency than in most other parts of the country.*

VISIT /friːˈkwent, ˈfriː·kwənt/ *v* [T] to often be in or often visit a particular place ○ *They go to clubs frequented by artists.*

WORD FAMILY frequent			
Nouns	frequency	*Verbs*	frequent
Adjectives	frequent infrequent	*Adverbs*	frequently infrequently

frequent flier, **frequent flyer** *n* [C] someone who can get special benefits for flying a lot on a particular company's aircraft

fresh RECENTLY GROWN/COOKED /freʃ/ *adj* [-*er*/-*est* only] **1** (of food or flowers) recently picked, made, or cooked ○ *fresh fruit/vegetables* ○ *fresh-baked bread* ○ *Elise is in the garden cutting some fresh flowers for the table.* ○ *There's a fresh pot of coffee on the stove.* **2** Fresh food is also food in a natural condition rather than artificially preserved by a process such as freezing.

RECENT /freʃ/ *adj* [-*er*/-*est* only] recently made or done, and not yet changed by time ○ *The events of last year are still fresh in people's minds.*
freshly /ˈfreʃ·li/ *adv* [not gradable] ○ *I just love the smell of freshly cut grass.*

DIFFERENT /freʃ/ *adj* different or additional; replacing what exists ○ *He's got a fresh way of looking at old material.*
freshen /ˈfreʃ·ən/ *v* [T] ○ *Can I freshen your drink* (= fill your glass again)*?*

COOL /freʃ/ *adj* [-*er*/-*est* only] (of air) clean and cool, in a way thought typical of air away from cities and outside buildings ○ *How can we keep the kids indoors when they want to play in the fresh air?*
freshen /ˈfreʃ·ən/ *v* [I/T] ○ [I] *The wind freshened* (= became stronger and cooler) *and dragged my hair across my eyes.*

CLEAN /freʃ/ *adj* [-*er*/-*est* only] clean and pleasant ○ *fresh bed linens* ○ *the fresh smell of pine trees*
freshen /ˈfreʃ·ən/ *v* [T] ○ *These mints are supposed to freshen your breath.*

NOT SALTY /freʃ/ *adj* [not gradable] (of water) from rivers and lakes and therefore not salty ○ *Rainfall is the sole source of the island's fresh water.*

NOT TIRED /freʃ/ *adj* [-*er*/-*est* only] energetic and enthusiastic; not tired ○ *I awoke feeling fresh and ready to go.*

TOO CONFIDENT /freʃ/ *adj* [-*er*/-*est* only] being too confident and showing a lack of respect ○ *Don't get fresh with me, young woman!*

WORD FAMILY fresh			
Nouns	freshness refresher refreshment	*Verbs*	freshen refresh
		Adverbs	freshly refreshingly
Adjectives	fresh refreshing		

IDIOMS with fresh

• **fresh out of** *something* having just finished or sold all of something ○ *We're fresh out of oranges, would you like an apple?*
• **fresh out of** *somewhere*, **fresh from** *somewhere* having just arrived from somewhere ○ *We hired her fresh out of college.*
• **fresh start** an opportunity to begin something again ○ *Ramirez is looking forward to a fresh start with his new team.*

PHRASAL VERB with fresh

• **freshen up** to do something to make yourself cleaner or neater, esp. to wash your face and hands and arrange your hair ○ *Velma disappeared into the ladies' lounge, saying that she needed to freshen up before supper.*

freshman /ˈfreʃ·mən/ *n* [C] *pl* **-men** a student in the first year of a program of study in a college, university, or HIGH SCHOOL (= a school for students aged 14 to 18) ○ *She is a freshman at Harvard.*

freshwater /ˈfreʃˌwɔːţ·ər, -ˌwɑţ·ər/ *adj* relating to, living in, or consisting of water that does not contain salt ○ *The village is near a freshwater pond.*

fret WORRY /fret/ *v* [I] **-tt-** to worry or be unhappy about something ○ *Don't fret – I'm sure we'll find the kitten.*

fretful /ˈfret·fəl/ *adj* ○ *She fell into a fretful sleep.*

RAISED BAR /fret/ *n* [C] a thin, slightly raised metal bar, several of which are positioned across the NECK (= long, narrow part) of some musical instruments, such as a guitar

Freudian /ˈfrɔɪd·iː·ən/ *adj* [not gradable] relating to the ideas or methods of Sigmund Freud about the way in which people's hidden thoughts and feelings influence their behavior

Freudian slip *n* [C] an act of saying something you do not mean to say that shows your hidden thoughts

friar /ˈfrɑɪ·ər, frɑɪr/ *n* [C] a member of a religious group of men who often work as teachers

friction FORCE /ˈfrɪk·ʃən/ *n* [U] ***physics*** the force that works against an object as it slides along the surface of another object or moves through a liquid or gas ○ *A gasoline engine loses over 70 percent of its energy to friction and heat.*

frictional /ˈfrɪk·ʃən·əl/ *adj* [not gradable] ***physics***

frictionless /ˈfrɪk·ʃən·ləs/ *adj* ***physics***

DISAGREEMENT /ˈfrɪk·ʃən/ *n* [U] disagreement or dislike caused by people having different opinions ○ *There's less friction in relationships when you use teamwork.*

Friday /ˈfrɑɪd·i, -eɪ/, *abbreviation* **Fri.** *n* [C/U] the day of the week after Thursday and before Saturday

fridge /frɪdʒ/ *n* [C] *infml* a REFRIGERATOR

friend /frend/ *n* [C] **1** a person you know well and like a lot, but who is usually not a member of your family ○ *I dreamed my school friends were being chased by a whale.* ○ *Today I got a call from a friend of mine.* ○ *Chloë was her best friend.* ○ *I moved to California, made friends* (= became friends with people), *and started dating.* **2** Friend can also be used when you are speaking to someone: *Well, friends, I think it's time to go.* **3** A person or organization that is a friend to/of a group or organization helps and supports it: *The president has been no friend to small business.* ○ *The Senator was a friend of business interests.*

friendly /ˈfren·dli/ *adj* **1** having an attitude or acting in a way that shows that you like people and want them to like and trust you ○ *They were friendly people.* ○ *She had a bright, friendly smile.* **2** If you describe a place as friendly, you mean that it is pleasant and comfortable: *It's a very friendly city.* **3** If countries or organizations are friendly, they are willing to help each other: *Sometimes an ambassador will get too friendly with the local dictator.* **4** Friendly is also used as a combining form to mean easy to be comfortable with or not damaging: *user-friendly technology* ○ *a family-friendly film*

friendship /ˈfrend·ʃɪp/ *n* [C/U] a friendly relationship, or the state of being friends ○ [C] *Their friendship goes back 25 years.* ○ [U] *I value friendship above all else.*

WORD FAMILY friend

Nouns	friend	Adjectives	friendly
	friendship		unfriendly
	unfriendliness	Verbs	befriend

WORD CHOICES friend

The words **chum** and **pal** are informal words for "friend."

*Pete was there with a couple of his **chums**.*

An **old friend** is someone you have known and liked for many years.

*Rachel is one of my **oldest friends**.*

An **acquaintance** is someone you know, but do not know well.

*He had a few business **acquaintances**.*

A confidant is a friend whom you can talk to about your feelings and secrets.

*Sarah was my **confidant** throughout this period and I told her everything.*

A group of friends with similar interests are sometimes described informally as a **crowd**.

*"Who was there?" "Oh, you know, Dave, Fiona, and all that **crowd**."*

The informal word **crony** is sometimes used disapprovingly to describe one of a group of friends who help each other in an unfair way.

*He always gives his **cronies** all the best jobs.*

fries /frɑɪz/ *pl n* FRENCH FRIES.

frieze /friːz/ *n* [C] a narrow strip of decoration, often cut from stone or wood and usually placed at the top of a wall

frigate /ˈfrɪg·ət/ *n* [C] a small, fast military ship

fright /frɑɪt/ *n* [C/U] the feeling of fear, esp. if felt suddenly, or an experience of fear which happens suddenly ○ [U] *When the rescue team reached him, he was shaking with fright.* ○ [C usually sing] *You gave her a fright turning the lights out like that.*

frighten /ˈfrɑɪt·ən/ *v* [T] ○ *Be quiet or you'll frighten the deer.*

frightened /ˈfrɑɪt·ənd/ *adj* ○ *She was too frightened to enter the room alone.*

frightening /ˈfrɑɪt·ən·ɪŋ/ *adj* **1** *a frightening situation* **2** Frightening can also mean extreme: *My car insurance payments are frightening.*

frighteningly /ˈfrɑɪt·ən·ɪŋ·li/ *adv* ○ *His heart rate changed frighteningly.*

frightful /ˈfrɑɪt·fəl/ *adj* shocking or extremely unpleasant ○ *People sometimes do frightful things to their pets.*

WORD FAMILY fright

Nouns	fright	Verbs	frighten
Adjectives	frightened	Adverbs	frighteningly
	frightening		frightfully
	frightful		

F

WORD CHOICES fright

Other common ways of saying "frightened" are **afraid** and **scared.**

If someone is extremely frightened, then you can use adjectives like **petrified, terrified, panic-stricken,** or the informal phrase **scared to death.**

*I'm **terrified** of flying.*

*She was **panic-stricken** when her little boy disappeared.*

*He's **scared to death** of having the operation.*

If someone is frightened because he or she is worrying about something, then you can use the adjectives **afraid** or **worried.**

*I'm **worried** that something will go wrong.*

If someone is frightened about something that might happen in the future, you can use the adjectives **apprehensive** or **uneasy.**

*He's a bit **apprehensive** about living away from home.*

To talk about things that make you feel uncomfortable and scared, you could use the phrase **give someone the creeps.**

*Being alone in that big house **gives me the creeps.***

To talk about something that is frightening in a shocking way, you could use the adjective **hair-raising.**

*The pilots are trained to do **hair-raising** stunts at low altitude.*

frightful /ˈfrɑɪt·fəl/ *adj* great or extreme ○ *The weather is just too frightful to go out.*

frightfully /ˈfrɑɪt·fə·li/ *adv* ○ *She's frightfully smart.*

frigid /ˈfrɪdʒ·əd/ *adj* extremely cold ○ *frigid weather/air/water* ○ *It's frigid in here – could you turn down the air-conditioning?*

frill DECORATION /frɪl/ *n* [C] a long, narrow strip of folded cloth that is sewn along the edge of a piece of clothing or material for decoration

frilly /ˈfrɪl·i/, **frilled** /frɪld/ *adj* ○ *She wore a frilly white dress.*

ADDITIONAL ITEM /frɪl/ *n* [C] something additional that is not necessary ○ *The frills on that car are nice, but except for air-conditioning, I don't want them.*

fringe EDGE /frɪndʒ/ *n* [C] the outer or less important part of an area, group, or activity ○ *There is some industry on the fringes of the city.* ○ *His organization is a fringe group* (= one that represents the views of a small number of people).

fringe /frɪndʒ/ *v* [T] ○ *The coast is fringed with islands and beaches.*

DECORATION /frɪndʒ/ *n* [C] a decorative edge of narrow strips of material or threads on a piece of clothing or material

fringed /frɪndʒd/ *adj* [not gradable] ○ *a fringed jacket/scarf* ○ *a fringed rug*

fringe benefit *n* [C usually pl] something useful you get because of your job in addition to your pay ○ *Fringe benefits here include health insurance, three weeks' vacation, and tuition reimbursement*

Frisbee /ˈfrɪz·bi/ *n* [C/U] *trademark* a plastic disk that is thrown between people as a game, or the game of throwing this disk ○ [U] *Do you want to play Frisbee?*

frisk /frɪsk/ *v* [T] to use your hands to search someone's clothes and body for hidden objects or weapons ○ *I was frisked when we went through security at the airport.*

frisky /ˈfrɪs·ki/ *adj* (of a person or an animal) playful or very active ○ *a frisky puppy*

frisk /frɪsk/ *v* [I] to move around in a happy, energetic way ○ *The dog ran ahead, frisking in the brush.*

fritter /ˈfrɪt̬·ər/ *n* [C] pieces of fried BATTER (= a mixture of flour, egg, and milk) usually containing fruit, vegetables, or meat ○ *corn/potato/apple fritters*

PHRASAL VERB with fritter

• **fritter away** *something* [M] *disapproving* to waste money, time, or an opportunity ○ *Retirees must plan how to fill their hours or they risk frittering the time away.*

frivolity /frɪ ˈvɑl·ət̬·i/ *n* [C/U] foolish behavior, or something silly or unimportant ○ [U] *You shouldn't treat such a serious subject with frivolity.*

frivolous /ˈfrɪv·ə·ləs/ *adj* (of people) behaving in a silly and foolish way, or (of activities or objects) silly or unimportant ○ *I'm very frivolous – I just like to have fun.* ○ *With our justice system there are a lot of frivolous cases that go to court.*

frivolously /ˈfrɪv·ə·lə·sli/ *adv* ○ *We don't have a monthly budget, but we don't spend frivolously either.*

frizzy /ˈfrɪz·i/ *adj* (of hair) having small, tight curls and not being smooth or shiny

frizz /frɪz/ *v* [I/T] *infml* ○ [T] *The rain frizzes my hair.*

frizz /frɪz/ *n* [U] ○ *She had a huge frizz of red hair.*

frog /frɔːɡ, frɑɡ/ *n* [C] a small animal that has smooth skin, lives in water and on land, has long powerful back legs with which it jumps from place to place, and has no tail

IDIOM with frog

• **a frog in** *your* **throat** difficulty speaking because your throat feels dry ○ *I had a frog in my throat, and I had to clear my throat several times before I could answer.*

frolic /ˈfrɑl·ɪk/ *v* [I] *pres. part.* **frolicking,** *past* **frolicked** to behave in a happy and playful way ○ *A group of children were frolicking on the beach.*

frolic /ˈfrɑl·ɪk/ *n* [C] ○ *Some people think of skiing as a wintertime frolic.*

from PLACE /frʌm, frɑm, frəm/ *prep* used to show the place where someone or something starts moving or traveling ○ *He took a handkerchief from his pocket.* ○ *She ran away from home.* ○ *The boy cried and cried, rocking* **from side to side** (= to the left and right).

TIME /frʌm, frɑm, frəm/ *prep* used to show the time when something starts or the time when it was made or first existed ○ *Here's a song from the 60s.* ○ *I'm leaving a week from Thursday* (= one week after Thursday). ○ *The class ends at 2:30 and* **from then on** (= starting at that time and then continuing) *I'll be at the library.*

DISTANCE /frʌm, frɑm, frəm/ *prep* used to show the distance between two places ○ *We're about a mile from home.*

ORIGIN /frʌm, frɑm, frəm/ *prep* used to show the origin of something or someone ○ *I heard music coming from my room.* ○ *Someone from the bank just called.* ○ *Where are you from?* ○ *US Route 1 runs from Maine to Florida.*

MATERIAL /frʌm, frɑm, frəm/ *prep* used to show the material of which something is made ○ *The desk is made from pine.*

RANGE /frʌm, frɑm, frəm/ *prep* used to show where a range of numbers, prices, or items begins ○ *Tickets will cost from $10 to $45.* ○ *Everyone from the oldest to the youngest had a good time.*

CHANGE /frʌm, frɑm, frəm/ *prep* used to show the original state of someone or something that is changing or has changed ○ *She has been promoted from manager to vice president.* ○ *Things went from bad to worse.*

CAUSE /frʌm, frɑm, frəm/ *prep* used to show the cause of something or the reason why something happens ○ *Your child will benefit from piano lessons.*

CONSIDER /frʌm, frɑm, frəm/ *prep* used to show the facts or opinions you consider before making a judgment or decision ○ *From looking at the clouds, I would say it's going to rain later.* ○ *It's cheap, but not very good from a quality standpoint.*

REDUCE /frʌm, frɑm, frəm/ *prep* used to show that a larger amount is being reduced by a smaller amount ○ *Three from sixteen is thirteen.*

DIFFERENCE /frʌm, frɑm, frəm/ *prep* used to show a difference between two people or things ○ *It's hard to tell one sister from the other.*

PROTECTION /frʌm, frɑm, frəm/ *prep* used to show what someone is being protected against ○ *They found shelter from the storm under a large oak tree.*

PREVENTION /frʌm, frɑm, frəm/ *prep* used to show what someone cannot do or know, or what cannot happen ○ *High rents keep us from moving to a larger apartment.*

IDIOMS with from

• **come from the heart**, **be from the heart** to be sincere ○ *Her speech came from the heart.*
• **from A to Z** including all the things involved ○ *I know that my parents will take care of everything from A to Z if I ask them.*
• **from far and wide** from many places ○ *People came from far and wide to see the parade.*
• **from head to toe** completely ○ *She was dressed in red from head to toe.*
• **from one day to the next** before each day happens ○ *I never know what I'll be doing from one day to the next.*
• **from scratch** completely from the beginning ○ *Can we fix the current computer system, or would it be better to start from scratch with a new system?*
• **from the bottom of** *your* **heart** very sincerely ○ *I'll always love you, and I mean it from the bottom of my heart.*
• **(straight) from the horse's mouth** directly from the person who has personal knowledge of the matter ○ *I know it's true, because I got it straight from the horse's mouth – Katie told me herself.*
• **from time to time** sometimes, but not regularly ○ *I still think of her from time to time.*
• **from top to bottom** completely ○ *They cleaned the house from top to bottom.*

frond /frɑnd/ *n* [C] a large, usually divided, leaf, esp. of a FERN or PALM TREE

front **PLACE** /frʌnt/ *n* [C] **1** the most forward position or most important side of an object or surface ○ *The front of the house faces Peach Street.* ○ *My little boy can't eat ice cream without most of it dripping down the front of his shirt.* ○ *You'll find the date of publication in the front of the book.* ○ *I like to sit near the front of the plane so that I can be among the first to get off.* ○ *Do you want me to lie on my front* (= the side of my body that faces forward) *or on my back?* ○ *Would you like me to sit in the front* (= most forward seat) *or the back of the car?* ○ *Dad pushed Matthew in the stroller while David and Stephen walked* **in front** (= farther forward than the others). **2** in a position close to the most forward or most important part ○ *They chatted for a while in front of the apartment house.* **3** Someone who is **in front of** someone else is in a position directly forward of that person: *Carla and Bob were sitting in front of me at the movie.*

front /frʌnt/ *adj* [not gradable] ○ *I'd like seats in the front row of the balcony.* ○ *Alice designed the front cover of the book.* ○ *I always go in through the front door instead of going around to the back.*

front /frʌnt/ *v* [I/T] to face or be next to something ○ [I/T] *Houses fronting (on) the ocean are the most expensive.*

frontal /ˈfrʌnt·əl/ *adj* [not gradable] at, from, or toward the front ○ *a frontal attack/assault*

AREA OF ACTIVITY /frʌnt/ *n* [C usually sing] **1** a particular area of activity ○ *Now let's take a look at news on the health front.* ○ *I'm not having much luck on the job front.* **2** During a war, a front is a particular place of directed military activity.

APPEARANCE /frʌnt/ *n* [U] **1** an appearance that a person chooses to show to others instead of showing his or her true feelings ○ *Even though he doesn't like his in-laws, he always puts on a cheerful front when they come to visit.* **2** A front can also be a person, group, or thing used to hide the real character of a secret or illegal activity: *The society was a front for making illegal political contributions.*

WEATHER /frʌnt/ *n* [C] ***earth science*** the advancing edge of a mass of cold or warm air ○ *a cold/warm front*

POLITICAL GROUP /frʌnt/ *n* [C usually sing] an organization of political groups united to put forward ideas or programs that they share ○ *The*

Animal Liberation Front promised to continue targeting the company until all animal testing stops.

IDIOMS with front

• **in front of** done or said when the person you are talking about is present ○ *Why did you have to embarrass me in front of all those people?*

• **on the front burner, on** *someone's* **front burner** getting or needing immediate attention ○ *A few important members of Congress are making an effort to keep human rights on the front burner.*

frontage /ˈfrʌnt·ɪdʒ/ *n* [C] the front part of a building or land that faces a road or river

frontier /frʌn ˈtɪr/ *n* [C] **1** a border between two countries, or (esp. in the past in the US) a border between developed land where white people live and land where Indians live or land that is wild ○ *It was a movie about the hardships of frontier life in the northwest.* **2** *fig.* A frontier is also a border between what is known and what is not known: *the frontiers of knowledge*

front-runner /ˈfrʌnt ˈrʌn·ər/ *n* [C] the person, idea, or product that seems most likely to succeed ○ *With polls showing Schaefer ahead by 20 percentage points, he's clearly the front-runner.*

frost **COLD** /frɔːst/ *n* [U] ***earth science*** water in the air that freezes when it touches a cold surface and forms a white, powdery layer ○ *There was frost on the grass in the early morning.* ○ *An early frost killed some of my tomatoes.*

frost /frɔːst/ *v* [I/T] ○ [I] *The windshield frosted up overnight.*

frosty /ˈfrɔː·sti/ *adj* covered with frost, or with something that looks like frost ○ *We each had a root beer served in a frosty glass with a big handle.*

COVER CAKE /frɔːst/, **ice** *v* [T] to cover a cake with a thin layer of sugar mixed with a liquid

frosting /ˈfrɔː·stɪŋ/ *n* [U] ○ *chocolate/vanilla frosting*

frostbite /ˈfrɔːst·bɑɪt/ *n* [U] injury to body tissues, esp. the fingers and toes, caused by freezing

frostbitten /ˈfrɔːst ˌbɪt·ᵊn/ *adj* (of body tissues) injured from having been frozen ○ *Rescuers found two of the mountain climbers alive but badly frostbitten.*

frosted /ˈfrɔː·stəd/ *adj* [not gradable] (of glass) having an uneven surface so that it is not transparent ○ *frosted glass*

frosty /ˈfrɔː·sti/ *adj* unfriendly or not welcoming ○ *a frosty manner*

froth /frɔːθ/ *n* [U] a mass of small bubbles, esp. on the surface of a liquid

frown /frɑʊn/ *v* [I] to bring your EYEBROWS together so that lines appear on your face above your eyes, in an expression of anger, disapproval, or worry ○ *For a moment he had frowned and looked annoyed.*

frown /frɑʊn/ *n* [C] ○ *Pierre's mouth tightened with a small frown.*

PHRASAL VERB with frown

• **frown on** *something/someone* to disapprove of something or someone ○ *You can wear jeans, but I think the restaurant frowns on shorts and sneakers.*

froze /froʊz/ *past simple of* FREEZE

frozen /ˈfroʊ·zən/ *past participle of* FREEZE

frugal /ˈfruː·gəl/ *adj* careful in spending money ○ *Lungren, a fiscal conservative when it comes to spending taxpayers' money, is frugal in his personal life as well.*

fruit **PLANT PART** /fruːt/ *n* [C/U] **1** an edible and usually sweet product of a plant or tree that contains seeds or a PIT (= large hard seed) ○ [C] *We eat a lot of fruits and vegetables at our house.* ○ [U] *I usually eat a piece of fresh fruit with my lunch.* **2** ***biology*** Fruit is also the part of a plant that contains the seed from which a new plant can grow.

fruity /ˈfruːt̬·i/ *adj* tasting or smelling like fruit ○ *The punch was pleasant and fruity.*

RESULT /fruːt/ *n* [C usually pl] the result of work or actions, esp. if pleasant or successful ○ *The fruits of economic growth are starting to make a difference in the lives of many workers.*

fruitful /ˈfruːt·fəl/ *adj* producing good results ○ *He had a long and fruitful career as a research chemist.*

fruitless /ˈfruːt·ləs/ *adj* unsuccessful or not productive ○ *After months of fruitless negotiations with team owners, the city withdrew its offer to build a new stadium.*

fruitcake **CAKE** /ˈfruːt·keɪk/ *n* [C] a cake containing small dried or sugar-covered fruit, nuts, and spices

PERSON /ˈfruːt·keɪk/ *n* [C] *slang* a crazy or unusual person ○ *His wife's a real fruitcake but they get along great.*

fruition /fruː ˈɪʃ·ən/ *n* [U] *fml* the state of having successfully completed an activity or plan ○ *The governor plans to use his considerable influence to bring the museum to fruition.*

fruity /ˈfruːt̬·i/ *adj* ○ See at FRUIT PLANT PART

frustrate **ANNOY** /ˈfrʌs·treɪt/ *v* [T] to annoy someone or cause someone to be disappointed or discouraged ○ *People are frustrated with the politicians.* ○ *Customer service is important, so businesses can't afford to frustrate customers.*

frustrated /ˈfrʌs ˌtreɪt̬·əd/ *adj* ○ *You just get so frustrated when everything in your vegetable garden is ripe and then the bugs get at them.* ○ *Frustrated residents protested the situation.*

frustrating /ˈfrʌs ˌtreɪt̬·ɪŋ/ *adj* ○ *I guess job opportunities at the top are improving for women, but it's such a slow process that it's frustrating.*

frustration /frʌs ˈtreɪ·ʃən/ *n* [C/U] disappointment or discouragement, or a discouraging situation ○ [U] *He finally quit in frustration.* ○ [U] *The teacher confirmed widespread frustration with the lack of up-to-date textbooks.* ○ [C] *You have to learn to cope with these frustrations.*

BLOCK /ˈfrʌs·treɪt/ *v* [T] to block something from being achieved; prevent the success of a plan or effort ○ *For now there are enough votes to frustrate the administration on issue after issue.*
frustrated /ˈfrʌsˌtreɪt̬·əd/ *adj* [not gradable] desiring something but not able to achieve it ○ *I'm a frustrated songwriter at heart.*
frustration /frʌsˈtreɪ·ʃən/ *n* [U] ○ *Our efforts to get funding to save the lighthouse met with frustration.*

fry /frɑɪ/ *v* [I/T] to cook food in hot oil or fat ○ [T] *She was frying eggs and getting the coffee ready.*
fried /frɑɪd/ *adj* [not gradable] ○ *We had fried chicken and mashed potatoes for supper.*
fries /frɑɪz/ *pl n short form of* FRENCH FRIES.

frying pan *n* [C] a flat metal pan with a long handle, used for frying food

ft. *n* [C] *pl* **ft.** *abbreviation for* FOOT MEASUREMENT

fudge CANDY /fʌdʒ/ *n* [U] a soft, creamy candy made from sugar, milk, butter, and chocolate or other flavoring

CHEAT /fʌdʒ/ *v* [I/T] to cheat about something slightly, esp. by not reporting facts accurately or not telling the exact truth ○ [T] *I think the company fudged the figures to make their losses look less than they were.*

fuel /ˈfjuː·əl, fjuːl/ *n* [C/U] a substance such as oil or gas that is used to provide heat or power, usually by being burned
fuel /ˈfjuː·əl, fjuːl/ *v* [T] to provide power to something ○ *The heating system is fueled by natural gas.*

fugitive /ˈfjuː·dʒət̬·ɪv/ *n* [C] a person who is running away, esp. from the police ○ *Three men escaped from the prison and were being sought as fugitives.*

fugue /fjuːg/ *n* [C] ***music*** a piece of music in which one tune is played or sung and then repeated in different ways to make HARMONY

fulcrum /ˈfʊl·krəm, ˈfʌl-/ *n* [C] ***physics*** the point of support for a LEVER (= bar used to move or raise something) ➤ Picture: **lever**

fulfill MAKE HAPPEN /fʊlˈfɪl/ *v* [T] to do something as promised or intended, or to satisfy your hopes or expectations ○ *She said the president had failed to fulfill his campaign promises.* ○ *He stayed an extra semester to fulfill his graduation requirements.* ○ *At the age of 45, she finally fulfilled her ambition to run a marathon.*
fulfillment /fʊlˈfɪl·mənt/ *n* [U] ○ *Morales said that owning his own home was the fulfillment of a dream.*

DEVELOP /fʊlˈfɪl/ *v* [T] to succeed in developing abilities or qualities to their fullest degree ○ *Her immediate goal was to complete her novel, but her long-term goal was to fulfill her potential as a writer.*
fulfilling /fʊlˈfɪl·ɪŋ/ *adj* ○ *I hope you can find a job that's really fulfilling.*
fulfillment /fʊlˈfɪl·mənt/ *n* [U] ○ *Workaholics can only find fulfillment in their work.*

full CONTAINING A LOT /fʊl/ *adj* having or containing a lot ○ *The glass is full, so be careful not to spill it.* ○ *This sweater is full of holes.* ○ *You're always so full of energy.* ○ *Don't talk with your mouth full* (= with food in your mouth)*!* ○ *I have a full schedule* (= a lot of activities planned) *next week.*

ATE ENOUGH /fʊl/ *adj* having eaten so much that you do not want to eat any more ○ *I'm so full I couldn't eat another bite.*

WHOLE /fʊl/ *adj* [not gradable] including all of something or everything; whole ○ *What should we do on our last full day in New York?*
full /fʊl/ *adv* [not gradable] ○ *The biting wind was blowing full in his face.*
fullness /ˈfʊl·nəs/ *n* [U] ○ *Life today doesn't have that fullness and beauty that it did when I was a young woman.*
fully /ˈfʊl·i, -li/ *adv* [not gradable] ○ *Have you fully recovered from your illness?* ○ *If you're not fully satisfied with your purchase, we'll refund your money.*

GREATEST POSSIBLE /fʊl/ *adj* [not gradable] the greatest possible; MAXIMUM ○ *We don't make full use of our basement.* ○ *My roommate's stereo was on* **full blast** (= as loudly as possible).
fully /ˈfʊl·i, -li/ *adv* [not gradable] ○ *Carrie has always participated fully in the life of the school.*

LARGE /fʊl/ *adj* [*-er/-est* only] (of clothing) loose or containing a lot of material, or (of the body) large and rounded ○ *full face/lips/mouth* ○ *The dress was tight at the waist with a very full skirt and puffy sleeves.*
fullness /ˈfʊl·nəs/ *n* [U] ○ *The ad claims you can increase the fullness of your hair naturally.*

STRONG /fʊl/ *adj* [*-er/-est* only] (of a flavor, sound, or smell) strong or deep ○ *A cello has a fuller sound than a violin.*

IDIOMS with full

• **full circle** returning to a previously held belief or position ○ *I left publishing, tried teaching and writing, and now I've come full circle back to publishing.*
• **full of** *your* **self** thinking that you are very important in a way that annoys other people ○ *I doubt he even thought about what you might need, he's so full of himself.*
• **(at) full throttle** moving or progressing as fast as possible ○ *She was roaring up the freeway at full throttle.* ○ *We're going ahead full throttle on this project.*
• *someone* **is full of it** *slang* someone is wrong or not telling the truth ○ *He's always saying he'll buy me things, but he's full of it.*
• **in full swing** at a stage when the level of activity is at its highest ○ *When we got there, the party was in full swing.* ○ *The economic recovery is now in full swing.*
• **know full well, understand/realize full well** to know something without a doubt ○ *You know full well that you're not supposed to take the car without asking me!* ○ **USAGE:** Used in a situation where someone knows something but does not act according to what they know.
• **on a full stomach** soon after you have eaten ○ *You might get sick if you go jogging on a full stomach.*

fullback /ˈfʊl·bæk/ *n* [C] **1** a player in some games who plays near the goal and tries to prevent the other team from scoring **2** In American football, a fullback sometimes catches the ball and runs with it to score a goal.

full-blown *adj* in its most developed or advanced form ○ *Aspirin reduces your chances of having a full-blown stroke.*

full-bodied *adj* having a lot of flavor ○ *These dark beans make a full-bodied cup of coffee.*

full-fledged *adj* completely developed or qualified ○ *She's a full-fledged member of the community.*

F

full grown *adj* completely grown ○ *This will be a big dog when it's full grown.*

full house *n* [C] a situation in which every seat in a room that is holding a public event has someone sitting in it ○ *For opening night we're expecting a full house.*

full-length **TALL** *adj* as tall as either a person or a room ○ *a full-length mirror* ○ *full-length windows*

CLOTHING *adj* designed to end just above your feet ○ *full-length coats*

COMPLETE *adj* giving complete treatment, or taking the usual amount of time ○ *a full-length biography* ○ *a full-length movie*

full moon *n* [C] a PHASE (= regular change in shape) of the moon in which all of its surface can be seen from the earth ➤ Picture: **moon**

full-scale *adj* using all the power and authority that is available ○ *The police have begun a full-scale investigation.*

full-sized *adj* larger than other things of the same type ○ *They bought a full-sized station wagon.*

full stop *n* [C] *Cdn, Br* a PERIOD MARK

full-time *adj* done for all the hours people usually work ○ *She was a full-time student.*

fumble /ˈfʌm·bəl/ *v* [I/T] **1** to feel around awkwardly, esp. with your hands ○ [I] *Jack fumbled in his pocket for the keys.* ○ [I] *My mind went blank, and I began to fumble for words.* **2** In some sports, esp. football, if you fumble the ball you fail to hold it after touching or carrying it.

fume /fjuːm/ *v* [I] to be very angry, sometimes without expressing it ○ *Days after the argument, he was still fuming.*

fumes /fjuːmz/ *pl n* harmful or strong-smelling gases or smoke ○ *Neighbors complain about fumes from the nearby sewage treatment plant.*

fumigate /ˈfjuː·məˌgeɪt/ *v* [I/T] to remove harmful insects, bacteria, or disease, using chemical gas or smoke ○ [T] *We had to fumigate the house to get rid of cockroaches.*

fumigation /ˌfjuː·məˈgeɪ·ʃən/ *n* [U]

fun /fʌn/ *n* [U] pleasure, enjoyment, amusement, or someone or something that causes this ○ *Everybody had a lot of fun at the party.* ○ *It's no fun having to work on Saturdays.* ○ *He studies French just for fun/for the fun of it.* ○ *I only said it* **in fun** (= as a joke).

fun /fʌn/ *adj* [not gradable] *infml* ○ *Going camping would be a really fun thing to do.* ○ *Cindy is a fun person* (= enjoyable to be with). ➤ Usage: **fun or funny?** at FUNNY AMUSING

IDIOM with fun

• **fun and games** enjoyable activities ○ *Being a comedian is not all fun and games.* ○ *These technological toys are more than just fun and games – they can teach kids things too.*

function Ⓐ **PURPOSE** /ˈfʌŋk·ʃən/ *n* [C/U] a purpose or duty, or the way something or someone works ○ [U] *The function of the veins is to carry blood to the heart.* ○ [C] *One of your functions as receptionist is to answer the phone.*

function Ⓐ /ˈfʌŋk·ʃən/ *v* [I] ○ *She quickly learned how the office functions.* ○ *I'm so tired today, I can barely function.* ○ *Our spare bedroom also* **functions as** *a study* (= is also used for that purpose).

functional Ⓐ /ˈfʌŋk·ʃən·əl, -ʃnəl/ *adj* intended to be used; practical rather than attractive ○ *Our furniture isn't very fancy, but it's functional.* ○ *Is the plumbing functional yet* (= does it work)?

functionally Ⓐ /ˈfʌŋk·ʃən·əl·i, -ʃnə·li/ *adv*

MATHEMATICAL RELATIONSHIP /ˈfʌŋk·ʃən/ *n* [C] ***mathematics*** a relationship between two sets in which each part of the first set is connected with just one member of the second set in number pairs

CEREMONY /ˈfʌŋk·ʃən/ *n* [C] a social event or official ceremony ○ *Morse went to the White House for a ceremonial function.*

fund Ⓐ /fʌnd/ *n* [C] a sum of money saved and made available for a particular purpose ○ *a scholarship fund for college students* ○ *the company's pension fund*

fund Ⓐ /fʌnd/ *v* [T] ○ *He plans to donate money to fund health centers.*

funder Ⓐ /ˈfʌn·dər/ *n* [C] ○ *It's the world's largest funder of education.*

funding Ⓐ /ˈfʌn·dɪŋ/ *n* [U] money made available for a particular purpose ○ *Doug is trying to get funding for his research.*

funds Ⓐ /ˈfʌndz/ *pl n* money, often money for a specific purpose ○ *I'm short of/low on funds at the moment.* ○ *The Brownies sold cookies to raise funds for their troop.*

WORD FAMILY fund

Nouns		Verbs	
	fund		fund
	funds		refund
	refund		
	funding		

fundamental Ⓐ /ˌfʌn·dəˈment·əl/ *adj* being the most basic or most important thing on which other things depend ○ *fundamental beliefs/principles* ○ *We need to make fundamental changes in the way we treat our environment.*

fundamentally Ⓐ /ˌfʌn·dəˈment·əl·i/ *adv* [not gradable] ○ *Their economy was fundamentally* (= basically) *in good shape.*

fundamentals /ˌfʌn·dəˈment·əlz/ *pl n* ○ *In the early grades, children learn the fundamentals of reading.*

Fundamental Counting Principle *n* [U] ***mathematics*** a rule that says if there are x ways in which one thing can be done, and y ways in which another thing can then be done, then there are x×y ways in which the two things can be done one after the other

fundamental force *n* [C] ***physics*** any of the four forces in nature that are responsible for the way that matter behaves: ELECTROMAGNETIC force GRAVITY, STRONG FORCE, and WEAK FORCE

fundamentalism /ˌfʌn·dəˈment·əlˌɪz·əm/ *n* [U] the belief that the traditional principles of a religion or set of beliefs should be maintained
fundamentalist /ˌfʌn·dəˈment·əl·əst/ *n* [C] ○ *She is religious but not a fundamentalist.*
fundamentalist /ˌfʌn·dəˈment·əl·əst/ *adj* ○ *fundamentalist groups*

fund-raiser *n* [C] a person or event that collects money, for example for a political organization or a CHARITY ○ *The Boy Scouts collect cans as a fund-raiser.*

fund-raising, **fundraising** /ˈfʌndˌreɪ·zɪŋ/ *n* [U] the activity of persuading people and organizations to give money for something ○ *The candidate raked in more than $4.9 million in cash from political fund-raising events.*

funeral /ˈfjuː·nə·rəl/ *n* [C] a ceremony honoring someone who has recently died, which happens before burying or burning the body

funeral home *n* [C] a place where the bodies of dead people are prepared to be buried or burned

fungus /ˈfʌŋ·gəs/ *n* [C/U] *pl* **fungi** ***biology*** a plant without leaves, flowers, or color that lives on other plants or on decaying matter

funk **UNHAPPY** /fʌŋk/ *n* [U] the state of being unhappy and without hope ○ *The team's been in a funk, losing three of the last four games.*

MUSIC /fʌŋk/ *n* [U] a style of music related to jazz, with a strong rhythm
funky /ˈfʌŋ·ki/ *adj* ○ *a funky beat*

funky /ˈfʌŋ·ki/ *adj* in a style that is informal and unusual ○ *Darcy usually wears really funky clothes.*

funnel **TUBE** /ˈfʌn·əl/ *n* [C] a tube with a wide opening at the top, sides that slope inward, and a narrow opening at the bottom, used for pouring liquids or powders into containers that have small openings ○ *Pour the batter through a funnel into hot oil.* ➤ Picture: **filtration**

MOVE /ˈfʌn·əl/ *v* [I/T] **-l-**, **-ll-** to move or be moved through a narrow space, or to put something in a place or use something for a particular purpose ○ [I] *The crowd funneled into the theater.* ○ [T] *We've been funneling our money into renovations.*

funnel cloud *n* [C] a TORNADO

funny **AMUSING** /ˈfʌn·i/ *adj* [*-er/-est* only] amusing; causing laughter ○ *Jerome is so funny.* ○ *She told me the funniest joke.*
funnies /ˈfʌn·iz/ *pl n* one or more pages in a newspaper that have groups of amusing drawings, each of which tell a story or joke ○ *the Sunday funnies* ○ Compare COMIC STRIP

USAGE

fun or funny?

If something is **fun**, you enjoy doing it.

I really liked the skating – it was such fun.

If something is **funny**, it makes you laugh.

It's a very funny film.

WORD CHOICES funny

The adjective **amusing** is a more formal alternative to "funny."

*I gave her an article that I thought she would find **amusing**.*

If a remark, story, piece of writing, etc., is funny, you can describe it as **humorous**.

*She wrote a **humorous** account of her teenage years.*

If something is extremely funny, you can use the adjectives **hilarious** or (*informal*) **hysterical**.

*I've just read his autobiography – it's absolutely **hilarious**.*

If someone talks in a way that is clever and funny, you can use the adjective **witty**.

*He was a very **witty** man.*

The adjective **comical** is sometimes used if someone or something looks funny.

*She looked so **comical** in that hat!*

You can describe a person or situation that is very funny informally as a **laugh** or a **scream**.

*You'd like Amanda – she's a real **scream**.*

STRANGE /ˈfʌn·i/ *adj* [*-er/-est* only] **1** strange or surprising, or difficult to explain or understand ○ *The washing machine is making funny noises again.* ○ *Something funny is going on next door.* ○ *That's funny – I'm sure I left my keys here, but now I can't find them.* ○ [+ question word] *It's funny how Pat always disappears whenever there's work to be done.* **2** If you feel funny, you feel slightly ill: *He felt a little funny after taking a pill on an empty stomach.*

funny bone /ˈfʌn·iːˌboʊn/ *n* [C usually sing] the part of the ELBOW that hurts a lot if it is hit even lightly

fur /fɜr/ *n* [C/U] the soft, thick hair that covers the bodies of some animals, or the hair-covered skin of animals, removed from their bodies ○ [U] *Persian cats have long fur.* ○ [U] *My jacket is lined with fur.* ○ [C] *She wore diamonds and furs and always looked glamorous.*
furry /ˈfɜr·i/ *adj* covered with fur, or feeling or looking like fur ○ *a furry animal* ○ *She was wearing her bathrobe and pink, furry slippers.*

furious **ANGRY** /ˈfjʊr·iː·əs/ *adj* extremely angry ○ *Sandy was furious with me for forgetting to pick her up.*

furiously /ˈfjʊr·iː·ə·sli/ *adv* ○ *She marched out of the house furiously.*

VIOLENT /ˈfjʊr·iː·əs/ *adj* violent or forceful ○ *Furious winds rocked the coastal town.*

furiously /ˈfjʊr·iː·ə·sli/ *adv* energetically ○ *I was furiously taking notes during the lecture.*

furl /ˈfɜrl/ *v* [T] (esp. of a flag, sail, or UMBRELLA) to roll or fold up and fasten ○ *He took down the flag and furled it carefully.*

furlong /ˈfɜr·lɔːŋ/ *n* [C] a unit of length equal to 1/8 mile or 201 meters, used esp. in horse racing ○ *a six-furlong race*

F

furlough /ˈfɜr·loʊ/ *n* [C] a time allowed for a person to be absent, esp. from the army or a prison ○ *I'm home on furlough.*

furnace /ˈfɜr·nəs/ *n* [C] a container for holding burning substances, usually to heat buildings or to melt metals and other materials

furnish **ADD FURNITURE** /ˈfɜr·nɪʃ/ *v* [T] to put furniture in a place ○ *They furnished their home with antiques.*

furnished /ˈfɜr·nɪʃt/ *adj* [not gradable] ○ *She's trying to rent a furnished apartment* (= one that has furniture in it).

furnishings /ˈfɜr·nɪ·ʃɪŋz/ *pl n* furniture and decorative items, such as curtains and floor coverings

SUPPLY /ˈfɜr·nɪʃ/ *v* [T] to supply or provide something needed ○ *Jeanne's catering company furnished all the food for the party.*

WORD FAMILY furnish

Nouns	furnishings furniture	*Adjectives*	furnished unfurnished
Verbs	furnish		

furniture /ˈfɜr·nɪ·tʃər/ *n* [U] items such as chairs, tables, and beds that are used in a home or office ○ *office/bedroom/lawn furniture*

furor /ˈfjʊr·ɔːr, -oʊr, -ər/ *n* [U] a sudden expression of excitement or anger by a lot of people, esp. in reaction to something ○ *The research results created a furor in the medical press.*

furrow /ˈfɜr·oʊ, ˈfʌ·roʊ/ *n* [C] a long, narrow cut or fold in the surface of something ○ *The plow sped along the furrow, turning over the earth.* ○ *He tried to smooth the furrow out of his jacket.*

furrow /ˈfɜr·oʊ, ˈfʌ·roʊ/ *v* [T] ○ *When Tony's deep in thought, he furrows his brow.*

furry /ˈfɜr·i/ *adj* ○ See at FUR

further **MORE** /ˈfɜr·ðər/ *adj, adv* more, extra, or additional; *comparative of* FAR **AMOUNT** ○ *Call your local library for further information.* ○ *To further complicate things, I locked my keys in the car.* ○ *Not only did I arrive at my conclusions after careful thought, I took a further step and tested them.*

GREATER DISTANCE /ˈfɜr·ðər/ *adj, adv* to a greater distance in space or time; *comparative of* FAR **DISTANCE** ○ *I can't run any further.* ○ *Read a little further and it will begin to make sense.*

CONFUSABLES

further or farther?

Further means the same as **farther** when you are talking about distance.

further/farther along the street

Only **further** is used to talk about something more or additional.

Are there any further questions?

Gas prices have increased further.

ENCOURAGE /ˈfɜr·ðər/ *v* [T] to help something to succeed; to advance something ○ *She says the money would be a great help in furthering their cause.*

furthermore Ⓐ /ˈfɜr·ðər ˌmɔːr, -ˌmoʊr/ *adv* [not gradable] (used to add information) also and more importantly ○ *I don't know what happened to Roberto, and furthermore, I don't care.*

furthest **DISTANCE** /ˈfɜr·ðəst/ *adj, adv superlative of* FAR **DISTANCE** ○ *The furthest west I've ever gotten is the Grand Canyon.* ○ **USAGE:** Both furthest and farthest are used as adverbs and adjectives. Farthest is more commonly used when referring to distances. Furthest is more often used when the intended meaning is figurative.

AMOUNT /ˈfɜr·ðəst/ *adj, adv superlative of* FAR **AMOUNT** ○ *At that time, the countries furthest along in terms of economic development were Chile, Mexico, and Venezuela.*

furthest /ˈfɜr·ðəst/ *pronoun* ○ *This is the furthest our soccer team has advanced in the playoffs.*

furtive /ˈfɜrt̬·ɪv/ *adj* done or acting secretly and quietly to avoid being noticed ○ *They exchanged furtive gestures and words of encouragement.*

furtively /ˈfɜrt̬·ɪv·li/ *adv* ○ *She glanced furtively at the papers on his desk.*

fury /ˈfjʊr·i/ *n* [C/U] extreme anger or force ○ [U] *The battle raged with mounting fury.*

fuse **SAFETY DEVICE** /fjuːz/ *n* [C] a safety device for protecting an electrical system which contains a material that will melt if too much electricity passes through the system

EXPLOSIVE DEVICE /fjuːz/ *n* [C] a cord or tube along which a flame moves to light FIREWORKS or bomb, or a device inside a bomb that causes it to explode at a particular time or when it hits something

JOIN /fjuːz/ *v* [I/T] to join or become combined, or to cause things to join ○ [I] *The two cells are fused with a jolt of electricity.* ○ [T] *The heat of the fire fused many of the machine's parts together.*

fusion /ˈfjuː·ʒən/ *n* [C/U] **1** [C] *His innovative albums feature a fusion of progressive rock and soul.* **2** ***physics*** Fusion is also the technique of joining atoms in a reaction that produces energy: [U] *nuclear fusion* ○ Compare FISSION

fuse box *n* [C] a container that holds several FUSES **SAFETY DEVICE**, for example for a home or vehicle

fuselage /ˈfjuː·səˌlɑʒ, -zə-/ *n* [C] the main part of an aircraft

fusillade /ˈfjuː·səˌlɑd, -zə-, -ˌleɪd/ *n* [C] a number of bullets fired at the same time or one after another quickly

fuss /fʌs/ *n* [U] the condition of being excited, annoyed, or not satisfied about something, esp. about something that is not very important ○ [U] *Let's see what all the fuss is about.* ○ [U] *She learned to make good food without too much fuss.* ○ [C] *Why are they suddenly making a fuss about this* (= becoming excited about it)*?*

fuss /fʌs/ *v* [I] to become upset or excited ○ *She was never one to fuss about insignificant things.* ○ *Some people like to be fussed over* (= receive a lot of attention). ○ *She sat there fussing with her bright red dress* (= touching and moving it nervously).

fussy **NOT SATISFIED** /ˈfʌs·i/ *adj disapproving* not easily satisfied or pleased; worried or careful about unimportant details ○ *She's really fussy about who she goes out with.* ○ *Kevin's a fussy eater.*

TOO DECORATED /ˈfʌs·i/ *adj* having too much decoration or too many details ○ *My new dress is sophisticated but not too fussy.*

futile /ˈfjuːt·əl, ˈfjuːˌtɑɪl/ *adj* [not gradable] achieving no result; not effective or successful ○ *The plane detoured north in a futile attempt to avoid the bad weather.*

futility /fjuːˈtɪl·əṭ·i/ *n* [U] ○ *A sense of futility and powerlessness infected her.*

futon /ˈfuː·tɑn/ *n* [C] a MATTRESS (= large, flat, firm bag filled with soft material and used for sleeping on) which is used on the floor or on a wooden frame that can often be folded to make a seat ○ *a futon sofa*

future **TIME** /ˈfjuː·tʃər/ *n* [C/U] time which is to come, or something that will happen or exist later ○ [U] *What are your plans for the future?* ○ [U] *We hope to buy a house in the foreseeable future.* ○ [C] *He faces an uncertain future.* ○ [U] *I really don't expect any change in the near future.* ○ *I'll be sure to observe the speed limit* **in the future** (= the next time).

future /ˈfjuː·tʃər/ *adj* [not gradable] ○ *She was aware that her writings might speak to future generations of African Americans.*

futuristic /ˌfjuː·tʃəˈrɪs·tɪk/ *adj* relating to the future, or very modern or advanced ○ *Her latest novel is a futuristic thriller, set in the twenty-first century.* ○ *The mall is noted for its futuristic, glass-steel-and-concrete construction.*

CONDITION /ˈfjuː·tʃər/ *n* [C/U] the conditions for success ○ [U] *In 1903, Ford realized that the future of automobiles lay in making them faster and cheaper.* ○ [C usually sing] *Candidates always promise a brighter future for Americans.*

GRAMMAR /ˈfjuː·tʃər/ *adj* [not gradable] ***grammar*** having the tense of the verb used to describe actions, events, or states that will happen or exist later ○ *In the sentence, "Who will look after the dog?", the phrase "will look" is in the future tense.*

future perfect *n* [U] ***grammar*** the tense formed using "will have" or "shall have" with a past participle to show that an action will be completed by a particular time in the future ○ *"I will have left by noon" is in the future perfect.*

fuzz /fʌz/ *n* [U] *infml* light, loose hairs or fibers, or a covering or mass of these ○ *He's got a little adolescent fuzz on his upper lip.* ○ *Nylon doesn't create fuzz like natural fibers.*

fuzzy /ˈfʌz·i/ *adj* ○ *I peel peaches because I don't like their fuzzy skins.*

fuzzy /ˈfʌz·i/ *adj* not clear or not easily heard, seen, or understood ○ *Is the picture always fuzzy on your TV?* ○ *The basic facts of the story are starting to emerge though the details are still fuzzy.*

FYI *abbreviation for* for your information ○ *FYI, tomorrow's staff meeting is scheduled for 10 A.M.*

G g

G **LETTER**, **g** /dʒiː/ *n* [C] *pl* **G's, Gs, g's, gs** the seventh letter of the English alphabet

MUSICAL NOTE /dʒiː/ *n* [C/U] *pl* **G's, Gs** ***music*** in Western music, the fifth note in the SCALE (= series of notes) that begins on the note C, or a set of notes based on this note

FORCE /dʒiː/ *n* [C] ***physics*** a unit of measure that is equal to the force of GRAVITY at the surface of the earth

MOVIE /dʒiː/ *adj abbreviation for* general ○ **USAGE:** Used in the US for movies considered suitable for all people, including children of any age. ○ Compare NC-17; PG; R MOVIE

MONEY /dʒiː/ *n* [C] *abbreviation for* GRAND MONEY

g **WEIGHT** *n* [C] *pl* **g** *abbreviation for* GRAM

gab /gæb/ *v* [I] **-bb-** *infml* to talk continuously and eagerly, esp. about unimportant matters ○ *The two of us were always gabbing away.*

gab /gæb/ *n* [U] ○ *Along with his gift for gab, he has a great grasp of human nature.*

gable /ˈgeɪ·bəl/ *n* [C] the triangular top end of the wall of a building where it meets the sloping parts of a roof

gadget /ˈgædʒ·ət/ *n* [C] a small device or machine with a particular purpose ○ *This handy gadget separates egg yolks from whites.*

gaffe /gæf/ *n* [C] an embarrassing mistake ○ *His failure to ask for his teacher's advice was a major gaffe.*

gag **PIECE OF CLOTH** /gæg/ *n* [C] a piece of cloth that is put over or in a person's mouth to stop the person from speaking, shouting, or calling for help ○ *The thieves tied him to a chair and put a gag over his mouth.*

gag /gæg/ *v* [T] **-gg-** ○ *He was left bound and gagged until the next morning.*

ALMOST VOMIT /gæg/ *v* [I] **-gg-** to experience the sudden, uncomfortable feeling in the throat and stomach that makes you feel you are going to vomit ○ *The smell of burning rubber made him gag.*

JOKE /gæg/ *n* [C] *infml* a joke, or an amusing trick ○ *He used to write gags for a talk-show host.*

gaggle /ˈgæg·əl/ *n* [C] a group of GEESE, or a group of people, esp. if they are noisy or silly ○ *A gaggle of kids followed him down the street.*

gag order, **gag rule** *n* [C] an official order not to discuss something, esp. a legal case

gaiety /ˈgeɪ·əṭ·i/ *n* [U] happiness and excitement ○ *She loved the gaiety of the holiday season.* ○ Related noun: GAY HAPPY

gaily /ˈgeɪ·li/ *adv* brightly, or in a happy manner ○ *gaily colored blouses*

gain **OBTAIN** /geɪn/ *v* [T] to obtain something useful, advantageous, or positive ○ *He gained control of the business.* ○ *You've got nothing to lose and everything to gain.* ○ *He hoped to gain an advantage by beginning his campaign early.*

gain /geɪn/ *n* [C/U] ○ [U] *The commissioner denied having used his office for personal gain.*

INCREASE /geɪn/ *v* [I/T] **1** to increase in weight, speed, height, or amount ○ [T] *I've gained weight, and I'm going on a diet.* ○ [T] *The campaign has been gaining momentum ever since the television ads started to run.* ○ [I] *Step on the gas – they're gaining on us* (= getting nearer to us). **2** If a clock or watch gains or gains time, it works too quickly and shows a time that is later than the real time.

gain /geɪn/ *n* [C/U] ○ [C] *Stock prices rose again today after yesterday's gains.*

gait /geɪt/ *n* [C] a particular way of walking ○ *He walked with a slow, stiff gait.*

gal /gæl/ *n* [C] *infml* a GIRL

gal. *n* [C] *pl* **gal., gals.** *abbreviation for* GALLON

gala /ˈgeɪ·lə, ˈgæl·ə/ *n* [C] a special public occasion at which there is a lot of entertainment ○ *a gala affair*

galaxy /ˈgæl·ək·si/ *n* [C] ***earth science*** **1** one of the large, independent groups of stars in the universe **2** A galaxy is sometimes used to describe a gathering of famous people: *a galaxy of Hollywood stars*

gale /geɪl/ *n* [C] a very strong wind

gall **ANNOY** /gɔːl/ *v* [T] to make someone annoyed ○ *It galls him to take orders from a less experienced colleague.*

galling /ˈgɔː·lɪŋ/ *adj* ○ *He found his reduced status galling.*

RUDE BEHAVIOR /gɔːl/ *n* [U] inability to understand that your behavior or what you say is rude and not acceptable to other people ○ [+ *to* infinitive] *I don't know how she can have the gall to accuse other people of being lazy when she comes in late every day!*

gallant **BRAVE** /ˈgæl·ənt/ *adj* showing no fear of dangerous or difficult things ○ *She made a gallant effort to win, even if her effort fell short.*

POLITE /gəˈlɑnt, gəˈlænt, ˈgæl·ənt/ *adj* (of a man) polite to women, esp. when in public ○ *He was always charming and gallant toward women.*

gall bladder /ˈgɔːlˌblæd·ər/ *n* [C] a small organ in the body connected to the LIVER that stores a liquid substance that helps you to digest food

gallery **BUILDING** /ˈgæl·ə·ri/ *n* [C] a room or building that is used for showing or selling works of art ○ *There are some contemporary art galleries you should visit.*

RAISED AREA /ˈgæl·ə·ri/ *n* [C] a raised area around the sides or at the back of a large room that provides extra space for people to sit or stand

galley /ˈgæl·i/ *n* [C] a kitchen in a ship or aircraft

gallivant /ˈgæl·əˌvænt/ *v* [I] *humorous* to visit or go to a lot of different places, enjoying yourself and having few worries or responsibilities ○ *I don't go gallivanting around like this every night.*

gallon /ˈgæl·ən/, *abbreviation* **gal.** *n* [C] a unit of measurement of volume of liquid equal to 4 quarts or 3.78 liters

gallop /ˈgæl·əp/ *v* [I/T] (of a horse) to run fast so that all four feet come off the ground together in each act of forward movement
gallop /ˈgæl·əp/ *n* [C] ○ *The horse suddenly broke into a gallop.*
galloping /ˈgæl·ə·pɪŋ/ *adj* [not gradable] increasing or developing at a very fast and often uncontrollable rate ○ *galloping inflation*

gallows /ˈgæl·oʊz/ *n* [C] *pl* **gallows** a raised, wooden structure used, esp. in the past, for hanging criminals

galore /gəˈlɔːr, -ˈloʊr/ *adj* [only after n] [not gradable] in great amounts or numbers ○ *Down South you get biscuits and gravy and fried foods galore.*

galoshes /gəˈlɑʃ·əz/ *pl n* large, waterproof shoes, usually made of rubber, for wearing over ordinary shoes esp. during snowy weather

galvanize /ˈgæl·vəˌnɑɪz/ *v* [T] to cause a person or group to suddenly take action, esp. by shocking or exciting them in some way ○ *Why not use the media to galvanize the community into action?*

galvanometer /ˌgæl·vəˈnɑm·əṱ·ər/ *n* [C] ***physics*** a device used to measure small amounts of electric current

gambit /ˈgæm·bət/ *n* [C] something that you do or say that is intended to achieve an advantage and usually involves taking a risk ○ *The arrest of the political leader was seen as the opening gambit in a move to take control of the government.*

gamble /ˈgæm·bəl/ *v* **1** to risk losing money in the hope of winning a lot more money, esp. if the result of a future event happens as you hope ○ [I] *Some people like to gamble even though the odds are against them.* ○ [M] *He gambled away most of his money.* **2** To gamble is also to do something that you think is worth doing although it might not succeed or you might lose money: [+ *that* clause] *We're gambling that enough people will show up at the concert to cover our expenses.*
gamble /ˈgæm·bəl/ *n* [C usually sing] ○ *Starting up a new business is always a gamble.*
gambler /ˈgæm·blər/ *n* [C] ○ *Gamblers can seek help from government-financed treatment programs.*
gambling /ˈgæm·blɪŋ/ *n* [U] ○ *Gambling in the form of state lotteries is used to raise money for education.*

game ENTERTAINMENT /geɪm/ *n* [C] **1** an entertaining activity, esp. one played by children, or a sports competition ○ *a baseball/basketball/football/soccer game* ○ *The kids are playing a computer game.* ○ *I told the children to put away their toys and games* (= equipment for an entertaining activity). ○ *Search dogs do an important job, but it's just a game to the dog* (= something that is done for fun). ○ *Not telling the whole truth is one of the games that people play* (= one of the ways in which they behave in order to get an advantage). **2** In some activities such as tennis, a game is one part of a competition: *I'm ahead, 3 games to 2.*
games /geɪmz/ *pl n* an organized competition consisting of different sporting events ○ *the Olympic Games*
gaming /ˈgeɪ·mɪŋ/ *n* [U] **1** the activity of playing games on computers and other electronic devices ○ *Alienware has actually branched out beyond the typical gaming market.* **2** Gaming is also a name for the industry in which people GAMBLE by playing cards and other games in CASINOS.

WILLING /geɪm/ *adj* willing to do something, esp something different, new, or slightly dangerous ○ *The ocean water's cold but I'm going in anyway – are you game?*

ANIMALS /geɪm/ *n* [U] wild animals and birds that are hunted for food or sport ○ *Deer and pheasant are types of game.*

game plan *n* [C] a plan for achieving success ○ *Cutting costs is part of our game plan.*

game show *n* [C] a television program in which people compete for money and prizes, often by answering questions

gamete /gəˈmiːt, ˈgæm·iːt/ *n* [C] ***biology*** a male or female cell that can unite with a cell of the opposite sex for the purpose of reproducing

gamma radiation /ˈgæm·ə ˌreɪd·iːˈeɪ·ʃən/ *n* [U] ***physics*** a type of powerful energy that travels in WAVES ENERGY FORM and can go through most solid objects

gamut /ˈgæm·ət/ *n* [U] the whole range of things that can be included in something ○ *Her stories express the gamut of emotions from joy to despair.*

gander BIRD /ˈgæn·dər/ *n* [C] a male GOOSE (= a large bird)

LOOK /ˈgæn·dər/ *n* [U] *infml* a quick look ○ *I heard she had a new car, so I went out to take a gander at it.*

gang CRIMINALS /gæŋ/ *n* [C] a group of criminals or of people, esp. young men and women, who spend time together and cause trouble ○ *The clubs present an alternative to becoming involved in a gang.*

GROUP /gæŋ/ *n* [C] a group of people who are friendly with each other or are involved in the same activity ○ *I went out with the usual gang on Friday night – all my friends from college.*

PHRASAL VERB with gang

• **gang up on** *someone* *infml* to unite as a group against someone ○ *Johnnie says the girls in his class are ganging up on him and teasing him.*

ganglion /ˈgæŋ·gliː·ən/ *n* [C] ***biology*** a group of nerve cells found outside the brain and SPINAL CORD

gangly /ˈgæŋ·gli/, **gangling** /ˈgæŋ·glɪŋ/ *adj* tall, thin, and awkward in movement ○ *Susan showed up with a tall, gangly boy.*

gangplank /ˈgæŋ·plæŋk/, **gangway** /ˈgæŋ·weɪ/ *n* [C] a board or similar object put between a ship and the land so that people can get on and off

gangrene /ˈgæŋ·griːn, gæŋˈgriːn/ *n* [U] decay of part of a person's body because the blood has stopped flowing there ○ *Doctors were afraid gangrene might set in.*

gangster /ˈgæŋ·stər/ *n* [C] a member of an organized group of violent criminals

gangway /ˈgæŋ·weɪ/ *n* [C] a passage for walking, esp. on a ship, or a GANGPLANK
gangway /ˈgæŋˈweɪ/ *exclamation* used to ask people to move so that you can go past quickly

gap /gæp/ *n* [C] **1** an empty space or opening in the middle of something or between two things ○ *Picking up speed, she closed the gap between them.* ○ *She has a gap between her front teeth.* **2** A gap can be a period in which something does not happen: *After a gap of five years, Juanita decided to go back to work full-time.* **3** A gap can also be something lacking: *Some people read to fill in gaps in their education.* **4** A gap can also be a difference between people: *He was trying to bridge the gap between elders and youth, the middle class and poor.*

gape /geɪp/ *v* [I] to look in great surprise at someone or something, esp. with an open mouth ○ *We all stood gaping at the bear in our backyard.*

gaping /ˈgeɪ·pɪŋ/ *adj* open wide ○ *He had a gaping wound and we called for an ambulance.*

garage /gəˈrɑʒ, -ˈrɑdʒ, *Cdn* gəˈræʒ, -ˈrædʒ/ *n* [C] **1** a building where a car or cars are kept, esp. one that is next to or part of a house ○ *The car wasn't in the garage so I thought you weren't home.* **2** A garage is also a place where you can have your car repaired.

garage sale *n* [C] an occasion when people sell things, often in a garage or outside a house, that are no longer wanted

garb /gɑrb/ *n* [U] *fml* clothes that are in a particular style ○ *She was dressed in Roman garb for the play.*

garbage WASTE /ˈgɑr·bɪdʒ/ *n* [U] waste material, esp. unwanted food, or a container in which waste is kept ○ *She threw the cheese in the garbage.* ○ *Take the garbage can/bags out to the curb to be picked up.* ○ *There will be no regular garbage collection Monday.* ○ *We were stuck in traffic behind a garbage truck* (= a large vehicle that collects garbage from containers outside buildings).
NONSENSE /ˈgɑr·bɪdʒ/ *n* [U] nonsense, or worthless ideas or things ○ *There's an awful lot of garbage on television and radio.*

garbage disposal *n* [C] an electrical device attached under a kitchen SINK that cuts unwanted food into very small pieces so that it can be washed away with water

garbageman /ˈgɑr·bɪdʒˌmæn/ *n* [C] *pl* **-men** a person whose job is to collect the garbage from containers outside houses and other buildings

garbanzo (bean) /gɑrˈbɑn·zoʊ (ˈbiːn)/ *n* [C] *pl* **garbanzos** a CHICKPEA

garbled /ˈgɑr·bəld/ *adj* (of something said) confused and unclear, or giving a false idea ○ *He left a garbled message on my answering machine.*

garden /ˈgɑrd·ən/ *n* [C] **1** a piece of land, usually near a home, where flowers and other plants are grown ○ *We have a vegetable garden.* **2** Gardens are also public places where flowers, trees, and other plants are grown for people to enjoy.
garden /ˈgɑrd·ən/ *v* [I] ○ *You've probably never gardened in your life.*
gardener /ˈgɑrd·nər, -ən·ər/ *n* [C] someone who takes care of a garden either as a hobby or as a regular job
gardening /ˈgɑrd·nɪŋ, -ən·ɪŋ/ *n* [U] the activity or hobby of taking care of a garden ○ *I don't do very much gardening.*

WORD FAMILY garden			
Nouns	garden	*Verbs*	garden
	gardener		
	gardening		

gardenia /gɑrˈdiːn·jə/ *n* [C] a plant with large white or yellow flowers that have a sweet smell

garden-variety *adj* very common or ordinary ○ *an ordinary, garden-variety mystery story*

gargantuan /gɑrˈgæn·tʃə·wən/ *adj* very large ○ *He has a gargantuan ego.*

gargle /ˈgɑr·gəl/ *v* [I] to wash your mouth or throat by holding liquid in your mouth, keeping your head back, and breathing out slowly through the mouth ○ *For a sore throat, gargle with warm salt water.*

gargoyle /ˈgɑr·gɔɪl/ *n* [C] a stone object in the shape of the head of an ugly creature, usually seen on the roofs of old churches and other buildings

garish /ˈgær·ɪʃ, ˈger-/ *adj* showy or too brightly colored ○ *The coffee shop, painted a garish pink, is a landmark in the neighborhood.*

garland /ˈgɑr·lənd/ *n* [C] a circle made of flowers and leaves worn around the neck or head as a decoration

garlic /ˈgɑr·lɪk/ *n* [U] a plant of the onion family that has a strong taste and smell and is used in cooking to add flavor

garlic bread *n* [U] bread that has been spread with a mixture of butter, garlic, and sometimes herbs before being heated

garment /ˈgɑr·mənt/ *n* [C] *fml* a piece of clothing ○ *He's fussy about how a garment fits him.*

garment bag *n* [C] a long, flat bag in which you can keep suits and other clothes neat while you travel

garner /ˈgɑr·nər/ *v* [T] to get or earn something valuable or respected, often with difficulty ○ *Coppola garnered several Oscars for his movie, "The Godfather."*

garnet /ˈgɑr·nət/ *n* [C] a dark red stone used in jewelry ○ *a garnet ring*

garnish /ˈgɑr·nɪʃ/ *v* [T] to decorate food with a small amount of a different food ○ *Garnish the dish with lemon wedges.*
garnish /ˈgɑr·nɪʃ/ *n* [C] ○ *Use chopped parsley for a garnish.*

garret /ˈgær·ət/ *n* [C] a small room at the top of a house

garrison /ˈgær·ə·sən/ *n* [C] a group of soldiers living in or defending a town or building, or the buildings that the soldiers live in

garrulous /ˈgær·ə·ləs, ˈgær·jə-/ *adj* having the habit of talking a lot, esp. about unimportant things ○ *I had talked too much about myself and felt like a garrulous old fool.*

garter /ˈgɑrt̬·ər/ *n* [C] a narrow piece of elastic used for holding up a STOCKING or sock

garter snake /ˈgɑrt̬·ər ˌsneɪk/ *n* [C] a small snake with a pattern of long, thin marks along its body whose bite is not poisonous

gas MATTER /gæs/ *n* [C/U] **1** *science* a form of matter that is neither solid nor liquid and can increase in size to fill any container **2** *science* Gas is also the usual word used to talk about NATURAL GAS. **3** Gas is also the feeling that you sometimes get after eating a lot and the air such eating produces in your stomach.
gas /gæs/ *v* [T] **-ss-** to kill or injure people or animals by making them breathe poisonous gas ○ *Hundreds of thousands of soldiers were gassed in World War I.*
gaseous /ˈgæs·i·əs, ˈgæʃ·əs/ *adj* ***science*** consisting of gases
gassy /ˈgæs·i/ *adj* feeling that your stomach is full of gas

LIQUID FUEL /gæs/, **gasoline** /ˈgæs·əˌliːn, ˌ--ˈ-/ *n* [U] a liquid obtained from PETROLEUM (= dark, thick oil), used esp. as a fuel for cars and other vehicles ○ *We're running low on gas.*

PHRASAL VERB with gas

• **gas up** *(something)* [M] , **gassed** to put fuel in a vehicle ○ *I want to gas up when we get to the next service area.*

gash /gæʃ/ *v* [T] to make a long deep cut in something ○ *She gashed her knee when she slipped on a rock.*
gash /gæʃ/ *n* [C] ○ *He suffered a deep gash on his hand from the broken glass.*

gasket /ˈgæs·kət/ *n* [C] a flat piece of soft material or rubber put between two joined metal surfaces to prevent gas, oil, or steam from escaping

gas mask *n* [C] a device a person wears over the face to protect against breathing in poisonous gases

gasoline /ˈgæs·əˌliːn, ˌgæs·əˈliːn/ *n* [U] GAS LIQUID FUEL

gasp /gæsp/ *v* [I/T] to take a short quick breath through the mouth, esp. because of surprise, pain, or shock ○ [I] *When he collapsed on stage, the audience gasped.* ○ [T] *"Help me!" he gasped.*
gasp /gæsp/ *n* [C] ○ *The circus acrobats drew gasps from the crowd.*

gas station *n* [C] a place where drivers can buy fuel and oil

gassy /ˈgæs·i/ *adj* ○ See at GAS MATTER

gastric /ˈgæs·trɪk/ *adj* [not gradable] *medical* of the stomach ○ *gastric juices* ○ *a gastric ulcer*

gastropod /ˈgæs·trəˌpɑd/ *n* [C] ***biology*** any of a group of animals with soft, flat bodies, no legs, and often a shell, for example, a SNAIL or SLUG CREATURE

gate /geɪt/ *n* [C] **1** a section of a fence or outer wall that can swing open to let you through ○ *I pushed open the gate and went into the backyard.* **2** A gate is also the door at an airport that you go through to get on an aircraft: *All passengers for flight 103 please proceed to gate D4.*

gate-crasher /ˈgeɪtˌkræʃ·ər/ *n* [C] a person who goes to a party without being invited to it ○ *The party was ruined by a couple of noisy, rude gate-crashers.*

gateway /ˈgeɪt·weɪ/ *n* [C] a place through which you have to go to get to another place, esp. a tall and wide entrance through a wall ○ *(fig.) The new airport is regarded as the most convenient gateway to southeast Asia.*

gather COLLECT /ˈgæð·ər/ *v* [T] **1** to collect or obtain things, esp. from different places ○ *I went to several libraries to gather information.* ○ *We gathered blackberries from the nearby fields.* **2** If something **gathers momentum/speed**, it gradually becomes faster or stronger: *Pressure for reform of the health-care system is gathering momentum.*

COME TOGETHER /ˈgæð·ər/ *v* [I] (of people or animals) to come together in a group ○ *A crowd gathered to hear her speak.*
gathering /ˈgæð·ə·rɪŋ/ *n* [C] ○ *We're having a little social gathering* (= meeting of people) *tonight and hope you can come.*

UNDERSTAND /ˈgæð·ər/ *v fml* to understand or believe something as a result of something that has been said or done ○ [+ (*that*) clause] *From the look on their faces, she gathered (that) they were annoyed with her.*

IDIOM with gather

• **gather dust** to be forgotten or not used ○ *My tennis racket has just been gathering dust since I hurt my back.*

gator /ˈgeɪt̬·ər/ *n* [C] *short form of* ALLIGATOR

GATT /gæt/, *abbreviation of* **General Agreement on Tariffs and Trade** *n* [U] ***world history*** an agreement made by 132 countries to improve trade from 1948 to 1994

G

gauche /goʊʃ/ *adj* behaving in a way that is offensive to other people, esp. because of not knowing what is correct or not caring about the feelings of others ○ *It was gauche to invite them just two days before the party.*

gaudy /ˈɡɔːd·i, ˈɡɑd·i/ *adj* having too many bright colors ○ *He was wearing a gaudy Hawaiian shirt.*

gauge /ɡeɪdʒ/ *v* [T] to calculate an amount by using a measuring device or by your own judgment, or to make a judgment about people's feelings ○ *It was not easy to gauge his height from this distance, but he seemed pretty tall.* ○ [+ question word] *It's difficult to gauge how they'll react when they hear the news.*

G

gauge /ɡeɪdʒ/ *n* [C] **1** a device for measuring the amount or size of something ○ *She used a pressure gauge to measure the air pressure in her bicycle tires.* ○ *The test is simply a gauge of* (= a way of judging) *how well they will do in college.* **2** A gauge is also a measure of the thickness of a wire or of the opening inside the BARREL (= long part) of a gun: *a 12-gauge shotgun*

gaunt /ɡɔːnt, ɡɑnt/ *adj* very thin, esp. because of illness or hunger ○ *He's always been thin, but now he looks gaunt, his skin stretched tight over his bones.*

gauntlet /ˈɡɔːnt·lət, ˈɡɑnt-/ *n* [C] a long thick GLOVE (= covering for the hand), worn for protection

gauze /ɡɔːz/ *n* [U] a very thin, light cloth used for making clothing and for covering cuts in the skin ○ *a gauze skirt* ○ *a sterile gauze bandage*

gave /ɡeɪv/ *past simple of* GIVE

gavel /ˈɡæv·əl/ *n* [C] a small hammer used by an official in charge of a meeting for hitting a wooden block or table in order to get people's attention ○ *The judge banged her gavel and said, "Quiet, please!"*

gawk /ɡɔːk/ *v* [I] to look at something or someone in a foolish way without thinking ○ *Don't stand there gawking at her, give her a hand!*

gay **HOMOSEXUAL** /ɡeɪ/ *adj* **1** homosexual ○ *gay rights* **2** **USAGE:** Sometimes gay refers only to men.
gay /ɡeɪ/ *n* [C] ○ *The law banned discrimination against gays.*
HAPPY /ɡeɪ/ *adj* [*-er/-est* only] *dated* (of a person) happy, or (of a place) bright and attractive ○ *Her gay, lively personality made her attractive to everyone who knew her.* ○ Related noun: GAIETY

gaze /ɡeɪz/ *v* [I] to look at something or someone for a long time, esp. in surprise, admiration, or because you are thinking about something else ○ *He spends hours gazing out of the window when he should be working.*
gaze /ɡeɪz/ *n* [U] ○ *I felt his gaze on me as I walked out the door.*

gazebo /ɡəˈziː·boʊ/ *n* [C] *pl* **gazebos** a small, often decorated shelter with no walls, usually in an open space, where people rest and relax

gazelle /ɡəˈzel/ *n* [C] an animal like a small deer that lives in Africa or Asia

gazette /ɡəˈzet/ *n* [C usually sing] (used only in the titles of newspapers) a newspaper ○ *the Montreal Gazette*

gazpacho /ɡəˈspɑtʃ·oʊ/ *n* [U] a spicy soup made from TOMATOES (= juicy, red fruit) and vegetables and eaten cold

GB *n* [C] *abbreviation for* GIGABYTE

GDP *n* [U] *abbreviation for* GROSS DOMESTIC PRODUCT

gear **MACHINE PART** /ɡɪr/ *n* **1** (in a machine) a wheel having pointed parts around the edge that come together with similar parts of other wheels to control how much power from an engine goes to the moving parts of a machine **2** In a vehicle, a gear is any of several limited ranges of power that are used for different speeds: [U] *Use second gear going up a steep hill.*
MAKE READY /ɡɪr/ *v* [always + adv/prep] to make something ready or suitable for a particular purpose ○ [T] *Our program is geared to the needs of children.*
EQUIPMENT /ɡɪr/ *n* [U] equipment or clothes used for a particular activity ○ *camping gear*

PHRASAL VERB with gear

• **gear up** to prepare for an activity or event ○ *Politicians are already gearing up for the next election.*

gearshift /n/ *n* [C] a metal rod or handle that you use to change from one GEAR to another in a vehicle

GED *n* [C] *abbreviation for* general equivalency diploma (= a document given to someone who did not complete HIGH SCHOOL but has passed an examination on those school subjects)

gee /dʒiː/ *exclamation* an expression of surprise, enthusiasm, annoyance, etc. ○ *Gee, I'm so glad you called!*

geek /ɡiːk/ *n* [C] someone who is extremely interested in computers, esp. someone whose only interest is computers ○ *Thanks to brilliant computer geeks, I can copy, scan, fax, and send photos all from a single machine.*

geese /ɡiːs/ *pl of* GOOSE **BIRD**

gee whiz /dʒiː ˈwɪz, -ˈhwɪz/ *exclamation* an expression of surprise, enthusiasm, annoyance, etc. ○ *Gee whiz, where'd you get that hat?*

geezer /ˈɡiː·zər/ *n* [C] an old man ○ **USAGE:** This word is sometimes considered offensive.

Geiger counter /ˈɡɑɪ·ɡər ˌkɑʊnt·ər/ *n* [C] an electronic device for finding and measuring the level of RADIOACTIVITY (= energy from atoms breaking)

geisha /ˈɡeɪ·ʃə, ˈɡiː-/ *n* [C] a Japanese woman trained in music and dancing whose job is entertaining men

gel /dʒel/ *n* [U] a thick, soft, partly liquid substance ○ *hair gel*

gel /dʒel/ *v* [I] **-ll-** (of a liquid) to become thick ○ *As the pudding cooled, it began to gel.*

gelatin /ˈdʒel·ət·ən/ *n* [U] a clear substance obtained by boiling animal bones, skin, etc., and used to make some foods and other substances such as glue

gelding /ˈgel·dɪŋ/ *n* [C] a male horse that has had its TESTICLES (= sexual organs that produce sperm) removed

gem /dʒem/ *n* [C] **1** a precious stone, esp. when cut into a regular shape; jewel ○ *The necklace was studded with diamonds, rubies, and other gems.* **2** If you say that something or someone is a gem, you mean that you value the quality or beauty of that person or thing highly: *The building was an architectural gem.*

Gemini /ˈdʒem·əˌnɑɪ/ *n* [C/U] the third sign of the ZODIAC, covering the period May 21 to June 21 and represented by TWINS, or a person born during this period

gender Ⓐ **SEX** /ˈdʒen·dər/ *n* [C/U] the male or female sex, or the state of being either male or female ○ [U] *Discrimination on the basis of gender is not allowed.*

GRAMMAR /ˈdʒen·dər/ *n* [C/U] ***grammar*** the divisions, usually MASCULINE, FEMININE, and NEUTER, into which nouns are separated in some languages ○ [C] *French has two genders and German has three.*

gene /dʒiːn/ *n* [C] ***biology*** a specific chemical pattern on a CHROMOSOME (= cell structure) that is received from the parents and controls the development of particular characteristics in an animal or plant

genealogy /ˌdʒiː·niːˈɑl·ə·dʒi, -ˈæl-/ *n* [C/U] the study of the history of the past and present members of a family, or a particular history of this type ○ [C] *He has produced a genealogy of his family going back to 1732.*
genealogical /ˌdʒiː·niː·əˈlɑdʒ·ɪ·kəl/ *adj* [not gradable]

gene pool *n* [C] ***biology*** all the GENES of a particular type of plant or animal

genera /ˈdʒen·ə·rə/ *pl of* GENUS

general **COMMON** /ˈdʒen·rəl, -ə·rəl/ *adj* involving or relating to most people, things, or conditions, esp. when these are considered as a unit; not particular or specific ○ *the general standard of living* ○ *This book is intended for the general reader* (= one who does not have special knowledge). ○ *He has only a general knowledge of anatomy* (= does not have detailed information about it). ○ **In general** (= In most cases), *women live longer than men.*
generality /ˌdʒen·əˈræl·əţ·i/ *n* [C usually pl] a statement without details and sometimes without much meaning ○ *The candidate's speech was full of generalities and never focused on the issues.*
generally /ˈdʒen·rə·li, -ə·rə·li/ *adv* ○ *It was generally believed at the time that both men were guilty.* ○ *The baby generally* (= usually) *wakes up twice during the night.*

generalize /ˈdʒen·rəˌlɑɪz, -ə·rə-/ *v* [I] to make a statement that relates to many people, things, or conditions, esp. when based on limited facts ○ *You can't generalize about a continent as varied as Africa.*
generalization /ˌdʒen·rə·ləˈzeɪ·ʃən, -ə·rə-/ *n* [C/U] ○ [C] *The report is full of sweeping generalizations* (= statements that lack facts or details and may be wrong).

OFFICER /ˈdʒen·rəl, -ə·rəl/ *n* [C] a military officer of the highest rank

WORD FAMILY general			
Nouns	generality generalization	*Verbs*	generalize
		Adverbs	generally
Adjectives	general		

general anesthetic *n* [C] a drug used for making a person unconscious so that the person does not feel pain during an operation

general delivery *n* [U] a department in a post office that will receive and hold mail for a person to pick up

general election *n* [C] a national or state election, not a local one

general store *n* [C] a store, usually in a rural area, that sells food and a large variety of other products

generate Ⓐ /ˈdʒen·əˌreɪt/ *v* [T] to cause to exist; produce ○ *The new construction project will generate 500 new jobs.* ○ *Her latest book has generated a lot of excitement.* ○ *The power plant generates electricity for the eastern part of the state.*
generation Ⓐ /ˌdʒen·əˈreɪ·ʃən/ *n* [U] ○ *the generation of electricity*
generator /ˈdʒen·əˌreɪţ·ər/ *n* [C] a machine that produces electricity

generation Ⓐ **GROUP** /ˌdʒen·əˈreɪ·ʃən/ *n* [C] **1** all the people of about the same age within a society or within a particular family, or the usual period of time from a person's birth to the birth of his or her children ○ *the last/next generation* ○ *There were three generations at the wedding – grandparents, parents, and children.* ○ *This farm has been in the family for generations.* **2** A generation is also a group of products or machines that are all at the same stage of development: *a new generation of cancer drugs* ○ *third-generation computers*
generational /ˌdʒen·əˈreɪ·ʃən·əl/ *adj* ○ *The poll found major generational differences in opinion.*

REPRODUCTION /ˌdʒen·əˈreɪ·ʃən/ *n* [U] ***biology*** (of living things) the act or process of reproducing

generation gap *n* [usually sing] a lack of understanding between older and younger people that results from different experiences of life

Generation X, *short form* **Gen X** *n* [U] the people born in the US in the second half of the 1960s or the early part of the 1970s

generic /dʒəˈner·ɪk/ *adj* **1** relating to or shared by a whole group of similar things; not specific to any particular thing ○ *Jazz is a generic term for a wide range of different styles of music.* **2** Generic also means not having a trademark: *a generic drug*

generic /dʒəˈner·ɪk/ *n* [C] a product, esp. a drug, that is no longer owned or legally controlled by a particular company

generosity /ˌdʒen·əˈrɑs·ət̬·i/ *n* [U] a willingness to give help or support, esp. more than is usual or expected ○ *She is admired for her generosity.*

generous /ˈdʒen·ə·rəs/ *adj* (of someone) willing to give help or support, esp. more than is usual or expected, or (of something) larger than usual or expected ○ *a generous donor* ○ *food in generous portions*

generously /ˈdʒen·ə·rə·sli/ *adv* ○ *Please give generously to those in need.*

WORD FAMILY generous			
Nouns	generosity	*Adverbs*	generously
Adjectives	generous		

genesis /ˈdʒen·ə·səs/ *n* [U] **1** the time when something came into existence; the beginning or origin ○ *the genesis of life on earth* **2** In the Bible, Genesis is the first book of the Old Testament, describing how God created the world.

genetic /dʒəˈnet̬·ɪk/ *adj* ***biology*** relating to the biological process by which the characteristics of living things are passed from parents to children

genetics /dʒəˈnet̬·ɪks/ *n* [U] the study in biology of how the characteristics of living things are passed through the GENES (= specific chemical patterns) from parents to children

genetically /dʒəˈnet̬·ɪ·kli/ *adv*

genetic code *n* [C] ***biology*** the pattern of chemicals inside the GENES (= cells which are passed from parent to child) which controls the characteristics and qualities of a living thing

genetic drift *n* [U] ***biology*** a situation in which the number of a particular GENE in a small population of living things changes without a known cause

genetic engineering *n* [U] ***biology*** the science of changing the structure of the GENES (= specific chemical patterns) of a living thing, used esp. in developing new food products and in medicine

genial /ˈdʒiːn·jəl/ *adj* friendly and pleasant ○ *a genial personality*

genie /ˈdʒiː·ni/ *n* [C] a spirit, esp. a magical spirit who will do whatever the person who controls it asks it to do

genitals /ˈdʒen·ət·əlz/, **genitalia** /ˌdʒen·əˈteɪl·jə/ *pl n* the sex organs

genital /ˈdʒen·ət·əl/ *adj* [not gradable] ○ *the genital organs*

genius /ˈdʒiːn·jəs/ *n* [C/U] a very great and rare natural ability of the mind, or a person having this ability ○ [C] *Einstein was a scientific genius.* ○ [U] *His idea was a stroke of genius!* ○ [U] *She has a genius* (= special skill) *for raising money.*

genocide /ˈdʒen·əˌsɑɪd/ *n* [C/U] ***politics & government*** the intentional killing of all of the people of a nation, religion, or racial group

genome /ˈdʒiː·noʊm/ *n* [C] the whole group of GENES in an organism

genotype /ˈdʒiː·nəˌtɑɪp, ˈdʒen-/ *n* [C] ***biology*** the type and arrangement of GENES that each living thing has

genre /ˈʒɑn·rə, ˈʒɑ̃·rə/ *n* [C] ***art, literature, music*** a particular subject or style of literature, art, or music ○ *the genre of landscape painting*

genteel /dʒenˈtiːl/ *adj* polite and correct in manner, or trying to be polite and correct in order to appear to be of a high social class ○ *When in company, they affected genteel table manners.*

gentile /ˈdʒen·tɑɪl/ *n* [C] a person who is not Jewish

gentle /ˈdʒent·əl/ *adj* calm, kind, or soft; not violent or severe ○ *a gentle smile* ○ *a gentle breeze* ○ *The path has a gentle* (= gradual) *slope.*

gently /ˈdʒent·li/ *adv* ○ *He gently lifted the baby out of the crib.*

gentleness /ˈdʒent·əl·nəs/ *n* [U]

USAGE

gentle

Be careful when using the word **gentle** to describe people. It does not mean exactly the same as **kind** or **nice**. **Gentle** tells you that someone behaves in a calm, quiet way that does not upset or hurt people.

She has a very gentle, loving personality.

If you simply mean that someone is helpful and nice you should use the word **kind**.

His sisters were very kind to me when I lost my job and needed somewhere to stay.

~~*His sisters were very gentle to me when I lost my job and needed somewhere to stay.*~~

WORD FAMILY gentle			
Nouns	gentleness	*Adverbs*	gently
Adjectives	gentle		

gentleman /ˈdʒent·əl·mən/ *n* [C] *pl* **-men 1** a man who is polite and behaves well toward other people ○ *a perfect gentleman* **2** Gentleman is often used as a polite way of referring to any man: *This gentleman has a question.* ○ *Ladies and gentlemen, may I have your attention.* **3** *infml* In speech, a gentleman often means simply a man: *The gentleman involved had a long history of this type of offense.*

gentrification /ˌdʒen·trə·fəˈkeɪ·ʃən/ *n* [U] the process by which a poor neighborhood in a city is changed by people who have money, including esp. the improvement or replacement of buildings ○ **USAGE:** This word is now sometimes used in a disapproving way, but was originally considered positive.

gentrify /ˈdʒen·trəˌfɑɪ/ *v* [T] ○ *The area where he grew up has been gentrified and lost all its old character.*

gentry /ˈdʒen·tri/ *pl n* people of high social class ○ *His diaries provide an intimate look at the life of the gentry in 18th-century Virginia.*

genuflect /ˈdʒen·jəˌflekt/ *v* [I] to bend one knee or touch one knee to the floor as a sign of worship or respect

genuflection /ˌdʒen·jəˈflek·ʃən/ *n* [C]

genuine /ˈdʒen·jə·wən, -ˌwɑɪn/ *adj* being what something or someone appears or claims to be; real, not false ○ *genuine leather* ○ *a genuine masterpiece* ○ *She showed genuine* (= sincere) *sorrow at the news.*

genuinely /ˈdʒen·jə·wən·li, -ˌwɑɪn·li/ *adv* ○ *I'm genuinely* (= sincerely) *sorry if I offended you.*

genuineness /ˈdʒen·jə·wən·nəs/ *n* [U] ○ *No one doubts the genuineness of your concern.*

genus /ˈdʒiː·nəs/ *n* [C] *pl* **genera** ***biology*** a group of animals or plants that share some characteristics in a larger biological group

geography /dʒiːˈɑg·rə·fi/ *n* [U] ***social studies*** the study of the features and systems of the earth's surface, including continents, mountains, seas, weather, and plant life, and of the ways in which countries and people organize life within an area

geographic /ˌdʒiː·əˈgræf·ɪk/, **geographical** /ˌdʒiː·əˈgræf·ɪ·kəl/ *adj* [not gradable] ○ *a geographic region*

geographically /ˌdʒiː·əˈgræf·ɪ·kli/ *adv* ○ *Japan is geographically close to North Korea.*

geology /dʒiːˈɑl·ə·dʒi/ *n* [U] ***earth science*** the study of the rocks and physical processes of the earth in order to understand its origin and history

geological /ˌdʒiː·əˈlɑdʒ·ɪ·kəl/, **geologic** /ˌdʒiː·əˈlɑdʒ·ɪk/ *adj* [not gradable] ○ *a geological survey*

geologist /dʒiːˈɑl·ə·dʒəst/ *n* [C] someone whose work or study is connected with geology

geometry /dʒiːˈɑm·ə·tri/ *n* [U] ***mathematics*** the area of mathematics relating to the study of space and the relationships between points, lines, curves, and surfaces

geometric /ˌdʒiː·əˈme·trɪk/, **geometrical** /ˌdʒiː·əˈme·trɪ·kəl/ *adj* ***mathematics*** consisting of shapes such as squares, triangles, or rectangles ○ *a geometric pattern* ➤ Picture: **solid; triangle**

geometrically *adv* ***mathematics*** ○ *solve the problem geometrically*

geophysical /ˌdʒiː·əˈfɪz·ɪ·kəl/ *adj* [not gradable] ***earth science, physics*** involving the study of physics as it relates to the earth and the environment of the earth

geothermal /ˌdʒiː·oʊˈθɜr·məl/ *adj* [not gradable] ***earth science*** involving or produced by the heat that is inside the earth

geranium /dʒəˈreɪ·niː·əm/ *n* [C] a plant with red, pink, or white flowers and round leaves

gerbil /ˈdʒɜr·bəl/ *n* [C] a small, furry animal that has long back legs and a thin tail, and is often kept as a pet

geriatric /ˌdʒer·iːˈæ·trɪk/ *adj* **1** relating to the medical care and treatment of old people ○ *geriatric medicine/patients* **2** *often disapproving* Geriatric also means old: *This place attracts a geriatric crowd.* ○ *Ballplayers are geriatric at 36.*

geriatrics /ˌdʒer·iːˈæ·trɪks/ *n* [U] the area of study in medicine that deals with the care and treatment of old people and the diseases of old age

germ **ORGANISM** /dʒɜrm/ *n* [C usually pl] a very small organism that causes disease ○ *The patient has little natural resistance to germs.*

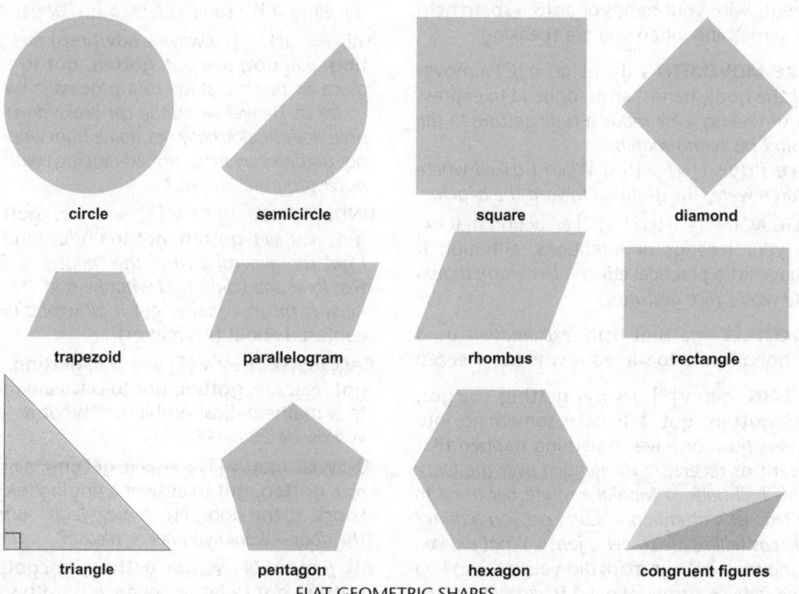

FLAT GEOMETRIC SHAPES

ORIGIN /dʒɜrm/ *n* [C] the origin of something that develops, esp. a cell from which grain grows or the beginning of an idea ○ *Alejandro's suggestion was the germ of an idea.*

German measles /ˈdʒɜr·mən ˈmiː·zəlz/, *medical* **rubella** *n* [U] an infectious virus that causes a fever, a cough, and small red spots on your skin

German shepherd /ˈdʒɜr·mən ˈʃep·ərd/ *n* [C] a type of dog that is large and is often used as a guard dog, for police work, and to lead the blind

germicide /ˈdʒɜr·məˌsɑɪd/ *n* [C] a substance that kills GERMS (= very small organisms that cause disease)

germinate /ˈdʒɜr·məˌneɪt/ *v* [I/T] to start growing, or to cause a seed to start growing ○ [I] *This community is where the seeds of Gandhi's philosophy germinated.*

germ warfare *n* [U] BIOLOGICAL WARFARE

gerrymander /ˈdʒer·iːˌmæn·dər/ *v* [T] ***politics & government*** to divide an area into election DISTRICTS (= areas that elect someone) in a way that gives an unfair advantage to one group or political party

gerrymandering /ˈdʒer·iːˌmæn·də·rɪŋ/ *n* [U] ○ *Enlarging the district to dilute the Latino vote is a blatant example of gerrymandering.*

gerund /ˈdʒer·ənd/ *n* [C] ***grammar*** a word ending in "-ing" that is made from a verb and is used like a noun ○ *In the sentence "Everyone enjoyed Tyler's singing," the word "singing" is a gerund.*

gestation /dʒeˈsteɪ·ʃən/ *n* [U] (the period of) the development of a child or young animal inside its mother's uterus ○ *The gestation period of rats is 21 days.*

gesticulate /dʒeˈstɪk·jəˌleɪt/ *v* [I] to make movements with your hands or arms, esp. to help express something when you are speaking

gesture MOVEMENT /ˈdʒes·tʃər/ *n* [C] a movement of the body, hands, arms, or head to express an idea or feeling ○ *He made a rude gesture to the crowd after his tennis match.*

gesture /ˈdʒes·tʃər/ *v* [I] ○ *When I asked where the children were, she gestured toward the beach.*

SYMBOLIC ACT /ˈdʒes·tʃər/ *n* [C] an action that expresses your feelings or intentions, although it might have little practical effect ○ *Her warm thank-you note was a nice gesture.*

gesundheit /gəˈzʊntˌhɑɪt/ *exclamation* used to wish good health to someone who has sneezed

get OBTAIN /get/ *v* [T] *pres. part.* **getting,** *past* **got,** *past part.* **gotten, got 1** to take something into your possession, or have something happen that you accept or receive ○ *He climbed over the fence to get his ball back.* ○ *Monique raised her hand to get the teacher's attention.* ○ *Can I get you a drink?* ○ *Dad keeps telling me to get a job.* ○ *What did you get on the test* (= What mark did you receive)? ○ *I think she gets* (= earns) *about $10 an hour.* ○ *We don't get much snow in this part of the country* (= It does not often snow). **2** To get something often means to buy or pay for it: *He went to the store to get milk.*

BECOME /get/ *v* [L] *pres. part.* **getting,** *past* **got,** *past part.* **gotten, got** to become or start to be ○ *Your coffee is getting cold.* ○ *He's gotten so big, I hardly recognized him.* ○ *They're getting married later this year.* ○ *Tom got lost in the woods.* ○ *What time do you get off work?* ○ *We'd better get going/moving or we'll be late.* ➤ Usage: **become or get?** at BECOME BE

BECOME ILL WITH /get/ *v* [T] *pres. part.* **getting,** *past* **got,** *past part.* **gotten, got** to become ill with a disease ○ *Everyone seems to be getting the flu.*

CAUSE /get/ *v* [T] *pres. part.* **getting,** *past* **got,** *past part.* **gotten, got** to cause something to be done or persuade someone to do something ○ *The bed is too wide – we'll never get it through the door.* ○ *I can't get this printer to work!*

PREPARE /get/ *v* [T] *pres. part.* **getting,** *past* **got,** *past part.* **gotten, got** to prepare a meal ○ *Why don't you get supper ready?*

MOVE /get/ *v* [always + adv/prep] *pres. part.* **getting,** *past* **got,** *past part.* **gotten, got 1** to move in a particular direction ○ [I] *Get away from that wet paint!* ○ [I] *He got down on his hands and knees to look for his contact lens.* ○ [T] *Her throat was so sore that she had trouble getting the medicine down* (= swallowing it). ○ [I] *I hit my head as I was getting into the car.* ○ [M] *Momma said we have to get these wet clothes off* (= remove them). ○ [T] *Get your feet off the couch* (= move them off it). **2** To get off a road when you are driving means to turn onto another road: [I] *Get off the expressway at exit 43.* **3** To get off a train, bus, or aircraft is to leave it: [I] *Get off at Union Station.*

TRAVEL /get/ *v* [T] *pres. part.* **getting,** *past* **got,** *past part.* **gotten, got** to go into a vehicle or aircraft for traveling ○ *We could call for a taxi or get the bus.*

ARRIVE /get/ *v* [I always + adv/prep] *pres. part.* **getting,** *past* **got,** *past part.* **gotten, got** to arrive at a place or reach a stage in a process ○ *We only got as far as Denver when the car broke down.* ○ *What time does he normally get home from work?* ○ *We're not getting very far* (= not advancing) *with this computer program, are we?*

UNDERSTAND /get/ *v* [T] *pres. part.* **getting,** *past* **got,** *past part.* **gotten, got** to understand ○ *I think I got the general idea of the chapter.* ○ *The music was loud and I didn't get what he said.* ○ *I never said he was mean – you've got it all wrong* (= you are confused about this matter).

CALCULATE /get/ *v* [T] *pres. part.* **getting,** *past simp.* **got,** *past part.* **gotten, got** to calculate the answer to a mathematical problem ○ *What do you get if you divide 20 by 4?*

ANSWER /get/ *v* [T] *pres. part.* **getting,** *past* **got,** *past part.* **gotten, got** to answer a ringing telephone, a knock at the door, etc. ○ *Hey, Juan, someone's at the door – would you get it, please?*

HIT /get/ *v* [T] *pres. part.* **getting,** *past* **got,** *past part.* **gotten, got** to hit someone, esp. with something thrown or a bullet ○ *My first throw missed, but the second got him in the leg.*

ANNOY /get/ *v* [T] *pres. part.* **getting,** *past* **got,** *past part.* **gotten, got** *infml* to cause someone to feel slightly angry ○ *It gets me when I have to both cook dinner and clean the dishes.*

CAUSE EMOTIONS /get/ *v* [T] *pres. part.* **getting,** *past* **got,** *past part.* **gotten, got** *infml* to have an emotional effect on someone ○ *That scene in the movie, when the father and daughter are reunited, always gets me.*

IDIOMS with get

• **get a feel for** *something* to begin to understand how to do something well ○ *I practiced for a few hours before I really got a feel for the best way to do it.*

• **get a grip on** *your* **self** to control your emotions ○ *Get a grip on yourself, and tell me what happened.*

• **get a jump on** *someone/something*, **get the jump on** *someone/something* to get an advantage over other people by doing something before they do ○ *The company is trying to get a jump on their competitors by putting a lot of money into research.*

• **get a life** *infml* stop being so boring or annoying and do something more interesting ○ *Dave kept trying to tell me what to do, and I just told him to get a life.*

• **get a move on** *infml* hurry ○ *Hey, Francine, get a move on or you'll be late!* ○ **USAGE:** Used to tell someone to do this.

• **get a word in edgewise** to have an opportunity to speak ○ *Brad talked so much that nobody could get a word in edgewise.*

• **get even** to punish someone who has done something bad to you by doing something equally bad to that person ○ *After she insulted me, all I thought about was how I could get even with her.*

• **get** *your* **feet wet** to become used to a new situation ○ *I worked as a substitute teacher for a while, just to get my feet wet.*

• **get** *your* **goat** to make you annoyed or angry ○ *When I park in her space, it really gets her goat.*

• **get hold of** *someone*, **get ahold of** *someone* to communicate with someone, esp. by telephone ○ *I haven't talked to her in years, so I wouldn't know how to get hold of her anymore.*

• **get hold of** *something*, **get ahold of** *something* to obtain something ○ *Where can I get hold of today's newspaper?*

• **get in** *your* **hair** to annoy you, usually by being present all the time ○ *The children have been getting in my hair all afternoon.*

• **get in on the act** to take advantage of something that someone else started ○ *We designed the Web page, and now everyone else in our class wants to get in on the act.*

• **get it, get what's coming to** *you* to be punished for something you did ○ *When Mom finds out you skipped school yesterday, you're going to get it.*

• **get it through** *your* **thick head, get it through** *your* **thick skull** *infml* to cause someone to understand something ○ *How can I get it through your thick head that it's dangerous to swim that far out in the ocean?*

• **get it together** to make a decision or take positive action ○ *We would have liked to have gone, but we couldn't get it together to drive there.*

• **get lost** *infml* go away ○ *The old man yelled at the kids playing in his yard to get lost.* ○ **USAGE:** Used to tell someone rudely to go away.

• **get** *your* **money's worth** to receive good value for something you have paid for ○ *Those sneakers lasted for four years – he really got his money's worth from them.*

• **get** *something* **off** *your* **chest** to express something that has been worrying you and that you have wanted to say ○ *I thought these meetings would help the kids get some of their worries off their chests.*

• **get off the ground** to start ○ *He and his friend tried to start a band but it never got off the ground.*

• **get on** *someone's* **nerves** to annoy someone a lot ○ *Stop whining. You're getting on my nerves.*

• **get** *something* **out of** *your* **system** to do something enough so that you do not want to do it any longer ○ *Let the kids run around a little longer, maybe they'll get it out of their system.*

• **get over** *something* to accept an unpleasant fact or situation after dealing with it for a while ○ *They're upset that you didn't call, but they'll get over it.*

• **get results** succeed ○ *She's an excellent coach, and she knows how to get results.*

• **get rid of** *someone* to find a way to make someone leave because you do not want the person to be with you any longer ○ *We finally got rid of my little sister by telling her scary stories.*

• **get rid of** *something* to remove something that you do not want any longer ○ *I can't wait to get rid of that ugly old couch.*

• **get somewhere** to make progress toward a goal ○ *After months of talks, negotiators think they're finally getting somewhere.*

• **get the better of** *someone*, **get the best of** *someone* to defeat someone ○ *She played well, but her opponent got the better of her.*

• **get the hang of** *something* to learn how to do something, esp. when it is not simple or obvious ○ *I'll teach you how to use the design program – you'll get the hang of it after a while.*

• **get the message** to understand what someone is trying to tell you even though the person does not say it directly ○ *I ignore him every time I see him, so you'd think he'd get the message and leave me alone.*

• **get this show on the road** *infml* to begin an activity that you have planned, esp. a trip ○ *If we're going to be on time, we'd better get this show on the road.*

• **get to the bottom of** *something* to discover the real but sometimes hidden reason that something exists or happens ○ *Investigators are trying to get to the bottom of what went wrong.*

• **get under** *your* **skin** to make you annoyed or angry ○ *I've noticed that little things have been getting under my skin lately – things that shouldn't upset me.*

• **get underway** to begin to happen ○ *The Democratic convention gets underway tomorrow in Chicago.*

• **get up on the wrong side of the bed** to wake up in a bad mood ○ *Dad got up on the wrong side of bed, and he's been grumpy all day.*
• **get wind of** *something* to learn a piece of information esp. when it has been a secret: *We have a crisis on our hands and don't want the press to get wind of it.*
• **get** *someone's* **wires crossed** to have a different understanding of the same situation ○ *We must have got our wires crossed – I thought she was arriving tomorrow, not today.* ○ **USAGE**: Used to talk about two or more people who fail to understand each other.
• **get** *someone* **wrong** to be offended because you do not understand someone correctly ○ *Don't get me wrong – I like your haircut, I'm just surprised you cut it so short.*
• **not get anywhere** to not make progress toward a goal ○ *His parents tried to talk him out of joining the army, but they didn't get anywhere.*
• **not get to first base** to not be able to start doing what you intend to do ○ *We need financing for this project, but we can't get to first base with the banks.*

PHRASAL VERBS with get

• **get across** *something* [M] to communicate an idea or message successfully ○ *I hoped to get across the idea that a community is more than just a bunch of people living in one place.* ○ *Our ideas are better and we need to find a different way of getting that across.*
• **get ahead** to achieve success, often in your work or in society ○ *You've got to take risks if you want to get ahead.*
• **get along/on** to have a good relationship or deal successfully with a situation ○ *Alexis and her roommate are getting along better.* ○ *She doesn't get on well with her father.*
• **get around** *something* **DEAL WITH** to find a way of dealing with or avoiding a problem ○ *The committee is looking for ways to get around the funding problem.*
• **get around** *(somewhere)* **TRAVEL** to travel or move from place to place ○ *You need a car to get around town.* ○ *During her last few years, Edna couldn't get around very well.* ○ *It didn't take long for that rumor to get around the office.*
• **get around to** *something* to find time to do something that you have intended or would like to do ○ *I wanted to see that movie but never got around to it.*
• **get at** *something* **SUGGEST** to suggest or express something in a way that is not direct or clear ○ *You mean I shouldn't come tonight – is that what you're getting at?*
• **get at** *something* **REACH** to reach something ○ *I keep cleaning supplies on a high shelf where my three-year-old can't get at them.*
• **get away** to leave or escape ○ *Wouldn't it be nice to get away for a weekend?* ○ Related noun: GETAWAY
• **get away with** *something* to escape blame or punishment when you do something wrong, or to avoid harm or criticism for something you did ○ *She thought she could get away with cheating on her taxes.*

• **get back RETURN** to return, esp. to your home ○ *When did you get back from Hawaii?*
• **get back** *something* **OBTAIN AGAIN** [M] to obtain something again after loss or separation ○ *She was thrilled to get her old job back.*
• **get back at** *someone* to punish someone because that person has done something wrong to you ○ *I think he's trying to get back at her for what she said in the meeting.*
• **get back to** *something* **START AGAIN** to continue doing something that you were doing or that you started earlier ○ *If you skip some days, it can be hard to get back to a regular bicycling routine.*
• **get back to** *someone* **COMMUNICATE** to communicate with someone at a later time ○ *He can't find the phone number right now, but promised to get back to me with it.*
• **get by** to manage or continue to exist in a state or situation where something is lacking ○ *When we were students we got by on very little money.* ○ *There is tremendous pressure on families trying to get by without health insurance.*
• **get** *someone* **down** to cause someone to feel unhappy and negative ○ *Mostly what gets him down is the incredibly long hours he works.*
• **get down to** *something* to start to direct your efforts and attention to something, esp. work ○ *We've got to get down to business, folks, or we'll never get the newsletter out on time.*
• **get in ARRIVE** to arrive at a place ○ *What time did you say his plane gets in?*
• **get in BE ELECTED** to be elected to a political position ○ *If Archer gets in as mayor, he's likely to raise taxes.*
• **get in** *something* **FIND TIME** [M] to manage to find time for doing something ○ *I'd like to get in some skiing while we're in Colorado.*
• **get in** *something* **SAY** [M] to succeed in saying something, often in a situation where other people talk a lot ○ *She tried to get her suggestion in at the start of the meeting.*
• **get in on** *something* to be involved in or benefit from something when there is an opportunity ○ *If you'd like to get in on this offer, call now.*
• **get** *(someone)* **off 1** to escape legal punishment, or to help someone escape legal punishment ○ *She was charged with fraud, but her lawyer got her off.* **2** If you get off with a particular punishment, or if someone gets you off, it means that the punishment could have been much more severe: *He got off with a suspended sentence of three years for practicing medicine without a license.*
• **get off on** *something* to become excited by something ○ *He really gets off on those little porcelain figurines.*
• **get on** to grow old ○ *Uncle Meade's getting on in years – he's 76.* ○ See also: GET ALONG/ON
• **get on with** *something* to continue doing something after stopping ○ *We don't have all day to finish this job, so can we just get on with it?*
• **get out of** *something* **AVOID** to avoid doing something that you do not want to do, or to escape responsibility for something ○ *If I can get out of going to the meeting tonight, I will.*

• **get out of** *something* **STOP** to stop doing an activity ○ *I used to work out every day, but I've gotten out of the habit.* ○ *Lately I've gotten out of reading novels.* ○ *Hey,* **get out of the way** (= move), *I want to put these boxes there.*

• **get** *something* **out of** *someone* **FORCE** to obtain something, esp. money or information, from someone by force or persuasion ○ *It was not easy to get the truth out of her.*

• **get** *something* **out of** *something* **OBTAIN** *infml* to obtain something, esp. a good feeling, by doing something ○ *Bob's sister would probably get a big kick out of visiting him.*

• **get over** *something* to return to your usual state of health or happiness after having a bad or unusual experience, or an illness ○ *She's just getting over the flu.* ○ *I can't get over how short he is* (= it surprised me).

• **get** *something* **over with** to finish or reach the end of some unpleasant work, experience, or duty ○ *I'll be glad to get these exams over with.*

• **get** *(someone)* **through** *something* **FINISH 1** to reach the end of or finish something ○ *Once we get through exams, we'll have three weeks off.* **2** To get someone through something is to make it possible for someone to deal successfully with a difficult or painful experience, and come to the end of it: *My friendship with Carla got me through those tough months just after we moved.*

• **get through COMMUNICATE** to communicate with someone, esp. by telephone ○ *I tried phoning her, but I couldn't get through.*

• **get** *something* **through** *(something)* **SUCCEED** to succeed in persuading a legislature or other group to accept new laws ○ *How would a Democratic president get those measures through a Republican Congress?*

• **get** *(something)* **through BE UNDERSTOOD** to be understood or believed, or to cause someone to understand or believe you ○ *I just don't seem to be able to get through to him.* ○ *Global warming is real: It's very critical to get that through to people.*

• **get to** *someone* **CAUSE BAD FEELINGS** *infml* to cause feelings, esp. suffering or disgust, in someone ○ *The heat was beginning to get to me so I went indoors.*

• **get** *(someone)* **together** to have a meeting or a party ○ *Why don't we all get together on Friday?* ○ *Lynn sent me an e-mail asking, "Can you get your committee together?"* ○ Related noun: GET-TOGETHER

• **get** *(someone)* **up RISE** to rise from bed, or to cause someone to rise from bed ○ *I get the boys up at 7 a.m.*

• **get up** *something* **MAKE STRONGER** [M] to make your feelings or your determination stronger in order to do something ○ *He finally got up his courage to climb the rock wall.*

get to HAVE CHANCE *auxiliary verb, pres. part.* **getting,** *past* **got,** *past part.* **gotten, got** to have an opportunity to do something ○ *I never get to see her now that she's moved to California.* ○ *I'd like to get to know you better – could we have dinner sometime?*

BEGIN *auxiliary verb* to begin to do or be ○ *You're getting to be just like your mother.*

getaway /ˈget̬·əˌweɪ/ *n* [C] **1** an escape, esp. from a dangerous situation ○ *The men made their getaway in a car parked outside the bank.* **2** A getaway is also a place where you go for a vacation: *a getaway in the Poconos* ○ Related verb: GET AWAY

get-together /ˈget·təˌgeð·ər/ *n* [C] a gathering of people, esp. for enjoyment ○ *She went home for a family get-together over the weekend.* ○ Related verb: GET (SOMEONE) TOGETHER

getup /ˈget̬·ʌp/ *n* [C] *infml* the particular clothing, esp. when strange or unusual, that someone is wearing ○ *He was in a weird getup with a red wig.*

get-up-and-go /ˌget̬ˌʌp·ənˈgoʊ/ *n* [U] *infml* the quality of being energetic, determined, and enthusiastic ○ *We need someone with real get-up-and-go to run this office.*

geyser /ˈgɑɪ·zər/ *n* [C] a pool of hot water that sends a column of water and steam into the air on a regular or irregular schedule

ghastly /ˈgæst·li/ *adj* frightening and shocking ○ *It was a ghastly crime.*

ghetto /ˈget̬·oʊ/ *n* [C] *pl* **ghettos, ghettoes** a very poor area of a city in which people of the same race or religion live, or a part of a society or group that is in some way set apart

ghost /goʊst/ *n* [C] the spirit of a dead person imagined as visiting the living and usually appearing as a pale, almost transparent form of the dead person ○ *There are lots of stories about ghosts.*

ghost town *n* [C] a town that was busy in the past but is now empty or nearly empty because the activities that kept people there have stopped

ghostwrite /ˈgoʊ·strɑɪt/, **ghost** /goʊst/ *v* [T] *pres. part.* **ghostwriting,** *past simp.* **ghostwrote,** *past part.* **ghostwritten** to write a book, article, or speech for another person to use as his or her own

ghostwriter /ˈgoʊˌstrɑɪt̬·ər/ *n* [C] ○ *Carol worked as a ghostwriter for that radio talk-show host.*

GI /dʒiːˈɑɪ/ *n* [C] *pl* **GI's, GIs** a soldier in the US army

giant LARGE PERSON/ORGANIZATION /ˈdʒɑɪ·ənt/ *n* [C] a person, either real or imaginary, who is extremely large and strong, or a very large or powerful organization ○ *He was a giant of a man, over six and a half feet tall.* ○ *The merger makes them a giant in the publishing business.*

giant /ˈdʒɑɪ·ənt/ *adj* [not gradable] ○ *a giant corporation* ○ *a giant-size box of cornflakes* ○ *Admitting the problem is a giant* (= large and important) *step forward in your recovery.* ○ See also: GIGANTIC

LEADING PERSON /ˈdʒɑɪ·ənt/ *n* [C] a person of great ability, power, or influence ○ *She was one of the intellectual giants of this century.*

STAR /ˈdʒɑɪ·ənt/ *n* [C] ***earth science*** a star that is ten to 100 times bigger than the sun, and much brighter

G

gibberish /ˈdʒɪb·ə·rɪʃ/ *n* [U] confused or meaningless speech or writing ○ *See if you can make out what he's saying – it sounds like gibberish to me.*

gibe, **jibe** /dʒɑɪb/ *n* [C] an insulting remark intended to make someone look foolish ○ *She made a gibe about how late I was.*

giblets /ˈdʒɪb·ləts/ *pl n* the neck and some other parts, such as the LIVER, of a bird that may be removed before the bird is cooked, or that may be cooked and eaten themselves or used as a flavoring

giddy /ˈgɪd·i/ *adj* having a slight feeling of spinning around or being unable to balance; slightly DIZZY ○ *When she got off the roller coaster, she felt giddy and lightheaded.*

G

gift PRESENT /gɪft/ *n* [C] something that is given, esp. to show your affection; a present ○ *I have to get my sister a gift for her birthday.*

ABILITY /gɪft/ *n* [C] a special or unusual ability; a TALENT ○ *He has a gift for music – he plays the piano and sings beautifully.*

gifted /ˈgɪf·təd/ *adj* **1** having a special ability ○ *a gifted artist* **2** Gifted can also be used more generally to mean intelligent or having a great range of abilities.

gift-wrap *v* [T] **-pp-** to cover (something intended as a present) with attractive paper

gig /gɪg/ *n* [C] a job, esp. one as a performer or one that lasts only a short time ○ *Now many of his gigs as a singer-saxophonist are being put on hold.*

gigabyte /ˈgɪg·ə,bɑɪt/, *abbreviation* **GB** *n* [C] a unit of measurement of computer storage space equal to 1,073,741,824 BYTES, which is about 1000 MEGABYTES

gigantic /dʒɑɪˈgænt·ɪk/ *adj* extremely large ○ *a gigantic shopping center*

giggle /ˈgɪg·əl/ *v* [I] to laugh quietly, esp. in a nervous way, often at something silly ○ *We couldn't stop giggling.*

giggle /ˈgɪg·əl/ *n* [C] ○ *There were a few nervous giggles from people in the audience.*

gill /gɪl/ *n* [C usually pl] the organ through which fish and other water creatures breathe

gilt /gɪlt/ *adj* [not gradable] covered with a thin layer of gold or a substance that looks like gold ○ *gilt-rimmed eyeglasses*

gilt-edged *adj* of the highest quality available ○ *gilt-edged bonds*

gimme /ˈgɪm·i/ *n* [C] *slang* something so easy to do that it seems as if you only have to reach out and take it ○ *Though everyone expected the victory by the world champions to be a gimme, in fact it was a close contest.*

gimmick /ˈgɪm·ɪk/ *n* [C] something invented esp. for the purpose of attracting attention and that has no other purpose or value ○ *The proposal to cut taxes was nothing but a campaign gimmick.*

gin /dʒɪn/ *n* [U] a type of colorless, strong alcoholic drink

ginger /ˈdʒɪn·dʒər/ *n* [U] the spicy root of a tropical plant, used esp. as a powder in cooking and baking

ginger ale *n* [U] a sweet, bubbly drink that has the flavor of GINGER

gingerbread /ˈdʒɪn·dʒər,bred/ *n* [U] a type of cake or cookie that contains GINGER ○ *a gingerbread man* (= a spicy gingerbread cookie shaped like a person)

gingerly /ˈdʒɪn·dʒər·li/ *adv* in a slow, careful way ○ *Gingerly, he moved the heavy vase.*

gingham /ˈgɪŋ·əm/ *n* [U] a cotton cloth that has a pattern of woven colored squares on a white background ○ *a gingham dress*

giraffe /dʒəˈræf/ *n* [C] a large African animal with a very long neck and long legs

girder /ˈgɜrd·ər/ *n* [C] a long, thick piece of steel or concrete that supports a roof, floor, bridge, or other large structure

girdle /ˈgɜrd·əl/ *n* [C] a piece of elastic underwear worn around the waist and buttocks, esp. in the past by women, to shape the body

girl /gɜrl/ *n* [C] **1** a female child or, more generally, a female of any age ○ *Two little girls showed us around the kindergarten.* ○ *The girls' basketball team is undefeated.* **2** Girl sometimes means daughter: *We have two girls, a six-year-old and an eight-year-old.* ○ **USAGE:** Many adult women consider it offensive to be called girls by other people, esp. men, although this was common in the past, and they might still call themselves or their friends girls.

girlhood /ˈgɜrl·hʊd/ *n* [U] ○ *She lived in Chicago during her girlhood* (= when she was a child).

girlfriend /ˈgɜrl·frend/ *n* [C] a woman with whom you have a romantic relationship, or a female friend ○ *I've never met his girlfriend.* ○ *Susan was going out to lunch with her girlfriends.* ○ Compare BOYFRIEND

Girl Scout *n* [C] a girl who is a member of an organization that encourages girls to take part in a variety of activities and to become responsible and independent

girth /gɜrθ/ *n* [U] the distance around the outside of a thick or fat object, like a tree or a body ○ *He was a man of massive girth.*

gist /dʒɪst/ *n* [U] the main subject, without details, of a piece of information ○ *The gist of what she said was that I didn't know what I was talking about.*

give OFFER /gɪv/ *v* [T] *pres. part.* **giving,** *past simp.* **gave,** *past part.* **given** to offer something of your own to another person or thing, or to allow something you own or control to be owned or used by another ○ *We're collecting for the Red Cross – please give what you can.* ○ *We're giving Helen a salad bowl/We're giving a salad bowl to Helen as a wedding present.* ○ *Give me back my book/Give my book back* (= Return my book). ○ *Give her enough time*

(= Allow her to have enough time) *to finish the exam.*

WORD CHOICES give

Very common alternatives to "give" are verbs such as **offer**, **provide**, and **supply**.

This booklet ***provides*** *useful information about local services.*

Your doctor should be able to ***offer*** *advice.*

The lake ***supplies*** *the whole town with water.*

The verb **donate** is often used when someone gives money or goods to an organization that needs help.

Four hundred dollars has been ***donated*** *to the school book fund.*

If one of many people gives something, especially money, in order to provide or achieve something, the verb **contribute** is used.

I ***contributed*** *twenty dollars toward Jamie's present.*

If you put something from your hand into someone else's hand, you can use verbs such as **pass** and **hand**.

Could you ***hand*** *me that book, please?*

He ***passed*** *a note to her during the meeting.*

The phrasal verb **hand in** is sometimes used when you give something to someone in a position of authority.

Have you ***handed in*** *your history essay yet?*

The phrasal verb **pass on** is often used when you ask someone to give something to someone else.

Could you ***pass*** *this* ***on*** *to Laura when you've finished reading it?*

If something like a prize or an amount of money is given in an official way, you can use verbs like **award** or **present**.

She was ***presented*** *with a bouquet of flowers and a check for $100.*

He was ***awarded*** *the Nobel Prize for Physics.*

PRODUCE /gɪv/ *v* [T] *pres. part.* **giving**, *past simp.* **gave**, *past part.* **given** to produce or cause something ○ *He gave me a hard push.* ○ *Give me a phone call when you get home.* ○ *The president is giving a speech tonight.* ○ *The fresh air gave us an appetite* (= made us hungry). ○ *We're giving a birthday party for Kareem.* ○ *He gave me the impression* (= He made me think) *that the deal would go through.* ○ *This car has given* (= caused) *me lots of trouble ever since I got it.*

STRETCH /gɪv/ *v* [I] *pres. part.* **giving**, *past simp.* **gave**, *past part.* **given** to stretch or become looser ○ *New shoes will give a little after you've worn them a few times.* ○ *(fig.) The negotiations are completely deadlocked, and neither side will give an inch* (= each refuses to change its position even a little).

give /gɪv/ *n* [U] ○ *A cotton sweater doesn't have much give.*

IDIOMS with give

• **give** *someone* **a break** *infml* stop criticizing or being angry with someone ○ *Give her a break – she was only five minutes late.*

• **give** *someone* **a heads up** to tell someone that something is going to happen ○ *I just wanted to give you all a heads up that we will be talking about the first two chapters of the book tomorrow.*

• **give a hoot** *slang* to care ○ *Many of my friends don't give a hoot about college basketball.*

• **give** *someone* **a piece of** *your* **mind** to tell someone why you are angry with that person ○ *I'd like to give her a piece of my mind.*

• **give** *someone* **a run for** *his or her* **money** to be as good at something as someone who is extremely good ○ *He'll give those professional players a run for their money.*

• **give** *something* **a whirl** to try something for the first time ○ *I've never done cross-country skiing before, but I thought I'd give it a whirl this winter.*

• **give** *someone* **hell** *slang* to criticize someone angrily ○ *The boss gave me hell for not telling him about it.*

• **give or take** a little more or a little less compared to the amount mentioned ○ *The building is 90 feet tall, give or take a few feet.*

• **give rise to** *something fml* to cause something to exist ○ *Heavy rains have given rise to flooding over a large area.*

• **give** *someone* **the benefit of the doubt** to decide that you will believe someone, even though you are not sure that what the person is saying is true ○ *She said she was late because her flight was canceled, and we gave her the benefit of the doubt.*

• **give** *someone* **the cold shoulder** to intentionally ignore someone or treat someone in an unfriendly way ○ *I thought she really liked me, but the next day she gave me the cold shoulder.*

• **give way** to break or fall down suddenly ○ *The wooden seats gave way under the weight of the crowd.*

• **give way to** *something* to be replaced by something ○ *My excitement gave way to fear when I drove a car for the first time.*

• **not give** *someone* **the time of day** to not be friendly to someone and not speak to or help that person ○ *He kept pestering me to go out with him, but I wouldn't give him the time of day.*

• *someone* **would give anything for** *something, someone* **would give anything to** *do something* to want something very much ○ *I'd give anything to see the pyramids of Egypt.*

• *someone* **would give** *someone* **the shirt off** *his or her* **back** someone would be willing to do anything to help another person ○ *Charlie is the nicest guy – he'd give you the shirt off his back if you were in trouble.*

PHRASAL VERBS with give

• **give away** *something* **TELL** [M] to tell a secret or show your feelings unintentionally ○ *I'm not giving away any plot surprises; read the review in the paper if you want to know them.* ○ *The look on her face gave her away* (= showed her real feelings). ○ Related noun: GIVEAWAY COMMUNICATION

• **give away** *something* **SUPPLY FREE** [M] to supply something at no charge ○ *They're giving away shopping bags.* ○ Related noun: GIVEAWAY SOMETHING FREE

G

•**give in** to decide to do what someone else wants ○ *Our kids kept begging us to take them to the beach, and finally we gave in.*
•**give off** *something* to produce something as a result of a natural process ○ *The forest fire gave off thick black smoke.*
•**give out** **NOT CONTINUE** to last no longer, or to work no longer ○ *Food supplies will give out by the end of the week.*
•**give out** *something* **SUPPLY** [M] to give something to each of a number of people ○ *They're giving out free tickets to the circus.*
•**give up** *(something)* [M] **1** to stop doing or to stop having something ○ *He gave up jogging after his heart attack.* **2** To give up also means to lose or be defeated: *Although behind in the chess match, he refused to give up.* ○ *"Can you guess what actor I'm pretending to be?" "No, I give up* (= I can't guess)*."*
•**give up on** *something/someone* to expect someone or something to fail ○ *Most people gave up on him when he quit school, but he went back and earned his degree two years later.*

give-and-take /ˌgɪv·ən ˈteɪk/ *n* [U] **1** a free exchange of ideas or opinions ○ *We were simply told what to do – there wasn't any give-and-take.* **2** A give-and-take is also the willingness to accept some of another person's ideas and give up some of your own: *Any successful negotiation involves some give-and-take.*

giveaway **COMMUNICATION** /ˈgɪv·əˌweɪ/ *n* [C usually sing] something that communicates information, esp. when there is no intention to do this ○ *The look on his face when her name is mentioned is a dead giveaway.* ○ Related verb: GIVE AWAY **TELL**
SOMETHING FREE /ˈgɪv·əˌwei/ *n* [C] something provided at no charge, or for which nothing is expected in return ○ *The tax cuts represent a giveaway by the government to these businesses.* ○ Related verb: GIVE AWAY **SUPPLY FREE**

given **GIVE** /ˈgɪv·ən/ *past participle of* GIVE
ACCEPTED FACT /ˈgɪv·ən/ *n* [C] something that is certain to happen or to be ○ *It's a given that if he is defeated for reelection, he'll be offered a position in the administration.*
KNOWING /ˈgɪv·ən/ *prep* considering ○ *Given his age, he's in excellent physical condition.*
ARRANGED /ˈgɪv·ən/ *adj* [not gradable] already decided, arranged, or agreed ○ *At any given time* (= at any particular time)*, the jury may reach a verdict, so we'd better stay nearby.*

given name *n* [C] your FIRST NAME

gizmo /ˈgɪz·moʊ/ *n* [C] *pl* **gizmos** *infml* any small device ○ *The store is full of gizmos like pagers and cellular telephones.*

glacier /ˈgleɪ·ʃər/ *n* [C] ***earth science*** a large mass of ice that moves slowly over land, esp. down the side of a mountain, often moving rocks with it and changing the shape of the land

glad /glæd/ *adj* [-er/-est only] **-dd-** pleased and happy ○ [+ *(that)* clause] *We were glad (that) she succeeded.* ○ [+ *to* infinitive] *You don't have to thank us – we were glad to help.* ○ *I'm glad of the opportunity to express my thanks.*
gladly /ˈglæd·li/ *adv* [not gradable] ○ *I'd gladly show her around, but I'll be on vacation next week.*
gladden /ˈglæd·ᵊn/ *v* [T] to make someone happy ○ *A visit to Disneyland is sure to gladden the heart of any 8-year-old.*

WORD FAMILY glad

Adjectives	glad	*Adverbs*	gladly
Verbs	gladden		

gladiator /ˈglæd·iːˌeɪţ·ər/ *n* [C] in ancient Rome, a man who fought another man or an animal as a public entertainment

gladiolus /ˌglæd·iːˈoʊ·ləs/, **gladiola** /ˌglæd·iːˈoʊ·lə/ *n* [C] *pl* **gladioli, gladiolas** a tall garden plant that has long, thin leaves and a stem with many brightly colored flowers

glamour, **glamor** /ˈglæm·ər/ *n* [U] a quality of someone or something that causes excitement and admiration because of its style or attractive appearance ○ *Hollywood glamour* ○ *The downhill race was one of the glamour events of the Winter Olympics.*
glamorous /ˈglæm·ə·rəs/ *adj* ○ *glamorous fashion models* ○ *a glamorous job*
glamorize /ˈglæm·əˌrɑɪz/ *v* [T] to make something more exciting and attractive ○ *The ad glamorized life on the island, emphasizing the beaches and warm weather.*

glance /glæns/ *n* [C] a quick look at someone or something ○ *The driver gave a glance back as he moved into the passing lane.*
glance /glæns/ *v* [I always + adv/prep] ○ *She glanced around the room to see who was there.*

IDIOM with glance

•**see** *something* **at a glance**, **tell** *something* **at a glance** almost immediately ○ *She could see at a glance that something was seriously wrong.*

glancing /ˈglæn·sɪŋ/ *adj* [not gradable] touching or hitting you quickly and lightly from the side rather than from the front, and usually not doing much damage ○ *He never saw the ball coming, but fortunately it gave him only a glancing blow.*

gland /glænd/ *n* [C] an organ of the body that produces chemicals that influence activities such as growth, and that has an important effect on health ○ *sweat glands*
glandular /ˈglæn·dʒə·lər/ *adj* [not gradable] ○ *glandular secretions*

glare **LOOK** /gler, glær/ *v* [I] to look at someone angrily and without moving your eyes ○ *He kept talking during the concert, and people were glaring at him.*
glare /gler, glær/ *n* [C] ○ *an angry glare*
SHINE /gler, glær/ *v* [I] to shine too brightly ○ *The sun glared on the snow and the effect was blinding.*

glare /gler, glær/ *n* [U] ○ *A tinted windshield cuts down on glare.*

glaring /ˈgler·ɪŋ, ˈglær-/ *adj* (of something bad) very obvious ○ *It was a glaring mistake.*

glasnost /ˈglæz·noʊst, ˈglæs-/ *n* [U] ***politics & government*** a Soviet political idea used by Mikhail Gorbachev to make the Soviet government more open to change and to create better relationships with other countries

glass /glæs/ *n* [C/U] **1** a hard, transparent material that is used to make windows, bottles, and other objects **2** A glass is a small container of glass, usually round and without a handle, for holding a liquid that you can drink, or the liquid held by such a container: [C] *She poured some milk into a glass.* ○ [C] *May I have a glass of water?*

glass /glæs/ *adj* [not gradable] made of glass ○ *a glass jar/bottle*

glasses /ˈglæs·əz/, **eyeglasses** *pl n* two small pieces of specially made glass or transparent plastic worn in front of the eyes to improve sight and held in place with a frame that reaches back over the ears ○ *a pair of glasses*

glassful /ˈglæs·fʊl/ *n* [C] the amount of something that is needed to fill a glass ○ *Drink a glassful of water with this medicine.*

glassy /ˈglæs·i/ *adj* [-*er*/-*est* only] **1** smooth and shiny like glass ○ *the glassy surface of the water* **2** Someone who has glassy eyes or a glassy stare has a fixed expression and seems unable to see anything: *When he arrived at the hospital, his eyes were glassy and he didn't seem to know where he was.*

WORD FAMILY glass

Nouns	glass	Adjectives	glass
	glasses		glassy
	glassful		

glass ceiling *n* [C] a limit that is unofficial but understood which prevents someone, esp. a woman, from advancing to a top position in a company or organization ○ *The fact that no woman has managed one of the branch offices is pretty strong evidence of a glass ceiling.*

glassware /ˈglæs·wer, -wær/ *n* [U] objects made of glass, esp. containers for drinking

glaucoma /glɑʊˈkoː·mə, glɔː-/ *n* [U] a disease in which pressure builds up inside the eye

glaze /gleɪz/ *n* [C] a shiny surface given to an object or a food, esp. by covering it with a liquid that shines when it dries ○ *The pottery was famous for the rich glaze of its vases and jugs.*

glaze /gleɪz/ *v* [I/T] **1** [T] *The cake was glazed with raspberry syrup.* **2** When someone's eyes glaze over, they become fixed and shiny, as if the person is not seeing anything: [I] *By the fourth act of the opera, his eyes had glazed over.*

gleam /gliːm/ *v* [I] to shine with a soft light ○ *Street lights gleamed brightly in the snow.*

gleam /gliːm/ *n* [C] ○ *the gleam of silver candlesticks*

IDIOM with gleam

• **a gleam in** *your* **eye** an expression in your eyes that shows that you are amused or that you have a secret ○ *"I can't tell you that yet, but I will soon," Grandpa said with a gleam in his eye.*

glean /gliːn/ *v* [T] to collect information in small amounts ○ *From what I was able to glean, the news isn't good.*

glee /gliː/ *n* [U] happiness or great pleasure ○ *Malone pumped his fist with glee after scoring the game-winner.*

gleeful /ˈgliː·fəl/ *adj* ○ *gleeful children*

gleefully /ˈgliː·fə·li/ *adv* ○ *She talks gleefully about her adventures.*

glee club /ˈgliː ˈklʌb/ *n* [C] a group organized to sing together, often at a school or university

glib /glɪb/ *adj* **-bb-** easy and confident in speech, with little thought or sincerity ○ *He's not flashy, and he doesn't know how to be glib.*

glide /glɑɪd/ *v* [I always + adv/prep] to move easily and continuously, as if without effort ○ *She glided along on her skates.*

glider /ˈglɑɪd·ər/ *n* [C] an aircraft without an engine that flies by using its long, fixed wings to ride on air currents

glimmer /ˈglɪm·ər/ *v* [I] (of light) to shine without strength or not continuously ○ *A candle glimmered faintly in the darkened room.*

glimmer /ˈglɪm·ər/ *n* [C] **1** *a glimmer of light* **2** A glimmer is also a slight sign: *The treaty offered a glimmer of hope to the region.*

glimpse /glɪmps/ *n* [C] a brief look at someone or something ○ *He caught a glimpse of her face.*

glimpse /glɪmps/ *v* [I/T] ○ [T] *I glimpsed her walking back from town.*

glint /glɪnt/ *v* [I] to produce or reflect small, bright flashes of light ○ *sun glinting off a windshield*

glint /glɪnt/ *n* [C] ○ *a glint in your eye*

glisten /ˈglɪs·ən/ *v* [I] (esp. of wet surfaces) to shine brightly ○ *His eyes glistened with tears.*

glitch /glɪtʃ/ *n* [C] *infml* a problem or fault ○ *a technical glitch* ○ *a minor glitch*

glitter /ˈglɪt̬·ər/ *v* [I] to shine with little, bright flashes of reflected light ○ *The grass glittered like jewels.*

glitter /ˈglɪt̬·ər/ *n* [U] **1** *the glitter of moonlight on the lake* **2** Glitter is also very small pieces of shiny material used to decorate a surface.

glitz /glɪts/ *n* [U] the showy quality of something ○ *the glitz and glamour of Hollywood*

glitzy /ˈglɪt·si/ *adj* ○ *a glitzy restaurant*

gloat /gloʊt/ *v* [I always + adv/prep] to feel or show much pleasure because of your own success or good luck, or because of someone else's misfortune ○ *You may have won, but don't gloat about it.*

glob /glɑb/ *n* [C] a round mass of a thick liquid or a soft substance ○ *a glob of wax*

globalization Ⓐ /ˌɡloʊ·bə·ləˈzeɪ·ʃən/ *n* [U] ***social studies*** the development of closer economic, cultural, and political relations among all the countries of the world as a result of travel and communication becoming easy ○ *Optimists say globalization means more cultural choices for everyone.*

global warming *n* [U] a gradual increase in the earth's temperature, caused by gases, esp. CARBON DIOXIDE, surrounding the earth

globe Ⓐ **WORLD** /ɡloʊb/ *n* [U] the world ○ *The Olympic Games will be seen around the globe.*
global Ⓐ /ˈɡloʊ·bəl/ *adj* ***politics & government*** relating to the whole world ○ *We hope an era of peace and global cooperation has begun.*
globally Ⓐ /ˈɡloʊ·bə·li/ *adv* ○ *The company is trying to compete globally.*

ROUND OBJECT /ɡloʊb/ *n* [C] an object shaped like a ball, or such an object having a map of the world on its outer surface

gloom **NO HOPE** /ɡluːm/ *n* [U] lack of hope ○ *Gloom and anger replaced her earlier upbeat mood.*
gloomy /ˈɡluː·mi/ *adj* ○ *Despite gloomy predictions, the stock market remains strong.*
gloomily /ˈɡluː·mə·li/ *adv* ○ *He watched gloomily as the bus drove off.*

DARKNESS /ɡluːm/ *n* [U] darkness or near darkness ○ *Up ahead they could see lights in the gloom.*
gloomy /ˈɡluː·mi/ *adj* ○ *It was another gray, gloomy day.*

glop /ɡlɑp/ *n* [U] *infml* a sticky, thick substance, such as food, that appears unpleasant ○ *I can't believe they served us this glop.*

glorify /ˈɡlɔːr·əˌfɑɪ, ˈɡloʊr-/ *v* [T] to praise or honor someone or something, or to make someone or something seem more excellent than is actually true ○ *The film glorifies the past too much.* ○ *He has been glorified in the press.*
glorification /ˌɡlɔːr·ə·fəˈkeɪ·ʃən, ˌɡloʊr-/ *n* [U] ○ *the glorification of wealth*

glory **ADMIRATION** /ˈɡlɔːr·i, ˈɡloʊr·i/ *n* [U] great admiration, honor, and praise that you earn by achieving something, or something which deserves admiration or honor ○ *He basked in the glory of his victory.* ○ *Winning the championship was the crowning glory of her career* (= it was her highest achievement).
glorious /ˈɡlɔːr·iː·əs, ˈɡloʊr-/ *adj* deserving admiration, praise, and honor ○ *She thought it was a grand and glorious country.*
gloriously /ˈɡlɔːr·iː·ə·sli, ˈɡloʊr-/ *adv* ○ *The meanings of his paintings are gloriously elusive.*

BEAUTY /ˈɡlɔːr·i, ˈɡloʊr·i/ *n* [C/U] great beauty, or something that is very beautiful or excellent ○ [U] *They are restoring the building to its former glory.* ○ [C usually pl] *the glories of ancient Egypt*
glorious /ˈɡlɔːr·iː·əs, ˈɡloʊr-/ *adj* ○ *July was a beautiful month of glorious sun.*

PHRASAL VERB with glory

• **glory in** *something* to be very pleased or proud about something ○ *Last week the Tulsa club gloried in its third U.S. Open tournament.*

gloss **SHINE** /ɡlɑs, ɡlɔːs/ *n* [U] a smooth shine on the surface of something ○ *The floor was waxed and buffed to a high gloss.*
glossy /ˈɡlɑs·i, ˈɡlɔː·si/ *adj* [-er/-est only] **1** *He has straight, glossy black hair.* **2** A glossy magazine or photograph is one printed on shiny paper.

EXPLANATION /ɡlɑs, ɡlɔːs/ *n* [C] an explanation of a word or phrase in a text
gloss /ɡlɑs, ɡlɔːs/ *v* [T] ○ *Special senses of words are glossed in this dictionary.*

PHRASAL VERB with gloss

• **gloss over** *something* to treat something in a way that fails to recognize its importance or its faults ○ *Popular writing sometimes glosses over important facts.*

glossary /ˈɡlɑs·ə·ri, ˈɡlɔː·sə-/ *n* [C] ***literature*** an alphabetical list of difficult, technical, or foreign words in a text along with explanations of their meanings

glove /ɡlʌv/ *n* [C] a covering for the hand and wrist, with separate parts for the thumb and each finger, that provides warmth or protection ○ *leather/rubber gloves* ○ *a pair of gloves*

glove compartment, **glove box** *n* [C] a small container facing the front passenger seat in a car which is used for storing small items

glow **LIGHT** /ɡloʊ/ *n* [U] continuous light, esp. light from something that is heated ○ *the glow of embers from a fire*
glow /ɡloʊ/ *v* [I] ○ *A nightlight glowed dimly in the bedroom.*
glowing /ˈɡloʊ·ɪŋ/ *adj* [not gradable] ○ *the glowing lights of a town in the distance*

LOOK /ɡloʊ/ *n* [U] **1** a red or warm look ○ *Her face has a natural, healthy glow.* **2** A glow is also a positive feeling: *The glow of romance seemed to have worn off.*
glow /ɡloʊ/ *v* [I] ○ *His cheeks glowed after the workout.*

glower /ˈɡlɑʊ·ər, ˈɡloʊ-/ *v* [I] to look angry or annoyed ○ *Grant glowered at the kids crossing his lawn.*

glowing /ˈɡloʊ·ɪŋ/ *adj* full of enthusiastic praise ○ *glowing reviews* ○ *a glowing evaluation*
glowingly /ˈɡloʊ·ɪŋ·li/ *adv* ○ *Engineers speak glowingly of the device.*

glucose /ˈɡluː·koʊs, -koʊz/ *n* [U] ***biology, chemistry*** a type of sugar that is found in many foods and that organisms use to get energy

glue /ɡluː/ *n* [U] a sticky substance used for joining things
glue /ɡluː/ *v* [T] ○ *I'll just glue the handle back on the cup.*

IDIOM with glue

• **glued to** *something* giving something your full attention ○ *During football season, he's glued to the TV.*

glum /ɡlʌm/ *adj* [-er/-est only] **-mm-** sad and discouraged ○ *a glum expression*

glumly /ˈɡlʌm·li/ *adv* ○ *Marty nodded glumly.*

glut /ɡlʌt/ *n* [C] a supply or amount that is much greater than necessary ○ *a glut of new housing* ○ *a glut of information*

glutton /ˈɡlʌt·ᵊn/ *n* [C] a person who regularly eats too much ○ *What a glutton – he ate a whole pizza by himself.*

glycerol /ˈɡlɪs·əˌrɔːl, -ˌroʊl/ *n* [U] ***biology*** a clear, thick liquid found in fats and oils, which is used in making many things, including explosives and medicines

glycogen /ˈɡlɑɪ·kə·dʒən/ *n* [U] ***biology*** a substance that is found in the LIVER (= organ that cleans the blood) and the muscles and that stores CARBOHYDRATE (= substance that provides energy) and helps to control the level of sugar in the blood

glycol /ˈɡlɑɪ·kɔːl, -koʊl/ *n* [U] ***chemistry*** a poisonous alcohol that is used as an ANTIFREEZE (= liquid that reduces the temperature at which water freezes) and in industry

gnarled /nɑrld/ *adj* rough and twisted in shape ○ *ancient gnarled trees* ○ *gnarled hands*

gnash /næʃ/ *v* [T] to bring your top and bottom teeth together quickly

IDIOM with gnash

• **gnash** *your* **teeth** to show that you are angry or annoyed about something bad that you can do nothing to stop ○ *Petersen is gnashing his teeth over his inability to prove his innocence.*

gnat /næt/ *n* [C] a small flying insect that bites

gnaw **BITE** /nɔː/ *v* [I/T] to bite or chew something repeatedly ○ [I] *The cat began to gnaw at the towel beneath him.*

FEEL ANXIOUS /nɔː/ *v* [I always + adv/prep] to cause someone to feel continual anxiety or pain

gnawing /ˈnɔː·ɪŋ/ *adj* ○ *He has gnawing doubts about his loyalties.*

gnome /noʊm/ *n* [C] (in children's stories) an imaginary, very small old man who lives underground and guards gold and other valuable objects

go **TRAVEL** /ɡoʊ/ *v* [I] **goes,** *pres. part.* **going,** *past simp.* **went,** *past part.* **gone** **1** to move or travel to another place ○ *Let's go home now.* ○ *Are you going away for your vacation?* ○ *He's going to his country house for the weekend.* ○ *We don't go to the movies much.* ○ *You go on (ahead) and I'll be along in a minute.* ○ *Are you planning to go by car or are you flying?* ○ *The payroll checks went out* (= were sent) *a week later than usual.* ○ *I'm just going over* (= making a visit) *to Pete's for half an hour.* ○ *My son is planning to go into* (= get a job in) *journalism.* ○ *Where did my keys go* (= I can't find them)*?* ○ *A considerable amount of money and effort has gone into* (= been used in preparing) *this exhibition.* **2** To **go back** is to return: *When do you go back to school?* **3** To **go back** is also to have existed since some time in the past: *Their friendship goes back to when they were in college together.* **4** To **go up** or **go down** is to increase or be reduced: *My rent is going up 6% this year.* **5** To be going or to **go for** a particular activity is to move to the place of the activity or to begin to do it: *to go for a walk/swim* ○ *Why don't we go for a drive* (= have a ride in a car)*?* ○ *We're going shopping at the mall.* **6** To have gone to do a particular activity is to have left to do it and not yet returned: *They've gone sailing on the lake.*

-goer /ˌɡoʊ·ər/ *suffix* a person who goes to the stated type of place ○ *Regular moviegoers like to compare notes about the latest movies.*

USAGE

gone or **been?**

The past participle of **go** is **gone**.

I'm sorry but she's gone away on business – she'll be back next week.

Sometimes, however, **been** is used to say that someone has gone somewhere and come back, or to say that someone has visited somewhere.

He's been to Chicago many times.

Been describes the past up through the present.

She's been away all week (= She left at the beginning of the week and she is not back yet).

~~*She's gone away all week.*~~

Gone describes the present and the future.

She's gone away for a month (= She is away now and will be back a month from the time she left).

MOVE TOWARD /ɡoʊ/ *v* [I] **goes,** *pres. part.* **going,** *past simp.* **went,** *past part.* **gone** **1** to be or continue moving, esp. in a particular way or direction ○ *We were going (at) about 65 miles an hour.* ○ *I had a wonderful weekend but it went awfully quickly.* ○ *If you take the bus, you go over the bridge, but the train goes through the tunnel.* ○ *There's still three months to go before he has surgery, but he's already nervous about it.* ○ *The flu is going around right now* (= It's moving from person to person). ○ *I was going up/down the stairs when the phone rang.* ○ *He went up to her* (= approached her) *and asked for her autograph.* ○ *On summer evenings we often sat on the porch and watched the sun go down.* **2** To **go by** is to move past or beyond: *We sat on the shore and watched the sailboats go by.* ○ *Several months went by, and still he had no word from her.*

going /ˈɡoʊ·ɪŋ/ *n* [U] ○ *It was slow going because of ice on the roads.*

LEAVE /ɡoʊ/ *v* [I] **goes,** *pres. part.* **going,** *past simp.* **went,** *past part.* **gone** **1** to leave a place, esp. in order to travel to somewhere else ○ *It's time to go.* ○ *Please close the door when you go.* ○ *She wasn't feeling well, so she went home early* (= left early to go home). ○ *She's gone off with my umbrella* (= She took it by accident). ○ *I always go out* (= leave my home and travel to another place, esp. for entertainment) *on Saturday night.* **2** If something is gone, none of it is left: *I can't believe the milk is gone already.*

going /ˈgoʊ·ɪŋ/ *n* [C] ○ *There were a lot of comings and goings at the apartment next door.*

LEAD /goʊ/ *v* [I always + adv/prep] **goes**, *pres. part.* **going**, *past simp.* **went**, *past part.* **gone 1** (of a road, path, etc.) to lead in a particular direction ○ *Does I-70 go to Denver?* **2** If something goes a particular length, it is that long: *The well goes down at least 30 feet.*

BECOME /goʊ/ *v* **goes**, *pres. part.* **going**, *past simp.* **went**, *past part.* **gone** to become or be in a certain condition ○ [L] *Her father is going blind.* ○ [L] *If anything goes wrong, you can call our emergency hotline.* ○ [L] *Because of lack of evidence, the police were forced to let him go free.* ○ [I] *If you keep applying ice, the swelling will go down* (= become smaller). ○ [I] *The computer went down* (= stopped operating) *twice last week.* ○ [I] *The electricity suddenly went off* (= stopped operating). ○ [I] *One of these days I'll have to go on a diet* (= start to be on one). ○ [I] *I was so exhausted I went to sleep* (= started sleeping) *immediately.* ○ [I] *It was feared for a while that the two countries would go to war* (= start to fight a war) *over this dispute.* ○ [I] *It wasn't a bad hospital, as hospitals go* (= compared with the usual standard of hospitals), *but I still hated being there.*

CHANGE /goʊ/ *v* [I always + adv/prep] **goes**, *pres. part.* **going**, *past simp.* **went**, *past part.* **gone** to do something to cause a change or create a new condition ○ *I'd love to come to dinner, but I don't want you to go to any trouble* (= do a lot of work).

WEAKEN /goʊ/ *v* [I] **goes**, *pres. part.* **going**, *past simp.* **went**, *past part.* **gone** to become weak or damaged, esp. from use, or to stop working ○ *Her hearing is starting to go, but otherwise she's in good shape.*

START /goʊ/ *v* [I] **goes**, *pres. part.* **going**, *past simp.* **went**, *past part.* **gone** to start doing or using something ○ *I'll just connect the printer to the computer and we'll be ready to go.*

OPERATE /goʊ/ *v* [I] **goes**, *pres. part.* **going**, *past simp.* **went**, *past part.* **gone** to operate ○ *My watch was going fine up until a few minutes ago, but then it stopped running.*

going /ˈgoʊ·ɪŋ/ *adj* [not gradable] operating successfully or without difficulty ○ *The advertising agency was a going concern when she headed it.*

MAKE SOUND /goʊ/ *v* [I/T] **goes**, *pres. part.* **going**, *past simp.* **went**, *past part.* **gone** to produce a noise ○ [I] *Somebody's car alarm went off at 3 in the morning and woke me up.*

MOVE BODY /goʊ/ *v* [I always + adv/prep] **goes**, *pres. part.* **going**, *past simp.* **went**, *past part.* **gone** to move a part of the body in a particular way or in the way that is shown ○ *Try making your foot go backwards and forwards.*

DIVIDE /goʊ/ *v* [I] **goes**, *pres. part.* **going**, *past simp.* **went**, *past part.* **gone** (of a number) to fit into another number, esp. resulting in a whole number ○ *Three goes into 12 four times.*

BE SITUATED /goʊ/ *v* [I always + adv/prep] **goes**, *pres. part.* **going**, *past simp.* **went**, *past part.* **gone** to belong in a particular place, esp. as the usual place ○ *Tell the moving men that the sofa goes against that wall.*

HAPPEN /goʊ/ *v* [I always + adv/prep] **goes**, *pres. part.* **going**, *past simp.* **went**, *past part.* **gone 1** to happen or develop ○ *The doctor said the operation went well.* ○ *What's going on here* (= Explain what is happening)? **2** If people have something going for them, that thing causes them to have a lot of advantages and to be successful: *They've got a happy marriage, great careers, and wonderful children – in fact they've got everything going for them.*

BE SOLD /goʊ/ *v* [I] **goes**, *pres. part.* **going**, *past simp.* **went**, *past part.* **gone** to be sold or be available ○ *The painting is expected to go for at least a million dollars.*

BE EXPRESSED /goʊ/ *v* [I] **goes**, *pres. part.* **going**, *past simp.* **went**, *past part.* **gone** to be expressed, sung, or played ○ *I can never remember how that song goes.*

BE SUITABLE /goʊ/ *v* [I] **goes**, *pres. part.* **going**, *past simp.* **went**, *past part.* **gone** to be acceptable or suitable ○ *Do you think my new brown scarf goes with my black coat?*

going /ˈgoʊ·ɪŋ/ *adj* [not gradable] (of a price or a charge) usual or suitable at the present time ○ *What's the going rate for this kind of work?*

BE KNOWN /goʊ/ *v* [I always + adv/prep] **goes**, *pres. part.* **going**, *past simp.* **went**, *past part.* **gone** to be known by a particular name ○ *He went under the name of Platt, but that was not his real name.*

DEPEND ON /goʊ/ *v* [I always + adv/prep] **goes**, *pres. part.* **going**, *past simp.* **went**, *past part.* **gone** to have an opinion, decision, or judgment depend on something ○ *There were no witnesses to the crime, and so far the police don't have much to go on.*

BE FINAL /goʊ/ *v* [I] **goes**, *pres. part.* **going**, *past simp.* **went**, *past part.* **gone** to be final; not to be questioned ○ *In my parents' day, nobody ever argued with their father – whatever he said went.*

PLAY /goʊ/ *v* [I] **goes**, *pres. part.* **going**, *past simp.* **went**, *past part.* **gone** to do something at a particular time or in a particular order, before or after other people; have a turn ○ *Who goes next?*

ENERGY /goʊ/ *n* [U] the condition of being energetic and active

IDIOMS with go

• **go easy on** *someone* to treat someone in a gentle way, esp. when you want to be or should be more severe ○ *Do you think judges should go easy on criminals if they're teenagers?*

• **go easy on** *something* to not take or use too much of something ○ *The doctor told me to go easy on the spicy food for a while.*

• **go from bad to worse** to become even more difficult or unpleasant ○ *Things went from bad to worse in the second game when we lost 38-0.*

• **go for it** *infml* to do what you need to do without additional thought ○ *If you want it, then stop worrying about it and go for it.*

• **go haywire** to stop working correctly ○ *They told us later in the hospital that his heart had gone haywire.*

• **go in one ear and out the other** to be heard but immediately forgotten ○ *You can give her advice, but it just goes in one ear and out the other.*

• **go it alone** to decide to do something by yourself, without help from other people ○ *I decided to go it alone and set up my own business at home.*

• **go out of** *your* **way** to try especially hard to do something good or helpful ○ *They really went out of their way to make us feel welcome.* ○ Compare BEND OVER BACKWARDS at BEND **IDIOMS**

• **go overboard** to do or say too much because you are so enthusiastic ○ *I think I went overboard cooking this dinner – there is enough to feed a dozen people.*

• **go public** to become a company in which anyone can invest ○ *The company went public in 2003.*

• **go public (with** *something***)** to make something known that was secret before ○ *If the teacher goes public with her story, the school's reputation will be damaged.*

• **go through the motions** to do something without believing it is important ○ *After his wife died, he went through the motions of living without really feeling anything.*

• **go to bat for** *someone* to support someone when the person needs help ○ *The government will go to bat for companies that pay lots of taxes.*

• **go to great lengths** to use a lot of effort to get or achieve something ○ *We went to great lengths to make sure the votes were counted correctly.*

• **go to** *someone's* **head 1** to damage or weaken your judgment ○ *The climate can go to your head.* **2** If success **goes to** *your* **head**, it makes you believe that you are more successful or powerful than you really are: *Don't let one win go to your head – you still have at least three more games to play.*

• **go to pot** *infml* to become worse or be spoiled because of lack of care or effort ○ *Our old neighborhood has gone to pot.*

• **go to the bathroom** to urinate or excrete waste from the bowels

• **go to the dogs** to become much worse in quality or character ○ *After Joe retired, the business went to the dogs.*

• **go to town (on** *something***)** to do something eagerly and as completely as possible ○ *Kayla and Josh really went to town on their wedding.*

• **go up in smoke** to be wasted ○ *When the business went bankrupt, twenty years of hard work went up in smoke.*

• **go with the flow** to do what other people are doing or agree with the opinions of others ○ *When you're new in a school, it's easiest to just go with the flow for a while, and see what people are like.*

• **go wrong 1** to make a mistake or a bad decision ○ *If you just follow the signs to the park, you can't go wrong.* **2** If a situation **goes wrong**, there are problems or there is a bad result: *I was so worried that something had gone wrong that I called the police.*

• *something* **goes for** *someone/something else* something is also true for someone or something else ○ *What Mary just said goes for me too* (= I agree with what she said). ○ *San Francisco will have a beautiful day on Friday, and that goes for Portland and Seattle too.*

• *something* **goes without saying, it goes without saying (that)** something is obviously true ○ *If you got an "A" in the class, it goes without saying that you did well on the final exam.*

• **(still) going strong 1** to still be successful after having existed for a long time ○ *After one hundred years of service as a public institution, the state university system is still going strong.* **2** Someone who is **still going strong** is healthy even though the person is old or has been ill: *He's still going strong at 94!*

• **on the go** very busy or active ○ *Elise is always on the go.*

• *someone* **is going places,** *someone* **will go places/far** someone will be successful ○ *Maria's a talented writer – she's definitely going places.*

• **(***something***) to go** packed or wrapped so that you can take it with you ○ *I'd like a cheeseburger and a strawberry milk shake to go, please.* ○ **USAGE:** Used to talk about restaurant food that you want to take with you.

G

PHRASAL VERBS with go

• **go about** *something* to begin to do something ○ *We'd like to help but we're not sure what's the best way to go about it.*

• **go against** *something/someone* to oppose or be in disagreement with something or someone ○ *What you're asking me to do goes against everything I believe in.* ○ *Anytime they go against each other, you know it's going to be a good fight.*

• **go ahead** to begin or continue with a plan or activity without waiting, esp. after a delay ○ *The meeting will go ahead as planned.* ○ Related noun: GO-AHEAD

• **go along** to agree or be willing to accept something ○ *Alex has already agreed, but it's going to be harder persuading Mike to go along.* ○ *The president would not feel obligated to go along with a deal he didn't like.*

• **go around** to be enough for everyone ○ *There won't be enough pizza to go around if you take two pieces.*

• **go at** *someone/something* **1** to attack someone or something violently, using either force or very strong language ○ *The candidates went at each other during the debate.* **2** To go at something is also to use all of your energy and effort to succeed: *The crowd showed up to see the two golfers go at it the final day of the tournament.*

• **go back on** *something* to fail to keep a promise, or to change a decision or agreement ○ *Jason is totally unreliable and always goes back on his word.*

• **go by** *something/someone* to follow or use information provided by something or someone ○ *Don't go by what she says – she's always wrong.*

• **go down as/in** *something* to be remembered or recorded in a particular way ○ *Hurricane Katrina will go down as one of the worst storms of this century.* ○ *He doesn't want to go down in the record books as the guy who walked away from his main responsibility.*

• **go for** *something/someone* **TRY TO GET** to try to achieve a goal, or try to attract someone's romantic interest ○ *He'll be going for his third straight Olympic gold medal in the 200-meter dash.*

• **go for** *someone/something* **CHOOSE** to choose something or someone ○ *Offered the choice be-*

tween a higher salary and more vacation time, I know which one I'd go for. ○ He can't even count on all the voters who went for him the last time.

•**go for** *something* **LIKE** *infml* to like or admire something ○ *I don't go for action movies or romances.*

•**go in for** *something* to do something regularly, or to enjoy something ○ *I've never gone in for spending all day at the beach.*

•**go in on** *something* to be involved in an activity that involves others ○ *He bought a jet for personal use, inviting three friends to go in on it.*

•**go into** *something* to discuss, describe, or explain something, esp. in a detailed or careful way ○ *This is the first book to go into her personal life as well as her work.*

G

•**go off 1** to explode, or to fire bullets ○ *The deer ran away just before the hunter's gun went off.* **2** If a special signal or an electronic device goes off, it warns people that there is danger or that something is wrong: *What do they do if the metal detector goes off?*

•**go on** to continue ○ *I won't go on working in this job forever.* ○ *Go on, tell me what happened next.* ○ *He could* **go on and on** (= continue talking for a long time) *about his adventures.*

•**go out BE WITH** to have a romantic relationship, esp. one that includes going places together ○ *We've been going out for five months.*

•**go out FLOW AWAY** (of the ocean TIDE) to be flowing to a lower level ○ *While we were gone the tide had gone out, leaving our boat sitting on a sandbar.* ○ Compare COME IN OCEAN

•**go out for** *something* to try to become part of a sports team ○ *Unable to play ball with his hand in a cast, he went out for track.*

•**go over** *something* **EXAMINE** to examine or look at something in a careful or detailed way ○ *Remember to go over your essay to check for grammar and spelling mistakes.* ○ Related noun: GOING-OVER

•**go over** *something* **STUDY** to study or explain something again ○ *Let's go over the rules once more before we begin.*

•**go over BE RECEIVED** to be received in a particular way ○ *Do you think my speech went over OK?*

•**go through** *something* **EXPERIENCE** to experience something, esp. something unpleasant or difficult ○ *She's been going through a difficult time since her brother's illness.*

•**go through** *something* **USE** to use something that cannot be used again ○ *She went through all the money from her paycheck in one day.*

•**go through BE ACCEPTED** to be officially accepted or approved ○ *We're hoping that the proposal for the new mall won't go through.*

•**go through** *something* **PRACTICE** to do something in order to practice or as a test ○ *Let's go through it once more to make sure you know what to say.*

•**go through** *something* **EXAMINE** to examine a collection of things carefully in order to organize them or find something ○ *I'm going through my clothes and throwing out all the stuff I don't wear any more.*

•**go through with** *something* to complete something that you have begun or promised ○ *He'd threatened to quit many times, but I never thought he'd go through with it.*

•**go together 1** to regularly exist at the same time, or often be found in the same place ○ *Movies and popcorn just seem to go together.* **2** If items of clothing, furniture, or food go together, they look or taste good when experienced at the same time: *His suit, shirt, and tie didn't really go together.*

•**go under** (of a business) to fail financially ○ *Nothing could be done to keep the bank from going under.*

•**go up** to be destroyed in a fire or explosion ○ *The wind was so strong, the house went up in flames almost immediately.*

•**go without** *(something)* to not have something or to manage to live despite not having something ○ *Many of the workers have gone without paychecks for months.*

goad /goʊd/ *v* [T] to cause someone to do something by being annoying ○ *His brother goaded him into a wrestling match.*

go-ahead /ˈgoʊ·əˌhed/ *n* [U] permission or notice that an activity may begin ○ *We're ready to start the project but we're still waiting for the go-ahead.* ○ Related verb: GO AHEAD

goal Ⓐ **AIM** /goʊl/ *n* [C] an aim or purpose ○ *My goal is to lose ten pounds before the summer.*

GAME /goʊl/ *n* [C] **1** (in many sports) a point scored when a player sends a ball or other object into a particular area of play or into a netted structure that is defended by the opposing team ○ *Lanzo missed scoring a goal by inches.* **2** In some sports, a goal is also the area or netted structure into which a player sends a ball or other object in order to score a point.

goalkeeper /ˈgoʊlˌkiː·pər/, *infml* **goalie** /ˈgoʊ·li/ *n* [C] in some sports such as SOCCER and HOCKEY, the player whose responsibility is to prevent the other team from scoring

goalpost /ˈgoʊl·poʊst/ *n* [C] in some sports, either of two vertical posts, often connected by a horizontal bar, between which a ball or other object must go in order to score points

goat ANIMAL /goʊt/ *n* [C] a horned animal related to the sheep, which is kept to provide milk, meat, or wool

PERSON BLAMED /goʊt/ *n* [C] *infml, disapproving* a person who is blamed for causing a failure or defeat, esp. in a team sports competition ○ *Jefferson's three errors made him the goat of last night's game.*

goatee /goʊˈtiː/ *n* [C] a small BEARD (= the hair on the lower part of a man's face) grown on the middle, but not the sides, of the lower part of the face

gob /gɑb/ *n* [C] a small piece or lump of something ○ *a gob of butter*

IDIOM with gob

•**gobs of** *something infml* large amounts of something ○ *He's got gobs of money.*

gobble **EAT** /ˈgɑb·əl/ *v* [T] to eat quickly and sometimes with a lot of noise ○ [M] *She gobbled up/down her lunch and hurried back.*

MAKE NOISE /ˈgɑb·əl/ *v* [I] to make the sound of a male TURKEY (= a large bird)

gobbledygook, **gobbledegook** /ˈgɑb·əl·di ˌguk, -ˌguːk/ *n* [U] *disapproving* language that sounds important and official but is difficult to understand ○ *This computer manual is gobbledygook.*

goblin /ˈgɑb·lən/ *n* [C] a small, imaginary, usually ugly creature who plays tricks on people

go-cart /ˈgoʊ·kɑrt/ *n* [C] a small, low racing car with an open frame

God /gɑd/ *n* [U] (esp. in Christian, Jewish, and Muslim belief) the being that created and rules the universe, the earth, and its people ○ *Do you believe in God?*

godless /ˈgɑd·ləs/ *adj* [not gradable] not showing belief in, or respect for, God

IDIOMS with God

• **God bless (you)** may good things happen to you ○ *Good night everyone, and God bless you.* ○ *"Achoo!" "God bless you!"* ○ **USAGE:** Used especially when saying goodbye to someone or when someone sneezes.

• **God only knows** *infml* it is impossible to say ○ *God only knows how he managed to find out where I lived.*

god /gɑd/, *female* **goddess** /ˈgɑd·əs/ *n* [C] **1** a spirit or being believed to control some part of the universe or life and often worshiped for doing so, or a representation of this being ○ *the god of war* **2** A god can also be someone who is admired a lot or too much: *Dr. Tay is a god to me.*

godchild /ˈgɑd·tʃɑɪld/ *n* [C] *pl* **godchildren** a child whose moral and religious development in the Christian religion is partly the responsibility of the child's GODPARENTS

goddaughter /ˈgɑd ˌdɔːt̬·ər/ *n* [C] a female GODCHILD

godfather **RESPONSIBLE ADULT** /ˈgɑd ˌfɑð·ər/ *n* [C] a male GODPARENT

FIRST PERSON /ˈgɑd ˌfɑð·ər/ *n* [C] *infml* a person who started or developed something new, esp. in music or art ○ *Mr. Brown became known as the godfather of soul music.*

God-fearing *adj dated* very religious and trying to live in the way you believe God would wish you to

godforsaken /ˈgɑd·fər ˌseɪ·kən/ *adj* (of places) not containing anything interesting or attractive, and far from other people ○ *Why would you come to this godforsaken place?*

godmother /ˈgɑd ˌmʌð·ər/ *n* [C] a female GODPARENT

godparent /ˈgɑd ˌpær·ənt, -ˌper-/ *n* [C] an adult who is partly responsible for the moral and religious development of his or her GODCHILD. ○ See also: GODFATHER

godsend /ˈgɑd·send/ *n* [C] something good that happens unexpectedly and at a time when it is especially needed ○ *That savings account was a real godsend when she lost her job.*

godson /ˈgɑd·sʌn/ *n* [C] a male GODCHILD

goes /goʊz/ *present simple of* GO, used with he/she/it

gofer /ˈgoʊ·fər/ *n* [C] *infml* a person whose job is to take messages or to collect and deliver things for other people

go-getter *n* [C] someone who is energetic and works hard to succeed ○ *We like go-getters who bring in new customers.*

goggle-eyed /ˈgɑg·ə ˌlɑɪd/ *adj* having eyes that are wide open, esp. in surprise ○ *Goggle-eyed tourists stared at the famous painting.*

goggles /ˈgɑg·əlz/ *pl n* special glasses that fit close to the face to protect the eyes ○ *safety goggles* ○ *swimming goggles*

going /ˈgoʊ·ɪŋ/ *n, adj* ○ See at GO **MOVE TOWARD**; GO **LEAVE**; GO **OPERATE**; GO **BE SUITABLE**

going on /ˌgoʊ·ɪŋ ˌɑn, -ˌɔːn/ *prep, adv* [not gradable] nearly; almost ○ *Leslie is 16 going on 17.*

going-over /ˌgoʊ·ɪŋ ˈoʊ·vər/ *n* [C usually sing] **goings-over** a careful look at all the parts of a thing or place, in order to find something ○ *Police gave the apartment a thorough going-over but failed to find any evidence.* ○ Related verb: GO OVER **EXAMINE**

goings-on /ˌgoʊ·ɪŋˈzɑn, -ˈzɔːn/ *pl n* unusual events or activities ○ *There were some strange goings-on in that house.*

going to /ˈgoʊ·ɪŋ ˌtuː, -tə/ *modal verb* intending to do something in the future, or being certain or expecting to happen in the future ○ *Are you going to go to Claire's party?* ○ *The radio said it was going to be hot and sunny tomorrow.*

gold **METAL** /goʊld/ *n* [U] a soft, yellow metal that is highly valued and used esp. in jewelry and as a form of wealth ○ *The price of gold reached a new high Thursday.*

gold /goʊld/ *adj* [not gradable] ○ *She wears lots of gold jewelry.*

golden /ˈgoʊl·dən/ *adj* [not gradable] ○ *a golden chain*

COLOR /goʊld/ *adj, n* [C/U] (of) a bright yellow color ○ *a gold dress* ○ [U] *His uniform was scarlet and gold.*

golden /ˈgoʊl·dən/ *adj* ○ *Bake about seven minutes, or until golden.*

golden /ˈgoʊl·dən/ *adj* advantageous, successful, or promising ○ *the golden days of youth* ○ *They had several golden opportunities (= especially good opportunities) to score.*

golden age *n* [C] a period of time in the past, sometimes imaginary, of great happiness and success ○ *the golden age of boxing*

golden anniversary *n* [C] a celebration of the 50th year of something, esp. a marriage ○ Compare SILVER ANNIVERSARY

goldfish /ˈgoʊld·fɪʃ/ *n* [C] *pl* **goldfish** a small, gold- or orange-colored fish often kept as a pet

gold medal *n* [C] a disk-shaped prize made of or covered with gold that is given to a person or team that wins a competition ○ Compare SILVER MEDAL; BRONZE MEDAL

gold mine PLACE *n* [C] a place where gold is removed from the ground

OPPORTUNITY *n* [C] an opportunity for making a lot of money ○ *In the eyes of real estate developers, this property was truly a gold mine.*

golf /gɑlf, gɔːlf/ *n* [U] a game in which players use a set of sticks to hit small, round, hard balls into a series of nine or 18 small holes on an area of grassy land using as few hits as possible ○ *Do you play golf?*

golfer /ˈgɑl·fər, ˈgɔːl-/ *n* [C] ○ *a professional golfer*

golf club STICK *n* [C] one of a set of wooden or metal sticks with long handles used for hitting the ball used in the game of golf

ORGANIZATION *n* [C] a private organization of people who play golf at the same place, or the place where they and their guests play golf and meet socially

golf course *n* [C] a large area of grassy land with a series of nine or 18 holes, used for playing golf

golly /ˈgɑl·i/ *exclamation infml* used to express surprise, or to emphasize what you are saying ○ *"He broke his arm and he'll be out for weeks." "Golly, that's terrible."*

gondola CONTAINER /ˈgɑn·də·lə, gɑnˈdoʊ-/ *n* [C] a container in which passengers travel, esp. one hung from a thick wire which moves up a mountain ○ *The gondolas seat 12 skiers and move at 14 miles per hour.*

BOAT /ˈgɑn·də·lə/ *n* [C] a long, narrow boat with a flat bottom and raised points at both ends, moved along by a person with a pole at the back end

gone GO /gɔːn, gɑn/ *past participle of* GO

DEAD /gɔːn, gɑn/ *adj* [not gradable] no longer living; dead ○ *Both her parents are gone.*

goner /ˈgɔː·nər, ˈgɑn·ər/ *n* [C usually sing] *infml* a person or thing that has no chance of succeeding or continuing to live or exist ○ *He reckoned he was a goner when he heard enemy soldiers approaching.*

gong /gɑŋ, gɔːŋ/ *n* [C] a piece of metal hanging from a frame which is hit with a stick to produce a hollow, ringing sound ○ *a dinner gong*

gonna /ˌgɔː·nə, ˌgoʊ·nə, gən·ə/ *modal verb not standard* (spelled the way it is often spoken) GOING TO ○ *What are you gonna do about it?* ○ USAGE: In written English "gonna" is usually used to report or approximate speech.

gonorrhea /ˌgɑn·əˈriː·ə/ *n* [U] a disease of the sex organs, caught during sexual activity

goo /guː/ *n* [U] *infml* a thick, sticky substance ○ *Mudslides left goo all over the highway.*

good SATISFACTORY /gʊd/ *adj comparative* **better**, *superlative* **best** of a kind that is pleasing or enjoyable, or of high quality ○ *Let's go on a picnic tomorrow if the weather's good.* ○ *That was a really good meal.* ○ *Dogs have a very good sense of smell.* ○ *Now would be a good time* (= a suitable time) *to talk to Andy about the promotion.* ○ *He's a good* (= able and skillful) *swimmer.* ○ *Did they have a good time on their vacation?* ○ *She makes good money* (= earns a high income) *in her new job.*

MORALLY RIGHT /gʊd/ *adj comparative* **better**, *superlative* **best** **1** morally right or admirable ○ *José is a genuinely good person.* ○ *If you're a good boy* (= if you behave well) *at the dentist, I'll buy you some ice cream later.* ○ *He's always been good to his mother.* **2** Good can be used as part of an exclamation: *Good heavens! You mean they still haven't arrived?*

good /gʊd/ *n* [U] ○ *Even a small donation can do a lot of good.*

goodness /ˈgʊd·nəs/ *n* [U] ○ *I believe in the basic goodness of human nature.* ○ See also: GOODNESS

GREETING /gʊd/ *adj* [not gradable] used in greetings

HEALTH /gʊd/ *adj comparative* **better**, *superlative* **best** useful for health, or in a satisfactory condition ○ *Make sure you eat plenty of good, fresh vegetables.*

LARGE /gʊd/ *adj* [not gradable] large in number or amount ○ *We had to walk a good way in the airport to reach our gate.* ○ *There was a good-sized crowd on hand.* ○ *There was a good deal of* (= a lot of) *discussion about how much the car was worth.*

WORD FAMILY good			
Nouns	good goodness goods	*Adjectives*	good

IDIOMS with good

• **a good** this much or more of a specific amount ○ *It's a good half hour's walk to the stadium from here.*

• **a good many** a lot of ○ *There were a good many people at the concert.*

• **good and** completely ○ *She won't drink coffee if it's not good and hot.*

• **(as) good as new** in very good condition again, after not working well ○ *Yaman fixed my computer, and now it's good as new.*

• **good for** *someone* I am pleased about someone's success or good luck ○ *She got her driver's license? Good for her!*

• **good riddance** I am happy that someone or something is gone ○ *Our neighbors and their nasty dogs have moved out – good riddance!*

• **(it's a) good thing** it is lucky ○ *Good thing they didn't go camping last weekend – the weather was terrible.*

• **no good, not any/much good** not very useful or effective ○ *It's no good trying to change his beliefs.* ○ *I'm not much good at explaining math problems.*

good afternoon *exclamation* used when greeting someone in the afternoon ○ *Good afternoon, Mr. Hopkins.*

Good Book *n* [C/U] the Bible

goodbye /gʊd ˈbɑɪ, gə-/, *short form* **bye** /ˈbɑɪ/, *infml* **bye-bye** /bɑɪ ˈbɑɪ/ *exclamation, n* [C/U] said when you are going away from someone else, or the act of saying this when you are going away ○ [U] *Goodbye, Roberto, and thanks again for a great dinner.* ○ [U] *Don't go without saying goodbye to me, will you?*

good evening *exclamation* used when greeting someone in the evening ○ *Good evening, Mr. Hopkins.*

good-for-nothing *n* [C] a person who is thought of as worthless ○ *She's a lazy good-for-nothing.*

Good Friday *n* [C usually sing] (in the Christian religion) the day Jesus is believed to have died; the Friday before Easter Sunday

good-hearted *adj* kind and willing to be helpful

good-humored *adj* behaving in a friendly and happy way

good-looking *adj* attractive and pleasant to look at

good morning *exclamation* used for greeting someone in the morning ○ *Good morning, how are you?*

good-natured *adj* friendly and welcoming toward other people

goodness /ˈgʊd·nəs/ *n* [U] used in many fixed expressions to show emotion, esp. surprise ○ *Goodness! I thought you'd gone home already!* ○ See also: GOODNESS at GOOD MORALLY RIGHT

good night *exclamation* used for saying goodbye to someone in the evening, or to someone before you go to bed or to sleep

goods /gʊdz/ *pl n* items for sale, or possessions that can be moved ○ *They sell leather goods such as wallets, purses, and briefcases.*

good Samaritan /səˈmær·ət·ᵊn/ *n* [C] someone who helps people in trouble

goodwill /ˈgʊd ˈwɪl/ *n* [U] a friendly attitude in which you wish that good things happen to people ○ *We hope the negotiations will take place in an atmosphere of openness and goodwill.*

goody FOOD /ˈgʊd·i/ *n* [C usually pl] *infml* something pleasant to eat, such as a piece of candy

EXPRESSION /ˈgʊd·i/ *exclamation* used, esp. by children, to show pleasure ○ *Oh goody! Chocolate cake.*

goody-goody /ˈgʊd·iˌgʊd·i/, **goody-two-shoes** /ˌgʊd·i ˈtuːˌʃuːz/ *n* [C] someone who is too ready to behave in a way intended to please people in authority ○ *She's a real goody-goody – I hate her!*

gooey /ˈguː·i/ *adj comparative* **gooier**, *superlative* **gooiest** (of a substance) thick and sticky ○ *a gooey dessert*

goof /guːf/ *v* [I] *infml* to make a foolish or embarrassing mistake ○ *The governor showed up and no one was there to meet him – somebody goofed!*

goof /guːf/ *n* [C] *infml* ○ *Forgetting to bring my driver's license was a major goof.*

goofy /ˈguː·fi/ *adj infml* silly, esp. in an amusing way ○ *The movie has talking skeletons and goofy stuff like that.*

PHRASAL VERB with goof

• **goof off** *infml* to avoid work or waste time ○ *You'd better not let the boss catch you goofing off!*

goon /guːn/ *n* [C] a man who is paid to threaten or hurt people ○ *The strikers were beaten by a bunch of hired goons.*

goop /guːp/ *n* [U] *infml* a messy, slightly liquid substance, esp. one whose contents are not known ○ *He puts this goop on his hair to make it stand up straight.*

goose /guːs/ *n* [C] *pl* **geese** a large bird that lives by water

goose bumps /ˈguːs·bʌmps/, **goose flesh** /ˈguːs·fleʃ/, **goose pimples** /ˈguːsˌpɪm·pəlz/ *pl n* a temporary condition in which small raised swellings appear on the skin because of cold, fear, or excitement ○ *Let's move out into the sun – I'm getting goose bumps.*

GOP *n* [U] *abbreviation for* Grand Old Party (= a name for the Republican Party) ○ *The symbol of the GOP is an elephant.*

gopher /ˈgoʊ·fər/ *n* [C] a North American animal that lives in holes it makes in the ground

gore INJURE /gɔːr, goʊr/ *v* [T] (of an animal) to cause an injury with the horns or TUSKS (= long, curved teeth) ○ *The bullfighter was almost gored to death.*

BLOOD /gɔːr, goʊr/ *n* [U] blood that has come from an injury and become thick

gory /ˈgɔːr·i, ˈgoʊr·i/ *adj* ○ *I'm afraid most operations look pretty gory.*

IDIOM with gore

• **gory details** the unpleasant but interesting facts about someone's private life ○ *Come on, I want to know all the gory details about why they split up.*

gorge VALLEY /gɔːrdʒ/ *n* [C] a deep, narrow valley with steep sides, usually formed by a river or stream cutting through rock ○ *The only way to cross the gorge was over a flimsy wooden bridge.*

EAT /gɔːrdʒ/ *v* [I/T] to eat or fill yourself with food until you are unable to eat any more ○ [T] *She sat in front of the television, gorging herself on chocolates.*

gorgeous /ˈgɔːr·dʒəs/ *adj* beautiful and attractive ○ *What a gorgeous dress!* ○ *The bride looked gorgeous.*

gorilla /gəˈrɪl·ə/ *n* [C] a large APE (= animal like a monkey) that comes from western and central Africa

gory /ˈgɔːr·i, ˈgoʊr·i/ *adj* ○ See at GORE **BLOOD**

gosh /gɑʃ, gɔːʃ/ *exclamation infml* used to express surprise ○ *Gosh, I didn't expect to see you here!*

G

gospel MUSIC /ˈgɑs·pəl/, **gospel music** /ˈgɑs·pəl ˈmjuː·zɪk/ *n* [U] a style of Christian religious music originally developed and performed by African-Americans ○ *gospel singers*

BOOK /ˈgɑs·pəl/ *n* [C] **1** any of the four books of the Bible that contain details of the life of Jesus **2** The gospel (truth) is the complete truth: *I don't know what happened to the money, that's the gospel truth.*

gossip /ˈgɑs·əp/ *n* [C/U] **1** talk about other people's private lives ○ [U] *Have you heard the latest gossip* (= what is being said about someone)*?* **2** A gossip is also someone who enjoys talking about other people's private lives: [C] *Charlie is a real gossip.*

gossip /ˈgɑs·əp/ *v* [I] ○ *Don't mind us – we're just gossiping!*

got /gɑt/ *past simple and past participle of* **1** GET **2** Got is also used with "have" or "has" to show that someone has or possesses something: *Brandon's got* (= now has) *a new pair of glasses.* ○ Compare GOTTEN

gotcha /ˈgɑtʃ·ə/ *exclamation not standard* **1** (spelled the way it is often spoken) got you ○ *"Gotcha* (= caught you)*, you little thief!" she cried, as I tried to snatch a cookie from the table.* **2** Gotcha also means I understand what you are trying to say: *"So be sure you get here by three." "Gotcha."*

Gothic /ˈgɑθ·ɪk/ *adj* (of buildings) built in an old style that uses stone, very high ceilings, and lots of decoration ○ *Gothic architecture*

gotta /ˈgɑt̬·ə/ *v* [I] *not standard* (spelled the way it is often spoken) got to ○ *"I gotta go now."* ○ *"He's gotta be kidding."*

gotten /ˈgɑt·ən/ *past participle of* **1** GET ○ *If you hadn't gotten sick, we'd be in Hawaii now.* ○ *She's gotten used to having me around.* **2** Gotten is also used with "have" to show that someone has recently come to possess something: *I've gotten* (= I recently bought) *a new pair of glasses.* ○ Compare GOT

gouge DIG /gaʊdʒ/ *v* [T] to make a hole in something, or remove something from a hole using a sharp, pointed object ○ *The bomb had gouged a huge hole in the roadway.*

CHEAT /gaʊdʒ/ *v* [T] to charge someone far too much money for something done or something sold ○ *We didn't know the value of the foreign money, and the taxi driver gouged us.*

goulash /ˈguː·lɑʃ/ *n* [U] a dish originally from Hungary consisting of meat cooked in a sauce with vegetables and PAPRIKA (= a red spice)

gourd /gɔːrd, goʊrd, gʊrd/ *n* [C] a round or bottle-shaped fruit that has a hard shell and that cannot usually be eaten, or the shell of this fruit used as a container

gourmet /ˈgʊr·meɪ, gʊrˈmeɪ/ *n* [C] a person who knows a lot about food and cooking, and who enjoys eating good food ○ *She is a gourmet cook.*

gout /gaʊt/ *n* [U] a painful disease of the joints, esp. in a toe or finger

gov /ˌdʒiː ˌoʊˈviː, gʌv/ *n* [U] used at the end of US INTERNET addresses to show that the address belongs to a federal or state government department ○ *info@hhs.gov*

govern RULE /ˈgʌv·ərn/ *v* [I/T] to control and be responsible for the public business of a country, state, city, or other organized group ○ [T] *The newly elected president will govern the country for four years.*

governance /ˈgʌv·ər·nəns/ *n* [U] the activity of governing something ○ *The Crow Indians have struggled to establish a new form of tribal governance.*

government /ˈgʌv·ərn·mənt, -ər·mənt/ *n* [C/U] **1** ***politics & government*** the offices, departments, and groups of people that control a country, state, city, or other political unit ○ [U] *She works for the government.* ○ [C] *The new tax law affects the budgets of both state and local governments.* **2** Government is also a particular system of managing a country, state, city, etc.: [U] *democratic government*

governmental /ˌgʌv·ərnˈment·əl, -ərˈment·əl/ *adj* ○ *The country has weak governmental institutions and no experience of democracy.*

governor /ˈgʌv·ə·nər, -ər·nər/ *n* [C] a person in charge of an organization or of a particular political unit, esp. a US state ○ *Governors from most of the 50 states will meet in Omaha this weekend.* ○ *The board of governors of the hospital meets every month.*

INFLUENCE /ˈgʌv·ərn/ *v* [T] to have a direct effect or controlling influence on something ○ *Prices of manufactured goods are governed largely by the cost of raw materials and labor.*

WORD FAMILY govern			
Nouns	governance government governor	*Adjectives* *Verbs* *Adverbs*	governmental govern governmentally

governess /ˈgʌv·ər·nəs/ *n* [C] (esp. in the past) a woman who lives with a family and educates the children at home

gown /gaʊn/ *n* [C] a woman's dress, esp. a long one worn on formal occasions, or a long, loose piece of clothing worn over other clothes for a particular purpose ○ *She wore a beautiful satin gown to the senior prom.* ○ *Students wore black gowns for the graduation ceremonies.*

GP *n* [C] *abbreviation for* general practitioner (= a doctor who provides general medical treatment)

GPA *n* [C] *abbreviation for* GRADE-POINT AVERAGE

grab /græb/ *v* [T] **-bb-** to take or take hold of something or someone suddenly ○ *I grabbed the rope and pulled myself out of the water.* ○ *We'd better get there early, or someone else will grab the best seats* (= take them first). ○ (*infml*) *Let's grab a sandwich* (= get it and eat it quickly) *before we leave.*

grab /græb/ *n* [C] ○ *The two children both made a grab for* (= made a sudden attempt to take) *the same piece of cake.*

grab bag *n* [C] any mixed collection of things, some of which may not be very attractive or useful ○ *The musical was a grab bag of old, tired songs and a few gems.*

grace **BEAUTY** /greɪs/ *n* [U] simple beauty of movement or form ○ *The skaters moved over the ice with effortless grace.*

graceful /ˈgreɪs·fəl/ *adj* ○ *The dancers formed graceful, whirling combinations.*

gracefully /ˈgreɪs·fə·li/ *adv* ○ *He gracefully skis down the slopes.*

PLEASANTNESS /greɪs/ *n* [U] the charming quality of being polite and pleasant, or a willingness to be fair and to forgive ○ *She always handles her clients with tact and grace.*

graceful /ˈgreɪs·fəl/ *adj* ○ *I want to make a graceful exit when it's time to leave.*

gracefully /ˈgreɪs·fə·li/ *adv* ○ *A lot of people grow old gracefully.*

RELIGION /greɪs/ *n* [U] **1** a prayer of thanks to God that is said before and sometimes after a meal ○ *Before we eat, I want to ask Cory to say grace.* **2** Grace is also approval or protection given by God: *By the grace of God, I hope to live for many years.*

TIME /greɪs/ *n* [U] an added period of time allowed before something must be done or paid ○ *The landlord gave us a week's grace to pay the rent.*

grace period *n* [C] extra time you are given to pay money you owe without losing something or paying an additional amount ○ *You have a 10-day grace period in which to pay your insurance premium.*

gracious **PLEASANT** /ˈgreɪ·ʃəs/ *adj* pleasant, kind, and polite ○ *You're a gracious host.*

graciously /ˈgreɪ·ʃə·sli/ *adv* ○ *You should learn to accept criticism graciously.*

COMFORTABLE /ˈgreɪ·ʃəs/ *adj* having the qualities great comfort and luxury made possible by wealth ○ *He was used to gracious living.*

SURPRISE /ˈgreɪ·ʃəs/ *exclamation dated* used to express surprise or to emphasize what is being said ○ *My goodness gracious, that was a huge repair bill.*

grad /græd/ *n, adj short form of* GRADUATE ○ *a Harvard grad* ○ *a grad student*

gradable /ˈgreɪd·ə·bəl/ *adj* ***grammar*** (of adjectives and adverbs) able to be used with words like "more" and "less," or having different forms that show this ○ *"Cold" is a gradable adjective and has the forms "colder" and "coldest."*

gradation /greɪˈdeɪ·ʃən, grə-/ *n* [C] a gradual change, or one stage in a series of changes ○ *There are many gradations of color in a rainbow.*

grade Ⓐ **MEASURE/MARK** /greɪd/ *n* [C] **1** a measure of the quality of a student's performance, usually represented by the letters A (the best) through F (the worst) ○ *She always gets good grades.* **2** A grade is also a measure or mark of quality, amount, or degree: *high-grade musicianship* ○ *He's suffering from a low-grade infection.*

grade Ⓐ /greɪd/ *v* [T] **1** to judge and give a mark to a student, exam, etc. ○ *The essays were graded on clarity of expression.* **2** To grade is also to separate things according to quality or size: *Eggs are usually graded by size.*

SCHOOL /greɪd/ *n* [C] a school class or group of classes in which all the children are of a similar age or ability ○ *James is in the seventh grade this year.*

-grader /ˈgreɪd·ər/ *n* ○ *Katy is a fifth-grader.*

SLOPE /greɪd/ *n* [C] the degree of slope of land or of a road or path ○ *In hilly San Francisco, many streets have a steep grade.*

grade-point average *n* [C] a number giving the average quality of a student's work, used to calculate rank in class ○ *To get into the best colleges you need a grade-point average between 3.0 and 4.0.*

grade school *n* [C] an ELEMENTARY SCHOOL

gradient /ˈgreɪd·iː·ənt/ *n* [C] ***earth science*** a measure of how steep a slope is, often expressed as a percentage

gradual /ˈgrædʒ·ə·wəl/ *adj* changing or developing slowly or by small degrees ○ *He has suffered a gradual decline in health over the past year.*

gradually /ˈgrædʒ·ə·wə·li/ *adv* ○ *Sales of the product are improving gradually.*

graduate /ˈgrædʒ·ə·wət/, *short form* **grad** /græd/ *n* [C] a person who has successfully completed studies at a school or received a degree from a college or university ○ *a Yale graduate/a graduate of Yale*

graduate /ˈgrædʒ·ə·wət/, *short form* **grad** /græd/ *adj* relating to or working toward a university degree beyond the one you receive after four years of study ○ *graduate school/student/studies*

graduate /ˈgrædʒ·əˌweɪt/ *v* [I/T] ○ [I] *Although he never graduated from high school, he became a successful businessman.*

graduation /ˌgrædʒ·əˈweɪ·ʃən/ *n* [C/U] the formal event at which a person who has successfully completed a course of study at a school, college, or university gets a document stating this fact, or the successful completion of a course of study ○ [C] *We'll be attending two graduations this weekend.*

○ [U] *After graduation, she wants to travel around Europe.*

graduated /ˈgrædʒ·əˌweɪt̬·əd/ *adj* arranged in regular small stages or degrees ○ *With a graduated income tax, people who make more money pay a higher rate.*

graduated cylinder *n* [C] a glass tube that is used in science LABORATORIES to measure liquids

graffiti /grəˈfiːt̬·i/ *n* [U] writings or drawings made on surfaces in public places ○ *Someone had painted graffiti on the entire wall.*

graft INFLUENCE /græft/ *n* [U] (esp. in politics) the obtaining of money or advantage through the dishonest use of power and influence ○ *His administration was marked by widespread graft and crime.*

TISSUE /græft/ *n* [C] ***biology*** **1** a piece of healthy skin or bone cut usually from a person's own body and used to repair a damaged part on that person **2** A graft is also a piece cut from a living plant and fixed to another plant so that it grows there.

graft /græft/ *v* [T]

Grail, **grail** /greɪl/ *n* [C] a HOLY GRAIL

grain SEED /greɪn/ *n* [C/U] a seed from a plant, esp. a grass such as wheat, or the crop from such a plant ○ [C] *Wheat and rye are two common grains used in making bread.* ○ [U] *Grain is one of the main exports of the American Midwest.*

SMALL PIECE/AMOUNT /greɪn/ *n* [C] a very small piece of a hard substance, or a small amount of something ○ *grains of sand* ○ *There was a grain of truth in what she said.* ○ *You haven't got a grain of sense.*

-grained /greɪnd/ *suffix* consisting of pieces of a specific size or type ○ *very fine-grained quartz*

grainy /ˈgreɪ·ni/ *adj* (of a picture) appearing to be made up of a lot of spots ○ *a grainy newspaper photo*

PATTERN /greɪn/ *n* [U] the natural pattern of lines in the surface of a material, such as wood or rock, or the direction in which the fibers that form these substances lie ○ *Polishing the wood brings out its grain.*

gram /græm/, *abbreviation* **g** *n* [C] a unit of measurement of weight equal to 0.001 kilogram

grammar /ˈgræm·ər/ *n* [U] ***grammar*** the study or use of the rules about how words change their form and combine with other words to express meaning ○ *She memorized the vocabulary but is having trouble with the grammar.*

grammatical /grəˈmæt̬·ɪ·kəl/ *adj* [not gradable] ○ *grammatical structure* ○ *Your sentence is not grammatical* (= the words it contains do not combine correctly).

grammar school *n* [C] *dated* an ELEMENTARY SCHOOL

Grammy /ˈgræm·i/ *n* [C] *trademark* one of a set of prizes given in the US each year to people in the music industry

grand IMPORTANT /grænd/ *adj* important and large in degree or size ○ *When I mess up, I mess up on a grand scale.* ○ *The ten top essayists will compete for the $10,000 grand prize* (= the largest prize in the competition). ○ *The new restaurant will hold its grand opening Saturday* (= a big celebration of the opening of its business).

ATTRACTIVE /grænd/ *adj* attractive in style and appearance ○ *A grand staircase leads to the second floor.*

MONEY /grænd/, *abbreviation* **G** *n* [C] *pl* **grand** *slang* $1000 ○ *He lost three grand in the stock market last week.*

grandchild /ˈgræn·tʃɑɪld/ *n* [C] *pl* **grandchildren** the child of a person's son or daughter

granddaughter /ˈgrænˌdɔːt̬·ər/ *n* [C] the daughter of a person's son or daughter

grandeur /ˈgræn·dʒər, -ˌdʒʊr/ *n* [U] a quality of great beauty and size which attracts admiration ○ *We were struck by the silent grandeur of the desert.*

grandfather /ˈgrændˌfɑð·ər/, *infml* **granddad** /ˈgræn·dæd/, *infml* **grandpa** /ˈgræm·pə, -pɑ/ *n* [C] the father of a person's mother or father

grandfather clock *n* [C] a clock in a tall wooden case that stands on the floor

grandiose /ˈgræn·diːˌoʊs, ˌgræn·diːˈoʊs/ *adj* very large or wonderful, or intended to seem great and important ○ *grandiose buildings* ○ *grandiose plans*

grand jury *n* [C] *law* a group of people who decide whether a person who has been accused of a crime should be given a trial in court or should be released

grandmother /ˈgrændˌmʌð·ər/, *infml* **grandma** /ˈgræm·ə, ˈgræn·mɑ/, *infml* **granny** /ˈgræn·i/ *n* [C] the mother of a person's father or mother

grandparent /ˈgrændˌpær·ənt, -ˌper-/ *n* [C] the father or mother of a person's father or mother

grand piano *n* [C] a large piano that has horizontal strings and is the type usually used in public performances

grand slam BASEBALL *n* [C] in baseball, the hitting of a HOME RUN with runners at all three BASES, so that four points are scored

TENNIS AND GOLF *n* [C] in tennis and golf, the act of winning all of a series of important competitions

grandson /ˈgrænd·sʌn/ *n* [C] the son of a person's son or daughter

grandstand /ˈgræn·stænd/ *n* [C] a large area containing many seats arranged in rising rows, sometimes covered by a roof, from which people can watch sports or other events

grandstanding /ˈgrænˌstæn·dɪŋ/ *n* [U] *disapproving* acting or speaking in a way intended to attract attention and to influence the opinion of people who are watching ○ *Experts criticized the program as mere grandstanding by corporations and local officials.*

grand total *n* [C] the complete amount after everything has been added up ○ *Andre's sold a grand total of 11 copies of the book.*

granite /ˈɡræn·ət/ *n* [U] a hard gray, pink, or black rock, used in buildings

granny /ˈɡræn·i/ *n* [C] *infml* GRANDMOTHER

granola /ɡrəˈnoʊ·lə/ *n* [U] a food made of grains, nuts, and dried fruit, often eaten for breakfast

grant Ⓐ **GIVE** /ɡrænt/ *v* [T] to give, agree to give, or do something that another person has asked for, esp. as an official or formal act ○ *She was granted American citizenship.*

MONEY /ɡrænt/ *n* [C] a sum of money given by the government, a university, or a private organization to another organization or person for a special purpose ○ *a research/study grant*

ACCEPT /ɡrænt/ *v* [T] to accept that something is true, often before expressing an opposite or disapproving opinion ○ [+ (*that*) clause] *I grant you (that) it must have been upsetting, but even so I think he made too big a deal of it.*

granulated /ˈɡræn·jəˌleɪt̬·əd/ *adj* [not gradable] (esp. of sugar) in small grains ○ *Granulated sugar is coarser than powdered sugar.*

grape /ɡreɪp/ *n* [C] a small, round fruit, usually pale green, purple, or red, that grows on a VINE and is eaten raw, made into juice, or used for making wine ○ *a bunch of grapes* ○ *grape juice*

grapefruit /ˈɡreɪp·fruːt/ *n* [C] **grapefruit, grapefruits** a yellow fruit that is larger than an orange but tastes less sweet

grapevine /ˈɡreɪp·vɑɪn/ *n* [C] the climbing plant that GRAPES grow on

IDIOM with grapevine

• **the grapevine** an unofficial, informal way of getting information by hearing about it from someone who heard it from someone else ○ *I heard through the grapevine that they fired him – is that true?*

graph /ɡræf/ *n* [C] ***mathematics*** **1** a drawing that shows lines or curves formed with two sets of measurements or amounts, or a such a drawing produced by the set of POINTS (= positions) that solve an EQUATION (= mathematical statement) ○ *a bar/line graph* ○ *A graph would show this information more clearly.* **2** Graph paper is paper with small squares printed on it that can be used for drawing some types of graphs. **3** The **graph of an equation** is the group of all points on a NUMBER LINE or the COORDINATE PLANE that are solutions of an EQUATION (= statement that two amounts are equal).

graph /ɡræf/ *v* [T] to show information in the form of a graph ○ *The global warming data will be graphed and the students will interpret it.*

graphical /ˈɡræf·ɪ·kəl/ *adj* [not gradable] represented by or relating to a graph

graphic **CLEAR** /ˈɡræf·ɪk/ *adj* producing very clear and detailed mental images ○ *a graphic description of the operation*

graphically /ˈɡræf·ɪ·kli/ *adv* in a very clear and detailed manner ○ *The accident graphically illustrates the importance of wearing seat belts.*

USAGE

graphic or striking?

To describe a very detailed and realistic image use **graphic**. To describe someone or something that is very impressive or unusual to look at use **striking**.

The film contains one very graphic scene of an accident.

The huge white tower on the waterfront is very striking.

~~*The huge white tower on the waterfront is very graphic.*~~

DRAWING /ˈɡræf·ɪk/ *adj* [not gradable] having to do with drawing or images ○ *She first worked as a graphic designer.* ○ *The network has upgraded the graphic look of the show.*

graphic /ˈɡræf·ɪk/ *n* [C] **1** *Choose a graphic from the clip-art file, add your text, and you've made your own birthday card.* **2** A graphic can also be printing shown on television that gives additional information: *Let's take a look at the graphic of that quote.*

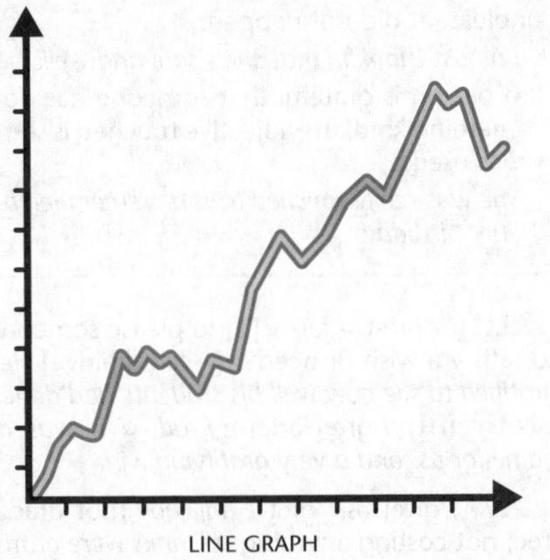
LINE GRAPH

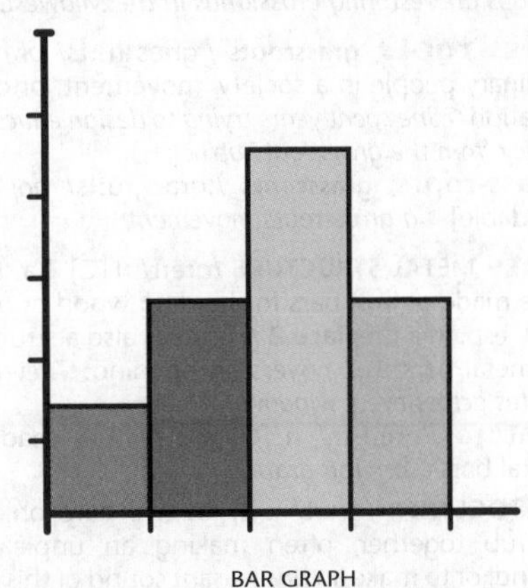
BAR GRAPH

graphic arts *pl n* the arts that include drawing and printing

graphite /ˈgræf·ɑɪt/ *n* [U] a soft, dark gray form of carbon used in the center of pencils which makes a mark when pressed against something

grapple /ˈgræp·əl/ *v* [I] to hold someone while fighting with him or her ○ *He briefly grappled with the police officer.* ○ *Bad news is something it becomes necessary to grapple with* (= deal with).

grasp **HOLD** /græsp/ *v* [I/T] to take something quickly, in your hand, and hold it firmly ○ [T] *I grasped his arm to keep from falling.*

grasp /græsp/ *n* [U] power to achieve or control something ○ *A full partnership at last seemed to be within her grasp.*

G

UNDERSTAND /græsp/ *v* [T] to understand, esp. something difficult ○ *It was hard to grasp what the professor was getting at.*

grasp /græsp/ *n* [U] ○ *I'm afraid my grasp of economics is weak.*

IDIOM with grasp

• **grasping at straws** **1** trying to find some way to succeed when nothing you choose is likely to work ○ *We searched all the backup tapes, trying to find the missing files, but we knew we were grasping at straws.* **2** If you are **grasping at straws**, you are trying to find a reason to feel hopeful in a bad situation: *I knew my mother was dying, but I was grasping at straws and denying reality.*

grasping /ˈgræs·pɪŋ/ *adj disapproving* always eager to get more of something, esp. money ○ *He's a grasping, insensitive executive.*

grass /græs/ *n* [C/U] a low, green plant with narrow leaves growing naturally over much of the earth's surface ○ [U] *Are you going to cut the grass?* ○ [C] *Wildflowers and grasses of the Great Plains thrive without chemicals or fertilizers.*

grassy /ˈgræs·i/ *adj* ○ *a grassy hillside*

grasshopper /ˈgræsˌhɑp·ər/ *n* [C] an insect that eats plants and has long back legs that make it able to jump high

grassland /ˈgræs·lænd, -lənd/ *n* [C/U] a large area of land covered with grass ○ *Conservation groups are restoring grasslands in the Midwest.*

grass roots, **grassroots** /ˈgræsˈruːts/ *pl n* the ordinary people in a society, movement, or organization ○ *She spent years trying to design education policy from the grass roots up.*

grass-roots, **grassroots** /ˌgræsˌruːts/ *adj* [not gradable] ○ *a grass-roots movement*

grate **METAL STRUCTURE** /greɪt/ *n* [C] **1** a structure made of iron bars for holding wood or other fuel, esp. in a fireplace **2** A grate is also a structure of metal bars that covers an opening: *They have grates across every window.*

grating /ˈgreɪt̬·ɪŋ/ *n* [C] a structure made of metal bars ○ *an iron grating*

RUB TOGETHER /greɪt/ *v* [I] (of two hard objects) to rub together, often making an unpleasant sound, or to make an unpleasant sound of this kind ○ *The trolley's wheels grated horribly as it went around the curve.*

grating /ˈgreɪt̬·ɪŋ/ *adj* ○ *I turned on the car's engine, and there was that familiar grating sound.*

ANNOY /greɪt/ *v* [I] to have an annoying or painful effect ○ *His constant whining for attention is beginning to grate on my nerves.*

COOKING /greɪt/ *v* [T] to rub food against the rough surface of a metal device having holes through which small pieces of the food fall as they break off ○ *Would you grate the cheese?* ○ *Add the grated carrots to the salad.*

grater /ˈgreɪt̬·ər/ *n* [C] a metal device with holes surrounded by sharp edges, used to cut food into small pieces ○ *a cheese grater*

grateful /ˈgreɪt·fəl/ *adj* showing or expressing thanks, esp. to another person ○ *I'm grateful for your love and support.*

gratefully /ˈgreɪt·fə·li/ *adv* ○ *We gratefully acknowledge the support of the Lincoln Fund.*

WORD FAMILY grateful

Nouns	gratitude ingratitude	*Adjectives*	grateful ungrateful
Adverbs	gratefully		

WORD CHOICES grateful

The adjective **appreciative** is sometimes used to show that someone is grateful, or you can use the verb **appreciate** to express the same idea.

*I'm really **appreciative** of all the help you've given me.*

*I really **appreciate** all the help you've given me.*

The expression **be glad of** is another alternative.

*We **were** very **glad of** some extra help.*

The expression **be indebted to** is a more formal way of saying that someone is very grateful for something.

***I'm indebted to** my parents for all their love and support.*

The adjectives **thankful** or **relieved** are often used when a person is grateful that something unpleasant did not happen.

*I'm just **thankful** that she's safe and well.*

If a person is grateful that someone has done something kind, the adjective **touched** is sometimes used.

*She was really **touched** that he remembered her birthday.*

gratify /ˈgræt̬·əˌfɑɪ/ *v* [T] to please someone, or to satisfy a wish or need ○ [+ *to* infinitive] *He was gratified to see how well his students had done.*

gratifying /ˈgræt̬·əˌfɑɪ·ɪŋ/ *adj* ○ *It was a big game for us, and a very gratifying win.*

gratis /ˈgræt̬·əs, ˈgrɑt̬-/ *adj, adv* [not gradable] free; not costing anything ○ *Drinks were gratis.*

gratitude /ˈgræt̬·əˌtuːd/ *n* [U] a strong feeling of appreciation to someone or something for what the person has done to help you ○ *Many of his patients gave works of art to Dr. Klein in gratitude.*

gratuitous /grəˈtuː·ət̬·əs/ *adj* not necessary; with no reasonable cause ○ *There were too many gratuitous personal insults throughout the debate.*

gratuity /grəˈtuː·ət̬·i/ *n* [C] *fml* an amount of money given as a reward for a service; TIP

grave BURYING PLACE /greɪv/ *n* [C] a place where a dead person or dead people are buried, esp. when under the ground and marked by a stone

SERIOUS /greɪv/ *adj* [*-er/-est* only] urgent and very bad; serious ○ *It was the gravest political crisis of his career.*

gravely /ˈgreɪv·li/ *adv* ○ *She is gravely ill.*

gravity /ˈgræv·ət̬·i/ *n* [U] ○ *I don't think you understand the gravity of the situation.* ○ See also: GRAVITY

gravel /ˈgræv·əl/ *n* [U] very small, rounded stones, often mixed with sand ○ *Gravel covers the driveway.*

gravelly /ˈgræv·ə·li/ *adj* (of a voice) low and rough

gravestone /ˈgreɪv·stoʊn/ *n* [C] a TOMBSTONE

graveyard /ˈgreɪv·jɑrd/ *n* [C] a place where dead people are buried

gravitate /ˈgræv·əˌteɪt/ *v* [I always + adv/prep] to be attracted to or move toward something ○ *People tend to gravitate to the beaches here.*

gravitation /ˌgræv·əˈteɪ·ʃən/ *n* [U] ***physics, earth science*** the natural attraction that any two masses have for each other; the force of GRAVITY

gravitational /ˌgræv·əˈteɪ·ʃən·əl/ *adj* ***physics*** **1** involving GRAVITY **2** A **gravitational field** is the area around a large object, such as a planet, where gravity has an effect. **3 Gravitational force** is the same as GRAVITY. **4 Gravitational potential energy** is the energy that an object has because it is in a situation where gravity could affect it.

gravity /ˈgræv·ət̬·i/ *n* [U] ***physics*** the force that makes objects fall toward the earth, or toward some other large object such as a planet or a star ○ See also: GRAVITY at GRAVE SERIOUS

gravy FOOD /ˈgreɪ·vi/ *n* [U] a sauce made from meat juices, often mixed with flour

EXTRA /ˈgreɪ·vi/ *n* [U] *infml* something extra that you welcome having and often did not expect to get ○ *This business took care of all our expenses, and the revenue from other ads and subscriptions was gravy.*

gray, *esp. Cdn, Br* **grey** /greɪ/ *adj, n* [C/U] **1** (of) the color that is a mixture of black and white, the color of clouds when it rains ○ *a gray coat* ○ [U] *She was dressed in gray.* **2** Hair that has changed color to gray: *He's already beginning to turn gray.* **3** If the weather is gray, there are a lot of clouds in the sky. **4** A gray area is an unclear situation, usually because the rules that relate to it are not known: *Criminal negligence is a gray area.*

graze HURT SLIGHTLY /greɪz/ *v* [T] to touch and rub against something while passing it, causing slight damage ○ *The bullet only grazed his leg.*

EAT /greɪz/ *v* [I/T] (of animals) to eat grass, or to cause animals to feed on grass ○ [I] *Cows grazed in the field.*

grease /griːs/ *n* [U] **1** animal fat that is soft after melting ○ *There's always a lot of grease when you cook lamb.* **2** Grease is also any thick, oily substance: *You ought to put some grease on that hinge.*

grease /griːs, griːz/ *v* [T] ○ *Grease the pan.*

greasy /ˈgriː·si, -zi/ *adj* covered with or full of grease ○ *These French fries are too greasy.*

greasepaint /ˈgriːs·peɪnt/ *n* [U] makeup as used by actors in the theater

greasy spoon *n* [C] *slang* a small, cheap restaurant, esp. one that sells a lot of fried food

great LARGE /greɪt/ *adj* [*-er/-est* only] large or unusually large in amount or degree ○ *the Great Lakes* ○ *He went on to great success as an actor.* ○ *There was a great deal of (= a lot of) excitement in the classroom before lunch.*

greatly /ˈgreɪt·li/ *adv* [not gradable] very much ○ *Her piano-playing has improved greatly.*

IMPORTANT /greɪt/ *adj* [*-er/-est* only] important, powerful, or famous ○ *a great president* ○ *a great athlete*

great /greɪt/ *n* [C] a famous person in a particular area of activity ○ *This sports facility is named after the tennis great Arthur Ashe.*

greatness /ˈgreɪt·nəs/ *n* [U] ○ *Her greatness as a writer is beyond question.*

GOOD /greɪt/ *adj* [*-er/-est* only] *infml* very good or very effective; excellent ○ *We had a great time.* ○ *She has a great voice.* ○ *This stuff is great for cleaning windows.*

great- FAMILIES /ˌgreɪt/ *prefix* used with a word for a family member, such as GRANDMOTHER, to mean one GENERATION older than that family member ○ *great-grandmother*

WORD FAMILY great			
Nouns	great greatness	*Adjectives* *Adverbs*	great greatly

Great Depression *n* [U] ***world history*** a period of decrease in wealth, industrial production, and employment from 1929 until the start of World War II

greater than, *symbol* > *adv* ***mathematics*** having a larger number or amount than ○ Compare LESS THAN

greatest common factor, *abbreviation* **GCF** *n* [C] ***mathematics*** the largest number that can be used to divide two other numbers

greed /griːd/ *n* [U] a strong desire to continually get more of something, esp. money ○ *He was motivated by pure greed.*

greedy /ˈgriːd·i/ *adj* ○ *He was greedy for power.*

green COLOR /griːn/ *adj, n* [C/U] (of) the color that is a mixture of blue and yellow; the color of grass ○ *a green dress* ○ [C] *I don't like that green.*

PLANTS /griːn/ *adj* [-*er*/-*est* only] of or relating to grass, trees, and other plants ○ *I'd like a green salad* (= made with leafy vegetables).

green /griːn/ *n* [C] *regional US* **1** an area planted with grass, esp. for use by the public ○ *The fair will be held on the green behind the library.* **2** A green is also an area of smooth grass surrounding a hole on a golf course.

greenery /ˈgriː·nə·ri/ *n* [U] green plants, or branches that have been cut off from plants, esp. when used as decoration

greens /griːnz/ *pl n* the leaves of green vegetables such as LETTUCE or SPINACH when eaten as food

POLITICAL /griːn/ *adj* [-*er*/-*est* only] relating to the protection of the environment ○ *green politics*

NOT READY /griːn/ *adj* [-*er*/-*est* only] not experienced or trained ○ *I was pretty green when I joined this company.*

WORD FAMILY green			
Nouns	green greenery greens	*Adjectives*	green

IDIOMS with green

• **a green thumb** the ability to make plants grow and be healthy ○ *My sister has a green thumb, but I kill most plants that I buy.*

• **green with envy** wishing very much that you had what someone else has ○ *When I heard about his new job I was green with envy.*

greenback /ˈgriːn·bæk/ *n* [C] any piece of US paper money ○ *He took out a thick wad of greenbacks.*

green bean, **string bean** *n* [C] a type of long, green, edible bean

green card *n* [C] a document giving a person from a foreign country permission to live and work in the United States

greenhorn /ˈgriːn·hɔːrn/ *n* [C] a person who is not experienced ○ *I'm a greenhorn when it comes to skiing.*

greenhouse /ˈgriːn·hɑʊs/ *n* [C] a building with a roof and sides made of glass or other transparent material, used for growing plants that need warmth and protection

greenhouse effect *n* [U] ***earth science*** the gradual warming of the earth because of heat trapped by CARBON DIOXIDE and other gases in the ATMOSPHERE

green light *n* [C] **1** a traffic signal with the green part lit as a signal that it is safe to go ○ *Wait for the green light before crossing the street.* ○ Compare RED LIGHT **2** *fig.* A green light is also permission to do something: *The developers were given a green light to go forward with the project.*

green revolution *n* [U] ***world history*** a large increase in food production around the world because of better farming TECHNOLOGY

greet /griːt/ *v* [T] to welcome someone with particular words or a particular action, or to react to something in the stated way ○ *The men greeted each other warmly.* ○ *The mayor was greeted with shouts of anger.*

greeting /ˈgriːt̬·ɪŋ/ *n* [C] ○ *Jennifer sends birthday greetings* (= good wishes for your birthday).

greeting card *n* [C] a card containing a message of good wishes, usually sent to someone to celebrate an event such as a birthday

gregarious /grɪˈgær·iː·əs, -ˈger-/ *adj* liking to be with other people ○ *Leo was an open, gregarious, kind individual, who loved people.*

gremlin /ˈgrem·lən/ *n* [C] an imaginary creature that gets inside things, esp. machines, and causes problems

grenade /grəˈneɪd/ *n* [C] a small bomb thrown by hand or shot from a gun

grew /gruː/ *past simple of* GROW

grey /greɪ/ *adj esp. Cdn, Br* GRAY

greyhound /ˈgreɪ·hɑʊnd/ *n* [C] a type of dog that has a thin body and long legs, and that can run very fast

grid /grɪd/ *n* [C] **1** a pattern of horizontal and vertical lines that cross each other to make a set of squares **2** A grid is also a system of wires through which electricity is connected to different parts of a region: *a power grid*

griddle /ˈgrɪd·əl/ *n* [C] a flat metal surface of a stove heated from below for cooking, or a flat metal pan ○ *Pancakes were cooking on the griddle.*

gridiron /ˈgrɪd,ɑɪ·ərn/ *n* [C] a football field

gridlock /ˈgrɪd·lɑk/ *n* [U] a situation where streets that meet and cross become so blocked by cars that it is impossible for any traffic to move

grief /griːf/ *n* [U] very great sadness, esp. at the death of someone ○ *It took her years to get over her grief at the death of her mother.* ○ (*fig.*) *I had no idea that forgetting my driver's license would cause me so much grief* (= trouble).

grievance /ˈgriː·vəns/ *n* [C] a complaint or a strong feeling that you have been treated unfairly ○ *A special committee investigates prisoners' grievances.*

grieve /griːv/ *v* [I/T] to feel a great sadness, esp. when someone dies ○ [I] *The entire community is grieving for the loss of the four children.*

grievous /ˈgriː·vəs/ *adj* having very serious effects or causing great pain ○ *It was a grievous head wound, and he was not expected to survive.*

grievously /ˈgriː·və·sli/ *adv* ○ *He was grievously injured.*

grill COOK /grɪl/ *v* [T] to cook something on a frame of metal bars, usually over a gas or coal fire

○ *We love to grill outside and eat on the back porch in the summer.*

grill /grɪl/ *n* [C] a frame of metal bars on which food is cooked over a fire

QUESTION /grɪl/ *v* [T] to ask someone a lot of questions for a long time ○ *After being grilled by the police for eight hours, Johnson signed a confession.*

grim **NOT GOOD** /grɪm/ *adj* [*-er/-est* only] **-mm-** not good; having no chance of a good result ○ *The outlook for a full recovery was grim.*

SERIOUS /grɪm/ *adj* [*-er/-est* only] **-mm-** very serious and sad ○ *The future looks grim for workers who are losing their jobs.* ○ *He looked at us with a grim expression.*

grimace /ˈgrɪm·əs, grɪˈmeɪs/ *n* [C] an expression of pain or disgust in which the muscles of the face are tightened and the face looks twisted

grimace /ˈgrɪm·əs, grɪˈmeɪs/ *v* [I] ○ *He grimaced in pain as the surgeon removed his bandages.*

grime /grɑɪm/ *n* [U] a layer of dirt on skin or a building ○ *The building is covered with grime.*

grimy /ˈgrɑɪ·mi/ *adj* ○ *a grimy face*

grin /grɪn/ *n* [C] a wide smile ○ *He flashed a big grin and gave us a thumbs up.*

grin /grɪn/ *v* [I] **-nn-** ○ *He grinned and waved to us.*

IDIOM with **grin**

• **grin and bear it** to accept something bad without complaining ○ *This cast will be on my arm for six weeks, so I'll just have to grin and bear it.*

grind **CRUSH** /grɑɪnd/ *v* [T] *past* **ground** to crush a substance between hard, moving surfaces into small pieces or a powder ○ *Every morning I go to the kitchen and grind some coffee.* ○ *Add a teaspoon of freshly ground black pepper.* ○ Related noun: GROUNDS

grinder /ˈgrɑɪn·dər/ *n* [C] a machine for crushing or cutting something into very small pieces ○ *a meat grinder*

RUB /grɑɪnd/ *v* [T] *past* **ground** **1** to rub an object against a hard surface in order to make it sharper, thinner, or smoother ○ *Laborers grind and shape steel bars into decorative fences.* **2** If you grind two sets of objects, you press and rub them together in a way that makes an unpleasant noise: *Ursula grinds her teeth at night.*

ACTIVITY /grɑɪnd/ *n* [U] *infml* difficult or unpleasant activity that is tiring or repeated too often ○ *Karen came to the hotel for a rest from the daily grind.*

grind /grɑɪnd/ *v* [I] *infml* ○ *The speeches ground on for hours.* ○ *They have been ground down by constant stress.*

grinding /ˈgrɑɪn·dɪŋ/ *adj* Something that is grinding causes people or activities to lose energy and spirit: *He was brought up in grinding poverty.*

IDIOM with **grind**

• **grind to a halt** to stop or no longer work well ○ *Traffic ground to a halt.* ○ *The country's economy is slowly grinding to a halt.*

grindstone /ˈgrɑɪn·stoʊn/ *n* a large, round stone that is turned by a machine and is used for making tools sharper

gringo /ˈgrɪŋ·goʊ/ *n* [C] *pl* **gringos** someone in a Latin American country who is not Latin American, esp. someone who speaks only English ○ **USAGE:** This word is usually considered offensive.

grip /grɪp/ *v* [I/T] *pres. part.* **gripping**, *past* **gripped** **1** to hold something tightly, or stick to something ○ [T] *The baby gripped my finger.* ○ [I] *Worn tires don't grip very well on wet roads.* **2** If an emotion grips you, you feel it strongly: [T] *Brady was gripped by fear.*

grip /grɪp/ *n* [C usually sing] a way of holding something, or a tight hold ○ *She has a strong/firm/weak grip.* ○ *He lost his grip on Nancy's arm.* ○ (*fig.*) *They were in the grip of a tropical storm* (= suffering its effects).

gripe /grɑɪp/ *n* [C] *infml* a strong complaint ○ *My biggest gripe about living here is the hot weather.*

gripe /grɑɪp/ *v* [I] ○ *People gripe about doing yard work.*

gripping /ˈgrɪp·ɪŋ/ *adj* interesting or exciting ○ *a gripping story*

grisly /ˈgrɪz·li/ *adj* extremely unpleasant or disgusting, and usually causing fear ○ *There were grisly pictures of an automobile accident on the evening news.*

gristle /ˈgrɪs·əl/ *n* [U] a part of a piece of meat that is very hard to chew

grit **STONES** /grɪt/ *n* [U] very small pieces of stone or sand ○ *I cleaned the grit off my bike.*

gritty /ˈgrɪţ·i/ *adj* ○ *gritty dust*

BRAVERY /grɪt/ *n* [U] bravery and strength of character ○ *Emma is enthusiastic, all grit and determination.*

gritty /ˈgrɪţ·i/ *adj* ○ *a gritty, no-nonsense approach*

PRESS /grɪt/ *v* [T] **-tt-** to press your top and bottom teeth together ○ *I grit my teeth because I'm trying not to moan.*

IDIOM with **grit**

• **grit** *your* **teeth** to deal with a difficult or unpleasant situation in a determined way ○ *I hate going to the gym, but I just grit my teeth and try to get through it.*

grits /grɪts/ *pl n* a dried, crushed type of corn, usually boiled in water and eaten esp. for breakfast

grizzly (bear) /ˈgrɪz·li (ˌber, ˌbær)/ *n* [C] a large, gray-brown bear from North America

groan /groʊn/ *n* [C] a low, sad sound that is continued for a while and that is made by someone who is suffering from pain or unhappiness ○ *Nick let out a groan.*

groan /groʊn/ *v* [I] ○ *He would often groan in his sleep.* ○ (*fig.*) *The tires of the pickup truck groaned under the weight* (= made sounds because of the pressure).

grocer /ˈgroʊ·sər/ *n* [C] a person who owns or works in a store selling food

groceries /ˈgroʊ·sə·riːz/ *pl n* the food and other items that you buy in a food store or SUPERMARKET ○ *My wife wrote a check to pay for groceries.*
grocery (store) /ˈgroʊ·sə·ri (ˌstɔːr, ˌstoʊr)/ *n* [C] a store where food and small items for the house are sold

groggy /ˈgrɑg·i/ *adj* weak and unable to think clearly or walk correctly, usually because of illness or being tired ○ *The drug treated her sypmtoms but left her groggy.*

groin /grɔɪn/ *n* [C] the place at the front of your body where your legs meet ○ *Jeff pulled a muscle in his groin.*

G

groom MAKE READY /gruːm, grʊm/ *v* [I/T] to make yourself ready to be seen; put in order ○ [T] *The girls groomed their hair.* ○ [I] *He's gone upstairs to finish grooming.* ○ [T] *They're grooming the ski runs at Snow Basin* (= preparing them for use).

PREPARE /gruːm, grʊm/ *v* [T] to prepare someone for a special job or activity ○ *The record company groomed performers to fit the music's image.*

MAN /gruːm, grʊm/, **bridegroom** *n* [C] a man who is about to get married or just got married ○ *The bride and groom were posing for pictures.*

CLEAN /gruːm, grʊm/ *v* [T] to clean an animal, often by brushing its fur ○ *I've groomed horses for years.*
groom /gruːm, grʊm/ *n* [C] a person whose job is to take care of and clean horses

groove /gruːv/ *n* [C] a long, narrow, hollow space cut into a surface ○ *The window slides along a groove in the frame.*

groovy /ˈgruː·vi/ *adj dated, slang* very fashionable and interesting ○ *groovy music*

grope /groʊp/ *v* [I/T] **1** to search for something you cannot see or find easily, esp. by feeling with your hands ○ [I] *She stands on her toes and gropes around on the closet shelf.* **2** *infml* Someone who gropes someone else touches that person's body without permission.

gross EXTREME /groʊs/ *adj* [*-er/-est* only] (esp. of something bad or wrong) extreme or obvious ○ *The birds die from hunger, thirst, and gross overcrowding.*
grossly /ˈgroʊ·sli/ *adj* ○ *Medical insurance can be grossly expensive.*

UNPLEASANT /groʊs/ *adj* [*-er/-est* only] *infml* rude or offensive ○ *She watches these really gross movies.* ○ *"Gross!" Pamela says as she wipes the goo off her fingers.*

TOTAL /groʊs/ *adj* [not gradable] (of earnings) total, before tax is paid or costs are subtracted ○ *Investors have earned gross income of $780 million.*
gross /groʊs/ *n* [C usually sing] ○ *On a gross of $28 million, the company netted $7 million.*
gross /groʊs/ *v* [T] ○ *The film grossed over $200 million.*

NUMBER /groʊs/ *n* [C] *pl* **gross** a group of 144 items

PHRASAL VERB with **gross**

• **gross** *someone* **out** [M] *infml* to make someone uncomfortable by saying or doing something very unpleasant ○ *It grosses people out when I show them my scar.*

gross domestic product, *abbreviation* **GDP** *n* [U] the total value of goods and services produced by a country in one year

grotesque /groʊˈtesk/ *adj* strange and often frightening in appearance or character ○ *Some deep-sea creatures look really grotesque.*
grotesquely /groʊˈtes·kli/ *adv* ○ *His face was grotesquely scarred.*

grotto /ˈgrɑţ·oʊ/ *n* [C] *pl* **grottoes, grottos** a small cave or an artificial structure that is like a cave, esp. one used for religious purposes

grouch /graʊtʃ/ *n* [C] a person who complains a lot even when there is little reason to complain
grouchy /ˈgraʊ·tʃi/ *adj* ○ *You're awfully grouchy today.*

ground CRUSH /graʊnd/ *past simple and past participle of* GRIND

LAND /graʊnd/ *n* [U] the surface of the earth or of a piece of land ○ *We laid a blanket on the ground for our picnic.*
ground /graʊnd/ *v* [T] to put or keep on the ground ○ *All flights have been grounded because of the snowstorm.*
grounds /graʊnz/ *pl n* land that surrounds a building ○ *We strolled around the hospital grounds.* ○ See also: GROUNDS

AREA OF KNOWLEDGE /graʊnd/ *n* [U] an area of knowledge or experience; a subject ○ *This teacher just keeps going over the same ground again and again.*

CAUSE /graʊnd/ *n* [C usually pl] a reason, cause, or argument ○ [+ *that* clause] *He refused to answer on the grounds that he'd promised to keep it secret.*
ground /graʊnd/ *v* [T] ○ *His beliefs are grounded in his experience.*
groundless /ˈgraʊn·dləs/ *adj* ○ *Your concerns are groundless.*

PUNISH /graʊnd/ *v* [T] *infml* to punish an older child by not allowing the child to go out or be involved in social activities ○ *My parents grounded me for a week.*

WIRE /graʊnd/ *n* [C] **1** a connection between a piece of electrical equipment and the earth, or a wire that makes this connection **2** A ground is also an object that holds a very large number of ELECTRONs, and can accept or supply more when there is an electric current.

WORD FAMILY ground			
Nouns	ground underground grounds	*Adjectives*	groundless underground
		Adverbs	underground
Verbs	ground		

IDIOM with **ground**

• **in on the ground floor** involved in something from its beginning ○ *Can someone tell me how you get in on the ground floor of a deal like that?*

groundbreaking /ˈgraʊnd ˌbreɪ·kɪŋ/ *adj* original and important; showing a new way of doing or thinking about things ○ *This groundbreaking work changed the way historians looked at slavery.*

ground floor, **first floor** *n* [U] the floor in a building that is nearest the level of the ground

groundhog /ˈgrɑʊnd ˌhɔːg, -ˌhɑg/, **woodchuck** *n* [C] a small North American mammal with short legs and rough, red-brown fur

Groundhog Day *n* [U] in the US, February 2nd, which according to an old story, is the day the groundhog wakes up after sleeping through the winter. If it sees its SHADOW on this day, there will be six more weeks of winter, and if it does not, spring will start early.

ground rules /ˈgrɑʊnd·ruːlz/ *pl n* the basic rules for doing something ○ *We set very strict ground rules for the interviews.*

grounds /grɑʊnz/ *pl n* the small pieces of solid material that sink to the bottom of a liquid, esp. coffee ○ See also: GROUNDS at GROUND LAND

ground state *n* [U] ***physics*** the lowest energy condition of an atom, NUCLEUS (= central part) of an atom, or MOLECULE

groundwater /ˈgrɑʊnd ˌwɔːt̬·ər, -ˌwɑt̬·ər/ *n* [U] water that collects below the surface of the earth

groundwork /ˈgrɑʊn·dwɜrk/ *n* [U] work done in preparation for something that will happen later ○ *The planning committee will lay the groundwork for the conference.*

group /gruːp/ *n* [C] **1** a number of people or things that are together or considered as a unit ○ *a group of trees* ○ *I'm meeting a group of friends for dinner.* **2** A group is also a number of people who play music together, especially popular music: *a rock/soul group* **3** ***chemistry*** A group is also any of the columns in the PERIODIC TABLE of chemical elements.

group /gruːp/ *v* [T] ○ *She grouped the children by height for the class photograph.*

groupie /ˈgruː·pi/ *n* [C] *infml* a person who admires and tries to meet someone famous, esp. a popular musician ○ *Groupies were hanging around the entrance while he was recording here.*

grouse COMPLAIN /grɑʊs/ *v* [I] *infml* to complain ○ *He's always grousing about how hard he has to work.*

BIRD /grɑʊs/ *n* [C/U] *pl* **grouse** a small, fat bird that is hunted, or the flesh of this bird eaten as meat

grove /groʊv/ *n* [C] a group of trees growing close together

grovel /ˈgrɑv·əl, ˈgrʌv·əl/ *v* [I] to lie facing the ground, esp. in fear, or to behave toward someone in a way that shows that you are small and unimportant and the other person is powerful ○ *My dog grovels at my feet when she's done something wrong.* ○ *I'll apologize, but I won't grovel just because I made a mistake.*

grow INCREASE /groʊ/ *v* [I/T] *past simp.* **grew**, *past part.* **grown** to increase in size or amount, or to allow or encourage something to increase in size or to become more advanced or developed ○ [I] *The population is growing rapidly.* ○ [I] *She's grown a lot since we last saw her.* ○ [T] *He began to grow a beard.* ○ [I] *The economy is expected to grow by 2% next year.*

growing /ˈgroʊ·ɪŋ/ *adj* [not gradable] increasing in size or amount ○ *There is a growing awareness of the seriousness of this disease.*

DEVELOP /groʊ/ *v* [I/T] *past simp.* **grew**, *past part.* **grown** to provide a plant with the conditions it needs to develop, or to develop from a seed or small plant ○ [I] *This plant grows best in the shade.* ○ [T] *We're growing some herbs on the windowsill.*

grower /ˈgroʊ·ər/ *n* [C] a person or company that cultivates a particular plant or crop in order to sell it ○ *citrus growers*

BECOME /groʊ/ *v past simp.* **grew**, *past part.* **grown** to develop gradually, or to start to do something gradually ○ [L] *I grew too old to be interested.* ○ [+ to infinitive] *She has grown to like him.*

WORD FAMILY grow			
Nouns	grower growth undergrowth	*Adjectives*	growing grown overgrown
Verbs	grow outgrow		

PHRASAL VERBS with grow

• **grow into** *something* DEVELOP to become a more completely developed type of person or thing ○ *We want these children to grow into responsible adults.* ○ *Founded by the Grand Trunk Pacific Railway, Kitimat grew into a sawmill town.*

• **grow into** *something* BEGIN TO FIT to become tall enough or big enough to wear or use something ○ *Never buy a bike that's too big and expect your child to grow into it.*

• **grow on** *someone* to become increasingly liked or enjoyed by someone ○ *Living in a small town was tough at first, but the place grows on you.*

• **grow out of** *something* DEVELOP to develop from something that happened or existed before ○ *The new law grew out of people's dissatisfaction with the election results.*

• **grow out of** *something* STOP LIKING to stop having an interest in something or stop doing something as you become older ○ *He wants to be a rapper, but I think he'll grow out of it.*

• **grow out of** *something* STOP FITTING to become too tall or too big to wear or use something ○ *Mom said she wasn't going to buy me something I was going to grow out of next week.*

• **grow up** **1** to change from being a child to being an adult ○ *She grew up on a Pennsylvania farm.* **2** If you say "grow up" to someone, you are telling the person to stop behaving like a child.

growing pains EMOTIONS *pl n* emotional difficulties or confusion experienced by a young

G

person during the time between being a child and an adult

PROBLEMS *pl n* temporary worries and problems experienced by an organization when it is new or becomes involved in a new activity

growl /graʊl/ *v* [I] **1** to make a low, rough sound, usually in anger ○ *The dog growled at her.* **2** If your stomach growls, it is making a low, continuous noise because you are hungry.

growl /graʊl/ *n* [C] ○ *I heard a growl outside our tent, and prayed that whatever was out there would go away.*

grown /groʊn/ *adj* [not gradable] adult ○ *a grown woman/man*

G

grown-up *n* [C] an adult ○ *The grown-ups sat inside while the children played in the yard.*

grown-up *adj* [not gradable] ○ *She has three grown-up sons.*

growth /groʊθ/ *n* [C/U] **1** the process of developing or of increasing in size ○ [U] *Plant growth is most noticeable in spring.* ○ [U] *His budget is designed to promote economic growth in this country.* **2** A growth is also tissue growing on the outside or inside of a person, animal, or plant which is caused by a disease.

grub **FOOD** /grʌb/ *n* [U] *slang* food ○ *The food was just good, greasy grub.*

ASK FOR /grʌb/ *v* [T] *pres. part.* **grubbing**, *past* **grubbed** *slang* to ask someone to give you something ○ *Can I grub a sandwich from you?*

INSECT /grʌb/ *n* [C] an insect in the stage when it has just come out of its egg

grubby /ˈgrʌb·i/ *adj* dirty or messy ○ *grubby old clothes*

grudge /grʌdʒ/ *n* [C] a strong feeling of anger and dislike for a person who treated you badly ○ *He wasn't one to hold a grudge, but he wasn't going to be friendly.*

grudging /ˈgrʌdʒ·ɪŋ/ *adj* done or offered unwillingly ○ *Her hard work won the grudging respect of her boss.*

grudgingly /ˈgrʌdʒ·ɪŋ·li/ *adv* ○ *Grudgingly, Congress approved the funds.*

grueling /ˈgruː·ə·lɪŋ, ˈgruː·lɪŋ/ *adj* extremely tiring and difficult, and demanding great effort and determination ○ *a grueling 50-mile run*

gruesome /ˈgruː·səm/ *adj* extremely unpleasant and shocking ○ *The movie was pretty gruesome.*

gruff /grʌf/ *adj* [*-er/-est* only] **1** dealing with people in a way that lacks patience and seems unfriendly ○ *He has that gruff exterior, but underneath he's very kind.* **2** If a person's voice is gruff, it sounds low and slightly damaged.

gruffly /ˈgrʌf·li/ *adv* ○ *"You drive," Casey gruffly told Jack.*

grumble /ˈgrʌm·bəl/ *v* [I] to complain in an annoyed way ○ *There's no point in grumbling about the hotel – we're only here for one night.*

grumpy /ˈgrʌm·pi/ *adj infml* being in a slightly angry mood because you are annoyed at something or are feeling tired ○ *Dad is always grumpy on Monday mornings.*

grunge /grʌndʒ/ *adj* connected with a type of ROCK music, popular in the early 1990s, or with a style of clothing that gives the appearance of being dirty and not cared for

grungy /ˈgrʌn·dʒi/ *adj slang* (of a person) feeling dirty and that you need to wash, or (of a thing) dirty ○ *After a 15-hour flight, I felt really grungy.*

grunt /grʌnt/ *v* [I] to make a short, low noise, esp. in surprise, pain, or pleasure, or to show that you do not want to talk ○ *I tried to start a conversation, but he just grunted and continued reading.*

grunt /grʌnt/ *n* [C] ○ *The weightlifter raised the bar over his head with a grunt.*

guacamole /ˌgwɑk·əˈmoʊ·li/ *n* [U] a thick mixture of AVOCADO (= an oily, green tropical fruit), TOMATO, onion, and spices, usually eaten cold with Mexican food and sometimes offered as a food before meals

guarantee Ⓐ /ˌgær·ənˈtiː, ˈgær·ənˌtiː/ *n* [C/U] **1** a promise that something will be done or will happen, esp. a written promise by a company to repair or change a product that develops a fault within a particular period of time ○ [C] *The vacuum cleaner comes with a two-year guarantee.* **2** Guarantee is also the state of being certain of a particular result: [U] *No matter how many stars you have in the show, there's no guarantee* (= it is not certain that) *it will be a success.*

guarantee Ⓐ /ˌgær·ənˈtiː, ˈgær·ənˌtiː/ *v* [T] **1** *The freezer is guaranteed for three years.* **2** If you guarantee something, you promise that a particular thing will happen or exist: [+ (*that*) clause] *I guarantee (you) that our team will play hard and have a shot at winning the championship.* **3** If something is guaranteed to happen or have a particular result, it is certain that it will happen or have that result: [+ *to* infinitive] *Eating all that rich food is guaranteed to give you indigestion.*

guard /gɑrd/ *n* [C] **1** a person or group of people whose job it is to protect a person, place, or thing from danger or attack, or to prevent a person such as a criminal from escaping ○ *prison guards* ○ *Armed guards were posted at every exit.* **2** In sports, a guard is a player who supports and defends other players of his or her team.

guard /gɑrd/ *v* [T] ○ *Soldiers guarded* (= protected) *the buildings against attack.*

guarded /ˈgɑrd·əd/ *adj* careful in speech in order to avoid giving information ○ *The president made a guarded, lawyerly response.*

IDIOM with guard

• **on** (*your*) **guard** careful and aware because a situation might be dangerous ○ *Passengers on public transportation were warned to be on their guard against pickpockets.*

guardian /ˈgɑrd·iː·ən/ *n* [C] **1** a person who has the legal right and responsibility of taking care of someone who is not responsible for his or her own care, such as a child whose parents have died **2** A guardian is also someone who protects something: *She characterized the department as the guardian of the nation's forests.*

guardian angel *n* [C] a spirit who is believed to protect and help a particular person

guava /ˈgwɑv·ə/ *n* [C] a round, yellow, tropical fruit with pink or white flesh and hard seeds

gubernatorial /ˌguː·bər·nəˈtɔːr·iː·əl, -ˈtoʊr-/ *adj* [not gradable] relating to a governor of a US state ○ *a gubernatorial election*

guerrilla /gəˈrɪl·ə/ *n* [C] a member of an unofficial military group that is trying to change the government by making sudden, unexpected attacks on the official army forces ○ *guerrilla warfare*

guess /ges/ *v* [I/T] **1** to give an answer to a question when you do not have all the facts and so cannot be certain if you are right ○ [I] *I didn't know the answer, so I had to guess.* ○ [+ (*that*) clause] *He guessed (that) she was about 50.* **2** To guess can also mean to give the correct answer: [T] *She guessed the right answer.* **3** To guess also means to think or believe: [T] *My plane leaves in an hour, so I guess I'd better be going.* ○ [T] *"Is he going to call you back?" "I guess so."*

guess /ges/ *n* [C] **1** an attempt to give the right answer when you are not certain if you are right ○ *Go on, take a guess.* **2** Someone's guess is also an opinion about something, formed without any knowledge of the situation: *I don't know why she's late, but my guess is she got off at the wrong exit.*

WORD CHOICES **guess**

Estimate can be used when someone guesses the cost, size, value, etc., of something, based on their knowledge.

*They **estimate** that the work will take at least ten weeks.*

Divine is a slightly formal word that means "guess."

*Mom, as moms tend to do, had **divined** my state of mind rather shrewdly.*

Surmise or **conjecture** are formal words that mean "to guess, based on the appearance of a situation and not on facts."

*From the expression on his face, she **surmised** that something bad had happened.*

*It would be reasonable to **conjecture** that lack of exercise contributed to his obesity.*

If someone guesses possible answers to a question without having enough information to be certain, you could use the verb **speculate**.

*A spokesperson declined to **speculate** on the cause of the plane crash.*

IDIOMS with **guess**

• *your* **guess is as good as mine** I have no way of knowing exactly what happened or what will happen ○ *"Do you think she'd go out with me if I asked her?" "Your guess is as good as mine."*

• *something* **is anyone's guess,** *something* **is anybody's guess** it is not possible for anyone to really know something ○ *He has a plan, but whether it will work or not is anyone's guess.*

guesstimate /ˈges·tə·mət/ *n* [C] a calculation of the size or amount of something when you do not know all the facts ○ *Current guesstimates are that the company's profits will increase by 10% this year.*

guesswork /ˈges·wɜrk/ *n* [U] the process of making a guess when you do not know all the facts ○ *She had to rely on pure guesswork in deciding how much food to order.*

guest /gest/ *n* [C] **1** a person who is staying with you in your home, or a person whom you have invited to a social occasion, such as a party or a meal ○ *dinner/wedding guests* **2** A person who is staying in a hotel is also called a guest. **3** If you are someone's guest, that person is paying for you: *Four senators and their families were flown to Martinique as guests of the oil company.*

guff /gʌf/ *n* [U] *infml* (of speech or writing) nonsense ○ *All that talk about an economic crisis is a lot of guff.*

guffaw /gəˈfɔː/ *v* [I] to laugh loudly but briefly ○ *Kruger guffawed as though Ray had told him a really funny joke.*

guffaw /gəˈfɔː/ *n* [C] ○ *a loud guffaw*

guide /gɑɪd/ *n* [C] **1** a person whose job it is to show a place or a route to visitors ○ *Our tour guide in Rome was a lovely young woman who spoke perfect English.* **2** A guide is also a book or piece of information that gives advice or help on how to do or understand something: *a travel guide* ○ *a guide to the best restaurants* ○ *a tax guide*

guide /gɑɪd/ *v* [T] **1** *She guided me into her living room and offered me a seat on her couch.* ○ *If you want to learn how to use the computer, it has a program that will guide you through it* (= show you how to use it). ○ *We took a guided tour of* (= A guide showed us) *the historic houses in Newport.* **2** To guide someone or something can also mean to control or influence that person or thing: *Public policy must be guided by the best information available.*

guidance /ˈgɑɪd·ᵊns/ *n* [U] help and advice about how to do something or about how to deal with problems ○ *She never got any guidance when she needed it.* ○ *The school district needs another guidance counselor to work with students* (= a person employed to give help and advice to students).

guidebook /ˈgɑɪd·bʊk/ *n* [C] a book that gives information for visitors about a place, such as a city or region of a country ○ *We bought a guidebook for the New England area.*

guided missile *n* [C] an explosive weapon whose direction is controlled by radio signals during its flight

guideline Ⓐ /ˈgɑɪd·lɑɪn/ *n* [C] a piece of information that suggests how something should be done ○ *The article gives guidelines on how to invest your money safely.*

guild /gɪld/ *n* [C] an organization of people who do the same job or have the same interests ○ *the Screen Actors Guild*

guile /gɑɪl/ *n* [U] *fml* the practice of deceiving people or using other dishonest methods to achieve your aims, or the ability to deceive people for this purpose ○ *He is a simple, honest man, totally lacking in guile.*

guileless /ˈgɑɪl·ləs/ *adj* honest and direct ○ *He was completely guileless and trusting.*

guillotine /ˈgɪl·əˌtiːn; ˈgiː·əˌtiːn/ *n* [C] a device, invented in France, consisting of a sharp blade in a tall frame that was used for killing a person by cutting off his or her head

guillotine /ˈgɪl·əˌtiːn; ˈgiː·əˌtiːn/ *v* [T] ○ *During the French Revolution, thousands of people were guillotined.*

guilt /gɪlt/ *n* [U] **1** the fact or state of having done something wrong or committed a crime ○ *In the US, people accused of a crime are presumed to be innocent until their guilt is proven.* **2** Guilt is also a feeling of anxiety or unhappiness that you have done something immoral or wrong, such as causing harm to another person: *She was tormented by feelings of guilt after putting her mother in a nursing home.*

guilty /ˈgɪl·ti/ *adj* **1** *He pleaded guilty* (= He formally admitted his guilt in court). **2** If you feel guilty, you feel that you have done something wrong: *I feel so guilty about forgetting your birthday.* **3** Someone who has a guilty conscience is unhappy because of something wrong that the person feels he or she has done.

WORD FAMILY guilt			
Nouns	guilt	*Adverbs*	guiltily
Adjectives	guilty		

guilt trip *n* [C] *infml* a strong feeling of having done something wrong in a particular situation ○ *Hector is going through a major guilt trip over losing his job.*

guinea pig /ˈgɪn·iːˌpɪg/ *n* [C] **1** a small, furry animal with rounded ears, short legs, and no tail, often kept as a pet and for use in scientific experiments **2** *fig.* A guinea pig is also a person used in a test, esp. one to discover how effective a new drug or process is: *Her own son accused her of having used him as a guinea pig to test her theories about the education of children.*

guise /gɑɪz/ *n* [U] the appearance of someone or something, esp. when intended to deceive ○ *The men who arrived in the guise of criminals were actually undercover police officers.*

guitar /gəˈtɑr, gɪ-, *esp. Southern* ˈgɪ·tɑr/ *n* [C/U] a musical instrument with usually six strings and a flat back that is held on the knee or by a strap worn over the shoulder and played by moving the fingers or a small piece of plastic across the strings, or this instrument generally ○ [C] *an acoustic/electric guitar*

guitarist /gəˈtɑr·əst, gɪ-, *esp. Southern* ˈgɪˌtɑr·əst/ *n* [C] a person who plays the guitar

gulch /gʌltʃ/ *n* [C] a narrow valley or channel with steep sides, made by a fast-flowing stream

gulf AREA /gʌlf/ *n* [C] an area of sea surrounded on three sides by land ○ *the Gulf of Mexico/the Gulf Coast* ○ *the Gulf Stream*

GULF

DIFFERENCE /gʌlf/ *n* [C] an important difference between two things or groups of people ○ *There is a widening gulf between the rich and the poor.*

gull /gʌl/, **sea gull** *n* [C] a large bird that is black or gray and white and that lives near the sea

gullible /ˈgʌl·ə·bəl/ *adj* easily deceived or tricked, and too willing to believe everything that other people say ○ *a gullible young man*

gully /ˈgʌl·i/ *n* [C] a channel cut by running water, which is usually dry except after heavy rain

gulp /gʌlp/ *v* [I/T] **1** to eat or drink food or liquid quickly by swallowing it in large amounts ○ [T] *Ray gulped the last of his coffee and pushed back his chair.* **2** to make a swallowing movement because of fear, surprise, or excitement ○ [I] *"I find this a very confusing conversation to have," he exclaimed, gulping.*

gulp /gʌlp/ *n* [C] ○ *He swallowed his drink in one gulp.*

PHRASAL VERB with gulp

• **gulp down** *something* [M] to eat or drink something quickly ○ *He hardly has time to gulp down a piece of pizza.*

gum MOUTH /gʌm/ *n* [C usually pl] either of the two areas of firm, pink flesh inside the mouth that covers the bones to which the teeth are attached

STICKY SUBSTANCE /gʌm/ *n* [U] **1** a sticky substance obtained from the stems of some trees and plants that is used in industry and for sticking things together **2** Gum is also CHEWING GUM: *Most teachers dont allow their students to chew gum in class.*

gum /gʌm/ *v* **-mm-**

PHRASAL VERB with gum

• **gum up** *something* [M] to cause something to slow down or stop working ○ *The volcanic ash can gum up a car's air filter.* ○ *Requiring every bill to have a hearing would* **gum up the works** (= cause a process to stop working).

gumbo /ˈɡʌm·boʊ/ *n* [C/U] *pl* **gumbos** a thick soup made with OKRA (= a green vegetable) and meat or fish

gumdrop /ˈɡʌm·drɑp/ *n* [C] a chewy candy that comes in many different colors and is usually fruit-flavored

gumption /ˈɡʌm·ʃən/ *n* [U] the strong will and determination to do something ○ *She had the gumption to write directly to the company president.*

gun **WEAPON** /ɡʌn/ *n* [C] a weapon from which bullets or SHELLS (= explosive containers) are fired through a metal tube
gunner /ˈɡʌn·ər/ *n* [C] a soldier or sailor in the armed forces who helps to operate a large gun

OPERATE ENGINE /ɡʌn/ *v* [T] **-nn-** to make an engine operate at high speed ○ *Tom gunned the engine and sped off into the night.*

PHRASAL VERBS with gun

• **gun down** *someone* [M] to shoot and kill or badly injure someone
• **gun for** *something* **TRY TO WIN** to make a great effort to win or obtain something ○ *Irwin is gunning for his third straight championship.*
• **gun for** *someone* **TRY TO HARM** **1** to make a great effort to defeat or hurt someone ○ *We know all the other teams are gunning for us.* **2** If someone is gunning for someone else, that person can also be trying to shoot or attack the other one.

gunfire /ˈɡʌn·fɑɪr/ *n* [U] the shooting of one or more guns, or the sound this makes ○ *We could hear gunfire but couldn't tell where it was coming from.*

gung-ho /ɡʌŋˈhoʊ/ *adj infml* extremely enthusiastic ○ *I have a grandson who is gung-ho for football.*

gunk /ɡʌŋk/ *n* [U] any thick, sticky, unpleasant substance ○ *There was a lot of gunk on my bike chain.*

gunman /ˈɡʌn·mən/ *n* [C] *pl* **-men** a criminal who uses a gun ○ *The gunman ordered the couple to toss their cash onto the floor.*

gunnysack /ˈɡʌn·iːˌsæk/ *n* [C] a large bag made of rough cloth ○ *She put the sticks in a gunnysack that she dragged along behind her.*

gunpoint **IDIOM** **at gunpoint** while threatening to use a gun ○ *He was robbed at gunpoint in his shop three years ago.*

gunpowder /ˈɡʌnˌpɑʊd·ər/ *n* [U] a substance in powder form that is used in making explosive devices

gunshot **SHOOTING** /ˈɡʌn·ʃɑt/ *n* [C] the shooting of a gun, or the sound this makes ○ *I hear gunshots in the forest sometimes.*

BULLETS /ˈɡʌn·ʃɑt/ *n* [U] the bullets shot from a gun ○ *He suffered a gunshot wound in the thigh.*

gurgle /ˈɡɜr·ɡəl/ *v* [I] to make a bubbling sound like water flowing over an uneven surface ○ *A stream gurgled over the rocks.*
gurgle /ˈɡɜr·ɡəl/ *n* [C] ○ *I said something that sounded like a gurgle.*

gurney /ˈɡɜr·ni/ *n* [C] a flat table, or a light frame covered with cloth, which has wheels and is used for moving people who are ill or injured ○ *A nurse wheeled the gurney away.*

guru /ˈɡʊr·uː, ˈɡuː·ruː/ *n* [C] an expert in a particular subject who gives advice ○ *I've become the computer guru in our department.*

gush **FLOW** /ɡʌʃ/ *v* [I] to flow or pour out suddenly in large amounts ○ *Water gushed out of the broken pipe.*
gush /ɡʌʃ/ *n* [U] ○ *There was a gush of water from the hose.*

EXPRESS /ɡʌʃ/ *v* to express admiration, praise, or pleasure, in such a strong and enthusiastic way that it does not seem sincere ○ *"This is the best party I've ever had," Taylor gushed.* ○ [I] *Mom gushed over the baby.*

gust /ɡʌst/ *n* [C] a sudden, strong wind that blows for a very short time ○ *A sudden gust lifted his trailer and tossed it on its side.*
gust /ɡʌst/ *v* [I] ○ *Winds are gusting up to 55 miles per hour.*
gusty /ˈɡʌs·ti/ *adj* ○ *gusty winds*

gusto /ˈɡʌs·toʊ/ *n* [U] eager enjoyment experienced when doing something ○ *We ate and drank with gusto.*

gut **STOMACH** /ɡʌt/ *n* [C/U] **1** the bowels or the stomach ○ [U] *I had a feeling of sickness deep in the gut.* **2** Your gut is also the front part of your body near the waist: [C usually sing] *He'd added a few extra pounds to his gut.* **3** The guts of a machine are its inner, necessary parts: [pl] *The front panel was attached to the guts of the unit by three color-coded wires.*

FEELING /ɡʌt/ *adj* [not gradable] coming from or having to do with your emotions, not from thought ○ *My gut reaction is we'd better not get involved.*

DESTROY /ɡʌt/ *v* [T] **-tt-** to destroy or remove the inside parts of a building ○ *The warehouse was gutted – only the charred walls remained.*

guts /ɡʌts/ *pl n infml* bravery and determination ○ [+ to infinitive] *I don't think I'd have the guts to say that to his face.*
gutsy /ˈɡʌt·si/ *adj infml* ○ *Suing your employer is a gutsy move.*

gutter **CHANNEL** /ˈɡʌt̬·ər/ *n* [C] a channel at the lower edge of a roof for carrying away rain, or a side of a road that is lower than the center of the road, where water and garbage collects ○ *Every fall we have to clean leaves out of the gutters.*

BAD MORALITY /ˈɡʌt̬·ər/ *n* [U] **1** a condition of very low moral standards ○ *The campaign went right into the gutter once the candidates started debating.* **2** Gutter talk is offensive language.

gut-wrenching *adj* emotionally painful ○ *The movie ends with a gut-wrenching scene where the friends part forever.*

G

guy /gaɪ/ *n* [C] *infml* **1** a man ○ *Who's that guy?* ○ *Three guys and three girls left the room.* **2** Sometimes guys means people, both men and women: *Are you guys coming to lunch?*

guzzle /ˈgʌz·əl/ *v* [T] *infml* to drink or eat something eagerly or in large amounts ○ *He sat in the shade, guzzling cold soda.*

gym BUILDING /dʒɪm/ *n* [C] *short form of* GYMNASIUM ○ *I work out at the gym every day.*

SCHOOL ACTIVITY /dʒɪm/ *n* [U] PHYSICAL EDUCATION ○ *We have gym after recess.*

gymnasium /dʒɪm ˈneɪ·ziː·əm/, *short form* **gym** /dʒɪm/ *n* [C] a building or room designed and equipped for various sports, physical training, and exercise

G

gymnast /ˈdʒɪm·næst, -nəst/ *n* [C] a person who is skilled at performing controlled physical exercises, often on special equipment, sometimes in sports competitions

gymnastics /dʒɪm ˈnæs·tɪks/ *n* [U] physical exercises that increase the body's strength, balance, and ability to move gracefully, often using special equipment, or the competitive sport of performing such exercises

gynecology /ˌgaɪ·nə ˈkal·ə·dʒi/ *n* [U] the area of medicine that deals with women's physical health and a woman's ability to reproduce

gynecological /ˌgaɪ·nə·kə ˈladʒ·ɪ·kəl/ *adj* [not gradable] ○ *a gynecological examination*

gynecologist /ˌgaɪ·nə ˈkal·ə·dʒəst/ *n* [C] a doctor who specializes in gynecology

gyp /dʒɪp/ *v* [T] **-pp-** *infml* to cheat someone ○ *I think the taxpayers are getting gypped.*

Gypsy /ˈdʒɪp·si/ *n* [C] a member of a group of people who travel from place to place esp. in Europe and who originally came from northern India, or anyone who travels often and does not live in one place for long

gyrate /ˈdʒaɪ·reɪt/ *v* [I] to swing repeatedly around a fixed point ○ *She recites a poem while a dancer gyrates next to her.*

gyration /dʒaɪ ˈreɪ·ʃən/ *n* [C/U] ○ [C] *The audience cheered at the gymnast's gyrations* (= twisting movements).

H h

H LETTER, **h** /eɪtʃ/ *n* [C] *pl* **H's, Hs, h's, hs** the eighth letter of the English alphabet

HUMAN /eɪtʃ/ *n* [C] ***biology*** *abbreviation for* HOMO

ha, hah /hɑ/ *exclamation* used to express surprise, interest, or victory ○ *Ha! So you see I was right after all!*

habeas corpus /ˈheɪ·biː·əs ˈkɔːr·pəs/ *n* [U] ***social studies*** a legal action demanding that a prisoner be brought before a judge to make sure that he or she is not being held illegally

habit /ˈhæb·ət/ *n* [C/U] a particular act or way of acting that you tend to do regularly ○ [U] *Judy is in the habit of sleeping late on Sundays.* ○ [U] *I have the habit of checking my e-mail as soon as I log on to my computer.* ○ [C] *Eating between meals is a bad habit.*

WORD FAMILY habit			
Nouns	habit	*Adverbs*	habitually
Adjectives	habitual		

habitable /ˈhæb·ət̬·ə·bəl/ *adj* suitable to be lived in ○ *The houses have been vacant and need repairs to make them habitable.*

habitat /ˈhæb·əˌtæt/ *n* [C] the natural surroundings in which an animal or plant usually lives

habitation /ˌhæb·əˈteɪ·ʃən/ *n* [U] *fml* the act of living in a place ○ *Wilderness areas are not intended for human habitation.*

habitual /həˈbɪtʃ·ə·wəl/ *adj* [not gradable] usual or repeated ○ *Longer prison sentences will help keep habitual criminals off the streets.*

habitually /həˈbɪtʃ·ə·wə·li/ *adv* [not gradable] ○ *She was habitually late.*

hack CUT /hæk/ *v* [I/T] to cut something or someone with rough or uneven movements ○ [T] *We hacked a path through the underbrush.* ○ [I] *He hacked away at the logs, splitting enough wood for a fire.*

PERSON /hæk/ *n* [C] **1** a person who willingly works or acts mostly for money or other rewards without worrying about independence, beliefs, or reputation ○ *a political/party hack* **2** A hack is also a writer who produces a lot of work for money without caring very much about its quality.

COMPUTING /hæk/ *v* [I] to access someone else's computer system without permission in order to obtain or change information ○ *Someone managed to hack into the company database.*

IDIOM with **hack**

• **can't hack it** *infml* to be no longer able to deal with a difficult situation ○ *I guess I'm burned out, and I just can't hack it anymore.*

hacker /ˈhæk·ər/ *n* [C] a person who is skilled in the use of computer systems, often one who illegally obtains access to private computer systems ○ *Hackers are a major defense department concern.*

hackneyed /ˈhæk·niːd/ *adj* used or said so often that it seems ordinary, meaningless, or not sincere ○ *a hackneyed plot*

hacksaw /ˈhæk·sɔː/ *n* [C] a small SAW (= a cutting tool with sharp points along a flat blade) used for cutting metal

had /hæd, həd, əd, d/ *past simple and past participle of* HAVE ○ *We had a dog when I was growing up.*

IDIOMS with **had**

• *someone* **had better** *do something* someone should do something ○ *You'd better get moving if you want to catch your train.*

• *someone* **was had**, *someone* **has been had** someone was tricked or made to look foolish ○ *If you paid more than $20 for that picture, you were had.* ○ *I think I've been had.*

haddock /ˈhæd·ək/ *n* [C/U] an edible sea fish

hadn't /ˈhæd·ᵊnt/ *contraction of* had not ○ *I hadn't seen Patty since we were in high school.*

hadron /ˌhæd·rɑn/ *n* [C] ***physics*** a very small piece of matter that is affected by the STRONG FORCE, such as a BARYON or a MESON.

hag /hæg/ *n* [C] an ugly old woman, esp. an unpleasant or cruel one

haggard /ˈhæg·ərd/ *adj* (of a person) having dark areas around the eyes and lines on the face, esp. from being tired or from suffering ○ *His face was haggard, and his eyes were bloodshot.*

haggle /ˈhæg·əl/ *v* [I] to argue, esp. about the price of something ○ *He hated to haggle over prices.*

ha ha /hɑˈhɑ, ˈhɑˈhɑ/ *exclamation* used in writing to represent laughter

hail ICE /heɪl/ *n* [U] **1** small, hard balls of ice that fall from the sky like rain **2** A hail of things is a lot of them directed toward someone: *After his speech he faced a hail of questions from reporters.*

hail /heɪl/ *v* [I] ○ *It hailed for a few minutes this morning.*

CALL /heɪl/ *v* [T] to call and attract the attention of someone ○ *You wait here with our bags while I hail a taxi.*

PRAISE /heɪl/ *v* [T] to publicly praise or show approval for a person or an achievement ○ *Heppner has been hailed as one of the finest tenors in the operatic world today.*

PHRASAL VERB with **hail**

• **hail from** *somewhere* to live somewhere or to have come from there originally ○ *Both John and Leeza hail from South Carolina.*

hailstorm /ˈheɪl·stɔːrm/ *n* [C] a storm that produces HAIL (= balls of ice that fall like rain)

hair /her, hær/ *n* the mass of thin structures on the head of a person, or any of these structures

H

that grow out of the skin of a person or animal ○ [U] *blond/curly/wavy hair* ○ [C] *I already have a few gray hairs.* ○ [U] *I have to get my hair cut this week.*

hairy /ˈher·i, ˈhær·i/ *adj* having a lot of hair, esp. on parts of the body other than the head ○ *hairy arms*

WORD FAMILY hair	
Nouns hair	*Adjectives* hairy

hairbrush /ˈher·brʌʃ, ˈhær-/ *n* [C] a brush used for making the hair on your head neat

haircut /ˈher·kʌt, ˈhær-/ *n* [C] an occasion when you have your hair cut, or the style in which it is cut

hairdo /ˈher·duː, ˈhær-/ *n* [C] *pl* **hairdos** a HAIRSTYLE

hairdresser /ˈher ˈdres·ər, ˈhær-/ *n* [C] a person whose job is cutting hair, esp. women's hair

hair dryer *n* [C] an electrical device that blows hot air for drying a person's hair

hairline HEAD /ˈher·lɑɪn, ˈhær-/ *n* [C] the edge of a person's hair where it joins the top of the face

NARROW /ˈher·lɑɪn, ˈhær-/ *adj* [not gradable] (of cracks or lines) very narrow ○ *a hairline fracture of a bone in the hand*

hairpiece /ˈher·piːs, ˈhær-/ *n* [C] an artificial covering of hair used to hide an area of the head where hair no longer grows

hair-raising *adj* frightening or shocking ○ *She told us a hair-raising story about suddenly meeting a bear on her camping trip.*

hair spray *n* [C/U] a substance that is sprayed onto the hair to hold it in position

hairstyle /ˈher·stɑɪl, ˈhær-/, **hairdo** *n* [C] the style in which a person's hair is arranged

hairy /ˈher·i, ˈhær·i/ *adj infml* difficult, dangerous, or frightening ○ *The roads were really icy, and it was definitely a hairy situation even going slow.*

halal /hæˈlæl/ *adj* [not gradable] (of food or places where food is kept) prepared or kept in conditions that follow the rules of Islamic law ○ *halal meat* ○ *a halal dining hall*

half /hæf/ *pronoun, n* [C/U] *pl* **halves 1** either of the two equal or nearly equal parts that together make up a whole ○ [U] *Half of 12 is 6.* ○ [U] *Half (of) the students are Spanish.* ○ [U] *Cut the apple in half* (= into two equal parts). ○ [C] *The recipe calls for a pound and a half of potatoes.* **2** In sports, a half is one of two equal periods of play, often with a short pause for rest between them.

half /hæf/ *adj, adv* [not gradable] **1** *Each talk should last about a half hour/half an hour* (= 30 minutes). ○ *We need half a dozen* (= six) *eggs.* **2** Half also means partly or not completely: *She was still sleepy and only half aware of what was happening.* ○ *I half expected* (= almost expected) *to see her at the party.*

IDIOM with half

• **half the battle** a large part of the effort or work that is needed ○ *With so many search engines on the Web, deciding which one is best is half the battle.*

halfback /ˈhæf·bæk/ *n* [C] (in football) a player who plays in the middle of the field, and (in SOCCER and FIELD HOCKEY) a player who plays near the forward line

half-baked *adj* not planned or considered carefully enough ○ *a half-baked scheme*

half brother *n* [C] a brother who has one of the same parents as you do, but whose other parent is different from yours

half-dollar *n* [C] a coin worth 50 cents

half-hearted *adj* showing a lack of enthusiasm ○ *He made a half-hearted attempt to keep up with us, but soon fell back.*

half-life /ˈhæf·lɑɪf/ *n* [C usually sing] ***physics, earth science*** the amount of time needed for the RADIOACTIVITY (= harmful form of energy) of a RADIOACTIVE substance to be reduced by half

half-mast *n* [U] the position half the way down a pole to which a flag is moved to show respect for someone who has died ○ *The flags were at half-mast all week.*

half moon, **first quarter**, **last quarter** *n* [C] a PHASE (= regular change in shape) of the moon in which half its surface can be seen from the earth ➤ Picture: **moon**

half note *n* [C] ***music*** a note that is typically equal to two times the length of a QUARTER NOTE ➤ Picture: **notation**

half sister *n* [C] a sister who has one of the same parents as you do, but whose other parent is different from yours

half step *n* [C] ***music*** the smallest difference in sound between two notes that are next to each other in a musical SCALE (= series of notes)

halftime /ˈhæf·tɑɪm/ *n* [U] a short rest period between the two parts of a sports game

half-truth *n* [C] a statement that is intended to deceive someone by telling only part of the truth

halfway /ˈhæf ˈweɪ/ *adj, adv* [not gradable] (being) at a place that is the same distance from two other places, or in the middle of something ○ *We're almost halfway there.* ○ *At the halfway point of the race, he began to pull away.* ○ *We're about halfway through the renovation.*

halibut /ˈhæl·ə·bət, ˈhɑl-/ *n* [C] a large, flat, edible sea fish

hall PASSAGE /hɔːl/, **hallway** /ˈhɔːl·weɪ/ *n* [C] a passage in a building, or the area just inside the main entrance of a building ○ *Her office is just down the hall.*

BUILDING /hɔːl/ *n* [C] **1** a building or large room used for events involving a lot of people ○ *a concert/lecture hall* **2** A hall can also be a building at a college or university.

hallelujah /ˌhæl·əˈluː·jə/ *exclamation* an expression of great happiness, praise, or thanks ○ *The worshipers raised their arms and shouted "Hallelujah!"*

hallmark /ˈhɔːl·mɑrk/ *n* [C] a typical characteristic or feature of a person or thing ○ *An independent press is one of the hallmarks of a free society.*

hall of fame *n* [C] a building where people can learn about a particular activity and the famous people who have been involved in it ○ *the Baseball Hall of Fame*

hallowed /ˈhæl·oʊd/ *adj fml* holy or highly respected ○ *hallowed traditions*

Halloween, Hallowe'en /ˌhæl·əˈwiːn, ˌhɑl-/ *n* [U] the evening of October 31, when children wear special clothes and often MASKS to hide their faces and go from house to house asking for candy

hallucinate /həˈluː·səˌneɪt/ *v* [I] to see or hear something that does not exist ○ *Police said the suspect was yelling incoherent statements as if he was hallucinating.*
hallucination /həˌluː·səˈneɪ·ʃən/ *n* [C/U] ○ [C] *His fever was so high he was having hallucinations.*

hallucinogen /həˈluː·sə·nə·dʒən/ *n* [C] a drug that causes people to HALLUCINATE (= see or hear things that do not exist)
hallucinogenic /həˌluː·sə·nəˈdʒen·ɪk/ *adj*

hallway /ˈhɔːl·weɪ/ *n* [C] a HALL PASSAGE

halo /ˈheɪ·loʊ/ *n* [C] *pl* **halos, haloes** a ring of light around or above the head of a holy person in a religious drawing or painting

halogen /ˈhæl·ə·dʒən/ *n* [C] ***chemistry*** any of a group of five chemical elements that combine with HYDROGEN to make substances from which SALTS (= substances made with an acid) can be made

halt /hɔːlt/ *v* [I/T] to stop something, or to bring something to a stop ○ [I] *"Halt!" ordered the guard.* ○ [T] *Congress voted additional funds in an effort to halt the spread of the disease.* ○ [T] *Nationwide, mail delivery was halted by the strike.*
halt /hɔːlt/ *n* [U] ○ *All work had come to a halt and everyone was standing silently at their desks.*
halting /ˈhɔːl·tɪŋ/ *adj* (esp. of speech or movement) slow, stopping and starting repeatedly, as if lacking confidence ○ *His mind is clear, but his speech is slow and halting.*

halve /hæv/ *v* [T] to divide something into two equal parts, or to reduce something to half of its original size, number, or degree ○ *The doctor decided to halve the dose of the drug.*

halves /hævz/ *pl of* HALF ○ *Cut the chicken breasts into halves.*

ham MEAT /hæm/ *n* [C/U] meat from a pig's leg or shoulder ○ [C] *a boiled ham* ○ [U] *ham and eggs*

ACTOR /hæm/ *n* [C] an actor who tends to perform with too much obvious expression
ham /hæm/ *v* **-mm-**

RADIO /hæm/ *n* [C] a person who operates a radio station as a hobby ○ *a ham radio operator*

IDIOM with ham

• **ham it up** to show expressions or emotions more obviously than is realistic ○ *Here's a picture of Philip hamming it up for grandma when he was three.*

hamburger /ˈhæmˌbɜr·gər/ *n* [C/U] very small pieces of BEEF (= meat from cattle), or this meat pressed into a round, flat shape, cooked, and usually eaten as a sandwich in a small, round ROLL (= piece of bread) ○ [U] *a pound of hamburger (meat)* ○ [C] *I'll take a hamburger and French fries, please.*

hamlet /ˈhæm·lət/ *n* [C] a small village

hammer /ˈhæm·ər/ *n* [C] a tool with a heavy metal top attached to a straight handle, used for hitting an object such as a nail into a substance that holds it firmly in place
hammer /ˈhæm·ər/ *v* [I/T] **1** to hit something repeatedly with, or as if with, a hammer ○ [T] *I hammered the nail into the wall.* **2** To hammer is also to repeat again and again esp. to persuade other people about something: [I always + adv/prep] *Martin Luther King, Jr., hammered at the theme that the civil rights movement must avoid violence.* ○ [I always + adv/prep] *His attorneys hammered away at the idea that the police department was incompetent.*

PHRASAL VERB with hammer

• **hammer out** *something* [M] to arrive at an agreement or solution after a lot of argument or discussion ○ *Eventually, a deal was hammered out between the government and the opposition to hold new elections.*

hammock /ˈhæm·ək/ *n* [C] a net or strong piece of cloth, wide enough for a person to lie on, hanging between two poles or trees to which it is attached

hamper MAKE DIFFICULT /ˈhæm·pər/ *v* [T] to make an action intended to achieve something more difficult ○ *High winds hampered efforts to put out the fire.*

CONTAINER /ˈhæm·pər/ *n* [C] a large container, often a BASKET (= container made of strips of wood), with a lid ○ *a laundry/picnic hamper*

hamster /ˈhæm·stər/ *n* [C] a small, furry animal with a short tail, often kept as a pet

hamstring PREVENT /ˈhæm·strɪŋ/ *v* [T] *past* **hamstrung** to prevent an activity, or to block the effectiveness of someone or something ○ *The company is hamstrung by its traditional but inefficient ways of doing business.*

MUSCLE /ˈhæm·strɪŋ/ *n* [C] a muscle at the back of the upper part of the leg ○ *I played the whole game with a pulled hamstring* (= injured muscle in the leg).

hand BODY PART /hænd/ *n* [C] the part of the body at the end of the arm that includes the fingers and is used for holding, moving, touching, and feeling things ○ *Keep both hands on the steering wheel.* ○ *When eating, most Americans hold the fork in their right hand.* ○ *He took my hand* (= held it with his hand) *as we walked along.*

hand /hænd/ *v* [T] to put something from your hand into someone else's hand ○ *Would you please hand me a pencil?*

CLOCK /hænd/ *n* [C] one of the two long narrow parts on a clock or watch that move to show the time ○ *the hour/minute hand*

CARDS /hænd/ *n* [C] the set of cards that a player is given in a game ○ *a winning/losing hand*

HELP /hænd/ *n* [C usually sing] help with doing something ○ *Can I give you a hand with those bags?*

WORKER /hænd/ *n* [C] a person who does physical work, esp. as one of a team or group ○ *a farm hand*

CLAPPING /hænd/ *n* [C usually sing] a period of clapping to show enjoyment of a performance ○ *Let's give this band a big hand.*

H

WORD FAMILY hand			
Nouns	hand handful	*Adjectives*	underhand handy
Verbs	hand		

IDIOMS with hand

•**at hand** happening or present at this time ○ *The space shuttle crew must stay completely focused on the task at hand.*

•**at the hands of** *someone* because of someone else's actions ○ *The old tennis player suffered an embarrassing defeat at the hands of Roger Federer.*

•**by hand** **1** by a person, not a machine ○ *All of our rugs are made by hand in Pakistan.* **2** Something that is delivered **by hand** is delivered by a person and given directly to the person it is addressed to: *Please deliver the message by hand.*

•**give** *someone* **a hand, lend** (*someone*) **a hand** to give someone help ○ *Could you give me a hand with these suitcases?* ○ *Marcia has taught her children to lend a hand when it comes to cleaning up after meals.*

•**hand in hand** holding each other's hand ○ *I saw Pat and Chris walking hand in hand the other day.*

•**hands down** definitely ○ *If we had a race, he'd win hands down.* ○ **USAGE:** Used to talk about someone or something that is definitely the best or most important.

•**hands off** (*something*) *infml* do not touch something ○ *Hey! Hands off my camera!*

•**in good hands, in safe hands** managed or cared for with great attention ○ *You'll be in good hands with her – she's a terrific lawyer.*

•**in hand** controlled by someone in a position of authority ○ *Don't worry – the police have the situation in hand.*

•**in the hands of** *someone*, **in** *someone's* **hands** controlled or owned by someone ○ *A large percentage of the nation's wealth is in the hands of a very, very few people.* ○ *Florida passed into American hands in 1821.*

•**on hand** ready and available ○ *He always kept a supply of firewood on hand for cold nights.*

PHRASAL VERBS with hand

•**hand back** *something* [M] to return something to the person who owns it after the person has given it to you ○ *You'll have to hand these books back at the end of the school year.*

•**hand down** *something* **GIVE** [M] to give something to a younger member of your family when you no longer need it, or to arrange for someone younger to get it after you have died ○ *My grandmother handed down this necklace to my mother.*

•**hand down** *something* **DECIDE** *law* to make a legal decision known to the public by making an official statement ○ *The appeals court handed down its decision yesterday.*

•**hand in** *something* [M] to give something to an authority or responsible person ○ *She handed her term paper in late.*

•**hand out** *something* [M] to give something to each of a number of people ○ *Would you please hand out the balloons to the children?* ○ Related noun: HANDOUT SOMETHING FREE; HANDOUT DOCUMENT

•**hand over** *something/someone* [M] to give something to someone, esp. after being asked or told to do this ○ *Tighter sanctions will be sought unless the suspects are handed over by the end of February.* ○ Related noun: HANDOVER

handbag /ˈhænd·bæg/ *n* [C] a bag, often with a handle or a strap going over the shoulder, used esp. by women for carrying money, keys, and small personal items such as makeup; PURSE

handbook /ˈhænd·bʊk/ *n* [C] a book that contains advice about how to do something or information about esp. an organization ○ *The student handbook describes all the campus activities.*

hand-crafted *adj* HANDMADE

handcuffs /ˈhænd·kʌfs/, *short form* **cuffs** *pl n* two metal rings, joined by a short chain, that are locked around a prisoner's wrists to prevent free movement ○ *She was taken away in handcuffs.*

handcuff /ˈhænd·kʌf/, *short form* **cuff** *v* [T] ○ *On the plane, he was handcuffed to an FBI agent.*

handful **VERY FEW** /ˈhænd·fʊl/ *n* [C usually sing] a very few, esp. when compared to a larger group ○ *A handful of professional athletes make millions, but most do not do so well.*

SMALL AMOUNT /ˈhænd·fʊl/ *n* [C] an amount of something that can be held in one hand ○ *He scooped up a handful of soil and examined it carefully.*

PROBLEM /ˈhænd·fʊl/ *n* [C usually sing] *infml* a person or thing that is difficult to control or manage ○ *Sam was an easygoing baby, but Rory is a real handful.*

handgun /ˈhænd·gʌn/ *n* [C] a small gun that is held in one hand when fired

handheld, **hand-held** /ˈhændˈheld/ *adj* small enough to hold in your hand ○ *a handheld computer*

handicap **PHYSICAL CONDITION** /ˈhæn·diːˌkæp/ *n* [C] a physical or mental condition that makes ordinary activities more difficult than they are for other people ○ *His loss of hearing was a severe handicap.*

handicapped /ˈhæn·diː ˌkæpt/ *adj* ○ *a handicapped person* ○ *Buildings have to provide access for the handicapped.* ○ **USAGE:** This word is considered offensive by some people, who prefer the words "challenged" or "impaired."

DIFFICULTY /ˈhæn·diː ˌkæp/ *n* [C] something that causes unusual difficulties ○ *Their lack of knowledge of computer programming was not much of a handicap for them.*

handicap /ˈhæn·diː ˌkæp/ *v* [T] **-pp-** ○ *Rescue efforts have been handicapped by bad weather.*

DISADVANTAGE /ˈhæn·diː ˌkæp/ *n* [C] (in a sports competition) a disadvantage given to a strong competitor in order to give weaker competitors a better chance of winning ○ *a golf handicap*

handiwork /ˈhæn·diː ˌwɜrk/ *n* [U] **1** work done skillfully with the hands ○ *He built his own telescope, and he was proud of his handiwork.* **2** Handiwork is also the effects of any action: *The damage to the house is the handiwork of termites.*

handkerchief /ˈhæŋ·kər·tʃəf, -tʃɪf, -ˌtʃiːf/ *n* [C] a square piece of cloth used for blowing the nose or for cleaning the face or eyes

handle **TOUCH** /ˈhæn·dᵊl/ *v* [T] to lift something and touch, hold, or move it with your hands ○ *Please handle the old photographs carefully.*

handle /ˈhæn·dᵊl/ *n* [C] a part of an object designed for holding, moving, or carrying the object ○ *the handle of a shovel* ○ *I can't pick the pot up – the handle's too hot.*

DEAL WITH /ˈhæn·dᵊl/ *v* [T] to deal with, have responsibility for, or be in charge of something ○ *Who handles the marketing in your company?* ○ *Some managers have no idea how to handle people.*

handler /ˈhæn·dlər, ˈhæn·dᵊl·ər/ *n* [C] a person who trains and takes care of animals, esp. as a job ○ *a dog handler*

WORD FAMILY handle			
Nouns	handle handler	*Verbs*	handle

handlebars /ˈhæn·dᵊl ˌbɑrz/ *pl n* the bar along the front of a bicycle or MOTORCYCLE that a rider holds in order to balance and turn

handmade /ˈhændˈmeɪd/, **hand-crafted** /ˈhænd ˌkræf·təd/ *adj* made by a person using just hands or tools, not by a machine ○ *handmade jewelry*

hand-me-down /ˈhænd·miː ˌdɑʊn/ *n* [C] a piece of clothing given to a younger family member or friend because the person who owns it no longer wants it or it no longer fits ○ *Claudia had three older sisters, so she wore a lot of hand-me-downs.*

handout **SOMETHING FREE** /ˈhæn·dɑʊt/ *n* [C] something such as food, clothing, or money that is given free to someone who needs it ○ *government handouts* ○ Related verb: HAND OUT

DOCUMENT /ˈhæn·dɑʊt/ *n* [C] a document given to each person who is present, usually to give information about a particular subject ○ *Her handout included a list of the books she referred to.* ○ Related verb: HAND OUT

handover /ˈhæn ˌdoʊ·vər/ *n* [C] the official act of giving something to someone after planning to do this ○ *After the election, there was a peaceful handover of power to the new government.* ○ Related verb: HAND OVER

handpicked /ˈhændˈpɪkt/ *adj* carefully chosen for a special job or purpose ○ *He was the mayor's hand-picked choice to lead the investigation.*

handshake /ˈhænd·ʃeɪk/ [C] a greeting or expression of agreement in which two people who are facing each other take hold of each other's right hands and move them up and down

handsome **ATTRACTIVE** /ˈhæn·səm/ *adj* (esp. of a man) physically attractive ○ *He was handsome, brilliant, witty, and generally the center of attention wherever he was.*

GENEROUS /ˈhæn·səm/ *adj* (esp. of money) large in amount ○ *a handsome salary*

hands-on **INVOLVED** *adj* actively involved with other people in making decisions and doing work ○ *She's a hands-on manager.*

DOING *adj* obtained by doing something, not by reading about it or by watching it done ○ *hands-on experience/training/education*

handstand /ˈhænd·stænd/ *n* [C] an action in which you put your hands on the ground and push your legs up so that they point straight up

handwriting /ˈhæn ˌdrɑɪ̬t·ɪŋ/ *n* [U] a person's style of writing done with a pen or pencil ○ *His handwriting is so sloppy it's hard to read.*

handwritten /ˈhæn ˌdrɪt·ᵊn/ *adj* [not gradable] written by someone using a pen or pencil ○ *a handwritten thank-you note*

handy **USEFUL** /ˈhæn·di/ *adj* useful or convenient ○ *We found it handy to have a cellular phone.* ○ *When I'm cooking something new, I like to keep the cookbook handy* (= in a convenient place).

SKILLFUL /ˈhæn·di/ *adj* skillful with the hands or with using tools, esp. in making or repairing things ○ *Eduardo is handy with power tools.*

handyman /ˈhæn·diː ˌmæn/ *n* [C] *pl* **-men** a man who works at many small jobs in and around a building, esp. repairing things

hang **ATTACH AT TOP** /hæŋ/ *v* [I/T] *past* **hung** to attach or support something at the top, leaving the other part parts free, or to be held in this way ○ [I] *There was no wind, and the flag hung straight down.* ○ [T] *I plan to hang this picture in the hall.*

KILL /hæŋ/ *v* [I/T] *past* **hanged, hung** to kill someone by fixing a rope around the neck and tying it to something above the person and then causing the body to drop down suddenly ○ [T] *He was sentenced to die and was hanged the next morning.*

hanging /ˈhæŋ·ɪŋ/ *n* [C/U] ○ [C] *He was present at the hangings of dozens of outlaws in the 1860s.*

STAY /hæŋ/ *v* [I] *past* **hung** to stay in the air ○ *Smoke from the campfires hung in the air.*

TURN /hæŋ/ *v* [T] *past* **hung** *infml* to turn to the left or right ○ *Hang a left/right at the next corner.*

WORD FAMILY hang

Nouns	overhang hanger hanging	*Adjectives*	hanging
		Verbs	hang overhang

IDIOMS with hang

• **hang** *your* **head** to be ashamed or unhappy ○ *We played a great game – we have no reason to hang our heads.*

• **hang in there** do not give up ○ *Hang in there – exams are almost over.*

• *something* **hangs in the balance** the result of a situation has not yet been decided yet ○ *The game hung in the balance until the last seconds.*

• *something* **hangs over** *your* **head** something makes you unable to relax or enjoy yourself ○ *I've got those darn credit card bills hanging over my head.*

PHRASAL VERBS with hang

• **hang around** *(somewhere)* to wait at a place, or to stay near a place or person, often for no particular reason ○ *We were just hanging around the mall.* ○ *She hangs around with some tough kids.*

• **hang back** to wait before doing something, esp. when others have already begun ○ *Most of them went up to their hotel rooms, but I hung back.*

• **hang on HOLD** to hold or continue holding onto something ○ *He was driving so fast I had to hang on tight whenever he turned.*

• **hang on WAIT** *infml* to wait ○ *Hang on – I'll be with you in a minute!*

• **hang on** *something* **LISTEN** to listen very carefully to someone's speech ○ *She hung on every word he said.*

• **hang onto** *something* to keep something, often when you must make an effort to do this ○ *Our team was just trying to hang onto the lead.*

• **hang out** *infml* to spend a lot of time in a place or with someone ○ *Who is he hanging out with these days?* ○ Related noun: HANGOUT

• **hang** *something* **up CLOTHING** [M] to place something, esp. clothing, on a hook or HANGER ○ *Hang your coat up and come on in.* ○ See also: HANG-UP

• **hang up TELEPHONE** to end a telephone conversation by ending the connection ○ *Don't hang up – there's something else I want to say.* ○ *She hung up on me* (= suddenly ended the connection between us) *in the middle of a sentence.* ○ See also: HANG-UP

hangar /ˈhæŋ·ər/ *n* [C] a large building in an airport in which aircraft are kept

hanger /ˈhæŋ·ər/ *n* [C] a frame of wire, wood, or plastic on which clothes are hung to keep them neat when you are not wearing them

hanger-on /ˈhæŋ·əˌrɔːn, -ˌrɑn/ *n* [C] *pl* **hangers-on** a person who tries to be friendly and spend time with rich or important people to get some advantage ○ *Wherever there are rock stars, there are always hangers-on.*

hang glider *n* [C] an aircraft consisting of a light frame over which cloth or similar material is stretched, so that a person can jump off from a high place and ride the air currents

hangout /ˈhæŋ·ɑʊt/ *n* [C] *infml* a place where someone or a particular group spends a lot of time ○ *a student hangout* ○ Related verb: HANG OUT

hangover /ˈhæŋˌoʊ·vər/ *n* [C] a feeling of illness you get the day after drinking too much alcohol

hang-up /ˈhæŋ·ʌp/ *n* [C] *infml* **1** a problem that causes a delay ○ *The doctor never got back to me with the test results – I guess there was some hang-up over the weekend.* **2** A hang-up is also a feeling of anxiety: *Everyone has their hang-up.* ○ See also: HANG UP CLOTHING; HANG UP TELEPHONE

hanker /ˈhæŋ·kər/ *v* [I] to have a strong desire for something ○ *I've been hankering for a hot dog.* ○ [+ *to* infinitive] *I always hankered to go to Nashville.*

hankering /ˈhæŋ·kə·rɪŋ/ *n* [C] ○ *She's got a hankering to write plays.*

hanky, **hankie** /ˈhæŋ·ki/ *n* [C] a small, often decorative HANDKERCHIEF (= square piece of cloth)

hanky-panky /ˌhæŋ·kiˈpæŋ·ki/ *n* [U] *infml* dishonest or immoral behavior ○ *financial hanky-panky*

Hanukkah /ˈhɑn·ə·kə, ˈxɑn-/, **Chanukah** *n* [U] a Jewish holiday celebrated for eight days in December

haphazard /hæpˈhæz·ərd/ *adj* lacking order or purpose; not planned ○ *Haphazard record-keeping made it difficult for the agency to keep track of its clients.*

hapless /ˈhæp·ləs/ *adj* unlucky ○ *hapless victims of the earthquake*

happen HAVE EXISTENCE /ˈhæp·ən/ *v* [I] **1** (of a situation or event) to come into existence; OCCUR ○ *If you want to know what is happening in the world, you have to read the newspapers.* ○ *No one knows exactly what happened, but several people have been hurt.* **2** If a situation or event happens to someone or something, it has an effect on that person or thing: *What happened to Phil? I thought he would be here by now.*

happening /ˈhæp·ə·nɪŋ/ *n* [C usually pl] ○ *Earl had been alerted to the happenings of the day before.*

happening /ˈhæp·ə·nɪŋ/ *adj* [not gradable] *slang* (of a place or event) newly exciting or fashionable ○ *a happening neighborhood*

CHANCE /ˈhæp·ən/ *v* [I] to do or be by chance ○ [+ *to* infinitive] *I happened to come across this book I think you would like.* ○ [+ *to* infinitive] *I happen to think he's right* (= I do, although others may not).

PHRASAL VERB with happen

• **happen on/upon** *something/someone* to meet or find someone or something when you were not looking for that person or thing ○ *I happened on the perfect dress for the party.*

happy **PLEASED** /ˈhæp·i/ *adj* **1** feeling, showing, or causing pleasure or satisfaction ○ *To tell the truth, I've never been happier in my whole life.* ○ *People want movies to have happy endings.* ○ [+ (*that*) clause] *I'm happy (that) everything is working out for you.* ○ *I've been very happy with* (= satisfied with) *the education that my boys have gotten through scouting.* **2** Happy is used as a polite way to express your willingness to do something: [+ *to* infinitive] *I'm driving that way and I'd be happy to drop you off at your home.* ○ [+ *to* infinitive] *It was no trouble at all – I was happy to be of help.* **3** Happy is also used in greetings for special occasions, expressing good wishes: *Happy birthday!* ○ *Happy New Year*

happily /ˈhæp·ə·li/ *adv* ○ *happily married*

happiness /ˈhæp·iː·nəs/ *n* [U] ○ *Our children have brought us so much happiness.*

WORD CHOICES happy

A person who seems happy may be described as **cheerful**.

*She's always very **cheerful**.*

If someone is happy at a particular time, you can describe them as being **in a good mood**.

*You're **in a good mood** this morning!*

Someone who is happy because of something may be described as **pleased** or **glad**, and someone who is extremely happy because of something may be described as **delighted**.

*He was **pleased** that she had come back.*

*I was so **glad** to see her.*

*They are **delighted** with their new car.*

Someone who is extremely happy and excited may be described as **ecstatic** or **elated**.

*The new president was greeted by an **ecstatic** crowd.*

*We were **elated** at the news.*

The expression **on cloud nine** can be used informally to say that someone is extremely happy because something good has happened.

*I was **on cloud nine** after being offered the job.*

Someone who seems to be happy most of the time can be described as **contented**.

*She's a very **contented** little baby.*

LUCKY /ˈhæp·i/ *adj* lucky ○ *By a happy coincidence, we found ourselves on the same flight.* ○ **USAGE:** said about a condition or situation

WORD FAMILY happy

Nouns	happiness unhappiness	*Adverbs*	happily unhappily
Adjectives	happy unhappy		

IDIOM with happy

• **not a happy camper** *infml* very annoyed or upset ○ *The dog is sick, Jessie sprained her ankle, and the car won't start – I am not a happy camper!*

happy-go-lucky *adj* not easily made worried or anxious

happy hour *n* [C] a period of time during which a restaurant or bar sells drinks at a reduced price

happy medium *n* [U] a way of acting or thinking that avoids being extreme and that is acceptable to everyone ○ *Somewhere in the debate over immigration, there has to be a happy medium.*

harangue /həˈræŋ/ *v* [T] to speak to someone or a group of people, often for a long time, in a forceful and sometimes angry way, esp. to persuade them or to express disapproval ○ *He harangued the class for half an hour about not paying attention.*

harangue /həˈræŋ/ *n* [C] ○ *The coach delivered his regular half-time harangue to the team.*

harass /həˈræs, ˈhær·əs/ *v* [T] to annoy or trouble someone repeatedly ○ *He claimed that the police continued to harass foreign journalists.* ○ *She felt she was being harassed by the coach's constant demands.*

harassment /həˈræs·mənt, ˈhær·ə·smənt/ *n* [U] ○ *Complaints of sexual harassment* (= offensive sexual suggestions or actions) *in the workplace have increased in recent years.*

harbor **WATER**, *Cdn, Br* **harbour** /ˈhɑr·bər/ *n* [C] a protected area of water next to the land where ships and boats can be safely kept

HAVE IN MIND, *Cdn, Br* **harbour** /ˈhɑr·bər/ *v* [T] to have in mind a thought or feeling, usually over a long period ○ *He harbored the suspicion that someone in the agency was spying for the enemy.*

HIDE, *Cdn, Br* **harbour** /ˈhɑr·bər/ *v* [T] to protect someone by providing a place to hide ○ *They were accused of harboring a fugitive.*

hard **SOLID** /hɑrd/ *adj* [*-er/-est* only] firm and solid, or not easy to bend, cut, or break ○ *It hadn't rained in a long time, and the ground was hard.* ○ *He chewed on something hard and was afraid he'd broken a tooth.*

harden /ˈhɑrd·ᵊn/ *v* [I/T] to become firm or solid, or to cause something to become firm or solid ○ [I] *In a few hours the cement will harden.*

hardness /ˈhɑrd·nəs/ *n* [U]

WORD CHOICES hard

You can use **stiff** when something is hard so that it does not bend very easily.

***stiff** cardboard*

If something is so hard that it cannot be bent at all, you could use the adjective **rigid**.

*a **rigid** steel and concrete structure*

Solid can be used when something is hard and keeps its shape.

*a **solid** object*

If something is not soft, you could describe it as **firm**.

*a **firm** mattress*

Food that is hard in a pleasant way can be described as **crisp**.

***crisp** crackers*

*a **crisp** apple*

H

DIFFICULT /hɑrd/ *adj* [*-er/-est* only] difficult to understand or do ○ *hard questions to answer* ○ [+ *to* infinitive] *It's hard to say which of them is lying.* ○ *It's hard being a working mother.* ○ [+ *to* infinitive] *Her handwriting is hard to read.* ○ *She always does things the hard way* (= makes things more difficult to do). ○ *I find her books hard going* (= difficult and tiring).

USING EFFORT /hɑrd/ *adj* [*-er/-est* only] needing or using a lot of physical or mental effort ○ *Qualifying as a surgeon is hard work.* ○ *We had fun cycling, but it was hard to go up the hills.*

hard /hɑrd/ *adv* [*-er/-est* only] **1** *You have to push the door hard to open it.* **2** If something is hard-earned or hard-won, it was achieved only after a lot of effort ○ *hard-earned money/knowledge/fame* ○ *hard-won freedoms/battles*

H

SEVERE /hɑrd/ *adj* [*-er/-est* only] **1** not pleasant or gentle; severe ○ *She's had a hard life.* ○ *His boss is giving him a hard time* (= is being unpleasant to him). ○ *Don't be too hard on her – she's just learning the job.* **2** Someone who is hard on a piece of clothing tends to damage it quickly: *I'm very hard on shoes.* **3** If water is hard, it contains MINERALS (= chemical substances) that prevent soap from producing bubbles and cleaning easily.

hard /hɑrd/ *adv* [*-er/-est* only] ○ *They took the defeat hard.* ○ *It's raining hard.* ○ *She stepped on my toe really hard.*

harden /ˈhɑrd·ᵊn/ *v* [I/T] to make or become stronger or more severe ○ [I] *As the war progressed, attitudes on both sides hardened.*

hardened /ˈhɑrd·ᵊnd/ *adj* ○ *The judge called him a hardened criminal* (= one who will not stop his criminal activity).

DRUG /hɑrd/ *adj* [*-er/-est* only] (of a drug) dangerous and ADDICTIVE (= giving you the habit of taking it), or (of a drink) containing a large amount of alcohol

BASED ON FACTS /hɑrd/ *adj* [*-er/-est* only] able to be proven ○ *hard evidence*

WORD FAMILY hard			
Nouns	hardship hardness	*Verbs*	harden
Adjectives	hard hardened	*Adverbs*	hard hardly

IDIOMS with hard

- **hard feelings** anger ○ *I'm sorry it didn't work out, but no hard feelings.* ○ *We may disagree, but let's not have any hard feelings.* ○ **USAGE:** Used only in questions and negative sentences.
- **hard to swallow, hard to take** difficult to believe or accept ○ *He said the news that the farm was being sold was hard to swallow at first.*

hard-and-fast *adj* not to be changed ○ *a hard-and-fast rule*

hardback /ˈhɑrd·bæk/ *n* [C] a HARDCOVER

hard-boiled EGG *adj* (of an egg) boiled in its shell until both the white and yellow parts are solid ○ Compare SOFT-BOILED

PERSON *adj* appearing not to have emotions or weaknesses ○ *a hard-boiled detective*

hard copy *n* [U] information from a computer that has been printed on paper

hard-core *adj* unlikely to change, or difficult to change ○ *hard-core poverty* ○ *a hard-core conservative*

hardcover /ˈhɑrdˌkʌv·ər/, **hardback** *n* [C] a book that has stiff covers ○ *This book was originally published in hardcover.* ○ *a hardcover book* ○ Compare PAPERBACK

hard disk, hard drive *n* [C] a disk with a magnetic covering on which a large amount of information can be stored and used by a computer

hard hat *n* [C] a hat made of a strong material which is worn to protect the head esp. of someone who builds buildings

hardheaded /ˈhɑrdˈhed·əd/ *adj* HARD-NOSED

hard-hearted *adj* not kind or sympathetic toward other people ○ Compare SOFTHEARTED

hardiness /ˈhɑrd·iː·nəs/ *n* [U] ○ See at HARDY

hard labor, *Cdn, Br* **hard labour** *n* [U] a punishment for criminals that involves tiring physical work

hard-line *adj* unwilling to change an opinion or position ○ *a hard-line opponent of reform*

hard line *n* [U] ○ *The president has taken a hard line on the budget.*

hard-liner *n* [C] ○ *The Senator is a hard-liner on law and order.*

hardly ONLY JUST /ˈhɑrd·li/ *adv* [not gradable] only just or almost not ○ *Hardly a day passes that I don't think about it.* ○ *You've hardly eaten anything.* ○ *Something is wrong with the phone – I can hardly hear you.* ○ *I can hardly wait for your visit.* ○ *We hardly ever see them anymore.*

CERTAINLY NOT /ˈhɑrd·li/ *adv* [not gradable] certainly not ○ *It's hardly surprising that he was angry.*

hard-nosed, hardheaded *adj* practical and determined ○ *He has a reputation as a hard-nosed negotiator.*

hard of hearing *adj* unable to hear well

hard-pressed, hard-put *adj* experiencing a lot of difficulty ○ *Most people would be hard-pressed to name all their elected officials.*

hard rock *n* [U] a type of ROCK music (= popular music) with a strong beat in which drums and electric guitars are played very loudly

hard sell *n* [U] **1** something that is difficult to get people to do or try ○ *A job in teaching can be a hard sell to young people who want to earn money.* **2** The **hard sell** is a way of trying to get someone to buy or do something by being very forceful: *When I told him I didn't think the car was right for me, he tried the hard sell on me.*

hardship /ˈhɑrd·ʃɪp/ *n* [C/U] a condition of life that causes difficulty or suffering ○ [U] *The 1930s* *were a time of high unemployment and economic hardship.*

hardware TOOLS /ˈhɑr·dwer, -dwær/ *n* [U] metal objects, materials, and equipment, such as tools ○ *a hardware store*

COMPUTER /ˈhɑr·dwer, -dwær/ *n* [U] the physical and electronic parts of a computer, rather than the instructions it follows ○ Compare SOFTWARE

hardwood /ˈhɑr·dwʊd/ *n* [U] the strong, heavy wood of particular trees such as OAK, used esp. to make furniture

hardworking /ˈhɑrd ˈwɜr·kɪŋ/ *adj* always putting a lot of effort and care into your work ○ *a hardworking employee*

hardy /ˈhɑrd·i/ *adj* **1** able to bear difficult or extreme conditions; strong and healthy ○ *a hardy group of campers* **2** A hardy plant can live through the winter without protection from the weather.
hardiness /ˈhɑrd·iː·nəs/ *n* [U]

hare /her, hær/ *n* [C] a small, furry animal with long ears that is like a large rabbit and can run fast

harebrained /ˈher·breɪnd, ˈhær-/ *adj* (of plans or people) foolish; not practical ○ *a harebrained scheme*

harem /ˈhær·əm, ˈher-/ *n* [C] esp. in the past, the women in a Muslim home, including the wives and other family members, servants, and female partners of a man, or the part of a house in which these women live

hark /hɑrk/, **hearken** /ˈhɑr·kən/ *v* [I] to listen closely or give attention to something ○ *Hark, I hear music.*

IDIOM with **hark**

• **hark back** to remember or to cause someone to remember something from the past ○ *The director's latest film harks back to the era of silent movies.*

harm /hɑrm/ *n* [U] physical or other injury or damage ○ *Missing a meal once in a while won't do you any harm.* ○ *Fortunately, she didn't come to any harm when the car skidded.* ○ *Maybe Jim can help you – there's no harm in asking* (= no one will be annoyed and you might benefit).
harm /hɑrm/ *v* [T] ○ *The tornado blew out the windows of a nearby school, but none of the children were harmed.*
harmful /ˈhɑrm·fəl/ *adj* ○ *This group of chemicals is known to be harmful to the environment.*
harmless /ˈhɑrm·ləs/ *adj* not able or likely to cause harm ○ *Some think television hurts children and others regard it as harmless entertainment.*

WORD FAMILY **harm**			
Nouns	harm	*Verbs*	harm
Adjectives	harmful harmless	*Adverbs*	harmlessly

harmonica /hɑrˈmɑn·ɪ·kə/ *n* [C/U] a small, rectangular musical instrument with spaces along one side that are blown into to play notes, or this type of instrument generally

harmony MUSIC /ˈhɑr·mə·ni/ *n* [C/U] ***music*** notes that are played or sung with the main tune and that make the piece more complicated and interesting
harmonize /ˈhɑr·məˌnɑɪz/ *v* [I/T] to add a harmony ○ [I] *I can sing a tune, but I find it hard to harmonize.*

AGREEMENT /ˈhɑr·mə·ni/ *n* [U] **1** agreement of ideas, feelings, or actions, or a pleasing combination of different parts ○ *He imagined a society in which all races lived together in harmony.* **2** ***art*** Harmony is the combination of separate but related parts in a way that uses their similarities to bring unity to a painting, drawing, or other art object.
harmonious /hɑrˈmoʊ·ni·əs/ *adj* ○ *a harmonious blend of colors*
harmonize /ˈhɑr·məˌnɑɪz/ *v* [I/T] ○ [T] *We need to harmonize the different approaches into a unified plan.*

harness /ˈhɑr·nəs/ *n* [C] a piece of equipment, including straps for fastening it, used to control an animal such as a horse or attach it to a load to be pulled, or a set of straps used to hold a person in place ○ *a horse's harness* ○ *a parachute harness*
harness /ˈhɑr·nəs/ *v* [T] ○ *He harnessed the baby into her car seat.* ○ *The dam harnesses water power* (= controls and uses it) *to generate electricity.*

harp INSTRUMENT /hɑrp/ *n* [C/U] a usually large, triangle-shaped musical instrument with strings stretched across it that you PLUCK (= pull with the fingers) to play notes, or this type of instrument generally

REPEAT /hɑrp/ *v* [I always + adv/prep] to repeat or esp. complain about something many times in an annoying way ○ *I'm tired of these people who keep harping on what is wrong with the country.*

harpoon /hɑrˈpuːn/ *n* [C] a long, sharp weapon that is fixed to a rope and shot from a gun or thrown, used for hunting WHALES and other sea animals

harpsichord /ˈhɑrp·sɪˌkɔːrd/ *n* [C/U] a large musical instrument, similar to a piano and used esp. in the 17th and 18th centuries, with a row of keys that are pressed with the fingers to play notes, or this type of instrument generally

harried /ˈhær·iːd/ *adj* anxious or worried because you have too many things to do ○ *I've been feeling very harried at work.*

harrowing /ˈhær·ə·wɪŋ/ *adj* extremely upsetting because connected with suffering ○ *His book tells the harrowing story of how they climbed Mt. Everest.*

harsh UNKIND /hɑrʃ/ *adj* [-er/-est only] unkind or cruel ○ *harsh criticism*
harshly /ˈhɑrʃ·li/ *adv* ○ *Violators are being dealt with harshly.*
harshness /ˈhɑrʃ·nəs/ *n* [U]

SEVERE /hɑrʃ/ *adj* [-er/-est only] severe and unpleasant ○ *a harsh winter* ○ *harsh lighting*
harshness /ˈhɑrʃ·nəs/ *n* [U] ○ *We weren't aware of the harshness of our condition.*

harshly /ˈhɑr∫·li/ *adv* ○ *harshly lit images*

harvest /ˈhɑr·vəst/ *n* [C/U] the activity or time of gathering a crop, or a crop that is gathered ○ [U] *We picked the corn that had been missed during harvest.* ○ [C] *He had a large garden and loved to share his harvest with others.*
harvest /ˈhɑr·vəst/ *v* [I/T] ○ [T] *They couldn't get anyone to harvest their crop.*

has /hæz, həz, əz/ *v* HAVE, used with he/she/it ○ **USAGE:** When used in the phrase "has to" it is often pronounced /hæs/.

has-been /ˈhæz·bɪn/ *n* [C] a person who was famous, important, admired, or good at something in the past, but is no longer any of these ○ *She's a has-been TV star.*

H

hash /hæ∫/ *n* [U] a mixture of meat and potatoes cut into small pieces and baked or fried ○ *hash and eggs*

PHRASAL VERB with hash

• **hash out** *something* [M] *infml* to talk about something with someone else in order to reach agreement about it ○ *You two hash out the details of the presentation.*

hash browns *pl n* small pieces of potato pressed flat and fried

hasn't /ˈhæz·ənt/ *contraction of* has not ○ *He hasn't visited in years.*

hassle /ˈhæs·əl/ *n* [C] *infml* a situation that causes difficulty or trouble, or an argument ○ *Bad weather was the major hassle during our trip.* ○ *I got into a hassle with my father about being late.*
hassle /ˈhæs·əl/ *v* [T] *infml* ○ *The kids keep hassling me about going to Disney World.*

haste /heɪst/ *n* [U] great speed ○ *In spite of all their haste, they didn't have time to finish.* ○ *Officials acted* **in haste** (= too quickly), *without understanding the situation.*
hasten /ˈheɪ·sən/ *v* to hurry, or to make something go or happen faster ○ [+ *to* infinitive] *They didn't get what they were after – thanks to you, I hasten to add.* ○ [T] *To hasten softening, place the cream cheese in the oven for a few minutes.*
hasty /ˈheɪ·sti/ *adj* ○ *Don't make a hasty decision.*
hastily /ˈheɪ·stə·li/ *adv* ○ *hastily constructed houses*

hat /hæt/ *n* [C] a piece of clothing for the head ○ *a straw/fur hat* ○ *a cowboy hat*

hatch BREAK EGG /hæt∫/ *v* [I/T] to break an egg so a baby animal can come out ○ [I] *The birds hatched out the next afternoon.*

PLAN /hæt∫/ *v* [T] to create or decide on a plan, esp. a secret plan ○ *They hatched a plan for a surprise birthday party.*

OPENING /hæt∫/ *n* [C] an opening through a floor or wall, or the cover for an opening, esp. on a ship ○ *a cargo hatch*

hatchback /ˈhæt∫·bæk/ *n* [C] a wide door in the back of a car that you open by lifting it up, or a car that has such a door

hatchet /ˈhæt∫·ət/ *n* [C] a tool with a blade that cuts which is attached to a short handle; a small AX

hatchet man *n* [C] *pl* **-men** *infml* someone who is employed to do unpleasant jobs, for example to reduce the number of employees or attack competitors unfairly

hate /heɪt/ *v* [I/T] to strongly dislike someone or something ○ [T] *Kelly hates her teacher.* ○ [T] *I have always hated speaking in public.* ○ [+ *to* infinitive] *I hate to say it, but I don't think Leo is the right man for the job.*
hate /heɪt/ *n* [U] ○ *Hate and bigotry can only make our lives more difficult.*
hateful /ˈheɪt·fəl/ *adj* filled with or causing strong dislike ○ *She said some hateful things about me.*

WORD CHOICES hate

Detest and **loathe** are strong words that can be used instead of "hate."

I ***detest*** *any kind of cruelty.*

"Do you like cabbage?" "No, I ***loathe*** *it."*

Despise is used when you hate someone and have no respect for them.

She ***despised*** *him for the way he treated her.*

A phrase which means the same as "hate" is **can't stand.**

I ***can't stand*** *the sight of blood.*

Abhor or **deplore** are formal words that mean the same as "hate" when someone hates a way of thinking or behaving.

I ***abhor*** *all forms of racism.*

He said that he ***deplored*** *all violence.*

If you want to say humorously that someone hates something, you can say that the person is **allergic to** it.

I'm ***allergic to*** *housework.*

In informal English if someone hates another person very much, you can use the phrase **hate** ***someone's*** **guts.**

I ***hate his guts*** *and wouldn't care if I never saw him again.*

IDIOM with hate

• **hate** *someone's* **guts** to hate someone very much ○ *She hates her ex-boyfriend's guts.*

hatred /ˈheɪ·trəd/ *n* [U] a strong feeling of dislike; hate ○ *He has an extreme hatred of taxes and tolls.*

haughty /ˈhɔːţ·i/ *adj* unreasonably proud and unfriendly ○ *They show a haughty contempt of others.*
haughtily /ˈhɔːt·əl·i/ *adv*

haul MOVE /hɔːl/ *v* [T] **1** to pull something heavy or transport something over long distances ○ *They use these trucks to haul freight.* **2** A person who is hauled somewhere is forced to go there: *She was arrested, fingerprinted, and hauled before a judge.* ○

If you even mention my name in public, I'll haul you right into court!

haul /hɔːl/ *n* [C usually sing] a distance over which something is transported ○ *short-haul flights* ○ *It's a long haul to Minnesota.*

AMOUNT /hɔːl/ *n* [C] an amount of something that was obtained illegally, esp. after it has been taken by the authorities ○ *Police say it is the largest haul of stolen art in years.*

PHRASAL VERB with haul

• **haul** *someone/something* **away**, **haul** *someone/something* **off** [M] to take someone or something somewhere ○ *Most of the buildings are simply flattened and hauled away to local dumps.* ○ *The police hauled him off to jail right in front of his whole family.*

haunch /hɔːntʃ, hɑntʃ/ *n* [C] the top part of the leg between the knee and the waist

haunt **APPEAR** /hɔːnt, hɑnt/ *v* [T] to often appear somewhere, or to appear to someone in the form of a GHOST (= spirit of a dead person)

haunted /ˈhɔːnt·əd, ˈhɑnt·əd/ *adj* [not gradable] ○ *a haunted house*

WORRY /hɔːnt, hɑnt/ *v* [T] to cause someone to worry or feel anxiety because of being thought about too often ○ *His experiences in Vietnam still haunt him.*

haunted /ˈhɔːnt·əd, ˈhɑnt·əd/ *adj* ○ *haunted eyes*

haunting /ˈhɔːnt·ɪŋ, ˈhɑnt·ɪŋ/ *adj* staying in the mind ○ *a haunting melody*

PLACE /hɔːnt, hɑnt/ *n* [C] a place often visited ○ *This restaurant was one of our old haunts.*

have **PERFECT TENSE** /hæv, həv, əv, v/ *auxiliary verb* **has**, *past* **had** used with the past participle of other verbs to form PERFECT tenses ○ *I have heard that story before.* ○ *"Have we been invited?" "Yes, we have."*

POSSESS /hæv, həv/, **have got** /hæv ˈgɑt, həv-/ *v* [T] **has**, *past* **had** **1** to own or possess something ○ *We have a dog.* ○ *Have you got a cold?* ○ *I've got a big nose.* ○ *Have you got any money on you* (= Are you carrying money with you)? **2** Have can also mean to be related to, or to know: *Carol has six sisters.* ○ *I've got a friend who could lend us a car.* **3** If a store has something, it is available to be bought: *While you're there, see if they have any toothpicks.* ○ **USAGE:** Have got is used only in the present tense.

CONTAIN /hæv, həv/, **have got** /hæv ˈgɑt, həv-/ *v* [T] **has**, *past* **had** to contain or include something ○ *The Chicago area has a population of about eight million.* ○ *Our house has three bedrooms and two baths.* ○ *We have a few minutes left before the end of class.*

DO /hæv/ *v* [T] **has**, *past* **had** **1** to do an action ○ *He didn't have a birthday party this year.* ○ *The baby is having her nap.* **2** Have can also mean eat or drink: *We're going to have lunch.* **3** To have a baby is to give birth: *Glennis had a girl.*

RECEIVE /hæv/ *v* [T] **has**, *past* **had** to receive or accept something, or to allow something to happen ○ *I'll have some more coffee.* ○ *I just had a phone call from Judy.* ○ *I won't have those kids running through my flower bed.*

CAUSE /hæv/ *v* [T] **has**, *past* **had** to cause something to happen, or to cause someone to do something ○ *We're having the house painted.* ○ *She had her parents come to her house for Thanksgiving.* ○ *We often have friends over.*

EXPERIENCE /hæv/ *v* [T] **has**, *past* **had** **1** to experience something ○ *We had a wonderful vacation.* ○ *She had her car stolen last week.* **2** If you say **have a good/great/nice** *something* you are saying that you hope someone enjoys a particular period of time ○ *Thanks for shopping with us, and have a good day!* ○ *Have a great trip, and drive safely!*

IDIOMS with have

• **have (got) a hand in** *something* to be involved with something or have influence on something ○ *Who planned the party – I bet you had a hand in it, didn't you?*

• **have a (good) head for** *something* to have a natural ability to do something well ○ *Kim has a head for numbers.*

• **have a heart** to show kindness and sympathy ○ *Please let me go to the party – have a heart!*

• **have a screw loose** *infml* to seem crazy ○ *Her brother definitely has a screw loose – I don't really trust him.*

• **have an ax to grind**, **have an axe to grind** to have a selfish reason or strong opinion that influences your actions ○ *The study should be conducted by a firm that has no axe to grind.*

• **have an eye for** *something* to have an ability to notice something ○ *She has a good eye for detail.*

• **have another think coming** *infml* to need to consider something again, because you made a mistake the first time ○ *If you expected him to pat you on the back, you had another think coming.*

• **have** *your* **cake and eat it too** to do or get two good things at the same time, esp. things that are not usually possible to have together ○ *I worked at home so I could raise my family and still earn money – I guess I wanted to have my cake and eat it too.*

• **have dibs on** *something* to have the first right to use something, before anyone else ○ *I've got dibs on the sofa.*

• **have** *your* **eye on** *something* to admire and want to have something ○ *She has her eye on that new bike at Miller's Toys.*

• **have** *your* **feet on the ground** to be practical and able to take care of yourself ○ *Don't worry about Kerry – she's a smart girl with her feet on the ground.*

• **have (just about) had it** **1** *infml* to not be willing or able to continue doing something ○ *We've been to three museums today and I've just about had it.* **2** *infml* If something has **had it**, it is not working any longer: *This old vacuum cleaner has had it.*

• **have had it with** *someone/something* to not be willing to continue to deal with someone or something ○ *I've had it with this job – I'm quitting.*

• **have (got)** *your* **hands full** to be very busy or involved with something ○ *I've got my hands full right now with a sick baby.*

• **have heard of** *someone/something* to have some knowledge about someone or something ○ *Have you heard of the artist Bazile?*

H

•**have (got)** *your* **heart set on** *something* to want something very much, so that you would be very disappointed if you do not get it ○ *She's got her heart set on ballet lessons.*
•**have it coming (to** *you***)** *infml* to deserve what happens to you, esp. something bad ○ *He got a ticket for speeding, but he had it coming.*
•**have it in** *you* to possess a particular ability ○ *His speech was really good – we didn't know he had it in him to be that funny.*
•**have it in for** *someone infml* to be determined to criticize or harm someone ○ *She's always had it in for me.*
•**have (got) it made 1** *infml* to be successful or rich ○ *Everyone thinks if you're in a hit movie, you've got it made.* **2** If you **have it made**, you are able to relax and do not have to worry about work or other problems: *You're taking all the easy classes this semester – you've got it made!*
•**have nothing to do with** *someone/something* to not involve someone or something ○ *This argument has nothing to do with me.* ○ *Much of the bill has nothing to do with civil rights.*
•**have nothing to lose** to be in a situation that could improve by doing something and that will not be any worse if you fail at it ○ *Since I had nothing to lose, I accepted the offer.*
•**have (got) only** *yourself* **to blame** to be responsible for something bad that has happened ○ *He didn't study, so he's got only himself to blame if he fails.*
•**have seen better days** to be old and in bad condition ○ *This jacket's seen better days.*
•**have (more than)** *your* **share of** *something* to have had a lot or too much of something ○ *We've had our share of problems with the new computer system.*
•**have the last word on** *something*, **have the final word on** *something* to be the person who makes a decision without asking anyone else ○ *Carol has the last word on whether we go.*
•**have to do with** *something* to be about something ○ *My question has to do with last week's assignment.*
•**have (got) to hand it to** *someone* to recognize that someone deserves respect for what the person did ○ *You've got to hand it to her, she built that cabin herself.*
•**have what it takes (to** *do something***)** to have the qualities or character needed to be successful ○ *She doesn't have a college degree, but I think she has what it takes to do the job.*
•**have** *your* **work cut out for** *you* to have something difficult to do ○ *If she has to finish that report by tomorrow, she has her work cut out for her.*
•**not have a clue** to have no knowledge about something, or to be unable to remember something ○ *I don't have a clue what I did with my baseball glove.* ○ *He doesn't have a clue about how to fix a car.*
•**not have a leg to stand on** to have no good arguments to support your position ○ *They settled the lawsuit because they did not have a leg to stand on.*
•**not have the heart (to** *do something***)** to lack the desire or strength to do something ○ *I didn't have the heart to tell him that his injury would prevent him from playing football.*

PHRASAL VERBS with have

•**have (got) on** *something* **WEAR** [M], **had** *infml* to be wearing particular clothes or items of clothing ○ *She had on a blue hat.*
•**have (got)** *something* **on** *someone* **KNOW** to know secret or damaging information about someone ○ *She threatened to go to the newspapers, but she hasn't got anything on me.*
•**have (got) on** *something* **OPERATE** [M], **had** (of machines, electric devices, and equipment) to be operating or in use ○ *She's always got the TV on while she irons.*

have to /ˈhæf·tuː, ˈhæv-, -tə/, **have got to** /hæv ˈɡɑtˌtuː, həv-, -tə/ *auxiliary verb* **has**, *past* **had** (used with the infinitive form of another verb) to need to or be forced to; must ○ *I have to go to Vermont tomorrow.*

haven /ˈheɪ·vən/ *n* [C] a safe or peaceful place

haven't /ˈhæv·ənt/ *contraction of* have not ○ *I haven't finished eating.*

havoc /ˈhæv·ək/ *n* [U] confusion and lack of order that result in damage or trouble ○ *The storm created complete havoc in the park.*

Hawaiian shirt /həˈwɑɪ·ən ˈʃɜrt, -ˈwɔɪ-/ *n* [C] a loose, informal shirt with colorful patterns on it

hawk **BIRD** /hɔːk/ *n* [C] a type of large bird that catches small birds and animals for food

SELL /hɔːk/ *v* [T] to sell goods in public places by calling out to people ○ *She was hawking flowers at the parking lot exit.*

hay /heɪ/ *n* [U] tall grass that is cut, dried, and used as animal food or as covering material ○ *a bale of hay*

hay fever *n* [U] a physical reaction to the POLLEN of plants which causes some people to have problems with their eyes, nose, throat, and lungs

hayride /ˈheɪ·rɑɪd/ *n* [C] a social event in which a group of people take a ride in an open vehicle filled with HAY

haystack /ˈheɪ·stæk/ *n* [C] a large pile of HAY in a field

hazard **DANGER** /ˈhæz·ərd/ *n* [C] something dangerous and likely to cause damage ○ *a health/fire hazard*

hazardous /ˈhæz·ərd·əs/ *adj* ○ *a hazardous road*

RISK /ˈhæz·ərd/ *v* [T] to risk making a guess or suggestion ○ *She wouldn't hazard a guess about the meaning of the word.*

haze **FOG** /heɪz/ *n* [C/U] fog caused by water, smoke, or dust, or an effect of heat that prevents things being seen clearly ○ [C] *A brownish haze hung over the field.*

hazy /ˈheɪ·zi/ *adj* **1** *a hazy day/sky* **2** Hazy also means not clear: *I'm hazy about what happened after the accident.*

TEST /heɪz/ *v* [T] to force people new to a group, esp. a sports team or college social group, to take part in activities that are silly, embarrassing, and sometimes harmful in order to be accepted as a member

hazing /ˈheɪ·zɪŋ/ *n* [U] ○ *Ten fraternity members had their heads shaved during hazing last week.*

hazel **TREE** /ˈheɪ·zəl/ *n* [C] a small tree that produces edible nuts

COLOR /ˈheɪ·zəl/ *adj* [not gradable] (esp. of eyes) a green-brown or yellow-brown color

H-bomb /ˈeɪtʃ·bɑm/ *n* [C] a HYDROGEN BOMB

HDTV [C/U] *pl* **HDTVs** *abbreviation for* **1** high-definition television (= a type of television that shows clear high-quality pictures on a wider screen than standard television) ○ [C] *Consumers have bought 10 million HDTVs but have found little to watch.* **2** HDTV is also the programs you watch or the business of broadcasting them: [U] *There's no HDTV on our local channels.*

he /hiː, iː/ *pronoun male* **1** the male being spoken about, who has already been mentioned ○ *Don't ask Andrew, he won't know.* **2** He is also used to refer to a person whose sex is not known: *Today a person can travel anywhere he likes.*

he /hiː/ *n* [C] *male* ○ *Is your turtle a he or a she?*

USAGE

he

Many people do not like the use of **he** to refer to a person whose sex is not known because it seems unfair to women. Instead, they prefer to use **they**.

"Someone's on the phone." "What do they want?"

He or she can be used, but this can be repetitive in normal conversation. **He/she** and **s/he** are sometimes used in writing, but **they** is also correct, even in formal writing. The same is true of **their** and **them**.

Somebody called and left their number.

If anybody needs to speak to me, tell them I'll be in the office this afternoon.

head **BODY PART** /hed/ *n* [C/U] **1** the part of the body that contains the eyes, nose, mouth, ears, and the brain ○ [C] *She nodded her head in agreement.* **2** A head is also the approximate length of a head used as a measurement: [C] *Carlos is almost a head taller than Manuel.*

MIND /hed/ *n* [C] the mind and mental abilities ○ *She has a good head for figures.* ○ *If you'd just use your head* (= think clearly and carefully), *you would realize that you are better off living where you are.* ○ *Someone offered me the ticket, and your name popped into my head.*

TOP /hed/ *n* [C/U] **1** a position or part at the top, front, or beginning ○ [U] *They were early enough to get a place at the head of the line.* ○ [U] *As the guest of honor, he sat at the head of the table* (= the more important end). **2** The head of a plant is the top part where a flower or leaves grow: [C] *I bought two heads of lettuce.*

head /hed/ *v* [T] ○ *Currently, her name heads* (= is at the top of) *the list of candidates for the job.*

heading /ˈhed·ɪŋ/ *n* [C] a word or words put at the top of a page or section of text as a title ○ *He looked at the listings under the heading, "Help wanted," hoping to find a job.*

LEADER /hed/ *n* [C] someone who leads or is in charge of an organization or group, or this position of leadership ○ *In 1990 he was made head of the engineering division.*

head /hed/ *adj* [not gradable] main or most important ○ *In his first season as head coach, McGuire guided his team to the regional championship.*

head /hed/ *v* [T] to lead or control something ○ *She headed a group that defended the senator against detractors.*

GO /hed/ *v* [I] to go in a particular direction ○ *I was heading out the door when the phone rang.* ○ *We decided to head back/home* (= return to where we started) *before it got too dark.* ○ (*fig.*) *He's headed for trouble if he gets involved with her.*

WORD FAMILY head

Nouns	head heading overhead	*Adjectives*	head heady overhead
Verbs	head behead	*Adverbs*	overhead

IDIOMS with head

• **head and shoulders above** *someone/something* much better than other people or things ○ *Natasha is head and shoulders above the other dancers in her age group.*

• **head over heels (in love)** completely in love with another person ○ *Laura fell head over heels in love with Chris.*

PHRASAL VERBS with head

• **head** *someone* **off** **STOP MOVEMENT** [M] to block someone's movement by getting in front of the person ○ *Police tried to head off the bank robbers at the next exit.*

• **head** *something* **off** **PREVENT ACTIVITY** [M] to stop something from happening ○ *The team would help developing countries head off such disasters.*

• **head up** *something* to lead or control a group ○ *He headed up a Miami-based legal team in 2006.*

headache **PAIN** /ˈhed·eɪk/ *n* [C] a pain you feel inside your head

PROBLEM /ˈhed·eɪk/ *n* [C] something that causes you difficulty or worry ○ *Finding a babysitter for New Year's Eve is going to be a real headache.*

headband /ˈhed·bænd/ *n* [C] a narrow strip of material you wear on your head, usually to keep your hair back from your face

head count *n* [C] the exact number of people in a place, or the act of counting them ○ *A quick head count revealed an audience of 56 people.*

headdress /ˈhed·dres/ *n* [C] a decorative covering for the head ○ *The Indian warrior wore an eagle-feather headdress.*

headfirst /ˈhed ˈfɜrst/ *adv* with your head in front of the rest of your body while you move forward ○ *She dived headfirst into the pool.*

headgear /ˈhed·gɪr/ *n* [U] any type of covering or protection for the head ○ *Protective headgear for hockey players is now required.*

headhunter /ˈhed ˌhʌnt·ər/ *n* [C] a person whose job is to find people qualified for and willing to take very important jobs ○ *She was contacted by a headhunter and invited to apply for the position.*

headlight /ˈhed·lɑɪt/ *n* [C] a light on the front of a vehicle, usually one of a pair of lights

headline LARGE PRINT /ˈhed·lɑɪn/ *n* [C] words printed in large letters at the top of a newspaper story that serve as its title

headline /ˈhed·lɑɪn/ *v* [T] ○ *She was judged fourth in a news story headlined: "New York's 100 Coolest People."*

PERFORM /ˈhed·lɑɪn/ *v* [I/T] to be the most famous or important performer or speaker to take part in an event ○ *Since last year, she has headlined at least 32 fundraising events.*

headlong /ˈhed ˈlɔːŋ/ *adj, adv* [not gradable] **1** very quick or quickly without considering what you are doing ○ *When you break up with someone, the temptation is to rush headlong into a new relationship.* **2** Headlong also means moving forward with your head first: *a headlong plunge into the lake*

headmaster /ˈhed ˌmæs·tər, hed ˈmæs-/, *female* **headmistress** /ˈhed ˌmɪs·trəs, hed ˈmɪs-/ *n* [C] a person who is the leader of a private school

head-on *adj, adv* **1** direct or directly ○ *We should have sat down and addressed the issues head-on.* **2** If two vehicles hit head-on, their fronts hit each other directly: *The head-on collision left three people dead.*

headphones /ˈhed·foʊnz/ *pl n* a device with parts that cover each ear through which you can listen to something, such as music, without other people hearing

headquarters /ˈhed ˌkwɔːrt̬·ərz/ *pl n* the main offices or center of operations of an organization, such as the army, police, or a company

headquartered /ˈhed ˌkwɔːrt̬·ərd/ *adj* ○ *The 15-person company will be headquartered in San Francisco.*

headroom /ˈhed·ruːm, -rʊm/ *n* [U] the space above your head when you are inside something, esp. a car or other vehicle ○ *There's not enough headroom to wear a hat.*

heads /hedz/ *pl n* the side of a coin that has a picture of the head of a person on it ○ Opposite: TAILS

headset /ˈhed·set/ *n* [C] an electrical device that consists of a part that fits over a person's ears and a part into which the person can speak, used for communicating over a telephone or by radio without using the hands

head start *n* [C] the advantage of beginning before others in a competition or other situation ○ *If we leave early, we can get a head start on the holiday traffic.*

headstone /ˈhed·stoʊn/ *n* [C] a TOMBSTONE

headstrong /ˈhed·strɔːŋ/ *adj* determined to do or think what you want despite opposition from others ○ *a headstrong teenager*

head-to-head *adj, adv* opposing each other in direct competition ○ *The two giant aircraft companies went head-to-head for the $2 billion order.* ○ *Tampa Bay has no head-to-head games with Boston this year.*

headwind /ˈhed·wɪnd/ *n* [C] a wind blowing directly against you as you move forward ○ *The boats had to battle a strong headwind over the last part of the race.*

heady /ˈhed·i/ *adj* producing a feeling of high energy, confidence, and excitement ○ *Home sales remained steady in August, although running slightly below July's heady pace.*

heal /hiːl/ *v* [I/T] to make or become healthy or whole again ○ [I] *As people age, they tend to heal more slowly.* ○ [T] *Steroids are produced by the body to help heal damaged tissue.*

healer /ˈhiː·lər/ *n* [C] a person or thing that heals ○ *Time is a great healer.*

health /helθ/ *n* [U] **1** the condition of the body or mind and the degree to which it is free from illness, or the state of being well ○ *Her health was much improved after she started exercising.* ○ (fig.) *The health of the economy is still causing concern.* **2** If you are in good/poor health, your physical condition is healthy or is not healthy: *He's in excellent health.*

healthy /ˈhel·θi/ *adj* **1** having, showing, or encouraging good health ○ *As long as the baby is healthy, I don't care if it's a boy or a girl.* **2** Healthy can mean positive: *She had a healthy attitude toward life and was fun to be with.* **3** Something is described as healthy if it is financially successful and strong: *The real-estate market is much healthier today than it was ten years ago.* **4** A healthy amount is a large amount: *Their business showed a healthy profit in its first year.*

healthful /ˈhelθ·fəl/ *adj* helping to produce good health ○ *A healthful diet includes plenty of green vegetables.* ➤ Usage: **condition or health?** at CONDITION STATE

WORD FAMILY health

Nouns	health	*Adjectives*	healthful
Adverbs	healthily		healthy
	unhealthily		unhealthy

health care, **health-care** *n* [U] the providing of medical services ○ *She claimed that women and minority-groups frequently receive inferior health care.* ○ *hospitals and other health-care providers*

health food *n* [C/U] food that is naturally grown or prepared, without artificial substances or processes

health maintenance organization, *abbreviation* **HMO** *n* [C] an organization that employs doctors and other medical people to provide health care to people who pay a fixed amount to the organization rather than an amount based on each service they get

heap /hiːp/ *n* [C] **1** a messy pile of things ○ *A heap of dirty laundry lay at the foot of his bed.* **2** *infml* A **heap of/heaps of** *something* is a lot of it: *Isako is making heaps of money now that she's in business for herself.*

heap /hiːp/ *v* [T] to put things in a pile ○ *They heaped their plates with food.*

heaping /ˈhiː·pɪŋ/ *adj* [not gradable] (of an amount of something esp. in a spoon) filling it to a rounded level above the top ○ *a heaping teaspoon of sugar*

PHRASAL VERB with **heap**

• **heap** *something* **on** *someone/something* to express a strong opinion by making many remarks about someone or something ○ *A parent-teachers organization heaped praise/scorn on Miller for the school's performance.*

hear RECEIVE SOUND /hɪr/ *v* [I/T] *past* **heard** to receive or become aware of sounds with your ears ○ [T] *I can't hear you with the TV on.* ○ [I] *After a long trip on a plane, I don't hear very well for a few hours.*

hearing /ˈhɪr·ɪŋ/ *n* [U] the ability to hear sounds ○ *Since he's gotten older, his hearing isn't what it used to be.* ➤ Usage: **listen, listen to, or hear?** at LISTEN

LISTEN /hɪr/ *v* [T] *past* **heard** to listen to what someone is saying or sounds being made ○ *I heard him interviewed on the radio this morning.* ○ *Have you heard the group's latest recording?*

hearing /ˈhɪr·ɪŋ/ *n* [C] an official meeting that is held to gather the facts about an event or problem ○ *A Senate subcommittee is holding hearings about the mortgage crisis.*

BE TOLD /hɪr/ *v* [I/T] *past* **heard** to be told or informed about ○ [T] *Have you heard the news?* ○ [I] *I hadn't heard about that.* ○ [+ (*that*) clause] *I hear (that) your house is up for sale.* ○ [T] *I've heard a lot about you from my sister and am glad to meet you.*

USAGE

hear

Remember to use the preposition **from** when you use **hear** to mean receive a letter, telephone call, or other message from someone.

I look forward to hearing from you.

~~*I look forward to hearing you.*~~

WORD FAMILY **hear**

Nouns	hearing	*Verbs*	hear overhear
Adjectives	unheard-of		

IDIOM with **hear**

• **never hear the end of it** to have to listen for a long time to embarrassing or annoying talk ○ *If Mary gets that promotion, we'll never hear the end of it.*

PHRASAL VERBS with **hear**

• **hear from** *someone* to get a letter, a telephone call, or message from someone ○ *We haven't heard from her in years.*

• **hear** *someone* **out** to listen to someone until the person is finished speaking ○ *Hear me out and then tell me what you think of the plan.*

hearing aid *n* [C] a small device that people who cannot hear well wear inside or next to the ear to make sounds louder

hearsay /ˈhɪr·seɪ/ *n* [U] information you have heard that might or might not be true ○ *The court cannot accept evidence based on hearsay and rumor.*

hearse /hɜrs/ *n* [C] a special car used to carry a body in a COFFIN (= long box) esp. to a funeral

heart ORGAN /hɑrt/ *n* [C] the organ inside the chest that sends the blood around the body ○ *heart disease* ○ *The paramedics took his pulse to see if his heart was still beating.*

EMOTIONS /hɑrt/ *n* [C/U] the center of a person's emotions, or the general character of someone ○ [C] *He has a good/kind heart* (= is a kind and generous person). ○ [C] *Our hearts were broken* (= We were very sad) *at the news of the accident.* ○ [C] *Homelessness is a subject close/near to her heart* (= is important to her and is a subject she feels strongly about). ○ [U] *In his heart* (= According to his true feelings), *he knew she was right.* ○ *She can be abrupt with people at times, but* **at heart** (= basically) *she's a good person.*

heartless /ˈhɑrt·ləs/ *adj* cruel or unkind ○ *She denounced the cutbacks on aid to the poor as heartless and shortsighted policies.*

CENTER /hɑrt/ *n* [C/U] **1** the central or most important part ○ [C usually sing] *Protestors marched through the heart of the city.* **2** The heart of a vegetable, esp. a leafy one, is its firm, central part: [C] *artichoke hearts*

SHAPE /hɑrt/ *n* [C] a shape used to represent the heart, esp. as a symbol of love

WORD FAMILY **heart**

Nouns	heart	*Verbs*	hearten
Adjectives	heartless hearty	*Adverbs*	heartily heartlessly

IDIOMS with **heart**

• **a heart of gold** a kind and generous character ○ *He plays the part of a tough cop on TV who really has a heart of gold.*

• *your* **heart goes out to** *someone* you feel sympathy for someone ○ *My heart goes out to Carla, with a sick husband and three kids to look after.*

• *someone's* **heart is in the right place** someone only has good intentions ○ *He is very strict with his students, but his heart is in the right place.*

• *your* **heart isn't in it** you do not feel that something is exciting or interesting enough to do ○ *I tried to make myself feel better by playing the guitar, but my heart wasn't in it.*

• *your* **heart sinks** you feel disappointed and discouraged ○ *My heart sank when I opened the letter and realized I had not been accepted into graduate school.*

heartache /ˈhɑrt̬·eɪk/ *n* [U] great sadness or worry ○ *Their son's illness has caused them so much heartache.*

heart attack *n* [C] a sudden and serious physical change in which the heart does not get enough blood, causing damage to the heart and sometimes death ○ *He'd survived two heart attacks and was very careful about what he ate.*

heartbeat /ˈhɑrt·biːt/ *n* [C] the regular movement or sound that the heart makes as it pushes blood around the body

heartbreak /ˈhɑrt·breɪk/ *n* [U] a feeling of great sadness ○ *They endured the heartbreak of watching two of their children die of the disease.*
heartbreaking /ˈhɑrt ˌbreɪ·kɪŋ/ *adj* ○ *The final scene, when they say goodbye for the last time, is heartbreaking.*

heartbroken /ˈhɑrt ˌbroʊ·kən/ *adj* feeling very sad or disappointed ○ *Alexis was heartbroken when she was dropped from the team.*

heartburn /ˈhɑrt·bɜrn/ *n* [U] an unpleasant burning feeling in the lower part of the chest caused by difficulty in digesting food

hearten /ˈhɑrt·ᵊn/ *v* [T] to encourage and make confident and happy ○ *We were heartened by the news that Jason is feeling so much better.*

heartfelt /ˈhɑrt·felt/ *adj* strongly felt and sincere ○ *He hugged her awkwardly as he said goodbye, but his good wishes were heartfelt.*

hearth /hɑrθ/ *n* [C] the floor of a fireplace, and often also the area in front of it

heartland /ˈhɑrt·lænd/ *n* [U] the central or most important part of an area ○ *The Midwest is the agricultural heartland of the US.*

heartrending /ˈhɑrt ˌren·dɪŋ/ *adj* making you feel great sympathy or sadness ○ *The pictures of starving children on television were heartrending.*

hearts /hɑrts/ *pl n* one of the four SUITS (= groups) of playing cards, the symbol for which is the shape used to represent the heart as a symbol of love

heartsick /ˈhɑrt·sɪk/ *adj* feeling very sad ○ *When the vet said that her cat was too badly hurt to survive, Keri was heartsick.*

heart-to-heart *n* [C] a talk or discussion in which two people talk honestly and in a serious way about their feelings ○ *We had a good, heart-to-heart talk about where our relationship was heading.*

heartwarming /ˈhɑrt ˌwɔːr·mɪŋ/ *adj* causing feelings of pleasure and happiness ○ *People have been so kind and helpful since Dan's been sick - it's really heartwarming to see.*

hearty ENTHUSIASTIC /ˈhɑrt̬·i/ *adj* enthusiastic and strong ○ *a hearty handshake* ○ *a hearty laugh*
heartily /ˈhɑrt·ᵊl·i/ *adv* ○ *He heartily approved of the changes in policy.*

LARGE /ˈhɑrt̬·i/ *adj* [-er/-est only] **1** generous or large ○ *We ate a hearty breakfast before we set off on our hike.* **2** Hearty is also used to mean satisfying to the taste: *a hearty vegetable soup*

heat TEMPERATURE /hiːt/ *n* [U] **1** warmth, esp. a lot of warmth ○ *the heat of the sun* **2** ***physics*** Heat is also a form of energy that a substance has because of the movement of its MOLECULES or atoms. **3** The heat can also mean hot weather: *I thought I'd like living in Florida, but the heat was too much for me.* **4** The heat is also the system in a building or a stove that controls the temperature: *I'm freezing – can you turn up the heat?* ○ *Lower the heat when the water starts to boil.*
heat /hiːt/ *v* [T] to make a place or thing warm ○ *It costs a lot to heat this house.* ○ *Heat the sauce in the microwave.*
heater /ˈhiːt̬·ər/ *n* [C] a device that heats esp. water or an enclosed space

POWER /hiːt/ *n* [U] ***physics*** a type of ENERGY that moves from one object or substance to another because of their difference in temperature

EMOTION /hiːt/ *n* [U] a state of strong emotion, esp. excitement or anger ○ *The heat of his own argument swept him away.* ○ *John apologized for the remarks he had made* **in the heat of the moment** (= while he was angry or excited).
heated /ˈhiːt̬·əd/ *adj* ○ *a heated argument/exchange*

RESPONSIBILITY /hiːt/ *n* [U] responsibility or blame ○ *We took a lot of heat for showing that on TV.*

COMPETITION /hiːt/ *n* [C] a competition, esp. a race, in which it is decided who will compete in the final event

BIOLOGY /hiːt/ *n* If an animal, esp. a female, is **in heat**, it is ready to breed.

WORD FAMILY heat

Nouns	heat heater heating	*Adjectives*	heated unheated
		Adverbs	heatedly
Verbs	heat		

PHRASAL VERB with heat

• **heat up** *something* [M] **1** to make something warm or hot ○ *Let's see what happens when I heat it up.* **2** If a situation heats up, it becomes more extreme: *With the political climate heating up, we can expect to hear a lot more from both candidates.*

heathen /ˈhiː·ðən/ *adj disapproving* (used, esp. in the past, of people or their way of life, activities, and ideas) having no religion, or belonging to a religion that is not Christianity, Judaism, or Islam
heathen /ˈhiː·ðən/ *n* [C] *pl* **heathen, heathens** *disapproving* ○ *Those folks are heathens.*

heating /ˈhiːt̬·ɪŋ/ *n* [U] the process of making something warm, esp. a building, or the equipment used for this ○ *heating costs/oil/efficiency* ○ *He takes care of the heating and air-conditioning.*

heat wave [C] a period of days during which the weather is much hotter than usual

heave MOVE /hiːv/ *v* [I/T] **1** to pull, push, lift, or throw something heavy ○ [T always + adv/prep] *He leaned his weight against the door and heaved it open.* **2** If something heaves, it moves up and down: [I] *After the race she was covered in sweat, her chest heaving.*

heave /hiːv/ *n* [C] ○ *With a great heave, they rolled the boulder out of the way.*

VOMIT /hiːv/ *v* [I] *infml* to feel as if you are going to vomit, or to vomit

heaven /ˈhev·ən/ *n* [U] **1** (in some religions) the place where God or the gods live or where good people are believed to go after they die, sometimes thought to be in the sky **2** Heaven is also something that gives you great pleasure: *It was heaven lying there in the sunshine listening to the birds sing.*

heavenly /ˈhev·ən·li/ *adj* of or from heaven, or giving great pleasure ○ *It was a good party and the food was heavenly.*

heavens /ˈhev·ənz/ *pl n* the sky ○ *They rolled their eyes toward the heavens.*

heavens /ˈhev·ənz/ *exclamation* an expression of surprise, anger, annoyance, or emphasis ○ *Good heavens – I didn't realize it was getting so late!*

heavy WEIGHING A LOT /ˈhev·i/ *adj* [*-er/-est* only] weighing a lot ○ *The piano's much too heavy for one person to lift.* ○ *Bob's much heavier than the last time I saw him.*

SOLID /ˈhev·i/ *adj* [*-er/-est* only] thick, strong, solid, or looking that way ○ *heavy clouds* ○ *heavy cream* ○ *It's too hot today for a heavy meal* (= a large, cooked meal that is hard to digest).

GREAT DEGREE /ˈhev·i/ *adj* [*-er/-est* only] of great amount, or degree, or force ○ *heavy snow/rain/fog* ○ *heavy traffic* ○ *a heavy workload* ○ *a heavy sleeper* ○ *heavy fighting*

heavily /ˈhev·ə·li/ *adv* ○ *heavily armed* ○ *She's heavily involved in politics.* ○ *The news weighed heavily on his mother.*

heavy-duty *adj* designed to be strong enough to do very difficult work for a long time ○ *heavy-duty tools*

heavy-handed *adj* done in an unnecessarily forceful way without considering the feelings of others ○ *Local people complained of the heavy-handed methods being used by the police.*

heavy industry *n* [U] the business of using large machines and materials such as coal and steel to produce large goods

heavy metal *n* [U] a style of ROCK music with a strong beat, played loudly on electric instruments

heavyset *adj* having a large, wide body ○ *He is a heavyset man with a beautiful tenor voice.*

heavy water *n* [U] ***chemistry, physics*** water in which ordinary HYDROGEN atoms have been replaced by DEUTERIUM atoms

heavyweight BOXING /ˈhev·iːˌweɪt/ *n* [C] in boxing, a competitor who weighs more than 175 pounds, or 79.5 kilograms, and is in the heaviest group

IMPORTANT PERSON /ˈhev·iːˌweɪt/ *n* [C] someone who has a lot of power in a particular business or activity ○ *a political heavyweight*

heck /hek/ *exclamation slang* an expression of annoyance or surprise, or a way of adding emphasis to a statement or question; HELL ○ *Where the heck have you been?*

IDIOM with **heck**

• **a heck of a** *someone/something*, **one heck of a** *someone/something* a surprisingly good person or thing ○ *You only paid 20 dollars for it? That's a heck of a good deal.* ○ *She's a heck of a writer – I think we should hire her.*

heckle /ˈhek·əl/ *v* [I/T] to interrupt a public speaker or entertainer with loud, unfriendly statements or questions

heckler /ˈhek·lər, ˈhek·ə·lər/ *n* [C] ○ *A heckler tried to disrupt the ceremony.*

hectic /ˈhek·tɪk/ *adj* busy, fast, and full of activity ○ *a hectic schedule* ○ *the hectic pace of city life*

he'd /hiːd, iːd/ *contraction of* he had or he would ○ *He'd* (= He had) *already spent all his money by the second day of the trip.* ○ *He'd* (= He would) *be able to do it if he would just try.*

hedge BUSHES /hedʒ/ *n* [C] a line of bushes or small trees planted close together, esp. along the edge of a yard or road

PROTECTION /hedʒ/ *n* [C] a means of protection, control, or limitation ○ *She invested in foreign companies as a hedge against inflation.*

hedge /hedʒ/ *v* [I/T] **1** [T] *Congressmen were warned against hedging their support for the missile program.* **2** To hedge is also to try to avoid giving an answer or taking any action: [I] *Officials continued to hedge on exactly when the program would begin.*

IDIOM with **hedge**

• **hedge** *your* **bets** to protect yourself against making the wrong choice ○ *The weather forecasters were hedging their bets, saying the storm might come into land or go out to sea.*

heed /hiːd/ *v* [T] to listen to and follow advice ○ *The airline failed to heed warnings about security.*

heed /hiːd/ *n* [U] ○ *Voters are dissatisfied, and Congress should take heed* (= consider this).

heedless /ˈhiːd·ləs/ *adj* not giving attention to a risk or difficulty ○ *Heedless of the hurricane warnings, they took the small boat out into open water.*

heel BODY PART /hiːl/ *n* [C] **1** the rounded back part of the foot ○ *I've got a splinter in my heel.* **2** The heel of your hand is the raised, inside part close to the wrist.

heel /hiːl/ *v* [I] If you say "Heel!" to a dog, you are ordering it to walk close to you.

FOOT COVERING /hiːl/ *n* [C] the part of a sock or shoe that covers the rounded back part of the foot,

H

or the part of the bottom of a shoe that lifts the back of the foot higher than the front

PERSON /hiːl/ *n* [C] *infml* a person who treats other people badly and unfairly ○ *I felt like a real heel when I saw how upset she was.*

IDIOMS with **heel**

• **(hot) on** *someone's* **heels, close on** *someone's* **heels** following closely behind someone ○ *The two men were running with a police officer hot on their heels.*

• **(hard) on the heels of** *something,* **hot/close on the heels of** *something* close behind or soon after something ○ *A second mistake followed hard on the heels of the first one.*

heft /heft/ *v* [T always + adv/prep] to lift, hold, or carry something heavy using your hands ○ *I watched him heft the heavy sack onto his shoulder.*

H

hefty /ˈhef·ti/ *adj* [-er/-est only] large in amount or size ○ *a hefty fine/bonus* ○ *a hefty steak dinner* ○ *a hefty, pink-faced baby*

heifer /ˈhef·ər/ *n* [C] a young cow that has not yet given birth to a CALF

height /hɑɪt, hɑɪtθ/ *n* [C/U] **1** the distance from the top to the bottom of something, or the quality of being tall ○ [C] *The heights of the two towers are equal.* ○ [U] *She's of average height* (= neither unusually short nor tall). **2** Height also refers to the distance that something is above a surface: [U] *You can adjust the height of the chair with this lever.* **3** **The height of** a condition or event is when it is most full of activity or when it is at its top level of achievement: *She was at the height of her career when they met.* **4** **The height of** also means an extreme example of: *the height of luxury/power/stupidity*

heights /hɑɪts/ *pl n* high places, or the tops of hills ○ *Don't go up there if you're afraid of heights.* ○ *(fig.) Stock prices reached new heights yesterday.*

WORD FAMILY **height**			
Nouns	height heights	*Verbs*	heighten

heighten /ˈhɑɪt·ᵊn/ *v* [I/T] to increase, esp. an emotion or effect ○ [I] *As the excitement heightened, the audience began stamping their feet.* ○ [T] *The high winds heightened concerns about forest fires.*

Heimlich maneuver /ˈhɑɪm·lɪk·məˈnuː·vər/ *n* [U] an emergency method of removing something that is stuck in a person's throat and is preventing that person from breathing, performed by putting sudden pressure on the person's stomach

heinous /ˈheɪ·nəs/ *adj* (esp. of a crime) extremely bad or evil ○ *heinous murders*

heir /er, ær/, *female* **heiress** /ˈer·əs, ˈær·əs/ *n* [C] a person who will receive or already has received money or property from another person at the time of that other person's death ○ *My cousin Robert is the only heir to my uncle's fortune.*

heirloom /ˈer·luːm, ˈær-/ *n* [C] a valuable object that has been given by an older member of a family to a younger member of the same family, esp. one given several times in this way ○ *family heirlooms*

heist /hɑɪst/ *n* [C] *slang* a crime in which property is taken illegally and often violently from a place or person

held **HOLD** /held/ *past simple and past participle of* HOLD

CARRIED /held/ *adj* [not gradable] carried, kept, or maintained ○ *a hand-held computer* ○ *firmly held beliefs*

helicopter /ˈhel·əˌkɑp·tər, ˈhiː·lə-/, *short form* **copter** *n* [C] a type of aircraft without wings but with large blades that spin on top

helium /ˈhiː·liː·əm/ *n* [U] a gas, one of the chemical elements, that is lighter than air and will not burn

helix /ˈhiː·lɪks/ *n* [C] **helix, helices** ***geometry*** a shape curving continuously around a center point as of a line wrapped around a cylinder or a cone; a SPIRAL

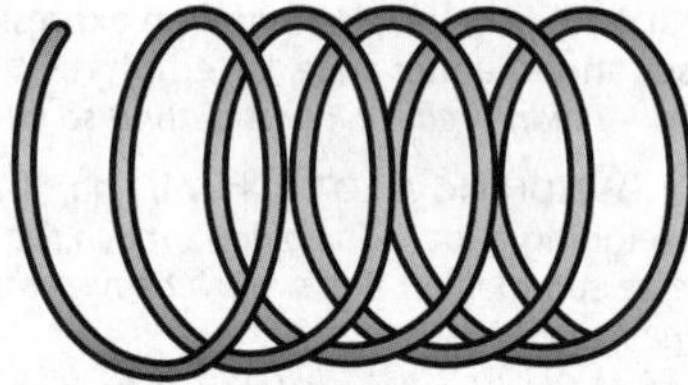

HELIX

hell **PLACE** /hel/ *n* [U] (in some religions) the place where some people are believed to go after death to be punished forever for the bad things they have done

CONDITION /hel/ *n* [U] an extremely unpleasant or difficult place, situation, or experience ○ *Holidays are hell for me.* ○ *We* **went through hell** *during the flood* (= had an extremely bad experience).

hellish /ˈhel·ɪʃ/ *adj* very bad or unpleasant ○ *a hellish experience*

EXPRESSION /hel/ *exclamation slang* used to express anger, or to give emphasis to an expression ○ *Oh hell, I forgot my keys!* ○ *Her dad was mad as hell.* ○ **USAGE:** This may be considered offensive by some people.

IDIOMS with **hell**

• **the hell out of** very much ○ *You scared the hell out of me!* ○ **USAGE:** This may be considered offensive by some people.

• **to hell with** *someone/something,* **the hell with** *someone/something* I do not care about someone or something ○ *I was ready to say to hell with it and leave.* ○ **USAGE:** This may be considered offensive by some people.

he'll /hiːl, iːl, hɪl,/ *contraction of* he will or he shall ○ *I'm sure he'll help you if he can.*

hello /həˈloʊ, helˈoʊ/ *exclamation, n* [C] *pl* **hellos** **1** used when meeting or greeting someone ○ *"Hello, Paul," she said, "I haven't seen you for* *months."* ○ *I know her vaguely – we've exchanged hellos a few times.* ○ *Come and say hello to my friends* (= meet them). **2** Hello is also said at the beginning of a telephone conversation. **3** Hello is also used to attract someone's attention: *She walked into the shop and called out, "Hello! Is anybody here?"*

helm /helm/ *n* [C] the handle or wheel that controls the direction in which a ship or boat travels

IDIOM with **helm**

• **at the helm (of** *something***)** in control ○ *She is the first woman to be at the helm of this corporation.*

helmet /ˈhel·mət/ *n* [C] a hard hat that covers and protects the head ○ *a soldier's helmet* ○ *a motorcycle/bicycle helmet*

help MAKE EASIER /help/ *v* [I/T] **1** to make it possible or easier for someone to do something ○ [T] *How can I help you?* ○ [T] *Please help those less fortunate than you are.* ○ [+ *to* infinitive] *Avoiding fatty foods and salt can help to bring down your blood pressure.* **2** If something helps a difficult or painful situation, it improves it or makes it easier or less painful: [T] *Aspirin will help relieve the pain.* **3** You shout "Help!" in an emergency when you need the immediate support of someone else.

help /help/ *n* [U] ○ *Do you need help with those boxes?* ○ *My parents gave us financial help when we bought our first house.*

helper /ˈhel·pər/ *n* [C] a person who helps ○ *The driver or a helper picks up the trash.*

helpful /ˈhelp·fəl/ *adj* giving help ○ *He made several helpful suggestions.*

helpless /ˈhel·pləs/ *adj* unable to care for yourself or protect yourself esp. against danger ○ *a helpless infant*

helplessly /ˈhel·plə·sli/ *adv* [not gradable]

helplessness /ˈhel·plə·snəs/ *n* [U]

USAGE

help

When you are are talking about **helping** *someone* **with** *something* such as a problem or task, remember to use the preposition **with**.

I try to help my parents with the housework and the shopping.

~~*I try to help my parents the housework and the shopping.*~~

WORD CHOICES help

The verbs **aid** and **assist** are more formal alternatives to "help."

The army arrived to ***assist*** *in the search.*

The project is designed to ***aid*** *poorer countries.*

If two or more people help each other in order to achieve the same thing, verbs such as **collaborate** or **cooperate** are sometimes used.

Several countries are ***collaborating/ cooperating*** *in the relief effort.*

The verb **benefit** is sometimes used when someone is helped by something.

The children have ***benefited*** *greatly from the new facilities.*

If someone is asking for help, in informal situations the expressions **give** someone **a hand** or **do** someone **a favor** are sometimes used.

Do you think you could ***give me a hand*** *with these heavy boxes?*

Could you ***do me a favor*** *and buy me some milk while you're out?*

GIVE/TAKE /help/ *v* [T] to serve something to someone, or to take something for yourself ○ *Help yourself to more cake.*

helping /ˈhel·pɪŋ/ *n* [C] an amount of food served to a person at one time ○ *He took another helping of dessert.*

WORD FAMILY help

Nouns	help helper helplessness helping	*Adjectives*	helpful unhelpful helpless
		Adverbs	helpfully helplessly
Verbs	help		

IDIOM with **help**

• **can't help, cannot help** *something* to not be able to control or stop something ○ *"Stop laughing!" "I can't help it!"*

PHRASAL VERB with **help**

• **help (***someone***) out** [M] to do work for someone or provide the person with something that is needed ○ *Blair helps us out at the store when we're busy.* ○ *We can help out by giving money to the Red Cross.*

helping verb *n* [C] an AUXILIARY VERB

helter-skelter /ˌhel·tərˈskel·tər/ *adj, adv* [not gradable] hurried and not organized ○ *People were running helter-skelter out of the building.*

hem /hem/ *n* [C] the bottom edge of a piece of cloth, folded up and sewn, on an item of clothing

hem /hem/ *v* [T] **-mm-** ○ *She was busy hemming her skirt.*

IDIOM with **hem**

• **hem and haw** to pause a lot and avoid saying something directly ○ *My sister hemmed and hawed and then finally admitted she'd worn my shoes.*

PHRASAL VERB with **hem**

• **hem in** *someone/something* [M] to surround someone or something closely ○ *Her car was hemmed in between two other vehicles.*

hemisphere /ˈhem·əˌsfɪr/ *n* [C] **1** ***earth science*** half of the earth ○ *The equator divides the earth into the northern and southern hemispheres.* **2** A hemisphere is also half of a ball-shaped object.

hemline /ˈhem·lɑɪn/ *n* [C] the bottom edge or the length of a skirt, dress, or coat

hemlock /ˈhem·lɑk/ *n* [C/U] **1** a poisonous plant that has small white flowers **2** Hemlock is also a type of evergreen tree or its wood.

H

hemoglobin /ˈhiː·məˌɡloʊ·bən/ *n* [U] ***biology*** a red substance in the red blood cells that contains iron and carries oxygen around the body

hemophilia /ˌhiː·məˈfɪl·iː·ə/ *n* [U] a rare blood disease, usually of males, in which the body lacks a chemical that stops the flow of blood when a BLOOD VESSEL is injured
hemophiliac /ˌhiː·məˈfɪl·iːˌæk/ *n* [C] a person who suffers from hemophilia

hemorrhage /ˈhem·ə·rɪdʒ/ *n* [C/U] a large flow of blood from a damaged BLOOD VESSEL (= tube that carries blood around the body)
hemorrhage /ˈhem·ə·rɪdʒ/ *v* [I] ○ *The car accident caused him to hemorrhage internally.* ○ *(fig.) The company was allowed to hemorrhage money* (= lose a lot of money) *for more than two years before the government closed it down.*

H

hemorrhoids /ˈhem·əˌrɔɪdz/ *pl n* swollen VEINS (= tubes carrying blood) at or near the ANUS (= the hole where solid waste is excreted), a condition that can be painful

hemp /hemp/ *n* [U] a plant used to make rope and strong, rough cloth

hen /hen/ *n* [C] an adult female chicken that is often kept for its eggs, or the female of any bird

hence Ⓐ **THEREFORE** /hens/ *adv* [not gradable] *fml* for this reason; therefore ○ *A better working environment improves people's performance, and hence productivity.*

FROM NOW /hens/ *adv* [not gradable] *fml* from this time ○ *The project should be completed by next March, six months hence.*

henceforth /ˈhensˌfɔːrθ, -ˌfoʊrθ/ *adv* [not gradable] *fml* starting from this time ○ *Henceforth, attendance will be taken in all classes.*

henchman /ˈhentʃ·mən/ *n* [C] *pl* **-men** *disapproving* a person who is loyal to and works for someone in a position of authority and is willing to help that person even by hurting others or by committing crimes ○ *Although the president kept himself above the fray, his henchmen were blaming everyone.*

hepatitis /ˌhep·əˈtɑɪt̬·əs/ *n* [U] a disease of the LIVER (= an organ in the body)

heptathlon /hepˈtæθ·lɑn/ *n* [C] a competition in which women ATHLETES compete in seven sporting events ○ Compare DECATHLON

her **POSSESSIVE** /hɜr, hər/ *pronoun female* belonging to or connected with the person mentioned; the possessive form of she, used before a noun ○ *Her name is Linda.* ○ *She met her husband in college.*

OBJECTIVE /hɜr, hər/ *pronoun female* the female being spoken about, who has already been mentioned; the objective form of she ○ *I saw her yesterday.*

herald /ˈher·əld/ *v* [T] to announce or signal that something is approaching ○ *The trade agreement heralded a new era of economic development.*

herb /ɜrb, hɜrb/ *n* [C] a type of plant with a soft stem, used in cooking and medicine

herbal /ˈɜr·bəl, ˈhɜr-/ *adj* [not gradable] relating to herbs, or made from herbs ○ *herbal tea*

herculean /ˌhɜr·kjəˈliː·ən, hərˈkjuː·liː·ən/ *adj* [not gradable] having or needing great strength or effort ○ *She had the herculean task of bringing up four children single-handedly.*

herd /hɜrd/ *n* [C] a large group of animals of the same type that feed, travel, or are kept together ○ *a herd of elephants*
herd /hɜrd/ *v* [T] to move together as a group, or to cause animals or people to move together in a group ○ *The teachers herded the children into buses.*

here /hɪr/ *adv* [not gradable] **1** in, at, or to this place ○ *I've lived here in Atlanta all my life.* ○ *Please step over here for a minute.* ○ *It hurts here, just above my ankle.* **2** Here can be used at the beginning of a statement to call attention to someone or something: *Here's the money I owe you.* ○ *Here she is now.*

IDIOMS with here

• **(right) here and now** in this place at this time ○ *We're going to solve this problem right here and now.*
• **here and there** in different places ○ *There are small towns here and there across this region, but there are no big cities.*
• **here goes** *infml* I am going to try this now ○ *I've never been on a surfboard before, but here goes!* ○ **USAGE:** Used before you try something new or difficult.
• **here to stay** permanent ○ *Higher oil prices are here to stay, so we'd better get used to them.*
• **here you go** this is the object you asked me to give you ○ *"Would you please pass the sugar?" "Here you go."*
• **here's to** *someone/something* let us drink to the health or success of someone or something ○ *Here's to the happy couple!*
• **the here and now** the present ○ *We have to look beyond the here and now and think about our future.*

hereafter **IN THE FUTURE** /hɪrˈæf·tər/ *adv* [not gradable] *fml* starting from this time; in the future ○ *I will let you in this time, but hereafter you have to get permission in advance.*

AFTER DEATH /hɪrˈæf·tər/ *n* [U] life after death

hereby /hɪrˈbɑɪ, ˈhɪr·bɑɪ/ *adv* [not gradable] *fml* by this statement, action, or law ○ *I hereby pronounce you man and wife.*

heredity /həˈred·ət̬·i/ *n* [U] ***biology*** the natural process by which parents pass on to their children through their GENES the characteristics that make them related
hereditary /həˈred·əˌter·i/ *adj* [not gradable] caused by or having to do with heredity

herein /hɪrˈɪn/ *adv* [not gradable] *fml* in this ○ *All opinions expressed herein are solely those of the author.*

heresy /ˈher·ə·si/ *n* [C/U] a belief opposed to the official belief of a church and that is considered wrong, or the condition of having such beliefs ○ [U] *(fig.) The concept of college athletes being paid to play sports was received as nothing short of* *heresy* (= unusual opinions considered completely wrong).

heretic /ˈher·əˌtɪk/ *n* [C] a person who has beliefs that are opposed to the official belief of a church and that the church considers wrong

herewith /hɪrˈwɪð, -ˈwɪθ/ *adv* [not gradable] *fml* with this letter or other official written material ○ *I enclose three documents herewith.*

heritage /ˈher·əṭ·ɪdʒ/ *n* [U] features belonging to the culture of a particular society, such as traditions, languages, or buildings, which come from the past and are still important ○ *The organization is devoted to preserving our cultural heritage.*

hermetically /hərˈmet·ɪ·kli/ *adv* [not gradable] tightly closed so that air cannot enter or escape ○ *The space vehicle must be hermetically sealed.*

hermit /ˈhɜr·mət/ *n* [C] a person who lives alone and apart from society

hernia /ˈhɜr·niː·ə/ *n* [C] a medical condition in which part of an organ, such as the INTESTINES, pushes through a layer of muscle that encloses it

hero /ˈhɪr·oʊ, ˈhiː·roʊ/, *female* **heroine** /ˈher·ə·wən/ *n* [C] *pl* **heroes 1** a person admired for bravery, great achievements, or good qualities **2** ***literature*** The hero is the main character of a story, play, or movie.

heroic /hɪˈroʊ·ɪk, hiː-/ *adj* [not gradable] ○ *The ceremony at City Hall honored the heroic acts of firefighters who lost their lives.*

heroics /hɪˈroʊ·ɪks, hiː-/ *pl n* unusual actions or achievements that are far greater than what is expected ○ *Her heroics in the last minute of the game gave the team a two-point victory.*

heroism /ˈher·əˌwɪz·əm, ˈhɪr-/ *n* [U] great bravery ○ *an act of heroism*

hero (sandwich) /ˈhɪr·oʊ, ˈhiː·roʊ/, *regional US* **submarine (sandwich),** *regional US* **hoagie,** *regional US* **grinder,** *regional US* **poor boy** *n* [C] *pl* **heroes** *regional US* a long, narrow sandwich filled with such things as meat, cheese, and vegetables

heroin /ˈher·ə·wən/ *n* [U] a powerful illegal drug

heroine /ˈher·ə·wən/ *n* [C] ○ See at HERO

heron /ˈher·ən/ *n* [C] a large bird with long legs and a long neck that lives near water

herpes /ˈhɜr·piːz/ *n* [U] any of several infectious diseases in which painful red sores appear on the skin

herring /ˈher·ɪŋ/ *n* [C/U] a long silver fish that swims in large groups in the sea and is used as food

hers /hɜrz/ *pronoun female* belonging to the person mentioned, or that which belongs to her ○ *I've been a friend of hers for years.* ○ *Hers is the second house.*

herself /hərˈself/ *pronoun female* **1** the female being spoken about, the reflexive form of she ○ *She kept telling herself that nothing was wrong.* **2** Herself is sometimes used to emphasize a female subject or object of a sentence: *She herself was to blame.* **3** If a woman or girl does something **(all) by herself**, she does it alone or without help from anyone: *Holly wrote her name all by herself.* **4** If a woman or girl is **not herself**, she is not in her usual mental or physical condition: *Janeen hasn't been herself recently.* **5** If a woman or girl has something **(all) to herself**, she has it for her own use only: *She's got the house all to herself while her husband is away.*

hertz /hɜrts/, *abbreviation* **Hz** *n* [U] ***physics*** the standard unit for measuring the frequency (= the rate of repetition) of a WAVE ENERGY FORM. One hertz equals one repetition per second.

he's /hiːz, iːz/ *contraction of* he is or he has ○ *He's* (= He is) *late.* ○ *He's* (= He has) *got $12 left.*

hesitate /ˈhez·əˌteɪt/ *v* [I] to pause before you do or say something, often because you are uncertain or nervous about it ○ [+ *to* infinitive] *If you need anything, don't hesitate to call me.*

hesitation /ˌhez·əˈteɪ·ʃən/ *n* [U] ○ *There was some hesitation about inviting him.*

hesitant /ˈhez·ə·tənt/ *adj* ○ [+ *to* infinitive] *The bank manager is hesitant to approve the loan.*

heterogeneous /ˌheṭ·ə·rəˈdʒiː·niː·əs, -njəs/ *adj fml* consisting of different parts or types ○ *With many ethnic groups represented, the student body is very heterogeneous.* ○ Compare HOMOGENEOUS

heterosexual /ˌheṭ·ə·rəˈsek·ʃə·wəl/, *infml* **hetero** /ˈheṭ·əˌroʊ/ *n* [C] a person who is sexually attracted to people of the opposite sex ○ Compare HOMOSEXUAL

heterosexual /ˌheṭ·ə·rəˈsek·ʃə·wəl/ *adj* [not gradable]

heterotroph /ˈheṭ·ə·roʊˌtroʊf, -ˌtrɑf/ *n* [C] ***biology*** a living thing that gets its food from other plants or animals

heterotrophic /ˌheṭ·ə·roʊˈtroʊ·fɪk/ *adj* [not gradable]

heterozygous /ˌheṭ·ə·roʊˈzaɪ·gəs/ *adj* [not gradable] ***biology*** having two different forms of a GENE that controls one characteristic, and therefore able to pass either form to the young

hew CUT /hjuː/ *v* [T] *past simp.* **hewed,** *past part.* **hewed, hewn** to cut something by hitting it repeatedly with a cutting tool ○ *The monument was hewn out of stone.*

OBEY /hjuː/ *v* [I] *past simp.* **hewed,** *past part.* **hewed** to obey or behave according to (rules, principles, or expectations) ○ *He never states his own opinion but hews to the party line.*

hexagon /ˈhek·səˌgɑn/ *n* [C] ***geometry*** a flat shape that has six straight sides ➤ Picture: **geometry**

hexane /ˈhek·seɪn/ *n* [C] ***chemistry*** any of several colorless liquids that burn easily and are found in PETROLEUM

hey /heɪ/ *exclamation infml* used to get someone's attention, or to express surprise, pleasure, or questioning ○ *Hey, you guys, wait for me!*

heyday /ˈheɪ·deɪ/ *n* [C usually sing] a period of great success, popularity, or power ○ *In its heyday, Pittsburgh was a center of the steel and coal industries.*

hi /hɑɪ/ *exclamation* used as an informal greeting ○ *Hi, how are you doing?*

hiatus /hɑɪ ˈeɪţ·əs/ *n* [C usually sing] a short pause in which nothing happens, or a space where something no longer is ○ *Peace talks resumed this week after a five-month hiatus.*

hibernate /ˈhɑɪ·bərˌneɪt/ *v* [I] (of some animals) to spend the winter months in a state like sleep
hibernation /ˌhɑɪ·bərˈneɪ·ʃən/ *n* [U]

hiccup, **hiccough** /ˈhɪk·ʌp, -əp/ *n* [C usually pl] one of a series of sudden, explosive releases of air from the throat, which are difficult to control but usually stop after a short time ○ *I've got the hiccups.*
hiccup, **hiccough** /ˈhɪk·ʌp, -əp/ *v* [I] **-p-**, **-pp-** ○ *She couldn't stop hiccuping.*

hick /hɪk/ *n* [C] *disapproving* **1** a person from a rural area who has little knowledge of culture and city life **2** A hick town is a rural town with few attractions.

hickory /ˈhɪk·ə·ri/ *n* [C/U] a small tree from North America or east Asia that has edible nuts, or the hard wood from this tree

hide PREVENT FINDING /hɑɪd/ *v* [I/T] *past simp.* **hid**, *past part.* **hidden 1** to put something or someone in a place where the person or thing cannot be seen or found, or to put yourself somewhere where you cannot be seen or found ○ [T] *She used to hide her diary under her pillow.* ○ [I] *Tommy ran and hid behind his dad.* **2** If you hide your feelings, you do not show them: [T] *She tried to hide her disappointment.* **3** If you hide information from someone, you do not let that person know it: [T] *He said nothing is wrong, but I think he's hiding something.*
hiding /ˈhɑɪd·ɪŋ/ *n* Someone who is **in hiding** or goes **into hiding** has secretly gone somewhere so he or she cannot be found. ○ *The family remained in hiding until they were rescued.*

SKIN /hɑɪd/ *n* [C/U] **1** the strong thick skin of an animal that is used for making leather ○ [C] *He began scraping the hide to prepare it for tanning.* **2** A person's hide is that person's self, esp. when in trouble: [C] *He expects me to save his hide every time he screws up.*

PHRASAL VERB with hide

• **hide out** to stay somewhere where you cannot be found ○ *Criminals often hide out in these empty apartments.*

hide-and-seek *n* [U] a game in which several children hide while one child counts to a particular number without watching the others and then tries to find them

hideaway /ˈhɑɪd·əˌweɪ/ *n* [C] a place where someone goes when the person wants to relax and get away ○ *a country hideaway*

hideous /ˈhɪd·iː·əs/ *adj* offensive, extremely ugly, or shocking ○ *The bathroom was pink and green and silver – it was absolutely hideous.*

hideout /ˈhɑɪd·ɑʊt/ *n* [C] a secret place where someone can go when the person does not want to be found by other people ○ *We made our hideout under the bushes.*

hierarchy Ⓐ /ˈhɑɪ·əˌrɑr·ki, ˈhɑɪˌrɑr-/ *n* [C] ***social studies*** a system in which people or things are put at various levels or ranks according to their importance ○ *He rapidly rose in the corporate hierarchy.*
hierarchical Ⓐ /ˌhɑɪ·əˈrɑr·kɪ·kəl/ *adj* arranged in an order from the most to the least important

hieroglyphics /ˌhɑɪ·ə·rəˈglɪf·ɪks, ˌhɑɪ·rə-/ *pl n* pictures or symbols that represent words, used in the writing system of ancient Egypt

hifalutin /ˌhɑɪ·fəˈluːt·ən/ *adj infml* HIGHFALUTIN

hi-fi /ˈhɑɪ ˈfɑɪ/ *n* [C/U] *dated* the sound produced by electronic equipment that plays recorded music very accurately, or the equipment itself

high DISTANCE /hɑɪ/ *adj* [*-er/-est* only] (esp. of things that are not living) being a large distance from top to bottom or a long way above the ground, or having the stated distance from top to bottom ○ *Mount Everest is the highest mountain in the world.* ○ *We had to climb over a wall that was ten feet high.*
high /hɑɪ/ *adv* [*-er/-est* only] ○ *The Concorde flies much higher than most airplanes.*

ABOVE AVERAGE /hɑɪ/ *adj* [*-er/-est* only] **1** greater than the usual level ○ *high standards of quality* ○ *high salaries* ○ *a high level of concentration* ○ *She was driving at high speed on a wet road.* ○ *The companies produce high-quality olive oils.* **2** Something's high point is the time when it is the most successful, enjoyable, important, or valuable: *The high point of my week is arriving home from work on a Friday evening.*
high /hɑɪ/ *n* [C] ○ *Interest rates have reached an all-time high.*
higher /ˈhɑɪ·ər/ *adj* [not gradable] more developed or advanced ○ *higher species of animals*
highly /ˈhɑɪ·li/ *adv* ○ *a highly paid job* ○ *We need a highly skilled, highly educated workforce.*

IMPORTANT /hɑɪ/ *adj* [*-er/-est* only] having power, great influence, or an important position ○ *He is an officer of high rank.* ○ *She has a lot of friends* **in high places** (= in positions of power).
highly /ˈhɑɪ·li/ *adv* ○ *The statement was made by a highly placed official* (= a person in an important position).

SOUND /hɑɪ/ *adj* [*-er/-est* only] near or at the top of the range of sounds ○ *Dog whistles play notes that are too high for human beings to hear.*

FEELING HAPPY /hɑɪ/ *adj* [*-er/-est* only] **1** feeling extremely happy, excited, or full of energy ○ *He was so high after winning the race that he couldn't sit still.* **2** Someone who is **in high spirits** is extremely happy and is enjoying the situation: *She was in high spirits after scoring the winning basket.*

high /haɪ/ *n* [C usually sing] ○ *There are lots of highs and lows in this job.*

WORD FAMILY high			
Nouns	high	*Adverbs*	high
Adjectives	high		highly
	higher		

IDIOMS with high

•**(it's) high time** *infml* (it is) past the time when something should have happened ○ *It's high time you got that bad knee looked at by a doctor!* ○ Compare (IT'S) ABOUT TIME at ABOUT IDIOM

•**in high gear** very active and productive ○ *The movie really goes into high gear when Williams appears on screen.*

high and low *adv* everywhere ○ *I searched high and low for my keys, and I still can't find them.*

high beams *pl n* the lights on the front of a car when they are switched to their brightest level ○ Compare LOW BEAMS

high blood pressure *n* [U] a medical condition in which the force of the blood against the walls of the ARTERIES as the blood travels through them is greater than is considered healthy

highbrow /ˈhɑɪ·brɑʊ/ *adj* (of literature, art, music, films, or plays) serious and intended for intelligent educated people who know a lot about these forms of art, or (of people) intelligent and knowing a lot about such things ○ *highbrow entertainment* ○ *a highbrow intellectual* ○ Compare LOWBROW; MIDDLEBROW

high chair *n* [C] a chair with long legs and usually with a small table connected to it for a baby or a small child to eat from

high-class *adj* of very good quality ○ *a high-class hotel*

high court *n* [U] *infml* the SUPREME COURT

higher education *n* [U] education at a college or university where subjects are studied in great detail and at an advanced level

highfalutin, **hifalutin** /ˌhɑɪ·fəˈluːt·ən/ *adj infml* trying to seem very important or serious without having a good reason for doing so; PRETENTIOUS ○ *highfalutin language*

high fidelity, *short form* **hi-fi** *n* [U] the sound produced by electronic equipment of very good quality that plays recorded music very accurately

high heels, **high-heeled shoes** *pl n* shoes usually worn by women that have a very tall piece on the bottom that lifts the back of the foot higher than the front

high jinks, **hijinks** /ˈhɑɪ·dʒɪŋks/ *n* [U] *dated* energetic behavior in which people do amusing or entertaining things or sometimes behave slightly badly ○ *The dancers let loose with some fancy footwork and high jinks.*

high jump *n* [U] a sport in which competitors try to jump over a bar that can be raised higher after each jump

highlands /ˈhɑɪ·ləndz/ *pl n* an area with mountains ○ *Melting snow in the highlands is causing flooding in the valley.*

high-level *adj* very important ○ *a high-level scientist/conference*

highlight Ⓐ **EMPHASIZE** /ˈhɑɪ·lɑɪt/ *v* [T] to attract attention to or emphasize something important ○ *The report highlights the need for increased funding.*

BEST PART /ˈhɑɪ·lɑɪt/ *n* [C] the best, most important, or most interesting part ○ *The highlight of our trip to New York was going to the top of the Empire State Building.*

BRIGHT AREA /ˈhɑɪ·lɑɪt/ *n* [C usually pl] a bright or lighter-colored area on the surface of something, esp. on a painting

highlighter /ˈhɑɪˌlɑɪt̬·ər/ *n* [C] a pen with a wide writing end and bright, transparent ink which is used to color parts of a text to make them easier to find later

high-minded *adj* having moral standards that are above average

Highness /ˈhɑɪ·nəs/ *n* [C] *fml* a title used when referring to an important member of a family that rules a country ○ *His Royal Highness Prince Michael*

high noon *n* [U] exactly twelve o'clock in the middle of the day, when the sun should be at its highest point in the sky

high-pitched *adj* having a high and sometimes also loud or unpleasant sound ○ *The combination of Pierce's tenor sax and Roney's high-pitched trumpet was exciting.*

high-powered **POWERFUL** *adj* having a lot of power or strength ○ *a high-powered microscope*

IMPORTANT *adj* having the skill, experience, knowledge, or authority needed to get important things done ○ *He's one of the most high-powered men in the capital.*

high-pressure **STRESS** *adj* involving a lot of stress because of the high expectations of others ○ *a high-pressure job*

FORCE *adj* **1** having or using a lot of force ○ *high-pressure hoses* **2** ***earth science*** High-pressure also means having a high BAROMETRIC PRESSURE (= amount of force on the earth's surface caused by the weight of the air).

high-profile *adj* attracting a lot of attention and interest from the public ○ *He has many high-profile clients.*

high-rise *n* [C] a tall, modern building with a lot of floors

high roller *n* [C] someone who risks a lot of money, esp. to win more money

high school /ˈhɑɪ·skuːl/ *n* [C/U] a school for children who are about 15 to 18 years old that is

H

usually divided into GRADES nine through twelve or ten through twelve ○ [U] *Cory will be starting high school in September.*

high-speed *adj* moving or operating at a fast rate ○ *a high-speed drill*

high-spirited *adj* full of energy and happiness ○ *a high-spirited young horse*

high-strung *adj* easily becoming worried or upset, and finding it difficult to relax ○ *As a teenager she was high-strung and restless.*

high-tech, **hi-tech** *adj* using the most advanced machines and methods ○ *Only a few teaching hospitals have those new, high-tech devices.*

high tide *n* [U] the time when the ocean reaches its highest level ○ Compare LOW TIDE

H

high-tops *pl n* a type of SNEAKERS (= cloth shoes esp. worn for sports) that cover the feet and the bottoms of the legs ○ *I got a new pair of high-tops yesterday.*

high treason *n* [U] the crime of making war against the government of your country, or attempting to help an enemy take control of your country

high-voltage *adj* having a very strong electric current moving through it

highway /ˈhɑɪ·weɪ/ *n* [C] a road, esp. a big road that joins cities or towns together ○ *The interstate highways are usually faster, but smaller roads can be more scenic.*

hijack /ˈhɑɪ·dʒæk/ *v* [T] **1** to force someone to give you control of a vehicle, aircraft, or ship that is in the middle of a trip ○ *Gunmen tried to hijack their truck.* **2** Someone who hijacks someone else's ideas or plans uses those ideas and claims to have created them: *The movie hijacks some of its style from "Blade Runner."*

hijacker /ˈhɑɪˌdʒæk·ər/ *n* [C] a person who takes control of a vehicle by force

hijacking /ˈhɑɪˌdʒæk·ɪŋ/ *n* [C/U] ○ [U] *He's a leading suspect in the hijacking of the jetliner.*

hike WALK /hɑɪk/ *v* [I] to walk a long distance, esp. in the countryside ○ *We plan to hike from lake to lake.* ○ *I've got to hike back to my car to get my jacket.*

hike /hɑɪk/ *n* [C] ○ *a 10-mile hike*

hiker /ˈhɑɪ·kər/ *n* [C] ○ *The wooded area is attractive to hikers and hunters.*

INCREASE /hɑɪk/ *n* [C] an increase in the cost of something, esp. a large or unwanted increase ○ *a tax hike*

hike /hɑɪk/ *v* [T] ○ *Dairies have hiked milk prices again.*

hilarious /hɪlˈer·iː·əs, -ˈær-/ *adj* extremely amusing and causing a lot of laughter ○ *Her jokes are absolutely hilarious.*

hill /hɪl/ *n* [C] **1** an area of land that slopes up to a point higher than the surrounding land and then slopes down again, but which is smaller than a mountain ○ *They built a house on the top of a hill, overlooking the town.* ○ *The highway runs through rolling hills* (= land that gradually slopes up and down). **2** *infml* **The Hill** is CAPITOL HILL.

hilly /ˈhɪl·i/ *adj* ○ *The plane crashed in a hilly, heavily wooded area.*

hillbilly /ˈhɪlˌbɪl·i/ *n* [C] *disapproving* a person from a rural area who lacks is not familiar with modern ideas and popular culture, esp. someone who lives in the mountains or far from cities or towns in the southeastern US

hillside /ˈhɪl·sɑɪd/ *n* [C] the sloping surface of a hill between its top and bottom

hilt /hɪlt/ *n* [C] the handle of a sharp, pointed weapon, esp. of a SWORD

IDIOM with hilt

• **to the hilt** as much as possible ○ *We're already being taxed to the hilt.*

him /hɪm, ɪm/ *pronoun male* **1** the male being spoken about, who has already been mentioned; the objective form of he ○ *Why don't you give him his present?* ○ *We've just got a new cat, but we haven't thought of a name for him yet.* **2** Him is also used to refer to a person whose sex is not known: *If anyone causes a problem, get rid of him.* ○ USAGE: Some people find this use of him to be offensive.

himself /hɪmˈself, ɪ—/ *pronoun male* **1** the male being spoken about; the reflexive form of he ○ *He bought himself a new coat.* **2** Himself is sometimes used to emphasize a male subject or object of a sentence: *I got to meet the president himself.* **3** Himself is also used to refer to a person whose sex is not known: *I hope nobody's hurt himself.* ○ USAGE: Some people find this use of him to be offensive. **4** If a man or boy does something **(all) by himself**, he does it alone or without help from anyone else: *Jamie made that snowman all by himself.* **5** If a man or boy is **not himself**, he is not in his usual mental or physical condition: *Hugh hasn't been himself since the accident.* **6** If a man or boy has something **(all) to himself**, he has it for his own use only: *He's got the house to himself tonight.*

hind /hɑɪnd/ *adj* [not gradable] at the back of an animal's body ○ *Phil's dog stands on her hind legs to greet me.*

hinder /ˈhɪn·dər/ *v* [T] *fml* to limit the ability of someone to do something, or to limit the development of something ○ *A poor diet can hinder mental and physical growth.* ○ *I don't know if these changes are going to help or hinder the team.*

hindrance /ˈhɪn·drəns/ *n* [C/U] *fml* ○ [C] *Often his training has proved a hindrance rather than a help.*

hindquarters /ˈhɑɪndˌkwɔːrt̬·ərz/ *pl n* the back part of an animal with four legs

hindsight /ˈhɑɪnd·sɑɪt/ *n* [U] the ability to understand, after something has happened, why or how it was done and how it might have been done better ○ *They are ideas that, in hindsight, often seem hair-brained.*

Hindu /ˈhɪn·duː/ *n* [C] a member of the main religion of India, which is based on four holy texts,

has a very long history, and supports the belief that when a person or creature dies, the spirit returns to life in another body ○ *There are more than 500 million Hindus in the world.*
Hindu /ˈhɪn·duː/ *adj* [not gradable] ○ *a Hindu god*
Hinduism /ˈhɪn·duːˌɪz·əm/ *n* [U] the Hindu religion

hinge /ˈhɪndʒ/ *n* [C] a folding device, usually made of metal, that is attached to a door, gate, or lid on one side, allowing it to open and close

PHRASAL VERB with **hinge**

• **hinge on/upon** *something* to depend on something, or to need something in order to be successful ○ *The case hinges on the evidence of a single eyewitness.*

hint **INDIRECT STATEMENT** /hɪnt/ *n* [C] **1** a statement or action that suggests what a person thinks or wants in an indirect way ○ [+ *that* clause] *When he yawned and looked at his watch, I took it as a hint that we should leave.* **2** A hint is also a piece of advice that helps you to do something: *hints on ways to save money*
hint /hɪnt/ *v* [I/T] ○ [+ *that* clause] *My parents have hinted that they'll pay for a European vacation after I graduate from college.*

SMALL AMOUNT /hɪnt/ *n* [C usually sing] a small amount of something ○ *It was the first cool day of September, and there was a hint of autumn in the air.*

hinterland /ˈhɪnt·ərˌlænd, -lənd/, **hinterlands** *n* [U] a region in the middle part of a country, esp. a large country, that is far from cities or the coast ○ *The touring theater group took its production into the hinterland.*

hip **BODY PART** /hɪp/ *n* [C] the part on either side of the body where the legs are attached to the upper part of the body, or either of the joints at the PELVIS (= bowl-shaped bones) where the legs are attached ○ *Arthritis is causing pain and stiffness in your hips.*

KNOWING /hɪp/ *adj* **-pp-** *approving slang* knowing a lot about what the most modern fashions are, esp. in music, social behavior, and styles of clothes

hip-hop /ˈhɪp·hɑp/ *n* [U] a type of popular, African-American music with songs about politics and society, and words spoken rather than sung

hippie, **hippy** /ˈhɪp·i/ *n* [C] a young person, esp. in the late 1960s and early 1970s, who typically had long hair, believed in peace, and opposed many accepted ideas about how to live

hippopotamus /ˌhɪp·əˈpɑt̬·ə·məs/, *short form* **hippo** /ˈhɪp·oʊ/ *n* [C] a large, dark gray animal of Africa that lives in or near rivers and that has a big head, short legs, and thick skin

hire /hɑɪr/ *v* [T] to start to employ someone ○ *You ought to hire a lawyer to handle your taxes.*
hire /hɑɪr/ *n* [C] an employee ○ *Those retiring will be replaced by new hires.*

his /hɪz, ɪz/ *pronoun male* **1** belonging to or connected with the person mentioned; the possessive form of he, often used before a noun ○ *Joe left his car parked with the lights on.* ○ *Isn't this Kevin's umbrella? I think it's his.* **2** His is also used to refer to a person whose sex is not known: *Anyone who drives his car that fast is asking for trouble.* ○ **USAGE**: Some people find this use of his to be offensive.

Hispanic /hɪˈspæn·ɪk/ *adj* [not gradable] connected with a person who lives in the US but who originally came from or whose family came from Spanish-speaking Latin America ○ *The US Hispanic population totaled more than 22 million in 1990.*
Hispanic /hɪˈspæn·ɪk/ *n* [C] ○ *Hispanics make up a large proportion of the population of Miami.*

Hispanic-American *n* [C] a US citizen of Hispanic origin

hiss /hɪs/ *v* [I] to make a noise like the sound of the letter "s"
hiss /hɪs/ *n* [C] ○ *We heard the loud hiss of escaping gas.*

histogram /ˈhɪs·tə·græm/ a type of GRAPH (= drawing) that shows how many items fall within each group

history **PAST EVENTS** /ˈhɪs·tə·ri, -tri/ *n* [C/U] (the study of) past events considered together, esp. events or developments of a particular period, country, or subject ○ [U] *I'm taking a course in American history.* ○ [C] *I'm reading a history of jazz* (= a book that describes the development of this music).
historian /hɪˈstɔːr·iː·ən, -ˈstoʊr-/ *n* [C] someone who writes about or studies history
historic /hɪˈstɔːr·ɪk, -ˈstɑr-/ *adj* [not gradable] (of a thing or event) important when studied as part of the past ○ *historic buildings and monuments*
historical /hɪˈstɔːr·ɪ·kəl, -ˈstɑr-/ *adj* [not gradable] connected with the study or representation of things from the past ○ *The library has an important collection of historical documents.*
historically /hɪˈstɔːr·ɪ·kli, -ˈstɑr-/ *adv* ○ *Many of the historically accurate costumes created for the show will eventually be in museums.*

CONFUSABLES

history or story?

History means all the events that happened in the past.

He's studying medieval history in college.

A **story** is a description of real or imaginary events, often told to entertain people.

The story is about two friends traveling across India.

~~*The history is about two friends traveling across India.*~~

WORD FAMILY history

Nouns	historian history	*Adjectives*	historic prehistoric historical
Adverbs	historically		

REPEATED HAPPENINGS /ˈhɪs·tə·ri, -tri/ *n* [C usually sing] something that has been done or experienced by a particular person or thing many times over a long period ○ *Our family has a history of diabetes.*

histrionic /ˌhɪs·triː ˈɑn·ɪk/ *adj* (of behavior) showing a lot of emotion in order to persuade others or attract attention ○ *a histrionic performance*

histrionics /ˌhɪs·triː ˈɑn·ɪks/ *pl n* loud, emotional behavior that does not seem sincere ○ *Both lawyers indulged in courtroom histrionics.*

hit **TOUCH FORCEFULLY** /hɪt/ *v* [T] *pres. part.* **hitting,** *past* **hit** **1** to touch quickly and forcefully, with the hand or an object ○ *Don't hit your little brother!* ○ *They were throwing rocks, and one of the rocks hit a window and broke it.* ○ *She must have fallen asleep, and the car hit a tree.* **2** If something hits part of your body, or you hit it, you come up against it by accident: *He's so tall he keeps hitting his head when he goes through a doorway.* **3** Someone who is hit by a bullet or explosive weapon is injured by it: *One journalist was hit in the leg by a stray bullet.*

hit /hɪt/ *n* [C] ○ *The hospital took a direct hit from a bomb.*

> **WORD CHOICES hit**
>
> **Whack** means the same as "hit" but is slightly more informal.
>
> *She* ***whacked*** *the water with her paddle.*
>
> **Bash** is an informal word that means to hit someone or something hard.
>
> *The swinging door* ***bashed*** *him in the face.*
>
> **Strike** can be used when someone hits a person or thing hard.
>
> *She had been* ***struck*** *on the head with a golf ball.*
>
> If someone hits someone or something repeatedly, you could use the word **beat.**
>
> *He was cruel to his dog and* ***beat*** *it with a stick.*
>
> **Punch** or **thump** are used when someone hits a person with a fist.
>
> *He* ***punched/thumped*** *me in the stomach.*
>
> If someone hits a person with the flat part of the hand, the words **slap** or **smack** are often used.
>
> *She* ***slapped*** *him across the face.*
>
> *You shouldn't* ***smack*** *a child for lying.*
>
> **Deck** is a slang word that you could use when someone hits a person so hard that the person falls over.
>
> *If you do that again, I'll* ***deck*** *you.*

HAVE EFFECT /hɪt/ *v* [T] *pres. part.* **hitting,** *past* **hit** **1** to have an unpleasant or negative effect on a person or thing ○ *Commuters are going to be hit hard by the rise in gasoline prices.* **2** *infml* If an important fact hits you, you suddenly understand the meaning of it: *It just hit me that once she leaves, I may never see her again.*

ARRIVE AT /hɪt/ *v* [T] *pres. part.* **hitting,** *past* **hit** *infml* to arrive at a place, position, or state ○ *The company's profits hit an all-time high last year.*

SUCCESS /hɪt/ *n* [C] someone or something that is very popular or successful ○ *The musical is one of the biggest hits on Broadway.*

BASEBALL /hɪt/ *v* [T] to make a thrown baseball move within the playing area by touching it with a BAT (= stick) ○ *Rodriguez hit a high fly ball that was caught by the shortstop.*

hit /hɪt/ *n* [C] a BASE HIT ○ *Jason had three hits in four times at bat.*

hitter /ˈhɪt̬·ər/ *n* [C] a player in baseball who hits the ball with the BAT (= stick) ○ *Babe Ruth is famous as one of the best hitters in baseball.*

IDIOMS with hit

• **hit home** to become completely understood ○ *The full horror of the war hit home when we started seeing pictures of the wounded soldiers on TV.*

• **hit it off (with** *someone***)** to be friendly with each other immediately ○ *We had similar ideas about the show, and the two of us hit it off right away.*

• **hit the books** *infml* to begin to study in a serious and determined way ○ *I have to hit the books this weekend — I have two exams next week.*

• **hit the deck** to lie down suddenly so that you are hidden or sheltered from something dangerous ○ *When we heard an explosion, everybody hit the deck.*

• **hit the ground running** to be ready to work immediately on a new activity ○ *She studied the reports over the weekend so she could hit the ground running when the meeting began.*

• **hit the jackpot** to succeed ○ *I think we hit the jackpot with the advertising — our sales have doubled.*

• **hit the nail on the head** to be exactly right about something ○ *I think David hit the nail on the head when he said that kids won't want to buy this product.*

• **hit the road** *infml* to leave a place or begin a trip ○ *I'd love to stay longer but it's really time to hit the road.*

• **hit the roof, hit the ceiling** to become extremely angry ○ *Dad will hit the roof when he finds out I dented the car.*

• **hit the sack, hit the hay** *infml* to go to bed in order to sleep ○ *I've got a busy day tomorrow, so I think I'll hit the sack.*

• **hit the skids** to fail ○ *His career hit the skids after his illness.* ○ Compare ON THE SKIDS at SKID IDIOM

• *something* **hits the spot** *infml* this is exactly what I needed or wanted ○ *That ice cream sandwich really hit the spot!*

PHRASAL VERBS with hit

• **hit back** to attack or criticize someone who has attacked or criticized you ○ *In tonight's speech, the attorney general is expected to hit back at his critics.*

• **hit on** *someone slang* to show someone in a direct way that you are attracted to him or her

• **hit on/upon** *something* to think of an idea unexpectedly or unintentionally ○ *When we first hit on the idea, everyone told us it would never work.*

•**hit up** *someone* [M] *infml* to ask someone for something, esp. money ○ *She tried to hit me up for a loan till payday, but I didn't have any money to give her.*

hit-and-run **ACCIDENT** *adj* involving a driver who hits and injures a person with a car and leaves without telling anyone about it ○ *a hit-and-run accident*

ATTACK *adj* involving an attack by a military group in which the group leaves immediately after attacking ○ *a hit-and-run mission*

hitch **DIFFICULTY** /hɪtʃ/ *n* [C] a difficulty or troubling fact esp. in a situation that is generally positive ○ *I finally did get a job offer that sounded perfect – the only hitch was the low salary.* ○ *The taping at Channel 4 went off without a hitch* (= perfectly).

RIDE /hɪtʃ/ *v* [T] to get a free ride in someone else's road vehicle as a way of traveling ○ *Nancy hitched a ride with her husband's cousin.*

FASTEN /hɪtʃ/ *v* [T] to fasten something to another thing, such as a vehicle ○ *We just need to hitch the trailer to the car and then we can go.*

hitchhike /ˈhɪtʃ·hɑɪk/ *v* [I] to travel by getting a free ride in someone else's road vehicle ○ *It took six days to hitchhike across Minnesota.*

hitchhiker /ˈhɪtʃˌhɑɪ·kər/ *n* [C]

hi-tech /ˈhɑɪ ˈtek/ *adj* HIGH-TECH

hither /ˈhɪð·ər/ *adv* [not gradable] *old use* to or toward this place ○ *Come hither!*

hitherto /ˈhɪð·ərˌtuː/ *adv* [not gradable] *fml* until now or until a particular time ○ *Economic aid has been offered to hitherto depressed people.*

hit list *n* [C] a list of people, groups, or organizations that someone, esp. in politics, intends to take unpleasant action against ○ *He's on the president's hit list because he helped defeat the tax bill.*

hit-or-miss, **hit-and-miss** *adj* as likely to be bad as to be good, esp. because of not being planned or organized well ○ *The service you get in these big stores can be hit-or-miss, depending on the salesperson you talk to.*

HIV *n* [U] *abbreviation for* **1** human immunodeficiency virus (= the virus that causes AIDS) **2** Someone who is **HIV-positive** is infected with HIV but might not have AIDS, or might not develop it for a long time.

hive /hɑɪv/ *n* [C] a place where bees live, esp. a BEEHIVE (= container), or the group of bees living there

hives /hɑɪvz/ *n* [U] a condition in which a person's skin develops swollen red areas, often suddenly, esp. as a reaction to something the person has eaten ○ *Eating shellfish makes me break out in hives.*

hm, **h'm**, **hmm** /həm/ *exclamation* a sound made when someone is thinking about something or needs more time to decide what to say

HMO *n* [C] *pl* **HMOs** *abbreviation for* HEALTH MAINTENANCE ORGANIZATION

hoard /hɔːrd, hoʊrd/ *v* [T] to collect a large supply of something, more than you need now, often because you think you will not be able to get it later ○ *Many people hoarded food in wartime.*

hoarse /hɔːrs, hoʊrs/ *adj* (of a voice) sounding weak and not very well controlled, often because it has been used too much or the speaker has a cold ○ *He was hoarse from shouting.*

hoax /hoʊks/ *n* [C] a plan to deceive a large group of people; a trick ○ *It is a cruel hoax, she said, to encourage people to think they have a real chance to win the lottery.*

hobble /ˈhɑb·əl/ *v* [I/T] to walk with difficulty in an awkward way, or to cause someone to walk in this way, usually because of an injury to the feet or legs ○ [I always + adv/prep] *He hobbled over on crutches.*

hobby /ˈhɑb·i/ *n* [C] an activity that you do for pleasure when you are not working ○ *Sonya's hobbies include traveling, sailing, and reading fiction.*

hobnob /ˈhɑb·nɑb/ *v* [I always + adv/prep] **-bb-** to spend time being friendly with someone who is important or famous ○ *She often gets her picture in the papers, hobnobbing with the rich and famous.*

hobo /ˈhoʊ·boʊ/ *n* [C] *pl* **hobos**, **hoboes** a person who does not have a job or a house to live in, and so moves from one place to another

hock /hɑk/ *v* [T] *infml* to exchange in return for borrowing money; PAWN ○ *to hock jewelry*

hock /hɑk/ *n* To be **in hock** is to have a debt: *The state is in hock already, with a $13 billion deficit.*

hockey /ˈhɑk·i/, **ice hockey** *n* [U] a game played on ice between two teams of eleven players who each have a curved stick with which the player tries to put the PUCK (= small, hard, rubber disk) into the other team's goal

hocus-pocus /ˌhoʊ·kəˈspoʊ·kəs/ *n* [U] tricks used to deceive or words used to hide what is happening, esp. by making the actual situation difficult to understand ○ *Like so many politicians, he relies on a lot of statistical hocus-pocus.*

hodgepodge /ˈhɑdʒ·pɑdʒ/ *n* [C usually sing] a confused mixture of different things ○ *It was a hodgepodge of theories.*

hoe /hoʊ/ *n* [C] a garden tool with a long handle and a short blade, used to remove WEEDS (= unwanted plants) and break up the surface of the ground

hog **ANIMAL** /hɑg, hɔːg/ *n* [C] a pig, esp. one allowed to grow large so that it can be used as food

PERSON /hɑg, hɔːg/ *n* [C] *infml, disapproving* a person who takes more than necessary of something, esp. food ○ *Don't be a hog – take only as much as you can eat.*

hog /hɑg, hɔːg/ *v* [T] **-gg-** *infml, disapproving* ○ *He's always hogging the newspaper* (= using it so that no one else can read it).

hogwash /ˈhɑg·wɑʃ, ˈhɔːg·wɔːʃ/ *n* [U] nonsense, or words intended to deceive ○ *His answer was pure hogwash.*

H

ho-hum /ˈhoʊˈhʌm/ *adj infml* not interesting; boring ○ *The chess match was a ho-hum affair, ending in a draw.*

hoist /hɔɪst/ *v* [T] to lift something heavy, often with special equipment ○ *Tomorrow the final section of the bridge will be hoisted into place.*

hokey /ˈhoʊ·ki/ *adj infml* too emotional or artificial to be believed ○ *The ending of the movie was hokey, but otherwise it was OK.*

hokum /ˈhoʊ·kəm/ *n* [U] nonsense ○ *This report on the causes of crime is pure hokum.*

hold TAKE FIRMLY /hoʊld/ *v* [I/T] *past* **held 1** to take and keep something in your hand or arms ○ [T] *The nurse held the child in her arms.* ○ [I] *Hold tight* (= firmly) *to the railing.* **2** If you hold your nose, you press your nose tightly between thumb and finger to close it. **3** When two people **hold hands**, each one takes the other person's hand in his or her hand, esp. to show affection.

hold /hoʊld/ *n* [U] ○ *Don't lose hold of the dog's leash.* ○ *If you can get/grab/take hold of that end of the box, I'll take this end and we'll lift it.*

> **WORD CHOICES hold**
>
> **Clasp** or **grip** can be used when you hold something very tightly.
>
> *The baby* ***gripped*** *my finger with her tiny hand.*
>
> *He reached out to* ***clasp*** *Lindsay's hand.*
>
> **Clutch** is often used when someone holds something tightly, especially because of fear, anxiety, or pain.
>
> *Silent and pale, she* ***clutched*** *her mother's hand.*
>
> If someone holds something and does not want to let go, you could use the verb **cling**.
>
> *One little girl was* ***clinging*** *onto a cuddly toy.*
>
> **Hang on** is used when someone continues holding something.
>
> *The child was* ***hanging on*** *to her mother's skirt.*
>
> If you hold someone or something gently, especially by supporting that person or thing in your arms, you could use the verb **cradle**.
>
> *She* ***cradled*** *him tenderly in her arms.*
>
> **Grasp** or **grab** can be used when someone suddenly reaches out and holds something.
>
> *She* ***grasped*** *his hand in a gesture of sympathy.*
>
> *He* ***grabbed*** *the rope and pulled it hard.*
>
> You could use the verb **wield** if someone is holding a weapon or tool and looks as if he or she is going to use it.
>
> *We found him* ***wielding*** *a power drill on the deck of his beach house.*

MOVE AWAY /hoʊld/ *v* [always + adv/prep] *past* **held** to move something away from your body ○ [M] *Rosie held an apple out to the horse.* ○ [M] *Close your eyes and hold out your hands.* ○ [M] *All those who agree, please hold your hand up.*

KEEP IN PLACE /hoʊld/ *v* [always + adv/prep] *past* **held** to keep something in a particular place or position ○ [M] *Could you hold the door open for me, please?* ○ [M] *I can't fasten this skirt unless I hold my stomach in* (= keep it tight with my muscles so that it does not stick out). ○ [M] *Each wheel is held on by/with four bolts.* ○ [M] *Individual parts are held together with glue.* ○ [I] *Hold still* (= Do not move)*!*

hold /hoʊld/ *n* [C] (in some sports) a position in which one person prevents another from moving ○ *In karate, beginners learn several simple holds.*

holder /ˈhoʊl·dər/ *n* [C] a device for putting objects in or for keeping them in place ○ *a cup/paper towel holder*

CONTINUE /hoʊld/ *v* [I/T] *past* **held 1** to continue or cause to continue in the same way as before ○ [I] *If the weather holds, we can go sailing.* ○ [T] *The ship held its course.* ○ [T] *She seemed to hold the note she was singing for more than a minute.* **2** If something **holds true**, it continues to be true: *Einstein's theories still hold true today.*

DELAY /hoʊld/ *v* [I/T] *past* **held 1** to stop something from happening, or to delay something temporarily ○ [T] *How long can you hold your breath?* **2** Someone on the telephone who asks you to hold wants you to wait until that person or someone else can speak to you: [I] *Her line is busy, would you like to hold?* **3** If you hold something that is usually included in food, you do not include it: [T] *I'd like a salad, but hold the dressing.*

hold /hoʊld/ *n* **1** If something is **on hold**, it is intentionally delayed: *The space launch is on hold until the weather clears.* **2** If you are **on hold** when using the telephone, you are waiting to speak to someone: *His line is busy – can I put you on hold?*

CONTAIN/SUPPORT /hoʊld/ *v* [T] *past* **held 1** to support or contain something or be able to contain or support it ○ *This bottle holds exactly one pint.* ○ *Modern computers can hold* (= store) *huge amounts of information.* ○ *Will the rope be strong enough to hold the weight?* **2** If something **holds promise**, it is likely to be successful: *The new drug holds promise for relieving arthritis.*

CONTROL /hoʊld/ *v* [T] *past* **held 1** to keep control or possession of something ○ *His speech held the audience's attention for over an hour.* ○ *He was held prisoner for three days.* ○ *After many days of fighting, the rebels now hold the town.* ○ *The champion held the lead until the last lap.* **2** If someone who committed a crime is held, that person is kept guarded in a police station. **3** If you hold a job or a financial account, you have it: *He currently holds the position of managing editor.* ○ *She holds three different accounts with the same bank.*

hold /hoʊld/ *n* [U] ○ *The team is strengthening its hold on first place.* ○ *She has a strong hold on her daughters.*

holder /ˈhoʊl·dər/ *n* [C] ○ *property holders* ○ *Competition benefits credit card holders.*

CAUSE TO HAPPEN /hoʊld/ *v* [T] *past* **held** to organize or cause a meeting, election, or social event to happen ○ *The election will be held on the 8th of November.* ○ *We're holding our annual New Year's Day party again.*

BELIEVE /hoʊld/ *v* [T] *past* **held** to believe an idea or opinion to be correct, or to state that something is true ○ *He holds unpopular views on many subjects.* ○ *I hold him responsible for the damage to my car.* ○ [+ *that* clause] *Murphy's law holds that if anything can go wrong, it probably will.*

SPACE /hoʊld/ *n* [C] the space in a ship or aircraft where goods are carried

WORD FAMILY **hold**			
Nouns	hold holder holdings holdover holdup	*Verbs*	hold

IDIOMS with hold

• **hold it** stop and do not continue what you are doing ○ *Hold it! You're putting too much pepper in the stew.*

• **hold** *your* **own** to maintain your position or condition despite difficulties ○ *She can hold her own in any argument.* ○ *He was very sick, but now he's holding his own.*

• **hold the fort** to have responsibility for something while someone else is absent ○ *I'm leaving my husband to hold the fort while I'm away.*

• **hold** *your* **tongue** to stop yourself from speaking ○ *I wanted to scream, "You're an idiot!" but I held my tongue.*

• **hold water** to seem to be true or reasonable ○ *The jury convicted her because her story just didn't hold water.*

• **not hold a candle to** *someone/something* to not be as good as someone or something else ○ *Her latest book can't hold a candle to her earlier works.*

PHRASAL VERBS with hold

• **hold** *something* **against** *someone/something* to consider something as a reason to have a bad opinion about someone or something ○ *He made a mistake, but I don't hold it against him – we all make mistakes.*

• **hold back** *(something)* [M] to stop something from happening or advancing, or to keep someone from doing something ○ *She held back from interfering in their arguments.* ○ *Sandbags will hold back the flood waters for a while.* ○ *He admitted that something had gone wrong, but he held back the details* (= stopped himself from telling the complete truth).

• **hold down** *something* **STAY WORKING** to stay working in a job ○ *He's never been able to hold down a steady job.*

• **hold down** *something* **MAINTAIN LEVEL** [M] to maintain something at a low level ○ *Hold down the noise in there, kids!*

• **hold forth** to express your opinions for a long time ○ *She held forth all through lunch on a variety of subjects.*

• **hold off** *(something)* [M] to stop something from happening, or to be delayed ○ *They're hoping to hold off surgery until he's stronger.* ○ *I hope the rain holds off until we get home.*

• **hold on** to wait, esp. for someone to speak ○ *She's on the other line – can you hold on?*

• **hold on/tight** *infml* to continue doing something or staying somewhere although it is difficult or unpleasant to do so ○ *Hold on and I'll go and get some help.*

• **hold onto** *something* to continue to keep something ○ *Two local representatives held onto their seats in yesterday's election.* ○ *The team held onto first place with a 4-3 win last night.*

• **hold out** *something* **OFFER AS POSSIBILITY** to offer or consider something as a possibility ○ *Few people hold out any hope of finding more survivors.*

• **hold out CONTINUE 1** to continue in a situation that is dangerous or difficult ○ *They won't be able to hold out much longer against these attacks.* **2** If something holds out, it continues to be useful or enough: *The sensors are designed to work as long as their batteries hold out.*

• **hold out for** *something* to continue to demand something, although you have been told you cannot have it ○ *The workers are holding out for a pay increase.*

• **hold out on** *someone* to refuse to give help, information, or something of value to someone ○ *Don't hold out on me – I need to know who did it.*

• **hold over** *something/someone* [M] to delay something, or delay someone from leaving ○ *The nomination was held over until the Senate adjourned, allowing a recess appointment.* ○ *The weather held us over in Denver for two days.* ○ Related noun: HOLDOVER

• **hold** *someone* **to** *something* to demand that someone act on a promise or agreement ○ *They're holding him to the exact terms of the contract.*

• **hold together** *(something)* [M] to keep (a group or organization) complete or in its original state or condition ○ *Social relationships held the Crow people together into the 20th century.* ○ *We ought to do everything we can to get marriages to hold together.*

• **hold up** *someone/something* **DELAY** [M] to delay someone or something ○ *Traffic was held up for several hours by the accident.* ○ *Sorry to hold you up – my train was late.* ○ Related noun: HOLDUP **DELAY**

• **hold up** *someone/something* **STEAL** [M] to try to steal money or property from a person, a bank, or a business by using violence or threats ○ *They held up the same store twice.* ○ Related noun: HOLDUP **CRIME**

• **hold up CONTINUE 1** to continue to operate or be able to do things, esp. after being repaired or being ill ○ *I hope the spare tire holds up until we can get to a garage.* ○ *She is holding up well despite her problems.* **2** If information holds up, it is proved to be true: *The evidence may not hold up in court.*

• **hold up** *someone/something* **GIVE EXAMPLE** [M] to offer something or someone as an example ○ *Her parents always held her sister up to her as the kind of person she should be.*

holdings /ˈhoʊl·dɪŋz/ *pl n* [C] something valuable that is owned, esp. investments in a company ○ *He's got several car dealerships and banks among his holdings.*

holdover /ˈhoʊlˌdoʊ·vər/ *n* [C] a person or thing that continues from an earlier time, esp. a person who continues in an organization after other people have been replaced ○ *The coach had*

H

a pointed message for newcomers to the team and a reminder for the holdovers. ○ *Freud explained it as a holdover from a childhood problem.* ○ Related verb: HOLD OVER

holdup DELAY /ˈhoʊl·dʌp/ *n* [C] a delay ○ *A likely reason for the holdup is political pressure from the fish-farming industry.* ○ Related verb: HOLD UP DELAY

CRIME /ˈhoʊl·dʌp/ *n* [C] a crime in which a person or group demands money, using weapons and threats of violence ○ *Robbers got away with $1000 in a holdup of the bank.* ○ Related verb: HOLD UP STEAL

hole SPACE /hoʊl/ *n* [C] **1** an empty space or opening in an object ○ *We dug a hole to plant the tree.* ○ *My sweater has a hole in it.* **2** A hole is also something that has been left out or not explained: *The new proposal is full of holes.* **3** In golf, a hole is one of the small hollow spaces in the ground into which the ball is hit, or one of the usually 18 areas of play: *the seventh hole*

DIFFICULTY /hoʊl/ *n* [C usually sing] a difficult situation ○ *Without their starting quarterback, the team is in a (bit of a) hole.*

IDIOM with **hole**

• **in the hole** owing money, rather than having extra money ○ *We're still in the hole on our credit cards.*

PHRASAL VERB with **hole**

• **hole up** to stay in a safe place, often as a way of escape ○ *While writing his book, he holed up for a year at a cabin in the woods.*

holiday /ˈhɑl·əˌdeɪ/ *n* [C] **1** a day for celebration when many people are allowed to stay away from work or school ○ *a national holiday* **2** *Cdn, Br* A holiday is a VACATION.

holiness /ˈhoʊ·liː·nəs/ *n* [U] ○ See at HOLY GOOD

holistic /hoʊˈlɪs·tɪk/ *adj* **1** relating to the whole of something or to the total system instead of just to its parts **2** Holistic medicine attempts to treat the whole person, including mind and body, not just the injury or disease.

holler /ˈhɑl·ər/ *v* [I/T] *infml* to shout or call loudly ○ [T] *She hollered "Stop!" just before the collision.*

holler /ˈhɑl·ər/ *n* [C] *infml* ○ *He let out a holler when he fell.*

hollow EMPTY /ˈhɑl·oʊ/ *adj* **1** having an empty space inside or on the surface of an object ○ *a hollow tree* ○ *His hollow cheeks and paleness made him look ill.* **2** If a sound is hollow, it sounds as if it were made by hitting an empty container: *the low, hollow rumble of thunder*

hollow /ˈhɑl·oʊ/ *n* [C] **1** an empty space inside something; a hole **2** A hollow is also a small valley: *We hiked along Bear Hollow last weekend.*

WITHOUT VALUE /ˈhɑl·oʊ/ *adj* (of situations, feelings, or words) lacking value; not true or sincere ○ *a hollow victory* ○ *hollow promises* ○ *Their objections had a hollow ring* (= did not seem sincere).

PHRASAL VERB with **hollow**

• **hollow out** *something* [M] to remove the inside of something ○ *We hollowed out the tree trunk to make a canoe.*

holly /ˈhɑl·i/ *n* [C/U] an evergreen bush with pointed, shiny green leaves and small, red fruit

Hollywood /ˈhɑl·iːˌwʊd/ *n* [U] an area in Los Angeles, California, that is considered the center of the movie industry in the US

holocaust /ˈhɑl·əˌkɔːst, ˈhoʊ·lə-, -ˌkɑst/ *n* [C] **1** a large amount of destruction, esp. by fire or heat, or the killing of large numbers of people ○ *a nuclear holocaust* **2 The Holocaust** was the systematic murder of many people, esp. Jews, by the NAZIS during World War II.

hologram /ˈhɑl·əˌɡræm, ˈhoʊ·lə-/ *n* [C] an image made with a LASER beam, in which the objects shown look like they have depth rather than appearing flat and can seem to move

holster /ˈhoʊl·stər/ *n* [C] a leather container that holds a gun, usually fixed on a belt or a strap

holy GOOD /ˈhoʊ·li/ *adj* considered to be pure or good because of being related to what a religion values ○ *holy scriptures* ○ *Jerusalem is a holy city to Christians, Muslims, and Jews.*

holiness /ˈhoʊ·liː·nəs/ *n* [U] **1** *This temple is a place of great holiness.* **2** Holiness is also a title used of or to the leader of the Roman Catholic Church: *We do not know the views of His Holiness on the subject.*

EMPHASIS /ˈhoʊ·li/ *adj infml* used to emphasize another word, and sometimes to avoid swearing ○ *My nephew is a holy terror* (= a child who behaves very badly).

IDIOM with **holy**

• **holy cow, holy mackerel/smoke** *infml* how surprising, or how wonderful ○ *"My friend won an Oscar for the music for that movie." "Holy cow! Really?"*

Holy Grail, holy grail *n* [C] **1** something that a person or a particular group of people want very much to have or achieve ○ *Earth-like planets - the holy grail of planet hunting - are too small to detect.* **2** The Holy Grail is also the cup Jesus was believed to have drunk from during his last meal with his DISCIPLES.

homage /ˈɑm·ɪdʒ, ˈhɑm-/ *n* [U] an expression of great respect and honor ○ *We pay homage to him for his achievements in medical research.*

home HOUSE /hoʊm/ *n* [C/U] **1** a structure in which a person lives, esp. a house or apartment ○ [U] *Phone me at home after four o'clock.* ○ [C] *We have a country home and a city home.* **2** A home also refers to the family that lives together there: [C] *a happy home* **3** A home is also a place where a group of people live who need special care: [C] *a nursing home* **4** Your home address is the address of the place where you live. ○ **USAGE:** "House" is the more usual word for a building that one family lives in. The word "home" also refers to the life that goes on in that building.

home /hoʊm/ *adj* [not gradable] **1** done or made in the place where you live ○ *home cooking* **2** For a sports team, home refers to the city or the building or STADIUM where that team usually plays: *a home game*

home /hoʊm/ *adv* [not gradable] to or toward the place where you live ○ *going home*

homeless /ˈhoʊm·ləs/ *adj* [not gradable] having no place to live ○ *a homeless person*

homeless /ˈhoʊm·ləs/ *pl n* ○ *The homeless sometimes have to sleep in the streets.*

homelessness /ˈhoʊm·lə·snəs/ *n* [U] ○ *Homelessness is a major problem in large cities.*

homeward /ˈhoʊm·wərd/, **homewards** /ˈhoʊm·wərdz/ *adv* toward home ○ *Now that our vacation is over, it's time to head homeward.*

USAGE

home

When you use verbs of movement, for example **go** or **come**, with the adverb **home**, you do not need to use a preposition.

What time did you go home?

I'll call you as soon as I get home.

~~*What time did you go at home?*~~

When you use the verbs **be** or **stay** with **home**, you can use the preposition **at**, although most US speakers use no preposition.

I was at home all afternoon.

I'll stay home with granny.

Will you be home when the mail comes?

ORIGIN /hoʊm/ *n* [C/U] **1** a place of origin, or the place where a person belongs ○ [C] *Australia is the home of the kangaroo.* ○ [U] *I've lived here for two years, but it still doesn't feel like home.* **2** When you are **at home** in a place or situation, you are comfortable and relaxed there: *She's beginning to feel at home in her new job.* ○ *Go into the living room and make yourself at home.*

WORD FAMILY home

Nouns	home homeless	Verbs	home
Adjectives	homeless homely	Adverbs	home homeward

IDIOM with home

• **home free** *infml* having finished the difficult or dangerous part of an activity and sure of finishing it successfully ○ *Once you get past the essay questions on the test, you're home free.*

PHRASAL VERB with home

• **home in on** *something/someone* *infml* to aim for and move directly toward something or someone ○ *The missile homed in on the ship.*

homeboy /ˈhoʊm·bɔɪ/, **homey** /ˈhoʊ·mi/ *n* [C] *slang* someone from your own town, or someone who is a close friend

homecoming /ˈhoʊm ˌkʌm·ɪŋ/ *n* [C] **1** a person's arrival home after being away for a long time ○ *We were all eagerly awaiting my brother's homecoming from the war.* **2** a celebration at a school or college, usually including a dance and a football game, when people who were students there at an earlier time can return to visit

home front *n* [U] ***world history*** the non-military people of a country at war and their activities in support of the war effort

homegrown, **home-grown** /ˈhoʊm ˈgroʊn/ *adj* **1** produced in or existing locally ○ *homegrown efforts/businesses/extremists* **2** Homegrown also means grown in your own garden.

homeland /ˈhoʊm·lənd, -lænd/ *n* [C] the country where you were born

homely /ˈhoʊm·li/ *adj* unattractive in appearance

homemade /ˈhoʊm ˈmeɪd/ *adj* made at home rather than bought from a store ○ *homemade bread*

homemaker /ˈhoʊm ˌmeɪ·kər/ *n* [C] someone who manages a home and family instead of earning money from employment ○ Compare HOUSEWIFE

homeopathy /ˌhoʊ·miːˈɑp·ə·θi/ *n* [U] a system of treating disease by giving extremely small amounts of natural substances that, if given in larger amounts to healthy people, would produce the same effects as the disease

homeopathic /ˌhoʊ·miː·əˈpæθ·ɪk/ *adj* [not gradable] ○ *homeopathic medicine*

homeostasis /ˌhoʊ·miː·oʊˈsteɪ·səs/ *n* [U] ***biology*** the process by which a living thing or a cell keeps the conditions inside it the same despite any changes in the conditions around it

homeowner /ˈhoʊm ˌoʊ·nər/ *n* [C] someone who owns the house or apartment in which that person lives

home page *n* [C] the first page of a WEBSITE ○ *Go to the home page, and click on the link that says women's shoes.*

home run /hoʊm ˈrʌn/, **homer** /ˈhoʊ·mər/ *n* [C] (in baseball) a play in which a player hits the ball and scores, usually by hitting the ball a long way so that it comes down beyond the playing area ○ *(fig.) The movie didn't just make money, it hit a home run* (= was extremely successful).

homesick /ˈhoʊm·sɪk/ *adj* unhappy because of being away from home ○ *She was homesick during her first semester at college.*

homesickness /ˈhoʊm ˈsɪk·nəs/ *n* [U] ○ *I was almost overcome with homesickness.*

homespun /ˈhoʊm·spʌn/ *adj* simple and ordinary ○ *homespun wisdom*

homestead /ˈhoʊm·sted/ *n* [C] a house and the surrounding area of land, esp. land obtained from the government which is lived on and used for farming

H

home stretch *n* [U] the last part of a race or other activity ○ *We've been on this project for three months, but we're in the home stretch now.*

hometown /ˈhoʊm ˈtɑʊn/ *n* [C] the town or city you are from, esp. the one in which you were born and lived while you were young

homework /ˈhoʊm·wɜrk/ *n* [U] studying that students do at home to prepare for school ○ *The teacher told us to read chapter five for homework.* ○ (*fig.*) *The travel agent's association suggests that travelers* **do their homework** (= study the available information closely)*to find the deal that is best for them.*

homey COMFORTABLE /ˈhoʊ·mi/ *adj* pleasant and comfortable ○ *It's a small hotel with a homey atmosphere.*

H

PERSON /ˈhoʊ·mi/ *n* [C] a HOMEBOY

homicide /ˈhɑm·əˌsɑɪd, ˈhoʊ·mə-/ *n* [C/U] the crime of killing a person; murder ○ [U] *He was convicted of homicide.*

homicidal /ˌhɑm·əˈsɑɪd·əl, ˌhoʊ·mə-/ *adj* likely to murder ○ *a homicidal maniac*

Homo /ˈhoʊ·moʊ/ *n* [C] the biological group that includes modern humans, or a member of that group ○ *The tools might have been made by an as-yet-undiscovered early species of the genus Homo.*

homogeneous /ˌhoʊ·məˈdʒiː·niː·əs/ *adj* consisting of parts or having qualities that are the same ○ *Like the other valley towns, this was once a fairly homogeneous Anglo community.* ○ Compare HETEROGENEOUS

homogenized /həˈmɑdʒ·əˌnɑɪzd/ *adj* [not gradable] (of a substance) mixed together so that it is equally thick in all parts ○ *homogenized milk*

homograph /ˈhɑm·əˌɡræf/ *n* [C] ***grammar*** a word which is spelled the same as another word, but that has a different meaning, origin, or pronunciation

homologous /həˈmɑl·ə·ɡəs, hoʊ-/ *adj* [not gradable] ***science*** similar in position, structure, or purpose

homologous series *n* [C] ***chemistry*** a series of ORGANIC substances (= substances containing the element carbon) with similar characteristics

homonym /ˈhɑm·əˌnɪm, ˈhoʊ·mə-/ *n* [C] ***grammar*** **1** a word that is spelled the same as another word but that does not have the same meaning ○ *"Close" as a verb and "close" as an adjective are homonyms.* **2** A homonym is also a HOMOPHONE.

homophobia /ˌhoʊ·məˈfoʊ·biː·ə/ *n* [U] fear and dislike of HOMOSEXUALS

homophobic /ˌhoʊ·məˈfoʊ·bɪk/ *adj*

homophone /ˈhɑm·əˌfoʊn, ˈhoʊ·mə-/ *n* [C] ***grammar*** a word which is pronounced the same as another word, but which has a different meaning or spelling ○ *The words "so" and "sew" are homophones.*

homosexual /ˌhoʊ·məˈsek·ʃə·wəl/ *n* [C] a person who is sexually attracted to people of the same sex ○ Compare HETEROSEXUAL

homosexual /ˌhoʊ·məˈsek·ʃə·wəl/ *adj* [not gradable]

homosexuality /ˌhoʊ·məˌsek·ʃəˈwæl·əţ·i/ *n* [U]

homozygous /ˌhoʊ·məˈzɑɪ·ɡəs/ *adj* [not gradable] ***biology*** having two of the same form of a GENE that controls one characteristic, and therefore able to pass on one form only to the young

hone /hoʊn/ *v* [T] **1** to direct something such as an ability to make it more effective ○ *He helps performers hone their skills as dancers and singers.* **2** To hone an object is to make it sharper: *to hone scissors*

honest /ˈɑn·əst/ *adj* (of a person) truthful or able to be trusted; not likely to steal, cheat, or lie, or (of actions, speech, or appearance) showing these qualities ○ *an honest man* ○ *an honest answer* ○ *To be honest* (= To tell the truth), *I didn't like the movie.*

honestly /ˈɑn·əs·tli/ *adv* ○ *We always try to deal honestly with our customers.*

honesty /ˈɑn·ə·sti/ *n* [U] the quality of being honest ○ *The judge praised the girl's honesty.*

WORD FAMILY honest

Nouns	honesty dishonesty	*Adjectives*	honest dishonest
Adverbs	honestly		

WORD CHOICES honest

See also: **sincere**

The adjective **straight** is often used instead of honest.

*Just be **straight** with her and tell her how you feel.*

*I don't think he is being entirely **straight** with me.*

If someone is honest and does not tell lies, you can describe that person as **truthful.**

*Are you being **truthful** with me?*

If someone is honest and not likely to steal or cheat, you can describe that person as **trustworthy.**

*In a small town, if someone isn't **trustworthy**, everyone knows it.*

The adjective **reputable** is often used for a business that is honest and will not try to cheat people.

*Make sure you insure your home with a **reputable** company.*

A business arrangement that is honest can be described as **aboveboard.**

*The deal was completely open and **aboveboard**.*

The adjectives **candid, frank,** or **open** are used when someone is honest about personal feelings even if they are embarrassing.

*We had a very **candid** discussion.*

*He's quite **open** about his weaknesses.*

To be **frank**, *I didn't really know what I was doing.*

honestly /ˈɑn·əs·tli/ *adv* [not gradable] used to emphasize that you are telling the truth ○ *I honestly don't know what I did to upset her.* ○ *Honestly, I wish I had time to do more reading.*

honey SWEET SUBSTANCE /ˈhʌn·i/ *n* [U] a sweet, sticky, yellow substance made by bees and used as food

PERSON /ˈhʌn·i/ *n* [C] *infml* used as an affectionate way to address a person ○ *Hi, honey, I'm home.*

honeybee /ˈhʌn·iː ˌbiː/ *n* [C] a bee that produces HONEY

honeycomb /ˈhʌn·iː ˌkoʊm/ *n* [C] a structure bees make in which to store HONEY, having many small separate areas, or *fig.* any space divided into many small, separate areas or paths ○ *The building was a honeycomb of private offices.*

honeymoon /ˈhʌn·iː ˌmuːn/ *n* [C] **1** a vacation or trip taken by two people who have just been married ○ *We went to Hawaii on our honeymoon.* **2** A honeymoon is also an early period in a relationship when criticism is not given: *The first year of the presidency is regarded as a honeymoon.*
honeymoon /ˈhʌn·iː ˌmuːn/ *v* [I always + adv/prep] ○ *They are honeymooning in Jamaica.*
honeymooners /ˈhʌn·iː ˌmuː·nərz/ *pl n* ○ *This resort is popular with honeymooners.*

honeysuckle /ˈhʌn·iː ˌsʌk·əl/ *n* [U] a climbing plant with white, yellow, or red flowers that smell sweet

honk /hɑŋk, hɔːŋk/ *v* [I/T] to make a short, loud noise, or to sound a horn to make such a noise ○ [I/T] *The cars honking (their horns) kept us awake half the night.*

honor RESPECT, *Cdn, Br* **honour** /ˈɑn·ər/ *n* [U] **1** great respect for someone, or the feeling of pride and pleasure resulting when respect is shown to you ○ *It is an honor to meet you.* ○ *The dinner is* **in honor of** (= to show respect for) *a colleague who is leaving.* **2 Your/His/Her Honor** is a title of respect for a judge or MAYOR (= elected official).
honor, *Cdn, Br* **honour** /ˈɑn·ər/ *v* [T] ○ *We are honored that you have come to speak to our students.*

CHARACTER, *Cdn, Br* **honour** /ˈɑn·ər/ *n* [U] a good character, or a reputation for honesty and fair dealing ○ *David has always been a man of honor.* ○ *On my honor* (= Asking you to trust my reputation for honesty), *I never said that.*
honorable, *Cdn, Br* **honourable** /ˈɑn·ə·rə·bəl/ *adj* ○ *The neighbors are decent, honorable people.*
honorably, *Cdn, Br* **honourably** /ˈɑn·ə·rə·bli/ *adv* ○ *The general served his country honorably for 32 years.*

REWARD, *Cdn, Br* **honour** /ˈɑn·ər/ *n* [C] a public reward to show appreciation for unusual achievement ○ *She received the Presidential Medal of Freedom, the country's highest civilian honor.*
honor, *Cdn, Br* **honour** /ˈɑn·ər/ *v* [T] ○ *Today we honor those who died defending our country.*

honorable, *Cdn, Br* **honourable** /ˈɑn·ə·rə·bəl/ *adj* **1** deserving public praise or reward **2** An honorable discharge from the armed forces is a release from your duties with praise from those in authority.

honorary /ˈɑn·əˌrer·i/ *adj* given as a reward, without qualifying in a standard way ○ *The university awards honorary degrees to various distinguished people each year.*

honors, *Cdn, Br* **honours** /ˈɑn·ərz/ *pl n* **1** *He was buried with full military honors.* **2** An honors course or program is one or more courses of a high standard for advanced students. **3** If a student qualifies for a degree **with honors** from a school, college, or university, that student has done work of an unusually high standard.

FULFILL, *Cdn, Br* **honour** /ˈɑn·ər/ *v* [T] to fulfill an existing agreement or promise, or to accept a form of payment ○ *The governor honored her pledge to cut taxes.*

honor roll, *Cdn* **honour roll** *n* [C] a list of students who have done the best work in a particular school

honor student, *Cdn* **honours student** *n* [C] a student whose work has earned that student a place on a school's HONOR ROLL

hood CLOTHING /hʊd/ *n* [C] a part of a coat or jacket that can be used to cover the head ○ *The raincoat comes with a detachable hood.*

CAR /hʊd/ *n* [C] the metal cover over the engine of a car

hoodlum /ˈhuːd·ləm, ˈhʊd-/, *infml* **hood** /ˈhʊd/ *n* [C] a criminal, esp. one who is a member of a group ○ *Hoodlums robbed two people in a convenience store, police said.*

hoodwink /ˈhʊd·wɪŋk/ *v* [T] to deceive or trick someone ○ *We were hoodwinked into believing that we had won a lot of money.*

hoof /hʊf, huːf/ *n* [C] *pl* **hooves, hoofs** the hard part of the foot of an animal such a horse

hook /hʊk/ *n* [C] a curved device used for catching hold of something or for hanging something on ○ *Hang your coat on one of the hooks in the hall.* ○ *I need to change the hook on my fishing line.*
hook /hʊk/ *v* [T] **1** to use something like a hook, or to put something so that it is supported at one end and hangs ○ *She hooked her arm through his.* ○ *He hooked his cane over the back of the chair.* **2** To hook fish means to catch them on hooks: *We hooked some bass.*

IDIOM with hook

• **hook, line, and sinker** completely ○ *I forged the note and the teacher fell for it hook, line, and sinker.* ○ USAGE: Used when you are you are surprised or pleased that someone believed something that was intended to deceive them.

PHRASAL VERBS with hook

• **hook up** *something* CONNECT [M] to connect something, usually to a system or to a piece of equipment ○ *We just moved and I haven't hooked* *up my stereo yet.* ○ *He hooked the trailer up to his car.* ○ Related noun: HOOKUP CONNECTION

•**hook up** **MEET** *infml* to meet with someone, or to begin a relationship, esp. for a particular purpose ○ *Give me a call if you'd like to hook up for lunch sometime.* ○ *The program is really an opportunity for college kids to hook up and get to know each other.*

hooked /hʊkt/ *adj* [not gradable] *infml* strongly attracted to something or someone ○ *We were afraid she was getting hooked on painkillers, so we changed the medication.* ○ *During the Olympics, we all got hooked on ice dancing.*

hooker /ˈhʊk·ər/ *n* [C] *slang* a PROSTITUTE

hookup /ˈhʊk·ʌp/ *n* [C] the connection between a supply of something and its user, or a connection between two or more pieces of equipment ○ *Each campsite has complete electric, water, and sewage hookups.* ○ *Millions were watching via a satellite hookup.* ○ Related verb: HOOK UP CONNECT

H

hoop /huːp, hʊp/ *n* [C] a ring of wood, metal, or plastic ○ *Dad put up a basketball hoop in the driveway on the front of the garage.*

hoopla /ˈhuː·plɑ, ˈhʊp·lɑ/ *n* [U] busy excitement or a lot of public attention for an event or activity ○ *She loved the thrill of the shows, the elegant parties, the attention, the hoopla.*

hooray /hʊˈreɪ, hə-/ *exclamation* HURRAH

hoot **SOUND** /huːt/ *n* [C] the sound an OWL (= type of bird) makes, or a shout showing anger or amusement ○ *There were some hoots from the audience at these so-called experts.*

hoot /huːt/ *v* [I/T] ○ [I] *He hooted with laughter.*

AMUSING PERSON/THING /huːt/ *n* [C] *infml* an amusing person or thing ○ *Matt's a real hoot.*

Hoover /ˈhuː·vər/ *v* [I/T] *Br* to VACUUM ○ **USAGE:** Hoover is a trademark for cleaning and other equipment.

hooves /hʊvz, huːvz/ *pl of* HOOF

hop /hɑp/ *v* [I/T] **-pp-** to make small jumps on one or two feet, or to move along in this way ○ [I] *A bird hopped across the lawn.* ○ [T] *Nikki hopped the fence* (= jumped over it). ○ [I] *(fig.) Come on, hop in* (= get in), *I've got plenty of room in the car.*

hop /hɑp/ *n* [C] ○ *(fig.) It's just a short hop to Pittsburgh by plane.*

hope /hoʊp/ *n* [C/U] the feeling that something desired can be had or will happen ○ [U] *We never entirely gave up hope.* ○ [U] *This research offers hope of developing better ways to treat cancer.* ○ [C] *He had hopes of being chosen for the leading part in the play.*

hope /hoʊp/ *v* to express the feeling or wish that something desired will happen ○ [I] *I'm hoping the company gives us a bonus this year.* ○ [+ to infinitive] *We hope to see you soon.* ○ [+ (*that*) clause] *I hope (that) his plane won't be delayed.*

hopeful /ˈhoʊp·fəl/ *adj* having hope or causing you to hope; believing or causing you to believe that something desired will happen ○ [+ *that* clause] *I'm hopeful that when both sides understand the situation better, they will agree to meet and cooperate.* ○ *The fact that he's eating with a good appetite is a hopeful sign.*

hopeful /ˈhoʊp·fəl/ *n* [C] a person who wants to achieve a position of power ○ *Five presidential hopefuls were invited to speak.*

hopefully /ˈhoʊp·fə·li/ *adv* ○ *"Do you have the tickets?" he asked hopefully.* ○ *Hopefully* (= I/we hope that), *dad will get home before his supper gets cold.*

hopeless /ˈhoʊ·pləs/ *adj* without hope ○ *We tried to save the building, but it was a hopeless task* (= it could not succeed).

hopelessly /ˈhoʊ·plə·sli/ *adv* completely ○ *We got hopelessly lost in Rome.*

WORD FAMILY hope

Nouns	hope hopeful	*Verbs*	hope
		Adverbs	hopefully hopelessly
Adjectives	hopeful hopeless		

horde /hɔːrd, hoʊrd/ *n* [C] a large group, esp. of people ○ *A horde of reporters waited on the lawn outside the White House.*

horizon /həˈraɪ·zən/ *n* **1** the place in the distance where the earth and sky seem to meet ○ [U] *We watched the horizon as the sun set.* **2** A person's horizons are the limit of that person's ideas, knowledge, and experience: [pl] *Spending her junior year abroad has broadened her horizons.*

horizontal /ˌhɔːr·əˈzɑnt·əl, ˌhɑr-/ *adj* [not gradable] flat or level; parallel with the ground ○ *Keep the patient in a horizontal position with her feet slightly raised.*

horizontally /ˌhɔːr·əˈzɑnt·əl·i, ˌhɑr-/ *adv* ○ Compare VERTICAL

hormone /ˈhɔːr·moʊn/ *n* [C] ***biology*** any of various chemicals in the body that are carried by the blood and that influence the body's growth and how it works

horn **ANIMAL** /hɔːrn/ *n* [C/U] a hard, pointed part, usually one of a pair, on the head of cows, goats, and other animals

horny /ˈhɔːr·ni/ *adj* consisting of, or feeling hard like horn ○ *Birds have horny beaks.*

MUSIC /hɔːrn/ *n* [C/U] any of various musical instruments consisting of a long curved metal tube that is narrow at the end you blow into and wider at the other end, or this type of instrument generally

VEHICLE /hɔːrn/ *n* [C] a device on a vehicle that is used to make a loud sound as a warning or signal ○ *Angry drivers were honking their horns.*

PHRASAL VERB with horn

•**horn in** to interrupt or try to become involved in something when you are not welcome ○ *Julie is always trying to horn in on our conversations.*

hornet /ˈhɔːr·nət/ *n* [C] a large flying insect that can give a severe sting

horoscope /ˈhɔːr·əˌskoʊp, ˈhɑr-/ *n* [C] a description of what is going to happen to you, based on the position of the stars and planets at the time of your birth

horrendous /həˈren·dəs/ *adj* so bad as to be shocking; extremely unpleasant ○ *Exhibits show how horrendous the living conditions there were.*

horrible /ˈhɔːr·ə·bəl, ˈhɑr-/ *adj* very bad, unpleasant, or disgusting ○ *There was a horrible smell outside the factory.*
horribly /ˈhɔːr·ə·bli, ˈhɑr-/ *adv* very badly ○ *They suffered horribly during the war.*

horrid /ˈhɔːr·əd, ˈhɑr-/ *adj* very bad or unpleasant ○ *It was a horrid purple color which she detested.*

horrify /ˈhɔːr·əˌfɑɪ, ˈhɑr-/ *v* [T] to cause someone to experience shock, fear, or disgust ○ *The public was horrified by the amount of pollution in the lake.* ○ (fig.) *He was horrified to find that I had never been to a county fair.*
horrifying /ˈhɔːr·əˌfɑɪ·ɪŋ, ˈhɑr-/ *adj* ○ *We saw some horrifying pictures of the effects of the storm.*
horrific /həˈrɪf·ɪk/ *adj* so bad as to be shocking ○ *The report detailed the horrific conditions in the prison.*

horror /ˈhɔːr·ər, ˈhɑr·ər/ *n* [C/U] a strong feeling of fear, shock, or disgust, or an event that produces such a feeling ○ [C] *the horrors of war* ○ [U] *People cried out in horror as they watched the building burn.*

horror story *n* [C] a situation that someone tells you about in which something bad happens ○ *I've heard a lot of horror stories about people driving their car and suddenly the steering wheel won't turn.*

hors d'oeuvre /ɔːrˈdɜrv/ *n* [C] a small amount of food served before a meal, or at a party

horse /hɔːrs/ *n* [C] a large animal with four legs that people ride on and which, esp. in the past, was used for pulling vehicles and carrying loads ○ *She taught him how to ride a horse.*

PHRASAL VERB with **horse**

• **horse around** *infml* to behave in a silly and noisy way ○ *This fellow at work keeps horsing around.*

horseback /ˈhɔːrs·bæk/ *adj, adv* sitting on a horse ○ *She taught him how to ride horseback.* ○ *I went horseback riding* (= riding on a horse for enjoyment) *with my brother.*

horsefly /ˈhɔːrs·flɑɪ/ *n* [C] any of various large, flying insects that bite

horseplay /ˈhɔːr·spleɪ/ *n* [U] noisy, physically active behavior, esp. when people push each other as a joke ○ *No running or horseplay in the halls.*

horsepower /ˈhɔːrˌspɑʊ·ər/ *n* [C/U] *pl* **horsepower** a unit for measuring the power of an engine ○ [C] *a 170-horsepower engine*

horseradish /ˈhɔːrsˌræd·ɪʃ/ *n* [U] a plant with a long, white root that has a strong taste

horseshoe /ˈhɔːrs·ʃuː/ *n* [C] a U-shaped metal object that is attached to the bottom of a horse's HOOF (= foot) to protect it
horseshoes /ˈhɔːrs·ʃuːz/ *n* [U] a game in which horseshoes are thrown at a metal rod in the ground

horticulture /ˈhɔːrt̬·əˌkʌl·tʃər/ *n* [U] the study or activity of growing plants, esp. for decoration

hose PIPE /hoʊz/ *n* [C] a long, usually plastic or rubber pipe that can be bent and is used to move water or other substances ○ *a fire hose* ○ *a garden hose* ○ *a radiator hose*
hose /hoʊz/ *v* [T always + adv/prep] to clean something with water ○ *They have to hose down the streets.* ○ *Just hose it off.*

CLOTHING /hoʊz/, **hosiery** /ˈhoʊ·ʒə·ri, -zə-/ *pl n* STOCKINGS or PANTYHOSE

hoser /ˈhoʊ·zər/ *n* [C] *Cdn, slang* a man, esp. one who works at a job that uses physical rather than mental skills and whose habits are slightly offensive but amusing ○ *You hoser – leave some food for the rest of us!*

hospice /ˈhɑs·pəs/ *n* [C] a place or an organization that provides care for people who are dying

hospitable /hɑsˈpɪt̬·ə·bəl/ *adj* friendly and welcoming to guests or visitors ○ *a hospitable host* ○ *She retired to a more hospitable climate* (= a more comfortable place).

hospital /ˈhɑsˌpɪt̬·əl/ *n* [C/U] a place where people who are very ill or injured are treated by doctors and nurses ○ [U] *She spent a week in the hospital last year.*
hospitalize /ˈhɑsˌpɪt̬·əlˌɑɪz/ *v* [T] to take someone to stay in a hospital because of illness or injury ○ *Did he have to be hospitalized?*
hospitalization /ˌhɑsˌpɪt̬·əl·əˈzeɪ·ʃən/ *n* [U]

hospitality /ˌhɑs·pəˈtæl·ət̬·i/ *n* [U] kindness and friendly behavior, esp. to guests ○ *Thank you for your hospitality.*

host PARTY ORGANIZER /hoʊst/, *female* **hostess** /ˈhoʊ·stəs/ *n* [C] someone who gives a party or has guests ○ *Lucy was a gracious host.* ○ *Vancouver played host to the conference* (= the event happened there).
host /hoʊst/ *v* [T] ○ *Which country is hosting the next Olympics?*

BROADCASTER /hoʊst/, *female* **hostess** /ˈhoʊ·stəs/ *n* [C] a person who introduces guests and performers on television or radio ○ *a talk-show host*

PLANT/ANIMAL /hoʊst/ *n* [C] a plant or animal that another plant or animal lives on as a PARASITE

LARGE NUMBER /hoʊst/ *n* [C usually sing] a large number ○ *They cared for wounded soldiers and performed a host of other duties.*

hostage /ˈhɑs·tɪdʒ/ *n* [C] someone who is made a prisoner in order to force other people to do something ○ *Inmates at the jail held 12 hostages and demanded to meet the governor.*

hostel /ˈhɑs·təl/ *n* [C] a large house where people can sleep for little money ○ *a youth hostel*

H

hostile UNFRIENDLY /ˈhɑs·tᵊl, -tɑɪl/ *adj* showing strong dislike; unfriendly ○ *Her parents were openly hostile to me.*

hostility /hɑsˈtɪl·ət̬·i/ *n* [U] ○ *He tried to hide his hostility.*

DIFFICULT /ˈhɑs·tᵊl, -tɑɪl/ *adj* difficult or not suitable for living or growing ○ *The Nevada desert is one of the most hostile regions in America.*

WARLIKE /ˈhɑs·tᵊl, -tɑɪl/ *adj* [not gradable] connected with an enemy or an act of war ○ *The enemy was preparing to take hostile action.*

hostilities /hɑˈstɪl·ət̬·iz/ *pl n fml* ○ *Both sides were trying to avoid further hostilities.*

hot VERY WARM /hɑt/ *adj* [*-er/-est* only] **-tt-** having a high temperature ○ *a hot day* ○ *a hot meal* ○ *It's hotter in Ohio than it is here.* ○ *Matt makes his little sister hot chocolate* (= a warm drink made with chocolate).

> **WORD CHOICES hot**
>
> If the weather outside or the temperature inside is very hot, you can use the adjectives **scorching, boiling (hot)**, or **sweltering**.
>
> *She won the race despite yesterday's* ***sweltering*** *heat.*
>
> *a* ***scorching*** *summer day.*
>
> If the temperature feels hot and unpleasant, you can say that it is **oppressive**.
>
> *The* ***oppressive*** *afternoon heat was making him feel tired.*
>
> Liquid that is extremely hot can be described as **scalding (hot)**.
>
> *She burned herself on* ***scalding*** *water from the kettle.*
>
> If food is pleasantly very hot, you could describe it as **piping hot**.
>
> *She gave us a bowl of* ***piping hot*** *soup.*
>
> If something is not as hot as it should be, it could be described as **lukewarm**.
>
> *Yuck! This coffee's* ***lukewarm***!

SPICY /hɑt/ *adj* [*-er/-est* only] **-tt-** (of food) causing a feeling in the mouth like burning or TINGLING (= as if a lot of sharp points are being put in quickly and lightly) ○ *If you like curry really hot, you can add some hot peppers and hot sauce.*

ANGRY /hɑt/ *adj* [*-er/-est* only] **-tt-** easily excited, or angry ○ *She's hot-tempered.* ○ *I got really hot about them not recycling.*

hotly /ˈhɑt·li/ *adv* ○ *She hotly denied having taken the money.* ○ *The race for district leader was hotly contested* (= the competition was strong).

GOOD /hɑt/ *adj* [*-er/-est* only] **-tt-** *infml* very good and having energy ○ *Right now the stock market is hot.* ○ *The show isn't so hot.* ○ *He doesn't feel so hot.*

STOLEN /hɑt/ *adj* [not gradable] *slang* (of goods) stolen and therefore difficult to sell ○ *Those CD players are so cheap, they must be hot.*

DANGEROUS /hɑt/ *adj* [*-er/-est* only] **-tt-** *infml* (of a situation) dangerous or difficult; RISKY ○ *Things got a lot hotter when the military took over.*

ATTRACTIVE /hɑt/ *adj* [*-er/-est* only] **-tt-** *slang* physically attractive

> **IDIOMS with hot**
>
> • **in hot pursuit** eagerly trying to get someone or something ○ *He drove off, with the police in hot pursuit.* ○ *Reporters from the Times were in hot pursuit of the story.*
>
> • **in hot water** in a difficult situation in which you are likely to be punished ○ *Emails that criticize others can land you in hot water, so be careful what you write.*

hot air *n* [U] *infml* words that do not really mean anything or are not sincere ○ *His promises turned out to be a lot of hot air.*

hot-air balloon *n* [C] an aircraft consisting of a very large bag filled with heated air, with a container hanging under it in which people can ride

hotbed /ˈhɑt·bed/ *n* [C] a place or situation where a lot of a particular activity is happening or might happen ○ *Seattle is a hotbed of software publishing.*

hotcake /ˈhɑt·keɪk/ *n* [C] a PANCAKE

hot dog /ˈhɑt·dɔːg/ *n* [C] a long, tube-shaped, cooked SAUSAGE (= meat), usually eaten in a long ROLL (= loaf of bread) ○ *a hot dog with mustard*

hotel /hoʊˈtel/ *n* [C] a building where you pay to have a room to sleep in ○ *a luxury hotel*

hot flash *n* [C] a hot and uncomfortable feeling that a woman has because of the effects of MENOPAUSE (= the time when she stops being able to have children)

hothead /ˈhɑt·hed/ *n* [C] *disapproving* someone who gets angry too quickly and reacts without thinking carefully first

hotheaded /ˈhɑtˈhed·əd/ *adj disapproving* ○ *a hotheaded young fool*

hotline /ˈhɑt·lɑɪn/ *n* [C] a special telephone number for emergencies or for a particular service ○ *a hotline for complaints*

hotplate /ˈhɑt·pleɪt/ *n* [C] a small, movable, electric device on which food is cooked

hot potato *n* [C] *infml* a situation or subject that people disagree strongly about and that no one wants to deal with ○ *The issue of immigration became a political hot potato.*

hotshot /ˈhɑt·ʃɑt/ *n* [C] someone who is skillful and successful at something ○ *He's a hotshot lawyer from New York.*

hot spot POPULAR PLACE *n* [C] a place that is popular, for example, for vacations or entertainment ○ *This summer's vacation hot spot is Alaska.*

VIOLENT PLACE *n* [C] a place where war or other fighting is likely to happen

CONNECTION *n* [C] a building or area where you can connect to the INTERNET at high speed without wires

hot tub *n* [C] a large container full of heated water in which more than one person can sit

hot water bottle *n* [C] a rubber container that you fill with hot water and use to warm a bed or part of your body

hot-wire /ˈhɑt·wɑɪr/ *v* [T] *slang* to start a car without using the key, by attaching together wires in the electrical system that starts the engine

hound /hɑʊnd/ *v* [T] to chase someone or refuse to leave someone alone, esp. because you want to get something from that person ○ *Socialists were hounded by the FBI in the 1950s.*

hound (dog) /ˈhɑʊnd (dɔːg)/ *n* [C] any of several types of dog used for hunting

hour /ɑʊr/, *abbreviation* **hr.** *n* [C] **1** a period of 60 minutes ○ *Take this an hour after eating.* ○ *It's open 24 hours a day.* ○ *He works long hours* (= starts work early and finishes late). ○ *He gets paid* **by the hour** (= for each hour worked). ○ *Buses pull out every hour* **on the hour** (= at the time an hour begins). **2** An hour can be a period of time, not necessarily 60 minutes, when you do something: *a lunch hour* **3** An hour can be the distance you can travel in 60 minutes: *San Francisco is only a couple of hours away.*

hourly /ˈɑʊr·li/ *adj* [not gradable] ○ *hourly pay* (= pay for every hour worked) ○ *hourly bus service* (= service once an hour)

hourly /ˈɑʊr·li/ *adv* [not gradable] ○ *Tours are offered hourly* (= once an hour).

USAGE

hour or time?

An **hour** is a period of 60 minutes.

The trip takes about three hours.

We went for a 2-hour walk.

Time is measured in hours and minutes. We use **time** to refer to a particular point during the day or night, or to say when something happens.

What time do you get up in the morning?

There's only one bus at that time of night.

Remember to use **time**, not **hour**, when you are talking about what time it is.

"What time is it?" "It's 2 o'clock."

~~*"What hour is it?" "It's 2 o'clock."*~~

IDIOMS with hour

• **hour after hour, hour upon hour** for a long time ○ *The dog just sits there hour after hour and watches the hamsters.*

• **hours (and hours)** *infml* a long time ○ *I spent hours filling out forms.*

hourglass /ˈɑʊr·glæs/ *n* [C] a glass container that contains sand that moves from an upper to a lower part through a narrow opening in the middle and is used for measuring time

hour-long, **hourlong** /ˈɑʊr ˈlɔːŋ/ *adj* continuing for one hour ○ *Last night's hour-long debate was broadcast live on TV.*

house HOME /hɑʊs/ *n* [C] *pl* **houses 1** a building in which people, usually one family, live ○ *to buy/rent a house* ○ *a brick/clapboard house* ○ *my/your/grandma's house* **2** A house can also be a building where animals are kept: *a dog house* **3** A house (also **household**) can also be all the people living in a house: *Try not to wake the whole house when you come in!*

house /hɑʊz/ *v* [T] ○ *Homeless families have been housed* (= given a place to live) *in motels.* ○ *The building houses the library* (= gives it space).

housing /ˈhɑʊ·zɪŋ/ *n* [U] buildings that people live in, or the providing of places for people to live ○ *affordable/expensive housing*

BUSINESS /hɑʊs/ *n* [C] *pl* **houses 1** a business or organization ○ *a publishing/fashion house* **2** A house can also be a building or part of a building which is used by an organization: *the Metropolitan Opera House*

POLITICS /hɑʊs/ *n* [C] *pl* **houses 1** an organization that makes laws, or its meeting place **2** *infml* The House is the US HOUSE OF REPRESENTATIVES.

THEATER /hɑʊs/ *n* [C] *pl* **houses** the seats in a theater, or the people watching a performance ○ *The opera played to a full/empty house.*

IDIOM with house

• **on the house** given to you free by a business ○ *Your meal is on the house tonight!*

house arrest *n* [U] the legal act of forcing someone to stay at home instead of in a prison ○ *Kitty's father was placed under house arrest.*

houseboat /ˈhɑʊs·boʊt/ *n* [C] a boat that people can use as their home

housebound /ˈhɑʊs·bɑʊnd/ *adj* unable to leave home, esp. because of illness or injury ○ *Ever since the accident she's been housebound.*

housebroken /ˈhɑʊs ˌbroʊ·kən/ *adj* (of a pet) taught to go outside to excrete waste matter ○ *The puppy is still not housebroken.*

housefly /ˈhɑʊs·flɑɪ/ *n* [C] a small, common FLY (= type of insect) often found in houses

household /ˈhɑʊs·hoʊld/ *n* [C] a group of people, often a family, who live together ○ *She became part of his household.*

CONFUSABLES

household or housework?

In English **household** is not used to mean the work that you do to keep your house clean. The name for this work is **housework**.

Traditionally women stayed at home to do the housework and raise the children.

~~*Traditionally women stayed at home to do the household and raise the children.*~~

IDIOM with household

• **a household name, a household word** a famous person or organization ○ *Overnight, his name be-*

came a household word and the movies he made afterward were instant successes.

housekeeper /ˈhɑʊsˌkiː·pər/ *n* [C] a person, usually a woman, whose job is to take care of another person's house, esp. by cleaning it

housekeeping /ˈhɑʊsˌkiː·pɪŋ/ *n* [U] ○ *She does some light housekeeping* (= cleaning) *for us.*

House of Commons, *infml* **Commons** *n* [U] in Canada, the group of elected government members that makes the laws

House of Representatives, *infml* **House** *n* [U] the larger of the two elected groups of the US CONGRESS (= the group of people who make the laws)

house-sit *v* [I] to stay in someone's house while the person is away in order to keep it safe

housewares /ˈhɑʊ·swerz, -swærz/ *pl n* equipment esp. for the kitchen that is sold in a store

housewarming /ˈhɑʊsˌwɔːr·mɪŋ/ *n* [C] a party that you give when you move into a new home

housewife /ˈhɑʊs·wɑɪf/ *n* [C] *pl* **-wives** someone who manages a home and family instead of earning money from employment ○ Compare HOMEMAKER

housework /ˈhɑʊs·wɜrk/ *n* [U] the work that you do around a house, for example cleaning, cooking, and washing clothes ➤ Usage: **household or housework?** at HOUSEHOLD

housing project, **project** *n* [C] a group of houses or apartments, usually provided by the government for families who have very low incomes

hovel /ˈhʌv·əl, ˈhɑv-/ *n* [C] a small home, esp. one that is dirty and in bad condition ○ *Their house was little more than a hovel.*

hover /ˈhʌv·ər, ˈhɑv-/ *v* [I] **1** to stay in the air in one place ○ *A helicopter hovered overhead.* **2** A person who hovers stands near someone, waiting for attention: *She hovered outside her boss's door.*

how /hɑʊ/ *adv* [not gradable] **1** in what way or state, to what amount or degree, or for what reason ○ *How do we get to the interstate highway from here?* ○ *How did you hear about the concert?* ○ *How is your mother?* ○ *How did you like the movie?* ○ *How much does this cost?* ○ *How old is his daughter?* ○ *She didn't say how far it is to her house.* ○ *How long are you going to be at the gym?* **2** How is sometimes used for emphasis: *How nice to see you!* **3 How are you?** is used as a greeting: *"Hi, how are you?" "Fine, thanks, how are you?"* **4 How are things?, How's everything?**, and **How's it going?** are informal greetings. ○ *Hi Deb! How's it going?* **5 How do you do?** is a formal greeting: *"I'm Jack Stewart." "How do you do, I'm Angela Black."*

how /hɑʊ/ *conjunction* the way or condition in which ○ *Do you know how this machine works?* ○ [+ to infinitive] *Roz doesn't know how to ride a bicycle.* ○ *I was horrified to hear about how she had been treated.*

USAGE

how or what?

Many people wrongly use **how** when they are talking about **what** something is called or **what** something or someone looks like. In these expressions remember to use **what**.

I don't know what it's called in English.

~~*I don't know how it's called in English.*~~

I'd like to see what it looks like before I buy it.

~~*I'd like to see how it looks like before I buy it.*~~

IDIOMS with how

• **how about** *something*, **how about** *doing something infml* I suggest this ○ *How about going out for a walk after dinner?*

• **how come** *something happened infml* why did something happen ○ *How come you got invited and I didn't?*

• **how dare you** *do something* I am very surprised and shocked by what you are doing ○ *How dare you question my authority?*

howdy /ˈhɑʊd·i/ *exclamation infml* used as a greeting; HELLO ○ *Howdy, folks! When did you all get here?*

however DEGREE /hɑʊˈev·ər/ *adv* [not gradable] to whatever amount or degree ○ *However fast we drive, we're not going to get there in time.* ○ *If Emma likes something she'll buy it, however much it costs.*

WAY /hɑʊˈev·ər/ *adv* [not gradable] in whatever way ○ *However you look at it, it's still a mess.*

however /hɑʊˈev·ər/ *conjunction* ○ *You can do it however you like, it really doesn't matter.*

DESPITE /hɑʊˈev·ər/ *adv* [not gradable] despite this; NEVERTHELESS ○ *There may, however, be other reasons that we don't know about.*

howl /hɑʊl/ *v* [I] to make a long, high, crying sound, like that of a dog ○ *Toby stepped on a nail, and he howled in pain.* ○ *The wind howled.* ○ [+ that clause] (*fig.*) *The senators kept howling* (= loudly complaining) *that there was not enough money in the budget to pay for the president's plan.*

howl /hɑʊl/ *n* [C] *fig.* A howl of a person or a group can mean a complaint that is strongly expressed: *The loudest howl seemed to come from farmers in the Midwest.*

hr. *n* [C] *abbreviation for* HOUR

HTML *n* [U] *abbreviation for* hypertext markup language (= a system for representing documents on computers)

hub /hʌb/ *n* [C] the central part of something, esp. of a wheel, or a center of activity ○ *Chicago is a major transportation hub, with the busiest airport in the US.*

hubbub /ˈhʌb·ʌb/ *n* [U] a mixture of continuing noises producing a feeling of busy activity or confused excitement ○ *There is always quite a hubbub in the hallways between class periods when students are moving from one room to another.*

hubcap /ˈhʌb·kæp/ *n* [C] a round cover that fits over the center of the outside of a car's wheel

hubris /ˈhjuː·brəs/ *n* [U] an extreme and unreasonable feeling of pride and confidence in yourself ○ *Hubris brought him down in the end.*

huckleberry /ˈhʌk·əlˌber·i/ *n* [C] a small, round, dark blue fruit, or the low North American bush on which it grows

huckster /ˈhʌk·stər/ *n* [C] *disapproving* a person who sells things or puts forward ideas in a very determined way that is often not completely honest

huddle /ˈhʌd·əl/ *v* [I always + adv/prep] to come close together in a group, or to hold your arms and legs close to your body, esp. because of cold or fear ○ *Everyone huddled around the fire to keep warm.*
huddle /ˈhʌd·əl/ *n* [C] ○ *The football players formed a huddle.*

hue /hjuː/ *n* [C] ***art*** a color, or the particular degree of light or dark of a color ○ *In the waters of the Caribbean there are fish of every hue.*

huff /hʌf/ *v* [I] to breathe loudly, esp. after physical exercise ○ *He huffed and puffed going up the stairs.*

IDIOM with **huff**

•**in a huff** feeling angry and upset ○ *When Julia criticized his art, Geraldo left in a huff.*

hug /hʌg/ *v* [I/T] **-gg-** to hold someone or something close to your body with your arms, esp. to show affection ○ [T] *Maria hugged her dog.* ○ [T] *As the verdict of not guilty was announced, he leaped up and hugged his lawyer.* ○ [T] *(fig.) Some fish hug* (= stay close to) *the bottom of the lake.*
hug /hʌg/ *n* [C] ○ *My little boy always gets a kiss and a hug before he goes to bed.*

huge /hjuːdʒ, juːdʒ/ *adj* [-*er*/-*est* only] extremely large in size or amount ○ *a huge forest* ○ *a huge parking lot* ○ *They made huge profits in real estate.*
hugely /ˈhjuːdʒ·li, ˈjuːdʒ-/ *adv* ○ *Their business has been hugely successful.*

huh /hʌ̃, hᵊm/ *exclamation* said to show that you have not heard or understood something, or used at the end of a statement to question it ○ *"Huh? What did you say?"* ○ *"You called right in middle of dinner." "Great timing, huh?"*

hulk BROKEN THING /hʌlk/ *n* [C] the body of an old ship, car, or large piece of equipment, which is broken and no longer used ○ *The rusted hulk of an abandoned car sat at the side of the road.*

LARGE PERSON /hʌlk/ *n* [C] a large, heavy person or thing ○ *He was a huge hulk of a man, about six and a half feet tall.*

hull SHIP /hʌl/ *n* [C] the body or frame of a ship, most of which lies under the water

PLANT COVERING /hʌl/ *n* [C] the outer covering of a seed or fruit, such as the shell of a nut

hullabaloo /ˌhʌl·ə·bəˈluː/ *n* [C] *pl* **hullabaloos** *infml* a loud noise made by people, often because they are angry, or a situation in which many people are angry or upset ○ *They finally stopped production of the play because of all the hullabaloo it caused.*

hum /hʌm/ *v* [I/T] **-mm- 1** to make a continuous, low sound, or to sing a tune with closed lips ○ [I] *Debbie always hums to herself when she listens to music.* ○ [T] *I've forgotten how that tune goes – could you hum it for me?* **2** *fig.* If something is humming, it is very busy and full of activity: [I] *Factories that make paper products are humming at 97% of capacity.*
hum /hʌm/ *n* [C usually sing] ○ *We could hear the constant hum of traffic outside the window.*

human /ˈhjuː·mən, ˈjuː-/ *adj* of or typical of people ○ *the human body* ○ *Of course I make mistakes, I'm only human* (= not perfect). ○ *The accident was due to human error* (= a person's mistake).
human (being) /ˈhjuː·mən (ˈbiː·ɪŋ), ˈjuː-/ *n* [C] a person
humanity /hjuːˈmæn·əţ·i, juː-/ *n* [U] all people in the world as a whole, or the qualities characteristic of people ○ *The former general was put on trial for crimes against humanity.* ○ See also: HUMANITY at HUMANE
humanize /ˈhjuː·məˌnɑɪz, ˈjuː-/ *v* [T] to make someone or something kinder, gentler, or more agreeable ○ *If people were just a little more courteous, it would humanize this city a lot.*
humanly /ˈhjuː·mən·li, ˈjuː-/ *adv* ○ *They did everything humanly possible to help her* (= They did everything they could).

WORD FAMILY **human**			
Nouns	human humanism humanity humanitarian inhumanity	*Adjectives*	human inhuman superhuman humane humanitarian
Adverbs	humanly humanely	*Verbs*	humanize

humane /hjuːˈmeɪn, juː-/ *adj* showing kindness, care, and sympathy toward others, esp. those who are suffering ○ *She felt it was more humane to kill the injured animal quickly than to let it suffer.*
humanity /hjuːˈmæn·əţ·i, juː-/ *n* [U] understanding and kindness toward other people ○ *He showed his humanity by giving generously to charities.* ○ See also: HUMANITY at HUMAN
humanely /hjuːˈmeɪn·li, juː-/ *adv*

humanism /ˈhjuː·məˌnɪz·əm, ˈjuː-/ *n* [U] ***social studies*** a system of thought and reasoning based on human values and interests, often without accepting the beliefs of religion

humanitarian /hjuːˌmæn·əˈter·iː·ən, juː-/ *adj* involved in or connected with improving people's lives and reducing suffering ○ *humanitarian aid in the form of food supplies*
humanitarian /hjuːˌmæn·əˈter·iː·ən, juː-/ *n* [C] ○ *She was regarded by many as a compassionate humanitarian.*

humanities /hjuːˈmæn·ət̬·iz, juː-/ *pl n* literature, language, history, PHILOSOPHY, and other subjects that are not a science, or the study of these subjects

humankind /ˈhjuː·mənˌkɑɪnd, ˈjuː-/ *n* [U] the whole of the human race, including both men and women

humanly /ˈhjuː·mən·li, juː-/ *adv* ○ See at HUMAN

human nature *n* [U] the behavior and feelings common to most people

human race *n* [U] all people ○ *This is the biggest health problem that faces the human race.*

human resources, **personnel** *n* [U] the department within a company or organization that is responsible for its relationship with its employees and for following employment laws

human rights *pl n* ***social studies*** the basic rights to fair and moral treatment that every person is believed to have

humble **NOT PROUD** /ˈhʌm·bəl/ *adj* tending to consider yourself as having no special importance that makes you better than others; not proud ○ *He's a humble man and he's not comfortable talking about his own achievements.*

humble /ˈhʌm·bəl/ *v* [T] ○ *Seeing the courage and skill of the disabled athletes was a humbling experience.*

humbly /ˈhʌm·bli/ *adv* ○ *I humbly ask your pardon.*

LOW IN RANK /ˈhʌm·bəl/ *adj* low in rank or position; poor ○ *She rose from humble origins to become one of the best-known political writers in the world.*

humbly /ˈhʌm·bli/ *adv* ○ *They live humbly* (= simply).

humdrum /ˈhʌm·drʌm/ *adj* lacking excitement and interest; ordinary ○ *We lead such a humdrum life/existence.*

humid /ˈhjuː·məd, juː-/ *adj* (of air and weather) containing extremely small drops of water in the air ○ *New York is very hot and humid in the summer.*

humidify /hjuːˈmɪd·əˌfɑɪ, juː-/ *v* [T] to make air wetter ○ *The doctor says we need to humidify the air in the baby's room because it's too dry.*

humidifier /hjuːˈmɪd·əˌfɑɪ·ər, juː-/ *n* [C] a machine that adds water to the air

humidity /hjuːˈmɪd·ət̬·i, juː-/ *n* [U] ***earth science*** a measure of how wet the air is ○ *Tomorrow will be hot, with high humidity.*

humiliate /hjuːˈmɪl·iːˌeɪt, juː-/ *v* [T] to make you feel ashamed or lose respect for yourself ○ *They called him an old fool in public just to humiliate him.*

humiliating /hjuːˈmɪl·iːˌeɪt̬·ɪŋ, juː-/ *adj* ○ [+ *to* infinitive] *It was humiliating to see all my possessions piled on the street.*

humiliation /hjuːˌmɪl·iːˈeɪ·ʃən, juː-/ *n* [C/U] ○ [U] *the humiliation of defeat*

humility /hjuːˈmɪl·ət̬·i, juː-/ *n* [U] the feeling or attitude that you have no special importance that makes you better than others; lack of pride ○ *Grandma was a religious woman of deep humility.*

hummed /hʌmd/ *past simple and past participle of* HUM

humming /ˈhʌm·ɪŋ/ *present participle of* HUM

hummingbird /ˈhʌm·ɪŋˌbɜrd/ *n* [C] a very small, brightly colored bird with a long beak that it uses to drink NECTAR (= sweet liquid) from flowers

humongous /hjuːˈmʌŋ·gəs, juː-/ *adj infml* very large ○ *We had our picture taken in New Mexico before a humongous cactus.*

humor **AMUSEMENT**, *Cdn, Br* **humour** /ˈhjuː·mər, ˈjuː-/ *n* [U] the ability to be amused by something seen, heard, or thought about, sometimes causing you to smile or laugh, or the quality in something that causes such amusement ○ *He has a wonderful sense of humor.* ○ *Fortunately, she saw the humor in the situation.*

humorist /ˈhjuː·mə·rəst, ˈjuː-/ *n* [C] a person who regularly writes or tells amusing stories, esp. as part of a job

humorous /ˈhjuː·mə·rəs, ˈjuː-/ *adj* ○ *Mark Twain was known for his humorous short sketches.*

humorless, *Cdn, Br* **humourless** /ˈhjuː·mər·ləs, ˈjuː-/ *adj* unable to see humor in things when most others do ○ *His father was humorless, embittered man.*

humorously /ˈhjuː·mə·rə·sli, ˈjuː-/ *adv*

AGREE WITH, *Cdn, Br* **humour** /ˈhjuː·mər, ˈjuː-/ *v* [T] to agree to someone's wishes in order to help improve that person's mood or to avoid upsetting him or her ○ *Phil seems a bit cranky today, so just humor him.*

hump /hʌmp/ *n* [C] **1** a large, round, raised lump or part ○ *The car swerved when it hit a hump in the road.* **2** A hump is also a round, raised part on a person's or animal's back: *a camel's hump*

hunch **IDEA** /hʌntʃ/ *n* [C] an idea that is based on feeling and for which there is no proof ○ [+ *that* clause] *I had a hunch that you'd be here.*

BEND /hʌntʃ/ *v* [I/T] to lean forward with your shoulders raised or to bend your back and shoulders into a rounded shape ○ [I] *We gathered in a circle and hunched over the fire to get warm.*

hunchback /ˈhʌntʃ·bæk/ *n* [C] a person who has a back with a large, round lump on it and therefore looks bent over even when standing upright

hundred /ˈhʌn·drəd/ *number* **1** 100 ○ *We've driven a/one hundred miles in the last two hours.* ○ *This area of the coast is home to hundreds of bird species.* **2 A/one hundred percent** means completely: *I agree with you a hundred percent.*

hundredth /ˈhʌn·drətθ/ *adj, adv, n* [C] **1** *She reached her hundredth birthday.* **2** A hundredth is one of a hundred equal parts of something.

USAGE

hundred or hundreds?

If you are using **hundred** to describe a particular number, use the singular form. Only use it in the plural form to refer to a large number that is not exact.

There are three hundred people employed here.

~~*There are over three hundreds people employed here.*~~

Hundreds of fans were waiting outside the theater.

hung /hʌŋ/ *past simple and past participle of* HANG

hunger **FOOD** /ˈhʌŋ·gər/ *n* [U] the uncomfortable or painful feeling in your stomach caused by the need for or lack of food ○ *Mother Teresa devoted her life to fighting hunger in the poorest parts of the world.*

DESIRE /ˈhʌŋ·gər/ *n* [U] a strong wish or desire ○ *a hunger for adventure/power*

hunger /ˈhʌŋ·gər/ *v* [I always + adv/prep] ○ *She had always hungered for a starring role in a musical.*

WORD FAMILY hunger

Nouns	hunger	*Verbs*	hunger
Adjectives	hungry	*Adverbs*	hungrily

hunger strike *n* [C] a period when someone such as a prisoner refuses to eat, usually to show strong opposition to something

hungry **NEEDING FOOD** /ˈhʌŋ·gri/ *adj* feeling the need to eat because there has been a period of time when you have not eaten ○ *The children are always hungry when they get home from school.* ○ *They were poor and often went to bed hungry* (= did not get enough to eat at night).

WORD CHOICES hungry

The adjective **ravenous** can be used to describe someone who is very hungry.

*I'm **ravenous**; when's dinner ready?*

Informal words which mean "very hungry" are **famished** or **starving.**

*I'm **famished**! I haven't eaten anything since this morning.*

*Is there anything to eat? I'm **starving**!*

The phrase **have a good appetite** can be used for someone who is often hungry and eats a lot of food.

*Both my children **have** very **good appetites**.*

EAGER /ˈhʌŋ·gri/ *adj* having a strong desire; eager ○ *Kim is so hungry for success that she'll do anything to achieve it.*

hung up /hʌŋˈʌp/ *adj infml* feeling unreasonably anxious, esp. about yourself ○ *Don't be so hung up about your weight – you look fine.*

hunk **PIECE** /hʌŋk/ *n* [C] a large, thick piece, esp. of food ○ *a hunk of bread/cheese/meat*

MAN /hʌŋk/ *n* [C] *slang* a large, strong man, esp. one who is attractive

hunker down /ˈhʌŋ·kər/ *phrasal verb* **1** to sit with your knees bent in front of you so that your buttocks are almost resting on your heels ○ *We hunkered down near the campfire.* **2** To hunker down is also to be prepared to stay in a particular place or situation for as long as necessary, esp. for protection or to achieve something: *We hunkered down in the cellar while the storm raged outside.* ○ *Members of Congress were hunkered down for weeks of debate on the health-care issue.*

hunky-dory /ˌhʌŋ·kiːˈdɔːr·i, -ˈdoʊr·i/ *adj infml* (esp. of a situation) satisfactory and pleasant ○ *You can't lose your temper with everyone like that and then expect everything to be hunky-dory.*

hunt **CHASE** /hʌnt/ *v* [I/T] to chase or search for a wild animal or bird with the intention of killing or catching it for food, sport, or profit ○ [I] *He hunts every weekend.* ○ [T] *Cats like to hunt mice and birds.*

hunt /hʌnt/ *n* [C] ○ *a deer hunt*

hunter /ˈhʌnt·ər/ *n* [C] a person or animal that hunts animals for food or sport

hunting /ˈhʌnt·ɪŋ/ *n* [U] ○ *My father and I both enjoy hunting.*

SEARCH /hʌnt/ *v* [I/T] to search for something or someone ○ [I] *I've hunted everywhere for the missing keys.*

hunt /hʌnt/ *n* [C] ○ *The hunt for the injured climber continued through the night.*

hunting /ˌhʌnt·ɪŋ/ *n* ○ *They spend their weekends house hunting.* ○ *Career counselors offer job-hunting strategies.*

PHRASAL VERB with hunt

• **hunt** *someone* **down** [M] to find someone after searching hard ○ *Detectives have finally managed to hunt down the thieves.*

hurdle /ˈhɜrd·əl/ *n* [C] **1** a frame for jumping over in a race **2** A hurdle is also a difficulty to be dealt with: *There are a lot of hurdles to overcome before the contract can be signed.*

hurdle /ˈhɜrd·əl/ *v* [I/T] ○ [T] *The boys hurdled the fence* (= jumped over it).

hurdler /ˈhɜrd·lər, -əl·ər/ *n* [C] a competitor in a race over a series of hurdles

hurl /ˈhɜrl/ *v* [T] to throw something forcefully ○ *The volcano hurled hundreds of tons of rock, ash, and dust into the air.* ○ *He hurled* (= shouted) *insults at his boss.*

hurrah, **hoorah** /həˈrɑ, -ˈrɔː/, **hooray** /hʊˈreɪ, hə-/ *exclamation* used to express excitement, pleasure, or approval ○ *Hurrah for the whole team!*

hurricane /ˈhɜr·əˌkeɪn, ˈhʌ·rə-/ *n* [C] ***earth science*** a violent storm with strong circular winds of at least 72 miles (or 118 kilometers) per hour, esp. in the western Atlantic Ocean

hurry /ˈhɜr·i, ˈhʌ·ri/ *v* [I/T] to move or act quickly, or to cause someone to move or act quickly ○ [I] *We have to hurry if we're going to make it there in time.* ○ [T] *I hurried the kids through their breakfasts.*

hurry /ˈhɜr·i, ˈhʌ·ri/ *n* [U] ○ *We've got plenty of time – what's the hurry* (= Why hurry)? ○ *He's **in a hurry** to get to a meeting* (= wants to get there quickly). ○ *I'm **in no hurry** for the book* (= I do not need it back quickly)*– keep it as long as you want.*

hurried /ˈhɜr·id, ˈhʌ·rid/ *adj* [not gradable] done quickly ○ *We left early, after a hurried breakfast.*
hurriedly /ˈhɜr·əd·li, ˈhʌ·rəd-/ *adv* ○ *The man hurriedly walked away.*

WORD FAMILY hurry			
Nouns	hurry	*Verbs*	hurry
Adjectives	hurried unhurried	*Adverbs*	hurriedly

IDIOM with hurry

• **hurry up and** *do something* to do something very soon ○ *All I wanted was for these very boring people to hurry up and leave.*

PHRASAL VERB with hurry

• **hurry up** do something more quickly ○ *Hurry up, or we'll miss the bus!*

H

hurt /hɜrt/ *v* [I/T] *past* **hurt 1** to feel pain, or to cause pain or injury to yourself or someone else ○ [I] *Tell me where it hurts.* ○ [I] *My leg hurts.* ○ [T] *Stop! You're hurting me!* ○ [T] *Emilio hurt his back when he fell off a ladder.* **2** To hurt also means to cause harm or difficulty: [T] *A lot of businesses are being hurt by high interest rates.* ○ [T] *His lack of experience may hurt his chances of getting the job.* **3** To hurt someone can also mean to make someone upset or unhappy: [T] *I didn't mean to* **hurt** *your* **feelings**.
hurt /hɜrt/ *adj* [not gradable] feeling pain or being upset ○ *I saw you fall – are you hurt?* ○ *Naomi was hurt by your criticism.*
hurt /hɜrt/ *n* [U] emotional pain ○ *It's a hurt that he has tried all his life to heal.*
hurtful /ˈhɜrt·fəl/ *adj* [not gradable] causing emotional pain ○ *a hurtful remark*

WORD FAMILY hurt			
Nouns	hurt	*Verbs*	hurt
Adjectives	hurtful	*Adverbs*	hurtfully

IDIOM with hurt

• **it doesn't hurt to** *do something*, **it doesn't hurt to** *have something* it is an advantage to do or have something ○ *It doesn't hurt to have money when you want to run for office.*

hurtle /ˈhɜrt̬·əl/ *v* [I always + adv/prep] to move very fast, esp. in what seems a dangerous way ○ *The truck hurtled along at breakneck speed.*

husband /ˈhʌz·bənd/ *n* [C] the man to whom a woman is married; a married man ○ Compare WIFE

hush /hʌʃ/ *n* [U] quiet or silence, esp. after noise ○ *A hush fell over the crowd.*
hush /hʌʃ/ *exclamation* ○ *Hush! You'll wake the baby!*
hushed /hʌʃt/ *adj* [not gradable] ○ *hushed tones/voices*

PHRASAL VERB with hush

• **hush up** *something* [M] to prevent something from becoming known ○ *The mayor tried to hush up the fact that he had been in prison.*

hush-hush *adj infml* secret ○ *I can't tell you anything about it – it's all hush-hush.*

husk /hʌsk/ *n* [C] the dry, outer covering of some fruits and seeds ○ *corn husks*

husky VOICE /ˈhʌs·ki/ *adj* (esp. of a person's voice) low and sounding slightly damaged ○ *The singer had a husky voice.*

STRONG /ˈhʌs·ki/ *adj* (esp. of boys or men) big and strong ○ *Rennett was a husky, broad-shouldered kid.*

DOG /ˈhʌs·ki/ *n* [C] a type of dog that is strong and furry and is used for pulling SLEDS in cold regions of the world

hustle ACT QUICKLY /ˈhʌs·əl/ *v* [I] to act quickly and with energy ○ *If we really hustle, we can finish the job by lunchtime.*
hustle /ˈhʌs·əl/ *n* [U] energetic action ○ *The team showed a lot of determination and hustle.* ○ *They love the* **hustle and bustle** *of the city* (= its energy and excitement).

PUSH /ˈhʌs·əl/ *v* [T always + adv/prep] to push or force someone along ○ *The demonstrators were hustled out of the hall.*

SELL /ˈhʌs·əl/ *v* [T] *infml* to forcefully encourage someone to buy something, or to cheat someone ○ *On weekends they hustle tourists on the waterfront.*
hustle /ˈhʌs·əl/ *n* [C] *infml* a dishonest way of making money ○ *Advertising turns every achievement into a hustle.*
hustler /ˈhʌs·lər/ *n* [C] someone who tries to get something, usually money, by deceiving others

hut /hʌt/ *n* [C] a small, simple house or shelter ○ *a thatched hut*

hutch CAGE /hʌtʃ/ *n* [C] a cage or box to keep small animals in

CABINET /hʌtʃ/ *n* [C] a cabinet with doors or drawers on the bottom and usually open shelves on the top

hyacinth /ˈhɑɪ·ə·sɪnθ/ *n* [C] a pleasant-smelling plant with a lot of small flowers growing closely around a thick stem

hybrid /ˈhɑɪ·brɪd/ *n* [C] **1** ***biology*** a plant or animal that has been produced from two different types of plant or animal **2** A hybrid is also anything that is a mixture of two or more things: *The architecture is a hybrid of classical and modern styles.* **3** A hybrid vehicle is one that is able to operate using either of two fuels: *US automakers are wrestling with how much to invest in hybrid gas-electric cars.*
hybridization /ˌhɑɪ·brɪd·əˈzeɪ·ʃən/ *n* [U] ***biology*** the process of producing a plant or animal from two different types of plant or animal

hydrant /ˈhɑɪ·drənt/ *n* [C] *short form of* FIRE HYDRANT.

hydrate GIVE WATER /ˈhɑɪ·dreɪt/ *v* [I/T] to provide someone or something with water or liquid ○ [T] *Drink lots of water and keep your body hydrated.*

CHEMICAL /ˈhɑɪ·dreɪt/ *v* [T] ***chemistry*** to chemically combine a substance or substances with water

hydrate /ˈhɑɪ·dreɪt/ *n* [C] ***chemistry*** a substance produced by chemically combining substances with water

hydraulic /hɑɪˈdrɔː·lɪk/ *adj* [not gradable] (of a device) operated by water pressure or by pressure from another liquid ○ *The plane's hydraulic systems can withstand incredibly high temperatures.*

hydrocarbon /ˌhɑɪ·drəˈkɑr·bən/ *n* [C] ***biology, chemistry*** a chemical combination of HYDROGEN (= a gas) and CARBON (= a chemical element that is in all animals and plants), found in fuels

hydroelectric /ˌhɑɪ·droʊ·ɪˈlek·trɪk/ *adj* [not gradable] of or related to electricity produced from the energy of fast-moving water ○ *a hydroelectric power plant*

hydrogen /ˈhɑɪ·drə·dʒən/ *n* [U] ***physics*** the lightest gas, one of the chemical elements, and having no color, taste, or smell

hydrogen bomb, **H-bomb** *n* [C] a type of nuclear bomb

hydrogen bond *n* [C] ***science*** a weak connection that is formed between an atom of HYDROGEN (= a gas) and an atom of another substance such as oxygen or NITROGEN (= a gas)

hydrogen peroxide *n* [U] a liquid chemical used for killing bacteria or making hair lighter in color

hydrology /hɑɪˈdrɑl·ə·dʒi/ *n* [U] ***earth science*** the study of water on the earth, for example, where it is and how it is used
hydrologic /ˌhɑɪ·drəˈlɑdʒ·ɪk/ *adj* [not gradable] ***earth science***

hydrolysis /hɑɪˈdrɑl·ə·səs/ *n* [U] ***chemistry*** a chemical reaction in which one substance reacts with water to produce another

hydronium /hɑɪˈdroʊ·niː·əm/ *n* [U] ***chemistry*** an ION of HYDROGEN that has been combined with water

hydrosphere /ˈhɑɪ·drəˌsfɪr/ *n* [U] ***earth science*** all of the water on the earth's surface, such as the seas, lakes, and ice, and sometimes also including water above the earth's surface, such as clouds

hydroxide /hɑɪˈdrɑk·sɑɪd/ *n* [C] ***chemistry*** a chemical that contains a combination of oxygen and HYDROGEN atoms with a negative electrical CHARGE

hyena /hɑɪˈiː·nə/ *n* [C] a wild animal of Africa and Asia that looks like a dog and makes a laughing sound

hygiene /ˈhɑɪ·dʒiːn/ *n* [U] the practice or principles of keeping yourself and your environment clean in order to maintain health and prevent disease ○ *He doesn't care much about personal hygiene.*
hygienic /hɑɪˈdʒiː·nɪk, -ˈdʒen·ɪk/ *adj* [not gradable] clean and unlikely to cause disease

hymn /hɪm/ *n* [C] a song of praise, esp. to God
hymnal /ˈhɪm·nəl/, **hymnbook** /ˈhɪm·bʊk/ *n* [C] a book of hymns

hype /hɑɪp/ *n* [U] *infml* information that makes something seem very important or exciting ○ *The big-name, big-money New York art world is full of hype.*
hype /ˈhɑɪp/ *v* [T] *infml* to make something seem more exciting or important than it is ○ *No sports event is more hyped than the Super Bowl.*

hyped (up) /hɑɪpt, ˈhɑɪpˈtʌp/ *adj infml* emotionally excited, nervous, or anxious ○ *I was really hyped about my new car, so it was disappointing when I had to keep bringing it in for repairs.*

hyper /ˈhɑɪ·pər/ *adj infml* extremely excited or nervous ○ *I was so hyper it took me over an hour to get to sleep.*

hyper- /ˌhɑɪ·pər/ *prefix* having a lot or too much of the stated quality ○ *hypercritical* ○ *hyper-intelligent*

hyperactive /ˌhɑɪ·pəˈræk·tɪv/ *adj* [not gradable] (esp. of children) extremely or unusually active ○ *She wanted to keep her hyperactive son busy.*

hyperbola /hɑɪˈpɜr·bə·lə/ *n* [C] ***mathematics*** a type of curve made up of two curves that are not connected

hyperbole /hɑɪˈpɜr·bə·li/ *n* [U] **1** a way of speaking or writing that makes someone or something sound much bigger, better, smaller, worse, more unusual, etc., than they are ○ *Although he's not given to hyperbole, Ron says we are light-years ahead of our time.* **2** ***literature*** Hyperbole is also the use of such language to express humor or great emotion.

hypersensitive /ˌhɑɪ·pərˈsen·sət̬·ɪv/ *adj* [not gradable] very easily changed or damaged by physical conditions, or easily upset ○ *He's hypersensitive about his height.*

hypertension /ˌhɑɪ·pərˈten·tʃən/ *n* [U] *medical* unusually high blood pressure

hyperventilate /ˌhɑɪ·pərˈvent·əlˌeɪt/ *v* [I] to breathe too quickly, causing too much oxygen to enter the blood

hyphen /ˈhɑɪ·fən/ *n* [C] the mark (-) used in writing to join two words together, or between the syllables of a word when it is divided at the end of a line of text
hyphenate /ˈhɑɪ·fəˌneɪt/ *v* [T] ○ *She hyphenates her first name, Anne-Marie.*

hypnosis /hɪpˈnoʊ·səs/ *n* [U] an artificially produced state of mind similar to sleep in which a person can be influenced to say or do things
hypnotic /hɪpˈnɑt̬·ɪk/ *adj* [not gradable] relating to or causing hypnosis ○ *a hypnotic trance* ○ *the hypnotic rhythm of the waves*
hypnotize /ˈhɪp·nəˌtɑɪz, -mə-/ *v* [T] to produce hypnosis in someone, or to completely influence someone ○ *The crowd sits hypnotized by Harper's trumpet.*
hypnotism /ˈhɪp·nəˌtɪz·əm, -mə-/ *n* [U] the act of causing hypnosis

H

hypochondria /ˌhɑɪ·pəˈkɑn·driː·ə/ *n* [U] unnecessary anxiety about and attention to your health

hypochondriac /ˌhɑɪ·pəˈkɑn·driːˌæk/ *n* [C] ○ *Elderly hypochondriacs were generally complainers in their youth.*

hypocrisy /hɪˈpɑk·rə·si/ *n* [U] *disapproving* pretending to be what you are not, or pretending to believe something that you do not ○ *Critics are accusing him of hypocrisy and deceit.*

hypocrite /ˈhɪp·əˌkrɪt/ *n* [C] ○ *The biggest hypocrites in sports are owners who yell about players' salaries.*

hypocritical /ˌhɪp·əˈkrɪt̬·ɪ·kəl/ *adj* [not gradable] ○ *It's hypocritical for him to criticize her for doing the same things that he does.*

H

hypodermic /ˌhɑɪ·pəˈdɜr·mɪk/ *adj* [not gradable] (of medical tools) used to INJECT drugs under a person's skin ○ *a hypodermic needle/syringe*

hypotenuse /hɑɪˈpɑt·ənˌuːs, -ˌuːz/ *n* [C] ***geometry*** the longest side of a triangle that has one angle of 90°

hypothalamus /ˌhɑɪ·pəˈθæl·ə·məs/ *n* [C usually sing] ***biology*** a small part in the front of the brain that controls body temperature and tells your body if you are hungry or need a drink of water

hypothermia /ˌhɑɪ·pəˈθɜr·miː·ə, -poʊ-/ *n* [U] *medical* a dangerous condition in which a person's body temperature is unusually low

hypothesis Ⓐ /hɑɪˈpɑθ·ə·səs/ *n* [C] *pl* **hypotheses** ***science*** an idea or explanation for something that is based on known facts but has not yet been proven ○ *Several hypotheses for global warming have been suggested.*

hypothesize Ⓐ /hɑɪˈpɑθ·əˌsɑɪz/ *v* [I/T] to give a possible but not yet proven explanation for something ○ *There's no point hypothesizing about how the accident happened, since we'll never really know.*

hypothetical Ⓐ /ˌhɑɪ·pəˈθet̬·ɪ·kəl/ *adj* [not gradable] of or based on a HYPOTHESIS ○ *He dismissed the questions as purely hypothetical.*

hypothetically Ⓐ /ˌhɑɪ·pəˈθet̬·ɪ·kli/ *adv* ○ *Any electronic voting system is hypothetically hackable.*

hysterectomy /ˌhɪs·təˈrek·tə·mi/ *n* [C] a medical operation to remove part or all of a woman's uterus

hysteria /hɪˈster·iː·ə, hɪˈstɪr-/ *n* [U] excitement or emotion that is uncontrollable ○ *One woman, close to hysteria, grabbed my arm.*

hysterical /hɪˈster·ɪ·kəl/ *adj* ○ *Calm down, you're getting hysterical.* ○ *She broke into hysterical laughter* (= laughter that is uncontrollable). ○ (*infml*) *That joke was hysterical* (= extremely amusing).

hysterically /hɪˈster·ɪ·kli/ *adv* [not gradable] ○ *Gillian was laughing/crying hysterically.*

hysterics /hɪˈster·ɪks/ *pl n* a state of uncontrollable excitement or emotion ○ *I told her she couldn't have it and she went into hysterics.*

Hz /hɜrts/ *n* [C] ***physics*** *abbreviation for* HERTZ

I i

I **LETTER**, **i** /ɑɪ/ *n* [C] *pl* **I's, i's** the ninth letter of the English alphabet

NUMBER, **i** /ɑɪ, wʌn/ *number* the ROMAN NUMERAL for the number 1

PERSON /ɑɪ/ *pronoun* the person speaking ○ *I can see her car.* ➤ Usage: **me or I?** at ME

iambic pentameter /ɑɪˈæm·bɪk penˈtæm·ət̬·ər/ *n* [U] ***literature*** a style of writing poems in lines of ten syllables with emphasis on the second, fourth, sixth, eighth, and tenth syllable ○ Compare BLANK VERSE

ice **FROZEN WATER** /ɑɪs/ *n* [U] water that has frozen solid, or pieces of this ○ *Don't slip on the ice.* ○ *I'd like a ginger ale with no ice.*

iced /ɑɪst/, **ice** /ɑɪs/ *adj* [not gradable] very cold, or with ice added ○ *iced tea* ○ **USAGE:** Used to describe drinks that are usually drunk hot.

icy /ˈɑɪ·si/ *adj* **1** covered with ice ○ *an icy sidewalk* **2** Icy also means extremely cold, like ice. ○ *icy winds* ○ See also: ICY

COVER CAKE /ɑɪs/ *v* [T] FROST **COVER CAKE**

WORD FAMILY ice

Nouns	ice icicle icing	*Adjectives*	iced icy
Verbs	ice	*Adverbs*	icily

iceberg /ˈɑɪs·bɜrg/ *n* [C] a very large mass of ice that floats in the sea

icebreaker **SHIP** /ˈɑɪsˌbreɪ·kər/ *n* [C] a strong ship that can move through ice

GAME OR JOKE /ˈɑɪsˌbreɪ·kər/ *n* [C] a game, joke, or story that makes people who do not know each other feel more comfortable together

ice-cold *adj* [not gradable] extremely cold ○ *The water off the coast here is always ice-cold.*

ice cream *n* [U] a sweet, frozen food made from milk and cream ○ *chocolate ice cream*

ice-cream cone, **cone** *n* [C] a small, cone-shaped, edible container that holds ice cream ○ *Who wants an ice-cream cone?*

ice cube *n* [C] a small block of ice, esp. one put into a drink to make it cold

ice hockey *n* [U] HOCKEY

ice skate /ˈɑɪs·skeɪt/ *n* [C usually pl] a special shoe with a metal blade attached to the bottom that you wear to slide over ice

ice-skate /ˈɑɪs·skeɪt/ *v* [I] ○ *Vivian loves to ice-skate.*

ice skating /ˈɑɪsˌskeɪt̬·ɪŋ/ *n* [U]

ice storm *n* [C] a storm in which frozen rain falls and covers everything with ice ○ *Northern New York is still recovering from last week's ice storm.*

ice water *n* [U] water that has been made very cold, esp. by putting ice in it

icicle /ˈɑɪˌsɪk·əl/ *n* [C] a pointed stick of ice that hangs down from something

icing /ˈɑɪ·sɪŋ/, **frosting** *n* [U] the sweet, thick mixture of sugar, liquid, and flavoring that is used to cover cakes

IDIOM with icing

• **icing on the cake** an unexpected additional good thing ○ *He was delighted to have his story published – getting paid for it was just icing on the cake.*

icky /ˈɪk·i/ *adj a child's word* unpleasant or disgusting ○ *Rory thinks peas are icky.*

icon **REPRESENTATION** /ˈɑɪ·kɑn/ *n* [C] a famous person or thing that represents something of importance ○ *The US Capitol building is an American icon.*

iconic /ɑɪˈkɑn·ɪk/ *adj* ○ *Scenes of Parisians dancing in the streets remain iconic images from World War II.*

COMPUTER SYMBOL /ˈɑɪ·kɑn/ *n* [C] a picture on a computer screen that represents a program, DISK DRIVE, file, or instruction ○ *Click on the icon to open the program.*

HOLY PAINTING /ˈɑɪ·kɑn/ *n* [C] a painting of Jesus Christ or of a holy person ○ **USAGE:** Used esp. in some Christian religions.

icy /ˈɑɪ·si/ *adj* unfriendly and showing dislike ○ *an icy stare* ○ See also: ICY at ICE **FROZEN WATER**

I'd /ɑɪd/ *contraction of* I had or I would ○ *I'd* (= I had) *just got in the shower when the phone rang.* ○ *I'd* (= I would) *love to see you.*

ID /ɑɪˈdiː/ *n* [C/U] any official card or document with your name and other information on it that you use to prove who you are ○ [U] *You need two pieces of ID to cash a check.*

idea **SUGGESTION** /ɑɪˈdiː·ə/ *n* [C] a suggestion, thought, or plan ○ *"Let's go swimming." "Good idea!"* ○ *She's full of bright ideas.*

WORD CHOICES idea

An idea about how to do something is often described as a **plan**, **thought**, or **suggestion**.

*The **plan** is to rent a car when we get there.*

*Have you got any **suggestions** for improvements?*

*Have you had any **thoughts** on presents for your mother?*

A sudden, clever idea is sometimes described as a **brainstorm**.

*I wasn't sure what to do and then I had a **brainstorm** – I could ask Anna for help.*

The noun **theory** is sometimes used to describe a set of ideas intended to explain something.

*He was giving a lecture on Einstein's **theory** of relativity.*

KNOWLEDGE /aɪˈdiː·ə/ *n* [C/U] knowledge or understanding about something ○ [C] *Can you give me a rough idea of the cost* (= tell me approximately how much it will cost)? ○ [U] *You have no idea what I just said, do you?*

BELIEF /aɪˈdiː·ə/ *n* [C] a belief about something ○ *They have some unusual ideas about parenting.*

PURPOSE /aɪˈdiː·ə/ *n* [C usually sing] a purpose or reason for doing something ○ *The idea behind the law is to raise money for education.*

ideal **PERFECT** /aɪˈdiːl/ *adj* [not gradable] perfect, or the best possible ○ *In an ideal world, no one would go hungry.*

ideal /aɪˈdiːl/ *n* [U] ○ *She's my ideal of beauty* (= perfectly beautiful).

ideally /aɪˈdiː·li/ *adv* [not gradable] ○ *This job is ideally suited to her skills.*

idealize /aɪˈdiː·əˌlɑɪz/ *v* [T] to think of or represent someone or something as perfect ○ *Thoreau seemed to idealize the women close to him.*

PRINCIPLE /aɪˈdiːl/ *n* [C] a principle that sets a high standard for behavior ○ *I think most people share the same ideals and basic beliefs.*

idealism /aɪˈdiː·əˌlɪz·əm/ *n* [U] ○ *He wrote about America's lost idealism* (= belief in principles).

idealist /aɪˈdiːl·əst/ *n* [C] a person who values principles above practical behavior

idealistic /aɪˌdiː·əˈlɪs·tɪk/ *adj* ○ *She sacrificed idealistic dreams for conventional reality.*

identical Ⓐ /aɪˈdent·ɪ·kəl/ *adj* [not gradable] exactly the same, or very similar ○ *The test is identical to the one you took last year.*

identically Ⓐ /aɪˈdent·ɪ·kli/ *adv* [not gradable] ○ *The two sisters dressed identically.*

identical twin *n* [C usually pl] either of two people who came from the same egg, are the same sex, and look extremely similar ○ Compare FRATERNAL TWIN

identification Ⓐ /aɪˌdent·ə·fəˈkeɪ·ʃən/ *n* [U] **1** the ability to name or recognize someone or something ○ *Identification of the victims of the plane crash still is not complete.* **2** Identification is also proof of who someone or something is, usually in the form of documents: *We were asked to show identification at the airport check-in.*

identify Ⓐ /aɪˈdent·əˌfɑɪ/ *v* [T] to recognize or be able to name someone or something, or to prove who or what someone or something is ○ *Small babies can identify their mothers.* ○ *The police officer refused to identify himself.*

identifiable Ⓐ /aɪˌdent·əˈfɑɪ·ə·bəl/ *adj* ○ *In her bright yellow coat, she was easily identifiable* (= you could recognize her).

WORD FAMILY identify			
Nouns	identification identity	*Adjectives*	identifiable unidentified
Verbs	identify		

PHRASAL VERBS with identify

• **identify with** *someone* **FEEL SIMILAR** to feel you are like someone and understand the way that person thinks ○ *I don't really identify with those beautiful, thin models in magazines.*

• **identify** *someone* **with** *something* **CONNECT** to connect someone with something in your mind ○ *The singer has become closely identified with raising awareness about poverty in Africa.*

identity Ⓐ **PERSON** /aɪˈdent·əṭ·i/ *n* [C] who a person is, or the qualities of a person or group that make them different from others ○ [U] *As a journalist she refuses to reveal the identity of her source.*

MATHEMATICAL STATEMENT /aɪˈdent·əṭ·i/ *n* [C] ***algebra*** an EQUATION (= mathematical statement) that is true for every value given to a VARIABLE (= number that can change)

identity crisis *n* [C] a feeling that you are not sure of who you are or what you should do

ideology Ⓐ /ˌɑɪd·iːˈɑl·ə·dʒi, ˌɪd-/ *n* [C/U] ***politics & government*** a theory or set of beliefs, esp. one on which a political system, party, or organization is based

ideological Ⓐ /ˌɑɪd·iː·əˈlɑdʒ·ɪ·kəl, ˌɪd-/ *adj* ○ *They voted along ideological lines.*

ideologically Ⓐ /ˌɑɪd·iː·əˈlɑdʒ·ɪ·kli, ˌɪd-/ *adv*

idiom /ˈɪd·iː·əm/ *n* [C] **1** a group of words whose meaning considered as a unit is different from the meanings of each word considered separately ○ *Mastering the use of idioms can be hard for a learner.* ○ *"Shoot yourself in the foot" is an idiom that means to do something that hurts yourself.* **2** An idiom is also the particular style or manner of expression used by a person or group: [C usually sing] *Anger and shouting simply aren't a part of his idiom.*

idiomatic /ˌɪd·iː·əˈmæṭ·ɪk/ *adj* **1** *an idiomatic expression* **2** ***English*** Idiomatic also means natural in expression, correct without being too formal: *His English is fluent and idiomatic.*

idiosyncrasy /ˌɪd·iː·əˈsɪŋ·krə·si/ *n* [C] a strange or unusual habit, way of behaving, or feature ○ *One of her many idiosyncrasies is always smelling a book before opening it.*

idiot /ˈɪd·iː·ət/ *n* [C] a foolish person, esp. someone who has done something stupid ○ *I felt like an idiot.*

idiotic /ˌɪd·iːˈɑṭ·ɪk/ *adj* ○ *Whose idiotic idea was it to go camping?*

idle /ˈɑɪd·əl/ *adj* **1** not working, not active, or doing nothing ○ *idle factories* ○ *The machines are standing idle because there are no spare parts.* **2** Idle also means not useful or not based on fact: *idle speculation*

idle /ˈɑɪd·əl/ *v* [I] If an engine idles, it is operating but not doing any work: *Let the engine idle for a minute before you put the car in gear.*

idly /ˈɑɪd·li, -əl·i/ *adv* ○ *I will not stand idly by while my business is being destroyed.*

idleness /ˈɑɪd·əl·nəs/ *n* [U]

idol /ˈɑɪd·əl/ *n* [C] **1** a person who is loved, admired, or respected a lot ○ *Basketball players are his idols.* **2** An idol is also an object or picture that is worshipped as a god.

idolize /ˈɑɪd·əlˌɑɪz/ *v* [T] ○ *Her young fans idolize her* (= admire her greatly).

i.e. *abbreviation for* id est (= Latin for "that is") ○ *The hotel is closed during the off season, i.e., from October to March.* ○ **USAGE:** Used esp. in writing after a general statement to introduce specific information or examples.

if IN THAT SITUATION /ɪf/ *conjunction* **1** used to say that a particular thing can or will happen when, only when, or after something else happens or becomes true ○ *We'll have the party in the backyard if the weather's good.* ○ *If anyone calls for me, just say I'll be back at 4 o'clock.* ○ *Would you mind if I opened the window* (= May I open it)? **2** If is also used to talk about the amount or degree of something: *This time of year we get little, if any, rain* (= almost none). **3** If can mean when: *If I don't have a cup of coffee in the morning, I'm useless.* **4** If can also mean in case it is true that: *I'm sorry if I've offended you.* **5** When you say **if it weren't for** or (**if it hadn't been for**) something, you mean if it were not true or had not happened, the situation would be different: *If it weren't for your help, we would never have finished in time.*

if /ɪf/ *n* [C] ○ *The plan contains a lot of ifs* (= arrangements that need to be made).

iffy /ˈɪf·i/ *adj* ○ *Our plans are iffy* (= uncertain). ➤ Usage: **when or if?** at WHEN CONSIDERING THAT

if WHETHER /ɪf/ *conjunction* (used to introduce a clause, often when reporting what someone else said) whether ○ *Mrs. Kramer called to ask if her cake was ready.*

IDIOMS with if

- **if all else fails** if what was planned cannot happen ○ *We could go to the beach or to my sister's house, and if all else fails, we can always find something to do at home.*
- **if and when** if ○ *We'll deal with that problem if and when it arises.* ○ **USAGE:** Used to emphasize that something is not likely to happen at all.
- **if I were you** putting myself in your situation ○ *If I were you, I'd accept his apology.* ○ **USAGE:** Used to give someone advice.
- **if need be** if it is necessary ○ *If need be, we can take two cars.*
- **if only 1** the reason for this is ○ *I think you should get a job, if only to have something to do.* **2 If only** also means that doing something simple would have made it possible to avoid something unpleasant: *If only she had listened to me, she wouldn't be in this mess.* **3 If only** is also used to mean "I wish": *If only I had more money.*
- **if the worst comes to the worst, if worse comes to worst** if a bad situation becomes even worse ○ *If the worst comes to the worst, we can ask Dad to send us some more money.*
- **if you will** this is one way of saying this ○ *I did very well in school, with a "genius IQ," if you will.* ○ Compare SO TO SPEAK at SO IDIOMS ○ **USAGE:** Used to suggest that some people may not think this is a good way to say something.

igloo /ˈɪɡ·luː/ *n* [C] *pl* **igloos** a circular house made of blocks of hard snow, esp. one built by the Inuit people of northern North America

igneous /ˈɪɡ·niː·əs/ *adj* [not gradable] ***earth science*** describes rocks made from MAGMA (= liquid rock) that has cooled and become solid

ignite /ɪɡˈnɑɪt/ *v* [I/T] to start burning, or to cause something to start burning ○ [T] *The forest fire began when a spark from a campfire ignited some dry grass nearby.* ○ [T] (*fig.*) *to ignite a controversy*

ignition /ɪɡˈnɪʃ·ən/ *n* [C/U] **1** the act of starting to burn **2** An engine's ignition is the electrical system that starts the engine.

ignominious /ˌɪɡ·nəˈmɪn·iː·əs/ *adj* (esp. of events or behavior) embarrassing ○ *an ignominious defeat*

ignorant Ⓐ /ˈɪɡ·nə·rənt/ *adj* having no knowledge or awareness of something or of things in general ○ *We were very young, ignorant, unskilled men.*

ignorance Ⓐ /ˈɪɡ·nə·rəns/ *n* [U] ○ *You have to assume that incoming students have an almost total ignorance of the rules of grammar.*

ignore Ⓐ /ɪɡˈnɔːr, -ˈnoʊr/ *v* [T] to give no attention to something or someone ○ *They ignored our warnings.* ○ *The mayor ignored the hecklers and went on with her speech.*

WORD CHOICES ignore

Disregard can sometimes be used instead of "ignore" when someone ignores suggestions, advice, rules, etc.

*He **disregarded** the advice of his doctor and went back to work.*

The phrase **turn a blind eye** to something can be used when someone ignores something bad and pretends it is not happening.

*Until now, the mayor has **turned a blind eye** to the city's homelessness problem.*

If you ignore or avoid something regularly, you could use the verb **shun**.

*As assistant to the president, he **shunned** the spotlight, but worked very hard behind the scenes.*

The phrase **give someone the cold shoulder** can also be used when someone ignores a person in an unfriendly way.

*I said hello to him and he just **gave me the cold shoulder**.*

iguana /ɪˈɡwɑn·ə/ *n* [C] a large, gray-and-green LIZARD (= animal)

ill NOT HEALTHY /ɪl/ *adj comparative* **worse**, *superlative* **worst** having a disease or feeling as if your body or mind has been harmed by not being able to work as it should ○ *I felt ill, so I went home.*

illness /ˈɪl·nəs/ *n* [C/U] a condition in which the body or mind is harmed because an organ or part is unable to work as it usually does; a disease or sickness ○ [U] *mental illness* ○ [C] *He died at home after a long illness.* ➤ Usage: **sick and ill** at SICK ILL

WORD CHOICES ill

A common alternative is the adjective **sick**.

*He was off work **sick** last week.* ➤

A more formal adjective meaning "ill" is **unwell**.

*I've felt a little **unwell** all week.*

If you want to say that someone feels slightly ill, in informal situations you can also use the expressions **be/feel under the weather** and **be/feel below par**.

*I don't think I'll be coming to the party – I'm **feeling a bit under the weather**.*

BADLY /ɪl/ *adv* [not gradable] badly, with great difficulty, or certainly not ○ *They could ill afford to lose all that money.*
ill /ɪl/ *adj* [not gradable] ○ *Did you experience any ill effects from the treatment?*

PROBLEM /ɪl/ *n* [C usually plural] a problem or difficulty ○ *We thought we could solve all the community's ills and we have failed.*

IDIOM with ill
• **ill at ease** feeling anxious and not relaxed ○ *He looked ill at ease in the room full of reporters.*

I'll /ɑɪl/ *contraction of* I will or I shall ○ *I'll want to see your tax records.* ○ *I'll be on vacation next week.*

ill-advised *adj* unwise or not carefully considered

illegal Ⓐ /ɪˈliː·ɡəl/ *adj* **1** against the law ○ *Fireworks are illegal in many places.* **2** An **illegal immigrant/alien** is a person who has entered a country without government permission.
illegality Ⓐ /ˌɪl·ɪˈɡæl·ət̬·i/ *n* [U] the quality of being against the law
illegally Ⓐ /ɪˈliː·ɡə·li/ *adv* ○ *illegally obtained passports*

illegible /ɪˈledʒ·ə·bəl/ *adj* (of writing or print) impossible or difficult to read because it is unclear ○ *illegible handwriting*

illegitimate /ˌɪl·ɪˈdʒɪt̬·ə·mət/ *adj* [not gradable] **1** born of parents not married to each other ○ *an illegitimate child* **2** Illegitimate can also mean not legal: *an illegitimate ruler*

ill-equipped *adj* lacking the ability or equipment necessary to do something well ○ *Young parents are sometimes ill-equipped to cope with a child.*

ill-fated *adj* unlucky or certain to experience failure that cannot be avoided

illicit /ɪˈlɪs·ət/ *adj* illegal or socially disapproved of ○ *illicit trade* ○ *illicit activities*

illiterate /ɪˈlɪt̬·ə·rət/ *adj* not knowing how to read and write
illiteracy /ɪˈlɪt̬·ə·rə·si/ *n* [U]

illness /ˈɪl·nəs/ *n* ○ See at ILL NOT HEALTHY

illogical Ⓐ /ɪˈlɑdʒ·ɪ·kəl/ *adj* not reasonable, wise, or practical ○ *It was an illogical decision, but I was in love.*
illogically Ⓐ /ɪˈlɑdʒ·ɪ·kli/ *adv*

illuminate /ɪˈluː·məˌneɪt/ *v* [T] **1** to put light in or on something ○ *The buildings were illuminated at night.* **2** If you illuminate a subject, you explain it: *This article illuminates the basic principles of economics.*
illuminating /ɪˈluː·məˌneɪt̬·ɪŋ/ *adj* ○ *She tells the story in illuminating detail* (= explaining it completely).
illumination /ɪˌluː·məˈneɪ·ʃən/ *n* [U] ○ *The only illumination* (= light) *was from a skylight in the roof.*

illusion /ɪˈluː·ʒən/ *n* [C] an idea or belief that is not true, or something that is not what it seems to be ○ *We have no illusions about how difficult the job will be.* ○ [+ *that* clause] *I was under the illusion that trains ran frequently on weekends* (= I wrongly believed this). ○ *They managed to create the illusion of space in a tiny apartment.*
illusory /ɪˈluː·sə·ri, -zə·ri/ *adj* ○ *Her fears were illusory.*

illustrate Ⓐ /ˈɪl·əˌstreɪt/ *v* [T] **1** to add pictures to something, such as a book ○ *She writes children's books and also illustrates them.* **2** To illustrate is also to show the meaning or truth of something more clearly by giving examples: *To illustrate her point, she told a story about how her family felt when they moved here.*
illustration Ⓐ /ˌɪl·əˈstreɪ·ʃən/ *n* [C/U] **1** a picture ○ [C] *Look at the illustration on page 37.* **2** An illustration is also an example that makes something easier to understand, or the giving of such examples: [C] *That's a perfect illustration of the problem.*
illustrative Ⓐ /ˈɪl·əˌstreɪ·t̬ɪv/ *adj* helping to explain or prove something ○ *Falling house prices are illustrative of the crisis facing the construction industry.*
illustrator /ˈɪl·əˌstreɪt̬·ər/ *n* [C] a person who draws pictures for books, magazines, etc.

illustrious /ɪˈlʌs·triː·əs/ *adj fml* famous because of its excellence ○ *an illustrious career*

IM /ɑɪˈem/, **instant message** *v* [T] **IM's**, *pres. part.* **IM'ing**, *past simp.* **IM'd** to communicate with someone over the INTERNET using a program that sends and receives messages without delay ○ *I finish my homework, take out the garbage, and then IM my friends.*

I'm /ɑɪm/ *contraction of* I am ○ *I'm sorry I'm late.*

image Ⓐ **IDEA** /ˈɪm·ɪdʒ/ *n* [C] **1** an idea, esp. a mental picture, of what something or someone is like ○ *I had an image of Texas in my head that was totally different from how it really is.* **2** Someone's image is the idea that other people have of that person, esp. an idea created by advertising and by newspaper and television stories: *He's trying to project a more presidential image.* **3** An image is also a description of something or someone: *The book presented an image of life on a farm in the 19th century.*
imagery Ⓐ /ˈɪm·ɪdʒ·ri/ *n* [U] the use of pictures or words to create images, esp. to create an impression or mood ○ *The film contains a lot of religious imagery.*

PICTURE /ˈɪm·ɪdʒ/ *n* [C] a picture, esp. one seen in a mirror or through a camera ○ *moving images on a TV screen*

imaginary number *n* [C] ***algebra*** a number that is the SQUARE ROOT (= number you multiply by itself to get a particular number) of a NEGATIVE number (= number less than zero), especially the square root of -1

imagine /ɪ'mædʒ·ən/ *v* [T] **1** to form or have a mental picture or idea of something or someone ○ *Imagine Tom as a child – that's what John looks like.* ○ [+ *that* clause] *I imagine* (= expect) *(that) they charge extra for dessert.* **2** If you imagine something that is not real or true, you think that it exists, has happened, or is true: *"Did you hear a noise?" "No, you're imagining things."*
imaginable /ɪ'mædʒ·ə·nə·bəl/ *adj* possible, or able to be imagined ○ *They sell every flavor of ice cream imaginable.*
imaginary /ɪ'mædʒ·ə,ner·i/ *adj* existing only in the mind; not real ○ *All her worries were imaginary.*
imagination /ɪ,mædʒ·ə'neɪ·ʃən/ *n* [U] ○ *Rafael has a very active imagination* (= has many ideas).
imaginative /ɪ'mædʒ·ə·nəţ·ɪv/ *adj* new, original, and showing a quick intelligence ○ *an imaginative little girl*
imaginatively /ɪ'mædʒ·ə·nəţ·ɪv·li/ *adv*

WORD FAMILY imagine

Nouns	imagination	*Verbs*	imagine
Adjectives	imaginable	*Adverbs*	unimaginably
	unimaginable		imaginatively
	imaginary		
	imaginative		

imbalance /ɪm'bæl·əns/ *n* [C] a condition in which two or more things are not equally or fairly divided or spread ○ *a trade imbalance*

imbecile /'ɪm·bə·səl, -,sɪl/ *n* [C] a stupid person

imbibe /ɪm'bɑɪb/ *v* [T] *fml* to drink ○ **USAGE:** usually said of drinking alcohol

imbue *something/someone* **with** *something* /ɪm'bju: ,wɪð, -wɪθ/ *phrasal verb* to fill something or someone with a quality or feeling ○ *Her poetry was imbued with a love of the outdoors.*

imitate /'ɪm·ə,teɪt/ *v* [T] to copy someone's speech or behavior, or to copy something as a model ○ *My four-year-old daughter is always trying to imitate her older sister.* ○ *He imitated her accent perfectly.*
imitation /,ɪm·ə'teɪ·ʃən/ *n* [C/U] something copied, or the act of copying ○ *Freya does a pretty good imitation of her science teacher.*
imitation /,ɪm·ə'teɪ·ʃən/ *adj* [not gradable] not real but produced as a copy of something real ○ [C] *imitation leather*

immaculate /ɪ'mæk·jə·lət/ *adj* perfectly clean or in perfect condition ○ *My aunt's kitchen was always immaculate.*
immaculately /ɪ'mæk·jə·lət·li/ *adv* ○ *She was immaculately dressed.*

immaterial /,ɪm·ə'tɪr·i:·əl/ *adj* [not gradable] not important; not likely to make a difference ○ *It's immaterial whether the trial is in San Diego or Los Angeles or anyplace else.*

immature Ⓐ /,ɪm·ə'tʃʊr, -'tʊr/ *adj* not completely developed physically, mentally, or emotionally, or lacking the expected type of responsible behavior for your age ○ *Some of the boys in my class are so immature – they're always doing silly things.*
immaturity Ⓐ /,ɪm·ə'tʃʊr·əţ·i, -'tʊr-/ *n* [U] ○ *physical/emotional immaturity*

immediate NO DELAY /ɪ'mi:d·i:·ət/ *adj* happening or done without delay or very soon after something else ○ *She made an immediate impact when she arrived to coach the team.* ○ *Emotional outbursts followed in the immediate aftermath of Stewart's death.*
immediately /ɪ'mi:d·i:·ət·li/ *adv* ○ *The plane began to turn to the left almost immediately after takeoff.*
immediacy /ɪ'mi:d·i:·ə·si/ *n* [U] the quality or feeling of being directly involved ○ *Recording before a live audience captures the immediacy of the performance.*

NEAREST /ɪ'mi:d·i:·ət/ *adj* **1** nearest in space or relationship ○ *There are three schools in the immediate area.* **2** Your **immediate family** includes your closest family members, such as your parents, children, husband or wife, and brothers and sisters.
immediately /ɪ'mi:d·i:·ət·li/ *adv* ○ *Turn left, and the bathroom is immediately on the right.*

immense /ɪ'mens/ *adj* extremely large; great in size or degree ○ *He inherited an immense fortune.* ○ *Did you see that guy? He was immense!*
immensely /ɪ'men·sli/ *adv* [not gradable] ○ *Country music is immensely popular.*
immensity /ɪ'men·səţ·i/ *n* [U] ○ *He realized the immensity of the risk he was taking.*

immerse /ɪ'mɜrs/ *v* [T] **1** to involve someone completely in an activity ○ *She immersed herself wholly in her work.* **2** To immerse something is also to put it completely under the surface of a liquid: *Immerse the egg in boiling water.*
immersion /ɪ'mɜr·ʒən, -ʃən/ *n* [U] ○ *The course offers total immersion in English.*

immigrant Ⓐ /'ɪm·ə·grənt/ *n* [C] ***social studies*** a person who has come into a foreign country in order to live there ○ *My grandparents arrived here as immigrants from Russia in 1910.* ○ Compare EMIGRANT at EMIGRATE
immigrate Ⓐ /'ɪm·ə,greɪt/ *v* [I] ○ *His family immigrated to the United States in 1928.* ○ Compare EMIGRATE
immigration Ⓐ /,ɪm·ə'greɪ·ʃən/ *n* [U] ***social studies*** the process by which people come in to a foreign country to live there, or the number of people coming in ○ *Immigration increased by 25% last year.*

imminent /'ɪm·ə·nənt/ *adj* (esp. of something unpleasant) likely to happen very soon ○ *A rain storm was imminent.*

immobile /ɪ'moʊ·bəl/ *adj* [not gradable] not moving, or not able to move or be moved ○ *He is in a cast to keep his spine immobile.*
immobilize /ɪ'moʊ·bə,lɑɪz/ *v* [T] ○ *The brace immobilized my elbow while the injury healed.*

immoral /ɪ'mɔ:r·əl, ɪ'mɑr-/ *adj* not following accepted standards of morally right behavior or thought ○ *Discrimination on the basis of race is immoral.*

immorality /ˌɪm·ɔːˈræl·əṭ·i/ *n* [U] ○ *the immorality of lying*

immortal /ɪˈmɔːrṭ·əl/ *adj* [not gradable] living or lasting forever, or so famous as to be remembered for a very long time ○ *Teenagers think they are immortal.* ○ *Churchill made his immortal speech about the Iron Curtain in Missouri.*

immortality /ˌɪm·ɔːrˈtæl·əṭ·i/ *n* [U] ○ *A place in history is the only kind of immortality open to us.*

immortalize /ɪˈmɔːrṭ·əlˌɑɪz/ *v* [T] to cause someone to be remembered for a very long time ○ *He was immortalized in song.*

immovable /ɪˈmuː·və·bəl/ *adj* [not gradable] fixed in place and impossible to move ○ *Without the help of heavy equipment, that large rock is immovable.*

immune /ɪˈmjuːn/ *adj* **1** ***biology*** protected against a particular disease or illness by particular substances in the blood ○ *The vaccine would make infants immune to bacteria that can cause middle ear infections.* **2** Immune also means protected from or unable to be influenced by something, esp. something bad: *She says her mother is immune to criticism from strangers.*

immunity /ɪˈmjuː·nəṭ·i/ *n* [U] **1** ***biology*** protection against a particular disease or illness by particular substances in the blood **2** *law* Immunity is also the condition of being protected from the law: *Rowe was promised immunity from prosecution if he cooperated.*

immunize /ˈɪm·jəˌnɑɪz/ *v* [T] to protect someone against a particular disease or infection by introducing special substances into the body, esp. by INJECTION ○ *All children should be immunized against childhood illnesses.*

immunization /ˌɪm·jə·nəˈzeɪ·ʃən/ *n* [U] ○ *immunization against polio*

immune system *n* [C] ***biology*** the body's cells and organs that fight illness and disease

immutable /ɪˈmjuːṭ·ə·bəl/ *adj* [not gradable] *fml* not changing or unable to be changed ○ *The laws of physics are assumed to be immutable.*

impact **A** **FORCE** /ˈɪm·pækt/ *n* [U] the force with which one thing hits another or with which two things hit each other ○ *The impact of the crash destroyed the car.* ○ *The bullet explodes* **on impact** (= at the moment when it hits something).

EFFECT /ˈɪm·pækt/ *n* [U] the strong effect or influence that something has on a situation or person ○ *These charges will have a damaging impact on the army's reputation.* ○ *The environmental impact of this project will be enormous.*

impact /ɪmˈpækt/ *v* [I/T] ○ [I/T] *A big decline in exports will impact (on) the country's economy.*

impair /ɪmˈper, -ˈpær/ *v* [T] to damage or weaken something so that it is less effective ○ *Lack of sleep impaired her ability to think clearly.*

impaired /ɪmˈperd, -ˈpærd/ *adj* ○ *She attended a school for the visually impaired* (= people who cannot see well). ○ *He was given a ticket for driving while impaired by alcohol.*

impairment /ɪmˈper·mənt, -ˈpær-/ *n* [C/U] ○ [C] *The law bans discrimination against anyone with a mental or physical impairment.*

impale /ɪmˈpeɪl/ *v* [T] to push a sharp pointed object through something, esp. an animal's or person's body ○ *Walruses sometimes use their tusks to impale seals for food.*

impart /ɪmˈpɑrt/ *v* [T] *fml* to give a feeling or quality to something, or to make information known to someone ○ *If the movie has any lesson to impart, it's that parents shouldn't aim for perfection.*

impartial /ɪmˈpɑr·ʃəl/ *adj* able to judge or consider something fairly without allowing your own interest to influence you ○ *The jury has to give an impartial verdict after listening to all of the evidence.*

impartially /ɪmˈpɑr·ʃə·li/ *adv* ○ *Many people do not believe that complaints against the police are impartially handled.*

impartiality /ɪmˌpɑr·ʃiːˈæl·əṭ·i/ *n* [U] ○ *scientific impartiality*

impassable /ɪmˈpæs·ə·bəl/ *adj* [not gradable] (esp. of a road) impossible to travel on or over ○ *Mudslides made the coast highway impassable.*

impasse /ˈɪm·pæs/ *n* [C usually sing] a point in a process at which further progress is blocked, esp. by disagreement ○ *We have reached an impasse in the negotiations—neither side will budge.*

impassioned /ɪmˈpæʃ·ənd/ *adj* expressed with strong feeling ○ *She went on television to make an impassioned plea for the release of her child.*

impassive /ɪmˈpæs·ɪv/ *adj* not showing or feeling any emotion ○ *Nick kept his face impassive but his mind was racing.*

impassively /ɪmˈpæs·ɪv·li/ *adv* ○ *Even as the guilty verdict was read, he stared impassively ahead.*

impatient /ɪmˈpeɪ·ʃənt/ *adj* **1** not willing to wait for something to happen and becoming annoyed at delays ○ *Don't be impatient, you'll get your turn.* ○ *She grew impatient with the others.* **2** Impatient can also mean eager for something to happen: [+ *to* infinitive] *He was impatient to become the new boss.*

impatience /ɪmˈpeɪ·ʃəns/ *n* [U] ○ *The horse snorted with impatience.*

impatiently /ɪmˈpeɪ·ʃənt·li/ *adv* ○ *Unable to sleep, he waited impatiently for the dawn to arrive.*

impeach /ɪmˈpiːtʃ/ *v* [T] *law* ***politics & government*** to formally accuse a public official of a serious crime in connection with their job

impeachment /ɪmˈpiːtʃ·mənt/ *n* [U] ○ *The federal judge faces impeachment.*

impeccable /ɪmˈpek·ə·bəl/ *adj* [not gradable] without mistakes or faults; perfect ○ *impeccable manners/taste*

impeccably /ɪmˈpek·ə·bli/ *adv* [not gradable] ○ *She was always impeccably dressed.*

impede /ɪmˈpiːd/ *v* [T] to slow something down or prevent an activity from making progress at its previous rate ○ *Shortages of medicine were impeding the effort to control diseases.*

impediment /ɪmˈped·ə·mənt/ *n* [C] ○ *The lack of funds is a major impediment to research.*

impel /ɪmˈpel/ *v* [T] **-ll-** *fml* to force someone to do something ○ [+ *to* infinitive] *When I see them eating, I feel impelled to eat, too.*

impending /ɪmˈpen·dɪŋ/ *adj* [not gradable] (esp. of something unpleasant) about to happen soon ○ *The impending crisis over trade made everyone nervous.*

impenetrable /ɪmˈpen·ə·trə·bəl/ *adj* **1** impossible to enter or go through ○ *an impenetrable jungle* **2** If language is described as impenetrable, it is impossible to understand: *Too many scholarly books are written in an impenetrable jargon.*

imperative URGENT /ɪmˈper·ət̬·ɪv/ *adj* extremely important or urgent ○ [+ *that* clause] *It is imperative that these medical supplies be delivered immediately.*
imperative /ɪmˈper·ət̬·ɪv/ *n* [C] ○ *The government has a moral imperative to provide equal access to high-quality education for all children.*

GRAMMAR /ɪmˈper·ət̬·ɪv/ *n* [U] ***grammar*** the MOOD (= form) of a verb used for giving orders ○ *In the phrase "Leave him alone," the verb "leave" is in the imperative.*

imperative sentence *n* [C] ***grammar*** a sentence that gives a command or gives a request to do something ○ *"Sit down" and "Hand me that bowl" are imperative sentences.*

imperceptible /ˌɪm·pərˈsep·tə·bəl/ *adj* [not gradable] (of an action or change) so slight that it cannot be noticed ○ *When they brought her in to the emergency room, her breathing was imperceptible.*
imperceptibly /ˌɪm·pərˈsep·tə·bli/ *adv* ○ *Imperceptibly, the day grew darker.*

imperfect /ɪmˈpɜr·fɪkt/ *adj* not perfect or not complete ○ *Our rule of law is still imperfect, but it's better than having no laws at all.*
imperfection /ˌɪm·pərˈfek·ʃən/ *n* [C/U] ○ [C] *Investigators suspect the engine broke because of a tiny imperfection in one of the parts.*

imperial /ɪmˈpɪr·iː·əl/ *adj* [not gradable] *usually disapproving* relating to a government or country that controls or rules other countries ○ *imperial expansion of American power* ○ *the imperial tradition of Britain*
imperialism /ɪmˈpɪr·iː·əˌlɪz·əm/ *n* [U] ***world history*** the attempt of one country to control another country, esp. by political and economic methods ○ *France was accused of economic imperialism because of its trade policies.*
imperialist /ɪmˈpɪr·iː·ə·ləst/ *n* [C] *usually disapproving* ○ *Roosevelt believed that he was a benevolent imperialist.*
imperialistic /ɪmˌpɪr·iː·əˈlɪs·tɪk/, **imperialist** /ɪmˈpɪr·iː·ə·ləst/ *adj usually disapproving* ○ *They denounced the war as an imperialistic exploitation of oppressed peoples.*

imperil /ɪmˈper·əl/ *v* [T] *fml* to put something or someone in danger ○ *Withdrawing the medical team would imperil the effort to control the spread of malaria.*

imperious /ɪmˈpɪr·iː·əs/ *adj fml* with an attitude of authority and expecting obedience ○ *She was a very imperious, arrogant woman.*

impermeable /ɪmˈpɜr·miː·ə·bəl/ *adj* ***science*** describes a substance that does not allow liquids or gases to go through it

impersonal /ɪmˈpɜr·sən·əl/ *adj* lacking or not showing any interest or feeling ○ *The congressman gave a short, impersonal speech and left soon afterward.*

impersonate /ɪmˈpɜr·səˌneɪt/ *v* [T] to intentionally copy another person's speech, appearance, or behavior ○ *to impersonate a movie star* ○ *He was charged with impersonating a police officer.*

impertinent /ɪmˈpɜrt·ən·ənt/ *adj* not showing enough respect; rude ○ *Don't be impertinent – you're in no position to tell your boss what to do.*

imperturbable /ˌɪm·pərˈtɜr·bə·bəl/ *adj fml* staying calm and controlled despite problems or difficulties ○ *He was imperturbable in a crisis.*

impervious /ɪmˈpɜr·viː·əs/ *adj* not able to be influenced, hurt, or damaged ○ *He seems to be impervious to pain.* ○ *Granite is almost impervious to acid-rain damage.*

impetuous /ɪmˈpetʃ·ə·wəs/ *adj* acting or done suddenly without much thought ○ *Then, impetuous as I was, I bought a new car before I even got a job.*

impetus /ˈɪm·pət̬·əs/ *n* [U] a force that encourages a particular action or makes it more energetic or effective ○ *Often the impetus for change in education has had to come from outside the school establishment.*

impinge on/upon *something* /ɪmˈpɪndʒ/ *phrasal verb* to have an effect on something, often by limiting it in some way ○ *The Supreme Court will decide if the new communications bill impinges on the Constitutional right to free speech.*

impish /ˈɪm·pɪʃ/ *adj* suggesting behavior that is playful but likely to upset other people ○ *He had an impish grin on his face.*

implacable /ɪmˈplæk·ə·bəl/ *adj* unable to be changed, satisfied, or stopped ○ *an implacable enemy*

implant /ɪmˈplænt/ *v* [T] to put an organ, group of cells, or device into the body in a medical operation ○ *He had a new heart valve implanted.* ○ (*fig.*) *Women's basketball must find a way to implant itself into* (= become a part of) *the sporting landscape.*
implant /ˈɪm·plænt/ *n* [C] ○ *dental implants*

implausible /ɪmˈplɔː·zə·bəl/ *adj* difficult to believe; not probable ○ *The plot of the movie, involving a 23-year-old brain surgeon, is implausible to begin with.*

implement Ⓐ USE /ˈɪm·plə,ment/ *v* [T] to put a plan or system into operation ○ *Congress refused to pass the bill that would implement tax reforms.*

implementation Ⓐ /ˌɪm·plə·mənˈteɪ·ʃən, -ˌmenˈteɪ-/ *n* [U] ○ *They've involved their workers in the development and implementation of the new program.*

TOOL /ˈɪm·plə·mənt/ *n* [C] a tool or other piece of equipment for doing work ○ *farm implements*

implicate Ⓐ /ˈɪm·plə,keɪt/ *v* [T] to show that someone is involved in a crime or partly responsible for something bad that has happened ○ *A lot of people were implicated in the scandal.*

implication Ⓐ /ˌɪm·pləˈkeɪ·ʃən/ *n* [U] ○ *Implication of his co-workers in the fraud was crucial to the defendant's case.*

implication Ⓐ /ˌɪm·pləˈkeɪ·ʃən/ *n* [C/U] a suggestion of something that is made without saying it directly ○ [U] *The implication was that the workers and management had already reached an agreement.* ○ [C] *What are the implications* (= possible effects) *of the new regulations?*

implicit Ⓐ SUGGESTED /ɪmˈplɪs·ət/ *adj* suggested but not communicated directly ○ *We interpreted his silence as implicit agreement.* ○ *Some reporters thought there was an implicit threat in the president's speech.* ○ Compare EXPLICIT

implicitly Ⓐ /ɪmˈplɪs·ət·li/ *adv* ○ *The report implicitly questioned his competence.*

COMPLETE /ɪmˈplɪs·ət/ *adj* [not gradable] (esp. of trust and belief) complete and without any doubts ○ *implicit faith*

implicitly /ɪmˈplɪs·ət·li/ *adv* ○ *He feels secure only with associates who obey him implicitly.*

implore /ɪmˈplɔːr, -ˈploʊr/ *v* [T] to ask someone in a determined, sincere, and sometimes emotional way to do or not to do something, or to ask for something in this way ○ *She implored him not to leave her.*

imply Ⓐ /ɪmˈplɑɪ/ *v* [T] to suggest something without saying it directly, or to involve something as a necessary part or condition ○ [+ (*that*) clause] *He implied (that) the error was mine.* ○ *Democracy implies free elections.*

impolite /ˌɪm·pəˈlɑɪt/ *adj* rude; not POLITE

import BRING IN /ɪmˈpɔːrt, -ˈpoʊrt/ *v* [T] **1** to bring in products, goods, etc. from another country for sale or use ○ *We import a large number of cars from Japan.* **2** To import information into a program or computer is to copy it from another program or form of storage. ○ Compare EXPORT

import /ˈɪm·pɔːrt, -poʊrt/ *n* [C] something bought and taken into a country from another ○ *Imports of foreign cars are at an all-time high.*

importation /ˌɪm·pɔːrˈteɪ·ʃᵊn, -poʊr-/ *n* [U] ○ *He opposed efforts to allow the importation of prescription drugs from other countries.*

IMPORTANCE /ˈɪm·pɔːrt, -poʊrt/ *n* [U] *fml* the importance given to something ○ *It is still too early to judge the political import of his speech.*

important /ɪmˈpɔːrt·ᵊnt/ *adj* **1** of great value, meaning, or effect ○ *an important discovery* ○ [+ *that* clause] *It's important that you tell the doctor all your symptoms.* **2** Important also means having great influence: *an important modern artist*

importantly /ɪmˈpɔːrt·ᵊnt·li/ *adv* ○ *She has a pleasant personality, but more importantly, she is well qualified for the job.*

importance /ɪmˈpɔːrt·ᵊns/ *n* [U] ○ *He stressed the importance of fruits and vegetables in the diet.*

WORD FAMILY important			
Nouns	importance	*Adjectives*	important
Adverbs	importantly		unimportant

WORD CHOICES important

Adjectives such as **big**, **major**, and **significant** are often used to mean "important."

*This is a **big** game tonight – if we lose, we won't be in the playoffs.*

*This is a **major** decision so we'd better get it right.*

*Did he make any **significant** changes to my suggestions?*

Someone or something **of note** is important or famous.

*Did she say anything **of note** at the meeting?*

A person who is important and famous is sometimes described as **eminent**, **prominent**, or **great**.

*Her father was an **eminent** historian.*

impose Ⓐ MAKE RULES /ɪmˈpoʊz/ *v* [T] to establish something as a rule to be obeyed, or to force the acceptance of something ○ *Settlers often imposed their culture on the peoples of the countries they conquered.*

INCONVENIENCE /ɪmˈpoʊz/ *v* [I] to cause inconvenience to someone or to try to spend time with them when do not want you to ○ *She's always imposing on people for favors.* ○ *I hope I'm not imposing by staying another night.*

imposing Ⓐ /ɪmˈpoʊ·zɪŋ/ *adj* noticeable because of large size, appearance, or importance ○ *an imposing mansion*

imposition Ⓐ INCONVENIENCE /ˌɪm·pəˈzɪʃ·ən/ *n* [C] something done that causes inconvenience to another person ○ *I hope the drive to the airport isn't an imposition.*

MAKING RULES /ˌɪm·pəˈzɪʃ·ən/ *n* [U] the act of establishing a rule or law to be obeyed ○ *the imposition of new taxes*

impossible NOT POSSIBLE /ɪmˈpɑs·ə·bəl/ *adj* [not gradable] unable to exist, happen, or be achieved; not possible ○ *an impossible goal* ○ [+ *to* infinitive] *It's almost impossible to get them to agree on anything.*

impossibility /ɪm,pɑs·əˈbɪl·əţ·i/ *n* [C] something that is not possible ○ *What you're asking for is an impossibility.*

VERY DIFFICULT /ɪmˈpɑs·ə·bəl/ *adj* very difficult to deal with ○ *Traffic at rush hour is just impossible.*

impossibly /ɪmˈpɑs·ə·bli/ *adv* [not gradable] ○ *She had to work impossibly long hours.*

impostor, **imposter** /ɪmˈpɑs·tər/ *n* [C] a person who pretends to be someone else in order to deceive others

impotent /ˈɪm·pət̬·ənt/ *adj* lacking the power or ability to change or improve a situation
impotence /ˈɪm·pət̬·əns/ *n* [U]

impound /ɪmˈpɑʊnd/ *v* [T] to take possession of something by legal right ○ *The police arrested the suspect and impounded his car.*

impoverished /ɪmˈpɑv·ə·rɪʃt/ *adj* extremely poor ○ *an impoverished family*

impractical /ɪmˈpræk·tɪ·kəl/ *adj* not effective or reasonable, or (of people) not able to provide effective or simple solutions ○ *an impractical plan* ○ *It's impractical to buy things just because they're on sale.*

imprecise Ⓐ /ˌɪm·prɪˈsɑɪs/ *adj* not accurate or exact ○ *As all the data have not yet been collected, the figures are still imprecise.*

impregnable /ɪmˈpreg·nə·bəl/ *adj* so strongly made that it cannot be broken into or taken by force ○ *an impregnable fortress*

impregnate MAKE PREGNANT /ɪmˈpreg ˌneɪt/ *v* [T] to make a woman or female animal pregnant
ABSORB /ɪmˈpreg ˌneɪt/ *v* [T] to cause a substance to absorb a liquid substance ○ *This cloth is impregnated with a cleaning solution.*

impress /ɪmˈpres/ *v* [T] **1** to cause someone to feel admiration or respect ○ *She impressed us with her sincerity.* **2** If you impress something on someone, you cause them to understand its importance or value: *He always impressed on us the need to do our best.*
impressive /ɪmˈpres·ɪv/ *adj* ○ *an impressive performance*
impressively /ɪmˈpres·ɪv·li/ *adv* ○ *an impressively large collection of medals*

WORD FAMILY impress

Nouns	impression	*Verbs*	impress
Adjectives	impressionable impressive	*Adverbs*	impressively

impression OPINION /ɪmˈpreʃ·ən/ *n* [C] an idea or opinion of what someone or something is like ○ *It makes a bad impression if you're late for an interview.* ○ [+ *that* clause] *I get the impression that she's rather shy.* ○ [+ *that* clause] *I was under the impression that you didn't like your job* (= I was wrong to think that you did not like your job).
EFFECT /ɪmˈpreʃ·ən/ *n* [U] effect or influence on the way someone feels or thinks ○ *All our warnings made little impression on him.*
impressionable /ɪmˈpreʃ·ə·nə·bəl/ *adj* easily influenced ○ *He's at an impressionable age.*
MARK /ɪmˈpreʃ·ən/ *n* [C] a mark made on the surface of something by pressing an object into it ○ *The bookcase had left an impression in the rug.*

imprint /ɪmˈprɪnt/ *v* [T] to mark a surface by pressing something into it, or to fix something firmly in the memory ○ *The terrible scene has been deeply imprinted on my mind.*
imprint /ˈɪm·prɪnt/ *n* [C] ○ *The children enjoyed leaving the imprints of their feet in the wet sand.*

imprison /ɪmˈprɪz·ən/ *v* [T] to put someone in prison or in a situation that is like prison ○ *If found guilty, he could be imprisoned for ten years.* ○ *After weeks of snow, she felt imprisoned in her own home.*
imprisonment /ɪmˈprɪz·ən·mənt/ *n* [U]

improbable /ɪmˈprɑb·ə·bəl/ *adj* not likely to be true or to happen; not PROBABLE ○ *an improbable excuse*
improbability /ɪmˌprɑb·əˈbɪl·ət̬·i/ *n* [C/U]
improbably /ɪmˈprɑb·ə·bli/ *adv*

impromptu /ɪmˈprɑm·tuː/ *adj* [not gradable] done or said without earlier planning or preparation ○ *an impromptu speech*

improper DISHONEST /ɪmˈprɑp·ər/ *adj* being against a law or a rule; dishonest or illegal ○ *The treasurer denied accepting any improper payments.*
WRONG /ɪmˈprɑp·ər/ *adj* not suitable or correct for a particular use or situation ○ *an improper choice of words*
improperly /ɪmˈprɑp·ər·li/ *adv* ○ *If handled improperly, some chemicals used for cleaning can cause severe skin irritation.*

impropriety /ˌɪm·prəˈprɑɪ·ət̬·i/ *n* [C/U] dishonest behavior, or a dishonest act ○ [U] *He said he regretted the appearance of impropriety and resigned.* ○ [C] *There have been charges of financial improprieties.*

improve /ɪmˈpruːv/ *v* [I/T] **1** to get better, or to make something better ○ [I] *Her grades have improved greatly this semester.* ○ [T] *He did a lot to improve conditions for factory workers.* **2** If you improve on something, you succeed in doing or making it better: [I] *The company is hoping to improve on last year's sales figures.*
improvement /ɪmˈpruːv·mənt/ *n* [C/U] ○ [C] *We made some improvements to the house before selling it.* ○ [U] *There's been no improvement in his condition.*

WORD FAMILY improve

Nouns	improvement	*Verbs*	improve
Adjectives	improved		

WORD CHOICES improve

A common alternative to "improve" is **get better**.

*The first part of the movie isn't very good but it **gets better**.*

If something improves after a period of doing badly, you can use the verbs **rally** and **recover**.

*The team played badly in the first half but **rallied** in the second.*

*We are still waiting for the economy to **recover**.* ➤

The phrasal verbs **look up** and **pick up** can be used informally to say that a situation is improving.

*Our financial situation is **looking up**.*

*Business is really beginning to **pick up**.*

The phrasal verb **work on** means "to try to improve something."

*You need to **work on** your technique.*

The verb **refine** can be used when someone improves something by making small changes.

*A team of experts spent several months **refining** the software.*

If someone or something improves very quickly, you can say that it is happening by/in **leaps and bounds.**

*The sport's popularity has grown by **leaps and bounds** in the past decade.*

improvise /ˈɪm·prəˌvɑɪz/ *v* [I/T] **1** to invent or provide something at the time when it is needed without having already planned it ○ [T] *We improvised a mattress from a pile of blankets.* **2** ***music*** To improvise music or speech is to invent it while you are performing it. ○ [I] *Hughes encourages young actors to improvise during rehearsals.*

improvisation /ɪmˌprɑv·əˈzeɪ·ʃən/ *n* [C/U] **1** ***music*** a performance that is not practiced and that is invented by the performers **2** Improvisation is also the activity of making or doing something that you have not planned, using whatever you find.

impudent /ˈɪm·pjəd·ənt/ *adj* rude and not showing respect ○ *an impudent child*

impudence /ˈɪm·pjəd·əns/ *n* [U]

impugn /ɪmˈpjuːn/ *v* [T] *fml* to cause people to doubt or not trust someone's character, honesty, or ability ○ *He could no longer work as a doctor because his reputation had been impugned.*

impulse DESIRE /ˈɪm·pʌls/ *n* [C/U] **1** a sudden, strong desire to do something ○ [+ *to* infinitive] *I had this impulse to dye my hair red.* **2** If you do something on impulse, you do it because you suddenly want to: [U] *I bought this expensive sweater on impulse.*

impulsive /ɪmˈpʌl·sɪv/ *adj* acting or done suddenly without any planning or consideration of the results ○ *She's an impulsive shopper and often buys things she doesn't need.*

impulsively /ɪmˈpʌl·sɪv·li/ *adv*

SIGNAL /ˈɪm·pʌls/ *n* [C] a short electrical signal that carries information or instructions between the parts of a system ○ *nerve impulses*

FORCE /ˈɪm·pʌls/ *n* [U] ***physics*** the force that is working on an object multiplied by the amount of time it is working

impunity /ɪmˈpjuː·nət̬·i/ *n* [U] *fml* freedom from punishment for something that has been done that is wrong or illegal ○ *She thought that her money and power gave her the right to ignore the law with impunity.*

impure /ɪmˈpjʊr/ *adj* mixed with other substances and therefore harmful or lower in quality ○ *impure drinking water*

impurity /ɪmˈpjʊr·ət̬·i/ *n* [C] ○ *Impurities are removed from the blood by the kidneys.*

in WITHIN /ɪn/ *prep, adv* [not gradable] **1** positioned inside or within the limits of something, or contained, surrounded, or enclosed by something ○ *There's a cup in the cabinet.* ○ *Anne is still in bed.* ○ *Don't stand in the driveway.* ○ *He's always looking at himself in the mirror.* ○ *Clarice lives in Orlando.* ○ *He was in prison* (= a prisoner). ○ *Erika is still in school* (= still a student). ○ *He has a pain in his shoulder.* **2** If you are **in and out** of a place, you go there and leave, often repeatedly: *Since the accident, she's been in and out of the hospital several times.*

USAGE

in or at?

The preposition **in** emphasizes "inside a place."

Mom doesn't like people wearing their shoes in the house.

The preposition **at** is used to talk about time spent at a place.

We had a really good time at your house last weekend.

~~*We had a really good time in your house last weekend.*~~

MOVING TOWARD /ɪn/ *prep* into or toward ○ *Get in the car.* ○ *She stepped in the batter's box.* ○ *He looked in my direction.*

FROM OUTSIDE /ɪn/ *adv* [not gradable] from outside, or toward the center ○ *Could you bring the clothes in for me?* ○ *The roof of their house caved in during a hurricane.*

INCLUSION /ɪn/ *prep, adv* [not gradable] being a member or forming a part of something ○ *Who's the woman in that painting?* ○ *Mr. Harper is in a meeting.* ○ *I've been waiting in line for two hours.* ○ *Do you take milk in your coffee?*

CONNECTED WITH /ɪn/ *prep* involved or connected with something, esp. with a job or subject ○ *I never knew you were in publishing.* ○ *I'm taking a course in economics next semester.*

WEARING /ɪn/ *prep* wearing, covering, or decorated with ○ *Do you recognize that man in the gray suit?* ○ *The living room is done in blue and green.*

USING /ɪn/ *prep* said, made, or done using something ○ *Fill out the application in ink.* ○ *They spoke in Russian the whole time.*

DURING /ɪn/ *prep* **1** during part or all of a period of time or an event ○ *We're going to Arizona in April.* ○ *What was it like to be a student in 1968?* ○ *See you in the morning.* ○ *How many people died in the war?* ○ *She's in her forties* (= between 40 and 49 years old). **2** In can also mean no longer than a particular period of time: *Can you finish the job in two weeks?* **3** In can also mean at the end of a particular period of time: *I should be there in half an hour.*

SITUATION /ɪn/ *prep, adv* [not gradable] experiencing a situation, condition, or feeling ○ *We watched* *in horror as the cars crashed.* ○ *I'd like to talk to you in private.* ○ *He left in a hurry.* ○ *Have you ever been in love?* ○ *He's always in a bad mood on Monday mornings.* ○ *Temperatures tomorrow will be in the 70s* (= between 70 and 79 degrees).

ARRANGEMENT /ɪn/ *prep* used to show how something is arranged or divided ○ *We sat in a circle around the campfire.* ○ *The potatoes will bake faster if you cut them in half.*

COMPARING AMOUNTS /ɪn/ *prep* used to compare a part of an amount of something with the total amount of it; out of ○ *The survey found that one person in ten has a reading problem.* ○ *The chance of that happening is one in a million.*

CHARACTERISTIC /ɪn/ *prep* used to show which characteristic of a person or thing is being described ○ *She's deaf in her left ear.* ○ *Canned vegetables are not very rich in vitamins.* ○ *I wasn't using the word "guarantee" in its strict legal sense.*

CAUSE /ɪn/ *prep* used to show that doing one thing is the cause of another thing happening ○ *I leaned out of the canoe and in doing so tipped it over.* ○ *It might be made of plastic, in which case it will be light enough to carry.*

AT PLACE /ɪn/ *adv* at a place, esp. at home or a place of work ○ *Why is it that whenever I call, you are never in?* ○ *Danielle was out sick last week – do you know if she'll be in today?*

PLACE /ɪn/ *adv* [not gradable] **1** used to show that a space or place exists where something can be put or added ○ *Just pencil in your answers on the attached sheet.* ○ *The text is finished, but the pictures need to be pasted in.* **2** For many sports, if a ball is in, it has not gone outside the edges of the area on which the game is played.

POLITICS /ɪn/ *adv* into an elected position or office ○ *She's been voted in for a second term as treasurer.*

FASHIONABLE /ɪn/ *adj, adv infml* fashionable or popular ○ *That new jazz club is the in place to go.* ○ *High heels came in again this season.*

ADVANTAGE /ɪn/ *n* [C] an advantage resulting from a good relationship with someone powerful ○ *Sal has an in with someone at the theater.*

IDIOMS with in

- **in for** *something* going to experience something ○ *It looks like we're in for rain.*
- **in on** *something* to take part in something ○ *I wasn't in on planning the party.*

in. *n* [C] *pl* **in.** *abbreviation for* INCH MEASUREMENT

in- /ɪn/ *prefix* used to add the meaning not, lacking, or the opposite of to adjectives and to words formed from adjectives ○ *incomplete/incompletely*

inability /ˌɪn·əˈbɪl·əṭ·i/ *n* [C/U] a lack of ability to do something ○ [C usually sing] *an inability to read and write*

inaccessible Ⓐ /ˌɪn·ɪkˈses·ə·bəl/ *adj* **1** difficult or impossible to reach ○ *The place is inaccessible except by trail.* **2** Language that is inaccessible is difficult or impossible to understand: *Environmental dialog has become the domain of experts, inaccessible to anyone without a PhD.*

inaccurate Ⓐ /ɪnˈæk·jə·rət/ *adj* not correct, or not exact ○ *Your information is inaccurate – I was born in 1956, not 1965.* ○ *inaccurate measurements*

inaccurately Ⓐ /ɪnˈæk·jə·rət·li/ *adv* ○ *an inaccurately worded question*

inaccuracy Ⓐ /ɪnˈæk·jə·rə·si/ *n* [C/U] ○ [C] *Rose says the story was loaded with inaccuracies.*

inaction /ɪnˈæk·ʃən/ *n* [U] failure to do anything that might provide a solution to a problem ○ *The mayor was criticized for his inaction on problems affecting the city's poor.*

inactive /ɪnˈæk·tɪv/ *adj* doing nothing ○ *Knee surgery will keep him physically inactive for two months.* ○ *About half of the club members are inactive.*

inactivity /ˌɪn·ækˈtɪv·əṭ·i/ *n* [U] ○ *The journey was long, and he found the inactivity boring.*

inadequate Ⓐ /ɪnˈæd·ɪ·kwət/ *adj* too low in quality or too small in amount; not enough ○ *an inadequate income/offer* ○ *I feel inadequate when I talk to Miranda about art because she knows so much.*

inadequately Ⓐ /ɪnˈæd·ɪ·kwət·li/ *adv* ○ *The research is inadequately funded.*

inadequacy Ⓐ /ɪnˈæd·ɪ·kwə·si/ *n* [C/U] ○ [C] *She's frustrated by the inadequacies of language.*

inadmissible /ˌɪn·ədˈmɪs·ə·bəl/ *adj* [not gradable] unable to be accepted, esp. in a law court ○ *The lie detector test was inadmissible as evidence in the case.*

inadvertent /ˌɪn·ədˈvɜrt·ənt/ *adj* done or happening unintentionally ○ *an inadvertent mistake*

inadvertently /ˌɪn·ədˈvɜrt·ənt·li/ *adv* ○ *I inadvertently gave her change for $20, but she'd only given me $10.*

inadvisable /ˌɪn·ədˈvɑɪ·zə·bəl/ *adj* likely to have unwanted results and therefore to be avoided ○ *It is inadvisable to generalize from the results of a single experiment.*

inalienable /ɪnˈeɪl·jə·nə·bəl/ *adj* unable to be taken away ○ *The right to survival has to be the first on any list of inalienable rights for every human being.*

inane /ɪˈneɪn/ *adj* extremely silly or lacking real meaning or importance ○ *There are so many inane programs on television!*

inanimate /ɪˈnæn·ə·mət/ *adj* [not gradable] possessing none of the characteristics of life that an animal or plant has ○ *an inanimate object*

inappropriate Ⓐ /ˌɪn·əˈproʊ·priː·ət/ *adj* unsuitable, esp. for the particular time, place, or situation ○ *His casual clothes were inappropriate for such a formal occasion.*

inappropriately Ⓐ /ˌɪn·əˈproʊ·priː·ət·li/ *adv* ○ *an effort to stop them spending money inappropriately*

inarticulate /ˌɪn·ɑrˈtɪk·jə·lət/ *adj* unable to express feelings or ideas in words, or communicated in a way that is difficult to understand ○ *He refers* *to them as inarticulate mountain people.* ○ *inarticulate cries of rage*

inasmuch as /ˌɪn·əzˈmʌtʃ·əz/ *conjunction fml* used to show why or in what limited way the other part of the sentence is true ○ *Inasmuch as funding is not available, building plans have been delayed.*

inattentive /ˌɪn·əˈtent·ɪv/ *adj* not listening to what is being said or giving your attention to what is happening ○ *Barbara has been inattentive in class lately.*

inaudible /ɪˈnɔːd·ə·bəl/ *adj* [not gradable] unable to be heard ○ *The noise of the machinery made her voice inaudible.*
inaudibly /ɪˈnɔːd·ə·bli/ *adv* ○ *Music was playing almost inaudibly backstage.*

inaugurate /ɪˈnɔːg·jəˌreɪt/ *v* [T] to put something into use or action, or to put a person into an official position with a ceremony ○ *He wants to inaugurate his museum with elaborate opening ceremonies.* ○ *The nation prepares to inaugurate its new president.*
inauguration /ɪˌnɔːg·jəˈreɪ·ʃən/ *n* [C/U] ○ [C] *She's a journalist who has covered six presidential inaugurations.*
inaugural /ɪˈnɔːg·jə·rəl/ *adj* [not gradable] ○ *What was the theme of her inaugural address?*

inauspicious /ˌɪn·ɔːˈspɪʃ·əs/ *adj* suggesting that success is not likely ○ *After an inauspicious start, our team went on to win the game 30 to 24.*

in-between *adj infml* having the qualities of two different things ○ *This suit isn't gray or blue, it's in between.* ○ See also: BETWEEN **SPACE**; BETWEEN **TIME**

inborn /ˈɪn·bɔːrn/ *adj* [not gradable] possessed as a characteristic from birth ○ *Research suggests that some people have an inborn tendency to develop certain types of cancer.*

in-box *n* [C] **1** a container where letters and other documents are put when they arrive in a person's office **2** An in-box is also a place in a computer E-MAIL program where new electronic messages are stored.

inbred **BASIC** /ˈɪn·bred/ *adj* [not gradable] having as a basic part of your character ○ *An inbred distrust of government is increasing across the nation.*
RELATED /ˈɪn·bred/ *adj* [not gradable] ***biology*** produced by breeding between closely related plants, animals, or people

Inc. /ɪŋk/ *adj short form of* INCORPORATED ○ *Automated Document Systems, Inc.*

incalculable /ɪnˈkæl·kjə·lə·bəl/ *adj* [not gradable] too large to be calculated or measured, or extremely large ○ *The consequences of a nuclear war are incalculable.*

incandescent /ˌɪn·kənˈdes·ənt/ *adj* [not gradable] producing a bright light after being heated to a high temperature ○ *an incandescent light/bulb*
incandescence /ˌɪn·kənˈdes·əns/ *n* [U] ○ *At night, Los Angeles looked like a vast carpet of incandescence.*

incantation /ˌɪnˌkænˈteɪ·ʃən/ *n* [C/U] the saying of words believed to have a magical effect when spoken or sung ○ [C] *She recited an incantation designed to protect the planet.*

incapable Ⓐ /ɪnˈkeɪ·pə·bəl/ *adj* unable to do something ○ *She's incapable of hurting a fly.*

incapacitate Ⓐ /ˌɪn·kəˈpæs·əˌteɪt/ *v* [T] to remove someone's ability to do something ○ *The accident incapacitated me for seven months.*
incapacitating /ˌɪn·kəˈpæs·əˌteɪt̬·ɪŋ/ *adj* ○ *an incapacitating illness*
incapacity /ˌɪn·kəˈpæs·ət̬·i/ *n* [U] ○ *The novel tells the story of a man's incapacity for love.*

incarcerate /ɪnˈkɑr·səˌreɪt/ *v* [T] to put or keep someone in prison ○ *The governor announced his plan to incarcerate repeat offenders.*
incarceration /ɪnˌkɑr·səˈreɪ·ʃən/ *n* [U] ○ *We're spending billions of dollars each year on incarceration.*

incarnation /ˌɪnˌkɑrˈneɪ·ʃən/ *n* [C/U] **1** the human form of a spirit, or the human representation of a principle or idea ○ [U] *When he dances, he's the incarnation of gracefulness.* **2** An incarnation is also, according to some religious beliefs, one of the several lives people have over time. ○ See also: REINCARNATION **3** An incarnation can also be a new or different form or condition of something: [C] *This movie is the latest incarnation of an old French fairy tale.*
incarnate /ɪnˈkɑr·nət, -ˌneɪt/ *adj* [not gradable] in human form ○ *Zhang is charisma incarnate, attracting your attention whenever she is on screen.*

incendiary **FIRE** /ɪnˈsen·diːˌer·i/ *adj* [not gradable] designed to cause fires ○ *an incendiary bomb/device* ○ *(fig.) Thai food often is incendiary* (= spicy hot).
CAUSING ANGER /ɪnˈsen·diːˌer·i/ *adj* likely to cause violence or strong feelings of anger ○ *He gave an incendiary speech at last night's rally.*

incense **SUBSTANCE** /ˈɪn·sens/ *n* [U] a substance that is burned to produce a sweet smell
ANGER /ɪnˈsens/ *v* [T] to cause someone to be extremely angry ○ *The editor felt readers would be incensed by my article.*

incentive Ⓐ /ɪnˈsent·ɪv/ *n* [C/U] something that encourages a person to do something ○ [C] *Tax incentives are sometimes effective in encouraging people to save money.* ○ [U] *These kids have no incentive to learn.*

inception /ɪnˈsep·ʃən/ *n* [U] the beginning of an organization or official activity ○ *Since its inception in 1968, the company has been at the forefront of computer development.*

incessant /ɪnˈses·ənt/ *adj* [not gradable] (esp. of something unpleasant) never stopping ○ *The region endured weeks of incessant rain.*
incessantly /ɪnˈses·ənt·li/ *adv* [not gradable] ○ *Bob talks incessantly about their new baby.*

incest /ˈɪn·sest/ *n* [U] sexual activity between people who are too closely related to marry

incestuous /ɪn ˈses·tʃə·wəs/ *adj* [not gradable]

inch MEASUREMENT /ɪntʃ/, *abbreviation* **in.**, *symbol* " *n* [C] a unit of measurement of length equal to 1/12 foot or 2.54 centimeters

MOVE /ɪntʃ/ *v* [always + adv/prep] to move very slowly, or in a lot of short stages ○ [I] *Stock prices inched higher throughout the afternoon.* ○ [T] *Mike inched the bookcase into position.*

incidence Ⓐ RATE /ˈɪn·səd·əns, -səˌdens/ *n* [U] the rate at which something happens ○ *There's been an increased incidence of cancer in the area.*

SURFACE /ˈɪn·səd·əns, -səˌdens/ *n* [C] **1** the falling or hitting of an object or beam of energy, such as light, on a surface **2** ***physics*** The **angle of incidence** is the angle that a beam of light or other energy hitting a surface makes with a line vertical to that surface.

incident Ⓐ EVENT /ˈɪn·səd·ənt, -səˌdent/ *n* [C/U] an event, esp. one that is either unpleasant or unusual ○ [C] *Many shipping companies do not report incidents of piracy, for fear of raising their insurance rates.* ○ [U] *The demonstration took place without incident.*

HITTING A SURFACE /ˈɪn·səd·ənt, -səˌdent/ *adj* [not gradable] **1** touching or hitting the surface of something **2** ***physics*** An **incident ray** or **incident wave** is a beam of light or other energy that hits a surface.

incidental /ˌɪn·səˈdent·əl/ *adj* happening by chance, or in connection with something of greater importance ○ *His influence on younger employees was incidental, not intentional.* ○ *Will I be reimbursed for incidental expenses at the conference?*

incidentally Ⓐ /ˌɪn·səˈdent·əl·i, -ˈdent·li/ *adv* [not gradable] **1** *"Ain't" was mentioned only incidentally in an article about nonstandard words.* **2** Incidentally is also used to introduce something additional that is not as important: *Incidentally, she was a very popular mayor.*

incidentals /ˌɪn·səˈdent·əlz/ *pl n* **1** unimportant facts ○ *She may be wrong on incidentals, but she's never wrong in substance.* **2** Incidentals are also small expenses: *I need money for incidentals like coffee.*

incinerate /ɪnˈsɪn·əˌreɪt/ *v* [T] to burn something completely ○ *The company is accused of incinerating hazardous waste without a license.*

incinerator /ɪnˈsɪn·əˌreɪţ·ər/ *n* [C] a device for burning waste material

incipient /ɪnˈsɪp·iː·ənt/ *adj fml* just beginning or just coming into existence ○ *He has a black mustache and an incipient potbelly.*

incision /ɪnˈsɪʒ·ən/ *n* [C] *medical* a cut made in the surface of the skin or in other body tissue

incisive /ɪnˈsɑɪ·sɪv/ *adj* expressing an idea or opinion clearly and in a persuasive manner ○ *The guide's incisive comments give us a new perspective on the painting.*

incisor /ɪnˈsɑɪ·zər/ *n* [C] one of the sharp teeth at the front of the mouth that cut food when you bite into it ○ Compare MOLAR

incite /ɪnˈsɑɪt/ *v* [T] to encourage someone to do or feel something unpleasant or violent, or to cause violent or unpleasant actions ○ *The ads were trying to incite public opinion against the government.*

incitement /ɪnˈsɑɪt·mənt/ *n* [U]

inclement /ɪnˈklem·ənt/ *adj* (of weather) unpleasant, esp. cold or stormy ○ *The concert in the park was postponed because of the inclement weather.*

inclination Ⓐ /ˌɪn·kləˈneɪ·ʃən/ *n* [C] a preference or tendency, or a feeling that makes a person want to do something ○ *Tony has a strong inclination toward the arts.* ○ *If I were in your situation, my inclination would be to look for another job.*

inclined Ⓐ /ɪnˈklɑɪnd/ *adj* ○ *I'm inclined to agree with you.*

incline Ⓐ /ɪnˈklɑɪn/ *v* [I/T] to lean down, or to place something with one part toward the ground and the opposite part raised ○ [T] *Marge inclined her head to whisper something to me.*

incline Ⓐ /ˈɪn·klɑin/ *n* [C] a slope ○ *The road has a steep incline for the next ten miles.*

inclined Ⓐ /ɪnˈklɑɪnd, ˈɪn·klɑind/ *adj* ○ *an inclined roof/roadway/surface*

include /ɪnˈkluːd/ *v* [T] (of something) to have something smaller as a part of it, or to make something smaller part of it ○ *The hotel room charge includes breakfast.* ○ *The encyclopedia includes the names of all Nobel Prize winners.* ○ *Sheila asked to be included among the people going on the tour.*

including /ɪnˈkluːd·ɪŋ/ *prep* ○ *The book has 360 pages, including the index.*

inclusion /ɪnˈkluː·ʒən/ *n* [U] the act of including something as a part of something else ○ *Twelve new stories were selected for inclusion in the book.*

inclusive /ɪnˈkluː·sɪv, -zɪv/ *adj* ○ *The governments want to reach a settlement that is as inclusive as possible* (= that includes as many people as possible). ➤ Usage: **contain or include?** at CONTAIN HAVE INSIDE

incoherent Ⓐ /ˌɪn·koʊˈhɪr·ənt/ *adj* not expressed in a way that can be understood, or not able to talk clearly ○ *He seemed dazed and incoherent, apparently from blood loss.*

incoherently Ⓐ /ˌɪn·koʊˈhɪr·ənt·li/ *adv*

income Ⓐ /ˈɪn·kʌm, -kəm/ *n* [C/U] money that is earned from doing work or received from investments ➤ Usage: **pay, wage, salary, or income?** at PAY GIVE EARNINGS

income tax *n* [C/U] ***social studies*** a tax on the money that a person earns from working ○ *federal, state, and local income taxes*

incoming /ˈɪnˌkʌm·ɪŋ/ *adj* [not gradable] arriving at, coming into, or entering a place ○ *Incoming flights are being delayed because of bad weather.*

incomparable /ɪnˈkɑm·pə·rə·bəl, ˌɪn·kəmˈpær·ə·bəl/ *adj* [not gradable] so good or great that nothing else could achieve the same standard ○ *the incomparable achievement of Einstein*

incompatible Ⓐ /ˌɪn·kəmˈpæţ·ə·bəl/ *adj* not able to exist or work with another person or thing

I

○ *Any new video system that is incompatible with existing ones has little chance of success.*

incompatibility Ⓐ /ˌɪn·kəmˌpæt·əˈbɪl·ət̬·i/ *n* [U]

incompetent /ɪnˈkɑm·pət̬·ənt/ *adj* lacking the skills or knowledge to do a job or perform an action correctly or to a satisfactory standard ○ *Cowden was incompetent and incapable of administering the duties of secretary of the association.*

incompetent /ɪnˈkɑm·pət̬·ənt/ *n* [C] ○ *The business failed because it was run by a bunch of incompetents.*

incompetence /ɪnˈkɑm·pət̬·əns/ *n* [U] ○ *Local politicians accused the federal government of incompetence in failing to respond more quickly to the emergency.*

incompetently /ɪnˈkɑm·pət̬·ənt·li/ *adv*

incomplete /ˌɪn·kəmˈpliːt/ *adj* lacking some parts, or not finished ○ *The polls have closed but the results of the election are still incomplete.*

incomplete /ˌɪn·kəmˈpliːt/ *n* [C] a mark, usually temporary, received when some of the work for a class has not been finished ○ *He failed to hand in his term paper, so he got an incomplete for the course.*

I

incomprehensible /ɪnˌkɑm·prɪˈhen·sə·bəl/ *adj* impossible or extremely difficult to understand ○ *The writing ability of some of the students was so poor that their essays were almost incomprehensible.*

inconceivable Ⓐ /ˌɪn·kənˈsiː·və·bəl/ *adj* impossible to imagine or think of ○ *Politicians always say that a tax increase is inconceivable.*

inconceivably Ⓐ /ˌɪn·kənˈsiː·və·bli/ *adv*

inconclusive Ⓐ /ˌɪn·kənˈkluː·sɪv, -zɪv/ *adj* not giving or having a result or decision; uncertain ○ *The evidence is inconclusive, and no arrest is warranted.*

inconclusively Ⓐ /ˌɪn·kənˈkluː·sɪv·li, -zɪv·li/ *adv*

incongruous /ɪnˈkɑŋ·grə·wəs/ *adj* appearing strange or wrong within a particular situation ○ *Such a modern office building looks incongruous in the quaint little town.*

inconsequential /ɪnˌkɑn·sɪˈkwen·tʃəl/ *adj* not important; able to be ignored ○ *Changes in the stock market were pretty inconsequential during the past week.*

inconsiderate /ˌɪn·kənˈsɪd·ə·rət/ *adj* not caring about other people or their feelings; selfish ○ *She thought it was inconsiderate of him not to have asked her friend to the party.*

inconsistent Ⓐ **NOT AGREEING** /ˌɪn·kənˈsɪs·tənt/ *adj* (of an argument or opinion) containing elements that are opposed and do not match, so that it is difficult to imagine how both can be true ○ *These findings are inconsistent with those of previous studies.*

inconsistency Ⓐ /ˌɪn·kənˈsɪs·tən·si/ *n* [C/U] a situation in which two things do not match and are opposed ○ [C] *There appear to be inconsistencies in her alibi.*

CHANGEABLE /ˌɪn·kənˈsɪs·tənt/ *adj disapproving* changing in character; not staying the same ○ *The team's play is inconsistent – winning one day and losing the next.*

inconspicuous /ˌɪn·kənˈspɪk·jə·wəs/ *adj* not easily noticed or seen; not attracting attention ○ *Agents placed the camera on a wall in an inconspicuous place.*

incontestable /ˌɪn·kənˈtes·tə·bəl/ *adj* [not gradable] impossible to question because obviously true ○ *There is now incontestable evidence that he is not guilty of the crime.*

incontinent /ɪnˈkɑnt·ən·ənt/ *adj* unable to control excretion

incontinence /ɪnˈkɑnt·ən·əns/ *n* [U]

incontrovertible /ɪnˌkɑn·trəˈvɜrt̬·ə·bəl/ *adj* [not gradable] *fml* impossible to doubt because obviously true ○ *incontrovertible proof*

inconvenience /ˌɪn·kənˈviːn·jəns/ *n* [C/U] something that causes trouble or difficulty and is annoying but not serious, or the condition of being in such an annoying situation ○ [C] *Changing planes was an inconvenience, but there were no direct flights.*

inconvenience /ˌɪn·kənˈviːn·jəns/ *v* [T] ○ *The postal strike inconvenienced many people.*

inconvenient /ˌɪn·kənˈviːn·jənt/ *adj* not convenient ○ *He scheduled the meeting for an inconvenient time, and few people could attend.*

incorporate Ⓐ **INCLUDE** /ɪnˈkɔːr·pəˌreɪt/ *v* [T] to include something within something else ○ *This aircraft incorporates several new safety features.*

incorporation Ⓐ /ɪnˌkɔːr·pəˈreɪ·ʃən/ *n* [U] ○ *the incorporation of black soldiers into Union ranks*

MAKE A COMPANY /ɪnˈkɔːr·pəˌreɪt/ *v* [I/T] to make a business into a CORPORATION (= business protected by specific laws)

incorporated Ⓐ /ɪnˈkɔːr·pəˌreɪt̬·əd/, *abbreviation* **Inc.** *adj* [only after n] [not gradable] ○ *McLaughlin Glass, Incorporated*

incorporation Ⓐ /ɪnˌkɔːr·pəˈreɪ·ʃən/ *n* [U]

incorrect /ˌɪn·kəˈrekt/ *adj* not CORRECT; not accurate ○ *He charged that the news story was factually incorrect and demanded an apology.*

incorrectly /ˌɪn·kəˈrekt·li/ *adv* ○ *For each question on the test that is answered incorrectly, you will lose two points.*

incorrigible /ɪnˈkɔːr·ɪ·dʒə·bəl, -ˈkɑr-/ *adj* [not gradable] (of people and their behavior) impossible to improve or correct ○ *an incorrigible liar*

increase /ɪnˈkriːs, ˈɪn·kriːs/ *v* [I/T] to become or make something larger or greater ○ [T] *They've increased the price of gas by two cents a gallon.* ○ [I] *Pressure is increasing to make health insurance more widely available.* ○ Opposite: DECREASE

increase /ˈɪn·kriːs/ *n* [C/U] ○ [C] *There was a slight increase in unemployment last month.* ○ *Homelessness is* **on the increase** (= increasing) *in many cities.*

increasingly /ɪnˈkriː·sɪŋ·li/ *adv* [not gradable] more often or to a greater degree ○ *She turned increasingly to radical diets to lose weight.*

USAGE

increase in or **increase of?**

The preposition **in** is used after the noun **increase** to say what is getting larger or greater.

an increase in profits/sales

The preposition **of** is used before numbers describing the size of an increase.

an increase of 10%

WORD FAMILY increase

Nouns	increase	*Adverbs*	increasingly
Verbs	increase		

WORD CHOICES increase

The verbs **grow** and **rise** are common alternatives to "increase."

The number of people living alone ***grows*** *each year.*

Prices ***rose*** *by 10 percent.*

The phrasal verb **go up** is often used when prices increase.

House prices keep ***going up****.*

The price of gas has ***gone up*** *another six cents a gallon.*

If something suddenly increases by a large amount, you can use verbs such as **escalate** or **soar**.

Crime in the city has ***escalated*** *in recent weeks.*

Building costs have ***soared*** *this year.*

If someone makes something increase in size or amount, you can use verbs like **expand** or **extend**.

We're hoping to ***expand/extend*** *our range of products.*

The verb **maximize** is sometimes used when someone tries to increase something as much as possible.

We need to ***maximize*** *profits.*

incredible /ɪnˈkred·ə·bəl/ *adj* **1** impossible or very difficult to believe ○ *She showed incredible courage and determination in coming back from her injuries to compete again at the international level.* **2** Incredible is also used to emphasize that something is unusually good or bad: *It was an incredible bargain.*

incredibly /ɪnˈkred·ə·bli/ *adv* **1** *Incredibly, no one was hurt in the accident.* **2** Incredibly also means extremely: *He was incredibly rude.*

incredulous /ɪnˈkredʒ·ə·ləs/ *adj* not wanting or not able to believe, and usually showing this ○ *"Why am I here?" the witness responded in an incredulous tone.*

increment /ˈɪŋ·krə·mənt, ˈɪn-/ *n* [C] one of a series of amounts that increase a total ○ *She was in the habit of saving in small increments each week.*

incremental /ˌɪŋ·krəˈment·əl, ˌɪn-/ *adj* [not gradable] ○ *Workers were promised two incremental pay increases a year.*

incriminate /ɪnˈkrɪm·əˌneɪt/ *v* [T] to seem to show that someone is guilty of a crime ○ *He refused to say anything on the grounds that he might incriminate himself.*

incriminating /ɪnˈkrɪm·əˌneɪt̬·ɪŋ/ *adj* ○ *incriminating evidence/statements*

incubate /ˈɪŋ·kjəˌbeɪt, ˈɪn-/ *v* [I/T] to keep something warm, causing it to develop, esp. to keep eggs warm until the young are born ○ *Condors incubate only one egg and raise one chick at a time.* ○ *Lyme disease is caused by bacteria that incubate in forest animals, such as mice.*

inculcate /ɪnˈkʌlˌkeɪt, ˈɪn·kʌl-/ *v* [T] *fml* to cause someone to have particular beliefs or values by repeating them frequently ○ *The goal is to inculcate in students a tolerance for people of other religions and races.*

incumbent PERSON /ɪnˈkʌm·bənt/ *n* [C] ***politics & government*** (referring to the present time) a person who has a particular office or position, esp. an elected one ○ *Senator Smith, the incumbent, faces a tough fight for reelection next year.*

NECESSARY /ɪnˈkʌm·bənt/ *adj fml* necessary ○ [+ *to* infinitive] *It is* **incumbent upon** (= necessary for) *all of us to create a safe community.*

incur /ɪnˈkɜr/ *v* [T] **-rr-** to experience something bad as a result of actions you have taken ○ *We incurred heavy expenses to repair the poor work done by the builder.*

incurable /ɪnˈkjʊr·ə·bəl/ *adj* [not gradable] **1** not able to be cured ○ *Before antibiotics the disease was incurable.* **2** If you describe someone as incurable, you mean that nothing that happens can change them: *Marjorie is an incurable optimist.*

incursion /ɪnˈkɜr·ʒən/ *n* [C] a sudden and unwanted entrance to a place or area controlled by others, esp. in a military attack

indebted GRATEFUL /ɪnˈdet̬·əd/ *adj* grateful to someone because of help that person has given you ○ *For her encouragement and support, I am especially indebted to my wife, Nancy.*

OWING /ɪnˈdet̬·əd/ *adj* owing money ○ *Heavily indebted farms are still struggling.*

indecent /ɪnˈdiː·sənt/ *adj* morally offensive, esp. in a sexual way ○ *Indecent language is not allowed on the radio between 6 a.m. and 10 p.m.*

indecency /ɪnˈdiː·sən·si/ *n* [C/U] ○ [U] *The network received the harshest fine ever imposed for indecency on TV.*

indecision /ˌɪn·dɪˈsɪʒ·ən/, **indecisiveness** /ˌɪn·dɪˈsɑɪ·sɪv·nəs/ *n* [U] the quality of being unable to make a decision or having a lot of difficulty in deciding something ○ *I tossed and turned all night in a frenzy of indecision.*

indecisive /ˌɪn·dɪˈsɑɪ·sɪv/ *adj* ○ *As a leader during the war, he was indecisive and ineffectual, and was eventually relieved of his command.*

indeed /ɪnˈdiːd/ *adv* [not gradable] **1** (used to emphasize something said or about to be said) re-

I

ally; truly ○ *If he has indeed quit his job, I asked myself, why is he still here?* ○ *From a medical standpoint, the discovery may turn out to be very big news indeed.* ○ *Indeed* (= When you really think about it), *why should you follow a doctor's advice to the letter when you feel like Superman?* **2** Indeed is also used to make something clear or add to something you have just said: *It was impossible to find work and, indeed, it became increasingly hard to keep looking for a job.*

indefatigable /ˌɪn·dɪˈfæt̬·ə·gə·bəl/ *adj fml* never becoming tired ○ *For many years Annie has been an indefatigable campaigner for human rights.*

indefensible /ˌɪn·dɪˈfen·sə·bəl/ *adj* (of behavior) so bad that it cannot be defended against criticism ○ *His actions in destroying the tapes were indefensible.*

indefinable /ˌɪn·dɪˈfɑɪ·nə·bəl/ *adj* impossible to clearly describe or explain ○ *She had about her an indefinable quality that charmed everyone.*

indefinite Ⓐ /ɪnˈdef·ə·nət/ *adj* not exact or not clear; without clear limits ○ *It was a wonderful opportunity, but it meant leaving family and friends for an indefinite period, perhaps forever.*
indefinitely Ⓐ /ɪnˈdef·ə·nət·li/ *adv* for an unlimited or unknown amount of time ○ *In the light of recent disclosures, the business deal has been postponed indefinitely.*

indefinite article *n* [C] ***grammar*** the words "a" and "an" in English, or words in other languages that have a similar use. ○ Compare DEFINITE ARTICLE

indelible /ɪnˈdel·ə·bəl/ *adj* [not gradable] impossible to remove by washing or by any other method ○ *an indelible mark* ○ *(fig.) His performance of Hamlet left an indelible impression on all who saw it.*

indelicate /ɪnˈdel·ɪ·kət/ *adj* showing a lack of awareness of socially correct behavior ○ *There was an embarrassed silence after his indelicate remark about her age.*

indemnity /ɪnˈdem·nət̬·i/ *n* [C/U] *law* protection against possible damage or loss, esp. a promise of payment, or the money paid if there is such damage or loss

indent /ɪnˈdent/ *v* [T] to begin a line of written or printed text after leaving extra space, compared with the place where other lines begin ○ *Normally each new paragraph is indented.*

indentation /ˌɪnˌdenˈteɪ·ʃən/ *n* [C] a part of a surface that curves inward ○ *If a surgeon takes out too much fat, he may leave indentations in the skin.*

Independence Day *n* [C usually sing] the FOURTH OF JULY

independent /ˌɪn·dɪˈpen·dənt/ *adj* **1** not influenced or controlled by other people but free to make your own decisions ○ *an independent thinker* ○ *Congress called for the appointment of an independent counsel to investigate the president.* ○ *Now that Jean's got a job, she's financially independent* (= she does not need money from other people). **2** ***social studies*** If a country becomes independent, it is no longer governed or ruled by another country. **3** An **independent contractor** is a person who agrees to do a particular job for someone else for an agreed amount of money but who is not an employee: *She used to be on staff, but now she's an independent contractor.*
independent /ˌɪn·dɪˈpen·dənt/ *n* [C] ***politics & government*** a voter or politician who does not belong to a political PARTY ○ *She is gaining support among independents who have no political preference or who lean Democratic.*
independence /ˌɪn·dɪˈpen·dəns/ *n* [U] ○ *Most college students who live on a campus are enjoying independence from their families for the first time in their lives.* ○ *Juan is in favor of Puerto Rican independence* (= the condition of not being governed by another country).
independently /ˌɪn·dɪˈpen·dənt·li/ *adv* ○ *The telephone was actually invented independently by two different people at almost the same time.*

WORD FAMILY independent			
Nouns	independence independent	*Adjectives* *Adverbs*	independent independently

independent clause *n* [C] ***grammar*** a clause in a sentence that would form a complete sentence by itself

independent variable *n* [U] ***algebra*** a number or amount in a mathematical statement that can change and which decides the value of the DEPENDENT VARIABLE

indescribable /ˌɪn·dɪˈskrɑɪ·bə·bəl/ *adj* [not gradable] impossible to describe, esp. because extremely good or bad ○ *The stench was indescribable.*

indestructible /ˌɪn·dɪˈstrʌk·tə·bəl/ *adj* [not gradable] impossible to destroy or break ○ *The fireproof material used is virtually indestructible.*

indeterminate /ˌɪn·dɪˈtɜr·mə·nət/ *adj* not clearly determined or established ○ *Juvenile criminals are sometimes sentenced to indeterminate prison terms rather than a fixed length of time.*

index Ⓐ **LIST** /ˈɪn·deks/ *n* [C] *pl* **indexes, indices** ***writing*** an alphabetical list, such as one printed at the back of a book showing on which page a name or subject appears, or computer information ordered in a particular way ○ *If you want to find the place in the text that Henry James is mentioned, look it up in the index.*
index Ⓐ /ˈɪn·deks/ *v* [T] ○ *He organized and indexed the material by computer.*

COMPARISON /ˈɪn·deks/ *n* [C] *pl* **indices, indexes** a number used to show the value of something by comparing it to something else whose value is known ○ *a wage/price index* ○ *(fig.) The rate of consumer spending is often thought to be an index of public confidence* (= show the state of the public's confidence) *in the health of the economy.*

index /ˈɪn·deks/ *v* [T] ○ *Social Security payments are indexed to* (= adjusted to allow for) *inflation every year.*

index finger /ˈɪnˌdeks ˈfɪŋ·gər/ *n* [C] the finger next to the thumb; FOREFINGER ○ *He pointed his index finger at me and cried out, "I mean you!"*

index fossil *n* [C] ***earth science*** a FOSSIL that is found in many places and comes from the same time in history, so that scientists can use it to decide how old certain rocks are

Indian /ˈɪn·diː·ən/ *n* [C] **1** an AMERICAN INDIAN; NATIVE AMERICAN **2** Indian also means a person from India.
Indian /ˈɪn·diː·ən/ *adj* [not gradable]

Indian summer *n* [C] a period of warm weather happening in the fall when you expect cooler weather

indicate Ⓐ /ˈɪn·dəˌkeɪt/ *v* to show or signal a direction or warning, or to make something clear ○ [T] *These statistics might indicate quality problems.* ○ [+ *that* clause] *She did not move or indicate that she had heard him.*
indication Ⓐ /ˌɪn·dəˈkeɪ·ʃən/ *n* [C/U] ○ [C] *Is that nod an indication of your agreement?* ○ [U] *The jury gave no indication of their decision as they came back into the courtroom.*
indicative Ⓐ /ɪnˈdɪk·ət̬·ɪv/ *adj* ○ *Resumption of the talks is indicative of an improved relationship between the countries.*
indicator Ⓐ /ˈɪn·dəˌkeɪt̬·ər/ *n* [C] ○ *Housing permits are an indicator of the state's economic health.* ○ *The car's speedometer and temperature indicator were broken.*

indicative /ɪnˈdɪk·ət̬·ɪv/ *n* [U] ***grammar*** the MOOD (= form) of a verb used in ordinary statements and questions ○ *In the sentence "We walked home," the verb "walked" is in the indicative.*

indices /ˈɪn·dəˌsiːz/ *pl of* INDEX

indict /ɪnˈdɑɪt/ *v* [T] *law* to accuse someone officially of a crime ○ *Five people were indicted on criminal charges.*
indictment /ɪnˈdɑɪt·mənt/ *n* [C] *law* **1** a formal statement of accusation **2** An indictment is also a reason for giving blame: *The high level of adult illiteracy is seen as an indictment of the country's education policy.*

indie /ˈɪn·di/ *adj* [not gradable] (music or a film) produced by a small, independent company ○ *indie filmmakers/rock/movies*
indie /ˈɪn·di/ *n* [C] music or a film produced by a such company, or a company that produces such music or films ○ *The film is a low-budget indie that grossed forty-two million dollars.*

indifferent NOT INTERESTED /ɪnˈdɪf·rənt/ *adj* [not gradable] lacking in interest or feeling ○ *an indifferent student* ○ *She was utterly indifferent to his irritation.*
indifference /ɪnˈdɪf·rəns/ *n* [U] ○ *Her indifference to sports bothered him.*
NOT GOOD OR BAD /ɪnˈdɪf·rənt/ *adj* [not gradable] neither very good nor very bad ○ *No matter how good or bad or indifferent Foster is, he'll always be my friend.*

indigenous /ɪnˈdɪdʒ·ə·nəs/ *adj* [not gradable] existing naturally or having always lived in a place; NATIVE ○ *The Navajos are among the indigenous people of North America.* ○ *Are there any species of frog indigenous to the area?*

indigent /ˈɪn·dɪ·dʒənt/ *adj* [not gradable] *fml* having no money or anything else of value ○ *an indigent family*

indigestible /ˌɪn·dəˈdʒes·tə·bəl, ˌɪn·dɑɪ-/ *adj* (of food) difficult or impossible to change into smaller forms that the body can absorb after eating it ○ *The meat was so tough, it was almost indigestible.*

indigestion /ˌɪn·dəˈdʒes·tʃən, ˌɪn·dɑɪ-/ *n* [U] an uncomfortable condition caused when your body cannot DIGEST food after you have eaten it ○ *Greasy food gives me indigestion.*

indignant /ɪnˈdɪg·nənt/ *adj* angry because of something that is wrong or not fair ○ *She wrote an indignant letter to the paper complaining about the mayor's actions.*
indignantly /ɪnˈdɪg·nənt·li/ *adv* ○ *"Your assumption is entirely incorrect," he declared indignantly.*
indignation /ˌɪn·dɪgˈneɪ·ʃən/ *n* [U] ○ *They reacted with shock and indignation when they were accused of cheating.*

indignity /ɪnˈdɪg·nət̬·i/ *n* [C/U] loss of respect, or something that causes this ○ [C] *She describes the indignities that victims suffer after the crime.*

indirect ADDITIONAL /ˌɪn·dəˈrekt, ˌɪn·dɑɪ-/ *adj* happening in addition to an intended result ○ *Several other people were hurt as an indirect result of his carelessness.*
NOT STRAIGHT /ˌɪn·dəˈrekt, ˌɪn·dɑɪ-/ *adj* not following a straight line, or not connected in a simple way ○ *an indirect route* ○ *Ransom thought the best approach in defending truth is the indirect one.*
indirectly /ˌɪn·dəˈrek·tli, ˌɪn·dɑɪ-/ *adv* ○ *She controls the company indirectly, through a hand-picked board of directors.*

indirect object *n* [C] ***grammar*** the person or thing that receives the effect of the action of a verb that has two objects ○ *In the sentence "Give Jason some cake," "Jason" is the indirect object.* ○ Compare DIRECT OBJECT ○ See also: OBJECT GRAMMAR

indirect speech *n* [U] REPORTED SPEECH

indiscreet Ⓐ /ˌɪn·dɪˈskriːt/ *adj* not careful in saying or doing things that should be kept secret ○ *It was indiscreet of you to mention the party – she hasn't been invited.*
indiscretion Ⓐ /ˌɪn·dɪˈskreʃ·ən/ *n* [C/U] ○ [C] *youthful indiscretions* ○ [U] *This sort of indiscretion is unforgivable!*

indiscriminate /ˌɪn·dɪˈskrɪm·ə·nət/ *adj* not showing careful thought or planning ○ *Cancer is completely indiscriminate in whom it strikes.*

indiscriminately /ˌɪn·dɪˈskrɪm·ə·nət·li/ *adv* ○ *Words like "organic" and "natural" are used so indiscriminately that they are often meaningless.*

indispensable /ˌɪn·dɪˈspen·sə·bəl/ *adj* too important not to have; necessary ○ *None of our players is indispensable.*

indisputable /ˌɪn·dɪˈspjuːt̬·ə·bəl/ *adj* [not gradable] obviously true ○ *an indisputable fact*
indisputably /ˌɪn·dɪˈspjuːt̬·ə·bli/ *adv* [not gradable] ○ *He is indisputably one of the finest baseball players ever.*

indistinct Ⓐ /ˌɪn·dɪˈstɪŋt/ *adj* not clear ○ *an indistinct shape/sound/recollection*
indistinctly Ⓐ /ˌɪn·dɪˈstɪŋk·tli, -ˈstɪŋk·li/ *adv*

indistinguishable /ˌɪn·dɪˈstɪŋ·gwɪʃ·ə·bəl, -wɪʃ-/ *adj* [not gradable] impossible to notice differences when compared to another similar thing ○ *The fish's markings make it virtually indistinguishable from the sand it swims over.*

I

individual Ⓐ /ˌɪn·dəˈvɪdʒ·ə·wəl/ *n* [C] a single person or thing, esp. when compared to the group or set to which it belongs ○ *We will remember him as an individual who always tried to make people happy.*
individual Ⓐ /ˌɪn·dəˈvɪdʒ·ə·wəl/ *adj* [not gradable] ○ *Every company has its own individual style.*
individually Ⓐ /ˌɪn·dəˈvɪdʒ·ə·wə·li/ *adv* [not gradable] ○ *The children will first sing individually and then as a group.*
individuality Ⓐ /ˌɪn·dəˌvɪdʒ·əˈwæl·ət̬·i/ *n* [U] ○ *His individuality* (= That which makes him different) *really comes out when he dances.*
individualism Ⓐ /ˌɪn·dəˈvɪdʒ·ə·wəˌlɪz·əm/ *n* [U] ***social studies*** the idea that each person should think and act independently rather than depending on others ○ *Many Americans believe strongly in individualism.*
individualist Ⓐ /ˌɪn·dəˈvɪdʒ·ə·wə·ləst/ *n* [C] a person who is different and original in his or her thoughts and actions ○ *Even though she's part of the mainstream, McCardell remains an individualist who thinks for herself.*
individualistic Ⓐ /ˈɪn·dəˌvɪdʒ·ə·wəˈlɪs·tɪk/ *adj* ○ *The company's individualistic, entrepreneurial style may not fit with its new owner's bureaucratic approach.*

indivisible /ˌɪn·dəˈvɪz·ə·bəl/ *adj* [not gradable] not able to be divided into parts

indoctrinate /ɪnˈdɑk·trəˌneɪt/ *v* [T] *esp. disapproving* to persuade someone to accept an idea by repeating it and showing it to be true ○ *They claimed the teacher was trying to indoctrinate his students with ideas that were not democratic.*

indolent /ˈɪn·də·lənt/ *adj fml* without real interest or effort; LAZY ○ *I was an indolent creature who could not imagine action.*

indomitable /ɪnˈdɑm·ət̬·ə·bəl/ *adj* (of a person) strong, brave, and impossible to defeat or make frightened ○ *an indomitable spirit/will*

indoor /ˌɪnˌdɔːr, -ˌdoʊr/ *adj* [not gradable] happening, used, or being inside a building ○ *indoor sports* ○ *indoor plumbing* ○ *an indoor swimming pool* ○ Opposite: OUTDOOR
indoors /ɪnˈdɔːrz, -ˈdoʊrz/ *adv* [not gradable] ○ *Come indoors, it's cold outside.* ○ Opposite: OUTDOORS

induce Ⓐ /ɪnˈduːs/ *v* [T] **1** to persuade someone to do something, or to cause something to happen ○ *They induced her to take the job by offering her a bonus.* **2** If doctors induce LABOR, they cause a baby to be born before its natural time.
inducement /ɪnˈduːs·mənt/ *n* [C] ○ *If you want me to stay, you're going to have to offer me some inducement.*

induced current /ɪnˈduːst ˈkɜr·ənt, ˈkʌ·rənt/ *n* [C] ***physics*** an electric current that results when a second CONDUCTOR (= substance that carries electricity) is placed in an area where there is already an electric current

induct /ɪnˈdʌkt/ *v* [T] to introduce someone formally or with a special ceremony to an organization or group ○ *She was inducted into the army.*
inductee /ɪnˌdʌkˈtiː/ *n* [C] ○ *Basketball Hall of Fame inductee Cheryl Miller will be there.*
induction /ɪnˈdʌk·ʃən/ *n* [C/U] ○ [U] *She is being considered for induction into the Soccer Hall of Fame.*

induction /ɪnˈdʌk·ʃən/ *n* [U] ***physics*** the process of establishing an electrical current in an object by placing it near another object that has current in it

indulge /ɪnˈdʌldʒ/ *v* [I/T] to allow yourself or someone else to have something enjoyable ○ [I] *When I get my first paycheck I'm going to indulge in a shopping spree.* ○ [T] *He indulged his passion for skiing whenever he could.*
indulgence /ɪnˈdʌl·dʒəns/ *n* [C/U] ○ [U] *Heavy indulgence in fatty foods should be avoided.* ○ [C] *I do not much like self-quotation, but I shall ask your indulgence.*
indulgent /ɪnˈdʌl·dʒənt/ *adj* ○ *He was indulgent to his grandchildren.*

industrialize /ɪnˈdʌs·triː·əˌlɑɪz/ *v* [I/T] ***social studies*** to increase the amount of industry in a place or region
industrialization /ɪnˌdʌs·triː·ə·ləˈzeɪ·ʃən/ *n* [U]

industrial revolution *n* [C] a period in which the development of machinery leads to major changes in AGRICULTURE, industry, transportation, and social conditions, esp. the Industrial Revolution in England in the 18th century

industry PRODUCTION /ˈɪn·də·stri, ˈɪnˌdʌs·tri/ *n* [U] the companies and activities involved in the production of goods for sale, esp. in a factory ○ *business and industry*
industrial /ɪnˈdʌs·triː·əl/ *adj* **1** *industrial output* ○ *It's an industrial city* (= one that has many factories). **2** An industrial park is a special area for factories and businesses.
industrialist /ɪnˈdʌs·triː·ə·ləst/ *n* [C] an owner or an employee in a high position in industry
industrialized /ɪnˈdʌs·triː·əˌlɑɪzd/ *adj* ○ *industrialized nations*

TYPE OF WORK /ˈɪn·də·stri, ˈɪnˌdʌs·tri/ *n* [C] a type of business ○ *She's worked in the banking and computer industries.*

HARD WORK /ˈɪn·də·stri, ˈɪnˌdʌs·tri/ *n* [U] the quality of working hard ○ *It takes industry and determination to complete a Ph.D.*

industrious /ɪnˈdʌs·triː·əs/ *adj* ○ *Every employee is expected to be competent and industrious.*

WORD FAMILY industry			
Nouns	industrialist industry	*Adjectives*	industrial industrialized industrious
Adverbs	industrially industriously		

inebriated /ɪˈniː·briːˌeɪt̬·əd/ *adj* having drunk too much alcohol

inedible /ɪˈned·ə·bəl/ *adj* not suitable as food ○ *The potato plant produces inedible fruit that looks like green tomatoes.*

ineffective /ˌɪn·əˈfek·tɪv/ *adj* not producing the results that are wanted; not effective ○ *Those pills were ineffective – I still have a headache.*

ineffectual /ˌɪn·əˈfek·tʃə·wəl/ *adj* not able to produce good results ○ *an ineffectual teacher*

inefficient /ˌɪn·əˈfɪʃ·ənt/ *adj* wasting time, money, energy, or other valuable possessions or qualities ○ *Many of their industries are hopelessly inefficient.*

inefficiently /ˌɪn·əˈfɪʃ·ənt·li/ *adv* ○ *He uses his time inefficiently.*

inefficiency /ˌɪn·əˈfɪʃ·ən·si/ *n* [U] ○ *She promised to end government inefficiency.*

inelegant /ɪnˈel·ɪ·gənt/ *adj* not graceful and attractive in character or appearance ○ *inelegant writing*

ineligible /ɪnˈel·ə·dʒə·bəl/ *adj* [not gradable] not allowed by the rules ○ [+ *to* infinitive] *After serving two terms, the president was ineligible to run again.*

inept /ɪˈnept/ *adj* not skilled or effective ○ *He was always pretty inept at sports.*

ineptitude /ɪˈnep·təˌtuːd/ *n* [U] ○ *political/social/economic ineptitude*

inequality /ˌɪn·ɪˈkwɑl·ət̬·i/ *n* [C/U] a lack of equality or fair treatment in the sharing of wealth or opportunities ○ [U] *social/racial inequality*

inequity /ɪˈnek·wət̬·i/ *n* [C/U] *fml* the quality of being unfair, or something that is not fair or equal ○ [C] *We're working to reduce the inequities in school funding.*

inert NOT MOVING /ɪˈnɜrt/ *adj* not moving or not able to move ○ *The inert figure of a man lay in the front of the car.*

CHEMISTRY /ɪˈnɜrt/ *adj* [not gradable] not reacting chemically with other substances ○ *an inert gas*

inertia /ɪˈnɜr·ʃə/ *n* [U] **1** the tendency not to change what is happening ○ *Many teachers were reluctant to use computers in their classrooms simply out of inertia.* **2** ***physics*** Inertia is the force that causes something moving to tend to continue moving, and that causes something not moving to tend to continue not to move.

inescapable /ˌɪn·əˈskeɪ·pə·bəl/ *adj* [not gradable] impossible to avoid or not to accept ○ *The evidence points to the inescapable conclusion that he is guilty of the crime.*

inevitable Ⓐ /ɪˈnev·ət̬·ə·bəl/ *adj* [not gradable] certain to happen ○ *Accidents are the inevitable result of carelessness.*

inevitability Ⓐ /ɪˌnev·ət̬·əˈbɪl·ət̬·i/ *n* [U] ○ *the inevitability of change*

inevitably Ⓐ /ɪˈnev·ət̬·ə·bli/ *adv* [not gradable] ○ *He inevitably orders iced tea with his lunch.*

inexact /ˌɪn·ɪgˈzækt/ *adj* not known in detail or not completely accurate ○ *Economics is an inexact science.*

inexcusable /ˌɪn·ɪkˈskjuː·zə·bəl/ *adj* (of behavior) too bad to be accepted ○ *It was inexcusable for them to leave so early.*

inexhaustible /ˌɪn·ɪgˈzɔː·stə·bəl/ *adj* [not gradable] existing in such large amounts that it cannot be used completely or cannot come to an end ○ *There's a nearly inexhaustible supply of people willing to buy those homes.*

inexorable /ɪˈnek·sə·rə·bəl, ɪˈneg·zə-/ *adj* [not gradable] continuing without any possibility of being stopped ○ *Aging is an inexorable process.*

inexpensive /ˌɪn·ɪkˈspen·sɪv/ *adj* costing little money ○ *an inexpensive hotel*

inexperience /ˌɪn·ɪkˈspɪr·iː·əns/ *n* [U] lack of practice in a particular activity ○ *He has been criticized for his inexperience in foreign affairs.*

inexperienced /ˌɪn·ɪkˈspɪr·iː·ənst/ *adj* ○ *She's relatively inexperienced with computers.*

inexplicable /ˌɪn·ɪkˈsplɪk·ə·bəl, ɪˈnek·splɪk-/ *adj* that cannot be explained or understood ○ *an inexplicable accident*

inexplicably /ˌɪn·ɪkˈsplɪk·ə·bli, ɪˈnek·splɪk-/ *adv* ○ *He inexplicably started to sing.*

inextricable /ˌɪn·ɪkˈstrɪk·ə·bəl, ɪˈnek·strɪk-/ *adj* [not gradable] unable to be separated, freed, or escaped from ○ *There's an inextricable bond between twins.*

inextricably /ˌɪn·ɪkˈstrɪk·ə·bli, ɪˈnek·strɪk-/ *adv* ○ *The Louis Armstrong legend is inextricably linked with his recordings.*

infallible /ɪnˈfæl·ə·bəl/ *adj* [not gradable] never wrong, or never failing ○ *Memory is not infallible.*

infallibly /ɪnˈfæl·ə·bli/ *adv* [not gradable] **1** *My car infallibly starts in cold weather.* **2** Infallibly also means always: *He is infallibly cheerful.*

infallibility /ɪnˌfæl·əˈbɪl·ət̬·i/ *n* [U] ○ *His stubborn belief in his own infallibility kept him from listening to others.*

infamous /ˈɪn·fə·məs/ *adj* well known for something bad; NOTORIOUS ○ *He is infamous for saying that cheating is the way the game is played.*

infamy /ˈɪn·fə·mi/ *n* [U] ○ *Franklin Roosevelt spoke of Japan's attack on Pearl Harbor as "a day that will live in infamy."*

infant /ˈɪn·fənt/ *n* [C] a baby
infancy /ˈɪn·fən·si/ *n* [U] the state or period of being a baby, or *fig.* the early stage of growth or development of something ○ (*fig.*) *Bird research on the island is still in its infancy.*

infantile /ˈɪn·fənˌtɑɪl/ *adj* **1** of or relating to babies ○ *infantile diseases* **2** If you describe the behavior of an older child or adult as infantile, you mean that it is foolish and is typical of a young child: *infantile humor*

infantry /ˈɪn·fən·tri/ *n* [U] soldiers who fight on foot

infatuated /ɪnˈfætʃ·əˌweɪt̬·əd/ *adj* having a strong but unreasonable feeling of love or attraction for someone or something ○ *Susan was infatuated with her friend's brother.*
infatuation /ɪnˌfætʃ·əˈweɪ·ʃən/ *n* [C/U] ○ [C] *It's just an infatuation – she'll get over it.*

infect /ɪnˈfekt/ *v* [T] to cause disease in someone by introducing organisms such as bacteria or viruses ○ *Mosquitoes can infect people with malaria.* ○ (*fig.*) *Fear of an attack infected the entire city.*
infected /ɪnˈfek·təd/ *adj* [not gradable] ○ *an infected toe*
infection /ɪnˈfek·ʃən/ *n* [C/U] ○ [C] *a sinus infection*
infectious /ɪnˈfek·ʃəs/ *adj* [not gradable] **1** *infectious diseases* **2** If something is infectious, it quickly spreads or influences others: *an infectious laugh*

WORD FAMILY infect			
Nouns	infection disinfectant	*Adjectives*	infected infectious
Verbs	infect disinfect		

infer Ⓐ /ɪnˈfɜr/ *v* [T] **-rr-** to reach an opinion from available information or facts ○ [+ *that* clause] *He inferred that she was not interested in a relationship from what she said in her letter.*
inference Ⓐ /ˈɪn·fə·rəns, -frəns/ *n* [C] a belief or opinion that you develop from the information that you know

inferior /ɪnˈfɪr·iː·ər/ *adj* worse than average, or not as good as others of the same type ○ *She felt inferior to her older sister.* ○ Compare SUPERIOR BETTER
inferiority /ɪnˌfɪr·iːˈɔːr·ət̬·i, -ˈɑr-/ *n* [U] ○ *feelings of inferiority*

inferiority complex *n* [C usually sing] a feeling that you are less important, intelligent, or skillful than other people.

infertile /ɪnˈfɜrt·əl/ *adj* [not gradable] (of people or animals) not able to produce young, or (of land) of poor quality for growing crops ○ *an infertile couple* ○ *infertile soil*
infertility /ˌɪn·fərˈtɪl·ət̬·i/ *n* [U]

infest /ɪnˈfest/ *v* [T] (of insects and some animals) to be present in large numbers, sometimes causing disease or damage ○ *When we first moved in, the apartment was infested with cockroaches.*

infidelity /ˌɪn·fəˈdel·ət̬·i/ *n* [C/U] the act of having sex with someone who is not your husband or wife

infield /ˈɪn·fiːld/ *n* [U] (in baseball) the part of the playing field enclosed by the BASES, or the four players whose positions are near the bases ○ Compare OUTFIELD
infielder /ˈɪnˌfiːl·dər/ *n* [C] any of the four players positioned in the infield

infighting /ˈɪnˌfɑɪt̬·ɪŋ/ *n* [U] arguments or competition between members of a group for power or influence ○ *Infighting continues among union and management representatives on the board.*

infiltrate JOIN SECRETLY /ɪnˈfɪlˌtreɪt, ˈɪn·fɪl-/ *v* [I/T] to become a member of a group or organization to secretly gather information about its activities

ENTER GROUND /ɪnˈfɪlˌtreɪt, ˈɪn·fɪl-/ *v* [I] ***earth science*** (of water) to flow slowly down into the earth from the earth's surface, for example, through cracks in rocks
infiltration /ˌɪn·fɪlˈtreɪ·ʃən/ *n* [U] ***earth science***

infinite Ⓐ /ˈɪn·fə·nət/ *adj* [not gradable] without limits; extremely large or great ○ *infinite space* ○ *There seemed to be an infinite number of paint colors to choose from.*
infinitely Ⓐ /ˈɪn·fə·nət·li/ *adv* [not gradable] very much ○ *Downtown traffic is infinitely worse than when we first moved to L.A.*

infinitesimal /ˌɪn·fɪn·əˈtes·ə·məl/ *adj* extremely small ○ *Even in infinitesimal amounts, this poison can kill you.*

infinitive /ɪnˈfɪn·ət̬·ɪv/ *n* [C] ***grammar*** the basic form of a verb, usually following "to" or another verb form ○ *In the sentences "I had to go" and "I must go," "go" is an infinitive.*

infinity /ɪnˈfɪn·ət̬·i/ *n* [C/U] unlimited space, time, or amount, or a number large beyond any limit

infirm /ɪnˈfɜrm/ *adj* physically or mentally weak, esp. because of old age or illness
infirmity /ɪnˈfɜr·mət̬·i/ *n* [C/U] (a) physical or mental weakness

infirmary /ɪnˈfɜr·mə·ri/ *n* [C] an office esp. in a school where someone can receive medical care

inflame /ɪnˈfleɪm/ *v* [T] to excite someone's strong feelings or make them stronger ○ *The defense objected to the graphic pictures, claiming they were meant merely to inflame the jury.*

inflamed /ɪnˈfleɪmd/ *adj* (of a part of the body) red, sore, and often swollen, esp. because of infection ○ *An inflamed tendon in his right shoulder kept him out of the game.*

inflammation /ˌɪn·fləˈmeɪ·ʃən/ *n* [C/U] ○ [C] *Tennis elbow is an inflammation of the ligaments below the elbow.*

inflammable /ɪnˈflæm·ə·bəl/ *adj* FLAMMABLE

inflammatory /ɪnˈflæm·əˌtɔːr·i, -ˌtoʊr·i/ *adj* likely to excite strong feelings, esp. of anger ○ *He thought his opponent's remarks were unfair and inflammatory.*

inflate FILL WITH AIR /ɪnˈfleɪt/ *v* [I/T] to cause an object to increase in size and shape by filling it with air or gas, or (of an object) to become larger as a result of this process ○ [T] *to inflate balloons* ○ [I] *Air bags in cars are designed to inflate automatically on impact.*

inflatable /ɪnˈfleɪţ·ə·bəl/ *adj* [not gradable] ○ *an inflatable mattress*

MAKE GREATER /ɪnˈfleɪt/ *v* [T] to make a number or value higher or greater than it should be, or to make something seem more important than it really is ○ *Company officials misled the public in order to inflate the value of the company's stock.* ○ *The story was inflated by the media.*

WORD FAMILY inflate			
Nouns	inflation	*Adjectives*	inflatable, inflationary
Verbs	inflate, deflate		

inflation /ɪnˈfleɪ·ʃən/ *n* [U] ***social studies*** a continuing rise in prices caused by an increase in the money supply and demand for goods

inflationary /ɪnˈfleɪ·ʃəˌner·i/ *adj* ○ *Inflationary pressures seem to be building in the economy.*

inflection SPEECH /ɪnˈflek·ʃən/ *n* [U] change in the quality of the voice, often showing an emotion ○ *Phyllis replies without any particular inflection in her voice, "I guess I'm lazy."*

GRAMMAR /ɪnˈflek·ʃən/ *n* [C] ***grammar*** a change in a word form or ending to show a difference in the word's meaning or use ○ *"Gets," "got," and "gotten" are inflections of the verb "get."*

inflexible Ⓐ NOT CHANGING /ɪnˈflek·sə·bəl/ *adj* fixed and unable or unwilling to change ○ *Some officials think the law is too harsh and inflexible, and they argue it should be changed.*

inflexibility Ⓐ /ɪnˌflek·səˈbɪl·əţ·i/ *n* [U] ○ *legitimate questions regarding the inflexibility of the sentencing guidelines*

STIFF /ɪnˈflek·sə·bəl/ *adj* [not gradable] (of a substance) stiff and hard, and not able to be bent ○ *an inflexible material*

inflexibility Ⓐ /ɪnˌflek·səˈbɪl·əţ·i/ *n* [U]

inflict /ɪnˈflɪkt/ *v* [T] to force someone or something to experience something unpleasant ○ *Why would anyone inflict harm on a helpless animal?*

in-flight *adj* [not gradable] done, available, or experienced during an aircraft flight ○ *The in-flight movie was "Shrek 2," in Spanish and English.*

influence /ˈɪnˌfluː·əns, *Southern also* ɪnˈfluː-/ *v* [T] to cause someone to change a behavior, belief, or opinion, or to cause something to be changed ○ *Businesses make large contributions to members of Congress, hoping to influence their votes on key issues.* ○ *She was influenced by the common-sense views of her grandparents.* ○ *That speech influenced the course of American history.*

influence /ˈɪnˌfluː·əns, *Southern also* ɪnˈfluː-/ *n* [C/U] the power to have an effect on people or things, or someone or something having such power ○ [C] *The kid next door is a bad/good influence on Kevin.* ○ [U] *She used her influence to get her son a summer job.*

influential /ˌɪn·fluːˈen·tʃəl/ *adj* having a lot of influence ○ *Dr. Carter is an influential member of the board.*

influenza /ˌɪn·fluːˈen·zə/ *n* [U] *esp. fml* FLU

influx /ˈɪn·flʌks/ *n* [U] the arrival of a large number of people or things ○ *The town's economy depends on the summer influx of tourists.*

info /ˈɪn·foʊ/ *n* [U] *short form of* INFORMATION ○ *For additional info, call this number.*

inform /ɪnˈfɔːrm/ *v* [T] to tell someone about something ○ *Keep me informed about any job opportunities.* ○ *She informed her tenants that she was raising the rent.*

informant /ɪnˈfɔːr·mənt/ *n* [C] a person who tells esp. the police or newspaper reporters about something ○ *He was working as an undercover informant for police.*

informative /ɪnˈfɔːr·məţ·ɪv/ *adj* providing useful knowledge or ideas ○ *The dietician's talk was very informative.*

informer /ɪnˈfɔːr·mər/ *n* [C] a person who tells esp. the police about someone's criminal activities

WORD FAMILY inform			
Nouns	informant, information, informer, misinformation	*Adjectives*	informative, uninformative
		Verbs	inform, misinform

informal /ɪnˈfɔːr·məl/ *adj* not formal or official, or not suitable for official or special occasions ○ *an informal gathering* ○ *Informal talks resumed today in an attempt to end the strike.*

informally /ɪnˈfɔːr·mə·li/ *adv* ○ *It's OK to dress informally for the dinner party.*

informality /ˌɪn·fɔːrˈmæl·əţ·i/ *n* [U]

information /ˌɪn·fərˈmeɪ·ʃən/, *short form* **info** *n* [U] news, facts, or knowledge ○ *an important piece of information* ○ *Can you give us some information on tours to Alaska?* ○ *Information about upcoming local events is printed in the newspaper.*

USAGE

information

Remember you cannot make **information** plural. Do not use **informations**.

Could you send me some information about your courses? ➤

For more information please contact our office.
We've been able to find out several pieces of information.
~~*For more informations please contact our office.*~~

WORD CHOICES information

The plural noun **details** is often used to describe facts or pieces of information grouped together.
*Please send me **details** of your training courses.*
The plural nouns **directions** and **instructions** are often used to talk about information which describes how to do something.
*Just follow the **directions** on the label.*
The plural noun **directions** is also used to mean "information about how to get to a place."
*We had to stop and ask for **directions**.*
The plural noun **guidelines** is used for information about the best way to do something.
*The government has issued new **guidelines** on health and safety at work.*
The noun **data** is sometimes used to describe information in the form of facts and numbers.
*Our consultants have been collecting financial **data**.*
The phrase **facts and figures** can be used for information which contains a lot of details which include facts and numbers.
*Check the website for **facts and figures** on skin cancer.*
Written information about a subject is sometimes described as **literature**.
*Some **literature** on our current policy is enclosed.*

infraction /ɪnˈfræk·ʃən/ *n* [C] *fml* a breaking of a rule or law ○ *a minor infraction*

infrared /ˌɪn·frəˈred/ *adj* [not gradable] ***science*** describing light at the red end of the SPECTRUM (= set of colors into which light is separated), which cannot be seen by human beings, and which gives out heat

infrastructure Ⓐ /ˈɪn·frəˌstrʌk·tʃər/ *n* [C] the basic structure of an organization or system which is necessary for its operation, esp. public water, energy, and systems for communication and transport

infrequent /ɪnˈfriː·kwənt/ *adj* not happening often; rare ○ *Wiggins made one of his infrequent trips into Manhattan.*
infrequently /ɪnˈfriː·kwənt·li/ *adv*

infringe /ɪnˈfrɪndʒ/ *v* [I/T] to act in a way that is against a law or that limits someone's rights or freedom ○ [T] *Copying videos infringes copyright law.* ○ [I always + adv/prep] *The senator is opposed to any laws that infringe on a citizen's right to free speech.*
infringement /ɪnˈfrɪndʒ·mənt/ *n* [C/U] ○ [U] *copyright/patent infringement*

infuriate /ɪnˈfjʊr·iːˌeɪt/ *v* [T] to make someone extremely angry ○ *The referee's calls infuriated the home team fans.*
infuriating /ɪnˈfjʊr·iːˌeɪţ·ɪŋ/ *adj* causing anger and annoyance ○ *It's infuriating to be kept waiting this long!*

infuse /ɪnˈfjuːz/ *v* [T] to cause someone or something to take in and be filled with a quality or a condition of mind ○ *His landscape paintings were infused with a warm, subtle light.*
infusion /ɪnˈfjuː·ʒən/ *n* [C] an inward flow that helps to fill something ○ *An infusion of funds is desperately needed.*

ingenious /ɪnˈdʒiːn·jəs/ *adj* (of a person) skilled at inventing new ways to do something, esp. to solve problems, or (of ideas or things) original, and showing esp. the ability to solve problems ○ *an ingenious engineer/songwriter* ○ *She devised an ingenious solution to the problem.*

ingenuity /ˌɪn·dʒəˈnuː·əţ·i/ *n* [U] the skill of thinking, performing, or using things in new ways, esp. to solve problems ○ *With a little ingenuity, meals can be tasty as well as inexpensive.*

ingest /ɪnˈdʒest/ *v* [T] *fml* to take food or liquid into the stomach ○ *These mushrooms are poisonous if ingested.*

ingrained /ˈɪn·greɪnd/ *adj* [not gradable] (of beliefs, attitudes, or habits) so established that they are difficult to change ○ *Saying "Thank You" became such a deeply ingrained habit that he never forgot to do it.*

ingratiate /ɪnˈgreɪ·ʃiːˌeɪt/ *v* [T] *disapproving* to try to make yourself especially pleasant in order to get someone to like or approve of you, and often to influence them to do something for you ○ *He tries to ingratiate himself with the boss by saying that all her ideas are brilliant.*

ingratitude /ɪnˈgræţ·əˌtuːd/ *n* [U] lack of appreciation for help that has been given

ingredient /ɪnˈgriːd·iː·ənt/ *n* [C] one of the parts in a mixture ○ *Combine all the ingredients for the stew.* ○ *(fig.) She viewed color as an essential ingredient of good design.*

in-group *n* [C usually sing] a social group whose members share interests or characteristics that people outside the group do not share

ingrown /ˈɪn·groʊn/ *adj* [not gradable] growing into the flesh ○ *an ingrown toenail*

inhabit /ɪnˈhæb·ət/ *v* [T] to live in a place ○ *These remote islands are inhabited only by birds and animals.*
inhabitant /ɪnˈhæb·əţ·ənt/ *n* [C] a person or animal living in a place

inhale /ɪnˈheɪl/ *v* [I/T] to breathe in something ○ [I/T] *She inhaled (the fresh air) deeply.*
inhalation /ˌɪn·həˈleɪ·ʃən, ˌɪn·əlˈeɪ-/ *n* [U] ○ *Two firefighters were treated for smoke inhalation.*

inhaler /ɪnˈheɪ·lər/ *n* [C] a small device for breathing in a medicine, used esp. by people who have ASTHMA (= disease that can make breathing difficult)

inherent Ⓐ /ɪnˈhɪr·ənt, -ˈher-/ *adj* [not gradable] existing as a natural and permanent quality of something or someone ○ *The drug has certain inherent side effects.*

inherently Ⓐ /ɪnˈhɪr·ənt·li, -ˈher-/ *adv* [not gradable] ○ *Some phenomena in physics are inherently uncertain.*

inherit /ɪnˈher·ət/ *v* [T] **1** to receive money, property, or possessions from someone after the person has died ○ *Who will inherit the house when he dies?* **2** ***biology*** To inherit particular characteristics is to receive them from the parents through the GENES (= chemical patterns).

inheritance /ɪnˈher·ət̬·əns/ *n* [C/U] **1** money, land, or possessions received from someone after the person has died **2** ***biology*** Inheritance also means the particular characteristics received from parents through the GENES.

inhibit Ⓐ /ɪnˈhɪb·ət/ *v* [T] to take an action that makes something less likely to happen, or that discourages someone from doing something ○ *The merger of the two corporations was not allowed because it would inhibit open competition.* ○ *Some states have a rule that inhibits lawyers from talking about their cases outside the courtroom.*

inhibited Ⓐ /ɪnˈhɪb·ət̬·əd/ *adj* not confident enough to say or do what you want ○ *The presence of strangers made her feel inhibited.*

inhibition Ⓐ /ˌɪn·həˈbɪʃ·ən, ˌɪn·ə-/ *n* [C/U] an inability to act naturally, esp. because of a lack of confidence

in-house *adj, adv* [not gradable] involving a company and its employees at the place where they work, and not other companies or people who are not regular employees ○ *Findory's technology was developed in-house.* ○ *in-house lawyers*

inhuman /ɪnˈhjuː·mən, -ˈjuː-/ *adj* [not gradable] extremely cruel; lacking in or not influenced by human feeling ○ *In those days war movies always portrayed the enemy as fanatical, even inhuman.*

inhumanity /ˌɪn·hjuːˈmæn·ət̬·i, -juː-/ *n* [U] inhuman treatment or behavior

inhumane /ˌɪn·hjuːˈmeɪn, -juː-/ *adj* [not gradable] cruel to people or animals in not caring about their suffering or about the conditions under which they live ○ *We have a responsibility to protect animals from inhumane treatment.*

inimitable /ɪˈnɪm·ət̬·ə·bəl/ *adj* [not gradable] *fml* impossible to copy because of being of very high quality or a particular style ○ *Louis Armstrong's inimitable gravelly voice*

initial Ⓐ **BEGINNING** /ɪˈnɪʃ·əl/ *adj* [not gradable] of or at the beginning; first ○ *She failed her driving test on the initial try, but passed the next time.* ○ *The president's initial popularity soon disappeared.*

initially Ⓐ /ɪˈnɪʃ·ə·li/ *adv* [not gradable] ○ *The ceremony, initially planned for this month, was postponed.*

FIRST LETTER /ɪˈnɪʃ·əl/ *n* [C] **1** the first letter of a name, esp. when used to represent a name **2** Your initials are the first letters of each of your names: *They will put your initials on the luggage for another $15.*

initial /ɪˈnɪʃ·əl/ *v* [T] to write your initials on something ○ *Please initial each document.*

initiate Ⓐ **BEGIN** /ɪˈnɪʃ·iːˌeɪt/ *v* [T] to cause something to begin ○ *The peace talks were initiated by a special envoy.*

initiation Ⓐ /ɪˌnɪʃ·iːˈeɪ·ʃən/ *n* [U] ○ *The initiation and carrying out of such a measure, he wrote, is absolutely necessary.*

initiative Ⓐ /ɪˈnɪʃ·ət̬·ɪv/ *n* [C] a new attempt to achieve a goal or solve a problem, or a new method for doing this ○ *The defense secretary announced a major initiative to upgrade our military preparedness.*

ACCEPT IN GROUP /ɪˈnɪʃ·iːˌeɪt/ *v* [T] to signal the acceptance of someone into a group by a special ceremony

initiation Ⓐ /ɪˌnɪʃ·iːˈeɪ·ʃən/ *n* [C/U] a special ceremony or responsibility that signals the acceptance of someone into a group ○ [C] *One fraternity's initiation required new members to wear their coats inside out for a day.* ○ [U] *Sailors who charter a boat must pay a $495 initiation fee to join the club.*

initiative Ⓐ /ɪˈnɪʃ·ət̬·ɪv/ *n* [U] the ability to judge what needs to be done and take action, esp. without suggestion from other people ○ *Lisa showed initiative on the job and was soon promoted.*

inject /ɪnˈdʒekt/ *v* [T] **1** to use a needle to put a drug into a person's body ○ *The morphine took effect almost as soon as it was injected.* **2** If you inject something into an organization, conversation, or exchange, you add it: *The contest was intended to inject some friendly competition into the proceedings.*

injection /ɪnˈdʒek·ʃən/ *n* [C/U] ○ [C] *an insulin injection* ○ [U] *vaccines given by injection*

in-joke *n* [C] a joke that is understood only by a small group of people

injunction /ɪnˈdʒʌŋ·ʃən/ *n* [C] *law* an official order given by a court, usually to stop someone from doing something ○ [+ *to* infinitive] *The court has issued an injunction to prevent distribution of the book.*

injure Ⓐ /ˈɪn·dʒər/ *v* [T] to hurt a living creature, esp. to cause physical harm to someone ○ *The bus careened out of control, injuring several people.*

injured Ⓐ /ˈɪn·dʒərd/ *adj* ○ *She was told to rest her injured back.*

injured Ⓐ /ˈɪn·dʒərd/ *pl n* people who are injured, considered as a group ○ *The injured were taken to several nearby hospitals.*

injury Ⓐ /ˈɪn·dʒə·ri/ *n* [C/U] physical harm or damage done to a living thing ○ [C] *He was removed from the game with a knee injury.* ○ [U] *They were lucky to escape injury.*

WORD FAMILY injure

Nouns	injury	*Adjectives*	injured
			uninjured
Verbs	injure		

injustice /ɪnˈdʒʌs·təs/ *n* [C/U] the condition of being unfair and lacking justice, or an action that is unfair ○ [U] *social injustice* ○ [C] *I was falsely arrested, so there was definitely an injustice done.* ○ Related adjective: UNJUST

ink /ɪŋk/ *n* colored liquid used for writing, printing, and drawing ○ [C] *colored inks* ○ [U] *Please write in ink, not pencil.*
inky /ˈɪŋ·ki/ *adj* colored or covered with ink, or having this appearance ○ *the inky blue of the night sky*

inkling /ˈɪŋ·klɪŋ/ *n* [U] a slight idea that something is true or likely to happen, although it is not certain ○ *She saw the look on Nick's face but had no inkling of what it meant.*

inland /ˈɪn·lænd, -lənd/ *adj, adv* away from the sea ○ *We left the coast and headed inland.*

in-law /ˈɪn·lɔː/ *n* [C] a person you are related to by marriage, esp. the parents and other members of your husband's or wife's family ○ *He's spending the holiday with his in-laws.*

inlay /ˈɪn·leɪ/ *n* [C/U] a decorative pattern made of pieces set into the surface of an object ○ [U] *a pine table with mahogany inlay*

inlet /ˈɪn·let, -lət/ *n* [C] a narrow channel of water that goes from a sea or lake into the land or between islands

in-line skate /ˌɪn ˌlɑɪn ˈskeɪt/, *trademark* **Rollerblade** *n* [C usually pl] a type of shoe with a single row of small wheels on the bottom which you wear in order to travel along quickly for enjoyment, sports, or exercise

inmate /ˈɪn·meɪt/ *n* [C] a person who is forced by law to stay in a prison or hospital ○ *The inmates were living in terrible conditions.*

inn /ɪn/ *n* [C] a hotel, esp. a small hotel, often with a restaurant

innards /ˈɪn·ərdz/ *pl n infml* the inner organs of a person or animal, or the inside parts of a machine ○ *the innards of radios* ○ *frogs' innards*

innate /ɪˈneɪt/ *adj* [not gradable] (of a quality) which you are born with, or which is present naturally ○ *Her dance expresses the innate beauty of the human spirit.*
innately /ɪˈneɪt·li/ *adv* ○ *Power is innately seductive.*

inner /ˈɪn·ər/ *adj* [not gradable] inside or contained within something else ○ *These islands lie between the bay's outer and inner sections.* ○ *She met life's challenges with courage and inner strength* (= the strength of her character or spirit). ○ *Simpson was part of the club's* **inner circle** (= the most powerful group).

inner-city *adj* [not gradable] found in or involving the older, central part of a city where there are poor people and bad housing ○ *There are more problems in large, inner-city school districts.*
inner city *n* [C] ○ *The program gives kids from the inner city a taste of the wilderness.*

innermost /ˈɪn·ər ˌmoʊst/ *adj* [not gradable] (of thoughts) most strongly felt and most private, or (of objects) nearest to the center ○ *They told her their innermost secrets.*

inner tube *n* [C] a round rubber tube filled with air that fits inside a car or bicycle tire

inning /ˈɪn·ɪŋ/ *n* [C] a numbered period of play in a game of baseball in which both teams BAT (= try to hit the ball), or one team's turn to bat in one of these periods ○ *Cleveland scored three times in the ninth inning.*

innkeeper /ˈɪn ˌkiː·pər/ *n* [C] *esp. old use* a person who owns or manages an INN (= a hotel)

innocent /ˈɪn·ə·sənt/ *adj* (of a person) not guilty of a particular crime, or having no knowledge of the unpleasant and evil things in life, or (of words or an action) not intended to cause harm ○ *He pleaded innocent to all charges against him.* ○ *It was a totally innocent kind of mistake.* ○ *Several innocent bystanders* (= people who were not involved but who were there by chance) *were injured when his car slid off the road.*
innocence /ˈɪn·ə·səns/ *n* [U] ○ *He acts like he doesn't have to prove his innocence* (= lack of guilt).
innocently /ˈɪn·ə·sənt·li/ *adv* ○ *Some people innocently drove into the contaminated area.*

WORD FAMILY innocent			
Nouns	innocence	*Adverbs*	innocently
Adjectives	innocent		

innocuous /ɪˈnɑk·jə·wəs/ *adj* completely without harm ○ *an innocuous statement* ○ *innocuous activities*

innovate Ⓐ /ˈɪn·əˌveɪt/ *v* [I] to introduce changes and new ideas ○ *The fashion industry is always desperate to innovate.*
innovator Ⓐ /ˈɪn·əˌveɪt̬·ər/ *n* [C] ○ *A fearless innovator, Ives liked to play music simultaneously in different meters and keys.*

innovative Ⓐ /ˈɪn·əˌveɪt̬·ɪv/ *adj* (of ideas and methods) new and different ○ *Gwen introduced a number of innovative solutions.*
innovation Ⓐ /ˌɪn·əˈveɪ·ʃən/ *n* [C/U] ○ [U] *The recording industry is driven by constant innovation.* ○ [C] *His latest innovation is a theater company that will perform for schools.*

innuendo /ˌɪn·jəˈwen·doʊ/ *n* [C/U] *pl* **innuendos, innuendoes** a remark that suggests something but does not refer to it directly, or this type of remark in general ○ [U] *The election campaign was marred by rumor and innuendo.*

innumerable /ɪˈnuː·mə·rə·bəl/ *adj* [not gradable] too many to be counted, or very many ○ *Roland sent her innumerable love letters.*

inoculate /ɪˈnɑk·jəˌleɪt/ *v* [T] to give a person or animal a VACCINE (= substance to prevent disease)
inoculation /ɪˌnɑk·jəˈleɪ·ʃən/ *n* [C/U] ○ [C] *a cholera inoculation*

inoffensive /ˌɪn·əˈfen·sɪv/ *adj* not causing any harm or offense ○ *Their music is upbeat and inoffensive.*

inoperable DISEASE /ɪˈnɑp·ə·rə·bəl/ *adj* [not gradable] (of an illness, esp. CANCER) that doctors are unable to treat or remove by an operation
NOT WORKING /ɪˈnɑp·ə·rə·bəl/ *adj* [not gradable] not able to be done or made to work ○ *Most of the machines were inoperable.*

inopportune /ɪˌnɑp·ərˈtuːn/ *adj fml* happening or done at a time that is not suitable or convenient ○ *Difficulties seem to crop up at the most inopportune times.*

inordinate /ɪˈnɔːrd·ən·ət/ *adj* unreasonably or unusually large in size or degree
inordinately /ɪˈnɔːrd·ən·ət·li/ *adv* ○ *She seemed to be inordinately fond of her dog.*

inorganic /ˌɪnˌɔːrˈgæn·ɪk/ *adj* [not gradable] not consisting of living material, or relating to substances that do not contain living material ○ *Rocks and metals are inorganic.* ○ *inorganic chemistry* ○ Compare ORGANIC LIVING

inpatient /ˈɪnˌpeɪ·ʃənt/ *n* [C] a person who stays one or more nights in a hospital in order to receive medical care ○ *His insurance company is unwilling to pay for inpatient treatment.* ○ Compare OUTPATIENT

input Ⓐ /ˈɪn·pʊt/ *n* [C/U] information, money, or energy that is put into a system, organization, or machine so it can operate ○ [U] *The city plans to get input from local community groups.* ○ [C] *This unit has three audio inputs* (= places to connect other devices).
input Ⓐ /ˈɪn·pʊt/ *v* [T] *pres. part.* **inputting**, *past* **input, inputted** ○ *keyboard operators inputting data*

inquest /ˈɪn·kwest/ *n* [C] an official examination of facts in an attempt to discover the cause of something, esp. of a sudden or violent death ○ *a coroner's inquest*

inquire, **enquire** /ɪnˈkwɑɪr/ *v* to ask for information ○ [I] *Officials from around the country have called to inquire about the program.* ○ [+ question word] *Phil inquired whether I wanted to meet his roommate.*
inquiring, **enquiring** /ɪnˈkwɑɪ·rɪŋ/ *adj* ○ *You have a very inquiring mind.*
inquiry, **enquiry** /ɪnˈkwɑɪ·ri, ˈɪn·kwə·ri/ *n* [C/U] **1** [C] *I've made inquiries about the cost of a ticket.* **2** An inquiry is also an official attempt to discover the facts about something.

PHRASAL VERB with inquire

• **inquire into** *something* to try to discover the facts about something ○ *The committee had no right to inquire into his politics.*

inquisition /ˌɪn·kwəˈzɪʃ·ən/ *n* [C usually sing] a detailed questioning, esp. of someone's beliefs

inquisitive /ɪnˈkwɪz·ət̬·ɪv/ *adj* (of a person or their behavior) eager to know a lot about people or things ○ *an inquisitive mind* ○ *Our neighbors are too inquisitive.*

inroads /ˈɪn·roʊdz/ *pl n* direct and noticeable effects on something ○ *Women have made major inroads into this profession over the last 20 years.*

ins and outs /ˈɪn·zəˈnɑʊts/ *pl n* the details or facts relating to something ○ *She knows the ins and outs of the law.*

insane /ɪnˈseɪn/ *adj* extremely unreasonable, or mentally ill ○ *You'd have to be insane to spend $200 on dinner!* ○ *Fisher went insane and had to be hospitalized.*
insanely /ɪnˈseɪn·li/ *adv* ○ *She's insanely* (= extremely unreasonably) *jealous of her husband.*
insanity /ɪnˈsæn·ət̬·i/ *n* [U] ○ *The jury found him innocent on the grounds of temporary insanity* (= mental illness).

insatiable /ɪnˈseɪ·ʃə·bəl/ *adj* (of a desire or need) too great to be satisfied ○ *an insatiable appetite* ○ *insatiable curiosity*

inscribe /ɪnˈskrɑɪb/ *v* [T] to write words in a book or cut words onto the surface of an object ○ *She inscribed the book, "To my number-one fan."*
inscription /ɪnˈskrɪp·ʃən/ *n* [C] ○ *Wind and rain wore away the inscriptions on the gravestones.*

inscrutable /ɪnˈskruːt̬·ə·bəl/ *adj* very difficult to understand or get to know ○ *an inscrutable smile* ○ *He believes that a certain portion of life must remain inscrutable.*

insect /ˈɪn·sekt/ *n* [C] ***biology*** a type of small animal with six legs, a body divided into three parts, and often two pairs of wings, for example, an ant, beetle, or butterfly

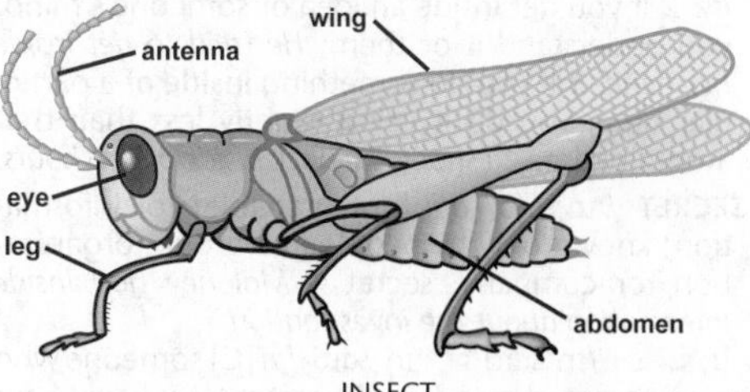

INSECT

insecticide /ɪnˈsek·təˌsɑɪd/ *n* [C/U] a chemical substance for killing insects ○ Compare PESTICIDE

insecure Ⓐ **NOT CONFIDENT** /ˌɪn·sɪˈkjʊr/ *adj* (of people) lacking confidence and doubting their own abilities ○ *Eleanor was shy and insecure as a child.*
insecurity Ⓐ /ˌɪn·sɪˈkjʊr·ət̬·i/ *n* [C/U] ○ [C] *I think he's trying to deal with his fears and insecurities.*
NOT SAFE /ˌɪn·sɪˈkjʊr/ *adj* (of objects or situations) not fixed or safe ○ *The stairs seemed kind of rickety and insecure.*
insecurity Ⓐ /ˌɪn·sɪˈkjʊr·ət̬·i/ *n* [C/U] ○ [U] *They experienced economic insecurity due to unemployment.*

inseminate /ɪnˈsem·əˌneɪt/ *v* [T] to put a male's sperm into a female and make her pregnant
insemination /ɪnˌsem·əˈneɪ·ʃən/ *n* [U]

insensitive /ɪnˈsen·sət̬·ɪv/ *adj* **1** not aware of other people's feelings, or not showing sympathy for the feelings of other people ○ *The governor apologized for his insensitive remarks about the homeless.* **2** Insensitive can also mean not noticing

the effects of something or unable to feel something: *His feet seem to be insensitive to pain.*
insensitivity /ɪnˌsen·səˈtɪv·ət̬·i/ *n* [U] ○ *I find your insensitivity to my needs insulting.*

inseparable /ɪnˈsep·ə·rə·bəl/ *adj* (of two or more people) such good friends that they spend most of their time together, or (of two or more things) so closely connected that they cannot be considered separately ○ *When we were kids Zoe and I were inseparable.*

insert Ⓐ /ɪnˈsɜrt/ *v* [T] to put something in something else ○ *Insert your ATM card in the slot to begin your transaction.*
insert Ⓐ /ˈɪn·sɜrt/ *n* [C] ○ *newspaper advertising inserts* (= extra pieces placed inside)
insertion Ⓐ /ɪnˈsɜr·ʃən/ *n* [U] ○ *Software can automate the insertion of SGML codes in texts.*

inset /ˈɪn·set/ *n* [C] something positioned within a larger object ○ *The city map has an inset in the corner showing the downtown area in more detail.*

I

inside INNER PART /ɪnˈsɑɪd, ˈɪn·sɑɪd/ *n* **1** the inner part, space, or side of (something) ○ [U] *the inside of a car* ○ [U] *the inside of your wrist* **2** *infml* Your insides are your stomach and other digestive organs. ○ Compare OUTSIDE OUTER PART
inside /ɪnˈsɑɪd, ˈɪn·sɑɪd/ *prep, adj, adv* [not gradable] **1** *What's inside the big box?* ○ *I'll work inside and you work outside.* ○ *People inside* (= working for) *the White House get an us versus them mentality.* **2** If you get inside an idea or someone's mind, you understand it or them: *He tried to get inside her mind.* **3** If you do something **inside of** a particular time, you do it using slightly less than that amount of time ○ *I should be back inside of two hours.*

SECRET /ˈɪn·sɑɪd/ *adj* [not gradable] (of information) known only by people in a group, organization, or company; secret ○ *Maloney had inside information about the investigation.*
insider /ɪnˈsɑɪd·ər, ˈɪnˌsɑɪd-/ *n* [C] someone who is an accepted member of a group ○ *His books have made him an insider in the music world.*

IDIOM with **inside**

• **inside out** **1** with the inside part facing out ○ *She put her sweater on inside out.* **2** If you know something **inside out**, you know it very well: *He's the best person to tell you how to get there because he knows the city inside out.*

insidious /ɪnˈsɪd·iː·əs/ *adj* (of something unpleasant or dangerous) gradually and secretly causing harm ○ *Cancer is an insidious disease.*
insidiously /ɪnˈsɪd·iː·ə·sli/ *adv* ○ *His negative attitude slowly and insidiously spoiled the atmosphere around the office.*

insight Ⓐ /ˈɪn·sɑɪt/ *n* [C/U] a clear, deep, and sometimes sudden understanding of a complicated problem or situation, or the ability to have such an understanding ○ [C] *Hurston's writings were recognized for their insights.* ○ [U] *His work shows originality and insight.*
insightful Ⓐ /ˈɪnˌsɑɪt·fəl, ɪnˈsɑɪt-/ *adj* ○ *an insightful observation*

insignia /ɪnˈsɪg·niː·ə/ *n* [C] an object or mark which shows that a person belongs to a particular organization or has a particular rank ○ *a Cub Scout insignia*

insignificant Ⓐ /ˌɪn·sɪgˈnɪf·ɪ·kənt/ *adj* not important or thought to be valuable ○ *Her problems seemed pretty insignificant compared to her brother's.*
insignificance /ˌɪn·sɪgˈnɪf·ɪ·kəns/ *n* [U] ○ *My colleagues despised this man for his insignificance.*
insignificantly Ⓐ /ˌɪn·sɪgˈnɪf·ɪ·kənt·li/ *adv*

insincere /ˌɪn·sɪnˈsɪr/ *adj disapproving* not feeling, believing, or meaning something although you pretend to; not sincere ○ *an insincere promise/offer*
insincerity /ˌɪn·sɪnˈser·ət̬·i/ *n* [U] ○ *There's often a bit of insincerity in these speeches.*

insinuate /ɪnˈsɪn·jəˌweɪt/ *v* [T] to express but not directly state something ○ *What exactly are you insinuating?* ○ [+ (*that*) clause] *She insinuated (that) I'm getting fat.*
insinuation /ɪnˌsɪn·jəˈweɪ·ʃən/ *n* [C/U] ○ [C] *Contrary to your insinuation, we are not being unreasonable.*

insipid /ɪnˈsɪp·əd/ *adj* (of food) lacking a strong taste or character, or (of people, activities, or entertainment) lacking in interest or energy ○ *an insipid flavor* ○ *insipid TV sitcoms*

insist /ɪnˈsɪst/ *v* to state or demand forcefully, esp. despite opposition ○ [I] *She insisted on seeing her lawyer.* ○ [+ (*that*) clause] *Greg still insists (that) he did nothing wrong.*
insistence /ɪnˈsɪs·təns/ *n* [U] ○ *At his insistence, I continued living with my mother.* ○ *Her insistence that he bring her took him by surprise.*
insistent /ɪnˈsɪs·tənt/ *adj* ○ *I heard a soft, insistent rapping at the door.*
insistently /ɪnˈsɪs·tənt·li/ *adv* ○ *She was insistently cheerful.*

WORD FAMILY insist			
Nouns	insistence	*Verbs*	insist
Adjectives	insistent	*Adverbs*	insistently

insofar as /ˌɪn·səˈfɑr·əz/ *adv* [not gradable] *fml* to the degree that ○ *She had done her best to comfort him, insofar as she was able.*

insolation /ˌɪn·soʊˈleɪ·ʃən/ *n* [U] ***earth science*** the amount of energy from the sun that reaches the earth

insolent /ˈɪn·sə·lənt/ *adj* (of a person or their behavior) intentionally and rudely showing no respect ○ *Students were often inattentive, sometimes even insolent, and showed relatively little interest in their work.*
insolently /ˈɪn·sə·lənt·li/ *adv*

insoluble DIFFICULT TO SOLVE /ɪnˈsɑl·jə·bəl/ *adj* [not gradable] (of a problem) so difficult that it is impossible to solve ○ *Traffic congestion in big cities seems to be an insoluble problem.*

IMPOSSIBLE TO MIX /ɪnˈsɑl·jə·bəl/ *adj* (of a substance) impossible to dissolve ○ *Sand is insoluble in water.*

insolvent /ɪnˈsɑl·vənt, -ˈsɔːl-/ *adj* (esp. of a company) unable to pay what you owe because you do not have enough money ○ *When it discovered the loans could not be repaid, the bank became insolvent.*

insomnia /ɪnˈsɑm·niː·ə/ *n* [U] the condition of being unable to sleep

inspect Ⓐ /ɪnˈspekt/ *v* [T] **1** to look at something or someone carefully in order to discover information, esp. about the quality or condition ○ *After the accident both drivers got out and inspected their cars for damage.* **2** If an official person inspects a thing, place, or a group of people, the official looks at it carefully in order to make certain it is in good condition and that rules are being obeyed: *Someone from the Health Department will inspect the restaurant this afternoon.*

inspection Ⓐ /ɪnˈspek·ʃən/ *n* [C/U] **1** [U] *At first she suspected that the letter was a forgery, but on closer inspection* (= looked at more carefully), *it appeared to be genuine.* **2** An inspection is also a careful examination by an official to make certain that something is in good condition, or that rules are being obeyed: [C] *He made an inspection of the elevators in the building.*

inspector Ⓐ /ɪnˈspek·tər/ *n* [C] **1** *a safety inspector* **2** An inspector is also a police officer of high rank.

inspire /ɪnˈspɑɪr/ *v* [T] **1** to fill someone with confidence and desire to do something ○ *She inspired her students to do the best they could.* **2** If something or someone inspires something else, it causes or leads to it: *A successful TV program inspires many imitations.*

inspiration /ˌɪn·spəˈreɪ·ʃən/ *n* [C/U] **1** [C usually sing] *She has been an inspiration to us all* (= a good example for all). **2** An inspiration is also a sudden good idea: [+ *to* infinitive] *She had the inspiration to turn the play into a musical.*

inspirational /ˌɪn·spəˈreɪ·ʃən·əl/ *adj* ○ *He gave an inspirational talk on overcoming obstacles in life.*

inspiring /ɪnˈspɑɪ·rɪŋ/ *adj approving* causing you to feel confident about yourself or eager to learn or do something ○ *She was an inspiring teacher and a gifted scientist.*

instability Ⓐ /ˌɪn·stəˈbɪl·ət̬·i/ *n* [U] the condition of being likely to change, esp. unexpectedly ○ *Teenagers often go through periods of emotional instability.*

install PUT IN /ɪnˈstɔːl/ *v* [T] **1** to put something in place so that it is ready for use ○ *We're having a new tile floor installed in the kitchen.* **2** When you install computer SOFTWARE, you copy it onto your computer so that it can be used.

installation /ˌɪn·stəˈleɪ·ʃən/ *n* [C/U] ○ [U] *Do you have to pay extra for installation?*

PLACE IN JOB /ɪnˈstɔːl/ *v* [T] to place someone formally in an official job of high rank ○ *The new president of the university was installed before the graduation ceremony.*

installment /ɪnˈstɔːl·mənt/ *n* [C] **1** one of a number of payments that you make over a period of time to pay for something that you can use while you are paying for it ○ *We paid for the car in monthly installments over two years.* **2** An installment is also one of the parts of something, such as a show, that is experienced as part of a series over a period of time: *a TV miniseries with five installments*

instance /ˈɪn·stəns/ *n* [C] a particular situation, event, or fact ○ *There were several instances of computer failure before we got the system to work properly.* ○ *Usually this kind of skin condition is caused by a food allergy, but in this instance it may be caused by the medicine you are taking.* ○ *Can you tell us a little about your background?* **For instance** (= As an example), *where were you born?*

instant /ˈɪn·stənt/ *n* [C usually sing] a very short moment of time, or a particular point in time ○ *At that instant, someone knocked on the door.* ○ *Call me the instant you get home* (= as soon as you get to your home).

instant /ˈɪn·stənt/ *adj* [not gradable] **1** happening immediately ○ *I took an instant liking to him.* **2** An instant food or drink is one, usually in dried or powdered form, that can be prepared easily and quickly, esp. by adding hot water: *instant coffee*

instantly /ˈɪn·stənt·li/ *adv* [not gradable] ○ *With e-mail you can send a message across the world almost instantly.*

WORD FAMILY instant			
Nouns	instance instant	*Adjectives*	instant instantaneous
Adverbs	instantly instantaneously		

instantaneous /ˌɪn·stənˈteɪ·niː·əs/ *adj* [not gradable] happening or completed immediately, without any delay ○ *TV has conditioned us to expect instantaneous answers to difficult questions.*

instantaneously /ˌɪn·stənˈteɪ·niː·ə·sli/ *adv* [not gradable]

instantaneous velocity *n* [U] ***physics*** a calculation that tells how far and in what direction an object would travel if it continued in the way it was going for one second

instant message *v* [T] IM

instant replay *n* [C] a short piece of film in a sports broadcast that shows a particular action in a game again, immediately after it has happened ○ *When they showed the instant replay, it looked like he had caught the ball out of bounds.*

instead /ɪnˈsted/ *adv* [not gradable] rather than; as an ALTERNATIVE ○ *If we don't go to Europe this summer, where would you like to go instead* (= what other place would you like to go)? ○ *We went by train instead of by car.*

instep /ˈɪn·step/ *n* [C] the curved upper part of the foot between the toes and the heel

instigate /ˈɪn·stəˌgeɪt/ *v* [T] to cause an event or situation to happen by your actions ○ *Changes in the orientation program were instigated by the new director.*

instigation /ˌɪn·stəˈgeɪ·ʃən/ *n* [U] ○ *The inquiry was begun at the instigation of Senator Hyde* (= he asked for it).

instill /ɪnˈstɪl/ *v* [T] to put a feeling, idea, or principle gradually into someone's mind, so that it has a strong influence on the way the person lives ○ *My parents instilled in me a love of reading.*

instinct /ˈɪn·stɪŋt/ *n* [C/U] **1** a natural ability that helps you decide what to do or how to act without thinking ○ [U] *He lacked the instinct for quick action.* ○ [C] *His biggest asset may be his political instincts.* **2** Instinct is also the ability to behave in a particular way that has not been learned: [U] *the maternal instinct*

instinctive /ɪnˈstɪŋ·tɪv/ *adj* ○ *My instinctive reaction was to walk away to avoid an argument.*

instinctively /ɪnˈstɪŋ·tɪv·li/ *adv* ○ *She instinctively understood how I felt.*

institute Ⓐ **START** /ˈɪn·stəˌtuːt/ *v* [T] to put into effect; cause to be used ○ *These are some of the safety guidelines we've instituted in our hotels.*

ORGANIZATION /ˈɪn·stəˌtuːt/ *n* [C] an organization whose purpose is to advance the study of a particular subject ○ *The National Institutes of Health fund medical research in many areas.*

institution Ⓐ **ORGANIZATION** /ˌɪn·stəˈtuː·ʃən/ *n* [C] **1** an organization that exists to serve a public purpose such as education or support for people who need help ○ *a charitable/educational/scientific institution* **2** An institution of higher learning is a college or university.

institutional Ⓐ /ˌɪn·stəˈtuː·ʃən·əl/ *adj* of or typical of an institution ○ *The hospital provides typically awful institutional food.*

institutionalize Ⓐ /ˌɪn·stəˈtuː·ʃən·əlˌɑɪz/ *v* [T] to send someone to stay or live in an institution, esp. a hospital for people who are mentally ill ○ *Martin had to be institutionalized for several months during his last depression.*

institutionally Ⓐ /ˌɪn·stəˈtuː·ʃən·əl·i, -ʃnə·li/ *adv*

CUSTOM /ˌɪn·stəˈtuː·ʃən/ *n* [C] a custom or practice that has existed for a long time and is accepted as an important part of a society ○ *the institution of marriage*

instruct Ⓐ **TEACH** /ɪnˈstrʌkt/ *v* [T] to teach someone how to do something ○ *I need someone to instruct me on how to use the computer.*

instruction Ⓐ /ɪnˈstrʌk·ʃən/ *n* [U] ○ *The course gives you basic instruction in car maintenance and repairs.*

instructional /ɪnˈstrʌk·ʃən·əl/ *adj* ○ *He taught himself the sport by watching online instructional videos.*

instructions Ⓐ /ɪnˈstrʌk·ʃənz/ *pl n* information about how to do, make, or use something ○ *Didn't the DVD player come with any instructions?*

instructive Ⓐ /ɪnˈstrʌk·tɪv/ *adj* giving useful or interesting information ○ *It would be instructive to follow up the opinion poll with another one after the election.*

instructor Ⓐ /ɪnˈstrʌk·tər/ *n* [C] **1** a person whose job is to teach people a skill ○ *a driving/ski/swimming instructor* **2** An instructor is also a teacher at a college or university, ranking lower than a PROFESSOR.

ORDER /ɪnˈstrʌkt/ *v* [T] to order or tell someone to do something, esp. in a formal way ○ [+ *to* infinitive] *The police have been instructed not to let anyone leave the area.*

instruction Ⓐ /ɪnˈstrʌk·ʃən/ *n* [C usually pl] ○ [+ *to* infinitive] *The general received instructions to return to the base.*

WORD FAMILY instruct

Nouns	instruction instructions instructor	*Adjectives*	instructional instructive
		Adverbs	instructively
Verbs	instruct		

instrument **MUSIC** /ˈɪn·strə·mənt/ *n* [C] an object, such as a piano, guitar, or FLUTE, which is played to produce musical sounds ○ *He plays saxophone, trumpet, and several other instruments.*

instrumental /ˌɪn·strəˈment·əl/ *adj* [not gradable] performed with musical instruments only and not voices

TOOL /ˈɪn·strə·mənt/ *n* [C] a tool or other device used for doing a particular piece of work ○ *surgical instruments*

instrumental /ˌɪn·strəˈment·əl/ *adj* important in causing something to happen ○ *As secretary of state, he was instrumental in the creation of NATO.*

insubordination /ˌɪn·səˌbɔːrd·ənˈeɪ·ʃən/ *n* [U] the refusal to obey someone who is in a higher position than you and who has the authority to tell you what to do ○ *She had recently been fired from her job for insubordination.*

insubstantial /ˌɪn·səbˈstæn·tʃəl/ *adj* of little value or importance, or not being strong, solid, or large ○ *He was popular during the early part of the 20th century, but today his work seems dated and insubstantial.*

insufferable /ɪnˈsʌf·ə·rə·bəl/ *adj* extremely unpleasant and therefore difficult to bear ○ *George is an insufferable bore, and you know it.*

insufficient Ⓐ /ˌɪn·səˈfɪʃ·ənt/ *adj* [not gradable] not enough in amount, strength, or quality; less than is needed ○ *There was insufficient evidence, so we had to find him not guilty.*

insufficiently Ⓐ /ˌɪn·səˈfɪʃ·ənt·li/ *adv* [not gradable] ○ *Many of the students got low grades because they were insufficiently prepared.*

insular /ˈɪn·sə·lər, -sjə-/ *adj* interested only in your own country or group and not willing to accept different or foreign ideas or people

insulate **COVER** /ˈɪn·səˌleɪt/ *v* [T] to use a material to cover or go around the surface of something in order to prevent heat, electricity, etc., from escaping or entering ○ *We've saved a lot on our heating bills by insulating the attic.*

insulator /ˈɪn·səˌleɪt̬·ər/ *n* [C] ***physics*** a substance that does not CONDUCT electricity (= allow it to pass through)

insulation /ˌɪn·səˈleɪ·ʃən/ *n* [U] the substance used in insulating ○ *Rubber is better insulation than cloth for electric wiring.*

PROTECT /ˈɪn·səˌleɪt/ *v* [T] to protect someone or something from outside influences ○ *As a member of a rich and powerful family, she was insulated from ordinary life.*

insulin /ˈɪn·sə·lən/ *n* [U] ***biology*** a HORMONE (= chemical substance) in the body that controls the amount of sugar in the blood

insult /ɪnˈsʌlt/ *v* [T] to act in a way or say something that is offensive or rude to someone ○ *Don't insult me just because I can't dance.*
insult /ˈɪn·sʌlt/ *n* [C] an offensive remark or action ○ *Offering me so little money was an insult.*
insulting /ɪnˈsʌl·tɪŋ/ *adj* ○ *an insulting remark*

insure MAKE CERTAIN, **ensure** /ɪnˈʃʊr/ *v* to make something certain, or to be certain about something ○ [+ (*that*) clause] *Because of the importance of the game, we wanted to insure (that) it would be televised.* ○ [T] *We had reporters check to insure the accuracy of the story.*

PROTECT /ɪnˈʃʊr/ *v* [T] to protect yourself or your property against damage or loss by making regular payments to a company that will pay for the damage or loss if it happens ○ *We've insured our house for $100,000.*
insurance /ɪnˈʃʊr·əns, *Southern also* ˈɪnˌʃʊr-/ *n* [U] the agreement in which you pay a company money and the company pays the cost if you have an accident, injury, or loss ○ *fire/health/life insurance*

insurgent /ɪnˈsɜr·dʒənt/ *n* [C] ***world history*** a person who is a member of a group that is fighting against the government of their country
insurgency /ɪnˈsɜr·dʒən·si/ *n* [C/U] ***world history*** the violent struggle of a group of people who refuse to accept their government's power ○ *The insurgency continues despite last week's assault on the rebel stronghold.*

insurmountable /ˌɪn·sərˈmaʊnt·ə·bəl/ *adj* [not gradable] (esp. of a problem or a difficulty) so great that it cannot be dealt with successfully ○ *As the election returns came in, it was clear that his opponent had an insurmountable lead.*

insurrection /ˌɪn·səˈrek·ʃən/ *n* [C/U] an organized attempt by a group of people to defeat their government or ruler and take control of the country, usually by violence

intact /ɪnˈtækt/ *adj* complete and in the original state ○ *He emerged from the investigation with his reputation largely intact* (= not damaged).

intake /ˈɪn·teɪk/ *n* [U] the amount of something such as food, breath, or a liquid that is taken in by someone or something ○ *the intake of fuel in a vehicle* ○ *a deep intake of breath*

intangible /ɪnˈtæn·dʒə·bəl/ *adj* influencing you but not able to be seen or physically felt ○ *There is the intangible benefit of playing a home game before a friendly crowd.*
intangible /ɪnˈtæn·dʒə·bəl/ *n* [C] ○ *Common sense and creativity are some of the intangibles we're looking for in the people we hire.*

integer /ˈɪnt·ə·dʒər/ *n* [C] ***mathematics*** a whole number and not a FRACTION ○ *The numbers 5, 3, and 0 are integers.*

integral Ⓐ /ˈɪnt·ə·grəl, ɪnˈteg·rəl/ *adj* necessary and important as a part of a whole, or contained within it ○ *Taking a ride on the canals of Venice is an integral part of experiencing that city.*

integrate Ⓐ /ˈɪnt·əˌgreɪt/ *v* [T] **1** to end the separation of people by race, sex, national origin, etc., in an organization or in society ○ *Until President Truman integrated the armed forces in 1948, African-American soldiers served in segregated army units.* **2** To integrate is also to combine two or more things to make something more effective: *We were taught how to integrate computer use into normal classroom procedures.*
integration Ⓐ /ˌɪnt·əˈgreɪ·ʃən/ *n* [U]

integrity Ⓐ HONESTY /ɪnˈteg·rət̬·i/ *n* [U] the quality of being honest and having strong moral principles ○ *He was a man of the highest personal integrity.*

UNITY /ɪnˈteg·rət̬·i/ *n* [U] wholeness and unity ○ *The integrity of the play would be ruined by changing the ending.*

intellect /ˈɪnt·əlˌekt/ *n* [C/U] a person's ability to think and understand esp. ideas at a high level ○ [C] *The stroke left her partially paralyzed, but her intellect was not affected.*
intellectual /ˌɪnt·əlˈek·tʃə·wəl/ *adj* relating to the ability to think and understand ideas at a high level, or involving ideas ○ *He was among the political and intellectual leaders of his time.*
intellectual /ˌɪnt·əlˈek·tʃə·wəl/ *n* [C] a person whose life or work centers around the study or use of ideas, such as in teaching or writing
intellectually /ˌɪnt·əlˈek·tʃə·wə·li/ *adv* ○ *It's fun and it's intellectually stimulating* (= encourages you to think at a high level).

intelligence Ⓐ THINKING ABILITY /ɪnˈtel·ə·dʒəns/ *n* [U] the ability to understand and learn well, and to form judgments and opinions based on reason ○ *He's a child of normal intelligence but he's emotionally immature.*
intelligent Ⓐ /ɪnˈtel·ə·dʒənt/ *adj* ○ *a highly intelligent woman*
intelligently Ⓐ /ɪnˈtel·ə·dʒənt·li/ *adv* ○ *She writes intelligently about the life of Mary Baker Eddy.*

WORD CHOICES intelligence

The adjective **smart** is a common alternative to "intelligent."

*She's a very **smart** woman.*

Young people who are intelligent are sometimes described as **bright**.

*Jacob was a very **bright** boy.*

Someone who is extremely intelligent is sometimes described as **brilliant**.

*William was a **brilliant** scholar.* ➤

> An intelligent person who has a natural ability to do a particular thing very well can be described as **gifted**.
>
> *a **gifted** mathematician*
>
> The adjective **intellectual** can be used about someone who studies and understands complicated subjects and ideas.
>
> *This course examines the most influential **intellectual** thinkers of modern times.*
>
> **Wise** can be used to describe someone who is intelligent as the result of experience.
>
> *a **wise** old teacher*

INFORMATION /ɪnˈtel·ə·dʒəns/ *n* [U] a government department or other group that gathers information about other countries or enemies, or the information that is gathered ○ *foreign intelligence*

intelligence test *n* [C] a test that measures the ability of a person to understand and learn by comparing it with the ability of other people. ○ Compare ACHIEVEMENT TEST

intelligible /ɪnˈtel·ə·dʒə·bəl/ *adj* (of speech and writing) clear enough to be understood ○ *It was a poor telephone connection, and only some of his words were intelligible.*

intend /ɪnˈtend/ *v* to have as a plan or purpose ○ [+ *to* infinitive] *We intend to go to Australia next year to visit our daughter.* ○ [T] *The remark was intended as a compliment.*

intent /ɪnˈtent/ *n* [U] *fml* something that you intend or intended to do ○ *There was clearly no intent to cause harm, and the judge ruled that the injury was accidental.* ○ See also: INTENT GIVING ATTENTION; INTENT DETERMINED

intention /ɪnˈten·ʃən/ *n* [C/U] something that you want and plan to do; an aim ○ [U] *I have no intention of selling this house.* ○ [C] *He had good intentions* (= He meant to be kind), *but unfortunately things just didn't work out.*

intentional /ɪnˈten·ʃən·əl/ *adj* ○ *Do you think the insult was intentional?*

intentionally /ɪnˈten·ʃən·əl·i/ *adv* ○ *The company was accused of intentionally dumping garbage into the river.*

intense Ⓐ /ɪnˈtens/ *adj* **1** extreme ○ *intense heat/cold* ○ *a look of intense joy* **2** Intense work or thought requires a lot of effort: *an intense 13-week course* **3** A person who is intense is very forceful and has strong emotions and opinions: *He was young and intense, and silly, too.*

intensely Ⓐ /ɪnˈten·sli/ *adv* ○ *intensely personal songs* ○ *He lives every aspect of life intensely.*

intensify Ⓐ /ɪnˈten·səˌfɑɪ/ *v* [I/T] ○ [T] *He intensified his training, running 45 miles a week.* ○ [I] *Fighting around the capital has intensified.*

intensity Ⓐ /ɪnˈten·sət̬·i/ *n* [U] **1** *Simone sings with emotional intensity.* ○ *The light hit us with such intensity that we ducked.* **2** ***art*** Intensity in a work of art describes the strength of the color, sound, light, or feeling.

intensive Ⓐ /ɪnˈten·sɪv/ *adj* **1** needing or using great energy or effort ○ *We're in the midst of intensive negotiations.* ○ *an intensive workout* **2** Intensive study or training deals with a lot of information in a short period of time: *a month-long intensive course in Spanish*

intensively Ⓐ /ɪnˈten·sɪv·li/ *adv*

intensifier /ɪnˈten·səˌfɑɪ·ər/, **intensive** /ɪnˈten·sɪv/ *n* [C] ***grammar*** a word, esp. an adverb, that is used to add force to another word or phrase ○ *In "extremely large" and "I strongly object," "extremely" and "strongly" are intensifiers.*

intensive care *n* [U] continuous treatment provided in a hospital for those who are extremely ill, or the department of a hospital that provides this care

intent GIVING ATTENTION /ɪnˈtent/ *adj* giving all your attention to something ○ *an intent look* ○ See also: INTENT atINTEND

intently /ɪnˈtent·li/ *adv* ○ *The boys played intently.*

DETERMINED /ɪnˈtent/ *adj* determined, esp. in a way that seems silly or harmful ○ *The climbers were* **intent on** *reaching the mountaintop despite the freezing temperatures.* ○ See also: INTENT at INTEND

WORD FAMILY intent

Nouns	intent, intention	Verbs	intend
Adjectives	intended, unintended, intentional, unintentional	Adverbs	intently, intentionally, unintentionally

IDIOM with intent

• **for all intents and purposes** almost completely ○ *Escape from the prison was, for all intents and purposes, impossible.*

intention /ɪnˈten·tʃən/ *n* ○ See at INTEND

intentional /ɪnˈten·tʃən·əl/ *adj* ○ See at INTEND

intentionally /ɪnˈten·tʃən·əl·i/ *adv* ○ See at INTEND

inter /ɪnˈtɜr/ *v* [T] **-rr-** *fml* to put a dead body in the earth; bury

inter- /ˌɪnt·ər/ *prefix* between or among ○ *intercollegiate sports*

interact Ⓐ /ˌɪnt·əˈrækt/ *v* [I] to communicate with or react to each other ○ *He does not interact well with the other students.*

interaction Ⓐ /ˌɪnt·əˈræk·ʃən/ *n* [C/U] ○ [C] *drug interactions*

interactive Ⓐ /ˌɪnt·əˈræk·tɪv/ *adj* **1** *The ocean and the atmosphere form an interactive system.* **2** An interactive computer program involves the user in the exchange of information while the computer is in operation: *interactive software/technology*

interactively Ⓐ /ˌɪnt·əˈræk·tɪv·li/ *adv*

intercede /ˌɪnt·ərˈsiːd/ *v* [I] to use your influence to persuade someone in authority not to punish or harm someone or to do something for someone ○ *Some pharmacists will intercede on your behalf with doctors.*

intercept /ˌɪnt·ərˈsept/ *v* [T] to stop or catch something or someone that is on the way from one place to another so that it does not reach the intended place ○ *to intercept a letter* ○ *The ball was intercepted by Grady.*

interception /ˌɪnt·ərˈsep·ʃən/ *n* [C] (esp. in football) the act of catching a ball intended for someone on the opposing team ○ *He's thrown 122 passes without an interception.*

interchange EXCHANGE /ˈɪnt·ərˌtʃeɪndʒ/ *n* [C/U] an exchange, esp. of ideas or information, between different people or groups ○ [U] *They hope to encourage the free interchange of ideas.*

interchangeable /ˌɪnt·ərˈtʃeɪn·dʒə·bəl/ *adj* able to be exchanged with each other without making any difference or without being noticed ○ *interchangeable machine parts*

ROAD /ˈɪnt·ərˌtʃeɪndʒ/ *n* [C] a connection between two roads that allows vehicles to move from one road to the other without crossing the flow of traffic

intercom /ˈɪnt·ərˌkɑm/ *n* [C] a set of communications devices that allows people in different parts of a building, aircraft, ship, etc., to speak to each other

intercontinental /ˌɪnt·ərˌkɑnt·ənˈent·əl/ *adj* [not gradable] between continents ○ *intercontinental flights*

intercourse /ˈɪnt·ərˌkɔːrs, -ˌkoʊrs/ *n* [U] the sexual activity in which the male's PENIS enters the female's VAGINA

interdependent /ˌɪnt·ər·dɪˈpen·dənt/ *adj* [not gradable] ***social studies*** depending on each other ○ *an interdependent relationship*

interdependence /ˌɪnt·ər·dɪˈpen·dəns/ *n* [U] **1** *our interdependence as a global society* **2** ***earth science*** Interdependence is also the idea that everything in nature is connected to and depends on every other thing.

interest INVOLVEMENT /ˈɪn·trəst, ˈɪnt·ə·rəst/ *n* [C/U] **1** a feeling of having your attention held by something, or of wanting to be involved with and learn more about something ○ [C] *an interest in chess* ○ [U] *I lost interest halfway through the book.* **2** Your interests are the activities that you enjoy doing and the subjects that you like to spend time learning about. **3** If something is **of interest**, it holds your attention and makes you want to learn more about it: *Nothing much of interest was discussed.*

interest /ˈɪn·trəst, ˈɪnt·ə·rəst/ *v* [T] ○ *Sailing has never really interested me.*

interested /ˈɪn·trə·stəd, ˈɪnt·ə·rə·stəd/ *adj* ○ *He didn't seem interested in coming.* ○ [+ to infinitive] *I'd be interested to learn why he likes her.*

interesting /ˈɪn·trə·stɪŋ, ˈɪnt·əˌres·tɪŋ/ *adj* holding one's attention ○ *An interesting thing happened on the trip back.*

interestingly /ˈɪn·trə·stɪŋ·li, ˈɪnt·əˌres·tɪŋ-/ *adv* Interestingly can introduce a piece of information that the speaker finds surprising and interesting: *Interestingly enough, he never actually said that he was innocent.*

USAGE

interested

The only prepositions that can be used after **interested** are **in** and **to**.

I'd be interested to hear other people's perspective.

Ben is very interested in his family history.

~~*Ben is very interested on his family history.*~~

USAGE

interesting

If something is **interesting** it is usually something that you will like or enjoy. Do not use **interesting** to describe something that will help you in a practical way. For that meaning you should use a word such as **important**, **profitable**, or **worthwhile**.

~~*This kind of experience could be very interesting for their future careers.*~~

This kind of experience could be very worthwhile for their future careers.

WORD CHOICES interest

You can use **absorbing**, **gripping**, or **riveting** to describe a game, book, movie, etc., that is so interesting that it keeps your attention completely.

*I found the book absolutely **gripping** – I couldn't put it down.*

*It was a very **absorbing** movie.*

*The performance was **riveting**.*

A game, book, TV program, etc., that is so interesting that you cannot stop playing, reading, or watching it, may be described as **compelling**.

*It was a **compelling** story.*

Fascinating is often used to describe someone or something you have seen or heard that you have found extremely interesting.

*The history of the place was absolutely **fascinating**.*

*He's **fascinating** on the subject.*

If something or someone is interesting and seems mysterious in a way that makes you want to know more about that thing or person, you can use the word **intriguing**.

*It's a very **intriguing** situation.*

ADVANTAGE /ˈɪn·trəst, ˈɪnt·ə·rəst/ *n* [C] something that gives you what is important or necessary or helps you in some way ○ *A union looks after the interests of its members.* ○ *I was only acting* **in** *your* **interest** (= to achieve what would help you).

MONEY /ˈɪn·trəst, ˈɪnt·ə·rəst/ *n* [U] money that is charged, esp. by a bank, when you borrow money,

I

or money that is paid to you for the use of your money ○ *My savings account is earning 5% interest.*

WORD FAMILY interest			
Nouns	interest disinterest	*Adjectives*	interested disinterested uninterested interesting
Verbs	interest		
Adverbs	interestingly		

IDIOM with interest

• **Can I interest** *you* **in** *something* Would you like to buy or take something ○ *Can I interest you in a cup of coffee?*

interface /ˈɪnt·ərˌfeɪs/ *n* [C] the place where two systems come together and have an effect on each other, or a connection between two computers or between a person and a computer ○ *Amphibians live at the interface of land and sea.* ○ *To simplify software, you improve its interface.*

interface /ˈɪnt·ərˌfeɪs/ *v* [I/T] to communicate or cause someone or something to communicate ○ [I] *Neighborhood groups here interface very well with police.*

interfere /ˌɪnt·ərˈfɪr/ *v* [I] **1** to involve yourself in matters connected with other people without being asked or needed ○ *Interfering in other people's arguments is always a mistake.* **2** If something or someone interferes with a situation or a process, it spoils it or prevents its progress: *Even a little noise interferes with my concentration.*

interference /ˌɪnt·ərˈfɪr·əns/ *n* [U] **1** *She seems to regard any advice from me as interference.* **2** On the radio, television, or telephone, interference is noise, lines, etc., that prevent a clear sound or picture from being received. **3** ***physics*** Interference between two waves happens when they have the same FREQUENCY and produce a force that is either stronger or weaker than one wave alone. **4** In sports, interference is an action that is against the rules which prevents an opposing player from completing a play.

interferon /ˌɪnt·ərˈfɪr·ɑn/ *n* [C] ***biology*** a substance produced in the body to fight against viruses

interim /ˈɪnt·ə·rəm/ *adj* [not gradable] temporary; intended for a short period only ○ *an interim government*

interim /ˈɪnt·ə·rəm/ *n* [U] ○ *I started writing two years ago, and other books on the subject have come out* **in the interim** (= during this period).

interior /ɪnˈtɪr·iː·ər/ *adj* [not gradable] inner; on or from the inside ○ *The interior surface of the seashell was smooth.* ○ Compare EXTERIOR

interior /ɪnˈtɪr·iː·ər/ *n* [C/U] the inside part of something ○ [U] *a car's interior* ○ Compare EXTERIOR

interior angle *n* [C] ***geometry*** an angle on the inside of a triangle or other POLYGON

interior decorator *n* [C] a person whose job is to decorate the inside of buildings and houses

interject /ˌɪnt·ərˈdʒekt/ *v* [T] to say something that interrupts someone who is speaking ○ *He interjected questions throughout the discussion.*

interjection /ˌɪnt·ərˈdʒek·ʃən/ *n* [C] ***grammar*** a word or phrase that is used as a short, sudden expression of emotion ○ *"Hey!" "Ouch!" and "Cut that out!" are interjections.*

interlock /ˌɪnt·ərˈlɑk/ *v* [I/T] to join together firmly, esp. by fitting one part into another

interlocking /ˌɪnt·ərˈlɑk·ɪŋ/ *adj* ○ *interlocking rings*

interloper /ˈɪnt·ərˌloʊ·pər/ *n* [C] someone who becomes involved in an activity or a social group without being asked or wanted, or who enters a place without being allowed ○ *We felt like interlopers when we tried to join the game.*

interlude /ˈɪnt·ərˌluːd/ *n* [C] a period or event that comes between two others and is different from them ○ *The ferry trip was a relaxing interlude during the drive.*

intermarriage /ˌɪnt·ərˈmær·ɪdʒ/ *n* [U] marriage between people who are of different groups

intermediary /ˌɪnt·ərˈmiːd·iːˌer·i/ *n* [C] someone who acts to arrange an agreement between people who are unwilling or unable to communicate directly

intermediate Ⓐ /ˌɪnt·ərˈmiːd·iː·ət/ *adj* [not gradable] being or happening between two other related things, levels, or points ○ *a student of English at the intermediate level*

interminable /ɪnˈtɜr·mə·nə·bəl/ *adj* continuing for too long and seeming never to end ○ *interminable arguments*

interminably /ɪnˈtɜr·mə·nə·bli/ *adv* ○ *They talked interminably.*

intermingle /ˌɪnt·ərˈmɪŋ·gəl/ *v* [I] to become mixed together ○ *The spices intermingle to produce an unusual flavor.*

intermission /ˌɪnt·ərˈmɪʃ·ən/ *n* [C/U] a brief period between the parts of a performance

intermittent /ˌɪnt·ərˈmɪt·ᵊnt/ *adj* not happening regularly or continuously; stopping and starting repeatedly or with long periods in between

intermittently /ˌɪnt·ərˈmɪt·ᵊnt·li/ *adv* ○ *It rained intermittently all day.*

intermolecular /ˌɪnt·ər·məˈlek·jə·lər/ *adj* [not gradable] ***chemistry*** happening among or between MOLECULES

intern PUNISH /ɪnˈtɜrn, ˈɪn·tɜrn/ *v* [T] ***world history*** to put someone in prison for political or military reasons

internment /ɪnˈtɜrn·mənt/ *n* [U]

STUDENT /ˈɪn·tɜrn/ *n* [C] someone who is receiving training by obtaining practical experience of a type of work

internship /ˈɪnˌtɜrnˌʃɪp/ *n* [C] ○ *He served his internship at a local hospital.*

internal Ⓐ /ɪn ˈtɜrn·əl/ *adj* [not gradable] existing, intended for, or happening inside a person, organization, place, country, etc. ○ *the internal organs of the body* ○ *The bank will conduct an internal investigation.* ○ Compare EXTERNAL
internally Ⓐ /ɪn ˈtɜrn·əl·i/ *adv* [not gradable] ○ *This medicine should not be taken internally.* ○ *Issues like this should be dealt with internally, and not discussed in public forums.*
internalize Ⓐ /ɪn ˈtɜrn·əlˌɑɪz/ *v* [T] **1** to accept an idea, attitude, belief, etc., so that it becomes part of your character ○ *He had not expected the people so readily to internalize the values of democracy.* **2** If you internalize your emotions or feelings, you do not express them openly: *He usually internalized his anger, rather than expressing it to anyone.*

internal energy *n* [U] ***physics*** the total amount of energy in a system, equal to the KINETIC energy added to the POTENTIAL energy

internal medicine *n* [U] the part of medical science that tries to cure illnesses inside the body, esp. of the organs

Internal Revenue Service *n* [U] the IRS

international /ˌɪnt·ərˈnæʃ·ən·əl/ *adj* [not gradable] involving more than one country ○ *international affairs/trade*
internationally /ˌɪnt·ərˈnæʃ·ən·əl·i/ *adv* [not gradable] ○ *an internationally acclaimed scientist*

internationalism /ˌɪnt·ərˈnæʃ·ən·əlˌɪz·əm/ *n* [U] ***politics & government*** the principle or practice of nations acting and working together, or a belief in this principle

International Phonetic Alphabet, *abbreviation* **IPA** *n* [U] a system of symbols for showing the speech sounds of a language

International System of Units *n* [U] ***science*** SI

Internet /ˈɪnt·ərˌnet/, **Net** *n* [U] the large system of connected computers around the world which people use to communicate with each other ○ *I learned about it on the Internet.*

internist /ˈɪnˌtɜr·nəst/ *n* [C] a doctor who specializes in INTERNAL MEDICINE (= medicine dealing with illnesses inside the body)

internship /ˈɪnˌtɜrnˌʃɪp/ *n* [C] ○ See at INTERN STUDENT

interpersonal /ˌɪnt·ərˈpɜr·sən·əl/ *adj* [not gradable] involving relationships between people

interphase /ˈɪnt·ərˌfeɪz/ *n* [C] ***biology*** the period of time between one cell division and the next

interplanetary /ˌɪnt·ərˈplæn·əˌter·i/ *adj* [not gradable] between planets ○ *interplanetary travel*

interplay /ˈɪnt·ərˌpleɪ/ *n* [U] the action between two or more things or the effect they have on each other ○ *the interplay of light and shadow in a photograph*

interpret Ⓐ FIND MEANING /ɪn ˈtɜr·prət/ *v* [T] to describe the meaning of something; examine in order to explain ○ *It's difficult to interpret these statistics without knowing how they were obtained.*
interpretation Ⓐ /ɪnˌtɜr·prəˈteɪ·ʃən/ *n* [C/U] **1** [C] *We had different interpretations of the survey results.* **2** An interpretation by actors or musicians is the expression by their performance of their understanding of the part or parts they are playing: [C] *Masur's interpretation of the Brahms symphony was masterful.*

CHANGE LANGUAGE /ɪn ˈtɜr·prət/ *v* [I/T] to change what someone is saying into the words of another language; TRANSLATE ○ [I] *I had to ask someone to interpret for me because I don't know any Italian.*
interpreter /ɪn ˈtɜr·prət̬·ər/ *n* [C] ○ *The Chinese witness testified with the help of an interpreter.*

interracial /ˌɪnt·əˈreɪ·ʃəl/ *adj* [not gradable] involving people of different races ○ *an interracial community*

interrelated /ˌɪnt·ə·rɪˈleɪt̬·əd/ *adj* connected in such a way that each thing has an effect on the others ○ *He saw all aspects of society as interrelated.*

interrogate /ɪn ˈter·əˌgeɪt/ *v* [T] to ask someone many questions in a formal situation, often in a forceful way that can be seen as threatening ○ *We were stopped at the border and interrogated for hours by the police.*
interrogation /ɪnˌter·əˈgeɪ·ʃən/ *n* [C/U] ○ [C] *Police brought in the suspect for a lengthy interrogation.*

interrogative sentence /ˌɪnt·əˈrɑg·ət̬·ɪv ˈsent·əns/ *n* [C] ***grammar*** a sentence that asks a question or makes a request for information

interrupt /ˌɪnt·əˈrʌpt/ *v* [T] to stop someone from speaking by saying or doing something, or to cause an activity or event to stop briefly ○ [I] *Please don't interrupt until I'm finished.* ○ [T] *The picnic was interrupted by a rain shower.*
interruption /ˌɪnt·əˈrʌp·ʃən/ *n* [C/U] ○ [U] *I need to get some work done without interruption this afternoon.*

WORD FAMILY interrupt	
Nouns interruption	*Verbs* interrupt

interscholastic /ˌɪnt·ər·skəˈlæs·tɪk/ *adj* [not gradable] involving two or more schools ○ *interscholastic sports*

intersect /ˌɪnt·ərˈsekt/ *v* [I/T] **1** to meet and go through or across ○ [T] *Weaver Street intersects Palmer Avenue at the next corner.* **2** ***geometry*** (of a line or surface) To intersect is to cross at a POINT or set of points.

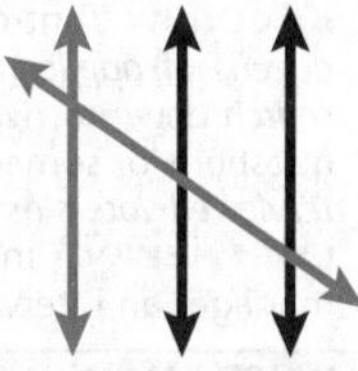
INTERSECTING LINES

intersection /ˈɪnt·ərˌsek·ʃən/ *n* [C] **1** ***geometry*** a POINT or set of points where two lines, planes, etc., cross **2** ***algebra*** An intersection is a group of items that belong to two different sets. **3** An intersecton is a place where streets meet or cross each other: *Times Square is one of New York's busiest intersections.*

intersperse /ˌɪnt·ər'spɜrs/ *v* [T] to put things of one type in different parts or places among other things ○ *Framed pictures of her children were interspersed among the books in the bookcase.*

interstate /ˌɪnt·ər'steɪt/ *adj* [not gradable] involving two or more US states ○ *interstate commerce*
interstate (highway) /'ɪnt·ərˌsteɪt ('hɑɪ·weɪ)/ *n* [C] one of the main roads that are part of a US system of large roads that go across states to connect many cities ○ *You'll get here quicker if you take the interstate, I-95.*

intertwined /ˌɪnt·ər'twɑɪnd/ *adj* twisted together or closely connected so as to be difficult to separate ○ *Our fates seemed to be intertwined.*

interval Ⓐ **TIME OR SPACE** /'ɪnt·ər·vəl/ *n* [C] **1** a period between two events or times, or the space between two points ○ *If there is a fire, the alarm will sound at 15-second intervals.* ○ *We've positioned guards around the embassy at intervals of 10 feet.* **2** *Br* An interval is an INTERMISSION.

MUSIC /'ɪnt·ər·vəl/ *n* [C] ***music*** the difference in PITCH between two notes

NUMBERS /'ɪnt·ər·vəl/ *n* [C] ***mathematics*** the set of all numbers between two the two particular numbers given

intervene Ⓐ **GET INVOLVED** /ˌɪnt·ər'viːn/ *v* [I] to become involved intentionally in a difficult situation in order to change it or improve it, or prevent it from getting worse ○ *The superpowers began to intervene in local struggles in Africa.*
intervention Ⓐ /ˌɪnt·ər'ven·tʃən/ *n* [C/U] ○ [C] *The intervention by UN troops prevented fighting from breaking out.*

COME BETWEEN /ˌɪnt·ər'viːn/ *v* [I] to happen between two events, or to prevent something from happening by happening first ○ *Two decades intervened between the completion of the design and the opening of the theater.*

interview /'ɪnt·ərˌvjuː/ *n* [C] **1** a formal meeting at which a person who is interested in getting a job or other position is asked questions to learn how well the person would be able to do it ○ *a job interview* **2** An interview is also a formal meeting at which reporters try to get information, esp. from a famous person or public official: *an interview with the British prime minister*
interview /'ɪnt·ərˌvjuː/ *v* [T] **1** *We interviewed dozens of applicants, and have narrowed the job search down to two.* **2** To interview is also to ask questions of someone to get information: *She interviewed voters as they left the polls.*
interviewer /'ɪnt·ərˌvjuː·ər/ *n* [C] a person who manages an interview and asks the questions

WORD FAMILY interview	
Nouns interview interviewer	*Verbs* interview

interweave /ˌɪnt·ər'wiːv/ *v* [T] *pres. part.* **interweaving**, *past simp.* **interwove**, *past part.* **interwoven** to put together or combine two or more things so that they cannot be separated easily ○ *The author skillfully interweaves fiction and history in her novel.*

intestines /ɪn'tes·tənz/, **bowels** *pl n* ***biology*** a long tube through which food travels while it is being digested after leaving the stomach
intestinal /ɪn'tes·tən·əl/ *adj* [not gradable]

intimate **PERSONAL** /'ɪnt·ə·mət/ *adj* **1** being a close, personal friend, or having a close, personal relationship ○ *an intimate friend* **2** An intimate relationship can also refer to a romantic relationship: *They had been good friends, but they had never in any way been intimate.* **3** Intimate can also mean private and personal: *She refused to discuss the intimate details of her life.*
intimacy /'ɪnt·ə·mə·si/ *n* [C/U] ○ [U] *He was always polite, but he shunned intimacy.*
intimate /'ɪnt·ə·mət/ *n* [C] a close friend ○ *George was never one of the president's intimates.*
intimately /'ɪnt·ə·mət·li/ *adv* ○ *I know him intimately and can assure you that he is the ideal man for the job.*

EXPERT /'ɪnt·ə·mət/ *adj* expert and detailed ○ *an intimate knowledge of cattle farming*
intimately /'ɪnt·ə·mət·li/ *adv* ○ *Local residents are intimately familiar with the area.*

SUGGEST /'ɪnt·əˌmeɪt/ *v* [T] to suggest that something will happen or is true, without saying so directly ○ [+ *that* clause] *He intimated that they had thought about getting married.*

intimidate /ɪn'tɪm·əˌdeɪt/ *v* [T] to frighten or threaten someone, usually in order to persuade the person to do something he or she does not wish to do ○ *Don't let those bullies intimidate you; just walk away from them.*
intimidation /ɪnˌtɪm·ə'deɪ·ʃən/ *n* [U] ○ *a campaign of intimidation against striking workers*

into **INSIDE** /'ɪn·tuː, -tə/ *prep* toward the inside or middle of something and about to be contained, surrounded, or enclosed by it ○ *Pour some sugar into the bowl.* ○ *They went into the backyard.*

CONNECTED WITH /'ɪn·tuː, -tə/ *prep* **1** connected with or involved in a condition or activity ○ *My father went into the army the day after the war began.* ○ *An investigation into the accident is underway.* ○ *I know I should do my taxes but I just don't want to get into it now.* **2** *infml* Into also means strongly interested in or involved with something: *Jeanne is heavily into organic food.* ○ *Ken is into long-distance running.*

CHANGE /'ɪn·tuː, -tə/ *prep* used to show when a person or thing is changing from one form or condition to another ○ *Peel the potatoes and chop them into small cubes.* ○ *We made the extra bedroom into an office.* ○ *Her novels have been translated into nineteen languages.*

MOVEMENT /'ɪn·tuː, -tə/ *prep* used to show movement that involves two things coming together with force ○ *The driver apparently fell asleep and his car slammed into a tree.* ○ (fig.) *Guess who I ran into* (= met unexpectedly) *at the shopping mall!*

DIVISION /'ɪn·tuː, -tə/ *prep* used when referring to the division of one number by another number ○ *5 into 10 is 2.*

intolerable /ɪnˈtɑl·ə·rə·bəl/ *adj* too bad or difficult to bear or to be accepted ○ *Living conditions were intolerable after the storm.* ○ *This hot weather is becoming intolerable.*

intolerant /ɪnˈtɑl·ə·rənt/ *adj* disapproving of or refusing to accept people, behavior, or ideas that are different from your own ○ *As a historian, she was intolerant of poorly done research.*
intolerance /ɪnˈtɑl·ə·rəns/ *n* [U] ○ *He began to speak out against racism and intolerance.*

intonation /ˌɪn·təˈneɪ·ʃən/ *n* [C/U] the sound changes produced by the rise and fall of the voice when speaking

intone /ɪnˈtoʊn/ *v* [I/T] to say something slowly and seriously in a voice that does not rise or fall much ○ [I] *"Say after me," he would intone, and the class dutifully repeated whatever he said.*

intoxicated /ɪnˈtɑk·səˌkeɪţ·əd/ *adj fml* drunk ○ *He was charged with driving while intoxicated.*
intoxicating /ɪnˈtɑk·səˌkeɪţ·ɪŋ/ *adj* making you feel happy, as if you are in a pleasant dream ○ *After being cooped up in the overheated room all day, we took a stroll and found the fresh air intoxicating.*

intracellular /ˌɪn·trəˈsel·jə·lər/ *adj* [not gradable] ***biology*** happening inside a cell or cells

intractable /ɪnˈtræk·tə·bəl/ *adj* difficult or impossible to manage or control ○ *intractable problems* ○ *an intractable child*

intramural /ˌɪn·trəˈmjʊr·əl/ *adj* [not gradable] happening within or involving the members of one school ○ *At college she was active in intramural sports.*

intransigent /ɪnˈtræn·zə·dʒənt/ *adj fml* refusing to change an opinion ○ *He was a man of strong views and intransigent positions.*

intransitive /ɪnˈtræn·zəţ·ɪv/ *adj* [not gradable] ***grammar*** (of a verb) needing no DIRECT OBJECT (= the thing the verb acts on) ○ *In the sentence "I ran with him to the store," "ran" is an intransitive verb.* ○ Compare TRANSITIVE

intravenous /ˌɪn·trəˈviː·nəs/, *abbreviation* **IV** *adj* [not gradable] put directly into a VEIN (= one of the tubes in the body that carry blood to the heart) ○ *an intravenous drug*
intravenously /ˌɪn·trəˈviː·nə·sli/ *adv* [not gradable] ○ *The antibiotic was given in a fluid intravenously.*

intrepid /ɪnˈtrep·əd/ *adj fml* very brave and willing to risk being in dangerous situations ○ *an intrepid explorer*

intricate /ˈɪn·trɪ·kət/ *adj* having a lot of small parts or pieces arranged in a complicated way, and therefore sometimes difficult to understand in detail ○ *The novel's intricate plot will not be easy to translate into a movie.*
intricately /ˈɪn·trɪ·kət·li/ *adv* ○ *The antique silver teapot is intricately engraved.*
intricacy /ˈɪn·trɪ·kə·si/ *n* [C usually pl] a detail that is part of something complicated ○ *No one could understand all the intricacies of the deal.*

intrigue INTEREST /ɪnˈtriːg/ *v* [T] to interest someone, often because of an unusual or unexpected quality ○ *I was intrigued by his slow, deliberate way of talking and the serious look in his eyes.*
intriguing /ɪnˈtriː·gɪŋ/ *adj* ○ *She has written an intriguing account of growing up on a farm as one of ten children.*

SECRET /ˈɪn·triːg, ɪnˈtriːg/ *n* [C/U] the making of a secret plan to do something, esp. something that will harm someone ○ [U] *In that tale of political intrigue, he combined great dialogue with an interesting plot and a surprise ending.*

intrinsic Ⓐ /ɪnˈtrɪn·zɪk/ *adj* basic to a thing, being an important part of making it what it is ○ *Each human being has intrinsic dignity and worth.*
intrinsically Ⓐ /ɪnˈtrɪn·zɪ·kli/ *adv*

intro /ˈɪn·troʊ/ *n* [C] *pl* **intros** *infml* an INTRODUCTION

introduce MEET SOMEONE /ˌɪn·trəˈduːs/ *v* [T] **1** to arrange for you to meet and learn the name of another person ○ *I'd like to introduce you to my friend, Sally.* ○ *George, I'd like to introduce my friend, Sally.* **2** To introduce is also to formally present someone to a group: *It's my distinct honor to introduce the president of the United States of America.*
introduction /ˌɪn·trəˈdʌk·ʃən/ *n* [C] ○ *Let me do the introductions* (= introduce everyone to each other).

BEGIN TO USE /ˌɪn·trəˈduːs/ *v* [T] to put something into use for the first time, or to put something into a new place ○ *When were music CDs first introduced?* ○ *These trees were introduced into New England from Europe.*
introduction /ˌɪn·trəˈdʌk·ʃən/ *n* [U] ○ *The introduction of express buses is scheduled for July.*

WORD FAMILY introduce			
Nouns	introduction	*Verbs*	introduce
Adjectives	introductory		

introduction /ˌɪn·trəˈdʌk·ʃən/ *n* [C] ***literature*** a short speech or piece of writing that comes before a longer speech or written text, usually giving basic information about what is to follow ○ *The author's introduction explains the organization of the book.*
introductory /ˌɪn·trəˈdʌk·tə·ri/ *adj* [not gradable] coming before something else ○ *introductory remarks*

intrude /ɪnˈtruːd/ *v* [I] to go into a place or be involved in a situation where you are not wanted or do not belong ○ *Sorry to intrude, but I wanted to insure that this got to your attention.* ○ *Students who live in a dorm regard any curfew as intruding on their rights.*
intruder /ɪnˈtruːd·ər/ *n* [C] someone who enters a place without permission, esp. in order to commit a crime
intrusion /ɪnˈtruː·ʒən/ *n* [C/U] ○ [U] *They complained that building a new airport nearby would be a noisy intrusion on their quiet lives.*
intrusive /ɪnˈtruː·sɪv, -zɪv/ *adj* ○ *He's fought for less intrusive government.*

intrusion /ɪn ˈtruː·ʒən/ *n* [U] ***earth science*** the flowing of hot melted rock into layers or cracks of rocks that already exist
intrusive /ɪn ˈtruː·sɪv, -zɪv/ *adj* ***earth science***

intuition /ˌɪn·təˈwɪʃ·ən/ *n* [C/U] an ability to understand or know something without needing to think about it or use reason to discover it, or a feeling that shows this ability ○ [U] *You should trust your intuition in making your decision.* ○ [C] *Hank's intuitions were right.*
intuitive /ɪn ˈtuː·ət̬·ɪv/ *adj* ○ *Most people have an intuitive sense of right and wrong.*
intuitively /ɪn ˈtuː·ət̬·ɪv·li/ *adv* ○ *People all over the world respond intuitively to the movie* (= understood it without using reason).

Inuit /ˈɪn·ə·wət, -jə-/ *n* [C] *pl* **Inuit, Inuits** *esp. Cdn* an ESKIMO

inundate /ˈɪn·ənˌdeɪt/ *v* [T] **1** to bring to a place or person too much of something, so that it cannot be dealt with ○ *After appearing on TV they were inundated with telephone calls for a week.* ○ *We were inundated with complaints when the show had to be canceled.* **2** To inundate is also to flood (an area) with water: *Floods inundated various Indian communities.*

invade /ɪn ˈveɪd/ *v* [I/T] to enter a place by force, often in large numbers ○ [T] *The Allies were poised to invade Germany.* ○ [T] *(fig.) I think that the opportunity is definitely there for people to invade your privacy when they want to* (= find out personal things about you against your wishes).
invasion /ɪn ˈveɪ·ʒən/ *n* [C] ○ *the invasion of the Normandy coast on D-day* ○ *(fig.) I certainly regarded the tapping of my phone as an invasion of (my) privacy.*

invalid Ⓐ **NOT ACCEPTABLE** /ɪn ˈvæl·əd/ *adj* [not gradable] not true or acceptable, or not correctly thought out ○ *The results of the election were declared invalid by the court.*
invalidate Ⓐ /ɪn ˈvæl·əˌdeɪt/ *v* [T] ○ *A few minor factual errors should not invalidate the theory* (= make it not true).

WEAK PERSON /ˈɪn·və·ləd, -ˌlɪd/ *n* [C] a person who is ill or injured for a long time and usually has to be cared for by others ○ *My dad's mother is an invalid, and she lives with my aunt and uncle.*

invaluable /ɪn ˈvæl·jə·bəl, -jə·wə·bəl/ *adj* [not gradable] extremely useful ○ *Alejandro said the tutoring he received was invaluable.*

invariable Ⓐ /ɪn ˈver·iː·ə·bəl, -ˈvær-/ *adj* [not gradable] never changing; staying the same ○ *an invariable response* ○ *an invariable rule*
invariably Ⓐ /ɪn ˈver·iː·ə·bli, -ˈvær-/ *adv* [not gradable] always ○ *There's no point in rushing – she's invariably late.* ○ *High blood pressure is almost invariably accompanied by high blood cholesterol.*

invasion /ɪn ˈveɪ·ʒən/ *n* ○ See at INVADE

invasive **SPREADING** /ɪn ˈveɪ·sɪv, -zɪv/ *adj* tending to spread in an uncontrollable way ○ *invasive plant species* ○ (*medical*) *invasive cancer cells*

MEDICAL PROCESS /ɪn ˈveɪ·sɪv, -zɪv/ *adj medical* done by cutting into or putting something into the body ○ *invasive surgery/tests/treatment*

inveigle /ɪn ˈveɪ·gəl/ *v* [T] to persuade someone to do something the person may not want to do ○ *Nomo meant to inveigle him into helping out.*

invent /ɪn ˈvent/ *v* [T] **1** to design or create something that did not exist before ○ *Gutenberg invented movable type in the 15th century.* **2** To invent is also to create a story or explanation which is not true: *I don't know what I really saw and what I've invented.*
invention /ɪn ˈven·tʃən/ *n* [C/U] something newly designed or created, or the activity of designing or creating new things ○ [C] *The mountain bike was a California invention.* ○ [U] *The invention of the pressure cooker provided a method for cooking quickly.* ○ [C] *His story of being kidnapped and held prisoner was an invention* (= something represented as being true which is not true).
inventive /ɪn ˈvent·ɪv/ *adj approving* having or showing the ability to design or create something new ○ *He is famous for his zany, inventive books for children.*
inventor /ɪn ˈvent·ər/ *n* [C] ○ *Alfred Nobel was the inventor of dynamite.*

WORD FAMILY invent			
Nouns	invention inventor	*Verbs*	invent reinvent
Adjectives	inventive	*Adverbs*	inventively

inventory /ˈɪn·vənˌtɔːr·i, -ˌtoʊr·i/ *n* [C/U] goods that are easily made available, or a detailed list of goods, property, etc. ○ [C] *large inventories of oil and gasoline* ○ [U] *The store is closed while we're taking inventory* (= counting and listing all the goods).

inverse /ɪn ˈvɜrs, ˈɪn·vɜrs/ *adj* [not gradable] changing in an opposite direction in relation to something else, esp. an amount ○ *in inverse proportion* ○ *an inverse relationship*
inversely /ɪn ˈvɜr·sli, ˈɪnˌvɜr-/ *adv* [not gradable] ○ *By and large, your ability to cope with change varies inversely with age.*

inversion /ɪn ˈvɜr·ʒən/ *n* [C/U] ***earth science*** a situation in which the temperature of the air high above the ground is warmer than the air near the ground

invert /ɪn ˈvɜrt/ *v* [T] to turn something so its top is at the bottom or put something in the opposite order or position ○ *Invert the cake onto a wire rack and let it cool.*

invest Ⓐ /ɪn ˈvest/ *v* [I/T] to put money or effort into something to make a profit or achieve a result ○ [T] *She tends to invest a lot of energy in her work.* ○ [I] *I think it's time to invest in* (= buy) *a new washing machine.*
investment Ⓐ /ɪn ˈvest·mənt/ *n* [C/U] ○ [C] *real estate investments* ○ [U] *There's an awful lot of foreign investment in the US.*

investor Ⓐ /ɪnˈves·tər/ *n* [C] a person or group of people that puts its money into a business or other organization in order to make a profit ○ *Many stock-market investors who wanted to sell couldn't find any buyers.*

investigate Ⓐ /ɪnˈves·təˌgeɪt/ *v* [I/T] to examine something carefully, esp. to discover the truth about it ○ [I] *There was a suspicious man near the playground, and we asked the police to investigate.* ○ [T] *The school created an independent review board to investigate charges of misconduct.*
investigation Ⓐ /ɪnˌves·təˈgeɪ·ʃən/ *n* [C/U] ○ [C] *a criminal investigation* ○ [U] *The cause of the fire is under investigation* (= is being examined).
investigative Ⓐ /ɪnˈves·təˌgeɪt̬·ɪv/ *adj* ○ *He's one of the paper's strongest investigative reporters* (= someone whose job is gathering facts to be published).
investigator Ⓐ /ɪnˈves·təˌgeɪt̬·ər/ *n* [C] ○ *She hired a private investigator to check into her husband's activities.*

inveterate /ɪnˈvet̬·ə·rət/ *adj usually disapproving* done as a habit and not likely to change ○ *an inveterate liar*

invidious /ɪnˈvɪd·iː·əs/ *adj fml* likely to cause unhappiness or offense ○ *We are not going to seek for invidious comparisons between governments.*

invigorate /ɪnˈvɪg·əˌreɪt/ *v* [T] to give new energy or strength to someone or something ○ *They argued that a cut in the tax rate would invigorate the economy.*
invigorating /ɪnˈvɪg·əˌreɪt̬·ɪŋ/ *adj* ○ *The fresh air was invigorating.*

invincible /ɪnˈvɪn·sə·bəl/ *adj* [not gradable] impossible to defeat or prevent from doing what is intended ○ *an invincible army* ○ *She seemed nearly invincible on the tennis court this year.*

invisible Ⓐ /ɪnˈvɪz·ə·bəl/ *adj* [not gradable] impossible to see ○ *Invisible bacteria can lead to food poisoning.* ○ *She was so unimportant in their lives that she was almost invisible to them.*
invisibility /ɪnˌvɪz·əˈbɪl·ət̬·i/ *n* [U]

invite ASK /ɪnˈvɑɪt/ *v* [T] to ask someone in a polite or friendly way to come somewhere, such as to a party, or to formally ask someone to do something ○ *Architects were invited to submit their designs for a new city hall.* ○ *I think we should invite her over to our place for coffee.*
invitation /ˌɪn·vəˈteɪ·ʃən/, *not standard* **invite** /ˈɪn·vɑɪt/ *n* [C] ○ *We received their wedding invitation today.* ○ *He accepted the invitation to join the committee.*

USAGE

invite

Remember that the usual preposition with the verb **invite** is **to**.

She invited me to her party.
~~*She invited me at her party.*~~
~~*She invited me for her party.*~~

ENCOURAGE /ɪnˈvɑɪt/ *v* [T] to do something that could cause something else to happen ○ *If you're scared of an animal, make a lot of noise, because running away usually invites problems.*
invitation /ˌɪn·vəˈteɪ·ʃən/ *n* [U] ○ *Leaving your house unlocked is an open invitation to burglars* (= encourages them).

WORD FAMILY invite

Nouns	invitation invite	*Verbs*	invite
		Adverbs	invitingly
Adjectives	inviting		

inviting /ɪnˈvɑɪt̬·ɪŋ/ *adj* attractive ○ *The kitchen is cheerful and inviting.*

invoice /ˈɪn·vɔɪs/ *n* [C] a statement listing goods or services provided and their prices, used in business as a record of sale ○ *You need to have a copy of your original invoice if you want a refund.*
invoice /ˈɪn·vɔɪs/ *v* [T] ○ *When they ship the CDs, the company will invoice you* (= send you a request for payment).

invoke Ⓐ CALL FOR HELP /ɪnˈvoʊk/ *v* [T] to call on something or someone, esp. God, for help
USE /ɪnˈvoʊk/ *v* [T] to cause something to be used; bring into effect ○ *Rather than answer the question, the witness invoked the Fifth Amendment against incriminating himself.*

involuntary /ɪnˈvɑl·ənˌter·i/ *adj* not done willingly, or not done intentionally ○ *A sharp tap beneath the knee usually causes an involuntary movement of the lower leg.* ○ *The driver of the vehicle was charged with involuntary manslaughter.*

involve Ⓐ INCLUDE /ɪnˈvɑlv, -ˈvɔːlv/ *v* [T] to include someone or something in an activity ○ *The accident involved two cars and a truck.* ○ *The operation involves inserting a small tube into the heart.*
involvement Ⓐ /ɪnˈvɑlv·mənt, -ˈvɔːlv-/ *n* [C/U] ○ [U] *He was accused of involvement in the robbery.*
MAKE INTERESTED /ɪnˈvɑlv, -ˈvɔːlv/ *v* [T] to make someone interested in taking part in something ○ *A good teacher tries to involve children in activities where they interact with each other.*
involved Ⓐ /ɪnˈvɑlvd, -ˈvɔːlvd/ *adj* **1** interested in or taking part in an activity or event ○ *The couple was having a loud argument, and I was afraid to get involved.* ○ *Maria was so involved in her work that she didn't hear me come in.* **2** If someone is **involved with** someone else, they have a romantic relationship.

WORD FAMILY involve

Nouns	involvement	*Adjectives*	involved uninvolved
Verbs	involve		

involved Ⓐ /ɪnˈvɑlvd, -ˈvɔːlvd/ *adj* difficult to understand or deal with; complicated ○ *His story was so involved that I couldn't follow it.*

inward /ˈɪn·wərd/ *adj* [not gradable] **1** on or toward the inside ○ *Hold out your hands and rotate your wrists inward.* **2** Inward also means directed toward your self, your mind, or your spirit: *an inward spiritual quest* ○ Compare OUTWARD AWAY FROM

inward /ˈɪn·wərd/, **inwards** /ˈɪn·wərdz/ *adv* [not gradable] ○ *Fold the edges of the paper inward.* ○ *We turned inward to our own thoughts.*

inwardly /ˈɪn·wərd·li/ *adv* [not gradable] ○ *She inwardly hoped he would fail.*

iodide /ˈɑɪ·əˌdɑɪd/ *n* [C] ***chemistry*** a chemical substance consisting of IODINE combined with another element

iodine /ˈɑɪ·əˌdɑɪn, -əd·ən/ *n* [U] ***chemistry, biology*** a chemical element found in small amounts in sea water, and used in medicine, PHOTOGRAPHY, and as a DYE (= substance for changing something's color) to discover whether there is STARCH (= substance found in plants) in cells

ion /ˈɑɪˌɑn, -ən/ *n* [C] ***physics, chemistry*** an atom that has a positive or negative electrical CHARGE as the result of adding or taking away an ELECTRON

ionic /ɑɪˈɑn·ɪk/ *adj* [not gradable] ***physics, chemistry*** relating to or containing ions

ionization /ˌɑɪ·ə·nəˈzeɪ·ʃən/ *n* [U] ***physics, chemistry*** the process by which an ion is produced

ionic bond *n* [C] ***chemistry*** a CHEMICAL BOND (= force that holds atoms together) in which two IONS are joined because one has a positive electrical CHARGE and the other a negative charge

iota /ɑɪˈoʊt̬·ə/ *n* [U] a very small amount ○ *All this bragging does not detract one iota from the fact that Henryk is an extraordinary man.*

IOU *n* [C] *pl* **IOUs, IOU's** *abbreviation for* I owe you (= a written promise to pay back money owed) ○ *I'll give you an IOU for the loan.*

IPA *n* [U] *abbreviation for* INTERNATIONAL PHONETIC ALPHABET.

iPod /ˈɑɪ·pɑd/ *n* [C] *trademark* an electronic device that fits in your hand and allows you to listen to music and view images that you get from the INTERNET

ipso facto /ˌɪp·soʊˈfæk·toʊ/ *adv* [not gradable] by that fact or act ○ *If he is right, then anyone who disagrees with him is, ipso facto, wrong.*

IQ *n* [C] *abbreviation for* intelligence quotient (= a person's level of intelligence measured by tests) ○ *a high/low IQ* ○ *an IQ test*

IRA /ˈɑɪ·rə/ *n* [C] *abbreviation for* individual retirement account (= a special bank account in which you invest money to use when you are older and stop working)

irascible /ɪˈræs·ə·bəl/ *adj* (of a person) easily made angry ○ *a cranky, irascible artist*

irate /ɑɪˈreɪt/ *adj* very angry ○ *We've been getting some irate calls from customers.*

ire /ɑɪr/ *n* [U] anger ○ *The team drew the ire of local politicians when it moved to a new stadium outside the city.*

iridium /ɪˈrɪd·iː·əm/ *n* [U] ***chemistry, earth science*** a rare metal element that is silver in color

iris **FLOWER** /ˈɑɪ·rəs/ *n* [C] a tall plant with large, colorful, often yellow or purple flowers and long pointed leaves

EYE /ˈɑɪ·rəs/ *n* [C] the colored, circular part of an eye surrounding the black PUPIL (= central part) ○ *When you say someone is blue-eyed, you are referring to the color of their irises.*

irk /ɜrk/ *v* [T] to annoy someone ○ *Her comments really irked me.*

iron **METAL** /ˈɑɪ·ərn/ *n* [U] a common, silver-colored, metal element that is magnetic and strong, is used in making steel, and is found in small amounts in blood and in all living things ○ *Iron rusts easily.* ○ *Liver is a rich source of dietary iron.*

iron /ˈɑɪ·ərn/ *adj* [not gradable] ○ *iron ore* ○ *an iron railing along the steps* ○ *(fig.) Her success depended on physical strength and an iron will* (= strong determination).

DEVICE /ˈɑɪ·ərn/ *n* [C] a device with a handle and a flat metal base that can be heated and pressed against cloth to make the cloth smooth

iron /ˈɑɪ·ərn/ *v* [T] ○ *I have to iron this skirt* (= make it smooth using an iron). ○ [M] *Let me iron out the wrinkles in this tablecloth.*

ironing /ˈɑɪ·ər·nɪŋ/ *n* [U] ○ *I do the ironing once a week.*

PHRASAL VERB with iron

• **iron out** *something* [M] to put something into a finished state by solving problems, removing differences, or taking care of details ○ *They met to iron out the details of the contract.*

ironclad /ˈɑɪ·ərnˌclad/ *adj* impossible to change or weaken ○ *The new contract provides employees with ironclad job security.*

ironing board *n* [C] a board covered with cloth, usually with folding legs, on which clothes and other items can be made smooth with an iron

irony /ˈɑɪ·rə·ni, ˈɑɪ·ər·ni/ *n* [C/U] **1** a type of usually humorous expression in which you say the opposite of what you intend ○ [U] *He had a powerful sense of irony, and you could never be absolutely sure when he was serious.* **2** Irony is also something that has a different or opposite result from what is expected: [C] *It is one of the ironies of life that by the time you have earned enough money for the things you always wanted, you no longer have the energy to enjoy them.* **3** ***literature*** Irony is a style of writing in which there is a noticeable, often humorous, difference between what is said and the intended meaning. ○ Compare SARCASM

ironic /ɑɪˈrɑn·ɪk/, **ironical** /ɑɪˈrɑn·ɪ·kəl/ *adj* ○ *The play was full of witty, ironic banter.* ○ [+ *that* clause] *It's really ironic that I would be asked to write about pets today because just yesterday our dog ran away.*

ironically /ɑɪˈrɑn·ɪ·kli/ *adv* in a way that is different or opposite from the result you would expect ○ *Ironically, his ability as an inventor made him a poor administrator, and he had one business failure after another.*

irradiate /ɪˈreɪd·iːˌeɪt/ *v* [T] ***biology*** to use RADIATION (= a form of energy) to destroy something, especially bacteria in food to keep it fresh
irradiation /ɪˌreɪd·iːˈeɪ·ʃən/ *n* [U]

irrational Ⓐ /ɪˈræʃ·ən·əl/ *adj* not based on reason or clear thinking; not reasonable ○ *One of her main themes is the irrational nature of love.*

irrational number *n* [C] ***algebra*** a number that cannot be expressed as the RATIO (= comparison of two numbers by division) of two whole numbers

irrefutable /ˌɪr·ɪˈfjuːt̬·ə·bəl, ɪˈref·jət̬-/ *adj* [not gradable] *fml* that cannot be proved wrong ○ *irrefutable proof*

irregardless /ˌɪr·ɪˈgɑrd·ləs/ *adv not standard* without attention to, or despite the conditions or situation; REGARDLESS ○ *Irregardless of whether he gives me a raise, I'm quitting at the end of this week.*

irregular SHAPE /ɪˈreg·jə·lər/ *adj* not regular in shape or form; having parts of different shapes or sizes ○ *an irregular surface*
irregularly /ɪˈreg·jə·lər·li/ *adv* ○ *This irregularly shaped lake is 4 miles long.*

TIME/SPACE /ɪˈreg·jə·lər/ *adj* not happening at regular times, or not having usual or regular spaces in between ○ *There are irregular spaces between the words.* ○ *He showed up at irregular intervals.*
irregularly /ɪˈreg·jə·lər·li/ *adv* ○ *He failed the exam because he only attended class irregularly.*

RULE /ɪˈreg·jə·lər/ *adj* **1** (of behavior or actions) not according to usual rules or what is expected **2** ***grammar*** An irregular verb, noun, adjective, or other type of word does not obey the usual rules in the language for changing word endings.
irregularly /ɪˈreg·jə·lər·li/ *adv* ○ *A stationary object in the sky can appear to move irregularly.*

irrelevant Ⓐ /ɪˈrel·ə·vənt/ *adj* not related to what is being discussed or considered ○ *These documents are totally irrelevant to the investigation.*
irrelevance Ⓐ /ɪˈrel·ə·vəns/, **irrelevancy** /ɪˈrel·ə·vən·si/ *n* [C/U] ○ *Many of these problems may simply fade into irrelevance when the new rules come into force.*

irreligious /ˌɪr·ɪˈlɪdʒ·əs/ *adj* not religious, or having no interest in religion

irreparable /ɪˈrep·ə·rə·bəl/ *adj* [not gradable] impossible to repair or make right again ○ *irreparable damage*
irreparably /ɪˈrep·ə·rə·bli/ *adv* [not gradable]

irreplaceable /ˌɪr·ɪˈpleɪ·sə·bəl/ *adj* [not gradable] too special, unusual, or valuable to replace with something else, or of which no others like it exist ○ *irreplaceable documents* ○ *No one on this team is irreplaceable, the new manager insisted.*

irrepressible /ˌɪr·ɪˈpres·ə·bəl/ *adj* full of energy and enthusiasm; impossible to hold back ○ *irrepressible high spirits*

irresistible /ˌɪr·ɪˈzɪs·tə·bəl/ *adj* impossible to refuse, oppose, or avoid because too pleasant, attractive, or strong ○ *an irresistible smile* ○ *I wasn't going to have dessert, but the pie proved irresistible.*

irrespective /ˌɪr·ɪˈspek·tɪv/ *adv* [not gradable] without considering; not needing to allow for ○ *The rules apply to everyone, irrespective of how long they have been with the company.*

irresponsible /ˌɪr·ɪˈspɑn·sə·bəl/ *adj* not thinking carefully enough or not caring about what might result from actions taken ○ [+ *to* infinitive] *It would have been irresponsible to let Claire drive home when she was so tired.*
irresponsibly /ˌɪr·ɪˈspɑn·sə·bli/ *adv*

irreverent /ɪˈrev·ə·rənt/ *adj* lacking the expected respect for official, important, or holy things ○ *The television program takes an irreverent look at the medical profession.*
irreverence /ɪˈrev·ə·rəns/ *n* [U]

irreversible Ⓐ /ˌɪr·ɪˈvɜr·sə·bəl/ *adj* [not gradable] impossible to change or to return to a previous condition ○ *Technology has had an irreversible impact on society.*

irrevocable /ɪˈrev·ə·kə·bəl, ˌɪr·ɪˈvoʊ·kə-/ *adj* [not gradable] (esp. of a decision) impossible to change ○ *The court's ruling is irrevocable.*

irrigate /ˈɪr·əˌgeɪt/ *v* [T] to supply land with water so that crops and plants will grow or grow better ○ *to irrigate farmland*
irrigation /ˌɪr·əˈgeɪ·ʃən/ *n* [U] ○ *an irrigation system*

irritate ANNOY /ˈɪr·əˌteɪt/ *v* [T] to annoy or make angry ○ *After a while the noise began to irritate him.*
irritable /ˈɪr·ət̬·ə·bəl/ *adj* ○ *The baby has really been irritable today.*
irritating /ˈɪr·əˌteɪt̬·ɪŋ/ *adj* ○ *There was one irritating delay after another.*
irritation /ˌɪr·əˈteɪ·ʃən/ *n* [C/U] ○ [C] *minor irritations*

MAKE SORE /ˈɪr·əˌteɪt/ *v* [T] to make something sore or painful, or to cause an uncomfortable physical reaction ○ *At first my contact lenses irritated my eyes.*
irritant /ˈɪr·ə·tənt/ *n* [C] a cause of an uncomfortable physical reaction ○ *Especially in the spring, plant pollen is an irritant that makes the eyes and throat itchy and can cause breathing problems.*
irritation /ˌɪr·əˈteɪ·ʃən/ *n* [C/U] a sore or reddened area on the skin or other part of the body ○ [C] *a skin irritation*

IRS *n* [U] *abbreviation for* Internal Revenue Service (= the part of the US Treasury Department that collects most taxes owed to the federal government, including income tax)

is /ɪz, əz/ *v* BE, used with he/she/it ○ *She is a lawyer.*

Islam /ɪzˈlɑm, ˈɪz·lɑm/ *n* [U] a religion based on a belief in one God and the teaching of Muhammad ○ *Islam is the religion of the Muslims.*
Islamic /ɪzˈlɑm·ɪk, -ˈlæm-/ *adj* [not gradable] ○ *Islamic art* ○ *an Islamic country*

island /ˈaɪ·lənd/ *n* [C] a piece of land completely surrounded by water ○ *Manhattan is an island.*

USAGE

island

Remember to use the preposition **on** before **island**.

They grew up on an island in the Pacific.

~~*They grew up in an island in the Pacific.*~~

ISLAND

isle /ɑɪl/ *n* [C] an ISLAND, esp. a small one

isn't /ˈɪz·ənt/ *contraction of* is not ○ *He isn't coming until tomorrow.*

isobar /ˈɑɪ·səˌbɑr/ *n* [C] ***earth science*** a line drawn on a weather map joining all the places that have the same air pressure

isolate Ⓐ /ˈɑɪ·səˌleɪt/ *v* [T] to separate something from other things, or to keep something separate ○ *They tried to isolate the cause of the problem.* ○ *A high wall isolated the house from the rest of the neighborhood.*

isolated Ⓐ /ˈɑɪ·səˌleɪt̬·əd/ *adj* ○ *Only a few isolated cases of measles have been reported.*

isolation Ⓐ /ˌɑɪ·səˈleɪ·ʃən/ *n* [U] ○ *The prisoner was kept in isolation for three days.*

isolationism Ⓐ /ˌɑɪ·səˈleɪ·ʃəˌnɪz·əm/ *n* [U] ***politics & government*** the political principle or practice of showing interest only in your own country and not being involved in international activities

isoline /ˌɑɪ·səˌlɑɪn/ *n* [C] ***earth science*** a line drawn on a map that connects things with the same value, such as temperature or height above the earth's surface

isomer /ˈɑɪ·sə·mər/ *n* [C] ***chemistry*** any one of a group of chemical substances which all have the same number and type of atoms but in which the arrangement of the atoms is slightly different between each substance

isomerism /ɑɪˈsɑm·əˌrɪz·əm/ *n* [U] ***chemistry*** the existence of two or more chemical substances that are isomers

isosceles triangle /ɑɪˈsɑs·əˌliːz ˈtrɑɪˌæŋ·gəl/ *n* [C] ***geometry*** a triangle that has two sides of equal length and two equal angles ➤ Picture: **triangle**

isotherm /ˈɑɪ·səˌθɜrm/ *n* [C] ***earth science*** a line on a weather map that connects areas with the same temperature

isotope /ˈɑɪ·səˌtoʊp/ *n* [C] ***physics, chemistry*** a form of an atom which has a different ATOMIC MASS from other forms of the same atom but the same chemical structure

issue Ⓐ **SUBJECT** /ˈɪʃ·uː, *esp. Southern* ˈɪʃ·ə/ *n* [C] a subject or problem that people are thinking and talking about ○ *There continues to be a great deal of debate over the property tax issue.* ○ *Isn't the need to hire more staff what's really at issue here* (= the subject of the disagreement)*?* ○ *I like my hair this way – I don't see why you have to make an issue of it* (= cause it to be a problem).

SUPPLY /ˈɪʃ·uː, *esp. Southern* ˈɪʃ·ə/ *v* [T] to give, supply, or produce something official ○ *Reporters gathered on the White House lawn, hoping that the president would issue a statement.*

issue /ˈɪʃ·uː, *esp. Southern* ˈɪʃ·ə/ *n* [C] a group or series, or one of a group or series, of things that are supplied, made available, or printed at the same time ○ *A new issue of postage stamps was released to honor women in the military.* ○ *He picked up an old issue of Life magazine.*

isthmus /ˈɪs·məs/ *n* [C] a narrow piece of land that has water on either side and joins two larger areas of land ○ *the Isthmus of Panama*

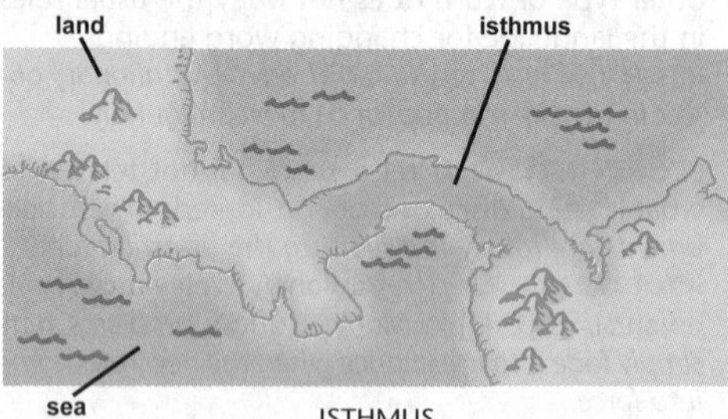

ISTHMUS

it /ɪt, ət/ *pronoun* **1** the thing or animal being spoken about, that has already been mentioned ○ *I can't find the newspaper. Do you know where it is?* ○ *Someone is at the door. Find out who it is.* **2** It is sometimes used to introduce a statement that does not involve a particular event or person: *It's supposed to rain tomorrow.*

italics /ɪˈtæl·ɪks, ɑɪ-/ *pl n* a style of printing in which the letters lean to the right ○ *This sentence is printed in italics.*

italic /ɪˈtæl·ɪk, ɑɪ-/ *adj* ○ *italic type*

italicize /ɪˈtæl·əˌsɑɪz, ɑɪ-/ *v* [T] ○ *Sometimes words are italicized for emphasis.*

itch /ɪtʃ/ *v* [I] to have an uncomfortable feeling on the skin that makes you want to rub it with something hard ○ *My insect bites are itching.*

itch /ɪtʃ/ *n* [C usually sing] ○ *I have an itch on the back of my neck.* ○ [+ *to* infinitive] *He has an itch* (= desire) *to travel.*

itchy /ˈɪtʃ·i/ *adj* [-er/-est only] ○ *an itchy sweater*

IDIOM with itch

• **itching to** *do something* wanting to do something very much ○ *The kids are itching to go out and play.*

it'd /ˈɪt̬·əd, ɪd/ *contraction of* it would or it had ○ *It'd* (= It would) *be great if we could finish today.* ○ *It'd* (= It had) *been left in the yard all week.*

item Ⓐ /ˈɑɪt̬·əm/ *n* [C] **1** one thing that is a part of a list or a collection of things ○ *There were several more items on the agenda.* **2** An item is also a particular thing considered as one among others of its type: *a news item in this morning's newspaper* ○ *basic food items such as butter*

itemize Ⓐ /ˈɑɪt̬·əˌmɑɪz/ *v* [T] to list particular things separately ○ *I always itemize deductions on my income tax.*

WORD FAMILY item	
Nouns item	*Verbs* itemize

itinerant /ɑɪˈtɪn·ə·rənt/ *adj* (of a person) traveling from one place to another, usually to work for a short period ○ *itinerant farm workers*

itinerary /ɑɪˈtɪn·əˌrer·i/ *n* [C] a detailed plan or route of a trip ○ *We planned our itinerary several weeks before the trip.*

it'll /ˈɪt̬·əl/ *contraction of* it will ○ *It'll be hard to find someone to help.*

its /ɪts, əts/ *pronoun* belonging to or connected with the thing or animal mentioned; the possessive form of it, used before a noun ○ *The horse flicked its tail at the flies.* ○ *The movie has its flaws, but it is interesting nevertheless.*

it's /ɪts, əts/ *contraction of* it is or it has ○ *It's* (= It is) *my turn to do it.* ○ *It's* (= It has) *been a long day and I'm tired.* ○ See also: ITS

itself /ɪtˈself, ət-/ *pronoun* **1** the thing or animal being spoken about; the reflexive form of it ○ *The cat licked itself all over.* **2** Itself can also used for emphasis: *The company itself is 15 years old, but the mail order business is new.* ○ *That in itself* (= without considering anything else) *was quite an achievement.*

IUPAC /ˌɑɪ ˌjuː ˌpiː ˌeɪ ˈsiː/ *n* [U] ***chemistry*** *abbreviation for* International Union of Pure and Applied Chemistry (= an international organization whose purpose is to advance chemistry).

I've /ɑɪv/ *contraction of* I have ○ *I've decided not to go.*

ivory /ˈɑɪ·və·ri, ˈɑɪv·ri/ *n* [U] **1** the hard white substance of the TUSKS (= long teeth growing outside the mouth) of some animals, such as ELEPHANTS ○ *an ivory statue* **2** Ivory is also a yellow-white color.

ivory tower /ˌɑɪv·riː ˈtɑʊ·ər/ *n* [C] an imaginary place where you are protected from unpleasant facts and have little practical knowledge of the real world ○ *They all live in their ivory towers and have no idea what it takes to win a football conference title.*

ivory-tower /ˌɑɪv·riː ˌtɑʊ·ər/ *adj* [not gradable] ○ *They were essentially realists, not ivory-tower dreamers.*

ivy /ˈɑɪ·vi/ *n* [C/U] an evergreen plant that often grows along the surface of trees or buildings

Ivy League *n* [U] a group of colleges and universities in the US that have a good reputation ○ *Yale and Harvard are Ivy League schools.*

J j

J **LETTER**, j /dʒeɪ/ *n* [C] *pl* **J's, Js, j's, js** the tenth letter of the English alphabet

MEASUREMENT /dʒeɪ/ *n* [C] ***science*** *abbreviation for* JOULE

jab /dʒæb/ *v* [I/T] **-bb- 1** to push at something hard and quickly with a finger or a thin, pointed object ○ [T] *I jabbed my finger on the needle.* ○ [I] *He jabbed at his food with his fork.* **2** To jab is also to hit someone hard and quickly with a tightly closed hand.

jab /dʒæb/ *n* [C] ○ *He gave his opponent a quick jab in the ribs.*

jabber /ˈdʒæb·ər/ *v* [I] to speak or say something quickly in a way that is difficult to understand ○ *Jay was jabbering on about this and that.*

jack **DEVICE** /dʒæk/ *n* [C] a device used to raise and hold something heavy off the ground, esp. one for raising a vehicle so that a tire can be changed

CARD /dʒæk/ *n* [C] a playing card that has a picture of a man on it and has a lower value than the cards showing a king or queen ○ *the jack of diamonds*

ELECTRICITY /dʒæk/ *n* [C] a hole into which a wire connected to a piece of electrical equipment can be plugged so that the equipment can operate ○ *a microphone jack*

PHRASAL VERBS with jack

• **jack up** *something* **RAISE** [M] to raise something heavy off the ground ○ *I had the car jacked up on blocks.*

• **jack up** *something* **INCREASE** [M] to increase a price ○ *Ad rates will be jacked up to $3600 a month.*

jackal /ˈdʒæk·əl/ *n* [C] any of several types of wild dog of Asia and Africa that hunt and travel in groups

jackass **PERSON** /ˈdʒæk·æs/ *n* [C] *infml* a silly, stupid person ○ *Why is Russ behaving like such a jackass?*

ANIMAL /ˈdʒæk·æs/ *n* [C] a male DONKEY

jacket **CLOTHING** /ˈdʒæk·ət/ *n* [C] a short coat ○ *a leather/denim jacket* ○ *a suit/sports jacket*

COVERING /ˈdʒæk·ət/ *n* [C] an outer cover that protects something ○ *the book jacket*

jackhammer /ˈdʒæk ˌhæm·ər/ *n* [C] a powerful tool, held in the hands and operated by air pressure, that is used for breaking hard surfaces such as rock and roads

jack-in-the-box /ˈdʒæk·ɪn·ðəˌbɑks/ *n* [C] a toy consisting of a box from which a model of a person suddenly appears when the top of the box is raised

jackknife **KNIFE** /ˈdʒæk·nɑɪf/ *n* [C] a knife with one or more blades that fold into the handle, which fits into a person's pocket

MAKE AN ANGLE /ˈdʒæk·nɑɪf/ *v* [I] to bend in half, or bend so the parts make a sharp angle ○ *A truck jackknifed on Route 80 this morning.*

jack-of-all-trades /ˌdʒæk·ə·vɔːlˈtreɪdz/ *n* [U] someone who can do many different jobs ○ *An artist with the right technology can become a jack-of-all-trades.*

jack-o'-lantern /ˈdʒæk·əˌlænt·ərn/ *n* [C] a PUMPKIN with its seeds removed and cut with holes shaped like eyes, a nose, and a mouth, and lit with a candle inside, which is made at HALLOWEEN

jackpot /ˈdʒæk·pɑt/ *n* [C] the largest prize offered in a competition, or a prize that is added to until it is won ○ *I dreamt that I won/hit the jackpot.*

jackrabbit /ˈdʒæk ˌræb·ət/ *n* [C] a type of large HARE (= animal like a rabbit) of North America, with long ears and long back legs

jacks /dʒæks/ *n* [U] a children's game in which the player bounces a small ball into the air and tries to pick up a number of small metal or plastic objects with the same hand before catching the ball again

Jacuzzi /dʒəˈkuː·zi/ *n* [C] *trademark* a bath or pool into which warm water flows through small holes, producing a pleasant, bubbling effect

jade /dʒeɪd/ *adj, n* [U] a precious, usually green stone from which jewelry is made, or a blue-green or yellow-green color

jaded /ˈdʒeɪd·əd/ *adj* [not gradable] lacking interest or desire because of experiencing too much of something ○ *Business travel is exciting at first, but you soon become jaded.*

jagged /ˈdʒæg·əd/ *adj* [not gradable] rough and uneven, with sharp points ○ *a jagged piece of glass* ○ *a jagged edge*

jaguar /ˈdʒæg·wɑr, -jəˌwɑr/ *n* [C] a large, wild cat of Central and South America with black spots

jail /dʒeɪl/ *n* [C/U] a place where criminals are kept as a punishment for their crimes or while waiting for trial ○ [C] *County jails are already overcrowded.* ○ [U] *He was sentenced to six months in jail.*

jail /dʒeɪl/ *v* [T] ○ *He was jailed for three years.*

jailer /ˈdʒeɪ·lər/ *n* [C] a person in charge of a jail or of the prisoners there

jalopy /dʒəˈlɑp·i/ *n* [C] *infml, humorous* an old car in bad condition

jam **PUSH** /dʒæm/ *v* [T always + adv/prep] **-mm-** to push something hard with sudden effort ○ [M] *She jammed on the brakes when the light turned red.*

PACK /dʒæm/ *v* [T always + adv/prep] **-mm-** to pack tightly into a small space ○ *He jammed the boxes into the trunk of the car.*

jammed /dʒæmd/, **jam-packed** /ˈdʒæm ˈpækt/ *adj* ○ *The room was jammed.* ○ *a jam-packed meeting*

BECOME STUCK /dʒæm/ *v* [I/T] **-mm-** to become stuck and unable to move, or to be stuck in some-

thing ○ [I] *My key jammed in the lock.* ○ [T] *Paper was jamming the printer.*
jammed /dʒæmd/ *adj* [not gradable] ○ *This drawer is jammed.*

SITUATION /dʒæm/ *n* [C] *infml* a difficult situation ○ *She expects her parents to bail her out whenever she gets in a jam.*

MUSIC /dʒæm/ *v* [I] **-mm-** to play popular music informally with other people, without planning it or practicing together ○ *He once jammed with Charlie Parker.*

FOOD /dʒæm/ *n* [U] a soft, sweet food made by cooking fruit with sugar ○ *strawberry/raspberry jam on toast*

jamboree /ˌdʒæm·bəˈriː/ *n* [C] a large social gathering ○ *a country music jamboree* ○ *a Boy Scout jamboree*

Jane Doe /ˈdʒeɪn ˈdoʊ/ *n* [C] *female* JOHN DOE.

jangle /ˈdʒæŋ·gəl/ *v* [I/T] to make a noise like metal hitting metal ○ [I] *The phone jangled insistently.*

janitor /ˈdʒæn·ət̬·ər/ *n* [C] a person whose job is to clean and take care of a building

January /ˈdʒæn·jəˌwer·i/, *abbreviation* **Jan.** *n* [C/U] the first month of the year, after December and before February

jar **CONTAINER** /dʒɑr/ *n* [C] a cylindrical container, usually made of glass, with a wide top opening, and used esp. for storing food, or the amount held by such a container ○ *a jar of pickles/mayonnaise* ○ *He poured half the jar into his cup.*

SHAKE /dʒɑr/ *v* [T] **-rr-** **1** to give a sudden shake to someone or something ○ *He kind of jars people when he tackles them.* **2** If a noise jars you, it shocks you: *The train's rumbling jarred them out of their sleep.*

CAUSE ACTION /dʒɑr/ *v* [I/T] to cause action or activity, or to have an effect ○ [T] *He was jarred into political action by events on the national scene.*

jargon /ˈdʒɑr·gən/ *n* [U] words and phrases used by particular groups of people, esp. in their work, that are not generally understood ○ *technical jargon* ○ *legal/computer jargon*

jarring /ˈdʒɑr·ɪŋ/ *adj* different from surrounding or usual things, or disagreeing with others, and therefore surprising or upsetting ○ *a jarring succession of images* ○ *The band took a new, if jarring, approach to this music.*

jaundice /ˈdʒɔːn·dəs, ˈdʒɑn-/ *n* [U] a disease of the blood that causes the skin and the white part of the eyes to turn yellow
jaundiced /ˈdʒɔːn·dəst, ˈdʒɑn-/ *adj*

jaundiced /ˈdʒɔːn·dəst, ˈdʒɑn-/ *adj* [not gradable] showing negative feelings or ideas ○ *He has a jaundiced view of middle-class life.*

jaunt /dʒɔːnt, dʒɑnt/ *n* [C] a short trip for pleasure ○ *a weekend jaunt*

jaunty /ˈdʒɔːnt·i, ˈdʒɑnt·i/ *adj* [-er/-est only] happy and confident
jauntily /ˈdʒɔːnt·əl·i, ˈdʒɑnt-/ *adv* ○ *He scampered jauntily down the stairs.*

Java /ˈdʒɑv·ə/ *n* [U] *trademark* a computer programming language used for writing programs for the INTERNET

javelin /ˈdʒæv·ə·lən/ *n* [C/U] a long, pointed stick that is thrown in sports competitions, or the sport in which this stick is thrown

jaw /dʒɔː/ *n* [C] either of the two bony parts bordering the mouth that hold your teeth in place ○ *the upper/lower jaw*
jaws /dʒɔːz/ *pl n* the mouth, including the teeth ○ *The lion opened its jaws and roared.*

IDIOM with jaw

• *someone's* **jaw drops** someone is very surprised ○ *When I saw him make that amazing shot, my jaw dropped.*

jawbone /ˈdʒɔː·boʊn/ *n* [C] either of the two bones that form the lower part of the mouth and face

jaywalk /ˈdʒeɪ·wɔːk/ *v* [I] to walk across a street at a place where you are not allowed to cross
jaywalking /ˈdʒeɪˌwɔː·kɪŋ/ *n* [U] ○ *You got ticketed for jaywalking?*

jazz /dʒæz/ *n* [U] a type of music of African-American origin with a strong rhythm in which the players IMPROVISE (= invent music that has not been written)
jazzy /ˈdʒæz·i/ *adj* [-er/-est only] ○ *There's a jazzy quality to her voice.*

PHRASAL VERB with jazz

• **jazz up** *something* [M] *infml* to make something more interesting or exciting ○ *He jazzed up the food with a spicy sauce.*

jazzy /ˈdʒæz·i/ *adj* [-er/-est only] *infml* exciting or showy ○ *a jazzy tie/dress*

jealous **WANTING QUALITIES** /ˈdʒel·əs/ *adj* unhappy and slightly angry because you wish you had someone else's qualities, advantages, or success ○ *Ron was jealous of his colleague's promotion.*
jealousy /ˈdʒel·ə·si/ *n* [C/U] ○ [C] *petty jealousies* ○ [U] *Jealousy over a colleague's success is considered unprofessional.*

WORD CHOICES jealous

Envious is a common alternative to "jealous."

*She was very **envious** of her brother's success.*

You could also use the phrase be **green with envy**.

*You'll be **green with envy** when you meet her new boyfriend.*

Someone who is **possessive** is jealous because that person does not want to share someone's love and attention with anyone else.

*a **possessive** boyfriend*

J

FEARFUL ABOUT LOVE /ˈdʒel·əs/ *adj* fearing that someone you love loves someone else or is loved by someone else

jealousy /ˈdʒel·ə·si/ *n* [C/U] ○ [U] *Grace felt the first pangs of jealousy when she saw them dancing.*

CAREFUL TO PROTECT /ˈdʒel·əs/ *adj* very careful to protect someone or something ○ *Her parents kept a jealous watch over her.*

jealously /ˈdʒel·ə·sli/ *adv* ○ *He jealously guarded his privacy.*

jeans /dʒiːnz/ *pl n* pants made of DENIM (= strong, cotton cloth) ○ *I don't usually wear blue jeans to work.*

Jeep /dʒiːp/ *n* [C] *trademark* a strongly built, four-wheeled motor vehicle designed for travel over rough ground

jeer /dʒɪr/ *v* [I/T] to laugh or shout insults at someone; to ridicule ○ [I] *Striking workers jeered at those who crossed the picket line.*

jeer /dʒɪr/ *n* [C] ○ *We were surprised to hear jeers from our own fans.*

J

jeez /dʒiːz/ *exclamation slang* used to express surprise, anger, or annoyance ○ *Jeez, what took you so long?*

Jehovah's Witness /dʒəˌhoʊ·vəz ˈwɪt·nəs/ *n* [C] a member of a Christian religious group who gives away religious literature at people's homes and on the street to try to persuade people to join the group

jell /dʒel/, **gel** *v* [I] (of a substance) to change from a liquid to a partly solid state, or (of ideas or plans) to become more clear and certain ○ *Refrigerate the mixture till it jells.* ○ *I'll let you know as soon as our plans jell.*

Jell-O, jello /ˈdʒel·oʊ/ *n* [U] *trademark* a soft, colored, sweet food made from GELATIN, sugar, and fruit flavoring

jelly /ˈdʒel·i/ *n* [U] **1** a soft, sweet, slightly solid food made by boiling fruit juice with sugar ○ *grape/apple jelly* ○ *a peanut butter and jelly sandwich* **2** Jelly is also a substance that is almost solid: *petroleum jelly*

jellybean /ˈdʒel·iːˌbiːn/ *n* [C] a small, brightly colored, bean-shaped candy that is soft in the middle and covered with hard sugar

jellyfish /ˈdʒel·iːˌfɪʃ/ *n* [C] *pl* **jellyfish** a sea animal with a soft, round, almost transparent body with TENTACLES that can sting

jeopardize /ˈdʒep·ərˌdɑɪz/ *v* [T] to cause something to be harmed or damaged, or to put something in danger ○ *She knew that failing her exams could jeopardize her whole future.*

jeopardy /ˈdʒep·ərd·i/ *n* [U] Something **in jeopardy** is in danger of being damaged or destroyed: *Bad investments have put the company's future in jeopardy.*

jerk MOVE /dʒɜrk/ *v* [always + adv/prep] to make a short, sudden movement, or to cause someone or something to move in this way ○ [T] *She jerked the phone out of his hands.* ○ [I] *The bus jerked to a halt.*

jerk /dʒɜrk/ *n* [C] ○ *He gave the dog's leash a jerk.*

jerky /ˈdʒɜr·ki/ *adj* ○ *jerky movements*

PERSON /dʒɜrk/ *n* [C] *slang* a foolish, annoying person ○ *What a jerk – he parked in my spot!*

PHRASAL VERB with jerk

• **jerk** *someone* **around** [M] *infml* to intentionally cause difficulty for someone ○ *I don't think she really likes Colten – she's just jerking him around.*

jerky /ˈdʒɜr·ki/ *n* [U] strips of dried, salty meat ○ *beef jerky*

jersey /ˈdʒɜr·zi/ *n* [C] **1** a shirt, esp. one that is part of a uniform ○ *I have to wash my daughter's softball jersey.* **2** Jersey is also a type of soft, KNITTED cloth: *She was dressed in a jersey top and jeans.*

jest /dʒest/ *n* [C] **1** a joke **2** If you say something **in jest**, you are not serious about it: *His remarks about the Beatles were in jest.*

jester /ˈdʒes·tər/ *n* [C] (in earlier times) a man whose job was to tell jokes and make people laugh ○ *a court jester*

Jesuit /ˈdʒeʒ·ə·wət, ˈdʒez-/ *n* [C] a Roman Catholic priest who is a member of the Society of Jesus (= a religious group begun in 1540)

Jesus (Christ) /ˈdʒiː·zəs (ˈkrɑɪst), -zəz/, **Christ** *n* [U] the Jewish religious teacher believed by those who follow him to be the son of God, whose teachings and life Christianity developed from

jet CONTINUOUS FLOW /dʒet/ *n* [C] a strong, narrow, continuous flow, esp. of water or gas, that is forced out of a small hole ○ *The whale blew a jet of water into the air.*

AIRCRAFT /dʒet/ *n* [C] a fast aircraft with a JET ENGINE ○ *He owns a private jet.*

jet /dʒet/ *v* [I always + adv/prep] **-tt-** to travel in a jet aircraft ○ *I'm jetting off to LA next week.*

STONE /dʒet/ *n* [U] a hard, black, shiny stone that is used to make jewelry

jet-black *adj* [not gradable] pure black in color ○ *jet-black hair*

jet engine *n* [C] an engine that moves an aircraft forward by sending hot air and gases under pressure out behind it

jet lag *n* [U] the feeling of being tired that you experience after a long flight to a place where the time is different from the place that you left

jet-propelled *adj* powered by a JET ENGINE, and so able to move very fast

jettison /ˈdʒet̬·ə·sən, -zən/ *v* [T] to throw away or get rid of something that is not wanted or needed ○ *Some of her material will probably be jettisoned for the TV show.* ○ *The bombs were jettisoned over the English Channel.*

jetty /ˈdʒet̬·i/ *n* [C] a structure built out from the land into the water as a landing place for boats or as protection from waves

Jew /dʒuː/ *n* [C] a person whose religion is Judaism, or a person related by birth to the ancient people of Israel

Jewish /ˈdʒuː·ɪʃ/ *adj* [not gradable] of or related to Jews

jewel /ˈdʒuː·əl/ *n* [C] a precious stone, such as a DIAMOND or RUBY, or a decorative object with such a stone or several stones in it ○ *a jewel necklace*

jeweler /ˈdʒuː·ə·lər, ˈdʒuː·lər/ *n* [C] a person who sells and sometimes repairs jewelry and watches

jewelry /ˈdʒuː·əl·ri, ˈdʒuːl·ri/, **jewels** *n* [U] decorative objects worn on clothes or on the body, such as rings and NECKLACES, often made from valuable metals and containing precious stones ○ *costume jewelry*

jibe **INSULT** /dʒɑɪb/ *n, v* GIBE

AGREE /dʒɑɪb/ *v* [I] to agree with something else ○ *Her story just doesn't jibe with what the other witnesses say.*

jiffy /ˈdʒɪf·i/ *n* [U] *infml* a very short time ○ *I'm on the phone, but I'll be with you in a jiffy.*

jig /dʒɪg/ *n* [C] an energetic, traditional dance of Great Britain and Ireland, or the music that is played for such a dance

jiggle /ˈdʒɪg·əl/ *v* [I/T] to move something or cause something to move from side to side or up and down with quick short movements ○ [T] *If the toilet won't stop flushing, jiggle the handle.*

jigsaw puzzle /ˈdʒɪg ˌsɔː ˌpʌz·əl/ *n* [C] a game consisting of a lot of differently shaped pieces of cardboard or wood that you try to fit together in order to show the complete picture that the pieces make when they are all used ○ *We spent the evening working on the jigsaw puzzle of the Monet painting.*

jihad /dʒɪˈhɑd/ *n* [C/U] an often violent effort by some MUSLIM people to defend their religion against those who they believe want to destroy it

jilt /dʒɪlt/ *v* [T] to end a romantic relationship with someone suddenly ○ *He jilted her for another woman.*

Jim Crow /ˈdʒɪm ˈkroʊ/ *n* [U] the US laws and customs that kept black people apart from white people and prevented them from having the opportunities available to white people from the 1800s to the 1960s

jingle **RING** /ˈdʒɪŋ·gəl/ *v* [I/T] to make a repeated gentle ringing sound, or to cause an object to make a ringing sound ○ [T] *He jingled the coins in his pocket.*

jingle /ˈdʒɪŋ·gəl/ *n* [U] ○ *the jingle of bells*

TUNE /ˈdʒɪŋ·gəl/ *n* [C] a short, simple tune, often with words, that is easy to remember and is used to advertise a product on radio or television

jinx /dʒɪŋks/ *v* [T] to cause a person or group to experience bad luck ○ *I didn't want to say anything to him – I was afraid I might jinx him.*

jinx /dʒɪŋks/ *n* [C usually sing] a person or thing that brings bad luck, or a period of bad luck ○ *There must be a jinx on our team – four of our best players were injured yesterday.*

jitney /ˈdʒɪt·ni/ *n* [C] a small bus that follows a regular route

jitters /ˈdʒɪt̬·ərz/ *pl n* a feeling of being nervous that you experience before something important happens ○ *I always get the jitters the morning before an exam.*

jittery /ˈdʒɪt̬·ə·ri/ *adj* ○ *Gwen always felt jittery when she got up on stage.*

jive /dʒɑɪv/ *n* [U] *slang* dishonest talk intended to deceive ○ *Don't give me this jive.*

job Ⓐ **EMPLOYMENT** /dʒɑb/ *n* [C] **1** the regular work that a person does to earn money ○ *a full-time/part-time/permanent/temporary job* ○ *to get/quit a job* ○ *The new supermarket will create 50 new jobs in the area.* ○ *She's applied for a job with an insurance company.* ○ *How long have you been out of a job* (= unemployed)? **2** If you do something **on the job**, you do it while at work: *He keeps falling asleep on the job.* ○ *The company provides on-the-job training* (= training while you work).

jobless /ˈdʒɑb·ləs/ *adj* [not gradable] without a job ○ *He's been jobless for more than six months.*

➤ Confusables: **work or job?** at WORK DO A JOB

WORD CHOICES job

A more formal alternative is the noun **occupation**.

Please fill in your name, age, and ***occupation****.*

The nouns **post** and **position** are often used to talk about a particular job within an organization.

She's applied for a part-time teaching ***position****.*

The noun **career** is sometimes used to describe a job that a person does for a long period in their life.

She's had a very successful ***career*** *in marketing.*

An **internship** is a job that someone does for a short time in order to learn more about a particular kind of work.

She's got a year's ***internship*** *before she can get her license to practice medicine.*

PIECE OF WORK /dʒɑb/ *n* [C] **1** a particular piece of work ○ *I should have this job done by lunchtime.* ○ *A microwave oven makes the job of preparing meals a lot easier.* **2** *infml* A job can be work done on or to something to improve or repair it: *a paint job* **3** If you do a good/bad job, you do a piece of work of that quality: *Jamie did a wonderful job on that sales presentation.*

DUTY /dʒɑb/ *n* [C] a responsibility or duty ○ [+ *to* infinitive] *I know it's not my job to tell you how to run your life, but I do think you've made a mistake.*

CRIME /dʒɑb/ *n* [C] *slang* a crime in which money or goods are stolen ○ *a bank job* ○ *an inside job* (=

a crime committed by someone who works for the company it was committed against)

jock /dʒɑk/ *n* [C] *infml* a person, esp. a young man, who is extremely enthusiastic about and good at sports ○ *Everyone on campus thought I was just another dumb jock.*

jockey **HORSE RIDER** /ˈdʒɑk·i/ *n* [C] a person whose job is riding horses in races

GET ADVANTAGE /ˈdʒɑk·i/ *v* [I always + adv/prep] to attempt to obtain power or get into a more advantageous position than other people by using any methods you can ○ *TV news cameramen jockeyed for position near the podium.*

jockstrap /ˈdʒɑk·stræp/ *n* [C] a tight piece of clothing worn by men under their pants or shorts to support and protect their sex organs, esp. while playing sports

jocular /ˈdʒɑk·jə·lər/ *adj* amusing or intended to cause amusement ○ *a jocular mood*

J

jog /dʒɑg, dʒɔːg/ *v* [I] **-gg-** to run at a slow regular speed, esp. as a form of exercise ○ *Bill jogs for 30 minutes every morning before breakfast.*

jog /dʒɑg, dʒɔːg/ *n* [U] ○ *I think I'll go out for a jog.*

jogger /ˈdʒɑg·ər, ˈdʒɔː·gər/ *n* [C] ○ *The park was full of joggers, bicyclists, and skaters.*

jogging /ˈdʒɑg·ɪŋ, ˈdʒɔː·gɪŋ/ *n* [U] ○ *The president goes jogging several times a week.*

IDIOM with jog

•**jog** *your* **memory** to cause you to remember something ○ *Seeing her again jogged my memory, and I recalled my life as a child on a farm in Minnesota.*

john /ˈdʒɑn/ *n* [C] *infml* a toilet or bathroom

John Doe /ˈdʒɑn ˈdoʊ/, *female* **Jane Doe** /ˈdʒeɪn ˈdoʊ/ *n* [U] *law* **1** a name used in a law court for a person whose real name is not known **2** John Doe is also an average or typical man, and Jane Doe is an average or typical woman.

johnny-come-lately /ˌdʒɑn·iː ˌkʌm ˈleɪt·li/ *n* [C] *disapproving* a person who starts a job or activity later than other people and sometimes uses the experience and knowledge of these people to obtain an advantage over them ○ *Riley, whose father founded the industry, calls her competitors johnny-come-latelies.*

join **DO WITH** /dʒɔɪn/ *v* [I/T] to do something with or be with someone or something ○ [T] *Why don't you ask your sister if she would like to join us for dinner?* ○ [T] *I'm sure everyone will join me in wishing you a very happy birthday.* ○ [I] *Won't you join with us in planning the party?*

BECOME A MEMBER /dʒɔɪn/ *v* [I/T] to become a member of an organization ○ [T] *I've decided to join a gym.* ○ [I] *It's a great club – why don't you join?*

FASTEN /dʒɔɪn/ *v* [I/T] **1** to cause something to be attached or fastened to another thing, or to bring two or more things together in this way; connect ○ [T] *A long suspension bridge joins the island with the mainland.* **2** If roads or rivers join, they meet at a particular point: [I] *The Missouri River and Mississippi River join north of St. Louis.* **3** If two or more people **join hands**, they hold each other's hands, esp. before doing some activity: *This folk dance begins with everyone joining hands to form a circle.*

IDIOM with join

•**join the club** *infml* I am in the same bad situation as you are ○ *"I've got no money till payday." "Join the club!"*

PHRASAL VERBS with join

•**join in** (*something*) to become involved with others in doing something ○ *Everyone can join in when I sing the National Anthem.*

•**join up** to become a member of the military or another group ○ *Levi was not the first member of his family to join up – his sister was already in the Navy.* ○ *Save the Seagulls is looking for volunteers to join up.*

joint **SHARED** /dʒɔɪnt/ *adj* [not gradable] **1** belonging to or shared between two or more people ○ *Do you and your husband have a joint bank account or separate accounts?* ○ *In court, the parents were awarded joint custody of their son* (= the right to care for him was shared between them). **2** A **joint venture** is a business that gets its money from two or more partners.

jointly /ˈdʒɔɪnt·li/ *adv* [not gradable] ○ *Construction of the new high school will be jointly funded by the city and the state.*

BODY PART /dʒɔɪnt/ *n* [C] a place in the body where two bones meet ○ *Good running shoes are supposed to reduce the stress on the ankle, knee, and hip joints.*

CONNECTION /dʒɔɪnt/ *n* [C] a place where two things are joined together ○ *Metal joints in the bridge allow it to expand or contract with changes in air temperature.*

PLACE /dʒɔɪnt/ *n* [C] *slang* **1** a cheap restaurant ○ *a hamburger joint* **2** A joint is also a place where people go for some type of entertainment: *a jazz joint*

Joint Chiefs of Staff, *short form* **Joint Chiefs** *n* [U] the leaders of the armed forces of the United States, who form an official group of six members to give advice to the president about military matters

joke **AMUSING** /dʒoʊk/ *n* [C] something, such as an amusing story or trick, that is said or done in order to make people laugh ○ *He told a joke about a farmer and a lawyer that made Nicholas burst into laughter.*

joke /dʒoʊk/ *v* to say things in an amusing or playful manner ○ [I] *He joked about how I was always cleaning.* ○ [+ *that* clause] *They've always joked that the place is so wet, the bullfrogs have to sit on the fences.*

RIDICULOUS /dʒoʊk/ *n* [U] *infml* something considered to be so bad or worthless that it is ridiculous

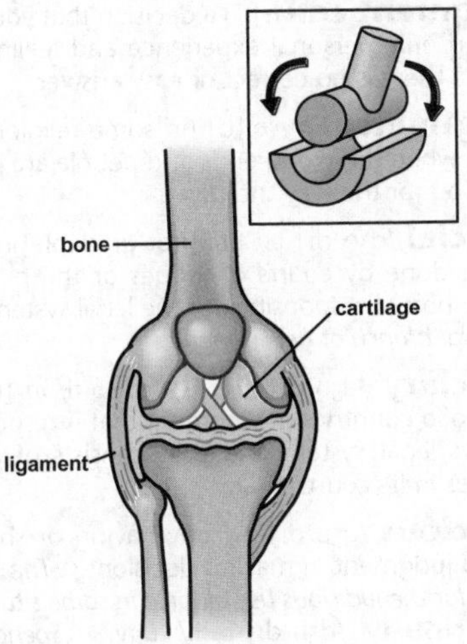

KNEE JOINT

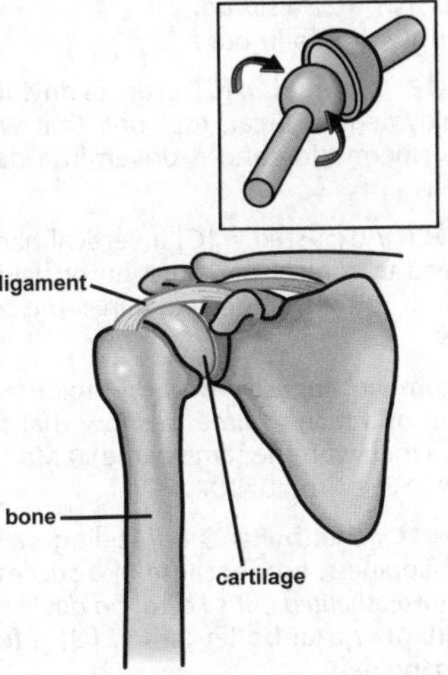

SHOULDER JOINT

○ *The playing conditions on the muddy field were a joke.* ○ *The midterm exam was a joke* (= too easy).

joker /ˈdʒoʊ·kər/ *n* [C] an annoying person ○ *We had to wait for an hour because some joker lost the key.*

WORD FAMILY joke			
Nouns	joke joker	*Verbs*	joke

joker /ˈdʒoʊ·kər/ *n* [C] (in some card games) a special playing card that can be given any value and used instead of any other card

jolly /ˈdʒɑl·i/ *adj* happy and pleasant ○ *That clown looks pretty jolly.*

jolt /dʒoʊlt/ *v* [T] to cause something or someone to move suddenly and violently, or to surprise someone in an unpleasant way ○ *I was jolted out of bed by the earthquake.* ○ *He was jolted by the sight of bodies lying in the lobby.*

jolt /dʒoʊlt/ *n* [C] a sudden, violent movement or force, or a large and unpleasant surprise ○ *jolts of electricity* ○ *She bumped into him, and the jolt sent his books to the ground.* ○ *Jack realized with a jolt of fear that he was helpless.*

jostle /ˈdʒɑs·əl/ *v* [I/T] to push against someone in order to move past that person or get more space when you are in a crowd of people ○ [T] *Someone jostled her from behind.*

jot /dʒɑt/ *v* [T] **-tt-** to write something quickly in a short note ○ [M] *The guard jotted down the van's license plate number.*

joule /dʒuːl/, *abbreviation* **J** *n* [C] ***science*** a unit for measuring ENERGY (= power) or work done

journal Ⓐ **MAGAZINE** /ˈdʒɜrn·ᵊl/ *n* [C] a magazine or newspaper, esp. one that deals with a particular subject ○ *a scientific journal* ○ *The Wall Street Journal*

RECORD /ˈdʒɜrn·ᵊl/ *n* [C] ***writing*** a record of what you have done, or of descriptions or thoughts, written each day or frequently over a long period; a DIARY ○ *He kept a journal for over 50 years.*

WORD FAMILY journal			
Nouns	journal journalism journalist	*Adjectives*	journalistic

journalism /ˈdʒɜrn·ᵊlˌɪz·əm/ *n* [U] the work of collecting, writing, and publishing or broadcasting news stories and articles ○ *broadcast journalism* ○ *print journalism*

journalist /ˈdʒɜrn·ᵊl·əst/ *n* [C] someone who collects and writes news stories and articles for newspapers, magazines, radio, and television ○ *a freelance journalist* ○ *a TV journalist* ○ *a Mexican journalist*

journalistic /ˌdʒɜrn·ᵊlˈɪs·tɪk/ *adj* [not gradable] ○ *Normal journalistic standards don't allow for this kind of abuse.*

journey /ˈdʒɜr·ni/ *n* [C] a trip, esp. over a long period or a great distance ○ *He was planning a six-week journey to China.*

journey /ˈdʒɜr·ni/ *v* [I always + adv/prep] ○ *As we journeyed north, the weather improved.* ➤ Usage: **travel, journey, or trip?** at TRAVEL

jovial /ˈdʒoʊ·viː·əl/ *adj* showing or feeling good humor; friendly ○ *a jovial smile*

jowls /dʒɑʊlz/ *pl n* loose skin and flesh that hangs below the JAW (= the lower part of the face)

joy /dʒɔɪ/ *n* [C/U] **1** great happiness or pleasure ○ [U] *My heart was full of pure joy.* **2** A joy is a person or thing that causes happiness: [C] *His daughters were the joys of his life.* ○ [C] *She's a joy to work with.*

joyful /ˈdʒɔɪ·fəl/ *adj* having or causing great happiness ○ *joyful news*

joyless /ˈdʒɔɪ·ləs/ *adj* being without happiness or pleasure ○ *a joyless marriage*

joyous /ˈdʒɔɪ·əs/ *adj* full of joy ○ *a joyous occasion*

joyously /ˈdʒɔɪ·ə·sli/ *adv*
joyfully /ˈdʒɔɪ·fə·li/ *adv*

joyride /ˈdʒɔɪ·rɑɪd/ *n* [C] an act of driving around for enjoyment in a car, esp. one that was taken without permission and is driven in a dangerous manner

joystick /ˈdʒɔɪ·stɪk/ *n* [C] a vertical handle that is moved to control the direction or height of an aircraft or to control the action in some computer games

Jr. /ˈdʒuːn·jər/ *adj abbreviation for* junior (= used at the end of a man's name to show that he is the son of a man with the same name) ○ *Martin Luther King, Jr.* ○ See also: JUNIOR

jubilant /ˈdʒuː·bə·lənt/ *adj* feeling or showing great happiness, esp. because of a success ○ *Jubilant crowds shouted, "It's liberation day!"*
jubilation /ˌdʒuː·bəˈleɪ·ʃən/ *n* [U] a feeling of great happiness

Judaism /ˈdʒuːd·əˌɪz·əm, -iːˌɪz-/ *n* [U] a religion based on a belief in a single God and on the TALMUD (= a collection of writings explaining Jewish law and customs) and parts of the Bible ○ Related adjective: JEWISH at JEW

judge LAW /dʒʌdʒ/ *n* [C] a person who is in charge of a court of law ○ *The judge dismissed the charge after a preliminary hearing.*
judgment, judgement /ˈdʒʌdʒ·mənt/ *n* [C/U] a decision in a court of law

DECIDE /dʒʌdʒ/ *v* [I/T] **1** to have or give an opinion, or to decide about something or someone, esp. after thinking carefully ○ [I] *He seems to be handling the job well, but it's really too soon to judge.* ○ [+ question word] *It's hard to judge how old he is.* ○ [T] *I'm hopeless at judging distances* (= guessing how far it is between places). ○ [T] *What gives you the right to judge people* (= decide how good or bad they are)*?* **2** To judge a competition is to decide officially who has won. **3 Judging by/from** or **to judge by/from** refers to the reasons you have for thinking something: *Judging by their home, they seem to be quite wealthy.*
judge /dʒʌdʒ/ *n* [C] **1** a person who is qualified to form or give an opinion about something ○ *a good judge of character* **2** A judge is also a person who officially decides who has won a competition.
judgment, judgement /ˈdʒʌdʒ·mənt/ *n* [C/U] **1** the ability to make decisions or to make good decisions, or the act of developing an opinion, esp. after careful thought ○ [U] *to show good/poor judgment* ○ [U] *They questioned his judgment in buying land he had never seen.* **2** A judgment is a decision: [C] *We were asked to make a number of difficult judgments.*
judgmental /dʒʌdʒˈment·əl/ *adj* tending to form opinions too quickly, esp. when disapproving of someone or something ○ *I'm trying not to be judgmental about my daughter's new boyfriend.*

WORD FAMILY judge			
Nouns	judge judgment	*Adjectives* *Verbs*	judgmental judge

judgment call *n* [C] a decision that you make based only personal experience and feelings because there is no correct or easy answer

Judgment Day *n* [U] (in some religions) the time when the world ends and people are judged by God for the way they lived

judicial /dʒʊˈdɪʃ·əl/ *adj* [not gradable] relating to or done by courts or judges or the part of a government responsible for the legal system ○ *the judicial branch of government*

judiciary /dʒʊˈdɪʃ·iːˌer·i, -ˈdɪʃ·ə·ri/ *n* [U] the part of a country's government that is responsible for its legal system and that consists of all the judges in its courts of law

judicious /dʒʊˈdɪʃ·əs/ *adv* having or showing good judgment in making decisions ○ *The law allows for the judicious use of force in some situations.*
judiciously /dʒʊˈdɪʃ·ə·sli/ *adv* ○ *Spend your money a little more judiciously.*

judo /ˈdʒuːd·oʊ/ *n* [U] a sport in which two people fight with their arms and legs, using skill more than strength, in trying to throw each other to the ground

jug /dʒʌg/ *n* [C] a large container for liquids that usually has a handle and a narrow opening at the top

juggle /ˈdʒʌg·əl/ *v* [I/T] to throw several objects into the air, catch them, and keep them moving so that at least one is always in the air ○ [T] *(fig.) Many women find it hard to juggle a family and a career* (= to arrange their lives so that they have time for both).
juggler /ˈdʒʌg·lər/ *n* [C]

jugular (vein) /ˈdʒʌg·jə·lər (ˌveɪn)/ *n* [C] any of several large VEINS (= tubes that carry blood to the heart) in the neck

juice LIQUID /dʒuːs/ *n* [C/U] the liquid that comes from fruits and vegetables ○ [U] *orange/tomato juice* ○ [C] *fruit juices*
juices /ˈdʒuː·səz/ *pl n infml* liquid in meat or in a person's body ○ *the digestive juices*
juicy /ˈdʒuː·si/ *adj* **1** full of juice or juices and therefore enjoyable to eat ○ *a juicy orange/steak* **2** *infml* Juicy can also mean very interesting or exciting: *a bit of juicy gossip*
juiciness /ˈdʒuː·siː·nəs/ *n* [U]

ELECTRICITY /dʒuːs/ *n* [U] *infml* electricity ○ *I've fixed the wiring, so you can turn the juice back on.*

WORD FAMILY juice			
Nouns	juice juices juiciness	*Adjectives*	juicy

jukebox /ˈdʒuːk·bɑks/ *n* [C] a machine that plays recorded music when a coin is put into it

July /dʒʊˈlɑɪ, dʒə-/, *abbreviation* **Jul.** *n* [C/U] the seventh month of the year, after June and before August

jumble /ˈdʒʌm·bəl/ *n* [U] a confused mixture or mass of things ○ *a jumble of papers on the desk*
jumble /ˈdʒʌm·bəl/ *v* [T] ○ *The events of the last few weeks are all jumbled up in my mind.*

jumbo /ˈdʒʌm·boʊ/ *adj* [not gradable] *infml* **1** extremely large ○ *a jumbo size box of cereal* **2** A jumbo jet is a very large aircraft that can fly long distances.

jump RAISE UP SUDDENLY /dʒʌmp/ *v* [I/T] **1** to push yourself off the ground and into the air using your legs and feet ○ [I] *The kids were jumping up and down with excitement.* ○ [I] *The cats jumped up onto the table.* **2** To jump sometimes means to lift yourself off the ground in order to go over something: [T] *Can you jump this fence?*
jump /dʒʌmp/ *n* [C] ○ *The skater's jump was high but not graceful.*
jumper /ˈdʒʌm·pər/ *n* [C] ○ *To dunk a basketball when you're just six feet tall, you have to be a great jumper.*

MOVE QUICKLY /dʒʌmp/ *v* [I] **1** to move suddenly or quickly ○ *A man jumped out of the bushes.* ○ *He jumped to his feet and ran out the door.* **2** If a noise or action causes you to jump, your body makes a sudden movement because of surprise or fear: *The thunder made us all jump.* **3** If a car **jumps the light**, it starts moving past a traffic light while the light is still red.

OMIT STAGES /dʒʌmp/ *v* [I/T] **1** to move up or go across suddenly from one point or stage to another without stopping at the stages in between ○ [I always + adv/prep] *Her book jumped from fifth place to first place on the best-seller list.* ○ [T] *The forest fire jumped the road and spread to the other side.* **2** If you **jump to conclusions**, you judge a situation quickly and emotionally without having all the facts: *It's not fair to jump to conclusions about a whole group of people based on one incident.*
jump /dʒʌmp/ *n* [C] ○ *He made a big jump from general manager to president of the company.*

INCREASE /dʒʌmp/ *v* [I] to increase suddenly by a large amount ○ *Home prices in the area have jumped to an all-time high.*

ATTACK /dʒʌmp/ *v* [T] *infml* to attack suddenly ○ *He was jumped and robbed by two guys on his way home from work.*

IDIOMS with jump

• **jump all over** *someone*, **jump on** *someone infml* to criticize someone suddenly and severely ○ *When I showed him my report card, Dad jumped all over me and said I wasn't working hard enough.*
• **jump the gun** to act too soon or before the right time ○ *They only met three weeks ago – isn't it jumping the gun to start talking about marriage?*
• **jump through hoops** to do a lot of extra things, esp. silly or difficult things, to achieve something ○ *We had to jump through hoops to get my Dad admitted to the hospital.*

PHRASAL VERB with jump

• **jump at** *something* to accept an opportunity eagerly ○ *She jumped at the chance to go to Paris.*

jumper /ˈdʒʌm·pər/ *n* [C] **1** a dress without sleeves that is usually worn over a shirt **2** *Br* A jumper is a SWEATER.

jumper cables /ˈdʒʌm·pər ˈkeɪ·bəlz/ *pl n* two wires that carry electrical power from one car's engine to help start another that has a BATTERY with no power

jump rope *n* [C] a rope that you pass over your head and under your feet while jumping, for exercise or amusement ○ *We grabbed our jump rope and headed for the playground.*

jump-start /ˈdʒʌmp·stɑrt/ *v* [T] **1** to start or improve something more quickly by giving it extra help ○ *These recordings jump-started her career.* **2** If you jump-start a car, you start its engine by using wires to carry electric power from another car's engine.

jumpy /ˈdʒʌm·pi/ *adj* nervous or anxious ○ *Stop watching him; it makes him jumpy.*

junction /ˈdʒʌŋ·ʃən/ *n* [C] a place where things, esp. roads and railroads, meet or join ○ *The shopping center is near the junction of the New Jersey Turnpike and Garden State Parkway.*

juncture /ˈdʒʌŋ·tʃər/ *n* [U] *fml* a particular point in time or stage in a series of events ○ *Negotiations are at a critical juncture.*

June /dʒuːn/, *abbreviation* **Jun.** *n* [C/U] the sixth month of the year, after May and before July

jungle /ˈdʒʌŋ·gəl/ *n* a forest in one of the hottest regions of the earth, where trees and plants grow very close together

junior LESS ADVANCED /ˈdʒuːn·jər/ *adj* less advanced, or lower in rank ○ *the junior varsity* ○ *Alfredo is a junior partner in the law firm.* ○ Compare SENIOR MORE ADVANCED

SCHOOL /ˈdʒuːn·jər/ *n* [C] a student in the third year of a program of study in a college, university, or HIGH SCHOOL (= a school for students aged 14 to 18)
junior /ˈdʒuːn·jər/ *adj* ○ *They met in their junior year of college and married soon after they graduated.*

YOUNGER /ˈdʒuːn·jər/ *adj* [not gradable] younger ○ *He was born in April, so he's three months my junior* (= he is three months younger). ○ See also: JR.

junior college *n* [C] a COMMUNITY COLLEGE

junior high school, *short form* **junior high** *n* [C] a school for children who are 12 to 15 years old

junk /dʒʌŋk/ *n* [U] things that are considered to be useless, worthless, or of low quality ○ *I cleared all the junk out of the garage.*
junk /dʒʌŋk/ *v* [T] *infml* to throw out something because it is does not work well or is worthless ○ *Why don't we junk this old TV and get a new one?*

junket /ˈdʒʌŋ·kət/ *n* [C] *disapproving* an unnecessary trip by a government official which is paid for with public money ○ *The senator is off on another junket to Hawaii at taxpayers' expense.*

junk food *n* [C/U] food that is not good for your health because it is high in fat, sugar, or artificial substances

junkie, **junky** /ˈdʒʌŋ·ki/ *n* [C] *slang* **1** a person who regularly takes and is dependent on illegal drugs, esp. HEROIN **2** *humorous* A junkie is also a person who enjoys or is interested in a particular activity to an extreme: *If you want to follow politics, basically you have to become a talk-show junkie.*

junk mail *n* [U] mail that advertises products and services and is sent to people although they have not asked to receive it ○ *There's a letter for you and the rest is junk mail.*

junkyard /ˈdʒʌŋk·jɑrd/ *n* [C] a place, often a large open area, where useless or unwanted items are left, and sometimes sold

junta /ˈhʊn·tə, ˈdʒʌnt·ə, ˈhʌn·tə/ *n* [C] ***world history*** a small group, esp. of military officers, that rules a country after taking power by force

Jupiter /ˈdʒuː·pəţ·ər/ *n* [U] the planet fifth in order of distance from the sun, after Mars and before Saturn ➤ Picture: **solar system**

jurisdiction /ˌdʒʊr·əsˈdɪk·ʃən/ *n* [U] ***politics & government*** the official authority to make (esp. legal) decisions and judgments ○ *The Supreme Court ruled that the US government had no jurisdiction over crimes committed on Indian lands.*

jurist /ˈdʒʊr·əst/ *n* [C] *fml* an expert in law, esp. a judge

jury /ˈdʒʊr·i/ *n* [C/U] **1** a group of people who have been chosen to listen to the facts of a trial in a law court and to decide whether a person is guilty or not guilty, or whether a claim has been proved ○ [U] *a trial by jury/a jury trial* ○ [C] *My husband served on a jury in a criminal case a few months ago.* **2** A jury is also a group of people chosen to judge a competition: [C] *The jury chose an unexpected winner for the literary prize.*

juror /ˈdʒʊr·ər, -ɔːr/ *n* [C] a member of a jury ○ *A majority of the jurors were women.*

IDIOM with jury

• **the jury is still out** no decision or agreement has been made about a situation, esp. because there is not enough information ○ *The jury is still out on whether the new healthcare system will work.*

just NOW /dʒʌst, dʒəst/ *adv* [not gradable] now or (almost) at the same time, or very soon, or very recently ○ *He just left – if you run, you can catch him.* ○ *It was just past* (= very soon after) *midnight.* ○ *We got the children off to school just as the bus was about to leave.* ○ *We're just about to begin* (= We will begin very soon). ○ *The doctor will see you in just a minute/moment/second* (= very soon).

EXACTLY /dʒʌst, dʒəst/ *adv* [not gradable] exactly ○ *Beth looks just like her mother.* ○ [+ question word] *It was just what I expected.*

ONLY /dʒʌst, dʒəst/ *adv* [not gradable] **1** only; simply ○ *I'll just check my e-mail, then we can go for coffee.* ○ *I just called to wish you a happy birthday.* ○ *We'll just have to wait and see what happens.* **2** Just can be used to make a statement stronger: *He just won't listen to me.*

ALMOST /dʒʌst, dʒəst/ *adv* [not gradable] almost not or almost ○ *We arrived at the airport just in time to catch the plane.* ○ *Matthew weighed just* (= slightly) *over seven pounds at birth.* ○ *"Are you finished yet?" "Just about."*

VERY /dʒʌst, dʒəst/ *adv* [not gradable] very; completely ○ *You look just wonderful!* ○ *It's just amazing how powerful the new computers are.*

FAIR /dʒʌst/ *adj* morally correct; fair ○ *a just verdict*

justly /ˈdʒʌs·tli/ *adv* **1** *We agreed that he was justly condemned to a long prison sentence.* **2** Justly also means with good reason or rightly: *Kenji Mizoguchi is justly recognized as one of Japanese cinema's greatest figures.*

IDIOMS with just

• **just a moment**, **just a minute/second** wait a short period of time ○ *Just a minute – I'm almost done.*

• **just in case** to protect against something bad that could happen ○ *I'll take my umbrella too, just in case.*

• **just now** a very short time ago ○ *Who was that at the door just now?*

• **just one of those things** something has happened that you must accept even if you do not like it ○ *The traffic was awful and I missed my flight – it was just one of those things.*

• *someone* **would just as soon** *do something* someone would rather do something ○ *He'd just as soon use the computer to play video games as go outside with his friends.* ○ *That was a journey I would just as soon forget.*

justice FAIRNESS /ˈdʒʌs·təs/ *n* [U] the condition of being morally correct or fair ○ *He accused the police of false arrest and demanded justice.*

LAW /ˈdʒʌs·təs/ *n* [U] the system of laws by which people are judged and punished ○ *the criminal justice system*

JUDGE /ˈdʒʌs·təs/ *n* [C] a judge, esp. of one of the higher courts of law ○ *a justice of the US Supreme Court*

justice of the peace *n* [C] a public officer who judges local and less important legal cases, and performs marriage ceremonies

justify Ⓐ /ˈdʒʌs·təˌfɑɪ/ *v* [T] to show that something is reasonable, right, or true ○ *Her fears of a low voter turnout were justified when fewer than half of the people voted.*

justifiable Ⓐ /ˈdʒʌs·təˌfɑɪ·ə·bəl/ *adj* able to be explained or shown to be reasonable; understandable ○ *The jury decided that the shooting was justifiable because Rogers thought his own life was in danger.*

justifiably Ⓐ /ˈdʒʌs·təˌfɑɪ·ə·bli/ *adv* ○ *His parents were justifiably proud of his achievements.*

justification Ⓐ /ˌdʒʌs·tə·fəˈkeɪ·ʃən/ *n* [C/U] ○ [U] *There is no justification for such rude behavior, she said.*

jut /dʒʌt/ *v* [I always + adv/prep] **-tt-** to stick out, esp. above or beyond the edge or surface of something ○ *A large ship was docked at the pier that jutted out into the harbor.*

juvenile /ˈdʒuː·vəˌnɑɪl, -vən·əl/ *adj esp. law* of, by, or for a young person who is not yet an adult ○ *He studied both adult and juvenile crime.*

juvenile delinquent *n* [C] a young person, usually under 18, who commits a crime

juvenile delinquency *n* [U] criminal activity by people under 18 years old

juxtapose /ˌdʒʌk·stəˈpoʊz/ *v* [T] to put things or people next to each other, esp. in order to compare them ○ *The exhibition juxtaposes architectural drawings with photographs of the buildings as constructed.*

juxtaposition /ˌdʒʌk·stə·pəˈzɪʃ·ən/ *n* [C/U] ○ [C] *The juxtaposition of the original painting with the fake clearly showed up the differences.*

J

K k

K **LETTER**, **k** /keɪ/ *n* [C] *pl* **K's, Ks, k's, ks** the eleventh letter of the English alphabet

SCHOOL /keɪ/ *n abbreviation for* KINDERGARTEN

TEMPERATURE /keɪ/ *n* [C] ***science*** *abbreviation for* KELVIN

kaleidoscope /kəˈlɑɪd·əˌskoʊp/ *n* [C] a tube-shaped device containing loose pieces of colored glass or plastic and mirrors which reflect changing patterns as the tube is turned

kangaroo /ˌkæŋ·gəˈruː/ *n* [C] *pl* **kangaroos** a type of large, Australian mammal with a long, thick tail, short front legs, and long powerful back legs, that moves by jumping

kaput /kəˈpʊt, kɑ-/ *adj* [not gradable] *infml* severely damaged, broken, or not working correctly ○ *His credibility is kaput.*

karat /ˈkær·ət/, *abbreviation* **kt.**, *abbreviation* **k.** *n* [C] a unit for measuring how pure gold is ○ Compare CARAT

K

karate /kəˈrɑt̬·i/ *n* [U] a method of fighting that uses fast, hard hits with the hands or feet

karma /ˈkɑr·mə/ *n* [U] (in the Buddhist and Hindu religions) the force produced by a person's actions in one life which influences what happens to that person in future lives

kayak /ˈkɑɪ·æk/ *n* [C] a small, light, narrow boat, pointed at both ends, with a covering over the top, which is moved by using a PADDLE (= short pole with a wide, flat part)

KB *n* [C] *pl* **KB** *abbreviation for* KILOBYTE

keel /kiːl/ *n* [C] the long piece of wood or steel put along the bottom of a boat from front to back that supports the frame

PHRASAL VERB with keel

• **keel over** to fall over suddenly ○ *After running the marathon, Jasper keeled over with exhaustion.*

keen **STRONGLY FELT** /kiːn/ *adj* [*-er/-est* only] (esp. of emotions and beliefs) strongly felt ○ *a keen interest in painting*

DEVELOPED /kiːn/ *adj* [*-er/-est* only] (of an awareness or ability) very developed, or (of the mind) very quick to understand ○ *a keen eye for detail* ○ *a keen sense of smell*

EAGER /kiːn/ *adj* [*-er/-est* only] eager, interested, and enthusiastic ○ *Theresa isn't too keen on pets.*

WORD FAMILY keen

Adjectives	keen	*Adverbs*	keenly

keep **POSSESS** /kiːp/ *v* [T] *past* **kept 1** to be in or continue to be in someone's possession ○ *Can I keep this photo?* ○ *"Keep the change," she told the driver.* ○ *We keep aspirin in the kitchen* (= have it there for future use). **2** If you keep a DIARY or record, you write about events or record information.

keeper /ˈkiː·pər/ *n* [C] someone responsible for guarding or taking care of a person, animal, or thing ○ *an animal keeper* ○ *Each of the contest judges was assigned a keeper.*

WORD CHOICES keep

If someone keeps something somewhere until it is needed, the verb **store** is sometimes used.

*I've **stored** all Helen's books in the attic.*

The verb **stash** is sometimes used if someone keeps a lot of something in a secret place.

*His money was **stashed** in a cupboard.*

The verb **save** is often used when someone keeps something to use in the future.

*I have some really good chocolates that I've been **saving** for a special occasion.*

The phrasal verbs **hang onto** and **hold onto** are also often used when someone keeps something that might be needed in the future.

*You should **hang/hold onto** that picture – it might be worth something.*

In formal situations, you can use the word **retain**.

*You should **retain** a copy of the receipt.*

DO /kiːp/ *v* [T] *past* **kept** to do something you promised or had scheduled ○ *I kept my promise.* ○ *Did she keep her appointment?* ○ *Can you* **keep a secret** (= not tell other people)*?*

keeping /ˈkiː·pɪŋ/ *n* ○ *We all get together for dinner once a month,* **in keeping with** (= following) *family tradition.*

STAY /kiːp/ *v past* **kept** to stay or cause to stay or continue in a particular place, direction, or condition ○ [L] *keep left* ○ [L] *keep quiet* ○ [L] *It's hard to keep cool in this weather.* ○ [T] *Sorry to keep you waiting.*

CONTINUE DOING /kiːp/ *v* [T] *past* **kept** to continue doing something without stopping, or to do it repeatedly ○ *I keep thinking I've seen her somewhere before.*

STAY FRESH /kiːp/ *v* [I] *past* **kept** (of food) to stay fresh and in good condition ○ *Milk keeps longer in the refrigerator.*

WORD FAMILY keep

Nouns	keep keeper keeping	*Adjectives* *Verbs*	kept keep

IDIOMS with keep

• **keep a tight rein on** *someone/something* to control someone or something carefully ○ *He doesn't earn very much, but he keeps a tight rein on his budget.*

• **keep an eye on** *someone/something*, **keep your eye on** *someone/something* to watch someone or something or stay informed about the person's be-

havior, esp. to keep someone out of trouble ○ *Keep an eye on your brother while I'm out, please.*
• **keep an eye out for** *something*, **keep your eyes open/peeled (for** *something*) to watch carefully for something ○ *Keep an eye out for spyware programs that install themselves on your computer.* ○ *I try to always keep my eyes open for good recipes.*
• **keep** *someone* **company** to stay with someone so the person is not alone ○ *I kept him company while he was waiting for the bus.*
• **keep count (of** *something*) to remember a total ○ *I've been keeping count of how many times he's called this week.* ○ Opposite: LOSE COUNT (OF SOMETHING) at LOSE **IDIOMS**
• **keep** *your* **fingers crossed** to hope strongly that something will happen ○ *We're keeping our fingers crossed that he'll be healthy again very soon.*
• **keep** *someone* **guessing** to cause someone to be uncertain ○ *The idea was to keep the enemy guessing until the attack had actually begun.*
• **keep** *your* **head above water** to just be able to continue doing what you do ○ *The business is in trouble, but we're keeping our heads above water.*
• **keep it down** to be quieter ○ *Hey you guys, keep it down in there – I'm on the phone!*
• **keep** *your* **mouth shut** to say nothing ○ *He told me to keep my mouth shut.*
• **keep** *your* **nose out of** *infml* to not become involved in something ○ *I know what I'm doing – just keep your nose out of it.*
• **keep** *your* **nose to the grindstone** to work very hard without resting ○ *After a year of keeping his nose to the grindstone, he finally got a vacation.*
• **keep** *someone* **posted** to make sure someone knows what is happening, esp. in a situation that is quickly changing ○ *The doctors kept me posted about her condition.*
• **keep** *something* **quiet, keep quiet about** *something* to say nothing about something ○ *She managed to keep the school's problems quiet for a while.*
• **keep** *your* **temper** not become angry ○ *It was hard to keep my temper with so many things going wrong.*
• **keep to** *your* **self** to often avoid other people ○ *I was very shy and pretty much kept to myself in school.*
• **keep** *something* **to** *your* **self** do not tell anyone about something ○ *The party's a surprise, so keep it to yourself!*
• **keep track (of** *someone/something*) to continue to be informed or know about someone or something ○ *My sister's had so many jobs, I can't keep track anymore.*

PHRASAL VERBS with **keep**

• **keep at** *something* to continue to do or work on something ○ *I kept at it and finally finished at three this morning.*
• **keep down** *something* **STOP INCREASING** [M] to prevent something from increasing ○ *We need to keep down our costs.*
• **keep down** *something* **NOT VOMIT** [M] to prevent something eaten from being vomited up ○ *After the operation I couldn't keep my food down.*
• **keep** *(yourself)* **from** *something* **PREVENT YOURSELF** to prevent yourself from doing something ○ *We couldn't keep from laughing.* ○ *He couldn't keep himself from grinning at Mrs. Crackitt.*
• **keep** *something* **from** *someone* **HIDE INFORMATION** to prevent someone from learning about something ○ *He's seriously ill, and I don't think it's right to keep it from the children.*
• **keep** *(something)* **off** *(something)* to prevent something from touching or being on something else ○ *He wears a hat to keep the sun off his head.* ○ *The sign says, Keep off.*
• **keep** *(something/someone)* **out (of** *somewhere*) [M] to prevent something or someone from entering a place ○ *Danger! Keep out!* ○ *You can't keep the dirt out of the tent.* ○ *Children without regular medical care are more likely to contract illnesses that keep them out of school.*
• **keep** *(someone/something)* **out of** *something* **1** to prevent yourself or someone else from involvement in something ○ *Carolyn keeps out of the public eye and away from Washington.* ○ *Don't use credit cards and you'll keep out of debt.* **2** If you keep one thing out of another thing, you prevent them from influencing each other: *You should keep your personal life out of your work.*
• **keep to** *something* **ONE SUBJECT** to limit yourself to a subject or activity ○ *I can never keep to a diet.*
• **keep** *something* **to** *yourself* **NOT SHARE** to not share information that you have ○ *I'm going to tell you something but I want you to keep it to yourself.*
• **keep up STAY LEVEL** to stay level or equal with someone or something ○ *You run too fast – I can't keep up.*
• **keep up** *something* **CONTINUE** [M] to continue to do or have something ○ *Keep up the good work.*
• **keep** *someone* **up PREVENT SLEEP** to prevent someone from sleeping ○ *I hope I'm not keeping you up.*
• **keep up with** *something* to continue to be informed about something ○ *He's never made an effort to keep up with current events.*

keepsake /ˈkiːp·seɪk/ *n* [C] something that helps you remember a person, place, or occasion ○ *Her aunt gave her a little wooden elephant as a keepsake.*

keg /keg/ *n* [C] a small BARREL (= container with a circular top and bottom and curved sides)

kelvin /ˈkel·vən/, *abbreviation* **K** *n* [C] ***science*** a standard unit of temperature

kennel /ˈken·əl/ *n* [C] a place where animals are bred and trained and where people pay to leave their dogs to be taken care of while they are away

kept /kept/ *past simple and past participle of* KEEP

kerb /kɜrb/ *n* [C] *Br for* CURB **EDGE**.

kerchief /ˈkɜr·tʃəf, -ˌtʃiːf/ *n* [C] a square piece of cloth worn on the head or around the neck

kernel /ˈkɜrn·əl/ *n* [C] the edible part of a nut that is inside the shell, or the whole seed of a grain plant ○ *(fig.) There's a kernel of truth in what he said* (= some small part of it is true).

kerosene /ˈker·əˌsiːn, ˌker·əˈsiːn/ *n* [U] a type of clear oil that is used as a fuel, esp. for heating and lighting

ketchup /ˈketʃ·əp, ˈkætʃ-/, **catsup** *n* [U] a thick, red sauce made from TOMATOES that is eaten on other foods ○ *Do you want ketchup for your French fries?*

ketone /ˈkiː·toʊn/ *n* [C] ***chemistry*** a chemical substance that contains carbon and oxygen, used in industry

kettle /ˈket̬·əl/ *n* [C] a covered container with a handle and a SPOUT (= opening for pouring), used for boiling water

key **METAL SHAPE** /kiː/ *n* [C] a piece of metal cut into a special shape to fit into a lock where it can be turned to open something, such as a door, or to start something, such as a car engine ○ *I put the key into the ignition.*

MOVABLE PART /kiː/ *n* [C] any of the set of movable parts that you press with your fingers on a computer or other machine to produce letters, numbers, or symbols, or on a musical instrument to produce sound ○ *piano keys* ○ *Press the shift key to write in capital letters.*

IMPORTANT PART /kiː/ *n* [U] the most important part of achieving something or explaining a situation ○ *Revision is the key to good writing.*
key /kiː/ *adj* ○ *Deception is a key element of military strategy.*

MUSICAL NOTES /kiː/ *n* [C] ***music*** a set of musical notes based on one particular note ○ *the key of C*

LIST OF SYMBOLS /kiː/ *n* [C] a list of the symbols used in a map or book with explanations of what they mean ○ *The key is printed at the bottom of the page.*

PHRASAL VERB with key

• **key in** *something* [M] to enter information into a computer or other device using a KEYBOARD or buttons ○ *It will take about two hours to key in all this data.*

keyboard **COMPUTER** /ˈkiː·bɔːrd, -boʊrd/ *n* [C] the set of keys arranged in rows that you use to operate a computer

MUSICAL INSTRUMENT /ˈkiː·bɔːrd, -boʊrd/ *n* [C] a musical instrument having keys like a piano, or the set of keys on this type of instrument ○ *Steve plays keyboards, drums, and saxophone.*

keyed up /ˈkiː ˈdʌp/ *adj* excited or nervous ○ *She was too keyed up to sleep.*

keyhole /ˈkiː·hoʊl/ *n* [C] a hole in a lock into which a key fits

keynote /ˈkiː·noʊt/ *n* [C] the most important part, esp. of an event, or something that is emphasized strongly ○ *a keynote speaker/speech* ○ *Luxury is the keynote here.*

key ring *n* [C] a metal ring used for keeping your keys together

keystroke /ˈkiː·stroʊk/ *n* [C] the act of pressing down on a key on a computer ○ *I can add the date with a single keystroke.*

kg *n* [C] *pl* **kg, kgs** *abbreviation for* KILOGRAM

khaki /ˈkæk·i, ˈkɑk·i, *Cdn often* ˈkɑr·ki/ *adj, n* [C/U] a pale yellow-brown color, or a type of cloth that is this color and is often used to make uniforms for soldiers ○ [pl] *I bought a new pair of summer khakis* (= pants made of this cloth).

kibbutz /kɪˈbʊts, -ˈbuːts/ *n* [C] *pl* **kibbutzim** (in Israel) a place, usually a farm, where a group of people live and work and where all duties are shared

kick **HIT** /kɪk/ *v* [I/T] to hit someone or something with the foot, or to move the feet and legs suddenly and violently ○ [T] *I kicked the ball as hard as I could.* ○ [I] *I kicked at the leaves, hoping to find the ring I dropped.*
kick /kɪk/ *n* [C] ○ *She gave him a kick in the shins.*
kicker /ˈkɪk·ər/ *n* [C] someone who kicks, esp. a player on a football team whose job is to kick the ball

EXCITEMENT /kɪk/ *n* [C] a strong feeling of excitement and pleasure ○ *We got a kick out of that show.*
kicker /ˈkɪk·ər/ *n* [C] *infml* something surprising ○ *And here's the real kicker, if you buy one you get the second one free.*

INTEREST /kɪk/ *n* [C usually sing] a new interest, esp. one that does not last long ○ *He's been on an exercise kick lately.*

IDIOMS with kick

• **a kick in the pants** something that makes you improve your behavior ○ *He needs a good kick in the pants.*
• **kick** *yourself* to be annoyed because you did something stupid or failed to act when you had an opportunity ○ *You know you'll kick yourself if you forget to do it, so just do it now!*
• **kick the bucket** *infml* to die
• **kick the habit, kick a habit** to give up something that you have done for a long time ○ *She used to bite her nails but she kicked the habit last year.*

PHRASAL VERBS with kick

• **kick back** to stop doing things and relax ○ *What good is life anyway if a guy can't kick back and watch a good movie?*
• **kick in** **HAVE AN EFFECT** to start to have an effect or to start operating ○ *The county will be able to spend more when a new tax kicks in next year.*
• **kick in** *something* **GIVE MONEY** [M] to give something, esp. money or help ○ *Another plan would require employers to kick in $20 per worker to set up the fund.*
• **kick off** *infml* to begin ○ *The three-day celebration kicks off tomorrow with a parade.*
• **kick** *something* **off (with** *something***)** [M] to begin an event or period of time, esp. with an activity ○ *We like to kick off the summer with a barbecue.*
• **kick** *someone* **out** [M] to make someone leave a place ○ *We should go home before they kick us out.*
• **kick up** *(something)* [M] to cause something to be much more active or noticeable ○ *Construction workers kicked up clouds of dust.* ○ *As the storm moves into the desert, the wind and rain start to kick up.*

kickback /ˈkɪk·bæk/ *n* [C] payment made to someone, esp. illegally, for providing help, a job, or a piece of business ○ *Bankhead got a contract to supply computers to the department in exchange for a kickback.*

kickoff /ˈkɪk·ɔːf/ *n* [C/U] the time when a football game starts, or a kick of the ball that starts play during a game ○ [U] *Kickoff is at 6:30.* ○ [C] *Patterson hurt his ankle on the opening kickoff.*

kid CHILD /kɪd/ *n* [C] **1** a child, or a young adult ○ *I took the kids to the park.* ○ *He's only 19, just a kid.* **2** A kid brother or kid sister is a younger brother or sister.

ANIMAL /kɪd/ *n* [C/U] a young goat, or very soft leather made from the skin of a young goat

JOKE /kɪd/ *v* [I/T] **-dd-** *infml* **1** to say something as a joke, often making someone believe something that is not true ○ [I] *You're kidding around, aren't you?* ○ [T] *Casey's just kidding you.* **2** If you **kid** *your***self**, you believe that something you want to be true is true although it probably is not: *He thinks she'll come back, but I think he's kidding himself.*

IDIOM with kid

• **you have got to be kidding**, **you must be kidding** I am very surprised and cannot believe you are serious ○ *You want me to drive into the city? You've got to be kidding.*

kiddie, **kiddy** /ˈkɪd·i/ *n* [C] *infml* a young child ○ *We have soda for the kiddies.*

kidnap /ˈkɪd·næp/ *v* [T] **-pp-**, **-p-** to illegally take a person away by force, usually in order to demand money in exchange for that person's release ○ *The wife of a prominent businessman was kidnapped today.*

kidnapper, **kidnaper** /ˈkɪd ˌnæp·ər/ *n* [C]

kidney /ˈkɪd·ni/ *n* [C] **1** ***biology*** either of a pair of small organs in the body that remove waste matter from the blood and produce urine **2** Kidney also means either of these organs from an animal used as food.

kidney bean /ˈkɪd·niː ˌbiːn/ *n* [C] a small, dark red, edible bean that is shaped like a KIDNEY

kid stuff *n* [U] something easy or suitable for children ○ *This class is kid stuff.*

kill /kɪl/ *v* [I/T] **1** to cause someone or something to die ○ [T] *Livestock are being killed by tigers in some areas.* ○ [I] *Just a tiny drop of this poison is enough to kill.* ○ [T] *(fig.) If you tell Mom, I'll kill you* (= I will be extremely angry with you). **2** To kill something can also mean to hurt, damage, remove, or destroy it: [T] *It wouldn't kill you to apologize.* ○ [T] *The doctor gave her something to kill the pain.* **3** If you **kill time** or have **time to kill**, you do something while you are waiting for something else to happen ○ *We killed some time playing cards while we waited for the flight.* ○ *I had a couple of hours to kill before dinner.*

kill /kɪl/ *n* [U] an animal that has been hunted and killed ○ *The leopard seized its kill and dragged it into the bush.*

killer /ˈkɪl·ər/ *n* [C] **1** *The police haven't found the killer yet.* ○ *Heart disease is a killer* (= cause of death). **2** *infml* If something is described as a killer, it is very difficult: *The test was a real killer.* **3** *infml* A killer is also someone or something that is very entertaining or skilled: *Dizzy was a killer on the trumpet.*

killing /ˈkɪl·ɪŋ/ *n* [C] ○ *She refused to take part in the killing of animals.*

WORD FAMILY kill			
Nouns	kill overkill killer killing	*Verbs*	kill

IDIOM with kill

• **kill two birds with one stone** to achieve two things at once ○ *I can bring your suit to the cleaners when I pick up the kids and kill two birds with one stone.*

PHRASAL VERB with kill

• **kill off** *someone/something* [M] to destroy or remove someone or something completely ○ *Killing off predators such as grizzly bears could throw the ecosystem out of balance.* ○ *The worship of celebrities has killed off common sense in America.*

K

kiln /kɪln, kɪl/ *n* [C] a type of large OVEN (= box in which things are cooked or heated) used for making bricks and clay objects hard after they have been shaped

kilo- *prefix* one thousand, used in units of measure ○ *kilometer* ○ *kilowatt*

kilobyte /ˈkɪl·əˌbɑɪt, ˈkiː·lə-/, *abbreviation* **KB** *n* [C] a unit of measurement of computer storage space equal to 1024 BYTES

kilogram /ˈkɪl·əˌɡræm/, *abbreviation* **kg**, *short form* **kilo** /ˈkiː·loʊ/ *n* [C] a unit of measurement of weight equal to 1000 grams or 2.2 pounds

kilojoule /ˈkɪl·əˌdʒuːl, ˈkiː·lə-/ *n* [C] ***physics*** a unit of ENERGY equaling 1000 JOULES

kilometer /kəˈlɑm·ət̬·ər, ˈkɪl·əˌmiːt̬·ər/, *abbreviation* **km** *n* [C] a unit of measurement of length equal to 1000 meters or 0.62 mile

kilowatt /ˈkɪl·əˌwɑt/, *abbreviation* **kW** *n* [C] a unit of power equal to 1000 WATTS

kilt /kɪlt/ *n* [C] a skirt with many folds, made from TARTAN cloth and traditionally worn by Scottish men and boys, but also worn by women and girls

kimono /kəˈmoʊ·nə, -noʊ/ *n* [C] *pl* **kimonos** a long, loose piece of outer clothing with very wide sleeves, traditionally worn by the Japanese

kin /kɪn/ *pl n* family ○ *They're not any kin of mine.*

kind GOOD /kɑɪnd/ *adj* [*-er/-est* only] generous, helpful, and caring about other people ○ *She's a kind, thoughtful person.* ○ *It was kind of you to give me your seat.*

kindly /ˈkɑɪn·dli/ *adj, adv* ○ *a kindly man* ○ *They treated me kindly.*

kindness /ˈkɑɪnd·nəs/ *n* [C/U] ○ [U] *Acts of kindness are rare.*

WORD CHOICES kind

The adjectives **nice** and **sweet** are common alternatives to "kind."

*It was really **nice** of you to come.*
*Wasn't it **sweet** of Heidi to call?*

If someone is **good to** you, that person does things to help you.

*Jay's mother has been very **good to** us.*

If someone is very willing to help, you can describe that person as **helpful**.

*The staff here are very **helpful**.*

Someone who is **caring** is kind to other people and tries to make them happy and well.

*I've always thought of Jack as a very **caring** person.*

You can describe someone who is kind and always thinks about other people's feelings as **thoughtful** or **considerate**.

*Thank you for phoning when I was ill – it was very **thoughtful** of you.*
*He's always very polite and **considerate**.*

The expression **mean well** is sometimes used to describe a person who tries to be kind and help but who does not improve a situation.

*I know my parents **mean well**, but I do wish they wouldn't interfere.*

TYPE /kɑɪnd/ *n* [C] a group with similar characteristics, or a particular type ○ *What kind of thing is it?* ○ *They talked about all kinds of stuff.* ○ *It's the largest organization of its kind in history.* ○ *Where books are concerned, Tyler and Chlo are two* **of a kind** (= similar).

WORD FAMILY kind

Nouns	kindness	*Adverbs*	kindly unkindly
Adjectives	kind unkind		

IDIOM with kind

• **kind of** *infml* in some way or to some degree ○ *"Did you like the movie?" "Kind of, but there were some weird things about it."* ○ *I guess I kind of forget to show her that I love her sometimes.* ○ Compare SORT OF at SORT IDIOM

kinda /ˈkɑɪn·də/ *adv* [not gradable] *not standard* (spelled the way it is often spoken) kind of (= slightly) ○ *I was kinda sorry to see him go.*

kindergarten /ˈkɪn·dərˌgɑrt·ən, -ˌgɑrd·ən/, *abbreviation* **K** *n* [C/U] a class for young children, usually children four and five years old, which is often the first year of formal education ○ [U] *Callie will start kindergarten in September.*

kind-hearted, **kindhearted** *adj* (of a person) showing a lot of care and kindness for other people

kindle /ˈkɪn·dəl/ *v* [T] to cause a fire to start burning ○ (*fig.*) *Great literature kindled their imaginations* (= made them work).

kindling /ˈkɪn·dlɪŋ, -lən/ *n* [U] small, dry sticks or other materials used to start a fire

kindred /ˈkɪn·drəd/ *adj* [not gradable] being related, esp. by having the same opinions, feelings, and interests ○ *We recognized each other as kindred spirits as soon as we met.*

kinetic /kəˈneţ·ɪk/ *adj* ***physics*** involving or producing movement

kinetic energy *n* [U] ***physics*** ENERGY (= power to do work) that an object or system has because it is moving

kinfolk /ˈkɪn·foʊk/, **kinfolks** /ˈkɪn·foʊks/ *pl n* family; KIN

king /kɪŋ/ *n* [C] **1** a man who rules a country because he has been born into a family which by tradition or law has the right to rule, or the title given to such a man ○ *King Philip IV of Spain* **2** A king is a playing piece in the game of CHESS and each player's most important piece. **3** A king is also a playing card with a picture of a king on it: *the king of hearts* **4** If someone or something is called the king of an activity, that person is the best or the most important in that activity: *He was baseball's home run king.*

kingdom /ˈkɪŋ·dəm/ *n* [C] **1** a country ruled by a king or queen ○ *She was queen of an ancient kingdom in Egypt.* **2** ***biology*** A kingdom is also one of the groups into which natural things can be divided, depending on their type.

kingpin /ˈkɪŋ·pɪn/ *n* [C] the most important person in an organization ○ *He was the kingpin of the Democratic organization in Chicago.*

king-sized, **king-size** *adj* [not gradable] larger than the ordinary size, and usually the largest size available ○ *a king-size bed* ○ Compare QUEEN-SIZED

kink /kɪŋk/ *n* [C] **1** a sharp twist or bend in something such as a wire or rope ○ *There was a kink in the hose and the water wouldn't come through.* **2** A kink is also a small problem: *The system will work fine once we work out a few kinks.*

kinky /ˈkɪŋ·ki/ *adj* [-er/-est only] ○ *kinky hair* (= hair with many small, tight bends in it)

kiosk /ˈkiː·ɑsk/ *n* [C] a small structure where things such as newspapers, magazines, and candy are sold

kiss /kɪs/ *v* [I/T] to touch or press your lips against another person, esp. another person's lips or CHEEK, as a greeting or to express love ○ [I/T] *The two women hugged and kissed (each other).* ○ [T] *He kissed the children goodbye.*

kiss /kɪs/ *n* [C] ○ *Give grandma a kiss and say goodnight.*

IDIOMS with kiss

• **kiss** *something* **goodbye** to lose something or lose the opportunity to have something ○ *If you lend him money, you can kiss it goodbye.*

• **the kiss of death (for** *something***)** something that will cause something else to fail ○ *The show's bad ratings were the kiss of death for his acting career.*

kit /kɪt/ *n* [C] **1** a set of things, such as tools or equipment, used for a particular purpose or activity ○ *We keep a first-aid kit in the office for emergencies.* **2** A kit is also a set of parts sold ready to be put together: *a model airplane kit*

kitchen /ˈkɪtʃ·ən/ *n* [C] a room where food is prepared and cooked

COMMON LEARNER ERROR

kitchen or cuisine?

A **kitchen** is a room in the house.

Chris is in the kitchen cooking dinner.

Cuisine is used to talk about a style of cooking.

Italian/Greek cuisine

The restaurant is famous for its French cuisine.

~~*The restaurant is famous for its French kitchen.*~~

kite /kɑɪt/ *n* [C] a light frame covered with plastic, paper, or cloth that is flown in the wind at the end of a long string, esp. for amusement ○ *On windy days the kids fly their kites in the park.*

kitsch /kɪtʃ/ *n* [U] showy art or cheap, decorative objects that are attractive to people who are thought to lack any appreciation of style or beauty ○ *She collects all sorts of kitsch, like these ceramic figurines of movie stars.*

kitten /ˈkɪt·ən/ *n* [C] a young cat ○ *Our cat just had six kittens.*

kitty **MONEY** /ˈkɪt̬·i/ *n* [C usually sing] money to be used for a particular purpose that has been collected from a number of people ○ *We each put $20 a week into the kitty to cover the cost of food.*

CAT /ˈkɪt̬·i/ *n* [C] a cat or KITTEN

kiwi (fruit) /ˈkiː·wiː (ˌfruːt)/ *n* [C] an oval fruit with brown, hairy skin and green flesh

Kleenex /ˈkliː·neks/ *n* [C/U] *trademark* a type of thin, soft paper that comes in separate sheets, or one of these sheets ○ [C] *She dried her eyes with a Kleenex.*

klutz /klʌts/ *n* [C] *infml* a person who moves awkwardly and often drops things ○ *Don't expect Mark to catch the ball – he's a klutz.*

km *n* [C] *pl* **km** *abbreviation for* KILOMETER

knack /næk/ *n* [U] an ability or special method for doing something easily and well ○ *There's a knack to using this quick-drying paint.*

knapsack /ˈnæp·sæk/ *n* [C] a small bag with straps that can hold it against a person's back, leaving the arms free

knead /niːd/ *v* [T] to press something, esp. clay or a mixture for making bread, firmly and repeatedly with the hands ○ *Knead the dough until it is smooth.*

knee /niː/ *n* [C] the middle joint of the leg ○ *I stood in the water up to my knees.* ○ *He got down on his hands and knees to look for his contact lens.*

kneecap /ˈniː·kæp/ *n* [C] the round bone at the front of the knee

knee-deep *adj* [not gradable] reaching from the ground up to your knees ○ *The snow was knee-deep.* ○ *(fig.) I'm knee-deep in work* (= have a lot of work).

knee-jerk *adj* happening or existing as a result of habit, rather than careful consideration ○ *When asked about crime, the mayor's knee-jerk reaction is to call for longer prison sentences.*

kneel /niːl/ *v* [I] *past* **knelt, kneeled** to go down into, or stay in, a position where one or both knees are on the ground ○ *She knelt down to look under the bed for her doll.* ○ *Gibbons kneeled next to the plant and started digging.*

knew /nuː/ *past simple of* KNOW

knickers /ˈnɪk·ərz/ *pl n* **1** short, loose pants that fit tightly below the knee, worn esp. in the past **2** *Br* Knickers are women's and girl's UNDERPANTS.

knickknack /ˈnɪk·næk/ *n* [C] a small, decorative object, esp. in a house ○ *The room was filled with knickknacks.*

knife /nɑɪf/ *n* [C] *pl* **knives** a tool or weapon used for cutting, usually consisting of a metal blade and a handle ○ *a sharp knife* ○ *We took plastic knives and forks on our picnic.*

knife /nɑɪf/ *v* [T] to push a knife into someone to hurt them

knight /nɑɪt/ *n* [C] **1** (in the past) a man of high rank who was trained to fight as a soldier on a horse ○ *I'm reading about King Arthur and his knights.* **2** A knight is a playing piece in the game of CHESS that is often shaped like a horse's head.

knight /nɑɪt/ *v* [T] in Britain, to give a person a rank of honor because of that person's special achievements ○ *He was knighted by Queen Elizabeth II.*

knighthood /ˈnɑɪt·hʊd/ *n* [C]

knit **MAKE CLOTHES** /nɪt/ *v* [I/T] *pres. part.* **knitting,** *past* **knitted, knit** to make cloth or clothing by connecting YARN (= fiber threads) into rows with two long needles, or to do this with a machine ○ [T] *She's knitting a scarf for her daughter.*

knitting /ˈnɪt̬·ɪŋ/ *n* [U] something being made by the act of knitting ○ *She takes her knitting with her everywhere.*

JOIN /nɪt/ *v* [I/T] *pres. part.* **knitting,** *past* **knitted, knit** to join together ○ [I] *She's got a break in this bone, but the ends of the bones will knit without the need for surgery.*

knitting needle *n* [C usually pl] a metal stick with a point on the end that is used with another one to KNIT

knob /nɑb/ *n* [C] a round handle or a small, round device for controlling a machine or electrical equipment ○ *Turn the knob on the left to start the washer.*

knobby /ˈnɑb·i/ *adj* having knobs on the surface, or shaped like a knob ○ *knobby knees*

knock **MAKE NOISE** /nɑk/ *v* [I] **1** to repeatedly hit something, producing a noise ○ *Someone is knocking at the door.* ○ *Jane knocked on the window to attract his attention.* **2** If an engine is knocking, it makes a repeated noise because of a mechanical problem.

knock /nɑk/ *n* [C] ○ *There was a loud knock at the door.*

knocker /ˈnɑk·ər/ *n* [C] a metal object attached to the outside surface of a door in such a way that it can be hit against the door to make a noise, getting the attention of those inside

MOVE /nɑk/ *v* [T] to push into something or someone, often forcefully, causing the thing or person to move ○ *Alice accidentally knocked the pot off the table.* ○ *The blast knocked him off his feet.*

knock /nɑk/ *n* [C] ○ *He got a nasty knock on the head from the side of the pool when he misjudged the turn.* ○ *(fig.) Joey has had a lot of hard knocks* (= bad luck).

CRITICIZE /nɑk/ *v* [T] *infml* to criticize, esp. unfairly ○ *She knocks every suggestion I make.*

IDIOMS with knock

•**knock it off** *infml* stop doing that ○ *Hey, knock it off – I'm tired of hearing you two fight!*

•**knock on wood** I hope my good luck will continue ○ *I never have trouble with my car, knock on wood.* ○ **USAGE**: Used when you think there could be difficulties.

PHRASAL VERBS with knock

•**knock down** *something/someone* **CAUSE TO FALL** [M] to hit someone or something forcefully so that it falls down, or falls to a lower place ○ *Try not to knock the fence down when you back out of the driveway.*

•**knock down** *something* **DESTROY** [M] **1** to destroy and remove a building, wall, or other structure ○ *The city is going to knock the old train station down and build a new library.* **2** To knock down a system, practice, rule, etc. means to get rid of it: *He wants to use the WTO to knock down trade barriers.*

•**knock down** *something* **REDUCE** [M] to reduce the price, amount, or value of something ○ *He wanted $300 for the ring, but we got him to knock it down to $250.* ○ *The SEC knocked down their $1.5 billion penalty to $500,000.*

•**knock off** *(something)* **STOP** to stop working or doing something ○ *The carpenter knocked off early to take his kid to baseball practice.*

•**knock off** *something* **REMOVE** to remove by pushing, hitting, or other forceful action ○ *A low branch knocked her off her horse.* ○ *One of the side mirrors on the truck got knocked off.*

•**knock** *something* **off** *(something)* **REDUCE** [M] to reduce the price or value of something by a particular amount ○ *The manager knocked off ten bucks because the dress had a few buttons missing.*

•**knock out** *someone* **HIT** [M] **1** to hit someone so that the person becomes unconscious, or to cause someone to go to sleep ○ *His fall from the ladder knocked him out.* ○ *Those sleeping pills knocked me out.* **2** If something such as a system or piece of equipment is knocked out by something else, it stops operating: *The lightning knocked out our electricity.* ○ Related noun: KNOCKOUT **BOXING**

•**knock out** *something/someone* **REMOVE** [M] **1** to remove something, esp. by hitting it with force ○ *Sean fell off his bike and knocked two teeth out.* **2** A person or team that is knocked out of a competition is defeated and no longer can take part: *A loss in today's game will knock our team out of the playoffs.*

•**knock over** *something/someone* [M] to hit something or someone so that the person falls down ○ *Who knocked over the chair?* ○ *Cyclists in the race have to worry about fans knocking them over.*

knock-down drag-out /ˈnɑk ˌdɑʊn ˈdræɡ ˌɑʊt/ *adj* [not gradable] *infml* (of an argument or physical fight) lasting a long time and energetically fought ○ *We had knock-down drag-out fights, but when I really needed him on the big issues, he was helpful.*

knockoff /ˈnɑk·ɔːf/ *n* [C] *infml* a cheaper copy of an expensive and popular product ○ *She bought a knockoff of a designer suit.*

knockout **BOXING** /ˈnɑk·ɑʊt/, *abbreviation* **KO** *n* [C] (in boxing) a situation in which a fighter falls after being hit and cannot get up in ten seconds ○ *He won by a knockout in the tenth round.* ○ Related verb: KNOCK OUT **HIT**

ATTRACTION /ˈnɑk·ɑʊt/ *n* [C] *slang* a very attractive person or thing ○ *She was a real knockout in her new dress.*

knoll /noʊl/ *n* [C] a small hill with a rounded top

knot **FASTENING** /nɑt/ *n* [C] a fastening made by tying together a piece or pieces of string, rope, cloth, etc. ○ *Wrap this string around the package and then tie a knot.* ○ *(fig.) She's so nervous, her stomach is in knots* (= feels tight and uncomfortable).

knot /nɑt/ *v* [I/T] **-tt-** ○ [T] *He knotted his tie carefully.*

GROUP /nɑt/ *n* [C] a group of people or things ○ *After the game, disappointed knots of people drifted away.*

WOOD /nɑt/ *n* [C] a hard, dark area on a tree or piece of wood where a branch was joined to the tree

knotty /ˈnɑt̬·i/ *adj* ○ *knotty pine*

MEASUREMENT /nɑt/ *n* [C] a measure of speed for ships, aircraft, or movements of water and air equal to approximately 6076 feet (1.85 kilometers) an hour

know **HAVE INFORMATION** /noʊ/ *v* [I/T] *past simp.* **knew**, *past part.* **known** **1** to have information in your mind; to be aware of something ○ [I] *"Where did he go?" "I don't know."* ○ [T] *Do you know the answer?* ○ [T] *She knows the name of every kid in school.* ○ [+ question word] *Do you know how to tap dance?* ○ [+ question word] *We don't know when he's arriving.* ○ [+ *(that)* clause] *I knew (that) something was wrong from the start.* ○ [+ question word] *I want to know how much this will cost.* **2** If you **know of** someone or something, you have experience of or information about the person or thing: *Do you know of a good doctor?*

know /noʊ/ *n* Someone who is **in the know** has information about something: *Ask Keith – he's always in the know about upcoming projects.*

knowing /ˈnoʊ·ɪŋ/ *adj* [not gradable] having or showing knowledge of private or secret information ○ *My mother gave me a knowing smile.*

knowingly /ˈnoʊ·ɪŋ·li/ *adv* [not gradable] while understanding the meaning of what you are doing ○ *Many of them knowingly broke the law.*

USAGE

know or find out?

If you **know** something, you already have the information.

Andy knows what time the train leaves.

Her parents already know about the problem.

If you **find** something **out**, you learn new information for the first time.

I'll check on the Internet to find out what time the train leaves.

~~*I'll check on the Internet to know what time the train leaves.*~~

HAVE UNDERSTANDING /noʊ/ *v* [I/T] *past simp.* **knew**, *past part.* **known 1** to agree with or understand the reasons for an action or opinion ○ [+ question word] *I don't know what all the fuss is about.* ○ [+ question word] *"What a stupid movie!" "I know what you mean."* **2** To **know what it is (like) to** be or do something is to understand because you have personally experienced it: *She knows what it's like to go bankrupt – it happened to her 20 years ago.*

known /noʊn/ *adj* [not gradable] generally understood or proven ○ *There is no known reason for the accident.* ○ *It is a known fact that he started out a poor man.* ○ [+ to infinitive] *These substances are known to cause skin problems.*

BE FAMILIAR WITH /noʊ/ *v* [I/T] *past simp.* **knew**, *past part.* **known** to be familiar with a person or place ○ [T] *I've known Vince since we were in elementary school.* ○ [T] *She grew up in Hawaii so she knows it well.* ○ [T] *Knowing Debbie* (= from my experience of her in the past), *she'll do a good job.*

USAGE

meet, get to know, or know?

When you **meet** someone, you see or speak to them for the first time. When you **get to know** someone, you learn more about them and after this you can say that you **know** them.

I met Nick in Key West.

~~*I knew Nick in Key West.*~~

We got to know each other and became good friends.

~~*We knew each other and became friends.*~~

How long have you known Nick?

~~*How long have you got to know Nick?*~~

FEEL CERTAIN /noʊ/ *v* [T] *past simp.* **knew**, *past part.* **known** to feel certain about something ○ *I know I'd enjoy myself if I went.* ○ [+ (*that*) clause] *I know (that) I took those library books back.* ○ [+ question word] *I don't know whether or not I should go to college.*

RECOGNIZE /noʊ/ *v* [T] *past simp.* **knew**, *past part.* **known** to recognize someone or something, or to recognize the difference between two people or things ○ *That's Pete – I'd know him anywhere.* ○ *I know a bargain when I see one!*

WORD FAMILY know

Nouns	knowledge unknown	*Verbs*	know
		Adverbs	knowingly unknowingly knowledgeably
Adjectives	knowing knowledgeable known unknown		

IDIOMS with know

• **know best** to have opinions that should be accepted and respected by other people ○ *Mom knows best when it comes to investing money.*

• **know better (than to do** *something*) to be wise enough to behave in a more responsible or acceptable way ○ *You know better than to interrupt when someone else is talking.*

• **know** *something* **like the back of your hand** to know a place very well ○ *She'll give you the name of a place to stay – she knows the area like the back of her hand.*

• **know** *your* **way around** *something* to be very familiar with a place, subject, or system, and therefore be able to act effectively ○ *Those two guys really know their way around an engine.*

• **know what** *you* **are doing** to have the knowledge or experience that is necessary to do something ○ *Don't worry about me – I know what I'm doing!*

• **know what** *you* **are talking about** to be able to speak in an informed way because of your experience or education ○ *He doesn't know what he's talking about – he's never even been to Alaska.*

• **know where** *you* **stand 1** to be certain about what someone thinks or feels about you ○ *He didn't even send me a birthday card, so I guess I know where I stand.* **2** to be certain about what your position and responsibilities are in a situation ○ *In the old days, the editor was completely in control, and we all knew where we stood.*

• **not know the first thing about** to know nothing about something ○ *I don't know the first thing about physics.*

• **not know what hit** *you* to be suddenly shocked and confused by something ○ *When he said I was fired, I didn't know what hit me.*

know-how *n* [U] *infml* knowledge and ability ○ *I don't have the technical know-how to repair a computer.*

know-it-all *n* [C] *infml, disapproving* people who think that they know everything

K

knowledge /ˈnɑl·ɪdʒ/ *n* [U] awareness, understanding, or information that has been obtained by experience or study, and that is either in a person's mind or possessed by people generally ○ *How will we use our increasing scientific knowledge?* ○ *A lack of knowledge on the part of teachers is a real problem.* ○ *He has a limited knowledge of French.* ○ *The owner claims the boat was being used without her knowledge.* ○ *It was common knowledge that Lucy was superstitious about the number 13.*
knowledgeable /ˈnɑl·ɪdʒ·ə·bəl/ *adj* [not gradable] ○ *He's very knowledgeable about Native American art.* ○ *She's a knowledgeable person.*

knuckle /ˈnʌk·əl/ *n* [C] one of the joints of the fingers

PHRASAL VERBS with knuckle

• **knuckle down** *infml* to start working hard ○ *You're going to have to knuckle down and catch up on your schoolwork.*

• **knuckle under** *infml* to give up power or control ○ *The other side is not ready to negotiate, but we won't knuckle under to their demands.*

KO *n* [C] *pl* **KOs** *abbreviation for* KNOCKOUT

koala (bear) /koʊˈɑl·ə (ˈber, ˈbær)/ *n* [C] an Australian animal like a small bear with gray fur which lives in trees and eats leaves

kook /kuːk/ *n* [C] *infml* a strange or crazy person ○ *There's some kook outside who says he's your long-lost brother.*
kooky /ˈkuː·ki/ *adj infml* ○ *I love her in spite of her kooky ways.*

Koran, **Quran** /kəˈræn, -ˈrɑn/ *n* [U] the holy book of the Islamic religion ○ *There are many verses in the Koran which emphasize that life is sacred.*

kosher /ˈkoʊ·ʃər/ *adj* [not gradable] **1** (of food or places where food is kept) prepared or kept in conditions that follow the rules of Jewish law ○ *kosher food* ○ *a kosher restaurant* **2** Kosher can also mean acceptable or correct: *It's kosher for a politician to make a fortune when he leaves office, but not when he's in office.*

kowtow /ˈkɑʊ ˌtɑʊ/ *v* [I] *disapproving* to show too much respect or obedience ○ *People say he kowtowed to the establishment to get elected.*

Kremlin /ˈkrem·lən/ *n* [U] the government of Russia and (in the past) of the Soviet Union, or the buildings where the Russian government meets ○ *They provided leaders in the Kremlin with information.*

kt. *n* [C] *abbreviation for* KARAT

kudos /ˈkuː·dɑs, -doʊs/ *n* [U] praise, admiration, and fame received for an achievement ○ *Women's organizations have been getting kudos for their service activities.*

kung fu /kʌŋˈfuː/ *n* [U] a method of fighting without weapons that involves using your hands and feet

kW *n* [C] *pl* **kW** *abbreviation for* KILOWATT

Kwanzaa, **Kwanza** /ˈkwɑn·zə/ *n* [C] an African-American cultural celebration lasting from December 26 to January 1

L l

L LETTER, **l** /el/ *n* [C] *pl* **L's, Ls, l's, ls** the twelfth letter of the English alphabet

NUMBER, **l** /el/ *number* the ROMAN NUMERAL for the number 50

SIZE /el/ *adj* [not gradable] *abbreviation for* LARGE ○ USAGE: Used esp. on clothing to show its size.

l VOLUME /el/ *n* [C] *pl* **l** *abbreviation for* LITER

lab /læb/ *n* [C] *short form of* LABORATORY ○ *a research lab* ○ *a lab technician*

label Ⓐ /ˈleɪ·bəl/ *n* [C] **1** a piece of paper or other material that gives information about the object it is attached to ○ *the address/mailing label* ○ *Follow the instructions on the label.* **2** A label can also mean the name or symbol of a company that produces goods for sale: *Everything we produce goes out under our own label.* **3** A label can also be a name or a phrase used to describe the characteristics or qualities of people, activities, or things: *It's hard to say whether to apply the label "jazz" or "rock" to her music.*

label Ⓐ /ˈleɪ·bəl/ *v* [T] **1** *She labeled all the packages and sent them out the same afternoon.* **2** To label something or someone is also to name that thing's or person's character: *He didn't want to be labeled a complainer, so he didn't raise any objection to the extra work.*

labor Ⓐ WORK, *Cdn, Br* **labour** /ˈleɪ·bər/ *n* [U] **1** practical work, esp. work that involves physical effort ○ *The car parts themselves are not expensive – it's the labor that costs so much.* **2** Labor also refers to the workers themselves, esp. those who do practical work with their hands: *skilled/unskilled labor* **3** A **labor-saving** device or method is one that saves a lot of effort and time.

labor Ⓐ, *Cdn, Br* **labour** /ˈleɪ·bər/ *v* [I] to do hard physical work ○ [+ *to* infinitive] *Hours after the explosion, rescue teams were still laboring to free those trapped.*

laborer, *Cdn, Br* **labourer** /ˈleɪ·bə·rər/ *n* [C] a person who does physical work ○ *a farm/factory laborer*

laborious /ləˈbɔːr·iː·əs, -ˈbour-/ *adj* needing a lot of time and effort ○ *a laborious task*

BIRTH, *Cdn, Br* **labour** /ˈleɪ·bər/ *n* [U] the last stage of pregnancy when the muscles of the uterus start to push the baby out of the body, usually lasting until the baby appears ○ *She went into* (= started) *labor at twelve o'clock last night.*

laboratory /ˈlæb·rəˌtɔːr·i, -ˌtour-/, *short form* **lab** *n* [C] a room or building with equipment for doing scientific tests or for teaching science, or a place where chemicals or medicines are produced ○ *a physics laboratory*

labor camp, *Cdn, Br* **labour camp** *n* [C] a place where people are kept as prisoners and forced to do hard physical work

Labor Day, *Cdn, Br* **Labour Day** *n* [C usually sing] a public holiday that honors workers, and is celebrated in the United States on the first Monday in SEPTEMBER

labor union, *Cdn, Br* **labour union**, *short form* **union** *n* [C] an organization of workers that protects their rights and represents them in discussions with employers over such matters as pay and working conditions

labyrinth /ˈlæb·əˌrɪnθ/ *n* [C] a confusing set of connecting passages or paths in which it is easy to get lost

lace MATERIAL /leɪs/ *n* [U] a decorative cloth that is made by weaving thin thread into delicate patterns having small spaces within them ○ *a lace curtain/handkerchief*

lacy /ˈleɪ·si/ *adj* ○ *a lacy white blouse*

CORD /leɪs/ *n* [C usually pl] a cord used to close a shoe or boot; SHOELACE ○ *Your laces are untied.*

lace (up) /leɪs (ʌp)/ *v* [T] ○ *She laced her boots.*

lacerate /ˈlæs·əˌreɪt/ *v* [T] to cut or tear something, esp. flesh ○ *His face and hands were lacerated by the flying glass.*

laceration /ˌlæs·əˈreɪ·ʃən/ *n* [C/U] ○ [C] *Justina was treated for a scalp laceration.*

lack /læk/ *n* [U] a condition of not having any or enough of something, esp. something necessary or wanted ○ *a lack of ambition/confidence/knowledge* ○ *a lack of money* ○ *She certainly has no lack of friends* (= She has a lot of friends).

lack /læk/ *v* [T] ○ *What we lack in this house is space to store things.* ○ *He's totally lacking a sense of humor.* ➤ Usage: **miss or lack?** at MISS NOT FIND

lackadaisical /ˌlæk·əˈdeɪ·zɪ·kəl/ *adj* lacking enthusiasm and effort ○ *The food wasn't bad but the service was lackadaisical.*

lackluster /ˈlækˌlʌs·tər/ *adj* lacking energy and effort ○ *a lackluster performance*

laconic /ləˈkɑn·ɪk/ *adj* using very few words to express what you mean ○ *"I might," was the laconic reply.*

lacquer /ˈlæk·ər/ *n* [U] a shiny, hard substance that is painted on wood or metal to protect its surface

lacrosse /ləˈkrɔːs/ *n* [U] a game played by two teams in which the players each use a long stick with a net at the end to catch, carry, and throw a small ball, and try to get the ball in the other team's goal

lacteal /ˈlæk·tiː·əl/ *n* [C] ***biology*** a tube that carries a liquid formed from digested food and that has the appearance of milk from the smaller of the INTESTINES (= tube through which food travels) into the blood

lacteal /ˈlæk·tiː·əl/ *adj* [not gradable] relating to, producing, or like milk

lacy /ˈleɪ·si/ *adj* ○ See at LACE MATERIAL

lad /læd/ *n* [C] *dated* a boy or young man

ladder /ˈlæd·ər/ *n* [C] a piece of equipment used for climbing up and down, and consisting of two vertical bars joined by a set of horizontal steps ○ (*fig.*) *In only a few years she managed to* **climb up the corporate ladder** (= achieve success in the business world) *to become a vice president.*

laden /ˈleɪd·ᵊn/ *adj* carrying or holding a lot of something ○ *a table laden with food*

ladies' room, women's room *n* [C] a toilet for women in a public building ○ Compare MEN'S ROOM

ladle /ˈleɪd·ᵊl/ *n* [C] a big spoon with a long handle and a deep, cup-shaped part ○ *a soup ladle*
ladle (out) /ˈleɪd·ᵊl (ɑʊt)/ *v* [T] to put liquids or food into bowls ○ *She ladled out hot food to the homeless.*

lady WOMAN /ˈleɪd·i/ *n* [C] **1** a woman who is polite and behaves well toward other people ○ *Try to act like a lady.* **2** Lady is often used as a polite way of addressing or referring to any woman: *This lady has a question.* ○ *Ladies and gentlemen, may I have your attention.* **3** Lady can be a form of address, sometimes considered rude, to a woman whose name you do not know: *Hey, lady, what's the rush?*
TITLE /ˈleɪd·i/ *n* [U] (in some countries) the title of a woman who has, or is the wife of a man who has, a specially high social rank, or the person herself ○ Compare LORD TITLE

L

ladybug /ˈleɪd·iːˌbʌg/ *n* [C] a small, round, red BEETLE (= type of insect) with black spots

ladylike /ˈleɪd·iːˌlɑɪk/ *adj* suitable for a LADY ○ *There are some things I won't talk about because it's not ladylike.*

lag /læg/ *v* [I] **-gg-** to move or advance so slowly that you are behind other people or things ○ *John's always lagging behind the others in the class.*
lag /læg/ *n* [C/U] a delay in the period of time in which events happen ○ [C] *There is often a lag between becoming infected and the first signs of the illness.*

lagoon /ləˈguːn/ *n* [C] an area of sea water separated from the sea by a SANDBAR (= raised area of sand) or REEF (= a line of rocks and sand)

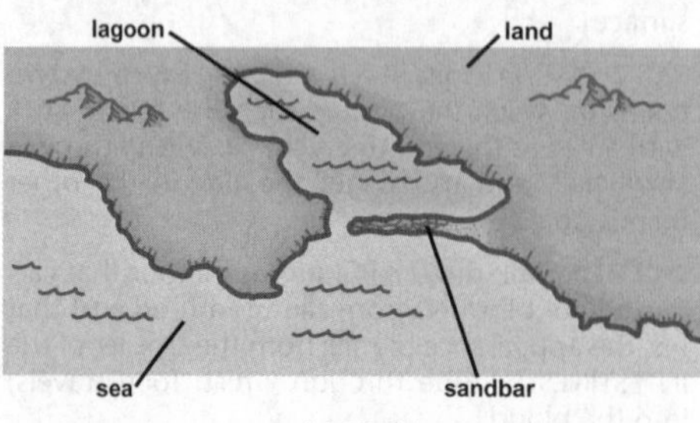

LAGOON

laid /leɪd/ *past simple, past participle of* LAY ○ *He laid the book on the table.* ○ **USAGE:** *not standard* In speech, many people use laid instead of lay as the past simple of lie: *He laid down and went to sleep.*

laid-back /ˈleɪdˈbæk/ *adj* not tending to get anxious about behavior or things that need to be done ○ *It's a laid-back company – you can choose your own hours and the dress is very casual.*

lain /leɪn/ *past participle of* LIE POSITION

lair /ler, lær/ *n* [C] a place where certain kinds of wild animals live, often underground and hidden, or a place where a person hides ○ *a fox's lair* ○ *a thieves' lair*

laissez-faire, laisser faire /ˌlesˌeɪˈfer, ˌleɪˌseɪ-, -ˈfær/ *n* [U] ***politics & government*** an economic theory or plan in which a government does not have many laws or rules to control the buying and selling of goods and services

laity /ˈleɪ·əţ·i/ *n* ○ See at LAY NOT TRAINED

lake /leɪk/ *n* [C] a large area of water that is not salty and is surrounded by land ○ *Lake Michigan*

lamb /læm/ *n* [C/U] a young sheep, or the flesh of a young sheep eaten as meat

lambaste /læmˈbeɪst, -ˈbæst/ *v* [T] to criticize someone or something severely ○ *His first novel was lambasted by the critics.*

lame UNABLE TO WALK /leɪm/ *adj* [*-er/-est* only] not able to walk correctly because of physical injury or weakness of the legs or feet
NOT SATISFACTORY /leɪm/ *adj* [*-er/-est* only] (esp. of an excuse or argument) weak and not deserving to be believed ○ *Saying she'd lost her homework was a pretty lame excuse, if you ask me.*

lame duck *n* [C] a person who still has time to serve in an elected position despite not being elected again in a recent election, with the result that the person has no real power

lament /ləˈment/ *v* [T] to express sadness and regret about something ○ *He lamented his students' lack of interest in the classics.*
lament /ləˈment/ *n* [C] an expression of sadness over something, or a complaint ○ *Baker's lament was that his schedule kept him away from his family too often.*
lamentable /ləˈment·ə·bəl, ˈlæm·ənt·ə-/ *adj fml* regrettable ○ *a lamentable failure of nerve*

laminated /ˈlæm·əˌneɪţ·əd/ *adj* [not gradable] consisting of several thin layers of wood, plastic, glass, etc., stuck together, or covered with a thin layer of plastic ○ *laminated plywood* ○ *laminated diplomas*

lamp /læmp/ *n* [C] a device for giving light, esp. one with a covering that the light shines through or around ○ *a floor lamp*

lampshade /ˈlæmp·ʃeɪd/ *n* [C] a covering over a light to reduce brightness or to direct the light

land DRY SURFACE /lænd/ *n* [U] **1** the surface of the earth that is not covered by water ○ *It is cheaper to drill for oil on land than at sea.* **2** Land is also a particular area of the earth's surface: *They just bought 150 acres of land in Idaho.* **3** The land refers to farms, farming, and the countryside: *My parents worked (on) the land all their lives.*
NATION /lænd/ *n* [C] a country ○ *Ireland was my mother's native land.* ➤ Usage: **country, land, nation, or state?** at COUNTRY POLITICAL UNIT

ARRIVE /lænd/ *v* [I/T] **1** to arrive or cause something to arrive at a place in an aircraft ○ [I] *The pilot said we would land in about 20 minutes.* **2** To land is also to arrive in a boat: [I] *We'd been sailing for three weeks by the time we landed at Miami.*

landed /ˈlæn·dəd/ *adj* [not gradable] *Cdn* officially living in Canada ○ *a landed immigrant*

landing /ˈlæn·dɪŋ/ *n* [C] ○ *We had a smooth take-off and the flight was great, but our landing was a bit rough.*

UNLOAD /lænd/ *v* [T] to unload people or things from a ship or aircraft onto the ground ○ *The general's plan involved landing troops behind enemy lines.*

ACHIEVE /lænd/ *v* [T] *infml* to get or achieve something desirable ○ *to land a job*

IDIOM with **land**

• **land on** *your* **feet** to be in good condition after a difficult experience ○ *She lost her job last year, but she landed on her feet and found another one a week later.*

landfall /ˈlænd·fɔːl/ *n* [U] a situation in which someone or something reaches land after being at sea ○ *Tropical storm Bonnie made landfall on Florida's Panhandle.*

landfill /ˈlænd·fɪl/ *n* [C/U] a place where garbage is buried ○ [U] *The shopping center was built on landfill.*

landform /ˈlænd·fɔːrm/ *n* [C] ***earth science*** a natural shape on the earth's surface, such as a mountain or a valley

landing /ˈlæn·dɪŋ/ *n* [C] a floor between two sets of stairs or at the top of a set of stairs ○ *There is another bathroom on the landing between the first and second floors.*

landlocked /ˈlænd·lɑkt, ˈlæn-/ *adj* [not gradable] surrounded by land and having no coast

landlord /ˈlænd·lɔːrd/, *female* **landlady** /ˈlænd ˌleɪd·i/ *n* [C] a person who owns a building or an area of land and is paid by other people for the use of it ○ *Heather's landlord actually lowered her rent when she said she might move out.*

landmark PLACE /ˈlænd·mɑrk/ *n* [C] **1** a building or place that is easily recognized, esp. one that you can use to judge where you are ○ *I couldn't pick out any familiar landmarks in the dark and got completely lost.* **2** A landmark is also a building or other structure that is considered especially important as an example of its type: *a landmark skyscraper*

STAGE /ˈlænd·mɑrk/ *n* [C] an important stage in the development of something ○ *The invention of the silicon chip is a landmark in the history of technology.*

land mine *n* [C] a bomb that is hidden in the ground and that explodes when a person steps on it or a vehicle drives over it

landowner /ˈlæn ˌdoʊ·nər/ *n* [C] someone who owns land, often a lot of land

landscape COUNTRYSIDE /ˈlænd·skeɪp/ *n* [C] **1** a large area of countryside, usually one without many buildings or other things that are not natural **2** A landscape is also a view or picture of the countryside: *She collects early twentieth century landscapes.*

AREA FEATURES /ˈlænd·skeɪp/ *n* [C] ***earth science*** the shape of the land and related features in a particular area ○ *a desert landscape*

CHANGE APPEARANCE /ˈlænd·skeɪp/ *v* [T] to change the appearance of an area of land, esp. by planting trees, flowers, and other plants ○ *The park was beautifully landscaped.*

landslide FALLING EARTH /ˈlænd·slɑɪd/ *n* [C] ***earth science*** a mass of rock and earth falling unexpectedly down a steep slope

ELECTION VICTORY /ˈlænd·slɑɪd/ *n* [C] the winning of an election with an extremely large number of votes ○ *a landslide victory* ○ *The senator won by a landslide last year.*

lane PATH /leɪn/ *n* [C] **1** one of two or more marked paths in a road to keep vehicles traveling in the same direction a safe distance apart ○ *That section of Interstate 95 is a four-lane highway, with two northbound lanes and two southbound lanes.* **2** A lane in a running track or swimming pool is a narrow section marked to keep the competitors apart.

ROAD /leɪn/ *n* [C] a narrow road, esp. in the countryside or in a small town

language /ˈlæŋ·gwɪdʒ, -wɪdʒ/ *n* [C/U] **1** a system of communication by speaking, writing, or making signs in a way that can be understood, or any of the different systems of communication used in particular regions ○ [C] *the English language* ○ [C] *American Sign Language* ○ [C] *He speaks six foreign languages.* ○ [U] *Her language skills are excellent.* **2** Language is also a particular type of expression: [U] *beautiful language* ○ [U] *foul language* (= offensive words) **3** In computer programming, a language is a system of writing instructions for computers.

languid /ˈlæŋ·gwəd/ *adj* lacking energy, or causing a lack of energy or enthusiasm ○ *He sat on the porch enjoying the delicious, languid warmth of a summer afternoon.*

languish /ˈlæŋ·gwɪʃ/ *v* [I] to exist in an unpleasant or unwanted situation, often for a long time ○ *Members of Congress have introduced plans, but those have languished.*

lanky /ˈlæŋ·ki/ *adj* [*-er/-est* only] tall and thin and often tending to move awkwardly as a result ○ *He shifted his lanky body uncomfortably in the cramped airplane seat.*

lantern /ˈlænt·ərn/ *n* [C] a light enclosed in a container that has a handle for holding it or hanging it up, or the container itself

lap LEGS /læp/ *n* [C usually sing] the top surface of the upper part of the legs of a person who is sitting down ○ *Come and sit on my lap and I'll read you a story.*

HIT GENTLY /læp/ *v* [I/T] **-pp-** (of waves) to hit something gently, producing low sounds ○ [I/T] *Waves lapped (at) the shore.*

L

RACING /læp/ *n* [C] one complete trip around a race track or from one end of a swimming pool to the other ○ *Each lap of the track is 400 meters.*

PHRASAL VERB with lap

• **lap up** *something* [M] to buy, listen to, or do something very enthusiastically ○ *Young people there are lapping up just about everything to do with pop culture from Japan.*

lapel /lə'pel/ *n* [C] a strip of cloth that is attached to the collar and front opening of a jacket or similar piece of clothing and is folded back over it ○ *wide lapels*

lapse **FAILURE** /læps/ *n* [C] a failure to do something that happens as a particular event at a particular time ○ *a memory lapse* ○ *She had a momentary lapse in concentration and lost the game.*

PERIOD /læps/ *n* [U] a period of time after an event or between two events ○ *Owing to the lapse of time since the crimes, none of the original witnesses could be found.*

END /læps/ *v* [I] to end something, either intentionally or accidentally, that might be continued or that should continue ○ *I must have let my subscription lapse, because I haven't received any issues of the magazine in months.*

PHRASAL VERB with lapse

• **lapse into** *something* **1** to change to a less active state ○ *The 84-year-old has lapsed into a coma.* **2** Someone who lapses into something chooses to do something that is easier: *He had difficulty with English and often lapsed into his native German.*

laptop (computer) /'læp·tɑp (kəm'pjuːt̬·ər)/ *n* [C] a computer small and light enough to be carried around ○ *If I had a laptop, I could work on the train.*

larceny /'lɑr·sə·ni/ *n* [C/U] *law* the crime of taking something that does not belong to you, but not in a way that involves force or the threat of force ○ [U] *As a pickpocket, he was charged with larceny.*

lard /lɑrd/ *n* [U] a soft, white, creamy substance made from the fat of pigs and used in cooking and baking

large /lɑrdʒ/ *adj* [-er/-est only] **1** of more than a typical or average size or amount ○ *They have a large house in the suburbs.* ○ *This apartment is much larger than our last one.* ○ *It was the largest bug I had ever seen.* ○ *This computer stores large amounts of data.* ○ *I'd like a large soda.* **2** If something is true **in large part** or **in large measure**, it is true to a great degree ○ *The rebirth of interest in cycling in this country was, in large part, a result of Lance Armstrong's success.* **3** Large (*abbreviation* **L**) is a size of clothing or other product that is bigger than average: *The shirt is available in small, medium, and large (sizes).* ○ Opposite: SMALL

WORD FAMILY large

Nouns	enlargement	*Verbs*	enlarge
Adjectives	large enlarged	*Adverbs*	largely

IDIOMS with large

• **at large 1** generally ○ *Society at large will benefit from this.* **2** A person who is **at large** is not in prison: *The escaped prisoners are still at large.*

• **by and large** when everything about a situation is considered together ○ *There are a few things that I don't like about my job, but by and large it's very enjoyable.*

• **larger than life** more obvious than usual ○ *His superhuman strength gives the story a larger-than-life quality, like a fable.*

largely /'lɑrdʒ·li/ *adv* [not gradable] to a great degree, or generally ○ *My advice was largely ignored.* ○ *His early novels went largely unnoticed.*

large-scale *adj* involving many people or things, or happening over a large area ○ *We must improve our response to large-scale natural disasters.*

lark **BIRD** /lɑrk/ *n* [C] a small, brown bird with a pleasant song

ACTIVITY /lɑrk/ *n* [C] an activity done for enjoyment or amusement ○ *He started hang-gliding years ago as a lark.*

larva /'lɑr·və/ *n* [C] *pl* **larvae** a young insect that has left its egg but has not yet developed wings, or the young of some animals

laryngitis /ˌlær·ən'dʒɑɪt̬·əs/ *n* [U] an infection of the LARYNX, which often makes speaking painful ○ *Carol's flu developed into laryngitis.*

larynx /'lær·ɪŋks/ *n* [C] *pl* **larynxes, larynges** an organ in the throat which contains the VOCAL CORDS (= tissue that moves to produce the voice) ○ *Changes in a teen's body cause the larynx to grow larger.*

lasagna, **lasagne** /lə'zɑn·jə/ *n* [U] a dish consisting of layers of thin, wide pasta combined with cheese, TOMATO sauce, and sometimes meat

lascivious /lə'sɪv·iː·əs/ *adj esp. disapproving* feeling or expressing strong sexual desire ○ *lascivious behavior*

laser /'leɪ·zər/ *n* [C] ***physics*** a device that produces a powerful, highly controlled, narrow beam of light ○ *a laser beam* ○ *Doctors destroyed the tumor with a laser.*

lash **HIT** /læʃ/ *v* [I/T] to hit someone or something with a lot of force, esp. using a stick or leather strip, or to move forcefully against something ○ [T] *The men lashed their horses into a run.* ○ [I] *Ice storms lashed across the state.*

lash /læʃ/ *n* [C] a thin strip of leather, or the act of hitting someone with such a strip

TIE /læʃ/ *v* [T always + adv/prep] to tie or fasten together tightly and firmly ○ *Lash the boat to the rail.*

HAIR /læʃ/ *n* [C] an EYELASH ○ *She has enormous wide-set eyes with thick lashes.*

lasso /'læs·oʊ, -uː/ *n* [C] *pl* **lassos, lassoes** a long rope with one end tied in a circle that can be tightened, used for catching horses and cattle

lasso /ˈlæs·oʊ, læˈsuː/ *v* [T] **lassoes,** *pres. part.* **lassoing,** *past* **lassoed** ○ *The terrified pony was finally lassoed* (= caught).

last FINAL /læst/ *n* [U] the person or thing after everyone or everything else ○ *Heather was the last to go to bed and the first to get up.*

last /læst/ *adj, adv* [not gradable] ○ *In math tests, American students came in last* (= ranked the lowest). ○ *He was last in line for tickets.* ○ *Our house is the last one on the left.* ○ *Despite recent wins, the team is still in last place* (= lowest in rank among it competitors).

last /læst/, **lastly** /ˈlæst·li/ *adv* [not gradable] (in ending a set of items or a series of thoughts) finally ○ *The men begin the dance, then the women enter, and last, the children join in.*

NO MORE /læst/ *n* [U] the only one or part that is left ○ *Mark ate the last of the ice cream.*

last /læst/ *adj* [not gradable] ○ *I need to borrow some money – I'm down to my last dollar.*

MOST RECENT /læst/ *n* [U] the most recent, or the one before the present one ○ *We had lunch together the week/month before last* (= two weeks/months ago). ○ *The last we heard, she was teaching English overseas.* ○ *Each of her novels seems better than the last.*

last /læst/ *adj, adv* [not gradable] ○ *last night/week/month/year* ○ *last spring/summer/fall/winter* ○ *These last five years have been very difficult for him.* ○ *Kristal said in her last letter that she might come to visit.* ○ *When was the last time you went to the movies?* ○ *We last saw Grandma in 1994.*

NOT DESIRABLE /læst/ *adj* [not gradable] being the least desirable or least likely ○ *Traveling across the country with two small children is the last thing I want to do.*

CONTINUE /læst/ *v* **1** to continue for a period of time, or to continue to exist ○ [I] *The tour lasts about an hour.* ○ [I] *She's into soccer at the moment, but it won't last.* **2** To last is also to continue in a situation although it is difficult: [L] *Her previous secretary only lasted a month.* **3** To last is also to continue to work well or stay in good condition: [I] *I'd rather pay a little more and buy clothing that's going to last.*

lasting /ˈlæs·tɪŋ/ *adj* continuing to exist or have an effect for a long time ○ *These poems have won him a lasting reputation as Puerto Rico's finest love poet.*

IDIOMS with last

• **have the last laugh, get the last laugh** to succeed when others thought you would not ○ *She was fired from the company last year, but she had the last laugh when she was hired by their main rival at twice the salary.*

• **last but not least** important, despite being mentioned at the end ○ *I would like to thank my publisher, my editor, and last but not least, my husband for his encouragement during the writing of my book.*

• **last resort** the only choice that remains after all others have been tried ○ *As a last resort, we could ask your mother to help.*

• **on its last legs** weak or in very bad condition ○ *My car is on its last legs, but I'll drive it until it won't go any farther.*

• **the last minute** the latest possible opportunity for doing something ○ *He always leaves his homework until the last minute.* ○ *At the last minute, we found our tickets.*

• **the last word in** *something* the best or most modern example of something ○ *In the 1970s, the magazine was considered the last word in humor by most young people.*

last-ditch *adj* [not gradable] happening or tried at the final opportunity, before it is too late ○ *In a last-ditch attempt to win the election, he promised sweeping tax cuts.*

last name *n* [C] your family name, which in English comes after other names you are given: *His first name is Julio, but I can't remember his last name.* ○ Compare FIRST NAME; MIDDLE NAME

last quarter *n* [C] a HALF MOON

latch /lætʃ/ *n* [C] a fastening device for a door or gate

latch /lætʃ/ *v* [I/T] ○ [T] *Make sure the cabinet door is latched so the cat can't get in.*

PHRASAL VERB with latch

• **latch onto** *something* *infml* **1** (esp. of living things) to become firmly attached to someone or something ○ *Antibodies latch onto proteins on the surfaces of the virus.* **2** Someone who latches onto an idea accepts it with enthusiasm: *In 1991, the company latched onto the idea of using its software to drive video-arcade games.*

late NEAR THE END /leɪt/ *adj, adv* [*-er/-est* only] (happening or being) near the end of a period or in the recent past ○ *I expect him home late this afternoon.* ○ *I'd better get going – I had no idea it was so late!* ○ [+ to infinitive] *It's too late to call now.* ○ *I think Jody's in her late twenties.* ○ *He is a celebrated painter of the late 19th century.* ○ See also: LATEST ○ Compare EARLY

lately /ˈleɪt·li/ *adv* [not gradable] recently ○ *My wife hasn't been feeling well lately.*

AFTER /leɪt/ *adj, adv* [*-er/-est* only] (happening or arriving) after the planned, expected, usual, or necessary time ○ *Sorry I'm late – I was caught in traffic.* ○ *You'll be later than you already are if you don't hurry up.* ○ *This is the latest she's ever worked.* ○ *Summer came late this year* (= The weather became warm after the usual time). ○ *It's too late to do anything about it now.* ○ See also: LATEST ○ Compare EARLY

lateness /ˈleɪt·nəs/ *n* [U] ○ *My boss doesn't tolerate lateness.*

DEAD /leɪt/ *adj* [not gradable] no longer alive, esp. having recently died ○ *She gave her late husband's clothes to charity.*

latecomer /ˈleɪtˌkʌm·ər/ *n* [C] a person who arrives late ○ *Latecomers will not be admitted until intermission.*

latent /ˈleɪt·ənt/ *adj* [not gradable] present, but not yet active, developed, or obvious ○ *Latent ethnic tensions exploded into the open yesterday.*

latent heat *n* [U] ***physics*** the heat that is absorbed or released by a substance when it changes form, for example, from a liquid to a gas, while the temperature of the substance stays the same

later NEAR THE END /ˈleɪt̬·ər/ *adv comparative of* LATE NEAR THE END ○ *He was successful later in his career.*

AFTER /ˈleɪt̬·ər/ *adv* after the present, expected, or usual time; *comparative of* LATE AFTER ○ *She said she would speak to me later.* ○ *Why don't you call back later on, when he's sure to be here?*

lateral /ˈlæt̬·ə·rəl/ *adj* [not gradable] relating to the sides of an object or to sideways movement ○ *The bird spread its wings for lateral stability.*

latest /ˈleɪt̬·əst/ *adj* [not gradable] newest, most recent, or most modern ○ *Did you see her latest movie?*

latest /ˈleɪt̬·əst/ *n* [U] the most recent news ○ *Have you heard* **the latest** *about Celine and Michael?*

latex /ˈleɪ·teks/ *n* [U] a white liquid produced by particular plants, esp. rubber trees, or an artificial substance similar to this, used esp. in paint, glue, and cloth ○ *latex paint* ○ *latex gloves*

lather /ˈlæð·ər/ *n* [U] a mass of small white bubbles produced esp. when soap is mixed with water

lather /ˈlæð·ər/ *v* [I/T] ○ [I] *I lathered and shaved quickly.*

L

Latina /læˈtiː·nə/ *n* [C] *pl* **Latinas** a woman who lives in the US whose family is from Latin America, or a woman who lives in Latin America ○ *a Latina activist* ○ *He appointed a Latina to the education committee.*

Latin American /ˈlæt·ən·əˈmer·ə·kən,-ˈmær-/, **Latin** /ˈlæt·ən/ *n* [C] a person of or coming from South America, Central America, or Mexico

Latin American /ˈlæt·ən·əˈmer·ə·kən, -ˈmær-/ *adj* [not gradable] ○ *Latin American coffee producers will be hurt by the embargo.*

Latino /læˈtiː·noʊ/ *n* [C] *pl* **Latinos** a person who lives in the US whose family is from Latin America, or a person who lives in Latin America ○ *a Latino leader* ○ *Small farming towns that were largely Anglo for more than 100 years are now as much as 98 percent Latino.*

latitude DISTANCE /ˈlæt̬·əˌtuːd/ *n* [C/U] the distance north or south of the equator measured from 0° to 90° ○ Compare LONGITUDE ➤ Picture: **earth**

latitudinal /ˌlæt̬·əˈtuːd·ən·əl/ *adj* [not gradable] ***earth science***

FREEDOM /ˈlæt̬·əˌtuːd/ *n* [U] freedom to behave, act, or think in the way you want to ○ *Judges now have considerable latitude in sentencing.*

latrine /ləˈtriːn/ *n* [C] a toilet, esp. a simple one such as a hole in the ground, used in a military area or when CAMPING (= living in a tent for a short period)

latter SECOND /ˈlæt̬·ər/ *n* [U] *fml* the second of two people, things, or groups previously mentioned ○ *He directed "The Wizard of Oz" and "Gone with the Wind," receiving an Oscar for the latter.* ○ Compare FORMER FIRST

END /ˈlæt̬·ər/ *adj* [not gradable] near or toward the end of something ○ *He was in the news during the latter part of the Watergate scandal.*

latter-day *adj* [not gradable] **1** being a new or recent form of a person or thing from the past ○ *He acts like a latter-day cowboy armed with ideas.* **2** Latter-day can also mean of the present time: *To many journalists, his stand against the newspaper made him a latter-day hero.*

laud /lɔːd/ *v* [T] *fml* to praise someone or something ○ *The president lauded the rise of market economies around the world.*

laudable /ˈlɔːd·ə·bəl/ *adj fml* ○ *Recycling is a laudable activity.*

laudatory /ˈlɔːd·əˌtɔːr·i, -ˌtoʊr·i/ *adj fml* expressing praise ○ *Patients speak of Dr. Goertzen in laudatory terms.*

laugh /læf/ *v* [I] **1** to make the sounds and movements of the face and body that express happiness or amusement, or that sometimes express ridicule or anxiety ○ *The audience just laughed and laughed.* ○ *That guy always makes me laugh.* ○ *When I made a face at Drew, he laughed out loud.* ○ *We were laughing at the clown.* **2** Sometimes when you laugh at someone, you are ridiculing that person: *I don't want to be laughed at by my classmates.*

laugh /læf/ *n* [C] **1** *Holly has a very strange laugh – it sounds like she's screaming.* **2** *infml* A laugh is also an amusing or ridiculous situation or person: *You should have seen Sean trying to stay on the skateboard – what a laugh!*

laughable /ˈlæf·ə·bəl/ *adj* amusing or ridiculous ○ *The movie was so far from accurate that it was laughable.*

WORD FAMILY laugh			
Nouns	laugh laughter	*Verbs*	laugh
		Adverbs	laughably
Adjectives	laughable		

WORD CHOICES laugh

If someone laughs quietly, the verb **chuckle** is sometimes used.

She was ***chuckling*** *as she read the letter.*

The verb **giggle** is often used when someone laughs in a quiet childish way, often at something silly or rude, or because he or she is nervous.

The girls were ***giggling*** *at the back of the classroom.*

If someone laughs in a childish and unkind way, you can use the word **snicker**.

They ***snickered*** *at what she was wearing.*

Chortle can be used when someone laughs because of being pleased, especially at someone else's bad luck.

She ***chortled*** *with glee at the news.*

The phrasal verb **crack up** or the phrase **burst out laughing** can be used when someone suddenly starts laughing.

I just ***cracked up*** *when I saw him in that ridiculous hat.*

I fell over the chair and everyone ***burst out laughing****.*

If someone is laughing so much that he or she cannot stop, in informal situations you can use the phrase **in stitches**.

His jokes had us all ***in stitches****.*

PHRASAL VERB with laugh

• **laugh off** *something* [M] to pretend that something is less serious than it is ○ *The coach laughed off the idea that his team wasn't ready to play.* ○ *She didn't get into the school she wanted, but she seemed to be able to laugh it off.*

laughingstock /ˈlæf·ɪŋˌstɑk/ *n* [C] a person or group that is ridiculed ○ *This team has become the laughingstock of the league.*

laughter /ˈlæf·tər/ *n* [U] the act or sound of laughing ○ *Laughter from the living room kept me awake past midnight.*

launch SEND /lɔːntʃ, lɑntʃ/ *v* [T] to send something out, esp. a vehicle into space or a ship onto water ○ *On the last shuttle mission, the crew launched a communications satellite.*

launch /lɔːntʃ, lɑntʃ/ *n* [C] ○ *The launch of the space shuttle was delayed by bad weather.*

BEGIN /lɔːntʃ, lɑntʃ/ *v* [I/T] to begin, or to introduce a new plan or product ○ [T] *We're planning to launch a new Internet services company next month.* ○ [I always + adv/prep] *He launched into a verbal attack on her handling of the finances.*

launch /lɔːntʃ, lɑntʃ/ *n* [C usually sing] ○ *Frank went to the launch* (= introduction) *of Hibichu's new flat-screen TV.*

BOAT /lɔːntʃ, lɑntʃ/ *n* [C] a large, open or partly enclosed motor boat

launch pad, **launching pad** *n* [C] a special area from which ROCKETS or MISSILES are sent up into the air

launder WASH CLOTHES /ˈlɔːn·dər, ˈlɑn-/ *v* [I/T] *fml* to clean clothes or other cloth items by washing them ○ [T] *The sweater should be laundered by hand or dry-cleaned.*

MOVE MONEY /ˈlɔːn·dər, ˈlɑn-/ *v* [T] to move money which has been obtained illegally through banks and other businesses to make it seem to have been obtained legally

Laundromat /ˈlɔːn·drəˌmæt, ˈlɑn-/ *n* [C] *trademark* a place where the public may wash and dry their clothes in machines that operate when coins are put in them

laundry /ˈlɔːn·dri, ˈlɑn-/ *n* [C/U] **1** clothing, bed sheets, etc., that have been or need to be washed ○ [U] *piles of dirty laundry* **2** A laundry is also a room in a house where clothes, etc., are washed, or a business that washes clothes, etc., for customers.

laundry list *n* [C] a long list of things ○ *There's a whole laundry list of things to do.*

laureate /ˈlɔːr·iː·ət, ˈlɑr-/ *n* [C] a person who has been given an important job or a prize because of an achievement in a particular subject ○ *a Nobel laureate*

laurel /ˈlɔːr·əl, ˈlɑr-/ *n* [C/U] a small evergreen tree that has shiny, dark green leaves and black BERRIES (= small round fruit)

lava /ˈlɑv·ə, ˈlæv·ə/ *n* [U] ***earth science*** hot liquid rock that comes out of a VOLCANO, or the solid rock formed when liquid rock cools

lavatory /ˈlæv·əˌtɔːr·i, -ˌtoʊr·i/ *n* [C] a room equipped with a toilet and sink ○ *The lavatories will be out of service for the rest of the flight.*

lavender PLANT /ˈlæv·ən·dər/ *n* [U] a plant with very thin, gray-green leaves and small, pale purple flowers that has a pleasant smell, or its dried flowers and stems which are sometimes kept with sheets and clothes to make them smell pleasant

COLOR /ˈlæv·ən·dər/ *adj, n* [U] (of) a pale purple color ○ *a lavender shirt*

lavish /ˈlæv·ɪʃ/ *adj* spending, giving, or using more than is necessary or reasonable; more than enough ○ *The team has the most lavish training facility in the league.*

lavishly /ˈlæv·ɪʃ·li/ *adv* ○ *They live in a lavishly furnished apartment overlooking Central Park.*

PHRASAL VERB with lavish

• **lavish** *something* **on** *someone/something* to give a lot or too much of something to someone or something ○ *She lavishes more attention on that dog than she does on her children.*

law RULE /lɔː/ *n* [C/U] **1** a rule made by a government that states how people may and may not behave in society and in business, and that often orders particular punishments if they do not obey, or a system of such rules ○ [U] *civil/criminal law* ○ [U] *federal/state law* ○ [C] *We have a law in this state that drivers must wear seatbelts.* ○ [U] *She's studying law at Georgetown University.* ○ [U] *Playing loud music late at night is against the law.* **2** The law is also the police: [U] *He got in trouble with the law as a young man.* **3 Law and order** is the condition of a society in which laws are obeyed, and social life and business go on in an organized way. **4 Law enforcement** is the government activity of keeping the public peace and causing laws to be obeyed: *Several law enforcement officers were sent to Mexico to bring the prisoner back.*

lawful /ˈlɔː·fəl/ *adj* [not gradable] permitted by law; legal ○ *The judge concluded that the search of the house had been lawful.*

lawless /ˈlɔː·ləs/ *adj* [not gradable] not permitted by law or not obeying the law; illegal ○ *The territory was once speckled with ranches and lawless towns.*

PRINCIPLE /lɔː/ *n* [C] a general rule that states what always happens when the same conditions exist ○ *the laws of physics*

WORD FAMILY law

Nouns	law lawyer outlaw	*Adjectives*	lawful lawless unlawful
Adverbs	lawfully unlawfully	*Verbs*	outlaw

L

law-abiding *adj* obeying and respecting the law ○ *a law-abiding citizen*

lawbreaker /ˈlɔːˌbreɪ·kər/ *n* [C] a person who does not obey the law, esp. intentionally and often

lawmaker /ˈlɔːˌmeɪ·kər/ *n* [C] someone, such as a politician, who is responsible for making and changing laws

lawn /lɔːn, lɑn/ *n* [C] an area of grass, esp. near a house or in a park, which is cut regularly to keep it short

lawnmower /ˈlɔːnˌmoʊ·ər, ˈlɑn-/ *n* [C] a machine used for cutting grass

lawsuit /ˈlɔː·suːt/ *n* [C] a disagreement between people or organizations that is brought to a court of law for a decision ○ *The lawsuit is aimed at protecting this species of salamander.*

lawyer /ˈlɔɪ·ər, ˈlɔː·jər/ *n* [C] someone whose job is to give advice to people about the law and speak for them in court ○ *Following his arrest, he demanded to see his lawyer before making any statement.*

USAGE

lawyer, counsel, or attorney?

Lawyer is the most general and common of these words. **Attorney** is slightly more formal but has the same meaning; it is used in some official titles, like **attorney general** and **district attorney**. **Counsel** refers to one or more lawyers who are representing a person in a court, legal case, or trial.

L

lax /læks/ *adj* lacking care, attention, or control; not severe or strong enough ○ *Security at the airport seemed lax.*

laxity /ˈlæk·sət̬·i/, **laxness** /ˈlæk·snəs/ *n* [U] ○ *Laxity in enforcing safety regulations can cost lives.*

laxative /ˈlæk·sət̬·ɪv/ *n* [C] a substance that helps a person excrete the contents of the bowels

lay PUT DOWN /leɪ/ *v* [T] *past* **laid 1** to put something down, esp. into a flat or horizontal position ○ *He laid his coat on a chair.* ○ *She laid the baby (down) in her crib.* **2** To lay is also to put down in a careful or systematic way for a particular purpose: *We're having a new carpet laid in the hall next week.* ○ Compare LIE POSITION

CONFUSABLES

lay or lie?

Be careful not to confuse these verbs.

Lay means "put down carefully" or "put down flat." This verb always has an object after it. **Laying** is the present participle. **Laid** is the simple past and the past participle.

She laid the papers on the desk.

Lie means "be in a horizontal position" or "be in a particular place." This verb is irregular and is never followed by an object. **Lying** is the present participle. **Lay** is the past simple and **lain** is the past participle.

The papers were lying on the desk.

~~*The papers were laying on the desk.*~~

I lay down and went to sleep.

~~*I laid down and went to sleep.*~~

The regular verb **lie** means "not tell the truth." **Lying** is the present participle. **Lied** is the past simple and the past participle.

He lied to me about his age.

PREPARE /leɪ/ *v* [T] *past* **laid** to prepare something ○ *The initial negotiations laid the groundwork for more detailed talks later on.*

NOT TRAINED /leɪ/ *adj* [not gradable] not trained in or not having a detailed knowledge of a particular subject ○ *To a lay audience, the mathematics would be difficult.*

laity /ˈleɪ·ət̬·i/ *n* [U] the ordinary people who are involved with a church but who do not hold official religious positions ○ *The clergy and the laity are both participating in the program.*

PRODUCE EGGS /leɪ/ *v* [I/T] *past* **laid** (of an animal or bird) to produce eggs from out of its body

RISK /leɪ/ *v* [T] *past* **laid** to risk something on the result of an event ○ *I'll lay odds* (= risk money) *that she won't show up.*

EXPRESS /leɪ/ *v* [T] *past* **laid** to put or express ○ *He laid emphasis on the fact that he had never been found guilty of a crime.* ○ *She's trying to lay the blame on someone else* (= blame someone else).

LIE /leɪ/ *past simple of* LIE POSITION

IDIOMS with lay

• **lay a finger on** *someone*, **lay a hand on** *someone* to touch someone as a threat ○ *If you lay a finger on her, you'll live to regret it!*

• **lay down** *your* **life** to die ○ *I hope you will never be asked to lay down your lives for your principles.*

• **lay down the law** to tell people what they must do, without caring about their opinions ○ *Some parents talk things through with their kids instead of simply laying down the law.*

• **lay** *someone* **to rest** to bury someone ○ *She was laid to rest in Mt. Zion Cemetery.*

• **lay** *something* **to rest** to remove or end something ○ *I hope the information I have given you has laid your fears to rest.*

PHRASAL VERBS with lay

• **lay down** *something* **STOP USING** [M] to put away or stop using something ○ *Lay down your weapons and surrender.*

• **lay down** *something* **STATE** to state something plainly esp. as an official rule ○ *The coach laid down the rules from the first day of practice.*

• **lay in** *something* [M] to obtain and store something for later use ○ *We'd better lay in plenty of food for the winter months.*

• **lay into** *someone infml* to attack someone physically or with words ○ *The critics laid into her for a weak and lackluster performance.*

• **lay off** *someone* **NOT EMPLOY** [M] to stop employing a worker, esp. for reasons that have nothing to do with the worker's performance ○ *She was* *laid off along with many others when the company moved to California.* ○ Related noun: LAYOFF

•**lay off** *(something/someone)* **STOP** *infml* to stop using or dealing with something, or to stop criticizing someone ○ *You're going to have to lay off salt.*

•**lay** *someone* **open** to put someone in a position where there is risk or danger, esp. of criticism ○ *The Senator's remarks were unkind and laid him open to criticism.*

•**lay out** *something* **ARRANGE** [M] to arrange in a pattern or design; to plan something by showing how its parts fit together ○ *The designer laid out the book with pictures on every page.* ○ Related noun: LAYOUT

•**lay out** *something* **SPEND** to spend money, esp. if it seems like a large amount ○ *He has laid out $40,000 to fund Little League teams in California.*

•**lay up** *someone* [M] to force someone to stay in bed ○ *She's been laid up with the flu for a week.*

layer Ⓐ /ˈleɪ·ər/ *n* [C] a thin sheet of a substance on top of a surface, or a level of material that is different from the material on either side ○ *We put on two layers of paint.* ○ *The road was built up with layers of crushed stone and asphalt.*

layer Ⓐ /ˈleɪ·ər/ *v* [T] to arrange something in layers ○ *Layer the pasta with slices of tomato.*

layered Ⓐ /ˈleɪ·ərd/ *adj*

layman /ˈleɪ·mən/, **layperson** /ˈleɪˌpɜr·sən/, **laywoman** /ˈleɪ·wʊm·ən/ *n* [C] **1** a person who is not trained in or does not have a detailed knowledge of a particular subject ○ *The book is supposed to be the layman's guide to home repair.* **2** A layman or layperson is also a member of a religion who is not a member of the CLERGY.

layoff /ˈleɪ·ɔːf/ *n* [C usually pl] an act of ending a worker's job, esp. when the worker has done nothing wrong ○ *Executives say no layoffs are expected as a result of the merger.* ○ Related verb: LAY OFF NOT EMPLOY

layout /ˈleɪ·ɑʊt/ *n* [C] the way something is designed or arranged ○ *His house has three bedrooms and ours has four, but otherwise the layout is much the same.* ○ *Each article in the journal has its own typeface and layout.* ○ Related verb: LAY OUT ARRANGE

layover /ˈleɪˌoʊ·vər/ *n* [C] a short stay at a place in the middle of a trip ○ *We had a three-hour layover in San Francisco and had to change planes on the way to Hawaii.*

lazy /ˈleɪ·zi/ *adj* [*-er/-est* only] **1** not willing or not wanting to work or use effort to do something ○ *If you weren't so lazy we could start fixing up the house.* **2** If you describe an activity as lazy, you mean that it is slow and gentle, or does not involve much effort: *a lazy breeze* ○ *We spent a lazy afternoon sunbathing on the beach.*

laziness /ˈleɪ·ziː·nəs/ *n* [U]

WORD FAMILY lazy

Nouns	laziness	*Adverbs*	lazily
Adjectives	lazy		

WORD CHOICES lazy

If someone is lazy for a period of time because of being tired and lacking in energy, the adjective **lethargic** can be used.

*I felt very **lethargic** after such a big lunch.*

You can say that someone who shows no interest in things is **indolent**.

*Some of my classmates are **indolent** in their health habits.*

Someone who watches a lot of television and does not do much else can be described as a **couch potato** in informal English.

*I was turning into a **couch potato**, watching TV and eating snacks all day.*

lb. *n* [C] *pl* **lb., lbs.** *abbreviation for* POUND WEIGHT

LCD *n* [C] *abbreviation for* **1** liquid crystal display (= a way of showing numbers or images on electronic devices using a liquid that reflects light when it receives an electric current) **2** An LCD is also the screen that shows the numbers or images: *With LCD monitors, the entire screen area is viewable.*

leach /liːtʃ/ *v* [I/T] (of a substance) to come out of or be removed from another substance, esp. dirt, by passing water through it

lead CONTROL /liːd/ *v* [T] *past* **led** to manage or control a group of people; to be the person who makes decisions that other people choose to follow or obey ○ *His sister is leading an effort to change this law.* ○ *I've asked George to lead the discussion.*

lead /liːd/ *n* [C] ○ *Who will play the lead* (= be the main actor) *in the show?*

leader /ˈliːd·ər/ *n* [C] a person who manages or controls other people, esp. because of his or her ability or position ○ *a business/financial/political leader*

leadership /ˈliːd·ərˌʃɪp/ *n* [U] **1** the quality or ability that makes a person a leader, or the position of being a leader ○ *The company was extremely successful under Murphy's leadership.* **2** Leadership is also the people who are in charge of a government or group: *the Democratic leadership in Congress*

SHOW WAY /liːd/ *v* [I/T] *past* **led 1** to show the way to someone or something, esp. by going first ○ [T] *She led the children along the path out of the forest.* ○ [T] *That research group leads the way in the development of new software.* ○ [T] *Just follow the signs and they will lead you to the exit.* **2** If something such as a road or sign leads somewhere, it goes toward something else or shows you how to get to a particular place: [I] *A flight of narrow stairs leads to the kitchen.*

lead /liːd/ *n* [C] a piece of information that allows a discovery to be made or a solution to be found ○ *The lead the detectives were following led to several arrests.*

CAUSE /liːd/ *v* [I/T] *past* **led** to prepare the way for something to happen; cause ○ [I] *Ten years of scientific research led to the development of the new drug.* ○ [T] *Discussions with lawyers led him to believe that the company would not sue him.*

BE FIRST /liːd/ *v* [I/T] *past* **led** (esp. in sports or other competitions) to be in front, be first, or be winning ○ [I/T] *With only three minutes to go in the football game, New Orleans led (Dallas), 24 to 21.*

lead /liːd/ *n* [U] **1** *She took the lead* (= went in front) *with ten meters to go in the race.* **2** A lead is also the amount or distance by which someone is in front: *After five games, she was still ahead by a point in the chess tournament, but her lead was shrinking.*

leader /ˈliːd·ər/ *n* [C] someone or something that is the first or the most important ○ *Her company is a leader in the women's clothing industry.*

leading /ˈliːd·ɪŋ/ *adj* first or most important ○ *She is a leading expert on the art of ancient Greece.*

METAL /led/ *n* [U] a dense, soft, dark gray metal, used esp. in combination with other metals and in BATTERIES (= devices that produce electricity) ○ *Lead pipes in many older houses have been replaced by copper ones.* ○ (*fig.*) *The day after running a marathon, my legs felt like lead* (= heavy and tired).

leaden /ˈled·ᵊn/ *adj* like lead in color or weight; gray or heavy ○ *They said goodbye under a leaden sky.*

PENCIL /led/ *n* [U] the black writing material made of GRAPHITE, used esp. in the center of a pencil

LIVE /liːd/ *v* [T] *past* **led** to live a particular type of life ○ *She retired to Florida and still leads a busy life.*

ANIMAL /liːd/ *n* [C] a LEASH

WORD FAMILY lead

Nouns	lead leader leadership	*Adjectives* *Verbs*	leading lead

IDIOMS with lead

• **lead the way** to be the best ○ *The company leads the way in developing new software.*

• **lead the way** *(somewhere)* to go first to show someone how to go somewhere ○ *We all walked down toward the beach with the kids leading the way.*

PHRASAL VERBS with lead

• **lead off** *(something)* to be the first of a series of people to do something ○ *"Who's the first speaker in the sales conference?" "Sally is leading off."* ○ *The 1998 expedition led off a series of annual ocean experiments.*

• **lead up to** *something* to happen, say, or do in preparation for something ○ *In the three games leading up to the Sugar Bowl, his team yielded 35, 35, and 42 points.* ○ *I thought you were leading up to a question at the end of that.*

• **lead with** *something* to put a particular story first or in the most important position in a news report or newspaper ○ *The Times leads with the coming mayoral elections.*

lead poisoning *n* [U] illness caused by eating or drinking something that that contains the metal LEAD

leaf PLANT /liːf/ *n* [C] *pl* **leaves** any of the flat, usually green parts of a plant that are joined at one end to the stem or branch ○ *By early November it's getting cold and the trees are starting to lose their leaves.*

leafy /ˈliː·fi/ *adj* ○ *You should include plenty of green leafy vegetables in your diet.*

PAPER /liːf/ *n* [C] *pl* **leaves 1** a thin flat substance, esp. a sheet of paper, or a layer of something ○ *Some of the leaves of the old book had come loose.* **2** A leaf of a table is an extra flat piece that can be added to the top surface to make the table larger.

PHRASAL VERB with leaf

• **leaf through** *something* to turn pages quickly and read only a little ○ *Three patients sat leafing through magazines in the doctor's waiting room.*

leaflet /ˈliː·flət/ *n* [C] a piece of paper, or several pieces of paper folded together, that gives information or advertises something ○ *They were handing out leaflets outside the supermarket about the school board election.*

league SPORTS /liːg/ *n* [C] **1** a group of teams or players in a sport who take part in competitions against each other ○ *Our team has the worst record in the league.* ○ *Do you belong to a bowling league?* **2** A league is also a group in which all the players, people, or things are on approximately the same level: *His new movie is just not in the same league as his last one* (= not as good as the one before).

ORGANIZATION /liːg/ *n* [C] **1** a group of people or countries that join together because they have the same interest ○ *the League of Nations* **2** *fml* If someone is **in league with** someone else, they have agreed secretly to do something together, esp. something illegal or wrong: *They were in league with their accountants to cheat the government by hiding their real income.*

leak /liːk/ *v* [I/T] **1** (of a liquid or gas) to escape from a hole or crack in a pipe or container, or (of a container) to allow liquid or gas to escape ○ [I] *He heard the sound of dripping and saw water leaking from a pipe overhead.* ○ [T] *The ship ran aground off the coast and began to leak oil.* **2** To leak is also to give out information privately, esp. when people in authority do not want it to be known: [T] *Someone had leaked the news of the ambassador's resignation to the press.*

leak /liːk/ *n* [C] **1** *Little jets of water shot out of the leaks in her garden hose.* **2** A leak is also the act of giving out information privately, esp. when people in authority do not want it to be known: *The Justice Department was investigating security leaks.*

leakage /ˈliː·kɪdʒ/ *n* [U] the condition of leaking ○ *The cause of the leakage of the chemical is under investigation, he said.*

leaky /ˈliː·ki/ *adj* [-er/-est only] ○ *There's a leaky radiator in the bedroom.*

lean SLOPE /liːn/ *v* [I/T] *past* **leaned** to move your body away from a vertical position so that it is bent forward or resting against something, or to place something in a sloping position against something ○ [I always + adv/prep] *The conductor leaned over us and asked for our tickets.* ○ [I always + adv/prep] *She paused for a moment to rest and leaned against a large rock.* ○ [T] *He leaned his bike against the wall.*

THIN /liːn/ *adj* [-er/-est only] **1** (of a person) thin and in good physical condition ○ *Her body is lean, taut, athletic.* **2** When you describe meat as lean, you mean that it does not have much fat in it: *lean hamburger meat* **3** A lean period is a time during which there is not enough of something, esp. money or food: *It is a particularly lean year for science funding.* **4** When you say that a company or business is lean, you mean that it has the fewest employees it needs to do its work.

PHRASAL VERBS with lean

• **lean on** *someone/something* to depend on someone or something ○ *They had leaned on the dictionary as the authority that answered all their questions.*

• **lean toward** *something* to be interested in something and be likely to do a particular activity ○ *He said he was leaning toward entering the race for governor.*

leaning /ˈliː·nɪŋ/ *n* [C usually pl] a tendency to have positive feelings or attitudes about beliefs or opinions of a particular kind ○ *Conservative groups rated Congressional members for their liberal leanings.*

leap /liːp/ *v* [I/T] *past* **leaped, leapt 1** to make a large jump or sudden movement, or to jump over something ○ [I] *He leaps to his feet when the phone rings.* ○ [I] *Flames were leaping into the sky.* ○ [T] *The dog leaped the fence.* ○ [I] *(fig.) Americans want change, but they don't want to leap into the unknown* (= move quickly into unknown situations). **2** If your heart leaps, you have a sudden, strong feeling of pleasure or fear: [I] *My heart leaps when I hear his voice.*

leap /liːp/ *n* [C] a large jump

IDIOMS with leap

• **by leaps and bounds** very quickly ○ *The company is growing by leaps and bounds this year.* ○ **USAGE:** Used to talk about how something increases or improves.

• **leap of faith** an act of believing something that is not easily believed ○ *It took a big leap of faith to decide to quit my job and try something new.*

PHRASAL VERB with leap

• **leap at** *something* to accept an opportunity quickly and eagerly ○ *I leapt at the chance to go to the concert.*

leapfrog /ˈliːp·frɔːg, -frɑg/ *n* [U] a children's game in which each player jumps over another who is bending over

leapfrog /ˈliːp·frɔːg, -frɑg/ *v* [I/T] **-gg-** to improve your position by moving quickly past or over something that blocks your way ○ [T] *We're going to leapfrog the rest of the market in technology.*

leap year *n* [C] a year, happening once every four years, that has 366 days and has February 29th as the extra day

learn /lɜrn/ *v* [I/T] to get knowledge or understanding of facts or ideas or of how to do things ○ [T] *We're learning algebra.* ○ [I] *He's not much of a cook, but he's learning.* ○ [I] *Parents learned of the budget cuts in a letter from the school superintendent.* ○ [I] *I hope you'll learn from your mistakes.* ○ [+ *to* infinitive] *I learned to drive when I was 16.* ○ [+ question word] *First you must learn how to use this computer.*

learned /ˈlɜr·nəd/ *adj fml* having or showing much knowledge ○ *a learned scholar*

learner /ˈlɜr·nər/ *n* [C] ○ *a fast/slow learner*

learning /ˈlɜr·nɪŋ/ *n* [U] the activity of getting knowledge ○ *This technique makes learning fun.*

USAGE

learn

Remember to use the preposition **from** when you are talking about **learning** something from someone or something.

I think I learned a lot from my three years in the Navy.

~~*I think I learned a lot with my three years in the Navy.*~~

USAGE

learn, teach, or study?

To **learn** is to get new knowledge or skills.

I want to learn how to drive.

When you **teach** someone, you give them new knowledge or skills.

My dad taught me how to drive.

~~*My dad learnt me how to drive.*~~

When you **study**, you go to classes and read books to try to understand new ideas and facts.

He is studying biology at Rutgers.

WORD FAMILY learn

Nouns	learner learning	*Adjectives*	learned unlearned
Verbs	learn		

WORD CHOICES learn

See also: **study**

You could use the verb **master** when someone learns how to do something well.

*She lived in Italy for several years but never quite **mastered** the language.*

If someone learns something by practicing it rather than by being taught, you could use the phrasal verb **pick up**.

*When you live in a country, you soon **pick up** the language.*

When you learn about something or how to do something, you can say that you **familiarize** yourself with it.

*He prepared for the interview by **familiarizing** himself with the company's work.*

Get the hang of something is an informal phrase that means "to learn how to do something, especially if it is not obvious or simple."

*"I've never used this software before." "Don't worry, you'll soon **get the hang of** it."*

IDIOMS with learn

• **learn a lesson**, **learn** *your* **lesson** to understand something because of an unpleasant experience, esp. when this means you will not do it again ○ *My computer crashed before I saved the document – I've learned my lesson, and now I save everything all the time.*

• **learn** *something* **the hard way** to discover what you need to know through experience or by making mistakes ○ *He doesn't want to take my advice, so I guess he'll have to learn the hard way.*

learning disability *n* [C] one of many conditions that can have an effect on someone's ability to learn easily

lease /liːs/ *v* [T] to use or allow someone else to use land, property, etc. for an agreed period of time in exchange for money ○ *I leased my new car instead of buying it.*

lease /liːs/ *n* [C] ○ *The lease on this office expires in two years.*

leash /liːʃ/, **lead** *n* [C] a strap, chain, etc., fastened to a dog or other animal, esp. at its collar, in order to lead or control it ○ *Dogs must be kept on a leash in this park.*

least /liːst/ *adj, adv, pronoun* less than anything or anyone else; (of) the smallest amount or number; *superlative of* LITTLE NOT MUCH ○ *I'm not the least bit concerned.* ○ *That's the answer I least wanted to hear.* ○ *Which car costs the least?*

L

IDIOMS with least

• **at least 1** used to emphasize that something is good in a bad situation ○ *The car was damaged, but at least he wasn't hurt.* **2 At (the very) least** means not less than: *It will cost at least $1000.* ○ *I'll be gone for two weeks, at the very least.* **3 At least** can also be used to reduce the effect of a statement: *I can handle it – at least, I think so.*

• **least of all** especially not ○ *No one believed her, least of all me.*

• **the least** *someone* **can do**, **the least** *someone* **could do** something someone should do ○ *"Do I have to go and say 'hi' to him?" "Yes – he's been very nice to you, so it's the least you can do."*

leather /ˈleð·ər/ *n* [U] animal skin that has been treated in order to preserve it and is used to make shoes, bags, clothes, equipment, etc. ○ *a leather jacket*

leathery /ˈleð·ə·ri/ *adj* ○ *His skin was tough and leathery.*

leave GO AWAY /liːv/ *v* [I/T] *past* **left 1** to go away from someone or something that stays in the same place ○ [I] *I'll be leaving tomorrow.* ○ [T] *He left the house by the back door.* ○ [I/T] *The bus leaves (the station) in five minutes.* **2** If you leave a job, you stop working at a place: [T] *He left work in June.* **3** If you leave home, you stop living in your parents' home.

NOT TAKE /liːv/ *v* [T] *past* **left 1** to not take something with you ○ *I mistakenly left my checkbook at home.* ○ *Hurry up or you'll get left behind the other hikers.* **2** You can leave something somewhere for a purpose: *I've left dinner for you on the stove.* **3** If you leave something to someone after you die, you have arranged for that person to receive it then: *She left all her money to her children.*

CAUSE TO STAY /liːv/ *v* [T] *past* **left 1** to allow or cause something to stay in a particular place, position, or state ○ *The dog left muddy tracks on the carpet.* ○ *He left a message for me at the office.* ○ *Leave the window open.* ○ *Her rudeness left us all speechless.* ○ *He left the engine running.* **2** If you leave some activity that involves work, you wait before you do it: *I'll leave the cleaning for tomorrow.*

MAKE AVAILABLE /liːv/ *v* [T] *past* **left 1** to make something available after some part has been taken or used ○ *There are only four cookies – please leave one for me.* ○ *Five from twelve leaves seven* (= Seven is the result of taking five from twelve). **2** If something is **left (over)**, it was not previously used or eaten: *There's some pasta left over from dinner.*

GIVE RESPONSIBILITY /liːv/ *v* [T] *past* **left** to allow someone to make a choice or decision about something, or to make someone responsible for something ○ *Leave it to me – I'll see what I can do.* ○ *I'll leave it up to you to choose the gift.*

VACATION /liːv/ *n* [U] time permitted away from work, esp. for a medical condition or illness or for some other special purpose ○ *maternity leave*

PERMISSION /liːv/ *n* [U] *fml* permission to do something ○ *He took it without my leave.*

IDIOMS with leave

• **leave a bad taste (in** *your* **mouth)** to cause an unpleasant memory ○ *The way the waitress treated us left a bad taste in my mouth and I never went back.*

• **leave a lot to be desired, leave something to be desired** to not be very good or not as good as you would like ○ *His taste in clothes leaves something to be desired.*

• **leave** *someone* **cold** to not make someone feel interested or excited ○ *The band's songs left me cold.*

• **leave** *someone* **hanging** to keep someone waiting for your decision or answer ○ *I was left hanging, waiting for the college to tell me whether I got a scholarship or not.*

• **leave** *someone* **high and dry** to leave someone in a difficult situation without any help ○ *We were left high and dry without any money or credit cards.*

• **leave** *someone* **in the lurch** to not do for someone what you had promised you would do ○ *He said he would help with the rent, but he left me in the lurch.*

• **leave it at that** to say no more about something ○ *He just said "I'm not going," and left it at that.*

• **leave** *your* **mark** to have an effect that changes someone or something ○ *The heart attack left its mark on him, and he was never quite the same after it.*

• **leave** *someone* **to** *his or her* **own devices** allow someone to make his or her own decisions about what to do

• **leave well enough alone** to allow something to stay as it is because doing more might make things worse ○ *I could rewrite it, but I decided to leave well enough alone.*

PHRASAL VERBS with leave

• **leave** *someone/something* **alone** to not annoy, change, or touch someone or something ○ *The*

Federal Reserve is leaving interest rates alone. ○ *This little girl won't leave Uncle Steve alone on the phone.*
• **leave behind** *something/someone* [M] to go away and not take something or someone with you ○ *The flood victims were forced to leave behind family photos and mementos.* ○ *We left him behind to continue to help out.* ○ *He left behind a wife and six-year-old twin boys* (= He died but they are still living).
• **leave out** *something/someone* [M] to fail to include something or someone; omit ○ *You left out the best parts of the story.*

leave of absence *n* [C] *pl* **leaves of absence** a permitted period of time away from work

leaves /liːvz/ *pl of* LEAF

Le Châtelier's principle /lə ˌʃæt·əl ˈjeɪz ˈprɪn·sə·pəl/ *n* [U] ***science*** the theory that if conditions in a system that is in a state of balance are changed, the system will adjust to return to a state of balance

lecherous /ˈletʃ·ə·rəs/ *adj disapproving* (esp. of men) too interested in sex

lectern /ˈlek·tərn/, **podium** *n* [C] a tall, narrow piece of furniture having a sloping part that holds a book or papers to be read from while standing

lecture Ⓐ **FORMAL TALK** /ˈlek·tʃər/ *n* [C] a formal, prepared talk given to a group of people, esp. students ○ *a lecture on astronomy* ○ Compare SEMINAR
lecture Ⓐ /ˈlek·tʃər/ *v* [I] ○ *She's lecturing on the geology of the region.*
lecturer /ˈlek·tʃə·rər/ *n* [C]
CRITICISM /ˈlek·tʃər/ *n* [C] a serious talk given to criticize someone or give someone advice ○ *She gave him a lecture about his table manners.*
lecture /ˈlek·tʃər/ *v* [T] ○ *He lectured me on the need to keep accurate records.*

led /led/ *past simple and past participle of* LEAD

LED *n* [C] *abbreviation for* light-emitting diode (= an electronic device that gives off light when it receives an electrical current) ○ *LED lamp technology is evolving at an incredible pace.*

ledge /ledʒ/ *n* [C] a narrow, flat area like a shelf that sticks out from a building, cliff, or other vertical surface ○ *a window ledge*

ledger /ˈledʒ·ər/ *n* [C] a book in which items are regularly recorded, esp. business activities and money received or paid

leech /liːtʃ/ *n* [C] **1** a fat WORM that lives in wet places and fastens itself onto the bodies of humans and animals to suck their blood **2** *disapproving* A leech is also a person who gets money or support from someone, giving little or nothing in return.

leek /liːk/ *n* [C] a vegetable in the onion family with long, straight leaves that are white at the bottom and dark green at the top

leer /lɪr/ *v* [I] to look at someone in an unpleasant or offensive way ○ *He was leering at her.*
leer /lɪr/ *n* [C]

leeward /ˈliː·wərd, ˈluː·ərd/ *adj, adv* ***earth science*** on the side away from the wind, or in the direction toward which the wind is blowing

leeway /ˈliː·weɪ/ *n* [U] **1** freedom to act within certain limits ○ [+ *to* infinitive] *The law gives companies more leeway to decide whether to accept or reject an offer.* **2** Leeway is also additional time or money: *Homeowners need some leeway to buy a new house after they sell the old one.*

left **DIRECTION** /left/ *adj, adv, n* [C/U] (in or toward) a position that is the opposite of right and on the side of your body that contains the heart ○ *He injured his left eye.* ○ *Turn left at the stop sign.* ○ [C] *Make a left at the corner.* ○ [U] *My sister is third from the left in the back row.* ○ Opposite: RIGHT DIRECTION
POLITICS /left/ *n* [U] political groups that believe governments should provide a higher level of social services and support laws to bring about greater economic and social equality ○ Compare RIGHT POLITICS
leftist /ˈlef·təst/ *n* [C] ○ *The university is a stronghold for traditional leftists and protests are frequent there.*
LEAVE /left/ *past simple and past participle of* LEAVE

IDIOM with left

• **(out) in left field** strange, unusual, or completely wrong ○ *I wouldn't vote for him – his ideas are way out in left field.*

left-hand *adj* [not gradable] on or to the left ○ *the left-hand column*

left-handed *adj, adv* [not gradable] **1** using the left hand for writing and for most other things **2** A thing is described as left-handed if it is done with the left hand or designed to be used by a person with the left hand: *left-handed scissors* ○ Compare RIGHT-HANDED

leftover /ˌlefˌtoʊ·vər/ *adj* [not gradable] that has not been eaten or used during a meal ○ *leftover meatloaf*
leftovers /ˈlefˌtoʊ·vərz/ *pl n* ○ *We ate the leftovers cold the next day.*

left-wing *adj* involved with or supporting political ideas on the left
left-winger *n* [C] a person who supports the political left

leg **BODY PART** /leg/ *n* [C/U] **1** one of the parts of a human or animal body that is used for standing or walking, or one of the thin, vertical parts on which a piece of furniture stands ○ [C] *He broke his leg skiing.* ○ [C] *The table has carved legs.* ○ [U] *We had leg of lamb for dinner.* ➤ Picture: **insect** **2** The leg of a piece of clothing is the part you put your leg into.
leggy /ˈleg·i/ *adj* [*-er/-est* only] having long legs
STAGE /leg/ *n* [C] a part of a trip, competition, or activity that has several stages ○ *the last leg of the race*
SIDE /leg/ *n* [C] ***geometry*** either one of the two sides that form the angle of 90° in a RIGHT TRIANGLE ➤ Picture: **triangle**

L

legacy /ˈleg·ə·si/ *n* [C] **1** something that is a result of events in the past ○ *the bitter legacy of a civil war* **2** A legacy is also money or property left to a person by someone who has died.

legal Ⓐ /ˈliː·gəl/ *adj* [not gradable] connected with or allowed by the law ○ *the legal profession* ○ *the legal right to vote*
legally Ⓐ /ˈliː·gə·li/ *adv* ○ *The contract is legally binding.*
legality Ⓐ /liːˈgæl·əṭ·i/ *n* [U] the fact or state of being allowed by law ○ *Attorneys questioned the legality of the police officer's actions.*
legalize /ˈliː·gəˌlɑɪz/ *v* [T] to allow by law; make legal
legalization /ˌliː·gə·ləˈzeɪ·ʃən/ *n* [U] ○ *Some kind of legalization plan is needed for temporary workers who have become permanent residents.*

WORD FAMILY legal

Nouns	legality illegality legalization	*Adjectives*	legal illegal
Verbs	legalize	*Adverbs*	legally illegally

legal holiday *n* [C] a day on which government offices and many businesses are not open

legal tender *n* [U] the official money used in a country

legend STORY /ˈledʒ·ənd/ *n* [C/U] ***literature*** an old story or set of stories from ancient times, or the stories that people tell about a famous event or person ○ [U] *Cajun legend suggests that white alligators are a symbol of prosperity.*
legendary /ˈledʒ·ənˌder·i/ *adj* [not gradable] ○ *legendary tales*
FAME /ˈledʒ·ənd/ *n* [C] someone who is very famous and admired, usually because of an ability in a particular area ○ *Louis Armstrong is a jazz legend.*
legendary /ˈledʒ·ənˌder·i/ *adj* ○ *the legendary magician Houdini*
EXPLANATION /ˈledʒ·ənd/ *n* [C] the words written on or next to a picture, map, coin, etc., that explain what it is about or what the symbols on it mean

leggings /ˈleg·ɪŋz/ *pl n* tight pants made from a material that stretches easily, usually worn by women

leggy /ˈleg·i/ *adj* ○ See at LEG BODY PART

legible /ˈledʒ·ə·bəl/ *adj* (of writing or print) able to be read easily ○ *The letter was faded and barely legible.*
legibly /ˈledʒ·ə·bli/ *adv*

legion /ˈliː·dʒən/ *n* [C] a very large group of soldiers who form part of an army, esp. of an ancient Roman army, or any large group of people ○ *Legions of fans attended the concert.*

legislate Ⓐ /ˈledʒ·əˌsleɪt/ *v* [I/T] ***politics & government*** to make laws ○ [T] *The Clean Air Act legislated a reduction of pollution from power plants.*
legislation Ⓐ /ˌledʒ·əˈsleɪ·ʃən/ *n* [U] ***politics & government*** a law or set of laws that is being created ○ *New legislation offers a tax break for young families.*
legislative Ⓐ /ˈledʒ·əˌsleɪṭ·ɪv/ *adj* [not gradable] ***politics & government*** relating to the making of laws ○ *Congress is the legislative branch of government.*
legislator Ⓐ /ˈledʒ·əˌsleɪṭ·ər/ *n* [C] ***politics & government*** a member of an elected group of people who have the power to make or change laws
legislature Ⓐ /ˈledʒ·əˌsleɪ·tʃər/ *n* [C] ***politics & government*** an elected group of people who have the power to make and change laws in a state or country

legitimate /ləˈdʒɪṭ·ə·mət/, *infml, short form* **legit** /ləˈdʒɪt/ *adj* allowed according to law, or reasonable and acceptable ○ *a legitimate tax deduction* ○ *legitimate concerns*
legitimacy /ləˈdʒɪṭ·ə·mə·si/ *n* [U]

legitimize /ləˈdʒɪṭ·əˌmɑɪz/, **legitimate** /ləˈdʒɪṭ·əˌmeɪt/ *v* [T] to make something legal or acceptable

legroom /ˈleg·ruːm, -rʊm/ *n* [U] the amount of space available for your legs when you are sitting

legwork /ˈleg·wɜrk/ *n* [U] *infml* practical work that needs to be done, as in gathering information, and that usually involves a lot of walking from place to place ○ *Months of legwork enabled detectives to uncover a new lead.*

leisure /ˈliː·ʒər, ˈleʒ·ər/ *n* [U] the time when you are free from work or other duties and can relax ○ *She has a limited amount of leisure time.*
leisurely /ˈliː·ʒər·li, ˈleʒ·ər-/ *adj* ○ *a leisurely stroll on the beach*

IDIOM with leisure

• **at *your* leisure** when you want to and have the time ○ *You can study the documents at your leisure.*

lemon /ˈlem·ən/ *n* [C/U] **1** a yellow, oval fruit whose juice has a sour taste **2** *infml* A lemon is a device or machine that does not work well: [C] *That car I bought is a real lemon.*

lemonade /ˌlem·əˈneɪd/ *n* [U] a drink made with the juice of lemons, water, and sugar

lend /lend/ *v* [T] *past* **lent** to give something to someone for a short period of time, expecting it to be given back ○ *Can you lend me a few dollars till payday?*
lender /ˈlen·dər/ *n* [C] a person or business, such as a bank, that lends money

USAGE

lend or borrow?

Lend means to give something to someone for a period of time.

It was raining so she lent me an umbrella.

Borrow means to receive something that belongs to someone else and to use it for a period of time.

Can I borrow your umbrella?

~~*Can I lend your umbrella?*~~

IDIOM with **lend**

• **lend itself to** *something fml* to be good for a particular use ○ *The book really lends itself to being turned into a film.*

length DISTANCE /leŋθ, lenθ/ *n* [C/U] **1** the measurement of something from end to end or along its longest side, or a measurement of a particular part of something ○ [C] *a length of rope* ○ [U] *The boat is 20 feet in length.* **2** The length of a piece of writing, such as a book or story, is a measure of the material it contains: [U] *The length of the poem was 30 lines.*

lengthen /ˈleŋ·θən, ˈlen-/ *v* [I/T] to make something longer, or to become longer ○ [T] *I'll have to lengthen this skirt.* ○ [I] *In the late afternoon, the shadows of the haystacks lengthened.*

lengthwise /ˈleŋθˌwɑɪz, ˈlenθ-/ *adv* [not gradable] in the direction of the longest side ○ *Cut the pickles lengthwise.*

TIME /leŋθ, lenθ/ *n* [U] an amount of time ○ *The movie is nearly three hours in length.* ○ *George went on about his illnesses at great/some length* (= for a long time).

lengthen /ˈleŋ·θən, ˈlen-/ *v* [I/T] to make something take longer to happen, or to become longer ○ [T] *There is a plan to lengthen the summer theater workshop to eight weeks.*

lengthy /ˈleŋ·θi, ˈlen-/ *adj* [*-er/-est* only] taking a long time ○ *a lengthy speech*

WORD FAMILY length

Nouns	length	*Adjectives*	lengthy
Adverbs	lengthily lengthwise	*Verbs*	lengthen

lenient /ˈliːn·jənt/ *adj* not as severe or strong in punishment or judgment as would be expected ○ *Some felt that five years in prison was lenient, considering the suffering he had caused.*

leniency /ˈliːn·jən·si/ *n* [U] ○ *The defense lawyer asked for leniency for her young client.*

leniently /ˈliːn·jənt·li/ *adv*

lens GLASS /lenz/ *n* [C] a piece of glass or plastic having a curved surface in order to change the images that are received after going through it, usually to make them larger, smaller, or clearer ○ *a camera lens* ○ *Her eyeglasses have thick lenses.*
➤ Picture: **microscope**

EYE /lenz/ *n* [C] a curved, transparent part of the eye that helps you to see clearly by directing images of light onto the RETINA (= the back surface of the eye)

lent /lent/ *past simple and past participle of* LEND

Lent /lent/ *n* [U] in Christian religions, the 40 days before Easter

lentil /ˈlent·əl/ *n* [C] a small, round, flat seed, cooked and eaten in soups and other dishes

Leo /ˈliː·oʊ/ *n* [C/U] *pl* **Leos** the fifth sign of the ZODIAC, covering the period July 23 to August 22 and represented by a lion, or a person born during this period

leopard /ˈlep·ərd/ *n* [C] a large, wild cat that has yellow fur with black spots and that lives in Africa and south Asia

leotard /ˈliː·əˌtɑrd/ *n* [C] a piece of clothing that fits tightly over the body from the shoulders to the tops of the legs, worn esp. by dancers and people exercising

leper /ˈlep·ər/ *n* [C] a person who has LEPROSY (= a disease of the nerves and skin)

leprosy /ˈlep·rə·si/ *n* [U] an infectious disease that damages a person's nerves and skin

lepton /ˈlep·tɑn/ *n* [C] ***physics*** any very small piece of matter that is influenced by the WEAK FORCE. ELECTRONS, MUONS, and NEUTRINOS are all leptons.

lesbian /ˈlez·biː·ən/ *n* [C] a woman who is physically attracted to other women

lesion /ˈliː·ʒən/ *n* [C] *medical* an injury to a person's body or to an organ

less SMALLER AMOUNT /les/ *adj, adv* a smaller amount of something, to a smaller degree, or not as much; *comparative of* LITTLE **NOT MUCH** ○ *We've got to spend less money.* ○ *It was less than a mile to the nearest gas station.* ○ *She had less reason to complain than I.* ○ *Skiing conditions this year are less than ideal* (= not good). ○ *There were* **no less than** (= as many as) *a thousand people buying tickets.*

lessen /ˈles·ən/ *v* [I/T] to become or make something smaller in amount or degree ○ [T] *Keeping your weight down can lessen the risk of heart disease.*

lesser /ˈles·ər/ *adj* [not gradable] not as great in size, amount, or importance as something else ○ *Texas and, to a lesser degree, Oklahoma will be affected by the drought.*

CONFUSABLES

less or fewer?

It is common for English speakers to use **less** before countable nouns, meaning "not so many."

The trees have produced less apples this year. ➤

L

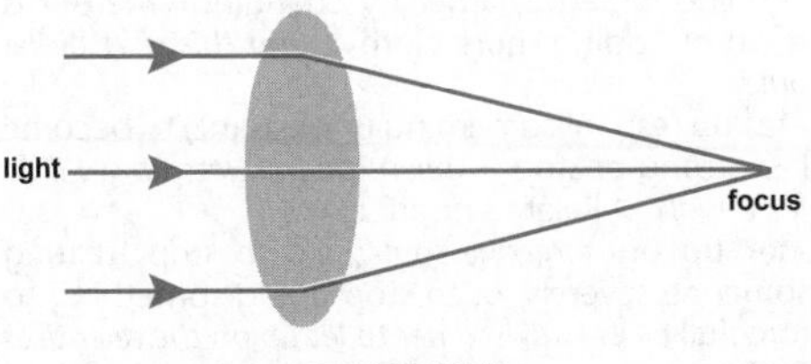

CONVEX LENS

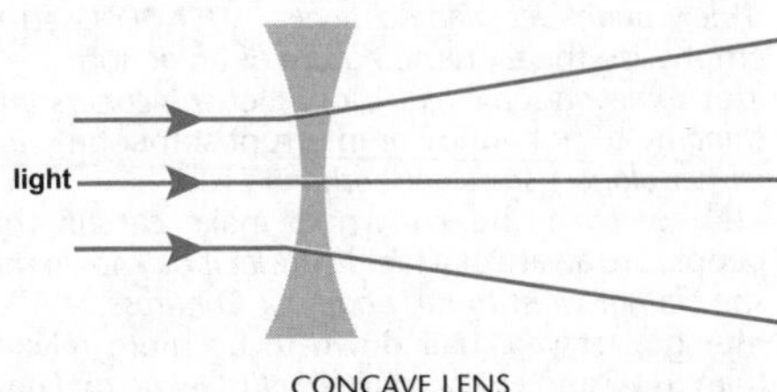

CONCAVE LENS

However, this is traditionally considered bad English. The standard word for "not so many" is **fewer**.
The trees have produced fewer apples this year.
The standard use of **less** is before uncountable nouns, meaning "not so much."
less money/time/food
The trees have produced less fruit this year.

SUBTRACT /les/ *prep* MINUS **SUBTRACTION**; after subtracting ○ *$30, less the discount of 15%, is $25.50.*

IDIOMS with **less**

• **less and less** gradually less or smaller ○ *I seem to see her less and less.*
• **the lesser of two evils** something that is bad, but not as bad as something else ○ *I had the choice of going with my parents to a concert or staying at my grumpy aunt's house – I chose my aunt's house as the lesser of two evils.*

lesson /ˈles·ən/ *n* [C] **1** a period of time during which something is taught ○ *Have you ever taken piano lessons?* **2** A lesson is also a useful piece of information learned through experience: *Losing his job was a lesson he never forgot.*

L

less than, *symbol* < ***mathematics*** having a smaller number or amount than ○ Compare GREATER THAN

lest /lest/ *conjunction fml* for fear that ○ *Gramps is too frightened to move, lest he disturb the infant.*

let **ALLOW** /let/ *v* [T] *pres. part.* **letting**, *past* **let** to allow something to happen or someone to do something by giving permission or by not doing anything to stop it from happening ○ *Fraya's parents let her go to the movie.* ○ *He decided to let his hair grow long.* ○ *She opened the door and let me in* (= allowed me to enter). ○ *After questioning him for six hours, the police finally let him go* (= released him). ➤ Usage: **allow or let?** at ALLOW **PERMIT**

CAUSE /let/ *v* [T] *pres. part.* **letting**, *past* **let** to cause something to happen or to be in a particular condition, or to cause someone to understand something ○ *He let the pool empty.* ○ *Let me know if you need help.* ○ *He let out a shout* (= He shouted).

SUGGEST /let/ *v* [T] *fml* **let us** I suggest that we ○ *For the sake of argument, let us assume that Rochelle is right.* ○ *After visiting the gift shop, let us proceed into Graceland itself.*

IDIOMS with **let**

• **let alone** *do something* and to an even greater degree do something ○ *Brian would never even read a newspaper, let alone a book.* ○ **USAGE:** Used to emphasize the extreme nature of an action.
• **let** *someone/something* **alone**, **let** *someone/something* **be** to not annoy or interrupt someone ○ *Just let her alone – she's not bothering you.*
• **let** *something* **be known** to make certain that people are aware of a fact ○ *She let it be known that she did not want to run again for Congress.*
• **let go**, **let** *your* **hair down** to be more relaxed than usual and enjoy yourself ○ *Just let go and have a little fun!* ○ *I like to let my hair down on the dance floor.*
• **let** *someone* **go** to end someone's employment ○ *We had to let fourteen employees go last month.*
• **let** *yourself* **go** to take less care of your appearance ○ *He's gained a lot of weight lately, and kind of let himself go.*
• **let go (of** *something/someone***)** to stop holding something or someone ○ *Brandon let go of her hand and ran across the street.*
• **let** *someone* **have it** to attack someone, either with words or physically ○ *When Joe finally got home three hours late, Lea let him have it.*
• **let nature take its course** to allow something to happen naturally ○ *Usually the Park Service lets nature take its course and does not replace dead trees.*
• **let off steam** to do or say something that helps you to get rid of strong feelings or energy ○ *She jogs after work to let off steam.* ○ Compare BLOW OFF STEAM at BLOW **IDIOMS**
• **let** *something/someone* **slide** to not do anything about something or someone when you should try to change or correct that thing or person ○ *I knew he wasn't telling me everything, but I decided to let it slide.* ○ *It's easy to let exercise slide in the suburbs where you have to drive your car all the time.*
• **let's face it** we should accept the truth ○ *Let's face it, I'm never going to be a great artist.*
• **let's see** **1** I am thinking about this ○ *"How many people will be there?" "Well, let's see – I think it's about 20."* ○ **USAGE:** Used in conversation when you are not sure what to say next. **2 Let's see** is also used when you want to discover something: *Now that we know what your interests are, let's see if we can match you to a job you'd like.*

PHRASAL VERBS with **let**

• **let down** *someone* [M] to cause someone to be disappointed, often because you have failed to do what you promised ○ *You'll be there tomorrow – you won't let me down, will you?* ○ Related noun: LETDOWN
• **let** *someone* **in on** *something* to tell someone something, esp. private information, that others already know ○ *My children never want to let me in on what they do in school.*
• **let off** *someone* [M] to fail to punish someone when the person expects to be punished, or to fail to punish someone severely enough ○ *The boys were let off with a reprimand.*
• **let on** to tell other people about something that you know, esp. when it is a secret ○ *If he did know the truth, he didn't let on.*
• **let out** **FINISH** (of a class or school) to end or be finished ○ *My history class lets out at 4:15.* ○ *When does your school let out for the summer?*
• **let out** *something* **WIDEN** [M] to make a piece of clothing wider or larger by changing where it is sewn or adding more cloth ○ *Can this skirt be let out?*
• **let up** (esp. of something unpleasant) to become less strong or stop ○ *When the rain lets up we'll go for a walk.* ○ Related noun: LETUP
• **let up on** *someone/something* to stop treating someone severely, or to stop doing something so forcefully ○ *He advised her to let up on the relentless criticism.*

letdown /ˈlet·dɑʊn/ *n* [C usually sing] an act of disappointing someone; DISAPPOINTMENT ○ *It was quite a letdown when Joyce only got a grade of C on the final exam.* ○ Related verb: LET DOWN

lethal /ˈliː·θəl/ *adj* able to cause or causing death; extremely dangerous ○ *a lethal weapon*

lethargic /ləˈθɑr·dʒɪk/ *adj* lacking in energy; feeling unwilling or unable to do anything
lethargy /ˈleθ·ər·dʒi/ *n* [U]

let's /lets/, *infml contraction of* **let us** ○ *Let's get out of here!* ○ See at LET SUGGEST

letter MESSAGE /ˈlet̬·ər/ *n* [C] a written or printed message from one person to another, usually put in an envelope and delivered as mail ○ *I got a letter from the bank this morning.*

SYMBOL /ˈlet̬·ər/ *n* [C] any of the set of symbols used to write a language, representing a sound in the language ○ *She wrote her name on the board in large letters.*
lettering /ˈlet̬·ə·rɪŋ/ *n* [U] written letters ○ *The perfume comes in a black box with gold lettering.*

letter carrier *n* [C] a person who delivers mail for the POST OFFICE

letterhead /ˈlet̬·ərˌhed/ *n* [U] **1** the printing at the top of a piece of writing paper telling the name and address of the person or business sending the letter **2** Letterhead is also the paper that this information is printed on.

lettuce /ˈlet̬·əs/ *n* [U] a plant of large, green leaves, eaten raw in salads

letup /ˈlet̬·ʌp/ *n* [U] the stopping or slowing down of something that is unpleasant ○ *Since the mall was built, there's been no letup in traffic.* ○ Related verb: LET UP

leukemia /luːˈkiː·miː·ə/ *n* [U] a disease in which the body produces too many white blood cells, causing weakness and sometimes death

levee /ˈlev·iː/ *n* [C] a wall made of land or other materials that is built to stop a river from OVERFLOWING (= flowing over its edges) ○ *Much of the city was under water after floods broke levees and forced the evacuation of 50,000 people.*

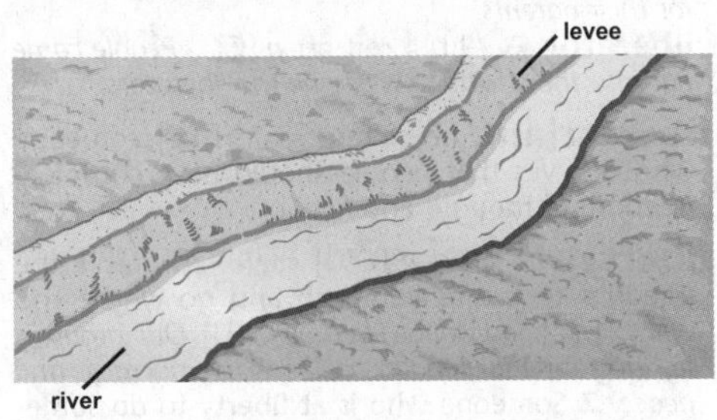

LEVEE

level HORIZONTAL /ˈlev·əl/ *adj* **1** (of a surface) not rising or falling or higher on one side, but even in all directions; horizontal or flat ○ *The table wobbles because the floor is not level.* **2** Something that is level with something else is at the same height: *The top of the tree is level with his bedroom window.* **3** A level spoon or cup is filled with something just to the top edge. **4** If you speak in a level voice, you speak in a calm and controlled way.
level /ˈlev·əl/ *v* [T] **1** to make something level ○ *We had to level the backyard before putting up the pool.* **2** To level buildings or other structures is to destroy them by causing them to fall down: *Her grandfather survived the 1906 earthquake that leveled San Francisco.*
level /ˈlev·əl/ *n* [C] a tool containing a tube of liquid with an air bubble in it, which shows whether a surface is horizontal by the position of the bubble

POSITION /ˈlev·əl/ *n* [C/U] **1** a particular position, degree, or amount of something, esp. compared with other possible positions, degrees, or amounts ○ [C] *The water level in the lake is higher after a heavy rain.* ○ [U] *The big debate is whether more decisions should be made at the local level or at the national level.* ○ [C] *He achieved a high level of skill as an interpreter.* ○ [U] *We publish a dictionary for intermediate level students.* **2** A level is also one of several floors at different heights in a building: [C] *The reception area is on the ground level.*

AIM /ˈlev·əl/ *v* [T] to aim or direct something at someone or something ○ *Soldiers leveled their weapons.* ○ *Criticism of the program was leveled by a number of politicians.*

IDIOMS with level

• **a level playing field** a situation in which everyone has the same advantages and disadvantages ○ *If the quality of high schools varies so much, how can everyone start college on a level playing field?*
• **on the level** being honest or speaking truthfully ○ *I know he's lied to you before, but I really think he's on the level this time.*

PHRASAL VERBS with level

• **level off** to stop increasing or being reduced ○ *The price of gas has finally leveled off after rising for several months.* ○ *The plane descended to 18,000 feet before leveling off.*
• **level with** *someone* to tell someone the truth, esp. when it may be unpleasant ○ *I'll level with you – the salary is not particularly good.*

level-headed *adj* able to be calm in difficult situations

lever /ˈlev·ər, ˈliː·vər/ *n* [C] **1** a handle that you move to control the operation of a machine ○ *He pushed the lever into the "on" position and started the machine.* **2** *physics* A lever is also a bar, moving over a fixed point, that when pressed down at one end can move or lift something at the other end.

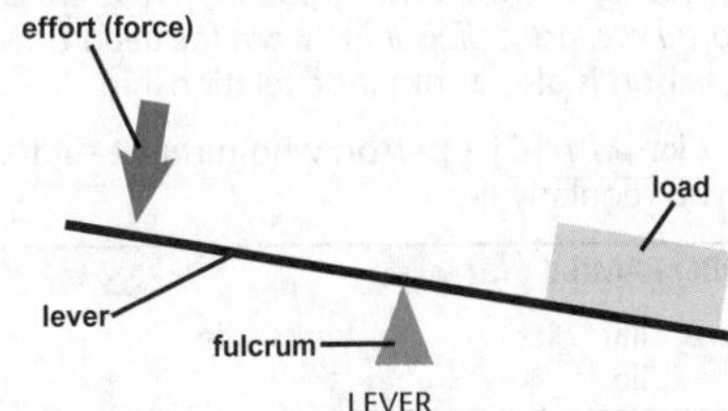

LEVER

leverage /ˈlev·ə·rɪdʒ, ˈliː·və-/ *n* [U] the power to influence results ○ *financial/political leverage* ○ *The US has very little leverage in that part of the world.*
leverage /ˈlev·ə·rɪdʒ, ˈliː·və-/ *v* [T] to use borrowed money for investments, esp. in order to buy a large enough part of a business so that you can control it ○ *They can leverage a very small investment into millions of dollars.*

levity /ˈlev·əţ·i/ *n* [U] amusement or lack of seriousness ○ *a moment of levity*

levy Ⓐ /ˈlev·i/ *n* [C] an amount of money, such as a tax, that you have to pay to a government or organization ○ *A levy was imposed on cotton imports.*
levy Ⓐ /ˈlev·i/ *v* [T] ○ *Taxes and fees levied on motorists would pay for the new highway.*

lewd /luːd/ *adj* [*-er/-est* only] (esp. of behavior or speech) sexual in an obvious and socially unacceptable way ○ *lewd remarks*

Lewis acid /ˈluː·əs ˈæs·əd/ *n* [C] ***chemistry*** a substance that can receive a pair of ELECTRONS from a BASE (= chemical substance)

Lewis base /ˈluː·əs ˈbeɪs/ *n* [C] ***chemistry*** a substance that can supply a pair of ELECTRONS to create a COVALENT BOND

Lewis structure /ˈluː·əs ˈstrʌk·tʃər/ *n* [C] ***chemistry*** a drawing that shows the way in which atoms are connected in a MOLECULE (= smallest unit of a substance)

lexicon /ˈlek·səˌkɑn/ *n* [C] all the words used in a particular language or subject, or a dictionary

liability /ˌlɑɪ·əˈbɪl·əţ·i/ *n* [C/U] **1** the responsibility of a person, business, or organization to pay or give up something of value ○ [U] *He denies any liability in the accident.* ○ [C usually pl] *The business has liabilities of $5 million.* **2** A liability is also anything that hurts your chances of success or that causes difficulties: [C] *Not having our own delivery trucks is a liability in our business.* ○ Compare ASSET

liable **LIKELY** /ˈlɑɪ·ə·bəl, ˈlɑi·bəl/ *adj* [+ *to* infinitive] likely to do, happen, or experience something ○ *If you don't take care of yourself, you're liable to get sick.* ○ *He's liable to say anything that comes into his head.*

RESPONSIBLE /ˈlɑɪ·ə·bəl/ *adj* [not gradable] *law* having legal responsibility for something ○ *He is still liable for repaying his student loan.*

liaison /liːˈeɪˌzɑn, ˈliː·ə-/ *n* [C/U] **1** communication between groups and the useful relationship that this creates, or a person who does the communicating between the groups ○ [U] *There is an unfortunate lack of liaison between the departments.* **2** A liaison is also a romantic relationship.

liar /ˈlɑɪ·ər/ *n* [C] a person who has just told a lie or who regularly lies

WORD FAMILY liar	
Nouns liar, lie	*Verbs* lie

libel /ˈlɑɪ·bəl/ *n* [C/U] a piece of writing that says bad, false, and harmful things about a person, or the legal claim you make when you accuse someone in court of writing such things about you ○ [C] *The whole story was a vicious libel.* ○ [U] *Angry at what the newspaper had printed, she sued for libel.* ○ Compare SLANDER
libel /ˈlɑɪ·bəl/ *v* [T] ○ *The general contends the network libeled him in a television broadcast.*
libelous /ˈlɑɪ·bə·ləs/ *adj* ○ *libelous articles*

liberal Ⓐ **SOCIAL** /ˈlɪb·ə·rəl/ *adj* allowing many different types of beliefs or behavior ○ *a liberal society/person*
liberalize Ⓐ /ˈlɪb·ə·rəˌlɑɪz/ *v* [I/T] ○ [T] *They have plans to liberalize the prison system* (= make it less severe).
liberalization Ⓐ /ˌlɪb·ə·rə·ləˈzeɪ·ʃən/ *n* [U] ○ *political/trade liberalization*

POLITICS /ˈlɪb·ə·rəl/ *adj* ***politics & government*** tending to emphasize the need to make new laws when necessary because of changing conditions and to depend on the government to provide social services ○ *a liberal policy/position* ○ Compare CONSERVATIVE POLITICS
liberal Ⓐ /ˈlɪb·ə·rəl/ *n* [C] ○ *Liberals in Congress support the bill.*
liberalism Ⓐ /ˈlɪb·ə·rəˌlɪz·əm/ *n* [U] ○ *She opposes liberalism and big-government solutions.*

GENEROUS /ˈlɪb·ə·rəl/ *adj* giving or given in a generous way ○ *Some merchants offer very liberal return policies, but others are strict.*
liberally Ⓐ /ˈlɪb·ə·rə·li/ *adv* ○ *The food was liberally seasoned with salt.*

NOT EXACT /ˈlɪb·ə·rəl/ *adj* without attention to or interest in small details ○ *Other teachers are a lot more liberal about spelling errors than Mr. Brady.*

liberal arts *n* [U] college or university subjects, including history, languages, and literature, that are not technical

liberate Ⓐ /ˈlɪb·əˌreɪt/ *v* [T] to release someone from control, duties, limits, or prison ○ *Muoz Rivera helped liberate Puerto Rico from Spain.*
liberated Ⓐ /ˈlɪb·əˌreɪţ·əd/ *adj* ○ *liberated nations/people*
liberation Ⓐ /ˌlɪb·əˈreɪ·ʃən/ *n* [U] ○ *Summer vacation means liberation for school children but not for their parents.*
liberator Ⓐ /ˈlɪb·əˌreɪţ·ər/ *n* [C] ○ *People came out into the streets to welcome the liberators.*

libertarian /ˌlɪb·ərˈter·iː·ən/ *n* [C] someone who believes that people should have complete freedom of thought and action

liberty /ˈlɪb·ərţ·i/ *n* [C/U] ***social studies*** **1** the freedom to live as you wish and go where you want ○ [C] *individual liberties* ○ [U] *Our group is fighting for independence, liberty, democracy, and peace.* **2** Someone who is **at liberty** to do something has permission to do it: *I'm not at liberty to discuss this with you.*

Libra /ˈliː·brə/ *n* [C/U] the seventh sign of the ZODIAC, covering the period September 23 to October 23 and represented by a pair of measuring SCALES, or a person born during this period

library /ˈlɑɪˌbrer·i, ˈlɑi·brər·i/ *n* [C] a building, room, or organization that has a collection esp. of books, music, and information that can be accessed by computer for people to read, use, or borrow ○ *a library book* ○ *a public library*
librarian /lɑɪˈbrer·iː·ən/ *n* [C] a person who works in a library, esp. someone with special training for this type of work

libretto /ləˈbret̬·oʊ/ *n* [C] *pl* **librettos** ***music*** the words that are sung or spoken in an opera or similar musical performance

lice /lɑɪs/ *pl of* LOUSE

license Ⓐ **DOCUMENT** /ˈlɑɪ·səns/ *n* [C] an official document that gives you permission to own, do, or use something ○ *a fishing/export/driver's license*
license Ⓐ /ˈlɑɪ·səns/ *v* [T] ○ *She's licensed to teach elementary school.*

FREEDOM /ˈlɑɪ·səns/ *n* [U] the freedom to break rules or principles, or to change facts, esp. when producing literature or works of art ○ *poetic/artistic license*

license plate *n* [C] a metal sign with numbers on it attached to the back, and sometimes the front of your car

lichen /ˈlɑɪ·kən/ *n* [C] ***biology*** a type of organism that consists of an ALGA (= plant without leaves or roots) and a FUNGUS (= plant without leaves, flowers, or color) growing together

lick **MOVE TONGUE** /lɪk/ *v* [T] to move the tongue across the surface of something as a way of eating it or making it wet or clean ○ [T] *to lick a stamp/lollipop*
lick /lɪk/ *n* [C] ○ *Can I have a lick of your ice cream cone?*

DEFEAT /lɪk/ *v* [T] *infml* to defeat someone or something, or to solve a difficult problem ○ *He has licked the cancer.*
licking /ˈlɪk·ɪŋ/ *n* [C] *infml* ○ *Our team really gave them a licking last night.*

SMALL AMOUNT /lɪk/ *n* [C] *infml* a small amount ○ *Chuck couldn't read a lick.*

IDIOM with **lick**

• **lick** *your* **wounds** to spend time getting back your strength or happiness after a defeat or bad experience ○ *Farmers were licking their wounds after crop prices dropped by 50%.*

licorice /ˈlɪk·ə·rɪʃ/ *n* [U] the dried root of a plant used for flavoring food, particularly candy, or candy with this flavor

lid /lɪd/ *n* [C] a cover that can be lifted up or removed from a container

IDIOM with **lid**

• **put a lid on** *something*, **keep a lid on** *something* to keep something under control and stop it from increasing ○ *We've got to keep a lid on our credit-card purchases.*

lie **POSITION** /lɑɪ/ *v pres. part.* **lying**, *past simp.* **lay**, *past part.* **lain** **1** to be in or move into a horizontal position on a surface ○ [I always + adv/prep] *The mechanic was lying on his back underneath my car.* ○ [I always + adv/prep] *I love to lie down in front of the fire and read.* ○ [L] *He lies awake at night, worrying.* **2** If something lies in a particular place, position, condition, or direction it is in that place, position, condition, or direction: [I always + adv/prep] *The river lies 40 miles to the south of us.* ○ [I always + adv/prep] *You shouldn't leave that check lying around* (= not in its place). ○ Compare LAY PUT DOWN ➤ Confusables: **lay or lie?** at LAY PUT DOWN

SPEAK FALSELY /lɑɪ/ *v* [I/T] *pres. part.* **lying**, *past* **lied** to say something that is not true in order to deceive ○ [I] *Both witnesses lied to the police about what happened.* ○ [T always + adv/prep] *She lied her way past the guards.* ○ See also: LIAR
lie /lɑɪ/ *n* [C] ○ *Her report is full of lies and misinformation.*

IDIOM with **lie**

• **lie low** to hide so you will not be found ○ *The gunmen were lying low until the sheriff left town.*

PHRASAL VERBS with **lie**

• **lie ahead (of** *someone***)** to be in the future ○ *We don't know what lies ahead.* ○ *You graduate today, and an exciting future lies ahead of you.*
• **lie behind** *something* to cause or be the reason for something ○ *I wonder what lay behind his decision to quit school.*

lie detector *n* [C] a piece of equipment used to try to discover if someone is lying

lieu **IDIOM** /luː/
• **in lieu of** instead of ○ *The company is allowing workers to receive cash in lieu of vacation time.*

lieutenant /luːˈten·ənt/ *n* [C] a naval officer of middle rank, above an ENSIGN; or a military officer of the lowest rank

lieutenant governor *n* [C] a state government official whose rank is just below the governor

life **TIME BEING ALIVE** /lɑɪf/ *n* [C/U] *pl* **lives** **1** the period between birth and death, or the state of being alive ○ [U] *Life is too short to worry about money!* ○ [C] *Cats are supposed to have nine lives.* **2** Life is also anything that is alive: [U] *animal/plant life* **3** If you believe in **life after death**, you believe that a person continues to exist in some way after dying.
lifeless /ˈlɑɪ·fləs/ *adj* dead or appearing to be dead ○ *a lifeless body* ○ (*fig.*) *The performance was boring and lifeless* (= lacking interest or energy).
lifelike /ˈlɑɪ·flɑɪk/ *adj* seeming real or seeming to be alive ○ *The mask was so lifelike it was frightening.*

EXPERIENCE /lɑɪf/ *n* [C/U] a particular type or part of someone's experience ○ [U] *She appreciates life in the United States.* ○ [U] *A vacation is a pleasant change from everyday life.* ○ [C] *He rarely talks about his private life.*

TIME SOMETHING WORKS /lɑɪf/ *n* [U] the period during which a machine or object that produces power works ○ *The newer batteries have a much longer life – up to 100 hours.*

L

ENERGY /lɑɪf/ *n* [U] energy or enthusiasm ○ *The show was full of life.*

WORD FAMILY life

Nouns	life	*Adjectives*	lifeless
Adverbs	lifelessly		lifelike
			lifelong

lifeblood /ˈlɑɪf·blʌd/ *n* [U] the thing that is most important to the continuing success and existence of something else ○ *Tourism is the lifeblood of Hawaii's economy.*

lifeboat /ˈlɑɪf·boʊt/ *n* [C] a large boat that is kept ready to take out to sea and save people who are in danger, or a smaller boat kept on a ship for people to leave in if the ship is not safe or might sink

life expectancy *n* [U] ***social studies*** the average length of the life of members of a group of people or animals

lifeguard /ˈlɑɪf·gɑrd/ *n* [C] a person on a beach or at a swimming pool whose job is to make certain that the people who swim are safe and to save them if they are in danger

life insurance *n* [U] a system in which you make regular payments to an INSURANCE company in exchange for a fixed amount of money that will be paid after you die to someone you chose

life jacket /ˈlɑɪf ˌdʒæk·ət/, **life vest** /ˈlɑɪf·vest/ *n* [C] a piece of equipment that looks like a jacket without sleeves and that is filled with air or light material designed to help someone float if the person falls into the water

lifeline /ˈlɑɪ·flɑɪn/ *n* [C] something, esp. a way of getting help, on which you depend ○ *Airplanes are this Alaskan town's lifeline.*

lifelong, **life-long** /ˈlɑɪf ˈlɔːŋ/ *adj* [not gradable] lasting for the whole of a person's life ○ *He's had a lifelong interest in science.*

life preserver /ˈlɑɪf·prɪˌzɜr·vər/ *n* [C] a large ring or jacket without sleeves made of material that floats and that you can put around your chest to keep you from sinking in the water

life-size, **life-sized** *adj* [not gradable] (of statues, models, etc.) having the same size as the person or thing that it represents: *a life-size plastic manikin*

lifestyle, **life-style** /ˈlɑɪf·stɑɪl/ *n* [C] the particular way that a person or group lives and the values and ideas supported by that person or group ○ *Ask yourself how much your job enhances your lifestyle.*

life support *n* [U] the equipment used to keep a dangerously ill person alive

life-threatening *adj* able to cause death ○ *a life-threatening experience/illness*

lifetime /ˈlɑɪf·tɑɪm/ *n* [U] the period of time during which someone lives or something exists ○ *The watch is high quality and should last a lifetime.*

lift RAISE /lɪft/ *v* [I/T] to move something from a lower to a higher position ○ [T] *I can't lift you up – you're a big boy now!* ○ [I always + adv/prep] *The top of the stool lifts off* (= can be removed) *so you can store things in it.* ○ [T] *She lifted the baby out of her chair.* ○ [T] (*fig.*) *Nothing, it seemed, could lift his spirits* (= make him feel happier).

lift /lɪft/ *n* [C] **1** [C] (*fig.*) *She'd been feeling depressed, but hearing that she got the job gave her spirits a lift* (= made her happier). **2** *Br* A lift is an ELEVATOR.

JOURNEY /lɪft/ *n* [C] *infml* a free trip in another person's vehicle, esp. a car ○ *Can I give you a lift home?*

GO AWAY /lɪft/ *v* [I] (of fog or rain) to go away until none is left ○ *The morning mist had lifted and the sun was shining.*

END /lɪft/ *v* [T] to end a rule or law ○ *They finally lifted the ban on baggy jeans at my school.*

STEAL /lɪft/ *v* [T] *infml* to steal something ○ *He lifted whole paragraphs verbatim from my book.*

IDIOM with lift

• **not lift a finger** to not make any effort ○ *He just watches TV and never lifts a finger to help with the dishes.*

liftoff, **lift-off** /ˈlɪft·ɔːf/ *n* [C] the moment when a space vehicle leaves the ground

ligament /ˈlɪg·ə·mənt/ *n* [C] any of the strong strips of tissue in the body that connect various bones together, that limit movements in joints, and that support muscles and other tissue ○ *She tore a ligament in her knee while she was playing basketball.* ➤ Picture: **joint**

ligation /lɑɪˈgeɪ·ʃən/ *n* [C/U] ***biology*** the process by which two pieces of DNA (= chemical in cells) are joined

light ENERGY /lɑɪt/ *n* [C/U] **1** the energy from the sun or fire and from electrical devices that allows you to see clearly ○ [U] *Light was streaming through the windows.* ○ [U] *The light was so bright that it hurt my eyes.* **2** A light is also anything that provides light, esp. an electric LAMP: [C] *Don't forget to turn off the lights when you leave.* **3** A light is also a TRAFFIC LIGHT: *Let's go – you've got a green light.*

light /lɑɪt/ *v* [T] *past* **lit**, **lighted** ○ *The house was lit with candles for the dinner party.*

light /lɑɪt/ *adj* [-er/-est only] ○ *It was still light out at eight in the evening.*

lighting /ˈlɑɪt̬·ɪŋ/ *n* [U] the lights in a room or on a stage, or the effects of those lights ○ *The lighting in the living room is too dim.*

FLAME /lɑɪt/ *n* [U] a device used to produce a flame, such as a MATCH ○ *Excuse me, have you got a light?*

light /lɑɪt/ *v* [I/T] *past* **lit**, **lighted** ○ [I] *I can't get the barbecue to light.* ○ [T] *I tried to light the fire, but the wood was wet.*

lighter /ˈlɑɪt̬·ər/ *n* [C] a small device that provides a flame

NOT HEAVY /lɑɪt/ *adj* [-er/-est only] **1** having little weight; not heavy ○ *This suitcase is pretty light.* ○ *Ty's a few pounds lighter than he used to be.* **2** Clothes that are light are made of thin material which allows you to be cool: *a light summer dress* **3** A light meal is a small one: *a light snack*

lighten /ˈlɑɪt·ᵊn/ *v* [T] **1** to reduce the weight of something ○ *He lost 30 pounds to lighten the burden on his knee.* **2** To lighten is also to make an amount of work or a responsibility less heavy: *To lighten the load, he decided to divide the job between two people.*

NOT FAT, **lite** /lɑɪt/ *adj* (of food) having less fat or fewer CALORIES than usual ○ *light cream cheese*

NOT SERIOUS /lɑɪt/ *adj* [-er/-est only] intended to entertain; not serious ○ *Take along some light reading for the trip.*

lighten /ˈlɑɪt·ᵊn/ *v* [T] to become or make someone happier and less anxious ○ *Being with friends lightened her mood.*

lightly /ˈlɑɪt·li/ *adv* without serious consideration ○ *Funding for public schools is something I don't take lightly.*

NOT A LOT /lɑɪt/ *adj* [-er/-est only] **1** not great in strength or amount; slight ○ *a light rain* ○ *light traffic* ○ *The doctor said it was OK to take light exercise, such as walking.* **2** A light sentence in prison is a short one. **3** Tastes and smells described as light are not obvious: *a light scent of wildflowers* **4** A **light eater/drinker** eats or drinks only a little.

lightly /ˈlɑɪt·li/ *adv* **1** *She patted the dog lightly on the head.* **2** If food is lightly cooked, it is cooked for only a short time.

PALE /lɑɪt/ *adj, adv* [-er/-est only] (of colors) pale ○ *a light-colored car* ○ *The walls were light green.*

lighten /ˈlɑɪt·ᵊn/ *v* [T] ○ *Do you think he lightens his hair?*

WORD FAMILY light

Nouns	light lighter lighting lightness	*Adjectives*	light
		Verbs	light lighten
		Adverbs	lightly

IDIOMS with light

- **in (the) light of** because or as a result of ○ *In light of the problems we're having, we have no choice but to close the business.*
- **light a fire under** *someone* to get someone to act quickly or forcefully, esp. someone who has not been doing enough before ○ *Coach tried to light a fire under the team in his halftime speech.*
- **(as) light as a feather** extremely light ○ *I can pick you up easily – you're as light as a feather.*
- **light at the end of the tunnel** hope of success, happiness, or help after a long period of difficulty ○ *After four years struggling as a grad student, Sujata could see the light at the end of the tunnel.*
- **lighten up** stop being so serious ○ *Why don't you just relax and enjoy yourself? Lighten up!*

PHRASAL VERBS with light

- **light up LOOK HAPPY** to look happy ○ *Rosa's face lit up when she saw the dog.*
- **light up** *something* **CIGARETTE** [M] to start a cigarette burning
- **light up** *something* **MAKE BRIGHT** [M] to make something bright or shiny ○ *When I'd say there was a letter for him you could see his eyes light up.*

light bulb, **lightbulb** /ˈlɑɪt·bʌlb/ *n* [C] a rounded glass container that produces light when an electric current is passed through it

lighter /ˈlɑɪt̬·ər/ *n* ○ See at LIGHT **FLAME**

lightheaded, **light-headed** /ˈlɑɪtˌhed·əd/ *adj* having a feeling that you may fall over or become unconscious ○ *If I don't eat something at lunchtime I start to feel lightheaded by midafternoon.*

lighthearted, **light-hearted** /ˈlɑɪtˌhɑrt̬·əd/ *adj* amusing and not serious ○ *The documentary takes a lighthearted look at the world of filmmaking.*

lighthouse /ˈlɑɪt·hɑʊs/ *n* [C] *pl* **lighthouses** a tall structure by the sea with a flashing light that warns ships of dangerous rocks or shows them the way into a port

lighting /ˈlɑɪt̬·ɪŋ/ *n* ○ See at LIGHT **ENERGY**

lightning ELECTRIC FLASH /ˈlɑɪt·nɪŋ/ *n* [U] **1** a flash of bright light in the sky produced by electricity moving within or between clouds, or between clouds and the ground ○ *That tree was struck by lightning in a recent thunderstorm.* **2** A **lightning bolt** or **bolt of lightning** is a particular flash of bright light seen in the sky.

FAST /ˈlɑɪt·nɪŋ/ *adj* [not gradable] very fast ○ *She moves at lightning speed.*

lightning bug *n* [C] a FIREFLY

lightning rod STRIP OF METAL *n* [C] a strip of metal that prevents lightning from damaging a building by directing the electricity into the ground

CRITICIZED PERSON *n* [C] someone who attracts criticism or anger that could be directed at someone else ○ *Darman continues to be the White House's lightning rod, drawing criticism from conservatives.*

lightweight LESS WEIGHT /ˈlɑɪt·weɪt/ *adj* (esp. of clothes) weighing little and therefore not warm ○ *a lightweight jacket*

NOT IMPORTANT /ˈlɑɪt·weɪt/ *adj* (of a person) of little importance, or (of ideas) without serious thought or purpose ○ *The movie was a lightweight comedy.*

lightweight /ˈlɑɪt·weɪt/ *n* [C] ○ *She's changed from a lightweight into a tough competitor.*

light year *n* [C] ***earth science*** **1** the great distance that light travels in one year; about 5,880,000,000,000 miles or 9,460,000,000,000 kilometers **2** People sometimes say light years to talk about an extremely long distance or time: *When I was a young man, being 50 seemed light years away.*

like ENJOY /lɑɪk/ *v* [T] **1** to enjoy or approve of something or someone, or to prefer something a particular way ○ *I like your new haircut.* ○ *Do you like fish?* ○ *I like taking my time in the morning.* ○ *I like my music loud.* **2** Like can be used with "how" when asking for someone's reaction to something: *How do you like my new shoes?*

likable, **likeable** /ˈlɑɪ·kə·bəl/ *adj* easy to like ○ *Cassius was a likable, friendly youngster.*

likes /laɪks/ *pl n* the things that you enjoy ○ *She knows her children's likes and dislikes.*
liking /ˈlɑɪ·kɪŋ/ *n* [U] ○ *The dessert was a bit sweet for my liking.*

WORD CHOICES like

If a person likes someone or something very much, you can use the verbs **love** and **adore**.

I ***adore/love*** *seafood.*

Oliver ***loves*** *animals.*

Kate ***adored*** *her grandfather.*

When a person likes someone very much, you could say that person **thinks the world of** someone or has a **soft spot for** someone.

I've always had a ***soft spot for*** *Rebecca ever since she was tiny.*

Annabel's like a daughter to him – he ***thinks the world of*** *her.*

The expression **be fond of** is sometimes used to talk about someone or something that you like.

She's very ***fond of*** *Chinese food.*

I think she's very ***fond of*** *you.*

The phrasal verbs **grow on, take to,** or **warm up to** can be used when someone starts to like someone or something.

I wasn't sure about the color at first, but it's ***growing on*** *me.*

For some reason, I just didn't ***take to/warm up to*** *him.*

The expressions **take a shine to** or **take a liking to** are sometimes used when someone immediately likes someone or something

I think he's ***taken a*** *bit of a* ***shine to*** *you.*

When someone likes something very much but knows it is not good to like it, you could say that the person has a **weakness** for it.

I have a ***weakness*** *for chocolate so I'm never going to lose weight.*

WANT /lɑɪk/ *v* [I/T] to want something ○ [T] *I'd like the chicken soup, please.* ○ [+ *to* infinitive] *The commissioner would like to say thanks to everyone who's helped.* ○ [T] *Would you like* (= Do you want) *something to drink?* ○ **USAGE:** Used with "would" to ask for something or express something in a polite way.

SIMILAR TO /lɑɪk/ *prep, conjunction* **1** similar to; in the same way or manner as ○ *I've got a sweater just like yours.* ○ *Stop acting like a jerk!* ○ *She looks just like her father.* ○ (*infml*) **Like I said** (= As I already said), *I'm not interested in buying insurance at the moment.* **2** If you ask what something is like, you are asking someone to describe it or compare it to something: *What's your new job like?* ○ *What does it taste like?*
-like /ˌlɑɪk/ *suffix* ○ *with catlike quickness* ○ *a ball-like shape*
likeness /ˈlɑɪk·nəs/ *n* [C] **1** a similarity ○ *Sandy bears a much stronger likeness to her mother than to her father.* **2** A painting, photograph, or other representation described as a good likeness looks very similar to the person or thing it represents.
like /lɑɪk/ *n* [U]

WILLING TO /lɑɪk/ *prep* willing to; in the mood for ○ *I don't feel like going out tonight.*

TYPICAL OF /lɑɪk/ *prep* typical or characteristic of; to be expected of ○ *It's not like you to be so quiet – are you all right?*

SUCH AS /lɑɪk/ *prep* such as; for example ○ *I prefer natural fabrics like cotton and wool.* ○ *Alonzo is not the kind of guy who would do something like this.*
likes /lɑɪks/, **like** /lɑɪk/ *pl n*

AS IF /lɑɪk/ *prep, conjunction* as if it will or was; in a way that suggests ○ *It looks like rain.* ○ *It sounds to me like you ought to change jobs.*

PAUSE /lɑɪk/ *adv* [not gradable] *not standard* **1** used in conversation to emphasize what follows, or when you cannot express your exact meaning ○ *He's, like, really friendly – someone you can talk to.* ○ *It was, like, getting pretty late but I didn't want to go home yet.* **2** Like is also used in conversation to introduce someone else's words or your own words: *So I'm telling Patti about my class and she's like, No way, and I'm like, It happened.*

WORD FAMILY like

Nouns	like likes liking likeness likelihood dislike	*Verbs*	like dislike
		Adverbs	like likely
		Prepositions	like
Adjectives	likeable likely	*Conjunctions*	like
		Suffixes	-like

IDIOMS with like

• **and the like** and other similar things ○ *There are courts for tennis and badminton and the like.*
• *something* **is like looking for a needle in a haystack** something is extremely difficult to find ○ *With 500 channels on TV, finding quality children's shows is like looking for a needle in a haystack.*
• **like clockwork** exactly as planned ○ *So far, everything had worked like clockwork.*
• **like crazy, like mad** a lot or very quickly ○ *Mark's working like crazy to get the house painted by the end of the week.*
• **like the sound of** *something* to feel happy or satisfied about a piece of information you have just heard ○ *"The radio says there'll be rain turning into snow." "Ooh, I don't like the sound of that."*
• **like there's no tomorrow** as much or as fast as possible, without planning or thinking first ○ *The minute he got paid, he started spending money like there's no tomorrow.*
• **like wildfire** quickly in a way that cannot be controlled ○ *News of the layoffs spread like wildfire through the company.*
• **the likes of** *someone/something* someone or something that is equal to or as important as the person or thing being mentioned ○ *We haven't seen the likes of Muhammad Ali since he retired.* ○ *They're competing with the likes of IBM and Unisys.*

likely /ˈlɑɪ·kli/ *adj* expected to happen; probable ○ [+ *to* infinitive] *If I don't write it down, I'm likely to forget.*
likely /ˈlɑɪ·kli/ *adv* probably ○ *I'll most likely get there at about ten o'clock.*

likelihood /ˈlɑɪ·kliːˌhʊd/ *n* [U] probability ○ *There's little likelihood of a compromise.*

WORD FAMILY likely			
Nouns	likelihood	*Adjectives*	likely
Adverbs	likely		unlikely

like-minded *adj* (of people) sharing the same opinions, ideas, or interests ○ *She is a football fan who started a magazine for like-minded women.*

likewise Ⓐ /ˈlɑɪ·kwɑɪz/ *adv* [not gradable] in the same way or manner; similarly ○ *We put up a fence, and other neighbors did likewise.*

lilac /ˈlɑɪ·lək, -læk, -lɑk/ *n* [C] a bush or small tree with sweet-smelling purple or white flowers

lilting /ˈlɪl·tɪŋ/ *adj* (of a voice or a piece of music) rising and falling in a regular or rhythmic way ○ *"It's about time you showed up," he says to Eddie in a lilting, teasing voice.*

lily /ˈlɪl·i/ *n* [C] a plant with large, usually bell-shaped flowers on long stems

lima bean /ˈlɑɪ·məˌbiːn/ *n* [C] an edible, flat, pale green bean

limb **ARM OR LEG** /lɪm/ *n* [C] *fml* an arm or leg of a person or animal, or an animal's wing

BRANCH /lɪm/ *n* [C] a large branch of a tree

limber /ˈlɪm·bər/ *adj* able to bend and move easily ○ *Good posture makes your muscles more limber.*

PHRASAL VERB with limber

• **limber up** *(something)* [M] to stretch your muscles by exercise, esp. in preparation for sports ○ *We limber up with a few tosses back and forth.* ○ *A short jog should limber you up.*

limbo **IDIOM** /ˈlɪm·boʊ/

• **in limbo** in a situation where you do not know what will happen or when something will happen ○ *We were in limbo for weeks while the jury tried to make a decision in the case.*

lime **FRUIT** /lɑɪm/ *n* [C/U] a green, oval fruit whose juice has a sour taste

CHEMICAL /lɑɪm/ *n* [U] a white powdery substance used in building materials and to improve earth for crops

limelight /ˈlɑɪm·lɑɪt/ *n* [U] public attention and interest ○ *He always tried to avoid the limelight.*

limerick /ˈlɪm·ə·rɪk/ *n* [C] a humorous poem with five lines, the first two lines having the same final sound as the last line

limestone /ˈlɑɪm·stoʊn/ *n* [U] a gray rock formed from the shells of sea animals, used in buildings and making CEMENT

limit /ˈlɪm·ət/ *n* [C] the greatest amount, number, or level allowed or possible ○ *There's a limit to her patience.* ○ *Two cups of coffee are my limit.* ○ *Spending limits were imposed by the mayor.*

limit /ˈlɪm·ət/ *v* [T] to control something so that it is not greater than a particular amount, number, or level ○ *I have to limit my talk to 20 minutes.*

limitation /ˌlɪm·əˈteɪ·ʃən/ *n* [C/U] the act of controlling, or something that controls ○ [C] *The major limitation of early record players was the short playing time of the records.* ○ [U] *They favor anything that involves limitation of government control.*

limited /ˈlɪm·ət̬·əd/ *adj* **1** *There are a limited (= small) number of bikes available in that store.* **2** Limited also means kept within a particular size, range, time, or group: *The advanced course is limited to those who have already taken the introductory course.*

WORD FAMILY limit			
Nouns	limit	*Adjectives*	limited
	limitation		unlimited
Verbs	limit		

limited monarchy *n* [C] ***politics & government*** a CONSTITUTIONAL MONARCHY

limousine /ˌlɪm·əˈziːn, ˈlɪm·əˌziːn/, *short form* **limo** /ˈlɪm·oʊ/ *n* [C] **limos** a large, comfortable car, or a small bus that takes people to and from an airport

limp **WALK** /lɪmp/ *v* [I] to walk with an irregular step, esp. because your foot or leg is hurt ○ *Jackson limped off the field after injuring his ankle.*

limp /lɪmp/ *n* [U] ○ *He walks with a slight limp.*

NOT FIRM /lɪmp/ *adj* [*-er/-est* only] not firm or stiff ○ *The lettuce in this salad is completely limp.*

linchpin /ˈlɪntʃ·pɪn/ *n* [C] a person or thing that is the most important part of a group or system's operation ○ *The city's River Park is the linchpin of its efforts to sell itself as a vacation destination.*

line **LONG MARK** /lɑɪn/ *n* [C] **1** a long, thin mark on the surface of something ○ *Draw a straight line.* ○ *You shouldn't drive across the double yellow lines.* ○ *As I grow older, lines and wrinkles show on my face.* **2** ***geometry*** A line is a row of POINTS that continues in both directions and is usually represented by a long thin mark.

linear /ˈlɪn·iː·ər/ *adj* [not gradable] consisting of or related to straight lines ○ *The garden has very linear paths.* ○ See also: LINEAR LENGTH; LINEAR REASONABLE

EDGE /lɑɪn/ *n* [C] **1** a real or imaginary mark that forms the edge, border, or limit of something ○ *The police caught him before he crossed the state line.* **2** A line is also a mark on a sports field which shows where things can or cannot happen, or which measures the field: *the foul line* ○ *the 50-yard line* ○ *the free-throw line*

STRING /lɑɪn/ *n* [C] a length of string, rope, or wire that is used to support something ○ *fishing line* ○ *Would you help me hang the wash out on the line?*

ROW /lɑɪn/ *n* [C] **1** a row of people or things ○ *There was a long line at the movie theater.* ○ *Just get* **in/on line** *and wait your turn.* **2** In football, the lines are the two front rows of opposing players who face one another at the start of a play: *the offensive/defensive line*

line /lɑɪn/ *v* [T] ○ *People lined the streets along the parade route.* ○ *The long driveway was lined with trees.*

L

SERIES /lɑɪn/ *n* [C usually sing] a series of people, esp. members of the same family, following one another in time ○ *He comes from a long line of doctors.*

COVER /lɑɪn/ *v* [T] to cover the inside surface of an object with another material ○ *I lined the kitchen cabinets with shelf paper.*

lining /ˈlɑɪ·nɪŋ/ *n* [C] material that covers the inside surface of something ○ *The lining of my jacket is torn.*

MILITARY /lɑɪn/ *n* [C] a row of military positions, particularly the ones closest to enemy positions ○ *the front line* ○ *behind enemy lines*

WIRE/CONNECTION /lɑɪn/ *n* [C] an electrical or telephone wire or connection ○ *Power lines were down after the storm.* ○ *That line is busy – may I take a message?*

PIPE /lɑɪn/ *n* [C] a system of pipes ○ *a water/gas line*

RAILROAD /lɑɪn/ *n* [C] a train route, or a railroad track ○ *rail/commuter lines*

COMPANY /lɑɪn/ *n* [C] a company that has an organized system of transport by ship, truck, aircraft, or bus ○ *a shipping line*

liner /ˈlɑɪ·nər/ *n* [C] a large ship operated by a transport company ○ *an ocean/cruise liner*

L

WORDS /lɑɪn/ *n* [C] **1** a row of words that form part of a text ○ *Limericks are humorous five-line poems.* **2** A line is also a short written message: *Drop me a line when you get a chance.* **3** A line is also a remark that is intended to amuse, persuade, or deceive: *He gave me some line about how his father is the mayor.* **4** Lines are also the words that actors speak when performing.

DIRECTION /lɑɪn/ *n* [C usually sing] a direction or path ○ *Fortunately, the pedestrian wasn't in the line of fire.*

WAY OF DEALING /lɑɪn/ *n* [C] a way of dealing with or thinking about something or someone ○ *I couldn't follow his line of reasoning.*

JOB /lɑɪn/ *n* [C] a job, interest, or activity ○ *"What line of work are you in?" "I'm a teacher."*

GOODS /lɑɪn/ *n* [C] a type of goods ○ *Our new swimwear line will be in stores shortly.*

IDIOMS with line

• **a fine line, a thin line** a very small difference between two things that may seem different ○ *There's sometimes a very thin line between love and hate.* ○ *As a comedian, I'm always walking that fine line between humor and sarcasm* (= finding a balance between them).

• **in line for** *something* likely to get a job or benefit ○ *I'm in line for a promotion.*

• **in line with** *something* similar to ○ *We try to keep our prices in line with our competitors.*

• **in the line of duty** while doing what was expected in a particular job ○ *A police officer was killed in the line of duty.* ○ **USAGE:** Used mostly about police officers, soldiers, and other people who do dangerous work.

• **line** *your* **pocket(s)** to make money esp. by using dishonest, immoral, or illegal methods ○ *Some of these lawyers are only interested in lining their pockets.*

• **on the line 1** at risk of failing or being harmed ○ *His job is on the line.* ○ *Firefighters regularly put their lives on the line.* **2 On the line** also means speaking on the telephone: *My mom was on the line, but I could hear my dad talking in the background.*

PHRASAL VERBS with line

• **line up** *(someone/something)* **FORM LINE** [M] to form a line, or form people or things into a line ○ *All the students were lining up for lunch.* ○ *The photographer lined the family members up for a picture.*

• **line** *someone/something* **up ORGANIZE** [M] to organize or arrange for something to be done ○ *Have you lined up a band to play at the party?*

lineage /ˈlɪn·iː·ɪdʒ/ *n* [U] ***biology*** all the living things that are related directly to the same living thing that existed long ago

linear LENGTH /ˈlɪn·iː·ər/ *adj* [not gradable] relating to length, rather than area or volume ○ *This carpet costs $12 per linear foot.* ○ See also: LINEAR at LINE LONG MARK

REASONABLE /ˈlɪn·iː·ər/ *adj* (esp. of stories or ideas) continuing in a clear and reasonable way from one part to the next ○ *The book offers excitement, linear plot development, and dramatic descriptions.* ○ See also: LINEAR at LINE LONG MARK

linear equation *n* [C] ***algebra*** an EQUATION (= mathematical statement) with a result that when it is put on a GRAPH (= drawing) forms a straight line

linebacker /ˈlɑɪn ˌbæk·ər/ *n* [C] (in football) a player on defense who tries to stop players from the other team from moving the ball along the field ○ *a middle/outside linebacker*

line-item veto *n* [C/U] ***politics & government*** the power to VETO (= not allow) a single item in a planned new law without vetoing the whole new law

lineman /ˈlɑɪn·mən/ *n* [C] *pl* **-men** (in football) a player on the forward line who protects other members of the team and stops plays by the opposing team

linen /ˈlɪn·ən/ *n* **1** strong cloth that is woven from plant fibers ○ [U] *a linen jacket* **2** Linens are cloth items for the home, such as sheets and TABLECLOTHS, made from linen or a similar material like cotton.

line of scrimmage *n* [C usually sing] an imaginary line along which football teams face each other at the start of each play

line segment *n* [C] ***geometry*** a section of a line between two POINTS

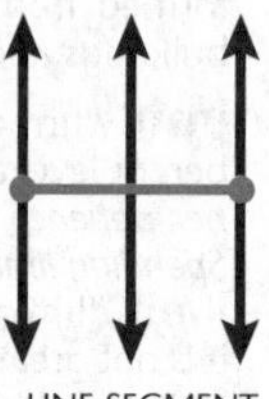
LINE SEGMENT

lineup /ˈlɑɪ·nʌp/ *n* [C] **1** a group of people that has been brought together to form a team or take part in an event ○ *the starting lineup for today's game* ○ *a star-*

studded lineup of guests on the show **2** A lineup is also a row of people brought together by the police so that a person who saw a crime can recognize the criminal among them.

linger /ˈlɪŋ·gər/ *v* [I] to take longer than usual to leave or disappear ○ *We went to small cafes where we could linger over cappuccino.* ○ *The smell lingered in the kitchen for days.*
lingering /ˈlɪŋ·gə·rɪŋ/ *adj* [not gradable] ○ *She has lingering doubts about his ability to do the job.*

lingerie /ˌlɑn·dʒəˈreɪ, ˌlɑ̃·ʒə-, -ˈriː/ *n* [U] women's underwear or clothing worn in bed

lingo /ˈlɪŋ·goʊ/ *n* [C] *pl* **lingoes** *infml* language containing SLANG (= informal language) or technical expressions, or a foreign language ○ *In typical Hollywood lingo, he said, "This is gonna be big."*

linguist /ˈlɪŋ·gwəst/ *n* [C] someone who studies the structure and development of language, or someone who knows several languages
linguistic /lɪŋˈgwɪs·tɪk/ *adj* [not gradable] connected with language or the study of language ○ *linguistic analysis*
linguistics /lɪŋˈgwɪs·tɪks/ *n* [U] the study of the structure and development of language in general or of particular languages

lining /ˈlɑɪ·nɪŋ/ *n* ○ See at LINE COVER

link Ⓐ CONNECTION /lɪŋk/ *n* [C] a connection between two things ○ *There is a clear link between poverty and malnutrition.* ○ *A high-speed rail link brings you to the airport.*
link Ⓐ /lɪŋk/ *v* [I/T] ○ [I] *Various activities have been linked to global warming.* ○ [T] *This is the only bridge linking the island with the mainland.*
linkage Ⓐ /ˈlɪŋ·kɪdʒ/ *n* [C/U] a connection, or the action of connecting ○ [C] *There's a direct linkage between cultural values and the way people live.*
CHAIN /lɪŋk/ *n* [C] one of the rings in a chain
WORD /lɪŋk/ *n* [C] a word or image on a WEBSITE that can take you to another document or website
link /lɪŋk/ *v* [I/T] ○ [T] *Linking your website to ours will benefit your site.*

PHRASAL VERB with link

• **link up** *(something)* [M] to connect or combine with something ○ *He's linking up small businesses in Harlem with big ones in midtown.*

linking verb *n* [C] a verb that connects the subject of a sentence to the properties in the PREDICATE ○ *In the sentence "My suitcase weighs 45 pounds," "weighs" is a linking verb.*

linoleum /ləˈnoʊ·liː·əm/ *n* [U] a hard, smooth floor covering

lint /lɪnt/ *n* [U] small, loose cloth fibers or pieces of thread ○ *My black sweater is covered with lint.*

Linux /ˈlɪn·əks/ *n* [U] *trademark* a program for operating a computer that users are allowed to change or improve as they choose

lion /ˈlɑɪ·ən/, *female* **lioness** /ˈlɑɪ·ə·nəs/ *n* [C] a large, strong animal of the cat family from Africa and Asia which has yellow-brown fur, the male having a large MANE (= long neck fur)

IDIOM with lion

• **the lion's share of** *something* the largest part of something ○ *She didn't do much, but she got the lion's share of the attention from the teachers.*

lip BODY PART /lɪp/ *n* [C] **1** either of the two edges of flesh around the opening of the mouth ○ *She licked/pursed/puckered her lips.* **2 Lip gloss** is a makeup put on the lips to make them shiny.
EDGE /lɪp/ *n* [C] the edge of a container or opening, esp. the part of the edge used for pouring
SPEECH /lɪp/ *n* [U] *slang* speech that is rude and shows a lack of respect ○ *Don't give me any more of your lip.*

IDIOM with lip

• *your* **lips are sealed** you will not talk about something ○ *"I want the party to be a surprise." "Don't worry, my lips are sealed."*

lipase /ˈlɑɪ·peɪs, -peɪz/ *n* [U] ***biology*** a substance that is produced mainly in the PANCREAS (= body organ) and helps the body to digest LIPIDS (= fats and oils)

lipid /ˈlɪp·əd/ *n* [C] ***biology*** a substance that is an important part of living cells, mainly in the form of fat or oil

lip-read *v* [I] to understand what someone is saying by watching the movements of the mouth

lip service *n* [U] to publicly support or approve of something, while actually taking no action to produce it ○ *A lot of adults pay lip service to the idea that it is important to listen to teenagers' ideas, but they tend to listen and then forget.* ○ *Is this a real promise, or is this just lip service?*

lipstick /ˈlɪp·stɪk/ *n* [C/U] a makeup for coloring a person's lips, usually enclosed in a tube

liquefy, **liquify** /ˈlɪk·wəˌfɑɪ/ *v* [I/T] to become or make something liquid ○ [I] *Gases liquefy under pressure.*

liqueur /lɪˈkɜr, -ˈkjʊr, -ˈkʊr/ *n* [C] any of several strong, sweet alcoholic drinks that are usually drunk in small amounts after a meal

liquid SUBSTANCE /ˈlɪk·wəd/ *n* [C/U] ***chemistry, earth science*** a substance that flows easily and is neither a gas nor a solid
liquid /ˈlɪk·wəd/ *adj* [not gradable] ***chemistry, earth science*** ○ *liquid oxygen/hydrogen* ○ *The metal mercury is liquid at room temperature.*
MONEY /ˈlɪk·wəd/ *adj* [not gradable] in the form of money, rather than investments or property, or able to be changed into money easily ○ *liquid assets*
liquidate /ˈlɪk·wəˌdeɪt/ *v* [T] **1** *Investors have started to liquidate their mutual funds* (= sell them). **2** Someone who liquidates a business closes it and sells what it owns.
liquidation /ˌlɪk·wəˈdeɪ·ʃən/ *n* [U] ○ *The company was forced into liquidation.*

liquify /ˈlɪk·wəˌfɑɪ/ *v* to LIQUEFY

L

liquor /ˈlɪk·ər/ *n* [U] an alcoholic drink, esp. one that has been DISTILLED (= heated to a gas, then cooled to a liquid)

lisp /lɪsp/ *v* [I/T] to pronounce "s" and "z" sounds like "th," so that "sin" sounds like "thin" and "Zen" sounds like "then"
lisp /lɪsp/ *n* [C] ○ *I was teased at school because I spoke with a lisp.*

list RECORD /lɪst/ *n* [C] a record of short pieces of information usually arranged one below the other so that they can be read easily or counted ○ *I have a long list of things we need to get for our new house.*
list /lɪst/ *v* [T] ○ *The professor gave us a handout in which she listed the books we were supposed to read for the course.*
listing /ˈlɪs·tɪŋ/ *n* [C] an item in a list of information that is published regularly ○ *To find the correct TV channel, check the listings in your local newspaper.*

LEAN /lɪst/ *v* [I] (esp. of a ship) to lean to one side ○ *The tanker is listing badly and may sink.*

listen /ˈlɪs·ən/ *v* [I] to give attention to something you can hear or to a person who is speaking ○ *Can you really listen to music while you do your homework?* ○ *Listen, we really need to do something about having this place painted.*
listener /ˈlɪs·ə·nər/ *n* [C] ○ *For many listeners, the music of the Beatles summed up the sentiments of the 1960s.*

USAGE
listen, listen to, or hear?
Use **hear** when you want to say that sounds, music, etc. come to your ears. You can **hear** something without wanting to.
I could hear his music through the wall.
Use **listen** to say that you pay attention to sounds or try to hear something.
The audience listened carefully.
Ssh! I'm listening!
Use **listen to** when you want to say what it is that you are trying to hear.
The audience listened to the singer.
Ssh! I'm listening to the radio!

WORD CHOICES **listen**
Hear can sometimes be used instead of "listen."'
*An audience gathered to **hear** him speak.*
If someone listens to another person's conversation without them knowing, the verb **eavesdrop** or the phrasal verb **listen in on** is often used.
*He was **eavesdropping** on our conversation.*
*I wish my brother would stop **listening in on** my phone calls.*
If you want someone to listen until you have said everything you want to say, you could use the phrasal verb **hear someone out**.
*At least **hear me out** before you make up your mind.*

If you suddenly start to listen to something carefully because you have heard something interesting, you could say that you **prick up your ears**.
*I heard my name mentioned and I **pricked up my ears**.*

PHRASAL VERB with listen
• **listen in (on** *something***)** to listen to someone's conversation when the person does not realize you are doing it ○ *She thinks her boss is listening in on her phone conversations.*

listless /ˈlɪst·ləs/ *adj* tired and weak, and lacking energy or interest ○ *As the tennis match continued in the 90° heat, his play grew listless and he made a number of errors.*

lit /lɪt/ *past simple and past participle of* LIGHT ○ *a dimly lit room* (= a room without much light)

litany /ˈlɪt·ᵊn·i/ *n* [C] a long list spoken or given to someone, esp. to someone who has heard or seen it before or finds it boring ○ *She had to hear once again his litany of complaints over how badly he was treated.*

lite /lɑɪt/ *adj* [not gradable] *infml* containing less fat or sugar than similar types of food and therefore less likely to make you increase your weight ○ *lite beer* ○ **USAGE:** This spelling of light is used in advertising products. If used otherwise, it is usually intended to be humorous.

liter /ˈliːt̬·ər/, *abbreviation* **l** *n* [C] a unit of measurement of volume equal to 1.057 quarts

literacy /ˈlɪt̬·ə·rə·si/ *n* [U] **1** the ability to read and write ○ *She was actively involved in programs to increase adult literacy.* **2** Literacy is also a basic skill or knowledge of a subject: *computer literacy*
literate /ˈlɪt̬·ə·rət/ *adj* **1** able to read and write ○ *The man was barely literate and took a long time to write his name.* **2** Literate also means having a good education or showing it in your writing: *He wrote a literate, colorful column and reviewed plays.* **3** Literate also means having a basic skill or knowledge of a subject: *They wanted to make sure their child was computer literate.*

literacy rate *n* [C] ***social studies*** the percentage of people who are able to read and write

literal /ˈlɪt̬·ə·rəl/ *adj* **1** having exactly the same meaning as the basic or original meaning of a word or expression ○ *a literal interpretation of the Constitution* **2** A literal translation of a phrase in another language gives the meaning of each separate word.
literally /ˈlɪt̬·ə·rə·li/ *adv* ○ *Beginning students tend to translate too literally.*

literally /ˈlɪt̬·ə·rə·li/ *adv* [not gradable] **1** used for emphasizing how large or great an amount is ○ *There were literally hundreds of pages to read in the contract.* **2** Literally is also used to emphasize a statement and suggest that it is surprising: *I literally* (= really) *had no idea you and Sophie were coming.*

literary /ˈlɪt̬·əˌrer·i/ *adj* ***literature*** **1** connected with literature ○ *She contributed poems to literary magazines.* **2** Literary analysis is the study of a work of literature by a critic, teacher, or student.

literature WRITING /ˈlɪt̬·ə·rə·tʃər, -ˌtʃʊr/ *n* [U] writing that has lasting value as art ○ *The course in English literature covers Shakespeare's plays.*

INFORMATION /ˈlɪt̬·ə·rə·tʃər, -ˌtʃʊr/ *n* [U] **1** all the information written about a subject ○ *The medical literature is full of examples of accidental discoveries that led to important advances in science.* **2** Literature is also printed material published by a company that informs people about its products or services: *They handed out literature at the meeting about their new software.*

lithe /lɑɪð, lɑɪθ/ *adj* (of a body) thin and attractive, and able to move easily and gracefully ○ *He was a fabulous athlete, full of lithe, quick movements.*

lithium /ˈlɪθ·iː·əm/ *n* [U] ***chemistry*** a soft, gray-white metal that is lighter than other metals

lithosphere /ˈlɪθ·əˌsfɪr/ *n* [C usually sing] ***earth science*** the solid outer layer of the earth
lithospheric /ˌlɪθ·əˈsfɪr·ɪk, -ˈsfer·ɪk/ *adj* [not gradable] ***earth science***

litigate /ˈlɪt̬·əˌgeɪt/ *v* [I/T] *law* to cause an argument between people or groups to be discussed in a law court so that a judgment can be made

litigation /ˌlɪt̬·əˈgeɪ·ʃən/ *n* [U] *law* the process of taking an argument between people or groups to a court of law ○ *Both sides agreed to the settlement to avoid the expense of litigation.*

litmus /ˈlɪt·məs/ *n* [U] ***chemistry*** a powder that is turned red by acid and blue by ALKALI (= substance with the opposite chemical reaction as acid)

litmus test CHEMICAL TEST *n* [C] ***chemistry*** a test of a chemical substance using paper treated with LITMUS, which tells whether a substance is acid or ALKALI

OPINION /ˈlɪt·məsˌtest/ *n* [C] an opinion or action that is thought to show more general opinions or likely future actions ○ *Analysts say the election is a litmus test for democracy in the region.*

litre /ˈliːt̬·ər/ *n* [C] a LITER

litter WASTE /ˈlɪt̬·ər/ *n* [U] pieces of paper and other small objects that have been thrown out and are left on the ground in public places
litter /ˈlɪt̬·ər/ *v* [T] ○ *The park was littered with bottles and soda cans after the concert.*

YOUNG ANIMALS /ˈlɪt̬·ər/ *n* [C] a group of animals born at the same time and having the same mother

litterbug /ˈlɪt̬·ərˌbʌg/ *n* [C] *disapproving* someone who leaves paper, plastic, etc., on the ground in public places

little SMALL /ˈlɪt̬·əl/ *adj* [-*er*/-*est* only] **1** small in size or amount, or brief in time ○ *She has a little room on the top floor where she works on her computer.* ○ *They have very little money.* ○ *It'll take me a little while longer to get ready.* **2** Little can be used with approving words for emphasis: *They have a nice little house.*

little /ˈlɪt̬·əl/ *pronoun, n* [U] **1** a small amount ○ *I could understand very little of what he said.* **2 A little** means a small amount of something: *"Do we have any sugar left?" "A little."* ➤ Usage: **small or little?** at SMALL LESS

> **GRAMMAR**
>
> **little**
>
> When **little** is used before a noun to show how much of the noun there is, remember that it can only be used with uncountable nouns.
>
> *There's very little sugar left.*
>
> ~~*There's very little sausages left.*~~
>
> For countable nouns, use **few** or **not many** instead.
>
> *There are very few sausages left.*

NOT MUCH /ˈlɪt̬·əl/ *adv comparative* **less**, *superlative* **least** **1** not much ○ *The county has done little to improve the traffic problem.* ○ *It's a little-known fact that technically ticks are not insects.* **2 A little** means slightly: *She was a little frightened.* ○ *You're walking a little too fast for me.*

YOUNG /ˈlɪt̬·əl/ *adj* [-*er*/-*est* only] young ○ *When you were little, you and your brother were always fighting.* ○ *My little brother/sister* (= younger brother or sister) *is seven years old.* ○ *He stayed home from work today because his little boy/girl* (= young son or daughter) *is sick.*

NOT IMPORTANT /ˈlɪt̬·əl/ *adj* [not gradable] not important or not serious ○ *I had a little problem with my car, but it's fixed now.*

little finger *n* [C] a PINKIE

Little League *n* [U] an organization of baseball teams in the US for children between the ages of 8 and 12

little toe *n* [C] the smallest of the five toes on your foot

liturgy /ˈlɪt̬·ər·dʒi/ *n* [C/U] a set of words, music, and actions regularly used in religious ceremonies
liturgical /ləˈtɜr·dʒɪ·kəl/ *adj* [not gradable]

livable, **liveable** /ˈlɪv·ə·bəl/ *adj* (esp. of a place) acceptable or good enough ○ *The apartment is far from perfect, but it's livable.*

live HAVE LIFE /lɪv/ *v* [I] to be alive or have life, or to continue in this state ○ *Rembrandt lived in the 17th century.* ○ *This oak tree has been living for over 200 years.*
live /lɑɪv/ *adj* [not gradable] ○ *There was a tank of live lobsters in the restaurant.*
living /ˈlɪv·ɪŋ/ *adj* [not gradable] **1** *Are any of your grandparents living* (= still alive)*?* **2** Living is also used in some expressions to make them stronger: *He's the living image of his father* (= looks exactly like his father).
living /ˈlɪv·ɪŋ/ *pl n* people who are still alive ○ *On this anniversary of the tragedy we remember the living as well as the dead.*

HAVE A HOME /lɪv/ *v* [I always + adv/prep] to have as your home or as the place where you stay or return, esp. to sleep ○ *Where do you live?* ○ *We live in St. Louis now but we used to live in Cincinnati.* ○

L

Freshmen are required to live on campus. ○ *My brother lives with four other people in a big house.*

STAY ALIVE /lɪv/ *v* [I] to stay alive by getting enough money to pay for food, a home, clothing, etc., or to stay alive by eating a particular food ○ *She's so poor – I wonder how she lives.* ○ *While he's studying for the finals, he lives on junk food.* ○ *He's living off the money he inherited from his father.*

living /ˈlɪv·ɪŋ/ *n* [C] the way you earn money; your job ○ *What do you do for a living?* ○ *She's not happy working at the hospital but at least it's a living.*

SPEND LIFE /lɪv/ *v* [always + adv/prep] **1** to spend your life in a particular way ○ [I] *After a while you get used to living alone.* ○ [I] *On his income, they can afford to live well.* ○ [T] *She lived her whole life in a little town in New Mexico.* **2** To live can also mean to have the full experience that life can offer: [I] *If you haven't been to Alaska, you haven't lived.*

AS IT HAPPENS /lɑɪv/ *adj, adv* [not gradable] (of a performance) shown or broadcast to people watching or listening as it is happening, rather than being recorded to be shown or broadcast later ○ *This evening at seven there will be a live telecast of the debate.* ○ *There will be live music* (= people playing music) *at the party.*

ELECTRICITY /lɑɪv/ *adj* [not gradable] carrying or charged with electricity ○ *You'd better test the electric outlet first to see if it's live.*

EXPLODE /lɑɪv/ *adj* [not gradable] able to explode ○ *The army is using live ammunition on these maneuvers.*

WORD FAMILY live			
Nouns	liveliness living	*Verbs*	live outlive relive
Adjectives	live lively living	*Adverbs*	live

IDIOMS with live

• **live and let live** to accept things as they are and not try to change them ○ *We think the best approach to having wolves here is to live and let live.*

• **live it up** to spend a lot of money to enjoy yourself because it is a special time ○ *The kids are away at camp, so we thought we'd live it up and go to Bermuda.*

PHRASAL VERBS with live

• **live down** *something* [M] to make people forget that you made a big mistake or did something very embarrassing in the past ○ *If you show up with green hair, your parents will never let you live it down.*

• **live for** *something* to enjoy something more than anything else that you do ○ *My son lives for sports.*

• **live through** *something* to experience something difficult or painful and continue to live ○ *He may not live through the operation, but it's his only chance.*

• **live together** to share a home ○ *She and her sister live together in Richmond.*

• **live up to** *something* to achieve what is expected, esp. high standards ○ *We expected a lot of her, and her performance lived up to our expectations.*

• **live with** *something* **ACCEPT** to experience and accept an unpleasant event, decision, or situation ○ *When you get arthritis at your age, it's just something you just have to live with.*

• **live with** *someone* **RELATIONSHIP** to share a home with someone ○ *How do you like living with your parents?*

liveable /ˈlɪv·ə·bəl/ *adj* LIVABLE

live-in *adj* [not gradable] living in the home of your employer ○ *We have a live-in nanny who takes care of the children.*

livelihood /ˈlɑɪv·liː ˌhʊd/ *n* [C/U] the way you earn the money you need to pay for food, a place to live, clothing, etc. ○ [C] *They earn their livelihood from farming.*

lively /ˈlɑɪv·li/ *adj* having or showing a lot of energy and enthusiasm, or showing interesting and exciting thought ○ *We have a lively group of seniors who meet to discuss the books they've read.* ○ *Imelda takes a lively interest in politics.*

liveliness /ˈlɑɪv·liː·nəs/ *n* [U]

liven up *something* /ˌlɑɪ·vəˈnʌp/ *phrasal verb* [M] to make something more interesting or attractive ○ *New wallpaper would help to liven up the kitchen.*

liver /ˈlɪv·ər/ *n* [C/U] **1** ***biology*** a large organ in the body that cleans the blood **2** Liver is also this organ from an animal used as meat.

lives /lɑɪvz/ *pl of* LIFE

livestock /ˈlɑɪv·stɑk/ *pl n* animals kept on a farm, such as cows, sheep, chickens, and pigs

live wire *n* [C] someone who is very energetic and has an enthusiastic personality ○ *My sister was the live wire and I was always called "the quiet one."*

livid ANGRY /ˈlɪv·əd/ *adj* extremely angry ○ *The rude letter from his mother-in-law made him livid.*

COLOR /ˈlɪv·əd/ *adj* (esp. of marks on the skin) of a purple or dark blue color, usually caused by an injury ○ *There was a livid bruise on her upper arm where she had fallen.*

living /ˈlɪv·ɪŋ/ *adj, n* ○ See at LIVE **HAVE LIFE**; LIVE **STAY ALIVE**

living room, livingroom *n* [C] the room in a house or apartment where people sit or relax together but do not usually eat or sleep

living will *n* [C] a written document in which you state the types of medical treatment you do not want if you become so ill that you will die soon

lizard /ˈlɪz·ərd/ *n* [C] a REPTILE (= a type of animal that produces eggs) that has a long body, four short legs, and a long tail

llama /ˈlɑm·ə/ *n* [C] a South American animal with a long neck and long hair, used to carry loads and to provide wool

LLC *n* [C] *abbreviation for* limited liability company (= a type of company in which the owners have specific tax advantages and no personal financial risk if the company should fail)

load WEIGHT CARRIED /loʊd/ *n* [C] **1** the amount or weight of something carried by a vehicle, a structure such as a bridge, or a person or animal ○ *The truck had a load of bricks.* ○ *The maximum load for this elevator is eight persons.* **2** ***physics*** Load is also the weight being moved by a LEVER. ➤ Picture: **lever**

load /loʊd/ *v* [T] to put something in or on a vehicle ○ *He could load more hay into the wagon.*

AMOUNT OF WORK /loʊd/ *n* [C] the amount of work to be done by a person ○ *The normal teaching load at this university is three courses each semester.*

PUT INTO /loʊd/ *v* [T] to put into a piece of equipment something it uses to make it work ○ *Bill loaded and aimed his crossbow.* ○ *The technician loaded a sample into the device.* ○ *You need to load the new software before you can use the computer.*

loaded /ˈloʊd·əd/ *adj* [not gradable] ○ *a loaded gun* (= one with bullets in it)

IDIOMS with **load**

• **loaded down with** *things* carrying or trying to carry a lot of things ○ *She had three children and was loaded down with two heavy suitcases.*

• **loads of** *something*, **a load of** *something* *infml* much or many ○ *There were loads of people standing around a TV set in the store.* ○ *Ellie's a good student, and she has a load of friends.*

PHRASAL VERBS with **load**

• **load up** *something* [M] to put things in or on a vehicle ○ *Let's load up the car and then we can go.*

• **load up on** *something* to gather a large amount of something ○ *The tourists started loading up on perfume and cosmetics.*

loaded NOT FAIR /ˈloʊd·əd/ *adj* not fair, esp. by being especially helpful to one side and not the other, or (of a question) by intentionally using words that will likely produce a particular answer ○ *The questions in this debate were so loaded that they always got the answers they expected.*

RICH /ˈloʊd·əd/ *adj infml* having a lot of money; rich ○ *The guy never spends a dime but believe me, he's loaded.*

loaf BREAD /loʊf/ *n* [C] *pl* **loaves** bread that is shaped and baked in a single piece and can be sliced for eating ○ *Get a loaf of white bread from the corner store.*

AVOID WORK /loʊf/ *v* [I] *infml* to avoid activity, esp. work ○ *He just wanted to loaf for a while before beginning the new job.*

loafer /ˈloʊ·fər/ *n* [C] a type of shoe with stitches around the top and without SHOELACES (= strings used to tie shoes)

loan /loʊn/ *n* [C/U] an act of lending something, esp. a sum of money that that has to be paid back with INTEREST (= an additional amount of money that is a percentage of the amount borrowed), or an amount of money that has been lent ○ [U] *Thanks for the loan of your bike.* ○ [C] *My brother repaid his student loan within five years.* ○ *The painting is* **on loan** *to the Metropolitan Museum of Art* (= has been lent to it, esp. for more than a short period of time).

loan /loʊn/ *v* [T] to lend something, esp. money ○ *Can you loan me $10 until payday?*

loan shark *n* [C] *infml, disapproving* a person who charges a very large amount of interest for lending money

loath /loʊθ, loʊð/ *adj* [+ *to* infinitive] unwilling; RELUCTANT ○ *She'd be loath to admit it, but she doesn't really like opera.*

loathe /loʊð/ *v* [T] to feel strong hate, dislike, or disgust for someone or something ○ *I loathe doing housework.* ○ *"Do you like fish?" "No, I loathe it."*

loathing /ˈloʊ·ðɪŋ/ *n* [U] ○ *He's full of loathing and despair.*

loaves /loʊvz/ *pl of* LOAF BREAD

lob /lɑb/ *v* [T] **-bb-** to hit or throw something, esp. a ball, in a high curve ○ *Smith lobbed a perfect pass over the basket to Watkins.*

lobby SPACE /ˈlɑb·i/ *n* [C] a large, open space just inside the main entrance of a public building such as a hotel, office building, or theater ○ *As you enter the lobby, you'll see the elevators on your right.*

PERSUADE /ˈlɑb·i/ *v* [I/T] ***politics & government*** to try to persuade an elected official to take a particular action or change a law ○ [T] *Council members have been lobbying colleagues on how to vote.*

lobby /ˈlɑb·i/ *n* [C] ***politics & government*** a group of people who represent a particular industry or interest in dealing with a politician, official, etc. ○ *the environmental lobby*

lobbyist /ˈlɑb·iː·əst/ *n* [C] ○ *lobbyists for the banking industry*

lobe /loʊb/ *n* [C] an EARLOBE

lobster /ˈlɑb·stər/ *n* [C/U] an animal that lives in the sea and has a shell-like covering on its body, two large CLAWS, and eight legs, or the flesh of this animal when used as food ○ [U] *We had lobster for dinner.*

local AREA /ˈloʊ·kəl/ *adj* [not gradable] **1** from, existing in, or serving a particular place or small area ○ *the local population* ○ *the local newspaper* ○ *local phone calls* ○ *local government* **2** *medical* Local also means limited to a particular part of the body: *a local anesthetic*

local /ˈloʊ·kəl/ *n* [C] a person who lives in the particular small area you are talking about ○ *If you're lost and need directions, just ask one of the locals.*

localize /ˈloʊ·kəˌlɑɪz/ *v* [I/T] ○ [I] *The infection seems to have localized in the foot.*

locally /ˈloʊ·kə·li/ *adv* [not gradable] ○ *locally grown vegetables*

VEHICLE /ˈloʊ·kəl/ *n* [C] a train or bus that stops at all or most of the places on its route where passengers can get on or off ○ Compare EXPRESS FAST

locale /loʊˈkæl/ *n* [C] an area or place, esp. one where something special happens ○ *The film's locale is Venice in the summer of 1957.*

locality /loʊˈkæl·ət̬·i/ *n* [C] a particular area or neighborhood ○ *The schools work with states, localities, teachers, and parents.*

locate Ⓐ **FIND POSITION** /ˈloʊ·keɪt, loʊˈkeɪt/ *v* [T] to find or discover the exact position of something ○ *Archeologists have located the remains of an ancient temple.*

PUT IN PLACE /ˈloʊ·keɪt, loʊˈkeɪt/ *v* [I/T] to put or establish something in a particular place ○ [T] *The company decided to locate its headquarters in Denver.*

WORD FAMILY locate			
Nouns	local location locale locality	*Verbs*	locate localize dislocate relocate
Adjectives	local	*Adverbs*	locally

location Ⓐ /loʊˈkeɪ·ʃən/ *n* [C] **1** a particular place or position ○ *a good location for a bookstore* ○ *The map showed the location of an old mine.* **2** If a movie is filmed **on location**, it is made in an actual place: *The documentary was filmed on location in San Francisco.*

lock DEVICE TO FASTEN /lɑk/ *n* [C] a device that keeps something, such as a door or drawer, fastened, usually needing a key to open it

lock /lɑk/ *v* [I/T] **1** [T] *Be sure to lock all the doors when you leave.* ○ [I] *The garage door doesn't lock.* **2** If you lock something somewhere, you make it safe by putting it in a special place and fastening it closed with a lock: [T] *He locked the documents in his filing cabinet.*

NOT ALLOW CHANGE /lɑk/ *v* [I/T] to be or hold something in a position or condition where movement, escape, or change is not possible ○ [T] *They're locked in a lawsuit with their former employer.* ○ [I] *The cars crashed and the bumpers locked, making it impossible to move.* ○ [M] *The bank won't lock in our mortgage rate.*

lock /lɑk/ *n* [C] ○ *The candidate has a lock on the nomination* (= has control of it).

WATER /lɑk/ *n* [C] a length of water with gates at either end where the level of water can be changed to allow boats to move between parts of a CANAL or river that are at different heights

HAIR /lɑk/ *n* [C] a curl of hair, or a group of hairs

IDIOM with lock

•**lock, stock, and barrel** including everything ○ *I'm selling my house, lock, stock, and barrel with all the furniture and appliances.*

PHRASAL VERBS with lock

•**lock** *someone* **out** to prevent someone from getting into a building, room, or vehicle ○ *I forgot that my dad didn't have keys, and I locked him out of the house.* ○ *The door slammed and our keys were inside – so we were locked out* (= unable to get in).

•**lock up DOOR** to make a building or room safe by locking the door and fastening the windows ○ *Don't forget to lock up when you leave the house.*

•**lock** *someone* **up IN PRISON** [M] to put someone in prison ○ *If found guilty, he could be locked up for life.*

locker /ˈlɑk·ər/ *n* [C] a cabinet, often tall and made of metal, in which someone can lock his or her possessions and leave them for a period of time

locker room *n* [C] a room with LOCKERS where people can leave their clothes while they exercise or play sports

locket /ˈlɑk·ət/ *n* [C] a small item of jewelry that opens to show a picture of someone or a piece of hair, which is usually worn on a chain around the neck

lockout /ˈlɑk·ɑʊt/ *n* [C] an action taken by an employer to stop workers from going into their place of work until they agree to particular conditions given by the employer

locksmith /ˈlɑk·smɪθ/ *n* [C] a person who makes and repairs locks and supplies keys

locomotion /ˌloʊ·kəˈmoʊ·ʃən/ *n* [U] the ability to move; movement

locomotive /ˌloʊ·kəˈmoʊt̬·ɪv/ *n* [C] the engine of a train that pulls it along

locust /ˈloʊ·kəst/ *n* [C] any of several types of large GRASSHOPPERS (= insects with wings and long back legs) found esp. in hot areas ○ *a swarm of locusts*

lodge BECOME FIXED /lɑdʒ/ *v* [always + adv/prep] to become fixed or cause something to become fixed in a place or position ○ [I] *A fish bone had lodged in her throat.* ○ [T] *The explosion lodged some metal fragments in his leg.*

MAKE /lɑdʒ/ *v* [T] to formally make a complaint to an official ○ *to lodge a complaint/protest*

STAY /lɑdʒ/ *v* [I always + adv/prep] to stay in a place temporarily, usually paying rent to do so ○ *Mrs. Brown rents rooms – you can lodge with her for a few weeks.*

lodging /ˈlɑdʒ·ɪŋ/ *n* [U] ○ *The price includes board and lodging* (= a room to sleep in).

BUILDING /lɑdʒ/ *n* [C] **1** a small building used by people during a particular sports season ○ *a hunting lodge* **2** A lodge is also a type of hotel in the countryside or mountains.

loft ROOF SPACE /lɔːft/ *n* [C] **1** a space at the top of a building under the roof, used for storage or sometimes made into a room, or a raised area built over part of a room that is used esp. for sleeping **2** A loft can also be an apartment in a building that was previously used for industry: *She lives in a converted loft.*

HIT /lɔːft/ *v* [T] to hit a ball high in the air ○ *The batter lofted the ball into right field.*

lofty /ˈlɔːf·ti/ *adj* **1** high ○ *lofty mountains* **2** If someone's ideas or words are lofty, they show high principles or standards: *lofty sentiments*

log WOOD /lɔːg, lɑg/ *n* [C] a thick piece of tree trunk or branch ○ *Stack the logs near the fireplace.*

log /lɔːg, lɑg/ *v* [I/T] **-gg-** to cut down trees for their wood ○ [T] *Timber companies logged these mountains for years.*
logging /ˈlɔː·gɪŋ, ˈlɑg·ɪŋ/ *n* [U] ○ *There's a lot of logging in the region.*

RECORD /lɔːg, lɑg/ *n* [C] a full, written record of a trip, a period of time, or an event ○ *a ship's log*
log /lɔːg, lɑg/ *v* [T] **-gg-** to put information into a written record ○ [T] *The police have logged several complaints about loud parties in that building.* ○ [T] *He has logged over 1500 hours of flying time* (= flown and recorded this amount).

PHRASAL VERBS with log

• **log off**, **log out** to stop using a computer system or program by giving a particular instruction ○ *The program lets you shut down, restart, or log off Windows at specific times and dates.*
• **log on**, **log in** to start using a computer system or program by giving a PASSWORD (= a secret word by which the system recognizes an approved user) ○ *About 40,000 gamers have been logging on every day since the website appeared last month.*

logarithm /ˈlɔː·gəˌrɪð·əm, ˈlɑg-/, *short form* **log** /lɔːg, lɑg/ *n* [C] ***algebra*** a number which shows how many times a particular number, called the base, has to be multiplied by itself to produce another number
logarithmic /ˌlɔː·gəˈrɪð·mɪk, ˌlɑg-/ *adj*

log cabin *n* [C] a small house made from tree trunks

loggerheads /ˈlɔː·gərˌhedz, ˈlɑg·ər-/ *pl n* strong disagreement ○ *The principal and the teachers were* **at loggerheads** *over some of the new school rules.*

logic Ⓐ **REASONABLE THINKING** /ˈlɑdʒ·ɪk/ *n* [U] a particular way of thinking, esp. one that is reasonable and based on good judgment ○ *I fail to see the logic of your argument.*
logical Ⓐ /ˈlɑdʒ·ɪ·kəl/ *adj* ○ *After the children were grown, moving to a smaller house was the logical thing to do.*
logically Ⓐ /ˈlɑdʒ·ɪ·kli/ *adv* ○ *Related material has been grouped logically.*

FORMAL THINKING /ˈlɑdʒ·ɪk/ *n* [U] a formal, scientific method of examining or thinking about ideas
logician Ⓐ /ləˈdʒɪʃ·ən/ *n* [C] someone who studies or is skilled in logic

logistics /ləˈdʒɪs·tɪks/ *pl n* the careful organization of a complicated military, business, or other activity so that it happens in a successful and effective way ○ *The logistics of getting five kids off to school in the morning are pretty complex.*
logistical /ləˈdʒɪs·tɪ·kəl/ *adj* ○ *Delays and logistical problems have become familiar concerns.*

logjam /ˈlɔːg·dʒæm, ˈlɑg-/ *n* [C] something that blocks the ability to do other things ○ *They broke the logjam by starting a series of discussions.*

logo /ˈloʊ·goʊ/ *n* [C] *pl* **logos** a small picture or design that a company or organization uses as its symbol ○ *Athletes are all wearing the sneaker company's logo.*

loin /lɔɪn/ *n* [C] a piece of meat from the back of an animal near the tail or from the top part of the back legs ○ *roast loin of venison*

loincloth /ˈlɔɪn·klɔːθ/ *n* [C] a piece of cloth that hangs down from the waist and covers the LOINS, sometimes worn by men in hot countries

loins /lɔɪnz/ *pl n* ***literature*** the reproductive organs

loiter /ˈlɔɪt̬·ər/ *v* [I] to stay in a public place without an obvious reason to be there ○ *The law prohibits loitering on a public street.*
loitering /ˈlɔɪt̬·ə·rɪŋ/ *n* [U] ○ *He was arrested for loitering.*

loll /lɑl/ *v* [I always + adv/prep] to lie or sit in a relaxed, informal way, or (esp. of the tongue) to hang loosely ○ *She lolled in an armchair.* ○ *The patient lay with her mouth open, her tongue lolling out.*

lollipop /ˈlɑl·iːˌpɑp/ *n* [C] a hard candy on the end of a small stick

lone /loʊn/ *adj* [not gradable] being the only one in a place or situation; standing alone ○ *Her singing is backed by a lone piano.*
loner /ˈloʊ·nər/ *n* [C] someone who prefers to be alone and to do things without other people

lonely /ˈloʊn·li/ *adj* **1** (of someone) feeling sad because you are alone, or (of something) causing this feeling ○ *a lonely child* ○ *my lonely room* **2** A lonely place has no people, buildings, etc.: *a lonely and deserted road*
loneliness /ˈloʊn·li·nəs/ *n* [U] ○ *Some elderly people live in isolation and loneliness.* ➤ Confusables: **alone or lonely?** at ALONE WITHOUT PEOPLE

lonesome /ˈloʊn·səm/ *adj* (of someone) feeling sad because you are alone or are apart from someone, or (of something) causing this feeling ○ *She was feeling lonesome for her family.* ○ *the lonesome whistle of a distant train*

long **DISTANCE** /lɔːŋ/ *adj* [*-er/-est* only] **1** being a distance between two points that is more than average or usual, or being of a particular length ○ *There was a long line at the post office.* ○ *When I was young I wore my hair long.* ○ *We're still a long way from the station* (= a great distance). **2** A long piece of writing, such as a book or story, has many words: *It's a long book – over 600 pages.* **3 Long underwear** is LONG JOHNS.

TIME /lɔːŋ/ *adj* [*-er/-est* only] **1** being an amount of time that is more than average or usual, or being of a particular amount of time ○ *The days are longer in summer than in winter.* ○ *We had to wait a long time to see the doctor.* ○ *We went away for a* **long weekend** *in April* (= Saturday, Sunday, and an extra day or days). **2** Something that is long-lost has not been seen for many years before appearing suddenly: *A long-lost diary was discovered among his papers.*
long /lɔːŋ/ *adv* [*-er/-est* only] ○ *Have you been waiting long?* ○ *I've known her longer than you have.* ○ *I don't want to stay any longer* (= for any more time).

WANT /lɔːŋ/ *v* [I] to want something very much ○ [+ *to* infinitive] *She longed to move out of the city.*

L

longing /ˈlɔːŋ·ɪŋ/ *n* [C] a strong desire ○ *a longing for peace and quiet*

IDIOMS with long

• **a long way to go** a large amount of time and effort ○ *You've got a long way to go before you're ready to compete at the national level.*

• **at long last** finally, after much waiting ○ *At long last the government is starting to listen to our problems.*

• **in the long run** at some time in the future ○ *You may want to quit school now, but in the long run, you'll regret it.* ○ Opposite: IN THE SHORT RUN at SHORT IDIOMS

• **the long haul** a period of years rather than days, weeks, or months ○ *I want to invest my money for the long haul, not just to get rich quick.*

long-distance *adj* traveling or separated by a large distance ○ *a long-distance phone call*

longevity /lɑnˈdʒev·ət̬·i, lɔːn-/ *n* [U] a long life ○ *He attributed his longevity to exercise and a healthy diet.*

longhand /ˈlɔːŋ·hænd/ *n* [U] writing done by hand usually with a pen or pencil ○ *He wrote the confession in longhand and signed it.*

L

longitude /ˈlɑn·dʒəˌtuːd/ *n* [C/U] the position to the east or west of an imaginary circle around the earth that goes through the North Pole, the South Pole, and Greenwich, England ○ Compare LATITUDE DISTANCE ➤ Picture: **earth**

longitudinal /ˈlɑn·dʒəˌtuː·dən·əl/ *adj* [not gradable] **1** LENGTHWISE ○ *a longitudinal section* **2** examined or done over time ○ *a longitudinal study of mental health* **3** ***earth science*** Longitudinal also means relating to LONGITUDE.

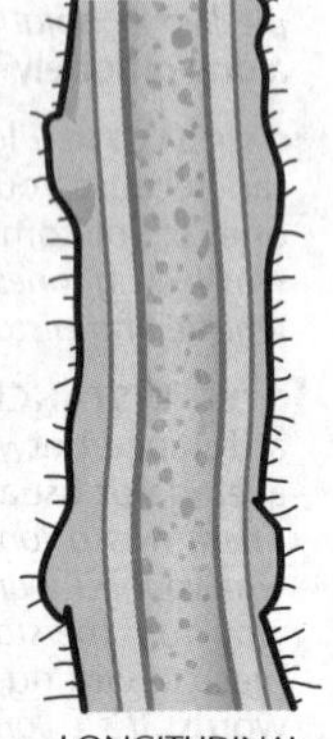

LONGITUDINAL SECTION

longitudinal wave *n* [C] ***physics*** a WAVE ENERGY FORM in which the substance the wave travels through moves in the same direction of the wave itself. Sound waves are longitudinal waves. ○ Compare TRANSVERSE WAVE

long johns, **long underwear** *pl n* warm, tight-fitting underwear reaching to the feet and hands

long-running *adj* continuing for a long period of time ○ *a long-running Broadway musical*

longshoreman /ˈlɔːŋˈʃɔːr·mən, -ˈʃoʊr-/ *n* [C] *pl* **-men** a person whose job is loading and unloading ships

long shot *n* [C] something that is not likely to succeed ○ *It's a long shot, but you could try calling him at home.*

long-standing *adj* having existed for a long time ○ *It's been our long-standing policy not to allow pets at the hotel.*

long-term *adj* happening, existing, or continuing for many years or far into the future ○ *Scientists warned of the long-term effects of global warming.*

longtime, **long-time** /ˈlɔːŋˈtɑɪm/ *adj* [not gradable] having existed or lasted for many years ○ *a longtime friend*

look SEE /lʊk/ *v* [I] to direct your eyes in order to see ○ *Come look at what I've found.* ○ *She looked at her brother.* ○ *He looked out (of) the window of the bus.* ○ Compare SEE USE EYES

look /lʊk/ *n* [C usually sing] ○ *Take a look at this picture and see if you recognize anyone.*

WORD CHOICES look

See also: **see**

Watch is used when someone looks at something for a period of time, especially something that is changing or moving.

I sat by the window and ***watched*** *people walking past.*

Glance is used when someone looks at a person or thing very quickly.

She ***glanced*** *around the room to see who was there.*

If you look very quickly and secretly, you can use the verbs **peep** or **peek**.

She ***peeped*** *through the curtains to see what was happening.*

He ***peeked*** *inside the box.*

The verb **stare** is used when someone looks for a long time, especially because of being surprised or frightened.

Don't ***stare*** *at people like that – it's rude.*

If you look at something or someone for a long time because you are admiring that thing or person or because you are thinking about something, you can use the verb **gaze**.

We sat there ***gazing*** *at the lake.*

Peer is used when someone looks at something with difficulty.

When no one answered the door, she ***peered*** *through the window.*

The verbs **examine**, **inspect**, or **scrutinize** are often used when someone looks at something very closely in order to find out more about it.

Police are ***examining*** *the house for clues.*

She ***inspected*** *the car for damage.*

He ***scrutinized*** *the woman's face to see if she was lying.*

SEARCH /lʊk/ *v* [I always + adv/prep] to try to find something ○ *Please help me look for my keys.* ○ *We looked everywhere but couldn't find it.* ○ *I'll look for a present for Tracy while I'm at the mall.*

look /lʊk/ *n* [C usually sing] ○ *I'll take a look and see if you left the keys in the kitchen.* ○ *After a brief look around, the police left.*

SEEM /lʊk/ *v* [L] to seem or appear to be ○ *The roads look icy.* ○ *That dress looks nice on you.* ○ *He looked friendly.* ○ *She looked like she hadn't slept all night.* ○ *He has started to look his age* (= appear as old as he really is). ○ *It looks like* (= It is likely that) *we'll be finished by January.* ○ *It looks like snow* (= It seems likely to snow).

look /lʊk/ *n* [C] an expression of the face, or a particular appearance ○ *a joyful/sad look* ○ *I didn't like the look of the place and left as soon as I could.* ○ [pl] *He had good looks and lots of money.*

looking /ˈlʊk·ɪŋ/ *adv* having a stated type of appearance ○ *an odd-looking man* ○ *A linen shirt is casual looking.*

EXAMINE /lʊk/ *v* [I always + adv/prep] to examine or study, often quickly or informally ○ *Would you look over these numbers to see if I've made a mistake?* ○ *I don't go there to shop – I just like to look around and see what they have.*

look /lʊk/ *n* [C usually sing] ○ *I'm worried about this skin rash and I want my doctor to have a look at it.*

FACE /lʊk/ *v* [I] to be in or view a particular direction; face ○ *The garden looks east.* ○ *The porch looks out over the lake.*

GETTING ATTENTION /lʊk/ *exclamation* used to get someone's attention, often to express anger or annoyance ○ *Look, I've already told you that I'm not lending you any more money.*

IDIOMS with **look**

• **look** *someone* **in the eye, look** *someone* **in the face** to talk to someone in an honest way that shows no doubts ○ *I wanted to look people in the eye and tell them I made a mistake.* ○ *I can't believe you can look me in the face and lie to me like that.*

• **look right through** *someone* to pretend not to see someone even while your eyes are directed toward that person ○ *I smiled at him, but he looked right through me.*

• **looking for trouble** behaving in a way that is likely to cause problems for you ○ *Parking illegally in front of the police station is looking for trouble.* ○ Compare ASKING FOR TROUBLE at ASK **IDIOM**

PHRASAL VERBS with **look**

• **look after** *someone/something* to care for or be in charge of someone or something ○ *He looks after his son during the day.* ○ *Annie can look after herself.*

• **look ahead** to think of and decide about the future ○ *We need to look ahead to when the children are grown.*

• **look back** to think of or remember what has happened in the past ○ *George looked back on his career in government with a great deal of satisfaction.*

• **look down on** *someone* to feel that someone is less important than you or does not deserve respect ○ *Homeowners often look down on plumbers.*

• **look forward to** *something* to feel pleasure because an event or activity is going to happen ○ *I'm looking forward to my vacation.*

• **look in on** *someone/something* to visit someone or something for a short time ○ *It helps if older people have a nearby relative who will look in on them.*

• **look into** *something* to try to find out about something ○ *I'll look into the reasons for the decision.*

• **look like** *someone/something* **SIMILAR APPEARANCE** to be similar in appearance to someone or something ○ *The twins look like their mother.* ○ *Inside is a computerized device that looks like a small turtle.*

• **look like** *something* **POSSIBLE FUTURE** to appear likely to happen ○ *It sure looks like snow today.*

• **look on/upon** *someone/something* to consider or think of someone or something in a stated way ○ *We looked on her as a daughter.*

• **look out** to watch what is happening and be careful ○ *Please look out when you're crossing streets.* ○ Related noun: LOOKOUT

• **look up** *someone* **VISIT** [M] to come and see someone; visit ○ *Look me up the next time you're in Los Angeles.*

• **look** *something* **up CHECK FACTS** [M] to check a fact or get information about something ○ *If you're not sure what the word means, look it up in a dictionary.* ○ *I looked up solar power on the Internet to find out more about it.*

• **look up IMPROVE** to get better; improve ○ *I hope things will start to look up in the new year.*

• **look up to** *someone* to admire and respect someone ○ *Kids look up to ballplayers, and we need to let kids know that it is not OK to cheat.*

look-alike, lookalike /ˈlʊk·əˌlɑɪk/ *n* [C] someone or something very similar in physical appearance to someone or something else ○ *an Elvis Presley lookalike*

lookout /ˈlʊk·ɑʊt/ *n* [C] **1** a person whose job is to watch for someone or something to appear ○ *Assign someone to be a lookout on the boat to keep an eye out for rocks.* **2** If you are **on the lookout** for something, you are watching for it to appear: *What kinds of behavior should parents be on the lookout for?* **3** A lookout is also a place where you can see a long distance: *Turner works at the fire lookout on Carey Dome.* ○ Related verb: LOOK OUT

loom APPEAR /luːm/ *v* [I] to appear, esp. when seeming large and threatening ○ *Record budget deficits, now running well above $200 billion a year, loom over the recovery.*

DEVICE /luːm/ *n* [C] a piece of equipment on which thread is woven into cloth

IDIOM with **loom**

• **loom large** to become or seem more important and often cause worry ○ *The question of how I had done on my finals loomed large in my mind.*

loonie /ˈluː·ni/ *n* [C] *Cdn, infml* a Canadian coin worth one dollar

loony /ˈluː·ni/ *adj* [-*er*/-*est* only] foolish or crazy ○ *He has loony ideas.*

loop /luːp/ *n* [C] a circular shape made by something long and narrow in which the two ends cross each other, leaving an open space within ○ *A loop of thread from my sweater caught on a nail.* ○ *The exit ramp makes a loop under the elevated highway.*

loop /luːp/ *v* [I/T] ○ [I always + adv/prep] *The nature trail loops around and comes back to where you start.*

loophole /ˈluːp·hoʊl/ *n* [C] an opportunity to legally avoid an unpleasant responsibility, usually because of a mistake in the way rules or laws have been written ○ *The new law is designed to close most of the tax loopholes.*

loose NOT ATTACHED /luːs/ *adj* [*-er/-est* only] **1** not firmly attached in place ○ *I'd better sew that loose button before it comes off.* ○ *A few loose sheets of paper were lying around.* **2** If an animal is loose, it is not tied up or caged in.

loosely /ˈluː·sli/ *adv* ○ *The package was loosely wrapped.*

loosen /ˈluː·sən/ *v* [I/T] to become or make something less firmly fixed ○ [I] *The screws holding the light fixture have loosened, and it's dangling from the ceiling.* ○ [T] (*fig.*) *When immigration laws were loosened, the number of immigrants shot up.*

> **CONFUSABLES**
>
> loose or lose?
>
> Be careful, these two words look and sound similar but have completely different meanings.
>
> **Loose** is an adjective, meaning not attached or not tight.
>
> *These trousers are a bit loose.*
>
> **Lose** is a verb, meaning "to not be able to find something" or "to have something taken away from you." Be careful not to use **loose** when you really mean **lose**.
>
> *I hope he doesn't lose his job.*
>
> ~~*I hope he doesn't loose his job.*~~

L

NOT TIGHT /luːs/ *adj* [*-er/-est* only] **1** not tight; not fitting closely to the body or the thing that is covered ○ *Wear comfortable, loose clothing to your exercise class.* **2** Loose can also mean not closely following something original, or not exact: *The film is a loose adaptation of Conrad's novel.*

loosely /ˈluː·sli/ *adv* ○ *a loosely knit sweater*

loosen /ˈluː·sən/ *v* [T] ○ *It was hot in the room so I loosened my tie.*

IDIOMS with loose

• **at loose ends** not knowing what to do, esp. because of an upsetting change ○ *I was at loose ends after finishing school and not being able to find a job.*

• **loosen up** **1** to stretch your muscles, esp. by doing special exercises before a hard physical activity ○ *He always spent 20 minutes loosening up before going for his morning run.* **2** To **loosen up** is also to relax, esp. after being nervous: *She was nervous at the beginning of the interview but loosened up after a while.*

loose end *n* [C usually pl] something that still needs to be done or explained ○ *My research is done, but I have some loose ends to tie up.*

loose-leaf *adj* [not gradable] having special paper that can be easily removed and replaced ○ *a loose-leaf notebook*

loot /luːt/ *v* [I/T] **1** (said esp. of large numbers of people) to steal from stores ○ [I] *Riot police were sent to prevent the mob from looting.* **2** To loot something is also to take a lot of money away from it that does not belong to you: [T] *The officers of the corporation looted the company of millions of dollars.*

loot /luːt/ *n* [U] money or valuable objects that have been stolen ○ *Three men have been sentenced to prison for taking part in the robbery, but the loot was never recovered.*

lop /lɑp/ *v* [T] **-pp-** to cut a piece from something with a single quick action ○ [M] *We've got to lop off the lower branches of this tree.* ○ (*fig.*) *The city council lopped thousands of dollars from the budget.*

lope /loʊp/ *v* [I] (of a person or animal) to run with long, relaxed steps

lopsided /ˈlɑp ˈsɑɪd·əd/ *adj* with one side or part much bigger or higher than the other; uneven ○ *The Yankees won by the lopsided score of 17 to 2.*

loquacious /loʊ ˈkweɪ·ʃəs/ *adj* having the habit of talking a lot

Lord /lɔːrd/ *n* [U] **1** (in the Christian and Jewish religions) God **2** Some people say Lord to express surprise, shock, or worry: *Oh Lord! I've forgotten the tickets!*

lord /lɔːrd/ *n* [C] **1** (in some countries) a title of a man who has a specially high social rank, or the person himself **2** A lord is also a man who has a lot of power in a particular area: *a feudal lord* ○ *a crime lord* ○ Compare LADY TITLE

IDIOM with lord

• **lord it over** *someone* to behave as if you are more important than someone and have a right to tell that person what to do ○ *He likes to lord it over his little sister.*

lore /lɔːr, loʊr/ *n* [U] knowledge and stories, usually traditional, about a subject ○ *He published several books on Indian lore and hunting.*

lorry /ˈlɔːr·i/ *n* [C] *Br* TRUCK

lose NOT BE ABLE TO FIND /luːz/ *v* [T] *past* **lost** to not be able to find something ○ *I lost my keys somewhere in the house.* ○ *Two officers chased the suspect, but he turned down an alley and they lost sight of him* (= could no longer see him). ➤ Confusables: **loose or lose?** at LOOSE NOT ATTACHED

> **USAGE**
>
> lose or miss?
>
> Usually you **miss** something that happens, such as an event, a train or plane leaving, or an opportunity.
>
> *I'm sorry I'm late, I missed the bus.*
>
> ~~*I'm sorry I'm late, I lost the bus.*~~
>
> Usually you **lose** a thing.
>
> *I've lost my umbrella.*

NO LONGER POSSESS /luːz/ *v* [T] *past* **lost** **1** to no longer have something, because it has been taken away from you, either by accident or purposely ○ *Workers will lose their jobs if the plant closes.* ○ *He lost his leg in a car accident.* **2** If you lose someone, that person dies: *George lost his wife in 1990.* **3** If you lose money you have risked, you do not make a profit and do not get your money back. **4** A business that is losing money is spending more money than it is receiving.

BE DEFEATED /luːz/ *v* [I/T] *past* **lost** to fail to succeed in a game or competition ○ [I] *If we lose again, we're out of the playoffs.* ○ [T] *Anderson lost the election by a narrow margin.*

loser /ˈluː·zər/ *n* [C] a person who is defeated, or someone who regularly fails ○ *When she found out she'd been accepted to the program because of her low scores, she felt like a loser.*

NOT MAINTAIN /luːz/ *v* [T] *past* **lost** **1** to not maintain or no longer have control over a quality or ability ○ *She used to play tennis regularly, but lately she's lost interest in it.* ○ *The driver lost control of her car.* ○ *The dog is losing her eyesight/hearing/sense of smell.* ○ *Carl lost his balance and fell down the stairs.* **2** If you lose time or an opportunity, you waste it. **3** If a clock loses time, it goes more slowly than it should.

HAVE LESS OF /luːz/ *v* [T] *past* **lost** to have less of something, esp. in the body ○ *to lose blood/weight*

CONFUSE /luːz/ *v* [T] *past* **lost** to confuse someone ○ *I'm sorry, you've lost me – would you go over that again?*

WORD FAMILY lose

Nouns	loser, loss	Adjectives	lost
		Verbs	lose

IDIOMS with lose

• **lose count of** *something* to not be able to remember a total ○ *I've lost count of how many times she's been late for work this month.* ○ Opposite: KEEP COUNT (OF SOMETHING) at KEEP **IDIOMS**

• **lose face** to become less respected by others ○ *She had to accept defeat without losing face.*

• **lose** *your* **head** to not have control of your emotions ○ *Everything went dark, and I just lost my head and couldn't think what to do.*

• **lose heart** to stop believing that you can succeed ○ *This is a difficult time, but don't lose heart – just remember how much you've already achieved.*

• **lose** *your* **mind** *infml* to become crazy ○ *I'm going to lose my mind if I have to stay here any longer.*

• **lose sight of** to not consider something, esp. because you have forgotten about it ○ *We cannot lose sight of the need to keep the public safe.*

• **lose sleep (over** *something***)** to worry about something so much that you cannot sleep ○ *I know you made a mistake, but I wouldn't lose sleep over it.*

• **lose** *your* **temper**, **lose your cool/lose it** to become very angry ○ *Michelle wanted everybody to like her so much that she just lost it if someone got mad at her.* ○ *When I feel like I'm about to lose my cool, I just leave the room.*

• **lose track** to not know any longer where someone or something is, or to not be able to remember something ○ *I've lost track of most of my old college friends, unfortunately.* ○ *Can you remember what number we were working on? I've lost track.*

• **lose** *your* **touch** to no longer be able to do something as well as you could before ○ *You only beat me once in the last five games – you're not losing your touch, are you?*

• **lose touch (with** *someone***)** to no longer communicate with someone ○ *I lost touch with Katie after she moved to Canada.*

• **lose touch (with** *something/someone***)** to no longer have recent knowledge of something or someone, so that you do not understand that thing or person well ○ *Politicians can easily lose touch with the real people if they spend too much time in Washington D.C.* ○ *He never lost touch with Mexican culture.*

loss **NOT HAVING** /lɔːs/ *n* [C/U] **1** the action or state of not having or keeping something any more ○ [C] *The company's losses over the last few years have been staggering.* **2** Loss may mean death: [U] *They never got over the loss of their son.*

NOT CONTROLLING /lɔːs/ *n* [C/U] the action or state of not maintaining or having control over something any more ○ [C] *He suffered a gradual loss of memory in his later years.*

IDIOM with loss

• **at a loss** to not know what to do ○ *I'm at a loss to explain what happened.* ○ *I was so embarrassed that I was at a loss for words* (= I didn't know what to say).

lost **CANNOT BE FOUND** /lɔːst/ *adj* (of a person) unable to find your way, or (of an item) not to be found ○ *a lost child/pet/earring* ○ *We got lost on the way home.* ○ (*fig.*) *I'd be lost without you* (= I would not know what to do).

CONFUSED /lɔːst/ *adj* confused, or not able to understand or appreciate ○ *His explanation was so complicated, I got lost after the first example.* ○ *Everyone else thought it was funny, but that joke was lost on me.*

LOSE /lɔːst/ *past simple and past participle of* LOSE

lost cause *n* [C] something that cannot be achieved ○ *It rained all weekend, so painting the house was a lost cause.*

lot **LARGE AMOUNT** /lɑt/ *n infml* **1** **A lot** can mean much or often: *You look a lot like your sister.* ○ *We eat out a lot.* **2** **A lot of** or **lots of** means a large amount or number of something: *I saved a lot of money with those coupons.* ○ *They want to have lots of children.* ➤ Usage: **many, much, or a lot of?** at MANY

USAGE

a lot

When you use a noun phrase after **a lot** or **lots,** remember to use the preposition **of** before the noun phrase.

There have been a lot of changes in recent years.

~~*There have been a lot changes in recent years.*~~

Lots of people hate the new computer system.

~~*Lots people hate the new computer system.*~~

LAND /lɑt/ *n* [C] an area of land ○ *They purchased a lot last summer and built a house on it the following year.*

lotion /ˈloʊ·ʃən/ *n* [C/U] a liquid that is put on your skin in order to protect it, improve its condi-

L

tion, or make it smell pleasant ○ [U] *She applied some hand/suntan lotion and rubbed it in.*

lottery /ˈlɑţ·ə·ri/ *n* [C] a system of selling numbered tickets and giving prizes to those people whose numbers are chosen by chance ○ *Even if she won the lottery, Paige says she'd still keep her job.*

loud NOISY /lɑʊd/ *adj, adv* [*-er/-est* only] having or producing a large amount of sound ○ *a loud noise* ○ *Would you speak a little louder, please?*
loudly /ˈlɑʊd·li/ *adv* ○ *"What does she want now?" he asked loudly.*
loudness /ˈlɑʊd·nəs/ *n* [U] ○ *Differences in loudness are measured in decibels.*

WORD CHOICES loud

An alternative to "loud" is **noisy**.
Our neighbors are very ***noisy***.
If something is extremely loud, you can use the words **deafening** or **thunderous**.
The music was ***deafening***.
Thunderous *cheers erupted from the fans during the final seconds of the game.*
A sound that is loud, unpleasant and high can be described as **piercing** or **shrill**.
a ***piercing*** *scream*
a ***shrill*** *whistle*

L

BRIGHT /lɑʊd/ *adj* [*-er/-est* only] (of colors) too bright ○ *a loud tie/pattern*

WORD FAMILY loud

Nouns	loudness	*Adverbs*	aloud loud loudly
Adjectives	loud		

IDIOM with loud

• **loud and clear** in a way that is easily understood ○ *We need to get our message through loud and clear.*

loudmouth /ˈlɑʊd·mɑʊθ/ *n* [C] someone who talks too much or too loudly, esp. in an offensive or stupid way

loudspeaker /ˈlɑʊd ˌspiː·kər/ *n* [C] a device that changes electrical signals into sounds loud enough to be heard at a distance

lounge ROOM /lɑʊndʒ/ *n* [C] a public room for relaxing or waiting in ○ *a faculty lounge*
RELAX /lɑʊndʒ/ *v* [I] to stand or sit in a relaxed way ○ *She was lounging on the beach.*

louse /lɑʊs/ *n* [C] *pl* **lice** a small insect that lives on the bodies of people and animals

PHRASAL VERB with louse

• **louse up** *something* [M] *infml* to spoil something or make it worse ○ *There isn't a mechanic alive who doesn't louse up a job once in a while.*

lousy /ˈlɑʊ·zi/ *adj* [*-er/-est* only] *infml* bad or unpleasant ○ *The city does a lousy job of snow removal.* ○ *I thought the movie was lousy.*

lout /lɑʊt/ *n* [C] *infml* a rude, stupid, or awkward man ○ *He's such a lout.*

love LIKE SOMEONE /lʌv/ *v* [T] to have a strong affection for someone, which can be combined with a strong romantic attraction ○ *Susan loved her brother dearly.* ○ *"I love you and want to marry you, Emily," he said.*
love /lʌv/ *n* [U] **1** *Our love will last forever.* ○ *Children need lots of love.* ○ *"I'm seeing Laura next week." "Oh, please give/send her my love* (= Tell her I am thinking about her with affection)." **2** If you **fall in love** you begin to love someone: *She's fallen in love and made plans to marry.* **3** You can write love/love from/all my love/lots of love before your name at the end of letters to family and friends. **4** A person who is **in love** is experiencing a romantic attraction for another person. ○ *I think he's in love with Anna.*
lovable, **loveable** /ˈlʌv·ə·bəl/ *adj* easy to love ○ *Owen's a lovable little kid with lots of energy.*
lover /ˈlʌv·ər/ *n* [C] a partner in a romantic or physical relationship
loving /ˈlʌv·ɪŋ/ *adj* ○ *a loving home/relationship*
lovingly /ˈlʌv·ɪŋ·li/ *adv* ○ *Grandma lovingly kissed the baby.*

WORD CHOICES love

A deep love that does not involve romantic feelings can be described as **adoration**.
She described her complete ***adoration*** *of her brother.*
The words **romance** or **passion** can be used when the love involves physical attraction.
The ***romance/passion*** *had gone out of their relationship.*
Infatuation is used when someone has a strong feeling of love which does not last very long.
No one expected their ***infatuation*** *with each other to last.*
If someone is very much in love, you can say that person is **head over heels (in love)**.
He fell ***head over heels in love*** *with his best friend's sister.*
Love between two people who are very young, which often disappears as they get older, can be described as **puppy love**.
It won't last, it's just ***puppy love***.

LIKE SOMETHING /lʌv/ *v* to like something very much ○ [T] *My kids love cartoons.* ○ [+ *to* infinitive] *We'd love to own our own home.*
love /lʌv/ *n* [C/U] ○ [U] *I don't share my boyfriend's love for sports.* ○ [C] *Music is Stephen's greatest love.*
lover /ˈlʌv·ər/ *n* [C] a person who likes or enjoys a particular thing ○ *The remote island is ideal for nature lovers.*
loving /ˈlʌv·ɪŋ/ *adj* ○ *He described his work in loving detail.*

WORD FAMILY love

Nouns	love lover loveliness	*Adjectives*	lovable unlovable lovely loving
Verbs	love	*Adverbs*	lovingly

love affair *n* [C] **1** a romantic and usually physical relationship between two people **2** A strong positive feeling between a person and an idea or activity can also be called a love affair: *The league launched the program in New Orleans because of Louisiana's love affair with football.*

lovely /ˈlʌv·li/ *adj* [*-er/-est* only] attractive and beautiful, or pleasant and enjoyable ○ *You look lovely in that dress.* ○ *Thank you for a lovely evening.*
loveliness /ˈlʌv·liː·nəs/ *n* [U]

love seat /ˈlʌvˈsiːt/ *n* [C] a small SOFA (= soft seat with a back and arms) that is only long enough for two people

loving /ˈlʌv·ɪŋ/ *adj* ○ See at LOVE **LIKE SOMEONE**; LOVE **LIKE SOMETHING**

lovingly /ˈlʌv·ɪŋ·li/ *adv* ○ See at LOVE **LIKE SOMEONE**

low NOT HIGH /loʊ/ *adj, adv* [*-er/-est* only] not high or tall; close to the ground, or near the bottom of something ○ *a low fence/ceiling* ○ *Until I'm a better skier, I'll stay on the lower slopes.* ○ *That plane is flying awfully low.*
lower /ˈloʊ·ər/ *v* [T] to let or bring someone or something down, or make something less high ○ *She lowered the blinds to block out the afternoon sun.*

SMALLER THAN USUAL /loʊ/ *adj, adv* [*-er/-est* only] **1** smaller than the usual or average size, number, value, or amount ○ *They have the lowest food prices in town.* ○ *Temperatures will dip lower near the end of the week.* ○ *Believe it or not, this dessert is low in calories.* **2** If a supply of something becomes low, you have very little of it left: *We're running low on gas.* **3** Low can also mean producing only a small amount of sound, heat, or light: *They spoke in low voices.* ○ *She turned the heat down low.* **4** Low can also mean of bad quality: *My test results were disappointingly low.*
low /loʊ/ *n* [C] a smaller than usual amount or level, or the smallest amount or level ○ *Enrollment at the college reached new lows this fall.* ○ *The temperature in Boston reached a record low last night.*
lower /ˈloʊ·ər/ *v* [I/T] to reduce something, or to become less ○ [T] *They lowered the asking price of their house.* ○ [T] *Please lower your voice* (= speak more softly).

NOT IMPORTANT /loʊ/ *adj* [*-er/-est* only] not important, or not of high rank ○ *low social status*
lowly /ˈloʊ·li/ *adj* not having importance or rank ○ *In chess it is possible for the lowly pawn to become the most powerful piece on the board.*

SOUND /loʊ/ *adj* **1** (of a sound or voice) near or at the bottom of the range of sounds ○ *a low voice/note* **2** If a sound is **low-pitched**, it is at the bottom of the range of sounds: *He gave a low-pitched whistle and his dog came running.*

NOT KIND /loʊ/ *adj* (of behavior or speech) mean or unfair ○ *What a cruel comment – how low can you get?*

UNHAPPY /loʊ/ *adj* [*-er/-est* only] unhappy or discouraged ○ *She's feeling pretty low because she failed her driver's test.*

WORD FAMILY low			
Nouns	low	*Verbs*	lower
Adjectives	low	*Adverbs*	low
	lowly		

low beams *pl n* the lights on the front of a car when they are on but not switched to their brightest level ○ Compare HIGH BEAMS

low blow *n* [C usually sing] a criticism or unkind act that is unexpected and unfair ○ *Criticizing his wife's family was a low blow.*

lowbrow /ˈloʊ·brɑʊ/ *adj disapproving* (of literature, art, music, movies, or plays) not serious and intended for people who do not know much about these forms of art, or (of people) not intelligent and not knowing a lot about such things ○ *lowbrow tastes* ○ *lowbrow readers* ○ Compare HIGHBROW; MIDDLEBROW

lowdown /ˈloʊ·dɑʊn/ *n* [U] the most important facts and information about something ○ *Our fashion editor gives you the lowdown on winter coats for this season.*

lowercase /ˌloʊ·ərˈkeɪs/ *n* [U] ***writing*** the small form of letters when they are printed or written ○ Compare UPPERCASE
lowercase /ˌloʊ·ərˈkeɪs/ *adj* [not gradable]

low-key *adj* simple and not attracting attention ○ *The wedding will be a low-key affair, with fewer than thirty guests.*

lowland /ˈloʊ·lənd, -lænd/ *n* [C] ***earth science*** an area of land that is not very high above the sea or that is lower than most of the land around it

low-level *adj* having little importance or rank ○ *a low-level job*

lowlife, low-life /ˈloʊ·lɑɪf/ *n* [C] someone of bad character

low-lying *adj* at a level that is not much higher than the level of the ocean

low-pressure *adj* [not gradable] ***earth science*** having a low BAROMETRIC PRESSURE (= amount of force on the earth's surface caused by the weight of the air)

low tide *n* [U] the time when the ocean reaches its lowest level ○ Compare HIGH TIDE

loyal /ˈlɔɪ·əl/ *adj* always giving help and encouragement ○ *People close to Woodruff are fiercely loyal and quick to shower her with superlatives.*
loyalty /ˈlɔɪ·əl·ti/ *n* [C/U] ○ [C] *My loyalties to my family come before my loyalties to my work.*

Loyalist /ˈlɔɪ·ə·ləst/ *n* [C] ***US history*** a person who supported the British government during the American Revolution: TORY. ○ Compare WHIG

lozenge /ˈlɑz·əndʒ, ˈlɑs-/ *n* [C] a small, flavored candy, often containing medicine, which dissolves when sucked in the mouth

LP /elˈpiː/ *n* [C] a record that plays for about 20 minutes a side

lubricate /ˈluː·brəˌkeɪt/, *infml* **lube** /luːb/ *v* [T] to put oil or an oily substance on or in something so that its parts move easily ○ *to lubricate gears/machinery*
lubricant /ˈluː·brə·kənt/, *infml* **lube** /luːb/ *n* [C/U] a substance that is used to make parts move easily
lubrication /ˌluː·brəˈkeɪ·ʃən/, *infml* **lube** /luːb/ *n* [U] ○ *engine lubrication*

lucid /ˈluː·səd/ *adj* (of speech or writing) clearly expressed and easy to understand, or (of a person) thinking or reasoning clearly ○ *He's 85 years old, but he's lucid and bright and amusing and clever.* ○ *He didn't seem very lucid after the accident.*

luck /lʌk/ *n* [U] **1** chance, or that which happens to you as the result of chance ○ *It was just by luck that she got the job.* **2** Luck is also the amount of success experienced: *She had bad luck in the last race, finishing fourth.* ○ *Jean had good luck in finding her great-grandmother's birth records.* **3** Luck is also success: *I've got a job interview today, so wish me luck.*
lucky /ˈlʌk·i/ *adj* [-*er*/-*est* only] having good things happen by chance ○ *For ten games, the Orioles have gotten every conceivable lucky break.* ○ *Today is my lucky day!*
luckily /ˈlʌk·ə·li/ *adv* ○ *I was late getting to the airport, but luckily for me, the plane was delayed.*
➤ Usage: **chance or lucky?** at CHANCE LUCK

L

WORD FAMILY luck

Nouns	luck	*Adverbs*	luckily unluckily
Adjectives	lucky unlucky		

WORD CHOICES luck

Fortunate is a common, slightly more formal alternative to "lucky."

It was ***fortunate*** *that he wasn't injured in the accident.*

If you want to say something is lucky, you could use the phrase **(it's a) good thing.**

It's a good thing *they didn't go camping this weekend – the weather's been awful.*

In informal English, the phrasal verb **luck out** can be used to say that someone is lucky.

The Giants really ***lucked out*** *in last night's game.*

People who are lucky, especially after a period of not being lucky, could be said to **land on *their* feet.**

She's really ***landed on her feet*** *with that job.*

IDIOMS with luck

• **in luck** experiencing a surprisingly good situation ○ *"Do you have any tickets for tonight's game?" "You're in luck – we have two left."*
• **out of luck** not having the success or good opportunities you wanted ○ *The bike only comes in large sizes, so if you're a short person you're out of luck.*

PHRASAL VERBS with luck

• **luck into** *something infml* to get or experience something good by chance ○ *I lucked into three empty seats on the flight over.*
• **luck out** *infml* to have something good happen by chance ○ *My wife lucked out – she left town just before the hurricane hit.*

lucrative /ˈluː·krət̬·ɪv/ *adj* producing much money or making a large profit ○ *The owner and general manager offered the player a lucrative lifetime contract.*

ludicrous /ˈluːd·ə·krəs/ *adj* ridiculous or foolish; unreasonable or unsuitable ○ *Some stories that initially seemed ludicrous turned out to be true.*

lug /lʌg/ *v* [T] **-gg-** to carry or pull something heavy with much effort ○ *I lugged my suitcase to the check-in counter.*

luggage /ˈlʌg·ɪdʒ/ *n* [U] the bags or other containers that you take your possessions in when traveling; BAGGAGE ○ *The luggage of our tour group was piled up next to the bus.*

lukewarm /ˈluːˈkwɔːrm/ *adj* [not gradable] **1** (esp. of a liquid) only slightly warm ○ *How can you drink lukewarm coffee?* **2** A reaction that is lukewarm is not enthusiastic: *His support for the voting measures was lukewarm.*

lull /lʌl/ *v* [T] to cause someone to feel calm, sleepy, or safe ○ *The music lulled the infant to sleep.* ○ *We were lulled into thinking they wouldn't do anything.*
lull /lʌl/ *n* [C] a period of quiet or reduced activity ○ *a lull in the conversation*

lullaby /ˈlʌl·əˌbɑɪ/ *n* [C] a quiet, gentle song sung to children to help them go to sleep

lumber WOOD /ˈlʌm·bər/ *n* [U] wood that has been cut into various lengths for building
MOVE /ˈlʌm·bər/ *v* [I always + adv/prep] to move in a slow, awkward, and heavy way ○ *A noisy, old, pickup truck lumbered past.*

lumberjack /ˈlʌm·bərˌdʒæk/ *n* [C] a person whose job is to cut down trees to be used in building and industry

lumberyard /ˈlʌm·bərˌjɑrd/ *n* [C] a place where wood used in building is stored and sold

lumen /ˈluː·mən/ *n* [C] ***physics, earth science*** the standard unit for measuring the brightness of a light, equal to the amount of light hitting one square foot of surface one foot away from the light

luminary /ˈluː·məˌner·i/ *n* [C] a person who is famous and important in a particular area of activity ○ *The speaker is a luminary in the field of cancer research.*

luminosity /ˌluː·məˈnɑs·ət̬·i/ *n* [C] ***earth science*** the total amount of energy produced by a star in one second

luminous /ˈluː·mə·nəs/ *adj* producing or reflecting light, esp. in the dark ○ *The snowy landscape was growing luminous in the late afternoon light.*

lump /lʌmp/ *n* [C] **1** a solid mass without a regular shape ○ *The gravy had lumps of flour in it.* **2** A lump is also a swelling under the skin: *She found a lump under her arm.*
lump /lʌmp/ *v* [T] to consider or deal with as a group ○ *Children of various abilities are lumped together in one class.*
lumpy /ˈlʌm·pi/ *adj* ○ *a lumpy pillow*

IDIOM with **lump**

• **a lump in** *your* **throat** a tight feeling in your throat because of a strong emotion, esp. sadness ○ *I had a huge lump in my throat as I watched my brother get on the plane.*

lump sum *n* [C] a single payment of an amount rather than several payments of smaller amounts ○ *The money can be paid to the winner in a lump sum or in yearly payments.*

lunar /ˈluː·nər/ *adj* [not gradable] of or relating to the moon ○ *a lunar eclipse*

lunar eclipse *n* [C] ***earth science*** ECLIPSE

lunatic /ˈluː·nəˌtɪk/ *n* [C] a foolish or crazy person ○ *He drives like a lunatic.*
lunacy /ˈluː·nə·si/ *n* [U] extreme foolishness or mental illness ○ *It would be lunacy to try and climb the mountain in this weather.*
lunatic /ˈluː·nəˌtɪk/ *adj* [not gradable]

lunatic fringe *n* [C usually sing] the members of a group whose opinions are extreme and different from those of the rest of the group ○ *Roosevelt attacked the reformers as a lunatic fringe.*

lunch /lʌntʃ/ *n* [C/U] a meal eaten in the middle of the day, or the food prepared for this meal ○ [U] *We had soup and sandwiches for lunch.* ○ [C] *I take my lunch to work.*
lunch /lʌntʃ/ *v* [I] ○ *We lunched on crackers and cheese.*

luncheon /ˈlʌn·tʃən/ *n* [C] a formal lunch ○ *The president hosted a luncheon for the press group.*

luncheonette /ˌlʌn·tʃəˈnet/ *n* [C] a small restaurant serving simple, light meals

lunchtime /ˈlʌntʃ·tɑɪm/ *n* [U] the time around the middle of the day when lunch is usually eaten

lung /lʌŋ/ *n* [C] ***biology*** either of the two breathing organs in the chest of people and some animals

lunge /lʌndʒ/ *v* [I always + adv/prep] to move forward with sudden force ○ *The goalkeeper lunged at the ball and knocked it away.*
lunge /lʌndʒ/ *n* [C] a sudden forward movement

lurch /lɜrtʃ/ *v* [I] to move in an irregular way, esp. making sudden movements forward or to the side ○ *When he put the truck into gear, it lurched forward.*

lure /lʊr/ *n* [C/U] **1** anything that attracts people or animals, or the qualities that make something attractive ○ [U] *The lure of the city for creative people has existed for centuries.* **2** A lure is an object used to attract fish or wild animals in order to catch them.

lure /lʊr/ *v* [T] to attract a person or animal ○ *The university hopes to lure a new coach with an attractive salary package.*

lurid /ˈlʊr·əd/ *adj* shocking because involving violence or sex ○ *She told me all the lurid details of her divorce.*

lurk /lɜrk/ *v* [I] to stay around a place secretly, or to stay hidden, waiting to attack or appear ○ *When I was four, I was convinced there was a monster lurking in my closet.*
lurking /ˈlɜr·kɪŋ/ *adj* [not gradable] ○ *(fig.) She had a lurking suspicion* (= a feeling that stayed in her mind) *that he wasn't telling the truth.*

luscious /ˈlʌʃ·əs/ *adj* [not gradable] **1** having a pleasant sweet taste or smell ○ *luscious fruit tarts and cream pies* **2** Luscious can also mean pleasing to see, hear, or feel: *She slipped into her luscious pale pink silk pajamas.*

lush /lʌʃ/ *adj* [-*er*/-*est* only] (of plants, or an area of land with plants) growing close together and in large numbers ○ *The lake, with its lush scenery, is a favorite with canoeists.*

lust /lʌst/ *n* [U] strong desire ○ *a lust for power and fame*
lust /lʌst/ *v* [I always + adv/prep] to have a strong desire for something ○ *Cathie has been lusting for my job for a long time.*

luster **BRIGHTNESS** /ˈlʌs·tər/ *n* [U] the brightness of a smooth or shiny surface ○ *The polished furniture had a rich luster.*
lustrous /ˈlʌs·trəs/ *adj* [not gradable] ○ *This conditioner will give your hair a lustrous glow.*

SPECIAL QUALITY /ˈlʌs·tər/ *n* [U] the quality of being attractive or special ○ *The commercial district around the theater had lost its luster, becoming a magnet for the homeless and driving moviegoers elsewhere.*

lusty /ˈlʌs·ti/ *adj* healthy, strong, and energetic ○ *Her lusty, alto voice has seldom sounded better.*
lustily /ˈlʌs·tə·li/ *adv* [not gradable] ○ *The baby cried lustily.*

Lutheran /ˈluː·θə·rən/ *n* [C] a member of a Christian religious group that is one of the Protestant churches
Lutheran /ˈluː·θə·rən/ *adj* [not gradable] ○ *a Lutheran church* ○ *a Lutheran minister*

luxuriant /ləgˈʒʊr·iː·ənt, ləkˈʃʊr-/ *adj* having a thick and healthy appearance ○ *Her luxuriant hair fell around her shoulders.*

luxury /ˈlʌk·ʃə·ri, ˈlʌg·ʒə-/ *n* [C/U] **1** great comfort, esp. as provided by expensive and beautiful possessions, surroundings, or food, or something enjoyable and often expensive but not necessary ○ [U] *a life of luxury* ○ [U] *a luxury hotel* ○ [C] *Having an extra bathroom was at first a luxury, but after we had children it became a necessity.* **2** A luxury is also any unusual, enjoyable activity: [C] *Sleeping late was a real luxury.*
luxurious /ləgˈʒʊr·iː·əs, ləkˈʃʊr-/ *adj* ○ *luxurious accommodations* ○ *a luxurious hotel/resort*

lying /ˈlɑɪ·ɪŋ/ *present participle of* LIE

lymph /lɪmf/ *n* [U] ***biology*** a colorless liquid that takes waste matter away from body tissue in order to prevent infection

lymphatic /lɪm ˈfæt̬·ɪk/ *adj* [not gradable]

lymph node *n* [C] ***biology*** one of many small organs in the body that produce white blood cells, which the body needs to fight infection

lymphocyte /ˈlɪm·fəˌsɑɪt/ *n* [C] ***biology*** a type of blood cell that fights disease in the body

lynch /lɪntʃ/ *v* [T] (of a group of people) to kill someone who has not been found guilty of a crime at a legal trial, esp. by HANGING (= killed using a rope around the neck)

lyric /ˈlɪr·ɪk/, **lyrical** /ˈlɪr·ɪ·kəl/ *adj* [not gradable] ***literature*** expressing emotions, and often having the quality of a song ○ *lyric poetry*

lyrics /ˈlɪr·ɪks/ *pl n* the words of a song

lysine /ˈlɑɪ·siːn/ *n* [U] ***biology*** an AMINO ACID (= chemical substance) that is necessary for growth and healthy bones

L

M m

M LETTER, **m** /em/ *n* [C] *pl* **M's, Ms, m's, ms** the 13th letter of the English alphabet

NUMBER, m /em/ *number* the ROMAN NUMERAL for the number 1000

m MEASUREMENT *n* [C] *pl* **m** *abbreviation for* METER MEASUREMENT

SIZE /em/ *adj* [not gradable] *abbreviation for* MEDIUM AVERAGE ○ **USAGE:** Used esp. on clothing to show its size.

ma /mɑ/ *n* [C] *infml* mother ○ *She was thrilled when her baby said, "Ma."*

M.A. *n* [C] *abbreviation for* MASTER OF ARTS ○ *My brother has an M.A. in linguistics.*

ma'am /mæm/ *contraction of* MADAM WOMAN ○ *Can I help you, ma'am?*

macabre /mə'kɑb·rə, -'kɑb/ *adj* causing shock and fear because connected with death, esp. strange or cruel death ○ *After the diagnosis, he said he just wanted to stay "above ground," she recalled, smiling at his macabre humor.*

macaroni /ˌmæk·ə'roʊ·ni/ *n* [U] a type of pasta in the shape of small tubes ○ *macaroni and cheese*

Mace /meɪs/ *n* [U] *trademark* a chemical in a container which, when sprayed into a person's face, causes the eyes to sting and become full of tears

machete /mə'ʃet̬·i/ *n* [C] a big knife with a wide blade ○ *You'd need a machete to clear a path through this undergrowth.*

machinations /ˌmæk·ə'neɪ·ʃənz, ˌmæʃ-/ *pl n* complicated and secret plans, esp. in obtaining or using power ○ *She complained about the machinations political candidates employed to win.*

machine /mə'ʃiːn/ *n* [C] **1** a device with moving parts that uses power to do work of a particular type ○ *a sewing/washing machine* ○ *an answering machine* **2** ***politics & government*** A machine is also a group of people who control a political organization: *He was a product of an old-line party machine.*

machinery /mə'ʃiː·nə·ri/ *n* [U] a group of machines, or the movable parts of a machine ○ *farm machinery* ○ *Some of the older machinery breaks down frequently.*

machinist /mə'ʃiː·nəst/ *n* [C] a person whose job is operating or repairing machines

WORD FAMILY machine			
Nouns	machine machinery machinist mechanic mechanics mechanism	*Adjectives* *Adverbs*	mechanical mechanically

machine gun *n* [C] an automatic gun that can fire a lot of bullets one after the other very quickly

machine-readable *adj* (of information or text) in a form that can be used by a computer

machismo /mə'tʃiːz·moʊ, -'kiːz-, -'kɪz-/ *n* [U] strong pride in behaving in a way that is thought to be typically male, esp. by showing strength and power

macho /'mɑtʃ·oʊ/ *adj* behaving in a way that is thought to be typical of a man, esp. by seeming strong and powerful but also seeming too determined to avoid showing weakness and sympathy ○ *He's too macho to admit that a woman can do his job as well as he can.*

mackerel /'mæk·rəl/ *n* [C/U] *pl* **mackerel** an edible sea fish

macro- /'mæk·roʊ/ *prefix* large, or relating to the whole of something and not just its parts ○ *macroeconomics* ○ Compare MICRO-

macromolecule /ˌmæk·roʊ'mɑl·əˌkjuːl/ *n* [C] ***biology, chemistry*** a large MOLECULE (= smallest unit of a substance), for example, a PROTEIN (= chemical substance in living things)

macroscopic /ˌmæk·rə'skɑp·ɪk/ *adj* ***science*** large enough to be seen without using any devices that make things look larger

mad ANGRY /mæd/ *adj* [-er/-est only] **-dd-** angry or annoyed ○ *I get so mad at her I sometimes start screaming.*

maddening /'mæd·ən·ɪŋ/ *adj* annoying ○ *Airlines make you wait in maddening ticket counter lines for hours on end.*

NOT CONTROLLED /mæd/ *adj* [-er/-est only] **-dd-** (of an activity) wild, fast, or excited and not well controlled ○ *We made a mad dash for the school bus.*

madly /'mæd·li/ *adv* ○ *Just before my in-laws arrived, I rushed around madly trying to clean the place up.*

ENTHUSIASTIC /mæd/ *adj* [-er/-est only] **-dd-** *infml* very enthusiastic and interested ○ *Jeanne's mad about old Woody Allen movies.*

madly /'mæd·li/ *adv* ○ *She says she's madly in love with him.*

MENTALLY ILL /mæd/ *adj* [-er/-est only] **-dd-** mentally ill, or unable to behave in a reasonable way; INSANE ○ *In his years as a prisoner of war, he often felt as if he might go mad.*

madness /'mæd·nəs/ *n* [U] ○ *There was a history of madness* (= mental illness) *in her family.* ○ *It would be sheer madness* (= crazy) *to ignore the symptoms and do nothing.*

madam /'mæd·əm/, *contraction* **ma'am** *n* [U] *fml* **1** a polite word used to address a woman, or a title for a woman used before a position ○ *"May I help you, madam?"* ○ *Madam President* **2** A madam can also be a woman who is in charge of a BROTHEL (= place where men pay to have sex with women) ○ Compare SIR MAN

Madame /mə'dæm, mæ-/ *n* [U] a title for a woman, esp. a married woman from France ○ *Madame Bovary*

M

madcap /ˈmæd·kæp/ *adj* silly and often amusing ○ *The madcap antics of the clowns made us laugh.*

made /meɪd/ *past simple and past participle of* MAKE

IDIOM with made

• **made for each other** perfectly matched ○ *The long cool drinks and the hot spicy food were made for each other.* ○ *The two of you were made for each other – I think you should get married!*

made-to-order /ˌmeɪd·təˈɔːrd·ər/ *adj* [not gradable] **1** (esp. of clothing) created especially for a particular person ○ *made-to-order boots* **2** A situation that is made-to-order is perfect: *The weather on this vacation has been made-to-order so far.*

made-up WEARING MAKEUP /ˈmeɪdˈʌp/ *adj* wearing esp. a lot of makeup ○ *She was heavily made-up and wearing a wig.*

INVENTED /ˈmeɪdˈʌp/ *adj* (of stories) created by the imagination, or invented and not true ○ *a made-up name* ○ *They complained about "made-up" data.*

madhouse /ˈmæd·hɑʊs/ *n* [C] a place that is wild and noisy, with too many activities going on ○ *I can't study here, this place is a madhouse!*

M

Madison Avenue /ˈmæd·ə·səˈnæv·əˌnuː, -ˌnjuː/ *n* [U] the advertising industry in the US

madly /ˈmæd·li/ *adv* ○ See at MAD NOT CONTROLLED; MAD ENTHUSIASTIC

madman /ˈmæd·mæn, -mən/ *n* [C] **-men** a man who is mentally ill, or who behaves in a way that seems strange, dangerous, or not controlled

madness /ˈmæd·nəs/ *n* ○ See at MAD MENTALLY ILL

Madonna /məˈdɑn·ə/ *n* [C/U] the mother of Jesus, or a picture or statue of her

maelstrom /ˈmeɪl·strəm, -ˌstrɑm/ *n* [C] a situation in which there is great confusion, disagreement, or violence ○ *It was a country in turmoil, caught up in a maelstrom of change.*

maestro /ˈmɑɪ·stroʊ/ *n* [C] *pl* **maestros** a person who is very skilled at CONDUCTING (= directing the performance of music) or writing music

Mafia /ˈmɑf·iː·ə, ˈmæf-/ *n* [U] a large criminal organization, esp. a secret criminal organization that is active in the US and Italy

mafic /ˈmæf·ɪk/ *adj* [not gradable] ***earth science*** describes rocks containing more dark-colored substances and iron than other rocks ○ Compare FELSIC

magazine /ˌmæg·əˈziːn/ *n* [C] **1** a type of thin book with a paper cover that is published regularly and usually contains articles and photographs ○ *a weekly/monthly magazine* **2** A magazine on television is a regularly broadcast program that reports about news events or other true stories.

magenta /məˈdʒent·ə/ *adj, n* [C/U] (of) a dark, purple-red color

maggot /ˈmæg·ət/ *n* [C] a creature like a very small WORM (= an animal with a soft body and no arms or legs) that later develops into a flying insect

magic IMAGINARY POWER /ˈmædʒ·ɪk/ *n* [U] **1** (esp. in stories for children) the use of special powers to make things happen that would usually be impossible ○ *a tale of witchcraft and magic* **2** Magic is also the skill of performing tricks to entertain people, such as making things seem to appear and disappear, or the tricks performed: *My daughter loves doing magic.*

magical /ˈmædʒ·ɪ·kəl/ *adj* ○ *It's a story about a timid schoolteacher who obtains magical powers after he's hit by a lightning bolt.*

magician /məˈdʒɪʃ·ən/ *n* [C] a person who performs tricks as entertainment, such as making things seem to appear and disappear

SPECIAL QUALITY /ˈmædʒ·ɪk/ *n* [U] a special, exciting quality that makes something or someone different and better than others ○ *As an actress, she has lost none of her magic, and she still is thrilling to watch.*

magical /ˈmædʒ·ɪ·kəl/ *adj* ○ *There was something magical about that evening that I will never forget.*

WORD FAMILY magic			
Nouns	magic magician	*Adjectives*	magical
		Adverbs	magically

Magic Marker *n* [C] *trademark* a type of pen available in many colors of ink that has a thick writing end made of fiber

magistrate /ˈmædʒ·əˌstreɪt/ *n* [C] a judge in a law court who deals with crimes that are not serious

magma /ˈmæg·mə/ *n* [U] ***earth science*** melted rock under the surface of the earth

magnanimous /mægˈnæn·ə·məs/ *adj* generous and kind, esp. toward a competitor or enemy ○ *The Yankees' manager was magnanimous in defeat, praising Seattle for its fine play.*

magnate /ˈmæg·nət, -neɪt/ *n* [C] a person who is very successful, powerful, and rich, esp. in a particular business ○ *a real estate/media magnate*

magnesium /mægˈniː·ziː·əm/ *n* [U] a silver-white metal that burns very brightly and is used in making FIREWORKS (= explosions producing colored patterns for entertainment)

magnet /ˈmæg·nət/ *n* [C] ***physics*** an object, esp. a piece of iron, that is able to attract iron and steel objects toward itself ○ *Magnets are used to attach the toy train's cars to the engine.* ○ *We use a refrigerator magnet* (= small decorative magnet that will stick to a steel door) *to hang our kids' latest drawings.* ○ (*fig.*) *New York City remains a magnet for tourists* (= it attracts them).

magnetic /mægˈneṭ·ɪk/ *adj* **1** *Leni was playing with the magnetic letters on the refrigerator.* ○ (*fig.*) *She has a magnetic personality* (= it is powerfully attractive). **2** ***physics*** A **magnetic field** is the area around a magnet that is affected by the power of the magnet.

magnetism /ˈmæg·nəˌtɪz·əm/ *n* [U] the power of a magnet to attract other objects ○ *(fig.) Elvis's animal magnetism* (= powerful physical attraction) *made him a beloved celebrity to millions.*

magnetic strip *n* [C/U] a plastic strip on which information can be recorded, for example on the back of a CREDIT CARD ○ *The state started issuing driver's licenses with magnetic strips on the back that contain data.*

magnet school *n* [C] a school that specializes in a particular subject in order to attract students from a wide area ○ *The Beebe School is a magnet school for the environmental sciences.*

magnificent /mægˈnɪf·ə·sənt/ *adj* causing admiration esp. because of an unusual quality such as great size or beauty ○ *New Orleans is famous for its magnificent old oak trees.*

magnificence /mægˈnɪf·ə·səns/ *n* [U] ○ *the magnificence of nature*

magnify /ˈmæg·nəˌfɑɪ/ *v* [T] **1** to make something look larger than it is, esp. by looking at it through a special piece of glass ○ *Although your skin looks smooth, when magnified you can see a lot of little bumps and holes.* **2** *fig.* To magnify something is also to make it seem more important or more serious than it really is: *He always magnifies the problems and inconveniences of travel.*

magnification /ˌmæg·nə·fəˈkeɪ·ʃən/ *n* [C/U] the act of making something look larger than it is, or the degree to which it does look larger

magnifying glass *n* [C] a special piece of glass, usually with a handle, that you hold over an object in order to make it appear larger

magnitude /ˈmæg·nəˌtuːd/ *n* [U] **1** large size or great importance ○ *The magnitude of the task would have discouraged an ordinary man.* **2** ***earth science*** Magnitude is also a measure of the brightness of a star as it appears from earth. **3** ***earth science*** The magnitude of an EARTHQUAKE is a measure of how strong or violent it is.

magnolia /mægˈnoʊl·jə/ *n* [C] a type of tree with large, sweet-smelling, usually white or pink flowers, esp. common in the southeastern US

magpie /ˈmæg·pɑɪ/ *n* [C] a bird with black-and-white feathers and a long tail

mahogany /məˈhɑg·ə·ni/ *n* [U] a type of tree that grows in hot regions of the earth, or its dark, red-brown wood used esp. to make furniture ○ *a mahogany chest of drawers*

maid /meɪd/ *n* [C] a woman who is employed to clean hotel rooms and make them neat, or a woman who is a servant in a person's home ○ *We left a note in our room for the maid to give us extra towels.*

maiden WOMAN /ˈmeɪd·ᵊn/, **maid** /meɪd/ *n* [C] ***literature*** *old use* a girl or young woman ○ *In the story, the prince woos the fair maiden.*

FIRST /ˈmeɪd·ᵊn/ *adj* [not gradable] (esp. of a trip by a ship or vehicle) first ○ *a maiden voyage/flight*

maiden name *n* [C usually sing] the family name of a woman before she gets married and begins to use her husband's family name

maid of honor /ˌmeɪd·əˈvɑn·ər/ *n* [C] (at a wedding) a girl or woman who is the most important BRIDESMAID (= woman who helps the woman getting married)

mail /meɪl/ *n* [U] the letters and packages that are transported and delivered to your home or the place you work, esp. those delivered by the government's system ○ *She spent the morning reading and answering mail.* ○ *The mail is usually delivered before noon.*

mail /meɪl/ *v* [T] to send esp. letters or packages by the mail system ○ *She mailed the letter last week but it still hasn't arrived.*

mailing /ˈmeɪ·lɪŋ/ *n* [C] ○ *The museum sent out a mailing* (= a lot of letters sent at one time) *asking for donations.*

mailbox /ˈmeɪl·bɑks/ *n* [C] **1** a metal container in a public place where you can put a letter you are sending by mail, or a box outside a person's house where letters are sent and delivered **2** A mailbox on a computer is the place where E-MAIL is received, sent, and stored.

mailing list *n* [C] a list of names and addresses kept by an organization of its members, customers, or other people to whom it sends letters or EMAILS

mailman /ˈmeɪl·mæn, -mən/ *n* [C] **-men** a male LETTER CARRIER

mail order *n* [C] a way of shopping in which you send payment and a form showing the product you want to buy to the company who makes the product, and it sends the product to you ○ *I often buy clothes by mail order.*

maim /meɪm/ *v* [I/T] to injure a person so severely that a part of that person's body will no longer work correctly or is completely lacking ○ [T] *Many civilians have been maimed by land mines.*

main MOST IMPORTANT /meɪn/ *adj* [not gradable] most important or larger ○ *The main thing is to keep calm and don't get angry.* ○ *The main social event of the summer was a dance and reception.*

mainly /ˈmeɪn·li/ *adv* [not gradable] usually, or to a large degree ○ *The group is mainly made up of young people.*

PIPE /meɪn/ *n* [C] a large pipe that is part of the system carrying water or gas from one place to another ○ *A water main burst and flooded the street.*

main drag *n* [C] *infml* a town's most important street, where most of the businesses are

mainframe /ˈmeɪn·freɪm/ *n* [C] a large computer that can be used to do several things at once and which is usually used by a number of people

mainland /ˈmeɪn·lənd/ *n* [U] the main part of a country or continent, not including the islands

M

around it ○ *The island is accessible by ferry from the mainland.*

mainstay /ˈmeɪn·steɪ/ *n* [C] the most important part of something, providing support for everything else ○ *In the early 1900s, farming was the mainstay of the national economy.*

mainstream /ˈmeɪn·stri:m/ *adj* (of beliefs or behavior) common and shared by most people, or representing such beliefs or behavior ○ *The story was largely ignored by the mainstream press.*

mainstream /ˈmeɪn·stri:m/ *n* [U] most of a society ○ *New laws will allow more disabled people to enter the mainstream.*

mainstream /ˈmeɪn·stri:m/ *v* [T] to place children with special needs in regular classes at school ○ *The district was ordered to mainstream more children with disabilities.*

Main Street *n* [U] **1** the street in a town with the most important stores and businesses **2** People often use Main Street to talk about average Americans and the most typical things about American life: *a Main Street jobs program*

maintain Ⓐ **CONTINUE TO HAVE** /meɪn ˈteɪn/ *v* [T] to continue to have; to keep in existence, or not allow to become less ○ *Despite living in different states, the two families have maintained a close friendship.* ○ *You have to maintain a minimum balance in your checking account.*

maintenance Ⓐ /ˈmeɪnt·ᵊn·əns/ *n* [U] the process of keeping or continuing something

PRESERVE /meɪn ˈteɪn/ *v* [T] to keep something in good condition ○ *A large house costs a lot to maintain.*

maintenance Ⓐ /ˈmeɪnt·ᵊn·əns/ *n* [U] the work needed to keep something in good condition ○ *Bridges require a lot of maintenance.*

EXPRESS /meɪn ˈteɪn/ *v* [T] to express strongly your belief that something is true ○ [+ (*that*) clause] *She maintains (that) she's being criticized simply for telling the truth.*

maize /meɪz/ *n* [U] corn

majestic /məˈdʒes·tɪk/ *adj* (of something) having the quality of causing you to feel great admiration and respect for it because of its size, power, or beauty ○ *We flew over the majestic Sierra Nevada mountains.*

majesty /ˈmædʒ·ə·sti/ *n* [U] ○ *A whale passed by in all its majesty.*

Majesty /ˈmædʒ·ə·sti/ *n* [C] a title used to speak to or about a king or queen or other ruler with a similar title ○ *Her Majesty, the Empress of Japan*

major Ⓐ **IMPORTANT** /ˈmeɪ·dʒər/ *adj* [not gradable] more important, bigger, or more serious than others of the same type ○ *Fresh fruits are a major source of vitamin C.* ○ *We awaited major new developments in the peace talks.* ○ Compare MINOR UNIMPORTANT

SPECIAL SUBJECT /ˈmeɪ·dʒər/ *n* [C] the most important subject that a college or university student is studying, or the student studying that subject ○ *an English major*

MUSIC /ˈmeɪ·dʒər/ *adj* ***music*** based on a SCALE (= series of musical notes) in which there is a WHOLE STEP (= sound difference) between each note except between the third and fourth notes and the seventh and eighth notes ○ *a major scale* ○ *a major chord* ○ Compare MINOR MUSIC

OFFICER /ˈmeɪ·dʒər/ *n* [C] a military officer of middle rank, above a CAPTAIN

PHRASAL VERB with major

• **major in** *something* to study something as your main subject in college or a university ○ *She majored in earth sciences at Arizona State.*

majority Ⓐ /məˈdʒɔ:r·əţ·i, -ˈdʒɑr-/ *n* [U] **1** more than half of a total number or amount; the larger part of something ○ *A majority of the people voted against the bill to raise school taxes.* **2** ***politics & government*** A majority is also the difference in the number of votes in an election between the winning person or group and the one that has the second highest number: [C] *The Republicans won by a small majority.* ○ Compare MINORITY

major league *n* [C] an organized group of sports teams that have the best players, who are paid for playing ○ *He's happy to finally be playing in the major leagues.* ○ (*fig.*) *She hired a major-league attorney* (= one who is highly paid and considered to be among the best).

make **PRODUCE** /meɪk/ *v* [T] *past* **made** to bring something into existence, esp. using a particular substance or material; produce ○ *Does that company make computers?* ○ *Butter is made from cream.* ○ *My wedding ring is made of gold.* ○ *He made us some coffee.*

make /meɪk/ *n* [C] a particular product, or the name of the company that made it ○ *What make of air conditioner do you recommend?*

maker /ˈmeɪ·kər/ *n* [C] ○ *The makers of music videos show a fantasy world.* ➤ Usage: **do or make?** at DO CAUSE TO HAPPEN

WORD CHOICES make

Produce is an alternative to "make."

*California **produces** a lot of grapes.*

*Red blood cells are **produced** in the bone marrow.*

The verb **create** is used when someone makes something new, especially something original.

*DaVinci **created** the masterpiece we know as "Mona Lisa."*

The verb **manufacture** is used when something is made in a factory.

*The product is **manufactured** in Germany.*

You can use the verbs **build** or **construct** when someone makes things by putting things together.

*The bird **built** its nest in a tree.*

*The walls are **constructed** of concrete.*

CAUSE /meɪk/ *v* [T] *past* **made** to cause something ○ *The kids made a mess in the kitchen.* ○ *Don't make any noise.*

CAUSE TO BE /meɪk/ *v* [T] *past* **made** to cause something to be, become, or appear in a particular way ○ *If you open some windows, you'll make it cooler.* ○ *He said something that made her angry.* ○ *We can sit closer together and make room* (= provide space) *for one more.* ○ *We're making our attic into a spare bedroom.*

PERFORM /meɪk/ *v* [T] *past* **made 1** to perform an action ○ *I've got to make a (phone) call to Ricardo.* ○ *We must make a decision by tomorrow.* ○ *Someone has made a mistake.* ○ *Latisha is making progress in her reading.* ○ *Can I make a suggestion?* ○ *We might as well make use of the car, since we've got it for the whole weekend.* **2** To **make the bed** is to put sheets and covers on a bed so that someone can sleep in it, or to straighten them after it has been slept in.

FORCE /meɪk/ *v* [T] *past* **made** to force someone or something to do something ○ *Ambition will make you get up off your sofa and go out and work for what you want.*

USAGE

make

Remember that if you use **make** with the meaning "cause something" or "force someone to do something" then you need to use the pattern **make** + *object* + **infinitive without to:**

They made him clean the house.

~~*They made him to clean the house.*~~

The exception to this rule is when **make** is in the passive, when you must use **to** with the infinitive.

We are made to feel these products are necessary.

BE OR BECOME /meɪk/ *v* [L] *past* **made** to be or become something, esp. by having the necessary characteristics ○ *I don't think he will ever make a good lawyer.* ○ *Hector and Wanda make a delightful couple.* ○ *He worked really hard, but he didn't make the team* (= was not chosen to be a member of it).

makings /ˈmeɪ·kɪŋz/ *pl n* ○ *I think the plan has (all) the makings of a disaster* (= is likely to be one).

TOTAL /meɪk/ *v* [L] *past* **made** to add up to (a total) ○ *6 and 6 make 12.*

EARN /meɪk/ *v* [T] *past* **made** to earn or get ○ *She makes $70,000 a year.* ○ *Can you make a living as a painter?*

ARRIVE /meɪk/ *v* [T] *past* **made** *infml* to arrive at or reach ○ *We should make Whitefish Bay by nightfall.* ○ *He made it to the bed and then collapsed.*

WORD FAMILY make

Nouns	make	*Verbs*	make
	remake		remake
	maker		
	makings		

IDIOMS with make

• **make a beeline for** *something* to move quickly and directly toward something ○ *When he saw me in the kitchen, he made a beeline for the door.*

• **make a (big) difference**, **make all the difference** to improve a situation or condition in an important way ○ *He's much happier now – his new school seems to have made a big difference.* ○ Opposite: MAKE NO DIFFERENCE

• **make a face (at** *someone/something***)**, **make faces (at** *someone/something***)** to move your mouth, nose, and eyes in strange ways to show emotion or make people laugh ○ *She stepped in something, made a face, and looked down.* ○ *My sister was making faces at me when my mom wasn't looking.*

• **make a fool (out) of** *someone* to do something that makes someone, esp. yourself, seem ridiculous ○ *I almost stood up and sang, but I decided I didn't want to make a fool out of myself.*

• **make a habit of** *something* to begin to do something regularly, often without thinking about it ○ *He made a habit of ignoring me whenever his friends were around.*

• **make a mountain out of a molehill** to cause something unimportant to seem important ○ *Stop worrying! You're making a mountain out of a molehill.*

• **make a point of** *doing something* to always do something or take particular care to do it ○ *She makes a point of calling her grandmother every week.*

• **make** *someone's* **acquaintance** *fml* to meet someone ○ *I'm very pleased to make your acquaintance.*

• **make allowances for** *something* to accept that a particular fact will change a situation ○ *We try to make allowances for our students' different backgrounds.*

• **make believe** to pretend ○ *Jake likes to make believe he's a pirate.*

• **make** *someone's* **blood boil** to cause someone to be very angry ○ *When I hear stories of cruelty to animals, it makes my blood boil.*

• **make** *someone's* **day** to make someone feel very happy ○ *Seeing those little kids having so much fun just made my day.*

• **make do (with** *something***)** to use what is available although it is not enough or what you wanted ○ *Can you make do with $5 for now and I'll give you the rest tomorrow?*

• **make ends meet** to have enough money to buy what you need to live ○ *It's not easy to make ends meet with a big family, but somehow we manage.*

• **make fun of** *someone* to be unkind to someone and laugh at or cause others to laugh at the person ○ *You're always making fun of me!*

• **make good** to become successful and usually rich ○ *He's a boy from a poor background who made good on Wall Street.*

• **make good on** *something* to do what you have said you would do ○ *My grandfather said he would pay for me to go to college, and he made good on that promise.*

• **make good time** to complete a trip quickly ○ *We made good time – I think it only took us an hour and fifteen minutes.*

• **make heads or tails of** *something* to not be able to understand something at all ○ *We couldn't make heads or tails of your directions.*

M

• **make headway** to begin to succeed ○ *Has the city made any headway in attracting new businesses?*

• **make it (big)** *infml* to become famous or successful ○ *By the time he was nineteen, he had made it big in the music business.*

• **make light of** *something* to act as if something is not serious, esp. when it is serious ○ *They've both had knee injuries, but the two friends make light of their weaknesses.*

• **make love** to have sex

• **make much of** *something* to give a lot of importance to something ○ *Don't make too much of the test results.*

• **make no apologies** to believe that what you have done is right or acceptable ○ *The network makes no apologies for broadcasting the controversial film.*

• **make no bones about** to not try to hide something or say you are sorry about it ○ *He makes no bones about the fact that his apartment is a mess.*

• **make no difference, not make any difference** to not change or improve a situation ○ *It doesn't make any difference now what he says – it's too late for apologies.* ○ Opposite: MAKE A (BIG) DIFFERENCE

• **make or break** *something* to cause something to succeed or fail ○ *She has the power to make or break your career.*

• **make sense 1** to be clear and easy to understand ○ *This last paragraph doesn't make any sense.* **2** Someone who **makes sense** is reasonable or shows good judgment: *Everything he said made sense – I'd definitely vote for him.* ○ *It makes sense to pay off your debts before you start trying to save money.*

• **make short work of** *someone/something* to deal with someone or something quickly and effectively ○ *We made short work of the food that was put in front of us.* ○ *The team made short work of their biggest rival last night.*

• **make sure 1** to take special care to do something ○ *Make sure you're home by midnight.* ○ *Make sure to tell them I said "hi."* **2** To **make sure** also means to find out whether something is really true or real: *Make sure he's honest before you lend him any money.*

• **make that** *something* *infml* I want to change what I just said to something else ○ *I'll have a steak – no, make that an omelet.*

• **make the grade (as** *something***)** to be good enough to be successful at something ○ *Do you think I will make the grade as a chef?*

• **make the most of** *something* to use or enjoy something as much as possible ○ *We're only in Paris for a day, so let's make the most of it.*

• **make time** to be certain there is enough time ○ *I try to make time to run twice a week.*

• **make up for lost time** to do something as much as possible because you were not able to do it before ○ *After seven years in prison, he's home with his kids and making up for lost time.*

• **make up** *your* **mind** to decide what to do or choose ○ *"Which one do you like best?" "I don't know – I can't make up my mind."* ○ *She made up her mind to call him again.*

• **make waves** to shock or upset people with something new or different ○ *When I started the job, a friend told me not to make waves because the managers didn't like people to disagree with them.*

• **make way for** *something* to provide a space or an opportunity for something else ○ *Some beautiful old buildings were torn down to make way for the new parking garage.*

• **on the make** trying hard to succeed, esp. in a way that is dishonest ○ *The movie is about a businessman on the make, who steals company funds.*

PHRASAL VERBS with make

• **make for** *something* **CREATE** to be one thing, or the most important thing, that causes something ○ *Everyone agreed that filming inside a chocolate factory would make for good television.*

• **make for** *somewhere/something* **MOVE TOWARD** to go directly toward someone or something ○ *They split up and the man made for the subway.*

• **make** *something* **of** *something/someone* to understand the meaning of a statement or action, or to have an opinion about something or someone ○ *What do you make of the new boss?*

• **make off with** *something* to steal something ○ *Thieves disguised as policemen made off with 13 pictures, including three Rembrandts.*

• **make out SUCCEED** to continue or succeed in life or in business ○ *How is Fran making out in her new job?*

• **make** *someone/yourself/something* **out CLAIM** to claim, usually falsely, that something is true ○ *He made himself out to be a millionaire.* ○ *You make it out as if the press can't tell the difference between image and reality.*

• **make out** *something/someone* **UNDERSTAND** [M] to see, hear, or understand something or someone with difficulty ○ *I couldn't make out what he said.*

• **make out** *something* **WRITE** [M] to write all the necessary information on an official form, document, etc. ○ *Make the check out to Hommocks School PTA.*

• **make out KISS** *infml* to kiss and hold someone romantically

• **make over** *someone/something* [M] to improve something or someone by working on or changing various parts ○ *Ed Carey has been chosen to make over the losing football team.* ○ Related noun: MAKEOVER

• **make up** *something* **INVENT** [M] to invent an excuse, a story, etc., often in order to deceive ○ *I was trying to make up a good excuse for being late.*

• **make up** *something* **PREPARE** [M] to prepare or arrange something by putting different things together ○ *Could you make up a list of what we need at the supermarket?* ○ *The maid will make up your room* (= clean it).

• **make up** *something* **PROVIDE** [M] to provide something, esp. an amount that reaches a total ○ *We're $5 short, but I'll make up the difference.*

• **make up** *something* **DO LATER** to do something at a different time because you cannot do it at the expected time ○ *She left work early and made up the time by staying late the next day.*

• **make up BECOME FRIENDS** to forgive someone and become friends again after an argument or disagreement ○ *We argue all right, but we always make up before long.*

M

• **make up** *something* **FORM** (of a number of things) to form something as a whole ○ *The book is made up of several different articles.* ○ Related noun: MAKEUP COMBINATION

• **make up for** *something* to use as a replacement for something missing, lost, or lacking ○ *What he lacks in size, Hayes makes up for in toughness on the basketball court.* ○ *Some of these horses have cost me a lot of money, but other ones have made up for it.* ○ *For all the skiers yet to make a trip to the mountains this winter, this is the perfect opportunity to* **make up for lost time** (= do what you did not have an opportunity to do earlier).

• **make** *something* **up to** *someone* to do something good for someone because the person has been good to you, or because you have been bad to the person ○ *You've done an awful lot for me, and I don't know how I can ever make it up to you.*

make-believe /ˈmeɪk·bəˌliːv/ *n* [U] a state of mind in which you pretend to believe that conditions are real, esp. because that reality would be more pleasant than the actual one ○ *Disneyland creates a world of make-believe.*

make-believe /ˈmeɪk·bəˌliːv/ *adj* [not gradable] (used esp. in children's play) representing something that you agree to pretend is real for the purpose of playing ○ *They dueled with make-believe swords and climbed make-believe cliffs.*

makeover /ˈmeɪkˌoʊ·vər/ *n* [C] a new or improved appearance that results from making many changes ○ *Honda unveiled the car's high-tech makeover this week.* ○ Related verb: MAKE OVER

makeshift /ˈmeɪk·ʃɪft/ *adj* temporary and of low quality, but used because of a sudden need ○ *We pulled into a makeshift parking area.*

makeup **SUBSTANCE** /ˈmeɪ·kʌp/ *n* [U] colored substances used on your face to improve or change its appearance ○ *She always wears a lot of makeup.*

COMBINATION /ˈmeɪ·kʌp/ *n* [C usually sing] a combination of things that form something ○ *The committee's membership does not reflect the city's racial makeup.* ○ Related verb: MAKE UP FORM

make-work *n* [U] unimportant work given to someone to keep that person busy

malady /ˈmæl·əd·i/ *n* [C] *fml* a disease, or a problem in the way something works ○ *She's suffering from a variety of maladies, including dizziness, weakness, and headaches.*

malaise /məˈleɪz, mæ-, -ˈlez/ *n* [U] a general feeling of bad health or lack of energy in a person, group, or society ○ *Many think there's a growing moral malaise in society.*

malaria /məˈler·iː·ə/ *n* [U] a disease, esp. of the hotter regions of the earth, caused by the bite of an infected MOSQUITO (= small flying insect)

male /meɪl/ *adj* [not gradable] of the sex that produces a natural substance that can make an egg develop into young ○ *a male gorilla* ○ *Male and female soldiers serve in the same units.* ○ Compare FEMALE

male /meɪl/ *n* [C] ○ *The target audience is young males 20 to 30 years old.*

malevolent /məˈlev·ə·lənt/ *adj* causing or wanting to cause harm or evil ○ *a malevolent juvenile delinquent*

malfunction /mælˈfʌŋk·ʃən/ *v* [I] (of a machine, piece of equipment, or organ) to fail to work correctly ○ *The equipment malfunctions at temperatures below freezing.*

malfunction /mælˈfʌŋk·ʃən/ *n* [C] ○ *a computer malfunction*

malice /ˈmæl·əs/ *n* [U] *law* the intention to do something wrong and esp. to cause injury ○ *An employee would have to prove an employer acted out of malice in order to sue.*

malicious /məˈlɪʃ·əs/ *adj* intending to cause harm, esp. by hurting someone's feelings or reputation ○ *He says she threatened him and spied on him, among other malicious activities.*

malign /məˈlɑɪn/ *v* [T] to say things about someone or something that are harmful and usually not true ○ *He said he had been unfairly maligned by a few board members who wanted him fired.*

malignant /məˈlɪg·nənt/ *adj medical* (of a disease or tissue growing because of a disease) leading to death ○ *The pathologist's report said the tumor was malignant.* ○ Compare BENIGN

malignancy /məˈlɪg·nən·si/ *n* [C/U] *medical* tissue that is growing because of a disease process and that is likely to cause death ○ [C] *If this type of malignancy is discovered early enough, the outlook is pretty good.*

mall /mɔːl/, **shopping mall** *n* [C] **1** a very large building or buildings containing a lot of stores and often restaurants, and usually with space around it outside for parking ○ *Judy likes to hang out at the mall with her friends.* **2** A mall is also a street in a city or town with a lot of stores and that is closed to traffic.

mallard /ˈmæl·ərd/ *n* [C] a common, wild DUCK (= type of water bird)

malleable /ˈmæl·iː·ə·bəl/ *adj* **1** easily influenced, trained, or controlled ○ *Mother wanted me to be a malleable girl who would take her advice.* **2** A substance that is malleable is easily bent and shaped.

malleability /ˌmæl·iː·əˈbɪl·əţ·i/ *n* [U]

mallet /ˈmæl·ət/ *n* [C] a hammer with a large, flat end made of wood or rubber

malnourished /mælˈnɜr·ɪʃt/ *adj* weak and in bad health because of a lack of food or a lack of food that is good for you ○ *By the time we saw the child, she was extremely malnourished.*

malnutrition /ˌmæl·nuːˈtrɪʃ·ən/ *n* [U] physical weakness and bad health caused by a lack of food or by a lack of food that is good for you

malpractice /mælˈpræk·təs/ *n* [U] *law* the failure of a doctor or other PROFESSIONAL to do his or her job with a reasonable degree of skill, esp. when that person's actions or failure to act causes injury or loss ○ *He was sued for medical malpractice.*

M

malt /mɔːlt/ *n* [U] grain, usually BARLEY, that has been left in water until it starts to grow and is then dried, used in making some types of alcoholic drinks

maltase /ˈmɔːl·teɪs, -teɪz/ *n* [U] ***biology*** an ENZYME (= substance that causes chemical change) that helps MALTOSE (= sugar made in the body) change to GLUCOSE (= sugar used for energy)

malted (milk) /ˈmɔːl·təd (ˈmɪlk)/ *n* [C] a drink made from milk, BARLEY, flavoring, and ice cream

maltose /ˈmɔːl·toʊs, -toʊz/ *n* [U] ***biology*** a type of sugar made in the body from starch by ENZYMES (= substances that cause chemical change)

mama, mamma, momma /ˈmɑm·ə/ *n* [C] *a child's word* mother

mama's boy *n* [C] *disapproving* a boy or man who others consider to be weak because he behaves as his mother tells him to

mammal /ˈmæm·əl/ *n* [C] ***biology*** any animal in which the female gives birth to babies, not eggs, and feeds them on milk from her own body

mammogram /ˈmæm·əˌgræm/ *n* [C] an X-RAY photograph of a woman's breasts, used to find signs of disease

M

mammoth /ˈmæm·əθ/ *adj* [not gradable] extremely large ○ *Building the dam was a mammoth construction project.*

man HUMAN MALE /mæn/ *n* [C] *pl* **men** **1** an adult male human being ○ *a young man* ○ *the men's 400-meter race* ○ *John can solve anything – the man's a genius.* **2** A man is also a male employee without particular rank or title, or a member of the military who has a low rank: *The gas company sent a man to fix the heating system.* **3** *infml* Man is sometimes used when addressing an adult male human being: *Hey, man, got a light?* **4** *infml* Man is sometimes used as an exclamation, esp. when the speaker is expressing a strong emotion: *Man, what a storm!* **5** When an official at a wedding says a man and a woman have become **man and wife**, it means they are now married to each other.

manhood /ˈmæn·hʊd/ *n* [U] **1** the condition or time of being a man ○ *a boy on the brink of manhood* **2** Manhood is also the qualities that are considered typical of a man: *He feels he has to do dangerous things to prove his manhood.*

manly /ˈmæn·li/ *adj* having qualities such as strength and bravery that people think a man should have ○ *The boy was told that it wasn't manly to cry.*

manliness /ˈmæn·liː·nəs/ *n* [U] ○ *We no longer equate aggression with manliness.*

mannish /ˈmæn·ɪʃ/ *adj* (of a woman) having characteristics typical of a man

PERSON /mæn/ *n* [C/U] *pl* **men** the human race, or any member or group of it ○ [U] *prehistoric man* ○ [U] *This poison is one of the most dangerous substances known to man.* ○ [C] *All men are equal in the sight of the law.* ○ **USAGE**: Some people dislike this use of man because it does not seem to give women equal importance with men. They prefer to use other words, such as humanity, humankind, people, and person.

OPERATE /mæn/ *v* [T] **-nn-** to be present in order to operate something, such as equipment or a service ○ *Man the pumps!* ○ *The phones are manned 24 hours a day.* ○ **USAGE**: Some people dislike this use of man because it does not seem to give women equal importance with men. They prefer to use other words, such as operate and staff.

PIECE /mæn/ *n* [C] *pl* **men** any of the pieces that are played with in games such as CHESS

WORD FAMILY man

Nouns	man manhood mankind	*Adjectives*	manly manliness mannish unmanned
Verbs	man		

IDIOMS with man

• **man's best friend** a dog ○ *The regulations would let man's best friend into public housing projects.*

• **the man in the street** a man or men who think like most other people ○ *To win the election she needs to understand what the man in the street wants.* ○ Compare THE WOMAN IN THE STREET at WOMAN IDIOM

manacles /ˈmæn·ə·kəlz/ *pl n* HANDCUFFS

manage SUCCEED /ˈmæn·ɪdʒ/ *v* [I/T] to succeed in doing something, esp. something difficult ○ [+ *to* infinitive] *The pilot managed to land the plane safely.* ○ [+ *to* infinitive] *We managed to live on very little money.* ○ [I] *Don't worry about us – we'll manage.*

manageable /ˈmæn·ɪdʒ·ə·bəl/ *adj* easy or possible to deal with ○ *The people at the workshop were divided into small, manageable groups.*

CONTROL /ˈmæn·ɪdʒ/ *v* [T] to control or organize someone or something, esp. a business ○ *Does she have any experience managing large projects?*

management /ˈmæn·ɪdʒ·mənt/ *n* [U] **1** the control and organization of something, esp. a business and its employees ○ *He assumed management of a large real-estate company.* **2** Management is also the people in charge of a business organization: *Negotiators tried all weekend to get labor and management back to the bargaining table.*

manager /ˈmæn·ɪdʒ·ər/ *n* [C] ○ *the manager of a supermarket* ○ *He is manager of the New York City Ballet.*

managerial /ˌmæn·əˈdʒɪr·iː·əl/ *adj* [not gradable] ○ *managerial skills* ➤ Usage: **chief or boss/manager?** at CHIEF PERSON IN CHARGE

WORD FAMILY manage

Nouns	management manager	*Adjectives*	manageable unmanageable managerial
Verbs	manage		

managed care *n* [U] a system in which medical costs are controlled by limiting the services that doctors and hospitals offer

mandate /ˈmæn·deɪt/ *n* [C] authority to act in a particular way given to a government or a person, esp. as a result of a vote or ruling ○ [+ *to* infinitive] *The president secured a congressional mandate to send troops to Bosnia.*
mandate /ˈmæn·deɪt/ *v* [T] to make something necessary, esp. as a rule ○ *The law mandated a minimum six-year sentence for violent crimes.*

mandatory /ˈmæn·dəˌtɔːr·i, -ˌtoʊr·i/ *adj* [not gradable] made necessary, usually by law or by some other rule ○ *The test includes a mandatory essay question.*

mandolin /ˌmæn·dəˈlɪn/ *n* [C/U] a musical instrument with eight strings and a rounded back that is held in the hands or on the knee and played by moving the fingers across the strings

mane /meɪn/ *n* [C] the long, thick hair that grows along the top of a horse's neck or around the face and neck of a male lion

maneuver MILITARY OPERATION /məˈnuː·vər/ *n* [C] a planned and controlled movement of military forces
maneuvers /məˈnuː·vərz/ *pl n* military operations by the armed forces for training purposes
PLANNED ACTION /məˈnuː·vər/ *n* [C] a planned action that is intended to obtain an advantage ○ *A clever maneuver by the chairman secured a valuable contract for the company.*
maneuver /məˈnuː·vər/ *v* [T] to cause someone to act in a particular way ○ *The management tried to maneuver her into resigning.*
HANDLE /məˈnuː·vər/ *v* [I/T] to handle and move something carefully or with difficulty ○ [T] *I maneuvered the grocery cart around piles of boxes to the checkout counter.*

manger /ˈmeɪn·dʒər/ *n* [C] an open box from which horses, cows, and other animals feed

mangle /ˈmæŋ·gəl/ *v* [T] to destroy something by twisting it with force or tearing it so that its original form is changed ○ *His car was mangled when it slammed head-on into a semitrailer truck.* ○ (fig.) *The text was so mangled in translation that it was impossible to be sure of the meaning.*

mango /ˈmæŋ·goʊ/ *n* [C] *pl* **mangoes, mangos** a fruit grown in the hotter parts of the earth, having an oval shape, a large seed, and juicy, orange-yellow flesh

mangy /ˈmeɪn·dʒi/ *adj* [-*er*/-*est* only] **1** (esp. of dogs and cats) having an infectious disease that makes hair fall out and causes areas of rough skin ○ *a mangy-looking dog* **2** Mangy also means old and dirty: *Throw away that mangy rug.*

manhandle /ˈmænˌhæn·dᵊl/ *v* [T] to handle someone with force or push someone around, often when taking the person somewhere ○ *Security guards had manhandled some of the fans.*

manhole /ˈmæn·hoʊl/ *n* [C] an opening in a street usually covered by a heavy, metal lid, for allowing workers to reach underground pipes and wires

manhood /ˈmæn·hʊd/ *n* ○ See at MAN HUMAN MALE

manhunt /ˈmæn·hʌnt/ *n* [C] an organized search for a person, esp. a criminal

mania STRONG INTEREST /ˈmeɪ·niː·ə/ *n* [C] a unusually strong and continuing interest in an activity or subject ○ *He was surprised by his wife's sudden mania for exercise.*
maniac /ˈmeɪ·niːˌæk/ *n* [C] a person who has an unusually strong interest in an activity or subject ○ *My brother is a maniac when it comes to football.*
MENTAL ILLNESS /ˈmeɪ·niː·ə/ *n* [U] *medical* a mental illness that causes a person to be in a state of extreme physical and mental activity
maniac /ˈmeɪ·niːˌæk/ *n* [C] a person who seems unable to control his or her behavior and may commit violent acts ○ *a homicidal maniac*

manic /ˈmæn·ɪk/ *adj* excited or anxious in a way that causes a lot of physical activity ○ *She was a manic talker.*

manicure /ˈmæn·əˌkjʊr/ *n* [C] a treatment for the hands that involves softening the skin and making the nails look better by cutting, smoothing, and possibly painting them

manifest /ˈmæn·əˌfest/ *v* [T] to show something clearly, through signs or actions ○ *Kipper manifested no joy or disappointment, but remained in his chair, calm and unconcerned.*
manifest /ˈmæn·əˌfest/ *adj* easily noticed or obvious ○ *His manifest joy in music is evident as soon as he starts to speak.*
manifestly /ˈmæn·əˌfest·li/ *adv* ○ *Her attorneys claimed the ruling was manifestly unfair.*
manifestation /ˌmæn·ə·fəˈsteɪ·ʃən, -ˌfesˈteɪ-/ *n* [C] a sign showing the existence of a particular condition ○ *His refusal to see us was a manifestation of his guilt.*

M

manifesto /ˌmæn·əˈfes·toʊ/ *n* [C] *pl* **manifestos, manifestoes** a written statement of the beliefs or aims esp. of a political party

manifold /ˈmæn·əˌfoʊld/ *adj* [not gradable] *fml* many and of different types ○ *Our organization's problems are manifold – too few members, too little money, and poor management.*

manila /məˈnɪl·ə/ *adj* [not gradable] made of strong, stiff, usually light brown paper ○ *She removed a manila folder from a desk drawer and handed it to me.*

manipulate Ⓐ INFLUENCE /məˈnɪp·jəˌleɪt/ *v* [T] to influence or control someone to your advantage, often without that person knowing it ○ *Her success is partly due to her ability to manipulate the media.*
manipulative Ⓐ /məˈnɪp·jə·ləṭ·ɪv, -ˌleɪṭ·ɪv/ *adj* ○ *He is resourceful, smart, skillful, ingenious, and savvy, but he also can be manipulative.*
manipulation Ⓐ /məˌnɪp·jəˈleɪ·ʃən/ *n* [U] ○ *They have been accused of illegal manipulation of the stock market.*

TOUCH /mə'nɪp·jə,leɪt/ *v* [T] to control something by using the hands ○ *The wheelchair is designed to be easy to manipulate.*

manipulation Ⓐ /mə,nɪp·jə'leɪ·ʃən/ *n* [C/U] ○ [U] *Often a dislocated finger can be fixed by manipulation.*

mankind /'mæn'kɑɪnd/ *n* [U] the whole of the human race, including both men and women ○ Compare WOMANKIND

manliness /'mæn·liː·nəs/ *n* ○ See at MAN **HUMAN MALE**

manly /'mæn·li/ *adj* ○ See at MAN **HUMAN MALE**

man-made *adj* [not gradable] produced or developed by humans rather than coming directly from nature ○ *man-made fibers*

mannequin /'mæn·ə·kɪn/ *n* [C] an artificial model made in the form of a human being, used esp. to show clothes in a store

manner **WAY** /'mæn·ər/ *n* [U] the way in which something is done ○ *Please exit the building in an orderly manner.*

BEHAVIOR /'mæn·ər/ *n* [U] the usual way in which you behave toward other people, or the way you behave on a particular occasion ○ *His manner was formal, though friendly.* ○ *She had a warm smile and an engaging manner.*

mannered /'mæn·ərd/ *adj* **1** *The children are well mannered.* **2** *disapproving* A mannered way of speaking or behaving is one that is artificial, or intended to achieve a particular effect: *He continued to write, but his mannered prose was not well received.*

IDIOM with manner

• **in a manner of speaking** in one way of expressing something or thinking about something ○ *His old self died, in a manner of speaking, and he was born again as a devout Christian.*

mannerism /'mæn·ə,rɪz·əm/ *n* [C] something that a person does repeatedly with the face, hands, or voice, esp. a habit that the person is not aware of ○ *We've spent so much time together that we've picked up each other's mannerisms.*

manners /'mæn·ərz/ *pl n* ways of behaving toward people that are socially correct and show respect for their comfort and their feelings ○ *He had the bad manners to keep interrupting whoever was speaking.*

mannish /'mæn·ɪʃ/ *adj* ○ See at MAN **HUMAN MALE**

manpower /'mæn,pɑʊ·ər, -,pɑʊr/ *n* [U] the supply of people who are able to work ○ *For years there was a shortage of manpower in engineering.*

mansion /'mæn·tʃən/ *n* [C] a very large and usually expensive house ○ *Mansions line the shore around the lake.*

manslaughter /'mæn,slɔːt̬·ər/ *n* [U] *law* the crime of killing someone unintentionally or without having planned to do it ○ *He was found guilty of manslaughter and sentenced to two years in prison.*

mantelpiece /'mænt·əl,piːs/, *short form* **mantel** /'mænt·əl/ *n* [C] a shelf above a fireplace, usually part of a frame that surrounds the fireplace

mantle **COVERING** /'mænt·əl/ *n* [C] ***literature*** a covering, or a layer of something that covers a surface ○ *They escaped under the mantle of darkness.*

EARTH /'mænt·əl/ *n* [U] ***earth science*** the part of the earth that is below the surface and that surrounds the smaller part in the center ➤ Picture: earth

POSITION /'mænt·əl/ *n* [C usually sing] a position of authority or responsibility ○ *He inherited the mantle of leadership at the Transit Authority in the early 1980s.*

man-to-man *adj* direct and honest, and done as equals ○ *I decided to have a man-to-man talk with my son.* ○ Compare WOMAN-TO-WOMAN

mantra /'mæn·trə, 'mɑn-/ *n* [C] **1** a word or sound that is repeated as a prayer **2** A mantra is also any word or expression used repeatedly: *"Moderate" is the new Republican mantra, he said.*

manual Ⓐ **DONE BY HAND** /'mæn·jə·wəl/ *adj* [not gradable] **1** done or operated with the hands ○ *The mail can be sorted faster by machine then by manual sorting.* ○ *He has callouses on his hands from years of manual labor.* **2** If a machine is manual, it does not use electricity to operate: *We all used manual typewriters in those days.*

manually Ⓐ /'mæn·jə·wə·li/ *adv* ○ *a manually operated pump*

BOOK /'mæn·jə·wəl/ *n* [C] a book that gives you practical instructions on how to do something or how to use something ○ *Get the computer manufacturer's operating manual.*

manufacture **PRODUCE** /,mæn·jə'fæk·tʃər/ *v* [T] to produce goods in large numbers, esp. in a factory using machines ○ *He works for a company that manufactures toys.*

manufacture /,mæn·jə'fæk·tʃər/ *n* [U] ○ *Oil is used in the manufacture of synthetic fabrics.*

manufacturer /,mæn·jə'fæk·tʃə·rər/ *n* [C] ○ *The company makes printed-circuit boards for manufacturers of electronic equipment.*

manufacturing /,mæn·jə'fæk·tʃə·rɪŋ/ *n* [U] the business of producing goods in factories

INVENT /,mæn·jə'fæk·tʃər/ *v* [T] to invent something such as a situation, story, or event, esp. to deceive someone ○ *The president said this is a political crisis manufactured by Republicans.*

manure /mə'nʊr, -'njʊr/ *n* [U] excrement from animals, esp. horses and cattle, often used as a FERTILIZER (= material added to earth to help plants grow)

manuscript /'mæn·jə,skrɪpt/ *n* [C] ***writing*** the original copy of a book or article before it is printed ○ *The author's manuscript ran to over 1000 pages.*

many /'men·i/ *adj, pronoun comparative* **more**, *superlative* **most** a large number (of), or a lot (of) ○ *Many people bought tickets for the concert.* ○ *Rachel has so many friends that I couldn't invite them all.* ○ *How many years have you worked here?* ○ *Not ev-*

eryone could get a seat, and many (of the people) were unhappy with having to stand. ○ **USAGE:** Many is used with countable nouns. ○ Compare MUCH GREAT

USAGE

many, much, or a lot of?

Many is used with countable nouns. It is more common in negative sentences and questions.

I haven't seen many films this year.

Much is used with uncountable nouns. It is more common in negative sentences and questions.

We haven't got much time left.

Many and **much** are both also used in formal positive sentences.

There is still much to do, if we are to be ready for the inspection.

In less formal positive sentences **a lot of** is generally used because **many** and **much** sound too formal. **A lot of** can be used with both countable and uncountable nouns.

a lot of people

There was a lot of enthusiasm for the project.

There was much enthusiasm for the project.

map /mæp/ *n* [C] a drawing that represents a region or place by showing the various features of it, such as rivers and roads, and the distances between them, so that people can get help in finding their way from one place to another ○ *a map of California* ○ *a New York City subway map* ○ *According to this road map, it's 740 miles from Charlotte, North Carolina to Miami, Florida.*

map /mæp/ *v* [T] **-pp-** to draw a representation of a place ○ *Archaeologists have mapped the old Roman city using aerial photography.*

PHRASAL VERB with map

• **map** *something* **out** [M] to plan an activity or process in detail ○ *She's mapped out her entire college career before she even started her first year.*

maple /ˈmeɪ·pəl/ *n* [C/U] a type of large tree that grows in northern areas of the world, or the wood of this tree

maple syrup *n* [U] a sticky, sweet liquid produced from maple trees and used to flavor foods ○ *pancakes with maple syrup*

maquette /mæˈket, mə-/ *n* [C] ***art*** a small model used by a SCULPTOR before beginning the real work of art

mar /mɑr/ *v* [T] **-rr-** to spoil something, making it less good or less enjoyable ○ *Water will mar the finish of polished wood.*

marathon /ˈmær·əˌθɑn/ *n* [C] **1** a long race, run on roads, of 26.2 miles or 42.2 kilometers ○ *The New York City marathon begins in Staten Island and ends in Manhattan's Central Park.* **2** A marathon is also an activity that continues for a very long time: *a dance marathon*

marathon /ˈmær·əˌθɑn/ *adj* [not gradable] **1** *a marathon runner* **2** A marathon activity is one that continues for a very long time: *The marathon negotiating session lasted all night.*

marble ROCK /ˈmɑr·bəl/ *n* [U] a type of hard stone, often with a pattern of irregular lines going through it, that is used as a building material and in statues ○ *polished marble floors*

GLASS BALL /ˈmɑr·bəl/ *n* [C] a small glass ball, often of various colors

marbles /ˈmɑr·bəlz/ *n* [U] a child's game in which marbles are rolled along the ground

march WALK /mɑrtʃ/ *v* [I] **1** to walk with regular steps of equal length, esp. with other people who are all walking in the same way ○ *The band marched through the downtown streets.* **2** If you march, you walk quickly with purpose and determination: *She marched up to the customer service desk and demanded her money back.*

march /mɑrtʃ/ *n* [C] (of a military unit) the act of walking together in formation

MUSIC /mɑrtʃ/ *n* [C] a piece of music with a strong, regular rhythm written for marching to ○ *The parade was led by the high school band, playing a series of marches.*

PUBLIC EVENT /mɑrtʃ/ *n* [C] an event in which many people walk through a public place to express their support of something, often in disapproval of an official position ○ *a protest march*

march /mɑrtʃ/ *v* [I] ○ *The group plans to march on City Hall today to bring attention to their cause.*

March /mɑrtʃ/, *abbreviation* **Mar.** *n* [C/U] the third month of the year, after February and before April

Mardi Gras /ˈmɑrd·iː ˌgrɑ, -ˌgrɔː/ *n* [C usually sing] the last day before Lent, or the large public celebration on this day ○ *In New Orleans, Mardi Gras marks the end of a carnival period.*

mare /mer, mær/ *n* [C] an adult female horse ○ Compare STALLION

margarine /ˈmɑr·dʒə·rən/ *n* [U] a yellow substance that is made from vegetable or animal fat and is often used instead of butter

margin Ⓐ AMOUNT/DEGREE /ˈmɑr·dʒən/ *n* [C] **1** the amount or degree of difference between a higher amount and a lower amount ○ *He was reelected by a wide margin.* **2** A **margin for error** is the amount by which you can make a mistake without risking complete failure: *There is no margin for error – it's got to work the first time.* **3** A **margin of error** is the degree to which a calculation can be wrong without changing how accurate the final result is: *The poll had a margin of error of plus or minus 4%.*

BORDER /ˈmɑr·dʒən/ *n* [C] the border of empty space around the written or printed text on a page ○ *She was in the habit of making notes in the margins of her textbooks.*

marginal Ⓐ /ˈmɑr·dʒən·əl/ *adj* small in amount or effect ○ *The difference between the two bids was marginal.*

marginally Ⓐ /ˈmɑr·dʒən·əl·i/ *adv* ○ *I think his guess is only marginally better than anybody else's.*

M

marigold /ˈmær·əˌgoʊld/ *n* [C] a plant with bright yellow or orange flowers

marijuana, **marihuana** /ˌmær·əˈwɑn·ə, -ˈhwɑn·ə/ *n* [U] an illegal drug that is made from the dried leaves and flowers of the HEMP plant

marina /məˈriː·nə/ *n* [C] a small port that is designed for small pleasure boats ○ *Our sailboat is docked at the marina.*

marinate /ˈmær·əˌneɪt/ *v* [T] to put fish, meat, or vegetables in a mixture of oil, vinegar or wine, and spices before cooking, in order to flavor it or make it softer

marine /məˈriːn/ *adj* [not gradable] of or near the sea ○ *a marine biologist* ○ *The oil slick threatened marine life around the islands.*

mariner /ˈmær·ə·nər/ *n* [C] ***literature*** a person who works on a ship; a SAILOR

Marine /məˈriːn/ *n* [C] a member of the United States Marine Corps, a part of the US military forces that consists of soldiers who operate on land and sea

marionette /ˌmær·iː·əˈnet/ *n* [C] a small model of a person or animal, controlled from above by strings attached to its movable body parts and used as characters on small stages as an entertainment

marital /ˈmær·əţ·əl/ *adj* [not gradable] connected with marriage ○ *marital problems*

maritime /ˈmær·əˌtɑɪm/ *adj* [not gradable] connected with ships or the sea, or being near the sea ○ *a maritime museum*

mark SMALL AREA /mɑrk/ *n* [C] a small area on the surface of something that is damaged, dirty, a different color, or in some other way not like the rest of the surface ○ *You've got paint marks on your shirt.* ○ *There were skid marks where the car had gone off the road.*

mark /mɑrk/ *v* [T] ○ *Sale items are marked in red on the tags.*

marking /ˈmɑr·kɪŋ/ *n* [C] noticeable spots or areas on a surface ○ *One of the fishes had blue and white markings.*

WORD CHOICES mark

If a dirty mark is difficult to remove, you could use the word **stain**.

*She had grass **stains** on her white jeans.*

Smear or **smudge** can be used for marks which look like someone has rubbed something dirty on a surface.

*He had **smears** of tomato ketchup on his shirt.*

A mark which has an irregular shape, especially on someone's skin is often called a **blotch**.

*He had **blotches** all over his face.*

A very small mark can be called a **speck** or **fleck**.

*There were a few **specks/flecks** of paint on the window.*

Spot can be used for a mark which is round.

*He had some grease **spots** on his tie.*

Streak can be used for long thin marks.

*There was a **streak** of dirt on her arm.*

If a mark has been made by blood, you could use the word **bloodstain**.

***Bloodstains** are difficult to get out of fabric.*

WRITING /mɑrk/ *n* [C] a written or printed symbol ○ *a punctuation mark* ○ *a check mark* ○ *Put a mark in the box that corresponds to the correct answer.*

mark /mɑrk/ *v* [T] ○ *The trail is marked by numbered signs.*

marker /ˈmɑr·kər/ *n* [C] **1** a symbol or object that gives information ○ *When the boats reached the halfway marker, the wind started to pick up.* **2** A marker is also a type of pen that makes a thick line: *She used a yellow, felt-tip marker to highlight certain words.*

SIGN /mɑrk/ *n* [C] an action that is understood to represent a characteristic or feeling ○ *As a mark of respect for those who died, there will be a minute of silence.*

REPRESENT /mɑrk/ *v* [T] to represent something that has happened in the past or is about to happen ○ *A guided tour will be held to mark the opening of the new school.* ○ *Today marks my tenth anniversary with this company.*

JUDGMENT /mɑrk/ *n* [C] **1** a letter or number used as a measure of how good a student's work is, usually given by a teacher; a GRADE ○ *I got a decent mark on my final exam and wound up with a B for the course.* **2** *fig.* If you give someone high/low marks for something, you judge that person to be good or bad in a particular way: *I'd certainly give him high marks for perseverance, but he doesn't have much talent.*

mark /mɑrk/ *v* [T] to put a number or letter on a student's work that shows how good it is ○ *I have a stack of exam papers to mark.*

PURPOSE /mɑrk/ *n* [C] an intended result or an object aimed at ○ *Mass marketing techniques very often miss their intended marks.* ○ *Her arrow hit the mark.*

WORD FAMILY mark

Nouns	mark	*Adjectives*	marked
	marker		unmarked
	marking	*Adverbs*	markedly
Verbs	mark		

PHRASAL VERBS with mark

• **mark down** *something* **REDUCE** [M] to reduce the price of something ○ *In August they begin to mark down summer suits.* ○ Related noun: MARKDOWN

• **mark down** *something/someone* **RECORD** [M] to record information about something or someone by writing it down ○ *She was marked down as having voted Republican in that primary.*

• **mark off** *something* [M] to make or draw a line that separates one thing from another ○ *Sheep graze on lush pastures marked off by centuries-old hedge rows.*

• **mark up** *something* [M] to increase the price of something, esp. because you are going to sell it again ○ *According to one study, hospitals mark up costs an average of 232%.* ○ Related noun: MARKUP

markdown /ˈmɑrk·dɑʊn/ *n* [C] a reduction in price ○ *a 25% markdown on swimsuits* ○ Related verb: MARK DOWN REDUCE

marked /mɑrkt/ *adj* obvious or noticeable ○ *There was a marked improvement in my health when I started exercising.*
markedly /ˈmɑr·kəd·li/ *adv* ○ *Eyewitness accounts differed markedly from police reports of the incident.*

market AREA /ˈmɑr·kət/ *n* [C] an open area, building, or event at which people gather to buy and sell goods or food
DEMAND /ˈmɑr·kət/ *n* [C] **1** the demand for products or services ○ *Are you sure there's a market for something like this?* **2** A market is also an area or particular group that goods can be sold to: *the teenage/adult market* ○ *domestic/foreign markets* **3** A market is also the business or trade in a particular type of goods or services: *the job/housing market*
ADVERTISE /ˈmɑr·kət/ *v* [T] to advertise and offer goods for sale ○ *It's a product that will sell if we can find the right way to market it.*
marketing /ˈmɑr·kəţ·ɪŋ/ *n* [U] ○ *marketing strategies* ○ *She's the director of marketing.*
marketable /ˈmɑr·kəţ·ə·bəl/ *adj* easily sold ○ *marketable products/skills*

WORD FAMILY market			
Nouns	market marketing	*Adjectives*	marketable
		Verbs	market

IDIOMS with market

• **in the market for** *something* interested in buying something ○ *Thanks for the offer, but I'm not in the market for another car at the moment.*
• **on the market** available for sale ○ *We put our house on the market last spring.*

market economy *n* [C] ***social studies*** an economic system in which goods and services are made, sold, and shared and prices set by the balance of supply and demand

marketplace PLACE TO SHOP /ˈmɑr·kət,pleɪs/ *n* [C] a place, usually in an open area, where things are sold; a market
TRADING SYSTEM /ˈmɑr·kət,pleɪs/ *n* [U] the system of buying and selling in competitive conditions ○ *Analysts question whether the company can survive in a highly competitive marketplace.*

market research *n* [U] the collection and study of information about what people prefer to buy

marksman /ˈmɑrk·smən/, *female* **markswoman** /ˈmɑrk,swʊm·ən/ *n* [C] *pl* **-men, -women** someone skilled at shooting accurately
marksmanship /ˈmɑrk·smən,ʃɪp/ *n* [U] skill in shooting ○ *The competitors display their marksmanship at targets along the ski route.*

markup /ˈmɑr·kʌp/ *n* [C] an increase in price, esp. the amount by which the cost of an item for sale is increased to provide a profit to the person selling it ○ *The markup on books has to be at least 30%.* ○ Related verb: MARK UP

marmalade /ˈmɑr·mə,leɪd/ *n* [U] a soft food made by cooking fruit, esp. oranges, with sugar ○ *She spread marmalade on her toast.*

maroon /məˈruːn/ *adj, n* [U] (of) a dark brown-red color ○ *a maroon tie*

marooned /məˈruːnd/ *adj* [not gradable] left in a place from which you cannot escape ○ *My flight was canceled because of a snowstorm and I was marooned at the Denver airport.*

marquee /mɑrˈkiː/ *n* [C] a covered entrance to a theater with a sign that shows the names of the movies or play that you can see

marrow /ˈmær·oʊ/, **bone marrow** *n* [U] the soft, fatty tissue in the center of bones

marry /ˈmær·i, ˈmer-/ *v* [I/T] **1** to become the legally accepted husband or wife of someone in an official or religious ceremony ○ [T] *He married Lori, his girlfriend from high school.* **2** To marry is also to perform the ceremony for two people that makes them legally married: [T] *Judge Wilcox married us at City Hall.*
married /ˈmær·iːd, ˈmer-/ *adj* [not gradable] ○ *a married couple* ○ *We plan to get married next June.*
marriage /ˈmær·ɪdʒ, ˈmer-/ *n* [C/U] a legally accepted relationship between a man and a woman in which they live as husband and wife, or the official ceremony which results in this ○ [C] *a long and happy marriage*

WORD FAMILY marry			
Nouns	marriage	*Adjectives*	married unmarried
Verbs	marry remarry		

Mars /mɑrz/ *n* [U] the planet fourth in order of distance from the sun, after the earth and before Jupiter ➤ Picture: **solar system**
Martian /ˈmɑr·ʃən/ *adj* [not gradable] relating to the planet Mars ○ *the Martian atmosphere*

marsh /mɑrʃ/ *n* [C/U] an area of low, wet land, usually covered with tall grasses ○ [C] *The marshes along the coast are home to many shorebirds.*
marshy /ˈmɑr·ʃi/ *adj* ○ *marshy ground*

marshal ORGANIZE /ˈmɑr·ʃəl/ *v* [T] to gather or organize people or things, esp. in order to achieve a particular aim ○ *The president is trying to marshal support for his plan.*
OFFICIAL /ˈmɑr·ʃəl/ *n* [C] an official who arranges and controls a public ceremony ○ *The mayor was the honorary grand marshal of the St. Patrick's Day parade.*
LAW /ˈmɑr·ʃəl/ *n* [C] **1** a government official who is responsible for putting the decisions of a law court into effect ○ *He was conducted to the airport by federal marshals and deported.* **2** In some parts of the US, marshal is also a title used for police or fire department officers of high rank.

marshmallow /ˈmɑrʃ,mæl·oʊ, -,mel-/ *n* [C/U] a soft, often white, candy made mainly of sugar ○ [C] *We roasted marshmallows over the campfire.*

marsupial /mɑrˈsuː·piː·əl/ *n* [C] ***biology*** a type of mammal from Australia, New Zealand, and

M

other islands in the South Pacific, or from South or Central America which is not completely developed when it is born and is carried around in a pocket on the mother's body

mart /mɑrt/ *n* [C] a market or place where goods are sold ○ *I'll pick up some snacks at the food mart on the corner.*

martial /ˈmɑr·ʃəl/ *adj* [not gradable] of or suitable for war

martial art *n* [C usually pl] a traditional method of fighting or defending yourself, such as JUDO or KARATE

martial law *n* [U] temporary rule by the military, esp. during a war or an emergency

Martian /ˈmɑr·ʃən/ *n* [C] ○ See at MARS

martini /mɑrˈtiː·ni/ *n* [C] an alcoholic drink usually made with GIN

martyr /ˈmɑrt̬·ər/ *n* [C] a person who suffers greatly or is killed, esp. because of political or religious beliefs

martyr /ˈmɑrt̬·ər/ *v* [T] to be killed or be made to suffer because of your beliefs

martyrdom /ˈmɑrt̬·ər·dəm/ *n* [U] a martyr's suffering or death ○ *the martyrdom of St. Catherine*

marvel /ˈmɑr·vəl/ *v* [I always + adv/prep] to show or experience great surprise or admiration ○ *Tourists marvel at the panoramic view.* ○ *I marvel at her patience with the children.*

marvel /ˈmɑr·vəl/ *n* [C] a person or thing that is very surprising or admirable ○ *This gadget is a technological marvel.*

marvelous /ˈmɑr·və·ləs/ *adj* [not gradable] extremely good ○ *This marvelous invention will help many disabled people.* ○ *We've had some marvelous results with this drug.*

marvelously /ˈmɑr·və·lə·sli/ *adv* ○ *Jackie is marvelously well organized.*

Marxism /ˈmɑrkˌsɪz·əm/ *n* [U] ***world history*** a social, political, and economic theory based on the writings of Karl Marx

Marxist /ˈmɑrk·səst/ *n* [C] ***world history*** a supporter of Marxism

mascara /mæsˈkær·ə/ *n* [U] makeup used to make EYELASHES appear darker and thicker

mascot /ˈmæs·kɑt/ *n* [C] a person, animal, or object used as a symbol and believed to bring good luck ○ *Their team's mascot is a goat.*

masculine MALE /ˈmæs·kjə·lən/ *adj* [not gradable] having qualities traditionally considered to be suitable for a man ○ *It was a movie likely to appeal to a masculine audience.* ○ Compare FEMININE FEMALE

masculinity /ˌmæs·kjəˈlɪn·ət̬·i/ *n* [U] ○ *Boys need to see a wide range of masculinity to pattern their lives after.*

GRAMMAR /ˈmæs·kjə·lən/, *abbreviation* **masc.** *adj* [not gradable] ***grammar*** being a noun or pronoun of a type that refers to males, or in some other languages, being a noun of a type that refers to things considered as male

mash /mæʃ/ *v* [T] to beat or crush something into a soft mass ○ *Mash the potatoes, adding warm milk and butter.*

mashed /mæʃt/ *adj* [not gradable] ○ *mashed potatoes*

mashup, **mash-up** /ˈmæʃ·ʌp/ *n* [C] a type of recorded music or VIDEO that consists of parts of different songs or images that have been combined ○ *The mash-up phenomenon is inspiring a wave of artist-approved, in-studio, legal mash-ups.*

mask /mæsk/ *n* [C] a covering for all or part of the face, worn for protection or to hide the face ○ *a gas mask* ○ *an exhibit of African masks* ○ *The children all wore Halloween masks that were supposed to frighten us.*

mask /mæsk/ *v* [T] to prevent something from being seen or noticed ○ *The tastelessness of the meat was masked by a heavy gravy.*

masking tape *n* [U] a narrow strip or roll of light brown, sticky material that is used esp. when painting, to cover surfaces on which you do not intend to paint

masochist /ˈmæs·ə·kəst/ *n* [C] a person who gets pleasure from being hurt by another person ○ Compare SADIST

masochistic /ˌmæs·əˈkɪs·tɪk/ *adj* [not gradable] ○ (*fig.*) *Running in ultramarathons seems somewhat masochistic to me.*

masochism /ˈmæs·əˌkɪz·əm/ *n* [U]

mason /ˈmeɪ·sən/ *n* [C] a person who is trained to work with bricks and stones used in buildings

masonry /ˈmeɪ·sən·ri/ *n* [U] something, esp. the walls of a building, made of bricks or stone

masquerade /ˌmæs·kəˈreɪd/ *n* [C] **1** a party or dance in which people wear MASKS (= coverings for the face) ○ *There were dozens of masquerade balls, parades, street dances, and fancy dress parties.* **2** A masquerade is also a false show or appearance: *I'm afraid we will not have a fair election but another masquerade.*

masquerade /ˌmæs·kəˈreɪd/ *v* [I always + adv/prep] to pretend or appear to be ○ *In this business, there are a lot of unqualified people masquerading as experts.*

mass LARGE AMOUNT /mæs/ *n* [C] a large amount or number ○ *A mass of earth and granite slid down into the narrow gorge.* ○ *We had to wade through masses of seaweed.*

mass /mæs/ *adj* [not gradable] involving or having an effect on a large number of people or things ○ *weapons of mass destruction* ○ *They hope the new movie will appeal to a mass audience.*

mass /mæs/ *v* [I/T] to come or bring together in large numbers ○ [I] *The crowd massed around the entrance to the exhibition.*

MATTER /mæs/ *n* [C] ***physics*** **1** the amount of matter in any solid object or in any volume of liquid or gas **2** ***physics*** The **mass number** is the total number of PROTONs and NEUTRONs in an atom. **3** ***physics*** The **mass defect** is the difference between the mass of a NUCLEUS (= central part of an atom) and the mass of the separate pieces that make up the nucleus.

ART /mæs/ *n* [U] ***art*** the outside size or shape of an object, or how big it appears to be

Mass /mæs/ *n* [C/U] (esp. in the Roman Catholic Church) a religious ceremony based on Jesus's last meal with his DISCIPLES (= the men who followed him), or music written for the parts of this ceremony

massacre /ˈmæs·ə·kər/ *n* [C] the killing of a large number of people, esp. people who are not involved in any fighting or have no way of defending themselves
massacre /ˈmæs·ə·kər/ *v* [T] ○ *Guerrilla troops are thought to have massacred the entire village.*

massage /məˈsɑʒ, -ˈsɑdʒ/ *v* [T] to rub or press someone's body, usually with repeated hand movements, in order to reduce stiffness or pain in that person's joints or muscles ○ *She massaged his aching neck.*
massage /məˈsɑʒ, -ˈsɑdʒ/ *n* [C/U] ○ [C] *A massage would do wonders for my back.*

masses /ˈmæs·əz/ *pl n* [C] the ordinary people who form the largest group in a society ○ *The candidate won the support of the masses.*

masseur /mæˈsɜr/, *female* **masseuse** /mæˈsuːz/ *n* [C] a person whose job it is to give MASSAGES to people

massive /ˈmæs·ɪv/ *adj* very large in size, amount, or degree ○ *a massive building* ○ *He took massive doses of vitamin C.* ○ *She died of a massive heart attack.*

mass media *pl n* the newspapers, magazines, television, and radio that reach large numbers of people

mass-produce *v* [T] to make a lot of a product, using machinery in a factory

mass transit *n* [U] a system of public transportation that includes such things as buses, trains, and SUBWAYS

mast /mæst/ *n* [C] a tall pole used to support a ship's sails

mastectomy /mæsˈtek·tə·mi/ *n* [C] the removal of a woman's breast by a medical operation

master **CONTROL** /ˈmæs·tər/, *female* **mistress** *n* [C] a person who controls something or someone ○ *I always wanted to start my own business, because I like being my own master.*
master /ˈmæs·tər/ *v* [T] ○ *Now that she's mastered* (= learned to control) *her fear of flying, she travels by air whenever possible.*
mastery /ˈmæs·tə·ri/ *n* [U] complete control ○ *Only a singer of Fitzgerald's mastery could have tackled such an immense project.*

SKILLED PERSON /ˈmæs·tər/ *n* [C] a person who is very skilled in a particular job or activity ○ *Everyone knew he was a master of compromise.* ○ *This painting is clearly the work of a master.* ○ *He is a master chef/craftsman.*
master /ˈmæs·tər/ *v* [T] to become skilled at something ○ *She quickly mastered the art of interviewing people.*
masterful /ˈmæs·tər·fəl/ *adj* ○ *It was a masterful analysis of the causes of the Civil War.*
mastery /ˈmæs·tə·ri/ *n* [U] ○ *Louis Armstrong's mastery of the trumpet is legendary.*

ORIGINAL /ˈmæs·tər/ *n* [C] an original of something, such as a document, recording, or film, from which copies can be made

master key *n* [C] a key that can be used to open a number of different locks

mastermind /ˈmæs·tərˌmɑɪnd/ *v* [T] to plan and direct a difficult activity ○ *Oliver masterminded the takeover of his top business competitor.*
mastermind /ˈmæs·tərˌmɑɪnd/ *n* [C] ○ *The mastermind behind the escape has never been identified.*

Master of Arts, **master's degree**, *abbreviation* **M.A.** *n* [C] a college or university degree in an art or SOCIAL SCIENCE that is higher than a BACHELOR'S DEGREE and below a DOCTOR'S DEGREE

master of ceremonies, *abbreviation* **MC** *n* [C] a person who is in charge of an official event and introduces the speakers or performers

Master of Science, **master's degree**, *abbreviation* **M.S.** *n* [C] a college or university degree in science that is higher than a BACHELOR'S DEGREE and below a DOCTOR'S DEGREE

masterpiece /ˈmæs·tərˌpiːs/, **masterwork** /ˈmæs·tərˌwɜrk/ *n* [C] something made or done with great skill, esp. an artist's greatest work

masthead /ˈmæst·hed/ *n* [C] a list of the names of the most important people involved in producing and writing for a magazine or newspaper ○ *Hirth, listed on the masthead as publisher, wrote several articles in each issue.*

masturbate /ˈmæs·tərˌbeɪt/ *v* [I/T] to rub or touch the sex organs of yourself or someone else for pleasure
masturbation /ˌmæs·tərˈbeɪ·ʃən/ *n* [U]

mat /mæt/ *n* [C] a flat piece of material that covers and protects part of a floor, or provides a soft surface ○ *The kids slept on straw mats on the floor of the den downstairs.*

matador /ˈmæt̬·əˌdɔːr/ *n* [C] the person in a BULLFIGHT who is skilled in killing the BULL (= male cow)

match **COMPETITION** /mætʃ/ *n* [C] a sports competition or event in which two people or teams compete against each other ○ *a tennis/wrestling match* ○ *(fig.) They got into a shouting/shoving match* (= they were arguing or fighting).

STICK /mætʃ/ *n* [C] a short, thin stick of wood or cardboard, covered at one end with a material that will burn when rubbed against a rough surface

SUITABLE /mætʃ/ *v* [I/T] to be similar to or the same as something, or to combine well with someone

M

or something else ○ [I] *The shirt and pants match perfectly.* ○ [T] *Her fingerprints matched the prints that were taken from the crime scene.*

match /mætʃ/ *n* [U] ○ *This tie is a perfect match for your shirt and suit.* ○ *I think Ross and Rhonda are a good match.*

EQUAL /mætʃ/ *v* [I/T] to be equal to another person or thing in some quality ○ [T] *It would be difficult to match the service this airline gives its customers.*

match /mætʃ/ *n* [U] ○ *The teams were a good match when it came to ability.*

matchless /ˈmætʃ·ləs/ *adj* [not gradable] of a standard or quality that cannot be equaled ○ *The museum has a matchless collection of Rembrandt etchings.*

WORD FAMILY match			
Nouns	match	Adjectives	matching
Verbs	match		matchless
			unmatched

PHRASAL VERB with match

• **match up to** *something* to be as good as something else ○ *The sequel didn't match up to the original movie.*

matchbook /ˈmætʃ·bʊk/, **book of matches** *n* [C] a small folded piece of cardboard containing cardboard matches

matchmaker /ˈmætʃˌmeɪ·kər/ *n* [C] a person who tries to arrange a relationship or a marriage between other people

matchup /ˈmætʃ·ʌp/ *n* [C] a competition between two teams or people ○ *The matchup turned out to be the premier race of the Olympics so far.*

mate FRIEND /meɪt/ *n* [C] *Br, infml* a friend, or a person you work with

PARTNER /meɪt/ *n* [C] **1** an animal's sexual partner ○ *Swans keep the same mate for life.* **2** A mate is also a husband or wife.

mate /meɪt/ *v* [I/T] to have sex and produce young, or to cause a male and female animal to do this ○ [I] *Zoo officials are hoping the pandas will mate.*

PAIR /meɪt/ *n* [C] either of a pair of matched objects ○ *I can't find the mate to this sock.*

material PHYSICAL THING /məˈtɪr·iː·əl/ *n* [C] a type of physical thing, such as wood, stone, or plastic, having qualities that allow it to be used to make other things ○ *a hard/soft material* ○ *The sculpture was made of various materials, including steel, copper wire, and rubber.*

CLOTH /məˈtɪr·iː·əl/ *n* [C/U] cloth that can be used to make clothes, curtains, etc. ○ [U] *What kind of material are you going to use for the curtains?*

SUPPLIES /məˈtɪr·iː·əl/ *n* [C/U] equipment or supplies needed for a particular activity ○ [C usually pl] *The money will be spent on educational materials.*

INFORMATION /məˈtɪr·iː·əl/ *n* [C/U] information used when writing something such as a book, or information produced to help people or to advertise products ○ [U] *He is working in the library gathering material for the article he is writing.*

WORD FAMILY material			
Nouns	material	Adjectives	material
	materialism		immaterial
Verbs	materialize		materialistic

materialism /məˈtɪr·iː·əˌlɪz·əm/ *n* [U] ***social studies*** the belief that money, possessions, and comfort are the most important things to obtain in life

materialistic /məˌtɪr·iː·əˈlɪs·tɪk/ *adj* ○ *I was a materialistic person, very career-oriented, with a large ego.*

materialize /məˈtɪr·iː·əˌlɑɪz/ *v* [I] **1** (of ideas and wishes) to become real or true ○ *Her hopes of owning her own restaurant never materialized.* **2** If a person or object materializes, it appears suddenly: *They listened to the footsteps, then watched the figure materialize in the doorway.*

maternal /məˈtɜrn·ᵊl/ *adj* **1** behaving or feeling as a mother does toward her child ○ *maternal instincts* **2** Maternal also means related by way of the mother: *Alice's maternal grandmother* (= her mother's mother) *will be 90 next month.* ○ Compare PATERNAL

maternity /məˈtɜr·nət̬·i/ *n* [U] **1** the state of being a mother ○ *issues of reproduction, maternity, and women's health* **2** Maternity leave is a period in which a woman is allowed to be absent from work in the weeks before and after she gives birth.

maternity /məˈtɜr·nət̬·i/ *adj* [not gradable] relating to a period during which a woman is pregnant and has a baby, and often to a period following this ○ *Anita passed along some used maternity clothes* (= clothes worn when she was pregnant). ○ *She asked about the company's maternity benefits.*

math /mæθ/ *n* [U] *short form of* MATHEMATICS

mathematics /ˌmæθ·əˈmæt̬·ɪks, mæθˈmæt̬-/, *short form* **math** /mæθ/ *n* [U] the science of numbers, forms, amounts, and their relationships

mathematical /ˌmæθ·əˈmæt̬·ɪ·kəl, mæθˈmæt̬-/ *adj* [not gradable] ○ *a mathematical formula*

mathematician /ˌmæθ·ə·məˈtɪʃ·ən/ *n* [C] a person skilled in mathematics

matinee, matineé /ˌmæt·ᵊnˈeɪ/ *n* [C] an afternoon performance of a movie or play

matriarch /ˈmeɪ·triːˌɑrk/ *n* [C] a powerful and usually older woman in charge of a family, or the female leader of a society in which women hold power ○ Compare PATRIARCH

matriarchal /ˌmeɪ·triːˈɑr·kəl/ *adj* ○ *a matriarchal society*

matriarchy /ˈmeɪ·triːˌɑr·ki/ *n* [C] ***social studies*** a society in which women have most of the authority and power, or a society in which property belongs to women rather than men

matriculate /məˈtrɪk·jəˌleɪt/ *v* [I] to be formally admitted to study at a university or college

○ *Are you just auditing the course or have you matriculated?*

matrimony /ˈmæ·trəˌmoʊ·ni/ *n* [U] *fml* the state of being married ○ *the bonds of matrimony*
matrimonial /ˌmæ·trəˈmoʊ·niː·əl/ *adj* [not gradable] ○ *matrimonial advice*

matrix /ˈmeɪ·trɪks/ *n* [C] *pl* **matrices, matrixes** ***algebra*** a group of numbers or other symbols arranged in a rectangle that can be used to solve particular mathematical problems

matron WOMAN /ˈmeɪ·trən/ *n* [C] *dated* a married woman who is old enough and of a high enough social class to have the respect of others
matronly /ˈmeɪ·trən·li/ *adj dated* looking like or typical of a matron ○ **USAGE:** said about a woman

MANAGER /ˈmeɪ·trən/ *n* [C] a woman who is in charge of women or children at a hospital, police station, prison, or school

matted /ˈmæt̬·əd/ *adj* twisted or pressed into a dense mass ○ *His hair was matted on his forehead.*

matter SITUATION /ˈmæt̬·ər/ *n* [C] a situation or subject that is being dealt with or considered ○ *Her arrival complicates matters even further.* ○ *I think this is a matter best left to the mayor to decide.*

BE IMPORTANT /ˈmæt̬·ər/ *v* to be important ○ [I] *"What did you say?" "Oh, it doesn't matter."* ○ [+ question word] *It no longer mattered what happened.*

PROBLEM /ˈmæt̬·ər/ *n* [U] the reason for pain or worry ○ *What's the matter? Why are you so upset?*

SUBSTANCE /ˈmæt̬·ər/ *n* [U] ***physics*** **1** physical substance in the universe **2** Matter is also a particular type of substance: *printed matter* ○ *waste matter*

IDIOMS with matter

- **a matter of** *something* only; just ○ *In a matter of seconds, the building was in flames.* ○ **USAGE:** Used to emphasize that an amount is small.
- **a matter of life and death** a situation that is extremely serious ○ *Don't worry about missing your bus – it's not a matter of life and death.*
- **a matter of opinion** something that depends on personal preference ○ *Choosing the best ballplayer of all time is really a matter of opinion.*
- *something* **is (just) a matter of** *doing something* solving a problem or performing a job has a simple solution ○ *Cooking lasagna isn't difficult – it's just a matter of following a recipe.*

matter-of-fact /ˌmæt̬·ə·rəˈfækt/ *adj* not showing feelings or emotion, esp. in a situation when emotion would be expected ○ *He spoke in a very matter-of-fact way about the accident.*
matter-of-factly /ˌmæt̬·ə·rəˈfæk·tli/ *adv* ○ *She announced the news matter-of-factly.*

mattress /ˈmæ·trəs/ *n* [C] the part of a bed that you lie on, made of a strong cloth cover filled with firm but comfortable material

maturation Ⓐ DEVELOP MENTALLY /mæt·jʊəˈreɪ·ʃᵊn/ *n* [U] the process of becoming completely developed mentally or emotionally

GROW PHYSICALLY /mæt·jʊəˈreɪ·ʃᵊn/ *n* [U] the process of becoming completely grown physically

mature Ⓐ GROW PHYSICALLY /məˈtʊr, -ˈtʃʊr/ *v* [I] to become completely grown ○ *Humans take longer to mature than most other animals.*
mature Ⓐ /məˈtʊr, -ˈtʃʊr/ *adj* **1** *The forest has a lot of mature oak trees.* **2** Mature can also be a polite way of saying older: *The jeans were marketed to mature women.*
maturity Ⓐ /məˈtʊr·ət̬·i, -ˈtʃʊr-/ *n* [U] ○ *How long does it take for the chicks to grow to maturity?*

DEVELOP MENTALLY /məˈtʊr, -ˈtʃʊr/ *v* [I/T] to become more developed mentally and emotionally and behave in a responsible way, or to cause someone to do this ○ [I] *When you are the oldest child of a large family, you mature pretty quickly, because you have to take care of your younger brothers and sisters.*
mature Ⓐ /məˈtʊr, -ˈtʃʊr/ *adj* mentally and emotionally well-developed, and therefore responsible ○ *He just wasn't mature enough to keep a dog.*
maturity Ⓐ /məˈtʊr·ət̬·i, -ˈtʃʊr-/ *n* [U] ○ *It takes maturity to be a leader.*

FINANCE /məˈtʊr, -ˈtʃʊr/ *v* [I] (of some types of investment) to become ready to be paid ○ *When her bonds matured, she moved the money into stocks.*

maul /mɔːl/ *v* [T] to physically attack and badly hurt a person or animal ○ *A jogger was mauled by a huge bear.*

mauve /moʊv, mɔːv/ *adj, n* [U] (of) a pale purple color

maven /ˈmeɪ·vən/ *n* [C] *infml* a person with good knowledge or understanding of a subject ○ *Walter's a baseball maven and knows Hank Aaron's statistics by heart.*

maverick /ˈmæv·ə·rɪk/ *n* [C] a person who thinks and acts independently of and differently from others ○ *She is considered a political maverick.*

max Ⓐ /mæks/ *adj, n slang* MAXIMUM ○ *"How much will it cost?" "Ten bucks max."*

IDIOM with max

- **to the max** to the highest degree or level ○ *Too many guys in the gym are pushing their bodies to the max and not using the weights correctly.*

PHRASAL VERB with max

- **max out** *(something)* [M] *slang* to reach the greatest level or amount of something ○ *We had seven credit cards and we maxed them all out.* ○ *My car maxes out at about 80 miles an hour.*

maxim /ˈmæk·səm/ *n* [C] a brief statement of a general truth, principle, or rule for behavior ○ *She lived by the maxim, "Do right, risk consequences."*

maximize Ⓐ /ˈmæk·səˌmɑɪz/ *v* [T] to make something as great in amount, size, or importance as possible ○ *Most people try to maximize their gains and minimize their losses.*
maximization Ⓐ /ˌmæk·sə·məˈzeɪ·ʃən/ *n* [C/U]

M

maximum Ⓐ /ˈmæk·sə·məm/ *adj* [not gradable] being the largest amount or number allowed or possible ○ *a maximum penalty/sentence* ○ *The stereo was turned up to maximum volume.* ○ Opposite: MINIMUM
maximum Ⓐ /ˈmæk·sə·məm/ *n* [C] ○ *The temperature will reach a maximum of 88 today.*

may POSSIBILITY /meɪ/ *modal verb* **may,** *past simp.* **might** used to express possibility ○ *She said she may decide to accept the job offer and may not.* ○ Compare MIGHT POSSIBILITY

PERMISSION /meɪ/ *modal verb* **may,** *past simp.* **might** used to ask or give permission ○ *May I use your telephone?*

SUGGESTION /meɪ/ *modal verb* **may,** *past simp.* **might** used to make a suggestion or suggest a possibility in a polite way ○ *You may want to have a bite to eat before you leave.* ○ Compare MIGHT SUGGESTION

IDIOM with may

• *someone* **may as well** *do something* there is no reason you should not do something ○ *I may as well go with you – I don't have anything else to do.*

May /meɪ/ *n* [C/U] the fifth month of the year, after April and before June

maybe /ˈmeɪ·bi/ *adv* [not gradable] **1** used to show that something is possible or that something might be true ○ *Maybe I can get the yard mowed before it rains.* ○ *There were maybe* (= approximately) *50 people there when I left.* **2** Maybe can also be used to avoid giving a clear or certain answer to a question: *"Are you still going to join me for dinner?" "Maybe."* **3** Maybe can also be used to introduce a possible explanation: *I thought maybe my phone message had scared him off.*

mayday /ˈmeɪ·deɪ/ *n* [C] a call for help sent from a ship or aircraft by radio, esp. in an emergency

mayhem /ˈmeɪ·hem/ *n* [U] confused activity or excitement, sometimes involving destructive violence ○ *The movie includes a considerable amount of violence and mayhem.*

mayonnaise /ˈmeɪ·əˌneɪz/, *short form* **mayo** /ˈmeɪ·oʊ/ *n* [U] a thick, creamy, cold sauce that is added to foods and is made from oil, vinegar, and the yellow part of eggs

mayor /meɪ·ər/ *n* [C] the elected leader of a city or town ○ *The mayor announced a reorganization of the police department.*
mayoral /ˈmeɪ·ə·rəl/ *adj* [not gradable] ○ *mayoral elections*

maze /meɪz/ *n* [C] a complicated and confusing network of passages ○ *He felt like a rat in a maze.* ○ (fig.) *You have to weed through the maze of complex rules in order to fill out your tax forms.*

MB *n* [C] *abbreviation for* MEGABYTE

M.B.A. *n* [C] *abbreviation for* Master of Business Administration (= an advanced university degree in business).

MC *n* [C] *abbreviation for* MASTER OF CEREMONIES ○ *Who's the MC for the awards ceremony?*

M.D. *n* [C] *abbreviation for* Doctor of Medicine (= an advanced university degree needed to work as a medical doctor) ○ *Steven Tay, M.D.*

me /miː/ *pronoun* the person speaking; the objective form of I ○ *Pass me that book/Pass that book to me.* ○ *"I want to go to the store." "***Me, too** (= I also want to go)*."* ○ *"I'd never go there alone at night." "***Me neither** (= I also would not)*."*

USAGE

me or I?

Me is used after **than, as,** or **to be**. It would be wrong or would sound very formal if you used **I**.

She's taller than me.
David is not as tall as me.
"Who's there?" "It's me."
"Who's there?" "It is I." (formal)

Sometimes **me** is used with another noun as the subject of a sentence, especially in informal English. **I** is usually considered more correct.

Jane and me went to the cinema yesterday. (informal)
Jane and I went to the cinema yesterday.

meadow /ˈmed·oʊ/ *n* [C] an area of land with grass and other wild plants in it ○ *We walked through fields and meadows.*

meager /ˈmiː·gər/ *adj* very small in amount or number; only as much or not as much as is needed or thought to be suitable ○ *The food at my grandmother's house was meager and barely edible.*

meal FOOD /miːl/ *n* [C] an occasion when food is served or eaten, esp. breakfast, lunch, or dinner, or the food itself on such an occasion ○ *I don't enjoy preparing three meals a day every day.*

POWDER /miːl/ *n* [U] a substance that has been crushed to make a rough powder, esp. plant seeds crushed to make flour or for animal food

meal ticket *n* [C usually sing] someone or something that provides you with the money you need to live ○ *The role has been a generous meal ticket for the actress.*

mealtime /ˈmiːl·tɑɪm/ *n* [C usually pl] a time of day when a meal is eaten ○ *Mealtimes were silent unless Dad had something to say.*

mean EXPRESS /miːn/ *v* [T] *past* **meant** to represent or express something intended, or to refer to someone or something ○ *"What does 'rough' mean?" "It means 'not smooth.'"* ○ [+ *that* clause] *These figures mean that almost 7% of the population is unemployed.* ○ *"Do you see that girl over there?" "Do you mean the one with short blond hair?"*
meaning /ˈmiː·nɪŋ/ *n* [C/U] what something represents or expresses ○ [C] *Do you know the meaning of this word?* ○ [C] *The word has several meanings.*
meaningless /ˈmiː·nɪŋ·ləs/ *adj* ○ *The leaflet was full of meaningless* (= not expressing anything) *information.*

M

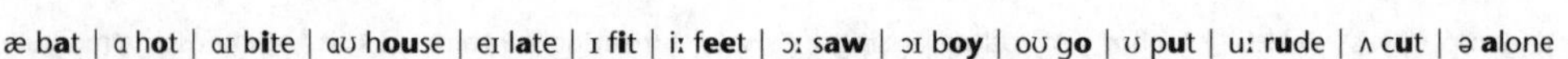

HAVE RESULT /miːn/ *v* [T] *past* **meant** to have as a result ○ *Lower costs mean higher profits.* ○ [+ (*that*) clause] *If she doesn't answer the phone, it means (that) she's out in the garden.*

AVERAGE /miːn/ *n* [C] ***mathematics*** a number that is the result of adding a group of numbers together and then dividing the result by how many numbers were in the group

HAVE IMPORTANCE /miːn/ *v* [T] *past* **meant** to have the importance or value of ○ *My grandmother's ring wasn't valuable, but it meant a lot to me.*

meaning /ˈmiː·nɪŋ/ *n* [U] importance or value ○ *Life had lost its meaning for her.*

meaningful /ˈmiː·nɪŋ·fəl/ *adj* ○ *She found it difficult to form meaningful relationships.*

meaningless /ˈmiː·nɪŋ·ləs/ *adj* without purpose; useless ○ *a meaningless gesture*

INTEND /miːn/ *v* [I/T] *past* **meant** **1** to say or do something intentionally; intend ○ [T] *I think she meant 8 o'clock, although she said 7 o'clock.* ○ [I] *I've been meaning to call you but I've been so busy I never got around to it.* **2** Mean can also be used to add emphasis to what you are saying: [T] *She means what she says.*

NOT KIND /miːn/ *adj* [*-er/-est* only] unkind or not caring ○ *I felt a little mean when I said I couldn't visit her in the hospital until Saturday.*

GOOD /miːn/ *adj* [*-er/-est* only] *slang* very good ○ *She plays a mean bass fiddle.*

WORD FAMILY mean

Nouns	meaning	*Verbs*	mean
Adjectives	meaningful meaningless	*Adverbs*	meaningfully

IDIOMS with mean

• **mean business** to be serious about taking action ○ *You've got to tell the students that you mean business – if they don't do work, they won't pass the class.*

• **mean well** to intend to be helpful, esp. when you unintentionally cause problems instead ○ *He means well, but he keeps trying to help with things he doesn't really understand.*

meander NOT DIRECT /miː ˈæn·dər/ *v* [I] to follow a route that is not straight or direct ○ *Hikers can meander along the path next to the river for several miles.*

RIVER BEND /miː ˈæn·dər/ *n* [C] ***earth science*** a bend in a river, esp. one of many

means METHOD /miːnz/ *pl n* **1** a method or way of doing something ○ *They had no means of letting him know that the flight was canceled.* **2 By means of** is used to show the method used: *Students are selected for scholarships by means of an open, national competition.* ➤ Usage: **way or method/means of?** at WAY MANNER

MONEY /miːnz/ *pl n* **1** money or income that allows you to buy things or services ○ [+ *to* infinitive] *They simply don't have the means to send their children to private schools.* **2** A person **of means** is rich.

IDIOMS with means

• **a means to an end** something you do in order to achieve something else ○ *For me, going to college is just a means to an end, a way to get a better job.*

• **by no means**, **not by any means** not in any way ○ *It is by no means clear what the president can do to end the strike.* ○ **USAGE:** Used to emphasize a negative statement.

meantime /ˈmiːn·tɑɪm/ *n* the time while something else is happening ○ *Rick wants to be an actor, but* **in the meantime** *he's working as a waiter.*

meanwhile /ˈmiːn·wɑɪl, -hwɑɪl/ *adv* [not gradable] until something expected happens, or while something else is happening ○ *It's going to take several days for my car to be repaired – meanwhile I'm renting one.*

measles /ˈmiː·zəlz/ *n* [U] an infectious disease, esp. of children, which produces small red spots all over the body

measly /ˈmiːz·li/ *adj* [not gradable] too small in size or amount; not generous ○ *We got a measly 2% raise last year.*

measure SIZE /ˈmeʒ·ər/ *v* to discover the exact size, amount, etc., of something, or to be of a particular size ○ [T] *"Will the table fit in here?" "I don't know – I'll measure it."* ○ [L] *The sofa measures* (= is of the size of) *3 feet by 7 feet.*

measure /ˈmeʒ·ər/ *n* [C/U] **1** a way of measuring, or a way of showing how much or how great something is ○ [C] *a system of weights and measures* ○ [U] *It is a measure of his popularity that he got over 70% of the vote.* **2** Measure can also mean amount or degree: [U] *There was a large measure of luck in his quick promotion to company vice president.* **3** ***music*** A measure is also one of the small equal parts into which a piece of music is divided, containing a fixed number of beats; a BAR.

measurable /ˈmeʒ·ə·rə·bəl/ *adj* ○ *a measurable amount of precipitation*

measurement /ˈmeʒ·ər·mənt/ *n* [C/U] **1** the act of measuring ○ [U] *The test is based on the measurement of blood sugar.* **2** A measurement is the length, height, width, etc., of something, which you discover by measuring it: [C] *The measurements of several of the drawings were identical.*

METHOD /ˈmeʒ·ər/ *n* [C] a way to achieve something; a method ○ *Medicare was a measure intended to guarantee health care for everyone over the age of 65.*

WORD FAMILY measure

Nouns	measure measurement	*Verbs*	measure

PHRASAL VERB with measure

• **measure up** to be as good as something else or as good as expected ○ *We compared the movie we made to some of the other students' films to see how it measured up.*

meat /miːt/ *n* [U] the flesh of an animal when it is used for food ○ *Get a pound of chopped meat from the supermarket on your way home.*

meaty /ˈmiːţ·i/ *adj* containing a lot of meat ○ *a meaty meal*

meat-and-potatoes *adj* basic and important ○ *Taxes are a meat-and-potatoes issue for most voters.*

meatball /ˈmiːt·bɔːl/ *n* [C] a small ball made of meat that has been cut into small pieces, pressed together, and cooked ○ *spaghetti and meatballs*

meat loaf, **meatloaf** /ˈmiːt·loʊf/ *n* [U] meat that has been cut into small pieces then shaped and baked

mecca /ˈmek·ə/ *n* [C] a place to which many people are attracted ○ *Historic Creek Street, lined with shops and restaurants, has become a tourist mecca.*

mechanical MACHINES /məˈkæn·ɪ·kəl/ *adj* [not gradable] **1** of machines or their parts ○ *a mechanical problem* **2** ***physics*** Mechanical forces are physical forces that cause objects or matter to move.

mechanic /məˈkæn·ɪk/ *n* [C] someone who repairs or works with machines, esp. as a job ○ *an auto mechanic*

WITHOUT THOUGHT /məˈkæn·ɪ·kəl/ *adj* without thinking about what you are doing, esp. because you do it often ○ *The garbagemen worked in a slow, mechanical way.*

mechanics OPERATION /məˈkæn·ɪks/ *n* [U] the particular way something works or happens ○ *The goals are the same, but the mechanics for achieving the goals differ greatly.*

PHYSICAL FORCES /məˈkæn·ɪks/ *n* [U] ***physics*** the study of the effect of physical forces on objects and their movement

mechanism Ⓐ MACHINE PART /ˈmek·əˌnɪz·əm/ *n* [C] a part of a machine, or a set of parts that work together ○ *Automatic cameras have a special focusing mechanism.*

SYSTEM /ˈmek·əˌnɪz·əm/ *n* [C] a way of doing something, esp. one that is planned or part of a system ○ *The mechanism for collecting taxes needs revising.*

medal /ˈmed·ᵊl/ *n* [C] a small metal disk given to someone to recognize a brave action or special service, or the winning of a competition esp. in sports ○ *She won three Olympic gold medals.*

medalist /ˈmed·ᵊl·əst/ *n* [C] a person who has won a medal in a sport ○ *She's the gold/silver/bronze medalist* (= She got the medal for finishing in first/second/third place) *in foil fencing.*

medallion /məˈdæl·jən/ *n* [C] **1** a metal disk worn as a decoration on a chain around the neck or attached to a vehicle to show that it can be legally used for a special purpose ○ *He drove a medallion taxi while he attended college at night.* **2** A medallion is also a round piece of meat: *medallions of lamb/veal*

Medal of Honor *n* [C] the highest military honor in the US

meddle /ˈmed·ᵊl/ *v* [I] *disapproving* to try to change or have an influence on things that are not your responsibility ○ *I don't want my parents meddling in my affairs by telling me how I should run my life.*

media Ⓐ NEWSPAPERS /ˈmiːd·iː·ə/ *pl n* newspapers, magazines, television, and radio, considered as a group ○ *the news media* ○ *There was a tremendous amount of media coverage of the funeral of Princess Diana.* ○ See also: MEDIUM METHOD

MEDIUM /ˈmiːd·iː·ə/ *pl of* MEDIUM METHOD

median LAND /ˈmiːd·iː·ən/, **median strip** /ˌmiːd·iː·ənˈstrɪp/ *n* [C] a narrow strip of land or concrete between the two sides of a large road, separating the vehicles moving in opposite directions ○ *The car went out of control, jumped the median, and hit a truck head on.*

NUMBER /ˈmiːd·iː·ən/ *n* [C] ***mathematics*** the middle number or amount in a series

mediate Ⓐ /ˈmiːd·iːˌeɪt/ *v* [I/T] to help solve a disagreement by talking to the separate people or groups involved, or to communicate information between people ○ [T] *to mediate a dispute*

mediation Ⓐ /ˌmiːd·iːˈeɪ·ʃən/ *n* [U] ○ *Last-minute attempts at mediation failed, and the workers went on strike.*

mediator /ˈmiːd·iːˌeɪţ·ər/ *n* [C] ○ *The governor appointed a mediator and asked both sides to return to the bargaining table.*

medic /ˈmed·ɪk/ *n* [C] *infml* a person who belongs to the part of the armed forces that gives medical help to soldiers

Medicaid /ˈmed·ɪˌkeɪd/ *n* [U] a government service in the US for poor people that pays for their medical treatment ○ Compare MEDICARE

medical Ⓐ /ˈmed·ɪ·kəl/ *adj* [not gradable] of or relating to medicine, or for the treatment of disease or injury ○ *She is in her final year of medical school.* ○ *Medical research has led to better treatment for diabetes patients.*

medically Ⓐ /ˈmed·ɪ·kli/ *adv* [not gradable] ○ *Staying another night in the hospital was not medically necessary, so she was discharged.*

WORD FAMILY medical			
Nouns	medical medication medicine	*Adjectives*	medical medicated medicinal
Verbs	medicate	*Adverbs*	medically

medical examiner *n* [C] a doctor, employed by the government, who examines dead bodies to discover the cause of death

Medicare /ˈmed·ɪˌker, -ˌkær/ *n* [U] a government service in the US for people who are 65 years old and older that pays for medical treatment ○ Compare MEDICAID

medicate /ˈmed·ɪˌkeɪt/ *v* [T] to treat someone with a medicine ○ *Patients are usually medicated with tranquilizers before having anesthesia.*

medication /ˌmed·ɪˈkeɪ·ʃən/ *n* [C/U] any substance used to treat an illness or disease, esp. a drug ○ [C] *Are you taking any medications now?* ○ [U] *I'm on medication for my heart condition.*

medicated /ˈmed·ɪˌkeɪt̬·əd/ *adj* [not gradable] containing a medical substance ○ *medicated shampoo*

medicine TREATMENT /ˈmed·ə·sən/ *n* [U] the science dealing with the preserving of health and with preventing and treating disease or injury ○ *Pediatrics is a branch of medicine.* ○ *She continued to practice medicine until she was in her eighties.*

SUBSTANCE /ˈmed·ə·sən/ *n* [C/U] a substance taken into the body in treating an illness ○ [U] *Take two spoonfuls of cough medicine.* ○ [C] *This antibiotic should not be taken with other medicines.*

medicinal /məˈdɪs·ən·əl/ *adj* ○ *The Indians used the plant as a medicinal substance.*

WORD CHOICES medicine

A common alternative to "medicine" is **drug**.

*The new **drug** has been shown to eliminate tumors.*

Medication is a medicine or set of medicines for a particular illness or condition.

*He's currently on **medication** for his heart.*

A small solid piece of medicine is a **pill** or **tablet**.

*He takes a sleeping **pill** at night.*

*Do you take any vitamin **tablets**?*

Ointment is medicine in the form of a cream that you rub into your skin.

*Apply the **ointment** to the sore area.*

Drops are a type of liquid medicine that you put into your eyes, ears, or nose in small amounts.

*These eye **drops** should clear up the infection.*

medicine cabinet, **medicine chest** *n* [C] a small cabinet, usually with a mirror on the front, which is attached to the wall in a bathroom

medieval /ˌmiːd·iːˈiː·vəl, medˈiː·vəl/ *adj* [not gradable] of or from the MIDDLE AGES (= the period in the past from about 500 to 1500) ○ *The tunnels were dug in medieval times as an escape route.*

mediocre /ˌmiːd·iːˈoʊ·kər/ *adj* [not gradable] just acceptable but not good; not good enough ○ *The movie's plot is predictable, the dialogue is second-rate, and the acting is mediocre.*

mediocrity /ˌmiːd·iːˈɑk·rət̬·i/ *n* [U] ○ *He urged educators to combat mediocrity in the classroom.*

meditate /ˈmed·əˌteɪt/ *v* [I] **1** to think seriously about something, esp. over a period of time ○ [always + adv/prep] *This exhibition does not attempt to meditate on the consequences of the disaster.* **2** If you meditate, you give your attention to one thing, and do not think about anything else, usually as a religious activity or as way of calming or relaxing your mind.

meditation /ˌmed·əˈteɪ·ʃən/ *n* [C/U]

medium Ⓐ AVERAGE /ˈmiːd·iː·əm/ *adj* [not gradable] **1** being in the middle between an upper and lower amount, size, or degree; average ○ *He was a man of medium height.* ○ *The shirt is available in small, medium, and large sizes.* **2** Medium also refers to a way of cooking meat or fish so that it is cooked in the middle: *Would you like your steak rare, medium, or well-done?*

METHOD /ˈmiːd·iː·əm/ *n* [C] *pl* **mediums, media** **1** a method or way of expressing something ○ *the broadcasting/print medium* **2** ***art*** The medium that an artist works in is the materials or method used to create things.

MATERIAL/SUBSTANCE /ˈmiːd·iː·əm/ *n* [C] ***physics*** the material through which a wave or other force travels

PERSON /ˈmiːd·iː·əm/ *n* [C] *pl* **mediums** a person who claims to receive messages from people who are dead

medley /ˈmed·li/ *n* [C] a mixture of different things, such as tunes put together to form a longer piece of music ○ *He played a medley of popular songs on the piano.*

medulla /məˈdʌl·ə/ *n* [C usually sing] ***biology*** the lowest part of the brain, which controls the body's automatic processes such as the way the heart works and the breathing

meek /miːk/ *adj* [*-er/-est* only] quiet and unwilling to disagree or fight or to strongly support personal ideas and opinions ○ *He's slight, meek, and balding, and hardly heroic.*

meekly /ˈmiː·kli/ *adv* ○ *Jennifer meekly suggested that maybe it won't happen.*

meet COME TOGETHER /miːt/ *v* [I/T] *past* **met** to come together with another person ○ [I] *We agreed to meet on Tuesday at six.* ○ [I] *They're meeting with their advisers to work out a new plan.* ○ [T] *The doctor unexpectedly met one of her patients in the supermarket.* ○ [T] *Will we meet Joyce's plane* (= be at the airport when she arrives)*?* ○ [I] *The teams met twice this season* (= competed against each other twice).

meeting /ˈmiːt̬·ɪŋ/ *n* [C] an occasion when people come together ○ *We scheduled the meeting for Friday.*

USAGE

meet, see, visit, or get to know?

Meet is only used about people. It is not used to mean "visit a place or thing." For this meaning use **see** or **visit**.

Annie and Paul met in college.

People love to travel and see different places.

~~*People love to travel and meet different places.*~~

When you **get to know** someone, you gradually learn more about them.

It's too soon to think about marriage, we're still getting to know each other.

BECOME FAMILIAR WITH /miːt/ *v* [I/T] *past* **met** to become familiar with someone for the first time ○ [I] *They met at work.* ○ [T] *I'd like you to meet my friend Laura.*

JOIN /miːt/ *v* [I/T] *past* **met** (esp. of objects) to join or touch ○ [I] *The curtains don't meet in the middle of the window.*

FULFILL /miːt/ *v* [T] *past* **met** to fulfill, satisfy, or achieve ○ *We haven't found office space that meets*

M

our needs. ○ *Do you think she'll be able to meet the deadline?*

SPORTS EVENT /miːt/ *n* [C] a sports event at which several teams or people compete ○ *a track meet* ○ *a swimming meet*

IDIOM with meet

• **meet** *someone* **halfway** to agree to do part of what someone wants if that person will do part of what you want ○ *The buyers wanted to bring the price down from $15,000 to $10,000, so I offered to meet them halfway at $12,500.*

PHRASAL VERBS with meet

• **meet up (with** *someone***)** to see and talk to someone after making an arrangement to do so ○ *I'm meeting up with some friends after work.*

• **meet with** *something* **EXPERIENCE** *fml* to experience something, esp. something unpleasant ○ *She met with an accident on her way to school.*

• **meet with** *something* **CAUSE REACTION** to cause a particular reaction ○ *The announcement met with applause from the audience.*

meeting /ˈmiːt̬·ɪŋ/ *n* ○ See at MEET COME TOGETHER

meeting house *n* [C] a Christian place of worship, esp. for QUAKERS

mega- /ˈmeg·ə/ *prefix* used to add the meaning "extremely big" or "a large amount" to nouns ○ *His last movie made him a megastar.* ○ *They're making megabucks* (= a lot of money).

megabyte /ˈmeg·əˌbɑɪt/, *abbreviation* **MB** *n* [C] a unit of measurement of computer storage space equal to 1,048,576 BYTES

megalomania /ˌmeg·ə·ləˈmeɪ·niː·ə/ *n* [U] the belief that you are much more important and powerful than you really are

megaphone /ˈmeg·əˌfoʊn/ *n* [C] a hollow, cone-shaped device, open at both ends, that makes your voice sound louder when you speak into its smaller end

meiosis /mɑɪˈoʊ·səs/ *n* [U] ***biology*** the type of cell division in which one cell divides into four GAMETES (= male or female cells that join to form an organism), each with a different mixture of CHROMOSOMES (= cell structures) and half the number as were in the original cell

meiotic /mɑɪˈɑt̬·ɪk/ *adj* [not gradable] ***biology*** relating to MEIOSIS (= a type of cell division)

melancholy /ˈmel·ənˌkɑl·i/ *adj* feeling or expressing sadness ○ *a melancholy song* ○ *Larry is in a very melancholy mood.*

melee /ˈmeɪˌleɪ, meɪˈleɪ/ *n* [C] a situation that is confused and not under control, esp. a fight involving a number of people ○ *A melee erupted in the stands near the end of the game.*

mellow SMOOTH /ˈmel·oʊ/ *adj* pleasing because of being smooth, soft, or well developed and not too sharp, bright, new, or rough ○ *a mellow flavor/tone*

mellow /ˈmel·oʊ/ *v* [I] ○ *The bright orange of the fresh paint mellowed as it dried.*

RELAXED /ˈmel·oʊ/ *adj* (of a person or mood) relaxed and pleasant ○ *He looks mellow on stage, but he's always tense before the show.*

mellow /ˈmel·oʊ/ *v* [I/T] ○ [I] *She used to be very impatient, but she's mellowed.*

PHRASAL VERB with mellow

• **mellow out** *slang* to become more relaxed ○ *My dad has definitely mellowed out as he's gotten older.*

melodrama /ˈmel·əˌdrɑm·ə, -ˌdræm·ə/ *n* [C/U] ***literature*** a play or style of acting in which the characters behave and show emotion in a more noticeable way than real people usually do

melodramatic /ˌmel·ə·drəˈmæt̬·ɪk/ *adj* tending to behave or show emotion in ways that are more extreme than usual ○ *I've always been a little melodramatic.*

melody /ˈmel·əd·i/ *n* [C] ***music*** the main tune in a piece of music that is often played or sung more than once ○ *Could you play the melody for me?*

melodic /məˈlɑd·ɪk/ *adj* relating to a tune, or having a pleasant tune ○ *a melodic theme*

melodious /məˈloʊd·iː·əs/ *adj* pleasant and relaxing to listen to

melon /ˈmel·ən/ *n* [C/U] any of several types of large, round, sweet fruit with a thick skin and seeds ○ [U] *I put orange, banana, and melon in the fruit salad.*

melt /melt/ *v* [I/T] to change something from solid to liquid by heating, or to dissolve a solid in a liquid ○ [T] *The sun was hot and melted the snow.* ○ [I] *The ice cream was starting to melt by the time I got it home.*

IDIOM with melt

• **melt in** *your* **mouth** (of food) to be prepared well and taste good ○ *The pie crust just melts in your mouth.*

PHRASAL VERBS with melt

• **melt away** to disappear ○ *Gradually her anger melted away, and she smiled.*

• **melt down** *something* [M] **1** to heat something until it loses its shape and becomes liquid ○ *Spaniards melted down Aztec jewelry for its gold.* **2** If an organization or system melts down, it loses its ability to operate in the way that it should: *The economic minister has kept the nation's economy from melting down.*

meltdown /ˈmelt·dɑʊn/ *n* [C/U] a dangerous accident in which the fuel melts in a nuclear REACTOR (= device that produces energy)

melting /ˈmel·tɪŋ/ *n* [U] ***chemistry*** the change or process of changing from a solid substance to a liquid

melting point *n* [C usually sing] ***chemistry*** the temperature at which a substance melts

melting pot *n* [C usually sing] a place or situation where the people and cultures of many different places mix together

member PERSON /ˈmem·bər/ *n* [C] a person or thing that is part of a group ○ *She's a member of our team.* ○ *The lion is a member of the cat family.*

membership /ˈmem·bərˌʃɪp/ *n* [C/U] **1** the state of belonging to an organization, or an agreement by which someone joins an organization ○ [U] *We applied for membership in the country club.* ○ [C] *Some fitness clubs sell lifetime memberships.* **2** The membership is all the members of an organization: [U] *We asked the membership to vote on the issue.*

BODY PART /ˈmem·bər/ *n* [C] a part or organ of a body, such as an arm, leg, or lung

membrane /ˈmem·breɪn/ *n* [C] a thin, soft layer of tissue that covers organs or connects parts of living things, or the outer covering of a cell ➤ Picture: **amoeba; cell**

memento /məˈment·oʊ/ *n* [C] *pl* **mementos, mementoes** an object that you keep to help you remember a person or a special event

memo /ˈmem·oʊ/ *n* [C] *pl* **memos** *short form of* MEMORANDUM ○ *He put his conclusions in a memo to Bethel.*

memoir /ˈmem·wɑr, -wɔːr/ *n* [C] ***writing*** a written record of a person's knowledge of events or of a person's own experiences ○ *She wrote a memoir about her years as a war correspondent.* ○ *He's writing his memoirs* (= the story of his life).

memorabilia /ˌmem·ə·rəˈbɪl·iː·ə/ *pl n* objects that are collected because they are connected with a person or event that you want to remember

memorable /ˈmem·ə·rə·bəl/ *adj* likely to be remembered or worth remembering ○ *a memorable song/story* ○ *Dizzy Dean was one of baseball's most memorable personalities.*
memorably /ˈmem·ə·rə·bli/ *adv* ○ *The part was played memorably by Humphrey Bogart.*

memorandum /ˌmem·əˈræn·dəm/, *short form* **memo** *n* [C] *pl* **memoranda, memorandums** a written report prepared especially for a person or group of people and containing information about a particular matter ○ *Ann will send a memorandum to the staff outlining the new procedures.*

memorial /məˈmɔːr·iː·əl, -ˈmoʊr-/ *n* [C] **1** an object made in order to honor a person or event ○ *The statue is a memorial to those who died in the war.* **2** A memorial service is an event held to remember a person who has died.

Memorial Day *n* [C] a US holiday on the last Monday in May honoring members of the military who died in war

memory **ABILITY TO REMEMBER** /ˈmem·ə·ri/ *n* [C/U] **1** the ability to remember things ○ [U] *After the accident he suffered from loss of memory.* ○ [C] *She has an excellent memory for names.* ○ [U] *Each of the children recited a short poem from memory* (= by remembering it). **2** A computer's memory is the part of a computer in which information is stored, or its ability to store information.
memorize /ˈmem·əˌrɑɪz/ *v* [T] to learn something so that you will remember it exactly ○ *She memorized her friends' phone numbers.* ➤ Usage: **remember or memory?** at REMEMBER

WHAT IS REMEMBERED /ˈmem·ə·ri/ *n* [C] something that you remember from the past ○ *She has vivid memories of her trip to Los Angeles 20 years ago.* ○ *That song brings back memories* (= makes me remember past events). ○ *A service was held* **in memory of** (= to remember) *those who died in the earthquake.*

WORD FAMILY memory			
Nouns	memorial memory	*Verbs*	memorize
Adjectives	memorable	*Adverbs*	memorably

men /men/ *pl of* MAN **MALE**

menace /ˈmen·əs/ *n* [C/U] danger, or someone or something that is likely to cause harm ○ [U] *There was an air of controlled menace about him.* ○ [C] *That boy is a menace to himself and his friends.*
menace /ˈmen·əs/ *v* [T] ○ *A hurricane menaced the east coast yesterday.*
menacing /ˈmen·ə·sɪŋ/ *adj* ○ *a menacing gesture*
menacingly /ˈmen·ə·sɪŋ·li/ *adv* ○ *She glared menacingly at him.*

menagerie /məˈnædʒ·ə·ri, -ˈnæʒ-/ *n* [C] a collection of different animals that are kept, usually for people to see

mend **REPAIR** /mend/ *v* [T] to repair cloth that is torn or something that is damaged ○ *Could you mend this hole in my shirt?* ○ *The country is seeking to mend relations with the US.*

BECOME WELL /mend/ *v* [I/T] to become well again after an illness or injury ○ [I] *The bones in my broken wrist took eight weeks to mend.*
mend /mend/ *n*

IDIOMS with mend

• **mend** *your* **ways** to behave better ○ *I was getting really bad grades, but I promised my parents I would mend my ways and work harder.*
• **on the mend** becoming healthy after an illness ○ *She's still in the hospital, but she's definitely on the mend.*

menial /ˈmiː·niː·əl/ *adj* (of work) needing little skill or education ○ *a menial job*

meningitis /ˌmen·ənˈdʒɑɪt̬·əs/ *n* [U] a swelling of the outer MEMBRANE (= thin layer of tissue) of the brain caused by an infection

meniscus /məˈnɪs·kəs/ *n* [C] ***chemistry*** the curved surface of a liquid in a container, which can be either in if the MOLECULES of the liquid are attracted to the container or out if the molecules are attracted to each other

menopause /ˈmen·əˌpɔːz/ *n* [U] the time in a woman's life, often between the ages of 45 and 55, when she gradually stops MENSTRUATING (= having a regular flow of blood from her uterus)

menorah /məˈnɔːr·ə, -ˈnoʊr·ə/ *n* [C] a base with seven branches for holding candles that is a symbol of the Jewish people, or one with nine branches used during the Jewish celebration of Hanukkah

M

men's room *n* [C] a toilet for men in a public building ○ Compare LADIES' ROOM

menstruate /ˈmen·strəˌweɪt/ *v* [I] to have a flow of blood from the uterus, usually for three to five days every four weeks, in women who are not pregnant
menstruation /ˌmen·strəˈweɪ·ʃən/ *n* [U] the flow of blood from a woman's uterus
menstrual /ˈmen·strəl, -strə·wəl/ *adj* [not gradable] ○ *a menstrual cycle/period*

menswear /ˈmenz·wer, -wær/ *n* [U] clothing for men ○ *designer menswear*

mental Ⓐ /ˈment·əl/ *adj* [not gradable] of or about the mind, or involving the process of thinking ○ *Stress can affect both your physical and mental health.* ○ *Many people suffer from some form of mental illness during their lives.* ○ *I made a mental note of her address* (= I will try to remember it).
mentally Ⓐ /ˈment·əl·i/ *adv* [not gradable] ○ *mentally ill*
mentality Ⓐ /menˈtæl·əṭ·i/ *n* [U] a person's or group's way of thinking about things ○ *They buy everything on credit – they have this play now, pay later mentality.*

WORD FAMILY mental			
Nouns	mentality	*Adverbs*	mentally
Adjectives	mental		

M

menthol /ˈmen·θɔːl/ *n* [U] a natural substance made from PEPPERMINT (= a plant with a fresh, strong smell) and used in medicines and as a flavoring

mention /ˈmen·tʃən/ *v* [T] to speak about someone or something, esp. briefly and without giving much detail ○ [+ (*that*) clause] *Has he mentioned (that) he's leaving his job?* ○ *I promised never to mention her again.*
mention /ˈmen·tʃən/ *n* [C/U] ○ [U] *There was no mention of the robbery in today's newspaper.*

mentor /ˈmenˌtɔːr/ *n* [C] an experienced and trusted person who gives another person advice and help, esp. related to work or school, over a period of time
mentoring /ˈmen·tə·rɪŋ/ *n* [U] ○ *The students' chances can be improved with more studying, mentoring, and intensive review.*

menu /ˈmen·juː/ *n* [C] **1** a list of the dishes served at a meal, esp. in a restaurant ○ *There are several vegetarian dishes on the menu.* **2** A menu is also a list of items shown on a computer screen from which the user can choose an operation for the computer to perform.

meow /miːˈɑʊ/ *n* [C] the crying sound a cat makes
meow /miːˈɑʊ/ *v* [I]

mercantilism /ˈmɜr·kənˌtiːˌlɪz·əm, -ˌtɑɪ-/ *n* [U] ***world history*** an economic theory developed in the 16th to 18th centuries holding that a government should control the economy and that a nation should increase its wealth by selling more than it buys from other nations

mercenary /ˈmɜr·səˌner·i/ *n* [C] a soldier who fights for a foreign country or group for pay
mercenary /ˈmɜr·səˌner·i/ *adj* interested only in the money that can be obtained from a situation ○ *I don't trust his motives – he's too mercenary.*

merchandise /ˈmɜr·tʃənˌdɑɪs/ *n* [U] goods that are bought and sold ○ *This store has a wide selection of merchandise for sale.*
merchandising /ˈmɜr·tʃənˌdɑɪ·zɪŋ/ *n* [U] the activity of advertising or selling goods

merchant /ˈmɜr·tʃənt/ *n* [C] a person whose business is buying and selling goods for profit

merchant marine *n* [U] a country's ships that are involved in trade

mercury /ˈmɜr·kjə·ri/ *n* [U] a heavy, silver-colored metal that is liquid at ordinary temperatures ○ *Mercury is used in thermometers.*

Mercury /ˈmɜr·kjə·ri/ *n* [U] the planet nearest in distance to the sun ➤ Picture: **solar system**

mercy KINDNESS /ˈmɜr·si/ *n* [U] kindness shown toward someone whom you have the right or power to punish ○ *He begged for mercy.* ○ *The soldiers showed no mercy toward their prisoners.*
merciful /ˈmɜr·sɪ·fəl/ *adj* kind and forgiving ○ *Judges are sometimes more merciful than a jury.*
merciless /ˈmɜr·sɪ·ləs/ *adj* showing no kindness; cruel ○ *a merciless enemy*
mercilessly /ˈmɜr·sɪ·lə·sli/ *adv* ○ *He was teased mercilessly at school.*

LUCK /ˈmɜr·si/ *n* [U] something that is considered lucky because it is not as bad as it had been or could have been ○ *It's a mercy that no one was hurt in the fire.*
mercifully /ˈmɜr·sɪ·fli, -fə·li/ *adv* luckily ○ *His speech was mercifully brief.*

mercy killing *n* [U] EUTHANASIA

mere /mɪr/ *adj* [not gradable] nothing more than; nothing more important than ○ *The mere fact that Greene plays for the Yankees gives him a lot of visibility.* ○ *The city receives a mere 20% of the parking revenues.*
merely /ˈmɪr·li/ *adv* [not gradable] only; and nothing more ○ *I merely said that I was tired.* ○ *These columns have no function and are merely decorative.*

merge /mɜrdʒ/ *v* [I/T] to combine or join together ○ [I] *Route 9A splits off from Route 9, but they merge after 5 more miles.*
merger /ˈmɜr·dʒər/ *n* [C] the combining of two or more companies or organizations into one

meridian /məˈrɪd·iː·ən/ *n* [C] ***earth science*** an imaginary line that passes from the North Pole to the South Pole through any place on the surface of the earth, used to show the position of places on a map

meringue /məˈræŋ/ *n* [C/U] a mixture of sugar and the beaten white part of eggs, baked until firm, or the light, sweet cake made of this

merit /ˈmer·ət/ *n* [C/U] the quality of being good and deserving praise, or a good quality ○ [U]

Judged on artistic merit, it was a success. ○ [C] *Being able to work at home has its merits.*
merit /ˈmer·ət/ *v* [T] to deserve something ○ *These recommendations merit careful attention.*

IDIOM with **merit**

• **on its (own) merits, on** *someone's* **(own) merits** based only on a person's or thing's qualities and not on what other people say about that person or thing ○ *Judge the product on its own merits, and not on what the ads say.*

mermaid /ˈmɜr·meɪd/ *n* [C] an imaginary creature with the upper body of a woman and the tail of a fish

merry /ˈmer·i/ *adj* **1** happy or showing enjoyment **2** You say **Merry Christmas** to wish people a happy time at Christmas.

merry-go-round /ˈmer·iː·goʊ ˌrɑʊnd/, **carousel** *n* [C] a circular stage with brightly colored artificial animals that children can ride on while it turns around and around as music plays

mesa /ˈmeɪ·sə/ *n* [C] ***earth science*** a mountain with a large flat top

mesh **NET** /meʃ/ *n* [U] a material loosely woven of wire, plastic, or thread so that it has spaces in it like a net ○ *Pour the liquid through a strainer of fine mesh.*

JOIN /meʃ/ *v* [I/T] (of two or more things) to fit together or be suitable for each other ○ [I] *The teeth of the smaller and larger gears mesh with each other.* ○ [I] *Their ideas on how to run the company never really meshed.*

mesmerize /ˈmez·məˌrɑɪz/ *v* [T] to hold completely the attention or interest of someone ○ *Her beautiful voice mesmerized the audience.*
mesmerizing /ˈmez·məˌrɑɪ·zɪŋ/ *adj* ○ *a mesmerizing performance*

meson /ˈmez·ɑn, ˈmes-; ˈmeɪ·zɑn, -sɑn/ *n* [C] ***physics*** a very small piece of matter that contains a QUARK and an ANTIQUARK.

mesosphere /ˈmez·əˌsfɪr, ˈmiː·zə-/ *n* [U] ***earth science*** the layer of gases surrounding the earth at a height of between 50 and 100 kilometers, above the STRATOSPHERE

mess **DISORDER** /mes/ *n* [C usually sing] **1** a condition of disorder and confusion, or something in that condition ○ *They left the kitchen a mess.* ○ *We sat in traffic for two hours while they cleaned up the mess from the accident.* **2** A mess is also a dirty condition: *The puppy's made a mess on the dining room rug.* **3** A mess is also a situation that is full of problems and difficulties: *Traffic was a mess.*
mess /mes/ *v* [I/T] *infml* ○ [I/T] *Don't mess up my hair – I just combed it.*
messed-up /mestˈʌp, ˈmest·ʌp/ *adj infml* unhappy and emotionally confused ○ *a messed-up teenager*
messy /ˈmes·i/ *adj* **1** dirty, unpleasant, or lacking order ○ *I hate a messy kitchen.* **2** A messy situation is one that is confused and unpleasant: *He's got a messy personal life.*

ROOM /mes/, **mess hall** /ˈmes·hɔːl/ *n* [C] a room or building in which members of the military eat their meals ○ *the officers' mess*

PHRASAL VERBS with **mess**

• **mess around** to waste time doing something without a particular purpose ○ *The kids were just messing around at the mall.*
• **mess (around) with** *something* **CHANGE** to make changes in something, esp. in a way that harms it ○ *Has someone been messing around with the settings on my computer again?*
• **mess (around) with** *something/someone* **DANGER** to become involved with someone or something dangerous ○ *You can't mess around with airport security.*
• **mess** *(something)* **up** **MISTAKE** to make a mistake or do something wrong ○ *I messed up – I'm sorry.* ○ *I really messed up on the second question on the test.* ○ *We had a chance to win the game and we messed it up.*
• **mess** *something* **up** **DAMAGE** [M] to break, damage, or spoil something ○ *I messed up my ankle playing soccer.* ○ *There are always a couple of kids who come to a party and try to mess things up.*

message **INFORMATION** /ˈmes·ɪdʒ/ *n* [C] a short piece of written or spoken information that is given or sent to someone ○ *If I'm not there when you phone, leave a message.* ○ *She's not here – can I take a message?*

IDEA /ˈmes·ɪdʒ/ *n* [C] the main idea that an artist, writer, speaker, or group is trying to communicate ○ *The message of the movie seems to be that only the most ruthless people can get ahead in politics.*

messaging /ˈmes·ə·dʒɪŋ/ *n* [U] a system or the process of sending and receiving messages or images on a computer or other electronic device ○ *Instant messaging alerts computer users when their friends are online.* ○ *It's not illegal in some states to drive while text messaging.*

messenger /ˈmes·ən·dʒər/ *n* [C] a person who carries a message

messenger RNA, *abbreviation* **mRNA** *n* [U] ***biology*** a type of RNA (= chemical in living cells) that provides the information needed to make PROTEIN (= a necessary part of all living cells)

messiah /məˈsɑɪ·ə/ *n* [C] **1** a person who is expected to come and save the world **2** In the Christian religion, the Messiah is Jesus. **3** In the Jewish religion, the Messiah has not yet come.

mestizo /mesˈtiː·zoʊ/, *female* **mestiza** *n* [C] *pl* **mestizos, mestizas** a person from Latin America who is part European and part American Indian

met /met/ *past simple and past participle of* MEET

metabolic /ˌmet̬·əˈbɑl·ɪk/ *adj* [not gradable] ***biology*** relating to METABOLISM (= processes by which the body uses food for energy and growth)

metabolism /məˈtæb·əˌlɪz·əm/ *n* [C] ***biology*** the chemical and physical processes by which a living thing uses food for energy and growth

metal /ˈmet̬·əl/ *n* [C/U] ***chemistry, physics*** a generally hard and shiny chemical element, such

M

as iron or gold, or a mixture of such elements, such as steel, which usually allows electricity and heat to travel through it
metallic /mə'tæl·ɪk/ *adj* ***chemistry, physics*** made of or similar to metal, or showing a quality of metal ○ *a loud metallic sound*

metal detector *n* [C] an electronic device that finds metal, used esp. to search people for weapons

metalloid /'met·əl,ɔɪd/ *n* [C] ***chemistry*** a chemical element with some of the characteristics of a metal and some of a substance that is not a metal, for example, SILICON and ARSENIC

metamorphic /,met̬·ə'mɔːr·fɪk/ *adj* [not gradable] ***earth science*** describes rocks changed to a new form as a result of physical processes, such as pressure or heat
metamorphism /,met̬·ə'mɔːr,fɪz·əm/ *n* [U] ***earth science***
metamorphosed /,met̬·ə'mɔːr·foʊzd, -foʊst/ *adj* ***earth science***

metamorphosis /,met̬·ə'mɔːr·fə·səs/ *n* [C/U] *pl* **metamorphoses 1** a complete change of character, appearance, or condition ○ [C] *She underwent a metamorphosis from a steady player into a ruthless aggressor on the court.* **2** ***biology*** Metamorphosis is the process by which the young form of insects, FROGS, etc., develops into the adult form.

metaphase /'met̬·ə,feɪz/ *n* [not gradable] ***biology*** the stage of cell division in which the CHROMOSOMES (= cell structures containing information) arrange themselves along the middle of the cell

metaphor /'met̬·ə,fɔːr, -fər/ *n* [C/U] ***literature*** an expression that describes a person or object by referring to something that is considered to possess similar characteristics ○ [C] *"A heart of stone" is a metaphor.*
metaphorical /,met̬·ə'fɔːr·ɪ·kəl, -'fɑr-/ *adj* ○ *metaphorical expressions*

metaphysical /,met̬·ə'fɪz·ɪ·kəl/ *adj* relating to the part of PHILOSOPHY that deals with existence and knowledge ○ *metaphysical questions about the nature of the universe*

mete out *something* /'miːt'ɑʊt/ *phrasal verb* [M] *fml* to give or order a punishment ○ *The prison sentence is the toughest meted out to any of the seven athletes who have pleaded guilty.*

meteor /'miːt̬·iː·ər, -,ɔːr/, **shooting star** *n* [C] a small piece of matter that falls from space with great speed, producing a bright light as it enters the earth's ATMOSPHERE (= the air surrounding it)
meteoric /,miːt̬·iː'ɔːr·ɪk, -'ɑr-/ *adj* [not gradable] **1** of or like a meteor ○ *meteoric rock* **2** If something is described as meteoric, it is sudden and usually brief: *a meteoric rise to fame*

meteorite /'miːt̬·iː·ə,rɑɪt/ *n* [C] ***earth science*** a piece of matter from space that has landed on earth ○ *Meteorites striking land usually vaporize instantly.*

meteorology /,miːt̬·iː·ə'rɑl·ə·dʒi/ *n* [U] the scientific study of the earth's ATMOSPHERE (= the air surrounding it) and how it causes changes in weather conditions
meteorological /,miːt̬·iː·ə·rə'lɑdʒ·ɪ·kəl/ *adj* [not gradable]
meteorologist /,miːt̬·iː·ə'rɑl·ə·dʒəst/ *n* [C]

meter MEASUREMENT /'miːt̬·ər/, *abbreviation* **m** *n* [C] a unit of measurement of length equal to 100 centimeters or 39.37 inches
metric /'me·trɪk/ *adj* [not gradable] of or using the meter or a system of measurement based on it
DEVICE /'miːt̬·ər/ *n* [C] **1** a device that measures the amount of gas, water, or electricity used **2** In a TAXI (= car whose driver you pay to take you somewhere), a meter is the device that measures the distance or the amount of time spent traveling and records how much you have to pay.
RHYTHM /'miːt̬·ər/ *n* [C/U] **1** ***literature*** the rhythm of a poem, produced by the arrangement of syllables according to the number and type of beats in each line **2** ***music*** Meter is the rhythm that organizes the beats in a piece of music into a pattern.

methane /'meθ·eɪn/ *n* [U] a gas having no color or smell which is often used as fuel

methanol /'meθ·ə,nɔːl, -,noʊl/ *n* [U] ***chemistry*** a poisonous chemical substance which is the most basic type of alcohol

method Ⓐ /'meθ·əd/ *n* [C] a way of doing something ○ *New teaching methods encourage children to think for themselves.* ○ *Automated telephone answering service is one method being used to cut business costs.*
methodical Ⓐ /mə'θɑd·ɪ·kəl/ *adj* controlled and systematic ○ *The economy's slow, methodical growth is likely to continue into next year.*
methodically /mə'θɑd·ɪ·kli/ *adv* ○ *We methodically recorded the details of how the new division would work.* ○ *He methodically ate the entire pie.*
➤ Usage: **way or method/means of?** at WAY MANNER

WORD FAMILY method			
Nouns	method methodology	*Adjectives* *Adverbs*	methodical methodically

Methodist /'meθ·əd·əst/ *n* [C] a member of a Christian religious group that is one of the Protestant churches
Methodist /'meθ·əd·əst/ *adj* [not gradable] ○ *a Methodist church* ○ *a Methodist minister*

methodology Ⓐ /,meθ·ə'dɑl·ə·dʒi/ *n* [C] a set of methods used in a particular area of study or activity ○ *The two researchers are using different methodologies.*
methodological Ⓐ /,meθ·əd·əl'ɑdʒ·ɪ·kəl/ *adj*

meticulous /mə'tɪk·jə·ləs/ *adj* giving or showing careful attention to every detail ○ *a meticulous housekeeper* ○ *meticulous research*
meticulously /mə'tɪk·jə·ləs·li/ *adv* ○ *She meticulously planned every decorating detail.*

metric /ˈme·trɪk/ *adj* ○ See at METER MEASUREMENT

metric system *n* [U] the system of measurement based on the meter, the gram, and the liter as the basic units of length, weight, and volume

metro /ˈme·troʊ/ *adj short form of* METROPOLITAN ○ *the Atlanta metro area* ○ *the metro section in today's newspaper*

metronome /ˈme·trəˌnoʊm/ *n* [C] a device that produces a regular beat at a desired speed to help musicians keep the correct rhythm

metropolis /məˈtrɑp·ə·ləs/ *n* [C] a large city, esp. the main city of a country or region ○ *Chicago is a major metropolis.*

metropolitan /ˌme·trəˈpɑl·ət·ən/ *adj* of or in a large city ○ *the Boston metropolitan area* ○ *the Metropolitan Museum of Art*

mettle /ˈmeţ·əl/ *n* [U] bravery and determination ○ *The climb to the summit in a blizzard would test their mettle.*

mezzanine /ˈmez·əˌniːn, ˌmez·əˈniːn/ *n* [C] a floor that comes between two other floors of a building, usually directly above the main floor

mg *n* [C] *pl* **mg** *abbreviation for* MILLIGRAM

mi. *n* [C] *pl* **mi.** *abbreviation for* MILE

mic /mɑɪk/ *n* [C] *short form of* MICROPHONE

mice /mɑɪs/ *pl of* MOUSE

Mickey Mouse /ˌmɪk·iː ˈmɑʊs/ *adj infml, disapproving* (of an organization, place, object, or activity) too small and simple; not to be taken seriously ○ *I don't get paid enough to put up with that Mickey Mouse sort of stuff.*

micro- /ˌmɑɪ·kroʊ, ˌmɑɪ·krə/ *prefix* very small ○ *a microbrewery* ○ Compare MACRO-

microbe /ˈmɑɪ·kroʊb/ *n* [C] ***biology*** a very small living thing, esp. one that causes disease, and which is too small to see without a MICROSCOPE (= device that makes very small objects look larger)

microbiology /ˌmɑɪ·kroʊ·bɑɪˈɑl·ə·dʒi/ *n* [U] the study of very small living things, such as bacteria

microcosm /ˈmɑɪ·krəˌkɑz·əm/ *n* [C/U] a small place, society, or situation that has the same characteristics as something much larger ○ [C] *What's happened to us is a microcosm of what's happened to industry in America.*

microcoulomb /ˌmɑɪ·kroʊˈkuː·lɑm, -loʊm/ *n* [C] ***physics*** a unit used to measure very small amounts of electricity, equal to a COULOMB divided by 1,000,000

microfiche /ˈmɑɪ·krəˌfiːʃ/ *n* [C/U] a small sheet of film on which information is photographed in a reduced size

microfilm /ˈmɑɪ·krəˌfɪlm/ *n* [C/U] (a length of) film containing photographed information in a reduced size

microfossil /ˈmɑɪ·kroʊˌfɑs·əl/ *n* [C] ***earth science*** a FOSSIL that is too small to see without using special equipment

micrometer /ˈmɑɪ·kroʊˌmiːţ·ər/, **micron** /ˈmɑɪ·krɑn/, *symbol* **µm** *n* [C] ***science*** a unit of measurement of distance equal to 0.000001 meter

micron /ˈmɑɪ·krɑn/ *n* [C] ***science*** **micrometer**

microorganism /ˌmɑɪ·kroʊˈɔːr·gəˌnɪz·əm/ *n* [C] ***biology*** a living thing which on its own is too small to be seen without a MICROSCOPE (= device that makes small objects look larger)

microphone /ˈmɑɪ·krəˌfoʊn/, *short form* **mike**, *short form* **mic** *n* [C] a device that records sound or increases the loudness of sounds by changing the sound waves into electrical waves

microscope /ˈmɑɪ·krəˌskoʊp/ *n* [C] ***science*** a device that makes very small objects look larger, esp. so that they can be scientifically examined and studied

microscopic /ˌmɑɪ·krəˈskɑp·ɪk/ *adj* extremely small, esp. so small that it can only be seen with a microscope

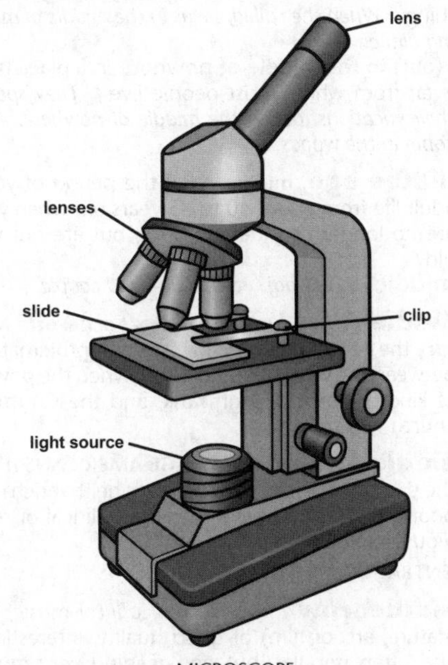

MICROSCOPE

microsecond /ˈmɑɪ·kroʊˌsek·ənd/ *n* [C] ***science*** a unit of time equal to one second divided by 1,000,000

microwave /ˈmɑɪ·krəˌweɪv/ *n* [C] **1** ***physics*** a very short, very fast WAVE ENERGY FORM of ELECTROMAGNETIC energy that causes heat in atoms of water and some other substances **2** A microwave or **microwave oven** is a machine that cooks food quickly using microwaves: *Heat up the leftover pizza in the microwave.*

microwave /ˈmɑɪ·krəˌweɪv/ *v* [I/T] ○ [I] *Microwave on high for 12 minutes.*

mid- /mɪd/ *prefix* the middle of ○ *midweek* ○ *mid-March* ○ *He's in his mid-thirties.*

midafternoon, **mid-afternoon** /ˈmɪd ˌæf·tər ˈnuːn/ *n* [U/C] the part of the afternoon half the way between 12 o'clock and the time when you last see the sun

midair /mɪd ˈer, -ˈær/ *n* [U] a point in the air, not on the ground ○ *She caught the ball in midair.*

midday /ˈmɪd·deɪ, -ˈdeɪ/ *n* [U] the middle of the day, at or near 12 o'clock; NOON

middle /ˈmɪd·əl/ *n* [C usually sing] **1** a point, position, or part that is not on one side or the other but is equally far from things on either side; the central point, position, or part ○ *This is my class photo – I'm the one in the middle.* **2** The middle of a period of time is a point between the beginning and the end of that period: *The noise woke us up in the middle of the night.* **3** *infml* Your middle is your waist.

middle /ˈmɪd·əl/ *adj* [not gradable] ○ *In the sequence a, b, c, d, e, the middle letter is c.*

IDIOMS with middle

- **in the middle of** *something* busy doing something ○ *When she called, I was in the middle of making dinner.*
- **(out) in the middle of nowhere** in a place that is far from where most people live ○ *They spend their vacations, out in the middle of nowhere, in a cabin in the woods.*

M

middle age, **midlife** *n* [U] the period of your adult life from about 40 to 65 years old when you are no longer considered young but are not yet old

middle-aged *adj* ○ *a middle-aged couple*

Middle Ages /ˌmɪd·əl ˈeɪ·dʒəz/ *pl n* ***world history*** the period in European history, approximately between the years 500 and 1400, when the power of kings, people of high rank, and the Christian church was strong

Middle America **AVERAGE AMERICANS** *n* [U] the part of American society that is neither rich nor poor and does not have extreme political or religious opinions

CENTRAL US *n* [U] the MIDWEST

middlebrow /ˈmɪd·əl ˌbrɑʊ/ *adj* (of music, literature, art, or film) of good quality, interesting, and often popular, but not needing very much thought to understand ○ Compare HIGHBROW; LOWBROW

middle class *n* [U] ***social studies*** the people in a society who are not of high social rank or extremely rich but are not poor

middle finger *n* [C] the longest finger on the hand

middle ground *n* [U] ***art*** the area in a painting or photograph that is between the FOREGROUND and the background

middleman /ˈmɪd·əl ˌmæn/ *n* [C] **-men** a person who buys goods from the person who makes or grows them and makes a profit by selling them to a store or a user

middle management *n* [U] the people within a company who are in charge of departments or groups but who are below those who are in control of the company as a whole

middle name *n* [C] the name that some people have between their first name and their last name ○ Compare FIRST NAME; LAST NAME

middle-of-the-road *adj* not extreme and acceptable to or liked by most people ○ *His views on social issues are pretty much middle-of-the-road.*

middle school *n* [C] a school for children between the ages of about 10 and 14

middling /ˈmɪd·lɪŋ, -lən/ *adj* [not gradable] medium or average; neither very good nor very bad ○ *a middling amount*

Mideast /mɪd ˈiːst/ *n* [U] the region of the world near and to the east and south of the Mediterranean Sea ○ *The President is on his way to the Mideast.* ○ *Mideast peace talks*

midget /ˈmɪdʒ·ət/ *n* [C] an unusually small person ○ **USAGE:** This word is usually considered offensive.

midlife /ˈmɪd·lɑɪf/ *n* [U] MIDDLE AGE

midlife crisis *n* [C] feelings of unhappiness and anxiety that some people experience, often when they are between 40 and 50 years old

midnight /ˈmɪd·nɑɪt/ *n* [U] 12 o'clock in the middle of the night

mid-ocean ridge *n* [C] ***earth science*** an area of mountains under an ocean where there are EARTHQUAKES and VOLCANOS

midpoint /ˈmɪd·pɔɪnt/ *n* [C usually sing] a point half the distance along something, esp. a line, or a point in the middle of a period of time ○ *the midpoint of the season*

midriff /ˈmɪd·rɪf/, **midsection** /ˈmɪd ˌsek·ʃən/ *n* [C] the part of the human body between the chest and the waist

midsize /ˈmɪd·sɑɪz/, **midsized** /ˈmɪd·sɑɪzd/ *adj* [not gradable] between large and small in size ○ *Their parents bought them a used midsize car as a graduation present.* ○ *It is beyond the budgets of most midsize and small businesses.*

midst /mɪdst, mɪtst/ *n fml* middle ○ *Long Beach is* **in the midst of** *a revival.* ○ *The pear tree stood* **in the midst of** *a rainbow of flowers.*

midstream /ˈmɪd ˈstriːm/ *n* [U] the middle of a river where the water flows fastest, or *fig.* the middle of an activity ○ (*fig.*) *Never switch software in midstream.*

midterm /ˈmɪd·tɜrm/ *adj* [not gradable] being at the end of the first half of a TERM (= fixed period of time) ○ *midterm elections* ○ *Midterm exams start next week.*

midterm /ˈmɪd·tɜrm/ *n* [C] a test given at the end of the first half of a school TERM

midtown /ˈmɪd·tɑʊn/ *n* [U] the part of a city near the center ○ *His company is in a suite of midtown offices overlooking Park Avenue.*

midway /ˈmɪd·weɪ, -ˈweɪ/ *adv* [not gradable] in the middle between two places, or in the middle of a process or period of time ○ *Milwaukee is about midway between Chicago and Green Bay.* ○ *She stopped working midway through her pregnancy.*

midweek /ˈmɪd·wiːk, -ˈwiːk/ *n* [U] the middle of the week

Midwest /mɪd ˈwest/, **Middle America, Middle West** *n* [U] the north central part of the US which includes Ohio, Indiana, Michigan, Illinois, Wisconsin, Iowa, Minnesota, Nebraska, Missouri, and Kansas ○ *The drought has destroyed grain crops across much of the Midwest.*
Midwestern /mɪd ˈwes·tərn/ *adj* ○ *midwestern states/farms/families*

midwife /ˈmɪd·wɑɪf/ *n* [C] *pl* **midwives** a person, usually a woman, who is not a doctor and who has been trained to help women when they are giving birth
midwifery /mɪd ˈwɪf·ə·ri, -ˈwɑɪ·fə-/ *n* [U] the techniques or activity of helping women give birth

miffed /mɪft/ *adj* annoyed, esp. at someone's behavior toward you ○ *I was miffed because she didn't call all week.*

might MAY /mɑɪt/ *past simple of* MAY
POSSIBILITY /mɑɪt/ *modal verb* **might** used to express the possibility that something will happen or be done or is true, although it may not be very likely ○ *We might come visit you in Atlanta in the spring.* ○ *He's very fast and he might even finish in the top three.* ○ *The Beach Boys might well have been the most talented act to perform at the Monterey Pop Festival.* ○ Compare MAY POSSIBILITY
SUGGESTION /mɑɪt/ *modal verb* **might** used to make a suggestion or suggest a possibility in a polite way ○ *I thought you might like to join me for dinner.* ○ Compare MAY SUGGESTION
SHOULD /mɑɪt/ *modal verb* **might** used to suggest, esp. angrily, what someone should do to be pleasant or polite ○ *You might at least try to look like you're enjoying yourself!*
POWER /mɑɪt/ *n* [U] power, strength, or force ○ *She struggled with all her might to lift the rock.*
mighty /ˈmɑɪt̬·i/ *adj, adv* ○ *a mighty* (= powerful) *river* ○ (*infml*) *I'd be mighty* (= very) *grateful if you looked in on my mother while I'm away.*

mightn't /ˈmɑɪt·ᵊnt/ *contraction of* might not ○ *I almost wondered if he mightn't be right.*

migraine /ˈmɑɪ·greɪn/ *n* [C/U] a severe continuous pain in the head, often with vomiting and difficulty in seeing

migrate Ⓐ /ˈmɑɪ·greɪt, mɑɪ ˈgreɪt/ *v* [I] ***social studies*** to move from one country or region to another, often temporarily ○ *Farm workers migrate at harvest time.* ○ *In September these birds migrate south.*
migrant Ⓐ /ˈmɑɪ·grənt/ *n* [C] ○ *migrant workers*
migration Ⓐ /mɑɪ ˈgreɪ·ʃən/ *n* [C/U] movement from one region to another and often back again, esp. according to the season of the year ○ [U] *She's interested in bat migration.*
migratory Ⓐ /ˈmɑɪ·grəˌtɔːr·i, -ˌtoʊr·i/ *adj* [not gradable] having the characteristic of moving regularly to another place ○ *migratory birds*

mike /mɑɪk/ *n* [C] *short form of* MICROPHONE

mild /mɑɪld/ *adj* [*-er/-est* only] **1** not violent, severe, or extreme; slight or gentle ○ *mild criticism* ○ *a mild case of the flu* ○ *She has a very mild temperament.* **2** If the flavor of food or a smell is described as mild, it is not very strong. **3** Mild weather is not very cold or not as cold as usual.
mildly /ˈmɑɪl·dli/ *adv* ○ *We were mildly surprised to see him again.* ○ *"I think you've made a mistake," he said mildly.*

mildew /ˈmɪl·duː/ *n* [U] a soft, usually white, green, or black area caused by a FUNGUS that sometimes grows on things such as plants, food, paper, or buildings, esp. if the conditions are warm and wet

mile /mɑɪl/, *abbreviation* **mi.** *n* [C] **1** a unit of measurement of distance equal to 1760 YARDS or 1.6 kilometers **2** Miles can mean a very long distance: *They live way out in the country, miles from anywhere.*
mileage, **milage** /ˈmɑɪ·lɪdʒ/ *n* [U] **1** the distance that a vehicle has traveled ○ *What's the mileage on your car?* **2** Mileage is also the distance a vehicle can travel using a particular amount of fuel: *Smaller cars get better mileage.*

milestone /ˈmɑɪl·stoʊn/ *n* [C] an important event in the development or history of something or in someone's life ○ *We've been married now for 20 years, a real milestone.*

milieu /mɪl ˈjʊ, -ˈjuː/ *n* [C] *pl* **milieus, milieux** the people and the physical and social conditions and events that provide a background in which someone acts or lives ○ *the Irish-Catholic milieu of Chicago* ○ *a cultural milieu*

militant /ˈmɪl·ə·tənt/ *adj* active, determined, and often willing to use force ○ *a militant group/leader*
militant /ˈmɪl·ə·tənt/ *n* [C] ○ *Security forces made it impossible for militants to carry out their threats.*

militarism /ˈmɪl·ə·təˌrɪz·əm/ *n* [U] ***politics & government*** the belief that it is necessary to have strong armed forces and that they should be used in order to win political or economic advantage
militaristic /ˌmɪl·ə·tə ˈrɪs·tɪk/ *adj* ○ *a hard-line militaristic regime*

military Ⓐ /ˈmɪl·əˌter·i/ *adj* [not gradable] **1** relating to or belonging to the armed forces ○ *military spending/intervention/forces* **2** A military academy is a place where soldiers are trained to become officers. **3** A military academy (or school) is also a private school or college that expects obedience to rules, has uniforms, and is generally run like the armed forces.
military Ⓐ /ˈmɪl·əˌter·i/ *n* [U] the armed forces of a country ○ *My Dad was in the military.*

M

militarily /ˌmɪl·əˈter·ə·li/ *adv* ○ *Washington is prepared to intervene militarily* (= with the use of its armed forces) *if the crisis is not resolved.*

WORD FAMILY military			
Nouns	militancy militant militarism military militia	*Adjectives*	military militant militaristic
		Adverbs	militantly militarily

militia /məˈlɪʃ·ə/ *n* [C] a military force that operates only some of the time and whose members are not soldiers in a permanent army ○ *Each militia represents one of the country's political factions.*

militiaman /məˈlɪʃ·ə·mən/ *n* [C usually plural] *pl* **-men** a man who belongs to a MILITIA ○ *Soldiers decided that the detainees were local militiamen.*

milk /mɪlk/ *n* [U] **1** the white liquid produced esp. by cows which people drink ○ *cookies and milk* **2** Milk is also the white liquid produced by female mammals as food for their young: *Breast milk is the best nourishment for a baby.* **3** The white liquid obtained from some plants is also called milk: *coconut milk*
milk /mɪlk/ *v* [T] **1** *Milking a cow by hand is harder than it looks.* **2** To milk something or someone is to get as much from that thing or person as possible: *The newspapers milked the story dry.*
milky /ˈmɪl·ki/ *adj* having the color or thickness of milk ○ *a milky white vase*

M

milk chocolate *n* [U] sweet chocolate that contains milk

milkshake, **milk shake** /ˈmɪlk·ʃeɪk/ *n* [C] a drink made of milk, ICE CREAM, and fruit, chocolate, or some other flavoring, all mixed together in a machine

Milky Way *n* [U] the pale strip of stars across the sky that forms part of the GALAXY (= star system) that includes the earth

mill /mɪl/ *n* [C] **1** a building with machinery for crushing grain into flour **2** A mill is also a factory where a particular materials or substances are processed: *a paper/steel mill* **3** A mill is also a device for crushing a solid substance into powder: *a coffee/pepper mill*

PHRASAL VERB with mill

• **mill around/about** (of a group of people) to move around with no obvious purpose ○ *There were people milling around the entrance to the stadium.*

millennium /məˈlen·iː·əm/ *n* [C] *pl* **millennia, millenniums** a period of 1000 years ○ *The area has experienced the worst drought in half a millenium.*
millennial /məˈlen·iː·əl/ *adj* [not gradable]

milli- /ˈmɪl·ə, ˌmɪl·ə ˌmɪl·iː/ *prefix* one THOUSANDTH, used in units of measure ○ *milliliter*

milliampere /ˌmɪl·iːˈæm·pɪr/ *n* [C] ***physics*** a unit for measuring small electric currents, equal to an AMPERE divided by 1,000

millibar /ˈmɪl·əˌbɑr/ *n* [C] ***earth science*** a unit that is used for measuring air pressure

milligram /ˈmɪl·əˌgræm/, *abbreviation* **mg** *n* [C] a unit of measurement of weight equal to 0.001 gram

milliliter /ˈmɪl·əˌliːt̬·ər/, *abbreviation* **ml** *n* [C] a unit of measurement of volume equal to 0.001 liter

millimeter /ˈmɪl·əˌmiːt̬·ər/, *abbreviation* **mm** *n* [C] a unit of measurement of length equal to 0.001 meter

millinery /ˈmɪl·əˌner·i/ *n* [U] women's hats and other related goods

million /ˈmɪl·jən/ *number* 1,000,000 ○ *The tourist attraction brings in over a million people a year.* ○ *a million-dollar project* ○ (*fig.*) *I have a million things* (= a lot of things) *to do tomorrow.*
millionth /ˈmɪl·jənθ/ *adj, n* [C] **1** *In 1988 Honda produced its millionth car in America.* **2** A millionth is one of a million equal parts of something.

millionaire /ˌmɪl·jəˈner, -ˈnær/ *n* [C] someone who has more than a MILLION dollars (= $1,000,000) in property, possessions, or money saved

millstone /ˈmɪl·stoʊn/ *n* [C] one of a pair of large, circular, flat stones used, esp. in the past, to crush grain into flour

mime /mɑɪm/ *n* [C/U] the art of acting without speech, or a person who is skilled at performing this art, esp. in a theater ○ [U] *In the game of charades, you have to convey the title of a movie or book through mime.*
mime /mɑɪm/ *v* [I/T] to use actions without speech to communicate something, or to pretend to speak by moving your lips but without making any sound ○ [I] *The illusion of live music was created by singers miming to their records.*

mimic /ˈmɪm·ɪk/ *v* [T] *pres. part.* **mimicking**, *past* **mimicked 1** to copy the way someone speaks and moves, esp. in order to amuse or insult people ○ *She was mimicking the various people in our office.* **2** To mimic is also to have the same or similar effect as something else: *This substance mimics calcium and can replace it in bones.*
mimic /ˈmɪm·ɪk/ *n* [C] ○ *He was a fine mimic.*
mimicry /ˈmɪm·ɪ·kri/ *n* [U] ○ *The mockingbird is known for its mimicry of other birds.*

min. *n* [C] *pl* **min.** *abbreviation for* MINUTE TIME

mince /mɪns/ *v* [T] to cut food into very small pieces ○ *Mince the onion and sauté it in butter.*
minced /mɪnst/ *adj* [not gradable] ○ *minced garlic/onions/parsley*

IDIOM with mince

• **not mince words** to say what you mean as clearly and directly as possible ○ *The report does not mince words, describing the situation as extremely serious.*

mincemeat /ˈmɪnˌsmiːt/ *n* [U] a sweet, spicy mixture of small pieces of apple, RAISINS, and other fruit that is cooked in pastry

mind THINKING /maɪnd/ *n* [C] **1** the part of you that has the ability to think, feel emotions, and be aware of things ○ *His mind was open to new ideas.* ○ *I just said the first thing that came into my mind.* **2** Your mind is also your attention or thoughts: *His mind began to wander during the lecture.* ○ *Joanna has a lot on her mind at the moment* (= has much to think about). **3** Your mind is also your intelligence and ability to reason: *a brilliant/logical mind* **4** Your mind is also your ability to remember: *My mind went blank on that exam question.*

mindless /ˈmɑɪn·dləs/ *adj* [not gradable] not reasonable or understandable ○ *People waste a lot of time doing mindless things.*

CARE FOR /maɪnd/ *v* [T] to watch carefully and care for someone or something ○ *She asked me if I'd mind the children for an hour.* ○ *Could you mind my bag while I go to the restroom?*

BE CAREFUL /maɪnd/ *v* [T] to be careful of; give attention to ○ [+ question word] *Mind how you cross the highway.* ○ *Mind your manners!* (= Be polite!) ○ *Don't mind him* (= Do not worry about him) – *he's harmless.*

mindful /ˈmaɪnd·fəl/ *adj* [not gradable] giving attention (to) ○ *Mindful of the poor road conditions, she drove slowly.*

OPPOSE /maɪnd/ *v* [I/T] (often used in requests and negative sentences) to find annoying or offensive, or to oppose ○ [T] *I wouldn't mind seeing a movie tonight* (= I would like to see a movie). ○ [T] *Would you mind turning the radio down* (= Please would you turn it down)? ○ [I] *Do you mind if I smoke* (= May I smoke)?

WORD FAMILY mind

Nouns	mind minder reminder	*Verbs*	mind remind
		Adverbs	mindlessly
Adjectives	mindless mindful		

IDIOMS with mind

• **a mind of your own** the ability to act or think independently ○ *I know she's only sixteen, but she has a mind of her own – she'll make the right decision.*

• **in** *your* **mind's eye** in your memory or your imagination ○ *In my mind's eye, I imagined the building painted white, with a beautiful garden around it.*

• **keep** *something* **in mind, bear** *something* **in mind** to remember a piece of information when you are doing something else or thinking about a matter ○ *"You're always welcome to stay with us when you're in town." "Thanks, I'll keep it in mind."* ○ *Now bear in mind that you don't have a lot of money, so you can't buy anything that you want.*

• **mind over matter** the power of the mind to control the body and the physical world generally ○ *My grandfather believed that he had cured his own cancer through mind over matter.*

• **mind** *your* **own business** do not be so interested in what other people are doing ○ *If she asks where we're going, tell her to mind her own business.*

mind-blowing, **mind-boggling** *adj* surprising, shocking, and often difficult to understand or imagine ○ *The movie's special effects are mind-blowing.*

mind-set, **mindset** /ˈmaɪnd·set/ *n* [C] a person's attitudes or opinions resulting from earlier experiences ○ *I try to keep a positive mind-set even when things are hard.*

mine BELONGING TO ME /mɑɪn/ *pronoun* belonging to me, or that which belongs to me ○ *"Whose bag is this?" "It's mine."* ○ *Your hair is longer than mine.* ○ *She's a friend of mine.*

HOLE /mɑɪn/ *n* [C] **1** a deep hole in the ground made for the removal of coal and other substances by digging ○ *a gold mine* **2** A mine is also where something can be found: *Belinda is a mine of information about home decorating.*

mine /mɑɪn/ *v* [I/T] ○ [T] *They mine copper in this area.*

miner /ˈmɑɪ·nər/ *n* [C] a person who works in a mine

mining /ˈmɑɪ·nɪŋ/ *n* [U] the industry or activity of removing coal and other substances from the earth

BOMB /mɑɪn/ *n* [C] **1** a bomb put underground or in the sea that explodes when vehicles, ships, or people go over or near it **2** A mine detector is a device used to discover whether there are mines in a particular area.

mine /mɑɪn/ *v* [T] to hide mines in an area ○ *The desert has been heavily mined.*

minefield /ˈmɑɪn·fiːld/ *n* [C] **1** an area of land or water that contains MINES (= small powerful bombs), **2** *fig.* A minefield can also be a situation that contains a lot of hidden problems and dangers ○ *Without a good lawyer, buying a house can be a minefield of legal problems.*

mineral /ˈmɪn·ə·rəl/ *n* [C] **1** ***chemistry*** a substance that exists naturally in foods, water, or the ground, and is not a living organism **2** ***earth science*** A mineral is also a natural substance such as coal, gold, or DIAMOND STONE that is obtained from the earth by MINING

mineral water *n* [C/U] natural water containing dissolved MINERALS that is used as drinking water

minesweeper /ˈmɑɪn ˌswiː·pər/ *n* [C] a ship that is used to discover and remove MINES (= small powerful bombs) that are under water

mingle MIX /ˈmɪŋ·gəl/ *v* [I/T] to mix with; combine ○ [T] *Her excitement at starting the new job was mingled with fear.*

BE WITH /ˈmɪŋ·gəl/ *v* [I] to be with or among other people, esp. talking to them ○ *He seems to be mingling with the other guests.*

mini /ˈmɪn·i/ *n* [C] short form of MINISKIRT

mini- /ˈmɪn·i/ *prefix* smaller than others of the same type ○ *a minivan*

miniature /ˈmɪn·iː·əˌtʃʊr, -tʃər/ *adj* [not gradable] very small ○ *She has dollhouse filled with miniature furniture.*

M

miniature /ˈmɪn·iː·əˌtʃʊr, -tʃər/ *n* [C/U] (of an object) the state of being much smaller than the thing it represents, or such an object ○ [U] *She bought a model of the Empire State Building in miniature.*

minibus /ˈmɪn·iːˌbʌs/ *n* [C] a small bus, usually for transporting people short distances

minimal Ⓐ /ˈmɪn·ə·məl/ *adj* [not gradable] as small as possible ○ *Fortunately, damage to the heart was minimal.*
minimalist Ⓐ /ˈmɪn·ə·mə·lɪst/ *adj* taking or showing as little action and involvement in a situation as possible ○ *a minimalist view of foreign policy*
minimally Ⓐ /ˈmɪn·ə·mə·li/ *adv* [not gradable] slightly ○ *The factory was only minimally damaged by the fire.*

minimize Ⓐ /ˈmɪn·əˌmɑɪz/ *v* [T] **1** to reduce something to the smallest possible level or amount ○ *We do all that we can to minimize the risk of infection.* **2** To minimize something is also to make it seem less important or smaller than it really is: *He minimized his involvement in the scandal.*

minimum Ⓐ /ˈmɪn·ə·məm/ *adj* [not gradable] being the smallest amount or number allowed or possible ○ *Her lawyer asked the judge to give her the minimum sentence.* ○ Opposite: MAXIMUM
minimum /ˈmɪn·ə·məm/ *n* [C] ○ *We need a minimum of ten people to play this game.* ○ *Expenses must be kept to a minimum.*

WORD FAMILY minimum			
Nouns	minimum	*Verbs*	minimize
Adjectives	minimal minimum	*Adverbs*	minimally

minimum wage *n* [U] the lowest pay for an hour's work that can legally be paid to a worker ○ *They want to raise the minimum wage to $8 an hour.*

mining /ˈmɑɪ·nɪŋ/ *n* ○ See at MINE HOLE

miniscule /ˈmɪn·əˌskjuːl/ *adj* [not gradable] MINUSCULE

miniseries /ˈmɪn·iːˌsɪr·iːz/ *n* [C] *pl* **miniseries** a television program broadcast in several parts over a short period of time

miniskirt /ˈmɪn·iːˌskɜrt/, *short form* **mini** *n* [C] a very short skirt

minister Ⓐ **PRIEST** /ˈmɪn·ə·stər/ *n* [C] (in various Christian churches) a person who leads religious ceremonies
minister Ⓐ /ˈmɪn·ə·stər/ *v* [I] to give help to or care for people ○ *He began ministering to prisoners.*
ministry Ⓐ /ˈmɪn·ə·stri/ *n* [U] the job of being a religious leader ○ *a youth ministry*
POLITICIAN /ˈmɪn·ə·stər/ *n* [C] (in many countries) a high government official who is in charge of or has an important position in a particular department ○ *the foreign minister*
ministerial Ⓐ /ˌmɪn·əˈstɪr·iː·əl/ *adj* [not gradable] ○ *Social justice has concerned him since his first ministerial assignment.*
ministry Ⓐ /ˈmɪn·ə·stri/ *n* [C] a government department led by a minister ○ *All the ministries were represented at the meeting – justice, foreign affairs, economic affairs, and the interior.*

minivan /ˈmɪn·iːˌvæn/ *n* [C] a large vehicle that looks like a small bus, usually with three rows of seats, the last of which can be removed or folded flat to transport large objects

mink /mɪŋk/ *n* [C] *pl* **minks, mink** a small brown animal from Europe, North America, and Asia, or its fur, used to make expensive coats and other items of clothing ○ *a mink coat*

minnow /ˈmɪn·oʊ/ *n* [C] a very small fish found in lakes and rivers

minor Ⓐ **UNIMPORTANT** /ˈmɑɪ·nər/ *adj* [not gradable] not great in size or importance ○ *She suffered minor injuries in the accident.* ○ *Waiting another half hour was only a minor inconvenience.* ○ Compare MAJOR IMPORTANT
YOUNG PERSON /ˈmɑɪ·nər/ *n* [C] a person under the age at which he or she legally becomes an adult
SPECIAL SUBJECT /ˈmɑɪ·nər/ *n* [C] the second most important subject that a college student is studying ○ *I'm taking two courses in my minor, chemistry.*
MUSIC /ˈmɑɪ·nər/ *adj* ***music*** based on a SCALE (= series of musical notes) in which there is a WHOLE STEP (= sound difference) between each note except between the second and third notes and between the fifth and sixth notes ○ *a minor scale* ○ *a minor chord* ○ Compare MAJOR MUSIC

PHRASAL VERB with minor

• **minor in** *something* to study something as your second most important subject in college or a university ○ *I minored in Spanish in college.*

minority Ⓐ **SMALLER AMOUNT** /məˈnɔːr·əṭ·i, mɑɪ-, -ˈnɑr-/ *n* [C/U] less than half of a total number or amount; the smaller part of something ○ [U] *Only a minority of people support military action.* ○ [U] *Traditional families are in the minority in this neighborhood* (= there are not many). ○ Compare MAJORITY
PEOPLE /məˈnɔːr·əṭ·i (ˌɡruːp), mɑɪ-, -ˈnɑr-/, **minority group** *n* [C] ***social studies*** a group of people who share some characteristic by birth that makes their group smaller than some other groups in a society and may cause others to treat them unfairly ○ *He argued that African Americans and other minorities were not getting a fair deal in sports and elsewhere in society.* ○ *Jews and Roman Catholics belonged to religious minorities.*

minstrel show /ˈmɪn·strəl/ *n* [C] a show of dance, song, and jokes intended to make black people seem simple and unimportant, popular before and after the American Civil War and performed by people who darkened their faces to amuse the white people who came to see it

mint **PLANT** /mɪnt/ *n* [C/U] **1** an herb whose leaves have a clean smell and taste, used to flavor food, drinks, and candy **2** A mint is also a candy with this strong, fresh flavor.

COIN FACTORY /mɪnt/ *n* [C] **1** a place where the new coins and paper money of a country are made **2** *infml* A mint is also a very large amount of money: *The new roof cost us a mint.*

mint /mɪnt/ *v* [T] to make a new coin

mint /mɪnt/ *adj* [not gradable]

IDIOM with mint

• **in mint condition** in excellent condition, as if new ○ *Alex's old Cadillac is in mint condition.*

minus **SUBTRACTION** /ˈmɑɪ·nəs/, *symbol* – *prep* **1** reduced by the stated number ○ *Five minus one is four.* **2** Minus can also mean without: *Tell me the story again, minus the cuteness.*

minus /ˈmɑɪ·nəs/, *symbol* – *adj* [not gradable] **1** less than zero ○ *Temperatures will be dropping to minus 10.* ○ **USAGE:** Used with a number or amount. **2** A mark such as B-minus (B–) or C-minus (C–) given to a student's work means that the work is slightly worse than if it were given the B or C mark.

DISADVANTAGE /ˈmɑɪ·nəs/ *n* [C] *pl* **minuses** a disadvantage ○ *Not having any experience is a big minus.*

minuscule /ˈmɪn·əˌskjuːl, məˈnʌsˌkjuːl/, **miniscule** /ˈmɪn·əˌskuːl/ *adj* extremely small ○ *Salaries are a minuscule part of the budget.*

minus sign *n* [C] a SUBTRACTION SIGN

minute **TIME** /ˈmɪn·ət/, *abbreviation* **min.** *n* [C] **1** any of the 60 parts that an hour is divided into; 60 seconds ○ *It takes me 20 minutes to get to work.* **2** **A minute** is also a very short time: *Just a minute – I'm almost ready.* ○ *When you've got a minute, I'd like to talk to you.*

SMALL /mɑɪˈnuːt, mə-/ *adj* extremely small ○ *minute amounts/quantities* ○ *She examined the contract* **in minute detail** (= looking at all the details of it).

IDIOM with minute

• **the minute (that)** as soon as ○ *The minute I saw him, I knew something was wrong.* ○ Compare THE SECOND (THAT) at SECOND IDIOMS

minutes /ˈmɪn·əts/ *pl n* the written record of what was said at a meeting ○ *Harry will take the minutes.*

miracle /ˈmɪr·ɪ·kəl/ *n* [C] **1** an unusual and mysterious event that is thought to have been caused by God **2** A miracle is also any surprising and unexpected event: [+ (*that*) clause] *It's a miracle (that) he wasn't killed in that car crash.*

miraculous /məˈræk·jə·ləs/ *adj* unusual and mysterious because of being caused by God, or very surprising and unexpected ○ *He made a miraculous recovery from heart disease.*

miraculously /məˈræk·jə·lə·sli/ *adv* ○ *Miraculously, all 25 crewmen aboard the eight planes survived their icy landings.*

mirage /məˈrɑʒ/ *n* [C] an image, produced by very hot air, of something that seems to be far away but does not really exist ○ *Up ahead she saw a slight shimmer that looked like water, a road mirage.*

Miranda /məˈræn·də/ *adj* [not gradable] involving statements that police must make to people they ARREST, so that the people do not say something that will hurt them later ○ *The Chief Justice's decisions weakened the Miranda rights and granted cops more leeway to conduct warrantless searches.*

mire /mɑɪr/ *n* [C usually sing] an area of deep, wet, sticky earth, or *fig.* any messy situation ○ *The cart's wheels sank in the red mire.*

mire /mɑɪr/ *v* [T] to cause something to sink in deep, wet, sticky earth, or *fig.* to cause someone or an activity to become trapped in a difficult situation ○ (*fig.*) *At the time the country was mired in the Great Depression.*

mirror **GLASS** /ˈmɪr·ər/ *n* [C] a piece of glass with a back that reflects light, producing an image of whatever is in front of it ○ *a rear-view mirror* ○ *a hand mirror*

REPRESENT /ˈmɪr·ər/ *v* [T] to be a copy of something; be similar to something

mirror /ˈmɪr·ər/ *n* [C] ○ *The law is a mirror of the nation's character.*

mirror image *n* [C] either of two things that look exactly the same except that the left and right sides have changed positions

mirth /mɜrθ/ *n* [U] ***literature*** laughter or amusement ○ *Chen could not contain his mirth.*

misadventure /ˌmɪs·ədˈven·tʃər/ *n* [C/U] bad luck, or an experience with a bad result

misapprehension /mɪsˌæp·rɪˈhen·tʃən/ *n* [C] a failure to understand something, or an understanding or belief about something that is not correct ○ *He was under the misapprehension that those chemicals were banned.*

misappropriate /ˌmɪs·əˈproʊ·priːˌeɪt/ *v* [T] to steal something that you have been trusted to manage and use it for your own benefit ○ *He misappropriated $30,000 to pay for personal travel.*

misbehave /ˌmɪs·bɪˈheɪv/ *v* [I] to behave badly ○ *There will always be some kids who misbehave.*

misbehavior, *Cdn, Br* **misbehaviour** /ˌmɪs·bɪˈheɪ·vjər/ *n* [U] ○ *You can be suspended from school for that sort of misbehavior.*

miscalculate /mɪsˈkæl·kjəˌleɪt/ *v* [I/T] to make a mistake when calculating an amount or judging someone or something ○ [T] *Swensen badly miscalculated the time it would take.*

miscalculation /mɪsˌkæl·kjəˈleɪ·ʃən/ *n* [C] ○ *They thought they could win the war, and that was a horrible miscalculation.*

miscarriage /ˈmɪsˌkær·ɪdʒ/ *n* [C/U] **1** an early, unintentional end to a pregnancy **2** **A miscarriage of justice** is a wrong decision in a court of law, or

M

any unfair decision: *He spent nine years in prison for a crime he didn't commit – it was a great miscarriage of justice.*

miscarry /ˌmɪsˈkær·i/ *v* [I] to unintentionally have a pregnancy end early

miscellaneous /ˌmɪs·əˈleɪ·niː·əs/ *adj* [not gradable] consisting of a mixture of various things that are not necessarily connected with each other ○ *His bedroom is full of guitars, keyboards, and miscellaneous instruments.*

mischief /ˈmɪs·tʃəf/ *n* [U] behavior, esp. of a child, that is slightly bad or causes trouble but is not intended to harm anyone ○ *Some of the neighborhood kids like to get into mischief.* ○ *She's a cute little girl, but full of mischief.*

mischievous /ˈmɪs·tʃə·vəs; *not standard* mɪsˈtʃiː·vəs, -viː·əs/ *adj* (of behavior) slightly annoying or slightly bad, esp. in a playful way, or (of someone's appearance) looking likely to do something bad ○ *a mischievous prank* ○ *a mischievous smile*

miscible /ˈmɪs·ə·bəl/ *adj* ***chemistry*** of a liquid, able to be mixed into another liquid without separating from it

misconception /ˌmɪs·kənˈsep·ʃən/ *n* [C] an idea that is wrong because it is based on a failure to understand a situation ○ [+ *that* clause] *It's a common misconception that Americans think only about money.*

M

misconduct /mɪsˈkɑnˌdʌkt/ *n* [U] wrong or immoral behavior of someone in a position of authority or responsibility ○ *criminal misconduct* ○ *official misconduct*

misconstrue /ˌmɪs·kənˈstruː/ *v* [T] *fml* to form a false understanding of the meaning or intention of something that someone does or says ○ *Johnson complained that his statements were misconstrued.*

misdeed /mɪsˈdiːd/ *n* [C usually pl] an act that is criminal or bad ○ *I cannot be held responsible for the misdeeds of others.*

misdemeanor /ˌmɪs·dəˈmiː·nər, ˈmɪs·dəˌmiː-/ *n* [C] a crime considered to be one of the less serious types of crime ○ *He was convicted in court on a misdemeanor charge.*

miser /ˈmɑɪ·zər/ *n* [C] someone who has a great desire to possess money and hates to spend it, sometimes living like a poor person because of this ○ *On environmental spending, the president is a miser.*

miserly /ˈmɑɪ·zər·li/ *adj* ○ *My father was pretty miserly.*

miserable UNHAPPY /ˈmɪz·ə·rə·bəl/ *adj* very unhappy, or causing much unhappiness ○ *They can make your life miserable if they want to.*

miserably /ˈmɪz·ə·rə·bli/ *adv* ○ *She groaned miserably and trembled with anger.*

LOW VALUE /ˈmɪz·ə·rə·bəl/ *adj* very low in quality or value ○ *The forecast is for miserable weather today.*

miserably /ˈmɪz·ə·rə·bli/ *adv* ○ *Our leaders have failed miserably* (= completely failed).

misery /ˈmɪz·ə·ri/ *n* [C/U] great unhappiness ○ [U] *With the rice harvest, hope is sprouting amid the misery.* ○ Related adjective: MISERABLE UNHAPPY

IDIOM with misery

• **misery loves company** people who are unhappy like to share their troubles with others ○ *We'd both just broken up with our boyfriends, so we decided to go see a movie together – misery loves company.*

misfire /mɪsˈfɑɪr/ *v* [I] (of a gun or other weapon) to fail to fire, or to fail to fire as intended ○ *Conchas's gun misfired after three shots.*

misfit /ˈmɪs·fɪt/ *n* [C] someone who is not accepted socially by other people because his or her behavior is unusual or strange ○ *I was a social misfit, the kind of kid no one played with.*

misfortune /mɪsˈfɔːr·tʃən/ *n* [C/U] bad luck, or an unlucky event ○ [C] *Never take delight in someone's personal misfortunes.* ○ [U] *The school nurse was as mean a lady as you'd ever have the misfortune to meet.*

misgiving /mɪsˈgɪv·ɪŋ/ *n* [C usually pl] a feeling of doubt, uncertainty, or worry about a future event ○ *Cheung spoke of his deep misgivings about graduate school.*

misguided /mɪsˈgɑɪd·əd/ *adj* unreasonable or unsuitable because of being based on a bad judgment of a situation or on information or beliefs that are wrong ○ *"The Red Shoes" was a misguided attempt to turn a ballet film into a musical.*

mishandle /mɪsˈhæn·dᵊl/ *v* [T] to deal with something without the necessary care or skill ○ *The administration completely mishandled this incident.*

mishap /ˈmɪs·hæp/ *n* [C/U] an accident or unlucky event ○ [U] *The parade took place without mishap.*

mishmash /ˈmɪʃ·mæʃ, -mɑʃ/ *n* [C usually sing] a badly organized mixture ○ *The movie is a mishmash of past and present.*

misinform /ˌmɪs·ənˈfɔːrm/ *v* [T] to tell someone information that is not correct ○ *I was misinformed about the meeting – it was yesterday, not today.*

misinformation /ˌmɪsˌɪn·fərˈmeɪ·ʃən/ *n* [U]

misinterpret Ⓐ /ˌmɪs·ənˈtɜr·prət/ *v* [T] to not understand or explain something correctly ○ *She felt that her comments had been misinterpreted.*

misinterpretation Ⓐ /ˌmɪs·ənˌtɜr·prəˈteɪ·ʃən/ *n* [C/U] ○ [C] *If a patient isn't honest, that can lead to misinterpretations of what is wrong with her.*

misjudge /mɪsˈdʒʌdʒ/ *v* [T] to form an unfair or wrong judgment about a person or thing ○ *He grabbed for her hand, but he misjudged her quickness.*

mislay /mɪsˈleɪ/ *v* [T] *past* **mislaid** to lose something temporarily by forgetting where you put it

○ *Could I borrow your pen? I seem to have mislaid mine.*

mislead /mɪsˈliːd/ *v* [T] *past* **misled** to cause someone to believe something that is not true ○ *We're not misleading people, and we're not pretending to be something we're not.*
misleading /mɪsˈliːd·ɪŋ/ *adj* ○ *misleading information* ○ *a misleading story*

mismanage /mɪsˈmæn·ɪdʒ/ *v* [T] to manage something badly ○ *Many of these health-care plans have been mismanaged.*
mismanagement /mɪsˈmæn·ɪdʒ·mənt/ *n* [U] ○ *Officials are facing charges of mismanagement.*

misnomer /mɪsˈnoʊ·mər/ *n* [C usually sing] a name that is not correct or does not suit what it refers to, or a use of such a name ○ *Dry cleaning is a misnomer, since the clothes are cleaned in a fluid.*

misogynist /məˈsɑdʒ·ə·nəst/ *n* [C] someone, usually a man, who hates women or believes that men are much better than women
misogyny /məˈsɑdʒ·ə·ni/ *n* [U] ○ *There's a disturbing misogyny in his films.*

misplace /mɪsˈpleɪs/ *v* [T] to lose something, esp. temporarily, by forgetting where you put it ○ *I am always misplacing my eyeglasses.*

misplaced /mɪsˈpleɪst/ *adj* directed toward someone or something for the wrong reasons ○ *Their life together was full of misplaced trust and repressed emotion.*

misprint /ˈmɪs·prɪnt/ *n* [C] a mistake in a printed text ○ *There was a misprint in the ad – it should have read $10,000, not $1000.*

mispronounce /ˌmɪs·prəˈnɑʊns/ *v* [T] to pronounce a word or sound the wrong way ○ *I always mispronounce his name.*

mispronunciation /ˌmɪs·prəˌnʌn·siːˈeɪ·ʃən/ *n* [C/U] a wrong sound used when saying a word, or the habit of pronouncing words or sounds the wrong way ○ [C] *I don't speak Russian well and when I made a slight mispronunciation, she didn't understand me.*

misquote /mɪsˈkwoʊt/ *v* [T] to repeat something someone has said or written in a way that is not accurate ○ *Lines from his essay were misquoted in the book.*

misread /mɪsˈriːd/ *v* [T] *past* **misread** to make a mistake when reading something, or *fig.* to form a wrong understanding or judgment of something ○ *Please correct me if I misread anything.* ○ *(fig.) I'm sorry I got angry – I simply misread the situation.*

misrepresent /mɪsˌrep·rɪˈzent/ *v* [T] to represent something or someone falsely, often in order to obtain an advantage ○ *He misrepresented facts about his legal experience on his application.*

miss NOT HIT /mɪs/ *v* [I/T] to fail to hit or to avoid hitting something ○ [T] *The plane narrowly missed power lines as it landed.* ○ [I] *He threw a snowball at me, but he missed.*

miss /mɪs/ *n* [C] ○ *Scurry blocked eight shots and caused misses on numerous others.*

NOT DO /mɪs/ *v* [T] to fail to do, see, or experience something, esp. something planned or expected when it is available ○ *I wanted to see that movie, but I missed it.* ○ *If you don't hurry you'll miss your plane* (= fail to get on it before it leaves). ○ *You should leave early if you want to miss rush hour* (= avoid it).

REGRET /mɪs/ *v* [T] to feel sad because you cannot see a person or place or do something ○ *Luis says he misses Puerto Rico very much.*

NOT FIND /mɪs/ *v* [T] to notice that something is lost or absent ○ *He didn't miss his wallet until the waiter brought the check.*
missing /ˈmɪs·ɪŋ/ *adj* [not gradable] (of a person or possession) not found where you expect to find someone or something; lost or absent ○ *He disappeared on his way to school and has been missing for over a year.* ○ *When did you realize the money was missing?* ➤ Usage: **lose or miss?** at LOSE NOT BE ABLE TO FIND

USAGE

miss or lack?

Be careful not to confuse the verb **lack** with **miss. Lack** means to not have something, or to not have enough of something.

Our town lacks a cinema.

~~*Our town misses a cinema.*~~

IDIOM with miss

• **miss the boat** *infml* to lose an opportunity to do something by being slow to act ○ *I decided not to go to college, but watching all my friends go off made me feel like I'd missed the boat.*

PHRASAL VERB with miss

• **miss out** to not use or to not have an opportunity to experience something good ○ *Having largely missed out on Pop Art, Russians seem hungry to catch up.*

Miss /mɪs/ *n* [U] **1** a title for a girl or a woman who has never been married, used before the family name or full name ○ *Miss Green* **2** Miss is also used as a form of address to get the attention of a girl or woman: *Hey, Miss, you dropped a glove!* **3** A woman who has won a beauty competition is often given the title "Miss" and the name of the place that she represents: *Miss Alaska/Miss America*

misshapen /mɪsˈʃeɪ·pən/ *adj* having a shape that is not natural ○ *His knee is badly misshapen from years of football and seven operations.*

missile /ˈmɪs·əl/ *n* [C] **1** a flying weapon that has its own engine and can travel a long distance before exploding at the place at which it has been aimed ○ *a nuclear missile* ○ *a guided missile* **2** A missile can also be any object that is thrown with the intention of causing injury or damage: *Rioters hurled missiles at the police.*

mission /ˈmɪʃ·ən/ *n* [C] **1** the action of sending someone to a place to do a particular job, esp. one

M

for a government or religious organization, or the job the person has been sent to do ○ *They were sent on a secret political mission to the Middle East.* ○ *(fig.) She's a woman on a mission* (= She is strongly determined) *to teach those children to read.* **2** A mission is also a group of people who are sent to another place to do a particular job or to represent their country, organization, or religion, or the place where they go to do this work: *A trade mission was sent to South Africa.* ○ *a Methodist mission*

missionary /ˈmɪʃ·əˌner·i/ *n* [C] a person who has been sent to a place, usually a foreign country, to teach a religion to the people who live there ○ *Pearl Buck was raised in China, where her parents were Christian missionaries.*

misspell /mɪsˈspel/ *v* [T] to spell a word the wrong way ○ *Edgar Allan Poe's middle name is often misspelled as Allen.*

misspelling /mɪsˈspel·ɪŋ/ *n* [C] ○ *This essay is full of misspellings.*

mist /mɪst/ *n* [C/U] a light rain or a collection of very small drops of water in the air that is like a fog ○ [C] *In the mornings, a mist covered the surface of the lake.*

misty /ˈmɪs·ti/ *adj* slightly wet ○ *His eyes grew misty as he remembered her.*

mistake /məˈsteɪk/ *n* [C] **1** an action or decision that is wrong or produces a result that is not correct or not intended ○ *We all make mistakes.* ○ [+ *to* infinitive] *It was a mistake to come to this restaurant without a reservation.* **2 By mistake** means unintentionally: *I'm sorry – I must have dialed your number by mistake.*

mistake /məˈsteɪk/ *v* [T] *past simp.* **mistook**, *past part.* **mistaken** to be wrong about or fail to recognize something or someone ○ [T always + adv/prep] *I called Karen and mistook her mother for her* (= I thought I was speaking to Karen when I was speaking to her mother).

mistaken /məˈsteɪ·kən/ *adj* [not gradable] wrong ○ *I was mistaken about how much it would cost.*

mistakenly /məˈsteɪ·kən·li/ *adv* ○ *Teens mistakenly believe that once they have a tan, their skin is protected against sunburn.* ➤ Usage: **fault or mistake/error?** at FAULT SOMETHING WRONG

USAGE

mistake

Be careful not to use the verb **do** with the noun **mistake**. The correct verb is **make**.

I never make mistakes in my essays.

~~*I never do mistakes in my essays.*~~

WORD FAMILY mistake

Nouns	mistake	*Verbs*	mistake
Adjectives	mistaken unmistakable	*Adverbs*	unmistakably mistakenly

WORD CHOICES mistake

A common alternative is the noun **error**.

*He admitted that he'd made an **error**.*

*The letter contained a number of typing **errors**.*

A stupid mistake is sometimes described as a **blunder**.

*The company was struggling after a series of financial **blunders**.*

A small mistake can be described as a **slip**.

*It was an understandable **slip**.*

A mistake which causes confusion is often described as a **mix-up**.

*There was a **mix-up** with the bags at the airport.*

An embarrassing mistake that someone makes when talking is sometimes described as a **gaffe**.

*I made a real **gaffe** by calling her "Emma" which is the name of his previous girlfriend.*

The noun **oversight** is sometimes used to describe a mistake which someone makes by forgetting to do something.

*The payment was delayed because of an **oversight** in the accounting department.*

A mistake in which you say something that you did not intend to say is described as **a slip of the tongue**.

*It was **a slip of the tongue** – I meant to say "painless" not "painful."*

A mistake in printed text is called a **misprint** or **typo**.

*The newspaper article was full of **misprints**.*

mister /ˈmɪs·tər/ *n* [U] **1** MR. **2** *infml* Mister is also of a way of getting the attention of a man you do not know: *Hey, Mister, do you know what time it is?*

mistletoe /ˈmɪs·əlˌtoʊ/ *n* [U] an evergreen plant with small white fruits and pale yellow flowers that is used esp. as a Christmas decoration

mistreat /mɪsˈtriːt/ *v* [T] to treat a person or animal badly or cruelly ○ *A state that mistreats its own people cannot be trusted by its neighbors.*

mistreatment /mɪsˈtriːt·mənt/ *n* [U] ○ *The sad condition of the horses suggested a long period of mistreatment and neglect.*

mistress /ˈmɪs·trəs/ *n* [C] a woman who has a sexual relationship over a long period of time with a man who is not her husband

mistrial /ˈmɪs·traɪl/ *n* [C] *law* a trial that is ended by a judge because no decision can be reached or because mistakes in law have been made that make a fair trial impossible ○ *After the jury had deliberated for two weeks without reaching a verdict, the judge declared a mistrial.*

mistrust /mɪsˈtrʌst/ *v* [T] to have doubts about the honesty of someone or be unable to trust something ○ *I've always mistrusted leaders who make too many promises.*

mistrust /mɪsˈtrʌst/ *n* [U] ○ *Their mistrust of lawyers remained with them long after the lawsuit was settled.*

misty /ˈmɪs·ti/ *adj* ○ See at MIST

misunderstand /mɪs,ʌn·dərˈstænd/ *v* [I/T] *past* **misunderstood** to fail to understand something or someone ○ [T] *I think she misunderstood what I meant.*

misunderstanding /mɪs,ʌn·dərˈstæn·dɪŋ/ *n* [C/U] a failure to understand, or an argument resulting from the failure of two people or two sides to understand each other ○ [C] *The whole thing was just a misunderstanding, he said, as he had no intention of breaking into the middle of the line.*

misuse /mɪsˈjuːz/ *v* [T] to use something in an unsuitable way or in a way that was not intended ○ *She's been accused of misusing federal funds to pay for her son's private school expenses.*

misuse /mɪsˈjuːs/ *n* [C/U] ○ [C] *This new computer system is completely unnecessary and a misuse of taxpayers' money.*

mitigate /ˈmɪt̬·ə,geɪt/ *v* [T] to make something less severe or less unpleasant ○ *Getting a lot of sleep and drinking plenty of fluids can mitigate the effects of the flu.*

mitochondrion /,maɪt̬·əˈkɑn·driː·ən/ *n* [C] *pl* **mitochondria** ***biology*** in a cell, a long or round structure found in the CYTOPLASM (= substance surrounding the central part) that produces energy for the cell by changing food into a form it can use ➤ Picture: **cell**

mitosis /maɪˈtoʊ·səs/ *n* [U] ***biology*** the type of cell division in which one cell divides into two cells exactly the same, each with the same number of CHROMOSOMES (= cell structures) as the original cell

mitotic /maɪˈtɑt̬·ɪk/ *adj* [not gradable] ***biology*** relating to MITOSIS (= a type of cell division)

mitt /mɪt/ *n* [C] a type of GLOVE used to protect the hand from injury under special conditions ○ *a baseball mitt* ○ *Use the mitt to take the pot out of the oven.*

mitten /ˈmɪt·ᵊn/ *n* [C] a type of GLOVE with a single part for all the fingers but the thumb, which is in a separate part ○ *She bought a pair of woolen mittens and a matching scarf.*

mix COMBINE /mɪks/ *v* [I/T] **1** to combine different substances, esp. so that the result cannot easily be separated into its parts, or to cause different substances to combine in this way ○ [I] *Oil and water don't mix.* ○ [T] *Mix two eggs into the flour.* ○ [T] *He mixed the blue paint with white to lighten it.* **2** To mix is also to combine or put in the same place: [T] *The report mixed together a lot of different ideas in a confusing way.*

mix /mɪks/ *n* [C/U] **1** a combination of different things or people ○ [C usually sing] *There was an interesting mix of people at Jean's party.* **2** A mix is also a food substance that you can buy and to which a liquid, such as water or milk, can be added later when preparing to cook something: [C] *a cake mix*

mixed /mɪkst/ *adj* **1** Mixed often means combining positive and negative features: *I have mixed emotions/feelings about moving across the country – it's exciting, but I'll miss my old friends.* **2** Mixed can also mean combining people of different races or religions: *The island's population is of mixed descent.*

mixer /ˈmɪk·sər/ *n* [C] a machine in which you mix things together ○ *Whip the cream by hand or with an electric mixer.*

SOCIALIZE /mɪks/ *v* [I] (of a person) to be comfortable being with or talking to other people in social situations, esp. people you do not know ○ *She is very shy and has trouble mixing at parties.*

WORD FAMILY mix			
Nouns	mix mixer mixture	*Adjectives* *Verbs*	mixed mix

PHRASAL VERB with mix

• **mix up** *someone/something* **MISTAKE** [M] to mistake someone or something for someone or something else; to confuse two people or things ○ *It's easy to mix up the twins.* ○ *I mix them up all the time.* ○ Related noun: MIX-UP

• **mix up** *something* **MESS** [M] to put objects in the wrong order or place ○ *If you mix up the photos in my family album, I'll never forgive you!*

mixed bag *n* [C usually sing] *infml* a situation that involves a variety of things, esp. good things mixed with bad things ○ *There's a real mixed bag of weather across the nation today – some hot weather, some fog, and some very big storms.*

mixed blessing *n* [C] an event or situation that has both advantages and disadvantages

mixed drink *n* [C] a drink made by mixing two or more liquids, one of which contains alcohol

mixed media *n* [U] ***art*** a way of making art that uses different substances mixed together ○ *The work of art was done in mixed media, and included wood shavings, pieces of metal, glue, and oil paint.*

mixed up CONFUSED /mɪkˈstʌp, ˈmɪk-/ *adj* temporarily confused ○ *I just got mixed up, and thought she wanted us to come early.*

INVOLVED /mɪkˈstʌp/ *adj* [not gradable] involved, esp. with someone or something bad or dangerous ○ *He was a great athlete at school, but he got mixed up with the wrong crowd and stopped training.*

mixture /ˈmɪks·tʃər/ *n* [C] **1** a combination of substances resulting from mixing them together so that they cannot be easily separated ○ *It's a highly explosive mixture and has to be handled carefully.* **2** A mixture is also any combination of different things: *Good fashion designers often rely on a mixture of the old and the new.*

mix-up *n* [C] a mistake ○ *She said that because of a mix-up, our check was sent to the wrong address.* ○ Related verb: MIX UP MISTAKE

M

ml /mɪl/ *n* [C] *pl* **ml** *abbreviation for* MILLILITER ○ *As little as 3 ml of this poison is enough to cause death.*

mm *n* [C] *pl* **mm** *abbreviation for* MILLIMETER

moan /moʊn/ *v* [I] to make a long, low sound because of pain or suffering, or to say something in a complaining way ○ *We could hear someone moaning within the rubble of the collapsed building.*
moan /moʊn/ *n* [C] ○ *We could hear moans and screams, but we couldn't tell where they were coming from.*

mob /mɑb/ *n* [C] **1** a large group of people gathered together and often uncontrollable or violent ○ *He arrived at the airport to find a mob of adoring fans waiting for him.* **2** The mob is also an organization of criminals, esp. the MAFIA.
mob /mɑb/ *v* [T] **-bb-** to gather in a large group around someone to express admiration, interest, or anger ○ *She was mobbed by her fans.* ○ *The stores are always mobbed* (= very crowded) *on Saturdays.*

mobile /ˈmoʊ·bəl, -bɑɪl/ *adj* able to move easily or be easily moved ○ *The Marines are a highly mobile force and can get anywhere fast.*
mobile /ˈmoʊ·biːl/ *n* [C] a decoration or work of art that has parts that move in the air, often because each one is hung by a thread ○ *We hung a mobile over the baby's crib, and she loves to look at it when it moves.*
mobility /moʊˈbɪl·ət̬·i/ *n* [U] the ability to move easily ○ *Because of severe arthritis, her mobility was limited.*

M

mobile home *n* [C] a long narrow home made in a factory that is brought to a permanent location

mobilize /ˈmoʊ·bəˌlɑɪz/ *v* [T] to organize people to support something or to make a part of an organization ready for a special purpose ○ *We're teaching people to mobilize and show their support for their libraries.*
mobilization /ˌmoʊ·bə·ləˈzeɪ·ʃən/ *n* [C/U] ○ [U] *Both parties have engaged in massive mobilization efforts.*

mobster /ˈmɑb·stər/ *n* [C] a person, esp. a man, who belongs to an organization of criminals

moccasin /ˈmɑk·ə·sən/ *n* [C] a light shoe made completely of soft leather and having stitches around the top

mock **INSULT** /mɑk, mɔːk/ *v* [T] to copy someone or a characteristic of someone in an amusing but unkind way that makes other people laugh, or to try to make someone or something seem foolish or ridiculous ○ *Some of the boys in the dorm loved to mock Roger's British accent.*
mockery /ˈmɑk·ə·ri, ˈmɔː·kə-/ *n* [U] unkind, critical remarks or actions, or something so foolish that it can be easily criticized ○ *The renewed fighting made a mockery of the peace agreement* (= made it look ridiculous).

ARTIFICIAL /mɑk, mɔːk/ *adj* [not gradable] intended to seem real; artificial or pretended ○ *She gave a little scream in mock surprise when she opened the door and saw us.*

mockingbird /ˈmɑk·ɪŋˌbɜrd, ˈmɔː·kɪŋ-/ *n* [C] a North American bird that copies the sounds made by other birds

modal verb /ˈmoʊd·əl ˈvɜrb/, **modal auxiliary** /ˈmoʊd·əlˌɔːgˈzɪl·jə·ri/ *n* [C] ***grammar*** a verb used with another verb to express an idea such as possibility that is not expressed by the main verb ○ *The modal verbs in English are "can," "could," "may," "might," "must," "ought," "shall," "should," "will," and "would."*

mode Ⓐ **WAY** /moʊd/ *n* [C] a way of operating, living, or behaving ○ *Good teachers get their students into a learning mode.* ○ *Each department has its own mode of operation.*

MUSIC /moʊd/ *n* [C] ***music*** an arrangement of half STEPS and whole STEPS (= differences in sound) in an OCTAVE (= series of eight notes)

NUMBER /moʊd/ *n* [C] ***mathematics*** the number or value that appears the most often in a particular set of numbers or values

model **REPRESENTATION** /ˈmɑd·əl/ *n* [C] **1** something built or drawn esp. to show how something much larger would look ○ *The architect showed us a model of the planned hotel.* **2** A model is also a representation of something in words or numbers that can be used to tell what is likely to happen if particular facts are considered as true: *a statistical model predicting population growth*
model /ˈmɑd·əl/ *v* [T] to form something from a plastic substance such as clay, or to use a plastic substance to make a form of something ○ *to model a face* ○ *She modeled the clay into a sculpture.*

GOOD EXAMPLE /ˈmɑd·əl/ *n* [C] someone or something that is an extremely good example of its type, esp. when a copy can be based on it ○ *She was a model of loyalty and stuck by him even after he went to jail.*
model /ˈmɑd·əl/ *adj* [not gradable] ○ *They were model parents and were loved by the whole community.*
model /ˈmɑd·əl/ *v* [T] to create something by basing its form or appearance on something else ○ *The state building was modeled on the US Capitol in Washington, D.C.*

PERSON /ˈmɑd·əl/ *n* [C] **1** a person employed to wear esp. new, fashionable clothes to show how the clothes look and to make them look attractive ○ *Models paraded down the ramp to show off the latest fashions of Paris and New York.* **2** A model is also a person employed to show his or her body to be drawn or photographed by those studying the human form.
model /ˈmɑd·əl/ *v* [T] ○ *She will be modeling the new line of spring coats.*

MACHINE /ˈmɑd·əl/ *n* [C] a particular type of device or machine that is different in quality, style, or some other feature from others that have the same use ○ *This car comes in a two-door and a four-door model.* ○ *We were shown large and small models of air conditioners.*

modem /ˈmoʊd·əm, ˈmoʊ·dem/ *n* [C] an electronic device that allows one computer to send information to another over telephone wires

moderate MEDIUM /ˈmɑd·ə·rət/ *adj* being within a middle range in size, amount, or degree; neither great nor little ○ *The rent has gone up over the years, but in moderate amounts.* ○ *The company was of moderate size, with about 50 employees.*
moderately /ˈmɑd·ə·rət·li/ *adv* ○ *The new apartment complex will be moderately priced for middle-income people.*
moderation /ˌmɑd·əˈreɪ·ʃən/ *n* [U] ○ *My doctor advised me to eat anything I want as long as it's in moderation.*

SOME /ˈmɑd·ə·rət/ *adj* some, but not as much or as great as desired ○ *There has been moderate improvement in her health since she began the treatment.*
moderately /ˈmɑd·ə·rət·li/ *adv* to some degree ○ *He was moderately successful, making a living but hardly getting rich.*

NOT EXTREME /ˈmɑd·ə·rət/ *adj* (of opinions) not extreme ○ *When she was young she was a radical, but her political views have become more moderate as she has gotten older.*
moderate /ˈmɑd·ə·rət/ *n* [C] ○ *Of the seven members of the committee, five were political moderates.*

LOSE STRENGTH /ˈmɑd·əˌreɪt/ *v* [I/T] to lose strength or force, or to make something less strong ○ [I] *The weather prediction is for strong winds, moderating by evening.*

MANAGE /ˈmɑd·əˌreɪt/ *v* [I/T] to manage a public discussion ○ [I/T] *The local TV anchorman is going to moderate (the debate).*
moderator /ˈmɑd·əˌreɪţ·ər/ *n* [C] ○ *The moderator allowed each side two minutes to sum up at the end of the televised debate.*

moderator /ˈmɑd·əˌreɪţ·ər/ *n* [C] ***physics*** a substance that slows NEUTRONS in a NUCLEAR REACTOR

modern /ˈmɑd·ərn/ *adj* existing in the present or a recent time, or using or based on recently developed ideas, methods, or styles ○ *modern life* ○ *modern architecture/art*
modernist /ˈmɑd·ər·nəst/ *n* [C] ○ *A large majority of traditionalists and modernists* (= people with modern ideas) *agree on the issues.*
modernistic /ˌmɑd·ərˈnɪs·tɪk/ *adj* designed in a way that is obviously modern ○ *The Denver airport has a modernistic design.*
modernity /məˈdɜr·nəţ·i/ *n* [U] ○ *Athens is a lively jumble of modernity* (= modern culture) *and the remnants of its glorious past.*
modernization /ˌmɑd·ər·nəˈzeɪ·ʃən, -ˌnɑɪˈzeɪ·ʃən/ *n* [U] ○ *The plan calls for the expansion and modernization of the airport facilities.*
modernize /ˈmɑd·ərˌnɑɪz/ *v* [I/T] to make or become more modern ○ [T] *We decided to modernize our kitchen and installed a new sink and dishwasher.*

WORD FAMILY modern

Nouns	modernist	*Adjectives*	modern
	modernity		modernistic
	modernization	*Verbs*	modernize

WORD CHOICES modern

Another way of saying "modern" is **up-to-date.**
The hospital has some of the most ***up-to-date*** *equipment in the country.*
Latest is a way of saying that something is the most modern.
She always wears the ***latest*** *fashions.*
The words **cutting-edge, high-tech**, or **state-of-the-art** can be used for things which use the most modern ideas, materials, features, etc.
Computers have brought ***cutting-edge*** *technology into the classroom.*
Divers with ***high-tech*** *equipment discovered the wreck of the ship.*
They've got a new ***state-of-the-art*** *kitchen.*
Someone or something which uses modern ideas and systems to encourage change can be described as **progressive.**
It's a very ***progressive*** *school.*
The word **contemporary** is used for art, literature, music, etc., which is modern.
The music was written a hundred years ago, but it still has a ***contemporary*** *feel to it.*
If something is modern but you do not like it, you can use the adjective **newfangled.**
I can't cope with all this ***newfangled*** *technology.*

M

modest NOT LARGE /ˈmɑd·əst/ *adj* not large in size or amount, or not great in value ○ *a modest increase in salary* ○ *a modest house*
modestly /ˈmɑd·əst·li/ *adv* ○ *He lives in a modestly furnished apartment.*

QUIETLY SUCCESSFUL /ˈmɑd·əst/ *adj* tending not to talk about or make obvious your own abilities and achievements ○ *Although an outstanding scientist, he's a modest man.*
modestly /ˈmɑd·əst·li/ *adv* ○ *She spoke modestly about her work.*
modesty /ˈmɑd·ə·sti/ *n* [U] ○ *Sosa's modesty and sportsmanship made him a fan favorite.*

CORRECT /ˈmɑd·əst/ *adj* (of behavior and clothes) correct or socially acceptable, representing traditional cultural values
modestly /ˈmɑd·əst·li/ *adv* ○ *She was modestly dressed in a full-length skirt.*
modesty /ˈmɑd·ə·sti/ *n* [U] ○ *The qualities Aristotle admired are moderation, common sense, restraint, and modesty.*

modicum /ˈmɑd·ɪ·kəm, ˈmoʊd-/ *n* [U] a small amount ○ *He achieved a modicum of success.*

modify CHANGE /ˈmɑd·əˌfɑɪ/ *v* [T] to change something slightly, esp. to improve it or make it more acceptable or less extreme ○ *The school board decided to modify its existing employment policy.*
modification /ˌmɑd·ə·fəˈkeɪ·ʃən/ *n* [C/U] ○ [U] *behavior modification* ○ [C] *Several modifications have been made in the proposals.*

GRAMMAR /ˈmɑd·əˌfɑɪ/ *v* [T] ***grammar*** to limit or add to the meaning of a word or phrase

modifier /ˈmɑd·əˌfɑɪ·ər/ *n* [C] ***grammar*** a word or phrase that limits or adds to the meaning of another word or phrase ○ *In the sentence "The little girl ran quickly," the adjective "little" and the adverb "quickly" are modifiers.*

modulate /ˈmɑdʒ·əˌleɪt/ *v* [T] to vary the strength, quality, or amount of something ○ *Teachers modulate the way they work in response to their students' needs.* ○ *Modulate your tone of voice when speaking in court.*

module /ˈmɑdʒ·uːl/ *n* [C] **1** one of a set of separate parts that can be joined together to form a larger object ○ *The reactor was built in modules that were assembled later at the site.* **2** A module is also a part of a spacecraft that can operate independently from the main part.
modular /ˈmɑdʒ·ə·lər/ *adj* [not gradable] ○ *modular homes* ○ *modular classrooms*

mogul /ˈmoʊ·gəl/ *n* [C] an important person who has great wealth or power ○ *a media mogul*

mohair /ˈmoʊ·her, -hær/ *n* [U] soft cloth made from ANGORA

Moho /ˈmoʊ·hoʊ/ *n* [U] ***earth science*** an area under the earth from 5 to 20 miles down, above the MANTLE

moist /mɔɪst/ *adj* slightly wet ○ *moist blueberry muffins* ○ *rich, moist soil*
moisten /ˈmɔɪ·sən/ *v* [I/T] ○ [T] *Moisten the shirts before ironing.*

moisture /ˈmɔɪs·tʃər/ *n* [U] very small drops of water, either in the air or on a surface ○ *It was a clear day with little moisture in the air.*
moisturize /ˈmɔɪs·tʃəˌrɑɪz/ *v* [T] ○ *This new makeup protects and moisturizes the skin.*
moisturizer /ˈmɔɪs·tʃəˌrɑɪ·zər/ *n* [C] a thick liquid put on the skin to make it soft and less dry

molar IN A LIQUID /ˈmoʊ·lər/ *adj* [not gradable] ***chemistry*** containing one MOLE of a substance in each liter of a liquid
molarity /moʊˈlær·ət̬·iː, -ˈler-/ *n* [U] ***chemistry*** a measure of the number of moles in each liter of a liquid

TOOTH /ˈmoʊ·lər/ *n* [C] any of the large teeth at the back of the mouth, used for crushing and chewing food ○ Compare INCISOR

molasses /məˈlæs·əz/ *n* [U] a thick, dark, sweet liquid made from sugar plants

mold SHAPE /moʊld/ *n* [C] a hollow container into which you pour a soft or liquid substance so that it will cool or harden into the shape of the container ○ *The pieces are made in a mold and I just paint them.*
mold /moʊld/ *v* [T] **1** to shape something into a particular form ○ *She molded the clay into little animals.* **2** Someone who molds someone else has an important influence on how that person develops: *Parents help mold a child's character.*
molding /ˈmoʊl·dɪŋ/ *n* [C/U] a line of wood, plastic, or PLASTER used as a decoration around the edge or along the top of something

GROWTH /moʊld/ *n* [U] a soft green, gray, or black growth that develops on old food or on objects that have been left too long in warm, slightly wet places
moldy /ˈmoʊl·di/ *adj* ○ *moldy cheese*

IDIOM with mold

• **in the mold of** *someone/something* sharing some important characteristics with someone or something ○ *Lewis was not an inventor in the mold of Edison.*

mole ANIMAL /moʊl/ *n* [C] a small, dark, furry mammal that lives in passages it digs under the ground

SPOT /moʊl/ *n* [C] a small, dark, permanent spot or lump on a person's skin

PERSON /moʊl/ *n* [C] a person who works within an organization, such as a government department, and secretly reports information about its activities to its enemy

MEASUREMENT /moʊl/ *n* [C] ***chemistry*** a unit of measurement of the amount of a substance expressed in grams
molal /ˈmoʊ·ləl/ *adj* [not gradable] ***chemistry***
molality /moʊˈlæl·ət̬·i/ *n* [U] ***chemistry***

molecule /ˈmɑl·əˌkjuːl/ *n* [C] ***science*** the smallest unit into which a substance can be divided without chemical change, usually a group of two or more atoms
molecular /məˈlek·jə·lər/ *adj* [not gradable]

molest /məˈlest/ *v* [T] to touch someone sexually when it is not wanted
molestation /ˌmoʊˌlesˈteɪ·ʃən/ *n* [U]
molester /məˈles·tər/ *n* [C]

mollify /ˈmɑl·əˌfɑɪ/ *v* [T] to make someone less angry or upset, or to make something less severe or more gentle ○ *She was not mollified by his apology.*

mollusk, **mollusc** /ˈmɑl·əsk/ *n* [C] any of a large group of animals that have soft bodies, no SPINE (= supporting bones), and usually a hard shell ○ *Oysters, clams, and snails are mollusks.*

molt /moʊlt/ *v* [I] (of a bird or animal) to lose feathers, skin, or hair as a natural process before a new growth of feathers, skin, or hair

molten /ˈmoʊlt·ən/ *adj* [not gradable] (esp. of metal or rock) melted or made liquid by being heated to very high temperatures

mom /mɑm/ *n* [C] *infml* MOTHER PARENT ○ *Can I borrow the car, Mom?*

moment SHORT TIME /ˈmoʊ·mənt/ *n* [C] a very short period of time ○ *Hold still for a moment while I tie your shoe.* ○ *I'll be ready in just a moment.*
momentary /ˈmoʊ·mənˌter·i/ *adj* [not gradable] ○ *There was a momentary lull in the conversation.*
momentarily /ˌmoʊ·mənˈter·ə·li/ *adv* [not gradable] ○ *I was momentarily confused.* ○ *The train will be leaving momentarily* (= very soon).

OCCASION /ˈmoʊ·mənt/ *n* [C] **1** a particular time or occasion ○ *I'm waiting for the right moment to tell her the good news.* ○ *Just at that moment, the phone rang.* ○ *Are you staying with your mother* **at the moment** (= now)? **2** A moment is also a special time or opportunity: *You know that when that curtain goes up, it's going to be your big moment.*

USAGE

moment

Remember to use the preposition **at** in the phrase **at that moment.**

At that moment all the lights went out.

~~*In that moment all the lights went out.*~~

WORD FAMILY moment

Nouns	moment	*Adjectives*	momentary momentous
Adverbs	momentarily		

momentous /moʊˈment·əs/ *adj* very important, esp. because of the effects on future events ○ *a momentous decision/event*

momentum /moʊˈment·əm/ *n* [U] ***physics*** the force or speed of an object in motion, or the increase in the rate of development of a process ○ *A falling object gains momentum as it falls.* ○ *Technology seems to create its own momentum – if something can be done, it will be.*

momma /ˈmɑm·ə/ *n* MAMA

mommy /ˈmɑm·i/ *n* [C] *infml* MOTHER **PARENT** ○ *The little girl misses her mommy.* ○ *Mommy, I want some candy.*

Mon. *n abbreviation for* MONDAY.

monarch /ˈmɑn·ərk, -ɑrk/ *n* [C] a nation's king or queen

monarchy /ˈmɑn·ər·ki, -ˌɑr·ki/ *n* [C/U] a system of government that has a king or queen, or a country that has this system of government

monastery /ˈmɑn·əˌster·i/ *n* [C] a building or group of buildings in which MONKS (= religious men) live and worship ○ Compare CONVENT

monastic /məˈnæs·tɪk/ *adj* of or related to MONASTERIES or MONKS

monatomic /ˈmɑn·əˈtɑm·ɪk/ *adj* [not gradable] ***chemistry*** having only one atom or group of atoms that can be replaced in a chemical reaction

Monday /ˈmʌn·di, -deɪ/, *abbreviation* **Mon.** *n* [C/U] the day of the week after Sunday and before Tuesday

monetary /ˈmɑn·əˌter·i/ *adj* [not gradable] relating to money, esp. the money supply of a country ○ *monetary policy*

money /ˈmʌn·i/ *n* [U] the coins or bills with their value on them that are used to buy things, or the total amount of these that someone has ○ *I need a dollar – have you got any money on you?* ○ *There's not much money in our savings account.* ○ *We spent a lot of money redecorating the house.* ○ *I save money on groceries by using coupons.* ○ *He makes a lot of money as a contractor.* ○ *The job wasn't exciting, but the money* (= amount of pay) *was good.*

IDIOMS with money

• **money talks** wealthy people receive special treatment or have more power and influence ○ *Unfortunately, in this town money talks, and if you don't have money you can forget it.*

• **(right) on the money** exact or correct ○ *Her prediction was right on the money.*

moneymaker /ˈmʌn·iːˌmeɪ·kər/ *n* [C] a person who is successful at obtaining large amounts of money, or something that produces a large profit

money market *n* [C] the system in which banks and other similar organizations buy, sell, lend, or borrow money for profit

money order *n* [C] a type of check that you buy at a bank or post office and use for paying someone

mongrel /ˈmɑŋ·grəl, ˈmʌŋ-/, *infml* **mutt** *n* [C] a dog of mixed breed

moniker /ˈmɑn·ɪ·kər/ *n* [C] *slang* a name or NICKNAME (= informal name)

monitor Ⓥ **WATCH** /ˈmɑn·əṭ·ər/ *v* [T] to watch and check something carefully over a period of time ○ *They hired an accountant to help monitor cash flow.* ○ *The nurse is monitoring his heart rate and respiration.*

monitor Ⓝ /ˈmɑn·əṭ·ər/ *n* [C] **1** a person who has the job of watching or checking particular things, or a machine that regularly tests or records things ○ *United Nations monitors were prevented from entering the area.* ○ *A fetal monitor records an unborn baby's heartbeat.* **2** In school, a monitor is a student with special duties who helps the teacher: *the attendance monitor*

SCREEN /ˈmɑn·əṭ·ər/ *n* [C] a device with a screen on which words or pictures can be shown ○ *a computer monitor*

monk /mʌŋk/ *n* [C] a man who is a member of a group of religious men who live a simple life apart from general society, usually in a MONASTERY

monkey /ˈmʌŋ·ki/ *n* [C] any of a group of mammals that usually have flat faces and long tails, esp. any of the smaller mammals in this group

monkey /ˈmʌŋ·ki/ *v infml*

PHRASAL VERBS with monkey

• **monkey around** to behave in a silly, playful way ○ *The kids were just monkeying around, throwing things at each other.*

• **monkey (around) with** *something* to play with or use something in a way that could damage it ○ *Who's been monkeying around with my tools?*

monkey business *n* [U] dishonest or illegal behavior ○ *There's been some monkey business connected with his tax returns.*

M

monkey wrench /ˈmʌŋ·kiː ˌrentʃ/ *n* [C] a tool that can be adjusted to hold or turn NUTS and BOLTS (= metal fasteners that screw together) of different widths

mono /ˈmɑn·oʊ/ *n* [U] *short form of* MONONUCLEOSIS

monochromatic /ˌmɑn·oʊ·kroʊˈmæt̬·ɪk/ *adj* ***art*** containing or using only one color

monogamy /məˈnɑg·ə·mi/ *n* [U] the condition or custom of being married to only one person at a time or of having only one sexual partner
monogamous /məˈnɑg·ə·məs/ *adj* ○ *a monogamous relationship*

monogram /ˈmɑn·əˌgræm/ *n* [C] a design made of two or more letters, usually the first letters of a person's names, used esp. on clothing and writing paper
monogrammed /ˈmɑn·əˌgræmd/ *adj* [not gradable] ○ *a monogrammed shirt*

monolingual /ˌmɑn·əˈlɪŋ·gwəl, -gjə·wəl/ *adj* [not gradable] speaking or using only one language ○ Compare BILINGUAL

monolithic /ˌmɑn·əˈlɪθ·ɪk/ *adj* **1** very large, united, and difficult to change ○ *People think of "the media" as this great monolithic thing that's out there.* **2** A monolithic building or rock is large and solid.

M

monologue /ˈmɑn·əlˌɔːg, -ˌɑg/ *n* [C] ***literature*** a long speech by one person, esp. in a play, movie, or television show

monomer /ˈmɑn·ə·mər/ *n* [C] ***chemistry*** a chemical substance whose basic MOLECULES can join together to form POLYMERS

monomial /mɑˈnoʊ·miː·əl/ *n* [C] ***algebra*** a number or VARIABLE (= mathematical symbol) or the result of multiplying two or more numbers or variables

mononucleosis /ˌmɑn·əˌnuː·kliːˈoʊ·səs/, *short form* **mono** *n* [U] a disease that causes a sudden fever, swelling of organs that produce white blood cells, and a sore throat, and which can make a person feel weak and ill for a long time

monoploid /ˈmɑn·əˌplɔɪd/ *adj* [not gradable] (of a cell or organism) having only one basic group of CHROMOSOMES (= cell structures containing chemical patterns)

monopoly /məˈnɑp·ə·li/ *n* [C] ***social studies*** complete control of the supply of particular goods or services, or a company or group that has such control ○ *The Postal Service is guaranteed a monopoly on all first-class letters.* ○ (*fig.*) *California has no monopoly on strangeness* (= is not the only strange place).
monopolistic /məˌnɑp·əˈlɪs·tɪk/ *adj* ○ *a monopolistic system*
monopolize /məˈnɑp·əˌlɑɪz/ *v* [T] ***social studies*** to have or take complete control of something so that others are prevented from sharing it ○ *Rockefeller monopolized oil refining in the 1800s.* ○ *She has a habit of monopolizing the conversation.*

monorail /ˈmɑn·əˌreɪl/ *n* [C] a railroad system in which trains travel along a single RAIL (= metal bar), usually above ground level

monosaccharide /ˌmɑn·əˈsæk·əˌrɑɪd/ *n* [C] ***biology*** a type of CARBOHYDRATE (= substance that provides energy) formed of only one MOLECULE (= smallest unit of a substance) of a sugar and therefore cannot be divided to form other sugars

monosodium glutamate /ˌmɑn·əˌsoʊd·iː·əm ˈgluːt̬·əˌmeɪt/, *abbreviation* **MSG** *n* [U] a chemical that is sometimes added to food to improve its taste

monotheism /ˈmɑn·əˌθiː ˌɪz·əm/ *n* [U] the belief that there is only one God

monotonous /məˈnɑt·ən·əs/ *adj* boring because of never changing ○ *She stood all day ironing a monotonous succession of clothes and sheets.*
monotony /məˈnɑt·ən·i/ *n* [U] boring sameness ○ *He drove for hours with nothing to break the monotony.*
monotone /ˈmɑn·əˌtoʊn/ *n* [U] a sound or voice that stays on the same note ○ *He spoke in a boring monotone.*

monsoon /mɑnˈsuːn/ *n* [C] the season of heavy rain, the wind that brings rain, or the heavy rain that falls during the summer in hot Asian countries

monster CREATURE /ˈmɑn·stər/ *n* [C] any imaginary frightening creature, esp. one that is large and strange

EVIL PERSON /ˈmɑn·stər/ *n* [C] a person who does very cruel and evil acts ○ *To the whole world, he was a monster.*
monstrous /ˈmɑn·strəs/ *adj* ○ *monstrous deeds*

BIG /ˈmɑn·stər/ *adj* [not gradable] very big, or too big ○ *a monster shark*
monster /ˈmɑn·stər/ *n* [C] ○ *a monster of a movie, over four hours long*
monstrous /ˈmɑn·strəs/ *adj* very bad, esp. because too big ○ *After the flood she was faced with monstrous repair bills.*

monstrosity /mɑnˈstrɑs·ət̬·i/ *n* [C] something that is very ugly and usually large ○ *That new office building is a real monstrosity.*

month /mʌnθ/ *n* [C] a period of about four weeks, esp. one of the twelve periods into which a year is divided ○ *I'll be away for the whole month of June.* ○ *The puppy is two months old.*
monthly /ˈmʌnθ·li/ *adj, adv* [not gradable] ○ *If you ride the bus a lot, you should buy a monthly ticket.* ○ *We're paid monthly.*
monthly /ˈmʌnθ·li/ *n* [C] a newspaper or magazine that is published once a month

monument /ˈmɑn·jə·mənt/ *n* [C] an object, esp. large and made of stone, built to remember and show respect for a person or group of people, or a special place made for this purpose ○ *While in Washington, D.C., we visited a number of historical monuments.* ○ (*fig.*) *The annual arts festival is a monument to* (= is a result of) *her vision and hard work.*

monumental /ˌmɑn·jəˈment·əl/ *adj* very big or very great ○ *Rebuilding the bridge proved to be a monumental job.*

moo /muː/ *n* [C] *pl* **moos** (esp. in children's books) a written representation of the noise that a cow makes

moo /muː/ *v* [I] **moos,** *pres. part.* **mooing,** *past* **mooed**

mood FEELING /muːd/ *n* [C] **1** the way you feel at a particular time ○ *She's in a good/bad mood today.* ○ *"Do you want to go to the movies?" "No, I'm not in the mood* (= not interested in that).*"* **2** ***art*** The mood of a work of art is the emotional features of it, or the way it makes you feel.

moody /ˈmuːd·i/ *adj* (of a person) often sad, or changing from being happy to sad, often for no clear reason

GRAMMAR /muːd/ *n* [C] ***grammar*** the forms of verbs used to show whether the person speaking intends to express a fact, an order, or a hope ○ *the indicative/imperative/subjunctive mood*

WORD FAMILY mood			
Nouns	mood moodiness	*Adjectives* *Adverbs*	moody moodily

moon OBJECT IN SPACE /muːn/ *n* [C/U] **1** the object, similar to a planet, that moves through the sky, circling the earth once every 28 days, and which can often be seen clearly at night when it shines with the light coming from the sun ○ [U] *the full moon* ➤ Picture: **lunar eclipse 2** A moon is also a similar object that moves around another planet: [C] *Jupiter has at least sixteen moons.*

moonless /ˈmuːn·ləs/ *adj* [not gradable] If a night is moonless, you cannot see the moon in the sky at night.

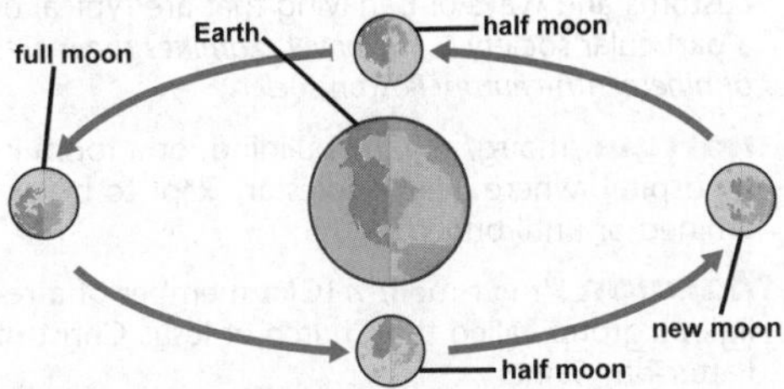

PHASES OF THE MOON

LACK PURPOSE /muːn/ *v* [I always + adv/prep] *infml* to move or spend time in a way that shows a lack of care and interest and no clear purpose ○ *She's been mooning around the house all weekend.*

moonlight LIGHT FROM MOON /ˈmuːn·lɑɪt/ *n* [U] the pale light of the moon

WORK SECRETLY /ˈmuːn·lɑɪt/ *v* [I] *past* **moonlighted** to work at an additional job, esp. without telling your main employer ○ *In addition to her teaching job, she moonlights as a waitress on weekends.*

moonshine /ˈmuːn·ʃɑɪn/ *n* [U] *slang* alcoholic drink made illegally

moor /mʊr/ *v* [I/T] to attach a boat or ship to something on land or to the surface under the water to keep it in place ○ [I/T] *We moored (the boat) further up the river.*

mooring /ˈmʊr·ɪŋ/ *n* [C usually pl] a place to tie a boat, ship, or aircraft

moose /muːs/ *n* [C] *pl* **moose** a type of large deer of North America and northern Europe, having large, flat horns

moot NOT WORTH CONSIDERING /muːt/ *adj* [not gradable] *law* having no practical use or meaning ○ *Because the claim of negligence was denied, seeking an award for damages was moot.*

NOT DECIDED /muːt/ *adj* [not gradable] (of a matter being considered) that has not been decided and can therefore still be discussed ○ *Whether or not to make the school coeducational is still a moot point, and we'll be discussing it over the next few months.*

mop /mɑp/ *n* [C] **1** a stick having at one end a mass of thick, cloth strings or a SPONGE (= soft substance) that you slide along a floor to spread or absorb a liquid in cleaning the floor **2** A mop of hair is a lot of hair in a thick mass: *The child's face was framed by a mop of brown curls.*

mop /mɑp/ *v* [I/T] **-pp- 1** [I/T] *I can go as soon as I finish mopping (the floor).* **2** If you mop the SWEAT (= liquid produced because you are hot) from your face, you use your hand or a piece of cloth to remove it.

PHRASAL VERB with mop

• **mop up** *(something)* [M] to finish the last part of a job after most of it has been completed ○ *The battle had been won, but two infantry units were left behind to mop up.* ○ *Twenty firefighters will be working on mopping up the fire today.*

mope /moʊp/ *v* [I] to be unhappy and unwilling to think or act in a positive manner, esp. because you are disappointed ○ *Don't sit in the house moping – go out and enjoy yourself.*

moped /ˈmoʊ·ped/ *n* [C] a small two-wheeled vehicle with a motor and PEDALS like those on a bicycle, which can be used when starting it or traveling up a hill

moraine /məˈreɪn/ *n* [C] ***earth science*** a large mass of rocks and dirt that is carried along with a GLACIER (= large mass of ice) and is left behind when the glacier melts

moral LESSON /ˈmɔːr·əl/ *n* [C] ***literature*** a lesson that can be learned from a story, esp. a FABLE, or other work of literature

RIGHT /ˈmɔːr·əl, ˈmɑr-/ *adj* relating to standards of good behavior, honesty, and fair dealing, or showing high standards of this type ○ *a highly moral man* ○ *It's her moral obligation to tell the police what she knows.*

morals /ˈmɔːr·əlz, ˈmɑr-/ *pl n* standards for good or bad character and behavior ○ *a man of low morals*

morality /məˈræl·əţ·i/ *n* [C/U] a personal or social set of standards for good or bad behavior and character, or the quality of being right and honest ○ [U] *Technology is neutral – its morality is determined by its political or social use.*

morally /ˈmɔːr·ə·li, ˈmɑr-/ *adv* **1** considered from a moral position ○ *morally wrong* **2** If you act morally, you act in a way that you or people in general consider to be right, honest, or acceptable.

moral /ˈmɔːr·əl, ˈmɑr-/ *n* [C] a message about how people should or should not behave, contained in a story, event, or experience ○ *The moral of the story is that honesty is the best policy.*

moralistic /ˌmɔːr·əˈlɪs·tɪk, ˌmɑr-/ *adj* involved with judging other people's morals and telling them how to behave ○ *American foreign policy had been rigidly moralistic.*

moralize /ˈmɔːr·əˌlɑɪz, ˈmɑr-/ *v* [I] *disapproving* to make judgments about right and wrong, esp. in a way that does not consider other people's ideas or opinions ○ *A good teacher manages to educate without moralizing.*

WORD FAMILY moral

Nouns	moral morals morality immorality	*Adjectives*	amoral immoral moral moralistic
Verbs	moralize	*Adverbs*	morally

M

morale /məˈræl/ *n* [U] the amount of confidence felt by a person or group of people, esp. when in a dangerous or difficult situation ○ *Low morale in the police department was a continuing problem.*

morass /məˈræs/ *n* [C usually sing] something that is extremely complicated and difficult to deal with, making any advance almost impossible ○ *The morass of rules and regulations is delaying the start of the project.*

moratorium /ˌmɔːr·əˈtɔːr·iː·əm, ˌmɑr-, -ˈtoʊr-/ *n* [C] a stopping of an activity for an agreed period of time ○ *They are proposing a five-year moratorium on whaling.*

morbid /ˈmɔːr·bəd/ *adj* too interested in unpleasant subjects, esp. death ○ *He has a morbid sense of humor.*

more /mɔːr, moʊr/ *adj, adv* **1** a larger or extra number or amount (of); *comparative of* MANY or MUCH ○ *You need to listen more and talk less.* ○ *There were no more seats on the bus, so we had to stand.* ○ *DisneyWorld was more fun than I expected.* ○ *Would you play the song once more* (= again)? **2** More is used to form the comparative of many adjectives and adverbs: *You couldn't be more wrong.* ○ *He finds physics much more difficult than biology.* ○ Compare MOST

more /mɔːr, moʊr/ *pronoun* ○ *She kept asking me if I wanted more to eat.* ○ *More than 20,000 people attended the concert.* ○ Compare MOST

USAGE

more

The opposite of **more** is **fewer** for countable nouns and **less** for uncountable nouns.

He asked more questions then.
He asks fewer questions now.
He made more progress today.
He made less progress yesterday.

IDIOMS with more

• **more and more** increasingly, or an increasing number of ○ *It gets more and more difficult to understand what is going on.* ○ *More and more people are becoming fed up with the corruption in government.*

• **more like it** *infml* more accurate or true ○ *I think he likes her – or maybe he's madly in love with her is more like it.*

• **more often than not** usually ○ *In winter it rains a lot, and more often than not, you're carrying an umbrella.*

• **more or less** approximately ○ *It weighs 50 pounds, more or less.*

• **more than** very ○ *It's more than likely that she got a ride home with Harry.* ○ *We will be more than happy to help you in any way we can.*

• **the more** *something happens*, **the less** *another thing happens* as one thing happens repeatedly, another thing happens less or becomes less likely ○ *The more he insisted he was innocent, the less they seemed to believe him.*

• **the more** *something happens*, **the more** *another thing happens* as one thing happens repeatedly, another thing happens more or becomes more likely ○ *The more he talked, the more I liked him.*

moreover /mɔːrˈoʊ·vər, moʊr-/ *adv* [not gradable] (used to add information) also and more importantly ○ *It was a good car and, moreover, the price was quite reasonable.*

mores /ˈmɔːr·eɪz, ˈmoʊr-/ *pl n* the traditional customs and ways of behaving that are typical of a particular society ○ *The novel examines the mores of nineteenth-century Boston society.*

morgue /mɔːrg/ *n* [C] a building, or a room in a hospital, where dead bodies are kept to be examined or until buried

Mormon /ˈmɔːr·mən/ *n* [C] a member of a religious group called the Church of Jesus Christ of Latter-day Saints

Mormon /ˈmɔːr·mən/ *adj* [not gradable] ○ *the Mormon church* ○ *a Mormon missionary*

morning /ˈmɔːr·nɪŋ/ *n* [C/U] the part of the day from the time when the sun rises until the middle of the day ○ [U] *Sunday/tomorrow morning* ○ [C] *I work three mornings a week at the bookstore.*

morning sickness *n* [U] a feeling of wanting to vomit soon after waking, experienced by some women, esp. early in pregnancy

moron /ˈmɔːr·ɑn, ˈmoʊr-/ *n* [C] a stupid person

morose /məˈroʊs/ *adj fml* unhappy or annoyed and unwilling to speak, smile, or be pleasant to people ○ *Michael became morose and withdrawn after he lost his job.*

morph /mɔːrf/ *v* [I/T] to change gradually in appearance or form ○ [I] *Cell phones have morphed into mini-computers with e-mail and Web access.*

morphine /ˈmɔːr·fiːn/ *n* [U] a drug used medically to stop people from feeling pain

morphology /mɔːrˈfɑl·ə·dʒi/ *n* [U] ***biology*** the scientific study of the structure and form of animals and plants

morsel /ˈmɔːr·səl/ *n* [C] a very small piece of food ○ *She ate every last morsel on her plate.*

mortal /ˈmɔːrt·ᵊl/ *adj* [not gradable] (of living things, esp. people) unable to continue living forever; having to die ○ *Humans are mortal and we all eventually die.* ○ *As the ship began to sink, they realized they were in mortal danger* (= they might die).

mortal /ˈmɔːrt·ᵊl/ *n* [C] a human, or an ordinary person ○ *mere mortals*

mortality /mɔːrˈtæl·ət̬·i/ *n* [U] **1** the condition of being mortal ○ *A sense of her own mortality overcame her.* **2** Mortality is also the number of deaths within a particular society and within a particular period of time: *infant mortality*

mortally /ˈmɔːrt·ᵊl·i/ *adv* ○ *He fell, mortally wounded.*

mortar MIXTURE /ˈmɔːrt̬·ər/ *n* [U] a mixture of sand, water, and CEMENT or LIME that is used to join bricks or stones to each other when building walls

GUN /ˈmɔːrt̬·ər/ *n* [C] a gun with a short, wide BARREL (= part shaped like a tube) that can fire bombs high in the air

mortarboard /ˈmɔːrt̬·ər ˌbɔːrd, -ˌbourd/ *n* [C] a black hat with a square, flat top, worn by some students and teachers on formal school occasions ○ *Following the ceremony, the graduating seniors all threw their mortarboards into the air.*

mortgage /ˈmɔːr·gɪdʒ/ *n* [C] an agreement that allows you to borrow money from a bank or similar organization by offering something of value, esp. in order to buy a house or apartment, or the amount of money itself ○ *They took out a $90,000 mortgage to buy the house.*

mortgage /ˈmɔːr·gɪdʒ/ *v* [T] to offer something of value in order to borrow money from a bank or similar organization ○ *They had to mortgage their home to borrow enough money to pay for their children's education.*

mortician /mɔːrˈtɪʃ·ən/ *n* [C] an UNDERTAKER

mortify /ˈmɔːrt̬·əˌfɑɪ/ *v* [T] to cause someone to feel extremely ashamed or embarrassed ○ *He's mortified by the fact that at 38 he still lives at home with his mother.*

mortuary /ˈmɔːr·tʃəˌwer·i/ *n* [C] a FUNERAL HOME

mosaic /mouˈzeɪ·ɪk/ *n* [C] a pattern or picture of many small pieces of colored stone or glass ○ *a mosaic floor*

mosey /ˈmou·zi/ *v* [I always + adv/prep] *infml* to walk or go slowly, usually without a special purpose ○ *I think I'll mosey on down to the beach for a while.*

Moslem /ˈmɑz·ləm, ˈmɑs-/ *n, adj* MUSLIM.

mosque /mɑsk/ *n* [C] a building for Islamic religious activities and worship

mosquito /məˈskiːt̬·ou/ *n* [C] *pl* **mosquitoes, mosquitos** a small flying insect that bites people and animals, and sucks their blood

moss /mɔːs/ *n* [U] a small green or yellow plant that grows esp. in wet earth or on rocks, walls, and tree trunks

most /moust/ *adj, adv* **1** the biggest number or amount (of), or more than anything or anyone else; *superlative of* MANY or MUCH ○ *Which of you earns the most money?* ○ *The kids loved the circus, and most of all the clowns.* **2** Most is used to form the superlative of many adjectives and adverbs: *Joanne is the most intelligent person I know.* **3** Most also means almost all: *I like most vegetables.* **4** Most also means very: *He argued his case most persuasively.* ○ Compare MORE

most /moust/ *pronoun* ○ *Most of the players are coming on the next bus.* ○ Compare MORE

mostly /ˈmous·tli/ *adv* [not gradable] in large degree or amount ○ *The story seemed to be mostly true.* ○ *The group is mostly teenagers, with a few younger children.*

motel /mouˈtel/ *n* [C] a hotel for people who arrive in their own cars, typically with all the rooms on one floor or a few floors, and with parking spaces near the rooms

moth /mɔːθ/ *n* [C] an insect with wings which is similar to a BUTTERFLY and flies esp. at night

mothball /ˈmɔːθ·bɔːl/ *n* [C] a small ball containing chemicals with a strong smell, used esp. to protect wool clothing from MOTHS

mother PARENT /ˈmʌð·ər/ *n* [C] a female parent ○ *My mother was 20 when I was born.* ○ *Mother, where's my red blouse?*

mother /ˈmʌð·ər/ *v* [T] to treat someone with kindness and affection and try to protect that person from danger or difficulty ○ *Leave me alone – I don't need to be mothered.*

motherhood /ˈmʌð·ərˌhʊd/ *n* [U] the state of being a mother

mother-in-law /ˈmʌð·ə·rɪnˌlɔː/ *n* [C] *pl* **mothers-in-law** the mother of someone's wife or husband

motherly /ˈmʌð·ər·li/ *adj* typical of a kind or caring mother

EXTREME THING /ˈmʌð·ər/ *n* [U] the largest or most extreme example of something ○ *They got caught in a mother of a storm.*

WORD FAMILY mother

Nouns	mother motherhood mother-in-law	*Verbs* *Adjectives*	mother motherly

Mother Nature *n* [U] nature or weather considered as a force that has power over human beings

mother-of-pearl /ˌmʌð·ə·rəvˈpɜrl/ *n* [U] a hard, shiny, white substance inside the shells of some sea animals that is used for decoration

Mother's Day *n* [C] the second Sunday in May in North America, when people express their love and appreciation for their mothers

mother-to-be *n* [C] a pregnant woman

motif /moʊˈtiːf/ *n* [C] **1** a pattern or design ○ *We chose curtains with a flower motif.* **2** ***art, literature, music*** A motif is also an idea that appears repeatedly in the work of an artist or in a piece of writing or music.

motion MOVEMENT /ˈmoʊ·ʃən/ *n* [C/U] **1** the act or process of moving, or a particular movement ○ [U] *The rocking motion of the ship upset her stomach.* ○ [C] *She moved her finger in a circular motion.* **2** Something **in motion** is moving or operating or has started: *The alarm rang and suddenly everyone was in motion.* ○ *The governor's request set in motion the process for receiving federal funds.*
motionless /ˈmoʊ·ʃən·ləs/ *adj* [not gradable] not moving

SIGNAL /ˈmoʊ·ʃən/ *v* [always + adv/prep] to make a signal to someone, usually with your hand or head ○ [T] *He motioned me to sit down.* ○ [I] *I saw him motion to the man at the door.*

FORMAL REQUEST /ˈmoʊ·ʃən/ *n* [C] **1** a formal request, usually one made, discussed, and voted on at a meeting ○ [+ *to* infinitive] *Someone made a motion to increase the membership fee.* **2** A motion is also a request made to a judge in court for something to happen.

motion picture *n* [C] *fml* a movie

motion sickness *n* [U] illness, esp. a need to vomit, caused by movement when traveling in a boat, car, or aircraft

motive Ⓐ /ˈmoʊt̬·ɪv/ *n* [C] a reason for doing something ○ *Does he have a motive for lying about where he was?* ○ *Judy moved to Florida because she likes it there, not for any ulterior motive* (= secret reason).
motivate Ⓐ /ˈmoʊt̬·əˌveɪt/ *v* [T] ○ *She's motivated by a desire to help people.*
motivated Ⓐ /ˈmoʊt̬·əˌveɪt̬·əd/ *adj* ○ *The lawsuit was politically motivated.* ○ *Heather is a highly motivated student* (= she works hard).
motivation Ⓐ /ˌmoʊt̬·əˈveɪ·ʃən/ *n* [C/U] **1** willingness to do something, or something that causes such willingness ○ [C] *One motivation for reducing the staff was the need to cut costs.* ○ [U] *You need a lot of motivation to succeed.* **2** ***literature*** Motivation in literature and film is the reason a character behaves a certain way.

motley /ˈmɑt·li/ *adj* consisting of many different types, parts, or colors that do not seem to belong together ○ *A motley crew of educators and students gathered at the seminar.*

motor ENGINE /ˈmoʊt̬·ər/ *n* [C] an engine that makes a machine work or a vehicle move ○ *an electric/diesel motor.*
motorized /ˈmoʊt̬·əˌrɑɪzd/ *adj* [not gradable] ○ *a motorized wheelchair/telescope*
motorist /ˈmoʊt̬·ə·rəst/ *n* [C] someone who drives a car or other road vehicle

BODY MOVEMENT /ˈmoʊt̬·ər/ *adj* [not gradable] relating to muscles that produce movement and the nerves and parts of the brain that control these muscles ○ *motor skills*

motorbike /ˈmoʊt̬·ərˌbɑɪk/ *n* [C] a small MOTORCYCLE

motorboat /ˈmoʊt̬·ərˌboʊt/ *n* [C] a small boat that is powered by an engine

motorcade /ˈmoʊt̬·ərˌkeɪd/ *n* [C] a group of cars or other vehicles traveling together, usually one behind the other ○ *a presidential motorcade*

motorcycle /ˈmoʊt̬·ərˌsɑɪ·kəl/ *n* [C] a two-wheeled vehicle powered by an engine

motor home *n* [C] an RV

motor neuron *n* [C] ***biology*** a nerve cell that sends messages to muscles or GLANDS (= organs that produce chemical substances in the body)

motor vehicle *n* [C] *fml* a car, bus, truck or other vehicle powered by a motor that uses roads

motorway /ˈmoʊt̬·ərˌweɪ/ *n* [C] *Br* EXPRESSWAY

mottled /ˈmɑt·ᵊld/ *adj* marked with areas of different colors in an irregular pattern ○ *mottled skin*

motto /ˈmɑt̬·oʊ/ *n* [C] *pl* **mottos, mottoes** a word, phrase, or sentence that expresses the principles or belief of a person, group, country, or organization ○ *The motto printed on US currency is "In God We Trust."*

mound /mɑʊnd/ *n* [C] **1** a rounded pile of dirt, sand, stones, or other material, or a raised area of earth ○ *We're using that mound of sand to level the ground for our new pool.* **2** A mound is also a rounded mass of something: *a mound of spaghetti*

mount GET ONTO /mɑʊnt/ *v* [I/T] to get onto something ○ [T] *The winners mounted the podium.* ○ [I] *When the horses were saddled we mounted up and rode away.*

GO UP /mɑʊnt/ *v* [T] to go up something ○ *Reaching the porch, he mounted the steps.*

INCREASE /mɑʊnt/ *v* [I] to increase, rise, or get bigger ○ *Excitement mounted as the racers neared the finish.* ○ *Watch what you eat, because those calories really mount up.*
mounting /ˈmɑʊnt·ɪŋ/ *adj* [not gradable] ○ *There's been mounting international criticism of the move.*

ORGANIZE /mɑʊnt/ *v* [T] to prepare and produce; to organize ○ *He has the support needed to mount a successful campaign.*

ATTACH /mɑʊnt/ *v* [T] to attach something to something else so that it can be seen ○ *Don's planning to mount these photographs.*

M

Mount /ˈmɑʊnt/, *abbreviation* **Mt.** *n* [U] (used esp. as part of the name of a place) a high hill or mountain ○ *Mount Saint Helens* ○ *Mt. Fuji*

mountain HIGH PLACE /ˈmɑʊnt·ən/ *n* [C] a raised part of the earth's surface, larger than a hill ○ *the Blue Ridge Mountains* ○ *We're spending the weekend in the mountains* (= an area with mountains). ○ *The Rockies form the biggest North American mountain range* (= group of mountains).
mountainous /ˈmɑʊnt·ən·əs/ *adj* having many mountains ○ *mountainous terrain*

LARGE AMOUNT /ˈmɑʊnt·ən/ *n* [C] a large amount of something ○ *I've got mountains of work to do.* ○ *You'll never eat that mountain of food.*

mountain bike *n* [C] a bicycle with thick tires that is made for riding on hills and rough ground

mountain lion *n* [C] a COUGAR

mountainside /ˈmɑʊnt·ənˌsɑɪd/ *n* [C] the sloping side of the mountain

Mountie /ˈmɑʊnt·i/ *n* [C] *infml* a member of the Royal Canadian Mounted Police

mourn /mɔːrn, moʊrn/ *v* [I/T] to feel or express deep sadness, esp. because of someone's death ○ [T] *Frank is mourning the death of his father.*
mourner /ˈmɔːr·nər, ˈmoʊr-/ *n* [C] a person who is feeling or expressing sadness, or who is at a funeral
mournful /ˈmɔːrn·fəl, ˈmoʊrn-/ *adj* ○ *We heard the mournful cry of a wolf.*
mournfully /ˈmɔːrn·fə·li, ˈmoʊrn-/ *adv* ○ *He gazed mournfully out the window.*
mourning /ˈmɔːr·nɪŋ, ˈmoʊr-/ *n* [U] ○ *The family is in morning.*

mouse ANIMAL /mɑʊs/ *n* [C] *pl* **mice** a type of small RODENT (= small mammal with sharp teeth) that has short, usually brown, gray, or white hair, a pointed face, and a long tail ○ *a field mouse* ○ *pet mice*

COMPUTER DEVICE /mɑʊs/ *n* [C] *pl* **mice** a small device with a ball inside that is moved by hand across a flat surface to control the movement of the CURSOR (= symbol that shows your position) on a computer screen

mousetrap /ˈmɑʊs·træp/ *n* [C] a small device used for catching and usually killing mice

mousse FOOD /muːs/ *n* [C/U] a light food made from eggs mixed together with cream and other things, such as fruit, chocolate, or fish, and served cold ○ [C] *a chocolate mousse*

BEAUTY SUBSTANCE /muːs/ *n* [U] a light, creamy substance that is put on the hair or skin to improve its appearance or condition ○ *styling/conditioning mousse*

moustache /ˈmʌs·tæʃ, məˈstæʃ/ *n* [C] a MUSTACHE

mousy, **mousey** /ˈmɑʊ·si, -zi/ *adj* (of hair) not shiny or attractive, or (of people) quiet and not interesting ○ *mousy brown hair* ○ *He's a meek, short, mousey man.*

mouth BODY PART /mɑʊθ/ *n* [C] the opening in the face used by a person or animal to eat food ○ *I wish you wouldn't chew with your mouth open.*
mouth /mɑʊð, mɑʊθ/ *v* [T] to move the lips as if speaking a word ○ *I mouthed a single word, "Please."*
mouthful /ˈmɑʊθ·fʊl/ *n* [C] **1** the amount of food or drink that fills your mouth, or that you put into your mouth at one time ○ *Marj forked up a mouthful of pie.* **2** *infml* A mouthful is also a long word or sentence, or something said that has a lot of meaning: *He has a mouthful to say on the subject.*

OPENING /mɑʊθ/ *n* [C usually sing] **1** the opening of a hole or cave ○ *We looked down into the mouth of the volcano.* **2** The mouth of a river is the place where it flows into the sea. **3** The opening of a bottle or JAR is also called a mouth.

PHRASAL VERB with mouth

• **mouth off** to express your opinions or complain, esp. loudly and in a way that shows no consideration or respect ○ *Clark was mouthing off in the locker room after we lost, and he started a fight.*

mouthpiece PLACE FOR MOUTH /ˈmɑʊθ·piːs/ *n* [C] the part of a musical instrument, telephone, or other device that goes near, on, or between the lips

OPINIONS /ˈmɑʊθ·piːs/ *n* [C] a person or a newspaper that expresses the opinions of others ○ *He's a mouthpiece for the pharmaceutical industry.*

mouth-to-mouth resuscitation, *short form* **mouth-to-mouth** *n* [U] a way to help get air into the lungs of a person who is not breathing by blowing into the person's mouth

mouthwash /ˈmɑʊθ·wɑʃ, -wɔːʃ/ *n* [C/U] a liquid used for keeping the mouth clean and smelling fresh

mouth-watering *adj* (of food) having a very good appearance or smell that makes you want to eat

move CHANGE BODY PLACE /muːv/ *v* [I/T] to change the place or position of your body or a part of your body, or to cause someone's body to do this ○ [I] *They moved out of the way to let us past.* ○ [T] *"Can you move your fingers?" the doctor asked.* ○ [I] *I could hear someone moving around upstairs.* ○ [T] *The police moved the crowd along.* ○ [I] *We should get moving* (= start to leave). ○ *There will be room for Joan, if you* **move over** (= go further to the side).
move /muːv/ *n* [U] ○ *I hate the way my boss watches my every move* (= everything I do).
movement /ˈmuːv·mənt/ *n* [C/U] ○ [C] *the movements of the dancers* ○ [U] *There was no movement in his legs.*

CHANGE POSITION /muːv/ *v* [I/T] (of a thing) to change position or place, or to cause something to change its position or place ○ [T] *Will you help me move this table?* ○ [I] *There was no wind, and the flags were not moving at all.*
move /muːv/ *n* [C] a change of the position of one of the pieces in a game, or a player's turn to move a piece ○ *It's your move.*

M

movable, **moveable** /ˈmuː·və·bəl/ *adj* [not gradable] able to be moved ○ *We have movable screens dividing our office into working areas.*
movement /ˈmuːv·mənt/ *n* [C/U] ○ [U] *Fire doors should be kept closed to prevent the movement of fire from one area to another.*
moving /ˈmuː·vɪŋ/ *adj* [not gradable] ○ *This machine has a lot of moving parts* (= parts that change their position).

GO /muːv/ *v* [I/T] **1** to go to live or work in a different place, or to cause someone to do this ○ [I] *We're moving next week.* ○ [I] *I've decided to move to the country.* **2** To move can mean to change a person's position in an organization or system, or to cause a person to be changed in this way: [I] *He's moving from the publicity department to sales.* ○ [T] *Carol has been moved (up) to a more advanced karate class.*
move /muːv/ *n* [C] the act or process of moving ○ *The office move is scheduled for March.*
mover /ˈmuː·vər/ *n* [C usually pl] a person or a company whose business is to move furniture and other possessions to a different place
moving /ˈmuː·vɪŋ/ *n* [U] ○ *Any moving expenses will be paid by the company.*

CHANGE CONDITIONS /muːv/ *v* [I/T] to change a situation or event, or to change the way something happens or is done ○ [T] *The meeting has been moved from Tuesday to Wednesday.* ○ [I] *People are moving toward buying products that don't harm the environment.*
movement /ˈmuːv·mənt/ *n* [C/U] ○ [C] *There has been a movement toward smaller families.*

M

ACT /muːv/ *v* [I/T] **1** to take action, or to cause someone to take action ○ [I] *OK, everybody, let's get things moving!* ○ [I] *If we don't move quickly on this deal, we'll lose it.* ○ [T] *I can't imagine what could have moved him to do such a thing.* **2** To move is also to progress, or to cause something to progress: [I] *The building project is finally moving ahead.*
move /muːv/ *n* [C] an action taken to cause something to happen ○ *What do you think our next move should be?* ○ *Buying that property was a good/smart move.*
movement /ˈmuːv·mənt/ *n* [C] a group of people with a particular set of aims ○ *The women's movement works for better job opportunities for women.*

FEEL /muːv/ *v* [T] to cause someone to have strong feelings, such as sadness or sympathy ○ *Their kindness really moved me.* ○ *The film moved him to tears* (= made him cry).
moving /ˈmuː·vɪŋ/ *adj* [not gradable] ○ *I found the novel deeply moving.*

SUGGEST /muːv/ *v* [T] *fml* to suggest something formally at a meeting or in a court of law ○ [+ *that* clause] *I move that the proposal be accepted.*

IDIOMS with move

• **move heaven and earth to** *do something* to do everything possible to make something happen ○ *If Brian wants something, his parents will move heaven and earth to get it for him.*
• **on the move 1** going to lots of different places ○ *I'm sorry I didn't call – I've been on the move all day.* **2 On the move** can also mean moving, esp. after having stopped ○ *The troops were on the move again, this time in a line of trucks moving west.*

PHRASAL VERBS with move

• **move away** to leave the place where you have been living to go to a different place ○ *My best friend moved away.*
• **move in** to begin to live in a new place ○ *When are you moving in to your new apartment?* ○ *We moved in in January.*
• **move in on** *someone/something* to threaten or attempt to take control of something or someone ○ *The big corporations began to move in on the action once they saw they could make money.*

mover and shaker *n* [C] *pl* **movers and shakers** someone who is willing to make big changes to get things done ○ *The new director of the company is a real mover and shaker.*

movie /ˈmuː·vi/ *n* [C] **1** a series of moving pictures, often telling a story, usually shown in a theater or on television; film **2** A movie theater is a building in which movies are shown.
movies /ˈmuː·viːz/ *pl n* the showing of movies at a theater ○ *We went to the movies last night.*

moviegoer /ˈmuː·viː ˌgoʊ·ər/ *n* [C] someone who goes to movies

mow /moʊ/ *v* [T] *past simp.* **mowed**, *past part.* **mown**, **mowed** to cut grass or grain with a machine or tool with a blade ○ [T] *You can't mow the grass if it's wet.*
mower /ˈmoʊ·ər/ *n* [C] ○ *The lawn still took a few hours, even with the riding mower.*

PHRASAL VERB with mow

• **mow** *someone* **down** [M] to hit and cause someone or something to fall ○ *The car didn't stay in its lane, and mowed down a whole row of traffic cones.*

mpg *pl n abbreviation for* miles per gallon (= the distance in miles that a vehicle can travel on one gallon of fuel) ○ *My car gets 29.7 mpg in the city.*

mph *n* [C] *pl* **mph** *abbreviation for* miles per hour (= the number of miles a vehicle travels in one hour, a measure of its speed) ○ *The speed limit is 55 mph.*

Mr. /ˈmɪs·tər/ *n* [U] a title for a man, used before the family name or full name, or sometimes before a position ○ *Mr. Kaplan/Mr. David Kaplan* ○ *Good afternoon, Mr. Mendoza.* ○ *I'm afraid I can't agree with what's just been said, Mr. Chairman.*

mRNA *n* [U] ***biology*** *abbreviation for* MESSENGER RNA

Mrs. /ˈmɪs·əz, -əs, *Southern also* mɪz, mɪs/ *n* [U] a title for a married woman, used before the family name or full name ○ *Mrs. Schultz/Mrs. Doris Schultz* ○ *Hello, Mrs. Taylor, how are you today?*

Ms. /mɪz/ *n* [U] a title for a woman, used before the family name or full name ○ *Ms. McCracken/Ms.*

Elizabeth McCracken ○ *What can I do for you, Ms. Jackson?*

M.S. *n* [C] *abbreviation for* MASTER OF SCIENCE ○ *Marj has an M.S. in biology.*

MSG *n* [U] *abbreviation for* MONOSODIUM GLUTAMATE

much GREAT /mʌtʃ/ *adj, adv comparative* **more**, *superlative* **most** great in amount, degree, or range ○ *Mark's got too much work to do.* ○ *I don't have much money to spend.* ○ *Jody doesn't eat very much.* ○ *It doesn't matter that much to me whether we go or not.* ○ *Thank you so/very much.* ○ *She doesn't go out much* (= often). ○ *He's feeling much better/worse* (= a lot better or worse). ○ *Rita would much rather have her baby at home than in a hospital* (= She would greatly prefer it). ○ **USAGE:** Much is used with singular, uncountable nouns. ○ Compare MANY

much /mʌtʃ/ *pronoun, n* [U] a great amount, degree, or range ○ *There's not much to do around here.* ○ *He's still recovering, and sleeps much of the time.* ➤ Usage: **many, much, or a lot of?** at MANY

AMOUNT /mʌtʃ/ *n* [U] an amount or degree of something ○ *How much sugar do you take in your coffee?* ○ *How much do these shoes cost?*

NEARLY /mʌtʃ/ *adv comparative* **more**, *superlative* **most** nearly; approximately ○ *The two schools are much the same.* ○ *She is so much like her mother.*

IDIOM with much

• **much less** *do something* and certainly not do something that is more difficult ○ *Tony can't boil an egg, much less cook dinner.*

muck /mʌk/ *n* [U] wet, sticky dirt ○ *It was hard to walk in the muck.*

mucus /ˈmjuː·kəs/ *n* [U] ***biology*** a sticky, wet liquid produced by GLANDS (= special organs) inside the nose, throat, and other parts of the body that help to protect them

mud /mʌd/ *n* [U] wet, sticky earth ○ *The car got stuck in the mud.*

muddy /ˈmʌd·i/ *adj* ○ *a muddy road*

IDIOM with mud

• **muddy the waters** to make a situation unnecessarily complicated and less clear ○ *His suggestions just muddied the waters further, rather than helping the situation.*

muddle /ˈmʌd·əl/ *n* [C] a messy and confused state ○ *Her life was in a muddle.*

muddled /ˈmʌd·əld/ *adj* confusing and not clearly reasoned ○ *muddled thinking* ○ *The book's message is hopelessly muddled.*

PHRASAL VERB with muddle

• **muddle through** to manage to do something although you are not organized or prepared to do it ○ *I don't know how to keep score – I'll just have to muddle through.*

mudslide /ˈmʌd·slɑɪd/ *n* [C] a large amount of wet dirt that moves down a hill or mountain and that can cause a lot of death and destruction ○ *The vice president surveyed the damage today from flooding and mudslides.*

mudslinging, mud-slinging /ˈmʌd ˌslɪŋ·ɪŋ/ *n* [U] the act of saying insulting or unfair things about someone else, esp. to damage that person's reputation ○ *It was a dirty, mud-slinging political campaign.*

muff /mʌf/ *v* [T] *infml* to fail to catch a ball, or do something badly ○ *She muffed her lines in her first stage appearance.*

muffin /ˈmʌf·ən/ *n* [C] a small, round, usually sweet bread, baked in a pan

muffle /ˈmʌf·əl/ *v* [T] to make a sound quieter and less clear ○ *Ted and I looked at each other with open mouths and muffled our laughs in our sleeves.*

muffled /ˈmʌf·əld/ *adj* [not gradable] ○ *I could hear muffled voices next door, but couldn't make out any words.*

muffler /ˈmʌf·lər/ *n* [C] a device on a vehicle which reduces noise

muffler /ˈmʌf·lər/ *n* [C] a long strip of cloth, often of wool, worn around the neck for warmth; SCARF

mug CUP /mʌg/ *n* [C] a large cup with a handle on the side, used esp. for hot drinks, and usually used without a SAUCER (= plate below it)

ATTACK /mʌg/ *v* [T] **-gg-** to attack a person, using force or threats of force to steal that person's money or possessions ○ *He was mugged in broad daylight.*

mugger /ˈmʌg·ər/ *n* [C] ○ *He helped police nab the mugger who jumped him.*

muggy /ˈmʌg·i/ *adj* (of weather) very warm and HUMID (= containing a lot of very small drops of water in the air)

mulatto /mʊˈlɑţ·oʊ, mjʊ-/ *n* [C] *dated* a person who has one black parent and one white parent or is of mixed black and white origin

mulberry /ˈmʌl ˌber·i/ *n* [C] a tree with wide, dark green leaves, or its small purple or white fruit

mulch /mʌltʃ/ *n* [C/U] a covering, esp. of decaying leaves, grass, or plant material, used to keep water in the earth near plants or to protect them from WEEDS (= unwanted plants)

mule /mjuːl/ *n* [C] an animal whose mother is a horse and whose father is a DONKEY, used esp. for transporting loads

mull over *something* /ˈmʌl ˈoʊ·vər/ *phrasal verb* [M] to think carefully about something for a period of time ○ *I need a few days to mull things over before I decide.*

mullah /ˈmʌl·ə, ˈmʊl·ə/ *n* [C] an Islamic religious teacher or leader

multi- /ˌmʌl·ti, ˌmʌl·tɑɪ/ *prefix* used to add the meaning "many" ○ *multiethnic* ○ *multimedia* ○ *multi-million dollar*

multicellular /ˌmʌl·tiː ˈsel·jə·lər, ˌmʌl ˌtɑɪ-/ *adj* [not gradable] ***biology*** made of many cells

M

multicultural /ˌmʌl·tiːˈkʌl·tʃə·rəl, ˌmʌlˌtɑɪ-/ *adj* [not gradable] relating to a number of different cultures, esp. to the traditions of people of different religions and races ○ *The school board strongly endorsed a curriculum that reflected a multicultural education.*
multiculturalism /ˌmʌl·tiːˈkʌl·tʃə·rəˌlɪz·əm, ˌmʌlˌtɑɪ-/ *n* [U]

multidimensional Ⓐ /ˌmʌl·tiː·dəˈmen·ʃən·əl, ˌmʌlˌtɑɪ-/ *adj* having many different features ○ *International terrorism poses a multidimensional threat.*

multilateral /ˌmʌl·tiːˈlæt̬·ə·rəl, ˌmʌlˌtɑɪ-/ *adj* [not gradable] involving more than two groups or countries ○ *a multilateral trade agreement*

multimedia /ˌmʌl·tiːˈmiːd·iː·ə, ˌmʌlˌtɑɪ-/ *n* [U] the use of a combination of pictures, sound, and words, used esp. in computers or entertainment ○ *a multimedia production*

multinational /ˌmʌl·tiːˈnæʃ·ən·əl, ˌmʌlˌtɑɪ-/ *adj* [not gradable] ***social studies*** involving or relating to different countries, or (of a business) operating in different countries ○ *multinational corporations*

multiple **MANY** /ˈmʌl·tə·pəl/ *adj* [not gradable] consisting of or involving many things or types of things ○ *Make multiple copies of the report.*
NUMBER /ˈmʌl·tə·pəl/ *n* [C] ***mathematics*** a number that results from multiplying one number by another when at least one of them is a WHOLE NUMBER (= a number with no part of a number after it) ○ *18 is a multiple of 3, because 6×3=18.*

multiple-choice *adj* [not gradable] (of questions or tests) giving you a list of possible answers that you have to choose from

multiplex /ˈmʌl·təˌpleks/ *n* [C] a large movie theater building that has several separate movie theaters inside it ○ *What's playing at the multiplex?*

multiplication sign *n* [C] ***mathematics*** the symbol × or the symbol · used between two numbers to show that they should be multiplied together

multiplicity /ˌmʌl·təˈplɪs·ət̬·i/ *n* [U] a large number or wide range of items ○ *She knew a multiplicity of languages.*

multiply **CALCULATE** /ˈmʌl·təˌplɑɪ/ *v* [I/T] ***mathematics*** to add a number to itself a particular number of times ○ [T] *If you multiply 7 by 15 you get 105.* ○ Compare DIVIDE CALCULATE; ADD CALCULATE
multiplication /ˌmʌl·tə·pləˈkeɪ·ʃən/ *n* [U] ***mathematics*** the process of multiplying numbers ○ *Emma's learning multiplication* (= how to multiply numbers) *in school.*
INCREASE /ˈmʌl·təˌplɑɪ/ *v* [I/T] to increase greatly in number ○ [I] *The viruses multiply within the body.*

multitude /ˈmʌl·təˌtuːd/ *n* a large number of things ○ [U] *Two large circles are surrounded by a multitude of small, colorful squares.* ○ [pl] *As manager of the restaurant, his job is to feed the multitudes* (= large numbers of people).

mum **SILENT** /mʌm/ *adj* [not gradable] silent in order not to tell anyone what you know ○ *The governor is keeping mum about his plans.*
FLOWER /mʌm/ *n* [C] *short form of* CHRYSANTHEMUM

mumble /ˈmʌm·bəl/ *v* [I/T] to speak quietly or in an unclear way so that the words are difficult to understand ○ [T] *She mumbled something about needing to be home, then left.* ○ [I] *He often mumbles, and I never know what he's asking me.*

mumbo jumbo /ˌmʌm·boʊˈdʒʌm·boʊ/ *n* [U] words or activities that are unnecessarily complicated or mysterious and seem meaningless ○ *Financial information is just mumbo jumbo to me.*

mummy /ˈmʌm·i/ *n* [C] (esp. in ancient Egypt) a dead body that has been preserved from decay, esp. by being treated with special substances before being wrapped in cloth

mumps /mʌmps/ *n* [U] an infectious disease that causes painful swellings in the neck and throat and a fever

munch /mʌntʃ/ *v* [I/T] to eat something with a loud chewing sound, or to SNACK (= eat a small amount of food between meals) ○ [I] *He was munching on an apple.*
munchies /ˈmʌn·tʃiːz/ *pl n* small, light foods eaten between meals, at a party, etc. ○ *Do you have any munchies – maybe potato chips or crackers?*

mundane /mʌnˈdeɪn, ˈmʌn·deɪn/ *adj* ordinary and not interesting in any way ○ *The show was just another mundane family sitcom.*

municipal /mjʊˈnɪs·ə·pəl/ *adj* [not gradable] of or belonging to a town or city ○ *municipal services*
municipality /mjʊˌnɪs·əˈpæl·ət̬·i/ *n* [C] a city or town with its own local government, or this local government itself

munitions /mjʊˈnɪʃ·ənz/ *pl n* military weapons such as guns and bombs

muon /ˈmjuː·ɑn/ *n* [C] ***physics*** a very small piece of matter with the same negative CHARGE STORE ENERGY as an ELECTRON, but much larger

mural /ˈmjʊr·əl/ *n* [C] a large picture painted on a wall

murder /ˈmɜrd·ər/ *n* [C/U] **1** the crime of intentionally killing a person ○ [C] *There were three murders in the town last year.* ○ [U] *He was convicted of murder.* **2** If you say that something is murder, you mean it is very difficult or takes a lot of work: [U] *It's murder finding a parking space in this neighborhood.*
murder /ˈmɜrd·ər/ *v* [T] ○ *Her husband was murdered.*
murderer /ˈmɜrd·ə·rər/ *n* [C] ○ *a convicted murderer*
murderous /ˈmɜrd·ə·rəs/ *adj* involving murder or violence ○ *the murderous reign of the emperor Caligula*

WORD FAMILY murder

Nouns	murder murderer	*Adjectives*	murderous
		Adverbs	murderously
Verbs	murder		

murk /mɜrk/ *n* [U] darkness or a thick cloud, which prevents you from seeing clearly ○ *a dense murk of smog*
murky /ˈmɜr·ki/ *adj* ○ *murky waters* ○ *The movie has dumb characters and a murky plot* (= it is difficult to understand).

murmur /ˈmɜr·mər/ *v* [I/T] to speak or say very quietly ○ *"I love you," she murmured.*
murmur /ˈmɜr·mər/ *n* [C] ○ *a murmur of voices*

muscle /ˈmʌs·əl/ *n* [C/U] **1** ***biology*** a mass of tissue in the body, often attached to bones, that can tighten and relax to produce movement **2** Muscle is also the power to do things or to make people behave in a certain way: [U] *Republicans are flexing some political muscle.*
muscle /ˈmʌs·əl/ *v* [always + adv/prep] to force your way into a place or situation ○ [T] *Starks muscled his way to the basket.* ○ [I] *Amanda muscled in on our meeting.*

muscle-bound *adj* having muscles that are too developed and make it difficult to move normally

muscular /ˈmʌs·kjə·lər/ *adj* having well-developed muscles ○ *muscular arms/legs*

muse THINK /mjuːz/ *v* [I/T] to think about something carefully and for a long time ○ [I always + adv/prep] *At breakfast, he allowed himself to muse about his presidency.*
IMAGINARY FORCE /mjuːz/ *n* [C/U] an imaginary force that gives you ideas and helps you to write, paint, or make music, or a physical representation of this force

museum /mjʊˈziː·əm/ *n* [C] a building where people can go to view works of art or objects of interest to science or history ○ *an art/science/natural history museum*

mush /mʌʃ/ *n* [U] any thick, soft substance, such as food that has been boiled too long ○ *The rain turned the ground into clay and then to mush.*
mushy /ˈmʌʃ·i/ *adj* [-er/-est only] ○ *The yard's still too mushy to mow the grass.*

mushroom PLANT /ˈmʌʃ·ruːm, -rʊm/ *n* [C] any one of many types of fast-growing FUNGUS (= plants without leaves or flowers) with a round top and short stem, many of which are used as food ○ *wild mushrooms* ○ *mushroom soup* ○ *a pizza with mushrooms*
GROW /ˈmʌʃ·ruːm, -rʊm/ *v* [I] to grow quickly ○ *If your business were to mushroom, would you be happy?*

music /ˈmjuː·zɪk/ *n* [U] a pattern of sounds made by instruments or by singing or by a combination of both, or the written symbols representing these sounds ○ *classical/folk/country/rap music* ○ *Music blared from a jukebox.* ○ *She started composing music when she was 14.*
musical /ˈmjuː·zɪ·kəl/ *adj* ○ *Musical instruments hang from the walls of the restaurant.* ○ *Everyone in our family is musical* (= can sing or play an instrument, or likes music a lot).

musician /mjʊˈzɪʃ·ən/ *n* [C] a person who is skilled in playing music, usually as a job ○ *a jazz/classical/rock musician*

WORD FAMILY music			
Nouns	music musical musician	*Adjectives* *Adverbs*	musical unmusical musically

IDIOM with music

• **music to *your* ears** something you are pleased to hear about ○ *When she said they would make a profit, it was music to Richard's ears.*

musk /mʌsk/ *n* [U] a natural substance with a strong, sweet smell
musky /ˈmʌs·ki/ *adj* ○ *a warm, musky odor*

musket /ˈmʌs·kət/ *n* [C] a type of gun with a long BARREL that was used in the past

Muslim /ˈmʌz·ləm, ˈmʊs-, ˈmʊz-/, **Moslem** *n* [C] a person who follows the religion of ISLAM
Muslim /ˈmʌz·ləm, ˈmʊs-, ˈmʊz-/ *adj* [not gradable] ○ *a Muslim mosque*

muslin /ˈmʌz·lən/ *n* [U] a type of thin cotton material ○ *a muslin shirt/blouse*

muss /mʌs/ *v* [T] to make messy ○ *Don't muss my hair (up) – I just had it styled.*

mussel /ˈmʌs·əl/ *n* [C] a small, edible sea animal that has a dark shell with two parts that close tightly together

must NECESSARY /mʌst, məst/ *modal verb* **must** **1** used to show that it is necessary or important that something happen in the present or future ○ *Seeing what others have and she lacks, she believes that she must have more.* ○ *We must not surprise them* (= it is wrong, dangerous, or forbidden). **2** If you say that you must do something, you can mean that you have a firm intention to do something in the future: *I must call my sister later.* **3** Must is sometimes used for emphasis: *I must admit I enjoy these movies.*
must /mʌst/ *n* [C] something that is necessary ○ *If you live in the suburbs a car is a must.*
PROBABLY /mʌst, məst/ *modal verb* **must** used to show that something is likely, probable, or certain to be true ○ *Death must be better than this.* ○ *"It must have been fun." "No, it wasn't."*

mustache /ˈmʌs·tæʃ, məˈstæʃ/, **moustache** *n* [C] hair that grows above the upper lip ○ *He's a slender man with a trim mustache.*

mustard /ˈmʌs·tərd/ *n* [U] a yellow or brown thick liquid that tastes spicy and is eaten in small amounts, esp. on meat and sandwiches ○ *a hot dog with mustard*

muster PRODUCE /ˈmʌs·tər/ *v* [T] to produce or encourage an emotion or support for something ○ *I shouted with all the lung power I could muster.*
GATHER /ˈmʌs·tər/ *v* [I/T] to gather together as a group or force, or to cause a force to gather, esp.

M

in preparation for a fight ○ [T] *Opponents will have to muster at least 23 votes to defeat the bill.*

musty /ˈmʌs·ti/ *adj* [*-er/-est* only] smelling old and slightly wet ○ *a musty room*

mutagenic /ˌmjuːt̬·əˈdʒen·ɪk/ *adj* [not gradable] ***biology*** having the ability to cause a permanent change in an organism's GENES

mutant /ˈmjuːt̬·ənt/ *n* [C] ***biology*** a new type of organism that is a result of the process of MUTATION

mutate /ˈmjuː·teɪt/ *v* [I] to become changed as a result of MUTATION

mutation /mjuːˈteɪ·ʃən/ *n* [C/U] ***biology*** the change that happens in an organism's GENES which produces differences that are passed to new organisms by reproduction, or the process of this change

mute /mjuːt/ *adj* [not gradable] (of a person) completely unable or unwilling to speak, or (of a place, object, or activity) silent ○ *He stood mute before the judge.* ○ *The decay of Dawson City bore mute testimony to the end of the gold rush era.*

muted /ˈmjuːt̬·əd/ *adj* **1** not loud, or not enthusiastic ○ *Her reaction was muted.* **2** Muted colors are not bright.

mutilate /ˈmjuːt̬·əlˌeɪt/ *v* [T] to damage very seriously, esp. by violently removing a part

mutilation /ˌmjuːt̬·əlˈeɪ·ʃən/ *n* [C/U] ○ [U] *Creatures living in the woods were blamed for the mutilation of animals in the village.*

mutiny /ˈmjuːt·ən·i/ *n* [C/U] refusal to obey orders, or a violent attempt to take control from people in authority, esp. in the military or on a ship ○ [U] *Walker's superiors charged him with mutiny.*

mutiny /ˈmjuːt·ən·i/ *v* [I] ○ *The crew mutinied and took over the ship.*

mutinous /ˈmjuːt·ən·əs/ *adj* ○ *Mutinous troops failed to overthrow the government.*

mutt /mʌt/ *n* [C] *infml* a MONGREL

mutter /ˈmʌt̬·ər/ *v* [I/T] to speak quietly and in a voice that is not easy to hear, often when you are anxious or complaining about something ○ [I] *He muttered to himself as he walked.* ○ [T] *I heard him mutter something.* ○ *"There has to be another way," he muttered.*

mutton /ˈmʌt·ən/ *n* [U] the meat from an adult sheep

mutual Ⓐ /ˈmjuː·tʃə·wəl/ *adj* [not gradable] **1** (of two or more people or groups) feeling the same emotion, or doing the same thing to or for each other ○ *The organization promotes mutual understanding between peoples.* ○ *We let the subject drop, by mutual agreement.* **2** A mutual friend is someone who is a friend of each of two or more other people: *They were gossiping about parties and mutual friends.*

mutually Ⓐ /ˈmjuː·tʃə·wə·li/ *adv* [not gradable] ○ *A lot of people still think brains and beauty are mutually exclusive* (= cannot exist together at the same time).

mutual fund /ˈmjuː·tʃə·wəlˌfʌnd/ *n* [C] a company that sells shares to the public and invests the money obtained in many different companies or lends it to governments

mutualism /ˈmjuː·tʃə·wəˌlɪz·əm/ *n* [U] ***biology*** a relationship between two organisms in which they live together and benefit each other

muzzle ANIMAL NOSE /ˈmʌz·əl/ *n* [C] the mouth and nose of an animal, esp. a dog or a horse, or a covering put over this in order to prevent the animal from biting

muzzle /ˈmʌz·əl/ *v* [T] ○ *Dangerous dogs should be muzzled.*

PREVENT EXPRESSION /ˈmʌz·əl/ *v* [T] to prevent someone from speaking or expressing his or her thoughts ○ *Frank will continue to muzzle his critics.*

GUN PART /ˈmʌz·əl/ *n* [C] the end of a gun BARREL (= the cylindrical part of a gun), where the bullets come out

MVP *n* [C] *abbreviation for* most valuable player (= an award given to a player in sports who is judged most important to the sport, team, or game) ○ *He was named the league's MVP two years in a row.*

my /mɑɪ/ *pronoun* **1** belonging to or connected with me; the possessive form of I, used before a noun ○ *I think about my father and my mother.* ○ *He wanted to be my friend.* ○ *My mind went absolutely blank.* **2 My own** is used to emphasize that something belongs to or is connected with me and no one else: *I bit my own hand.*

IDIOMS with my

• **be my guest** yes, definitely; I do not mind ○ *"Can I take this seat?" "Be my guest."*

• **my, (oh, my), my, my** used to express surprise or pleasure ○ *My, this food is wonderful.* ○ *My, oh, my, what a strange haircut!*

myopic /mɑɪˈɑp·ɪk, -ˈoʊ·pɪk/, **near-sighted** *adj* unable to see clearly things that are far away

myriad /ˈmɪr·iː·əd/ *n* [C usually sing] a very large number ○ *There's a myriad of insects on the island.*

myriad /ˈmɪr·iː·əd/ *adj* [not gradable] ○ *A cloud of dust was raised by their myriad feet.*

myself /mɑɪˈself, mə-/ *pronoun* **1** the person speaking; the reflexive form of I ○ *I found myself addressing a tall elegant man in his mid-forties.* **2** Myself is sometimes used to emphasize I as the subject of a sentence: *I myself prefer to skip lunch.* **3** Myself is sometimes used instead of I or me: *They very kindly invited my sister and myself to the party.* ○ *I live* **by myself** (= alone) *in a small apartment in Brooklyn.* ○ *I had to do the whole job* **(all) by myself** (= alone and without help from anyone). ○ *I just need some time* **to myself** (= for my own use).

mystery /ˈmɪs·tə·ri, -tri/ *n* [C/U] **1** something strange or unknown which has not yet been explained or understood ○ [C] *Despite years of study, sleepwalking remains a mystery.* ○ [U] *The details of the scandal are shrouded in mystery.* **2** A mystery is also a book, movie, or play about a crime or other event that is difficult to explain: [C] *a murder mystery*

mysterious /mɪsˈtɪr·iː·əs/ *adj* ○ *He tried to convince this mysterious woman to go out with him.*
mysteriously /mɪsˈtɪr·iː·ə·sli/ *adv* ○ *The light mysteriously came on, although no one was near the switch.*

IDIOM with mystery

• **a mystery to me** something I do not understand ○ *It's a mystery to me why she married him in the first place!*

mysticism /ˈmɪs·tə,sɪz·əm/ *n* [U] the belief that it is possible to directly obtain truth or achieve communication with God or other forces controlling the universe by prayer and CONTEMPLATION (= serious, quiet consideration)
mystic /ˈmɪs·tɪk/ *n* [C] a person who tries to communicate directly with God or other forces controlling the universe
mystical /ˈmɪs·tɪ·kəl/, **mystic** /ˈmɪs·tɪk/ *adj* ○ *a mystical experience*

mystify /ˈmɪs·tə,fɑɪ/ *v* [T] to confuse someone or make someone uncertain by doing or involving the person in something difficult to explain ○ *Doctors were mystified by her high fever and headaches.*

mystique /mɪsˈtiːk/ *n* [U] a quality of mysterious attraction ○ *The specialty shop creates a mystique for tea like the one surrounding coffee.*

myth /mɪθ/ *n* [C/U] **1** ***literature*** a traditional story, esp. one which explains the early history or a cultural belief or practice of a group of people, or explains a natural event ○ [C] *Kids like the stories about the gods and goddesses of Greek and Roman myths.* **2** A myth is also a commonly believed but false idea: [C] *Equal opportunity continues to be a myth for many.*
mythical /ˈmɪθ·ɪ·kəl/ *adj* **1** *Grandpa tells stories about dragons and other mythical creatures.* **2** Mythical also means imaginary or not real: *I'd like to see that mythical girlfriend he's always talking about.*
mythology /mɪθˈɑl·ə·dʒi/ *n* [U] myths in general ○ *We're studying classical mythology in English.*
mythological /,mɪθ·əˈlɑdʒ·ɪ·kəl/ *adj* [not gradable] ○ *mythological tales*

M

N n

N, n /en/ *n* [C] *pl* **N's, Ns, n's, ns** the 14th letter of the English alphabet

N., No. *adj, n* [U] *abbreviation for* NORTH or NORTHERN

NAACP *n* [U] *abbreviation for* National Association for the Advancement of Colored People (= an organization whose goal is to make certain that people of all races are treated equally).

nab /næb/ *v* [T] **-bb-** *infml* to catch someone or take something suddenly ○ *The thief was nabbed as he left the store.*

nag /næg/ *v* [I/T] **-gg-** to annoy a person by making continual criticisms or suggestions ○ [T] *My mom's always nagging me to get my hair cut.*
nagging /ˈnæg·ɪŋ/ *adj* ○ *She has a nagging cough* (= a cough that worries you because it does not completely stop).

nah /næ, nɑ/ *adv infml* no ○ *Nah, it doesn't work that way.*

nail METAL /neɪl/ *n* [C] a thin piece of metal having a pointed end that is forced into wood or another substance by hitting the other end with a hammer, and is used esp. to join two pieces or to hold something in place
nail /neɪl/ *v* [T] **1** to attach or fasten with a nail or nails ○ [M] *Workmen were nailing down the carpet.* **2** If you nail something shut, you put nails in it to fasten it so that it cannot easily be opened: *He nailed the box shut.* **3** *infml* To nail someone is to catch someone in a dishonest or illegal act: *We finally nailed the guys dumping garbage in the park.*
BODY PART /neɪl/ *n* [C] the hard, smooth part at the upper end of each finger and toe

IDIOM with **nail**

• **(as) tough as nails, (as) hard as nails** strong and very determined ○ *She is a warm and friendly person, but she is also as tough as nails at work.*

PHRASAL VERB with **nail**

• **nail** *something* **down** [M] to make something certain or final ○ *He's traveling all over the state to nail down support for his senate campaign.*

nailbrush /ˈneɪl·brʌʃ/ *n* [C] a small, stiff brush used for cleaning your nails

nail file *n* [C] a strip of metal with a rough surface, for smoothing and shaping the ends of your nails

nail polish *n* [U] a shiny liquid substance used to decorate the nails of your fingers or toes

naive /nɑɪˈiːv/ *adj* too ready to believe someone or something, or to trust that someone's intentions are good, esp. because of a lack of experience ○ *It was naive of her to think that she would ever get her money back.*

naked /ˈneɪ·kəd/ *adj* [not gradable] not wearing any clothes

name /neɪm/ *n* [C] **1** a word or words that a person or thing is known by ○ *Hello, my name is Beth.* ○ *Do you remember the name of that town we visited in Maine?* ○ *I'm looking for someone* **by the name of** (= who has the name) *Stephen Weinberg.* **2** A name is also a reputation, esp. a good one: *She had made a name for herself as an architect by the time she was thirty.* **3** A name is also a famous person or thing: *He's a big name in the field of fashion.* ○ *They wanted a name band for the wedding.*
name /neɪm/ *v* [T] **1** to give a name to someone or something ○ *They decided to name their first child Benjamin.* **2** To name is also to choose or to state publicly: *The president has yet to name a new ambassador to Russia.*
nameless /ˈneɪm·ləs/ *adj* [not gradable] (of a person's name) unknown or not given publicly ○ *We are pleased to report a large gift to the school from someone who wishes to remain nameless.*

WORD FAMILY name

Nouns	name	*Verbs*	name
Adjectives	named		rename
	unnamed	*Adverbs*	namely
	nameless		

IDIOMS with **name**

• **in name only** having a particular title or name without the characteristics or duties that usually come with that title ○ *It's an island in name only, since it's been joined to the mainland now by landfill.*
• **in the name of** *something*, **in** *something's* **name** in order to do or become something ○ *In the name of being cool, kids miss out on a lot of fun activities.* ○ *Are you willing to be worked to death in the name of competition?*
• **name names** to tell the names of people who are involved in something bad or illegal ○ *She said she would never name names, even if she were offered money.*
• **the name of the game** the main purpose of an activity ○ *In professional sports, winning is the name of the game.*

name-dropping *n* [U] *disapproving* the habit of mentioning the names of famous or important people that you know or pretend to know, in order to make yourself seem more important

namely /ˈneɪm·li/ *adv* [not gradable] to be specific ○ *He suggested that these so-called contributions are something else, namely taxes.*

namesake /ˈneɪm·seɪk/ *n* [C usually sing] a person or thing with the same name as another person or thing

nanny /ˈnæn·i/ *n* [C] a woman employed to take care of children in the children's home ○ *She relied on a nanny to care for her baby during the week.*

nanotechnology /ˌnæn·oʊˌtekˈnɑl·ə·dʒi/ *n* [U] the science of making extremely small devices the size of atoms and MOLECULES

nap /næp/ *n* [C] a brief sleep, esp. during the day
nap /næp/ *v* [I] **-pp-** ○ *While the children nap after lunch, their teachers will get a break.*

nape /neɪp/ *n* [C usually sing] the back of the neck ○ *Her hair was gathered at the nape of her neck.*

napkin /ˈnæp·kən/, *Cdn, Br* **serviette** *n* [C] a piece of cloth or paper used at meals to protect your clothes and to clean your lips or fingers

nappy /ˈnæp·i/ *n* [C] *Br* DIAPER

narcotic /nɑrˈkɑt̬·ɪk/ *n* [C] a type of drug that causes sleep and that is used medically to reduce the strength of pain, and that in some forms is also used illegally
narcotic /nɑrˈkɑt̬·ɪk/ *adj* ○ *narcotic painkillers*

narrative /ˈnær·ət̬·ɪv/ *n* [C] ***literature*** a story or a description of events ○ *The novel is a wonderful narrative of wartime adventure.*

narrator /ˈnær·eɪt̬·ər/ *n* [C] ***literature*** a person who tells a story, or a person who speaks during a film or television program not as an actor but to describe or discuss the pictures being shown ○ *Michael Caine is the narrator in the documentary film.*
narrate /ˈnær·eɪt, nærˈeɪt/ *v* [I/T] to act as a narrator for something shown ○ [T] *We have to hire a professional to narrate the video.*
narration /nærˈeɪ·ʃən/ *n* [C/U] ***literature*** the telling of a story, or the work of a narrator

narrow SMALL /ˈnær·oʊ/ *adj* **1** having a small distance from one side to the other ○ *Scenes from the movie were filmed in some of Rome's ancient, narrow streets.* **2** Narrow also means slight, esp. as a measure of difference: *He was defeated in the election by a narrow margin.* ○ *It was a narrow victory, with the golf tournament decided by a single stroke.* **3** Narrow also means only just successful: *He had a narrow escape, getting out of the car just before it burst into flames.*
narrow /ˈnær·oʊ/ *v* [I/T] to become or make something narrower or smaller ○ [I] *The road narrows from four lanes to two when you leave town.* ○ [T] *Senate leaders met again to try to narrow the budget deficit.*
narrowly /ˈnær·ə·li/ *adv* ○ *Voters narrowly defeated the proposed school budget* (= a small number of votes defeated it).

LIMITED /ˈnær·oʊ/ *adj* limited in range ○ *The local newspaper tends to focus on narrow regional issues.*

narrow-minded *adj* [not gradable] unwilling to accept or consider other people's different ideas and behavior

NASA /ˈnæs·ə/ *n* [U] *abbreviation for* National Aeronautics and Space Administration (= the US government organization that plans and controls space travel and the scientific study of space).

nasal /ˈneɪ·zəl/ *adj* **1** of or related to the nose ○ *This medicine is supposed to relieve nasal congestion.* **2** If a person's voice is nasal, the sound is produced through the nose: *He had a high, unpleasant, nasal voice.*

nascent /ˈneɪ·sənt/ *adj* in the earliest stages of development ○ *Everyone in this nascent business is still struggling with basic issues.*

nasty /ˈnæs·ti/ *adj* mean, unpleasant, or offensive ○ *He was, to be honest, a nasty man, with never a kind word for anyone.* ○ *I got a rather nasty* (= severe) *cut from the garage door.*

nation /ˈneɪ·ʃən/ *n* [C] **1** a country, esp. when thought of as a large group of people living in one area with their own government, language, and traditions ○ *Most industrialized nations of the world will be represented at the conference.* ○ *Throughout the nation today people will go to the polls to elect a new government.* **2** A nation is also an American Indian group, esp. one that is a member of an American Indian FEDERATION.
national /ˈnæʃ·ən·əl/ *adj* [not gradable] relating to all parts of a nation or to a nation as a whole rather than to any part of it ○ *National headquarters of the company are in Atlanta, with branches throughout the country.* ○ *National news goes on the front page of the newspaper, with local news in the second section.*
national /ˈnæʃ·ən·əl/ *n* [C usually pl] a citizen of a particular or different country ○ *Irish/Mexican nationals* ○ *a foreign national*
nationality /ˌnæʃ·əˈnæl·ət̬·i/ *n* [C/U] the state of belonging to a particular country or being a citizen of a particular nation ○ [C] *"What's your nationality?" "I'm from Brazil."* ○ [C] *New York City is home to people of many nationalities.*
nationally /ˈnæʃ·ən·əl·i/ *adv* ○ *The football game, to be nationally televised, will begin at 9.*
nationalism /ˈnæʃ·ən·əlˌɪz·əm/ *n* [U] **1** ***social studies*** the feelings of affection and pride that people have for their country **2** ***politics & government*** Nationalism is also the desire for political independence in a country that is controlled by or part of another country: *The government is alarmed at the rise of nationalism among its ethnic minorities.*
nationalist /ˈnæʃ·ən·əl·əst/ *adj* ***politics & government*** supporting political independence for a group within a nation ○ *His views were those of the nationalist Quebec government.*
nationalistic /ˌnæʃ·ən·əlˈɪs·tɪk/ *adj* ***politics & government*** strongly supporting your country or its political independence ○ *A series of nationalistic speeches prepared the country for going to war.*
➤ Usage: **country, land, nation, or state?** at COUNTRY POLITICAL UNIT

WORD FAMILY nation

Nouns	nation national multinational nationalism nationalist nationality	*Adjectives*	national international multinational nationalistic
		Adverbs	nationally internationally
Verbs	nationalize		

national anthem *n* [C] a country's official song, often played on public occasions

National Guard *n* [U] the state military force that is available for service in state and federal emergencies

nationalize /ˈnæʃ·ən·əlˌɑɪz/ *v* [T] ***social studies*** to bring business, industry, or land under the control or ownership of the government ○ *The program's huge cost makes it unlikely that Congress will try to nationalize health care in the near future.*
nationalization /ˌnæʃ·ən·əl·əˈzeɪ·ʃən, -ɑɪˈzeɪ·ʃən/ *n* [U]

national park *n* [C] an area that is owned and maintained by the government because of its natural beauty or importance to history ○ *Yellowstone National Park*

nationwide /ˌneɪ·ʃənˈwɑɪd/ *adj* [not gradable] existing or happening in all parts of a particular country ○ *A nationwide survey of mothers revealed some very interesting things about what mothers want from fathers.*
nationwide /ˌneɪ·ʃənˈwɑɪd/ *adv* [not gradable] ○ *The performances were taped for telecasting nationwide.*

native /ˈneɪt̬·ɪv/ *adj* [not gradable] **1** of or relating to the place where you were born ○ *This was his first visit to his native land in 30 years.* ○ *Larry is a native Texan* (= He was born in Texas). ○ *His native language is Spanish, but he speaks English without a trace of an accent.* **2** Someone or something native to a place was born or started to develop there: *Corn is native to North America.*
native /ˈneɪt̬·ɪv/ *n* [C] **1** a person born in a particular place ○ *He was a native of Indianapolis and a graduate of Indiana University.* **2** *dated* A native is also a person who was born and lived in a country before Europeans began to visit and live there: *Raleigh wanted the cooperation of the natives and treated the Indians with respect.* ○ **USAGE:** This use is considered offensive.

Native American, **American Indian** *n* [C] a member of any of the groups of people that lived in North America before the Europeans arrived

Nativity /nəˈtɪv·ət̬·i/ *n* [U] the birth of Jesus, celebrated by Christians at Christmas ○ *the Nativity story*

NATO, **Nato** /ˈneɪt̬·oʊ/ *n* [U] *abbreviation for* North Atlantic Treaty Organization (= an international organization that includes the US, Canada, and several European countries, formed in 1949 for military defense).

natural NOT ARTIFICIAL /ˈnætʃ·ə·rəl/ *adj* **1** from nature; not artificial or involving anything made or caused by people ○ *Cotton is a natural fiber.* ○ *He died of natural causes* (= because he was old or ill). ○ *Floods and earthquakes are natural disasters.* **2** If food or drink is described as natural, it means it has no artificial chemical substances added to it.
naturally /ˈnætʃ·ə·rə·li/ *adv* ○ *naturally curly hair*
naturalness /ˈnætʃ·ə·rəl·nəs/ *n* [U] ○ *I admire his naturalness on stage.*

BORN WITH /ˈnætʃ·ə·rəl/ *adj* having an ability or characteristic because you were born with it ○ *a natural athlete* ○ *a natural blonde*
natural /ˈnætʃ·ə·rəl/ *n* [C] *infml* a person born with the characteristics or abilities needed for doing something ○ *She won't have any trouble learning to ride a horse – she's a natural.*
naturally /ˈnætʃ·ə·rə·li/ *adv* ○ *a naturally talented artist*

EXPECTED /ˈnætʃ·ə·rəl/ *adj* to be expected; usual ○ *a natural reaction* ○ [+ to infinitive] *It's only natural to be upset when your dog dies.*
naturally /ˈnætʃ·ə·rə·li/ *adv* ○ *Exercising should come as naturally as brushing your teeth.* ○ *Naturally, we have to arrive early to get the best seats.* ○ *"You will be polite when you speak to her, won't you?" "Naturally* (= Yes, obviously)."

MUSIC /ˈnætʃ·ə·rəl/ *n* [C] ***music*** a mark in written music that shows that a note should return to its original PITCH ➤ Picture: **notation**
natural /ˈnætʃ·ə·rəl/ *adj* [not gradable] ***music*** (of written music) having no SHARP or FLAT ○ *a B natural* ○ *a natural scale*

WORD FAMILY natural

Nouns	nature natural naturalist naturalization naturalness supernatural	*Adjectives*	natural supernatural unnatural naturalistic
Verbs	naturalize	*Adverbs*	naturally unnaturally

natural childbirth *n* [U] a method of giving birth in which there is little or no use of pain medicine and other medical involvement

natural gas *n* [U] gas found underground that is used as a fuel

naturalist /ˈnætʃ·ə·rə·ləst/ *n* [C] a person who studies plants and animals

naturalize /ˈnætʃ·ə·rəˌlɑɪz/ *v* [T] to make someone a legal CITIZEN of a country that the person was not born in
naturalization /ˌnætʃ·ə·rə·ləˈzeɪ·ʃən/ *n* [U] ○ *She's applied for naturalization.*

natural resource *n* [C] any of the materials such as water, coal, and wood that exist in nature and can be used by people

natural selection *n* [U] the process by which animals and plants that are best suited to their environment have the best success at reproduction
n [U] ***biology*** the theory that organisms with characteristics that allow them to live successfully in a particular environment will reproduce organisms with the same characteristics

nature LIFE /ˈneɪ·tʃər/ *n* [U] **1** all the animals and plants in the world and all the features, forces, and processes that exist or happen independently of people, such as the weather, the sea, mountains, reproduction, and growth ○ *As a young man he loved hiking and being close to nature.* ○ *This technique of growing cells copies what actually happens in nature.* **2** The force that is responsible for physical life is often called nature, and is sometimes spoken of as a person: *Feeling stressed is Nature's way of telling you to relax.*

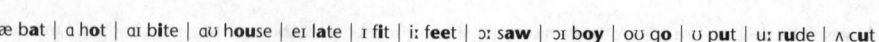

USAGE

nature, the environment, or the countryside?

Nature means all the things in the world that exist naturally and were not created by people.

He's fascinated by wildlife and anything to do with nature.

The environment means the land, water, and air that animals and plants live in. It is usually used when talking about the way people use or damage the natural world.

The government has introduced new policies to protect the environment.

Countryside means land where there are no towns or cities.

I love walking in the countryside.

TYPE /ˈneɪ·tʃər/ *n* [C/U] the type or main characteristic (of something) ○ [U] *The problem is delicate in nature.* ○ [C] *Nothing of a secret nature can happen in that household.*

CHARACTER /ˈneɪ·tʃər/ *n* [C/U] the character of a person, or the characteristics a person is born with ○ [C] *She's always had a sunny nature.* ○ [U] *She is by nature a gentle soul.*

IDIOM with nature

• **the nature of things** the usual and expected characteristics of life ○ *There are problems in every relationship – it's in the nature of things.*

nature reserve, **nature preserve** *n* [C] an area of land protected by the government so that plants and animals can live there without being harmed

naught /nɔːt, nɑt/ *n* [U] *old use* nothing ○ *All our effort was for naught.*

naughty /ˈnɔː·t̬i, ˈnɑt̬·i/ *adj* (esp. of children) behaving badly and not being obedient, or (esp. of behavior or language) not socially acceptable ○ *a naughty girl* ○ *a naughty word*

nausea /ˈnɔː·ziː·ə, ˈnɔː·ʒə, ˈnɔː·ʃə/ *n* [U] a feeling of illness in the stomach that makes you think you are going to vomit

nauseated /ˈnɔː·ziː ˌeɪt̬·əd/ *adj* ○ *He didn't become nauseated by the treatments at all.*

nauseating /ˈnɔː·ziː ˌeɪt̬·ɪŋ/ *adj* ○ *The TV news can be pretty nauseating at times.*

nauseous /ˈnɔː·ʃəs, ˈnɔː·ziː·əs/ *adj* feeling that you are likely to vomit, or causing this feeling ○ *He felt nauseous and dehydrated.* ○ *unpleasant, nauseous odors*

nautical /ˈnɔːt̬·ɪ·kəl, ˈnɑt̬-/ *adj* [not gradable] relating to ships, sailing, or people who work on ships

nautical mile *n* [C] a unit of distance used at sea which is equal to 6076 feet in the US system ○ Compare MILE

naval /ˈneɪ·vəl/ *adj* [not gradable] belonging to a country's navy, or relating to military ships ○ *A major naval battle was fought near here.*

navel /ˈneɪ·vəl/, *infml* **belly button** *n* [C] the small round part or hollow place in the middle of the stomach which is left after the UMBILICAL CORD (= long tube of flesh joining the baby to its mother) has been cut at birth

navigable /ˈnæv·ɪ·gə·bəl/ *adj* deep and wide enough for a ship to go through ○ *a navigable stretch of river*

navigate /ˈnæv·əˌgeɪt/ *v* [I/T] to direct the way that a vehicle, esp. a ship or aircraft will travel, or to find a direction across, along, or over an area of water or land ○ [T] *He learned to navigate these waters.* ○ [I] *Whales navigate by visual means.* ○ [I] *(fig.) Cyberspace is an environment in which computers navigate.*

navigation /ˌnæv·əˈgeɪ·ʃən/ *n* [U] ○ *a satellite navigation system*

navigator /ˈnæv·əˌgeɪt̬·ər/ *n* [C] a person in a vehicle who decides on the direction in which the vehicle travels

navy /ˈneɪ·vi/ *n* [C] the part of a country's armed forces that is trained to operate at sea

navy (blue) /ˈneɪ·vi (ˈbluː)/ *adj, n* [U] dark blue

Nazi /ˈnɑt·si, ˈnæt-/ *n* [C] a member of the National Socialist German Workers' Party that controlled Germany from 1933 to 1945 under Adolf Hitler, or someone who believes in FASCISM (= state control of social and economic life and extreme pride in country and race, with no political disagreement allowed)

Nazi /ˈnɑt·si, ˈnæt-/ *adj* [not gradable]

NBA *n* [U] *abbreviation for* National Basketball Association (= the main organized group of US BASKETBALL teams that have players who are paid for playing).

NC-17 /ˌenˌsiːˌsev·ənˈtiːn/ *adj* [not gradable] used in the US for movies that no one under the age of 17 will be admitted to see ○ Compare G MOVIE; PG; R MOVIE

N.E. *adj, n* [U] *abbreviation for* NORTHEAST or NORTHEASTERN

Neanderthal, **Neandertal** /niːˈæn·dərˌtɔːl, -ˌθɔːl/ *n* [C] **1** one of the ancient people who lived in Europe and Asia from approximately 30,000 to 150,000 years ago **2** *fig.* someone who behaves in a rude or offensive way

Neanderthal, **Neandertal** /niːˈæn·dərˌtɔːl, -ˌθɔːl/ *adj* ○ *a Neanderthal skeleton*

near /nɪr/, **near to** /ˈnɪr·tə, -tuː/ *prep* close to; not far away from in distance, time, or relationship ○ *We live near the school.* ○ *She asked to sit nearer the front of the classroom.* ○ *It will probably be near midnight by the time we get home.* ○ *We couldn't park anywhere near the theater.*

near /nɪr/ *adv* [-er/-est only] ○ *I wish we lived nearer.* ○ *I was standing near enough to hear what they were saying.*

near /nɪr/ *adj* [-er/-est only] ○ *in the near future* ○ *The nearest library is in the next town.*

near /nɪr/ *v* [I/T] to come closer to something, or to approach ○ [I] *As the big day nears, I'm starting*

N

to get nervous. ○ [T] *The project is nearing completion.*

nearly /ˈnɪr·li/ *adv* [not gradable] almost but not quite; close to ○ *I've nearly finished that book you lent me.* ○ *She's nearly as tall as her father now.* ○ *The problem isn't nearly as bad as you think.*

nearness /ˈnɪr·nəs/ *n* [U] ○ *I'm surprised by the nearness of her.*

nearby /nɪrˈbɑɪ, ˈnɪr·bɑɪ/ *adj, adv* [not gradable] not far away in distance; close ○ *A police officer was standing nearby.* ○ *We walked to a nearby park.*

near miss *n* [C] a situation in which an accident almost happened ○ *That was a near miss – he must have come within 50 feet of the other plane.*

nearsighted /ˈnɪrˌsɑɪt̬·əd/ *adj* [not gradable] able to see clearly only objects that are close up ○ Compare FARSIGHTED

neat ARRANGED /niːt/ *adj* [*-er/-est* only] **1** arranged well, with everything in its place ○ *neat handwriting* ○ *She keeps her room neat and clean.* **2** A neat person likes everything to be clean and well arranged. **3** Neat can also mean skillful or effective: *a neat trick/solution*

neatly /ˈniːt·li/ *adv* ○ *neatly folded clothes*

neatness /ˈniːt·nəs/ *n* [U]

NOTHING ADDED /niːt/ *adj* [not gradable] (of alcoholic drinks) with nothing added; STRAIGHT

GREAT /niːt/ *adj* [*-er/-est* only] *infml* great ○ *The party was really neat.* ○ *What a neat bike!*

N

nebula /ˈneb·jə·lə/ *n* [C] *pl* **-las, -lae** ***earth science*** a cloud of dust or gas in outer space ○ *The Orion Nebula is visible to the naked eye under dark skies.*

nebular /ˈneb·jə·lər/ *adj* [not gradable] ***earth science***

nebulous /ˈneb·jə·ləs/ *adj* (esp. of ideas) unclear and lacking form; VAGUE ○ *a nebulous concept*

necessary /ˈnes·əˌser·i/ *adj* **1** needed in order to achieve a particular result ○ *Don't take any more luggage than is strictly necessary.* ○ *He lacks the necessary skills for the job.* ○ *If necessary, we can always change the date of our trip.* **2** A **necessary evil** is something unpleasant that must be accepted in order to achieve a particular result: *Most Americans accept taxes as a necessary evil.* **3** Necessary can be used in negatives and questions to show that you disapprove of something and do not think it should be done: [+ *to* infinitive] *Was it really necessary to say that?*

necessarily /ˌnes·əˈser·ə·li/ *adv* [not gradable] (esp. in negatives) in all cases; as an expected result ○ *Money doesn't necessarily buy happiness.* ○ *"These cheap glasses will break easily." "Not necessarily."*

WORD FAMILY necessary

Nouns	necessity	*Verbs*	necessitate
Adjectives	necessary unnecessary	*Adverbs*	necessarily unnecessarily

WORD CHOICES necessary

The verbs **need** and **require** and the modal verb **must** are very commonly used to show that something is necessary.

*The meat **must** be cooked thoroughly.*

*Does she have the skills **needed/required** for work of that sort?*

If something is very important and necessary, you can use adjectives such as **essential, fundamental**, and **indispensable**.

*Some understanding of grammar is **essential/fundamental** to learning a language.*

*This book is an **indispensable** resource for teachers.*

The expression **be a must** is sometimes used in informal situations to describe things that are very necessary to have or do.

*This book **is a must** for anyone who loves history.*

necessitate /nəˈses·əˌteɪt/ *v* [T] to make something necessary ○ *An important meeting necessitates my being in Houston on Friday.*

necessity /nəˈses·ət̬·i/ *n* [C/U] the need for something, or something that is needed ○ [U] *Don't you understand the necessity of eating a balanced diet?* ○ [U] *She was forced to take the job out of necessity.* ○ [C] *In my work, a computer is a necessity.*

neck BODY PART /nek/ *n* [C] **1** the part of the body that joins the head to the shoulders ○ *She rubbed her neck.* **2** The neck of a piece of clothing is the part that goes around a person's neck: *His shirt was open at the neck.* **3** A neck is also a narrow part near the top of an object such as a bottle: *a vase with a long neck* **4** A neck is also the long, narrow part of a string instrument, such as a guitar, on which the strings are pressed in order to produce different notes.

KISS /nek/ *v* [I] *dated, infml* to kiss someone for a long time

IDIOMS with neck

• **neck and neck** very close or equal ○ *The two boys ran toward the finish line neck and neck.*

• *someone's* **neck of the woods, this neck of the woods** *infml* the area someone comes from, or the area where you are ○ *I'm surprised to see you in this neck of the woods.*

necklace /ˈnek·ləs/ *n* [C] a piece of jewelry worn around the neck, such as a chain or a string of decorative stones or BEADS

neckline /ˈnek·lɑɪn/ *n* [C] the shape made by the edge of a dress or shirt at the front of the neck or on the chest ○ *a ruffled/square neckline*

necktie /ˈnek·tɑɪ/ *n* [C] a TIE (= long, thin piece of material worn that fits under a shirt collar)

nectar /ˈnek·tər/ *n* [U] **1** a sweet liquid produced by flowers and collected by bees ○ *The bee turns* *nectar into honey.* **2** Nectar is also a drink made from some fruits: *apricot nectar*

nectarine /ˌnek·təˈriːn/ *n* [C] a type of PEACH (= a fruit) with a smooth skin

neé /neɪ/ *adj* [not gradable] used after a woman's married name to show the family name by which she was known before she married ○ *Anne Timberlake, neé Logan*

need **MUST HAVE** /niːd/ *v* [T] **1** to be necessary to have something, or to want something very much ○ *To make pastry, you need flour, fat, and water.* ○ *Do we need anything from the store?* ○ *Will I be needed in the office tomorrow?* ○ *I need you to advise me on what to wear.* ○ *I need a rest.* **2** *infml* If you say that you don't need something, it can mean that you do not want it because it is causing you trouble: *I don't need all this arguing.* **3** If you say that someone needs something, you can mean that the person should have it or would benefit from having it: *What you need is some hot soup to warm you up.* ○ *She needs her hair washed.*

need /niːd/ *n* [U] **1** something that you must or should have, or the lack of this ○ *There's a growing need for low-cost housing.* **2** Need can be a reason: [+ *to* infinitive] *I don't think there's any need to worry.* **3** Need is also a feeling or state of greatly wanting something: [+ *to* infinitive] *a desperate need to be loved* ○ *We have no need for your sympathy.* **4** Need is also the state of being necessary: *Help yourself to supplies as the need arises.* ○ [+ *to* infinitive] *There's no need to buy any more food.* **5** People who are **in need** do not have enough money or need some type of help: *The money will go to those who are most in need.* **6** Someone who is **in need of** something must or should have it: *They're in need of help.*

needs /niːdz/ *pl n* the things you must have for a satisfactory life ○ *the special needs of the disabled*

needy /ˈniːd·i/ *adj* If people are needy, they are very poor.

MUST DO /niːd/ *v* **needs, need** to have to take an action ○ [+ *to* infinitive] *He needs to lose weight.* ○ [+ *to* infinitive] *Before we make a decision, we need to consider our options.* ○ [+ *to* infinitive] *I need to do some shopping on my way home.* ○ *I don't think we need ask him.* ○ *Nothing need be done about this before next week.* ○ [+ *to* infinitive] *As it turned out, I didn't need to buy any extra material* (= I did it, although I didn't have to).

WORD FAMILY need

Nouns	need needs	*Adjectives*	needless needy
Verbs	need	*Adverbs*	needlessly

IDIOM with need

• **need I say more** you know what would happen next if I were to tell you more ○ *Mike did the cooking – need I say more?*

needle **TOOL** /ˈniːd·əl/ *n* [C] **1** a thin, solid, metal piece with a sharp point at one end, esp. one used for sewing that has a hole to hold thread ○ *Can you thread this needle for me?* **2** A needle is also a small stick with a point or hook, used to make stitches: *knitting needles* **3** A needle is also a thin metal tube with a sharp, pointed end, used to put a liquid, such as a medicine, into the body or to remove a liquid, such as blood, from the body.

POINTER /ˈniːd·əl/ *n* [C] the thin, moving part on a COMPASS (= device for finding direction) or measuring instrument that points in a particular direction or to a particular value

LEAF /ˈniːd·əl/ *n* [C] one of the thin, stiff, green leaves of some evergreen trees ○ *pine needles*

ANNOY /ˈniːd·əl/ *v* [T] *infml* to purposely annoy someone by making critical remarks or jokes ○ *I hate to be needled about my weight.*

needless **UNNECESSARY** /ˈniːd·ləs/ *adj* [not gradable] completely unnecessary ○ *a needless waste of time*

needlessly /ˈniːd·lə·sli/ *adv* [not gradable] ○ *You're worrying needlessly – they'll be fine.*

IDIOM with needless

• **needless to say** obviously ○ *Needless to say, because of the accident he won't be at work for a while.*

needn't /ˈniːd·ənt/ *contraction of* need not ○ *You needn't be shy.*

needs /niːdz/ *pl n* ○ See at NEED **MUST HAVE**

needy /ˈniːd·i/ *adj* ○ See at NEED **MUST HAVE**

negate Ⓐ /nɪˈgeɪt/ *v* [T] to show something to be wrong or to be the opposite of what was thought, or to cause something to have no effect ○ *The increase in sales was negated by the rising cost of materials.*

negative Ⓐ **NO** /ˈneg·ət̬·ɪv/ *adj* **1** expressing no or not, or expressing refusal ○ *We received a negative answer to our request.* ○ Compare AFFIRMATIVE **2** A negative sentence or phrase is one that contains a word such as no, not, nor, never, or nothing. **3** A medical test that is negative shows that you do not have that disease or condition. ○ Compare POSITIVE **MEDICAL TEST**

negative Ⓐ /ˈneg·ət̬·ɪv/ *n* [C/U] ○ [U] *The governor replied in the negative.* ○ Opposite: AFFIRMATIVE

negatively Ⓐ /ˈneg·ət̬·ɪv·li/ *adv* ○ *This time, she answered both questions negatively* (= by saying "no").

NOT HAPPY /ˈneg·ət̬·ɪv/ *adj* not happy, hopeful, or approving; tending to consider only bad things ○ *a negative attitude* ○ *All the candidates in the mayoral campaign ran negative ads* (= advertising saying bad things about each other). ○ Opposite: POSITIVE **HAPPY**

negatively Ⓐ /ˈneg·ət̬·ɪv·li/ *adv* ○ *The public reacts negatively* (= shows its disapproval) *when told health benefits may be cut.*

LESS THAN ZERO /ˈneg·ət̬·ɪv/ *adj* [not gradable] ***algebra*** (of a number or amount) less than zero ○ *negative numbers* ○ Opposite: POSITIVE **MORE THAN ZERO**

ART /ˈneg·ət̬·ɪv/ *adj* ***art*** (of spaces and shapes in a painting, statue, drawing, etc.) empty space, or areas lacking objects or other particular features; background

ELECTRICITY /ˈneg·ət̬·ɪv/ *adj* [not gradable] ***physics*** of the type of electrical CHARGE that an ELECTRON has ○ Compare POSITIVE ELECTRICITY

negatively Ⓐ /ˈneg·ət̬·ɪv·li/ *adv* ***physics***

PHOTOGRAPH /ˈneg·ət̬·ɪv/ *n* [C] a piece of film in which light areas appear dark and dark areas appear light, the opposite of how they will appear in the photograph made from it

neglect /nɪˈglekt/ *v* [I/T] to fail to give needed care or attention to someone or something ○ [T] *She had neglected the program and allowed student interest in it to fall off.* ○ [I] *He neglected to tell his employer that he would be taking the day off.*

neglect /nɪˈglekt/ *n* [U] ○ *The park was in a sorry state of neglect.*

negligent /ˈneg·lə·dʒənt/ *adj* failing to be careful enough or to give enough attention to your responsibilities, esp. when this results in harm or loss to others

negligence /ˈneg·lə·dʒəns/ *n* [U] ○ *She charged her landlord with negligence for not repairing leaks that ruined her rugs.*

negligible /ˈneg·lɪ·dʒə·bəl/ *adj* too slight or small in amount to be important ○ *The effect on sales was negligible.*

N

negotiate **DISCUSS** /nɪˈgoʊ·ʃiːˌeɪt/ *v* [I/T] to have formal discussions with someone in order to reach an agreement ○ [T] *We want to negotiate a settlement that is fair to both sides.*

negotiation /nɪˌgoʊ·ʃiːˈeɪ·ʃən/ *n* [C/U] ○ [C usually pl] *Negotiations remained at a standstill.*

negotiable /nɪˈgoʊ·ʃə·bəl, -ʃiː·ə-/ *adj* ○ *At this stage, everything is negotiable* (= can be discussed or changed).

negotiator /nɪˈgoʊ·ʃiːˌeɪt̬·ər/ *n* [C]

MOVE /nɪˈgoʊ·ʃiːˌeɪt/ *v* [T] to move carefully or with difficulty past, through, or along something ○ *She was able to negotiate the climb with some help from younger campers.*

Negro /ˈniː·groʊ/ *n* [C] *pl* **Negroes** *dated* a person of African origin with dark skin ○ **USAGE:** "Negro" is now considered offensive by most people, and "African-American" is used instead. See the usage note at BLACK DARK SKIN.

neigh /neɪ/ *n* [C] a long, loud, high sound that horses make when excited or frightened

neigh /neɪ/ *v* [I]

neighbor, *Cdn, Br* **neighbour** /ˈneɪ·bər/ *n* [C] someone who lives near you ○ *Elie is my next-door neighbor.*

neighborhood, *Cdn, Br* **neighbourhood** /ˈneɪ·bərˌhʊd/ *n* [C] **1** an area with characteristics that make it different from other areas, or the people who live in a particular area ○ *This is a nice, quiet neighborhood, with modest single-family homes.* **2** the approximate amount of something ○ *We hope to get* **something in the neighborhood of** (= a price that is close to) *$200,000 for our house.*

neighboring, *Cdn, Br* **neighbouring** /ˈneɪ·bə·rɪŋ/ *adj* [not gradable] (of places) next or near to each other ○ *Kentucky and Tennessee are neighboring states.*

neighborly, *Cdn, Br* **neighbourly** /ˈneɪ·bər·li/ *adj* friendly and helpful, esp. to those living near you

neither /ˈniː·ðər, ˈnaɪ-/ *pronoun, conjunction, adj* [not gradable] not one and not the other of two things or people ○ *They have two TVs but neither one works.* ○ *Neither of my brothers could come to the party.* ○ (infml) *"I don't feel like going out tonight." "Me neither."*

> **USAGE**
>
> **neither . . . nor**
>
> The phrase **neither** *someone* **nor** *someone else* is usually used with a singular verb, but it can also be used with a plural verb.
>
> *Neither Ricky nor Lucy like television.*
>
> *Neither Ricky nor Lucy likes television.*

IDIOM with **neither**

• **neither here nor there** not important, or not connected with the subject being discussed ○ *Her age is neither here nor there – the real question is, can she do the job?*

neon /ˈniː·ɑn/ *n* [U] a colorless gas, one of the chemical elements, that is often used in signs because it produces a bright light when an electric current goes through it ○ *a neon sign*

neonatal /ˌniː·oʊˈneɪt̬·əl/ *adj* [not gradable] *medical* of or for babies that were just born ○ *a nurse specializing in neonatal care*

neophyte /ˈniː·əˌfaɪt/ *n* [C] someone who has recently become involved in an activity and is still learning about it ○ *This computer course is for neophytes.*

nephew /ˈnef·juː/ *n* [C] a son of someone's brother or sister, or a son of someone's husband's or wife's sister or brother ○ Compare NIECE

nepotism /ˈnep·əˌtɪz·əm/ *n* [U] the activity of unfairly giving good jobs or advantages to members of your family

Neptune /ˈnep·tuːn/ *n* [U] the planet eighth in order of distance from the sun, after Uranus and before Pluto ➤ Picture: **solar system**

nerd /nɜrd/ *n* [C] *infml* a person who lacks social skills, esp. someone interested in technical things ○ *Gina's brother is a complete nerd.*

nerdy /ˈnɜrd·i/ *adj infml* ○ *He was a short, nerdy guy with glasses.*

nerve **BODY FIBER** /nɜrv/ *n* [C] ***biology*** a group of long, thin fibers in the body, esp. in the brain, which send and receive messages that control how the body reacts to signals it receives, such as to changes in temperature or pressure against the skin

nervous /ˈnɜr·vəs/ *adj* [not gradable] relating to or controlled by the nerves

BRAVERY /nɜrv/ *n* [U] **1** bravery or confidence necessary to do something difficult or unpleasant ○ *It takes a lot of nerve to get up in front of a class when you're not used to it.* **2** Nerve also means the ability to do something rude without caring about other people's feelings: *She has some nerve.* ○ *I can't believe she* **had the nerve to** *call me fat!*

WORD FAMILY nerve			
Nouns	nerve nerves nervousness	*Adjectives* *Adverbs*	nervous nervously

nerve-racking, **nerve-wracking** *adj* [not gradable] difficult to do and causing a lot of worry or anxiety ○ *I had to go out and find a new job, which is always a nerve-racking experience.*

nervous /ˈnɜr·vəs/ *adj* worried or slightly frightened ○ *I was nervous during my driving test.*

nerves /nɜrvz/ *pl n* [C] worry or anxiety ○ *an attack of nerves*

nervously /ˈnɜr·və·sli/ *adv* ○ *He laughed nervously.*

nervousness /ˈnɜr·və·snəs/ *n* [U] ○ *There's nervousness about what the future will hold.*

nervous breakdown *n* [C] an illness that causes a person to suffer from anxiety and to have difficulty living and working as usual

nervous system *n* [C] ***biology*** (in animals and people) the brain and all the nerves in the body that together make movement and feeling possible ○ Compare AUTONOMIC NERVOUS SYSTEM

nest /nest/ *n* [C] a structure or other place where creatures, esp. birds, give birth or leave their eggs to develop

nest /nest/ *v* [I] ○ *Swallows are nesting in our apple tree.*

nest egg *n* [C usually sing] money saved or kept for a special purpose ○ *I have a little nest egg that I'm saving for college.*

nestle /ˈnes·əl/ *v* [I/T] to be in or put someone or something into a comfortable or protected position ○ [I] *She nestled the cat in her arms.*

net MATERIAL /net/ *n* [C] a piece of material made of long, narrow strips woven so that there are spaces between them ○ *fishing nets* ○ *a volleyball net*

net /net/ *v* [T] **-tt- 1** (in sports) to hit the ball into a net instead of over it ○ *He netted an easy backhand in the fifth game to lose the tennis match.* **2** To net is also to catch something in a net: *They netted five crabs.*

LEFT OVER /net/ *adj* [not gradable] **1** (of money received from selling something) left after you have subtracted the cost of what you are selling, and other expenses related to it ○ *net income/profit* ○ *(fig.) The net result* (= result after everything has been considered) *of the changes will be fewer trains for most suburban commuters.* **2** Net weight is the weight of something contained in a package, without including the weight of the package. **3** ***physics*** Net force is the total amount of force that is in effect on an object at a particular time.

net /net/ *v* [T] **-tt-** ○ *Smithsonian, on a gross of $28 million, netted $7 million with one magazine.*

GET /net/ *v* [T] **-tt-** to succeed in getting something of value, esp. as the result of a plan of action ○ *The deal netted the online video company $23 million.*

Net /net/ *n* [U] **1** *short form of* INTERNET **2** Net is also used at the end of a US INTERNET address to show that the address belongs to a network: *info@sover.net*

network Ⓐ /ˈnet·wɜrk/ *n* [C] **1** a group formed from parts that are connected together ○ *a transportation network* **2** A network is also a company that provides programs to a group of television or radio stations, or this company and the group considered together: *the ABC television network* **3** A network is also a group of computers that are connected and can share information. **4** A network is also a group of people with the same interests: *a network of political advisers*

network Ⓐ /ˈnet·wɜrk/ *v* [I/T] To network is also to make an effort to meet and talk to a lot of people, esp. in order to get information that can help you.

networking Ⓐ /ˈnet ˌwɜr·kɪŋ/ *n* [U] Networking is also the process of meeting and talking to a lot of people, esp. in order to get information that can help you: *Students find networking essential to finding the right job.*

neurology /nʊrˈɑl·ə·dʒi/ *n* [U] the study of the structure and diseases of the brain and the nervous system

neurological /ˌnʊr·əˈlɑdʒ·ɪ·kəl/ *adj* [not gradable] ○ *a neurological disorder*

neuron /ˈnʊr·ɑn/ *n* [C] ***biology*** (in animals and people) a type of cell that sends and receives messages within the brain and the nerves of the body

neurosis /nʊˈroʊ·səs/ *n* [C] *pl* **neuroses** a mental condition resulting in unreasonable anxiety and unusual behavior

neurotic /nʊˈrɑt̬·ɪk/ *adj* related to or having unreasonable anxiety or unusual behavior ○ *a deep-seated neurotic fear of flying*

neurotic /nʊˈrɑt̬·ɪk/ *n* [C] a neurotic person

neurotransmitter /ˌnʊr·oʊ·trænzˈmɪt̬·ər/ *n* [C] ***biology*** a chemical substance that carries messages from one nerve cell to another in the body

neuter GRAMMAR /ˈnuːt̬·ər/ *adj* [not gradable] ***grammar*** being a noun or pronoun of a type that refers to things; not MASCULINE or FEMININE

PREVENT REPRODUCTION /ˈnuːt̬·ər/ *v* [T] to remove part of the sex organs of an animal so that it cannot reproduce

neutral Ⓐ **NO OPINION** /ˈnuː·trəl/ *adj* ***world history*** not expressing an opinion or taking ac-

N

tions that support either side in a disagreement or war ○ *Switzerland remained neutral during the war.*
neutrality Ⓐ /nuː ˈtræl·ət̬·i/ *n* [U] ***world history*** the condition of being neutral

NOT SOMETHING /ˈnuː·trəl/ *adj* **1** (of colors) not bright, and therefore not likely to attract attention ○ *He wanted the office painted in neutral colors.* **2** ***chemistry*** A neutral substance is neither an acid nor a BASE. **3** ***physics*** A neutral wire in an electrical CIRCUIT is a wire with no electrical CHARGE.
neutralize Ⓐ /ˈnuː·trə ˌlɑɪz/ *v* [T] ***science***

neutralization Ⓐ /ˌnuː·trə·ləˈzeɪ·ʃən/ *n* [U] ***chemistry*** the reaction between an acid and a BASE, which produces a SALT and water

neutralize Ⓐ /ˈnuː·trə ˌlɑɪz/ *v* [T] to produce an effect that removes the effect of something else ○ *Raising the sales tax will neutralize the tax cut.*
neutralization Ⓐ /ˌnuː·trə·ləˈzeɪ·ʃən/ *n* [U]

neutrino /nuː ˈtriː·noʊ/ *n* [C] ***physics*** a very small piece of matter that has no electrical CHARGE, that is produced during some types of nuclear reactions, and exists for a very short time

neutron /ˈnuː ˌtrɑn/ *n* [C] ***physics, chemistry*** the part of an atom that has no electrical CHARGE and is part of the atom's NUCLEUS (= central part) ○ Compare ELECTRON; PROTON ➤ Picture: **atom**

never /ˈnev·ər/ *adv* [not gradable] not at any time, or not on any occasion ○ *I've never been to Europe.* ○ *He was never seen again.* ○ *She never had acting lessons* ○ *We've never had a chance to sit down and talk.* ○ *Hal Willner? Never heard of him.* ○ *I never forget a face.*

N

USAGE
never
Never has a negative meaning, so you do not need to use the adverb **not** with it to make a sentence negative.
I'll never do that again.
~~*I'll not never do that again.*~~

IDIOM with never

• **never mind** do not worry about it ○ *"I lost that wallet you gave me." "Well, never mind, I can always buy you another one."*

nevertheless Ⓐ /ˌnev·ər·ðəˈles/, **nonetheless** *adv* [not gradable] despite what has just been said or referred to ○ *Their team hadn't lost a game the entire season. Nevertheless, we beat them by a huge margin last night.*

new RECENTLY CREATED /nuː/ *adj* [-*er*/-*est* only] recently created or having started to exist recently ○ *His newest book will be out next month.* ○ *She's always coming up with new ideas.*
newly /ˈnuː·li/ *adv* [not gradable] ○ *a newly waxed floor* ○ *She plans to begin touring with a newly formed band in July.*
newness /ˈnuː·nəs/ *n* [U] ○ *Kids lose their enthusiasm for things when the sense of newness wears off.*

WORD CHOICES new
If something is completely new and has not been used, you can describe it as **brand-new**.
*How can he afford to buy a **brand-new** car?*
Fresh can be used when something is new and therefore interesting or exciting.
*We need a **fresh** approach to the problem of crime.*
The adjectives **novel** or **innovative** can be used when something involves new and unusual ideas or methods.
*The bank has introduced a **novel** way of detecting fraud.*
*The project uses **innovative** ideas for recycling.*

DIFFERENT /nuː/ *adj* [-*er*/-*est* only] different from the one that existed earlier ○ *Have you met Carlos's new assistant?* ○ *"What's new* (= What is different in your life)*?" "Not much, what's new with you?"*

NOT FAMILIAR /nuː/ *adj* [-*er*/-*est* only] not yet familiar or experienced ○ *Don't ask me how to get there, I'm new around here.*

NOT USED /nuː/ *adj* [-*er*/-*est* only] not previously used or owned ○ *They sell new and used cars/books/clothing.*

RECENTLY DISCOVERED /nuː/ *adj* [-*er*/-*est* only] recently discovered or made known ○ *This new treatment offers hope to many sufferers.* ○ *Astronomers reported finding millions of new stars.*

WORD FAMILY new

Nouns	news newness renewal	*Adjectives*	new newsy renewable renewed
Verbs	renew	*Adverbs*	newly

New Age *adj* relating to a way of life and thinking that stresses awareness of your spirit ○ *They are New Age types – into yoga and strict vegetarianism.*

new blood *n* [U] people who have just started working or living somewhere who are energetic, enthusiastic, and often, young ○ *The new boss brought in some new blood.*

newborn /ˈnuː·bɔːrn/ *adj* [not gradable] having recently been born ○ *a newborn baby*
newborn /ˈnuː·bɔːrn/ *n* [C] a child or animal that has recently been born

newcomer /ˈnuː ˌkʌm·ər/ *n* [C] someone who has recently arrived in a place, or a person or organization that has recently become involved in an activity ○ *The company is a relative newcomer to the personal computer industry.*

newfangled /ˈnuː ˈfæŋ·gəld/ *adj* [not gradable] *esp. disapproving* recently created or invented ○ *I hate those newfangled alarm clocks that buzz.*

newfound, **new-found** /ˈnuː ˈfɑʊnd/ *adj* [not gradable] only recently happening, discovered, or beginning to exist ○ *Scientists believe the newfound planets are mostly solid.* ○ *She seemed to be enjoying her newfound celebrity.*

newlywed /ˈnuː·liː ˌwed/ *n* [C] someone who has recently married

new moon *n* [C] a PHASE (= regular change in shape) of the moon in which none of its surface can be seen from the earth ➤ Picture: **moon**

news INFORMATION /nuːz/ *n* [U] recent information about people you know ○ *Why don't you call them and see if there's any news?* ○ *I've got some bad news for you.* ○ *We just heard the good news – congratulations on your engagement!*

newsy /ˈnuː·zi/ *adj* full of news ○ *a long, newsy letter*

REPORTS /nuːz/ *n* [U] a printed or broadcast report of information about important events in the world, the country, or the local area ○ *the nightly news* ○ *I'm pretty disgusted with TV news coverage.* ○ *Where were you when the news of the assassination broke?*

IDIOM with news

• **news to** *someone* to be very surprising to someone ○ *She's expecting a baby? That's news to me.*

newscast /ˈnuːz·kæst/ *n* [C] a radio or television program consisting of news reports

newscaster /ˈnuːz ˌkæs·tər/ *n* [C] someone who reads the reports on a television or radio news program

news conference *n* [C] a meeting in which someone makes a statement to reporters or answers questions from them

newsletter /ˈnuːz ˌlet̬·ər/ *n* [C] a printed document with information about the activities of a group, sent regularly to members or friends

newspaper /ˈnuːz ˌpeɪ·pər, nuːs-/ *n* [C] a document published regularly, consisting of news reports, articles, photographs, and advertisements that are printed on large sheets of paper folded together

newsroom /ˈnuːz·ruːm, -rʊm/ *n* [C] a room in a newspaper office or television or radio station where the news is prepared before it is published or broadcast ○ *The newsroom just received a press release.*

newsstand /ˈnuːz·stænd/ *n* [C] a small structure where newspapers and magazines are sold

newsworthy /ˈnuːz ˌwɜr·ði/ *adj* [not gradable] considered important enough to be in news reports, newspapers, etc.

newt /nuːt/ *n* [C] a small animal with a long body and tail, short, weak legs, and cold, wet skin; a type of SALAMANDER

New Testament *n* [U] the second of the two main parts of the Christian Bible ○ *The New Testament describes the life and work of Jesus Christ.* ○ Compare OLD TESTAMENT

newton /ˈnuːt·ᵊn/ *n* [C] ***physics*** the standard unit for the measure of force, equal to the force that produces a movement of one meter in a second on an object that weighs one kilogram

New World *n* [U] North, Central, and South America, as they were considered by the Europeans after Christopher Columbus traveled there ○ **USAGE:** The phrase "Western Hemisphere" is generally preferred. ○ Compare OLD WORLD

New Year *n* [C usually sing] the beginning of the year that is about to begin or has just begun

New Year's Day *n* [C usually sing] the first day of the year, which is a public holiday in many countries

New Year's Eve *n* [C usually sing] the last day of the year, and esp. the evening of the last day, when many people celebrate

next /nekst/ *pronoun, adj* [not gradable] being the first one after the present one or after the one just mentioned, or being the first after the present moment ○ *Go straight at the traffic light and then take the next right.* ○ *The next time you want to borrow my dress, ask me first.* ○ *She was next in line after me.* ○ *They're getting married next week/month/year.* ○ *The next day/morning we left for Calgary.*

next /nekst/ *adv* [not gradable] **1** immediately following in time ○ *What happened next?* **2** Two people or things that are **next to** each other are very close to each other with nothing in between them: *My friend and I sat next to each other on the bus.* **3** Sometimes **next to** means almost: *They pay me next to nothing but I really enjoy the work.*

IDIOM with next

• **the next best thing** something that is almost as good ○ *If I can't have cake, ice cream is the next best thing.*

next door *adj, adv* [not gradable] beside a building, house, apartment, or other place ○ *next-door neighbors* ○ *Danny lived next door to me when we were kids.*

next of kin *n* [U] a very close family member or family members

NFL *n* [U] *abbreviation for* National Football League (= the main organized group of US football teams that have players who are paid for playing).

NHL *n* [U] *abbreviation for* National Hockey League (= the main organized group of US and Canadian HOCKEY teams that have players who are paid for playing).

nibble /ˈnɪb·əl/ *v* [I/T] **1** to eat something by taking a lot of small bites ○ [T] *Ben stopped nibbling his apple.* ○ [I] *Keep vegetables handy to nibble on.* **2** You can nibble something by moving your teeth against it without eating it: [T] *Fish were nibbling at their hands.*

nibble /ˈnɪb·əl/ *n* [C] ○ *(fig.) The real-estate agent says she's gotten some nibbles for our house* (= some people have expressed interest in it).

N

nice PLEASANT /nɑɪs/ *adj* [*-er/-est* only] pleasant, enjoyable, or satisfactory ○ *Have a nice day!* ○ *It was nice talking to you.* ○ *That's a really nice restaurant.* ○ *She plans to start running more when the weather gets nicer.*
nicely /ˈnɑɪ·sli/ *adv* ○ *That's a nicely tailored jacket.* ○ *Elise and her new baby are both doing nicely* (= They are healthy).

KIND /nɑɪs/ *adj* [*-er/-est* only] kind or friendly ○ *I wish you'd be nice to your brother.* ○ *He's very smart, but he isn't very nice.*
nicely /ˈnɑɪ·sli/ *adv* ○ *Even though I was new at school, they treated me very nicely.*

WORD CHOICES nice

If people are nice because they are generous and helpful to other people, you can say that they are **kind** or **sweet**.

*She's a very **kind** person.*

*Thank you so much for the card – it was very **sweet** of you!*

If something that you do is nice, you can describe it as **fun**, **enjoyable**, or **lovely**.

*We had a really **lovely** day at the beach.*

*You'd have liked the party – it was **fun**.*

If something is nice to look at, then adjectives such as **attractive**, **beautiful**, **pleasant**, **lovely**, and **pretty** are often used.

*There's some **beautiful** mountain scenery in Idaho.*

*That's a **pretty** dress you're wearing.*

If food tastes nice, you can say that it is **delicious** or **tasty**.

*This chicken soup is absolutely **delicious**.*

niche POSITION /nɪtʃ/ *n* [C] **1** a job, position, or place that is very suitable for someone ○ *She's never quite found her niche on television.* **2** ***biology*** A niche is also an organism's specific position or purpose within the group of organisms with which it lives

HOLLOW /nɪtʃ/ *n* [C] a hollow made in a wall, esp. one designed to put a statue in so that it can be seen

nick /nɪk/ *n* [C] a small cut in a surface or an edge ○ *The car was covered with nicks and scratches.*
nick /nɪk/ *v* [T] ○ *He nicked himself shaving.*

IDIOM with nick

• **(just) in the nick of time** at the last possible moment ○ *She fell in the river and was rescued in the nick of time.*

nickel COIN /ˈnɪk·əl/ *n* [C] (in the US and Canada) a coin worth five cents
nickel /ˈnɪk·əl/ *v*

METAL /ˈnɪk·əl/ *n* [U] a silver-white metal ○ *Nickel is useful because of its resistance to corrosion.*

nickname /ˈnɪk·neɪm/ *n* [C] an informal name for someone or sometimes something, used esp. to show affection, and often based on the person's name or a characteristic of the person
nickname /ˈnɪk·neɪm/ *v* [T] ○ *He was so optimistic that his staff nicknamed him Twinkletoes.*

nicotine /ˈnɪk·əˌtiːn/ *n* [U] a poisonous chemical found in tobacco

niece /niːs/ *n* [C] a daughter of someone's brother or sister, or a daughter of someone's husband's or wife's brother or sister ○ Compare NEPHEW

nifty /ˈnɪf·ti/ *adj infml* good, pleasing, or effective ○ *What a nifty little gadget – you can use it for all kinds of things.*

niggling /ˈnɪg·lɪŋ/ *adj* (of thoughts, worries, or details) unimportant but demanding one's attention in an annoying way ○ *She had no niggling doubts like the ones that plagued me.*

nigh /nɑɪ/ *prep, adv* [not gradable] ***literature*** *dated* near in time or space ○ *She believes that the end of the world is nigh.*

night /nɑɪt/ *n* [C/U] the part of every 24-hour period when it is dark because there is no direct light from the sun ○ [C] *I'll be in Pittsburgh on Tuesday night.* ○ [C] *There was a fire last night in the Tremont section of the Bronx.* ○ [U] *It often gets cold here at night.*
nightly /ˈnɑɪt·li/ *adj, adv* [not gradable] happening every night ○ *a nightly news program*
nights /nɑɪts/ *adv* [not gradable] ○ *She works nights* (= at night) *at the hospital.*

WORD FAMILY night

Nouns	night midnight	*Adverbs*	overnight nightly
Adjectives	overnight		

IDIOMS with night

• **night after night** repeatedly for many nights ○ *The howling of the neighbors' dogs kept him awake night after night.*

• **night and day** all the time ○ *He says he wants to be with me night and day.*

nightclub /ˈnɑɪt·klʌb/ *n* [C] a place where people go in the evening to eat and drink, dance, listen to music, or watch entertainment

nightfall /ˈnɑɪt·fɔːl/ *n* [C] the time at the end of the day when it becomes dark

nightgown /ˈnɑɪt·gɑʊn/ *n* [C] a comfortable piece of clothing like a loose dress that women and girls wear in bed

nightlife /ˈnɑɪt·lɑɪf/ *n* [U] the music, entertainment, dancing, and other activities that happen in a city or town in the evening

nightlight /ˈnɑɪt·lɑɪt/ *n* [C] a light that is not bright and is left on through the night to allow you to see if you wake up

nightmare /ˈnɑɪt·mer, -mær/ *n* [C] a very upsetting or frightening dream, or an extremely unpleasant event or experience
nightmarish /ˈnɑɪtˌmer·ɪʃ, -ˌmær-/ *adj* ○ *a nightmarish traffic jam*

night owl *n* [C] someone who prefers to be awake and active at night ○ *My wife's a night owl, but I like to be in bed by 10 o'clock.*

night school *n* [C] a series of classes held in the evening, esp. for adults who work during the day

nighttime /ˈnɑɪt·tɑɪm/ *n* [U] the time in every 24-hour period when it is dark ○ Opposite: DAYTIME

nil /nɪl/ *n* [U] nothing ○ *Investment in the industry has dropped to virtually nil.*

nimble /ˈnɪm·bəl/ *adj* quick and exact in movement or thought; AGILE ○ *a nimble mind* ○ *He tried to catch his friend, but she was too nimble.*

nincompoop /ˈnɪŋ·kəm ˌpuːp/ *n* [C] *infml* a foolish or stupid person

nine /nɑɪn/ *number* **1** 9 ○ *My sister is nine.* ○ *a nine-month prison sentence* **2** Nine can also mean nine o'clock.

ninth /nɑɪnθ/ *adj, adv, n* [C] **1** *She currently ranks ninth in the world.* ○ [C] *Election day falls on the ninth of November this year.* **2** A ninth is one of nine equal parts of something.

nineteen /nɑɪn ˈtiːn, nɑɪnt-/ *number* 19 ○ *Nineteen of the passengers were injured.* ○ *a nineteen-car train*

nineteenth /nɑɪn ˈtiːnθ, nɑɪnt-/ *adj, adv, n* [C] **1** *I was nineteenth in line to renew my driver's license.* ○ [C] *Our next meeting is on the nineteenth of June.* **2** A nineteenth is one of nineteen equal parts of something.

ninety /ˈnɑɪnt·i, ˈnɑɪn·di/ *number* 90 ○ *Grandma just turned ninety.* ○ *a ninety-year-old woman*

nineties, **90s, 90's** /ˈnɑɪnt·iːz, ˈnɑɪn·diːz/ *pl n* the numbers 90 through 99 ○ *It's expected to be in the nineties* (= between 90° and 99°) *tomorrow.* ○ *Inflation was held in check in the nineties* (= between 1990 and 1999). ○ *I know only two people in their nineties* (= between 90 and 99 years old).

ninetieth /ˈnɑɪnt·iː·əθ, ˈnɑɪn·diː-/ *adj, adv, n* [C] **1** *He finished ninetieth in the marathon.* ○ *Mine was the ninetieth signature on the petition.* **2** A ninetieth is one of ninety equal parts of something.

ninny /ˈnɪn·i/ *n* [C] *infml* a foolish person

ninth /nɑinθ/ *adj, adv, n* ○ See at NINE

nip /nɪp/ *v* [I/T] **-pp-** to press something hard between two often sharp objects, such as teeth or the nails on fingers ○ [I/T] *The puppy kept nipping (at) her ankles.*

IDIOMS with nip

- **a nip in the air** a feeling of cold ○ *There's a real nip in the air this morning.*
- **nip and tuck** in a situation in which one side seems to be winning and then the other, so that the result is uncertain ○ *The election was nip and tuck at first, but then Roberts pulled ahead and won.*
- **nip** *something* **in the bud** to stop something before it has an opportunity to develop ○ *We have to nip these money problems in the bud before we get into real trouble.*

nipple /ˈnɪp·əl/ *n* [C] **1** the dark part of the skin in the middle of a human breast, or the similar part of an animal, and through which females can supply milk to their young **2** A nipple is also the part of a bottle used for feeding babies through which liquid comes out.

nippy /ˈnɪp·i/ *adj* [*-er/-est* only] cold ○ *It's a bit nippy outside.*

nit /nɪt/ *n* [C] the egg of an insect, esp. a LOUSE

nite /nɑɪt/ *n* [C] NIGHT

nitpicking /ˈnɪt ˌpɪk·ɪŋ/ *n* [U] the tendency to look for slight mistakes or faults ○ *This constant nitpicking is hard on your friends.*

nitrate /ˈnɑɪ·treɪt/ *n* [C/U] a chemical that is used esp. as a FERTILIZER (= substance that helps plants grow)

nitric acid /ˈnɑɪ·trɪk ˈæs·əd/ *n* [U] ***chemistry*** a clear, colorless liquid that is used in making many chemicals, especially explosives and FERTILIZERS (= substances that help plants to grow)

nitrifying bacteria /ˈnɑɪ·trə ˌfɑɪ·ɪŋ bæk ˈtɪr·iː·ə/ *n* [pl] bacteria in the dirt on the surface of the earth that change the NITROGEN (= gas) in dead plants into a form that growing plants can use for food

nitrogen /ˈnɑɪ·trə·dʒən/ *n* [U] ***biology, chemistry*** a gas, one of the chemical elements, that has no color or taste, is a part of all living things, and forms about 78 percent of the earth's ATMOSPHERE (= mixture of gases surrounding it)

nitrogen cycle *n* [U] ***biology*** the process by which NITROGEN is exchanged between different living organisms on earth and between living organisms and the environment, for example, when plants take it from the air and animals eat the plants

nitrogen-fixing bacteria *n* [pl] ***biology*** bacteria that can absorb NITROGEN from the air and change it into a form that plants can use for food

nitrogenous /nɑɪ ˈtrɑdʒ·ə·nəs/ *adj* [not gradable] ***biology, chemistry*** containing the gas NITROGEN

nitty-gritty /ˌnɪt̬·iː ˈgrɪt̬·i/ *n* [U] *infml* the basic facts of a situation ○ *Let's get down to the nitty-gritty of the actual building costs.*

nitwit /ˈnɪt·wɪt/ *n* [C] a foolish or stupid person

nix /nɪks/ *v* [T] *infml* to stop, forbid, or refuse to accept something ○ *I hoped to get the day off, but the boss nixed it.*

no NOT ANY /noʊ/ *adj* [not gradable] **1** not any; not one; not a ○ *There's no butter left.* ○ *No trees grow near the top of the mountain.* ○ *There's no chance of us getting there by eight.* ○ *She no longer writes to me* (= does not continue to write to me). **2** In signs and official notices, "no" is used to show that something is not allowed: *No hunting/trespassing/swimming*

NEGATIVE ANSWER /noʊ/ *adv* [not gradable] used to give negative answers ○ *"Are you hurt?" "No, I'm OK."* ○ *"Would you like some coffee?" "No, thank you."*

no /noʊ/ *n* [C] *pl* **noes** ○ *The answer is no.*

NOT /noʊ/ *adv* [not gradable] not ○ *It's no colder today than it was yesterday.*

IDIOMS with no

• **in no time (at all)** very quickly ○ *Now that we're on the highway, we'll be there in no time.*

• **in no uncertain terms** very clearly and often unkindly ○ *She was told in no uncertain terms that the magazine had no interest in her short stories.*

• *someone* **is no fool** someone is not easily deceived ○ *The teacher won't believe your little brother took your homework – he's no fool.*

• *something* **is no joke** something is a difficult or serious matter ○ *It's no joke when a virus gets into your computer.*

• *something* **is no object** something is not a difficulty that will prevent something from happening ○ *When he really wanted something, money was no object.*

• *someone* **is no stranger to** *something* someone is familiar with something, esp. something difficult or unpleasant ○ *She's no stranger to hard work.*

• **it's no use** (*doing something*), **there's no use (***doing something*) the thing someone tries cannot be or was not successful ○ *People tried to stop her, but it was no use.* ○ *There's no use asking me about it, because I don't know anything.*

N

• **no doubt** certainly ○ *He will no doubt tell you all about his vacation.*

• **no end of** *something* a lot of something ○ *The twins were no end of trouble.*

• **no go** not allowed or not acceptable ○ *Shorts are no go here – you have to wear long pants and shoes.*

• **no hard feelings** no feeling of being upset ○ *"I'm really sorry." "Don't worry – No hard feelings."* ○ *Yvonne wanted to show there were no hard feelings after I won the contest.*

• **no ifs, ands, or buts** no excuses or doubts ○ *I want no ifs, ands, or buts – give Sam his game back right now.*

• **no kidding** really or honestly ○ *No kidding, there were about a hundred people at Latisha's party.*

• **no laughing matter** very serious ○ *Being late for a job interview is no laughing matter.*

• **no mean** *something* something that is very good ○ *Getting the job finished so quickly was no mean achievement.*

• **no news is good news** if something bad had happened, you would have been told ○ *We haven't heard that they got home safely, but I guess no news is good news.*

• **no problem** *infml* yes, I can do that without any trouble ○ *"Can you pick me up at noon?" "No problem."*

• **no questions asked** without asking questions, esp. in a situation where you would expect questions ○ *If you are not satisfied with your purchase, we will refund your money, no questions asked.*

• **no sooner** *does something happen* **than** *something else happens* a second thing happens immediately after the first ○ *No sooner had I started mowing the lawn, than it started raining.*

• **no sweat** *infml* this is not difficult for me ○ *"Will you be able to fix the light?" "Yeah, no sweat."*

• **no thanks to** *someone* despite someone ○ *We finished the painting, no thanks to Sandra, who decided she had to go away for the weekend.*

• **(there's) no two ways about it** there is no doubt about something ○ *My mom is going to have to come live with us – there's no two ways about it.*

• **no way** *infml* no or not in any way ○ *No way was I going to pay that much for an old, beat-up car.* ○ *"Can I go with you guys?" "No way – this is just for big kids."* ○ **USAGE:** Used to emphasize that you really mean no. ○ Compare NOT A CHANCE at NOT IDIOMS

• **to no avail** *fml* without any success or any effect ○ *The students asked the school to help them raise the money, but to no avail.*

no. /ˈnʌm·bər/ *n* [C] *pl* **nos.** *abbreviation for* number

No. *adj, n* [U] *abbreviation for* NORTH or NORTHERN

Nobel /noʊˈbel, ˈnoʊ·bel/, **Nobel prize** *n* [C] an international prize given each year for achievements in literature, physics, chemistry, medicine, ECONOMICS, and world peace

noble MORAL /ˈnoʊ·bəl/ *adj* having or showing high moral qualities or character ○ *It was a noble effort to achieve a peaceful settlement to the conflict.*

HIGH RANK /ˈnoʊ·bəl/ *adj* [not gradable] having a high social rank, esp. from birth ○ *a noble family related to the queen*

noble /ˈnoʊ·bəl/ *n* [C] a person of high social rank, esp. from birth

nobility /noʊˈbɪl·ət̬·i/ *n* [U] the class or group of people who have a high social rank, esp. from birth

noble gas *n* [C] ***chemistry*** any of a group of gases, such as HELIUM, that do not react with other chemicals

nobody /ˈnoʊ·bəd·i, -ˌbɑd·i/ *pronoun, n* [C] **1** not anyone; no person ○ *Nobody was around to answer the phone.* ○ *If he can't fix your computer, nobody can.* **2** A nobody is also someone who is considered unimportant: *There were celebrities there, but I sat between two nobodies.*

no-brainer /noʊˈbreɪ·nər/ *n* [C] *slang* something so simple or obvious that you do not need to think much about it ○ *Taking that job over the one I had was a no-brainer.*

nocturnal /nɑkˈtɜrn·əl/ *adj* of the night, or active during the night ○ *Most bats and owls are nocturnal.*

nod MOVE HEAD /nɑd/ *v* [I/T] **-dd-** to move the head down and then up again quickly, esp. to show agreement, approval, or greeting ○ [I/T] *The teacher nodded (his head) in agreement.*

nod /nɑd/ *n* [C usually sing] ○ *He gave her a nod of recognition.*

SLEEP /nɑd/ *v* [I] **-dd-** to let your head fall forward when you are beginning to sleep

PHRASAL VERB with nod

• **nod off** to begin to sleep, esp. while sitting up ○ *I nodded off once or twice during the movie.*

node TISSUE /noʊd/ *n* [C] a lump of tissue ○ *a lymph node*

WAVE PATTERN /noʊd/ *n* [C] ***physics*** the point that represents the lowest AMPLITUDE in a pattern of DESTRUCTIVE INTERFERENCE ○ Compare ANTI-NODE

noes /noʊz/ *pl of* NO NEGATIVE ANSWER

no-fault *adj* [not gradable] (of agreements, contracts, etc.) stating that blame does not have to be proved before action can be taken ○ *no-fault insurance*

no-frills *adj* [not gradable] basic, without details or extras ○ *He opted for a no-frills flight to save on expenses.*

no-holds-barred *adj* [not gradable] without limits or controls ○ *She had no regrets about what she said in her no-holds-barred speech.*

noir /nwɑr/, **film noir** *n* [C/U] a type of movie, usually filmed in a city, that shows the world as an unhappy, violent place in which many unpleasant people live, or a film of this type ○ *The film is a classic noir with an unusual mix of political satire.*

noise /nɔɪz/ *n* [C/U] (a) sound, esp. when it is unwanted, unpleasant, or loud ○ [U] *I heard background noise on the phone line.* ○ [C] *If the washing machine gets out of balance, it makes a horrible noise.*

noisy /ˈnɔɪ·zi/ *adj* [*-er/-est* only] ○ *The garbage truck is so noisy it wakes me up in the morning.*

WORD FAMILY noise

Nouns	noise	*Adverbs*	noisily
Adjectives	noisy		

nomad /ˈnoʊ·mæd/ *n* [C] a member of a group of people who move from one place to another, rather than living in one place all of the time

nomadic /noʊˈmæd·ɪk/ *adj* ○ *nomadic people*

no-man's-land *n* [C usually sing] an area or strip of land that no one owns or controls, such as a strip of land between two countries' borders

nomenclature /ˈnoʊ·mənˌkleɪ·tʃər/ *n* [C] a system for naming things, esp. in a particular area of science ○ *the nomenclature of nuclear physics*

nominal NOT IN REALITY /ˈnɑm·ən·əl/ *adj* [not gradable] in name or thought, but not in reality ○ *He's the nominal head of the university.*

SMALL /ˈnɑm·ən·əl/ *adj* [not gradable] (of a sum of money) very small compared to an expected price or value ○ *There is a nominal fee for the workshop.*

nominate /ˈnɑm·əˌneɪt/ *v* [T] **1** to officially suggest someone for a position, an honor, or election ○ *She was nominated by the president to serve on the Supreme Court.* **2** If someone or something is nominated for a prize, it is one of the official competitors for it.

nomination /ˌnɑm·əˈneɪ·ʃən/ *n* [C/U] ○ [U] *Three candidates are seeking the Democratic nomination for the presidency.*

nominative /ˈnɑm·ə·nət̬·ɪv/ *adj* [not gradable] ***grammar*** having or relating to the CASE (= form) of a noun, pronoun, or adjective used to show that a word is the subject of a verb

nominee /ˌnɑm·əˈniː/ *n* [C] a person who has been officially suggested for a position, an honor, or election ○ *He is a nominee for best actor.*

non- /nɑn/ *prefix* used to add the meaning "not" to adjectives and nouns ○ *nonexistent* ○ *nonflammable* ○ *nonpartisan*

nonchalant /ˌnɑn·ʃəˈlɑnt/ *adj* [not gradable] behaving in a calm manner, showing that you are not worried or frightened ○ *She waited her turn to audition, trying to look nonchalant.*

nonchalantly /ˌnɑn·ʃəˈlɑnt·li/ *adv* [not gradable] ○ *Once on a safari Charles found 14 female lions walking nonchalantly across an open field.*

nonchalance /ˌnɑn·ʃəˈlɑns/ *n* [U]

noncombatant /ˌnɑn·kəmˈbæt·ənt/ *n* [C] a person who is part of a military group, but whose job does not include fighting ○ *Medics, chaplains, and other noncombatants were part of the regiment.*

noncommittal /ˌnɑn·kəˈmɪt̬·əl/ *adj* [not gradable] not expressing a clear opinion or decision ○ *The ambassador was noncommittal about the introduction of further sanctions.*

nonconformist Ⓐ /ˌnɑn·kəmˈfɔːr·məst/ *n* [C] a person who does not live and think according to accepted customs and standards

nonconformity Ⓐ /ˌnɑn·kəmˈfɔːr·mət̬·i/ *n* [U] the condition of not acting or not thinking like other people, esp. in relation to religion ○ *William Penn was expelled from Oxford for nonconformity.*

nondescript /ˌnɑn·dɪˈskrɪpt/ *adj* [not gradable] having no interesting or unusual features; ordinary ○ *A nondescript couple sat next to her in the waiting room.*

none /nʌn/ *pronoun* not one, or not any ○ *None of my children has blue eyes.* ○ *"Is there any more orange juice?" "I'm sorry, there's none left."*

none /nʌn/ *adv* [not gradable]

IDIOMS with none

• **none other than** *someone/something* the very famous or important person or thing ○ *The speech was given by none other than the vice president.*

• **none the wiser**, **not be any the wiser 1** to not understand something ○ *I read the computer manual, but I'm still none the wiser.* **2** To be **none the wiser** means to not be aware of something: *The health department gave the restaurant a warning, but the customers were none the wiser.*

• **none the worse (for** *something***)** not damaged or harmed despite something ○ *It was cold and windy during the parade but we were none the worse for the weather.*

N

• **none too** not very ○ *He seemed none too happy at the prospect of meeting the family.*

nonelectrolyte /ˌnɑn·ɪˈlek·trəˌlɑɪt/ *n* [C] ***chemistry*** a substance that dissolves in water to produce a liquid that electricity does not go through

nonentity /nɑn ˈent·ət̬·i/ *n* [C] a person or thing of no importance ○ *It's a low-budget film full of nonentities.*

nonetheless Ⓐ /ˌnʌn·ðəˈles/ *adv* [not gradable] despite what has just been said or referred to; NEVERTHELESS ○ *There are possible risks, but nonetheless, we feel it's a sound investment.*

nonexistent /ˌnɑn·ɪɡˈzɪs·tənt/ *adj* [not gradable] completely absent ○ *Crime is virtually nonexistent around here.*

nonfiction /ˈnɑnˈfɪk·ʃən/ *n* [U] ***literature*** the type of book or other writing that deals with facts about real people or events, not imaginary stories ○ Compare FICTION

nonflammable /nɑnˈflæm·ə·bəl/ *adj* not able to burn ○ *nonflammable clothing*

nongovernmental /ˌnɑnˌɡʌv·ərnˈment·əl, -ˌɡʌv·ər-/ *adj* not part of or controlled by the government ○ *a nongovernmental organization*

nonmetal /nɑnˈmet·əl/ *n* [C] ***chemistry*** a chemical element that is not a metal

no-no *n* [C] *infml* something that is thought to be unsuitable or unacceptable ○ *Wearing shorts to work is a no-no.*

no-nonsense *adj* [not gradable] serious and practical ○ *Barnes has a quiet, no-nonsense manner of doing business.*

nonpartisan /nɑnˈpɑrt̬·ə·zən, -sən/ *adj* not a member of or connected with a group or political party ○ *a nonpartisan organization/voter/watchdog group*

nonpayment /ˈnɑnˈpeɪ·mənt/ *n* [U] failure to pay an amount that is expected ○ *He has a long record of nonpayment of traffic violations.*

nonplacental /ˌnɑn·pləˈsent·əl/ *adj* [not gradable] ***biology*** relating to mammals such as MARSUPIALS whose babies, which are not fully developed at birth, continue to develop outside the mother's uterus

nonplussed /nɑnˈplʌst/ *adj* surprised, confused, and not certain how to react ○ *The aggressive questioning at the job interview left her nonplussed.*

nonpolar /ˌnɑnˈpoʊ·lər/ *adj* [not gradable] ***chemistry*** describes a substance whose MOLECULES do not have opposite positive and negative POLES ELECTRICITY

nonprofit /ˈnɑnˈprɑf·ət/ *adj* [not gradable] not established to make a profit ○ *nonprofit organizations*

nonprofit /ˈnɑnˈprɑf·ət/ *n* [C] an organization whose most important goal is something that does not involve making a profit ○ *We can help by making donations to nonprofits that serve the homeless.*

nonproliferation /ˌnɑn·prəˌlɪf·əˈreɪ·ʃən/ *n* [U] the effort to stop the increase in nuclear weapons

nonsectarian /ˌnɑnˌsekˈter·iː·ən/ *adj* [not gradable] not connected with any specific religion ○ *About 1,500 students attend 23 nonsectarian private schools.*

nonsense /ˈnɑn·sens, -səns/ *n* [U] **1** foolish words or actions ○ *Those accusations are pure/sheer nonsense.* ○ *What's all this nonsense about quitting school?* **2** Nonsense is also language that cannot be understood or that has no meaning.

nonsensical /nɑnˈsen·sɪ·kəl/ *adj* [not gradable]

non sequitur /nɑnˈsek·wət̬·ər/ *n* [C] a statement that does not relate in a clear, reasonable way to the previous statement

nonsmoker /nɑnˈsmoʊ·kər/ *n* [C] a person who does not smoke cigarettes or other tobacco products

nonsmoking /nɑnˈsmoʊ·kɪŋ/ *adj* [not gradable] (of a place) where smoking is not permitted

nonstandard /nɑnˈstæn·dərd/ *adj* [not gradable] not standard; different from a standard, and often considered not correct ○ *"Drownded" is a nonstandard pronunciation for "drowned."*

nonstop /ˈnɑnˈstɑp/ *adj, adv* [not gradable] (of travel) without any stops, or (of an action) done without stopping ○ *We got on a nonstop flight from New York to Denver.* ○ *He talked nonstop about his new book.*

nontraditional Ⓐ /ˌnɑn·trəˈdɪʃ·ən·əl/ *adj* different from what was considered usual or typical in the past ○ *nontraditional families/medicine/methods*

nonviolent /nɑnˈvɑɪ·ə·lənt/ *adj* [not gradable] not using violent methods, esp. to cause a political or social change ○ *The protest demonstration was nonviolent, although the marchers were heckled throughout by onlookers.*

nonviolence /nɑnˈvɑɪ·ə·ləns/ *n* [U] the use of methods that are not violent to cause a political or social change

nonwhite /nɑnˈhwɑɪt, -ˈwɑɪt/ *adj* [not gradable] not belonging to a race that has pale skin

noodle /ˈnuːd·əl/ *n* [C usually pl] a long, thin strip of pasta made from flour, water, and sometimes eggs, and cooked esp. in boiling water or soup

nook /nʊk/ *n* [C] a small space that is hidden or partly sheltered

noon /nuːn/ *n* [U] 12 o'clock in the middle of the day; MIDDAY ○ *My first class is at noon.*

no one /ˈnoʊ·wən, -wʌn/ *pronoun* not any person ○ *I called twice, but no one answered.*

noontime /ˈnuːn·tɑɪm/ *n* [U] 12 o'clock in the middle of the day; NOON ○ *He frequents the restaurant at noontime.*
noontime /ˈnuːn·tɑɪm/ *adj* [not gradable]

noose /nuːs/ *n* [C] one end of a rope tied to form a circle which can be tightened around something, such as a person's neck to HANG (= kill) the person

nope /noʊp/ *adv* [not gradable] *infml* (esp. used in spoken answers) no ○ *"Are you coming along?" "Nope."*

nor /nɔːr, nər/ *conjunction* used before the second or last of a series of negative possibilities that usually begin with "neither" ○ *Neither Michael nor his wife was injured in the crash.*

nor'easter /nɔːrˈiː·stər/ *n* [C] a NORTHEASTER (= a storm with northeast winds)

norm Ⓐ /nɔːrm/ *n* [C] an accepted standard or a way of being or doing things ○ *Illness has become the norm for her.*

normal Ⓐ **NOT UNUSUAL** /ˈnɔːr·məl/ *adj* ordinary or usual; as would be expected ○ *He seemed perfectly normal to me.* ○ *The temperature is above/below normal today.*
normality Ⓐ /nɔːrˈmæl·ət̬·i/, **normalcy** /ˈnɔːr·məl·si/ *n* [U] the state of being normal
normalize Ⓐ /ˈnɔːr·məˌlɑɪz/ *v* [I/T] to return to the usual or generally accepted situation ○ [T] *They hope to normalize relations with the US.*
normalization Ⓐ /ˌnɔːr·mə·ləˈzeɪ·ʃən, -lɑɪ-/ *n* [U]
normally Ⓐ /ˈnɔːr·mə·li/ *adv* usually or regularly ○ *She doesn't normally stop working to have lunch.*

WORD CHOICES normal

The word **natural** can be used instead of "normal" when talking about feelings.

*It's completely **natural** to feel anxious on your first day at a new school.*

If you are talking about what is normal because it happens most often, you can use the word **usual**.

*I went to bed at my **usual** time.*

If someone or something is normal because that person or thing is not different in any way, the word **ordinary** can be used.

*The magazine has stories about **ordinary** people rather than celebrities.*

Standard describes something that is normal because it is correct or acceptable in a particular job or situation.

*It's **standard** practice for surgeons to wear gloves.*

If something or someone is normal because that thing or person shows the characteristics you would expect, you can use the word **typical**.

*He was a **typical** teenager – arguing with his parents and staying out late.*

LINE /ˈnɔːr·məl/ *n* [C] ***physics*** a line that is PERPENDICULAR (= at an angle of 90 degrees) to a surface

WORD FAMILY normal

Nouns	normality/normalcy abnormality	*Adjectives*	normal abnormal
Adverbs	normally abnormally		

normal force *n* [U] ***physics*** the amount of force that keeps two surfaces touching, but does not let them come apart or press further together

north /nɔːrθ/, *abbreviation* **N.**, *abbreviation* **No.** *n* [U] **1** the direction that is opposite south, or the part of an area or country which is in this direction ○ *The points of the compass are north, south, east, and west.* **2** In the US, the North is the part of the country in the north and east: *Ken grew up in Mississippi but settled in the North after college.* **3** ***US history*** In the US Civil War, the North was the group of states that fought to keep the US together.
north /nɔːrθ/, *abbreviation* **N.**, *abbreviation* **No.** *adj, adv* [not gradable] **1** *the north coast* ○ *She lives about forty miles north of here.* **2** A north wind is a wind coming from the north.
northerly /ˈnɔːr·ðər·li/ *adj* toward or near the north ○ *a northerly route*
northern /ˈnɔːr·ðərn/, *abbreviation* **N.**, *abbreviation* **No.** *adj* [not gradable] ○ *Tom lives in the northern part of the state.*
northerner /ˈnɔːr·ðər·nər, -ðə·nər/ *n* [C] a person from the northern part of a country, or (in the US) a person from the part of the country in the north and east
northward /ˈnɔːrθ·wərd/ *adj* [not gradable] toward the north ○ *northward migration*
northward /ˈnɔːrθ·wərd/, **northwards** /ˈnɔːrθ·wərdz/ *adv* [not gradable] ○ *He headed northward.*

WORD FAMILY north

Nouns	north northerner	*Adjectives*	north northerly northern northward
Adverbs	north northward		

northeast /nɔːrˈθiːst/, *abbreviation* **N.E.** *n* [U] the direction between north and east, or the part of an area or country which is in this direction ○ *A snowstorm brought an inch of snow to the northeast.*
northeast /nɔːrˈθiːst/, *abbreviation* **N.E.** *adj, adv* [not gradable] ○ *Betsy lives in the northeast corner of Vermont.*
northeastern /nɔːrˈθiː·stərn/, *abbreviation* **N.E.** *adj* [not gradable] ○ *northeastern Arizona*
northeaster /nɔːrˈiː·stər, nɔːrθ-/, **nor'easter** /nɔːrˈiː·stər/ *n* [C] a storm with northeast winds, or a strong wind coming from the northeast

Northern Lights *pl n* patterns of colors in the sky that can be seen at night in extreme northern parts of the world

North Pole *n* [U] the point on the earth's surface that is farthest north

northwest /nɔːrθˈwest/, *abbreviation* **N.W.** *n* [U] the direction between north and west, or the part of an area or country which is in this direction ○ *Seattle is in the northwest.*

northwest /nɔːrθˈwest/, *abbreviation* **N.W.** *adj, adv* [not gradable] ○ *The plane crashed six miles northwest of the airport.*

northwestern /nɔːrθˈwes·tərn/, *abbreviation* **N.W.** *adj* [not gradable] ○ *northwestern Mexico*

nose BODY PART /noʊz/ *n* [C] the part of a person's or animal's face above the mouth through which the person or animal breathes and smells ○ *He fractured a wrist and broke his nose in a fall.* ○ *I have a runny nose* (= liquid coming out of the nose). ○ *She blew her nose* (= breathed out through the nose to clear it). ○ Related adjective: NASAL

FRONT /noʊz/ *n* [C] the front of a vehicle, esp. an aircraft or spacecraft

nose /noʊz/ *v* [always + adv/prep] to move forward slowly and carefully ○ [I] *The car nosed out into traffic.*

SEARCH /noʊz/ *v* [I always + adv/prep] *infml* to look around or search in order to discover something, esp. something that other people do not want you to find ○ *I don't want you nosing around in my closet.*

IDIOMS with nose

• **on the nose** exactly correct or the exact amount ○ *He weighs 175 pounds on the nose.*

• **stick** *your* **nose into** *something*, **poke/put** *your* **nose into** *something infml* to try to discover things which do not involve you ○ *You're always sticking your nose into my business.*

N

nosebleed /ˈnoʊz·bliːd/ *n* [C] a period of bleeding from the nose

nosedive /ˈnoʊz·dɑɪv/ *n* [C] (esp. of an aircraft) a fast and sudden fall to the ground with the front pointing down ○ (*fig.*) *Stock prices took a nosedive* (= a sudden fall in value).

nosedive /ˈnoʊz·dɑɪv/ *v* [I] ○ (*fig.*) *Profits nosedived in the last quarter.*

nosh /nɑʃ/ *n* [U] *infml* a small amount of food eaten between meals or as a meal

nosh /nɑʃ/ *v* [I] *infml* ○ *We noshed on pretzels during the game.*

no-show *n* [C] a person who is expected but does not arrive ○ *Airlines overbook some flights because they count on a certain number of no-shows.*

nostalgia /nɑˈstæl·dʒə, nə-; nəˈstɑl-/ *n* [U] a feeling of pleasure and sometimes slight sadness at the same time as you think about things that happened in the past ○ *Hearing her voice again filled him with nostalgia.*

nostalgic /nɑˈstæl·dʒɪk, nə-; nəˈstɑl-/ *adj* ○ *Jenny grew nostalgic for home on Thanksgiving Day.*

nostril /ˈnɑs·trəl/ *n* [C] either of the two openings in the nose through which air moves

nosy, **nosey** /ˈnoʊ·zi/ *adj* too interested in what other people are doing and wanting to discover too much about them ○ *I was a nosy kid.*

not /nɑt/ *adv* [not gradable] **1** used to make a word or group of words negative, or to give a word or words an opposite meaning ○ *Her life was not happy.* ○ *If it's not yours, whose is it?* ○ *He's not bad-looking* (= He is attractive). ○ *She was* **not only** *an excellent teacher* **but (also)** *a brilliant researcher* (= she was both these things). ○ **Not that** *I mind* (= I do not mind), *but why didn't you call yesterday?* **2 Not-too-distant** refers to a time in the near future or recent past: *They plan to have children in the not-too-distant future.*

USAGE

not...either

The words **not...either** are used to add another piece of negative information.

I do not have my credit card with me and I do not have any cash either.

~~*I do not have my credit card with me and I do not have any cash neither.*~~

Shona didn't like the movie, and Helen didn't enjoy it either.

~~*Shona didn't like the movie, and Helen didn't enjoy it too.*~~

IDIOMS with not

• **not a chance** there is no possibility ○ *"Do you think I could pass for a 21-year-old?" "Not a chance!"* ○ Compare NO WAY at NO IDIOMS ○ **USAGE**: Used as an answer to a question.

• **not at all** I do not mind ○ *"Do you mind if I sit here?" "Not at all."* ○ **USAGE**: Used to answer a question.

• **not** *your* **day** a bad day when things do not happen as you would like them to ○ *I missed my bus and forgot my glasses – I guess it's just not my day.* ○ Compare ONE OF THOSE DAYS at ONE IDIOMS

• **not** *yourself* not feeling well or not acting in your usual way ○ *I'm sorry for crying – I'm not myself today.*

• **not to mention** (*someone/something*) and something else, even more than the first thing ○ *Bananas were scarce, not to mention mangoes.*

notable /ˈnoʊt̬·ə·bəl/ *adj* important and deserving attention ○ *She worked with many notable musicians.*

notably /ˈnoʊt̬·ə·bli/ *adv* ○ *Other sports have had work stoppages, most notably baseball.*

notary (public) /ˈnoʊt̬·ə·ri (ˈpʌb·lɪk)/ *n* [C] *pl* **notaries (public)** *law* an official who has the legal authority to say that documents are correctly signed or truthful

notarize /ˈnoʊt̬·əˌrɑɪz/ *v* [T] *law* ○ *Do these signatures have to be notarized?*

notation /noʊˈteɪ·ʃən/ *n* [C/U] **1** ***mathematics*** the system of written symbols used esp. in mathematics **2** ***music*** Musical notation is the system of symbols used to write music.

notch CUT /nɑtʃ/ *n* [C] a cut in a hard surface ○ *The rope had jammed in a V-shaped notch.*

notch /nɑtʃ/ *v* [T] ○ *He notched the end of the beam.*

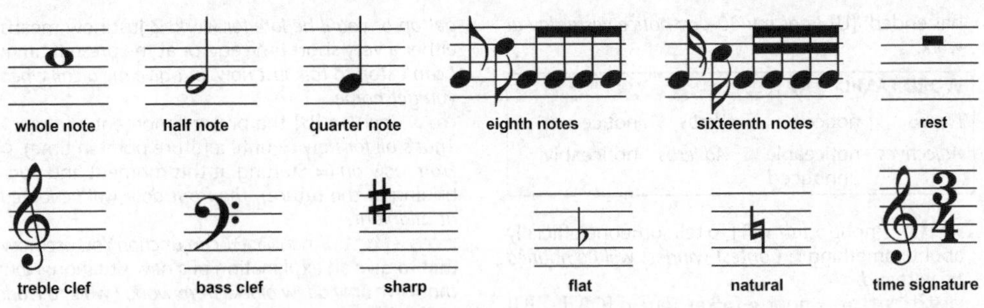

MUSICAL NOTATION

POSITION /nɑtʃ/ *n* [C] an imaginary point or position in a comparison of amounts or values; degree ○ *Suddenly he raised his voice a notch.*

RECORD /nɑtʃ/ *v* [T] to achieve or keep a record of something ○ *Her band notched another Grammy Award last night.*

note **WRITING** /noʊt/ *n* [C] **1** a short piece of writing ○ *a handwritten note* ○ *Make a note to phone him* (= Write it down so you remember). **2** A note is a piece of information that you write down while something is happening: [C usually pl] *Be sure to take notes in class* (= write down information).

SOUND /noʊt/ *n* [C] **1** a single sound, esp. in music, or a written symbol which represents this sound ○ *Her soprano voice intoned the low, first notes of the song.* **2** *fig.* Note also means the particular quality of an emotion or feeling: *The meeting ended on an optimistic note.*

NOTICE /noʊt/ *v* [T] to take notice of, give attention to, or make a record of something ○ [+ *that* clause] *Please note that we will be closed on Saturday.*

IMPORTANCE /noʊt/ *n* importance or fame ○ *There was nothing* **of note** *in the report.*

noted /ˈnoʊt̬·əd/ *adj* ○ *a noted scholar*

notebook **BOOK OF PAPER** /ˈnoʊt·bʊk/ *n* [C] a book of paper for writing on ○ *She wrote everything down in her notebook.*

SMALL COMPUTER /ˈnoʊt·bʊk/ *n* [C] a small, light computer

noteworthy /ˈnoʊtˌwɜr·ði/ *adj* deserving attention because of being important or interesting ○ *Two noteworthy films open this week.*

nothing /ˈnʌθ·ɪŋ/ *pronoun* **1** not anything ○ *There's nothing in the drawer – I took everything out.* ○ *Money means nothing to him* (= is not important). ○ *The score is Yankees three, Red Sox nothing* (= no points). ○ *The story was* **nothing but** (= only) *lies.* **2** If something is **nothing to** someone, it has little meaning or value to the person: *Losing a thousand bucks is nothing to him.* **3** Someone or something that has **nothing to do with** something else is not involved with it: *That has nothing to do with me.* **4** People say something is nothing as a polite answer when they are thanked: *"Thanks for the tickets." "Oh, it's nothing."*

nothingness /ˈnʌθ·ɪŋ·nəs/ *n* [U] a state or place where nothing is present, or where nothing important is present

IDIOMS with nothing

• **nothing could be further from the truth** what has been suggested is completely untrue ○ *I'm certainly not in love with him – nothing could be further from the truth!*

• **nothing less than** *something*, **nothing short of** *something* **1** only a particular quality in something, and not worse ○ *The chef will accept nothing less than perfection from his kitchen staff.* **2 Nothing less than** is also used to show something is very important or serious: *The president proposed nothing less than a complete overhaul of the tax system.* ○ **USAGE:** Used to emphasize how important or difficult an activity is.

• **nothing like** *something* not nearly as good as ○ *Instant coffee is OK, but it's nothing like the real thing.*

• **nothing much** very little ○ *"What's up?" "Nothing much."* ○ *I had nothing much to do that day.*

• **nothing special** neither very good nor very bad ○ *Dinner was nothing special.*

• **nothing to sneeze at** something that deserves serious attention, esp. an amount of money ○ *An extra two thousand bucks a year is nothing to sneeze at.*

notice **SEE** /ˈnoʊt̬·əs/ *v* to become aware of, esp. by looking; to see ○ [I] *Mary waved but he didn't seem to notice.* ○ [+ *that* clause] *He noticed that she was staring at him.*

notice /ˈnoʊt̬·əs/ *n* [U] ○ *Twain first attracted notice* (= attention) *as a humorist.*

noticeable /ˈnoʊt̬·ə·sə·bəl/ *adj* easy to see or recognize ○ *There's a noticeable improvement in your grades.*

noticeably /ˈnoʊt̬·ə·sə·bli/ *adv* ○ *It's gotten noticeably colder this week.*

INFORMATION /ˈnoʊt̬·əs/ *n* [C/U] **1** something written or printed that gives information or instructions ○ [C] *We got a notice about recycling in the mail.* ○ [U] *This building is closed until further notice* (= until official instructions are given). **2** Notice is also warning that something will happen or needs to happen: [U] *I can't cancel my plans on such short notice/at a moment's notice* (= immediately). **3** Notice is also an official statement saying you are leaving your job or telling you your job

N

has ended: [U] *I got my 30-day notice yesterday at work.*

WORD FAMILY notice			
Nouns	notice	*Verbs*	notice
Adjectives	noticeable unnoticed	*Adverbs*	noticeably

notify /ˈnoʊt̬·əˌfɑɪ/ *v* [T] to tell someone officially about something ○ *Contest winners will be notified by postcard.*

notification /ˌnoʊt̬·ə·fəˈkeɪ·ʃən/ *n* [C/U] ○ [U] *Final notification should reach teachers by March 15.*

notion Ⓐ /ˈnoʊ·ʃən/ *n* [C] a belief or idea ○ *Nast helped form the American notion of Santa Claus.*

notoriety /ˌnoʊt̬·əˈrɑɪ·ət̬·i/ *n* [U] the state of being famous for doing something, esp. something immoral or bad ○ *She isn't happy about the notoriety of the mayor.*

notorious /nəˈtɔːr·iː·əs, -ˈtoʊr-/ *adj* famous for something immoral or bad ○ *The canal is notorious for its pollution.*

notoriously /nəˈtɔːr·iː·ə·sli, -ˈtoʊr-/ *adv*

notwithstanding Ⓐ /ˌnɑt·wɪθˈstæn·dɪŋ, -wɪð-/ *prep, adv* not considering or being influenced by; despite ○ *Injuries notwithstanding, this season has been a disappointment to me.*

noun /nɑʊn/ *n* [C] ***grammar*** a word that refers to a person, place, thing, event, substance, or quality ○ *"Doctor," "party," and "beauty" are nouns.*

N

nourish /ˈnɜr·ɪʃ, ˈnʌ·rɪʃ/ *v* [T] to provide people or animals with food in order to make them grow and keep them healthy

nourishing /ˈnɜr·ɪ·ʃɪŋ, ˈnʌ·rɪ·ʃɪŋ/ *adj* ○ *Candy isn't very nourishing.*

nourishment /ˈnɜr·ɪʃ·mənt, ˈnʌ·rɪʃ-/ *n* [U] ○ *A young baby gets its nourishment from its mother's milk.*

novel **BOOK** /ˈnɑv·əl/ *n* [C] ***literature*** a long, printed story about imaginary characters and events ○ *literary/romance novels*

novelist /ˈnɑv·əl·əst/ *n* [C] ***writing*** a person who writes novels

NEW /ˈnɑv·əl/ *adj* new and original; not like anything seen before ○ *a novel idea/suggestion*

novelty /ˈnɑv·əl·ti/ *n* [C/U] the quality of being new or unusual, or a new or unusual experience ○ [U] *The novelty of the toys soon wore off.*

November /noʊˈvem·bər/, *abbreviation* **Nov.** *n* [C/U] the eleventh month of the year, after October and before December

novice /ˈnɑv·əs/ *n* [C] a person who is beginning to learn a job or an activity and has little or no experience or skill in it ○ *I'm just a novice at making videos.*

now **AT PRESENT** /nɑʊ/ *adv* [not gradable] **1** at the present time rather than in the past or future, or immediately ○ *She used to work in an office, but now she works at home.* ○ *It's now 7 o'clock, time to get up or you'll be late for work.* **2** Just now means either a very short time ago or at the present time: *I can't stop to talk just now, but give me a call when you get home.*

now /nɑʊ/ *n* [U] the present moment or time ○ *That's all for now* (= until a future point in time). ○ *From now on* (= Starting at this moment and continuing in the future)*, the front door will be locked at midnight.*

now (that) /ˈnɑʊ (ðət)/ *conjunction* You use now that to give an explanation of a new situation: *Now that I live only a few blocks from work, I walk to work and enjoy it.*

IN SPEECH /nɑʊ/ *adv* [not gradable] used in statements and questions to introduce or give emphasis to what you are saying ○ *Now where was I before you interrupted me?*

IDIOM with now

• **(every) now and then, (every) now and again** sometimes but not very often ○ *We still meet for lunch now and then, but not as often as we used to.* ○ Compare EVERY ONCE IN A WHILE at EVERY IDIOMS

nowadays /ˈnɑʊ·əˌdeɪz/ *adv* [not gradable] at the present time, in comparison to the past ○ *Nowadays people don't dress up as much as they used to.*

nowhere /ˈnoʊ·hwer, -wer, -hwær, -wær/ *adv* [not gradable] in, at, or to no place; not anywhere ○ *Nowhere in the statement did he apologize for what he had done.* ○ *Nowhere else will you find such wonderful beaches.*

IDIOMS with nowhere

• **get nowhere (fast), go nowhere (fast)** to completely fail to achieve something ○ *He was trying to persuade her to let him drive, but he was getting nowhere fast.*

• **nowhere near** not in any way ○ *The operation had already been going on for eight hours, and it was nowhere near finished.*

• **nowhere to be found** not able to be seen ○ *We looked for her everywhere, but she was nowhere to be found.*

no-win *adj* [not gradable] not allowing for success ○ *a no-win situation*

noxious /ˈnɑk·ʃəs/ *adj* (esp. of a gas) poisonous or harmful ○ *noxious gases*

nozzle /ˈnɑz·əl/ *n* [C] a narrow piece attached to the end of a tube so that the liquid or air that comes out can be directed in a particular way ○ *Attach the nozzle to the garden hose before turning on the water.*

nuance /ˈnuː·ɑns/ *n* [C] a quality of something that is not easy to notice but may be important ○ *Actors have to study the nuances of facial expression to show the whole range of emotions.*

nuanced /ˈnuː·ɑnst/ *adj* ○ *He gives a beautifully nuanced performance in a tricky role.*

nuclear Ⓐ **OF ATOMS** /ˈnuː·kliː·ər, *not standard* ˈnuː·kjə·lər/ *adj* [not gradable] **1** ***physics*** of or relating to a process by which the NUCLEUS (= central part) of an atom is divided or joined to another nucleus, resulting in the release of energy **2** relating to weapons, or the use of weapons, in which an atom is divided or joined to another nucleus to release energy in a destructive way ○ *nuclear war* ○ *nuclear disarmament* (= giving up or removing a country's nuclear weapons)

OF CELLS /ˈnuː·kliː·ər/ *adj* [not gradable] ***biology*** of or relating to the NUCLEUS of a cell

nuclear family *n* [C] a social unit of two parents and their children ○ *We average fewer than two children per nuclear family.* ○ Compare EXTENDED FAMILY

nuclear reactor *n* [C] a large device that produces nuclear energy

nuclear waste *n* [C/U] the unwanted RADIOACTIVE material that is created when producing nuclear power

nuclease /ˈnuː·kliːˌeɪs, -ˌeɪz/ *n* [C] ***biology*** a type of ENZYME (= chemical in cells) that can divide a NUCLEIC ACID into its basic parts

nucleic acid /nuːˈkliː·ɪk ˈæs·əd, -ˈkleɪ-/ *n* [C/U] ***biology*** a type of acid, for example, DNA and RNA, that is found in all living cells and contains the GENETIC information passed from parents to children

nucleus /ˈnuː·kliː·əs/ *n* [C] *pl* **nuclei 1** the central part of something **2** People or things that form the nucleus of something are the most important part of it: *These two people will form the nucleus of a new management team to promote sales in South America.* **3** ***physics*** A nucleus is the central part of an atom. ➤ Picture: **atom 4** ***biology*** A nucleus is the central part of a cell that controls its growth. ➤ Picture: **amoeba; cell**

nuclear /ˈnuː·kliː·ər, *not standard* ˈnuː·kjə·lər/ *adj*

nuclide /ˈnuː·klɑɪd/ *n* [C] ***chemistry, physics*** a type of atom having a specific number of PROTONS and NEUTRONS

nude /nuːd/ *adj* [not gradable] not wearing any clothes

nude /nuːd/ *n* [C] **1** a picture or other piece of art showing a person who is not wearing any clothes **2** If you are **in the nude**, you are not wearing any clothes: *The first Olympians of ancient Greece competed in the nude.*

nudist /ˈnuːd·əst/ *n* [C] a person who believes that not wearing clothes is healthy and who is often part of a group of people who meet to practice their belief

nudity /ˈnuːd·ət̬·i/ *n* [U] the state of wearing no clothes

nudge /nʌdʒ/ *v* [T] to push someone or something gently, sometimes to get someone's attention ○ *My wife nudged me to tell me to get off the phone so that she could use it.*

nudge /nʌdʒ/ *n* [C] ○ *I gave him a nudge to wake him up.*

nugget /ˈnʌɡ·ət/ *n* [C] a small, rough lump, esp. of gold ○ *a gold nugget*

nuisance /ˈnuː·səns/ *n* [C] something or someone that annoys you or causes trouble for you ○ *It's a nuisance filling out all these forms.*

nuke /nuːk/ *v* [T] *infml* **1** to bomb with nuclear weapons **2** *slang* To nuke food is to cook it in a MICROWAVE.

nuke /nuːk/ *n* [C] *infml* a nuclear weapon ○ *Signs reading "No nukes!" were everywhere.*

null and void /ˈnʌl·ənd ˈvɔɪd/ *adj* [not gradable] *law* (of an agreement or contract) having no legal effect and to be considered therefore as if it did not exist

nullify /ˈnʌl·əˌfɑɪ/ *v* [T] to cause an agreement or result to be no longer effective or consider it as not existing ○ *The referee nullified the goal.*

numb /nʌm/ *adj* [-er/-est only] **1** (of a part of the body) unable to feel anything ○ *My fingers are so cold, they're numb.* **2** If you are numb with a strong emotion, you are not able to feel anything else or to think clearly: *At the sound of breaking glass, she went numb with fear.*

numbness /ˈnʌm·nəs/ *n* [U]

number SYMBOL /ˈnʌm·bər/, *abbreviation* **no.** *n* [C] *pl* **nos. 1** a unit or its symbol that forms part of a system of counting and calculating, and that represents an amount or position in a series ○ *You can write numbers in words, such as six, seven, and eight, or with symbols, such as 6, 7, and 8.* **2** A number is also a specific set of symbols in a particular order that represent someone or something: *Please write down your Social Security number.* **3** A number can also be a position in a series: *We're up to 10 – who has the next number?*

number /ˈnʌm·bər/ *v* [T] to give a different number to each of two or more things, esp. in a particular order ○ *The software automatically numbers the footnotes.*

AMOUNT /ˈnʌm·bər/ *n* [C/U] **1** an amount or total ○ [C] *A large number of tickets were sold almost immediately.* ○ [C] *Large numbers of people* (= A lot of people) *crowded the streets.* ○ [U] *Quite a number of* (= Many) *cases of the flu have been reported already.* **2** A number of things is several of them: [U] *There were a number of causes for the accident.* **3** Any number of things is a lot of them: [U] *He'd already heard any number of excuses.*

number /ˈnʌm·bər/ *v* [L] to be (a total) ○ *The crowd numbered over 100,000.* ➤ Usage: **amount of or number of?** at AMOUNT

GRAMMAR /ˈnʌm·bər/ *n* [U] ***grammar*** the forms of words, esp. nouns, pronouns, and verbs, that show whether they are singular or plural

SONG /ˈnʌm·bər/ *n* [C] a song, dance, or other part in a performance ○ *The last number she sang was a beautiful, slow ballad.*

WORD FAMILY number

Nouns	number numeral	*Verbs*	number enumerate outnumber
Adjectives	innumerable numerical numerous		

N

IDIOM with number

• *someone's* **number is up** *infml* someone is going to die ○ *When the plane started to shake, Charles thought his number was up.*

number line *n* [C] ***mathematics*** a drawing that represents all the numbers that exist, including those greater than and less than zero and IRRATIONAL NUMBERS such as π

number one *n* [C] the best or highest ranking person or thing ○ *She's still number one in tennis.*

number theory *n* [U] ***mathematics*** the study of the qualities and characteristics of numbers

numeral /ˈnuː·mə·rəl/ *n* [C] a symbol that represents a number ○ *the numeral 5*

numerator /ˈnuː·məˌreɪt̬·ər/ *n* [C] ***mathematics*** a number above the line in a FRACTION (= a division of a whole number) ○ *In the fraction, 3 is the numerator.* ○ Compare DENOMINATOR

numerical /nuːˈmer·ɪ·kəl/ *adj* [not gradable] involving or expressed in numbers ○ *numerical ability* ○ *Keep your files in numerical order.*

numerous /ˈnuː·mə·rəs/ *adj* many ○ *She is the author of three books and numerous articles.*

nun /nʌn/ *n* [C] a member of a female religious group whose members promise to obey the orders of the leader of the group, to be poor, and not to marry

N

nuptial /ˈnʌp·ʃəl, -tʃəl/ *adj* [not gradable] *fml* relating to marriage ○ *nuptial vows*

nuptials /ˈnʌp·ʃəlz, -tʃəlz/ *pl n fml* a marriage ceremony; a wedding ○ *The nuptials will take place in the home of the bride's parents.*

nurse PERSON /nɜrs/ *n* [C] a person trained to care for people who are ill or not able to care for themselves because of injury or old age, and who may also help doctors in treating people ○ *The hospital has at least five nurses on duty in the pediatrics ward all the time.*

nurse /nɜrs/ *v* [T] **1** to care for people who are sick or cannot care for themselves because of injury or old age ○ *After my mother's operation, she stayed with us for a while until we nursed her back to health.* **2** If you nurse an injury, you rest it to help it get better: *Robert stayed home today, nursing a bad back.*

nursing /ˈnɜr·sɪŋ/ *n* [U] the job of being a nurse ○ *She studied nursing at Northwestern University.*

FEED A BABY /nɜrs/ *v* [I/T] to feed a baby from the breast, or of a baby, to drink from a woman's breast ○ [I/T] *I'm planning to nurse (the baby) for at least three months.*

LAST LONGER /nɜrs/ *v* [T] to make something continue to exist ○ *Oklahoma was nursing a 7–3 lead over Texas with two minutes left.*

WORD FAMILY nurse			
Nouns	nurse	*Verbs*	nurse
	nursery		
	nursing		

nursery CHILD CARE /ˈnɜr·sə·ri/ *n* [C] **1** a place where young children and babies are cared for while their parents are somewhere else ○ *The store has a nursery where you can leave your children while you shop.* **2** *dated* A nursery is also a child's room in a house.

PLANTS /ˈnɜr·sə·ri/ *n* [C] a place where plants and trees are grown, usually for sale

nursery rhyme *n* [C] a short poem or song for young children

nursery school *n* [C] a PRESCHOOL

nursing home *n* [C] a place where old people live and receive care when they can no longer care for themselves

nurture /ˈnɜr·tʃər/ *v* [T] to feed and care for a child, or to help someone or something develop by encouraging that person or thing ○ *As a record company director, his job is to nurture young talent.*

nut FOOD /nʌt/ *n* [C] the dry fruit of some trees, consisting of an edible seed within a hard, outer shell, or the seed itself

nutty /ˈnʌt̬·i/ *adj* [-er/-est only] ○ *a nutty flavor*

METAL OBJECT /nʌt/ *n* [C] a small ring of metal that a BOLT (= screw without a pointed end) can be screwed into to hold something in place ○ *a wing nut* (= a nut with flat edges for turning)

PERSON /nʌt/ *n* [C] *infml* **1** a person who is crazy, foolish, or strange ○ *What kind of nut would leave a computer in his car overnight with the doors unlocked?* **2** A nut is also a person who is extremely enthusiastic about a particular activity or thing: *Joyce is a nut for antiques – we've got a house full of them.*

nuts /nʌts/ *adj* [not gradable] *infml* **1** crazy, foolish, or strange ○ *You're nuts if you think you can go mountain climbing in a snowstorm.* **2** If you are nuts about or nuts over someone or something, you are very enthusiastic about that person or thing: *He's nuts about his new granddaughter.*

nutty /ˈnʌt̬·i/ *adj* [-er/-est only] very foolish, or not practical ○ *It sounds nutty, but she can make it work.*

IDIOM with nut

• **the nuts and bolts of** *something* the basic facts or practical things that need to be understood or done ○ *He was a genius on paper, but when it came to the nuts and bolts of running a business he was a failure.*

nutcracker /ˈnʌtˌkræk·ər/ *n* [C] a tool for breaking the shell of a nut

nutmeg /ˈnʌt·meg/ *n* [U] a brown powder made from the fruit of a tree and used as a spice

nutrient /ˈnuː·triː·ənt/ *n* [C] ***biology*** any substance that plants or animals need in order to live and grow

nutrition /nuːˈtrɪʃ·ən/ *n* [U] ***biology*** the process by which the body takes in and uses food, esp. food that it needs to stay healthy, or the scientific study of this process

nutritional /nuː'trɪʃ·ən·ᵊl/, **nutritive** /'nuː·trəţ·ɪv/ *adj* [not gradable] relating to nutrition, or containing a food substance your body can use

nutritious /nuː'trɪʃ·əs/ *adj* containing substances your body needs and can use to stay healthy

nuts /nʌts/ *adj* ○ See at NUT PERSON

nutshell /'nʌt·ʃel/ *n* [U] the hard, outer covering of a nut of a tree

IDIOM with nutshell

• **in a nutshell** very briefly, giving only the main points ○ *"What went wrong?" "In a nutshell, everything."*

nutty /'nʌţ·i/ *adj* ○ See at NUT FOOD; NUT PERSON

nuzzle /'nʌz·əl/ *v* [I/T] to touch, rub, or press someone gently and affectionately, esp. with the head or nose ○ [T] *She loved to nuzzle her dog and scratch him behind the ears.*

N.W. *adj, adv* [not gradable] *abbreviation for* NORTHWEST or NORTHWESTERN

nylon /'nɑɪ·lɑn/ *n* [U] **1** an artificial substance used esp. to make clothes, ropes, and brushes ○ *The fishing line is made of nylon and it's very strong.* **2** Nylons are women's nylon STOCKINGS: [pl] *Most women these days wear pantyhose instead of nylons.*

N

O o

O **LETTER**, **o** /oʊ/ *n* [C] *pl* **O's, Os, o's, os** the 15th letter of the English alphabet

EMOTION /oʊ/ *exclamation old use* used when addressing someone or something, or when expressing strong emotion ○ *"O! Canada" is the Canadian national anthem.* ○ Compare OH

ZERO /oʊ/ *n* [U] (spelled the way it is often spoken) ZERO **NUMBER**

oaf /oʊf/ *n* [C] a big, stupid, awkward person, esp. a man

oak /oʊk/ *n* [C/U] a large tree common in northern countries, or the hard wood of this tree ○ [U] *The floors in their home are made from oak.*

oar /ɔːr, oʊr/ *n* [C] a long pole with a wide, flat part at one end which is used to ROW a boat (= move it through water) ○ Compare PADDLE

oasis /oʊˈeɪ·səs/ *n* [C] *pl* **oases** an area in a desert where there is water and trees can grow

oath **PROMISE** /oʊθ/ *n* [C] a serious promise that you will tell the truth or that you will do what you have said ○ *Presidents take an oath to uphold the Constitution.*

RUDE WORD /oʊθ/ *n* [C] ***literature*** *dated* an offensive word, esp. one that uses a name for God

oatmeal /ˈoʊt·miːl/ *n* [U] crushed OATS, esp. cooked as a breakfast food

oats /oʊts/ *pl n* a tall plant grown for its grain, or the grain from this plant used for food
oat /oʊt/ *adj* ○ *oat bran*

obedient /oʊˈbiːd·iː·ənt/ *adj* doing or willing to do what you have been asked or ordered to do by someone in authority ○ *an obedient child* ○ Related verb: OBEY
obedience /oʊˈbiːd·iː·əns/ *n* [U] ○ *She demands absolute obedience to the rules.*

obese /oʊˈbiːs/ *adj* extremely fat
obesity /oʊˈbiː·sət̬·i/ *n* [U] ○ *Obesity and lack of exercise are bad for the heart.*

obey /oʊˈbeɪ/ *v* [I/T] to do what you are told or expected to do according to someone in authority or a rule or law ○ [I] *The toddler refused to obey.* ○ [T] *Residents are expected to obey the house rules.* ○ Related adjective: OBEDIENT

WORD FAMILY obey

Nouns	obedience disobedience	*Verbs*	obey disobey
Adjectives	obedient disobedient		

WORD CHOICES obey

Follow can sometimes be used instead of "obey."

All religions guide youths to ***follow*** *the teachings of elders and parents.*

Comply can be used in formal English when someone obeys an order, rule, or request.

There are serious penalties for failure to ***comply*** *with the regulations.*

Observe is often used in formal English when someone obeys a law or custom.

People must ***observe*** *the law.*

If someone continues to obey a rule, you could use the phrasal verb **adhere to.**

They failed to ***adhere to*** *the terms of the agreement.*

Abide by can be used when someone accepts and obeys a decision, agreement, etc.

Players must ***abide by*** *the referee's decision.*

OB-GYN /ˌoʊˌbiːˌdʒiːˌwɑɪˈen/ *n* [U] *medical, abbreviation for* OBSTETRICS and GYNECOLOGY (= a part of medicine that manages pregnancy, birth, and a woman's ability to reproduce)

obituary /oʊˈbɪtʃ·əˌwer·i/, *infml* **obit** /oʊˈbɪt, ˈoʊ·bət/ *n* [C] a notice, esp. in a newspaper, of a person's death, usually with details about his or her life

object **THING** /ˈɑb·dʒɪkt/ *n* [C] a thing that can be seen, held, or touched, usually not a living thing ○ *Distant objects look blurry to me.*

PURPOSE /ˈɑb·dʒɪkt/ *n* [C] a purpose or aim of some effort or activity ○ *The object of the game of chess is to checkmate your opponent.*

PERSON DIRECTED TO /ˈɑb·dʒɪkt/ *n* [C] a person or thing to which thoughts, feelings, or actions are directed ○ *The court has been the object of recent criticism.*

GRAMMAR /ˈɑb·dʒɪkt/ *n* [C] ***grammar*** a noun, pronoun, or noun phrase that represents the person or thing toward which the action of a verb is directed or to which a preposition relates ○ *In the sentence, "Give the book to me," "book" is the direct object of the verb "give," and "me" is the indirect object.*

OPPOSE /əbˈdʒekt/ *v* to feel or express opposition, dislike, or disapproval ○ [I] *I don't think anyone will object to leaving early.* ○ [+ *that* clause] *She objected that the price was too high.*
objection /əbˈdʒek·ʃən/ *n* [C] ○ *A couple of people raised/voiced objections to the plan.* ○ *Does anyone have any objections?*
objectionable /əbˈdʒek·ʃə·nə·bəl/ *adj* causing offense or opposition ○ *objectionable behavior*

objective Ⓐ **FAIR OR REAL** /əbˈdʒek·tɪv, ɑb-/ *adj* not influenced by personal beliefs or feelings; fair or real ○ *an objective opinion* ○ Opposite: SUBJECTIVE
objectively Ⓐ /əbˈdʒek·tɪv·li, ɑb-/ *adv* ○ *Jurors must weigh the evidence in the case objectively.*
objectivity Ⓐ /ɑbˌdʒekˈtɪv·ət̬·i/ *n* [U] ○ *The newspaper has a reputation for objectivity and fairness.*

AIM /əbˈdʒek·tɪv, ɑb-/ *n* [C] something that you aim to do or achieve ○ *long-term objectives* ○ *His main objective this semester is to improve his grades.*

GRAMMAR /əbˈdʒek·tɪv, ɑb-/ *adj* [not gradable] ***grammar*** having or relating to the CASE (= form) of a noun, pronoun, or adjective used to show that a word is the object of a verb

obligate /ˈɑb·ləˌgeɪt/ *v* [T] to make someone feel morally or legally forced to do something ○ *I'm in favor of obligating welfare recipients to do more.*

obligated /ˈɑb·ləˌgeɪt̬·əd/ *adj* ○ [+ *to* infinitive] *I felt obligated to speak up and defend my friend's reputation.*

obligation /ˌɑb·ləˈgeɪ·ʃən/ *n* [C/U] something that a person feels morally or legally forced to do ○ [C] *The government has an obligation to assist relief efforts.* ○ [U] *You can just look – you're under no obligation to buy.*

oblige **FORCE** /əˈblɑɪdʒ/ *v* [T] *fml* to force or make it expected for someone to do something ○ *Circumstances obliged him to leave town.*

obligatory /əˈblɪg·əˌtɔːr·i, -ˌtoʊr·i/ *adj* [not gradable] ○ *Everybody who goes to England makes the obligatory trip to Stonehenge.*

obliged /əˈblɑɪdʒd/ *adj* ○ [+ *to* infinitive] *He was obliged to call the nurse to help him up again.*

HELP /əˈblɑɪdʒ/ *v* [I/T] to please or help someone, esp. by doing something the person has asked you to do ○ [I] *We needed a guide and he was only too happy to oblige.*

obliging /əˈblɑɪ·dʒɪŋ/ *adj* willing or eager to help ○ *An obliging neighbor helped her shovel the snow.*

obligingly /əˈblɑɪ·dʒɪŋ·li/ *adv* ○ *She obligingly offered us a lift.*

oblique **INDIRECT** /oʊˈbliːk, ə-, -ˈblɑɪk/ *adj* not clear or direct ○ *He made an oblique reference to their relationship.*

DIAGONAL /oʊˈbliːk, ə-, -ˈblɑɪk/ *adj* having a sloping direction, angle, or position ○ *the oblique rays of the afternoon sun*

obliterate /əˈblɪt̬·əˌreɪt, oʊ-/ *v* [T] to remove all signs of something; destroy ○ *The hurricane virtually obliterated this small coastal town.*

oblivion **MENTAL STATE** /əˈblɪv·iː·ən, oʊ-/ *n* [U] the state of being unconscious or lacking awareness of what is happening around you

FORGOTTEN BY OTHERS /əˈblɪv·iː·ən, oʊ-/ *n* [U] the state of being completely forgotten by the public ○ *He wrote one extraordinary book and then faded into oblivion.*

oblivious /əˈblɪv·iː·əs, oʊ-/ *adj* not aware of or not noticing something, esp. what is happening around you ○ *She was often oblivious to the potential consequences of her actions.*

oblong /ˈɑb·lɔːŋ/ *n* [C] a shape that is longer than it is wide, esp. a rectangle that is not a square

obnoxious /əbˈnɑk·ʃəs, ɑb-/ *adj* very unpleasant or offensive ○ *Can't you express your opinions without being obnoxious?*

oboe /ˈoʊ·boʊ/ *n* [C/U] a tube-shaped musical instrument that is played by blowing through two REEDS (= thin pieces of wood), or this type of instrument generally; a WOODWIND

obscene /əbˈsiːn, ɑb-/ *adj* offensive, rude, or disgusting according to accepted moral standards

obscenity /əbˈsen·ət̬·i, ɑb-/ *n* [C/U] behavior or language that is offensive, rude, or disgusting

obscure **UNKNOWN** /əbˈskjʊr, ɑb-/ *adj* not known to many people ○ *an obscure 18th-century painter*

obscurity /əbˈskjʊr·ət̬·i, ɑb-/ *n* [U] ○ *She worked in obscurity for years.*

UNCLEAR /əbˈskjʊr, ɑb-/ *adj* unclear and difficult to understand or see ○ *Official policy has changed for reasons that remain obscure.*

obscure /əbˈskjʊr, ɑb-/ *v* [T] ○ *Bad writing just obscures your point.* ○ *Two large trees obscured the view.*

obscurity /əbˈskjʊr·ət̬·i, ɑb-/ *n* [U] ○ *Many movie reviewers confuse obscurity with quality.*

obsequious /əbˈsiː·kwiː·əs, ɑb-/ *adj* too eager to serve or obey someone ○ *She is embarrassingly obsequious to anyone in authority.*

observatory /əbˈzɜr·vəˌtɔːr·i, -ˌtoʊr·i/ *n* [C] a building equipped for studying the planets and the stars

observe **WATCH** /əbˈzɜrv/ *v* [T] to watch something or someone carefully ○ *She spent her career observing animal behavior.* ○ [+ question word] *On their field trip, the students observed how a newspaper was put together.*

observation /ˌɑb·zərˈveɪ·ʃən/ *n* [C/U] ○ [U] *He was admitted to the hospital for observation after complaining of chest pains.*

observer /əbˈzɜr·vər/ *n* [C] a person who watches what happens but has no active part in it ○ *Political observers say it's going to be a close election.*

NOTICE /əbˈzɜrv/ *v* [T] to notice something or someone ○ [T] *Jack observed a look of panic on his brother's face.*

observable /əbˈzɜr·və·bəl/ *adj* [not gradable] ○ *There's no observable connection between the two events.*

observant /əbˈzɜr·vənt/ *adj* quick to notice things ○ *Carrie has a clear, observant eye.*

observation /ˌɑb·zərˈveɪ·ʃən/ *n* [U] ○ *He has remarkable powers of observation.*

EXAMINE /əbˈzɜrv/ *v* [T] ***science*** to study and record information about a scientific event

observation /ˌɑb·zərˈveɪ·ʃən/ *n* [C] ***science*** the recorded information that results from studying a scientific event

REMARK /əbˈzɜrv/ *v* [I] to remark about something ○ *"It's raining again," he observed.*

observation /ˌɑb·zərˈveɪ·ʃən/ *n* [C] ○ *She made an interesting observation about the poet's intentions.*

OBEY /əbˈzɜrv/ *v* [T] to obey a law or rule, or celebrate a holiday or religious event in a traditional way ○ *You must observe the law.*

observance /əbˈzɜr·vəns/ *n* [C/U] ○ [U] *Financial markets will be closed Monday in observance of Labor Day.*

O

observant /əbˈzɜr·vənt/ *adj* careful in obeying laws, rules, or customs ○ *observant of cultural traditions*

obsessed /əbˈsest, ɑb-/ *adj* unable to stop thinking about something ○ *The kids are obsessed with video games.*

obsession /əbˈseʃ·ən, ɑb-/ *n* [C/U] the control of one's thoughts by a continuous, powerful idea or feeling, or the idea or feeling itself ○ [C] *They have an obsession with making money.*

obsessive /əbˈses·ɪv, ɑb-/ *adj* ○ *She is obsessive about punctuality.*

obsessively /əbˈses·ɪv·li, ɑb-/ *adv* ○ *Sue exercises obsessively.*

obsolescence /ˌɑb·səˈles·əns/ *n* [U] the process of becoming no longer useful or needed ○ *Older versions had passed into obsolescence and a new version was already on the market.*

obsolete /ˌɑb·səˈliːt/ *adj* [not gradable] no longer used or needed, usually because something newer and better has replaced it ○ *Typewriters have been rendered obsolete by computers.*

obstacle /ˈɑb·stɪ·kəl/ *n* [C] something that blocks your way so that movement or progress is prevented or made more difficult ○ *We suddenly encountered an obstacle along the trail.* ○ *Money seems to be no obstacle.*

obstacle course *n* [C] an area with a series of difficult objects that people climb over or go under or through as a form of exercise or in a race

O

obstetrics /əbˈste·trɪks, ɑb-/ *n* [U] the area of medicine that deals with pregnancy and the birth of babies

obstetrician /ˌɑb·stəˈtrɪʃ·ən/ *n* [C] a doctor with special training in how to care for pregnant women and help in the birth of babies

obstinate /ˈɑb·stə·nət/ *adj* **1** unwilling to change your opinion or action despite argument or persuasion; STUBBORN ○ *an obstinate two-year-old* **2** An obstinate thing or problem is difficult to deal with, remove, or defeat.

obstinately /ˈɑb·stə·nət·li/ *adv* ○ *The engine obstinately refused to start.*

obstinacy /ˈɑb·stə·nə·si/ *n* [U] ○ *the obstinacy of the human spirit*

obstruct /əbˈstrʌkt, ɑb-/ *v* [T] to block or get in the way of something or someone, or to prevent something from happening or progressing by causing difficulties ○ *Demonstrators obstructed the entrance to the building.* ○ *Trees obstructed our view of the ocean.*

obstruction /əbˈstrʌk·ʃən, ɑb-/ *n* [C/U] **1** [C] *Doctors found an obstruction in one of his arteries* (= something was blocking it). **2** *law* Obstruction of justice is the act of preventing the police or law courts from doing their job.

obtain Ⓐ /əbˈteɪn, ɑb-/ *v* [T] to get something, esp. by a planned effort ○ *to obtain knowledge* ○ *She was finally able to obtain legal possession of the house.*

obtainable Ⓐ /əbˈteɪ·nə·bəl, ɑb-/ *adj* [not gradable] ○ *That drug is now obtainable without a prescription.*

obtrusive /əbˈtruː·sɪv, ɑb-, -zɪv/ *adj* noticeable in a way that is unpleasant or unwanted ○ *The soldiers wore civilian clothes to make their presence less obtrusive.*

obtuse ANGLE /əbˈtuːs, ɑb-/ *adj* ***geometry*** (of an angle) more than 90° and less than 180°, or (of a triangle) containing an angle of more than 90° and less than 180° ○ Compare ACUTE ANGLE ➤ Picture: **angle**

STUPID /əbˈtuːs, ɑb-/ *adj* stupid or slow to understand ○ *I'm not trying to be obtuse, but I don't get it.*

obvious Ⓐ /ˈɑb·viː·əs/ *adj* easily seen, recognized, or understood ○ *an obvious solution* ○ *For obvious reasons, he needs to find work soon.*

obviously Ⓐ /ˈɑb·viː·ə·sli/ *adv* ○ *They were obviously exhausted after the game.* ○ *Obviously, you won't be needing my help.* ➤ Usage: **evident or obvious?** at EVIDENT

WORD CHOICES obvious

Clear, **apparent**, and **plain** are common alternatives to "obvious."

*It was **clear** that he was unhappy.*

*Her joy was **apparent** to everyone.*

*His disappointment was **plain** to see.*

A more formal way of saying "obvious" is by using the word **evident** or **manifest**.

*The company president was impressed by her **evident** ambition.*

*His **manifest** lack of interest has provoked severe criticism.*

An obvious change can be described as **marked**.

*There has been a **marked** improvement in his behavior.*

If someone or something is very different from everything or everyone else, you can describe them as **conspicuous**.

*I felt very **conspicuous** in a suit when everyone else was in jeans.*

When something is very obvious and bad, you can describe it as **blatant** or **glaring**.

*It was a **blatant** attempt to gain publicity.*

*They made some **glaring** errors.*

occasion PARTICULAR TIME /əˈkeɪ·ʒən/ *n* [C] a particular time when something happens ○ *Sarah loves dressing up for special occasions.* ○ *She has lied on several occasions.* ○ *This meeting provides an occasion* (= a suitable time) *to discuss the issues affecting our school.*

REASON /əˈkeɪ·ʒən/ *n* [U] a reason or cause ○ *I've never had occasion to worry about my children's school work.*

WORD FAMILY occasion

Nouns	occasion	*Adverbs*	occasionally
Adjectives	occasional		

IDIOM with occasion

• **on occasion** sometimes but not often ○ *He has, on occasion, told a small lie.*

occasional /ə'keɪ·ʒən·əl/ *adj* [not gradable] not happening often or regularly ○ *occasional snowstorms* ○ *His job requires occasional trips to the West Coast.*

occasionally /ə'keɪ·ʒən·əl·i/ *adv* [not gradable] ○ *Stir occasionally while the pasta is cooking.* ○ *I occasionally watch TV.*

occluded front /ə'kluːd·əd 'frʌnt/ *n* [C] ***earth science*** a situation in the weather when a mass of cold air reaches warm air and pushes the warm air up off the earth's surface

occult /ə'kʌlt, 'ɑk·ʌlt/ *adj* [not gradable] relating to mysterious or SUPERNATURAL powers and activities

occult /ə'kʌlt, 'ɑk·ʌlt/ *n* [U]

occupancy Ⓐ /'ɑk·jə·pən·si/ *n* [U] *fml* the act or state of living in or using a particular place ○ *Her occupancy of the apartment lasted only six months.*

occupant Ⓐ /'ɑk·jə·pənt/ *n* [C] **1** someone who lives in a particular place ○ *The occupants of the building are unhappy about the rent increase.* **2** An occupant of a car, room, seat, or other space is a person who is in it.

occupation Ⓐ **JOB** /ˌɑk·jə'peɪ·ʃən/ *n* [C] *fml* **1** a person's job ○ *He listed his occupation on the form as "teacher."* **2** An occupation is also a regular activity: *Sailing was his favorite weekend occupation.*

occupational Ⓐ /ˌɑk·jə'peɪ·ʃən·əl/ *adj* [not gradable] relating to or caused by a person's work or activity ○ *Occupational training is absolutely essential.*

CONTROLLING FORCE /ˌɑk·jə'peɪ·ʃən/ *n* [U] the act of controlling a foreign country or region by armed force ○ *the occupation of France during World War II*

occupy Ⓐ **TAKE CONTROL** /'ɑk·jəˌpɑɪ/ *v* [T] (of an army or group of people) to move into and take control or possession of a place ○ *Nationalist forces now occupy more than 70% of the country.*

occupied Ⓐ /'ɑk·jəˌpɑɪd/ *adj* [not gradable] ○ *occupied territories*

occupier Ⓐ /'ɑk·jəˌpɑɪ·ər/ *n* [C]

FILL /'ɑk·jəˌpɑɪ/ *v* [T] to fill, use, or exist in a place or a time ○ *A large couch occupies most of the space in the living room.*

occupied Ⓐ /'ɑk·jəˌpɑɪd/ *adj* full, in use, or busy ○ *Every room in the hotel is occupied.* ○ *Organized sports can keep teenagers occupied.*

occur Ⓐ **HAPPEN** /ə'kɜr/ *v* [I] **-rr-** (esp. of unexpected events) to happen ○ *The incident occurred shortly after the plane took off.*

occurrence Ⓐ /ə'kɜr·əns/ *n* [C] ○ *Break-ins are an everyday occurrence in this neighborhood.*

EXIST /ə'kɜr/ *v* [I] **-rr-** to exist or be present ○ *The condition occurs primarily in older adults.* ○ *Helium occurs as a byproduct of natural gas.*

occurrence Ⓐ /ə'kɜr·əns/ *n* [U] ○ *The tests can detect the occurrence of certain cancers.*

PHRASAL VERB with occur

• **occur to** *someone* (of a thought or idea) to come into someone's mind ○ *Didn't it occur to you to phone the police?* ○ *It never occurred to her that her parents might be worried.*

ocean /'oʊ·ʃən/ *n* [C/U] **1** the large mass of salt water that covers most of the earth's surface ○ [U] *These mysterious creatures live at the bottom of the ocean.* **2** Ocean is also used in the name of the world's five main divisions of this mass of water: [C] *the Atlantic/Pacific/Indian/Arctic/Antarctic Ocean*

oceanic /ˌoʊ·ʃiː'æn·ɪk/ *adj* [not gradable] ○ *oceanic conditions*

oceanography /ˌoʊ·ʃə'nɑg·rə·fi/ *n* [U] ***earth science*** the scientific study of the oceans and seas and the organisms that live in them

oceanographer /ˌoʊ·ʃə'nɑg·rə·fər/ *n* [C] ***earth science***

o'clock /ə'klɑk/ *adv* [not gradable] used after a number from one to twelve to state the time ○ *She called at nine o'clock this morning.*

octagon /'ɑk·təˌgɑn/ *n* [C] ***geometry*** a flat shape with eight straight sides and eight angles

octagonal /ɑk'tæg·ən·əl/ *adj* [not gradable]

octane /'ɑk·teɪn/ *n* [C] a chemical substance in GASOLINE (= liquid fuel) which is used as a measure of its quality

octave /'ɑk·tɪv/ *n* [C] ***music*** the space between two musical notes that are eight musical notes apart

October /ɑk'toʊ·bər/, *abbreviation* **Oct.** *n* [C/U] the tenth month of the year, after September and before November

octopus /'ɑk·tə·pəs, -ˌpʊs/ *n* [C] *pl* **octopuses, octopi** a sea creature with a soft oval body and eight TENTACLES (= arms)

odd Ⓐ **STRANGE** /ɑd/ *adj* [-er/-est only] strange or unexpected ○ *an odd person* ○ *That's odd – I thought I left my glasses on the table but they're not here.*

oddity /'ɑd·əṭ·i/ *n* [C] someone or something that is strange and unusual ○ *As one of the few women in engineering in the 1950s, she was considered an oddity.*

oddly /'ɑd·li/ *adv* ○ *an oddly shaped house* ○ *Oddly enough, despite the sizzling heat, scientists suspect there could be water frozen on Mercury.*

SEPARATED /ɑd/ *adj* [not gradable] (of something that should be in a pair or set) separated from its pair or set ○ *He's got a whole drawer full of odd socks.*

NUMBER /ɑd/ *adj* [not gradable] (of numbers) not able to be divided exactly by 2 ○ *Some examples of odd numbers are 1, 3, 5, and 7.* ○ Compare EVEN NUMBER

APPROXIMATELY /ɑd/ *adv* [not gradable] used after a number, esp. a number that can be divided by 10, to show that the exact number is not known ○ *He holds another 50-odd acres of land in reserve, providing plenty of room for expansion.*

O

oddball /ˈɑd·bɔːl/ *n* [C] a person whose behavior is unusual and strange

odd jobs *pl n* small jobs of different types, esp. those that involve repairing or cleaning things ○ *He's been doing odd jobs this summer to earn a little extra money.*

odds Ⓐ /ɑdz/ *pl n* the likelihood that a particular thing will or will not happen ○ *She was sick yesterday, so the odds are she won't be in today.*

IDIOM with **odds**

• **at odds (with** *someone/something***)** in disagreement ○ *The two brothers were always at odds.* ○ *His behavior is clearly at odds with what the college expects from its students.*

odds and ends /ˌɑd·zəˈnenz/ *pl n* various items of different types, usually small and unimportant or of little value ○ *We've moved most of the furniture to the new house, but there are still a few odds and ends to bring over.*

ode /oʊd/ *n* [C] ***literature*** a poem that deals with thoughts and feelings about an idea or subject and that is written in lines and STANZAs (= groups of lines) varying in length

odious /ˈoʊd·iː·əs/ *adj* extremely unpleasant; causing and deserving hate ○ *an odious person/task*

odometer /oʊˈdɑm·ət̬·ər/ *n* [C] a device in a vehicle that measures and shows the distance the vehicle travels

odor, *Cdn, Br* **odour** /ˈoʊd·ər/ *n* [C] a particular smell, esp. a bad one ○ *the musty odor of a damp cellar*

odorless, *Cdn, Br* **odourless** /ˈoʊd·ər·ləs/ *adj* [not gradable] having no smell ○ *an odorless gas*

odyssey /ˈɑd·ə·si/ *n* [C usually sing] a long trip or period involving a lot of different and exciting activities, esp. while searching for something ○ *The movie follows one man's odyssey to find the mother he was separated from at birth.*

of **POSSESSION** /ʌv, ɑv, əv/ *prep* used to show possession, belonging, or origin ○ *She is a friend of mine.* ○ *The color of his tie matches his suit.* ○ *Have you read the novels of John Updike?*

CONTAINING /ʌv, ɑv, əv/ *prep* containing or consisting of ○ *a bag of groceries* ○ *a book of short stories* ○ *a forest of pine trees* ○ *a bunch of grapes*

AMOUNT /ʌv, ɑv, əv/ *prep* used after words or phrases expressing amount, number, or a particular unit ○ *a drop of rain* ○ *two pounds of potatoes* ○ *hundreds of people*

POSITION /ʌv, ɑv, əv/ *prep* used in expressions showing position ○ *I left the book on top of my desk.* ○ *I've never been north of Montreal.*

RESULT /ʌv, ɑv, əv/ *prep* resulting from or having to do with ○ *the joy of family* ○ *the fear of failure*

RELATING TO /ʌv, ɑv, əv/ *prep* about, or relating to ○ *Speaking of Elizabeth, here she is.* ○ *There's a chapter on the use of herbs for medicinal purposes.*

CAUSED BY /ʌv, ɑv, əv/ *prep* used to show the cause of something ○ *He died of a heart attack.* ○ *Penny is frightened of spiders.* ○ *I'm tired of all this criticism.*

THAT IS/ARE /ʌv, ɑv, əv/ *prep* that is/are ○ *Sales tax of 7% is included in the price.* ○ *She could read by the age of five.*

COMPARING /ʌv, ɑv, əv/ *prep* used when comparing related things ○ *He's the oldest of three brothers.* ○ *Of all his films, this one is my favorite.*

DONE TO /ʌv, ɑv, əv/ *prep* done to or involving ○ *the destruction of the rain forests* ○ *the graduation of the class of 2001*

DISTANCE FROM /ʌv, ɑv, əv/ *prep* used in expressions showing distance from something in place or time ○ *We live within a mile of the school.* ○ *She came within two seconds of beating the world record.*

TIME /ʌv, ɑv, əv/ *prep* used in saying what the time is ○ *It's ten (minutes) of five* (= ten minutes before five o'clock).

DAYS /ʌv, ɑv, əv/ *prep* used to describe a particular day ○ *the eleventh of March* ○ *the first of the month*

off **NOT OPERATING** /ɔːf/ *adj, adv* [not gradable] (esp. of machines, electrical devices, lights, etc.) not operating because they are not switched on ○ *Was the computer on or off when you left?* ○ *Turn the engine off.*

AWAY FROM /ɔːf/ *prep, adj, adv* [not gradable] away from a place or position, esp. the present place or position ○ *He drove off at high speed.* ○ *She's off to Canada next week.* ○ *The sign says, "Keep off the grass."*

REMOVED /ɔːf/ *prep, adv* [not gradable] used with actions in which something is removed or removes itself from another thing ○ *I think I'll take my jacket off.* ○ *I can't get the lid off this jar.* ○ *He fell off his bike.* ○ *Did you leave the phone* **off the hook** (= not put back in such a way that a call is ended)*?*

NOT AT /ɔːf/ *adj, adv* [not gradable] **1** not at work or school, esp. being at home or on vacation ○ *I'm going to take a week off to work on my house.* ○ *I'm off next week.* ○ *The kids get off early from school today.* **2** To be **off duty** is to not be working, usually because you have finished work for the day: *She goes off duty at midnight.* ○ *An* **off-duty** *police officer on his way home interrupted a crime in progress.*

NEAR TO /ɔːf/ *prep* near to ○ *The island is just off the coast of Florida.*

TAKEN AWAY /ɔːf/ *adv* [not gradable] in such a way as to be taken away or removed, esp. because of having been used or killed ○ *to pay off debts* ○ *Exercise burns off fat.* ○ *They were all killed off by disease.*

BELOW USUAL LEVEL /ɔːf/ *adj, adv* [not gradable] below the usual standard or rate ○ *Sales have been off this month.* ○ *He's a good tennis player but had an off day and lost in straight sets.* ○ *They took 10% off* (= below the usual price) *because I paid in cash.*

FAR AWAY /ɔːf/ *prep, adv* [not gradable] far away in time or space ○ *Graduation is still a long way off.* ○ *That's not the right answer, but you're not far off.*

STOPPED /ɔːf/ *adj, adv* [not gradable] (of an arranged event) stopped or given up in advance ○ *Last night's baseball game was called off because of rain.*

CLOSED /ɔːf/ *adv* [not gradable] in such a way as to be separated ○ *to mark off 10 feet* ○ *The children's play area is fenced off for safety reasons.*

IDIOMS with **off**

• **off balance** surprised or confused, so that it is difficult to behave or react as you usually would ○ *He walked up and said I was fat, which really threw me off balance* (= made me feel confused). ○ *Her remark seemed to catch her mother off balance* (= surprise her).

• **off the beaten path, off the beaten track** not known or popular with many people ○ *We wanted to find a camping site that was a little bit off the beaten path.*

off and on, on and off *adj, adv* happening or existing only some of the time ○ *He worked off and on as a bicycle messenger, but he never found permanent work.*

offbeat /ˈɔːf·biːt, ɔːfˈbiːt/ *adj* unusual and therefore surprising or noticeable ○ *an offbeat sense of humor*

off-color *adj* (of remarks, jokes, etc.) rude or offensive to some people

offend /əˈfend/ *v* [T] to cause to be upset or to hurt the feelings of someone, esp. by being rude or showing a lack of respect ○ *I think she was offended that she wasn't invited to the party.*

offender /əˈfen·dər/ *n* [C] a person who is guilty of a crime ○ *Because he is a first-time offender, he is unlikely to receive jail time.*

offense **BAD FEELINGS** /əˈfens/ *n* [U] the condition of having your feelings hurt esp. because someone has been rude or showed a lack of respect ○ *Do you think he took offense* (= was upset) *at the joke about his age?*
offensive /əˈfen·sɪv/ *adj* **1** causing someone to be upset or to have hurt feelings ○ *offensive comments/jokes* **2** Offensive can be used more generally to mean unpleasant: *an offensive odor*

CRIME /əˈfens/ *n* [C] an illegal act; crime ○ *He was charged with the offense of driving without a license.*

SCORING ABILITY /ˈɔː·fens, ˈɑf·ens, əˈfens/ *n* [U] (in sports) the ability to score points in a competition, or, esp. in football, the team that has the ball and is trying to score points ○ Compare DEFENSE SPORTS
offensive /ˈɔːˌfen·sɪv, ˈɑfˌen-, əˈfen-/ *adj* [not gradable] ○ *Bob made the team as an offensive guard.*

WORD FAMILY offense

Nouns	offense offender offensive	*Adjectives*	offensive inoffensive
Verbs	offend	*Adverbs*	offensively

offensive /əˈfen·sɪv/ *n* [C] a planned military attack ○ *They launched the land offensive in the middle of the night.*
offensive /əˈfen·sɪv/ *adj* ○ *an offensive action*

offer **AGREE TO GIVE** /ˈɔː·fər, ˈɑf·ər/ *v* [I/T] to ask someone if the person would like to have something or would like you to do something ○ [T] *She was offered a new job.* ○ [T] *Can I offer you* (= Would you like) *something to drink?* ○ [I] *My father offered to take us to the airport.*
offer /ˈɔː·fər, ˈɑf·ər/ *n* [C] ○ [+ *to* infinitive] *I appreciate your offer to help.* ○ *The offer of $5000 was too good to refuse.*
offering /ˈɔː·fə·rɪŋ, ˈɑf·ə-/ *n* [C] something that a person gives, often during a religious ceremony

PROVIDE /ˈɔː·fər, ˈɑf·ər/ *v* [T] to provide or supply something ○ *The organization offers free legal advice to low-income people.* ○ *He offered excuses but no real explanation.*

offhand /ˈɔːfˈhænd/ *adv* now, without looking for information or without taking the time to consider carefully ○ *I can't tell you the exact number offhand, but it was something like $25,000.*
offhand /ˈɔːfˈhænd/ *adj* not showing or not done with much thought or consideration ○ *offhand remarks* ○ *His offhand manner disturbed us.*

office **WORK PLACE** /ˈɔː·fəs, ˈɑf·əs/ *n* [C] **1** a place in a building where a business is carried on by people working at DESKS (= special tables) used for writing and for holding telephones and computers ○ *an office building* ○ *I didn't leave the office until nearly 8 o'clock.* **2** An office is also the place of business where a doctor, lawyer, or other PROFESSIONAL sees people: *The doctor's office was filled with people.*
officer /ˈɔː·fə·sər, ˈɑf·ə-/ *n* [C] a person who has an important job in a company ○ *the chief financial officer* ➤ Usage: **cabinet or office?** at CABINET FURNITURE

GOVERNMENT DEPARTMENT /ˈɔː·fəs, ˈɑf·əs/ *n* [C] a part of a government department ○ *the Office of Management and Budget* ○ *the Patent Office*

RESPONSIBILITY /ˈɔː·fəs, ˈɑf·əs/ *n* [C/U] a position of authority and responsibility in a government or other organization ○ [U] *elective office* ○ [C] *the office of executive vice president* ○ [U] *The governor retired after 12 years in office.*
officer /ˈɔː·fə·sər, ˈɑf·ə-/ *n* [C] **1** a person in the armed forces who has a position of authority ○ *Mike's father was an officer in the US Marines.* **2** An officer is also a member of a police force.

WORD FAMILY office

Nouns	office officer official	*Adjectives*	official unofficial
		Adverbs	officially unofficially

official /əˈfɪʃ·əl/ *n* [C] a person who has a position of responsibility in an organization ○ *a senior official*
official /əˈfɪʃ·əl/ *adj* connected with or arranged by someone in a position of responsibility ○ *an official announcement*
officially /əˈfɪʃ·ə·li/ *adv* ○ *The name of the new director will be officially announced in June.*

O

officiate /ə'fɪʃ·iː ˌeɪt/ *v* [I] to be in charge of a sports event and make decisions about the rules of play, or to lead a ceremony or other public event ○ *Lambert was a football official for three decades and officiated in ten postseason games.* ○ *A judge officiated at the wedding.*

offing IDIOM /'ɔː·fɪŋ, 'ɑf·ɪŋ/
• **in the offing** going to happen soon ○ *With an election in the offing, the mayor is getting nervous.*

off-key /'ɔːf 'kiː/ *adv* singing the wrong notes ○ *He was singing off-key, and it was painful to hear.*

off-season *n* [U] a period of the year when there is less activity in business ○ *The ski resort closes completely in the off-season.*

offset Ⓐ /ɔːf 'set/ *v* [T] *pres. part.* **offsetting**, *past* **offset** to balance one influence against an opposing influence so that no great difference results ○ *The extra cost of commuting to work from the suburbs is offset by cheaper rents.*

offshoot /'ɔːf·ʃuːt/ *n* [C] something that has developed from something larger that already existed ○ *Cyber cafes are just the latest offshoot of the Internet craze.*

offshore /'ɔːf 'ʃɔːr, -'ʃoʊr/ *adj, adv* **1** away from or at a distance from the land ○ *an offshore oil rig* **2** Offshore businesses, banks, or accounts are located in an island country or a country away from your own country.

offspring /'ɔːf·sprɪŋ/ *n* [C] *pl* **offspring** the young of an animal, or a person's children ○ *Champion horses have numerous offspring.*

offstage /'ɔːf 'steɪdʒ/ *adv* [not gradable] behind or at the side of the stage, so that people who are watching cannot see ○ *We could hear someone shouting offstage.*

off the record *adj, adv* said without the intention of being published or officially noted ○ *An aide told reporters, off the record, that the senator had been lying.* ○ *My off-the-record remarks were printed in the paper the next day.*

off the wall *adj* strange or very different, often intentionally ○ *Teenagers love his off-the-wall comedy.*

often /'ɔː·fən, 'ɔːf·tən/ *adv* a lot or many times; frequently ○ *She was often late for class.* ○ *I don't see my parents as often as I'd like to.*

ogle /'oʊ·gəl/ *v* [I/T] to look at someone with obvious sexual interest

ogre /'oʊ·gər/ *n* [C] a frightening, fierce, or ugly person

oh /oʊ/ *exclamation* used to express a variety of emotions, such as surprise and pleasure, often as a reaction to something someone has said ○ *Oh, I didn't know they were married.* ○ *Oh, really?*

ohm /oʊm/ *n* [C] ***science*** the standard unit of electrical RESISTANCE (= the degree to which electrical flow is prevented)

oil FAT /ɔɪl/ *n* [C/U] thick, liquid fat obtained from plants which does not mix with water and is used esp. in cooking ○ [U] *vegetable/corn/olive oil* ○ [U] *I like oil and vinegar on my salad.* ○ [C] *These cookies are made with soybean and palm oils.*

oil /ɔɪl/ *v* [T] to put oil on a pan or other surface that you cook on to keep things from sticking to it ○ *Lightly oil the grill.*

oily /'ɔɪ·li/ *adj* like oil, or containing or covered with oil ○ *an oily liquid* ○ *oily skin/hair*

FUEL /ɔɪl/ *n* [U] a thick, liquid substance that burns and is used as fuel or as a LUBRICANT (= substance that helps connecting parts move easily), or the thick liquid taken from under the ground which oil, GASOLINE, and other products are made from ○ *motor oil* ○ *fuel/heating oil* ○ *Change your car's oil every 12,000 miles.*

oil /ɔɪl/ *v* [T] to add oil to something so it works better ○ *Oil the door hinges so they stop squeaking.*

oily /ɔɪ·li/ *adj* covered in or containing a lot of oil ○ *an oily rag*

LIQUID SUBSTANCE /ɔɪl/ *n* [C] any of a number of thick liquid substances that do not dissolve in water and are used in beauty products, paints, medicines, etc.

oil paint *n* [C/U] a type of paint made by adding color to oil, used for painting pictures

oil painting *n* [C/U] the activity of painting with oil paint, or a painting made with oil paint

oil slick *n* [C] a layer of oil floating on water, esp. on the surface of the ocean

oink /ɔɪŋk/ *n* [C] the sound made by a pig

oink /ɔɪŋk/ *v* [I] *infml*

ointment /'ɔɪnt·mənt/ *n* [C/U] a thick, oily substance, usually containing medicine, that is put on skin where you feel sore or on an injury ○ [U] *germicidal ointment*

OJ /'oʊ·dʒeɪ/ *n* [U] *abbreviation for* orange juice

OK AGREED, **okay** /oʊ'keɪ/ *exclamation, adj* [not gradable] agreed or acceptable; ALL RIGHT AGREED ○ *Is it OK if I bring a friend to the party?* ○ *"Will you lend me ten bucks?" "OK."*

OK, **okay** /oʊ'keɪ/ *v* [T] *singular* **OK's**, *pres. part.* **OK'ing, okaying**, *past* **OK'd, okayed** ○ *Did the boss OK your proposal?*

OK, **okay** /oʊ'keɪ/ *n* [C] agreement about or permission to do something ○ *We'll start building as soon as we get the OK from the owner.*

SATISFACTORY, **okay** /oʊ'keɪ/ *adj, adv* **1** in a satisfactory state or of a satisfactory quality; ALL RIGHT SATISFACTORY ○ *Are you OK? You look pale.* ○ *I hope you got home OK.* **2** OK is used to mean not bad but also not very good: *Her voice is OK, but it's nothing special.*

EXPRESSION, **okay** /oʊ'keɪ, 'oʊ'keɪ/ *exclamation infml* used as a way of showing that you are going to take action or start doing or saying something new ○ *OK, let's go.*

okra /'oʊ·krə/, **gumbo** *n* [U] a plant with long, green PODS (= seed containers) that are used as a vegetable

old EXISTING A LONG TIME /oʊld/ *adj* [*-er/-est* only] having lived or existed for a long time in comparison to others of the same kind ○ *An old man lives there with his dog.* ○ *They have a beautiful old farm house in the country.* ○ *She got very depressed in her old age* (= the time of her life when she was old). ○ Compare ELDERLY at ELDER

> **USAGE**
>
> **old** or **elderly?**
>
> It is considered more polite to use **elderly** instead of **old** when describing a person.
>
> *an elderly gentleman*

KNOWN A LONG TIME /oʊld/ *adj* [*-er/-est* only] **1** (esp. of a friend) known for a long time ○ *She's one of my oldest friends.* **2** *infml* Old is also used to show that you know and like someone: *Poor old Frank broke his arm.*

AGE /oʊld/ *adj* [*-er/-est* only] having a particular age, or an age suited to a particular activity or condition ○ *a 14-year-old* ○ *Charlie is older than I.* ○ *You're old enough to know better.* ➤ Usage: **elder/eldest or older/oldest?** at ELDER

> **USAGE**
>
> **x years old** or **x-year-old?**
>
> You can give someone's age in two different ways.
>
> You can write the age as three separate words, using the word **years**, when the age follows a verb.
>
> *My daughter is three years old.*
>
> However, when you someone's age is used as a compound noun or adjective, you should write the age using **year** with hyphens.
>
> *I've got a three-year-old daughter.*

> **WORD CHOICES old**
>
> When we are talking about old people, we can use the following words.
>
> **Elderly** is a polite way of describing someone who is old.
>
> *A large number of **elderly** people live alone.*
>
> **The elderly** is used for describing the group of people who are old.
>
> *Many among **the elderly** cannot afford to pay their electric bills.*
>
> **Aged** and **aging** can be used to describe people who are old.
>
> *He has to look after his **aged** aunt.*
>
> *The **aging** chairman was forced to retire.*
>
> An informal way of saying that someone is old is to use the phrase **be getting on**.
>
> *He's **getting on** in years. He'll be eighty next birthday.*
>
> **Geriatric** is used to talk abut medicine, services, etc., for old people, and it is also an informal and disapproving way of describing someone who is old and weak.
>
> *She specializes in **geriatric** medicine.*
>
> *Who's going to elect a **geriatric** president?*
>
> If someone is too old to do something, in informal or humorous situations you can say they are **over the hill**.
>
> *I'm only forty, you know. I'm not **over the hill** yet!*
>
> When we are talking about old things, we can use the following words.
>
> The word **ancient** can be used for things that have existed for a very long time.
>
> *We need to protect **ancient** monuments.*
>
> **Ancient** can also be used informally for anything that is old.
>
> *That computer's **ancient**.*
>
> **Archaic** is used to describe things that are old and no longer used or existing.
>
> ***archaic** language*
>
> Something that is old and valuable, rare, or beautiful can be described as **antique**.
>
> *The shop sells **antique** furniture.*
>
> **Age-old** is a literary word for stories, beliefs, customs, etc., which are very old.
>
> *It's an **age-old** story of love and betrayal.*

PREVIOUS /oʊld/ *adj* [*-er/-est* only] from a previous time or a period in the past; FORMER EARLIER ○ *Our old house in Lakewood burned down.* ○ *Sharon gave her old skates to her younger cousin.*

olden /ˈoʊl·dən/ *adj* [not gradable] from a long time ago ○ *olden times/days*

old-fashioned /ˈoʊldˈfæʃ·ənd/ *adj* not modern; belonging to or typical of a time in the past ○ *old-fashioned clothes/ideas/music* ○ *She's old-fashioned* (= her views are typical of the past, not the present).

> **WORD CHOICES old-fashioned**
>
> **Antiquated, dated,** and **outdated** are alternatives to "old-fashioned."
>
> *The school wants to update its **antiquated** computer system.*
>
> *The hotel's décor is starting to look **dated**.*
>
> *Many hospitals struggle with **outdated** equipment and facilities.*
>
> Something that is attractive because it is old-fashioned can be described as **quaint**.
>
> *The area is full of **quaint** little villages.*
>
> **Behind the times** is a phrase that can be used to describe a person or thing that is thought old-fashioned in modern society.
>
> *Her grandfather was **behind the times** and thought that women shouldn't work outside the home.*

old hat *adj* [not gradable] *infml* not interesting because of being familiar ○ *The winter coats and jackets we saw in the fashion show looked like old hat to me.*

oldie /ˈoʊl·di/ *n* [C] *infml* someone or something, esp. a song, movie, or joke, that was popular long ago ○ *That radio station plays only golden oldies.*

old maid *n* [C] *dated* a woman who is not young and has not married ○ **USAGE:** This word is likely to be considered offensive.

old-school *adj* old-fashioned; not modern ○ *This videogame offers chunky old-school graphics with a bizarre story line that involves a giant sticky ball.*

Old Testament *n* [U] the holy writings of the Jewish people that form the first part of the Christian Bible ○ Compare NEW TESTAMENT

old-timer *n* [C] *infml* someone who has lived a long time, or who has lived or worked in a place for a long time

old wives' tale *n* [C] a traditional story or belief, esp. one that is not true

Old World *n* [U] the part of the world consisting of Europe, Asia, and Africa that Europeans knew about before Christopher Columbus traveled to the Americas ○ Compare NEW WORLD

Olestra /oʊˈles·trə/ *n* [U] *trademark* an artificially produced substance that replaces fat in some foods

oligarchy /ˈɑl·əˌɡɑr·ki, ˈoʊ·lə-/ *n* [C] ***world history*** a government in which power is held by a small group of people

olive /ˈɑl·ɪv/ *n* [C/U] **1** a small, oval fruit eaten raw or cooked or pressed to make oil, or the evergreen tree on which this fruit grows **2** Olive is also a dark, yellow-green color.

Olympics /əˈlɪm·pɪks, oʊ-/, **Olympic Games** /əˌlɪm·pɪk ˈɡeɪmz, oʊ-/ *pl n* international winter and summer sports competitions, each taking place every four years, but not in the same year ○ *She won a gold medal at the Winter Olympics in Nagano, Japan, in 1998.*

Olympic /əˈlɪm·pɪk, oʊ-/ *adj* [not gradable] ○ *Olympic athletes/competitions* ○ *an Olympic gold medalist*

Olympian /əˈlɪm·piː·ən, oʊ-/ *n* [C] a competitor in the Olympics

ombudsman /ˈɑmˌbʊdz·mən, -bədz-/ *n* [C] *pl* **-men** someone who works for a government or large organization and deals with the complaints made against it

omelet, **omelette** /ˈɑm·lət/ *n* [C] eggs with their yellow and transparent parts mixed together, cooked in a pan, and usually folded over some other food ○ *a cheese/mushroom omelet*

omen /ˈoʊ·mən/ *n* [C] an event that is thought to tell something about the future ○ *Scoring that goal was an omen of things to come.*

ominous /ˈɑm·ə·nəs/ *adj* suggesting something unpleasant will happen ○ *a ominous silence*

ominously /ˈɑm·ə·nə·sli/ *adv* ○ *Clouds had gathered ominously.*

omit /oʊˈmɪt, ə-/ *v* [T] **-tt-** to fail to include or do something ○ *I'd be upset if my name were omitted from the list of contributors.*

omission /oʊˈmɪʃ·ən, ə-/ *n* [C/U] ○ [U] *Parents are upset by the omission of music from the school's courses.*

omnipotent /ɑmˈnɪp·əţ·ənt/ *adj* [not gradable] having the power to do anything ○ *The people overthrew the once omnipotent dictator.*

omnipotence /ɑmˈnɪp·əţ·əns/ *n* [U] ○ *America had illusions of omnipotence in the 1950s.*

omniscient /ɑmˈnɪʃ·ənt/ *adj* [not gradable] having or seeming to have unlimited knowledge ○ *They give the impression that the magazine is omniscient.*

omniscience /ɑmˈnɪʃ·əns/ *n* [U]

omniscient narrator *n* [C] ***literature*** the voice in which a story is written that is outside the story and that knows everything about the characters and events in the story

omnivore /ˈɑm·nəˌvɔːr/ *n* [C] ***biology*** an organism that eats both plant and animal matter

omnivorous /ɑmˈnɪv·ə·rəs/ *adj* [not gradable] eating both plants and meat ○ *Bears are omnivorous.*

on SUPPORTED BY /ɔːn, ɑn/ *prep, adv* [not gradable] supported by or resting at the top of another thing ○ *There is snow on the ground.* ○ *You put pudding in the pie crust and then put whipped cream on.*

ATTACHED TO /ɔːn, ɑn/ *prep, adj, adv* [not gradable] attached to or forming a part of another thing ○ *Read the instructions on the bag.* ○ *Hang your coat on that hook.* ○ *Don't screw the lid on so tight.*

COVERING /ɔːn, ɑn/ *prep, adj, adv* [not gradable] covering or wrapping another thing ○ *The child had no shoes on her feet.* ○ *You should put a coat on.* ○ *The baby's got nothing on* (= is not wearing anything).

AT /ɔːn, ɑn/ *prep* at, near, or next to a particular place, thing, or person ○ *They live on Carlisle Street.* ○ *Which page is that cheesecake recipe on?* ○ *El Paso is on the Mexican border.* ○ *Princess Caroline was seated on my left.*

STORED AS /ɔːn, ɑn/ *prep* used to show the form in which information is stored or recorded for use with an electronic device ○ *How much data can you store on your hard disk?* ○ *That movie just came out on video.*

BROADCAST /ɔːn, ɑn/ *prep, adj, adv* [not gradable] being broadcast ○ *What's on TV tonight?* ○ *I wish there were more jazz on the radio.*

USING /ɔːn, ɑn/ *prep* showing what tool, instrument, system, etc., is used to do or achieve something ○ *I made this chart on my computer.* ○ *I'm on the telephone.* ○ *You'll cut yourself on that knife if you're not careful.*

TAKING /ɔːn, ɑn/ *prep* showing that a drug is taken or used ○ *My doctor put me on antibiotics.*

NEEDING HELP FROM /ɔːn, ɑn/ *prep* used after some verbs and adjectives to show that help is needed from a person or thing ○ *We're counting on you to drive us to the airport.*

EXISTING /ɔːn, ɑn/ *prep* used to show that a condition or process exists or is being experienced ○ *The musicians are on strike.* ○ *Are winter coats on sale?*

INVOLVED IN /ɔːn, ɑn/ *prep* **1** involved in or doing a particular thing ○ *I'm working on a new book.* ○ *She's on a diet.* **2** On is also used to show that someone is doing something he or she was chosen to do: *There was a guard on duty.*

CONNECTED WITH /ɔːn, ɑn/ *prep* connected with or part of a group or process ○ *Have you ever served on a jury?* ○ *There are two women on the committee.*

ABOUT /ɔːn, ɑn/ *prep* about or having something as a subject ○ *Did you see that documentary on volcanoes last night?* ○ *Sarita's thesis is on George Crumb.*

PAYING FOR /ɔːn, ɑn/ *prep* showing that something is paid for or how something is paid for ○ *I've wasted a lot of money on this car.* ○ *Lunch is on me.*

WHEN /ɔːn, ɑn/ *prep* used to show when something happens ○ *What are you doing on Friday?* ○ *My birthday's on May 30th.* ○ *The flight arrived on time* (= at the time it was expected).

TRAVEL BY /ɔːn, ɑn/ *prep, adj, adv* [not gradable] **1** used to show a method of travel; VIA ○ *It's easy to get to the beach on foot.* ○ *Two people rode by on horseback.* **2** On is also sometimes used to show you are getting in a vehicle: *It's time to get on the bus.*

COMPARED WITH /ɔːn, ɑn/ *prep* used to make a comparison ○ *This week's sales figures are down on last week's.* ○ *He's got two inches on me* (= is two inches taller).

HAVING AN EFFECT /ɔːn, ɑn/ *prep* used to show that something has happened to someone ○ *Marty is always playing jokes on people.* ○ *My car broke down on me this morning.*

POSSESSING /ɔːn, ɑn/ *prep* possessing, carrying, or having something with you now ○ *Do you have any money on you?* ○ *I don't have my driver's license on me.*

NOT STOPPING /ɔːn, ɑn/ *adv* [not gradable] continuing or not stopping ○ *If her line's busy, keep on trying.*

TOWARD /ɔːn, ɑn/ *adv* [not gradable] toward or to something or someone ○ *You go on and I'll meet you at the lake.* ○ *Pass the newsletter on to Emily.*

OPERATING /ɔːn, ɑn/ *adj, adv* [not gradable] **1** operating or made to start operating ○ *Would you turn the TV on?* ○ *The electricity hasn't been turned back on yet.* **2** *infml* Someone who is on is either performing very well or is in a situation where the person must be aware of everything that is happening and ready to act: *Andy was really on last night – I haven't heard him sing like that in months.*

HAPPENING /ɔːn, ɑn/ *adj* [not gradable] happening or planned ○ *I have nothing on for tomorrow.* ○ *Is the party still on?*

on and off *adj, adv* OFF AND ON

on and on *adv* continuing for a long time ○ *The noise just went on and on.*

on-board /ˌɔːnˌbɔːrd, ˌɑn-, -ˌbourd/ *adj* [not gradable] existing among the parts that make up or come with a vehicle ○ *an on-board computer*

once **AT ONE TIME** /wʌns/ *adv* [not gradable] on or at a single time ○ *I went to Disney World once.* ○ *The book club meets once a month.* ○ *Going to the Olympics is a once-in-a-lifetime opportunity* (= a rare and valuable one).

IN THE PAST /wʌns/ *adv* [not gradable] in the past, but not now ○ *I lived in Milwaukee once.* ○ *Computers are much cheaper now than they once were.*

AS SOON AS /wʌns/ *conjunction* as soon as, or when ○ *Once you've tried their ice cream, you'll be back for more.*

IDIOMS with once

• **at once** **1** immediately ○ *You have to call him at once.* **2** **At once** also means at the same time: *Everything happened at once – she graduated, got a job, and got married, all in June!*
• **once and for all** completely and finally ○ *We have to decide, once and for all, whether we want to ask Dad for money.*
• **once in a blue moon** rarely ○ *Once in a blue moon he'd call, but for months at a time we heard nothing.*
• **(every) once in a while** sometimes but not often ○ *We see each other every once in a while.* ○ Compare (EVERY) NOW AND THEN at NOW IDIOM
• **once more, once again** another time ○ *I'll explain it once more, but listen this time.*

once-over /ˈwʌnˌsouˑvər/ *n* [C usually sing] *infml* a quick examination of someone or something ○ *The security guards gave me the once-over.*

oncoming /ˈɔːnˌkʌm·ɪŋ, ˈɑn-/ *adj* [not gradable] moving toward or approaching you ○ *His car was struck by an oncoming vehicle.*

one **NUMBER** /wʌn/ *number* **1** 1 ○ *I have one brother and two sisters.* ○ *Paula rented a one-room studio apartment.* **2** One can also mean one o'clock. ○ Related Number: FIRST

SINGLE /wʌn/ *pronoun, adj* [not gradable] not two or more ○ *There are too many of us to fit in just one car.*

ONLY /wʌn/ *adj* [not gradable] used when saying there is no other person or thing ○ *He's the one person you can rely on in an emergency.*

PARTICULAR THING/PERSON /wʌn/ *pronoun, adj* [not gradable] **1** used to refer to a particular thing or person within a group or range of things or people ○ *There are lots of flavors – which one would you like?* ○ *He advised workers around him, especially the younger ones, to be patient.* ○ *Kayla is the one with dark brown hair.* ○ *Make sure the ones that we've got there do what you want them to do.* ○ *She is one beautiful woman* (= she is very beautiful). ○ *Why don't we meet for lunch one day next week?* **2** To be **one of** a group of people or things is to be a member of that group: *It's one of the most popular songs.*

O

ANY PERSON /wʌn/ *pronoun fml* any person, but not a particular person ○ *One ought to make the effort to vote.*

IDIOMS with one

• **one after another, one after the other** first one person or thing and then another, followed by more ○ *He ate one chocolate after another until the box was finished.*

• **one and only** only ○ *This may be your one and only opportunity to meet her.*

• **one by one** one person or thing following another in order ○ *The children filed out of the bus, one by one.*

• **one day** at some time in the future ○ *I'd like to go to Mexico again one day.*

• **one of a kind** the only person or thing of a particular type ○ *In the world of ballet, she was one of a kind.*

• **one of the boys** someone who is accepted as part of a social group, esp. a group of boys or men ○ *She hangs out with her brothers' friends, like one of the boys.*

• **one of those days** a bad day when things do not happen as you would like them to ○ *I forgot to call her again - it's just been one of those days.* ○ Compare NOT YOUR DAY at NOT IDIOMS

• **one step at a time** slowly and carefully, doing just a little at a time ○ *He wanted to rush through the job, but I encouraged him to take it one step at a time.*

• **one thing leads to another** an event or activity results in another that you have usually not planned ○ *I agreed to help him paint the house, and one thing led to another until I ended up helping him fix his kitchen.*

O

• **one way or another** using any method possible ○ *These bills have to be paid one way or another.*

• **one way or the other 1** which of two possibilities will be chosen ○ *They've had two weeks to think about it, and now they have to decide one way or the other.* **2** whatever method is used ○ *One way or the other, this project has to be finished by Tuesday.*

• **on the one hand** *but* **on the other hand** the first thing to consider is this, but a second and different thing to consider is this ○ *On the one hand, I'd like a job that pays more, but on the other hand I enjoy the work I'm doing now.*

• **the one and only** the only person or thing of this type ○ *And now I'd like to introduce, the one and only Stevie Wonder!*

one another *pronoun* EACH OTHER

one-man, one-woman *adj* [not gradable] created or performed by only one man or woman

one-on-one *adj, adv* [not gradable] having direct, personal communication ○ *Smaller class sizes mean that children get more one-on-one teacher attention.*

onerous /ˈɑn·ə·rəs, ˈoʊ·nə-/ *adj* causing great difficulty or trouble ○ *The tax bill was aimed at lifting the onerous tax burden from the backs of the middle class.*

oneself /wʌn ˈself, wə-/ *pronoun fml* the person speaking; the reflexive form of one ○ *One needs to take care of oneself.*

one-shot *adj* [not gradable] happening or possible only once ○ *The tryouts are a one-shot deal, so you either you get the part or you don't.*

one-sided NOT FAIR *adj* [not gradable] not balanced or fair ○ *The book presents a one-sided view of history.*

NOT EQUAL *adj* [not gradable] benefiting one side, group, or team much more than the other ○ *It was a one-sided victory - we won 10-3.*

one-time ONLY ONCE *adj* [not gradable] only once ○ *The gym charges a separate, one-time fee to join.*

IN THE PAST *adj* [not gradable] at some time in the past, but no longer ○ *The one-time Olympic track star is now a coach.*

one-track mind *n* [C] someone's tendency to think about or be interested in a single subject

one-upmanship /wʌn ˈʌp·mən ˌʃɪp/, **one-upsmanship** /wʌn ˈʌp·smən ˌʃɪp/ *n* [U] an effort to show that you are better than someone you are competing with ○ *We heard the usual boasting and one-upsmanship before the boxers entered the ring.*

one-way *adj, adv* [not gradable] traveling or allowing travel in only a single direction ○ *a one-way street* ○ *He bought a one-way ticket to Miami.*

ongoing Ⓐ /ˈɔːn ˌgoʊ·ɪŋ, ˈɑn-/ *adj* [not gradable] continuing to exist, happen, or develop ○ *The investigation is ongoing.*

onion /ˈʌn·jən/ *n* [C] a plant with a round, edible root having a strong smell and flavor

online /ˈɔːn ˈlɑɪn, ˈɑn-/, **on-line** *adj, adv* [not gradable] using a computer to communicate with other computers, or of or about a computer that is connected to another computer ○ *I went online to see if I got any e-mail.* ○ *The computer isn't online now, so the phone line is available.*

onlooker /ˈɔːn ˌlʊk·ər, ˈɑn-/ *n* [C] someone who watches something happening but is not involved in it ○ *The building was demolished before a crowd of nearly 200 onlookers.*

only SINGLE /ˈoʊn·li/ *adj* [not gradable] being a particular one or that one and no other; single ○ *As the only surviving relative, he will someday inherit a lot of money.* ○ *The only solution is to buy a whole new computer.*

NO MORE THAN /ˈoʊn·li/ *adv* [not gradable] **1** no more than or no other than; as much or as great as (something) but no more; just ○ *She was only 27 when she died.* ○ *These shoes only cost $40.* ○ *I was only trying to help.* ○ *I was only going to say that I was sorry.* ○ *I got paid only* (= as recently as) *yesterday.* **2** Only can mean "and no one else": *Only she knew the truth.* ○ *This club is for members only.*

IN THIS WAY /ˈoʊn·li/ *adv* [not gradable] for this reason or in this way and no other ○ *You only said* that to annoy me. ○ It only happened because he forgot to lock the front door.

BUT /ˈoʊn·li/ *conjunction* but; except that ○ *This fabric is similar to wool, only cheaper.* ○ *I would have left earlier, only you didn't want to.*

IDIOMS with only

• **only just** very recently ○ *She only just arrived in town.*

• **only too** very ○ *There are some people who would be only too happy to cheat on their tax returns.*

only child *n* [C usually sing] someone who has no sisters or brothers

onomatopoeia /ˌɑn·əˌmɑţ·əˈpiː·ə/ *n* [U] ***grammar*** the naming of something with a word whose sound suggests the thing itself, such as "buzz" and "zip"

on-screen *adj, adv* [not gradable] on the screen of a television or computer ○ *I easily adjusted the colors by using the on-screen menu.*

onset /ˈɔːn·set, ˈɑn-/ *n* [U] the beginning of something ○ *We have to get the roof fixed before the onset of winter.*

onslaught /ˈɑn·slɔːt, ˈɔːn-/ *n* [C] a violent and forceful attack ○ *(fig.) With the nice weather, the beach towns are expecting an onslaught of tourists.*

onstage /ɑnˈsteɪdʒ/ *adj, adv* [not gradable] on the STAGE of a theater or other place where people are performing ○ *Rock stars usually show up onstage looking just the way you want them to.*

onto /ˈɔːn·tə, ˈɑn-, -tuː/ *prep* **1** into a position on ○ *Gennaro tossed his newspaper onto the table.* **2** To **be onto** something or someone is to be aware of other information relating to the situation, esp. when someone is trying to deceive you: *Everybody is onto you – why don't you admit you lied?*

onus /ˈoʊ·nəs/ *n* [U] the responsibility or duty to do something ○ *The onus is on the administration to come up with a balanced budget.*

onward /ˈɔːn·wərd, ˈɑn-/, **onwards** /ˈɔːn·wərdz, ˈɑn-/ *adj, adv* [not gradable] further on in place or time ○ *The geese continued onward, heading south.*

oodles /ˈuːd·əlz/ *pl n infml* very large amounts ○ *She inherited oodles of money.*

ooh /uː/ *exclamation infml* used to express surprise, pleasure, or approval ○ *Ooh, I like that sauce they put on the fish.*

oops /ʊps, uːps/ *exclamation infml* used to express surprise or regret about a mistake or slight accident

ooze /uːz/ *v* [I/T] to flow slowly out through a small opening, or to slowly produce a liquid through such an opening ○ [I always + adv/prep] *Sap oozed from the pine tree.* ○ [T] *The wound oozed blood.* ○ [T] *(fig.) The golfer was oozing confidence* (= had a lot of confidence).

ooze /uːz/ *n* [U] soft, sticky earth

opaque /oʊˈpeɪk/ *adj* [not gradable] **1** (of a substance) preventing light from traveling through, and therefore not allowing you to see through it ○ *opaque watercolors* **2** Opaque also means difficult to understand: *The majority of readers found his poetry difficult, even opaque.* ○ Compare TRANSLUCENT; TRANSPARENT

op-ed /ˈɑpˈed/ *n* [U] a page or section of a newspaper with signed articles expressing personal opinions, usually opposite the page of EDITORIALS (= statements of the newspaper's opinions)

open **POSITIONED FOR ACCESS** /ˈoʊ·pən/ *adj, adv* [not gradable] being in a position that allows things to pass through or that allows for immediate use; not closed or fastened ○ *The window was wide open.* ○ *The trunk of his car had been pried open.*

open /ˈoʊ·pən/ *v* [I/T] ○ [T] *She opened a window to let in some air.* ○ [T] *You can open your eyes now.* ○ [I] *These cans open easily.* ○ [I] *That door opens (out) onto the porch.*

opener /ˈoʊ·pə·nər/ *n* [C] a device for opening closed containers ○ *a bottle/can opener*

opening /ˈoʊ·pə·nɪŋ/ *n* [C] a hole or space ○ *The children crawled through an opening in the fence.*

READY FOR USE /ˈoʊ·pən/ *adj* [not gradable] ready to be used or to provide a service ○ *The supermarket is open till 9 p.m.*

open /ˈoʊ·pən/ *v* [I/T] to become or make something ready to provide a service ○ [I] *The cleaners opens (up) around seven.* ○ [T] *They opened the exhibit to the public yesterday.*

opening /ˈoʊ·pə·nɪŋ/ *n* [C] ○ *A huge crowd turned out for the opening of the new show.*

COMMON LEARNER ERROR

open/close or turn on/turn off?

In some languages the verbs **open** and **close** are used with electrical devices such as TVs and lights. In English, however, you must use the phrasal verbs **turn on** and **turn off** or **shut off**.

She turned on the light and looked around the room.
~~*She opened the light and looked around the room.*~~
I asked him to turn off the light.
~~*I asked him to close the light.*~~
Please shut off the TV and go to bed.
~~*Please close the TV and go to bed.*~~

CONFUSABLES

open and close

Be careful not to confuse the adjective and verb forms of these words.

The adjectives are **open** and **closed**.
Is the supermarket open on Sunday?
The museum is closed today.
The verbs are **open** and **close**.
The supermarket opens at 8 a.m.
The museum closes at 5 p.m. tomorrow.

O

NOT DECIDED /ˈoʊ·pən/ *adj* not decided or certain ○ *I want to keep my options open until I have all the facts.* ○ *Whether we'll go is still an open question.* ○ *You should keep an open mind about your new school* (= not form any opinions) *until you've been there.*

NOT SECRET /ˈoʊ·pən/ *adj* **1** not secret ○ *Open warfare had broken out in Yugoslavia.* **2** A person who is open is honest and not trying to hide something: *He is quite open about his weaknesses.*

openly /ˈoʊ·pən·li/ *adv* ○ *She talked about her cancer quite openly.*

openness /ˈoʊ·pən·nəs/ *n* [U] ○ *The agency released detailed plans for greater openness and stronger standards in the international marketplace.*

BEGIN /ˈoʊ·pən/ *v* [I/T] to begin something or cause it to begin ○ [T] *I would like to open the meeting by asking each of you to introduce yourself.* ○ [M] *They're opening up a new restaurant in about a month.* ○ [I] *The film opens* (= will be shown for the first time) *next week.*

opening /ˈoʊ·pə·nɪŋ/ *adj* [not gradable] ○ *He made some opening remarks, then introduced the main speaker.*

opening /ˈoʊ·pə·nɪŋ/ *n* [C] ○ *The opening* (= beginning) *of the symphony is by far the best part.*

opener /ˈoʊ·pə·nər/ *n* [C] *infml* the first in a series of competitions or items ○ *The team played their season opener a couple of nights ago.*

NOT COVERED /ˈoʊ·pən/ *adj* not enclosed or covered ○ *The park is one of the city's largest open spaces.*

open /ˈoʊ·pən/ *n* [U] ○ *After being at work all day, it's good to get (out) in the open* (= somewhere outside a building).

AVAILABLE /ˈoʊ·pən/ *adj* [not gradable] available; not limited ○ *Are there any positions open in the marketing department?* ○ *This library is open to the general public.* ○ *Their behavior at these negotiations is open to criticism* (= can be criticized). ○ *I'm open to* (= willing to consider) *any reasonable suggestion.*

opening /ˈoʊ·pə·nɪŋ/ *n* [C] an available position or job ○ *I hear you have an opening in sales.*

WORD FAMILY open

Nouns	open opener opening openness	*Adjectives*	open opening unopened
Verbs	open reopen	*Adverbs*	open openly

IDIOMS with open

• **in the open** no longer secret ○ *Now that her feelings are out in the open, she says she feels relieved.*

• **open** *someone's* **eyes** to show someone something, esp. something surprising or shocking that the person had not known about or understood before ○ *She opened my eyes to how stupid I'd been.*

• **open fire** start shooting a gun ○ *Do not open fire until you hear the command.*

• **open** *your* **mouth** *infml* to say something ○ *I was so scared that I never opened my mouth.*

• **open the floodgates** to make it possible for something to happen in great numbers ○ *The court's decision could open the floodgates for many similar cases.*

PHRASAL VERBS with open

• **open up LET IN** (used as an exclamation) let me in; open the door ○ *"Open up!" Sam shouted, banging on the door.*

• **open up** *something* **MAKE AVAILABLE** [M] to make something available ○ *Robinson, the first black player, opened up a wealth of opportunity for others.*

• **open up** *something* **MAKE LARGER** [M] to make something larger or less enclosed ○ *We're going to open up the kitchen by knocking down that wall.*

• **open up SPEAK** to talk about your personal thoughts or feelings ○ *I felt I couldn't open up to anybody.*

open air *n* [U] anywhere that is not inside a building ○ *It's nice to get out in the open air.*

open-and-shut *adj* easy to prove or answer ○ *Our lawyer thinks that we have an open-and-shut case.*

open-heart surgery *n* [C/U] a medical operation in which the heart is repaired while the body's blood is kept flowing by a machine

open house PARTY *n* [C usually sing] a party at which visitors are welcome in your home ○ *We're having an open house on Sunday.*

HOUSE FOR SALE *n* [C usually sing] a time when a house or apartment that is being sold or is available for rent can be looked at by the public

PUBLIC EVENT *n* [C] an occasion when an organization such as a school or college allows members of the public in to see what happens there

opening night *n* [C] the first night that a play or other entertainment is performed or shown

open market *n* [C/U] a trading situation in which anyone can be involved and prices are not controlled ○ *New apartments will be built and sold on the open market to those who can afford them.*

open-minded *adj* willing to listen to other people and consider new ideas, suggestions, and opinions

open season *n* [C usually sing] the period in the year when it is legal to hunt particular animals ○ *If wolves are taken off the endangered list, does that mean it's open season for hunters?* ○ *(fig.) The mayor has declared open season on jaywalkers.*

opera /ˈɑp·rə, ˈɑp·ə·rə/ *n* [C/U] ***music*** a formal play in which all or most of the words are sung, or this type of play generally

operatic /ˌɑp·əˈræţ·ɪk/ *adj*

operate WORK /ˈɑp·əˌreɪt/ *v* [I/T] to work or cause something to work, be in action, or have an effect ○ [T] *How do you operate the remote control unit?* ○ [I] *Changes are being introduced to make the department operate more efficiently.*

operation /ˌɑp·əˈreɪ·ʃən/ *n* [C/U] **1** [U] *Several printing presses are in operation* (= working) *at the moment.* ○ [C] *Setting a mousetrap is a delicate operation* (= act of doing something). **2** An operation is also an activity planned to achieve something: [C] *a rescue operation*

operational /ˌɑp·əˈreɪ·ʃən·əl/ *adj* [not gradable] ○ *Repairs have already begun and we expect the plant to soon be fully operational* (= working correctly and completely).

operative /ˈɑp·ə·rət̬·ɪv/ *adj* working, or in existence ○ *Our computerized stock-control system is now operative.* ○ *I'm looking for a large, affordable apartment – and "affordable" is the operative word* (= it has special importance).

operator /ˈɑp·əˌreɪt̬·ər/ *n* [C] **1** a person who makes something work or puts something into action ○ *a computer/machine operator* **2** An operator is also a person who works on a telephone SWITCHBOARD: *Dial zero for the operator.* **3** *usually disapproving* An operator is a person who is often successful but seems too intelligent or speaks and acts too quickly and may not always be honest: *He's a smooth operator.*

MEDICAL PROCESS /ˈɑp·əˌreɪt/ *v* [I] to cut a body open in order to repair, remove, or replace an unhealthy or damaged part ○ *Doctors will operate on her tomorrow morning.*

operation /ˌɑp·əˈreɪ·ʃən/ *n* [C] ○ *She underwent a six-hour open-heart operation.*

WORD FAMILY operate

Nouns	operation cooperation cooperative operator	*Adjectives*	operational operative cooperative
		Verbs	operate cooperate

operating room, *abbreviation* **OR** *n* [C] a special room in a hospital in which doctors perform medical operations

operating system, *abbreviation* **OS** *n* [C] the set of programs that a computer uses to operate, store files, and communicate with devices and other computers

operation /ˌɑp·əˈreɪ·ʃən/ *n* [C] ***mathematics*** a mathematical process, such as addition, in which one set of numbers is produced from another ○ See also: OPERATION at OPERATE

operetta /ˌɑp·əˈret̬·ə/ *n* [C/U] an amusing play in which many or all of the words are sung and which often includes some dancing, or this type of play generally

ophthalmologist /ˌɑf·θəlˈmɑl·ə·dʒəst, ˌɑp-/ *n* [C] *medical* a doctor who specializes in treatment of the eyes

opinion /əˈpɪn·jən/ *n* [C/U] the ideas that a person or a group of people have about something or someone, which are based mainly on their feelings and beliefs, or a single idea of this type ○ [C] *When you're a teenager you've got strong opinions on/about everything.* ○ [C] *McGuinness was expressing his personal opinion.* ○ [U] *Her writings influenced public opinion.* ○ [C] *I think you're wrong, though you're certainly entitled to your opinion.*

opinionated /əˈpɪn·jəˌneɪt̬·əd/ *adj* having strong opinions that you feel free to express ○ *She's seven years old and she's already pretty opinionated.*

WORD CHOICES opinion

The words **view, feeling,** and **thoughts** can be used instead of "opinion."

*In my **view**, her criticisms were justified.*

*My **feeling** is that we should wait a while.*

*What are your **thoughts** on the matter?*

Point of view or **viewpoint** are used especially when someone's opinion depends on that person's situation.

*We interviewed a lot of people in order to get several **points of view**.*

*Try to understand my **viewpoint**.*

The word **attitude** is used especially when someone's opinion causes that person to behave in a particular way.

*It can be very difficult to change people's **attitudes**.*

If you want to talk about a person's or organization's official opinion, the words **position** or **stance** can be used.

*What's the company's **position** on recycling?*

*The president's **stance** on global warming has been criticized.*

opium /ˈoʊ·piː·əm/ *n* [U] a drug made from POPPY plants and used in medicine to control pain or help people sleep

opossum /əˈpɑs·əm/, *short form* **possum** *n* [C] a small animal that lives in trees and has thick fur, a long nose, and no hair on its tail

opponent **OPPOSING POSITION** /əˈpoʊ·nənt/ *n* [C] a person who disagrees with something and speaks against it or tries to change it ○ *Opponents of the project fear it will attract undesirables.*

COMPETITOR /əˈpoʊ·nənt/ *n* [C] a person you are competing against, esp. in politics or sports ○ *His chief opponent in the November election will be Jim Crowley.*

opportune /ˌɑp·ərˈtuːn/ *adj* happening at a time which is likely to give success or which is convenient ○ *You couldn't have arrived at a more opportune time.*

opportunist /ˌɑp·ərˈtuː·nəst/ *n* [C] *disapproving* a person who takes advantage of every chance for success without thinking about the effects on other people ○ *There will always be opportunists ready to play on the public's fears and prejudices.*

opportunistic /ˌɑp·ər·tuːˈnɪs·tɪk/ *adj* ○ *Our team was pretty opportunistic and took advantage of some mistakes.*

opportunity /ˌɑp·ərˈtuː·nət̬·i/ *n* [C/U] an occasion or situation which makes it possible to do something that you want to do or have to do, or the possibility of doing something ○ [C] *She was given the opportunity to manage a day-care center.* ○ [C] *The university is not providing enough recreational opportunities for the community.* ○ [U] *He had ample opportunity to examine the car.*

oppose /ə'poʊz/ *v* [T] to disagree with something, often by speaking or fighting against it ○ *The governor adamantly/vehemently opposes raising taxes.* ○ Related noun: OPPONENT OPPOSING POSITION

opposed /ə'poʊzd/ *adj* ○ *Mom's strongly opposed to my learning to drive.* ○ *I'd prefer to go in May,* **as opposed to** (= rather than) *September.*

opposing /ə'poʊ·zɪŋ/ *adj* [not gradable] ○ *The opposing sides failed to reach agreement today.*

WORD CHOICES oppose

If someone opposes something, you can say that the person **objects**.

*No one **objected** to the decision.*

Defy can be used when someone opposes something by refusing to do it.

*A few workers **defied** the decision to strike and went in to work.*

If someone opposes something in a public way, you could use the phrase **speak out against**.

*More and more people are **speaking out against** this unpopular law.*

If someone opposes a particular thing, you can say that the person is **against** it or use the prefix **anti-**.

*His parents were completely **against** the idea.*

*A group of **anti**-war demonstrators were marching in the street.*

Hostile and **antagonistic** can be used when someone opposes something strongly in an angry way.

*Many people were **hostile** to the idea of change.*

*Management was **antagonistic** toward the workers' demands.*

WORD FAMILY oppose

Nouns	opposition opposite	*Adjectives*	opposed opposing opposite
Verbs	oppose		
		Adverbs	opposite

opposite DIFFERENT /'ɑp·ə·zət/ *adj* [not gradable] completely different ○ *We turned and walked in the opposite direction.* ○ *People often believe the exact opposite of what you tell them.* ○ *His efforts to intimidate his enemies produced just the opposite effect* (= made them braver).

opposite /'ɑp·ə·zət/ *n* [C/U] ○ [U] *My father is a very calm person, but my mother is just the opposite.* ○ [C] *Do you think it's true that opposites are attracted to each other?*

FACING /'ɑp·ə·zət/ *prep, adj, adv* [not gradable] being in a position on the other side; facing ○ *The two settlements are on opposite sides of the river.* ○ *We're in the building opposite the gas station.* ○ *She asked the man sitting opposite if she could borrow his newspaper.*

opposition /ˌɑp·ə'zɪʃ·ən/ *n* [U] disagreement with something, often by speaking or fighting against it, or (esp. in politics) the people or group who are not in power ○ *The proposal faces strong opposition.* ○ *They expect to defeat the opposition.*

oppress RULE /ə'pres/ *v* [T] to govern people in an unfair and cruel way and prevent them from having opportunities and freedom ○ *In his speech he spoke against those who continue to oppress the poor.*

oppression /ə'preʃ·ən/ *n* [U] ○ *There's less oppression and freer speech here now.*

oppressive /ə'pres·ɪv/ *adj* ○ *an oppressive government*

oppressor /ə'pres·ər/ *n* [C] ○ *They're not the powerful oppressors that society says they are.*

MAKE UNCOMFORTABLE /ə'pres/ *v* [T] to make a person feel uncomfortable or anxious ○ *He's feeling oppressed by the approach of a deadline.*

oppressive /ə'pres·ɪv/ *adj* **1** *an oppressive sense of guilt* **2** Oppressive weather is hot, with a lot of wetness in the air.

oppressively /ə'pres·ɪv·li/ *adv* ○ *It was oppressively hot on the bus.*

opt /ɑpt/ *v* [I] to make a choice, esp. for one thing or possibility in preference to any others ○ *Instead of a soft drink, she opted for water.* ○ *He opted out of the health insurance plan* (= chose not to be a part of it).

WORD FAMILY opt

Nouns	option	*Verbs*	opt
Adjectives	optional	*Adverbs*	optionally

optical /'ɑp·tɪ·kəl/ *adj* [not gradable] connected with the eyes or sight, or connected with or using light ○ *an optical telescope*

optic /'ɑp·tɪk/ *adj* [not gradable] *medical* referring to the eyes ○ *the optic nerve*

optician /ɑp'tɪʃ·ən/ *n* [C] a person who makes LENSES for eyeglasses or sells eyeglasses

optics /'ɑp·tɪks/ *n* [U] the study of light

optical illusion *n* [C] something that you think you see, but that is not really there ○ *Some sort of optical illusion makes these things seem to travel faster than they really do.*

optimal /'ɑp·tə·məl/ *adj* OPTIMUM

optimism /'ɑp·təˌmɪz·əm/ *n* [U] the tendency to be hopeful and to emphasize or think of the good part in a situation rather than the bad part, or the feeling that in the future good things are more likely to happen than bad things ○ *There was a note of optimism in his voice as he spoke about his recovery.* ○ Opposite: PESSIMISM

optimist /'ɑp·tə·məst/ *n* [C] ○ *She was an optimist in the face of adversity.*

optimistic /ˌɑp·təˈmɪs·tɪk/ *adj* ○ *I'm optimistic that they can work things out.*
optimistically /ˌɑp·təˈmɪs·tɪ·kli/ *adv* ○ *White optimistically predicted success.*

optimum /ˈɑp·tə·məm/, **optimal** *adj* [not gradable] being the best or most likely to bring success or advantage ○ *For optimum flavor, prepare just before serving.*

option Ⓐ /ˈɑp·ʃən/ *n* [C] **1** one thing that can be chosen from a set of possibilities, or the freedom to make a choice ○ *The program helps students explore career options.* **2** An option is also a part of a contract that allows for something to happen in the future: *He decided to exercise an option to break the team's lease on the stadium.*
optional Ⓐ /ˈɑp·ʃən·əl/ *adj* [not gradable] not necessary or demanded but possible or available; depending on what you decide to do ○ *I think military service should be completely optional.*

IDIOM with **option**

• **keep** *your* **options open, leave** *your* **options open** to wait before making a choice ○ *I haven't signed a contract – I'm leaving my options open.*

optometrist /ɑpˈtɑm·ə·trəst/ *n* [C] a person trained to test the sight of people and to decide how best to improve their sight, if necessary, by ordering glasses or CONTACT LENSES for them
optometry /ɑpˈtɑm·ə·tri/ *n* [U] ○ *She decided to study optometry.*

opulent /ˈɑp·jə·lənt/ *adj* rich in appearance; showing great wealth ○ *He lived an opulent lifestyle that included sports cars and enormous homes.*
opulence /ˈɑp·jə·ləns/ *n* [U]

or POSSIBILITIES /ɔːr, ər/ *conjunction* **1** used to connect different possibilities ○ *Is today Tuesday or Wednesday?* ○ *You can get that blouse in blue, gray, or white.* ○ *There were ten or twelve people in the room* (= approximately that number of people). ○ *We'd better make a decision soon or the whole deal will fall through.* **2** After a negative verb, or can also continue the negative meaning of the verb: *He won't eat meat or fish* (= and will not eat fish either).
EXPLAIN /ɔːr, ər/ *conjunction* used to show that a word or phrase means the same as, or explains or corrects, another word or phrase ○ *Photons, or individual particles of light, travel huge distances in space.* ○ *Things were going well, or seemed to be, but the relationship had already begun to change.*

IDIOMS with **or**

• **or else 1** or ○ *We'd better be there by eight or else we'll miss the beginning.* **2** When **or else** is spoken at the end of a demand, it can also be a mild threat: *You'd better remember to bring the baby bottles this time, or else!*
• **or so** approximately ○ *We raised $500 or so for charity.*

OR *n* [C] *abbreviation for* OPERATING ROOM

oral SPOKEN /ˈɔːr·əl, ˈoʊr-, ˈɑr-/ *adj* [not gradable] spoken; not written ○ *an oral agreement/exam*
orally /ˈɔːr·ə·li, ˈoʊr-, ˈɑr-/ *adv* [not gradable] ○ *She decided to give the report orally rather than in writing.*
MOUTH /ˈɔːr·əl, ˈoʊr-, ˈɑr-/ *adj* [not gradable] of, taken by, or done to the mouth ○ *oral medication* ○ *oral surgery*
orally /ˈɔːr·ə·li, ˈoʊr-, ˈɑr-/ *adv* [not gradable] ○ *This medicine is to be taken orally.*

oral history *n* [U/C] ***English, social studies*** recorded information about the past that has been collected from the speech of people who were there, or a book based on such information

orange COLOR /ˈɑr·əndʒ, ˈɔːr-/ *adj, n* [U] (of) the color that is a mixture of red and yellow ○ *an orange jacket* ○ *The setting sun made the sky orange.*
FRUIT /ˈɑr·əndʒ, ˈɔːr-/ *n* [C/U] a round, orange-colored fruit that is valued mainly for its sweet juice

orangutan, **orangutang** /əˈræŋ·əˌtæŋ, -ˌtæn/ *n* [C] a large APE (= animal like a monkey) with red-and-brown hair and long arms

oratorio /ˌɔːr·əˈtɔːr·iːˌoʊ, ˌɑr-, -ˈtoʊr-/ *n* [C] ***music*** a long piece of music for singers and instruments in which a religious story is told in songs

oratory /ˈɔːr·əˌtɔːr·i, ˈɑr-, -ˌtoʊr·i/ *n* [U] the activity of giving skillful and effective speeches in public
oration /ɔːˈreɪ·ʃən/ *n* [C] a formal public speech about a serious subject ○ *a funeral oration*
orator /ˈɔːr·əṭ·ər, ˈɑr-/ *n* [C] ○ *Daniel Webster was famous as an orator.*

orbit /ˈɔːr·bət/ *n* [C/U] **1** ***physics*** the curved path through which objects in space move around a planet or star that has GRAVITY (= a pulling force) **2** ***physics*** An orbit is also the path an ELECTRON takes around the NUCLEUS (= central part) of an atom. **3** ***biology*** Orbit also means the round hollow area surrounding the eye.
orbit /ˈɔːr·bət/ *v* [I/T] ***physics***

orbital /ˈɔːr·bət·əl/ *n* [C] ***physics*** the path that an ELECTRON or electrons take around the NUCLEUS (= central part) of an atom

orchard /ˈɔːr·tʃərd/ *n* [C] an area of land where fruit trees are grown ○ *an apple orchard*

orchestra /ˈɔːr·kə·strə, -ˌkes·trə/ *n* [C] **1** a large group of musicians playing different instruments and usually organized to play together and led by a CONDUCTOR ○ *the New York Philharmonic Orchestra* **2** The orchestra of a theater is the part on the main floor: *We've got seats in the fifth row of the orchestra.*
orchestral /ɔːrˈkes·trəl/ *adj* [not gradable] ○ *an orchestral arrangement*
orchestrate /ˈɔːr·kəˌstreɪt/ *v* [T] to arrange or write a piece of music to be played by an orchestra
orchestration /ˌɔːr·kəˈstreɪ·ʃən/ *n* [C/U]

orchestrate /ˈɔːr·kəˌstreɪt/ *v* [T] to plan and organize something carefully and sometimes secretly in order to achieve a desired result ○ *The White House orchestrated a series of events to showcase the president on the global stage.*

orchid /ˈɔːr·kəd/ *n* [C] a plant with three-part flowers, or one of its flowers, which can be white or of several different colors

ordain /ɔːrˈdeɪn/ *v* [T] to make someone officially a priest, minister, or rabbi in a religious ceremony ○ Related noun: ORDINATION

ordeal /ɔːrˈdiːl/ *n* [C] an experience that is very painful, difficult, or tiring ○ *Her seven-month stay in the hospital was quite an ordeal.*

order **INSTRUCTION** /ˈɔːrd·ər/ *n* [C] something you are told to do by someone else and which you must do ○ [+ *to* infinitive] *The company has received an order to stop releasing pollution into the air.* ○ *His defense was that he was only obeying orders.*

order /ˈɔːrd·ər/ *v* [T] (esp. of a person in authority) to tell someone to do something ○ *They ordered him to leave the room.*

REQUEST /ˈɔːrd·ər/ *v* [I/T] to ask for something to be made, supplied, or delivered ○ [I] *Are you ready to order, or do you need a little more time?* ○ [T] *I ordered some pasta and a mixed salad.* ○ [T] *After looking through the catalog, she called the store and ordered new sheets and towels.*

order /ˈɔːrd·ər/ *n* [C] **1** *Can I take your order now or would you like to have a drink first?* ○ *I would like to place* (= make) *an order for the new software.* **2** An order is also the thing that has been requested: *The store phoned to say your order has come in.* **3** If something is **on order**, you have asked for it to be obtained but have not yet received it: *The lamp has been on order for several weeks.*

ARRANGEMENT /ˈɔːrd·ər/ *n* [U] **1** the way in which people or things are arranged in relation to one another or according to a particular characteristic ○ *Please arrange the books in alphabetical order by author.* ○ *I can't find the files I need because they're all out of order* (= they are not arranged in the correct way). **2** If you leave/put things in order, you make them neat: *I want to leave my desk in order before I go on vacation.*

order /ˈɔːrd·ər/ *v* [T] ○ *The records are ordered by date.*

orderly /ˈɔːrd·ər·li/ *adj* well arranged or organized ○ *During the fire drill, the children were asked to proceed in an orderly way down the stairs and out of the building.*

CORRECT BEHAVIOR /ˈɔːrd·ər/ *n* [U] a situation in which rules are obeyed and people do what they are expected to do ○ *Observers were present to preserve order during the voting.*

USABLE CONDITION /ˈɔːrd·ər/ *n* [U] the state of working correctly or of being suitable for use ○ *The set of power tools are all in good working order.* ○ *Are your immigration papers in order* (= legally correct)*?* ○ *The elevator is out of order* (= not working).

SYSTEM /ˈɔːrd·ər/ *n* [C] a social or political system ○ *a new economic order*

WORD FAMILY order

Nouns	order disorder orderly	Adjectives	orderly disorderly
		Verbs	order

IDIOMS with order

• **in order** right for the occasion ○ *I think congratulations are in order for the new graduates in the room!*

• **in order for** *something to happen* if you want a particular result ○ *In order for us to win, we'll all have to try a little harder.*

• **in order to** *do something* with the aim or purpose of doing something ○ *He came home early in order to see the children before they went to bed.*

PHRASAL VERB with order

• **order around** *someone* [M] to tell someone what to do in an annoying way ○ *The older waitresses didn't talk to her except to order her around.*

orderly /ˈɔːrd·ər·li/ *n* [C] a hospital worker who does jobs for which no training is necessary, such as helping nurses or carrying heavy things

ordinal (number) /ˈɔːrd·ən·əl (ˈnʌm·bər)/ *n* [C] a number like 1st, 2nd, 3rd, that shows the position of something in a list of items ○ *In "She was fifth in the race," "fifth" is an ordinal number.* ○ Compare CARDINAL (NUMBER)

ordinance /ˈɔːrd·ən·əns/ *n* [C] ***social studies*** a law or rule made by a government or authority ○ *A city ordinance forbids the parking of cars in this area.*

ordinary /ˈɔːrd·ənˌer·i/ *adj* not different, special, or unexpected in any way; usual ○ *His music was of the sort that ordinary Americans could relate to.* ○ *Computers are now widely available in ordinary school settings.*

ordinarily /ˌɔːrd·ənˈer·ə·li/ *adv* usually; most often ○ *We ordinarily get paid on Friday, but because Friday is a holiday, we're getting paid on Thursday instead.*

ordinate /ˈɔːrd·ən·ət/ *n* [C] ***mathematics*** the second number in a pair; a number on a Y-AXIS (= line) that shows the COORDINATE (= place along that line) of a point ○ Compare ABSCISSA

ordination /ˌɔːrd·ənˈeɪ·ʃən/ *n* [C/U] a religious ceremony at which someone is officially made a priest, minister, or rabbi ○ Related verb: ORDAIN

ore /ɔːr, oʊr/ *n* [C/U] a substance formed naturally in the ground and from which metal can be obtained ○ [U] *iron ore*

oregano /əˈreg·əˌnoʊ/ *n* [U] an herb whose dried leaves are used in cooking

org /ˌoʊˌɑrˈdʒiː, ɔːrg/ *n* [U] used at the end of US INTERNET addresses to show that the address belongs to a group or company that is not established to make a profit ○ *dictionaries@cup.org*

organ **BODY PART** /ˈɔːr·gən/ *n* [C] ***biology*** a part of the body of a person, animal, or plant that performs a special job

INSTRUMENT /ˈɔːr·gən/ *n* [C/U] a musical instrument with one or more rows of keys that are pressed with the fingers to play notes produced by forcing air through pipes of different sizes, or a similar electronic instrument ○ [U] *Fred taught his wife to play the organ.*

organist /ˈɔːr·ɡə·nəst/ *n* [C] ○ *He is the organist at Washington Cathedral.*

organelle /ˌɔːr·ɡəˈnel/ *n* [C] ***biology*** any of the parts inside a living cell that have a particular purpose, such as a NUCLEUS (= central part) or a CHLOROPLAST (= part in a plant cell)

organic **LIVING** /ɔːrˈɡæn·ɪk/ *adj* [not gradable] **1** consisting of or relating to living plants and animals, or the substances of which they are made **2** ***biology, chemistry*** Organic also means relating to, or belonging to a group of substances containing the chemical element carbon. ○ Compare INORGANIC

NO CHEMICALS /ɔːrˈɡæn·ɪk/ *adj* not using artificial chemicals in the production of plants and animals for food ○ *organic fruits and vegetables*

organism /ˈɔːr·ɡəˌnɪz·əm/ *n* [C] ***biology*** a single living plant, animal, or other living thing

organization /ˌɔːr·ɡə·nəˈzeɪ·ʃən/ *n* [C] a group whose members work together for a shared purpose in a continuing way ○ *the National Organization of Women* ○ *Labor organizations have contributed heavily to the Democratic campaigns.*

organizational /ˌɔːr·ɡə·nəˈzeɪ·ʃən·əl/ *adj* [not gradable] ○ *The new campaign promotes our organizational effectiveness.*

organize **PLAN** /ˈɔːr·ɡəˌnɑɪz/ *v* [T] to make the necessary plans for something to happen; arrange ○ *The group organizes theater trips once a month.* ○ *They organized a meeting between the students and teachers.*

organization /ˌɔːr·ɡə·nəˈzeɪ·ʃən/ *n* [U] ○ *He didn't want to be involved in the organization of the conference.*

organizational /ˌɔːr·ɡə·nəˈzeɪ·ʃən·əl/ *adj* [not gradable] ○ *Her networking and organizational skills came in handy for a charity boxing event she hosted.*

organizer /ˈɔːr·ɡəˌnɑɪ·zər/ *n* [C] ○ *a union organizer*

MAKE A SYSTEM /ˈɔːr·ɡəˌnɑɪz/ *v* [T] to do or arrange something according to a particular system ○ *She had organized her work so that she could do some of it at home.*

organization /ˌɔːr·ɡə·nəˈzeɪ·ʃən/ *n* [U] arrangement according to a particular system ○ *An organization by subject rather than by date seems to make sense.*

organizational /ˌɔːr·ɡə·nəˈzeɪ·ʃən·əl/ *adj* [not gradable] ○ *The White House Office of Management and Budget issued a revised organizational chart.*

organized /ˈɔːr·ɡəˌnɑɪzd/ *adj* **1** able to plan things carefully and keep things neat ○ *We are looking for a person who is well organized.* **2** Organized also means relating to groups or people who are members of large and often powerful organizations in a particular area of activity: *organized labor* ○ *organized sports* ○ *organized crime*

WORD FAMILY organize			
Nouns	organization disorganization reorganization organizer	*Adjectives*	organizational organized disorganized
		Verbs	organize reorganize

organized labor *n* [U] ***social studies*** LABOR UNIONs (= organizations of workers) considered as a group

orgasm /ˈɔːrˌɡæz·əm/ *n* [C/U] the moment of greatest pleasure in sexual activity

orient Ⓐ **FIND DIRECTION** /ˈɔːr·iː·ənt, ˈoʊr-, -ˌent/, *esp. Br* **orientate** /ˈɔːr·iː·ənˌteɪt, ˈoʊr-/ *v* [T] to discover the position of yourself in relation to your surroundings ○ *After she came out of the station, she paused to orient herself.*

orientation Ⓐ /ˌɔːr·iː·ənˈteɪ·ʃən, ˌoʊr-/ *n* [U] the position of something in relation to its surroundings ○ *The church has an east-west orientation* (= has one main side facing east and the opposite side facing west).

MAKE FAMILIAR /ˈɔːr·iː·ənt, ˈoʊr-, -ˌent/, *esp. Br* **orientate** /ˈɔːr·iː·ənˌteɪt, ˈoʊr-/ *v* [T] to make someone familiar with a new place ○ *Incoming freshmen have advisers to help orient them to the university.*

orientation Ⓐ /ˌɔːr·iː·ənˈteɪ·ʃən, ˌoʊr-/ *n* [C/U] ○ [C] *There's an orientation* (= meeting to help you become familiar with a new place) *for freshmen tonight.*

Orient /ˈɔːr·iː·ənt, ˈoʊr-/ *n* [U] the countries in the east and southeast of Asia

oriental /ˌɔːr·iːˈent·əl, ˌoʊr-/ *adj* [not gradable] ○ *oriental cuisine/art*

orientation Ⓐ /ˌɔːr·iː·ənˈteɪ·ʃən, ˌoʊr-/ *n* [U] the particular interests, activities, or aims of a person or an organization ○ *He has never tried to hide his political orientation.*

oriented Ⓐ /ˌɔːr·iːˌent·əd, ˌoʊr-/ *adj* showing the direction in which something is aimed ○ *Hotels are a service-oriented industry.*

origin /ˈɔːr·ə·dʒən, ˈɑr-/ *n* [C/U] **1** the thing from which something comes, or the place where it began ○ [C] *the origins of language* ○ [U] *He studied the origin and development of the nervous system.* **2** A person's origin is the country from which the person comes: [U] *The population is of Indian or Pakistani origin.* **3** ***mathematics*** The origin is the zero point on a NUMBER LINE (= drawing that represents all the numbers that exist), or the point where the horizontal and vertical lines on a GRAPH (= drawing) cross.

original /əˈrɪdʒ·ən·əl/ *n* [C] **1** the first one made and not a copy ○ *Send a copy of your receipt, but keep the original.* **2** An original is also a piece of work by an artist or designer and not a copy by someone else. **3** Someone who is an original behaves or speaks in a way that is not like other people.

original /əˈrɪdʒ·ən·əl/ *adj* [not gradable] **1** in the earliest form of something, or in the form that existed at the beginning ○ *The original plans have been changed.* **2** Original can also mean different from anything or anyone else and therefore new and interesting: *Our teacher said we'd better come up with something original.* **3** An original piece of work, such as a painting or drawing, is produced by the artist or writer and is not a copy.

originality /əˌrɪdʒ·əˈnæl·ət̬·i/ *n* [U] ○ *The essays will be judged on the basis of style and originality* (= the degree to which they are new and different).

O

originally /əˈrɪdʒ·ən·əl·i/ *adv* [not gradable] ○ *It was a bedroom originally* (= in the beginning), *but we turned it into a study.* ○ *They now live in California, but originally they came from Mexico.*
originate /əˈrɪdʒ·əˌneɪt/ *v* [I] to come from or begin in a particular place or situation ○ *Jazz originated in the US and is now popular throughout the world.*
originator /əˈrɪdʒ·əˌneɪt·ər/ *n* [C] ○ *Morton was the originator of Arbor Day.*

WORD FAMILY origin			
Nouns	origin original originality originator	*Adjectives*	original unoriginal
		Verbs	originate
		Adverbs	originally

original jurisdiction *n* [U] ***social studies*** the right of a court to be the first to hear a legal case ○ Compare APPELATE JURISDICTION

oriole /ˈɔːr·iː·əl, ˈoʊr-/ *n* [C] a bird found in many parts of North America, the male of which has bright black and orange or black and yellow feathers

ornament /ˈɔːr·nə·mənt/ *n* [C] an object that is decorative rather than useful ○ *They spent decades collecting these colorful, Victorian-era ornaments.*
ornament /ˈɔːr·nəˌment/ *v* [T] ○ *Climbing plants ornamented the wall.*
ornamental /ˌɔːr·nəˈment·əl/ *adj* ○ *The buttons on the sleeves are just ornamental.*

O

ornate /ɔːrˈneɪt/ *adj* having a lot of decoration ○ *ornate jewelry/buildings*

ornery /ˈɔːr·nə·ri/ *adj infml* tending to get angry and argue with people ○ *He's ornery and opinionated, but he doesn't lie.*

ornithology /ˌɔːr·nəˈθɑl·ə·dʒi/ *n* [U] the study of birds
ornithologist /ˌɔːr·nəˈθɑl·ə·dʒəst/ *n* [C] someone who scientifically studies birds

orphan /ˈɔːr·fən/ *n* [C] a child whose parents are dead
orphan /ˈɔːr·fən/ *v* [T] ○ *She was orphaned at an early age.*
orphanage /ˈɔːr·fə·nɪdʒ/ *n* [C] a home for children whose parents are dead or unable to care for them

orthodontist /ˌɔːr·θəˈdɑnt·əst/ *n* [C] a DENTIST who specializes in correcting the position of the teeth

orthodox /ˈɔːr·θəˌdɑks/ *adj* (of beliefs, ideas, or activities) following generally accepted beliefs or standards ○ *orthodox methods of teaching*
orthodoxy /ˈɔːr·θəˌdɑk·si/ *n* [C/U] ○ *Any questioning of conservative orthodoxy was viewed as an act of betrayal.*

Orthodox Church *n* [C/U] a Christian religious group with many members in Greece and eastern Europe, or any particular church belonging to this group

orthopedics /ˌɔːr·θəˈpiːd·ɪks/ *n* [U] the medical specialty that deals with the treatment of bones that did not grow correctly or are damaged
orthopedic /ˌɔːr·θəˈpiːd·ɪk/ *adj* [not gradable] ○ *an orthopedic surgeon*

OS *n* [C] *abbreviation for* OPERATING SYSTEM

Oscar /ˈɑs·kər/ *n* [C] *trademark* an ACADEMY AWARD ○ *He won an Oscar for best supporting actor.*

oscillate /ˈɑs·əˌleɪt/ *v* [I] to move repeatedly from side to side or up and down between two points, or to vary between two feelings or opinions ○ *She oscillates between cooperation and hostility.*
oscillation /ˌɑs·əˈleɪ·ʃən/ *n* [C/U]

osmoregulatory /ˌɑz·məˈreg·jə·ləˌtɔːr·i, -ˌtoʊr·i/ *adj* ***biology*** relating to the process by which the amount of water in living things and the substances it contains are controlled

osmosis /ɑzˈmoʊ·səs, ɑs-/ *n* [U] **1** ***biology*** the process in animals and plants by which a liquid passes gradually from one part to another through a MEMBRANE (= tissue that covers cells) **2** Osmosis is also the process by which ideas and information are absorbed without conscious effort: *Children often learn by osmosis.*

ostensible /ɑˈsten·sə·bəl/ *adj* [not gradable] appearing or claiming to be one thing when it is really something else ○ *Rous published 60 scientific papers after his ostensible retirement.*
ostensibly /ɑˈsten·sə·bli/ *adv* [not gradable] ○ *If the engine on an ostensibly low-mileage car is filthy, it may have higher mileage than it seems.*

ostentation /ˌɑs·tənˈteɪ·ʃən/ *n* [U] a show of wealth, possessions, or power intended to attract admiration or notice

ostentatious /ˌɑs·tənˈteɪ·ʃəs/ *adj* intended to attract admiration or notice ○ *ostentatious jewelry* ○ *ostentatious gestures*
ostentatiously /ˌɑs·tənˈteɪ·ʃə·sli/ *adv* ○ *She waved her hand about, ostentatiously displaying her large diamond ring.*

osteoporosis /ˌɑs·tiːˌoʊ·pəˈroʊ·səs/ *n* [U] a medical condition that causes the bones to weaken and become easy to break

ostracize /ˈɑs·trəˌsɑɪz/ *v* [T] to prevent someone from being part of a group because you dislike the person or disapprove of something the person has done ○ *She was ostracized by fellow officers after bringing charges against her partner.*
ostracism /ˈɑs·trəˌsɪz·əm/ *n* [U] ○ *Those who refused to conform risked ostracism.*

ostrich /ˈɑs·trɪtʃ/ *n* [C] a very large bird from Africa that has a long neck and long legs and cannot fly

other PART OF A SET /ˈʌð·ər/ *pronoun* **1** the second of two things or people, or the item or person that is left from a group or set of things ○ *Hold the* *racket in one hand and the ball in the other.* ○ *Some people like living in big cities, but others prefer the suburbs.* **2 Or other** is used after words such as some, someone, something, or somewhere when you cannot be exact about what you are saying: *The event will be held in some park or other.*

other /ˈʌð·ər/ *adj* [not gradable] **1** *Where's the other key to the back door?* ○ *I've found one glove – have you seen the other one?* **2** The other end/side means the opposite end or side: *Put this chair at the other end of the table.* ○ *Jeanne was waiting on the other side of the street.*

MORE /ˈʌð·ər/ *adj* [not gradable] **1** more of the same kind as the item or person already mentioned ○ *In addition to the microwave oven, the kitchen has several other modern appliances.* ○ *There is one other point I would like to discuss with you.* ○ *Are there any other people you want to invite?* **2** Other can be used at the end of a list to show that there are more items without being exact about what they are: *milk, cheese, and other dairy products*

others /ˈʌð·ərz/ *pronoun* **1** *I only know about this book, but there might be others* (= other books). ○ *This one is broken – can you find any others?* **2** Others also refers to people in general, not the person you are talking to or about: *You shouldn't expect others to do your work for you.*

DIFFERENT /ˈʌð·ər/ *adj* [not gradable] different from the item or person already mentioned ○ *I'm going to have to take the car – there's no other way to get there.* ○ *Ask me some other time, when I'm not so busy.* ➤ Usage: **another or other?** at ANOTHER ADDITIONAL

IDIOMS with other

• **in other words** to explain it more clearly ○ *He was economical with the truth – in other words, he lied.*

• **on the other hand** in a way that is different from the first thing you mentioned ○ *My husband likes classical music – I, on the other hand, like all kinds.*

• **other than** except ○ *The form cannot be signed by anyone other than you.*

• **the other day, the other night/week** recently ○ *I saw him the other day.* ○ *She called the other night.*

otherwise /ˈʌð·ərˌwɑɪz/ *adv* [not gradable] **1** differently, or in another way ○ *Samuel Clemens, otherwise known as Mark Twain* ○ *Parts of the company will be sold or otherwise dismantled.* **2** Otherwise also means except for what was just referred to: *I like working outside when it's warm, but otherwise I stay indoors.*

otherwise /ˈʌð·ərˌwɑɪz/ *conjunction* if not; or else ○ *Tell me if you want it, otherwise I'll give it to Freya.*

otter /ˈɑţ·ər/ *n* [C] a water mammal with four legs and dark brown fur, which eats fish and is related to the WEASEL

ouch /ɑʊtʃ/ *exclamation* used to express sudden pain ○ *Ouch, you're hurting me!*

ought DUTY /ɔːt, ɑt/ *modal verb* [+ *to* infinitive] **ought** used to say that it is necessary or desirable to perform the action expressed in the verb ○ *We ought to clean up before we go home.* ○ *She really ought to apologize.*

PROBABLE /ɔːt, ɑt/ *modal verb* [+ *to* infinitive] **ought** used to say that the action expressed in the verb is probable or expected ○ *He ought to be home by seven o'clock.* ○ *The curtains ought to be ready on Monday.* ○ *At his age, he ought to have known better.*

ounce WEIGHT /ɑʊns/, *abbreviation* **oz.** *n* [C] **1** a unit of measurement of weight equal to 1/16 pound or 28 grams **2** An ounce is also a very small amount: *If he's got an ounce of common sense, he'll realize that this project is bound to fail.*

VOLUME /ɑʊns/, *abbreviation* **oz.** *n* [C] a FLUID OUNCE

our /ɑʊr, ɑr/ *pronoun* [pl] belonging to or connected with us; the possessive form of we, used before a noun ○ *These are our children.* ○ *Our plans have changed.*

ours /ɑʊrz, ɑrz/ *pronoun* [pl] belonging to, or that which belongs to us ○ *He's a cousin of ours.* ○ *That's their problem – not ours.* ○ *I think these seats are ours.*

ourselves /ɑʊrˈselvz, ɑr-/ *pronoun* [pl] the person speaking and one or more others; the reflexive form of we ○ *We promised ourselves a long vacation this year.* ○ *It's a big garden, but we do the gardening* **by ourselves** (= without help). ○ *Everyone else is busy, so we'll have to go* **all by ourselves** (= without other people). ○ *We had the swimming pool all* **to ourselves** (= we did not have to share it).

oust /ɑʊst/ *v* [T] to force someone out of a job or position ○ *The school board voted to oust the school superintendent.*

ouster /ˈɑʊ·stər/ *n* [U] ○ *She publicly called for his ouster as chairman.*

out FROM INSIDE /ɑʊt/ *prep, adv* [not gradable] from within to a place or position that is not inside a building or not enclosed or contained ○ *I'm going out for a walk.* ○ *He leaned out the window and waved.* ○ *Our office looks out on a public park.* ○ See also: OUT OF OUTSIDE

BEYOND /ɑʊt/ *adv* [not gradable] in the area beyond a building or room, or OUTDOORS (= not in a building) ○ *It's cold out today.* ○ *They camped out.* ○ *Keep out* (= Do not enter). ○ See also: OUT OF OUTSIDE

AWAY /ɑʊt/ *prep, adv* [not gradable] **1** away or absent from your home or place of work ○ *I'll be out tomorrow.* ○ *Leo went out to lunch.* ○ *We often eat out* (= at restaurants). ○ *Bill asked me out* (= to go somewhere enjoyable together). ○ See also: OUT TO LUNCH at OUT IDIOMS **2** If something is out, it is not where it is usually kept or belongs: *I checked at the library and that book is out.* ○ See also: OUT OF OUTSIDE

REMOVED /ɑʊt/ *adv* [not gradable] to the point where something is removed or disappears ○ *The stain on my tie won't come out.* ○ *Cross out the second number.*

O

FROM A PLACE /aʊt/ *prep, adv* [not gradable] away from a place or starting point, or far away ○ *They moved out to the country.* ○ *Have you sent out the invitations yet?* ○ See also: OUT OF OUTSIDE

COMPLETELY /aʊt/ *adv* [not gradable] completely, or as much as possible ○ *She stretched out on the bed.* ○ *We were tired out.*

ALOUD /aʊt/ *adv* [not gradable] aloud, so other people can hear ○ *Her mother called out to us.*

AVAILABLE /aʊt/ *adj, adv* [not gradable] (esp. of a book, movie, or recording) available to the public ○ *Is his new novel out yet?*

MADE KNOWN /aʊt/ *adj, adv* [not gradable] made known to the public ○ *The secret's out about her retirement.*

SEEN /aʊt/ *adj, adv* [not gradable] able to be seen ○ *It stopped raining and the sun came out.*

NOT OPERATING /aʊt/ *adj, adv* [not gradable] **1** no longer operating or working ○ *The electricity went out during the storm.* **2** If something that burns is out, it is no longer burning: *Be sure the fire is out.* ○ See also: OUT OF NOT IN A STATE OF

NOT AWARE /aʊt/ *adj, adv* [not gradable] unconscious, sleeping, or not aware ○ *He passed out* (= became unconscious). ○ *Matt was so tired, he's out cold* (= in a deep sleep). ○ See also: OUT OF NOT IN A STATE OF

COMPLETELY USED /aʊt/ *adj, adv* [not gradable] (coming) into a condition in which something has been used and no more of it is left ○ *Our money ran out.* ○ *His luck was running out.* ○ *Renew your membership before the month is out.* ○ See also: OUT OF NOT HAVE

NOT ACCEPTABLE /aʊt/ *adj* [not gradable] not acceptable, not possible, or not allowed ○ *Thursday is out so let's meet Friday.* ○ See also: OUT OF NOT IN A STATE OF

NOT FASHIONABLE /aʊt/ *adj, adv* [not gradable] *infml* not fashionable or popular ○ *Long hair is out.* ○ See also: OUT OF NOT IN A STATE OF

INTENDING /aʊt/ *adj* [not gradable] *infml* intending to do or get something ○ *He's just out for a good time.* ○ *The mayor is out to get some publicity.*

BASEBALL /aʊt/ *adj* [not gradable] failing or having failed to reach a BASE ○ *He was out on a close play at second base.* ○ Compare SAFE BASEBALL

out /aʊt/ *n* [C] ○ *He made an out on a fly ball.*

EXCUSE /aʊt/ *n* [C usually sing] *infml* an excuse or reason for avoiding an unpleasant situation ○ *The kids need to get home, so we have an out if we need it.*

IDIOMS with **out**

• **out of commission** not working or no longer in use ○ *My car is out of commission again.*

• **out of it** not aware of what is happening ○ *I'm sorry I forgot to call you back – I'm completely out of it today.*

• **out of** *your* **league** doing something that you are not skilled enough to do, esp. compared to other people doing the same thing ○ *She has been working very hard on the project, but I think she's a little out of her league.*

• *someone/something* **is out of** *someone's* **league** someone or something is too good or expensive for someone to have ○ *She was the most beautiful girl in school, and I knew she was out of my league.*

• **out of line** beyond what is considered acceptable behavior ○ *You can disagree with her, but calling her dishonest was out of line.*

• **out of** *your* **mind** crazy or behaving in a crazy way ○ *You have to be out of your mind to go swimming when it's below freezing outside.*

• **out of order** not operating because it is broken ○ *I'm afraid we have to walk up the stairs – the elevator is out of order.*

• **out of place** not comfortable in or not suitable for a situation ○ *The picture looks out of place here.* ○ *I felt out of place in my huge new school.*

• **out of shape** not physically healthy enough for difficult exercise because you have not been involved in physical activities ○ *I'm so out of shape that I get out of breath climbing the stairs.*

• **out of sight, out of mind** not able to be seen, and so not thought about ○ *Problems in remote places can be out of sight, out of mind for many people.*

• **out of sorts** in an unhappy mood ○ *Peter overslept this morning and has been out of sorts all day.*

• **out of step with** *someone/something* not having the same ideas or beliefs as other people, or not being aware of other people's beliefs ○ *The governor's remarks show that she is seriously out of step with the voters.*

• **out of the blue** unexpectedly ○ *My old roommate called me out of the blue.*

• **out of the corner of** *your* **eye** without looking at something directly ○ *I was watching TV when I saw something move out of the corner of my eye.*

• **out of the frying pan into the fire** from a bad or difficult situation to one that is even worse ○ *Many kids who try to run away from unhappy homes discover that they've jumped out of the frying pan into the fire when they try to live on their own.*

• **out of the question** not possible or not allowed ○ *The class ends at 2, and leaving before then is out of the question.*

• **out of the running** having no chance of being successful in a competition or election ○ *He wasn't able to raise enough money for his campaign and declared himself out of the running.* ○ Compare IN THE RUNNING at RUN IDIOMS

• **out of the way 1** completed ○ *I can relax when this term paper is out of the way.* **2** A place that is **out of the way** is far away from areas that are central: *The post office is a bit out of the way.*

• **out of the woods** not having a problem or difficulty any longer ○ *It's too soon to say if either airline is out of the woods yet.*

• **out of thin air** from nowhere or from nothing ○ *She seemed to appear out of thin air.*

• **out of this world** extremely good ○ *The food at that restaurant is out of this world.*

• **out of touch** not informed or not having the same ideas as most people about something, so that you make mistakes ○ *A few of the older teachers are completely out of touch with their students.*

• **out to lunch** *infml* slightly crazy or not thinking clearly ○ *You must have thought I was completely out to lunch when I forgot about meeting you.*

out of **OUTSIDE** /ˈ--/ *prep* **1** from a place or position inside something to a place or position that is beyond it or not part of it ○ *I jumped out of bed and ran downstairs.* ○ *My daughter just got out of the hospital.* **2** If you are out of an activity, you are no longer involved in it: *He decided to get out of teaching.* **3** If something is **out of sight** it is hidden or too far away to be seen.

NOT IN A STATE OF /ˈ--/ *prep* **1** not in the best or in a correct state, or not in a particular state or condition ○ *The picture was out of focus.* ○ *James has been out of work for over a month.* ○ *This dress is* **out of style** (= no longer fashionable). **2** If a person's behavior is **out of character**, it is very different from the usual way that person behaves: *It was out of character for Charles not to offer to help.* **3** Someone or something **out of control** is difficult to manage: *The weeds in the garden are out of control.* **4** A book that is **out of print** is no longer available. **5** When a fruit or vegetable is **out of season**, it is a time of the year when it does not usually grow locally and must be obtained from another region or country: *Tomatoes are out of season now.*

WITH /ˈ--/ *prep* with the help of ○ *I paid for the computer out of my savings.*

BY USING /ˈ--/ *prep* (of a material or substance) by using, to produce something ○ *The dress was made out of velvet.*

NOT HAVE /ˈ--/ *prep* in a condition in which you have no more of something, esp. because it has all been used ○ *We'll soon be out of gas.* ○ *I'm out of patience with her.* ○ *We're out of time – we've got to leave right now.*

COMING FROM /ˈ--/ *prep* coming from ○ *She copied the pattern out of a magazine.*

BECAUSE OF /ˈ--/ *prep* because of ○ *She volunteered out of a sense of duty.*

FROM AMONG /ˈ--/ *prep* from among a group or a particular number ○ *The poll showed that six out of ten people approved of the job the president is doing.*

out-and-out /ˈɑʊt·ᵊn ˌɑʊt/ *adj* [not gradable] complete; in all ways ○ *He's an out-and-out fraud.*

outbreak /ˈɑʊt·breɪk/ *n* [C] a sudden appearance of something, esp. of a disease or something else dangerous or unpleasant ○ *an outbreak of cholera* ○ *the outbreak of war*

outburst /ˈɑʊt·bɜrst/ *n* [C] a sudden, violent expression of emotion, esp. anger

outcast /ˈɑʊt·kæst/ *n* [C] a person who is not accepted or has no place in society or in a particular group ○ *a social outcast*

outclass /ɑʊtˈklæs/ *v* [T] to be much better than someone or something ○ *Jason outclasses everyone on the team.*

outcome Ⓐ /ˈɑʊt·kʌm/ *n* [C] **1** the result or effect of an action, situation, or event ○ *It's too early to predict the outcome of the election.* **2** ***mathematics*** An outcome is one of the possible results in a PROBABILITY (= likelihood) experiment.

outcrop /ˈɑʊt·krɑp/ *n* [C] ***earth science*** an area of BEDROCK (= solid rock that supports the earth above it) that can be seen at the surface of the earth

outcry /ˈɑʊt·krɑɪ/ *n* [C] a strong expression of public anger and disapproval ○ *Plans to tear down the old courthouse led to a public outcry.*

outdated /ɑʊtˈdeɪt̬·əd/, **out-of-date** *adj* no longer useful or modern ○ *an outdated computer system* ○ *This handbook is outdated.*

outdistance /ɑʊtˈdɪs·təns/ *v* [T] to go faster or farther than other competitors, esp. in a race ○ *He easily outdistanced the other runners.*

outdo /ɑʊtˈduː/ *v* [T] **outdoes,** *past simp.* **outdid,** *past part.* **outdone** to do more or be better than someone else ○ *He always tries to outdo his teammates.*

outdoor /ˌɑʊt ˌdɔːr, -ˌdoʊr/ *adj* [not gradable] existing, happening, or done outside a building ○ *The city's outdoor pools open June 19th.*

outdoors /ɑʊtˈdɔːrz, -ˈdoʊrz/, **out of doors** *adv* [not gradable] out in the air, not in a building ○ *We'll eat outdoors.* ○ *The kids are playing outdoors.*

outdoors /ɑʊtˈdɔːrz, -ˈdoʊrz/, **out-of-doors** *n* [U] ○ *Mike enjoys the outdoors.*

outer /ˈɑʊt̬·ər/ *adj* [not gradable] on the outside, or at a greater distance from the center or inside ○ *an outer covering/layer* ○ *A line of trees marks the outer edge of the property.*

outermost /ˈɑʊt̬·ər ˌmoʊst/ *adj* [not gradable] farthest away, or farthest from the center or from the inside ○ *We took a ferry ride to the outermost island.*

outer space *n* [U] the universe beyond the earth's ATMOSPHERE (= the air surrounding the earth).

outfield /ˈɑʊt·fiːld/ *n* [C/U] (in baseball) the part of the playing field beyond the BASES, or the three players whose positions are in this area ○ Compare INFIELD

outfielder /ˈɑʊt ˌfiːl·dər/ *n* [C]

outfit **CLOTHES** /ˈɑʊt·fɪt/ *n* [C] **1** a set of clothes worn for a particular occasion or activity ○ *Susan wore a black outfit.* **2** An outfit is also a set of equipment for a particular purpose: *She got a complete ski outfit as a gift from her parents.*

outfit /ˈɑʊt·fɪt/ *v* [T] to provide someone with clothes or other equipment ○ *I found a place that can outfit us for the canoe trip.*

ORGANIZATION /ˈɑʊt·fɪt/ *n* [C] an organization or group ○ *Our company merged with another consulting outfit.*

outflow /ˈɑʊt·floʊ/ *n* [C] the flow from something ○ *an outflow of waste water*

outgas /ˈɑʊt·gæs, ɑʊtˈgæs/ *v* [I/T] ***earth science*** to release gases and water in the form of gas from hot liquid rock into the air

outgoing FRIENDLY /ˈɑʊtˌɡoʊ·ɪŋ/ *adj* friendly and willing to meet new people ○ *Sherry is a very outgoing person.*

LEAVING /ˈɑʊtˌɡoʊ·ɪŋ/ *adj* [not gradable] leaving a particular job, office, or position ○ *the outgoing chairman*

outgrow /ɑʊtˈɡroʊ/ *v* [T] *past simp.* **outgrew**, *past part.* **outgrown** to grow too large for something ○ *Our teenager has outgrown most of his clothes.* ○ *The company outgrew its office space.*

outgrowth /ˈɑʊt·ɡroʊθ/ *n* [C usually sing] a result or further development of something ○ *The new emphasis on science teaching is an outgrowth of a report that criticized the way science had been taught.*

outhouse /ˈɑʊt·hɑʊs/ *n* [C] *pl* **outhouses** a small building containing a seat over a hole that is used as a toilet, used esp. by people who live in houses that do not have water moving in pipes

outing /ˈɑʊt̬·ɪŋ/ *n* [C] a short trip, taken for pleasure or entertainment ○ *a family outing* ○ *an outing to the beach*

outlandish /ɑʊtˈlæn·dɪʃ/ *adj* strange and unusual ○ *She liked to dress in outlandish clothes.*

outlast /ɑʊtˈlæst/ *v* [T] to exist or operate longer than someone or something ○ *This type of battery outlasts the ordinary kind.*

outlaw /ˈɑʊt·lɔː/ *n* [C] a criminal, esp. one who is trying to avoid being caught

outlaw /ˈɑʊt·lɔː/ *v* [T] to make something illegal ○ *Only one state has outlawed the use of cell phones while driving.*

outlay /ˈɑʊt·leɪ/ *n* [C] an amount of money spent, esp. at the beginning of a planned activity or business ○ *This year's advertising outlay was over $250,000.*

outlet OPENING /ˈɑʊt·lət, -let/ *n* [C] an opening through which something, usually a liquid or gas, can come out ○ *an outlet to the sea* ○ *The plumber tightened the outlet valve.*

METHOD OF EXPRESSION /ˈɑʊt·lət, -let/ *n* [C] a method by which emotions, energy, or abilities can be expressed ○ *Drawing classes provided an outlet for her creativity.*

STORE /ˈɑʊt·lət, -let/ *n* [C] a store selling the goods of a particular company or goods of a particular type, often one selling goods at prices that are lower than usual ○ *a factory outlet* ○ *The company has more than 1200 retail outlets nationwide.*

ELECTRICITY /ˈɑʊt·lət, -let/ *n* [C] a device connected to the electricity system that a plug fits into in order to supply electricity to something ○ *a wall outlet*

outline STATEMENT /ˈɑʊt·lɑɪn/ *n* [C] a statement of the main facts, ideas, or items ○ *The House approved the broad outlines of the president's budget.*

outline /ˈɑʊt·lɑɪn/ *v* [T] ○ *I've outlined my research paper and begun writing the first draft.*

LINE /ˈɑʊt·lɑɪn/ *n* [C] a line or lines showing the main shape of something ○ *She drew the outline of a face.*

outlive /ɑʊtˈlɪv/ *v* [T] to live or exist longer than someone or something ○ *At 90, I've outlived most of my friends.*

outlook FUTURE SITUATION /ˈɑʊt·lʊk/ *n* [C usually sing] the likely future situation ○ *The economic outlook is good.*

ATTITUDE /ˈɑʊt·lʊk/ *n* [C usually sing] a person's general attitude or way of thinking about something ○ *He has a positive outlook on life.*

outlying /ˈɑʊtˌlɑɪ·ɪŋ/ *adj* away from the center or main area ○ *Many of the students come from outlying areas.*

outmaneuver /ˌɑʊt·məˈnuː·vər/ *v* [T] to obtain an advantage over someone, esp. a competitor, in a skillful or intelligent way ○ *He outmaneuvered the competition.*

outmoded /ɑʊtˈmoʊd·əd/ *adj* old-fashioned; no longer modern, useful, or necessary ○ *The city is replacing its outmoded sewage-treatment plant.*

outnumber /ɑʊtˈnʌm·bər/ *v* [T] to be greater in number than someone or something ○ *Girls outnumbered boys by a margin of 2 to 1.*

out-of-bounds, **out of bounds** *adj, adv* [not gradable] **1** (in sports) not within the playing area ○ *The ball was ruled out of bounds.* ○ *The ball went out-of-bounds.* **2** If something is **out-of-bounds**, it is beyond the usual limits of acceptable behavior or the usual standards: *The President claimed the Senator's comments were out of bounds and damaging to reform.*

out-of-date *adj* [not gradable] OUTDATED ○ *The information in the book is out of date.* ○ *out-of-date fashions*

out-of-doors, **out of doors** *n, adj, adv* [not gradable] OUTDOORS ○ *On nice days in summer, we sometimes eat out-of-doors in the backyard.* ○ See at OUTDOOR

out-of-the-way *adj* away from where people usually go ○ *We had dinner at a little, out-of-the-way place.*

outpace /ɑʊtˈpeɪs/ *v* [T] to increase, move, or grow faster than another thing ○ *Aging boomers will outpace the supply of nurses who could help care for them at home.*

outpatient /ˈɑʊtˌpeɪ·ʃənt/ *n* [C] a person who receives medical care from a hospital but who does not stay in the hospital for one or more nights ○ *Anna had foot surgery as an outpatient.* ○ Compare INPATIENT

outperform /ˌɑʊt·pərˈfɔːrm/ *v* [T] to perform better or do better than someone or something ○ *Technology stocks are outperforming the rest of the market.*

outplay /ɑʊtˈpleɪ/ *v* [T] to play better than another person or team

outpost /ˈɑʊt·poʊst/ *n* [C] a small town or group of buildings in a place that is far away, usually established as a center for military or trade operations

outpouring /ˈɑʊtˌpɔːr·ɪŋ, -ˌpoʊr·ɪŋ/ *n* [C] something that flows out in large amounts or with strong force, esp. emotion ○ *an outpouring of love/sympathy*

output Ⓐ /ˈɑʊt·pʊt/ *n* [U] an amount that a person, machine, or organization produces ○ *agricultural/industrial output*

outrage /ˈɑʊt·reɪdʒ, ɑʊtˈreɪdʒ/ *v* [T] to cause someone to feel very angry, shocked, or upset ○ *The proposed pay cut outraged the staff.*

outrage /ˈɑʊt·reɪdʒ/ *n* [C/U] a strong feeling of anger and shock, or an act or event that causes these feelings ○ [C] *The terrible living conditions of migrant workers, he said, were an outrage.*

outrageous /ɑʊtˈreɪ·dʒəs/ *adj* unacceptable, offensive, violent, or unusual ○ *He made outrageous claims.*

outrageously /ɑʊtˈreɪ·dʒə·sli/ *adv*

outrank /ɑʊtˈræŋk/ *v* [T] to have greater importance than someone or something, or to have a higher rank than someone ○ *She outranks the other officers involved in the investigation.*

outreach /ˈɑʊt·riːtʃ/ *n* [U] an effort to bring services or information to people where they live or spend time ○ *The center was awarded a grant for counseling and outreach to the homeless.*

outright /ɑʊtˈrɑɪt/ *adv* [not gradable] directly and plainly, or immediately instead of in stages ○ *They bought their car outright.* ○ *I told him outright that I think he is making a mistake.*

outright /ˈɑʊt·rɑɪt/ *adj* [not gradable] ○ *Environmentalists are asking for an outright ban on logging in the old-growth forest.*

outrun /ɑʊtˈrʌn/ *v* [T] *pres. part.* **outrunning,** *past simp.* **outran,** *past part.* **outrun** to run faster than someone, or to increase faster or do better than something ○ *Martha can outrun everyone on the team.*

outs IDIOM /ɑʊts/

•**on the outs** in a state of disagreement or unfriendliness ○ *Dick is on the outs with his father.*

outset /ˈɑʊt·set/ *n* [C usually sing] the start or beginning ○ *From the outset we planned to conduct our research together.*

outside OUTER PART /ɑʊtˈsɑɪd, ˈɑʊt·sɑɪd/ *n* [U] the outer part of something, or the area or side that faces out or can be seen ○ *She stood in the snow on the outside, watching him.* ○ Compare INSIDE INNER PART

outside /ɑʊtˈsɑɪd, ˈɑʊt·sɑɪd/ *prep, adj, adv* [not gradable] ○ *Hordes of cats howled outside the window.*

NOT PART OF SOMETHING /ɑʊtˈsɑɪd, ˈɑʊt·sɑɪd/ *prep, adj, adv* [not gradable] **1** not within or part of something ○ *I live just outside (of) Baltimore.* ○ *Cars, movies, and radio linked small towns to the outside world.* **2 Outside of** means other than or except for: *There are few cities outside of Boston, New York, and Chicago where baseball fans get this excited.*

outside /ɑʊtˈsɑɪd, ˈɑʊt·sɑɪd/ *n* [U] ○ *People looking from the outside would say I had a dream childhood.*

outsider /ɑʊtˈsɑɪd·ər/ *n* [C] a person who is not involved with a particular group of people or an organization, or who does not live in a particular place ○ *I moved here three years ago, but I still feel like an outsider.*

SLIGHT /ɑʊtˈsɑɪd, ˈɑʊt·sɑɪd/ *adj* slight, small, or unlikely ○ *There's an outside chance that Boston will make it to the playoffs.*

outskirts /ˈɑʊt·skɜrts/ *pl n* (of cities and towns) the areas that form the edge ○ *the outskirts of town*

outsmart /ɑʊtˈsmɑrt/ *v* [T] to obtain an advantage over someone by using your intelligence and often by using a trick; to OUTWIT ○ *You think you can outsmart me?*

outsource /ˈɑʊt·sɔːrs, -soʊrs/ *v* [I/T] to get work done by making a contract with another company to do it, often in another country, rather than in your own company ○ *The candidate talks about working-class issues, particularly about jobs being outsourced overseas.*

outsourcing /ˈɑʊtˌsɔːr·sɪŋ, -ˌsoʊr·sɪŋ/ *n* [U] ○ *Outsourcing might be inevitable, but that doesn't make it any more attractive to American workers.*

outspoken /ɑʊtˈspoʊ·kən/ *adj* (of a person) expressing strong opinions very directly without worrying if other people will be upset by them ○ *an outspoken critic of corruption*

outstanding EXCELLENT /ɑʊtˈstæn·dɪŋ, ˈɑʊtˌstæn-/ *adj* very much better than usual; excellent ○ *You've done an outstanding job.*

NOT FINISHED /ɑʊtˈstæn·dɪŋ, ˈɑʊtˌstæn-/ *adj* not yet done, solved, or paid ○ *My credit cards usually have an outstanding balance.*

outstretched /ɑʊtˈstretʃt/ *adj* stretched as far as possible or held out in front ○ *outstretched arms*

outstrip /ɑʊtˈstrɪp/ *v* [T] **-pp-** to be or become greater than something or someone in amount, degree, or success ○ *Car dealers worry that demand will outstrip their supply.*

outta /ˈɑʊt̬·ə/ *prep not standard* (spelled the way it is often spoken) out of ○ *I gotta get outta here.*

outward SEEMING /ˈɑʊt·wərd/ *adj* [not gradable] relating to how people, situations, or things seem to be, rather than how they are inside ○ *There were no outward signs that she was injured.*

outwardly /ˈɑʊt·wərd·li/ *adv* [not gradable] ○ *Outwardly, he seemed confident, but he was full of doubt.*

AWAY FROM /ˈɑʊt·wərd/, **outwards** /ˈɑʊt·wərdz/ *adv* [not gradable] away from a particular place or toward the outside ○ *The door opens outward.* ○ Compare INWARD

O

outweigh /ɑʊt ˈweɪ/ *v* [T] to be likely to be more important than or have an effect on something else ○ *The benefits of increased immigration outweigh the costs.*

outwit /ɑʊt ˈwɪt/ *v* [T] **-tt-** to obtain an advantage over someone by being more intelligent; to OUTSMART ○ *It is impossible to negotiate if one side feels that the other side is trying to outwit them.*

oval /ˈoʊ·vəl/ *adj* shaped like a circle that is flattened with two long, straight sides and round ends, or shaped like an egg ○ *an oval table*
oval /ˈoʊ·vəl/ *n* [C] ○ *The sculptor created patterns of cylinders, cones, and ovals.*

ovary /ˈoʊ·və·ri/ *n* [C] ***biology*** either of the pair of organs in a woman's body that produce eggs, or the part of any female animal or plant that produces eggs or seeds
ovarian /oʊ ˈver·iː·ən/ *adj* [not gradable]

ovation /oʊ ˈveɪ·ʃən/ *n* [C] loud clapping that expresses a crowd's great enjoyment or approval of something ○ *At the end of the program, the dancers received a thunderous ovation.*

oven /ˈʌv·ən/ *n* [C] part of a stove that is box-shaped with a door, in which food is baked or heated, or a separate device with this shape and use ○ *Roast the turkey in a 325° oven for four hours.* ○ *a toaster/microwave oven*

over **ABOVE** /ˈoʊ·vər/ *prep* in, to, on, or at a position above or higher than something else, sometimes so that one thing covers the other; above ○ *The sign over the door said, "Private."* ○ *He put a sweater on over his shirt.* ○ *The horse jumped over the fence.* ○ *I couldn't hear what she said over the sound of the music* (= The music was louder than her voice). ○ Compare UNDER LOWER POSITION
over /ˈoʊ·vər/ *adv* [not gradable] ○ *We repaired the cracks in the wall and painted over them.*

ACROSS /ˈoʊ·vər/ *prep* **1** across from one side to the other, esp. by going up and then down ○ *Once we get over the bridge we'll stop for lunch.* ○ *She tripped over the rug.* ○ *The car went over the cliff* (= across the edge of it). **2** Over also means on the other side of: *Their house is just over the river.*
over /ˈoʊ·vər/ *adv* [not gradable] **1** *She leaned over and kissed the baby.* ○ *Who's that man over there?* ○ *When is Howard coming over* (= coming to your house)? **2** Over also describes the way an object moves or is moved so that a different part of it is facing up: *The dog rolled over onto its back.*

MORE THAN /ˈoʊ·vər/ *prep* **1** more than ○ *Most of these rugs cost over $1000.* ○ *Children over 12* (= older than 12) *pay full price.* **2** If someone or something goes over a limit or point, it increases beyond it: *Construction costs are already $25 million over budget.* ○ Compare UNDER LESS THAN
over- /ˌoʊ·vər/ *prefix* too much or more than usual ○ *overpriced* ○ *overdressed* ○ *He's always been an overachiever.*

CALCULATE /ˈoʊ·vər/ *prep* ***mathematics*** *infml* divided by

DOWN /ˈoʊ·vər/ *adv* [not gradable] from a higher to a lower position; down ○ *The little boy fell over and started to cry.*

USING /ˈoʊ·vər/ *prep* using a device such as a telephone ○ *They spoke over the phone.* ○ *We transfer files over the Internet.*

DURING /ˈoʊ·vər/ *prep* during a period of time, or while doing something ○ *She made a lot of changes over the past six months.* ○ *Can we discuss this over lunch?*

AUTHORITY /ˈoʊ·vər/ *prep* greater in authority, power, or position than ○ *Parents want to have control over their children.*

ABOUT /ˈoʊ·vər/ *prep* about or connected with ○ *There's no point in arguing over this.*

FINISHED /ˈoʊ·vər/ *adj* [not gradable] (esp. of an event) finished, completed, or ended ○ *I'll be glad when the meeting is over.* ○ *The game was over by 5 o'clock.* ○ *I'm worried about the test, but at least it will be all over* (= completely finished) *in an hour.*
over /ˈoʊ·vər/ *prep* (esp. of illness) no longer suffering from ○ *Is he over the flu yet?* ○ *His wife died last year and he's still not over it.*

AGAIN /ˈoʊ·vər/ *adv* [not gradable] again or repeatedly ○ *You've ruined it – now I'll have to do it over.*

IDIOMS with over

• **over** *your* **head** too difficult for someone to understand ○ *Most of that lecture was over my head.*
• **over the hill** no longer able to do something well because of age ○ *I don't think of myself as being over the hill yet.*

overall Ⓐ /ˌoʊ·vəˈrɔːl/ *adj, adv* [not gradable] in general rather than in particular, or including all the people or things in a particular group or situation ○ *The overall situation is good.* ○ *The second act was a little long, but overall it was a good performance.*

overalls /ˈoʊ·vəˌrɔːlz/ *pl n* a pair of pants with an extra piece of cloth that covers the chest and is held in place by a strap over each shoulder

over and over *adv* repeating many times ○ *We have to explain the same thing over and over before he understands.*

overbearing /ˌoʊ·vər ˈber·ɪŋ, -ˈbær-/ *adj* too confident and too determined to tell other people what to do, in a way that is unpleasant and not easy to like ○ *an overbearing father*

overblown /ˌoʊ·vər ˈbloʊn/ *adj* made to seem more important or bigger than what is really true ○ *As for the wage gap, Davis says it's overblown.*

overboard /ˈoʊ·vərˌbɔːrd, -ˌboʊrd/ *adv* [not gradable] over the side of a boat or ship and into the water ○ *Someone fell overboard.*

overburdened /ˌoʊ·vər ˈbɜrd·ənd/ *adj* having too much to carry, contain, or deal with ○ *We're trying to stop development in areas with overburdened roads and schools.*

overcast /ˈoʊ·vərˌkæst, ˌoʊ·vər ˈkæst/ *adj* cloudy and therefore not bright and sunny ○ *an overcast sky/day*

overcoat /ˈoʊ·vərˌkoʊt/ *n* [C] a long coat, esp. a thick one used in cold weather

overcome DEAL WITH /ˌoʊ·vərˈkʌm/ *v* [I/T] *past simp.* **overcame**, *past part.* **overcome** to defeat or succeed in controlling or dealing with something ○ [T] *I eventually overcame my shyness in class.* ○ [I] *I believe that we will overcome in the end.*

UNABLE TO ACT /ˌoʊ·vərˈkʌm/ *v* [T] *past simp.* **overcame**, *past part.* **overcome** to prevent someone from being able to act or think in the usual way ○ *He was overcome by smoke before he could get out of the apartment.*

overcompensate /ˌoʊ·vərˈkɑm·pənˌseɪt/ *v* [I] to try too hard to produce a usual or correct state from one that is not usual, and therefore produce a new difficulty or lack of balance ○ *Chris overcompensates for his lack of height by being a clown.*

overcrowded /ˌoʊ·vərˈkrɑʊd·əd/ *adj* containing too many people or things ○ *The prisons are overcrowded.*

overcrowding /ˌoʊ·vərˈkrɑʊd·ɪŋ/ *n* [U] ○ *Overcrowding in classrooms is an important issue in this election.*

overdo /ˌoʊ·vərˈduː/ *v* [T] **overdoes**, *past simp.* **overdid**, *past part.* **overdone** to do, use, or say something in a way that is too extreme ○ *They should get the attention they need without overdoing it.*

overdone /ˌoʊ·vərˈdʌn/ *adj* (esp. of meat) cooked too long ○ *The steak was dry and overdone.*

overdose /ˈoʊ·vərˌdoʊs/ *n* [C] an amount of a medicine or drug that is too large

overdose /ˌoʊ·vərˈdoʊs/ *v* [I]

overdrawn /ˌoʊ·vərˈdrɔːn/ *adj* (of a person) having taken more money out of a bank account than the account contained, or (of a bank account) having had more money taken from it than was originally in it ○ *Your account is overdrawn.*

overdrive /ˈoʊ·vərˌdrɑɪv/ *n* [U] a state of great activity, effort, or hard work ○ *The show's cast went into overdrive to prepare for the first performance.*

overdue /ˌoʊ·vərˈduː/ *adj* not done or happening when expected or when needed; late ○ *She feels she's overdue for a promotion.*

overeat /ˌoʊ·vəˈriːt/ *v* [I] *past simp.* **overate**, *past part.* **overeaten** to eat more food than your body needs, esp. so that you feel uncomfortable ○ *You're supposed to overeat on Thanksgiving.*

overestimate Ⓐ /ˌoʊ·vəˈres·təˌmeɪt/ *v* [I/T] to think that something is or will be greater, more extreme, or more important than it really is ○ [T] *I'm afraid Theresa is forever overestimating her strength.*

overflow /ˌoʊ·vərˈfloʊ/ *v* [I/T] (of a liquid) to flow over the edges of a container because there is too much, or to contain more of something then can be held ○ [T] *Because of the heavy rains, the river overflowed its banks.* ○ [I] *The sink quickly overflowed, flooding the room.* ○ [I] *The train platform was overflowing with passengers.*

overflow /ˈoʊ·vərˌfloʊ/ *n* [C] ○ *There is sewer overflow due to the storm.* ○ *(fig.) The old barn is being used to house the overflow of guests.*

overgrown COVERED /ˌoʊ·vərˈgroʊn/ *adj* having a thick, dense covering of plants growing in a wild way ○ *The playground is overgrown with weeds.*

TOO LARGE /ˌoʊ·vərˈgroʊn/ *adj disapproving* (of people) grown large or too large ○ *Even Professor Adams looked like an overgrown schoolboy beside him.*

overhand /ˈoʊ·vərˌhænd/ *adj, adv* [not gradable] (esp. of a throw) made with the hand and part or all of the arm moving above the shoulder ○ *an overhand pitch* ○ *Throw the ball overhand.*

overhang /ˌoʊ·vərˈhæŋ/ *v* [T] *past* **overhung** (of something at a high level) to stick out farther than something at a lower level and therefore not to have any support from below, or to hang over ○ *The balcony overhangs the patio, creating a shady place to sit.*

overhang /ˈoʊ·vərˌhæŋ/ *n* [C] ○ *The house has a deep overhang facing the southern sun.*

overhaul /ˌoʊ·vərˈhɔːl/ *v* [T] to repair or improve something so it works well ○ *They repaired and maintained aircraft and overhauled their engines.* ○ *Congressional leaders are considering overhauling the Clean Air Act.*

overhaul /ˈoʊ·vərˌhɔːl/ *n* [C] ○ *I think our justice system needs a major overhaul.*

overhead IN AIR /ˈoʊ·vərˌhed/ *adj, adv* [not gradable] at a level higher than a person's head; in the air or the sky above the place where you are ○ *overhead lighting* ○ *A flock of geese flew overhead.*

EXPENSES /ˈoʊ·vərˌhed/ *n* [U] the regular and necessary costs, such as rent, heat, electricity, and telephone, involved in operating a business ○ *overhead expenses*

overhear /ˌoʊ·vərˈhɪr/ *v* [I/T] *past* **overheard** to hear what other people are saying unintentionally and without their knowledge ○ [T] *I overheard a funny conversation on the bus this morning.* ○ [I] *They were so loud, I couldn't help overhearing.*

overjoyed /ˌoʊ·vərˈdʒɔɪd/ *adv* extremely pleased and happy ○ [+ *to* infinitive] *They were overjoyed to learn that their son had not been injured in the accident.*

overkill /ˈoʊ·vərˌkɪl/ *n* [U] much more of something than is needed or suitable ○ *Running so fast with the competition so far behind might seem like overkill, but that's Gardner.*

overland /ˈoʊ·vərˌlænd, -lənd/ *adj, adv* [not gradable] (of travel) across the land, and not by sea or air ○ *They're taking an overland trip across Canada.*

overlap Ⓐ PARTLY COVER /ˌoʊ·vərˈlæp/ *v* [I/T] **-pp-** to partly cover something with a layer of something else ○ [I] *The edges of the wallpaper should overlap slightly.*

SHARE FEATURES /ˌoʊ·vərˈlæp/ *v* [I] **-pp-** to have some parts or features that are the same ○ *Their core businesses do not overlap much.*

O

overlap Ⓐ /ˌoʊ·vərˈlæp/ *n* [C] ○ *There's little overlap between James's playlist and ours.*

overload /ˌoʊ·vərˈloʊd/ *v* [T] **1** to put too great a load in or on something ○ *Don't overload the washer or it won't work properly.* ○ *(fig.) I can't go out tonight – I'm overloaded with work* (= I have a lot of work to do). **2** If you overload an electrical system, you put too much electricity through it.

overlook VIEW /ˌoʊ·vərˈlʊk/ *v* [T] to have or give a view of something from above ○ *Our hotel room overlooked the harbor.*

overlook /ˈoʊ·vərˌlʊk/ *n* [C] a place that provides a good view of what is below, esp. an area of natural beauty ➤ Usage: **oversee or overlook?** at OVERSEE

NOT NOTICE /ˌoʊ·vərˈlʊk/ *v* [T] **1** to fail to notice something ○ *His film was nominated for an Oscar, but Reiner himself was overlooked as best director.* **2** To overlook is also to forgive bad behavior: *We'll overlook your absence this time, but don't let it happen again.*

overly /ˈoʊ·vər·li/ *adv* [not gradable] too; very ○ *Sales forecasts were overly optimistic.*

overnight /ˌoʊ·vərˈnɑɪt/ *adj, adv* [not gradable] for or during the night ○ *You can stay overnight with us if you want to.* ○ *(fig.) The book was an overnight success* (= a sudden success).

overpass /ˈoʊ·vərˌpæs/ *n* [C] a bridge that carries a road or railroad over another road

overpopulated /ˌoʊ·vərˈpɑp·jəˌleɪţ·əd/ *adj* having too many people or animals for the amount of food, materials, and space available

overpopulation /ˌoʊ·vərˌpɑp·jəˈleɪ·ʃən/ *n* [U]

overpower /ˌoʊ·vərˈpɑʊ·ər, -ˈpɑʊr/ *v* [T] to defeat someone by having greater strength or power ○ *The team's forward is strong enough to overpower smaller defenders and quick enough to drive past bigger ones.*

overpowering /ˌoʊ·vərˈpɑʊ·ə·rɪŋ, -ˈpɑʊ·rɪŋ/ *adj* ○ *His overpowering laugh made him immediately identifiable, even in a crowded room.*

overpriced /ˌoʊ·vərˈprɑɪst/ *adj* offered for sale at too high a price ○ *I think these coats are overpriced.*

overran /ˌoʊ·vərˈræn/ *past simple of* OVERRUN

overrated /ˌoʊ·vərˈreɪţ·əd/ *adj* (of something) considered to be better than it really is ○ *After seeing the award-winning movie, we decided it was overrated.*

overreact /ˌoʊ·vər·riːˈækt/ *v* [I] to react too strongly ○ *She overreacted when I said she'd made a mistake.*

overreaction /ˌoʊ·vər·riːˈæk·ʃən/ *n* [C/U]

override /ˌoʊ·vərˈrɑɪd/ *v* [T] *past simp.* **overrode**, *past part.* **overridden** to ignore or refuse to accept a suggestion, idea, or method that already exists or operates ○ *The legislature voted to override the presidential veto.*

overriding /ˌoʊ·vərˈrɑɪd·ɪŋ/ *adj* [not gradable] most important; main ○ *The government's overriding concern is to reduce inflation.*

overrule /ˌoʊ·vərˈruːl/ *v* [T] to make a decision that opposes and changes another decision or suggestion from a position of higher authority ○ *The judge was constantly overruling the objections of the prosecution.*

overrun /ˌoʊ·vərˈrʌn/ *v* [T] *pres. part.* **overrunning**, *past simp.* **overran**, *past part.* **overrun** to spread over an area quickly and in large numbers ○ *The city has become increasingly unpleasant because it is overrun with tourists.*

overseas Ⓐ /ˌoʊ·vərˈsiːz/ *adj, adv* [not gradable] in, from, or to countries that are across the sea ○ *The Air Force was recalling troops from overseas bases.* ○ *I've had to travel overseas fairly often.*

oversee /ˌoʊ·vərˈsiː/ *v* [T] *past simp.* **oversaw**, *past part.* **overseen** to watch and manage a job or activity ○ *As marketing manager, her job is to oversee all the company's advertising.*

> **USAGE**
>
> **oversee or overlook?**
>
> **Oversee** cannot be used to mean "to fail to notice or consider something." The correct word for this meaning is **overlook**.
>
> *Two important facts have been overlooked in this case.*
>
> ~~*Two important facts have been overseen in this case.*~~

overshadow /ˌoʊ·vərˈʃæd·oʊ/ *v* [T] to cause someone or something to seem less important or noticeable ○ *Karen has always been overshadowed by her older sister.*

overshoot /ˌoʊ·vərˈʃuːt/ *v* [T] *past* **overshot** to go past or beyond a limit or stopping place ○ *The plane overshot the runway and wound up in a cornfield.*

oversight MISTAKE /ˈoʊ·vərˌsɑɪt/ *n* [C] a mistake caused by a failure to notice or do something ○ *Because of a bank oversight, the money had not been credited to my account.*

MANAGEMENT /ˈoʊ·vərˌsɑɪt/ *n* [U] management of an operation or process ○ *The FBI provided technical expertise and general oversight to the investigation.*

oversimplify /ˌoʊ·vərˈsɪm·pləˌfɑɪ/ *v* [I/T] to state something in such a simple way that it is no longer accurate ○ [T] *The issue has been oversimplified for political purposes.*

oversimplification /ˌoʊ·vərˌsɪm·plə·fəˈkeɪ·ʃən/ *n* [C/U]

oversized /ˈoʊ·vərˌsɑɪzd/, **oversize** /ˈoʊ·vərˌsɑɪz/ *adj* bigger than the usual size ○ *The house is a Spanish-style mansion with two tennis courts and an oversized ballroom.*

oversleep /ˌoʊ·vərˈsliːp/ *v* [I] *past* **overslept** to sleep longer or later than you intended to ○ *I missed the bus because I overslept.*

overstate /ˌoʊ·vər'steɪt/ *v* [T] to state something too strongly, or to state that it is greater than it really is ○ *The prospect of a trade war is vastly overstated.*

overstep /ˌoʊ·vər'step/ *v* [T] **-pp-** to go beyond what is permitted or acceptable ○ *He overstepped his authority in agreeing to those terms.*

overt /oʊ'vɜrt/ *adj* [not gradable] done or shown obviously or publicly; not hidden or secret ○ *There are no overt signs of damage.*
overtly /oʊ'vɜrt·li/ *adv* [not gradable] ○ *He refrained from overtly criticizing his opponent.*

overtake GO PAST /ˌoʊ·vər'teɪk/ *v* [T] *past simp.* **overtook**, *past part.* **overtaken** to go beyond something by being a greater amount or degree, or to come from behind and move in front of ○ *In the 1500-meter race, he finished with a late rush to overtake Barbosa in 1 minute, 44.84 seconds.* ○ *The Bruins got within three points late in the game but just couldn't overtake the Cowboys.*

HAPPEN /ˌoʊ·vər'teɪk/ *v* [T] *past simp.* **overtook**, *past part.* **overtaken** (esp. of unpleasant emotions or events) to happen suddenly and unexpectedly ○ *The family was overtaken by tragedy several years ago.*

over-the-counter /ˌoʊ·vər·ðə'kaʊnt·ər/ *adj* [not gradable] (of drugs) legally sold without a PRESCRIPTION (= special written instruction from a doctor) ○ *The painkiller is available as an over-the-counter drug.*

overthrow /ˌoʊ·vər'θroʊ/ *v* [T] *past simp.* **overthrew**, *past part.* **overthrown** to remove from power, esp. by force ○ *He allegedly plotted to overthrow the government.*
overthrow /'oʊ·vərˌθroʊ/ *n* [C] ○ *The overthrow of the dictatorship occurred in 1922.*

overtime /'oʊ·vərˌtaɪm/ *n* [U] **1** time worked in addition to your usual job hours **2** Overtime is also the period of time in a game, such as football or BASKETBALL, in which play continues if neither team has won in the usual time allowed for the game.
overtime /'oʊ·vərˌtaɪm/ *adj, adv* [not gradable] ○ *I'm working overtime this week.*

overtly /oʊ'vɜrt·li/ *adv* ○ See at OVERT

overtone /'oʊ·vərˌtoʊn/ *n* [C usually pl] a quality, attitude, or emotion that is suggested in addition to what is stated ○ *His music has been called R&B with jazz overtones.*

overtook /ˌoʊ·vər'tʊk/ *past simple of* OVERTAKE

overture MUSIC /'oʊ·vərˌtʃʊr, -tʃər/ *n* [C] a piece of music that is an introduction to a longer piece, such as an opera

APPROACH /'oʊ·vərˌtʃʊr, -tʃər/ *n* [C] an approach made to someone in order to discuss or establish something ○ *The country's leaders rejected all overtures for a peace settlement.*

overturn /ˌoʊ·vər'tɜrn/ *v* [I/T] **1** to turn over, or to cause something to turn over ○ [I] *The truck overturned, spilling its cargo.* **2** To overturn a decision or judgment is for a court to change it so it will not be in effect: [T] *The court of appeals overturned her conviction and ordered a new trial.*

overuse /ˌoʊ·vər'juːz/ *v* [T] to use something too often or too much ○ *We all tend to overuse certain expressions.*
overuse /ˌoʊ·vər'juːs/ *n* [U] ○ *You can strain your muscles from sudden twisting or overuse.*

overview /'oʊ·vərˌvjuː/ *n* [C] a short description of something that provides general information but no details ○ *I'll give you a brief overview of what the job involves.*

overweight /ˌoʊ·vər'weɪt/ *adj* too heavy or too fat ○ *He's at least 20 pounds overweight.*

overwhelm /ˌoʊ·vər'welm, -'hwelm/ *v* [T] **1** to be too much to deal with ○ *The number of refugees overwhelmed the relief agencies in the area.* **2** To overwhelm is also to cause someone to feel sudden strong emotion: *He was overwhelmed by feelings of remorse for what he had done.*
overwhelming /ˌoʊ·vər'wel·mɪŋ, -'hwel·mɪŋ/ *adj* very great or strong ○ *An overwhelming majority voted in favor of the proposal.* ○ *I felt an overwhelming sense of relief when the semester was over.*
overwhelmingly /ˌoʊ·vər'wel·mɪŋ·li, -'hwel-/ *adv* [not gradable]

overwork /ˌoʊ·vər'wɜrk/ *v* [I/T] to work or make a person or animal work too hard or too long ○ [T] *She overworks her staff.*
overwork /ˌoʊ·vər'wɜrk/ *n* [U] ○ *Her headaches are likely caused by overwork.*
overworked /ˌoʊ·vər'wɜrkt/ *adj* ○ *I feel overworked and underpaid.*

ovule /'ɑv·juːl, 'oʊv-/ *n* [C] ***biology*** the part inside the OVARY of a plant that contains the egg cell and will develop into a seed

ovum /'oʊ·vəm/ *n* [C] ***biology*** an egg in a female animal or plant that can grow into a baby or new plant

ow /ɑʊ/ *exclamation* used to express sudden pain ○ *Ow, stop it, you're hurting me!*

owe HAVE A DEBT /oʊ/ *v* [I/T] to have the responsibility to pay or give back something you have received from someone ○ [T] *Don't forget – you owe me ten dollars.*

BE GRATEFUL /oʊ/ *v* [T] to be grateful to someone or something because of what the person or thing provided or made possible ○ *I owe a lot to my parents, who have always supported and encouraged me.*

IDIOMS with owe

• **owe it to** *someone* **to** *do something* to have a duty to do something for someone ○ *We owe it to our students to prepare them well for college.*
• *you* **owe it to** *yourself* **to** *do something* you deserve to do something ○ *You owe it to yourself to take a long vacation.*

O

owing to /ˈ---/ *prep fml* because of ○ *The performance has been canceled owing to the strike.*

owl /ɑʊl/ *n* [C] a bird with a flat face, large round eyes, a hook-shaped beak, and strong, curved nails, that hunts small mammals at night

own /oʊn/ *adj* belonging to or done by a particular person or thing ○ *Mary has her own car.* ○ *You'll have to fix your own dinner.* ○ *The police testified that the woman left* **of her own accord** (= she chose to do it without being forced).
own /oʊn/ *v* [T] to have or possess something ○ *We own some property in Texas.*
owner /ˈoʊ·nər/ *n* [C] ○ *Will the owner of the gray Ford parked in front of the restaurant please move it?*
ownership /ˈoʊ·nərˌʃɪp/ *n* [U] the right or state of being an owner ○ *His business interests include ownership of a county newspaper.*

WORD FAMILY own			
Nouns	owner ownership	*Verbs*	own disown
Adjectives	own		

IDIOMS with own

• **in** *your* **own right, in** *its* **own right** because of your own ability, effort, or situation and not because of anyone or anything else ○ *Her husband has money, but she's wealthy in her own right.* ○ *This hospital is an advanced critical care center in its own right.*
• **on** *your* **own 1** alone ○ *I don't mind going to the movies on my own.* **2** If you do something **on** *your* **own**, you do it without help from anyone else: *Bridget learned to tie her shoes on her own when she was three.*

PHRASAL VERB with own

• **own up** to tell the truth or to admit that you are responsible for something ○ *A young nurse looked at the two men and waited for one of them to own up.*

ox /ɑks/ *n* [C] *pl* **oxen** an adult animal of the cattle family, esp. a male that has had its sexual organs removed

oxidation /ˌɑk·səˈdeɪ·ʃən/ *n* [U] ***chemistry*** **1** the process by which iron and steel RUST **2** Oxidation is also the chemical process by which an atom or group of atoms loses ELECTRONS.

oxide /ˈɑk·sɑɪd/ *n* [C/U] ***chemistry*** a chemical combination of oxygen and one other element ○ [U] *nitrogen/iron oxide*

oxidize /ˈɑk·səˌdɑɪz/ *v* [I/T] ***chemistry*** **1** to react with oxygen and RUST **2** Oxidize also means to cause an atom or group of atoms to lose ELECTRONS during a chemical reaction.

oxygen /ˈɑk·sə·dʒən/ *n* [U] ***biology, chemistry*** a colorless gas, one of the chemical elements, that forms a large part of the air on earth and is needed to keep most living things alive and to create fire

oxygenate /ˈɑk·sə·dʒəˌneɪt/ *v* [T] ***biology, chemistry*** to get oxygen into a substance

oxyhemoglobin /ˌɑk·siːˈhiː·məˌgloʊ·bən/ *n* [U] ***biology*** the bright red form of HEMOGLOBIN (= substance in red blood cells) that contains oxygen and gives blood its bright red color

oxymoron /ˌɑk·siˈmɔːr·ɑn/ *n* [C] ***grammar*** a phrase or statement that seems to say two opposite things, as in "jumbo shrimp" and "agree to disagree"

oyster /ˈɔɪ·stər/ *n* [C] a water creature that grows within a shell, some types of which can be eaten, and other types of which produce PEARLS (= small, round, white stones used in jewelry)

oz. *n* [C] *pl* **oz., ozs.** *abbreviation for* OUNCE

ozone /ˈoʊ·zoʊn/ *n* [U] a colorless gas that is a form of oxygen

ozone layer *n* [U] a layer of OZONE (= a form of oxygen) above the earth that protects the earth from the sun's ULTRAVIOLET light

P p

P, p /piː/ *n* [C] *pl* **P's, Ps, p's, ps** the 16th letter of the English alphabet

p. *n* [C] *pl* **pp.** *abbreviation for* PAGE **PAPER** ○ *See "Sleepwalking Through History," p. 368.*

pa /pɑ, pɔː/ *n* [C] *infml* father ○ *Do you know where pa went?*

Pa *n* [C] ***physics*** *abbreviation for* PASCAL

PAC /pæk/ *n* [C] *pl* **PACs** *abbreviation for* POLITICAL ACTION COMMITTEE

pace SPEED /peɪs/ *n* [U] the speed at which someone or something moves, or with which something happens or changes ○ *She walks four miles every day at a brisk pace.* ○ *You seem to be working at a slower pace than normal.* ○ *(fig.) The Orioles won their ninth straight game to keep pace with Boston* (= stay in the same position compared to them).

pace /peɪs/ *v* [T] **1** *It was a cheaply produced film, sluggishly paced and poorly acted.* **2** To pace a group is to lead them: *Smith scored 17 points to pace North Springs to a 78-38 victory.*

WALK /peɪs/ *v* [I/T] to walk in one direction and then in the opposite direction, often because you are worried or waiting for something to happen ○ [I] *She paced back and forth outside the courtroom.*

pacemaker /ˈpeɪsˌmeɪ·kər/ *n* [C] a small, electronic device that is put near a person's heart, usually under the skin, in order to control the rate at which the heart beats

pacifier /ˈpæs·əˌfɑɪ·ər/ *n* [C] a rubber or plastic object with a part that sticks out like a NIPPLE and that is given to a baby to suck, usually to calm the baby

pacifism /ˈpæs·əˌfɪz·əm/ *n* [U] the belief that war and violence are wrong

pacifist /ˈpæs·ə·fəst/ *n* [C] ○ *Einstein was an ardent pacifist who promoted the cause of world peace.*

pacify /ˈpæs·əˌfɑɪ/ *v* [T] **1** to cause someone who is angry or upset to be calm and satisfied ○ *The governor later apologized, but union members weren't pacified.* **2** To pacify a place is to bring peace there or end a war: *The US plans to send troops to pacify the country.*

pack PUT INTO /pæk/ *v* [I/T] to put items into a container, esp. for transporting them or for storage ○ [I] *You'd better start packing.* ○ [T] *I forgot to pack my socks.* ○ [T] *Pack your bag, we're leaving tonight.*

pack /pæk/ *n* [C] **1** a number of things usually of the same kind that are tied together or stored in a container, or the container itself ○ *a pack of bubble gum* ○ *a pack of cards* **2** A pack is also a BACKPACK.

packer /ˈpæk·ər/ *n* [C] a person whose job is wrapping or tying items or putting them in containers ○ *a meat packer*

packing /ˈpæk·ɪŋ/ *n* [U] the act of putting things in containers for travel or storage ○ *We still have a lot of packing to do before our trip.*

FILL /pæk/ *v* [T] to fill a space, or to crowd people or things together, esp. in large numbers ○ [T] *People packed Times Square, waiting for the new year to begin.* ○ *The cooler was packed with cans of soda.* ○ *(fig.) How much can you pack into a short vacation?*

packed /pækt/ *adj* ○ *Several people in the packed courtroom were crying.*

PRESS TOGETHER /pæk/ *v* [T] to press something consisting of a lot of small pieces together so that they form a solid mass ○ *Nina packed the snow into a hard snowball.*

GROUP /pæk/ *n* [C] a group of animals ○ *Wolves live and hunt in packs.*

WORD FAMILY pack

Nouns	pack packer packing package packaging packet	Adjectives Verbs	packed pack unpack package

IDIOM with pack

• **pack it in** *infml* to stop doing something ○ *When it started to rain again, we decided to pack it in and go home.*

PHRASAL VERBS with pack

• **pack** *someone* **in** [M] to attract large numbers of people ○ *A movie depicting the country's top war criminal as a hero is packing them in.*

• **pack off** *someone* [M] to send someone somewhere else ○ *We packed the kids off to their grandparents for the weekend.*

• **pack up** to stop doing an activity ○ *It's 5:30, time to pack up and head home.*

package /ˈpæk·ɪdʒ/ *n* [C] **1** a box or container in which something is put, esp. to be sent or sold, or a group of objects wrapped together ○ *a package of frozen spinach* ○ *She went to the post office to mail a package.* ○ *a five-night ski package* **2** A package is also a group of objects, plans, or arrangements that are related and offered as a unit: *a retirement package*

package /ˈpæk·ɪdʒ/ *v* [T] **1** to put something in a box or container, or to wrap things together, esp. to be sold ○ *The book and CD are packaged together.* **2** To package someone or something is also to represent it in a way to make it seem attractive: *You have an idea, but how do you package it?*

packaging /ˈpæk·ɪ·dʒɪŋ/ *n* [U] ○ *frozen food packaging* ○ *It came shrink-wrapped in its original packaging.*

packed /pækt/ *adj* ○ See at PACK **FILL**

packer /ˈpæk·ər/ *n* [C] ○ See at PACK **PUT INTO**

packet /ˈpæk·ət/ *n* [C] **1** a small package or envelope, or a collection of things in it ○ *a packet of stamps* **2** A packet is also a piece of information that is exchanged between computers or over the Internet: *The device converts speech into digital packets that scatter and reassemble at their destination.*

packing /ˈpæk·ɪŋ/ *n* [U] ○ See at PACK PUT INTO

pact /pækt/ *n* [C] a formal agreement between two people or groups of people ○ *a peace pact*

pad **PAPER** /pæd/ *n* [C] a number of sheets of paper glued along one edge so that they can be easily carried about together but separated as needed ○ *He gave me a pencil and laid a pad on my bed for me to write on.*

SOFT MATERIAL /pæd/ *n* [C] a flat piece of soft material used to protect a surface, to prevent injury to a person, or to give a fuller shape to clothing ○ *Hockey players wear these pillow-thick leg pads.* ○ *A carpet and pad on the floor help insulate against the cold.*

pad /pæd/ *v* [T] **-dd-** **1** *Old-fashioned Valentine's cards were often padded with satin.* **2** If you pad a document or report, you add something extra that is unnecessary or not correct: *Lawyers occasionally pad their hours.*

padding /ˈpæd·ɪŋ/ *n* [U] ○ *We put some padding around the sides of the baby's crib.*

WALK /pæd/ *v* [I] **-dd-** to walk with a soft, light step ○ *She padded silently into his bedroom.*

HOUSE /pæd/ *n* [C] *slang* a person's house or apartment ○ *a bachelor pad*

paddle /ˈpæd·əl/ *n* [C] **1** a short pole with a wide, flat part at one or both ends, used for moving a small boat through the water **2** A paddle is also a flat blade held with a short handle that is used in some games such as TABLE TENNIS for hitting a small ball.

paddle /ˈpæd·əl/ *v* [I/T] ○ [T] *She paddled her canoe across the lake.*

padlock /ˈpæd·lɑk/ *n* [C] a movable lock with a U-shaped part that is pushed into another part to close and is usually opened with a key ○ *One of the gates has a padlock on it.*

padlock /ˈpæd·lɑk/ *v* [T] ○ *After 10 p.m. the doors are padlocked.*

pagan /ˈpeɪ·gən/ *adj* belonging to or used in a religion that worships many gods ○ *Those altars were used in pagan worship.*

page **PAPER** /peɪdʒ/, *abbreviation* **p.** *n* [C] one side of a sheet of paper in a book, newspaper, magazine, etc. ○ *What page are the baseball standings on?* ○ *It's a terrific novel, but it's over 800 pages long.* ○ *The article is continued on page 43* (= a side of a sheet of paper numbered 43).

COMPUTER /peɪdʒ/ *n* [C] a group of text and images shown together on a computer screen ○ *Do you have a home page?* ○ *It took her only 20 minutes to customize a Web page.*

COMMUNICATE /peɪdʒ/ *v* [T] to communicate with a person by having the person's name announced publicly or by sending a signal to an electronic device the person is carrying ○ *Doctors are paged by their answering services at all hours.*

pager /ˈpeɪ·dʒər/ *n* [C] a small electronic device that you carry or wear that makes a noise or shows a message to tell you that someone is trying to contact you; a BEEPER

pageant /ˈpædʒ·ənt/ *n* [C] a show, celebration, or PARADE (= a large number of people walking or marching together), esp. one in which people wear special clothing or act out events from the past ○ *the Miss Chinatown pageant* ○ *Our school held a Pageant of Great Women.*

pageantry /ˈpædʒ·ən·tri/ *n* [U] ○ *Between games, the traditional pageantry includes the Parade of Champions.*

pagoda /pəˈgoʊd·ə/ *n* [C] a tall building that is used for religious worship in Asia, each floor of which has its own curved and decorated roof

paid /peɪd/ *past simple and past participle of* PAY

pail /peɪl/ *n* [C] a container, usually with a curved handle attached to opposite sides of the top edge ○ *She carried a pail of water.*

pain /peɪn/ *n* [C/U] a bad or unpleasant physical feeling, often caused by injury or illness, that you want to stop, or an emotional feeling of this type ○ [U] *Your whole perspective on life changes when you're in pain.* ○ [C] *He was admitted to the hospital with chest pains.*

pain /peɪn/ *v* [T] *fml* ○ *It pained him when he did not make the high school football team.*

painful /ˈpeɪn·fəl/ *adj* ○ *A painful leg injury forced her to withdraw from the competition.*

painfully /ˈpeɪn·fə·li/ *adv* **1** *We were painfully* (= unpleasantly but clearly) *aware of the money that we had lost already.* **2** Painfully is also used to emphasize a quality or situation that is unpleasant or not desirable: *He's a bright boy, but painfully shy.*

painless /ˈpeɪn·ləs/ *adj* without pain, or causing no pain ○ *Laser treatments for this condition are simple and painless.* ○ *The company tried to make the layoffs as painless as possible.*

WORD FAMILY pain

Nouns	pain	*Verbs*	pain
Adjectives	pained painful painless	*Adverbs*	painfully painlessly

WORD CHOICES pain

Ache is used for a pain which is continuous and unpleasant but not very strong.

I've got a dull (= slight) ***ache*** *in my back.*

If you have a pain in a particular part of your body, you can say that it **hurts**.

My leg ***hurts***.

Sore can be used when you feel pain because of an injury or infection.

I've got a ***sore*** *throat.*

If you feel pain when you touch a part of your body, you can use the word **tender**.

The glands in my neck feel really ***tender***.

You can say that someone who is in extreme pain is in **agony**.

*He was lying on the floor in **agony**, clutching his stomach.*

In informal situations, if you feel a lot of pain in part of your body, you can say that it is **killing you**.

*I must take my shoes off, my feet are **killing me**.*

IDIOM with **pain**

• **a pain (in the neck)** *infml* someone or something that is annoying or difficult to deal with ○ *One of my students is a real pain in the neck.*

painkiller /ˈpeɪn ˌkɪl·ər/ *n* [C] a pill or other medicine used to reduce or remove physical pain

painstaking /ˈpeɪn ˌsteɪ·kɪŋ/ *adj* (esp. of work) very careful and needing a lot of attention ○ *It took many months of painstaking research, but he was now ready to write the book.*

paint /peɪnt/ *n* [C/U] a colored liquid that is put on a surface to protect or decorate it ○ [C] *acrylic/oil paints* ○ [U] *We need some white paint for the kitchen.*

paint /peɪnt/ *v* [I/T] **1** [T] *We hired three men to paint the outside of our house.* **2** Someone who paints may make a picture by using paints: [I] *She always loved to paint.*

painter /ˈpeɪnt·ər/ *n* [C] an artist who uses paint to create pictures, or a worker whose job is to cover parts of buildings with paint

painting /ˈpeɪnt·ɪŋ/ *n* [C/U] a picture created by putting paint on a surface, or the activity or skill of creating pictures by using paint ○ [C] *oil paintings* ○ [U] *In later years, he took up painting as a hobby.*

WORD FAMILY paint

Nouns	paint, painter, painting
Verbs	paint

IDIOM with **paint**

• **paint a picture (of *something*)** to describe something in a particular way ○ *The statistics do not paint an optimistic picture.*

paintbrush /ˈpeɪnt·brʌʃ/ *n* [C] a brush used for putting paint on a surface

pair /per, pær/ *n* [C] *pl* **pairs**, **pair** two things of the same appearance and size that are intended to be used together, or something that consists of two parts joined together ○ *a pair of gloves/shoes* ○ *a pair of pants/scissors* ○ *Each package contains three pairs of socks.*

pair /per, pær/ *v* [I/T] to make or become one of a pair ○ [T] *Famous paintings have been paired with poems by Sandburg, Angelou, and others.*

PHRASAL VERB with **pair**

• **pair off** to form a group of two ○ *The skaters, six girls and six boys, paired off and started across the ice.*

paisley /ˈpeɪz·li/ *adj* [not gradable] (esp. of cloth) having a pattern of curved, colored shapes ○ *a paisley tie*

pajamas /pəˈdʒɑm·əz, -ˈdʒæm·əz/, *infml* **pj's** *pl n* clothes worn in bed, consisting of a loosely fitting shirt and pants ○ *I need a new pair of pajamas.*

pal /pæl/ *n* [C] *infml* a friend ○ *The two politicians were never really pals.*

palace /ˈpæl·əs/ *n* [C] a large, highly decorated house, esp. one that is the official home of a king or queen ○ *Most of the palace is open to the public as a museum.* ○ Related adjective: PALATIAL

palatable /ˈpæl·əţ·ə·bəl/ *adj* **1** good enough to eat or drink ○ *They could make powdered eggs into palatable omelets.* **2** If something is palatable, it is acceptable: *The city council has tried to make property taxes more palatable by giving homeowners more time to pay them.*

palate /ˈpæl·ət/ *n* [C] **1** the top part of the inside of your mouth **2** A person's palate is also the ability to taste and judge good food and drink: *I let my palate dictate what I eat.*

palatial /pəˈleɪ·ʃəl/ *adj* (of a house or other property) large and highly decorated; like a PALACE ○ *They lived in a palatial apartment.*

pale /peɪl/ *adj* [-er/-est only] (of a person's face) having less color than usual, or (of a color or light) not bright or strong ○ *a pale blue scarf* ○ *A pale young man answered the door.*

pale /peɪl/ *v* [I] to become lighter than usual in color ○ *Madeleine sickened and paled during the next two days.*

IDIOM with **pale**

• **pale in comparison (with *something/someone*)**, **pale by comparison (with *something/someone*)** to be not nearly as good as something or someone else ○ *The paintings he made later pale in comparison with his earlier work.*

paleontology /ˌpeɪ·liː·ənˈtɑl·ə·dʒi, ˌpæl·iː-/ *n* [U] ***earth science*** the scientific study of organisms that lived on earth before there were written records, esp. by examining FOSSILS

paleontologist /ˌpeɪ·liː·ənˈtɑl·ə·dʒəst, ˌpæl·iː-/ *n* [C] ***earth science***

palette /ˈpæl·ət/ *n* [C] a thin board that artists use to hold and mix paints before putting them on the picture surface, or a range of colors, esp. those typically used by an artist ○ *Van Gogh's palette included brilliant yellows and blues.*

palisade /ˌpæl·əˈseɪd/ *n* [C] ***earth science*** a long row of CLIFFS (= high area of rock with a steep side)

palisade layer /ˌpæl·əˈseɪd ˈleɪ·ər/ *n* [C] ***biology*** a layer of long cells between two thin surface layers of a leaf, that contains a lot of CHLOROPLASTS (= parts of a cell where energy from the sun is turned into food)

pall COVERING /pɔːl/ *n* [C] **1** a dark, thick covering or cloud that blocks light ○ *A heavy pall of* *smoke from the forest fires blotted out the sun.* **2** A pall can also be a feeling of being unhappy or hopeless: *News of his death cast a pall over the evening.*

BECOME LESS GOOD /pɔːl/ *v* [I] to become less interesting or enjoyable ○ *The joy of being his own boss began to pall after working 70-hour weeks.*

pallbearer /ˈpɔːlˌber·ər, -ˌbær·ər/ *n* [C] a person who helps to carry a COFFIN (= a box that holds a dead body) at a funeral or who walks beside it

pallid /ˈpæl·əd/ *adj* pale and looking unhealthy ○ *He looked pallid and bloated a few years ago.*

pallor /ˈpæl·ər/ *n* [U] the condition of being pale ○ *The pallor of his skin contrasted with his dark hair.*

palm /pɑm, pɑlm/ *n* [C] the inside part of your hand from your wrist to the base of your fingers ○ *I wiped my palm on my shirt.*

IDIOM with palm

• **in the palm of** *your* **hand** under your complete control ○ *The audience was fascinated by his performance – he had them in the palm of his hand.*

PHRASAL VERB with palm

• **palm off** *something* [M] to persuade someone to accept something that you do not want or something that has no value ○ *They produced fake stamps and palmed them off as genuine.*

palm (tree) /ˈpɑm (ˌtriː), ˈpɑlm/ *n* [C] a tree growing in warm regions and having a tall, straight trunk, no branches, and a mass of long, pointed leaves at the top

Palm Sunday /ˈpɑm ˈsʌn·di, ˈpɑlm-, -deɪ/ *n* [C/U] the Sunday before Easter in the Christian year

palpable /ˈpæl·pə·bəl/ *adj* so obvious that it can easily be seen or known, or (of a feeling) so strong that it seems as if it can be touched or physically felt ○ *The tension in the room was palpable during the exam.*

palpitations /ˌpæl·pəˈteɪ·ʃənz/ *pl n* fast and strong beating of the heart

paltry /ˈpɔːl·tri/ *adj* less than expected or needed; too small or slight ○ *I don't think my paltry student grants are enough for us to live on.*

pamper /ˈpæm·pər/ *v* [T] to treat with too much kindness and attention ○ *Our children are pampered by their grandparents.*

pamphlet /ˈpæm·flət/ *n* [C] a few sheets of paper folded together to form a thin magazine that contains information or opinions about something ○ *a voter's information pamphlet* ○ *She wrote the pamphlet, "Grow Your Own Vegetables."*

pan **CONTAINER** /pæn/ *n* [C] any of various types of metal containers, usually not deep, used for cooking food ○ *a frying pan* ○ *Louise moved around some pots and pans on the stove.*

CRITICIZE /pæn/ *v* [T] **-nn-** *infml* to severely criticize something ○ *Critics panned the concert.*

MOVE SLOWLY /pæn/ *v* [I] **-nn-** (of a movie camera) to move gradually in one direction ○ *Opening scenes panned the crowded, cluttered street.*

PHRASAL VERB with pan

• **pan out** to develop or be successful ○ *Not all his ideas have panned out as he would have liked.*

panacea /ˌpæn·əˈsiː·ə/ *n* [C] something that will solve all problems or cure all illnesses ○ *Books are not meant to be a panacea for an illness or loss.*

Pan-Africanism /pæn ˈæfrɪ·kəˌnɪz·əm/ *n* [U] ***world history*** a belief that people from Africa and their DESCENDANTs (= younger related people) should be united, or a movement to achieve such unity

Pan-Arabism /pæn ˈær·əbˌɪz·əm/ *n* [U] ***world history*** a belief that Arab people and nations should be united, or a movement to achieve such unity

pancake /ˈpæn·keɪk/, **flapjack, hot cake** *n* [C] a thin, flat, usually round cake made from a mixture of flour, milk, and egg that is fried on both sides and usually eaten for breakfast ○ *He poured the maple syrup on his stack of pancakes.*

pancreas /ˈpæŋ·kriː·əs/ *n* [C] ***biology*** an organ in the body that produces INSULIN (= a chemical substance that controls the amount of sugar in the blood) and substances that help to digest food

panda /ˈpæn·də/ *n* [C] a large black-and-white mammal, similar to a bear, that lives in forests in China and eats BAMBOO (= stems of a type of grass)

pandemic /pænˈdem·ɪk/ *n* [C] a dangerous disease that infects many people at one time ○ *What can be done to prevent a bird flu pandemic?*

pandemic /pænˈdem·ɪk/ *adj* [not gradable] ○ *Scientists who study viruses say they don't know what a pandemic strain would look like.*

pandemonium /ˌpæn·dəˈmoʊ·niː·əm/ *n* [U] noisy confusion and wild excitement ○ *Pandemonium erupted in the courtroom when the verdict was read.*

pander to *someone/something* /ˈpæn·dər ˌtuː, -ˌtʊ, -tə/ *phrasal verb* to please other people by doing or saying what you think they want you to do or say ○ *She accused the other candidate of pandering to radical environmental groups.*

pane /peɪn/ *n* [C] a flat piece of glass used in a window or door ○ *a window pane* ○ *a pane of glass*

panel Ⓐ **TEAM** /ˈpæn·əl/ *n* [C] a small group of people chosen to give advice, make a decision, or publicly discuss their opinions ○ *A panel of experts was formed to look into the causes of the fire.*

panelist /ˈpæn·əl·əst/ *n* [C] a member of a panel, esp. on a television or radio show ○ *He was a panelist on the popular television show "Meet the Press."*

PART /ˈpæn·əl/ *n* [C] a flat section in the shape of a rectangle that is part of or fits into something larger ○ *We sanded down the insides of the door panels.*

panel /ˈpæn·əl/ *v* [T] ○ *The hall has been tastefully paneled in cherrywood.*
paneling /ˈpæn·əl·ɪŋ/ *n* [U] ○ *My den had dark wood paneling at one end.*

CONTROL DEVICE /ˈpæn·əl/ *n* [C] a surface with devices that a person uses to control or get information about the operation of one or more machines ○ *The car's instrument panel has buttons that give off a little blue-green light at night.*

pang /pæŋ/ *n* [C] a sudden, sharp feeling of pain or painful emotion ○ *hunger pangs* ○ *pangs of remorse*

Pangea /pænˈdʒiː·ə/ *n* [U] ***earth science*** the name given the one large area of land that, in theory, broke apart to create the present continents

panhandle **ASK** /ˈpænˌhæn·dəl/ *v* [I] to ask for money, esp. in a public place; to BEG ○ *A homeless man often panhandles in front of the bank.*

AREA /ˈpænˌhæn·dəl/ *n* [C] a long, narrow piece of land joined to a larger area ○ *The Oklahoma panhandle extends over Texas.*

panic /ˈpæn·ɪk/ *n* [C/U] **1** a sudden, strong feeling of anxiety or fear that prevents reasonable thought and action and may spread to influence many people ○ [U] *When fire broke out, 602 people died in the panic that ensued.* **2** Panic is also used to describe any behavior that is sudden, extreme, and results from fear: [C] *A brief panic overtook the financial markets in October.*
panic /ˈpæn·ɪk/ *v* [I/T] *pres. part.* **panicking**, *past* **panicked** ○ [I] *The driver who hit him panicked and fled.*
panicky /ˈpæn·ɪ·ki/ *adj* ○ *a panicky feeling*

IDIOM with panic

• **hit the panic button**, **press/push the panic button** to react to a situation with fear and confusion ○ *The coach isn't going to hit the panic button just because we lost two games.*

panic-stricken *adj* [not gradable] very frightened

panorama /ˌpæn·əˈræm·ə, -ˈrɑm·ə/ *n* [C] a view from a great distance that covers a very large area ○ *From the top floor of the hotel you get a panorama of the whole city.*
panoramic /ˌpæn·əˈræm·ɪk/ *adj* ○ *a panoramic view of the city*

pansy /ˈpæn·zi/ *n* [C] a small garden plant with flowers of many different colors

pant /pænt/ *v* [I] to breathe quickly and loudly through your mouth, usually because you have been doing something energetic ○ *Blake was panting hard after running up the hill.*

panther /ˈpæn·θər/ *n* [C] a black LEOPARD (= large wild cat) or a COUGAR

panties /ˈpænt·iːz/ *pl n* underwear worn by women and girls that covers the area between the waist and the tops of the legs

pantomime /ˈpænt·əˌmɑɪm/ *n* [C/U] the art or act of expressing thoughts and emotions with movement rather than speech; MIME

pantry /ˈpæn·tri/ *n* [C] a small room or storage area near a kitchen, where food is kept

pants /pæns/ *pl n* **1** a piece of clothing covering the lower part of the body from the waist to the foot, and including separate sections, joined at the top, for each leg ○ *I need a new pair of gray pants to go with this jacket.* **2** *Br* Pants are UNDERPANTS. **3** A pants/pant leg is either of the separate sections covering a leg in a pair of pants.

pantsuit /ˈpænt·suːt/ *n* [C] a matching jacket and pair of pants worn by women

pantyhose /ˈpænt·iːˌhoʊz/ *pl n* a piece of clothing made of a thin material that stretches to cover the body below the waist, including the legs and feet, and that is usually worn under dresses or skirts by women and girls ○ *She bought a new pair of pantyhose.*

papa /ˈpɑp·ə/ *n* [C] *dated, infml* father; DAD

papacy /ˈpeɪ·pə·si/ *n* [U] the position of the POPE (= leader of the Roman Catholic Church)
papal /ˈpeɪ·pəl/ *adj* [not gradable] ○ *a papal audience/Mass*

papaya /pəˈpɑɪ·ə/ *n* [C/U] a large, oval fruit that grows on trees in hotter regions of the world, having a yellow skin and sweet, orange flesh

paper /ˈpeɪ·pər/ *n* [C/U] **1** a thin, flat material made from crushed wood or cloth used esp. for writing and printing on and in packaging ○ [U] *a piece/sheet of paper* ○ [U] *a paper bag/towel* ○ [U] *paper cups/napkins/plates* ○ *Let's put some of your good ideas down* **on paper** (= write them down) **2** A paper is also a newspaper: [C] *I read it in the paper.* **3** A paper is also a piece of writing by a student for a course: [C] *One of the course requirements is a 20-page paper.*
paper /ˈpeɪ·pər/ *v* [T] to put WALLPAPER (= decorative paper) on a surface, esp. a wall ○ *We plan to paper the dining room.*
papers /ˈpeɪ·pərz/ *pl n* ○ *The guard asked to see my papers* (= official documents).

IDIOM with paper

• **on paper** according to a theory or idea as opposed to something that has been tried ○ *On paper it looks like it could work, but I won't believe it until I see it in operation.*

paperback /ˈpeɪ·pərˌbæk/ *n* [C] a book with a cover made of thick paper ○ *I want to get a paperback to read on the plane.* ○ Compare HARDCOVER

paper clip *n* [C] a small piece of bent wire or plastic used for holding pieces of paper together

paper-thin *adj* [not gradable] very thin ○ *The walls are paper-thin – you can hear every word our neighbors say.*

paperweight /ˈpeɪ·pərˌweɪt/ *n* [C] a small, heavy object, often decorative, placed on papers to keep them together

paperwork /ˈpeɪ·pərˌwɜrk/ *n* [U] the activity of keeping records and writing reports ○ *She liked everything about her job except the paperwork.*

P

papier-mâché /ˌpeɪ·pər·məˈʃeɪ, ˌpɑpˌyeɪ·mə-/ *n* [U] paper mixed with glue or flour and water that can be shaped to make decorative objects or models that become hard when dry ○ *a papier-mâché mask*

paprika /pəˈpriː·kə, pæ-/ *n* [U] a red powder used as a spice to give a slightly hot flavor to food, esp. in meat dishes

Pap test /ˈpæp·test/, **Pap smear** /ˈpæp·smɪr/ *n* [C] an examination of cells contained in the thick liquid on the surface of a woman's CERVIX (= entrance to the uterus) to discover if there is CANCER (= a disease)

par /pɑr/ *n* [U] **1** the usual standard or condition ○ *About half the teachers are good, and the rest are clearly below par.* **2** In golf, par is the expected number of times a good player should have to hit the ball in order to get it into a hole or into all the holes: *Walker shot a par 72 for the victory.*

IDIOMS with par

• **on (a) par with** *someone/something* equal or similar to someone or something ○ *In my opinion, none of the new jazz trumpeters are on a par with Miles Davis.*
• **par for the course** what should be expected because of past experience ○ *The school budget is going to be cut again this year, but that's par for the course.*

par. *n* [C] *abbreviation for* PARAGRAPH

parable /ˈpær·ə·bəl/ *n* [C] a simple story told because it represents a basic moral truth or religious principle

parabola /pəˈræb·ə·lə/ *n* [C] ***geometry*** **1** a U-shaped curve **2** A parabola is the GRAPH (= drawing) of a QUADRATIC EQUATION.

parachute /ˈpær·əˌʃuːt/ *n* [C] a large, usually circular piece of special cloth fastened to someone or something so that when dropped from an aircraft, it will catch the wind like a sail to make the person or thing fall slowly and safely to the ground
parachute /ˈpær·əˌʃuːt/ *v* [I/T] ○ [I] *When the plane went down, three of the crewmen parachuted to safety.*

parade /pəˈreɪd/ *n* [C] **1** a large number of people marching, walking, or riding in vehicles, all moving in the same direction, usually in a formal way as part of a public celebration ○ *We used to go and see the Thanksgiving Day parade in New York.* **2** A parade is also a military ceremony in which soldiers march in front of important officials or as part of a public celebration.
parade /pəˈreɪd/ *v* [I/T] ○ [I] *The Saint Patrick's Day marchers paraded up Fifth Avenue.* ○ [T] *The owners paraded their dogs in front of the audience before the winners were announced.* ○ [I] *We all paraded down to the cellar to carry up boxes of books* (= went there together).

paradigm Ⓐ /ˈpær·əˌdɑɪm/ *n* [C] *fml* a very clear or typical example used as a model ○ *His ruthless accumulation of wealth stands as a paradigm of greed in the business world.*

paradise /ˈpær·əˌdɑɪs, -ˌdɑɪz/ *n* [U] **1** a place or condition of great happiness where everything is exactly as you would like it to be ○ *His idea of paradise is to spend the day sailing.* ○ (*infml*) *This place is a shopper's/children's/pickpocket's paradise* (= a place where the conditions are exactly right for them). **2** Paradise is another word for heaven.

paradox /ˈpær·əˌdɑks/ *n* [C] a statement or situation that may be true but seems impossible or difficult to understand because it contains two opposite facts or characteristics ○ *It's a strange paradox that people who say you shouldn't criticize the government criticize it as soon as they disagree with it.*
paradoxical /ˌpær·əˈdɑk·sɪ·kəl/ *adj* ○ *a paradoxical quality*
paradoxically /ˌpær·əˈdɑk·sɪ·kli/ *adv* ○ *The hot thing in video equipment is, paradoxically, sound.*

paragon /ˈpær·əˌgɑn, -gən/ *n* [C] a person or thing that is perfect or has a large amount of a particular good characteristic ○ *a paragon of virtue*

paragraph Ⓐ /ˈpær·əˌgræf/, *abbreviation* **par.** *n* [C] a short part of a text that begins on a new line and consists of one or more sentences dealing with a single idea

parakeet /ˈpær·əˌkiːt/ *n* [C] a small PARROT (= type of tropical bird) with a long tail

parallel Ⓐ POSITION /ˈpær·əˌlel, -ləl/ *adj* [not gradable] ***geometry*** (of two or more straight lines) being the same distance apart along all their length ○ *The wood was marked with parallel dark bands.*

PARALLEL LINES

parallel Ⓐ /ˈpær·əˌlel, -ləl/ *n* [C] ***earth science*** one of the imaginary latitude lines around the earth that are parallel to the equator ○ *the 40th parallel* ➤ Picture: **earth**
parallel Ⓐ /ˈpær·əˌlel, -ləl/ *adv* [not gradable] ○ *Maple Street runs parallel to State Street.*
parallel Ⓐ /ˈpær·əˌlel, -ləl/ *v* [T] ○ *The highway parallels the river for about 20 miles.*

SIMILARITY /ˈpær·əˌlel, -ləl/ *n* [C] something very similar to something else, or a similarity between two things ○ *There's an incredible parallel between the talking blues of 50 years ago and today's rap music.* ○ *The black experience in America has been without parallel in the experience of other peoples.*
parallel Ⓐ /ˈpær·əˌlel, -ləl/ *adj* similar or matching ○ *Parallel experiments are being conducted in Europe and the United States.*
parallel Ⓐ /ˈpær·əˌlel, -ləl/ *v* [T] ○ *Her account of the incident closely parallels what others have reported.*

parallel circuit *n* [C] ***physics*** an electrical CIRCUIT in which current flows in more than one path at the same time

parallelism /ˈpær·ə·lelˌɪz·əm, -ləˌlɪz·əm/ *n* [U] ***writing*** the use of matching sentence structure, phrases, or longer parts so as to balance ideas of equal importance

parallelogram /ˌpær·əˈlel·əˌgræm/ *n* [C] ***geometry*** a flat shape with four sides, with opposite sides parallel and equal in length ➤ Picture: **geometry**

paralysis /pəˈræl·ə·səs/ *n* [U] the state of being unable to move or act ○ *Some spinal cord injuries can cause permanent paralysis.*

paralyze /ˈpær·əˌlɑɪz/ *v* [T] to cause a person or animal to lose the ability to move or feel part of the body, or to cause someone or something to be unable to act or operate correctly ○ *He was paralyzed from the waist down.* ○ *Commuter traffic paralyzes the city's roads every morning.*

paramecium /ˌpær·əˈmiː·ʃiː·əm, -ʃəm, -siː·əm/ *n* [C] *pl* **paramecia, parameciums** ***biology*** a type of PROTOZOAN (= organism with only one cell) that lives in water and swims by moving structures similar to hairs that are attached to its body

paramedic /ˌpær·əˈmed·ɪk/ *n* [C] a person who is trained to give medical help, especially in an emergency, but who is not a doctor or a nurse

parameter Ⓐ /pəˈræm·əţ·ər/ *n* [C usually pl] a fixed limit that establishes how something should be done ○ *Aspin outlined the parameters of the debate between Congress and the Pentagon.*

paramilitary /ˌpær·əˈmɪl·əˌter·i/ *adj* [not gradable] similar to an army, but not official and sometimes not legal ○ *paramilitary forces*

paramount /ˈpær·əˌmɑʊnt/ *adj* [not gradable] more important than anything else ○ *Everybody agrees that education is the paramount issue.*

paranoia /ˌpær·əˈnɔɪ·ə/ *n* [U] a strong tendency to feel that you cannot trust other people or that other people have a bad opinion of you, or *medical* a mental illness that causes extreme feelings that others are trying to harm you

paranoid /ˈpær·əˌnɔɪd/ *adj* anxious because you do not feel you can trust others, or *medical* suffering from PARANOIA ○ *My husband is very paranoid about making sure everything's locked.*

paraphernalia /ˌpær·ə·fəˈneɪl·jə, -fər-/ *n* [U] a collection of objects, esp. equipment needed for or connected with a particular activity ○ *photography paraphernalia*

paraphrase /ˈpær·əˌfreɪz/ *v* [T] to state something written or spoken in different words, esp. in a shorter and simpler form to make the meaning clearer ○ *I'll have to paraphrase it because I didn't get a chance to memorize it.*

paraplegic /ˌpær·əˈpliː·dʒɪk/ *n* [C] a person who has lost the ability to move the legs and lower part of the body, usually because of a severe injury to the SPINE (= bones in the back)

parasite /ˈpær·əˌsɑɪt/ *n* [C] **1** ***biology*** an animal or plant that lives on or in another animal or plant of a different type and feeds from it **2** A parasite is also a person who uses others to obtain an advantage without doing anything in exchange.

parasitism /ˈpær·ə·səţˌɪz·əm, -ˌsɑɪţˌɪz·əm/ *n* [U] ***biology*** the relationship that exists between parasites

parasol /ˈpær·əˌsɔːl, -ˌsɑl/ *n* [C] a type of UMBRELLA (= round cloth-covered frame on a stick) carried by women, esp. in the past, for protection from the sun

paratrooper /ˈpær·əˌtruː·pər/ *n* [C] a soldier who is trained to be dropped from an aircraft with a PARACHUTE ○ *French paratroopers held war games last week.*

parcel /ˈpɑr·səl/ *n* [C] **1** an object or collection of objects wrapped in paper; a package ○ *a food parcel* **2** A parcel of land is an area of it: *a 50-acre parcel on Lake Mead*

PHRASAL VERB with **parcel**

• **parcel out** *something* [M] , **-ll-** to divide something and give it in parts to different people ○ *More than $13,000 in awards will be parceled out, with $6000 going to the first-prize winner.*

parcel post *n* [U] the cheapest way to send packages through the mail

parched /pɑrtʃt/ *adj* dried out because of too much heat ○ *My lips were parched.*

parchment /ˈpɑrtʃ·mənt/ *n* [C/U] the dried, pale skin of some animals which was used in the past for writing on, or a paper made to look like this ○ [U] *I found a scrap of parchment dating from the 17th century.*

pardon /ˈpɑrd·ᵊn/ *v* [T] **1** to forgive someone for something ○ *Satellite radio is about to – pardon the expression* (= forgive me for using this phrase) *– go into orbit.* **2** If someone who has committed a crime is pardoned, the person is officially forgiven and punishment is stopped: *He was convicted of murder, but was later pardoned by the governor.*

pardon /ˈpɑrd·ᵊn/ *n* [C] forgiveness ○ *He had actively sought a pardon* (= official forgiveness) *from the president.*

pardon /ˈpɑrd·ᵊn/ *exclamation* said when you have not heard what someone has said to you and you want the person to repeat it ○ *"The train leaves at 2:15." "Pardon?"*

pardonable /ˈpɑrd·ᵊn·ə·bəl/ *adj* able to be forgiven ○ *a pardonable mistake*

IDIOM with **pardon**

• **pardon me** **1** please repeat what you just said ○ *Pardon me? I didn't hear you.* **2** **Pardon me** is sometimes used to say you are sorry when you do something slightly rude, such as BURP or accidentally push someone. **3** **Pardon me** is also polite way of attracting someone's attention: *Pardon me, does this train go to Oakland?* **4** **Pardon me** can also be used to show respect before disagreeing with someone: *Pardon me, but I think you have that wrong.*

pare /per, pær/ *v* [T] to cut away the thin outer layer of something, esp. food, or to reduce the size of something ○ [M] *He turned the blade to pare off a piece of cheese.* ○ [M] *We have to pare down and eliminate the waste and inefficiency.* ○ [T] *Simon had to pare the play.*

parent /ˈpær·ənt, ˈper-/ *n* [C] **1** a person who gives birth to or raises a child ○ *His parents live in*

P

New York. **2** ***biology*** A parent is also any animal or plant that produces another.

parentage /ˈpær·ənt·ɪdʒ, ˈper-/ *n* [U] one's parents or origins ○ *She's of Puerto Rican parentage.*

parental /pəˈrent·əl/ *adj* [not gradable] ○ *parental guidance*

parenthood /ˈpær·ənt ˌhʊd, ˈper-/ *n* [U] ○ *Just barely newlyweds, they now have to confront the harsh realities of parenthood.*

parenting /ˈpær·ənt·ɪŋ, ˈper-/ *n* [U] the raising of children and all the responsibilities and activities involved in it ○ *parenting skills*

parents-in-law /ˈpær·ən·sən ˌlɔː/ *pl n* the parents of someone's husband or wife

parenthesis /pəˈren·θə·səs/ *n* [C usually pl] *pl* **parentheses** either of a pair of marks ( ), or the information inside them, used in a piece of writing to show that what is inside these marks should be considered as separate from the main part ○ *Dates in parentheses indicate when the film was reviewed.*

parenthetical /ˌpær·ən ˈθet̬·ɪ·kəl/, **parenthetic** /ˌpær·ən ˈθet̬·ɪk/ *adj* [not gradable] written in PARENTHESES, or said in addition to the main part of what you are saying ○ *He added a parenthetical comment to his original statement.*

Parent-Teacher Association, *abbreviation* **PTA** *n* [C] an organization of parents and teachers of children at a school that tries to help the school, esp. by arranging activities that raise money for it

par excellence /ˌpɑr ˌek·səˈlɑns, -ˈlɑ̃s/ *adj* [only after n] [not gradable] of the best quality of its type ○ *He praised her as the teacher par excellence.*

pariah /pəˈrɑɪ·ə/ *n* [C] a person who is avoided or not accepted by a social group, esp. because he or she is not liked, respected, or trusted; an OUTCAST ○ *Because of its poor human rights record, the country was treated as a pariah by other nations.*

parish /ˈpær·ɪʃ/ *n* [C] **1** an area that a church provides for ○ *She lived her whole life in this parish.* **2** A parish is also a political division within the state of Louisiana. ○ Related adjective: PAROCHIAL OF A CHURCH

parishioner /pəˈrɪʃ·ə·nər/ *n* [C] a member of a particular parish, esp. one who frequently goes to its church

parity /ˈpær·ət̬·i/ *n* [U] **1** equality, esp. of pay or position ○ *Washington, DC, hopes to achieve political parity with the states.* **2** ***US history*** Parity is also the ability of farmers to buy things at the same level as during a past time set as a standard and maintained by government price support.

park AREA OF LAND /pɑrk/ *n* [C] a large area of land with grass and trees which is maintained for the pleasure of the public ○ *a picnic in the park* ○ *Central Park*

STOP /pɑrk/ *v* [I/T] to leave a vehicle in a place where it can stay for a period of time, or *fig., infml* to put yourself or something in a particular place for a period of time ○ [I] *Where did you park?* ○ [T] *Just park your car out front.* ○ [T] (*fig.*) (*infml*) *He parked himself in front of the TV.*

parking /ˈpɑr·kɪŋ/ *n* [U] **1** the act of parking, or the spaces in which cars are parked ○ *There's lots of parking available at the theater.* **2** A parking garage is a building, or an area under a building, where cars can be parked.

parka /ˈpɑr·kə/ *n* [C] a long, often waterproof, warm jacket with a HOOD (= covering for the head)

parking lot *n* [C] an open area where cars can be parked

parking meter *n* [C] a device in the street or in a PARKING LOT that you put money into so that you can park your car next to it for a particular period of time

parkway /ˈpɑr·kweɪ/ *n* [C] a wide, usually divided, road with an area of grass and trees on both sides

parliament /ˈpɑr·lə·mənt/ *n* [C/U] ***world history*** **1** the group of people who make the laws in some countries **2** Parliament often refers to the legislature of the United Kingdom of Great Britain and Northern Ireland.

parliamentary /ˌpɑr·ləˈment·ə·ri, -ˈmen·tri/ *adj* [not gradable] ○ *a parliamentary election*

parlor STORE, *Cdn, Br* **parlour** /ˈpɑr·lər/ *n* [C] a store that sells a stated product, or a business that provides a stated service ○ *an ice cream parlor* ○ *a beauty parlor*

ROOM, *Cdn, Br* **parlour** /ˈpɑr·lər/ *n* [C] *dated* a room in a private house used esp. for entertaining guests ○ *the front parlor*

Parmesan (cheese) /ˈpɑr·məˌzɑn (ˈtʃiːz), -ˌʒɑn/ *n* [U] a hard, dry, Italian cheese that is usually GRATED (= broken into small pieces)

parochial OF A CHURCH /pəˈroʊ·kiː·əl/ *adj* [not gradable] connected with a PARISH (= an area that a church provides for) or with a church ○ *a parochial school*

LIMITED /pəˈroʊ·kiː·əl/ *adj* limited to a narrow or local range of matters ○ *The US coverage of the summit has been extremely parochial.*

parody /ˈpær·əd·i/ *n* [C/U] ***literature*** a piece of writing or music that copies the style of a serious piece in a way that is intentionally humorous ○ [C] *Brando did a parody of the character he played in "The Godfather."*

parody /ˈpær·əd·i/ *v* [T] ○ *Downey started the show by parodying a performance artist.*

parole /pəˈroʊl/ *n* [U] the release of a prisoner before that person's period in prison is finished, with the agreement that the person will behave well ○ *a life sentence without parole*

parole /pəˈroʊl/ *v* [T] ○ *He was paroled after serving ten years.*

paroxysm /ˈpær·əkˌsɪz·əm, pəˈrɑk-/ *n* [C] a sudden and powerful expression of strong feeling ○ *The mention of his name can send people into paroxysms of anger.*

parquet /pɑrˈkeɪ/ *n* [U] floor covering that consists of small blocks of wood arranged in a pattern

parrot BIRD /ˈpær·ət/ *n* [C] a tropical bird with a curved beak and usually colorful feathers, some of which can be taught to repeat words

REPEAT WORDS /ˈpær·ət/ *v* [T] to repeat something said by someone else without thought or understanding ○ *She just parrots anything he says.*

parsley /ˈpɑr·sli/ *n* [U] an herb with curly or flat green leaves, used to add flavor to food or to decorate it

parsnip /ˈpɑr·snəp/ *n* [C] a long, cream-colored root eaten as a vegetable

part SOME /pɑrt/ *n* [C/U] some but not all of something larger or greater ○ [U] *I could only eat part of my dinner.* ○ [C] *Parts of the movie were good.* ○ [U] *Surgeons had to remove part of his lung.* ○ [U] *Part of the problem is that she doesn't like her boss very much.*

part /pɑrt/ *adj, adv* [not gradable] ○ *She's part scientist and part artist.* ○ *Al is a part owner of a restaurant* (= one of the owners).

partly /ˈpɑrt·li/ *adv* [not gradable] ○ *The house is partly owned by her father.*

SEPARATE PIECE /pɑrt/ *n* [C] **1** a separate piece or unit of something, esp. a piece that combines with other pieces to form the whole of something ○ *The garage stocks auto parts from all current car models.* **2** A part is also one of two or more equal measures of something: *Mix one part vinegar with three parts olive oil.* **3** A part is also a single broadcast of a series of television programs or a division of a story: *Part three will be broadcast Tuesday.*

SEPARATE /pɑrt/ *v* [I/T] to cause to separate, or to come apart ○ [I] *The curtains parted, revealing a darkened stage.*

parting /ˈpɑrt̬·ɪŋ/ *n* [C/U] the act of leaving or of moving apart ○ [C] *It was a sad parting, because we knew it was the last time we would see each other.*

parting /ˈpɑrt̬·ɪŋ/ *adj* [not gradable] ○ *She gave him a parting wave.*

INVOLVEMENT /pɑrt/ *n* [C usually sing] **1** involvement in or responsibility for an activity or action ○ *He admitted his part in the robbery.* ○ *It was a mistake on Julia's part* (= she was responsible). **2** A part in a movie or play is one of its characters, or the words written for that character: *She plays the part of Lady Macbeth.* ○ *Ben is learning his part for the school play.*

WORD FAMILY part			
Nouns	part counterpart parting partiality partition	*Adjectives*	part partial parting
		Adverbs	part partially partly
Verbs	part partition		

HAIR /pɑrt/ *n* [C] a line formed by the hair on a person's head where the hair is divided

part /pɑrt/ *v* [T] ○ *I've always parted my hair on the left side.*

IDIOM with part

• **a parting of the ways** different ideas or a disagreement about something that make two people or groups decide they cannot work together any longer ○ *We had a parting of the ways over when we couldn't agree on how to manage the company.*

PHRASAL VERB with part

• **part with** *something* **1** to give away or get rid of something, esp. a possession that you enjoy having ○ *I just couldn't part with my old car, even though it uses too much gas.* **2** If you part with money, you spend it or give it to someone, although you may not want to: *You really have to be a Dylan fan to part with $50 for "Highway 61 Interactive," released earlier this year.*

partake /pɑrˈteɪk/ *v* [I] *past simp.* **partook**, *past part.* **partaken** *fml* **1** to become involved with or take part in something with other people **2** To partake of food or drink is to eat or drink some of it: *Feel free to partake of the food and drink displayed on tables.*

partial NOT COMPLETE /ˈpɑr·ʃəl/ *adj* [not gradable] not complete ○ *He made a partial repayment of the loan.*

partially /ˈpɑr·ʃə·li/ *adv* [not gradable] ○ *The accident left him partially paralyzed.*

PREFERENCE /ˈpɑr·ʃəl/ *adj* to have a particular preference or liking for someone or something ○ *I'm partial toward the larger dogs.*

partiality /ˌpɑr·ʃiːˈæl·ət̬·i/ *n* [U] an unfair preference for one person or group over another ○ *Some parents complained about the partiality of the teacher toward certain students.*

participant Ⓐ /pɑrˈtɪs·ə·pənt/ *n* [C] a person who takes part in or becomes involved in a particular activity ○ *Participants in the experiment also keep track of what they eat and drink over three days so their eating habits can be evaluated.*

participate Ⓐ /pɑrˈtɪs·əˌpeɪt/ *v* [I] to be or become involved in an activity ○ *The teacher tries to get everyone to participate in the classroom discussion.*

participation Ⓐ /pɑrˌtɪs·əˈpeɪ·ʃən/ *n* [U] ○ *Participation in the program was voluntary.*

participatory Ⓐ /pɑrˈtɪs·ə·pəˌtɔːr·i, -ˌtoʊr·i/ *adj* ○ *Participatory sports are becoming more popular.*

participle /ˈpɑrt̬·əˌsɪp·əl/ *n* [C] ***grammar*** a form of a verb, often ending in "-ed" or "-ing" and used with auxiliary verbs to make verb tenses, or to form adjectives

particle /ˈpɑrt̬·ɪ·kəl/ *n* [C] **1** an extremely small piece of something ○ *dust particles* **2** ***physics*** A particle is also any of the smallest pieces of matter that make up atoms or the parts of atoms.

particular SPECIAL /pərˈtɪk·jə·lər, pəˈtɪk-/ *adj* special or single, or this and not any other ○ *Is there a particular restaurant you'd like to eat at?* ○ *What in particular* (= special things) *did you like about the last apartment that we saw?*

particularly /pərˈtɪk·jə·lər·li, pəˈtɪk-/ *adv* very or very much; especially ○ *We're particularly interested in hearing from people who are fluent in both Spanish and English.*

P

particulars /pərˈtɪk·jə·lərz, pəˈtɪk-/ *pl n* details or information about a person or an event ○ *We're going to discuss a little bit more about the particulars of the case.*

CAREFUL /pərˈtɪk·jə·lər, pəˈtɪk-/ *adj* wanting to make choices carefully because you are not easily satisfied ○ *She's very particular about what she eats.*

particulate /pɑrˈtɪk·jə·lət/ *adj* [not gradable] ***science*** relating to or consisting of very small pieces of a substance

parting shot *n* [C] a remark made as you are leaving, so that it has a stronger effect ○ *"And the dress that you bought me doesn't fit either!" was her parting shot.*

partisan /ˈpɑrt̬·ə·zən, -sən/ *adj* involving loyal support of a person, principle, or political party ○ *partisan politics*

partisanship /ˈpɑrt̬·ə·zənˌʃɪp, -sən-/ *n* [U] ○ *The political parties are more divided by partisanship than ever before.*

partition /pɑrˈtɪʃ·ən/ *n* [C/U] **1** the division of something into smaller parts, or something that divides a space ○ [U] *The partition of the building into separate apartments brought in enough income that she could retire from her job.* **2** ***world history*** Partition is also the division of a country or region into two or more separate political units: [U] *Both sides agreed to the partition of the disputed territory.* **3** A partition is also a wall that separates one part of a room or building from another: [C] *These partitions between our desks allow us to work in relative privacy.*

partition /pɑrˈtɪʃ·ən/ *v* [T] ○ *Germany was partitioned after World War II.*

partly /ˈpɑrt·li/ *adv* ○ See at PART **SOME**

partner Ⓐ /ˈpɑrt·nər/ *n* [C] **1** one of two people who do something together or are closely involved in some way ○ *Children, hold your partner's hand when you cross the street.* **2** A partner in a company is one of the owners. **3** A partner is also one of two people who dance together or who play a sport or a game together, esp. when they play as a team. **4** A person's partner can also be the person to whom someone is married, or to whom the person is not married but with whom they have a close relationship.

partnership Ⓐ /ˈpɑrt·nərˌʃɪp/ *n* [C/U] ○ [C] *a business partnership*

part of speech *n* [C] ***grammar*** any of the groups into which words are divided depending on their use, such as verbs, nouns, and adjectives

partook /pɑrˈtʊk/ *past simple of* PARTAKE

part-time /ˈpɑrtˈtɑɪm/ *adj, adv* [not gradable] (of an activity or work) done for periods of time shorter than the usual hours or schedule ○ *She got a part-time job working three days a week.* ○ *Joe works part-time.*

part-timer /ˈpɑrtˈtɑɪ·mər/ *n* [C] ○ *We have a full-time staff of three, plus two part-timers.*

party **SOCIAL GATHERING** /ˈpɑrt̬·i/ *n* [C] a social gathering at which people talk, eat, drink, and enjoy themselves ○ *a birthday party* ○ *Sally is having a party at her place tonight.*

party /ˈpɑrt̬·i/ *v* [I] *infml* to enjoy yourself at a party with others, esp. by drinking alcohol, dancing, etc.

POLITICAL GROUP /ˈpɑrt̬·i/ *n* [C] ***social studies*** a political group with particular beliefs and aims and which supports members who are trying to get elected to public office ○ *the Democratic/Republican Party* ○ *a political party*

PARTICULAR GROUP /ˈpɑrt̬·i/ *n* [C] a particular group of people who are involved in an activity ○ *I made a dinner reservation for a party of eight.*

ONE INVOLVED /ˈpɑrt̬·i/ *n* [C] one of the people or sides involved in a formal agreement or argument, esp. a legal one ○ *The UN called on all parties to lay down their arms.*

pascal /pæsˈkæl, pɑsˈkɑl/, *abbreviation* **Pa** *n* [C] ***physics*** the standard unit for measuring pressure

pass **GO PAST** /pæs/ *v* [I/T] to go past or move beyond something or someone ○ [T] *A car passed us doing 70 miles per hour.* ○ [I] *I was just passing by and stopped to say hello.*

passable /ˈpæs·ə·bəl/ *adj* able to be traveled on or through ○ *It's snowing, but the roads are passable.*

passing /ˈpæs·ɪŋ/ *adj* [not gradable]

GO THROUGH /pæs/ *v* [I/T] to cause something to go around, across, through, etc., something else, or to be positioned in such a way ○ [T] *Pass the wire through the slot and pull it out from the other side.* ○ [I always + adv/prep] *The causeway passes across the bay and takes you to the mainland.*

passage /ˈpæs·ɪdʒ/ *n* [U] ○ *Passage through the Panama Canal will take a number of hours.* ○ See also: PASSAGE **CONNECTING WAY**; PASSAGE **PART**; PASSAGE **TRAVEL**

GIVE /pæs/ *v* [I/T] **1** to give something to someone ○ [T] *Please pass the bread.* **2** In team sports played with a ball, if you pass, you throw, kick, or hit the ball to someone on your team.

pass /pæs/ *n* [C] the act of giving or sending the ball to another player on your own team ○ *The receiver dropped the pass.*

DO WELL /pæs/ *v* [I/T] to be successful in a test, exam, or course, or to judge someone as having been successful in it ○ [T] *The professor said that if I passed the final exam, she'll pass me.*

pass /pæs/ *n* [C] a mark given to show that a student has successfully completed a course or an exam

passable /ˈpæs·ə·bəl/ *adj* satisfactory but not excellent ○ *Angie can speak passable Russian.*

TIME /pæs/ *v* [I/T] to go past or through a period of time ○ [I] *The hours passed quickly.*

passage /ˈpæs·ɪdʒ/ *n* [U] ○ *Memory fades with the passage of time.* ○ See also: PASSAGE **CONNECTING WAY**; PASSAGE **PART**; PASSAGE **TRAVEL**

APPROVE /pæs/ *v* [I/T] to approve or be approved by a group having authority, esp. by voting ○ [T] *The bill passed both houses of Congress and was signed by the president.* ○ [I] *The bill passed unanimously.*

passage /ˈpæs·ɪdʒ/ *n* [U] ○ *The speaker urged passage of the tax bill.* ○ See also: PASSAGE CONNECTING WAY; PASSAGE PART; PASSAGE TRAVEL

NOT DO /pæs/ *v* [I] to choose not to do, have, take part in, or take a turn at something ○ *I think I'll pass on going to the movies.*

DOCUMENT /pæs/ *n* [C] an official document or ticket showing that you have the right to go somewhere or do something ○ *We bought three-day passes to the amusement park.* ○ *The children get bus passes to travel to and from school.*

BE ACCEPTED /pæs/ *v* [I] to be accepted as being something that you are not, esp. something better or more attractive ○ *Marion looks so young she could pass for 30.* ○ *Do this jacket and skirt match well enough to pass as a suit?*

WORD FAMILY pass			
Nouns	pass overpass underpass passage	*Adjectives*	passable passing
		Verbs	pass

IDIOMS with pass

•**in passing** while talking or thinking about something else ○ *Leo mentioned in passing that you are going on vacation next week.*
•**pass the buck** to leave a difficult problem for someone else to deal with ○ *Don't try to pass the buck - this is your responsibility, not mine.*
•**pass the hat** to ask a number of people to give money for something, esp. to help pay for something or reward someone ○ *They're passing the hat around the company to get money for charity.*
•**pass the time** to do something to keep busy while waiting ○ [T] *We passed the time in the airport playing cards.*
•**pass judgment on** *someone/something* to express a strong opinion about someone or something ○ *Don't pass judgment on Lori until you hear what happened.*

PHRASAL VERBS with pass

•**pass around** *something* [M] to give something to someone, who will then give it to others ○ *Journalists had been passing around the link to the photo all week.*
•**pass away** to die ○ *Her father passed away last week.*
•**pass down** *something* [M] **1** to give something to someone who is younger, less important, or at a lower level than you ○ *The word being passed down from the leadership is that the polls are showing good results.* **2** If property, diseases, or biological conditions **pass down**, they go from parents to children: *Should I pass down wealth now or wait until I die?*
•**pass** *someone/something* **off as** *something* [M] to try to make others believe that someone or something is something other than what the person or thing is ○ *Maurice is trying to pass himself off as a journalist to get admitted to the press conference.*
•**pass on DIE** to die ○ *It's important to remember friends and family who have passed on.*
•**pass on** *something* **RECEIVE AND GIVE** [M] **1** to give something to someone, after someone else gave it to you ○ *Some organizations passed on substantially less money to the candidates.* **2** If you pass on information, you tell it to someone else after you have heard it: *No one passed the news on to me.*
•**pass on** *something* **WITHIN FAMILIES** [M] **1** to give something to someone who lives after you die, usually a person in your family ○ *You may want a way to pass on money to your children or to cover the taxes on your estate.* **2** If you **pass on** a biological condition, you have it and your children also have it: *There are some diseases that a woman might pass on to her child.*
•**pass on** *something/someone* **SAY NO** *infml* to refuse an opportunity involving something or someone; DECLINE REFUSE ○ *Many stars passed on the sequins and glitz for simple satin at this year's awards.*
•**pass out UNCONSCIOUS** to become unconscious ○ *He passed out from the heat.*
•**pass out** *something* **GIVE** [M] to give something to each person in a group ○ *Jeff, please pass out the test booklets.*
•**pass over** *someone/something* [M] to ignore or to not give attention to someone or something ○ *They passed Sal over for promotion.*
•**pass up** *something* [M] to fail to take advantage of an opportunity ○ *I can't believe she passed up the chance to go to South America.*

passage CONNECTING WAY /ˈpæs·ɪdʒ/, **passageway** /ˈpæs·ɪdʒˌweɪ/ *n* [C] **1** a usually long and narrow part of a building with rooms on one or both sides, or an enclosed path that connects places ○ *A narrow passage led through the house to the yard.* **2** A passage is also an entrance or opening: *the nasal passages* ○ See also: PASSAGE at PASS GO THROUGH; PASSAGE at PASS TIME; PASSAGE at PASS APPROVE

PART /ˈpæs·ɪdʒ/ *n* [C] a short piece of writing or music that is part of a larger piece ○ *a short passage for a trumpet solo* ○ See also: PASSAGE at PASS GO THROUGH; PASSAGE at PASS TIME; PASSAGE at PASS APPROVE

TRAVEL /ˈpæs·ɪdʒ/ *n* [U] the right to travel or to leave a place ○ *We booked passage on a cruise ship.* ○ *He was guaranteed safe passage to the border.* ○ See also: PASSAGE at PASS GO THROUGH; PASSAGE at PASS TIME; PASSAGE at PASS APPROVE

passé /pæˈseɪ/ *adj* no longer fashionable ○ *Writing personal letters, unfortunately, is passé.*

passenger /ˈpæs·ən·dʒər/ *n* [C] a person who is traveling in a vehicle but is not operating it or working as an employee in it ○ *airline passengers* ○ *Taxis are allowed to carry no more than four passengers.*

passerby, **passer-by** /ˌpæs·ərˈbɑɪ/ *n* [C] *pl* **passersby** someone who is going past a particular place ○ *A passer-by saw smoke and called the fire department.*

pass-fail *adj* [not gradable] (of college and university courses) having only two marks, one for passing and one for failing

P

passing /ˈpæs·ɪŋ/ *n* [U] *fml* someone's death ○ *We note with sorrow the passing of Raymond Wilson, a member of the board.*

passion EMOTION /ˈpæʃ·ən/ *n* [C/U] a powerful emotion or its expression, esp. the emotion of love, anger, or hate ○ [U] *romantic passion* ○ [C] *Passions were running high in the aftermath of the accident.*
passionate /ˈpæʃ·ə·nət/ *adj* full of emotion ○ *a passionate speech*
passionately /ˈpæʃ·ə·nət·li/ *adv* ○ *He really cares passionately about getting students to stay in school.*
STRONG INTEREST /ˈpæʃ·ən/ *n* [C] something that you are strongly interested in and enjoy ○ *She has two passions in life – her cats and opera.*

passive Ⓐ BEHAVIOR /ˈpæs·ɪv/ *adj* not reacting to what happens, or not acting or taking part ○ *They attack people who are too weak or too passive to resist.*
passively Ⓐ /ˈpæs·ɪv·li/ *adv* ○ *She watched passively as the children ran wild.*
passivity Ⓐ /pæsˈɪv·əṭ·i/ *n* [U] ○ *Unemployment leads to political passivity, according to a study in Sweden.*
GRAMMAR /ˈpæs·ɪv/ *adj* [not gradable] ***grammar*** describing a verb or sentence in which the subject is the person or thing to which something stated is done ○ *In the sentence "I was given a gift by Alex," the verb "give" is passive, or in the passive voice.* ○ USAGE: In English, passive verbs or sentences are formed with a form of the verb "to be" and a past participle. ○ Compare ACTIVE GRAMMAR

passive immunity *n* [U] ***biology*** protection against disease in the form of ANTIBODIES (= substances in the blood that fight disease) that come from someone else, for example, from the mother's milk

passive resistance *n* [U] a way of showing your opposition to a law or official activity without acting violently

passive voice *n* [U] ***grammar*** the relationship between a subject and a verb in which the subject receives the action of the verb, or the verb forms which show this relationship ○ *In the sentence "He was hit by the ball," "was hit" is in the passive voice.* ○ Compare ACTIVE VOICE; VOICE

Passover /ˈpæsˌoʊ·vər/ *n* [U] a Jewish celebration in March or April, lasting seven or eight days, in memory of the escape of the Jews from Egypt

passport /ˈpæs·pɔːrt, -poʊrt/ *n* [C] an official document provided by the government of a particular country which shows that the owner is a citizen of that country and allows that person to travel to foreign countries

password /ˈpæs·wɜrd/ *n* [C] a secret word or phrase that is used to obtain access to a place, information, or a computer system

past TIME BEFORE /pæst/ *n* [C/U] **1** the period before and until, but not including, the present time ○ [U] *In the past, a streetcar line ran down 13th Avenue.* **2** Your past is your life before the present time: [C] *He never talks about his past.*
past /pæst/ *adj* [not gradable] ○ *I've been working out regularly for the past six months.* ○ *Rising temperatures signal that the worst of winter is past* (= finished).
GRAMMAR /pæst/ *adj* [not gradable] ***grammar*** having the tense used to describe actions, events, or states that happened or existed before the present time ○ *The past tense of "change" is "changed."*
FAR SIDE /pæst/ *prep, adv* [not gradable] on the far side of something, or from one side to the other ○ *They live just past the post office.* ○ *Three boys went past us on bikes.*
BEYOND /pæst/ *prep, adv* [not gradable] beyond or above a particular point ○ *Melissa is past the age where she needs a babysitter.* ○ *It's already past noon.*

pasta /ˈpɑs·tə, ˌˈpæs-/ *n* [U] a food made of flour, water, and sometimes egg which is formed into a variety of shapes that are hard when dry and soft when cooked

paste /peɪst/ *n* [U] a thick, wet substance used for sticking things together, or any soft, wet mixture of powder and liquid ○ *Use paste, glue, or tape to attach the pictures.* ○ *tomato paste*
paste /peɪst/ *v* [T always + adv/prep] to stick something to something else ○ *She pasted a heart onto the valentine.*

pastel COLOR /pæsˈtel/ *adj* (of colors) pale and soft
pastel /pæsˈtel/ *n* [C] ○ *Her room is decorated in pink and pastels.*
COLORED STICK /pæsˈtel/ *n* [C] a soft, powdery, coloring material that is pressed into a stick and is used for drawing, or a picture made using these sticks

pasteurize /ˈpæs·tʃəˌrɑɪz/ *v* [T] to heat something, esp. milk, at a high temperature for a fixed period of time in order to kill bacteria
pasteurization /ˌpæs·tʃə·rəˈzeɪ·ʃən/ *n* [U] ○ *ultra-high temperature pasteurization*

pastime /ˈpæs·tɑɪm/ *n* [C] an activity that is done for enjoyment ○ *Hockey is Canada's national pastime.*

pastor /ˈpæs·tər/ *n* [C] a minister of a Christian church, esp. one that is Protestant
pastoral /ˈpæs·tə·rəl/ *adj* ○ *pastoral work/duties*

pastoral /ˈpæs·tə·rəl/ *adj* (of a piece of art, writing, or music) having or representing the pleasant, traditional features of the countryside ○ *a pastoral scene*

past participle *n* [C] ***grammar*** a form of a verb that is used to show past action or to make PERFECT tenses and adjectives ○ *"Sung" is the past participle of the verb "sing."*

past perfect *n* [U] ***grammar*** a tense usually formed with "had" that is used to refer to the earlier of two different times in the past ○ *The sentence "She had broken her leg once before," is in the past perfect.*

pastrami /pəˈstɑm·i/ *n* [U] spicy smoked BEEF (= meat from a cow), usually cut in slices ○ *a pastrami sandwich on rye*

pastry /ˈpeɪ·stri/ *n* [C/U] **1** a mixture of flour, fat, and water which is used as a base or covering for other foods and baked ○ [U] *pie pastry* **2** A pastry is a sweet, baked food made of a mixture of flour, fat, and water and often filled with fruit or cream: [C] *We were offered a selection of pastries for dessert.*

pasture /ˈpæs·tʃər/ *n* [C/U] land covered with grass or similar plants suitable for animals, such as cows and sheep, to eat ○ [C] *The best places to find bluebirds are open pastures.*

pasty /ˈpeɪ·sti/ *adj* (of someone's skin) pale and unhealthy looking ○ *a pasty face*

pat TOUCH /pæt/ *v* [T] **-tt-** to touch someone or something lightly and repeatedly with an open hand ○ *He patted me on the shoulder.* ○ *Pat the vegetables dry with a paper towel.*

pat /pæt/ *n* [C]

PIECE /pæt/ *n* [C] a small, flat piece of butter

WITHOUT THINKING /pæt/ *adj, adv* [not gradable] *usually disapproving* (esp. of an answer) having been already prepared and therefore said without thinking much about the question ○ *You've got a pat response to every question that comes along.*

IDIOM with pat

• **a pat on the back** praise ○ *You've done a great job, and you deserve a pat on the back.*

patch AREA /pætʃ/ *n* [C] a small part of a surface that is different in some way from the area around it ○ *Watch for patches of ice on the road.* ○ *We have a small vegetable patch* (= area for growing vegetables).

patchy /ˈpætʃ·i/ *adj* **1** happening or existing in small areas ○ *patchy rain/fog* **2** If information is patchy, only small parts of it are known: *My knowledge of physics is pretty patchy.*

PIECE OF MATERIAL /pætʃ/ *n* [C] a piece of material put over a damaged area or hole to repair, strengthen, or cover it ○ *His old jeans are covered with patches.*

patch /pætʃ/ *v* [T] ○ *to patch a tire*

PHRASAL VERB with patch

• **patch up** *something* [M] to fix the problems in a relationship ○ *The couple are working on patching up their differences.*

patchwork /ˈpætʃ·wɜrk/ *n* [U] cloth consisting of smaller pieces of differently patterned cloth that are sewn together ○ *a patchwork quilt* ○ (*fig.*) *We looked down at the patchwork of fields below us.*

pate /peɪt/ *n* [C] *dated, humorous* the top of a person's head ○ *A hat covered his bald pate.*

pâté /pɑˈteɪ, pæ-/ *n* [C/U] a thick, smooth, soft mixture made from ground meat, fish, or vegetables

patent LEGAL RIGHT /ˈpæt·ənt/ *n* [C] the legal right to be the only one who can make, use, or sell an invention for a particular number of years

patent /ˈpæt·ənt/ *v* [T] ○ *Otis patented a steam elevator in 1861.*

OBVIOUS /ˈpæt·ənt, ˈpeɪt-/ *adj* (of ideas or characteristics) obvious ○ *He felt the notion of beginner's luck was patent nonsense.*

patently /ˈpæt·ənt·li, ˈpeɪt-/ *adv* ○ *Your entire argument is patently ridiculous.*

patent leather /ˈpæt·ənt ˈleð·ər/ *n* [U] leather with a hard, shiny surface ○ *black patent-leather shoes*

paternal /pəˈtɜrn·əl/ *adj* **1** behaving or feeling as a father does toward his child ○ *His father gave him a good-humored, paternal smile.* **2** Paternal also means related by way of the father: *paternal grandparents* ○ Compare MATERNAL

paternity /pəˈtɜr·nət̬·i/ *n* [U] the fact or state of being a father

paternalism /pəˈtɜrn·əlˌɪz·əm/ *n* [U] the practice of controlling esp. employees or citizens in a way that is similar to that of a father controlling his children, by giving them what is beneficial but not allowing them responsibility or freedom of choice

paternalistic /pəˌtɜrn·əlˈɪs·tɪk/ *adj* ○ *a paternalistic employer*

path /pæθ/ *n* [C] **1** a way or track made by or for people walking on the ground, or a line along which something moves ○ *a bike path* ○ *The forest fire burned everything in its path.* **2** A path is also a set of actions that lead to a result or goal: *Ashe pioneered the path of black tennis players to the top of the game.* **3** ***physics*** The path of an ELECTRON is the space it travels in around the center of an atom.

P

pathetic SAD /pəˈθet̬·ɪk/ *adj* causing feelings of sadness or sympathy ○ *I think it's pathetic that only half of the eligible voters tend to vote.*

pathetically /pəˈθet̬·ɪ·kli/ *adv* ○ *a pathetically small dog*

UNSUCCESSFUL /pəˈθet̬·ɪk/ *adj* unsuccessful, useless, or worthless ○ *a pathetic excuse* ○ *Bernie's hitting was pretty pathetic!*

pathogen /ˈpæθ·ə·dʒən/ *n* [C] ***biology*** any small organism that can cause disease

pathological /ˌpæθ·əˈlɑdʒ·ɪ·kəl/ *adj* (of a person) unreasonable, or unable to control part of his or her behavior ○ *a pathological fear of heights* ○ *a pathological liar*

pathology /pəˈθɑl·ə·dʒi, pæ-/ *n* [U] the scientific study of disease

pathological /ˌpæθ·əˈlɑdʒ·ɪ·kəl/ *adj* of or caused by disease ○ *a pathological laboratory*

pathologist /pəˈθɑl·ə·dʒəst, pæ-/ *n* [C] a doctor who has expert knowledge of pathology

pathos /ˈpeɪ·θɑs, -θoʊs, -θɔːs/ *n* [U] a quality in life or art that causes feelings of sadness or sympathy ○ *The dying girl's speech generates genuine pathos.*

pathway /ˈpæθ·weɪ/ *n* [C] a PATH ○ *a rough pathway on the mountainside*

patience /ˈpeɪ·ʃəns/ *n* [U] the ability to accept delay, suffering, or annoyance without complaining or becoming angry ○ *He's a man of great patience.* ○ *Her constant complaining was beginning to test/try my patience.*
patient /ˈpeɪ·ʃənt/ *adj* ○ *Just be patient – dinner's almost ready.*
patiently /ˈpeɪ·ʃənt·li/ *adv* ○ *He waited patiently for his name to be called.*

patient /ˈpeɪ·ʃənt/ *n* [C] a person who is receiving medical care, esp. in a hospital, or who is cared for by a particular doctor or DENTIST when necessary

WORD FAMILY patient			
Nouns	patience impatience patient	*Adjectives*	patient impatient
		Adverbs	patiently impatiently

patina /pəˈtiː·nə, ˈpæt·ən·ə/ *n* [C usually sing] a thin layer of a substance, usually green, that develops on the surface of some metals, caused by their reaction to air

patio /ˈpæt̬·iː ˌoʊ/ *n* [C] *pl* **patios** an outside area with a solid floor next to a house, where people can sit

patriarch /ˈpeɪ·triː ˌɑrk/ *n* [C] a powerful and usually older man in charge of a family, or the male leader of a society in which men hold power ○ Compare MATRIARCH
patriarchal /ˌpeɪ·triːˈɑr·kəl/ *adj* ○ *a patriarchal society*
patriarchy /ˈpeɪ·triː ˌɑr·ki/ *n* [C/U] ***social studies*** **1** a form of social organization in which fathers or other males control the family, clan, tribe, or larger social unit, or a society organized in this way **2** Patriarchy is also the control by men, rather than women or both men and women, of most of the power and authority in a society.

P

patrician /pəˈtrɪʃ·ən/ *n* [C] **1** a person of high social class ○ *She is descended from a long line of patricians* **2** ***world history*** In ancient Rome, a patrician was a member of one of the families of original citizens of the city

patriot /ˈpeɪ·triː·ət, -ˌɑt/ *n* [C] **1** a person who loves his or her country and defends it when necessary **2** ***US history*** A patriot during the American Revolution was a person who believed in or fought for independence from Britain.
patriotic /ˌpeɪ·triːˈɑt̬·ɪk/ *adj* ○ *Candidates love to associate themselves with patriotic values.*
patriotism /ˈpeɪ·triː·əˌtɪz·əm/ *n* [U] ○ *This really calls into question his patriotism.*

patrol /pəˈtroʊl/ *v* [I/T] **-ll-** to go around an area or a building to check that it is free from trouble or danger ○ [T] *Security guards patrol the building at night.*
patrol /pəˈtroʊl/ *n* [C/U] ○ [C] *State troopers make regular patrols of the highway.* ○ [U] *Aircraft are on patrol in the region.*

patrol car, **squad car** *n* [C] a car used by police officers that has radio equipment for communicating with other police officers

patron SUPPORTER /ˈpeɪ·trən/ *n* [C] a person or group that gives money or support to a person, an activity, or an organization ○ *Auchincloss is a long-time patron of the arts.*
CUSTOMER /ˈpeɪ·trən/ *n* [C] a customer of a store, restaurant, hotel, etc., esp. a regular customer
patronage /ˈpæ·trə·nɪdʒ, ˈpeɪ-/ *n* [U] ○ *We would like to thank all of our customers for their patronage.*
patronize /ˈpeɪ·trəˌnɑɪz, ˈpæ-/ *v* [T] ○ *Local writers and artists patronize the coffee house.*

patronage /ˈpæ·trə·nɪdʒ, ˈpeɪ-/ *n* [U] *esp. disapproving* the power to give someone an important job or advantages in exchange for help or support ○ *New rules would minimize the effects of political patronage.*

patronize /ˈpeɪ·trəˌnɑɪz, ˈpæ-/ *v* [T] *disapproving* to treat others in a manner that shows you consider yourself to be better or more important than they are ○ *She's angry, smart, and not about to be patronized.*
patronizing /ˈpeɪ·trəˌnɑɪ·zɪŋ, ˈpæ-/ *adj disapproving* ○ *a patronizing manner/attitude*

patsy /ˈpæt·si/ *n* [C] *slang* a person who is easily cheated or made to suffer ○ *He claimed he was a patsy being framed by the police.*

patter TALK /ˈpæt̬·ər/ *n* [U] fast, continuous talk, esp. that of an entertainer or someone trying to sell things ○ *Phinizy's clever patter kept his audience in a good mood.*
SOUND /ˈpæt̬·ər/ *n* [U] the sound of quick, light hits or steps ○ *Now that she's older, we have the patter of little feet in our hallways.*

pattern WAY /ˈpæt̬·ərn/ *n* [C] a particular way in which something is done or organized, or in which something happens ○ *Our weather pattern comes from the northwest.* ○ *A whole variety of behavior patterns affect infants.*
SHAPES /ˈpæt̬·ərn/ *n* [C] **1** a regular arrangement of lines, shapes, or colors ○ *A human fingerprint can be viewed as a geometric pattern.* **2** A pattern is also a design or set of shapes that show how to make something: *a dress pattern*
patterned /ˈpæt̬·ərnd/ *adj* ○ *a rose and black patterned skirt*

patty /ˈpæt̬·i/ *n* [C] pieces of food, esp. meat, formed into a thin, circular shape and then usually cooked ○ *hamburger patties*

paucity /ˈpɔː·sət̬·i/ *n* [U] *fml* the condition of having very little or not enough of something ○ *The authorities had to cope with the paucity of information about the effects of the storm.*

paunch /pɔːntʃ, pɑntʃ/ *n* [C] a fat stomach

pauper /ˈpɔː·pər/ *n* [C] *dated* a very poor person

pause /pɔːz/ *n* [C] a moment in which something, such as a sound or an activity, stops before

starting again ○ *There was a long pause during which we all wondered what he would say next.*
pause /pɔːz/ *v* [I] ○ *She paused to catch her breath.*

pave /peɪv/ *v* [T] to cover an area of ground or a road with materials such as stone, concrete, or bricks that will form a hard, level surface

IDIOM with pave

• **pave the way (for** *something/someone*) to make it possible or easier for something or someone to follow ○ *Data from the space flight should pave the way for a more detailed exploration of Mars.*

pavement /ˈpeɪv·mənt/ *n* [C/U] the hard surface of a road, a SIDEWALK (= path next to a road), or other area of ground ○ [U] *The umbrella fell to the pavement with a clatter.*

pavilion /pəˈvɪl·jən/ *n* [C] **1** a large, open structure or tent, providing shelter esp. in a park or at a FAIR (= temporary public event) **2** A pavilion is also one of a group of related buildings, such as a hospital.

paw /pɔː/ *n* [C] the foot of an animal, such as a cat, dog, or bear, that has CLAWS or nails
paw /pɔː/ *v* [I/T] **1** [I/T] *The dog was pawing (at) the door to be let in.* **2** *infml* A person who paws someone else feels or touches the other person, often in a sexual way that is too forceful.

pawn MONEY /pɔːn/ *v* [T] to leave a possession with someone in order to borrow money from that person, with the understanding that if you do not pay it back within the agreed time, the person can keep your possession and sell it
GAME PIECE /pɔːn/ *n* [C] **1** any of the eight least valuable pieces in the game of CHESS **2** A pawn is also a person who is controlled by others and used for their own advantage: *She felt she had been used as a political pawn.*

pawnshop /ˈpɔːn·ʃɑp/ *n* [C] a store where you can leave possessions in order to borrow money, or buy objects that others have left there and that are now for sale

pay GIVE MONEY FOR /peɪ/ *v* [I/T] *past* **paid** **1** to give money to someone for goods or services ○ [T] *We paid a lot of money for that table.* ○ [I] *Would you prefer to pay by credit card?* ○ [I] (*fig.*) *We all eventually pay for our mistakes* (= suffer or are punished because of our mistakes). **2** To pay is also to give someone or something money for an amount you owe: [T] *We've got to pay the rent.* ○ [T] *We have so many bills to pay.*
payable /ˈpeɪ·ə·bəl/ *adj* [not gradable] ○ *Please make your check payable to Broadway Antiques.*
payee /peɪˈiː/ *n* [C] a person to whom money is given or owed
payer /ˈpeɪ·ər/ *n* [C] a person who pays or owes money that should be paid
payment /ˈpeɪ·mənt/ *n* [C/U] an amount of money paid, or the act of paying ○ [C] *When is the first payment due?* ○ [U] *Usually we ask for payment when the order is placed.*

USAGE

pay for

Remember that **pay** is usually followed by the preposition **for** if there is a direct object and the money is being paid to obtain something.

You have to pay for the tickets in advance, I'm afraid.

~~*You have to pay the tickets in advance, I'm afraid.*~~

If you pay an amount you owe, **pay** is not followed by a preposition.

Did you pay the electric bill this month?

GIVE EARNINGS /peɪ/ *v* [I/T] *past* **paid** to give money to someone that the person has earned for work done ○ [T] *We pay our salespeople a salary plus a bonus based on their sales.* ○ [I] *Construction jobs generally pay well.*
pay /peɪ/ *n* [U] ○ *I asked the boss for a raise in pay.*

USAGE

pay, wage, salary, or income?

Pay is a general word which means the money that you receive for working.

Olive was suspended without pay from her job.

A **wage** or **wages** is an amount of money you receive each hour, day, or week that you work, and is often based on a certain rate of pay per hour.

We spent a week's wages on one dinner out.

A **salary** is the total amount of money you receive in a year, part of which is usually paid once or twice a month.

His salary is $70, 000.

Your **income** is the total amount of money that you earn by working or investing money.

She has a monthly income of $2,400.

PROFIT /peɪ/ *v* [I] *past* **paid** to give a profit, advantage, or benefit ○ [+ *to* infinitive] *It never pays to take risks where human safety is concerned.* ○ *The moral is, "Crime doesn't pay."*

PROVIDE /peɪ/ *v* [T] *past* **paid** to provide or do something ○ *Please pay attention.* ○ *It's always nice to be paid a compliment.*

WORD FAMILY pay

Nouns	pay payee payer payment repayment	*Adjectives*	unpaid payable underpaid
		Verbs	pay repay

IDIOMS with pay

• **pay** *someone* **a visit** to visit someone ○ *Why don't you pay us a visit next time you're in town?*
• **pay** *your* **dues** to earn the right to have something because you worked hard ○ *I've paid my dues for the last 25 years, and now I'm ready for a comfortable retirement.*

•**pay through the nose (for** *something***)** to pay too much money for something ○ *If you drive into the city, you have to pay through the nose for parking.*

PHRASAL VERBS with pay

•**pay back** *something* [M] to return money to someone from whom you have borrowed it ○ *I'll pay you back as soon as I get my next paycheck.* ○ Related noun: PAYBACK MONEY RETURN
•**pay down** *something* [M] to reduce a debt ○ *She plans to live at home with her mother while she pays down her student loan.*
•**pay off** *something* **GIVE MONEY OWED** [M] to give all of or the last part of an amount that you owe ○ *I expect to pay the debt off within two years.*
•**pay off HAVE SUCCESS** to result in success ○ *I hope all this work pays off.* ○ Related noun: PAYOFF REWARD
•**pay off** *someone* **MONEY FOR HELP** [M] to give someone money, often illegally, after the person has done something to help you ○ *He paid off the inspectors with bribes of $500.* ○ Related noun: PAYOFF MONEY
•**pay out** *(something)* to spend money ○ *The federal government paid out $7.7 billion as a result of damage caused by hurricanes this year.* ○ Related noun: PAYOUT
•**pay up** to give all the money that is owed or asked for ○ *Some ballplayers charge fans $10 for autographs, and the fans, incredibly enough, pay up.*

payback **PUNISHMENT** /ˈpeɪ·bæk/ *n* [C/U] an action that punishes someone for something bad that the person did to you; REVENGE ○ [U] *They view the proposed initiative as payback to those senators who have not shown enough Republican loyalty.*

MONEY RETURN /ˈpeɪ·bæk/ *n* [C usually sing] the activity of giving money that is owed, or of getting back something for money spent ○ *He'll have a 20-year payback on his investment, and the improvements should last another 20 years after that.* ○ Related verb: PAY BACK

paycheck /ˈpeɪ·tʃek/ *n* [C] a check used to pay an employee the amount of money the employee has earned

payday /ˈpeɪ·deɪ/ *n* [C] the day on which employees receive their pay

payload /ˈpeɪ·loʊd/ *n* [C] the amount of explosive that a MISSILE carries, or the equipment carried in a spacecraft

payment /ˈpeɪ·mənt/ *n* [C/U] ○ See at PAY GIVE MONEY FOR

payoff **REWARD** /ˈpeɪ·ɔːf/ *n* [C] *infml* a result that rewards you for your effort or work ○ *After years of study, the payoff is supposed to be a good job.* ○ Related verb: PAY OFF HAVE SUCCESS

MONEY /ˈpeɪ·ɔːf/ *n* [C] money paid to someone for something that you want done or to not cause you trouble ○ *He denied receiving any kickbacks or payoffs for giving a large contract to the company.* ○ Related verb: PAY OFF MONEY FOR HELP

payout /ˈpeɪ·ɑʊt/ *n* [C] an amount of money paid to someone ○ *The payout was increased from 10 cents to 11 cents a share.* ○ Related verb: PAY OUT

pay phone *n* [C] a public telephone that you operate by putting coins into it or by using a special card

payroll /ˈpeɪ·roʊl/ *n* [C] a list of a company's employees and the amount each earns, or the total earnings a business gives to its employees

PC **COMPUTER, pc** /piːˈsiː/ *n* [C] *abbreviation for* PERSONAL COMPUTER (= a small computer used in homes and offices)

CORRECT *adj abbreviation for* POLITICALLY CORRECT

pct *adv abbreviation for* PERCENT

PDA *n* [C] *abbreviation for* personal digital assistant (= a very small computer that you can carry with you to store information and to do simple computer jobs)

PDF *n* [C/U] *abbreviation for* **1** portable document format (= an electronic way to store pictures and text so they can be printed on any computer or looked at on the Internet) **2** A PDF is also a computer file that contains information in PDF form: *The printable PDF includes six papers and an introduction.*

pea /piː/ *n* [C] an edible, round, green seed, that grows with others in a POD (= outer covering), from which they are removed to be cooked as a vegetable

peace **NO VIOLENCE** /piːs/ *n* [U] (a period of) freedom from war or violence, esp. when people live and work together without violent disagreements ○ *People don't like to think about spending money on the military in a time of peace.* ○ *The country has been* **at peace** *for 25 years* (= not involved in war during this period).
peaceful /ˈpiːs·fəl/ *adj* [not gradable] ○ *The US is promoting a peaceful and rapid solution to the present crisis.*
peaceable /ˈpiː·sə·bəl/ *adj* [not gradable] not liking or involving fighting or argument ○ *The group supports peaceable, nonviolent protest.*
peaceably /ˈpiː·sə·bli/ *adv*

CALM /piːs/ *n* [U] calm and quiet; freedom from worry or annoyance ○ *I need peace and quiet to study.*
peaceful /ˈpiːs·fəl/ *adj* [not gradable] ○ *It's so peaceful by the lake.*
peacefully /ˈpiːs·fə·li/ *adv* [not gradable] ○ *She died peacefully in her sleep at the age of 90.*
peacefulness /ˈpiːs·fəl·nəs/ *n* [U]

WORD FAMILY peace

Nouns	peace peacefulness	*Adverbs*	peacefully peaceably
Adjectives	peaceful peaceable		

IDIOMS with peace

•**at peace with** *something/yourself* feeling calm and relaxed about something or yourself ○ *She seems at peace with herself.*

•**peace of mind** a feeling of calm or not being worried ○ *For my peace of mind, please check that the door is locked.*

peacekeeping /ˈpiːsˌkiː·pɪŋ/ *n* [U] the maintaining of peace, esp. the use of armed forces not involved in the disagreement to prevent fighting in an area

peacekeeper /ˈpiːsˌkiː·pər/ *n* [C] a special soldier whose only job is to stop violence in a troubled area ○ *U.N. peacekeepers were brought in to the troubled area.*

peacemaker /ˈpiːsˌmeɪ·kər/ *n* [C] a person who tries to influence people, organizations, or countries to stop fighting or arguing

peacetime /ˈpiːs·tɑɪm/ *n* [U] a period when a country is not at war

peach FRUIT /piːtʃ/ *n* [C] a round fruit with sweet, juicy, yellow flesh, soft red and yellow skin, and a large seed in its center

COLOR /piːtʃ/ *adj*, *n* [U] (of) a pink-orange color ○ *a set of peach towels*

peacock /ˈpiː·kɑk/ *n* [C] a large bird with long, bright, showy, blue and green tail feathers that it can spread out

peak REACH HIGHEST POINT /piːk/ *v* [I] to reach the highest point, value, or level ○ *Official figures show unemployment peaked in November.*

peak /piːk/ *n* [C] ○ *Kelly is at the peak of her skating career.*

peak /piːk/ *adj* [not gradable] ○ *During the peak season, the population swells with over 50,000 tourists.*

MOUNTAIN TOP /piːk/ *n* [C] the pointed top of a mountain, or the mountain itself

peaked /ˈpiː·kəd/ *adj* [not gradable] (of a person) looking slightly ill and often pale

peal /piːl/ *v* [I] to sound loudly ○ *The bells pealed from the town hall tower.*

peal /piːl/ *n* [C] a loud sound ○ *A peal of thunder woke him up.*

peanut /ˈpiː·nət, -nʌt/ *n* [C] a small nut that grows in a shell under the ground

peanut butter *n* [U] a soft food made of crushed, ROASTED PEANUTS, that is often spread on bread

peanuts /ˈpiː·nəts, -nʌts/ *pl n infml* a very small amount of money ○ *They expect us to work for peanuts.*

pear /per, pær/ *n* [C] a sweet, juicy, yellow or green fruit with a round base and slightly pointed top

pearl /ˈpɜrl/ *n* [C] a small, shiny, hard ball, usually white or blue-gray, that forms around a grain of sand inside some OYSTER shells and is valued as a jewel ○ *a string of pearls*

peasant /ˈpez·ənt/ *n* [C] ***world history*** a member of a low social class of farm workers and owners of small farms

peat /piːt/ *n* [U] partly decayed plant matter, used to improve garden dirt or as fuel

pebble /ˈpeb·əl/ *n* [C] a small stone, made smooth by the action of water

pecan /pɪˈkɑːn, -ˈkæn/ *n* [C] an edible nut with a smooth shell

peck /pek/ *v* [I/T] (of a bird) to hit, bite, or pick up something with the beak

peck /pek/ *n* [C] A peck is also a quick kiss: *Aunt Velma gave me a peck on the cheek.*

pecking order *n* [C usually sing] *infml* the order of importance of people in a group ○ *The teachers are so low in the social and economic pecking order that nobody listens to them.*

peculiar STRANGE /pɪˈkjuːl·jər/ *adj* [not gradable] unusual and strange ○ *The copy editor will check type size and technical details to see if anything looks peculiar.*

peculiarity /pɪˌkjuː·liːˈær·əţ·i/ *n* [C/U] ○ [C] *The owners love the house in spite of its peculiarities* (= strange characteristics).

BELONGING TO /pɪˈkjuːl·jər/ *adj* [not gradable] characteristic especially of a particular person, group, or thing ○ *Katherine Hepburn's way of talking was peculiar to her.*

peculiarly /pɪˈkjuːl·jər·li/ *adv* [not gradable] ○ *He identifies this social practice as peculiarly Irish.*

peculiarly /pɪˈkjuːl·jər·li/ *adv* [not gradable] very or specially ○ *Her complex writing style makes this book peculiarly difficult to read.*

pedagogical /ˌped·əˈgɑdʒ·ɪ·kəl, -ˈgoʊdʒ-/ *adj* relating to the practice of teaching and its methods ○ *The book describes current pedagogical methods used in teaching reading.*

pedal /ˈped·ᵊl/ *n* [C] a small part of a machine or vehicle that you can press down with your foot to operate the machine or make the vehicle move ○ *bicycle pedals* ○ *You have to press down hard on the gas pedal to get this car up hills.*

pedal /ˈped·ᵊl/ *v* [I/T] ○ [I/T] *He struggled to pedal (his bike) up the hill.*

pedantic /pɪˈdænt·ɪk/ *adj* caring too much about unimportant rules or details and not enough about understanding or appreciating a subject ○ *Professor Harris had a narrow, pedantic approach to history that put us to sleep.*

peddle /ˈped·ᵊl/ *v* [T] to sell things, esp. by taking them to different places ○ *Mrs. Cawthorn peddled vegetables out of the back of a pickup truck to earn a living.*

peddler /ˈped·lər/ *n* [C] a person who sell things on the street or by going to people's houses ○ *His grandfather was a street peddler on NY's Lower East Side.*

pedestal /ˈped·ə·stəl/ *n* [C] a base for a statue, or a base for a column ○ *Museum staff plan to replace the cracked pedestal under the statue.*

P

IDIOM with pedestal

•**put** *someone/something* **on a pedestal** to behave as if one person is more important than others ○ *We put athletes and movie stars on a pedestal.*

pedestrian WALKER /pəˈdes·triː·ən/ *n* [C] a person who is walking, esp. in an area where vehicles go ○ *Bicyclists and pedestrians use the path.*

NOT INTERESTING /pəˈdes·triː·ən/ *adj* showing little imagination; not interesting ○ *The lyrics are pretty pedestrian.*

pediatrics /ˌpiːd·iːˈæ·trɪks/ *n* [U] the area of medicine that deals with children

pediatric /ˌpiːd·iːˈæ·trɪk/ *adj* [not gradable] ○ *a pediatric nurse*

pediatrician /ˌpiːd·iː·əˈtrɪʃ·ən/ *n* [C] a doctor with special training in medical care for children

pedicure /ˈped·ɪˌkjʊr/ *n* [C] a treatment for the feet that involves cutting and sometimes painting the nails, and softening or MASSAGING (= rubbing) the skin

pedigree /ˈped·əˌgriː/ *n* [C] **1** the parents and other family members of a particular animal, or a record of them ○ *a dog's pedigree* **2** The pedigree of a person, idea, or activity is its history: *Populism and conservatism have strong Southern pedigrees.*

pee /piː/ *v* [I] *infml* to excrete urine; to URINATE

pee /piː/ *n* [U] *infml*

peek /piːk/ *v* [I] **1** to look, esp. for a short time or while trying to avoid being seen ○ *Close your eyes and don't peek.* **2** If something peeks out or up, it can be partly seen: *The dog's head peeked out from behind the tree.*

peek /piːk/ *n* [C] ○ *She took a peek down the hall.*

P

peek-a-boo /ˈpiː·kəˌbuː/ *exclamation, n* [U] a game played with very young children in which you hide your face, esp. with your hands, and then suddenly take your hands away, saying "peek-a-boo"

peel REMOVE VEGETABLE SKIN /piːl/ *v* [T] to remove the skin of fruit and vegetables ○ *Peel, core, and chop the apples.*

peel /piːl/ *n* [C/U] ○ [C] *banana peels* ○ [U] *strips of lemon peel*

peeler /ˈpiː·lər/ *n* [C] a utensil for removing the skin of fruit and vegetables ○ *a vegetable peeler*

REMOVE COVERING /piːl/ *v* [I/T] **1** to remove a covering slowly and carefully, or of a covering to come off ○ [T always + adv/prep] *We peeled the wallpaper off the walls.* ○ [I] *My back is peeling from that sunburn I got last weekend.* **2** If you peel off clothing, you take it off: [M] *Ramon peeled his sweaty shirt off and hung it on a chair to dry.*

peep LOOK /piːp/ *v* [I] **1** to look quickly and often secretly ○ *He peeped over his shoulder to see if anyone was watching.* **2** If something peeps up or out, it has just begun to appear: *Daisies were peeping through the turf.*

peep /piːp/ *n* [C usually sing] ○ *Take a peep at this* (= Look quickly at it).

SOUND /piːp/ *n* [C] a sound, or a spoken word ○ *She's too scared to make a peep.*

peephole /ˈpiːp·hoʊl/ *n* [C] a small hole in a door or a wall through which you can see to the other side

peer LOOK /pɪr/ *v* [I always + adv/prep] to look carefully or with difficulty ○ *The judge peered over his glasses at the jury.*

EQUAL /pɪr/ *n* [C] a person of the same age, the same social position, or having the same abilities as other people in a group ○ *Getting help from a peer is easier than asking a teacher.*

peerless /ˈpɪr·ləs/ *adj* [not gradable] *fml* better than all others ○ *peerless beauty*

peer pressure *n* [U] the pressure that you feel to behave in a certain way because your friends or people in your group expect it ○ *There is tremendous peer pressure among teenagers to dress a certain way.*

peg HANGING DEVICE /peg/ *n* [C] a small, shaped piece of wood or other material on which objects can be hung ○ *She hung her apron on the peg.*

ATTACHING TOOL /peg/ *n* [C] a device used to attach something or hold it in place

FIX AMOUNT /peg/ *v* [T] **-gg-** to fix the amount or value of something in relation to something else ○ *There's talk of trying to peg the value of the peso to the dollar.*

DISCOVER /peg/ *v* [T] **-gg-** *infml* to recognize or discover what something is; IDENTIFY ○ *They had you pegged as a sucker the minute you walked in.*

PHRASAL VERB with peg

•**peg down** [M] to fix something in place ○ *The tent's ropes were pegged down by two-foot stakes.*

pejorative /pɪˈdʒɔːr·ət̬·ɪv, -ˈdʒɑr-/ *adj fml* insulting, disapproving, or suggesting that something is not good or is of no importance ○ *Is "Yankee" a pejorative term?* ○ **USAGE**: said of words

pelican /ˈpel·ɪ·kən/ *n* [C] a large, fish-eating bird with a long beak and a throat that is like a bag

pellet /ˈpel·ət/ *n* [C] a small, hard, ball-shaped or tube-shaped piece of any substance ○ *shotgun pellets* ○ *plastic pellets*

pelt THROW /pelt/ *v* [I/T] to throw a number of things quickly at someone or something ○ [T] *Youths tried to pelt them with stones.*

SKIN /pelt/ *n* [C] the skin and fur of a dead animal, or the skin with the fur removed ○ *rabbit pelts*

pelvis /ˈpel·vəs/ *n* [C] the bones that form a bowl-shaped structure in the area below the waist at the top of the legs, to which the leg bones and SPINE (= row of bones in the back) are joined

pelvic /ˈpel·vɪk/ *adj* [not gradable]

pen WRITING DEVICE /pen/ *n* [C/U] a thin device with a point used for writing or drawing with ink ○ [C] *a fountain/ballpoint/felt-tip pen* ○ [U] *You must fill out the application in pen* (= using a pen).

pen /pen/ *v* [T] **-nn-** ○ *She penned* (= wrote) *a thank-you note.*

ENCLOSED SPACE /pen/ *n* [C] a small area surrounded by a fence in which animals are kept, or *slang* a prison or JAIL
pen /pen/ *v* [T] **-nn-** ○ *Sheep are penned behind the barn.*

penal /ˈpiːn·əl/ *adj* [not gradable] of or connected with punishment given by law ○ *the penal system*
penalize /ˈpiːn·əlˌɑɪz, ˈpen-/ *v* [T] to punish someone, esp. for breaking the law or a rule ○ *The new law penalizes the taxpayers who can least afford to pay.* ○ *Boone was penalized for unnecessary roughness and thrown out of the game.*
penalty /ˈpen·əl·ti/ *n* [C] **1** a punishment, esp. the usual one, for breaking a law ○ *Repeat offenders should face stiff/tough penalties.* **2** A penalty is also a type of punishment for breaking an agreement or not following rules: *If you pay off the loan early, they'll charge an extra month's interest as a prepayment penalty.* ○ *When a football team gives up 143 yards in penalties, they deserve to lose.*

penal code *n* [C] the system of legal punishment in a particular place ○ *the Swedish Penal Code*

penance /ˈpen·əns/ *n* [C/U] activity that shows you regret some previous action, sometimes for religious reasons ○ [U] *They are doing penance for their sins.*

penchant /ˈpen·tʃənt/ *n* [C usually sing] a liking for or a habit of doing something, esp. something that other people might not like ○ *Ives had a penchant for musical experimentation.*

pencil /ˈpen·səl/ *n* [C/U] a thin, usually wooden, tube-shaped device for writing or drawing which has colored material in the center and a point at one end ○ [C] *colored pencils* ○ [U] *Make your corrections in pencil* (= using a pencil).
pencil /ˈpen·səl/ *v* [T] **-l-**, **-ll-** ○ [T] *She penciled* (= wrote) *the name "Sloan" inside a circle.* ○ [M] *Bill spent a couple of hours penciling in corrections.*

pencil sharpener *n* [C] an electric, mechanical, or small hand-held device for making a sharp point on pencils

pendant /ˈpen·dənt/ *n* [C] a piece of jewelry worn around the neck consisting of a long chain with an object hanging from it, or the object itself

pending /ˈpen·dɪŋ/ *adj* [not gradable] about to happen or waiting to happen ○ *His application for citizenship was still pending.*
pending /ˈpen·dɪŋ/ *prep* until after ○ *Flights were suspended pending an investigation of the crash.*

pendulum /ˈpen·dʒə·ləm/ *n* [C] **1** a device consisting of a weight hanging on a rod or cord that moves from one side to the other, esp. one that forms a part of a clock **2** A pendulum is also power or control of an activity that changes from one group to another: *In labor-management relations, the pendulum has swung wildly in the direction of the players.*

penetrate **MOVE** /ˈpen·əˌtreɪt/ *v* [I/T] to move into or through something ○ [I] *The drill isn't sharp enough to penetrate into the rock.* ○ [T] *Women have begun to penetrate a lot of fields that were dominated by men for centuries.*
penetration /ˌpen·əˈtreɪ·ʃən/ *n* [U] ○ *The program's penetration in Utah schools varies from district to district.*

UNDERSTAND /ˈpen·əˌtreɪt/ *v* [I/T] to understand something, or to be understood as a result of study or INVESTIGATION ○ [I] *Her writing penetrated to the heart of contemporary life.*
penetrating /ˈpen·əˌtreɪt·ɪŋ/ *adj* showing a very good understanding ○ *a penetrating critique* ○ *penetrating observations*

penetrating /ˈpen·əˌtreɪt·ɪŋ/ *adj* **1** very loud ○ *I heard a penetrating scream.* **2** Someone with penetrating eyes or a penetrating gaze seems able to understand or know you just by looking at you.

penguin /ˈpen·gwən, ˈpeŋ-/ *n* [C] a black-and-white sea bird found in cold, southern parts of the world which cannot fly and swims using its small wings

penicillin /ˌpen·əˈsɪl·ən/ *n* [U] a type of ANTIBIOTIC (= medicine that kills bacteria)

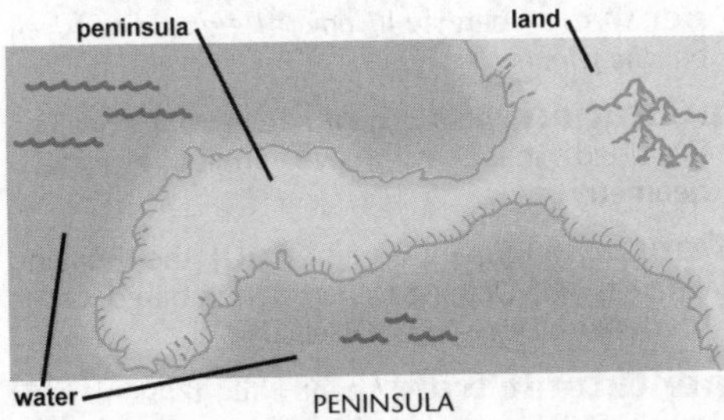

PENINSULA

peninsula /pəˈnɪn·sə·lə/ *n* [C] an area of land mostly surrounded by water but connected to a larger piece of land ○ *the Monterey Peninsula*

penis /ˈpiː·nəs/ *n* [C] an organ of male mammals that is used to excrete urine and for sex

penitence /ˈpen·ə·təns/ *n* [U] regret for a mistake and willingness to correct it ○ *He expressed his penitence for what he had done.*

penitentiary /ˌpen·əˈten·tʃə·ri/ *n* [C] a prison ○ *a federal/state penitentiary*

penknife /ˈpen·nɑɪf/ *n* [C] a small knife with a blade that folds into its handle

penmanship /ˈpen·mənˌʃɪp/ *n* [U] the ability to write neatly, or the activity of learning to do this

pen name *n* [C] an invented name used by a writer when he or she publishes something ○ *C. L. Dodgson published under the pen name Lewis Carroll.*

pennant /ˈpen·ənt/ *n* [C] a flag shaped like a triangle

penny /ˈpen·i/ *n* [C] **1** in the US and Canada, a coin worth 1/100th of a dollar; a cent ○ *I keep pennies in a jar.* **2** A penny can also mean the smallest

P

amount of money possible or the total cost of something: *Our insurance didn't cover a penny of our medical bills.* ○ *It was an expensive meal but worth every penny.*

penniless /ˈpen·iː·ləs/ *adj, adv* without any money at all ○ *a penniless youth*

IDIOM with penny

• **a penny for your thoughts** I would like to know what you are thinking ○ *You haven't said very much – a penny for your thoughts.*

pen pal *n* [C] someone with whom you exchange letters as a hobby, esp. someone in another country

pension /ˈpen·tʃən/ *n* [C] a sum of money paid regularly to a person who has RETIRED (= stopped working because of having reached a certain age)

pension fund *n* [C] a supply of money that many people pay into, which is invested in order to provide them with a PENSION

pension plan *n* [C] a system of investment that allows a person or group to receive a PENSION

pensive /ˈpen·sɪv/ *adj* quiet and thinking seriously ○ *James was more pensive than usual.*

pensively /ˈpen·sɪv·li/ *adv* ○ *He gazed pensively out the window.*

pentagon /ˈpent·əˌɡɑn/ *n* [C] ***geometry*** a flat, five-sided shape with five angles ➤ Picture: **geometry**

Pentagon /ˈpent·əˌɡɑn/ *n* [U] the building where the US Defense Department is based, or the US Defense Department itself

P

pentatonic scale /ˌpent·əˈtɑn·ɪk ˈskeɪl/ *n* [C] ***music*** a SCALE based on five notes, such as the one that uses only the black keys on a piano

penthouse /ˈpent·hɑʊs/ *n* [C] *pl* **penthouses** a comfortable, expensive apartment or set of rooms at the top of a hotel or tall building

pent-up /ˈpentˈʌp/ *adj* (of feelings) not expressed or released ○ *His pent-up anger and frustration burst forth.*

peony /ˈpiː·ə·ni/ *n* [C] a plant with large red, pink, or white flowers

people PERSONS /ˈpiː·pəl/ *pl n* **1** men, women, and children generally; *pl of* PERSON ○ *There were a lot of people there.* ○ *Some people were hurt.* **2** People can refer to a particular group mentioned: *young/old people* ○ *poor/rich people* ○ *Those people look as if they're lost.* **3** When you say the people, you mean the large number of ordinary men and women who do not have positions of power: *The president wanted to take his message directly to the people.* ○ **USAGE:** See the usage note at PERSON.

people /ˈpiː·pəl/ *v* [T] If a place is peopled by a particular type of people, they have moved there or live there: *Honolulu is peopled by native Hawaiians, Japanese, Chinese, Filipinos, white Americans, and others.*

NATION /ˈpiː·pəl/ *n* [C] a culture or nation ○ *It is a custom shared by many Native American peoples.*

pep /pep/ *n* [U] *infml* energy or enthusiasm ○ *That morning she felt full of pep and decided to go for a long walk.*

PHRASAL VERB with pep

• **pep up** *(something/someone)* [M] **1** to make something more exciting or interesting ○ *Add cheese and horseradish to pep up the flavor of mashed potatoes.* **2** If you **pep up** someone, or if someone peps up, the person starts behaving with more energy and enthusiasm: *The sight and smell of a rose will pep you up.*

pepper SPICE /ˈpep·ər/ *n* [U] a black or cream-colored spice, often used in powdered form, that gives a spicy hot taste to food

VEGETABLE /ˈpep·ər/ *n* [C] a vegetable that is green, red, or yellow, having a rounded shape, that is hollow with seeds in the middle

ATTACK /ˈpep·ər/ *v* [T] **1** to direct something suddenly and repeatedly at someone, as if attacking the person ○ *The mayor was peppered with questions from reporters about the municipal corruption scandal.* **2** To pepper is also to add to something in many places: *He peppered his speech with jokes.*

peppermint /ˈpep·ərˌmɪnt/ *n* [C/U] **1** a strong, fresh flavoring from a type of MINT plant **2** A peppermint is a candy that has the flavor of peppermint.

pepperoni /ˌpep·əˈroʊ·ni/ *n* [U] a type of Italian SAUSAGE ○ *Do you want pepperoni on your pizza?*

pep rally *n* [C] a gathering of people who want to show their support and enthusiasm, esp. for a sports team before a game

pep talk *n* [C] a short speech intended to encourage someone to make more effort or to think more positively ○ *The coach gave them a pep talk at halftime.*

peptide /ˈpep·tɑɪd/ *n* [C] ***biology*** a chemical that is made of two or more AMINO ACIDS, which combine to make PROTEIN (= chemicals that are a necessary part of cells)

per /pɜr, pər/ *prep* for each ○ *The speed limit is 55 miles per hour.* ○ *This dish is 225 calories per serving.*

per capita /pər ˈkæp·əṭ·ə/ *adj, adv* [not gradable] for each person, esp. when considering all of the people in a group ○ *New Hampshire ranks second per capita in the percentage of National Guard members who served in Iraq.* ○ *Texas has the most state and local government employees on a per-capita basis.*

perceive Ⓐ THINK OF /pərˈsiːv/ *v* [T] to think of something in a particular way ○ *The way people perceive the real world is strongly influenced by the language they speak.* ○ *In those days, crime wasn't even perceived as a problem.*

NOTICE /pərˈsiːv/ *v* [T] to notice something or someone by using sight, sound, touch, taste, or smell ○ *I perceived something moving in the shadows.*

percent Ⓐ, **per cent** /pərˈsent/, *abbreviation* **pct**, *symbol* **%** *adv* [not gradable] for or out of every 100 ○ *You got 20 percent of the answers right.* ○ *Only 48% of registered voters actually voted in the election.*
percentage Ⓐ /pərˈsent·ɪdʒ/ *n* [C] an amount of something, often expressed as a number out of 100 ○ *TV ratings are based on the percentage of sets tuned to a particular program.*

percentage /pərˈsent·ɪdʒ/ *n* [U] an improvement or advantage, esp. when considered against other possibilities ○ *There's no percentage in working long hours if you don't plan to stay in that job.*

perceptible /pərˈsep·tə·bəl/ *adj* that can be seen, heard, felt, tasted, smelled, or noticed ○ *His pulse was barely perceptible* (= difficult to feel) *upon arrival at the hospital.*

perception Ⓐ **BELIEF** /pərˈsep·ʃən/ *n* [C] a thought, belief, or opinion, often held by many people and based on appearances ○ *Even though he had done nothing illegal, the public's perception was that he had acted dishonestly, and he was forced to resign.*
AWARENESS /pərˈsep·ʃən/ *n* [U] an awareness of things through the physical SENSES, esp. sight
perceptive /pərˈsep·tɪv/ *adj* able to notice and understand things that many other people do not notice ○ *Her books are full of perceptive insights.*

perch /pɜrtʃ/ *v* [I/T] (of a bird) to rest on a branch or other object, or of a person or thing to sit or be on the edge or top of something ○ [T] *A baseball cap, turned backwards, was perched on his head.*
perch /pɜrtʃ/ *n* [C] ○ *From their perches in the towers, the prison guards could see the entire prison yard.*

percolate /ˈpɜr·kəˌleɪt/ *v* [I] (of a liquid) to move through a substance by going through very small spaces within it ○ *Underground water had percolated through the soil to form puddles.*
percolator /ˈpɜr·kəˌleɪt̬·ər/ *n* [C] a device for making coffee that boils water and forces it up a tube and through crushed coffee beans held in a container

percussion /pərˈkʌʃ·ən/ *n* [U] musical instruments, such as drums, that are played by being hit with an object or with the hand

peremptory /pəˈremp·tə·ri/ *adj fml* having the expectation of immediate and complete obedience, or to be obeyed without explanation ○ *In his usual peremptory manner, he ordered us all into the conference room.*

perennial **TIME** /pəˈren·iː·əl/ *adj* lasting a long time, or happening repeatedly or all the time ○ *Each year, the nation's marketers try to answer the perennial question, What do consumers really want?*

PLANT /pəˈren·iː·əl/ *n* [C] a plant that lives for more than two years ○ Compare ANNUAL PLANT; BIENNIAL

perestroika /ˌper·əˈstrɔɪ·kə/ *n* [U] ***world history*** economic and government REFORMs (= changes to make things better) established in the Soviet Union in the 1980s

perfect **RIGHT** /ˈpɜr·fɪkt/ *adj* **1** complete and right in every way; having nothing wrong ○ *The car is two years old but it's in perfect condition.* **2** You can also use perfect to mean complete and emphasize the noun that comes after it: *I felt like a perfect fool when I forgot her name.*
perfect /pərˈfekt/ *v* [T] to make something perfect ○ *She practices tennis whenever she can, hoping to perfect her serve.*
perfectly /ˈpɜr·fɪk·tli/ *adv* **1** extremely well; in a perfect way ○ *He managed everything perfectly.* **2** Perfectly can also mean very or completely: *I want to make it perfectly clear that I have no intention of selling this company.*
perfection /pərˈfek·ʃən/ *n* [U] **1** *She is a superb violinist, and combines technical perfection with an exciting performance style.* **2** If something is done to perfection, it is done very well and happens exactly as planned: *In the last few minutes of the football game, they tried a trick play, and it worked to perfection.*
perfectionist /pərˈfek·ʃə·nəst/ *n* [C] a person who wants very much to get every detail exactly right ○ *As a film director, Alfred Hitchcock had the reputation of a perfectionist.*

> **WORD CHOICES perfect**
>
> If something is perfect because it has no mistakes or anything bad, you can use adjectives such as **faultless**, **flawless**, **immaculate**, and **impeccable**.
>
> *They gave a **faultless** performance.*
> *The house was always in **immaculate** condition.*
> *His English is **impeccable**.*
> *She has a **flawless** complexion.*
>
> The adjective **ideal** is sometimes used to describe something that is perfect for a particular purpose.
>
> *The book is **ideal** for children aged between four and six.*
>
> In informal situations, if you want to describe something such as a job, house, etc., which is perfect for you, you can describe it as a **dream** job, **dream** house, etc.
>
> *A pretty cottage on the lake – that would be my **dream** home.*

BEST /ˈpɜr·fɪkt/ *adj* exactly right for a particular purpose or situation; being the best possible ○ *It was a warm, sunny day, a perfect afternoon for a ballgame.*
GRAMMAR /ˈpɜr·fɪkt/ *adj* [not gradable] ***grammar*** having the tense of a verb that shows action that

has happened in the past or before another time or event and has continued up to the present or up to a particular point ○ See also: PRESENT PERFECT; FUTURE PERFECT; PAST PERFECT

WORD FAMILY perfect			
Nouns	perfection imperfection perfectionist	*Adjectives*	perfect imperfect
		Adverbs	perfectly
Verbs	perfect		

perforated /ˈpɜr·fəˌreɪt̬·əd/ *adj* [not gradable] (of a surface) having a hole or holes in it ○ *He was taken to the hospital to have emergency surgery for a perforated stomach ulcer.*

perforation /ˌpɜr·fəˈreɪ·ʃən/ *n* [C] ○ *The perforations* (= very small holes) *make it easy to remove checks from your checkbook.*

perform DO /pərˈfɔːrm/ *v* [I/T] **1** to do an action or piece of work ○ [T] *The operation was performed with the patient under general anesthesia.* **2** If something performs well or badly, it operates satisfactorily or does not operate satisfactorily: [I] *The car performed poorly during the tests.*

performance /pərˈfɔːr·məns/ *n* [U] **1** the act of doing something, such as your job ○ *If the accident happened during the performance of his regular duties, he's covered by disability insurance.* **2** Performance also refers to how well an activity or job is done: *With a record of 2 wins and 3 defeats, the team's performance has been disappointing.*

ENTERTAIN /pərˈfɔːrm/ *v* [I/T] to entertain people by singing, dancing, playing music, etc. ○ [T] *The magician performed a number of tricks that had us gasping in surprise.*

performance /pərˈfɔːr·məns/ *n* [C] ○ *Her performance in the play won rave reviews.*

performer /pərˈfɔːr·mər/ *n* [C] ○ *By the age of 12, she was a seasoned circus performer.*

performing /pərˈfɔːr·mɪŋ/ *adj* [not gradable]

WORD FAMILY perform			
Nouns	performance performer	*Adjectives*	performing
		Verbs	perform

performance art *n* [U] ***art*** art that consists only of a person or group performing something and that does not exist apart from when it is being performed

performing arts *pl n* acting, singing, dancing, and other forms of public entertainment ○ *Season tickets to the theater are a perfect gift for someone who loves the performing arts.*

perfume /ˈpɜr·fjuːm, pərˈfjuːm/ *n* [C/U] a liquid produced and sold for its strong, pleasant smell, often used on the skin ○ [U] *She put a few drops of perfume on the back of her neck.*

perfunctory /pərˈfʌŋ·tə·ri/ *adj* done quickly and without showing that you care or have much interest ○ *She asked a few perfunctory questions about my family and then ended the conversation.*

perhaps /pərˈhæps, pəˈræps/ *adv* [not gradable] used to show that something is possible or that you are not certain about something; MAYBE ○ *Perhaps the greatest swimming coach in history, Kiphuth retired after 41 years at Yale.* ○ *Soon, perhaps as early as this week, she is to testify in the trial.*

peril /ˈper·əl/ *n* [C/U] *fml* danger, or something that is dangerous ○ [U] *The president said that we are entering a time of great peril.*

perilous /ˈper·ə·ləs/ *adj fml* dangerous

perimeter /pəˈrɪm·ət̬·ər/ *n* [C] **1** the outer edge of an area or the border around it ○ *Several bombs landed near the perimeter of the airport.* **2** ***geometry*** The perimeter is the outer edge of a flat shape or area. **3** ***geometry*** Perimeter is also the distance around the outer edge of a flat shape.

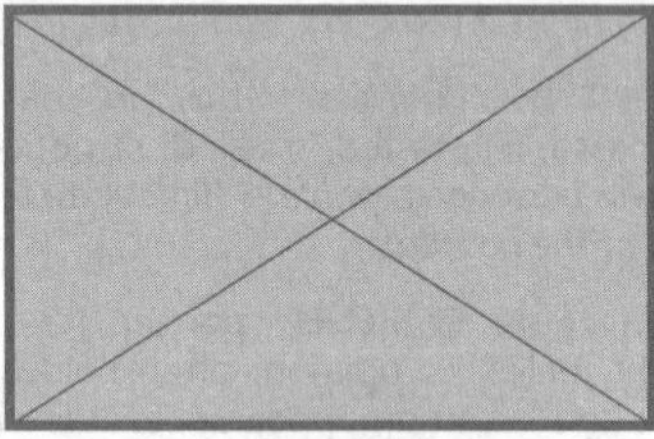

PERIMETER

period Ⓐ TIME /ˈpɪr·iː·əd/ *n* [C] **1** a length of time ○ *The study will be carried out over a six-month period.* **2** A period in the life of a person or in history is a particular time during that life or history: *The period after World War II was marked by rapid economic growth.* **3** A period is a division of time in an event of fixed length, such as a day at school or a game: *There was no scoring in the second period.* **4** ***physics*** A period is the time it takes for one complete repetition of a pattern that repeats. A second is used as the standard unit in most areas of science. **5** Period costume/dress/furniture is the clothing or furniture of a particular time in history: *At the Revolutionary War theme park, everyone was wearing period costumes.*

periodic Ⓐ /ˌpɪr·iːˈɑd·ɪk/, **periodical** /ˌpɪr·iːˈɑd·ɪ·kəl/ *adj* [not gradable] **1** happening repeatedly although not necessarily frequently ○ *He suffers periodic mental breakdowns.* **2** ***physics*** A pattern or other event is periodic if it repeats at periods of time that are equal.

periodically Ⓐ /ˌpɪr·iːˈɑd·ɪ·kli/ *adv* [not gradable] ○ *The equipment should be tested periodically* (= repeatedly at regular times).

MARK /ˈpɪr·iː·əd/ *n* [C] **1** a mark (.) used in writing to show where the end of a sentence is, or to show that the letters before it are an ABBREVIATION (= short word form) **2** *infml* You can say period at the end of a statement as a way of adding emphasis: *There will be no more shouting, period!*

BLEEDING /ˈpɪr·iː·əd/, **menstrual period** /ˈmen·strəlˌpɪr·iː·əd, -strə·wəl-/ *n* [C] the bleeding from a woman's uterus that happens approximately every four weeks when she is not pregnant

REPEATED EVENT /ˈpɪr·iː·əd/ *n* [C] ***science*** the time needed to complete a regularly repeating event or series of events

periodic /ˌpɪr·iː'ɑd·ɪk/ *adj* [not gradable] ***science*** happening repeatedly in a fixed pattern
periodicity /ˌpɪr·iː·ə'dɪs·ət̬·i/ *n* [U] ***science*** the tendency of an event or series of events to happen repeatedly in a fixed pattern
ROW /'pɪr·iː·əd/ *n* [C] ***chemistry*** any of the rows in the PERIODIC TABLE of chemical elements

periodical /ˌpɪr·iː'ɑd·ɪ·kəl/ *n* [C] a magazine that is published regularly ○ *The library subscribes to a number of periodicals dealing with the arts and sciences.*

periodic table *n* [U] ***chemistry*** a list of the symbols of all the chemical elements arranged in rows and COLUMNS down a page

peripheral nervous system /pə'rɪf·ə·rəl 'nɜr·vəs ˌsɪs·təm/ *n* [C] ***biology*** the part of the NERVOUS SYSTEM that includes all the nerves in the body outside the brain and the SPINAL CORD

periphery /pə'rɪf·ə·ri/ *n* [C usually sing] the outer edge of an area ○ *We've planted 50 small trees around the periphery of the property.*
peripheral /pə'rɪf·ə·rəl/ *adj* **1** not central or of main importance ○ *First of all, we had to find out who the thief was – getting the money back was a peripheral issue.* **2** Peripheral vision is what you can see to the sides of what you are looking at.
peripheral /pə'rɪf·ə·rəl/ *n* [C] a piece of equipment, such as a printer, that can be connected to a computer

periscope /'per·əˌskoʊp/ *n* [C] a vertical tube containing mirrors that can give you a view of what is above you when you look through the bottom of the tube ○ *The periscope of the submarine was visible just above the surface of the water.*

perish /'per·ɪʃ/ *v* [I] to die, esp. as a result of an accident, violence, or war ○ *Without this assistance, thousands of refugees would perish from hunger and neglect.*
perishable /'per·ɪ·ʃə·bəl/ *adj* Food that is perishable has to be used quickly or it will decay so that you cannot eat it: *He owns one of the largest distributors of perishable foods.*

peristalsis /ˌper·ə'stɑl·səs, -'stɔːl-, -'stæl-/ *n* [U] ***biology*** the repeated movements made in the tube that carries food away from the stomach, which push food and waste through the body

perjury /'pɜr·dʒə·ri/ *n* [U] *law* the crime of telling a lie in court after promising formally to tell the truth
perjure /'pɜr·dʒər/ *v* [T] *law* ○ *Perjuring yourself* (= Telling a lie in court) *is a criminal offense.*

perk ADVANTAGE /pɜrk/ *n* [C] *infml* a special advantage or benefit, in addition to the money you are paid, that you are given because of your job ○ *Free child care for preschool children of employees was a popular perk.*
MAKE COFFEE /pɜrk/ *v* [I/T] (of boiling water or coffee) to move up a tube in a PERCOLATOR (= a type container for making coffee) when the coffee is being made ○ [I] *The coffee had begun to perk.*

PHRASAL VERB with perk

• **perk up** *(something/someone)* [M] **1** to make something more interesting or exciting, or to become this way ○ *The city is trying to perk up the business district by planting trees.* **2** If someone perks up or you perk someone up, the person becomes more energetic and happier: *She perked up considerably when her sister arrived.*

perky /'pɜr·ki/ *adj* showing a lot of energy in a happy, confident way ○ *Kimberly burst in with a crowd of perky teenagers.*

perm /pɜrm/, **permanent (wave)** /'pɜr·mə·nənt ('weɪv)/ *n* [C] a chemical process that makes a person's hair curly
perm /pɜrm/ *v* [T] ○ *Tiffany got her hair permed.*

permanent /'pɜr·mə·nənt/ *adj* [not gradable] lasting for a long time or forever ○ *Are you looking for a temporary job or something permanent?* ○ *He entered the United States in 1988 as a permanent resident with a green card.*
permanently /'pɜr·mə·nənt·li/ *adv* [not gradable] ○ *The accident left him permanently paralyzed.*
permanence /'pɜr·mə·nəns/ *n* [U]

permeable /'pɜr·miː·ə·bəl/ *adj* [not gradable] ***science*** allowing liquids or gases to go through
permeability /ˌpɜr·miː·ə'bɪl·ət̬·i/ *n* [U] ***science***

permeate /'pɜr·miːˌeɪt/ *v* [T] to spread through something and be present in every part of it ○ *The smell of detergent and bleach permeated the air.*

permission /pər'mɪʃ·ən/ *n* [U] the act of allowing someone to do something, or of allowing something to happen ○ *Parents have to give their permission for their children to go on school trips.* ○ [+ *to* infinitive] *We had to get permission* (= approval) *from the city to build an extension to our house.*
permissible /pər'mɪs·ə·bəl/ *adj* ○ *It is no longer permissible for athletic programs in universities to give a lot more money for men's sports than for women's sports.*
permissive /pər'mɪs·ɪv/ *adj esp. disapproving* allowing a wide range of choices, esp. in an area where there have traditionally been rules that had to be obeyed ○ *The neighbors thought they were too permissive with their children, letting them stay up so late at night.*
permissiveness /pər'mɪs·ɪv·nəs/ *n* [U]

permit /pər'mɪt/ *v* [T] **-tt-** to allow something, or make something possible ○ *Playing loud music is not permitted after 10 pm.*
permit /'pɜr·mɪt, pər'mɪt/ *n* [C] an official document that allows you to do something ○ *Do you have a permit to park here?*
permitting /pər'mɪt̬·ɪŋ/ *adj* [only after n] used to show that an activity depends on an uncertain condition ○ *Weather permitting* (= if the weather is good enough), *the picnic will be next Saturday.*

WORD FAMILY permit

Nouns	permissiveness	*Adjectives*	permissible
	permission		impermissible
	permit		permissive
Verbs	permit		permitting

P

permutation /ˌpɜr·mjuːˈteɪ·ʃən/ *n* [C] ***mathematics*** any of the various arrangements in which a set of objects can be organized

pernicious /pərˈnɪʃ·əs/ *adj* having a very harmful effect or influence ○ *The book focuses on the pernicious effects of slavery.*

peroxide /pəˈrɑkˌsɑɪd/ *n* [U] HYDROGEN PEROXIDE

perpendicular /ˌpɜr·pənˈdɪk·jə·lər/ *adj* [not gradable] **1** ***geometry*** at an angle of 90° to another line or surface ○ *Two perpendicular lines form a right angle.* **2** Perpendicular is also standing or rising straight up: *The cliff was nearly perpendicular and impossible to climb.*

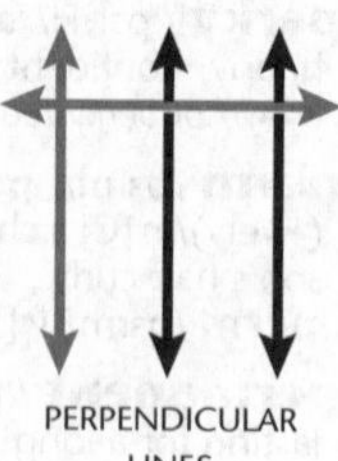

PERPENDICULAR LINES

perpetrate /ˈpɜr·pəˌtreɪt/ *v* [T] to commit a crime or other harmful act ○ *We will find the person who perpetrated this crime.*

perpetrator /ˈpɜr·pəˌtreɪţ·ər/ *n* [C] ○ *He promised vigorous action against the perpetrators of this crime.*

perpetual /pərˈpetʃ·ə·wəl/ *adj* [not gradable] continuing forever, or happening all the time ○ *They lived in perpetual fear of being discovered.* ○ *She resented his perpetual complaining about her cooking.*

perpetually /pərˈpetʃ·ə·wə·li/ *adv* [not gradable] ○ *She is perpetually late.*

perpetuate /pərˈpetʃ·əˌweɪt/ *v* [T] to cause something to continue ○ *The movie perpetuates stereotypes of small-town life.*

perpetuity /ˌpɜr·pəˈtuː·əţ·i/ *n fml* forever ○ *Wildlife areas have to be maintained* **in perpetuity**.

perplex /pərˈpleks/ *v* [T] to cause someone to be confused or uncertain over something that is not understood ○ *The symptoms of the disease have continued to perplex her doctors.*

perplexed /pərˈplekst/ *adj* ○ *Just when it appeared that interest rates were headed up, they fell, leaving some analysts clearly perplexed.*

per se /pɜrˈseɪ/ *adv* [not gradable] by or of itself ○ *It is not a pretty town per se, but it is where my family comes from, so I like it.*

persecute /ˈpɜr·sɪˌkjuːt/ *v* [T] to treat people unfairly or cruelly over a period of time because of their race, religion, etc. ○ *She claimed the government was persecuting its opponents.*

persecution /ˌpɜr·sɪˈkjuː·ʃən/ *n* [U] ○ *political/religious persecution*

persecutor /ˈpɜr·sɪˌkjuːţ·ər/ *n* [C] ○ *Given the chance, victims may seek revenge on their persecutors.*

persevere /ˌpɜr·səˈvɪr/ *v* [I] to try to do or continue doing something in a determined way, despite difficulties ○ *If I had persevered, I probably would have gotten the job.*

perseverance /ˌpɜr·səˈvɪr·əns/ *n* [U] ○ *Perseverance accounts for much of their success.*

persist Ⓐ /pərˈsɪst, -ˈzɪst/ *v* [I] to continue to exist past the usual time, or to continue to do something in a determined way even when facing difficulties or opposition ○ *If the pain persists, consult a doctor.* ○ *Although the meeting had ended, she persisted in trying to question the mayor.*

persistence Ⓐ /pərˈsɪs·təns, -ˈzɪs-/ *n* [U] ○ *A problem with pesticides is the persistence of chemicals in the soil.* ○ *His persistence paid off – he won the contract.*

persistent Ⓐ /pərˈsɪs·tənt, -ˈzɪs-/ *adj* ○ *a persistent cough* ○ *persistent rumors*

persistently Ⓐ /pərˈsɪs·tənt·li, -ˈzɪs-/ *adv* ○ *The rains persistently fell.*

person /ˈpɜr·sən/ *n* [C] *pl* **people, persons 1** a man, woman, or child ○ *Neil Armstrong was the first person to set foot on the moon.* ○ *The auditorium can seat about 500 people.* ○ *The plane crashed just after takeoff, killing all 29 persons aboard.* **2** Person is also used when describing someone's character or personality: *I don't think of him as a book person* (= someone who likes books). ○ *She's nice enough as a person, but she's not right for the job.* ○ **USAGE:** In formal writing, the plural "persons" is sometimes preferred over "people," but "persons" is also used in news reports – *At least 30 persons are dead or missing* – and in the phrase "person or persons" when the number of people is not known – *We expect to catch the person or persons responsible.*

IDIOM with person

• **in person** by meeting with someone rather than talking on the phone, e-mailing, or writing to the person ○ *You must apply for the license in person.*

persona /pərˈsoʊ·nə/ *n* [C] *pl* **personas, personae 1** the particular type of character that a person seems to have, which is often different from the real or private character that person has ○ *the senator's public persona* **2** ***literature*** A persona is also the voice in which an author writes a story or poem

personable /ˈpɜr·sə·nə·bəl/ *adj* having a pleasing and attractive manner ○ *She is an intelligent and personable young woman.*

personal /ˈpɜr·sən·əl/ *adj* **1** relating or belonging to a single or particular person ○ *I think you have a personal responsibility to know when to stop.* ○ *That's my personal opinion.* ○ *He was given one hour to pack his personal belongings and leave.* **2** Personal is also used to refer to your body: *Students are taught about personal hygiene.* **3** A personal action is one that is done by someone directly rather than by someone else: *The governor made a personal appearance at the hospital.* **4** Personal also means private or relating to someone's private life: *Simon's songs are intensely personal.* ○ *He's got problems in his personal life.* **5** Personal also refers to an intentionally offensive or critical remark about someone's character or appearance: *There's no need to get personal.*

personalize /ˈpɜr·sən·əlˌɑɪz/ *v* [T] **1** to make something specially suitable for a particular person ○ *We try to personalize these stories for the people* *who are listening.* **2** If you personalize an issue, you talk about how it relates to particular people: *In his description, he personalizes the plight of the homeless.* **3** Objects that are personalized have your name or something else you choose on them: *personalized checks* ○ *personalized license plates* **4** If you personalize an argument or discussion, you start to criticize the other person's faults instead of discussing the facts: *We shouldn't personalize these negotiations.*

personally /ˈpɜr·sən·əl·i/ *adv* **1** Personally can refer to yourself or your own opinion: *Personally, I think their marriage won't last.* ○ */I haven't been there personally, but I've read a lot about it.* **2** If you do something personally, you do it yourself rather than asking someone else to do it: *He plans to personally direct the fund-raising drive.* ○ *He believes that parents should be made personally responsible for their children's behavior.* **3** Personally also refers to an intentionally offensive remark about someone's character or appearance or which is understood as being critical: *Please don't take this personally, but I think you need to brush your teeth.*

WORD FAMILY personal

Nouns	person personality personification	*Adjectives*	personal impersonal
		Verbs	personalize personify
Adverbs	personally		

personal ad, *short form* **personal** *n* [C] a short advertisement about yourself that you put in a newspaper or magazine in order to meet a romantic partner

personal computer, *abbreviation* **PC** *n* [C] a small computer used in homes and offices

personality /ˌpɜr·səˈnæl·əṭ·i/ *n* [C/U] **1** the special combination of qualities in a person that makes that person different from others, as shown by the way the person behaves, feels, and thinks ○ [C] *She has a cheerful, attractive personality.* ○ [U] *Personality is formed at a very early age.* **2** A personality is also a famous person, esp. in popular entertainment or sports: [C] *a TV personality*

personal pronoun *n* [C] (in grammar) a word such as "I," "you," or "they," that refers to a person in speech or in writing

personify /pərˈsɑn·əˌfɑɪ/ *v* [T] **1** to be a person who is a perfect example of a thing or quality ○ *The senator personifies Washington, DC, to many people.* **2** If a particular quality or idea is personified, it is represented in the form of a person: *In Greek myth, love is personified by the goddess Aphrodite.*

personification /pərˌsɑn·ə·fɪˈkeɪ·ʃən/ *n* [U] ***literature*** the description of an object or an idea as if it had human characteristics ○ *They paid tribute to the artist as "the personification of excellence."*

personnel /ˌpɜr·səˈnel/ *pl n* the people working in an organization or for a particular type of employer ○ *Saturday was the most convenient day for students, parents, and school personnel.* ○ *military personnel*

personnel /ˌpɜr·səˈnel/ *n* [U] HUMAN RESOURCES

perspective Ⓐ **VIEW** /pərˈspek·tɪv/ *n* [C/U] **1** a particular way of viewing things that depends on one's experience and personality ○ [C] *He brings a new perspective to the job.* ○ [C] *From a social perspective, I am very much a liberal, although my economic policies are very conservative.* **2** Perspective also means the ability to consider things in relation to one another accurately and fairly: [U] *With more maturity and experience, you will gradually acquire perspective.* **3** If something is **in perspective**, it is considered as part of a complete situation so that you have an accurate and fair understanding of it: *Let's try to talk about both sides of the issue and put it in perspective.*

ART /pərˈspek·tɪv/ *n* [U] ***art*** the method by which solid objects drawn on a flat surface are given the appearance of depth and distance

perspire /pərˈspɑɪr/ *v* [I] *fml* to excrete a salty, colorless liquid through the skin which cools the body; SWEAT

perspiration /ˌpɜr·spəˈreɪ·ʃən/ *n* [U] *fml* ○ *Beads of perspiration glistened on his forehead.*

persuade /pərˈsweɪd/ *v* [T] to cause people to do or believe something, esp. by explaining why they should ○ *The government is trying to persuade consumers to save more.* ○ *She tried to persuade them that they should leave.*

persuasion /pərˈsweɪ·ʒən/ *n* [U] **1** *Most of the time he gets what he wants with gentle persuasion.* **2** ***writing*** Persuasion is also a form of speech or writing that uses argument or emotion to make the listener or reader believe what the author is saying.

persuasive /pərˈsweɪ·sɪv, -zɪv/ *adj* ○ *a persuasive argument*

WORD FAMILY persuade

Nouns	persuasion	*Verbs*	persuade dissuade
Adjectives	persuasive		

P

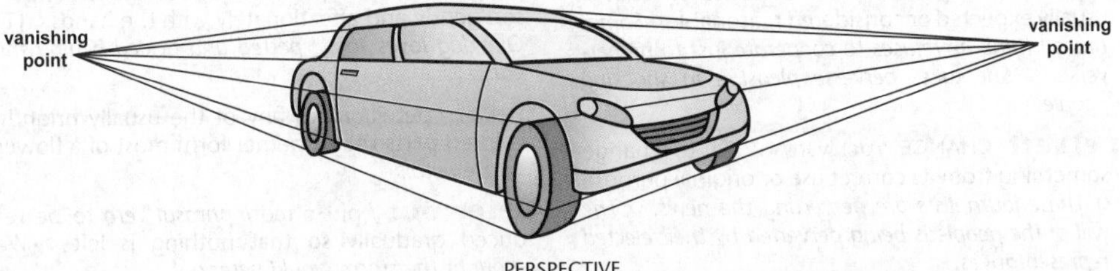

PERSPECTIVE

WORD CHOICES persuade

The phrasal verb **talk *someone* into** doing something can be used instead of "persuade."

She managed to ***talk me into*** *going along.*

The verbs **cajole** or **coax** are often used when someone persuades a person to do something by saying nice things to that person.

He really knows how to ***cajole*** *people into doing what he wants.*

A mother was ***coaxing*** *her reluctant child to get into the water.*

If someone persuades a person that something is true, you could use the verb **convince**.

The lawyer ***convinced*** *the jury of the man's innocence.*

The verb **dissuade** means "to persuade someone not to do something."

I tried to ***dissuade*** *her from leaving.*

persuasion /pər'sweɪ·ʒən/ *n* [C] a particular set of beliefs, esp. religious or political ones ○ *People of all religious persuasions are welcome.*

pert /pɜrt/ *adj* [not gradable] **1** (esp. of a young woman) energetic, enthusiastic, and confident **2** Pert can also mean small and attractive: *a pert nose* **3** Pert can also mean too confident and not showing respect: *a pert reply*

pertain to *something* /pər'teɪn ˌtuː, -ˌtʊ, -tə/ *phrasal verb* to relate to or have a connection with something ○ *regulations pertaining to high-tech industries* ○ *Seaweed's properties, as they pertain to skin care, are still in dispute.*

P

pertinent /'pɜrt·ən·ənt/ *adj* relating directly to the subject being considered; RELEVANT ○ *a pertinent question*

perturbed /pər'tɜrbd/ *adj fml* worried or troubled ○ *Ms. McCurdy was too perturbed to pay attention.*

peruse /pə'ruːz/ *v* [T] **1** to read or look at something in a relaxed way ○ *He opened the newspaper and perused the sports pages.* **2** Peruse can also mean to read carefully in a detailed way.

pervade /pər'veɪd/ *v* [T] to spread through all parts of something ○ *The influence of the early jazz musicians pervades American music.*

pervasive /pər'veɪ·sɪv, -zɪv/ *adj* ○ *a pervasive smell of insecticide* ○ *pervasive political corruption*

perverse /pər'vɜrs/ *adj* having the effect of being, or intended to be, the opposite of what is usually expected or considered reasonable ○ *Sometimes I think he refuses to cooperate just to be perverse.* ○ *She takes perverse pleasure in shocking people.*

pervert CHANGE /pər'vɜrt/ *v* [T] to change something from its correct use or original purpose ○ *These journalists are perverting the news.* ○ *The will of the people is being perverted by their elected representatives.*

perverted /pər'vɜrt̬·əd/ *adj* ○ *He used a perverted form of nationalism to incite anger among the crowd.*

perversion /pər'vɜr·ʒən/ *n* [C/U] ○ [C] *What we're being shown here is not normal family life, it's a perversion of that.*

UNNATURAL PERSON /'pɜr·vɜrt/ *n* [C] a person whose sexual behavior is considered unnatural and morally wrong

perverted /pər'vɜrt̬·əd/ *adj*

perversion /pər'vər·ʒən/ *n* [C/U] sexual behavior that is considered unnatural and morally wrong

pesky /'pes·ki/ *adj infml* annoying or causing trouble ○ *No matter how often I weed the garden, those pesky weeds keep coming back.*

pessimism /'pes·əˌmɪz·əm/ *n* [U] the tendency to see the bad side of things or to expect the worst in any situation ○ *There has been a mood of growing pessimism about the nation's economy.* ○ Compare OPTIMISM

pessimist /'pes·ə·məst/ *n* [C] ○ *How come you're such a pessimist?*

pessimistic /ˌpes·ə'mɪs·tɪk/ *adj* ○ *She's pretty pessimistic about her chances* (= thinks her chances are not good).

pest /pest/ *n* [C] **1** an insect or small animal that is harmful or damages crops ○ *The aphid is a garden pest.* **2** *infml* A pest is also an annoying person, esp. a child: *My brother is such a pest.*

pester /'pes·tər/ *v* [T] to annoy someone by doing or asking for something repeatedly ○ *The kids keep pestering me to buy them a new video game.*

pesticide /'pes·təˌsɑɪd/ *n* [C] a chemical substance used to kill harmful insects, small animals, wild plants, and other unwanted organisms ○ Compare INSECTICIDE

pestilence /'pes·tə·ləns/ *n* [C/U] *fml* a disease that spreads quickly and kills large numbers of people

pestle /'pes·əl, 'pes·təl/ *n* [C] a tool used for crushing substances into a powder

pesto /'pes·toʊ/ *n* [U] a green sauce used in Italian cooking, esp. on pasta

pet ANIMAL /pet/ *n* [C] an animal that is kept in the home as a companion and treated affectionately ○ *She has several interesting pets, including a couple of snakes.*

LIKED /pet/ *adj* [not gradable] especially liked or personally important ○ *The legislation will face strong opposition from senators whose pet projects would be cut back.*

TOUCH /pet/ *v* [I/T] **-tt-** to touch an animal or person gently and affectionately with the hands ○ [T] *Our dog loves to be petted and tickled behind the ears.*

petal /'pet·əl/ *n* [C] any of the usually brightly colored parts that together form most of a flower ○ *rose petals*

peter out /ˌpiːt̬·ə'rɑʊt/ *phrasal verb* to be reduced gradually so that nothing is left ○ *We thought the storm would peter out.*

petite /pəˈtiːt/ *adj* **1** of smaller than average height **2** Petite is also a size of clothing for small women.

petition /pəˈtɪʃ·ən/ *n* [C] a document signed by a large number of people requesting some action from the government or another authority, or *law* a formal letter to a court of law requesting a particular legal action ○ *More than 2000 people signed a petition to protect a wildlife area from development.* ○ (*law*) *She's filing a petition for divorce.*
petition /pəˈtɪʃ·ən/ *v* [I/T] ○ [T] *They plan to petition the governor to increase funding for the project.*

pet name *n* [C] an informal, affectionate name given to someone by family or friends ○ *Bruce's pet name for Noelle is "Otter," which can be embarrassing when other people hear it.*

pet peeve /ˈpet· ˈpiːv/ *n* [C] something that especially annoys you ○ *Weak coffee is one of my pet peeves.*

petrified /ˈpet·rəˌfɑɪd/ *adj* very frightened ○ *As soon as they got on the stage they were petrified with fright.*

petrochemical /ˌpe·troʊˈkem·ɪ·kəl/ *n* [C] any chemical substance obtained from PETROLEUM or natural gas

petrol /ˈpe·trəl/ *n* [U] *Br* GAS LIQUID FUEL

petroleum /pəˈtroʊ·liː·əm/ *n* [U] a dark, thick oil obtained from under the ground and made into fuels such as GAS and heating oil, and used in making plastics

petty SMALL /ˈpet̬·i/ *adj* small or of little importance ○ *a petty thief* ○ *I don't have time for petty matters like that.*
SELFISH /ˈpet̬·i/ *adj* selfish and mean, esp. because of having too much interest in small and unimportant matters ○ *The women in the story are petty and hateful.*
pettiness /ˈpet̬·iː·nəs/ *n* [U]

petty cash *n* [U] a small amount of money kept for buying cheap items, esp. in an office

petulant /ˈpetʃ·ə·lənt/ *adj* easily angered or annoyed, esp. in a rude way ○ *He plays the part of a petulant young man in the film.*

petunia /pɪˈtuːn·jə/ *n* [C] a plant with white, pink, or purple, bell-shaped flowers

pew /pjuː/ *n* [C] a long, wooden seat with a back in a church, usually forming one of a number of rows facing the ALTAR in the front

pewter /ˈpjuːt̬·ər/ *n* [U] a blue-gray metal that is a mixture of TIN and LEAD

PG *adj abbreviation for* parental guidance ○ **USAGE:** Used in the US for movies that some parents might think unsuitable for their children. ○ Compare G MOVIE; NC-17; R MOVIE

PG-13 *adj* [not gradable] (of movies) possibly unsuitable for children under the age of 13 because of sex, violence, or bad language ○ Compare G MOVIE; NC-17; R MOVIE

pH /piː ˈeɪtʃ/ *n* [C usually sing] ***chemistry, biology*** a number in a range from 0 to 14 that shows how strong an acid or an ALKALI a substance is

phagocyte /ˈfæg·əˌsɑɪt/ *n* [C] ***biology*** a cell that gets rid of bacteria and other cells that cause harm by absorbing them

phagocytosis /ˌfæg·əˌsɑɪˈtoʊ·səs/ *n* [U] ***biology*** the process by which PHAGOCYTES absorb and get rid of harmful bacteria

phantom /ˈfænt·əm/ *n* [C] **1** something that appears or seems to exist but is not real or is imagined **2** A phantom is also a GHOST.

pharmaceutical /ˌfɑr·məˈsuːt̬·ɪ·kəl/ *adj* [not gradable] connected with the science, preparation, and production of medicines ○ *the pharmaceutical industry*
pharmaceutical /ˌfɑr·məˈsuːt̬·ɪ·kəl/ *n* [C] **1** a drug that is made by a big drug company ○ *Dozens of pharmaceuticals have been detected in minute quantities in treated wastewater.* **2** *infml* A pharmaceutical is also a big drug company: *Don't expect major pharmaceuticals to let reforms pass without a well-funded political fight.*

pharmacist /ˈfɑr·mə·səst/, **druggist** *n* [C] a person who is trained in the preparation of medicines ○ *Rachel is studying to be a pharmacist.*
pharmacy /ˈfɑr·mə·si/ *n* [C] a store or a part of a store where medicines are prepared and sold

pharynx /ˈfær·ɪŋks/ *n* [C] *pl* **pharynges** ***biology*** the soft part at the top of the throat which connects the mouth and nose to the throat

phase /feɪz/ *n* [C] **1** any stage in a series of events or in a process of development ○ *The project is only in its first phase of planning, so we haven't yet established the cost.* **2** The phases of the moon are the regular changes in its shape as it appears to people on earth. **3** ***physics*** A phase is one of the forms in which matter can exist, such as solid, liquid, or a gas. **4** ***physics*** A phase is also one of the stages or points in a repeating process measured from a specific starting point.

PHRASAL VERBS with phase

• **phase** *something* **in** [M] to introduce something gradually in stages ○ *We start phasing in the new software this week.*
• **phase** *something* **out** [M] to gradually stop using something ○ *The airlines are phasing out any aircraft that is more than 20 years old.*

Ph.D. *n* [C] *abbreviation for* doctor of philosophy (= the highest college degree or a person having this) ○ *He earned a Ph.D. in physics from Northwestern University.*

pheasant /ˈfez·ənt/ *n* [C/U] a large bird with a rounded body and long tail, sometimes hunted as a sport and eaten as food

P

phenolphthalein /ˌfiː·nəlˈθæl·iː·ən, -ˈθæl ˈiːn, -ˈθeɪl-/ *n* [U] ***science*** a substance that is colorless when it is mixed with an acid and pink or red when mixed with an ALKALI

phenomenon Ⓐ **EXPERIENCE** /fɪˈnɑm·əˌnɑn, -nən/ *n* [C] *pl* **phenomena** anything that is or can be experienced or felt, esp. something that is noticed because it is unusual or new ○ *We discussed the ever-growing popularity of talk radio, and wondered how to explain this phenomenon.*

SPECIAL PERSON/THING /fɪˈnɑm·əˌnɑn, -nən/ *n* [C usually sing] *pl* **phenomenons** someone or something special, esp. because it is completely different or extremely unusual ○ *He was a kind of phenomenon, an actor running for president.*

phenomenal Ⓐ /fɪˈnɑm·ən·əl/ *adj* unusually great; much more or much better ○ *Angela can do a phenomenal amount of work in one day.* ○ *He has a phenomenal memory.*

phenomenally /fɪˈnɑm·ən·əl·i/ *adv* ○ *Her first play was phenomenally successful.*

phenotype /ˈfiː·nəˌtɑɪp/ *n* [C] ***biology*** all the characteristics of a living thing, especially the qualities that you can see, for example the color of the hair and eyes, the weight, etc.

philanthropy /fəˈlæn·θrə·pi/ *n* [U] the giving away of money, esp. in large amounts, to organizations that help people ○ *Minnesota has long been considered a beacon of philanthropy.*

philanthropic /ˌfɪl·ənˈθrɑp·ɪk/ *adj* ○ *a philanthropic organization*

philanthropist /fəˈlæn·θrə·pəst/ *n* [C] ○ *As a philanthropist he donated substantial sums to many educational and charitable institutions.*

P

philistine /ˈfɪl·əˌstiːn, fəˈlɪsˌtiːn/ *n* [C] *disapproving* a person who enjoys only popular entertainment but does not appreciate art, literature, or music of high quality

philodendron /ˌfɪl·əˈden·drən/ *n* [C] a climbing plant with leaves that are usually green and heart-shaped

philosophy Ⓐ /fəˈlɑs·ə·fi/ *n* [C/U] **1** the study of the nature of reality and existence, of what it is possible to know, and of right and wrong behavior, or a particular set of beliefs of this type ○ [C] *the philosophy of Kant* ○ [U] *I'd like to take a course in philosophy next semester.* **2** The philosophy of a subject is a group of theories and ideas related to the understanding of that subject: [U] *the philosophy of language/science* **3** A philosophy is also the beliefs you have about how you should behave in particular situations in life: [C] *It was always my philosophy to pay my debts promptly.*

philosopher Ⓐ /fəˈlɑs·ə·fər/ *n* [C] ○ *Plato, Aristotle, and the other Greek philosophers*

philosophize Ⓐ /fəˈlɑs·əˌfɑɪz/ *v* [I] ○ *That's when she'll start philosophizing about the notion of time.*

philosophical Ⓐ /ˌfɪl·əˈsɑf·ɪ·kəl/ *adj* **1** relating to philosophy ○ *Pragmatism is a philosophical theory.* **2** To be philosophical about something, esp. something disappointing, is to accept it calmly: *You just have to be philosophical about losing some games, because you can't win them all.*

philosophically Ⓐ /ˌfɪl·əˈsɑf·ɪ·kli/ *adv*

phlegm /flem/ *n* [U] a thick, liquid substance produced in the throat and nose esp. when you have a cold

phlegmatic /flegˈmæt̬·ɪk/ *adj* not easily excited or emotional; calm ○ *He is a retired lawyer with a solid, phlegmatic manner.*

phloem /ˈfloʊ·em/ *n* [U] ***biology*** the part of a plant that carries food from the leaves to other parts where the food is needed

phobia /ˈfoʊ·biː·ə/ *n* [C] an extreme fear of a particular thing or situation, esp. one that does not have a reasonable explanation ○ *a phobia about heights*

phone /foʊn/ *n* [C] *short form of* TELEPHONE ○ *The phone is ringing – would you answer it?*

phone /foʊn/ *v* [I/T] ○ [I] *Fernando phoned just after lunch.*

phone book *n* [C] a book containing the telephone numbers of people and businesses in a particular area

phone card *n* [C] a card that you buy and use to pay for telephone calls from a public and sometimes from a private telephone

phone number *n* [C] a series of numbers which you use to call a particular telephone

phonetic /fəˈnet̬·ɪk/ *adj* [not gradable] ***English, grammar*** relating to the sounds made in speaking

phonetics /fəˈnet̬·ɪks/ *n* [U] ***English, grammar*** the study of the sounds made by the human voice in speech

phonics /ˈfɑn·ɪks/ *n* [U] ***English*** a method of teaching how to read that emphasizes the relationship between letters and sounds

phony /ˈfoʊ·ni/ *adj* represented as real but actually false; intended to deceive ○ *They were accused of submitting phony claims to insurers, including Medicare.*

phony /ˈfoʊ·ni/ *n* [C] *infml* a person who falsely pretends to be something ○ *I think he's a phony.*

phosphate /ˈfɑs·feɪt/ *n* [C] a chemical COMPOUND (= substance consisting of at least two elements) that contains PHOSPHORUS ○ *a phosphate-free detergent* ○ *The plant fertilizer contains phosphates.*

phosphorescent /ˌfɑs·fəˈres·ənt/ *adj* giving off or shining with light, and giving off little or no heat

phosphorescence /ˌfɑs·fəˈres·əns/ *n* [U]

phosphorus /ˈfɑs·fə·rəs/ *n* [U] a poisonous, yellow-white chemical element that shines in the dark and burns when in the air

photo /ˈfoʊt̬·oʊ/ *n* [C] *pl* **photos** *short form of* PHOTOGRAPH ○ *Giraldo takes a lot of photos.*

photochemical /ˌfoʊt̬·oʊˈkem·ɪ·kəl/ *adj* [not gradable] ***biology***, ***chemistry*** relating to the effect of light on some chemicals

photocopier /ˈfoʊt̬·əˌkɑp·iː·ər/ *n* [C] a machine to make copies of pages with printing, writing, or drawing on them by a process using light and electricity
photocopy /ˈfoʊt̬·əˌkɑp·i/ *n* [C] a copy of a document made on a photocopier
photocopy /ˈfoʊt̬·əˌkɑp·i/ *v* [T]

photoelectric /ˌfoʊt̬·oʊ·ɪˈlek·trɪk/ *adj* [not gradable] ***physics*** involving the production of electricity from light

photo finish *n* [C] a race in which competitors finish so close together that a photograph must be examined to decide who won

photogenic /ˌfoʊt̬·əˈdʒen·ɪk, -ˈdʒiː·nɪk/ *adj* having an appearance that is attractive in photographs

photograph /ˈfoʊt̬·əˌɡræf/, *short form* **photo** *n* [C] an image of a person, object, or view that is produced by using a camera and film ○ *color/black-and-white photographs*
photograph /ˈfoʊt̬·əˌɡræf/ *v* [T] ○ *We photographed the house to document the damage done by the storm.*
photographer /fəˈtɑɡ·rə·fər/ *n* [C] ○ *a fashion/newspaper photographer*
photographic /ˌfoʊt̬·əˈɡræf·ɪk/ *adj* [not gradable] ○ *photographic equipment* ○ *You can store photographic images on your computer's hard drive.*
photography /fəˈtɑɡ·rə·fi/ *n* [U] the skill or activity of taking or processing photographs

WORD FAMILY **photograph**			
Nouns	photo photograph photographer photography	*Adjectives*	photogenic photographic
		Verbs	photograph

photon /ˈfoʊ·tɑn/ *n* [C] ***physics*** a very small piece of matter that is the basic unit of ELECTROMAGNETIC energy, and that travels in waves and carries light and other forms of RADIATION

photosynthesis /ˌfoʊt̬·əˈsɪn·θə·səs/ *n* [U] ***biology*** the process by which a plant uses the energy from the light of the sun to make its own food

phrasal verb /ˈfreɪ·zəl ˈvɜrb/ *n* [C] ***grammar*** a combination of a verb and an adverb or a verb and a preposition, or both, in which the combination has a meaning different from the meaning of the words considered separately ○ *"Catch on" is a phrasal verb meaning to understand.*

phrase /freɪz/ *n* [C] **1** a group of words expressing a particular idea or meaning ○ *I think the phrase "bundle of energy" describes Mara very well.* **2** ***grammar*** A phrase is a group of words forming a part of a sentence: *In "He was a man of great wealth," "of great wealth" is a prepositional phrase.* **3** ***music*** A phrase is also a group of notes with a clear beginning and ending within a larger piece of music.
phrase /freɪz/ *v* [T] to express something in a particular way when speaking or writing ○ *The wording of his resignation was carefully phrased to avoid any admission of guilt.*
phrasal /ˈfreɪ·zəl/ *adj*

phylum /ˈfɑɪ·ləm/ *n* [C] ***biology*** one of the groups into which animals are divided, mainly based on the shape of the animal's body and the way that the body is arranged

physical Ⓐ MATERIAL /ˈfɪz·ɪ·kəl/ *adj* existing as or connected with things that can be seen or touched ○ *The physical dimensions of the theater are smaller than I thought.*

BODY /ˈfɪz·ɪ·kəl/ *adj* connected with the body ○ *physical strength/disabilities* ○ *She tries to keep herself in good physical condition.* ○ See also: PHYSICAL at PHYSICS ○ Compare MENTAL
physical (examination) /ˈfɪz·ɪ·kəl (ɪɡˌzæm·əˈneɪ·ʃən)/ *n* [C] a careful look at a person's body by a doctor in order to discover if that person is healthy, sometimes done before a person can be accepted for a particular job ○ *They found the cancer during a routine physical.*
physically Ⓐ /ˈfɪz·ɪ·kli/ *adv* **1** *She works out at a gym and is very physically fit.* **2** People who are physically disabled/handicapped/challenged lack the full use of their body.

physical education, *abbreviation* **PE**,, **phys. ed.** *n* [U] school classes in which children exercise and learn to play sports, or the area of study relating to such classes

physical science *n* [C usually pl] any of the sciences such as physics, chemistry, and ASTRONOMY that examine matter and energy and the way the universe behaves

physical therapy, **physiotherapy** /ˌfɪz·iː·oʊˈθer·ə·pi/ *n* [U] the treatment of stiffness, muscle weakness, and pain, esp. by rubbing and moving the sore parts and through exercise
physical therapist, **physiotherapist** /ˌfɪz·iː·oʊˈθer·ə·pəst/ *n* [C] a person whose job is treating people using physical therapy

physician /fəˈzɪʃ·ən/ *n* [C] a medical doctor, esp. one who is not a SURGEON

physics /ˈfɪz·ɪks/ *n* [U] ***science*** the scientific study of matter and energy and the effect that each has on the other ○ *nuclear/particle/theoretical physics*
physical /ˈfɪz·ɪ·kəl/ *adj* connected with physics ○ See also: PHYSICAL BODY
physicist /ˈfɪz·ə·səst/ *n* [C] a person who studies physics or whose job is connected with physics

physiology /ˌfɪz·iːˈɑl·ə·dʒi/ *n* [U] the scientific study of the way in which the bodies of animals and plants work ○ *the physiology of the brain*

physiotherapy /ˌfɪz·iː·oʊˈθer·ə·pi/ *n* [U] PHYSICAL THERAPY

P

physiotherapist /ˌfɪz·iː·oʊˈθer·ə·pəst/ *n* [C] a PHYSICAL THERAPIST

physique /fəˈziːk/ *n* [C] the appearance, esp. shape and size, of a human body ○ *a small/large physique* ○ *a dancer's physique*

phytoplankton /ˌfaɪt̬·oʊˈplæŋk·tən, -tɑn/ *n* [U] ***biology*** very small plants that float near the surface of water

pi /paɪ/, *symbol* π *n* [U] ***geometry*** a number that is the RATIO (= comparison) of the distance around a circle to the distance across the circle, equal to about 3.14159

piano /piːˈæn·oʊ/ *n* [C/U] *pl* **pianos** a large musical instrument with a row of black and white keys that are pressed with the fingers to play notes, or this type of instrument generally ○ [C] *a grand/upright piano* ○ [U] *I play piano.*
pianist /piːˈæn·əst, ˈpiː·ə·nəst/ *n* [C] someone who plays the piano ○ *a concert/jazz pianist*

piccolo /ˈpɪk·əˌloʊ/ *n* [C/U] *pl* **piccolos** a very small musical instrument that is like a FLUTE and plays high notes, or this type of instrument generally

pick **CHOOSE** /pɪk/ *v* [T] to take some things and leave others ○ *She's been picked for the Olympic team.* ○ *We finally picked February 14 as the date for our wedding.*
pick /pɪk/ *n* [C/U] a choice, or something that is chosen ○ [U] *Mick gets first pick of where to sit.* ○ [C] *Here are my picks for the ten best restaurants.*
picky /ˈpɪk·i/ *adj* liking only a few things and therefore difficult to please ○ *a picky eater*
REMOVE /pɪk/ *v* [T] to remove or move something with your fingers or hands ○ *I picked a piece of lint off my suit.* ○ *We picked apples yesterday.*
picker /ˈpɪk·ər/ *n* [C] a person or machine that picks crops ○ *fruit pickers*
MUSIC TOOL /pɪk/ *n* [C] a thin piece of plastic or metal used to pull at the strings of a guitar
DIGGING TOOL /pɪk/ *n* [C] a PICKAX, or a sharp, pointed tool ○ *They worked with a pick and shovel.*

IDIOMS with pick

•**pick a fight** to intentionally start a fight ○ *Some kids were teasing him, trying to pick a fight.*
•**pick and choose** to take only the things you want from a group ○ *You can't pick and choose which rules you want to follow and which ones you don't.*
•**pick** *someone's* **brain** to ask someone's advice about a subject the person knows a lot about ○ *Can I pick your brain about how you got rid of those weeds?*
•**pick** *someone's* **pocket** to steal small objects, esp. money, from someone's pockets or bag ○ *One of the kids tried to pick my pocket.*
•**pick up steam** to start working or producing at a faster rate or more effectively ○ *After a slow start, the project began to pick up steam.*
•**pick up the tab (for** *something***)**, **pick up the bill (for** *something***)** to pay for something, esp. for what someone else has bought or used ○ *The company will pick up the tab for this trip.*
•**pick** *your way somewhere* to walk carefully and slowly ○ *Charlie picked his way through the muddy field.*
•**the pick of** *something* the best of a group ○ *This puppy was the pick of the litter.*

PHRASAL VERBS with pick

•**pick at** *something* to eat food in small pieces and without enjoyment ○ *She only picked at her dinner.*
•**pick off** *someone/something* [M] to shoot a person or animal chosen out of a group, esp. from a distance
•**pick on** *someone* to criticize, annoy, or punish someone repeatedly and unfairly ○ *He gets picked on because he's small.*
•**pick out** *something/someone* [M] to choose, find, or recognize something or someone in a group ○ *From all the puppies, we picked out the smallest one to take home.* ○ *We could pick our parents out easily in the old photos.*
•**pick over** *something* [M] to examine a group of things carefully in order to choose the ones you want ○ *She picked over the strawberries, selecting the largest ones.*
•**pick through** *something* to look at the things in a group and take only what you want ○ *I had to pick through the trash to find my electric bill.*
•**pick up** *something/someone* **LIFT** [M] to lift something or someone ○ *He picked his briefcase up and headed for the door.* ○ *She picked up the little boy and kissed him.*
•**pick up** *someone/something* **TAKE** [M] **1** to get or bring someone or something from somewhere ○ *Whose turn is it to pick up the kids from school?* ○ *A truck picks up the recycling once a week.* **2** If the police pick someone up, they catch the person: *Cops picked up the suspect a few miles away.* ○ Related noun: PICKUP GETTING
•**pick up** *something* **OBTAIN** [M] to obtain or receive something ○ *While you're in town, would you pick up a book for me?* ○ *Can you pick up the Yankees game up here* (= receive broadcasts of it)? ○ *She picked up her soccer skills from her older brother* (= learned them informally). ○ *Gwen picked up a cold on her trip* (= started to suffer from it).
•**pick up** *someone* **MEET** [M] *infml* to meet someone for the first time and begin having a romantic relationship
•**pick up** **IMPROVE/INCREASE** to improve an activity or increase an amount ○ *Retailers are starting to see sales pick up again.* ○ *The truck picked up speed slowly.* ○ Related noun: PICKUP INCREASE
•**pick up** *(something)* **START AGAIN** [M] to start again after an interruption ○ *The author picks up the theme again on page ten.* ○ *In tomorrow's class we'll pick up where we left off.*
•**pick up on** *something* **GIVE ATTENTION** to give particular attention to something that someone has said or done ○ *I want to pick up on a point that Susan made about role models.* ○ *Sporting-goods makers were quick to pick up on surfers' innovations like foot straps for leaping giant waves.*
•**pick up on** *something* **UNDERSTAND** to understand something that is not communicated di-

rectly ○ *He obviously didn't pick up on her lack of interest in the subject.*

pickax, **pickaxe** /ˈpɪk·æks/, **pick** *n* [C] a tool with a long wooden handle fitted into the middle of a curved metal bar with a sharp point

picket /ˈpɪk·ət/, **picketer** /ˈpɪk·ət̬·ər/ *n* [C] a person or group of people who have a disagreement with a company, usually the one where they work, and who walk around in a line outside the place of business to tell other people not to enter until the problem is solved ○ *Three pickets stood at the factory gate.*

picket /ˈpɪk·ət/ *v* [I/T] ○ [I/T] *The women picketed (outside) the factory for three months.*

picket fence /ˈpɪk·ət ˈfens/ *n* [C] a low fence made of a row of flat, vertical sticks, pointed at the top, usually with space between them and connected by a few horizontal sticks

picket line *n* [C] a group of people holding signs to show that they are not working and are having a disagreement with their employer ○ *Truck drivers refused to cross the picket line.*

pickle /ˈpɪk·əl/ *n* [C] a CUCUMBER (= a green, tube-shaped vegetable) that has been preserved in a liquid containing salt and other spices or vinegar ○ *a sweet/dill pickle*

pickle /ˈpɪk·əl/ *v* [T] to preserve in a liquid containing salt or vinegar

pickled /ˈpɪk·əld/ *adj* ○ *pickled tomatoes/herring*

pick-me-up /ˈpɪk·miː ˌʌp/ *n* [C] *infml* something, often food or drink, that gives you more energy or makes you feel better ○ *I need a little pick-me-up in the middle of the afternoon.*

pickpocket /ˈpɪkˌpɑk·ət/ *n* [C] a thief who steals things out of pockets or bags, esp. in a crowd

pickup **GETTING** /ˈpɪk·ʌp/ *n* [C] the act of getting something or someone ○ *Trash pickups are on Tuesdays and Fridays.* ○ *We arranged the pickup for ten o'clock.* ○ Related verb: PICK UP TAKE

INCREASE /ˈpɪk·ʌp/ *n* [U] **1** an increase in something that has different levels at different times ○ *Next year is expected to show some pickup in inflation.* **2** Pickup in a vehicle is its power to increase its rate of speed: *The car is easy to turn but it lacks pickup.* ○ Related verb: PICK UP IMPROVE/INCREASE

INFORMAL /ˈpɪk·ʌp/ *adj* (of games) not officially organized ○ *The basketball courts bustled with pickup games.*

pickup truck, *short form* **pickup** *n* [C] a vehicle with an open part at the back in which things can be carried

picky /ˈpɪk·i/ *adj* See at PICK CHOOSE.

picnic /ˈpɪk·nɪk/ *n* [C] **1** a meal you take to a place outside to be eaten there in an informal way, or an occasion on which such a meal is eaten ○ *a church picnic* **2** *infml* A picnic is also any pleasant activity: *Did you think law school would be a picnic?* ○ *Filing tax returns is no picnic.*

picnic /ˈpɪk·nɪk/ *v* [I] *pres. part.* **picnicking**, *past* **picnicked** ○ *We can picnic in the park.*

pictorial /pɪkˈtɔːr·iː·əl, -ˈtoʊr-/ *adj* [not gradable] consisting of or having the form of a picture or pictures ○ *a pictorial history of America*

picture **REPRESENTATION** /ˈpɪk·tʃər/ *n* [C] **1** a representation of someone or something produced by drawing, painting, or photographing ○ *He drew/painted a picture of my dog.* ○ *Brian takes lots of pictures* (= photographs). **2** A picture is also an image seen on a television or movie screen: *It's an old set, and the picture is a little fuzzy.* **3** A picture is also a movie: *It won an Academy Award for best picture.*

picture /ˈpɪk·tʃər/ *v* [T] to imagine how something looks ○ *Try to picture yourself lying on a beach in the hot sun.*

DESCRIPTION /ˈpɪk·tʃər/ *n* [C/U] **1** a description of a situation, or the situation itself ○ [C] *Do news reports give an accurate picture of events?* ○ [U] *They're looking at individuals and not at the overall picture.* ○ [U] *Don't say any more – I get the picture* (= understand the situation). ○ [U] *Marilyn's mother more or less stayed out of the picture* (= was not involved). **2** To paint a picture is to describe a situation: [C] *The statistics do not paint an optimistic picture.*

WORD FAMILY picture

Nouns	picture	*Adjectives*	pictorial
Verbs	picture		picturesque

IDIOM with picture

• **the picture of** *something* a very good example of a particular condition or attitude ○ *He's the picture of health.*

picturesque /ˌpɪk·tʃəˈresk/ *adj* (esp. of a place) attractive in appearance ○ *We strolled through the picturesque streets of the old city.*

piddling /ˈpɪd·lɪŋ, -lən/ *adj infml* very small or unimportant ○ *a piddling amount/figure*

pidgin /ˈpɪdʒ·ən/ *n* [C] a language that has developed from a mixture of two or more languages and is used for communicating by people who do not speak each other's language

pie /pɑɪ/ *n* [C/U] a round pastry with a filling such as fruit, meat, or vegetables ○ [C] *a blueberry pie* ○ [U] *We're having sweet potato pie for dinner.*

IDIOM with pie

• **pie in the sky** something good that is unlikely to happen ○ *I wanted to be a major league baseball player, but I knew it was probably pie in the sky.*

piece **PART** /piːs/ *n* [C] a part of something ○ *a piece of cake/chicken/pizza* ○ *The vase lay on the floor* **in pieces** (= broken into small parts). ○ *She was so mad that she ripped the letter* **to pieces** (= into small parts).

ITEM /piːs/ *n* [C] **1** a single item that is one of other similar items ○ *a piece of furniture/equipment/luggage/paper* ○ *I have an important piece of informa-*

tion for you. **2** A piece can be something created by an artist, writer, or musician: *He's written a new piece of music.*

COMMON LEARNER ERROR

piece

Piece cannot be used to mean one of the rooms in a building. You should use the word **room** instead.

~~*The house needed redecorating in every piece.*~~

The house needed redecorating in every room.

IDIOMS with piece

• **go to pieces, fall to pieces** to become unable to think clearly and control your emotions because of something unpleasant or difficult that you have experienced ○ *She went to pieces at the funeral.*

• **a piece of cake** *infml* something that is easy to do ○ *For him, taking tests is a piece of cake.*

• **a piece of the action** *infml* a part of the profits or advantages that come from an activity ○ *When it comes to lawsuits, everyone seems to want a piece of the action.*

• **a piece of the pie** a share of something ○ *When the business started making money, everyone in his family wanted a piece of the pie.*

PHRASAL VERB with piece

• **piece together** *something* [M] **1** to put the parts of something into place ○ *Archeologists have pieced together fragments of the pottery.* **2** If you **piece together** facts or information, you collect them in order to understand a situation: *Investigators are trying to piece together what happened just before the accident.*

P

piecemeal /ˈpiːˑsmiːl/ *adj, adv* [not gradable] not done according to a plan but done at different times in different ways ○ *Do we fix it all now, or do we approach it piecemeal over time?*

piecework /ˈpiːsˑwɜrk/ *n* [U] work for which the amount of pay depends on the number of items completed rather than the time spent making them

pie chart *n* [C] a circle that is divided into parts to show how a total amount is divided

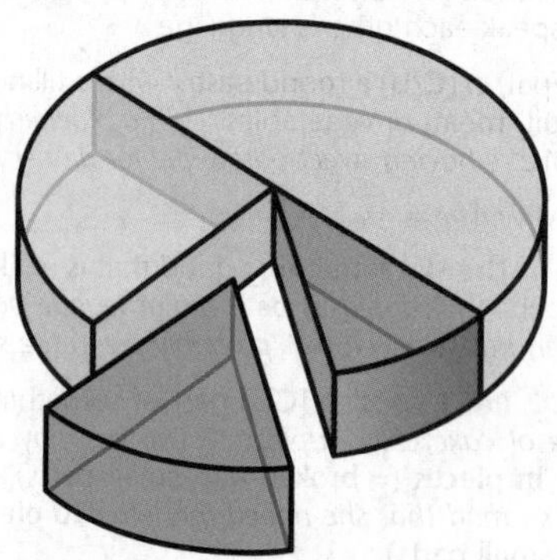

PIE CHART

piecrust /ˈpɑɪˑkrʌst/ *n* [C/U] the pastry on the top or bottom of a PIE

pier STRUCTURE /pɪr/ *n* [C] a structure built out over the water on posts, along which boats can land ○ *a fishing pier*

COLUMN /pɪr/ *n* [C] a thick, strong column used to support a structure such as a bridge

pierce /pɪrs/ *v* [T] to go in or through something, esp. with a pointed object, making a hole ○ *Pierce the potatoes with a fork to see if they're done.* ○ *She got her ears pierced.*

piercing /ˈpɪrˑsɪŋ/ *adj* feeling or seeming very sharp or powerful ○ *He had piercing blue eyes.* ○ *She let out a piercing* (= loud) *shriek.*

piety /ˈpɑɪˑəṭˑi/ *n* [U] a strong belief in God or a religion, shown by your worship and behavior ○ Related adjective: PIOUS

pig ANIMAL /pɪg/ *n* [C] a farm or wild animal with pink, brown, or black skin, short legs, and a SNOUT (= flat nose)

piggy, piggie /ˈpɪgˑi/ *n* [C] *a child's word* pig

PERSON /pɪg/ *n* [C] *infml* a person who is messy, selfish, or rude, or someone who eats too much

PHRASAL VERB with pig

• **pig out** *infml* to eat too much ○ *We just pigged out on potato chips while we watched the movie.*

pigeon /ˈpɪdʒˑən/ *n* [C] a large, usually gray-and-white bird that lives esp. in cities ○ *We fed the pigeons in the park.*

pigeonhole /ˈpɪdʒˑən ˌhoʊl/ *v* [T] to put someone or something into a group or type, often unfairly ○ *He's was pigeonholed early on in his career as a gospel singer.*

pigeon-toed *adj* (of a person) having feet that point in toward each other

piggyback /ˈpɪgˑiː ˌbæk/ *adj, adv* [not gradable] on someone's back ○ *Uncle Sean loves to give Tyler piggyback rides.*

piggy bank *n* [C] a container, sometimes in the shape of a pig, that holds coins and is used esp. by children for saving money

pigheaded /ˈpɪg ˌhedˑəd/ *adj* unwilling to change very strong opinions ○ *Not even somebody as pigheaded as Ira could argue about it.*

piglet /ˈpɪgˑlət/ *n* [C] a young pig

pigment /ˈpɪgˑmənt/ *n* [C/U] **1** ***biology*** a natural substance that produces color in animals and plants, such as of skin, hair, and leaves **2** Pigment is also the substance in a paint or DYE that gives it its color.

pigmentation /ˌpɪgˑmənˈteɪˑʃən/ *n* [U]

pigpen /ˈpɪgˑpen/, **pigsty** /ˈpɪgˑstɑɪ/ *n* [C] **1** an enclosed area where pigs are kept **2** A pigpen is also a dirty or messy place: *Your bedroom is a pigsty!*

pigtail /ˈpɪgˑteɪl/ *n* [C usually pl] one of usually two lengths of hair gathered at each side of the head, either hanging loose or in a BRAID ○ *a little girl in pigtails*

pike FISH /paɪk/ *n* [C] *pl* **pike** a large fish with sharp teeth that lives in lakes and rivers

ROAD /paɪk/ *n* [C] *short form of* TURNPIKE ○ *Traffic is slow along Rockville Pike.*

pile THINGS /paɪl/ *n* [C] **1** a number of things lying on top of each other ○ *a pile of newspapers* ○ *After dinner there is always a pile of dishes to be washed.* **2** *infml* A pile or piles can also be a lot of something: *I've got piles of homework.*

pile /paɪl/ *v* [always + adv/prep] to put (things) near or on top of each other, or to collect in this way ○ [I] *Magazines just pile up on my desk at work.* ○ [M] *I asked her to pile on extra potatoes.*

MOVE /paɪl/ *v* [I always + adv/prep] (of a group of people) to move together, esp. in a way that is not organized ○ *About ten kids piled into the room, all talking at once.* ○ *Someone yelled "Fire!" and we all piled out into the street.*

SURFACE /paɪl/ *n* [U] the soft surface of short threads on a CARPET (= material for covering a floor) or on some types of cloth ○ *carpets with a deep pile*

PHRASAL VERB with pile

• **pile up** to increase in amount ○ *The work was piling up, and I decided I had to go in to the office on the weekend.*

pileup /ˈpaɪl·ʌp/ *n* [C] a traffic accident involving several vehicles ○ *Police reported a ten-car pileup on an icy road.*

pilfer /ˈpɪl·fər/ *v* [I/T] to steal things of little value or in small amounts ○ [I/T] *Neighborhood kids were pilfering (candy) from the corner store.*

Pilgrim /ˈpɪl·grəm/ *n* [C] ***US history*** a member of the group of English people who sailed to America and began living in Plymouth, Massachusetts, in 1620

pilgrim /ˈpɪl·grəm/ *n* [C] a person who travels to a holy place as a religious act

pilgrimage /ˈpɪl·grə·mɪdʒ/ *n* [C/U] a trip, often a long one, made to a holy place for religious reasons

pill /pɪl/ *n* [C] a small, solid substance that a person swallows whole, esp. as medicine ○ *a sleeping pill*

pillage /ˈpɪl·ɪdʒ/ *v* [I/T] *fml* to steal something from a place or a person by using violence, esp. during war ○ [T] *Rioters pillaged and set fire to downtown buildings.*

pillar /ˈpɪl·ər/ *n* [C] **1** a strong vertical column made of stone, metal, or wood that supports part of a building or stands alone for decoration **2** A pillar is also someone or something that is an important part of a group, place, or activity: *He's a pillar of the Dallas business community.*

pillow /ˈpɪl·oʊ/ *n* [C] a cloth bag filled with feathers or soft artificial fibers that supports a person's head while resting or sleeping ○ *I was asleep the minute my head hit the pillow.*

pillowcase /ˈpɪl·oʊˌkeɪs, ˈpɪl·ə-/ *n* [C] a cloth cover for a bed PILLOW

pilot PERSON /ˈpaɪ·lət/ *n* [C] a person who flies an aircraft, or someone who directs a ship safely through an area of water ○ *an airline pilot* ○ *a harbor pilot*

pilot /ˈpaɪ·lət/ *v* [T] ○ *He piloted the ship through the busy harbor.*

TEST /ˈpaɪ·lət/ *adj* [not gradable] (of a plan, product, or system) done as a test before introducing it ○ *From the pilot episode, this looks to be one of the best new shows we'll see this fall.*

pilot /ˈpaɪ·lət/ *v* [T] ○ *Our district is piloting a daycare program.*

pilot (light) /ˈpaɪ·lət (ˈlaɪt)/ *n* [C] a small flame that lights gas in a BURNER of a stove, or a device that heats a home, water, etc.

pimp /pɪmp/ *n* [C] a man who controls PROSTITUTES (= people who are paid to have sex)

pimple /ˈpɪm·pəl/ *n* [C] a small, raised spot on the skin

pimply /ˈpɪm·pə·li/ *adj* ○ *a pimply teenager*

pin FASTENER /pɪn/ *n* [C] **1** a thin piece of stiff wire with a pointed end that you can stick through two things to fasten them together ○ *Mary put a pin in her hair to hold her hat on.* **2** A pin can also be decorative and used as jewelry: *She wore a beautiful gold pin on her coat.*

pin /pɪn/ *v* [T] **-nn-** ○ *She kept a map of Manhattan pinned on the wall.*

HOLD FIRMLY /pɪn/ *v* [T always + adv/prep] **-nn-** to hold someone or something firmly in the same position or place ○ *After the earthquake there were several people pinned in the wreckage.* ○ (*fig.*) *No one could pin the label of "conservative" on him* (= call him that).

IDIOM with pin

• **on pins and needles** worried or excited about something that is going to happen ○ *Don't keep Margaret on pins and needles – give her a call.*

PHRASAL VERBS with pin

• **pin down** *something* **DISCOVER** [M] to discover the exact details about something ○ *The fire department is trying to pin down the cause of Wednesday's fire.*

• **pin** *someone* **down** **QUESTION** [M] to force someone to be specific or make his or her intentions known, esp. by asking a lot of questions ○ *I tried to pin him down on where the money would come from.*

• **pin down** *someone* **LIMIT** [M] to limit someone's ability to move or act, esp. by using force ○ *Soldiers were pinned down by enemy fire.*

• **pin** *something* **on** *someone/something* **1** to blame someone for something ○ *He tried to pin the mess on his brother, but it didn't work.* **2** If you pin hopes or expectations on something, you want that thing to bring success: *They pinned their hopes on the new technology.*

PIN /pɪn/ *n* [C] *abbreviation for* personal identification number (= a secret number that can be read by a computer to prove who you are) ○ *I punched my PIN into the ATM machine and took out $100.*

pinball /ˈpɪn·bɔːl/ *n* [U] a game played on a machine in which the player tries to prevent a ball from rolling off the end of a sloping surface by causing the ball to bounce between devices that score points ○ *a pinball machine*

pinch PRESS /pɪntʃ/ *v* [I/T] to tightly press something, esp. someone's skin, between your finger and thumb or between two surfaces ○ [T] *He pinched his nose together and breathed through his mouth.* ○ [T] *I had to pinch myself so I'd know I wasn't dreaming.*
pinch /pɪntʃ/ *n* [C usually sing] ○ *He gave her a playful pinch on the cheek.*

AMOUNT /pɪntʃ/ *n* [C] a small amount of something, esp. the amount that you can hold between your finger and thumb ○ *a pinch of nutmeg/pepper*

IDIOM with pinch

• **in a pinch** if necessary ○ *You should use lime juice, but in a pinch lemon juice will work.*

pinched /pɪntʃt/ *adj* **1** (of someone's face) thin and anxious, or (of clothing) narrow ○ *Nora was short, with a pinched face, and wore thick glasses with wire rims.* ○ *Her dress was pinched at the waist.* **2** A person or organization that is pinched does not have enough money: *The space program is pinched.*

pinch-hit /ˈpɪntʃˈhɪt/ *v* [I] (in baseball) to take another player's turn to hit
pinch hitter /ˈpintʃˈhɪt̬·ər/ *n* [C] ○ *They took me out for a pinch hitter.*

pincushion /ˈpɪnˌkʊʃ·ən/ *n* [C] a small bag filled with soft material into which pins are pushed until they are needed

P

pine TREE /pɑɪn/ *n* [C/U] an evergreen tree that has thin leaves like needles and that grows in cool northern regions, or the wood of these trees

DESIRE /pɑɪn/ *v* [I always + adv/prep] to strongly desire esp. something that is difficult or impossible to obtain ○ *Bradley pined for his wife, who was far away.*

pineapple /ˈpɑɪˌnæp·əl/ *n* [C/U] a large, juicy fruit that grows in hotter regions, having a rough skin, a short stem, and pointed leaves on the top, or its sweet, yellow flesh

pinecone, **pine cone** /ˈpɑɪn·koʊn/ *n* [C] a hard, oval fruit from a pine tree that opens and releases seeds

ping /pɪŋ/ *n* [C] a short, often electronic, ringing sound

Ping-Pong /ˈpɪŋ·pɔːŋ, -pɑŋ/ *n* [U] *trademark* TABLE TENNIS

pinhole /ˈpɪn·hoʊl/ *n* [C] a very small hole made by a pin or by something like it

pinion /ˈpɪn·jən/ *v* [T] to hold or tie someone by the arms to prevent the person from moving ○ *He was pinioned to the wall by the two men.*

pink /pɪŋk/ *adj, n* [C/U] (of) a pale red color ○ *a pink hat* ○ [U] *The bridesmaid wore pink.*

pinkeye /ˈpɪŋ·kɑɪ/ *n* [U] an infectious illness of the eyes in which the eye and the surrounding area become red and swollen, a condition that is easily spread from one person to another

pinkie, **pinky** /ˈpɪŋ·ki/ *n* [C] the smallest finger of a person's hand

pink slip *n* [C] a notice from an employer informing employees that they no longer have jobs ○ *Management started issuing pink slips yesterday.*

pinnacle SUCCESSFUL POINT /ˈpɪn·ɪ·kəl/ *n* [C usually sing] the most successful point ○ *The Olympics represent the pinnacle of athletic achievement.*

TOP /ˈpɪn·ɪ·kəl/ *n* [C usually pl] a small pointed structure on top of a building, or a pointed top on a mountain ○ *The volcanic range is extremely rugged, with many cliffs, gorges, canyons, and pinnacles.*

pinpoint /ˈpɪn·pɔɪnt/ *v* [T] to discover or establish something exactly ○ *They were unable to pinpoint the source of the noise.*

pinstripe /ˈpɪn·strɑɪp/ *n* [C] a narrow line of a light color in the design of a cloth, or the cloth itself with such parallel lines ○ *a dark blue suit and pants with gray pinstripes*
pin-striped /ˈpɪn·strɑɪpt/, **pin-stripe** /ˈpɪn·strɑɪp/ *adj* [not gradable] ○ *a pin-striped suit*

pint /pɑɪnt/, *abbreviation* **pt.** *n* [C] a unit of measurement of volume equal to 1/2 quart or about 0.47 liter

pint-sized, **pint-size** *adj* [not gradable] *infml* smaller than usual or expected ○ *The school library was full of pint-sized scientists setting up their science experiments.*

pin-up /ˈpɪn·ʌp/ *n* [C] a picture of an attractive, usually famous person, suitable for hanging on a wall, or a person shown in such a picture

pioneer /ˌpɑɪ·əˈnɪr/ *n* [C] **1** a person who is among the first to study or develop something ○ *He was a pioneer in big-band jazz.* **2** ***US history*** A pioneer is also a person who is among the first to enter and live in an area, esp. European Americans in the western US: *The pioneers made their way across the desert.*
pioneer /ˌpɑɪ·əˈnɪr/ *v* [T] ○ *He pioneered the design of the Internet.*

pious /ˈpɑɪ·əs/ *adj* strongly believing in God or a particular religion, and living in a way that shows this belief ○ Related noun: PIETY

pipe TUBE /pɑɪp/ *n* [C] a tube through which liquids or gases can flow ○ *You have to remember to shut off the water in winter or the pipes will freeze and burst.*
pipe /pɑɪp/ *v* [T always + adv/prep] ○ *Hot water is piped to all the apartments from the boiler.*
piping /ˈpɑɪ·pɪŋ/ *n* [U] pipes, or a system of pipes ○ See also: PIPING

DEVICE FOR SMOKING /pɑɪp/ *n* [C] a short, narrow tube with a small bowl at one end, used for smoking esp. tobacco

MUSICAL INSTRUMENT /pɑɪp/ *n* [C] **1** a musical instrument consisting of a short, narrow tube that is played by blowing through it **2** Pipes are also the metal or wood tubes in an ORGAN (= musical instrument played by pressing keys) that produce sound.

PHRASAL VERBS with **pipe**

• **pipe down** *infml* to stop making noise; become quieter ○ *You kids better pipe down in there!*

• **pipe up** to speak suddenly, esp. in an excited way ○ *"I'll bet you dropped it," Cherry piped up.*

pipe dream *n* [C] an idea or plan that is not practical or possible ○ *Many people still believe that traveling to Mars is just a pipe dream.*

pipeline /ˈpɑɪp·lɑɪn/ *n* [C] a series of connected tubes for transporting gas, oil, or water, usually over long distances

IDIOM with **pipeline**

• **in the pipeline** being developed ○ *Twenty-eight lawsuits were filed this week, and another 200 cases are in the pipeline.*

piping /ˈpɑɪ·pɪŋ/ *n* [U] a folded strip of cloth, often enclosing a cord, used to decorate the edges of clothes or furniture ○ *Contrasting fabric was used for the cushion's piping.* ○ See also: PIPING at PIPE TUBE

piping hot /ˈpɑɪ·pɪŋ ˈhɑt/ *adj* [not gradable] (of food or drinks) very hot ○ *I like my soup piping hot.*

pipsqueak /ˈpɪp·skwiːk/ *n* [C] *infml* a small or unimportant person ○ *I'm not afraid of that little pipsqueak!*

piquant /ˈpiː·kənt, piːˈkɑnt/ *adj* having a strong, slightly sour, slightly spicy taste or smell ○ *a piquant sauce*

pique **EXCITE** /piːk/ *v* [T] to excite or cause interest ○ *Labor law piqued his interest in law school.*

ANGER /piːk/ *n* [U] anger or annoyance ○ *He stormed from the room in a fit of pique.*

pique /piːk/ *v* [T] ○ *Something piqued him and he had words with our coach.*

piranha /pəˈrɑn·ə/ *n* [C] *pl* **piranha, piranhas** a small, South American river fish with sharp teeth, that attacks and eats small animals

pirate **COPY** /ˈpɑɪ·rət/ *v* [T] to illegally copy and sell something, such as recorded music, a film, etc., without permission ○ *A lot of this software is pirated.*

pirate /ˈpɑɪ·rət/ *n* [C] ○ *Video pirates are stealing movie company revenues.*

piracy /ˈpɑɪ·rə·si/ *n* [U] ○ *The agency tries to halt piracy of copyrighted recordings.*

SEA THIEF /ˈpɑɪ·rət/ *n* [C] a person who sails on the sea and attacks and steals from other ships

piracy /ˈpɑɪ·rə·si/ *n* [U] the practice of attacking and stealing from ships at sea

pirouette /ˌpɪr·əˈwet/ *n* [C] a fast turn of the body on the toes or the front part of the foot, performed esp. by a BALLET dancer

pirouette /ˌpɪr·əˈwet/ *v* [I] ○ *Dancers pirouetted across the stage.*

Pisces /ˈpɑɪ·siːz, ˈpɪs·iːz/ *n* [C/U] *pl* **Pisces** the twelfth sign of the ZODIAC, covering the period February 19 to March 20 and represented by two fish, or a person born during this period

pistachio /pəˈstæʃ·iː·oʊ/ *n* [C/U] *pl* **pistachios** **1** an edible green nut with a hard shell **2** Pistachio is also a pale green color.

pistil /ˈpɪs·tᵊl/ *n* [C] ***biology*** the female part of a flower, consisting of one or more of the organs that produce seeds

pistol /ˈpɪs·tᵊl/ *n* [C] a small gun which can be held in and fired from one hand

piston /ˈpɪs·tən/ *n* [C] an engine part, usually a short, solid tube or round, flat object, which moves up and down or forward and backward inside a cylinder, and causes other parts of an engine or machine to move

pit **HOLE** /pɪt/ *n* [C] **1** a large hole in the ground, or a hollow in any surface ○ *The trash had been buried in a six-foot-deep pit.* ○ *a fire pit* **2** A pit is also the area in the front of a theater where the musicians perform. **3 The pit of** *your* **stomach** is the center of your body, where you feel esp. fear and anxiety: *I got a sick feeling in the pit of my stomach before the performance.*

pitted /ˈpɪt̬·əd/ *adj* (of a surface) covered with holes ○ *Their cars have been pitted by acid rain.*

SEED /pɪt/ *n* [C] a large, hard seed that grows inside some types of fruit and vegetables ○ *a peach/plum/cherry pit*

pitted /ˈpɪt̬·əd/ *adj* [not gradable] having the seed removed ○ *pitted cherries/olives*

REPAIR AREA /pɪt/ *n* [C] an area on the side of a TRACK on which cars race, where the cars are given fuel or repaired during a race

UNDERGROUND METALS /pɪt/, **pit mine** *n* [C] a hole from which natural substances, such as rocks and MINERALS, are dug; MINE

IDIOM with **pit**

• **the pits** *infml* a very bad or unpleasant thing ○ *When I first came to the college, this place was the pits, but it's improved a lot.*

PHRASAL VERB with **pit**

• **pit** *someone/something* **against** *someone/something* to put someone or something in opposition or competition with someone or something else ○ *That talk show is always pitting men against women.*

pita (bread) /ˈpiːt̬·ə (ˈbred)/ *n* [C] a round or oval flat bread that is hollow and can be filled with other food

pit bull (terrier) /ˈpɪt·bʊl (ˈter·iː·ər)/ *n* [C] a type of small dog with a wide chest and short hair, known for its strength and sometimes trained to fight

P

pitch **THROW** /pɪtʃ/ *v* [T] to throw something, esp. forcefully ○ *She pitched a stone into the river.*

THROW BASEBALL /pɪtʃ/ *v* [I/T] (in baseball) to throw a baseball toward a player from the opposing team who tries to hit it with a baseball BAT

pitch /pɪtʃ/ *n* [C] ○ *Wait for a good pitch before you swing.*

pitcher /ˈpɪtʃ·ər/ *n* [C] a person who pitches the baseball to a BATTER ○ See also: PITCHER

FALL /pɪtʃ/ *v* [always + adv/prep] to fall suddenly ○ [T] *The bus stopped suddenly, pitching everyone forward.*

SOUND QUALITY /pɪtʃ/ *n* [C/U] ***music*** the degree to which a sound or a musical note has a high or low quality

pitch /pɪtʃ/ *v* [T] ○ *He pitched his voice just so, making them pay attention.*

PERSUASION /pɪtʃ/ *n* [C] a speech that attempts to persuade someone to buy or do something ○ *a sales pitch*

RAISE /pɪtʃ/ *v* [T] to raise a tent and fix it in place ○ *We pitched our tent in a sheltered area.*

SLOPE /pɪtʃ/ *n* [U] the degree of slope, esp. of a roof

pitched /pɪtʃt/ *adj* [not gradable] ○ *a pitched roof*

BLACK SUBSTANCE /pɪtʃ/ *n* [U] a thick, black, sticky substance used to make ships and roofs waterproof, and to cover cracks in roads

SPORTS FIELD /pɪtʃ/ *n* [C] *Br* FIELD SPORTS

PHRASAL VERB with **pitch**

• **pitch in** to become involved in esp. something helpful ○ *If we all pitch in, the cleanup shouldn't take long.*

pitch-black *adj* [not gradable] completely black ○ *a moonless, pitch-black night*

pitch-dark *adj* [not gradable] completely dark ○ *In winter it was already pitch-dark by 5.*

pitcher /ˈpɪtʃ·ər/ *n* [C] a container for liquids with a handle on one side and a shaped opening at the top of the other side for pouring ○ See also: PITCHER at PITCH THROW BASEBALL

pitchfork /ˈpɪtʃ·fɔːrk/ *n* [C] a tool with a long handle and two or three large points used for moving HAY (= cut dried grass) or STRAW (= cut dried stems of crops)

pitfall /ˈpɪt·fɔːl/ *n* [C] an unexpected danger or difficulty ○ *Who knows what kind of pitfalls they're going to run into.*

pithy /ˈpɪθ·i/ *adj* (of speech or writing) brief and full of meaning ○ *pithy comments* ○ *a pithy quote*

pit stop **CAR REPAIR** *n* [C] a brief stop for fuel or repairs in a car race

STOP FOR NEEDS *n* [C] *infml* a brief stop during a car trip to get food or fuel, or to use the bathroom

pittance /ˈpɪt·ᵊns/ *n* [C usually sing] a very small amount of money ○ *He couldn't live on the pittance his mother sent him.*

pituitary gland /pəˈtuː·əˌter·i ˌglænd/ *n* [C usually sing] ***biology*** a small organ at the bottom of the brain which controls how the body grows and develops by producing HORMONES (= chemicals that influence the body's processes)

pity /ˈpɪt̬·i/ *n* [U] **1** sympathy and understanding for someone else's suffering or troubles ○ *She did not want his pity.* **2** If something is described as a pity, it is a cause for regret: *It's a pity you can't come to the party.*

pity /ˈpɪt̬·i/ *v* [T] ○ *I pity people who have to work with statistics.*

pitiful /ˈpɪt̬·ɪ·fəl/, **pitiable** /ˈpɪt̬·iː·ə·bəl/ *adj* **1** *She made a pitiful plea for acceptance.* **2** Something described as pitiful is not considered to be satisfactory or deserving of respect: *The party is a pitiful example of an opposition party.*

pitifully /ˈpɪt̬·ɪ·fə·li, -fli/, **pitiably** /ˈpɪt̬·iː·ə·bli/ *adv* [not gradable] ○ *I was pitifully ill-informed.*

pitiless /ˈpɪt·ɪ·ləs/ *adj* [not gradable] having or showing no pity ○ *a pitiless dictator*

pivot /ˈpɪv·ət/ *n* [C] a fixed point supporting something which turns or balances, or a person or thing on which something else depends ○ *Boston was the pivot of his emotional and intellectual life.*

pivot /ˈpɪv·ət/ *v* [I/T] **-tt-** to turn or twist ○ [T] *She pivots her left foot.* ○ [I] *He pivoted on his heels and headed out.* ○ [I] *Future deals will pivot on easing commercial conflicts* (= they will depend on this).

pivotal /ˈpɪv·ət̬·ᵊl/ *adj* [not gradable] important because other things depend on it ○ *She played a pivotal role in the civil rights movement.*

pixel /ˈpɪk·səl/ *n* [C] *technology* the smallest unit of an image on a television or computer screen

pixie /ˈpɪk·si/ *n* [C] (esp. in children's stories) a small, imaginary person

pizazz, pizzazz /pɪˈzæz/ *n* [U] *infml, approving* excitement, energy, or style ○ *I want food that's low in fat but that has some pizazz.*

pizza /ˈpiːt·sə/ *n* [C/U] a flat, usually round bread that is baked covered with TOMATO sauce, cheese, and often pieces of vegetables or meat ○ [U] *a slice of pizza* ○ [C] *I phoned for a pizza.*

pj's /ˈpiː·jeɪz/ *pl n infml* PAJAMAS

placard /ˈplæk·ərd, -ɑrd/ *n* [C] a notice or sign hung in a public place or carried by people ○ *Foley's placard read, "Go home."*

placate /ˈpleɪ·keɪt, ˈplæk·eɪt/ *v* [T] to stop someone from feeling angry ○ *She's more easily placated than her husband.*

place **AREA** /pleɪs/ *n* [C] **1** an area, a building, or a city, town, or village ○ *Airports are usually busy places.* ○ *Larchmont is a nice place to live.* **2** Your place is your home: *We can meet at my place.* **3** A place is also an area or building used for a specific purpose: *a place of worship*

POSITION /pleɪs/ *n* [C] **1** a particular position ○ *That's the best place for the piano.* ○ *The librarian put the book back in its place* (= in the right position). **2** A place is also a space for a person, as in a theater, at a table, or in a line: *Will you hold my place in line for a minute?* **3** If plans are **in place**,

they have been made: *I think everything's in place for the wedding.* **4 In place** can also be used to talk about something that is being used now ○ *The new building code will replace the rules that are currently in place.*
place /pleɪs/ *v* [T] ○ *Flowers had been placed on all the tables.*
placement /ˈpleɪ·smənt/ *n* [U] ○ *The placement of the furniture makes it hard to walk around.*

RANK /pleɪs/ *n* [C] the rank someone or something has ○ *Our team finished in second place.*
place /pleɪs/ *v* [I] ○ *She placed high on the tests.*
placement /ˈpleɪ·smənt/ *n* [U]

JOB /pleɪs/ *n* [C] a job, or a position in an organization, at a school, etc. ○ *Ann just got a place at Yale.*
place /pleɪs/ *v* [T] ○ *The agency is usually able to place temporary workers for the summer.*
placement /ˈpleɪ·smənt/ *n* [U] ○ *There are students for whom this school is not the best possible placement.*

RECOGNIZE /pleɪs/ *v* [T] to recognize someone or something because of memory or past experience ○ *She looks familiar, but I can't place her.*

DUTY /pleɪs/ *n* [U] a person's duty or position of authority ○ [+ *to* infinitive] *It's not your place to tell me what to do.*

PUT /pleɪs/ *v* [T] to put someone in a situation ○ *They placed him in a nursing home.* ○ *She was placed under arrest.*

INVEST /pleɪs/ *v* [T] to invest or risk money ○ *They placed a significant amount in stocks.*

GIVE /pleɪs/ *v* [T] to arrange to get something by telling someone who will supply it ○ *I placed an order for three CDs.*

WORD FAMILY place

Nouns	place placement replacement	*Adjectives*	misplaced
		Verbs	place displace replace

IDIOM with place

• **trade places (with** *someone***)**, **change places (with** *someone***)** to exchange positions with someone ○ *We traded places so he could sit near the window.* ○ *He might be rich, but I wouldn't change places with him for anything.*

placebo /pləˈsiː·boʊ/ *n* [C] *pl* **placebos** a substance that is not medicine, but that is given to someone who is told that it is a medicine, used to test the effect of a drug or to please a patient

place mat, **placemat** /ˈpleɪs·mæt/ *n* [C] a piece of cloth, paper, or plastic put on a table under someone's plate and eating utensils

placement test *n* [C] a test that measures someone's ability in order to put that person in a particular class or group

placenta /pləˈsent·ə/ *n* [C] *pl* **placentas** ***biology*** an organ that develops inside the uterus of a pregnant woman or animal and provides food for the developing baby
placental /pləˈsent·əl/ *adj* [not gradable]

place setting *n* [C] the arrangement of dishes and utensils that a person uses when eating at a table

placid /ˈplæs·əd/ *adj* calm and peaceful ○ *a placid child* ○ *The placid lake was perfect for canoeing.*

plagiarize /ˈpleɪ·dʒəˌrɑɪz/ *v* [I/T] to use another person's idea or a part of that person's work and pretend that it is your own
plagiarism /ˈpleɪ·dʒəˌrɪz·əm/ *n* [U] ○ *She's been accused of plagiarism.*

plague **CAUSE DIFFICULTY** /pleɪg/ *v* [T] to cause someone or something difficulty or suffering, esp. repeatedly or continually ○ *Financial problems have been plaguing the company.* ○ *That pain in my shoulder is plaguing me again.*

DISEASE /pleɪg/ *n* [C/U] **1** a serious disease which kills many people **2** ***world history*** **The plague** refers to a disease that appeared several times in the 14th century and later and that killed more than one-third of the people in Europe and many people in Africa and Asia; BLACK DEATH. **3** A plague is also a large number of insects or animals which cause damage or unpleasant conditions in an area: [C] *Trees throughout the Northeast are being attacked by a plague of gypsy moths.*

plaid /plæd/ *n* [U] a pattern of different colored straight lines crossing each other at 90° angles, or a cloth with this pattern

plain **WITH NOTHING ADDED** /pleɪn/ *adj* [-*er*/-*est* only] not decorated in any way; with nothing added ○ *The catalog was sent in a plain brown envelope.* ○ *The food is pretty plain* (= prepared simply and without strong flavors), *but there's lots of it.*
plainly /ˈpleɪn·li/ *adv* ○ *a plainly furnished room*

CLEAR /pleɪn/ *adj* [-*er*/-*est* only] obvious, or clear and easy to see or understand; not complicated ○ *A group of wild horses was in plain view* (= We could see them clearly). ○ *Why can't they write these instructions in plain English?*
plain /pleɪn/ *adv* [not gradable] *infml* ○ *It was just plain stupid to give him your telephone number.*
plainly /ˈpleɪn·li/ *adv* clearly or obviously ○ *Plainly, the new tax rules are a major headache.*

NOT ATTRACTIVE /pleɪn/ *adj* [-*er*/-*est* only] (esp. of a woman or girl) not attractive ○ *She always thought of herself as plain.*

LAND /pleɪn/ *n* [C usually pl] ***earth science*** a large area of flat land at low ELEVATION (= height above the surface of the earth) ○ *A number of paintings by Western artists show Indian settlements in the plains.*

plainclothes /ˈpleɪn·kloʊðz, -kloʊz/ *adj* [not gradable] not wearing the uniform that is connected with a job ○ *plainclothes detectives/policemen*

plaintiff /ˈpleɪnt·əf/ *n* [C] *law* a person who accuses someone else in a law case of having done

P

something illegal ○ Compare DEFENDANT at DEFEND PROTECT

plaintive /ˈpleɪnt·ɪv/ *adj* (esp. of a sound) having a sad quality ○ *I love the plaintive sound of the bagpipes.*

plait /pleɪt, plæt/ *v, n esp. Br* BRAID HAIR

plan METHOD /plæn/ *n* [C/U] **1** a method for doing or achieving something, usually involving a series of actions or stages, or something you have arranged to do ○ [C] *The financial plan calls for growth of 5% next year.* ○ [C] *They had plans to have dinner at a local restaurant.* **2** A plan is also an arrangement for investment: [C] *a pension/savings plan* **3** If something goes according to plan, it happens the way you wanted it to: [U] *Producing a new movie rarely goes exactly according to plan.*

plan /plæn/ *v* [I/T] **-nn-** to think about and decide on a method for doing or achieving something ○ [+ *to* infinitive] *She's planning to visit her sister in Australia next year.* ○ [I always + adv/prep] *He planned on taking his vacation in July.* ○ [I always + adv/prep] *You've got to plan ahead and save your money for your retirement.*

MAP /plæn/ *n* [C] a drawing that shows the shape, size, and position of important details of a building or other structure, or of objects within it ○ *The floor plan showed us exactly where everyone's office would be.*

plan /plæn/ *v* [T] **-nn-** ○ *Few American cities were planned – they just grew larger in all directions.*

planner /ˈplæn·ər/ *n* [C] a person whose job is to plan something, esp. how land in a particular area is to be used and what should be built on it ○ *a city planner* ○ *an urban planner*

WORD FAMILY plan			
Nouns	plan planner	Verbs	plan

Planck's constant /ˈplæŋks ˈkɑn·stənt, ˈplɑŋks-/ *n* [U] ***physics*** a number that never changes and that expresses the relationship between the energy of a PHOTON and its FREQUENCY

plane AIRCRAFT /pleɪn/, **airplane** *n* [C] a vehicle that is designed for air travel and that has wings and one or more engines ○ *Shelley's plane is due in at 10, but it's a half-hour late.*

SURFACE /pleɪn/ *n* [C] ***geometry*** a flat surface that continues in all directions ➤ Picture: **geometry**; **triangle**

LEVEL /pleɪn/ *n* [C] a level or standard ○ *Once we got a new financial manager, our business meetings were conducted on a much higher plane.*

TOOL /pleɪn/ *n* [C] a tool with a blade in a flat surface that is rubbed against wood to cut away rough parts and make it smooth

planet /ˈplæn·ət/ *n* [C] ***earth science*** an extremely large, round mass of matter, such as Earth or Mars, that moves in a circular path around the sun or another star

planetary /ˈplæn·əˌter·i/ *adj* [not gradable] ***earth science*** ○ *planetary scientists*

planetarium /ˌplæn·əˈter·iː·əm/ *n* [C] a building specially equipped to show images of the stars in the sky and other objects in space on a curved ceiling

plank FLAT PIECE /plæŋk/ *n* [C] a long, flat piece of wood or other material, esp. one wide enough and strong enough to walk on ○ *They walked across the creaky, wooden-plank floor of the old house.*

PRINCIPLE /plæŋk/ *n* [C] an important principle on which the activities of a political or other group are based ○ *He prepared the peace plank in the Democrats' 1864 presidential platform.*

plankton /ˈplæŋk·tən, -tɑn/ *n* [U] ***biology, earth science*** very small organisms that float in water, esp. near the surface, and are food for fish and other animals that live in water

plant LIVING THING /plænt/ *n* [C] a living thing that usually produces seeds and typically has a stem, leaves, roots, and sometimes flowers ○ *We brought a house plant as a gift when we spent the weekend with our friend Sylvia.*

plant /plænt/ *v* [T] to put a seed or plant into the ground or into a container of earth so that it will grow ○ *We've planted some trees along the back of our property.*

planter /ˈplænt·ər/ *n* [C] **1** a large container in which esp. decorative plants are grown ○ *The sidewalk is lined with planters overflowing with flowers.* **2** A planter is also someone who owns a PLANTATION (= large farm in a hot part of the world).

GROUP /plænt/ *n* [U] ***biology*** one of five KINGDOMS (= groups) into which living things are divided, the members of which have many cells, are unable to control their own movement, and get their energy from the light of the sun

PUT /plænt/ *v* [T always + adv/prep] **1** to put something firmly in a particular place ○ *He planted a kiss on her forehead.* **2** To plant an idea or story is to cause it to exist: *Defense lawyers try to plant doubts in the minds of the jurors about what actually happened.*

PUT SECRETLY /plænt/ *v* [T] to put something or someone in a position secretly, esp. in order to deceive ○ *She insisted that the real thief had planted the evidence in her car.*

FACTORY /plænt/ *n* [C] a factory and the machinery in it used to produce or process something ○ *a manufacturing plant*

WORD FAMILY plant			
Nouns	plant planter transplant plantation	Verbs	plant transplant

plantain /ˈplænt·ən/ *n* [C] a fruit of the hotter regions that looks like a BANANA and is usually cooked before being eaten

plantation /plænˈteɪ·ʃən/ *n* [C] a large farm, esp. in a hot part of the world, on which a particular crop is grown ○ *a coffee/rubber plantation*

plaque RECORD /plæk/ *n* [C] a flat object, often of stone or metal, with text that records information about a person, place, or event ○ *The plaque on the building pays tribute to the founder's generosity.*

SUBSTANCE /plæk/ *n* [C/U] **1** a substance that grows on your teeth if you do not brush them regularly **2** Plaque is also a substance that may grow inside the body with certain diseases: *About 20 companies are working on treatments for Alzheimer's that would interfere with plaque formation.*

plasma /ˈplæz·mə/ *n* [U] ***biology*** the liquid part of blood that carries the blood cells

plaster WALL COVERING /ˈplæs·tər/ *n* [U] a substance that is used esp. for spreading on walls and ceilings because it makes a smooth, hard surface after it dries
plaster /ˈplæs·tər/ *v* [T] **1** *Someone will come in tomorrow to plaster the wall where the plumber had to make a hole.* **2** *infml* To plaster a surface or an object with something is to cover it completely or thickly: *She has plastered her bedroom walls with posters of pop singers.*

INJURY PROTECTION /ˈplæs·tər/ *n* [C] *Br* BAND-AID.

plaster of Paris *n* [U] a mixture of a white powder and water that becomes hard as it dries and is used to make statues, MOLDS, and other objects

plastic MATERIAL /ˈplæs·tɪk/ *n* [C/U] any one of a group of materials made chemically and shaped into different forms for different uses ○ [U] *The cover of the book is actually made of plastic, though it looks like cloth.* ○ [C] *Plastics can be produced in the form of fibers or sheets and are used in building materials as well as in consumer goods.*
plastic /ˈplæs·tɪk/ *adj* [not gradable] ○ *a plastic bag/bottle/container*

SOFT /ˈplæs·tɪk/ *adj* soft enough to be shaped into different forms ○ *Clay is a plastic material.*

plastic surgery *n* [U] medical operations to repair a damaged or badly formed area of skin or bone, or to improve a person's appearance

plate DISH /pleɪt/ *n* [C] **1** a flat dish on which food is served or from which it is eaten **2** A plate (also **plateful**) is an amount of food on a plate: *Dominic helped himself to a plate of spaghetti.*

FLAT PIECE /pleɪt/ *n* [C] a flat piece of something that is hard, does not bend, and is usually used to cover something ○ *Large, metal plates covered the trench in the roadway.*

ADD THIN LAYER /pleɪt/ *v* [T] to cover a metal object with a thin layer of another metal, esp. gold or silver ○ *gold plated*
plate /pleɪt/ *n* [U] ○ *The knives and forks are silver plate.*

LAYER /pleɪt/ *n* [C] ***earth science*** one of the large moving layers of rock that the earth's surface is believed to be made of ➤ Picture: **tectonic plate**

plateau /plæˈtoʊ/ *n* [C] **1** ***earth science*** a large, flat area of land that is higher than the land around it **2** A plateau is also a period during which there are no big changes: *The crime rate in the city reached a plateau in the 1980s and then declined.*
plateau /plæˈtoʊ/ *v* [I] to reach a level and stay there, rather than rising or falling ○ *The population increase is expected to plateau in the year 2007.*

plate glass *n* [U] large sheets of glass used esp. as windows and doors in stores and offices ○ *a plate-glass window*

platelet /ˈpleɪt·lə/ *n* [C] ***biology*** a very small cell in the blood that makes the blood thicker and stops it from flowing when you cut yourself

plate tectonics /ˈpleɪt tekˈtɑn·ɪks/ *n* [U] ***earth science*** the theory that the earth's surface is made of large layers of rock that are always moving, causing EARTHQUAKES and VOLCANOES, and explaining the creation of the varied features of the earth's surface ➤ Picture: **tectonic plate**

platform /ˈplæt·fɔːrm/ *n* [C] **1** a flat, raised area or structure ○ *We waited on the platform for the train to arrive from Boston.* **2** Politicians' or political partys' platforms are the things they say they believe in and that they will achieve if they are elected: *He campaigned on a platform of reducing taxes and cutting the costs of government.*

platinum /ˈplæt·ᵊn·əm/ *n* [U] a valuable metal that is silver in color, does not react easily with other elements, and is used in jewelry and in industry

platitude /ˈplæt̬·əˌtuːd/ *n* [C] a statement that has been repeated so often that it is meaningless ○ *They nodded at every platitude about making sacrifices today for a better tomorrow.*

platonic /pləˈtɑn·ɪk/ *adj* (of a relationship or emotion) affectionate but not sexual

platoon /pləˈtuːn/ *n* [C] a military unit consisting of a group of about 20 soldiers who are all members of a COMPANY

platter /ˈplæt̬·ər/ *n* [C] **1** a large plate used for serving food **2** In a restaurant, a platter is a dish with a variety of foods on it: *I'd like the seafood platter, please.*

plaudit /ˈplɔːd·ət/ *n* [C usually pl] *fml* an expression of approval; praise ○ *She won plaudits for her toughness during tense labor negotiations.*

plausible /ˈplɔː·zə·bəl/ *adj* possibly true; able to be believed ○ *a plausible excuse/explanation*

play ENJOY /pleɪ/ *v* [I] to spend time doing something enjoyable or amusing ○ *The children spent the afternoon playing.*
playful /ˈpleɪ·fəl/ *adj* done as a form of play rather than intended seriously, or wanting to have a good time and not feeling serious ○ *She gave him a playful push.* ○ *My mother was in a playful mood that day.*

COMPETE /pleɪ/ *v* [I/T] **1** to take part in a game or other organized activity ○ [T] *He loves playing football.* ○ [I] *What team does she play for?* **2** If you play

P

a person or team, you compete against them: [T] *We're going to the stadium to see New York play Chicago.* **3** If you play the ball or a shot, you hit or kick the ball: [T] *In golf, you have to take time to decide how to play difficult shots.* **4** In a card game, to play a card is to choose it from the ones you are holding and put it down on the table.

play /pleɪ/ *n* **1** [U] *Play was suspended because of a heavy rainstorm.* **2** If a ball or something else is **in play**, it is in a position where it can be used as part of the regular action in a game or sport, and if it is **out of play**, it is not in such a position: [U] *She put the ball in play in midfield.* **3** In sports, a play can also be a particular action or a plan for a specific set of actions: [C] *The school football team has been practicing new plays all week.*

player /ˈpleɪ·ər/ *n* [C] someone who takes part in a sport or game ○ *This basketball team has a lot of talented players.* ○ *(fig.) The company is one of the leading players* (= organizations taking part) *in the deal.*

ACT /pleɪ/ *v* **1** to perform as a character in a play or movie, or (of a performance) to be shown ○ [T] *She played the part of a beautiful and brilliant scientist.* ○ [I] *What's playing at* (= being shown at) *the local movie theaters?* **2** To play is also to behave or pretend in a particular way, esp. to produce an effect or result: [L] *Don't play dumb with me* (= pretend you don't know anything) *– you know very well what happened!* **3** To play can mean to influence or have an effect on: [T] *The president denied that politics played any part in his decision to appoint a woman to the Supreme Court.* **4** To **play a joke on** *someone* or **play a trick on** *someone* is to deceive someone for amusement or in order to get an advantage: *She loves to play jokes on her friends.*

play /pleɪ/ *n* [C] ***literature*** a story that is intended to be acted out before people who have come to see it ○ *She starred in many Broadway plays in her career.*

PRODUCE SOUNDS/PICTURES /pleɪ/ *v* [I/T] to perform music on an instrument, or to cause something that produces sound or a picture to operate ○ [I/T] *She plays (the piano) beautifully.* ○ [T] *I was just playing my stereo.* ○ *I learned how to* **play** *the guitar* **by ear** (= by listening rather than by reading music).

player /ˈpleɪ·ər/ *n* [C] **1** someone who plays a musical instrument ○ *a cello/flute player* **2** A player is also a machine: *a CD/record player*

RISK MONEY /pleɪ/ *v* [T] to risk money, esp. on the results of races or business deals, hoping to win money ○ *He plays the stock market.*

WORD FAMILY play

Nouns	play interplay replay player	*Verbs*	play outplay replay
Adjectives	playful	*Adverbs*	playfully

IDIOMS with play

• **a play on words** an amusing use of a word or phrase that has more than one meaning

• **play ball** *infml* to agree to work with or help someone in the way the person has suggested ○ *The family wanted a full-time nurse but the insurance company refused to play ball* (= would not pay for one).

• **play** *your* **cards right** to do the correct things to achieve the desired result ○ *If you play your cards right, you could make a lot of money out of this.*

• **play games** to behave in a way that is not serious or honest enough ○ *I'm not interested in playing games with people at city hall on the tax issue.* ○ *Stop playing games with me, or you will not be allowed to go out this weekend.*

• **play hardball** *infml* to behave in an unpleasant, threatening way so that you get what you want ○ *He's a nice guy, but he can play hardball when he has to.*

• **play havoc with 1** to make a situation much more difficult or confusing ○ *The snowstorm is really playing havoc with rush-hour traffic.* **2** to damage something ○ *The acid rain plays havoc with marine life.*

• **play hooky, play hookey** to stay away from school without permission ○ *They played hooky and went fishing.*

• **play it by ear** to decide what to do when you know what is happening, rather than planning in advance ○ *"I can't tell you what to expect." "Don't worry, I'll play it by ear."*

• **play it safe** to avoid any risks ○ *Let's play it safe and allow an extra ten minutes to get there.*

• **play with fire** to do something that could cause you trouble later ○ *You're playing with fire if you try to cheat on the test.*

PHRASAL VERBS with play

• **play along** to act as if you agree with something that is happening, esp. if it is something wrong ○ *She claims she was fired because she refused to play along with the coverup.*

• **play around** to have a sexual relationship with someone other than your husband or wife

• **play back** *something* [M] to hear a sound recording or see a film that has been previously recorded ○ *She taped the Olympic speed skating final so that she could play it back later.* ○ Related noun: PLAYBACK

• **play down** *something* [M] to make something seem less important than or not as bad as it really is ○ *The doctor tried to play down the seriousness of my father's illness, but we weren't fooled.*

• **play up CAUSE TROUBLE** to behave or operate in a way that causes difficulty ○ *Is your ulcer playing up again?*

• **play up** *something* **GIVE IMPORTANCE** [M] to make something seem more important or better than it really is, esp. to get an advantage ○ *The report plays up the benefits of the plan, but doesn't say much about the costs.*

• **play with** *something* to use something in a way that is not serious or careful ○ *You're not really making a budget, you're just playing with numbers.* ○ *Stop playing with your food.*

playback /ˈpleɪ·bæk/ *n* [C/U] the act of listening to or watching something that was previously recorded ○ [C] *Each playback will sound as pure as the original.* ○ Related verb: PLAY BACK

playboy /ˈpleɪ·bɔɪ/ *n* [C] a rich man who spends his time and money on luxuries and a life of pleasure

playful /ˈpleɪ·fəl/ *adj* ○ See at PLAY ENJOY

playground /ˈpleɪ·ɡrɑʊnd/ *n* [C] an outside area designed for children to play in

playhouse THEATER /ˈpleɪ·hɑʊs/ *n* [C] a theater

CHILD'S TOY /ˈpleɪ·hɑʊz/ *n* [C] a small house that is a model of a real house, designed for children to play in

playing card *n* [C] one of a set of 52 small, rectangular pieces of stiff paper, each with a number or face and one of four signs printed on it, used in games

playing field PLACE FOR SPORTS *n* [C] an open, outside area for sports, esp. one that is marked with lines for playing a sport

COMPETITION *n* [C usually sing] a situation where there is competition ○ *All we ask is that there be a level playing field* (= equal opportunities) *for everyone bidding for the work.*

playmate /ˈpleɪ·meɪt/ *n* [C] a friend, esp. another child, with whom a child often plays ○ *We were childhood playmates.*

playoff, **play-off** /ˈpleɪ·ɔːf/ *n* [C] one of a series of games played after the regular season to decide which teams will advance to play for the CHAMPIONSHIP (= compete to be recognized as the best team) ○ *the basketball playoffs* ○ *a playoff game*

playpen /ˈpleɪ·pen/ *n* [C] a small structure with bars or a net around the sides but open at the top, for a baby to play in

plaything TOY /ˈpleɪ·θɪŋ/ *n* [C] a child's toy, or something used like a toy ○ *Fancy cars were the playthings of the rich.*

PERSON /ˈpleɪ·θɪŋ/ *n* [C] a person who is not treated with care or respect

playwright /ˈpleɪ·rɑɪt/ *n* [C] a person who writes plays

plaza /ˈplæz,ə, ˈplɑz·ə/ *n* [C] an open, public area in a city or town, or a group of buildings with stores, often including an open, public area ○ *New York City's Rockefeller Plaza*

plea REQUEST /pliː/ *n* [C] an urgent and emotional request ○ *The president made a strong plea to Congress to vote on the health-care bill.*

STATEMENT /pliː/ *n* [C] *law* the answer that a person gives in court to the accusation of having committed a crime ○ *He received a sentence of 5 to 10 years for his guilty plea to the robbery.*

plea bargain *n* [C] ***social studies*** an agreement to allow someone accused of a crime to admit to being guilty of a less serious crime in order to avoid being tried for the more serious one

plea bargaining *n* [C] ***social studies*** the legal discussion that may result in a plea bargain

plead REQUEST /pliːd/ *v* [I] *past* **pleaded, pled** to make an urgent, emotional statement or request for something ○ *She appeared on television to plead for help in finding her child.*

STATE /pliːd/ *v* [T] *past* **pleaded, pled** *fml* to give an official answer to an accusation in a law court ○ *to plead guilty/not guilty*

pleasant /ˈplez·ənt/ *adj* enjoyable or attractive, or (of a person) friendly and easy to like ○ *We spent a pleasant afternoon at the beach.* ○ *She had a pleasant manner and was popular with everyone.*

pleasantly /ˈplez·ənt·li/ *adv* ○ *Mohammed was pleasantly surprised to get a B in history.*

pleasantry /ˈplez·ən·tri/ *n* [C usually pl] a polite remark, usually made by people when they first meet to show they are friendly ○ *The officials shook hands and exchanged pleasantries about the weather before getting down to business.*

please POLITE REQUEST /pliːz/ *exclamation* commonly used in order to make a request more polite, or, sometimes, to make it stronger or urgent ○ *Could I please have some ketchup for my hamburger?* ○ *Please be sure to take all your personal belongings when you leave the train.* ○ *Please do as I say and don't ask questions.* ○ *"Would you like some more salad?" "Please* (= yes, I would).*"*

MAKE HAPPY /pliːz/ *v* [I/T] to make someone feel happy or satisfied, or to give someone pleasure ○ [I/T] *He did what he could to please her, but she was hard to please.* ○ [T] *I'm pleased to report that sales have increased by 15%.* ○ [I] *She'll listen to what you say, but in the end she'll do as/what she pleases* (= what she wants to do).

pleased /pliːzd/ *adj* **1** happy or satisfied ○ *a pleased expression* ○ *Mom was not pleased when she saw my grades.* **2** A person may say **(I'm) pleased to meet you** as a polite way of greeting someone when they meet for the first time.

pleasing /ˈpliː·zɪŋ/ *adj* giving a feeling of satisfaction or enjoyment ○ *a pleasing performance/design*

WORD FAMILY please

Nouns	pleasure pleasantry displeasure	*Adjectives*	pleasant unpleasant pleased pleasing pleasurable
Verbs	please displease		
Adverbs	pleasantly unpleasantly	*Exclamations*	please

pleasure /ˈpleʒ·ər/ *n* [C/U] a feeling of enjoyment or satisfaction, or something that produces this feeling ○ [U] *The boy's visits gave his grandparents a great deal of pleasure.* ○ [C usually sing] *It's always a pleasure to see you.*

pleasurable /ˈpleʒ·ə·rə·bəl/ *adj* pleasant ○ *The hotels were not so good, but on the whole the trip was a pleasurable experience.*

pleat /pliːt/ *n* [C] a flat, usually narrow, fold made in a piece of cloth by pressing or sewing two parts of the cloth together

pleated /ˈpliːt̬·əd/ *adj* ○ *a pleated skirt*

pled /pled/ *past simple and past participle of* PLEAD

pledge /pledʒ/ *n* [C] a formal promise, or something that is given as a sign that you will keep a promise ○ *a pledge of friendship* ○ *The telethon raised $150,000 in pledges for leukemia research.*
pledge /pledʒ/ *v* ○ [T] *Many countries have pledged food and funds to aid the region.* ○ [+ *to* infinitive] *The police pledged to arrest those responsible.*

Pledge of Allegiance *n* [U] a promise to be loyal to the US that is said esp. by children at school at the start of each day ○ *The teacher asked the children to stand and recite the Pledge of Allegiance.*

plenary /ˈpliː·nə·ri, ˈplen·ə-/ *adj* [not gradable] *fml* having all the members of a group or organization present ○ *a plenary session*

plenty /ˈplent·i/ *n* [U] an amount or supply that is enough or more than enough, or a large number or amount ○ *This car has plenty of power.* ○ *I didn't eat them all – there's plenty left for you.* ○ (*infml*) *This car cost me plenty* (= a lot of money). ○ *Have another sandwich – there's* **plenty more where** *that* **came from** (= a lot more available).
plenty /ˈplent·i/ *adv* [not gradable] *infml* ○ *He was plenty mad.*
plentiful /ˈplent·ɪ·fəl/ *adj* ○ *Strawberries are in plentiful supply this year.*

plethora /ˈpleθ·ə·rə/ *n* [U] a very large amount of something, esp. a larger amount than you need, want, or can deal with ○ *a plethora of excuses/agencies/diet books*

pliable /ˈplɑɪ·ə·bəl/, **pliant** /ˈplɑɪ·ənt/ *adj* (of a substance) easily bent without breaking or cracking, or (of a person) easily influenced or controlled by others ○ *soft, pliable materials* ○ *A more pliant leader would compromise.*

pliers /ˈplɑɪ·ərz/ *pl n* a small tool used for pulling, holding, or cutting that has two handles that you press together in order to bring together two specially shaped pieces of metal at the other end

plight /plɑɪt/ *n* [C usually sing] an unpleasant condition, esp. a serious, sad, or difficult one ○ *My problems aren't much compared with the plight of the storm victims.*

PLO /ˌpiː·elˈoʊ/ *n* [U] ***world history*** abbreviation for Palestine Liberation Organization (= an organization formed to protect and to represent Palestinians and that seeks to establish an independent Palestinian state).

plod WALK /plɑd/ *v* [I always + adv/prep] **-dd-** to walk taking slow steps as if your feet are heavy ○ *Danny plodded through the store behind his wife.*
WORK /plɑd/ *v* [I always + adv/prep] **-dd-** to work or do something slowly and continuously in a tiring or boring way ○ *I sat at my desk, plodded ahead doggedly, and finished the paper before noon.*
plodding /ˈplɑd·ɪŋ/ *adj* ○ *I'll try not to bore you with a lot of plodding details.*

plop SOUND /plɑp/ *n* [C] a soft sound like that of something dropping lightly into a liquid
PUT /plɑp/ *v* [always + adv/prep] **-pp-** to sit down or land heavily, or to put something down heavily without taking care ○ [I] *He came over and plopped down next to me.* ○ [T] *He plopped the sandwich into the pan.*

plot SECRET PLAN /plɑt/ *n* [C] a secret plan to do something that is wrong, harmful, or illegal ○ *The police discovered a plot to rob the bank.*
plot /plɑt/ *v* **-tt-** ○ [T] *They were accused of plotting the removal of the king.* ○ [+ *to* infinitive] *They were plotting to blow up the dam.*
plotter /ˈplɑt̬·ər/ *n* [C]
STORY /plɑt/ *n* [C] ***literature*** the plan or main story of a book, film, play, etc. ○ *The novel has a complicated plot that is sometimes difficult to follow.*
MARK /plɑt/ *v* [T] **-tt- 1** ***mathematics*** to mark a paper or use a computer to show the position of a number or represent a solution to an EQUATION (= mathematical statement) and create a GRAPH (= drawing) **2** To plot something is also to mark or draw lines showing a route on a piece of paper or a map, or to put numbers on a piece of paper to show how amounts are related: *He plotted a course between Hawaii and Tahiti.* ○ *We measured and plotted the amounts of chemicals that were released in the countryside.*
GROUND /plɑt/ *n* [C] a small piece of land that has been marked or measured for a particular purpose ○ *a garden plot*

plow TOOL /plɑʊ/ *n* [C] a large farming tool with blades that dig into the earth, or a large, curved blade fixed to the front of a vehicle that moves snow or sand
plow /plɑʊ/ *v* [I/T] ○ [T] *It rained so much I thought I'd have to plow the crops under.* ○ [I] *I won't be able to drive to the store until they plow.*
FORCE /plɑʊ/ *v* [always + adv/prep] to force your way, or to advance slowly although it is difficult ○ [I] *His truck left the road and plowed through some small trees.* ○ [T] *He picked the book up again and plowed his way through two more chapters.*
INVEST /plɑʊ/ *v* [T always + adv/prep] to invest money in a business to make it successful ○ *If we're hit by higher taxes, we'll have a little less to plow back into the business.*

ploy /plɔɪ/ *n* [C] something that is done or said, often dishonestly, in order to get an advantage; a trick ○ *a marketing ploy*

pluck REMOVE /plʌk/ *v* [T] **1** to remove something, esp. with a sudden movement ○ *Astronauts plan to use the shuttle's robot arm to pluck the satellite out of space.* **2** If you pluck something, you remove hair or feathers from it by pulling: *She plucked her eyebrows.* ○ *I don't think I could pluck a chicken.*
BRAVERY /plʌk/ *n* [U] bravery and a strong desire to succeed ○ *Her 80-plus years have not dulled her pluck.*
plucky /ˈplʌk·i/ *adj* brave ○ *Terriers are plucky little dogs with independent spirits and reckless courage.*

PULL AT /plʌk/ *v* [I/T] to pull at something with your fingers and then release it ○ [T] *Jenkins's idea of swinging is plucking violins.* ○ [I] (*fig.*) *Her stories are designed to pluck at your heartstrings.*

plug **ELECTRICAL DEVICE** /plʌg/ *n* [C] **1** a small plastic or rubber device with metal pins that connects the end of a wire on a piece of electrical equipment to a supply of electricity **2** A plug is also a SPARK PLUG.

plug /plʌg/ *v* [I/T] **-gg-** ○ [M] *All you have to do is plug in the computer.* ○ [T] *I'd like to plug the stereo into that outlet.* ○ [I] *These systems plug into TV sets and run games.*

HOLE BLOCK /plʌg/ *n* [C] a small piece of esp. rubber or plastic that fits into a hole in order to block it ○ *I was trying to fill the bathtub, but Matthew kept pulling out the plug.*

plug /plʌg/ *v* [T] **-gg-** ○ *Workers finished plugging the hole in the dam.*

ADVERTISE /plʌg/ *v* [T] **-gg-** to advertise something by talking about it or praising it, esp. on television or radio

plug /plʌg/ *n* [C] ○ *He took the opportunity to put in a plug for his new book.*

PHRASAL VERB with **plug**

• **plug away** to keep working hard in a determined way, esp. at something that you find difficult ○ *She's been plugging away at that novel for years.*

plug-in *n* [C] a small device or computer program that is designed to be used with and fits into a larger one

plum **FRUIT** /plʌm/ *n* [C] a small, round fruit with a smooth, usually red-purple skin, sweet flesh, and a single large seed

SOMETHING GOOD /plʌm/ *n* [C] something that is very good and worth having

plum /plʌm/ *adj* [not gradable] ○ *Senior staff members get all the plum assignments.*

plumbing /ˈplʌm·ɪŋ/ *n* [U] the system of pipes and other devices that carry water in a building ○ *bathroom plumbing*

plumber /ˈplʌm·ər/ *n* [C] someone whose job is to supply, connect, and repair water pipes and devices

plume /pluːm/ *n* [C] **1** a long, large feather ○ *She wore a hat with a tall white plume.* **2** A plume of something like smoke, steam, or dust is a long mass of it that rises up into the sky: *A black plume of smoke rose from the ship.*

plumage /ˈpluː·mɪdʒ/ *n* [U] the feathers that cover a bird ○ *a parrot with bright plumage*

plummet /ˈplʌm·ət/ *v* [I] to fall very quickly and suddenly ○ *Temperatures plummeted last night.* ○ *The parachute failed to open and he plummeted to the ground.*

plump /plʌmp/ *adj* [-*er*/-*est* only] having a soft, rounded shape; slightly fat ○ *plump hands* ○ *a plump, middle-aged woman* ○ *The berries are plump and juicy.*

plump /plʌmp/ *v* [T] ○ *The nurse plumped the pillows* (= shook them to make them bigger and softer).

PHRASAL VERB with **plump**

• **plump for** *something/someone* *infml* to support something or someone enthusiastically ○ *Marcy had been writing campaign speeches and plumping for McCarthy since December.*

plunder /ˈplʌn·dər/ *v* [I/T] to steal goods forcefully from a place, esp. during a war ○ [I] *After the battle the soldiers began looting and plundering.* ○ [T] (*fig.*) *He plundered* (= took from) *his ballet scores in writing his later operas.*

plunder /ˈplʌn·dər/ *n* [U] ○ *We met after school and divided our plunder so each boy would have about the same amount.*

plunge /plʌndʒ/ *v* [I/T] **1** to move or fall suddenly forward, down, or into something ○ [I] *Her car plunged off the cliff.* ○ [I] *He plunged into the crowd, smiling and shaking hands.* ○ [T always + adv/prep] *She suddenly plunged the knife into the cake.* **2** If a value or price plunges, it suddenly becomes less: [I] *Rumors on Wall Street have caused stock prices to plunge.* **3** If a person or group plunges into an activity, or a place plunges into a condition, it suddenly experiences it: [I always + adv/prep] *The economy was in danger of plunging into a depression.* ○ [T always + adv/prep] *The storm cut power lines, plunging the town into darkness.*

plunge /plʌndʒ/ *n* [C] ○ *A tree broke his plunge downhill.* ○ *The rapid plunge of the stock market caused panic among investors.*

plunger /ˈplʌn·dʒər/ *n* [C] a device consisting of a cup-shaped piece of rubber on the end of a stick, used to remove substances blocking a pipe, esp. in a kitchen or bathroom

plunk **PUT** /plʌŋk/ *v* [T always + adv/prep] **1** to put something down heavily or suddenly ○ [M] *She plunked the trashcan down in the driveway.* **2** If you plunk money down, you pay it: [M] *She plunked down most of her savings to buy the house.*

SOUND /plʌŋk/ *n* [U] a sound like that made when a hollow object is dropped ○ *The stone dropped in the lake with a satisfying plunk.*

pluperfect /pluːˈpɜr·fɪkt/ *n, adj* ***grammar*** the PAST PERFECT

plural /ˈplʊr·əl/ *adj* [not gradable] ***grammar*** being the form of a word used to talk about more than one thing ○ *a plural verb* ○ *"Cats" and "cattle" are plural nouns.* ○ Compare SINGULAR GRAMMAR

plural /ˈplʊr·əl/ *n* [C/U] ***grammar*** ○ [U] *"Geese" is the plural of "goose."*

pluralize /ˈplʊr·əˌlɑɪz/ *v* [T] ***grammar*** to make a word plural in form ○ *Certain nouns, such as "information," cannot be pluralized.*

pluralism /ˈplʊr·əˌlɪz·əm/ *n* [U] ***social studies*** the existence of people of different races, religious beliefs, and cultures within the same society, or the belief that this is a good thing ○ *religious pluralism* ○ *political pluralism*

pluralistic /ˌplʊr·əˈlɪs·tɪk/, **pluralist** /ˈplʊr·ə·ləst/ *adj* ***social studies*** ○ *the pluralistic American system*

plurality /plʊˈræl·ət̬·i/ *n* [C/U] ***social studies*** (in elections involving three or more people) the difference between the number of votes received by the person who won and the number received by the person who is second, or a number of votes or places in a legislature that is more than any other party has but less than half the total number ○ [C] *Jenson won by a plurality of 2000 votes over her nearest rival.*

plus Ⓐ **ADDITION** /plʌs/, *symbol* + *prep* added to, or and in addition ○ *Six plus four is ten.* ○ *That will be $16.99, plus tax.*
plus Ⓐ /plʌs/, *symbol* + *adj* [not gradable] **1** *They earn $100 an hour, plus or minus 10%.* ○ *Those cars cost $30,000 plus* (= more than that amount). **2** A mark such as B-plus (B+) or C-plus (C+) given to a student's work means that the work is slightly better than if it were given the B or C mark.
plus Ⓐ /plʌs/ *conjunction* and also ○ *The four of us, plus my son's girlfriend, went out to dinner.*
ADVANTAGE /plʌs/ *n* [C] *pl* **pluses, plusses** an advantage or a good feature ○ *Your teaching experience will be a plus in this job.*

plush COMFORTABLE /plʌʃ/ *adj* [-er/-est only] expensive, comfortable, and of high quality ○ *a plush hotel room*
CLOTH /plʌʃ/ *n* [U] thick, soft cloth, with a surface like short fur, that is used esp. for covering furniture

plus sign *n* [C] *infml* an ADDITION SIGN

Pluto /ˈpluːt̬·oʊ/ *n* [U] a large, round mass of matter ninth in order of distance from the sun, after Neptune, considered in the past to be a planet

plutonium /pluːˈtoʊ·niː·əm/ *n* [U] a metal that is used esp. as a fuel in the production of nuclear power, and in nuclear weapons

ply LAYER /plɑɪ/ *n* [U] a layer of something such as wood or paper, or a thread that is wrapped with other threads to form YARN (= wool cord) or rope ○ *two-ply facial tissue*
WORK /plɑɪ/ *v* [T] to work at something regularly ○ *New buses plied the city's bus routes this week.*
TRAVEL /plɑɪ/ *v* [I/T] to travel over distances regularly by boat or other form of transport ○ [T] *Large numbers of vessels plied the waters between New York and Cape Hatteras.*

PHRASAL VERB with **ply**

• **ply** *someone* **with** *something* **1** to give large amounts of something to someone ○ *We were plied with coffee, doughnuts, and refreshments.* **2** If you ply someone with questions, you ask that person many questions: *Anxious to hear firsthand the latest about the outside world, they plied us with questions.*

plywood /ˈplɑɪ·wʊd/ *n* [U] wood in sheets that is made of several thin layers glued together ○ *plywood bookshelves*

p.m., P.M. /piːˈem/ *adv* [not gradable] used when referring to a time between twelve o'clock in the middle of the day and twelve o'clock at night; in the afternoon or evening or at night ○ *Our plane is due to arrive at 8:30 p.m.* ○ Compare A.M.

PMS *n* [U] *abbreviation for* PREMENSTRUAL SYNDROME

pneumatic /nʊˈmæt̬·ɪk/ *adj* [not gradable] operated by air pressure, or containing air ○ *pneumatic tires*

pneumatic drill *n* [C] a JACKHAMMER

pneumonia /nʊˈmoʊn·jə/ *n* [U] a serious illness in which one or both lungs become red and swollen and filled with liquid ○ *The patient died of pneumonia.*

P.O. *n* [U] *abbreviation for* POST OFFICE

poach COOK /poʊtʃ/ *v* [T] to cook something in water or another liquid that is almost boiling ○ *poached eggs*
TAKE ILLEGALLY /poʊtʃ/ *v* [I/T] to catch or kill an animal without permission on someone else's property, or to kill animals illegally to get valuable parts of them ○ [T] *Anybody you see with a piece of ivory has poached it.* ○ [I] *Foreign fishing boats were caught poaching offshore.*
poacher /ˈpoʊ·tʃər/ *n* [C]

P.O. Box *n* [C] a POST OFFICE BOX

pocket BAG /ˈpɑk·ət/ *n* [C] **1** a small bag, usually made of cloth, sewn on the inside or outside of a piece of clothing and used to hold small objects ○ *coat/pants/shirt pockets* ○ *She took her keys out of her pocket.* ○ *I paid for my ticket out of my own pocket* (= with my own money). **2** A pocket is also a small container that is part of or attached to something else: *The map is in the pocket on the car door.* **3** In the game of POOL, the pockets are the holes around the edge of the table into which the balls are hit.
pocket /ˈpɑk·ət/ *v* [T] to put something in your pocket, or (fig.) to take money esp. when it has been obtained unfairly or illegally ○ *He pocketed his change.* ○ *(fig.) Some sold nonexistent land and pocketed all the cash.*
pocket /ˈpɑk·ət/ *adj* [not gradable] small enough to be kept in a pocket ○ *a pocket diary* ○ *a pocket watch*
pocketful /ˈpɑk·ətˌfʊl/ *n* [C] ○ *a pocketful of coins*
PART /ˈpɑk·ət/ *n* [C] a small part of something larger that is considered separate because of a particular quality ○ *It remained a pocket of poverty within a generally affluent area.*

pocketbook /ˈpɑk·ətˌbʊk/, **bag, handbag, purse** *n* [C] **1** a bag, often with a handle or a strap going over the shoulder, used esp. by women for carrying money and small items such as keys ○ *I have a map in my pocketbook.* **2** Someone's pocketbook is that person's finances or ability to pay for something: *The sales tax hits consumers in the pocketbook.*

pocketknife /ˈpɑk·ətˌnɑɪf/ *n* [C] a small knife with one or more blades that can be folded into its handle

pocket money *n* [U] a small amount of money for small expenses

pocket-size, pocket-sized *adj* small enough to fit in a pocket ○ *a pocket-size book*

pocket veto *n* [C] ***social studies*** an indirect VETO (= refusal) of a new law by leaving it unsigned until the legislature has finished its work

pockmark /ˈpɑk·mɑrk/ *n* [C] a small hollow on the skin caused by a disease
pockmarked /ˈpɑk·mɑrkt/ *adj* **1** *a pockmarked face* **2** A surface that is pockmarked has a lot of hollows in it: *a pockmarked wall*

pod /pɑd/ *n* [C] a long seed container that grows on some plants ○ *a pea/bean pod*

podcast /ˈpɑd·kæst/ *n* [C] a broadcast that is placed on the INTERNET for anyone who wants to listen to it or watch it ○ *Some radio stations already are posting their talk shows on websites to reach podcast audiences.*
podcasting /ˈpɑdˌkæs·tɪŋ/ *n* [U] ○ *Podcasting represents the next wave of do-it-yourself peer-to-peer broadcasting.*

podiatrist /pəˈdɑɪ·ə·trəst/ *n* [C] a person trained in the treatment of problems and diseases of people's feet
podiatry /pəˈdɑɪ·ə·tri/ *n* [U]

podium /ˈpoʊd·iː·əm/ *n* [C] **1** a small, low box or stage that someone stands on in order to be seen by a group of people, esp. to speak or CONDUCT music ○ *The conductor mounted the podium.* **2** A podium is also a LECTERN.

poem /ˈpoʊ·əm, ˈpɔː·ɪm/ *n* [C] ***literature*** a piece of writing in which the words are carefully chosen for the images and ideas they suggest, and in which the sounds of the words when read aloud often follow a particular rhythmic pattern

WORD FAMILY poem			
Nouns	poem poet poetry	*Adjectives*	poetic

poet /ˈpoʊ·ət/ *n* [C] ***literature*** someone who writes poems
poetic /poʊˈeţ·ɪk/ *adj* ***literature*** of or suggesting poets or poems ○ *poetic language*
poetry /ˈpoʊ·ə·tri/ *n* [U] ***literature*** poems, esp. as a form of literature ○ *the poetry of John Donne* ○ Compare PROSE

poetic justice /poʊˌeţ·ɪk ˈdʒʌs·təs/ *n* [U] a punishment or a reward that you feel is just, esp. when it is unexpected or unusual

poetic license *n* [U] changes by a writer to facts or rules of good writing to make the work more interesting or effective

pogrom /pəˈgrɑm, -ˈgrʌm; ˈpoʊ·grəm/ *n* [C] ***world history*** organized killing of a large group of people, esp. Jews, because of their religion or race

poignant /ˈpɔɪn·jənt/ *adj* causing a feeling of sadness ○ *The monument is a poignant reminder of those who died in the war.*
poignantly /ˈpɔɪn·jənt·li/ *adv*

poinsettia /ˌpɔɪnˈseţ·ə, -ˈseţ·iː·ə/ *n* [C] a Central American plant with groups of bright red leaves that look like flowers

point SHARP END /pɔɪnt/ *n* [C] **1** the sharp or narrow end of something, such as a knife or pin ○ *I stuck myself with the point of the needle.* **2** A point is also a narrow piece of land that stretches out into the sea.
pointed /ˈpɔɪnt·əd/ *adj* ○ *a pointed arch* ○ See also: POINTED
pointy /ˈpɔɪnt·i/ *adj* [-er/-est only] ○ *pointy shoes*

SHOW /pɔɪnt/ *v* [I/T] **1** to direct other people's attention to something by signaling toward it with your finger ○ [I] *"Look," she said, pointing at the sign.* ○ [M] *Which one is your sister – would you point her out to me?* **2** If something points in a particular direction, it is turned toward that direction: [I] *The arrow points left.*
pointer /ˈpɔɪnt·ər/ *n* [C] **1** any of various things used for pointing, esp. a long, thin stick ○ *The lecturer used a pointer to show what part or the diagram he was referring to.* **2** A pointer is also a helpful piece of advice or information: *The booklet gives some useful pointers for getting around in Washington.*

IDEA EXPRESSED /pɔɪnt/ *n* [C] **1** an idea, opinion, or piece of information that is said or written ○ *He made some good points in his speech.* ○ *The lawyers reviewed the issues point by point.* ○ *You have a point* (= What you say is reasonable). **2** The point is the main or most important idea: *He doesn't have much money, but that's not the point.*

POSITION /pɔɪnt/ ***geometry*** an exact position in space that has no size and is usually represented by a small, round mark

CHARACTERISTIC /pɔɪnt/ *n* [C] a particular quality or characteristic ○ *Truthfulness is not one of his strong points.*

TIME OR PLACE /pɔɪnt/ *n* [C] a particular time, place, or stage reached in a process ○ *She felt that they were at a critical point in their marriage.*

ADVANTAGE /pɔɪnt/ *n* [U] purpose or usefulness ○ *What's the point of leaving at six in the morning?*
pointless /ˈpɔɪnt·ləs/ *adj* having no useful purpose ○ *a pointless argument* ○ *The trip seemed pointless.*

UNIT /pɔɪnt/ *n* [C] a unit for measuring or counting ○ *Our team won by seven points.* ○ *Interest rates dropped two percentage points.*

POSITION /pɔɪnt/ *n* [C] an exact position, or a small mark showing an exact position ○ *Find the point in the map where Broadway intersects 15th Street.*

WORD FAMILY point			
Nouns	point pointer	*Verbs*	point
		Adverbs	pointlessly pointedly
Adjectives	pointy pointed pointless		

IDIOMS with point

• **point the finger at** *someone* to say that someone should be blamed ○ *I just tried to do what was right, and now everyone's pointing the finger at me.*

• **point the way (to** *something***)** to be among the first to show how something can be done ○ *The new research points the way to the development of better vaccines.*

P

PHRASAL VERBS with point

•**point out** *something* [M] to direct attention toward something ○ *Angela pointed out some spelling errors in my paper.*

•**point up** *something* to make something clearer; show ○ *The program teaches tolerance but also points up cultural similarities.*

point-blank /ˈpɔɪnt ˈblæŋk/ *adv* [not gradable] aimed or fired directly at from a close position ○ *He was shot in the back, point-blank.* ○ *(fig.) He asked me point-blank* (= directly) *if I was lying.*

point charge *n* [C] ***physics*** a point in space that has an electrical CHARGE that exists only in theory and that cannot be measured

pointed /ˈpɔɪnt·əd/ *adj* intending criticism ○ *He made a pointed remark about her unwillingness to volunteer.* ○ See also: POINTED at POINT SHARP END

pointedly /ˈpɔɪnt·əd·li/ *adv* in an obvious and intentional way ○ *She pointedly ignored him.*

pointer /ˈpɔɪnt·ər/ *n* ○ See at POINT SHOW

pointless /ˈpɔɪnt·ləs/ *adj* ○ See at POINT ADVANTAGE

point of no return *n* [C usually sing] the stage in a process when it is too late to change what you are doing so that you must continue ○ *Once the contract is signed, we've reached the point of no return.*

point of view, **viewpoint** *n* [C] **1** a person's opinion or particular way of thinking about something ○ *We're interested in hearing all points of view.* **2** ***literature*** Point of view is also the voice in which a story is told and its relationship to the events in the story. **3** ***art*** In a painting or photograph, the point of view is the place where the artist chooses to stand and what this tells you about the subject.

P

pointy /ˈpɔɪnt·i/ *adj* ○ See at POINT SHARP END

poise /pɔɪz/ *n* [U] behavior or a way of moving that shows calm confidence ○ *"I think it was a credit to our team that we kept our poise," the coach said, "even when we were down by 21 points."*

poised /pɔɪzd/ *adj* ○ *Angela is a polite, poised young woman.*

poised /pɔɪzd/ *adj* [not gradable] ready to move, or prepared and waiting for something to happen ○ *The lion was poised to strike.*

poison SUBSTANCE /ˈpɔɪ·zən/ *n* [C/U] a substance that causes illness or death if swallowed, absorbed, or breathed into the body ○ [U] *poison gas* ○ [C] *Some cleaning products are poisons.* ○ [U] *He sprayed the weeds with poison.*

poison /ˈpɔɪ·zən/ *v* [T] to cause a person or animal to take in poison, or to add poison to food or a liquid ○ *He thinks someone is trying to poison him.* ○ *Her tea was poisoned.*

poisonous /ˈpɔɪ·zə·nəs/ *adj* ○ *The mushrooms they picked were poisonous.*

CAUSE HARM /ˈpɔɪ·zən/ *v* [T] to cause serious harm to something ○ *Jealousy poisoned our relationship.* ○ *I don't see why you think TV poisons people's minds* (= influences them in a bad way).

poison /ˈpɔɪ·zən/ *n* [U] ○ *the poison of hatred*

poison ivy *n* [U] a North American plant that can cause your skin to become red and ITCH if the leaves touch you

poke PUSH /poʊk/ *v* [I/T] to push a finger or other object into someone or something, or to push something through or past someone or something ○ [T] *Quit poking me to move ahead – there are people in front of me.* ○ [T] *Josie poked her head around the corner to see what made the noise.*

poke /poʊk/ *n* [C] ○ *He gave his brother a poke in the arm.*

INVOLVE /poʊk/ *v* [I always + adv/prep] to involve yourself or take part in (something) that is not your responsibility or does not involve you ○ *He's always poking into other people's business.*

IDIOM with poke

•**poke fun at** *someone/something* to make someone or something seem ridiculous by making jokes about the person or thing ○ *Late night comedy shows often poke fun at politicians.*

PHRASAL VERB with poke

•**poke around/about** to search through something, esp. without permission or without any particular idea of what you might find ○ *He loves going to auctions and poking around antique shops.*

poker GAME /ˈpoʊ·kər/ *n* [U] a game played with cards in which people try to win money from each other

TOOL /ˈpoʊ·kər/ *n* [C] a long, metal pole that you can stick in a fire to move wood or coal so that it will burn better

poker face *n* [C] an expression on someone's face that does not show what the person is thinking or feeling

poker-faced *adj, adv* ○ *He stared at us poker-faced.*

polar bear *n* [C] a large, white bear that lives in the cold regions of the north

Polaris /pəˈler·əs, -ˈlɑr-, -ˈlær-/ *n* [U] ***earth science*** the bright star almost directly above the North Pole

polarize DIVIDE OPINIONS /ˈpoʊ·ləˌrɑɪz/ *v* [I/T] to cause people in a group to have opposing positions ○ [T] *The property tax issue polarized the city council.*

LIGHT /ˈpoʊ·ləˌrɑɪz/ *v* [T] ***physics*** to cause light to travel in a particular pattern, rather than going in all directions at once

polarization /ˌpoʊ·lə·rəˈzeɪ·ʃən/ *n* [U]

Polaroid /ˈpoʊ·ləˌrɔɪd/ *n* [C] *trademark* a camera that takes a picture and prints it after a few seconds, or a photograph taken with this type of camera

pole STICK /poʊl/ *n* [C] a long, usually round, piece of wood or metal, often used to support something ○ *a telephone pole* ○ *a tent pole*

PLACE /poʊl/ *n* [C] either of the two points at the most northern and most southern ends of the earth or another planet, around which the planet turns ○ *the North/South Pole*

polar /ˈpoʊ·lər/ *adj* [not gradable] of or near the area around the most northern or most southern points of the earth ○ *the polar ice cap* ○ *a polar expedition*

ELECTRICITY /poʊl/ *n* [C] either of the two ends of a magnet or two parts of a BATTERY (= device that produces electricity) which have opposite CHARGES

polar /ˈpoʊ·lər/ *adj* **1** (*fig.*) *The play's main characters are polar opposites* (= They are completely opposite). **2** ***chemistry*** Polar also describes a substance whose MOLECULES have opposite positive and negative poles

polarity /poʊˈlær·əţ·i/ *n* [U] ***physics*** the quality in an object that produces opposite magnetic or electric charges

polemic /pəˈlem·ɪk/ *n* [C] *fml* a piece of writing or a speech in which a person argues forcefully for or against someone or something

polemical /pəˈlem·ɪ·kəl/ *adj fml* ○ *a series of polemical essays*

pole vault *n* [U] a sports competition in which you hold a long, stiff pole near one end and force it to bend so that when it straightens, it pushes you up over a high bar

police /pəˈliːs/ *pl n* an official force whose job is to maintain public order, deal with crime, and make people obey the law, or the members of this force ○ *I think you should call the police.* ○ *Police arrested two people in connection with the robbery.*

police /pəˈliːs/ *v* [T] to control or maintain order, esp. with police ○ *Security forces policed the border.* ○ *It's up to the government to police the financial markets.*

police department *n* [C] an organization of police in a city, region, or state

police force *n* [C] the group of people who are employed as police in a city, region, or state

police officer, *male* **policeman** /pəˈliː·smən/, *female* **policewoman** /pəˈliːˌswʊm·ən/ *n* [C] *pl* **policemen**, *pl* **policewomen** a member of the police force

police state *n* [C] *disapproving* a country controlled by the government police

police station *n* [C] the office of the local police force

policy Ⓐ **PLAN** /ˈpɑl·ə·si/ *n* [C] a set of ideas or a plan for action followed by a business, a government, a political party, or a group of people ○ *The White House said there will be no change in policy.*

DOCUMENT /ˈpɑl·ə·si/ *n* [C] a document showing an agreement you have made with an INSURANCE company ○ *a life-insurance policy*

policyholder /ˈpɑl·ə·siːˌhoʊl·dər/ *n* [C] a person who owns INSURANCE for a car, home, life, etc. ○ *Each of the company's 12 million policyholders will see premium increases of about 6%.*

policymaker, **policy-maker** /ˈpɑl·ə·siːˌmeɪ·kər/ *n* [C] a member of a government department, legislature, or other organization who is responsible for making new rules, laws, etc. ○ *U.S. policymakers are forced to make hard choices between national security and domestic priorities.*

policymaking, **policy-making** /ˈpɑl·ə·siːˌmeɪ·kɪŋ/ *n* [U] ○ *The Bundesbank said Thursday its policy-making council left the German discount rate unchanged.*

polio /ˈpoʊ·liːˌoʊ/, *medical* **poliomyelitis** /ˌpoʊ·liː·oʊˌmɑɪ·əˈlɑɪţ·əs/ *n* [U] a serious, infectious disease of the nerves of the SPINE (= row of bones in the back) that can cause temporary or permanent PARALYSIS (= inability to move the body)

polis /ˈpɑl·əs/ *n* [C] *pl* **poleis** ***world history*** a city-state in ancient Greece

polish /ˈpɑl·ɪʃ/ *v* [T] **1** to make something smooth and shiny by rubbing ○ *He polished the hardwood floor.* **2** If you polish your nails, you paint them with a colored or colorless liquid to make them shine.

polish /ˈpɑl·ɪʃ/ *n* [U] **1** *I'll just give my shoes a quick polish.* **2** Polish is a cream or other substance that you use to clean or shine something: *shoe/furniture/silver polish* **3** Someone or something with polish has great skill or perfect style: *The rest of the cast comes nowhere near equaling his polish onstage.*

polished /ˈpɑl·ɪʃt/ *adj* [not gradable] **1** *highly polished furniture* **2** Someone who is polished is polite, graceful, and stylish: *He's suave, polished, and charming.* **3** Something that is polished shows great skill: *a polished performance*

PHRASAL VERBS with polish

• **polish off** *something* [M] *infml* to finish something quickly and easily ○ *He polished off two burgers and a mountain of French fries.*

• **polish up** *something* [M] to improve something ○ *I write a rough draft on the computer and then polish it up a bit.*

polite /pəˈlɑɪt/ *adj* behaving in a way that is socially correct and shows respect for other people's feelings ○ *She was too polite to point out my mistake.*

politely /pəˈlɑɪt·li/ *adv* ○ *He politely asked them to leave.*

politeness /pəˈlɑɪt·nəs/ *n* [U] ○ *With unfailing politeness he answered their questions.*

WORD FAMILY polite

Nouns	politeness	*Adverbs*	politely impolitely
Adjectives	polite impolite		

WORD CHOICES polite

The adjectives **courteous**, **respectful**, and **well-mannered** are sometimes used when someone is polite and shows respect for other people.

*Although she often disagreed with me, she was always **courteous**.*

*They were quiet, **well-mannered** children.*

A man who is polite to a woman is sometimes described as **chivalrous**. ➤

*He held open the door in that **chivalrous** way of his.*

Someone who is polite but in a formal and not very friendly way can be described as **civil**.

*Try to at least be **civil** toward him even if you don't like him.*

Conversation which is polite and calm is sometimes described as **civilized**.

*Let's discuss this in a **civilized** manner.*

politic /ˈpɑl·əˌtɪk/ *adj* wise or practical ○ *It would not be politic for you to be seen there.*

political /pəˈlɪt̬·ɪ·kəl/ *adj* [not gradable] ***politics & government*** relating to politics ○ *political parties* ○ *a political speech* ○ *Free trade is an ongoing political issue because it affects local employment rates.*

politically /pəˈlɪt̬·ɪ·kli/ *adv* [not gradable] ***politics & government*** ○ *They encourage young people to become more politically active.*

political action committee, *abbreviation* **PAC** *n* [C] an organization that gives money and support to politicians in order to influence them

politically correct, *abbreviation* **PC** *adj disapproving* avoiding language or behavior that any particular group of people might feel is unkind or offensive ○ *The politically correct term "firefighter" is used instead of "fireman."*

political prisoner *n* [C] a person who has been put in prison for criticizing the government

political science *n* [U] the study of government and political systems

politics /ˈpɑl·əˌtɪks/ *n* ***politics & government*** **1** the activities of the government, politicians, or political parties, or the study of these activities ○ [U] *She got involved in local politics.* **2** A person's politics are that person's opinions about how a country should be governed: [pl] *His politics are becoming increasingly liberal.* **3** Politics are also the activities of people who are trying to obtain an advantage within a group or organization: [pl] *I don't like to get involved in office politics.*

politician /ˌpɑl·əˈtɪʃ·ən/ *n* [C] ***politics & government*** a person who is active in politics, esp. as a job

politicize /pəˈlɪt̬·əˌsɑɪz/ *v* [T] ***politics & government*** to make an organization, individual, or activity political or more aware of political matters ○ *Law enforcement should not be politicized.*

WORD FAMILY politics

Nouns	politician politics	*Adjectives*	political apolitical politicized
Verbs	politicize	*Adverbs*	politically

polka /ˈpoʊl·kə, ˈpoʊ-/ *n* [C] a fast, active dance from eastern Europe, or a piece of music for this dance

polka dot /ˈpoʊ·kəˌdɑt/ *n* [C usually pl] one of many round spots that form a pattern on cloth ○ *a polka-dot bow tie*

poll OPINION /poʊl/ *n* [C] a study of a group's opinion on a subject, in which people are questioned and their answers examined ○ *an opinion poll* ○ *We took a poll this week.*

poll /poʊl/ *v* [T] ○ *Almost 86% of the parents polled said yes, and only 7% said no.*

RECEIVE VOTES /poʊl/ *v* [T] to receive a particular number of votes in an election ○ *Bob Friedman polled 67% of the vote.*

polls /poʊlz/ *pl n* the places where people vote in a political election ○ *The polls close in an hour.*

pollen /ˈpɑl·ən/ *n* [U] ***biology*** a powder produced by the male part of a flower that causes the female part of other flowers of the same type to produce seeds

pollen count *n* [C] a measurement how much POLLEN is in the air in a particular place or on a particular day

pollinate /ˈpɑl·əˌneɪt/ *v* [T] ***biology*** to carry POLLEN from a male part of a flower to the female part of another flower of the same type

pollination /ˌpɑl·əˈneɪ·ʃən/ *n* [U]

pollster /ˈpoʊl·stər/ *n* [C] a person whose job is to ask people their opinions on a subject, as part of a POLL (= opinion study)

poll tax *n* [C] ***social studies*** a tax of a set amount that must be paid by each adult, esp. in order to vote

pollute /pəˈluːt/ *v* [T] to make air, water, or earth dirty or harmful to people, animals, and plants, esp. by adding harmful chemicals or waste ○ *Chemical fertilizers and pesticides are polluting the groundwater.*

pollutant /pəˈluːt·ənt/ *n* [C] ○ *Maybe there's some kind of chemical pollutant in their drinking water.*

polluter /pəˈluːt̬·ər/ *n* [C] a person or organization that pollutes

pollution /pəˈluː·ʃən/ *n* [U] the act of polluting, or the substances that pollute ○ *air pollution* ○ *Pollution from the factory could be contaminating nearby wells.*

polo /ˈpoʊ·loʊ/ *n* [U] a game in which players riding horses use wooden hammers with long handles to hit a ball into the opposing team's goal

polo shirt /ˈpoʊ·loʊˌʃɜrt/ *n* [C] a shirt with short sleeves, a collar, and some buttons at the neck

polyatomic /ˌpɑl·iː·əˈtɑm·ɪk/ *adj* [not gradable] ***physics, chemistry*** containing more than two atoms

polychromatic /ˌpɑl·iː·kroʊˈmæt̬·ɪk/ *adj* ***physics*** involving or producing light in all colors

polyester /ˌpɑl·iːˈes·tər/ *n* [U] a cloth made from artificial substances ○ *polyester pants*

polygamy /pəˈlɪg·ə·mi/ *n* [U] the custom or condition of being married to more than one person at the same time ○ Compare MONOGAMY

polygon /ˈpɑl·ɪˌgɑn/ *n* [C] ***geometry*** a flat shape with three or more straight sides ○ *Triangles and squares are polygons.*

polygonal /pə·ˈlig·ə·nᵊl/ *n* [C] ***geometry***

polygraph /ˈpɑl·ɪˌgræf/ *n* [C] *fml* a LIE DETECTOR

polyhedron /ˌpɑl·iːˈhiː·drən/ *n* [C] *pl* **polyhedrons, polyhedra** ***geometry*** a solid shape with four or more flat surfaces

polymer /ˈpɑl·ə·mər/ *n* [C] ***chemistry*** a natural or artificial substance made from many smaller MOLECULES (= groups of combined atoms)

polymerization /pəˌlɪm·ə·rəˈzeɪ·ʃən, ˌpɑl·ə·mə·rə-/ *n* [U] ***chemistry*** a chemical reaction in which many small molecules join to make a polymer

polynomial /ˌpɑl·əˈnoʊ·miː·əl/ *n* [C] ***algebra*** a number or VARIABLE (= mathematical symbol), or the result of adding or subtracting two or more numbers or variables

polyp /ˈpɑl·əp/ *n* [C] a small mass of tissue that grows in the body

polysaccharide /ˌpɑl·iːˈsæk·əˌrɑɪd/ *n* [U] ***biology*** a type of CARBOHYDRATE (= substance that provides energy), whose MOLECULES (= smallest units of a substance) are groups of sugar molecules joined together

polytechnic /ˌpɑl·əˈtek·nɪk/ *n* [C] a college where students study scientific and technical subjects ○ Compare UNIVERSITY

polytheism /ˌpɑl·ɪˈθiːˌɪz·əm/ *n* [U] the belief in or worship of more than one god

polyunsaturated fat /ˌpɑl·iːˌʌnˈsætʃ·əˌreɪṭ·əd/ *n* [C] a fat or oil with a chemical structure that does not easily change into CHOLESTEROL (= a fatty substance that can cause heart disease) in the blood

pomegranate /ˈpɑm·əˌgræn·ət, ˈpʌmˌgræn-/ *n* [C] a round, thick-skinned fruit with a center full of large, juicy, edible seeds

pomp /pɑmp/ *n* [U] showy, formal ceremony, esp. on public occasions ○ *Pomp and pageantry accompanied the royal couple on their state visit.*

pompom /ˈpɑm·pɑm/, **pompon** /ˈpɑm·pɑn/ *n* [C] a small ball of loose strings or pieces of YARN used as a decoration, esp. on the top of a hat, or a ball of loose strips of paper or plastic waved at sports events

pompous /ˈpɑm·pəs/ *adj disapproving* feeling or showing that you think you are better or more important than other people ○ *I regarded him as somewhat pompous and opinionated.*

pomposity /pɑmˈpɑs·əṭ·i/, **pompousness** /ˈpɑm·pə·snəs/ *n* [U] *disapproving* ○ *the pomposity of New York society*

poncho /ˈpɑn·tʃoʊ/ *n* [C] *pl* **ponchos** an outer piece of clothing without sleeves which hangs from your shoulders, made of a large piece of material with a hole in the middle for your head

pond /pɑnd/ *n* [C] a still area of water smaller than a lake, often artificially made

ponder /ˈpɑn·dər/ *v* [I/T] to consider something carefully for a long time ○ [T] *She ponders the reaction she'll receive.* ○ [I] *The back porch is a quiet place where I can ponder.*

ponderous /ˈpɑn·də·rəs/ *adj* slow and awkward because of being very heavy or large, or (esp. of speech or writing) boring and difficult ○ *a ponderous pace* ○ *ponderous dialogue*

pontiff /ˈpɑnt·əf/ *n* [C] a POPE (= leader of the Roman Catholic Church)

pontificate /pɑnˈtɪf·ɪˌkeɪt/ *v* [I] to speak in an important manner as if only your opinion was correct ○ *Experts get on the tube and pontificate about the economy.*

pontoon /pɑnˈtuːn/ *n* [C] a small, flat boat or similarly shaped metal structure used esp. to form or support a temporary floating bridge

pony /ˈpoʊ·ni/ *n* [C] a small type of horse

pony express *n* [U] a system for carrying mail using horses and riders, which existed in the American West in the 1800s

ponytail /ˈpoʊ·niːˌteɪl/ *n* [C] a hairstyle in which the hair is gathered and fastened at the back of the head so that it hangs down loosely

pooch /puːtʃ/ *n* [C] *infml* a dog

poodle /ˈpuːd·ᵊl/ *n* [C] a type of dog with curly hair that is usually cut only on parts of its body

pool LIQUID /puːl/ *n* [C] **1** a small area of usually still water, or a small amount of liquid ○ *pools of water in the gutter* ○ *a pool of blood* **2** A pool is also a SWIMMING POOL.

COLLECTION /puːl/ *n* [C] **1** an amount of money or a number of people or things collected together for shared use by several people or organizations ○ *Their profits get plowed back into a pool to pay subscribers' claims.* **2** A pool is also the total amount of money risked by people on the result of a card game or sports event: *an office Super Bowl pool*

pool /puːl/ *v* [T] ○ *The kids pooled their money to buy their parents plane tickets.*

GAME /puːl/ *n* [U] a game played by two or more people in which a CUE (= long, round stick) is used to hit a white ball against other balls in order to roll them into one of six holes around the edge of a special table ○ *a pool table*

poop /puːp/ *n* [U] *infml* excrement

poop /puːp/ *v* [I] *infml*

poop out /ˈpuːpˈɑʊt/ *v* [I] *infml* to become very tired ○ *I just poop out if I stay up too late.*

pooped /puːpt/ *adj infml* very tired ○ *Students are pooped because they're juggling classes, studying, and jobs.*

pooper-scooper /ˈpuː·pərˈskuː·pər/ *n* [C] a small tool used for picking up dog excrement from public places

poor NO MONEY /pʊr, poʊr/ *adj* [*-er/-est* only] having little money or few possessions, or lacking something important ○ *He came from a poor, immigrant family.* ○ *Most of the world's poorest countries are in Africa.* ○ *The country is poor in natural resources.*

poor /pʊr, poʊr/ *pl n* poor people ○ *She gives a lot of money to the poor.*

WORD CHOICES poor

Penniless or **impoverished** are more formal alternatives to "poor."

*I was a **penniless** student.*

*Benefits should be targeted at the most **impoverished** families.*

In informal English, **broke** or the phrase **strapped (for cash)** are ways of saying that someone has very little money at a particular time.

*I'm not going away this year. I'm **broke**.*

*Most schools are pretty **strapped for cash**.*

Needy people are poor and do not have enough food, clothes, etc.

*Your donations will make a difference to **needy** children all over the world.*

If a person or place is **poverty-stricken**, that person or place is suffering very badly from the effects of being poor.

*He visited **poverty-stricken** countries where people are starving.*

Destitute is used when someone is extremely poor and has no house or possessions.

*The floods left thousands of people **destitute**.*

The adjectives **deprived** or **disadvantaged** are often used when people are poor and do not have the good living conditions and opportunities that other people have.

*It's one of the most **deprived** areas of the city.*

*The program was set up to help **disadvantaged** children.*

BAD /pʊr, poʊr/ *adj* [*-er/-est* only] of a very low quality or standard; not good ○ *poor eyesight* ○ *poor grades* ○ *He's in very poor health.*

poorly /ˈpʊr·li, ˈpoʊr-/ *adv* [not gradable] ○ *Critics say the plan was poorly conceived.* ○ *The kids are doing poorly at school.*

DESERVING SYMPATHY /pʊr, poʊr/ *adj* [not gradable] deserving sympathy ○ *That poor dog looks like it hasn't been fed in a while.*

pop **SOUND** /pɑp/ *v* [I/T] **-pp-** to make a short little explosive sound, often by bursting something, or to cause this to happen ○ [T] *The kids were popping all the birthday balloons.*

pop /pɑp/ *n* [C] ○ *There was a loud pop as the cork came out of the bottle.*

MOVE /pɑp/ *v* [I always + adv/prep] **-pp-** to move or appear quickly, suddenly, or when not expected ○ *McEnroe hits it and the ball pops over his shoulder.* ○ *There are lots of good young players popping up these days.*

POPULAR /pɑp/ *adj* [not gradable] of or for the general public ○ *pop art* ○ *pop culture* ○ *pop music*

FATHER /pɑp/ *n* [C] *infml* a father ○ *Hey Pop, can I borrow the car?*

DRINK /pɑp/, *dated* **soda pop** *n* [C/U] *regional US* a SOFT DRINK

IDIOM with pop

• **a pop** *infml* for each one ○ *The tickets cost $200 a pop.* ○ **USAGE:** Used after an amount of money, esp. a large one.

PHRASAL VERBS with pop

• **pop in/into** *(somewhere)* **VISIT** *infml* **1** to visit briefly ○ *Why don't you pop in and see us this afternoon?* **2** If you pop into a place, you visit there briefly, usually for some purpose: *All I have to do on the way home is pop into the drugstore.*

• **pop** *(something)* **in/into** *something* **MOVE QUICKLY** *infml* **1** to put something quickly into something else ○ *Pop the CD-ROM into a personal computer.* ○ *Just pop your supper in the microwave.* **2** Something that **pops into your head/mind** is an idea that you suddenly have: *He jotted down story ideas that popped into his head.*

• **pop off** to say something quickly and without thinking, esp. because of anger ○ *Rice popped off about his teammate on a TV interview.*

pop. *n* [U] *abbreviation for* POPULATION (= the number of people living in a place) ○ *Devil's Lake, N.D. (pop. 7442)*

popcorn /ˈpɑp·kɔːrn/ *n* [U] seeds of corn that are heated until they burst, becoming light, white balls that are usually eaten with salt and butter or a sweet covering on them

pope /poʊp/ *n* [C/U] the leader of the Roman Catholic Church ○ [U] *Pope John Paul II*

poplar /ˈpɑp·lər/ *n* [C] a tall, straight, fast-growing tree with soft wood

poplin /ˈpɑp·lən/ *n* [U] a plain, closely woven cloth with a slightly shiny surface

poppy /ˈpɑp·i/ *n* [C] a plant with large, usually red flowers, and small, black, edible seeds

Popsicle /ˈpɑp ˌsɪk·əl/ *n* [C] *trademark* a sweet, flavored ice on a stick

populace /ˈpɑp·jə·ləs/ *n* [U] the people who live in a particular country or place, or ordinary people ○ *It seemed as if the town's entire populace had turned out for the parade.*

popular **LIKED** /ˈpɑp·jə·lər/ *adj* liked, enjoyed, or admired by many people or by most people in a particular group ○ *In-line skating is increasingly popular.*

popularity /ˌpɑp·jəˈlær·ət̬·i/ *n* [U] ○ *The governor's popularity will probably guarantee his reelection.*

popularize /ˈpɑp·jə·ləˌrɑɪz/ *v* [T] to cause something to become known, admired, or used by many people ○ *He helped to popularize the hard-bop style of jazz in the mid-1950s.*

GENERAL /ˈpɑp·jə·lər/ *adj* involving or relating to ordinary people or to all the people who live in a country or area ○ *Contrary to popular belief, air travel is less dangerous than travel by car.*

popularize /ˈpɑp·jə·ləˌrɑɪz/ *v* [T] to make something known or understood to ordinary people ○ *His books helped popularize the study of language.*

popularly /ˈpɑp·jə·lər·li/ *adv* by most people ○ *In the 1970s, so many Russian immigrants came to live in Brighton Beach that it became popularly known as Little Odessa.*

WORD FAMILY popular			
Nouns	popularity unpopularity popularization	*Adjectives*	popular unpopular
Verbs	popularize	*Adverbs*	popularly

popular music, *short form* **pop music**, *short form* **pop** *n* [U] the kind of music with words and a strong rhythm that many young people enjoy listening and dancing to

population /ˌpɑp·jəˈleɪ·ʃən/, *abbreviation* **pop.** *n* [C/U] **1** all the people living in a particular country, area, or place ○ [U] *What is the population of Toronto* (= how many people live there)? **2** ***biology*** Population is also used to refer to all the living things of a particular type or group who live in a particular area or environment.

populated /ˈpɑp·jəˌleɪṭ·əd/ *adj* lived in ○ *densely populated cities*

populous /ˈpɑp·jə·ləs/ *adj* (of a country, area, or place) having a lot of people living there ○ *populous metropolitan areas*

populist /ˈpɑp·jə·ləst/ *n* [C] ***social studies*** a person or a politician who is mainly interested in the problems and needs of ordinary people ○ *His populist ideas appeal to both poor and middle class workers.*

populism /ˈpɑp·jəˌlɪz·əm/ *n* [U] ***social studies*** ○ *American populism has always had two faces: economic and cultural.*

porcelain /ˈpɔːr·sə·lən/ *n* [U] a hard but delicate, shiny, white substance made by heating a special type of clay to a high temperature, used esp. to make cups, plates, and small, decorative objects ○ *a porcelain figurine*

porch /pɔːrtʃ/ *n* [C] a covered area next to the entrance of a house, sometimes open to the air and sometimes surrounded by a SCREEN (= wire net) ○ *The back porch looks out on our garden.*

porcupine /ˈpɔːr·kjəˌpɑɪn/ *n* [C] a small, brown mammal with a covering of QUILLS (= long, sharp points) on its back

pore /pɔːr, pour/ *n* [C] one of many very small holes in the skin of people or other animals or on the surface of plants

PHRASAL VERB with pore

• **pore over** *something* to look at and study a book, document, etc. carefully ○ *She spends a lot of time poring over the historical records of the church.*

pork /pɔːrk/ *n* [U] meat from a pig, eaten as food ○ *pork chops*

pork barrel, **pork** /pɔːrk/ *n* [U] the spending of federal or state government money for local improvements to help a politician win popularity with local voters ○ *pork-barrel politics*

pornography /pɔːrˈnɑg·rə·fi/ *n* [U] pictures, movies, or writing that show or describe sexual behavior for the purpose of exciting people sexually

pornographer /pɔːrˈnɑg·rə·fər/ *n* [C] a person who makes or sells pornography

pornographic /ˌpɔːr·nəˈgræf·ɪk/ *adj*

porous /ˈpɔːr·əs, ˈpour·əs/ *adj* allowing liquid or air to pass through ○ *porous soil*

porpoise /ˈpɔːr·pəs/ *n* [C] a large mammal that lives in the sea and swims in groups

porridge /ˈpɔːr·ɪdʒ, ˈpɑr-/ *n* [U] *dated* a thick, soft food made from OATS (= a type of grain) boiled in water or milk; OATMEAL

port **CITY** /pɔːrt, pourt/ *n* [C/U] a city or town that has a HARBOR (= sheltered area of water where ships can load or unload) on the sea or a river, or the harbor itself ○ [C] *a fishing/naval port*

CONNECTION /pɔːrt, pourt/ *n* [C] *technology* a part of a computer where wires can be connected in order to control other pieces of equipment, such as a printer

LEFT /pɔːrt, pourt/ *n* [U] the left side of a ship or aircraft as you are facing forward ○ Compare STARBOARD

portable /ˈpɔːrṭ·ə·bəl, ˈpourṭ-/ *adj* [not gradable] small and light enough to be carried or moved easily, and not attached by electric wires ○ *a portable phone/radio*

portal **BUILDING** /ˈpɔːrt·ᵊl, ˈpourṭ-/ *n* [C] *fml* a large and often highly decorated entrance to a building ○ *We entered the side portal of the cathedral.*

INTERNET /ˈpɔːrt·əl, ˈpourṭ-/ *n* [C] a page on the WORLD WIDE WEB that users can change so it shows information they want to see ○ *The portal lets you access specific information from anywhere in the site.*

portend /pɔːrˈtend, pour-/ *v* [T] *fml* to be a sign that something is likely to happen in the future ○ *It was a major scandal whose full exposure portended the end of a popular presidential reign.*

porter /ˈpɔːrṭ·ər, ˈpourṭ-/ *n* [C] **1** a person whose job is to carry bags at railroad stations and airports **2** A porter is also a person whose job is to clean, esp. in a large building.

portfolio **CONTAINER** /pɔːrtˈfou·liːˌou, pourt-/ *n* [C] *pl* **portfolios** **1** a large, flat container used for carrying large drawings, documents, or other papers **2** ***art*** A portfolio is also a collection of drawings, designs, or other papers that represent a person's work.

INVESTMENTS /pɔːrtˈfou·liːˌou, pourt-/ *n* [C] *pl* **portfolios** a collection of investments that are

P

owned by a particular person or organization ○ *a stock portfolio*

porthole /ˈpɔːrt·hoʊl, ˈpoʊrt-/ *n* [C] a small, usually round, window in the side of a ship

portico /ˈpɔːrt̬·ɪˌkoʊ, ˈpoʊrt̬-/ *n* [C] *pl* **porticoes, porticos** an open structure with a roof supported by columns, which serves as an entrance, usually to a large house or a public building

portion Ⓐ /ˈpɔːr·ʃən, ˈpoʊr-/ *n* [C] **1** a part or share of something larger ○ *She read large portions of the manuscript and offered many useful suggestions.* ○ *A portion of my paycheck was withheld for taxes.* **2** A portion is also the amount of food served to or suitable for a person: *They serve children's portions at half-price.*

portly /ˈpɔːrt·li, ˈpoʊrt-/ *adj* slightly fat ○ *a tall portly man*

portrait /ˈpɔːr·trət, ˈpoʊr-/ *n* [C] **1** a painting, photograph, or drawing of a person **2** A portrait is also a description or representation of something: *The book paints a grim portrait of wartime suffering.*

portray /pɔːrˈtreɪ, poʊr-/ *v* [T] **1** to represent or describe someone or something in a book, movie, etc. ○ *The book portrayed him as somebody who was uncaring, even bigoted.* ○ *The writer portrays life in a working-class community at the turn of the century.* **2** To portray is also to act the part of someone in a movie or play: *Michael Douglas portrays the president of the United States.*

portrayal /pɔːrˈtreɪ·əl, poʊr-/ *n* [C] ○ *A lot of people felt the film wasn't quite an accurate portrayal.*

pose Ⓐ **CAUSE** /poʊz/ *v* [T] **1** to cause something, esp. a problem or difficulty ○ *Does this defendant really pose a threat to the community?* **2** To pose a question is to bring attention to a problem, often in the form of a question: *Joanna poses the question, "How do we accomplish these goals?"*

POSITION /poʊz/ *v* [I] to move into and stay in a particular position, usually so that you can be photographed or have your picture drawn or painted ○ *We all posed for our photographs in front of the Lincoln Memorial.*

pose Ⓐ /poʊz/ *n* [C] the position in which someone stands or sits when posing ○ *Can you hold that pose?*

PRETEND /poʊz/ *v* [I] to pretend to be someone else in order to deceive others ○ *The detective posed as a sailor to try to catch the smugglers.*

posh /pɑʃ/ *adj* expensive, comfortable, and of high quality ○ *a posh hotel/restaurant*

position PLACE /pəˈzɪʃ·ən/ *n* [C/U] **1** the place where something or someone is, often in relation to other things ○ [C] *I've switched the positions of the sofa and the chair.* **2** In sports, a position is the place where you play on your team, or the responsibilities of someone who plays in that place: [C] *He played the shortstop position when he started in baseball.*

position /pəˈzɪʃ·ən/ *v* [T] ○ *The Secret Service men quickly positioned themselves around the president.*

RANK /pəˈzɪʃ·ən/ *n* [C] **1** a rank or level in a company, competition, or society ○ *She's devoted her life to improving the position of women in society.* **2** A position in a company or organization is also a job: *He applied for the position of marketing manager.*

SITUATION /pəˈzɪʃ·ən/ *n* [C usually sing] **1** a situation or condition ○ *a shaky financial position* ○ *She found herself in a difficult position and didn't know what to say.* **2** If you are in a position to do something, you are able to do it, usually because you have the necessary power or money: [+ *to* infinitive] *Do you think she's in a position to help you?*

OPINION /pəˈzɪʃ·ən/ *n* [C] a way of thinking about a particular matter; opinion ○ *Our position is that we've made a very fair offer to settle this dispute.*

ARRANGEMENT OF BODY /pəˈzɪʃ·ən/ *n* [C] the way in which the body is arranged ○ *My knees get stiff when I sit in the same position for a long time.*

positive Ⓐ **CERTAIN** /ˈpɑz·ət̬·ɪv/ *adj* without any doubt; certain ○ *I'm absolutely positive that he's the man I saw.*

positively Ⓐ /ˈpɑz·ət̬·ɪv·li/ *adv* ○ *I positively will be there.*

HAPPY /ˈpɑz·ət̬·ɪv/ *adj* happy or hopeful, or giving cause for happiness or hope ○ *It's important to have a positive attitude when you have a serious illness.* ○ Opposite: NEGATIVE **NOT HAPPY**

positively Ⓐ /ˈpɑz·ət̬·ɪv·li/ *adv* ○ *I just don't respond positively to being bossed around.*

MORE THAN ZERO /ˈpɑz·ət̬·ɪv/ *adj* [not gradable] ***algebra*** (of a number or amount) more than zero ○ *Two is a positive number.* ○ Opposite: NEGATIVE **LESS THAN ZERO**

ELECTRICITY /ˈpɑz·ət̬·ɪv/ *adj* [not gradable] ***physics*** of the type of electrical CHARGE that a PROTON has ○ Compare NEGATIVE **ELECTRICITY**

positively /ˈpɑz·ət̬·ɪv·li, ˌpɑz·əˈtɪv·li/ *adv* ***physics*** ○ *positively charged*

MEDICAL TEST /ˈpɑz·ət̬·ɪv/ *adj* [not gradable] (of a medical test) showing that the disease or condition for which the person is being tested does exist ○ *Her TB test was positive.* ○ Compare NEGATIVE **NO**

COMPLETE /ˈpɑz·ət̬·ɪv/ *adj* [not gradable] (used to add force to an expression) complete ○ *She was a positive joy to have around.*

positively /ˈpɑz·ət̬·ɪv·li/ *adv* [not gradable] ○ *You look positively gorgeous in that outfit!*

positron /ˈpɑz·əˌtrɑn/ *n* [C] ***physics*** a very small piece of matter with a positive electrical CHARGE, and with the same size as an ELECTRON

posse /ˈpɑs·i/ *n* [C] a group of people following a person in order to catch him or her ○ *In a lot of old westerns, the sheriff gathers a posse to chase the bad guy.*

possess OWN /pəˈzes/ *v* [T] to have or own something, or to have a particular quality ○ *Those states are the countries that possess nuclear weapons.* ○ *She possesses the unusual talent of knowing when to say nothing.*

possession /pə'zeʃ·ən/ *n* [C/U] **1** something that you own, or the condition of owning something ○ [U] *She couldn't take possession of the house until the current occupants moved out.* ○ [C] *Meanwhile, all her possessions were in storage.* **2** *fml* If you are **in possession of** something, you have it with you: *He was in possession of two tickets to the concert.*

possessive /pə'zes·ɪv/ *adj* **1** If you are possessive about something that you own, you do not like sharing it: *He's very possessive about his car.* **2** Someone who is possessive in feelings and behavior toward another person wants all of that person's love and attention. ○ See also: POSSESSIVE

possessor /pə'zes·ər/ *n* [C usually sing] ○ *I am now the proud possessor of a driver's license!*

CONTROL /pə'zes/ *v* [T] (of a desire or an idea) to take control over a person's mind, making that person behave in a strange way ○ *I don't know what possessed me to start yelling like that.*

possessive /pə'zes·ɪv/ *adj* [not gradable] ***grammar*** having or relating to the CASE (= form) of a word used to show who or what something belongs to ○ See also: POSSESSIVE at POSSESS OWN

possible **ACHIEVABLE** /'pɑs·ə·bəl/ *adj* [not gradable] that can be done or achieved, or that can exist ○ [+ *to* infinitive] *Is it possible to get an earlier flight?* ○ *If possible I'd like to get there before noon.* ○ *We need to send that letter off as soon as possible.*

possibly /'pɑs·ə·bli/ *adv* [not gradable] ○ *He can't possibly mean what he says.*

possibility /ˌpɑs·ə'bɪl·ət̬·i/ *n* [C] ○ *One possibility is to hire more people.*

NOT CERTAIN /'pɑs·ə·bəl/ *adj* [not gradable] that might or might not happen or exist ○ [+ (*that*) clause] *It's possible (that) Mary will turn up tonight.*

possibly /'pɑs·ə·bli/ *adv* [not gradable] ○ *"Do you think this skirt might be too small for her?" "Possibly, she has put on weight."*

possibility /ˌpɑs·ə'bɪl·ət̬·i/ *n* [U] ○ *There's a possibility of snow tonight.*

WORD FAMILY possible

Nouns	possibility impossibility	*Adverbs*	possibly impossibly
Adjectives	possible impossible		

possum /'pɑs·əm/ *n short form of* OPOSSUM

post **POLE** /poʊst/ *n* [C] a vertical pole stuck in the ground, usually to support something or to mark a position ○ *Al leaned against a fence post.*

JOB /poʊst/ *n* [C] a job, esp. one in which someone is performing an official duty ○ *Novello was the first woman and first Hispanic to hold the post of surgeon general.*

post /poʊst/ *v* [T] ○ *Police officers will be posted at every intersection during the march.*

MAKE KNOWN /poʊst/ *v* [T] **1** to make information known to the public, or to put up signs on land or other property ○ *Snow advisories were posted for Ohio and Pennsylvania.* ○ *All over town, for-sale signs are posted in front of houses.* **2** To post something is also to put it on the Internet where others can see it: *The earnings release also will be posted on the Company's website.*

posting /'poʊ·stɪŋ/ *n* [C] a single act of putting information on the Internet, or the information itself ○ *A hoaxer wrote a widely publicized posting in Ms. Hilton's name.*

PAY /poʊst/ *v* [T] to pay money to a law court, as a formal promise that a person released from prison will return for trial ○ *McLaughlin posted $3000 bail after his arrest.*

WORD FAMILY post

Nouns	post postage posting	*Adjectives* *Verbs*	postal post

post- /poʊst/ *prefix* after (a time or event) ○ *post-9/11* ○ *post-election*

postage /'poʊ·stɪdʒ/ *n* [U] the money charged or paid for sending letters and parcels by mail

postal /'poʊ·stəl/ *adj* [not gradable] relating to the delivery of mail, or to or about the POST OFFICE ○ *Two postal workers were accused of theft.*

postcard /'poʊst·kɑrd/ *n* [C] a small, rectangular card, often with a picture on one side, that can be sent in the mail without an envelope ○ *a picture postcard*

postcode /'poʊst·koʊd/ *n* [C] *Br* a ZIP CODE

postdate /poʊs'deɪt/ *v* [T] to write a DATE (= day, month, and year) that is later than the present on (a check, letter, or document)

poster /'poʊ·stər/ *n* [C] a large printed picture or notice put up for advertising or decoration ○ *She had a poster of some rock star on the wall.*

posterior /pɑ'stɪr·iː·ər, poʊ-/ *n* [C] *infml, usually humorous* a person's buttocks ○ *Park your posterior on that seat.*

posterity /pɑ'ster·ət̬·i/ *n* [U] the people who will exist in the future ○ *Their recollections were recorded for posterity.*

postgraduate /ˌpoʊst'grædʒ·ə·wət/ *n* [C] a student who is doing advanced studies after already obtaining one degree

postgraduate /ˌpoʊst'grædʒ·ə·wət/, **graduate** *adj* [not gradable] ○ *postgraduate studies*

posthumous /'pɑs·tʃə·məs/ *adj* [not gradable] happening after a person's death

posthumously /'pɑs·tʃə·mə·sli/ *adv* [not gradable] ○ *Dillon was posthumously awarded a Silver Star.*

Post-It (note) /'poʊ·stət ('noʊt)/ *n* [C] *trademark* a piece of paper with a sticky strip on the back that allows it to be stuck temporarily to smooth surfaces

postmark /'poʊst·mɑrk/ *n* [C] an official mark on letters or packages, showing the place and day, month, and year of mailing

P

postmark /ˈpoʊst·mɑrk/ *v* [T] ○ *Contest entries must be postmarked no later than July 16.*

postmaster /ˈpoʊstˌmæs·tər/, *female* **postmistress** /ˈpoʊstˌmɪs·trəs/ *n* [C] a person in charge of a POST OFFICE ○ *He's the local postmaster.*

postmodern, **post-modern** /poʊstˈmɑd·ərn/ *adj* involving a view of society or a style in art that is very recent but different from what came immediately before ○ *The book reassures adherents of postmodern culture that they are on the cutting edge of change.*

post-mortem /poʊstˈmɔːrt̬·əm/ *n* [C] a medical examination of a dead body to discover the cause of death, or a discussion of an event after it has happened ○ *The disease can be confirmed only in a post-mortem.* ○ *a post-mortem on Harkin's presidential campaign*

postnatal /poʊstˈneɪt·ᵊl/ *adj* [not gradable] relating to the period of time immediately after a baby has been born ○ *a postnatal exercise program* ○ Compare PRENATAL

post office *n* [C] a place where you can mail letters or packages and buy stamps, or *infml* the US Postal Service

post office box, *abbreviation* **P.O. Box** *n* [C] a small, numbered, locked box at a post office to which letters are delivered

postpartum /poʊstˈpɑrt̬·əm/ *adj* [not gradable] following the birth of a child ○ *They offer the full package of prenatal, delivery, and postpartum care.*

postpone /poʊstˈpoʊn/ *v* [T] to delay an event or arrange for it to take place at a later time ○ *The trip has been postponed twice.*
postponement /poʊstˈpoʊn·mənt/ *n* [C/U] ○ [C/U] *Rain forced (a) postponement of the match.*

postscript /ˈpoʊs·skrɪpt/ *n* [C] an extra message added at the end of a story or letter ○ *There is a postscript to this story.*

post-traumatic stress disorder, *abbreviation* **PTSD** *n* [C usually sing] *medical* a mental condition in which a person suffers severe anxiety and illness after a very frightening or shocking experience, such as a war or an accident

postulate /ˈpɑs·tʃəˌleɪt/ *v* [T] *fml* to suggest or accept that a theory or idea is true as a starting point for reasoning or discussion ○ [+ *that* clause] *Astronomers postulate that the comet will reappear in 4000 years.*
postulate /ˈpɑs·tʃə·lət, -ˌleɪt/ *n* [C] *fml* ○ *He suggested an original and interesting postulate.*

posture POSITION OF BODY /ˈpɑs·tʃər/ *n* [C/U] a position of the body, or the way in which someone holds the body when standing, sitting, or walking ○ [C] *Newton sat back in a reclining posture.* ○ [U] *She's got good/bad posture.*

ACT FALSELY /ˈpɑs·tʃər/ *v* [I] to act falsely in order to attract attention or achieve an effect ○ *This trial turned into a carnival, with everybody posturing and playing to the camera.*

postwar /ˈpoʊs·twɔːr/ *adj* [not gradable] happening or existing in the period after a war, esp. World War II

pot CONTAINER /pɑt/ *n* [C] **1** a round container used for cooking, serving, storing, and other purposes ○ *a clay/brass pot* ○ *a flower pot* ○ *We need space for our pots and pans.* **2** A pot is also the substance contained in a pot: *The pot was simmering.* ○ *He made a new pot of coffee.*
pot /pɑt/ *v* [T] **-tt-** to put a plant into a pot ○ *We should be potting the roses.*

AMOUNT /pɑt/ *n* [C] *infml* **1** a large amount, esp. of money ○ *There are pots of money involved in this deal.* **2** A pot is also all the money being risked at a single time in a card game.

IDIOM with pot

• **the pot calling the kettle black** a situation in which one person criticizes another for a fault the first person also has ○ *Sean called me a liar – that's the pot calling the kettle black!*

potassium /pəˈtæs·iː·əm/ *n* [U] a soft, silver-white metal that burns quickly in the air and is used in special hard glasses and FERTILIZERS (= substances that help crops grow better)

potato /pəˈteɪt̬·oʊ/ *n* [C/U] *pl* **potatoes** a white vegetable with a brown or reddish skin which grows underground and is used for food, or the plant on which this grows ○ [C] *a baked potato* ○ [U] *mashed potato*

potato chip *n* [C usually plural] a very thin slice of potato fried until stiff, and sometimes flavored

potbellied stove *n* [C] an old-fashioned round stove that uses wood or COAL for fuel

potbelly /ˈpɑtˌbel·i/ *n* [C] a fat, round stomach
potbellied /ˈpɑtˌbel·iːd/ *adj* ○ *a small, potbellied old man*

potent /ˈpoʊt·ᵊnt/ *adj* powerful, persuasive, or effective ○ *This is the most potent headache remedy you can get without a prescription.* ○ *Her voice has been a potent force on concert stages for more than 30 years.*
potency /ˈpoʊt·ᵊn·si/ *n* [U] ○ *Scientists are testing the potency of the new drug.*

potential Ⓐ /pəˈten·tʃəl/ *adj* [not gradable] possible but not yet achieved ○ *He was eager to talk with potential customers.*
potential Ⓐ /pəˈten·tʃəl/ *n* [U] **1** *He saw little potential* (= possibility) *for change.* **2** Someone's potential is an ability the person has not yet developed: *She keeps saying I should live up to my potential.* **3** ***physics*** Potential energy is the energy that something has because of its position and structure, not because of its movement. **4** ***physics*** Electric potential is a measure of the power of electrical energy, measured in VOLTS.
potentially Ⓐ /pəˈten·tʃə·li/ *adv* [not gradable] ○ *Potentially dangerous products are often recalled by their manufacturers.*

potential energy *n* [U] ***physics*** the energy stored by something because of its position compared with other objects, its condition, or its electrical CHARGE

potholder /ˈpɑtˌhoʊl·dər/ *n* [C] a small piece of thick material for protecting your hands when holding hot pots or pans

pothole /ˈpɑt·hoʊl/ *n* [C] a hole in the surface of a road caused by traffic and bad weather

potion /ˈpoʊ·ʃən/ *n* [C] a drink that is believed to be poisonous, to have magical power, or to be able to cure an illness ○ *We don't have a magic potion to make you tell the truth.*

pot luck /ˈpɑtˈlʌk/ *adj* [not gradable] offering whatever is available or what others bring ○ *We invited all the neighbors over for a pot luck supper last night.*

pot pie *n* [C] a pastry filled with vegetables and usually meat ○ *a chicken pot pie*

potpourri /ˌpoʊ·pəˈriː/ *n* [C/U] **1** a mixture of dried flower petals and spices, used to make a room or drawer smell pleasant ○ [U] *She liked the scent of floral potpourri.* **2** A potpourri is also a mixed grouping of things: [C] *a potpourri of scenes*

pot roast *n* [C] a piece of BEEF (= meat from cattle) cooked whole in a covered pot

potshot /ˈpɑt·ʃɑt/ *n* [C] a criticism made without careful thought ○ *Her opponent has taken potshots at her for not being tough enough.*

pottery /ˈpɑt̬·ə·ri/ *n* [U] dishes, bowls, and other objects made from baked clay

potty /ˈpɑt̬·i/ *n* [C] a small toilet used by children when they are being trained to use a toilet

pouch /pɑʊtʃ/ *n* [C] **1** a bag or soft container ○ *The raincoat is folded inside a small waterproof pouch.* **2** A pouch is also a pocket of skin on the lower part of the body of some female animals, such as KANGAROOS, in which they carry their young.

poultry /ˈpoʊl·tri/ *n* [U] birds, such as chickens, kept for their meat or eggs, or the meat from these birds ○ *Mediterranean diets favor fish and poultry over red meat.*

pounce /pɑʊns/ *v* [I] to attack suddenly, esp. by jumping or flying down to catch or take hold of something or someone ○ *The mountain lion pounced onto the back of an elk.*

pound **WEIGHT** /pɑʊnd/, *abbreviation* **lb.**, *symbol* # *n* [C] a unit of measurement of weight equal to 0.453 kilogram

HIT /pɑʊnd/ *v* [I/T] **1** to hit repeatedly with force, or to crush by hitting repeatedly ○ [T] *The speaker pounded his fists on the table.* ○ [I] *Waves were pounding at the rocks.* **2** If your heart pounds, it beats very strongly: [I] *My heart was still pounding after we nearly crashed on the Interstate.*

pounding /ˈpɑʊn·dɪŋ/ *n* [C/U] the sound, feeling, or action of something beating repeatedly ○ [U] *The pounding in her chest was loud.* ○ [U] *All that pounding from running really isn't good for your knees.* ○ [C] (*fig.*) *The dollar's going to take a pounding* (= its value will be damaged).

PLACE /pɑʊnd/ *n* [C] a place where pets that are lost or not wanted are kept ○ *We got this mutt at the pound.*

MONEY /pɑʊnd/, *symbol* **£** *n* [C] the standard unit of money in the United Kingdom and some other countries

pound cake /ˈpɑʊnd·keɪk/ *n* [C] a type of cake made with flour, butter, sugar, and eggs

pound sign **TELEPHONE KEY** *n* [C] the symbol # on a telephone or computer key ○ *Enter your Social Security number, then press the pound sign.*

MONEY *n* [C] the symbol £, which is put in front of amounts of money in pounds

pour **CAUSE TO FLOW** /pɔːr, poʊr/ *v* [T] to make a substance flow, esp. out of a container and usually into another container ○ [T] *Pour the sugar into the bowl.* ○ [T] *Would you like me to pour you some coffee?*

FLOW QUICKLY /pɔːr, poʊr/ *v* [always + adv/prep] **1** to flow quickly and in large amounts, or to cause (something) to flow in large amounts ○ [I] *Water poured into the basement.* ○ [I] *When the movie ended, the crowd poured into the street.* **2** If you say about the weather that it is pouring, you mean that it is raining heavily: [I] *You'd better take an umbrella – it's pouring out there.*

PHRASAL VERBS with **pour**

• **pour** *something* **into** *something* to give a lot of money or effort to something with the idea of making it successful ○ *Most of the money raised by the new taxes will be poured into the arena project.*

• **pour** *something* **out** [M] to give many details about your feelings in speech or writing ○ *He could tell her everything, pour out his soul and let her sponge it up.*

pout /pɑʊt/ *v* [I] to show annoyance esp. by pressing the lips together or pushing out the lower lip ○ *Our four-year-old pouts whenever she doesn't get what she wants.*

poverty /ˈpɑv·ərt·i/ *n* [U] the condition of being poor ○ *He grew up in poverty.*

poverty line, **poverty level** *n* [U] the amount of income a person or family needs in order to maintain an acceptable standard of living, and below which they are considered poor

poverty-stricken *adj* [not gradable] extremely poor ○ *My grandparents arrived in this country as poverty-stricken immigrants.*

pow /pɑʊ/ *exclamation* (a word representing) a sudden loud noise, as that of an explosion or of a gun being fired ○ *All of a sudden we heard pow! pow! pow! – like shots being fired.*

POW *n* [C] *abbreviation for* PRISONER OF WAR

powder /ˈpɑʊd·ər/ *n* [C/U] **1** a loose, dry substance of extremely small pieces, usually made by breaking up something into smaller parts and crushing them **2** Powder is also any of various

P

loose, dry, usually pleasant-smelling substances that people put on their skin as a help in healing or as makeup: [U] *talcum powder* **3** Powder is also GUNPOWDER.

powdered /ˈpɑʊd·ərd/ *adj* [not gradable] being in the form of a powder ○ *powdered milk*

powdery /ˈpɑʊd·ə·ri/ *adj* having the form of powder

powder keg *n* [C] a situation that is dangerous and that could become violent ○ *Tension was high following the protest and several city leaders called the inner city a powder keg.*

powder room *n* [C] *dated* a bathroom for women

power CONTROL /ˈpɑʊ·ər/ *n* [U] the ability or right to control people and events, or to influence the way people act or think in important ways ○ *The election results showed that the Democrats had lost power, with Republicans taking over five more Democratic seats.*

powerful /ˈpɑʊ·ər·fəl/ *adj* having a lot of power ○ *He's in a powerful position as an adviser of the president.*

powerless /ˈpɑʊ·ər·ləs/ *adj* without the power to do something or to prevent something from happening ○ [+ *to* infinitive] *The government seems powerless to do anything about the rising price of oil.*

STRENGTH /ˈpɑʊ·ər/ *n* [U] physical strength or force ○ *He's a good baseball player – he hits with a lot of power.*

power /ˈpɑʊ·ər/ *v* [T] ○ *At the start of the race, she dived into the pool and quickly powered her way into the lead.*

powerful /ˈpɑʊ·ər·fəl/ *adj* **1** strong ○ *The picture quality is bad because the TV signal isn't powerful enough.* **2** Things that are powerful have a strong effect: *a powerful drug*

powerfully /ˈpɑʊ·ər·fə·li, -fli/ *adv* ○ *Dewayne is powerfully built* (= has a strong body).

ENERGY /ˈpɑʊ·ər/ *n* [U] **1** the ability to produce energy, or the energy produced ○ *electrical/nuclear/solar power* **2** ***physics*** Power is also the rate at which work is done or at which energy is produced, measured in WATTS. **3** Power is also electricity: *Whenever there's a storm in these parts, you can expect a power outage* (= a loss of electrical power).

power /ˈpɑʊ·ər/ *v* [T] to provide something with the energy it needs to operate ○ [T] *Many buses and trucks are powered by diesel fuel.*

powerful /ˈpɑʊ·ər·fəl/ *adj* ○ *Do you really need a car with such a powerful engine?*

MATHEMATICS /ˈpɑʊ·ər/ *n* [U] ***mathematics*** the number of times that a number is to be multiplied by itself, or the number that is the result of multiplying a number by itself ○ *Three to the fourth power can be written* 3^4.

NATION /ˈpɑʊ·ər/ *n* [C] ***world history*** an independent nation

PERSON WHO CONTROLS /ˈpɑʊ·ər/ *n* [C] someone or something, such as an organization or country, that has control over others, often because of authority, importance, or wealth ○ *She is a power in the field of medical education.*

NATURAL ABILITY /ˈpɑʊ·ər/ *n* [C/U] a natural skill or ability to do something ○ [U] *She was so shocked that for a moment she lost the power of speech.* ○ [C] *The doctor did everything in her power to save him.*

WORD FAMILY power			
Nouns	power superpower empowerment	*Verbs*	power empower overpower
Adjectives	powerful overpowering powerless	*Adverbs*	powerfully

PHRASAL VERB with power

• **power up** (*something*) [M] to provide something with energy so that it can begin to operate ○ *The phone sits in the stand to power up.* ○ *Warm water acts as fuel for a hurricane's engine, powering it up.*

powerboat /ˈpɑʊ·ərˌboʊt/ *n* [C] a small, fast boat often used in racing

powerhouse /ˈpɑʊ·ərˌhɑʊs/ *n* [C] a person, organization, or country with a lot of energy, power, or influence ○ *The country is the economic powerhouse of the European Union.*

power of attorney *n* [C/U] *law* a legal document in which you give another person the right to act for you, esp. in financial or legal matters

power plant *n* [C] a building where electricity is produced

power steering *n* [U] a system that lets the driver of a vehicle easily change the direction in which it is moving by using power from the engine

powwow /ˈpɑʊ·wɑʊ/ *n* [C] an American Indian meeting or gathering for making decisions or for ceremonies or celebrations ○ *In South Dakota each summer, a Sioux powwow attracts dancers from all over the US.* ○ (*fig.*) *I'm going home for a family powwow* (= discussion) *this weekend.*

pp. *pl n abbreviation for* PAGES ○ *There is a detailed discussion on pp. 101–123.*

ppm *n* [U] ***chemistry*** *abbreviation for* parts per million (= a unit for measuring the amount of a substance that is mixed with a liquid or another substance)

PR *n* [U] *abbreviation for* PUBLIC RELATIONS

practicable /ˈpræk·tɪ·kə·bəl/ *adj* able to be done or put into action ○ *A detailed report on the cause of the accident will be made public as soon as practicable.*

practical ACTUAL/REAL /ˈpræk·tɪ·kəl/ *adj* **1** relating to actual experience or to the use of knowledge in activities rather than to knowledge only or ideas ○ *I know you've been trained as a teacher, but do you have any practical teaching experience?* **2** If you say that a person is practical, you mean the person behaves in ways that relate more to the realities of the world than to ideas or desires: *You've got to learn to be practical and save your money.*

practicalities /ˌpræk·tɪˈkæl·əṭ·iːz/ *pl n* the particular conditions of a situation; the actual facts ○ *I know you have to be in Paris tomorrow, but you have to understand the practicalities of arranging transportation on such short notice.*

EFFECTIVE /ˈpræk·tɪ·kəl/ *adj* **1** fitting the needs of a particular situation in a helpful way; helping to solve a problem or difficulty; effective or suitable ○ *We didn't want to spend the night at a motel, but it just wasn't practical to do the trip in one day.* ○ *In some cities, it isn't practical to keep the subways operating all night because there aren't enough passengers.* **2** When used of objects such as clothes, practical can mean directed only to the goal of doing their intended work, and often plain in style or character: *I wear clothes that are practical rather than fashionable.*

practically /ˈpræk·tɪ·kli/ *adv* ○ *Many people have offered help, but there's little they can practically do.*

WORD FAMILY practical

Nouns	practicalities practicality	*Adjectives*	practicable practical impractical
Adverbs	practically		

practical joke *n* [C] a joke intended to make someone seem foolish that involves a physical action rather than words ○ *She glued the cup and saucer together as a practical joke.*

practically /ˈpræk·tɪ·kli/ *adv* [not gradable] almost or very nearly ○ *Practically everybody will be at the party.* ○ *It's practically impossible to get home in less than an hour.*

practical nurse *n* [C] a NURSE who has limited medical training ○ Compare REGISTERED NURSE

practice ACTION /ˈpræk·təs/ *n* [U] [not gradable] action rather than thought or ideas ○ *It seemed like a good idea, but in practice it was a disaster.* ○ *How soon will the new procedures be put into practice?*

REGULAR ACTIVITY /ˈpræk·təs/ *n* [C/U] something that is usually or regularly done, often as a habit, tradition, or custom ○ [U] *It was his usual practice to buy a newspaper every morning on the way to the office.*

practice, *esp. Cdn, Br* **practise** /ˈpræk·təs/ *v* [T] ○ *The right to practice religion as you choose is guaranteed by the US Constitution.*

practicing, *esp. Cdn, Br* **practising** /ˈpræk·tə·sɪŋ/ *adj* [not gradable] following the rules esp. of a religion ○ *a practicing Catholic/Jew/Muslim*

TRAIN, *esp. Cdn, Br* **practise** /ˈpræk·təs/ *v* [I/T] to do or play something regularly or repeatedly in order to become skilled at it ○ [T] *I'm good at tennis but I need to practice my serve.*

practice /ˈpræk·təs/ *n* [C/U] ○ [U] *I need more practice before I take my driving test.*

WORK, *esp. Cdn, Br* **practise** /ˈpræk·təs/ *v* [I/T] to do work of a particular type for which a lot of training is necessary ○ [T] *The firm has been practicing law for over a hundred years.*

practice /ˈpræk·təs/ *n* [C] ○ *He gave up the practice of medicine when he came to the United States.*

practicing, *esp. Cdn, Br* **practising** /ˈpræk·tə·sɪŋ/ *adj* [not gradable] ○ *He remained a practicing architect until he died at the age of 89.*

WORD FAMILY practice

Nouns	practice practitioner	*Adjectives*	practicing
		Verbs	practice

IDIOM with practice

• **practice what** *you* **preach** to behave in the way you tell other people to behave ○ *She's always telling me to exercise, but she should practice what she preaches.*

practitioner Ⓐ /prækˈtɪʃ·ə·nər/ *n* [C] someone whose regular work has involved a lot of training ○ *Dr. Goldstein is a family/general practitioner* (= a medical doctor who treats general conditions).

pragmatic /prægˈmæṭ·ɪk/ *adj* based on practical judgments rather than principles ○ *He made a pragmatic decision to settle the lawsuit because in the end it would cost more to try it in court.*

pragmatism /ˈpræg·məˌtɪz·əm/ *n* [U] ***social studies*** an approach to problems and situations that is based on practical solutions

prairie /ˈprer·i/ *n* a wide area of flat land, covered with grass, esp. a large area in central North America that was originally covered by grass and is now mainly farming land

prairie dog *n* [C] a small animal found in western North American that is a kind of SQUIRREL that lives in large groups underground

praise SHOW APPROVAL /preɪz/ *v* [T] to express strong admiration for or approval of a person or something done ○ *The "Times" praised the mayor's decision to reappoint the parks commissioner.*

praise /preɪz/ *n* [U] ○ *His economic policies have won praise from fellow Republicans.*

WORD CHOICES praise

If you **congratulate** someone, you praise that person and say that you are pleased for his or her success or because something special has happened.

*I **congratulated** him on passing his driving test.*

Compliment can be used when someone praises what someone has done or the way that person looks.

*I was just **complimenting** Robert on the wonderful meal he has cooked.*

If someone praises a person publicly or officially, you can use the verb **commend** or the phrase **pay tribute to**.

*The judge **commended** her for her bravery.*

*He **paid tribute to** the firefighters who had saved his daughter's life.* ➤

Flatter means "to make someone feel important or attractive, or to praise someone in order to please him or her."

*I knew he was only **flattering** me because he wanted to borrow some money.*

In informal English, the verb **rave** is used when someone praises someone or something a lot.

*Everyone's **raving** about the new band.*

GOD /preɪz/ *v* [T] to honor, worship, and express admiration for (God or a god) ○ *Praise God/the Lord.*

prance /præns/ *v* [I] to walk or dance in an energetic way, with high, kicking steps ○ *In the square dance, each couple took turns prancing together under the linked arms of the other couples.*

prank /præŋk/ *n* [C] a trick that is intended to be amusing and often to make someone look foolish ○ *She's always playing pranks on her little brother.*

pray /preɪ/ *v* **1** to speak to God or a god either privately or in a religious ceremony esp. to express thanks or to ask for help ○ [I] *Then the minister said, "Let us pray."* ○ [+ (*that*) clause] *We often prayed (that) the war would end.* **2** To pray also means to hope: [+ (*that*) clause] *I prayed (that) she wouldn't discover my secret.*

prayer /prer, prær/ *n* [C/U] the act or ceremony of speaking to God or a god, esp. to express thanks or to ask for help, or the words used in this act ○ [C] *an evening prayer* ○ [C] *a prayer of thanks* ○ [U] *She knelt in prayer.*

praying mantis /ˈpreɪ·ɪŋˈmænt·əs/ *n* [C] a large, green insect that holds its front legs in a way that makes it look as if it is praying

P

pre- /ˌpriː/ *prefix* before (a time or an event) ○ *precooked food* ○ *a preexisting condition*

preach **SPEAK IN CHURCH** /priːtʃ/ *v* [I/T] to give a religious speech ○ [T] *The minister preached a sermon on the need for forgiveness.*

preacher /ˈpriː·tʃər/ *n* [C] a person who gives a religious speech, esp. one whose job is to do this

PERSUADE /priːtʃ/ *v* [I/T] **1** to try to persuade other people to do or accept something ○ [T] *Should Liddy be allowed to preach hatred?* **2** To preach is also to try to persuade other people to have particular beliefs or behave in particular ways: [I] *My mother's always preaching at me about studying harder.*

IDIOM with preach

• **preach to the choir, preach to the converted** to try to persuade people who already agree with you ○ *The men who really need to hear the message don't come to the meetings, so I'm just preaching to the choir.*

preamble /ˈpriːˌæm·bəl/ *n* [C] an introduction to a speech or piece of writing ○ *the preamble to the Constitution*

prearranged /ˌpriː·əˈreɪndʒd/ *adj* [not gradable] arranged in advance ○ *a prearranged plan*

precarious /prɪˈkær·iː·əs, -ˈker-/ *adj* in danger because not firmly fixed; likely to fall or suffer harm ○ *I climbed onto a precarious platform to get a better view.*

precariously /prɪˈkær·iː·ə·sli, -ˈker-/ *adv* ○ *The vase was precariously perched on a narrow shelf next to the door.*

precaution /prɪˈkɔː·ʃən/ *n* [C] an action taken to prevent something unpleasant or dangerous from happening ○ *Homeowners should take the basic precaution of locking their doors and windows.*

precautionary /prɪˈkɔː·ʃəˌner·i/ *adj* [not gradable] ○ *The company has withdrawn the drug as a precautionary measure while further testing is done.*

precede Ⓐ /prɪˈsiːd/ *v* [T] to be or go before someone or something in time or space ○ *John Adams preceded Thomas Jefferson as president.* ○ *Nouns are often preceded by adjectives*

preceding Ⓐ /prɪˈsiːd·ɪŋ/ *adj* [not gradable] ○ *The table on the preceding page shows the test results.*

precedence Ⓐ /ˈpres·əd·əns/ *n* [U] the condition of being dealt with before other things or of being considered more important than other things ○ *What takes precedence here, environmental cost or consumer convenience?*

precedent Ⓐ /ˈpres·əd·ənt/ *n* [C/U] a previous action, situation, or decision that can be used as a reason or example for a similar action or decision at a later time ○ [C] *Conditions have changed enormously, and the past is not much of a precedent.* ○ [U] *Precedent indicated that a change would take place sooner rather than later.*

precept /ˈpriː·sept/ *n* [C] a rule for action or behavior, esp. one based on moral consideration ○ *common precepts of decency*

precinct /ˈpriː·sɪŋt/ *n* [C] **1** a division of a city or town, esp. an area protected by one police station, or a division used for elections **2** The precincts of a place are the areas that surround it, esp. when enclosed: *the private precincts of the university*

precious **VALUABLE** /ˈpreʃ·əs/ *adj* **1** of very great value or worth ○ *precious memories* ○ *Children are our most precious resource.* **2** Precious metals are gold, silver, and PLATINUM. **3** A precious stone is a jewel: *Diamonds and rubies are precious stones.*

VERY /ˈpreʃ·əs/ *adv infml* very ○ *He earns precious little money.*

precipice /ˈpres·ə·pəs/ *n* [C] a very steep side of a cliff or mountain ○ *We stood at the edge of the precipice and looked down at the sea.*

precipitate **MAKE HAPPEN** /prɪˈsɪp·əˌteɪt/ *v* [T] *fml* to make something happen suddenly or sooner than expected ○ *An invasion would certainly precipitate a war.*

precipitate /prɪˈsɪp·ət̬·ət/ *adj fml* ○ *We were alarmed by his precipitate actions.*

SEPARATE /priːˈsɪp·əˌteɪt/ *v* [I/T] ***chemistry*** to separate, or cause a substance to separate from a liquid as a solid

precipitate /priː'sɪp·ət̬·ət, -əˌteɪt/ *n* [C] ***chemistry*** a substance that separates from a liquid as a solid

precipitation /priːˌsɪp·ə'teɪ·ʃən/ *n* [U] ***chemistry*** the chemical process that causes a substance to precipitate

precipitation /prɪˌsɪp·ə'teɪ·ʃən/ *n* [U] water that falls from the clouds toward the ground, esp. as rain or snow

precipitous /prɪ'sɪp·ət̬·əs/ *adj* very steep, or falling a long way very fast ○ *precipitous cliffs* ○ *New fads could result in a precipitous drop in sales.*

précis /'preɪ·si, preɪ'siː/ *n* [C] *pl* **précis** *fml* a short form of a text that gives only the important parts

precise Ⓐ /prɪ'sɑɪs/ *adj* exact and accurate in form, time, detail, or description ○ *The precise recipe is a closely guarded secret.* ○ *Years of doing this research had made her very precise in her working methods.* ○ *There was a good turnout for the meeting – twelve of us, to be precise.*

precisely Ⓐ /prɪ'sɑɪ·sli/ *adv* **1** *Tell me precisely what happened.* ○ *He works slowly and precisely, whereas I tend to rush things and make mistakes.* **2** Precisely is also used to emphasize the accuracy of what you are saying: *Armed conflict is precisely what the government is trying to avoid.*

precision Ⓐ /prɪ'sɪʒ·ən/ *n* [U] **1** *Great precision is required to grind the lenses accurately.* ○ *She writes with clarity and precision.* **2** ***science*** Precision is also the level of agreement of a particular measurement with itself when it is repeated. ○ Compare ACCURACY

COMMON LEARNER ERROR

precise

You cannot use **precise** as a verb. It is only an adjective. If you want to use a verb with a similar meaning, you can use words such as **specify, explain,** or **make clear**.

~~*Your advertisement doesn't precise whether flights are included in the price.*~~

Your advertisement doesn't explain whether flights are included in the price.

WORD FAMILY precise

Nouns	precision	*Adjectives*	precise imprecise
Adverbs	precisely		

preclude /prɪ'kluːd/ *v* [T] *fml* to prevent something or make it impossible ○ *Although your application was not accepted, it doesn't preclude the possibility of your applying again later.*

precocious /prɪ'koʊ·ʃəs/ *adj* showing unusually early mental development or achievement ○ *Lucy was a verbally precocious child.*

preconceived /ˌpriː·kən'siːvd/ *adj* [not gradable] (of an idea or opinion) formed too early, esp. without enough consideration or knowledge ○ *Since I'm new, I have no preconceived notions about how it should be done.*

preconception /ˌpriː·kən'sep·ʃən/ *n* [C] an idea or opinion formed before enough information is available to form it correctly ○ *Many people still have preconceptions about how Native Americans live.*

precondition /ˌpriː·kən'dɪʃ·ən/ *n* [C] something that must happen or be true before it is possible for something else to happen ○ *Sound financial policies are a precondition for economic growth.*

precursor /prɪ'kɜr·sər, 'priːˌkɜr-/ *n* [C] something that comes before another and may lead to it or influence its development ○ *Opponents fear this would be a precursor to development of the entire canyon.*

predate /priː'deɪt/ *v* [T] to have existed or happened before another thing ○ *These burial mounds predated the arrival of Europeans in North America.*

predator /'pred·ət̬·ər/ *n* [C] an animal that hunts and kills other animals for food

predatory /'pred·əˌtɔːr·i, -ˌtoʊr-/ *adj* **1** *a predatory bird* **2** People or organizations who are predatory tend to use others for their own advantage: *Larger companies, which played a predatory role, swooped down to cash in on the new fad.*

predecessor /'pred·əˌses·ər, 'priːd-/ *n* [C] a person who had a job or position before someone else, or a thing that comes before another in time or in a series ○ *My predecessor worked in this job for twelve years.* ○ *The latest model is faster and sleeker than its predecessors.*

predestination /priːˌdes·tə'neɪ·ʃən/ *n* [U] the belief that events in life are decided in advance by God or by FATE and cannot be changed

predicament /prɪ'dɪk·ə·mənt/ *n* [C] an unpleasant or confusing situation that is difficult to get out of or solve ○ *With no money and no job, he found himself in a real predicament.*

predicate GRAMMAR /'pred·ɪ·kət/ *n* [C] ***grammar*** the part of a sentence that gives information about the subject ○ *In the sentence "We went to the airport," "went to the airport" is the predicate.*

STATE /'pred·əˌkeɪt/ *v* [T] *fml* **1** to state that something is true ○ [+ *that* clause] *One cannot predicate that the disease is caused by a virus on the basis of current evidence.* **2** If an idea or argument is **predicated on** something, it depends on the existence or truth of that thing: *The sales forecast is predicated on a growing economy.*

predict Ⓐ /prɪ'dɪkt/ *v* to say that an event or action will happen in the future ○ [T] *Astronomers can predict the exact time of an eclipse.* ○ [+ *that* clause] *Who could have predicted that she would win the election?* ○ [+ *to* infinitive] *The storm is predicted to reach the Florida coast tomorrow morning.* ○ [+ question word] *No one can predict when the disease will strike again.*

predictable Ⓐ /prɪ'dɪk·tə·bəl/ *adj* acting or happening in a way that is expected ○ *Comets usually appear at predictable times.* ○ *She's so predict-*

P

able – she always wants to go to the same old restaurant.

predictably Ⓐ /prɪˈdɪk·tə·bli/ *adv* ○ *Predictably, the movie was a hit.*

predictability Ⓐ /prɪˌdɪk·təˈbɪl·əṭ·i/ *n* [U] ○ *Can the predictability of these results be improved?*

prediction Ⓐ /prɪˈdɪk·ʃən/ *n* [C/U] ○ [C] *We are not yet able to make accurate predictions about earthquakes.*

predilection /ˌpred·əlˈek·ʃən, ˌpriːd-/ *n* [C] a strong liking or preference ○ *a predilection for spicy foods*

predispose /ˌpriːd·ɪˈspoʊz/ *v* [T] to influence someone to behave or think in a particular way or to have a particular condition ○ *Individualism predisposes many people to look for individual solutions to social problems.* ○ *Your family history can help a doctor determine if you are predisposed to developing heart disease.*

predisposition /ˌpriːˌdɪs·pəˈzɪʃ·ən/ *n* [C] ○ *She has an annoying predisposition to find fault with everything.* ○ *There is evidence that a predisposition toward asthma runs in families.*

predominant Ⓐ /prɪˈdɑm·ə·nənt/ *adj* [not gradable] being the most noticeable or largest in number, or having the most power or influence ○ *Women have a predominant role as health care professionals.*

predominantly Ⓐ /prɪˈdɑm·ə·nənt·li/ *adv* [not gradable] ○ *This neighborhood is now predominantly Hispanic.*

predominance Ⓐ /prɪˈdɑm·ə·nəns/ *n* [U] ○ *The predominance of white males in powerful school positions sends a signal to youngsters about who is going to be successful in life.*

P

predominate Ⓐ /prɪˈdɑm·əˌneɪt/ *v* [I] to be the most important or the greatest in number ○ *We live in an area in which livestock, poultry, and dairy farming predominate.*

preeminent /priːˈem·ə·nənt/ *adj* [not gradable] more important or powerful than all others ○ *He was the preeminent scientist of his day.*

preeminence /priːˈem·ə·nəns/ *n* [U] ○ *Before the 19th century, China's preeminence in Asia was never challenged.*

preempt /priːˈempt/ *v* [T] **1** to prevent something from happening by taking action first ○ *State laws preempted local governments from restricting newspaper displays.* **2** If a broadcast is preempted, it is replaced by another, usually more important broadcast: *One station preempted its Friday night schedule to televise the high school playoffs.*

preemptive, **pre-emptive** /priːˈemp·tɪv/ *adj* [not gradable] ○ *a preemptive air strike on an enemy base*

preen /priːn/ *v* [I/T] **1** (of a bird) to clean and arrange its feathers using its beak **2** People who preen make themselves more attractive: [I] *As they preened in the sun, Evelyn snapped photos of them.*

prefabricated /priːˈfæb·rəˌkeɪṭ·əd/, *infml* **prefab** /ˈpriː·fæb/ *adj* [not gradable] built from parts that have been made in a factory and can be put together quickly ○ *Our school is using prefabricated buildings for extra classrooms.*

preface /ˈpref·əs/ *n* [C] ***literature*** something that comes before and introduces a more important thing, esp. an introduction at the beginning of a book that explains its aims ○ *an author's preface*

preface /ˈpref·əs/ *v* [T] ○ *He didn't preface the bad news with "I don't know how to tell you this, but."*

prefer /prɪˈfɜr/ *v* **-rr-** to choose or want one thing rather than another ○ [T] *We have tea and coffee, but perhaps you'd prefer a cold drink.* ○ [T] *He prefers watching baseball to playing it.* ○ [+ *that* clause] *She prefers that we meet at the station.* ○ [+ *to* infinitive] *Would you prefer to leave?*

preferable /ˈpref·ə·rə·bəl/ *adj* [not gradable] better or more desirable ○ *We could take a later flight if it would be preferable.* ○ *Surely a diplomatic solution is preferable to war.*

preferably /ˈpref·ə·rə·bli/ *adv* [not gradable] ○ *We're looking for a new house, preferably one closer to the school.*

preference /ˈpref·ə·rəns/ *n* [C/U] **1** [C] *What are your preferences in music?* **2** A preference is also an advantage given to someone: [U] *The city gives preference to job applicants who live there.*

preferential /ˌpref·əˈren·tʃəl/ *adj* better than that given to others ○ *Some prisoners had apparently received preferential treatment.*

WORD FAMILY prefer

Nouns	preference	*Verbs*	prefer
Adjectives	preferable preferential	*Adverbs*	preferably

prefix /ˈpriː·fɪks/ *n* [C] ***grammar*** a letter or group of letters added to the beginning of a word to change the meaning or make a new word ○ *In the words "unknown" and "unusual," "un-" is a prefix meaning "not."* ○ Compare SUFFIX

pregnant DEVELOPING YOUNG /ˈpreg·nənt/ *adj* [not gradable] (of female mammals) having young developing in the uterus ○ *She's seven months pregnant.*

pregnancy /ˈpreg·nən·si/ *n* [C/U] ○ [U] *She experienced morning sickness during her first months of pregnancy.*

HAVING MEANING /ˈpreg·nənt/ *adj* filled with meaning that has not been expressed ○ *There followed a pregnant pause in which each knew what the other was thinking but neither knew what to say.*

preheat /priːˈhiːt/ *v* [T] to heat something before using it ○ *Preheat the oven to 350°F.*

prehistoric /ˌpriː·hɪsˈtɔːr·ɪk, -ˈtɑr-/ *adj* [not gradable] ***world history*** happening in the period of human history before there were written records ○ *Painting originated in prehistoric times with murals drawn on cave walls.*

prejudge /priːˈdʒʌdʒ/ *v* [T] to form an opinion about someone or something before knowing or examining all the facts ○ *I am not prejudging your guilt or innocence.*

prejudice /ˈpredʒ·əd·əs/ *n* [C/U] an unfair and unreasonable opinion or feeling formed without enough thought or knowledge ○ [U] *racial prejudice* ○ [C] *The experience merely confirmed all his prejudices about living in the city.*
prejudice /ˈpredʒ·əd·əs/ *v* [T] to unfairly influence a person or matter so that an unreasonable opinion or decision results ○ *Both sides pledged not to do anything to prejudice the final outcome.*1
prejudicial /ˌpredʒ·əˈdɪʃ·əl/ *adj* ○ *An official investigation would have a prejudicial effect on the company's reputation.*
prejudiced /ˈpredʒ·əd·əst/ *adj*

preliminary Ⓐ /prɪˈlɪm·əˌner·i/ *adj* [not gradable] coming before a more important action or event, esp. introducing or preparing for it ○ *preliminary talks* ○ *a preliminary investigation* ○ *The preliminary rounds of negotiation went well.*
preliminary Ⓐ /prɪˈlɪm·əˌner·i/ *n* [C usually pl] ○ *Her time of 12:32 took four seconds off the mark she set in Friday's preliminaries.*

prelude INTRODUCTION /ˈprel·juːd, ˈpreɪ·luːd/ *n* [C usually sing] something that comes before a more important event or action and introduces or prepares for it ○ *The dinner was only a prelude to a much larger meeting.*
MUSIC /ˈprel·juːd, ˈpreɪ·luːd/ *n* [C] ***music*** a piece of music that introduces a longer piece of music, or a short piece of music written esp. for the piano

premarital /priːˈmær·əţ·əl/ *adj* [not gradable] before marriage ○ *premarital counseling*

premature /ˌpriː·məˈtʊr, -ˈtʃʊr/ *adj* happening or done too soon, esp. before the natural or desired time ○ *a premature death at age 50* ○ *A spokesman said it was premature to comment on the negotiations.*
prematurely /ˌpriː·məˈtʊr·li, -ˈtʃʊr-/ *adv* ○ *Twins often are born prematurely.* ○ *Tony is getting prematurely gray* (= his hair is becoming gray).

premed /priːˈmed/ *adj* [not gradable] being in a university course that prepares students for medical school ○ *He was a premed student at the University of California.*

premeditated /priːˈmed·əˌteɪţ·əd/ *adj* [not gradable] thought of or planned before being done ○ *The police believe the crime was premeditated.*

premenstrual /priːˈmen·strə·wəl/ *adj* [not gradable] of the time just before a woman's PERIOD (= bleeding each month from her uterus)

premenstrual syndrome, *abbreviation* **PMS** *n* [U] pains and feelings of unhappiness or anxiety that some women experience a few days before their PERIOD (= flow of blood each month from the uterus) begins

premier BEST /prɪˈmɪr, ˈpriː·mɪr, ˈprem·ɪr/ *adj* [not gradable] best or most important ○ *He was widely regarded as one of the world's premier authorities on heart disease.*
LEADER /prɪˈmɪr, ˈpriː·mɪr, ˈprem·ɪr/ *n* [C] the leader of the government of some countries, or the leader of the government of a part of a country ○ *the premier of Ontario*

premiere, **première** /prɪmˈjer, prɪˈmɪr/ *n* [C] the first public showing of a play, opera, movie, television program, or other entertainment ○ *The season premieres of two of my favorite TV shows are on Wednesday.*
premiere /prɪmˈjer, prɪˈmɪr/ *v* [I] ○ *The three-part BBC program will premiere in the United States on the Discovery Channel on Sunday.*

premise /ˈprem·əs/ *n* [C] an idea or theory on which a statement or action is based ○ [+ *that* clause] *We don't accept the premise that cutting taxes will necessarily lead to increased economic productivity.*

premises /ˈprem·ə·səz/ *pl n* a house or other building and the land on which it is built ○ *The bread sold here is baked on the premises.*

premium PAYMENT /ˈpriː·miː·əm/ *n* [C] an amount of money paid at regular times to INSURE (= protect against risk) your health or life, or your home or possessions ○ *That could mean higher Medicare premiums for retirees.*
EXTRA /ˈpriː·miː·əm/ *n* [C] **1** something extra given or an extra amount charged ○ *You get a lipstick as a premium with the purchase of this makeup.* ○ *Our customers are willing to pay a premium for a superior product.* **2** If you get something **at a premium**, you pay a high price for it, esp. because it is not easily available: *It's possible to get a large apartment, but only at a premium.* **3** A premium is also a great amount of importance: *The admissions office places a premium on a student's character in the selection process.*
premium /ˈpriː·miː·əm/ *adj* [not gradable] of higher than usual quality or value ○ *premium gasoline*

premonition /ˌprem·əˈnɪʃ·ən, ˌpriː·mə-/ *n* [C] a feeling that something, esp. something unpleasant, is going to happen ○ *a premonition of danger*

prenatal /priːˈneɪţ·əl/ *adj* [not gradable] happening or existing before birth ○ *prenatal care*

prenuptial /priːˈnʌp·ʃəl, -tʃəl/ *adj* [not gradable] before getting married

prenuptial agreement *n* [C] a legal document signed by two people before they marry stating what will happen to their money and possessions if they DIVORCE (= legally end their marriage)

preoccupy /priːˈɑk·jəˌpɑɪ/ *v* [T] to be the main thought in someone's mind, causing other things to be forgotten ○ *The wedding next month preoccupied her.*
preoccupied /priːˈɑk·jəˌpɑɪd/ *adj* ○ *He's been preoccupied lately because of problems at school.*
preoccupation /priːˌɑk·jəˈpeɪ·ʃən/ *n* [C/U] the thing you think about most ○ [U] *His preoccupation with sports is affecting his grades.*

P

prep /prep/ *v* [T] **-pp-** *infml* **1** to prepare ○ *The president's advisers are busy prepping him for the debate.* **2** *medical* To prep is also to get a person in a hospital ready for an operation.

preparatory school, *short form* **prep school**, *short form* **prep** *n* [C] a private school for children over the age of eleven that prepares them to go to college ○ *He went to St. John's Prep.*

prepare /prɪˈper, -ˈpær/ *v* [I/T] to make or get something or someone ready for something that will happen in the future ○ [T] *Keane is preparing a film version of the play.* ○ [I] *The Southeast prepared for the worst as the hurricane turned toward the Atlantic coast.*

prepared /prɪˈperd, -ˈpærd/ *adj* ○ *Everything looked prepared for the party.* ○ *The press representative read a prepared statement* (= one already written).

preparedness /prɪˈper·əd·nəs, -ˈpær·əd-/ *n* [U] ○ *earthquake preparedness*

preparation /ˌprep·əˈreɪ·ʃən/ *n* [C/U] the state of being ready for something that will happen, or an action taken to become ready ○ [U] *The teacher said my preparation for the exam was inadequate.* ○ [C] *By the next morning our preparations for the storm were complete.* ○ [U] *A platform had been set up in preparation for the ceremony.*

preparatory /prɪˈpær·əˌtɔːr·i, -ˈper-, -ˌtoʊr·i/ *adj* [not gradable] ○ *Plans for building a new school are under way, but so far only in the preparatory stage.*

WORD FAMILY prepare			
Nouns	preparation preparations preparedness	*Adjectives*	prepared unprepared preparatory
Verbs	prepare		

P

IDIOM with prepare

• **be prepared to** *do something* to be willing to do something ○ *I don't mind explaining it to you, but I'm not prepared to do it for you.*

preponderance /prɪˈpɑn·də·rəns/ *n* [U] the largest part or greatest amount ○ *The preponderance of evidence suggests the crash was an accident.*

preposition /ˌprep·əˈzɪʃ·ən/ *n* [C] ***grammar*** a word that connects a noun, a noun phrase, or a pronoun to another word, esp. to a verb, another noun, or an adjective ○ *In the sentence, "We jumped in the lake," "in" is a preposition, and in the sentence, "I heard the sound of loud music," "of" is a preposition.*

prepositional phrase *n* [C] a combination of a PREPOSITION followed by a noun or pronoun

preposterous /priˈpɑs·tə·rəs/ *adj* completely unreasonable and ridiculous; not to be believed ○ *It was a preposterous idea, and no one took it seriously.*

preppie, **preppy** /ˈprep·i/ *n* [C] a person who is or was a student at a PREPARATORY SCHOOL (= private school that prepares students for college), or someone who dresses in the traditional style of such students ○ *Dressed like a preppie, she wears a pleated skirt, cotton shirt, and knee socks.*

prep school /ˈprep·skuːl/ *n short form of* PREPARATORY SCHOOL

prerequisite /priːˈrek·wə·zət/ *n* [C] something that must exist or happen before something else can exist or happen ○ *Introductory physics is a prerequisite for any of the advanced courses in physics.*

prerogative /prɪˈrɑg·əṭ·ɪv/ *n* [C] a special advantage that allows some people the freedom to do or have something that is not possible or allowed for everyone ○ *It's the president's prerogative to nominate judges who share his political philosophy.*

Pres. /prez/ *n* [C] *abbreviation for* PRESIDENT **POLITICS**

Presbyterian /ˌprez·bəˈtɪr·iː·ən/ *n* [C] a member of a Christian religious group that is one of the Protestant churches

Presbyterian /ˌprez·bəˈtɪr·iː·ən/ *adj* [not gradable] ○ *a Presbyterian church* ○ *a Presbyterian minister*

preschool /ˈpriː·skuːl/ *n* [C/U] a school for children who are between about three and five years old

preschooler /ˈpriːˌskuː·lər/ *n* [C]

prescribe **GIVE MEDICAL TREATMENT** /prɪˈskrɑɪb/ *v* [T] to order treatment for someone, or to say what someone should do or use to treat an illness or injury ○ *Many doctors prescribe aspirin to forestall second heart attacks.* ○ *My doctor prescribed rest and gave me a painkiller for my knee.*

GIVE RULE /prɪˈskrɑɪb/ *v* [T] to tell people what they must have or do, or to give as a rule ○ *A secretary of education cannot and should not prescribe the curriculum of the nation's colleges.*

prescription **MEDICINE** /prɪˈskrɪp·ʃən/ *n* [C] a doctor's written direction for the medicine that someone needs and how it is to be used, or the medicine itself ○ *The doctor gave me prescriptions for antibiotics and cough syrup.* ○ *The drugstore called to say your prescription is ready to be picked up.*

RULES /prɪˈskrɪp·ʃən/ *n* [C] rules or a situation that will have a particular effect ○ *The company's reorganization could be a prescription for disaster.*

prescriptive /prɪˈskrɪp·tɪv/ *adj* tending to say what someone should do or how something should be done ○ *His basic attitude toward language is highly prescriptive.*

preseason /ˈpriːˌsiː·zən/ *n* [C usually sing] the period before a sports team begins its official competition ○ *He has played three preseason games, averaging 4.3 points.*

presence of mind *n* [U] the ability to make good decisions and to act quickly in a difficult situation

present **SOMETHING GIVEN** /ˈprez·ənt/ *n* [C] something that is given without being asked for, esp. on a special occasion or to say thank you; a GIFT ○ *a birthday present* ○ *Did you wrap the present?*

PROVIDE /prɪˈzent/ *v* [T] **1** to give, show, provide, or make known ○ *The mayor presented five firefighters with medals for saving people's lives.* ○ *Two clubs in the neighborhood present jazz on Thursdays.* ○ *Dr. Gottlieb will present her research in a series of lectures this spring.* **2** If you present yourself, you go to someone or make yourself known to someone: *Paul Groncki presented himself to the receptionist on the 41st floor.* **3** If something presents itself, it happens or takes place: *An opportunity suddenly presented itself.*

CAUSE /prɪˈzent/ *v* [T] to cause something ○ *Falling tax revenues present a problem for the city.*

NOW /ˈprez·ənt/ *n* [U] this period of time, not the past or the future; now ○ *The story moves back and forth between the past and the present.*

present /ˈprez·ənt/ *adj* [not gradable] ○ *the present situation*

presently /ˈprez·ənt·li/ *adv* [not gradable] at this time ○ *Three of the ten boats are presently being repaired.* ○ See also: PRESENTLY

GRAMMAR /ˈprez·ənt/ *adj* [not gradable] ***grammar*** having the tense of a verb used to describe actions, events, or states that are happening or existing at this time ○ *Her book is written entirely in the present tense.*

PLACE /ˈprez·ənt/ *adj* [not gradable] in a particular place ○ *The mayor was present during the entire meeting.*

presence /ˈprez·əns/ *n* [C/U] **1** [U] *We shouldn't discuss Jeff's progress in the presence of the other students* (= when the other students are there). ○ [U] *Those who disagreed with the funding proposal made their presence felt* (= made their opinions known). **2** Presence is also a person's ability to make his or her character known to others: [U] *He writes better, he reports better, and his presence on camera is better.* **3** If a country or organization has a presence somewhere, some of its members are there.

INTRODUCE /prɪˈzent/ *v* [T] *fml* to introduce a person ○ *I'm pleased to present my son, Charles.*

WORD FAMILY present

Nouns	presence present presentation representation representative presenter	*Adjectives*	present presentable representative
		Verbs	present represent
		Adverbs	presently

presentable /prɪˈzent·ə·bəl/ *adj* looking suitable or good enough, esp. in the way you are dressed ○ *You need to look presentable for the interview.* ○ *A coat of paint made the house presentable.*

presentation /ˌprez·ənˈteɪ·ʃən, ˌpriːˌzen-/ *n* [C/U] the act of giving or showing something, or the way in which something is given or shown ○ [C] *a multimedia presentation* ○ [C] *After the sales presentation, the board had a number of questions.* ○ [U] *Presentation of the awards takes place at a banquet in June.* ○ [U] *Both the food and its presentation were excellent.*

present-day *adj* [not gradable] modern; of today rather than of earlier times ○ *The setting is present-day London.*

presently /ˈprez·ənt·li/ *adv* [not gradable] soon; not at this time but after a short time in the future ○ *We will be leaving presently.* ○ See also: PRESENTLY at PRESENT NOW

present participle *n* [C] ***grammar*** a form of a verb that ends in "ing" and comes after another verb to show continuous action ○ *In the sentence "The children are watching television," "watching" is a present participle.*

present perfect *n* [U] ***grammar*** the tense you use to talk about actions or events that happen in both the past and the present ○ *The sentence "She has broken her leg" is in the present perfect.*

preserve **KEEP** /prɪˈzɜrv/ *v* [T] **1** to keep something as it is, esp. in order to prevent it from decaying or to protect it from being damaged or destroyed ○ *The committee will suggest ways to preserve historically important buildings in the downtown area.* **2** To preserve food is to treat it in a particular way so it can be kept for a long time without going bad: *My grandmother preserved cherries in syrup.*

preserve /prɪˈzɜrv/ *n* [C usually pl] fruit cooked with sugar ○ *apricot preserves*

preservative /prɪˈzɜr·vəţ·ɪv/ *n* [C/U] ○ [C] *artificial/natural preservatives*

preservation /ˌprez·ərˈveɪ·ʃən/ *n* [U] ○ *Janet is very interested in historic preservation* (= protecting places of historic importance).

preservationist /ˌprez·ərˈveɪ·ʃə·nəst/ *n* [C] ○ *Preservationists were outraged at the proposal to tear down a historic theater.*

SEPARATE ACTIVITY /prɪˈzɜrv/ *n* [C] an activity that only one person or a particular type of person does or is responsible for ○ *The gardening is Jeanne's special preserve.*

SEPARATE PLACE /prɪˈzɜrv/ *n* [C] an area of land kept in its natural state, esp. for hunting and fishing or for raising animals and fish ○ *a wildlife preserve*

preside /prɪˈzɑɪd/ *v* [I] to be in charge of or to control a meeting or event ○ *The vice president will preside at today's meeting.*

president **POLITICS** /ˈprez·əd·ənt, -əˌdent/, *abbreviation* **Pres.** *n* [C] ***politics & government*** the highest political position in the United States and some other countries, usually the leader of the government ○ *Several people are considering running for president, but none have announced their candidacy yet.*

presidential /ˌprez·əˈden·tʃəl/ *adj* ○ *a presidential candidate*

presidency /ˈprez·əd·ən·si, -əˌden-/ *n* [C] ***politics & government*** the position of being presi-

P

dent, or the length of time during which someone is president ○ *the office of the presidency* ○ *Franklin D. Roosevelt's presidency lasted more than 12 years.*

ORGANIZATION /ˈprez·əd·ənt, -əˌdent/ *n* [C] a person who has the highest position in a company or organization ○ *The company's board of directors will name a new president at its next meeting.*

press PUSH /pres/ *v* [I/T] **1** to push firmly against something that is fixed in position ○ [T] *I pressed the volume button on the remote.* ○ [I always + adv/prep] *The crowd pressed up against the doors.* ○ [I always + adv/prep] *He pressed down hard on the accelerator, and the car shot ahead.* **2** When you press clothes, you use an IRON (= a heavy device with a flat base) to make them smooth.

PERSUADE /pres/ *v* [T] to try to persuade or cause someone to do something, or to act in a determined way to cause something to be accepted ○ *The police pressed her to identify the man she had seen.* ○ *Marquez will visit Washington to press his country's case.* ○ *She decided not to press charges against him* (= make an official complaint).

DEVICE /pres/ *n* [C] any of various devices that use force ○ *a pants press* ○ *a garlic press* ○ *a printing press*

NEWSPAPERS /pres/ *n* [U] **1** newspapers, magazines, and other businesses that communicate news to the public by print, television, or radio, or the people who work to prepare and present the news ○ *Is the press too conservative?* **2** Good/bad press is the positive or negative reaction of newspapers, magazines, etc., to a person or thing: *At some point, every president has complained about bad press.*

PUBLISHER /pres/ *n* [C] a business that prints and produces books or other printed material ○ *Cambridge University Press*

WORD FAMILY press

Nouns	press pressure	*Verbs*	press pressure
Adjectives	pressed pressing		

PHRASAL VERBS with press

• **press ahead (with** *something***)** to continue to do something although there is opposition to it ○ *The company pressed ahead with plans to build the skyscraper.*

• **press for** *something* to work hard to win support for a plan so that it will succeed ○ *He will press for stricter pollution controls.*

• **press on** to continue traveling or doing something ○ *We didn't have time to stop, and pressed on into Arizona.* ○ *The witness started crying, but the lawyer pressed on.*

press conference *n* [C] a meeting at which government or business officials make a public statement and reporters can ask questions

pressing /ˈpres·ɪŋ/ *adj* urgent or needing to be dealt with immediately ○ *a pressing need/issue*

press release *n* [C] a written statement from a person or group that is given to newspapers and broadcasting organizations to become part of the news

pressure FORCE /ˈpreʃ·ər/ *n* [C/U] **1** the force produced by pressing against something ○ [U] *air/blood/water pressure* **2** ***physics*** Pressure is also the force that is put on a surface with reference to the area of the surface.

INFLUENCE /ˈpreʃ·ər/ *n* [C/U] **1** a strong, often threatening influence on an organization or person ○ [C] *Competitive pressures will force the company to sell off its factories.* **2** If you put pressure on someone, you try to cause that person to do something by persuading or threatening them: [U] *They put a lot of pressure on him to resign.*

pressure /ˈpreʃ·ər/ *v* [T] ○ *She was pressured into signing the agreement.*

WORRY /ˈpreʃ·ər/ *n* [U] worry and fear caused by the feeling that you have too many responsibilities and cares ○ *I like this job – there's not so much pressure to produce every day.*

pressure cooker *n* [C] a container with a tightly fitting lid that cooks food quickly in steam

prestige /presˈtiːʒ, -ˈtiːdʒ/ *n* [U] respect and admiration given to someone or something, usually because of a reputation for high quality, success, or social influence ○ *No one would go into this sort of work for the prestige.*

prestigious /presˈtɪdʒ·əs/ *adj* ○ *a prestigious school*

presume Ⓐ **BELIEVE** /prɪˈzuːm/ *v* [T] to believe something to be true because it is likely, although not certain ○ [+ (*that*) clause] *I presume (that) they're not coming, since they haven't replied to the invitation.* ○ *People accused of a crime are presumed innocent until proven guilty.*

presumably Ⓐ /prɪˈzuː·mə·bli/ *adv* [not gradable] ○ *Presumably they can afford to buy an apartment, or they wouldn't be looking.*

BE RUDE /prɪˈzuːm/ *v* [I] to be rude by doing something you know that you do not have a right to do ○ [+ *to* infinitive] *How can you presume to criticize me when you did the same thing yourself?*

presumption Ⓐ **BELIEF** /prɪˈzʌmp·ʃən/ *n* [C] a belief that something is true because it is likely, although not certain ○ *There is no scientific evidence to support such presumptions.*

RUDENESS /prɪˈzʌmp·ʃən/ *n* [U] behavior that is rude or shows that you expect too much ○ *What presumption, to assume that I'd pay for everyone!*

presumptuous Ⓐ /prɪˈzʌmp·tʃə·wəs/ *adj* rude because of doing something although you know you do not have a right to do it ○ *It would be presumptuous of me to speak for the others.*

presuppose /ˌpriː·səˈpoʊz/ *v* [T] *fml* to think that something is true in advance without having any proof, or to consider that something is necessarily true if something else is true ○ [+ *that* clause] *You're presupposing that he told her – but he may not have.* ○ *Teaching presupposes a formal education.*

pretax /ˈpriːˈtæks/ *adj* [not gradable] before tax is paid ○ *pretax income/earnings/profit*

pretend /prɪˈtend/ *v* [I/T] to behave as if something is true when you know that it is not, esp. in order to deceive people or as a game ○ [+ *to* infinitive] *Tom pretends to care.* ○ [+ (*that*) clause] *The children pretended (that) they were dinosaurs.*
pretend /prɪˈtend/ *adj* [not gradable] ○ *a pretend tea party*
pretense /ˈpriː·tens, prɪˈtens/ *n* [U] a way of behaving that is intended to deceive people ○ *He made no pretense of looking for work.* ○ [pl] *Money was collected* **under false pretenses** (= by deceiving people).

pretension /prɪˈten·tʃən/ *n* [C/U] **1** the appearance of being more important or more serious than there is reason for ○ [U] *Leonard's paintings have a real freedom from pretension.* **2** A pretension is also a claim or belief that you can succeed or that you are important or have serious value: [C usually pl] *He has no pretensions for higher office.*

pretentious /prɪˈten·tʃəs/ *adj disapproving* trying to give the appearance of great importance, esp. in a way that is obvious ○ *pretentious restaurants* ○ *pretentious, silly poetry*

pretext /ˈpriː·tekst/ *n* [C] a pretended reason for doing something that is used to hide the real reason ○ *He called her on the pretext of needing help with his homework.*

pretrial, **pre-trial** /ˈpriː·traɪl/ *adj, adv* [not gradable] happening in or involving the period before a trial begins ○ *Cooper failed to testify in a March 1 pretrial hearing.*

pretty PLEASANT /ˈprɪt̬·i/ *adj* [*-er/-est* only] pleasant to look at, or (esp. of girls or women or things connected with them) attractive or charming in a delicate way ○ *a pretty view* ○ *My older sister is prettier than I am.*
prettiness /ˈprɪt̬·iː·nəs/ *n* [U] ○ *Her prettiness was matched by her intelligence.*
TO A LARGE DEGREE /ˈprɪt̬·i/ *adv* [not gradable] (used to give emphasis) to a large degree; to some degree ○ *I've got a pretty clear idea of what's going on.* ○ *She was pretty tired.* ○ *"How are you feeling?" "Pretty good, thanks."*

IDIOM with **pretty**

• **pretty much**, **pretty well** almost completely ○ *I've pretty much finished packing now.* ○ *I've pretty well decided I'm not going to go.*

pretzel /ˈpret·səl/ *n* [C] a kind of hard or chewy bread, usually with salt on it, that is baked in the shape of a loose knot or stick

prevail /prɪˈveɪl/ *v* [I] to exist and be accepted among a large number of people, or to get a position of control and influence ○ *Let's hope that common sense prevails.* ○ *In spite of injuries, our team prevailed and went on to win.*
prevailing /prɪˈveɪ·lɪŋ/ *adj* [not gradable] existing and accepted ○ *The prevailing view is that economic growth is likely to slow down.*

PHRASAL VERB with **prevail**

• **prevail on/upon** *someone* **to** *do something* to persuade someone to do something ○ *My father prevailed on some friends to let us stay with them.*

prevalent /ˈprev·ə·lənt/ *adj* existing commonly or happening frequently ○ *Drought conditions have been prevalent across the area for several years.*
prevalence /ˈprev·ə·ləns/ *n* [U] ○ *He was surprised by the prevalence of middle-aged women among the job seekers.*

prevent /prɪˈvent/ *v* [T] to stop something from happening or someone from doing something ○ *The police tried to prevent him from leaving.* ○ *Can this type of accident be prevented?*
preventable /prɪˈvent·ə·bəl/ *adj* ○ *Fortunately, the suffering caused by ulcers is entirely preventable.*
prevention /prɪˈven·tʃən/ *n* [U] ○ *crime prevention*
preventive /prɪˈvent·ɪv/, **preventative** /prɪˈvent·ət̬·ɪv/ *adj* [not gradable] intended to stop something before it happens ○ *preventive measures* ○ *preventative health care*

USAGE

prevent or protect?

Prevent means to stop something from happening.

Wearing sunscreen can help prevent skin cancer.

Protect means to keep someone or something safe from bad things.

The police wear bulletproof vests to protect themselves.

WORD FAMILY **prevent**

Nouns	prevention	*Adjectives*	preventable
Verbs	prevent		preventive preventative

WORD CHOICES **prevent**

Two common alternatives to "prevent" are **avoid** or **stop**.

Label the boxes to ***avoid*** *confusion.*

This should ***stop*** *any further trouble.*

They've put barriers up to ***stop*** *people from getting through.*

To talk about preventing something bad from happening, the verb **avert** can be used.

We had to act quickly to ***avert*** *disaster.*

If something prevents something else by making it impossible, you can use the verb **prohibit**.

Behavioral problems in the classroom ***prohibit*** *learning.*

Check can be used when something prevents another thing from continuing or increasing.

Children are being vaccinated in an attempt to ***check*** *the spread of the disease.*

The verbs **foil** and **thwart** mean to prevent someone or something from being successful.

The attempted kidnapping was ***foiled*** *by some undercover police.*

My trip to London was ***thwarted*** *by a pilots' strike.*

P

preview /ˈpriː·vjuː/ *n* [C] an advance showing of something such as a movie or play before its formal opening, or the showing of a few parts of a movie or television program as an advertisement
preview /ˈpriː·vjuː/ *v* [T] ○ *Members got a chance to preview the new show at the museum.*

previous Ⓐ /ˈpriː·viː·əs/ *adj* [not gradable] happening or existing before the one mentioned ○ *The previous owner of the house added a back porch.*
previously Ⓐ /ˈpriː·viː·ə·sli/ *adv* [not gradable] ○ *She was previously employed as a tour guide.*

prewar /priː ˈwɔːr/ *adj* [not gradable] existing or happening before a war, esp. World War II ○ Compare POSTWAR

prewriting /ˈpriː ˌrɑɪt̬·ɪŋ/ *n* [U] ***writing*** the first stage in writing, in which you gather ideas and information and plan how to organize them

prey /preɪ/ *n* [U] a creature that is hunted and killed for food by another animal ○ *The prey had been sighted.*

IDIOM with prey

• **fall prey to** *someone/something*, **be prey to** *someone/something* to be influenced by someone or something ○ *We worry that our children will fall prey to the influence of bad kids.*

PHRASAL VERB with prey

• **prey on** *something/someone* **1** to kill and eat an animal ○ *Lions prey on huge herds of wildebeest and zebra.* **2** Someone who **preys on** a group of people tries to get something from them illegally or unfairly: *These telemarketers prey on the elderly and call them 5 or 10 times a day.*

price /prɑɪs/ *n* [C] the amount of money for which something is sold or offered for sale ○ *high/low prices* ○ *The price of gas went up five cents a gallon.*
price /prɑɪs/ *v* [T; not gradable] ○ *The car is priced at $24,000.*
priceless /ˈprɑɪ·sləs/ *adj* more valuable than any amount of money; precious ○ *He has a priceless collection of antique silver.*
pricey /ˈprɑɪ·si/ *adj comparative* **pricier**, *superlative* **priciest** expensive ○ *That restaurant's too pricey for me.*

WORD FAMILY price

Nouns	price	*Adjectives*	overpriced
Verbs	price		priceless
			pricey

COMMON LEARNER ERROR

price or prize?

These two words sound similar but have different spellings and very different meanings.

Price means "the amount of money that you pay to buy something."

The price of oil has risen by 20%.
~~*The prize of oil has risen by 20%.*~~

Prize means "something valuable that is given to someone who wins a competition or who has done good work."

She won first prize in the competition.
~~*She won first price in the competition.*~~

IDIOM with price

• **at a price** for a lot of money ○ *She'll decorate your house however you want it – at a price.* ○ Compare FOR A PRICE at FOR IDIOMS

price tag *n* [C] a piece of paper attached to something for sale that shows how much it costs, or the cost of something ○ *The price tag for restoring the building will be around $150 million.*

prick /prɪk/ *v* [T] to make a small hole or holes in the surface of something ○ *The nurse pricked his finger to draw blood.*

IDIOM with prick

• **prick up** *your* **ears** to listen carefully ○ *The children pricked up their ears when they heard the word "candy."*

prickle /ˈprɪk·əl/ *n* [C] **1** a stinging feeling as if made by a sharp point ○ *A prickle of fear ran up the back of my neck.* **2** A prickle is also a sharp point that sticks out of a plant or animal.
prickle /ˈprɪk·əl/ *v* [I/T] ○ [T] *She lay on the dry grass, which prickled the back of her legs.*
prickly /ˈprɪk·li/ *adj* having sharp points that stick out, or causing a stinging feeling ○ *a prickly cactus* ○ *The wool felt prickly and itchy against his skin.*

pride FEELING OF SATISFACTION /prɑɪd/ *n* [U] a feeling of pleasure and satisfaction that you get because you or people connected with you have done something good ○ *Their son's outstanding academic record was a source of great pride to them.* ○ *We take pride in the high quality of our food.* ○ Related adjective: PROUD SATISFIED

FEELING OF WORTH /prɑɪd/ *n* [U] **1** your feelings of your own worth and respect for yourself ○ *Out of pride, he refused an offer to take over his business.* **2** *disapproving* Pride is also the belief that you are better or more important than other people. ○ Related adjective: PROUD RESPECTING YOURSELF

GROUP /prɑɪd/ *n* [C] a group of lions

IDIOMS with pride

• *someone's* **pride and joy** a person or thing that gives someone great joy and satisfaction ○ *Those flowers are her pride and joy.*
• **pride** *yourself* **on** *something* to value a special quality or ability that you have ○ *He prides himself on his singing.*

priest /priːst/ *n* [C] a person, usually a man, who has been trained to perform religious duties in some Christian churches, esp. the Roman Catholic Church, or (*female* **priestess**) a person with particular duties in some other religions ○ *a Catholic priest*
priesthood /ˈpriːst·hʊd/ *n* [U] the position of being a priest ○ *He entered the priesthood after three years of study.*

prim /prɪm/ *adj* formal, neat, and socially correct ○ *She wore a silk gown and prim white gloves.*

primacy Ⓐ /ˈprɑɪ·mə·si/ *n* [U] the state of being important or most important ○ *Satellite television,* *boasting 300 digital channels, was threatening the primacy of cable TV.*

prima donna /ˌprim·əˈdɑn·ə, ˈpriː·mə-/ *n* [C] *pl* **prima donnas** the most important woman singing in an opera company, or *disapproving* a person who is difficult to please and who expects to be treated better than anyone else ○ *The performance was met with enough applause to please the most demanding prima donna.*

primal /ˈprɑɪ·məl/ *adj* [not gradable] characteristic of the earliest time in the existence of a person or thing; basic ○ *The appeal of music is primal.*

primary Ⓐ **MOST IMPORTANT** /ˈprɑɪˌmer·i, -mə·ri/ *adj* [not gradable] more important than anything else; main ○ *The primary goal of the space flight was to recover a satellite.*

primarily Ⓐ /prɑɪˈmer·ə·li/ *adv* [not gradable] mainly ○ *The company's failure was primarily due to weak sales.*

EDUCATION /ˈprɑɪˌmer·i, -mə·ri/ *adj* [not gradable] relating to the first part of a child's education ○ *the primary grades*

EARLIEST /ˈprɑɪˌmer·i, -mə·ri/ *adj* [not gradable] happening first ○ *the primary stages of development*

ELECTION /ˈprɑɪˌmer·i, -mə·ri/ *n* [C] ***politics & government*** an election in which people who belong to a political party choose who will represent that party in an election for political office

primary care *n* [U] *medical* basic medical care that is available when someone first goes to a doctor to be helped ○ *a primary care physician*

primary color *n* [C] ***art*** one of the three colors – red, yellow, or blue – that can be mixed together in various ways to make any other color

primary school *n* [C] a school for children from the ages of about five to nine, or an ELEMENTARY SCHOOL

primate /ˈprɑɪ·meɪt/ *n* [C] ***biology*** a member of the most developed and intelligent group of mammals, including humans, monkeys, and APES

prime Ⓐ **MAIN/BEST** /prɑɪm/ *adj* [not gradable] most important, or of the best quality ○ *You're a prime candidate to be spending money on foolish things.* ○ *This is a prime example of native Utah architecture.* ○ *The hospital is located on prime Upper East Side property.*

PREPARE /prɑɪm/ *v* [T] **1** to prepare someone or something for the next stage in a process ○ *Their teachers are getting those kids primed for the tests.* **2** To prime a surface is to cover it with a special paint before the main paint is put on.

primer /ˈprɑɪ·mər/ *n* [C/U] a type of paint put on a surface before putting on the main paint

IDIOMS with prime

• **in** *your/its* **prime**, **in the prime of** *your* **life** in the best, most successful, most productive stage ○ *The horse retired from racing while still in his prime.* ○ *She was in the prime of her working life when she retired, but she continued as a consultant.*

• **past** *your/its* **prime** after the best, most successful, most productive stage ○ *He can still play, but he's past his prime.*

prime minister *n* [C] the leader of the government in some countries

prime number *n* [C] ***mathematics*** a number that cannot be divided by any other number except itself and the number 1

primer /ˈprɪm·ər/ *n* [C] a basic text for teaching something ○ *As a primer for Navaho thinking, this book is a good place to start.*

prime time *n* [U] the period between 8 and 11 at night when the largest number of people are watching television ○ *prime time programs*

primeval /prɑɪˈmiː·vəl/ *adj* existing at or from a very early time; ancient ○ *primeval forests*

primitive /ˈprɪm·ət̬·ɪv/ *adj* of or typical of an early stage of development; not advanced or complicated in structure ○ *primitive art/tools* ○ *The pioneers who settled the west had to cope with primitive living conditions.*

primordial /prɑɪˈmɔːrd·iː·əl/ *adj* existing at or since the beginning of the world or the universe ○ *primordial gases*

primrose /ˈprɪm·roʊz/ *n* [C] a wild plant with pale yellow flowers

prince /prɪns/ *n* [C] **1** a member of a ROYAL family, esp. a son of a king or queen **2** A prince is also a male ruler of a small country.

princely /ˈprɪn·sli/ *adj* [not gradable] (esp. of money) very large in amount ○ *Advertisers pay a princely sum for prime-time commercials.*

princess /ˈprɪn·səs, -ses/ *n* [C] **1** a member of a ROYAL family, esp. a daughter of a king or queen **2** A princess is also the wife of a PRINCE.

principal Ⓐ **MAIN** /ˈprɪn·sə·pəl/ *adj* [not gradable] first in order of importance ○ *Iraq's principal export is oil.*

principally Ⓐ /ˈprɪn·sə·pli/ *adv* [not gradable] more than anything or anyone else; mainly ○ *The advertising campaign is aimed principally at women.*

PERSON /ˈprɪn·sə·pəl/ *n* [C] a person in charge of a school

MONEY /ˈprɪn·sə·pəl/ *n* [C usually sing] an amount of money that is lent, borrowed, or invested, apart from any additional money such as INTEREST

principality /ˌprɪn·səˈpæl·ət̬·i/ *n* [C] a country ruled by a PRINCE

principle Ⓐ **MORAL RULE** /ˈprɪn·sə·pəl/ *n* [C/U] **1** a moral rule or standard of good behavior or fair dealing ○ [C] *His guiding principle is that everyone should have equal access to high-quality health care.* ○ [C] *He refused to compromise his principles.* **2** If you believe or act **on principle**, you are following a personal standard of behavior: *On principle, I never eat meat.*

principled Ⓐ /ˈprɪn·sə·pəld/ *adj* based on principles, or (of a person) having good personal standards of behavior ○ *She was known among her colleagues as a principled professional.*

P

BASIC TRUTH /ˈprɪn·sə·pəl/ *n* [C often pl] **1** a basic truth that explains or controls how something happens or works ○ *the principles of Newtonian physics* **2** Someone who agrees to something **in principle**, agrees with the idea, but may not agree with using the idea to bring about practical changes: *In principle I agree that mothers should spend as much time as possible with their young children, but it isn't easy.*

print **MAKE TEXT** /prɪnt/ *v* [T] **1** to put letters or images on paper or another material using a machine, or to produce books, magazines, newspapers, etc., in this way ○ *The newspaper printed my letter to the editor.* **2** To print is also to write without joining the letters together: *Please print your name clearly below your signature.* **3** To print something out is to print text or images from a machine attached to a computer: [M] *Just print out the first two pages.*

print /prɪnt/ *n* [U] **1** text or images that are produced on paper or other material by printing **2** If something is **in print**, it is published and available to buy. ○ *Is the book still in print?* **3** If a book is **out of print**, it is no longer available from a publisher ○ *I'm afraid you can't get that book – it's out of print.*

printing /ˈprɪnt·ɪŋ/ *n* [C/U] **1** the process or business of producing printed material **2** A printing is the number of copies of a book printed at one time: [C] *The first printing will be 25,000 copies.*

printer /ˈprɪnt·ər/ *n* [C] **1** a machine connected to a computer that prints onto paper using ink ○ *a laser printer* **2** A printer is also a person whose job is to print material.

PICTURE /prɪnt/ *n* [C] **1** a single photograph made from film, or a photograph of a painting or other work of art ○ *We made extra prints of the baby to send out with the birth announcement.* **2** A print is also a picture made by pressing paper or other material against a special surface covered with ink: *woodcut prints*

print /prɪnt/ *v* [T] ○ *Photographs are better if they are printed from the original negative.*

PATTERN /prɪnt/ *n* [C] a pattern produced on a piece of cloth, or cloth having such a pattern ○ *a print dress*

MARK /prɪnt/ *n* [C] **1** a mark left on a surface where something has been pressed on it ○ *The dog left prints all over the kitchen floor.* **2** A print is also a FINGERPRINT.

WORD FAMILY print			
Nouns	print printer printing	*Verbs*	print

printing press *n* [C] a machine that prints text or images, esp. to produce books, magazines, and newspapers

printout /ˈprɪnt·ɑʊt/ *n* [C] a paper copy of computer text and images produced by a PRINTER attached to the computer

prior Ⓐ /ˈprɑɪ·ər/ *adj, adv* [not gradable] coming before in time, order, or importance ○ *She denied prior knowledge of the meeting.* ○ *Passengers may board the plane twenty minutes* **prior to** (= before) *departure.*

priority Ⓐ /prɑɪˈɔːr·ət̬·i, -ˈɑr-/ *n* [C/U] **1** something that is considered more important than other matters ○ [C] *The president vowed to make education one of his top priorities.* **2** If something **takes priority over** something else, it is more important: [U] *Getting fresh water and food to the flood victims takes priority over dealing with their insurance claims.*

prioritize Ⓐ /prɑɪˈɔːr·əˌtɑɪz, -ˈɑr-/ *v* [I/T] to arrange in order of importance so that you can deal with the most important things before the others ○ [I] *You have to prioritize in this job because you can't do everything.*

prioritization Ⓐ /prɑɪˌɔːr·ət̬·əˈzeɪ·ʃən, -ˌɑr-/ *n* [U]

prism /ˈprɪz·əm/ *n* [C] a transparent object, often glass, that separates white light into different colors

prison /ˈprɪz·ən/ *n* [C/U] a building where criminals are kept as a punishment ○ [U] *He was sent to prison for life.*

prisoner /ˈprɪz·ə·nər/ *n* [C] **1** a person who is kept in prison as punishment **2** Prisoners are also people who are not physically free because they are under the control of someone else: *Two security guards were held/taken prisoner during the robbery.*

WORD FAMILY prison			
Nouns	prison prisoner imprisonment	*Verbs*	imprison

prisoner of war, *abbreviation* **POW** *n* [C] a member of the armed forces who has been caught by enemy forces during a war

pristine /ˈprɪs·tiːn, prɪˈstiːn/ *adj* [not gradable] original and pure; not spoiled or worn from use ○ *The car seemed to be in pristine condition.*

private **PERSONAL** /ˈprɑɪ·vət/ *adj* **1** for the use of or belonging to one particular person or group only, or not shared or available to other people ○ *The sign on the gate said "Private Property – Keep Out."* ○ *Let's go somewhere private so we can talk freely.* **2** If you do something **in private**, you do it without other people present: *I asked if I could talk to her in private.*

privately /ˈprɑɪ·vət·li/ *adv* [not gradable] ○ *Could I speak with you privately* (= without other people present)? ○ *Despite his public support, privately* (= in his own mind) *he was worried.*

privacy /ˈprɑɪ·və·si/ *n* [U] the state of being alone, or the right to keep one's personal matters and relationships secret ○ *A fence would give us more privacy in the backyard.*

INDEPENDENT /ˈprɑɪ·vət/ *adj* [not gradable] belonging to or managed by a person or independent company rather than the government ○ *The governor visited Ireland as a private citizen* (= not as an official).

privately /ˈprɑɪ·vət·li/ *adv* [not gradable] ○ *She was privately educated at an exclusive girls' school.*

privatize /ˈprɑɪ·vəˌtɑɪz/ *v* [T] ***social studies*** (of an industry, company, or service) to change from being owned by a government to being owned and controlled independently

privatization /ˌprɑɪ·vəţ·əˈzeɪ·ʃən/ *n* [U]

RANK /ˈprɑɪ·vət/ *n* [C] a person in the military of the lowest rank, below a CORPORAL

WORD FAMILY private

Nouns	privacy private privatization	*Adjectives*	private
		Verbs	privatize
		Adverbs	privately

private enterprise *n* [C/U] a business owned and controlled independently and not by government, or the system that encourages such businesses

private investigator, **private detective**, *infml* **private eye** *n* [C] a person whose job it is to discover information about people, but who is not a member of a police force

private parts *pl n* someone's sexual organs

private school *n* [C] a school that does not receive its main financial support from the government

private sector *n* [C usually sing] all the businesses that are not owned and controlled by the government ○ *The project will be financed by the government and two companies in the private sector.*

privilege /ˈprɪv·ə·lɪdʒ/ *n* [C/U] a special advantage or authority possessed by a particular person or group ○ [C] *As a senior executive, you will enjoy certain privileges.* ○ [C] *I had the privilege* (= the honor) *of interviewing the prime minister of Canada.*

privileged /ˈprɪv·ə·lɪdʒd/ *adj* [not gradable] **1** *As an old friend of the president, he enjoys privileged status.* **2** *law* Information that is privileged is secret: *A person's medical history is privileged information.*

privy /ˈprɪv·i/ *adj* [not gradable] *fml* having secret knowledge ○ *Only top management was* **privy to** (= knew about) *the proposed merger.*

prize /prɑɪz/ *n* [C] a reward for victory in a competition or game ○ *David won first prize in the school science fair.*

prize /prɑɪz/ *adj* [not gradable] given as a prize, or having won or deserving to win a prize ○ *prize money*

prize /prɑɪz/ *v* [T] **1** to value greatly ○ *The Japanese prize personal relationships in doing business.* **2** A prized possession is one that is very important to you. ➤ Learner error: **price or prize?** at PRICE

prizefight /ˈprɑɪz·fɑɪt/ *n* [C] a boxing competition between fighters who get paid

pro **SPORTS PERSON** /proʊ/ *n* [C] *pl* **pros** *infml* **1** a person who receives money for playing a sport ○ *a tennis pro* **2** A pro is also someone who is very good at something: *Debbie is a real pro at arranging flowers.*

ADVANTAGE /proʊ/ *n* [C] *pl* **pros** an advantage or a reason for doing something ○ *I made a list of all* **the pros and cons** (= advantages and disadvantages) *of each school before I made my decision.*

pro- /proʊ/ *prefix* supporting or approving of something ○ *pro-American* ○ Compare ANTI-

proactive, **pro-active** /proʊˈæk·tɪv/ *adj* intending or intended to produce a good result or avoid a problem, rather than waiting until there is a problem ○ *The agency decided to take a proactive approach to better serve its clients.*

probability /ˌprɑb·əˈbɪl·əţ·i/ *n* [C/U] ***mathematics*** **1** a number that represents how likely it is that a particular thing will happen **2** Probability is the study of the mathematics of calculating the likelihood that particular events will happen.

probable /ˈprɑb·ə·bəl/ *adj* likely to be true or likely to happen ○ *The doctor said that the most probable cause of death was heart failure.*

probably /ˈprɑb·ə·bli/ *adv* [not gradable] ○ *I'll probably be home about midnight.*

probability /ˌprɑb·əˈbɪl·əţ·i/ *n* [C/U] the likelihood of something happening or being true ○ [C] *There's a higher probability of now having a state income tax* (= the tax is more likely now). ○ **In all probability** *he would never see her again* (= very likely he would not see her again).

WORD FAMILY probable

Nouns	probability improbability	*Adverbs*	probably improbably
Adjectives	probable improbable		

probation /proʊˈbeɪ·ʃən/ *n* [U] **1** a period during which a person's behavior or performance on a job or in a school is watched closely to see whether the person is good enough to stay ○ *I'm on probation this semester, so I've really got to study hard.* **2** Probation for criminals is the condition of being allowed freedom if they commit no more crimes and follow certain rules.

probation officer *n* [C] an officer whose job is to manage criminals who are on PROBATION

probe /proʊb/ *v* [I/T] **1** to search into or examine something ○ [I] *Investigators are probing into new evidence in the case.* **2** To probe something with a tool is to examine it: [T] *Using a special instrument, the doctor probed the wound for the bullet.*

probe /proʊb/ *n* [C] **1** a careful and detailed examination ○ *The probe explored allegations of corruption in the police department.* **2** A probe is also a long, thin tool used by doctors in medical examinations or operations.

probing /ˈproʊ·bɪŋ/ *adj* (of a question) difficult to answer without telling the truth ○ *probing questions*

problem /ˈprɑb·ləm/ *n* [C] **1** something that causes difficulty or that is hard to deal with ○ *Financing the camp's athletic program is a problem.* ○ *He has a serious health problem.* ○ *I'm having prob-*

P

lems with my in-laws again. **2** ***mathematics*** A problem is also a question to be answered or solved, esp. by reasoning or calculating: *math problems*

problematic /ˌprɑb·lə'mæt̬·ɪk/ *adj* ○ *Social interactions are really problematic with a lot of children.* ➤ Usage: **trouble or problem?** at TROUBLE DIFFICULTIES

WORD CHOICES problem

The noun **difficulty** is a common alternative to "problem."

The company is having some financial ***difficulties*** *at the moment.*

You can describe several problems as **trouble**.

We've had a lot of ***trouble*** *with the new computer system.*

A small, temporary problem may be described informally as a **hitch**.

The ceremony went without a ***hitch****.*

A **glitch** is a problem that stops something from working properly.

We've had a few technical ***glitches****, but I'm confident we'll be ready on time.*

A **hurdle** or **obstacle** is a problem that you need to deal with so that you can continue to make progress.

Getting a work permit is only the first ***hurdle****.*

There may be too many ***obstacles*** *in the way of progress.*

A **pitfall** is a problem that is likely to happen in a particular situation.

It's just one of the ***pitfalls*** *of buying a house.*

A **setback** is a problem that makes something happen less quickly than it should.

The project has suffered a series of ***setbacks*** *this year.*

A **snag** is a small problem in something which is mostly good.

The only ***snag*** *is the cost.*

P

procedure Ⓐ /prə'siː·dʒər/ *n* [C/U] an order or method of doing something ○ [U] *It's standard procedure for those at the top of the list to be called first.*

procedural Ⓐ /prə'siː·dʒə·rəl/ *adj* [not gradable] ○ *Defense lawyers most often challenge test results based on procedural grounds.*

proceed Ⓐ /prə'siːd, proʊ-/ *v* [I] **1** to start or continue an action or process ○ *The building project is proceeding smoothly.* ○ *You should ask a lawyer for advice on how to proceed.* **2** To proceed is also to move forward or travel in a particular direction: *The warning signs said "Proceed with caution."*

proceedings Ⓐ /prə'siːd·ɪŋz, proʊ-/ *pl n* a series of actions that happen in a planned and controlled way ○ *As the president was sworn in, the nation watched the proceedings on TV.*

proceeds Ⓐ /'proʊ·siːdz/ *pl n* the amount of money received from a particular sale or event ○ *All proceeds from the auction will be donated to charity.*

process Ⓐ /'prɑs·es, 'proʊ·ses/ *n* [C] **1** a series of actions or events performed to make something or achieve a particular result, or a series of changes that happen naturally ○ *Completing his degree at night was a long process.* ○ *Graying hair is part of the aging process.* ○ *We are still* **in the process of** *redecorating the house* (= working to decorate it). **2** A process is also a method of doing or making something, as in industry: *A new process has been developed for removing asbestos.*

process Ⓐ /'prɑs·es, 'proʊ·ses/ *v* [T] **1** to deal with something according to a particular set of actions ○ *Your insurance claim will take about a month to process.* **2** If a computer processes information, it performs a series of operations on it. **3** To process food or raw materials is to prepare, change, or treat them as part of an industrial operation.

processed Ⓐ /'prɑs·est, 'proʊ·sest/ *adj* [not gradable] (of food) treated with chemicals that preserve it or give it extra taste or color ○ *processed cheese/meat*

processor /'prɑsˌes·ər, 'proʊˌses-/ *n* [C] a person, device, or business that processes things ○ *a food processor*

WORD FAMILY process

Nouns	process procession processor	*Adjectives*	processed
		Verbs	process

procession /prə'seʃ·ən/ *n* [C] a line of people, vehicles, or objects moving forward in an organized manner, esp. as part of a ceremony ○ *a funeral procession*

processional /prə'seʃ·ən·əl/ *adj* [not gradable] ○ *There was tight security along the processional route.*

pro-choice /'proʊ'tʃɔɪs/ *adj* [not gradable] supporting the belief that a pregnant woman should have the freedom to choose an ABORTION (= an operation to end a pregnancy) if she does not want to have a baby ○ Compare PRO-LIFE

proclaim /prə'kleɪm, proʊ-/ *v* [T] to announce something publicly or officially ○ *She confidently proclaimed victory even as the first few votes came in.*

proclamation /ˌprɑk·lə'meɪ·ʃən/ *n* [C] a public announcement, or the act of making it

procrastinate /prə'kræs·təˌneɪt/ *v* [I] to delay doing something ○ *When it comes to housework, I tend to procrastinate.*

procreate /'proʊ·kriːˌeɪt/ *v* [I] to reproduce sexually

procreation /ˌproʊ·kriː'eɪ·ʃən/ *n* [U]

procure /prə'kjʊr, proʊ-/ *v* [T] to obtain something, esp. after an effort ○ *We procured maps and directions from the tourist office.*

procurement /prə'kjʊr·mənt, proʊ-/ *n* [U] ○ *the city's procurement process*

prod /prɑd/ *v* [I/T] **-dd-** to push something or someone with your finger or with an object, or to

encourage someone to take action, esp. when the person is slow or unwilling ○ [T] *The barber prodded the back of Ray's head.* ○ [I] *No matter how much I prod he will not tell me what happened.*
prod /prɑd/ *n* [C] ○ *The protests were a prod for Congress to debate the issue.*

prodigal /ˈprɑd·ɪ·gəl/ *adj esp. fml* tending to spend or use something without thinking of the future ○ *He was prodigal with his talents.*

prodigious /prəˈdɪdʒ·əs/ *adj* extremely great in ability, amount, or strength ○ *Americans are the world's most prodigious consumers.*
prodigiously /prəˈdɪdʒ·ə·sli/ *adv* ○ *a prodigiously gifted artist*

prodigy /ˈprɑd·ə·dʒi/ *n* [C] a child who shows a great ability at a young age ○ *a child prodigy on the piano*

produce MAKE /prəˈduːs/ *v* [T] to create something or bring into existence ○ *Bukowski produced poetry and novels.* ○ *Dairy goods and beef are produced locally.*
producer /prəˈduː·sər/ *n* [C] a company, country, or person that makes things, usually for sale, esp. things made by an industrial process or grown or obtained from the ground ○ *a producer of automobiles/wheat*
ORGANIZE A SHOW /prəˈduːs/ *v* [T] to organize the financial and other practical matters connected with the making of a movie, play, television show, or other entertainment program ○ *He produced a couple of wonderful films.* ○ Compare DIRECT CONTROL
producer /prəˈduː·sər/ *n* [C] ○ *a movie/record producer*
BRING OUT /prəˈduːs/ *v* [T] to bring something out and show it ○ *He walked up and produced his passport.*
CAUSE /prəˈduːs/ *v* [T] to cause a reaction or result ○ *Too much coffee can produce unwanted side-effects.*
FOOD /ˈprɑd·uːs, ˈproʊd·uːs/ *n* [U] food that is grown or raised through farming, esp. fruits and vegetables ○ *local produce*

WORD FAMILY produce			
Nouns	produce producer product production reproduction productivity	*Adjectives*	productive counterproductive reproductive unproductive
		Adverbs	productively unproductively
Verbs	produce reproduce		

product THING MADE /ˈprɑd·əkt, -ʌkt/ *n* [C] something that is made to be sold, esp. something produced by an industrial process or something that is grown or raised through farming ○ *industrial products* ○ *A new product can require two years to develop.*
production /prəˈdʌk·ʃən/ *n* [U] the process of making or growing goods to be sold, or the amount of goods made or grown ○ *mass production* ○ *Agricultural production has increased dramatically this year.*
RESULT /ˈprɑd·əkt, -ʌkt/ *n* [C] **1** a result obtained from experiencing something ○ *She's a product of the city's public schools.* **2** ***mathematics*** A product is the number you get when you multiply numbers: *The product of 6 and 3 is 18.* **3** ***chemistry*** A product is also the substance that results from a chemical reaction between other substances.

production ENTERTAINMENT /prəˈdʌk·ʃən/ *n* [C/U] a movie, television program, play, or other entertainment, or the work of organizing the practical matters involved in a show ○ [C] *a terrific production of "The Wizard of Oz"* ○ [U] *She's hoping to get into television production.*
PROCESS /prəˈdʌk·ʃən/ *n* [U] ***biology*** (of living things) the process of making a natural substance, such as a HORMONE

productive /prəˈdʌk·tɪv/ *adj* causing or providing a good result or a large amount of something ○ *We had a very productive meeting – a lot of problems were solved.* ○ *What was once desert has become productive farmland.*
productively /prəˈdʌk·tɪv·li/ *adv* ○ *Her students worked less productively than the teacher hoped.*
productivity /ˌproʊ.dʌkˈtɪv·əṭ·i, ˌprɑd·ək-/ *n* [U] the rate at which a person, company, or country does useful work ○ *A pleasant working environment increases productivity.*

Prof. /prɑf/ *n abbreviation for* PROFESSOR ○ *Prof. Linda Chen* ○ **USAGE:** Used in writing before a name.

profane /prəˈfeɪn, proʊ-/ *adj* (esp. of words) offensive because of not respecting religion, or offensive because of being rude ○ *profane language* ○ *His letter is too profane to print, but it is very funny, too.* ○ Compare SACRED
profanity /prəˈfæn·əṭ·i, proʊ-/ *n* [C/U] ○ [U] *The film contains profanity and violence.* ○ [C usually pl] *They shouted profanities at us.*

profess /prəˈfes, proʊ-/ *v* to claim something, sometimes falsely ○ [+ *to* infinitive] *They professed to have no knowledge of the event.* ○ [T] *She continues to profess her innocence.*
professed /prəˈfest/ *adj* [not gradable] ○ *a professed belief*
profession /prəˈfeʃ·ən/ *n* [C] ○ *His professions of regret were not sincere.*

profession /prəˈfeʃ·ən/ *n* [C/U] any type of work, esp. one that needs a high level of education or a particular skill ○ [C] *the medical/teaching profession* ○ [U] *I'm a writer by profession.*
professional Ⓐ /prəˈfeʃ·ən·əl/ *adj* **1** done as a job, or relating to a skilled type of work ○ *a professional athlete* ○ *professional sports* ○ *He spent his professional career at the University of Pennsylvania.* **2** Professional also means having the qualities of skilled and educated people, such as effectiveness and seriousness of manner: *Wearing jeans to work is not looked upon as being professional.* ○ Compare AMATEUR

P

professional Ⓐ /prəˈfeʃ·ən·əl/ *n* [C] a person who has a job that needs skill, education, or training ○ *Don't you wish you had hired a professional to paint your house?* ○ *Many of these homes have been restored by young professionals.*
professionally Ⓐ /prəˈfeʃ·ən·əl·i/ *adv* ○ *I always wanted to sing professionally.*
professionalism Ⓐ /prəˈfeʃ·ən·əlˌɪz·əm/ *n* [U] the qualities connected with trained and skilled people ○ *We were impressed with the professionalism of the staff.*

SPELLING

profession

Many people make mistakes when spelling this word and related words. The correct spelling has one "f" and two "s's."

Engineering was her chosen profession.

WORD FAMILY profession

Nouns	profession professional professionalism	*Adjectives*	professional unprofessional
		Adverbs	professionally

professor /prəˈfes·ər/, *abbreviation* **Prof.** *n* [C] a teacher of high rank in an American university or college ○ *Professor W. B. Ofuatey-Kodjoe* ○ *a history professor/professor of history*

proficient /prəˈfɪʃ·ənt/ *adj* skilled and experienced ○ *a proficient swimmer* ○ *He studied Chinese and became proficient in the language.*
proficiency /prəˈfɪʃ·ən·si/ *n* [U] ○ *Morgan has great proficiency as a jazz saxophonist.*

P

profile SIDE VIEW /ˈproʊ·fɑɪl/ *n* [C/U] a side view of a person's face ○ [C] *I'd seen her profile on a billboard.* ○ [U] *A face in profile never looks at the viewer.*

DESCRIPTION /ˈproʊ·fɑɪl/ *n* [C] a description of someone containing all the most important or interesting facts about that person ○ *There's a profile of producer Hal Willner in "New York" magazine.*
profile /ˈproʊ·fɑɪl/ *v* [T] ○ *Gilbert was recently profiled by a Washington business magazine.*

ATTENTION /ˈproʊ·fɑɪl/ *n* [C usually sing] the amount of public attention that someone or something receives ○ *He keeps a low profile and doesn't go after headlines.* ○ *She has had a high profile in the world of fashion for many years.*

profit /ˈprɑf·ət/ *n* [C/U] **1** money that a business earns above what it costs to produce and sell goods and services ○ [U] *Any profit made on the sale is taxable.* ○ [C] *A lot of businesses are reaping huge profits.* **2** Profit can also mean benefit: [U] *He could see little profit in arguing with them.*
profit /ˈprɑf·ət/ *v* [I/T] ○ [I] *It's sickening that somebody would profit* (= earn money) *from her misfortune.* ○ [T] *(fml) What will it profit us to make this bargain* (= How will we benefit)?
profitable /ˈprɑf·ət̬·ə·bəl/ *adj* resulting in or likely to result in a profit or a benefit ○ *a profitable business* ○ *I try to make profitable use of my time.*
profitably /ˈprɑf·ət̬·ə·bli/ *adv* ○ *We can operate profitably within that market.*
profitability /ˌprɑf·ət·əˈbɪl·ət̬·i/ *n* [U] ○ *He revealed plans to restore the magazine's profitability.*

WORD FAMILY profit

Nouns	profit profitability	*Adjectives*	profitable unprofitable
Verbs	profit	*Adverbs*	profitably

profit margin *n* [C] the amount that is made in a business after the costs have been subtracted ○ *Many farmers claim that the profit margin for growing trees remains slim.*

profit sharing *n* [U] a system in which the people who work in a company are given part of the profits in addition to their regular pay

profligate /ˈprɑf·lɪ·gət, -ˌgeɪt/ *adj* wasting something, esp. money ○ *profligate spending*

profound EXTREME /prəˈfɑʊnd/ *adj* felt or experienced strongly; extreme ○ *The speech had a profound influence on her.*
profoundly /prəˈfɑʊn·dli/ *adv* ○ *The operation can profoundly improve patients' lives.*

SHOWING UNDERSTANDING /prəˈfɑʊnd/ *adj* showing a clear and deep understanding of serious matters ○ *You're touching on a very profound question.*

profuse /prəˈfjuːs/ *adj* large in amount
profusely /prəˈfjuː·sli/ *adv* ○ *a profusely illustrated book* ○ *Quinn was bleeding profusely.*
profusion /prəˈfjuː·ʒən/ *n* [U] ○ *a profusion of beautiful flowers*

progeny /ˈprɑdʒ·ə·ni/ *n* [U] the young of a person, animal, or plant; OFFSPRING ○ *Housewives chased their progeny out-of-doors.*

progesterone /prəˈdʒes·təˌroʊn/ *n* [U] ***biology*** a female HORMONE (= chemical that influences growth and development) which causes the uterus to prepare for pregnancy

prognosis /prɑgˈnoʊ·səs/ *n* [C] *pl* **prognoses** a doctor's judgment of the likely or expected development of a disease, or a statement of what the likely future situation is ○ *After successful surgery his prognosis was good.*

program ACTIVITIES /ˈproʊ·græm, -grəm/ *n* [C] a group of activities or things to be achieved ○ *a training program* ○ *the university basketball program* ○ *a pilot recycling program*

BROADCAST /ˈproʊ·græm, -grəm/ *n* [C] a broadcast or series of broadcasts on television or radio ○ *What's your favorite program?*

COMPUTER /ˈproʊ·græm, -grəm/ *n* [C] a series of instructions that make a computer perform an operation ○ *a word processing program*
program /ˈproʊ·græm, -grəm/ *v* [T] **-mm-** to instruct a computerized device or system to operate in a particular way or at a particular time ○ *The CD player can be programmed to play the songs in any order.*

programmer /ˈproʊˌɡræm·ər/ *n* [C] a person whose job is to write computer programs
programmable /ˈproʊˌɡræm·ə·bəl/ *adj* ○ *a programmable thermostat*

THIN BOOK /ˈproʊ·ɡræm, -ɡrəm/ *n* [C] a thin book or piece of paper giving information about a play or musical or sports event

progress /ˈprɑɡ·rəs, -res/ *n* [U] **1** movement toward an improved or more developed state, or to a forward position ○ *The talks failed to make any progress toward a settlement.* **2** If something is **in progress**, it is happening or being done now: *The construction work is already in progress.*
progress /prəˈɡres/ *v* [I] ○ *Construction is progressing well.* ○ *As the game progressed I was bouncing in my chair.*
progression /prəˈɡreʃ·ən/ *n* [U] ○ *The show examines one woman's progression from youth to old age.*
progressive /prəˈɡres·ɪv/ *adj* **1** *His papers show a progressive* (= gradually advancing) *change in style.* **2** A progressive disease is one that gets increasingly worse. **3** Progressive ideas or systems encourage change in society or in the way things are done: *She worked for women's rights, labor reforms, and other progressive causes.*
progressively /prəˈɡres·ɪv·li/ *adv* ○ *My eyesight has gotten progressively worse over the years.*

WORD FAMILY progress

Nouns	progress progression	*Verbs*	progress
		Adverbs	progressively
Adjectives	progressive		

progressivism /prəˈɡres·ɪˌvɪz·əm/ *n* [U] ***social studies*** a social or political movement that aims to represent the interests of ordinary people through political change and the support of government actions

prohibit Ⓐ /prəˈhɪb·ət, proʊ-/ *v* [T] **1** to officially forbid something ○ *The law prohibits smoking in restaurants.* **2** To prohibit is also to prevent something by making it impossible: *Loud music prohibited serious conversation.*
prohibition Ⓐ /ˌproʊ·həˈbɪʃ·ən, ˌproʊ·ə-/ *n* [C/U] **1** [C] *Are you proposing a prohibition on bilingual signs?* ○ [U] *Prohibition of free speech is forbidden by the Constitution.* **2** ***US history*** In the US, Prohibition was the period from 1920 to 1933 when the production and sale of alcohol was illegal.
prohibitive Ⓐ /prəˈhɪb·əṭ·ɪv/ *adj* (of costs) too expensive to pay ○ *The cost of a nursing home is prohibitive.*
prohibitively /prəˈhɪb·əṭ·ɪv·li/ *adv* ○ *Fees are prohibitively expensive.*

project Ⓐ **PIECE OF WORK** /ˈprɑdʒ·ekt, -ɪkt/ *n* [C] a piece of planned work or activity that is completed over a period of time and intended to achieve a particular aim ○ *a research project* ○ *construction projects* ○ *Painting the bedroom is Steve's next project.*

BUILDING /ˈprɑdʒ·ekt, -ɪkt/ *n* [C usually pl] a HOUSING PROJECT

CALCULATE /prəˈdʒekt/ *v* [T] to calculate an amount or result expected in the future from information already known ○ *The hotels are projecting big profits.* ○ [+ (*that*) clause] *They project (that) 31 billion people will watch the World Cup.*
projected Ⓐ /prəˈdʒek·təd/ *adj* [not gradable] ○ *The projected population growth will keep doctors busy.*
projection Ⓐ /prəˈdʒek·ʃən/ *n* [C] ○ *Sales projections made last year were too optimistic.*

STICK OUT /prəˈdʒekt/ *v* [I] to stick out beyond the edge of something ○ *The hotel dining room projects (out) over the water.*
projection Ⓐ /prəˈdʒek·ʃən/ *n* [C] ○ *It was a strange-looking house, with little projections off the sides.*

MAKE AN IMAGE /prəˈdʒekt/ *v* [T] to cause a picture or light to appear on a surface ○ *We don't have a screen but we can project the slides onto the back wall.*
projection /prəˈdʒek·ʃən/ *n* [C/U] ○ [C] *A projection of his face appeared on the back wall.*
projector /prəˈdʒek·tər/ *n* [C] a device for showing movies or other images on a screen or other surface
projectionist /prəˈdʒek·ʃə·nəst/ *n* [C] a person whose job is to operate a projector in a movie theater

THROW /prəˈdʒekt/ *v* [T] **1** to throw something forward or into the air ○ *The device allows you to scoop up a ball and project it some 140 feet.* **2** To project is also to speak or sing loudly and clearly: *Singers are used to projecting their voices.*

IDIOM with project

• **project an image** to represent yourself in a particular way through your speech, behavior, and appearance ○ *He's trying to project a more confident image by dressing better.*

projectile /prəˈdʒek·təl, -ˌtaɪl/ *n* [C] an object that is thrown or fired, esp. from a weapon

prokaryotic /ˌproʊˌkær·iːˈɑṭ·ɪk/ *adj* [not gradable] ***biology*** of or relating to organisms such as bacteria that have only one cell, which lacks a NUCLEUS

proletariat /ˌproʊ·ləˈtær·iː·ət/ *n* [U] ***world history*** the people in a society who do not control production and must work in order to live, or the lowest social and economic group in a society

pro-life /proʊˈlaɪf/ *adj* [not gradable] supporting the belief that it is immoral for a pregnant woman to have the freedom to choose to have an ABORTION (= an operation to end a pregnancy) if she does not want to have a baby ○ Compare PRO-CHOICE

proliferate /prəˈlɪf·əˌreɪt/ *v* [I] to increase greatly in number or amount, usually quickly ○ *Amusement and theme parks are proliferating across the country.*
proliferation /prəˌlɪf·əˈreɪ·ʃən/ *n* [U] ○ *The proliferation of cell phones has changed the ways we communicate.*

P

prolific /prəˈlɪf·ɪk/ *adj* producing a great number or amount of something ○ *He was probably the most prolific songwriter of his generation.*

prologue /ˈproʊ·lɔːg, -lɑg/ *n* [C] ***literature*** a part at the beginning of esp. a play, story, or long poem that introduces it ○ *The essay provides a prologue to the book.*

prolong /prəˈlɔːŋ/ *v* [T] to make something last a longer time ○ *They're trying to prolong their lives.*
prolonged /prəˈlɔːŋd/ *adj* ○ *Grasslands were damaged by the prolonged drought.*

prom /prɑm/ *n* [C] a formal party held at the end of the school year for older students in HIGH SCHOOL ○ *Who are you taking to the senior/junior prom?*

promenade /ˌprɑm·əˈneɪd, -ˈnɑd/ *n* [C] a wide path for walking on, esp. one built next to a sea, lake, or river ○ *We strolled along the promenade.*
promenade /ˌprɑm·əˈneɪd, -ˈnɑd/ *v* [I] *dated* to walk slowly along a street or path, usually where you can be seen by many people, for relaxation and pleasure

prominent /ˈprɑm·ə·nənt/ *adj* **1** very noticeable, important, or famous ○ *She plays a prominent role in the organization.* **2** If something is prominent, it sticks out from a surface or can be seen easily: *She has a prominent chin/nose.*
prominently /ˈprɑm·ə·nənt·li/ *adv* ○ *prominently displayed pictures*
prominence /ˈprɑm·ə·nəns/ *n* [U] ○ *Despite his prominence, he was never able to make a living.*

promiscuous /prəˈmɪs·kjə·wəs/ *adj disapproving* (of a person) having a lot of different sexual partners
promiscuity /ˌprɑm·əˈskjuː·ət̬·i/ *n* [U]

promise STATE CERTAINLY /ˈprɑm·əs/ *v* [I/T] to state to someone that you will certainly do something ○ [T] *We promised the kids (that) we'd take them to the zoo.* ○ [+ *to* infinitive] *She promised to be careful.*
promise /ˈprɑm·əs/ *n* [C] a statement that you will certainly do something ○ *I'll try to get back in time, but I'm not making any promises.* ○ *He broke his promise to* (= said he would but did not) *give his art collection to the county museum.*

USAGE
promise

When you use the expression **promise** *someone something* or **promise** *you* **will** *do something* no preposition is needed after the verb.

He promised his mom he would clean his room.
He promised he would clean his room.
~~*He promised to his mom he would clean his room.*~~

To plus an *infinitive* is needed in the expression **promise to** *do something.*

He promised to clean his room.
~~*He promised clean his room.*~~

WORD CHOICES promise

Guarantee is an alternative to "promise."

I can't ***guarantee*** *that the operation will be successful.*

To **give someone your word** is a formal way of saying "promise."

He ***gave me his word*** *that the job would be finished on time.*

If someone promises a person something in order to make that person feel less worried, the word **assure** is often used.

"Don't worry, your car will be ready tomorrow," the mechanic ***assured*** *him.*

Swear can be used when someone promises in a strong way that he or she is telling the truth or will do something or behave in a particular way.

I didn't know anything about what happened, I ***swear****.*

Pledge is used when someone formally promises to give or do something.

We are asking people to ***pledge*** *their support for our campaign.*

If you make a promise to yourself that you will do something, you can use the verbs **resolve** or **vow**.

I ***vowed*** *I would never speak to him again after the way he treated me.*
I have ***resolved*** *to lose ten pounds.*

LIKELY SUCCESS /ˈprɑm·əs/ *n* [U] the likelihood of success or achievement ○ *She shows great promise as a fiction writer.*
promise /ˈprɑm·əs/ *v* to seem likely ○ [+ *to* infinitive] *The new movie promises to be one of the biggest money-makers of all time.*
promising /ˈprɑm·ə·sɪŋ/ *adj* showing signs of future success or achievement ○ *a promising career*

promote Ⓐ ENCOURAGE /prəˈmoʊt/ *v* [T] to encourage or support something, or to help something become successful ○ *A new campaign has been launched to promote safe driving.*
promoter Ⓐ /prəˈmoʊt̬·ər/ *n* [C] a person or company that organizes or finances a sports event or a performance, esp. of musical entertainment

ADVERTISE /prəˈmoʊt/ *v* [T] to advertise something in order to sell it ○ *The new model cars are being heavily promoted on television.*
promotion Ⓐ /prəˈmoʊ·ʃən/ *n* [C/U] advertising intended to increase the sales of a product or service
promotional /prəˈmoʊ·ʃən·əl/ *adj* [not gradable] ○ *We picked up some promotional material on holiday tours to Europe.*

ADVANCE /prəˈmoʊt/ *v* [T] **1** to advance someone to a more important rank or position ○ *She was promoted to division manager last year.* **2** A student who is promoted advances to the next GRADE (= level of schooling). ○ Opposite: DEMOTE
promotion Ⓐ /prəˈmoʊ·ʃən/ *n* [C/U] ○ [C/U] *She's been recommended for a promotion.*

prompt QUICK /prɑmt/ *adj* [*-er/-est* only] (of an action) done quickly and without delay, or (of a person) acting quickly or arriving at an arranged time ○ *The agency sent back a prompt reply to my inquiries.*

promptly /ˈprɑm·tli/ *adv* ○ *She arrived promptly at 9 o'clock.*

CAUSE /prɑmt/ *v* [T] **1** to cause someone to say or do something ○ [+ *to* infinitive] *What prompted you to say that?* **2** If you prompt an actor or speaker, you help by quietly saying the next word or phrase if it has been forgotten.

prompt /prɑmt/ *n* [C] **1** a sign from the computer that shows it is ready to receive your instructions **2** ***writing*** A prompt is also a set of directions or a passage from a book, poem, or play to give you ideas for writing something

prone LIKELY /proʊn/ *adj* likely to do, get, or suffer from something ○ *As a child, he was prone to ear infections.* ○ *Carol's kind of accident-prone* (= seems to have a lot of accidents).

LYING DOWN /proʊn/ *adj* [not gradable] lying on your chest, with your face looking down ○ *The injured player was lifted into a cart and driven off the field in a prone position.*

prong /prɔːŋ, prɑŋ/ *n* [C] one of two or more long pointed parts at the end of a tool, electric plug, or other object

pronged /prɔːŋd, prɑŋd/ *adj* [not gradable] A two/three-pronged plan involves two/three different ways of achieving the same aim: *The government has launched a two-pronged attack against poverty.*

pronoun /ˈproʊ·nɑʊn/ *n* [C] ***grammar*** a word that is used instead of a noun or a noun phrase ○ *Pronouns are often used to refer to a noun that has been previously mentioned.* ○ *"She," "it," "them," and "who" are all examples of pronouns.*

pronounce MAKE SOUND /prəˈnɑʊns/ *v* [T] ***English*** to say a word or a letter in a particular way or in a correct way ○ *Around here, "aunt" is not pronounced the same as "ant."* ○ *How do you pronounce your last name?* ○ Related noun: PRONUNCIATION

TO STATE /prəˈnɑʊns/ *v* [T] to state something officially or formally ○ *Dewey was mistakenly pronounced the winner of the election.*

pronouncement /prəˈnɑʊn·smənt/ *n* [C] an official or formal statement

pronounced /prəˈnɑʊnst/ *adj* easily noticeable; obvious ○ *The need for strong leadership is more pronounced* (= clearer) *during wartime.*

pronto /ˈprɑn·toʊ/ *adv* [not gradable] *infml* quickly and without delay ○ *When you get fresh corn, eat it pronto.*

pronunciation /prəˌnʌn·siːˈeɪ·ʃən/ *n* [C/U] the way in which a word or letter is said, or said correctly, or the way in which a language is spoken ○ [U] *Her pronunciation of English is improving.* ○ [C] *There are two acceptable pronunciations for the word "either."* ○ Related verb: PRONOUNCE MAKE SOUND

proof FACTS /pruːf/ *n* [U] facts or documents that can be used to show that something is true ○ *You will need to have proof of citizenship in order to get a passport.*

PRINTED COPY /pruːf/ *n* [C] a printed copy of written material that is examined and corrected before final copies are printed ○ *Page proofs went out yesterday to all the contributors to the book.*

CALCULATION /pruːf/ *n* [C] ***mathematics*** the calculations that show how the solution to a mathematical problem or EQUATION was reached

AMOUNT OF ALCOHOL /pruːf/ *n* [U] [not gradable] a measure of the percentage of alcohol in an alcoholic drink, equal to twice the actual percentage of alcohol ○ *Liquor that is 50 proof is 25% alcohol.*

proofread /ˈpruː·friːd/ *v* [I/T] to read and correct a piece of written work ○ [I/T] *Tondra proofreads (books) for a small publishing company.*

prop SUPPORT /prɑp/ *v* [T] **-pp- 1** to support something by putting something else under or against it ○ *She propped the door open with a footstool.* ○ *He was reading in bed, propped up by pillows.* **2** *fig.* To prop up something/prop something up is to support something that would fail or become weaker without such help: [M] *The US joined with other nations in a coordinated effort yesterday to prop up the value of the dollar.*

prop /prɑp/ *n* [C] an object used to support something or hold it in position

THEATER/MOVIES /prɑp/ *n* [C usually pl] an object that is used on a theater stage or in a movie ○ *The only props used in the show are a table, a chair, and a glass of water.*

propaganda /ˌprɑp·əˈgæn·də/ *n* [U] information or ideas that are spread by an organized group or government to influence people's opinions, esp. by not giving all the facts or by secretly emphasizing only one way of looking at the facts

propagate /ˈprɑp·əˌgeɪt/ *v* [I/T] **1** to produce a new plant from a parent plant, or of a plant or animal to reproduce **2** To propagate ideas, opinions, or customs is to spread them among people, or to spread them to other places.

propane (gas) /ˈproʊ·peɪn (ˈgæs)/ *n* [U] a colorless gas used as a fuel ○ *Camps for mobile homes usually provide propane gas for cooking and heating.*

propanone /ˈproʊ·pəˌnoʊn/ *n* [U] ***chemistry*** a colorless liquid that burns easily and is used in paints, glues, etc., to make them flow

propel /prəˈpel/ *v* [T] **-ll-** to cause something to move forward ○ *Seals use their fins and flippers to propel them through the water with great force.* ○ *(fig.) If the team won the next two games, they would be propelled into the number one ranking in collegiate football.*

propeller /prəˈpel·ər/ *n* [C] a device with two or more blades that spin around to produce a force for moving the ship or aircraft to which it is attached

propensity /prəˈpen·sət̬·i/ *n* [U] *fml* a tendency to behave in a particular way ○ [+ *to* infinitive] *The*

P

poll confirmed Americans' growing propensity to invest in the stock market.

proper SUITABLE /ˈprɑp·ər/ *adj* fitting or right for a particular situation; suitable ○ *We didn't have the proper tools to do the job right.* ○ *With proper treatment she should recover completely.*

properly /ˈprɑp·ər·li/ *adv* ○ *If the plants are tended properly, they'll thrive in this climate.*

CORRECT /ˈprɑp·ər/ *adj* [not gradable] correct, or considered to be correct ○ *The coach showed him the proper way to hold a bat.*

properly /ˈprɑp·ər·li/ *adv* [not gradable] ○ *To learn to speak a language properly, you have to live in the country where that language is spoken.*

SOCIALLY ACCEPTABLE /ˈprɑp·ər/ *adj* according to socially accepted standards of behavior ○ *I didn't think it was proper to just invite myself in.*

properly /ˈprɑp·ər·li/ *adv* ○ *I expect you to behave properly at the restaurant.*

CENTRAL /ˈprɑp·ər/ *adj* [only after n] [not gradable] being in the central or main part or place ○ *They live in the suburbs, not in Boston proper.*

proper noun *n* [C] ***grammar*** (in grammar) the name of a particular person, place, or thing that is spelled with a beginning capital letter ○ *"San Francisco" and "White House" are proper nouns.* ○ Compare COMMON NOUN

property THINGS OWNED /ˈprɑp·ərt̬·i/ *n* [C/U] **1** a thing or things owned by someone; a possession or possessions ○ [U] *The books are the property of the public library.* **2** Property is also land and buildings: [C] *He owns some valuable waterfront properties.*

QUALITY /ˈprɑp·ərt̬·i/ *n* [C] **1** a quality that something has ○ *Wool has excellent properties for clothing, since it can keep you warm while letting air in.* **2** ***science*** A property is also a particular physical or chemical characteristic of a substance.

prophase /ˈproʊ·feɪz/ *n* [U] ***biology*** the first stage in cell division

prophecy /ˈprɑf·ə·si/ *n* [C] a statement that tells what will happen in the future ○ *biblical prophecies*

prophesy /ˈprɑf·əˌsɑɪ/ *v* [T] to say what will happen in the future ○ *He prophesied a Democratic defeat in the next election.*

prophet /ˈprɑf·ət/ *n* [C] a person who speaks for God or a god, or a person who tells what will happen in the future

prophetic /prəˈfet̬·ɪk/ *adj* accurately saying what will happen ○ *His predictions about how computer technology would revolutionize the workplace were prophetic* (= true).

propitious /prəˈpɪʃ·əs/ *adj* likely to result in success, or showing signs of success ○ *With economic conditions so uncertain, he felt it was not a propitious time to make a big investment.*

proponent /prəˈpoʊ·nənt/ *n* [C] a person who supports an idea, plan, or cause ○ *Long a proponent of government health insurance, he pointed out that millions of Americans have no health insurance at all.*

proportion Ⓐ /prəˈpɔːr·ʃən/ *n* [C/U] **1** a part or share of the whole, or the relationship between one thing and another in size, amount, or degree ○ [C] *The proportion of the population that is over 65 has been growing.* ○ [pl] *The occurrence of the disease has reached epidemic proportions.* **2** Proportion is also the right relationship between one thing and another: [U] *His anger was out of all proportion to the offense* (= was much too strong). **3** ***art*** Proportion is also the correct relationship of the parts of a work of art to each other, especially in their size. **4** ***mathematics*** A proportion is also a EQUATION (= mathematical statement) that shows two RATIOS (= comparisons) are equal.

proportional Ⓐ /prəˈpɔːr·ʃən·əl/, **proportionate** /prəˈpɔːr·ʃə·nət/ *adj* **1** in correct relation to ○ *The degree of punishment is meant to be proportional to the seriousness of the crime.* **2** ***mathematics*** Proportional also means that two things have the same size relationship or RATIO.

proportionally Ⓐ /prəˈpɔːr·ʃən·əl·i/, **proportionately** /prəˈpɔːr·ʃə·nət·li/ *adv*

propose SUGGEST /prəˈpoʊz/ *v* **1** to suggest or state (a possible plan or action) for consideration ○ [+ *to* infinitive] *She proposed to keep the schools open all summer.* ○ [+ *that* clause] *It has often been proposed that the president be elected by direct popular vote.* **2** If you propose to someone, you ask that person to marry you: [I] *She felt sure he was going to propose.*

proposal /prəˈpoʊ·zəl/ *n* [C] a suggestion for a possible plan or action ○ *The president's proposal was to tax a percentage of Social Security benefits for high-income people.*

USAGE

propose/proposal

Propose and **proposal** are more formal words that are usually only used when suggesting a plan or idea in politics, business, or in a college or university.

The housing project is an ambitious $6 million proposal with a nursing home, assisted living quarters, and apartments.

Suggest or **recommend** are the normal words used when suggesting a plan or idea.

Since you don't have much time, I suggest you fly to Seattle.

~~*Since you don't have much time, I propose you fly to Seattle.*~~

Propose and **proposal** are not usually used when you are giving something to someone or asking someone to do something with you. The normal words here are **offer** and **invite**.

She invited me to come for the weekend, and I accepted her offer.

~~*She proposed to me that I come for the weekend and I accepted her proposal.*~~

Propose is not used to talk about the services which are available somewhere. The normal verb here is **offer**.

Does your resort offer any fitness facilities?

~~*Does your resort propose any fitness facilities?*~~

INTEND /prəˈpoʊz/ *v fml* to intend to do something ○ [+ *to* infinitive] *How do you propose to complete the project in such a short time?*

proposition /ˌprɑp·əˈzɪʃ·ən/ *n* [C] a suggestion or statement for consideration ○ *The chairman was advised that it was a risky business proposition.*

proprietor /prəˈprɑɪ·ət̬·ər/ *n* [C] a person who owns and usually manages a business ○ *He is the proprietor of one of the best hotels in Orlando.*

proprietary /prəˈprɑɪ·əˌter·i/ *adj* [not gradable] owned and legally controlled by a particular company ○ *This is proprietary software, and you have no right to copy it without a license from the owner.*

propriety /prəˈprɑɪ·ət̬·i/ *n* [U] correct moral behavior or actions ○ *Critics questioned the propriety of the senator's appearance at a political fundraiser with a convicted criminal.*

props /ˈprɑps/ *pl n slang* respect for someone ○ *I've got to give her her props for being such a great athlete.*

propulsion /prəˈpʌl·ʃən/ *n* [U] the force produced by a system for moving a vehicle or other object ○ *jet propulsion*

prosaic /proʊˈzeɪ·ɪk/ *adj* ordinary and not especially interesting or unusual ○ *Only a few prosaic tables and chairs remained by the time we got to the auction.*

proscribe /proʊˈskrɑɪb/ *v* [T] to forbid an action or practice officially ○ *The sale of materials that could be used in making nuclear weapons is proscribed by US law.*

prose /proʊz/ *n* [U] ***English*** written language in its ordinary form rather than in the form of poems ○ Compare POETRY at POET

prosecute /ˈprɑs·ɪˌkjuːt/ *v* [I/T] to officially accuse someone of committing an illegal act, and to bring a case against that person in a court of law ○ [T] *The banker was prosecuted for fraud.*

prosecution /ˌprɑs·ɪˈkjuː·ʃən/ *n* [C/U] **1** [U] *She was granted full immunity from prosecution by the state in return for her testimony.* **2** *law* The prosecution refers to the lawyers in a trial who try to prove that a person accused of committing a crime is guilty of that crime.

prosecutor /ˈprɑs·ɪˌkjuːt̬·ər/ *n* [C] a legal representative who officially accuses someone of committing a crime in a court of law ○ *Federal prosecutors intend to retry the case.*

proselytize /ˈprɑs·ə·ləˌtɑɪz/ *v* [I/T] to try to persuade someone to change their religious beliefs, political party, etc., to your own ○ [I] *Missionaries were sent to proselytize in rural areas of the country.*

prose poem *n* [C] ***literature*** a poem that is written on the page like PROSE, but that has rhythm, images, and patterns of sound

prospect Ⓐ **POSSIBILITY** /ˈprɑs·pekt/ *n* [C/U] the possibility or likelihood that something will happen ○ [C] *Losing the elections is a prospect that still appears unlikely.* ○ [U] *She smiled at the prospect of seeing him again.* ○ [pl] *Prospects* (= Chances for success) *in the computer industry are excellent.*

prospective Ⓐ /prəˈspek·tɪv/ *adj* [not gradable] possible ○ *There were offers from several prospective buyers.*

SEARCH /ˈprɑs·pekt/ *v* [I] to search for gold, oil, or other valuable substances on or under the surface of the earth

prospector /ˈprɑsˌpek·tər/ *n* [C] ○ *a prospector searching for gold*

prospectus /prəˈspek·təs/ *n* [C] a small book that describes a college, school, etc., and its activities, or a document that advertises a planned business, investment opportunity, etc.

prosper /ˈprɑs·pər/ *v* [I] to be successful, esp. financially ○ *As the company prospered, we prospered.*

prosperity /prɑsˈper·ət̬·i/ *n* [U] ○ *a period of increasing prosperity*

prosperous /ˈprɑs·pə·rəs/ *adj* ○ *a prosperous business*

prostate (gland) /ˈprɑs·teɪt (ˈglænd)/ *n* [C] an organ in males that surrounds the URETHRA

prosthesis /prɑsˈθiː·səs/ *n* [C] *pl* **prostheses** an artificial body part, such as an arm or leg

prosthetic /prɑsˈθet̬·ɪk/ *adj* [not gradable] ○ *prosthetic devices*

prostitute /ˈprɑs·təˌtuːt/ *n* [C] someone, usually a woman, who has sex with people for money

prostitute /ˈprɑs·təˌtuːt/ *v* [T] ○ *(fig.) Some critics say that he is prostituting his writing talent* (= using it in a way that does not deserve respect, esp. to earn money).

prostitution /ˌprɑs·təˈtuː·ʃən/ *n* [U] the business of having sex for money

prostrate /ˈprɑs·treɪt/ *adj* lying flat with the face down ○ *She lay there prostrate, exhausted after a long day's work.*

protagonist /proʊˈtæg·ə·nəst/ *n* [C] ***literature*** an important character in a story or play

protease /ˈproʊt̬·iːˌeɪs, -ˌeɪz/ *n* [U] ***biology*** an ENZYME (= substance made by living cells) that causes PROTEINS to break into smaller pieces

protect /prəˈtekt/ *v* [T] to keep someone or something safe from injury, damage, or loss ○ *He says he was protecting his home and family.* ○ *A citizens' group worked to protect forest areas.*

protected /prəˈtek·təd/ *adj* ○ *a protected environment* ○ *a protected species*

protection /prəˈtek·ʃən/ *n* [C/U] ○ [U] *Their tent offered little protection against the storm.* ○ [C] *The proposed law is intended to provide legal protections for farm workers.* ○ [U] *These laws may not provide enough protection for some endangered species.*

protective /prəˈtek·tɪv/ *adj* ○ *Firefighters wear protective clothing to reduce the risk of being burned.* ○ *She is fiercely protective of her family.*

protector /prəˈtek·tər/ *n* [C] ○ *After his parents died, he became the protector of his sisters.* ○ *A $20*

P

surge protector can save your computer. ➤ Usage: **prevent or protect?** at PREVENT

WORD FAMILY protect			
Nouns	protection protector	*Adjectives*	protected unprotected protective
Verbs	protect	*Adverbs*	protectively

protectorate /prə'tek·tə·rət/ *n* [C] ***world history*** **1** a region or political unit that is controlled by another, or the government by which it is ruled **2** The Protectorate refers to the government of England from 1653 to 1659.

protégé /'proʊt̬·əˌʒeɪ/ *n* [C] someone who is helped, taught, or protected by an important or more experienced person

protein /'proʊ·tiːn/ *n* [C/U] ***biology*** any of a large group of chemicals that are a necessary part of the cells of all living things

protest /'proʊ·test/ *n* [C/U] a strong complaint expressing disagreement, disapproval, or opposition ○ [U] *Three board members walked out of the meeting in protest.* ○ [C] *A protest against capital punishment was held outside the courthouse.* ○ [U] *He paid the tax under protest to avoid a penalty.*

protest /prə'test, 'proʊ·test/ *v* [I/T] ○ [I/T] *Groups of students have been protesting (against) the tuition increase.*

Protestant /'prɑt̬·ə·stənt/ *n* [C] a member of one of the major Christian divisions to which a number of different religious groups belong ○ *Methodists, Baptists, and Lutherans are all Protestants.*

Protestant /'prɑt̬·ə·stənt/ *adj* [not gradable] ○ *a Protestant minister*

Protestantism /'prɑt̬·ə·stəntˌɪz·əm/ *n* [U] the beliefs of the Protestant religions

protista /proʊ'tɪs·tə/ *pl n* one of five KINGDOMS (= groups) into which living things are divided, the members of which usually have only one cell which contains a NUCLEUS (= central part)

protocol Ⓐ **RULES** /'proʊt̬·əˌkɔːl, -ˌkɑl/ *n* [C/U] **1** the formal system of rules for correct behavior on official occasions ○ [U] *According to protocol, the new ambassador will present his credentials to the president.* **2** ***science*** A protocol is also the rules to be followed when doing a scientific study or an exact method for giving medical treatment: [U] *medical protocol* ○ [C] *a treatment protocol*

AGREEMENT /'proʊt̬·əˌkɔːl, -ˌkɑl/ *n* [C] a formal international agreement

proton /'proʊ·tɑn/ *n* [C] ***physics, chemistry*** the part of an atom that has a positive electrical CHARGE and is part of the atom's NUCLEUS (= central part) ○ Compare ELECTRON; NEUTRON ➤ Picture: **atom**

protoplasm /'proʊt̬·əˌplæz·əm/ *n* [U] ***biology*** the transparent liquid that is inside all living cells

prototype /'proʊt̬·əˌtɑɪp/ *n* [C] the original model of something from which later forms are developed

prototypical /ˌproʊt̬·ə'tɪp·ɪ·kəl/ *adj* [not gradable] ○ *a prototypical jazz singer*

protozoan /ˌproʊt̬·ə'zoʊ·ən/ *n* [C] *pl* **protozoans, protozoa** ***biology*** a very small organism with only one cell

protracted /proʊ'træk·təd/ *adj* lasting for a long time, or made to continue longer than necessary ○ *Their protracted legal battle may soon be resolved.*

protractor /proʊ'træk·tər/ *n* [C] a device for measuring and drawing angles, usually shaped in a half circle and marked with degrees

protrude /prə'truːd/ *v* [I/T] to stick out from something ○ [I] *Tufts of gray hair protruded from under his hat.* ○ [T] *The snake protruded its tongue and hissed loudly.*

protrusion /prə'truː·ʒən/ *n* [C/U] ○ [C] *A protrusion on the cliffs looks like a human head.*

proud **SATISFIED** /prɑʊd/ *adj* [*-er/-est* only] feeling satisfaction and pleasure because of something that you have achieved, possess, or are a part of ○ *He's very proud of his daughters.* ○ *The company is proud of its environmental record.* ○ [+ *to infinitive*] *I am proud to have played a part in what this team achieved.*

proudly /'prɑʊd·li/ *adv* ○ *We proudly announce the birth of our son, Logan.*

RESPECTING YOURSELF /prɑʊd/ *adj* [*-er/-est* only] **1** having respect for yourself, or showing feelings of your own worth ○ *Americans are a proud people.* ○ *He might be poor but he's too proud to accept charity.* **2** People may also be proud in an unpleasant way and have too high an opinion of themselves: [+ *to infinitive*] *She is too proud to admit that she could ever be wrong.* ○ Related noun: PRIDE FEELING OF WORTH

proudly /'prɑʊd·li/ *adv* ○ *Crow warriors rode proudly through the village.*

prove **SHOW** /pruːv/ *v past part.* **proved, proven** to show after a time or by experience that something or someone has a particular quality ○ [L] *The dispute over rights to the song could prove impossible to resolve.* ○ [+ *to infinitive*] *The new safety procedures have so far proven to be satisfactory.* ○ *As a newcomer, I felt I had to* ***prove myself*** (= show I am skilled).

proven /'pruː·vən/ *adj* [not gradable] ○ *You can't trust him – he's a proven liar.*

MAKE CLEAR /pruːv/ *v* [T] *past part.* **proved, proven** to make it clear that something is or is not true ○ *They suspected she cheated, but they could never prove it.* ○ [+ (*that*) *clause*] *I had to take all my records to the bank to prove (that) the mistake was theirs.* ○ *Under our legal system, you're innocent until proven guilty.*

WORD FAMILY prove			
Nouns	proof	*Verbs*	prove disprove
Adjectives	proven		

proverb /ˈprɑv·ɜrb/ *n* [C] ***literature*** a short statement, usually known by many people for a long time, that gives advice or expresses some common truth ○ *A Chinese proverb says that the longest journey begins with a single step.*
proverbial /prəˈvɜr·biː·əl/ *adj* [not gradable] ○ *Yelling at me was the proverbial straw that broke the camel's back.*

provide GIVE /prəˈvɑɪd/ *v* [T] to give something that is needed or wanted to someone ○ *The company provides medical benefits to all employees.* ○ *I can provide you with directions to their house.*
provider /prəˈvɑɪd·ər/ *n* [C] ○ *The company's medical plan allows you to choose your health-care provider.* ○ *He is the main provider in the family* (= earns most of the family's money).

> **USAGE**
> **provide**
> Remember to use the preposition **with** in the phrase **provide** *someone* **with** *something.*
> *Could you provide us with a list of hotels in the area?*
> ~~*Could you provide us a list of hotels in the area?*~~

STATE /prəˈvɑɪd/ *v* (of a law or contract) to state that something must happen or be done ○ [I] *The new statute provides for life imprisonment without parole.* ○ [+ *that* clause] *Many loan agreements provide that the interest rate will change.*

WORD FAMILY provide

Nouns	provider provision	*Verbs*	provide
		Adverbs	provisionally
Adjectives	provisional		

PHRASAL VERB with provide

• **provide for** *someone* to give someone the things needed to live ○ *The men must learn to provide for themselves once they've left the halfway house.*

provided (that) /prəˈvɑɪd·əd (ðət, ˌðæt)/, **providing (that)** /prəˈvɑɪd·ɪŋ (ðət, ˌðæt)/ *conjunction* if; only if ○ *I know what to do, provided that nobody asks me.*

providence /ˈprɑv·əd·əns, -əˌdens/ *n* [U] the care and control of God or of a force that is not human in origin ○ *He trusts in divine providence.*

province REGION /ˈprɑv·əns/ *n* [C] **1** a division of a country that has its own government ○ *The province of Quebec has voted several times on independence from Canada.* **2** The provinces are the parts of a country outside its capital or most important city.
provincial /prəˈvɪn·tʃəl/ *adj* **1** of or relating to a province, or to the parts of a country outside its capital or most important city ○ *provincial governments* **2** *disapproving* A provincial person has limited ideas and is not willing to understand or accept new ideas or ways of behaving.

SUBJECT /ˈprɑv·əns/ *n* [U] *fml* a subject or activity of special interest, knowledge, or responsibility ○ *Architecture is within the province of the art department.*

provision SOMETHING NEEDED /prəˈvɪʒ·ən/ *n* [C/U] **1** something that is needed or wanted, or the act of considering the need for something and arranging for it ○ [U] *When designing buildings in California, you have to make some provision for earthquakes.* ○ [C] *Ample provisions for aircraft stability have been made.* **2** Provisions are also supplies of food and other necessary items: [pl] *Provisions had to be flown in by helicopter.*

AGREEMENT /prəˈvɪʒ·ən/ *n* [C] a statement in an agreement or a law that a particular thing must happen or be done ○ *Her contract contains a provision covering additional expenses.*

provisional /prəˈvɪʒ·ən·əl/ *adj* for the present time but likely to change; temporary ○ *a provisional government*
provisionally /prəˈvɪʒ·ə·nə·li/ *adv* ○ *I was provisionally accepted at Stanford.*

provocation /ˌprɑv·əˈkeɪ·ʃən/ *n* [C/U] an action that is intended to cause a reaction, esp. anger or annoyance ○ [U] *a deliberate act of provocation*
provocative /prəˈvɑk·əţ·ɪv/ *adj* **1** *a provocative speech* ○ *provocative advertisements* **2** If behavior or clothing is provocative, it is likely to cause sexual desire.
provocatively /prəˈvɑk·əţ·ɪv·li/ *adv*

provoke ANGER /prəˈvoʊk/ *v* [T] to try to make a person or an animal angry or annoyed ○ *He was trying to provoke me into a fight.*

CAUSE REACTION /prəˈvoʊk/ *v* [T] to cause a particular reaction or feeling ○ *I'm trying to make people think, provoke their emotions.* ○ *His death provoked huge demonstrations.*

provost /ˈproʊ·voʊst/ *n* [C] an official of high rank at a college or university

prow /prɑʊ/ *n* [C] the front part of a boat or ship; BOW

prowess /ˈprɑʊ·əs/ *n* [U] great ability or skill ○ *athletic prowess*

prowl /prɑʊl/ *v* [I/T] to move around an area quietly and secretly, as when hunting ○ [T] *At night, scorpions prowl the desert for insects.* ○ [I] *There have been reports of a man prowling in the neighborhood.*
prowl /prɑʊl/ *n* [U]

IDIOM with prowl

• **on the prowl** moving around an area and looking for something or someone ○ *On the way home I saw a raccoon on the prowl.*

proximity /prɑkˈsɪm·əţ·i/ *n* [U] the state of being near in space or time ○ *Mexico is a popular vacation spot because of its proximity to California.*

proxy /ˈprɑk·si/ *n* [C/U] authority given to someone to act for you, as by voting for you in an election, or the person to whom this authority is given

prude /pruːd/ *n* [C] *disapproving* a person who is easily shocked by rude things

P

prudish /ˈpruːd·ɪʃ/ *adj disapproving*

prudent /ˈpruːd·ᵊnt/ *adj* showing good judgment in avoiding risks and uncertainties; careful ○ *His decision was prudent and timely.*

prudence /ˈpruːd·ᵊns/ *n* [U] ○ *A little prudence would be appropriate.*

prune CUT /pruːn/ *v* [T] to cut off unwanted branches from a tree, bush, or other plant ○ *They advise growers not to prune fruit trees heavily.*

FRUIT /pruːn/ *n* [C] a dried whole PLUM (= fruit)

prurient /ˈprʊr·iː·ənt/ *adj* having or showing too much sexual interest in things

pry OPEN /praɪ/ *v* [T always + adv/prep] **1** to open, move, or lift something by putting one end of a tool under it and pushing down on the other end ○ *She pried the oyster open.* **2** *fig.* To pry is also to get something with much effort: *They pried the information out of him.*

ASK QUESTIONS /praɪ/ *v* [I] to try to obtain private facts about a person ○ *Reporters were prying into her personal life.*

P.S. *n abbreviation for* POSTSCRIPT ○ *P.S. Best wishes to your father.* ○ **USAGE:** Added at the end of a letter when you want to write something more.

psalm /sɑm, sɑlm/ *n* [C] a religious poem or song

pseudonym /ˈsuːd·ᵊn ˌɪm/ *n* [C] a name someone uses instead of his or her real name, esp. on a written work ○ *Samuel Clemens used the pseudonym Mark Twain.*

pseudopod /ˈsuːd·əˌpɑd/ *n* [C] ***biology*** a part that temporarily sticks out of the PROTOPLASM (= liquid inside a cell) of some organisms that have only one cell, used for movement and to get food ➤ Picture: **amoeba**

P

psych STUDY OF THE MIND /saɪk/ *n short form of* PSYCHOLOGY

PREPARE MENTALLY /saɪk ʌp/ *v* [T] *infml* to prepare yourself mentally to do something difficult ○ *I really tried to psych myself up to do it.*

PHRASAL VERB with psych

• **psych** *someone* **out** [M] *infml* to cause someone to lose confidence in dealing with a difficult situation ○ *He hit a couple of bad shots at the start and I think it just psyched him out.*

psyche /ˈsɑɪ·ki/ *n* [C] the mind, or the deepest thoughts, feelings, or beliefs of a person or group ○ *the male/female psyche*

psychedelic /ˌsɑɪ·kəˈdel·ɪk/ *adj* **1** causing unusually strong experiences of color, sound, smell, taste, and touch, and other mental effects such as feelings of deep understanding or HALLUCINATION (= imagining things that do not exist) **2** Psychedelic also means likely to produce a strong effect because of having bright colors or patterns.

psychiatry /sɑɪˈkɑɪ·ə·tri/ *n* [U] the medical study and treatment of mental illness

psychiatric /ˌsɑɪ·kiːˈæ·trɪk/ *adj* [not gradable] ○ *psychiatric treatment*

psychiatrist /sɑɪˈkɑɪ·ə·trəst/ *n* [C] a doctor with special training in treating mental illness

psychic /ˈsɑɪ·kɪk/ *adj* **1** having to do with the mind and the emotions rather than with the body ○ *Regular exercise has psychic as well as physical benefits.* **2** If a person, experience, or event is said to be psychic, the person's abilities or the nature of the experience or event cannot be explained by modern science: *psychic phenomena*

psychic /ˈsɑɪ·kɪk/ *n* [C] a person believed to have abilities, esp. involving a knowledge of the future, that cannot be explained by modern science

psycho /ˈsɑɪ·koʊ/ *n pl* **psychos** *infml* a PSYCHOPATH

psychoanalysis /ˌsɑɪ·koʊ·əˈnæl·ə·səs/ *n* [U] a theory and method of treating mental illness in which a person is encouraged to talk about private thoughts and events to someone trained in this method

psychoanalyst /ˌsɑɪ·koʊˈæn·ᵊl·əst/, *short form* **analyst** *n* [C] a person with special training in psychoanalysis

psychology Ⓐ /sɑɪˈkɑl·ə·dʒi/, *short form* **psych** *n* [U] the scientific study of how the mind works and how it influences behavior, or the influence of character on a particular person's behavior ○ *She took a course in abnormal psychology.*

psychological Ⓐ /ˌsɑɪ·kəˈlɑdʒ·ɪ·kəl/ *adj* **1** relating to the study of the mind ○ *psychological testing* ○ *Her problems were psychological.* **2** Psychological also means having an effect on or involving the mind: *psychological stress/well-being* ○ *Her new novel is a psychological thriller.*

psychologically Ⓐ /ˌsɑɪ·kəˈlɑdʒ·ɪ·kli/ *adv* ○ *Gifted children are well-adjusted, popular and psychologically healthy.*

psychologist Ⓐ /sɑɪˈkɑl·ə·dʒəst/ *n* [C] someone who studies the mind and emotions and their relationship to behavior

psychopath /ˈsɑɪ·kəˌpæθ/, *infml* **psycho** *n* [C] a person who is likely to commit violent criminal acts because of a mental illness that causes the person to lack any feelings of guilt

psychopathic /ˌsɑɪ·kəˈpæθ·ɪk/ *adj* ○ *psychopathic tendencies*

psychosis /sɑɪˈkoʊ·səs/ *n* [C/U] *pl* **psychoses** *medical* a severe mental illness

psychotic /sɑɪˈkɑt̬·ɪk/ *adj medical* ○ *psychotic delusions*

psychosomatic /ˌsɑɪ·koʊ·səˈmæt̬·ɪk/ *adj* relating to a physical problem caused by emotional anxiety and not by illness, infection, or injury ○ *The doctor thinks Leo's symptoms are psychosomatic.*

psychotherapy /ˌsɑɪ·koʊˈθer·ə·pi/ *n* [C/U] any of various methods of treating mental illness in which the people who are ill are encouraged to talk about themselves to each other or to a person trained in the method being used

psychotherapist /ˌsɑɪ·koʊˈθer·ə·pəst/ *n* [C]

pt. *n* [C] *pl* **pt.** *abbreviation for* PINT

PTA *n* [C] *abbreviation for* PARENT-TEACHER ASSOCIATION.

PTSD *n abbreviation for* POST-TRAUMATIC STRESS DISORDER

pub /pʌb/ *n* [C] a BAR DRINKING PLACE

puberty /ˈpjuː·bərt̬·i/ *n* [U] the stage in a person's life when the person develops from a child into an adult because of changes in the body that make the person able to have children

pubic /ˈpjuː·bɪk/ *adj* [not gradable] on or in the body near the sexual organs

public INVOLVING PEOPLE /ˈpʌb·lɪk/ *adj* [not gradable] relating to or involving people in general, rather than being limited to a particular group of people ○ *public opinion* ○ *They're trying to raise public awareness of the benefits of early-childhood education.* ○ *His ideas have very little public support.* ○ *The results won't be made public* (= told to people in general).

public /ˈpʌb·lɪk/ *n* [U] **1** all the people, esp. all those in one place or country ○ *The park is open to the public from sunrise to sunset.* **2** The public is also the people who do not belong to a particular group or organization: *The book is not yet available to the general public.* **3** Your public is the people involved with you or your organization, esp. in a business relationship: *The newspapers publish the stories they know their public wants to read.*

publicly /ˈpʌb·lɪ·kli/ *adv* [not gradable] by or among ordinary people ○ *publicly traded stock*

OPEN /ˈpʌb·lɪk/ *adj* **1** allowing anyone to see or hear what is happening ○ *a public performance* ○ *a public display of temper* **2** Something done **in public** is done where anyone can see or hear it: *He was afraid to be seen in public for some time after the incident.*

publicly /ˈpʌb·lɪ·kli/ *adv* ○ *She spoke out publicly in opposition to US participation in the war.*

BY THE GOVERNMENT /ˈpʌb·lɪk/ *adj* [not gradable] **1** involving or provided by the government, usually for the use of anyone ○ *public transportation* ○ *a public park* ○ *public housing* **2** Public also means supported by government funds, sometimes also by money given by private citizens: *public broadcasting/radio/television*

publicly /ˈpʌb·lɪ·kli/ *adv* [not gradable] ○ *The new airport will not be publicly funded.*

WORD FAMILY public

Nouns	public publication publicist publicity	*Adjectives* *Verbs* *Adverbs*	public publicize publicly

publication Ⓐ /ˌpʌb·ləˈkeɪ·ʃən/ *n* [C/U] a book, magazine, newspaper, or document, or the act of making information or writing available, esp. in a printed form ○ [C] *His writing appears frequently in French, Mexican, and Canadian publications.* ○ [U] *The publication of the marathon finishers will be in next Sunday's newspaper.*

public defender *n* [C] a lawyer paid for by the government to represent an accused person who cannot pay for a private lawyer

public health *n* [U] the government system for providing for the health needs and services of all the people of a country or region ○ *The county's public health officer urged parents to keep their children home from school when they have the flu.*

publicity /pəˈblɪs·ət̬·i/ *n* [U] the activity of making certain that someone or something attracts a lot of interest or attention from many people, or the attention received as a result of this activity ○ *The publicity surrounding the case made jury selection difficult.* ○ *His speech attracted a lot of publicity.*

publicist /ˈpʌb·lə·səst/ *n* [C] someone whose job is to draw attention to events and give information to reporters and broadcasters

publicize /ˈpʌb·ləˌsɑɪz/ *v* [T] to make information available about someone or something ○ *Luna has helped publicize the problem of homelessness.*

public relations, *abbreviation* **PR** *n* [U] the activity of keeping good relationships between an organization and the people outside it

public school *n* [C] a free school, supported by taxes, and managed by local representatives

public sector *n* [C usually sing] the offices and responsibilities of government ○ *She worked in the public sector for years before returning to private practice in her old law firm.*

public servant *n* [C] an elected official or someone employed by local or national government

public service *n* [U] the work that elected officials and government employees do for the benefit of the public

publish Ⓐ /ˈpʌb·lɪʃ/ *v* [I/T] to make available to the public, usually by printing, a book, magazine, newspaper, or other document ○ [T] *She was 29 when her first novel was published.* ○ [T] *We plan to begin publishing a newsletter on the Internet.*

publisher Ⓐ /ˈpʌb·lɪʃ·ər/ *n* [C] **1** an organization that publishes books, magazines, or newspapers **2** Publisher is also the title of a person in a company who is responsible for publishing particular books, magazines, or newspapers.

publishing Ⓐ /ˈpʌb·lɪʃ·ɪŋ/ *n* [U] the buiness of makeing books, magazines, or newspapers available to the public ○ *She hopes to pursue a career in publishing.*

WORD FAMILY publish

Nouns	publisher publishing	*Adjectives* *Verbs*	unpublished publish

puck /pʌk/ *n* [C] a small, hard, rubber disk used in HOCKEY (= a game played on ice)

pucker /ˈpʌk·ər/ *v* [T] to press together and form small folds in something such as cloth or skin ○ *She* *puckered her lips and gave her grandma a kiss.* ○ [M] *This hem is all puckered up.*

pucker /ˈpʌk·ər/ *n* [C] ○ *Puckers were sewn in the sleeves of the blouse.*

pudding /ˈpʊd·ɪŋ/ *n* [C/U] a sweet dish, often made from sugar, milk, flour, and flavoring, and usually eaten after a meal ○ [U] *I'll make rice pudding for dessert.*

puddle /ˈpʌd·əl/ *n* [C] a pool of liquid on the ground or floor, formed by filling up the holes in uneven surfaces ○ *You have to step around the puddles in the street after a rain shower.*

pudgy /ˈpʌdʒ·i/ *adj* short and fat ○ *He jabbed a pudgy finger at me.*

pueblo /ˈpweb·loʊ, puːˈeb-/ *n* [C] *pl* **pueblos** a group of flat-roofed, connected buildings made of pressed, dried earth or stone, built by American Indians in the southwestern US ○ *While in New Mexico we visited the ruins of an ancient pueblo.*

puff BREATHE /pʌf/ *v* [I] **1** to breathe quickly and with a lot of force, usually as a result of an activity that needs a lot of physical effort ○ *Ricardo was puffing hard after he raced up five flights of stairs.* **2** To puff is also to breathe in and blow out smoke from a cigarette, CIGAR (= rolled tobacco), or PIPE (= device for smoking).

puff /pʌf/ *n* [C] an act of breathing in and blowing out smoke

SMALL BURST /pʌf/ *n* [C] a small burst of smoke, air, or something that can rise into the air in a small cloud ○ *We felt a puff of wind as the door open and closed.*

puff /pʌf/ *v* [I] ○ *The volcano continued to puff out poisonous gases.*

SWELL /pʌf/ *v* [I/T] to swell or increase in size ○ [T] *One eye was puffed and her cheek was bruised dark as a coal smear.* ○ [T] *The child held a deep breath and puffed her cheeks until they turned red.*

puffy /ˈpʌf·i/ *adj* swollen to a size slightly larger than usual ○ *His eyes were red and puffy.*

CAKE /pʌf/ *n* [C] a small, round cake or other food, esp. one made from pastry with a filling inside ○ *a cream puff*

puffin /ˈpʌf·ən/ *n* [C] a sea bird that lives in northern parts of the world and has a large, brightly colored beak

puff pastry *n* [U] a light pastry made in layers with butter between them

pugnacious /pʌɡˈneɪ·ʃəs/ *adj* ready to fight or to argue very forcefully ○ *a pugnacious politician*

puke /pjuːk/ *v* [I/T] *slang* to vomit ○ [I] *It makes me want to puke, just thinking about it.*

puke /pjuːk/ *n* [U] *slang* vomit

pull MOVE TOWARD YOU /pʊl/ *v* [I/T] to move something toward yourself, sometimes with great physical effort ○ [I] *Could you help me move this bookcase over there? You pull and I'll push.* ○ [T] *Alice lay down and pulled a blanket over her.* ○ [I] *The little girl pulled at his sleeve* (= moved it slightly and repeatedly toward her).

pull /pʊl/ *n* [C/U] ○ [C] *Give the rope a hard pull.*

WORD CHOICES pull

If someone is pulling something heavy, you could use the verbs **drag** or **haul**.

*She **dragged** the canoe down to the water.*

*They **hauled** the boat out of the water.*

If a vehicle is pulling another vehicle behind it, the word **tow** is used.

*You shouldn't drive fast when your car is **towing** a trailer.*

Yank is used in informal language when someone pulls something very quickly and hard.

*She marched to the door and **yanked** it open.*

You could use the verb **wrench** when someone pulls something violently from its position.

*The phone had been **wrenched** from the wall.*

If you pull something several times with your fingers, the verbs **pull at** or **pluck at** are often used. If you do it hard, you could use **tug at**.

*The child **pulled at** my sleeve to catch my attention.*

*I felt a small hand **plucking at** my jacket.*

*Tom **tugged at** the doorknob.*

REMOVE /pʊl/ *v* [T] **1** to take something out of or away from a place, esp. using physical effort ○ [M] *The dentist had to pull two of my teeth out.* ○ [M] *I spent the morning pulling up weeds in the garden.* ○ *She's asking companies to pull their ads from the program.* **2** Someone who **pulls a** *weapon* **on** you takes it from a hidden place and points it at you.

BRING BEHIND YOU /pʊl/ *v* [I/T] to hold or be attached to the front of something and cause it to move with you ○ [T] *The car was pulling a trailer.* ○ [I] *Elise sat on the sled while Carol pulled.*

MOVE IN A DIRECTION /pʊl/ *v* [I always + adv/prep] **1** to move or move something in the stated direction ○ *Her car pulled out into traffic.* ○ *The sun was so strong we had to pull down the blinds.* ○ *He pulled off his wet clothes and laid them out to dry.* **2** If you **pull up a chair**, you move a chair so you can sit with other people: *Pull up a chair and join us.*

MOVE YOUR BODY /pʊl/ *v* [I/T] to move your body or a part of your body ○ [I] *He started yelling at the referee and had to be pulled away by teammates.* ○ [T always + adv/prep] *He pulled his arm out just as the doors were closing.* ○ [T always + adv/prep] *She pulled herself up onto the rock.*

OPERATE A DEVICE /pʊl/ *v* [T] to operate a device that makes a piece of equipment work ○ *She took out a quarter, dropped it into the slot machine, and pulled the lever.*

ATTRACT /pʊl/ *v* [T] to attract a person or people ○ *She was able to pull more votes than the other candidates.* ○ [M] *The networks are grabbing for any edge that pulls in viewers.*

pull /pʊl/ *n* [U] ○ *Our bodily processes are influenced by the moon's gravitational pull.*

INFLUENCE /pʊl/ *n* [U] *infml* influence, esp. with important people ○ *The manufacturer used political pull to get the application approved.*

INJURE /pʊl/ *v* [T] to injure a muscle by stretching it too much ○ *Marie pulled a hamstring and couldn't play in the finals.*
pull /pʊl/ *n* [C] ○ *a muscle pull*

BE DISHONEST /pʊl/ *v* [T] *slang* to perform an action that is dishonest or intended to deceive ○ *Mikey was pulling his usual stunt of feeding most of his lunch to the cat.* ○ *Why would you try to pull a trick/prank like that on her?*

IDIOMS with **pull**

• **pull a fast one** to trick someone ○ *I don't think he was being truthful – I think he was just trying to pull a fast one.*
• **pull** *someone's* **leg** *infml* to tell someone something that is not true as a way of joking with the person ○ *Stop pulling my leg – you didn't have lunch with Bono!*
• **pull out all the stops** to make a lot of effort to do something well ○ *The kids pulled out all the stops and organized a really great party.*
• **pull strings** to use your influence over important people to get something or help someone else ○ *I may be able to pull a few strings for you if you need the document urgently.*
• **pull the plug** to stop something from continuing ○ *The network pulled the plug on the show after three weeks.*
• **pull the rug out (from under** *someone***)** to suddenly take away important support from someone ○ *The school pulled the rug out from under the city soccer league when they asked them to pay for using their field.*
• **pull the wool over** *someone's* **eyes** to decieve someone ○ *He doesn't have any special powers – he's just trying to pull the wool over your eyes.*
• **pull** *yourself* **together** to get control of your emotions or actions after being very upset ○ *I blew my nose and tried to pull myself together.*
• **pull** *your* **weight** to do your fair share of work that a group of people is doing together ○ *If he doesn't start pulling his weight, he'll lose his job.*

PHRASAL VERBS with **pull**

• **pull away** to increase a score or improve a rank ○ *The Cowboys hit five shots in a row to pull away from Marquette.* ○ **USAGE:** Used to describe a game or team in sports.
• **pull back STOP SUPPORTING** to stop supporting or doing something ○ *Both parties indicate they will not pull back from a new peace deal.*
• **pull back** *(something)* **REDUCE** [M] to reduce or remove something ○ *Stock prices pulled back Tuesday, as investors continued to worry about interest rates.* ○ *She criticized his proposal to pull back security forces from the province.*
• **pull down** *something* **DESTROY** [M] to destroy something, esp. a building ○ *Many of those old buildings will soon be pulled down.*
• **pull down** *something* **EARN** *infml* to earn an amount of money ○ *She's pulling down over $100,000 a year.*
• **pull off** *something* [M] *infml* to succeed in doing something difficult or unexpected ○ *He won five straight games and pulled off one of the tournament's biggest upsets.*
• **pull out** *(someone/something)* [M] to leave or no longer be involved in something ○ *They'll be pulling the rest of the troops out by next spring.* ○ *She's considering a run for governor but is stalling to see who else may jump in or pull out.* ○ Related noun: PULLOUT
• **pull over** *(someone/something)* [M] to stop your car at the side of the road, or to force another car or driver to do this ○ *Be sure you're in an area where a taxi can safely and legally pull over to pick you up.* ○ *The police officer pulled him over for changing lanes without signaling.*
• **pull** *(someone/something)* **through** *(something)* to help someone or something to continue to exist or live after a serious problem or illness ○ *He pulled the city through a financial crisis.* ○ *I didn't think he'd survive, but he pulled through.* ○ *Some people pull through things that seem impossible.*
• **pull together WORK EFFECTIVELY** to work well with others in a group to achieve a particular result ○ *I think the team won because they really made an effort to pull together.*
• **pull** *something* **together FORM A GROUP** [M] to bring various people or things together in a group for a particular purpose ○ *Bradford pulled together a group of experts to help him research his idea.* ○ *The website pulls several independent electronic book libraries together into a new archive.*
• **pull up STOP A VEHICLE** to cause a vehicle to stop ○ *The boat pulled up at the dock.* ○ *I was at the gas station, and he pulled up next to me.*
• **pull up** *something* **GET INFORMATION** [M] to get information, esp. on a computer screen ○ *Click on a square to pull up an overview of the site with name, description, location, and domain.*

pulley /ˈpʊl·i/ *n* [C] a piece of equipment for moving heavy objects up or down, consisting of a small wheel over which a rope or chain attached to the object can be easily pulled or released slowly

pullout /ˈpʊl·ɑʊt/ *n* [C] the act of ending involvement in something, esp. in military action ○ *a troop pullout* ○ *His pullout from the race leaves her the likely winner.* ○ Related verb: PULL OUT

pullover /ˈpʊlˌoʊ·vər/ *n* [C] a piece of clothing, esp. made of warm material, that is worn on the top part of the body and put on by pulling it over your head

pulmonary /ˈpʊl·məˌner·i/ *adj* [not gradable] *medical* relating to the lungs ○ *a test of pulmonary function*

pulp /pʌlp/ *n* [U] **1** a soft, wet mass, often produced by crushing something ○ *Mash the bananas to a pulp and then mix in the yogurt.* **2** Pulp is also a mixture of water and small pieces of paper, cloth, or wood that is used for making paper: *wood pulp*

pulpit /ˈpʊl·pət, ˈpʌl-/ *n* [C] a raised place in a church, with steps leading up to it, from which a minister or priest speaks

pulsate /ˈpʌl·seɪt/ *v* [I] to make sounds or movements with a regular rhythm ○ *A light pulsates in the distance.*

P

pulse /pʌls/ *n* [C] **1** ***biology*** a regular rhythm made by blood being moved through your body by your heart, esp. when it is felt at the wrist or side of the neck **2** ***physics*** A pulse is also a single burst of light or some other form of energy that is sudden and strong.

pulse /pʌls/ *v* [I] to move with a regular beat ○ *The music pulses with soul, Creole, and Cuban rhythms.*

pulverize /ˈpʌl·vəˌrɑɪz/ *v* [T] to press or crush something until it becomes powder or a soft mass ○ *Seashells were pulverized by the ocean's waves.* ○ (*infml*) *Our team aims to pulverize the competition* (= badly defeat them).

puma /ˈpjuː·mə, ˈpuː-/ *n* [C] a COUGAR (= large wild cat)

pummel /ˈpʌm·əl/ *v* [T] **-l-, -ll-** to hit someone or something repeatedly, esp. with your FISTS ○ *She hates watching boxers pummel and be pummeled in the ring.* ○ (*fig.*) *The region was pummeled by its second storm in less than a week.*

pump **DEVICE** /pʌmp/ *n* [C] a piece of equipment used to cause liquid, air, or gas to move from one place to another ○ *a gas/water pump*

pump /pʌmp/ *v* [T] **1** *You have to pump your own gasoline at that station.* ○ *He ran toward us, pumping his arms* (= moving them up and down energetically). ○ [M] *She pumped her bike tires up* (= filled them with air). **2** If you pump money into something, you spend a lot of money trying to make it successful: *We're pumping millions into this new program.* **3** *infml* When you pump someone, you ask for information, esp. in an indirect way: *I pumped him for details about the deal.*

SHOE /pʌmp/ *n* [C usually pl] a women's shoe with no fasteners

IDIOM with **pump**

• **pump iron** *infml* to lift heavy weights for exercise ○ *I usually pump iron at the gym for an hour in the morning.*

PHRASAL VERBS with **pump**

• **pump** *something* **into** *something* to direct large amounts of money toward a particular organization or cause ○ *The federal program has pumped $14 million into Texas for care for the elderly.*

• **pump up** *someone* [M] *infml* to make someone more confident or more enthusiastic ○ *Myerson spent a lot of time trying to pump up his partners.*

pumpernickel /ˈpʌm·pərˌnɪk·əl/ *n* [U] a type of dark brown bread made from RYE

pumpkin /ˈpʌmp·kən, ˈpʌŋ·kən/ *n* [C] a large, round vegetable with hard yellow or orange flesh

pun /pʌn/ *n* [C] an amusing use of a word or phrase that has several meanings or that sounds like another word ○ *People groan at a pun if it's told correctly.*

pun /pʌn/ *v* [I] **-nn-** ○ *She kept punning on "whole" and "hole."*

punch **HIT** /pʌntʃ/ *n* [C] a forceful hit with a FIST (= hand with the fingers closed tight)

punch /pʌntʃ/ *v* [I/T] ○ [T] *She punched the pillow, trying to fluff it up.*

EFFECT /pʌntʃ/ *n* [U] the power to be interesting and have a strong effect on people ○ *His acting gives the show its emotional punch.*

DRINK /pʌntʃ/ *n* [C/U] a cold or hot drink made by mixing fruit juices, pieces of fruit, and sometimes alcohol ○ [U] *Would you like a glass of punch?*

TOOL /pʌntʃ/ *n* [C] a piece of equipment that cuts holes in a material by pushing a piece of metal through it ○ *a hole/leather punch*

punch /pʌntʃ/ *v* [T] ○ *The rod came loose, punching a hole in the box.*

PHRASAL VERBS with **punch**

• **punch in** *something* **ENTER INFORMATION** [M] to enter information into a computer or other device, using keys or buttons ○ *Trev lifted the receiver and punched in the telephone number.*

• **punch in** **RECORD HOURS** to use a special clock to record the time you start working ○ *I punched in on the time clock.*

• **punch out** to record the time you finish working on a special clock ○ *I punched out and walked out the door.*

punching bag *n* [C] a bag filled with material that is hung from a frame or attached to a stand and hit for exercise or boxing practice

punch line *n* [C] the last part of a joke or a story that explains the meaning of what has happened previously or makes it amusing

punctual /ˈpʌŋ·tʃə·wəl/ *adj* arriving, doing something, or happening at the expected or correct time; not late ○ *Please try to be punctual, so we can start the meeting on time.*

punctually /ˈpʌŋ·tʃə·wə·li/ *adv* ○ *We arrived punctually at 8.*

punctuality /ˌpʌŋ·tʃəˈwæl·ət̬·i/ *n* [U] ○ *He's obsessive about punctuality.*

punctuate /ˈpʌŋ·tʃəˌweɪt/ *v* [T] to regularly interrupt something that is happening ○ *His comments were punctuated by shouts from hecklers.*

punctuated equilibrium *n* [U] ***biology*** a theory of EVOLUTION (= change in the development of living things) that claims that change happens suddenly over short periods of time followed by long periods of no change

punctuation /ˌpʌŋ·tʃəˈweɪ·ʃən/ *n* [U] special marks that are placed in a text to show the divisions between phrases and sentences, or the use of these marks ○ *Check your spelling and punctuation.*

punctuate /ˈpʌŋ·tʃəˌweɪt/ *v* [T] ○ *I would punctuate that sentence differently.*

punctuation mark *n* [C] ***writing*** a mark that you add to a text to show the divisions between different parts of it ○ *Periods, commas, semicolons, question marks, and parentheses are all punctuation marks.*

puncture /ˈpʌŋ·tʃər/ *n* [C] a small hole made by a sharp object

puncture /ˈpʌŋ·tʃər/ *v* [I/T] ○ [I] *Hot-air balloons are made so that they won't puncture easily.* ○ [T] *The bullet hadn't punctured any vital organs.*

pundit /ˈpʌn·dət/ *n* [C] a person who knows a lot about a particular subject, or someone who gives opinions in a way that sounds intelligent or wise ○ *Wall Street pundits are divided over whether the economy is slowing down.*

pungent /ˈpʌn·dʒənt/ *adj* (of a smell or taste) very strong, sometimes in an unpleasant way ○ *pungent odors*

punish /ˈpʌn·ɪʃ/ *v* [T] to cause people who have done something wrong or committed a crime to suffer by making them do something they don't want to do or sending them to prison ○ *She was punished for being late to school.*
punishable /ˈpʌn·ɪʃ·ə·bəl/ *adj* ○ *Swimming in the Potomac is punishable by a fine.*
punishment /ˈpʌn·ɪʃ·mənt/ *n* [C/U] ○ [C] *Serving your community is seen as a punishment these days.*

WORD FAMILY punish			
Nouns	punishment	*Adjectives*	punishable
Verbs	punish		punishing

punishing /ˈpʌn·ɪʃ·ɪŋ/ *adj* extremely difficult or tiring ○ *a punishing schedule*

punitive /ˈpjuː·nəţ·ɪv/ *adj* intended as a punishment ○ *No punitive action was taken against Dawkins after he smashed the backboard during warmups.*

punk CULTURE /pʌŋk/ *n* [U] a style or culture popular among young people, esp. in the late 1970s, expressing opposition to authority through shocking behavior, clothes, and hair, and through fast, loud music ○ *punk music/rock*
CRIMINAL /pʌŋk/ *n* [C] *slang* a young person who fights and is involved in criminal activities ○ *Some punk tried to steal my coat.*

punt /pʌnt/ *v* [T] (in football) to kick the ball after you have dropped it from your hands and before it touches the ground
punt /pʌnt/ *n* [C] ○ *I caught the punt and started running.*

puny /ˈpjuː·ni/ *adj* [-er/-est only] small and weak, or not effective ○ *Don't tell me you're afraid of that puny little kid.* ○ *In 1981, computers were puny compared with today's machines.*

pup /pʌp/ *n* [C] the young of particular animals, or a PUPPY DOG ○ *a seal pup*

pupil STUDENT /ˈpjuː·pəl/ *n* [C] a person who is being taught, esp. a child at school
EYE PART /ˈpjuː·pəl/ *n* [C] the circular, black area in the center of the eye that gets larger and smaller and lets in light

puppet /ˈpʌp·ət/ *n* [C] **1** a type of toy that looks like a person or animal and is moved by a person using strings or putting a hand inside it **2** *disapproving* A puppet is also a person or group whose actions are controlled by someone else: *The mayor is a puppet who does what business leaders tell him to.*
puppeteer /ˌpʌp·əˈtɪr/ *n* [C] a person who makes or uses puppets

puppy (dog) /ˈpʌp·i (ˌdɔːg)/, **pup** *n* [C] a young dog

puppy love /ˈpʌp·iː ˌlʌv/ *n* [U] romantic love that a young person feels for someone else

purchase Ⓐ /ˈpɜr·tʃəs/ *v* [T] to buy something ○ *To qualify for this fare, you must purchase your ticket 21 days in advance.*
purchase Ⓐ /ˈpɜr·tʃəs/ *n* [C/U] **1** [C] *The makeover is free with a $50 purchase.* **2** Purchase can also mean the act of buying: [U] *You can apply the value of your old car to the purchase of a new one.*
purchaser Ⓐ /ˈpɜr·tʃə·sər/ *n* [C] ○ *Software purchasers have reported problems with the product.*

pure NOT MIXED /pjʊr/ *adj* [*-er/-est* only] not mixed with anything else ○ *The scarf is pure silk.* ○ *It was a moment of pure joy.* ○ *The mountain air was fresh and pure* (= not polluted).
purify /ˈpjʊr·əˌfɑɪ/ *v* [T] to rid something of dirty or harmful substances ○ *Flower growers here are required to purify all their runoff water.*
purist /ˈpjʊr·əst/ *n* [C] a person who believes that it is important to speak, write, or do things in a correct or traditional way ○ *Some purists complain that the buildings are not being accurately restored.*
purity /ˈpjʊr·əţ·i/ *n* [U] ○ *The purity of the city's water is checked regularly at its reservoirs.*
purification /ˌpjʊr·ə·fəˈkeɪ·ʃən/ *n* [U]
MORALLY GOOD /pjʊr/ *adj* [*-er/-est* only] morally good, or relating to someone's inner character ○ *His motives were pure, but his approach was tactless.*
purify /ˈpjʊr·əˌfɑɪ/ *v* [T] ○ *White sage is sometimes burned to purify people and places.*
purity /ˈpjʊr·əţ·i/ *n* [U] ○ *purity of heart*
COMPLETE /pjʊr/ *adj* [not gradable] complete; only ○ *Getting the job was pure luck.*
purely /ˈpjʊr·li/ *adv* [not gradable] only; just ○ *Meeting Gail in the airport was purely coincidental.*

WORD FAMILY pure			
Nouns	purification	*Adjectives*	pure
	purist		impure
	purity	*Verbs*	purify
	impurity	*Adverbs*	purely

puree, **pureé** /pjʊˈreɪ, -ˈriː/ *v* [T] to crush food into a thick, soft sauce ○ *Puree the bananas thoroughly in a blender.*
puree, **pureé** /pjʊˈreɪ, -ˈriː/ *n* [C/U] ○ [U] *Add two tablespoons of tomato puree.*

purge RID /pɜrdʒ/ *v* [T] to rid a group or organization of unwanted people ○ *They purged the senior ranks of the department by offering them generous retirement packages.*
purge /pɜrdʒ/ *n* [C] ○ *The purge of alleged Communists and progressives had started as early as April.*

REMOVE /pɜrdʒ/ *v* [T] to remove something bad or wrong ○ *The system is designed to purge impurities from the city's drinking water.*

Puritan, **puritan** /ˈpjʊr·ət·ᵊn/ *n* [C] a member of an English religious group in the 16th and 17th centuries who wanted to make church ceremonies simpler and emphasized moral behavior that forbid many pleasures

puritanical /ˌpjʊr·əˈtæn·ɪ·kəl/ *adj* [not gradable] having standards of moral behavior that forbid many pleasures ○ *His coach believes in rules and regulations and has puritanical standards for behavior.*

purple /ˈpɜr·pəl/ *adj, n* [C/U] (of) the color that is a mixture of red and blue ○ *a purple dress* ○ [C] *The walls are a pale purple.*

purport /pərˈpɔːrt, -ˈpoʊrt/ *v* [+ *to* infinitive] *fml* to claim that something is true, but without proof ○ *The story purports to explain the origin of the game of chess.*

purported /pərˈpɔːrt̬·əd, -ˈpoʊrt̬-/ *adj* [not gradable] claimed but not proved to be true ○ [+ *to* infinitive] *The new brand of potato chips is purported to be lower in cholesterol, fat, and calories.*

purpose **REASON** /ˈpɜr·pəs/ *n* [C/U] **1** an intention or aim; a reason for doing something or for allowing something to happen ○ [C] *For budgeting purposes, you really have to start estimating costs now.* ○ [C] *The delay really served no good purpose and may have harmed the negotiation.* **2** If you do something **on purpose**, you do it intentionally: *This is the second time in a row that he didn't show up, and I believe he did it on purpose.* **3** Purpose is also determination: [U] *The project gave him a renewed sense of purpose.*

purposeful /ˈpɜr·pəs·fəl/ *adj* **1** aimed at achieving something; determined ○ *He desired to lead a more purposeful life.* **2** Purposeful also means intentional: *the purposeful destruction of historic sites*

purposely /ˈpɜr·pə·sli/ *adv* [not gradable] with a specific intent ○ *I purposely spoke loud enough to be overheard.*

RESULT /ˈpɜr·pəs/ *n* [C] an intended result or use ○ *This budget is designed to meet one purpose and one purpose only, to do what is best for the economy.*

WORD FAMILY purpose			
Nouns	purpose	*Adverbs*	purposefully purposely
Adjectives	purposeful		

purr /pɜr/ *v* [I] (of a cat) to make a soft, low, continuous sound, or (of a machine) to make a similar sound ○ *After a tune-up, the car just purred like new.*

purr /pɜr/ *n* [C]

purse **BAG** /pɜrs/ *n* [C] a bag, often with a handle or a strap going over the shoulder, used esp. by women for carrying money, keys, and small personal items such as makeup; a POCKETBOOK

AMOUNT OF MONEY /pɜrs/ *n* [C] an amount of money offered as a prize in a sporting competition, or the total amount of money available for spending ○ *Yesterday's race had a purse worth over $100,000.*

MOVE LIPS /pɜrs/ *v* [T] to bring your lips tightly together so that they form a rounded shape ○ *She pursed her lips and said nothing.*

purse strings *pl n* control over how much money is spent ○ *Retailers are hoping that American consumers will loosen their purse strings next year.*

pursue Ⓐ **FOLLOW** /pərˈsuː/ *v* [I/T] to follow or search for someone or something, in order to catch or attack that person or thing ○ [I] *The police pursued on foot, but lost him in the crowd.*

ATTEMPT /pərˈsuː/ *v* [T] to try to achieve ○ *She single-mindedly pursued her goal of earning a law degree.*

CONTINUE /pərˈsuː/ *v* [T] **1** to continue to do ○ *The hobbies that I pursue in my spare time are crafts – woodworking, mainly.* **2** To pursue is also to continue to consider: *I don't think the idea is worth pursuing.*

pursuit Ⓐ **ACT OF FOLLOWING** /pərˈsuːt/ *n* [C/U] the act of following or searching for someone or something, in order to catch or attack the person or thing ○ [U] *The two children ran through the field in pursuit of their puppy.*

ATTEMPT /pərˈsuːt/ *n* [U] an attempt to achieve something ○ *The Declaration of Independence states that life, liberty, and the pursuit of happiness are basic human rights.*

ACTIVITY /pərˈsuːt/ *n* [C usually pl] an activity that you spend time and energy doing ○ *scholarly pursuits*

purvey /pərˈveɪ/ *v* [T] *fml* to provide food, services, or information as a business ○ *The two mall shops purvey nearly identical merchandise.*

purveyor /pərˈveɪ·ər/ *n* [C] *fml* ○ *Radio stations are purveyors of music, information, and companionship.*

pus /pʌs/ *n* [U] thick, yellow liquid that forms in and comes out from infected body tissue

push **USE FORCE AGAINST** /pʊʃ/ *v* [I/T] **1** to put a continuing force against something to cause it to move forward or away from you ○ [I] *We should be able to move this table if we both push together.* ○ [T] *She pushed her plate away.* **2** To push is also to cause something to move or change in a stated direction: [M] *Rising demand tends to push prices up.*

push /pʊʃ/ *n* [C] ○ *She gave her daughter a push on the swing.*

MOVE FORCEFULLY /pʊʃ/ *v* [I/T] to move forcefully through a group of people or things ○ [I] *Stop pushing and wait your turn!* ○ [T always + adv/prep] *Rescuers pushed their way through the rubble to reach survivors.*

PERSUADE FORCEFULLY /pʊʃ/ *v* [T] to persuade someone forcefully to do or accept something ○ *She's pushing me for an answer.* ○ *The administration is pushing its new trade agreement with Mexico.* ○ (*infml*) *This restaurant is pushing its carrot soup today* (= trying to get people to order it).

push /pʊʃ/ *n* [C] ○ [+ *to* infinitive] *Florida is making a major push to attract more tourists.*

pushy /ˈpʊʃ·i/ *adj disapproving* trying too hard to persuade someone to do something ○ *The salesman was a little too pushy, and we felt uncomfortable.*

WORD FAMILY push			
Nouns	push pusher	Adjectives Verbs	pushy push

IDIOM with push

• **when push comes to shove, if push comes to shove** when all the easy answers to a problem have not worked, and something else must be tried ○ *Only a few people were there to help me when push came to shove.*

PHRASAL VERBS with push

• **push** *someone* **around** [M] to use greater strength or power to treat someone in a rude and threatening way ○ *When we were kids, my older brother liked to push me around.*

• **push back** *something* [M] to delay something; POSTPONE ○ *The target date for construction has been pushed back at least until fall.*

• **push for** *something* to demand that something be done or to take strong action to cause something to happen ○ *The unions are pushing for job security even if it means settling for modest wage increases.*

• **push off** *infml* to leave ○ *I'd better be pushing off now – I've got work to do.*

• **push on** to continue in a determined way ○ *We decided to push on to the top of the mountain while there was still daylight.*

pushchair /ˈpʊʃ·tʃer, -tʃær/ *n* [C] *Br* a STROLLER.

pushover /ˈpʊʃˌoʊ·vər/ *n* [C] *infml* something easy to do or win, or someone who is easily persuaded, influenced, or defeated ○ *Krista gets whatever she wants – her parents are real pushovers.*

push-up *n* [C] a physical exercise performed by lying with your face down and using only your arms to raise and lower your body

pussy /ˈpʊs·i/, **pussycat** /ˈpʊs·iːˌkæt/ *n* [C] *a child's word* a cat

pussyfoot /ˈpʊs·iːˌfʊt/ *v* [I] to be careful about expressing an opinion or taking action, esp. because you might hurt someone's feelings ○ *Quit pussyfooting around and tell me what you really think.*

pussy willow /ˈpʊs·iːˌwɪl·oʊ/ *n* [C] a small tree that has gray, furry flowers in the spring

put MOVE /pʊt/ *v* [T always + adv/prep] *pres. part.* **putting,** *past* **put 1** to move something or someone into the stated place, position, or direction ○ *She put her arm around him.* ○ *Put your clothes in the closet.* ○ *When you set the table, put the soup spoons next to the knives.* ○ *She put her coffee cup on the table.* ○ *The movie was so scary that she put her hands over her eyes.* **2** If you **put** *someone* **to bed**, you dress the person in the clothes worn for sleeping and see that the person gets into bed: *I'll call back after I put the kids to bed.*

WRITE /pʊt/ *v* [T always + adv/prep] *pres. part.* **putting,** *past* **put** to write down or record ○ *Put your name on the list if you want to go.* ○ *Put an answer in the space provided.*

EXPRESS /pʊt/ *v* [T] *pres. part.* **putting,** *past* **put 1** to express something in words ○ *She wanted to tell him that she didn't want to see him any more, but she didn't know how to put it.* ○ *He has difficulty putting his feelings into words.* **2** If you put something in a particular way, you express it that way: *To put it bluntly, Pete, you're just no good at the job.* ○ *Dad was annoyed, to put it mildly.*

CONDITION /pʊt/ *v* [T] *pres. part.* **putting,** *past* **put** to cause something to be in the stated condition or situation ○ *Are you prepared to put your children at risk?* ○ *This puts me in a very difficult position.* ○ *What put you in such a bad mood?*

JUDGE /pʊt/ *v* [T always + adv/prep] *pres. part.* **putting,** *past* **put** to judge something or someone in comparison with other similar things or people ○ *I'd put him among the top six tennis players of all time.* ○ *The value of the painting has been put at $1.5 million.* ○ *He always puts his family first.*

IDIOMS with put

• **I wouldn't put it past** *someone* **(to** *do something***)** *infml* I would not be surprised if someone did something ○ *I wouldn't put it past Helena to tell a secret, especially if it helped her in some way.*

• **put a damper on** *something* to make something less enjoyable ○ *The bad weather put a damper on this year's New Year celebrations.*

• **put down roots** to feel that you belong in a place ○ *Very quickly, settlers in Oregon built towns and put down roots.*

• **put an end to** *something* to cause something to stop existing or happening ○ *Mrs. Carroll said she was going to put an end to all the talking and fooling around in our class.*

• **put** *your* **feet up** to relax and do very little ○ *After working all week, you deserve to put your feet up.*

• **put** *your* **finger on** *something* to know or understand something, and be able to say exactly what it is ○ *Something seemed to be wrong, but I couldn't put my finger on it.*

• **put** *your* **foot down** to use your authority to stop something from happening ○ *When she started borrowing my clothes without asking, I had to put my foot down.*

• **put** *your* **foot in** *your* **mouth** to say or do something that you should not have, esp. something that embarrasses someone else ○ *I really put my foot in my mouth – I asked her if Jane was her mother, but she said Jane is her sister.*

• **put in a good word for** *someone* to say positive things about someone to other people ○ *I'm applying for a job in your department, so put in a good word for me.*

• **put** *your* **heads together** to share ideas in trying to solve a problem ○ *If we can put our heads together we'll figure out a way to deal with this.*

P

•**put** *someone* **in** *his/her* **place** to let someone know that the person is less important than he or she thinks ○ *When he tried to take charge, she immediately put him in his place.*
•**put** *yourself* **in** *someone's* **place, put** *yourself* **in** *someone's* **position/shoes** to imagine that you are someone in a difficult situation, and imagine how that person feels ○ *Put yourself in my place – I was scared, and I had nobody to talk to.*
•**put** *someone* **on** to joke with someone by saying something that is hard for the person to believe ○ *"I hear Joe's quit his job." "You're putting me on!"*
•**put** *someone/something* **out of** *your* **mind** to not think about someone or something ○ *I tried hard to put the conversation with my mom out of my mind.*
•**put the brakes on** *something/someone* to slow or stop the progress of something or someone ○ *Raising taxes now would put the brakes on economic recovery.*
•**put the squeeze on** *something/someone* to put pressure on someone or something to spend more money or to cause the person to earn less money ○ *Budget cuts are putting the squeeze on scientific research.*
•**put** *someone/something* **through** *his/her/its* **paces** to test the ability or skill of a person or thing ○ *I like to put a new car through its paces.*
•**put** *someone/something* **to the test** to test how good someone or something is, esp. in difficult conditions ○ *Those icy roads certainly put my driving to the test.*
•**put two and two together** to understand something by using the information you have ○ *I didn't tell her George had left, but she noticed his car was gone and put two and two together.*
•**put words in** *someone's* **mouth** to say that someone means one thing when the person really meant something else ○ *I never said you should leave – don't put words in my mouth.*

P

PHRASAL VERBS with **put**

•**put** *something* **across** [M] to communicate an idea or opinion ○ *What's the most important thing you try to put across in your book?*
•**put aside** *something* **IGNORE** [M] to ignore or not deal with something ○ *Let's put aside our differences.*
•**put aside** *something* **SAVE** [M] to save something, esp. money, for a purpose ○ *We're putting aside $20 a week for our vacation.* ○ *He puts some time aside each evening to read to his children.*
•**put away** *something* **EAT** [M] *infml* to eat a lot of food ○ *He put away a whole pie in one sitting.*
•**put away** *something* **STORE** [M] to store things where they are usually stored ○ *You never put away your toys.*
•**put away** *someone* **MOVE INTO CARE** [M] *infml* to move someone into prison, a mental hospital, or a home for old people ○ *He deserves to be put away for life.*
•**put back** *something* [M] to move something to a place or position it was in before ○ *Will you put the books back when you're finished with them?*
•**put** *something* **before** *someone/something* to offer an idea or law to a group for a decision or vote ○ *Our panel can put the proposal before the Executive Committee in July.*
•**put** *something* **behind** *someone* to try to forget or ignore something unpleasant ○ *I'm going to put all this behind me and think about the future.*
•**put down** *something/someone* **STOP CARRYING** [M] to stop carrying or holding someone or something ○ *I have to put this bag down – it's too heavy.* ○ *Put me down, Daddy!*
•**put down** *something* **PAY** [M] to pay money, esp. part of a total payment ○ *She put $1000 down on an apartment this afternoon.*
•**put down** *someone* **INSULT** [M] *infml* to make someone feel foolish and unimportant ○ *They never put down other companies in their commercials.* ○ *Did you have to put me down in front of everybody?* ○ Related noun: PUT-DOWN
•**put down** *something* **STOP** [M] to stop or limit forces opposing an authority or government, usually by using force ○ *He helped put down the rebellion.*
•**put** *someone* **down RECORD** [M] to record someone in a particular way ○ *Put down my sister as agreeing with the Democrats.* ○ *Lauren accidentally put me down for five boxes of cookies, but I only wanted one.*
•**put** *something* **down KILL** [M] to kill an animal that is ill or injured and cannot be made healthy
•**put forward/forth** *something* [M] to suggest an idea for consideration ○ *None of the ideas that I put forward have been accepted.* ○ *He put forth a clear, logical argument.*
•**put in** *something* **INCLUDE** [M] to include something, esp. in a piece of writing or a broadcast ○ *Kids like this computer program because they can put in images that they create.* ○ *We put an ad in the paper to sell our car.*
•**put in** *(something)* **OFFER OR REQUEST** [M] **1** to offer something for consideration ○ *She put in an application to the college.* **2** If you put in for something, or put in to do something, you make a request for it: *I am putting in for a transfer to Washington.*
•**put in** *something* **MAKE READY** [M] to take a device somewhere and make it ready to operate ○ *They're putting Paul's new stove in next week.*
•**put in** *something* **DO** [M] to do work, make effort, or spend time ○ *She's put in a lot of effort on this proposal.*
•**put** *something* **into** *something* to give money or effort to an activity ○ *We put all our profits back into the company.* ○ *She's put a lot of energy into making the house look nice.*
•**put off** *something/someone* **DELAY** [M] to delay or move an activity to a later time, or to stop or prevent someone from doing something ○ *The meeting has been put off for a week.* ○ *He keeps asking me out, and I keep putting him off.*
•**put** *someone* off **DISLIKE** [M] to discourage someone from doing something, or from liking someone or something ○ *I was put off by his appearance.* ○ *The experience put me off politics.*
•**put on** *something* **WEAR** [M] to move something you wear onto your body ○ *Put your shoes on.* ○ *She put on too much makeup.*

• **put on** *something* **ADD** [M] to add or increase an amount or action ○ *I put on weight when I went away to college.* ○ *The school puts a lot of emphasis on music and art.*

• **put on** *something* **START** [M] to start a piece of equipment, or to place a recording in a device that will play it ○ *I put on the brakes too fast, and the car skidded.* ○ *I put the heat on, but it will take a minute for the car to warm up.* ○ *Put on that Ella Fitzgerald CD.*

• **put on** *something* **DO** [M] to do an activity, esp. one that others can watch ○ *The second graders want to put a play on.* ○ *The experience of putting on a campaign was exciting.*

• **put** *someone* **on** *something* **DOCTOR'S ORDER** to order that someone start taking a particular medicine or eating or avoiding certain foods ○ *Doctors put her on antibiotics after discovering an infection.* ○ *He's putting me on a liquid protein diet.*

• **put on** *someone/something* **PRETEND** [M] **1** to appear to have a feeling or way of behaving that is not real or not natural for you ○ *I can't tell whether he's really upset or if he's just putting it on.* **2** If you put someone on, you deceive someone, often in a joking way: *He said they wanted me to do a show for the president, and I thought he was putting me on.*

• **put out** *something* **MOVE AWAY** [M] to move a part of your body away from the rest of you ○ *She put out her hand to shake mine.*

• **put out** *something* **INJURE** [M] to injure a part of the body by pulling or twisting it ○ *I put my back out last week when I fell.*

• **put out** *something* **STOP BURNING** [M] to stop something that is burning from continuing to burn ○ *Be sure to put out your campfire before you go to sleep.*

• **put out** *something* **PUBLISH** [M] to publish something or make information generally known ○ *The senator has put out a statement denying the allegations.*

• **put** *someone* **out** **ANNOY** [M] to annoy, upset, or inconvenience someone ○ *Would you be put out if we came tomorrow instead of today?*

• **put out** *something* **SPEND** [M] to spend money ○ *I'll be putting a lot of money out when I buy my house.*

• **put** *something* **over on** *someone* *infml* to persuade someone to believe something that is not true ○ *My dad's really smart – you can never put anything over on him.*

• **put** *someone* **through** *something* **CAUSE TO EXPERIENCE** to cause, allow, or pay for someone to experience or do something ○ *I'm sorry to have to put you through this.* ○ *She's putting herself through college.*

• **put** *someone* **through** **CONNECT TELEPHONES** [M] to connect a person's telephone call ○ *I expect someone to either answer or at least put me through to somebody who I can talk to.*

• **put** *someone* **to** *something* **CAUSE EXPERIENCE** to cause someone to experience something ○ *Your generosity puts me to shame.* ○ *He was put to death.* ○ **USAGE:** Used to describe negative emotions or events.

• **put** *something* **to** *someone* **EXPLAIN** [M] to tell someone your explanation of something ○ *Let me put it to you this way – you'll fail the test if you don't study.* ○ *The suspects answered a series of questions which authorities had put to them.*

• **put together** *something* **COMBINE** [M] to combine people or things, or organize something ○ *Put two and two together and you get four.* ○ *She earns more than all three of us put together.* ○ *After his first band failed, he put together a second orchestra.*

• **put together** *something* **MAKE WHOLE** [M] to repair something broken or make something out of parts ○ *The bowl broke into so many pieces that I can't put it back together again.*

• **put** *something* **toward** *something* to use money to help pay the cost of something ○ *Grandma told me to put that money toward my college education.*

• **put up** *something* **ATTACH** [M] to attach something, esp. to a wall ○ *We put up some new pictures in the living room.*

• **put up** *something* **RAISE** [M] to raise something to a higher position ○ *I put my hands up.* ○ *A statue of him was put up in Gramercy Park.*

• **put up** *something* **BUILD** [M] to build a structure in an empty space ○ *They're planning to put a hotel up where the museum used to be.*

• **put up** *something* **SHOW FEELINGS** to show or express your feelings about something ○ *I'm not going to let them build a road here without putting up a fight.* ○ *Little Rory always puts up such a fuss around bedtime.* ○ **USAGE:** Used when the feelings expressed are negative.

• **put up** *someone* **PROVIDE HOUSING** [M] to provide someone with a place to stay temporarily ○ *Sally is putting me up for the weekend.*

• **put up** *something* **PROVIDE MONEY** [M] to provide money so that an aim can be achieved ○ *Dad put $1000 up to help me buy a car.*

• **put** *someone* **up to** *something* to encourage someone to do something, esp. something wrong ○ *She never stole anything before – maybe her friends put her up to it.*

• **put up with** *someone/something* to be willing to accept someone or something that is unpleasant or not desirable ○ *I don't know why she puts up with him.*

put-down, **putdown** /ˈpʊt·dɑʊn/ *n* [C] *infml* a negative statement about someone; insult ○ *Calling American workers lazy was a mean-spirited put-down.* ○ Related verb: PUT DOWN INSULT

putrefy /ˈpjuː·trəˌfɑɪ/ *v* [I] *fml* to decay, producing a strong, unpleasant smell

putrid /ˈpjuː·trəd/ *adj* very decayed and having an unpleasant smell ○ *a putrid garbage dump*

putt /pʌt/ *v* [I/T] to hit a golf ball gently across an area of short and even grass toward or into a hole
putt /pʌt/ *n* [C] ○ *She won with an impressive six-yard putt.*

putter /ˈpʌt̬·ər/ *v* [I] to move around without hurrying and in a relaxed and pleasant way ○ *He really enjoys puttering in the garden.*

putty /ˈpʌt̬·i/ *n* [U] a thick, soft material that becomes hard when it dries and is used esp. for fixing

P

glass into window frames or for filling small holes in wood

put-upon /ˈpʊt̬·əˌpɑn/ *adj infml* treated unfairly by others who want you to help them ○ *Parents often feel put-upon by the school fund-raisers.*

puzzle /ˈpʌz·əl/ *n* [C] **1** something that is difficult to understand ○ *Their son is a puzzle to them.* ○ *The police are trying to solve the puzzle of who sent them the letter.* **2** A puzzle is also a game or toy in which you have to fit separate pieces together, or a problem or question which you have to answer by using your skill or knowledge: *a jigsaw/crossword puzzle*

puzzle /ˈpʌz·əl/ *v* [I/T] ○ [T] *It puzzles me why she said that.* ○ [I always + adv/prep] *We puzzled over what it meant.*

puzzled /ˈpʌz·əld/ *adj* ○ *She looked puzzled, then suspicious.*

Pygmy, Pigmy /ˈpɪg·mi/ *n* [C] a member of one of several groups of very small people who live in central Africa

pygmy, pigmy /ˈpɪg·mi/ *adj* [not gradable] (of an animal or bird) one of a type which is smaller than animals or birds of that type usually are ○ *a pygmy hippopotamus*

pylon /ˈpɑɪ·lɑn/ *n* [C] a tall, metal structure used as a support ○ *power pylons*

pyramid /ˈpɪr·əˌmɪd/ *n* [C] **1** ***geometry*** a solid shape with a flat, square base and four flat, triangular sides which slope inward and meet to form a point at the top ➤ Picture: **solid** **2** A pyramid is also a pile of things that has a triangular shape: *The acrobats formed a pyramid by standing on each other's shoulders.* **3** ***biology*** A pyramid is also a representation of a system with more items at the bottom and fewer at the top, for example, of the effect that one living thing has on another in the FOOD CHAIN.

pyre /pɑɪr/ *n* [C] a large pile of wood on which a dead body is burned in some types of funerals

Pyrex /ˈpɑɪ·reks/ *n* [U] *trademark* a type of glass that is used to make containers for cooking because it does not break when it is heated

Pythagorean theorem /pəˌθæg·əˈriː·ən ˈθɪr·əm/ *n* [U] ***geometry*** a statement that in a RIGHT TRIANGLE (= triangle with a 90° angle) the SQUARE (= number obtained by multiplying a number by itself) of the length of the side opposite the 90° angle is equal to the squares of each of the other two sides added together

python /ˈpɑɪ·θɑn, -θən/ *n* [C] a very large snake that kills animals for food by wrapping itself around them and crushing them

P

Q q

Q, q /kjuː/ *n* [C] *pl* **Q's, Qs, q's, qs** the 17th letter of the English alphabet

qt. *n* [C] *pl* **qt.** *abbreviation for* QUART

Q-tip /ˈkjuː·tɪp/ *n* [C] *trademark* a short stick with a small amount of cotton on each end, used for cleaning esp. the ears

quack SOUND /kwæk/ *v* [I] to make the sound DUCKS make ○ *The ducks started quacking.*

FALSE DOCTOR /kwæk/ *n* [C] a person who falsely pretends to have medical skills or knowledge

quad /kwɑd/, **quadrangle** /ˈkwɑd ˌræŋ·ɡəl/ *n* [C] a square or rectangular outside area with buildings on all four sides, often part of the land of a college or university

quadrangle /ˈkwɑd ˌræŋ·ɡəl/ *n* [C] ***geometry*** a flat shape with four straight sides ○ *Squares and rectangles are forms of quadrangles.*

quadrant /ˈkwɑ·drənt/ *n* [C] ***mathematics*** one of four rectangular areas that a COORDINATE PLANE (= area with vertical and horizontal measures) is divided into

quadratic equation /kwɑˈdræţ·ɪk ɪˈkweɪ·ʒən/ *n* [C] ***algebra*** an EQUATION (= mathematical statement) that includes an unknown value multiplied by itself only once, and does not include an unknown value multiplied by itself more than once; an equation that can be expressed as ($ax^2+bx+c=0$), when "a" does not equal zero

quadrilateral /ˌkwɑ·drəˈlæţ·ər·əl/ *n* [C] ***geometry*** a flat shape with four straight sides

quadriplegic /ˌkwɑd·rəˈpliː·dʒɪk/ *n* [C] a person who is permanently unable to move any of his or her arms or legs ○ *The riding accident injured his spine and left him a quadriplegic.*

quadruped /ˈkwɑd·rəˌped/ *n* [C] ***biology*** any animal that has four feet ○ *Horses and dogs are quadrupeds.*

quadruple /kwɑˈdruː·pəl, -ˈdrʌp·əl/ *v* [I/T] to become or make something four times greater ○ [I] *The number of students at the college quadrupled in the last ten years.*

quadruple /kwɑˈdruː·pəl, -ˈdrʌp·əl/ *adj* [not gradable] consisting of four parts, or four times greater in amount, number, or size ○ *My father had quadruple bypass heart surgery.*

quadruplet /kwɑˈdruː·plət, -ˈdrʌp·lət/, *short form* **quad** /kwɑd/ *n* [C] any of four children who are born to the same mother at the same time

quagmire /ˈkwæɡ·mɑɪr, ˈkwɑɡ-/ *n* [C] a situation that can easily trap you so that you become involved with problems from which it is difficult to escape ○ *When I tried to get my tax situation straightened out with the government, I ran into a bureaucratic quagmire.*

quail /kweɪl/ *n* [C/U] a small brown bird with a short tail, sometimes hunted as a sport and eaten as a food

quaint /kweɪnt/ *adj* [-er/-est only] attractive because of being unusual and esp. old-fashioned ○ *In Spain, we visited a cobblestone plaza with quaint little cafés around its perimeter.*

quake SHAKE /kweɪk/ *v* [I] to shake, esp. because you are frightened ○ *He quaked with fear at the thought.*

EARTH MOVEMENT /kweɪk/ *n* [C] *short form of* EARTHQUAKE

Quaker /ˈkweɪ·kər/ *n* [C] a member of a Christian group called the Society of Friends, which believes that a person can experience God directly and which does not have formal ceremonies or ministers, and whose meetings often include periods of silence

qualification SKILL /ˌkwɑl·ə·fəˈkeɪ·ʃən/ *n* [C usually pl] **1** knowledge, skill, or some other characteristic that gives a person the ability or the right to do or have something ○ *I assume my qualifications for the job will be considered along with theirs.* **2** A qualification is also a level of skill or ability that you have to achieve to be allowed to do something: *Passing the advanced Red Cross life-saving course is a qualification for all our lifeguards.*

LIMITATION /ˌkwɑl·ə·fəˈkeɪ·ʃən/ *n* [C/U] the act of limiting the use or range of a statement you make, or a particular limitation to a statement ○ [U] *I can recommend Helen Hefferman for this position without qualification.*

qualify REACH A STANDARD /ˈkwɑl·əˌfɑɪ/ *v* [I/T] **1** to achieve or have the standard of skill, knowledge, or ability that is necessary for doing or being something, or to cause someone to reach that standard ○ [+ *to* infinitive] *She was qualified to teach high school mathematics and physics.* ○ [I] *Derrick won his tennis match and qualified for the semifinals.* ○ [I] *James hopes to qualify as a nurse practitioner.* **2** To qualify is also to have the legal right to have or do something: [I] *She doesn't qualify for maternity leave because she hasn't worked there long enough.*

qualified /ˈkwɑl·əˌfɑɪd/ *adj* ○ *She was extraordinarily well qualified to run the State Department.*

LIMIT /ˈkwɑl·əˌfɑɪ/ *v* [T] to limit the strength or meaning of a statement ○ *The press secretary later qualified the president's remarks by saying he hadn't been aware of all of the facts.*

WORD FAMILY qualify			
Nouns	qualification disqualification	*Verbs*	qualify disqualify
Adjectives	qualified unqualified		

qualitative Ⓐ /ˈkwɑl·əˌteɪţ·ɪv/ *adj* relating to the quality of an experience or situation rather

Q

than to facts that can be measured ○ *There's a qualitative difference between seeing a live performance in a theater and watching a movie.*
qualitatively Ⓐ /ˌkwɑl·əˈteɪt̬·ɪv·li/ *adv* ○ Compare QUANTITATIVE

quality **EXCELLENCE** /ˈkwɑl·ət̬·i/ *n* [U] **1** the degree of excellence of something, often a high degree of it ○ *Our company guarantees the quality of our merchandise.* **2** Quality often refers to how good or bad something is: *The fabric was of the highest quality.*
quality /ˈkwɑl·ət̬·i/ *adj* ○ *This is a quality product* (= an excellent product).

CHARACTERISTIC /ˈkwɑl·ət̬·i/ *n* [C] a characteristic or feature of someone or something ○ *We're looking for someone who loves children and has the qualities of a good teacher.*

quality of life *n* [U] the level of satisfaction and comfort that a person or group enjoys ○ *Our quality of life improved tremendously once we finished paying for our kid's college education.*

qualm /kwɑm, kwɑlm/ *n* [C usually pl] an uncomfortable feeling of doubt about whether you are doing the right thing ○ *Unfortunately, he said, there are people who have no qualms about bringing in replacement workers for strikers.*

quandary /ˈkwɑn·dri/ *n* [C usually sing] a state of not being able to decide what to do about a situation in which you are involved ○ *I've had two job offers, and I'm in a real quandary about/over which one to accept.*

quantify /ˈkwɑnt·əˌfɑɪ/ *v* [T] to measure or judge the amount or number of something ○ *It's difficult to quantify how many people will have to pay higher taxes.*
quantifier /ˈkwɑnt·əˌfɑɪ·ər/ *n* [C] ***grammar*** a word or phrase that is used before a noun to show the amount of it that is being considered ○ *"Some," "many," "a lot of," and "a few" are examples of quantifiers used in English.*

quantitative /ˈkwɑnt·əˌteɪt̬·ɪv/ *adj* relating to an amount that can be measured ○ *Our employees receive a quantitative rating based on the dollar value of their sales.* ○ Compare QUALITATIVE

quantity /ˈkwɑnt·ət̬·i/ *n* [C/U] the amount or number of something, or a particular amount or number ○ [C] *a large/small quantity* ○ [C] *She served each of us a vast quantity of spaghetti.*

quantum /ˈkwɑnt·əm/ *n* [C] *pl* **quanta** ***physics*** the smallest amount of energy that can be measured

quantum leap /ˈkwɑnt·əm ˈliːp/, **quantum jump** /ˈkwɑnt·əm ˈdʒʌmp/ *n* [C] a great improvement or important advance in something ○ *It was a revolutionary generation of computers that was a quantum leap beyond anything on the market.*

quarantine /ˈkwɑr·ənˌtiːn, ˈkwɔːr-/ *n* [U] a period of time during which a person or animal that might have a disease is kept away from other people or animals so that the disease cannot spread ○ *The horse had to spend several months in quarantine when it reached this country.*
quarantine /ˈkwɑr·ənˌtiːn, ˈkwɔːr-/ *v* [T] ○ *He was quarantined with mumps, which is highly contagious.*

quark /kwɑrk, kwɔːrk/ *n* [C] ***physics*** one of the most basic forms of matter that make up atoms

quarrel /ˈkwɑr·əl, ˈkwɔːr-/ *n* [C] an angry disagreement between people, groups, or countries ○ *A big family quarrel left Judith and me in tears.*
quarrel /ˈkwɑr·əl, ˈkwɔːr-/ *v* [I] **1** *We often heard our neighbors quarreling about/over money.* **2** If you quarrel with facts or judgments, you do not accept them as true: *While we may quarrel with his conclusions, there is no reason to doubt his sincerity.*

quarry **PLACE** /ˈkwɑr·i, ˈkwɔːr·i/ *n* [C] a large hole in the ground that workers dig in order to use the stone and sand for building material
quarry /ˈkwɑr·i, ˈkwɔːr·i/ *v* [T] ○ *The gray limestone in this area was once quarried for use in bridges and buildings.*

PERSON/ANIMAL /ˈkwɑr·i, ˈkwɔːr·i/ *n* [U] a person, animal, or group being hunted or looked for ○ *Using video cameras can be tricky for researchers trying to blend in with their quarry.*

quart /kwɔːrt/, *abbreviation* **qt.** *n* [C] a unit of measurement of volume equal to 2 PINTS or about 0.95 liter

quarter **FOURTH PART** /ˈkwɔːrt̬·ər/ *n* [C] **1** one of four equal or almost equal parts of something ○ *My house is one and three-quarter miles/a mile and three-quarters from here.* **2** A quarter of/to the hour means 15 minutes before the stated hour: *It's a quarter to three.* **3** A quarter past/after the hour means 15 minutes after the stated hour: *I'll meet you at a quarter past five.* **4** A quarter is one of four equal or nearly equal periods of time into which an activity is divided: *Many universities divide the school year into quarters rather than two semesters.*
quarter /ˈkwɔːrt̬·ər/ *v* [T] to divide something into four pieces of approximately the same size ○ *Peel and quarter the tomatoes and put them in the stew.*
quarterly /ˈkwɔːrt̬·ər·li/ *adj, adv* [not gradable] (happening) four times a year ○ *a quarterly journal* ○ *It's published quarterly.*
quarterly /ˈkwɔːrt̬·ər·li/ *n* [C] a magazine that is published four times a year

MONEY /ˈkwɔːrt̬·ər/ *n* [C] in the US and Canada, a coin worth 25 cents

AREA /ˈkwɔːrt̬·ər/ *n* [C] an area of a city or place having a special history or character ○ *We stayed in the French Quarter in New Orleans.*

WORD FAMILY quarter

Nouns	quarter quarters quarterly	*Adjectives*	quarterly
		Verbs	quarter
		Adverbs	quarterly

quarterback /ˈkwɔːrt̬·ərˌbæk/ *n* [C] (in football) the player who receives the ball at the start of every play and tries to move it along the field by carrying it or throwing or handing it to other members of the team

quarterfinal /ˈkwɔːrt̬·ərˌfɑɪn·əl/ *n* [C] any of the four games in a competition that decides which players or teams will play in the two SEMIFINALS

quarter note *n* [C] ***music*** a note that is typically equal to one beat ➤ Picture: **notation**

quarters /ˈkwɔːrt̬·ərz/ *pl n* a place where someone lives or has a business ○ *In 1998 he moved his company to larger quarters on State Street.*

quartet /kwɔːrˈtet/ *n* [C] four people who sing or play musical instruments together, or a piece of music written for four people ○ *A string quartet was playing Mozart.* ○ Compare DUET; QUINTET; TRIO

quartz /ˈkwɔːrts/ *n* [U] a MINERAL (= hard substance formed naturally in the ground) used in making electronic equipment and watches and clocks

quash /kwɑʃ/ *v* [T] to stop or block something from happening ○ *The Secretary of Defense tried to quash speculation that he was planning to resign following the disastrous military defeat.*

quasi- /ˌkweɪˌzɑɪ, ˌkwɑz·iː/ *prefix* to a degree, but not completely ○ *Do companies need to be quasi-monopolies to survive in this new global economy?*

quaver /ˈkweɪ·vər/ *v* [I] (of a person's voice) to sound nervous, esp. because of emotion ○ *Her voice quavered for moment before she gained control.*

quay /kiː, keɪ, kweɪ/ *n* [C] a long, usually stone structure beside water, where boats can be tied up and their goods can be loaded or unloaded

queasy /ˈkwiː·zi/ *adj* feeling as if you are going to vomit ○ *I'm a little queasy this morning.*

queen /kwiːn/ *n* [C] **1** a woman who rules a country because she has been born into a family which by tradition or law has the right to rule, or the title given to such a woman ○ *Queen Elizabeth II* **2** A queen is also a woman who is considered to be the best in some way: *the reigning queen of crime writers* ○ *a beauty queen* **3** In the game of CHESS, the queen is the most powerful piece on the board. **4** A queen is also a playing card with a picture of a queen on it: *the queen of hearts* **5** In a group of insects, a queen is a large female that produces eggs: *a queen bee*

queen-sized, **queen-size** *adj* [not gradable] larger than the ordinary size, but not the largest size ○ *a queen-sized bed* ○ Compare KING-SIZED

queer /kwɪr/ *adj* [*-er/-est* only] *dated* unusual or strange ○ *She had a queer expression on her face.*

quell /kwel/ *v* [T] **1** to completely stop or end something ○ *The police were called in to quell the riot.* **2** If you quell doubts, fears, etc., you calm them: *He's been unable to quell his wife's suspicions.*

quench /kwentʃ/ *v* [T] to satisfy a need to drink by drinking liquid, or to stop fire from burning ○ *We quenched our thirst at a mountain spring.* ○ *Heavy rains quenched the fire.*

query /ˈkwɪr·i, ˈkwer·i/ *n* [C] a question, often one expressing doubt about something or looking for information

query /ˈkwɪr·i, ˈkwer·i/ *v* [T] ○ *Lawyers queried Ann about what she wore that day.*

quest /kwest/ *n* [C] a long search for something that is difficult to find ○ *a quest for the meaning of life*

question SOMETHING ASKED /ˈkwes·tʃən/ *n* [C] a word or words used to find out information ○ *May I ask you a personal question?* ○ *Our help line will answer your questions about patient care.*

question /ˈkwes·tʃən/ *v* [T] **1** *Mom's always questioning me about my friends.* ○ *The police questioned several men about the burglary.* **2** If you question something, you express doubt or uncertainty about it: [+ question word] *The book questions whether people today are better off than their parents were.*

questionable /ˈkwes·tʃə·nə·bəl/ *adj* not certain, or probably wrong in some way ○ [+ question word] *It is questionable whether that investment will pay off.* ○ *His comments were in questionable taste.*

questioner /ˈkwes·tʃə·nər/ *n* [C] a person who asks a question

> **USAGE**
> **question**
> Remember to use the verb **ask** with the noun **question.**
> *We weren't allowed to ask any questions.*
> ~~*We weren't allowed to make any questions.*~~

PROBLEM /ˈkwes·tʃən/ *n* [C/U] **1** a matter to be dealt with or discussed, or a problem to be solved ○ [C] *Your article raises the question of human rights.* ○ [C] *It's simply a question of getting your priorities straight.* ○ [C] *The question is, are they telling the truth?* ○ [U] *I was at home on the night in question.* **2** In an exam, a question is a problem that tests a person's knowledge: [C] *Answer as many questions as you can.*

DOUBT /ˈkwes·tʃən/ *n* [U] doubt or uncertainty ○ *He's competent – there's no question about that.* ○ *Her loyalty is beyond question.*

WORD FAMILY question			
Nouns	question questioner	*Adjectives*	questionable unquestioned unquestionable
Verbs	question		
Adverbs	unquestionably		

question mark *n* [C] a symbol (?) used in writing at the end of a word or group of words to show that it is a question

questionnaire /ˌkwes·tʃəˈner, -ˈnær/ *n* [C] a written list of questions that people are asked so that information can be collected

queue /kjuː/ *n* [C] *esp. Br* a line of people or things waiting for something ○ *There was a long queue for tickets at the theater.*

queue /kjuː/ *v* [I] ○ *Fans queued up to buy tickets.*

Q

quibble /ˈkwɪb·əl/ *v* [I] to argue or complain about small and unimportant details ○ *The issue is too important to quibble over.*
quibble /ˈkwɪb·əl/ *n* [C] ○ *My only quibble with the movie is that it's too long.*

quiche /kiːʃ/ *n* [C/U] an open pastry filled with a mixture of eggs, cheese, and other foods ○ [C] *a spinach quiche*

quick /kwɪk/ *adj* [-er/-est only] done, happening, or moving fast; lasting only a short time ○ *She cast a quick glance in the mirror.* ○ *You're back already – that was quick!* ○ *He made a quick profit.* ○ [+ to infinitive] *John was quick to point out the error.*
quick /kwɪk/ *adv not standard* ○ *We bought it quick, before someone else could.*
quick /kwɪk/ *exclamation* ○ *Quick! Close the door before the dog gets out!*
quicken /ˈkwɪk·ən/ *v* [I/T] to become or make faster or more active ○ [I] *His pulse quickened when he saw her.* ○ [T] *Computers have quickened the pace of communications.*
quickly /ˈkwɪk·li/ *adv* ○ *Emergency workers were on the scene quickly.*
quickness /ˈkwɪk·nəs/ *n* [U] ○ *She moves with quickness, balance, and grace.*

WORD CHOICES quick

A very common alternative is **fast**.

*I tried to catch him, but he was too **fast** for me.*

If something is done quickly, without waiting, you can use the adjectives **prompt, speedy**, or **swift**.

*A **prompt** reply would be very much appreciated.*

*He made a **speedy** recovery.*

*His plea for aid resulted in a **swift** response.*

If something is done too quickly, without thinking carefully, the adjectives **hasty** and **hurried** are often used.

*I don't want to make a **hasty** decision.*

*We left early after a **hurried** breakfast.*

A quick walk is often described as **brisk**.

*We took a **brisk** walk through the park.*

The adjective **rapid** is often used to describe quick growth or change.

*The 1990s were a period of **rapid** growth.*

quick fix *n* [C] an easy but temporary solution to a problem ○ *Managers are looking for a quick fix.*

quicksand /ˈkwɪk·sænd/ *n* [U] a mass of wet sand into which people and objects can sink

quick-witted *adj* [not gradable] able to react quickly and skillfully

quid pro quo /ˌkwɪd ˌproʊ ˈkwoʊ/ *n* [C] *pl* **quid pro quos** something that is given or received in return for something else ○ *Contributors expect a quid pro quo for their donations.*

quiet NO NOISE /ˈkwaɪ·ət/ *adj* **1** making very little or no noise ○ *Our new dishwasher is very quiet.* ○ **Be quiet** (= Stop making noise)! **2** A quiet person is one who does not talk much: *a shy, quiet child*
quiet /ˈkwaɪ·ət/ *v* [I/T] ○ [T] *He quieted the crowd by raising his hand.* ○ [I] *After a great deal of crying, the baby quieted down.* ○ [M] *I tried to quiet him down.*
quietly /ˈkwaɪ·ət·li/ *adv* ○ *"It's time," he said quietly.*
quiet /ˈkwaɪ·ət/ *n* [U] ○ *Let's have some quiet in here!*
quietness /ˈkwaɪ·ət·nəs/ *n* [U] ○ *I need sustained quietness to write.*

CONFUSABLES

quiet or **quite**?

Be careful, these two words look similar, but they are spelled differently and have completely different meanings.

Quiet means "making little or no noise."

The house was very quiet without the children around.

~~*The house was very quite without the children around.*~~

Quite is used in combination with "not" or followed by nouns. See the entry about it for examples.

WORD CHOICES quiet

If there is no noise or sound at all, the word **silent** is often used.

*The stadium fell **silent** after the goal was scored.*

Voices or sounds which are quiet can be described as **soft**.

*"Come here!" he said in a **soft** voice.*

*The restaurant had nice **soft** music playing in the background.*

If a sound is quiet and not clear you could describe it as **muffled**.

*I could hear **muffled** voices from the next room.*

If a sound is so quiet you can only just hear it, the adjective **faint** can be used.

*There was the **faint** sound of traffic in the distance.*

Hushed is usually used when people are quiet because they are afraid that someone might hear them or because they are waiting for something important to happen.

*The judge delivered his decision to a crowded but **hushed** courtroom.*

Quiet places where not much happens can be described as **peaceful, sleepy**, or **tranquil**.

*He needed a **peaceful** place to write his novels.*

*They retired to a **sleepy** little village.*

*The hotel is in a **tranquil** rural setting.*

A person who is quiet and does not often talk very much can be described as **taciturn**.

*Her father was a shy, **taciturn** man.*

NO ACTIVITY /ˈkwaɪ·ət/ *adj* [-er/-est only] without much activity or many people ○ *a quiet neighborhood* ○ *a quiet candlelit dinner*

Q

quiet /ˈkwɑɪ·ət/ *n* [U] ○ *After a hard day at work, all she wanted was some peace and quiet.*
quietly /ˈkwɑɪ·ət·li/ *adv* without attracting attention ○ *The airline quietly increased fares by 10 percent.*

WORD FAMILY quiet			
Nouns	quiet quietness	*Adjectives*	quiet disquieting
Verbs	quiet	*Adverbs*	quietly

quill /kwɪl/ *n* [C] a long, sharp point on a PORCUPINE, or a large feather with the end cut to a sharp point that was used, esp. in the past, as a pen

quilt /kwɪlt/ *n* [C] a covering for a bed, made of two layers of cloth with a layer of soft filling between them, and stitched in lines or patterns through all the layers ○ *a patchwork quilt*
quilted /ˈkwɪl·təd/ *adj* ○ *a quilted coat*

quintessential /ˌkwɪnt·əˈsen·tʃəl/ *adj* [not gradable] representing the most perfect or most typical example of something ○ *a quintessential small town* ○ *a quintessential athlete*
quintessentially /ˌkwɪnt·əˈsen·tʃə·li/ *adv* [not gradable] ○ *She is quintessentially American.*

quintet /kwɪnˈtet/ *n* [C] a group of five people who sing or play musical instruments together, or a piece of music written for five people ○ Compare DUET; QUARTET; TRIO

quintuplet /kwɪnˈtʌp·lət, -ˈtuː·plət/ *n* [C] any of five children born at the same time to the same mother ○ Compare QUADRUPLET; TRIPLET; TWIN

quip /kwɪp/ *n* [C] a quick, intelligent, and often amusing remark
quip /kwɪp/ *v* [T] **-pp-** ○ *The piano mover quipped, "Of course I love piano – I picked it up as a child!"*

quirk /kwɜrk/ *n* [C] an unusual habit or type of behavior, or something that is strange and unexpected ○ *a personality quirk* ○ *It's just one of the quirks of living there.*
quirky /ˈkwɜr·ki/ *adj* [*-er/-est* only] ○ *a quirky, offbeat sense of humor*

quit /kwɪt/ *v* [I/T] **quitting**, *past* **quit** to leave a job or a place, or to stop doing something ○ [I] *Her assistant quit without an explanation.* ○ [T] *I quit working to be at home with the kids.* ○ [T] *Quit worrying about him – he'll be fine!*

quite **VERY** /kwɑɪt/ *adv* [not gradable] **1** to a large degree ○ *School is quite different from what it once was.* **2 Quite a** is used before some nouns to emphasize the large number, amount, or size of the subject referred to: *We've had quite a lot of rain this year.* ○ *There were quite a few* (= a lot) *of people waiting in line.* ○ *She had quite a bit* (= a lot) *to say to him when he finally showed up.* ○ *I hadn't seen Rebecca in quite a while* (= for a long time). ➤ Confusables: **quiet or quite?** at QUIET NO NOISE
COMPLETELY /kwɑɪt/ *adv* [not gradable] completely ○ *Quite frankly, the thought of performing terrifies me.* ○ *I'm not quite done yet.* ○ *I'm not quite sure I understand.*
REALLY /kwɑɪt/ *adv* [not gradable] really or truly ○ *Winning this contest was quite an accomplishment.* ○ *It was quite a remarkable speech.*

quiver /ˈkwɪv·ər/ *v* [I] to shake slightly; TREMBLE ○ *The dog quivered with fear.*
quiver /ˈkwɪv·ər/ *n* [C] ○ *A quiver of excitement ran through the crowd.*

quixotic /kwɪkˈsɑt̬·ɪk/ *adj* ***literature*** having intentions or ideas that are admirable but not practical ○ *Many think these attempts to make lawyers behave are quixotic.*

quiz /kwɪz/ *n* [C] a short, informal test ○ *We had a history quiz today.*
quiz /kwɪz/ *v* [T] **-zz-** ○ *Reporters quizzed the jurors about their verdict.*

quizzical /ˈkwɪz·ɪ·kəl/ *adj* expressing slight uncertainty or amusement ○ *a quizzical look/smile*

quorum /ˈkwɔːr·əm, ˈkwoʊr-/ *n* [C] the number of members who must be present at a meeting in order for decisions to be officially made

quota /ˈkwoʊt̬·ə/ *n* [C] a number, amount, or share that is officially allowed or necessary ○ *A bill before Congress would impose import quotas that might save 3700 jobs.*

quotation mark, **quote** /kwoʊt/ *n* [C usually pl] ***grammar*** either of a pair of symbols (" ") used in writing before and after a word or group of words to show that they are spoken or that someone else originally wrote them

quote Ⓐ **SAY** /kwoʊt/ *v* [I/T] **1** to repeat words that someone else has said or written ○ [T] *She quoted him as saying he couldn't care less.* ○ [I] *He illustrated by quoting from Winston Churchill's speech.* **2** If you quote a fact or example, you refer to it to provide proof of something: [T] *The judge quoted several cases to support his opinion.* **3** You say quote or **quote, unquote** to show you are repeating the words of someone else: *He hailed the performance as, quote, an extraordinary achievement.* ○ *She moved to New York City knowing that that's where she had to live to, quote, unquote, make it in the music world.*
quotation Ⓐ /kwoʊˈteɪ·ʃən/, **quote** /kwoʊt/ *n* [C] ***literature*** a group of words from a book, play, speech, etc., that are repeated by someone who did not write them ○ *A quotation from Shakespeare prefaces the novel.*
STATE A PRICE /kwoʊt/ *v* [T] to state a price or amount that something will cost ○ *The roofer quoted $3000 to fix the roof.*
quotation /kwoʊˈteɪ·ʃən/, **quote** /kwoʊt/ *n* [C] ○ *He called back to say the price quotes were "not accurate."*

quotient /ˈkwoʊ·ʃənt/ *n* [C] **1** the degree, rate, or amount of something ○ *King had a full quotient of faults.* **2** ***mathematics*** A quotient is also the result you get when you divide one number by another.

Qur'an /kəˈræn, -ˈrɑn/ *n* [U] the KORAN

R r

R LETTER, **r** /ɑr/ *n* [C] *pl* **R's, Rs, r's, rs** the 18th letter of the English alphabet

MOVIE *adj* [not gradable] *abbreviation for* RESTRICTED ○ **USAGE:** Used in the US for movies that people under the age of 17 will not be allowed in to see except if they are with an adult. ○ Compare G MOVIE; NC-17; PG

rabbi /ˈræb·ɑɪ/ *n* [C] (the title of) a Jewish religious leader or a teacher of Jewish law

rabbit /ˈræb·ət/ *n* [C] a small animal with long ears and a short tail, that lives in holes in the ground

rabble /ˈræb·əl/ *n* [U] *disapproving* the mass of people who are ordinary, unimportant, and poor, and sometimes threatening

rabble-rouser /ˈræb·əl ˌrɑʊ·zər/ *n* [C] a person who excites others to anger, hate, or violence

rabid /ˈræb·əd, ˈreɪ·bəd/ *adj* **1** having RABIES (= serious disease of the nervous system) **2** A person who is described as rabid is extremely enthusiastic or has extreme feelings or opinions: *rabid fans of baseball* ○ *rabid anticommunists*

rabies /ˈreɪ·biːz/ *n* [U] a disease of the nervous system of animals that can be spread to humans, usually by a bite of an infected animal, and that causes death if not treated quickly

raccoon /ræˈkuːn/ *n* [C] a North American animal whose fur is mainly gray and brown, but black around the eyes, and with a thick tail

race COMPETITION /reɪs/ *n* [C] **1** a competition between people or animals to see who can get from the starting place to the finish before all the others ○ *a horse race* ○ *She won the 100-meter race in 11.06 seconds.* **2** *fig.* A race is also an urgent effort: [+ *to* infinitive] *It was a race against time to get the project finished by Friday's deadline.* **3** ***politics & government*** A race is also a competition to be elected to a political position: *The governor of California plans to enter the presidential race.*

race /reɪs/ *v* [I/T] **1** to compete in a race or run a race with someone ○ [I/T] *He's been racing (cars) for over ten years.* **2** *fig.* To race is also to move fast or to happen quickly: [I always + adv/prep] *The boys came racing across the playground.* ○ [I always + adv/prep] *Last summer seemed to race by.*

racer /ˈreɪ·sər/ *n* [C] ○ *The average racer completed the race in 13 hours last year.*

racing /ˈreɪ·sɪŋ/ *n* [U] ○ *thoroughbred/harness racing*

PEOPLE /reɪs/ *n* [C/U] any group into which humans can be divided according to their shared physical or GENETIC characteristics ○ [U] *Discrimination because of race is against the law.*

racial /ˈreɪ·ʃəl/ *adj* [not gradable] of or involving a particular race or different races ○ *racial discrimination/equality*

racially /ˈreɪ·ʃə·li/ *adv* [not gradable] ○ *They lived in a racially mixed neighborhood.*

racism /ˈreɪ ˌsɪz·əm/ *n* [U] ***social studies*** the belief that some races are better than others, or the unfair treatment of someone because of his or her race

racist /ˈreɪ·səst/ *n* [C] ***social studies*** a person who believes that some races are better than others, or who acts unfairly to someone because of his or her race

racist /ˈreɪ·səst/ *adj* ○ *a racist society*

WORD FAMILY race

Nouns	race racism racist	*Adjectives*	racial multiracial racist
		Adverbs	racially

racehorse /ˈreɪs·hɔːrs/ *n* [C] a horse that is bred and trained for racing

racetrack /ˈreɪs·træk/ *n* [C] a usually oval path on which esp. horses or cars compete

rack FRAME /ræk/ *n* [C] a frame, often with bars or hooks, for holding or hanging things ○ *a bike rack* ○ *a towel rack*

CAUSE PAIN /ræk/ *v* [T] to cause someone great physical or mental pain ○ *Even near the end, when cancer racked his body, he remained hopeful.*

IDIOM with rack

• **rack** *your* **brain** to try very hard to think of or remember something ○ *I've been racking my brain all day trying to remember her name.*

PHRASAL VERB with rack

• **rack up** *something* [M] *infml* to obtain or achieve something, or to score goals or points ○ *The airline was racking up losses of $1.5 million a day.* ○ *Miller racked up 28 points in the first half, and kept racking them up in the second.*

racket SPORTS, **racquet** /ˈræk·ət/ *n* [C] an object consisting of a net fixed tightly to an oval frame with a long handle, used in various sports for hitting a ball ○ *a tennis/squash racket*

NOISE /ˈræk·ət/ *n* [U] *infml* a loud, annoying noise ○ *Who's making such a racket?*

ILLEGAL ACTIVITY /ˈræk·ət/ *n* [C] *infml* a dishonest or illegal activity that makes money

racketeer /ˌræk·əˈtɪr/ *n* [C] a person who makes money through dishonest or illegal activities

racketeering /ˌræk·əˈtɪr·ɪŋ/ *n* [U]

racquetball /ˈræk·ət ˌbɔːl/ *n* [U] a game played in an enclosed playing area between two or four people who use RACKETS to hit a small rubber ball against a wall

racy /ˈreɪ·si/ *adj* [*-er/-est* only] causing slight shock because sex is mentioned or suggested ○ *a racy story*

radar /ˈreɪ·dɑr/ *n* [C/U] a device or system for finding the position or speed of objects, such as aircraft, that cannot be seen, by measuring the direction and timing of short radio waves that are sent out and reflect back from the objects

radial (tire) /ˈreɪd·iː·əl (ˈtɑɪr)/ *n* [C] a tire that has cords arranged across the edge of the wheel at an angle of 90 ○ *Radials make a vehicle easier to control on wet surfaces.*

radian *n* [C] ***geometry*** the measure of an angle at the center of a circle opposite an ARC (= part of the edge of a circle) that is the same length as the RADIUS (= line from the center to the edge of the circle)

radiant energy *n* [U] ***physics*** ENERGY POWER such as heat, light, and sound in the continuous repeating pattern of WAVES ENERGY FORM

radiate SEND OUT HEAT/LIGHT /ˈreɪd·iː ˌeɪt/ *v* [I/T] to send out heat or light, or (of heat or light) to be sent out ○ [T] *The little stove radiated a surprising amount of heat.*
radiant /ˈreɪd·iː·ənt/ *adj* ○ *Plants absorb radiant energy from sunlight.*
radiance /ˈreɪd·iː·əns/ *n* [U] ○ *We basked in the radiance of the afternoon sun.*
radiation /ˌreɪd·iː ˈeɪ·ʃən/ *n* [U] (the sending out of) heat, light, or energy in waves ○ *solar radiation*
EXPRESS /ˈreɪd·iː ˌeɪt/ *v* [I/T] to express strongly an emotion or quality, or of an emotion or quality to be expressed strongly by someone ○ [T] *He simply radiates integrity.*
radiant /ˈreɪd·iː·ənt/ *adj* expressing great happiness, hope, or beauty ○ *The bride looked radiant on her wedding day.*
radiance /ˈreɪd·iː·əns/ *n* [U]
SPREAD /ˈreɪd·iː ˌeɪt/ *v* [I always + adv/prep] to spread out from a central point ○ *The major avenues of the city all radiate from this point.*

radiation /ˌreɪd·iː ˈeɪ·ʃən/ *n* [U] ***physics*** energy in the form of WAVES or PARTICLES (= any of the smallest pieces of matter that make up atoms) ○ *Residents argued that electromagnetic radiation emitted by the radar towers might pose a health hazard.*

radiator /ˈreɪd·iː ˌeɪt̬·ər/ *n* [C] **1** a device for heating rooms in buildings, consisting of a series of pipes through which steam or hot water passes **2** In a motor vehicle, a radiator is a device for cooling the engine.

radical Ⓐ SUPPORTING CHANGE /ˈræd·ɪ·kəl/ *adj* believing or expressing the belief that there should be great or extreme social, economic, or political change ○ *White's political orientation was decidedly liberal, but hardly radical.*
radical Ⓐ /ˈræd·ɪ·kəl/ *n* [C] a person who supports great social, economic, or political change
EXTREME /ˈræd·ɪ·kəl/ *adj* causing or being an example of great change; extreme ○ *During bad economic times, radical steps may be necessary to restore the confidence of the consumer.*
radically Ⓐ /ˈræd·ɪ·kə·li/ *adv* ○ *Her views are not radically different from my own.*

radii /ˈreɪd·iː ˌɑɪ/ *pl of* RADIUS

radio /ˈreɪd·iː ˌoʊ/ *n* [C/U] *pl* **radios 1** a device for receiving, and sometimes broadcasting, sound messages, or the receiving or sending of sound messages ○ [C] *I listen to the radio in the morning to get the weather report.* **2** Radio is also the work of broadcasting sound programs for the public to listen to. **3** ***physics*** Radio WAVES are the energy waves of a certain length that are used in radio broadcasts.
radio /ˈreɪd·iː ˌoʊ/ *v* [I/T] *pres. part.* **radioing**, *past* **radioed** to send a message to someone by radio ○ [I/T] *They radioed (their base) for help.*

radioactive /ˌreɪd·iː·oʊ ˈæk·tɪv/ *adj* ***physics*** possessing or producing energy from the breaking up of atoms, or resulting from the production of such energy ○ *radioactive waste*
radioactivity /ˌreɪd·iː ˌoʊ·æk ˈtɪv·ət̬·i/ *n* [U] ***physics***

radiocarbon dating /ˌreɪd·iː·oʊ ˈkɑr·bən ˈdeɪt̬·ɪŋ/ *n* [U] ***science*** CARBON DATING

radioisotope /ˌreɪd·iː·oʊ ˈɑɪ·sə ˌtoʊp/ *n* [C] ***chemistry, physics*** an ISOTOPE that gives off RADIATION (= form of energy)

radiology /ˌreɪd·iː ˈɑl·ə·dʒi/ *n* [U] the scientific study of the medical use of RADIATION (= type of energy), esp. X-RAYS
radiologist /ˌreɪd·iː ˈɑl·ə·dʒəst/ *n* [C] a doctor who specializes in the medical use of RADIATION, esp. X-RAYS

radiotherapy /ˌreɪd·iː·oʊ ˈθer·ə·pi/ *n* [U] the use of controlled amounts of RADIATION (= type of energy), aimed at a particular part of the body, to treat disease

radish /ˈræd·ɪʃ/ *n* [C] a small, red or white vegetable that grows as a root and is eaten raw, esp. in salads

radium /ˈreɪd·iː·əm/ *n* [U] a chemical element that is RADIOACTIVE (= producing energy from the breaking up of atoms)

radius /ˈreɪd·iː·əs/ *n* [C] *pl* **radii** ***geometry*** (the length of) a straight line from the center of a circle to its edge ○ *The supermarket, shopping mall, and school are all within a one-mile radius of the house* (= are all less than a mile away from it). ➤ Picture: **circle**

radon /ˈreɪ·dɑn/ *n* [U] a colorless RADIOACTIVE gas that is formed when RADIUM (= a chemical element) and some other substances break down

raffle /ˈræf·əl/ *n* [C] a system of selling numbered tickets and then giving prizes to those people whose numbers are chosen by chance

PHRASAL VERB with raffle

• **raffle off** *something* [M] to sell chances to win something ○ *Players signed footballs, which were raffled off along with a mink coat.*

raft FLOATING STRUCTURE /ræft/ *n* [C] **1** a flat, floating structure made of pieces of wood tied together, often attached to the bottom of a river or

R

lake for use when swimming **2** A raft is also a small rubber or plastic boat that can be filled with air.

rafting /ˈræf·tɪŋ/ *n* [U] the use of a rubber raft to travel with the current of a river, esp. as a sport ○ *The camp offered bicycle tours, river rafting, fishing, and hiking.*

A LOT /ræft/ *n* [C] a large number or collection; a lot ○ *We've identified a whole raft of problems affecting traffic flow.*

rafter /ˈræf·tər/ *n* [C] any of the large, specially shaped pieces of wood that support a roof

rag /ræg/ *n* [C] a piece of usually old, torn cloth ○ *I use these rags for cleaning.* ○ *They were dressed* **in rags** (= in old, torn pieces of clothing).

rag doll *n* [C] a child's DOLL (= toy in the shape of a person) made of cloth filled with a soft material

rage /reɪdʒ/ *n* [C/U] extreme or violent anger, or a period of feeling such anger ○ [C] *I had never seen him in such a rage before.*

rage /reɪdʒ/ *v* [I always + adv/prep] **1** *He raged at me for sending the letter out before he had seen it.* **2** If something destructive rages, it happens in a way that cannot be controlled: *The fire broke out and raged for four days, destroying most of the old city.*

ragged **IN BAD CONDITION** /ˈræg·əd/ *adj* (of clothes) torn and usually in bad condition from too much use, or (of people) wearing clothes in this condition ○ *A group of ragged children appeared, begging for coins.*

UNEVEN /ˈræg·əd/ *adj* not straight or even ○ *His scalp had a ragged gash.*

rags-to-riches *adj* [not gradable] involving a change from being poor to becoming rich ○ *her rags-to-riches success story*

ragtag /ˈræg·tæg/ *adj* consisting of parts or pieces that are in no particular order or system ○ *They put together a ragtag team for a third of the cost of the Yankees and they won it all.*

R

ragtime /ˈræg·tɑɪm/ *n* [U] a type of popular music, developed about 1900, with a strong beat

raid /reɪd/ *n* [C] **1** a planned attack by a military group that is done suddenly and unexpectedly and is intended to destroy or damage something ○ *an air raid* ○ *a bombing raid* **2** A raid is also a planned but sudden and unexpected entering of a place by the police in order to search for something or to stop an illegal activity.

raid /reɪd/ *v* [T] **1** to enter a place suddenly and unexpectedly in order to search for something or to stop an illegal activity ○ *The FBI said it had no plans to raid the suspect's farm.* **2** To raid is also to unfairly or secretly take something for your own use or benefit: *The movie company was accused of raiding talent from other studios.*

rail **TRAINS** /reɪl/ *n* [C/U] **1** one of the two metal bars fixed to the ground on which trains travel **2** Rail also means railroad: [U] *rail transportation* ○ [U] *Commuter rail and subway lines will be linked.*

ROD /reɪl/ *n* [C] a straight bar or rod fixed in position, esp. to a wall or to vertical posts, used to enclose something or as a support ○ *The car swerved out of control and crashed through a guard rail on the bridge.*

COMPLAIN /reɪl/ *v* [I always + adv/prep] to complain angrily ○ *He railed against the injustices of the system.*

railing /ˈreɪ·lɪŋ/ *n* [C] a type of fence made of one of more usually metal or wooden bars attached to posts, often along the edge of a path or at the side of stairs for safety and to provide support ○ *The iron railing at the edge of the boardwalk was some six feet above the beach.*

railroad **TRANSPORTATION** /ˈreɪl·roʊd/, **railway** /ˈreɪl·weɪ/ *n* [C] a system of transportation using special vehicles whose wheels turn on metal bars fixed to the ground, or a particular company using such a system ○ *railroad tracks* ○ *a railroad station* ○ *the Pennsylvania Railroad*

FORCE /ˈreɪl·roʊd/ *v* [T always + adv/prep] to force something to happen or force someone to do something, esp. quickly and unfairly ○ *We feel our client was railroaded into pleading guilty.*

rain /reɪn/ *n* [U] drops of water that fall from clouds ○ *It looks like rain* (= as if rain is going to fall).

rain /reɪn/ *v* [I] **1** *It's raining hard* (= heavily). ○ *The tennis match was* **rained out** (= stopped because of rain). **2** Rain can also mean to fall in a large amount: *Debris from the explosion rained down.*

rainy /ˈreɪ·ni/ *adj* ○ *a rainy afternoon*

IDIOMS with rain

• **rain cats and dogs** to rain very heavily ○ *Don't forget to take your umbrella - it's raining cats and dogs out there.*

• **a rainy day** a time when money might unexpectedly be needed ○ *She had saved some money for a rainy day.*

rainbow /ˈreɪn·boʊ/ *n* [C] an arch of many colors sometimes seen in the sky for a short time when it rains and the sun is shining

rain check **TICKET FOR LATER** *n* [C] a part of a ticket to a game, activity, etc., that can be used later if bad weather prevents the original event from happening

DELAY IN ACCEPTING *n* [C usually sing] an offer or request to do or get something at a later time than was originally intended ○ *I'm busy now, but can I take a rain check on that cup of coffee?*

raincoat /ˈreɪn·koʊt/ *n* [C] a coat worn for protection from the rain

rainfall /ˈreɪn·fɔːl/ *n* [C] the amount of rain that falls ○ *Heavy rainfall is expected in the northwest.*

rain forest, **rainforest** /ˈreɪn ˌfɔːr·əst, -ˌfɑr·əst/ *n* [C] a forest in a hot area of the world that receives a lot of rain

rainstorm /ˈreɪn·stɔːrm/ *n* [C] a period with strong winds and heavy rain

rainwater /ˈreɪnˌwɔːt̬·ər, -ˌwɑt̬·ər/ *n* [U] water that has fallen as rain

raise LIFT /reɪz/ *v* [T] to cause something to be lifted up or become higher ○ *He raised the window shades.* ○ *Stephie raised her hand to ask the teacher a question.* ➤ Confusables: **rise or raise?** at RISE

INCREASE

BECOME BIGGER /reɪz/ *v* [T] to cause something to become bigger or stronger; increase ○ *I had to raise my voice to be heard over the noise in the classroom.* ○ *There are no plans to raise taxes, the president said.* ○ *I don't want to raise your hopes too much, but I think the worst of the flooding is over.*

raise /reɪz/ *n* [C] an increase in the amount money you earn ○ *She asked her boss for a raise.*

DEVELOP /reɪz/ *v* [T] to take care of children or young animals until completely grown ○ *They raised a family and now want to enjoy their retirement.*

BRING ABOUT /reɪz/ *v* [T] **1** to bring something to your attention; cause to be noticed ○ *This raises a number of important issues.* **2** To raise money is to succeed in getting it: *I want to start my own business if I can raise enough money.*

IDIOM with **raise**

• **raise hell** **1** to behave in a way that is not controlled and causes trouble **2** **Raise hell** can also mean to argue loudly or make demands.

raisin /ˈreɪ·zən/ *n* [C] a dried GRAPE (= a small, round fruit)

rake /reɪk/ *n* [C] a garden tool with a long handle and pointed parts sticking out in a row at the bottom, used for making earth level or for gathering leaves or cut grass

rake /reɪk/ *v* [T] ○ *Some workers raked leaves in the park.*

PHRASAL VERB with **rake**

• **rake in** *something* [M] to earn a lot of money ○ *These huge websites rake in $20 million in a year.*

rally MEETING /ˈræl·i/ *n* [C] a public meeting of a large group of people, esp. to show support for a particular opinion, political party, or sports team ○ *He helped organize the first national rally against the war.*

rally /ˈræl·i/ *v* [I/T] to bring or come together in order to provide support or make a shared effort ○ [I] *African-American groups rallied around the president when he was under attack.*

IMPROVE /ˈræl·i/ *v* [I/T] to return or bring to a better condition; improve or cause to succeed ○ [I] *Cleveland rallied in the fourth quarter to beat Washington, 111-102.* ○ [I] *The dollar rallied against the yen in trading today.*

rally /ˈræl·i/ *n* [C] **1** *Stock prices fell again today after yesterday's rally.* **2** In baseball, a rally is a period during which a team scores a lot of RUNS (= points), esp. when it has been losing.

ram PUSH /ræm/ *v* [I/T] **-mm-** to hit or push with force ○ [I/T] *Someone rammed (into) my car in the parking lot.* ○ [T] (*fig.*) *The governor tried to ram the budget through in the last days of the legislative session.*

ANIMAL /ræm/ *n* [C] an adult male sheep

RAM /ræm/ *n* [U] *abbreviation for* random-access memory (= a type of computer memory that can be searched in any order and changed as necessary)

Ramadan /ˈrɑm·əˌdɑn, ˈræm-/ *n* [C] the ninth month in the Islamic year, during which Muslims take no food or drink during the day from the time the sun appears in the morning until it can no longer be seen in the evening

ramble WALK /ˈræm·bəl/ *v* [I] to walk for pleasure, esp. in the countryside ○ *I love to ramble through the woods.*

ramble /ˈræm·bəl/ *n* [C] ○ *We took a ramble through the park.*

TALK /ˈræm·bəl/ *v* [I] to talk or write in a confused way, often for a long time ○ *It was hard to listen to her ramble on and on about her vacation.*

rambunctious /ræmˈbʌŋ·ʃəs/ *adj* full of energy and difficult to control ○ *Driving a long distance with four rambunctious children is not exactly fun.*

ramification /ˌræm·ə·fəˈkeɪ·ʃən/ *n* [C usually pl] the possible result of a decision or action ○ *Have you considered all the ramifications of changing careers at this stage of your life?*

ramp /ræmp/ *n* [C] **1** a surface connecting a higher and a lower level; a slope ○ *Wide ramps flanked the stairs at the entrance.* **2** A ramp is also a road that lets you drive onto or leave a large road, such as an EXPRESSWAY: *an entrance/exit ramp*

rampage /ˈræm·peɪdʒ/ *v* [I] to move, run, and do things in a wild, violent way ○ *Youths rampaged through the downtown district.*

rampage /ˈræm·peɪdʒ/ *n* [C] ○ *The hurricane continues its rampage through the Caribbean.*

rampant /ˈræm·pənt/ *adj* [not gradable] happening a lot or becoming worse, usually in a way that is out of control ○ *Weeds are growing rampant in the garden.*

ramshackle /ˈræmˌʃæk·əl/ *adj* badly made and likely to break or fall down easily ○ *a ramshackle building with a sagging roof*

ran /ræn/ *past simple of* RUN

ranch /ræntʃ/ *n* [C] a type of large farm on which animals are kept ○ *a cattle ranch*

rancher /ˈræn·tʃər/ *n* [C] someone who owns or works on a ranch

ranch house, **ranch** /ræntʃ/ *n* [C] a house built on one level and usually in the shape of a long rectangle, or this style of house

rancid /ˈræn·səd/ *adj* (of food containing a fat such as butter or oil) tasting or smelling unpleasant because it is not fresh

R

rancor, *Cdn, Br* **rancour** /ˈræŋ·kər/ *n* [U] *fml* bitter anger or unfriendly feelings ○ *Can we settle this disagreement without rancor?*

rancorous /ˈræŋ·kə·rəs/ *adj fml* ○ *a rancorous debate*

random Ⓐ /ˈræn·dəm/ *adj* **1** happening, done, or chosen by chance rather than according to a plan or pattern ○ *a random sample* ○ *He was stopped at the border in a random check.* **2 At random** means by chance, or without any organization or plan: *Dylan picked several books at random.*

randomly Ⓐ /ˈræn·dəm·li/ *adv* ○ *The people I interviewed were chosen randomly.*

randomness Ⓐ /ˈræn·dəm·nəs/ *n* [U]

rang /ræŋ/ *past simple of* RING **SOUND**

range Ⓐ **LIMIT** /reɪndʒ/ *n* [C/U] **1** the level to which something is limited, or the area within which something operates ○ [C] *a wide range of subjects* ○ [C] *The coat was beautiful, but way out of my price range.* ○ [C] *I like temperatures in the 60s and 70s, somewhere in that range.* **2** Range is also the period of time within which something happens, or the distance something travels: [U] *the short/intermediate/long range* ○ [U] *He was shot at very close range.* **3** A vehicle's or aircraft's range is the distance that it can travel without having to stop for more fuel.

range Ⓐ /reɪndʒ/ *v* [I always + adv/prep] ○ *Prices range from $50 to $250.* ○ *Our discussions ranged over many issues.*

SET /reɪndʒ/ *n* [C] **1** a set of similar or related things ○ *We offer a wide range of options.* ○ *The clinic provides a full range of medical services.* **2** A range (also (**line**)) is a group of products of a particular type.

MOUNTAINS /reɪndʒ/ *n* [C] a group of mountains or hills ○ *the San Juan Range*

PRACTICE AREA /reɪndʒ/ *n* [C] an area where people can practice shooting guns or hitting golf balls, or where weapons can be tested

LAND /reɪndʒ/ *n* [C] a large area of land for animals to feed on, or the region a type of animal or plant comes from and is most often found in

R

range Ⓐ /reɪndʒ/ *v* [I always + adv/prep] to move or travel with complete freedom ○ *The hikers ranged over the hills all day.*

STOVE /reɪndʒ/ *n* [C] a stove used for cooking that has a top surface with BURNERs (= devices for controlling flames or heat) for heating food and usually an OVEN (= enclosed cooking space) ○ *gas/electric range*

ranger /ˈreɪn·dʒər/ *n* [C] a person whose job is to care for or protect a forest, park, or public lands

rank **POSITION** /ræŋk/ *n* [C/U] a position in relation to others higher or lower, showing the importance or authority of the person having it ○ [C] *You get more privileges if you have a higher rank.* ○ [U] *He rose quickly in rank.*

rank /ræŋk/ *v* [I/T] ○ [I] *Sylvia ranks in the top 5 percent in her class.* ○ [T] *The tennis association ranks her second.*

ranking /ˈræŋ·kɪŋ/ *adj* [not gradable] having the highest rank or standing in relation to others of the same kind ○ *The Senator is the ranking Republican on the committee.*

rankings /ˈræŋ·kɪŋz/ *pl n* ○ *She has been near the top of the 800-meter rankings for the past 13 years.*

ranks /ræŋks/ *pl n* the members of a group or organization, or members of the armed service who are not officers ○ *He rose through the ranks to become a director of the company.*

SMELLY /ræŋk/ *adj* smelling very unpleasant ○ *a rank odor*

rank and file *n* [U] soldiers who are not officers, or the members of an organization who are not part of the leadership

rankle /ˈræŋ·kəl/ *v* [I/T] to cause annoyance or anger that lasts a long time ○ [I] *The way she left him still rankles.*

ransack /ˈræn·sæk/ *v* [T] to completely search a place in a way that causes mess and damage ○ *Burglars ransacked the house.*

ransom /ˈræn·səm/ *n* [C/U] a sum of money demanded in exchange for someone or something that has been taken ○ [C] *The kidnappers demanded a huge ransom.* ○ [U] *The man's brother was held for ransom.*

ransom /ˈræn·səm/ *v* [T] to free someone who has been taken away by paying money ○ *The executive was ransomed for a million dollars.*

rant /rænt/ *v* [I] to speak or shout in a loud or angry way ○ *I got really wound up and started ranting and raving.*

rap **HIT** /ræp/ *v* [I/T] **-pp-** to hit suddenly and forcefully ○ [I] *We heard him rap on the door.* ○ [T] *She rapped the table to get everyone's attention.*

rap /ræp/ *n* [C] ○ *He got a nasty rap on the head.*

MUSIC /ræp/ *n* [U] a type of popular music of African-American origin that features rhythmic speaking set to a strong beat

rap /ræp/ *v* [I] **-pp-** ○ *On his new album he raps about his hard life and hard times.*

rapper /ˈræp·ər/ *n* [C] ○ *The rapper will release two albums on Sept. 14.*

ACCUSATION /ræp/ *n* [C usually sing] *slang* an accusation that someone has committed a crime, or punishment for a crime

REPUTATION /ræp/ *n* [C usually sing] *slang* a judgment, report, or reputation ○ *The smell of the Great Salt Lake has given it a bad rap.*

rape /reɪp/ *v* [T] **1** to force someone to have sex when he or she is unwilling **2** Rape also means to damage or destroy something by using it in an unsuitable way: *Developers are raping the countryside.*

rape /reɪp/ *n* [C/U] ○ [U] *He was convicted of rape.*

rapist /ˈreɪ·pəst/ *n* [C] a man who rapes someone

rapid /ˈræp·əd/ *adj* quick or sudden ○ *rapid growth* ○ *There's been rapid change in China.* ○ *We kept up a rapid pace.*

rapidly /ˈræp·əd·li/ *adv* ○ *Males grow more rapidly than females.*

rapids /ˈræp·ədz/ *pl n* a fast-flowing part of a river

rapport /ræˈpɔːr, rə-, -ˈpoʊr/ *n* [U] agreement or sympathy between people or groups ○ *She has a good rapport with her staff.*

rapprochement /ˌræp ˌroʊʃˈmɑ̃, -ˌrɔːʃ-/ *n* [C/U] *fml* agreement reached by opposing groups or people ○ [C] *Both countries have agreed to seek a rapprochement.*

rap sheet *n* [C] a list of crimes a person has committed or been accused of that is kept by the police

rapt /ræpt/ *adj* receiving someone's full interest, or complete ○ *I haven't been following the conversation with rapt attention.*

rapture /ˈræp·tʃər/ *n* [C/U] extreme pleasure and happiness ○ [U] *Life was rapture for a little while.*

rare NOT COMMON /rer, rær/ *adj* not common and therefore sometimes valuable ○ *rare species of birds* ○ *Success like that is extremely rare.* ○ *She's usually positive, but on rare occasions disappointment shows through.* ○ *With rare exceptions, the families in this town have lived here for generations.*

rarely /ˈrer·li, ˈrær-/ *adv* ○ *I rarely have time to read the newspaper.*

rarity /ˈrer·ət̬·i, ˈrær-/ *n* [C/U] something rare, or the state of being rare ○ [C] *Snow in Florida is a rarity.*

SLIGHTLY COOKED /rer, rær/ *adj* [-er/-est only] (esp. of meat) not cooked for very long and still red inside ○ *rare steak*

WORD FAMILY rare			
Nouns	rarity	*Adverbs*	rarely
Adjectives	rare		

rarefied /ˈrer·əˌfɑɪd, ˈrær-/ *adj* not ordinary, esp. because of being related to wealth, high social position, art, or literature ○ *You get a very rarefied view of things living on a college campus.*

raring /ˈrer·ɪŋ, ˈrær-, -ən/ *adj* [+ *to* infinitive] *infml* very enthusiastic or eager ○ *Everyone is raring to go.*

rascal /ˈræs·kəl/ *n* [C] a person who behaves badly or dishonestly but who is usually likable ○ *The group includes thieves, politicians, and rascals of every sort.*

rash WITHOUT THOUGHT /ræʃ/ *adj* without thought for what might happen or result; unwise in your actions ○ *a rash statement* ○ *It was rash of them to get married so quickly.*

SKIN CONDITION /ræʃ/ *n* [C] a group of spots or a raised area on the skin resulting from illness or from touching a harmful substance ○ *an itchy rash*

LARGE NUMBER /ræʃ/ *n* [C usually sing] a large number, esp. of something happening in a short period of time ○ *There's been a rash of robberies in the valley.*

rasp /ræsp/ *n* [U] an unpleasant sound, like something with a rough surface being rubbed

raspy /ˈræs·pi/ *adj* [-er/-est only] ○ *His voice had dwindled to a raspy croak.*

raspberry /ˈræz ˌber·i, -bə·ri/ *n* [C] a small, soft, red fruit that grows on a bush

rat ANIMAL /ræt/ *n* [C] a small animal that looks like a large mouse ○ *A rat was sniffing around the trash.*

PERSON /ræt/ *n* [C] *infml* an unpleasant person who deceives or is not loyal

ratchet /ˈrætʃ·ət/ *v* [I/T] to change an activity, amount, or feeling by degrees ○ [I] *Interest rates always ratchet down in an election year.* ○ [M] *Critics are trying to ratchet up public pressure on lawmakers.*

rate MEASUREMENT /reɪt/ *n* [C] a measurement of the speed at which something happens or changes, or the number of times it happens or changes, within a particular period ○ *the rate of change/decay* ○ *rates of digestion/oxygenation* ○ *We have relatively low unemployment rates these days.* ○ *If we improve students' self-esteem, we could reduce the dropout rate.*

PAYMENT /reɪt/ *n* [C] an amount or level of payment ○ *Interest rates may rise soon.* ○ *Rental rates vary depending on the size of the car.*

VALUE /reɪt/ *v* **1** to judge the value or worth of something ○ [T] *Half of those surveyed rated his work as good.* ○ [L] *The movie is rated R.* ○ [I] *Mark Twain has rated as an enduring author for 100 years.* **2** *disapproving* If you say someone or something doesn't rate, you mean it is of poor quality or not worth consideration.

rating /ˈreɪt̬·ɪŋ/ *n* [C] **1** *Chez Paul got a three-star rating from our restaurant reviewer.* **2** A rating is a record of the number of people who watch or listen to a particular broadcast: *Advertisers are interested in ratings.*

WORD FAMILY rate			
Nouns	rate rating	*Verbs*	rate underrate
Adjectives	overrated underrated		

rather PREFERABLY /ˈræð·ər, ˈrɑð-, ˈrʌð-/ *adv* [not gradable] in preference to, or as a preference ○ *She wants us to meet her here rather than go to her apartment.* ○ *I'd rather wear the black shoes.* ○ *She's saying things that many would rather not hear.*

TO SOME DEGREE /ˈræð·ər, ˈrɑð-, ˈrʌð-/ *adj, adv* [not gradable] to a noticeable degree; SOMEWHAT ○ *It all seems rather unimportant.*

MORE EXACTLY /ˈræð·ər, ˈrɑð-, ˈrʌð-/ *adv* [not gradable] more accurately; more exactly ○ *These were not common criminals, but rather enemies of the state.*

ratify /ˈræt̬·əˌfɑɪ/ *v* [T] (esp. of governments or organizations) to agree in writing to a set of rules, or to officially approve a decision or plan ○ *Four countries have now ratified the agreement.*

ratification /ˌræt̬·ə·fəˈkeɪ·ʃən/ *n* [U] ○ *The Senate will consider ratification of the treaty in July.*

R

ratio Ⓐ /ˈreɪ·ʃiː ˌoʊ/ *n* [C] *pl* **ratios 1** ***mathematics*** a comparison of two numbers calculated by dividing **2** Ratio is also a relationship between two groups or amounts that expresses how much bigger one is than the other: *a low student-teacher ratio* ○ *The ratio of men to women at the conference was ten to one.*

ration /ˈræʃ·ən, ˈreɪ·ʃən/ *n* [C] a limited amount (of something) that one person is allowed to have, esp. when there is not much of it available ○ *Rations of rice were distributed to the refugees.*
ration /ˈræʃ·ən, ˈreɪ·ʃən/ *v* [T] ○ *Even their clothing is rationed.*
rationing /ˈræʃ·ə·nɪŋ, ˈreɪ·ʃə-/ *n* [U] ○ *food rationing*
rations /ˈræʃ·ənz, ˈreɪ·ʃənz/ *pl n* the food given to someone at one time, esp. to soldiers ○ *He fed prisoners the same rations he fed his own troops.*

rational Ⓐ /ˈræʃ·ən·əl/ *adj* showing clear thought or reason ○ *a rational decision* ○ *Obviously, he wasn't rational.*
rationally Ⓐ /ˈræʃ·ən·əl·i/ *adv* [not gradable] ○ *It's hard to behave rationally at such times.*
rationality Ⓐ /ˌræʃ·əˈnæl·əṭ·i/ *n* [U] ○ *You have too much faith in rationality* (= reason).

rationale /ˌræʃ·əˈnæl/ *n* [C/U] the reasons or intentions for a particular set of thoughts or actions ○ [C] *I don't understand your rationale.*

rationalism Ⓐ /ˈræʃ·ən·əl·ɪ·zəm/ *n* [U] the belief or principle that actions and opinions should be based on reason

rationalize Ⓐ /ˈræʃ·ən·əlˌɑɪz/ *v* [I/T] to create a reason, explanation, or excuse for something ○ [T] *You can rationalize your way out of anything.*
rationalization Ⓐ /ˌræʃ·ən·əl·əˈzeɪ·ʃən/ *n* [C/U] ○ [C] *Parents are fed up with rationalizations about why schools don't work.*

R

rational number *n* [C] ***mathematics*** a number that can be expressed as the RATIO (= relationship expressed in numbers showing how much bigger one thing is than the other) of two whole numbers

rat race *n* [C usually sing] a situation or way of life in which there is severe competition ○ *I love the city, but sometimes it's a rat race.*

rattle /ˈræṭ·əl/ *v* [I/T] to make a noise consisting of quickly repeated knocks ○ [I] *The windows rattled when the wind blew.* ○ [T] *Manny slammed the door, rattling the cups on the shelf.*
rattle /ˈræṭ·əl/ *n* [C/U] **1** [U] *We could hear the rattle of stones as they fell down the well.* **2** A rattle is also a baby's toy that rattles when it is shaken.

PHRASAL VERB with rattle

• **rattle off** *something* [M] to say something quickly ○ *She rattled off the names of everyone coming to the party.*

rattled /ˈræṭ·əld/ *adj* worried or nervous ○ *Walter got rattled when they didn't call.*

rattlesnake /ˈræṭ·əlˌsneɪk/, **rattler** /ræt·lər/ *n* [C] a poisonous snake of the southwestern US and Mexico that produces a noise by shaking its tail

raucous /ˈrɔː·kəs/ *adj* loud, excited, and not controlled, esp. in an unpleasant way ○ *raucous laughter*

raunchy /ˈrɔːn·tʃi, ˈrɑn-/ *adj infml* rude or offensive because of showing or talking about sex in an obvious way ○ *raunchy language/humor*

ravage /ˈræv·ɪdʒ/ *v* [T] to cause great damage to something or someone ○ *Hurricane Mitch ravaged the tiny Central American country.*
ravages /ˈræv·ɪ·dʒəz/ *pl n* ○ *They survived the ravages of disease and malnutrition.*

rave ENTHUSIASTIC /reɪv/ *adj* admiring; giving praise ○ *The show has received rave reviews.*
rave /reɪv/ *n* [C] ○ *Her speech drew raves from everyone.*
rave /reɪv/ *v* [I] *infml* ○ *Everyone is raving about that new Vietnamese restaurant.*
SPEAK FOOLISHLY /reɪv/ *v* [I] to speak or shout in a way that is out of control, usually because of anger or mental illness ○ *She was wild and raving, tearing up her books.*

raven /ˈreɪ·vən/ *n* [C] a large, black bird that is bigger than a CROW

ravenous /ˈræv·ə·nəs/ *adj* [not gradable] extremely hungry ○ *We were ravenous after hiking all day.*

ravine /rəˈviːn/ *n* [C] a deep, narrow valley with steep sides

raving /ˈreɪ·vɪŋ/ *adj, adv* [not gradable] complete or extreme, or completely or extremely ○ *He was raving mad near the end of his life.*

ravioli /ˌræv·iːˈoʊ·li/ *pl n* small squares of pasta, often filled with meat or cheese, that are cooked in boiling water

raw NOT COOKED /rɔː/ *adj* [not gradable] not cooked ○ *raw fish/oysters*
NOT PROCESSED /rɔː/ *adj* [not gradable] **1** not processed or treated; in its natural condition ○ *raw milk* ○ *raw silk* ○ *Raw sewage ran in ditches along the streets of the village.* **2** If people or their qualities are raw, they have not been developed or trained: *Even when she first started skating, you could see the determination and the raw talent.* ○ *Alex was just a raw recruit when he was handed this job.*
SORE /rɔː/ *adj* sore because the skin has been rubbed or damaged
COLD /rɔː/ *adj* [not gradable] (of weather) cold and wet ○ *It was a raw, wintry day with a cold wind.*

IDIOM with raw

• **a raw deal** unfair treatment or arrangements ○ *He felt he had gotten a raw deal but didn't complain.*

raw material *n* [C] any material, such as oil, cotton, or sugar, in its natural condition, before it has been processed for use ○ *The cost of raw materials was going up.*

ray BEAM /reɪ/ *n* [C] ***physics*** a narrow beam of light, heat, or energy

LINE /reɪ/ *n* [C] ***geometry*** half of a line

AMOUNT /reɪ/ *n* [C] a slight amount or signal of something good ○ *One couple seems interested in buying our house, which is a ray of hope after all these months.*

rayon /ˈreɪ·ɑn/ *n* [U] smooth, shiny material made from CELLULOSE (= wood fibers)

raze /reɪz/ *v* [T] to destroy a building, structure, etc. completely ○ *Developers razed the old buildings on the site to make way for new construction.*

razor /ˈreɪ·zər/ *n* [C] a device with a sharp blade for removing hair from the skin's surface ○ *an electric razor*

razor blade *n* [C] a very thin, sharp blade that can be used in a RAZOR ○ *She used a razor blade to cut out newspaper articles.*

razor-sharp *adj* [not gradable] very sharp ○ *These animals have razor-sharp teeth.*

razor-thin *adj* [not gradable] very thin or small ○ *The administration's economic program was approved by a razor-thin margin in the Senate.*

razzle-dazzle /ˌræz·əlˈdæz·əl/ *n* [U] *infml* showy appearance or performance, intended to attract attention or cause confusion ○ *The razzle-dazzle in this movie doesn't make up for the lack of plot.*

RCMP *n* [U] *abbreviation for* Royal Canadian Mounted Police (= a Canadian police force known for special police services and for ceremonial appearances in red uniform and on horses).

Rd. *n* [U] *abbreviation for* road ○ *The center is located at 1065 Edwards Rd.*

re /reɪ, riː/ *prep* (esp. in business letters) about; on the subject of ○ *Re your memo July 10, I have indeed received the order.*

re- /riː/ *prefix* used esp. with verbs to add the meaning "do again" ○ *reactivate; reactivation; reassess; reassessment; reassign; recommence; re-create; redistribute; redistribution; redraft; reevaluate; reevaluation; refocus; reformulate; reformulation; reinterpret; reinterpretation; reinvest; reinvestment; reoccur; reorient; reorientation*

reach ARRIVE /riːtʃ/ *v* [T] to arrive somewhere ○ *The storm continues to move west and is expected to reach the east coast of Florida tomorrow.*

> **USAGE**
>
> **reach**
>
> When **reach** means "arrive somewhere" or "get to a particular level" it is not normally followed by a preposition.
>
> *We finally reached the hotel just after midnight.*
>
> *The project has now reached the final stage.*
>
> ~~*The project has now reached to the final stage.*~~

BECOME HIGHER /riːtʃ/ *v* [T] **1** to become higher or greater so as to equal a particular level ○ *The temperature is expected to reach 90° today.* ○ *The government fears unemployment will reach 10%.* **2** To reach is also to develop to a stage in order to achieve a particular result: *We hope to reach agreement soon on the new trade policy.* ○ *They reached the conclusion that nothing further could be done.*

STRETCH /riːtʃ/ *v* [I/T] **1** to stretch out your arm to its full length in order to take or touch something ○ [T] *Our little girl isn't tall enough to reach the light switches.* ○ [I always + adv/prep] *The receptionist reached for the phone.* ○ [I always + adv/prep] *She reached across the table and took his hand.* **2** If an object reaches something, the top or bottom of it touches that thing: [T] *The ladder won't quite reach the roof.*

reach /riːtʃ/ *n* [U] the distance to which you can put out your arm and touch something ○ *All medicines should be kept out of the reach of children.*

COMMUNICATE /riːtʃ/ *v* [T] to communicate with someone in another place, usually by telephone ○ *I've been trying to reach you all afternoon, but your phone was busy.*

> PHRASAL VERB with **reach**
>
> • **reach out to** *someone* to make an effort to communicate with people or to give them your support ○ *The Democrats have to reach out to these people to win this election.*

react Ⓐ /riːˈækt/ *v* [I] **1** to act in a particular way as a direct result of something else ○ *How do you think she'll react when she hears the news?* ○ *The State Department reacted favorably to the proposal.* **2** ***chemistry*** If substances react, they change when brought together.

reaction Ⓐ /riːˈæk·ʃən/ *n* [C] **1** behavior, a feeling, or an action that is a direct result of something else ○ *My initial reaction was to call off the party.* ○ *Senator, what is your reaction to the proposal to cut Medicare benefits?* **2** A reaction is also a change that opposes a previous opinion or behavior: *His art is a reaction against photographic realism.* **3** ***biology*** A reaction can also be an unpleasant effect on the body resulting from something eaten or taken, such as a drug. **4** ***chemistry*** A chemical reaction is the change that happens when two or more substances are mixed with each other.

WORD FAMILY react

Nouns		Adjectives	
	reaction		reactionary
	reactor	Verbs	react
	reactionary		overreact
	overreaction		

reactant /riːˈæk·tənt/ *n* [C] ***chemistry*** a chemical substance that reacts with another

reactionary Ⓐ /riːˈæk·ʃəˌner·i/ *n* [C] ***social studies*** a person who opposes political or social change

reactionary Ⓐ /riːˈæk·ʃəˌner·i/ *adj* [not gradable] ○ *Reactionary forces opposed to the president's reforms could move to oust him.*

reactivity /ˌriː·ækˈtɪv·əţ·i/ *n* [U] ***chemistry*** a measure of how much a substance reacts when it is mixed with another substance

R

reactor /riː ˈæk·tər/ *n* [C] a NUCLEAR REACTOR

read OBTAIN MEANING /riːd/ *v* [I/T] *past* **read 1** to obtain meaning or information by looking at written words or symbols ○ [T] *I read the book over the weekend.* ○ [I] *She couldn't read or write.* ○ [I] *Did you read about the plan to build a new road to the airport?* ○ [+ *that* clause] *I read that the job market for teachers is excellent.* ○ [T] *He reads music.* **2** To read is also to say aloud the written words: [I/T] *She read the story to the class.*

readable /ˈriːd·ə·bəl/ *adj* easy or enjoyable to read ○ *Reviewers praised it as a highly readable and rewarding book.*

reader /ˈriːd·ər/ *n* [C] a person who reads ○ *Both of my parents were great readers* (= they read a lot). ○ *The local newspaper welcomes comments from its readers.*

reading /ˈriːd·ɪŋ/ *n* [C/U] **1** the skill of activity of getting information from written words ○ [U] *Reading is my favorite pastime.* **2** Reading is also text to be read: [U] *These books are required reading for architecture students.* **3** A reading is an occasion when a literary work or formal text is read aloud to a group of people: [C] *a poetry reading*

UNDERSTAND /riːd/ *v* [I/T] to understand the meaning or intention of something ○ [T] *If I've read the situation right, we'll soon have agreement on a contract.*

reading /ˈriːd·ɪŋ/ *n* [C] the way in which you understand something ○ *My reading of the situation is that John wanted an excuse to resign.*

SHOW/STATE /riːd/ *v past* **read 1** to show or state information ○ [L] *The sign read, "No parking here to corner."* **2** If you read a device, you look at the measurement it shows: [T] *The gas company sends someone to read the meter every month.*

reading /ˈriːd·ɪŋ/ *n* [C] ○ *Temperature readings in the area are in the 30s.*

WORD FAMILY read

Nouns	read reader reading	*Adjectives*	readable unreadable
		Verbs	read

IDIOMS with read

•**read between the lines** to find meanings that are intended but that are not directly expressed in something said or written ○ *She said she could afford it, but reading between the lines I don't think she has enough money.*

•**read** *someone's* **mind** to know what someone is thinking without being told ○ *How did you know I wanted that CD for my birthday – you must have read my mind.*

PHRASAL VERBS with read

•**read** *something* **into** *something* [M] to give your own meaning to something rather than what was intended ○ *I think you're reading too much into his comments – he's not trying to trick anyone.* ○ *Too much shouldn't be read into the city rankings.*

•**read out** *something* [M] to read something to people so that it becomes officially known ○ *The three-judge panel read out the verdict to a packed courtroom.*

•**read up on** *something* to learn about something by reading ○ *I don't know much about Malawi – I'll go home and read up on it.*

readjust Ⓐ /ˌriː·əˈdʒʌst/ *v* [I/T] **1** to change the way you live or behave to fit a new or different situation ○ [I] *The government program was established to help soldiers returning from World War II readjust to civilian life.* **2** To readjust something is to change it, move it, or correct it: [T] *It's time to readjust income taxes so the more well-to-do pay a higher percent of tax.*

readjustment Ⓐ /ˌriː·əˈdʒʌs·mənt/ *n* [C] ○ *Retirement is a readjustment – no question about it.*

readout /ˈriːd·ɑʊt/ *n* [C] information produced by electronic equipment and shown in print on a screen

ready PREPARED /ˈred·i/ *adj* [not gradable] prepared and suitable for action or use ○ *Dinner is ready.* ○ *The twins are getting ready for bed.* ○ [+ *to* infinitive] *I'm ready to go now.* ○ [+ *to* infinitive] *"Are you ready to order?" the waiter asked.*

readily /ˈred·əl·i/ *adv* quickly or easily ○ *The complete collection is now readily available to researchers through the Internet.*

readiness /ˈred·iː·nəs/ *n* [U] the state of being ready or prepared ○ *Military readiness is the country's overriding concern.*

WILLING /ˈred·i/ *adj* [not gradable] willing ○ *My friends are always ready to help me out.*

readily /ˈred·əl·i/ *adv* [not gradable] ○ *Cory readily admits he was hired because of his contacts.*

QUICK /ˈred·i/ *adj* [not gradable] quick, esp. in answering or in thinking of what to say ○ *He had a ready reply to every question.*

WORD FAMILY ready

Nouns	readiness	*Adverbs*	readily
Adjectives	ready		

ready-made *adj* [not gradable] in finished form, or available to use immediately ○ *I didn't sew the curtains – they came ready-made.*

reaffirm /ˌriː·əˈfɜrm/ *v* [T] to state something as true again, or to state your support for something again ○ *This album reaffirms his reputation as a splendid songwriter and guitarist.*

real ACTUAL /riːl/ *adj* existing in fact; not imaginary ○ *There is a real possibility that he will lose his job.* ○ *This is a true story about real people.*

realism /ˈriː·əˌlɪz·əm/ *n* [U] **1** a tendency to accept and deal with people and situations as they are **2** ***literature*** Realism is also a style of writing, art, or film that shows things as they are in life.

realist /ˈriː·ə·ləst/ *n* [C] a person who tends to accept and deal with people and situations as they are

realistic /ˌriː·əˈlɪs·tɪk/ *adj* **1** having or showing a practical awareness of things as they are ○ *She is realistic about her chances of winning.* **2** Realistic also means appearing to be existing or happening

in fact: *The scene in the movie where the dinosaur hatches from the egg is incredibly realistic.*
realistically /ˌriː·əˈlɪs·tɪ·kli/ *adv* [not gradable] ○ *Realistically, we can't afford a piano.*
reality /riːˈæl·əţ·i/ *n* [C/U] **1** the actual state of things, or the facts involved in such a state [U] *The reality is I'm not going to be picked for the team.* ○ [C] *The realities of parenthood were overwhelming at first.* **2 In reality** means what actually happened or what the actual situation is: *He told the police he was out of town, but in reality, he never went anywhere.*
really /ˈriː·li/ *adv* [not gradable] ○ *What really happened that day?* ○ *I just don't know if we would really use it that much.* ○ See also: REALLY SINCERELY; REALLY EXPRESSING SURPRISE; REALLY at REAL VERY GREAT

NOT FALSE /riːl/ *adj* being what it appears to be; GENUINE ○ *Are those flowers real or fake?* ○ *The chest of drawers is a real antique.*

VERY GREAT /riːl/ *adj* [not gradable] very great or to a great degree ○ *He's a real gentleman.* ○ *The current situation is a real mess.*
real /riːl/ *adv* [not gradable] *infml* ○ *I get cold real easy.* ○ *It's real nice to meet you.*
really /ˈriː·li/ *adv* [not gradable] ○ *That was a really good movie.* ○ *This room is really hot.* ○ See also: REALLY SINCERELY; REALLY EXPRESSING SURPRISE; REALLY at REAL ACTUAL

WORD FAMILY real

Nouns	realism realist reality unreality realization	*Adjectives*	real unreal realistic unrealistic
Verbs	realize	*Adverbs*	real really realistically

IDIOM with real

• **the real McCoy** the original or true person or thing, and not a copy ○ *We've seen so many reproductions of the Mona Lisa, but when we were in Paris we saw the real McCoy.*

real estate /ˈriː·ləˌsteɪt/ *n* [U] property in the form of land or buildings

real estate agent *n* [C] a person whose business is to arrange the selling or renting of houses, land, offices, or buildings for their owners

reality check *n* [C] an occasion when someone must consider the unpleasant truth about something rather than trying to ignore it ○ *The disappointing results of the last election were a reality check for the Republicans.*

realize BECOME AWARE /ˈriː·əˌlɑɪz/ *v* [T] to become aware of or understand a situation ○ *He realized the store would be closing in a few minutes.* ○ [+ *(that)* clause] *Suddenly I realized (that) I was lost.*
realization /ˌriː·ə·ləˈzeɪ·ʃən/ *n* [C usually sing] ○ *You soon come to the horrible realization that the flat skinny letters mean, No, you are not accepted.*

ACHIEVE /ˈriː·əˌlɑɪz/ *v* [T] to achieve things you hope for or plan for ○ *They finally realized their goal of buying a summer home.*
realization /ˌriː·ə·ləˈzeɪ·ʃən/ *n* [U] ○ *Playing in the major leagues was the realization of his dreams.*

really SINCERELY /ˈriː·li/ *adv* [not gradable] sincerely; truly ○ *I'm really telling the truth this time.* ○ *If she really cared about me, she would have called by now.* ○ See also: REALLY at REAL ACTUAL; REALLY at REAL VERY GREAT

EXPRESSING SURPRISE /ˈriː·li/ *exclamation* used to express interest, surprise, or annoyance ○ *"Debbie and I are getting married." "Really? When?"* ○ *Really, Jen, you should have let me know sooner.* ○ See also: REALLY at REAL ACTUAL; REALLY at REAL VERY GREAT

realm /relm/ *n* [C] an area of interest or activity ○ *the economic/political realm* ○ *the realm of art/literature/music*

real number *n* [C] ***mathematics*** a number that can represented using a NUMBER LINE (= drawing that represents all the numbers that exist)

realtor /ˈriːl·tər, ˈriː·ləţ·ər/ *n* [C] **1** a REAL ESTATE AGENT (= a person sells or rents houses, land, offices, or buildings) **2** *trademark* A Realtor is also a member of the National Association of Realtors, an organization of REAL ESTATE AGENTS.

ream /riːm/ *n* [C] a standard measure of paper equal to 500 sheets

reams /riːmz/ *pl n infml* a very large amount of something ○ *They had reams of data to prove their point.*

reap /riːp/ *v* [I/T] **1** to obtain or receive something as a result of your own actions ○ [T] *They didn't reap any benefits from that deal.* **2** If you reap a crop, you cut and collect it.
reaper /ˈriː·pər/ *n* [C] a machine that cuts and collects crops, or a person who cuts and collects crops by hand

rear AT THE BACK /rɪr/ *adj* [not gradable] at or near the back of something ○ *I had the rear brakes on the car redone.* ○ *She entered the school through an unlocked rear door.* ○ *Our dog hurt his rear left leg.*
rear /rɪr/ *n* [C/U] **1** [U] *The bus driver told us to move to the rear.* **2** *infml* Your buttocks are sometimes called your rear.

CARE FOR /rɪr/ *v* [T] to care for young children or animals until they are able to care for themselves ○ *She reared eight children.*

RISE /rɪr/ *v* [I/T] to rise up or to lift up ○ [I] *The horse suddenly reared (up) on its hind legs.*

IDIOM with rear

• *something* **rears its (ugly) head** something unpleasant appears ○ *Racism once again reared its ugly head in our town.*

rear end /rɪrˈend/ *n* [C] the back of something ○ *the rear end of the car* ○ (infml) *The cow rose from the ground rear end first.*
rear-end /rɪrˈend/ *v* [T] to hit esp. the back of a vehicle from behind ○ *A truck rear-ended a car stopped in traffic on the expressway.*

rearguard action, **rear-guard action** *n* [C] an effort to do something effective or get an advantage after the main effort has failed ○ *Supporters trying to keep the museum open are fighting a rear-guard action.*

rearrange /ˌriː·əˈreɪndʒ/ *v* [T] to change the order, position, or time of arrangements already made ○ *Our bedrooms are so small we can't rearrange the furniture.*
rearrangement /ˌriː·əˈreɪndʒ·mənt/ *n* [C/U] ○ [C] *There was a last-minute rearrangement of the schedule.*

rearview mirror, **rear-view mirror** *n* [C] a mirror inside a car in which the driver can see what is happening behind the car

reason EXPLANATION /ˈriː·zən/ *n* [C/U] the cause of an event or situation, or something suggested as an explanation ○ [C] *She had never stopped by before for any reason.* ○ [C] *There must be a reason why she's not here yet.* ○ [U] *Adams had good reason to fire Pickering.*

JUDGMENT /ˈriː·zən/ *n* [U] the ability to think and make judgments, esp. good judgments ○ *Meditation seemed to have improved her ability to reason.*
reason /ˈriː·zən/ *v* **1** [+ (*that*) clause] *He reasoned (that) he had only four or five years left as an athlete.* **2** To reason with someone is to argue with and try to persuade someone: [I] *Grace kept her voice gentle, as if she were reasoning with a child.*
reasonable /ˈriː·zə·nə·bəl/ *adj* **1** based on or using good judgment, and therefore fair and practical ○ *Johnson was a reasonable man.* ○ *It seemed like a reasonable question/explanation.* **2** Reasonable also means not expensive: *You can still get a good house for a very reasonable price.* **3** Reasonable also means satisfactory or not bad: *He could read French with reasonable fluency.*
reasonably /ˈriː·zə·nə·bli/ *adv* ○ *He kept talking slowly and reasonably* (= in a way that showed good judgment). ○ *I was reasonably certain she would be home* (= it seemed likely).
reasoned /ˈriː·zənd/ *adj* using judgment ○ *He offered reasoned responses to our questions.*
reasoning /ˈriː·zə·nɪŋ/ *n* [U] ○ *I didn't follow her reasoning.*

R

WORD FAMILY reason			
Nouns	reason reasoning	*Adjectives*	reasoned reasonable unreasonable
Adverbs	reasonably unreasonably	*Verbs*	reason

reassure /ˌriː·əˈʃʊr/ *v* [T] to comfort someone and stop that person from worrying ○ *Her smile didn't reassure me.*
reassuring /ˌriː·əˈʃʊr·ɪŋ/ *adj* ○ *His reassuring manner convinced her she was safe.*
reassuringly /ˌriː·əˈʃʊr·ɪŋ·li/ *adv* ○ *I bent down and patted the dog reassuringly.*
reassurance /ˌriː·əˈʃʊr·əns/ *n* [C/U] ○ [C] *We need reassurances our company isn't going to be closed.* ○ [U] *The boy looked at his parents for reassurance.*

rebate /ˈriː·beɪt/ *n* [C] money that is returned to you after you pay for goods or services, done in order to make the sale more attractive ○ *Chrysler announced cash rebates of $1000 on some trucks.*

rebel /ˈreb·əl/ *n* [C] **1** a person who refuses to accept the government's power and uses force to oppose it, or a person who opposes authority and thinks or behaves differently ○ *The government tried to set up talks with the rebels.* ○ *Though he dressed unusually, he never meant to be a rebel.* **2** ***US history*** Soldiers fighting for the southern states in the American Civil War were called rebels.
rebel /rəˈbel/ *v* [I] **-ll-** ○ *Children often rebel against being forced to eat certain foods.*
rebellion /rəˈbel·jən/ *n* [C/U] **1** violent action organized by a group of people who refuse to accept their government's power and are willing to use force to oppose it ○ [C] *The African-American Nat Turner led an 1831 rebellion.* **2** Rebellion is also a feeling of strong disagreement with an organization or with people in authority: [U] *Many students were in rebellion against the older generation.*
rebellious /rəˈbel·jəs/ *adj* ○ *A peace agreement was signed yesterday between the republic and its rebellious region.* ○ *He was a rebellious young man.*

rebirth /riːˈbɜrθ/ *n* [U] a new period of growth of something or an increase in popularity of something that was popular in the past ○ *Spring is the season of rebirth.* ○ *This production was hailed as a rebirth of Swedish theater.*

rebound /ˈriː·bɑʊnd, rɪˈbɑʊnd/ *v* [I] **1** to return to an earlier and better condition; improve ○ *Older athletes find it harder to rebound from injuries.* **2** If a ball or other object rebounds, it bounces back after hitting a hard surface.
rebound /ˈriː·bɑʊnd/ *n* [C/U] ○ [U] *The artist is on the rebound from his midcareer slump.*

rebuff /rɪˈbʌf/ *v* [T] to refuse to accept a suggestion or an offer to help, often in an unfriendly way ○ *Our request for assistance has been rebuffed.*
rebuff /rɪˈbʌf/ *n* [C] ○ *Boren's idea took a sharp rebuff.*

rebuild /riːˈbɪld/ *v* [I/T] *past* **rebuilt 1** to build something again that has been damaged or destroyed ○ [T] *The historic building was completely rebuilt after it had burned down.* **2** If you rebuild a system or organization, you develop it so that it works effectively: [I] *The company is rebuilding under new management.*

rebuke /rɪˈbjuːk/ *v* [T] *fml* to criticize someone strongly because you disapprove of what the person has said or done ○ *He was publicly rebuked for his involvement in the scandal.*
rebuke /rɪˈbjuːk/ *n* [C/U] *fml* ○ [C] *a sharp rebuke*

rebut /rɪˈbʌt/ *v* [T] **-tt-** *fml* to argue that a statement or claim is not true ○ *He appeared on TV to rebut the charges against him.*

rebuttal /rɪˈbʌt̬·əl/ *n* [C] *fml* a statement that a claim or criticism is not true ○ *She issued a rebuttal of the charges.*

recalcitrant /rɪˈkæl·sə·trənt/ *adj* unwilling to do what you are asked or ordered to do, even if it is reasonable ○ *Tenants petitioned their recalcitrant landlord to finish repairs to their building.*

recall REMEMBER /rɪˈkɔːl/ *v* [T] to bring the memory of a past event into your mind ○ *I can vividly recall our first kiss.* ○ [+ *that* clause] *He recalled that he had sent the letter over a month ago.* ○ [+ question word] *Can you recall what happened last night?*
recall /rɪˈkɔːl, ˈriː·kɔːl/ *n* [U] the ability to remember things ○ *He has perfect/total recall.*
ASK TO RETURN /rɪˈkɔːl/ *v* [T] to order the return of a product made by a company because of a fault in the product
recall /ˈriː·kɔːl/ *n* [C usually sing] ○ *The government ordered a recall of the garment, saying it could burst into flames.*

recant /rɪˈkænt/ *v* [I/T] to announce in public that your past beliefs or statements were wrong or not true and that you no longer agree with them ○ [I] *Anderson recanted, saying his brother had told him to lie.*

recap /ˈriː·kæp, rɪˈkæp/ *v* [I/T] **-pp-** *short form of* RECAPITULATE ○ [T] *We saw a video recapping her early career.* ○ [I] *To recap, we expect sunny skies in the morning, rain by nightfall.*
recap /ˈriː·kæp/ *n* [C] ○ *They give a quick recap of the top news stories.*

recapitulate /ˌriː·kəˈpɪtʃ·əˌleɪt/ *v* [I/T] *fml* to repeat the main points of an explanation or description ○ [T] *The passage recapitulates the version he offers in his prologue.*

recapture /riːˈkæp·tʃər/ *v* [T] **1** to take something into your possession again, esp. by force ○ *American troops recaptured Guam in July 1944.* **2** If something recaptures an emotion, it allows you to experience that emotion again: *They're bent on recapturing their past glory.*

recede /rɪˈsiːd/ *v* [I] **1** to move further away into the distance, or to become less clear ○ *McLaughlin expects to go home again when the flood waters recede.* **2** If a man has a receding hairline, he is losing the hair from the front of his head.

receipt PAPER /rɪˈsiːt/ *n* [C] a piece of paper which proves that money or goods have been received ○ *Ask the taxi driver for a receipt.*
RECEIVING /rɪˈsiːt/ *n* [U] *fml* the act of receiving something, esp. of money or goods ○ *We are awaiting receipt of your check.*

WORD FAMILY receipt

Nouns	receipt receipts receiver reception	*Adjectives* *Verbs*	receptive receive

receipts /rɪˈsiːts/ *pl n* the amount of money received during a particular period by a business or government ○ *tax receipts* ○ *box-office receipts*

receive GET /rɪˈsiːv/ *v* [T] **1** to get or be given something ○ *She received a letter from her son.* ○ *I'll receive my bachelor's degree in the spring.* **2** When a radio or television receives signals, it changes them into sounds or pictures. ○ Related noun: RECEPTION RADIO/TELEVISION
receiver /rɪˈsiː·vər/ *n* [C] **1** a piece of equipment that changes radio and television signals into sounds and pictures, or that changes electrical signals into sound ○ *a telephone receiver* ○ *a stereo receiver* **2** In football, a receiver is one of the players who can catch the ball on the team that is trying to score points. ○ See also: RECIPIENT
WELCOME /rɪˈsiːv/ *v* [T] *fml* to welcome someone or something ○ *The president received Fulbright cordially.* ○ Related noun: RECEPTION WELCOME

IDIOM with receive

• **on the receiving end of** *something*, **at the receiving end of** *something* suffering from something unpleasant when you have done nothing to deserve it ○ *She was on the receiving end of a lawsuit.*

recent /ˈriː·sənt/ *adj* having happened or having been done a short time ago ○ *He sent me a copy of his most recent article.* ○ *A recent study shows that most of the country-music audience is female.*
recently /ˈriː·sənt·li/ *adv* ○ *We just recently moved to Texas.*

receptacle /rɪˈsep·tɪ·kəl/ *n* [C] *fml* a container for holding things or that you can put things in ○ *a trash receptacle*

reception WELCOME /rɪˈsep·ʃən/ *n* [C] **1** the way in which people react to something or someone ○ *The proposed jail has received a cool/lukewarm reception from local residents.* ○ *American musicians found a warm reception in Europe in the 1960s.* **2** A reception is also a formal party: *a cocktail/wedding reception* ○ Related verb: RECEIVE WELCOME
RADIO/TELEVISION /rɪˈsep·ʃən/ *n* [U] the degree to which radio or television sounds and pictures are clear ○ *We get poor reception around here.* ○ Related verb: RECEIVE GET

receptionist /rɪˈsep·ʃə·nəst/ *n* [C] a person who works in an office, store, or hotel, helping visitors or giving information

receptive /rɪˈsep·tɪv/ *adj* willing to listen to and accept new ideas and suggestions ○ *I think you're more receptive to new ideas when you're younger.*

receptor /rɪˈsep·tər/ *n* [C] ***biology*** a nerve ending that reacts to a change, such as heat or cold, in the body by sending a message to the CENTRAL NERVOUS SYSTEM

recess PAUSE /ˈriː·ses, rɪˈses/ *n* [C] a period of time in which an organized activity such as study or work is temporarily stopped ○ *Congress returns from its August recess next week.* ○ *After lunch, the kids have recess.*
SECRET PLACE /ˈriː·ses, rɪˈses/ *n* [C usually pl] **1** a secret or hidden place ○ *He pointed his flashlight into the dark recesses of the cave.* **2** A recess is also an ALCOVE.

recession /rɪˈseʃ·ən/ *n* [C/U] ***social studies*** a period when the economy of a country is not do-

R

ing well, industrial production and business activity are at a low level, and there are many people unemployed ○ [U] *The country is mired in recession.* ○ [C] *The Japanese economy is experiencing its worst recession in 20 years.*

recessive /rɪˈses·ɪv/ *adj* ***biology*** of or relating to a GENE (= chemical pattern) that causes a particular characteristic only when it is passed on by both parents

recharge /riːˈtʃɑrdʒ/ *v* [T] to give (a BATTERY) the ability to supply electricity again by connecting it to a piece of electrical equipment and filling it with electricity

rechargeable /riːˈtʃɑr·dʒə·bəl/ *adj* [not gradable] ○ *a rechargeable electric razor*

recipe /ˈres·ə·piː/ *n* [C] a set of instructions telling you how to prepare and cook a particular food, including a list of what foods are needed for this ○ *When I make pies, I don't need to follow a recipe.*

IDIOM with **recipe**

• **a recipe for** *something* an idea, situation, or method that is likely to result in something ○ *Treating teenagers like six-year-olds is a recipe for disaster.*

recipient /rɪˈsɪp·iː·ənt/ *n* [C] a person who receives something ○ *Lund was the first female recipient of an artificial heart.* ○ See also: RECEIVER at RECEIVE GET

reciprocal SIMILIAR /rɪˈsɪp·rə·kəl/ *adj fml* operating for both, esp. equally or to a similar degree ○ *They share a truly reciprocal relationship.* ○ **USAGE:** said about two people or things

reciprocate /rɪˈsɪp·rəˌkeɪt/ *v* [I/T] *fml* to do something for someone because the person has done something similar for you ○ [I] *We gave them information, but they didn't reciprocate.* ○ [T] *Hemingway loved Stein and she reciprocated his love.*

NUMBER /rɪˈsɪp·rə·kəl/ *n* [C] ***mathematics*** a number that when multiplied by another number results in 1

R

recital /rɪˈsɑɪt̬·əl/ *n* [C] a performance of music or dance, usually given by one person or a small group of people ○ *a piano recital*

recite /rɪˈsɑɪt/ *v* [I/T] to say a piece of writing aloud from memory ○ [I] *He was nervous about reciting in front of the class.* ○ [T] *The children recite the Pledge of Allegiance every morning.*

recitation /ˌres·əˈteɪ·ʃən/ *n* [C] *fml* ○ *a recitation of the "Gettysburg Address"*

reckless /ˈrek·ləs/ *adj* showing a lack of care about risks or danger, and acting without thinking about the results of your actions ○ *These punks have a reckless disregard for the law.* ○ *He pleaded innocent to reckless driving charges.*

recklessly /ˈrek·lə·sli/ *adv* ○ *She spends her money recklessly.*

recklessness /ˈrek·lə·snəs/ *n* [U] ○ *The accident was a result of recklessness.*

reckon CALCULATE /ˈrek·ən/ *v* [T] to calculate an amount based on facts or on your expectations ○ *Do you reckon this watch has a little value?* ○ [+ *that* clause] *Brusca reckons that the value of all goods and services produced declined last quarter.*

reckoning /ˈrek·ə·nɪŋ/ *n* [U] ○ *By my reckoning, we should get there in another hour or so.*

CONSIDER /ˈrek·ən/ *v* [T] to consider or have the opinion that something is as stated ○ *She reckoned they were both equally responsible.* ○ *She was widely reckoned to be the best actress of her generation.* ○ *I reckon I better get goin' now.*

PHRASAL VERB with **reckon**

• **reckon with** *something/someone* to consider the effect something or someone will have ○ *Experts did not reckon with his determination.* ○ *Bening is a force to be reckoned with.*

reclaim /rɪˈkleɪm/ *v* [T] to take back something that was yours ○ *Students whose averages drop can reclaim their scholarships if they raise their grades.* ○ *The team reclaimed the lead and increased it to 13.*

recline /rɪˈklɑɪn/ *v* [I/T] **1** to lean or lie back with the upper part of your body in a nearly horizontal position, or to cause (something) to lean back ○ [I] *Hacker was reclining leisurely in an office chair, his legs propped up on a desk.* **2** If a seat reclines, you can change the position of its back so that it is in a leaning position: [I] *The bus has air conditioning and seats that recline/reclining seats.*

recluse /ˈrek·luːs, rəˈkluːs/ *n* [C] a person who lives alone and avoids going outside or talking to other people

recognition KNOWLEDGE /ˌrek·ɪgˈnɪʃ·ən/ *n* [U] the fact of knowing who a person is or what a thing is because of having seen or experienced that person or thing before ○ *Dole obviously had the greatest name recognition of all the Republican candidates.* ○ Related verb: RECOGNIZE KNOW

APPRECIATION /ˌrek·ɪgˈnɪʃ·ən/ *n* [U] **1** public appreciation for a person's or group's achievements ○ *She gained recognition as an expert in energy conservation.* **2** Recognition also refers to the accepting of something as true: *Charges were dropped in recognition of the fact that there simply wasn't enough evidence.* ○ Related verb: RECOGNIZE ACCEPT AS TRUE

recognize KNOW /ˈrek·ɪgˌnɑɪz/ *v* [T] to know someone or something because you have seen or experienced that person or thing before ○ *I recognized my old high school teacher from the photograph.* ○ *Doctors are trained to recognize the symptoms of different diseases.* ○ Related noun: RECOGNITION KNOWLEDGE

recognizable /ˈrek·ɪgˌnɑɪ·zə·bəl/ *adj* familiar because of having been seen or experienced before ○ *The cartoon character was instantly recognizable to millions of children.*

recognizably /ˈrek·ɪgˌnɑɪ·zə·bli/ *adv* ○ *a recognizably American name*

ACCEPT AS TRUE /ˈrek·ɪgˌnɑɪz/ *v* [T] **1** to accept that something is true, important, or legal ○ [T] *We recognize the problems you've faced and sympathize with you.* ○ [+ *that* clause] *He recognized that it was* *unlikely he would ever see her again.* **2** To recognize is also to show public appreciation for the achievements of someone, or a person or group: [T] *With this medal, we would like to recognize Lynn Jennings for excellence in women's running.* ○ Related noun: RECOGNITION APPRECIATION

WORD FAMILY recognize			
Nouns	recognition	*Verbs*	recognize
Adjectives	recognizable unrecognizable	*Adverbs*	recognizably

recoil /rɪˈkɔɪl/ *v* [I] to make a sudden movement away from something esp. because of fear or disgust ○ (*fig.*) *Sun-worshipers might recoil in horror at the chilling winds and rough seas, but we loved the place.*

recoil /ˈriː·kɔɪl, rɪˈkɔɪl/ *n* [U] the sudden, backward movement that a gun makes when it is fired

recollect /ˌrek·əˈlekt/ *v* [I/T] to remember something ○ [I] *There were five young men in the car, as near as I can recollect.*

recollection /ˌrek·əˈlek·ʃən/ *n* [C/U] a memory of something, or the ability to remember past events ○ [C] *I have fond recollections of the times our families vacationed together in Vermont.*

recombinant DNA /riːˈkɑm·bə·nənt ˌdiː ˌenˈeɪ/ *n* [U] ***biology*** DNA (= chemical that controls the structure and purpose of cells) that is produced artificially by combining DNA from different organisms or cells.

recombination /ˌriː ˌkɑm·bəˈneɪ·ʃən/ *n* [C/U] ***biology*** the process of creating new combinations of GENES with characteristics different from those in either parent

recommend /ˌrek·əˈmend/ *v* [T] to suggest that someone or something would be good or suitable for a particular job or purpose, or to suggest that a particular action should be done ○ *Can you recommend a hotel in San Francisco?* ○ [+ that clause] *I recommend that you go on a diet.*

recommendation /ˌrek·ə·mənˈdeɪ·ʃən, -ˌmen-/ *n* [C/U] a statement that someone or something would be good or suitable for a particular job or purpose, or the act of making such a statement ○ [U] *I have to get five letters of recommendation to support my application to medical school.*

SPELLING

recommend

Many people make mistakes when spelling this word. The correct spelling has one "c" and two "m's." One way to remember this is that the word is made up of "re" + "commend."

I can recommend the cheeseburger – it's excellent.

recompense /ˈrek·əm ˌpens/ *n* [U] *fml* payment given to someone for an injury suffered, or for the loss of or damage to property ○ *The government seized the land without recompense to the owners.*

reconcile /ˈrek·ən ˌsɑɪl/ *v* [T] **1** to adjust the way you think about a fact or situation that is opposed to another fact or situation so that you can accept both ○ *How do we reconcile the seemingly contradictory notions of cutting taxes and balancing the budget?* **2** If two people are reconciled, they become friendly again after having argued so seriously that they kept apart: *After two years of not speaking to one another, the two brothers were finally reconciled.* **3** To reconcile yourself to a situation is to accept it even if it is unpleasant or painful, because it cannot be changed: *He has reconciled himself to the loss of the election and is moving on.*

reconciliation /ˌrek·ən ˌsɪl·iːˈeɪ·ʃən/ *n* [C/U] the process of making two people or groups of people friendly again after they have argued seriously or fought and kept apart from each other, or a situation in which this happens

reconnaissance /rɪˈkɑn·ə·səns, -zəns/ *n* [U] the process of obtaining information about enemy forces or positions by sending out small groups of soldiers or by using aircraft ○ *Aerial reconnaissance showed the location of the enemy's tanks.*

reconsider /ˌriː·kənˈsɪd·ər/ *v* [I/T] to think again about (a decision or opinion) and decide whether you want to change it ○ [I] *He begged her to reconsider.*

reconstruct Ⓐ /ˌriː·kənˈstrʌkt/ *v* [T] **1** to build or create again something that has been damaged or destroyed **2** If you reconstruct something that happened in the past, you combine a lot of details to try to get a clear idea of what happened: *Detectives tried to reconstruct the crime by comparing all the statements of the eyewitnesses.*

reconstruction Ⓐ /ˌriː·kənˈstrʌk·ʃən/ *n* [C/U]

Reconstruction /ˌriː·kənˈstrʌk·ʃən/ *n* [U] ***US history*** the period after the US Civil War from 1863 to 1877 when the southern states were brought back into the nation

record STORE INFORMATION /rɪˈkɔːrd/ *v* [T] **1** to keep information for the future by writing it down or storing it on a computer ○ *She carefully recorded the events of the meeting.* **2** To record is also to use a device to measure an amount, rate of speed, etc. and show it: *Wind gusts of up to 50 miles per hour were recorded.*

record /ˈrek·ərd/ *n* [C/U] **1** a piece of information or a description of an event that is written on paper or stored in a computer ○ [C] *Did anyone make a record of what the president said at that meeting?* ○ [C] *All medical records are kept confidential.* ○ [C] *She has a long criminal record* (= there is official information about many crimes she has done). ○ [U] *This summer has been the hottest on record* (= the hottest summer known about). **2** A person's or organization's record is the actions that have been done in the past, and esp. how well or badly those actions have gone: [C] *During his twenty years as a football coach, he compiled an outstanding record.*

STORE SOUNDS/IMAGES /rɪˈkɔːrd/ *v* [T] to put sounds or pictures onto magnetic TAPE or a computer using electronic equipment so that they can

R

be heard or seen later ○ *The Beatles recorded many terrific albums over the years.* ○ *When I tried to phone her, all I got was a recorded message.*

record /ˈrek·ərd/ *n* [C] a flat, plastic disk on which music is recorded

recording /rɪˈkɔːrd·ɪŋ/ *n* [C] a group of sounds or pictures on a disk or TAPE that can be heard or seen when played in a machine

BEST /ˈrek·ərd/ *n* [C] the best or fastest ever done ○ *She set a new world record in the high jump.* ○ *Sales this season broke/shattered the record* (= were better than ever before).

record /ˈrek·ərd/ *adj* [not gradable] at a higher level than ever achieved before ○ *Farmers in the Midwest are reporting a record harvest this year.*

WORD FAMILY record			
Nouns	record	*Adjectives*	record
	recorder		recorded
	recording		unrecorded
Verbs	record		

record-breaking *adj* [not gradable] better or more extreme than anything that has come before ○ *This is going to be a record-breaking year for the company.*

recorder /rɪˈkɔːrd·ər/ *n* [C/U] a musical instrument consisting of a wooden tube with holes along its length that are covered by the fingers to vary the notes and played by blowing into one end, or this type of instrument generally

record player *n* [C] a machine on which records can be played

recount **DESCRIBE** /rɪˈkɑʊnt/ *v* [T] to describe the particular events of an experience, or to tell a story ○ *She recounted some of her experiences working as a nurse in a hospital emergency room.*

COUNT /ˈriː·kɑʊnt/ *n* [C] a second or another count, esp. of the number of votes in an election ○ *The final vote was so close that they demanded a recount.*

R

recoup /rɪˈkuːp/ *v* [T] to get back money that has been spent or lost ○ *It takes a while to recoup your initial costs when you begin a new business.*

recourse /ˈriː·kɔːrs, -koʊrs/ *n* [U] *fml* a way of dealing with a difficult or unpleasant situation ○ *If the company won't pay me, the only recourse left to me is to sue them.*

recover Ⓐ /rɪˈkʌv·ər/ *v* [I/T] **1** to get better after an illness or a period of difficulty or trouble ○ [I] *It took her a while to recover after the operation.* **2** To recover something is to find or get back the use of something lost or taken away: [T] *The police recovered her handbag, but her wallet was gone.*

recovery Ⓐ /rɪˈkʌv·ə·ri/ *n* [C/U] the act or process of getting better; improvement ○ [U] *The economy is showing signs of recovery.* ○ [U] *The story deals with the recovery of* (= getting back) *stolen jewelry.*

recreation /ˌrek·riːˈeɪ·ʃən/ *n* [C/U] something done for pleasure or to relax, or such activities generally ○ [C] *Sarah's favorite recreation is shopping for antiques.*

recreational /ˌrek·riːˈeɪ·ʃən·əl/ *adj* ○ *Recreational facilities include a swimming pool, gym, and fully-equipped exercise center.*

recreational vehicle, *abbreviation* **RV** *n* [C] a large motor vehicle in which you can sleep and often cook, used for traveling and CAMPING

recrimination /rɪˌkrɪm·əˈneɪ·ʃən/ *n* [C/U] argument between people who are blaming each other, or the particular way they blame each other ○ [U] *Western leaders, instead of presenting a coherent policy, have repeatedly lapsed into finger-pointing and recrimination.*

recruit /rɪˈkruːt/ *v* [T] to persuade someone to become a new member of an organization ○ *The coach spends a lot of time recruiting the top high school athletes.*

recruit /rɪˈkruːt/ *n* [C] a new member of an organization, esp. a military organization

recruiter /rɪˈkruːt̬·ər/ *n* [C] ○ *He worked as a military recruiter in Texas.*

rectal /ˈrek·təl/ *adj* ○ See at RECTUM

rectangle /ˈrekˌtæŋ·gəl/ *n* [C] ***geometry*** a flat shape with four sides and four 90° angles, with opposite sides of equal length and two sides longer than the other two ➤ Picture: **geometry**

rectangular /rekˈtæŋ·gjə·lər/ *adj* ***geometry*** having the shape of a rectangle ○ *The painting consists of four rectangular blocks of color.*

rectify /ˈrek·təˌfɑɪ/ *v* [T] to correct or make right ○ *I hadn't meant to cause trouble, and asked what I could do to rectify the situation.*

rector /ˈrek·tər/ *n* [C] **1** (in some Christian groups) a priest in charge of a PARISH (= area) **2** A rector can also be the person in charge of a university or school.

rectory /ˈrek·tə·ri/ *n* [C] a house in which a rector or other priest lives

rectum /ˈrek·təm/ *n* [C] the lowest end of the bowels, through which excrement passes as it leaves the body

rectal /ˈrek·təl/ *adj* [not gradable] ○ *She took the baby's temperature with a rectal thermometer.*

recuperate /rɪˈkuː·pəˌreɪt/ *v* [I] to become stronger and better again after an illness or injury ○ *After leaving the hospital, he continued to recuperate at home.*

recuperation /rɪˌkuː·pəˈreɪ·ʃən/ *n* [U] ○ *a lengthy recuperation*

recur /rɪˈkɜr/ *v* [I] **-rr-** to happen again or happen many times ○ *If the problem recurs, I'll see my doctor about it.*

recurring /rɪˈkɜr·ɪŋ/, **recurrent** /rɪˈkɜr·ənt/ *adj* [not gradable] ○ *He suffered recurring nightmares that someone was chasing him.*

recurrence /rɪˈkɜr·əns/ *n* [C/U]

recycle /riːˈsɑɪ·kəl/ *v* [I/T] to collect and treat used objects and materials that are ready to be thrown out in order to produce materials that can be used again ○ [T] *The law requires us to recycle paper products, glass bottles, soda cans, and some kinds of plastic.*

recyclable /riːˈsɑɪ·klə·bəl/ *adj* able to be recycled ○ *Are plastic bottles recyclable or do they go in the garbage?*

red /red/ *adj, n* [C/U] **-dd- 1** (of) the color of fresh blood ○ *red gloves* ○ [U] *She wore red.* ○ [C] *These reds don't match.* **2** ***physics*** Red is also the color of light with the longest WAVES that humans can see.
reddish /ˈred·ɪʃ/ *adj* slightly red ○ *The leaves turn bright yellow or reddish-orange in the fall.*
redden /ˈred·ᵊn/ *v* [I/T] to make or become red ○ [I] *His face reddened with embarrassment.*

IDIOM with red

• **in the red** spending more money than you earn ○ *The company has been in the red for the last three quarters.* ○ Compare IN THE BLACK at BLACK IDIOMS

Red /red/ *n* [C] ***world history*** a COMMUNIST (= a person who believes in shared ownership of property and control of the methods of production)

red blood cell *n* [C] ***biology*** any of the cells that carry oxygen around the body ○ Compare WHITE BLOOD CELL

Red Crescent *n* [U] a group belonging to an international organization that takes care of people suffering because of war, storms, or other events

Red Cross *n* [U] a group belonging to an international organization that takes care of people suffering because of war, storms, or other events ○ *There are 185 national Red Cross and Red Crescent societies in the world.*

redeem IMPROVE /rɪˈdiːm/ *v* [T] to improve yourself, or to take action to improve the way other people think of you or something you have done ○ *After his poor performance in the golf tournament two weeks before, he was determined to redeem himself by playing well.* ○ *Very few TV talk shows have any redeeming values* (= have good qualities that make their bad qualities less important).

BUY BACK /rɪˈdiːm/ *v* [T] to buy back something, or to exchange something for money or for goods or services ○ *You can redeem the bond at any time, but you will lose some interest.*

redefine Ⓐ /ˌriː·dɪˈfɑɪn/ *v* [T] to give something a new meaning ○ *Researchers have called for the government to redefine dietary guidelines.*

redemption /rɪˈdem·ʃən/ *n* [U] the state of being kept from evil or of improving morally ○ *The political leadership in that state is so corrupt that it's beyond redemption* (= it will always be morally bad).

redesign /ˌriː·dɪˈzɑɪn/ *n* [C/U] a change in the design of something ○ [C] *Major redesigns come once a decade.* ○ [U] *That meant further redesign to add additional support.*
redesign /ˌriː·dɪˈzɑɪn/ *v* [T] ○ *In 1993 NASA redesigned the planned space station.*

redevelopment /ˌriː·dɪˈvel·əp·mənt/ *n* [C/U] the improvement of an area that is in bad condition, esp. an area of old buildings in a city ○ [U] *Parking is something many plans for downtown redevelopment now recognize as critical.*

redhead /ˈred·hed/ *n* [C] a person whose hair is red or a brown color that is partly red

red herring *n* [C] something that takes attention away from a more important subject ○ *Racism was not a factor in the case – that was a red herring thrown in by the defense lawyers.*

red light *n* [C] a red traffic light, where vehicles have to stop ○ Compare GREEN LIGHT

red meat *n* [U] meat from animals with four legs such as cows, pigs, and sheep

redneck /ˈred·nek/ *n* [C] *slang* a poor, white person without education, esp. one living in the countryside in the southern US, who is believed to have PREJUDICED (= unfair and unreasonable) ideas and beliefs ○ **USAGE**: This word is usually considered offensive.

redouble /riːˈdʌb·əl/ *v* [T] to make something much stronger; increase ○ *We must redouble our efforts to provide help quickly.*

redox /ˈriː·dɑks/ *n* [U] ***chemistry*** a chemical process in which an atom, MOLECULE, etc., either gains or loses ELECTRONS

redress /rɪˈdres/ *v* [T] *fml* to correct a wrong ○ *Affirmative action to help minorities is intended to redress wrongs.*

redshift /ˈredˈʃɪft/ *n* [U] ***physics*** a change in the way that light reaches the earth from stars and other objects in space because they are moving away from the earth

red tape *n* [U] official rules and processes that seem unnecessary and delay results ○ *Rescue work is often hampered by red tape at national borders.*

reduce /rɪˈduːs/ *v* [T] **1** to make something less in size, amount, degree, importance, or price ○ *A low-fat diet can reduce the risk of heart disease.* ○ *Grunn employs 17,900 people, but that number will be reduced by 500 workers.* ○ *All electronic equipment in the store has been reduced* (= lowered in price). **2** To reduce someone or something to a particular state is to cause that person or thing to be in that state: *Without any information, we've been reduced to guessing what happened.* ○ *The town was reduced to rubble in the fighting.*
reduction /rɪˈdʌk·ʃən/ *n* [C/U] ○ [C] *a 2% reduction in the budget* ○ [U] *There will be no reduction in services.*

reducing agent *n* [C] ***chemistry*** a substance that adds one or more ELECTRONS to another substance

redundant /rɪˈdʌn·dənt/ *adj* **1** more than what is usual or necessary, esp. using extra words that mean the same thing ○ *My English teacher was merciless if what we wrote was abstract, sentimental, or redundant.* **2** *Br* People who are redundant have become unemployed because they are no longer needed at their place of work.

R

redundancy /rɪˈdʌn·dən·si/ *n* [U] ○ *They're trying to cut the redundancy of some federal programs.*

redwood /ˈred·wʊd/ *n* [C/U] an evergreen tree that grows esp. in California and can become very tall, or the valuable brown-red wood of this tree

reed /riːd/ *n* [C] **1** a type of tall, stiff grass that grows near water **2** A reed is also a thin strip of wood in some musical instruments, such as the CLARINET or OBOE, that produces sound when air is blown over it.

reef /riːf/ *n* [C] a line of rocks or sand at or near the surface of the sea ○ *a coral reef*

reek /riːk/ *v* [I] to have a strong, unpleasant smell ○ *The locker room reeked of gym clothes.*
reek /riːk/ *n* [U] ○ *the reek of dead fish*

reel **HOLDER** /riːl/ *n* [C] a round or cylindrical device on which a rope, wire, film, or other long, thin strip or object is rolled, or the amount of something stored on this ○ *a reel of film*

MOVE /riːl/ *v* [I] **1** to move from side to side as if you are going to fall while walking or standing ○ *Reeling a bit, he tripped and fell.* **2** If you reel, or your mind or brain reels, you feel very confused or shocked: *Our team is reeling from five straight losses.*

PHRASAL VERBS with reel

• **reel in/out** *something* [M] to move something by using a REEL ○ *Gibson reeled in a 10-pound largemouth bass.* ○ *The firemen reeled the hoses out.*
• **reel in** *something/someone* [M] to get control of something or someone, sometimes by offering something in exchange ○ *The article offers tips on how computer users can avoid being reeled in by internet hustlers.*
• **reel off** *something* [M] to do something quickly and easily ○ *He reeled off the names of his grandchildren.* ○ *The Hawks reeled off nine straight points.*

reelect /ˌriː·əˈlekt/ *v* [T] to elect someone again ○ *He was reelected despite some concerns about his personal life.*
reelection /ˌriː·əˈlek·ʃən/ *n* [C/U] ○ [U] *Reelection seemed unlikely after her arrest.*

R

reenact /ˌriː·əˈnækt/ *v* [T] to repeat the actions of an event that happened in the past as a hobby or as a performance ○ *The show reenacts medical emergencies.*
reenactment /ˌriː·əˈnækt·mənt/ *n* [C] ○ *a reenactment of Civil War battles*

reenter /riːˈent·ər/ *v* [I/T] to enter a place again, or to join an activity again ○ [T] *She reentered the game shortly after being injured.*
reentry /riːˈen·tri/ *n* [C/U] ○ [U] *The highest risks in space flight are on launch and during reentry into Earth's atmosphere.*

ref /ref/ *n* [C] short form of REFEREE

refer /rɪˈfɜr/ *v* **-rr-**

PHRASAL VERBS with refer

• **refer to** *someone/something* **MENTION** to mention or talk about someone or something ○ *I don't know which of his sisters he was referring to.* ○ Related noun: REFERENCE **MENTIONING**
• **refer to** *someone/something* **RELATE** to relate to or involve someone or something ○ *The town's name may refer to a nearby underground spring.* ○ Related noun: REFERENCE **CONNECTION**
• **refer to** *something* **LOOK AT** to look at something for information or help ○ *He referred to the dictionary for the correct spelling of the word.* ○ Related noun: REFERENCE **AUTHORITY**
• **refer** *someone/something* **to** *someone/something* **SEND** to send someone or something to a different place or person for help ○ *First see your pediatrician, who may refer you to a pediatric allergist.* ○ Related noun: REFERRAL

WORD FAMILY refer			
Nouns	referee reference referral	*Verbs*	refer referee

referee /ˌref·əˈriː/, short form **ref** *n* [C] (in some sports) a person who controls a game and makes sure the rules are followed, or more generally a person who helps to find a fair solution to a disagreement ○ *Fans booed the referee's call.*
referee /ˌref·əˈriː/ *v* [I/T] ○ [T] *He volunteered to referee the game.*

reference **MENTIONING** /ˈref·rəns/ *n* [C/U] the act of mentioning someone or something in speech or writing ○ [U] *Avoid making any reference to his accident.* ○ Related verb: REFER TO **MENTION**

STATEMENT /ˈref·rəns/ *n* [C] a written statement describing your character and abilities, or the person who writes this statement ○ *She has excellent references.* ○ *Could I list you as a reference on my application?*

CONNECTION /ˈref·rəns/ *n* [U] the act of making a connection between subjects ○ *His comments were* **in reference to** *a stupid question someone asked.* ○ Related verb: REFER TO **RELATE**

AUTHORITY /ˈref·rəns/ *n* [C/U] **1** a text that records facts and information ○ [C] *There is a list of the author's references at the end of the article.* **2** A reference is also the act of looking at a text: [U] *These books are for reference only and may not be checked out of the library.* **3** A reference can also mean a REFERENCE BOOK: [C] *What references did you use for this research?* ○ Related verb: REFER TO **LOOK AT**

reference book *n* [C] a book of facts, such as a dictionary or an ENCYCLOPEDIA, which you look at to get information

referendum /ˌref·əˈren·dəm/ *n* [C] *pl* **referendums, referenda** a vote in which all the people in a country or an area decide on an important question

referral /rɪˈfɜr·əl/ *n* [C] an act of sending someone or something to a person or place where what is wanted or needed can be obtained ○ *Her doctor gave her a referral to a specialist.* ○ Related verb: REFER TO **SEND**

refill /riːˈfɪl/ *v* [T] to fill something again with more of the same thing ○ *He refilled their glasses with ice-cold lemonade.*

refill /ˈriː·fɪl/ *n* [C] A refill is also a container or an amount of what is needed to fill something again: *a prescription refill* ○ *The waitress asked if I wanted a refill of coffee.*

refine Ⓐ /rɪˈfɑɪn/ *v* [T] **1** to make a substance pure by removing unwanted material ○ *Sugar and oil are refined before use.* **2** To refine something also means to improve it by making small changes: *We haven't finished refining the plan yet.*

refined Ⓐ /rɪˈfɑɪnd/ *adj* **1** *Regional exports include refined oil and copper.* **2** Someone who is refined is polite, graceful, and aware of quality and style: *The hotel lobby reflects the refined taste of the owners.*

refinement Ⓐ /rɪˈfɑɪn·mənt/ *n* [C/U] the process of improving something ○ [C] *The accuracy of the machine has been increased through a number of refinements.* ○ [U] *The refinement of sugar cane produces sugar.* ○ [U] *She grew up in a home environment of culture and refinement* (= politeness and quality).

refinery /rɪˈfɑɪ·nə·ri/ *n* [C] a factory where raw substances, such as sugar, oil, or metal, are made pure

reflect SEND BACK /rɪˈflekt/ *v* [I/T] ***physics*** to send back light, heat, energy, or sound from a surface ○ [T] *Light-colored clothing reflects the sun's heat rather than absorbing it.* ○ [I] *Moonlight reflected off the surface of the lake.*

reflective /rɪˈflek·tɪv/ *adj* ○ *Joggers should wear reflective clothing at night.* ○ See also: REFLECTIVE at REFLECT THINK

reflection /rɪˈflek·ʃən/ *n* [C/U] **1** ***physics*** the return of light, heat, sound, or energy from a surface **2** A reflection is also an image seen in a mirror or other shiny surface ○ *Standing on the dock, we could see the reflection of the sky in the still water.* **3** ***physics*** The **angle of reflection** is the angle that a beam of light or other energy that is reflected from a surface makes with a line vertical to that surface.

reflector /rɪˈflek·tər/ *n* [C] ○ *His new lighting system uses lamps and reflectors.*

SHOW /rɪˈflekt/ *v* [T] to show, express, or be a sign of something ○ *His blank face reflected his boredom.*

reflection /rɪˈflek·ʃən/ *n* [C] ○ *Their finely decorated home is a reflection of their good taste.* ○ *The team's losses of late seem to be a reflection on the coaching.*

THINK /rɪˈflekt/ *v* [I] to think carefully ○ *She felt she needed time to reflect on what to do next.*

reflection /rɪˈflek·ʃən/ *n* [C/U] ○ [C] *Her reflections on life are recorded in her journal.* ○ [U] *After much reflection, he decided to return to teaching.*

reflective /rɪˈflek·tɪv/ *adj* ○ *In my more reflective moments, I write poetry.* ○ See also: REFLECTIVE at REFLECT SEND BACK

WORD FAMILY reflect

Nouns	reflection reflector	*Adjectives* *Verbs*	reflective reflect

IDIOM with reflect

• **reflect on** *someone/something* to influence people's opinion of a person, group, or organization ○ *When one player behaves badly, it reflects on the whole team.* ○ *The outstanding work of our scientists reflects well on the entire university* (= influences people to have a good opinion of the university). ○ *Trash in the streets reflects badly on the community* (= influences people to have a bad opinion of the community).

reflex /ˈriː·fleks/ *n* [C usually pl] **1** a sudden, automatic reaction to something ○ *He's strong, always has good positioning, and his reflexes are fantastic.* **2** ***biology*** A reflex is also an automatic reaction involving nerve cells that is not controlled by the brain, and, therefore, does not involve choice, for example, sneezing or vomiting

reflexive /rɪˈflek·sɪv/ *adj* [not gradable] ***grammar*** showing that the action of the verb is directed back on the subject ○ *In the sentence "He hurt himself," "hurt" is a reflexive verb and "himself" is a reflexive pronoun.*

reform /rɪˈfɔːrm/ *v* [I/T] ***social studies*** to become better, or to make something better by making corrections or removing any faults ○ [T] *As governor, he reformed election procedures.* ○ [I] *She insists that she has finally reformed.*

reform /rɪˈfɔːrm/ *n* [C/U] ○ [U] *The administration is proposing welfare reform.*

reformation /ˌref·ərˈmeɪ·ʃən/ *n* [C/U] ○ [U] *reformation of the health care system*

reformed /rɪˈfɔːrmd/ *adj* ○ *I'm a reformed guy – I eat a low-fat diet and exercise every day.*

reformer /rɪˈfɔːr·mər/ *n* [C] ***social studies*** a person who works for political, social, or religious change

refract /rɪˈfrækt/ *v* [T] ***physics*** to change the direction of light, sound, heat, or other energy as it travels across or through something

refraction /rɪˈfræk·ʃən/ *n* [U] ***physics*** **1** The **absolute index of refraction** is a calculation of the relationship between the speed of light moving through a MEDIUM (= a substance) and the speed of light in a VACUUM (= place with no matter in it). **2** The **angle of refraction** is the angle that a beam of light or other energy that is refracted by a surface makes with a line vertical to that surface.

refrain NOT DO /rɪˈfreɪn/ *v* [I] to not let yourself do something ○ *Please refrain from talking during the lecture.*

SONG /rɪˈfreɪn/ *n* [C] a short part of a song or poem that is repeated, esp. at the end of each longer part, or any phrase that is often repeated ○ *Every year we hear the same refrain, that women are making great strides in business.*

refresh /rɪˈfreʃ/ *v* [T] to give new energy and strength to someone ○ *A good night's sleep will refresh you.*

refresher /rɪˈfreʃ·ər/ *n* [C] ○ *Lemonade is a good refresher on a hot summer day.*

refreshing /rɪˈfreʃ·ɪŋ/ *adj* ○ *a refreshing breeze on a hot day* ○ [+ to infinitive] *It's refreshing to see*

so many young families moving into the neighborhood.
refreshingly /rɪˈfreʃ·ɪŋ·li/ *adv* ○ *a refreshingly honest statement*
refreshment /rɪˈfreʃ·mənt/ *n* [C/U] a small amount of food or drink ○ [C] *Light refreshments will be available after the meeting.*

IDIOM with **refresh**

• **refresh** *someone's* **memory** help someone remember something ○ *She reread her notes to refresh her memory.*

refresher course *n* [C] a training course that keeps people informed about new developments in their area of interest or skill

refrigerate /rɪˈfrɪdʒ·əˌreɪt/ *v* [T] to make or keep something, esp. food or drink, cold so that it stays fresh, usually in a REFRIGERATOR ○ *Refrigerate the mayonnaise after opening the jar.*
refrigeration /rɪˌfrɪdʒ·əˈreɪ·ʃən/ *n* [U] ○ *The food will spoil without refrigeration.*
refrigerator /rɪˈfrɪdʒ·əˌreɪt̬·ər/, *infml* **fridge** *n* [C] a large piece of equipment that uses electricity to preserve food at a cold temperature ○ Compare FREEZER at FREEZE

refuge /ˈref·juːdʒ, -juːʒ/ *n* [C/U] protection or shelter from danger, trouble, etc., or a place that provides this ○ [U] *Residents took refuge in their basements during the tornado.* ○ [C] *The bay is also a wildlife refuge for large numbers of birds.*
refugee /ˌref·jʊˈdʒiː, ˈref·jʊˌdʒiː/ *n* [C] a person who leaves his or her home or country to find safety, esp. during a war or for political or religious reasons

refund /rɪˈfʌnd, ˈriː·fʌnd/ *v* [T] to pay back money received or spent ○ *The theater refunded our money when the performance was canceled.*
refund /ˈriː·fʌnd/ *n* [C] ○ *If you overpaid, you should demand a refund.*

refurbish /rɪˈfɜr·bɪʃ/ *v* [T] to make a room or building look fresh and new again ○ *You've refurbished the kitchen.*

refuse SAY NO /rɪˈfjuːz/ *v* [I/T] to say or show that you are not willing to do, accept, or allow something ○ [I] *She asked him for a loan, but he refused.* ○ [T] *We were refused admission to the building.* ○ [+ *to* infinitive] *On cold mornings, the car may refuse to start.*
refusal /rɪˈfjuː·zəl/ *n* [C/U] ○ [C] *His refusal to contribute money angered the organizers.*
GARBAGE /ˈref·juːs, -juːz/ *n* [U] worthless or unwanted objects or materials; garbage ○ *We separate refuse from recyclables.*

refute /rɪˈfjuːt/ *v* [T] to prove a statement, opinion, or belief to be wrong or false ○ *Are you refuting the evidence?*

regain /rɪˈgeɪn/ *v* [T] to get something back again ○ *I had to move out to regain my sanity.*

regal /ˈriː·gəl/ *adj* suitable for or in the manner of a king or queen ○ *a regal bearing*

regale /rɪˈgeɪl/ *v* [T] to entertain someone with stories or jokes ○ *Grandpa regaled us with tales of his small-town childhood.*

regalia /rɪˈgeɪl·jə/ *n* [U] special clothes and decorations, esp. those used at official ceremonies ○ *He wore the full regalia of a Kiowa chieftain.*

regard /rɪˈgɑrd/ *v* [T always + adv/prep] to consider or think about something in a particular way, or to look carefully at someone or something ○ *Laura is highly regarded by her colleagues.* ○ *The dog regarded me with suspicion as I approached the door.*
regard /rɪˈgɑrd/ *n* [U] ○ *She has no regard for other people's feelings.* ○ *The boss holds her opinions in high regard.*
regarding /rɪˈgɑrd·ɪŋ/ *prep* in relation to; about ○ *I have a question regarding your last statement.*
regardless /rɪˈgɑrd·ləs/ *adv* [not gradable] despite what has been said or done ○ *We want tax cuts, but regardless, we need to limit expenditures.*

IDIOMS with **regard**

• **in regard to** *someone/something*, **with regard to** *someone/something* in relation to someone or something ○ *I am calling in regard to your recent inquiry.*
• **regardless of** *something* without being influenced by any other events or conditions ○ *I tell them the truth, regardless of what they want to hear.*

regards /rɪˈgɑrdz/ *pl n* greetings and expressions of affection ○ *Please give my regards to your sister.*

regatta /rɪˈgɑt̬·ə, -ˈgæt̬·ə/ *n* [C] a boat race or series of races

regenerate IMPROVE /riːˈdʒen·əˌreɪt/ *v* [T] to improve a place or system so that it is active or producing good results again ○ *As president of the college, he regenerated a failing institution.*
GROW AGAIN /riːˈdʒen·əˌreɪt/ *v* [I/T] ***biology*** to grow again, or to make something grow again, for example, new tissue or a new part
regeneration /riːˌdʒen·əˈreɪ·ʃən/ *n* [U]

regent /ˈriː·dʒənt/ *n* [C] (in the US) a member of the governing group of a university or educational system ○ *the Board of Regents*

reggae /ˈreg·eɪ, ˈreɪ·geɪ/ *n* [U] a type of popular music from Jamaica with a strong second and fourth beat

regime Ⓐ /reɪˈʒiːm, rə-/ *n* [C] a particular government, or a system or method of government ○ *a Communist/totalitarian regime*

regimen /ˈredʒ·ə·mən/, **regime** /reɪˈʒiːm, rə-/ *n* [C] a set of rules about food, exercise, or behavior that you follow, esp. in order to improve your health ○ *His doctor put him on a strict regimen of exercise and low-fat food.*

regiment /ˈredʒ·ə·mənt/ *n* [C] a large group of soldiers combining several BATTALIONS

regimented /ˈredʒ·əˌment·əd/ *adj* extremely controlled ○ *They lead a very regimented life.*
regimentation /ˌredʒ·ə·mənˈteɪ·ʃən, -ˌmen-/ *n* [U] ○ *He hated the regimentation of boarding school.*

region Ⓐ /ˈriː·dʒən/ *n* [C] **1** a particular area or part of a state, country, or the earth's surface ○ *Wheat is the major crop of this region.* **2** A region is also a particular area or part of the body: *He's complaining of pain in the lower abdominal region.*

regional Ⓐ /ˈriː·dʒən·əl/ *adj* [not gradable] ○ *a regional trade and rail center*

regionally Ⓐ /ˈriː·dʒən·əl·i/ *adj*

IDIOM with **region**

• **(somewhere) in the region of** approximately ○ *The temperature yesterday was somewhere in the region of 30°.*

regionalism /ˈriː·dʒən·əlˌɪz·əm/ *n* [C] a word or expression characteristic of a particular area ○ *"Spider" is a New England regionalism for a type of frying pan.*

register Ⓐ RECORD /ˈredʒ·ə·stər/ *v* [I/T] **1** to record someone's name or ownership of property on an official list ○ [T] *I registered the car in my name.* ○ [+ to infinitive] *Voters have until February 16 to register to vote in the primary.* ○ [I] *Students are currently registering for summer courses.* **2** If you register a letter or package when you mail it, you pay extra to have it recorded and receive special care in delivery.

register Ⓐ /ˈredʒ·ə·stər/ *n* [C] a book containing an official list or record ○ *The American Film Institute drew up a register of the 100 greatest American films ever made.*

registered Ⓐ /ˈredʒ·ə·stərd/ *adj* [not gradable] ○ *Only registered voters can be picked for jury selection.*

registration Ⓐ /ˌredʒ·əˈstreɪ·ʃən/ *n* [C/U] ○ [C] *Keep your car registration with the vehicle.* ○ [U] *With an election approaching, both political parties are encouraging voter registration.*

registry /ˈredʒ·ə·stri/ *n* [C] an official list or record, or a place where official records are kept ○ *a voter registry*

MEASURE /ˈredʒ·ə·stər/ *v* [I/T] (of an instrument) to measure and record an amount ○ [T] *The thermometer registered 79°F.* ○ [I] *The tremor barely registered on the Richter scale.*

SHOW /ˈredʒ·ə·stər/ *v* [T] to show an emotion by the expression on your face ○ *Her face registered shock at the news.*

HAVE EFFECT /ˈredʒ·ə·stər/ *v* [I] to have some effect ○ *The loss of her home has not really registered on her yet.*

RANGE /ˈredʒ·ə·stər/ *n* [C] all the notes that a voice or musical instrument can produce, from the highest to the lowest

MONEY /ˈredʒ·ə·stər/ *n* [C] *short form of* CASH REGISTER

DEVICE /ˈredʒ·ə·stər/ *n* [C] a device that controls the flow of air from a heating or cooling system through an opening into a room

registered mail *n* [U] a way to send a letter in which you pay extra to have a record of when it was delivered and who received it

registered nurse, *abbreviation* **R.N.** *n* [C] a nurse who has formally trained and passed an exam and is officially qualified to perform all nursing duties ○ Compare PRACTICAL NURSE

registered trademark, *symbol* ® *n* [C] a TRADEMARK that is officially recorded by a government office

registrar /ˌredʒ·əˈstrɑr/ *n* [C] a person who keeps records, esp. a college or university official who is responsible for students' records of classes and marks

regress /rɪˈgres/ *v* [I] to return to a previous and less advanced or worse state ○ *Our team improved in the second half, while our opponents regressed.*

regression /rɪˈgreʃ·ən/ *n* [U] ○ *Learning a language requires regression to childlike simplicity.*

regret /rɪˈgret/ *v* **-tt- 1** to feel sorry or unhappy about something you did or were unable to do ○ [T] *He regretted his decision to leave school.* ○ [+ (*that*) clause] *I regret (that) I didn't buy more when they were on sale.* ○ [T] *I'm going to regret eating all those nachos.* **2** *fml* Regret is also used to express in a polite way that you feel sorry about something: [+ (*that*) clause] *My husband regrets (that) he couldn't be here tonight.* ○ [+ *to* infinitive] *The weather, I regret to say, is getting worse.*

regret /rɪˈgret/ *n* [C/U] ○ [C] *I have no regrets about quitting.* ○ [U] *She expressed regret for letting her friends down.*

regretful /rɪˈgret·fəl/ *adj* feeling or expressing sadness or disappointment ○ *a regretful sigh*

regretfully /rɪˈgret·fə·li/ *adv* ○ *"We never spoke of it," Anne regretfully acknowledged.*

regrettable /rɪˈgreţ·ə·bəl/ *adj* causing or deserving sadness or disappointment ○ *The omission of a sponsor's name on the program was a regrettable error.*

regrettably /rɪˈgreţ·ə·bli/ *adv* ○ *Regrettably, he died before he could see her again.*

WORD FAMILY regret

Nouns	regret	*Verbs*	regret
Adjectives	regrettable regretful	*Adverbs*	regrettably regretfully

regroup /riːˈgruːp/ *v* [I/T] to organize again in order to make a new effort, esp. after a defeat ○ [I] *They lost their first game, but then regrouped and beat Detroit and Hartford.*

regular REPEATED /ˈreg·jə·lər/ *adj* happening repeatedly in a fixed pattern, with equal or similar amounts of space or time between one and the next ○ *a regular heartbeat* ○ *working regular hours* ○ *Trees were planted at regular intervals along the avenue.*

regularly /ˈreg·jə·lər·li/ *adv* ○ *We meet regularly each morning for coffee.* ○ See also: REGULARLY at REGULAR OFTEN

regularity /ˌreg·jəˈlær·əţ·i/ *n* [U] ○ *The regularity of the design gets boring after a while.* ○ See also: REGULARITY at REGULAR OFTEN

USUAL /ˈreg·jə·lər/ *adj* **1** usual or ordinary; NORMAL ○ *He drove his regular route to work.* ○ *Her regular assistant is on vacation.* **2** Regular also means of an average or standard size: *That minivan is longer than a regular station wagon.* **3** The regular

R

army is the permanently organized army of a country. **4** ***grammar*** A regular verb, noun, adjective, or other type of word follows the usual rules in the language for changing word endings. **5** If you describe a man as a regular guy, you mean that he is an ordinary, likable person: *He wanted to prove he was a regular guy by going fishing.*

OFTEN /ˈreg·jə·lər/ *adj* doing the same thing or going to the same place often ○ *a regular contributor to the magazine* ○ *a regular customer*

regular /ˈreg·jə·lər/ *n* [C] ○ *He's one of the regulars at the club.*

regularly /ˈreg·jə·lər·li/ *adv* ○ *She appears regularly on national TV.* ○ See also: REGULARLY at REGULAR **REPEATED**

regularity /ˌreg·jəˈlær·ət̬·i/ *n* [U] ○ *She watches those shows with amazing regularity.* ○ See also: REGULARITY at REGULAR **REPEATED**

EQUAL /ˈreg·jə·lər/ *adj* shaped equally on all sides ○ *Her teeth are small and regular.*

WORD FAMILY regular

Nouns		Adjectives	
	regular		regular
	regularity		irregular
	irregularity	Adverbs	regularly
			irregularly

regulate Ⓐ /ˈreg·jəˌleɪt/ *v* [T] **1** to control an activity or process by rules or a system ○ *A computer system regulates production.* ○ [+ question word] *Their parents regulate how much TV the children can watch.* **2** Regulate also means to adjust something to a desired level or standard: *As a diabetic, she regulates her sugar intake carefully.*

regulation Ⓐ /ˌreg·jəˈleɪ·ʃən/ *n* [C/U] ○ [C] *federal safety regulations* ○ [U] *She favors government regulation of health-care systems.*

regulation Ⓐ /ˌreg·jəˈleɪ·ʃən/ *adj* [not gradable] ○ *Soldiers wear a regulation uniform.*

regulator Ⓐ /ˈreg·jəˌleɪt·ər/ *n* [C] a person or organization whose job is to control an activity or process and make certain that it operates as it should ○ *Federal regulators prepare to set stricter rules for cars and fuel.*

regulatory Ⓐ /ˈreg·jə·ləˌtɔːr·i, -ˌtour·i/ *adj* ○ *a regulatory agency* ○ *federal regulatory standards*

regulation /ˌreg·jəˈleɪ·ʃən/ *n* [U] ***biology*** the chemical and nerve processes that allow people to adjust to changes in themselves and their environment so that they can continue to live

regurgitate /rɪˈgɜr·dʒəˌteɪt/ *v* [I/T] **1** to repeat information without understanding it ○ [+ question word] *People are just regurgitating what they see on TV.* **2** Regurgitate also means to vomit.

rehabilitate /ˌriː·həˈbɪl·əˌteɪt, ˌriː·ə-/, *short form* **rehab** /ˈriː·hæb/ *v* [T] to return someone to a healthy or usual condition or way of living, or to return something to good condition ○ *The aim is to rehabilitate the prisoners so that they can lead productive lives when they are released.* ○ *That builder rehabilitates older housing which he then sells for a profit.*

rehabilitation /ˌriː·həˌbɪl·əˈteɪ·ʃən, ˌriː·ə-/, *short form* **rehab** /ˈriː·hæb/ *n* [U] ○ *How much rehabilitation will your knee require?*

rehash /ˈriː·hæʃ/ *v* [T] to present something old in a new way or form without any real change or improvement ○ *The kids keep rehashing the same old argument about whose turn it is.*

rehash /ˈriː·hæʃ/ *n* [C] ○ *The new season's fashions seem like a rehash of last year's.*

rehearse /rɪˈhɜrs/ *v* [I/T] to practice something, such as music or a speech, or lead a person or group in practicing it, in order to prepare for a public performance ○ [I] *We rehearse all day and do the show that evening.*

rehearsal /rɪˈhɜr·səl/ *n* [C/U] ○ [C] *Zubin Mehta will conduct several rehearsals as well as the actual concert.* ○ [U] *The play is in rehearsal.*

reign /reɪn/ *v* [I] to rule a country, or to have power or control

reign /reɪn/ *n* [C] ○ *the reign of Louis XIV*

reimburse /ˌriː·əmˈbɜrs/ *v* [T] to give back the amount of money that someone has spent ○ *They're going to reimburse me for the airfare.*

reimbursement /ˌriː·əmˈbɜr·smənt/ *n* [C/U] the act of paying back, or the money that is paid back

rein /reɪn/ *n* [C usually pl] a long thin piece of material, esp. leather, used to control a horse

PHRASAL VERB with rein

• **rein in** *something/someone* [M] to control undesirable activity or growth, or control someone who is behaving badly ○ *The federal government is attempting to rein in health care costs.* ○ *The premier will soon rein in his new security chief.*

reincarnation /riːˌɪn·kɑrˈneɪ·ʃən/ *n* [C/U] the belief of some people that the spirit of a dead person returns to life in another body or form, or a person or thing believed to have returned or been brought back in this way

reincarnate /ˌriː·ɪnˈkɑrˌneɪt/ *v* [T] to live again in a different body or form

reindeer /ˈreɪn·dɪr/ *n* [C] *pl* **reindeer** a type of deer that has horns like branches and lives in colder, northern parts of the world

reinforce Ⓐ /ˌriː·ənˈfɔːrs, -ˈfours/ *v* [T] **1** to make something stronger, usually by adding more material or another piece ○ *Building codes in California required that steel rods be used to reinforce cinder-block construction.* **2** Something that reinforces an idea or opinion provides proof or support: *But let me just cite one other fact to reinforce what you're saying.* **3** To reinforce an army is to provide it with more soldiers or weapons.

reinforcement Ⓐ /ˌriː·ənˈfɔːr·smənt, -ˈfour-/ *n* [U] **1** something added to provide more strength or support ○ *The dam urgently needs reinforcement.* **2** Reinforcements are soldiers sent to join an army to make it stronger. **3** Reinforcement is also a way of influencing behavior through rewards and punishments: *positive/negative reinforcement*

reinstate /ˌriː·ənˈsteɪt/ *v* [T] to put someone back in a job or position previously held, or to put a law or rule back into effect ○ *She will be reinstated to her full professorship and receive back pay and benefits.* ○ *The hospital suspended Goldstein during the investigation but reinstated him when the report cleared him of any wrongdoing.*

reinvent /ˌriː·ən ˈvent/ *v* [T] to change someone or something so much that the person or thing seems completely new ○ *He promised to reinvent government if elected.*

IDIOM with **reinvent**

• **reinvent the wheel** to waste time learning how to do something when it is already known how to do it ○ *We don't need to reinvent the wheel, we just need to hire someone who already knows how to make the system work.*

reissue /riːˈɪʃ·uː/ *v* [T] to print or produce again ○ *The recording was reissued on CD.*

reiterate /riːˈɪt̬·əˌreɪt/ *v* [T] *fml* to say something again ○ *He reiterated his view that it was time to withdraw from the region.*

reject Ⓐ /rɪˈdʒekt/ *v* [T] **1** to refuse to accept, use, or believe something or someone ○ *The school rejects a third of all applicants.* **2** To reject someone is also to treat someone in a way that shows you do not feel affection for that person: *As a child, she had felt rejected by her mother.* **3** *medical* If your body rejects tissue or an organ that comes from another person, your body has a dangerous physical reaction to it.

reject Ⓐ /ˈriː·dʒekt/ *n* [C] a damaged or faulty object, or a person who has had many jobs because of not being successful at any of them ○ *In desperation the hockey team picked up a 35-year-old reject as a backup goalie.*

rejection Ⓐ /rɪˈdʒek·ʃən/ *n* [C/U] ○ [U] *fear of rejection* ○ [C] *I applied for ten jobs and got ten rejections.*

rejoice /rɪˈdʒɔɪs/ *v* [I] *fml* to feel or show great happiness ○ *Everyone rejoiced at the news of his safe return.*

rejoin /riːˈdʒɔɪn/ *v* [T] to return to a person or group ○ *She rejoined her husband in Toronto.*

rejoinder /rɪˈdʒɔɪn·dər/ *n* [C] *fml* a quick answer, often given in a way that is competitive or amusing ○ *The reviewer's mistakes were so flagrant that Gove drafted a strong rejoinder.*

rejuvenate /rɪˈdʒuː·vəˌneɪt/ *v* [T] **1** to make someone look or feel young and energetic again ○ *She felt rejuvenated by her vacation.* **2** To rejuvenate an organization or place is to improve the way it works or looks and make it seem fresh: *They can do much to rejuvenate old neighborhoods and keep the city from declining again.*

relapse /rɪˈlæps/ *v* [I] to return to a previous bad condition or a worse way of life after making an improvement ○ *She briefly relapsed twice after being released from the hospital.*

relapse /rɪˈlæps, ˈriː·læps/ *n* [C] the return of an illness suffered previously

relate CONNECT /rɪˈleɪt/ *v* [I/T] to be connected with something, or to show that something is connected with something else ○ [I always + adv/prep] *The point I'm making now relates to what I said before.* ○ [T] *She relates rising unemployment rates directly to government policies.*

related /rɪˈleɪt̬·əd/ *adj* [not gradable] connected ○ *We discussed inflation, unemployment, and related issues.* ○ *They invested in technology-related companies.* ○ See also: RELATED

relation /rɪˈleɪ·ʃən/ *n* **1** connection or similarity ○ [U] *There was little relation between the book and the movie.* **2** Relations are the connections between people, groups, organizations, or countries: [pl] *diplomatic relations* ○ [pl] *business/economic relations*

relationship /rɪˈleɪ·ʃənˌʃɪp/ *n* [C] **1** the way in which things are connected or work together ○ *Write an essay on the economic relationship between farming and transportation.* **2** A relationship is the way two or more people are connected, or the way they behave toward each other: *"What is your relationship to the soloist?" "She's my daughter."* ○ *The two men have a good working relationship.* **3** A relationship is also a close romantic friendship between two people.

USAGE

relationship

Be careful to use the preposition **with** when the expression "have a relationship" is followed by a name or pronoun.

I have a good relationship with my parents.

~~I have a good relationship to my parents.~~

TELL /rɪˈleɪt/ *v* [T] to tell a story or describe a series of events ○ *She related the story over dinner.* ○ [+ question word] *In this article, the author relates what it felt like to return to school at the age of 47.*

WORD FAMILY **relate**

Nouns	relation relations relationship relative	*Adjectives*	related unrelated relative
		Adverbs	relatively
Verbs	relate		

IDIOM with **relate**

• **in relation to** *something* **1** in connection with something ○ *The drug is being studied for possible beneficial effects in relation to migraine headaches.* **2 In relation to** also means compared with: *She checked the map to see where Miami is in relation to Orlando.*

PHRASAL VERB with **relate**

• **relate to** *someone/something* to understand and appreciate someone or something ○ *The kids need a teacher who can relate to them.* ○ *"Malcolm thought people should learn to live together." "I can relate to that."*

related /rɪˈleɪt̬·əd/ *adj* [not gradable] belonging to the same family ○ *Of course Elise and Linda are related – they're cousins.* ○ *José and Alfonso are related by marriage.* ○ See also: RELATED at RELATE CONNECT

R

relation /rɪˈleɪ·ʃən/ *n* [C] a person who is a member of the same family as another person ○ *On our trip, we visited friends and relations on both sides of the family.*

relative COMPARED WITH /ˈrel·ət̬·ɪv/ *adj* [not gradable] as judged or measured in comparison with something else ○ *We considered the relative merits of flying to Washington or taking the train.* ○ *Relative to* (= Considering) *birthweight, the newborns were doing well.*
relatively /ˈrel·ət̬·ɪv·li/ *adv* [not gradable] ○ *The stereo was relatively inexpensive.*
FAMILY /ˈrel·ət̬·ɪv/ *n* [C] a member of your family ○ *All her relatives came to the wedding.*

relative clause *n* [C] ***grammar*** a clause in a sentence that cannot exist independently, begins with a RELATIVE PRONOUN, and describes a noun that comes before it ○ *In the sentence "The movie that we saw was very good," "that we saw" is a relative clause.*

relative pronoun *n* [C] (in grammar) a pronoun such as "which," "who," or "that," that is used to begin a RELATIVE CLAUSE ○ *In the sentence "The movie that we saw was very good," "that" is a relative pronoun.*

relativity /ˌrel·əˈtɪv·ət̬·i/ *n* [U] ***physics*** a two-part theory in physics describing motion and the relationships between space, time, and energy ○ *Einstein's theory of relativity*

relax Ⓐ /rɪˈlæks/ *v* [I/T] **1** to become or cause someone to become calm and comfortable, and not worried or nervous, or to become or cause a muscle or the body to become less tight ○ [I] *She saw a need for a downtown club where women could relax.* ○ [T] *This exercise will help you to relax your neck muscles.* ○ [T] *He relaxed his grip on my arm* (= held it less tightly). **2** When rules or controls are relaxed, they are made less severe.
relaxation Ⓐ /ˌriːˌlækˈseɪ·ʃən/ *n* [U] ○ *The senator and his family flew to West Palm Beach for golf and relaxation.*
relaxed Ⓐ /rɪˈlækst/ *adj* comfortable and informal ○ *It's a very relaxed atmosphere on campus.*

WORD FAMILY relax

Nouns	relaxation	*Verbs*	relax
Adjectives	relaxed		

WORD CHOICES relax

The phrasal verb **chill out** is a common, informal way of saying "relax."

*We spent the whole week **chilling out** on the beach.*

The verb **unwind** means "to start to relax after working or doing something difficult."

*Music helps me to **unwind**.*

If a person relaxes and doesn't use much energy, the expression **take it easy** is often used.

*You'll need to spend a few days **taking it easy** after the operation.*

The fixed expression **put your feet up** is also often used to mean "sit down and relax."

*I'm going to make myself a cup of coffee and **put my feet up** for half an hour.*

relay /riːˈleɪ, ˈriː·leɪ/ *v* [T] to tell something you heard ○ *I relayed the news to the others.*

relay (race) /ˈriː·leɪ (ˈreɪs)/ *n* [C] a running or swimming race between two or more teams usually of four members, each of whom goes a part of the distance ○ *the Penn Relays*

release Ⓐ MAKE FREE /rɪˈliːs/ *v* [T] **1** to give freedom to someone ○ *Agents questioned the men, then released them because they had done nothing wrong.* **2** If you release a device, you move it from a locked position and allow it to move freely: *She released the brake and the car rolled forward.*
release Ⓐ /rɪˈliːs/ *n* [C usually sing] ○ *Diplomatic efforts were underway to secure the release of the two journalists.*
STOP HOLDING /rɪˈliːs/ *v* [T] to drop, or to stop carrying, holding, or containing something ○ *The dog brought the ball back to us but wouldn't release it.* ○ *The company was charged with releasing toxic gases into the atmosphere.*
MAKE PUBLIC /rɪˈliːs/ *v* [T] to let something be shown in public or made available for use ○ *The police released a drawing of the suspect.*
release /rɪˈliːs/ *n* [C] ○ *The release of the movie was delayed for several months.*

relegate /ˈrel·əˌɡeɪt/ *v* [T] *fml* to put something or someone into a lower or less important rank or position ○ *In the past when African-American men worked as sailors aboard ships, they were often relegated to jobs as cooks and stewards.*

relent /rɪˈlent/ *v* [I] to do something you had refused to do before, or to allow someone to do something that you had refused to allow before ○ *For days we begged him to see a doctor about his cough, and finally he relented.*

relentless /rɪˈlent·ləs/ *adj* continuing in a determined way without any interruption ○ *the relentless pursuit of wealth and power*
relentlessly /rɪˈlent·lə·sli/ *adv* ○ *He is campaigning relentlessly, trying to build support.*

relevant Ⓐ /ˈrel·ə·vənt/ *adj* related to a subject or to something happening or being discussed ○ *We turned over relevant documents to the investigating team.*
relevance Ⓐ /ˈrel·ə·vəns/, **relevancy** /ˈrel·ə·vən·si/ *n* [U] ○ *the relevance of railroads to the development of the American west*

reliable Ⓐ /rɪˈlɑɪ·ə·bəl/ *adj* deserving trust; DEPENDABLE ○ *My car is old but it's reliable.*
reliably Ⓐ /rɪˈlɑɪ·ə·bli/ *adv* ○ *His whereabouts were unknown, but he was reliably reported to be alive.*
reliability Ⓐ /rɪˌlɑɪ·əˈbɪl·ət̬·i/ *n* [U] ○ *The reliability of this smoke detector is guaranteed.*

reliance Ⓐ /rɪˈlɑɪ·əns/ *n* [U] the condition of depending on something or someone ○ *She said that there is too much reliance on meat in our diet.*
reliant Ⓐ /rɪˈlɑɪ·ənt/ *adj* ○ *The nation is still reliant on imported oil.*

relic /ˈrel·ɪk/ *n* [C] **1** an object from the past, esp. one that has no modern use but is often valued for its meaning or importance in history ○ *The ship was a relic of the Spanish-American War.* **2** A relic is also a part of the body or clothing of a SAINT (= holy person), or something that belonged to a saint.

relief HAPPINESS /rɪˈliːf/ *n* [U] **1** a feeling of happiness that something unpleasant has not happened or has ended ○ *She breathed a sigh of relief when she finished her exams.* **2** Relief also means the reduction or end of pain: *Aspirin may give you some relief.*

HELP /rɪˈliːf/ *n* [U] food, money, or services for people in need ○ *disaster relief*

WORK OF ART /rɪˈliːf/ *n* [C/U] the building up of parts of a surface to form a picture or design that can be seen above the background, or a work of art made by this method ○ [C] *the reliefs of the Parthenon*

relieve LESSEN PAIN /rɪˈliːv/ *v* [T] **1** to make something bad or painful less severe ○ *The addition to the school will relieve overcrowding.* ○ *She was given morphine to relieve the pain.* **2** To relieve yourself is to excrete urine.
relieved /rɪˈliːvd/ *adj* happy that something unpleasant has not happened or has ended ○ *She was immensely relieved when the medical test proved to be negative.*

REPLACE /rɪˈliːv/ *v* [T] to arrive or come in order to take the place of another person ○ *The guard is relieved at 6 p.m. by the night watchman.*

PHRASAL VERB with **relieve**

• **relieve** *someone* **of** *something* to take a responsibility or job from someone ○ *After the story appeared in the newspaper, the captain was relieved of his command.*

religion /rɪˈlɪdʒ·ən/ *n* [C/U] the belief in and worship of a god or gods, or any such system of belief and worship
religious /rɪˈlɪdʒ·əs/ *adj* ○ *a religious holiday* ○ *He is deeply religious.*
religiously /rɪˈlɪdʒ·ə·sli/ *adv* If you do something religiously, you do it regularly: *I exercise religiously, I really do.*

relinquish /rɪˈlɪŋ·kwɪʃ/ *v* [T] to give up something, such as a responsibility or claim ○ *He refused to relinquish control of his company.*

relish ENJOY /ˈrel·ɪʃ/ *v* [T] to like or enjoy something ○ *I enjoyed our vacation, but didn't relish the twenty-hour trip back home.*
relish /ˈrel·ɪʃ/ *n* [U] the enjoyment you get from doing something

SAUCE /ˈrel·ɪʃ/ *n* [C/U] a type of sauce, usually made of vegetables cut into small pieces, vinegar, and spices, that adds flavor to food ○ [U] *We have relish for the hamburgers and hot dogs.*

relive /riːˈlɪv/ *v* [T] to remember an experience clearly ○ *She and I like to reminisce and relive the good-old days.*

relocate Ⓐ /riːˈloʊˌkeɪt/ *v* [I/T] to move to a new place ○ [I] *The company will relocate, but a new home has not been chosen yet.*
relocation Ⓐ /ˌriː ˌloʊˈkeɪ·ʃən/ *n* [C/U] ○ *Big contracts make the relocation of those players unlikely.*

reluctant Ⓐ /rɪˈlʌk·tənt/ *adj* not wanting to do something and therefore slow to do it ○ [+ *to* infinitive] *She had trouble sleeping but was reluctant to take sleeping pills.*
reluctantly Ⓐ /rɪˈlʌk·tənt·li/ *adv* ○ *He reluctantly resigned.*
reluctance Ⓐ /rɪˈlʌk·təns/ *n* [U]

rely on/upon *something/someone* Ⓐ /rɪˈlɑɪˌɔːn, -ˌɑn; -əˌpɔːn, -əˌpɑn/ *phrasal verb* to depend on or trust someone or something ○ *You can't rely on good weather for the whole trip.* ○ *The system relies too heavily on one person.*

remain /rɪˈmeɪn/ *v* **1** to stay in the same place or in the same condition ○ [I] *The doctor said he should remain in bed for a few days.* ○ [L] *She remained silent.* **2** If something remains, it continues to exist when other parts or things no longer do: [I] *Only the foundation of the ancient temple remains.*
remainder /rɪˈmeɪn·dər/ *n* [C usually sing] **1** the part that is left after the other parts are gone, used, or taken away ○ *It rained the first day but was sunny for the remainder of the trip.* **2** ***mathematics*** A remainder is the amount left when one number cannot be exactly divided by another.
remaining /rɪˈmeɪ·nɪŋ/ *adj* [not gradable] ○ *Use half the dough and keep the remaining half covered.*
remains /rɪˈmeɪnz/ *pl n* **1** *Rescue workers searched the remains of the house.* **2** A person's remains are that person's dead body. ➤ Usage: **rest, stay, or remain?** at REST RELAX

WORD FAMILY remain			
Nouns	remainder remains	*Adjectives* *Verbs*	remaining remain

IDIOM with **remain**

• *something* **remains to be seen** something is still unknown or unclear ○ *Whether the Republican candidate can still win the election remains to be seen.* ○ *It remains to be seen what the students think of their teachers' ideas.*

remake /riːˈmeɪk/ *v* [T] *past* **remade** to make something again as new ○ *The President is slipping in the polls and he is trying to remake his image.* ○ *Hollywood studios often remake foreign films*
remake /ˈriː·meɪk/ *n* [C] ○ *Have you seen the remake of "King Kong"?*

remark /rɪˈmɑrk/ *v* **1** to give a spoken statement of an opinion or thought ○ [+ (*that*) clause] *She remarked (that) she'd be home late.* **2** If you remark on something, you notice it and say something

R

about it: [I] *All his friends remarked on the change in him.*

remark /rɪˈmɑrk/ *n* [C] ○ *I think if you read his remarks, you'll find them very fair.*

WORD FAMILY remark			
Nouns	remark	*Verbs*	remark
Adjectives	remarkable unremarkable	*Adverbs*	remarkably

remarkable /rɪˈmɑr·kə·bəl/ *adj approving* unusual and surprising ○ *He's a remarkable young man.*

remarkably /rɪˈmɑr·kə·bli/ *adv approving* ○ *They were remarkably calm after the crash.*

rematch /ˈriː·mætʃ/ *n* [C] a second competition or game between competitors ○ *The teams meet in a rematch of last season's conference finals.*

remedial /rɪˈmiːd·iː·əl/ *adj* [not gradable] (of an activity) intended to correct or improve something, esp. skills ○ *Students can enroll in remedial English classes.*

remedy /ˈrem·əd·i/ *n* [C] a substance or method for curing an illness, or a way of dealing with a problem or difficulty ○ *cold remedies*

remedy /ˈrem·əd·i/ *v* [T] ○ *We're working to remedy these shortcomings.*

remember /rɪˈmem·bər/ *v* [I/T] to be able to bring a piece of information back into your mind, or to keep a piece of information in your memory ○ [T] *Naomi vividly remembers the day her daughter was born.* ○ [I] *I've been a Tiger fan as long as I can remember.* ○ [T] *Williams will be remembered for his generosity.* ○ [+ question word] *Can you remember where we parked the car?* ○ [+ *that* clause] *You have to remember that these things take time.* ○ [+ *to* infinitive] *Remember to buy some stamps.*

remembrance /rɪˈmem·brəns/ *n* [C/U] ○ [C] *The video makes a nice remembrance of the party.*

➤ Usage: **remind or remember?** at REMIND

R

USAGE

remember or memory?

Remember is a verb. Use **remember** when you think about or bring thoughts into your mind about a person, place, or event from the past.

I can remember when I went skiing in Colorado for the first time.

Memory is a noun. Use **memory** to talk about the person, place, or event from the past that you think about.

I have many good memories of when I was a child.

WORD CHOICES remember

More formal alternatives are verbs such as **recall** and **recollect**.

I don't ***recall*** *arranging a time to meet.*

I didn't ***recollect*** *having seen him.*

Remind means "to make someone remember something," or "to make someone remember to do something."

Every time we meet he ***reminds*** *me about the money he lent me.*

Will you ***remind*** *me to buy some eggs?*

The phrasal verb **come back** is often used when someone suddenly remembers something.

I'd forgotten his name but it's just ***come back*** *to me.*

To **reminisce** is to remember and talk about pleasant things that happened in the past.

We were just ***reminiscing*** *about our school days.*

To **keep/bear** something **in mind** is to remember someone or something that may be useful in the future.

When you book your flight, ***keep/bear in mind*** *that the holidays are the busiest period.*

If something **sticks in your mind**, you can remember it easily, often because it is strange or exciting.

His name ***stuck in my mind*** *because it was very unusual.*

remind /rɪˈmɑɪnd/ *v* [T] to make someone aware of something forgotten or possibly forgotten, or to bring back a memory to someone ○ *Remind him to call me.* ○ *Anna reminds me of her mother.*

reminder /rɪˈmɑɪn·dər/ *n* [C] something that helps someone remember ○ *She kept the shells as a reminder of our days together.* ○ [+ *that* clause] *The park serves as a reminder that nature is worth preserving.*

USAGE

remind or remember?

If you **remember** a fact or something from the past, you keep it in your mind or bring it back into your mind.

I can't remember the name of that film.

Did you remember to bring your passport?

When you **remind** someone to do something, you make them remember it.

Can you remind me to phone Anna tomorrow?

~~*Can you remember me to phone Anna tomorrow?*~~

reminisce /ˌrem·əˈnɪs/ *v* [I] to talk or write about past experiences that you remember with pleasure ○ *Grandpa likes to reminisce about his years in the navy.*

reminiscence /ˌrem·əˈnɪs·əns/ *n* [C/U] ○ [C] *She published reminiscences of her life in China.*

reminiscent /ˌrem·əˈnɪs·ənt/ *adj* ○ *That tune is reminiscent of a song my mother used to sing.*

remiss /rɪˈmɪs/ *adj* not doing a duty carefully or well enough ○ *I would be remiss if I didn't mention it.*

remission /rɪˈmɪʃ·ən/ *n* [C/U] a period of time when an illness is less severe ○ [U] *Her leukemia is in remission.*

remit /rɪˈmɪt/ *v* [T] **-tt-** *fml* to send money to someone ○ *Please remit payment by the 15th of the month.*

remnant /ˈrem·nənt/ *n* [C] a small piece or amount of something that is left from a larger, original piece or amount ○ *a carpet remnant*

remodel /riːˈmɑd·əl/ *v* [I/T] **-l-, -ll-** to give a new shape or form to something, esp. a room or house ○ [T] *We remodeled the kitchen.*

remorse /rɪˈmɔːrs/ *n* [U] a strong feeling of guilt and regret about something you have done ○ *Judges took account of the prisoner's remorse.*
remorseful /rɪˈmɔːrs·fəl/ *adj* ○ *I'm still remorseful for having broken it.*
remorseless /rɪˈmɔːr·sləs/ *adj* ○ *a remorseless tyrant*

remote /rɪˈmoʊt/ *adj* **1** far away in distance, time, or relation; not close ○ *Ben grew up in a remote part of Montana.* ○ *It happened in the remote past.* ○ *There is a remote possibility* (= slight chance) *that we won't be able to make the trip.* **2** Someone whose behavior is remote is not friendly or interested in others.
remotely /rɪˈmoʊt·li/ *adv* [not gradable] ○ *He isn't even remotely* (= in any way) *like his brother.* ○ *a remotely operated car*

remote control, *short form* **remote** *n* [C/U] a device or a system for controlling something from a distance ○ *Is this remote for the TV or the DVD player?* ○ *The robot, standing about 3 feet tall, can be operated by remote control.*
remote-controlled *adj* [not gradable] ○ *Remote-controlled cameras monitor the entrance.*

remove Ⓐ /rɪˈmuːv/ *v* [T] to take something away from an object, group, or place ○ *Please remove your books from the counter.* ○ *Club soda will remove that stain.* ○ *He was removed from office* (= forced to leave an official position). ○ *Space flight is pretty far removed from* (= not part of) *most people's experience.*
removal Ⓐ /rɪˈmuː·vəl/ *n* [U] ○ *He ordered the immediate removal of the troops.*
removable Ⓐ /rɪˈmuː·və·bəl/ *adj* able to be removed ○ *This jacket has a removable collar.*
remover /riˈmuː·vər/ *n* [U] ○ *paint remover*

remuneration /rɪˌmjuː·nəˈreɪ·ʃən/ *n* [U] *fml* pay for work or services

renaissance /ˈren·əˌsɑns, -ˌzɑns/ *n* [C] **1** a new growth or interest in something, esp. art, literature, or music ○ *a poetry renaissance* **2** ***world history*** The Renaissance was a period of growth and activity in the areas of art, literature, and ideas in Europe during the 14th, 15th, and 16th centuries.

rename /riːˈneɪm/ *v* [T] to give something a new name ○ *Upon completion, the fort was renamed in honor of its commander.*

rend /rend/ *v* [T] *past* **rent** *dated* to break something violently; tear

render CAUSE /ˈren·dər/ *v* [T] to cause someone or something to be in a particular state ○ *New technology renders a computer obsolete in a year.*

REPRESENT /ˈren·dər/ *v* [T] to represent something in a work of art or a performance ○ *The drawing was rendered in muted pastels.*
rendering /ˈren·də·rɪŋ/ *n* [C] ○ *a watercolor rendering*

GIVE /ˈren·dər/ *v* [T] *fml* to give something to someone ○ *An employee is someone who renders his or her services in exchange for pay.*

rendezvous /ˈrɑn·dɪˌvuː, -deɪ-/ *n* [C] *pl* **rendezvous** **1** a meeting at a particular place and time ○ *a secret rendezvous* **2** A rendezvous is also a particular place where people often meet: *This restaurant is a popular rendezvous for local artists.*
rendezvous /ˈrɑn·dɪˌvuː, -deɪ-/ *v* [I] ○ *Shall we rendezvous around 6 p.m.?*

rendition /renˈdɪʃ·ən/ *n* [C] a particular way in which music is performed or a drawing or painting is produced or appears ○ *new renditions of old Beatles tunes*

renegade /ˈren·ɪˌgeɪd/ *n* [C] a person who has changed from supporting esp. one political, religious, or national group to supporting another ○ *a renegade state* ○ *She's always been a renegade.*

renege /rɪˈnɪg, -ˈneg/ *v* [I] to not do what you previously agreed to do; to fail to keep a promise or agreement ○ *He reneged on his offer.*

renew INCREASE ACTIVITY /rɪˈnuː/ *v* [T] to begin doing something again or with increased strength ○ *She renewed her efforts to contact her sister.*
renewed /rɪˈnuːd/ *adj* [not gradable] ○ *renewed interest/enthusiasm*

CONTINUING USE /rɪˈnuː/ *v* [T] to increase the period of time that something can be used or is in effect ○ *to renew a passport/subscription*
renewable /rɪˈnuː·ə·bəl/ *adj* [not gradable] **1** *a renewable agreement* **2** Renewable substances can be used and easily replaced: *renewable energy resources*
renewal /rɪˈnuː·əl/ *n* [C/U] ○ [U] *renewal of a license*

renounce /rɪˈnɑʊns/ *v* [T] to say publicly that you no longer own, support, believe in, or have a connection with something ○ *Gandhi renounced the use of violence.* ○ Related noun: RENUNCIATION

renovate /ˈren·əˌveɪt/ *v* [T] to repair and improve something, esp. a building
renovation /ˌren·əˈveɪ·ʃən/ *n* [C/U] ○ [C] *The museum is closed for renovations.*

renown /rɪˈnɑʊn/ *n* [U] *fml* the state of being famous ○ *an artist of national renown*
renowned /rɪˈnɑʊnd/ *adj* ○ *The region is renowned for its natural beauty.*

rent PAYMENT /rent/ *n* [C/U] a fixed amount of money paid or received regularly for the use of usually an apartment, house, or business space ○ [C] *Rents in this building are ridiculously high.* ○ [U] *How much rent do you pay?* ○ [U] *Are there any apartments for rent* (= available) *there?*
rent /rent/ *v* [T] ○ *I rented a car for the trip to Boston.*

R

rental /ˈrent·ᵊl/ *n* [C/U] the act of renting, an amount paid in rent, or something rented ○ [U] *boat/car rental*

USAGE

rent

This verb can be confusing because people sometimes use it to mean two different things. Usually if you **rent** an apartment or house, you pay someone so that you can live there.

I rent a 2-bedroom apartment.

If you **rent** or **rent out** an apartment or house that you own, you accept money from someone else who is living there.

We usually rent out the cabin during hunting season.

We thought we should look for a house that had apartments that we could rent to pay the mortgage.

TORN /rent/ *past simple and past participle of* REND

renunciation /rɪˌnʌn·siːˈeɪ·ʃən/ *n* [C] the act of RENOUNCING (= no longer supporting) something ○ *the renunciation of the use of force*

reopen /riːˈoʊ·pən/ *v* [I/T] **1** to open something again after it has been closed for a period of time ○ [I] *Restaurant and hotel owners were wondering when they could reopen.* ○ [T] *He said he would reopen the road during morning and evening rush hours.* **2** If a process or discussion reopens, it begins again after it has stopped for a period of time: [T] *This may present an opportunity to reopen peace talks.*

reorganize /riːˈɔːr·ɡəˌnɑɪz/ *v* [I/T] to organize something differently ○ [I] *After the battle, the platoon reorganized on the edge of the town.* ○ [T] *The IRS has proposed a new plan to reorganize the agency.*

reorganization /ˌriːˌɔːr·ɡə·nəˈzeɪ·ʃən/ *n* [C/U] ○ [U] *The company may announce a reorganization of management before the end of this year.*

R

rep SALES /rep/ *n* [C] *short form of* SALES REPRESENTATIVE

REPUTATION /rep/ *n* [C usually sing] *short form of* REPUTATION ○ *I wouldn't spend time with him – he's got a bad rep.*

Rep. *n* [C] *abbreviation for* REPRESENTATIVE

repaid /rɪˈpeɪd/ *past simple and past participle of* REPAY

repair /rɪˈper, -ˈpær/ *v* [T] to put something damaged, broken, or not working correctly back into good condition or make it work again ○ *Surgeons repaired the severed artery.*

repair /rɪˈper, -ˈpær/ *n* [C/U] ○ [C] *My car is in the garage for repairs.* ○ [U] *Our building is in poor repair* (= bad condition).

WORD FAMILY repair

Nouns	repair disrepair	*Verbs*	repair
Adjectives	irreparable	*Adverbs*	irreparably

WORD CHOICES repair

The verbs **fix** and **mend** are common alternatives.

*I must get my bike **fixed**.*

*Can you **mend** that hole in my trousers?*

The phrasal verb **fix up** is often used when someone repairs something and improves it.

*Nick loves **fixing up** old cars.*

The verb **service** is often used when examining and repairing cars or other machines.

*I'm taking the car to the garage to have it **serviced** this afternoon.*

The verb **patch** can be used when someone fixes something in a basic and temporary way.

*We managed to **patch** the hole in the roof.*

repairman /rɪˈper·mən, rɪˈpær-, -ˌmæn/ *n* [C] someone whose job is to make things that are broken work correctly ○ *a TV repairman*

reparation /ˌrep·əˈreɪ·ʃən/ *n* [C/U] payment for harm or damage ○ [C] *The company paid reparations to the victims of the explosion.*

reparations /ˌrep·əˈreɪ·ʃənz/ *pl n* ***world history*** payments made by a defeated nation after a war to pay for damages or expenses it caused to another nation

repatriate /riːˈpeɪ·triːˌeɪt, -ˈpæ·triː-/ *v* [T] to send or bring someone or something back to the country that person or thing came from

repatriation /riːˌpeɪ·triːˈeɪ·ʃən, -ˌpæ·triː-/ *n* [U] ○ *Repatriation of refugees is essential to rebuilding the country.*

repay /rɪˈpeɪ/ *v* [T] *past* **repaid** to pay someone money that was borrowed, or to reward (someone) ○ *How can I ever repay you for your kindness?*

repayment /riːˈpeɪ·mənt/ *n* [C/U] ○ [U] *They expect repayment of the loan over three years.*

repeal /rɪˈpiːl/ *v* [T] (of a government) to make a law no longer a law ○ *Legislators repealed the sales tax.*

repeal /rɪˈpiːl/ *n* [U] ○ *Senators called for the law's repeal.*

repeat /rɪˈpiːt/ *v* [T] to say, tell, or do something again ○ *She repeated the question.* ○ *Listen to the tape and repeat each word.*

repeat /rɪˈpiːt, ˈriː·piːt/ *n* [C] ○ *We're hoping to avoid a repeat of last year's disaster.*

repeated /rɪˈpiːt̬·əd/ *adj* [not gradable] happening again and again ○ *repeated attempts/warnings*

repeatedly /rɪˈpiːt̬·əd·li/ *adv* [not gradable] ○ *He has repeatedly denied being there.*

WORD FAMILY repeat

Nouns	repeat repetition	*Adjectives*	repeated repetitive repetitious
Adverbs	repeatedly repetitively	*Verbs*	repeat

repel /rɪˈpel/ *v* [T] **-ll- 1** to force away something unwanted ○ *This coat repels moisture.* **2** Repel can also mean disgust: *Even the idea of him repels her.*

repellent /rɪˈpel·ənt/ *n* [C/U] ○ [U] *Bring insect repellent along on the hike.*

repent /rɪˈpent/ *v* [I/T] to be sorry you did or did not do something ○ [I] *Jenkins returned, to repent and face justice.*

repercussion /ˌriː·pərˈkʌʃ·ən, ˌrep·ər-/ *n* [C usually pl] the usually bad effect of an event, action, or decision ○ *The repercussions of her comments could be serious.*

repertoire /ˈrep·ərˌtwɑr/ *n* [C] all the music, plays, dances, operas, etc., that a person or a group can perform, or that exist in a particular type of activity related to the arts ○ *Americans don't know the American repertoire, aside from Gershwin.*

repertory /ˈrep·ərˌtɔːr·i, -ˌtoʊr·i/ *n* [C/U] a series of performances by a group of actors or dancers presenting several different works during a particular period, or a REPERTOIRE

repetitive /rɪˈpet̬·ət̬·ɪv/ *adj* expressed or happening in the same way many times ○ *a repetitive task* ○ *a series of repetitive motions* ○ Related verb: REPEAT

repetitious /ˌrep·əˈtɪʃ·əs/ *adj* ○ *The movie got a little repetitious after the third car chase.*

repetition /ˌrep·əˈtɪʃ·ən/ *n* [C/U] ○ [U] *It takes time, patience, and repetition to learn a language.*

rephrase /riːˈfreɪz/ *v* [T] to say or write something again in a different way ○ *Could you rephrase your question?*

replace CHANGE FOR /rɪˈpleɪs/ *v* [T] to take the place of something or put in the place of something or someone else ○ *We replaced our old air conditioners.* ○ *The ailing actress was replaced by her understudy.*

replacement /rɪˈpleɪs·mənt/ *n* [C/U] ○ [U] *The replacement of typewriters by computers happened quickly.*

PUT BACK /rɪˈpleɪs/ *v* [T] to put something back where it was before ○ *After dusting the vase, she replaced it on the shelf.*

replay REPETITION /ˈriː·pleɪ/ *n* [C usually sing] a repetition of an earlier event ○ *Interest rates were lowered to avoid a replay of the stock market crash.*

REPEAT PLAYING /ˈriː·pleɪ/ *n* [C] a playing for a second time, sometimes at a slower speed, of a recording, esp. of an event shown on television ○ *News programs broadcast endless replays of the shooting.*

replay /riːˈpleɪ/ *v* [T] ○ *I replayed the night in my mind.*

replenish /rɪˈplen·ɪʃ/ *v* [T] to fill something again, or return something to its earlier condition ○ *We need to replenish our cookie supply.*

replete /rɪˈpliːt/ *adj fml* full ○ *a heart* **replete with** (= full of) *affection*

replica /ˈrep·lɪ·kə/ *n* [C] a copy of an object

replicate /ˈrep·ləˌkeɪt/ *v* [I/T] **1** to copy or repeat something ○ [T] *Researchers tried to replicate the original experiment.* **2** ***biology*** To replicate an organism, cell, or DNA means to produce an exact copy of it.

replication /ˌrep·ləˈkeɪ·ʃən/ *n* [C]

reply /rɪˈplɑɪ/ *v* to answer a question ○ [I] *She asked him how old he was but he didn't reply.* ○ [+ that clause] *He replied that he wasn't interested.*

reply /rɪˈplɑɪ/ *n* [C/U] ○ [C] *Mary's reply was carefully considered.* ○ [U] *When he made no reply, she continued.*

report TELL /rɪˈpɔːrt, -ˈpoʊrt/ *v* [T] to give a description of something or information about something to someone ○ *We called the police to report the theft.* ○ *The accident was reported in all the newspapers.* ○ [+ that clause] *The crew reported that the situation was normal.*

report /rɪˈpɔːrt, -ˈpoʊrt/ *n* [C] ○ *a financial report* ○ *I have to write a report on immigration.* ○ *According to reports there has been an earthquake in Los Angeles.*

reportedly /rɪˈpɔːrt̬·əd·li, -ˈpoʊrt̬-/ *adv* [not gradable] ○ *New York is reportedly a very exciting place to live* (= People say that it is).

reporter /rɪˈpɔːrt̬·ər, -ˈpoʊrt̬·ər/ *n* [C] a person whose job is to discover information about news events and describe them for a newspaper or magazine or for radio or television

GO SOMEWHERE /rɪˈpɔːrt, -ˈpoʊrt/ *v* [I always + adv/prep] to go to a place and say that you are there or inform someone about what you are doing ○ *I report for work/duty at 8 a.m. every morning.* ○ *In this job you'll be reporting directly to* (= working for) *the president.*

WORD FAMILY report			
Nouns	report reporter	*Verbs*	report
		Adverbs	reportedly
Adjectives	unreported		

report card *n* [C] **1** a teacher's written statement about a student's performance at school ○ *Sam got three A's and a B on his report card.* **2** A report card can also be a report about the performance of an organization or program that is made public: *The report card evaluates the performance of private and public universities.*

R

reported speech, **indirect speech** *n* [U] ***English*** a description of what someone has said without using the exact words used ○ *The sentence "He told me that he would like to go" is an example of reported speech.*

repository /rɪˈpɑz·əˌtɔːr·i, -ˌtoʊr·i/ *n* [C] a place where things are stored ○ *a nuclear waste repository* ○ (*fig.*) *The proverbs amounted to a repository of wisdom.*

reprehensible /ˌrep·rɪˈhen·sə·bəl/ *adj* [not gradable] deserving blame; recognized as bad ○ *His conduct, though morally reprehensible, is not a crime.*

represent ACT FOR /ˌrep·rɪˈzent/ *v* [T] to speak, act, or be present officially for a person or group ○ *His law firm is representing a dozen of the families involved in that disaster.*

representation /ˌrep·rɪ·zenˈteɪ·ʃən, -zən-/ *n* [U] ○ *People too poor to pay for legal representation get a public defender.*

representative /ˌrep·rɪˈzent·ət̬·ɪv/ *adj* [not gradable] ○ *Democracy is a representative system of government.*

representative /ˌrep·rɪˈzent·ət̬·ɪv/ *n* [C] **1** a person who represents another person or a group ○ *The company has representatives in most European capitals.* **2** ***politics & government*** A representative is also a member of a law-making group. ○ See also: REPRESENTATIVE

DESCRIBE /ˌrep·rɪˈzent/ *v* [T] to show or describe something, or to be a sign or symbol of something ○ *The memorial represents the sacrifice of men and women who gave their lives in the war.*

representative /ˌrep·rɪˈzent·ət̬·ɪv/ *adj* [not gradable] serving to describe, esp. a larger group of the same type ○ *A good political poll is based on a representative sampling of voters.* ○ See also: REPRESENTATIVE

BE /ˌrep·rɪˈzent/ *v* [L] to be the result of something, or to be something ○ *This represents years of work.* ○ *China and India represent 40% of the world's population.*

WORD FAMILY represent	
Nouns representation representative	*Adjectives* representative unrepresentative
Verbs represent	

representative, **Representative** /ˌrep·rɪˈzent·ət̬·ɪv/, *abbreviation* **Rep.** *n* [C] ***politics & government*** a member of the US House of Representatives; a CONGRESSMAN or CONGRESSWOMAN ○ See also: REPRESENTATIVE at REPRESENT ACT FOR

repress /rɪˈpres/ *v* [T] to prevent feelings, desires, or ideas from being expressed ○ *In the end, it was impossible to repress her emotions.* ○ *The government repressed all reports from the region.*

repressed /rɪˈprest/ *adj* ○ *repressed memories*

repression /rɪˈpreʃ·ən/ *n* [U] ○ *The report dealt with the repression of civil liberties during the period.*

repressive /rɪˈpres·ɪv/ *adj* ○ *The military regime was repressive and corrupt.*

reprieve /rɪˈpriːv/ *n* [C] **1** an official order to delay or stop a prisoner's punishment, esp. the punishment of death ○ *The warden notified Shaw of his reprieve.* **2** A reprieve is also any delay that is welcomed: *The play, about to close, was granted a four-week reprieve.*

reprieve /rɪˈpriːv/ *v* [T]

reprimand /ˈrep·rəˌmænd/ *v* [T] to tell someone, esp. officially, that his or her behavior is wrong and not acceptable ○ *The committee reprimanded and censured him for his uncooperative attitude.*

reprimand /ˈrep·rəˌmænd/ *n* [C] ○ *His boss gave him a severe reprimand for being late again.*

reprint /riːˈprɪnt/ *v* [T] to print a book again ○ *The first edition sold out, so it is being reprinted.*

reprint /ˈriː·prɪnt/ *n* [C]

reprisal /rɪˈprɑɪ·zəl/ *n* [C/U] an act of damage or injury against an enemy in reaction to an act of damage or injury done to you ○ [C] *Employees didn't speak out about the company's pollution for fear of reprisal.*

reprise /rɪˈpriːz/ *n* [C] a repeat of something ○ *The actor is planning a reprise of his role in the play.*

reprise /rɪˈpriːz/ *v* [T] to repeat a song, performance, or set of actions ○ *I was to play the doctor, reprising a role I'd done years earlier.*

reproach /rɪˈproʊtʃ/ *v* [T] to criticize or find fault with someone ○ *He's still reproaching himself for the accident.*

reproach /rɪˈproʊtʃ/ *n* [C/U] ○ [U] *The child's behavior was above/beyond reproach* (= blameless).

reproduce **PRODUCE NEW LIFE** /ˌriː·prəˈduːs/ *v* [I/T] ***biology*** (of living things) to produce a new living thing of the same type as itself

reproduction /ˌriː·prəˈdʌk·ʃən/ *n* [U] the act or process of producing new life

reproductive /ˌriː·prəˈdʌk·tɪv/ *adj* [not gradable] relating to the production of new life

COPY /ˌriː·prəˈduːs/ *v* [I/T] to produce a copy of something, or to show or do something again ○ [T] *The design was reproduced on T-shirts.*

reproduction /ˌriː·prəˈdʌk·ʃən/ *n* [C/U] ○ [C] *The poster is a reproduction of a Monet painting.*

reptile /ˈrep·təl, -tɑɪl/ *n* [C] any of various animals whose blood temperature changes with the outside temperature and whose bodies are covered by SCALES or PLATES (= hard material) ○ *Snakes, turtles, and crocodiles are all reptiles.*

republic /rɪˈpʌb·lɪk/ *n* [C] ***politics & government*** a country that is governed by elected representatives and an elected leader

republican /rɪˈpʌb·lɪ·kən/ *n* [C] ***politics & government*** a person who supports or believes in representative government

Republican Party *n* [U] one of the two main political parties in the US. Traditionally it supports lower taxes and smaller government, and is supported by wealthy people and businesses.

repudiate /rɪˈpjuːd·iːˌeɪt/ *v* [T] *fml* to refuse to accept or obey something or someone; REJECT ○ *The evidence presented at the trial has since been repudiated.*

repudiation /rɪˌpjuːd·iːˈeɪ·ʃən/ *n* [U]

repugnant /rɪˈpʌg·nənt/ *adj* [not gradable] causing a feeling of strong dislike or disgust ○ *The trade in wild animals was repugnant to most people.*

repulse /rɪˈpʌls/ *v* [T] **1** to push someone or something back or away, esp. to successfully stop an attack ○ *The enemy attack was quickly repulsed.* **2** If something repulses you, it causes you to have a strong feeling of dislike and want to avoid it.

repulsion /rɪˈpʌl·ʃən/ *n* [U] ○ *When she was pregnant, certain foods produced a feeling of repulsion in her.*

repulsive /rɪˈpʌl·sɪv/ *adj* causing a feeling of strong dislike or disgust ○ *a repulsive odor/crime*

reputation /ˌrep·jəˈteɪ·ʃən/ *n* [C] the general opinion that people have about someone or something ○ *a good/bad reputation* ○ *His work in Congress won him a reputation as reliable and industrious.*

reputable /ˈrep·jət̬·ə·bəl/ *adj* having a good reputation ○ *Call a reputable heating contractor to inspect your furnace.*

reputed /rɪˈpjuːt̬·əd/ *adj* [not gradable] generally reported or believed ○ [+ *to* infinitive] *The restaurant is reputed to be the best of its kind in the city.*

reputedly /rɪˈpjuːt̬·əd·li/ *adv* [not gradable] ○ *At one time he was reputedly the richest man in America.*

WORD FAMILY reputation

Nouns	reputation disrepute	*Adjectives*	reputable disreputable reputed
Adverbs	reputedly		

request /rɪˈkwest/ *n* [C/U] an act of asking for something, or the thing asked for ○ [C] *The library gets a lot of requests for books about new babies.* ○ [U] *An application will be sent to you upon request* (= if you ask).

request /rɪˈkwest/ *v* [T] ○ [+ *that* clause] *The caller requested that his name not be mentioned on the air.* ➤ Confusables: **require or request?** at REQUIRE NEED

require Ⓐ **NEED** /rɪˈkwɑɪr/ *v* [T] to need something, or to make something necessary ○ *If you require assistance with your bags, I'll be glad to get someone to help you.* ○ *This game requires total concentration.*

requirement Ⓐ /rɪˈkwɑɪr·mənt/ *n* [C] something needed or necessary ○ *Previous experience is one of the requirements for the job.*

CONFUSABLES

require or **request?**

The main meaning of **require** is "need."

Learning a language requires time and effort.

Request means "ask for."

I wrote a letter to request more information.

~~*I wrote a letter to require more information.*~~

ORDER /rɪˈkwɑɪr/ *v* to order or demand something, or to order someone to do something, esp. because of a rule or law ○ [+ *to* infinitive] *We're required to check your identification before letting you in.* ○ [T] *A building permit is required.*

requisite /ˈrek·wə·zət/ *adj* [not gradable] *fml* needed for a particular purpose or result ○ *I worked to develop the requisite skills for a managerial position.*

requisition /ˌrek·wəˈzɪʃ·ən/ *n* [C/U] a formal or official request for something needed ○ [C] *The staff made a requisition for new desks.*

requisition /ˌrek·wəˈzɪʃ·ən/ *v* [T] to officially request or take (something) ○ *The army requisitioned all the trucks in the region.*

reroute /riːˈruːt, -ˈrɑʊt/ *v* [T] to change the route of someone or something ○ *Traffic is being rerouted due to construction.*

rerun /riːˈrʌn/ *v* [T] *pres. part.* **rerunning**, *past simp.* **reran**, *past part.* **rerun** to show again a television program or movie

rerun /ˈriː·rʌn/ *n* [C] ○ *There's nothing on TV but reruns.*

reschedule Ⓐ /riːˈskedʒ·uːl, -əl/ *v* [T] to arrange something for a different time ○ *I rescheduled my doctor's appointment for later in the week.*

rescind /rɪˈsɪnd/ *v* [T] *fml* to make a law, order, or decision no longer have any legal effect ○ *The vote rescinds zoning decisions made earlier in the decade.*

rescue /ˈres·kjuː/ *v* [T] to save someone or something from a dangerous, harmful, or difficult situation ○ *Medical teams immediately rushed in to rescue persons trapped in buildings and give medical aid.*

rescue /ˈres·kjuː/ *n* [C/U] ○ [U] *Rescue workers arrived at the scene within minutes.*

rescuer /ˈres·kjuː·ər/ *n* [C] ○ *Rescuers in helicopters and on foot continued their search for survivors.*

research Ⓐ /ˈriː·sɜrtʃ, rɪˈsɜrtʃ/ *n* [U] a detailed study of a subject in order to discover information or achieve a new understanding of it ○ *medical/scientific research* ○ *The US government has funded some research on high-speed trains.* ○ *I like doing research.*

research Ⓐ /rɪˈsɜrtʃ, ˈriː·sɜrtʃ/ *v* [I/T] ○ [T] *Obviously they didn't research it and get enough information.*

researcher Ⓐ /ˈriːˌsɜr·tʃər, rɪˈsɜr-/ *n* [C]

resell /riːˈsel/ *v* [T] *past* **-sold** to sell something that you previously bought ○ *The buyer hoped to fix up the car and resell it.*

resemble /rɪˈzem·bəl/ *v* [T] to be similar to someone or something ○ *Several of the women resemble one another closely enough to be sisters.*

resemblance /rɪˈzem·bləns/ *n* [C/U] ○ [C] *There is a clear resemblance between the two breeds of dogs.*

resent /rɪˈzent/ *v* [T] to dislike or be angry at something or someone because you have been hurt or not treated fairly ○ *She resented being treated like a child.*

resentful /rɪˈzent·fəl/ *adj* ○ *Marshall was resentful that he had made almost nothing from his discovery.*

resentment /rɪˈzent·mənt/ *n* [U] ○ *There is some community resentment toward the school's new policy.*

reservation /ˌrez·ərˈveɪ·ʃən/ *n* [C/U] a doubt or reason for not accepting or agreeing with something completely ○ [C] *We have reservations about letting the children stay home alone.*

reserve /rɪˈzɜrv/ *v* [I/T] **1** to keep something for a particular purpose or time ○ [T] *He reserved the right to veto any future plans.* **2** If you reserve something such as a table in a restaurant or a room in a hotel, you arrange for it to be kept for your use

R

at a later time: [I] *It's a popular restaurant, and you'll have to reserve well in advance.* ○ [T] *I'm sorry, this seat is reserved.*

reservation /ˌrez·ərˈveɪ·ʃən/ *n* [C] **1** an arrangement to have something kept for a person or for a special purpose ○ *I made a reservation at the restaurant for 7 o'clock.* **2** A reservation is also an area of land set apart for a particular group of people to live on, esp. American Indians.

reserve /rɪˈzɜrv/ *n* [C/U] **1** [C] *I have a reserve of food in case of emergency.* ○ [U] *The book is on reserve and can't be checked out.* ○ *She keeps a little money* **in reserve** (= for use if and when needed). **2** A reserve (also **preserve**) is also an area of land kept for the protection of animals and plants: [C] *a nature/game reserve* **3** The reserves are a part of a country's armed forces that are not always on active duty but are available in an emergency.

reserved /rɪˈzɜrvd/ *adj* tending to keep your feelings or thoughts private rather than showing them ○ *Marcus is more reserved than his brother.*

reservoir /ˈrez·ərˌvwɑr, -ərˌvwɔːr/ *n* [C] **1** a natural or artificial lake for storing and supplying water for an area **2** A reservoir is also a large supply of something that could be used if needed: *There's a tremendous reservoir of goodwill out there.*

reshape /riːˈʃeɪp/ *v* [T] to change the character or organization of something ○ *Baby boomers continue to reshape society as they age.* ○ *Governments have sought to reduce or reshape health programs.*

reshuffle /riːˈʃʌf·əl/ *v* [T] to change the positions of people or things within a group ○ *It is rumored that the president will reshuffle his Cabinet.*

reside Ⓐ /rɪˈzɑɪd/ *v* [I always + adv/prep] *fml* to live in a place ○ *The family resides in Arkansas.*

residence Ⓐ /ˈrez·əd·əns/ *n* [C/U] the place where someone lives, or the condition of living somewhere ○ [C] *That big building is the Governor's official residence* (= home). ○ [U] *She took up residence in Boston* (= began living there).

residency /ˈrez·əd·ən·si/ *n* [C/U] **1** [U] *You have to meet residency requirements* (= live in a place long enough) *before you can apply for citizenship.* **2** A residency is also a period of work, usually in a hospital, for a doctor to get practical experience and training in a special area of medicine.

resident Ⓐ /ˈrez·əd·ənt/ *n* [C] **1** someone who lives in a place ○ *The local residents were angry at the lack of parking spaces.* **2** A resident is also a doctor who is working, usually in a hospital, to get practical experience and training in a special area of medicine.

residential Ⓐ /ˌrez·əˈden·tʃəl/ *adj* [not gradable] of or relating to houses where people live rather than to places where they work ○ *Glen Oaks is a residential neighborhood.*

residue /ˈrez·əˌduː/ *n* [C] something that is left after the main part is no longer present ○ *Pesticide residue is present in many fruits and vegetables, even after proper washing.*

residual /rɪˈzɪdʒ·ə·wəl/ *adj* [not gradable] resulting or left from something that was previously present ○ *Residual oil has to be cleaned up.*

resign /rɪˈzɑɪn/ *v* [I/T] to give up a job or position ○ [I] *He resigned from the committee.*

PHRASAL VERB with resign

• **resign** *yourself* **to** *something* to make yourself accept something unpleasant that cannot be changed ○ *He was resigned to living alone.* ○ Related noun: RESIGNATION ACCEPTING DIFFICULTY ○ Related adjective: RESIGNED

resignation LEAVING POSITION /ˌrez·ɪgˈneɪ·ʃən/ *n* [C/U] the act of leaving a job or position and making a statement that you are doing this ○ [U] *a letter of resignation* ○ [C] *Protesters took to the streets in massive numbers to demand the president's resignation.*

ACCEPTING DIFFICULTY /ˌrez·ɪgˈneɪ·ʃən/ *n* [U] the attitude of accepting something unpleasant because you cannot change it ○ *She received the disappointing news with resignation.*

resigned /rɪˈzɑɪnd/ *adj* [not gradable] willing to accept something unpleasant ○ *They are resigned and a little depressed at the thought of losing money for at least the first year.*

resilient /rɪˈzɪl·jənt/ *adj* [not gradable] able to improve quickly after being hurt or being ill ○ *Life is hard there, but the people are resilient.*

resilience /rɪˈzɪl·jəns/, **resiliency** /rɪˈzɪl·jən·si/ *n* [U]

resin /ˈrez·ən/ *n* [U] a clear, yellow, sticky substance produced by some trees and plants and used to make VARNISH, medicine, or plastics, or a similar substance produced chemically for use in industry

resist /rɪˈzɪst/ *v* [I/T] **1** to fight against or oppose something or someone ○ [T] *Students want to discover the truth themselves, and they resist having conclusions forced upon them.* **2** To resist is also to keep or stop yourself from doing something: [T] *I couldn't resist laughing at him.*

resistance /rɪˈzɪs·təns/ *n* [U] **1** *A good diet helps the body to build up resistance to disease.* **2** ***science, physics*** Resistance is the degree to which a substance prevents the flow of electricity through it: *Copper has low resistance.*

resistivity /rɪˌzɪsˈtɪv·ət̬·i, ˌriː-/ *n* [U] ***physics*** a measure of the electrical resistance of a substance

resistant /rɪˈzɪs·tənt/ *adj* not easily changed or damaged, or not accepting of (something) ○ *fire resistant* ○ *Why are you so resistant to change?*

resistor /rɪˈzɪs·tər/ *n* [C] ***physics*** a device used to stop the flow of electricity in a particular place

resolute /ˈrez·əˌluːt/ *adj* determined in character, action, or ideas ○ *I admired her resolute optimism in those difficult times.*

resolutely /ˈrez·əˌluːt·li, ˌrez·əˈluːt-/ *adv* ○ *She resolutely refuses to lower her standards.*

resolution Ⓐ SOLUTION /ˌrez·əˈluː·ʃən/ *n* [C/U] **1** the act of solving a problem or finding a way to improve a difficult situation ○ [C] *Negotiators are working tirelessly for a swift resolution of this crisis.* **2** ***physics*** Resolution is also the process of finding out the direction and strength of a VECTOR.

DECISION /ˌrez·əˈluː·ʃən/ *n* [C] **1** a formal statement of decision or opinion ○ *The chairing officer called for a vote on the resolution.* **2** If you make a resolution, you promise yourself to do something: [+ *to* infinitive] *I made a New Year's resolution to lose ten pounds.*

resolve Ⓐ **SOLVE** /rɪˈzɑlv, -ˈzɔːlv/ *v* [T] to solve or end a problem or difficulty ○ *The couple resolved their differences.*

DECIDE /rɪˈzɑlv, -ˈzɔːlv/ *v* to make a determined decision ○ [+ *that* clause] *They resolved that they would never argue over money.* ○ [+ *to* infinitive] *I resolved to run a mile a day.*

resolve /rɪˈzɑlv, -ˈzɔːlv/ *n* [U] strong determination ○ *The experience increased her resolve to change careers.*

resolved /rɪˈzɑlvd, -ˈzɔːlvd/ *adj* ○ [+ *to* infinitive] *We're resolved to get together more often.*

resonate /ˈrez·əˌneɪt/ *v* [I] **1** to produce or be filled with clear, continuing sound ○ *The noise of the bell resonated through the building.* **2** ***physics*** An object that resonates reflects sound waves and makes them seem louder.

resonant /ˈrez·ə·nənt/ *adj* (of sound) clear and continuing ○ *a resonant voice*

resonance /ˈrez·ə·nənts/ *n* [U] ***physics***

resort /rɪˈzɔːrt/ *n* [C] a place where people can go on vacations to relax or for an activity they enjoy ○ *a ski resort*

PHRASAL VERB with resort

• **resort to** *something* to do or use something because it is the only thing available ○ *There's hope the countries will reach a settlement without resorting to armed conflict.*

resound /rɪˈzɑʊnd/ *v* [I] to sound loudly or for a long time, or (of a place) to be filled with sound ○ *The air resounds with the delightful music of birds.*

resounding /rɪˈzɑʊn·dɪŋ/ *adj* very great; complete ○ *The remake of the movie was a resounding success.*

resource Ⓐ /ˈriː·sɔːrs, -zɔːrs/ *n* [C] **1** something that can be used to help you ○ *The library was a valuable resource, and he frequently made use of it.* **2** Resources are natural substances such as water and wood which are valuable in supporting life: [pl] *The earth has limited resources, and if we don't recycle them we use them up.* **3** Resources are also things of value such as money or possessions that you can use when you need them: [pl] *The government doesn't have the resources to hire the number of teachers needed.*

resourceful Ⓐ /rɪˈsɔːrs·fəl, -ˈzɔːrs-/ *adj* able to find and use different ways to help achieve your goals ○ *She plays the part of a tough, resourceful newspaper reporter.*

respect **ADMIRATION** /rɪˈspekt/ *n* [U] admiration for someone or something that you believe has good ideas or qualities ○ *I believe people had more respect for teachers back then.*

respect /rɪˈspekt/ *v* [T] to admire an ability or good quality, or to admire someone for the ability or qualities that person has ○ *While I respected his deep knowledge of American history, he wasn't a very effective teacher.*

POLITE ATTITUDE /rɪˈspekt/ *n* [U] **1** the polite attitude shown toward someone or something that you consider important ○ *Some drivers don't have any respect for other motorists.* **2** Respects are polite expressions of greeting or sympathy: [pl] *Give my respects to your parents.* ○ [pl] *We stopped by the funeral home to pay our respects.*

respect /rɪˈspekt/ *v* [T] ○ *We should try to respect one another no matter what we believe.*

respectful /rɪˈspekt·fəl/ *adj* ○ *The protestors were respectful and polite.*

respectfully /rɪˈspekt·fə·li/ *adv* ○ *Most old acquaintances address him respectfully as "Governor."*

FEATURE /rɪˈspekt/ *n* [C] a particular feature or detail ○ *In some respects, I had to admit, I had behaved foolishly.*

WORD FAMILY respect

Nouns	respect disrespect respectability	*Adjectives*	respectable respectful disrespectful respective
Adverbs	respectfully disrespectfully respectively	*Verbs*	respect

respectable /rɪˈspek·tə·bəl/ *adj* **1** socially acceptable because of having a good character or appearance or behaving in a way that is approved of ○ *It was hard to find a clean shirt that looked respectable enough to be seen in.* **2** Respectable also means large enough or good enough to be acceptable: *a respectable income* ○ *Her school has a respectable basketball program.*

respectability /rɪˌspek·təˈbɪl·ət̬·i/ *n* [U] ○ *Everything in the hotel had an air of old-time respectability.*

respectively /rɪˈspek·tɪv·li/ *adv* [not gradable] (of two or more items) with each relating to something previously mentioned, in the same order as first mentioned ○ *George and Kenneth were married in 1980 and 1985, respectively.*

respective /rɪˈspek·tɪv/ *adj* [not gradable] ○ *Barkley and Jordan are the two best players on their respective* (= separate) *teams.*

respiratory /ˈres·pə·rəˌtɔːr·i, -ˌtoʊr·i/ *adj* [not gradable] ***biology*** of or relating to breathing

respirator /ˈres·pəˌreɪt̬·ər/ *n* [C] a device that forces air into a person's lungs when the person cannot breathe independently and needs help to breathe ○ *Miya was hooked up to a respirator at University Hospital.*

respiration /ˌres·pəˈreɪ·ʃən/ *n* [U] ***biology*** the process of breathing

respite /ˈres·pət, rɪˈspɑɪt/ *n* [C/U] a pause or rest from something difficult or unpleasant ○ [C usually sing] *The center provides a respite for teens in trouble.*

resplendent /rɪˈsplen·dənt/ *adj fml* beautiful and seeming to shine ○ *a white hat resplendent with*

R

red velvet flowers ○ **USAGE:** said esp. about a person's clothes or jewelry, usually because they are fashionable and expensive

respond Ⓐ /rɪˈspɑnd/ *v* [I] **1** to say or do something as a reaction to something that has been said or done ○ *I want to respond to something that Norman said.* **2** If a disease responds to treatment, the harmful effects of the disease begin to lessen.

respondent Ⓐ /rɪˈspɑn·dənt/ *n* [C] **1** someone who responds to a question or offer ○ *Most respondents in the survey voiced an unfavorable attitude toward the policy.* **2** In the legal system, a responent is the person against whom a case is brought.

WORD FAMILY respond			
Nouns	response responsiveness	*Adjectives*	responsive unresponsive
Verbs	respond		

response Ⓐ /rɪˈspɑns/ *n* [C/U] **1** something said or done as a reaction to something that has been said or done; an answer or reaction ○ [C] *She's applied for admission and is still waiting for a response from the school.* ○ *The law was passed by the town council* **in response to** (= as a result of) *complaints from residents.* **2** ***biology*** A response is also a reaction of an organism to a change in its environment.

responsive Ⓐ /rɪˈspɑn·sɪv/ *adj* quick to act, esp. to meet the needs of someone or something ○ *He had promised a government responsive to the people.*

responsiveness Ⓐ /rɪˈspɑn·sɪv·nəs/ *n* [U]

responsible DUTY /rɪˈspɑn·sə·bəl/ *adj* **1** having the duty of taking care of something ○ *The government's Energy Regulatory Board is responsible for nuclear safety.* **2** A responsible job/position is an important one involving control and authority over something.

responsibility /rɪˌspɑn·səˈbɪl·ət̬·i/ *n* [C/U] ○ [C] *With this promotion, Jorge's responsibilities will be increased.* ○ [U] *Parents must assume responsibility for their children.*

BLAME /rɪˈspɑn·sə·bəl/ *adj* being the cause of a particular action or situation, esp. a harmful or unpleasant one ○ *We are not responsible for things getting lost in the mail.*

responsibility /rɪˌspɑn·səˈbɪl·ət̬·i/ *n* [U] ○ *The oil company has denied responsibility for the leak.*

GOOD JUDGMENT /rɪˈspɑn·sə·bəl/ *adj* having good judgment and the ability to act correctly and make decisions on your own ○ *We want to be responsible citizens.*

responsibly /rɪˈspɑn·sə·bli/ *adv* ○ *Parties are permitted, so long as everyone behaves responsibly.*

WORD FAMILY responsible			
Nouns	responsibility	*Adverbs*	responsibly irresponsibly
Adjectives	responsible irresponsible		

rest RELAX /rest/ *v* [I/T] to stop being active for a period of time in order to relax and get back your strength, or to cause someone or something to stop doing an activity in order to get back strength ○ [I] *We hiked for five miles and then rested for a while.* ○ [T] *The coach decided to rest some of the team's starters tomorrow night.* ○ [T] *I just need to sit down and rest my legs.*

rest /rest/ *n* [C/U] **1** [C] *What you need is a nice long rest.* ○ [U] *The doctor told him to get plenty of rest and drink lots of fluids.* **2 At rest** means not doing anything active or not moving: *The cat seemed coiled to spring, even when it was at rest.*

restful /ˈrest·fəl/ *adj* causing a feeling of calmness ○ *The island was quiet and restful and so beautiful.*

restless /ˈrest·ləs/ *adj* **1** moving because you are unable to relax, esp. because you are worried or bored, or (of an activity) having a lot of movement as a characteristic ○ *He dozed off to a restless sleep.* ○ *The audience began to get restless.* **2** Restless can also mean not satisfied with your situation and wanting a change: *The opposition parties provide no clear alternative for restless voters.*

restlessly /ˈrest·lə·sli/ *adv* ○ *I wandered restlessly around the apartment.*

restlessness /ˈrest·lə·snəs/ *n* [U] ○ *He paced back and forth out of sheer restlessness.*

USAGE

rest, stay, or remain?

Rest means to relax or sleep because you are tired or ill.

The doctor told him to rest.

Stay means to continue to be in the same place, job, or particular state.

It was raining, so we stayed home.

~~*It was raining, so we rested home.*~~

Remain means to continue to be in the same state, or to continue to exist when everything or everyone else has gone.

He remained unconscious for a week after the accident.

After the earthquake, nothing remained of the village.

MUSIC /rest/ *n* [C] ***music*** a mark in written music that shows when and for how long an instrument should be silent ➤ Picture: **notation**

STAY /rest/ *v* [I] to be or stay under the control of a particular person or organization ○ *The final decision rests with the City Council.*

SUPPORT /rest/ *v* [I/T] to lie or lean on something, or to put something on something else so that its weight is supported ○ [T] *She rested her elbows on the table.*

OTHER PART /rest/ *n* [U] the other things, people, or parts that are left ○ *I want to do something else with the rest of my life.*

WORD FAMILY rest			
Nouns	rest unrest restlessness	*Adjectives*	restless restful
		Adverbs	restlessly
Verbs	rest		

R

IDIOMS with rest

• **rest assured** to be certain that something will happen ○ *You can rest assured that you're going to get a good deal.* ○ **USAGE:** Used to make someone feel safe or less worried about something.

• **rest in peace** to be free from trouble ○ *the late Pat McLaughlin, may he rest in peace* ○ **USAGE:** Used only about dead people.

• **rest on *your* laurels** to feel comfortable because you have been successful in the past ○ *The company can't just sit back and rest on its laurels – we have to move on to something new.*

rest area, **rest stop** *n* [C] a place beside a large road where a vehicle can stop and where toilets and sometimes food and fuel are available

restart /riː'stɑrt/ *v* [I/T] to begin or start something again after it has stopped for a period of time ○ [I] *Sometimes the computer wouldn't restart at all.* ○ [T] *He offered to restart the talks which broke down last year.*

restaurant /'res·tə·rənt, -tə,rɑnt/ *n* [C] a place of business where people can choose a meal to be prepared and served to them at a table, and for which they pay, usually after eating ○ *a Chinese/Italian/Mexican restaurant*

SPELLING

restaurant

Be careful with the "au" vowel combination in the middle of this word.

*First Wok is a wonderful rest**au**rant.*

restaurateur /,res·tə·rə'tɜr/ *n* [C] a person who owns or manages a restaurant

restitution /,res·tə'tuː·ʃən/ *n* [U] *law* payment for damage or loss of property, or the return of items stolen or lost ○ *The company has agreed to make restitution of $44,930 and to pay an equal fine.*

restive /'res·tɪv/ *adj fml* unwilling to be controlled or be patient ○ *The crowd began to get restive during the long wait for the concert to begin.*

restore Ⓐ /rɪ'stɔːr, -'stoʊr/ *v* [T] to return something or someone to an earlier condition or position, or to bring something back into existence ○ *Power company crews were working yesterday to restore electrical service to homes in the area.* ○ *Surgeons restored the sight in her right eye.*

restoration Ⓐ /,res·tə'reɪ·ʃən/ *n* [C/U] the act or the process of returning something to its original condition, or to a state similar to its original condition ○ [U] *She is in charge of the restoration of paintings in the collection.* ○ [C] *Elise has worked on a number of 19th-century building restorations.*

restrain Ⓐ /rɪ'streɪn/ *v* [T] **1** to control the actions or behavior of someone by force, esp. in order to stop that person from doing something ○ *Seamons got into a shouting match and had to be restrained by his teammates.* ○ *I could hardly restrain my laughter.* **2** To restrain is also to limit the growth or force of something: *Politicians are reluctant to restrain spending.*

restrained Ⓐ /rɪ'streɪnd/ *adj* ○ *Considering the abuse they receive from fans, athletes are remarkably restrained* (= calm and controlled).

restraint Ⓐ /rɪ'streɪnt/ *n* [C/U] **1** determined control over behavior in order to prevent the strong expression of emotion or any violent action ○ [U] *You really have to show a lot of restraint to stay out of debt.* **2** A restraint is something that limits freedom of movement, action, or growth: [C] *Social restraints seem to have become dangerously unrestrictive.*

restrict Ⓐ /rɪ'strɪkt/ *v* [T] to limit someone's actions or movement, or to limit the amount, size, etc., of something ○ *The government has so sharply restricted his fishing that he can barely pay his crew.* ○ *The state legislature voted to restrict development in the area.*

restricted Ⓐ /rɪ'strɪk·təd/ *adj* ○ *Many events are free, so families on restricted budgets can participate.*

restriction Ⓐ /rɪ'strɪk·ʃən/ *n* [C/U] ○ [C] *You can get a discount fare, but some restrictions* (= rules about limits) *apply.*

restrictive Ⓐ /rɪ'strɪk·tɪv/ *adj* ○ *She campaigned against restrictive immigration laws.*

restrictively Ⓐ /rɪ'strɪk·tɪv·li/ *adv*

restroom /'rest·ruːm, -rʊm/ *n* [C] a room in a public building in which there are toilets ➤ Usage: **toilet, bathroom, or restroom?** at TOILET

restructure Ⓐ /riː'strʌk·tʃər/ *v* [T] to change the jobs and responsibilities within an organization, usually in order to make the organization operate more effectively ○ *The commission developed guidelines for restructuring the city's police department.*

result /rɪ'zʌlt/ *n* [C] **1** something that happens or exists because of something else ○ *The mayor says crime is lower as a result of good police work.* ○ *A lot of people survived the crash as a direct result of the excellent training our pilots and flight attendants receive.* **2** Results are what you discover after examining something: *The election results show that the governor is not as popular as she was two years ago.* ○ *Results of the medical tests showed no sign of cancer.*

result /rɪ'zʌlt/ *v* [I] ○ *Weeks of negotiations resulted in an agreement.* ○ *The flight delay resulted from mechanical problems.*

WORD CHOICES result

The result of a particular influence is an **effect**.

*The radiation leak has had a disastrous **effect** on the environment.*

Consequence is used especially when the result of an action or situation is bad or inconvenient.

*Failure to do proper safety checks may have serious **consequences**.*

Outcome or **upshot** are alternatives to "result."

*It's too early to predict the **outcome** of the meeting.*

*The **upshot** of the discussions is that there will be no layoffs.* ➤

The result of a process or series of events is the **end result**.

*The **end result** of these changes should be a more efficient system for dealing with complaints.*

Fallout is also used when a result is very bad.

*The political **fallout** of the revelations was very damaging for the President.*

A **byproduct** is something unexpected that happens as a result of something else.

*Unpleasant noises in the head can be a distressing **byproduct** of some forms of deafness.*

resultant /rɪˈzʌlt·ənt/ *n* [C] ***physics*** the total when two or more VECTORS are added

resume /rɪˈzuːm/ *v* [I/T] to start something again after a pause or period of time ○ [T] *The director hopes to resume filming next week.* ○ [I] *Government officials hoped talks will resume.*

résumé, **resume** /ˈrez·əˌmeɪ/ *n* [C] a written statement of your educational and work experience ○ *He looked at her résumé, asked her a few questions, and then offered her the job.*

resumption /rɪˈzʌm·ʃən/ *n* [U] the act of starting something again after a pause or period of time ○ *He worked for the resumption of economic ties between Vietnam and the US.*

resurface COVER /riːˈsɜr·fəs/ *v* [T] to put a new surface on a road ○ *Expect delays while they resurface the highway.*

APPEAR /riːˈsɜr·fəs/ *v* [I] to appear again after not being seen or heard ○ *The tax issue is likely to resurface next year.*

resurgence /rɪˈsɜr·dʒəns/ *n* [C/U] an increase of activity or interest in a particular subject or idea which had been forgotten for some time ○ [C usually sing] *There's been a resurgence of criticism of the president.*

resurrect /ˌrez·əˈrekt/ *v* [T] to bring someone back to life, or bring something back into use or existence after it disappeared ○ *Buckley enjoys resurrecting some of the more obscure words of the English language.*

resurrection /ˌrez·əˈrek·ʃən/ *n* [U] **1** *the resurrection of his political career* **2** In the Christian religion, the Resurrection is Jesus Christ's return to life after his death.

resuscitate /rɪˈsʌs·əˌteɪt/ *v* [I/T] to bring someone who is dying back to life, wake someone who is unconscious, or bring something back into use or existence ○ [T] *You should learn how to resuscitate a person whose breathing has stopped.* ○ [T] *He led the effort to resuscitate the local newspaper.*

retail /ˈriː·teɪl/ *n* [U] the activity of selling goods to the public, usually in small amounts, for their own use ○ Compare WHOLESALE SELLING

retail /ˈriː·teɪl/ *adj, adv* [not gradable] ○ *Retail sales are rising.* ○ *The company has three retail outlets/stores in the Washington area.*

retail /ˈriː·teɪl/ *v* [I/T] to sell goods to the public, usually in small amounts, for their own use ○ [T] *Country Miss makes and retails sportswear.* ○ [I] *The software retails for $69.*

retailer /ˈriː·teɪ·lər/ *n* [C] ○ *If you bought it there, you can't take it back to another retailer.*

retain Ⓐ /rɪˈteɪn/ *v* [T] to keep or continue to have something ○ *Francis retained control of the company.* ○ *His capacity to retain* (= remember) *facts was as keen as ever, but he had trouble remembering people's names.*

retainer Ⓐ /rɪˈteɪ·nər/ *n* [C] **1** an amount of money that you pay to someone in advance so that the person will work for you when needed ○ *He was on a $150,000 retainer from Lloyd's of London.* **2** A retainer is also a device that holds something in place. **3** A retainer that you wear in your mouth helps to straighten your teeth.

retake /riːˈteɪk/ *v* [T] *past simp.* **retook**, *past part.* **retaken** to take something into possession again, esp. by force ○ *He ordered his troops to prepare to retake the town.*

retaliate /rɪˈtæl·iːˌeɪt/ *v* [I] to hurt someone or do something harmful to someone because that person has done or said something harmful to you ○ *His first instinct was to retaliate against the attacks.*

retaliation /rɪˌtæl·iːˈeɪ·ʃən/ *n* [U] ○ *She said she was fired in retaliation for her reports of illegal business practices earlier this year.*

retard /rɪˈtɑrd/ *v* [T] to make something slower ○ *Reductions in pollution levels could retard global warming.*

retarded /rɪˈtɑrd·əd/ *adj* having a slower mental development than other people of the same age ○ *mentally/emotionally retarded* ○ **USAGE**: Because "retarded" has sometimes been used as an insult, the term is now less often used to describe people with slow mental development.

retardation /ˌriːˌtɑrˈdeɪ·ʃən/ *n* [U] *fml* the process of making something happen or develop slower than it should

retch /retʃ/ *v* [I] to make the sound and action of vomiting, esp. when nothing is actually vomited

retention Ⓐ /rɪˈten·tʃən/ *n* [U] the ability to keep or continue having something ○ *Officials are focusing on job creation, not job retention.*

retentive Ⓐ /rɪˈtent·ɪv/ *adj* ○ *a retentive memory*

rethink /riːˈθɪŋk/ *v* [T] *past* **rethought** to think again about something, such as a plan in order to change or improve it ○ *It's time to rethink whether we need a part-time or full-time mayor.*

reticent /ˈret̬·ə·sənt/ *adj* unwilling to speak about your thoughts or feelings ○ *At first she was reticent, but later she relaxed and was more forthcoming.*

reticence /ˈret̬·ə·səns/ *n* [U] ○ *Due to his reticence, little is known about his personal life.*

retina /ˈret·ən·ə/ *n* [C] the area at the back of the eye that receives light and sends an image to the brain so that seeing can happen

retinue /ˈret·ən ˌuː/ *n* [C] *fml* a group of people who help and who travel with an important person ○ *He jets around the country with a retinue of aides and attorneys.*

retire STOP WORKING /rɪˈtɑɪr/ *v* [I/T] to leave your job or stop working because of having reached a particular age or because of ill health, or to cause someone or something to stop being employed or used ○ [I] *He worked in television after retiring from baseball.* ○ [I] *I'll be retiring soon.* ○ [T] *The aircraft was retired in 1990.*
retired /rɪˈtɑɪrd/ *adj* [not gradable] ○ *He is a retired airline pilot.*
retirement /rɪˈtɑɪr·mənt/ *n* [C/U] the point at which someone stops working, esp. because of having reached a particular age or because of ill health, or the period in someone's life after the person has stopped working ○ [C] *He announced his retirement in September.*
retiree /rɪˌtɑɪˈriː/ *n* [C] ○ *Florida and Arizona are the most popular states for retirees* (= people who have stopped working).
LEAVE A PLACE /rɪˈtɑɪr/ *v* [I] *fml* **1** to leave a room or group of people and go somewhere quiet or private ○ *The judge retired to her study to review the case.* **2** To retire also means to go to bed.

WORD FAMILY retire			
Nouns	retiree retirement	*Adjectives*	retired retiring
Verbs	retire		

retiring /rɪˈtɑɪr·ɪŋ/ *adj* unwilling to be noticed or to be with other people ○ *He's a shy, retiring sort of person.*

retort /rɪˈtɔːrt/ *v* [T] to make a quick answer that is often amusing and sometimes expresses anger or annoyance ○ *When the telephone operator called him boy, he retorted, "That's Mr. Boy to you!"*
retort /rɪˈtɔːrt/ *n* [C]

retort stand /rɪˈtɔːrt ˌstænd, ˈriː·tɔːrt-/ *n* [C] ***science*** a device that is used to hold glass containers esp. during a chemistry experiment

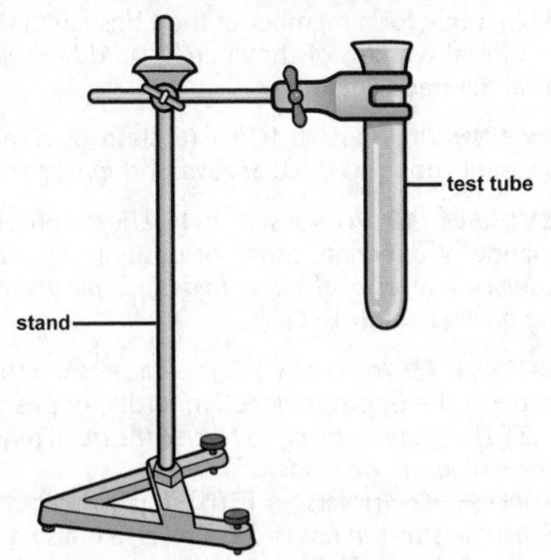

RETORT STAND

retouch /riːˈtʌtʃ/ *v* [T] to make small changes to something, such as a picture or photograph, in order to improve it ○ *Photographs do not lie, unless they are retouched.*

retrace /riːˈtreɪs/ *v* [T] to go back over a path or a series of past actions ○ *This trail is not circular, so you have to retrace your steps back to the start.*

retract /rɪˈtrækt/ *v* [I/T] **1** to say publicly that you will not do something you had said you would do, or to admit that something that you had said was true is false ○ [T] *She had to retract statements in published articles.* **2** To retract is also to pull something back or in: [T] *The pilot retracted the landing gear soon after takeoff.*
retractable /rɪˈtræk·tə·bəl/ *adj* [not gradable] ○ *Cats have retractable claws* (= they can be pulled back).

retread /ˈriː·tred/ *n* [C] a worn tire that has had a new rubber surface joined to its outer part

retreat /rɪˈtriːt/ *v* [I] **1** to move back and away from someone or something, esp. because you are frightened or want to be alone ○ *She burst into tears and retreated to the bedroom.* **2** To retreat is also to go away from a person or place because you are unwilling to fight any more: *Under heavy fire, the soldiers retreated.*
retreat /rɪˈtriːt/ *n* [C/U] **1** the act of going away from a person or place because you are unwilling to fight any more or are frightened ○ [U] *Rebel soldiers were in (full) retreat.* **2** A retreat is also a private and safe place where you can be alone.

retrial /ˈriː·trɑɪl/ *n* [C] a new trial of a law case ○ *The appeals court ordered a retrial.*

retribution /ˌre·trəˈbjuː·ʃən/ *n* [U] *fml* deserved punishment ○ *He was seeking retribution for the crime committed against him.*

retrieve /rɪˈtriːv/ *v* [T] to find and bring back something ○ *Important historic documents were retrieved from a dumpster last week.*
retrieval /rɪˈtriː·vəl/ *n* [U] ○ *information storage and retrieval*

retro /ˈre·troʊ/ *adj* having the appearance of something that existed in the past ○ *a stylish retro look* ○ *retro fashions/cars/clothing*

retroactive /ˌre·troʊˈæk·tɪv/ *adj* [not gradable] (of a law or other agreement) having effect from the time before the law or agreement was approved ○ *I'm getting a retroactive salary increase.*
retroactively /ˌre·troʊˈæk·tɪv·li/ *adv* [not gradable] ○ *The courts cannot apply a new rule retroactively.*

retrospect /ˈre·trəˌspekt/ *n* an act of thinking about the past ○ **In retrospect**, (= thinking about the past now) *I think their marriage was doomed from the beginning.*
retrospective /ˌre·trəˈspek·tɪv/ *adj* looking back over the past ○ *He was the subject of a retrospective exhibit.*

return GO BACK /rɪˈtɜrn/ *v* [I] to come or go back to a previous place, subject, activity, or condition ○ *He returned to New York last week.* ○ *He* *worked at other jobs but kept returning to mining.* ○ *She was returning home from a business trip when the plane crashed.*

return /rɪˈtɜrn/ *n* [C] ○ *She looked forward to the return of spring.* ○ *On her return* (= When she came back), *she decided to take a few days off.*

return /rɪˈtɜrn/ *adj* [not gradable] **1** *return postage* **2** A return address is the address from which a letter is being sent.

PUT BACK /rɪˈtɜrn/ *v* [T] to put, send, or give something back to where it came from ○ *Emily returned the blouse because it didn't fit.*

EXCHANGE /rɪˈtɜrn/ *v* [T] to give, do, or get something in exchange ○ *She just doesn't return phone calls.*

return /rɪˈtɜrn/ *n*

DECIDE /rɪˈtɜrn/ *v* [T] *fml* to decide on something such as a judgment or decision ○ *The jury returned a verdict of not guilty.*

IDIOM with return

• **in return for** *something* as an exchange for something ○ *The farmer offered us food in return for our work.*

returns /rɪˈtɜrn/ *pl n* the results of voting in an ELECTION (= a political competition) ○ *Officials haven't finished counting the returns yet.*

reunification /ˌriːˌjuː·nɪ·fɪˈkeɪ·ʃən/ *n* [U] the process of joining two parts of something, esp. a country, that were previously divided ○ *The reunification of Germany meant that East Germany no longer existed as a legal entity.*

reunion /riːˈjuːn·jən/ *n* [C] a gathering of people who have been together before, esp. as a special event at a planned time ○ *a family reunion* ○ *a high school reunion*

reunite /ˌriː·jʊˈnɑɪt/ *v* [I/T] to bring together again ○ [T] *He was reunited with his sister after 14 years.*

R

reuse /riːˈjuːz/ *v* [T] to use something again ○ *We reuse our grocery bags.*

reusable /riːˈjuː·zə·bəl/ *adj* [not gradable] ○ *reusable containers*

rev /rev/ *v* [I/T] **-vv-** to increase the speed of the engine of a vehicle while the vehicle is not moving ○ [T] *The pilot moved the plane into position and revved its engines.*

PHRASAL VERB with rev

• **rev up** *something* [M] **1** to increase the speed of the engine of a vehicle while the vehicle is not moving ○ *He revved up the engine of the sportscar.* **2** If people rev up, they become more excited: *The art world is revving up for the Jackson Pollock show at the Museum of Modern Art.*

revamp /riːˈvæmp/ *v* [T] to change something, or to make or arrange something differently, in order to improve it ○ *This country's health care system needs revamping.*

reveal Ⓐ /rɪˈviːl/ *v* to make known or show something usually secret or hidden ○ *She revealed her history to him because she thought it was important.* ○ [+ that clause] *X-rays revealed that my ribs had been cracked but not broken.*

revealing Ⓐ /rɪˈviː·lɪŋ/ *adj* **1** showing more than is usual ○ *The dress code bans revealing clothing.* **2** Revealing also means explaining more than you might expect: *The book provides a revealing glimpse of how the organization works.*

revel /ˈrev·əl/ *v* [I] **-l-**, **-ll-** to dance, sing, and enjoy yourself with others in a noisy way

revelry /ˈrev·əl·ri/ *n* [C] the activity of a noisy party or other celebration

PHRASAL VERB with revel

• **revel in** *something* to get great pleasure from a situation or activity ○ *They reveled in their success.*

revelation Ⓐ /ˌrev·əˈleɪ·ʃən/ *n* [C/U] the act of making known something that was secret, or a fact that has been made known ○ [C] *The first planet discovered around an ordinary star was a strange and unexpected revelation.*

revenge /rɪˈvendʒ/ *n* [U] harm that you do to someone as a punishment for harm that the person has done to you ○ *He had been seeking a chance for revenge against those who had helped oust him from his leadership position in Congress.*

revenue Ⓐ /ˈrev·əˌnuː/ *n* [C/U] the income that a business or government receives regularly, or an amount representing such income ○ [C usually pl] *state/federal revenues* ○ [U] *Company revenue rose 4% last year.*

reverberate /rɪˈvɜr·bəˌreɪt/ *v* [I] (of sound) to continue to be heard; to ECHO repeatedly ○ *The loud music reverberated off the walls.*

revere /rɪˈvɪr/ *v* [T] to greatly respect and admire someone or something ○ *Nelson Mandela is widely revered for his courage and leadership.*

reverence /ˈrev·ə·rəns/ *n* [U] ○ *Most Americans have little reverence for their political leaders.*

Reverend /ˈrev·rənd, -ə·rənd/, *abbreviation* **Rev.** *n* [C] a title for a member of the Christian CLERGY (= official workers of the church) ○ *I'd like you to meet Reverend Smith.*

reverie /ˈrev·ə·ri/ *n* [C/U] (a state of having) pleasant thoughts ○ [U] *She was lost in reverie.*

reversal Ⓐ /rɪˈvɜr·səl/ *n* [C/U] a complete change of direction, order, or position ○ [C] *In a significant reversal of earlier trends, people are moving back to Salt Lake City.*

reverse Ⓐ /rɪˈvɜrs/ *v* [I/T] to cause something to go in the opposite direction, order, or position ○ [T] *The group is trying to reverse the trend toward developing the wetlands.*

reverse Ⓐ /rɪˈvɜrs/ *n* [C/U] **1** [U] *A car came down the street in reverse.* **2** A reverse is also a defeat or failure: [C] *He suffered a series of financial reverses in the 1980s.*

reverse Ⓐ /rɪˈvɜrs/ *adj* [not gradable] ○ *Repeat the steps in reverse order to shut the system off.*

reversible Ⓐ /rɪˈvɜr·sə·bəl/ *adj* **1** *a reversible condition* **2** Something that is reversible can be placed or worn with either side out: *a reversible jacket*

reverse discrimination *n* [U] the practice of giving unfair preference to people from groups such as African-Americans or women who were treated unfairly in the past so that someone else is at a disadvantage ○ Compare AFFIRMATIVE ACTION

reversion /rɪˈvɜr·ʒən/ *n* [U] *fml* a change back to a previous and often worse condition ○ *Reversion to the wild isn't easy for a captive animal.*

revert to *something* /rɪˈvɜrtˌtuː/ *phrasal verb* to go back to a previous condition ○ *The money will revert to the state general fund if it isn't claimed.*

review /rɪˈvjuː/ *v* [T] to consider something in order to make changes in it, study it, or give an opinion about it ○ *Officials have to review the text before it's made public.* ○ *Pauline Kael reviewed movies* (= wrote opinions about movies) *for "The New Yorker."* ○ *She spent half the night reviewing her notes for the French test* (= studying them again).
review /rɪˈvjuː/ *n* [C/U] ○ [U] *The proposed budget is under review.* ○ [C] *Cash's work got rave reviews* (= published opinions of it were good). ○ [C/U] *The teacher devoted the last week of the semester to review* (= studying again what was taught).
reviewer /rɪˈvjuː·ər/ *n* [C] someone who writes articles expressing an opinion about a book, play, movie, etc. ○ *She's the restaurant reviewer for the "New York Times."*

revile /rɪˈvɑɪl/ *v* [T] to criticize someone strongly ○ *Works of art are often reviled when they are first produced.*

revise Ⓐ /rɪˈvɑɪz/ *v* [I/T] **1** to change or correct something, esp. a piece of writing ○ [T] *With the final exam, you don't revise it after the teacher reads it.* **2** *Br* To revise is to study again what you have been learning in order to prepare for an exam.
revised Ⓐ /rɪˈvɑɪzd/ *adj* [not gradable] ○ *Her book is available in a new revised edition.*
revision Ⓐ /rɪˈvɪʒ·ən/ *n* [C/U] the act of changing or correcting something, or the thing that has been changed or corrected ○ [U] *The Senate is expected to act on tax revision.*

revisit /riːˈvɪz·ət/ *v* [T] to examine or consider something again, for example a subject or rule ○ *Justices have repeatedly refused to revisit issues raised by their 1980 decision.*

revitalize /riːˈvɑɪţ·əlˌɑɪz/ *v* [T] to put new life or energy into something ○ *to revitalize a city/the economy*

revival meeting, *short form* **revival** *n* [C] a Christian religious meeting that is intended to make people enthusiastic about Christianity

revive /rɪˈvɑɪv/ *v* [I/T] to come back to life, health, existence, or use, or bring something back to such a state ○ [T] *She tried to revive the unconscious woman.* ○ [I] *My plants revived as soon as I gave them a little water.*
revival /rɪˈvɑɪ·vəl/ *n* [C/U] **1** [C] *There's been a revival of ancient disputes in the region.* **2** A revival is also a performance of a play which has not been seen for a long time: [C] *a revival of Pinter's 1960 play*

revoke /rɪˈvoʊk/ *v* [T] to say officially that an agreement, permission, or law is no longer effective ○ *Licenses can be revoked for up to five years.*

revolt FIGHT /rɪˈvoʊlt/ *v* [I] to take violent action against authority, or to refuse to be controlled or ruled ○ *Californians may be ready to revolt against broad cuts in government services.*
revolt /rɪˈvoʊlt/ *n* [C/U] ○ [U] *a spirit of revolt* ○ [C] *The punk movement was a revolt against both the sound and the system of popular music.*
DISGUST /rɪˈvoʊlt/ *v* [T] to make someone feel disgusted ○ *I was revolted by his cruelty.*
revolting /rɪˈvoʊl·tɪŋ/ *adj* ○ *I've never eaten such revolting food!*

revolution Ⓐ /ˌrev·əˈluː·ʃən/ *n* [C/U] ***social studies*** a sudden and great change, esp. the violent change of a system of government ○ [U] *The country seems to be heading toward revolution.* ○ [C] *The discovery of penicillin produced a revolution in medicine.* ○ See also: REVOLUTION at REVOLVE
revolutionary Ⓐ /ˌrev·əˈluː·ʃəˌner·i/ *adj* ***social studies*** relating to a complete change in a system of government, or bringing or causing great change ○ *a revolutionary leader/program/idea* ○ *Computers have brought revolutionary changes to publishing.*
revolutionary Ⓐ /ˌrev·əˈluː·ʃəˌner·i/ *n* [C] ***social studies*** a person who supports or takes part in a revolution
revolutionize Ⓐ /ˌrev·əˈluː·ʃəˌnɑɪz/ *v* [T] to produce a very great or complete change in something ○ *Newton's discoveries revolutionized physics.*

revolve /rɪˈvɑlv, -ˈvɔːlv/ *v* [I/T] to move in a circle or a curve around a central point, or to cause something to do this ○ [T] *The plane revolved 162 degrees onto its back.* ○ [I] *The earth revolves around the sun, roughly in a circle.* ○ [I] *(fig.) His life revolves around* (= He is only interested in) *football.*
revolution /ˌrev·əˈluː·ʃən/ *n* [C/U] ○ [C] *The moon makes one revolution around the earth in about 29.5 days.* ○ See also: REVOLUTION

revolver /rɪˈvɑl·vər, -ˈvɔːl-/ *n* [C] a small gun that is held in one hand and can be fired several times before needing more bullets

revolving door *n* [C] **1** a set of doors that you go through by pushing them around in a circle **2** If you say that a situation is a revolving door, you mean that people or other things are continuously coming and going, rather than staying somewhere: *The department was a revolving door for top leaders, as 10 directors came and went over a dozen years.*

revue /rɪˈvjuː/ *n* [C] a theater show with songs, dances, jokes, and short plays, often about recent events

R

revulsion /rɪˈvʌl·ʃən/ *n* [U] a strong, often sudden, feeling of dislike or disgust ○ *Most of us feel only revulsion from such crimes.*

reward /rɪˈwɔːrd/ *n* [C/U] **1** something given in exchange for a useful idea, good behavior, excellent work, etc. ○ [U] *Students hoped for more reward than an announcement in the school paper of their achievement.* ○ [C] *The rewards* (= benefits) *of motherhood outweigh the difficulties.* **2** A reward is also an amount of money given to someone who gives information about a crime to the police or who helps to return lost or stolen property to its owner.

reward /rɪˈwɔːrd/ *v* [T] ○ *He was rewarded for his bravery with a medal from the president.*

rewarding /rɪˈwɔːrd·ɪŋ/ *adj* satisfying or beneficial ○ *a rewarding experience*

WORD FAMILY reward			
Nouns	reward	*Adjectives*	rewarding unrewarding
Verbs	reward		

rewind /riːˈwɑɪnd/ *v* [T] *past* **rewound** to put a TAPE recording back to the beginning

rework /riːˈwɜrk/ *v* [T] to change a speech, other writing, or a drawing to make it better or more suitable for a particular purpose

rewrite /riːˈrɑɪt/ *v* [T] *past simp.* **rewrote**, *past part.* **rewritten** ***writing*** to write a book, speech, etc. again to improve or change it or to correct information in it

rewrite /ˈriː·rɑɪt/ *n* [C] ***writing*** ○ *The producer says the last scene in the play needs a rewrite.*

rhapsody /ˈræp·səd·i/ *n* [C] a piece of music written without a formal structure that expresses powerful feelings and emotional excitement ○ *Gershwin's "Rhapsody in Blue"*

rhetoric /ˈreṭ·ə·rɪk/ *n* [U] **1** speech or writing that is effective and persuasive **2** ***literature*** Rhetoric is also the art of speaking and writing effectively, or the study of this art.

rhetorical /rɪˈtɔːr·ɪ·kəl, -ˈtɑr-/ *adj*

rhetorically /rɪˈtɔːr·ɪ·kli, -ˈtɑr-/ *adv* [not gradable] without expecting or needing an answer ○ *"Why did this happen to me?" she asked rhetorically.*

rhetorical question *n* [C] a statement made in the form of a question with no expectation of an answer

rhetorical strategy *n* [C] ***English*** one of four forms of writing and speech: DESCRIPTION, EXPOSITION EXPLANATION, NARRATION, PERSUASION

rheumatism /ˈruː·məˌtɪz·əm/ *n* [U] a medical condition that causes stiffness and pain in the joints or muscles

rhinestone /ˈrɑɪn·stoʊn/ *n* [C] a bright, colorless, artificial jewel that looks like a DIAMOND

rhinoceros /rɑɪˈnɑs·ə·rəs/, *short form* **rhino** /ˈrɑɪ·noʊ/ *n* [C] *pl* **rhinoceroses, rhinoceros** a very large, thick-skinned animal that eats plants and has one or two horns on its nose

rhizoid /ˈrɑɪ·zɔɪd/ *n* [C] ***biology*** a part similar to a root that provides food to some types of plants such as ALGAE and FUNGI

rhododendron /ˌroʊd·əˈden·drən/ *n* [C] a large evergreen bush with flat, shiny leaves and bright pink, purple, or white flowers

rhombus /ˈrɑm·bəs/ *n* [C] *pl* **rhombuses, rhombi** ***geometry*** a flat shape with four sides of equal length and four angles that usually are not 90° ○ Compare: PARALLELOGRAM; SQUARE ➤ Picture: **geometry**

rhubarb /ˈruː·bɑrb/ *n* [U] the long red stems of a plant that are prepared in a pie or as a sweet fruit dish

rhyme /rɑɪm/ *v* [I/T] ***literature*** (of words) to have the same final sound, or to use words that have the same final sound ○ [I] *"Love" and "above" rhyme.*

rhyme /rɑɪm/ *n* [C/U] ***literature*** ○ [C] *Can you think of a rhyme for "orange"?* ○ [U] *She does not use rhyme in her poems.*

rhyme scheme *n* [C] ***literature*** a regular pattern of rhyme at the end of the lines in a poem

rhythm /ˈrɪð·əm/ *n* [C/U] **1** ***music*** a regularly repeated pattern of sounds or beats used in music, poems, and dances ○ [C] *a jazz rhythm* ○ [U] *You need a sense of rhythm to be a good dancer.* **2** Rhythm is also a regular movement: [C] *The rhythm of a boat rocking in the water lulled him to sleep.* **3** Rhythm is also a regular pattern of change: [C] *Waking and sleeping are examples of biological rhythms.*

rhythmic /ˈrɪð·mɪk/, **rhythmical** /ˈrɪð·mɪ·kəl/ *adj* ○ *The rhythmic sound of the rain on the roof put the child to sleep.*

rhythm and blues, *abbreviation* **R&B** *n* [U] a type of popular music with a strong beat and jazz influence, developed by African-Americans in the 1940s and 1950s

rib BONE /rɪb/ *n* [C] **1** one of the bones that curve around from the SPINE (= the line of bones down the center of the back) on each side of the upper part of the body to form the chest **2** A rib is also a piece of meat taken from this part of an animal: *barbecued ribs* **3** Ribs are also the thin, curved pieces of metal or wood that shape and support the sides and bottom of a boat or the top of an UMBRELLA (= a cover that protects from rain or sun).

JOKE /rɪb/ *v* [T] **-bb-** *infml* to laugh at or joke about someone in a friendly way; TEASE ○ *The two leaders ribbed each other good-naturedly during the press conference.*

ribbon /ˈrɪb·ən/ *n* [C/U] **1** a long, narrow strip of material used to tie things together or as a decoration ○ [U] *He tied the present with ribbon.* ○ [C] *(fig.) A ribbon of road stretched before us.* **2** A ribbon

R

is also the narrow strip of material that contains the ink for a TYPEWRITER or computer PRINTER.

rib cage *n* [C] the structure in the body formed by the RIBS (= bones in the chest that protect the heart, lungs and other organs)

ribonucleic acid /ˌrɑɪ·boʊ·nʊˌkliː·ɪk ˈæs·əd, -ˌkleɪ·ɪk-/ *n* [C/U] ***biology*** RNA.

ribosomal RNA /ˌrɑɪ·bəˈsoʊ·məl ˌɑrˌenˈeɪ/, *abbreviation* **rRNA** *n* [U] ***biology*** the type of RNA (= a chemical in all living cells) that forms the RIBOSOME

ribosome /ˈrɑɪ·bəˌsoʊm/ *n* [C] ***biology*** a small structure in cells that produces PROTEIN from AMINO ACIDS

rice /rɑɪs/ *n* [U] the small brown or white seeds produced by a grass plant that are a major food source in many countries, or the plant itself, which is grown in warm, wet places

rice paddy *n* [C] a flooded field in which rice is grown

rice pudding *n* [C/U] a sweet dish made by cooking rice in milk and sugar

rich **WEALTHY** /rɪtʃ/ *adj* [*-er/-est* only] **1** having a lot of money or valuable possessions; wealthy ○ *a rich man* ○ *The United States is one of the world's richest nations.* **2** Rich also means made of something beautiful and expensive or valuable: *a rich brocade jacket*

rich /rɪtʃ/ *pl n* people who have a lot of money or valuable possessions ○ *The resort is crowded with the rich and famous in winter.*

riches /ˈrɪtʃ·əz/ *pl n* great wealth

WORD CHOICES rich

The adjectives **wealthy** and **well-off** are common alternatives to "rich."

*Oliver's parents are very **wealthy/well-off**.*

If someone is very rich, in informal situations you can use the adjective **loaded**.

*They don't have any money worries – they're **loaded**.*

If someone is richer than he or she was previously, the adjective **better off** is often used.

*We're a lot **better off** now that Jane's working again.*

The adjectives **affluent** and **prosperous** are sometimes used to describe areas where people are rich.

*It's a very **affluent** neighborhood.*

*In a **prosperous** country like this, no one should go hungry.*

HAVING A LOT /rɪtʃ/ *adj* [*-er/-est* only] **1** having or containing a large amount of something desirable or valuable ○ *The country is rich in oil, minerals, and timber.* ○ *Orange juice is rich in vitamin C.* ○ *The island has a rich and complex history* **2** Earth that is rich contains a large amount of substances that help plants to grow. **3** If the style or decoration of something, such as a piece of furniture or a building, is rich, it has a large amount of valuable and beautiful decoration.

riches /ˈrɪtʃ·əz/ *pl n* a large amount of something desirable or valuable ○ *oil/mineral/cultural riches*

richly /ˈrɪtʃ·li/ *adv* [not gradable] to a great degree ○ *richly decorated gowns of scarlet and gold* ○ *a richly deserved reward*

richness /ˈrɪtʃ·nəs/ *n* [U] ○ *the richness of detail* ○ *the richness of Mexico's history*

FOOD /rɪtʃ/ *adj* [*-er/-est* only] (of food) containing a large amount of oil, butter, eggs, or cream ○ *This chocolate butter cream is too rich for me.*

richness /ˈrɪtʃ·nəs/ *n* [U] ○ *The richness of the food made him feel slightly ill.*

COLOR/SOUND /rɪtʃ/ *adj* [*-er/-est* only] (of a color, sound, smell, or taste) strong in a pleasing or attractive way ○ *The fields were bathed in a rich, red-gold light from the setting sun.* ○ *He has a rich, resonant voice.*

WORD FAMILY rich

Nouns	rich riches richness enrichment	*Adjectives* *Verbs* *Adverbs*	rich enrich richly

Richter scale /ˈrɪk·tər/ *n* [U] a system that uses the numbers one through ten and that measures how severe an EARTHQUAKE is

rickety /ˈrɪk·ət̬·i/ *adj* in bad condition or weak and therefore likely to break ○ *a rickety old chair*

ricochet /ˈrɪk·əˌʃeɪ/ *v* [I] (of a ball, bullet, or other small object) to bounce off a surface ○ *The ball ricocheted off the goalie's foot and into the net.*

ricochet /ˈrɪk·əˌʃeɪ/ *n* [C] ○ *Carey bent a free kick that took three ricochets before landing in the goal.*

ricotta /rəˈkɑt̬·ə/ *n* [U] soft, white Italian cheese that does not have a strong flavor

rid /rɪd/ *v* [T] *past* **rid** to free a person or place of something unwanted or harmful ○ *In the city, it is hard to rid a building permanently of pests.*

riddle **QUESTION** /ˈrɪd·əl/ *n* [C] a question that has a surprising or amusing answer, or something that is a mystery or is hard to explain ○ *Scholars have not completely solved the riddle of the sphinx.*

MAKE HOLES /ˈrɪd·əl/ *v* [T] to make a lot of holes in something ○ *By the end of the game we had riddled the wall around the dartboard with a dozen little holes.*

riddled /ˈrɪd·əld/ *adj* [not gradable] full of something unwanted ○ *an old sweater riddled with holes* ○ *a book riddled with errors*

ride /rɑɪd/ *v* [I/T] *past simp.* **rode**, *past part.* **ridden** **1** to sit on a horse, bicycle, etc. and travel on it while controlling its movements, or to travel in a vehicle, such as a car, bus, or train ○ [I] *I ride to work on my bike.* ○ [T] *We rode the subway from Coney Island to the Bronx.* **2** To ride someone is to criticize someone, esp. to forcefully persuade that person to do more or to do what you want: [T] *Your boss rides you much too hard.*

R

ride /raɪd/ *n* [C] **1** a trip on an animal or bicycle, etc., or in a vehicle ○ *It's a short bus ride to the airport.* **2** A ride is also a machine in an amusement park which spins or moves people for entertainment: *My favorite ride is the Ferris wheel.*
rider /ˈraɪd·ər/ *n* [C] a person in a vehicle, or on an animal, bicycle, etc.
ridership /ˈraɪd·ərˌʃɪp/ *n* [U] the number of passengers on a transportation system ○ *This month, ridership on the Chicago subway went down again.*
riding /ˈraɪd·ɪŋ/ *n* [U] the sport or activity of riding horses ○ See also: RIDING ➤ Usage: **drive or ride?** at DRIVE USE VEHICLE

WORD FAMILY ride			
Nouns	ride rider riding ridership	*Adjectives* *Verbs*	overriding ride override

IDIOMS with ride

• **ride a wave of** *something*, **ride the wave of** *something* to be helped by being connected to something attractive or interesting ○ *The president was riding a wave of good feeling about the economy, but it didn't last long.*
• **riding high** doing very well ○ *The soccer team was riding high after winning four straight games.*

PHRASAL VERBS with ride

• **ride on** *something* to need something to make a result happen ○ *The future of the company is riding on the new management.*
• **ride out** *something* [M] to stay and experience a difficult situation, rather than trying to escape it ○ *Some of the children have fears about riding out another storm.*
• **ride up** **CHANGE POSITION** (of a piece of clothing) to move toward the top of the body ○ *That sweater rides up in the back.*
• **ride up** **TRAVEL TOWARD** [M] to travel toward someone or something on an animal, bicycle, or MOTORCYCLE ○ *Julie rode up on a mustang.* ○ *The boys rode up close to the group, then got off their bikes and walked.*

R

ridge /rɪdʒ/ *n* [C] **1** a long, narrow, raised part of a surface, esp. a high edge of a hill or mountain ○ *a mountain ridge* ○ *Plowed ridges looked like stripes across the field.* **2** A ridge of high pressure is a narrow air mass that brings good weather. **3** The ridge of a roof is where the sloping parts or sides come together at the top.

ridicule /ˈrɪd·əˌkjuːl/ *n* [U] words or actions that make someone or something seem foolish or stupid ○ *He was an unhappy figure of ridicule, not a figure of fun, among his colleagues.*
ridicule /ˈrɪd·əˌkjuːl/ *v* [T] to laugh at someone or something in an unkind way ○ *She was ridiculed for her old-fashioned ideas.*
ridiculous /rəˈdɪk·jə·ləs/ *adj* foolish or unreasonable and deserving to be laughed at ○ *Don't be ridiculous – there's no way I can buy a car.*

riding /ˈraɪd·ɪŋ/ *n* [C] *Cdn* a particular area of a country which is represented by an elected official ○ See also: RIDING at RIDE

rife /raɪf/ *adj* [not gradable] **1** (of something unpleasant) very common or frequent ○ *Graft and corruption were rife in city government.* **2** If a place is rife with something unpleasant, it is full of it: *The office is rife with rumors that many of us will be fired.*

riff /rɪf/ *n* [C] (in popular music) a simple tune that is used as a pattern for creating more complicated musical patterns

riffraff /ˈrɪf·ræf/ *pl n disapproving* people with a bad reputation or of a low social class ○ *She warned her son to keep away from such riffraff.*

rifle **GUN** /ˈraɪ·fəl/ *n* [C] a type of gun with a long BARREL (= cylindrical part) which is fired from the shoulder

SEARCH /ˈraɪ·fəl/ *v* [I/T] to search quickly through something, esp. in order to steal something ○ [I] *He rifled through the safe, but the diamonds were gone.*

HIT OR THROW /ˈraɪ·fəl/ *v* [T] to hit or throw a ball very hard ○ *By the game's end, he had rifled two balls out of the ball field.*

rift /rɪft/ *n* [C] something that divides partners or friends ○ *The border dispute caused a rift between Canada and the US.*

rig **ARRANGE** /rɪg/ *v* [T] **-gg-** to arrange an event or amount in a dishonest way ○ *The station had rigged gasoline prices.* ○ *Until this year, all elections were rigged by the ruling party.*

FIX IN PLACE /rɪg/ *v* [T] to fix a piece of equipment in place, or to put something together quickly, for temporary use ○ [M] *I rigged up a TV antenna from a coat hanger.*

STRUCTURE /rɪg/ *n* [C] a structure used to support machinery and equipment for a particular purpose ○ *an oil rig* ○ *a camera/plow rig*
rigging /ˈrɪg·ɪŋ/ *n* [U] the ropes that hold and control the sails on a boat or ship

TRUCK /rɪg/ *n* [C] a large truck consisting of at least two sections, including an engine to drive it and another part to hold a load ○ *A huge rig, a sixteen-wheeler, rolling downhill, flew right by me.*

rigamarole /ˈrɪg·ə·məˌroʊl/ *n* [U] RIGMAROLE

right **CORRECT** /raɪt/ *adj, adv* correct, true, or exact ○ *He said the trip would take two hours and he was absolutely/exactly right.* ○ *My watch has stopped – do you have the right time?* ○ *Ellen is the right person for the job.* ○ *She got every answer right.* ○ Opposite: WRONG NOT CORRECT
rightly /ˈraɪt·li/ *adv* [not gradable] ○ *I think these people don't rightly know what they're doing.* ➤ Usage: **correct or right?** at CORRECT

CONFUSABLES

right or true?

Right is usually used to say something is correct or to agree with something someone has said.
He gave the right answer.
"That's right, they live in downtown Minneapolis."
True is usually used to say that something is based on facts.

> *Is it true that she's leaving?*
> *Everything I've told you is true.*

WISE /rɑɪt/ *adj* having or showing good judgment; wise ○ [+ *to* infinitive] *The president was right to veto that bill.* ○ *I think we reached the right conclusion.*

rightly /ˈrɑɪt·li/ *adv* [not gradable] ○ *You did have the opportunity, and rightly or wrongly, you didn't follow up on it.*

SUITABLE /rɑɪt/ *adj, adv* suitable or desirable, or as it should be ○ [+ *to* infinitive] *He thought the time was right to expand his new business.* ○ *That hat looks just right on you.* ○ Opposite: WRONG NOT SUITABLE

MORAL RULE /rɑɪt/ *n* [U] **1** what is considered to be morally good or acceptable or fair ○ *You know the difference between right and wrong.* ○ [+ *to* infinitive] *You have no right* (= You are wrong) *to criticize me.* **2** Someone who is **in the right** is morally or legally correct. ○ *The jury had a hard time agreeing about which side was in the right.* ○ Opposite: WRONG IMMORAL

right /rɑɪt/ *adj, adv* [not gradable] considered fair or morally acceptable by most people ○ *It isn't right to tell a lie.*

right /rɑɪt/ *v* [T] ○ *Lawsuits were brought to right wrongs* (= to correct unfair situations) *in the workplace.*

rightly /ˈrɑɪt·li/ *adv* [not gradable] ○ *She rightly protested against the idea that women can't succeed in politics.*

LEGAL OPPORTUNITY /rɑɪt/ *n* [C] ***social studies*** your opportunity to act and to be treated in particular ways that the law promises to protect for the benefit of society ○ *civil/human rights* ○ *You have a right to a trial by jury.* ○ [+ *to* infinitive] *Patients have a right to keep their medical records confidential.* ○ *The dispute is over fishing rights.*

rightful /ˈrɑɪt·fəl/ *adj* [not gradable] ○ *The stolen property was returned to the rightful owners.*

rightfully /ˈrɑɪt·fə·li/ *adv* [not gradable] ○ *This portion of land is rightfully theirs.*

rights /rɑɪts/ *pl n* the legal authority to publish, copy, or make available a work such as a book, movie, recording, or work of art ○ *electronic/reprint rights*

DIRECTION /rɑɪt/ *adj, adv, n* [C/U] the side of the body opposite the side that contains the heart, or the direction that is the opposite of left ○ *Most people throw a ball with their right hand.* ○ *Our house is on the right.* ○ [C] *After you go over the bridge, make a right* (= turn to the right). ○ Opposite: LEFT DIRECTION

POLITICS /rɑɪt/ *n* [U] ***politics & government*** political groups that believe in limited government and economic controls, private ownership of property and wealth, and traditional social attitudes ○ Compare LEFT POLITICS

HEALTHY /rɑɪt/ *adj, adv* [not gradable] healthy, or working correctly ○ *I haven't felt right all day.*

AGREEMENT /rɑɪt/ *exclamation* used to express agreement with someone or to show that you have understood what someone has said ○ *"Robert, be sure to pick up Susan on your way home." "Right."*

EXACTLY /rɑɪt/ *adv* [not gradable] exactly; just ○ *I'm too busy to talk right now but I'll get back to you later.* ○ *He sat right behind me.* ○ *I'll be right back* (= I will return very soon).

WORD FAMILY right

Nouns	right	*Adjectives*	right
	rightness		righteous
	rights		rightful
	righteousness	*Adverbs*	right
Verbs	right		rightly
			rightfully

IDIOMS with right

• **get off on the right foot, start off on the right foot** to make a successful start ○ *He really got off on the right foot with my mother.*

• **right away** immediately ○ *I need someone to help me right away.*

• **right on** *slang* exactly correct ○ *I heard them talking about how we needed to change the way things work around here, and I was thinking to myself "right on!"* ○ **USAGE**: Used to agree with someone and show approval.

• **right on (the money)** exactly correct ○ *Shania guessed there were 126 jelly beans, and she was right on the money.*

right angle *n* [C] ***geometry*** an angle of 90° ○ *Join the two pieces of wood at a right angle.* ➤ Picture: **angle**

righteous /ˈrɑɪ·tʃəs/ *adj* behaving in a morally correct way, or considered morally correct ○ *a righteous man*

right-hand *adj* [not gradable] on or to the right ○ *The picture is on the right-hand page.*

right-handed *adj* [not gradable] using the right hand for writing and for most other things ○ Compare LEFT-HANDED

right triangle *n* [C] ***geometry*** a triangle with an angle of 90° ➤ Picture: **triangle**

right-wing *adj* supporting the political opinions of the right

right-winger *n* [C] a person who supports the political right

rigid Ⓐ **NOT VARYING** /ˈrɪdʒ·əd/ *adj* not permitting any change ○ *rigid rules of behavior* ○ *I keep to a rigid schedule.*

rigidly Ⓐ /ˈrɪdʒ·əd·li/ *adv* ○ *rigidly defined terms*

rigidity Ⓐ /rəˈdʒɪd·əţ·i/ *n* [U]

STIFF /ˈrɪdʒ·əd/ *adj* not able to be bent ○ *rigid plastic*

rigidly /ˈrɪdʒ·əd·li/ *adv*

rigidity /rəˈdʒɪd·əţ·i/ *n* [U]

rigmarole /ˈrɪg·məˌroʊl/, **rigamarole** *n* [U] a long, complicated, or silly process ○ *You have to go through this whole rigmarole before you can register for a course.*

rigor, *Cdn, Br* **rigour** /ˈrɪg·ər/ *n* [U] high standards ○ *She studied ways to improve academic rigor in high schools.*

R

rigorous /ˈrɪg·ə·rəs/ *adj* severe or difficult, esp. because at a high level ○ *rigorous standards of accuracy* ○ *The Manhattan district attorney's office had a pretty rigorous training program.*

rigors /ˈrɪg·ərz/ *pl n* difficult conditions ○ *Chan shows how the rigors of big-city American life can affect a new immigrant.*

rile /rɑɪl/ *v* [T] to annoy or make angry ○ *Many farmers have been riled by Department of Agriculture fines.* ○ [M] *Your loud parties rile up the neighbors.*

rim /rɪm/ *n* [C] the outer edge of something, esp. of something curved or circular ○ *The rim of this cup is chipped.*

rind /rɑɪnd/ *n* [C/U] the hard outer layer or covering of some fruits and foods ○ [U] *lemon/orange/melon rind*

ring **CIRCLE** /rɪŋ/ *n* [C] **1** a circular piece, esp. of jewelry worn on a finger ○ *a gold wedding ring* **2** A ring is also any group of things or people in a circular shape or arrangement: *a key ring* ○ *A ring of people joined hands in the dance.* **3** ***earth science*** A ring is also the small pieces of matter that circle around a planet.

ring /rɪŋ/ *v* [T] to surround something ○ *The island is ringed with rocks.*

SOUND /rɪŋ/ *v* [I/T] *past simp.* **rang**, *past part.* **rung** to make a sound, esp. the sound made when metal is hit, or to cause a bell to make a sound ○ [I] *The telephone rang.* ○ [T] *I rang the doorbell but nobody answered.* ○ [I] *My ears are ringing* (= I hear a noise that is not really there).

ring /rɪŋ/ *n* [C usually sing] a telephone call ○ *I'll give Sophia a ring.*

ringer /ˈrɪŋ·ər/ *n* [C usually sing] ○ *I turned the ringer off on my phone so I could get some sleep.*

GROUP /rɪŋ/ *n* [C] a group of people who work together, often secretly in criminal activities ○ *a spy ring*

R

SPACE /ˈrɪŋ/ *n* [C] a space where people perform or compete that is separated from, and usually at the center of, the space where people can watch the event ○ *a boxing ring* ○ *a one-ring/three-ring circus*

IDIOM with **ring**

• *something* **rings a bell** something, esp. a name, is familiar to you ○ *His name rang a bell, but I don't know where I met him.*

PHRASAL VERBS with **ring**

• **ring up** *something* **SELL** [M] to record items being bought and calculate the cost, using a CASH REGISTER ○ *He finished ringing up a sale and handed Mrs. Drummond her change.*

• **ring up** *someone* **TELEPHONE** [M] to telephone someone ○ *She rang me up at home.*

ringleader /ˈrɪŋˌliːd·ər/ *n* [C] the leader of a group of people who cause trouble or commit crimes

ringside /ˈrɪŋ·sɑɪd/ *n* [U] the area just outside the space where people compete or perform ○ *They had ringside seats.*

ringworm /ˈrɪŋ·wɜrm/ *n* [U] a disease caused by a FUNGUS that leaves red rings on the skin

rink /rɪŋk/ *n* [C] a large, separate area having a flat surface specially prepared, sometimes with ice, for SKATING, or a building having such an area ○ *an ice-skating/roller-skating rink*

rinse /rɪns/ *v* [T] to use water to clean soap or dirt from something ○ *Rinse the silverware before drying it.* ○ [M] *Don't forget to rinse the dishes off.* ○ [M] *Did you rinse out your bathing suit?*

rinse /rɪns/ *n* [C usually sing] **1** *I put the clothes through a cold rinse in the washing machine.* **2** A rinse is also a temporary coloring for hair.

riot /ˈrɑɪ·ət/ *n* [C] **1** a noisy and violent public gathering ○ *The streets in this district include South Central Los Angeles, where the riots broke out two years ago.* **2** *infml* A riot is also something very amusing: [C usually sing] *The show was a riot.*

riot /ˈrɑɪ·ət/ *v* [I] ○ *Inmates rioted yesterday at the prison.*

rioter /ˈrɑɪ·ət̬·ər/ *n* [C] ○ *The police said 80 rioters had been arrested.*

rip **TEAR** /rɪp/ *v* [I/T] **-pp-** **1** to tear something quickly and with force, or to break apart something ○ [T] *I ripped my sleeve.* ○ [T] *The wind ripped the flag to shreds.* ○ [M] *The letter made me so angry, I ripped it up.* ○ [M] *He lost control of the car and it ripped down a fence.* **2** To rip out something is to remove it: [M] *The previous owner ripped out the fireplace.*

MOVE QUICKLY /rɪp/ *v* [I always + adv/prep] to move quickly or violently ○ *A hurricane ripped through Rhode Island yesterday.*

rip into *someone/something* to attack or criticize someone or something with great force ○ *Riker was not going to give her lawyer a chance to rip into his witnesses before the trial.*

PHRASAL VERB with **rip**

• **rip off** *someone/something* [M] *infml* to cheat someone by charging too much money, or to steal something ○ *We got ripped off buying our new car.* ○ *Some accuse the company of ripping off the programming language from its competitor.* ○ Related noun: RIP-OFF

ripe /rɑɪp/ *adj* **1** wholly developed, esp. of fruit ready to be collected or eaten ○ *The tomatoes aren't ripe.* **2** *fig.* A ripe old age is a very old age: *My grandmother lived to the ripe old age of 95.*

ripen /ˈrɑɪ·pən/ *v* [I/T] ○ [I] *Mangoes need to ripen at room temperature until the fruit yields to the touch.*

IDIOM with **ripe**

• **ripe for** *something* ready or in a good condition for something to happen ○ *The city is ripe for an explosion in the film industry.*

rip-off *n* [C] *slang* an act of cheating someone by charging too much or not giving anything of value for money spent ○ *Don't eat in the museum restaurant – it's a rip-off.* ○ Related verb: RIPOFF

ripple /ˈrɪp·əl/ *n* [C] **1** a small wave or a slight movement of a surface, esp. the surface of water

○ *The stone hit the water and caused a ring of ripples to spread out.* **2** A ripple is also a sound or feeling that is slight but is noticed: *A ripple of laughter ran through the crowd.* ○ *The story created ripples of alarm here in Washington.*

ripple /ˈrɪp·əl/ *v* [I/T] **1** [T] *A breeze rippled the water.* **2** Something that ripples moves in a way that is not obvious but is noticeable: [I always + adv/prep] *A shy smile rippled nervously over his features.*

ripple effect *n* [C] a series of things that happen as the result of a particular action or event ○ *It is hoped the arts center will have a ripple effect by attracting more shops and other arts-related activities.*

rise MOVE UP /rɑɪz/ *v* [I] *past simp.* **rose**, *past part.* **risen 1** to move up from a lower to a higher position, or to become higher ○ *Smoke rose from the campfire.* ○ *The trail rises gently to the top of the ridge.* ○ *We watched the sun rise over the bay.* ○ *New buildings are rising* (= becoming higher as they are built) *throughout the city.* ○ *On a clear day, you can see the mountains rising* (= appearing high) *in the distance.* **2** To rise is also to stand up: *She rose to welcome us.* **3** To rise is also to get out of bed, esp. in the morning.

rise /rɑɪz/ *n* [C] a small hill or slope ○ *The house is built on a rise.*

riser /ˈrɑɪ·zər/ *n* [C] ○ *Paul is an early riser* (= gets out of bed early).

INCREASE /rɑɪz/ *v* [I] *past simp.* **rose**, *past part.* **risen 1** to become more or greater in amount, size, or degree; increase ○ *Real estate prices have risen rapidly.* ○ *The temperature rose to 80° by midday.* ○ *Our hopes rose when the doctors told us that she was conscious and alert.* ○ *A murmur rose from the crowd* (= began to be heard). **2** To rise is also to move into a more important rank or position: *He rose to fame in the 1940s.*

rise /rɑɪz/ *n* [C/U] ○ [C] *a rise in temperature* ○ [U] *Inflation is on the rise* (= increasing).

CONFUSABLES

rise or raise?

Be careful not to confuse these two verbs. **Rise** means to increase or move up. This verb cannot be followed by an object.

The price of energy is rising.

~~*The price of energy is raising.*~~

Raise means to lift something to a higher position or to increase an amount or level. This verb must always be followed by an object.

Power companies keep raising the price of energy.

~~*Power companies keep rising the price of energy.*~~

FIGHT /rɑɪz/ *v* [I always + adv/prep] *past simp.* **rose**, *past part.* **risen** to begin to oppose or fight (esp. a bad government or ruler) as a group ○ *He urged his followers to rise up against the oppressive regime.*

PHRASAL VERBS with **rise**

• **rise above** *something* to not allow something unpleasant to influence your behavior ○ *She rose above the personal tragedy in her life and became a senator.*

• **rise to** *something* to react to a difficult situation by working hard to succeed ○ *There were some other very good competitors, but Megan rose to the challenge and sang beautifully.*

risk /rɪsk/ *n* [C/U] **1** danger, or the possibility of danger, defeat, or loss ○ [C] *There's a risk of an accident happening in this fog.* ○ [C] *I was afraid to take the risk of quitting my job before I had another one lined up.* ○ [U] *We want clean rivers and lakes, where you can swim without risk to your health.* ○ [U] *It was a high/low risk situation* (= a situation with a lot of/very little danger). **2** A risk is also someone or something that could cause a problem or loss: [C] *Teenage drivers are considered higher risks.* **3** To be **at risk** is to be in danger: *A child who hasn't been vaccinated is at risk.*

risk /rɪsk/ *v* [T] to do something or to enter a situation where there is a possibility of being hurt or of a loss or defeat ○ *He risked his life helping another man escape the fire.* ○ *We risk losing the business if we don't pay off the loan on time.*

risky /ˈrɪs·ki/ *adj* ○ *The business investment was a risky proposition.*

risqué /rɪˈskeɪ/ *adj* slightly shocking, usually because of being connected with sex

rite /rɑɪt/ *n* [C] a set of fixed words and actions, often said and done as part of a religious ceremony ○ *the marriage rite*

ritual /ˈrɪtʃ·ə·wəl/ *n* [C/U] **1** a set of actions or words performed in a regular way, often as part of a religious ceremony **2** A ritual is also any act done regularly, usually without thinking about it: [C] *My morning ritual includes reading the newspaper while I drink my coffee.*

ritzy /ˈrɪt·si/ *adj* [*-er/-est* only] *infml* expensive and showy ○ *They had a ritzy wedding.*

rival /ˈrɑɪ·vəl/ *n* [C] a person, group, or organization competing with others for the same thing or in the same area ○ *business/political rivals*

rival /ˈrɑɪ·vəl/ *adj* [not gradable] ○ *rival political organizations* ○ *rival claims*

rival /ˈrɑɪ·vəl/ *v* [T] to equal or be as good as ○ *No computer can rival a human brain.*

rivalry /ˈrɑɪ·vəl·ri/ *n* [C/U] a serious and often continuing competition ○ [C] *Jerusalem was the scene of more passions and rivalries than any other city on earth.*

river /ˈrɪv·ər/ *n* [C] **1** water that flows naturally through a wide channel that is surrounded by land ○ *the Mississippi River* ○ *We went swimming in the river.* **2** A river is also any large flow of a liquid: *Rivers of sweat ran down his back.*

riverbank /ˈrɪv·ərˌbæŋk/ *n* [C] the land at either side of a river

riverbed /ˈrɪv·ərˌbed/ *n* [C] the low ground over which a river flows

riverside /ˈrɪv·ərˌsɑɪd/ *n* [U] the land along either side of a river

R

rivet /ˈrɪv·ət/ *n* [C] a metal pin used to fasten together flat pieces of metal or other thick materials such as leather
rivet /ˈrɪv·ət/ *v* [T] **1** *Parts of the aircraft are riveted together.* **2** If something rivets someone, it attracts and keeps someone's attention: *Her performance riveted the audience.*
riveting /ˈrɪv·ət̬·ɪŋ/ *adj* extremely interesting ○ *a riveting TV show*

R.N. *n* [C] *abbreviation for* REGISTERED NURSE ○ *Ruth Retallack, R.N.*

RNA *n* [U] ***biology*** *abbreviation for* ribonucleic acid (= an important chemical present in all living cells)

roach /roʊtʃ/ *n* [C] *short form of* COCKROACH

road /roʊd/ *n* [C/U] **1** a route for traveling between places by vehicle, esp. one that has been specially surfaced and made flat ○ [C] *a gravel/dirt/paved road* **2** Road (*abbreviation* **Rd.**) is often used in the names of roads: [U] *82 Mill Road*

IDIOMS with road

• **on the road** traveling to different places ○ *The band spends three months a year on the road.*
• **on the road to** *something* likely to achieve something ○ *The doctors say she's on the road to recovery.*

roadblock /ˈroʊd·blɑk/ *n* [C] **1** a temporary structure put across a road to stop traffic, esp. to try to stop illegal activity ○ *a police roadblock* **2** *fig.* A roadblock can also be anything that stops progress: *There have been several roadblocks in the peace process.*

road rage *n* [U] dangerous behavior by people who become angry while driving a vehicle

roadrunner /ˈroʊdˌrʌn·ər/ *n* [C] a fast-running bird from the southwestern US, Mexico, and Central America which has a long tail and feathers that stand up on the top of its head

roadside /ˈroʊd·sɑɪd/ *n* [C] the edge of a road

R

road test DRIVING TEST *n* [C] an official test of driving skill that must be passed in order to obtain a DRIVER'S LICENSE

VEHICLE TEST *n* [C] a test of a new vehicle, machine, or idea to see how well it works ○ *The truck currently is undergoing a seven-day road test and initial reports are good.*

road trip *n* [C] a long trip taken for pleasure or business in which the travel is on roads

roadway /ˈroʊd·weɪ/ *n* [C] the part of the road on which vehicles drive

roadworthy /ˈroʊdˌwɜr·ði/ *adj* (of vehicles) in good condition for driving

roam /roʊm/ *v* [I/T] to walk or travel without any real purpose or direction ○ [I] *Our dog just likes to roam.*

roar /rɔːr, roʊr/ *v* [I] **1** to make a long, loud, deep sound ○ *Lions were roaring in their cages.* ○ *The crowd roared with laughter.* **2** If a vehicle roars somewhere, it moves there quickly making a lot of noise: *His truck roared down the steep mountain.*
roar /rɔːr, roʊr/ *n* [C/U] ○ [U] *Living near the highway, we hear the constant roar of traffic.*
roaring /ˈrɔːr·ɪŋ, ˈroʊr-/ *adj, adv* **1** *a roaring river* **2** A roaring fire is very large, noisy, and bright.

roast /roʊst/ *v* [I/T] to cook meat or other food by dry heat in an OVEN or over a fire
roast /roʊst/, **roasted** /ˈroʊ·stəd/ *adj* [not gradable] ○ *roast beef/turkey*
roast /roʊst/ *n* [C] **1** a large piece of meat cooked in an OVEN ○ *a beef roast* **2** A roast is also an outside event at which food is cooked over a fire: *a lobster roast*

rob /rɑb/ *v* [T] **-bb- 1** to take money or property from a person or place illegally ○ *Two men robbed the store last night.* **2** If someone is robbed of a quality, that quality is taken away: *Elderly people should not be robbed of their dignity.*
robber /ˈrɑb·ər/ *n* [C] a person who takes money or property illegally
robbery /ˈrɑb·ə·ri/ *n* [C/U] ○ [U] *armed robbery* ○ [C] *He's accused of several bank robberies.*

robe /roʊb/ *n* [C] a long, loose-fitting piece of clothing, esp. one worn at home ○ *I had on pajamas and a robe.*

robin /ˈrɑb·ən/ *n* [C] a brown North American bird with a red chest

robot /ˈroʊ·bɑt, -bət/ *n* [C] a mechanical device that works automatically or by computer control ○ *Industrial robots are replacing people.*
robotic /roʊˈbɑt̬·ɪk/ *adj* ○ *He spoke in a robotic monotone.*
robotics /roʊˈbɑt̬·ɪks/ *n* [U] the science of designing and operating ROBOTS

robust /roʊˈbʌst/ *adj* (of a person, animal, or plant) strong and healthy, or (of food or drink) full of flavor ○ *She was in robust health.* ○ *The house blend of coffee is particularly robust.*

rock STONE /rɑk/ *n* [C/U] **1** a large mass of stone that sticks up out of the ground or the sea, or a separate piece of stone ○ [U] *This is some of the oldest rock on the earth's surface.* ○ [C] *Waves crashed against the rocks.* ○ [C] *Bees poured into the neighborhood when boys threw rocks at the hives.* ○ Compare MINERAL; SOIL EARTH **2** *slang* A rock is also a DIAMOND or other jewel.
rocky /ˈrɑk·i/ *adj* covered with, or consisting of, stones ○ *a rocky path* ○ See also: ROCKY

MOVE /rɑk/ *v* [I/T] **1** to move something or cause something to move backward and forward or from side to side ○ [T] *He rocked the baby to sleep.* ○ [I] *If you rock back on that chair, you're going to break it.* **2** If a building or area rocks, it shakes it violently: [T] *An earthquake rocked the downtown area today.* **3** If a person or place is rocked, it is surprised, upset, or excited: [T] *The university was rocked by the scandal.*
rocker /ˈrɑk·ər/ *n* [C] a ROCKING CHAIR (= a chair built on two pieces of curved wood), or one of the two curved pieces under the chair that allow it to move forward and backward

MUSIC /rɑk/, **rock-and-roll** /ˌrɑk·ənˈroʊl/, **rock 'n' roll** *n* [U] a type of popular music with a strong beat, which is usually played with electric guitars and drums

rocker /ˈrɑk·ər/ *n* [C] *infml* someone who performs or likes ROCK music

BE EXCELLENT /rɑk/, *n* [I/T] to be extremely good ○ [I] *She's such a great role model for young women – she really rocks!*

IDIOMS with **rock**

• **on the rocks** **1** *infml* failing ○ *Their marriage is on the rocks.* **2** If an alcoholic drink is **on the rocks**, it is served with ice.

• **rock the boat** *infml* to do or say something that upsets people or causes problems ○ *It's better not to rock the boat when you first start a job.*

rock-bottom *adj infml* at the lowest possible level or in the worst situation ○ *rock-bottom prices* ○ *The team hit rock bottom, losing 12 games in a row.*

rocket /ˈrɑk·ət/ *n* [C] a cylindrical device containing material that explodes, sending the device through the air ○ *The rocket was launched yesterday.*

rocket /ˈrɑk·ət/ *v* [I/T] to travel by rocket, or to rise, increase, or move very quickly ○ [T] *The astronauts were rocketed into space.* ○ [I] *A train rocketed by.* ○ [I] *Anna rocketed to fame in the late 1980s.*

IDIOM with **rocket**

• **it doesn't take a rocket scientist to** *do something*, **you don't have to be a rocket scientist to** *do something humorous* it is easy to do or understand something ○ *It doesn't take a rocket scientist to figure out that if you treat her well, she'll be happier.*

rocking chair, *short form* **rocker** /ˈrɑk·ər/ *n* [C] a chair built on two pieces of curved wood so that you can move forward and backward when you sit in it

rocking horse *n* [C] a toy horse that a child sits on and goes backward and forward

rocky /ˈrɑk·i/ *adj* difficult or uncertain ○ *Their season got off to a rocky start with three straight losses.* ○ See also: ROCKY at ROCK **STONE**

rod /rɑd/ *n* [C] a long, thin pole made of wood, metal, or other material ○ *a fishing/curtain rod*

rode /roʊd/ *past simple of* RIDE

rodent /ˈroʊd·ᵊnt/ *n* [C] a type of small mammal with sharp front teeth ○ *They expect to catch rodents, mostly mice.*

rodeo /ˈroʊd·iːˌoʊ, rəˈdeɪ·oʊ/ *n* [C] *pl* **rodeos** a public performance or competition in which COWBOYS (= people who take care of cattle) show their skill at riding cattle and wild horses and at catching cattle with ropes

roe /roʊ/ *n* [U] the mass of eggs inside a female fish, which is eaten as food

rogue /roʊg/ *n* [C] a person, organization, or country that does not behave in the usual or acceptable way ○ *Buzzy's a fun-loving teenage rogue.*

rogue /roʊg/ *adj* [not gradable] ○ *A rogue employee might tap into the computer.*

role Ⓐ **DUTY** /roʊl/ *n* [C] the duty or use that someone or something usually has or is expected to have ○ *Bouchard hopes to play a pivotal/major/key role in Quebec's future.*

REPRESENTATION /roʊl/ *n* [C] the person whom an actor represents in a movie or play ○ *Astin plays the role of Radford, the store's owner.*

role model *n* [C] a person whose behavior is copied by others

roll **MOVE** /roʊl/ *v* [I/T] **1** to move in a direction by turning over and over or by traveling on wheels, or to cause something to move in this way ○ [I] *The coin rolled off the table.* ○ [T] *I rolled the spare tire around to the side of the car.* ○ [I] *Tears rolled down his cheeks.* ○ *Bob* **rolled over** (= turned his body while lying down) *onto his stomach.* **2** If you roll a car window up or down, you turn a handle or press a button that opens or closes the window.

roll /roʊl/ *n* [C/U] ○ [C] *You have to allow for the roll of the ball when it lands after you hit it.*

roller /ˈroʊ·lər/ *n* [C] a cylinder or wheel that turns over and over in order to move something along

FORM ROUNDED SHAPE /roʊl/ *v* [T] to form something soft into a rounded shape ○ *He rolled the clay into a ball.* ○ [M] *She rolled up her pants so they wouldn't get wet.*

roll /roʊl/ *n* [C] **1** a long piece of something that bends, formed into a cylinder ○ *a roll of film/tape/aluminum foil* **2** A roll is also a rounded mass of something: *rolls of fat*

SOUND /roʊl/ *v* [I/T] to make a continuous repeated sound ○ [I] *Thunder rolled in the distance.*

roll /roʊl/ *n* [C usually sing] ○ *a drum roll*

LIST /roʊl/ *n* [C] an official list of names ○ *a roll of eligible voters*

BREAD /roʊl/ *n* [C] a small loaf of bread

WORD FAMILY **roll**			
Nouns	roll roller	*Verbs*	roll unroll

IDIOMS with **roll**

• **on a roll** *infml* experiencing a period of success or good luck ○ *They've won nine games in a row, so they're obviously on a roll.*

• **(all) rolled into one** combined ○ *He is a businessman, community leader, and family man all rolled into one.* ○ **USAGE:** Used esp. to talk about someone or something that has many good qualities.

• **roll** *your* **eyes** to move your eyes around in a circle because someone has said or done something stupid or strange ○ *"Don't pay any attention to what he says," Carrie said rolling her eyes.*

• **rolling in the aisles** *infml* laughing very hard ○ *The comedian had the audience rolling in the aisles.*

• **roll out the red carpet (for** *someone***)** to give a guest special treatment ○ *New York rolled out the red carpet for the astronauts.*

• **roll up** *your* **sleeves** *infml* to prepare for hard work ○ *We've planned everything – now it's time to roll up our sleeves and get started.*

R

PHRASAL VERBS with roll

• **roll around** (of a time or event) to happen ○ *Will you still be here when spring rolls around?*

• **roll back** *something* [M] to reduce something to an earlier level or standard ○ *The president's plan to roll back environmental protections was not popular.* ○ *The governor plans to roll property taxes back.* ○ **USAGE:** Usually said about a price or rate

• **roll in 1** to arrive ○ *Fog rolled in overnight.* **2** *infml* If you say someone rolls in, you mean that person has arrived late or unexpectedly: *What time did you roll in last night?* **3** *infml* If something such as money rolls in, it arrives in large amounts: *Business was great, and the money was rolling in.*

• **roll out** *something* **MAKE SMOOTH** [M] to make something smooth and flat, by pushing a cylindrical object or tool over it ○ *Roll out the cookie dough between two sheets of wax paper.*

• **roll out** *something* **MAKE AVAILABLE** [M] to make something available or known to people for the first time ○ *The company has rolled out new services faster than any other in the field.* ○ Related noun: ROLLOUT

roll call *n* [C] the act of reading aloud the names of people on a list to check whether they are present

roller /ˈroʊ·lər/ *n* [C] a cylinder used for shaping something, or for spreading something over a surface ○ *hair rollers* ○ *a paint roller*

Rollerblade /ˈroʊ·lərˌbleɪd/ *n* [C] *trademark* an IN-LINE SKATE

roller coaster /ˈroʊ·lərˌkoʊ·stər/ *n* [C] *pl* **roller coasters 1** a small railroad, esp. in an AMUSEMENT PARK, with open cars that travel quickly along a steep, curved track **2** A roller coaster is also a feeling, situation, or experience that changes very quickly: *an emotional roller coaster*

roller skate /ˈroʊ·lərˌskeɪt/ *n* [C usually pl] a boot with wheels on the bottom that lets you roll quickly over a smooth surface

roller-skate /ˈroʊ·lərˌskeɪt/ *v* [I] ○ *Jessica loves to roller-skate in the park.*

R

rollicking /ˈrɑl·ɪ·kɪŋ/ *adj* [not gradable] (esp. of an experience or story) happening with a lot of fast action and good humor and often noise ○ *a rollicking adventure movie*

rolling /ˈroʊ·lɪŋ/ *adj* [not gradable] (of hills) gently rising and falling

rolling pin *n* [C] a cylinder that you roll over DOUGH or pastry to make it flat

rollout /ˈroʊ·lɑʊt/ *n* [C] **1** the act of making something, esp. a product or service, available for the first time ○ *Since its rollout in fall of 1999, PayPal has gained millions of members.* **2** A rollout of proposals, laws, or information is the first time they are made known to the public. ○ Related verb: ROLL OUT

Roman Catholic /ˌroʊ·mən ˈkæθ·ə·lɪk/ *n* [C] a member of the largest Christian religion

Roman Catholic /ˌroʊ·mən ˈkæθ·ə·lɪk/ *adj* [not gradable] ○ *a Roman Catholic priest* ○ *the Roman Catholic church*

Roman Catholicism /ˌroʊ·mən·kəˈθɑl·əˌsɪz·əm/ *n* [U] the beliefs of the Roman Catholic religion

romance /roʊˈmæns, ˈroʊ·mæns/ *n* [C/U] **1** a close relationship between two people who are in love with each other ○ [C] *Their three-year romance never went smoothly.* **2** Romance is also the feeling of comfort and pleasure you experience in a relationship with someone you love: [U] *Without romance, marriage is a lot like an old habit.* **3** Romance is also a quality of excitement or mystery connected with an experience or place: [U] *He loves the romance of traveling by train.* **4** ***literature*** A romance is a story of love between two people, often containing exciting events or magic: [C] *He is the successful author of rollicking historical romances.*

WORD FAMILY romance

Nouns	romance romantic	*Adjectives*	romantic unromantic romanticized
Verbs	romance romanticize	*Adverbs*	romantically

Roman numeral /ˈroʊ·mən ˈnuː·mə·rəl/ *n* [C] one of the letters that the ancient Romans used to write numbers ○ *Written in Roman numerals, 14=XIV and 2001=MMI.* ○ Compare ARABIC NUMERAL

romantic /roʊˈmænt·ɪk/ *adj* **1** relating to love or to an affectionate, loving relationship ○ *a romantic comedy/novel* **2** If something is romantic, it is exciting and mysterious and has a strong effect on your emotions: *I think Egypt is an incredibly romantic country.* **3** Romantic ideas and people are not practical or related to real life: *She has a romantic idea of what it's like to be an actor.*

romantic /roʊˈmænt·ɪk/ *n* [C] ○ *You're such an old-fashioned romantic, always bringing me flowers.*

romantically /roʊˈmænt·ɪ·kli/ *adv* ○ *Their names have been romantically linked.*

romanticize /roʊˈmænt·əˌsɑɪz/ *v* [T] to believe that something is better, more interesting, or more exciting than it really is ○ *He romanticized the life of a spy, not knowing how boring and lonely it can be.*

romp /rɑmp, rɔːmp/ *v* [I] **1** to play or run in a happy, excited, and noisy way ○ *The puppy and children romped together in the yard.* **2** To romp is also to succeed or win easily: *The unbeaten Charlottesville Crackers romped past the Beantown Beanies 68-26.*

romp /rɑmp, rɔːmp/ *n* [C usually sing] **1** *The film is a comic romp.* **2** A romp is also an easy victory over an opponent: *Nothing could stop his romp to the nomination.*

roof /ruːf, rʊf/ *n* [C] **1** the covering that forms the top of a building, vehicle, or other object ○ *The school has a flat roof.* **2** The roof of your mouth is the mouth's upper, inside surface: *Peanut butter sticks to the roof of your mouth.*

roof /ruːf, rʊf/ *v* [T] ○ *They roofed the house with old-fashioned shingles.*

roofing /ˈruː·fɪŋ, ˈrʊf·ɪŋ/ *n* [U] material used for roofs, or the process of building roofs

IDIOM with **roof**

• **a roof over** *your* **head** a place to live ○ *It is hard to keep a roof over your head and food in the fridge when you get paid $6.50 an hour.*

roof rack *n* [C] a device attached to the roof of a car to hold bicycles, boxes, etc.

rooftop /ˈruːf·tɑp, ˈrʊf-/ *n* [C] the top surface of the roof of a building

rook /rʊk/, **castle** *n* [C] (in the game of CHESS) a piece that can move in a straight line in any direction but not on a diagonal

rookie /ˈrʊk·i/ *n* [C] a person with little experience who is just starting to work in a job or to play on a sports team ○ *a rookie goalie/cop*

room PLACE /ruːm, rʊm/ *n* [C] an area within a building that has its own walls, floor, ceiling, and door ○ *The house has a laundry room.*
room /ruːm, rʊm/ *v* [I always + adv/prep] to share a room with someone, esp. a rented room ○ *I roomed with Anita in college.*

SPACE /ruːm, rʊm/ *n* [U] space available for something ○ *Is there any room for me in the car?* ○ *(fig.) She writes better, but there is still room for improvement.*
roomy /ˈruː·mi, ˈrʊm·i/ *adj* [not gradable] having a lot of space ○ *Her new apartment is very roomy.*

room and board *n* [U] a charge for renting a room and the cost of meals ○ *I pay each semester for room and board at college.*

roommate /ˈruːm·meɪt, ˈrʊm-/ *n* [C] a person with whom you share a room, apartment, or house

room service *n* [U] a hotel service that provides food and drink to guests in their rooms

roost /ruːst/ *n* [C] a place, such as a branch of a tree, where birds rest or sleep
roost /ruːst/ *v* [I] ○ *In the city, pigeons roost on the ledges of buildings.*

rooster /ˈruː·stər/, **cock** *n* [C] an adult male chicken

root PLANT PART /ruːt, rʊt/ *n* [C] ***biology*** **1** the part of a plant which grows down into the earth **2** The root of a hair, tooth, or nail is the part of it that is inside the body.
root /ruːt, rʊt/ *v* [I/T] (of a plant) to develop roots and begin to grow

ORIGIN /ruːt, rʊt/ *n* [C] the origin or source of something ○ *We must get to the root of this problem.*
rooted /ˈruːt̬·əd, ˈrʊt̬-/ *adj* [not gradable] ○ *deeply rooted loyalty*
roots /ruːts, rʊts/ *pl n* family origins, or the particular place you come from and the experiences you have had living there ○ *Somehow, I had forgotten my roots in Kansas.*
rootless /ˈruːt·ləs, ˈrʊt-/ *adj* [not gradable] having no family origins or connections, or having no feeling of belonging to a particular place

WORD /ruːt, rʊt/ *n* [C] the basic form of a word, to which prefixes or endings can be added ○ *The root of the word "sitting" is "sit."*

NUMBER /ruːt, rʊt/ *n* ***algebra*** a number that is the solution of an EQUATION (= mathematical statement)

PHRASAL VERB with **root**

• **root for** *someone/something* to express your support for the success of someone or something ○ *The crowds have been large, with the vast majority of the fans rooting for Mexico.*

root beer *n* [U] a sweet, bubbly drink, flavored with the roots of various plants, that is not alcoholic

root canal *n* [C] a treatment for a tooth where the infected roots are removed and replaced by a hard substance

rope /roʊp/ *n* [C/U] a strong, thick cord made of twisted fibers
rope /roʊp/ *v* [T] **1** to tie something with rope ○ *We roped the box to the top of the car.* **2** To rope something off is to put rope or cord around it to keep it separate: [M] *The site has been marked with "no trespassing" signs and areas have been roped off.*

IDIOMS with **rope**

• **on the ropes** in serious trouble or likely to fail ○ *For a while, our business was on the ropes.*
• **the ropes** the practices or rules you need to know in order to get something done ○ *I spent a day in our warehouse showing the new guy the ropes.*

PHRASAL VERBS with **rope**

• **rope** *someone* **in** [M] to force or persuade someone to join a group or become involved in something ○ *The National Guard roped him in for another two years of service.*
• **rope** *someone* **into** *something* to persuade a person or group to do something ○ *I was roped into playing softball last night.*

rosary /ˈroʊ·zə·ri/ *n* [C] a series of prayers said by Roman Catholics, or a string of BEADS (= little balls) used to count prayers

rose RISE /roʊz/ *past simple of* RISE

PLANT /roʊz/ *n* [C] a plant with pleasant-smelling flowers and THORNS (= sharp points) on its stems, or a flower from this plant ○ *a bunch of roses* ○ *I am planting roses this year.*

COLOR /roʊz/ *adj, n* [U] (of) a light red-purple color ○ *a rose dress* ○ [U] *painted in rose*
rosy /ˈroʊ·zi/ *adj* [-er/-est only] **1** of a pale red or pink color ○ *sunset's rosy glow* **2** Rosy also means optimistic, bright, happy: *Our future looks rosy.*

rose-colored glasses *pl n* a happy or positive attitude that fails to notice negative things, leading to a view of life that is not realistic

rosemary /ˈroʊzˌmer·i/ *n* [U] an herb whose leaves are used to flavor foods and to make PERFUME (= pleasant-smelling liquid)

R

Rosh Hashanah /ˌroʊʃ·hə'ʃoʊ·nə, ˌrɑʃ-, -'ʃɑn·ə/, **Rosh Hashana** *n* [U] the Jewish New Year, celebrated in early fall, either on the first or second day of the first month of the Jewish year

roster /'rɑs·tər/ *n* [C] a list of people's names and sometimes their work schedules, esp. for a military unit or a sports team

rostrum /'rɑs·trəm/ *n* [C] a PODIUM

rot /rɑt/ *v* [I/T] **-tt-** to decay, or to cause something to decay or weaken ○ [I] *The fallen apples rotted on the ground.* ○ [T] *Dampness rotted the old wood.*
rot /rɑt/ *n* [U] ○ *Rot weakened the beams in the house.*
rotten /'rɑt·ən/ *adj* **1** *The room smelled of rotten eggs.* **2** Rotten also means bad: *a rotten trick* ○ *rotten behavior*

rotary /'roʊţ·ə·ri/ *adj* [not gradable] turning in a circle around a fixed point, or having one or more parts that turns in this way ○ *a rotary motor/mower*
rotary /'roʊţ·ə·ri/ *n* [C] a TRAFFIC CIRCLE

rotate TURN /'roʊ·teɪt/ *v* [I/T] to turn around a fixed point, or to cause something to do this ○ [I] *The wheel rotates on an axle.*
rotation /roʊ'teɪ·ʃən/ *n* [C/U] ○ [C] *Two rotations of the dial opens the lock.*
rotational /roʊ'teɪ·ʃən·əl/ *adj* [not gradable]

TAKE TURNS /'roʊ·teɪt/ *v* [I/T] to happen in turns, or to cause something to happen in a particular order ○ [T] *Every 30 days we rotate shifts.*
rotation /roʊ'teɪ·ʃən/ *n* [U] ○ *crop rotation*

rote /roʊt/ *n* [U] the process of learning something by repetition, rather than by really understanding it ○ *She learned multiplication by rote.*

rotisserie /roʊ'tɪs·ə·ri/ *n* [C] a device that turns meat around slowly to cook it over a flame or in an OVEN (= enclosed cooking space)

rotten /'rɑt·ən/ *adj* See at ROT.

rotund /roʊ'tʌnd/ *adj* rounded or fat ○ *a rotund piglet/man*

R

rotunda /roʊ'tʌn·də/ *n* [C] a building or part of a building that is round in shape, and often has a DOME (= rounded roof)

rouge /ru:ʒ, *esp. Southern* ru:dʒ/ *n* [U] BLUSH MAKEUP

rough UNEVEN /rʌf/ *adj* [*-er/-est* only] (of a surface) not even or smooth ○ *It was a rough road, full of potholes.* ○ *Her laugh was rough and loud.*
roughen /'rʌf·ən/ *v* [T] to make or become rough ○ *I roughened the edges and glued them together.*

VIOLENT /rʌf/ *adj* [*-er/-est* only] violent or stormy ○ *The sea was too rough for sailing.* ○ *They live in a rough neighborhood.*
rough /rʌf/ *adv* [not gradable] ○ *The team had a reputation for playing rough.*
roughly /'rʌf·li/ *adv* [not gradable] ○ *He pushed the luggage roughly to the side.*

DIFFICULT /rʌf/ *adj* [*-er/-est* only] difficult or unpleasant ○ *She's had a rough year – she lost her job, then her father died.*

NOT EXACT /rʌf/ *adj* [*-er/-est* only] not exact or detailed; approximate ○ *I quickly made a rough table from some boards.* ○ *Can you give us a rough estimate of the cost?*
roughly /'rʌf·li/ *adv* [not gradable] ○ *The town's population has roughly doubled.*

WORD FAMILY rough			
Adjectives	rough	*Adverbs*	rough
Verbs	rough		roughly
	roughen		

IDIOM with rough

• **rough it** to live without comforts, esp. running water, heat, etc. ○ *We roughed it until our house was repaired.*

PHRASAL VERB with rough

• **rough up** *someone* [M] to attack someone physically ○ *Who roughed this guy up in the parking lot?*

rough-and-tumble *adj* very competitive and failing to pay attention to rules ○ *rough-and-tumble politics*

rough-hewn OBJECT *adj* looking not finished or not smooth ○ *The students sang on a rough-hewn stage.*

PERSON /'rʌf·hju:n/ *adj* not very polite and having a lack of grace and style ○ *The hero in the film is a rough-hewn detective.*

roughhouse /'rʌf·hɑʊs, -hɑʊz/ *v* [I] to play in a rough and noisy way ○ *The boys roughhoused outdoors.*

roughshod IDIOM /'rʌf·ʃɑd/
• **run roughshod over** *someone*, **ride roughshod over** *someone* to act without caring how you will affect someone or something ○ *He ran roughshod over his employees when he thought they weren't working hard enough.*

round CIRCULAR /rɑʊnd/ *adj* [*-er/-est* only] shaped like a circle or having a surface like part of a ball ○ *They sat at a round table.* ○ *She held up a round mirror.* ○ *Carlos was a round-cheeked boy.*
rounded /'rɑʊn·dəd/ *adj* curved ○ *rounded pebbles*

APPROXIMATE /rɑʊnd/ *adj* [not gradable] (of a number) not exact but approximate, and ending in zero ○ *In round numbers, about three million tourists visit each year.*

MOVE AROUND /rɑʊnd/ *v* [T] to go around something and arrive on the other side ○ *The car rounded the corner and stopped in front of the house.*
round /rɑʊnd/ *adv* around

SINGLE EVENT /rɑʊnd/ *n* [C] **1** a single event or a small group of similar events that are part of a larger series of events ○ *The first round of negotiations got nowhere.* **2** In many sports, a round is a stage in a competition: *They lost in the first round of the tournament.* **3** In golf, a round is a complete game. **4** In boxing, a round is one of the periods during which the competitors fight. **5** A **round of applause** is a period of clapping to show approval:

Let's give the band a nice round of applause. **6** A **round (of drinks)** is a drink for each person in a group.

BULLET /raʊnd/ *n* [C] a bullet or other piece of AMMUNITION (= something that can be shot from a weapon or exploded) ○ *They fired several rounds, then fled.*

WORD FAMILY round			
Nouns	round	*Verbs*	round
Adjectives	round rounded	*Adverbs*	round roundly

IDIOMS with round

• **round and round** moving in circles ○ *The children spun round and round until they made themselves dizzy.* ○ Compare AROUND AND AROUND at AROUND IDIOMS

• **round the clock** all day and all night without stopping ○ *He studied round the clock, losing forty pounds during that time.* ○ *He requires round-the-clock care.* ○ Compare AROUND THE CLOCK at AROUND IDIOMS

PHRASAL VERBS with round

• **round out** *something* [M] to complete something ○ *A bit more research is needed to round out the article.*

• **round up** *something/someone* [M] to gather people, animals, or things into one place ○ *The brothers set about rounding up the horses.* ○ Related noun: ROUNDUP

roundabout NOT DIRECT /ˈraʊn·dəˌbaʊt/ *adj* not simple, direct, or quick ○ *You took the roundabout way to get here.*

CIRCLE /ˈraʊn·dəˌbaʊt/ *n* [C] *Br* a TRAFFIC CIRCLE

round-robin *n* [C] a competition in which everyone competes at least once against each other competitor ○ *a round-robin tennis tournament*

rounds /raʊndz/ *pl n* a work activity that regularly involves going to several different places ○ *Doctors made their daily rounds, visiting patients in the hospital.*

roundtable, **round-table** /ˈraʊndˌteɪ·bəl/ *adj* [not gradable] involving several people who talk about something as equals ○ *The writers will take part in round-table discussions and read from their works.*

round trip *n* [C] a trip from one place to another and back to where you started ○ *I drive 45 miles round trip every day for work.*
round-trip *adj* [not gradable] ○ *I'd like a round-trip ticket to Baltimore, please.*

roundup /ˈraʊn·dʌp/ *n* [C] the act of gathering together people, animals, or things ○ *a cattle roundup* ○ *a roundup of local news stories* ○ Related verb: ROUND UP

rouse /raʊz/ *v* [T] to wake someone or make someone more active or excited ○ *She roused him from his sleep.*

rousing /ˈraʊ·zɪŋ/ *adj* enthusiastic, or causing enthusiasm ○ *a rousing speech* ○ *They gave him a rousing welcome.*

rout /raʊt/ *v* [T] to defeat an enemy or competitor completely
rout /raʊt/ *n* [C usually sing] ○ *Washington defeated Orlando in a 141-104 rout.*

route Ⓐ /ruːt, raʊt/ *n* [C] **1** a particular way or direction between places ○ *The most direct route is to take the expressway.* **2** A route is also a fixed path for regularly moving or delivering people or things: *bus routes* ○ *a supply route*
route Ⓐ /ruːt, raʊt/ *v* [T always + adv/prep] ○ *The airline thinks my bags were routed* (= sent) *to Portland, Oregon instead of Portland, Maine.*

router /ˈraʊt̬·ər/ *n* [C] an electronic device that deals with communications between two or more computer networks

routine /ruːˈtiːn/ *n* [C/U] **1** a usual set of activities or way of doing things ○ [C] *Getting coffee and a bagel was part of my daily routine.* **2** A routine is also a particular set of activities performed to entertain others: [C] *a comedy/skating routine*
routine /ruːˈtiːn/ *adj* [not gradable] ○ *The test is part of a routine six-month checkup.*
routinely /ruːˈtiːn·li/ *adv* [not gradable] ○ *She routinely works out at the gym.*

rove /roʊv/ *v* [I/T] to move, travel, or look around an area, without having a particular place you intend to go to ○ [I] *He roved around town, looking for work.*

row LINE /roʊ/ *n* [C] **1** a line of things arranged next to each other ○ *Everybody lined up in a neat little row.* ○ *I want to sit in the front row.* **2** If something happens a number of times **in a row**, it happens that many times without interruption: *They've won six games in a row.*

USAGE

row

Remember to use the preposition **in** when you say that something or someone is in a particular **row**.

We had seats in the last row.

~~*We had seats at the last row.*~~

MOVE IN WATER /roʊ/ *v* [I/T] to cause a boat to move by pushing against the water with OARS (= long poles with flat ends), or to move people in a boat in this way ○ [T] *Dad rowed us back to shore.*
rowing /ˈroʊ·ɪŋ/ *n* [U] ○ *Sarah won an Olympic medal in rowing.*

rowboat /ˈroʊ·boʊt/ *n* [C] a small boat that is moved by using OARS

rowdy /ˈraʊd·i/ *adj* noisy and seeming likely to become violent ○ *The theater was full of rowdy teenagers throwing popcorn and yelling.*

row house, **rowhouse** /ˈroʊ·haʊs/ *n* [C] a house in a city that is joined to others like it on either side

R

royal /ˈrɔɪ·əl/ *adj* [not gradable] belonging or connected to a king or queen ○ *Sweden's royal family*

WORD FAMILY royal			
Nouns	royal royalty	*Adjectives* *Adverbs*	royal royally

Royal Canadian Mounted Police, *infml* **Mounties** *pl n* Canada's national police force.

royalty PEOPLE /ˈrɔɪ·əl·ti/ *n* [U] kings or queens and their families as a group, or the rank or power of these people ○ *They treated her like royalty.*

PAYMENT /ˈrɔɪ·əl·ti/ *n* [C usually pl] a payment made esp. to writers and musicians every time their books or songs are bought or used by others

rpm *n abbreviation for* revolutions per minute (= a measurement of the number of times something goes around during a minute) ○ *a 78 rpm record*

rRNA *n* [U] ***biology*** *abbreviation for* RIBOSOMAL RNA

RSS *n* [U] *abbreviation for* really simple syndication (= a way of sending electronic information that changes often to people who ask to receive it) ○ *Hundreds of websites now offer RSS feeds on every subject imaginable.*

RSVP *v* [I] *abbreviation for* répondez s'il vous plaît (= French for "please answer") ○ *RSVP by October 9th.* ○ **USAGE:** Often used on written invitations.

rub /rʌb/ *v* [I/T] **-bb-** to press or be pressed against something with a repeated circular, side to side, or up and down movement ○ [T] *I rubbed the place where I bumped my head.* ○ [T] *If you rub linseed oil into the wood, it will protect it.*

rub /rʌb/ *n* [C] **1** *Give my neck a rub.* **2** The rub is something that prevents success: *She got good reviews for her original cooking, but the rub was that people wanted very traditional dishes.*

R

IDIOMS with rub

•**rub it in** to make someone feel worse about something the person already feels embarrassed about ○ *I know I shouldn't have paid that much for the poster – don't rub it in, OK?*

•**rub shoulders with** *someone* **rub elbows with** *someone* to meet or spend time with someone socially, esp. someone important or famous ○ *He loved his job because he got to rub shoulders with high-powered Hollywood stars.*

•**rub** *someone* **the wrong way** to annoy someone ○ *He was known as an arrogant player who rubbed his teammates the wrong way.*

PHRASAL VERBS with rub

•**rub down** *someone* [M] to rub or press someone's body in order to dry it or reduce muscle stiffness or pain ○ *After the game the trainer was rubbing my arm down.* ○ Related noun: RUBDOWN

•**rub off on** *someone* to become part of someone because that person has been in a place where it was present ○ *I like to think that our love of reading will rub off on our children.* ○ **USAGE:** Usually said about a quality, skill, condition, or interest.

•**rub out** *something/someone* [M] *infml* to get rid of something, or to kill someone

rubber /ˈrʌb·ər/ *n* [C/U] **1** an elastic, waterproof substance made either from the juice of a tree that grows in hotter parts of the world or artificially ○ [U] *rubber boots/gloves* ○ [U] *Tires are made of rubber.* **2** *Br* A rubber is an ERASER. **3** Rubbers are waterproof shoes made of rubber, which are worn over regular shoes to keep them dry: [pl] *Wear your rubbers – it's raining.*

rubbery /ˈrʌb·ə·ri/ *adj* **1** elastic and difficult to break, like rubber ○ *I don't like squid, it's too rubbery.* **2** Rubbery also means feeling weak: *His legs were rubbery.*

rubber band *n* [C] a thin ring of rubber used for holding things together ○ *She brought five or six pencils and put a rubber band around them.*

rubbernecking /ˈrʌb·ərˌnek·ɪŋ/ *n* [U] the act of slowing down while driving to look at something interesting, esp. an accident ○ *There are delays due to rubbernecking at the scene of the accident.*

rubber stamp /ˈrʌb·ər ˈstæmp/ *n* [C] **1** a device used for printing with raised letters, numbers, or pictures made of an elastic substance such as rubber that you cover with ink and press against a surface, or the printed letters, etc., made in this way ○ *The guard marked my pass with a rubber stamp.* **2** *disapproving* A rubber stamp is also an approval given without much thought: *The mayor has a lot of power, and city counselors provide a rubber stamp.*

rubber-stamp /ˈrʌb·ər ˈstæmp/ *v* [T] *disapproving* to approve something without giving it much thought ○ *Congress is not going to simply rubber-stamp any policy the president proposes.*

rubbish /ˈrʌb·ɪʃ/ *n* [U] worthless and unwanted things or ideas; garbage ○ *All that was left of the property was a pile of rubbish nine feet high.* ○ *I can't believe they broadcast such rubbish.*

rubble /ˈrʌb·əl/ *n* [U] broken wood, stones, bricks, etc., that are left when a building falls down or is destroyed

rubdown /ˈrʌb·dɑʊn/ *n* [C] the act of rubbing someone's body to dry it or to make it feel better ○ *I got a rubdown after my workout.* ○ Related verb: RUB DOWN

rubella /ruːˈbel·ə/ *n* [U] *medical* GERMAN MEASLES.

ruby /ˈruː·bi/ *n* [C] a dark red jewel ○ *a ruby ring*

ruckus /ˈrʌk·əs/ *n* [C usually sing] *infml* a noisy situation or argument ○ *He caused quite a ruckus.*

rudder /ˈrʌd·ər/ *n* [C] a flat blade at the back of a boat or aircraft that is moved from side to side in order to control the direction of travel

ruddy /ˈrʌd·i/ *adj* (of a white person's skin) having a red color, often suggesting good health ○ *a ruddy-cheeked girl*

rude NOT POLITE /ruːd/ *adj* [-*er*/-*est* only] behaving in a way that hurts other people's feelings; not polite ○ *I apologized for Ted's rude behavior.* ○ *I thought it was rude of him not to introduce me.*
rudeness /ˈruːd·nəs/ *n* [U] ○ *He asked too many questions, and his curiosity verged on rudeness.*
rudely /ˈruːd·li/ *adv*

WORD CHOICES rude

A more formal alternative to "rude" is the word **impolite**.

She asks direct questions without being in any way ***impolite.***

If someone is rude or does not show respect to a person who is older or has more authority, that person might be described as **impertinent** or **insolent**.

It was clear that they found his questions ***impertinent.***

The adjective **abrasive** describes someone's manner when being rude and unfriendly.

I thought he was kind of ***abrasive.***

A person who is rude and unpleasant is sometimes described as **uncouth**.

She considers him loud-mouthed and ***uncouth.***

Language which is rude, often because it refers to the body in an unpleasant way, can be described as **vulgar** or **crude**.

He told a pretty ***vulgar*** *joke over dinner.*

SUDDEN /ruːd/ *adj* [-*er*/-*est* only] sudden and unpleasant ○ *I've lived in Texas most of my life, so it was a rude awakening when I moved to New York.*

WORD FAMILY rude

Nouns	rudeness	*Adverbs*	rudely
Adjectives	rude		

rudimentary /ˌruːd·əˈment·ə·ri, -ˈmen·tri/ *adj* only basic, and not deep or detailed ○ *She has only a rudimentary grasp of the language.*
rudiments /ˈruːd·ə·mənts/ *pl n* the simplest and most basic facts ○ *the rudiments of grammar*

rue /ruː/ *v* [T] to feel sorry about an event and wish it had not happened; regret
rueful /ˈruː·fəl/ *adj* ○ *She gave him a rueful smile.*

ruffle MAKE UPSET /ˈrʌf·əl/ *v* [I/T] to make someone upset or nervous or reduce someone's confidence ○ [T] *It ruffled her composure, and she did not know how to respond.*
ruffled /ˈrʌf·əld/ *adj* [not gradable] ○ *We spent a lot of time soothing the author's ruffled feelings.*

MAKE UNEVEN /ˈrʌf·əl/ *v* [T] to make something that is smooth uneven ○ *A sudden, strong breeze ruffled the women's skirts in the stands.*

FOLD /ˈrʌf·əl/ *n* [C] a series of small folds made in a piece of cloth or sewn into it as decoration ○ *lace ruffles*
ruffled /ˈrʌf·əld/ *adj* [not gradable] ○ *a blouse with a ruffled neck*

IDIOM with ruffle

• **ruffle** (*someone's*) **feathers** to cause someone to be upset ○ *David ruffled a few feathers when he suggested cutting the teachers' salaries.*

rug /rʌg/ *n* [C] a shaped piece of thick cloth for covering part of a floor ○ *The rug we bought for the living-room has a beautiful red and gold pattern.*

rugby /ˈrʌg·bi/ *n* [U] a game played between two teams using an oval-shaped ball that is kicked or carried to goals at either end of a field

rugged STRONG /ˈrʌg·əd/ *adj* **1** strong or powerful; not delicate ○ *rugged individualism* **2** If you describe a man's face as rugged, you mean it is strong and rough: *rugged good looks*

UNEVEN /ˈrʌg·əd/ *adj* (of land) uneven and wild; not easy to travel over ○ *rugged terrain/cliffs*

ruin /ˈruː·ən, -ɪn/ *v* [T] to spoil or destroy something ○ *It would be a shame to ruin such a beautiful place.* ○ *That guy isn't going to ruin my life.*
ruin /ˈruː·ən, -ɪn/ *n* [C/U] ○ [C] *an ancient Mayan ruin* (= destroyed building) ○ *The city lies* **in ruins** (= destroyed).
ruinous /ˈruː·ə·nəs/ *adj* [not gradable] causing permanent and severe harm ○ *ruinous costs*

rule INSTRUCTION /ruːl/ *n* [C] an accepted principle or instruction that states the way things are or should be done, and tells you what you are allowed or are not allowed to do ○ *The company's chief executive failed to enforce federal workplace rules.* ○ *If you broke the rule, you're going to be punished for it.* ○ *It's against the rules to kick someone.*

DECIDE /ruːl/ *v* [I/T] to decide officially ○ [I] *A lower court ruled in favor of the society.* ○ [+ *that* clause] *The judge ruled that the defendant be taken back to Virginia.*
ruling /ˈruː·lɪŋ/ *n* [C] an official decision ○ *The US Supreme Court refused to review the state court's ruling.*

CONTROL /ruːl/ *v* [I/T] ***politics & government*** to control, or be the person in charge of a country ○ [I] *The prince ruled wisely and well.*
rule /ruːl/ *n* [U] ○ *This area was under Polish rule until the start of World War II.*
ruler /ˈruː·lər/ *n* [C] ○ *a military ruler*
ruling /ˈruː·lɪŋ/ *adj* [not gradable] ***politics & government*** ○ *the ruling party*

WORD FAMILY rule

Nouns	rule	*Adjectives*	ruling
	ruler		unruly
	ruling	*Verbs*	rule
			overrule

PHRASAL VERB with rule

• **rule out** *something* [M] to stop considering something as a possibility ○ *It's unlikely that he'll run for president, but you can never rule anything out.*

rule of thumb *n* [C] *pl* **rules of thumb** a method of judging a situation or condition that is

R

not exact but is based on experience ○ *As a rule of thumb, the ice on the lake should be at least two inches thick to support one person.*

ruler /ˈruː·lər/ *n* [C] a narrow, flat object with straight edges you can use to draw straight lines and having marks you can use to measure things

rum /rʌm/ *n* [U] a strong alcoholic drink made from MOLASSES (= sweet liquid from sugar plants)

rumble /ˈrʌm·bəl/ *v* [I] to make a continuous, low sound, or to move slowly while making such a sound ○ *My stomach is rumbling.* ○ *The trucks rumbled across the field.*

rumble /ˈrʌm·bəl/ *n* [C usually sing] ○ *We could hear the rumble of distant thunder.*

ruminate /ˈruː·məˌneɪt/ *v* [I] *fml* to think slowly and carefully ○ *He ruminated over his loss.*

rummage /ˈrʌm·ɪdʒ/ *v* [I always + adv/prep] to search for something by moving things around without care and looking into, under, and behind them ○ *She rummaged through the drawer, looking for a pen.*

rummage sale /ˈrʌm·ɪdʒ ˈseɪl/ *n* [C] a sale of used clothing, books, toys, etc.

rummy /ˈrʌm·i/ *n* [U] any of various card games in which two or more players try to collect cards that have the same value or whose numbers follow an ordered series

rumor, *Cdn, Br* **rumour** /ˈruː·mər/ *n* [C/U] an unofficial, interesting story or piece of news that might be true or invented, and that is communicated quickly from person to person ○ [C] *Rumors about her are circulating at school.*

rumored, *Cdn, Br* **rumoured** /ˈruː·mərd/ *adj* [not gradable] ○ *The rumored plan to sell the company never actually took place.*

rump /rʌmp/ *n* [C] the back end of an animal, or a person's buttocks ○ *a rump steak*

rumple /ˈrʌm·pəl/ *v* [T] to cause something smooth to become messy with unwanted folds ○ *You'll rumple your jacket if you don't hang it up.*

rumpled /ˈrʌm·pəld/ *adj* ○ *a rumpled suit*

run GO QUICKLY /rʌn/ *v* [I/T] *pres. part.* **running**, *past simp.* **ran**, *past part.* **run** to move your legs faster than when walking, with the weight of your body pressing forward ○ [I] *They ran for the bus and got there just in time.* ○ [T] *Hugh runs five miles a day.* ○ [I] *We want a place with a big backyard with room for the kids to run around.* ○ [I] (*fig.*) *I've got to run now* (= hurry away) *because I'm late for my appointment.*

run /rʌn/ *n* [C] ○ *She goes for a three-mile run every evening after work.*

runner /ˈrʌn·ər/ *n* [C] ○ *Distance runner Gwyn Coogan is a favorite in the marathon.* ○ See also: RUNNER SHOE; RUNNER BLADE

running /ˈrʌn·ɪŋ/ *n* [U] ○ *Running is a very popular form of exercise.* ○ See also: RUNNING at RUN OPERATE; RUNNING at RUN POLITICS

WORD CHOICES run

If someone runs very fast over a short distance, you can use the verb **sprint**.

I had to ***sprint*** *to catch the bus.*

Jog is used when someone runs at a slow regular speed, especially as a form of exercise.

"What do you do to keep fit?" "I ***jog*** *and go swimming."*

If someone goes somewhere very quickly on foot, you can use the verbs **race, rush, dash**, or **hurry**.

He ***raced*** *up the stairs to answer the phone.*

Everyone ***rushed*** *to the door when the alarm went off.*

The verb **hurtle** can be used when someone is running so fast that it seems dangerous.

A little boy came ***hurtling*** *down the stairs.*

Bolt can be used when someone runs because he or she is frightened or is trying to escape.

He ***bolted*** *out of the door as soon as he saw her.*

If an animal runs somewhere with small short steps, you can use the verbs **scamper** or **scurry**.

The dog ***scampered*** *off into another room.*

The mouse ***scurried*** *across the floor.*

TRAVEL/GO /rʌn/ *v* [I/T] *pres. part.* **running**, *past simp.* **ran**, *past part.* **run** **1** to travel or go, to move something, or to be positioned in a particular way ○ [I] *The bus runs three times a day between here and Albuquerque.* ○ [I] *I'm going to run down to the bank to cash my check.* ○ [I] *Trains are running twenty minutes late because of the weather.* ○ [I] *The car skidded on the ice and ran off the road.* ○ [I] *A shiver of fear ran through her.* ○ [T] *John said he'd run me back to school* (= take me there in his car). ○ [I] *A deep creek runs through the property.* ○ [I] *The road runs along the coast.* **2** If you run your finger or hand over something, you move it quickly: [T] *She ran her fingers along the edge of the desk.* **3** If you run something through your hair, you move it quickly and easily: [T] *He ran a comb through his hair.* **4** If a driver or a vehicle runs a sign or signal to stop, the vehicle continues without stopping: [T] *Our taxi ran a red light and a truck rammed us in the side.*

run /rʌn/ *n* [C] a trip ○ *The train made its final run in 1986.*

OPERATE /rʌn/ *v* [I/T] *pres. part.* **running**, *past simp.* **ran**, *past part.* **run** **1** to manage or operate something ○ [T] *She runs the business out of her home.* ○ [I] *She left the engine running while she went into the store.* ○ [T] *Can you run both of these programs at once?* ○ [T] *They're running tests on his heart functions.* **2** If something runs on a particular type of energy, it uses that type of energy to operate: [I] *Some calculators run on solar power.*

running /ˈrʌn·ɪŋ/ *n* [U] the management or operation of something ○ *The running of a large household is not easy.* ○ See also: RUNNING at RUN GO QUICKLY; RUNNING at RUN POLITICS

FLOW /rʌn/ *v* [I/T] *pres. part.* **running,** *past simp.* **ran,** *past part.* **run** to cause a liquid to flow, or to produce a liquid that flows ○ [T] *He ran a little cold water into the sink.* ○ [I] *He has a cold and his nose is running.* ○ [I] *Tears were running down her face.*
runny /ˈrʌn·i/ *adj infml* producing a lot of liquid, or of a substance partly liquid ○ *a runny nose* ○ *runny eggs*

LOSE COLOR /rʌn/ *v* [I] *pres. part.* **running,** *past simp.* **ran,** *past part.* **run** (of colors) to come out of material and mix with other colors, so that the original colors are lost ○ *If you wash the dress in hot water, the colors will run.*

POLITICS /rʌn/ *v* [I] *pres. part.* **running,** *past simp.* **ran,** *past part.* **run** to try to get elected; be a CANDIDATE ○ *Kutukas ran unsuccessfully for sheriff.*
run /rʌn/ *n* [C] ○ *Gunter made a run for the US Senate.*
running /ˈrʌn·ɪŋ/ *n* [U] ○ See also: RUNNING at RUN GO QUICKLY; RUNNING at RUN OPERATE

BE/CONTINUE /rʌn/ *v pres. part.* **running,** *past simp.* **ran,** *past part.* **run** to be, become, or continue in a particular way ○ [L] *The doctor is running a bit late.* ○ [L] *We're running low on gas.* ○ [I always + adv/prep] *Inflation is running at 4%.* ○ [I always + adv/prep] *The show ran on Broadway for six weeks before closing.*
run /rʌn/ *n* [C] a period during which something happens or continues ○ *The movie starts a two-week run tonight.*

SHOW /rʌn/ *v* [T] *pres. part.* **running,** *past simp.* **ran,** *past part.* **run** to show something in a newspaper or magazine, or on television ○ *Both parties are already running campaign ads.*

POINT /rʌn/ *n* [C] (in baseball) a single point, scored by touching each of the four BASES (= positions on a square) in the correct order

HOLE /rʌn/ *n* [C] a long, vertical hole in particular types of cloth, esp. STOCKINGS (= thin, tight-fitting clothing for a woman's feet and legs)
run /rʌn/ *v* [I] *pres. part.* **running,** *past simp.* **ran,** *past part.* **run** ○ *My stockings ran!*

WORD FAMILY run

Nouns	run rerun runner running	*Adjectives*	running runny
		Verbs	run outrun overrun

IDIOMS with run

• **in the running** having a chance of being successful, esp. in a competition or election ○ *She's still in the running for Treasurer.* ○ Compare OUT OF THE RUNNING at OUT IDIOMS
• **on the run 1** while busy doing something else ○ *He ate on the run, downing an apple in his car.* **2** If criminals are **on the run,** they are trying to avoid being caught. ○ *The two men were on the run for three weeks before being caught by police.* **3** Someone or something **on the run** is at a disadvantage in a competitive situation: *Competition from Internet retailers has some big department stores on the run.*
• **run afoul of** *something* to do something you are not allowed to do, esp. breaking a rule or law ○ *Foreigners who run afoul of the law are punished severely.*
• **run amok** to behave without control in a wild or dangerous manner ○ *There were 50 little kids running amok at the snack bar.*
• **run out the clock, run down the clock** to use all the available time ○ *He was supposed to fall on the ball, allowing San Jose to run out the clock.* ○ *The president's strategy is to run the clock down until the elections, then win control of Congress.*
• *something* **runs in** *someone's* **family** a skill or quality is present in many of your relatives ○ *I guess a love of music runs in the family.*
• **run the gamut** to include the whole range of possible things within a group or type ○ *Their projects run the gamut from mobile homes to luxury condos.*
• **run the risk of** *doing something* to make a particular result possible ○ *When doctors do not follow government guidelines, they run the risk of being sued.*
• **run with it** *infml* to work independently to achieve something ○ *The Japanese took that technology and ran with it.*

PHRASAL VERBS with run

• **run across** *someone/something* to meet someone unexpectedly, or to experience something unexpected ○ *You don't run across many people who don't own a TV.*
• **run after** *someone/something* to chase someone or something ○ *I ran after her, trying to get her attention.*
• **run around** to exist or do something in the stated condition ○ *I'm tired of running around on crutches.* ○ Compare RUNAROUND
• **run around with** *someone* to spend a lot of time with someone ○ *Mom likes to know what kind of crowd I'm running around with.*
• **run away** to leave a place or person secretly and suddenly ○ *Vinnie ran away from home when he was 16.* ○ Related noun: RUNAWAY
• **run** *something* **by** *someone* to tell something to someone ○ *Would you run that by me again?*
• **run down** *something/someone* **HIT** [M] to hit and hurt a person or animal with a vehicle, esp. intentionally ○ *Some people drive like they're trying to run you down.*
• **run down** *(someone/something)* **WEAKEN** [I] to lose energy, power, or strength ○ *By 1923 the radio boom seemed to be running down.* ○ Related adjective: RUN-DOWN
• **run down** *something* **FIND** [M] to learn the facts about something after searching for them ○ *The police are running down several leads related to the crime.* ○ Related noun: RUNDOWN
• **run down** *something* **EXAMINE** to look at, examine, think of, or deal with a set of things, esp. quickly ○ *The safety inspector ran down the list of hazards present in a transit system.*
• **run down** *something/someone* **CRITICIZE** [M] to criticize something or someone, often unfairly ○ *Those people are always running down our country and our values.*

R

•**run** *(something)* **into** *something* **HIT** to unintentionally drive a vehicle into something ○ *He ran his car into a ditch.*
•**run into** *someone* **MEET** to meet someone by chance ○ *I ran into Mike on Seventh Avenue.*
•**run into** *something* **EXPERIENCE** to experience something unexpectedly ○ *The center ran into some financial trouble and had to borrow money.* ○ **USAGE:** usually said about an unpleasant experience
•**run off** *(somewhere)* **LEAVE** to leave a place suddenly and unexpectedly ○ *She ran off before I had a chance to talk to her.*
•**run** *someone/something* **off** *(somewhere)* **FORCE TO LEAVE** to cause someone or something to leave ○ *When the moose didn't leave, I tried to run him off.* ○ *His business partner ran him off the road on purpose.*
•**run off** *something* **PRODUCE** [M] **1** to make copies of something ○ *She downloaded it, printed it, and ran off copies for her friends.* ○ *McKennitt ran off 5,000 copies of her CD and sold them on the streets of Toronto.* **2** A person or team who runs off points in a competition scores quickly: *Iowa ran off 12 straight points to take the lead.*
•**run off with** *something/someone* **1** to borrow, steal, or take something that does not belong to you ○ *The dog ran off with my shoe.* **2** If a person runs off with someone else, the two people leave together secretly and suddenly.
•**run out** to use something completely so that nothing is left ○ *He just ran out of ideas.* ○ *Time is running out* (= There is only a little time left).
•**run over** *something/someone* **HIT** [M] to hit and drive over someone or something with a vehicle
•**run over** *something* **EXAMINE** to look at, examine, think of, or deal with a set of things, esp. quickly ○ *They ran over the list to make sure there were no mistakes.*
•**run** *(someone)* **through** *something* **PRACTICE** [M] **1** to practice something; to REHEARSE ○ *The director wants us to run through the first act this morning.* **2** If you run someone through something, you practice it or talk about it so the person will know it better: *A technician ran me through the data recovery process.*
•**run through** *something* **EXAMINE** to look at, examine, think of, or deal with a set of things, esp. quickly ○ *I mentally ran through what I had eaten since Thursday.*
•**run through** *something* **EXIST** to be present in something, or in a group of people ○ *The blues runs through all of Ned Hayden's music.* ○ **USAGE:** said about a quality or feeling
•**run to** *something* to reach a particular amount, level, or size ○ *Its 2006 budget ran to over $1 billion.*
•**run up** *something* [M] to increase a debt by spending more ○ *He ran up huge bills on clothes.*
•**run up against** *something/someone* to experience an unexpected difficulty, or to meet someone who is difficult to deal with ○ *He's the slickest talker I've ever run up against.*

runaround /ˈrʌn·əˌrɑʊnd/ *n* [U] a series of actions or answers to questions that prevent someone from achieving something ○ *He expected to get the runaround, but surprisingly, the store offered him a refund.*

runaway **NOT CONTROLLED** /ˈrʌn·əˌweɪ/ *adj* [not gradable] being or seeming to be out of control, or happening suddenly and strongly ○ *runaway health-care costs* ○ *From the moment he launched the Boy Scout movement in 1908, it was a runaway success.*
PERSON /ˈrʌn·əˌweɪ/ *n* [C] a young person who has left home without permission ○ Related verb: RUN AWAY

rundown /ˈrʌn·dɑʊn/ *n* [C] a report that provides the most important information about something ○ *This guide gives a rundown on the basics of backpacking.* ○ Related verb: RUN DOWN **FIND**

run-down *adj* weak or in bad condition ○ *an old run-down factory* ○ *She was run-down, thin, with no appetite.* ○ Related verb: RUN DOWN **WEAKEN**

rung **RING** /rʌŋ/ *past participle of* RING **SOUND**
STEP /rʌŋ/ *n* [C] any of the short bars that form the steps of a LADDER (= a device used for climbing), or *fig.* a level or stage of progress ○ (*fig.*) *Community colleges occupy the lower rung of the state's higher education system.*

run-in /ˈrʌn·ɪn/ *n* [C] *infml* an argument, disagreement, or fight ○ *She'd had a run-in with the dog before.*

runner **BLADE** /ˈrʌn·ər/ *n* [C] a long, narrow blade designed to slide over ice easily, fixed to the bottom of SKATES (= a type of boot) or snow vehicles ○ See also: RUNNER at RUN **GO QUICKLY**
SHOE /ˈrʌn·ər/ *n* [C usually pl] a SNEAKER ○ See also: RUNNER at RUN **GO QUICKLY**

runner-up /ˈrʌn·əˌrʌp/ *n* [C] *pl* **runners-up** a person or team that finishes second in a race or competition ○ *Madison is the Eastern Region champion and last year's state runner-up.*

running /ˈrʌn·ɪŋ/ *n* ○ See at RUN **GO QUICKLY**; RUN **OPERATE**; RUN **POLITICS**

running back *n* [C] a football player who carries the ball from the line where the play starts

running mate *n* [C] someone who is trying to get elected to the second of two top positions ○ *It will soon be time for the presidential candidates to choose their running mates.*

running water *n* [U] water supplied by pipes to a house or building ○ *The summer homes on the island have no running water.*

runny /ˈrʌn·i/ *adj* ○ See at RUN **FLOW**

runoff **ELECTION** /ˈrʌn·ɔːf/ *n* [C] a second or final election held when no one got enough votes to win an earlier election
LIQUID /ˈrʌn·ɔːf/ *n* [U] ***earth science*** **1** water that flows away from high areas to low areas ○ *Houses and subdivisions can disturb spring water runoff from the mountains.* **2** Runoff is also chemicals and ani-

mal excrement that flow into rivers and lakes and pollute the environment: *Stormwater runoff is a major source of water pollution.*

run-up /ˈrʌn·ʌp/ *n* [U] the period before an important event ○ *Wolfson is playing a key role in the run-up to the elections.*

runway /ˈrʌn·weɪ/ *n* [C] a long, level piece of ground at an airport, having a smooth, hard surface on which aircraft can take off and land

rupture /ˈrʌp·tʃər/ *v* [I/T] to burst or break, or to cause something to burst or break ○ [I] *High winds caused the oil tank to rupture.*
rupture /ˈrʌp·tʃər/ *n* [C] ○ *There is a rupture in confidence in government.*

rural /ˈrʊr·əl/ *adj* in, of, or like the COUNTRY (= land not in cities) ○ *She grew up in rural Utah.* ○ Compare URBAN

ruse /ruːz/ *n* [C] a trick intended to deceive someone ○ *You didn't fall for my ruse.*

rush /rʌʃ/ *v* [I/T] to do something or move very quickly, or to cause someone to act in such a way; hurry ○ [I] *She rushed toward me, talking and laughing.* ○ [I] *You shouldn't rush out and buy one.* ○ [T] *We rushed her to the hospital.* ○ [T] *She never rushes her students.*
rush /rʌʃ/ *n* [C/U] **1** something moving quickly, or the need for quick action ○ [C] *a rush of cold air* ○ [U] *There's no rush, I can wait.* ○ *"It's like this," she said in a rush* (= quickly). **2** A rush is also a sudden strong emotion or physical feeling: [C] *a rush of excitement*

rush hour *n* [C] one of the busy parts of the day, either when people are traveling to work in the morning or when they are traveling home from work in the evening ○ *Take alternate routes during the morning rush hour.*

rust /rʌst/ *n* [U] a red-brown substance that forms on the surface of iron and steel as a result of decay caused by reacting with air and water
rust /rʌst/ *v* [I/T] ○ [I] *Stainless steel won't rust.*
rusty /ˈrʌs·ti/ *adj* ○ *People would toss their soda cans into rusty old barrels.* ○ See also: RUSTY

rustic /ˈrʌs·tɪk/ *adj* typical of the COUNTRY (= land not in cities), esp. because of being attractively simple ○ *We stayed in rustic cabins, with no electricity.*

rustle MAKE NOISE /ˈrʌs·əl/ *v* [I/T] to make soft sounds, or to cause something, such as cloth, paper, or leaves, to make soft sounds ○ [T] *A sudden breeze rustled the leaves.*
rustle /ˈrʌs·əl/ *n* [C usually sing] ○ *We heard the rustle of her dress.*
rustling /ˈrʌs·ə·lɪŋ/ *n* [C/U] ○ [U] *the rustling of papers on the desk*
STEAL /ˈrʌs·əl/ *v* [T] to steal cattle, horses, etc., from a farm or RANCH
rustler /ˈrʌs·lər, -ə·lər/ *n* [C] ○ *Some rustlers had made off with half of their horses during the night.*

PHRASAL VERB with **rustle**

• **rustle up** *something* [M] *infml* to make, find, or prepare something quickly ○ *Give me a minute and I'll rustle up some scrambled eggs.*

rusty /ˈrʌs·ti/ *adj* (esp. of a person) not as good at knowing or doing something as you once were, because you have not practiced it in a long time ○ *We're a little rusty after having the summer off.* ○ See also: RUSTY at RUST

rut /rʌt/ *n* [C] a narrow channel, esp. one that has been unintentionally cut into the ground by a wheel

IDIOM with **rut**

• **be in a rut** to not have changed what you do or how you do it for a very long time so that it is not interesting any longer ○ *I was in a rut and couldn't get out of it.*

ruthless /ˈruːθ·ləs/ *adj* cruel, or determined to succeed without caring about others ○ *a ruthless ruler* ○ *To compete abroad requires ruthless cost-cutting at home.*

RV *n* [C] *abbreviation for* RECREATIONAL VEHICLE (= a large motor vehicle in which you can sleep and often cook, used for traveling and CAMPING)

Rx /ˈɑrˈeks/ *n* [C] *symbol* a medical PRESCRIPTION (= a doctor's written order for a person's medicine)

rye /rɑɪ/ *n* [U] **1** a type of plant, the grain of which is used to feed animals and to make flour for bread **2** Rye is a type of strong alcoholic drink made from this grain.

R

S s

S LETTER, s /es/ *n* [C] *pl* **S's, Ss, s's, ss** the 19th letter of the English alphabet

SIZE *adj* [not gradable] *abbreviation for* SMALL **LESS** ○ **USAGE:** Used esp. on clothing to show its size.

S., **So.** *adj, n* [U] *abbreviation for* SOUTH or SOUTHERN

Sabbath /ˈsæb·əθ/ *n* [C] the day of the week used by some religions as a day of rest and worship

sabbatical /səˈbæt̬·ɪ·kəl/ *n* [C/U] time away from work given to college or university teachers, esp. to study, write, or travel ○ [U] *Professor Logan will be on sabbatical this term.*

saber /ˈseɪ·bər/ *n* [C] a weapon with a sharp blade, used esp. in the past by soldiers on horses

sable /ˈseɪ·bəl/ *n* [C] *pl* **sables, sable** a small animal from cold regions that has very soft, dark brown fur, or the fur of this animal used esp. to make expensive coats

sabotage /ˈsæb·əˌtɑʒ/ *v* [T] to intentionally damage or destroy property ○ *Enemy agents had sabotaged the bridge.* ○ *(fig.) The bombing was meant to sabotage the peace talks.*
sabotage /ˈsæb·əˌtɑʒ/ *n* [U] ○ *The explosion was not an accident, it was sabotage.*

sac /sæk/ *n* [C] ***biology*** a part inside a plant or animal which is like a small bag and contains liquid or air

saccharin /ˈsæk·ə·rən/ *n* [U] a chemical with a sweet taste, used to replace sugar

saccharine /ˈsæk·ə·rən, -əˌrɑɪn/ *adj disapproving* too pleasant or charming, with too much feeling to be believed ○ *Longfellow's later poems are regarded as saccharine.*

sack BAG /sæk/ *n* [C] a bag, or the amount contained in a bag ○ *plastic sacks* ○ *a sack of flour*

FOOTBALL /sæk/ *v* [T] (in football) to bring the other team's QUARTERBACK to the ground before he can complete a play

STEAL /sæk/ *v* [T] to steal all the valuable things from a place and destroy it, usually during a war ○ *Villages were sacked and burned by the raiders.*

PHRASAL VERB with sack

• **sack out** *infml* to go to sleep ○ *She sacked out in the front seat of the car.*

sacrament /ˈsæk·rə·mənt/ *n* [C] (in Christianity) an important religious ceremony, such as marriage, BAPTISM, or CONFIRMATION

sacred /ˈseɪ·krəd/ *adj* holy and deserving respect ○ *sacred writings/music* ○ *(fig.) Art was sacred to her* (= extremely important and deserving respect). ○ Compare PROFANE

sacred cow *n* [C] something that people accept or believe to be good or necessary without ever questioning their belief ○ *Defense spending is a sacred cow in Congress.*

sacrifice GIVE UP /ˈsæk·rəˌfɑɪs/ *v* [T] to give up something for something else considered more important ○ *He sacrificed his vacations to work on his book.*
sacrifice /ˈsæk·rəˌfɑɪs/ *n* [C/U] ○ [C] *My parents made many sacrifices to pay for my college education.*

OFFER A LIFE /ˈsæk·rəˌfɑɪs/ *v* [I/T] to offer the life of an animal or a person to a god or gods in the hope of pleasing them, usually as part of a ceremony
sacrifice /ˈsæk·rəˌfɑɪs/ *n* [C/U] ○ [U] *animal/ritual sacrifice*

sacrilege /ˈsæk·rə·lɪdʒ/ *n* [C/U] the failure to treat something holy with the respect it should have, or an example of this ○ [U] *Many thought it was sacrilege to move the bones to another place.*
sacrilegious /ˌsæk·rəˈlɪdʒ·əs/ *adj* ○ *He considered the artwork to be sacrilegious.*

sacrosanct /ˈsæk·roʊˌsæŋt/ *adj* so important that there cannot be any change or question ○ *His time with his children was sacrosanct.*

sad NOT HAPPY /sæd/ *adj* **-dd-** showing, feeling, or causing unhappiness or regret ○ *I've just heard the saddest news.*
sadly /ˈsæd·li/ *adv* ○ *She spoke sadly about the loss of her home.*
sadness /ˈsæd·nəs/ *n* [U] ○ *There was a look of great sadness in his eyes.*
sadden /ˈsæd·ən/ *v* [T] ○ *It saddened me to learn of your father's death.*

WORD CHOICES sad

Unhappy and **miserable** can mean the same as "sad."

*She'd had a very **unhappy** childhood.*

*I just woke up feeling **miserable**.*

Someone who is **upset** is unhappy because something bad has happened.

*They'd had an argument and he was still **upset** about it.*

*Mike got very **upset** when I told him the news.*

If you are **broken-hearted** or **heartbroken** you are very sad, often because someone you love has ended a relationship with you.

*She was **broken-hearted** when Richard left.*

If you are **devastated** or **distraught**, you are extremely upset.

*He was **devastated** when he lost his house.*

*She was **distraught** over the article and feared losing her job.*

The adjectives **depressed**, **down**, or **low** are often used when someone is very unhappy for a long time.

*It makes her **depressed** to think about the injury.*

*I've been feeling a little **down** recently.*

*He was very **low** for months after he lost his job.*

UNPLEASANT /sæd/ *adj* **-dd-** very bad or regretted ○ *The sad fact is that all the trees have got the virus.*
sadly /ˈsæd·li/ *adv* ○ *If you think she doesn't care, you're sadly mistaken.*

WORD FAMILY sad

Nouns	sadness	*Verbs*	sadden
Adjectives	sad	*Adverbs*	sadly

IDIOM with sad

• **sad to say** it is sad, regrettable, or embarrassing that this fact is true ○ *Sad to say, the violin was never found.* ○ *Yes, sad to say, I've seen the movie fifteen times.*

saddle /ˈsæd·əl/ *n* [C] **1** a seat, usually made of leather, fastened on the back of a horse for a rider **2** A saddle is also a seat on a bicycle or MOTORCYCLE.
saddle /ˈsæd·əl/ *v* [T] ○ *She saddled her pony and went riding.*

PHRASAL VERBS with saddle

• **saddle up** *something* [M] to fasten a seat on the back of a horse, or to ride a horse ○ *Fred saddled up a horse and set out for Kingston to pick up the mail.*
• **saddle** *someone* **with** *something* to give a job or responsibility to someone who does not want it ○ *They saddled me with cleaning up after the party.*

sadist /ˈseɪd·əst, ˈsæd-/ *n* [C] a person who gets pleasure from hurting another person ○ Compare MASOCHIST
sadistic /səˈdɪs·tɪk/ *adj* ○ *a sadistic act*
sadism /ˈseɪˌdɪz·əm, ˈsædˌɪz-/ *n* [U]

sadly /ˈsæd·li/ *adv* ○ See at SAD NOT HAPPY; SAD UNPLEASANT

sadness /ˈsæd·nəs/ *n* ○ See at SAD NOT HAPPY

safari /səˈfɑr·i/ *n* [C] *pl* **safaris** a trip to watch, photograph, or hunt wild animals in their natural environment ○ *For his vacation, he plans to go on safari in Kenya.*

safe FREE FROM DANGER /seɪf/ *adj* **1** free from danger or harm, or not causing danger or harm ○ *Have a safe trip.* ○ *Is this medicine safe for children?* ○ *I feel safe here.* **2** Safe also means not involving any risk or disagreement: *She's looking for some safer investments.* ○ [+ *to* infinitive] *With most of the votes counted now, I think it's safe to say that we won.*
safely /ˈseɪ·fli/ *adv* ○ *The plane landed safely in the storm.*

BOX /seɪf/ *n* [C] a strong box, usually made of steel, with a door and lock, where valuable things, esp. money or jewels, can be kept

BASEBALL /seɪf/ *adj* [not gradable] (of a player in the game of baseball) having successfully reached a BASE ○ Compare OUT BASEBALL

WORD FAMILY safe

Nouns	safe safety	*Adjectives*	safe unsafe
Adverbs	safely		

IDIOMS with safe

• **safe and sound** not hurt or damaged ○ *Three days later, the hikers were found safe and sound.*
• **to be on the safe side** to avoid risk ○ *Maybe it won't rain, but to be on the safe side, take your umbrella.*

safe deposit box, **safety deposit box** *n* [C] a strong box in a bank where you can keep valuable things, esp. documents or jewelry

safeguard /ˈseɪf·gɑrd/ *v* [T] to protect someone or something from harm or destruction ○ *Judges have an obligation to safeguard our right to free speech and a free press.*
safeguard /ˈseɪf·gɑrd/ *n* [C] ○ *The best safeguard against someone stealing your car is to lock it.*

safe haven *n* [C] an officially protected place in an area of military activity, or any safe or peaceful place in a dangerous area

safekeeping /ˈseɪfˈkiː·pɪŋ/ *n* [U] protection from harm or loss ○ *My friend left her jewelry with me for safekeeping when she went on vacation.*

safely /ˈseɪ·fli/ *adv* ○ See at SAFE FREE FROM DANGER

safe sex *n* [U] the use of CONDOMS or other methods to avoid catching a sexual disease, esp. AIDS

safety /ˈseɪf·ti/ *n* [U] the condition of not being in danger or of not being dangerous ○ *For your safety, keep your seat belt securely fastened.* ○ *Fire officials worry about the safety of those heaters.*

USAGE

safety or security?

Safety is when you are safe or how safe something is.

There have been some safety issues with the tires.

Children should have lessons in road safety.

Security means activities or people that protect you from harm, or that try to stop crime.

He works as a security guard.

airport security

safety belt *n* [C] a SEAT BELT

safety deposit box *n* [C] a SAFE DEPOSIT BOX

safety net *n* [C usually sing] something, esp. a government program, that protects or helps people ○ *Unemployment insurance is a safety net for people who lose their jobs.*

safety pin *n* [C] a pin with a round end to hold the sharp point, so that it will not stick you and will stay fastened

safety valve *n* [C] a device on a machine that allows steam or gas to escape if there is too much pressure ○ (*fig.*) *For people with stressful jobs, weekends in the country can be a good safety valve.*

S

sag /sæg/ *v* [I] **-gg- 1** to bend or sink lower ○ *It was a ramshackle building and its roof sagged.* ○ *Her shoulders sagged wearily.* **2** Sag also means to become weaker or less firm: *Muscles sag when you reach your 50s.* ○ *The economy is sagging.*

saga /ˈsɑɡ·ə/ *n* [C] ***literature*** a long, detailed story of connected events ○ *The Gold Rush was just one chapter in the saga of the old West.*

sage WISE /seɪdʒ/ *adj* [not gradable] wise, esp. as a result of long experience ○ *sage advice*
sage /seɪdʒ/ *n* [C] a wise person, esp. an old man
PLANT /seɪdʒ/ *n* [U] an herb with gray-green leaves that is used to flavor foods in cooking

Sagittarius /ˌsædʒ·əˈter·iː·əs/ *n* [C/U] the ninth sign of the ZODIAC, covering the period November 22 to December 21 and represented by a creature with a human upper body and horse's lower body, or a person born during this period

said /sed/ *past simple and past participle of* SAY

sail /seɪl/ *v* [I/T] **1** to travel across water in a boat or ship, or to operate a boat or ship on the water ○ [I] *He is not fun to sail with.* ○ [T] *I sail a small racing boat.* **2** Sail also means to leave on a boat or ship: [I] *When do we sail?*
sail /seɪl/ *n* [C] a sheet of material used to catch the wind and move a boat or ship ○ *I restored an old wooden boat and got a new canvas sail for it.*
sailing /ˈseɪ·lɪŋ/ *n* [U] the sport or activity of using boats with sails ○ *I never really got into sailing.*
sailor /ˈseɪ·lər/ *n* [C] a person who operates or works on a boat or ship, or a person in the navy who is not an officer ○ *My dad is a sailor.*

PHRASAL VERB with sail

- **sail through** *(something)* to do something easily and confidently ○ *She sailed through her final exams.*

sailboat /ˈseɪl·boʊt/ *n* [C] a boat with one or more sails used to move it

saint /seɪnt/, *abbreviation* **St.** *n* [C] **1** a holy person, esp. one who has been officially honored with this title by a Christian church ○ *Elizabeth Seton was the first person born in the US to be made a saint by the Roman Catholic Church.* **2** A saint is also a good, kind, and patient person: *His mother was a saint to everyone who knew her.*
saintly /ˈseɪnt·li/ *adj* ○ *He seemed the gentle, saintly man everyone said he was.*

sake ADVANTAGE /seɪk/ *n* [C] an advantage or benefit ○ *For his sake, I hope he has some protection.* ○ *She tried to look healthy, for her husband's sake.*
PURPOSE /seɪk/ *n* [U] purpose or reason ○ *He is unwilling to oppose it just for the sake of opposing.*

salacious /səˈleɪ·ʃəs/ *adj* causing or showing too much interest in sexual matters

salad /ˈsæl·əd/ *n* [C/U] **1** a mixture of raw vegetables, usually covered with a SALAD DRESSING ○ [C] *a green salad* ○ [U] *Lunches include soup or salad.* **2** A salad is also a dish of small pieces of cold food, usually mixed with a sauce such as MAYONNAISE (= a thick sauce of oil, vinegar, and eggs): [U] *tuna/egg/potato/macaroni salad*

salad bar *n* [C] a table in a restaurant or store where you serve yourself from a variety of salads

salad dressing *n* [C] a liquid mixture such as oil, vinegar, and spices, added to vegetable salads to give them flavor

salamander /ˈsæl·əˌmæn·dər/ *n* [C] a small AMPHIBIAN (= animal that lives in water and on land) that has a long, narrow body, four short legs, a long tail, and soft, wet skin

salami /səˈlɑm·i/ *n* [U] a large, strongly flavored SAUSAGE (= meat cut into small pieces and shaped in a tube) that is usually eaten cold in slices

salary /ˈsæl·ə·ri/ *n* [C] a fixed amount of money paid to people for the work they are employed to do, esp. the amount paid every year ○ *a meager/generous salary* ○ *Teachers' salaries would rise an average of $1000 under the proposal.*
salaried /ˈsæl·ə·riːd/ *adj* [not gradable] ○ *All our salaried employees have agreed to take a pay cut.*
➤ Usage: **pay, wage, salary, or income?** at PAY GIVE EARNINGS

sale SELL /seɪl/ *n* [C/U] an act of exchanging something for money ○ [U] *You pay tax on the profits from the sale of buildings.* ○ [C] *The school raised money from book sales, bake sales, and individual contributors.* ○ [U] *When I bought this house, there were many, many homes* **for sale** (= available to be bought).
sales /seɪlz/ *pl n* **1** the number of items sold ○ [C] *US car sales got off to a hot start in January.* **2** Sales is also the department that sells a company's products: *He works in sales.*

> **USAGE**
>
> **sale or sales?**
>
> Remember that when you are talking about an amount of something that is sold, you use the plural noun **sales.**
>
> *This could have a considerable effect on our sales in Europe.*
>
> ~~*This could have a considerable effect on our sale in Europe.*~~

LOWER PRICE /seɪl/ *n* [C] an occasion when goods are sold at a lower price than usual ○ *a clearance sale* ○ *Are these dresses* **on sale** (= reduced in price)*?*

salesclerk *n* [C] someone who works in a store and sells products to customers

salesperson /ˈseɪlzˌpɜr·sən/, *male* **salesman** /ˈseɪlz·mən/, *female* **saleswoman** /ˈseɪlzˌwʊm·ən/ *n* [C] someone whose job is to sell something

sales representative, *short form* **sales rep, rep** *n* [C] someone whose job is to sell a company's products, often by traveling to different places

sales tax *n* [U] a tax on things that people buy in stores, collected by many states and some cities

salient /ˈseɪ·liː·ənt/ *adj* [not gradable] most noticeable or important ○ *The salient fact about the case is that it involves an American.*

saline /ˈseɪ·liːn, -lɑɪn/ *adj medical* containing or consisting of salt ○ *a saline solution*

salinity /səˈlɪn·əṭ·i, seɪ-/ *n* [U] ***chemistry, earth science*** a measure of the amount of salt dissolved in water, esp. sea water

saliva /səˈlɑɪ·və/ *n* [U] ***biology*** the natural, watery liquid in the mouth that keeps it wet and helps prepare food for digestion
salivate /ˈsæl·əˌveɪt/ *v* [I] to produce saliva

salivary gland /ˈsæl·əˌver·i ˌglænd/ *n* [C] ***biology*** one of the body parts that produce SALIVA (= liquid in the mouth)

sallow /ˈsæl·oʊ/ *adj* pale yellow and unhealthy looking ○ *a sallow face*

salmon /ˈsæm·ən/ *n* [C/U] *pl* **salmon** a medium-size fish with pink flesh which lives in the sea ○ [U] *smoked/canned salmon* ○ [U] *They went salmon fishing.*

salmonella /ˌsæl·məˈnel·ə/ *n* [C/U] *pl* **salmonella** a group of bacteria, some types of which live in food and cause illness in people who eat the food, or the illness caused by this bacteria

salon STORE /səˈlɑn, ˈsæl·ɑn/ *n* [C] a store where you can obtain esp. a beauty service or fashionable clothes ○ *a beauty/tanning/hair salon*
MEETING /sæˈlɔ̃ː, səˈlɑn/ *n* [C] a regular meeting of important or influential people, esp. of writers or artists at the house of someone famous ○ *the Paris salon of Gertrude Stein*

saloon /səˈluːn/ *n* [C] a place where alcoholic drinks are sold and drunk; a bar

salsa /ˈsɔːl·sə/ *n* [C/U] a spicy sauce made esp. of TOMATOES, onions, and CHILIES, that you put on Mexican foods

salt FOOD /sɔːlt/ *n* [U] a common, white substance, found in sea water and in the ground, used to add flavor to food or to preserve it ○ *a grain of salt* ○ *Please pass the salt and pepper.* ○ *Add a pinch of salt* (= small amount of it).
salt /sɔːlt/ *v* [T] ○ *She salted and peppered her stew.*
salt /sɔːlt/ *adj* [not gradable] containing or tasting of salt, or preserved with salt ○ *a salt pond/lake* ○ *salt pork/cod*
salted /ˈsɔːl·təd/ *adj* [not gradable] ○ *salted nuts/pretzels*
salty /ˈsɔːl·ti/ *adj* tasting or smelling like salt ○ *salty popcorn* ○ *salty sea air*
CHEMICAL /sɔːlt/ *n* [C] ***chemistry*** **1** a chemical substance made with an acid **2** Salt is used to melt ice on roads and SIDEWALKS in the winter.
salt /sɔːlt/ *v* [T] ○ *Work crews were busy plowing and salting roads.*

PHRASAL VERB with salt

• **salt away** *something* [M] to save something, esp. money, to use at a later time ○ *She's salting away more money for retirement.*

saltshaker /ˈsɔːltˌʃeɪ·kər/ *n* [C] a small container for salt with holes in the top so the salt can be shaken out of it

saltwater /ˈsɔːltˌwɔːṭ·ər, -ˌwɑṭ·ər/ *n* [U] water containing salt, esp. when it comes from an ocean or sea ○ *saltwater fish/plants*

salutary /ˈsæl·jəˌter·i/ *adj fml* causing improvement of behavior or character ○ *The effects of such a decision would not be salutary.*

salutation /ˌsæl·jəˈteɪ·ʃən/ *n* [C/U] a greeting in words or actions, or the words used at the beginning of a letter or speech ○ [C] *Start your letter with the salutation "Dear Friends."*

salute RECOGNIZE /səˈluːt/ *v* [I/T] to recognize or show respect for a member of the armed forces of higher rank than yourself, usually by raising the right hand to the side of the head ○ [I] *When you see an officer, you must salute.*
salute /səˈluːt/ *n* [C] **1** *Uniformed soldiers gave him a salute.* **2** A salute is also the firing of guns by a military organization to show respect for someone: *a 21-gun salute*
HONOR /səˈluːt/ *v* [T] to honor or express admiration publicly ○ *We salute the important work done by the association.*
salute /səˈluːt/ *n* [C] ○ *The Film Institute held a salute to Jack Nicholson.*

salvage /ˈsæl·vɪdʒ/ *v* [T] to save something valuable from damage, destruction, or loss ○ *After the storm, we were able to salvage some of our belongings, but the house was destroyed.*

salvation /sælˈveɪ·ʃən/ *n* [U] **1** something that prevents danger, loss, or harm ○ *That blanket was my salvation when my car broke down in the snow.* **2** In some religions, salvation is the state of complete belief in God that will save those who believe from the punishment of God for evil or immoral acts.

Salvation Army *n* [U] an international Christian organization whose members work to help poor people

salvo /ˈsæl·voʊ/ *n* [C] *pl* **salvos, salvoes** a firing of several guns at the same time, either in a war or in a ceremony, or a statement in an exchange of opinions ○ *His opening salvo in the debate sparked a war of words.*

samba /ˈsæm·bə, ˈsɑm-/ *n* [C/U] a rhythmic style of dance from Brazil, or the music for this dance ○ [U] *Fans jumped up and danced the samba.*

same EXACTLY LIKE /seɪm/ *adj* [not gradable] exactly like another or each other ○ *My sister and I have the same color hair.* ○ *Our grades were exactly the same.* ○ *They are all the same, these "in-town" events.*
same /seɪm/ *pronoun* ○ *Life was never the same again once the children started school.* ○ *It took longer to lose weight the second time, even though my diet was exactly the same.*
sameness /ˈseɪm·nəs/ *n* [U] ○ *The fall TV lineup promises another season of sameness.*

S

NOT ANOTHER /seɪm/ *adj* [not gradable] this one; not another, different one ○ *She keeps saying the same thing over and over.* ○ *Production is down by 80% from the same period last year.* ○ *She started studying languages and became interested in travel at the same time.*

IDIOMS with **same**

• **at the same time** despite what was just said ○ *She's optimistic that she can get results, but at the same time, she knows it's a very hard job.*
• **in the same boat** in the same difficult situation as someone else ○ *None of us has any money, so we're all in the same boat.*
• **in the same league (as** *someone/something***), in the same league (with** *someone/something***)** having qualities or achievements that are similar to someone or something ○ *The new charity will be giving away $55 million a year, putting it in the same league as other well-known charities.* ○ *He's very good at his job, but he's not in the same league as Gerry.*
• **on the same wavelength** thinking in the same way as someone else ○ *Luckily, my husband and I are on the same wavelength about how to raise our kids.*
• **same difference** *infml* the same thing ○ *Either he's a genius or he's crazy - same difference really.*
• **same here** I agree ○ *"I thought that movie was awful." "Same here."*
• **the same old thing, the same old, same old** something that has not changed, with the result that it seems boring ○ *You get tired of eating the same old thing for breakfast.*

sample /ˈsæm·pəl/ *n* [C] **1** a small amount of something which shows what the rest is or should be like ○ *a free sample* ○ *a blood/tissue sample* ○ *The booklet contains sample questions and answers.* **2** A sample of people is a small group that is tested to obtain information about the larger group: *The poll is based on a random sample of Montgomery voters.*

sample /ˈsæm·pəl/ *v* [T] to take or try a small amount of something ○ *He sampled a little of each dish.* ○ *Buma sampled opinions from people in both countries.*

sanatorium /ˌsæn·əˈtɔːr·iː·əm, -ˈtour-/ *n* a SANITARIUM

sanctify /ˈsæŋk·təˌfɑɪ/ *v* [T] to make holy ○ *a relationship sanctified by marriage*

sanctimonious /ˌsæŋk·təˈmoʊ·niː·əs/ *adj disapproving* showing that you believe you are morally better or more religious ○ *sanctimonious remarks*

sanction **APPROVAL** /ˈsæŋk·ʃən/ *n* [U] *fml* approval or permission ○ *To be just, a government must have the sanction of the governed.* ○ **USAGE:** usually describes formal or legal approval

sanction /ˈsæŋk·ʃən/ *v* [T] ○ *The UN sanctioned intervention in the crisis.*

PUNISHMENT /ˈsæŋk·ʃən/ *n* [C usually pl] an official action taken against a government to force it to behave in a particular way or as punishment for not doing so ○ *trade/economic sanctions*

sanctity /ˈsæŋk·təţ·i/ *n* [U] the condition of being holy or of deserving great respect ○ *the sanctity of life*

sanctuary /ˈsæŋk·tʃəˌwer·i/ *n* [C/U] ***social studies*** **1** protection or a safe place, esp. for someone or something being chased or hunted ○ [U] *The storm's survivors took sanctuary in the church.* ○ [C] *Soldiers attacked an enemy sanctuary.* **2** A sanctuary is a place where birds or animals can live and be protected: [C] *a wildlife/bird sanctuary* **3** A sanctuary is the part of a church where religious ceremonies happen: [C] *Nan and her parents found seats in the sanctuary for the service.*

sand **SMALL GRAINS** /sænd/ *n* [U] a mass of very small grains that at one time were rock and now form deserts and beaches

sandy /ˈsæn·di/ *adj* **1** *Cactuses grow well in sandy soil.* **2** Sandy hair is pale brown.

MAKE SMOOTH /sænd/ *v* [T] to make a surface smooth by rubbing it with SANDPAPER (= strong, rough paper) or with a special tool ○ *The bookcase has to be sanded and stained.*

sandal /ˈsæn·dᵊl/ *n* [C] a light shoe consisting of a bottom part held onto the foot by straps ○ *a pair of sandals*

sandbag /ˈsænd·bæg, ˈsæn-/ *n* [C] a strong cloth bag filled with sand that is used as a defense against flooding and explosions ○ *Thousands of sandbags were piled along the riverbank.*

sandbar /ˈsænd·bɑr/ *n* [C] a BANK (= raised area) of sand that exists just below the surface or a sea or river ➤ Picture: **lagoon**

sandbox /ˈsænd·bɑks, ˈsæn-/ *n* [C] a square area filled with sand in which children can dig and play

sandcastle /ˈsændˌkæs·əl/ *n* [C] a model building of sand, often made by children on the beach

sand dune *n* [C] a DUNE

sandman /ˈsænd·mæn/ *n* [C usually sing] an imaginary man who puts sand in children's eyes to make them go to sleep

sandpaper /ˈsændˌpeɪ·pər/ *n* [U] strong paper with a layer of sand or a similar rough substance stuck to one side, used for rubbing a surface in order to make it smooth

sandpaper /ˈsændˌpeɪ·pər/ *v* [T] to rub a surface, esp. wood with sandpaper to make it smooth

sandstone /ˈsænd·stoʊn/ *n* [U] a soft, yellow or red rock, often used as a building material

sandstorm /ˈsænd·stɔːrm, ˈsæn-/ *n* [C] a strong wind in a desert carrying a large amount of sand

sandwich /ˈsæn·dwɪtʃ/ *n* [C] slices or pieces of meat, cheese, salads, etc., put between two pieces of bread that are held together by the person who picks them up when ready to eat ○ *a bacon, lettuce, and tomato sandwich* ○ *My kids always eat peanut butter and jelly sandwiches for lunch.*

sandwich /ˈsæn·dwɪtʃ/ *v* [T always + adv/prep] to put something or someone in a small space between two other, usually bigger, things or people ○ *She lived in a skinny Victorian house sandwiched between two brownstones in Cambridge.*

sandy /ˈsæn·di/ *adj* ○ See at SAND SMALL GRAINS

sane /seɪn/ *adj* [*-er/-est* only] having a reasonable or healthy mind, or showing good judgment and understanding ○ *Your work, he said, is the one thing that keeps you sane in this crazy world.*
sanity /ˈsæn·ət̬·i/ *n* [U] ○ *He was beginning to doubt his own sanity.*

sang /sæŋ/ *past simple of* SING

sanguine /ˈsæŋ·gwən/ *adj* (of someone or someone's character) positive and hopeful ○ *Some people expect the economy to continue to improve, but others are less sanguine.*

sanitarium /ˌsæn·əˈter·iː·əm/, **sanatorium** /ˌsæn·əˈtɔːr·iː·əm, -ˈtour-/ *n* [C] (esp. in the past) a type of hospital for people who needed long periods of rest and treatment for their illnesses ○ *She died of tuberculosis at a sanitarium in Saranac Lake, N.Y., in 1914.*

sanitary /ˈsæn·əˌter·i/ *adj* relating to being clean and healthy, esp. to the protection of health by the removal of dirt and waste, including human waste ○ *He worked to improve sanitary conditions in New Orleans.*
sanitation /ˌsæn·əˈteɪ·ʃən/ *n* [U] the system used to keep healthy standards in a place where people live, esp. by removing waste products and garbage safely ○ *the Department of Sanitation* ○ *Sanitation workers are picking up the garbage.*

sanitary napkin *n* [C] a soft paper product worn by a woman during her MENSTRUAL period (= bleeding each month from her uterus)

sanitize CLEAN /ˈsæn·əˌtɑɪz/ *v* [T] to make something completely clean ○ *The majority of public swimming pools are sanitized with chlorine.*
CHANGE /ˈsæn·əˌtɑɪz/ *v* [T] to change something to make it less upsetting or unpleasant and more acceptable ○ *The new text sanitizes early American history.*

sanity /ˈsæn·ət̬·i/ *n* ○ See at SANE

sank /sæŋk/ *past simple of* SINK

Santa Claus /ˈsænt·əˌklɔːz/, **Santa** /ˈsænt·ə/ *n* [C] an imaginary old man with white hair, a long white BEARD, and a red coat who, children are told, brings them presents at Christmas

sap WEAKEN /sæp/ *v* [T] **-pp-** to gradually weaken someone's strength ○ *Depression can sap the energy and self-esteem from an individual.*
LIQUID /sæp/ *n* [U] the liquid within a plant that carries food to all parts of it
PERSON /sæp/ *n* [C] *dated* a foolish person

sapling /ˈsæp·lɪŋ/ *n* [C] a young tree

saponification /səˌpɑn·ə·fəˈkeɪ·ʃən/ *n* [U] ***chemistry*** the chemical reaction between a fat or oil and an ALKALI which produces soap

sapphire /ˈsæf·ɑɪr/ *n* [C] a transparent precious stone that is usually bright blue

saprophyte /ˈsæp·rəˌfɑɪt/ *n* [C] ***biology*** an organism that lives and feeds on dead and decaying plant and animal matter

sarcasm /ˈsɑrˌkæz·əm/ *n* [U] ***literature*** remarks that mean the opposite of what they say, made to criticize someone or something in a way that is amusing to others but annoying to the person criticized ○ *biting/heavy sarcasm*
sarcastic /sɑrˈkæs·tɪk/ *adj* ○ *sarcastic comments*

sardine /sɑrˈdiːn/ *n* [C] a small, edible fish, often packed in large numbers in flat metal containers ○ *The train was so crowded, we were packed in like sardines* (= too close together).

sardonic /sɑrˈdɑn·ɪk/ *adj* showing an amused attitude toward someone or something that suggests a criticism but does not express it ○ *a sardonic smile* ○ *Mildly sardonic, the chairman's soft-spoken cross-examination embarrassed hostile witnesses without humiliating them.*

sari /ˈsɑr·i/ *n* [C] a dress consisting of a very long piece of cloth wrapped around the body, worn esp. by Indian and Pakistani women

SASE *n* [C] *abbreviation for* self-addressed stamped envelope (= an envelope that has a stamp on it and the address of the person who sends it)

sash CLOTHING /sæʃ/ *n* [C] a long, narrow piece of cloth worn around the waist, or a strip of cloth worn over the shoulder and across the chest
WINDOW /sæʃ/ *n* [C] the frame of a window or door around a piece of glass

sassy /ˈsæs·i/ *adj* [*-er/-est* only] rude but not seriously offensive ○ *I was a sassy kid who sometimes talked back to my mother.*

SAT /ˌesˌeɪˈtiː/ *n* [C] *trademark* one of two tests for entering college that measure students' abilities and skills

sat /sæt/ *past simple and past participle of* SIT

Sat. *n* [U] *abbreviation for* SATURDAY.

Satan /ˈseɪt·ən/ *n* the main evil spirit; the DEVIL (= the origin of evil and the enemy of God)
satanic /səˈtæn·ɪk, seɪ-/ *adj* evil, or done in worship of Satan

satellite /ˈsæt·əlˌɑɪt/ *n* [C] ***physics*** a natural object moving around a larger object in space, or an artificial object sent up into space to travel around the earth ○ *a spy/weather satellite* ○ *The moon is a satellite of the earth.*

satellite dish *n* [C] a round dish-shaped object that receives television or other electronic signals

satin /ˈsæt·ən/ *n* [U] a type of cloth that is shiny on one side but not on the other ○ *a satin dress*

satire /ˈsæ·tɑɪr/ *n* [C/U] ***literature*** a humorous way of criticizing people or ideas to show that they have faults or are wrong, or a piece of writing or

S

a play that uses this style ○ [C] *The play is a satire on corporate culture.*
satirical /sə'tɪr·ɪ·kəl/ *adj* ○ *satirical humor*
satirist /'sæt̬·ə·rəst/ *n* [C] ***literature*** a person who writes or performs satires
satirize /'sæt̬·ə,rɑɪz/ *v* [T] ○ *Garry Trudeau would satirize him in his Doonesbury comic strip.*

satisfaction /,sæt̬·əs'fæk·ʃən/ *n* [C/U] **1** the pleasant feeling you get when you receive something you wanted, or when you have done or are doing something you wanted to do ○ [U] *She looked at the finished painting with satisfaction.* ○ [U] *He had the satisfaction of knowing he had done the right thing.* ○ [U] *The job had to be done to our satisfaction* (= to a standard that we approved). **2** Satisfaction is also the condition of having a desire or need fulfilled.

satisfactory /,sæt̬·əs'fæk·tə·ri/ *adj* good or good enough, esp. for a particular need or purpose ○ *We did not feel the response was satisfactory and asked for more information.* ○ *Her progress so far has been satisfactory, and we expect a full recovery.*
satisfactorily /,sæt̬·əs'fæk·tə·rə·li/ *adv* ○ *The heating system is working satisfactorily now.*

satisfy /'sæt̬·əs,fɑɪ/ *v* [T] **1** to please someone by giving the person something that is wanted or needed, or to make someone feel pleased because a particular desirable result has happened ○ *Giving the baby her bottle seemed to satisfy her, and she stopped crying.* ○ *I am not really satisfied with the job you did.* **2** To satisfy a standard is to show that you are qualified for it: *I'd like to go to that college if I can satisfy the entrance requirements.* **3** To be satisfied is also to be sure, with all your doubts removed: [+ *that* clause] *I'm satisfied that the doctors did all they could to save her.*
satisfying /'sæt̬·əs,fɑɪ·ɪŋ/ *adj* giving pleasure, esp. by taking care of a need or desire ○ [+ *to* infinitive] *It's very satisfying to know that we were the ones who brought Sarah and Stephen together.*

S

WORD FAMILY satisfy			
Nouns	satisfaction dissatisfaction	Adjectives	satisfactory unsatisfactory dissatisfied satisfying
Verbs	satisfy		
Adverbs	satisfactorily		

saturate /'sætʃ·ə,reɪt/ *v* [T] **1** to make something or someone completely wet, or to make a place completely full of something ○ *Water thoroughly to saturate the soil.* ○ *Contemporary U.S. culture is completely saturated with technology.* **2** ***chemistry*** Saturate also means to cause a substance to combine with as much of another substance as is possible.
saturated /'sætʃ·ə,reɪt̬·əd/ *adj* [not gradable] ***chemistry*** **1** containing all of a substance that can be absorbed **2** Saturated also describes a HYDROCARBON in which the carbon atoms are joined to as many HYDROGEN atoms as possible.
saturation /,sætʃ·ə'reɪ·ʃən/ *n* [U]

Saturday /'sæt̬·ər·di, -,deɪ/, *abbreviation* **Sat.** *n* [C/U] the day of the week after Friday and before Sunday ○ [U] *Do you want to go out Saturday night?* ○ [C] *Saturdays are the only days I get to sleep late.*

Saturn /'sæt̬·ərn/ *n* [U] the planet sixth in order of distance from the sun, after Jupiter and before Uranus ➤ Picture: **solar system**

sauce /sɔːs/ *n* [C/U] a thick liquid prepared and served with food to add flavor ○ [U] *barbecue/tomato sauce*

saucepan /'sɔːs·pæn/ *n* [C] a deep cooking pan with a long handle

saucer /'sɔː·sər/ *n* [C] a small plate that goes under a cup ○ *a cup and saucer*

saucy /'sɔː·si, 'sæs·i/ *adj* [*-er/-est* only] **1** rude and lacking respect ○ *a saucy child* **2** Saucy also means confident and full of energy in an entertaining, exciting way: *a saucy musical*

sauerkraut /'saʊr·kraʊt/ *n* [U] CABBAGE (= large, leafy vegetable) that has been cut into small pieces and preserved in its own salted juice ○ *Do you want sauerkraut on your frankfurter?*

sauna /'sɔː·nə, 'saʊ·nə/ *n* [C] a room or small building, often with wooden walls, that is heated to a high temperature and in which people sit for their health

saunter /'sɔːnt·ər, 'sɑnt-/ *v* [I always + adv/prep] to walk in a slow and relaxed way ○ *My cousin stood up, yawning, and sauntered away toward the door.*

sausage /'sɔː·sɪdʒ/ *n* [C/U] a food made of meat that has been cut into very small pieces, mixed with spices, and put into a thin and usually edible tube

sauté /sɔː'teɪ/ *v* [T] to fry food in a little oil or fat, usually until it is brown

savage FIERCE /'sæv·ɪdʒ/ *adj* (of an animal) wild and fierce, or (of a remark or action) violently cruel ○ *savage beasts* ○ *He writes about people who are savage and cruel.*
savage /'sæv·ɪdʒ/ *v* [T] to criticize someone cruelly ○ *The performance was savaged by the media.*
savagely /'sæv·ɪdʒ·li/ *adv* ○ *savagely attacked*
savagery /'sæv·ɪdʒ·ri/ *n* [U] violent cruelty

PERSON /'sæv·ɪdʒ/ *n* [C] *dated* someone who is thought to be in a wild state and to have no experience of a CIVILIZED society (= highly developed society) ○ **USAGE:** This word is often considered offensive.

save MAKE SAFE /seɪv/ *v* [T] to make or keep someone or something safe from danger or harm, or to bring something back to a satisfactory condition ○ *She jumped into the pool and saved the child from drowning.* ○ *His leg was partly crushed in the accident but the surgeon was able to save it.* ○ *Smoke detectors can save lives.*

KEEP /seɪv/ *v* [I/T] **1** to keep money or something else for use in the future ○ [I] *I'm saving (up) for a new bike and I've got almost $100.* ○ [T] *If you save* *the receipts from your business trip, the company will reimburse you.* ○ [T] *I forgot to get milk – will you save my place in line while I get it?* **2** *technology* To save information on a computer is to store it in a computer file.

savings /ˈseɪ·vɪŋz/ *pl n* the money you keep, esp. in a bank or other financial organization ○ *I'm going to put some of my savings into a down payment on a car.*

NOT WASTE /seɪv/ *v* [I/T] to prevent time, money, or effort from being lost or spent, or to help someone by taking an action to prevent time, money, etc., from being lost ○ [T] *You'll save time if you take the car.* ○ [T] *The governor claims he can save the taxpayers $10 million a year.* ○ [T] *If you'd stop and pick up the kids on your way home, it will save me from having to do it later.*

SPORTS /seɪv/ *n* [C] (in some sports) the stopping of the ball or other object from going into the goal you are defending ○ *We watched a soccer game on TV, and the goalie made several spectacular saves.*

EXCEPT /seɪv/, **save for** /ˈseɪv·fɔːr, -fər/ *prep* but or except (for) ○ *They found all the lost documents save one.* ○ *The walls were bare save for a poster.*

WORD FAMILY save

Nouns		Verbs	
	save		save
	saving		
	savings		
	savior		

IDIOMS with save

• **save** *your* **breath** to not say anything ○ *I don't know why I bother trying to explain this to you – I might as well save my breath.*

• **save face** to keep your reputation and avoid others losing respect for you ○ *We said he left "to pursue other interests" to let him save face, but actually we fired him.*

PHRASAL VERB with save

• **save on** *something* **1** to spend less money for something ○ *The city dimmed its street lights after 9 p.m. to save on its electric bill.* **2** If you save on something that can be used up, you use less of it: *Smaller private planes will be used to save on fuel.*

savings account *n* [C] an account in a bank or similar financial organization that earns INTEREST (= a kind of profit)

savior, *Cdn, Br* **saviour** /ˈseɪv·jər/ *n* [C] **1** a person who saves someone from danger or harm **2** In Christianity, the Savior is a name for Jesus.

savor, *Cdn, Br* **savour** /ˈseɪ·vər/ *v* [T] to enjoy food or an experience slowly, in order to appreciate it as much as possible ○ *He wanted to savor his time with Henrietta and their grown children.*

savvy /ˈsæv·i/ *n* [U] *infml* practical knowledge and ability ○ *She has a lot of marketing savvy.*

savvy /ˈsæv·i/ *adj infml* ○ *He's a politically savvy guy.*

saw SEE /sɔː/ *past simple of* SEE

TOOL /sɔː/ *n* [C] a tool that has a blade with sharp points along one edge, used for cutting hard materials, such as wood or metal ○ *a circular saw* ○ *a hand-held saw*

saw /sɔː/ *v* [I/T] *past simp.* **sawed,** *past part.* **sawn, sawed** to cut with a saw ○ [M] *I sawed off the end of the plank.*

sawdust /ˈsɔː·dʌst/ *n* [U] the very small grains that are produced when you cut wood

sawmill /ˈsɔː·mɪl/ *n* [U] a place where wood is cut into boards or other forms, usually with heavy machinery

saxophone /ˈsæk·səˌfoʊn/, *short form* **sax** /sæks/ *n* [C/U] a musical instrument that is played by blowing through a REED (= thin piece of wood), or this instrument generally

say SPEAK /seɪ/ *v* [T] *past* **said, says** to speak or pronounce words ○ *How do you say your name?* ○ *The child could say her ABCs when she was still a baby.*

USAGE

say or tell?

Say can refer to any type of speech.

"Good night," she said.

She said she was unhappy.

Jim said to meet him here.

Say is never followed directly by a person as an object. You must use "say something to someone" for this.

She said goodbye to me at the airport.

~~*She said me goodbye at the airport.*~~

Tell is used to report that someone has given information or an order. The verb **tell** is always followed by the person that the information or order is given to.

Simon told them all to stay inside the house.

Oscar told the boys a wonderful story about a giant.

~~*Oscar told to the boys a wonderful story about a giant.*~~

WORD CHOICES say

See also: **tell**

Utter is a slightly formal word which means "say."

He sat through the meeting without ***uttering*** *a word.*

Remark or **comment** can be used instead of "say" to talk about an opinion or thought, or in formal English you could use **observe.**

He ***remarked/commented*** *that she was looking thin.*

"I've always found German-made cars very reliable," he ***observed.***

If someone says something, especially clearly and carefully, you could use the verb **state.**

Union members ***stated*** *that they were unhappy with the proposal.* ➤

S

Announce or **declare** are often used when someone says something publicly.

*He suddenly **announced** in the middle of dinner that they were getting married.*

*She **declared** that it was the best chocolate cake she had ever tasted.*

Claim can be used when someone says that something is true but cannot be proven.

*He **claimed** that he was not responsible for the accident.*

If someone says something suddenly and unexpectedly, you could use the phrase **come out with**.

*Young children **come out with** very funny things sometimes.*

If you say something although it is difficult because other people are talking too, you could use the phrasal verb **get *something* in**.

*She couldn't **get** a word **in** because he just loves to talk.*

EXPRESS /seɪ/ *v* [I/T] *past* **said**, **says** **1** to express something in words, or to tell someone something ○ [T] *What did you say to him?* ○ [I] *Mom said to meet her in front of the building.* **2** To say also means to communicate without using words, esp. in music and art: [T] *What do you think the artist said in this painting?*

STATE AN OPINION /seɪ/ *v* [I/T] *past* **said**, **says** **1** to state an opinion ○ [+ (*that*) clause] *If they're late, I say (that) we go without them.* **2** Say can also mean imagine: [+ (that) clause] *Let's say (that) you are a planner and that you think far ahead.*

say /seɪ/ *n* [U] the right or opportunity to give your opinion or be involved in making decisions ○ *I have no say in hiring and firing.*

GIVE INFORMATION /seɪ/ *v* [I/T] *past* **said**, **says** to provide information or instructions in writing ○ [T] *What does that sign say?*

IDIOMS with say

• **say a lot about** *something/someone* to clearly show or express something about someone or something ○ *It says a lot about her that she's willing to help people she doesn't even know.* ○ *I think the way someone dresses says a lot about their character.*

• **say** *something* **to** *yourself* to think something ○ *I said to myself, I'd better take care of that now.*

• **say when** decide when to stop or end something ○ *She started pouring the water and told me to "say when."* ○ **USAGE:** Used esp. when giving someone food or drink.

• **to say the least** to not describe something in the strongest way you could, often in order to be polite ○ *The dinner was not tasty, to say the least.*

saying /ˈseɪ·ɪŋ/ *n* [C] a well-known expression or wise statement ○ *I hate T-shirts with sayings on them.*

say-so /ˈseɪ·soʊ/ *n* [U] *infml* authority or approval to do something ○ *A coach's responsibility is to have the final say-so on any subject.*

scab **SKIN COVERING** /skæb/ *n* [C] a hard covering of dry blood that forms over a cut or sore ○ *Don't pick at your scab!*

WORKER /skæb/ *n* [C] someone who takes the place of a worker who is STRIKING (= joining in an organized refusal to work)

scads /skædz/ *pl n infml* a large number or amount ○ *There were scads of dogs, all sizes, shapes, and colors.*

scaffold /ˈskæf·əld, -oʊld/ *n* [C] a structure workers can stand on while working on a building, or a structure from which to HANG (= kill by hanging from a rope around the neck) criminals sentenced to death

scaffolding /ˈskæf·əl·dɪŋ, -ˌoʊl·dɪŋ/ *n* [U] a raised structure that supports workers and materials during work on a building ○ *The scaffolding rises 10 stories above the street.*

scalar /ˈskeɪ·lər/ *adj* [not gradable] ***mathematics, physics*** having MAGNITUDE (= strength) but not direction

scalawag /ˈskæl·əˌwæg/ *n* [C] someone who causes trouble in a playful way, or a charming person who is slightly dishonest ○ *That's the last time that scalawag is going to steal from me.*

scald /skɔːld/ *v* [T] **1** to burn someone with very hot liquid or steam ○ *The liquid spilled out and scalded his hand.* **2** To scald a liquid is to heat it until it almost boils: *scald the milk*

scalding /ˈskɔːl·dɪŋ/ *adj, adv* ○ *You can wash off the wax with scalding water.*

scale **MEASURING SYSTEM** /skeɪl/ *n* [C] a range of numbers used as a system to measure or compare things ○ *Restaurant ratings are on a scale of zero to five stars.*

SERIES OF MARKS /skeɪl/ *n* [C] a series of marks in a line with regular spaces between them for measuring, or an object for measuring marked in this way ○ *The two scales show inches and centimeters.*

SIZE/LEVEL /skeɪl/ *n* [U] ***art*** the size or level of something in comparison to what is average ○ *Our problems are like those in the city, just on a smaller scale.*

WEIGHING DEVICE /skeɪl/ *n* [C] a device for weighing people or things ○ *a baby scale* ○ *a postal scale*

SIZE RELATIONSHIP /skeɪl/ *n* [C/U] the relationship of the size of a map, drawing, or model of something to the size of the actual thing ○ [C] *The model was built at a 1-inch-to-1-foot scale.*

MUSIC /skeɪl/ *n* [C] ***music*** a set of musical notes in which each note is higher or lower than the previous one by a particular amount ○ *Tyler practices scales on the piano every day.*

SKIN /skeɪl/ *n* [C usually pl] any of the thin pieces of hard skin covering the bodies of fish, snakes, and LIZARDS

scaly /ˈskeɪ·li/ *adj* [-er/-est only] **1** *Reptiles have scaly skin.* **2** If a person's skin is scaly, it is very dry.

CLIMB /skeɪl/ *v* [T] to climb up something steep, such as a cliff or wall ○ *He scaled a steep cliff beside the river.*

S

PHRASAL VERBS with scale

• **scale back/down** *(something)* [M] to reduce something in size, amount, or production ○ *Sid will have to scale back his plans.*

• **scale up** *(something)* [M] to increase something in size, amount, or production ○ *This research on seaweed could be scaled up at low cost.*

scalene triangle *n* [C] ***geometry*** a triangle in which all three sides are different lengths

scallion /ˈskæl·jən/ *n* [C] a small, thin onion with a white bottom and a green stem and leaves, which is eaten in salads and other dishes

scallop /ˈskɑl·əp, ˈskæl-/ *n* [C] a sea creature with two joined, flat, round shells, or the thick, round muscle of this animal eaten as food

scalp HEAD /skælp/ *n* [C] the skin on the top of the head where the hair grows ○ *His hair was cut so short you could see his scalp.*

scalp /skælp/ *v* [T] to cut the hair and skin off someone's head

SELL /skælp/ *v* [T] to sell tickets increased prices without official permission

scalper /ˈskæl·pər/ *n* [C] ○ *We tried to get tickets, but the scalpers wanted $150 per ticket.*

scalpel /ˈskæl·pəl/ *n* [C] a small, very sharp knife used for exact cutting, esp. for an operation

scam /skæm/ *n* [C] *infml* a dishonest or illegal plan or activity, esp. one for making money ○ *She was involved in an insurance scam, collecting on false accident claims.*

scamper /ˈskæm·pər/ *v* [I always + adv/prep] (esp. of small children and animals) to run with small, quick steps ○ *The kitten scampered around the kitchen, chasing a ball.*

scan /skæn/ *v* [I/T] **-nn- 1** to examine something carefully ○ [I] *This technique is used to scan for defective genes.* **2** If an image or text on paper is scanned into a computer, it is changed into electronic information by a special device: [T] *A little hand-held device beeps as soon as it has scanned a bar code.* **3** If you scan a text you read it quickly: [T] *I scanned a few pages of the book and thought it looked interesting.*

scan /skæn/ *n* [C] **1** *A quick scan of my calendar shows that I'm pretty busy this week.* ○ *a security scan of passengers' bags* **2** A scan is an examination of the inside of something, such as part of the body or a package, using a computerized device to produce an image of what cannot be seen with the eyes: *a medical scan of the head*

scanner /ˈskæn·ər/ *n* [C] a device that changes images or text into electronic form ○ *a supermarket checkout scanner* ○ *An MRI scanner makes images of the brain, spinal cord, and other organs.*

scandal /ˈskæn·dᵊl/ *n* [C/U] an action or event that is considered immoral, causing the public to react with shock or anger ○ [C] *People withdrew their money from banks caught up in the scandal.*

scandalize /ˈskæn·dəˌlɑɪz/ *v* [T] to shock someone with an action or opinion thought of as immoral or wrong ○ *His novel scandalized readers with his description of Washington power brokers.*

scandalous /ˈskæn·də·ləs/ *adj* ○ *She has a reputation for spreading scandalous gossip.*

scant /skænt/ *adj* [not gradable] **1** very little or not much ○ *I paid scant attention to the movie's plot.* **2** Scant can also mean not quite a full measure of something: *Pour the batter by scant 1/4 cups onto the hot griddle.*

scanty /ˈskænt·i/ *adj* smaller in size or amount than what is considered necessary or desirable ○ *scanty food supplies*

scantily /ˈskænt·ᵊl·i/ *adv*

scapegoat /ˈskeɪp·goʊt/ *n* [C] someone who is blamed or punished for another's faults or actions ○ *When things don't go well, people always look for a scapegoat.*

scar /skɑr/ *n* [C] a mark left on the skin by a cut or burn that has healed ○ (*fig.*) *The loss of a parent causes permanent scars for many children.*

scar /skɑr/ *v* [T] **-rr-** ○ *She was badly scarred by the fire.*

scarce /skers, skærs/ *adj* [*-er/-est* only] not available in necessary amounts, or rare ○ *Jobs are scarce.*

scarcity /ˈsker·sət̬·i, ˈskær-/ *n* [C/U] a lack of something ○ [C] *A scarcity of flour makes bread, cake, and other baked goods more expensive.*

scarcely ONLY JUST /ˈsker·sli, ˈskær-/ *adv* [not gradable] only just or almost not ○ *I could scarcely move my arm after the accident.*

NOT /ˈsker·sli, ˈskær-/ *adv* [not gradable] *fml* certainly not ○ *He would scarcely have broken it on purpose.*

scare /sker, skær/ *v* [I/T] to feel frightened, or to cause someone to feel frightened ○ [T] *Snakes scare me.* ○ [I] *Jesse doesn't scare easily.*

scare /sker, skær/ *n* [C] ○ *You gave me a real scare.*

scared /skerd, skærd/ *adj* ○ *I was scared, and I wanted to go home.*

scary /ˈsker·i, ˈskær·i/ *adj* [*-er/-est* only] ○ *New York isn't very scary.*

WORD FAMILY scare

Nouns	scare	*Adjectives*	scared
Verbs	scare		scary

WORD CHOICES scare

Other common ways of saying "scared" are **afraid** or **frightened**.

If someone is extremely scared, then you can use the adjectives **petrified**, **terrified**, **panic-stricken** or the informal phrase **scared to death**.

I'm ***petrified/terrified*** *of spiders.*

She was ***panic-stricken*** *when her little boy disappeared.*

He's ***scared to death*** *of having the operation.*

If someone is scared because of worrying about something, then you can use adjectives like **afraid** or **worried**.

I'm ***afraid/worried*** *that something will go wrong.*

➤

To talk about things that make you feel uncomfortable and scared, you could use the idiom **give *me* the creeps.**

Being alone in that big house ***gives me the creeps.***

IDIOM with scare

• **scare *someone* to death, scare the (living) daylights out of *someone*** to frighten someone very much ○ *Thunderstorms scare her to death.*

PHRASAL VERBS with scare

• **scare away/off *someone/something*** [M] to cause a person or animal to go or stay away ○ *I wish I could scare those crows away.* ○ *A show like that could scare off advertisers.*

• **scare up *something*** [M] *infml* to find or obtain something that is not easily available ○ *She's campaigning hard, trying to scare up votes.* ○ *I'll scare up something for us to eat.*

scarecrow /ˈsker·kroʊ, ˈskær-/ *n* [C] an object that looks like a person dressed in old, torn clothes and that stands in a garden or field to frighten birds away

scare tactics *pl n* ways of achieving a particular result by frightening people so much that they do what you want them to do ○ *Some of the companies selling anti-spyware tools employ scare tactics.*

scarf CLOTH /skɑrf/ *n* [C] *pl* **scarves, scarfs** a piece of cloth that covers the shoulders, neck, or head for warmth or appearance ○ *A heavy woolen scarf hid most of his face.*

EAT /skɑrf/ *v* [I/T] *infml* to eat a lot of food quickly ○ [I] *In no time, I scarfed down two hamburgers, French fries, and something to drink.*

scarlet /ˈskɑr·lət/ *adj, n* [U] (of) a bright red color ○ *scarlet roses* ○ [U] *She was dressed in scarlet.*

scary /ˈsker·i, ˈskær·i/ *adj* ○ See at SCARE

scat /skæt/ *exclamation infml* said to make an animal go away quickly ○ *Go on – scat! Get off my chair!*

scathing /ˈskeɪ·ðɪŋ/ *adj* severely critical and unkind ○ *He delivered a scathing attack on the president.*

scatter /ˈskæt̬·ər/ *v* [I/T] to move apart in many directions, or to throw something in different directions ○ [I] *We grew up in a small town, but now we're scattered all over the country.*

scattered /ˈskæt̬·ərd/ *adj* ○ *There will be scattered showers throughout the afternoon.*

scatterplot /skæt̬·ər·plɑt/, **scatter diagram** *n* [C] ***mathematics*** a graph in which each mark represents a pair of values relating two sets of DATA (= numbers) drawn on a COORDINATE PLANE (= area with vertical and horizontal measures)

scavenge /ˈskæv·əndʒ/ *v* [I/T] to search for and collect unwanted food or objects, or of animals or birds to feed on decaying flesh ○ [T] *We scavenged a table and chairs someone had thrown out.* ○ [I] *The crows scavenged on the dead carcass.*

scavenger /ˈskæv·ən·dʒər/ *n* [C] an animal, bird, or person who scavenges

scavenger hunt *n* [C] a game in which people must collect a number of items in a given period of time without buying them

scenario Ⓐ /səˈnær·iːˌoʊ, -ˈner-, -ˈnɑr-/ *n* [C] *pl* **scenarios 1** a description of possible events, or a description of the story of a movie, play, or other performance **2** The worst-case scenario is the worst situation that can be imagined: *In the worst-case scenario, the whole coast would be under water.*

scene PLAY/MOVIE /siːn/ *n* [C] a part of a play or movie in which the action stays in one place for a continuous period ○ *The opening scene of the movie was filmed in New York City.*

VIEW /siːn/ *n* [C] a view or picture of a place ○ *The scene from the mountaintop was breathtaking.* ○ *He painted a street scene.*

PLACE /siːn/ *n* [C usually sing] a place where an actual or imagined event happens ○ *He was convicted of leaving the scene of an accident.* ○ *Dozens of firefighters converged on the scene* (= they arrived at the place quickly).

EVENT /siːn/ *n* [C] an event, actual or imaginary ○ *The novel recalls scenes from an era that's vanished.*

AREA /siːn/ *n* [U] a particular area of activity or way of life ○ *the fashion/music scene* ○ *He disappeared from the political scene after failing to win reelection.*

SHOW /siːn/ *n* [C] a show of emotion or anger ○ *She made a scene at the checkout when I wouldn't buy her any candy.*

scenery COUNTRYSIDE /ˈsiː·nə·ri/ *n* [U] the general appearance of natural surroundings, esp. when these are beautiful ○ *We stopped at the top of the hill to admire the scenery.*

scenic /ˈsiː·nɪk/ *adj* [not gradable] having or showing beautiful natural surroundings ○ *They took the scenic route on the way home.*

THEATER /ˈsiː·nə·ri/ *n* [U] the painted backgrounds used on a theater stage to represent the place where the action is

scent /sent/ *n* [C/U] **1** a smell, esp. when pleasant, or a smell left behind by an animal or person ○ [C] *The scent of lilacs permeated the air.* ○ [C] *The dogs were onto the lost boy's scent* (= were following his smell). **2** Scent is also PERFUME (= liquid with a pleasant smell).

scent /sent/ *v* [T] **1** *Perfume scented the air* (= filled the air with a smell). ○ *The dogs eventually scented the fox* (= discovered it by smelling). **2** If you scent something, you have a feeling that something exists or is present: *We could scent danger/trouble/success.*

scented /ˈsent·əd/ *adj* [not gradable] ○ *scented perfume/soap/candles*

scepter /ˈsep·tər/ *n* [C] a decorated stick that is carried by a queen or king as a symbol of authority, esp. at official ceremonies

schedule Ⓐ /ˈskedʒ·uːl, -əl; *Cdn often* ˈʃedʒ-/ *n* [C/U] **1** a list of planned activities or things to be done at or during a particular time ○ [C] *Amid her*

S

hectic schedule, she found time to stop by. ○ [C] *The work schedule for this month is posted on the staff bulletin board.* ○ [U] *The construction was completed ahead of/on/behind schedule* (= early/on time/late). ○ [U] *Everything went according to schedule* (= as planned). **2** An airline/bus/train schedule (also (**timetable**)) is a list of days and times that aircraft/buses/trains leave and arrive at particular places.

schedule Ⓐ /ˈskedʒ·uːl, -əl; *Cdn often* ʃedʒ-/ *v* [T] to plan something for a particular time ○ *The meeting has been scheduled for tomorrow afternoon.* ○ *The film is scheduled to begin production in August.*

schematic Ⓐ /skɪˈmæţ·ɪk/ *adj* showing the main form and features of something, usually in the form of a drawing, which helps people to understand it ○ *a schematic diagram*

schematic Ⓐ /skɪˈmæţ·ɪk/ *n* [C] a drawning or plan that shows the details of how something operates or is put together

schematically Ⓐ /skɪˈmæţ·ɪk·li/ *adv*

scheme Ⓐ /skiːm/ *n* [C] **1** a plan for doing or organizing something ○ *The committee came up with a creative fundraising scheme.* ○ *The yellow and white color scheme brightened up the kitchen.* **2** A scheme is also a secret and dishonest plan: [+ *to* infinitive] *They devised a scheme to defraud the government of millions of dollars.*

scheme Ⓐ /skiːm/ *v* [I] to make a plan, esp. a secret and dishonest one ○ [+ *to* infinitive] *He was scheming to get the top job from the moment he joined the company.*

schemer /ˈskiː·mər/ *n* [C] *disapproving*

IDIOM with scheme

• **in the (grand) scheme of things** considering everything ○ *In the scheme of things, having lots of money isn't as important as having friends.*

schism /ˈsɪz·əm, ˈskɪz-/ *n* [C] a division of a group into two opposing groups, esp. in a church

schizo /ˈskɪt·soʊ/ *adj, n short form of* SCHIZOPHRENIC

schizophrenia /ˌskɪt·səˈfriː·niː·ə/ *n* [U] *medical* a mental illness in which a person's thoughts and feelings are not related to reality

schizophrenic /ˌskɪt·səˈfren·ɪk/, *short form* **schizo** /ˈskɪt·soʊ/ *n* [C] a person who has schizophrenia

schizophrenic /ˌskɪt·səˈfren·ɪk/, *short form* **schizo** /ˈskɪt·soʊ/ *adj* [not gradable]

schlep CARRY /ʃlep/, **schlepp, shlep** *v* [T] **-pp-** *infml* to carry an object with effort ○ [I] *We schlepped our suitcases into the airport.*

GO /ʃlep/ *v* [I] to go or move around with effort ○ *I've been schlepping all over town looking for just the right present.*

schlock /ʃlɑk/ *n* [U] *slang* anything cheap or of low quality ○ *The jewelry she bought on the street was real schlock.*

schmaltzy, **schmalzy** /ˈʃmɔːlt·si, ˈʃmɑlt-/ *adj infml, disapproving* causing extreme emotions of love or sadness, esp. in the arts ○ *They spend a lot of time together listening to schmaltzy love songs.*

schmaltz, **schmalz** /ʃmɔːlts, ʃmɑlts/ *n* [U] *infml* ○ *His writing is full of schmaltz.*

schmooze, **shmooze** /ʃmuːz/ *v* [I] *infml* to talk informally with someone ○ *Mike's out on the porch schmoozing with the neighbors.*

schnapps /ʃnæps, ʃnɑps/ *n* [U] a colorless alcoholic drink, usually made from grain, potato, or fruit

scholar /ˈskɑl·ər/ *n* [C] **1** a person with great knowledge, usually of a particular subject **2** A scholar is also a student who has been given a college or university SCHOLARSHIP (= money to pay for studies).

scholarly /ˈskɑl·ər·li/ *adj* relating to, or typical of scholars ○ *John is more serious and scholarly than his brother.* ○ *Her research was published in a scholarly journal.*

scholarship /ˈskɑl·ərˌʃɪp/ *n* [C/U] **1** the qualities, methods, or achievements of a scholar ○ [U] *Recent scholarship has addressed this scientific issue.* **2** A scholarship is also money given to someone to help pay for that person's education.

scholastic /skəˈlæs·tɪk/ *adj* [not gradable] relating to school and education ○ *Laura's scholastic achievements won her acceptance into Harvard.*

school EDUCATION /skuːl/ *n* [C/U] **1** a place where people, esp. young people, are educated ○ [C] *a nursery/grade/elementary/secondary/graduate school* ○ [C] *What school do you go to?* ○ [U] *The kids walk to school.* ○ [C] *The whole school knew about the incident* (= all the students and teachers at the school knew about it). **2** School also means the time spent in school: [U] *School is out early today.* **3** School also means the process of being educated in a school: [U] *Krista starts school in the fall.* ○ [U] *I've got one more year of school left.* **4** A school is also a part of a college or university specializing in a particular subject or group of subjects: [C] *Johns Hopkins School of Advanced International Studies* **5** A school is also a place where a particular subject or skill is taught: [C] *a driving/dancing/art school* **6** School is also a college or university: [U] *We went to school together in Atlanta.*

school /skuːl/ *v* [T] to train or teach ○ *She was schooled locally and then went away to college.*

schooling /ˈskuː·lɪŋ/ *n* [U] training or education ○ *He had little formal schooling* (= education at school).

GROUP /skuːl/ *n* [C] a group of artists, writers, or PHILOSOPHERS (= people with theories about existence) whose styles, methods, or ideas are similar ○ *Her painting belongs to the Impressionist school.*

SEA ANIMALS /skuːl/ *n* [C] a large number of fish or other sea animals swimming in a group

WORD FAMILY school

Nouns	school preschool schooling preschooler	*Adjectives*	preschool
		Verbs	school

schoolchild /'sku:l·tʃaɪld/ *n* [C] *pl* **-children** a child who goes to school ○ *American schoolchildren are taught that everyone must obey the laws.*

school of thought *n* [C] a set of ideas or opinions about a matter that are shared by a group of people ○ *There are two schools of thought on reducing unemployment.*

schoolteacher /'sku:lˌti:·tʃər/ *n* [C] a teacher in a school

schoolwork /'sku:l·wɜrk/ *n* [U] studying done at school or at home

schooner /'sku:·nər/ *n* [C] a sailing ship with two or more MASTS, and sails parallel to the length of the ship

science /'sɑɪ·əns/ *n* [C/U] **1** the systematic study of the structure and behavior of the natural and physical world, or knowledge obtained about the world by watching it carefully and experimenting ○ [U] *Advances in medical science mean that people are living longer.* ○ [U] *She shows a talent for math and science.* **2** Sciences are also particular areas of science, such as biology, chemistry, and physics. **3** Science also refers to subjects which are studied like a science: [U] *political/computer science*

WORD FAMILY science			
Nouns	science scientist	*Adjectives*	scientific unscientific
Adverbs	scientifically		

science fiction, *short form* **sci-fi** /'sɑɪ 'fɑɪ/ *n* [U] a type of writing about imagined developments in science and their effect on life esp. in the future

scientific /ˌsɑɪ·ən 'tɪf·ɪk/ *adj* **1** relating to science ○ *The biotechnology center is on the cutting edge of scientific research.* **2** Scientific also means using organized methods, like those of science: *I haven't been very scientific about the design of the garden.*

scientifically /ˌsɑɪ·ən 'tɪf·ɪ·kli/ *adv*

scientific notation *n* [U] ***mathematics, science*** a way of writing very large or very small numbers by multiplying power of 10 and a number between 1 and 10 ○ 3.6×10^3

scientist /'sɑɪ·ən·təst/ *n* [C] an expert in science

sci-fi /'sɑɪ 'fɑɪ/ *n* [U] *short form of* SCIENCE FICTION

scintillating /'sɪnt·əlˌeɪt̬·ɪŋ/ *adj* exciting and intelligent ○ *It was a superb script and a scintillating production.*

scion /'sɑɪ·ən/ *n* [C] *fml* a young member of a rich and famous family

scissors /'sɪz·ərz/ *pl n* a cutting device consisting of two blades, each with a ring-shaped handle, which are joined in the middle so that their sharp edges move against each other, used esp. for cutting paper or cloth ○ *a pair of scissors*

sclerosis /sklə'roʊ·səs/ *n* [U] *medical* a medical condition that causes the soft organs and TISSUES of the body to become hard

scoff /skɑf, skɔ:f/ *v* [I] to speak about someone or something in a way which shows that you have no respect for that person or thing ○ *The coach scoffed at the notion that he was about to resign.*

scold /skoʊld/ *v* [T] to criticize angrily someone who has done something wrong ○ *His mother scolded him for breaking the window.*

scolding /'skoʊl·dɪŋ/ *n* [C/U] ○ [C] *I got a scolding for coming home late.*

scone /skoʊn, skɑn/ *n* [C] a small, usually round, soft bread made with flour, milk, and fat

scoop **TOOL** /sku:p/ *n* [C] **1** a tool with a handle and a curved, open end, used to dig out and move an amount of something ○ *an ice-cream scoop* **2** A scoop is also the amount held by a scoop: *Just one scoop of mashed potatoes for me, please.*

scoop /sku:p/ *v* [T] ○ *Scoop out the melon with a spoon.* ○ *He scooped the sand into a bucket.*

NEWS /sku:p/ *n* [C usually sing] **1** a news story discovered and published by one newspaper before all the others **2** The scoop is also the most recent information or details: *What's the scoop on the new boss?*

scoop /sku:p/ *v* [T] ○ *Another paper scooped the story, just as we were about to publish it.*

scoot /sku:t/ *v* [I] *infml* **1** to go quickly ○ *I need to scoot over to the post office.* **2** To scoot is also to slide while sitting: *Scoot over and make room for your sister.*

scooter **TOY** /'sku:t̬·ər/ *n* [C] a child's vehicle with two or three small wheels joined to the bottom of a narrow board and a long vertical handle fixed to the front wheel. The rider stands with one foot on the board and pushes against the ground with the other foot, while turning the handle to direct movement.

MOTOR VEHICLE /'sku:t̬·ər/ *n* [C] a motor vehicle with two wheels, that is similar to, but smaller than, a MOTORCYCLE

scope Ⓐ **RANGE** /skoʊp/ *n* [U] the range of matters considered or dealt with ○ *We are going to widen the scope of the investigation.*

OPPORTUNITY /skoʊp/ *n* [U] the opportunity for activity ○ *There is limited scope for further reducing the workforce.*

DEVICE /skoʊp/ *infml* a device you look through to see something that is difficult to see directly, such as a MICROSCOPE or a TELESCOPE

scorch /skɔ:rtʃ/ *v* [I/T] to burn a surface slightly, causing it to change color ○ [T] *The iron was too hot and scorched the shirt.*

scorch /skɔ:rtʃ/ *n* [C] a burn mark on a surface

scorcher /'skɔ:r·tʃər/ *n* [C] *infml* an extremely hot day ○ *Yesterday was a real scorcher.*

scorching /'skɔ:r·tʃɪŋ/ *adj, adv* [not gradable] (of the weather) very hot ○ *I don't want to be outside in this scorching heat.* ○ *It was scorching hot at the beach.*

score **WIN** /skɔ:r, skoʊr/ *v* [I/T] to win or obtain a point or something else that gives you an advantage in a competitive activity, such as a sport, game, or test ○ [I] *Has either team scored yet?* ○ [T] *The Packers scored a touchdown with two minutes to go in the football game.* ○ [T] *A student from Gettysburg scored a perfect 1600 points on the college entrance exam.* ○ [T] (*fig.*) *He scored* (= obtained) *a deal with a recording label two years ago.*

score /skɔːr, skoʊr/ *n* [C] the number of points achieved or obtained in a game or other competition ○ *The final score was 103–90.* ○ *Who's going to keep score when we play bridge?* ○ (*infml*) *So what's the score* (= what are the facts of this situation), *doctor? Is it serious?*

scoreless /ˈskɔːr·ləs, ˈskoʊr-/ *adj* [not gradable] ○ *After eight innings, the game was still a scoreless tie* (= neither team had made any points).

scorer /ˈskɔːr·ər, ˈskoʊr-/ *n* [C] someone who scores a point or points ○ *Patrick is his team's leading scorer.*

MUSICAL TEXT /skɔːr, skoʊr/ *n* [C] ***music*** a piece of written music showing the parts for all the different instruments and voices, or the music written for a movie or other entertainment

MATTER /skɔːr, skoʊr/ *n* [C usually sing] a particular matter among others related to it ○ *I'll let you have the money, so there's nothing to worry about on that score.*

NUMBER /skɔːr, skoʊr/ *n* [C] (a set or group of) 20 ○ *Brandon received cards from scores of* (= many) *local well-wishers.*

WORD FAMILY score

Nouns	score	Adjectives	scoreless
	scorer	Verbs	score
			underscore

IDIOM with score

• **score points (with** *someone***)** to do something that will make someone like you ○ *He tried really hard to be funny and cool to try to score points with Amanda.*

scoreboard /ˈskɔːr·bɔːrd, ˈskoʊr·boʊrd/ *n* [C] a large board or screen, sometimes electronic, on which the score of a game is shown

scorn /skɔːrn/ *n* [U] a strong feeling that someone or something is of little or no worth and deserves no respect ○ *These countries deserve our respect, not the scorn of a politician.*

scorn /skɔːrn/ *v* [T] to treat with a great lack of respect, or to refuse something because you think it is wrong or not acceptable ○ *He was scorned by his classmates for his bad behavior.*

scornful /ˈskɔːrn·fəl/ *adj* ○ *a scornful laugh/look*

Scorpio /ˈskɔːr·piː ˌoʊ/ *n* [C/U] *pl* **Scorpios** the eighth sign of the ZODIAC, covering the period October 24 to November 21 and represented by a SCORPION, or a person born during this period

scorpion /ˈskɔːr·piː·ən/ *n* [C] a small creature that lives in hot, dry areas of the world and has a long body and a curved tail with a poisonous sting

scotch /skɑtʃ/ *v* [T] to prevent something from being believed or being done ○ *The company hoped to scotch the rumors of a takeover.*

Scotch (whiskey) /ˈskɑtʃ (ˈwɪs·ki, ˈhwɪs-)/ *n* [C/U] a strong alcoholic drink made in Scotland

Scotch tape /ˈskɑːtʃ ˈteɪp/ *n* [U] *trademark* a long, usually transparent strip of material with a sticky substance on one side, used for attaching two pieces of paper or fixing a torn place

scot-free /ˈskɑt ˈfriː/ *adv* [not gradable] without receiving the punishment deserved ○ *She agreed to testify against her boyfriend and got off scot-free.*

scoundrel /ˈskɑʊn·drəl/ *n* [C] a person, esp. an elected official, who treats others badly and cannot be trusted

scour CLEAN /skɑʊr/ *v* [T] to clean something by rubbing it hard with rough cleaning material ○ *We scoured the pots and pans with pads of steel wool.*

SEARCH /skɑʊr/ *v* [T] to search a place or thing very carefully ○ *Police are scouring the countryside for the missing child.*

scourge /skɜrdʒ/ *n* [C] someone or something that causes harm, evil, or destruction ○ *Smallpox, that scourge of previous generations, now is effectively extinct.*

scout BOY/GIRL /skɑʊt/ *n* [C] a BOY SCOUT or GIRL SCOUT

SEARCH /skɑʊt/ *v* [I/T] **1** to go to look in various places for something you want or to check for possible danger ○ [I] *Retired folks were scouting for homes in Florida.* ○ [I] *When not traveling worldwide to scout out ideas, they visit with their daughter Sarah.* **2** In sports, to scout is to have the job of trying to find young players with the ability to play the sport well: [I] *I scouted for the Angels baseball team for about 15 years.*

scout /skɑʊt/ *n* [C] **1** someone whose job is to look for people with particular skills, esp. in sports or entertainment **2** A scout is also a person, esp. a soldier, sent out to get information about the enemy.

scowl /skɑʊl/ *v* [I] to use the face to express anger, esp. at someone ○ *When I asked the boss for a day off, he just scowled and told me to get back to work.*

scowl /skɑʊl/ *n* [C] ○ *She is clearly annoyed, as you can tell from the scowl on her face.*

scrabble /ˈskræb·əl/ *v* [I] to move your hands or fingers quickly to find and pick up something, esp. something that you cannot see ○ *She scrabbled around in her bag, trying to find her keys.*

scram /skræm/ *v* [I] **-mm-** *infml* to leave quickly; get away ○ *We'd better scram!*

scramble MOVE QUICKLY /ˈskræm·bəl/ *v* [I] to move or climb quickly but with difficulty, often using the hands ○ *She scrambled to safety away from the fighting.* ○ [+ *to* infinitive] (*fig.*) *Poultry farmers scrambled* (= worked hard and fast) *to provide water to their flocks as pipes burst in Georgia's coldest weather this century.*

scramble /ˈskræm·bəl/ *n* [U] ○ (*fig.*) *There was a mad scramble* (= many people moving at once) *for the best seats in the theater.*

S

MIX EGGS /ˈskræm·bəl/ *v* [T] to mix together and cook the transparent and yellow parts of eggs ○ *We had bacon and scrambled eggs for breakfast.*

CHANGE SIGNAL /ˈskræm·bəl/ *v* [T] to change a radio or telephone signal while it is being sent so that it cannot be understood without a special device

scrap **THROW AWAY** /skræp/ *v* [T] **-pp-** to get rid of something no longer useful or wanted ○ *Over 60% of all Georgians want to keep the present flag and only 29% want to scrap it.*

MATERIALS /skræp/ *n* [U] old or used material, esp. metal, that has been collected in one place, often in order to be treated so that it can be used again ○ *He was charged with stealing copper tubing, which he then sold as scrap metal.*

SMALL PIECE /skræp/ *n* [C] a small and often irregular piece of something, or a small amount of something ○ *He jotted it down on a scrap of paper.* ○ [pl] *She picked up scraps of information about her husband's whereabouts, but nothing definite.*

scrapbook /ˈskræp·bʊk/ *n* [C] a book with empty pages where you can stick newspaper articles, pictures, etc., that you have collected and want to keep

scrape /skreɪp/ *v* [I/T] to remove something by rubbing something rough or sharp against it, or to rub part of your body against something rough that tears away or injures your skin ○ [T] *Jackie scraped her knee on the wall as she was climbing over it.* ○ [T] *Sheila scraped the snow off the windshield of her car.* ○ [I] *The metal gate scraped along the ground when I opened it.*

scrape /skreɪp/ *n* [C] **1** a slight injury caused by having your skin rubbed against something rough ○ *She had a few scrapes from the accident in the parking lot, but nothing serious.* **2** *infml* A scrape is also a difficult situation that you are in because of your own actions: *Oh, he's had a few scrapes with the law when he was younger, but he's straightened his life out now.*

PHRASAL VERBS with scrape

• **scrape by** to have only enough money to pay for the basic things you need ○ *Even with both of us working, we earn just enough to scrape by.*

• **scrape together/up** *something* [M] to gather something with difficulty ○ *He's trying to scrape together enough money to buy a computer.*

scrappy /ˈskræp·i/ *adj* [-er/-est only] *approving* very competitive and willing to oppose others without fear to achieve something ○ *They were a scrappy team – you had to go all out to beat them.*

scratch **CUT** /skrætʃ/ *v* [I/T] **1** to cut or damage a surface with something sharp or rough, or to rub a part of your body with something sharp or rough ○ [T] *He used a penknife to scratch his initials into the bark of the tree.* ○ [I] *You can hold the cat – she won't scratch.* **2** If you scratch your skin, you rub it with the nails of your fingers: [T] *I know they itch, but don't scratch your mosquito bites.*

scratch /skrætʃ/ *n* [C] ○ *Tiny particles of car wax fill in the little scratches on the car.*

REMOVE /skrætʃ/ *v* [I/T] **1** to remove yourself or another person or an animal from a competition before the start ○ [I] *Mary Slaney scratched from the 1500-meter run because of an Achilles tendon problem.* **2** To scratch is also to decide not to do something that you had planned to do; to CANCEL: [T] *We were going to remodel our kitchen, but we had to scratch that when I lost my job.*

IDIOMS with scratch

• **scratch** *your* **head** to have difficulty understanding something ○ *All I can do is scratch my head and ask why.*

• **scratch the surface** to deal with only a small part of a subject or a problem ○ *All the payments we've made have hardly scratched the surface of the amount we borrowed.*

scrawl /skrɔːl/ *v* [T] to write something in a fast, messy way ○ *Someone had scrawled graffiti on the side of our garage.*

scrawl /skrɔːl/ *n* [C] ○ *I had trouble reading the uneven scrawl of his signature.*

scrawny /ˈskrɔː·ni/ *adj* (of a person's or animal's body) very thin because not fed enough, so that you can see the shape of the bones under the skin ○ *The store had only a few scrawny chickens left.*

scream /skriːm/ *v* [I/T] to cry or say something loudly and usually on a high note, esp. because of strong emotions such as fear, excitement, or anger ○ [I] *The children screamed in delight as they sledded down the hill.* ○ [I] *Some people still trapped in the wreckage screamed for help.*

scream /skriːm/ *n* [C] **1** *screams of joy/laughter/pain* **2** *slang* A scream is someone or something that is very entertaining: *Josie's a real scream – she's never serious.* ➤ Usage: **cry, scream, or shout?** at CRY SHOUT

screech /skriːtʃ/ *v* [I] to make a long, loud, high noise ○ *They clapped their hands and screeched with laughter.* ○ *A semitrailer truck screeched to a halt* (= stopped suddenly with a long, loud, high noise of its BRAKES).

screech /skriːtʃ/ *n* [C] ○ *The truck stopped with a screech of brakes.*

screen **PICTURE** /skriːn/ *n* [C] **1** a flat surface in a theater, on a television, or on a computer system on which pictures or words are shown ○ *I spend most of the day working in front of a computer screen.* **2** The screen sometimes means the movies: *Her ambition is to write for the screen.* ○ *a screen actor/actress*

screen /skriːn/ *v* [T] to show or broadcast a movie or television program ○ *His new movie got rave reviews when it was screened at Cannes.*

EXAMINE /skriːn/ *v* [T] to test or examine people or things to discover if there is anything wrong with them ○ *Airport security staff have to screen and check millions of bags a year.* ○ *The company president's secretary screens all his calls* (= answers them first to prevent some from getting through).

THING THAT SEPARATES /skriːn/ *n* [C] **1** something that blocks you from seeing what is behind it, esp. a stiff piece of material that you can stand up like part of a wall and move around ○ *Jennifer has a beautiful screen decorated with Japanese art.* **2** A screen is also a stiff, wire net that has very small holes and is fixed within a frame, put in windows esp. in warm weather to let in air and keep insects out.

screen /skriːn/ *v* [T] ○ *She raised her hand to screen her eyes from the sun.*

PHRASAL VERB with screen

• **screen out** *something/someone* [M] to prevent something or someone undesirable from coming in ○ *Home water filtration systems are supposed to screen out toxins and other contaminants.*

screen door *n* [C] a door fitted on the outside of a regular door that lets in air but keeps out insects

screenplay /ˈskriːn·pleɪ/ *n* [C] a story written with the words to be spoken by actors on television or in a movie

screenwriter /ˈskriːnˌrɑɪt̬·ər/ *n* [C] someone who writes the story for a movie

screw METAL FASTENER /skruː/ *n* [C] a thin piece of metal, usually with a pointed end and a flat top shaped to hold a tool, that is forced into wood or metal by turning, and is used esp. to join two pieces or to hold something in place

screw /skruː/ *v* [T] **1** to fasten objects with a screw ○ *The shelves were screwed to the wall.* **2** To screw also means to attach to something by turning: *Screw the lid onto the jar.* ○ [M] *Just screw in that loose bulb.*

CHEAT /skruː/ *v* [T] *slang* to cheat or deceive someone ○ *He really got screwed on that stock tip.*

IDIOMS with screw

• **screw it** *slang* I do not care what happens ○ *It takes a lot of work to be successful, but most people are lazy and say screw it.*

• **screw up** *your* **courage** to make a feeling of bravery stronger ○ *I screwed up my courage and tried to eat the stuff.*

PHRASAL VERBS with screw

• **screw around** *slang* to waste time ○ *Stop screwing around and finish your work.*

• **screw up** *(something/someone)* DAMAGE [M] *infml* **1** to do very badly or fail at something ○ *You couldn't screw up much worse than I did.* **2** If you screw someone up, you cause someone to become anxious, confused, or mentally ill.

• **screw up** *something* TWIST to twist a part of the face ○ *"This milk is sour," she said, screwing up her face.*

screwball /ˈskruː·bɔːl/ *n* [C] *slang* a person who is strange and amusing

screwball /ˈskruː·bɔːl/ *adj* [not gradable] ○ *screwball ideas*

screwdriver /ˈskruːˌdrɑɪ·vər/ *n* [C] a tool for turning screws that has a handle at one end and a metal rod at the other end, shaped to fit in the top of a screw

screw top *n* [C] a lid that fastens by being turned

screwy /ˈskruː·i/ *adj* [-er/-est only] *infml* very strange, foolish, or unusual ○ *She had some weird ideas, but her brother was even screwier.*

scribble /ˈskrɪb·əl/ *v* [I/T] to write or draw something quickly or without thought, or to make meaningless marks ○ [T] *I scribbled a few words to her on a postcard.*

scribble /ˈskrɪb·əl/ *n* [C/U] ○ [U] *His scribble is completely illegible.*

scribe /skrɑɪb/ *n* [C] a person who made written copies of documents, before the invention of printing

scrimp /skrɪmp/ *v* [I] to spend as little money as possible ○ *She scrimped and saved to care for her two younger sisters.*

script TEXT /skrɪpt/ *n* [C] a text that is written for a movie, play, broadcast, or speech ○ *They gave me the script and I only had five lines.*

scripted /ˈskrɪp·təd/ *adj* [not gradable] (of a speech, conversation, meeting, or public appearance) written or arranged in advance ○ *The meeting was scripted, which means there was no real discussion.*

WRITING /skrɪpt/ *n* [C/U] **1** writing, esp. writing done by hand in which the letters of a word are joined to each other ○ [C] *a neat, legible script* **2** Script is also the special set of letters used in writing a language: [U] *Arabic/Hebrew script*

scripture /ˈskrɪp·tʃər/ *n* [C/U] **1** the holy writings of a religion ○ [C] *sacred Scriptures* **2** Scripture or the Scriptures refers to the Bible, including the Old and New Testaments.

scriptwriter /ˈskrɪpt·rɑɪt̬·ər/ *n* [C] someone who writes stories for movies, television programs, etc.

scroll MOVE TEXT /skroʊl/ *v* [I] to move text or pictures up or down on a computer screen to view different parts of them ○ *Scroll to the end of the document.*

PAPER /skroʊl/ *n* [C] a long roll of paper or similar material, usually with official writing on it ○ *parchment/ancient scrolls* ○ *a painted Japanese scroll*

scrotum /ˈskroʊt̬·əm/ *n* [C] (in most male mammals) a bag of skin near the PENIS which contains the TESTICLES (= male sex organs)

scrounge /skrɑʊndʒ/ *v* [I/T] *infml* to get something by asking for it instead of buying it or working for it, or to gather something you want or need from what is available ○ [T] *Baxter scrounged furniture and equipment from local businesses.* ○ [I] *A black cat scrounged through piles of litter.*

scrub CLEAN /skrʌb/ *v* [I/T] **-bb-** to clean something by rubbing it hard ○ [T] *After the tomato sauce boiled over, I had to scrub the stove.* ○ [I] *You scrub and scrub, but those marks never come off.*

PLANTS /skrʌb/ *n* [U] low trees and bushes that grow in dirt that is not especially good or where it is windy and dry

S

scruff /skrʌf/ *n* **the scruff of** *your* **neck** the back of your neck ○ *She grabbed the dog by the scruff of his neck and hung on to him.*

scruffy /ˈskrʌf·i/ *adj* old and dirty; messy ○ *a scruffy denim jacket*

scrumptious /ˈskrʌm·ʃəs/ *adj* tasting extremely good; DELICIOUS ○ *a scrumptious breakfast*

scrunch /skrʌntʃ/ *v* [I/T] to press or crush something together ○ [I] *He scrunched down to hide in a nearby doorway.*

scruple /ˈskruː·pəl/ *n* [C/U] a strong belief about what is right or wrong that governs your actions ○ [C] *He has scruples about going out with his students.*

scrupulous /ˈskruː·pjə·ləs/ *adj* **1** extremely careful to do what is right or moral ○ *She managed to get a copy of the report through a friend who wasn't so scrupulous about sharing information.* **2** Scrupulous also means extremely accurate and exact: *Her report is scrupulous in its detail.*

scrutinize /ˈskruːt·ᵊnˌɑɪz/ *v* [T] to examine someone or something very carefully ○ *All new products are scrutinized by the laboratory.*
scrutiny /ˈskruːt·ᵊn·i/ *n* [U] ○ *Will the candidates stand up under all that scrutiny?*

scuba diving /ˈskuː·bəˌdɑɪ·vɪŋ/ *n* [U] the sport of swimming under water with special equipment for breathing

scuff /skʌf/ *v* [T] **1** to make a mark on a smooth surface, esp. on a shoe or floor ○ *Always wear sneakers in the gym to avoid scuffing the floor.* **2** If you scuff your feet, you do not lift them as you walk.

scuffle /ˈskʌf·əl/ *n* [C] a short fight that is filled with confusion ○ *He had gotten into a scuffle with another employee.*
scuffle /ˈskʌf·əl/ *v* [I/T] ○ [I] *Two men were scuffling on the sidewalk.*

S

sculpture /ˈskʌlp·tʃər/ *n* [C/U] ***art*** the art of creating objects out of material such as wood, clay, metal, or stone, or a work of art of this type ○ [C] *In the ruins they found ancient stone sculptures.*
sculpt /skʌlpt/, **sculpture** /ˈskʌlp·tʃər/ *v* [T] ○ *Picasso sculpted the "Venus of Lapigue."*
sculpted /ˈskʌlp·təd/, **sculptured** /ˈskʌlp·tʃərd/ *adj* ○ *Dramatically sculpted red and gray sandstone cliffs came into view.*
sculptor /ˈskʌlp·tər/ *n* [C] ○ *The sculptor supervised the placement of his newest sculpture in the garden.*

scum /skʌm/ *n* [U] a thin layer that forms on the surface of a liquid ○ *The tea was nasty-tasting stuff that looked like pond scum.* ○ *I wish you wouldn't leave soap scum in the bathtub.*

scurrilous /ˈskɜr·ə·ləs/ *adj* rude and cruel, and sometimes damaging ○ *scurrilous remarks*

scurry /ˈskɜr·i, ˈskʌ·ri/ *v* [I always + adv/prep] to move quickly, esp. with small running steps ○ *Mice scurried around the attic.*

scuttle RUN /ˈskʌt̬·əl/ *v* [I always + adv/prep] to move quickly, with small, short steps ○ *We heard rats scuttling by in the dark.*
GIVE UP /ˈskʌt̬·əl/ *v* [T] to give up a plan or activity, or spoil a possibility for success ○ *Angry workers scuttled all hope of quick agreement on a new contract.*
SINK /ˈskʌt̬·əl/ *v* [T] to intentionally sink a ship by opening a hole in the bottom or sides

scuttlebutt /ˈskʌt̬·əlˌbʌt/ *n* [U] *infml* information that may or may not be true; RUMOR ○ *Scuttlebutt around the office has it that he's been fired.*

scythe /sɑɪð, sɑɪ/ *n* [C] a tool with a long curved blade and a long handle, used esp. to cut down tall grass

S.E. *adj, adv, n* [C] *abbreviation for* SOUTHEAST or SOUTHEASTERN

sea /siː/ *n* [C/U] **1** a large area of salt water that is partly or completely surrounded by land, or the salt water that covers most of the surface of the earth ○ [C] *the Caribbean/Mediterranean Sea* ○ [C] *The seas are filled with creatures we know nothing about.* **2** If you travel by sea, you go in a ship.

IDIOMS with sea

- **at sea** confused ○ *With no data they could depend on, they were completely at sea.*
- **sea of** *something* a lot of something ○ *She looked out at the sea of faces in the audience.*

seabed /ˈsiː·bed/ *n* [U] the land at the bottom of an ocean or sea

seaboard /ˈsiː·bɔːrd, -bourd/ *n* [C usually sing] a country's area of land next to the sea ○ *the eastern seaboard*

seacoast /ˈsiː·koust/ *n* [C] the edge of the land next to the sea

seafood /ˈsiː·fuːd/ *n* [C/U] fish or SHELLFISH eaten as food

sea gull *n* [C] a large bird that usually lives near an ocean or other large body of water

sea horse *n* [C] a type of fish whose head and neck look like those of a horse

seal ANIMAL /siːl/ *n* [C] a large, fish-eating mammal that has very thick fur and lives in the sea ○ *Seals are sometimes hunted for their valuable fur.*
OFFICIAL MARK /siːl/ *n* [C] **1** an official mark on a document which shows that it is legal or actually what it claims to be ○ *Diplomas are stamped with the state seal.* **2** A seal of approval means that something has been proven to be good or is very pleasing: *My brother's girlfriend got my mom's seal of approval.*
seal /siːl/ *v* [T] If you seal an agreement, you formally approve or agree to it: *They sealed the agreement with their signatures.*
COVERING /siːl/ *n* [C] anything that prevents the escape of liquid or gas from a container or pipe ○ *The oil seal broke, and all the oil leaked from the*

engine. ○ *Don't use that jar of baby food if the seal is broken.*

seal /siːl/ *v* [T] **1** *Rubber seals jars tightly.* ○ *He sealed the envelope and put a stamp on it.* ○ [M] *Broiling with high heat seals in the flavor of the meat.* ○ [M] *The police sealed off the area to search it.* **2** If official documents are sealed, they cannot be seen or are not available to the public.

sea level *n* [U] the average level of the sea where it meets the land ○ *The town is 300 feet above sea level.*

sea lion *n* [C] a large SEAL **ANIMAL** that has ears

seam **JOINT** /siːm/ *n* [C] a line where two things join, esp. where two pieces of cloth or other material have been sewn together ○ *My jacket came apart at the back seam.*

seamless /ˈsiːm·ləs/ *adj* [not gradable] **1** *seamless tube socks* **2** Seamless can also mean without noticeable change from one part to the next: *The department hopes this will be a seamless transition from one computer system to another.*

LAYER /siːm/ *n* [C] a long, thin layer of rock or another substance that formed between layers of other rocks ○ *a coal seam*

seaman /ˈsiː·mən/ *n* [C] **1** a man who lives and works mostly on ships at sea **2** A seaman is also a SAILOR in the US Coast Guard or Navy who is not an officer.

seamstress /ˈsiːm·strəs/ *n* [C] a woman whose job is sewing, esp. clothes

seamy /ˈsiː·mi/ *adj* [-er/-est only] unpleasant and sometimes illegal, immoral, or violent ○ *Every city has its seamy neighborhood.*

séance /ˈseɪ·ɑns, -ɑ̃s/ *n* [C] a meeting where people try to communicate with the dead, often with the help of someone who claims to have special powers to do this

seaplane /ˈsiː·pleɪn/ *n* [C] an aircraft that can land on and take off from water

seaport /ˈsiː·pɔːrt, -pourt/ *n* [C] a town or city on the water where ships load and unload freight

sear /sɪr/ *v* [T] to burn the surface of something with very high heat, or to cook meat quickly at a high temperature to keep in the juices and flavor ○ *He seared the steaks on the grill.*

searing /ˈsɪr·ɪŋ/ *adj* **1** very hot ○ *searing temperatures* **2** Searing also means very powerful: *Gary felt searing pain in his leg.*

search /sɜrtʃ/ *v* [I/T] to look somewhere carefully in order to find something ○ [T] *Dogs were brought in to search the area for survivors.* ○ [I] *Teens are often searching for their identity.*

search /sɜrtʃ/ *n* [C/U] ○ [C] *After a long search, they finally found the lost child.* ○ [U] *It's a book about the search for love.*

USAGE

search or search for?

If you **search** a place or person, you look for something in that place or on that person:

The police searched the man/the house for weapons.

If you **search for** something or someone, you look for that thing or person.

The police searched for the stolen computers but they were never recovered.

~~*The police searched the stolen computers but they were never recovered.*~~

WORD FAMILY search

Nouns		Adjectives	
	search		searching
	research	Verbs	search
	researcher		research

WORD CHOICES search

Look and **hunt** are very common alternatives to "search."

*She was **looking** in her handbag for a pen.*

*I'm **looking** for my keys. Have you seen them?*

*I've **hunted** all over the place but I can't find that book.*

Rummage can be used when someone searches in a drawer, bag, etc., for something.

*He **rummaged** through his pockets, looking for a pen.*

The phrasal verb **ferret out** can be used when someone searches for information, especially information that other people do not want known.

*The inspector general has broad powers to **ferret out** fraud on the state and local level.*

If someone searches a place very carefully in order to find something or someone, the words **comb** or **scour** are often used.

*Police **combed** the area for evidence.*

*Police **scoured** the countryside looking for the missing child.*

If someone searches a place in a violent and careless way, you could use the verb **ransack**.

*Burglars had **ransacked** the house and stolen three watches.*

If you are **on the lookout for** something, you are continuously searching for it.

*He is always **on the lookout for** a bargain.*

search engine *n* [C] a computer program used for finding specific information on the INTERNET

searching /ˈsɜr·tʃɪŋ/ *adj* intended to discover the hidden truth ○ *Fran stared hard, her searching gaze trying to get him to admit what he knew.*

searchlight /ˈsɜrtʃ·lɑɪt/ *n* [C] a device that puts out a very bright beam of light and can turn in any direction

search party *n* [C] a group of people who look for someone who is lost

search warrant *n* [C] an official document that gives the police the authority to search a place

seashell /ˈsiː·ʃel/ *n* [C] the empty shell of a sea animal

seashore /ˈsiː·ʃɔːr, -ʃoʊr/ *n* [C/U] the land at the edge of the sea

seasick /ˈsiː·sɪk/ *adj* feeling like vomiting as a result of traveling in a boat

seaside /ˈsiː·saɪd/ *n* [C usually sing] a place near the ocean or sea ○ *a seaside resort*

season PART OF YEAR /ˈsiː·zən/ *n* [C] one of the four parts a year is divided into; spring, summer, fall, or winter

seasonable /ˈsiː·zə·nə·bəl/ *adj* expected at or suitable for a particular season ○ *seasonable weather*

seasonal /ˈsiː·zən·əl/ *adj* ○ *seasonal jobs/work*

seasonally /ˈsiː·zən·əl·i/ *adv* ○ *Sage grouse migrate seasonally from summer to winter habitat.*

PERIOD /ˈsiː·zən/ *n* [C] **1** a period of time during the year, esp. a period that happens every year at the same time ○ *flu season* ○ *the holiday season* ○ *The baseball season lasts from April to October.* **2** A fruit or vegetable that is **in season** is available fresh locally at that time: *Strawberries are in season.*

seasonal /siː·zən·əl/ *adj* ○ *seasonal fruits and vegetables* ○ *seasonal decorations*

seasonally /ˈsiː·zən·əl·i/ *adv* ○ *New homes sold at a seasonally adjusted annual rate of 671,000 units.*

FLAVOR /ˈsiː·zən/ *v* [T] to improve the flavor of food by adding small amounts of salt, herbs, or spices ○ *Season the soup with fresh tarragon, salt, and pepper.*

seasoning /ˈsiː·zə·nɪŋ/ *n* [C/U] ○ [U] *Adjust the seasoning to taste.*

seasoned /ˈsiː·zənd/ *adj* having much experience and knowledge of a particular activity ○ *seasoned travelers/journalists*

seat PLACE TO SIT /siːt/ *n* [C] **1** a piece of furniture or other place for someone to sit ○ *She left her jacket on the back of her seat.* ○ *I got a seat on the flight to New York.* ○ *Please take a seat* (= sit down). **2** A seat is a part of something on which a person sits: *a bicycle seat* ○ *There's a piece of gum stuck under the seat of the chair.* ○ *He stood up and brushed the sand off the seat of his pants.*

seat /siːt/ *v* [T] to have or be given a place to sit ○ *I was seated between Jasmine and Emily.* ○ *The concert hall seats 350.* ○ *Our group is still waiting to be seated for dinner.* ○ *Please be seated* (= sit down).

seating /ˈsiːt̬·ɪŋ/ *n* [U] the seats provided in a place ○ *The seminars are free but seating is limited.* ○ *The kids couldn't agree on the seating arrangement in the car* (= where they would sit).

OFFICIAL POSITION /siːt/ *n* [C] an official position as a member of a legislature or group of people who control an organization ○ *She decided to run for a seat on the school board.*

PLACE /siːt/ *n* [C] a place that is a center for an important activity, esp. government ○ *Pittsburgh is the county seat of Alleghany County.*

WORD FAMILY seat			
Nouns	seat seating	*Adjectives*	seated
		Verbs	seat unseat

IDIOM with seat

• **by the seat of** *your* **pants** without the necessary experience or ability ○ *We started a magazine by the seat of our pants, without any of the market testing that's done today.*

seat belt, **seatbelt** /ˈsiːt·belt/ *n* [C] a strap in a vehicle or aircraft that fastens around you, holding you in your seat to reduce the risk of injury in an accident

seaweed /ˈsiː·wiːd/ *n* [U] a green, brown, or dark red plant that grows in the sea

sec /sek/ *n* [C] short form of SECOND TIME ○ *Hang on a sec, Brian, I've got another call.*

secant *n* [C] **1** ***trigonometry*** in a triangle that has one angle of 90°, the RATIO (= comparison) of the HYPOTENUSE (= length of the side opposite the 90° angle) to the length of the side next to an angle less than 90° **2** ***geometry*** A secant is also a line that crosses a circle at two places.

secede /sɪˈsiːd/ *v* [I] ***US history*** to decide not to continue to be part of a larger group or organization ○ *The American Civil War began when the South seceded from the Union.*

secession /sɪˈseʃ·ən/ *n* [U] ***US history*** the act of leaving an organization or government, esp. the decision of a state to separate from the government of the United States ○ *Dabney had opposed secession at first.*

secluded /sɪˈkluːd·əd/ *adj* away from people and busy activities, and often hard to reach ○ *a secluded area/beach*

seclusion /sɪˈkluː·ʒən/ *n* [U] ○ *She spent her days in the seclusion of her room.*

second POSITION /ˈsek·ənd/ *adj, adv, n* [C] (a person or thing) coming immediately after the first ○ *He missed only 2 of 11 shots in the second half.* ○ [C] *Rent is due the second of every month.* ○ Related Number: TWO

seconds /ˈsek·ənz/ *pl n* an extra serving of food given after the first serving has been eaten ○ *Would anybody like seconds?*

secondly /ˈsek·ən·dli/, **second** *adv* [not gradable] ○ *First, what does it cost? And secondly, who's it for?*

TIME /ˈsek·ənd/, short form **sec** *n* [C] **1** any of the 60 parts that a minute is divided into ○ *She won by 22 seconds.* **2** A second is also any short period of time: *I'll be back in a second.*

SUPPORT /ˈsek·ənd/ *v* [T] to make a formal statement of support for a suggestion made by someone else during a meeting in order to allow a discussion or vote ○ *I second the motion to adjourn.*

IDIOM with second

• **the second (that)** as soon as ○ *The second I saw him, I knew he was going to be a star.* ○ Compare THE MINUTE (THAT) at MINUTE IDIOM

secondary LESS IMPORTANT /ˈsek·ən ˌder·i/ *adj* [not gradable] less important than related things ○ *A coach's first responsibility is to the team – everything else is secondary.*

EDUCATION /ˈsek·ən ˌder·i/ *adj* [not gradable] relating to the education of children approximately between the ages of 12 and 18 ○ *The secondary curriculum will have to be drastically improved.*

COMING AFTER /ˈsek·ən ˌder·i/ *adj* [not gradable] developing from something similar that existed earlier ○ *Someone who's been treated for cancer can get a secondary tumor 20 years later.*

secondary color *n* [C] ***art*** one of the three colors – orange, green, or purple – that can be made by mixing together two of the PRIMARY COLORS

secondary school *n* [C] a HIGH SCHOOL

second base, *short form* **second** *n* [C usually sing] the second place a baseball player has to touch in order to score, or a position near this place played by a member of the team on the field

second-class *adj* [not gradable] considered to be less important or of lower quality than others ○ *The poor are treated as second-class citizens.*

second-guess CRITICIZE *v* [T] to criticize someone's decision after it has been made, and say what you think is wrong with it ○ *It doesn't help to second-guess their decision.*

GUESS *v* [T] to guess what someone will do or what will happen

secondhand OWNED BEFORE, **second-hand** /ˈsek·ənd ˈhænd/ *adj, adv* [not gradable] owned or used in the past by someone else ○ *a secondhand car* ○ *I bought it second-hand at that bookstore on Elm Street.*

LEARNED INDIRECTLY, **second-hand** /ˈsek·ənd ˈhænd/ *adj, adv* [not gradable] learned or heard about from someone else rather than directly from the person involved ○ *She said she had heard second-hand reports of officers sleeping on the job.*

secondhand smoke, **second-hand smoke** *n* [U] tobacco smoke that you breathe in because someone else is smoking

second nature *n* [U] something that is so familiar that it is done without having to think about it ○ *Using the computer is second nature to me now.*

second person *n* [U] ***grammar*** the form of pronouns and verbs that people use when speaking or writing to someone else ○ *"You" and "your" are second person pronouns.* ○ Compare FIRST PERSON; THIRD PERSON

second-rate *adj* [not gradable] not of good quality ○ *a second-rate hotel*

seconds /ˈsek·ənz/ *pl n* ○ See at SECOND POSITION

second thought *n* [C] a change in a decision or opinion ○ *He apparently* **had second thoughts** *about that remark.* ○ **On second thought** (= after thinking about it further), *I would like a glass of water.*

second wind *n* [U] a return of strength or energy that makes it possible to continue in an activity or start again ○ *I was tired, but I ignored it until I got my second wind.*

secret /ˈsiː·krət/ *n* [C] a piece of information that is not generally known or is not known by someone else and should not be told to others ○ *We don't keep secrets from each other.* ○ *Don't tell anyone – it's a secret.* ○ *What's* **the secret of** *your success* (= How was it achieved)?

secret /ˈsiː·krət/ *adj* known, done, or kept without others knowing ○ *secret information* ○ *The peace process began with secret talks in Norway.*

secretive /ˈsiː·krəţ·ɪv/ *adj* not wanting others to know, or done privately so that others do not know ○ *secretive dealings* ○ *She's secretive about her age.*

secretly /ˈsiː·krət·li/ *adv* ○ *They secretly took photographs of Jack.*

secrecy /ˈsiː·krə·si/ *n* [U] ○ *What's the reason for all this secrecy?*

WORD FAMILY secret

Nouns	secrecy secret	*Adverbs*	secretly secretively
Adjectives	secret secretive		

WORD CHOICES secret

Covert is an alternative to "secret," especially when talking about military or police actions.

The government was accused of ***covert*** *military operations.*

Clandestine is a formal word for "secret," especially describing something that is not officially allowed.

He arranged a ***clandestine*** *meeting between his client and the candidate.*

If information is **confidential**, it is secret, especially in a formal or business situation, and should not be told to anyone else.

All the information you give us will treated as strictly ***confidential***.

Official government information that is secret is described as **classified**.

These documents contain ***classified*** *information.*

Innermost or **private** can be used for thoughts or feelings which someone keeps secret.

She never told anyone her ***innermost*** *thoughts.*

She kept her views on the subject ***private***.

If someone does something in a secret way because he or she does not want other people to see that action, you could use the adjectives **furtive** or **surreptitious**.

He kept giving her ***furtive*** *glances.*

She took a ***surreptitious*** *look at her watch.* ➤

S

If something is **under wraps**, it is secret and you are deliberately not telling anyone about it yet.
*He is doing some research for a new book which is **under wraps** at the moment.*

secretary OFFICE WORKER /ˈsek·rəˌter·i/ *n* [C] a person who works in an office and prepares letters, keeps records, schedules meetings, and makes other arrangements for a particular person or for an organization
secretarial /ˌsek·rəˈter·iː·əl/ *adj* [not gradable] ○ *She does mostly secretarial work.*

GOVERNMENT OFFICIAL /ˈsek·rəˌter·i/ *n* [C] the head of a government department ○ *the Secretary of the Treasury*

WRITER /ˈsek·rəˌter·i/ *n* [C] an official in an organization who is responsible for writing notes about what happens at meetings and sending official letters ○ *Freya is running for secretary of the student council.*

secrete /sɪˈkriːt/ *v* [T] ***biology*** to produce and release liquid, esp. from the cells or body ○ *The thyroid gland secretes hormones that affect growth.*
secretion /sɪˈkriː·ʃən/ *n* [C/U] ***biology*** ○ [C] *nasal secretions*

secretive /ˈsiː·krət̬·ɪv/ *adj* ○ See at SECRET

secretly /ˈsiː·krət·li/ *adv* ○ See at SECRET

secret police *n* [U] a government police organization that keeps information about a country's citizens and prevents opposition to the government

Secret Service *n* [U] a US government organization responsible for the safety of important politicians, esp. the president

sect /sekt/ *n* [C] **1** a religious group with beliefs that make it different from a larger or more established religion it has separated from ○ *a Christian sect* **2** A sect is also a small group of people who share a particular set of political beliefs.
sectarian /sekˈter·iː·ən/ *adj* [not gradable] relating to a sect, or happening between sects ○ *sectarian fighting*

section Ⓐ /ˈsek·ʃən/ *n* [C] a part of something ○ *Dad always reads the sports section of the newspaper.* ○ *He lived in a poor section of town.* ○ *You'll find ice cream in the frozen food section of the supermarket.*
section Ⓐ /ˈsek·ʃən/ *v* [T] ○ *If the tooth is sectioned lenghtwise, ridges of alternating dark and light rings can be seen.*

PHRASAL VERB with section

• **section off** *something* [M] to separate one thing from another, or to divide into equal or similar parts ○ *Security agents sectioned off the area where she shopped.*

sector Ⓐ /ˈsek·tər/ *n* [C] **1** a part of society that can be separated from other parts because of its own special character ○ *the farm sector* ○ *the nonprofit sector* ○ *She works in the private/public sector* (= for a business/government) **2** A sector is also an area of land or sea that has been divided from other areas: *The buildings are in an industrial sector in the southern part of the city.*

secular /ˈsek·jə·lər/ *adj* not having any connection with religion ○ *secular society/music/education*

secure Ⓐ FREE FROM RISK /sɪˈkjʊr/ *adj* **1** free from risk and the threat of change for the worse ○ *a secure job* ○ *People want to feel secure economically.* ○ *The museum has a large endowment, so its future is relatively secure.* **2** Secure can also mean confident and free from worry: *Children need to feel secure in order to do well at school.*
security Ⓐ /sɪˈkjʊr·ət̬·i/ *n* [U] ○ *financial/job security* ○ See also: SECURITY INVESTMENT; SECURITY MONEY; SECURITY at SECURE FREE FROM DANGER

FREE FROM DANGER /sɪˈkjʊr/ *adj* free from danger or the threat of harm or unwanted access; safe ○ *Troops were sent to make the border secure.* ○ *He questioned whether the government's computer database was secure from hackers.* ○ *For some time after the robbery we could not feel secure, even in our own home.*
secure Ⓐ /sɪˈkjʊr/ *v* [T] ○ *The wall was originally built to secure the town from attack.*
security Ⓐ /sɪˈkjʊr·ət̬·i/ *n* [U] ***social studies*** **1** freedom from danger; safety ○ *For security reasons, for the protection of the White House and the president, they felt it necessary to close the avenue.* ○ *A convicted spy, he sold information that may have damaged our national security.* **2** Security is also the group of people responsible for keeping buildings or other areas safe: *If anyone gives you trouble, just call security.* ○ See also: SECURITY INVESTMENT; SECURITY MONEY; SECURITY at SECURE FREE FROM RISK ➤ Usage: **safety or security?** at SAFETY

FIXED /sɪˈkjʊr/ *adj* fixed, fastened, or locked into a position that prevents movement ○ *That ladder doesn't look very secure to me.* ○ *Just check that the door is secure – the lock doesn't always work.*
secure Ⓐ /sɪˈkjʊr/ *v* [T] to fasten something firmly ○ *Secure the boat to the dock.*
securely Ⓐ /sɪˈkjʊr·li/ *adv* ○ *Please make sure that your seatbelts are securely fastened.*

OBTAIN /sɪˈkjʊr/ *v* [T] to obtain something, sometimes with difficulty ○ *She managed to secure a loan from the bank.*

security Ⓐ INVESTMENT /sɪˈkjʊr·ət̬·i/ *n* [C usually pl] an investment in a company or in government debt that can be traded on the financial markets ○ See also: SECURITY MONEY; SECURITY at SECURE FREE FROM RISK; SECURITY at SECURE FREE FROM DANGER

MONEY /sɪˈkjʊr·ət̬·i/ *n* [U] money you pay someone that can be legally used by that person if your actions cause the person to lose money, but that will be returned to you if it is not used ○ *You have give the landlord an extra month's rent as security when you sign the lease.* ○ See also: SECURITY INVESTMENT; SECURITY at SECURE FREE FROM RISK; SECURITY at SECURE FREE FROM DANGER

security blanket *n* [C] **1** a small BLANKET (= bed cover) sometimes carried by a child to provide a feeling of safety **2** A security blanket is also anything that you use or keep to make you feel safe: *Having my brother at the same college gave me the security blanket I needed to leave home.*

sedan /sɪˈdæn/ *n* [C] a type of car with two or four doors and seats for at least four people

sedate /sɪˈdeɪt/ *adj* calm and controlled, and often traditional in habit or manner ○ *She preferred standard ballads and sedate pop tunes to rock music.*

sedative /ˈsed·ət̬·ɪv/ *n* [C] a drug that has a calming effect ○ *If your pet is unaccustomed to car travel, consider a mild sedative to help relieve its anxiety.*

sedentary /ˈsed·ən ˌter·i/ *adj* involving little exercise or physical activity ○ *Marilyn leads a more sedentary lifestyle now that she works at home.*

sediment /ˈsed·ə·mənt/ *n* [C/U] solid material, such as dirt or MINERALS, that falls to the bottom of a liquid

sedimentary /ˌsed·əˈment·ə·ri, -ˈmen·tri/ *adj* [not gradable] ***earth science*** describes rock made from solid material left by the action of water, ice, or wind

sedition /sɪˈdɪʃ·ən/ *n* [U] ***social studies*** language or behavior intended to persuade other people to oppose their government and change it, sometimes by using violence ○ *He himself was tried for sedition and sentenced to ten years in jail.*
seditious /sɪˈdɪʃ·əs/ *adj*

seduce /sɪˈduːs/ *v* [T] **1** to persuade or trick someone into doing something by making it very attractive ○ *Nowadays you have to seduce students into learning through colorful graphics or exciting adventure themes.* **2** If you seduce someone, you persuade that person to have sex with you.
seduction /sɪˈdʌk·ʃən/ *n* [C/U] ○ [U] *The movie is an advertisement for the seduction of flight.*
seductive /sɪˈdʌk·tɪv/ *adj* ○ *Their marketing campaign was slick and seductive.*

see USE EYES /siː/ *v* [I/T] *past simp.* **saw**, *past part.* **seen** to be aware of what is around you by using your eyes; look at something ○ [T] *From the kitchen window, I can see the kids playing in the backyard.* ○ [+ question word] *Can you see what is happening?* ○ [T] *The agent said they could see the house at 3 p.m.* ○ [T] *Did you see that documentary about homelessness on TV last night?*

WORD CHOICES see

See also: **look**

If you see or become aware of something, the verbs **notice** or **perceive** are often used, or in formal English, **observe**.

*I **noticed** a crack in the ceiling.*

*Bill **perceived** a tiny figure in the distance.*

*A teacher **observed** her climbing over the gate.*

Spot is used when you see someone or something, especially when you are looking hard for them.

*We **spotted** several dolphins swimming nearby.*

The phrases **catch sight of** and **catch a glimpse of** are used when you suddenly see something for a moment.

*He **caught sight of/caught a glimpse of** his reflection in the glass.*

You use the verb **witness** when someone sees an event such as a crime or an accident.

*Did anyone **witness** the attack?*

The phrasal verb **make something out** is used when you see something but with difficulty.

*I could just **make out** a figure standing in the doorway.*

UNDERSTAND /siː/ *v* [I/T] *past simp.* **saw**, *past part.* **seen** to understand, know, or be aware ○ [I] *"It's easier if you hold it this way." "Oh, I see."* ○ [T] *I can't see any reason why they would object.* ○ [+ question word] *I can see why you didn't want to go out with him.*

CONSIDER /siː/ *v* [I/T] *past simp.* **saw**, *past part.* **seen** to consider someone or something in a particular way, or to imagine someone doing a particular activity ○ [T] *Under the circumstances, I can't see her accepting the job* (= I do not think she will accept it). ○ [T] *I can't see my brother as a businessman.* ○ [T] *As I see it/the situation, we'll have to get extra help.* ○ [I] *"Do you think there'll be time to stop for lunch?" "We'll see* (= I will consider it)*."* ○ [+ question word] *I'll see how I feel tomorrow.*

MEET /siː/ *v* [T] *past simp.* **saw**, *past part.* **seen** to meet, visit, or spend time with someone ○ *I saw Darlene last week.* ○ *Mom is seeing the doctor tomorrow.* ○ *They see each other on weekends* (= they are often together then). ○ *How long have they been seeing each other* (= having a romantic relationship)? ➤ Usage: **meet, see, visit, or get to know?** at MEET COME TOGETHER

TRY TO DISCOVER /siː/ *v* [+ question word] *past simp.* **saw**, *past part.* **seen** to try to discover ○ *Will you see who is at the door?*

MAKE CERTAIN /siː/ *v* [+ *that* clause] *past simp.* **saw**, *past part.* **seen** to make certain (that something happens) ○ *She said she'd see that her boss gets the message.*

EXPERIENCE /siː/ *v* [T] *past simp.* **saw**, *past part.* **seen** **1** to experience something ○ *This coat has seen a lot of wear.* ○ *She's seen a lot of changes in this office over the years.* **2** If a time or place has seen something, it happened or existed there or then: *This summer has seen unusually high temperatures.*

IDIOMS with see

• **see eye to eye** (*with someone*) to agree with someone ○ *My sister didn't see eye to eye with me about the how to tell my parents about the problem.*
• **see fit (to do** *something*) to think it is good or necessary to do something ○ *You can leave it here or take it home with you, whichever you see fit.*
• **seeing is believing** if you see something yourself, you will believe it to exist or be true, despite the

fact that it is unlikely ○ *I never thought he'd shave off his beard, but seeing is believing!*
• **seeing that**, **seeing as (how)** considering that ○ *We might as well go, seeing as we've already paid for the tickets.*
• **seeing things** imagining that things are present or happening when they are not ○ *Didn't Maria come in just now? I must be seeing things.*
• **see red** to become very angry ○ *The corruption in government is making voters see red.*
• **see stars** to see bright flashes in front of your eyes, esp. because you hit your head ○ *The fall made me see stars and left me with a huge bump on my head.*
• **see the light** to understand something you did not understand before ○ *It wasn't until I was in my thirties that I saw the light and started to work hard.*
• **see the point of** *something* to understand the reason for something ○ *Most of the employees couldn't see the point of further training.*
• **see you (later)** *infml* goodbye ○ *"Ok, see you later." "Yeah, I'll see you tomorrow."*

PHRASAL VERBS with see

• **see about** *something* to get information or knowledge of whether something can be done ○ *I'll see about movie times and call you back.*
• **see off** *someone* [M] to watch someone leave on a trip ○ *My parents saw me off at the airport.*
• **see through** *someone/something* **NOT BE DECEIVED** to understand the truth about someone or something and not allow yourself to be deceived ○ *She saw through his excuse – he was trying to put the blame on someone else.*
• **see** *someone* **through** *something* **SUPPORT** to support someone during a difficult time ○ *He was a real friend to see me through my long illness.*
• **see** *something* **through** **CONTINUE DOING** to continue until something is finished ○ *She saw the project through to the end.*
• **see to** *something fml* to do something that has to be done ○ *They hired an event planner to see to all of the details of the party.* ○ *Please see to it that no one comes in without identification.*

S

seed **PLANT** /siːd/ *n* [C/U] ***biology*** a small, usually hard part of a plant from which a new plant can grow
seed /siːd/ *v* [T] to plant seeds in the ground ○ *We seeded the lawn with a different grass this year.*
seeded /ˈsiː·dəd/, **seedless** /ˈsiːd·ləs/ *adj* [not gradable] with the seeds removed ○ *seeded grapes*

BEGINNING /siːd/ *n* [C usually pl] the beginning or cause of something ○ *A good defense lawyer knows how to plant these little seeds of doubt in the minds of jurors.*

SPORTS /siːd/ *n* [C] any of the players or teams ranked among the best in a particular competition
seeded /ˈsiːd·əd/ *adj* [not gradable] ranked as one of the better players or teams, in order to arrange that these do not compete early in a competition ○ *Michigan State University, seeded first in the Southeast, also plays today.*

seed money *n* [U] money that is used to start a business or activity

seedy /ˈsiːd·i/ *adj* [-*er*/-*est* only] in bad condition, esp. because not cared for and therefore unattractive ○ *We had quarters in a rather seedy hotel near the railroad tracks.*

seek Ⓐ **SEARCH** /siːk/ *v* [T] *past* **sought** **1** to search for something or try to find or obtain something ○ *She is actively seeking work.* ○ *The government is seeking ways to reduce the cost of health care.* **2** If you seek advice/approval/help/permission, you ask for it: *They suggested she seek advice from the legal department.*
seeker /ˈsiː·kər/ *n* [C] ○ *job/thrill/ fortune seekers*

TRY /siːk/ *v* [+ *to* infinitive] *past* **sought** to try or attempt ○ *They sought to reassure people that their homes would be safe from the flood.*

seem /siːm/ *v* to appear to be ○ [L] *You seem very quiet today.* ○ [L] *He's 16, but he seems younger.* ○ [L] *The news seemed too good to be true.* ○ [L] *She didn't seem (to be) particularly happy.* ○ [I always + adv/prep] *They seemed like such a nice couple.* ○ [+ *to* infinitive] *I can't seem to stay awake.*
seeming /ˈsiː·mɪŋ/ *adj* [not gradable] appearing true or obvious, although it might not be ○ *Their seeming reluctance to demand better treatment was puzzling.*
seemingly /ˈsiː·mɪŋ·li/ *adv* [not gradable] ○ *He is seemingly untroubled by our recent problems.*

seen /siːn/ *past participle of* SEE

seep /siːp/ *v* [I always + adv/prep] (of liquids) to flow slowly through something ○ *The flood water seeped into the basement.*
seepage /ˈsiː·pɪdʒ/ *n* [U]

seesaw /ˈsiː·sɔː/, **teeter-totter** *n* [C] a device for children's play that consists of a board balanced at the center, with a place at each end for a child to sit on and push away from the ground with their feet, causing the other end to go down
seesaw /ˈsiː·sɔː/ *v* [I] to change direction or move backward and forward or up and down repeatedly ○ *The lead seesawed* (= first one side was winning, then the other) *throughout the game.*

seethe /siːð/ *v* [I] to feel very angry ○ *She was still seething, remembering how rudely she was treated.*

see-through *adj infml* transparent or almost transparent ○ *see-through material*

segment /ˈseg·mənt/ *n* [C] **1** any of the parts into which something can be divided ○ *The news program contained a brief segment on white-collar crime.* **2** A segment is also one of several parts of an orange, lemon, or similarly divided fruits. **3** ***biology*** A segment is also one of the parts of the body of an insect. **4** ***mathematics*** A segment is also one part of a line that has two end points. ➤ Picture: **line segment**

segregate /ˈseg·rəˌgeɪt/ *v* [T] ***social studies*** to keep one group of people apart from others because of race, religion, sex, etc. ○ *Most people wouldn't remember that some ballparks were segregated* (= black people were kept apart) *in the early years.* ○ *The boys and girls were segregated into different classes.*

segregation /ˌseg·rəˈɡeɪ·ʃən/ *n* [U] ○ *racial segregation* ○ *Almost every community has laws prohibiting segregation in housing.*

seismic /ˈsɑɪz·mɪk/ *adj* [not gradable] ***earth science*** relating to, or caused by an EARTHQUAKE (= sudden violent movement of the earth's surface)

seismograph /ˈsɑɪz·məˌɡræf/ *n* [C] ***earth science*** a piece of equipment which measures and records the strength of an EARTHQUAKE (= sudden movement of the earth's surface)
seismographic /ˌsɑɪz·məˈɡræf·ɪk/ *adj* [not gradable] ***earth science***

seize /siːz/ *v* [T] **1** to take something quickly and hold it ○ *He seized her arm to lead her through the crowd.* ○ *(fig.) While she was distracted, I seized the opportunity to take a cookie.* **2** Seize can also mean to take by force: *Rebel forces seized control of six towns.* **3** If police or other officials seize something, they take possession of it by legal authority: *The goods that were seized had been hidden in a shipment of paint.*
seizure /ˈsiː·ʒər/ *n* [C/U] **1** the act of taking hold or possession of something ○ [U] *Violators of the fishing regulations face seizure of the boat's catch.* **2** A seizure is also a medical condition that can cause you to lose control of your muscles and, often, cause you to become unconscious: [C] *The cat suffered several seizures after eating some poison.*

PHRASAL VERB with **seize**

• **seize on/upon** *something* to use or bring attention to something for your advantage ○ *Immigration issues have been seized on by conservative politicians.*

seldom /ˈsel·dəm/ *adv* almost never ○ *I seldom drive my car into the city.*

select Ⓐ **CHOOSE** /səˈlekt/ *v* [I/T] to choose something, or to make a choice ○ [T] *They have the option of selecting the school that they want their kids to go to.* ○ [I] *You can select from among the offerings shown on this screen.*
selection Ⓐ /səˈlek·ʃən/ *n* [C/U] **1** the act of choosing, or the person or thing chosen ○ [C] *They performed a mix of old hits and selections from their new CD.* **2** A selection can also be a range and variety of something from which to choose: [C] *That bookstore has a wide selection of mystery novels.* ○ [U] *Shop early for the best selection.*
selective Ⓐ /səˈlek·tɪv/ *adj* [not gradable] careful in choosing ○ *The school is very selective and accepts only those students who are extremely motivated.*
selectively Ⓐ /səˈlek·tɪv·li/ *adv* ○ *Purebred dogs have been selectively bred for thousands of years in some cases.*
BEST QUALITY /səˈlekt/ *adj* [not gradable] the best of its type or highest in quality ○ *select fruit/school* ○ *a select group of people*

selective breeding *n* [U] ***biology*** the process of choosing only plants and animals with desirable characteristics to reproduce

selenium /səˈliː·niː·əm/ *n* [U] ***chemistry*** a chemical element that is used in electronic devices and is also necessary in small amounts in the body

self /self/ *n* [C/U] *pl* **selves** who a person is, including the qualities such as personality and ability that make one person different from another ○ [C] *Now I'm feeling better, and I'm back to my old self again.* ○ [U] *I still assert the validity of self over social convention.*
selfish /ˈsel·fɪʃ/ *adj* caring only about what you want or need without any thought for the needs or wishes of other people ○ *Am I being selfish to want more?*
selfless /ˈsel·fləs/ *adj* caring more about other people's needs and interests than about your own ○ *She's a selfless person who is deeply concerned about social justice.*

self-absorbed /ˌsel·fəbˈsɔːrbd, -ˈzɔːrbd/ *adj* so involved with yourself that you do not think about anyone else; SELF-CENTERED ○ *Henry is so self-absorbed it's a miracle anyone bothers with him at all.*

self-addressed /ˌsel·fəˈdrest/ *adj* [not gradable] (of an envelope) having the name and address of the person who originally sent it on it ○ *a self-addressed, stamped envelope* ○ See also: SASE

self-appointed /ˌsel·fəˈpɔɪnt·əd/ *adj* [not gradable] behaving as if you had special knowledge or authority without actually having it ○ *Mrs. McElvey was the self-appointed spokeswoman for the group.*

self-assured /ˌsel·fəˈʃʊrd/ *adj* having confidence in yourself ○ *She moves with self-assured grace.*
self-assurance /ˌsel·fəˈʃʊr·əns/ *n* [U] ○ *His calm self-assurance had vanished.*

self-centered /selfˈsent·ərd/ *adj* caring only about yourself; SELF-ABSORBED ○ *Angela is a good kid who is also, at times, whiny and self-centered.*

self-confident /selfˈkɑn·fəd·ənt, -fəˌdent/ *adj* certain that you can manage any situation by yourself ○ *She's one of the most self-confident young women I've ever met.*
self-confidence /selfˈkɑn·fəd·əns, -fəˌdens/ *n* [U] ○ *the self-confidence of an experienced professional*

self-conscious /selfˈkɑn·ʃəs/ *adj* uncomfortable about yourself and worried about disapproval from other people ○ *She was self-conscious about her weight.*
self-consciously /selfˈkɑn·ʃə·sli/ *adv* ○ *She blushed self-consciously when I complimented her.*

self-contained /ˌself·kənˈteɪnd/ *adj* (of someone or something) having everything necessary to be independent or to work independently ○ *a self-contained environment* ○ *a self-contained, independent person*

self-control /ˌself·kənˈtroʊl/ *n* [U] control over your emotions and actions; SELF-RESTRAINT ○ *They try to teach teamwork, self-control, and how to deal with adversity.*

self-defeating /ˌself·dɪˈfiːt̬·ɪŋ/ *adj* [not gradable] done in a way that keeps you from succeeding ○ *He raises the issue in a way that is self-defeating.*

S

self-defense /ˌself·dɪˈfens/ *n* [U] the protection of yourself ○ *She says she shot him in self-defense.*

self-denial /ˌself·dɪˈnɑɪ·əl/ *n* [U] a decision not to do or have something you want, esp. because it is good for you not to do or have it ○ *He felt he had wasted his youth in self-denial.*

self-destructive /ˌself·dɪˈstrʌk·tɪv/ *adj* (of behavior or actions) likely to harm or kill you ○ *Freedom is not an excuse to indulge in self-destructive behavior.*
self-destruction /ˌself·dɪˈstrʌk·ʃən/ *n* [U] ○ *Barrymore was a brilliant actor bent on self-destruction.*

self-discipline /ˌselfˈdɪs·ə·plən/ *n* [U] the ability to make yourself do things when you should, even if you do not want to do them ○ *He lacked self-discipline and seemed unable to finish anything.*

self-employed /ˌsel·fɪmˈplɔɪd/ *adj* [not gradable] having your own business and working for yourself rather than for an employer

self-esteem /ˌsel·fəˈstiːm/ *n* [U] respect for yourself ○ *The program is intended to build students' self-esteem.* ○ *Does he suffer from low self-esteem?*

self-evident /selˈfev·əd·ənt, -əˌdent/ *adj* [not gradable] so clear or obvious that no proof or explanation is needed ○ *self-evident facts*

self-fulfilling IDIOM /ˌself·fʊlˈfɪl·ɪŋ/
• **a self-fulfilling prophecy** a situation in which something happens because you expected or said it would happen: *Sales predictions determine how a book is published, and a prediction of poor sales is often a self-fulfilling prophecy.*

self-help /ˈselfˈhelp/ *adj* [not gradable] providing ways to help you solve a problem, end a habit, learn a skill, etc. by yourself ○ *self-help books* ○ *a self-help organization*

self-image /ˈselˈfɪm·ɪdʒ/ *n* [C] your opinion of yourself, esp. how you appear to other people ○ *Her self-image doesn't depend entirely on professional success.*

self-importance /ˌsel·fɪmˈpɔːrt·ᵊns/ *n* [U] the belief that you are more important or valuable than other people ○ *He strutted into the room, self-importance written all over his face.*
self-important /ˌsel·fɪmˈpɔːrt·ᵊnt/ *adj* ○ *You are a self-important little twerp.*

self-improvement /ˌsel·fɪmˈpruːv·mənt/ *n* [U] learning new things on your own that make you a more skilled or able person ○ *In the interest of self-improvement, I took a course in Spanish.*

self-indulgent /ˌsel·fɪnˈdʌl·dʒənt/ *adj* allowing yourself to have or do anything you want ○ *A lot of the poetry is just self-indulgent nonsense.*
self-indulgence /ˌsel·fɪnˈdʌl·dʒəns/ *n* [U] ○ *My parents' trip to Hawaii was an unusual self-indulgence for them.*

self-inflicted /ˌsel·fɪnˈflɪk·təd/ *adj* [not gradable] (of something bad) done to yourself ○ *a self-inflicted wound*

self-interest /selˈfɪn·trəst, -ˈfɪnt·ə·rəst/ *n* [U] consideration of advantages for yourself in making a decision, usually without worrying about its effect on others ○ *Each side was thinking only of their own self-interest.*

selfish /ˈsel·fɪʃ/ *adj* [not gradable] ○ See at SELF

selfless /ˈsel·fləs/ *adj* [not gradable] ○ See at SELF

self-made /ˈselfˈmeɪd/ *adj* [not gradable] successful as a result of your own effort ○ *a self-made man*

self-pity /ˈselfˈpɪt̬·i/ *n* [U] care and sadness about your own problems ○ *It's not easy to face serious illness without self-pity.*

self-pollination /ˌselfˌpɑl·əˈneɪ·ʃən/ *n* [U] ***biology*** the process by which POLLEN from the male part of a flower is carried to the female part of the same flower or to another flower of the same type

self-portrait /ˈselfˈpɔːr·trət, -ˈpoʊr-/ *n* [C] a picture you make of yourself ○ *How accurate is his self-portrait?*

self-possession /ˌself·pəˈzeʃ·ən/ *n* [U] the quality of being calm and in control of your emotions ○ *She shows remarkable self-possession for a child.*
self-possessed /ˌself·pəˈzest/ *adj*

self-preservation /ˌselfˌprez·ərˈveɪ·ʃən/ *n* [U] the ability of animals or people to protect themselves from danger or destruction ○ *an instinct for self-preservation*

self-proclaimed /ˌself·prəˈkleɪmd/ *adj* [not gradable] said or announced by yourself about yourself ○ *He is a self-proclaimed literary genius.*

self-reliance /ˌself·rɪˈlɑɪ·əns/ *n* [U] the ability to depend on yourself or your own abilities ○ *Learning self-reliance is a slow, hard process.*
self-reliant /ˌself·rɪˈlɑɪ·ənt/ *adj* ○ *She's cool, determined, and self-reliant.*

self-respect /ˌself·rɪˈspekt/ *n* [U] positive thoughts and feelings about yourself; SELF-ESTEEM ○ *His self-respect is based on solid achievement.*
self-respecting /ˌself·rɪˈspek·tɪŋ/ *adj* [not gradable] ○ *No self-respecting person would tolerate that.*

self-restraint /ˌself·rɪˈstreɪnt/ *n* [U] control over your emotions and actions; SELF-CONTROL. ○ *You need to exercise a little self-restraint.*

self-righteous /selˈfrɑɪ·tʃəs/ *adj* believing that you are better and more moral than other people, often expressed in an annoying or offensive way ○ *Spare us from your self-righteous nonsense.*

self-sacrifice /ˈselfˈsæk·rəˌfɑɪs/ *n* [U] a decision to give up something you want or need so that others can have what they want or need ○ *Heroism and self-sacrifice inspired the young men and women.*

self-satisfied /ˈselfˈsæt̬·əsˌfɑɪd/ *adj* too pleased with yourself and what you have achieved ○ *an annoyingly self-satisfied person*

self-service /ˈselfˈsɜr·vəs/ *adj* [not gradable] (of a business or machine) operated without employees to help you, so that you take items for yourself and then pay someone for whatever you have taken ○ *a self-service gas station/cafeteria*

self-starter /ˈselfˈstɑrt̬·ər/ *n* [C] someone who can work well alone ○ *Applicants must be self-starters.*

self-sufficient /ˌself·səˈfɪʃ·ənt/ *adj* able to provide what is necessary without the help of others ○ *a self-sufficient economy/person*

self-sufficiency /ˌself·səˈfɪʃ·ən·si/ *n* [U] ○ *They showed their self-sufficiency by growing their own vegetables.*

self-supporting /ˌself·səˈpɔːrt̬·ɪŋ, -ˈpoʊrt̬-/ *adj* [not gradable] having enough money to take care of yourself ○ *Children eventually become self-supporting.*

self-taught /ˈselfˈtɔːt/ *adj* [not gradable] (of a skill or knowledge) learned or trained by yourself ○ *a self-taught artist/musician*

sell EXCHANGE FOR MONEY /sel/ *v* [I/T] *past* **sold** to give a thing or perform a service in exchange for money ○ [T] *The children sold lemonade.* ○ [I] *These baskets sell well* (= people buy a lot of them). ○ See also: SALE SELL

seller /ˈsel·ər/ *n* [C] **1** *The seller of the painting was kept secret.* **2** A seller is also something that is sold: *That CD is our best seller.*

WORD CHOICES sell

Retail is a word that means "sell" when talking about companies selling things in stores or by mail.

*The company makes and **retails** moderately priced sportswear.*

The phrasal verb **deal in** can be used when someone sells and buys things as part of a business.

*They mainly **deal in** rare books.*

Divest or **sell off** means "to sell something, especially a business or part of a business."

*The company is **divesting/selling off** the less profitable parts of its business.*

If a company or country sells goods to other countries, you could use the word **export**.

*France **exports** a lot of cheese.*

Hawk can be used when someone sells things informally in public places.

*There were lots of street vendors **hawking** candy.*

Peddle is a usually disapproving word when someone goes from place to place to sell things.

*They were caught on the street **peddling** counterfeit CDs.*

If you **auction (off)** something, you sell it at a public sale to the person who offers the most money.

*The family is **auctioning off** its art collection.*

Sell out (of) means to sell all of the supply that you have of something.

*We **sold out of** the T-shirts within two hours.*

PERSUADE /sel/ *v* [I/T] *past* **sold** to persuade someone to accept an idea or plan, or to cause something to be accepted ○ [T] *That is a plan we can easily sell to the school board.*

IDIOM with sell

• **sell** *someone* **short** to value someone too little ○ *It's a mistake to sell your audience short – they're more intelligent than you think they are.*

PHRASAL VERBS with sell

• **sell off** *something* to exchange all or a large part of something for money ○ *Farmers have had to sell off cattle because of the drought.*

• **sell** *someone* **on** *something* to persuade someone that something is good, valuable, or useful ○ *The filmmakers sold me on the idea that my book would work on the screen.*

• **sell out** *(something)* EXCHANGE ALL [M] **1** to get rid of all of an item in exchange for money ○ *We sold out (of) the T-shirts in the first couple of hours.* ○ *Ten of the Huskies' 15 home games are already* **sold out** (= all the tickets have been bought). **2** If a business sells out, it receives money in exchange for control of it: *The owners of the Meadowlark Inn said they would be willing to sell out at a fair price.* ○ Related noun: SELLOUT SUCCESSFUL SALES

• **sell out** *(something)* DO FOR MONEY [M] to give up support for a person or belief for money or personal advantage ○ *He wouldn't sell out the cause to serve his own interests.* ○ Related noun: SELLOUT MONEY OPPORTUNITY

sellout SUCCESSFUL SALES /ˈsel·ɑʊt/ *n* [C] the selling of all the tickets to an event, or of all available items ○ *Saturday's show was a sellout.* ○ Related verb: SELL OUT EXCHANGE ALL

MONEY OPPORTUNITY /ˈsel·ɑʊt/ *n* [C] the act of doing something selfishly for money, without considering principles or damage to others ○ *The peace deal was praised by some as a courageous breakthrough while others condemned it as a sellout.* ○ Related verb: SELL OUT DO FOR MONEY

seltzer /ˈselt·sər/ *n* [C/U] bubbly water

selves /selvz/ *pl of* SELF

semantic /səˈmænt·ɪk/ *adj* [not gradable] ***English*** (of words and language) connected with meaning ○ *Words are semantic units that convey meaning.*

semantics /səˈmænt·ɪks/ *n* [U] ***English*** the study of meaning in language

semblance /ˈsem·bləns/ *n* [U] a similarity to something, or the appearance of being or having something ○ *She's raising two kids, holding down a full-time job, and trying to maintain some semblance of a personal life.*

semen /ˈsiː·mən/ *n* [U] ***biology*** a sticky, white liquid containing sperm which is produced by men and male animals

semester /səˈmes·tər/ *n* [C] either of the two periods into which a year is divided at a school or university ○ *fall/spring semester*

S

semi TRUCK /ˈsem·i, -ɑɪ/, **semitrailer** *n* [C] *pl* **semis** *infml* a large truck with a separate TRAILER (= vehicle without an engine) for carrying freight, or such a trailer itself ○ *The semi screeched to a halt.*

COMPETITION /ˈsem·i, -ɑɪ/ *n* [C] *pl* **semis** short form of SEMIFINAL

semi- /ˌsem·i, -ɑɪ/ *prefix* half or partly ○ *semiretired* ○ *semiserious*

semiautomatic /ˌsem·iːˌɔːt̬·əˈmæt̬·ɪk, ˌsem·ɑɪ-/ *adj* [not gradable] (of a gun) having a bullet in position and ready for firing when the TRIGGER is pulled ○ *a semiautomatic pistol/rifle*

semicircle /ˈsem·iːˌsɜr·kəl/ *n* [C] ***geometry*** half of a circle, or something in this shape ○ *Our tents were set in a semicircle.* ➤ Picture: **geometry**

semicircular /ˌsem·iːˈsɜr·kjə·lər/ *adj* [not gradable] having the shape of half a circle ○ *a semicircular table*

semicolon /ˈsem·ɪˌkoʊ·lən/ *n* [C] ***grammar*** a mark (;) used in writing for separating large or important independent parts of a sentence or items in a list

semiconductor /ˈsem·iː·kənˌdʌk·tər, ˈsemˌɑɪ-/ *n* [C] a substance, such as SILICON, that allows some electricity to flow through it, used in making electronic devices

semifinal /ˈsem·ɪˌfɑɪn·əl/, short form **semi** *n* [C] the game or set of games before the final game in a competition ○ *France was eliminated in Saturday's semifinal.* ○ Compare FINAL COMPETITION

seminal /ˈsem·ən·əl/ *adj* containing important new ideas that influence later developments ○ *"The Adventures of Huckleberry Finn" is regarded as a seminal work of American literature.*

seminar /ˈsem·əˌnɑr/ *n* [C] a meeting of a group of people with a teacher or expert for training, discussion, or study on a particular subject ○ *Police officers attended a seminar on relieving rush-hour traffic jams.*

S

seminary /ˈsem·əˌner·i/ *n* [C] a college where people are trained to become priests, ministers, or rabbis

semipermeable /ˌsem·iːˈpɜr·miː·ə·bəl/ *adj* [not gradable] ***biology, chemistry*** allowing some liquids and gases, but not others, to pass through

Semitic /səˈmɪt̬·ɪk/ *adj* [not gradable] being or having to do with the Arabs and Jews of the Middle East

semitrailer /ˈsem·ɪˌtreɪ·lər, ˈsemˌɑɪ-/ *n* [C] a SEMI TRUCK

senate /ˈsen·ət/ *n* [U] ***politics & government*** **1** the group of politicians who have the most power to make laws in a government ○ *The US Senate has 100 members.* ○ *He served in the state senate.* **2** In Canada, members of the Senate give advice about laws but do not make laws.

senator /ˈsen·ət̬·ər/, abbreviation **Sen.** *n* [C] ***politics & government*** a member of a senate, esp. of the US Senate ○ *Write to your senator about your concerns.*

senatorial /ˌsen·əˈtɔːr·iː·əl, -ˈtoʊr-/ *adj* [not gradable] ○ *senatorial candidates* ○ *a Senatorial committee*

send HAVE DELIVERED /send/ *v* [T] *past* **sent** to cause something to go or be taken somewhere without going yourself ○ *Send a letter to my office.* ○ *I like to send e-mail to my friends.*

MAKE SOMEONE GO /send/ *v* [T] *past* **sent** to cause or arrange for someone to leave or go ○ *The UN sent relief workers to the region.* ○ *My parents want to send me back to Argentina when I finish my studies.* ○ *Who can afford to send their kids to college these days?*

MAKE SOMETHING MOVE /send/ *v* [T] *past* **sent** to make something move quickly by force ○ *Wind sent clouds skittering across the sky.* ○ *The researcher sent the particles flying apart.*

CAUSE TO HAPPEN /send/ *v* [T] *past* **sent** to cause someone to feel or behave in a particular way, or to cause something to happen ○ *Final exams always send me into a panic.*

IDIOMS with send

• **send a message, send a signal** to do or say something in order to try to influence someone else's attitudes or behavior ○ *We need to send a clear message that pollution will not be tolerated.*

• **send** *someone's* **love (to** *someone***), send** *someone's* **regards (to** *someone***)** to express someone's good feelings to someone else ○ *Maggie sends her love to you and the kids.*

• **send shivers down** *your* **spine, send shivers up** *your* **spine** to feel very frightened or excited ○ *The thought of what might have happened to us sent shivers down my spine.* ○ *Hearing that song still sends shivers up my spine.*

PHRASAL VERBS with send

• **send away for** *something* to request something by mail ○ *Carson sent away for a magic kit.*

• **send back** *something* [M] to return something to the place it came from ○ *Send your steak back if it's undercooked.*

• **send for** *someone/something* to request or demand that someone or something come ○ *Once he was settled in America, he sent for his wife.*

• **send in** *something* MAIL [M] to mail something to a place ○ *I sent in my entry form, but I don't expect to win anything.*

• **send in** *something/someone* CAUSE TO GO [M] to cause a group of people to go to a place ○ *The commissioner sent in a team of investigators.*

• **send off** *something* MAIL [M] to mail something ○ *She sent the manuscript off to her publisher.*

• **send off** *someone* CAUSE TO GO [M] to ask or tell someone to leave, usually for a particular purpose ○ *Companies sometimes send a troubled boss off for counseling.*

• **send out** *something* MAIL [M] to mail something ○ *Frank sent out about 400 invitations to his party.* ○ USAGE: usually said about mailing many things that go to different places

• **send out** *someone/something* **CAUSE TO GO** [M] **1** to ask or demand that someone go somewhere ○ *Mom sent me out to weed the garden.* **2** If energy or a signal is sent out, it is produced: *The laser sends out a long red beam of light.*

send-off /ˈsen·dɔːf/ *n* [C] an occasion at which people express good wishes to someone who is leaving ○ *Friends gave them a rousing send-off.*

senile /ˈsiː·nɑɪl, ˈsen·ɑɪl/ *adj* mentally confused as a result of old age ○ *Her children couldn't cope with her because she's somewhat senile.*
senility /səˈnɪl·ət̬·i/ *n* [U] ○ *Miller suffers from senility.*

senior MORE ADVANCED /ˈsiːn·jər/ *adj* more advanced, or higher in rank ○ *Senior officials denied that a problem exists.* ○ Compare JUNIOR LESS ADVANCED
seniority /siːnˈjɔːr·ət̬·i, -ˈjɑr-/ *n* [U] higher rank or advantage obtained as a result of the length of job service ○ *Most of these workers have 20 to 30 years of seniority.*
SCHOOL /ˈsiːn·jər/ *n* [C] a student in the fourth and final year of a program of study in a college, university, or HIGH SCHOOL (= a school for students 15 to 18 years old)
senior /ˈsiːn·jər/ *adj* [not gradable] ○ *Alanna's in her senior year of high school.*
OLDER /ˈsiːn·jər/ *adj* older ○ *The senior Griffey played on the same baseball team as his son, Ken Griffey, Jr.*
senior /ˈsiːn·jər/ *n* [U] ○ *She married a man almost 40 years her senior.*

senior citizen, *short form* **senior** *n* [C] an older person, usually over the age of 60 or 65, esp. one who is no longer employed ○ *Senior citizens get a discount.*

senior high school *n* [C] a HIGH SCHOOL

sensation FEELING /senˈseɪ·ʃən, sən-/ *n* [C/U] a feeling in your body resulting from something that happens or is done to it, or the ability to feel as the result of touch ○ [C] *He felt a sinking sensation in the pit of his stomach.* ○ [U] *This part of your body doesn't have a lot of sensation.*
EXCITEMENT /senˈseɪ·ʃən, sən-/ *n* [C] great excitement or interest, or someone or something that causes excitement ○ *His first recordings caused a sensation and became classics of rock.*
sensational /senˈseɪ·ʃən·əl, sən-/ *adj* **1** very exciting, or extremely good ○ *She was absolutely sensational in that movie.* **2** *disapproving* Something or someone sensational purposely shocks people and attracts their interest: *Readers love sensational crime stories.*
sensationalism /senˈseɪ·ʃən·əlˌɪz·əm, sən-/ *n* [U] the use of shocking or exciting subjects, language, or style in order to interest the public ○ *Kids tend to watch news for its sensationalism.*

sense JUDGMENT /sens/ *n* the ability to make reasonable judgments ○ [U] *If the boy had any sense he would be scared.* ○ [U] *You ought to have more sense than to get involved with him.* ○ [pl] *Have you taken leave of your senses?*
sensible /ˈsen·sə·bəl/ *adj* **1** having or using good judgment; reasonable ○ *She was sensible and easy to deal with.* ○ *The only sensible thing to do is recycle.* **2** If an object is sensible, it is practical but not exciting: *a sensible family car* ○ *sensible shoes*
sensibly /ˈsen·sə·bli/ *adv* ○ *You have to eat more sensibly.*
senseless /ˈsen·sləs/ *adj* lacking purpose or meaning ○ *a senseless prank* ○ *It was senseless to treat me like that.*

> **CONFUSABLES**
>
> **sensible or sensitive?**
>
> Remember that **sensible** does not mean "easily upset" or "able to understand what people are feeling." The word you need to express these two meanings is **sensitive**.
>
> *Don't criticize her too much. She's very sensitive.*
>
> *He's very sensitive to atmosphere and other people's feelings.*
>
> ~~*He's very sensible to atmosphere and other people's feelings.*~~

BODY POWER /sens/ *n* [C] ***biology*** any of the five physical abilities to see, hear, smell, taste, and feel ○ Related adjective: SENSORY
senseless /ˈsen·sləs/ *adj* unconscious ○ *They beat him senseless.*
AWARENESS /sens/ *n* [C usually sing] **1** an awareness of something, or an ability to do or understand something ○ *I have a very bad sense of direction.* **2** A sense of humor is the ability to understand and enjoy jokes and amusing situations, or to make people laugh: *Matt has a great sense of humor.*
FEELING /sens/ *n* [C] a feeling about something ○ *They move with a sense of confidence.* ○ *Students need some sense of responsibility.*
sense /sens/ *v* [T] to feel or be aware of something ○ *Although she said nothing, I could sense her anger.* ○ *I sensed someone was approaching me from behind.*
MEANING /sens/ *n* [C] ***English*** a meaning of a word or phrase ○ *This isn't a travel book in the usual sense of the word.*

WORD FAMILY sense

Nouns	sense nonsense sensibility sensitivity insensitivity	*Adjectives*	sensible senseless sensitive insensitive nonsensical
Adverbs	sensibly sensitively insensitively	*Verbs*	sense

sensibility /ˌsen·səˈbɪl·ət̬·i/ *n* the ability to feel and react to something ○ [U] *Those attitudes are offensive to the modern sensibility.* ○ [pl] *He*

S

launched a crusade against publicly funded art that offended his moral sensibilities.

sensitive UNDERSTANDING /ˈsen·sə̬t·ɪv/ *adj* having or showing awareness and understanding, esp. of other people's feelings and needs ○ *My experience made me very sensitive to the suffering of others.*

sensitively /ˈsen·sə̬t·ɪv·li/ *adv* ○ *How can I say this sensitively?*

sensitivity /ˌsen·səˈtɪv·ə̬t·i/ *n* [U] ○ *A good teacher has enthusiasm, intelligence, and sensitivity to students' needs.* ➤ Confusables: **sensible or sensitive?** at SENSE JUDGMENT

UPSET /ˈsen·sə̬t·ɪv/ *adj* (of a person) easily upset ○ *Tom is extremely sensitive about his hair.* ○ *She's very sensitive to criticism.*

sensitivity /ˌsen·səˈtɪv·ə̬t·i/ *n* the tendency to be upset ○ [U] *He didn't want to say anything because of the sensitivity of the issue.* ○ [pl] *He tried to avoid offending their sensitivities.*

REACTING EASILY /ˈsen·sə̬t·ɪv/ *adj* easily influenced, changed, or damaged, esp. by a physical activity or effect ○ *an environmentally sensitive river* ○ *Their products include cleansers and moisturizers for sensitive skin.*

sensitivity /ˌsen·səˈtɪv·ə̬t·i/, **sensitiveness** /ˈsen·sə̬t·ɪv·nəs/ *n* [U] ○ *Many people have food sensitivities or allergies.*

NEEDING CAREFUL TREATMENT /ˈsen·sə̬t·ɪv/ *adj* needing to be treated with care ○ *Raising fuel prices can be a sensitive issue.*

sensitivity /ˌsen·səˈtɪv·ə̬t·i/ *n* [U] ○ *Discussions about co-workers' salaries need to be approached with special sensitivity.*

sensor /ˈsen·sər/ *n* [C] a device that discovers and reacts to changes in such things as movement, heat, and light ○ *motion/radiation/humidity sensors*

sensory /ˈsen·sə·ri/ *adj* [not gradable] ***biology*** of or related to the physical SENSES of touch, smell, taste, sight, and hearing

sensory neuron *n* [C] ***biology*** a nerve cell that receives messages from the environment or outer part of the body and carries them to the brain or SPINAL CORD

sensual /ˈsen·tʃə·wəl/ *adj* expressing or suggesting physical pleasure ○ *a sensual mouth* ○ *They shared the sensual satisfaction of French food.*

sensuality /ˌsen·tʃəˈwæl·ə̬t·i/ *n* [U]

sensuous /ˈsen·tʃə·wəs/ *adj* **1** pleasing to the physical SENSES ○ *Her flower garden is a totally sensuous environment.* **2** Sensuous can also mean SENSUAL: *He's won critical raves for his sensuous designs.*

sent /sent/ *past simple and past participle of* SEND

sentence GRAMMAR /ˈsent·ᵊns/ *n* [C] ***grammar*** a group of words, usually containing a subject and a verb, expressing a statement, question, instruction, or exclamation, and, when written, starting with a capital letter and ending with a PERIOD or other mark ○ *Your sentences are too long and complicated.*

PUNISHMENT /ˈsent·ᵊns/ *n* [C] a punishment given by a law court to a person or organization that is guilty of a crime ○ *She served a three-year prison sentence.*

sentence /ˈsent·ᵊns/ *v* [T] ○ *He was sentenced to three years in jail and fined $40,000.*

sentiment GENERAL FEELING /ˈsent·ə·mənt/ *n* [C/U] a general feeling, attitude, or opinion about something ○ [C] *Writers learn that sentiments and ideas must serve the story, and not the other way around.* ○ [U] *Boyd tried to turn community sentiment against the program.*

USAGE

sentiments or **feelings?**

Feelings is the normal word used for talking about the way someone feels.

She couldn't find the words to express her feelings.

~~*She couldn't find the words to express her sentiments.*~~

Sentiments is a more formal word used especially for the way a person feels or thinks about a particular subject.

Many other people have expressed similar sentiments about the new plan.

EMOTION /ˈsent·ə·mənt/ *n* [U] *often disapproving* gentle emotions such as love, sympathy, or caring ○ *The film wallows in sentiment.* ○ *There was little room for compassion or sentiment in his world.*

sentimental /ˌsent·əˈment·ᵊl/ *adj* **1** related to feelings rather than reason ○ *When you ask which team will win, my sentimental favorite would have to be Philadelphia.* **2** Sentimental also means expressing or causing gentle emotions: *He gets sentimental and starts crying when we talk about his mother.*

sentimentally /ˌsent·əˈment·ᵊl·i/ *adv* ○ *Children get sentimentally attached to their pets.*

sentimentality /ˌsent·əˌmenˈtæl·ə̬t·i, -mən-/ *n* [U] ○ *She had never liked that song's sentimentality.*

sentry /ˈsen·tri/ *n* [C] a soldier who guards a place and prevents those who are not allowed in from entering ○ *Sentries stood guard at the palace.*

sepal /ˈsiː·pəl/ *n* [C] ***biology*** one of the parts of the outer part of a flower, which surround the petals and are usually small and green

separate /ˈsep·ə·rət, ˈsep·rət/ *adj* existing or happening independently or in a different physical space ○ *The middle school and the high school are in two separate buildings.* ○ *I have my public life and my private life, and as far as possible I try to keep them separate.*

separate /ˈsep·əˌreɪt/ *v* [I/T] **1** to cause two or more people or things to stop being with or near each other, or to be positioned between two or more things ○ [T] *A six-foot-high wall separates ticket holders from those hoping to get tickets.* ○ [T] *Fighting broke out between two hockey players, and it took nearly five minutes to separate them.* **2** If two married people separate, they stop living together as husband and wife, often as a part of a legal arrangement.

separately /ˈsep·ə·rət·li, ˈsep·rət-/ *adv* ○ *You have to wash dark clothes and white stuff separately.*

separation /ˌsep·əˈreɪ·ʃən/ *n* [C/U] **1** [U] *The laws now require the separation of garbage that can be recycled, such as newspapers and glass bottles.* **2** A separation is an arrangement, often a legal one, by which two married people stop living together as husband and wife.

WORD FAMILY separate			
Nouns	separation separatist	*Verbs*	separate
Adjectives	inseparable separate	*Adverbs*	inseparably separately

separatist /ˈsep·rət̬·əst, ˈsep·ə·rə·tɪst/ *n* [C] someone who supports an effort to become independent of the country or group to which the person belongs ○ *Albanian/Basque/Chechen separatists*

September /sepˈtem·bər, səp-/, *abbreviation* **Sept.** *n* [C/U] the ninth month of the year, after August and before October

sequel /ˈsiː·kwəl/ *n* [C] a book, movie, or play that continues the story of a previous work ○ *Sequels to movies like "Jaws" and "Superman" have become big business in the film industry.*

sequence Ⓐ /ˈsiː·kwəns, -ˌkwens/ *n* [C/U] **1** a series of related things or events, or the order in which things or events follow each other ○ [C] *The first chapter describes the strange sequence of events that led to his death.* ○ [C] *The test papers were not in the correct alphabetical sequence.* **2** ***biology*** A gene sequence is the order in which the BASES (= chemical substances) in DNA are arranged in a particular GENE (= chemical pattern the controls the characteristics of living things).

sequential Ⓐ /sɪˈkwen·tʃəl/ *adj* following a particular order ○ *a sequential exposition of the war's events*

sequentially Ⓐ /sɪˈkwen·tʃə·li/ *adv* ○ *It stores the voting records sequentially on a strip of paper.*

sequester /sɪˈkwes·tər/ *v* [T] *law* to keep the people on a JURY (= group deciding a legal case) separate from everyone else, even from their families, while deciding a case ○ *The judge refused to have the jury sequestered.*

sequin /ˈsiː·kwən/ *n* [C] a small, shiny metal or plastic disk sewn on clothes for decoration ○ *Her dress sparkled with sequins.*

sequoia /sɪˈkwɔɪ·ə/ *n* [C] an evergreen tree that can reach a height of more than 300 feet and grows in California and Oregon

serenade /ˌser·əˈneɪd/ *v* [T] to play music or sing for someone ○ *On Saturdays, shoppers at the mall are serenaded with live piano music.*

serenade /ˌser·əˈneɪd/ *n* [C] a piece of music or song performed for someone, esp. outside at night

serene /səˈriːn/ *adj* peaceful and calm, or (of a person) not worried or excited ○ *He approached the job with the serene confidence that he could succeed where others had failed.*

serenity /səˈren·ət̬·i/ *n* [U] ○ *He wrote of the beauty and serenity of the great river.*

serf /sɜrf/ *n* [C] ***world history*** a member of a low social class of farm workers who cannot leave the land where they work and who are ruled by the owner of the land

sergeant /ˈsɑr·dʒənt/ *n* [C] a person in the military below the rank of a LIEUTENANT (= an officer of the lowest rank)

serial /ˈsɪr·iː·əl/ *adj* [not gradable] happening one after another in time or order ○ *She's the librarian in charge of serial publications* (= magazines, newspapers, etc., that appear at regular periods).

serial /ˈsɪr·iː·əl/ *n* [C] a story printed in a newspaper or magazine or broadcast on television or radio in several parts

serial music *n* [U] ***music*** music that is based on an arrangement of the notes in the TWELVE-TONE SCALE

serial number *n* [C] a number on a product, esp. electronic or electrical goods, that is different from all the other product numbers, used to prove who it belongs to if it is stolen or damaged

series Ⓐ /ˈsɪr·iːz/ *n* [C] *pl* **series** a number of similar or related events or things, one following another ○ *A series of scandals over the past year has not helped public confidence in the administration.*

series circuit *n* [C] ***physics*** an electrical CIRCUIT in which electricity flows in only one path

serious NOT JOKING /ˈsɪr·iː·əs/ *adj* not joking; not intended to amuse ○ *You can never tell when he's serious.*

seriously /ˈsɪr·iː·ə·sli/ *adv* ○ *Seriously* (= Without joking), *now, did he really say that?* ○ *You're not seriously* (= really) *thinking of quitting, are you?*

NEEDING ATTENTION /ˈsɪr·iː·əs/ *adj* needing complete attention ○ *That's an interesting job offer – I'd give it serious consideration if I were you.*

seriously /ˈsɪr·iː·ə·sli/ *adv* ○ *The police have to take crowd control seriously.*

BAD /ˈsɪr·iː·əs/ *adj* severe in effect; bad ○ *Fortunately, there were no serious injuries.*

seriously /ˈsɪr·iː·ə·sli/ *adv* ○ *Uncooked shellfish can make you seriously ill.*

seriousness /ˈsɪr·iː·ə·snəs/ *n* [U] ○ *I don't think he has any idea of the seriousness of the situation.*

DETERMINED /ˈsɪr·iː·əs/ *adj* **1** determined to follow a particular plan of action ○ *Is she serious about moving to Nevada?* ○ *You have to start getting serious about your studies.* **2** If two people who have a romantic relationship are serious about each other, they intend to continue the relationship and possibly marry.

WORD FAMILY serious			
Nouns	seriousness	*Adverbs*	seriously
Adjectives	serious		

S

sermon /ˈsɜr·mən/ *n* [C] a talk on a religious or moral subject, esp. one given by a religious leader during a religious ceremony

serpent /ˈsɜr·pənt/ *n* [C] a snake

serrated /səˈreɪţ·əd, ˈserˌeɪţ-/ *adj* having a row of sharp points along the edge ○ *You need a knife with a serrated edge for cutting bread.*

serum /ˈsɪr·əm/ *n* [C/U] the watery, colorless part of the blood, or this liquid taken from blood, used for medical purposes

servant /ˈsɜr·vənt/ *n* [C] **1** a person who is employed to do work for another person, esp. to work in another person's home doing jobs such as cooking and cleaning **2** Servant is also used in combination to mean someone working for the public: *a civil/public servant*

serve HELP /sɜrv/ *v* [I/T] **1** (esp. of a person working in a restaurant or store) to help a customer by getting what someone needs or by showing or selling goods, or to provide food or drinks to a customer or guest ○ [T] *We've been in the restaurant for half an hour and we're still waiting to be served.* ○ [T] *Breakfast is served between seven and nine every morning.* ○ [I/T] *We'll be ready to serve (lunch) soon.* **2** To serve is also to provide an area or group of people with something that is needed: [T] *As long as I am your representative, I will continue to serve the needs of this community.*

serving /ˈsɜr·vɪŋ/ *n* [C] the amount of one type of food given to one person ○ *This recipe makes enough for four servings.*

WORK /sɜrv/ *v* [I/T] to work for, or to carry out your duty ○ [I] *He served in the US Navy for twelve years.* ○ [T] *If memory serves me right* (= If I am remembering correctly), *I was 13 at the time.*

SPEND TIME /sɜrv/ *v* [T] to spend a period of time in a job or activity ○ *He served three terms in the senate.*

HELP ACHIEVE /sɜrv/ *v* [I/T] to help achieve something, or to be useful as something ○ [+ *to* infinitive] *Those discussions only served to reinforce her fears.* ○ [I] *The sofa can serve as* (= be used as) *a bed for a couple of nights.*

HIT BALL /sɜrv/ *v* [I/T] (in tennis and other sports) to hit the ball to the other player or team as a way of starting play

serve /sɜrv/ *n* [C] ○ *He's got a powerful serve.*

IDIOM with serve

• **it serves** *someone* **right** *infml* someone deserves the punishment given ○ *People think this game is so important, and it would serve them right if it was rained out.*

PHRASAL VERBS with serve

• **serve out** *something* [M] to continue to work or hold a position for a determined period ○ *Should Mr. Murphy simply serve out the rest of his contract?*

• **serve up** *something* [M] *infml* to make something available to people; provide ○ *The search engine serves up a list of Web sites that contain the user's query.*

WORD FAMILY serve

Nouns	servant serve server service serviceman servicewoman servitude disservice serving	*Adjectives*	serviceable servile
		Verbs	serve service

server /ˈsɜr·vər/ *n* [C] a central computer from which other computers obtain information

service HELP /ˈsɜr·vəs/ *n* [U] the help provided to a customer by someone who works in esp. a restaurant or store ○ *The service in this restaurant is terrible – I've been waiting fifteen minutes.*

WORK /ˈsɜr·vəs/ *n* work done or help provided, esp. for the public or for a person or an organization ○ [U] *She was given the award for a lifetime of public service.* ○ [U] *The airplane had been in service* (= used) *for fifteen years.* ○ [pl] *You should have the services of a lawyer.*

SYSTEM /ˈsɜr·vəs/ *n* [C/U] **1** a system, organization, or business that provides for a public need, or the operation of such a system ○ [C] *the diplomatic/postal service* ○ [C] *medical/social services* ○ [U] *There is bus service to Newark Airport every twenty minutes.* **2** A service is a business that provides something for people but does not produce goods: [U] *My brother runs a car service* (= business that rents cars with drivers). **3** The service is the armed forces: [U] *He spent ten years in the service.*

RELIGIOUS CEREMONY /ˈsɜr·vəs/ *n* [C] a formal religious ceremony

REPAIR /ˈsɜr·vəs/ *v* [T] to examine a machine and repair any parts that are not working ○ *I'm taking the car in to have it serviced this afternoon.*

EMPLOYMENT /ˈsɜr·vəs/ *n* [U] **1** work done for others, such as cleaning or repairing, caring for a building, or making deliveries ○ *This building has five service employees including the super.* **2** A service entrance is an entrance to a building that is used for deliveries.

BALL HIT /ˈsɜr·vəs/ *n* [U] the act of hitting a ball to put it in play in tennis and some other sports

serviceable /ˈsɜr·və·sə·bəl/ *adj* (of an object or activity) able to do the work intended ○ *If this fan is still serviceable, we could use it in the office.*

service charge *n* [C] an amount of money added to the basic price of something you buy which pays for a service you used when buying it ○ *There is a $4 service charge added to the price of each ticket if you order by phone.*

serviceman /ˈsɜr·vəˌsmæn, -smən/ *n* [C] *pl* **-men** a man who is a member of the armed forces

service station *n* [C] a business that sells gas for vehicles and sometimes repairs them

servicewoman /ˈsɜr·vəˌswʊm·ən/ *n* [C] *pl* **-women** a woman who is a member of the armed forces

serviette /ˌsɜr·viː ˈet/ *n* [C] *Cdn, Br* a NAPKIN

servile /ˈsɜr·vəl, -vɑɪl/ *adj* eager to serve and please someone else in a way that shows a lack of respect for yourself ○ *As a waiter, you want to be pleasant to people without appearing servile.*

servitude /ˈsɜr·vəˌtuːd/ *n* [U] the state of being under the control of someone else and of having no freedom; the condition of a SLAVE

sessile /ˈses·ɑɪl, -əl/ *adj* [not gradable] ***biology*** **1** describes a leaf or flower that has no stem of its own but is attached directly to the main stem of the plant **2** Sessile also describes animals that are permanently attached to one spot and cannot move around: *sessile sponges*

session **FORMAL MEETING** /ˈseʃ·ən/ *n* a formal meeting of an organization, esp. of a legislature or law court ○ [C] *He wanted to introduce the bill before the present session of the state legislature adjourned.* ○ [U] *Congress is in session* (= continuing to have meetings) *until the end of the month.*

ACTIVITY /ˈseʃ·ən/ *n* [C] **1** a period of time or a meeting arranged for a particular activity ○ *The musicians gathered in the studio, waiting for the start of the recording session.* **2** At a college or university, a session is any of the periods of time into which a teaching year is divided: *The first summer session starts June 3rd.*

set **GROUP** /set/ *n* [C] **1** a group of things that belong together or are used together ○ *a chess set* ○ *She has a strange set of symptoms.* **2** ***mathematics*** A set is a group of numbers or things with particular characteristics: *a number set* **3** A set is also a group of people who have similar interests and spend time together: *the golf-playing set* **4** In tennis, a set is a group of games between the same competitors: *The match was over quickly, four sets to two.*

PUT /set/ *v* [T always + adv/prep] *pres. part.* **setting,** *past* **set** **1** to put something in a particular place or position ○ *Set the box on its end.* ○ *Our house is set back from the road.* **2** If you set something down, you put it on a surface: [M] *She set down her teacup and leaned forward.* **3** If you set a story in a particular place or time, the events happen then or there: *Banks's novel is set in the years before the Civil War.*

setting /ˈset̬·ɪŋ/ *n* [C] the surroundings or place in which something is put ○ *The house has a beautiful setting overlooking the river.* ○ *The setting of the novel is Paris in the 1920s.*

CAUSE A CONDITION /set/ *v pres. part.* **setting,** *past* **set** to cause someone or something to be in a particular condition, or to begin doing something ○ [T] *He carelessly dropped a match and set the grass on fire.* ○ [T] *His remarks set me thinking.* ○ [L] *The wildness in her paintings is what sets them apart.* ○ [+ *to* infinitive] *With the deadline only a few weeks away, I set to work right away.*

ARRANGE /set/ *v* [T] *pres. part.* **setting,** *past* **set** to arrange or adjust something so it is ready to work or be used ○ *I've set the clock to daylight savings time.* ○ *To get rid of mice, set a trap – or get a cat.* ○ *My job is to set the table before dinner* (= arrange the plates, utensils, etc.).

set /set/ *adj* [not gradable] with everything arranged; ready ○ [+ *to* infinitive] *Katy is set to go to college in September.* ○ *Is everything all set for the party?*

setting /ˈset̬·ɪŋ/ *n* [C] a position of the controls on a machine or instrument ○ *If the image is dark or fuzzy, adjust the settings.*

ESTABLISH /set/ *v* [T] *pres. part.* **setting,** *past* **set** to establish a pattern or example to follow ○ *Parents should try to set a good example.* ○ *The governor wants to set spending limits.* ○ *She set a new world record at the Wannamaker Games.*

BECOME FIXED /set/ *v* [I/T] *pres. part.* **setting,** *past* **set** **1** to cause something to become fixed or firm ○ [T] *Have they set a date for the wedding yet?* ○ [I] *Glue that sets quickly makes it easier to repair things.* ○ [T] *The old man's face was set in a continual scowl.* **2** If you have your hair set, you have it arranged while it is wet so that it will stay in a particular style when it is dry. **3** If a stone is set, it is fixed in a piece of jewelry: [T] *The blue stone was set in a gold ring.* **4** When a broken bone is set, it is kept in a fixed position so that it can heal.

set /set/ *adj* [not gradable] **1** fixed or firm ○ *There wasn't a set time for us to get there.* **2** If you are set on something, you have firmly decided about it: *HMOs are good if you aren't set on one specific doctor.*

set /set/ *n* [C/U] a position or an arrangement, esp. of the hair or body ○ [U] *I could tell from the set of his jaw that he was angry.* ○ [C] *Could you give my hair a set like the one in the picture in this magazine?*

setting /ˈset̬·ɪŋ/ *n* [C] the part of a piece of jewelry designed to hold a stone ○ *It was her grandmother's ring – a single diamond in a gold setting*

PLAY BACKGROUND /set/ *n* [C] something built or put together to represent a place where the action happens in a play or movie ○ *The set looks just like a real subway car.*

set /set/ *v*

MOVE DOWN /set/ *v* [I] *pres. part.* **setting,** *past* **set** (esp. of the sun or moon) to sink in the sky until it cannot be seen ○ *The sun sets with a great show of color.* ○ Opposite: RISE MOVE UP

TELEVISION /set/ *n* [C] a television ○ *I walked in the room and turned off the set.*

IDIOMS with set

• **set foot in** (*some place*) to enter a place ○ *Can you believe she's never set foot in a McDonald's?* ○ **USAGE:** Used in questions and negative sentences.

• **set** *something* **in motion** to begin something ○ *Newly discovered evidence set a second investigation in motion.*

• **set in stone** to be very difficult or impossible to change ○ *The schedule isn't set in stone, but we'd like to stick to it pretty closely.*

• **set in** *your* **ways** not liking change in your life ○ *They're very set in their ways – they always eat dinner exactly at 6:00.*

• **set** *your* **mind to** *something* to be determined to do or have something ○ *You can lose weight if you set your mind to it.*
• **set sail** to begin a trip on a ship or boat ○ *The ship set sail on January 2, 1589.*
• **set** *your* **sights on** *something* to decide on a goal that you want to achieve or something you want to have ○ *She set her sights on becoming the first woman president of the United States.*
• **set** *someone* **straight, set the record straight** to tell someone the true facts about a situation that the person had not understood ○ *I had to set him straight about what really happened.* ○ *The article about the trial really set the record straight.*
• **set** *your* **teeth on edge** to annoy you very much ○ *The kids screaming in the next room really set my teeth on edge.*
• **set the stage (for** *something***)** to make it possible for something else to happen ○ *The new evidence sets the stage for a long and interesting trial.*
• **set the tone (for** *something***)** to establish a particular mood or character for something ○ *The governor's speech set the tone for the whole conference.* ○ *The good financial news set an optimistic tone for the year.*
• **set** *something* **to music** to write or provide music for a poem, story, or other words so that it can be performed ○ *The poem was set to music in 1888.*
• **set up shop** to establish a business ○ *Several chain stores have announced that they will set up shop in the new mall.*

PHRASAL VERBS with set

• **set about** *something* to begin to do or deal with something ○ *After putting up the tent, she set about making a fire.*
• **set** *something* **against** *something* **COMPARE** to consider one thing in relation to another ○ *He describes the major discoveries in the field, set against the backdrop of how scientists work together.*
• **set** *someone* **against** *someone/something* **OPPOSE** to cause a person or group to oppose another or to be opposed to something ○ *It's easy to learn, but most people just have their minds set against it.* ○ *Generational differences have now set family members against each other.*
• **set** *someone/something* **apart** to show someone or something to be different or special ○ *Her original ideas set her apart from other students.*
• **set aside** *something* **SAVE** [M] to save for a particular purpose ○ *He sets aside some time every day to read to his children.* ○ *After melting the chocolate, set it aside and beat the eggs.*
• **set aside** *something* **IGNORE** [M] **1** to decide not to consider something ○ *We need to set aside our differences and begin to cooperate.* **2** To set aside a legal decision or a judgment is to state that it is no longer in effect: *The court of appeals set aside his conviction.*
• **set back** *someone/something* **DELAY** [M] to delay or stop the progress of someone or something ○ *Then I needed a second operation, which really set me back.* ○ Related noun: SETBACK
• **set** *someone* **back** *(something)* **COST** *infml* to cost someone an amount of money ○ *Our vacation set us back over $3000.*
• **set down** *something* [M] to write or print words, ideas, or information ○ *It's often a lot of work to set your thoughts down on paper.*
• **set forth** *something* [M] *fml* to explain ideas, or make rules or suggestions ○ *She set forth her views in "The Art of Making Dance."* ○ *The board set forth the conditions for her release.*
• **set in** to begin ○ *If the wound is untreated, infection may set in.* ○ *In winter, darkness sets in so early!* ○ **USAGE:** said about conditions or situations that last for a period of time
• **set off BEGIN TRIP** to start on a trip ○ *What time do we set off tomorrow?*
• **set off** *something* **CAUSE** [M] , **set** to cause a device to explode or a signal to start ○ *I accidentally set the alarm off.*
• **set** *someone* **off MAKE ANGRY** [M] to make someone angry or upset ○ *Two things set them off – fear of losing their jobs or feeling constantly picked on.*
• **set** *someone/something* **on** *someone* to cause someone or something to attack someone ○ *The security guards set their dogs on the intruders.*
• **set out START ACTION** to begin to carry out a plan of action ○ *So many young people set out to change the world.*
• **set out** *something* **GIVE DETAILS** [M] to give the details of or explain something, esp. in writing ○ *Your contract sets out the terms and conditions of your employment.*
• **set out** *something* **ARRANGE** [M] to arrange or prepare something for others to see or use ○ *The market was filled with fresh vegetables set out on tables.*
• **set up** *something/someone* **ESTABLISH** [M] **1** to establish or create something ○ *I'd be willing to set up a seminar if I thought people would come.* ○ *We were so impressed that we set up a second interview for him.* **2** If you set someone up, you establish someone on a particular path through life esp. by paying for something or supplying money: *His father set him up in the family business.* ○ *Thomson set himself up in an off-campus lab so he could do the research.* ○ Related noun: SETUP SITUATION
• **set up** *something* **PREPARE** [M] to prepare or arrange something for use ○ *We have a little area set up for serving food.* ○ Related noun: SETUP ARRANGEMENT
• **set up** *someone* **DECEIVE** [M] to create the appearance that someone has done something wrong, or to trick someone ○ *The documents support his claim that he was set up and wasn't anywhere near there that night.* ○ Related noun: SETUP TRICK

setback /ˈset ˌbæk/ *n* [C] something that causes delay or stops progress ○ *Democrats suffered a serious setback in yesterday's election, losing all three contested seats.* ○ Related verb: SET BACK DELAY

setter /ˈset̬·ər/ *n* [C] a type of dog with long hair, sometimes trained to help people who hunt find birds or animals

settle MAKE COMFORTABLE /ˈset̬·əl/ *v* [always + adv/prep] to get or to become comfortable ○ [T]

Campbell settled herself in front of a blazing fire. ○ [I] *He settled back in his chair and took out a book.*
settled /ˈset̬·əld/ *adj* ○ *Although I lived there for over a year, I never really felt settled in that apartment.*

AGREE /ˈset̬·əl/ *v* [I/T] **1** to reach a decision or an agreement about something, or to end a disagreement ○ [T] *Rogers paid $2 million to settle the lawsuit.* ○ [T] *Americans turn to a dictionary to settle questions of language.* ○ [I] *Negotiators are hopeful the two sides will settle.* **2** If you **settle out of court**, you reach an agreement in a legal case without holding a trial in court. ○ *The defendant agreed to settle out of court.*
settlement /ˈset̬·əl·mənt/ *n* [C] **1** *Both sides are working to negotiate a peace settlement.* **2** A settlement is also an arrangement, often with payment of money, to end a legal disagreement without taking it to court.

PAY /ˈset̬·əl/ *v* [T] to pay money owed ○ *He sold his photographs to settle some old debts.*
settlement /ˈset̬·əl·mənt/ *n* [C/U] ○ [U] *We enclose a check in settlement* (= as payment) *of your claim.*

LIVE /ˈset̬·əl/ *v* [I/T] to live in a place or to go somewhere to live, esp. permanently ○ [I] *After they got married, they settled in Virginia.* ○ [T] *Immigrants settled this island two hundred years ago.* ○ [I] (*fig.*) *An early-evening glow settles on the city* (= the city has begun to glow).
settled /ˈset̬·əld/ *adj* ○ *After living in several countries, we're now enjoying a more settled life.*
settlement /ˈset̬·əl·mənt/ *n* [C/U] ○ [C] *Permanent European settlements were established here in the 1830s.* ○ [U] *Early settlement developed around a copper mine.*
settler /ˈset·lər, ˈset̬·əl·ər/ *n* [C] ○ *The first settlers of this area were Germans.*

MOVE LOWER /ˈset̬·əl/ *v* [I] to move to a lower level and stay there; drop ○ *Dust can settle into the wet paint and spoil the finish.* ○ *Unused farm machinery settled in high weeds behind the house.*

IDIOMS with settle

• **settle** *your* **nerves** to make yourself feel calmer ○ *After the accident, he went for a walk to try to settle his nerves.*
• **settle** *your* **stomach** to make you feel less sick ○ *Drink this tea, it'll help to settle your stomach.*
• **settle the score, settle a score** do something to someone because that person did something harmful or insulting to you in the past ○ *After being embarrassed in front of the class, Dan was determined to settle the score.*

PHRASAL VERBS with settle

• **settle down 1** to become quieter ○ *OK, everybody, settle down.* **2** Someone who settles down accepts responsibilities and lives a calmer life: *He settled down after he married Vicki.*
• **settle down to** *something* to give all of your attention to something you are doing ○ *When the work was done, we settled down to a home-cooked meal.*
• **settle for** *something* to agree to or accept something, although it is not what you want ○ *They were hoping to sell their car for $2000 but settled for $1500.*
• **settle in** to arrange yourself and the things you own so you feel more comfortable in a new place ○ *Once we've settled in, you'll have to come for dinner.*
• **settle into** *somewhere/something* to become comfortable in a place or doing an activity ○ *Students settled into their desks and took out their notebooks.* ○ *After moving frequently during his first 14 years, he settled into a normal high school life.*
• **settle on** *something* to make a final decision about something, or to agree to accept something ○ *Have you settled on a name for the baby yet?* ○ *We wanted to buy a house, but at these prices we had to settle on an apartment.*
• **settle up** to pay all of an amount you owe ○ *I've finished eating – just let me settle up and we can go.*

setup **ARRANGEMENT** /ˈset̬·ʌp/ *n* [C/U] an arrangement of things that allows something to happen, or the process that prepares this arrangement ○ [C] *The novel's setup smacks of stereotype, but its heroine has a strong voice and a spine of steel.* ○ [U] *This television's excellent on-screen display make setup a breeze.* ○ Related verb: SET UP **PREPARE**

SITUATION /ˈset̬·ʌp/ *n* [C] a situation that has been arranged for some purpose ○ *He's in the sign business and has a nice setup with that.* ○ Related verb: SET UP **ESTABLISH**

TRICK /ˈset̬·ʌp/ *n* [C] an action that deceives someone in order to profit or get an advantage ○ *His family claims the trial was a setup from beginning to end.* ○ Related verb: SET UP **DECEIVE**

seven /ˈsev·ən/ *number* **1** 7 ○ *I have seven sisters.* ○ *a seven-week course* **2** Seven can also mean seven o'clock.
seventh /ˈsev·ənθ/ *adj, adv, n* [C] **1** *Our team came in seventh.* ○ [C] *It's the seventh of May today.* **2** A seventh is one of seven equal parts of something.

IDIOM with seven

• **in seventh heaven** extremely happy ○ *Since they got married, they're in seventh heaven.*

seventeen /ˌsev·ən ˈtiːn/ *number* 17 ○ *It is seventeen days until my birthday.* ○ *a seventeen-story building*
seventeenth /ˌsev·ən ˈtiːnθ/ *adj, adv, n* [C] **1** *the seventeenth century* ○ [C] *Her birthday is on the seventeenth.* **2** A seventeenth is one of 17 equal parts of something.

Seventh-Day Adventist *n* [C] a member of a Christian religious group that has Saturday as its day of worship

seventy /ˈsev·ən·ti, -di/ *number* 70 ○ *Grandpa turned seventy last week.* ○ *a seventy-room hotel*
seventies, 70s, 70's /ˈsev·ən·tiz, -diz/ *pl n* **1** the numbers 70 to 79 ○ *The temperature was in the seventies* (= between 70° and 79°). ○ *Ginny must be in her seventies* (= between 70 and 79 years old).

S

2 The seventies are the years between 1970 and 1979.

seventieth /ˈsev·ən·tiː·əθ, -diː-/ *adj, adv, n* [C] **1** *Today is his seventieth birthday.* **2** A seventieth is one of 70 equal parts of something.

sever /ˈsev·ər/ *v* [T] to separate or break something, esp. by cutting ○ *He severed a finger in the accident.* ○ *An explosion severed the plane's hydraulic systems.* ○ *The US severed diplomatic relations with Cuba in 1961.*

several /ˈsev·rəl, -ə·rəl/ *adj* [not gradable] (of an amount or number) more than two and fewer than many; some ○ *I've seen "Star Wars" several times.*

several /ˈsev·rəl, -ə·rəl/ *pronoun* ○ *Several* (= some of the people) *in the building have complained about the fumes.*

severance /ˈsev·ə·rəns/ *n* [U] money paid by an employer to an employee ordered to give up a job ○ *a severance package* ○ *severance pay* ○ *The company offered severance to everyone who was let go.*

severe VERY SERIOUS /səˈvɪr/ *adj* causing great pain, difficulty, damage, etc.; very serious ○ *a severe earthquake* ○ *The family faced severe challenges when he lost his job.*

severely /səˈvɪr·li/ *adv* ○ *Several people were severely injured in the accident.*

severity /səˈver·əţ·i/ *n* [U] ○ *You can't imagine the severity of the heat here during the summer.*

NOT KIND /səˈvɪr/ *adj* not kind or sympathetic; HARSH ○ *severe criticism*

severely /səˈvɪr·li/ *adv* ○ *The teacher spoke severely to the noisy children.*

severity /səˈver·əţ·i/ *n* [U] ○ *The severity of her comments surprised everyone.*

sew /soʊ/ *v* [I/T] *past simp.* **sewed**, *past part.* **sewn, sewed** to join together pieces of cloth by putting thread through it with a needle ○ [I] *Do you like to sew?* ○ [T] *She sewed her outfit by hand.* ○ [M] *Would you sew on these buttons?* ○ [M] *I had to sew up* (= repair) *a hole in my jeans.*

sewing /ˈsoʊ·ɪŋ/ *n* [U] **1** *I have some sewing I need to finish.* **2** A sewing circle is a group, usually of women, that meets regularly to sew.

S

PHRASAL VERB with sew

• **sew up** *something* [M] *infml* to complete an arrangement or event successfully or control it completely ○ *The basketball team sewed up the championship this week with their ninth consecutive win.*

sewer /ˈsuː·ər, sʊr/ *n* [C] an artificial passage or pipe, usually underground, that carries waste and used water from sinks and toilets away from buildings to a place where they can be safely gotten rid of ○ *The county is putting in new sewers.*

sewage /ˈsuː·ɪdʒ/ *n* [U] waste and liquid from toilets ○ *The storm caused raw sewage to flow into the bay.*

sewing machine *n* [C] a machine you use to sew pieces of cloth together

sex Ⓐ MALE OR FEMALE /seks/ *n* [C/U] the state of being either male or female, or all males or all females considered as a group; GENDER ○ [C] *List the name, age, and sex of each of your children.* ○ [U] *Employment discrimination on the basis of sex is illegal.* ○ Related adjective: SEXUAL BEING MALE OR FEMALE

sexism Ⓐ /ˈsekˌsɪz·əm/ *n* [U] actions based on a belief that particular jobs and activities are suitable only for women and others are suitable only for men ○ *Sexism continues to keep girls out of plumbing, electrical, and construction trades.*

sexist /ˈsek·səst/ *adj* ○ *sexist stereotypes* ○ *a sexist joke*

sexist /ˈsek·səst/ *n* [C] ○ *The girls said I was a sexist.*

ACTIVITY /seks/ *n* [U] the activity of sexual INTERCOURSE

sexy /ˈsek·si/ *adj* **1** attractive in a physical way ○ *a sexy movie star* **2** Sexy also means interesting and exciting: *a sexy job/car*

sex appeal *n* [U] the quality of being physically attractive

sex chromosome *n* [C] ***biology*** a CHROMOSOME (= structure in living cells) that controls what sex an organism will be

sex education *n* [U] a school course about sexual reproduction and sexual feelings

sex symbol *n* [C] someone whom many people find physically attractive or exciting

sexual Ⓐ MALE OR FEMALE /ˈsek·ʃə·wəl/ *adj* connected with being male or female ○ *the sexual characteristics of butterflies* ○ *He's always believed in sexual equality.* ○ Related noun: SEX MALE OR FEMALE

ACTIVITY /ˈsek·ʃə·wəl/ *adj* connected with the activity of sex

sexually Ⓐ /ˈsek·ʃə·wə·li/ *adv* ○ *The research focused on sexually mature birds.* ○ *Three women in the neighborhood were sexually assaulted.*

sexuality Ⓐ /ˌsek·ʃəˈwæl·əţ·i/ *n* [U] attitudes and activities relating to sex ○ *human sexuality*

sexual harassment *n* [U] unwanted or offensive sexual attention, suggestions, or talk, esp. from an employer or other person in a higher position

sexually transmitted disease, *abbreviation* **STD** *n* [C] any disease that infects people during sexual activity

sexual orientation, sexual preference *n* [U] the tendency to have feelings of physical attraction for a person of the opposite or the same sex

sexual reproduction *n* [U] ***biology*** the method of producing plants, animals, and people in which a male seed or SPERM cell and a female egg join ○ Compare ASEXUAL REPRODUCTION

sh /ʃ/ *exclamation* SHH

shabby BAD CONDITION /ˈʃæb·i/ *adj* looking old and in bad condition because of wear or lack of care ○ *The man wore a long, shabby coat.* ○ *We parked near Bobby's shabby trailer.*

shabbily /ˈʃæb·ə·li/ *adv* ○ *A shabbily dressed man lay sleeping in the park.*

NOT FAIR /ˈʃæb·i/ *adj* not fair or showing respect; unacceptable ○ *Her salary is $305,000 this year – not too shabby* (= very generous).

shabbily /ˈʃæb·ə·li/ *adv* ○ *Lawsuits arise when people feel that they were treated shabbily.*

shack /ʃæk/ *n* [C] a simple, small building ○ *The family lived in a one-room shack.*

shackle /ˈʃæk·əl/ *n* [C usually pl] one of a pair of metal rings connected by a chain and fastened to a person's wrists or the bottoms of the legs to prevent the person from escaping ○ *The prisoner was led away in shackles.*

shackle /ˈʃæk·əl/ *v* [T] ○ *The convicts were shackled and led onto the bus.* ○ *(fig.) She was no longer shackled by her memories* (= they did not prevent her from doing what she wanted to do).

shade **DARKNESS** /ʃeɪd/ *n* [C/U] **1** darkness and cooler temperatures caused by something blocking the direct light from the sun ○ [U] *The truck was parked in the shade.* **2** A shade is a covering that is put over a light to make it less bright: [C] *The lamps had matching shades.* **3** A shade is also a cover, usually attached at the top of a window, that can be pulled over a window to block the light or to keep people from looking in.

shade /ʃeɪd/ *v* [T] ○ *She shaded her eyes with her hand.* ○ *The backyard is shaded by tall oaks.*

shady /ˈʃeɪd·i/ *adj* ○ *It's nice and shady in front of the house.* ○ See also: SHADY

shades *pl n infml* SUNGLASSES

DEGREE /ʃeɪd/ *n* [C] **1** ***art*** a degree of darkness of a color ○ *He painted the room a beautiful shade of red.* **2** A shade can also mean one type among several: *Simple yes-or-no questions can't reveal all shades of opinion.*

shade /ʃeɪd/ *v* [I/T] ○ [T] *Students shade* (= darken) *the ovals on multiple-choice tests.* ○ [I] *Use adjectives to shade in the mood of your sentences.*

IDIOM with shade

• **a shade** slightly ○ *He weighs a shade under 300 pounds.*

shadow **DARKNESS** /ˈʃæd·oʊ/ *n* [C/U] an area of darkness caused when light is blocked by something, usually in a shape similar to the object that is blocking the light ○ [C] *Chloë kept jumping on Tyler's shadow.* ○ [U] *This corner of the room is always in shadow.* ○ [C] *He was standing in the shadows* (= a dark area). ➤ Picture: **eclipse**

shadowy /ˈʃæd·ə·wi/ *adj* **1** causing or covered by shadows ○ *Orchids hung from shadowy trees.* **2** Shadowy can also mean mysterious: *These criminals have built a shadowy network of hard-to-trace bank accounts.*

SMALL AMOUNT /ˈʃæd·oʊ/ *n* [C] a small amount ○ *He saw a shadow of malice in her dark eyes.* ○ *Are you convinced beyond a shadow of a doubt?*

FOLLOW /ˈʃæd·oʊ/ *v* [T] to follow someone closely ○ *Matsuoka was shadowed by a security officer.*

WORD FAMILY shadow			
Nouns	shadow	*Verbs*	shadow
Adjectives	shadowy		overshadow

IDIOMS with shadow

• **a shadow of** *your* **former self, a shadow of** *its* **former self** someone or something that is not as strong, powerful, or useful as it once was ○ *Since her accident, she's become a shadow of her former self.*

• **in the shadow of** *someone* receiving little attention because someone else is better known or more skillful ○ *DeMarco plays a lawyer living in the shadow of a famous father.*

shadowboxing /ˈʃæd·oʊˌbɑk·sɪŋ/ *n* [U] the exercise of boxing without a partner by hitting at the air with your hands as if another person were boxing with you

shady /ʃeɪd·i/ *adj* dishonest or illegal ○ *They'd been involved in shady real estate deals.* ○ *He has a shady reputation.* ○ See also: SHADY at SHADE DARKNESS

shaft **POLE** /ʃæft/ *n* [C] **1** a long pole or rod ○ *Energy from the wheels turns the shafts and produces electricity.* ○ *The feathers at the end of the arrow's shaft help it travel in a straight line.* ○ *Sliced beef was curled around a scallion shaft, then fried.* **2** A shaft of light is a single beam.

PASSAGE /ʃæft/ *n* [C] a long vertical or sloping passage through a building or through the ground ○ *a mine shaft* ○ *an elevator shaft* ○ *The window looks out on an air shaft.*

UNFAIR TREATMENT /ʃæft/ *n* [U] *slang* bad or unfair treatment ○ *Corporations pay almost nothing while taxpayers get the shaft.*

shaggy /ˈʃæg·i/ *adj* having or covered with long, messy hair, or (of hair) long and messy ○ *a large, shaggy dog* ○ *His gray hair was shaggy.*

shaggy-dog story *n* [C] a long story that is intended to be amusing and that has an intentionally silly or meaningless ending

shake **MOVE** /ʃeɪk/ *v* [I/T] *past simp.* **shook**, *past part.* **shaken** **1** to move something backward and forward or up and down in quick, short movements ○ [T] *Shake the can.* ○ [T] *She shook Dana gently.* ○ [T] *Cory shook some powdered sugar on her French toast.* ○ [I] *The explosion made the ground shake.* ○ [M] *Lily shook her long hair out* (= moved her hair to make it fall loosely around her shoulders). ○ [M] *She shook out the tablecloth* (= shook it so anything on it fell off). **2** If you or part of your body shakes, you make quick, short movements, or you feel as if you are doing this, because you are cold, frightened, or upset: [I] *She was soaking wet and shaking when she when she finally got home.* ○ [I] *Her hands shook as she opened the letter.* **3** If someone's voice shakes, its sound frequently changes because of fear or other emotions. **4** If you **shake** *your* **fist**, you hold your hand up with your fingers and thumb closed and move it backward and forward to show you are angry: *They*

S

stood at the gate, shaking their fists and shouting. **5** If two people **shake hands**, they greet or say goodbye by briefly joining hands and moving them slightly up and down: *We shook hands and left.* **6** If you **shake** *your* **head**, you move it from side to side to say "no" or show disagreement, sympathy, sadness, or that you do not believe something: *Frank shook his head in disbelief.* ○ *My dad shook his head, "No, you can't go."*

shake /ʃeɪk/ *n* [C] **1** *Give the bottle a shake.* ○ *Maria answered no with a shake of her head.* **2** *infml* A shake is a MILKSHAKE. **3** *infml* **The shakes** is a condition in which most or all of your body moves slightly from cold, fear, or illness: *Just thinking about the upcoming interview gave him the shakes.*

shaker /ˈʃeɪ·kər/ *n* [C] **1** a container with holes in its lid from which spices and other powders can be shaken onto food ○ *a salt/pepper shaker* **2** A shaker is also a container with a tight-fitting lid in which liquids can be mixed together by moving the container quickly.

shaky /ˈʃeɪ·ki/ *adj* ○ *His hands were shaky.* ○ *She spoke in a shaky voice.*

UPSET /ʃeɪk/ *v* [T] *past simp.* **shook**, *past part.* **shaken** to cause someone to feel upset and troubled ○ *Juanita was shaken and tried not to cry.* ○ *The instructor was shaken by the angry e-mails she received.*

shaky /ˈʃeɪ·ki/ *adj* ○ *This was my fourth time in a plane, but I still felt shaky.*

WEAKEN /ʃeɪk/ *v* [T] *past simp.* **shook**, *past part.* **shaken** to make someone's beliefs less certain or strong; to weaken ○ *Nothing shook her conviction that there was no substitute for hard work.* ○ *The defense failed to shake Powell's testimony.*

shaky /ˈʃeɪ·ki/ *adj* **1** *It was a shaky marriage from the start.* ○ *The building's foundations are pretty shaky.* **2** Shaky also means uncertain: *The agreement is still shaky and hasn't been approved yet.* **3** Someone whose performance is shaky is not performing well: *After a shaky start, the team started moving the ball and communicating.*

GET RID OF /ʃeɪk/ *v* [T] *past simp.* **shook**, *past part.* **shaken** to get rid of something, or escape from something ○ *He couldn't shake the feeling that Tony had another motive.* ○ *I've had this cold all week and just can't seem to shake it.*

WORD FAMILY shake			
Nouns	shake shaker	*Verbs*	shake
		Adverbs	shakily
Adjectives	shaky		

IDIOMS with shake

• **on shaky ground** likely to fail ○ *At least one factory is on shaky ground, and the town expects more to shut down.*

• **shake a leg** to hurry ○ *Better shake a leg, we leave in ten minutes.*

PHRASAL VERBS with shake

• **shake down** *someone* [M] *infml* to get money from someone by using threats ○ *They tried to shake him down for five bucks.* ○ Related noun: SHAKEDOWN

• **shake off** *something* [M] to get rid of something bad ○ *The team is trying to shake off its early-season losses and start winning again.*

• **shake** *something* **up** CAUSE CHANGE [M] to cause changes to something, esp. in order to make improvements ○ *He's running for senator as an outsider who will shake things up.* ○ Related noun: SHAKEUP

• **shake** *someone* **up** UPSET [M] to upset someone ○ *It really shook Gerry up when his best friend moved away.*

shakedown /ˈʃeɪk·dɑʊn/ *n* [C] *infml* the act of getting money from someone by using threats ○ *Her lawyers say the suit is a shakedown, an attempt to get her to pay them off.* ○ Related verb: SHAKE DOWN

shaken /ˈʃeɪ·kən/ *past participle of* SHAKE

shakeup /ˈʃeɪ·kʌp/ *n* [C] a new arrangement of something, esp. people's jobs, that is intended to be an improvement ○ *CBS announced a shakeup of its Friday night TV schedule.* ○ Related verb: SHAKE UP CAUSE CHANGE

shale /ʃeɪl/ *n* [U] ***earth science*** a type of rock consisting of solid material that has been pressed into thin layers

shall /ʃæl, ʃəl/ *modal verb fml* used when referring to the future instead of "will," esp. in questions ○ *Shall we go?* ○ (*law*) *Nothing in this letter shall be construed as a license to use our property.* ○ **USAGE:** In the past, as taught in schools, the future tense in English was formed with "shall" in the first person – *I shall go, we shall go* – and "will" in the second and third persons – *you will go, Mary will go, they will go.* In modern American English, "will" is commonly used in speech and writing for all three persons – *I will go*, etc. "Shall" is used mainly in formal situations with the first person – *We shall be pleased to accept your invitation* – and in legal documents.

shallow NOT DEEP /ˈʃæl·oʊ/ *adj* [*-er/-est* only] having only a short distance from the top to the bottom ○ *shallow water* ○ *Transfer the tofu and broccoli to a shallow bowl.*

NOT SERIOUS /ˈʃæl·oʊ/ *adj* [*-er/-est* only] not showing serious or careful thought or real understanding ○ *Reviewers called the book lightweight, shallow, and simplistic.*

sham /ʃæm/ *n* [C usually sing] someone or something that is falsely represented, esp. as being important or powerful ○ *I thought the meeting was a total sham and a waste of time.*

sham /ʃæm/ *adj* [not gradable] pretended; not real ○ *a sham battle*

shambles /ˈʃæm·bəlz/ *n* [U] **1** a place or situation that is in a state of confusion or disorder ○ *The morning after the party, the house was a complete shambles.* ○ *The strike-shortened basketball season* *was a shambles.* **2** Shambles is also a messy or confused state: *The candidate claimed that the economy was in (a) shambles.*

shame **GUILT** /ʃeɪm/ *n* [U] an uncomfortable feeling of guilt or of being ashamed because of your own or someone else's bad behavior ○ *He pointed out that society needed to restore a sense of shame about certain things.*

shame /ʃeɪm/ *v* [T] ○ *My aunt told us that in her day women who weren't married by the age of 25 were considered "old maids" and were so shamed by their families that they would do anything to get married.*

shameful /ˈʃeɪm·fəl/ *adj* causing you to feel guilty or ashamed, or being a cause for feeling ashamed ○ [+ *that* clause] *It's shameful that his own country did not fully appreciate his talent until it was recognized abroad.*

shameless /ˈʃeɪm·ləs/ *adj* **1** being something you should be ashamed of ○ *It was a shameless display of cowardice.* **2** Shameless also means done without worrying about whether your actions are right or wrong: *When the senator wanted something from a colleague, he first resorted to shameless flattery.* ○ *shameless manipulation of the press*

shamelessly /ˈʃeɪm·lə·sli/ *adv*

MISFORTUNE /ʃeɪm/ *n* [U] an unlucky or disappointing situation ○ *What a shame that they left just before we arrived.* ○ [+ *to* infinitive] *Have some more vegetables – it would be a shame to waste them.*

WORD FAMILY shame

Nouns	shame	*Verbs*	shame
Adjectives	ashamed shameful shameless	*Adverbs*	shamefully shamelessly

IDIOM with shame

• **shame on you** you should feel ashamed of what you have done ○ *I can't believe you lied to her - shame on you!*

shampoo /ʃæmˈpuː/ *n* [C/U] *pl* **shampoos** **1** a liquid soap used for washing the hair, or the act of washing the hair with this liquid ○ [U] *a bottle of shampoo* ○ [C] *The dog needs a shampoo.* **2** A shampoo is also a liquid used to clean certain thick materials: [C] *a rug shampoo*

shampoo /ʃæmˈpuː/ *v* [T] **shampoos**, *pres. part.* **shampooing**, *past* **shampooed** ○ *He took a shower and shampooed his hair.*

shamrock /ˈʃæm·rɑk/ *n* [C] a plant with three round leaves on each stem, known as the plant that represents Ireland

shanty /ˈʃænt·i/ *n* [C] a small, badly built house, usually made from pieces of wood, metal, or cardboard, in which poor people live ○ *He lived in a little shanty in the desert, miles from anything else.*

shantytown /ˈʃænt·iːˌtɑʊn/ *n* [C] an area in or near a city in which poor people live in small, badly built houses

shape **APPEARANCE** /ʃeɪp/ *n* [C/U] **1** the particular way something looks as a whole ○ [U] *Our table is oval in shape.* ○ [C] *The birthday cake for Luis was in the shape of a heart.* ○ [U] *These old sweatpants are all stretched out of shape* (= changed from their original form). **2** ***art*** A shape is also an arrangement that is formed by joining lines together in a particular way: [C] *A triangle is a shape with three sides.* ➤ Picture: **geometry; solid; triangle** **3** A shape is also a person or object that you cannot see clearly because it is too dark, or because the person or object is too far away.

shape /ʃeɪp/ *v* [T] to make something look a particular way ○ *Shape the dough into balls.*

-shaped /ʃeɪpt/ *adj* ○ *an L-shaped room* ○ *heart-shaped leaves*

shapeless /ˈʃeɪp·ləs/ *adj* *disapproving* (of an object) not having an appearance that you consider clear, pleasing, or correct ○ *Summer and winter she wore the same array of faded gingham dresses and shapeless sweaters.*

shapely /ˈʃeɪ·pli/ *adj* *approving* having an attractive appearance ○ *Businesswomen are wearing shapely suits.*

FORM /ʃeɪp/ *v* [T] to cause something to have a particular character or nature; form ○ *We're worried that they will try to shape the issue in a way that doesn't reflect what's really going on.* ○ *He had a major influence in shaping the government's economic policies.*

shape /ʃeɪp/ *n* [U] the way something is organized; the general character or nature of something ○ *The governor's new program is finally beginning to take shape* (= become better organized).

CONDITION /ʃeɪp/ *n* [U] **1** (of a thing) condition, or (of a person) state of health ○ *The city's finances are in bad shape.* ○ *I keep myself in good shape by running five miles a day.* **2** Shape can also mean good physical condition: *He's in/out of shape* (= in good/not in good condition). ○ *I try to stay in shape.*

WORD FAMILY shape

Nouns	shape	*Adjectives*	-shaped
Verbs	shape		shapeless shapely

PHRASAL VERBS with shape

• **shape up** **DEVELOP** to develop ○ *It's shaping up to be a fierce battle for the leadership of Congress.*

• **shape up** **IMPROVE** to improve your behavior or performance ○ *The coach told him to shape up and start practicing more.*

shard /ʃɑrd/ *n* [C] a sharp broken piece of a hard substance ○ *shards of glass/metal/pottery*

share **PART** /ʃer, ʃær/ *n* [C] one of the parts into which something has been divided ○ *The total bill comes to $200, so our share is $40.* ○ *She's not doing her fair share of the work.*

share /ʃer, ʃær/ *v* [I/T] to divide or use something with others ○ [T] *Why don't we share the salad?* ○ [I/T] *All the employees in the company share (in) the profits.* ○ [T] *She shares an office with Anne.* ○ [T] *It's a long trip – why don't we share the driving* (= each do some of it)? ○ [T] *Our whole family shares*

S

an interest in hiking (= We all like it). ○ [T] *I have an idea I'd like to share with you* (= tell you).

PART OWNERSHIP /ʃer, ʃær/ *n* [C] one of the equal parts into which the ownership of a company is divided ○ *She owns 2000 shares of General Electric.*

sharecropper /ˈʃerˌkrɑp·ər, ˈʃær-/ *n* [C] ***US history*** a member of a low social class of farm workers who receive a share of the value of the crop and who must pay the farm owner for seed, tools, food, and a place to live

shareholder /ˈʃerˌhoʊl·dər, ˈʃær-/ *n* [C] someone who owns SHARES in a company

shark /ʃɑrk/ *n* [C] **1** a type of large fish that has rows of sharp teeth **2** *infml* A shark is also a person who cheats other people, esp. if they seem trusting: *a loan shark*

sharp **ABLE TO CUT** /ʃɑrp/ *adj* [*-er/-est* only] having a thin edge or point that can cut something ○ *a sharp blade/knife* ○ *She put a sharp point on the pencil.*

sharpen /ˈʃɑr·pən/ *v* [T] ○ *We just had these knives/scissors sharpened.* ○ *He sharpened his pencil* (= made the end used for writing come to a point). ○ See also: SHARPEN ; SHARPEN at SHARP CLEAR

sharpener /ˈʃɑr·pə·nər/ *n* [C] a device or tool for making something sharper, esp. pencils or knives ○ *a pencil sharpener*

sharpness /ˈʃɑrp·nəs/ *n* [U]

SUDDEN /ʃɑrp/ *adj* [*-er/-est* only] sudden and immediately noticeable ○ *a sharp drop in temperature* ○ *a sharp increase in prices* ○ *There's a sharp curve in the road up ahead.*

sharply /ˈʃɑr·pli/ *adv* ○ *Interest rates rose sharply last month.*

sharpness /ˈʃɑrp·nəs/ *n* [U]

STRONGLY FELT /ʃɑrp/ *adj* [*-er/-est* only] strongly felt ○ *As he leaned over, he felt a sudden, sharp pain in his lower back.* ○ *This sauce is pretty sharp* (= It has a strong taste).

sharply /ˈʃɑr·pli/ *adv* ○ *The movie is sharply funny in these scenes.*

SEVERE /ʃɑrp/ *adj* [*-er/-est* only] intended to be strong enough to be felt as painful ○ *The candidate delivered a sharp attack on her opponent's voting record.* ○ *Leonard has a sharp tongue* (= often speaks in a severe and critical way).

sharply /ˈʃɑr·pli/ *adv* ○ *The current government has sharply criticized the court.*

CLEAR /ʃɑrp/ *adj* [*-er/-est* only] easy to see or understand; clear ○ *High-definition television produces a very sharp picture.* ○ *Sales this month were up, in sharp contrast to the dismal sales of the last few months.*

sharpen /ˈʃɑr·pən/ *v* [T] to make something clearer ○ *Turn the knob to sharpen the focus of the slide projector.* ○ See also: SHARPEN; SHARPEN at SHARP ABLE TO CUT

sharply /ˈʃɑr·pli/ *adv* ○ *We have sharply differing views on this issue.*

sharpness /ˈʃɑrp·nəs/ *n* [U]

QUICK /ʃɑrp/ *adj* [*-er/-est* only] able to understand or see quickly and easily ○ *She has a really sharp mind and a great sense of humor.*

FASHIONABLE /ʃɑrp/ *adj* [*-er/-est* only] *infml* fashionable ○ *a sharp dresser*

MUSIC /ʃɑrp/ *adj, adv* [*-er/-est* only] ***music*** higher in PITCH than a particular or the correct note ○ Compare FLAT MUSIC

sharp *n* [C] ***music*** a mark in written music showing that a note should be played a HALF STEP higher ➤ Picture: **notation**

EXACTLY /ʃɑrp/ *adv* [not gradable] exactly at the stated time ○ *The tour bus will leave at 8:30 a.m. sharp.*

WORD FAMILY sharp

Nouns	sharpener sharpness	*Verbs*	sharpen
		Adverbs	sharp sharply
Adjectives	sharp		

sharpen /ˈʃɑr·pən/ *v* [T] to make stronger or improve ○ *The dollar's decline in value sharpened fears of another recession.* ○ *I'm taking a course that should help me sharpen my computer skills.* ○ See also: SHARPEN at SHARP ABLE TO CUT; SHARPEN at SHARP CLEAR

shatter /ˈʃæt̬·ər/ *v* [I/T] **1** to break suddenly or cause something to break suddenly into small pieces ○ [T] *The earthquake shattered all the windows in the building.* **2** *fig.* To shatter can also mean to end or damage: [T] *The defeat shattered her confidence.*

shave /ʃeɪv/ *v* [I/T] **1** to remove hair from the face or body by cutting it close to the skin with a RAZOR (= a device with a blade) ○ [T] *He shaved his face.* ○ [I] *He carefully shaved around the cut on his cheek.* ○ [M] *I was amazed to see he had shaved off his beard.* **2** If you shave an amount off or from an object or surface, you cut a thin layer from it: [M] *She shaved about an eighth of an inch off the door, and now it closes.*

shave /ʃeɪv/ *n* [C] ○ *After three days of camping, he needed a good shave.*

shaver /ˈʃeɪ·vər/ *n* [C] a device, esp. an electric one, used to shave ○ Compare RAZOR

shawl /ʃɔːl/ *n* [C] a large piece of cloth worn esp. by women or girls over their shoulders or head

she /ʃiː/ *pronoun female* **1** the female being spoken about, who has already been mentioned ○ *I asked Barb if she'd lend me some money, but she said no.* ○ *She's such a cute dog!* **2** She is sometimes used instead of "it" to refer to something, such as a country, vehicle, or ship, that has already been mentioned: *Look at my new car – isn't she a beauty?*

she /ʃiː/ *n* [C] *female* ○ *The kitten is a she, not a he.*

sheaf /ʃiːf/ *n* [C] *pl* **sheaves** a number of things held or tied together ○ *A sheaf of papers lay on her desk.* ○ *Sheaves of dry corn stalks leaned against the fence.*

shear **CUT** /ʃɪr/ *v* [T] *past simp.* **sheared,** *past part.* **sheared, shorn** to cut off the hair of an animal or a person ○ *The barber sheared Jim's hair, just like you'd shear a sheep.*

MOVEMENT /ʃɪr/ *n* [U] ***earth science*** movement in the PLATES LAYER in the surface of the earth that causes them to change shape or break

shears /ʃɪrz/ *pl n* large SCISSORS (= cutting tool), or a similar tool for cutting ○ *kitchen shears* ○ *pruning shears for the garden*

sheath /ʃiːθ/ *n* [C] a close-fitting covering ○ *The cable is a copper wire with a heavy plastic sheath.*
sheathe /ʃiːð/ *v* [T] to put something, esp. a knife, in its cover

sheaves /ʃiːvz/ *pl of* SHEAF

shed BUILDING /ʃed/ *n* [C] a small building usually used for storage or shelter ○ *The lawn mower is kept in the shed.*

GET RID OF /ʃed/ *v* [T] *pres. part.* **shedding**, *past* **shed** to get rid of something ○ *As the day warmed up, she shed her sweater.*

FALL OFF /ʃed/ *v* [I/T] to lose hair, leaves, or skin, or to cause hair, skin, or leaves to drop ○ [I] *My cat shed all over the couch.* ○ [T] *By November, the trees had shed their leaves.*

FLOW /ʃed/ *v* [T] to make blood or tears flow ○ *He didn't shed one tear when his old car was stolen.*

SPREAD /ʃed/ *v* [T] *pres. part.* **shedding**, *past* **shed** to spread light ○ *A single bulb shed a harsh light on the table.*

IDIOM with shed

• **shed light on** *something* to help to explain a situation ○ *Experts hope the plane's flight recorders will shed light on the cause of the crash.*

she'd /ʃiːd/ *contraction of* she had or she would ○ *She'd* (= She had) *already left.* ○ *I think she'd* (= she would) *like to go to the dance with you.*

sheen /ʃiːn/ *n* [U] a smooth shine or brightness ○ *The polished floor had a beautiful sheen to it.*

sheep /ʃiːp/ *n* [C] *pl* **sheep** a farm animal with thick curly hair that eats grass and is kept for its wool, skin, and meat ○ Compare LAMB; MUTTON; RAM

sheepish /ˈʃiː·pɪʃ/ *adj* embarrassed because you realize you have done something wrong or silly ○ *a sheepish grin*
sheepishly /ˈʃiː·pɪʃ·li/ *adv* ○ *He sheepishly admitted he hadn't done his homework.*

sheer COMPLETE /ʃɪr/ *adj* [not gradable] not mixed with anything else; pure or complete ○ *Some of those books are sheer magic.*

EXTREME /ʃɪr/ *adj* [not gradable] (of size or weight) very large ○ *The sheer size of the engine makes it difficult to transport.*

STEEP /ʃɪr/ *adj* rising almost straight up or down; very steep ○ *She hauled herself up the sheer slope of the mountain.*

sheet /ʃiːt/ *n* [C] **1** a large rectangular piece of cloth used to cover a bed, or a rectangular piece of any material, such as paper, glass, or metal ○ *She made up the bed with clean sheets.* ○ *Do you have a sheet of paper I could use?* ○ *She put the dough onto cookie sheets.* **2** A sheet is also a thin layer of something: *A sheet of ice formed on the puddles.*

sheik, **sheikh** /ʃiːk, ʃeɪk/ *n* [C] an Arab leader

shelf /ʃelf/ *n* [C] *pl* **shelves** a long, flat board hung on a wall or supported by a frame or cabinet, used to hold objects ○ *Her shelves are filled with books and photographs.* ○ Related verb: SHELVE PUT ON SHELF

IDIOM with shelf

• **on the shelf** delayed ○ *Plans to start a free film series have been put on the shelf.*

shelf life *n* [U] the length of time that something stays in good condition and can be used ○ *Because it is vacuum-packed, it has a much longer shelf life than regular beef.*

shell COVERING /ʃel/ *n* [C/U] the hard outer covering of nuts, eggs, a few vegetables, and some animals ○ [C] *Turtles, snails, and crabs all have shells to protect them.*
shell /ʃel/ *v* [T] to remove the hard outer covering of nuts and other foods ○ *He sits in front of the TV, shelling peanuts.*

EXPLOSIVE /ʃel/ *n* [C] a tube filled with explosives that is fired from a large gun
shell /ʃel/ *v* [T] to fire shells at something ○ *Military forces began shelling areas north of the city.*

PHRASAL VERB with shell

• **shell out** *something* [M] *infml* to pay money ○ *I hope we don't have to shell out a lot of money for tickets.*

she'll /ʃiːl, ʃɪl/ *contraction of* she will or she shall ○ *She'll be there tomorrow, I'm sure.*

shellfish /ˈʃel·fɪʃ/ *n* [C/U] *pl* **shellfish** an animal that lives in water and has a shell ○ [C] *Lobsters, crabs, shrimp, mussels, and oysters are all shellfish commonly eaten as food.*

shell shock *n* [U] mental illness caused by experiences of war
shell-shocked *adj*

shelter /ˈʃel·tər/ *n* [C/U] something that gives protection, such as a building or tent, or the protection provided ○ [C] *We took the stray dog to an animal shelter.* ○ [U] *The wall gave us some shelter from the wind.* ○ [U] *The program offers shelter to runaway teens.*
shelter /ˈʃel·tər/ *v* [I/T] ○ [T] *The city feeds, clothes, and shelters the orphans.* ○ [I] *We were caught in a thunderstorm and sheltered in a cave.*
sheltered /ˈʃel·tərd/ *adj* **1** *We found a sheltered spot to have our picnic.* **2** If you have a sheltered life, you are protected from harmful, unpleasant, or frightening experiences: *I wonder how well she will do on her own after leading such a sheltered life.*

shelve PUT ON SHELF /ʃelv/ *v* [T] to put something on a shelf or shelves ○ *Would you shelve these books while I unpack the rest?*

DELAY /ʃelv/ *v* [T] to delay action on something ○ *I shelved plans to buy a new car, because I can't afford it right now.*

shelves /ʃelvz/ *pl of* SHELF

S

shenanigans /ʃəˈnæn·ɪ·gənz/ *pl n* humorous or dishonest tricks ○ *I don't know how he puts up with their shenanigans.*

shepherd /ˈʃep·ərd/, *female* **shepherdess** /ˈʃep·ərd·əs/ *n* [C] a person who takes care of sheep
shepherd /ˈʃep·ərd/ *v* [T always + adv/prep] to move and care for sheep, or to lead people somewhere ○ *Visitors are shepherded through the mansion by volunteers.* ○ *Roberti shepherded the legislation through Congress* (= made sure it was approved).

sherbet /ˈʃɜr·bət, ˈʃɜr·bərt/ *n* [U] a sweet, fruit-flavored ice, usually made with milk

sheriff /ˈʃer·əf/ *n* [C] an elected law officer in a COUNTY (= an area of local government)

sherry /ˈʃer·i/ *n* [C/U] a type of strong wine, usually brown in color, originally from Spain

she's /ʃiːz/ *contraction of* she is *or* she has ○ *She's* (= She is) *about to have her baby.* ○ *I think she's* (= she has) *already left the house.*

shh, **sh** /ʃ/ *exclamation* used to tell someone to be quiet; SHUSH ○ *Shh, you'll wake the baby.*

shied /ʃɑɪd/ *past simple and past participle of* SHY

shield /ʃiːld/ *n* [C] a piece of metal or other material, carried to protect the front of the body when being attacked, or a person or thing that provides protection ○ *The police held up their riot shields.* ○ *The ozone layer is the earth's shield against radiation from the sun.*
shield /ʃiːld/ *v* [T always + adv/prep] ○ *When the lights came on, I shielded my eyes with my hands,* ○ *Mom tried to shield us from the bad news.*

shies /ʃɑɪz/ *present participle of* SHY

shift Ⓐ **MOVE OR CHANGE** /ʃɪft/ *v* [I/T] **1** to change direction or move from one person, position, or place to another ○ [I] *The wind shifted to the east.* ○ [T] *She shifted her weight from one foot to the other.* ○ [T] *He tried to shift the blame onto his sister.* **2** If you shift your emphasis or attitude, you change it: [T] *Our attention has shifted from baseball to the election.* **3** When you shift the GEARS of a vehicle, you move them into different positions to change the speed of the vehicle.
shift Ⓐ /ʃɪft/ *n* [C] ○ *There's been a substantial shift in doctors' methods.*

PERIOD /ʃɪft/ *n* [C] the period that a person is scheduled to work, or a group of workers who work during the same period of time ○ *I'm working the day shift this month.* ○ *The night shift is finished at 7 a.m.*

IDIOM with shift

• **shift gears**, **switch gears** to suddenly change what you are doing ○ *The first half is a comedy, but then the movie shifts gears.*

shiftless /ˈʃɪft·ləs/ *adj* [not gradable] not having determination or purpose ○ *He says only the shiftless are unemployed.*

shifty /ˈʃɪf·ti/ *adj* [-er/-est only] *disapproving* intelligent and skilled in deceiving others ○ *His shifty eyes make him look like a used-car salesman.*

Shiite /ˈʃiː·ɑɪt/ *n* a member of an ISLAMIC religious group
Shiite /ˈʃiː·ɑɪt/ *adj* [not gradable] ○ *a Shiite mosque* ○ *a Shiite cleric*

shimmer /ˈʃɪm·ər/ *v* [I] to shine with a soft light that changes strength ○ *The stars shimmered in the night sky.*
shimmer /ˈʃɪm·ər/ *n* [U] ○ *the shimmer of moonlight on the lake*

shin /ʃɪn/ *n* [C] the front part of your leg between your knee and your foot

shine **SEND OUT LIGHT** /ʃɑɪn/ *v* [I/T] *past* **shone**, **shined** to send out or reflect light ○ [T] *Cops shone their flashlights into the car window.* ○ [I] *The area shines like Times Square.* ○ [I] *(fig.) Her dark eyes shone with happiness* (= she looked very happy).
shiny /ˈʃɑɪ·ni/ *adj* ○ *Who owns the shiny new car?* ○ *(slang) Chloë's new job is really shiny* (= interesting and attractive).

MAKE BRIGHT /ʃɑɪn/ *v* [T] to make something smooth and bright by rubbing ○ *He used all my polish to shine his shoes!*
shine /ʃɑɪn/ *n* [C usually sing] ○ *The stone was polished to a glossy shine.*

SHOW ABILITY /ʃɑɪn/ *v* [I] to show great ability in an activity ○ *Shaw is an underrated actor who truly shines in this movie.*

WORD FAMILY shine

Nouns	shine	*Verbs*	shine
Adjectives	shiny		

shingle /ˈʃɪŋ·gəl/ *n* [C] a thin, flat piece of wood or other material, many of which are attached in rows to the outside of a roof or a wall

Shinto /ˈʃɪn·toʊ/, **Shintoism** /ˈʃɪn·toʊˌɪz·əm/ *n* [U] ***world history*** a religion of Japan that emphasizes the spirits of nature and being loyal to the Japanese EMPEROR (= ruler)

ship /ʃɪp/ *n* [C] **1** a boat, esp. one that is large enough to travel on the sea ○ *a cruise/cargo ship* **2** A ship is also an aircraft or spacecraft.
ship /ʃɪp/ *v* [T] **-pp-** to transport something or someone by air, train, boat, or truck ○ *They shipped our furniture from Tennessee.* ○ *Parts for the space station are being shipped out there by spacecraft.*
shipping /ˈʃɪp·ɪŋ/ *n* [U] **1** ships as a group, or the business of transporting things ○ *Shipping along the St. Lawrence River takes goods from the Atlantic Ocean to the heart of Canada.* **2** Shipping or shipping and handling is the cost of sending something: *You'll be billed $15.95 plus shipping.*
shipment /ˈʃɪp·mənt/ *n* [C/U] goods transported together, or the act of transporting them ○ [C] *A shipment of vegetables arrived last week.* ○ [U] *It was taken to the airport for shipment to Hawaii.*

PHRASAL VERB with ship

• **ship** *someone/something* **off** [M] to send someone somewhere, esp. to an unpleasant place ○ *When she was eight, her father shipped her off to Baltimore to live with her aunt.*

shipwreck /ˈʃɪp·rek/, **wreck** *n* [C/U] the destruction or sinking of a ship at sea, or a ship destroyed this way ○ [C] *Fog in the area caused many shipwrecks.*
shipwreck /ˈʃɪp·rek/ *v* [T] ○ *The crew was shipwrecked off the coast of Newfoundland.*

shirk /ʃɜrk/ *v* [I/T] to avoid work or a duty ○ [T] *Town officials shirked their responsibilities by failing to follow up on residents' complaints.*

shirt /ʃɜrt/ *n* [C] a piece of clothing worn on the upper part of the body, made of cloth and often having a collar and buttons at the front ○ *a short-sleeved/long-sleeved shirt* ○ *Her shirt was untucked.*

shirtsleeves *pl n* **1** the parts of a shirt that cover the arms ○ *Baker sat on the edge of his chair and rolled up his shirtsleeves.* **2** People who are in their shirtsleeves have rolled them up so that their arms are showing.

shish kebab, **shish kabob** /ˈʃɪʃ·kəˌbɑb/ *n* [C/U] small pieces of meat, esp. LAMB, and vegetables cooked on a stick or metal rod

shiver /ˈʃɪv·ər/ *v* [I] (esp. of a person or animal) to shake slightly and quickly because of feeling cold, ill, or frightened ○ *Your creepy look makes me shiver.* ○ *Robbins shivered in the chill air.*
shiver /ˈʃɪv·ər/ *n* [C] ○ *"The temperature is down to 12 degrees," she said with a shiver.*

shoal LAND /ʃoʊl/ *n* [C] a raised bank of sand or rocks under the surface of the water

FISH /ʃoʊl/ *n* [C] a large group of fish swimming together ○ *shoals of mackerel*

shock SURPRISE /ʃɑk/ *n* [C/U] **1** a sudden, unexpected, and often unpleasant or offensive event, or the emotional or physical reaction to such an event ○ [C] *It was kind of a shock to hear they wanted to throw it out.* **2** Shock is also a medical condition caused by severe injury, pain, loss of blood, or fright that slows down the flow of blood around the body: [U] *She was going into shock – her flesh was becoming chilled and her muscles were contracting.*
shock /ʃɑk/ *v* [I/T] to make someone suddenly feel very upset or surprised ○ [T] *Her painting might shock viewers.* ○ [I] *The ads were designed to shock.*
shocked /ʃɑkt/ *adj* ○ [+ *to* infinitive] *He was shocked to discover that he had no money left in his account.*
shocking /ˈʃɑk·ɪŋ/ *adj* ○ *The book was considered shocking when it was first published.*

EFFECT FROM HITTING /ʃɑk/ *n* [U] the effect, often including damage or slight movement, of one object hitting another forcefully ○ *Running shoes lose their ability to absorb shock.*

ELECTRIC CURRENT /ʃɑk/ *n* [C] a current of electricity going through the body ○ *If that cord is pulled loose, you'll get a shock from the plug.*

WORD FAMILY shock			
Nouns	shock	*Verbs*	shock
Adjectives	shocked shocking	*Adverbs*	shockingly

shock absorber, *short form* **shock** /ʃɑk/ *n* [C usually pl] a device that is attached to each of the wheels on a vehicle to reduce the effects of traveling over rough ground

shock wave REACTION TO NEWS *n* [C] a strong reaction within a group of people to an upsetting piece of news ○ *The president's sudden illness sent shock waves around the world.*

INCREASE IN PRESSURE *n* [C] a sudden increase in pressure or temperature caused by an explosion or other violent or fast movement ○ *The bomb's shock wave tore the windshield off the truck.*

shoddy /ˈʃɑd·i/ *adj* [-*er*/-*est* only] made or done without care ○ *The furniture is shoddy and cheap.*

shoe /ʃuː/ *n* [C] **1** one of a pair of covers for your feet, with an upper part made of a strong material such as leather and a base made usually of thick leather or rubber ○ *tennis shoes* ○ *high-heeled shoes* ○ *patent leather shoes* ○ *He said he couldn't afford a new pair of shoes.* **2** A shoe is also a HORSESHOE.
shoe /ʃuː/ *v* [T] *pres. part.* **shoeing**, *past* **shod**, **shoed 1** to wear shoes, or to put shoes on someone ○ *She was shod in loafers with soles as thin as paper.* **2** If you shoe a horse, you nail a curved piece of metal to its foot.

IDIOMS with shoe

• **in** *someone else's* **shoes** experiencing the same condition or situation as someone else, so that you know how the other person feels ○ *Try to put yourself in her shoes, and think about what she might want.* ○ *What would you do if you were in my shoes?*
• **on a shoestring** with a very small amount of money ○ *The theater company operates on a shoestring.*

shoehorn /ˈʃuː·hɔːrn/ *n* [C] a smooth, curved piece of plastic or metal that is placed in the back of a shoe when putting it on in order to help the foot slide in more easily
shoehorn /ˈʃuː·hɔːrn/ *v* [T] to fit something or someone into a tight place ○ *We'd have to build another school to shoehorn all our students in.*

shoelace /ˈʃuː·leɪs/ *n* [C] a thin cord of cloth or leather used to fasten shoes ○ *Your shoelace is untied.*

shogun /ˈʃoʊ·gən/ *n* [C] ***world history*** a military governor in Japan before 1867

shone /ʃoʊn/ *past simple and past participle of* SHINE

shoo /ʃuː/ *exclamation infml* said to animals or to people to make them go away quickly ○ *"Shoo! Get out of here!"*
shoo /ʃuː/ *v* [T] **shoos**, *pres. part.* **shooing**, *past* **shooed** *infml* ○ *My husband shooed me out of the car.*

shoo-in /ˈʃuː·ɪn/ *n* [C] *infml* something that is certain to happen, or someone who is certain to win a competition ○ *If that election were held today, Kitzhaber would be a shoo-in.*

shook /ʃʊk/ *past simple of* SHAKE

S

shoot **FIRE WEAPON** /ʃuːt/ *v* [I/T] *past* **shot 1** to fire a gun or other weapon, or to hit, injure, or kill someone or something by firing a gun or other weapon ○ [I] *We'd take our bows and arrows and shoot at targets.* ○ [T] *A long time ago the sergeant learned how to shoot a gun.* ○ [T] *An unidentified man was shot yesterday afternoon.* **2** *infml* If you say that someone or something should be shot, you are very annoyed by it: [T] *This computer should be shot.*

shooter /ˈʃuːt̬·ər/ *n* [C] ○ *Large-caliber rifles allow a shooter to hit targets at a great distance.*

shooting /ˈʃuːt̬·ɪŋ/ *n* [C/U] **1** [U] *She heard shooting* (= guns being fired) *in the distance.* **2** A shooting is also an occasion on which someone is injured or killed by a bullet fired from a gun.

SPORTS /ʃuːt/ *v* [I/T] *past* **shot 1** to throw, hit, or kick a ball or other object toward a goal in order to score points ○ [T] *Both teams shoot the ball well.* ○ [I] *When you shoot as poorly as we did, you can't expect to win.* **2** *slang* If you **shoot baskets** or **shoot hoops** you play BASKETBALL. **3** *slang* If you **shoot pool** you play that game: *Patrick and I were shooting pool after work.*

shooter /ˈʃuːt̬·ər/ *n* [C] ○ *She is a great outside shooter and gets the offensive rebounds.*

MOVE QUICKLY /ʃuːt/ *v* [I always + adv/prep] *past* **shot** to move in a particular direction quickly and without unnecessary turns or stops ○ *The ambulance was shooting around the corner, its tires squealing.* ○ *Grace's eyebrows shot up when she heard his voice.*

PLANT /ʃuːt/ *n* [C] the first part of a plant to appear above the ground as it develops from a seed, or a new growth on an already existing plant ○ *Little green shoots appeared in the spring.*

FILM /ʃuːt/ *v* [I/T] *past* **shot** to film or photograph something ○ [T] *The movie will be shot in the fall.*

shoot /ʃuːt/ *n* [C] ○ *I remember doing a shoot there.*

SPEAK /ʃuːt/ *exclamation infml* used to tell someone else they should speak ○ *"Dad, I need to talk to you." "Shoot."*

IDIOMS with shoot

• **shoot** *yourself* **in the foot** to do or say something that causes problems for you ○ *I think you might be shooting yourself in the foot if you don't take his offer.*

• **shoot** *your* **mouth off** *infml* to talk too much about things other people should not know ○ *Don't go shooting your mouth off about how much money you earn.*

• **shoot the breeze** *infml* to talk with someone about unimportant things for a long time ○ *We sat on the porch until late at night, just shooting the breeze.*

PHRASAL VERBS with shoot

• **shoot down** *something/someone* [M] **1** to destroy an aircraft or kill a person with guns ○ *A Navy missile may have shot down the aircraft.* **2** To shoot down an idea or suggestion is to prevent it from being accepted: *A proposal to require high school students to take at least one AP course was shot down by concerned parents.*

• **shoot for** *something infml* to try to achieve something ○ *Our football team will shoot for its first victory today.*

• **shoot off** *something* to write and send a message quickly ○ *My daughter will shoot off an e-mail before she'll sit down and write a letter.*

• **shoot up** **INCREASE** to increase very quickly in size or amount ○ *Kerry shot up, growing something like six inches in six months.* ○ *If he lost his temper, his blood pressure would shoot up.*

• **shoot up** *something* **FIRE GUNS** [M] *infml* to fire guns in a place, causing a lot of damage

shooting star *n* [C] a METEOR

shootout **GUNS** /ˈʃuːt̬·ɑʊt/ *n* [C] a fight using guns

SPORTS /ˈʃuːt̬·ɑʊt/ *n* [C] a competition in making goals, used in some sports to decide who will win when a game ends with both teams having the same number of points

shop **BUY THINGS** /ʃɑp/ *v* [I] **-pp-** to look for and buy (things) ○ *We shop in malls because they're convenient.*

shop /ʃɑp/ *n* [C] a place where you can buy goods or services; store ○ *a gift shop* ○ *a barber shop* ○ *a coffee shop*

shopper /ˈʃɑp·ər/ *n* [C] a person who is looking for things to buy ○ *Shoppers stroll through the stores.*

shopping /ˈʃɑp·ɪŋ/ *n* [U] the activity of looking for things to buy ○ *I was out shopping this afternoon.* ○ *My daughter and I go shopping together.*

WORK AREA /ʃɑp/ *n* [C] a place where a particular type of thing is made or repaired ○ *a bicycle repair shop* ○ *I work in a machine shop making wire.*

WORD FAMILY shop			
Nouns	shop shopper shopping	*Verbs*	shop

PHRASAL VERB with shop

• **shop around** to compare the price and quality of items in different stores before you decide which one to buy ○ *Did you shop around when you were looking for your car?*

shoplift /ˈʃɑp·lɪft/ *v* [I/T] to take goods illegally from a store without paying for them

shoplifting /ˈʃɑp ˌlɪf·tɪŋ/ *n* [U] ○ *He was charged with shoplifting.*

shoplifter /ˈʃɑp ˌlɪf·tər/ *n* [C] ○ *Shoplifters will be arrested.*

shopping cart *n* [C] a large container with wheels that you push around a store and fill with things you want to buy

shopping center *n* [C] a group of stores with a common area for parking ○ *There's a little shopping center next door with a bank and a dry-cleaning place.*

shopping mall *n* [C] a very large building or buildings containing a lot of stores and restaurants, usually with space outside for parking ○ *A shopping mall is no longer just a place to go to buy something, it's a community and entertainment center.*

shore /ʃɔːr, ʃoʊr/ *n* [C/U] the land along the edge of the sea, a lake, or a wide river ○ [U] *We rode into the city along the shore of Lake Washington.* ○ [pl] *Although it happened far from our shores* (= this country)*, the disaster has affected many Americans.*

PHRASAL VERB with **shore**

• **shore up** *something* [M] to make something stronger by supporting it ○ *The plan will enable his company to shore up its financial position.* ○ *After the earthquake we had to shore up ceilings and walls.*

shoreline /ˈʃɔːr·lɑɪn, ˈʃoʊr-/ *n* [C] the edge of the sea, a lake, or a wide river ○ *Most of the shoreline is swamp.*

shorn /ʃɔːrn, ʃoʊrn/ *past participle of* SHEAR

short LENGTH /ʃɔːrt/ *adj* [*-er/-est* only] having little length, distance, or height ○ *Short hair is back in style.* ○ *It's only a short walk to the store.*

short /ʃɔːrt/ *adv* [*-er/-est* only] ○ *She decided to cut her hair short.*

shorts /ʃɔːrts/ *pl n* pants that end above the knee or reach to the knee, or men's underwear worn below the waist ○ *He put on a pair of shorts and a T-shirt.* ○ *The doctor told him to strip to his shorts.*

shorten /ˈʃɔːrt·ᵊn/ *v* [T] ○ *I'd like to have this jacket shortened by about two inches.*

TIME /ʃɔːrt/ *adj* [*-er/-est* only] of a small amount of time, or less than the average or usual amount of time ○ *Mary Lou was here a short while ago.* ○ *There will be a short delay in the flight while we load a few more bags.*

short /ʃɔːrt/ *adv* [not gradable] ○ *I started to say something, but he cut me short* (= stopped me from continuing).

shorten /ˈʃɔːrt·ᵊn/ *v* [T] ○ *A high school knee injury probably shortened his football career.*

shortly /ˈʃɔːrt·li/ *adv* [not gradable] soon ○ *Shortly after you left the office, your wife called.* ○ *We will be landing shortly.*

LACKING /ʃɔːrt/ *adj* [not gradable] not reaching a desired amount or level; lacking ○ *The bill comes to $85, but we're $15 short.*

shortage /ˈʃɔːrt̬·ɪdʒ/ *n* [C] a lack of something needed ○ *There is a severe shortage of low-cost housing in the city.*

WORD FAMILY **short**			
Nouns	short shortage shorts	*Verbs*	shorten
		Adverbs	short shortly
Adjectives	short		

IDIOMS with **short**

• **be short with** *someone* to speak to someone rudely without saying much ○ *You could tell Dad was worried about something because he was short with everyone.*

• **in short** briefly ○ *In short, we have to decide whether to continue losing money or change the way we do business.*

• **in the short run** for a short period of time ○ *This may save money in the short run, but it will eventually cost you more.* ○ Opposite: IN THE LONG RUN at LONG IDIOMS

• **short for** *something* as a less long form of a word or name ○ *Their baby's name is Libby, short for Elizabeth.*

• **in short supply** only available in small amounts ○ *Money was in short supply.*

• **short of** *something* **1** not having enough of something ○ *I'm a little short of cash right now, so I can't lend you anything.* ○ *She ran a little farther and then stopped, feeling short of breath* (= felt as if she did not have enough air). **2 Short of** something also means not including something: *There must be some punishment you can give him short of expelling him from school.*

shortchange /ˈʃɔːrtˈtʃeɪndʒ/ *v* [T] to give someone or something less money, time, or attention than is deserved ○ *The report claimed that girls were being shortchanged in public education, particularly in math and science.*

short circuit, *infml* **short** *n* [C] an electrical connection that not working correctly and allows too much current to flow into a CIRCUIT (= a closed system of wires), causing a dangerous condition

shortcoming /ˈʃɔːrt ˌkʌm·ɪŋ/ *n* [C usually pl] a fault of someone or something ○ *My father had some shortcomings as a businessman, but he was a good father.*

shortcut /ˈʃɔːrt·kʌt/ *n* [C] a route that is more direct than the usual route, or a quicker way of doing something ○ *The kids take a shortcut through the parking lot to get to school.* ○ *Don't use shortcuts to solve the problem, or the answer is likely to be wrong.*

shorten /ˈʃɔːrt·ᵊn/ *v* ○ See at SHORT LENGTH; SHORT TIME

shortening /ˈʃɔːrt·nɪŋ/ *n* [U] butter or other fat used in cooking, esp. to make pastry

shortfall /ˈʃɔːrt·fɔːl/ *n* [C] an amount that is less than what was expected or needed ○ *The county had to close three of its four libraries because of a budget shortfall.*

shorthand /ˈʃɔːrt·hænd/ *n* [U] a system of fast writing, using lines and symbols to represent letters, words, and phrases

short-handed *adj, adv* not having the usual or necessary number of workers ○ *We've got two people out sick so we're short-handed today.*

short-lived /ˈʃɔːrt·lɪvd, -lɑɪvd/ *adj* lasting only for a brief time ○ *He got angry easily, but his anger was always short-lived.*

shortly /ˈʃɔːrt·li/ *adv* ○ See at SHORT TIME

S

shorts /ʃɔːrts/ *pl n* ○ See at SHORT LENGTH

shortsighted, **short-sighted** /ˈʃɔːrtˈsɑɪt̬·əd/ *adj* showing a lack of thought for what might happen in the future ○ *It's shortsighted to spend all your money on having a good time.*

shortstop /ˈʃɔːrt·stɑp/ *n* [C] (in baseball) the position of the player on the inner field between second and third BASE (= a position on a square that a player must touch), or the player at that position

short story *n* [C] ***literature*** an invented written story that is shorter than a NOVEL

short-tempered *adj* tending to become angry quickly and easily

short-term *adj* happening, existing, or continuing for only a little time ○ *Short-term interest rates are going down.*

shortwave /ˈʃɔːrt·weɪv/ *n* [C/U] a radio wave that is smaller than that used in standard broadcasting and that can only be broadcast using a special radio

shot **SHOOT** /ʃɑt/ *past simple and past participle of* SHOOT

WEAPON /ʃɑt/ *n* [C] the action of firing a gun or another weapon ○ *Several shots were fired.*

SPORTS /ʃɑt/ *n* [C] an attempt to score a point by throwing, hitting, or kicking a ball or other object ○ *Roberts sank two foul shots to win the game.*

FILM /ʃɑt/ *n* [C] a photograph, or a short piece in a movie in which there is a single action or a short series of actions ○ *I got some really good shots of the harbor at sunset.*

DRUG /ʃɑt/ *n* [C] an amount of a drug that is put into the body by a single INJECTION ○ *The doctor gave him a shot of cortisone.*

METAL BALL /ʃɑt/ *n* [C/U] a heavy metal ball thrown in a sports competition, or small metal balls fired from a gun

ATTEMPT /ʃɑt/ *n* [U] *infml* an attempt to do or achieve something that is difficult, when success is uncertain ○ *I'm not sure they'll consider me for the job, but I'll give it a shot.*

DESTROYED /ʃɑt/ *adj* [not gradable] *infml* no longer working or effective ○ *The brakes are shot – you'd better take the car in to the garage.*

AMOUNT OF DRINK /ʃɑt/ *n* [C] a small amount of an alcoholic drink ○ *a shot of whiskey*

IDIOM with **shot**

• **a shot in the arm** something that has a sudden, strong, positive effect on something ○ *Winning this award has been a big shot in the arm for the students.*

shotgun /ˈʃɑt·ɡʌn/ *n* [C] a long gun that fires a large number of small metal bullets at one time, used esp. for hunting

shot put *n* [U] a sports competition in which each competitor throws a heavy metal ball as far as possible

S

should **DUTY** /ʃʊd, ʃəd/ *modal verb* used to express that it is necessary, desirable, or important to perform the action of the following verb ○ *He should have told me about the change in plans.* ○ *People like that should go to jail.* ○ *Where should we meet tonight?*

PROBABLE /ʃʊd, ʃəd/ *modal verb* used to express that the action of the main verb is probable ○ *She should be back at any minute.* ○ *If you follow these directions, you shouldn't have any trouble finding our house.* ○ *That should be enough food for five people.*

OPINION /ʃʊd, ʃəd/ *modal verb fml* used to express a desire or opinion ○ *I should think he'd be happy just to have a job.* ○ *I shouldn't worry about that if I were you.*

ASKING WHY /ʃʊd, ʃəd/ *modal verb* used after a question word, such as "how" or "why," when asking a reason for something ○ *How should I know where you put the car keys?*

shoulder **BODY PART** /ˈʃoʊl·dər/ *n* [C] **1** one of the two rounded, bony parts of a person's body on either side of the neck where the top of the arm is joined ○ *She put her head on my shoulder.* **2** A shoulder of a road is an edge just beyond the part you drive along, where you can stop safely.

shoulder /ˈʃoʊl·dər/ *v* [T] ○ *Shouldering her pack* (= putting it on her shoulders to carry it)*, she strode off up the road.*

ACCEPT RESPONSIBILITY /ˈʃoʊl·dər/ *v* [T] to accept responsibility for something ○ *It is usually women who shoulder the responsibility for the care of elderly relatives.*

shoulder bag *n* [C] a bag carried by a long strap over the shoulder

shoulder blade *n* [C] either of the two large, flat bones on the upper part of the back

shouldn't /ˈʃʊd·ənt/ *contraction of* should not ○ *I shouldn't have said that.* ○ *Shouldn't we call and make a reservation?*

should've /ˈʃʊd·əv/ *contraction of* should have ○ *I should've known better.*

shout /ʃɑʊt/ *v* [I/T] to say something in a loud voice ○ [I] *If anyone's up there," he shouted sternly, "come out now!"*

shout /ʃɑʊt/ *n* [C] a loud call ○ *When nominated for the presidency the entire audience came to its feet with a shout.* ➤ Usage: **cry, scream, or shout?** at CRY SHOUT

WORD CHOICES shout

An alternative to "shout" is **yell** or **bellow**.

"What are you doing?" he ***yelled***.

"Listen to me!" he ***bellowed***.

Holler is an informal word for shout.

"Dinner's ready!" ***hollered*** *Mrs. Jackson from the kitchen.*

Call or **cry** are used when someone shouts something to attract attention.

"I'm up here," he ***called***.

"Look out!" she ***cried***.

Scream is often used when someone shouts because of a strong emotion such as fear or anger.

*My sisters were always **screaming** at each other.*

*"Let go of me!" she **screamed**.*

When someone shouts to show approval or encouragement, you could use the verb **cheer**.

*The audience **cheered** as he came on stage.*

shove /ʃʌv/ *v* [I/T] **1** to push someone or something forcefully and with a lot of energy ○ [T] *The opposing player said something, and Chris went over and shoved him.* **2** To shove is also to slide something along a surface by moving or pushing it: [T] *She got into her coat and shoved her hands deep into her pockets.* ○ [M] *Jim shoved open the door* (= pushed the door to open it), *and invited his visitor in.* **3** A shoving match is an angry disagreement in which two people push each other in the chest: *The discussion in the jury room got so heated that at one point two jurors got into a shoving match.*

shove /ʃʌv/ *n* [C] ○ *Someone in the crowd gave me a shove in the back, and I almost went sprawling.*

shovel /ˈʃʌv·əl/ *n* [C] a tool consisting of a wide blade attached to a long handle, used for digging up or moving loose material, such as earth or snow

shovel /ˈʃʌv·əl/ *v* [T] ○ *Sally is outside shoveling snow away from the driveway.*

show MAKE SEEN /ʃoʊ/ *v* [T] *past simp.* **showed**, *past part.* **shown** to cause or allow something to be seen ○ *You should show that rash to your doctor.* ○ *These trees show the effects of acid rain.* ○ *He's starting to show his age.*

show /ʃoʊ/ *n* [C/U] ○ [C] *Ray made a show of reaching for his wallet.* ○ [U] *Does this fireplace work or is it just for show?* ○ [U] *Half for show and half in real anger, I stood up and shouted, "I'm not your friend!"*

showy /ˈʃoʊ·i/ *adj* attracting attention, sometimes by being extreme in color, design, or materials ○ *We saw several showy insects that have colored patterns on their wings.*

EXPRESS /ʃoʊ/ *v* [T] *past simp.* **showed**, *past part.* **shown** to express your feelings or opinion by your actions or words ○ *I do not know how to show my thanks for all your help.* ○ *He is a scrappy lawyer and shows no mercy to any opponent.*

EXPLAIN /ʃoʊ/ *v* [T] *past simp.* **showed**, *past part.* **shown** to explain something to someone by helping to do it or by giving instructions or examples to copy ○ [+ question word] *The diagram shows how to fit the pieces together.*

PROVE /ʃoʊ/ *v* [T] *past simp.* **showed**, *past part.* **shown** to make something clear or prove something to be true ○ *Your writing shows you can be a good writer.* ○ *He has shown himself to be unreliable.*

BE NOTICEABLE /ʃoʊ/ *v* [I/T] *past simp.* **showed**, *past part.* **shown** to be able to be seen or noticed, or to make something noticeable ○ [I] *I've been working for hours, and I've got nothing to show for it.*

LEAD /ʃoʊ/ *v* [T] *past simp.* **showed**, *past part.* **shown** to lead someone somewhere or to point out something ○ *Could you show me the way to the post office?* ○ *Show me which cake you want.*

RECORD /ʃoʊ/ *v* [T] *past simp.* **showed**, *past part.* **shown** to record or express an amount, number, or measurement ○ *My barometer shows a change in the weather is coming.*

ENTERTAINMENT /ʃoʊ/ *n* [C] a performance in a theater, a movie, or a television or radio program ○ *a stage/talk show*

PUBLIC EVENT /ʃoʊ/ *n* [C] an event at which the public can view a particular collection of things ○ *a flower show* ○ *a fashion show*

show /ʃoʊ/ *v* [I/T] *past simp.* **showed**, *past part.* **shown 1** [T] *This gallery is a place where young artists can show their work.* **2** To show a movie is to offer it for viewing in a movie theater or on television: [T] *That channel often shows foreign films.*

showing /ˈʃoʊ·ɪŋ/ *n* [C] ○ *This is the first showing of his paintings in this country.* ○ See also: SHOWING

ACTIVITY /ʃoʊ/ *n* [U] *infml* an activity, business, or organization, considered in relation to who is managing it ○ *Who will run the show when the boss retires?*

APPEAR /ʃoʊ/ *v* [I] to appear at a gathering or event ○ *Jenny said she'd be here, but she never showed.*

IDIOMS with show

• **show** *your* **face** to go somewhere where you are not expected or wanted, usually because you have done something offensive to someone else ○ *I don't know how he can show his face here after the way he talked to my brother.*

• **show** *someone* **the door** to tell someone to leave or make it clear you want someone to leave ○ *Your boss isn't going to show you the door just because you made a mistake.*

PHRASAL VERBS with show

• **show** *someone* **around** to lead someone through a place ○ *Phil had never seen Chicago, so I offered to show him around.*

• **show off** ATTRACT ATTENTION to do something to attract attention to yourself ○ *My parents were in town and I wanted to show off.* ○ Related noun: SHOW-OFF

• **show off** *something/someone* MAKE SEEN [M] to make it possible for others to see and admire something or someone ○ *She brought her baby pictures so she could show them off.* ○ *That shirt shows off the color of your eyes.*

• **show up** ARRIVE to arrive for a gathering or event ○ *He showed up late for the meeting.*

• **show up** APPEAR to appear or be seen ○ *The virus does not show up in blood tests.*

• **show up** *someone* EMBARRASS [M] to do something that embarrasses someone or makes someone seem stupid ○ *She's always trying to show up her colleagues to make herself look smarter.*

show-and-tell *n* [U] a school activity in which a child brings an object to class and talks to the other children about it

show business, *infml* **show biz** *n* [U] the industry that produces entertainment such as mov-

S

ies and popular music, and the people who work in that industry

showcase CABINET /ˈʃoʊ·keɪs/ *n* [C] a cabinet, usually of glass, in which objects are kept that are valuable or easily broken ○ *a jeweler's showcase*

OPPORTUNITY /ˈʃoʊ·keɪs/ *n* [C] a place or event where something, esp. something new, can be shown or performed ○ *The Sundance Film Festival is an especially sympathetic showcase for unusual films.*

showcase /ˈʃoʊ·keɪs/ *v* [T] ○ *In the opening set, he showcased his own songs.*

showdown /ˈʃoʊ·daʊn/ *n* [C] an event, such as a meeting or fight, that ends a disagreement or decides who will win ○ *a military showdown* ○ *Sunday's showdown will decide whether Mexico or Italy is the world soccer champion.*

shower RAIN /ˈʃaʊ·ər, ʃaʊr/ *n* [C] **1** a brief rain, or a light fall of snow ○ *a snow shower* **2** A shower is also something that falls like rain: *a shower of sparks* ○ *a shower of confetti*

shower /ˈʃaʊ·ər, ʃaʊr/ *v* [I] ○ *It showered on and off all afternoon.*

GIVE /ˈʃaʊ·ər, ʃaʊr/ *v* [T always + adv/prep] to give a lot of something to someone ○ *His family showers him with love.*

shower /ˈʃaʊ·ər, ʃaʊr/ *n* [C] a party held to give presents to someone who will soon be married or will become a parent ○ *a bridal shower* ○ *a baby shower*

DEVICE /ˈʃaʊ·ər, ʃaʊr/ *n* [C] a device that sprays water on your body while you wash yourself, or an act of washing using such a device ○ *He stays in the shower until there is no more hot water!* ○ *Have I got time to take a shower before we go out?*

shower /ˈʃaʊ·ər, ʃaʊr/ *v* [I] ○ *I usually shower in the morning.*

shower curtain *n* [C] a usually plastic curtain that you pull across an opening when you are having a SHOWER to prevent the spray of water from getting out

showing /ˈʃoʊ·ɪŋ/ *n* [C] a performance in a competitive activity ○ *A poor showing by the team's offense led to a 22-17 loss.* ○ See also: SHOWING at SHOW PUBLIC EVENT

showman MAKER OF SHOWS /ˈʃoʊ·mən/ *n* [C] **-men** someone who produces movies, stage shows, or other entertainment ○ *P.T. Barnum, a founder of the circus, was a great showman.*

PERFORMER /ˈʃoʊ·mən/ *n* [C] **-men** someone who is a skilled performer ○ *The President is a great showman and a clever politician.*

showmanship /ˈʃoʊ·mən ˌʃɪp/ *n* [C] skill in making people feel entertained ○ *His televised speeches demonstrate his showmanship.*

shown /ʃoʊn/ *past participle of* SHOW

show-off *n* [C] a person who has a habit of attracting attention ○ *David's a showoff in the kitchen – he loves having dinner guests.* ○ Related verb: SHOW OFF ATTRACT ATTENTION

showpiece /ˈʃoʊ·piːs/ *n* [C] an extremely good example of something that attracts attention or admiration ○ *This painting will be the showpiece of the exhibit.*

showroom /ˈʃoʊ·ruːm, -rʊm/ *n* [C] a room in which goods for sale are arranged ○ *a car dealer's showroom*

showy /ˈʃoʊ·i/ *adj* ○ See at SHOW MAKE SEEN

shrank /ʃræŋk/ *past simple of* SHRINK

shrapnel /ˈʃræp·nəl/ *n* [U] small pieces of metal blown through the air when a bomb or other device explodes ○ *Most of the injuries were caused by flying shrapnel.*

shred CUT /ʃred/ *v* [T] **-dd-** to cut or tear something into small pieces ○ *Shred some lettuce into the salad bowl.* ○ *He shredded documents to get rid of them.*

shred /ʃred/ *n* [C usually pl] ○ *My silk blouse was ripped to shreds in the washing machine.*

shredder /ˈʃred·ər/ *n* [C] a machine used for cutting things into very small pieces

SMALL AMOUNT /ʃred/ *n* [C usually sing] a very small amount of something ○ *There isn't a shred of evidence to support her accusation.*

shrewd /ʃruːd/ *adj* [*-er/-est* only] able to judge a situation accurately and turn it to your own advantage ○ *He's a very shrewd businessman.* ○ *Barbara made some shrewd investments.*

shriek /ʃriːk/ *n* [C] a loud, high cry ○ *the shriek of sea gulls* ○ *She heard a high-pitched shriek.*

shriek /ʃriːk/ *v* [I/T] ○ [I] *We shrieked with laughter.*

shrill /ʃrɪl/ *adj* [*-er/-est* only] not pleasant to hear; loud and high ○ *a shrill voice*

shrilly /ˈʃrɪl·li/ *adv* ○ *The terrified woman shrilly ordered the goat out of her kitchen.*

shrimp ANIMAL /ʃrɪmp/ *n* [C/U] *pl* **shrimp** a small sea creature with a shell, ten legs, and a long tail, or its flesh eaten as food

PERSON /ʃrɪmp/ *n* [C] *infml* a short or small person ○ *It's hard to believe this sculpted athlete was once a shrimp.* ○ **USAGE:** This word can be offensive unless you are using it humorously with someone you know well.

shrine /ʃraɪn/ *n* [C] **1** a place where people come to worship, usually because of a connection with a holy person or a mysterious religious event or object **2** A shrine can also be a place that is honored because of some connection with a famous person or event.

shrink BECOME SMALLER /ʃrɪŋk/ *v* [I/T] *past simp.* **shrank**, **shrunk**, *past part.* **shrunk**, *past part.* **shrunken** to become smaller or cause something to become smaller ○ [I] *The show's audience has shrunk in the last few months.* ○ [T] *I shrank my sweater by putting it in the dryer!*

shrinkage /ˈʃrɪŋ·kɪdʒ/ *n* [U] ○ *Financial support for the university has undergone substantial shrinkage.*

MOVE AWAY /ʃrɪŋk/ *v* [I always + adv/prep] *past simp.* **shrank**, **shrunk**, *past part.* **shrunk**, **shrunken**

S

1 to move away from something unpleasant or frightening ○ *My first reaction was to shrink in disgust at the sight of it.* **2** If you shrink from something, you avoid it: *Kate's a good worker, but she seems to shrink from responsibility.*

DOCTOR /ʃrɪŋk/ *n* [C] *slang* a PSYCHIATRIST, PSYCHOTHERAPIST, or PSYCHOANALYST

shrivel /ˈʃrɪv·əl/ *v* [I/T] **-l-**, **-ll-** to become dried out and smaller, appearing crushed or folded, or to make something do this ○ [T] *The hot sun shriveled the flowers I put in the window.*

shroud /ʃrɑʊd/ *n* [C] **1** a cloth used to wrap a dead body before it is buried **2** A shroud is also anything that covers: *He cleared the leafy shroud covering the sign.*

shroud /ʃrɑʊd/ *v* [T] to cover or hide something ○ *The mountains were shrouded in fog.* ○ *The fate of the explorer is shrouded in mystery.*

shrub /ʃrʌb/ *n* [C] a plant with a wooden stem and many small branches that usually does not grow very tall

shrubbery /ˈʃrʌb·ə·ri/ *n* [U] low-growing plants considered as a group, or an arrangement of such plants in a garden

shrug /ʃrʌg/ *v* [I/T] **-gg-** to raise your shoulders to express that you do not know, do not care, or are not sure about something ○ [I] *My brother just shrugged in reply, too lazy to answer in words.*

shrug /ʃrʌg/ *n* [C] ○ *Bill's only explanation was a careless shrug of his shoulders.*

shrunk /ʃrʌŋk/ *past simple and past participle of* SHRINK

shrunken /ˈʃrʌŋ·kən/ *past participle of* SHRINK

shucks /ʃʌks/ *exclamation dated* used to express slight regret or to show you are disappointed, or sometimes to show that something is not very important ○ *Shucks, I wish I could have been there.* ○ *Shucks, it wasn't that hard to do.*

shudder /ˈʃʌd·ər/ *v* [I] to shake suddenly and briefly, esp. because of an unpleasant thought or feeling ○ *I shuddered, remembering the frightening stories I had heard.*

shudder /ˈʃʌd·ər/ *n* [C] ○ *When the car flipped over, a shudder went through the crowd watching the race.* ○ *Just thinking about that film sends shudders down my spine.*

shuffle WALK /ˈʃʌf·əl/ *v* [I/T] **1** to walk by sliding your feet, rather than lifting them as you step ○ [I always + adv/prep] *Grandfather shuffled into the kitchen, leaning on his cane.* **2** If you **shuffle** *your* **feet**, you move your feet slightly because you are uncomfortable or embarrassed: [T] *When I asked where he'd been, he just stared at the ground and shuffled his feet.*

shuffle /ˈʃʌf·əl/ *n* [U] ○ *the shuffle of shoes on city sidewalks*

MOVE AROUND /ˈʃʌf·əl/ *v* [T] to move things to different positions or into a different order ○ *She shuffled papers on her desk as she waited for the phone to ring.* ○ *The software lets you shuffle all of your songs or albums with a single click.*

shuffle /ˈʃʌf·əl/ *n* [C] **1** *She gave her papers a quick shuffle.* **2** A shuffle is also a change in people or their positions in an organization: *The top-level shuffle brought Groncki into the White House.*

shun /ʃʌn/ *v* [T] **-nn-** to avoid or refuse to accept someone or something ○ *She shunned publicity after she retired from the stage.*

shunt /ʃʌnt/ *v* [T always + adv/prep] to move someone or something to the side or away ○ *Seals can shunt blood away from their skin to maintain body temperature.* ○ *You can't just shunt your problems aside.*

shush /ʃʌʃ, ʃʊʃ/ *exclamation infml* used to tell someone to be quiet ○ *Shush! You're too loud.*

shush /ʃʌʃ, ʃʊʃ/ *v* [T] *infml* ○ *Marge put a finger to her lips to shush us.*

shut /ʃʌt/ *v* [I/T] *pres. part.* **shutting,** *past* **shut** to close something ○ [T] *Would you shut the door, please?* ○ [I] *I can't get this window shut.* ○ [T] *I shut the book* (= closed it) *and put it back on the shelf.*

shut /ʃʌt/ *adj* [not gradable] ○ *Her office door was shut all day.* ○ *Her eyes were shut, but she was still awake.*

IDIOM with **shut**

• **shut** *your* **mouth** *(infml)* to stop talking ○ *Just shut your mouth and stop whining!*

PHRASAL VERBS with **shut**

• **shut down** *(something)* [M] to stop operating ○ *The company announced plans to shut down two factories.* ○ *Our town's only grocery store shut down last year.* ○ Related noun: SHUTDOWN

• **shut off** *(something)* **STOP** [M] to stop the operation of a machine or system ○ *Did you shut off the light in the bedroom?* ○ *Shut the engine off and take the keys.* ○ *Lift your foot and the water shuts off.*

• **shut off** *something/someone/yourself* **SEPARATE** [M] to separate something or someone from other parts, places, or people ○ *Railroad tracks shut off the area from the rest of the city.* ○ *On cooler evenings we shut the living room off and stay warm by the fireplace.* ○ *These countries could suffer more if they shut themselves off from their neighbors.*

• **shut out** *someone/something* **PREVENT ENTRANCE** [M] to prevent someone or something from entering a place ○ *The double windows shut most of the traffic noise out.* ○ *(fig.) She can't shut out the memory of the accident* (= stop remembering it).

• **shut out** *someone* **PREVENT SCORING** [M] to prevent a competitor from scoring any points ○ *The White Sox shut out the Orioles today at Comiskey Park.* ○ Related noun: SHUTOUT

• **shut up** *(someone/something)* **STOP TALKING** [M] *infml* to stop talking or making a noise, or to make a person or animal stop making noise ○ *I wish you'd shut up and listen.* ○ *Can you shut that dog up?*

• **shut up** *something/someone* **KEEP LOCKED** [M] to keep people or animals in a locked place, or to completely close a place ○ *The zoo keepers shut the animals up in cages at the end of the day.* ○ *They shut up the country house for the winter.*

S

shutdown /ˈʃʌt·dɑʊn/ *n* [C] the act of closing a factory or business or of stopping a machine ○ *The shutdown of the military base is scheduled for next summer.* ○ Related verb: SHUT DOWN

shuteye /ˈʃʌt̬·ɑɪ/ *n* [U] *infml* sleep ○ *Try to get some shuteye.*

shutout /ˈʃʌt̬·ɑʊt/ *n* [C] a competition in which one team or player fails to score any points ○ *He pitched a shutout.* ○ Related verb: SHUT OUT **PREVENT SCORING**

shutter **CAMERA OPENING** /ˈʃʌt̬·ər/ *n* [C] the part of a camera that opens briefly to allow light to reach the film when a photograph is being taken

WINDOW COVER /ˈʃʌt̬·ər/ *n* [C] a wooden cover like a door on the outside of a window

shuttered /ˈʃʌt̬·ərd/ *adj* [not gradable] ○ *In the midday heat, all the houses were shuttered* (= their shutters were closed). ○ *Most of the region's factories are shuttered* (= not operating).

shuttle /ˈʃʌt̬·əl/ *n* [C] **1** a vehicle or aircraft that travels regularly between two places, carrying people or things ○ *You can take the shuttle across town.* ○ *The New York to Boston shuttle is usually on time.* **2** A shuttle is also a SPACE SHUTTLE.

shuttle /ˈʃʌt̬·əl/ *v* [always + adv/prep] ○ [I] *A van shuttles between the hotel and the airport every ten minutes.*

shuttlecock /ˈʃʌt̬·əlˌkɑk/, *infml* **birdie**, *infml* **shuttle** *n* [C] a small, light object with a rounded end to which real or artificial feathers are attached and which is hit over a net in the game of BADMINTON

shut up *exclamation* stop talking or making noise ○ *Shut up! I'm trying to think.* ○ **USAGE:** Often used in an angry way. ○ Related verb: SHUT UP

shy /ʃɑɪ/ *adj* [-er/-est only] *comparative* **shyer**, *superlative* **shyest** uncomfortable with other people and unwilling to talk to them ○ *He was too shy to ask her to dance with him.*

shy /ʃɑɪ/ *v* [I] If a horse shies, it moves back suddenly, esp. from fear or surprise.

shyly /ˈʃɑɪ·li/ *adv* ○ *She smiled shyly.*

shyness /ˈʃɑɪ·nəs/ *n* [U] ○ *They have no shyness about telling you what they think.*

IDIOMS with shy

• **shy away from** *something* to move away from or try to avoid something ○ *He never shied away from a fight, no matter how powerful the foe.*

• **shy of** *something* to lack something ○ *The bill was four votes shy of a majority.*

shyster /ˈʃɑɪ·stər/ *n* [C] *infml* a dishonest person, esp. a lawyer

SI /esˈɑɪ/ *n* [U] ***science*** *abbreviation for* International System of Units (= an international system of units used for measurement in scientific work).

sibling /ˈsɪb·lɪŋ/ *n* [C] a brother or sister ○ *I have four siblings.*

sibling rivalry *n* [U] competition and arguments among brothers and sisters

sic /sɪk/ *adv* [not gradable] used in BRACKETS after a word or phrase copied from somewhere else to show the writer knows it appears to be wrong but this is intentional or exactly as in the original ○ *The sign said, "Closed on Wendsday"* [sic].

PHRASAL VERB with sic

• **sic** *something* **on** *someone*, **sicced or sicked** to order an animal, esp. a dog, to attack someone ○ *The police will sic their dogs on you if they have to.*

sick **ILL** /sɪk/ *adj* physically or mentally ill; not well or healthy ○ *We've got a sick cat.* ○ *I feel sick.* ○ *Only a sick mind could think of such things.* ○ *He's out sick* (= absent because of illness). ○ *Samantha called in sick* (= called to say she was ill and not coming to work).

sicken /ˈsɪk·ən/ *v* [I] ○ *The animals sickened and died.* ○ See also: SICKEN at SICK **UNPLEASANT**

sickly /ˈsɪk·li/ *adj* weak and unhealthy ○ *He was a sickly child.*

sickness /ˈsɪk·nəs/ *n* [C/U] the state or condition of being ill, or a disease ○ [U] *No one escapes occasional sickness.* ○ [C] *Raymond has a rare sickness.*

> **USAGE**
>
> **sick and ill**
>
> These two words mean the same thing, but **ill** is more formal.
>
> *He went home early because he felt sick.*
>
> *She's never been ill for more than a day in her life.*
>
> When nouns are used, however, **illness** and **disease** are both more common than **sickness.**

VOMITING /sɪk/ *adj* [-er/-est only] feeling as if you are going to vomit ○ *She was so nervous she got sick.* ○ *I feel* **sick to** *my* **stomach** (= likely to vomit).

UNPLEASANT /sɪk/ *adj* [-er/-est only] causing or experiencing unpleasant feelings ○ *Michelle is sick about not getting that job.* ○ *I can't believe she lost the election – it just makes me sick.*

sicken /ˈsɪk·ən/ *v* [T] ○ *I was sickened by the attitude of people who could take enjoyment in the building's destruction.* ○ See also: SICKEN at SICK **ILL**

sickening /ˈsɪk·ə·nɪŋ/ *adj* ○ *She slipped and fell with a sickening thud.*

WORD FAMILY sick

Nouns	sick sickness	*Adjectives*	sick sickening sickly
Verbs	sicken		
		Adverbs	sickeningly

IDIOM with sick

• **sick (and tired) of** *someone/something* to have experienced too much of someone or something with the result that you are annoyed ○ *I'm sick of him whining about money.*

sick day *n* [C] a day for which an employee receives pay while absent from work because of illness

sickle /ˈsɪk·əl/ *n* [C] a tool with a short handle and a curved blade, used for cutting grass and other plants

sick leave *n* [U] permitted absence from work because of illness

sickle cell *n* [C] ***biology*** a RED BLOOD CELL with a curved shape that is produced in people with SICKLE CELL ANEMIA

sickle cell anemia *n* [U] ***biology*** a form of ANEMIA (= condition in which the blood cannot carry enough oxygen) that is caused by a GENE (= chemical pattern) that is received from both parents

side **SURFACE** /sɑɪd/ *n* [C] **1** a surface of something that is not the top or the bottom, or a surface of a flat object ○ *Label all four sides of the box.* ○ *I painted one side of the boat green to see if we like the color.* ○ *The trail leads up the side of the mountain.* ○ *Please write on only one side of the paper.* **2** A side is also a surface that is not the front or the back: *There's a scratch on the side of my new bookcase.*

side /sɑɪd/ *adj* [not gradable] at, on, of, or in the side of something ○ *a side view* ○ *Please use the side entrance.*

EDGE /sɑɪd/ *n* [C] **1** an edge or border of something ○ *A square has four sides.* ○ *We rested by the side of the river.* ○ *There are trees on both sides of the road.* **2** ***geometry*** A side is one of the edges of a flat surface.

NEXT POSITION /sɑɪd/ *n* [U] **1** a place next to something ○ *I have a small table by the side of my bed.* **2 a side of** some type of food is a small serving of food, esp. vegetables, served in addition to the main dish. ○ *I'll have a side of onion rings.*

LESS IMPORTANT /sɑɪd/ *adj* less important or smaller than the thing it is connected with ○ *a side issue* ○ *We parked on a side street.*

PART /sɑɪd/ *n* [C] a part of something, esp. in relation to a real or imagined central line ○ *the right/left side* ○ *The swimming pool is on the other side of town.* ○ *I'm Irish on my mother's side* (= her family is from Ireland). ○ *Children came running from all sides* (= from many directions).

OPPOSING GROUP /sɑɪd/ *n* [C] one of two or more opposing groups or people ○ *This is a war which neither side can win.* ○ *Which side are you on* (= Whom do you support)? ○ (*fig.*) *The other candidate had experience on his side* (= as an advantage).

side /sɑɪd/ *v* [I always + adv/prep] ○ *Peter always sides with you* (= supports you).

OPINION /sɑɪd/ *n* [C] an opinion held in an argument, or a way of considering something ○ *There are two sides to every argument.*

PERSONAL QUALITY /sɑɪd/ *n* [C] a part of someone's character ○ *He has a gentle side.*

IDIOMS with side

• **on the side 1** in addition ○ *He drives a bus, but he's a tour guide on the side.* **2** Food that is served **on the side** is served separate from other food ○ *I'll have the salad with the dressing on the side.*

• **side by side** next to each other ○ *The children sat side by side.*

sideboard /ˈsɑɪd·bɔːrd, -boʊrd/ *n* [C] a piece of furniture with a flat top and enclosed shelves at the bottom, usually used for holding such things as glasses, plates, knives, and forks

sideburns /ˈsɑɪd·bɜrnz/ *pl n* areas of hair grown down the sides of a man's face in front of the ears

side dish *n* [C] a small serving of food, esp. vegetables, served in addition to the main dish

side effect *n* [C usually pl] an unwanted or unexpected result or condition that comes along with the desired effects of something ○ *Does this drug have any side effects?*

sidekick /ˈsɑɪd·kɪk/ *n* [C] *infml* a friend, or a person who works with someone more important ○ *The course will focus on fictional master sleuth Sherlock Holmes and his sidekick Dr. Watson.*

sideline **ACTIVITY** /ˈsɑɪd·lɑɪn/ *n* [C] an activity that is less important than the main one ○ *Jean teaches French in the evening as a sideline.*

MARK ON GROUND /ˈsɑɪd·lɑɪn/ *n* [C] (in some sports, esp. football) a line marking the side of the area of play ○ *The ball fell just outside the sideline.* ○ (*fig.*) *I don't like dancing, I'd rather watch from the sidelines* (= not to be directly involved).

sideline /ˈsɑɪd·lɑɪn/ *v* [T] to remove a player from a game ○ *He was sidelined because of injuries.*

IDIOM with sideline

• **on the sidelines** not taking part in an activity ○ *Several countries chose to remain on the sidelines during the war.*

sidelong /ˈsɑɪd·lɔːŋ/ *adj, adv* [not gradable] directed to or from the side ○ *a sidelong glance*

side order, **side** *n* [C] a small serving of food sold at a restaurant, usually to be eaten with other food

sideshow /ˈsɑɪd·ʃoʊ/ *n* [C] a small show in addition to the main one, esp. at a CIRCUS (= traveling entertainment)

sidestep /ˈsɑɪd·step/ *v* [I/T] **-pp- 1** to avoid something ○ [T] *The developer tried to sidestep city building rules.* ○ [T] *She skillfully sidestepped questions about her past.* **2** A person or animal who sidesteps moves quickly to the side.

sideswipe /ˈsɑɪd·swɑɪp/ *v* [T] to hit a vehicle on the side while passing in another vehicle ○ *My car was sideswiped in the parking lot.*

sidetrack /ˈsɑɪd·træk/ *v* [I] to direct (someone) away from an activity or subject toward another one that is often less important ○ *Rhonda was looking for an envelope and got sidetracked reading some old letters.*

sidewalk /ˈsɑɪd·wɔːk/ *n* [C] a path with a hard surface on which people walk along one or both sides of a road

sideways /ˈsɑɪd·weɪz/ *adj, adv* [not gradable] **1** from one side to another, or with a side to the front ○ *If you'd move sideways I could see better.* ○ *Turn the table sideways.* **2** If you look at something sideways, you do not look at it directly.

S

siding /ˈsɑɪd·ɪŋ/ *n* [U] material that covers the outer walls of a building ○ *vinyl/aluminum/wood siding*

sidle /ˈsɑɪd·əl/ *v* [I always + adv/prep] to move in an uncertain manner with one side facing forward ○ *Jordan sidled over to the girl and asked if she'd like to dance.*

siege /siːdʒ, siːʒ/ *n* [C/U] the act of surrounding a place by an armed force in order to defeat those defending it ○ [C] *After a month-long siege, they gave themselves up to federal agents.* ○ [U] *The town was under siege.*

siesta /siːˈes·tə/ *n* [C] a rest or sleep taken at the beginning of the afternoon, esp. in hot countries

sieve /sɪv/ *n* [C] a bowl-shaped tool with many very small holes in it, used to separate larger from smaller pieces or solids from a liquid

sift SEPARATE /sɪft/ *v* [T] to shake a powdered substance through a SIEVE in order to break lumps into very small grains ○ *Sift some powdered sugar on top of the cake.*

EXAMINE /sɪft/ *v* [I/T] to make a close examination of something ○ [T] *The police are carefully sifting the evidence.* ○ [I] *I had to sift through all my papers.*

sigh /sɑɪ/ *v* [I] to breathe out a deep breath that can be heard, esp. because you are tired, sad, pleased, or bored ○ *Angelica sighed in relief.* ○ *She sighs again, looking bored.* ○ *(fig.) A soft breeze sighed through the trees.*

sigh /sɑɪ/ *n* [C] ○ *You could hear an occasional sigh from the crowd.*

IDIOM with **sigh**

• **a sigh of relief** a feeling of comfort after worrying about something ○ *Residents in coastal areas are breathing a sigh of relief now that the storm has passed.*

sight SEEING /sɑɪt/ *n* [U] the ability to see, or the act of seeing something ○ *Machines don't have a sense of sight.* ○ *The sight of sick children disturbs her.* ○ *I know David* **by sight** (= I know what he looks like). ○ *Officers arrested the looters* **on sight** (= as soon as they saw them).

sightless /ˈsɑɪt·ləs/ *adj* [not gradable] blind

VIEW /sɑɪt/ *n* [C/U] **1** something that is in someone's view, or the view someone has ○ [C] *The finish line was a welcome sight for the runners.* ○ [C] *Don't let the children out of your sight.* ○ [U] *Keep your bags in sight.* **2** A sight is also an interesting place: [C] *No sights in Moscow are more historic than the Kremlin.*

sight /sɑɪt/ *v* [T] ○ *After several days at sea, the sailors finally sighted land.*

sighting /ˈsɑɪt̬·ɪŋ/ *n* [C] ○ *This is the first sighting of an eastern bluebird in this part of the country.*

➤ Usage: **sightseeing or sight?** at SIGHTSEEING; **view or sight?** at VIEW SIGHT

GUN PART /sɑɪt/ *n* [C] a device, esp. on a gun or TELESCOPE (= device for looking at objects that are far away), through which you look to help you aim at something ○ *Locate the target in your sight.*

IDIOMS with **sight**

• **a sight for sore eyes** someone or something that you are happy to see ○ *After twenty hours of driving, my family was a sight for sore eyes.*

• **sight unseen** without seeing or examining something ○ *I never buy anything sight unseen.*

WORD FAMILY sight

Nouns	sight insight oversight sighting	*Adjectives*	sightless insightful unsightly
		Verbs	sight

sight-read *v* [I/T] to play or sing written music the first time you see it

sightseeing /ˈsɑɪtˌsiː·ɪŋ/ *n* [U] the act of visiting interesting places, esp. while on vacation ○ *Are you going to go sightseeing this afternoon?*

sightseer /ˈsɑɪtˌsiː·ər/ *n* [C] someone who visits interesting places

sign MARK /sɑɪn/ *n* [C] a written or printed mark that has a standard meaning ○ *The symbol for subtraction is the minus sign.*

PUBLIC INFORMATION /sɑɪn/ *n* [C] a device that gives information to people who see it ○ *a stop sign* ○ *A neon sign marked the entrance to the parking garage.*

BODY MOVEMENT /sɑɪn/ *n* [C] a movement of the hands or body that gives information or an instruction ○ *He kept giving me the cut-throat sign to end the speech.*

sign /sɑɪn/ *v* to communicate by using hand movements ○ [+ *that* clause] *He signed that he'd be ready in five minutes.*

SIGNAL /sɑɪn/ *n* [C] a signal that something exists or that shows what might happen in the future ○ *She was at least sharing her problems with me, and that was a sign of progress.* ○ *There was nobody in the place, and I thought that was a bad sign.* ○ *There are signs that he is thinking of running for president.*

WRITE /sɑɪn/ *v* [I/T] **1** to write your name on a document to show that you agree with it or that you have written it yourself ○ [T] *to sign a letter/contract/check* ○ [I] *Please sign for the package when it arrives* (= write your name on a form to show that you have received it). **2** If an organization signs someone, that person has officially become a member of the organization by agreeing to a contract: [T] *The team signed four new players this week.*

WORD FAMILY sign

Nouns	sign signal signatory signature signing	*Adjectives*	signed unsigned
		Verbs	sign signal

PHRASAL VERBS with **sign**

• **sign away** *something* [M] to give up your rights to something or ownership of it by formally signing a document ○ *She signed away her rights to the book before it became a best-seller.*

•**sign in** to write your name on a form when entering or leaving a place ○ *Messengers are required to sign in at the front desk when they make a delivery.*
•**sign off** to end a conversation or a television or radio broadcast
•**sign off (on** *something***)** to approve something officially ○ *Both sides signed off on a legally binding agreement last month.*
•**sign on 1** to agree to take part ○ *Several corporations have signed on to sponsor the tournament.* **2** If you sign on to an agreement, law, or idea, you state that you will support it: *Nearly every state has signed on, agreeing to drop their lawsuits and accept a settlement.*
•**sign** *something* **over (to** *someone***)** [M] to give up something by signing a formal document that gives it to someone else ○ *He signed the land over to the city before he died.*
•**sign up** to join a group or organization ○ *Kathy signed up for the soccer team this year.*
•**sign with** *someone* to start working for an organization or become a member of a sports team ○ *Some teams have let players sign with other teams because they could not afford to keep them.*

signal ACTION /ˈsɪg·nəl/ *n* [C] **1** an action, movement, or sound that gives information, a message, a warning, or an order ○ *I tried to call but kept getting a busy signal.* ○ *When the lieutenant gave the signal, five police officers charged into the apartment.* ○ *In retrospect, looking at how she was acting, we should have been able to recognize the danger signals.* **2** A signal is also a device, often with lights, that shows people or vehicles whether to stop, go, or move carefully.
signal /ˈsɪg·nəl/ *v* [I/T] ○ [I] *When you learn to drive, you are told that you have to signal before you turn right or left.* ○ [T] *The police officer signaled us to stop.*

WAVE /ˈsɪg·nəl/ *n* [C] a series of energy waves that carry a sound, picture, or other information ○ *a low-frequency radio signal*

IMPORTANT /ˈsɪg·nəl/ *adj fml* unusual and important ○ *You performed a signal service to our people, and we wish to express our gratitude.*

signatory /ˈsɪg·nəˌtɔːr·i, -ˌtoʊr·i/ *n* [C] a person, organization, or country that signs an agreement ○ *Canada was a signatory to the Geneva Convention.*

signature /ˈsɪg·nə·tʃər, -ˌtʃʊr/ *n* [C] your name written in the particular way you write it, esp. on a printed document to show that you have written it yourself ○ *I need your signature on the credit card receipt.* ○ *We collected hundreds of signatures on our petition.*

significant Ⓐ /sɪgˈnɪf·ɪ·kənt/ *adj* important, large, or great, esp. in leading to a different result or to an important change ○ *This election reaffirms a significant shift of the center of power.* ○ *Marriage is a significant commitment.*
significance Ⓐ /sɪgˈnɪf·ɪ·kəns/ *n* [U] ○ *The full significance of space exploration may not be understood for many years to come.*
significantly Ⓐ /sɪgˈnɪf·ɪ·kənt·li/ *adv* by a large amount ○ *Our prison population has significantly increased in the last ten years.* ○ *Men are making significantly more money than women at the same professional level.*

signify Ⓐ MEAN /ˈsɪg·nəˌfɑɪ/ *v* [T] to mean something, or be a sign of ○ *In this picture, red represents sulfur and green signifies hydrogen.*

MAKE KNOWN /ˈsɪg·nəˌfɑɪ/ *v* to make (something) known; to show ○ [I] *All those in favor, please signify by raising your hands.* ○ [+ *that* clause] *I need a letter from you signifying that this matter is closed.*

WORD FAMILY signify			
Nouns	significance insignificance	*Verbs*	signify
		Adverbs	significantly insignificantly
Adjectives	significant insignificant		

sign language *n* [C/U] a system of communication for people who cannot hear that uses hand and finger movements

signpost /ˈsɑɪn·poʊst/ *n* [C] **1** a pole with a sign on it, esp. showing the way to a place or the name of a road ○ *The camp roads had signposts that read Sparks Street, Portage Avenue, Yonge Street, and the like.* **2** *fig.* A signpost is also a clear signal that something will happen: *a signpost of progress*

Sikh /siːk/ *n* a member of a religion based on the belief in one God and the equality of all people
Sikh /siːk/ *adj* [not gradable] ○ *a Sikh temple*
Sikhism /ˈsiːˌkɪz·əm/ *n* [U] the Sikh religion

silence QUIET /ˈsɑɪ·ləns/ *n* [U] an absence of sound; complete quiet ○ *A profound silence spread itself through the sleeping house.*
silent /ˈsɑɪ·lənt/ *adj* ○ *Madeleine turned back down the empty, silent street.*
silently /ˈsɑɪ·lənt·li/ *adv* ○ *Silently, he crept up the stairs.*
silencer /ˈsɑɪ·lən·sər/ *n* [C] a part that can be attached to a gun to reduce the noise when it is fired

NO SPEAKING /ˈsɑɪ·ləns/ *n* [C/U] a state of not speaking or making noise ○ [U] *The two men ate in silence and listened to traffic swishing past on the highway.* ○ [C] *Her question was followed by a long silence* (= a long period of time in which no one spoke).
silence /ˈsɑɪ·ləns/ *v* [T] to stop someone from speaking or from criticizing ○ *Successful action could silence the administration's critics.*
silent /ˈsɑɪ·lənt/ *adj* **1** *I have remained silent till now, Mike, but I have to tell you what I think.* **2** If a letter in a word is silent, it is not pronounced: *The "b" in doubt is silent.*
silently /ˈsɑɪ·lənt·li/ *adv* without speaking, or only in the mind ○ *After losing, the US players walked off the field silently.*

WORD FAMILY silence			
Nouns	silence silencer	*Verbs*	silence
		Adverbs	silently
Adjectives	silent		

S

silent partner *n* [C] someone who owns part of a business but does not make decisions about how it operates

silhouette /ˌsɪl·əˈwet/ *n* [C/U] a dark shape seen against a light background ○ [U] *An unidentified witness was shown on camera in silhouette.*
silhouette /ˌsɪl·əˈwet/ *v* [T] ○ *Kate was silhouetted in the pale light of the porch.*

silicon /ˈsɪl·ɪ·kən, -əˌkɑn/ *n* [U] a common chemical element that is used in electronic devices, such as computers, and in making materials such as glass, concrete, and steel

silicone /ˈsɪl·əˌkoʊn/ *n* [U] a chemical substance that is not easily damaged by heat or water, used for making many things including oils, plastics, and artificial body parts

Silicon Valley *n* [U] an area in northern California where there are many companies that make or use computer materials and electronic devices

silk /sɪlk/ *n* [U] a smooth, shiny cloth made from a thread produced by a type of CATERPILLAR (= small, tube-shaped insect), or the thread itself ○ *a silk shirt*
silky /ˈsɪl·ki/, **silken** /ˈsɪl·kən/ *adj* made of silk, or soft and smooth like silk ○ *a silky nightgown* ○ *silky fabrics*

silkworm /ˈsɪlkˌwɜrm/ *n* [C] a CATERPILLAR that produces threads which are used to make silk

sill WINDOW BASE /sɪl/ *n* [C] a flat, horizontal piece, usually of wood, forming the base of the frame of a window ○ *She leaned on the sill and looked out through the open window.*

ROCK LAYER /sɪl/ *n* [U] ***earth science*** a layer of rock that is created when hot melted rock forces itself into spaces between other rock, then cools and becomes solid

silly /ˈsɪl·i/ *adj* showing a lack of thought or judgment; not serious and not showing much intelligence ○ *a silly grin* ○ *I watched another silly movie last night.*
silliness /ˈsɪl·iː·nəs/ *n* [U] ○ *It's time to stop the silliness and get serious.*

silo /ˈsɑɪ·loʊ/ *n* [C] *pl* **silos 1** a large structure, usually cylindrical, used for storing grain or winter food for farm animals **2** A silo is also an underground structure for storing and firing MISSILES (= flying weapons).

silt /sɪlt/ *n* [U] sand or earth that has been carried along by flowing water and then left esp. at a bend in a river or at a river's opening

silver METAL /ˈsɪl·vər/ *n* [U] a white metal that is highly valued and used esp. in utensils, jewelry, coins, and decorative objects
silver /ˈsɪl·vər/ *adj* ○ *a silver tray*

COLOR /ˈsɪl·vər/ *adj, n* [U] (of) a bright gray-white color ○ *silver hair* ○ *The book jacket was printed in silver and black.*

silver anniversary *n* [C] a celebration of the 25th year of something, esp. a marriage

silver medal *n* [C] a disk-shaped prize made of or covered with silver, given to a person or team that is second in a competition ○ Compare GOLD MEDAL; BRONZE MEDAL

silverware /ˈsɪl·vərˌwer, -ˌwær/ *n* [U] knives, forks, and spoons used for eating and serving food, which may or may not be made of silver

similar Ⓐ /ˈsɪm·ə·lər/ *adj* looking or being almost the same, although not exactly ○ *They both went to Ivy League schools and have similar backgrounds.* ○ *He used similar tactics to win the last election.*
similarity Ⓐ /ˌsɪm·əˈlær·əṭ·i/ *n* [C/U] the state of being almost the same, or a particular way in which something is almost the same ○ [C] *Even though there are many similarities between men and women, there still remain many differences.*
similarly Ⓐ /ˈsɪm·ə·lər·li/ *adv* ○ *The disease affects both sexes similarly.*

WORD FAMILY similar			
Nouns	similarity	*Adjectives*	similar dissimilar
Adverbs	similarly		

simile /ˈsɪm·ə·liː/ *n* [C/U] ***English*** an expression including the words "like" or "as" to compare one thing with another ○ [U] *She was good at capturing a passing figure with an apt simile or comparison.*

simmer /ˈsɪm·ər/ *v* [I/T] to cook a liquid or something with liquid in it at a temperature slightly below boiling ○ [I] *Add broth and simmer for 15 minutes.*
simmer /ˈsɪm·ər/ *n* [U] ○ *Bring the water to a simmer.*
simmering /ˈsɪm·ə·rɪŋ/ *adj* [not gradable] **1** *a pot of simmering water* **2** *fig.* Something that is simmering is controlled but may burst out at any time, often violently: *simmering tensions* ○ *The simmering controversy now appears to be coming to an end.*

simple PLAIN /ˈsɪm·pəl/ *adj* [-*er*/-*est* only] without unnecessary or extra things or decorations; plain ○ *a simple black dress* ○ *It's a simple Boston lettuce salad.*
simplicity /sɪmˈplɪs·əṭ·i/ *n* [U] ○ *What fascinated us was the simplicity and usefulness of the design.*
simply /ˈsɪm·pli/ *adv* ○ *He lived in a simply furnished apartment.* ○ *She lived simply, alone with her cat and her books.* ○ See also: SIMPLY ; SIMPLY at SIMPLE EASY; SIMPLY at SIMPLE CONSIDERED ALONE

EASY /ˈsɪm·pəl/ *adj* [-*er*/-*est* only] easy to understand or do; not difficult or complicated ○ *The recipe is very simple.* ○ *There's a simple solution if you don't like what's on TV – change the channel.*
simplicity /sɪmˈplɪs·əṭ·i/ *n* [U] ○ *A flat tax has the virtue of simplicity, but I question how fair it would be.*
simplify /ˈsɪm·pləˌfɑɪ/ *v* [T] ○ *We're looking for ways to simplify the process of applying for US citizenship.*
simply /ˈsɪm·pli/ *adv* ○ *To put it simply, we won't pay until we've received the goods we ordered.* ○ See

also: SIMPLY; SIMPLY at SIMPLE PLAIN; SIMPLY at SIMPLE CONSIDERED ALONE

simplification /ˌsɪm·plə·fɪˈkeɪ·ʃən/ *n* [C/U]

CONSIDERED ALONE /ˈsɪm·pəl/ *adj* [not gradable] without considering or including anything else ○ *The simple fact is the fee is high because the rights are valuable.*

simply /ˈsɪm·pli/ *adv* [not gradable] ○ *Bowman said simply that "everything was OK."* ○ See also: SIMPLY; SIMPLY at SIMPLE PLAIN; SIMPLY at SIMPLE EASY

COMMON /ˈsɪm·pəl/ *adj* [*-er/-est* only] common or ordinary ○ *I've got simple tastes, and I'm too old and cranky to change.*

FOOLISH /ˈsɪm·pəl/ *adj* [*-er/-est* only] *dated* foolish; easily deceived ○ *He's a very simple young man.*

WORD FAMILY simple			
Nouns	simplicity simplification	*Adjectives*	simple simplistic
Verbs	simplify	*Adverbs*	simply

simple-minded *adj* unable to deal with complicated matters

simplistic /sɪmˈplɪs·tɪk/ *adj disapproving* simple but not effectively dealing with a real situation or problem, which is more complicated ○ *a simplistic idea/plan*

simply /ˈsɪm·pli/ *adv* [not gradable] **1** just; only ○ *I simply don't trust him.* ○ *We simply go to camp, set it up, and spend the weekend.* ○ *They voted not simply for him and his party, but against Boris Yeltsin.* **2** Simply is sometimes used for emphasis: *That simply isn't so!* ○ See also: SIMPLY at SIMPLE PLAIN; SIMPLY at SIMPLE EASY; SIMPLY at SIMPLE CONSIDERED ALONE

simulate Ⓐ /ˈsɪm·jəˌleɪt/ *v* [T] to create conditions or processes similar to something that exists ○ *Researchers are developing new techniques to simulate crashes.*

simulated Ⓐ /ˈsɪm·jəˌleɪt̬·əd/ *adj* [not gradable] made to look like something else; artificial ○ *simulated leather*

simulation Ⓐ /ˌsɪm·jəˈleɪ·ʃən/ *n* [C/U] a model of a real activity, created for training purposes or to solve a problem ○ [U] *Astronauts are trained using space flight simulation.*

simultaneous /ˌsɑɪ·məlˈteɪ·niː·əs, ˌsɪm·əl-/ *adj* [not gradable] happening or existing at exactly the same time ○ *The report will be broadcast in Russian with simultaneous English translation.*

simultaneously /ˌsɑɪ·məlˈteɪ·niː·ə·sli, ˌsɪm·əl-/ *adv* [not gradable] ○ *To drive a car, you've got to learn to do several things simultaneously.*

sin /sɪn/ *n* [C/U] **1** an act of breaking a religious law, or such acts considered together ○ [C] *In most religions, stealing is regarded as a sin.* **2** A sin is also anything considered wrong: [C] *It is not a sin to drop your kid off at soccer practice and stay in the car to read a book.*

sin /sɪn/ *v* [I] **-nn-** ○ *I don't think there's a good way to say I have sinned.*

sinful /ˈsɪn·fəl/ *adj* **1** *We all know that what he did is sinful, but it may not be illegal.* **2** Sinful also means wrong: *It's sinful to waste food.*

sinner /ˈsɪn·ər/ *n* [C] a person who commits sins

SIN (number) /ˈsɪn (ˈnʌm·bər)/ *n* [C] *Cdn, abbreviation for* SOCIAL INSURANCE NUMBER.

since TIME /sɪns/ *adv* [not gradable] from a particular time in the past until now ○ *Alfredo left the house at six this morning, and we haven't seen him since.* ○ *I got my first job in 1973 and I've been working ever since* (= from then until now).

since /sɪns/ *prep* ○ *A lot has happened since 1980.*

since /sɪns/ *conjunction* ○ *It's been more than two years since we moved back to New York.*

BECAUSE /sɪns/ *conjunction* because; as ○ *Since you've asked, I'll tell you what I really think.*

IDIOM with since

• **since when** for how long have you believed ○ *Since when do you have the right to tell me what to do?* ○ **USAGE**: Used in questions to show anger because you do not believe something is right or true.

sincere /sɪnˈsɪr/ *adj* (esp. of feelings, beliefs, opinions, or intentions) honest; not false or invented ○ *sincere modesty/belief/statement* ○ *More than sincere words of support, we need action.*

sincerely /sɪnˈsɪr·li/ *adv* [not gradable] **1** *I sincerely hope she's happy with her decision.* **2** Sincerely or **Sincerely yours** is a common way to end a letter to someone who is not a friend or family member, before you sign your name.

sincerity /sɪnˈser·ət̬·i, -ˈsɪr-/ *n* [U] ○ *She spoke with such sincerity, you had to believe her.*

WORD CHOICES sincere

See also: **honest**

An alternative to "sincere" is **genuine**.

*His surprise was perfectly **genuine**.*

*He's a very **genuine** person.*

True or **real** can be used about feelings which are sincere.

*He showed **true** concern for his students.*

*She didn't show any **real** regret for what she had done.*

If a feeling is strong and sincere, you could use the adjective **heartfelt**.

*His **heartfelt** desire is to end world hunger.*

sine /sɑɪn/, *abbreviation* **sin** *n* [C] ***trigonometry*** in a triangle that has one angle of 90°, the RATIO (= relationship) of the length of the side opposite an angle less than 90° divided by the length of the HYPOTENUSE (= the side opposite the 90° angle)

sinew /ˈsɪn·juː/ *n* [C usually pl] a strong cord of muscle found in meat; a TENDON

sinewy /ˈsɪn·jə·wi/ *adj* ○ *lean, sinewy thighs*

sinful /ˈsɪn·fəl/ *adj* See at SIN.

sing /sɪŋ/ *v* [I/T] *past simp.* **sang, sung,** *past part.* **sung 1** to make musical sounds with the voice ○

S

[T] *She sings really terrible songs in the shower.* ○ [I] *At dawn, the birds began to sing.* ○ [I] *We sang along to* (= sang with) *the radio while driving.* **2** If you **sing** *someone* **to sleep**, you sing until the person goes to sleep: *She sang her baby to sleep.*

singer /ˈsɪŋ·ər/ *n* [C] a person who sings, esp. someone whose job is singing

WORD FAMILY sing			
Nouns	singer	*Verbs*	sing
Adjectives	unsung		

IDIOM with sing

• **sing** *someone's/something's* **praises, sing the praises of** *someone/something* to praise someone or something with enthusiasm ○ *The review in the paper sings the movie's praises.*

singe /sɪndʒ/ *v* [T] *pres. part.* **singeing** to burn something slightly, or to be burned slightly ○ *The candle singed his arm hairs.*

single ONE /ˈsɪŋ·gəl/ *adj* [not gradable] **1** one only ○ *A single customer was left in the shop.* ○ Compare DOUBLE TWICE **2** A single bed is a bed for one person.

singly /ˈsɪŋ·gli/ *adv* [not gradable] ○ *Students can work singly or in pairs.*

single /ˈsɪŋ·gəl/ *n* [C] **1** A single is a one-dollar bill. **2** A single is also a room for only one person.

singles /ˈsɪŋ·gəlz/ *n* [C] *pl* **singles** (esp. in tennis) a game played with one player on each side

SEPARATE /ˈsɪŋ·gəl/ *adj* [not gradable] considered by itself or separate from other things ○ *Taxes are the single most important source of funds for the government.*

NOT MARRIED /ˈsɪŋ·gəl/ *adj* [not gradable] not married ○ *He's been single for so long, I don't think he'll ever marry.*

single /ˈsɪŋ·gəl/ *n* [C] a person who is not married ○ *Singles pay more in income tax than married people do.*

S

WORD FAMILY single			
Nouns	single	*Adjectives*	single
	singles		singular
	singular	*Adverbs*	singly
Verbs	single		singularly

PHRASAL VERB with single

• **single out** *someone/something* [M] to choose someone or something for special attention ○ *You can't just single out young people when you talk about what's wrong with the country.*

single file *n* [U] a line with one person behind another ○ *The children walked single file down the hall.*

single-handed *adj* [not gradable] involving only one person's work or effort ○ *The round-the-world single-handed race is sailing's ultimate challenge.*

single-handedly *adv* ○ *She single-handedly supported the family after her husband's death.*

single-minded *adj* only doing things that relate to one activity or interest ○ *She is single-minded in her pursuit of her studies.*

singsong /ˈsɪŋ·sɔːŋ/ *adj* [not gradable] becoming higher and lower in a regular, boring way when speaking ○ *Her singsong reading of that report actually put me to sleep.*

singular GRAMMAR /ˈsɪŋ·gjə·lər/ *adj* [not gradable] ***grammar*** being the form of a word used to talk about only one thing ○ *a singular noun/verb* ○ *"Woman" is singular, but "women" is plural.* ○ Compare PLURAL

singular /ˈsɪŋ·gjə·lər/ *n* [C/U] ***grammar*** ○ [U] *The singular of "clouds" is "cloud."*

NOTICEABLE /ˈsɪŋ·gjə·lər/ *adj* [not gradable] unusual and easily noticed ○ *His campaign was singular because he talked about issues and did not attack his opponents' personal lives.*

singularly /ˈsɪŋ·gjə·lər·li/ *adv* [not gradable] obviously or particularly ○ *New England has some singularly beautiful towns.*

sinister /ˈsɪn·ə·stər/ *adj* [not gradable] evil, or suggesting that something evil is going to happen ○ *She has dark, sinister eyes that make you nervous when she looks at you.*

sink GO BELOW WATER /sɪŋk/ *v* [I/T] *past simp.* **sank, sunk,** *past part.* **sunk** to move below the surface of water ○ [I] *The boat filled with water and began to sink.* ○ [T] *It isn't clear exactly what sank the ship.* ○ Related adjective: SUNKEN

FALL /sɪŋk/ *v* [I/T] *past simp.* **sank, sunk,** *past part.* **sunk 1** to fall or move to a lower level ○ [I] *The sun sank slowly below the horizon.* ○ [I] *Exhausted after the race, she sank to the ground.* ○ [I] *My feet sink into the sand with every step.* ○ [I] *Gasoline prices sank last year.* ○ [I] *Relations between the countries have sunk to a new low.* **2** To sink a ball is to hit it into a hole, as in golf and POOL, or throw it through a HOOP (= ring with a net) in BASKETBALL. **3** People or animals who **sink** *their* **teeth into** something bite hard: *I sank my teeth into the sandwich.*

sinking /ˈsɪŋ·kɪŋ/ *adj* **1** *He throws a sinking fastball* (= one that moves down). **2** A **sinking feeling** is a feeling that something bad is happening or will happen: *He had a sinking feeling that he would not make the team.*

DESTROY /sɪŋk/ *v* [T] *past simp.* **sank, sunk,** *past part.* **sunk** to cause something to fail ○ *A price war sank the company.* ○ *I thought these issues would sink his career.*

CONTAINER /sɪŋk/ *n* [C] a container for water in a kitchen or bathroom used for washing and connected to pipes that bring and carry off water

IDIOMS with sink

• **sink or swim** a situation in which you will fail if you do not make a lot of effort ○ *When we started the business, it was sink or swim.*

• **sink** *your* **teeth into** *something* to become completely involved in something ○ *It was a story you could really sink your teeth into.*

PHRASAL VERBS with sink

• **sink back** to move into a relaxed, comfortable position ○ *He sank back in his chair and closed his eyes.*
• **sink in** BECOME KNOWN to become understood or known ○ *It took a while for the reality of my situation to sink in.*
• **sink in** BE ABSORBED (of liquid) to be absorbed ○ *Wait a few minutes to let the moisturizer sink in.*
• **sink into** *something* BECOME WORSE to change to a worse state or condition ○ *He sank into a coma.* ○ *The play starts well, then sinks into melodrama.*
• **sink** *something* **into** *something* SPEND MONEY to spend money on something or invest money in something ○ *No developer is going to sink millions of dollars into something he can't sell.*
• **sink into** *something* UNDERSTAND to realize or understand something ○ *Finally the full extent of his words sank into her brain.*
• **sink into** *something* BECOME COVERED to be covered or absorbed by something ○ *My feet sank into the sand with every step.*

sinus /ˈsɑɪ·nəs/ *n* [C] any of the hollow spaces in the bones of the head that open into the nose

sip /sɪp/ *v* [T] **-pp-** to drink a liquid slowly by taking in small amounts at a time ○ *He sipped the hot coffee.*
sip /sɪp/ *n* [C] ○ *He took another sip of tea.*

siphon, **syphon** /ˈsɑɪ·fən/ *n* [C] a tube for moving a liquid from one container to another or to a lower level, using the weight of air to keep the liquid flowing through the tube
siphon, **syphon** /ˈsɑɪ·fən/ *v* [T always + adv/prep] ○ *We had to siphon some gas into the tank before the car would start.*

PHRASAL VERB with siphon

• **siphon off** *something* [M] to gradually steal money or goods, usually from a business or government ○ *Over the years, she siphoned off hundreds of thousands of dollars from various accounts.*

sir /sɜr/ *n* [C] **1** a polite word used to address a man ○ *Excuse me, sir, do you know what time it is?* **2** Sir is used at the beginning of a formal letter to a man you do not know: *Dear Sir* ○ Compare MADAM WOMAN

Sir /sɜr/ *n* [U] used as a title with the first or full name of a man given a rank of honor by a king or queen

sire MALE PARENT /sɑɪr/ *n* [C] the male parent of an animal with four feet
sire /sɑɪr/ *v* [T] to be the male parent of an animal ○ *The large bay colt was sired by Pleasant Colony.*

KING /sɑɪr/ *n* [C] *old use* used as a form of address to a king

siren DEVICE /ˈsɑɪ·rən/ *n* [C] a device that makes a loud warning noise ○ *The terrible wail of sirens signaled a disaster.*

WOMAN /ˈsɑɪ·rən/ *n* [C] (in ancient Greek literature) a creature who was half woman and half bird, whose singing brought ships into dangerous waters

siren call, **siren song** *n* [C] a powerful attraction ○ *I responded to the siren call of the road and left home to drive across the country.*

sirloin (steak) /ˈsɜr·lɔɪn (ˈsteɪk)/ *n* [C/U] the best meat from the lower back of cattle

sis /sɪs/ *n* [C] *short form of* SISTER

sissy /ˈsɪs·i/ *n* [C] *infml* a boy who seems to be easily frightened and not brave, or who is not interested in things boys usually like ○ *Dancing was for sissies when I was a kid.*

sister /ˈsɪs·tər/ *n* [C] **1** a female who has the same parents as another person ○ *an older/younger sister* **2** A sister is also a member of the same race, church, religious group, or organization: *a sorority sister* **3** Sister may be used as a form of address to a woman.
sisterhood /ˈsɪs·tərˌhʊd/ *n* [U] a feeling of shared interests and support among women
sister-in-law /ˈsɪs·tə·rənˌlɔː/ *n* [C] *pl* **sisters-in-law** the wife of someone's brother, or the sister of someone's husband or wife, or the wife of the brother of someone's husband or wife
sisterly /ˈsɪs·tər·li/ *adj* like or characteristic of a sister ○ *sisterly love*

sit REST /sɪt/ *v* [I/T] *pres. part.* **sitting**, *past* **sat** to be in a position with your buttocks on a surface that supports your body, or to cause someone to be in this position ○ [I] *Andrea was sitting on the couch, watching TV.* ○ [T] *Dad sat her on a chair and told her not to move.* ○ **Sit still** (= sit without moving) *while I comb your hair!*
sitting /ˈsɪt̬·ɪŋ/ *n* [C] ○ *I read the book in one sitting.* ○ *It took several sittings for the artist to paint her portrait.*

BE IN A POSITION /sɪt/ *v* [I] *pres. part.* **sitting**, *past* **sat** to be or stay in a position or place ○ *That book is still sitting on my shelf unread.* ○ *The college sits on top of a hill.*

MEET /sɪt/ *v* [I] *pres. part.* **sitting**, *past* **sat** (of a legislature or court) to have an official meeting or series of meetings ○ *The Supreme Court sits from October to June.*

TAKE CARE /sɪt/ *v* [I/T] *short form of* BABY-SIT
sitter /ˈsɪt̬·ər/ *n* [C] *short form of* BABY-SITTER

IDIOMS with sit

• **not sit well with** *someone* to be difficult for someone to agree with or accept ○ *The principal's decision did not sit well with many parents.*
• **sit on** *your* **hands** to do nothing ○ *The President sat on his hands for three years and blamed Congress.*
• **sit tight** to wait patiently and take no action ○ *You sit tight, and I'll go get help.*
• **sitting pretty** in a good situation ○ *Our apartment isn't expensive, so we're sitting pretty.*
• **sit up and take notice** to suddenly give attention to something when you had not done so before ○ *The losses in the election have made party leaders finally sit up and take notice.*

PHRASAL VERBS with sit

• **sit around** *(somewhere)* to sit somewhere and do nothing or do nothing in particular ○ *He just sits around the house watching TV.*

• **sit back** **1** to rest in a comfortable position ○ *Sit back, relax, and enjoy the flight.* **2** To sit back is also to take no action: *You can't just sit back and let them close the library.*

• **sit by** to do nothing when something bad is happening or about to happen ○ *The community will not sit by while others attack their freedom of expression.*

• **sit down** to move from a standing position to a sitting position ○ *They sat down on a park bench.* ○ *She slipped on the ice and sat down with a thump.*

• **sit in** **BE PRESENT** to be present at an event without being involved ○ *Do you mind if I sit in on your class?*

• **sit in** **ACT FOR SOMEONE** **1** to fulfill a responsibility for another person ○ *The vice president will sit in for the president at today's meeting.* **2** A musician who sits in plays music with someone the musician does not usually play with: *Jeanne needed a drummer and asked if I could sit in.*

• **sit on** *something* **NOT USE** to not use something ○ *The supervisors want a tax increase for law enforcement when they are sitting on a huge budget surplus.* ○ *It's hard to imagine how the government could have sat on this information.*

• **sit on** *something* **BE A MEMBER** to be a member of an official group ○ *Our senator sits on the subcommittee for foreign relations.*

• **sit out** *something* [M] to not be involved in something ○ *He sat out the football season because of a contract dispute.* ○ *She knew she couldn't sit this election out, as she had the last one.*

• **sit through** *something* to stay until something is completed ○ *It's hard for little kids to sit through a whole baseball game.*

• **sit up** **STRAIGHTEN** to straighten your body or move into a sitting position ○ *She was finally strong enough to sit up in bed.*

• **sit up** **STAY AWAKE** to stay awake late, esp. past the time that you usually go to bed ○ *We sat up talking until 2 a.m.*

• **sit with** *someone* to be considered by someone ○ *When someone calls you "a woman of letters," how does that sit with you?* ○ *Their long conversations didn't sit well with the boss.*

S

sitcom /ˈsɪt·kɑm/, **situation comedy** *n* [C] a television series in which the same characters are involved in amusing situations in each show

site Ⓐ /sɑɪt/ *n* [C] a place where something is, was, or will be ○ *The fort is now a historic site.* ○ *The fan club has its own Web site.*

sit-in /ˈsɪt̬·ɪn/ *n* [C] ***social studies*** a public event in which a person or group enters a place and refuses to leave until certain demands have been agreed to ○ *Students carried out a sit-in at the governor's office to protest higher tuition costs.*

sitting duck *n* [C] a person or thing in a situation that is easy to attack ○ *A car without side-impact airbags is a sitting duck if it's hit broadside by an SUV.*

situate /ˈsɪtʃ·əˌweɪt/ *v* [T always + adv/prep] to put something in a particular position ○ *The restaurant is situated near the Hudson River.*

situation /ˌsɪtʃ·əˈweɪ·ʃən/ *n* [C] a condition or combination of conditions that exist at a particular time ○ *I was in a situation where I didn't have cash handy.*

situation comedy *n* [C] a SITCOM

sit-up /ˈsɪt̬·ʌp/ *n* [C] an exercise that strengthens your stomach muscles, in which you lie down and lift yourself into a sitting position without using your arms

six /sɪks/ *number* **1** 6 ○ *My sister is six.* ○ *a six-sided figure* **2** Six can also mean six o'clock.

sixth /sɪksθ/ *adj, adv, n* [C] **1** *This skater is ranked sixth in the world.* ○ [C] *We leave on the sixth of June.* **2** A sixth is one of six equal parts of something.

six-pack **DRINKS**, **six pack** *n* [C] a set of six cans or bottles of a drink sold together

MUSCLES, **six pack** *n* [C] a set of well-developed muscles on someone's stomach ○ *I train to be fit for football, but I bare my six-pack on the beach in San Diego.*

sixteen /sɪkˈstiːn/ *number* 16 ○ *Jamie just turned sixteen.* ○ *a sixteen-piece picnic set*

sixteenth /sɪkˈstiːnθ/ *adj, adv, n* [C] **1** *On this list, my name is sixteenth.* ○ [C] *This is the sixteenth of August.* **2** A sixteenth is one of sixteen equal parts of something.

sixteenth note *n* [C] ***music*** a note that is typically equal to half the length of an EIGHTH NOTE ➤ Picture: **notation**

sixth sense *n* [C usually sing] an ability to know something without using the ordinary five SENSES of sight, hearing, smell, touch, and taste ○ *My sixth sense told me something awful was going to happen.*

sixty /ˈsɪk·sti/ *number* 60 ○ *My uncle is sixty.* ○ *a sixty-foot boat*

sixties, **60s**, **60's** /ˈsɪk·stiːz/ *pl n* the numbers 60 through 69 ○ *The temperature is expected to be in the sixties* (= between 60° and 69°). ○ *This building was a concert hall in the sixties* (= between 1960 and 1969). ○ *Uncle Buddy is in his sixties* (= between 60 and 69 years old).

sixtieth /ˈsɪk·stiː·əθ/ *adj, adv, n* [C] **1** *He finished sixtieth in the marathon.* **2** A sixtieth is one of sixty equal parts of something.

size **DEGREE** /sɑɪz/ *n* [C/U] the degree to which something or someone is large or small ○ [C] *an average size* ○ [U] *to double in size* ○ [U] *Have you seen the size of their house?* ○ [C] *Skirts come in many colors and sizes.* ○ [U] *The camera is roughly the size of a business-card case.*

sizable /ˈsɑɪ·zə·bəl/ *adj* large ○ *Emanuel already has a sizable amount of money saved up for college.*

size /ˌsɑɪz/, **sized** /ˌsɑɪzd/ *adj* of a particular size ○ *The house is tiny, just three medium-size rooms and a kitchen.* ○ *We can give you a special rental rate on a full-sized car* (= a large car).

MEASURE /sɑɪz/ *n* [C] one of the standard measures according to which goods are made or sold ○ *She generally wears a size 12.* ○ *What is your shoe size?* ○ *The boxes come in many sizes.*

PHRASAL VERB with **size**

• **size up** *something* [M] to examine something in order to make a judgment or form an opinion ○

After sizing up the opposition, Abe suggested a strategy.

sizzle /ˈsɪz·əl/ *v* [I] to make the sound of food frying ○ *Doughnuts sizzled in the hot fat.* ○ *(fig.) This movie sizzles with excitement.*
sizzle /ˈsɪz·əl/ *n* [U] ○ *(fig.) Their reporting lacks sizzle* (= excitement).

skate /skeɪt/ *n* [C] a special shoe or boot with wheels for moving quickly over a smooth surface, or an ICE SKATE (= shoe with a metal blade for sliding over ice) ○ *I caught my skates in a rut and fell.*
skate /skeɪt/ *v* [I] ○ *She skated over to me.*
skater /ˈskeɪt̬·ər/ *n* [C] ○ *Skaters glided across the ice.*
skating /ˈskeɪt̬·ɪŋ/ *n* [U] ○ *She loves to go skating.*

skateboard /ˈskeɪt·bɔːrd, -bourd/ *n* [C] a short, flat board with small wheels under each end which a person stands on and moves forward by pushing one foot on the ground
skateboard /ˈskeɪt·bɔːrd, -bourd/ *v* [I] ○ *He skateboards to school sometimes.*

skeletal /ˈskel·ət̬·əl/ *adj* of or like a SKELETON (= frame of bones) ○ *skeletal injuries*

skeletal muscle *n* [C] ***biology*** any of the muscles that are connected to the bones and work to create movement of the bones and joints

skeleton /ˈskel·ət·ən/ *n* [C] the frame of bones supporting a human or animal body ○ *We found a deer skeleton.*

IDIOM with **skeleton**

• **a skeleton in the closet** a secret that would cause embarrassment if it were known ○ *Almost everybody has a skeleton in the closet.*

skeleton crew, **skeleton staff** *n* [C] the smallest number of people needed to keep a business or organization operating ○ *On weekends the hospital has a skeleton staff.*

skeptic /ˈskep·tɪk/ *n* [C] a person who doubts the truth or value of an idea or belief
skeptical /ˈskep·tɪ·kəl/ *adj* ○ *They're very skeptical of his motives.*
skepticism /ˈskep·təˌsɪz·əm/ *n* [U] ○ *He displays a healthy skepticism toward his own beliefs.*

sketch DRAWING /sketʃ/ *n* [C] a simple, quickly made drawing ○ *a pen and ink sketch*
sketch /sketʃ/ *v* [I/T] ○ [I] *I like to sketch.*
HUMOROUS PERFORMANCE /sketʃ/ *n* [C] a short, humorous part of a stage, television, or radio show ○ *She helped write a sketch for a comedy show.*
DESCRIPTION /sketʃ/ *n* [C] a short description that does not give many details ○ *a biographical sketch*
sketchy /ˈsketʃ·i/ *adj* not detailed or not complete ○ *Officials provided only sketchy details of the trip.*

PHRASAL VERB with **sketch**

• **sketch in/out** *something* [M] to give some details about something ○ *Sketch out the situation for me.*

skew /skjuː/ *v* [T] to cause information or results to be changed ○ *Biased questions can skew the results.*
skewed /skjuːd/ *adj* ○ *Maybe your world view is a little skewed* (= not accurate). ○ *Her smile is slightly skewed* (= not straight).

skewer /ˈskjuː·ər, skjʊr/ *n* [C] a long, thin rod that is put through pieces of food, esp. meat, for cooking
skewer /ˈskjuː·ər, skjʊr/ *v* [T] ○ *He skewered the onion with a toothpick.*

ski /skiː/ *n* [C] either of a pair of long, narrow pieces of wood or other material which curve up at the front and are fastened to boots so the person wearing them can move quickly and easily over snow
ski /skiː/ *v* [I] **skis**, *pres. part.* **skiing**, *past* **skied** ○ *We skied a lot when we were younger.*
skier /ˈskiː·ər/ *n* [C] ○ *There are lots of skiers on the slopes today.*
skiing /ˈskiː·ɪŋ/ *n* [U] ○ *I'm going skiing.*

skid /skɪd/ *v* [I] **-dd-** (esp. of a vehicle) to slide unintentionally on a surface ○ *His car skidded on a patch of ice.* ○ *(fig.) Stock prices skidded again today* (= they dropped suddenly).
skid /skɪd/ *n* [C] ○ *The roads were slick, and we went into a skid.* ○ *(fig.) They won three games, then went into a skid* (= begin to lose frequently).

IDIOM with **skid**

• **on the skids** failing ○ *Both of the government programs were on the skids.* ○ Compare HIT THE SKIDS at HIT IDIOMS

Skid Row /ˈskɪd ˈroʊ/ *n* [C usually sing] *infml* a street or part of a town that is poor and dirty, where many people who have no jobs or homes spend time

skill /skɪl/ *n* [C/U] a special ability to do something ○ [C] *Schools often do not provide students with marketable skills.* ○ [U] *He lacked skill as a painter.*
skillful /ˈskɪl·fəl/ *adj* ○ *Kraft was a skillful composer.*
skillfully /ˈskɪl·fə·li/ *adv* ○ *Some students are unable to use dictionaries skillfully.*
skilled /skɪld/ *adj* ○ *Many companies depend on skilled labor.*

WORD FAMILY **skill**

Nouns	skill	*Adjectives*	skillful skilled unskilled
Adverbs	skillfully		

WORD CHOICES **skill**

A common phrase which means the same as "skillful" is **good at**.

She's very ***good at*** *dealing with people.*

If someone is skillful and seems to have a special natural ability you could describe that person as **able, gifted,** or **talented.**

She's a very ***able*** *student.*

She's a ***gifted*** *musician.*

He's a very ***talented*** *actor.*

Adept and **deft** are used when someone is very skillful and clever at doing something. ➤

S

*Her movements were **deft** and quick.*
*She's very **adept** at dealing with all management issues.*
Accomplished means skillful, especially when talking about someone who writes, plays music, etc.
*He's an **accomplished** pianist.*
Someone who is skillful because he or she has practiced something a lot can be described as **competent** or **proficient**.
*She's a very **competent** skier.*
*He's a **proficient** horseback rider.*

skillet /ˈskɪl·ət/ *n* [C] a FRYING PAN

skim MOVE ABOVE /skɪm/ *v* [I/T] **-mm-** to move quickly just above or on a surface, or to cause something to move above or on a surface ○ [I] *Skaters skim over the ice.* ○ [T] *I skimmed a pebble across the lake.*

READ QUICKLY /skɪm/ *v* [I/T] **-mm-** to read or look at something quickly to understand the main points, without studying it in detail ○ [T] *You can't just skim the tax forms.* ○ [I] *Skim through this report.*

REMOVE /skɪm/ *v* [T] **-mm-** to remove something solid from the surface of a liquid ○ *Stew the chicken, then skim the fat.*

skim milk, **skimmed milk** *n* [U] milk from which the fat has been removed

skimp /skɪmp/ *v* [I] to use less of something than is necessary ○ *The district skimps on staff training.*

skimpy /ˈskɪm·pi/ *adj* [*-er/-est* only] **1** *skimpy knowledge* **2** Skimpy clothing is made with only a small amount of material: *skimpy swimsuits*

skin BODY COVER /skɪn/ *n* [C/U] the natural outer layer that covers a person or animal ○ [C] *leopard skins* ○ [U] *He had dark, leathery skin.*

skin /skɪn/ *v* [T] **-nn-** to remove skin from an animal, or to rub skin off a part of the body ○ *Bridget fell off her bike and skinned her knee.*

FRUIT/VEGETABLE COVER /skɪn/ *n* [C] the outer covering of some fruits and vegetables ○ *potato skins*

SURFACE /skɪn/ *n* [C/U] a thin, solid surface ○ [C] *Those airplanes have titanium skins to survive the heat.*

IDIOM with **skin**

• **skin and bones** extremely thin ○ *Your brother is just skin and bones - has he been sick?*

skin-deep /ˈskɪn ˈdiːp/ *adj* powerful or strong only in appearance ○ *Her confidence was only skin-deep.*

skinhead /ˈskɪn·hed/ *n* [C] *disapproving* a young person, esp. a man, who has very short hair or no hair, refuses to accept society, and may behave violently toward others

skinny THIN /ˈskɪn·i/ *adj* [*-er/-est* only] very thin ○ *She's shorter and skinnier than me.* ○ *My bike has skinny tires.*

INFORMATION /ˈskɪn·i/ *n* [U] *slang* the true information about someone or something ○ *Get the skinny on hundreds of celebs in our "People Profiles" section.*

skin-tight *adj* (of clothes) fitting very tightly

skip MOVE /skɪp/ *v* [I] **-pp-** to move lightly and quickly, esp. with small dancing or jumping steps ○ *He skipped off to school.*

LEAVE /skɪp/ *v* [I/T] **-pp-** *infml* to leave a place quickly ○ [T] *Mark took the money and then skipped town.*

AVOID /skɪp/ *v* [T] to not do or have something; avoid ○ *Martin skipped fifth grade.* ○ *I skipped lunch today.*

PHRASAL VERBS with **skip**

• **skip out (on** *something/someone***)** to avoid a responsibility, esp. by leaving or not appearing ○ *He explained why he skipped out on a live radio appearance.* ○ *I was hoping I might be able to skip out at 4 o'clock, but my boss wants this done by Monday.*

• **skip over** *something* [M] to avoid reading or looking at something ○ *I usually skip over the boring stuff.*

skipper /ˈskɪp·ər/ *n* [C] *infml* the person in charge of a ship or boat

skirmish /ˈskɜr·mɪʃ/ *n* [C] (in wars) a short fight that is usually not planned and happens away from the main area of fighting, or any short fight ○ *Government troops lost a minor skirmish.* ○ *The court skirmish over video rights to the movie continues.*

skirt CLOTHING /skɜrt/ *n* [C] a piece of women's clothing that hangs from the waist and does not have material between the legs, or the part of a dress below the waist ○ *She looked good in a skirt and blouse.*

GO AROUND /skɜrt/ *v* [T] to go around or move along the edge of something ○ *We were skirting the highways and taking the back roads.*

skit /skɪt/ *n* [C] a short, amusing play ○ *I wrote a skit for my English class.*

skittish /ˈskɪt̬·ɪʃ/ *adj* (of people and animals) nervous and easily frightened ○ *The kitten was really skittish.*

skulk /skʌlk/ *v* [I] to hide or move around as if trying not to be seen, usually with bad intentions ○ *Dogs were skulking in the alleys.*

skull /skʌl/ *n* [C] the bones of the head that surround the brain, or *infml* someone's mind or head ○ *He fractured his skull in an automobile accident.* ○ *(infml) Cartoons will fill your skull full of mush.*

skullcap /ˈskʌl·kæp/ *n* [C] a small, round hat that fits closely on the top of the head, worn esp. by some religious men

skunk /skʌŋk/ *n* [C] a small, furry, black-and-white animal with a large tail, which makes a strong, unpleasant smell as a defense when it is attacked

S

sky /skaɪ/ *n* the area above the earth in which clouds, the sun, and the stars can be seen ○ [U] *White clouds dotted the sky.* ○ [pl] *They strolled beneath clear blue skies.*

IDIOM with sky

• **the sky is the limit** there is no limit ○ *Houseboats can be inexpensive, but on prices for bigger boats the sky is the limit.*

skydiving /ˈskaɪˌdaɪ·vɪŋ/ *n* [U] the sport of jumping from an aircraft and falling through the air before opening a PARACHUTE (= a circular cloth with ropes)

sky-high *adj* at a very high level ○ *Our expectations of him were sky-high.*

skylight /ˈskaɪ·lɑɪt/ *n* [C] a window built into a roof

skyline /ˈskaɪ·lɑɪn/ *n* [C] the shape of objects against the sky, esp. buildings in a city

skyrocket /ˈskaɪˌrɑk·ət/ *v* [I] (esp. of amounts) to rise extremely quickly ○ *The value of their business skyrocketed last year.*

skyscraper /ˈskaɪˌskreɪ·pər/ *n* [C] a very tall building ○ *The restaurant is at the top of one of the big downtown skyscrapers.*

slab /slæb/ *n* [C] a thick, flat, usually square or rectangular piece of a solid substance ○ *a marble slab*

slack NOT TIGHT /slæk/ *adj* [-*er*/-*est* only] not tight; loose ○ *His jaw went slack, and he looked puzzled.*
slacken /ˈslæk·ən/ *v* [I/T] to loosen something, or to become loose ○ [I] *His muscles slackened under the steaming shower.*
slack /slæk/ *n* [U] ○ *There was too much slack in the cable.*

NOT ACTIVE /slæk/ *adj* [-*er*/-*est* only] showing a lack of activity; not busy or happening in a positive way ○ *The teachers are kind of slack about enforcing rules.*
slacken /ˈslæk·ən/ *v* [I/T] to become slower or less busy ○ [T] *Let's slacken our pace a little.*
slacker /ˈslæk·ər/ *n* [C] *infml, disapproving* a person who does not work hard ○ *Dad says my boyfriend's a slacker.*
slack /slæk/ *n*

IDIOM with slack

• **pick up the slack, take up the slack** to improve a situation by doing something that someone else has not done or not completed ○ *With our best player injured, other players have to pick up the slack.*

PHRASAL VERB with slack

• **slack off** to work less hard or to be less than is usual or necessary ○ *Workers tend to slack off on Mondays and Fridays.*

slacks /slæks/ *pl n* a pair of pants ○ *They both wore gray slacks and white shirts.*

slag /slæg/ *n* [U] waste material produced when removing unwanted substances from metals

slain /sleɪn/ *past participle of* SLAY

slake /sleɪk/ *v* [T] to satisfy a need to drink or a desire for something ○ *Two new natural-gas plants should help slake the country's demand for power.*

slalom /ˈslɑl·əm/ *n* [C/U] a race, esp. down a mountain on SKIS, in which the competitors follow a path that curves around a series of poles ○ [C] *He competed in his last World Cup slalom last March.*

slam /slæm/ *v* [I/T] **-mm-** to move against a hard surface with force and usually a loud noise, or to cause something to move this way ○ [I] *The truck slammed into an oncoming car.* ○ [T] *Ray slammed the door shut.*
slam /slæm/ *n* [C usually sing] ○ *He closed the door with a slam.*

slammer /ˈslæm·ər/ *n* [U] *slang* prison ○ *He's doing ten years in the slammer.*

slander /ˈslæn·dər/ *n* [C/U] a false, spoken statement about someone which damages that person's reputation, or the making of such a statement ○ [U] *Political campaigns are full of shameless slander.* ○ Compare LIBEL
slander /ˈslæn·dər/ *v* [T] ○ *Her statement was not meant to slander anybody – it's just descriptive.*
slanderous /ˈslæn·də·rəs/ *adj* ○ *McCarthy unleashed slanderous accusations in every direction.*

slang /slæŋ/ *n* [U] ***English*** very informal language that is used esp. in speech by particular groups of people and which sometimes includes words that are not polite ○ *computer/teenage slang*
slangy /ˈslæŋ·i/ *adj* ○ *a slangy style of writing*

slant LEAN /slænt/ *v* [I] to lean in a diagonal direction, or to cause (something) to slope ○ *Rays of sunlight slanted down on her.*
slant /slænt/ *n* [U] ○ *Most ocean beaches are on a slant.*

OPINION /slænt/ *n* [C] someone's opinion about a subject that is expressed by ignoring or hiding some information and emphasizing other information ○ *He put his own liberal slant on the general's writings.*
slant /slænt/ *v* [T] ○ *He was known to slant reports, writing what his boss wanted to hear.*

slap HIT /slæp/ *v* [T] **-pp-** to hit someone quickly with the flat part of the hand ○ *In the movie, he kisses her and she slaps his face.*
slap /slæp/ *n* [C] ○ *She testified that she had only given her child a slap and had not meant to hurt her.*

PUT QUICKLY /slæp/ *v* [T always + adv/prep] to put or move something quickly or with force ○ *Once I got to the counter, I slapped down my passport.*

IDIOMS with slap

• **a slap in the face** an insult, esp. when it comes as a surprise ○ *It was a real slap in the face when they didn't invite me to the wedding.*
• **a slap on the wrist** a small punishment when a more severe punishment is deserved ○ *They rob someone on the street and they get a slap on the wrist – thirty days in jail.*

S

PHRASAL VERB with slap

• **slap down** *something/someone* [M] to severely criticize or defeat something or someone ○ *She showed no regrets after being slapped down by a panel of judges.*

slapdash /ˈslæp·dæʃ/ *adj* done or made in a hurry and without care

slapstick /ˈslæp·stɪk/ *n* [U] a type of acting intended to be amusing because of the timing of fast physical actions, typically of someone falling or being hit by something or someone

slash REDUCE /slæʃ/ *v* [T] to reduce an amount by a lot ○ *Airfares have been slashed on most domestic routes.*
slash /slæʃ/ *n* [C] ○ *a slash in prices*

CUT /slæʃ/ *v* [I/T] to cut someone or something with a sharp blade in a quick, swinging action ○ [I] *Arauz slashed through brush with a machete.*

SLOPING LINE /slæʃ/ *n* [C] a mark in the form of a sloping line (/), used in signs to mean not permitted, and to separate numbers or words ○ *The no-parking sign had a red slash through a picture of a car.* ○ *Fractions are often written with slashes, for example 2/3.*

slat /slæt/ *n* [C] a thin, narrow piece of wood, plastic, or metal used to make such things as floors, furniture, or window coverings ○ *She closed the slats of the Venetian blinds.*

slate ROCK /sleɪt/ *n* [U] a dark gray rock that can be divided into wide, flat, thin pieces

SCHEDULE /sleɪt/ *v* [T] to schedule or expect to happen ○ *The festival is slated to run here January 28th to February 7th.*

POLITICS /sleɪt/ *n* [C] the people of a particular political party who are trying to be elected to offices in government in an election ○ *The Republicans are expected to announce their slate tomorrow.*

slaughter KILLING ANIMALS /ˈslɔːt̬·ər/ *n* [U] the killing of animals for their meat, or the killing of large numbers of animals in a cruel manner
slaughter /ˈslɔːt̬·ər/ *v* [T] to kill animals, esp. for their meat

KILLING PEOPLE /ˈslɔːt̬·ər/ *n* [U] the killing of large numbers of people ○ *We must find ways of reducing the slaughter on the highways* (= deaths of many people in car accidents).
slaughter /ˈslɔːt̬·ər/ *v* [T] **1** to kill large numbers of people **2** *infml* In sports and other competitions, to slaughter is to defeat easily: *The Red Sox slaughtered the Yankees in last night's baseball game, winning 12 to 0.*

slaughterhouse /ˈslɔːt̬·ərˌhɑʊs/ *n* [C] a place where animals are killed for their meat

slave /sleɪv/ *n* [C] ***social studies*** a person who is legally owned by someone else and has no personal freedom ○ *Born a slave in 1760, he was sold as a child to a farmer in Delaware.*
slavery /ˈsleɪ·və·ri/ *n* [U] ***social studies*** the condition of being legally owned by someone else, or the system in which some people are owned by others
slavish /ˈsleɪ·vɪʃ/ *adj* completely obedient ○ *He was criticized for his slavish devotion to rules and regulations.*

slaw /slɔː/ *n* [U] *short form of* COLESLAW

slay /sleɪ/ *v* [T] *past simp.* **slew**, *past part.* **slain** to kill someone violently ○ *They believe he was slain for organizing workers.*

sleazy /ˈsliː·zi/ *adj* morally bad and low in quality, but trying to attract people by a showy appearance or false manner ○ *He's a sleazy politician who ignored his responsibilities in order to make his friends rich.*

sled /sled/ *n* [C] a vehicle used for carrying people or goods over snow and ice, having narrow strips of wood or metal on the bottom instead of wheels ○ *The children are playing in the snow with their sleds.*
sled /sled/ *v* [I] **-dd-** to ride on a sled over snow or ice, esp. in play

sledgehammer /ˈsledʒˌhæm·ər/ *n* [C] a large, heavy hammer with a long handle, used for jobs like breaking stones or hitting posts into the ground

sleek /sliːk/ *adj* [-er/-est only] (esp. of hair or shapes) smooth, usually curved and shiny, and therefore looking healthy and attractive ○ *The two horses paused, their sleek sides heaving gently as they waited.*

sleep /sliːp/ *n* [U] the resting state in which the body is not active and the mind is unconscious ○ *I usually sit up in bed and watch the TV news before going to sleep.*
sleep /sliːp/ *v* [I/T] *past* **slept** ○ [I] *I was too excited to sleep much that night.* ○ [T] *The boat sleeps four* (= has space for four people to sleep) *comfortably.*
sleeper /ˈsliː·pər/ *n* [C] **1** Someone who is a light sleeper wakes easily, and someone who is a heavy sleeper does not. **2** A sleeper is also a person or thing that is unexpectedly successful: *We almost gave up on this line of merchandise, but it's a real sleeper – it keeps selling.*
sleepless /ˈsliː·pləs/ *adj* [not gradable] without sleeping, or without being able to sleep ○ *I've spent so many sleepless nights worrying about him.*
sleepy /ˈsliː·pi/ *adj* tired and needing sleep
sleepily /ˈsliː·pə·li/ *adv* [not gradable] ○ *She stumbled sleepily into the bathroom.*

WORD FAMILY sleep

Nouns	sleep sleeper	*Adjectives*	asleep sleepless sleepy
Verbs	sleep		
Adverbs	sleepily		

IDIOMS with sleep

• **sleep it off** to stop the bad effects of having too much of something by sleeping for as long as it takes to end those effects ○ *The police let him sleep it off in the cell.*

• **sleep like a log** *infml* to sleep very well, without being woken by any noises ○ *I slept like a log – I didn't even hear the thunderstorm.*
• **sleep on it** to wait before making a decision ○ *Don't give me an answer now – sleep on it and tell me whenever you're ready.*

PHRASAL VERBS with sleep

• **sleep over** to stay the night in someone else's home ○ *If you don't want to drive home this late, you're welcome to sleep over.* ○ Related noun: SLEEPOVER
• **sleep in** to sleep later than you usually do, or later than most people do ○ *Amelia is an early riser, but Gorda sleeps in whenever she can.*

sleeping bag *n* [C] a large bag for sleeping in outside that has layers of material to keep you warm in cold weather

sleeping pill *n* [C] a pill that you take to help you sleep better

sleepover /ˈsliː ˌpoʊ·vər/ *n* [C] a visit to another person's home to spend the night ○ *Games, DVDs, and junk food are sleepover mainstays for both boys and girls.* ○ Related verb: SLEEP OVER

sleepwalking /ˈsliːp ˌwɔː·kɪŋ/ *n* [U] the activity of walking in the night while still sleeping

sleepyhead /ˈsliː·piː ˌhed/ *n* [C] a person, esp. a child, who is tired and looks ready to sleep ○ *Come on, sleepyhead, it's time for bed.*

sleet /sliːt/ *n* [U] rain that is partly frozen ○ *The snow and sleet made driving hazardous.*

sleeve /sliːv/ *n* [C] the part of a piece of clothing that covers some or all of the arm ○ *I wore the black dress with the short sleeves.*
sleeveless /ˈsliːv·ləs/ *adj* [not gradable] (of clothing) without sleeves ○ *a sleeveless blouse/T-shirt*

sleigh /sleɪ/ *n* [C] a large SLED (= vehicle for traveling over snow and ice) pulled by animals, esp. horses ○ *a sleigh ride*

sleight of hand /ˌslɑɪt̬·əv ˈhænd/ *n* [U] speed and skill with the hands when performing tricks that seem to be magic

slender /ˈslen·dər/ *adj* thin ○ *The slender book runs all of 150 pages.* ○ *Sarane is a tall, slender man.*

slept /slept/ *past simple and past participle of* sleep

sleuth /sluːθ/ *n* [C] someone who discovers information about crimes

slew KILL /sluː/ *past simple of* SLAY
LARGE AMOUNT /sluː/ *n* [C usually sing] *infml* a large amount or number ○ *There's a whole slew of new movies that I want to see.*

slice /slɑɪs/ *n* [C] **1** a flat, often thin piece of food that has been cut from a larger piece ○ *a slice of bread/cake/pizza* **2** *fig.* A slice is also any small part that has been separated from something larger: *She demanded a slice of the profits.* **3** If you describe a story as a **slice of life**, you mean that it shows ordinary details of the lives of the people mentioned: *The drama is a slice of life about Puerto Ricans living in the Bronx.*
slice /slɑɪs/ *v* [T] to cut something into thin pieces, or to cut one or more thin pieces from something ○ *Slice the onions and fry them in butter.*

IDIOM with slice

• **any way you slice it, no matter how you slice it** there is only one possible result ○ *Any way you slice it, there are going to be a lot of unhappy people when the winner is announced.*

slick SKILLFUL /slɪk/ *adj* **1** operating or performing skillfully and effectively and without seeming to try hard ○ *Maz was such a slick fielder, one of the best in baseball.* **2** Slick can sometimes mean skillful and effective but lacking in sincerity: *He was a slick politician with an answer for everything.*
SMOOTH /slɪk/ *adj* having a smooth, shiny surface so that you tend to slide when walking or riding on it ○ *roads slick with ice*
slick /slɪk/ *v* [T] to cause hair to be smooth and shiny ○ *His hair was slicked back.*

slicker /ˈslɪk·ər/ *n* [C] a waterproof coat used in wet weather

slide MOVE EASILY /slɑɪd/ *v past* **slid** to cause something to move easily over a surface, or to move in this way ○ [I] *My mother slid into the car seat next to me.* ○ [T] *He slid his hand into his back pocket.*
slide /slɑɪd/ *n* [C] a structure used by children in their play that has a smooth, sloping side which lets them move down quickly from the top to the ground
GET WORSE /slɑɪd/ *v* [I] *past* **slid** to go into a worse state, often through lack of control or care ○ *The stock market crashed in October 1929 and the nation slid into a depression.*
slide /slɑɪd/ *n* [C usually sing] ○ *He felt he was on a downward slide in which nothing was going right in his life.*
PHOTOGRAPH /slɑɪd/ *n* [C] **1** a small piece of film in a frame which, when light is passed through it, shows a photograph on a screen ○ *The art history professor showed us slides of the Parthenon today.* **2** ***science*** In scientific study, a slide is a small piece of glass on which you put something in order to look at it through a MICROSCOPE (= device that makes small objects look larger) and see its structure. ➤ Picture: **microscope**

slide projector *n* [C] a machine that shines a light through a photograph made into a SLIDE to produce a larger image on a screen

slight SMALL IN AMOUNT /slɑɪt/ *adj* [*-er/-est* only] small in amount or degree ○ *He speaks with a slight French accent.* ○ *She had a slight cold, but wasn't feeling too bad.*
slightly /ˈslɑɪt·li/ *adv* ○ *She's slightly taller than her sister.*
THIN /slɑɪt/ *adj* [*-er/-est* only] (of people) thin and delicate ○ *He was a young man of slight build with sensitive eyes and expressive hands.*

S

INSULT /slɑɪt/ *v* [T] to insult someone by not paying attention or by treating the person as unimportant ○ *He slighted his wife by neglecting to introduce her.*

WORD FAMILY slight			
Nouns	slight	*Adverbs*	slightly
Adjectives	slight		

slim /slɪm/ *adj* [-*er*/-*est* only] **-mm- 1** thin, or (esp. of people) attractively thin ○ *She's published several slim volumes of poetry.* **2** Slim also means only a little or not much: *Coaches told him his chances of making the team were slim at best.*

PHRASAL VERB with slim

• **slim down** (of people) to become thinner, or (of things) to become smaller ○ *Regular exercise has helped him slim down considerably.* ○ *Many firms have slimmed down, consolidating some offices and closing others.*

slime /slɑɪm/ *n* [U] a smooth, sticky, liquid substance usually considered unpleasant ○ *A greenish slime covered the surface of the water near the sewer pipe.*

slimy /ˈslɑɪ·mi/ *adj* [-*er*/-*est* only] **1** *slimy seaweed* **2** If you describe a person as slimy, you mean that the person appears to be friendly but cannot be trusted and is not sincere: *He was really a slimy character.*

sling **THROW** /slɪŋ/ *v* [T always + adv/prep] *past* **slung** to throw or drop something quickly and not very carefully ○ *She came in and slung her coat over a chair.*

SUPPORTING DEVICE /slɪŋ/ *n* [C] **1** a device used to support, lift, or carry objects, often by ropes or straps ○ *The helicopter lowered a sling to the boat and rescued the sailor.* **2** *medical* A sling is a piece of material tied around the neck and providing support for a broken or damaged arm while it heals: *They put his arm in a sling.*

slingshot /ˈslɪŋ·ʃɑt/ *n* [C] a Y-shaped stick with a piece of elastic fixed to the top parts, used esp. by children for shooting small stones

S

slink /slɪŋk/ *v* [I always + adv/prep] *past* **slunk** to walk or leave quietly, esp. because you do not want to be noticed or are ashamed of something ○ *I was so embarrassed that I tried to slink away.*

slinky /ˈslɪŋ·ki/ *adj* (of women's clothes) fitting the body closely ○ *I like simple, slinky long dresses.*

slip **SLIDE** /slɪp/ *v* [I] **-pp-** to slide suddenly and without intending to ○ *He slipped on an icy sidewalk and broke his hip.* ○ *The blanket began to slip off my shoulders.*

slippery /ˈslɪp·ə·ri/ *adj* **1** *The sidewalks were slippery with ice.* **2** Slippery also means not certain: *Choosing the perfect juror can be a slippery matter.* **3** *infml* A person who is slippery is someone you feel you cannot trust: *He is a slippery fellow, full of schemes.*

MOVE EASILY /slɪp/ *v* [I/T] **-pp- 1** to move easily and quietly so you are not noticed, or to move something easily into position ○ [I always + adv/prep] *He was able to slip out of the room without disturbing anyone.* ○ [T always + adv/prep] *Ben slipped the credit card into the machine.* ○ [I always + adv/prep] (*fig.*) *While I napped in my chair, the hours slipped by.* **2** If you slip something to someone, you give it to that person without attracting attention: [T always + adv/prep] *I slipped some money to the maitre d' to get a table.* ○ [T always + adv/prep] *She slipped her hand into his.*

GET WORSE /slɪp/ *v* [I] **-pp-** to change to a worse state or condition ○ *We've slipped even further behind schedule.* ○ *After slipping into a coma, he never woke up.*

PIECE OF PAPER /slɪp/ *n* [C] a small piece of paper ○ *You get a slip from the cash machine when you take out money.*

MISTAKE /slɪp/ *n* [C] a mistake that someone makes when the person is not being careful ○ *She has made some slips lately that show she's thinking about other things.*

slip /slɪp/ *v* [I/T] **-pp-** ○ [I] *They slipped up and ordered the wrong part for the car.* ○ [+ *that* clause] *My daughter let the news slip that she is going to get married.*

UNDERWEAR /slɪp/ *n* [C] women's underwear that is shaped like a skirt or a dress

ESCAPE /slɪp/ *v* [I/T] **-pp-** to get away from or get free from something ○ [T] *The dog slipped its leash and ran off.* ○ [I always + adv/prep] *The ball slipped through my fingers.*

WORD FAMILY slip			
Nouns	slip	*Adjectives*	slippery
	slipper	*Verbs*	slip

IDIOMS with slip

• **a slip of the tongue** a mistake made when what someone says is different from what was meant ○ *That one slip of the tongue caused me a lot of trouble.*

• *something* **slips** *your* **mind** to forget something ○ *I was supposed to go to basketball practice, but it completely slipped my mind.*

• *something* **slips through** *your* **fingers** an opportunity to achieve or have something is wasted ○ *This is the best thing that's happened to my career – I can't let it slip through my fingers.*

• *someone* **slips through** *your* **fingers** someone escapes from you ○ *The police let the prisoners slip through their fingers.*

PHRASAL VERBS with slip

• **slip away** **LEAVE** to leave without being noticed ○ *Shortly before midnight, he slipped away to meet her.*

• **slip away** **OPPORTUNITY** (of an opportunity) to no longer be available ○ *His chance at the medal slipped away as his Olympic teammate took the gold.*

• **slip into** *something* to put clothing on quickly and easily ○ *Nancy slipped into her pajamas.*

• **slip off** *something* [M] to remove clothing quickly and easily ○ *She slipped off her gloves.*

• **slip on** *something* [M] to put clothing on quickly and easily ○ *After breakfast, we slipped on our coats.*
• **slip out** *(something)* **LEAVE QUIETLY** to leave quietly or quickly so that no one will notice ○ *He slipped out to make a phone call.* ○ *Before I could say anything she had gathered her books and slipped out the door* (= left quickly through the door).
• **slip out** **BECOME KNOWN** to become known or be spoken unexpectedly ○ *These rude and unappreciated remarks just slipped out when he introduced me.*
• **slip out of** *something* to remove clothing quickly and easily ○ *Rose slipped out of her work clothes.*
• **slip up** to make a small mistake, often as a result of not thinking carefully ○ *It's easy for a journalist to slip up and use somebody else's idea without crediting him or her.* ○ Related noun: SLIP-UP

slipcover /ˈslɪpˌkʌv·ər/ *n* [C] a cover for a chair or SOFA (= seat for two or more people) that is easily removed

slipper /ˈslɪp·ər/ *n* [C] a soft, comfortable shoe worn inside the house

slippery /ˈslɪp·ə·ri/ *adj* ○ See at SLIP **SLIDE**

slipshod /ˈslɪp·ʃɑd/ *adj* showing lack of effort and attention ○ *slipshod repairs*

slip-up *n* [C] a mistake that someone makes by not giving something enough attention ○ *That slip-up cost a lot of money.* ○ Related verb: SLIP UP

slit /slɪt/ *v* [T] *pres. part.* **slitting**, *past* **slit** to make a straight, narrow cut in something ○ *I slit open the envelope with a knife.*
slit /slɪt/ *n* [C] ○ *Cut slits in the piecrust.* ○ *Her eyes are like little slits.*

slither /ˈslɪð·ər/ *v* [I always + adv/prep] to move by twisting or sliding ○ *A long snake slithered toward them.*

sliver /ˈslɪv·ər/ *n* [C] **1** a thin, sharp piece, usually broken off something larger ○ *The glass smashed into slivers.* **2** A sliver is also any narrow or thin piece: *I just want a sliver of cake.*

slob /slɑb/ *n* [C] *infml* **1** a person who is messy, unattractive, and rude ○ *Some guys are real slobs.* **2** A slob is also someone who is just an ordinary person: *a working slob*

slobber /ˈslɑb·ər/ *v* [I] to let SALIVA (= the liquid in the mouth) or other liquid run out of the mouth ○ *No one likes to have a dog slobber on them.*

slog /slɑg, slɔːg/ *v* [always + adv/prep] **-gg-** to walk heavily and with difficulty, or to work hard on something difficult ○ [I] *I slogged through a mess of paperwork.* ○ [T] *We slogged our way through the mud.*

slogan /ˈsloʊ·gən/ *n* [C] a short, easily remembered phrase used to describe the character of something, esp. a political idea or a product ○ *That old campaign slogan really means that there should be jobs and enough food for all citizens.*

slop /slɑp/ *v* [I/T] **-pp-** (of a liquid) to flow or fall over the edge of a container, or to cause a liquid to do this ○ [I] *The coffee slopped onto the tablecloth.*

slope **SURFACE** /sloʊp/ *n* [C] a surface that rises at an angle, esp. a hill or mountain, or the angle at which something rises ○ *Students learn to ski on gentle slopes in a straight line.* ○ *Snow had settled on some of the higher slopes.*
slope /sloʊp/ *v* [I] ○ *The path slopes down to the house.*

MEASURE /sloʊp/ *n* [C] ***geometry*** a measure of how steep an angle a line has

sloppy **CARELESS** /ˈslɑp·i/ *adj* messy or lacking care or attention ○ *sloppy clothes* ○ *a sloppy administrator*
sloppily /ˈslɑp·ə·li/ *adv* ○ *We played sloppily and lost the game.*
sloppiness /ˈslɑp·iː·nəs/ *n* [U] ○ *Such remarkable sloppiness was the result of too much hurry.*

TOO WET /ˈslɑp·i/ *adj* too wet to be pleasant ○ *sloppy weather* ○ *Her grandchildren nearly smothered her with sloppy kisses.*

slosh /slɑʃ, slɔːʃ/ *v* [always + adv/prep] (of a liquid) to hit against the inside of a container, or to cause liquid to move around in this way ○ [I] *Water sloshed over the sides of the pool as the children jumped in.* ○ [T] *John sloshed juice on his jacket by pouring too fast.*

slot **HOLE** /slɑt/ *n* [C] a narrow hole or opening ○ *Drop the letter in the mail slot.*

POSITION /slɑt/ *n* [C] a place or position available to someone or something ○ *Perry will fill one of the open slots on the commission.* ○ *Shaap's program can be heard in the same time slot every morning.*
slot /slɑt/ *v* [T] **-tt-** to put someone or something in a particular position ○ *Weather reports are slotted between commercials.*

sloth /slɔːθ, sloʊθ/ *n* [C] an animal that moves very slowly and spends much of its time hanging by its feet from trees

slot machine *n* [C] a machine on which you play a game of chance each time you put a coin in it

slouch /slɑʊtʃ/ *v* [I] to stand, sit, or walk with the shoulders and head bent forward ○ *In a bad mood, the boy slouched off to the beach.*
slouch /slɑʊtʃ/ *n* [C] ○ *He's developed a slouch from leaning over his books all day.*

slough off *something* /ˈslʌfˈɔːf/ *phrasal verb* [M] **1** to get rid of something, esp. a skin or shell **2** If you slough something off, you treat it as unimportant or do not take it seriously: *Politicians sloughed off the issue.*

slovenly /ˈslʌv·ən·li/ *adj* messy, dirty, or not careful ○ *slovenly work* ○ *a slovenly housekeeper*

slow /sloʊ/ *adj* [-er/-est only] **1** lacking speed; not fast or quick ○ *He was far too slow to catch me.* ○ *We were slow to understand how we could use computers in our work.* **2** A clock or watch that is slow shows a time that is earlier than the correct time.

S

3 A person who is slow does not understand or learn things quickly: *a class for slower students*

slow /sloʊ/ *v* [I/T] ○ [I] *Traffic slowed to a crawl.* ○ [T] *There's still a chance to slow the spread of the disease.*

slow /sloʊ/ *adv* [-*er*/-*est* only] ○ *You're driving too slow.*

slowly /ˈsloʊ·li/ *adv* ○ *The medication took effect slowly.*

PHRASAL VERB with slow

• **slow down** *(something)* [M] to move slower, or to cause someone or something to move slower ○ *The car slowed down, then suddenly pulled away.* ○ *We tried to slow the guy down.* ○ Related noun: SLOWDOWN

slowdown /ˈsloʊ·dɑʊn/ *n* [C] a reduction in speed or activity ○ *Consumer buying has picked up again after a summer slowdown.* ○ Related verb: SLOW DOWN

slow motion *n* [U] action on film that is made to appear slower than it was when it happened ○ *a slow motion replay*

sludge /slʌdʒ/ *n* [U] wet dirt, or any other thick, wet substance ○ *The dirty water left a layer of sludge in the bottom of the pail.*

slug **CREATURE** /slʌg/ *n* [C] **1** a small animal with a soft body like a SNAIL without a shell **2** If you say that someone is a slug, you mean that the person would rather do very little or nothing at all: *I suppose you think I'm a slug for not helping.*

sluggish /ˈslʌg·ɪʃ/ *adj* moving, acting, or working with less than usual speed or energy ○ *a sluggish economy* ○ *a sluggish drain*

BULLET /slʌg/ *n* [C] *infml* a bullet

DRINK /slʌg/ *n* [C] *infml* an amount of a drink that fills your mouth ○ *She took a huge slug of very cold water.*

HIT /slʌg/ *v* [T] **-gg-** *infml* **1** to hit someone hard; PUNCH ○ *He made me so mad I wanted to slug him.* **2** If you slug a baseball, you hit it very hard.

S

COIN /slʌg/ *n* [C] a piece of metal used instead of a coin in a machine ○ *The new toll machines will reject slugs.*

IDIOM with slug

• **slug it out, slug this out** to argue or compete with someone fiercely ○ *The two groups have been slugging it out for years.*

slugger /ˈslʌg·ər/ *n* [C] a baseball player who hits the ball very hard

slum /slʌm/ *n* [C] a very poor and crowded area of a city ○ *She works with children in a rough New Jersey slum.*

slum /slʌm/ *v* [I] **-mm-** *infml* to visit a slum, or to work doing something that is not suitable ○ *Did you feel you were slumming by writing this kind of popular fiction?*

slumber /ˈslʌm·bər/ *n* [C/U] sleep ○ [C] *She felt as if she had awakened from a long slumber.*

slumber /ˈslʌm·bər/ *v* [I] ○ *The small town slumbered in the moonlight.*

slumber party *n* [C] a party in which a group of friends, esp. girls, sleep at one friend's home

slump **FALL** /slʌmp/ *v* [I always + adv/prep] to fall heavily and suddenly ○ *She slumped to the floor in a faint.*

BEND /slʌmp/ *v* [I always + adv/prep] to stand or sit bent over, with the head and shoulders forward; SLOUCH ○ *The old man slumped in his chair, asleep.* ○ *We both slumped against the wall.*

REDUCE SUDDENLY /slʌmp/ *v* [I] to fall suddenly in price, amount, or value ○ *Home computer sales slumped dramatically last year.*

slump /slʌmp/ *n* [C] ○ *a slump in the economy* ○ *The team is in a slump this year.*

slung /slʌŋ/ *past simple and past participle of* SLING

slunk /slʌŋk/ *past simple and past participle of* SLINK

slur **PRONOUNCE BADLY** /slɜr/ *v* [I/T] **-rr-** to pronounce words in a way that is not clear ○ [T] *How can you possibly understand someone who slurs his speech?*

slur /slɜr/ *n* [C] ○ *The injury made her speak with a slur.*

INSULT /slɜr/ *n* [C] words intended to insult someone or injure someone's reputation ○ *He apologized for shouting an ethnic slur at a fan.*

slurp /slɜrp/ *v* [I/T] to make sucking noises while eating or drinking ○ [T] *I wanted to tell him not to slurp his soup.*

slush /slʌʃ/ *n* [U] snow or ice that has started to melt ○ *The city's streets were covered with dirty, gray slush.*

slushy /ˈslʌʃ·i/ *adj* ○ *Slushy snow can be very slippery.*

sly /slɑɪ/ *adj comparative* **slyer**, *superlative* **slyest** not letting others know true opinions or intentions, or dishonest ○ *She thought that by being sly, she could fool people.* ○ *A cat can be a very sly animal.*

slyly /ˈslɑɪ·li/ *adv* ○ *He winked slyly and lowered his voice, as if he had some secret to reveal.*

sly /slɑɪ/ *n* [U]

IDIOM with sly

• **on the sly** secretly ○ *On the sly, Dave was adding chilies to the desserts he made.*

smack **HIT FORCEFULLY** /smæk/ *v* [I/T] to hit someone or something forcefully, usually making a loud noise ○ [T] *I was afraid she was going to smack me.* ○ [I] *The car spun around and smacked into a tree.* ○ [T] *She smacked the ball over the fence.* ○ [M] *He smacked his hand down on the table to get our attention.*

smack /smæk/ *n* [C] ○ *The men were keeping the volleyballs in the air with sure-handed smacks.*

DIRECTLY /smæk/ *adv* [not gradable] directly and with force ○ *He stopped the car so suddenly, the car behind ran smack into him.*

IDIOM with **smack**

• **smack** *your* **lips** to make a noise to show that something is good by opening and closing your lips ○ *The dogs were smacking their lips at the smell of the meat.*

PHRASAL VERB with **smack**

• **smack of** *something* to show or seem to have a characteristic or quality ○ *Their behavior smacks of very bad judgment.*

smack dab, **smack-dab** *adv* exactly in a place or at a time ○ *You called smack dab in the middle of dinner.*

small LESS /smɔːl/ *adj* [*-er/-est* only] **1** not big; less in size or amount than is average ○ *a small business* ○ *small lunches* ○ *He's small for his age.* ○ *Those jackets come in small, medium, and large sizes.* **2** Small (*abbreviation* **S**) is a size of clothing or other product that is smaller than average: *Those sweaters are available in small, medium, and large (sizes).* **3** The **small of your back** is the back below the waist where it curves in slightly.
small /smɔːl/ *adv* [*-er/-est* only] ○ *The ingredients are printed so small I can hardly read them.*

USAGE

small or **little**?

Small refers to size and is the usual opposite of **large**.

Could I have a hamburger and a small Coke please?

Our house is pretty small.

Little refers to size and is the usual opposite of **big** but when used with other adjectives also expresses the speaker's feelings.

They live in a beautiful little town on the river.

Rats are horrible little animals.

WORD CHOICES **small**

Little is a very common alternative to "small," and can describe things or people.

If someone is extremely small, you can say that the person is **tiny**, and if something is extremely small, you can say that it is **minute**, **tiny**, or, in more formal contexts, **microscopic** or **minuscule**.

The Chihuahua is the ***tiniest*** *breed of dog in the world.*

The phone he pulled out of his pocket was ***minute.***

The cost of vaccination is ***minuscule*** *compared to the cost of treatment.*

The adjectives **dwarf** and **miniature** are sometimes used to describe things that are smaller than the normal size.

There were ***dwarf*** *fir trees in pots on the patio.*

It's a ***miniature*** *bath for the doll's house.*

If a person or thing is small in an attractive way, you can use the adjectives **dainty** or **petite**.

She had ***dainty*** *feet.*

Emma was dark and ***petite.***

The adjective **slight** is sometimes used with abstract nouns to describe things that are small and not important.

There was a ***slight*** *difference in color.*

YOUNG /smɔːl/ *adj* [*-er/-est* only] (of children) very young ○ *His mother died when he was small.*

LACKING IMPORTANCE /smɔːl/ *adj* [*-er/-est* only] not having much importance or effect ○ *a small problem* ○ *a small part in a movie*

LETTER SIZE /smɔːl/ *adj* [not gradable] (of a letter of the alphabet) LOWERCASE ○ Compare CAPITAL (LETTER)

IDIOM with **small**

• **a small fortune** an amount of money that seems to be a lot ○ *Getting the car fixed will cost a small fortune.*

small change *n* [U] coins of little value, or a small amount of money ○ *I only had some small change in my pocket.* ○ *The cost of this project is small change compared to the one we'll be starting next year.*

small claims court *n* [C] a court where legal action can be taken against a person who owes a small amount of money

small-minded *adj disapproving* unable to accept different ideas or things that are not familiar

small potatoes *pl n infml* someone or something that is unimportant ○ *Compared to her problems, mine seem like small potatoes.*

smallpox /ˈsmɔːl·pɑks/ *n* [U] an extremely infectious viral disease that causes fever, spots on the skin, and often death ○ *smallpox vaccinations*

small-scale *adj* small, esp. when compared to other things like it ○ *The house is like a small-scale castle.*

small screen *n* [U] television ○ *His novel has been adapted for the small screen.*

small talk *n* [U] social conversation about unimportant things, often between people who do not know each other well ○ *I hate conversation that is nothing but small talk.*

small-time *adj* not very important or successful ○ *a small-time football team* ○ Compare BIG TIME

small-town *adj* of or from a small town, and sometimes having a simple or limited quality ○ *a small-town girl* ○ *small-town politics*

smart INTELLIGENT /smɑrt/ *adj* [*-er/-est* only] **1** intelligent, or able to think and understand quickly in difficult situations ○ *Jed's smart enough to get A's in this class.* ○ *Her daughter is smarter than she is.* ○ *Ginny is a very smart kid.* ○ *Quitting that job was a smart move.* **2** Smart devices are ones that operate using computers: *smart phones* ○ *a smart card*

STING /smɑrt/ *v* [I] to feel a stinging pain ○ *Abby's eyes smarted from the smoke.* ○ *(fig.) Sacramento is still smarting from the loss* (= is upset by it).

STYLISH /smɑrt/ *adj* [-er/-est only] *dated* having a clean, neat, stylish appearance ○ *She wore smart dresses and dashing hats.*

smartly /ˈsmɑrt·li/ *adv dated* **1** *Sid dresses very smartly.* **2** Smartly also means quickly: *Soldiers marched smartly up the avenue.*

smart-aleck *n* [C] *infml* an annoying person who thinks that other people are less intelligent ○ *That kid's a real smart-aleck.*

smart money *n* [U] money invested by experienced people who know a lot about investing money

smash BREAK /smæʃ/ *v* [I/T] to break into small pieces, esp. by hitting or throwing ○ [T] *Some kids smashed her bedroom window.* ○ [I] *Her cup fell and smashed to pieces on the stone floor.* ○ [M] *Police had to smash the door down to get into the house.* ○ [M] *The band reportedly smashed up their hotel room.*

smash /smæʃ/ *n* [U] ○ *I heard a smash and glass breaking.*

HIT /smæʃ/ *v* [I/T] to hit or move with force against something hard, usually causing damage or injury ○ [T] *She smashed her right knee in the accident.* ○ [I] *His car flipped over and smashed into a tree.*

smash /smæʃ/ *n* [C] a forcefully hit ball ○ *Robinson hit a smash to my left.*

DESTROY /smæʃ/ *v* [T] to defeat or destroy completely ○ *The government smashed the rebellion.*

smash (hit) /ˈsmæʃ (ˈhɪt)/ *n* [C] a popular and successful song, play, or movie ○ *a smash hit album* ○ *His first movie was a box-office smash.*

smattering /ˈsmæt̬·ə·rɪŋ/ *n* [C usually sing] a slight knowledge of something, or a small amount ○ *I know a smattering of German.* ○ *There was a smattering of boos when he was introduced.*

smear SPREAD /smɪr/ *v* [T always + adv/prep] to spread something soft or wet over a surface ○ *Mom smeared peanut butter and grape jelly on bagels for lunch.*

smear /smɪr/ *n* [C] ○ *He had a smear of paint on his shirt.*

ACCUSATION /smɪr/ *n* [C] an accusation made publicly with the intention of harming a person's reputation ○ *Throughout the election he had to contend with smears about his personal life.* ○ *She was upset by the smear tactics used by her opponents.*

smear /smɪr/ *v* [T] ○ *He was smeared in the newspapers.*

smell ABILITY /smel/ *n* [U] the ability to notice or discover a substance in the air by using the nose ○ *Smell is one of the five senses.* ○ *Dogs have a very good sense of smell.*

smell /smel/ *v* [I/T] ○ [T] *I have a cold and I can't smell anything.*

CHARACTERISTIC /smel/ *n* [C] the characteristic of something that can be recognized or noticed using the nose ○ *a sweet/strong/unpleasant smell* ○ *the smell of flowers/perfume/coffee/paint* ○ *I woke up to the smell of bacon and eggs.* ○ *I wish we could get rid of that smell in the garage.*

smell /smel/ *v* ○ [I] *My hands smell of onions.* ○ [I] *It smells like you've been baking in here.* ○ [L] *That soup smells good.* ○ [I] *Your feet smell* (= have an unpleasant smell).

smelly /ˈsmel·i/ *adj* having an unpleasant smell ○ *smelly feet* ○ *The basement is damp and smelly.*

> **WORD CHOICES smell**
>
> **Aroma** is often used when a smell is strong and pleasant, especially a smell from food or drink.
>
> *The delicious **aroma** of fresh bread wafted out of the bakery.*
>
> A sweet or pleasant natural smell is a **fragrance**, **perfume**, or **scent**.
>
> *the delicate **fragrance** of the roses*
> *The **perfume** of the flowers filled the room.*
> *She smelled the sweet **scent** of the lilies.*
>
> **Odor** is a slightly more formal word meaning "smell" and is often used when the smell is unpleasant.
>
> *There was the unmistakable **odor** of sweaty feet.*
>
> The word **stench** and the informal words **reek** and **stink** can all be used when a smell is very unpleasant.
>
> *the **stench** of rotting fish*
> *The noisy engines filled the air with the **reek** of gasoline.*
> *There was a bad **stink** in the kitchen.*
>
> If a smell just lasts for a short time, carried on a current of air, you could use the word **whiff**.
>
> *He leaned towards me and I got a **whiff** of garlic.*

DISCOVER /smel/ *v* [T] to become aware of or to discover something using the nose ○ *Just smell this perfume!* ○ *She smelled something burning.* ○ *(fig.) Brenda can smell trouble a mile off.* (= knows when there will be trouble.)

smell /smel/ *n* [U] ○ *Have a smell of this thyme.*

IDIOMS with smell

• **smell fishy** to not seem to be truthful or honest ○ *His excuses smell fishy to me.*

• **smell a rat** to believe something is wrong ○ *When I got an e-mail asking for my password, I should have smelled a rat.*

smelt /smelt/ *v* [T] to obtain a metal from rock by heating it to a very high temperature

smidgen /ˈsmɪdʒ·ən/ *n* [U] *infml* a very small amount ○ *I have a smidgen of hope that things will turn out all right.*

smile /smɑɪl/ *n* [C] an expression on the face in which the ends of the mouth curve up slightly, often with the lips moving apart so that the teeth can be seen, expressing esp. happiness, pleasure, amusement, or a friendly feeling ○ *a big/happy/*

pretty smile ○ *a smile of joy/satisfaction/amusement* ○ *We exchanged smiles as we passed in the hallway.*
smile /smɑɪl/ *v* [I/T] ○ [I] *I couldn't help smiling.* ○ [I] *When he smiled at me, I knew everything was OK.* ○ [I] *She smiled to herself.* ○ [T] *He smiled a happy smile.*
smiley /ˈsmɑɪ·li/ *adj infml* ○ *He's a very smiley, friendly baby.*

USAGE
smile
Be careful to use the preposition **at** after the verb **smile** if you are smiling in someone's direction.
She smiled at the little girl.
~~*She smiled to the little girl.*~~

smiley face *n* [C] *infml* a drawing that represents a person smiling, using a simple circle for the head and two spots and a curve for the eyes and mouth

smirk /smɜrk/ *v* [I] to smile in a way that expresses satisfaction with yourself or pleasure about having done something or knowing something that is not known by someone else ○ *When she told him he was cool, he just smirked.*
smirk /smɜrk/ *n* [C] ○ *Her lips curled into a smirk.*

smithereens /ˌsmɪð·əˈriːnz/ *pl n* a lot of small, broken pieces ○ *The vase smashed to smithereens when it fell.*

smitten /ˈsmɪt·ᵊn/ *adj* [not gradable] strongly influenced by someone or feeling the effects of something ○ *He's clearly smitten with publicity.* ○ *Howard was smitten by her beauty.*

smock /smɑk/ *n* [C] a piece of clothing like a long shirt that is worn loosely over other clothing to protect it when working ○ *an artist's smock* ○ *a painting/gardening smock*

smog /smɑg, smɔːg/ *n* [C/U] air POLLUTION caused by smoke or chemicals mixing with fog ○ [U] *We get a lot of smog downtown.* ○ [C] *A poisonous smog killed 20 people.*
smoggy /ˈsmɑg·i, ˈsmɔː·gi/ *adj* ○ *a smoggy city/day*

smoke CLOUDY AIR /smoʊk/ *n* [U] a cloudy gray or black mixture of air and very small pieces of carbon produced by something that is burning ○ *The building filled with smoke.* ○ *Nobody died in the fire, but three people were treated for smoke inhalation.*
smoke /smoʊk/ *v* [I] to produce or give off smoke ○ *The oil in the frying pan started smoking.*
smokeless /ˈsmoʊ·kləs/ *adj* ○ *smokeless candles*
smoky, **smokey** /ˈsmoʊ·ki/ *adj* ○ *The chicken has a nice smoky flavor.*

BREATHE SMOKE /smoʊk/ *v* [I/T] to breathe smoke into the mouth or lungs from burning tobacco
smoke /smoʊk/ *n* [C] an act of smoking
smokeless /ˈsmoʊ·kləs/ *adj* (of tobacco) chewed and not burned or smoked
smoker /ˈsmoʊ·kər/ *n* [C] someone who smokes
smoking /ˈsmoʊ·kɪŋ/ *n* [U] the action or activity of smoking ○ *Smoking is not permitted.*
smoky, **smokey** /ˈsmoʊ·kɪ/ *adj* filled with smoke

PRESERVE /smoʊk/ *v* [T] to preserve and add a smoky flavor to meat, fish, or cheese using smoke from burning wood ○ *They smoke the fish over wood chips.*

WORD FAMILY smoke

Nouns	smoke smoker nonsmoker smoking	*Adjectives*	smoked smoking smokeless nonsmoking smoky
Verbs	smoke		

PHRASAL VERB with smoke

• **smoke** *someone* **out** [M] to force someone to leave a hiding place ○ *He didn't just walk in and surrender, we had to smoke him out.*

smoke detector *n* [C] a device that makes a loud noise when smoke is present to warn of a possible fire

smoke screen *n* [C] something that hides the truth about a person's actions or intentions ○ *The story served as a useful smoke screen to conceal where he really got the money.*

smokestack /ˈsmoʊk·stæk/ *n* [C] a tall, vertical pipe through which smoke or steam leaves a building or engine

smoking gun *n* [C] information that proves who committed a crime ○ *The tapes provided prosecutors with the smoking gun they needed.*

smolder /ˈsmoʊl·dər/ *v* [I] **1** to burn slowly with smoke but without flames ○ *The fire was still smoldering the next morning.* **2** If a strong emotion smolders, it continues to exist but is not expressed: *This issue has been smoldering all week.*

smooch /smuːtʃ/ *v* [I] *infml* to kiss someone
smooch /smuːtʃ/ *n* [C usually sing] *infml* ○ *She gave her husband a smooch on the way out.*

smooth REGULAR /smuːð/ *adj* [-er/-est only] having a surface or substance that is perfectly regular and has no holes or lumps or areas that rise or fall suddenly ○ *a smooth surface* ○ *Mix together the butter and sugar until smooth.* ○ *The baby's skin is so smooth!*
smooth /smuːð/ *v* [T] ○ *Use fine sandpaper to smooth the surface before varnishing.* ○ *She smoothed the wrinkles from her skirt.*
smoothness /ˈsmuːð·nəs/ *n* [U] ○ *I love the smoothness of silk.*

NOT INTERRUPTED /smuːð/ *adj* [-er/-est only] happening without any sudden changes, interruption, inconvenience, or difficulty ○ *a smooth ride/flight* ○ *The bill had a smooth passage through both houses of Congress.*
smooth /smuːð/ *v* [T] ○ *We must do more to smooth the country's path to democratic reform.*
smoothly /ˈsmuːð·li/ *adv* ○ *Oil is used to make the parts of a machine move smoothly when they*

rub together. ○ *It's nice to work in such a smoothly run office.*

smoothness /ˈsmuː·ð·nəs/ *n* [U] ○ *The car delivers power with the smoothness of a jet engine.*

POLITE /smuːð/ *adj* [-er/-est only] polite, confident, and persuasive, esp. in a way that lacks sincerity ○ *I trust an honest face more than a smooth talker.*

WORD FAMILY smooth			
Nouns	smoothness	*Verbs*	smooth
Adjectives	smooth	*Adverbs*	smoothly

PHRASAL VERBS with smooth

• **smooth down** *something* [M] to make something flat ○ *He straightened his tie nervously and smoothed down his hair.*

• **smooth out** *something* [M] to reduce or remove differences or changes in something ○ *You can use a sander to smooth out any small dents in the frame.* ○ *They're working to smooth out the wild swings in the cost of oil.*

• **smooth over** *something* [M] to make less serious or easier to solve ○ *Negotiators have been able to smooth over differences in one area of disagreement.*

smooth muscle *n* [C] ***biology*** a VISCERAL MUSCLE

smorgasbord /ˈsmɔːr·gəsˌbɔːrd, -ˌbourd/ *n* [C] a mixture of many different hot and cold dishes that are arranged so that you can serve yourself as much as you want; a BUFFET ○ *We'll have a smorgasbord at the party.* ○ *(fig.) Candidates offered a smorgasbord of reforms* (= a large variety of them).

smother **PREVENT BREATHING** /ˈsmʌð·ər/ *v* [T] **1** to prevent a person or animal from getting oxygen ○ *Several animals were smothered by smoke from the fire.* **2** To smother someone is to kill someone by covering the person's face, making it impossible to breathe.

COVER /ˈsmʌð·ər/ *v* [T] to cover most or all of a surface ○ *The pasta was smothered with a creamy sauce.*

STOP FIRE /ˈsmʌð·ər/ *v* [T] to stop a fire from burning by covering it with something that prevents air from reaching it ○ *Firefighters smothered the blaze with chemical foam.*

GIVE LOVE /ˈsmʌð·ər/ *v* [T] to give someone you love too much attention and make the person feel less independent ○ *He felt smothered by her love.*

smudge /smʌdʒ/ *n* [C] a mark left on a surface, usually unintentionally, from having touched something wet or sticky ○ *Trev wiped a smudge of chocolate from the side of his mouth.*

smudge /smʌdʒ/ *v* [T] **1** *She was sweaty and her face was smudged with dirt.* **2** If you smudge something that is neat, you make it messy: *She draws a line and then smudges it with her finger.*

smug /smʌg/ *adj* [-er/-est only] **-gg-** *disapproving* very pleased and satisfied with yourself, and having no doubt about the value of what you know or have done ○ *His attitude showed a smug indifference to the hardships others faced.*

smuggle /ˈsmʌg·əl/ *v* [T] to take things or people to or from a country or place illegally and secretly ○ *He caught trying to smuggle goods across the border.*

smuggler /ˈsmʌg·lər/ *n* [C] ○ *drug smugglers*

smut /smʌt/ *n* [U] pictures, writing, language, or performances that deal with sex and are offensive

smutty /ˈsmʌţ·i/ *adj*

snack /snæk/ *n* [C] a small amount of food, esp. when eaten between meals

snack bar *n* [C] a place where you can buy small amounts of food that are packaged or ready to eat ○ *The snack bar on the train is open now.*

snafu /snæˈfuː/ *n* [C] a situation in which nothing happens as planned and everything goes wrong ○ *The snowstorm created a terrible snafu at the airport, with hundreds of passengers waiting for flights to be rescheduled.*

snag **PROBLEM** /snæg/ *n* [C] a problem or difficulty that stops or slows the progress of something ○ *The team was close to signing him to a long-range contract, but talks have hit a snag.*

BECOME CAUGHT /snæg/ *v* [I/T] **-gg-** to catch on something sharp or rough and become damaged ○ [T] *Be careful not to snag your sweater on the rose bushes.*

snag /snæg/ *n* [C] a tear, hole, or loose fiber in a piece of clothing or cloth caused by a sharp or rough object ○ *a snag in a stocking*

OBTAIN /snæg/ *v* [T] **-gg-** *infml* to obtain or catch something by acting quickly ○ *I hoped to snag a good job.*

snail /sneɪl/ *n* [C] a small animal that has a shell and moves very slowly

IDIOM with snail

• **at a snail's pace** extremely slowly ○ *The roads were jammed with cars, and we were moving at a snail's pace.*

snail mail *n* [U] *infml* mail that is sent through the post office, esp. in comparison with E-MAIL

snake **ANIMAL** /sneɪk/ *n* [C] an animal with a long, cylindrical body and no legs

TWIST /sneɪk/ *v* [I always + adv/prep] to move along a route that includes a lot of twists or bends ○ *People spent hours waiting in lines that snaked around the stadium to get tickets.*

snap **BREAK** /snæp/ *v* [I/T] **-pp-** **1** to break something quickly with a cracking sound ○ [I] *High winds caused some power lines to snap, and we lost our electricity.* **2** *fig.* People who snap suddenly lose control of their behavior when they experience very strong emotions: [I] *His lawyer said he just snapped.*

snap /snæp/ *n* [C usually sing] the act of breaking something stiff, or the cracking sound made when it breaks ○ *The plastic handle broke with a loud snap.*

MOVE QUICKLY /snæp/ *v* **-pp-** **1** to move (something) or change into a new position quickly ○ [M]

The sudden stop of the car snapped his head back. **2** If you snap your fingers, you make a sudden, cracking noise by pushing a finger against the base of your thumb, usually in order to get someone's attention.

FASTEN/CLOSE /snæp/ *v* [I/T] **-pp- 1** to make a quick, cracking sound by suddenly bringing together the two parts of something ○ [T] *She snapped her briefcase shut and marched out of the room.* **2** If a dog snaps at you, it suddenly tries to bite you.

snap /snæp/ *n* [C usually pl] ○ *The shirt fastens with snaps.*

SPEAK /snæp/ *v* [I/T] **-pp-** to speak or say something suddenly in anger ○ [I] *Don't snap at your brother like that.*

TAKE PHOTOGRAPHS /snæp/ *v* [T] **-pp-** to use a camera to take a photograph without spending a lot of time doing it ○ *Washington is full of tourists snapping pictures of each other.*

SOMETHING EASY /snæp/ *n* [C usually sing] *infml* something that can be done without any difficulty ○ *Thinking that the exam would be a snap, she didn't bother to study for it.*

SUDDEN /snæp/ *adj* done suddenly without allowing time for careful thought or preparation ○ *Don't make a snap decision – take some time to think it over.*

IDIOM with **snap**

• **snap out of it, snap out of** *something* to stop experiencing something unpleasant or stop behaving in a negative way ○ *I was depressed, and I couldn't snap out of it.* ○ *Johnson has finally snapped out of a four-week hitting slump.*

PHRASAL VERB with **snap**

• **snap up** *something* [M] to buy or obtain something quickly and enthusiastically ○ *Tickets for the concert were snapped up within three hours of going on sale.*

snapdragon /ˈsnæpˌdræg·ən/ *n* [C] a garden plant with white, yellow, pink, or red flowers that open like a pair of lips when they are pressed

snapper /ˈsnæp·ər/ *n* [C] an edible fish that lives in warm seas

snappy /ˈsnæp·i/ *adj* **1** immediately effective in getting people's attention or communicating an idea ○ *The music video was full of snappy editing and atmospheric lighting.* **2** Snappy also means stylish and attractive: *a snappy dresser/outfit*

snapshot /ˈsnæp·ʃɑt/ *n* [C] an informal photograph

snare /sner, snær/ *n* [C] **1** a device for catching small animals, usually with a rope or wire that tightens around the animal **2** A snare is also a trick or situation that deceives you or involves you unexpectedly in a problem: *The legal system is full of snares for the unwary.*

snare /sner, snær/ *v* [T] to get or achieve something that is difficult to get ○ *Arriving in Nashville, she had hopes of snaring a country-music record contract.*

snarl **THREATEN** /snɑrl/ *v* [I/T] (esp. of dogs) to make a fierce sound while showing the teeth, or (of people) to speak or say something in an angry and fierce way ○ [I] *"What do you want?" he snarled.*

snarl /snɑrl/ *n* [C]

STOP MOVEMENT /snɑrl/ *v* [I/T] to make or become stuck, knotted, or blocked, and so unable to move easily ○ [T] *The collision snarled traffic for 10 miles on the Interstate.*

snatch /snætʃ/ *v* [T] **1** to take hold of something suddenly and without warning ○ [M] *They snatched up their coats and hats and ran outside.* ○ *Somebody snatched her purse when she wasn't looking.* **2** To snatch something is to do it in the short amount of time available: *We rushed in and snatched the best seats we could get.*

snatch /snætʃ/ *n* [C] a brief part (of something) ○ *I could hear snatches of conversation from the people in the booth next to ours.*

snazzy /ˈsnæz·i/ *adj infml* modern and stylish in a way that attracts attention ○ *snazzy computer graphics*

sneak /sniːk/ *v* [always + adv/prep] *past* **sneaked, snuck** to go or do something secretly, or take someone or something somewhere secretly ○ [I always + adv/prep] *He sneaked out of the house, going out through the back way.* ○ [T] *I sneaked a look at my watch.* ○ [T] *Make sure you sneak a little bit of protein into your snacks.* ○ [I always + adv/prep] *He snuck out of the budget meeting and went back to the lab.*

sneaky /ˈsniː·ki/ *adj* secretive or dishonest ○ *sneaky tricks* ○ *a sneaky way to raise taxes*

PHRASAL VERB with **sneak**

• **sneak up (on** *someone***) 1** to approach someone quietly and surprise that person ○ *Overton sneaked up behind Brown and knocked the ball out of bounds.* **2** If an event or day sneaks up on you, it arrives before you are ready for it.

sneaker /ˈsniː·kər/ *n* [C] a light shoe that has a top made of cloth and a bottom made of rubber, worn esp. for sports

sneaking /ˈsniː·kɪŋ/ *adj* [not gradable] (of feelings or thoughts) slowly becoming stronger ○ *I have a sneaking suspicion that I need more memory in my computer.*

sneer /snɪr/ *v* [I/T] to show in an expression on your face or in your manner of speaking that someone or something is so foolish that it deserves to be ridiculed ○ [I] *You may sneer (at it), but a lot of people like this kind of music.*

sneer /snɪr/ *n* [C] ○ *"Is that the best you can do?" he asked with a sneer.*

sneeze /sniːz/ *v* [I] to send air out from the nose and mouth in an explosive way that you cannot control ○ *I don't know why, but I couldn't stop sneezing.*

sneeze /sniːz/ *n* [C]

snicker /ˈsnɪk·ər/ *v* [I] *infml* to laugh quietly at someone or something that you think is silly or

S

slightly ridiculous ○ *The audience of sportswriters tried to keep from snickering, but failed miserably.*
snicker /ˈsnɪk·ər/ *n* [C]

snide /snɑɪd/ *adj* containing indirect and unkind criticism ○ *snide remarks*

sniff **SMELL** /snɪf/ *v* [I/T] **1** to smell something by taking in air through the nose ○ [T] *Jack crushed a bit of dried grass between his fingers and sniffed its scent.* **2** To sniff is also to quickly take in a breath through the nose.
sniff /snɪf/ *n* [C]

SHOW DISAPPROVAL /snɪf/ *v* [I/T] to express a bad opinion of something or someone; to show disapproval ○ [I] *The museum's front lawn does not need to be cluttered with silly pop art, sniffed a newspaper editorial.*

PHRASAL VERB with **sniff**

• **sniff out** *something* [M] to discover something, usually only after a special effort ○ *Professors are always trying to sniff out plagiarized term papers.*

sniffle /ˈsnɪf·əl/ *v* [I] to take in air through the nose repeatedly in a way that others can hear, usually because you are crying or because you have a cold ○ *I could hear her sniffling into her handkerchief.*
sniffle /ˈsnɪf·əl/ *n* [C] The sniffles is a slight cold.

snip /snɪp/ *v* [T] **-pp-** to cut something, usually with a few quick actions using SCISSORS (= cutting device with two blades) or a similar device ○ *I asked the barber just to snip the ends of my hair.*
snip /snɪp/ *n* [C]

snipe /snɑɪp/ *v* [I] to criticize, esp. in a mean way because you are annoyed or angry ○ *Frustrated by the war, Republicans and southern Democrats contented themselves with sniping at the president.*

sniper /ˈsnɑɪ·pər/ *n* [C] someone who, while hidden, tries to shoot a person with a gun

snippet /ˈsnɪp·ət/ *n* [C] a small bit or part of something ○ *I'll watch snippets of baseball games, but I just don't have that much time to sit and watch the whole thing.*

S

snit /snɪt/ *n* [C] *infml* an angry mood ○ *He's in a snit because his train was late.*

snitch **TELL SECRETLY** /snɪtʃ/ *v* [I] *infml* to secretly tell someone in authority that someone else has done something bad, often in order to cause trouble ○ *If you keep snitching on your friends, you won't have many left.*
snitch /snɪtʃ/ *n* [C] *infml* ○ *Don't be a snitch.*

STEAL /snɪtʃ/ *v* [T] *infml* to steal, or to take without permission ○ *I snitched a pencil from your desk – hope you don't mind.*

snob /snɑb/ *n* [C] **1** a person who judges the importance of people mainly by their social position or wealth, and who believes social position or wealth make one person better than others **2** Snobs can also be people who give a very high value to any quality which they believe they have that makes them better than other people: *intellectual snobs*

snobbish /ˈsnɑb·ɪʃ/, **snobby** /ˈsnɑb·i/ *adj* ○ *a snobbish remark*
snobbery /ˈsnɑb·ə·ri/, **snobbishness** /ˈsnɑb·ɪʃ·nəs/ *n* [U]

snoop /snuːp/ *v* [I] *infml* to look around a place secretly in order to discover things about it or the people connected with it ○ *You have no business snooping around my office.*
snoop /snuːp/ *n* [C] *infml*

snooty /ˈsnuːt̬·i, ˈsnʊt̬·i/ *adj infml* seeming by your manner to think that you are better than everyone else ○ *Some snooty kid opened the door and told me to use the side entrance.*

snooze /snuːz/ *v* [I] *infml* to sleep lightly for a short time ○ *The dog was snoozing in front of the fire.*
snooze /snuːz/ *n* [C] *infml*

snore /snɔːr, snoʊr/ *v* [I] to make loud noises as you breathe while you are sleeping ○ *My husband snores so loudly it keeps me awake at night.*
snore /snɔːr, snoʊr/ *n* [C]

snorkel /ˈsnɔːr·kəl/ *n* [C] a tube that lets you breathe while swimming under water by keeping one end in the mouth while the other end sticks up above the surface of the water
snorkeling /ˈsnɔːr·kə·lɪŋ/ *n* [U] ○ *We went snorkeling off the coast of Key West.*

snort /snɔːrt/ *v* [I/T] **1** to make an explosive sound by forcing air quickly through the nose **2** To snort is also to express strong negative feelings, esp. by making a sound: [T] *She snorted her disapproval and walked away.*
snort /snɔːrt/ *n* [C] ○ *The teacher's explanation drew snorts of laughter from the students.*

snot /snɑt/ *n* [U] *slang* a green or yellow substance sometimes produced in the nose, esp. when a person has a cold

snotty /ˈsnɑt̬·i/ *adj infml* rude and showing a lack of respect for others, esp. because you think you are better than they are ○ *He has three snotty teenage daughters.*
snot /snɑt/ *n* [C] *infml* a person who is disliked for being rude and lacking respect for others ○ *I remember this one little snot in my class who always talked back to the teacher.*

snout /snɑʊt/ *n* [C] the nose and mouth that stick out from the face of some animals ○ *a dog's snout*

snow **WEATHER** /snoʊ/ *n* [C/U] water that falls from clouds as soft, white FLAKES (= thin pieces) of ice when it is cold, or an amount of these flakes ○ [U] *Six inches of snow fell overnight.* ○ [C] *We have had several snows in the past week.*
snow /snoʊ/ *v* [I] ○ *It snowed all weekend.*
snowy /ˈsnoʊ·i/ *adj* ○ *It was one of the snowiest winters on record.*

DECEIVE /snoʊ/ *v* [T] *infml* to deceive someone with charming, persuasive talk ○ *This guy is very smooth and can snow anybody.*

IDIOM with **snow**

• **snowed under** having too much to do ○ *I am totally snowed under at school*

PHRASAL VERB with snow

• **snow** *someone/something* **in** [M] to be unable to leave because of too much snow ○ *Many people were snowed in by Tuesday's storm.*

snowball **BALL OF SNOW** /ˈsnoʊ·bɔːl/ *n* [C] snow pressed into a ball

INCREASE QUICKLY /ˈsnoʊ·bɔːl/ *v* [I] to grow quickly in size or importance ○ *Public support for military action has snowballed.*

snowboard /ˈsnoʊ·bɔːrd, -boʊrd/ *n* [C] a board shaped like a wide SKI that you stand on to slide on the snow

snowbound /ˈsnoʊ·bɑʊnd/ *adj* [not gradable] unable to go anywhere because the snow is too deep

snowdrift /ˈsnoʊ·drɪft/ *n* [C] a hill of snow created by the wind ○ *There were some snowdrifts as high as twenty feet.*

snowfall /ˈsnoʊ·fɔːl/ *n* [U] the amount of snow that falls during a period of time or in a place

snowflake /ˈsnoʊ·fleɪk/ *n* [C] a single piece of snow that falls from the sky

snowmobile /ˈsnoʊ·moʊˌbiːl/ *n* [C] a small motor vehicle for traveling over snow

snowplow /ˈsnoʊ·plɑʊ/ *n* [C] a large blade attached to the front of a truck that pushes snow off roads

snowstorm /ˈsnoʊ·stɔːrm/ *n* [C] a storm that brings a lot of snow and usually strong winds

snow tire *n* [C] a vehicle tire designed to prevent sliding on ice or snow

snub /snʌb/ *v* [T] **-bb-** to treat someone rudely, esp. by ignoring that person ○ *They're likely to snub people who aren't just like them.*

snub /snʌb/ *n* [C] ○ *She was annoyed by their snubs.*

snuck /snʌk/ *past simple and past participle of* SNEAK

snuff /snʌf/ *n* [U] tobacco in the form of a powder that people breathe in through their noses

PHRASAL VERBS with snuff

• **snuff out** *something* **STOP FLAME** [M] to stop a flame from burning, usually by covering it ○ *The child was allowed to snuff out the candles.*

• **snuff out** *something* **END** [M] to end something ○ *There is concern that overfishing could snuff out some species.* ○ *His political career was snuffed out in its prime.*

snug **WARM** /snʌg/ *adj* [-er/-est only] **-gg-** warm, comfortable, and protected ○ *Are you nice and snug in that sleeping bag?*

snugly /ˈsnʌg·li/ *adv* [not gradable] ○ *The cat curled up snugly in the armchair.*

CLOSE FITTING /snʌg/ *adj* fitting closely or tightly ○ *snug blue jeans*

snugly /ˈsnʌg·li/ *adv* [not gradable] ○ *His vest fitted snugly.*

snuggle /ˈsnʌg·əl/ *v* [I always + adv/prep] to move close to someone for affection, warmth, or comfort, or to arrange something around yourself ○ *They snuggled together on the couch.*

so **TO SUCH A DEGREE** /soʊ, sə/ *adv* [not gradable] to such a great degree; very ○ *He's so stupid he'd believe anything you tell him.* ○ *Our families live so far away.*

SIMILARLY /soʊ/ *adv* [not gradable] (used usually before the verbs have, be, do, and other auxiliary verbs) in the same way; similarly ○ *He was interested, and so were a lot of other people.*

IN ORDER THAT /soʊ/ *conjunction* in order that, or with the result that ○ *They moved so they could be closer to her family.*

THEREFORE /soʊ, sə/ *conjunction* and for that reason; therefore ○ *My knee started hurting, so I stopped running.*

IT IS THE SITUATION /soʊ/ *adj, adv* [not gradable] (used instead of repeating something that has just been mentioned) it is the situation ○ *"I hope our paths cross again." "I hope so too."*

TRUE /soʊ/ *adv* [not gradable] true, or truly ○ *He thinks I'm out to get him, but that simply isn't so.*

IN THIS WAY /soʊ/ *adv* [not gradable] **1** more or less like this or in this way ○ *Grandpa could be generous when he so desired.* **2** So is also used to suggest the approximate size of someone or something: *The box is about so big.*

IDIOMS with so

• **in so many words** directly ○ *I have never lied to him in so many words.*

• **so much** to a great degree or very much ○ *She wanted to go so much.*

• **so much as** but rather ○ *I didn't listen so much as survive the conversation.*

• **so much so** to such a great degree ○ *It was a great project, so much so that it won first prize.*

• **so what** *infml* it is of no importance ○ *"We are not supposed to be here." "So what?"*

• **so there** *infml* it cannot be doubted or questioned ○ *I said that book would be a hit, and it was. So there!*

• **so be it** it is necessary to accept the situation as it exists ○ *If she spends all her money on clothes, so be it!*

• **so far** at this particular time ○ *So far, only two Democrats have entered the race for governor.*

• **so far, so good** satisfactory up to this particular time ○ *"How's your new job?" "So far, so good."*

• **so help me** this is true ○ *So help me, they were having so much fun they didn't hear me come in.*

• **so long** goodbye ○ *So long, see you Thursday.*

• **so long as** only if ○ *I'll lend you the money so long as you'll pay me back.*

• **so much for** that is the end of ○ *"It's raining." "So much for our day at the beach."*

• **so to speak** this is one way to say it ○ *I am a writer, so to speak.* ○ **USAGE:** Used to suggest that some people may not think this is a good way to say something. ○ Compare IF YOU WILL at IF IDIOMS

So. *adj, n* [U] *abbreviation for* SOUTH *or* SOUTHERN

S

soak MAKE WET /soʊk/ *v* [I/T] **1** to make something very wet, or of a liquid to be absorbed ○ [T] *The hikers got soaked in the downpour.* ○ [I] *Water soaked through my shoes.* **2** To soak something means to leave it in liquid for a period of time, esp. to clean or soften it: [T] *Let's just soak the dishes.*
soaking /ˈsoʊ·kɪŋ/, **soaking wet** /ˌsoʊ·kɪŋ ˈwet/ *adj* ○ *It's so humid that my shirt is soaking wet before I leave the house.*

CHARGE /soʊk/ *v* [T] *slang* to charge someone too much money ○ *I got soaked for the cab ride.*

PHRASAL VERB with soak

• **soak up** *something* [M] to absorb or enjoy something that exists around you ○ *I just want to lie on the beach and soak up the sun.* ○ *She soaks up everything that's said in class.*

so-and-so /ˈsoʊ·ənˌsoʊ/ *n* [C] *pl* **so-and-sos** *infml* **1** (used instead of an actual name) a particular person or thing ○ *He asked if I knew where so-and-so lives.* **2** If you say that someone is a so-and-so, you do not have a good opinion of that person: *You can't trust that so-and-so.*

soap /soʊp/ *n* [U] a substance used with water for washing or cleaning, or a block of this substance ○ *liquid soap*
soap /soʊp/ *v* [I/T] to rub or cover someone or something with soap ○ [I] *He soaped up and then rinsed off.*
soapy /ˈsoʊ·pi/ *adj* containing soap ○ *Wash your hands in soapy water.*

soap opera /ˈsoʊp ˌɑp·rə/, *infml* **soap** /soʊp/ *n* [C] a television program, usually broadcast five days a week, about the lives of a particular group of characters

soapsuds /ˈsoʊp·sʌdz/ *pl n* bubbles that form when soap is mixed with water

soar INCREASE QUICKLY /sɔːr, soʊr/ *v* [I] to increase or go up quickly to a high level ○ *temperatures/prices soared* ○ *My spirits soared when I heard the good news.*

RISE IN AIR /sɔːr, soʊr/ *v* [I] **1** (esp. of a bird or aircraft) to rise or fly high in the air ○ *Planes soared overhead.* **2** If you say that a mountain, building, or other object soars, you mean that it has great height: *The mountain soars 10,000 feet above the village.*

S

sob /sɑb/ *v* [I/T] **-bb-** to cry in a noisy way, taking in sudden, short breaths
sob /sɑb/ *n* [C] ○ *I never heard such sobs.*

sober NOT DRUNK /ˈsoʊ·bər/ *adj* having had no alcohol; not drunk ○ Related noun: SOBRIETY

SERIOUS /ˈsoʊ·bər/ *adj* serious and calm ○ *The sober expression had not left Martin's face.*
soberly /ˈsoʊ·bər·li/ *adv* ○ *The jury soberly considered the evidence.*
sobering /ˈsoʊ·bə·rɪŋ/ *adj* ○ *Jail has had a sobering effect on Hicks.*

PHRASAL VERB with sober

• **sober** *(someone)* **up** [M] to stop drinking alcohol, or to cause someone to stop drinking

sobriety /səˈbrɑɪ·ət̬·i/ *n* [U] **1** the state or quality of being SOBER (= not drunk) **2** Sobriety also means the state of being serious and calm: *This judge is known for his sobriety and fairness.*

sob story *n* [C] *infml, disapproving* a long excuse or explanation that is meant to make you feel sorry for someone

so-called Ⓐ /ˈsoʊˈkɔːld/ *adj* [not gradable] **1** named or called in a particular way ○ *Married taxpayers are hit hard by the so-called marriage penalty.* **2** People or things that are so-called may not fit their name: *These so-called experts don't know anything.*

soccer /ˈsɑk·ər/ *n* [U] a game in which two teams of eleven players try to send a ball into the goal of the opposing side without using their arms or hands

sociable /ˈsoʊ·ʃə·bəl/ *adj* liking to be with people; friendly ○ *The new sales rep is savvy and sociable.*

WORD FAMILY sociable

Nouns	society	*Adjectives*	sociable
	sociologist		unsociable
	sociology		social
Verbs	socialize		anti-social
Adverbs	socially		unsocial

social OF HUMAN SOCIETY /ˈsoʊ·ʃəl/ *adj* [not gradable] related to the way people live together or to the rank a person has in a society ○ *social conditions/position*
socially /ˈsoʊ·ʃə·li/ *adv* ○ *Certain behavior is socially unacceptable.*

OF MEETING PEOPLE /ˈsoʊ·ʃəl/ *adj* [not gradable] related to meeting and spending time with other people for pleasure ○ *He had almost no social life.*
socially /ˈsoʊ·ʃə·li/ *adv* [not gradable] ○ *We first met socially and later worked together.*
socialize /ˈsoʊ·ʃəˌlɑɪz/ *v* [I] ○ *Although he works a lot, Manny still finds time to socialize with friends.*

social climber *n* [C] *disapproving* someone who tries to move into a higher social rank

social contract *n* [C/U] ***social studies*** agreement among the members of a society or between a society and its rulers about the rights and duties of each

Social Insurance Number /ˈsoʊ·ʃəl·ɪn ˈʃʊr·əns·ˈnʌm·bər/, *abbreviation* **SIN** *n* [C] *Cdn* a number given to each citizen and used by the Canadian federal government to provide citizens with government services or to collect taxes

socialism /ˈsoʊ·ʃəˌlɪz·əm/ *n* [U] ***social studies*** any economic or political system based on government ownership and control of important businesses and methods of production ○ Compare CAPITALISM; COMMUNISM
socialist /ˈsoʊ·ʃə·ləst/ *adj* [not gradable] ○ *Socialist ideas are not as radical as we once thought.* ○ Compare COMMUNIST

socialist /ˈsoʊ·ʃə·ləst/ *n* [C] ○ *He is a dedicated socialist.* ○ Compare COMMUNIST
socialized /ˈsoʊ·ʃəˌlɑɪzd/ *adj* [not gradable] ○ *Political leaders are opposed to socialized medicine* (= government control of medical care).

social mobility *n* [U] ***social studies*** the ability to move from one level of society to another

social science *n* [C/U] the study of the customs and culture of a society, or a particular part of this subject, such as history, politics, or economics

Social Security *n* [U] the US government program that provides financial help and services for old people, people whose husbands or wives have died, and people who are unable to work

social service *n* [C usually pl] any of the services provided by governments or other organizations to people with particular needs

social studies *pl n* a course for younger students that includes many of the SOCIAL SCIENCES

social welfare *n* [U] ***social studies*** services provided by the government or private organizations to help poor, ill, or old people

social worker *n* [C] a person who is trained to help people who are at a mental, physical, economic, or social disadvantage

societal /səˈsɑɪ·ət̬·əl/ *adj* [not gradable] of or relating to human society ○ *societal concerns/issues/problems* ○ *Rapid societal changes have complicated parents' task.*

society PEOPLE /səˈsɑɪ·ət̬·i/ *n* [C/U] **1** people considered as a group, or a group of people who live together in a particular social system ○ [U] *Society is changing little by little.* ○ [C] *Societies change over the course of time.* **2** Society also refers to that group of people who are rich, powerful, or fashionable: [U] *He's a part of Boston society.*

ORGANIZATION /səˈsɑɪ·ət̬·i/ *n* [C] an organization for people who have special interests or who want to support particular activities ○ *Zoological societies protect and study wild animals.*

USAGE

society or company?

Society is used to mean an organization of people with similar interests or one whose most important goal is doing something other than make a profit.

the Baltimore Choral Society

the National Geographic Society

Company is the correct word for a business organization whose most important goal is making money.

I work for a large company.

~~*I work for a large society.*~~

socioeconomic /ˌsoʊ·siː·oʊˌek·əˈnɑm·ɪk, ˌsoʊ·ʃiː·oʊ-, -ˌiː·kə-/ *adj* [not gradable] involving both social and economic matters ○ *socioeconomic backgrounds/factors/resources*

sociology /ˌsoʊ·siːˈɑl·ə·dʒi/ *n* [U] the study of human societies
sociologist /ˌsoʊ·siːˈɑl·ə·dʒəst/ *n* [C] ○ *He trained as a sociologist at the university.*

sock FOOT COVERING /sɑk/ *n* [C] *pl* **socks, sox** a covering for your foot, worn inside a shoe and made of soft material

HIT /sɑk/ *v* [T] to hit someone ○ *He socked his brother in the eye.*

PHRASAL VERB with sock

• **sock in** *something/somewhere* to stop all travel or movement of vehicles in an area because of fog ○ *The entire coast was socked in all week.*

socket /ˈsɑk·ət/ *n* [C] a hollow or curved part into which something fits ○ *The bulb screwed easily into a socket.* ○ *Somehow the bone was pulled from its socket.*

sod /sɑd/ *n* [U] dirt with grass rooted in it ○ *Truckloads of sod were needed to make the new lawn.*

soda /ˈsoʊd·ə/, *dated* **soda pop** /ˈsoʊd·əˌpɑp/ *n* [C/U] *regional US* a SOFT DRINK

soda water, *short form* **soda** *n* [U] plain water containing air bubbles

sodden /ˈsɑd·ən/ *adj* [not gradable] extremely wet as a result of absorbing liquid ○ *The carpet was a sodden mess.*

sodium /ˈsoʊd·iː·əm/ *n* [U] a soft, silver-white chemical element that is found only combined with other elements

sodium chloride /ˈklɔːr·ɑɪd/ *n* [U] ***chemistry*** salt

sofa /ˈsoʊ·fə/ *n* [C] a long, soft seat with a back and usually arms, large enough for two or more people to sit on; a COUCH

sofa bed *n* [C] a bed that folds out of a SOFA

soft NOT HARD /sɔːft/ *adj* [*-er/-est* only] not hard or firm; changing its shape when pressed ○ *The crabs are plucked from the water before their soft shells have had a chance to harden.* ○ *The baby's skin feels so soft* (= smooth and enjoyable to touch).
soften /ˈsɔː·fən/ *v* [I/T] ○ [I] *The butter will soften if you leave it out.*
softness /ˈsɔːft·nəs/ *n* [U] ○ *I sank into the softness of my bed.*

GENTLE /sɔːft/ *adj* [*-er/-est* only] not forceful, loud, or easily noticed ○ *a soft voice* ○ *She likes soft pastel colors.*
soften /ˈsɔː·fən/ *v* [I/T] ○ [T] *He made an effort to soften his tone.*
softly /ˈsɔːf·tli/ *adv* ○ *She spoke so softly it was hard to hear her.*
softness /ˈsɔːft·nəs/ *n* [U] ○ *There was a softness in her voice.*

WEAK /sɔːft/ *adj* [*-er/-est* only] **1** not strong; weak ○ *Car sales were soft last year.* **2** If someone is said to be **soft on crime**, that person is thought to be not forceful enough in punishing criminals.

soften /ˈsɔː·fən/ *v* [T] ○ *Congress will move to soften the law's impact.*

softness /ˈsɔːft·nəs/ *n* [U] ○ *A lot of people think that kindness is a sign of softness.*

EASY /sɔːft/ *adj* [*-er/-est* only] not difficult; easier than other things of the same type ○ *She asked some soft questions.*

WORD FAMILY soft

Nouns	softness	*Verbs*	soften
Adjectives	soft	*Adverbs*	softly

IDIOM with soft

• **soften the blow** to make a difficult experience less unpleasant ○ *I put my arm around her before I gave her the bad news to try to soften the blow.*

PHRASAL VERB with soft

• **soften** *someone/something* **up** [M] to weaken someone or something ○ *She tried to soften me up by saying nice things about me, and then asked for the week off.*

softball /ˈsɔːft·bɔːl/ *n* [C/U] a game similar to baseball but played with a larger, softer ball, or the ball used in this game

soft-boiled *adj* [not gradable] (of an egg) boiled with its shell on and removed from the water while the yellow part is still soft ○ Compare HARD-BOILED EGG

soft drink *n* [C] a drink, usually flavored, that does not contain alcohol

soft-hearted, **softhearted** *adj* kind and willing to help other people ○ Compare HARD-HEARTED

soft-pedal *v* [T] to treat something unpleasant as less important, because you want to avoid angering or hurting people ○ *The movie soft-pedals the more sensational aspects of his life.*

soft-spoken *adj* usually speaking in a quiet voice ○ *a soft-spoken, understated style*

soft spot *n* [C usually sing] a strong liking for something or someone ○ *I'll always have a soft spot in my heart for Denver.*

soft touch *n* [C usually sing] *infml* someone who is easy to control or get money from ○ *The chief, obviously a soft touch, gave him ten bucks.*

software /ˈsɔːfˌtwer, -ˌtwær/ *n* [U] the instructions that control what a computer can do; computer programs ○ *educational software* ○ Compare HARDWARE COMPUTER

soggy /ˈsɑg·i, ˈsɔː·gi/ *adj* (of a substance) very wet from having absorbed liquid ○ *They played on a wet, soggy field.*

soil EARTH /sɔɪl/ *n* [C/U] **1** the material on the surface of the ground in which plants grow; earth ○ [U] *Plant the seeds in potting soil.* **2** Soil is sometimes a country: [U] *At the Olympics he was competing on foreign soil for only the third time in his life.*

MAKE DIRTY /sɔɪl/ *v* [T] to make something dirty

soiled /sɔɪld/ *adj* ○ *soiled diapers*

sojourn /ˈsoʊ·dʒɜrn/ *n* [C] a temporary stay at one place, esp. while traveling

sojourn /ˈsoʊ·dʒɜrn, soʊˈdʒɜrn/ *v* [I always + adv/prep] ○ *They sojourned in Memphis to celebrate Elvis Presley's birthday.*

solace /ˈsɑl·əs/ *n* [U] help and comfort when you are feeling sad or worried ○ *She found solace in her memories of her grandmother.*

solar /ˈsoʊ·lər/ *adj* [not gradable] of or from the sun, or using the energy from the sun to produce electric power ○ *solar energy* ○ *solar power*

solar eclipse *n* [C] ***earth science*** ECLIPSE

solar system *n* [C usually sing] ***earth science*** the sun and the group of planets that move around it, or a similar system somewhere else in the universe

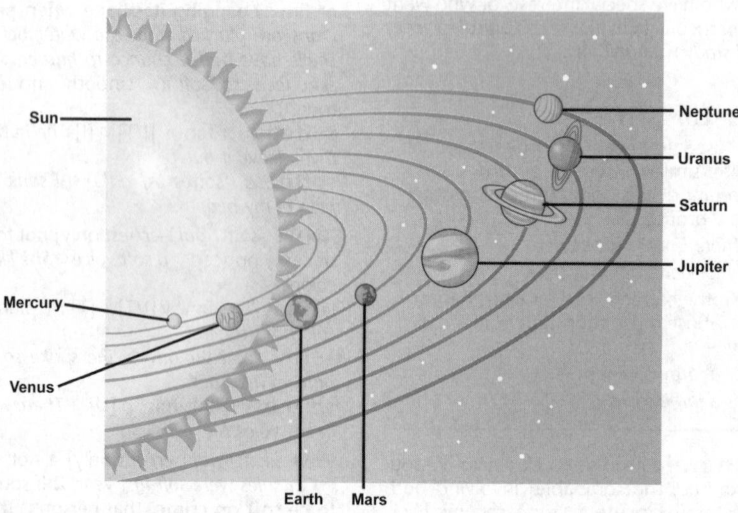

SOLAR SYSTEM

sold /sould/ *past simple and past participle of* SELL

solder /ˈsɑd·ər/ *n* [U] a type of soft metal that is melted to join separate metal parts which are then permanently attached when the metal cools
solder /ˈsɑd·ər/ *v* [T] ○ *Wrap metal foil around the glass pieces and solder them together.*

soldier /ˈsoul·dʒər/ *n* [C] a person who is in an army and wears its uniform, esp. someone who fights when there is a war ○ *American/Italian/Chinese soldiers*

sole Ⓐ **ONLY** /soul/ *adj* [not gradable] **1** being the only one; single ○ *She is the sole survivor of the accident.* **2** Sole also means belonging to one person or group: *The team moved into sole possession of first place.*
solely Ⓐ /ˈsoul·li/ *adv* [not gradable] ○ *These industries aren't solely responsible for hazardous wastes.*

BOTTOM PART OF FOOT /soul/ *n* [C] the bottom part of a foot which touches the ground when you stand or walk, or the front part of the bottom of a shoe ○ *shoes with leather/rubber soles*

FISH /soul/ *n* [C/U] *pl* **sole** a flat, round fish that is eaten as food

solemn /ˈsɑl·əm/ *adj* having or showing serious purpose and determination ○ *He looked stern and solemn, and rarely spoke.* ○ *The memorial was a very solemn occasion.*
solemnly /ˈsɑl·əm·li/ *adv* ○ *Borden solemnly promised that he would take care of it.*
solemnity /səˈlem·nət̬·i/ *n* [U] ○ *There was an air of solemnity in the room.*

solenoid /ˈsou·ləˌnɔɪd, ˈsɑl·ə-/ *n* [C] ***physics*** a device consisting of a wire wrapped in the shape of a cylinder, which acts like a magnet when electricity goes through it

solicit /səˈlɪs·ət/ *v* [T] to ask for something in a persuasive and determined way ○ *He's soliciting funds to keep the library open.* ○ *Grace has run an online campaign to solicit employee suggestions.*
solicitation /səˌlɪs·əˈteɪ·ʃən/ *n* [C/U] ○ [C] *I get a lot of phone solicitations from banks.*

solicitor **LAWYER** /səˈlɪs·ət̬·ər/ *n* [C] the official in a local government who deals with legal matters ○ *He served as city solicitor.*

SELL /səˈlɪs·ət̬·ər/ *n* [C] someone who asks for money or tries to sell you something ○ *Beware of telephone solicitors who say, "All proceeds will go to charity."*

solicitous /səˈlɪs·ət̬·əs/ *adj fml* eager to help ○ *Carla becomes angry at her overly solicitous mother.*

solid **FIRM/NOT LIQUID** /ˈsɑl·əd/ *adj* **1** having a fixed shape that cannot be changed easily ○ *After flying all night, he was glad to be on solid ground.* **2** ***chemistry*** A substance that is solid is not a liquid or a gas.
solid /ˈsɑl·əd/ *n* [C] ○ *After the operation, Mrs. Groncki couldn't eat solids* (= food that is not liquid).
solidify /səˈlɪd·əˌfɑɪ/ *v* [I/T] to make something firm, or to become firm ○ [T] *A chemical reaction solidifies the resin.* ○ [I] *Lava solidifies as it cools.*
solidity /səˈlɪd·ət̬·i/ *n* [U] ○ *For solidity, glue the strip in place.*

SHAPE /ˈsɑl·əd/ *n* [C] ***geometry*** an object with three DIMENSIONS (= height, width, and length) ○ *A cube is a solid.*

DENSE /ˈsɑl·əd/ *adj* **1** completely packed with material; not hollow ○ *solid rock* ○ *a solid oak table* **2** A solid metal or color is pure and does not have anything else mixed together with it: *solid gold* ○ *a solid blue background*
solid /ˈsɑl·əd/ *adv* [not gradable] with no openings; full ○ *He has 54 tin boxes, packed solid with baseball cards.*
solidly /ˈsɑl·əd·li/ *adv* ○ *The holes are solidly filled with concrete.*

STRONG /ˈsɑl·əd/ *adj* (of objects) made in a way that is strong, or (of a person) strong ○ *It's a solid house.* ○ *David has a solid, muscular body.*
solidly /ˈsɑl·əd·li/ *adv* ○ *The rocking chair is solidly built.*

CERTAIN /ˈsɑl·əd/ *adj* being of a good quality that can be trusted; certain or safe ○ *All the performers showed solid musicianship and technique.* ○ *Rela-*

S

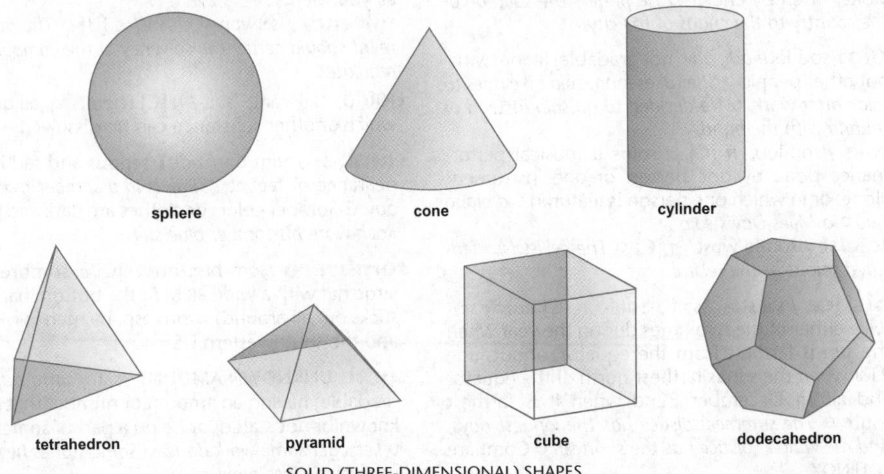

SOLID (THREE-DIMENSIONAL) SHAPES

tions between them are based on a solid foundation of friendship and trust.

solidly /ˈsɑl·əd·li/ *adv* completely; safely ○ *He appears to be solidly in control of the organization.*

solidify /səˈlɪd·əˌfɑɪ/ *v* [I/T] to make something complete, or to become more certain or safer ○ [T] *The play solidified his reputation as a serious writer.* ○ [I] *Her voice strengthened and solidified as she sang.*

WORD FAMILY solid			
Nouns	solid solidarity solidity solids	Adjectives	solid
		Verbs	solidify
		Adverbs	solidly

solidarity /ˌsɑl·əˈdær·ət̬·i/ *n* [U] agreement between and support for the members of a group ○ *Hundreds of supporters gathered to show solidarity for the three men.*

Solidarity /ˌsɑl·əˈder·ət̬·i, -ˈdær-/ *n* [U] ***world history*** a TRADE UNION (= an organization of workers) in Poland that began in 1980 and that was important in establishing free elections in 1989

soliloquy /səˈlɪl·ə·kwi/ *n* [C/U] ***literature*** a speech in a play which the character speaks to himself or herself or to the people watching rather than to the other characters ○ [C] *Hamlet's soliloquy begins, "To be or not to be."*

solitaire **JEWEL** /ˈsɑl·əˌter, -ˌtær/ *n* [C] a single jewel that is part of a piece of jewelry, esp. a ring, or the ring itself ○ *a diamond solitaire*

CARDS /ˈsɑl·əˌter, -ˌtær/ *n* [U] a game played with cards by one person

solitary /ˈsɑl·əˌter·i/ *adj* being the only one, or not being with other similar things, often by choice ○ *I live a solitary life.* ○ *He enjoys solitary walks in the wilderness.*

solitary confinement *n* [U] the condition of being kept alone in a room in prison

solitude /ˈsɑl·əˌtuːd/ *n* [U] the situation of being alone, often by choice ○ *He prefers the solitude of the country to the chaos of the city.*

solo /ˈsoʊ·loʊ/ *adj, adv* [not gradable] alone; without other people ○ *She takes long, solo bike rides to relax after work.* ○ *He decided to go solo instead of touring with the band.*

solo /ˈsoʊ·loʊ/ *n* [C] *pl* **solos** a musical performance done by one person or one instrument alone, or in which one person is featured ○ *a piano solo* ○ *a Miles Davis solo*

soloist /ˈsoʊ·lə·wəst/ *n* [C] ○ *The cellist is a featured soloist at the recital.*

solstice /ˈsɑl·stəs, ˈsɔːl-, ˈsoʊl-/ *n* [C] ***earth science*** either of the two times during the year when the sun is farthest from the equator, about June 21st when the sun is farthest north of the equator and about December 22nd when it is farthest south ○ *The summer solstice has the longest days, and the winter solstice has the shortest.* ○ Compare EQUINOX

solubility /ˌsɑl·jəˈbɪl·ət̬·i/ *n* [U] ***chemistry*** a quality a substance has of being able to dissolve in another substance, or of being able to dissolve another substance

soluble /ˈsɑl·jə·bəl/ *adj* ***chemistry***

solute /ˈsɑl·juːt/ *n* [C] ***chemistry*** a substance that has been dissolved in another substance

solution **ANSWER** /səˈluː·ʃən/ *n* [C] an answer to a problem ○ *It seemed a reasonable solution to a difficult problem.* ○ Related verb: SOLVE

USAGE

solution

The correct preposition after **solution** is usually **to** if what follows the preposition is the problem.

The ambassador is still trying to find a diplomatic solution to the crisis.

~~*The ambassador is still trying to find a diplomatic solution of the crisis.*~~

LIQUID /səˈluː·ʃən/ *n* [C/U] ***chemistry*** a liquid in which other substances have been mixed and dissolved

soluble /ˈsɑl·jə·bəl/ *adj* able to be dissolved when mixed with a liquid ○ *Sugar is soluble in water.*

solve /sɑlv, sɔːlv/ *v* [T] to find an answer to a problem ○ *The arrests have not solved the mystery of what happened to the stolen cash.* ○ Related noun: SOLUTION ANSWER

solvable /ˈsɑl·və·bəl, ˈsɔːl-/, **soluble** /ˈsɑl·jə·bəl/ *adj* ○ *Hunger in this city is a solvable problem.*

WORD FAMILY solve			
Nouns	solution solvent	Adjectives	soluble solvable insoluble unsolved solvent
Verbs	dissolve solve		

solvent **HAVING MONEY** /ˈsɑl·vənt, ˈsɔːl-/ *adj* (esp. of companies) having enough money to pay all your debts

solvency /ˈsɑl·vən·si, ˈsɔːl-/ *n* [U] ○ *The government should certify the solvency of the companies it regulates.*

LIQUID /ˈsɑl·vənt, ˈsɔːl-/ *n* [C] ***chemistry*** a liquid in which another substance can be dissolved

somber /ˈsɑm·bər/ *adj* **1** serious and sad in appearance or feeling ○ *Raji is in a somber mood today.* **2** Somber colors or clothes are dark and plain: *Koch wore his somber blue suit.*

sombrero /səmˈbrer·oʊ/ *n* [C] *pl* **sombreros** a large hat with a wide BRIM (= the bottom part that sticks out all around), worn esp. by men in Mexico and the southwestern US

some **UNKNOWN AMOUNT** /sʌm, səm/ *adj* [not gradable] having an amount or number that is not known or not stated, or being a part of something ○ *Let's get some work done.* ○ *Some stories he wrote were made into movies.*

S

some /sʌm, səm/ *pronoun* **1** *If you want more spaghetti, please take some.* ○ *I like some of the people in my class.* **2** Some can also mean some people: *Some have compared him to President Kennedy.* ○ **USAGE**: In negative sentences, you use "any" or "no" instead of "some." In questions, you usually use "any" instead of "some."

some /sʌm/ *adv* [not gradable] *infml* ○ *I slept some in the car on the way home.*

USAGE

some or any?

Some is used in positive sentences. **Any** is used in questions and negative sentences.

There are some flowers in front of the house, but there aren't any trees.

Does he have any brothers or sisters?

Some is sometimes used in offers or requests, or other polite questions.

Would you like some more coffee?

The same rules are true for **something** and **anything**, **someone** and **anyone**, and **somewhere** and **anywhere**.

LARGE AMOUNT /sʌm/ *adj* [not gradable] being a large amount or number of something ○ *She was married to him for some years.* ○ *These things have been going on for some time.*

PERSON OR THING /sʌm, səm/ *adj* [not gradable] used to refer to a person or thing when you cannot say exactly who or what it is ○ *Some jerk backed into my car in the parking lot.* ○ *There's got to be some way out of here.*

UNUSUAL /sʌm/ *adj* [not gradable] *infml* used before a noun and spoken with emphasis to show that something is unusual ○ *Some party that turned out to be – nobody showed up.* ○ *Margo is really a terrific cook – that was some dinner!*

APPROXIMATELY /sʌm, səm/ *adv* [not gradable] (used in front of a number) approximately; about ○ *Some 200 people applied for the job.*

IDIOM with some

• **some** *thing* **or other** something that is not known exactly ○ *For some reason or other, these people have no place to go.* ○ *You must have met her at some time or other if you were both working in the same office.*

somebody /ˈsʌm ˌbɑd·i, -bəd·i/ *pronoun* a person; someone ○ *I'd rather take care of my own kids than let somebody I don't know raise them.* ○ *You don't have the right to interfere in somebody else's life.*

someday /ˈsʌm·deɪ/ *adv* [not gradable] at some time in the future which is not yet known or not stated ○ *I keep thinking that maybe someday we'll move.*

somehow /ˈsʌm·hɑʊ/ *adv* [not gradable] in a way which is not known or not stated ○ *Money has been extremely tight, but we've managed somehow.* ○ *He felt that everything was somehow connected.*

IDIOM with somehow

• **somehow or other** in a way that you do not know or understand ○ *I'm afraid that somehow or other we spoiled the kids.* ○ Compare SOMETHING OR OTHER at SOMETHING IDIOMS

someone /ˈsʌm·wən, -wʌn/ *pronoun* a person ○ *I'm not interested in someone else's experience.* ○ *I hate cutting the lawn, so I pay someone to do it.* ○ **USAGE**: "Anyone" is usually used instead of "someone" in negative sentences and questions.

someplace /ˈsʌm·pleɪs/ *adv* [not gradable] in, to, or at a place which is not known or not stated; somewhere ○ *The only time I've been to Florida I was on the way someplace else.*

somersault /ˈsʌm·ərˌsɔːlt/ *n* [C] a rolling movement or jump, either forward or backward, in which you turn over completely, with your body above your head, and finish on your feet ○ *She turned somersaults on the lawn.*

somersault /ˈsʌm·ərˌsɔːlt/ *v* [I] ○ *The bus plunged down the hill, somersaulted twice, and landed on its side.*

something /ˈsʌm·θɪŋ/ *pronoun* **1** a thing which is not known or stated ○ *I was anxious to do something.* ○ *Can I read you something else?* ○ *I was sure something had happened to him.* ○ *The ball and bat arrive at the same place at the same time, and the rest has* **something to do with** (= is in some way connected with) *the laws of physics.* **2** Something can be used to describe a situation or an event that is good, although it is not everything you had hoped for: *I exercise three times a week – it's not enough, but at least it's something.* ○ **USAGE**: "Anything" is usually used instead of "something" in negative sentences and questions.

IDIOMS with something

• **something else** unusual, esp. extremely good or extremely bad ○ *"He sang better than anyone I've ever heard." "Yeah, I know, he's really something else."*

• **something like** **1** similar to but not exactly like ○ *The town's Algonquian name means something like "water over a white bottom."* **2 Something like** also means approximately when used about an amount or a number: *She's on page 285 or something like that.*

• **something or other** something whose exact nature you do not know or have forgotten ○ *He's a professor of something or other, and now he's living in China.* ○ Compare SOMEHOW OR OTHER at SOMEHOW IDIOM

S

sometime /ˈsʌm·tɑɪm/ *adv* [not gradable] at a time in the future or the past which is not known or stated ○ *I'm having lunch with an old friend sometime next week.*

sometimes /ˈsʌm·tɑɪmz/ *adv* [not gradable] on some occasions but not all the time ○ *Sometimes you think you can't really trust anybody.*

somewhat Ⓐ /ˈsʌm·hwʌt, -wʌt, -hwɑt, -wɑt/ *adv* [not gradable] to some degree ○ *Washington, D.C., is somewhat smaller than Baltimore.* ○ *I was* *somewhat disappointed.* ○ **USAGE**: "Somewhat" is usually not used in negative phrases or sentences.

somewhere **PLACE** /ˈsʌm·hwer, -wer, -hwær, -wær/ *adv* [not gradable] in, to, or at a place which is not known or not stated ○ *I want to live somewhere else.* ○ *Can we go somewhere and talk?* ○ **USAGE**: "Anywhere" is usually used instead of "somewhere" in negative sentences and questions.

APPROXIMATELY /ˈsʌm·hwer, -wer, -hwær, -wær/ *adv* [not gradable] (used esp. before a number) approximately; about ○ *CDs cost somewhere around $15 apiece.*

IDIOM with **somewhere**

• **somewhere between** with the qualities of each of two things ○ *He made a sound somewhere between a gurgle and a cough.*

son /sʌn/ *n* [C] a male child in relation to his parents ○ *I have two sons.*

son-in-law /ˈsʌn·ən ˌlɔː/ *n* [C] *pl* **sons-in-law** the husband of a person's daughter

sonar /ˈsoʊ·nɑr/ *n* [U] a device on a ship that uses sound to show the position of objects under the water

sonata /səˈnɑt̬·ə/ *n* [C] a piece of music in three or four parts, either for a piano or for another instrument, such as a VIOLIN, sometimes also with a piano

song /sɔːŋ/ *n* [C/U] **1** a usually short piece of music with words that are sung ○ [C] *We bought a CD of Cole Porter songs.* **2** Song is also the act of singing, or singing when considered generally: [U] *He was so happy he wanted to burst into song* (= start singing). **3** The song of a bird is the musical sound it makes.

song form *n* [U] ***music*** a form of music often used for songs that consists of two parts that repeat, such as the VERSE and the CHORUS

songwriter /ˈsɔːŋˌrɑɪt̬·ər/ *n* [C] a person who writes songs

sonnet /ˈsɑn·ət/ *n* [C] ***literature*** a poem that has 14 lines and a particular pattern of RHYME and word arrangement

soon /suːn/ *adv* [-er/-est only] in or within a short time; before long; quickly ○ *We'll soon be there.* ○ *How soon* (= When) *can we sign the contract?* ○ *"When would you like to meet?" "The sooner the better."*

IDIOM with **soon**

• **sooner or later** at some time in the future ○ *Don't worry, sooner or later the cat will come home.*

soot /sʊt/ *n* [U] a black powder produced when coal, wood, etc., is burned

soothe /suːð/ *v* [T] to cause someone to be less upset or angry, or to cause something to hurt less ○ *I picked up the crying child and tried to soothe her.*

soothing /ˈsuː·ðɪŋ/ *adj* ○ *a soothing ointment for sunburn*

sop /sɑp/ *n* [C] something unimportant or of little value that is offered to stop complaints or unhappiness ○ *He regarded third prize as just a sop.*

PHRASAL VERB with **sop**

• **sop up** *something* [M] to absorb a liquid ○ *She spilled some orange juice and sopped it up with paper towels.*

sophisticated /səˈfɪs·təˌkeɪt̬·əd/ *adj* **1** having an understanding of the world and its ways, so that you are not easily fooled, and having an understanding of people and ideas without making them seem simple ○ *Sophisticated readers understood the book's hidden meaning.* **2** If a way of thinking, a system, or a machine is sophisticated, it is complicated or made with great skill: *sophisticated computer systems*

sophistication /səˌfɪs·təˈkeɪ·ʃən/ *n* [U] ○ *The level of sophistication in the cameras has grown tremendously.* ○ *I longed for the wit and sophistication of New York City.*

sophomore /ˈsɑfˌmɔːr, -ˌmoʊr/ *n* [C] a student in the second year of a program of study in a college, university, or HIGH SCHOOL (= a school for students aged 14 to 18)

sophomoric /sɑfˈmɔːr·ɪk, -ˈmoʊr-/ *adj* (of an adult) typical of someone acting like a child ○ *sophomoric behavior*

sopping /ˈsɑp·ɪŋ/ *adj* [not gradable] extremely wet ○ *You're sopping wet – go put some dry clothes on.*

soprano /səˈpræn·oʊ, -ˈprɑn-/ *n* [C] *pl* **sopranos** a woman's or young boy's singing voice in the highest range, or a person or musical instrument with this range

sorbet /sɔːrˈbeɪ/ *n* [C/U] a food made from frozen fruit juice and water ○ [C/U] *(a) raspberry sorbet*

sorcery /ˈsɔːr·sə·ri/ *n* [U] a type of magic that is used esp. to harm someone or make things happen

sordid **MORALLY BAD** /ˈsɔːrd·əd/ *adj* morally ugly, so that being involved makes you feel dirty ○ *a sordid story* ○ *sordid details*

DIRTY /ˈsɔːrd·əd/ *adj* dirty and in bad condition ○ *The sordid condition of many of the city school buildings was shocking.*

sore **PAINFUL** /sɔːr, soʊr/ *adj* painful and uncomfortable, esp. (of a body part) because of injury or infection or (of a muscle) from being used too much ○ *If you have a sore throat, take aspirin.* ○ *I went rowing yesterday for the first time in years, and my arms are sore today.*

sore /sɔːr, soʊr/ *n* [C] a painful area on the surface of a body, esp. an infected area

soreness /ˈsɔːr·nəs, ˈsoʊr-/ *n* [U]

ANGRY /sɔːr, soʊr/ *adj* [-er/-est only] *infml* angry, esp. because you feel you have been unfairly treated ○ *Chris wants to win, but he's not a sore loser.*

sorely /ˈsɔːr·li/ *adv* very much ○ *She will be sorely missed.*

sorority /sə'rɔːr·əṭ·i, -'rɑr-/ *n* [C] a social organization for female students at a college or university ○ Compare FRATERNITY

sorrow /'sɑr·oʊ, 'sɔːr-/ *n* [C/U] a feeling of great sadness or regret, or something that causes this feeling ○ [U] *The English language does not contain the words to express the sorrow I feel.*

sorry **ASKING FORGIVENESS** /'sɑr·i, 'sɔːr·i/ *adj* **1** feeling bad because you have caused trouble or difficulty to someone else ○ [+ (*that*) clause] *I'm really sorry (that) I forgot about our appointment yesterday.* **2** Sorry is also used as a polite way to show your sympathy to someone because of a loss, problem, or trouble the person has had: [+ *to* infinitive] *We were sorry to learn about the death of your grandmother.* **3** Sorry is also used as a polite way of asking someone to excuse you for having done something that might have annoyed the person: *The train will be moving shortly – we are sorry for the inconvenience.*

POLITE REFUSAL /'sɑr·i, 'sɔːr·i/ *adj* used as a polite way of expressing refusal or disagreement ○ *I'm sorry, but I think you've made a mistake in our check.* ○ *Sorry, you can't go in there.*

BAD CONDITION /'sɑr·i, 'sɔːr·i/ *adj* [-er/-est only] *dated* so bad as to cause feelings of sympathy ○ *They were a sorry sight, dressed in rags and so weak they could hardly stand up.* ○ **USAGE:** describing a situation or condition

sort **TYPE** /sɔːrt/ *n* [C] **1** a group of things that are of the same type or that share similar qualities ○ *What sort of equipment will she need?* ○ *He was squinting through the eyepiece of some sort of navigational device.* **2** Sort can sometimes refer to a person of a particular type: *What sort of person do you think I am?* **3** A person might say **a sort of** or **sort of** when describing something about which the person does not have a clear or exact knowledge: *He's a sort of agent for athletes, but not officially.* ○ *She's sort of running the company, I think, but her parents are still involved.*

WORD CHOICES sort

Kind, **type**, and **form** are alternative ways of saying "sort."

*What **kind** of job are you looking for?*

*He's the **type** of man who never listens to what you're saying.*

*Swimming is the best **form** of exercise.*

If you are talking about the sort of design that something has, you could use the word **style**.

*The street is full of buildings in different **styles** of architecture.*

If you want to talk about the different sorts of something, you could use the word **variety**.

*The article was about the different **varieties** of Spanish spoken in South America.*

*This **variety** of rose is particularly hardy.*

If you are talking about a sort of animal, you could use the word **breed**.

*What **breed** of dog do you have?*

The words **brand** or **make** are used for talking about sorts of products.

*She always buys expensive **brands** of chocolate.*

*What is the **make** of your car?*

If things that are of the same sort are considered as a group, you could use the word **category**.

*There are three **categories** – standard, executive, and deluxe.*

PUT IN ORDER /sɔːrt/ *v* [I/T] to put things in a particular order or separate them into groups according to a principle ○ [T] *We have to sort the job applications into groups based on their qualifications.* ○ [T] *Paper, plastic, and cans are sorted for recycling.* ○ [M] *Sort out the clothes that you don't want, and we'll donate them to a charity.* ○ [I always + adv/prep] *He spent hours sorting through the photos* (= searching them to find one).

IDIOM with sort

• **sort of** in some way or to some degree ○ *I feel sort of sorry for him, even though I know he's not a nice person.* ○ Compare KIND OF at KIND **IDIOM**

PHRASAL VERB with sort

• **sort out** *something* [M] to deal successfully with a problem or a situation ○ *Her financial records are a mess, but we'll sort them out.*

SOS /ˌesˌoʊ'es/ *n* [C] (esp. from a boat or ship) an urgent request for help

so-so /'soʊ'soʊ/ *adj, adv* [not gradable] not very good but not very bad either ○ *"You had a bad time with the flu – how are you feeling?" "So-so, I'm still pretty weak."*

sought /sɔːt/ *past simple and past participle of* SEEK

sought-after *adj* wanted or desired by many people ○ *He was one the most sought-after speakers at political rallies.*

soul **SPIRIT** /soʊl/ *n* [C] **1** the part of a person that some people believe continues to exist in some form after the body has died, or the part of a person or thing that expresses the basic qualities that make it what it is ○ *May her soul rest in peace.* **2** If you say that someone is the soul of a quality, you mean the person has that quality in a high degree: *He is the soul of honor, and would never intentionally try to deceive you.*

BLACK CULTURE /soʊl/ *n* [U] a deep understanding of and pride in the culture of African-Americans

PERSON /soʊl/ *n* [C] **1** a person of a stated type ○ *a happy soul* **2** Soul can also mean any person, and is usually used in negative statements: *There wasn't a soul around when we arrived at the beach.*

soul food *n* [C/U] food that comes from the African-American culture in the southern US ○ *Corn bread, black-eyed peas, ham hocks, and sweet potato pie are all soul food.*

S

soulful /ˈsoʊl·fəl/ *adj* expressing feeling or emotion ○ *The dog looked at me with her big, soulful, brown eyes.*

soul music *n* [U] a type of popular music with a strong beat and rhythm that developed from GOSPEL music

soul-searching *n* [U] deep and careful consideration of inner thoughts ○ *After much soul-searching, she decided not to run for reelection.*

sound SOMETHING HEARD /sɑʊnd/ *n* [C/U] something heard or that may be heard ○ [C] *They could hear the sound of an airplane overhead.*
sound /sɑʊnd/ *v* [I/T] ○ [I] *A bell sounds* (= makes a noise) *after fifty minutes to signal the end of the class period.* ○ [T] *Sound the alarm – a prisoner has escaped!*

SEEM /sɑʊnd/ *v* to suggest a particular feeling, state, or thing by the way something is said or a noise is made ○ [L] *He sounded rather discouraged when I called him yesterday.* ○ [I always + adv/prep] *You sound as if you have a sore throat.* ○ [I always + adv/prep] *From what you told me, she sounds like* (= seems to be) *a nice person.* ○ [I always + adv/prep] *That sounds like fun* (= seems likely to be enjoyable).

HEALTHY /sɑʊnd/ *adj* [*-er/-est* only] **1** in good condition; (of a person) healthy, or (of a thing) not broken or damaged ○ *a person of sound mind* ○ *Engineers had to close the bridge because it was not sound.* **2** Sound also describes sleep that is deep and peaceful: *She was sound asleep when the phone rang.*

GOOD /sɑʊnd/ *adj* [*-er/-est* only] good because based on good judgment or correct methods ○ *It was a sound approach to investing money.*

WATER PASSAGE /sɑʊnd/ *n* [C] a passage of sea connecting two larger areas of sea, or an area of sea mostly surrounded by land ○ *Puget Sound* ○ *Long Island Sound*

PHRASAL VERBS with sound

• **sound off** *infml* to express opinions forcefully, esp. without being asked for them ○ *He's always sounding off about having to pay so much in taxes.*
• **sound out** *someone* [M] to discover someone's opinions or intentions ○ *Why don't you sound her out before the meeting, to see which way she's going to vote?*

sound bite *n* [C] a short sentence or phrase said publicly, esp. by a politician, to be broadcast

sound effects *pl n* the sounds in a radio or television program or a movie that are added to make it seem more real

sounding board *n* [C] someone you use to test a new idea or suggestion to see if it is liked ○ *President Johnson said he used his wife as a sounding board for many of his ideas.*

soundly /ˈsɑʊn·dli/ *adv* completely ○ *She always sleeps soundly.* ○ *He was soundly defeated in his bid for reelection.*

soundproof /ˈsɑʊnd·pruːf/ *adj* not allowing sound to go outside or come inside ○ *a soundproof television studio*

soundtrack /ˈsɑʊnd·træk, ˈsɑʊn-/ *n* [C] a recording of the music from a movie or a play

soup /suːp/ *n* a liquid food made esp. by cooking vegetables and sometimes also meat or fish in water and usually served hot ○ [U] *chicken/tomato/vegetable soup*

PHRASAL VERB with soup

• **soup up** *something* [M] to make mechanical changes to something, esp. a vehicle, in order to make it unusually powerful ○ *He souped it up so that it could go at speeds of over 150 mph.* ○ Related adjective: SOUPED-UP

souped-up *adj* (of a vehicle or machine) made to go faster or be more powerful ○ *a souped-up motorcycle* ○ Related verb: SOUP UP

soup kitchen *n* [C] a place where free food is given to people with no money or no homes

sour TASTE /sɑʊr/ *adj* (esp. of food) having a sharp taste ○ *The four basic tastes are sweet, salty, bitter, and sour.*
sour /sɑʊr/ *v* [I] to become sour ○ *I'm afraid the milk has soured.*

UNPLEASANT /sɑʊr/ *adj* unfriendly or unpleasant in manner or attitude ○ *The team's perfect season went/turned sour after they lost their second straight game.*
sour /sɑʊr/ *v* [I/T] to become bad or unpleasant, or cause someone to feel bad or unhappy ○ [T] *When the economy soured, donations to the charity dried up.*

source Ⓐ /sɔːrs, soʊrs/ *n* [C] **1** something or someone that causes or produces something, or is the origin of it ○ *a source of energy/light* ○ *Spinach is a good source of vitamins.* ○ *His wife was a constant source of inspiration to him.* **2** A source is also someone or something from which you obtain information: *The reporter refused to cite the names of her sources.*
source Ⓐ /sɔːrs, soʊrs/ *v* [T] to get something from a particular place ○ *Where possible the produce used in our restaurant is sourced locally.*

sour cream *n* [U] cream that is made sour by adding special bacteria, used in cooking

sour grapes *n* [U] bad behavior that happens because someone else is more successful ○ *Are his criticisms justified, or is this a case of sour grapes from a less successful artist?*

south /sɑʊθ/, *abbreviation* **S.**, *abbreviation* **So.** *n* [U] **1** the direction opposite north, or the part of an area or country in this direction ○ *The points of the compass are north, south, east, and west.* **2** In the US, the South is the southeastern part of the country: *We moved to the South when I was a child.* **3** ***US history*** In the US Civil War, the South was the group of states that fought to become separate from the federal government.

south /saʊθ/, *abbreviation* **S.**, *abbreviation* **So.** *adj, adv* [not gradable] ○ *The University is on the south side of town.* ○ *We drove south.*

southerly /ˈsʌð·ər·li/ *adj* ○ *a southerly direction*

southern /ˈsʌð·ərn/, *abbreviation* **S.**, *abbreviation* **So.** *adj* [not gradable] ○ *Louisiana is in the southern part of the US.*

southerner /ˈsʌð·ər·nər/ *n* [C] a person from the southern part of a country, or (in the US) a person from the South

southward /ˈsaʊθ·wərd/ *adj* [not gradable] toward the south ○ *a southward direction*

southward /ˈsaʊθ·wərd/, **southwards** /ˈsaʊθ·wərdz/ *adv* [not gradable] toward the south ○ *They drove southward toward the Mexican border.*

WORD FAMILY south			
Nouns	south southerner	*Adjectives*	south southerly southern
Adverbs	south southward(s)		

IDIOM with south

• **south of the border** Mexico and the other countries south of the US border with Mexico.

southeast /saʊˈθiːst/, *abbreviation* **S.E.** *n* [U] [not gradable] the direction between south and east, or the part of an area or country in this direction ○ *The house faces northwest, so southeast is behind us.*

southeast /saʊˈθiːst/, *abbreviation* **S.E.** *adj, adv* [not gradable] ○ *She lives on the southeast side of town.* ○ *They drove southeast.*

southeastern /saʊˈθiː·stərn/, *abbreviation* **S.E.** *adj* [not gradable] ○ *There will be rain in southeastern Massachusetts.*

southpaw /ˈsaʊθ·pɔː/ *n* [C] *infml* a left-handed person, esp. in sports and particularly a PITCHER (= person who throws the ball in baseball)

South Pole *n* [U] the point on the earth's surface that is farthest south

southwest /saʊθˈwest/, *abbreviation* **S.W.** *n* [U] the direction between south and west, or the part of an area or country that is in this direction ○ *He's currently living in the Southwest.*

southwest /saʊθˈwest/, *abbreviation* **S.W.** *adj, adv* [not gradable] ○ *The district is in the southwest corner of the state.* ○ *We drove southwest.*

southwestern /saʊθˈwes·tərn/, *abbreviation* **S.W.** *adj* [not gradable] ○ *She grew up in southwestern Ohio.*

souvenir /ˌsuː·vəˈnɪr/ *n* [C] something you keep or give to remember a special visit or event ○ *I'll keep this as a souvenir of my trip to New York.*

USAGE

souvenir

A **souvenir** is a thing, not a feeling. If you want to talk about a feeling or memory that you have about something in the past, you should use the noun **memory**.

~~*I have a lot of happy souvenirs of staying at my grandparents' house.*~~

I have a lot of happy memories of staying at my grandparents' house.

sovereign /ˈsɑv·rən/ *n* [C] ***world history*** a king or queen, or a person having the power to govern a country

sovereign /ˈsɑv·rən/ *adj* [not gradable] ○ *Algeria was a colony but now is a sovereign nation.*

sovereignty /ˈsɑv·rən·ti/ *n* [U] ***social studies*** the power or authority to rule

soviet /ˈsoʊ·viːˌet, -viː·ət/ *n* [C] ***world history*** **1** a group elected to govern a region or area in a COMMUNIST country (= one based on public ownership of property and control of production) **2** ***world history*** the people and esp. the leaders of the U.S.S.R.

sow PLANT /soʊ/ *v* [I/T] *past simp.* **sowed,** *past part.* **sown, sowed** to put seeds in the ground so that plants will grow ○ [T] *Settlers sowed the seeds they had brought with them.*

ANIMAL /saʊ/ *n* [C] an adult female pig

soy /sɔɪ/ *adj* [not gradable] made from SOYBEANS ○ *soy milk/burgers/margarine*

soybean /ˈsɔɪ·biːn/ *n* [C] a type of bean grown esp. in Asia and the US, used as a food for people and animals

soy sauce /ˈsɔɪ·sɔːs/ *n* [U] a salty, dark brown liquid made from SOYBEANS, used as a flavoring esp. in Chinese and Japanese cooking

spa /spɑ/ *n* [C] a place where people can stay to improve their appearance or health by eating well and exercising and sometimes also by drinking or bathing in water with natural substances in it

space EMPTY PLACE /speɪs/ *n* [C/U] **1** an empty place ○ [C] *a parking/storage space* ○ [U] *He was staring into space, seeing nothing.* **2** Open space is land that has nothing built on it: [C] *Out west there are lots of wide open spaces.* **3** ***art*** In a painting, space is the appearance of depth even though the painting only has width and height.

space /speɪs/ *v* [T] to arrange the distance between things ○ *Try to space the stitches evenly as you sew.*

spacing /ˈspeɪ·sɪŋ/ *n* [U] ○ *Make sure there is equal spacing between you.*

spacious /ˈspeɪ·ʃəs/ *adj* having a lot of space ○ *A spacious house is comfortable.*

BEYOND EARTH /speɪs/ *n* [U] the area beyond the ATMOSPHERE (= air) of the earth ○ *space travel* ○ *The rocket blasted off to outer space.*

TIME /speɪs/ *n* [U] an amount of time ○ *Within the space of three weeks, I felt much better.*

space /speɪs/ *v* [T] ○ *The moves are spaced about eight to ten seconds apart.*

spacing /ˈspeɪ·sɪŋ/ *n* [U] ○ *The plan offered several options for the spacing of payments* (= the amount of time between them).

space-age *adj* very modern and using complicated electronics or equipment ○ *DNA testing gives investigators a space-age tool to tackle crimes.*

S

space bar *n* [U] a long key on a computer or TYPEWRITER that you press to make an opening between words

spacecraft /ˈspeɪs·kræft/, **spaceship** /ˈspeɪs·ʃɪp/ *n* [C] a vehicle designed for travel in space ○ *an unmanned spacecraft*

spaced out /speɪs ˈdɑʊt/, **spacey** /ˈspeɪ·si/ *adj slang* not aware of or paying attention to what is happening around you ○ *I just got home from work and I'm kind of spaced out.*

space shuttle *n* [C] a vehicle that takes people into space and comes back to Earth again

space station *n* [C] a structure in space where people can live and work

spacious /ˈspeɪ·ʃəs/ *adj* See at SPACE **EMPTY PLACE**.

spade /speɪd/ *n* [C] a tool with a blade for digging, esp. one with a long handle

spades /speɪdz/ *pl n* one of the four SUITS (= groups) of playing cards, the symbol for which is a black pointed leaf with a small stem

spaghetti /spəˈget̬·i/ *n* [U] pasta made in long, thin, round strips

spam /spæm/ *n* [U] E-MAIL that is sent to a lot of people, esp. e-mail that is not wanted ○ *Some Internet service providers block spam to subscribers.*
spam /spæm/ *v* [I/T] **-mm-** ○ *He denies he's spamming anyone.*

span /spæn/ *n* [C] **1** the length of something ○ *A lifetime is a span of about seventy years.* ○ *The Rangers scored three goals in the span of five minutes.* **2** A span is also the distance between two points, esp. between the structures that hold up a bridge: *In 1855, an 850-foot span was built to carry trains across the gorge.*
span /spæn/ *v* [T] **-nn-** ○ *An old bridge spans the river just outside the town.*

spangle /ˈspæŋ·gəl/ *n* [C] a small piece of shiny metal or plastic, used esp. to decorate clothes
spangled /ˈspæŋ·gəld/ *adj* ○ *She wore a spangled top and a striped skirt.*

S

spaniel /ˈspæn·jəl/ *n* [C] a type of dog of small or medium size with soft hair and long ears that hang down

spank /spæŋk/ *v* [T] to hit someone, esp. a child, with the hand on the buttocks, usually as a punishment
spanking /ˈspæŋ·kɪŋ/ *n* [C/U] ○ [U] *My parents didn't believe in spanking.*

spanner /ˈspæn·ər/ *n* [C] *Br* WRENCH **TOOL**

spar /spɑr/ *v* [I] **-rr- 1** to practice the sport of boxing without hitting hard ○ *Dexter sparred with his partner for about an hour.* **2** To spar also means to argue: *State officials are still sparring over funding.*

spare **SAVE** /spær, sper/ *v* [T] to decide not to hurt or destroy something or someone ○ *By reducing workers' hours, the company spared some people's jobs.*

AVOID /spær, sper/ *v* [T] to avoid something ○ *A quiet chat about this would spare everyone embarrassment.*
sparing /ˈspær·ɪŋ, ˈsper-/ *adj* ○ *He certainly is sparing in his praise* (= avoids giving much of it).
sparingly /ˈspær·ɪŋ·li, ˈsper-/ *adv* ○ *Apply the lotion sparingly.*

GIVE /spær, sper/ *v* [T] to give or use something because you have enough available ○ *Can you spare a dollar?* ○ *I'd love to come, but I'm afraid I can't spare the time.*

EXTRA /spær, sper/ *adj* [not gradable] not being used, or more than what is usually needed ○ *I keep my spare change in a jar.*
spare /spær, sper/ *n* [C] ○ *In case I lose my key, I keep a spare in the garage.*

THIN /spær, sper/ *adj* [*-er/-est* only] (of people) thin with no extra fat on the body ○ *He had the spare build of a runner.*

IDIOMS with spare

• **spare no effort**, **spare no expense** to achieve something by working as hard as possible or spending as much money as is necessary ○ *She spared no expense in decorating her office.*
• **to spare** still available ○ *I caught the plane with only five minutes to spare.*

spare part *n* [C usually plural] an extra piece that can be used to replace a piece that breaks, esp. in a machine

spareribs /ˈspær·rɪbz/, *short form* **ribs** *pl n* the RIBS (= chest bones) of a pig, with most of the meat removed ○ *Barbecued spareribs are a Texas specialty.*

spare time *n* [U] time when you are not working or do not have anything you must do ○ *What do you like to do in your spare time?*

spare tire **EXTRA TIRE**, **spare** *n* [C] an extra tire for a car

FAT *n* [C] a layer of fat around a person's waist ○ *I was determined to get some exercise and lose my growing spare tire.*

spark /spɑrk/ *n* [C] **1** a very small bit of something burning that flies out from a fire, or a flash of light seen when an electric current crosses an open space ○ *Flame, smoke, and sparks climbed into the dark sky.* ○ *Sparks from the old wiring started the fire.* ○ *(fig.) No one can light the spark that will make you a writer* (= the thing that causes you to write). **2** A spark of something is a small amount of it: *When students show a spark of interest, I try to give them extra encouragement.*
spark /spɑrk/ *v* [T] ○ *Downed power lines sparked fires in several parts of town.* ○ *Parks's actions in 1955 sparked the Civil Rights Movement.* ○ *We try to find stories that will spark our students' imaginations.*

IDIOM with spark

• **sparks fly** there is an angry argument ○ *The sparks really fly when my mother and her sister get together.*

sparkle /ˈspɑr·kəl/ *v* [I] **1** to shine brightly ○ *The lake sparkled in the sunlight.* **2** *fig.* Someone or something that sparkles is energetic, interesting, and exciting: *His writings sparkle with intelligence.*
sparkle /ˈspɑr·kəl/ *n* [U] ○ *We could tell she was happy by the sparkle in her eyes.*
sparkling /ˈspɑr·kə·lɪŋ, ˈspɑr·klɪŋ/ *adj* **1** *His writing is known for its sparkling dialogue.* ○ *The whole house was sparkling clean.* **2** A sparkling drink has bubbles in it: *sparkling water*

sparkler /ˈspɑr·klər/ *n* [C] a wire stick held in your hand and covered with a substance that produces SPARKS as it burns

spark plug *n* [C] a device in an engine that produces the electricity needed to start the fuel on fire

sparrow /ˈspær·oʊ/ *n* [C] a common, small, gray-brown bird

sparse /spɑrs/ *adj* [-er/-est only] small in number or amount and not dense or close together ○ *plants with sparse foliage* ○ *sparse attendance* ○ *a sparse vocabulary*
sparsely /ˈspɑr·sli/ *adv* ○ *This area is very sparsely settled because there isn't much water.*

spartan /ˈspɑrt·ən/ *adj* simple and not particularly comfortable ○ *Our spartan way of life included hard beds, hard work, and no TV.*

spasm /ˈspæz·əm/ *n* [C] a sudden, uncontrollable tightening of a muscle, or a sudden, burst of activity or energy ○ *He left the game because of back spasms.* ○ *The rebels' spasm of resistance was short-lived.*

spat FORCE OUT /spæt/ *past simple and past participle of* SPIT FORCE OUT
ARGUMENT /spæt/ *n* [C] an argument about something not important ○ *This was a spat, not a serious fight.*

spate /speɪt/ *n* [U] an unusually large number of events that happen suddenly and at about the same time ○ *We have had a spate of burglaries recently.*

spatter /ˈspæt̬·ər/ *v* [I/T] to scatter small drops or bits of liquid on a surface, or of liquid to fall in small drops ○ [T] *The taxi hit a puddle and spattered us with mud.*
spatter /ˈspæt̬·ər/ *n* [C] ○ *You left paint spatters on the floor!*

spatula /ˈspætʃ·ə·lə/ *n* [C] a kitchen utensil with a wide, flat blade, used esp. for lifting and spreading foods

spawn /spɔːn/ *n* [U] the eggs of fish
spawn /spɔːn/ *v* [I/T] (esp. of fish) to lay eggs ○ [I] *Salmon swim up rivers and streams to spawn.* ○ [T] (*fig.*) *Generous loans have spawned hundreds of small businesses* (= caused them to be started).

spay /speɪ/ *v* [T] to remove the organs that produce eggs from an animal

speak SAY WORDS /spiːk/ *v* [I/T] *past simp.* **spoke**, *past part.* **spoken** **1** to say words, to use the voice, or to have a conversation with someone ○ [I] *I heard someone speaking in the hallway.* ○ [I] *Please speak louder.* ○ [I] *"I'll never speak to you again," he said angrily.* ○ [T] *No one spoke a word* (= No one said anything). ○ [I] *She spoke in a whisper* (= very quietly). **2** Speaking is used with adverbs ending in -ly to show that you are talking from a particular point of view: [I] *Generally speaking, this is what happens when you see a nutritionist.*
speaker /ˈspiː·kər/ *n* [C] **1** a person who speaks or is speaking ○ *Will the speaker please identify herself?* **2** ***literature*** The speaker in a work of literature is the person who is imagined to be saying the written words, or the character who speaks a MONOLOGUE (= a long speech) ○ Related noun: SPEECH TALKING

KNOW A LANGUAGE /spiːk/ *v* [T] *past simp.* **spoke**, *past part.* **spoken** to talk in a language ○ *How many languages do you speak?* ○ *He speaks fluent Italian.* ○ *When I arrived in Canada, I didn't speak a word of English* (= I did not know any English).
speaker /ˈspiː·kər/ *n* [C] someone who speaks a particular language ○ *a French/Chinese speaker* ○ See also: SPEAKER ; SPEAKER at SPEAK FORMAL TALK

FORMAL TALK /spiːk/ *v* [I] *past simp.* **spoke**, *past part.* **spoken** to give a formal talk ○ *Will you be speaking at the conference?* ○ *Ted will speak about careers in education.* ○ Related noun: SPEECH FORMAL TALK
speaker /ˈspiː·kər/ *n* [C] **1** a person who gives a speech at a public event ○ *There will be three speakers at the graduation ceremony.* ○ *She's not a good public speaker.* **2** A speaker is also the person who controls the way in which business is done in an organization which makes laws, such as the US House of Representatives: *the Speaker of the House* ○ See also: SPEAKER ; SPEAKER at SPEAK KNOW A LANGUAGE
speaking /ˈspiː·kɪŋ/ *n* [U] ○ *She looks on public speaking as an opportunity to share information.* ○ *He has several speaking engagements* (= occasions when he will give a talk) *next month.*

SUGGEST /spiːk/ *v* [I/T] *past simp.* **spoke**, *past part.* **spoken** to show or express something without using words ○ [I always + adv/prep] *The incident spoke of shady financial dealings between the partners.* ○ [T] *Her face spoke volumes* (= showed clearly what she thought).

IDIOMS with speak

• **speak for** *yourself* I disagree with what you have just said ○ *"None of us like the hotel." "Speak for yourself – I think it's OK."*
• **on speaking terms** friendly enough to talk ○ *We had an argument, but we're back on speaking terms now.*
• **speaking as** *someone* with the experience of being this type of person ○ *Speaking as a mother of four, I can tell you that children are exhausting.*
• **speaking of** *someone/something* **1** related to the subject being discussed **2** *Casey is at a birthday party – speaking of birthdays, Abe's is Friday.*
• *something* **speaks for itself** something is clear and needs no further explanation ○ *The senator's record speaks for itself - he has always voted for what is best for this state.*

S

• **speak too soon** to say something which is quickly proven not to be true ○ *It looks like Hanna will be late – I spoke too soon, here she comes now.*
• **no** *something* **to speak of, nothing/not anything to speak of** not enough of something to make it worth talking about ○ *There was no snow to speak of this winter.*

PHRASAL VERBS with speak

• **speak for** *someone* to express the opinions or wishes of someone ○ *I can't speak for the others.*
• **speak out** to say in public what you think about something such as a law or an official plan or action ○ *He spoke out against the school's admissions policy.*
• **speak up** **TALK LOUD** to speak louder ○ *Speak up! We can't hear you in the back.*
• **speak up** **EXPRESS OPINION** to express your opinion ○ *If you disagree, please speak up.*
• **speak up for** *someone/something* to express support for a person or idea ○ *Many employees wouldn't speak up for themselves.* ○ *There is no one in the capital speaking up for this part of Ohio.*

WORD FAMILY speak			
Nouns	speaker speech speaking	*Adjectives*	unspeakable speechless outspoken unspoken
Verbs	speak		
Adverbs	unspeakably		

speaker /ˈspiː·kər/ *n* [C] a piece of electrical equipment through which recorded or broadcast sound can be heard ○ *We bought new speakers for our stereo system.* ○ See also: SPEAKER at SPEAK **KNOW A LANGUAGE**; SPEAKER at SPEAK **FORMAL TALK**

spear /spɪr/ *n* [C] a pole with a sharp point at one end, used as a weapon that is either thrown or held in the hand

spear /spɪr/ *v* [T] ○ *They catch the fish by spearing them.* ○ *(fig.) She speared the steak with her fork and lifted it off the grill.*

spearhead /ˈspɪr·hed/ *v* [T] to lead something such as a course of action or an attack ○ *Joe will spearhead our new marketing campaign.*

spearmint /ˈspɪr·mɪnt/ *n* [U] a strong, sweet flavoring, or the plant from which this flavoring comes ○ *spearmint gum/toothpaste/tea*

spec /spek/ *n* [C usually pl] *short form of* SPECIFICATION ○ *We're drawing up the specs for your new bathroom this week.*

special **NOT USUAL** /ˈspeʃ·əl/ *adj* **1** not ordinary or usual ○ *a special occasion* ○ *special attention/treatment* ○ *The car has a number of special safety features.* ○ *Is there anything special you'd like to do today?* ○ *The magazine published a special anniversary issue.* **2** Special can also mean unusually great or important: *You're very special to me.*

special /ˈspeʃ·əl/ *n* [C] **1** *There's a two-hour special* (= a television program that is not regularly shown) *on the Olympics tonight.* ○ *Our restaurant's specials today are pasta primavera, baked chicken with rice, and shrimp scampi* (= these foods are not always sold). **2** A special is also the sale of goods at a reduced price: *The store had a special on lawn furniture this week.*

specialty /ˈspeʃ·əl·ti/, *Br* **speciality** /ˌspeʃ·iː·ˈæl·əṭ·i/ *n* [C] a product that is unusually good in a particular place ○ *Oysters are a local specialty.* ○ *Paella is the specialty of the house at this restaurant.*

WORD CHOICES special

See also: **unusual**

If someone or something is special because of being better than usual, you can describe that person or thing as **exceptional** or **outstanding**.

Their standard of acting was very high but there was one ***exceptional/outstanding*** *performance.*

The adjective **extraordinary** is sometimes used to describe someone or something that is special in a surprising way.

Her capacity to remember things is ***extraordinary.***

She has an ***extraordinary*** *talent.*

The adjectives **deluxe** and **superior** are sometimes used to describe things you can buy that are special because they are particularly good quality.

The clerk tried to sell us the ***deluxe*** *model.*

The adjective **rare** is sometimes used instead of "special" when it means "unusual."

This is a ***rare*** *opportunity to see inside the building.*

PARTICULAR /ˈspeʃ·əl/ *adj* [not gradable] having a particular purpose ○ *Kevin goes to a special school for the blind.* ○ *She's a special correspondent for National Public Radio.*

specialist /ˈspeʃ·ə·ləst/ *n* [C] **1** someone who limits his or her studying or work to a particular area of knowledge, and who is an expert in that area ○ *She's a specialist in financial management.* **2** A specialist is also a doctor who works in and knows a lot about one particular area of medicine: *an eye/heart/joint specialist*

specialty /ˈspeʃ·əl·ti/, *Br* **speciality** /ˌspeʃ·iː·ˈæl·əṭ·i/ *n* [C] the subject of one's study or work, or a particular skill ○ *Her specialty is heart surgery.* ○ *The company's specialty is high-performance cars.*

specialize /ˈspeʃ·əˌlɑɪz/ *v* [I] ○ *She's a lawyer who specializes in accident cases.* ○ *The store specializes in Asian antiques.*

specialization /ˌspeʃ·ə·ləˈzeɪ·ʃən/ *n* [C/U] **1** the limiting of one's study or work to one particular area, or a particular area of knowledge ○ [C] *My main specialization was literature.* **2** ***biology*** Specialization is also the development in organisms of cells that have particular purposes.

specialized /ˈspeʃ·əˌlɑɪzd/ *adj* ○ *Her job is very specialized.*

specially /ˈspeʃ·ə·li/ *adv* [not gradable] in a particular way or for a particular purpose ○ *Her wheelchair was specially designed for her.*

CONFUSABLES

specially or especially?

Sometimes these two words both mean "for a particular purpose."

I cooked this meal specially/especially for you.

Specially is often used before an adjective made from a past participle.

specially prepared/specially trained.

He uses a specially adapted wheelchair.

Especially is used to give emphasis to a person or thing. This word is usually used at the beginning of a phrase but not at the beginning of a sentence.

I like all kinds of films, especially horror films.

~~*Especially I like horror films.*~~

WORD FAMILY special

Nouns	special specialist specialty specialization	*Adjectives*	special specialized
		Verbs	specialize
		Adverbs	specially

special education, *short form* **special ed** *n* [U] education for children with physical or mental problems, who need to be taught in a different way

special effects *pl n* artificial images, esp. in a film, that appear real but are created by artists and technical experts ○ *The movie won several awards for its special effects.*

special interest *n* [C] ***social studies*** a person, group, or organization that tries to influence government decisions to benefit itself

speciation /ˌspiː·siː'eɪ·ʃən, ˌspiː·ʃiː-/ *n* [U] ***biology*** the process by which new types of living things are thought to develop from existing ones during EVOLUTION

species /'spiː·ʃiːz, -siːz/ *n* [C] *pl* **species** ***biology*** a set of animals or plants, members of which have similar characteristics to each other and which can breed with each other

specific Ⓐ **PARTICULAR** /spɪ'sɪf·ɪk/ *adj* relating to one thing and not others; particular ○ *The virus attacks specific cells in the body.* ○ *The meeting is for the specific purpose of discussing the merger.*

specifically Ⓐ /spɪ'sɪf·ɪ·kli/ *adv* ○ *These jeans were designed specifically for women.* ○ *We went to New York specifically to visit the Metropolitan Museum.*

specificity Ⓐ /ˌspes·ə'fɪs·əṭ·i/ *n* [U] the quality of being particular to one person or thing

EXACT /spɪ'sɪf·ɪk/ *adj* clear and exact ○ *The report makes specific recommendations.* ○ *Can you be more specific?*

specifically Ⓐ /spɪ'sɪf·ɪ·kli/ *adv* ○ *I specifically asked you not to be late.* ○ *She mentioned you specifically.*

specificity Ⓐ /ˌspes·ə'fɪs·əṭ·i/ *n* [U] the quality of being clear and exact ○ *There was a dramatic lack of specificity in his answer.*

specifics Ⓐ /spɪ'sɪf·ɪks/ *pl n* exact details ○ *The proposal lacked specifics.* ○ *The specifics of the plan need to be worked out.*

specification Ⓐ /ˌspes·ə·fə'keɪ·ʃən/, *short form* **spec** *n* [C usually pl] a clear, detailed plan or description of how something will be made ○ *Specifications have been drawn up for the new aircraft.* ○ *The house was built to the architect's specifications.*

specify Ⓐ /'spes·əˌfɑɪ/ *v* [T] to state or describe something clearly and exactly ○ *The treaty specified terms for the withdrawal of troops.* ○ [+ question word] *He didn't specify how much was spent on advertising.*

specifiable Ⓐ /ˌspes·ə'fɑɪ·ə·bəl/ *adj*

specimen /'spes·ə·mən/ *n* [C] **1** something shown or examined as an example; a typical example ○ *He has a collection of rare insect specimens.* **2** *medical* A specimen is a small amount of something, such as urine or blood, taken for testing.

specious /'spiː·ʃəs/ *adj fml* seeming to be right or true, but really wrong or false ○ *a specious distinction* ○ *His whole argument is specious.*

speck /spek/ *n* [C] a very small mark, piece, or amount ○ *There are paint specks all over the floor.* ○ *These small islands are just specks on the map.* ○ *There's not a speck of dust in their house.*

speckled /'spek·əld/ *adj* having very small marks of a different color from the surface on which they are found ○ *We saw some speckled goose eggs.*

spectacle **UNUSUAL EVENT** /'spek·tɪ·kəl/ *n* [C] an unusual or unexpected event or situation that attracts attention ○ *an amazing/terrible spectacle* ○ *The trial became a public spectacle.* ○ *She made a spectacle of herself* (= behaved in a way that attracted attention and made her look ridiculous).

PUBLIC SHOW /'spek·tɪ·kəl/ *n* [C] a large public event or show ○ *The fireworks were a magnificent spectacle.*

spectacles /'spek·tɪ·kəlz/, *short form* **specs** /speks/ *pl n* glasses ○ *You could just see his eyes behind the thick lenses of his spectacles.*

spectacular /spek'tæk·jə·lər/ *adj* exciting and interesting because of being large or extreme ○ *a spectacular sunset* ○ *The scenery is spectacular.* ○ *He scored a spectacular touchdown.* ○ *The raffle was a spectacular success.*

spectacularly /spek'tæk·jə·lər·li/ *adv* ○ *The city is spectacularly lit at night.* ○ *She is spectacularly well paid.*

spectacular /spek'tæk·jə·lər/ *n* [C] a large, exciting event, show, or performance ○ *a television spectacular*

spectator /'spekˌteɪṭ·ər/ *n* [C] a person who watches an activity, esp. a public event, without taking part ○ *The stadium was packed with cheering spectators.*

spectator ion *n* [C] ***chemistry***, ***physics*** an ION that does not join in a chemical reaction

S

spectator sport *n* [C] a sport that people go to watch ○ *Swimming is a popular form of recreation but not a popular spectator sport.*

specter, **spectre** /ˈspek·tər/ *n* [C] **1** something that causes fear or worry ○ *The specter of inflation concerns many voters.* ○ *The familiar specter of adversity continues to accompany him.* **2** A specter is also a GHOST (= the spirit of a dead person that can be seen).

spectroscope /ˈspek·trəˌskoʊp/ *n* [C] ***science*** a piece of equipment that separates light into its colors

spectrum RANGE /ˈspek·trəm/ *n* [C] a range of objects, ideas, or opinions ○ *There's agreement across the political spectrum.* ○ *A wide spectrum of opinion was represented at the meeting.*

COLORS /ˈspek·trəm/ *n* [C] *pl* **spectra, spectrums** ***physics*** **1** the set of colors into which a beam of light can be separated **2** Spectrum also means a range of WAVES such as light waves or radio waves.

speculate GUESS /ˈspek·jəˌleɪt/ *v* [I] to form opinions about something without having the necessary information or facts; to make guesses ○ *I'm just speculating about what happened.* ○ *Officials refused to speculate on the cause of the crash.*

speculation /ˌspek·jəˈleɪ·ʃən/ *n* [C/U] ○ [U] *The rumors were dismissed as mere speculation.* ○ [U] *There is widespread speculation that the company is about to collapse.* ○ [C] *Len kept his speculations to himself.*

speculative /ˈspek·jə·lət̬·ɪv/ *adj* ○ *Our forecast for next year is speculative.*

TRADE /ˈspek·jəˌleɪt/ *v* [I] ***social studies*** to buy and sell with the hope that the value of what you buy will increase and that it can then be sold at a higher price in order to make a profit ○ *He made his money speculating in the gold and silver markets.*

speculation /ˌspek·jəˈleɪ·ʃən/ *n* [C/U] ○ [U] *currency/land speculation*

speculative /ˈspek·jə·lət̬·ɪv/ *adj* ○ *a speculative venture*

speculator /ˈspek·jəˌleɪt̬·ər/ *n* [C] ○ *a real estate speculator*

S

sped /sped/ *past simple and past participle of* SPEED

speech TALKING /spiːtʃ/ *n* [U] **1** the ability to talk, or the activity of talking ○ *People who suffer a stroke may experience a loss of speech.* **2** Your speech is also your way of talking: *His speech became slurred and indistinct.* **3** Speech can also mean the language used when talking: *Some expressions are used more in speech than in writing.* ○ Related verb: SPEAK SAY WORDS

speechless /ˈspiːtʃ·ləs/ *adj* [not gradable] temporarily unable to talk or to know what to say, esp. because of having strong feelings ○ *Her remark left me speechless.*

FORMAL TALK /spiːtʃ/ *n* [C] a formal talk given usually to a large number of people on a special occasion ○ *an acceptance speech* ○ *I'm nervous about the speech I'm making tomorrow.* ○ Related verb: SPEAK FORMAL TALK

USAGE

speech

The correct verb to use with **speech** is usually **make** or **give**.

I have to make a speech.
~~*I have to do a speech.*~~
He gave a speech at the conference.
~~*He said a speech at the conference.*~~

speechwriter /ˈspiːtʃˌrɑɪt̬·ər/ *n* [C] a person whose job is to write formal talks for someone else

speed /spiːd/ *n* [C/U] **1** (a) rate at which something moves or happens ○ [C] *a speed of 25 miles per hour* ○ [U] *Both cars were traveling at high speed.* ○ [U] *They came racing down the hill at top speed* (= as fast as they could go). ○ [U] *The processing speed of my new computer is much faster.* ○ [C] *This electric drill has two speeds* (= rates at which it turns). **2** ***physics*** Speed is also the rate at which something travels, expressed as the number of meters in a second. **3** A speed is also a GEAR (= part that controls the rate at which a vehicle moves): [C] *I have a ten-speed bicycle.*

speed /spiːd/ *v* [I/T] *past* **sped, speeded** to move, go, or happen fast, or to cause something to happen fast ○ [I] *The train sped along at over 120 miles per hour.* ○ [I] *This year seems to be speeding by/past.* ○ [T] *Ambulances sped the injured people* (= moved them quickly) *away from the scene.*

speeding /ˈspiːd·ɪŋ/ *n* [U] the act of driving a vehicle faster than is legally allowed ○ *He was fined $75 for speeding.*

speedy /ˈspiːd·i/ *adj* very quick or fast ○ *They hope to bring a speedy end to the conflict.*

speedily /ˈspiːd·əl·i/ *adv* ○ *The error can be speedily corrected.*

WORD FAMILY speed

Nouns	speed speeding	*Verbs* *Adverbs*	speed speedily
Adjectives	speedy		

PHRASAL VERB with speed

• **speed up** *(something)* [M] to go or happen faster, or to cause something to happen faster ○ *The car suddenly sped up and went through a red light.* ○ *He developed a new system to help speed up the work.*

speedboat /ˈspiːd·boʊt/ *n* [C] a small boat that has a powerful engine and can travel very fast

speed limit *n* [C] the fastest rate at which vehicles can legally travel on a particular road ○ *They raised the speed limit on the interstate to 65 miles per hour.*

speedometer /spɪˈdɑm·ət̬·ər/ *n* [C] a device in a vehicle that shows how fast the vehicle is moving

spell FORM WORDS /spel/ *v* [I/T] to form a word or words with the letters in the correct order ○ [I] *As a child he never learned to spell.* ○ [T] *Send it to Dr. Mikolajczyk – I'll spell that name for you* (= say the letters that form the word).

spelling /ˈspel·ɪŋ/ *n* [C/U] the forming of words with the letters in the correct order, or the way in which a word is formed ○ [C] *I shouldn't be marked wrong just because I used British spellings rather than American.*

RESULT /spel/ *v* [T] to have usually something unpleasant as a result ○ *This cold weather could spell trouble for gardeners.*

PERIOD /spel/ *n* [C] a period of time during which an activity or condition lasts ○ *a spell of wet weather* ○ *She lived in London for a short spell in the 1980s.*

POWER /spel/ *n* [C] a magic power produced by speaking a set of words or taking a specific set of actions ○ *He was placed under a spell that could be broken only when the princess kissed him.*

WORD FAMILY spell

Nouns	spelling misspelling	*Verbs*	spell misspell

PHRASAL VERBS with spell

•**spell** *something* **out SAY LETTERS** [M] to say or show letters ○ *They spelled out the letters Y, M, C, and A with their arms and bodies.*

•**spell** *something* **out EXPLAIN** [M] to explain something in detail ○ *The mayor has so far refused to spell out how he intends to raise the money.*

spellbound /ˈspel·bɑʊnd/ *adj* having your attention completely held by something, so that you cannot think about anything else ○ *At the circus, the children are spellbound, watching the acrobats perform.*

spelling bee *n* [C] a competition in which people, often students, try to spell increasingly difficult words until all but one make a mistake

spend MONEY /spend/ *v* [I/T] *past* **spent** to give money as a payment for something ○ [T] *We spent a lot of money on our vacation but we had a great time.*

spending /ˈspen·dɪŋ/ *n* [U] the act of giving money for goods and services ○ *Government spending for scientific research will be increased in next year's budget.* ○ *We have to find ways to cut spending and keep down costs.*

USAGE

spend

Remember to use the preposition **on** when you are talking about money or time you **spend** to do something.

Schools should spend more money on new technology.

~~*Schools should spend more money in new technology.*~~

You're spending too long on these tasks, Jon.

~~*You're spending too long for these tasks, Jon.*~~

WORD CHOICES spend

The most common alternative is the verb **pay**.

*When you booked the tickets, how much did you **pay**?*

*I **paid** an extra $30 to get a double room.*

The verb **invest** is used when someone spends money on something and hopes to get a profit.

*She's **invested** all her savings in the business.*

If someone spends a lot of money on something, the phrasal verb **pay out** is sometimes used.

*I've just **paid out** $700 to get the car fixed.*

If someone spends a lot of money on something that he or she wants but does not need, you can use the verb **splurge**.

*We've just **splurged** on new kitchen appliances.*

If someone spends a lot of money on something that seems like a waste of money, in informal English you can use the verb **blow**.

*We won a $15 million settlement in court and we **blew** it all in six years.*

The phrasal verb **dip into** is sometimes used when someone spends part of a supply of money that has been kept or saved.

*We had to **dip into** our savings to pay for the repairs.*

If someone spends money on something but does not want to, the phrasal verbs **fork over** and **shell out** are often used.

*We had to **shell out** $2000 to get the roof fixed.*

*I'm not going to **fork over** another $20 for their tickets.*

TIME /spend/ *v* [T] *past* **spent** to use time; to allow time to go past ○ *It doesn't look as if you spent very long on your homework.* ○ *I've spent many years building up my collection.* ○ *You can spend the night here if you like* (= stay here for the night).

FORCE /spend/ *v* [T] *past* **spent** to use energy, effort, force, etc., until there is no more left ○ *For the past month he's been spending all his energy trying to find a job.*

spent /spent/ *adj* [not gradable] **1** completely used to the point of no longer having any power or effectiveness ○ *Radio signals enabled recovery of the spent rocket 25 miles from the launch site.* **2** Spent also means having no energy left: *After doing her shopping, she was spent.*

spendthrift /ˈspend·θrɪft/ *n* [C] *disapproving* a person who wastes money, or spends more than is necessary ○ *I'm not a spendthrift and I really have to think about my purchases.*

sperm /spɜrm/ *n* [C/U] *pl* **sperm** ***biology*** **1** a cell produced by a male animal for the purpose of reproducing **2** Sperm is also SEMEN (= liquid containing the cells of male animals for reproducing).

spew /spjuː/ *v* [I/T] to flow or let out in large amounts ○ [I/T] *The volcano spewed (out) a giant cloud of ash, dust, and gases into the air.*

SPF *n* [U] *abbreviation for* sun protection factor (= the level of protection that a substance gives against damage to your skin from the sun) ○ *The American Cancer Society recommends people use sunscreen with at least 15 SPF.*

S

sphere Ⓐ **ROUND OBJECT** /sfɪr/ *n* [C] ***geometry*** a solid shape like a round ball ○ *This changes the shape of the cornea from a spoonlike form to a sphere.* ➤ Picture: **solid**

spherical Ⓐ /ˈsfɪr·ɪ·kəl, ˈsfer-/ *adj* ○ *The earth is not perfectly spherical.*

spherically Ⓐ /ˈsfɪr·ɪ·kli, ˈsfer-/ *adv*

AREA /sfɪr/ *n* [C] a range or area of activity ○ *In the foreign policy sphere, Li also indicated that China is ready to include human rights in its diplomacy.* ○ *When the children played they always remained within the sphere of their own little group.*

sphere of influence *n* [C] ***world history*** an area in which the power or interests of a country or an organization are of greatest importance

sphinx /sfɪŋks/ *n* [C] *pl* **sphinxes** an ancient, imaginary creature with a lion's body and a human head

spice /spɑɪs/ *n* [C/U] **1** a flavoring for food made from part of a plant, such as its fruit, seeds, or root, usually dried and often made into a powder ○ [C] *Cinnamon, ginger, and cloves are all spices.* ○ [U] *This curry needs a little more spice.* **2** Spice can also mean excitement or interest: [U] *"Variety is the spice of life" is a common expression.*

spicy /ˈspɑɪ·si/ *adj* flavored with spices that are hot to the taste ○ *spicy Mexican food*

PHRASAL VERB with spice

• **spice up** *something* [M] **1** to add spice to food to make it more interesting ○ *Ty is always looking for ways to spice up a recipe.* **2** If you spice up something you add excitement or interest to it: *That bluesy sound really spices up Hargrove's music.*

spick-and-span /ˌspɪk·ənˈspæn/ *adj* [not gradable] very clean and neat

spider /ˈspɑɪd·ər/ *n* [C] a small creature that looks like an insect with eight thin legs

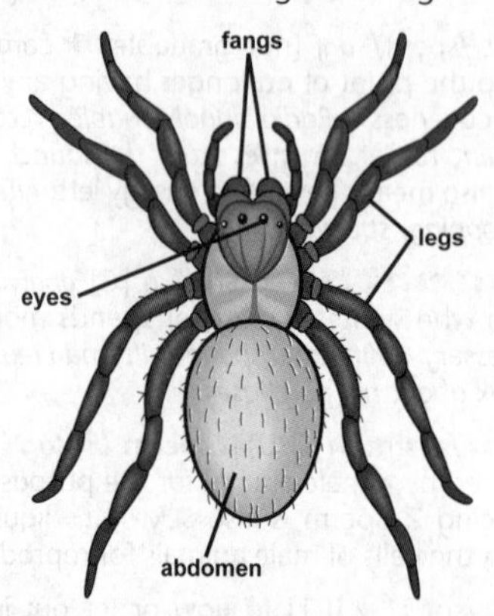

SPIDER

spiel /spiːl, ʃpiːl/ *n* [C] a speech, esp. one that is long and spoken quickly and is intended to persuade the listener about something ○ *a sales/marketing spiel*

spiffy /ˈspɪf·i/ *adj* [*-er/-est* only] *infml* stylish, attractive, or pleasing ○ *She got a spiffy haircut.*

spigot /ˈspɪɡ·ət, ˈspɪk-/ *n* [C] a device used to control a flow of liquid, esp. from a container or pipe ○ *(fig.) When an industry decides to lobby Congress, the money spigot is always open.*

spike **POINT** /spɑɪk/ *n* [C] **1** a long metal nail used to hold something in place, or a shape that is long and narrow and comes to a point at one end ○ *railroad spikes* **2** Spikes are also pointed pieces of metal fixed on the bottom of special shoes, used in some sports to catch in the ground and prevent falling or sliding, or the shoes themselves. **3** A spike is also a sudden increase, often shown on a GRAPH (= type of drawing) by a long, narrow shape that comes to a point at the top: *The upward spike in prices was attributed to bad weather in farm areas.*

MAKE STRONGER /spɑɪk/ *v* [T] to add a strong or dangerous substance, usually to a drink or to food ○ *In Italy you would find yourself eating a local dish of goulash copiously spiked with paprika.* ○ *(fig.) Their writing is spiked with a dry, cutting wit.*

spill /spɪl/ *v* [I/T] to cause a liquid to flow or fall over the edge of a container or beyond the limits of something, or of a liquid to flow or fall in this way ○ [T] *I just spilled gravy on my shirt.* ○ [T] *He tried to fill the sugar bowl and managed to spill sugar all over the floor.* ○ [I] *Some milk spilled on the floor.*

spill /spɪl/ *n* [C] **1** *The tanker started to leak oil and officials worried about a major oil spill.* **2** A spill is also a fall: *Jockey Luis Ortega suffered a broken ankle in a spill at Hollywood Park yesterday.*

IDIOM with spill

• **spill the beans** to let secret information become known ○ *We'll all be there at 6 for the surprise party – now don't spill the beans!*

PHRASAL VERB with spill

• **spill over** to reach or influence a larger area; spread ○ *The conflict threatens to spill over into neighboring regions.* ○ Related noun: SPILLOVER

spillover /ˈspɪl ˌoʊ·vər/ *n* [U] an effect that results from a problem spreading ○ *Chemotherapy poisons the bad cells, but we know there's spillover, and sometimes the treatment hurts patients.* ○ Related verb: SPILL OVER

spin **TURN** /spɪn/ *v* [I/T] *pres. part.* **spinning**, *past* **spun** to turn around and around, or to cause something or someone to turn ○ [I] *The earth spins on its axis.* ○ [I] *She heard footsteps behind her, and spun around to see who was there.* ○ [T] *The slight contact spun Joyce around.*

spin /spɪn/ *n* [C/U] a fast turning movement ○ [C] *I hit a patch of ice in the road, which sent the car into a spin.*

WAY OF REPRESENTING /spɪn/ *n* [U] a particular way of representing an event or situation to the public so that it will be understood in a way that you want it to be understood ○ *They tried to put a positive/negative spin on the story* (= They tried to make it seem better or worse), *but nobody was fooled.* ○ *To understand spin, he said, is to understand that you get your story told without getting your fingerprints on it.*

MAKE THREAD /spɪn/ *v* [T] *pres. part.* **spinning,** *past* **spun** to make thread by twisting fibers, or to produce something using thread ○ *Cotton is spun into thread.* ○ *Spiders spin webs.*

TRIP /spɪn/ *n* [C] a short trip taken for pleasure, usually in a car ○ *We went for a spin in Bill's new car.*

IDIOM with spin

• **spin** *your* **wheels** to use a lot of effort without achieving anything ○ *I sat in front of the computer all night trying to write, but I felt like I was just spinning my wheels.*

PHRASAL VERBS with spin

• **spin off** *something* [M] **1** to produce something additional, often something not originally planned ○ *The space program has spun off many new commercial technologies.* **2** To spin off something is also to form a separate company from parts of an existing company: *The corporation will spin its maintenance department off as an independent business.* ○ Related noun: SPINOFF

• **spin out** *something* [M] to describe the details of something ○ *Jay-Z spins out his raps over forceful grooves.*

spinach /ˈspɪn·ɪtʃ/ *n* [U] a vegetable that has wide, dark green leaves that are eaten cooked or raw ○ *a spinach salad*

spinal cord *n* [C] ***biology*** the set of nerves inside the SPINE that connect the brain to other nerves in the body

spin control *n* [U] an effort to control the damage done by a bad situation ○ *Various spokespersons attempted a desperate exercise in spin control to deny that Reagan ever made such a promise.*

spindly /ˈspɪn·dli/ *adj* long or tall and thin, and not appearing to be very solid or strong ○ *Carrie, almost six, was all spindly arms and legs.*

spin doctor *n* [C] *slang* a person who represents esp. a political situation in a way that is likely to help one side and hurt another ○ *News coverage of the campaign can be influenced to a candidate's advantage by spin doctors.*

spine **BONE** /spɑɪn/, **backbone, spinal column** *n* [C] the line of bones down the center of the back that provides support for the body

spinal /ˈspɑɪn·ᵊl/ *adj* [not gradable] ○ *He suffered a spinal injury from the fall.*

POINT /spɑɪn/ *n* [C] one of the thin, pointed objects that are part of the outer surface of some animals and plants ○ *Be careful of the cactus spines.*

BOOK PART /spɑɪn/ *n* [C] the end of a book where the pages are attached and which usually shows the writer's name and title on its outer part

spineless /ˈspɑɪn·ləs/ *adj disapproving* lacking determination and the willingness to take risks ○ *It upset me to realize how spineless I was.*

spinoff /ˈspɪn·ɔːf/ *n* [C] **1** a result that is produced in addition to the main result of a process ○ *The research has spinoffs in the development of medical equipment.* **2** A spinoff is also a separate company formed from parts of an existing company. ○ Related verb: SPIN OFF

spinster /ˈspɪn·stər/ *n* [C] *dated* a woman who is not married, esp. a woman who is no longer young and seems unlikely ever to marry ○ **USAGE:** This word is likely to be offensive except if it is used about people in the past.

spiral /ˈspɑɪ·rəl/ *n* [C] a shape of a continuous, curving line that forms circles around a center point ○ *A corkscrew is made in a spiral.* ○ (*fig.*) *Roy was bitter about the downward spiral of his life* (= it was becoming continuously worse).

spiral /ˈspɑɪ·rəl/ *adj* [not gradable] ○ *New playground equipment includes a large spiral slide.*

spiral /ˈspɑɪ·rəl/ *v* [I] **-l-, -ll-** ○ *The engine quit, and my beautiful model airplane spiraled downward.* ○ *High winds spiraled around the storm center.*

spiral notebook *n* [C] a book of paper for writing that is held together by a wire that curves around and around through small holes at the edge of the paper

spire /spɑɪr/ *n* [C] a tall, narrow structure that rises to a point, esp. on a church ○ *The mountains' rocky spires surrounded us.*

spirit **STATE OF MIND** /ˈspɪr·ət/ *n* [U] a state of mind or attitude ○ *It's very important to play the game in the right spirit.* ○ *Rock music in the 1960s expressed the spirit of the times.*

spirits /ˈspɪr·əts/ *pl n* a mood ○ *I've been in low spirits all day.* ○ See also: SPIRITS

INNER CHARACTER /ˈspɪr·ət/ *n* [C/U] **1** the inner character of a person, thought of as different from the material person we can see and touch ○ [U] *All her life she remained young in spirit, bubbling with ideas.* ○ [C] *It is a belief of many religions that your spirit lives on after your body dies.* **2** A spirit is also something that can be felt to be present but cannot be seen, similar to a GHOST.

ENTHUSIASM /ˈspɪr·ət/ *n* [U] enthusiasm and energy ○ *The orchestra performed the symphony with great spirit.*

spirited /ˈspɪr·ət̬·əd/ *adj* ○ *It was an unusually spirited performance of the play.*

MOVE /ˈspɪr·ət/ *v* [T always + adv/prep] to move someone or something secretly ○ [M] *Everyone wonders who spirited away the body.*

spirits /ˈspɪr·əts/ *pl n fml* strong alcoholic drink; LIQUOR ○ *Sale of beer, wine, or spirits to anyone under 21 is illegal.* ○ See also: SPIRITS at SPIRIT STATE OF MIND

spiritual **SONG** /ˈspɪr·ətʃ·ə·wəl/ *n* [C] a kind of religious song, originally developed by African-Americans

OF THE SPIRIT /ˈspɪr·ətʃ·ə·wəl/ *adj* of or relating to the inner character of a person ○ *Religion focuses on the spiritual side of life.* ○ *He's the group's spiritual leader.*

spirituality /ˌspɪr·ətʃ·əˈwæl·ət̬·i/ *n* [U] ○ *Researchers are delving into the roots of human spirituality.*

spiritually /ˈspɪr·ətʃ·ə·wə·li/ *adv* ○ *He seemed to be a rare person, both spiritually and physically.*

S

spit **FORCE OUT** /spɪt/ *v* [I/T] *pres. part.* **spitting,** *past* **spat, spit** to force out liquid in the mouth, esp. SALIVA (= liquid produced in the mouth) ○ [I] *He spat on the ground and stared straight ahead.* ○ [M] *(fig.) He angrily spat an insult out* (= said it quickly).
spit /spɪt/ *n* [U] *infml* SALIVA (= liquid produced in the mouth) ○ *Spit dribbled down his chin.*

ROD /spɪt/ *n* [C] a long, thin rod put through meat to hold it while it cooks over a fire

LAND /spɪt/ *n* [C] a long, thin point of land that sticks out into water ○ *Our hotel was perched on a spit of land in the harbor.*

IDIOM with spit

• **spit it out** *infml* tell me what you want to say without waiting any longer ○ *Come on, spit it out – I can't do anything if you don't tell me what's going on.*

PHRASAL VERB with spit

• **spit up** *(something)* [M] to bring food up from the stomach out of the mouth, or cough something up out of the mouth ○ *A lot of babies spit up after eating.*

spite /spɑɪt/ *n* [U] the desire to annoy, upset, or hurt someone ○ *He let the air out of your tires just for spite.*
spite /spɑɪt/ *v* [T] ○ *I think he died without making a will just to spite his family.*
spiteful /ˈspɑɪt·fəl/ *adj* ○ *They were just spiteful gossips spreading rumors.*

IDIOM with spite

• **in spite of** *something* even though there is something unpleasant or bad happening ○ *In spite of his injury, Ricardo will play in Saturday's game.*

splash **HIT WITH LIQUID** /splæʃ/ *v* [I/T] to scatter liquid or to cause liquid to scatter through the air or onto something ○ [T] *She splashed her face with cold water.* ○ [I] *Kids love to splash around in mud puddles.*
splash /splæʃ/ *n* [C] an amount of liquid scattered, or the sound made by liquid being scattered ○ *I wiped up the splashes from the floor.* ○ *Jimmy jumped into the pool with a splash.*

AREA OF BRIGHTNESS /splæʃ/ *n* [C] a bright area of color or light ○ *a splash of sunlight* ○ *The child's red dress brought a splash of color to the picture.*
splashy /ˈsplæʃ·i/ *adj* attracting attention, particularly colorful or showy ○ *Her dress was made of a bright, splashy print.*

splat /splæt/ *n* [U] *infml* the sound of something wet hitting a surface ○ *The tomato hit the window with a splat.*

splatter /ˈsplæt̬·ər/ *v* [I/T] (esp. of something wet) to hit and scatter onto a surface in small drops, or to cause this to happen ○ [T] *The bike was splattered with mud.*
splatter /ˈsplæt̬·ər/ *n* [C] ○ *Splatters of paint covered the floor.*

splay /spleɪ/ *v* [I/T] to spread wide apart ○ [I] *He lay on the floor, his legs splayed out beneath him.*

splendid /ˈsplen·dəd/ *adj* extremely good, large, or important ○ *Our splendid weather ended with a terrible storm.* ○ *The splendid old opera house was torn down.*
splendidly /ˈsplen·dəd·li/ *adv* very well; admirably ○ *Although we were very different, we got along splendidly.*

splendor, *Cdn, Br* **splendour** /ˈsplen·dər/ *n* [C/U] great beauty, or something that causes admiration and attention ○ [U] *It took several years to restore the building to its original splendor.* ○ [C] *We can only imagine the splendors of ancient Rome.*

splice /splɑɪs/ *v* [T] to join the ends of something so that they become one piece ○ *Scientists splice genes to produce the protein.*

splint /splɪnt/ *n* [C] a flat piece of material that does not bend, used to support a broken bone and to keep it in one position

splinter /ˈsplɪnt·ər/ *n* [C] a small, sharp, piece of wood, glass, or similar material that has broken off a larger piece ○ *She tried to ignore the splinter in her foot.*
splinter /ˈsplɪnt·ər/ *v* [I] ○ *The old tree cracked and splintered as it fell.*

splinter group *n* [C] a group of people who have left a political party or other organization to form a new, separate organization

split /splɪt/ *v* [I/T] *pres. part.* **splitting,** *past* **split** **1** to divide into two or more parts, esp. along a particular line ○ [T] *I suggest we split the profits between us.* ○ [T] *The teacher split the class into three groups.* ○ [I] *His pants split when he jumped the fence.* **2** *slang* To split also means to leave a place: [I] *The movie was boring, so I split.*
split /splɪt/ *n* [C] a long, thin tear, or a division ○ *There's a split in this sheet.* ○ *Peace talks are threatened by a split among rebel leaders.*

IDIOM with split

• **split the difference** to accept only part of what you originally wanted when making an agreement with someone, esp. an agreement involving money ○ *You want $50 for the bike and I say it's worth $30 – let's split the difference and I'll pay you $40.*

PHRASAL VERB with split

• **split up** to end a marriage or relationship

split-level *adj* [not gradable] (of houses, buildings, or rooms) having floors on slightly different levels with a few stairs connecting them ○ *a split-level living room*

split second *n* [C] a very short period of time ○ *For a split second we thought the bus would crash.*

splitting /ˈsplɪt̬·ɪŋ/ *adj* [not gradable] very strong, severe, or painful ○ *a splitting headache* ○ *an ear-splitting noise*

splotch /splɑtʃ/ *n* [C] a mark or spot with an irregular shape ○ *The rash showed as red splotches on her face.*

S

splurge /ˈsplɜrdʒ/ *v* [I/T] to spend money on something that is more expensive than you usually buy ○ [I] *We could save the money or splurge on a new car*
splurge /ˈsplɜrdʒ/ *n* [C] ○ *We go to that restaurant for our big end-of-the-year splurge.*

spoil DESTROY /spɔɪl/ *v* [I/T] *past* **spoiled, spoilt** to destroy or damage something, or to become destroyed or damaged ○ [T] *The oil spill spoiled five miles of coastline.* ○ [T] *Don't tell me how it ends, you'll spoil the movie for me.* ○ [I] *Food spoils quickly in hot weather.*
spoiled /spɔɪld/ *adj* [not gradable] ○ *spoiled meat*

WORD CHOICES spoil

Ruin is a very common alternative to "spoil."

*I put too much salt in the sauce and **ruined** it.*

The verb **deface** is sometimes used when someone spoils the appearance of something by writing or drawing on it.

*Many of the library books had been **defaced**.*

The verb **disfigure** is sometimes used when a person's physical appearance has been spoiled.

*Her face was **disfigured** by the scar.*

If something spoils a friendship or other relationship, you can use the verbs **sour** or **poison**.

*The long dispute has **poisoned/soured** relations between the two countries.*

In informal situations you can use the phrasal verbs **mess up** and **screw up** to say that something has been spoiled.

*Laurie's illness has completely **messed up** all our holiday plans.*

*That new software has really **screwed up** my computer.*

TREAT TOO WELL /spɔɪl/ *v* [T] *past* **spoiled, spoilt** to treat someone very well, esp. by being too generous ○ *My vacation spoiled me.* ○ *"We're spoiling you," he said, handing her another cookie.*
spoiled /spɔɪld/ *adj* [not gradable] ○ *You're acting like a spoiled brat.*

WORD FAMILY spoil

Nouns	spoils	*Adjectives*	spoiled
Verbs	spoil		unspoiled

spoils /spɔɪlz/ *pl n* goods, advantages, or profits obtained by winning a war or being in a particular position or situation ○ *Only one competitor wins and gets the spoils of victory.*

spoke SPEAK /spoʊk/ *past simple of* SPEAK
WHEEL PART /spoʊk/ *n* [C] any of the rods that join the edge of a wheel to its center to strengthen it

spoken /ˈspoʊ·kən/ *past participle of* SPEAK

spokesman /ˈspoʊk·smən/ *n* [C] *pl* **-men** a male SPOKESPERSON

spokesperson /ˈspoʊkˌspɜr·sən/ *n* [C] *pl* **-people** a person who makes official, public statements for a group or organization ○ *a government spokesperson*

spokeswoman /ˈspoʊkˌswʊm·ən/ *n* [C] *pl* **-women** a female SPOKESPERSON

sponge SUBSTANCE /spʌndʒ/ *n* [C/U] a substance that is full of holes, soft when wet, and able to absorb a lot of liquid, used for washing and cleaning ○ [C] *He wiped off the table with a soapy sponge.*
sponge /spʌndʒ/ *v* [T] to wash or clean, esp. by using a wet sponge or cloth ○ *Sponge the stain promptly with cold water.* ○ [M] *She's always sponging off the kitchen counter.*
spongy /ˈspʌn·dʒi/ *adj* ○ *The ground was damp and spongy* (= soft).
GET MONEY /spʌndʒ/ *v* [I/T] to get money, food, or other needs from other people rather than by taking care of yourself, or to live by getting help from other people ○ [I] *He's been sponging off her for years.*

sponge cake *n* [C] a soft, light cake made with eggs, sugar, and flour but without fat

sponsor /ˈspɑn·sər/ *v* [T] to support a person, organization, or activity by giving money, encouragement, or other help ○ *The Rotary Club sponsors Little League baseball in the summer.*
sponsor /ˈspɑn·sər/ *n* [C] ○ *Corporate sponsors support many public TV programs.*
sponsorship /ˈspɑn·sərˌʃɪp/ *n* [C/U] ○ [U] *corporate sponsorship of the arts*

spontaneous /spɑnˈteɪ·niː·əs/ *adj* happening naturally, without planning or encouragement ○ *a spontaneous performance* ○ *spontaneous affection*
spontaneously /spɑnˈteɪ·niː·ə·sli/ *adv* ○ *The children spontaneously gave us hugs and kisses.*

spoof /spuːf/ *n* [C] an original work that copies the style of another work in a way meant to be ridiculous or humorous ○ *The book ends with a hilarious spoof of an academic conference.*
spoof /spuːf/ *v* [I/T] ○ [T] *The funniest part of the show spoofed TV news.*

spook FRIGHTEN /spuːk/ *v* [T] to frighten a person or animal ○ *That car wreck spooked me badly.*
spooky /ˈspuː·ki/ *adj infml* ○ *I think it's very spooky sleeping in a dark and creaky house.*
SPIRIT /spuːk/ *n* [C] *infml* GHOST
PERSON /spuːk/ *n* [C] *slang* SPY PERSON

spool /spuːl/ *n* [C] a cylinder that is wider at each end, around which esp. thread, wire, or film is wrapped ○ *TV cables were unwound from huge spools.*

spoon /spuːn/ *n* [C] a utensil that is a small, flat bowl with a handle, used for mixing, serving, and eating food ○ *a wooden cooking spoon* ○ *a silver baby spoon*
spoon /spuːn/ *v* [T always + adv/prep] ○ *Spoon a little gravy over the meat.*
spoonful /ˈspuːn·fʊl/ *n* [C] *pl* **spoonfuls, spoonsful** the amount that a spoon will hold ○ *a spoonful of mustard*

spoon-feed PROVIDE INFORMATION *v* [T] *past* **spoon-fed** to give someone so much help or information that the person has no opportunity to act or think independently ○ *I was being spoon-fed friendly audiences that wouldn't give me trouble.*

FEED *v* [T] *past* **spoon-fed** to feed someone with a spoon ○ *The zookeepers were spoon-feeding the baby chimpanzees.*

sporadic /spəˈræd·ɪk/ *adj* not happening or appearing in a pattern; not continuous or regular ○ *She makes sporadic trips to Europe.* ○ *The storm caused sporadic flooding throughout the region.*
sporadically /spəˈræd·ɪ·kli/ *adv* ○ *I've been working sporadically this year.*

spore /spɔːr, spour/ *n* [C] ***biology*** a cell produced by plants without seeds and by some other organisms and that is able to grow into a new plant or organism

sport GAME /spɔːrt, spourt/ *n* [C/U] a game, competition, or similar activity, done for enjoyment or as a job, that takes physical effort and skill and is played or done by following particular rules ○ [C] *Football, baseball, and basketball are all team sports.* ○ [U] *Do you hunt for sport or in order to eat?*
sporting /ˈspɔːrt̬·ɪŋ, ˈspourt̬-/ *adj* connected with sports ○ *The Olympics is the biggest sporting event in the world.*
sports /spɔːrts, spourts/ *adj* [not gradable] connected with sports ○ *He only reads the sports section of the newspaper.*
sportsmanship /ˈspɔːrt·smən,ʃɪp, ˈspourt-/ *n* [U] the quality of showing fairness, respect, and generosity toward the opposing team or player and for the sport itself when competing

PERSON /spɔːrt, spourt/ *n* [C] *infml* a person who has a good attitude about playing a game or having to do something ○ *He was a very bad sport when he lost a game.* ○ *Be a sport and take your little sister to the movies with you.*

WEAR /spɔːrt, spourt/ *v* [T] to wear or be decorated with something ○ *Back in the 1960s he sported bell-bottoms and long hair.*

WORD FAMILY sport			
Nouns	sport sportsmanship	*Adjectives*	sporting sports sporty
Verbs	sport		

sports car *n* [C] a fast, low car, often big enough for only two people

sportscaster /ˈspɔːrt,skæs·tər/ *n* [C] someone who describes sporting events and news about sports for broadcast

sports jacket, **sport coat** *n* [C] a man's jacket, which is worn with pants of a different color or cloth

sportswear /ˈspɔːrt·swer, -swær/ *n* [U] informal clothing designed for comfort ○ *Sportswear has become popular around the world.*

sport utility vehicle, *abbreviation* **SUV** *n* [C] a very large car with a truck engine and two or three rows of seats

sporty /ˈspɔːrt̬·i, ˈspourt̬·i/ *adj* stylish and suitable for active people ○ *They drive a sporty red car.* ○ *You're looking very sporty in your new jacket.*

spot MARK /spɑt/ *n* [C] **1** a mark, usually round, that is different esp. in color from the area around it ○ *You got a spot on your new blouse.* **2** *esp. Cdn, Br* A spot is a PIMPLE.

SEE /spɑt/ *v* [T] **-tt-** to see or notice someone or something ○ *Darryl spotted a woodpecker high on the tree.*

PLACE /spɑt/ *n* [C] **1** a particular place ○ *a vacation spot* ○ *Our cat has a favorite spot where he loves to sleep.* **2** A spot is also a job in a particular organization or a position within a group, esp. in sports: *When Sain was injured, they asked me to fill his spot.*

BROADCAST /spɑt/ *n* [C] **1** a period of time during which a broadcast takes place ○ *NBC put the show on in the 7 p.m. spot.* **2** A spot is also an advertisement: *a 30-second spot*

WORD FAMILY spot			
Nouns	spot	*Verbs*	spot
Adjectives	spotted spotless	*Adverbs*	spotlessly

IDIOM with spot

• **on the spot 1** at that moment or place ○ *He was arrested on the spot.* **2** Someone who is put **on the spot** is forced to do or say something the person would rather not do or say: *I'm not trying to put you on the spot, but could you explain why you did that?*

spot check *n* [C] a close look at a few items in a group ○ *A spot check revealed that many students are out with flu.*

spotless /ˈspɑt·ləs/ *adj* **1** extremely clean ○ *Her kitchen counters were spotless.* **2** If someone's behavior or reputation is spotless, it is extremely good: *a spotless career*

spotlight /ˈspɑt·lɑɪt/ *n* [C] a circle of strong light that comes from a LAMP whose beam can be directed ○ *Spotlights followed the two dancers around the stage.* ○ (*fig.*) *The incident brought toxic waste into the national spotlight* (= directed attention to it).
spotlight /ˈspɑt·lɑɪt/ *v* [T] ○ (*fig.*) *Special-interest groups are effective at spotlighting neglected issues* (= directing attention to them).

spouse /spɑus, spɑuz/ *n* [C] a person's husband or wife

spout FLOW /spɑut/ *v* [I/T] to send out liquid or flames quickly and with force, or of liquid or flame to flow quickly ○ [T] *The volcano spouted flames and red-hot rocks.*

OPENING /spɑut/ *n* [C] a tube-shaped opening that allows liquids to be poured out of a container ○ *Fruit is put into the blender and juice comes out the spout.*

SPEAK /spɑut/ *v* [I/T] to say or repeat something, often in a way that is annoying for other people ○

[T] *The man was spouting nonsense about people trying to spy on him.*

sprain /spreɪn/ *v* [T] to stretch or tear the tissue that limits the movement of a joint in the body ○ *My dad fell and sprained his knee.*

sprain /spreɪn/ *n* [C] ○ *He twisted his ankle and suffered a bad sprain.*

sprang /spræŋ/ *past simple of* SPRING

sprawl /sprɔːl/ *v* [I] to spread out esp. awkwardly over a large area ○ *Jamie came home from school and sprawled on the couch.*

sprawling /ˈsprɔː·lɪŋ/ *adj* existing or reaching over a large area ○ *the sprawling city of Los Angeles*

sprawl /sprɔːl/ *n* [C usually sing] ○ *A massive sprawl of high-rise buildings fills the site.*

spray **LIQUID** /spreɪ/ *n* [C/U] a mass of very small drops of liquid forced through the air, or a container from which small drops of liquid are forced out ○ [U] *As the waves crashed over the rocks, some of the ocean spray reached them where they stood.* ○ [C] *When my nose is stuffy, I use a nasal spray.*

spray /spreɪ/ *v* [I/T] ○ [T] *Store employees offer to spray you with perfume.* ○ [T] (*fig.*) *They were sprayed with flying glass from the shattered windows.*

FLOWERS /spreɪ/ *n* [C] a single, small branch or stem with leaves and flowers on it, or a small arrangement of cut flowers ○ *On the table was a spray of fresh flowers.*

spread **COVER** /spred/ *v* [I/T] *past* **spread** to cover or cause something to cover an object or an area ○ [T] *Pianist Eubie Blake could spread his fingers over 20 keys.* ○ [M] *She spread out the tablecloth.* ○ [I] *I had toast spread with strawberry jam.* ○ [I] *A strange look spread over his face.*

spread /spred/ *n* [C] **1** A spread is a cover for a bed. **2** A spread is also a soft food put on bread or other food: *a cheese spread* **3** A spread is also a meal, esp. one with a lot of different foods arranged on a table: *This is quite a spread.*

MOVE /spred/ *v* [I/T] to move from one place to another, or to cause something to move or be communicated ○ [I] *The flames quickly spread to the next room.* ○ [I] *Obesity is spreading in many countries.* ○ [I] *Doctors fear the cancer may spread to other organs.* ○ [T] *She's been spreading lies about him.* ○ [T] *Neighbors have been spreading the word* (= communicating information) *about the proposed building project.*

spread /spred/ *n* [U] ○ *Jazz records fostered the spread of American culture.* ○ *More should be done to stop the spread of this disease.*

IDIOM with spread

• **spread** *yourself* **(too) thin** to try to do too many different things at the same time ○ *The company has expanded into many different areas and has probably spread itself too thin.*

PHRASAL VERBS with spread

• **spread out** to cover a larger area ○ *Soldiers spread out among the trees.* ○ *Dark clouds began to spread out across the sky.*

• **spread** *something* **out (over** *something***)** [M] to cause something to happen over a period of time, usually in stages ○ *You can spread the payments out over six months if you want to.*

spree /spriː/ *n* [C] a short period of doing something in an extreme way without control ○ *a shopping/spending spree*

sprig /sprɪg/ *n* [C] a small branch of a plant with leaves on it ○ *a sprig of mint*

spring **SEASON** /sprɪŋ/ *n* [C/U] the season of the year between winter and summer, lasting from March to June north of the equator and from September to December south of the equator, when the weather becomes warmer and leaves and plants start to grow again ○ [C] *last/this/next spring* ○ [U] *It was a beautiful spring day.*

CURVED METAL /sprɪŋ/ *n* [C] a piece of curved or bent metal that can be pressed into a smaller space but will return to its usual shape if released ○ *I could feel the springs of the lumpy mattress.*

MOVE QUICKLY /sprɪŋ/ *v past simp.* **sprang, sprung,** *past part.* **sprung** to move quickly and suddenly toward a particular place or to a new condition ○ [I always + adv/prep] *She sprang out of bed and ran to the window.* ○ [L] *A single kick made the door spring open.*

APPEAR SUDDENLY /sprɪŋ/ *v* [always + adv/prep] *past simp.* **sprang, sprung,** *past part.* **sprung** to appear or exist suddenly, or to cause something to happen suddenly ○ [I always + adv/prep] *Little patches of weeds seem to spring up everywhere in my backyard.* ○ [T always + adv/prep] *Mr. Pollack likes to spring quizzes on the class.*

WATER /sprɪŋ/ *n* [C] a place where water flows out from the ground ○ *The lake is fed by underground springs.*

IDIOMS with spring

• *someone* **is no spring chicken,** *someone* **is not a spring chicken** someone is no longer young ○ *I think I look pretty good, considering I'm no spring chicken.*

• **spring to life** to become active ○ *By nine o'clock, the town had sprung to life with shoppers in the streets.*

• **spring to mind** to be quickly thought of ○ *Mention fashion and Kate's name immediately springs to mind.*

PHRASAL VERB with spring

• **spring for** *something infml* to pay for or buy something ○ *To increase the radio's performance, spring for a powered antenna.*

springboard /ˈsprɪŋ·bɔːrd, -bourd/ *n* [C] **1** a board that bends when you jump on the end of it, used to help you jump higher in some sports or physical exercises **2** A springboard is also something that provides an opportunity to achieve something: *Many young women hope modeling will be a springboard to stardom.*

spring break *n* [C] a school vacation in the spring

S

spring chicken *n* [C] *infml* a young person ○ *I think I look pretty good, considering I'm no spring chicken.*

spring constant *n* [U] ***physics*** the force needed to to stretch or press a spring, divided by the distance that the spring gets longer or shorter

spring fever *n* [U] a feeling of excitement because the weather suddenly becomes warmer in spring

springtime /ˈsprɪŋ·tɑɪm/ *n* [U] the season of spring

sprinkle /ˈsprɪŋ·kəl/ *v* [I/T] **1** to scatter a few drops or small pieces of something ○ [T] *Sprinkle cheese on the pizza.* **2** Someone who says that it is sprinkling means it is raining lightly.
sprinkle /ˈsprɪŋ·kəl/, **sprinkling** /ˈsprɪŋ·klɪŋ/ *n* [C] ○ *We might get a sprinkle today* (= a light rain).
sprinkler /ˈsprɪŋ·klər/ *n* [C] a device used in gardens and areas of grass for scattering drops of water over the ground

sprinkler system *n* [C] a set of pipes and devices that carry water through a building in order to spray it on a fire

sprint /sprɪnt/ *v* [I] to run very fast esp. for a short distance, either as a competitor in a sport or because you are in a hurry to get somewhere ○ *Clark sprinted past Smith and caught the ball in the end zone.* ○ *He sprinted off to meet his girlfriend.*
sprint /sprɪnt/ *n* [C] a short race run at full speed, or any short period of fast running
sprinter /ˈsprɪnt·ər/ *n* [C] ○ *Carl Lewis was a world-class sprinter for many years.*

sprout /sprɑʊt/ *v* [I/T] to begin to grow, or to produce new growth ○ [I] *Our new seedlings have begun to sprout.*
sprout /sprɑʊt/ *n* [C] a new growth of a plant ○ *a bean sprout*

spruce /spruːs/ *n* [C/U] an evergreen tree with thin, pointed leaves, or the wood of this tree

PHRASAL VERB with spruce

• **spruce up** *something* [M] to improve the appearance of something by making it neater or by adding decorations ○ *She'd spruce the place up with plastic flowers.*

sprung /sprʌŋ/ *past simple and past participle of* SPRING

spry /sprɑɪ/ *adj* (esp. of an old person) active and able to move quickly and energetically ○ *A spry elderly lady was pulling weeds in a large garden.*

spud /spʌd/ *n* [C] *infml* a potato

spun /spʌn/ *past simple and past participle of* SPIN

spunk /spʌŋk/ *n* [U] *approving* brave determination and confidence even in discouraging situations ○ *The kid showed lots of spunk to compete with her arm in a cast.*
spunky /ˈspʌŋ·ki/ *adj approving* ○ *a spunky nine-year-old*

spur ENCOURAGE /spɜr/ *v* [T] **-rr-** to encourage an activity or development, or to cause something to develop faster ○ *The huge new factory spurred economic growth in the entire region.*
spur /spɜr/ *n* [C]

SHARP OBJECT /spɜr/ *n* [C] a sharp metal object sticking out of a U-shaped device that is attached to the heel of a boot and used by a rider to encourage a horse to go faster

IDIOM with spur

• **on the spur of the moment** suddenly without any planning ○ *On the spur of the moment, we decided to go to the beach.*

PHRASAL VERB with spur

• **spur** *someone* **on** [M] to encourage someone ○ *Ambition spurred him on.*

spurious /ˈspjʊr·iː·əs/ *adj fml* based on false reasoning or information that is not true, and therefore not to be trusted ○ *They made spurious claims of personal injury.*

spurn /spɜrn/ *v* [T] to refuse to accept something ○ *She spurned his attentions and refused to see him.*

spurt /spɜrt/ *v* [I/T] to flow out suddenly and with force ○ [I] *Water spurted from the faucet into the sink.*
spurt /spɜrt/ *n* [C] **1** *There was a sudden spurt of flame.* **2** A spurt is also a sudden and brief period of increased activity, effort, or speed: *a child's growth spurt* ○ *Penn State ended the game with a 10–4 spurt* (= period of scoring).

sputter /ˈspʌt̬·ər/ *v* [I/T] **1** to make repeated explosive sounds ○ [I] *The plane's engine began to sputter.* **2** To sputter is also to speak in a way that is not clear, esp. because you are angry: [I] *He sputtered and flapped his hands in response.*

spy PERSON /spɑɪ/, *slang* **spook** *n* [C] a person employed by a country or organization to secretly gather and report information about another country or organization
spy /spɑɪ/ *v* [I] ○ *Bazoft confessed on television that he spied for Israel.*

SEE /spɑɪ/ *v* [T] to see or notice someone or something ○ *He kept on their trail until he spied firelight from a camp nestled in the rocks.*

spyware /ˈspɑɪ·wer, -wær/ *n* [U] a program that is put on a computer that is connected to the INTERNET without the knowledge of the user and that gathers information about the user ○ *Viruses are bad, and spyware is even worse.*

sq. *adj abbreviation for* SQUARE

squabble /ˈskwɑb·əl/ *n* [C] a disagreement, often about an unimportant matter ○ *family squabbles with your brothers and sisters*
squabble /ˈskwɑb·əl/ *v* [I] ○ *They squabbled about how the money would be spent.*

squad /skwɑd/ *n* [C] a small group of people trained to work together as a unit ○ *The rescue squad managed to free the child.*

squad car *n* [C] a PATROL CAR

squadron /ˈskwɑd·rən/ *n* [C] a unit of one of the armed forces ○ *a squadron of Navy jets*

squalid /ˈskwɑl·əd/ *adj* extremely dirty, poor, and unpleasant ○ *The squalid apartment was her first home in the city.*

squalor /ˈskwɑl·ər/ *n* [U] ○ *He lived in dreadful squalor despite having a small fortune in the bank.*

squall /skwɔːl/ *n* [C] a sudden, strong wind or brief storm, esp. over water ○ *Occasional rain squalls blow furiously across the sea.*

squander /ˈskwɑn·dər/ *v* [T] to waste money, or to use something valuable that you have a limited amount of in a bad or foolish way ○ *Government should not squander the taxpayers' money.* ○ *Don't squander your opportunities when you are young.*

square **SHAPE** /skwer, skwær/ *n* [C] ***geometry*** a flat shape with four sides of equal length and four angles of 90°, or an area or object having this shape ➤ Picture: **geometry**

square /skwer, skwær/ *adj* [-*er*/-*est* only] **1** *They set up the square card tables for the bridge players.* **2** (*abbreviation* **sq**) A square unit of measurement is an area that is a particular distance wide and the same distance long: *The box was three feet square.* ○ *The correct figure is 900 sq miles.*

MULTIPLY /skwer, skwær/ *v* [T] ***mathematics*** to multiply a number by itself ○ *Ten squared equals a hundred.*

square /skwer, skwær/ *n* [C] the result of multiplying a number by itself ○ *The square of 7 is 49.*

PLACE /skwer, skwær/ *n* [C] a small area of open land in a city or town, often one in the shape of a square

EQUAL /skwer, skwær/ *adj* [-*er*/-*est* only] **1** having all debts paid or other matters arranged fairly ○ *I paid last time, so if you pay now, we're square.* **2** A **square deal** is a fair agreement: *All I want is a square deal.*

PERSON /skwer, skwær/ *n* [C] *dated, slang* a person who is old-fashioned

PHRASAL VERBS with square

• **square away** *something/someone* [M] *infml* to complete all necessary arrangements for something or someone ○ *I've got my tickets and hotel squared away.* ○ *The dishes are done and the kids are all squared away.*

• **square off** to oppose someone in a competition or prepare to fight someone ○ *Bradley is expected to square off with Cook in the next election.*

• **square** *something* **with** *something* to accept one idea or fact as able to exist with something else ○ *It's hard to square his honest record in the past with these charges.*

square dance /ˈskwer·dæns, ˈskwær-/ *n* [C] an active, often fast-moving dance in which each of four pairs of dancers takes a position opposite another pair and at the same distance, forming a square

squarely /ˈskwer·li, ˈskwær-/ *adv* [not gradable] **1** directly and with no doubt ○ *We have to face these issues squarely and honestly.* ○ *The blame for Wade's death rests squarely on him.* **2** Squarely also means in a direct way and esp. with force: *Williams hit the ball squarely, sending it over the fence.*

square meal *n* [C] a satisfying meal with enough to eat

square root *n* [C] ***mathematics*** of a particular number, a number that is SQUARED (= multiplied by itself) to produce that particular number ○ *the square root of 25 is 5*

squash **VEGETABLE** /skwɑʃ/ *n* [C/U] *pl* **squash, squashes** a vegetable with a hard skin and many seeds at its center

CRUSH /skwɑʃ/ *v* [T] **1** to press down or crush something so that it becomes flat ○ *Kate squashed the paper cup and dropped it into the trash can.* **2** If you squash a plan or idea, you stop it completely and suddenly: *Republican leaders will probably try to squash the tax cut.*

PUSH /skwɑʃ/ *v* [I/T] to push a person or thing into a small space ○ [T] *Four of us were squashed into the back seat of his car.*

SPORT /skwɑʃ/ *n* [U] a game played in an enclosed playing area between two or four people who use RACKETS (= tightly fixed nets in frames attached to long handles) to hit a hard rubber ball against a wall

squat **SIT** /skwɑt/ *v* [I] **-tt-** to position yourself close to the ground by bending your legs under you and balancing on the front part of your feet ○ *He squatted down and picked up some pebbles.*

SHORT /skwɑt/ *adj* [-*er*/-*est* only] **-tt-** short and wide ○ *Mickey was a squat, dark man with a ragged beard.*

squatter /ˈskwɑt̬·ər/ *n* [C] a person who lives in an empty building or area of land without the permission of the owner

squawk /skwɔːk/ *v* [I] **1** to make a loud, unpleasant cry ○ *Sea gulls squawked overhead.* **2** *infml* Someone who squawks about something complains about it in a way that gets attention: *Employers have begun to squawk because of rising health insurance costs.*

squawk /skwɔːk/ *n* [C] ○ *The owl flew off with a squawk.*

S

squeak **MAKE SOUND** /skwiːk/ *v* [I/T] to make a short, very high sound or cry ○ [I] *Her expensive shoes squeaked when she walked.*

squeak /skwiːk/ *n* [C] ○ *Every time I stepped on the brakes I'd hear a little squeak.*

squeaky /ˈskwiː·ki/ *adj* ○ *The door swung open on its squeaky hinges.*

JUST DO /skwiːk/ *v* [I always + adv/prep] to just manage to do something ○ *Our team squeaked out a victory in Sunday's game.*

squeaky-clean *adj infml* **1** extremely clean **2** A person who is described as squeaky-clean is completely correct, esp. in public behavior, and has never done anything immoral.

squeal **MAKE SOUND** /skwiːl/ *v* [I/T] to make a long, very high sound or cry ○ [I] *The tires squealed*

as I sped away. ○ [T] *"This is awesome," Mary Lou squealed in her coach's ear.*
squeal /skwiːl/ *n* [C] ○ *She collapsed into giggles and squeals when her sister tickled her.*

GIVE INFORMATION /skwiːl/ *v* [I] *slang* to give the authorities information about people you know who have committed crimes or done something wrong ○ *He refused to squeal on his buddies.*

squeamish /ˈskwiː·mɪʃ/ *adj* easily upset or disgusted by things or actions you find unpleasant ○ *Dad was squeamish about killing roaches.*

squeeze **PRESS TOGETHER** /skwiːz/ *v* [T] to press something firmly, or to force something out, esp. a liquid, by pressing ○ *Bake for 15 minutes, then squeeze the cloves to get the softened garlic out.* ○ *I squeezed her shoulder* (= pressed it affectionately with a hand).
squeeze /skwiːz/ *n* [C] ○ *I gave his shoulder a squeeze.* ○ *(fig.) State parks will feel the squeeze from budget cuts* (= the cuts will have a limiting effect).

FORCE INTO /skwiːz/ *v* [always + adv/prep] to force someone or something into a small space or a short period of time ○ [I] *I'm just not able to squeeze into last year's swimsuit.* ○ [T] *She's asking me to squeeze a shopping trip into my day off.* ○ [M] *You can squeeze in six people at the table.*
squeeze /skwiːz/ *n* [C usually sing] ○ *It'll be a tight squeeze with four other people in the car, but I'll give you a lift.*

PHRASAL VERB with squeeze

• **squeeze** *something* **out of** *someone/something* to get or obtain something from someone with difficulty, or to cause something to happen by a continuous and difficult effort ○ *He used various tricks to squeeze money out of his father in England.* ○ *Small businesses are being squeezed out of the neighborhood by developers.*

squelch /skweltʃ/ *v* [T] to stop something quickly and completely ○ *One professor claimed that the university tried to squelch his criticisms.*

S

squid /skwɪd/ *n* [C/U] *pl* **squid** an edible sea creature that has a long body with eight arms and two TENTACLES (= arm-like parts) around the mouth ○ [U] *deep-fried squid*

squiggle /ˈskwɪɡ·əl/ *n* [C] a short line written or drawn in an irregular, curving way ○ *To my eye this picture just looks like squiggles.*
squiggly /ˈskwɪɡ·li/ *adj* ○ *squiggly lines*

squint /skwɪnt/ *v* [I] to look with your eyes partly closed ○ *He squinted into the morning sun.*

squire **OWNER** /skwɑɪr/ *n* [C] *old use* (in the past in England) a man who owned most of the land around a village

TAKE /skwɑɪr/ *v* [T always + adv/prep] *fml* to take someone places; ESCORT ○ *Skinner uses the plane to squire around bureaucrats.*

squirm /ˈskwɜrm/ *v* [I] to make twisting movements with the body, esp. because of embarrassment, pain, or excitement ○ *The kids squirmed in their chairs.*

squirrel /ˈskwɜr·əl, ˈskwʌ·rəl/ *n* [C] a small furry animal with a long tail which climbs trees and feeds on nuts and seeds

squirt /skwɜrt/ *v* [I/T] to quickly force a liquid out of something, or of liquids to flow through a narrow opening ○ [T] *Squirt lemon juice on the clams and enjoy them.* ○ [I] *(fig.) The ball squirted free* (= moved quickly away) *and bounced out of bounds.*
squirt /skwɜrt/ *n* [C] **1** *A squirt of glue should fix it.* **2** *infml* A squirt is also a small person you consider unimportant. ○ **USAGE:** This use is usually intended to be insulting.

squish /skwɪʃ/ *v* [I/T] to crush something, or to make the sound you make when you walk through something soft and wet ○ [I always + adv/prep] *We squished through the mud.*
squishy /ˈskwɪʃ·i/ *adj* soft and easily crushed or shaped ○ *squishy white bread*

St. **STREET** /striːt/ *n abbreviation for* street ○ *19 East 17th St.* ○ **USAGE:** Used in writing after the name or number of a street.

PERSON *n abbreviation for* SAINT ○ *St. Bartholomew's Church*

stab /stæb/ *v* [T] **-bb-** to injure someone using a sharp, pointed object ○ *He was stabbed with a fork.*
stab /stæb/ *n* [C] **1** *He's recovering from stab wounds.* **2** A stab is also a sudden feeling: *Cheri felt a sudden stab of guilt.* **3** A stab is also an attempt to do something that you may not be able to do: *I wouldn't even take a stab at estimating its cost.*
stabbing /ˈstæb·ɪŋ/ *n* [C] ○ *Police said they did not know what led to the stabbing.*

IDIOM with stab

• **stab** *someone* **in the back** to harm someone who trusts you ○ *A lot of people in this business think they have to stab each other in the back to succeed.*

stable Ⓐ **FIXED** /ˈsteɪ·bəl/ *adj* firmly fixed or not likely to move or change ○ *Don't climb the ladder until you're sure it's stable.* ○ *She's in the hospital in stable condition.* ○ *The country needs a stable government that is free of corruption.*
stability Ⓐ /stəˈbɪl·əṭ·i/ *n* [U] ○ *economic and political stability* ○ *I'm worried about his mental stability.*
stabilize Ⓐ /ˈsteɪ·bəˌlɑɪz/ *v* [I/T] to cause something to become fixed and stop changing, esp. in order to keep it from becoming worse, or to become fixed and stop changing ○ [T] *These medicines stabilize your heart rate and lower blood pressure.* ○ [I] *Once your salary stabilizes you can start to save a little money.*
stabilization Ⓐ /ˌsteɪ·bə·ləˈzeɪ·ʃən/ *n* [U] ○ *stabilization of the economy*

BUILDING /ˈsteɪ·bəl/ *n* [C] a building in which horses or cattle are kept ○ *The horses in the stable have plenty of straw.*

staccato /stəˈkɑṭ·oʊ/ *adj, adv* **1** (of music) played as short, separate notes **2** If a noise is described as staccato, it consists of a series of short, quick sounds: *The sudden staccato burst of fireworks startled us.*

stack /stæk/ *n* [C] **1** a pile of things arranged one on top of another ○ *a stack of pancakes* ○ *stacks of newspapers* **2** In a LIBRARY (= a building with a collection of books and study materials), **the stacks** are the area where books are stored: *I found the book in the stacks, but it was in the wrong place.*
stack /stæk/ *v* [T] ○ *The cases were stacked neatly in the middle of the room.*

IDIOM with stack

• **stack the deck (against** *someone/something***)** to arrange something so that the results are unfair ○ *Critics say that having so many businessmen on the panel stacks the deck against the environment.*

stadium /ˈsteɪd·iː·əm/ *n* [C] a large structure consisting of many rows of seats surrounding an area of land on which sports are played and where sometimes other public events happen ○ *a football stadium* ○ *Yankee Stadium*

staff PEOPLE /stæf/ *n* [C] a group of people who work for an organization, often for a special purpose, or who work for a manager within an organization ○ *The coaching staff felt we needed more defense.* ○ *She joined the staff of the Smithsonian Institution in 1954.*
staff /stæf/ *v* [T] ○ *The after-school program is staffed entirely by volunteers.*

USAGE

staff or employee?

Staff always refers to a group of people who work for a store, company, or organization. If you want to refer to a single person, you can use **employee**.

The company has 17 full-time staff.
~~*The company has 17 full-time staffs.*~~
Is there an employee who speaks Spanish?
~~*Is there a staff who can speak Spanish?*~~

MUSIC /stæf/, **stave** /steɪv/ *n* [C] ***music*** the five lines and four spaces between them on which musical notes are written

staffer /ˈstæf·ər/ *n* [C] someone who is a member of the group of people who work for an organization ○ *a Senate staffer*

stag /stæg/ *n* [C] an adult male deer

stage PART /steɪdʒ/ *n* [C] **1** a part of an activity, or a period of development ○ *The software is in the early stages of development.* ○ *At that stage of my life, I was married but didn't have any children.* **2** If you do something **in stages**, you divide the activity into parts and complete each part separately: *We're repairing the house in stages – first the roof and chimney, then the windows.*

COMMON LEARNER ERROR

stage

Stage cannot be used to mean a training course.

He took a course in web design.
~~*He took a stage in web design.*~~

THEATER /steɪdʒ/ *n* [C/U] **1** the area in a theater, often raised above ground level, on which actors or entertainers perform ○ [C] *When you're sitting in the balcony, you see more of the ceiling than the stage.* ○ [U] *Berlin's most successful stage musical was "Annie Get Your Gun."* ○ [U] *She was a popular star of the musical stage* (= of this type of theater). ○ *As a child, he appeared on stage* (= performing in theaters). **2** A stage is also a particular area of public life: [C] *His novel includes such actors on the world stage as Fidel Castro and the Pope.*
stage /steɪdʒ/ *v* [T] **1** to arrange the performance of a play or other entertainment ○ *Bejart was staging his own ballets.* **2** If you stage an event, you organize it: *Bus drivers are planning to stage a 24-hour strike.*
staging /ˈsteɪ·dʒɪŋ/ *n* [C] ○ *The theater produced the first staging of any of Eugene O'Neill's works.*

stagecoach /ˈsteɪdʒ·koʊtʃ/ *n* [C] (in the past) a covered vehicle pulled by horses that carried passengers and goods on regular routes ○ *The coming of the stagecoach was once a major event in remote American settlements.*

stage fright *n* [U] feeling nervous because you are about to perform or talk to a large group of people

stagger MOVE /ˈstæg·ər/ *v* [I/T] to walk or move awkwardly, as if you have lost your balance, or to cause someone to move awkwardly or to lose his or her balance ○ [T] *When he hit his head on a shelf, it momentarily staggered him.* ○ [I] *She staggered out of bed to answer the phone.*

ARRANGE /ˈstæg·ər/ *v* [T] to arrange events or schedules so that they happen at different times, or to arrange objects so they are not regular ○ *The clinics will try to stagger vaccination times to minimize waits and confusion.*
staggered /ˈstæg·ərd/ *adj* [not gradable] ○ *staggered payments* ○ *Cabinets can be hung at staggered heights.*

staggering /ˈstæg·ə·rɪŋ/ *adj* shocking because of being extremely large ○ *Nursing care costs a staggering $15,000 per week!*

staging /ˈsteɪ·dʒɪŋ/ *n* [C] ○ See at STAGE THEATER

staging area *n* [C] a place where people gather before going somewhere or doing something ○ *Bangalore is a comfortable staging area for several South India tours.*

stagnant NOT FLOWING /ˈstæg·nənt/ *adj* (of liquids or air) not flowing or moving, and often smelling unpleasant ○ *Hot, stagnant air filled the subway.*

NOT BUSY /ˈstæg·nənt/ *adj* not growing or developing ○ *Jobs become scarce in a stagnant economy.*
stagnate /ˈstæg·neɪt/ *v* [I] ○ *The local economy stagnated when the factories closed.*
stagnation /stægˈneɪ·ʃən/ *n* [U] ○ *High costs have caused stagnation in the building industries.*

staid /steɪd/ *adj* not exciting or fashionable; serious ○ *She never adjusted to her husband's staid lifestyle.*

stain /steɪn/ *v* [I/T] **1** to leave a mark on something that is difficult to remove, or to become colored or spoiled by a mark ○ [T] *Strawberry juice stained my shirt.* ○ [I] *This carpet is practical because it doesn't stain easily.* **2** If you stain wood, you put a substance on it that changes its color: [T] *Instead of painting the woodwork, she stained it dark brown.*
stain /steɪn/ *n* [C] **1** *The tomato sauce left a stain on the tablecloth.* **2** A stain is also a thin, oily liquid used to change the color of wood. **3** ***biology*** A stain is also a chemical used to color cells to make them easier to see when studying them under a MICROSCOPE.
stainless /ˈsteɪn·ləs/ *adj*

stained glass /steɪnd ˈglæs/ *n* [U] pieces of colored glass that have been joined to form a picture or pattern, used esp. in the windows of churches

stainless steel *n* [U] a type of steel which does not chemically react with air or water and does not change color

staircase /ˈster·keɪs, ˈstær-/ *n* [C] a set of stairs inside a building, including the bars and posts that people to hold on to as they go up or down

stairs /sterz, stærz/ *pl n* a set of steps that lead from one level to another, esp. in a building ○ *Her office is at the top of the stairs.*
stair /ster, stær/ *n* [C] a step in a set of stairs ○ *The top stair creaked loudly as she stepped on it.*

stairway /ˈster·weɪ, ˈstær-/ *n* [C] a passage that contains a set of steps

stake **SHARE** /steɪk/ *n* [C] **1** a share in something, esp. a financial share in a business, or an emotional investment in something ○ *He holds a 20% stake in the company.* ○ *Parents have a large stake in their children's education.* **2** In an activity or competition, the stakes are the costs or risks involved in competing: *Global competition has raised the stakes of doing business.*

RISK /steɪk/ *n* [C] the amount of money that you risk on the result of a game or competition ○ *Almost everyone has a stake in the global economy these days.*
stake /steɪk/ *v* [T] ○ *He has talent and ambition, and I'd stake my reputation on his success.*

POLE /steɪk/ *n* [C] a thick, strong, pointed wood or metal pole pushed into the ground and used to mark a spot or to support something ○ *Stakes in the ground marked the outline of the new building.*
stake /steɪk/ *v* [T] to fasten something to a stake ○ *Tomato plants should be staked soon after they are planted.*

IDIOMS with **stake**

• **at stake** in danger of being lost ○ *About 3000 jobs are at stake if the company closes down.*
• **stake a claim (to** *something***)** to announce that something belongs to you ○ *Stacy staked her claim to to her uncle's fortune.*

PHRASAL VERBS with **stake**

• **stake out** *something* **CLAIM** [M] to claim ownership of or a particular interest in something ○ *All politicians will stake out lowering taxes as their very own idea.*
• **stake out** *something* **WATCH** [M] to secretly watch a place, esp. for illegal activity ○ *A group of reporters staked out the hallway, hoping to catch the singer on her way out.* ○ Related noun: STAKEOUT

stakeout /ˈsteɪ·kaʊt/ *n* [C] an act of secretly watching a place or person, esp. to see if any illegal activity is taking place ○ *The stakeout did not provide much help to investigators.* ○ Related verb: STAKE OUT

stalactite /stæˈlʌk ˌtɑɪt/ *n* [C] a solid mass hanging from the top of a CAVE (= large hole in the ground) that is thicker at the top and thinner at the bottom and is formed by drops of water ○ Compare STALAGMITE

STALACTITE

stalagmite /stəˈlæg ˌmɑɪt/ *n* [C] a solid mass rising from the bottom of a CAVE (= large hole in the ground) that is thicker at the bottom and thinner at the top and is formed by drops of water ○ Compare STALACTITE

STALAGMITE

stale /steɪl/ *adj* [*-er/-est* only] not fresh or new ○ *stale bread* ○ *Stale air smells very bad.* ○ *I used to like that sitcom, but it's getting kind of stale.*

stalemate /ˈsteɪl·meɪt/ *n* [C/U] a situation in which nothing can change or no action can be taken ○ [U] *Stalemate in Congress over education reform has made voters angry.* ○ [C] *The arrival of fresh troops broke the military stalemate.*

stalk PLANT PART /stɔːk/ *n* [C] any stem on a plant, esp. the main stem ○ *Cynthia says those flowers have pretty tall stalks.*

FOLLOW /stɔːk/ *v* [T] to follow an animal or person as closely as possible without being seen or heard ○ *He spent the weekend stalking deer to photograph them.* ○ *Celebrities are often stalked by photographers and reporters.*

stalker /ˈstɔː·kər/ *n* [C] someone who follows a person, usually intending to hurt that person ○ *The idea of a stalker on the loose is quite frightening.*

stalking /ˈstɔː·kɪŋ/ *n* [U] ○ *The writer accused this one fan of stalking.*

WALK /stɔːk/ *v* [I always + adv/prep] to walk in an angry or proud way ○ *She didn't say anything but stalked furiously out of the room.*

stall DELAY /stɔːl/ *v* [I/T] to delay or put off action ○ [I] *They're just stalling, trying to avoid making a decision.* ○ [T] *I can stall him for a few minutes.*

STOP WORKING /stɔːl/ *v* [I/T] to cause a vehicle or engine to stop suddenly, or of a vehicle or engine to stop suddenly ○ [I] *My car stalled at the traffic light.*

AREA /stɔːl/ *n* [C] **1** a separate area in which an animal is kept **2** A stall is also a small enclosed space used for a particular purpose: *The bathroom had a tiled shower stall.*

stallion /ˈstæl·jən/ *n* [C] an adult male horse, esp. one used for breeding ○ Compare MARE

stalwart /ˈstɔːl·wərt/ *adj* very loyal to someone or something ○ *She has always been a stalwart supporter of the arts.*

stamina /ˈstæm·ə·nə/ *n* [U] the physical or mental strength to do something for a long time, esp. something difficult ○ *The triathlon is a great test of stamina.*

stammer /ˈstæm·ər/ *v* [I/T] to speak or say something with unusual pauses or repeated sounds; STUTTER ○ [I] *He stammers when he is nervous.*

stammer /ˈstæm·ər/ *n* [U] ○ *Robert has a slight stammer which was much worse when he was younger.*

stamp HIT WITH FOOT /stæmp, stɑmp/ *v* [I/T] to hit the floor or ground hard with a foot, usually making a loud noise ○ [T] *She stood by the road, stamping her feet to stay warm.* ○ [I] *I wish those people upstairs would stop stamping around.* ○ Compare STOMP

stamp /stæmp, stɑmp/ *n* [C] ○ *With a stamp of her foot she hurried out.*

MAIL /stæmp/, **postage stamp** *n* [C] a small piece of paper, usually with a colorful design, that is attached to a package or envelope to show that the charge for sending it through the mail has been paid ○ *The new stamps depict blues singers.*

stamped /stæmpt/ *adj* [not gradable] ○ *Send a stamped, self-addressed envelope.*

MARK /stæmp/ *n* [C] a tool for printing or cutting a mark into an object, or the mark made by such a tool ○ *The guard examined the permit, then reached for his rubber stamp.* ○ *The stamp on the rim shows that Paul Revere made this mug.*

stamp /stæmp/ *v* [T] ○ *An immigration official stamped his passport.* ○ *(fig.) That scene will be stamped in my memory forever.*

QUALITY /stæmp/ *n* [U] a particular quality or character ○ *This painting clearly bears the stamp of genius.*

PHRASAL VERB with stamp

• **stamp** *something* **out** [M] to stop or destroy something ○ *Our first goal is to stamp out hunger.*

stampede /stæmˈpiːd/ *n* [C] a situation where a large group of frightened animals, esp. horses or cattle, all run in the same direction ○ *(fig.) A stampede of fans tried to enter the stadium at once.*

stampede /stæmˈpiːd/ *v* [I/T] ○ [T] *A loud clap of thunder stampeded the herd.*

stance OPINION /stæns/ *n* [C] an opinion about something, esp. one that is publicly expressed ○ *The governor's stance on the issue of tax cuts is well known.*

WAY OF STANDING /stæns/ *n* [C] a way of standing ○ *He had the stance of a baseball player focusing on the ball.*

stanch /stɔːntʃ, stɑntʃ/ *v* [T] STAUNCH STOP

stand BE VERTICAL /stænd/ *v* [I/T] *past* **stood 1** to be on your feet or get into a vertical position, or to put someone or something into a vertical position ○ [I] *I stood motionless as the snake slithered by.* ○ [I] *Please stand back so the paramedics can get through.* ○ [T always + adv/prep] *I stood the ironing board against the wall.* **2** If you **stand on** *your* **hands** or **head**, you hold yourself with your head near or on the ground and your feet in the air.

standing /ˈstæn·dɪŋ/ *adj* [not gradable] ○ *Only one building was left standing after the earthquake.* ○ See also: STANDING PERMANENT; STANDING RANK

BE IN SITUATION /stænd/ *v past* **stood 1** to be or get into a particular state or situation ○ [I] *As things stand right now, there's no telling who will win.* ○ [I] *Let the mixture stand for fifteen minutes.* ○ [L] *Some of these older houses have stood empty for years.* ○ [L] *He stands accused of tax evasion.* ○ [L] *Even without her shoes, she stands over six feet tall.* **2** If someone **stands trial**, accusations against that person are examined in a court of law. ○ *Berenson will stand trial next month in the county court.*

BE IN PLACE /stænd/ *v* [I] *past* **stood** to be in a particular place ○ *A desk stood in the middle of the room.* ○ *A taxi stood at the curb, waiting for a fare.* ○ *(fig.) If you want to apply for promotion, I won't stand in your way.*

ACCEPT /stænd/ *v* [T] *past* **stood** to be able to accept or bear something unpleasant or difficult ○ *Our tent won't stand another storm like the last one.* ○ *How can you stand all that pressure at work?*

S

OPINION /stænd/ *n* [C] an opinion, esp. one publicly expressed ○ *What's his stand on health care reform?* ○ *She'll no doubt take a strong stand against raising taxes.*

stand /stænd/ *v* [I always + adv/prep] *past* **stood** ○ *On foreign policy, the president seems to stand to the left of his party.*

COURT /stænd/ *n* [C] *short form of* WITNESS STAND

STRUCTURE /stænd/ *n* [C] a small structure where food, newspapers, candy, and other small items are sold ○ *Hot dog stands with colorful umbrellas always attract a crowd.*

GROUP /stænd/ *n* [C] a group of trees or tall plants ○ *Stands of spruce trees dotted the hills.*

FRAME /stænd/ *n* [C] a pole or frame designed to hold something ○ *a coat stand* ○ *He mounts the baseballs on marble stands.*

WORD FAMILY stand			
Nouns	stand standing	*Adjectives*	standing outstanding
Verbs	stand	*Adverbs*	outstandingly

IDIOMS with stand

• **I stand corrected** I admit that I said something that was not correct ○ *I stand corrected – the company was founded in 1927, not 1926.*

• **it stands to reason (that)** something seems likely to be true ○ *It stands to reason that with all his experience, he would not make such a simple mistake.*

• **on standby** ready to work or be used if necessary ○ *Hospitals are on standby to care for casualties of the crash.*

• **stand a chance** to have a chance of success ○ *He doesn't stand much of a chance in the election.*

• **stand** *your* **ground** to refuse to change your opinion or give in to an argument ○ *I kept trying to get my grandmother to find a smaller house, but she stood her ground.*

• **stand guard** to guard someone or something ○ *Soldiers stood guard over the prisoner.*

• **stand on** *your* **own (two) feet** to provide yourself with all the things that you need without asking for help ○ *Ever since college, Jim has stood on his own two feet.*

PHRASAL VERBS with stand

• **stand around** to stay in one place doing little or nothing ○ *We stood around in the cold for an hour.*

• **stand by LET HAPPEN** to let something happen or to be unable to prevent something ○ *How could anyone simply stand by while the man was robbed?* ○ *We stood by helplessly while the fire destroyed our barn.*

• **stand by** *someone/something* **SUPPORT** to support or be loyal to someone or something ○ *The editors stand by the story.* ○ *The boy's friends stood by him, firmly convinced of his innocence.*

• **stand by BE PREPARED** to be prepared for something ○ *The general ordered his troops to stand by for a possible attack.* ○ Related noun: STANDBY

• **stand for** *something* **REPRESENT** to represent something ○ *She explained that DIN stands for "do it now."* ○ *Uncle Sam stands for the US.*

• **stand for** *something* **SUPPORT** to support or accept particular principles or values ○ *I'm not sure what the Republican candidate stands for.* ○ *Maybe you think his behavior is OK, but I won't stand for it.*

• **stand out** to be easily seen or noticed ○ *The black lettering really stands out against that background.* ○ *The applicant we hired was so well qualified, she stood out from all the rest.* ○ Related noun: STANDOUT

• **stand over** to watch someone closely ○ *When you stand over me all the time, it makes me nervous.*

• **stand up** *someone* **NOT MEET** [M] *infml* to fail to meet someone you had arranged to see ○ *He was supposed to be here at seven, so by seven thirty I began to think that he stood me up.*

• **stand up PROVE TRUE 1** to prove to be true when closely examined ○ *The evidence is weak and will not stand up in court.* ○ *Good research will stand up under any criticism.* **2** To stand up also means to continue to be strong even after receiving severe treatment: *This fabric will stand up well even if it gets lots of wear.*

• **stand up for** *someone/something* to defend or support someone or something ○ *Don't be bullied – stand up for yourself and your beliefs.*

• **stand up to** *someone/something* to deal effectively with a person or situation ○ *She stood up to her boss when he accused her of arriving late and leaving work early.*

stand-alone /ˈstæn·dəˌloʊn/ *adj* [not gradable] single, complete by itself ○ *Stand-alone houses have become too expensive for many people.*

standard USUAL /ˈstæn·dərd/ *adj* **1** usual or expected; not involving something special or extra ○ *a standard contract* ○ *I don't work a standard, 35-hour week.* ○ *The car came with an air conditioner and tape player as standard equipment.* ○ *This is a standard medical text* (= a commonly used medical book). **2** A standard unit of measurement is an accepted method of measuring things of a similar type.

standardize /ˈstæn·dərdˌɑɪz/ *v* [T] to make one thing the same as others of that type, or to compare one thing to something accepted as a model ○ *Governor Vizard wants to standardize school spending throughout the state.*

standardized /ˈstæn·dərdˌɑɪzd/ *adj* [not gradable] ○ *Standardized tests will be used to measure their progress.*

standardization /ˌstæn·dərd·əˈzeɪ·ʃən/ *n* [U] ○ *At first, they made no attempt at standardization.*

LEVEL OF QUALITY /ˈstæn·dərd/ *n* [C] something that others of a similar type are compared to or measured by, or the expected level of quality ○ *moral/ethical/community standards* ○ *That's not their usual standard of service.* ○ *The new standard will allow data to be sent over telephone wires at higher speeds.*

SONG /ˈstæn·dərd/ *n* [C] a song or piece of music that has been popular for many years and that musicians often perform

FLAG /ˈstæn·dərd/ *n* [C] a flag used as the symbol of a person, group, or organization ○ *Pete carried the troop's standard in the parade.*

S

WORD FAMILY standard			
Nouns	standard standardization	*Adjectives*	standard standardized substandard
Verbs	standardize		

standard-bearer *n* [C] a person who leads a group or a political party ○ *Is he qualified to be the UN's standard-bearer for democracy and freedom?*

standard of living *n* [C usually sing] the level of wealth and comfort people have in a particular society ○ *Our country has a very high standard of living.*

standard operating procedure *n* [C/U] the usual method followed in doing a particular thing ○ *Running a credit check before opening new accounts is standard operating procedure.*

standard time *n* [U] the time that is officially used in a region in the fall, winter, and spring ○ Compare DAYLIGHT SAVING TIME

standby /ˈstændˌbɑɪ/ *n* [C/U] *pl* **standbys 1** something available for use when needed, or the state of being ready for use ○ *I have several meals I use as standbys for unexpected company.* ○ *Cary also has sought to put more contractors on standby for major storms.* **2** If you fly standby, you hold a ticket and are ready to travel when space becomes available on a flight. ○ Related verb: STAND BY BE PREPARED

stand-in /ˈstæn·dɪn/ *n* [C] a person who takes the place or does the job of another person ○ *Critics serve as a kind of stand-in for the average person.*

standing PERMANENT /ˈstæn·dɪŋ/ *adj* [not gradable] permanent or always continuing to exist or happen ○ *African-Americans headed five standing committees in the House of Representatives.* ○ See also: STANDING at STAND BE VERTICAL

RANK /ˈstæn·dɪŋ/ *n* **1** rank, position, or reputation in an area of activity, system, or organization ○ [U] *Financial scandal will affect the institute's standing in the academic community.* ○ [U] *You must pay dues to remain a member in good standing.* **2** Standings are ranked lists of people or things: [pl] *the league standings* ○ See also: STANDING at STAND BE VERTICAL

standing ovation *n* [C] the activity of people standing and clapping to show their appreciation ○ *What began as applause turned into a long standing ovation.*

standing room *n* [U] **1** a place for standing rather than sitting in a theater or other performance place ○ *He buys standing room for whatever is playing because the tickets are cheaper.* **2** If something is standing room only, it means that all seats are filled: *Last night, every bus was standing room only.*

standing wave *n* [C] ***physics*** a WAVE ENERGY FORM that appears to not move at certain points, between which are areas of the greatest possible movement

standoff /ˈstæn·dɔːf/ *n* [C] a situation in which neither side has won a competition or argument, or an occasion when someone prevents officials from acting, usually by threatening violence ○ *The battle of wills between teacher and student was a standoff.* ○ *She locked herself in the house, but after a brief standoff, police convinced her to come out.*

standout /ˈstæn·dɑʊt/ *n* [C] someone or something that is easily noticed, usually because of being much better than others ○ *Phelps is clearly the standout in a bright galaxy of American swimmers.* ○ Related verb: STAND OUT

standpoint /ˈstænd·pɔɪnt/ *n* [C] a set of beliefs and ideas from which opinions and decisions are formed ○ *He looks at things from a technological standpoint.* ○ *From a fundraising standpoint, he's been very successful.*

stands /stændz/ *pl n* the large area containing many seats arranged in rising rows from which people can watch sports or other events ○ *Gordon was sitting in the stands, eating hot dogs and watching the game.* ○ Compare GRANDSTAND

standstill /ˈstænd·stɪl/ *n* [U] a condition in which all movement or activity has stopped ○ *Bad weather brought construction to a standstill.* ○ *The truck came to a standstill in the muddy field.*

stand-up /ˈstæn·dʌp/ *adj* [not gradable] related to a type of performance in which someone stands in front of a group of people and tells jokes ○ *stand-up comedy*
standup /ˈstæn·dʌp/ *n* [U] ○ *She doesn't do a lot of standup anymore.*

stank /stæŋk/ *past simple of* STINK

stanza /ˈstæn·zə/ *n* [C] ***literature*** a related group of lines in a poem or song; a VERSE

staple WIRE /ˈsteɪ·pəl/ *n* [C] **1** a short, thin, U-shaped piece of wire with ends that bend to fasten sheets of paper together ○ *Put a staple in the upper left-hand corner.* **2** A staple is also a small, thick, U-shaped piece of metal with sharp ends that is hammered into a surface to hold something in place.
staple /ˈsteɪ·pəl/ *v* [T] ○ *Please staple the reports together.*
stapler /ˈsteɪ·plər/ *n* [C] a device used to attach papers together with staples

BASIC ITEM /ˈsteɪ·pəl/ *n* [C] a basic food, or a main product or material ○ *Because of the storm, most stores were low on staples such as bread and milk.* ○ *Scandals are a newspaper staple.*
staple /ˈsteɪ·pəl/ *adj* [not gradable] ○ *staple foods*

staple gun *n* [C] a tool used to push STAPLES (= thin wires) into a surface such as wood

star OBJECT IN SPACE /stɑr/ *n* [C] a large ball of burning gas in space that is usually seen from earth as a point of light in the sky at night ○ *Stars twinkled in the night sky.* ○ Related adjective: STELLAR OF OBJECTS-IN SPACE
starry /ˈstɑr·i/ *adj* ○ *a starry night/sky*

SHAPE /stɑr/ *n* [C] **1** a shape having four or more pointed parts coming out from a center at equal distances ○ *The children were cutting stars out of paper to make decorations.* **2** A star is sometimes used as a symbol of quality: *The Times gave this*

S

restaurant three stars. **3** A star is also used as a symbol of rank or position: *a four-star general* **4** A star is also an ASTERISK (= the symbol *).

PERFORMER /stɑr/ *n* [C] **1** a famous and successful person, esp. a performer such as a musician, actor, or sports player ○ *a rock/movie/basketball star* **2** A star is also someone who is especially good at something: *Janet is our star math student.*

star /stɑr/ *v* [I/T] **-rr-** to be one of the most important performers in a show ○ [I] *He has starred in several recent movies.* ○ [T] *The school play stars children in the seventh and eighth grades.*

stardom /ˈstɑrd·əm/ *n* [U] ○ *He was destined for stardom* (= fame).

starboard /ˈstɑr·bərd/ *n* [U] the right side of a ship or aircraft as you are facing forward ○ Opposite: PORT LEFT

starch FOOD /stɑrtʃ/ *n* [C/U] **1** ***biology*** a substance that exists in large amounts in many plants **2** Starches are foods containing a large amount of starch, such as potatoes, rice, bread, pasta, and CEREAL.

starchy /ˈstɑr·tʃi/ *adj* [*-er/-est* only] ○ *starchy foods*

CLOTH /stɑrtʃ/ *n* [U] a chemical that is used to make cloth stiff

starch /stɑrtʃ/ *v* [T] ○ *I starch all my dress shirts.*

stare /ster, stær/ *v* [I/T] to look directly at someone or something for a long time ○ [I] *Don't stare at people.* ○ [M] *The fighters tried to stare each other down* (= cause the other to turn away).

stare /ster, stær/ *n* [C] ○ *She tried to silence him with a hard stare.*

IDIOMS with stare

• **stare** *you* **in the face** to be obvious ○ *The answer was staring us in the face.*

• **stare** *something* **in the face** to deal with something unpleasant directly ○ *We are trying to deal with the reality staring us in the face.*

starfish /ˈstɑr·fɪʃ/ *n* [C] *pl* **starfish** a sea animal with five pointed parts growing out from around a circular body

S

stark /stɑrk/ *adj* [*-er/-est* only] **1** empty or without decoration ○ *stark white walls* **2** Stark also means completely clear: *The dim halls made a stark contrast with the bright, sun-drenched apartment.* **3** Someone who is **stark naked** is not wearing any clothes.

starlet /ˈstɑr·lət/ *n* [C] a young female actor who hopes to be or is thought likely to be famous in the future

starlight /ˈstɑr·lɑɪt/ *n* [U] the light produced by stars ○ *We ate on the terrace by starlight.*

starling /ˈstɑr·lɪŋ/ *n* [C] a common bird with dark-colored feathers that lives in large groups in many parts of the world

starlit /ˈstɑr·lɪt/ *adj* [not gradable] lit by stars in the sky

Star of David *n* [C] a star with six points that represents Judaism

starry /ˈstɑr·i/ *adj* ○ See at STAR OBJECT IN SPACE

start BEGIN /stɑrt/ *v* [I/T] **1** to begin to do something or go somewhere, or to begin or happen ○ [T] *When do you start your new job?* ○ [I] *We started with nothing when we got married.* ○ [I] *Classes start next month.* ○ [I] *Work starts at 9:00 a.m.* ○ [I] *Ticket prices start at $20* (= these are the cheapest prices). ○ [T] *I just started this book* (= began to read it). ○ [I] *We'll start out with Lucy* (= She will be the first). **2** *infml* If you tell someone not to start, you are warning that person not to begin complaining or annoying you: [I] *Don't start – I said no!*

start /stɑrt/ *n* [C/U] the time where something begins, or the act of beginning ○ [U] *We were worried from the start.* ○ [U] *They announced the start of the race.* ○ [C] *The play got off to a bad start.*

starter /ˈstɑrt̬·ər/ *n* [C] a person, thing, or organization that is involved at the beginning of an activity, esp. a race ○ *Only four of the ten starters finished the race.*

CAUSE /stɑrt/ *v* [T] to cause something to be or happen ○ *His mother started the craft market at the community center.* ○ *You've been starting trouble all morning.*

MOVE SUDDENLY /stɑrt/ *v* [I] to move your body suddenly because something has surprised you ○ *He started when the car backfired.*

start /stɑrt/ *n* [U] ○ *He woke with a start when the alarm sounded.*

OPERATE /stɑrt/ *v* [I/T] to cause something to operate, or to begin to work or operate ○ [T] *Annie went outside to start the car.* ○ [I] *I heard a lawnmower start.*

WORD FAMILY start			
Nouns	start	*Verbs*	start
	starter		restart

IDIOMS with start

• **start something** *infml* to begin an argument or fight ○ *You could tell the guy wanted to start something, so we just walked away.*

• **to start with** first ○ *We'll need a half cup of sugar to start with, and then we'll need another cup later.* ○ Compare TO BEGIN WITH at BEGIN IDIOM

PHRASAL VERBS with start

• **start** *(something)* **off** [M] to begin doing something ○ *I knew almost nothing when I started off in this business.* ○ *He started the meeting off by welcoming the new members.*

• **start** *(something)* **over** [M] to begin something again ○ *I decided to throw out what I'd written and start over.* ○ *We had to start the whole thing over when we realized our mistake.*

• **start up** *(something)* **OPERATE ENGINE** to cause an engine to begin to operate ○ *I didn't even hear the vacuum cleaner start up when Jose began cleaning the carpets.* ○ *He heard the stranger start up a motorcycle.*

• **start up** *something* **BEGIN COMPANY** [M] to begin a new company, organization, or activity ○ *We started up an opera theater company that toured all over the South.* ○ Related noun: START-UP

startle /ˈstɑrt̬·əl/ *v* [T] to surprise a person or animal ○ *She startled him when she said hello.*
startling /ˈstɑrt̬·əl·ɪŋ/ *adj* ○ *We've made some startling discoveries.*

start-up, **startup** /ˈstɑrt̬·ʌp/ *n* [C] a new business, or the activities involved in starting a new business ○ *Start-ups need to generate revenue quickly.* ○ Related verb: START UP
start-up, **startup** /ˈstɑrt̬·ʌp/ *adj* [not gradable] ○ *startup costs*

starve /stɑrv/ *v* [I/T] **1** to become weak or die because there is not enough food to eat ○ [I] *Many people could starve because of the drought.* **2** If you say you are starving, you want to eat: [I] *I'm starved because I missed lunch today.*
starvation /stɑrˈveɪ·ʃən/ *n* [U] ○ *The animals died of starvation.*

stash /stæʃ/ *v* [T] to store or hide something ○ *Extra blankets are stashed in the closet.*
stash /stæʃ/ *n* [C] ○ *He has a stash of old comic books in the attic.*

state WAY OF BEING /steɪt/ *n* [C] a condition or way of being ○ *The stable was preserved in its original state.* ○ *Your room is in a terrible state.* ○ *It's a sad* **state of affairs** (= a bad situation) *when our rivers are so endangered.*

PLACE /steɪt/ *n* [C] ***politics & government*** **1** one of the political units that some countries, such as the US, are divided into ○ *New York State* ○ *the State of Arizona* **2** A state is also a country or its government: *the member states of the United Nations* **3** ***US history*** **The States** is another way of referring to the United States: *When will you be visiting the States?*
state /steɪt/ *adj* [not gradable] **1** *a state legislature/law* ○ *state police* **2** ***politics & government*** State also refers to formal or official government activities: *a state dinner*
statewide /ˈsteɪt·wɑɪd/ *adj* [not gradable] ***politics & government*** in every part of a state ○ *statewide elections* ➤ Usage: **country, land, nation, or state?** at COUNTRY POLITICAL UNIT

EXPRESS /steɪt/ *v* [T] to express information clearly and carefully ○ *His will states the property is to be sold.* ○ *Please state your preference.*
statement /ˈsteɪt·mənt/ *n* [C] **1** something that is said, esp. formally and officially ○ *The candidate made a statement to the press.* **2** A statement is also an act or object that expresses an idea or opinion: *a fashion statement* ○ *They wore the armbands as a political statement.* **3** A statement is also a piece of paper that lists financial details: *a bank/credit card statement*

WORD FAMILY state

Nouns	state statement understatement	*Adjectives*	statewide understated
		Verbs	state overstate

State Department *n* [U] the part of the US government that deals with other nations

statehood /ˈsteɪt·hʊd/ *n* [U] ***social studies*** **1** the condition of being a political unit within a country, for example within the U.S. ○ *Both Alaska and Hawaii achieved statehood in 1959.* **2** Statehood is also the condition of being a country: *the struggle for Palestinian statehood*

statehouse /ˈsteɪt·hɑʊs/ *n* [C] the building in which a state legislature meets in any of the US states ○ *the California statehouse*

stately /ˈsteɪt·li/ *adj* formal in style and appearance ○ *a stately old hotel*

state of emergency *n* [U] an extreme condition caused by severe weather or war in which a government allows itself special powers ○ *The governor declared a state of emergency in two counties hit by the hurricane.*

state of mind *n* [C] a person's mood and the effect that mood has on the person's thinking and behavior ○ *I was not in the right state of mind to laugh at his jokes.*

state-of-the-art *adj* the best and most modern of its type ○ *a state-of-the-art computer system*

statesman /ˈsteɪt·smən/, *female* **stateswoman** /ˈsteɪtˌswʊm·ən/ *n* [C] *pl* **-men, -women** a politician or government official who is respected and experienced
statesmanlike /ˈsteɪts·mənˌlɑɪk/ *adj* ○ *a statesmanlike speech*

states' rights *n* [U] ***US history*** the powers and authority that are neither held by the federal government nor forbidden by the CONSTITUTION of the United States and that therefore belong to the state governments

static /ˈstæt̬·ɪk/ *adj* staying in one place without moving, or not changing for a long time ○ *Oil prices remained static worldwide.*

static (electricity) /ˈstæt̬·ɪk (ɪˌlekˈtrɪs·ət̬·i)/ *n* [U] **1** an electrical charge that collects esp. on the surfaces of some objects ○ *There's a lot of static in here – I keep getting shocks when I touch things.* **2** Static is also noise that interrupts radio or television signals.

static equilibrium *n* [U] ***physics*** the energy condition of an object when no outside force is used on it

station BUILDING /ˈsteɪ·ʃən/ *n* [C] a building or buildings and the surrounding area where a particular service or activity takes place ○ *a train/bus station* ○ *a gas station* ○ *a police/fire station*

USAGE

station or stop?

Station is used for trains and buses.

I'll meet you at the train station in an hour.
Denver's main bus station
a subway station

Stop and **bus stop** are used mainly for buses, but people sometimes use **stop** for local trains in cities. ➤

S

I stood at the bus stop for over half an hour. Isn't Diversey a stop on the Brown Line in Chicago?

BROADCAST ORGANIZATION /ˈsteɪ·ʃən/ *n* [C] a place or organization that sends out radio or television broadcasts, or the broadcasts sent out ○ *At our house in the mountains we only get two TV stations.* ○ *I can't tune in that radio station.*

POSITION /ˈsteɪ·ʃən/ *v* [T] to cause someone, esp. a soldier, to be in a particular place to do a job ○ *I hear your son's in the army – where's he stationed?*
station /ˈsteɪ·ʃən/ *n* [C] ○ *The honor guard took their stations at the side of the road.*

stationary /ˈsteɪ·ʃəˌner·i/ *adj* [not gradable] not moving, or not changing ○ *House prices have been stationary for months.*

stationery /ˈsteɪ·ʃəˌner·i/ *n* [U] paper, esp. that used for writing letters, or writing materials such as pens, pencils, and books for writing in ○ *business/personal stationery* ○ *I got these folders at the stationery store.*

station house *n* [C] a place where police or fire fighters keep their equipment and where they go to work

station wagon *n* [C] a type of car with a large area behind the back seats for carrying things

statistics Ⓐ /stəˈtɪs·tɪks/, *infml* **stats** /stæts/ *pl n* a collection of NUMERICAL facts or measurements, as about people, business conditions, or weather ○ *The statistics show that, in general, women live longer than men.*
statistics Ⓐ /stəˈtɪs·tɪks/ *n* [U] the science of using information discovered from collecting, organizing, and studying numbers
statistic Ⓐ /stəˈtɪs·tɪk/ *n* [C] a single number in a range of STATISTICS ○ *The city's most shocking statistic is its infant mortality rate.*
statistical Ⓐ /stəˈtɪs·tɪ·kəl/ *adj* ○ *There is little statistical evidence to support the idea that stocks do better in summer than in other seasons.*
statistician Ⓐ /ˌstæt̬·əˈstɪʃ·ən/ *n* [C] a person who studies or works with statistics
statistically Ⓐ /stəˈtɪs·tɪ·kli/ *adv*

statue /ˈstætʃ·uː/ *n* [C] a large art object, often representing a person or an animal, that is made from a hard material, esp. stone or metal
statuette /ˌstætʃ·əˈwet/ *n* [C] a very small statue

Statue of Liberty *n* [U] a large statue of a woman holding a lighted TORCH above her head in New York City

stature **REPUTATION** /ˈstætʃ·ər/ *n* [U] reputation and importance based on admirable qualities or achievements ○ *He is a philosopher of great stature in the academic community.*

HEIGHT /ˈstætʃ·ər/ *n* [C usually sing] the height of a person or an animal ○ *Although short in stature, his voice and stage presence were remarkable.*

status Ⓐ **POSITION** /ˈsteɪt̬·əs, ˈstæt̬-/ *n* [U] **1** position or rank, esp. in a social group or legal system ○ *The association works to promote the status of retired people as active and useful members of the community.* **2** Status can also mean state or condition at a particular time: *The type of treatment used will depend on the patient's health status.*

RESPECT /ˈsteɪt̬·əs, ˈstæt̬-/ *n* [U] the position of respect and importance given to someone or something ○ *The leaders often seemed to be more concerned with status and privilege than with the problems of the people.*

status quo /ˌsteɪt̬·əˈskwoʊ, ˌstæt̬-/ *n* [U] the present situation or condition ○ *Are you in favor of statehood, independence, or the status quo for Puerto Rico?*

status symbol *n* [C] something that people want to have or do because they think other people will respect or admire them for it ○ *The newest of these electronic gaming systems are the latest status symbols among teenagers.*

statute /ˈstætʃ·uːt/ *n* [C/U] a law that has been formally approved and written down ○ [U] *The salaries of most federal workers are set by statute.*
statutory /ˈstætʃ·əˌtɔːr·i, -ˌtoʊr·i/ *adj* [not gradable]

statutory rape *n* [U] *law* the crime of having sex with a person younger than the age at which she or he can legally have sex

staunch **LOYAL** /stɔːntʃ, stɑntʃ/ *adj* [-er/-est only] strongly loyal to a person, organization, or set of beliefs or opinions ○ *a staunch defender of free speech*
staunchly /ˈstɔːntʃ·li, ˈstɑntʃ-/ *adv* ○ *She staunchly supports the party's candidates.*

STOP /stɔːntʃ, stɑntʃ/, **stanch** *v* [T] **1** to stop liquid, esp. blood, from flowing out ○ *Mike pressed hard on the wound and staunched the flow of blood.* **2** To staunch is also to keep something from continuing: *The company abandoned the plan to staunch the departure of more managers.*

stave /steɪv/ *n* a STAFF MUSIC

PHRASAL VERB with stave

• **stave off** *something/someone* [M] to prevent something, or prevent someone from doing something, esp. until a later time ○ *The Federal Reserve lowered interest rates to stimulate the economy and stave off a recession.* ○ *Els staved off Woods by a shot after entering the final day eight ahead.*

stay **NOT LEAVE** /steɪ/ *v* [I] to not move away from or leave a place ○ *I have a meeting at three so I can't stay long.* ○ *They need an assistant who is willing to stay for six months.* ○ *Can you stay for dinner?* ○ *James had to stay after school to complete the assignment.* ○ *Because of the snow, he stayed home from school today.* ○ *She's come back home to stay* (= She will not move away again). ➤ Usage: **rest, stay, or remain?** at REST RELAX

CONTINUE /steɪ/ *v* to continue to be in a particular state or position, or to continue doing something ○ [I always + adv/prep] *Stay away from the edge of the cliff.* ○ [I always + adv/prep] *His boss asked him*

to stay on as manager for another year. ○ [I always + adv/prep] *Mom told me not to stay out/up too late.* ○ [L] *I found it difficult to stay awake/calm/warm.* ○ [L] *The store stays open until 9 p.m.* ○ [L] *They stayed friends, even after they moved to different countries.* ○ [L] *For further news of the hurricane, stay tuned* (= keep listening to this program).

LIVE TEMPORARILY /steɪ/ *v* [I] to live in a place for a short time as a visitor, or just sleep there ○ *We stayed in San Francisco for a few days before flying to Hawaii.* ○ *I'll be staying overnight at my sister's house.*

stay /steɪ/ *n* [C] ○ *They plan a short stay at a motel while the house is being painted.*

USAGE

stay

When you use **stay** to describe living temporarily in a place, such as a hotel, remember to use the prepositions **at** or **in** or use the adverb **where**.

I was really impressed by the hotel we were staying at.

~~*I was really impressed by the hotel we were staying.*~~

She prefers the cottage where we stayed last year.

IDIOM with stay

• **stay put** do not move from here ○ *Just stay put, and I'll get the car.*

STD *n* [C] *abbreviation for* SEXUALLY TRANSMITTED DISEASE

steadfast /ˈsted·fæst/ *adj* staying the same for a long time; not changing or losing purpose ○ *steadfast beliefs* ○ *a steadfast friend*

steady GRADUAL /ˈsted·i/ *adj* happening or developing in a gradual, regular way over a period of time ○ *steady improvement* ○ *steady growth in profits* ○ *His recovery has been slow but steady.*

steadily /ˈsted·ᵊl·i/ *adv* ○ *Prices have risen steadily.*

FIRM /ˈsted·i/ *adj* not moving or changing suddenly; continuing in the same condition ○ *a steady job/relationship* ○ *I'll hold the boat steady while you climb in.* ○ *We drove at a steady 65 mph for most of the trip.*

steady /ˈsted·i/ *v* [I/T] ○ [T] *He wobbled a little on the bike and then steadied himself.* ○ [I] *The stock market has steadied after a sharp fall in prices.*

CONTROLLED /ˈsted·i/ *adj* calm and under control ○ *Her voice was steady as she described the accident.*

steady /ˈsted·i/ *v* [T] ○ *He took a deep breath to steady his nerves.*

steak /steɪk/ *n* [C/U] a thick, flat slice of meat or fish that is cooked quickly

steal TAKE AWAY /stiːl/ *v* [I/T] *past simp.* **stole**, *past part.* **stolen 1** to take something without the permission or knowledge of the owner and keep it or use it ○ [T] *They broke into cars to steal the radios.* ○ [T] *He never paid me back, so basically he ended up stealing a hundred dollars from me.* **2** To steal is also to do something quickly while trying not to be seen doing it: [I always + adv/prep] *to steal out of a room* ○ [T] *She stole a glance at her watch.*

WORD CHOICES steal

Take is often used instead of "steal."

*Someone **took** their car from outside the house.*

If someone steals something from a store, you could use the verb **shoplift**.

*He was caught **shoplifting** by a store detective.*

If someone steals something from a place or person, often in a violent way, you could use the verb **rob**.

*He **robbed** a bank of about $5000.*

Burglarize is used when someone illegally enters a building and steals things.

*When she got home from work, she discovered that her house had been **burglarized**.*

Pilfer is used when people steal things that are not very valuable.

*Employees **pilfering** paper, pens, etc., can cost employers a lot.*

If large numbers of people steal things from stores and houses during a violent event, you could use the word **loot**.

*During the riots, stores were **looted** and cars set on fire.*

Embezzle can be used when someone steals money that belongs to the company or organization they work for.

*She **embezzled** thousands of dollars from the charity.*

CHEAP ITEM /stiːl/ *n* [C] *infml* something obtained at a much lower price than its true value ○ *At half the original price, that designer dress is a steal.*

stealth /stelθ/ *n* [U] movement that is quiet and careful in order to avoid notice, or secret or indirect action

stealthy /ˈstel·θi/ *adj* ○ *a stealthy burglar*

stealthily /ˈstel·θə·li/ *adv*

stealth bomber, **stealth fighter** *n* [C] an aircraft designed so that it cannot be seen on enemy RADAR (= equipment used for watching aircraft when they cannot be seen with the eyes)

steam /stiːm/ *n* [U] **1** the hot gas that is produced when water boils **2** Steam can be used to provide power: *a steam engine*

steam /stiːm/ *v* [I/T] **1** [I] *The ship steamed* (= moved by steam power) *out of the harbor.* **2** If food is steamed, it is cooked by steam.

steamy /ˈstiː·mi/ *adj* **1** *By the time Hannah finished her shower, the bathroom was all steamy.* **2** *infml* Steamy also means having to do with sex.

S

WORD FAMILY steam			
Nouns	steam	*Verbs*	steam
Adjectives	steamy		

PHRASAL VERB with steam

• **steam** *something* **up** [M] to become covered with a thin layer of steam ○ *Going into the warm room steamed my glasses up.*

steamroller VEHICLE /ˈstiːm ˌroʊ·lər/ *n* [C] a vehicle whose wheels are large, heavy cylinders that roll over a road surface to make it flat

FORCE /ˈstiːm ˌroʊ·lər/, **steamroll** /ˈstiːm·roʊl/ *v* [T] to use great force to make someone do something or to make (something) happen ○ *He steamrollered the bill through Congress.*

steel METAL /stiːl/ *n* [U] a strong metal that is made by processing iron to remove some of the carbon ○ *steel doors/girders* ○ *the steel industry*

steely /ˈstiː·li/ *adj* (of a person's behavior or character) hard and strong as steel ○ *Only their steely determination to survive kept them going.*

PREPARE /stiːl/ *v* [T] to prepare yourself to be able to do something unpleasant or difficult ○ *She steeled herself to face her accusers.*

steel wool *n* [U] a mass of thin steel threads twisted together and used to clean a surface or rub it smooth

steep NOT GRADUAL /stiːp/ *adj* [-*er*/-*est* only] **1** (of a slope) rising or falling at a sharp angle ○ *The train slowed as it went up a steep incline.* **2** A steep rise or fall is one that goes very quickly from low to high or from high to low: *Yesterday's steep decline in the value of the dollar was unexpected.*

steeply /ˈstiː·pli/ *adv* ○ *The beach slopes steeply down to the sea.*

TOO HIGH /stiːp/ *adj* [-*er*/-*est* only] (esp. of prices) too high; more than is reasonable ○ *We enjoyed our stay at the hotel, but the charges were a bit steep.*

MAKE WET /stiːp/ *v* [I/T] **1** to stay or cause to stay in a liquid, esp. in order to improve flavor or to become soft or clean ○ [I] *Let the tea steep for five minutes.* ○ [T] *This stain will come out if you steep the cloth in cold water.* **2** To be steeped in something is to be filled with it or to know a lot about it: [T] *The college is steeped in tradition.*

WORD FAMILY steep			
Nouns	steepness	*Verbs*	steep
Adjectives	steep	*Adverbs*	steeply

steeple /ˈstiː·pəl/ *n* [C] a tall, narrow structure, esp. on a church, having a pointed top

steer DIRECT /stɪr/ *v* [I/T] **1** to control the direction of a vehicle ○ [T] *It's not easy to steer the car through these narrow streets.* ○ [I] (*fig.*) *The speech steered clear of* (= avoided) *controversial issues.* **2** If you steer people, you cause them to go in a particular direction: [T] *She steered her guests into the dining room.* **3** If you steer an activity, you cause it to deal with a particular feature or topic: [T] *I'd like to steer the discussion back to our original topic.*

MALE COW /stɪr/ *n* [C] a young male of the cattle family that has had its sex organs removed and that is usually raised for meat

IDIOM with steer

• **steer clear of** *someone/something* to avoid someone or something because you think the person or thing may cause trouble or be dangerous ○ *Davis steered clear of politics because of all the problems his father had had as governor.*

steering wheel *n* [C] the wheel in a vehicle that the driver turns in order to make the vehicle go in a particular direction

stellar OF OBJECTS IN SPACE /ˈstel·ər/ *adj* [not gradable] of a star or stars ○ *stellar light*

HIGH IN QUALITY /ˈstel·ər/ *adj* [not gradable] (of people or their activities) extremely high in quality; excellent ○ *The cellist gave a stellar performance before an enthusiastic audience.*

stem CENTRAL PART /stem/ *n* [C] **1** a central part of something from which other parts can develop or grow, or which forms a support **2** The stem of a plant is the straight part that grows above the ground and from which leaves and flowers grow. **3** The stem of a glass is the narrow, vertical part that supports the container into which you put liquid.

STOP /stem/ *v* [T] **-mm-** to stop something unwanted from spreading or increasing ○ *The bank tried to stem the currency's recent decline against the dollar.*

PHRASAL VERB with stem

• **stem from** *something* to develop or come from something ○ *These practices stem from traditional Chinese medicine.*

stem cell *n* [C] ***biology*** a type of cell that is able to divide to produce more cells, or to develop into a cell that has a particular purpose

stench /stentʃ/ *n* [U] a strong, unpleasant smell ○ *the stench of rotting fish*

stencil /ˈsten·səl/ *n* [C] a piece of flat material in which shapes or letters have been cut out, so that when you paint or draw over it, images of the shapes or letters that have been cut out will be left on the surface below, or the patterns or letters made by this method

stencil /ˈsten·səl/ *v* [T] ○ *The back of the chair was painted solid black with designs stenciled in gold.*

stenographer /stəˈnɑg·rə·fər/ *n* [C] a person who does SHORTHAND (= system of fast writing) in an office or records speech using a special machine in a court

stenography /stəˈnɑg·rə·fi/ *n* [U] a system for recording speech quickly by writing it down in SHORTHAND or by using a special machine

step MOVE FOOT /step/ *v* [I always + adv/prep] **-pp-** to lift one foot and put it down in front of the other foot, as in walking or running ○ *He stepped*

S

to his left, picked up the ball, and threw. ○ *We stepped carefully along the slippery path.*

step /step/ *n* [C] **1** *He took a couple of steps into the room.* **2** A step is the distance covered by one step: *I'd only gone about three steps before I fell.* **3** A step is also the sound of making such a movement: *I heard my father's step on the stairs.* **4** A step is also a particular movement that you make with your feet when you dance: *I've finally learned some dance steps.* **5** If you move **in step with** *someone*, you move your feet at the same time and in the same way: *Three angry women marched in step down the hall.*

STAGE /step/ *n* [C] a stage in a process ○ *The first step in fixing our house is to put on a new roof.* ○ *Let's make these changes carefully, a step at a time.*

MUSIC /step/, **tone** *n* [C] ***music*** the largest difference in sound between two notes next to each other in a musical SCALE (= series of notes) ○ *Tones in a scale are arranged in steps and half steps.*

ACTION /step/ *n* [C] one action in a series, taken for a particular purpose ○ *As a first step, both sides agreed to a cease-fire.*

FLAT SURFACE /step/ *n* [C] a flat surface on which you put your foot when going up or down from one level to another ○ *Mom took a picture of us sitting on the front steps of the house.* ○ Compare STAIRS

IDIOMS with **step**

• **step on** *someone's* **toes** to upset someone, esp. by getting involved in something that is that person's responsibility ○ *It's a very competitive business – you can't afford to step on too many toes.*

• **in step with** *someone/something* **1** in agreement with someone or something ○ *She is very much in step with the times.* **2 In step with** can also mean at the same speed or level as someone or something: *Gasoline prices rose in step with oil prices.* ○ *He found it hard to keep in step with the changes.*

PHRASAL VERBS with **step**

• **step back** to stop being involved in something ○ *We need to step back and look at all our options.*

• **step down**, **step aside** to give up a job or position ○ *She stepped down as captain of the team.*

• **step in** to become involved ○ *An outside buyer stepped in to save the company.*

• **step out** to leave a place, esp. for a short time ○ *Mr. Taylor just stepped out of the office to get the mail.*

• **step up** *something* **INCREASE** [M] to make something more effective, or to increase the size or speed of something ○ *Efforts were stepped up in Congress to pass the bill.*

• **step up** **TAKE ACTION** to take action when there is a need or opportunity for it ○ *Investors have to step up and assume more responsibility for their assets.*

step-by-step *adj, adv* one at a time in a particular order ○ *a step-by-step guide to installing the software* ○ *She followed the instructions step-by-step.*

stepchild /ˈstep·tʃɑɪld/ *n* [C] *pl* **stepchildren** a child of a previous marriage of either a husband or a wife

stepdaughter /ˈstep ˌdɔːţ·ər/ *n* [C] a daughter of a previous marriage of either a husband or a wife

stepfather /ˈstep ˌfɑð·ər/ *n* [C] a man who is married to the mother of a child but is not the biological father

stepladder /ˈstep ˌlæd·ər/ *n* [C] a piece of equipment for climbing up and down that can stand on its own or be folded for storage

stepmother /ˈstep ˌmʌð·ər/ *n* [C] a woman who is married to the father of a child but is not the biological mother

stepping stone /ˈstep·ɪŋ ˌstoʊn/ *n* [C] **1** something that helps someone advance or achieve something ○ *I hope this job will be a stepping stone to something better.* **2** A stepping stone is also a stone that you step on to cross a stream or wet area: *Flat stepping stones crossed the stream.*

stepson /ˈstep·sʌn/ *n* [C] a son of a previous marriage of either a husband or a wife

stereo /ˈster·iː ˌoʊ/ *n* [C/U] *pl* **stereos** a device that plays recorded sound through two or more SPEAKERS, or sound produced in this way ○ [C] *Music was blaring from her car stereo.*

stereo /ˈster·iː ˌoʊ/, **stereophonic** /ˌster·i·əˈfɑn·ɪk/ *adj* [not gradable] ○ *stereo sound* ○ *stereo equipment*

stereotype /ˈster·iː·ə ˌtɑɪp/ *n* [C] *disapproving* an idea that is used to describe a particular type of person or thing, or a person or thing thought to represent such an idea ○ *All jobs can be made to fit stereotypes, but accountants are particularly easy targets.*

stereotype /ˈster·iː·ə ˌtɑɪp/ *v* [T] *disapproving* ○ *That unfortunate statement stereotypes all men as wimps.*

stereotypical /ˌster·iː·əˈtɪp·ɪ·kəl/ *adj disapproving* ○ *I'm not your stereotypical Texan.*

sterile **UNABLE TO PRODUCE** /ˈster·əl/ *adj* [not gradable] (of a person or animal) unable to produce young, or of land unable to produce plants or crops ○ *It was a small oasis surrounded by sterile desert.*

sterility /stəˈrɪl·əţ·i/ *n* [U] ○ *Certain chemicals cause sterility in farm animals.*

sterilize /ˈster·ə ˌlɑɪz/ *v* [T] ○ *The clinic will sterilize your cat for free.*

sterilization /ˌster·ə·ləˈzeɪ·ʃən/ *n* [U] ○ *The compound causes sterilization in certain types of flies.*

WITHOUT BACTERIA /ˈster·əl/ *adj* [not gradable] free from bacteria ○ *Medical equipment must be kept sterile.*

sterilize /ˈster·ə ˌlɑɪz/ *v* [T] ○ *Dental instruments are routinely sterilized.*

sterilization /ˌster·ə·ləˈzeɪ·ʃən/ *n* [U] ○ *Sterilization of milk products kills dangerous bacteria.*

LACKING /ˈster·əl/ *adj* [not gradable] lacking in imagination, ideas, or enthusiasm ○ *Suburban housing developments are often sterile environments.*

sterling /ˈstɜr·lɪŋ/ *adj* [not gradable] of the highest quality ○ *McCoy had a sterling season last year.*

S

sterling (silver) /ˈstɜr·lɪŋ (ˈsɪl·vər)/ *adj* [not gradable] silver that is very pure ○ *The bracelet is made of sterling silver.*

stern SEVERE /ˈstɜrn/ *adj* [-*er*/-*est* only] severe ○ *Sterner punishment may produce better behavior, but I doubt it.*

sternly /ˈstɜrn·li/ *adv* ○ *He sternly reminded his son to drive carefully.*

SHIP PART /ˈstɜrn/ *n* [C] the back end of a ship ○ *A rope over the stern towed the little boat.* ○ Compare BOW SHIP PART

steroid /ˈstɪr·ɔɪd, ˈster-/ *n* [C] ***biology, chemistry*** any of a large group of chemical substances produced in the body or in a plant, or an artificial form of these substances used to treat various medical conditions or to illegally improve sports performance

stethoscope /ˈsteθ·əˌskoʊp/ *n* [C] a medical device that allows a doctor to listen to your heart, lungs, or other part of your body

stew COOK /stuː/ *v* [I/T] to cook food slowly in liquid or to cook slowly in liquid ○ [T] *It tastes good if you boil it, fry it in oil, and then stew it with chilies.*

stew /stuː/ *n* [C/U] a dish consisting usually of meat or fish and vegetables cooked slowly in a small amount of liquid

BE ANXIOUS /stuː/ *v* [I always + adv/prep] *infml* to be anxious or upset about something ○ *You're not still stewing over the election results, are you?*

stew /stuː/ *n* [C] ○ *She has been in a stew over plans for her wedding.*

steward /ˈstuː·ərd/ *n* [C] **1** a person who is responsible for an event or for the management of a place ○ *a race steward* ○ *He has been a careful steward of our parks.* **2** A steward is also a person who is responsible for food or drink at a restaurant. **3** A steward (*female* **stewardess**) on an aircraft, ship, or train, is someone who helps and serves passengers.

stewardship /ˈstuː·ərdˌʃɪp/ *n* [U] care or management ○ *The team has fallen to new lows under his stewardship.*

S

stick THIN PIECE /stɪk/ *n* [C] **1** a thin piece of wood ○ *The campers collected sticks to start a fire.* **2** A stick is also a long, thin handle with a specially shaped end, used esp. to play HOCKEY and LACROSSE. **3** A stick can also be a long, thin piece of something: *sticks of dynamite* ○ *a stick of chewing gum*

PUSH INTO /stɪk/ *v* [always + adv/prep] *past* **stuck** to push something pointed into or through something, or to be pushed into or through something ○ [T] *I simply cannot watch when someone sticks a needle in my arm.* ○ [I] *He throws the knife, and the blade sticks in the wall.*

ATTACH /stɪk/ *v* [I/T] *past* **stuck** to attach or become attached ○ [T] *Stick the tape to the back of the picture.* ○ [I] *It was so hot that my clothes stuck to me.*

sticky /ˈstɪk·i/ *adj* **1** tending to stick, or covered with a substance that sticks ○ *You had better wash your sticky fingers.* **2** If the weather is sticky, it is hot and the air feels wet. ○ See also: STICKY

sticker /ˈstɪk·ər/ *n* [C] a small piece of paper with a picture or writing on one side and a sticky substance on the other ○ *Dana collects stickers of cartoon characters.*

PUT /stɪk/ *v* [T always + adv/prep] *past* **stuck** *infml* **1** to put something somewhere, usually temporarily ○ *Stick the packages under the table for now.* **2** If you **stick out** *your* **tongue**, you push your tongue out of your mouth, usually as an insult: *She stuck her tongue out at him and smiled.* ○ **USAGE**: This action is usually done by children.

UNABLE TO MOVE /stɪk/ *v* [I] *past* **stuck** to be fixed in position and unable to move ○ *The window sticks, making it hard to shut it.* ○ Related adjective: STUCK FIXED

WORD FAMILY stick			
Nouns	stick sticker	*Adjectives*	sticky stuck unstuck
Verbs	stick		

IDIOMS with stick

• *something* **sticks in** *your* **mind** you remember something ○ *Her angry remarks stuck in my mind for a long time.*

• **stick** *your* **neck out** to take a risk ○ *I'm really sticking my neck out by investing my money in this idea.*

• **stick to** *your* **guns** to refuse to change your beliefs or actions ○ *My parents didn't want me to be an actor, but I stuck to my guns.*

PHRASAL VERBS with stick

• **stick around** *infml* to stay somewhere and wait for someone or for something to happen ○ *You go ahead – I'll stick around until Candice shows up.*

• **stick by** *someone/something* to continue to support someone, or to not change your mind about something ○ *He stuck by his earlier statements and never changed his story.*

• **stick out** *(something)* GO BEYOND [M] to reach beyond the surface or edge of something ○ *They built the house on a little peninsula that sticks out into the lake.* ○ *He stuck his arm out to hail a cab.*

• **stick** *something* **out** CONTINUE to continue to do something to its end ○ *I didn't really like the movie, but I stuck it out.*

• **stick out** BE NOTICEABLE to be very noticeable because of being different ○ *Dye your hair orange and you'll really stick out in a small town like this.* ○ *My colorful clothes stuck out like a sore thumb.*

• **stick to** *something* to continue with a subject, activity, or plan without changing ○ *Would you stick to the point, please?*

• **stick together** to support each other ○ *If we all stick together, we can succeed.*

• **stick up** GO ABOVE to reach above the surface of something ○ *A few green shoots were sticking up out of the ground.*

• **stick** *something* **up** STEAL [M] *infml* to use a gun to steal something from a person or place ○ *Did you hear that someone stuck the post office up?* ○ Related noun: STICKUP

• **stick up for** *something/someone* *infml* to support or defend something or someone ○ *Her friends* *stuck up for her when other people said she was guilty.*

• **stick with** *someone/something* **STAY CLOSE** *infml* to stay close to someone, or to continue to do something ○ *Stick with me, and we'll do lots of interesting things.* ○ *Once Stephen takes up a hobby, he sticks with it.*

• **stick** *someone* **with** *something* **FORCE TO HAVE** to force someone to have or do something less desirable ○ *Big power companies grab cheap supplies and stick everyone else with more expensive ones.*

sticker /ˈstɪk·ər/ *n* [C] See at STICK ATTACH.

stick figure *n* [C] a drawing of a person with the body made of single lines

sticking point *n* [C] a subject that is very difficult to reach agreement about ○ *Dividing up the land is the main sticking point of the peace talks.*

stickler /ˈstɪk·lər/ *n* [C] someone who believes in closely following rules or in maintaining a high standard of behavior ○ *He was a stickler when it came to office manners.*

sticks /stɪks/ *pl n infml, disapproving* The sticks is a humorous way of referring to a place in the country: *My parents live out in the sticks.*

stick shift *n* [C] a GEARSHIFT in the floor of a car, or a car that has one of these

stickup /ˈstɪk·ʌp/ *n* [C] *infml* an act of stealing in which a gun is used ○ *The stickup at the bank was carried out in broad daylight.* ○ Related verb: STICK UP STEAL

sticky /ˈstɪk·i/ *adj* difficult to deal with or solve ○ *a sticky situation* ○ *a sticky issue* ○ See also: STICKY at STICK ATTACH

stiff **FIRM** /stɪf/ *adj* [-*er*/-*est* only] **1** firm or hard and not bending or moving easily ○ *He had stiff leather shoes on.* ○ *If the dough is stiff, add more sour cream.* **2** If your body is stiff, you cannot move easily and your muscles hurt when moved: *He was unable to turn his head because of a stiff neck.*

stiffen /ˈstɪf·ən/ *v* [I/T] ○ [T] *To paint on linen, you first have to stiffen the fabric with a glue mixture.* ○ [I] *His back stiffened up after the game.*

stiffly /ˈstɪf·li/ *adv* ○ *The gown is constructed so stiffly that it could stand up on its own.*

stiffness /ˈstɪf·nəs/ *n* [U] ○ *I had some muscle stiffness after the bike ride.*

NOT RELAXED /stɪf/ *adj* [-*er*/-*est* only] not relaxed or friendly; formal ○ *The performance was stiff and rather predictable.* ○ *You can't be stiff with a guy who takes you into his confidence.*

stiffen /ˈstɪf·ən/ *v* [I] to become nervous and less relaxed ○ *I stiffened when I saw him coming toward me.*

stiffly /ˈstɪf·li/ *adv* ○ *"I don't think it has anything to do with you," he said stiffly.*

stiffness /ˈstɪf·nəs/ *n* [U] ○ *His early stiffness and formality evolved into friendliness.*

SEVERE /stɪf/ *adj* [-*er*/-*est* only] severe; difficult to deal with or do ○ *The penalties for corruption are stiff.* ○ *Most of the team's losses have come against stiff competition.*

stiffen /ˈstɪf·ən/ *v* [I/T] ○ [T] *The measure would stiffen the penalties for driving without a license.* ○ [I] *Competition will stiffen considerably if another store opens in town.*

STRONG /stɪf/ *adj* strong or powerful ○ *A stiff wind beat against the house.*

VERY MUCH /stɪf/ *adv* [not gradable] *infml* very much; to a great degree ○ *I was scared stiff during the air raids.*

PERSON /stɪf/ *n* [C] *slang* **1** a person of the type described ○ *I'm just a working stiff.* ○ *You lucky stiff!* **2** *slang* A stiff is also a dead person's body.

CHEAT /stɪf/ *v* [T] to cheat someone out of money ○ *She stiffed the taxi driver.*

WORD FAMILY stiff			
Nouns	stiffness stiff	*Adjectives*	stiff
		Adverbs	stiff stiffly
Verbs	stiffen stiff		

stifle /ˈstɑɪ·fəl/ *v* [T] to prevent something from happening, being expressed, or continuing ○ *It is the responsibility of schools to encourage learning, not to stifle it.*

stifling /ˈstɑɪ·flɪŋ/ *adj* extremely hot, with a lack of fresh air ○ *Summers in Virginia have always had stifling humidity.*

stigma **DISAPPROVAL** /ˈstɪg·mə/ *n* [C/U] a strong lack of respect for a person or group of people or a bad opinion of them because they have done something society does not approve of ○ [C usually sing] *There's a stigma associated with low-income food programs.*

stigmatize /ˈstɪg·məˌtɑɪz/ *v* [T] to make people feel that they are not respected ○ *Gabrielle felt stigmatized in math class because she was not seen as one of "the smart kids."*

FLOWER /ˈstɪg·mə/ *n* ***biology*** the part of the PISTIL (= female part) of a flower that receives the POLLEN (= powder produced by the male part)

still **UNTIL NOW** /stɪl/ *adv* [not gradable] continuing until now or until a particular time ○ *The universe is still expanding.* ○ *Two years later she still had scars on her knees.*

DESPITE /stɪl/ *adv* [not gradable] despite that ○ *He was diagnosed with cancer but still returned to work.* ○ *I'm a mother of two and I still hold down a job.*

EVEN GREATER /stɪl/ *adv* [not gradable] to an even greater degree or in an even greater amount ○ *Lulu's apartment is crammed with papers and boxes that hold still more papers.*

NOT MOVING /stɪl/ *adj, adv* [-*er*/-*est* only] not moving; staying in the same position ○ *Just hold still – you've got a little cut on your head.* ○ *Time seems almost to stand still here, doesn't it?*

still /stɪl/ *n* [U] ○ *In the still (= quiet) of the night, nothing moved.*

S

WORD CHOICES still

Motionless means the same as "still."

*He stood **motionless** when he saw the snake.*

The expression **not move a muscle** can also be used when someone is completely still.

*He sat there the whole time and **didn't move a muscle**.*

Immobile or **inert** can be used when someone is still or unable to move.

*She sat **immobile**, wondering what to do next.*

*The **inert** figure of a man could be seen lying in front of the car.*

If something is still and firm, you could use the adjective **steady**.

*I'll hold the boat **steady** while you climb in.*

Stationary is usually used for vehicles which are not moving.

*We sat **stationary** in heavy traffic for close to an hour.*

If someone becomes completely still because of being frightened, you can say that the person **freezes**.

*She saw someone outside the window and **froze**.*

EQUIPMENT /stɪl/ *n* [C] a piece of equipment used for making alcohol

stillbirth /ˈstɪl·bɜrθ/ *n* [C] the birth of a baby who has already died inside the mother

stillborn /ˈstɪl·bɔːrn/ *adj* [not gradable] dead at the time of birth ○ *Her first child was stillborn.*

still life *n* [C] ***art*** a painting or drawing of an arrangement of objects that do not move, such as flowers or fruit

stilted /ˈstɪl·təd/ *adj* (of behavior, speech, or writing) too formal and not smooth or natural ○ *Legal language tends to be very stilted.*

stilts /stɪlts/ *pl n* long pieces of wood with supports for the feet on which someone can stand and walk, or long pieces of wood that support small buildings above the ground or above water

stimulate /ˈstɪm·jəˌleɪt/ *v* [T] to encourage something to grow, develop, or become active ○ *Tax cuts will stimulate the economy.* ○ *Read books to stimulate your child's imagination.* ○ *Some vegetables stimulate cells to manufacture a cancer-fighting enzyme.*

stimulant /ˈstɪm·jə·lənt/ *n* [C] a drug or chemical substance that encourages growth or increases activity

stimulating /ˈstɪm·jəˌleɪt̬·ɪŋ/ *adj* causing enthusiasm and interest ○ *The conversation was stimulating, witty, and learned.*

stimulation /ˌstɪm·jəˈleɪ·ʃən/ *n* [U] ○ *I need the intellectual stimulation of work.*

stimulus /ˈstɪm·jə·ləs/ *n* [C/U] *pl* **stimuli** something that causes growth, activity, or reaction ○ [C] *Scientists are studying the cell's response to stimuli.* ○ [U] *The aid package would provide very little fiscal stimulus.*

sting **HURT** /stɪŋ/ *v* [I/T] *past* **stung** **1** (esp. of insects, plants, and animals) to produce a small but painful injury by making a very small hole in the skin ○ [I] *Why do bees sting?* **2** If something stings, it causes you to feel pain: [T] *Cold air stung Jack's lungs.* ○ [I] *The soap made his eyes sting.* **3** If someone's remarks sting you, they make you feel upset and annoyed: [T] *Managers were stung by criticism from environmentalists.*

sting /stɪŋ/ *n* [C] ○ *Bee stings covered his hands.*

stinger /ˈstɪŋ·ər/ *n* [C] the pointed part of an insect, plant, or animal that stings

POLICE ACTIVITY /stɪŋ/ *n* [C] an operation in which police officers or others pretend to be criminals so they can catch people committing crimes ○ *Officers set up a sting in which they sold him the jewels, and when he drove off with them they arrested him.*

stingy /ˈstɪn·dʒi/ *adj* [*-er/-est* only] not generous, or unwilling to spend money ○ *Some bankers are stingy in lending to small businesses.*

stink **SMELL** /stɪŋk/ *v* [I] *past simp.* **stank**, **stunk**, *past part.* **stunk** *infml* to smell very unpleasant ○ [I] *Your feet stink.*

stink /stɪŋk/ *n* [C] ○ *I can't stand the stink of rotten meat.*

stinking /ˈstɪŋ·kɪŋ/ *adj* [not gradable] ○ *Houses were built along stinking drainage ditches.*

BE BAD /stɪŋk/ *v* [I] *past simp.* **stank**, **stunk**, *past part.* **stunk** *infml* to be extremely bad or unpleasant ○ *The music scene here stinks.*

stink /stɪŋk/ *n* [U] *infml* a negative reaction from a group of people or from the public ○ *City employees are raising a stink over the plan.*

stinker /ˈstɪŋ·kər/ *n* [C] *infml* an unpleasant person, thing, or situation ○ *Don was punished for calling his mother a stinker.*

stinking /ˈstɪŋ·kɪŋ/ *adj infml* ○ *I hate this stinking job!*

PHRASAL VERB with stink

• **stink up** *something* [M] *infml* to make a place smell unpleasant ○ *That perfume stunk up the whole store.*

stint **PERIOD** /stɪnt/ *n* [C] a period of time spent doing a particular job or activity ○ *He took up boxing during his stint in the army.*

LIMIT /stɪnt/ *v* [I] to give, take, or use only a small amount of something ○ *She doesn't stint when it comes to buying new clothes.*

stipend /ˈstɑɪ·pend, -pənd/ *n* [C] a fixed, regular income that is usually not based on an amount of work done ○ *As a student advisor, she gets a monthly stipend from the college.*

stipulate /ˈstɪp·jəˌleɪt/ *v* [T] to state exactly what must be done ○ [+ *that* clause] *State laws stipulate that public education be free.*

stipulation /ˌstɪp·jəˈleɪ·ʃən/ *n* [C] ○ *There was a stipulation that the land be used as a park.*

stir **MIX** /stɜr/ *v* [I/T] **-rr-** to mix liquids or other substances, or to move an object such as a spoon in a circular movement ○ [T] *Chad stirred the thick paint in the buckets.* ○ [I] *Add tomatoes, stir, and bring to boil.* ○ [M] *Let the rice sit, and then stir it up.*

stir /stɜr/ *n* [C] ○ *Give the onions a stir.*

MOVE /stɜr/ *v* [I/T] **-rr-** to move slightly, or to cause something to move ○ [T] *A breeze stirred the palm trees.* ○ [I] *The old man stirred in his chair.* ○ [M] *Her boat went ahead of mine, so she'd stir up the fish and I'd catch them.*

CAUSE /stɜr/ *v* [T] to cause feelings or emotions to be felt ○ *That music stirred some old emotions.* ○ [M] *He was just trying to stir up unrest.*

stir /stɜr/ *n* [U] ○ *He caused a stir at the music awards by emptying a glass of water over the presenter's head.*

stir-fry /ˈstɜr·frɑɪ/ *v* [T] to cook pieces of meat or vegetables quickly in very hot oil, moving them around all the time ○ *She stir-fried the vegetables.*

stir-fry /ˈstɜr·frɑɪ/ *n* [C] ○ *Tomatoes add color to a stir-fry.*

stirrup /ˈstɜr·əp, ˈstɪr-/ *n* [C] one of a pair of metal pieces that hangs from the side of a horse's SADDLE (= seat), which you put your foot in when riding

stitch **THREAD** /stɪtʃ/ *n* [C] **1** a piece of thread sewn in cloth, or the single movement of a needle and thread into and out of the cloth that produces this ○ *She sewed neat, firm stitches.* **2** A stitch is also a length of special thread used to join the edges of a deep cut in the flesh: *A cut on his left ankle required six stitches.*

stitch /stɪtʃ/ *v* [T] **1** *His name is stitched onto the back of his boxing trunks.* **2** Someone who has been stitched up has had a deep cut closed with stitches: [M] *The operation started at 8 a.m., and Bobby was stitched up by midafternoon.*

stitching /ˈstɪtʃ·ɪŋ/ *n* [U] ○ *I sew it on so you can't see the stitching.*

PAIN /stɪtʃ/ *n* [C] a sharp pain in the side of your stomach or chest ○ *I got a stitch while I was running.*

IDIOM with **stitch**

• **in stitches** laughing very hard ○ *He was telling jokes at the dinner table that had us all in stitches.*

stock **SUPPLY** /stɑk/ *n* [C/U] **1** a supply of something for use or sale ○ [C] *New regulations should preserve stocks of haddock and other fish.* ○ [U] *The company won't let you return unsold stock.* **2** Stock is also the total amount of goods or the amount of a particular type of goods available in a store: [U] *New Video has 4000 titles in stock.* ○ [U] *That CD is out of stock.*

stock /stɑk/ *v* [T] ○ *They stock all sorts of gifts for travelers.*

INVESTMENT /stɑk/ *n* [C/U] ***social studies*** a part of the ownership of a company that people buy as an investment ○ [C] *There is more risk with stocks than with bonds.* ○ [U] *Stock prices fell this week.*

USUAL /stɑk/ *adj* [not gradable] (of an idea, expression, or action) usual or typical ○ *a stock phrase/response*

FLAVORED LIQUID /stɑk/ *n* [U] a liquid made by boiling vegetables or the bones from meat or fish in water which is used to add flavor to soups and other food ○ *vegetable/beef/chicken stock*

ANIMALS /stɑk/ *pl n* short form of LIVESTOCK (= animals, such as cows or sheep, kept on a farm)

ORIGIN /stɑk/ *n* [U] the family, country, or group from which a person comes ○ *He's an American of Irish stock.*

GUN PART /stɑk/ *n* [C] the part of a RIFLE (= long gun) that rests against the shoulder

IDIOM with **stock**

• **stock up (on** *something***)** to buy a large amount of something so that you will have enough for the future ○ *I hadn't stocked up on food, so I wasn't ready to feed Kate and her friends.*

stockade /stɑˈkeɪd/ *n* [C] a strong wooden fence built around an area to defend it against attack

stockbroker /ˈstɑkˌbroʊ·kər/ *n* [C] a person or company that buys and sells investments for other people

stock exchange, **stock market** *n* [C] a place where SHARES (= parts of the ownership of companies) are bought and sold, or the organization of people whose job is to do this buying and selling ○ *The company's shares fell sharply on the London stock exchange.*

stockholder /ˈstɑkˌhoʊl·dər/ *n* [C] a person or group that owns part of a company in the form of SHARES

stocking /ˈstɑk·ɪŋ/ *n* [C usually pl] one of a pair of tight-fitting, thin, cloth covers for the feet and legs worn esp. by women

stock in trade *n* [C usually sing] a person's typical way of behaving, or a skill that is usual for someone ○ *He spoke with the humor and warmth that has become his stock in trade.*

stock market *n* [C] **1** the value of all investments that are traded ○ *Rumors about the president's illness caused the stock market to go down yesterday.* **2** A stock market is also another word for a STOCK EXCHANGE..

stockpile /ˈstɑk·pɑɪl/ *n* [C] a large amount of goods kept ready for future use ○ *a stockpile of wheat*

stockpile /ˈstɑk·pɑɪl/ *v* [T] ○ *She stockpiled chocolate bars in her car.*

stock-still /ˈstɑkˈstɪl/ *adv* [not gradable] without moving; completely still ○ *He stood stock-still, waiting for them to pass.*

stocky /ˈstɑk·i/ *adj* (esp. of a man) wide and strong-looking ○ *He was shorter and stockier than I expected.*

stockyard /ˈstɑk·jɑrd/ *n* [C] a set of enclosed areas where farm animals are kept before being sold or killed

S

stodgy /ˈstɑdʒ·i/ *adj* acting according to old, established methods and unwilling to change or consider new ideas ○ *one of the stodgiest and most private of the nation's banks*

stoic /ˈstoʊ·ɪk/, **stoical** /ˈstoʊ·ɪ·kəl/ *adj* not showing or not feeling any emotion, esp. in a situation in which the expression of emotion is expected ○ *He is somewhat stoic as he speaks of his past.*

stoke /stoʊk/ *v* [T] to add fuel to a large enclosed fire and move the fuel around so that it burns well and produces a lot of heat ○ *Returning to the camp, he stoked the fire.* ○ (fig.) *The flag is a symbol used to stoke the flames of* (= increase) *national pride.*

stole /stoʊl/ *past simple of* STEAL **TAKE AWAY**

stolen /ˈstoʊ·lən/ *past participle of* STEAL **TAKE AWAY**

stolid /ˈstɑl·əd/ *adj* showing little or no emotion or imagination ○ *Stolid and impassive, the customs inspector listened to her explanation.*

stomach /ˈstʌm·ək/ *n* [C] *pl* **stomachs 1** ***biology*** an organ in the body where food is digested **2** Your stomach is also the front part of your body near the waist. **3** Stomach can also mean desire or an interest in doing something: *I used to watch the TV news all the time, but I no longer have the stomach for it.*
stomach /ˈstʌm·ək/ *v* [T] to accept or be able to deal with something that causes you difficulty ○ *Vernon was simply too unreliable, and after awhile we couldn't stomach his behavior.*

stomachache, **stomach ache** /ˈstʌm·ɪkˌeɪk/ *n* [C] a pain in the stomach

stomp /stɑmp, stɔːmp/ *v* [I/T] to put your foot down so that it hits the ground with a lot of force, or to walk with heavy steps ○ [I always + adv/prep] *She had waited hours already and was about to stomp away furiously.*

stone HARD SUBSTANCE /stoʊn/ *n* [C/U] **1** the hard, solid substance found in the ground that is often used as a building material, or a small piece of this substance ○ [U] *The museum was made of stone.* **2** A stone is also a jewel: [C] *He wore a ring with a black stone on his little finger.* **3** A stone is also a piece of hard material that can form in an organ in the body: [C] *kidney stones*
stone /stoʊn/ *v* [T] to throw rocks or other hard objects at someone or something
stone /stoʊn/ *adv* [not gradable] completely ○ *By the time he was 80, he was stone deaf.*
stony /ˈstoʊ·ni/ *adj* **1** *The ground was too stony to be used as a farm.* **2** Stony also means not showing any emotion, esp. sympathy, when you might expect it to be shown: *Though we begged him, he gave us a stony look and turned away.*

SEED /stoʊn/ *n* [C] a PIT **SEED** ○ *a cherry stone*

WORD FAMILY stone

Nouns	stone	*Verbs*	stone
Adjectives	stoned stony	*Adverbs*	stone

IDIOM with stone

• **a stone's throw (away)** a short distance ○ *The animal was sitting just a stone's throw away from us.* ○ *The lodge is within a stone's throw of the ski slopes.*

stone-faced *adj* not showing any emotion

stonewall /ˈstoʊn·wɔːl/ *v* [I/T] to prevent someone from discovering information by not being helpful or by refusing to answer questions ○ [I] *If you refuse to be interviewed, or stonewall and make it difficult for us to do our job, you might face punishment later.*

stood /stʊd/ *past simple and past participle of* STAND

stool SEAT /stuːl/ *n* [C] a seat without any support for the back or arms ○ *a piano stool* ○ *Sarah sat on a kitchen stool.*

SOLID WASTE /stuːl/ *n* [C] *medical* a piece of excrement

stoop BEND /stuːp/ *v* [I] to bend the top half of the body forward and down ○ *The mother stooped to button up the coat of her little girl.*
stoop /stuːp/ *n* [U] ○ *He walks with a stoop because of arthritis.*

STEPS /stuːp/ *n* [C] a structure that is part of the front of a house consisting of a few steps leading up from ground level, often with a raised, flat area near the door

stop FINISH /stɑp/ *v* [I/T] **-pp-** to finish doing something or end, or to cause someone or something to finish ○ [I] *When do you think the snow will stop?* ○ [T] *When will it stop snowing?* ○ [T] *Please stop pushing.* ○ [T] *Fortunately, police stopped the fight before anyone got hurt.*
stop /stɑp/ *n* [C] ○ *Please wait until the plane comes to a complete stop before leaving your seat.*

USAGE

stop *doing* or stop *to do*?

Stop *doing something* means "not continue with an activity."

Suddenly, everyone stopped talking.

~~*Suddenly, everyone stopped to talk.*~~

Stop to *do something* means "stop one activity so that you can do something else."

We stopped to look at the map.

PREVENT /stɑp/ *v* [T] **-pp-** to prevent someone from doing something ○ *Lifeguards stopped them from going into the water because sharks had been spotted in the area.*

PAUSE /stɑp/ *v* [I/T] **-pp-** to pause or stay in a place, or cause someone to pause ○ [I] *We stopped for gas and had something to eat.* ○ [+ to infinitive] *We'd better stop at the next rest area to let the kids go to the bathroom.* ○ [T] *Naomi was stopped at the gate and asked to show identification.*
stop /stɑp/ *n* [C] **1** *It was a five-hour drive including a 30-minute stop for lunch.* **2** A stop is a place where a bus or train pauses to allow passengers to get off and on: *I'm getting off at the next stop.*

stoppage /ˈstɑp·ɪdʒ/ *n* [C] ○ *After a two-day work stoppage in early July, another strike started in September.* ➤ Usage: **station or stop?** at STATION BUILDING

WORD FAMILY stop			
Nouns	stop stoppage	*Verbs*	stop
Adjectives	nonstop	*Adverbs*	nonstop

IDIOMS with stop

• **stop on a dime** to be able to stop almost immediately, even when moving very quickly ○ *He runs up the field and stops on a dime to catch the ball.*

• **stop (dead) in** *your* **tracks** to suddenly stop moving or doing something ○ *I stopped dead in my tracks when I heard the scream.*

PHRASAL VERBS with stop

• **stop by/in/off** to visit a place or a person for a short time, esp. when you are on the way to somewhere else ○ *A group of friends stopped by to say hello.* ○ *I'll stop off on my way home and pick up some pop.*

• **stop over** to stay at a place for a short period of time on the way to somewhere else or before returning home ○ *Marj decided to stop over in Pittsburgh to see an old friend.* ○ Related noun: STOPOVER

stopgap /ˈstɑp·ɡæp/ *n* [C] something that can be used until something better or more permanent can be obtained ○ *Housing the homeless in shelters has to be seen as a stopgap measure.*

stoplight /ˈstɑp·lɑɪt/ *n* [C] a TRAFFIC LIGHT

stopover /ˈstɑpˌoʊ·vər/ *n* [C] a short stay at a place while in the middle of a trip ○ *The tour included a stopover in Pisa on the way to Florence.* ○ Related verb: STOPˈ OVER

stopper /ˈstɑp·ər/ *n* [C] a round object that fits into or covers a hole, such as in a sink, to prevent liquids from escaping it ○ *a rubber sink stopper*

stop sign *n* [C] a red, eight-sided sign at the side of a road that signals drivers to stop before continuing

stopwatch /ˈstɑp·wɑtʃ, -wɔːtʃ/ *n* [C] a watch that you can start and stop to measure exactly how much time has passed

store PLACE TO BUY THINGS /stɔːr, stoʊr/ *n* [C] a place where you can buy goods or services ○ *a grocery/hardware/video store* ○ *convenience/department stores*

KEEP /stɔːr, stoʊr/ *v* [T] to put or keep things for use in the future ○ *We store the garden tools in a shed in the backyard.* ○ *All the information is stored on a hard disk.*

storage /ˈstɔːr·ɪdʒ, ˈstoʊr-/ *n* [U] ○ *Fire broke out in a basement storage area.* ○ *Much of the art they've acquired is still in storage* (= being kept in a safe place and not yet in use).

store /stɔːr, stoʊr/ *n* [C] a supply of something ○ *energy stores* ○ *She has a store of anecdotes* (= a large number of them) *that she could draw on whenever she needed one.*

IDIOM with store

• **in store (for** *someone/something***)** planned or likely to happen ○ *We have a big surprise in store for you.*

storefront /ˈstɔːr·frʌnt, ˈstoʊr-/ *n* [C] the part of a store that faces the street, usually a glass front ○ *In the downtown area, there are dozens of boarded-up storefronts.* ○ *Volunteers are working out of a storefront office* (= an office that uses the space of a store).

storehouse /ˈstɔːr·hɑʊs, ˈstoʊr-/ *n* [C] a WAREHOUSE

storekeeper /ˈstɔːrˌkiː·pər, ˈstoʊr-/ *n* [C] a person who owns or operates a store

storeroom /ˈstɔːr·ruːm, ˈstoʊr-, -rʊm/ *n* [C] a room in which things that are not being used can be kept ○ *You can get a mop from the school's storeroom downstairs.*

storied /ˈstɔːr·iːd, ˈstoʊr-/ *adj* famous, esp. because of being interesting or an important part of history ○ *a storied career* ○ *storied buildings*

stork /stɔːrk/ *n* [C] a large bird with long legs, a long neck, and a long beak that walks in water to find its food

storm VIOLENT WEATHER /stɔːrm/ *n* [C] an extreme weather condition with strong winds and heavy rain or snow ○ *The storm left over a foot of snow on the ground.*

stormy /ˈstɔːr·mi/ *adj* ○ *I remember one stormy afternoon when Marcelle and I were kept indoors by the weather.* ○ *(fig.) The new president's promise of dramatic change has already run into some stormy weather* (= difficult problems) *on Capitol Hill.*

STRONG FEELING /stɔːrm/ *n* [C] a strong expression of feeling, esp. in reaction to a statement or event ○ *The new rent regulations raised a storm of criticism from both renters and landlords.*

storm /stɔːrm/ *v* [I always + adv/prep] to move quickly and forcefully to show you are angry ○ *Henry stormed into Giffen's office waving a copy of the newspaper and yelling at the top of his lungs.*

stormy /ˈstɔːr·mi/ *adj* full of difficulties or fights ○ *He is best remembered for his stormy marriage to actress Bette Davis.*

ATTACK /stɔːrm/ *v* [T] to attack a place or building suddenly ○ *Officers stormed the building the demonstrators had occupied.*

WORD FAMILY storm			
Nouns	storm	*Verbs*	storm
Adjectives	stormy		

story DESCRIPTION /ˈstɔːr·i, ˈstoʊr·i/ *n* [C] **1** a description of events that actually happened or that are invented ○ *There was a news story on television about flooding on the west coast.* ○ *My daugh-*

S

ter won't go to bed without hearing a bedtime story. **2** A story can also be a lie: *Don't tell me any stories – I want to know what really happened.* ➤ Confusables: **history or story?** at HISTORY PAST EVENTS

WORD CHOICES story

Tale is an alternative to "story," especially when it might be invented or difficult to believe.

*The book is a well-told **tale** about life during the Civil War.*

Narrative is a formal word for a story.

*It's a moving **narrative** of wartime adventure.*

If a story is someone's description of an event, you could use the word **account**.

*She gave a thrilling **account** of her life in the jungle.*

A short amusing story, especially about something that someone has done, is an **anecdote**.

*He told one or two amusing **anecdotes** about his years as a police officer.*

The story of a book, film, etc., is its **plot**.

*The movie has a very simple **plot**.*

If a story is ancient and about famous people or events, the word **legend** is often used.

*The dance was based on several Hindu **legends**.*

Myths are ancient stories that explain the history of a group of people or are about natural events.

*Greek **myths***

A **fable** is a story that tells a general truth or is only partly based on facts.

*the **fable** of the hare and the tortoise*

Stories for children which involve magic and imaginary creatures are often called **fairy tales**.

LEVEL /ˈstɔːr·i, ˈstoʊr·i/ *n* [C] a level of a building ○ *She lived on the third floor of a seven-story building.*

storybook /ˈstɔːr·iːˌbʊk, ˈstoʊr-/ *n* [C] a book containing stories for children

storyteller /ˈstɔːr·iːˌtel·ər, ˈstoʊr-/ *n* [C] a person who tells or reads stories to others

storytelling /ˈstɔːr·iːˌtel·ɪŋ, ˈstoʊr-/ *n* [U] the art of telling stories ○ *The celebration will include dance, song, and storytelling.*

stout FAT /stɑʊt/ *adj* [*-er/-est* only] (of people) fat and solid-looking, esp. around the waist, or (of things) thick and strong ○ *He was seen as a pleasant man – short, a bit stout and balding, with a radiant smile.* ○ *There is much to be said for having a stout fence to protect your flower beds.*

DETERMINED /stɑʊt/ *adj* [*-er/-est* only] determined and strong, esp. in opinion ○ *He was the brains and the stout heart behind the best of these stories.*

stove /stoʊv/ *n* [C] **1** a piece of kitchen equipment having a top for cooking food in containers placed over gas flames or circles of metal heated by electricity, and that usually has an OVEN below ○ *She got some eggs out and heated a pan on the stove.* **2** A stove is also a piece of equipment for heating a space inside a room, often using wood or a form of COAL as a fuel: *a potbellied stove*

stow /stoʊ/ *v* [T] to put something in a place where it can be kept safely ○ *Please stow your carry-on bags under the seat in front of you.*

stowaway /ˈstoʊ·əˌweɪ/ *n* [C] someone who hides on a ship or aircraft to travel without having to pay

straddle /ˈstræd·əl/ *v* [T] **1** to have or put your legs on either side of something ○ *Grace straddled her chair.* **2** To straddle something is also to be unable to decide which of two opinions about something is better, and so to partly support both opinions: *The president has tried to straddle the issue of political fund-raising.*

straggle /ˈstræg·əl/ *v* [I] to move alone or in small groups slowly and usually separated in distance or time from those who went earlier ○ *The players straggled in for the morning practice session.*

straggler /ˈstræg·lər/ *n* [C] ○ *I want all you children to stay together and hold hands when crossing a street – no stragglers!*

straight NOT CURVING /streɪt/ *adj, adv* [*-er/-est* only] not bending or curving ○ *Draw a straight line between the two dots.* ○ *Stand up straight.* ○ *The car seemed to be coming straight at me.*

straighten /ˈstreɪt·ən/ *v* [I/T] to make something so that it does not bend ○ [I] *Her shoulders straightened, and she cleared her throat.* ○ [T] *First bend and then straighten your leg.* ○ [M] *You must straighten out the pipe.*

LEVEL /streɪt/ *adj, adv* [*-er/-est* only] not leaning to either side; level ○ *Since the wall is crooked, how can the picture hang straight?*

straighten /ˈstreɪt·ən/ *v* [T] ○ *Please straighten the lampshade – it tilts to the right.*

IMMEDIATELY /streɪt/ *adv* [not gradable] **1** without delay; immediately or directly ○ *I got to the hotel and went straight to bed.* **2** If you get straight to the point, you say immediately what is on your mind: *My boss simply said, "I'll get straight to the point. You're fired!"*

BASIC /streɪt/ *adj, adv* [*-er/-est* only] **1** without anything added or changed; basic or true ○ *Things have gotten so bad, I think it's time for some straight talk.* ○ *She couldn't give a straight answer to any question.* ○ *It's important to tell the story straight, exactly as it happened.* **2** If an alcoholic drink is taken straight, it has no water, ice, or other liquid added to it.

DIRECTLY /streɪt/ *adv* [not gradable] **1** clearly or directly ○ *This valentine comes straight from my heart.* **2** If you tell someone something **straight out**, you say it immediately and without a long explanation or any excuses: *I walked in, and she told me straight out what had happened.*

CLEARLY /streɪt/ *adv* [not gradable] clearly; plainly ○ *I'm so tired I can't think straight anymore.*

FOLLOWING /streɪt/ *adj, adv* [not gradable] following one after another without an interruption; CONSECUTIVE ○ *The team had won four straight* *games before they lost this one.* ○ *Sometimes we work 16 hours straight.*

NOT HOMOSEXUAL /streɪt/ *adj* [not gradable] *infml* not homosexual; HETEROSEXUAL

IDIOM with straight

•**the straight and narrow (path)** a course of behavior that is correct ○ *Ray runs an after-school program meant to keep young people on the straight and narrow.*

PHRASAL VERB with straight

•**straighten** *someone* **out IMPROVE** [M] to cause someone to improve his or her behavior or character ○ *I thought marriage would straighten him out.*
•**straighten** *something* **out ORGANIZE** [M] to organize or correct something ○ *It took me a while to straighten out my father's accounts.*
•**straighten** *something* **up** [M] to organize a place or make it neat ○ *You need to straighten up your room before your friends come over.*

straight angle *n* [C] ***geometry*** an angle of 180°

straight face *n* [C usually sing] an expression on your face that shows on emotion in order to hide what you really think or feel ○ *It's hard to argue that point of view with a straight face.*

straightforward Ⓐ **UNDERSTANDABLE** /streɪtˈfɔːr·wərd/ *adj* easy to understand; clear ○ *The doctor explained the operation in straightforward English.*

HONEST /streɪtˈfɔːr·wərd/ *adj* honest and without unnecessary politeness ○ *She's a straightforward, no-nonsense teacher.*

straightjacket /ˈstreɪtˌdʒæk·ət/ *n* [C] a STRAITJACKET

strain WORRY /streɪn/ *n* [C/U] something that causes anxiety, worry, or difficulty ○ [U] *Loss of funding has put a lot of strain on the day-care center.* ○ [C] *The benefits of keeping our daughter at home make the strains of having only one income worthwhile.*

strain /streɪn/ *v* [T] to cause anxiety or problems ○ *This relationship has been strained almost to the breaking point.* ○ *These extra costs have strained our financial resources.*

strained /streɪnd/ *adj* ○ *She had a strained expression on her face.*

PRESSURE /streɪn/ *n* [U] physical pressure ○ *The bookcase collapsed under the strain.*

strain /streɪn/ *v* [I] to create pressure or use effort ○ *The dog strained at the leash, pulling his master along.* ○ [+ to infinitive] *I had to strain to hear the audio.*

INJURY /streɪn/ *n* [C] an injury caused by working the muscles too hard ○ *Running puts a strain on your heart.*

strain /streɪn/ *v* [T] ○ *I strained my back carrying those boxes.*

strained /streɪnd/ *adj* ○ *a strained knee*

SEPARATE /streɪn/ *v* [I/T] to separate solid pieces from a liquid by pouring it through a utensil with small holes at the bottom of it or through a cloth ○ [T] *Strain the liquid and discard the vegetables.*

strainer /ˈstreɪ·nər/ *n* [C] ○ *Force the cooked fruit through a strainer*

DIFFERENT TYPE /streɪn/ *n* [C] **1** an animal or plant that is only slightly different from other animals or plants of the same type ○ *A new strain of the virus has been found.* **2** A strain is also a quality that gives something a particular character: *There has long been a populist strain in American politics.* **3** A strain is also a particular sound: *Strains of piano music drifted across the room.*

strait /streɪt/ *n* [C] a narrow area of water that connects two larger areas of water ○ *The strait lies between the Atlantic Ocean and the Mediterranean Sea.*

straitjacket, **straightjacket** /ˈstreɪtˌdʒæk·ət/ *n* [C] a special item of clothing like a coat that ties the arms to the body and limits the movement of a violent or mentally ill person

strand /strænd/ *n* [C] a fiber or group of fibers twisted together that form one part of a length of rope, cord, thread, etc., or a single string, hair, or line of objects ○ *a strand of hair* ○ *She wore three strands of beads around her neck.* ○ (fig.) *There are many strands* (= types) *of pacifism.*

stranded /ˈstræn·dəd/ *adj* [not gradable] lacking what is necessary to leave a place or to get out of a situation ○ *During the storm, stranded passengers slept at the airport.*

strange UNUSUAL /streɪndʒ/ *adj* [-*er*/-*est* only] not familiar, or difficult to understand; different ○ *We kept hearing strange noises coming from the attic.* ○ *I had a strange feeling that we had met before.* ○ *That's strange – I thought I had locked this door when we left.*

strangely /ˈstreɪndʒ·li/ *adv* **1** *It seemed to me that she was acting strangely.* **2 Strangely enough** means that something is unusual or hard to explain: *Strangely enough, my father was the last one to know about my mother's illness.*

WORD CHOICES strange

See also: **unusual**

Other ways of saying "strange" are **odd**, **bizarre**, and **weird**.

I always thought there was something a bit ***odd*** *about her.*

I had a really ***bizarre/weird*** *dream last night.*

If something is strange because it is not what you usually expect, you can use the adjectives **curious**, **funny**, or **peculiar**.

This lemonade tastes ***funny****.*

The chicken had a ***peculiar*** *smell.*

A ***curious*** *thing happened to me yesterday.*

If someone always behaves strangely, you might describe that person as **eccentric**.

The whole family is ***eccentric****.*

NOT FAMILIAR /streɪndʒ/ *adj* [-*er*/-*est* only] not known or familiar ○ *I really don't like strange people coming to my door.*

S

stranger /ˈstreɪn·dʒər/ *n* [C] **1** someone not known or not familiar ○ *After being away so long, my sister seemed like a stranger.* **2** A stranger in a particular place is someone who has never been there before: *Sorry, I can't direct you – I'm a stranger here myself.*

USAGE

strange or foreign?

Strange means unusual, unexpected, or not familiar. **Foreign** means coming from another country which is not your country.

There are a lot of foreign students in Los Angeles.

~~*There are a lot of strange students in Los Angeles.*~~

WORD FAMILY strange			
Nouns	stranger	*Adverbs*	strangely
Adjectives	strange		

strangle /ˈstræŋ·gəl/ *v* [T] to kill someone by pressing the throat so that the person cannot breathe
strangulation /ˌstræŋ·gjəˈleɪ·ʃən/ *n* [U] ○ *An autopsy showed that he had died of strangulation.*

strap /stræp/ *n* [C] a narrow piece of strong material, esp. leather, used for holding or fastening something ○ *Her bag hung from its shoulder strap.* ○ *I lost my watch when the strap broke.*
strap /stræp/ *v* [T always + adv/prep] **-pp-** ○ *I strapped on my helmet and rode off.* ○ *We had to strap the mattress to the top of our car.*
strapless /ˈstræp·ləs/ *adj* [not gradable] without straps

strapped /stræpt/ *adj* not having enough money ○ *In the early days, we were strapped.*

IDIOM with strapped

• **strapped for** *something* lacking something ○ *Busy executives are strapped for time.*

strapping /ˈstræp·ɪŋ/ *adj* [not gradable] healthy, big, and strong ○ *The sickly child grew up to be a strapping six-footer.*

strata /ˈstræţ·ə, ˈstreɪţ·ə/ *pl of* STRATUM

stratagem /ˈstræţ·ə·dʒəm, -ˌdʒem/ *n* [C] a plan or trick to achieve something ○ *Barry devised several stratagems for escape.*

strategic weapon *n* [C usually pl] a weapon that is designed to attack an enemy from a distance

strategy Ⓐ /ˈstræţ·ə·dʒi/ *n* [C/U] a long-range plan for achieving something or reaching a goal, or the skill of making such plans ○ [U] *Chess is a game that requires strategy.*
strategic Ⓐ /strəˈtiː·dʒɪk/ *adj* ○ *The hill was of strategic importance for control of the countryside.*
strategically Ⓐ /strəˈtiː·dʒɪk·li/ *adv* ○ *The cameras are strategically placed in areas with the most criminal activity.*

strategist Ⓐ /ˈstræţ·ə·dʒəst/ *n* [C] someone who is skilled in planning, esp. in military, political, or business matters ○ *Democratic/Republican strategists*

stratified /ˈstræţ·əˌfɑɪd/ *adj* [not gradable] arranged in separate layers ○ *stratified rock* ○ *a stratified society*

stratosphere /ˈstræţ·əˌsfɪr/ *n* [U] ***earth science*** the layer of gases that surrounds the earth from about seven to 30 miles above it

stratum /ˈstræţ·əm, ˈstreɪţ-/ *n* [C usually pl] *pl* **strata** a single layer of something ○ *the upper strata of society* ○ ***earth science*** *Engineers could inject seawater into sandy strata* (= layers of the earth) *beneath the city.*

straw DRIED STEMS /strɔː/ *n* [U] the dried yellow stems of crops such as wheat, used for animals or for weaving ○ *straw hats/baskets* ○ *The horse had a warm bed of fresh straw.*

TUBE /strɔː/ *n* [C] a thin tube, usually made of plastic, used to suck a drink from a container

IDIOM with straw

• **the last straw, the final straw** the latest problem in a series of problems, that makes a situation impossible to accept ○ *The last straw was when the company fired most of the managers.*

strawberry /ˈstrɔːˌber·i, -bə·ri/ *n* [C] a small, juicy, red fruit shaped like a cone with seeds on its surface, or the plant on which this fruit grows

stray MOVE AWAY /streɪ/ *v* [I] to move away from a place where you should be or from a direction in which you should go ○ *The children were told to stay together and not to stray.* ○ *The plane disappeared after straying several hundred miles off course.*

LOST /streɪ/ *adj* [not gradable] **1** (of an animal) having no home, or lost ○ *Eric and Lise rescued the stray cat and named her Pashmina.* **2** Stray also means happening by chance and lacking direction: *It was just a stray thought I had while washing the dishes.*
stray /streɪ/ *n* [C] ○ *We have given a home to a number of strays.*

streak MARK /striːk/ *n* [C] a mark of a color that is different from what surrounds it, or a thin strip of light ○ *Streaks of gray and black colored the marble.* ○ *The comet appeared as a dazzling streak in the sky.*
streak /striːk/ *v* [T] ○ *Her cheeks were streaked with sweat and dirt.*

CHARACTERISTIC /striːk/ *n* [C] an obvious characteristic in a personality ○ *He seems to have a mean streak that I hadn't noticed before.*

PERIOD /striːk/ *n* [C] a period during which a series of things happens ○ *What will the team do after this memorable eight-game winning streak?*

MOVE FAST /striːk/ *v* [I always + adv/prep] to move quickly ○ *The space shuttle rose from its launching pad and streaked into the sky.*

stream SMALL RIVER /striːm/ *n* [C] a small river that flows on or below the surface of the ground ○ *Rivers are wider, deeper, and longer than streams.*

S

FLOW /striːm/ *n* [C] a continuous flow ○ *The faucet leaked in a steady stream.* ○ *An endless stream of traffic clogged the roads today.*
stream /striːm/ *v* [I] to move continuously ○ *Record numbers of applications were streaming into our offices.* ○ *Tears streamed down her cheeks.* ○ *Sunlight was streaming through the window.*

SEND /striːm/ *v* [T] to send continuous sound or moving images using computers ○ *Wi-fi networking allows you to stream music from a PC to the device.*
streaming /ˈstriː·mɪŋ/ *adj* [not gradable] ○ *Jeff's new cell phone receives streaming video.*

streamline **SHAPE** /ˈstriːm·lɑɪn/ *v* [T] to shape something so that it moves as easily as possible through air or water ○ *Designers streamlined the boat, hoping to improve its performance.*
streamlined /ˈstriːm·lɑɪnd/ *adj* ○ *a streamlined shape/appearance*

IMPROVE /ˈstriːm·lɑɪn/ *v* [T] to change something so that it works better, esp. by making it simpler ○ *The company streamlined its operations and increased its profits.*
streamlined /ˈstriːm·lɑɪnd/ *adj* ○ *a streamlined system*

street /striːt/ *n* [C] **1** a road in a city or town, usually with buildings along one or both sides ○ *Our daughter lives across the street from us.* ○ *Look both ways when you cross the street.* **2** A street sometimes means a road and the SIDEWALKS (= paths) along it: *The streets were full of people.* ○ *A group of laughing children ran down the street.*

streetcar /ˈstriːt·kɑr/ *n* [C] a TROLLEY

streetlight /ˈstriːt·lɑɪt/, **streetlamp** /ˈstriːt·læmp/ *n* [C] a light, usually on a tall post, that lights a road at night

street people *pl n* people who have no homes and live on the streets

strength **PHYSICAL POWER** /streŋθ, strenθ/ *n* [U] **1** the ability to do things that demand physical effort, or the degree to which something is strong or powerful ○ *After having surgery, it takes a while to get your strength back.* ○ *Making baskets requires skill more than physical strength.* ○ *The storm is gathering/gaining strength.* **2** The strength of a drug is its ability to have an effect.
strengthen /ˈstreŋ·θən, ˈstren-/ *v* [I/T] to become more powerful or more difficult to break, or to make something stronger ○ [T] *If something isn't done to strengthen the railroad bridge, it may collapse.* ○ [I] *The tone of her voice strengthened suddenly.* ○ [T] *Exercise will strengthen your legs.*

BRAVERY /streŋθ, strenθ/ *n* [U] bravery in dealing with difficulties ○ *He showed real strength in refusing to change his vote in spite of the call from the president.*

GOOD FEATURE /streŋθ, strenθ/ *n* [C/U] **1** a positive quality that makes you more effective ○ [C] *The plan had both strengths and weaknesses.* ○ [C] *Her drive to succeed was a real strength.* **2** The strength of a company or economy is its ability to produce goods, profits, and jobs: [U] *a period of continuing economic strength*
strengthen /ˈstreŋ·θən, ˈstren-/ *v* [I/T] ○ [T] *Somehow his illness strengthened their marriage and brought them closer together.* ○ [T] *Parents can strengthen ties with their children.*

NUMBER /streŋθ, strenθ/ *n* [U] the number of people in a group ○ *Estimates of enemy troop strengths differed.*

WORD FAMILY strength

Nouns	strength	*Verbs*	strengthen
Adjectives	strong	*Adverbs*	strongly

IDIOM with strength

• **on the strength of** *something* because of something ○ *I invested in the company on the strength of my brother's advice.*

strenuous /ˈstren·jə·wəs/ *adj* needing or using a lot of effort or energy ○ *I think football is much more strenuous than baseball.*
strenuously /ˈstren·jə·wə·sli/ *adv* ○ *He strenuously denies that he is guilty.*

strep (throat) /ˈstrep (ˈθroʊt)/ *n* [C] an infection of the throat caused by bacteria

stress Ⓐ **IMPORTANCE** /stres/ *v* [T] to give special importance or emphasis to something ○ *I'd like to stress the differences between our opinions.*
stress Ⓐ /stres/ *n* [U] ○ *There's constant stress on status in this community.*

WORRY /stres/ *n* [C/U] worry caused by a difficult situation, or something that causes this condition ○ [U] *Luis is under a lot of stress right now.* ○ [C] *It's hard to cope with the stresses of raising a family.*
stressed Ⓐ /strest/, **stressed-out** /ˈstrest ˈɑʊt/ *adj* ○ *The kids are sick, I just lost my baby-sitter, and our toilet doesn't work – no wonder I feel stressed-out!*
stressful Ⓐ /ˈstres·fəl/ *adj* ○ *Working in the emergency room of a major hospital is highly stressful work.*

PRONOUNCE /stres/ *v* [T] ***English*** to pronounce a word or syllable with greater force than other words in the same sentence or other syllables in the same word ○ *In the word "engine," you should stress the first syllable.*
stress /stres/ *n* [C/U] ***English*** ○ [C] *The main stress in the word "command" is on the second syllable.*

FORCE /stres/ *n* [C/U] a force that tends to change the shape or strength of an object ○ [U] *If a metal object experiences constant stress, it may bend or break.*

WORD FAMILY stress

Nouns	stress	*Adjectives*	stressed
Verbs	stress		stressful

stress fracture *n* [C] a thin crack in a bone, esp. in the leg or foot

stretch **BECOME LONGER** /stretʃ/ *v* [I/T] **1** to reach across a distance or become longer or wider, or to cause something to do this ○ [I] *Rubber* *stretches when you pull it.* ○ [T] *The banner was stretched across the street.* ○ [M] *He removed his hat and stretched out his arms to embrace her.* **2** If you stretch your body, your arms, or your legs, you straighten them so that they are as long as possible: [T] *"I'm so tired," she said, yawning and stretching her arms.*

stretch /stretʃ/ *n* [C] ○ *Before jogging, you should always do some stretches* (= stretch parts of your body).

BREAK LIMITS /stretʃ/ *v* [T] to go beyond, or almost beyond, the usual limit of something ○ *Buying a new dishwasher will really stretch our budget.* ○ *We try to stretch ourselves in our reading group, picking books we wouldn't ordinarily read.*

stretch /stretʃ/ *n* [C usually sing] an unusual and sometimes difficult situation ○ *Playing two games in two days is a bit of a stretch for us, but I think we'll make it.*

SPREAD OVER AREA /stretʃ/ *v* [I always + adv/prep] to spread over a large area or distance ○ *A huge cloud of dense smoke stretched across the sky.*

stretch /stretʃ/ *n* [C usually sing] an area of land or water ○ *Traffic is at a standstill along a five-mile stretch of Route 17 just south of Bridgeport.*

EXIST OVER TIME /stretʃ/ *v* [I always + adv/prep] to spread over a long period of time ○ [I] *The dispute stretches back over many years.* ○ [M] *I'd like to stretch my mortgage payments out for 30 years.*

stretch /stretʃ/ *n* [C usually sing] a continuous period of time ○ *We had a long stretch of days with sub-zero temperatures last month.*

IDIOMS with stretch

• **at a stretch** continuously ○ *Sometimes I work for ten hours at a stretch.* ○ Compare ON END at END IDIOMS

• **not by any stretch of the imagination, by no stretch of the imagination** even if you try, it is still difficult to accept ○ *By no stretch of the imagination could you think of her as a real artist.*

• **stretch *your* legs** to stand or walk after sitting for a long time ○ *We drove there in five hours, including a couple of stops to stretch our legs.*

S

stretcher /ˈstretʃ·ər/ *n* [C] a light bed made of cloth with poles for a frame, used for carrying people who are injured or dead

strew /struː/ *v* [T] *past simp.* **strewed,** *past part.* **strewn, strewed** to scatter things over a surface ○ *The park was strewn with litter after the concert.*

striation /straɪˈeɪ·ʃən/ *n* [C] a pattern of lines or GROOVES on the surface of something

strict /strɪkt/ *adj* [-*er*/-*est* only] limiting people's freedom to behave as they wish beyond what is usual ○ *The school is an old-fashioned institution with strict discipline.* ○ *Do you think stricter laws would help reduce automobile accidents?* ○ *He's not a vegetarian* **in the strictest sense** (= if you are exact about the word's meaning).

strictly /ˈstrɪk·tli/ *adv* completely or entirely ○ *Photography is strictly forbidden.* ○ *Public assistance is strictly limited to those who are willing to work.* ○ **Strictly speaking** (= Being completely accurate), *pollen is like a virus in that both are not alive and cannot reproduce.*

WORD CHOICES strict

If someone is very strict in the way he or she deals with others, you can describe that person as **firm**.

*I was always very **firm** with my children.*

If someone is very strict in the way he or she deals with a particular thing, you could say that person **takes a hard line on** something.

*The school **takes a hard line on** bullying.*

A person, government, system, etc., that is strict in a way you disapprove of can be described as **authoritarian**.

*His manner is extremely **authoritarian**.*

Rules, laws, etc., which are strict can be described as **stringent, tough,** or **tight**.

***Stringent** safety regulations were introduced after the accident.*

*We need some **tough** new measures to combat crime.*

***Tighter** security has resulted in longer waits at airports.*

If you think rules are unreasonably strict, you can use the adjective **draconian**.

*He criticized the **draconian** measures used by the police in controlling the demonstrators.*

stride WALK /straɪd/ *v* [I always + adv/prep] *past* **strode,** *past part.* **stridden** to walk somewhere quickly with long steps ○ *She strode across the room and demanded to speak to the manager.*

stride /straɪd/ *n* [C] a step, esp. a long step ○ *He reached me in one long stride.*

DEVELOPMENT /straɪd/ *n* [C usually pl] an important positive development ○ *They have already made great strides in improving service.*

strident /ˈstraɪd·ənt/ *adj* forceful, or very loud ○ *strident criticism* ○ *a strident voice*

strife /straɪf/ *n* [U] angry disagreement or violent actions ○ *civil/ethnic/political strife* ○ *He led the union through several years of labor strife.*

strike HIT /straɪk/ *v* [I/T] *past* **struck 1** to hit or physically attack someone or something ○ [T] *A car struck the man trying to cross a major highway.* ○ [T] *She was struck in the back of the head by a ball that was thrown across the field.* **2** If you strike a match, you cause it to burn by rubbing it against a rough surface.

strike /straɪk/ *n* [C] a brief military attack ○ *air/military strikes*

CAUSE HARM /straɪk/ *v* [I/T] *past* **struck,** *past part.* **stricken** to bring sudden harm, damage, or injury to a person or thing ○ [T] *It was a disease that struck mainly young people.* ○ [I] *Many public health officials fear that a similar flu virus will one day strike again.* ○ [T] *He was stricken with polio at the age of 13 and lost the use of his legs.*

stricken /ˈstrɪk·ən/ *adj* suffering severely from the effects of something ○ *She grew up in a poverty-*

stricken area of the state. ○ *The little boy got absolutely panic-stricken when his mother left the doctor's office.*

STOP WORK /strɑɪk/ *v* [I/T] *past* **struck** ***social studies*** to refuse to continue working because workers or their LABOR UNION (= employees' organization) cannot come to an agreement with an employer over pay or other conditions of the job ○ [I] *Flight attendants are threatening to strike to get more flexible schedules.*

strike /strɑɪk/ *n* [C/U] ○ [U] *If the teachers go on strike again and close the schools down, I don't know what I'll do with the kids.*

striker /ˈstrɑɪ·kər/ *n* [C] ***social studies*** a person, esp. a member of a LABOR UNION, who refuses to work until a satisfactory agreement with their employer has been reached

CAUSE AN IDEA /strɑɪk/ *v* [T] *past* **struck** **1** to cause someone to have a feeling or idea about something ○ *From what you've said, it strikes me that you would be better off working for someone else.* ○ *I was struck by her sincerity.* **2** To strike also means to suddenly cause someone to think of something: *I was immediately struck by the similarities in their appearance.*

DISCOVER /strɑɪk/ *v* [T] *past* **struck** to discover something such as oil, gas, gold, etc., underground at a particular place ○ *to strike gold/oil*

AGREE /strɑɪk/ *v* [T] *past* **struck** **1** to agree to or achieve a solution ○ *My children and I have struck a deal – they can play any kind of music they want as long as I don't hear it.* **2** If you strike a balance between two things, you try to give an equal amount of attention or importance to each: *It's a question of striking the right balance between quality and productivity.*

SHOW THE TIME /strɑɪk/ *v* [I/T] *past* **struck** (esp. of a clock) to make a sound or a series of sounds that show the time ○ [T] *The clock struck midnight.*

WORD FAMILY strike

Nouns	strike striker	*Adjectives*	stricken striking
Verbs	strike	*Adverbs*	strikingly

IDIOMS with strike

• **strike a chord (with** *someone***)** to cause you to remember that something is connected to you in some way ○ *The healthcare reforms struck a chord with voters.*

• **strike it rich** to become suddenly and unexpectedly rich ○ *He struck it rich on the stock market when he was only twenty-four.*

PHRASAL VERBS with strike

• **strike back** to attack someone who has attacked you; RETALIATE ○ *When you bully people long enough they are going to strike back.*

• **strike down** *something* (of a court) to decide that a law or rule is illegal and should be ignored ○ *The court struck down the law on the grounds that it was unconstitutional.*

• **strike out BEGIN** to begin a new and independent activity ○ *I needed to strike out on my own.* ○ *Next year I'm hoping to strike out and find a job where I could make some money.*

• **strike out** *(someone)* **BASEBALL** [M] **1** (in baseball) to be called OUT (= lose your chance to hit) because you have failed or did not try to hit the ball three times ○ *After Buhner struck out, Sorrento singled.* **2** If you strike someone out, you PITCH (= throw) the ball in a way that the person cannot hit it three times: *The relief pitcher struck out the first two batters he faced.* ○ Related noun: STRIKEOUT

• **strike out FAIL** to try without success; fail ○ *"How did you do at the auction?" "We really struck out – there wasn't anything worth getting."*

• **strike out at** *someone/something* to violently attack or criticize someone or something ○ *She struck out at the royal family in her famous TV interview.*

• **strike up** *something* **START FRIENDSHIP** to create or establish a relationship or conversation with someone ○ *She struck up a relationship with an artist soon after she arrived in Paris.*

• **strike up** *(something)* **START MUSIC** to start to play music ○ *The band struck up a medley of Cole Porter tunes.*

strikeout /ˈstrɑɪk ˌɑʊt/ *n* [C] (in baseball) the act of failing three times to hit the ball or of causing a player to do this ○ *Nolan Ryan was a great pitcher, and usually led the league in strikeouts.* ○ Related verb: STRIKE OUT BASEBALL

striking /ˈstrɑɪ·kɪŋ/ *adj* obvious, interesting, and (esp. of a person) often attractive ○ *Perhaps the most striking feature of this computer is that it is so easy to use.* ○ *There was a striking physical resemblance between the two men.* ○ *He was a striking figure with full beard and flowing, collar-length hair.*

strikingly /ˈstrɑɪ·kɪŋ·li/ *adv* ○ *a strikingly beautiful landscape* ○ *They came to strikingly different conclusions about what should be done.* ➤ Usage: **graphic, graphical, or striking?** at GRAPHIC CLEAR

string CORD /strɪŋ/ *n* [C/U] a thin length of cord ○ [U] *a piece of string*

string /strɪŋ/ *v* [T] *past* **strung** to attach a length of string or something similar by the ends, so that the middle hangs ○ *They strung ribbons of bright paper around the room in preparation for the party.*

stringy /ˈstrɪŋ·i/ *adj* [-er/-est only] having the appearance of strings, or (of food) hard to chew ○ *stringy meat* ○ *His black hair was stringy and brushed his shoulders.*

MUSIC /strɪŋ/ *n* [C] **1** a thin wire or cord that is stretched across a musical instrument and produces musical notes when pulled or hit ○ *Guitar strings are made from steel or nylon.* **2** The strings in an ORCHESTRA is a group of instruments that produce sound with strings: *Violins, cellos, and double basses are all strings.*

SET /strɪŋ/ *n* [C] a set of objects joined together in a row on a single cord or thread ○ *a string of pearls*

string /strɪŋ/ *v* [T] *past* **strung** to put a thread or cord through each of a set of things ○ *The child sat on the floor, stringing wooden beads.* ○ (fig.) *I can just barely string together* (= say) *a couple of sentences in Japanese.*

S

SERIES /strɪŋ/ *n* [C] a series of related things or events ○ *He told the committee a string of lies.* ○ *Her new novel is the latest in a string of successes.*

IDIOM with **string**

• **strings attached** special demands or limitations that affect something such as an agreement ○ *You don't get anything for free - there are always strings attached.* ○ *I really wanted to give this money to my family with no strings attached.*

PHRASAL VERBS with **string**

• **string along** *something* **POSITION** [M] to arrange things in a line ○ *Occasional gas stations and small markets are strung along the roads.*
• **string** *someone* **along ENCOURAGE** [M] to falsely encourage someone to believe there is hope of a good result ○ *He was stringing along a rep from one TV show while trying to book his client on a higher-rated program.*
• **string out** *something* **POSITION** [M] to arrange things in a line ○ *A set of 10 powerful radio telescopes were strung out from the Virgin Islands to Hawaii.*
• **string out** *something* **LENGTHEN** [M] to cause something to last longer than it usually would ○ *That ruling could string out the dispute for months.*

string bean *n* [C] a GREEN BEAN

stringent /ˈstrɪn·dʒənt/ *adj* extremely limiting or difficult; severe ○ *Members of the organization have to be willing to abide by the stringent rules.* ○ *The city has stringent fire-safety standards.*

string quartet *n* [C] a group of four people who play music together on instruments with strings

string theory *n* [C] ***physics*** a theory explaining the character of matter and the forces of the universe, based on the idea that they behave more like closed circles of string than like points

string tie *n* [C] a length of cord, worn with a shirt, that goes under the collar and down the front and is held by a decorative device at the neck

strip REMOVE COVERING /strɪp/ *v* [T] **-pp- 1** to remove, pull, or tear the covering or outer layer from something ○ *I have this cabinet that had about eight layers of paint on it, and I stripped it down to refinish it.* **2** If you strip someone of something, you remove it from that person: *Canada wants to strip Luitjens, a retired University of British Columbia botany instructor, of his citizenship.*

REMOVE CLOTHING /strɪp/ *v* [I/T] **-pp-** to remove your clothes, or to remove the clothes from someone else ○ [M] *It was so hot that we stripped off our shirts.* ○ [I] *We were told to strip to the waist* (= remove our clothes above the waist). ○ [I] *The nurse told me to strip down to my underwear* (= remove all of my clothes except my underwear).
stripper /ˈstrɪp·ər/ *n* [C] someone whose job is removing all of his or her clothes to entertain other people
strip /strɪp/ *n* [U]

PIECE /strɪp/ *n* [C] a long, flat, narrow piece ○ *a strip of land* ○ *He didn't have a bandage, so he ripped up his shirt into thin strips.* ○ *To prolong the working life of your credit card, keep the magnetic strip protected from scratches, heat, and moisture.*

stripe /strɑɪp/ *n* [C] **1** a line on a surface that is a different color from the rest of the surface ○ *a blue tie with gray stripes* **2** A stripe is also a particular type, esp. when there are many possible types: *Governments of every stripe* (= of all political opinions) *have a tendency to try to control the press.*
striped /strɑɪpt/ *adj* [not gradable] ○ *a striped red-and-white shirt*

strip search *n* [C] the act of searching for illegal items hidden on or in someone's body, in which authorities force the person to remove all of his or her clothes

striptease /ˈstrɪp·tiːz/ *n* [C/U] a performance in which someone, usually a woman, takes off clothes to entertain people watching, or this activity

strive /strɑɪv/ *v* [I] *past simp.* **strove, strived**, *past part.* **striven, strived** to try hard to do something or make something happen, esp. for a long time or against difficulties ○ [+ *to* infinitive] *Neither Jefferson nor Madison was a pacifist, though both strove to keep America at peace.*

strode /stroʊd/ *past simple of* STRIDE WALK

stroke TOUCH /stroʊk/ *v* [T] to move your hand or an object gently over something, usually repeatedly ○ *Asked another question, she stroked her chin and closed her eyes before answering.*

MARK /stroʊk/ *n* [C] a movement of a pen or pencil when writing, or by a brush when painting, or the line or mark made by such a movement ○ *With a stroke of his pen, the governor signed the bill into law.*

ILLNESS /stroʊk/ *n* [C] a sudden change in the blood supply to a part of the brain, which can result in a loss of some mental or physical abilities, or death ○ *He suffered a stroke and died two days later.*

SWIMMING ACTION /stroʊk/ *n* [C/U] a particular type of repeated movement used in a method of swimming ○ [U] *He swims the breast stroke competitively, but for his ads he did the butterfly stroke.*

EVENT /stroʊk/ *n* [C] an unexpected but important event or experience ○ *The bid to take over the company was seen as a bold stroke.* ○ *To get a job in those years was an incredible stroke of luck.*

TIME /stroʊk/ *n* [C] an exact time, or a sound or series of sounds that show this time ○ *The fireworks will start at the stroke of 10.*

stroll /stroʊl/ *v* [I] to walk in a slow, relaxed manner, esp. for pleasure ○ *We could stroll into town if you like.*
stroll /stroʊl/ *n* [C] ○ *Sometimes he would take a stroll before dinner.*

stroller /ˈstroʊ·lər/ *n* [C] a small chair having wheels, suitable for a small child to sit in and be pushed around

strong PHYSICALLY POWERFUL /strɔːŋ/ *adj* [*-er/ -est* only] physically powerful or energetic ○ *You* *must be strong to be able to lift all that weight.* ○ *I feel a little stronger every day.* ○ *Strong winds blew down a number of trees.* ○ *The doctor prescribed a stronger pain-killer.* ○ Related noun: STRENGTH PHYSICAL POWER

DIFFICULT TO BREAK /strɔːŋ/ *adj* [-*er*/-*est* only] not easily broken or damaged ○ *The swings are strong enough for any of the kids.* ○ Related noun: STRENGTH PHYSICAL POWER

strongly /ˈstrɔːŋ·li/ *adv* ○ *The castle walls were strongly constructed of stone.*

DETERMINED /strɔːŋ/ *adj* [-*er*/-*est* only] having a forceful and determined personality ○ *He has a strong personality, but don't let him intimidate you.* ○ Related noun: STRENGTH GOOD FEATURE

IMPORTANT /strɔːŋ/ *adj* [-*er*/-*est* only] having a lot of influence or importance ○ *My grandmother had a strong influence on me as a child.* ○ *He is a strong supporter of the arts in the city.*

strongly /ˈstrɔːŋ·li/ *adv* ○ *Beliefs are strongly tied to culture.*

PERSUASIVE /strɔːŋ/ *adj* [-*er*/-*est* only] believed or expressed without any doubt; persuasive ○ *She has strong opinions about many things.* ○ *There are strong arguments to support both sides.*

strongly /ˈstrɔːŋ·li/ *adv* [not gradable] ○ *He is strongly opposed to censorship.* ○ *Voters strongly supported the candidate.*

OBVIOUS /strɔːŋ/ *adj* [-*er*/-*est* only] easily noticed, felt, tasted, or smelled; obvious ○ *He bears a strong likeness to his brother.* ○ *This coffee is too strong!* ○ *There was a strong smell of gas.*

REALISTIC /strɔːŋ/ *adj* [-*er*/-*est* only] likely or realistic ○ *There's a strong possibility that the naval base will close next year.*

strong acid *n* [C] ***chemistry*** an acid with a PH of between 1 and 3, whose MOLECULES break down into smaller molecules or atoms in water

strong-arm *adj* [not gradable] *disapproving* involving force and threats to get people to do something ○ *The curfew is just another of the city's strong-arm policies.*

strong base *n* [C] ***chemistry*** a BASE CHEMICAL whose MOLECULES break down into smaller molecules or atoms in water

strong force *n* [U] ***physics*** the force that holds together the PARTICLES (= small pieces of matter) in the center of an atom

stronghold /ˈstrɔːŋ·hoʊld/ *n* [C] a place that is well defended or is a center for particular beliefs or activities ○ *Bears could return to the area that was once their last stronghold in Texas.* ○ *That county has always been a Democratic stronghold.*

strong-minded *adj* (of people) determined and independent in the way they think

strong-willed *adj* (of people) determined to do what they want, even if other people disagree or disapprove ○ *a strong-willed woman*

strove /stroʊv/ *past simple of* STRIVE

struck /strʌk/ *past simple and past participle of* STRIKE

structure Ⓐ **ARRANGEMENT** /ˈstrʌk·tʃər/ *n* [C/U] the arrangement or organization of parts in a system ○ *molecular structure* ○ [U] *Grammatical structure changes from language to language.* ○ [C] *When the United States broke away from England, the social structure did not change very much.*

structure Ⓐ /ˈstrʌk·tʃər/ *v* [T] ○ *Office hours are structured to accommodate individual workers' needs.*

structural Ⓐ /ˈstrʌk·tʃə·rəl/ *adj* [not gradable] ○ *Private ownership of companies was the greatest structural change that occurred in the economy.*

structurally Ⓐ /ˈstrʌk·tʃə·rə·li/ *adv* ○ *We don't have evidence that the brain is structurally changed by stress.*

BUILDING /ˈstrʌk·tʃər/ *n* [C] something built, such as a building or a bridge ○ *The bridge is the longest steel structure in the world.*

structural Ⓐ /ˈstrʌk·tʃə·rəl/ *adj* [not gradable] ○ *Many of the city's buildings suffered structural damage as a result of the earthquake.*

structurally Ⓐ /ˈstrʌk·tʃə·rə·li/ *adv* ○ *The vast majority of buildings remain structurally sound* (= they are not in danger of fallling down).

WORD FAMILY structure

Nouns	structure restructuring	*Verbs*	structure restructure
Adjectives	structural	*Adverbs*	structurally

struggle **TRY HARD** /ˈstrʌg·əl/ *v* [I] to work hard to do something ○ *We watched boys on skateboards struggle to keep their balance.*

struggle /ˈstrʌg·əl/ *n* [C] ○ *Central banks everywhere are still fighting the struggle against inflation.*

FIGHT /ˈstrʌg·əl/ *v* [I] to fight, esp. physically ○ *He struggled with his cousin, and his uncle had to step in to calm things down.*

struggle /ˈstrʌg·əl/ *n* [C] ○ *Both men were arrested after their struggle in the street.*

MOVE /ˈstrʌg·əl/ *v* [I] to move with difficulty ○ *She struggled out of her chair.*

strum /strʌm/ *v* [I/T] **-mm-** to play a guitar or similar instrument by moving the fingers lightly across all of the strings together

strung /strʌŋ/ *past simple and past participle of* STRING

strut **WALK** /strʌt/ *v* [I] **-tt-** to walk with your chest pushed forward and your shoulders back to show you are proud ○ *The boys strutted around like peacocks, showing off to some girls nearby.*

SUPPORT /strʌt/ *n* [C] a support for a structure such as an aircraft wing, roof, or bridge

IDIOM with strut

• **strut** *your* **stuff** *infml* to show other people what you can do well ○ *Winnie loves to dance and has been strutting her stuff since she was very young.*

stub **SHORT END** /stʌb/ *n* [C] the short end which is left after the main part of something has been

S

used or removed, as of a pencil ○ *I put the ticket stubs in my pocket after we went into the theater.*

stubby /ˈstʌb·i/ *adj* ○ *A toddler's legs are short and stubby.*

HURT /stʌb/ *v* [T] **-bb-** to hit your foot or toe against a hard object ○ *I stubbed my toe on a rock.*

PHRASAL VERB with stub

• **stub out** *something* [M] to stop the end something, such as a CIGAR, from burning by pressing it against something else

stubble **HAIR** /ˈstʌb·əl/ *n* [U] the short hair that grows on a man's face if he has not recently SHAVED (= cut the hair)

STEMS /ˈstʌb·əl/ *n* [U] the stems left in the ground after a crop has been cut

stubborn /ˈstʌb·ərn/ *adj* [not gradable] **1** opposed to change or suggestion ○ *He's sick, but he's too stubborn to see a doctor.* **2** If something is stubborn, it is hard to fix or deal with: *stubborn stains* ○ *a stubborn problem*

stucco /ˈstʌk·oʊ/ *n* [U] a material that is soft and wet when it is spread on a surface and is hard when it dries, used esp. for covering walls

stuck **STICK** /stʌk/ *past simple and past participle of* STICK

FIXED /stʌk/ *adj* [not gradable] unable to move from a particular position or place, or unable to change a situation ○ *This door seems to be stuck.* ○ *I hate being stuck at a desk all day.* ○ *Ty got stuck with doing the laundry.* ○ Related verb: STICK UNABLE TO MOVE

IDIOM with stuck

• **stuck on** *someone* *infml* strongly attracted to someone ○ *Mark's wife was stuck on him from the day they met.*

stuck-up /ˈstʌkˈʌp/ *adj* *infml, disapproving* too proud or satisfied with yourself

stud **MALE ANIMAL** /stʌd/ *n* [C] a male animal kept esp. for breeding

S

DECORATION /stʌd/ *n* [C] a small, bright-colored nail, often specially shaped, that is fixed esp. to cloth or leather as decoration

studded /ˈstʌd·əd/ *adj* [not gradable] ○ *a studded jacket*

JEWELRY /stʌd/ *n* [C] a small ball fixed to a metal post that fits through a hole made in the body, esp. in the ear

POST /stʌd/ *n* [C] any of the vertical wood or metal posts used to make the frame of a wall

IDIOM with stud

• **studded with something** having a lot of something ○ *a hillside studded with trees*

student /ˈstuːd·ᵊnt, *Southern also* -ənt/ *n* [C] **1** a person who is studying at a school, college, or university ○ *He is a student at the University of California.* **2** Someone who is a student of a particular subject is very interested in it: *As a nurse, you get to be a student of human nature.*

WORD FAMILY student

Nouns	student study studies	*Adjectives*	studious
		Verbs	study
		Adverbs	studiously

student body *n* [C] all of the students in a school ○ *Chatsworth School's student body raised $5,000 for the charity.*

studied /ˈstʌd·iːd/ *adj* [not gradable] carefully prepared or considered, esp. to create an effect ○ *He showed a studied disregard for her concerns.*

studies /ˈstʌd·iːz/ *pl n* ○ See at STUDY LEARN

studio **ROOM** /ˈstuːd·iːˌoʊ/ *n* [C] *pl* **studios** a room where an artist paints or a musician practices ○ *an artist's studio*

RECORDING PLACE /ˈstuːd·iːˌoʊ/ *n* [C] *pl* **studios** a specially equipped place where television or radio programs are made or music is recorded

MOVIE PRODUCTION /ˈstuːd·iːˌoː/ *n* [C] a place where movies are produced, or a company that produces movies ○ *Most of the big studios are in Hollywood.*

studio apartment, *short form* **studio** *n* [C] an apartment with only one room, a bathroom, and a kitchen area

study **LEARN** /ˈstʌd·i/ *v* [I/T] to learn a particular subject or subjects, esp. in a school or college or by reading books ○ [T] *Next semester we'll be studying biology.* ○ [I] *I've got to study tonight.*

study /ˈstʌd·i/ *n* [C/U] **1** the activity of studying ○ [U] *He began the study of violin when he was only three.* **2** A study is a room used for reading and writing in a person's home.

studies /ˈstʌd·iːz/ *pl n* the work a student does at school ○ *His studies will suffer if he has to stay home for too long.*

studious /ˈstuːd·iː·əs/ *adj* liking to study ○ *She was a studious child who spent hours reading.* ➤ Usage: **learn, teach, or study?** at LEARN

WORD CHOICES study

If someone is studying something as his or her main subject at a college or university, you can use the verb **major in**.

*She **majored in** philosophy at Harvard.*

Cram or **review** can be used when someone is studying very hard just before an exam.

*She's **cramming** for her history exam.*

*I'm **reviewing** for the test tomorrow.*

If someone is studying a subject in order to discover new facts, the verb **research** is often used.

*Scientists are **researching** possible new treatments for breast cancer.*

EXAMINE /ˈstʌd·i/ *v* [T] to look at something carefully to learn about it ○ *She studied the embroidery to see how it was done.*

study /ˈstʌd·i/ *n* [C] ○ *Studies show that exercise is important to health.*

stuff SUBSTANCE /stʌf/ *n* [U] a substance or material ○ *What's the black stuff on the rug?* ○ *This stuff tastes good.*

THINGS /stʌf/ *n* [U] a group of different things, activities, or matters ○ *We helped him move his stuff to the new apartment.* ○ *I've got a lot of stuff to do this weekend.* ○ *They'd heard all this stuff before.*

FILL /stʌf/ *v* [T] **1** to fill the inside of something ○ *I can't stuff another thing into this suitcase.* **2** To stuff a TURKEY, or other meat or vegetable, is to fill it with other food before cooking it. **3** If you stuff yourself, you eat a large amount of food: *The kids stuffed themselves with snacks.*

stuffed /stʌft/ *adj* [not gradable] filled with some material ○ *Children love stuffed animals.*

stuffing /ˈstʌf·ɪŋ/ *n* [U] **1** material that is used to fill something ○ *The stuffing was coming out of the mattress.* **2** Stuffing is also food, usually a mixture of bread, onions, and herbs, which is used as a filling for TURKEY or other meats or vegetables.

stuffed-up *adj* having difficulty breathing through your nose because of an illness or ALLERGY

stuffy FORMAL /ˈstʌf·i/ *adj* formal, boring, and not modern ○ *a stuffy, arrogant man*

LACKING AIR /ˈstʌf·i/ *adj* lacking fresh air ○ *The office gets so stuffy in the afternoon.*

stumble FALL /ˈstʌm·bəl/ *v* [I] to hit your foot against something while walking and almost fall, or to walk awkwardly as if you might fall ○ *She stumbled over a toy.* ○ *He stumbled around in the dark.*

MAKE A MISTAKE /ˈstʌm·bəl/ *v* [I] to make a mistake, or to pause unexpectedly when speaking ○ *He stumbled through several early career choices.* ○ *Several times the reader stumbled over lines in the poem.*

PHRASAL VERBS with stumble

- **stumble across/on** *something/someone* to discover or find something or someone by chance ○ *Look at what I stumbled across at the flea market!*
- **stumble into** *something* to start doing something by chance and without an intention ○ *Fry says he stumbled into guitarmaking.*

stumbling block *n* [C] a difficulty that prevents progress, understanding, or agreement ○ *Several major stumbling blocks must be resolved.*

stump PART LEFT /stʌmp/ *n* [C] the part of a tree, arm, etc. that is left after another part has been removed

CONFUSE /stʌmp/ *v* [T] to confuse or cause someone to be unable to understand or explain something ○ *He seemed stumped by our questions.*

SPEAK /stʌmp/ *v* [I] to talk in support of a politician or idea ○ *Taylor stumped for him throughout the state.*

stun SHOCK /stʌn/ *v* [T] **-nn-** to shock someone so much that the person does not know how to react ○ *She was stunned by his generous offer.*

stunning /ˈstʌn·ɪŋ/ *adj* ○ *a stunning victory*

MAKE UNCONSCIOUS /stʌn/ *v* [T] **-nn-** to make a person or animal unconscious or confused, esp. by hitting their head hard ○ *He was stunned by the sudden blow to his head.*

stung /stʌŋ/ *past simple and past participle of* STING

stunk /stʌŋk/ *past simple and past participle of* STINK

stunning /ˈstʌn·ɪŋ/ *adj* [not gradable] extremely beautiful or attractive ○ *They make a stunning couple.*

stunt DANGEROUS ACT /stʌnt/ *n* [C] an exciting and often dangerous act, usually performed for use in a movie by someone specially trained

ACTIVITY /stʌnt/ *n* [C] something done mainly to attract attention ○ *This was not just some publicity stunt.*

PREVENT GROWTH /stʌnt/ *v* [T] to slow or prevent the growth or development of someone or something ○ *Drought has stunted this year's corn crop.*

stunt man *n* [C] a person whose job is performing STUNTS (= difficult physical actions) that are too dangerous for the actors in a movie or television show to do

stupefy TIRE /ˈstuː·pəˌfɑɪ/ *v* [T] to tire or bore someone so much that the person cannot think or do anything ○ *His classes totally stupefied me.*

SURPRISE /ˈstuː·pəˌfɑɪ/ *v* [T] to shock someone; STUN SHOCK ○ *He was stupefied to learn that he was fired.*

stupendous /stuːˈpen·dəs/ *adj* very great in amount or size ○ *He ran up stupendous debts.*

stupid /ˈstuː·pəd/ *adj* **1** lacking thought or intelligence ○ *I just made another stupid mistake.* **2** *infml* You might say something is stupid because it annoys you: *Turn off that stupid program!*

stupidity /stuːˈpɪd·ət̬·i/ *n* [U] ○ *Can you believe my stupidity? I locked my keys in the car!*

WORD CHOICES stupid

Some common alternatives to "stupid" are **foolish** or **silly**.

She was really ***foolish*** *to quit her job like that.*

It was ***silly*** *of you to go out in the sun without a hat.*

If something or someone is stupid enough to be funny or strange, you can use the words **absurd**, **ridiculous**, or **ludicrous**.

What an ***absurd*** *thing to say!*

Do I look ***ridiculous*** *in this hat?*

I think giving young children such expensive jewelry is a ***ludicrous*** *idea.*

You can describe a stupid person as a **fool** or an **idiot**.

You were a ***fool*** *not to take that job.*

Some ***idiot*** *dropped a lighted match in the wastepaper basket.*

In informal situations, if you think people have been stupid, you can say that they are **out of *their* minds**. ➤

S

You must be ***out of your mind*** *spending so much money on a car.*

WORD FAMILY stupid			
Nouns	stupidity	*Adverbs*	stupidly
Adjectives	stupid		

stupor /ˈstuː·pər/ *n* [C usually sing] a state in which a person is almost unconscious

sturdy /ˈstɜrd·i/ *adj* strong or solid ○ *That ladder doesn't look sturdy enough to hold you.*

stutter /ˈstʌt̬·ər/ *v* [I/T] to speak or say part of a word with difficulty, esp. by repeating it several times or by pausing before it ○ [I] *He doesn't normally stutter when he speaks.*

stutter /ˈstʌt̬·ər/ *n* [C] ○ *I type up tapes of people talking, all the stutters and everything.*

style Ⓐ **WAY** /stɑɪl/ *n* [C/U] **1** a way of doing something that is typical of a person, group, place, or time ○ [C] *Puente fused Latin with other musical styles.* ○ [C] *The book is written in the style of an 18th-century novel.* ○ [U] *His portraits were awkward in style.* **2** Style is also a special quality that makes a person or thing seem different and attractive: [U] *I like this team – the players have style.*

stylistic /stɑɪˈlɪs·tɪk/ *adj* ○ *The first major stylistic change in popular music after rock was punk.*

stylize Ⓐ /ˈstɑɪl·ɑɪz/ *v* [T] to show or do something in a particular style ○ *Looking for ways to rearrange, stylize and add inspiration to your work area?*

stylized Ⓐ /ˈstɑɪlˌɑɪzd/ *adj* ***art*** represented in a way that simplifies details rather than trying to show naturalness or reality ○ *Curtis took stylized photographs of Native Americans.*

DESIGN /stɑɪl/ *v* [T] to arrange or design hair, clothes, a room, etc., so that it looks attractive ○ *Most women style their hair.*

style Ⓐ /stɑɪl/ *n* [C] **1** *They had hundreds of styles* (= designs) *of light fixtures in stock.* **2** Style also means fashion: [C] *I keep up with the latest styles.* ○ [U] *The classic black dress is always in style.* **3** ***art*** Style also refers to particular features of art that are found in a group of artists who lived and worked at the same time.

stylish Ⓐ /ˈstɑɪ·lɪʃ/ *adj* ○ *stylish people* ○ *stylish clothing*

stylist /ˈstɑɪ·ləst/ *n* [C] ○ *She gave up a career as a fashion stylist to rear two daughters.*

WORD FAMILY style			
Nouns	style stylist	*Adjectives*	stylish stylistic stylized
Verbs	style		
Adverbs	stylishly		

stymie /ˈstɑɪ·mi/ *v* [T] *pres. part.* **stymieing** to prevent someone from achieving a goal or doing something that had been planned ○ *Students were stymied by the test.*

Styrofoam /ˈstɑɪ·rəˌfoʊm/ *n* [U] *trademark* a light, usually white plastic used to make containers that prevent foods and liquids from changing temperature or to protect delicate objects inside containers ○ *a Styrofoam cup/cooler* ○ *Styrofoam packing materials*

suave /swɑv/ *adj* (esp. of men) having a pleasant and charming manner that may not be sincere ○ *He's a suave Texas-bred lawyer.*

sub **REPLACEMENT** /sʌb/ *n* [C] *short form of* SUBSTITUTE TEACHER

sub /sʌb/ *v* [I] **-bb-** ○ *She subs at three schools.*

SHIP /sʌb/ *n* [C] *short form of* SUBMARINE ○ *a nuclear sub*

FOOD /sʌb/ *n* [C] *short form of* SUBMARINE (SANDWICH)

subatomic /ˌsʌb·əˈtɑm·ɪk/ *adj* [not gradable] ***physics*** smaller than or within an atom

subcommittee /ˈsʌb·kəˌmɪt̬·i/ *n* [C] a number of people chosen from a COMMITTEE (= a small group of people who represent a larger organization) to study or manage a particular subject

subcompact /sʌbˈkɑmˌpækt/ *n* [C] a very small car ○ *We're renting a subcompact.*

subconscious /sʌbˈkɑn·tʃəs/ *adj* [not gradable] relating to thoughts and feelings that exist in the mind and influence your behavior although you are not aware of them ○ *On some subconscious level he wants to make her miserable.*

subconscious /sʌbˈkɑn·tʃəs/ *n* [U] ○ *My subconscious works on things while I'm asleep.*

subconsciously /sʌbˈkɑn·tʃə·sli/ *adv* [not gradable] ○ *When people see these pictures, they subconsciously think of their childhoods.*

subcontractor /sʌbˈkɑn·træk·tər, ˌsʌb·kənˈtræk-/ *n* [C] a person or company that a CONTRACTOR pays to do part of the work that the contractor has agreed to do ○ *an electrical subcontractor*

subculture /ˈsʌbˌkʌl·tʃər/ *n* [C] the way of life, customs, and ideas of a particular group of people within a society, which are different from the rest of that society ○ *An entire subculture grew up around female bodybuilding.*

subdivide /ˈsʌb·dɪˌvɑɪd/ *v* [T] to divide something into smaller parts

subdivision /ˈsʌb·dɪˌvɪʒ·ən/ *n* [C] **1** *The book's chapters have major subdivisions.* **2** A subdivision is also an area of land containing many homes built at about the same time: *We moved to a brand-new subdivision in 1965.*

subduction /səbˈdʌk·ʃən, sʌb-/ *n* [U] ***earth science*** a situation in which one of the earth's PLATES (= large layer of rock that the earth's surface is made of) slides under another, often causing an EARTHQUAKE or VOLCANO

subdue /səbˈduː/ *v* [T] to reduce the force of (someone or something) ○ *She'd be hard to subdue if she got mad.*

S

subdued /səbˈduːd/ *adj* **1** (of color or light) not very bright, or (of sound) not very loud ○ *a subdued voice* ○ *a subdued chalk-stripe suit* **2** A person who is subdued is unusually quiet: *Most of the fans were subdued, quietly waiting for the race to start.*

subgroup /ˈsʌb·gruːp/ *n* [C] a smaller group that is in some way different from the larger group to which it belongs ○ *The Chinese make up the largest Asian subgroup.*

subject AREA OF DISCUSSION /ˈsʌb·dʒɪkt, -dʒekt/ *n* [C] something that is being discussed or considered ○ *School officials broached the subject of extending the school year.* ○ *It seemed like a good idea to change the subject.*

SCHOOL COURSE /ˈsʌb·dʒɪkt, -dʒekt/ *n* [C] an area of knowledge that is studied in school or college ○ *My favorite subjects are history and geography.*

PERSON /ˈsʌb·dʒɪkt, -dʒekt/ *n* [C] a person who lives or who has the right to live in a particular country, esp. a country with a king or queen ○ *a British subject* ○ Compare CITIZEN

GRAMMAR /ˈsʌb·dʒɪkt, -dʒekt/ *n* [C] ***grammar*** the person or thing that performs the action of a verb, or which is joined to a description by a verb ○ *"Bob" is the subject of the sentence, "Bob threw the ball."* ○ Compare OBJECT GRAMMAR

IDIOM with **subject**

• **subject to** *something* **1** likely to experience or suffer from something ○ *The bay is subject to heavy fog in summer.* ○ *If the plants are growing well, they'll be less subject to pests.* **2** If an action or event is **subject to** something, it needs something to happen before it can take place ○ *The agreement is still subject to approval by the League's 30 teams and the players.*

PHRASAL VERB with **subject**

• **subject** *someone/something* **to** *something* to cause someone or something to experience something, esp. something unpleasant ○ *I hate being subjected to boring lectures.*

subjective /səbˈdʒek·tɪv/ *adj* influenced by or based on personal beliefs or feelings, rather than based on facts ○ *Whether something is objectionable is a subjective question.* ○ Opposite: OBJECTIVE FAIR OR REAL

subject matter *n* [U] the subject of a program, movie, book, article, etc. ○ *Critics were upset by the subject matter of the book.*

subjugate /ˈsʌb·dʒəˌgeɪt/ *v* [T] *fml* ***social studies*** to defeat people or a country and rule them in a way that allows them no freedom

subjugation /ˌsʌb·dʒəˈgeɪ·ʃən/ *n* [U] *fml*

subjunctive /səbˈdʒʌŋk·tɪv/ *n* [U] ***grammar*** the MOOD (= form) of a verb used to refer to actions that are possibilities rather than facts ○ *In the sentence "I wish I were rich," the verb "were" is in the subjunctive.*

sublet /ˈsʌbˈlet/ *v* [I/T] *pres. part.* **subletting**, *past* **sublet** to rent all or part of a rented apartment, house, or other building to someone else

sublet /ˈsʌb·let/ *n* [C] ○ *a summer sublet*

sublime SATISFYING /səˈblɑɪm/ *adj* extremely good, beautiful, or enjoyable, and therefore satisfying ○ *sublime food/scenery*

CHANGE /səˈblɑɪm/ *v* [I/T] ***chemistry*** to change a solid directly into a gas without the solid first becoming a liquid

sublimation /ˌsʌb·ləˈmeɪ·ʃən/ *n* [U]

subliminal /səbˈlɪm·ən·əl/ *adj* not recognized or understood by the conscious mind, but still having an influence on it ○ *a subliminal message*

submarine /ˈsʌb·məˌriːn, ˌsʌb·məˈriːn/, *short form* **sub** *n* [C] a ship that can travel under water ○ *a nuclear submarine*

submarine (sandwich) /ˈsʌb·məˌriːn (ˈsæn·dwɪtʃ)/, *short form* **sub** *n* [C] *Cdn, regional US* a long, narrow sandwich filled with such things as meat, cheese, and vegetables; a HERO (SANDWICH)

submerge /səbˈmɜrdʒ/ *v* [I/T] to go below the surface of an area of water ○ [T] *Take a normal breath and completely submerge yourself.* ○ [I] *Seals exhale so they can submerge more easily.*

submit Ⓐ OFFER FOR DECISION /səbˈmɪt/ *v* [T] **-tt-** to give or offer something for a decision to be made by others ○ *Companies are required to submit monthly financial statements to the board.*

submission Ⓐ /səbˈmɪʃ·ən/ *n* [C/U] ○ [C] *The films were chosen from 350 submissions.*

GIVE POWER /səbˈmɪt/ *v* [I/T] **-tt-** to give power or authority over a person or group to someone, or to accept something unwillingly ○ [T] *He had never been able to submit himself to that sort of discipline.* ○ [I] *All newly hired employees must submit to a background check.*

submission Ⓐ /səbˈmɪʃ·ən/ *n* [U] ○ *We raised our arms in submission.*

submissive /səbˈmɪs·ɪv/ *adj* showing a willingness to be controlled by other people ○ *a submissive gesture*

subordinate Ⓐ /səˈbɔːrd·ən·ət/ *adj* having a lower or less important position ○ *I'm happy in a subordinate role.*

subordinate Ⓐ /səˈbɔːrd·ən·ət/ *n* [C] ○ *You need to assign this job to a subordinate.*

subordinate Ⓐ /səˈbɔːrd·ənˌeɪt/ *v* [T] to treat someone or something as less important than something else ○ *Japan has a tradition of subordinating individual desires to group goals.*

subordination Ⓐ /səˌbɔːrd·ənˈeɪ·ʃən/ *n* [U] ○ *She studies patterns of domination and subordination among orangutans.*

subordinate clause *n* [C] ***grammar*** a DEPENDENT CLAUSE

subpoena /səˈpiː·nə, -ni/ *v* [T] ***social studies*** *law* to order someone to go to a court of law to answer questions, or to order the appearance of documents in a court of law ○ *to subpoena a witness*

subpoena /səˈpiː·nə, -ni/ *n* [C] *law* ○ *The judge issued a subpoena.*

subscribe /səbˈskrɑɪb/ *v* [I] to pay money to an organization in order to receive a product or use a

S

service regularly ○ *She subscribes to a couple of magazines.*
subscriber /səbˈskrɑɪ·bər/ *n* [C] ○ *cable TV subscribers*
subscription /səbˈskrɪp·ʃən/ *n* [C] ○ *a magazine subscription*

PHRASAL VERB with subscribe

• **subscribe to** *something* to agree with or support an opinion, belief, or theory ○ *They all believe the same rumors, subscribe to the same theories, and write the same stories.*

subsequent Ⓐ /ˈsʌb·sɪ·kwənt, -ˌkwent/ *adj* [not gradable] happening after something else ○ *Everything I do makes me better at each subsequent thing.*
subsequently Ⓐ /ˈsʌb·sɪ·kwənt·li, -ˌkwent·li/ *adv* [not gradable] ○ *He was made a partner, but he subsequently retired.*

subservient /səbˈsɜr·viː·ənt/ *adj disapproving* willing to do what other people want, or considering your wishes as less important than those of other people ○ *In the past, women were viewed as subservient to men.*
subservience /səbˈsɜr·viː·əns/ *n* [U] *disapproving* ○ *Your subservience to your boss disgusts me.*

subset *n* [C] ***mathematics*** a set of numbers or things that is part of another, larger set

subside BECOME WEAKER /səbˈsɑɪd/ *v* [I] (of a condition) to become less strong, or (of an activity or disagreement) to become less violent ○ *When her pain didn't subside, Matt drove her to the hospital.* ○ *Friction between the groups subsided gradually.*

GO DOWN /səbˈsɑɪd/ *v* [I] (of a building, area of land, or level of water) to go down to a lower level ○ *Forecasters predict the high tides will subside today.*

subsidiary Ⓐ /səbˈsɪd·iːˌer·i, -ˈsɪd·ə·ri/ *n* [C] a company that is owned by a larger company
subsidiary Ⓐ /səbˈsɪd·iːˌer·i, -ˈsɪd·ə·ri/ *adj* ○ *All the major record companies had subsidiary labels under their control.*

subsidy Ⓐ /ˈsʌb·səd·i/ *n* [C] money given as part of the cost of something to help or encourage it to happen ○ *export subsidies* ○ *farm subsidies*
subsidize Ⓐ /ˈsʌb·səˌdɑɪz/ *v* [T] to pay part of the cost of something ○ *Taxpayers shouldn't subsidize a golf course.* ○ *The tenants live in federally subsidized apartments.*

subsist /səbˈsɪst/ *v* [I] to obtain enough food or money to stay alive ○ *These people subsist on rice, beans, fruits, and vegetables.*
subsistence /səbˈsɪs·təns/ *n* [U] what a person needs in order to stay alive ○ *Art satisfies a need beyond mere subsistence.* ○ *Palau's economy is based on subsistence agriculture* (= producing enough food to feed themselves).

subsoil /ˈsʌb·sɔɪl/ *n* [U] ***earth science*** the layer of earth under the TOPSOIL (= the layer of earth in which plants grow)

substance MATERIAL /ˈsʌb·stəns/ *n* [C] a material with particular physical characteristics ○ *The pesticide contains a substance that is toxic to insects.*

IMPORTANCE /ˈsʌb·stəns/ *n* [U] importance, seriousness, or relationship to real facts ○ *Surprisingly, these filmmakers opted for substance over style.*

WORD FAMILY substance

Nouns	substance	*Adjectives*	substantial
Verbs	substantiate		insubstantial
Adverbs	substantially		substantive

substance abuse *n* [U] *medical* the use of drugs or alcohol in a way that damages a person's life
substance abuser *n* [C] *medical*

substandard /sʌbˈstæn·dərd/ *adj* below a satisfactory standard ○ *There's plenty of substandard child care available.*

substantial /səbˈstæn·tʃəl/ *adj* large in size, value, or importance ○ *He took a substantial amount of money.* ○ *They do a substantial portion of their business by phone.*
substantially /səbˈstæn·tʃə·li/ *adv* to a large degree ○ *Serious crime is down substantially.*

substantiate /səbˈstæn·tʃiːˌeɪt/ *v* [T] *fml* to show something to be true, or to support a claim with facts ○ *They have enough evidence to substantiate complaints of vandalism.*

substantive /ˈsʌb·stən·tɪv/ *adj* having real importance or value ○ *a substantive issue/matter* ○ *substantive talks/negotiations*

substitute Ⓐ /ˈsʌb·stəˌtuːt/ *v* [I/T] to use someone or something instead of another person or thing ○ [T] *You can substitute oil for butter in this recipe.* ○ [I] *He was called on to substitute for the ailing star last night.*
substitute Ⓐ /ˈsʌb·stəˌtuːt/ *n* [C] ○ *Talk is a poor substitute for action.*
substitution Ⓐ /ˌsʌb·stəˈtuː·ʃən/ *n* [C/U] ○ [U] *Substitution of less costly materials for bricks will hurt brick-makers.* ○ [C] *People who have difficulty digesting beans can make substitutions.*

substitute teacher, *short form* **sub**, **substitute** *n* [C] a teacher who replaces another teacher who is absent from work ○ *We had a substitute in math yesterday.*

substrate /ˈsʌb·streɪt/ *n* [C] ***biology*** **1** a substance or surface which an organism grows and lives on and uses as food **2** A substrate is also a substance which an ENZYME (= substance produced by living cells) acts on to produce a chemical reaction.

subsume /səbˈsuːm/ *v* [T] to include something in a larger group or a group in a higher position

subterfuge /ˈsʌb·tərˌfjuːdʒ/ *n* [C/U] an action taken to hide something from someone ○ [U] *His excuse sounded more like subterfuge than a real reason.*

subterranean /ˌsʌb·təˈreɪ·niː·ən/ *adj* [not gradable] under the ground ○ *a subterranean passage/river*

subtitle /ˈsʌbˌtɑɪt̬·əl/ *n* [C] ***writing*** a word, phrase, or sentence that is used as the second part of a book title and is printed under the main title at the front of the book, or the words shown at the bottom of a film or television picture to explain what is being said in another language
subtitle /ˈsʌbˌtɑɪt̬·əl/ *v* [T] ○ *The novel is subtitled "A Fable."*

subtle /ˈsʌt̬·əl/ *adj* **1** not loud, bright, noticeable, or obvious ○ *subtle flavors* ○ *a subtle shade of pink* ○ *The subtle nuances of English pronunciation are hard to master.* **2** Subtle can also mean small but important: *There are subtle differences between the two.*
subtly /ˈsʌt̬·əl·i, ˈsʌt·li/ *adv* ○ *He subtly affects the lives of everyone he encounters.*
subtlety /ˈsʌt̬·əl·ti/ *n* [C/U] ○ [U] *Her acting was full of subtlety.* ○ [C] *He's baffled by the subtleties of modern life.*

subtotal /ˈsʌbˌtoʊt̬·əl/ *n* [C] the total of one set of numbers to which other numbers will be added ○ *Add the tax to the subtotal.*

subtract /səbˈtrækt/ *v* [T] ***mathematics*** to take a number or amount away from another number or amount ○ *Four subtracted from ten equals six.* ○ Compare ADD CALCULATE; DIVIDE CALCULATE
subtraction /səbˈtræk·ʃən/ *n* [C/U] ***mathematics*** the process of taking one number or amount away from another number or amount ○ [U] *The test involves simple addition and subtraction.*

subtraction sign *n* [C] ***mathematics*** the symbol -, used to represent subtraction or show that a number is less than zero

subtropical /sʌbˈtrɑp·ɪ·kəl/, **subtropic** /sʌbˈtrɑp·ɪk/ *adj* [not gradable] of or characteristic of the areas bordering the TROPICS (= hottest area of the earth)

subunit /ˈsʌbˌjuː·nət/ *n* [C] ***biology*** a part of a MOLECULE, esp. a molecule of PROTEIN (= chemical in all living cells)

suburb /ˈsʌb·ɜrb/ *n* [C] an area outside a city but near it and consisting mainly of homes, sometimes also having stores and small businesses ○ [pl] *Most of the people who live in the suburbs work in the city.*
suburban /səˈbɜr·bən/ *adj* ○ *He grew up in a wealthy suburban community near Chicago.*
suburbia /səˈbɜr·biː·ə/ *n* [U] the suburbs of a city, or suburbs in general

subversion /səbˈvɜr·ʒən/ *n* [U] ***world history*** an attempt to change or weaken a government or to remove it from power by working secretly within it

subversive /səbˈvɜr·sɪv, -zɪv/ *adj* tending to weaken or destroy an established political system, organization, or authority ○ *The FBI had the duty of obtaining evidence of subversive activity.*
subvert /səbˈvɜrt/ *v* [T] *fml* ○ *The book describes the techniques that Hitler used to subvert democracy in the Weimar Republic.*

subway /ˈsʌb·weɪ/ *n* [C] **1** an underground, electric railroad in a city ○ *Take the subway to Times Square.* **2** *Br* A subway is an underground passage that people who are walking can use to cross under a busy street.

succeed ACHIEVE SOMETHING /səkˈsiːd/ *v* [I] to achieve something that you have been aiming for, or (of a plan or piece of work) to have the desired results ○ *She's been trying to pass her driving test for years and she finally succeeded.* ○ *He succeeded in building the business into one the leaders in its field.*

> **USAGE**
> **succeed**
> Remember that **succeed** is often followed by the preposition **in** and a verb in the present participle (the **-ing** form). It is never followed by an infinitive.
> *Two prisoners succeeded in escaping.*
> ~~*Two prisoners succeeded to escape.*~~

FOLLOW /səkˈsiːd/ *v* [T] *fml* to take the place of another person or thing ○ [T] *Kamen was named company chairman, succeeding Robert Schwartz, who is retiring after 44 years.*

WORD FAMILY succeed

Nouns	success succession successor	*Adjectives*	successful unsuccessful successive
Verbs	succeed	*Adverbs*	successfully unsuccessfully

success /səkˈses/ *n* [C/U] the achieving of desired results, or someone or something that achieves positive results ○ [U] *We've tried to contact him, but so far without success.* ○ [C] *The dinner party was a great success.*
successful /səkˈses·fəl/ *adj* achieving desired results, or achieving the result of making a lot of money ○ *a successful architect/doctor/lawyer* ○ *Fortunately, my second attempt at starting a business was more successful than my first.*
successfully /səkˈses·fə·li/ *adv* ○ *A number of patients have been successfully treated with the new drug.*

> **USAGE**
> **success**
> Be careful to choose the correct verb with this noun.
> *The evening* ***was*** *a great success.*
> *They tried for weeks but* ***had*** *little success.*
> *They are determined to* ***make*** *a success of the plan.*
> ~~*She reached success as a writer.*~~

succession Ⓐ /səkˈseʃ·ən/ *n* [C/U] a series of things coming one after another ○ [U] *In rapid succession he lost his job, his wife, and his health.* ○ [U] (*fml*) *At that time, the secretary of state followed the vice president in line of presidential succession* (= the order of taking over a position of authority).

S

successive Ⓐ /sək'ses·ɪv/ *adj* [not gradable] happening one after the other ○ *It was the team's third successive defeat.*
successively /sək'ses·ɪv·li/ *adv*

successor Ⓐ /sək'ses·ər/ *n* [C] someone or something that next has the job, place, or position that was held by another ○ *The company will announce the appointment of a successor to its retiring chairman at the next board meeting.*

success story *n* [C] something or someone who achieves an unusual degree of success ○ *My mother's sister, Karla, was a doctor and the success story in her family.*

succinct /sək'sɪŋkt, sə'sɪŋkt/ *adj* (of writing or speech) clear and short; expressing what needs to be said without unnecessary words ○ *Keep your letter succinct and to the point.*

succulent /'sʌk·jə·lənt/ *adj* (of food) pleasantly juicy ○ *The sirloin is a quality piece of meat, tender and succulent.*

succumb /sə'kʌm/ *v* [I] **1** to lose the determination to oppose something, or to give up and accept something that you first opposed ○ *She succumbed to temptation and had a second helping of ice cream.* **2** If you succumb to an illness, you die from it.

such SO GREAT /sʌtʃ, sətʃ/ *adj* used before a noun or noun phrase to add emphasis ○ *I've never in my life had such delicious food.* ○ *It seems like such a long way to drive.* ○ *It was such a pity they missed the show.* ○ [+ *that* clause] *It was such a large fire that over 100 firefighters were on the scene.*

OF THAT TYPE /sʌtʃ, sətʃ/ *adj, pronoun* of that or a similar type ○ *With such evidence, they should have no difficulty getting a conviction.* ○ *Small companies such as ours are having a hard time.* ○ *They'll pay our expenses, such as food and lodging.* ○ *(infml) We talked about the kids and the weather and such* (= and that type of thing).

such and such /'sʌtʃ·ən ˌsʌtʃ/ *adj, pronoun* used to represent a specific person or thing when you cannot or do not want to give the actual information ○ *If they tell you to arrive at such and such a time, get there about ten minutes early.*

suck PULL IN /sʌk/ *v* [I/T] **1** to pull liquid or air into your mouth without using your teeth, or to move the tongue and muscles of the mouth around something inside your mouth, often in order to dissolve it ○ [T] *The two-year-old sucked his thumb.* ○ [I] *Sometimes a baby will hold the pacifier in her mouth without really sucking.* ○ [I/T] *We were all sucking (on) lollipops.* **2** Something that sucks something in a particular direction pulls it with great force: [T] *The vacuum cleaner sucks dirt into a disposable bag.*

BE BAD /sʌk/ *v* [I] *slang* to be bad or worthless ○ *We all thought the movie sucked.*

IDIOM with **suck**

• **get sucked into** *something*, **be sucked into** *something* to become involved in a situation when you do not want to be involved ○ *I got sucked into the argument because I was a friend of the family.*

PHRASAL VERB with **suck**

• **suck up to** *someone disapproving* to try to win the approval and good opinion of someone in authority ○ *She's always sucking up to the boss, telling him how wonderful he is.*

sucker FOOLISH PERSON /'sʌk·ər/ *n* [C] *infml* **1** a person who believes everything you say and is therefore easy to deceive **2** If you are a sucker for something, you like it so much that you cannot refuse it: *Josie's a sucker for burnt almond ice cream.*

THING /'sʌk·ər/ *n* [C] *infml* used to refer to a thing that is surprising or that is causing trouble ○ *My car won't start again, and hopefully between the two of us we can figure out how to make that sucker work.*

CANDY /'sʌk·ər/ *n* [C] a LOLLIPOP

suction /'sʌk·ʃən/ *n* [U] the process of reducing air pressure by removing air or liquid from an enclosed space, or the force created by this reduction that causes two surfaces to stick together ○ *Cylinder vacuum cleaners work entirely by suction.*

sudden /'sʌd·ən/ *adj* happening or done quickly or unexpectedly ○ *The cyclist lowered his head and put on a sudden burst of speed.*
suddenly /'sʌd·ən·li/ *adv* ○ *Suddenly, from somewhere behind us, a loud voice spoke out.* ○ *Carpenter suddenly felt dizzy.*

WORD FAMILY **sudden**	
Adjectives sudden	*Adverbs* suddenly

sudden death *n* [C usually sing] a method of deciding who will win a game when the score for each team is equal, in which the first player or team to score wins ○ *The game went into sudden death overtime, and Cleveland's field goal won the game.*

suds /sʌdz/ *pl n* the mass of small bubbles that forms on the surface of a liquid, esp. on water mixed with soap

sue /suː/ *v* [I/T] to take legal action against a person or organization, esp. by making a legal claim for money because of some harm that the person or organization has caused you ○ [T] *She was hit by a city bus and is suing the city for $2 million.*

suede /sweɪd/ *n* [U] leather whose surface has been made slightly rough so that it is soft but not shiny ○ *She decided to wear her brown suede shoes.*

suffer EXPERIENCE /'sʌf·ər/ *v* [I/T] to experience or show the effects of something bad ○ [T] *About 50,000 bicyclists suffer serious head injuries each year.* ○ [T] *Block's own farm has suffered large financial setbacks.* ○ [I] *If you and your husband have jobs in different cities, your marriage is likely to suffer.*

FEEL PAIN /'sʌf·ər/ *v* [I] to experience physical or mental pain ○ *She suffers in cold weather when her joints get stiff.* ○ *He suffers from migraine headaches.*
sufferer /'sʌf·ə·rər/ *n* [C] someone who experi-

S

ences physical or mental pain of a type that is mentioned ○ *High pollen counts are bad news for allergy sufferers.*

suffering /ˈsʌf·ə·rɪŋ/ *n* [U] ○ *The prolonged drought and famine caused widespread suffering.*

WORD FAMILY suffer			
Nouns	sufferer suffering	*Verbs*	suffer
		Adverbs	insufferably
Adjectives	insufferable		

suffice /səˈfɑɪs/ *fml* to be enough ○ *The problems were of global importance, and only an international effort would suffice to deal with them.*

sufficient Ⓐ /səˈfɪʃ·ənt/ *adj* [not gradable] enough for a particular purpose ○ [+ *to* infinitive] *The company did not have sufficient funds to pay for the goods it had received.*

sufficiency Ⓐ /səˈfɪʃ·ən·si/ *n* [U] an amount of something that is enough for a particular purpose

sufficiently Ⓐ /səˈfɪʃ·ənt·li/ *adv* [not gradable] ○ [+ *to* infinitive] *Kulkowski hopes to have recovered sufficiently from his knee injury to play in the semifinals next week.*

suffix /ˈsʌf·ɪks/ *n* [C] ***grammar*** a letter or group of letters added at the end of a word to make a new word ○ *In the word "quickly," "-ly" is a suffix meaning "in the specified manner."* ○ Compare PREFIX

suffocate /ˈsʌf·əˌkeɪt/ *v* [I/T] to die because of a lack of oxygen, or to kill someone by preventing that person from breathing ○ [I] *The government warned parents yesterday not to let infants sleep on small plastic pillows because the babies could suffocate.*

suffrage /ˈsʌf·rɪdʒ/ *n* [U] ***social studies*** *fml* the right to vote in an election ○ *She wrote a book about the women's suffrage movement in America.*

sugar /ˈʃʊg·ər/ *n* [U] ***biology*** a sweet substance obtained esp. from particular plants and used to make food and drinks sweet

suggest MENTION /səgˈdʒest, sə-/ *v* [T] to mention an idea, possible plan, or action for other people to consider ○ *They were wondering where to hold the office party and I suggested the Italian restaurant on Main Street.* ○ [+ *that* clause] *I suggest that we ask someone for directions, or we'll never find the place.*

suggestion /səgˈdʒes·tʃən, sə-/ *n* [C/U] ○ [C] *She made some helpful suggestions on how to cut our costs.* ○ [C] *They didn't like my suggestion that we should all share the cost.* ○ [U] *We're open to suggestion* (= willing to listen to other people's ideas).

WORD CHOICES suggest

If someone suggests a plan or action, especially in business, you can use nouns such as **proposal** or **proposition**.

*The **proposal** for a new stadium has been rejected.*

*He wrote to me with a very interesting business **proposition**.*

A suggestion about what to do is sometimes described as a **thought** or **idea**.

*Rebecca has a few **ideas** about how we could improve things.*

*I've had a **thought** about what we might do this summer.*

SHOW /səgˈdʒest, sə-/ *v* [T] to communicate or show an idea or feeling without stating it directly ○ *His manner suggested a lack of interest in what we were doing.* ○ [+ *that* clause] *She's applied for a lot of jobs recently, which suggests that she's not altogether happy with her position.*

suggestive /səgˈdʒes·tɪv, sə-/ *adj* causing you to think about something ○ *They said they had no intention of hiding the facts, but their behavior was suggestive of the opposite.*

suggestion /səgˈdʒes·tʃən, sə-/ *n* [C] something that shows the existence of something but is not obvious ○ *Police said there was no suggestion of foul play and that the death was the result of an accident.*

suicide /ˈsuː·əˌsɑɪd/ *n* [C/U] **1** the act of killing yourself intentionally ○ [U] *She threatened to commit suicide.* **2** Suicide can also refer to any act that has the effect of causing defeat: [U] *It would be political suicide for him to refuse to support his own party's platform.*

suicidal /ˌsuː·əˈsɑɪd·əl/ *adj* **1** having the tendency to want to kill yourself **2** Suicidal also means likely to cause your own defeat: *The union leader argued that a strike now would be suicidal.*

suit WORK WELL /suːt/ *v* [T] **1** to be convenient or work well for someone or something ○ *What time suits you best?* ○ *The job of a salesman seems to suit him.* **2** To suit also means to make someone look more attractive: *That new hairstyle really suits you – you look terrific.*

suitable /ˈsuːt̬·ə·bəl/ *adj* being right or correct for a particular situation or person ○ *The book is suitable as a text for a course in beginning chemistry.* ○ *The movie may not be suitable for very young children.*

suitability /ˌsuːt̬·əˈbɪl·ət̬·i/ *n* [U] ➤ Usage: **fit or suit?** at FIT CORRECT SIZE

WORD CHOICES suitable

A common alternative to "suitable" is the adjective **appropriate**.

*Is this film **appropriate** for young children?*

*You should bring **appropriate** footwear.*

If an action is suitable for a particular situation, you can use the adjectives **apt** or **fitting**.

*"Unusual," yes, that's a very **apt** description.*

*The promotion was a **fitting** reward for all his hard work.*

The adjective **right** can also be used to show that someone or something is suitable for a particular situation.

*I'm not sure that she's the **right** person for the job.* ➤

S

Is this the **right** *way to do it?*

If someone or something is very suitable, you can use the adjective **perfect**.

It's a **perfect** *day for a picnic.*

She'd be **perfect** *for the job.*

The expression **in keeping with** is sometimes used when something is suitable for a particular style or tradition.

The antique desk was very much **in keeping with** *the rest of the furniture in the room.*

CLOTHES /suːt/ *n* [C] **1** a set of clothes made of the same material and usually consisting of a jacket and pants or skirt **2** A suit is also a set of clothes or a piece of clothing to be worn in a particular situation or for a particular activity: *a bathing suit* **3** *slang* A suit is also someone in business, esp. when compared with an artist or ordinary worker: *The network suits don't care about the fans who show up at the ballpark.*

LEGAL CASE /suːt/ *n* [C] a LAWSUIT ○ *She brought a suit against the HMO for medical malpractice.*

CARD TYPE /suːt/ *n* [C] any of the four types of cards in a set of playing cards, each having a different symbol printed on it ○ *The four suits in a deck of cards are hearts, spades, clubs, and diamonds.*

PHRASAL VERB with suit

• **suit up** to prepare to take part in something, esp. a sport, by putting on a uniform ○ *Anderson suited up only in Games 3 and 4 because of an injured right shoulder.*

suitcase /ˈsuːt·keɪs/ *n* [C] a large container with a handle and often with wheels for carrying clothes and possessions while traveling ○ *Have you packed your suitcase yet?*

suite ROOMS/FURNITURE /swiːt/ *n* [C] **1** a set of connected rooms, esp. in a hotel ○ *Guests were invited to the publisher's hospitality suite to meet the author.* **2** A suite is also a set of matching furniture for one room: *They bought a living room suite consisting of a sofa and two easy chairs.*

S

MUSIC /swiːt/ *n* [C] ***music*** a piece of music that consists of a set of related pieces, all for the same instruments

suitor /ˈsuːt̬·ər/ *n* [C] **1** a man who wants a particular woman to agree to marry him **2** A suitor is also a person or company that wants to take control of another company.

sulfate /ˈsʌl·feɪt/ *n* [C] ***chemistry*** a substance formed from SULFUR, oxygen, and another element

sulfide /ˈsʌl·faɪd/ *n* [C] ***chemistry*** a chemical formed from SULFUR and another element

sulfur, **sulphur** /ˈsʌl·fər/ *n* [U] a pale yellow chemical element with a strong smell that is found in various physical forms and burns with a blue flame

sulfuric acid /sʌlˈfjʊr·ɪk ˈæs·əd/ *n* [U] ***chemistry*** a STRONG ACID with no color

sulk /sʌlk/ *v* [I] to be silent and unpleasant because you are angry or annoyed ○ *She pouts and sulks, and she almost never smiles or laughs.*

sullen /ˈsʌl·ən/ *adj* silent and unpleasant ○ *They stared at him with an expression of sullen dislike.* ○ *(fig.) The skies looked very sullen* (= dark and unpleasant).

sulphur /ˈsʌl·fər/ *n* [U] SULFUR

sultan /ˈsʌlt·ən/ *n* [C] a title of someone who rules or governs in some Muslim countries

sultry HOT /ˈsʌl·tri/ *adj* (of weather) very hot and HUMID (= with air that contains very small drops of water) ○ *It was a sultry night, and I was walking home.*

ATTRACTIVE /ˈsʌl·tri/ *adj* sexually attractive ○ *a sultry dance*

sum Ⓐ **AMOUNT OF MONEY** /sʌm/ *n* [C] a particular amount of money ○ *The sum involved in the sale was not reported.*

TOTAL /sʌm/ *n* [U] **1** ***mathematics*** a total found by the addition of two or more numbers ○ *The sum of seven and twelve is nineteen.* **2 In sum** is said before giving a final, brief statement describing something: *In sum, the American public did not perceive global warming as urgent.*

PHRASAL VERB with sum

• **sum up** *(something/someone)* Ⓐ [M] to express briefly the important facts about something or the characteristics of someone ○ *The oral report should sum up the main points of the written essay.* ○ *He's a man with a big ego – that about sums him up.*

summary Ⓐ /ˈsʌm·ə·ri/ *n* [C] **1** a brief, clear statement giving the most important facts about something ○ *The assignment was to write a summary of the news.* **2 In summary** is said before giving a final, brief statement: *In summary, Chen's book is a good introduction to the subject.*

summarize Ⓐ /ˈsʌm·əˌrɑɪz/ *v* [I/T] ○ [T] *Before each episode, the narrator summarizes earlier events in the story.*

summarization Ⓐ /ˌsʌm·ə·rəˈzeɪ·ʃən/ *n* [U] the act of providing a clear statement of the important points

summation Ⓐ /sʌmˈeɪ·ʃən/ *n* [C/U] a short statement of the main points of what someone has done, said, or written ○ *Marylanders deserve a complete and accurate summation of the facts in this debate.*

summer /ˈsʌm·ər/ *n* [C/U] the season of the year between spring and fall, lasting from June to September north of the equator and from December to March south of the equator, when the weather is warmest ○ [C] *We always spend our summers on the island.*

summer school *n* [C] classes that students at a school, college or university can take during the summer

summertime /ˈsʌm·ərˌtɑɪm/ *n* [U] the season of summer ○ *We get quite a few tourists here in the summertime.*

summer vacation *n* [C] a vacation during the summer, esp. the time when students are not in school ○ *We took several short trips during summer vacation.*

summit TOP /ˈsʌm·ət/ *n* [C] the top or highest point, esp. of a mountain ○ *We climbed to the summit of Mount Rainier.*

MEETING /ˈsʌm·ət/ *n* [C] a meeting of government leaders from several countries ○ *The economic summit did not accomplish all that the President had hoped it would.*

summon /ˈsʌm·ən/ *v* [T] **1** to order someone come to a particular place, or to officially tell someone to be present ○ *The president summoned an emergency meeting of his advisers.* ○ *I have been summoned to appear in court.* **2** To summon is also to find, call, or gather together something for use: *I couldn't summon any strength.* ○ *He summoned up enough energy to prepare a revision of his novel.* **3** To summon is also to remember or imagine something: *He recollects the streets of Paris when he was a student and summons up the faces of fellow students.*

summons /ˈsʌm·ənz/ *n* [C] *pl* **summonses** a demand to appear in a particular place, esp. in a court of law ○ *I received a summons to appear in court on June 25th.*

sumptuous /ˈsʌm·tʃə·wəs/ *adj* of high quality, and often expensive ○ *I had never seen such a sumptuous apartment.*

sum total *n* [C] the whole amount ○ *That's the sum total of our knowledge about this.*

sun /sʌn/ *n* [U] **1** the star around which the earth moves and that provides light and heat for the earth ○ *The sun is the center of our solar system.* ➤ Picture: **eclipse; solar system 2** Sun also means the light or heat that the earth receives from this star: *Sit in the sun where it's a lot warmer.*

sun /sʌn/ *v* [I/T] **-nn-** ○ [T] *All morning, the cat sunned herself on the stone wall.*

sunny /ˈsʌn·i/ *adj* **1** *Flowers filled a sunny corner of the garden.* **2** A person who is sunny is happy and pleasant.

Sun. *n abbreviation for* SUNDAY.

sunbathe /ˈsʌn·beɪð/ *v* [I] to sit or lie in the sun

sunburn /ˈsʌn·bɜrn/ *n* [U] sore, red skin caused by too much time in the sun ○ *A long day at the beach gave him a bad sunburn.*

sundae /ˈsʌn·di, -deɪ/ *n* [C] ice cream with a topping of sweet sauce, nuts, and cream

Sunday /ˈsʌn·di, -deɪ/, *abbreviation* **Sun.** *n* [C/U] the day of the week after Saturday and before Monday

Sunday school *n* [C] a religious school for children held on Sunday by many Christian churches

sundial /ˈsʌn·daɪl/ *n* [C] a device that uses the light of the sun to show the time of day

sundry /ˈsʌn·dri/ *adj* [not gradable] several and different types of; various ○ *Diaz is surrounded by sundry laboratory equipment.*

sunflower /ˈsʌnˌflaʊ·ər, -flaʊr/ *n* [C] a tall plant having a large, round, flat, yellow flower whose seeds can be eaten or used to make cooking oil

sung /sʌŋ/ *past participle of* SING

sunglasses /ˈsʌnˌglæs·əs/ *pl n* dark glasses you wear to protect your eyes from the light of the sun

sunk SINK /sʌŋk/ *past simple and past participle of* SINK

IN TROUBLE /sʌŋk/ *adj* [not gradable] *infml* experiencing serious trouble, or unable to solve a problem ○ *If I had to pay off that debt, I'd be sunk.*

sunken /ˈsʌŋ·kən/ *adj* [not gradable] lying at the bottom of the sea or below a surrounding surface ○ *A few steps below the path lay a beautiful sunken garden.* ○ Related verb: SINK GO BELOW WATER

sunlight /ˈsʌn·lɑɪt/ *n* [U] light that comes from the sun ○ *These flowers need bright sunlight.*

sunlit /ˈsʌn·lɪt/ *adj* lit up by light from the sun ○ *a sunlit room/meadow*

Sunni /ˈsʊn·ni, ˈsʊn·i, ˈsuː·ni/ *n* a member of an ISLAMIC religious group

Sunni /ˈsʊn·ni, ˈsʊn·i, ˈsuː·ni/ *adj* ○ *a Sunni mosque* ○ *a Sunni cleric*

sunny /ˈsʌn·i/ *adj* [*-er/-est* only] See at SUN

sunrise EARLY MORNING /ˈsʌn·rɑɪz/, **sunup** /ˈsʌn·ʌp/ *n* [U] the time in the morning when you first see the sun ○ *In winter, I leave the house before sunrise.*

SKY APPEARANCE /ˈsʌn·rɑɪz/ *n* [C] the appearance of the sky when the sun comes up ○ *a beautiful sunrise*

sun roof *n* [C] an opening like a window in the roof of a car

sunscreen /ˈsʌn·skriːn/, **sunblock** /ˈsʌn·blɑk/ *n* [U] a substance you put on your skin to prevent it from being burned by the sun

sunset EVENING /ˈsʌn·set/, **sundown** /ˈsʌn·daʊn/ *n* [U] the time in the evening when you last see the sun

SKY APPEARANCE /ˈsʌn·set/ *n* [C] the appearance of the sky when the sun goes down ○ *a brilliant purple sunset*

sunshine /ˈsʌn·ʃɑɪn/ *n* [U] the light and heat that come from the sun ○ *The towels dried quickly in the sunshine.*

suntan /ˈsʌn·tæn/, *short form* **tan** *n* [C] a darker skin color that results from being in the sun

super EXCELLENT /ˈsuː·pər/ *adj* [not gradable] *infml* excellent; extremely good ○ *She's done a super job and deserves to be promoted.* ○ *Your new haircut looks super.*

super /ˈsuː·pər/ *adv* [not gradable] *infml* very; extremely ○ *Todd's a super nice guy.*

PERSON /ˈsuː·pər/ *n* [C] *short form of* SUPERINTENDENT BUILDING MANAGER

superb /sʊˈpɜrb/ *adj* [not gradable] of the very best quality; excellent ○ *superb seafood* ○ *The cast is superb, especially Philip Bosco.*

S

superbly /sʊˈpɜr·bli/ *adv* ○ *a superbly illustrated book*

Super Bowl *n* [C] an important football game that is played once a year between the two US teams that are the best in their divisions

superficial NOT DEEP /ˌsuː·pərˈfɪʃ·əl/ *adj* **1** on the surface only; not deep ○ *a superficial wound* **2** If something written or said is superficial, it does not show any real understanding of the subject and does not include many details: *Her book on the history of cars in America was extremely superficial.* **3** A person who is described as superficial does not want to think seriously about anything, even important matters.

superficially /ˌsuː·pərˈfɪʃ·ə·li/ *adv* ○ *Superficially, these books are very different.*

NOT MUCH /ˌsuː·pərˈfɪʃ·əl/ *adj* slight; not much ○ *The storm was not bad, and most property damage was superficial.*

superficially /ˌsuː·pərˈfɪʃ·ə·li/ *adv* ○ *Half asleep, I was only superficially aware of what was going on.*

superfluous /sʊˈpɜr·flə·wəs/ *adj* more than is needed; extra and not necessary ○ *Our new mayor plans to eliminate superfluous programs.* ○ *Much of the school day is wasted on superfluous activities.*

supergiant /ˈsuː·pərˌdʒɑɪ·ənt/ *n* [C] ***earth science*** an extremely large star that is from 10,000 to 100,000 times brighter than the sun

superhero /ˈsuː·pərˌhɪr·oʊ, -ˌhiː·roʊ/ *n* [C] **-heroes 1** a character in stories or movies who has special powers, such as the ability to fly, that are used for fighting evil or helping people **2** A superhero is also a person whose actions or achievements are far greater than what people expect: *Police officers are the real superheroes.*

superhighway /ˌsuː·pərˈhɑɪˌweɪ/ *n* [C] a wide road with two or more LANES (= parallel divisions) in each direction, usually separated, and on which traffic travels at high speeds

superhuman /ˌsuː·pərˈhjuː·mən, -ˈjuː-/ *adj* [not gradable] having or needing powers or abilities that are greater than those of most people ○ *Cops say he exhibited superhuman strength in resisting arrest.*

superimpose /ˌsuː·pər·ɪmˈpoʊz/ *v* [T] to position an image over another image so that both images can be seen together

superintendent PERSON IN CHARGE /ˌsuː·pə·rɪnˈten·dənt/ *n* [C] a person who is in charge of work done and who manages the employees in a particular office, department, or area ○ *She was appointed superintendent of schools in Tacoma, Washington.*

BUILDING MANAGER /ˌsuː·pə·rɪnˈten·dənt/, *short form* **super** *n* [C] a person in charge of keeping a building in good condition ○ *Ask the superintendent to check the boiler – we're not getting any hot water.*

superior BETTER /sʊˈpɪr·iː·ər/ *adj* [not gradable] **1** better than average, or better than others of the same type ○ *They were clearly the superior team.* ○ *Some people think acoustic recordings are superior to digital ones.* **2** *disapproving* People who are superior or behave in a superior way believe that they are better than other people: *I can't stand Bill's superior attitude.* ○ Compare INFERIOR

superiority /sʊˌpɪr·iːˈɔːr·ət̬·i, -ˈɑr·ət̬·i/ *n* [U] ○ *Advertisements are designed to show the superiority of one product over its competitors.*

HIGHER /sʊˈpɪr·iː·ər/ *adj* [not gradable] higher in rank or position than others ○ *When your superior officer gives you an order, you do it.*

superior /sʊˈpɪr·iː·ər/ *n* [C] ○ *We will need a letter of recommendation from one of your superiors.*

superlative GRAMMAR /sʊˈpɜr·lət̬·ɪv/ *n* [C] ***grammar*** the form of an adjective or adverb that shows the thing or action described has more of the quality than all others of the same type ○ *"Funniest" is the superlative of "funny."* ○ *"Most" is the superlative of "more" and "many."* ○ Compare COMPARATIVE

superlative /sʊˈpɜr·lət̬·ɪv/ *adj* [not gradable] ○ *The superlative form of "slow" is "slowest."*

BEST /sʊˈpɜr·lət̬·ɪv/ *adj* [not gradable] of the highest quality; the best ○ *a superlative performance*

supermarket /ˈsuː·pərˌmɑr·kət/ *n* [C] a large store where many different foods and other goods used in the home are sold ○ *I have to stop at the supermarket on the way home.*

supernatural /ˌsuː·pərˈnætʃ·ə·rəl/ *adj* (of something's cause or existence) not able to be explained by the laws of science ○ *From the center of the tree, a supernatural light began to glow.*

supernatural /ˌsuː·pərˈnætʃ·ə·rəl/ *n* [U] forces or events that cannot be explained by science

superpower /ˈsuː·pərˌpɑʊ·ər, -ˌpɑʊr/ *n* [C] any of the few countries considered to be among the most powerful in the world ○ *a military/economic superpower*

supersaturated /ˌsuː·pərˈsætʃ·əˌreɪt̬·əd/ *adj* [not gradable] ***chemistry*** containing more of a substance than can be absorbed

supersede /ˌsuː·pərˈsiːd/ *v* [T] to replace something older, less effective, or less important or official ○ *Wireless broadband could supersede satellite radio one day.* ○ *The state law was superseded by the federal Family and Medical Leave Act.*

supersonic /ˌsuː·pərˈsɑn·ɪk/ *adj* [not gradable] faster than the speed of sound, or able to fly faster than sound travels ○ *a supersonic plane* ○ *supersonic speed*

superstar /ˈsuː·pərˌstɑr/ *n* [C] an extremely famous person, esp. esp someone who performs or plays a sport ○ *She is definitely one of the superstars of country music.*

superstition /ˌsuː·pərˈstɪʃ·ən/ *n* [C/U] a belief that is not based on reason or scientific thinking and that explains the causes for events in ways that are connected to magic ○ [C] *Do you have any superstitions about cutting your hair?*

superstitious /ˌsuː·pərˈstɪʃ·əs/ *adj* ○ *Supersti-*

S

tious baseball players will wear the same shirt every day when they are on a hitting streak.

superstructure /ˈsuː·pərˌstrʌk·tʃər/ *n* [C] a structure built on top of something else, esp. the part of a building above the ground or the part of a ship above the main DECK (= floor)

supervise /ˈsuː·pərˌvɑɪz/ *v* [T] to be responsible for the good performance of an activity or job, or for the correct behavior or safety of a person ○ *The Red Cross supervised the distribution of food to refugees.* ○ *She supervises 75 employees in our order department.*

supervision /ˌsuː·pərˈvɪʒ·ən/ *n* [U] ○ *City schools were placed under state supervision last week.*

supervisor /ˈsuː·pərˌvɑɪ·zər/ *n* [C] ○ *a nursing/construction supervisor* ○ *I have to get off the phone – my supervisor just walked into the office.*

supervisory /ˌsuː·pərˈvɑɪ·zə·ri/ *adj* [not gradable] ○ *He applied for a supervisory position in the bank.*

supper /ˈsʌp·ər/ *n* [C/U] a meal eaten in the evening, esp. when eaten at home and usually the main meal of the day ○ [C] *I usually heat a quick supper in the microwave when I get home from work.* ○ [U] *She has supper on the table* (= it is ready to eat). ○ Compare DINNER

suppertime /ˈsʌp·ərˌtɑɪm/ *n* [U] the time in the evening when people have a meal ○ *I got home well past suppertime.*

supplant /səˈplænt/ *v* [T] to take the place of (something or someone) ○ *Travel videos do not supplant guidebooks, but they can be useful when planning a trip.*

supple /ˈsʌp·əl/ *adj* bending or able to be bent easily; not stiff ○ *His supple fingers manipulated the needle with the utmost delicacy.* ○ (fig.) *Adams brings a supple* (= easily changing) *voice to Mayfield's songs.*

supplement Ⓐ /ˈsʌp·lə·mənt/ *n* [C] **1** something that is added to something else in order to improve it or complete it; something extra ○ *hormone/vitamin supplements* **2** A supplement is also an extra part of a magazine or newspaper: *an advertising supplement*

supplement Ⓐ /ˈsʌp·ləˌment/ *v* [T] to add to something ○ *She got a second job to supplement her income.*

supplementary Ⓐ /ˌsʌp·ləˈment·ə·ri, -ˈmen·tri/, **supplemental** /ˌsʌp·ləˈment·ᵊl/ *adj* [not gradable] ○ *Teachers often create supplementary materials for their classes.* ○ *Some workers are eligible for supplemental unemployment benefits.*

supplementary angles *pl n* ***geometry*** two angles that together add up to 180° ➤ Picture: **angle**

supply /səˈplɑɪ/ *v* [T] to provide something that is needed or wanted, or to provide someone with what the person needs or wants ○ *Fran Gebus supplied the recipe for these muffins.* ○ *The dam supplies San Francisco with water and power.*

supply /səˈplɑɪ/ *n* [C/U] an amount of something that is available for use ○ [U] *In New York, demand for housing far outstrips supply.* ○ [C] *Medical supplies were desperately needed in the war zone.*

supplies /səˈplɑɪz/ *pl n* food and other ordinary goods needed by people every day ○ *On their fourth day out, the climbers began to run low on supplies.*

supplier /səˈplɑɪ·ər/ *n* [C] a person, company, or country that provides goods of a particular kind ○ *They are the world's largest supplier of baby foods.*

WORD FAMILY supply			
Nouns	supplier	*Verbs*	supply
	supplies		
	supply		

supply and demand *n* [U] the balance between the amount of goods available and the amount that people want to buy ○ *Oil prices should be set by supply and demand, and not artificially regulated.*

support ENCOURAGE /səˈpɔːrt, -ˈpoʊrt/ *v* [T] to give encouragement and approval to someone or something because you want that person or thing to succeed ○ *The president strongly supported Egypt's role in the negotiations.*

support /səˈpɔːrt, -ˈpoʊrt/ *n* [U] ○ *The senator voiced his support for making health care available to all.*

supporter /səˈpɔːrt̬·ər, -ˈpoʊrt̬·ər/ *n* [C] ○ *He is a strong supporter of states' rights.*

supportive /səˈpɔːrt̬·ɪv, -ˈpoʊrt̬·ɪv/ *adj* ○ *They were supportive of immigration reform* (= They encouraged it).

HELP /səˈpɔːrt, -ˈpoʊrt/ *v* [T] to help someone or something in an emotional or practical way ○ *My family always supported me in whatever I wanted to do.* ○ *Many companies support public television very generously.*

support /səˈpɔːrt, -ˈpoʊrt/ *n* [U] ○ *I got a lot of support from my friends and colleagues.*

supporter /səˈpɔːrt̬·ər, -ˈpoʊrt̬·ər/ *n* [C] a person who actively helps someone ○ *Supporters of the bill expect it to pass.*

supportive /səˈpɔːrt̬·ɪv, -ˈpoʊrt̬·ɪv/ *adj* giving help and encouragement, esp. to someone who needs it ○ *Housing is part of the growth of the neighborhood, and I'm generally supportive of that.*

PROVIDE /səˈpɔːrt, -ˈpoʊrt/ *v* [T] to provide someone with money or physical things that are needed ○ *She has to work at two jobs to support her family.*

support /səˈpɔːrt, -ˈpoʊrt/ *n* [U] ○ *The government promised financial support to the areas affected by the flooding.*

PROVE /səˈpɔːrt, -ˈpoʊrt/ *v* [T] to show or seem to prove something to be true ○ *New research supports the theory.*

support /səˈpɔːrt, -ˈpoʊrt/ *n* [U] ○ *He produced charts and graphs in support of his argument.*

STOP FROM FALLING /səˈpɔːrt, -ˈpoʊrt/ *v* [T] to hold something firmly or bear its weight, esp. from below, to stop it from falling ○ *The pole is supported by wires.*

S

support /sə'pɔːrt, -'pourt/ *n* [C/U] ○ [C] *The floor is held up by wooden supports.* ○ [U] *You may have to use crutches for support while your ankle heals.*

WORD FAMILY support			
Nouns	support supporter	*Adjectives* *Verbs*	supportive support

support group *n* [C] a group of people who meet regularly to give and receive help for a problem by talking about it among themselves

suppose THINK LIKELY /sə'pouz/ *v* [I/T] **1** to expect or believe ○ [I] *"Will you be going with them?" "Yes, I suppose (so)."* ○ [+ (*that*) clause] *"You don't suppose (that) they forgot about meeting us, do you?"* **2** Suppose can also show that you are guessing about something: [T] *I suppose it's about six months since I last had the brakes checked.*

WHAT IF /sə'pouz/, **supposing** /sə'pou·zɪŋ/ *conjunction* (used at the beginning of a sentence or clause) what would happen if ○ *Suppose we miss the train – what would we do then?* ○ *Supposing that you had that opportunity, Mrs. Gallagher, what would you say?*

WORD FAMILY suppose			
Nouns	supposition	*Verbs*	suppose presuppose
Adjectives	supposed	*Adverbs*	supposedly

supposed POSSIBLY TRUE /sə'pou·zəd, -'pouzd/ *adj* [not gradable] believed by many people to be true, but not proven and often doubted by the person who is speaking or writing ○ *Nighttime experiments demonstrated that supposed eyewitnesses could not have seen anyone clearly enough to identify them at the distances described.* ○ *The cost of the plan far outweighs its supposed benefits.*
supposedly /sə'pou·zəd·li/ *adv* [not gradable] ○ *The tickets are supposedly in the mail.* ○ *I've been down to the south of England where supposedly King Arthur's castle was.*
supposition /ˌsʌp·ə'zɪʃ·ən/ *n* [C] *fml* an idea that something may be true, although it is not certain ○ [+ *that* clause] *The investment was based on the supposition that there was adequate demand for a new modern office building.*

RESPONSIBLE FOR /sə'pouzd/ *adj* [not gradable] responsible ○ *The children are* **supposed to** *be at school by 8:45 a.m.*

INTENDED /sə'pouzd/ *adj* **1** intended ○ *These batteries are* **supposed to** *last for a year.* **2** if you are **not supposed to** do something you are not allowed to do it: *You're not supposed to park here.*

CONSIDERED /sə'pouzd/ *adj* [not gradable] considered by many people ○ *Her new book is* **supposed to** *be excellent.*

suppress END BY FORCE /sə'pres/ *v* [T] to end something by force ○ *He either has to begin reforms, or he has to suppress the opposition.*
suppression /sə'preʃ·ən/ *n* [U]

KEEP HIDDEN /sə'pres/ *v* [T] to prevent something from being expressed or known ○ *He was accused of suppressing evidence.* ○ *She could barely suppress a smile.*
suppression /sə'preʃ·ən/ *n* [U] ○ *the suppression of human rights*

supreme /sə'priːm, suː-/ *adj* [not gradable] at the highest level ○ *The dictionary was called the supreme authority on all matters relating to the language.*
supremely /sə'priːm·li, suː-/ *adv* [not gradable] ○ *He was supremely self-confident.*
supremacy /sə'prem·ə·si, suː-/ *n* [U] the highest authority or greatest power ○ *He approved the supremacy of a strong federal government over the demands of states.*

Supreme Being *n* [U] GOD

Supreme Court *n* [U] the highest court in the US, consisting of nine judges

surcharge /'sɜr·tʃardʒ/ *n* [C] a charge in addition to the usual amount paid for something ○ *If you order the tickets by mail, there is a $5.00 surcharge.*

sure /ʃur, Southern also ʃour/ *adj* [*-er/-est* only] **1** certain; without any doubt ○ *"No more dessert for me, thank you." "Are you sure?"* ○ [+ (*that*) clause] *I'm sure (that) I left my keys on the table.* ○ [+ question word] *I'm not sure where they live.* ○ *If there's anything you're not sure of/about, just ask.* ○ *He said that he wasn't completely sure of his facts* (= not certain that his information was correct). ○ *We arrived early, to be sure of getting a good seat.* ○ [+ *to* infinitive] *She's sure to win.* **2** If you are sure of yourself, you are confident: *She's much more sure of herself since she started work.*
sure /ʃur, Southern also ʃour/ *adv* [*-er/-est* only] ○ *"Do you want to come swimming with us?" "Sure* (= Yes, certainly)*."* ○ *I sure am hungry* (= I am very hungry).
surely /'ʃur·li, Southern also 'ʃour·li/ *adv* [not gradable] **1** *She is slowly but surely getting her strength back.* **2** Surely can be used to express surprise, doubt, or disagreement: *Surely you're joking!* ○ *Surely they could have done better than that* (= I believe they could have done better).

IDIOM with sure

• **sure enough** as expected ○ *He said he left the book on the desk, and sure enough, there it was.*

sure thing *n* [C usually sing] something certain to win or succeed ○ *Your promotion is a sure thing – you're the best person for the job.*

surf WAVES /sɜrf/ *n* [U] the waves on the sea when they approach the coast or hit against rocks
surf /sɜrf/ *v* [I] to use a SURFBOARD (= long, narrow board) to ride waves toward a beach ○ *They go surfing every weekend.*
surfer /'sɜr·fər/ *n* [C] ○ *When the waves are big, the surfers come out.*
surfing /'sɜr·fɪŋ/ *n* [U] ○ *Dale took up surfing after his family moved to Los Angeles.*

MOVE QUICKLY /sɜrf/ *v* [T] to move quickly from one place to another within a system to learn what each place is offering ○ *You can turn on your com-*

puter now and go surfing on the Web. ○ *He spends a lot of time surfing TV channels.*

surface /ˈsɜr·fəs/ *n* [C] **1** the outer or top part or layer of something ○ *the earth's surface* ○ *a rough/smooth surface* ○ *Try to find a level surface on the ground where you can spread out your sleeping bags.* ○ *There was very little wind, and the surface of the water was calm.* **2** ***mathematics*** A surface is also a flat shape or area. **3** The surface can also be what is obvious about a person or situation rather than truer or more important facts that are hidden or hard to see: *But the fear that lurks just below the surface emerges quickly in talks with villagers.* ○ *That may seem absurd on the surface, but in a few years it will seem like wisdom.*

surface /ˈsɜr·fəs/ *v* [I] **1** *The ducks would dive to the bottom of the lake and surface* (= appear at the surface) *a minute or two later yards away.* **2** If a feeling or information surfaces, it becomes known: *This story first surfaced about a week ago.*

surface /ˈsɜr·fəs/ *adj* [not gradable] Surface means using the surface of the land or sea: *When you land in the airport, look for signs directing you to surface transportation to get a bus to the city.* ○ *If you send it overseas by surface mail it will take forever.*

WORD FAMILY surface			
Nouns	surface	*Verbs*	surface, resurface
Adjectives	surface		

surfboard /ˈsɜrf·bɔːrd, -boʊrd/ *n* [C] a long, narrow board made of wood or plastic that you can stand on to ride on waves as they come toward the beach

surge /sɜrdʒ/ *n* [C] a sudden and great increase ○ *a surge in sales* ○ *a surge in the stock market* ○ *The young American's victory touched off a surge of interest in golf across the country.*

surge /sɜrdʒ/ *v* [I] (of a large group) to move suddenly forward ○ *The crowd surged onto the field after the game ended.*

surgeon /ˈsɜr·dʒən/ *n* [C] a doctor who performs medical operations ○ *a brain/heart surgeon*

surgery /ˈsɜr·dʒə·ri/ *n* [C/U] **1** the treatment of injuries or diseases by cutting open the body and removing or repairing the damaged part, or an operation of this type ○ [U] *He had undergone open-heart surgery two years ago.* ○ [U] *I'm recovering from back surgery, so it's going to be awhile before I can ride a horse again.* ○ [C] *She has undergone several surgeries and will require more.* **2** *Br* The surgery is a doctor's office where you go to be examined.

surgical /ˈsɜr·dʒɪ·kəl/ *adj* [not gradable] ○ *surgical equipment/procedures*

surly /ˈsɜr·li/ *adj* not wanting to please you or to be friendly ○ *The clerks in this post office are sullen, surly, and inefficient.*

surmise /sərˈmɑɪz/ *v* [T] to decide that something is true without having complete information or proof ○ [+ (*that*) clause] *I quickly surmised (that) my dinner companion was something of a bore.*

surmount /sərˈmɑʊnt/ *v* [T] to deal successfully with a difficulty or problem ○ *She had to surmount the difficulties of bringing up five children on her own.*

surname /ˈsɜr·neɪm/ *n* your LAST NAME

surpass /sərˈpæs/ *v* [T] to do or be better or more than something else ○ *Our team's achievements surpass those of teams in earlier years.*

surplus /ˈsɜr·pləs, -plʌs/ *n* [C] **1** an amount that is more than is needed ○ *The world is now producing large food surpluses.* ○ *The government is forecasting a budget surplus this year* (= all the money available to be spent will not be spent). **2** A surplus is also the amount of money you have left when you sell more than you buy: *a trade surplus*

surplus /ˈsɜr·pləs, -plʌs/ *adj* [not gradable] ○ *Farmers are feeding their surplus wheat to pigs.*

surprise /sərˈprɑɪz, sə-/ *n* [C/U] an unexpected event, or the feeling caused when something unexpected happens ○ [C] *Don't tell Ann we're having a party for her – I want it to be a surprise.* ○ [C] *Last night's heavy snow came as a complete surprise.* ○ [U] *To my great surprise, they gave us everything we asked for.*

surprise /sərˈprɑɪz, sə-/ *adj* [not gradable] ○ *The basketball player paid a surprise visit to the campus on Thursday.*

surprise /sərˈprɑɪz, sə-/ *v* [T] **1** (of an event you did not expect) to cause you to feel excitement over a sudden discovery ○ *She surprised a lot of tennis fans by winning the Canadian Open.* **2** If you say that you are not surprised or would not be surprised if something happened, you mean that you almost expect it: *I'm not surprised that their parents don't want them to get married.* ○ *I would not be surprised to see the economy slow down next year.* **3** To surprise someone is also to find the person unexpectedly: *She jumped out and surprised her sister, who ran out into the hall.*

surprised /sərˈprɑɪzd, sə-/ *adj* ○ *He seemed surprised by the question.* ○ [+ to infinitive] *We were pleasantly surprised to find that the hotel was so comfortable.* ○ [+ question word] *You'd be surprised how quickly the time passes.*

surprising /sərˈprɑɪ·zɪŋ, sə-/ *adj* unexpected and causing surprise ○ *The election results were surprising for a number of reasons.* ○ *There was a surprising amount of talk about resignations.*

surprisingly /sərˈprɑɪ·zɪŋ·li, sə-/ *adv* ○ *These chairs are surprisingly comfortable.*

WORD FAMILY surprise			
Nouns	surprise	*Adjectives*	surprise, surprised, surprising
Verbs	surprise		
Adverbs	surprisingly		

WORD CHOICES surprise

A strong way of saying "surprise" is **amaze**.

*It would **amaze** me if they win the competition.*

Things that are very surprising can be described as **incredible** or **amazing**. ➤

S

*After missing so much school, it was **incredible** that she passed her exams.*

*The team has made an **amazing** comeback after last season's poor showing.*

Something that is so surprising that it is almost difficult to believe is sometimes described as a **miracle**.

*It's a **miracle** that she survived the accident.*

An unpleasant surprise is often described as a **shock**.

*It will be a terrible **shock** if their income is cut in half.*

The expression **a rude awakening** is sometimes used if someone has an unpleasant surprise when he or she discovers the truth about a situation.

*She'll be in for **a rude awakening** when she has to pay her own bills.*

If you want to say informally that an event is a surprise to you, you can use the expression **be news to**.

*Sarah is leaving? Well that's **news to** me.*

You can use the idiom **a bolt from the blue** for something that is a surprise because you were not expecting it at all.

*The news of his marriage was **a bolt from the blue**.*

surreal /sə'riːl/ *adj* strange, esp. because of combining items that are never found together in reality ○ *a surreal landscape/painting*
surrealistic /səˌriː·ə'lɪs·tɪk/ *adj*

surrender ACCEPT DEFEAT /sə'ren·dər/ *v* [I] to stop fighting and accept defeat ○ *They would rather die than surrender.*
surrender /sə'ren·dər/ *n* [C/U] ○ [C] *Robert E. Lee's surrender, which ended the Civil War, was one of the most important events in American history.*
GIVE /sə'ren·dər/ *v* [T] to give something that is yours to someone else, usually because you have been forced to do so ○ *U.S. Magistrate Celeste Bremer restricted Gruenwald's travel and ordered that he surrender his passport.*

surreptitious /ˌsɜr·əp'tɪʃ·əs/ *adj* done secretly, without anyone seeing or knowing ○ *a surreptitious glance*

surrogate /'sɜr·ə·gət, -ˌgeɪt/ *n* [C] someone or something that replaces or is used instead of someone or something else; a SUBSTITUTE for another ○ *She seems to regard him as a surrogate for her father.*

surround /sə'rɑʊnd/ *v* [T] **1** to be around something on all sides ○ *Snow-capped mountains surround the city.* ○ *The house was surrounded by dense woods.* **2** To surround something also means to have to do with it or to result from it: *I'm interested in the circumstances surrounding the accident.* ○ *The controversy that surrounded the police action led to a number of investigations.*
surrounding /sə'rɑʊn·dɪŋ/ *adj* [not gradable] ○ *Hundreds of people fled from the city and are now living in the surrounding countryside.*

surroundings /sə'rɑʊn·dɪŋz/ *pl n* the place where you live and the conditions in which you live ○ *Everyone wants safe, comfortable surroundings.*

CONFUSABLES

surroundings or **surrounding**?

Do not confuse the plural noun **surroundings** with the adjective **surrounding**.

It's much better to see animals in their natural surroundings.

~~*It's much better to see animals in their natural surrounding.*~~

WORD FAMILY surround

Nouns	surroundings	*Verbs*	surround
Adjectives	surrounding		

surveillance /sər'veɪ·ləns/ *n* [U] the act of watching a person or a place, esp. a person believed to be involved with criminal activity or a place where criminals gather ○ *The parking lot is kept under video surveillance.*

survey Ⓐ QUESTIONS /'sɜr·veɪ/ *n* [C] a set of questions people are asked to gather information or find out their opinions, or the information gathered by asking many people the same questions ○ *A recent survey found that working women want better child care and flexible hours.*
survey /sər'veɪ, 'sɜr·veɪ/ *v* [T] ○ *Researchers surveyed the political opinions of 2000 college students.*
LOOK AT /sər'veɪ, 'sɜr·veɪ/ *v* [T] to look at or examine all of something ○ *After we'd finished painting the kitchen, we stood back and surveyed our work.*
survey /'sɜr·veɪ/ *n* [C] ○ *His new book is a survey of contemporary Latin American architecture.*
MEASURE /sər'veɪ, 'sɜr·veɪ/ *v* [T] to measure and describe the details of an area of land ○ *The property must be surveyed before you can buy it.*
survey /'sɜr·veɪ/ *n* [C] ○ *Geological surveys are an important tool used in locating oil reserves.*
surveyor /sər'veɪ·ər/ *n* [C] ○ *It took a team of surveyors about three months to lay out this part of the new highway.*

survive Ⓐ /sər'vɑɪv/ *v* [I/T] **1** to continue to live or to exist, esp. after a dangerous event ○ [I] *The baby was born with a defective heart and survived for only a few hours.* ○ [T] *The building survived the earthquake with little damage.* **2** If someone is survived by family members, those family members are still alive when that person dies: [T] *He is survived by his wife and two children.*
survival Ⓐ /sər'vɑɪ·vəl/ *n* [U] ○ *Doctors told my wife I had a 50/50 chance of survival.*
survivor Ⓐ /sər'vɑɪ·vər/ *n* [C] **1** *a Holocaust survivor* ○ *He was the sole survivor of the crash.* ○ *Business is bad, but she's a survivor, she'll deal with it.* **2** A survivor is also a person who continues to live after a close relative dies: *Her survivors include two children and five grandchildren.*

WORD FAMILY survive

Nouns	survival survivor	Verbs	survive

IDIOM with survive

• **survival of the fittest** the belief that only the people with a strong desire to succeed and the ability to change as conditions change will achieve success ○ *Survival of the fittest will determine which farms make it.*

susceptible /sə'sep·tə·bəl/ *adj* easily influenced or likely to be hurt by something ○ *Some people are more susceptible to peer pressure than others.* ○ *He's very susceptible to colds.*

sushi /'suː·ʃi/ *n* [U] a type of food, originally from Japan, made from cold, boiled rice pressed into a ball or square with small pieces of raw fish or other food on top

suspect THINK LIKELY /sə'spekt/ *v* [T] to think or believe something is likely ○ *Medical investigators suspect the outbreak was caused by bacteria in the water supply.* ○ Related noun: SUSPICION FEELING OR BELIEF

THINK GUILTY /sə'spekt/ *v* [T] to think or believe that someone is guilty of something ○ *Authorities have the power to evict residents when they suspect criminal activity.* ○ Related noun: SUSPICION BELIEF IN GUILT

suspect /'sʌs·pekt/ *n* [C] ○ *After the robbery, the usual suspects were rounded up.*

DOUBT /sə'spekt/ *v* [T] to doubt or not believe in something ○ *There is no reason to suspect their loyalty.* ○ Related noun: SUSPICION DOUBT

suspect /'sʌs·pekt, sə'spekt/ *adj* ○ *I can't understand why my reasons seem suspect to a number of people.*

WORD FAMILY suspect

Nouns	suspect suspicion	Adjectives	suspect suspected unsuspecting suspicious
Verbs	suspect		
Adverbs	suspiciously		

suspend Ⓐ STOP /sə'spend/ *v* [T] **1** to stop doing an activity ○ *Relief agencies suspended aid yesterday.* **2** A person who is suspended from a job, school, or an activity, is not allowed to be involved in it, usually as a punishment: *Two students were suspended for damaging school property.*

suspension Ⓐ /sə'spen·tʃən/ *n* [C/U] ○ [C] *Stevens will begin his three-day suspension Tuesday.* ○ [U] *Students who are warned twice may face suspension.*

HANG /sə'spend/ *v* [T always + adv/prep] to hang down from something ○ *The lights were suspended from long cords.*

suspenders /sə'spen·dərz/ *pl n* a pair of straps that hold up a pair of pants, which are attached to the waist of the pants and stretch over the shoulders

suspense /sə'spens/ *n* [U] a feeling of excitement or anxiety while waiting for something uncertain to happen ○ *The suspense of waiting for her answer nearly drove him crazy.*

suspension (system) /sə'spen·tʃən ('sɪs·təm)/ *n* [C] a system connected with the wheels in a vehicle that reduces the effects of traveling over an uneven surface ○ *The suspension can be raised for driving in snow.*

suspension bridge /sə'spen·tʃən ˌbrɪdʒ/ *n* [C] a bridge supported by strong steel ropes hung from a tall structure at each of its ends

suspicion FEELING OR BELIEF /sə'spɪʃ·ən/ *n* [C] a feeling or belief that something is likely or true ○ [+ *that* clause] *There are suspicions that he may not be able to play at all.* ○ Related verb: SUSPECT THINK LIKELY

suspiciously /sə'spɪʃ·ə·sli/ *adv* ○ *The envelope contained something that looked suspiciously like airline tickets* (= seemed likely to be airline tickets).

BELIEF IN GUILT /sə'spɪʃ·ən/ *n* [C/U] the belief that someone is guilty of something ○ [C] *His strange behavior raised suspicions among his co-workers.* ○ Related verb: SUSPECT THINK GUILTY

suspicious /sə'spɪʃ·əs/ *adj* ○ *Last night's fire at the bank is being treated as suspicious.* ○ *Neighbors were asked if they had noticed anything suspicious.*

DOUBT /sə'spɪʃ·ən/ *n* [U] lack of belief in someone or something; doubt ○ *Because he was a new arrival, other workers looked at him with suspicion.* ○ Related verb: SUSPECT DOUBT

suspicious /sə'spɪʃ·əs/ *adj* ○ *Many of the workers were suspicious of the labor agreement.*

suspiciously /sə'spɪʃ·ə·sli/ *adv* ○ *Our mayor won election by a suspiciously narrow margin.* ○ *Her eyes narrowed suspiciously* (= in a way that expresses doubt).

sustain Ⓐ MAINTAIN /sə'steɪn/ *v* [T] to keep something in operation; maintain ○ *It is hard to see what will sustain them when they have no income.*

sustainable Ⓐ /sə'steɪ·nə·bəl/ *adj* ○ *The growth momentum is likely to be sustainable* (= continued) *into next year.*

sustainability Ⓐ /səˌsteɪ·nə'bɪl·ət̬·i/ *n* [U] ○ *We remain committed to ensuring sustainability of our social security system.*

sustained /sə'steɪnd/ *adj* continuing for a time ○ *sustained applause* ○ *We'll have to make a sustained effort to finish this job on time.*

SUFFER /sə'steɪn/ *v* [T] *fml* to suffer or experience damage or loss ○ *She sustained serious injuries in the accident.*

SUPPORT /sə'steɪn/ *v* [T] to support someone emotionally ○ *Throughout the ordeal, he was sustained by the belief that he would get home.*

sustenance Ⓐ /'sʌs·tə·nəns/ *n* [U] food, or the energy and other things food provides people and animals to keep them strong and healthy *The ranch animals get a lot of their sustenance from grazing.*

SUV *n* [C] *abbreviation for* SPORT UTILITY VEHICLE

S.W. *adj, adv* [not gradable] *abbreviation for* SOUTHWEST or SOUTHWESTERN

swab /swɑb/ *n* [C] a small piece of soft material at the end of a thin stick, used esp. for cleaning something or for putting on medicine ○ *a cotton swab*

swagger /ˈswæg·ər/ *v* [I] to walk, esp. with a swinging movement, in a way that shows that you are confident and think you are important ○ *He swaggered into the room just like any bully would.*
swagger /ˈswæg·ər/ *n* [C/U] ○ [C] *He walked out of the room with a swagger that made me dislike him.*
swaggering /ˈswæg·ə·rɪŋ/ *adj* [not gradable] ○ *Such swaggering self-confidence irritates a lot of people.*

swallow MOVE FOOD /ˈswɑl·oʊ/ *v* [I/T] to force food or liquid in your mouth to move into your stomach by use of the muscles of your throat ○ [I] *My throat is so sore that it really hurts when I swallow.*
swallow /ˈswɑl·oʊ/ *n* [C] ○ *He said he only wanted one swallow of milk – but it was a big one!*

ACCEPT /ˈswɑl·oʊ/ *v* [T] *infml* to accept something without question or without expressing disagreement ○ *Not surprisingly, this excuse was too much for them to swallow.*

NOT EXPRESS /ˈswɑl·oʊ/ *v* [T] not to express or show feelings or emotions ○ *I swallowed my anger and tried to be friendly.*

BIRD /ˈswɑl·oʊ/ *n* [C] any of various types of small bird with pointed wings and a tail shaped like a fork, which flies quickly, catching insects

PHRASAL VERB with swallow

• **swallow up** *something/someone* [M] to take someone or something in so that it is destroyed or no longer independent ○ *The company was swallowed up by a competitor.* ○ *A house in Florida disappeared Thursday, as a 40-foot-wide sinkhole began swallowing it up.*

swam /swæm/ *past simple of* SWIM

swamp WET LAND /swɑmp, swɔːmp/ *n* [C/U] an area of very wet, soft land ○ [C] *Alligators live in these swamps.*
swampy /ˈswɑm·pi, ˈswɔːm-/ *adj* ○ *a low-lying, swampy region*

COVER WITH WATER /swɑmp, swɔːmp/ *v* [T] to cover a place or thing with a large amount of water ○ *The boat was swamped by an enormous wave.*

BE TOO MUCH /swɑmp, swɔːmp/ *v* [T] to have too many of something, or to give someone too much to do ○ *Foreign cars have swamped the market.* ○ *We've been swamped with emergencies today.*

swan /swɑn/ *n* [C] any of various types of a large, usually white bird with a long neck that lives on rivers and lakes

swanky /ˈswæŋ·ki/, **swank** /swæŋk/ *adj* [-er/-est only] *infml* expensive and fashionable, and therefore admirable or desirable ○ *a swanky new restaurant*

swap /swɑp/ *v* [I/T] **-pp-** *infml* to exchange one thing for another ○ [T] *The two computers can easily swap data.*
swap /swɑp/ *n* [C] ○ *They proposed a straight swap of food for tools.*

swarm /swɔːrm/ *n* [C] a large group of insects, esp. bees, or any large, busy group ○ *Swarms of reporters descended on the little town.*
swarm /swɔːrm/ *v* [I always + adv/prep] to move in a large group ○ *In summer, mosquitoes swarm around that pond.* ○ *The playground swarmed with little kids.*

swarthy /ˈswɔːr·ði, -θi/ *adj* [not gradable] having a dark or slightly dark skin ○ *His companion was skinny, with a swarthy complexion.*

swastika /ˈswɑs·tɪ·kə/ *n* [C] an ancient symbol in the form of a cross with each of its arms bent in the middle at a 90° angle, used as a symbol by NAZIS in the 20th century

swat /swɑt/ *v* [T] **-tt-** to hit something hard by suddenly swinging your hand or an object ○ *I swatted the fly with a folded newspaper.*
swat /swɑt/ *n* [C] ○ *A buddy took a swat at him* (= tried to hit him).

swath /swɑθ, swɔːθ/ *n* [C] a strip or belt, or a long area of something ○ *The sheriff's department polices a wide swath of the county.*

sway MOVE /sweɪ/ *v* [I] to move slowly from side to side ○ *The trees sway in the wind.*
sway /sweɪ/ *n* [U] ○ *The car showed lots of sway in crosswinds.*

PERSUADE /sweɪ/ *v* [T] to persuade someone to believe or to do something ○ *Were you swayed by her arguments?*
sway /sweɪ/ *n* [U] the ability to persuade ○ *As a young musician, he fell under the sway of Louis Armstrong.* ○ *Large corporations hold sway with Congress.*

swear USE RUDE WORDS /swer, swær/ *v* [I] *past simp.* **swore**, *past part.* **sworn** to use rude or offensive language for emphasis or as an insult ○ *He started swearing for no good reason.*

PROMISE /swer, swær/ *v* [I/T] *past simp.* **swore**, *past part.* **sworn** to state or promise that you are telling the truth or that you will do something or behave in a particular way ○ [I] *I swear to you I'll take care of them.* ○ [T] *All the soldiers swore allegiance to the republic.* ○ [I] *(infml) I think she's upstairs, but I wouldn't swear to it* (= I am not completely sure).

WORD FAMILY swear

Nouns	swearing	*Verbs*	swear
Adjectives	sworn		

PHRASAL VERBS with swear

• **swear by** *something* to strongly believe in the effectiveness of something ○ *Some moms swear by storybook tapes from the library to entertain kids.*
• **swear in** *someone* [M] to formally give someone a new position or responsibility by promising to be

loyal or truthful ○ *A ceremony to swear in the new government took place Wednesday.*
• **swear off** *something*, **sworn** to make a decision to stop using something, esp. something that harms you ○ *He has sworn off coffee completely.*

swear word *n* [C] a rude or offensive word

sweat /swet/, *fml* **perspire** *v* [I] *past simp.* **sweat, sweated,** *pres. part.* **sweated 1** to excrete a salty, colorless liquid through the skin, esp. when you are hot or frightened ○ *He was sweating profusely.* **2** If something sweats, it has drops of liquid on the outside: *The soda cans sweat in this humidity.* **3** You may say you sweat if you feel worried: *We have to sweat about money because we don't have much of it.*
sweat /swet/, *fml* **perspiration** *n* [U] **1** the salty, colorless liquid that you excrete through your skin ○ *beads of sweat* **2** Sweat is also effort or work: *They lived off the sweat and toil of others.*
sweaty /ˈswet̬·i/ *adj* ○ *His face was sweaty* (= covered in sweat).

sweater /ˈswet̬·ər/ *n* [C] a warm piece of clothing with long sleeves, made of KNITTED wool or other material and worn on the upper part of the body ○ *a turtleneck sweater*

sweat gland *n* [C] ***biology*** a gland in the skin that produces sweat

sweatpants /ˈswet·pænts/ *pl n* pants made of thick cotton and worn esp. for exercising

sweats /swets/ *pl n* SWEATPANTS, a SWEATSHIRT, or both of these

sweatshirt /ˈswet·ʃɜrt/ *n* [C] a shirt made of thick cotton that you pull over your head, worn for exercise or to keep warm ○ *He threw on a sweatshirt and jeans.*

sweatshop /ˈswet·ʃɑp/ *n* [C] a small factory where workers are paid very little and work many hours under bad conditions

sweep CLEAN /swiːp/ *v* [I/T] *past* **swept** to clean a floor or other surface by using a brush to collect the dirt into one place from which it can be removed ○ [T] *She sweeps the street in front of her house.* ○ [M] *The classroom is filthy – could you sweep it out?* ○ [I] *I swept under every piece of furniture.*

REMOVE /swiːp/ *v* [T always + adv/prep] *past* **swept** to remove or take something in a particular direction, esp. suddenly and with force ○ *She paused, sweeping a hair from her brow.* ○ [M] *Floodwaters were sweeping away gardens and driving residents to higher ground.*

MOVE /swiːp/ *v* [I/T] *past* **swept** to move quickly and sometimes forcefully ○ [I always + adv/prep] *A stiff breeze swept across the parking lot.* ○ [I always + adv/prep] *He would sweep through the room shaking hands with everyone.* ○ [T] *Our headlights were sweeping the trees ahead.*
sweep /swiːp/ *n* [C] **1** a large movement across an area ○ *the sweep of the clock's hour hand* ○ *a police sweep* **2** The sweep of an idea or piece of writing is the range of its subject: *He is aware of the epic sweep of this project.*
sweeping /ˈswiː·pɪŋ/ *adj* having great effect or range ○ *The proposal calls for sweeping changes in public land use.*

WIN /swiːp/ *v* [T] *past* **swept** to win all the parts of a competition ○ *New York swept their series with Vancouver, 3-0.*
sweep /swiːp/ *n* [C] ○ *She prevented Republicans from making a clean sweep of the election by winning the race in District 27.*

IDIOMS with sweep

• **sweep** *something* **under the rug** to hide something damaging or unpleasant and try to keep it secret ○ *This scandal can't be swept under the rug.*
• **sweep** *someone* **off** *their* **feet** to cause someone to fall suddenly and completely in love with you ○ *He brought me flowers, kissed my hand, and swept me off my feet.*

sweepstakes /ˈswiːp·steɪks/ *pl n* a competition for a prize, esp. for money, in which those who win are chosen by chance ○ *She won $5000 in a charity sweepstakes.*

sweet /swiːt/ *adj* [-er/-est only] **1** (esp. of food or drink) having a taste similar to that of sugar or HONEY ○ *The four basic tastes are sweet, salty, bitter, and sour.* ○ *I like sweet cherries.* ○ *The desserts were not overly sweet.* **2** If a smell or sound is sweet, it is pleasant and enjoyable: *a sweet-smelling rose bush* ○ *These singers are known for their sweet voices.* **3** Sweet can be used, esp. of something or someone small, to mean charming and attractive: *What a sweet baby!* **4** Sweet can also mean kind, generous, and likable: *He was very sweet to her.*
sweets /swiːts/ *pl n* sweet food, such as candy or cake ○ *Rosie tries to avoid sweets.*
sweeten /ˈswiːt·ᵊn/ *v* [T] ○ *Sweeten the nut bread by adding dried fruit.* ○ (*infml*) *If they want to settle the strike, the owners still must sweeten their offer* (= make it more valuable and attractive).
sweetener /ˈswiːt·ᵊn·ər/ *n* [C/U] an artificial substance that tastes sweet ○ [C] *Excessive use of any artificial sweetener is unwise.*
sweetly /ˈswiːt·li/ *adv* ○ *The birds sang sweetly.*
sweetness /ˈswiːt·nəs/ *n* [U] ○ *Melons have more sweetness in the summer.*

WORD FAMILY sweet

Nouns	sweet	*Adjectives*	sweet
	sweetener	*Verbs*	sweeten
	sweetness	*Adverbs*	sweetly
	sweets		

sweet-and-sour *adj* [not gradable] (of food) flavored with a sauce usually containing sugar and vinegar

sweetheart /ˈswiːt·hɑrt/, *infml* **sweetie** /ˈswiːt̬·i/ *n* [C] **1** a person you love, esp. one with whom you have a romantic relationship ○ *Jeanne was my high school sweetheart.* ○ *Hi, sweetheart.* **2** A sweetheart is also a kind, generous person: *She's a sweetheart.*

S

sweet pepper *n* [C] a PEPPER VEGETABLE that is not spicy

sweet potato, **yam** *n* [C] a brown or orange-colored vegetable with yellow or orange flesh

sweet talk *v* [T] *infml* to talk to someone in a very kind or pleasant way because you want to persuade that person to do, allow, or believe something ○ *I tried to sweet talk my way out of going.*

sweet tooth *n* [C usually sing] a strong liking for sweet foods ○ *I have a sweet tooth - I can't say no to cookies.*

swell INCREASE /swel/ *v* [I/T] *past simp.* **swelled**, *past part.* **swollen**, **swelled** to become larger and rounder ○ [I] *It's spring, and the buds on the trees are beginning to swell.* ○ [I] *One of his eyes swelled shut.* ○ [T] *Immigrants swelled the city's population* (= increased it). ○ [I] (*fig.*) *His chest swelled with pride at being chosen* (= He felt extremely proud).
swelling /ˈswel·ɪŋ/ *n* [C/U] ○ [U] *We won't know how serious the injury is until the swelling subsides.*

WAVE MOVEMENT /swel/ *n* [C] the slow up and down movement of a long, smooth wave or series of waves in the sea ○ *ocean swells*

EXCELLENT /swel/ *adj* [-er/-est only] *dated*, *infml* excellent; very good ○ *The food was good and the service was swell.*

sweltering /ˈswel·tə·rɪŋ/ *adj* extremely hot ○ *a sweltering summer day*

swept /swept/ *past simple and past participle of* SWEEP

swerve /swɜrv/ *v* [I/T] to turn suddenly to one side while moving forward ○ [I] *The cab slowed down and swerved towards the curb.*

swift /swɪft/ *adj* [-er/-est only] moving or able to move at great speed, or happening within a very short time; fast or quick ○ *A swift current carried him downstream.* ○ *Public reaction has been swift and negative.*
swiftly /ˈswɪf·tli/ *adv* ○ *The sky was swiftly becoming dark.*

S

swig /swɪg/ *v* [I/T] **-gg-** *infml* to drink something in large swallows
swig /swɪg/ *n* [C] *infml* ○ *He took a swig of coffee.*

swill DRINK /swɪl/ *v* [T] *infml* to drink something, usually alcohol, in large amounts

PIG FOOD /swɪl/ *n* [U] waste food used for feeding pigs, or *fig.* bad or unpleasant food

swim /swɪm/ *v* [I/T] *pres. part.* **swimming**, *past simp.* **swam**, *past part.* **swum** to move through water by moving parts of the body ○ [I] *He jumped in the river and swam.* ○ [T] *Gertrude Ederle was the first woman to swim the English Channel.*
swim /swɪm/ *n* [C] ○ *Let's go for a swim this afternoon.*
swimmer /ˈswɪm·ər/ *n* [C] ○ *Katy is a good swimmer.*
swimming /ˈswɪm·ɪŋ/ *n* [U] ○ *Swimming is excellent exercise.*

WORD FAMILY swim	
Nouns swim, swimmer, swimming	*Verbs* swim

IDIOM with swim

• **be swimming in** *something* to have too much of something ○ *This salad was swimming in oil.* ○ *The company is swimming in cash and trying to figure out what to do with it.*

swimming pool, *short form* **pool** *n* [C] an artificial area of water for swimming

swimsuit /ˈswɪm·suːt/ *n* [C] a piece of clothing for swimming; a BATHING SUIT

swindle /ˈswɪn·dᵊl/ *v* [T] to obtain money or property from people by deceiving or cheating them ○ *She tried to swindle him out of the tickets.*
swindle /ˈswɪn·dᵊl/ *n* [C] ○ *a stock swindle*
swindler /ˈswɪn·dlər/ *n* [C] ○ *a convicted swindler*

swine PERSON /swɑɪn/ *n* [C] *pl* **swine** a person whom you consider to be extremely unpleasant and unkind ○ *He can be such a swine sometimes.*

ANIMAL /swɑɪn/ *n* [C usually pl] *pl* **swine** a pig, esp. when raised for food

swing MOVE SIDEWAYS /swɪŋ/ *v* [I/T] *past* **swung** to move easily to one direction and then to the other from a fixed point, or to cause something to move this way ○ [I] *He hung upside down and swung back and forth.* ○ [I] *The heavy door swung open.* ○ [T] *Campanella knew how to swing a bat.* ○ [T] *He swung the car into the garage.*
swing /swɪŋ/ *n* [C] **1** *Scott took a big swing at the ball and missed.* **2** A swing is also an attempt to hit someone: *This guy took a swing at me.* **3** A swing is also a seat that moves backward and forward and hangs from ropes or chains. **4** A swing can also be a brief trip: *Ed took a 10-day swing through France.*

CHANGE /swɪŋ/ *v* [I] *past* **swung** to change from one condition or attitude to another ○ *The company swung from record profits last year to huge losses this year.*
swing /swɪŋ/ *n* [C] ○ *He's very creative but prone to mood swings.*

BE EXCITING /swɪŋ/ *v* [I] *past* **swung** *dated*, *slang* to be exciting, enjoyable, and active
swinging /ˈswɪŋ·ɪŋ/ *adj dated*, *slang* ○ *a swinging party*

MUSIC /swɪŋ/ *n* [U] a form of jazz music that was popular esp. in the 1930s and 1940s

ARRANGE /swɪŋ/ *v* [T] *past* **swung** *infml* to arrange to obtain or achieve something ○ *The kids need new clothes, and I don't see how I can swing it.*

PHRASAL VERBS with swing

• **swing around** to turn quickly to face another direction ○ *Juan swung around to look at her.*
• **swing at** *someone/something* to try to hit someone or something ○ *They were arguing, and then I saw him swing at Brian.*

•**swing by/past** (*somewhere*) to briefly go somewhere, esp. on your way to another place ○ *I told Paul we'd swing by his place around 7:30.* ○ *We can swing past the store on the way to the party.*

swipe HIT /swɑɪp/ *v* [I/T] to hit or try to hit something, esp. with a sideways movement of the arm ○ [I always + adv/prep] *Ray swiped at a tear running down his cheek.*

swipe /swɑɪp/ *n* [C] ○ *No one took a swipe at the ball or tried to knock it away from me.* ○ *(fig.) Thomas took a swipe at the competition* (= criticized them).

STEAL /swɑɪp/ *v* [T] *infml* to steal ○ *He was trying to swipe a sweatshirt.*

swirl /swɜrl/ *v* [always + adv/prep] to move quickly with a twisting circular movement, or to cause something to move this way ○ [I] *Snowflakes swirled down from the sky.* ○ [I] *(fig.) Accusations continue to swirl around him.* ○ [T] *I swirled cocoa through the dough.*

swirl /swɜrl/ *n* [C] ○ *We arrived in a swirl of jet fumes.*

swish /swɪʃ/ *v* [I/T] to move quickly through the air making a high, soft sound, or to cause something to move this way ○ [I] *The elevator doors swished open.* ○ [T] *Vizard swished the ball through the hoop.*

swish /swɪʃ/ *n* [C] ○ *the swish of tires on wet pavement*

switch DEVICE /swɪtʃ/ *n* [C] a device that controls an electric current and turns it on or off ○ *Flip a switch and the coffee makes itself.*

CHANGE /swɪtʃ/ *v* [I/T] to change suddenly or completely from one thing to another, or to exchange one person or thing with another ○ [T] *Jeff decided to switch his major from engineering to medicine.* ○ [I] *I used to have tapes, but I switched to CDs.*

switch /swɪtʃ/ *n* [C] ○ *The team made a switch to a smaller, quicker lineup.*

STICK /swɪtʃ/ *n* [C] a thin stick that bends easily and is used esp. for hitting animals

IDIOM with switch

•**switch gears** to suddenly change what you are doing esp. the way you think about a particular activity ○ *First they threatened us, then they switched gears and started acting nice.*

PHRASAL VERBS with switch

•**switch on/off** *something* [M] to start or stop a device powered by electricity ○ *She switched the light off.* ○ *Switch on the video camera, please.* ➤ Usage: **open or switch/turn on?** at OPEN READY FOR USE

•**switch over** to stop doing or using one thing and start another ○ *The system switched over to the backup generator when the power went out.* ○ Related noun: SWITCHOVER

switchblade /ˈswɪtʃ·bleɪd/ *n* [C] a knife having a blade hidden inside its handle which springs out when a button is pressed

switchboard /ˈswɪtʃ·bɔːrd, -boʊrd/ *n* [C] a piece of equipment that is used to direct all the telephone calls esp. in an office or hotel

switchover /ˈswɪtʃˈoʊ·vər/ *n* [C] a change from using or doing one thing to another ○ *The switchover to daylight-savings time represents a 1 percent saving of electricity annually.* ○ Related verb: SWITCH OVER

swivel /ˈswɪv·əl/ *v* [I/T] **-l-**, **-ll-** to turn around from a fixed point in order to face in another direction, or to turn something in this way ○ [I] *Kennedy swiveled around in his seat.* ○ [T] *He swiveled his face toward Jack.*

swollen /ˈswoʊ·lən/ *adj, past participle of* SWELL INCREASE ○ *a swollen lip* ○ *swollen glands*

swoon /swuːn/ *v* [I] **1** to have a feeling of extreme pleasure or happiness ○ *Sarah swooned when her baby was handed to her.* **2** *dated* to FAINT (= become unconscious)

swoop /swuːp/ *v* [I] to move quickly in a smooth path, esp. through the air ○ *Swarms of birds swooped down from the sky.*

swoop /swuːp/ *n* [C] ○ *He lifted the baby up in one swoop.*

sword /sɔːrd, soʊrd/ *n* [C] a weapon with a long, sharp, metal blade and a handle, used esp. in the past

swordfish /ˈsɔːrd·fɪʃ, ˈsoʊrd-/ *n* [C/U] a large fish, often eaten as food, having a long, pointed part at the front of its head

swore /swɔːr, swoʊr/ *past simple of* SWEAR

sworn /swɔːrn, swoʊrn/ *adj, past participle of* **1** SWEAR; formally or officially stated to be true ○ *He was asked to give a sworn statement* (= statement formally and officially stated as true) *for the trial.* **2** Sworn enemies are people who are completely opposed to each other.

swum /swʌm/ *past participle of* SWIM

swung /swʌŋ/ *past simple and past participle of* SWING

sycamore /ˈsɪk·əˌmɔːr, -ˌmoʊr/, **plane tree** *n* [C] a tree with divided leaves, spreading branches, and round fruit

syllable /ˈsɪl·ə·bəl/ *n* [C] a single unit of speech, in English usually containing a vowel, consisting of either a whole word or one of the parts into which a word is separated when it is spoken or printed ○ *There are two syllables in the word silver and three in appetite.*

syllabus /ˈsɪl·ə·bəs/ *n* [C] *pl* **syllabi**, **syllabuses** a plan showing the subjects or books to be studied in a particular course

symbiosis /ˌsɪm ˌbɑɪ ˈoʊ·səs, ˌsɪm·biː-/ *n* [U] ***biology*** a close connection between different types of organisms in which they live together and benefit from each other

symbol Ⓐ /ˈsɪm·bəl/ *n* [C] **1** anything used to represent something else, such as a sign or mark,

S

a person, or an event ○ *Five interlocking rings is the symbol of the Olympic games.* ○ *She's a symbol of hope for people living with this condition.* **2** Symbols are used in mathematics, music, and science and also have various practical uses: *The symbol on this label means that the shirt is washable.*

symbolic Ⓐ /sɪm ˈbɑl·ɪk/ *adj* ○ *The Oval Office in the White House has come to be regarded as symbolic of the presidency.*

symbolism Ⓐ /ˈsɪm·bəˌlɪz·əm/ *n* [U] the use of symbols to represent ideas, or the meaning of something as a symbol ○ *poetic symbolism*

symbolize Ⓐ /ˈsɪm·bəˌlɑɪz/ *v* [T] ○ *The lighting of the Olympic torch symbolizes* (= represents) *peace and friendship.*

symbolically Ⓐ /sɪm ˈbɑl·ɪ·kli/ *adv*

WORD FAMILY symbol

Nouns	symbol symbolism	*Verbs*	symbolize
Adjectives	symbolic		

symmetry /ˈsɪm·ə·tri/ *n* [U] ***geometry*** the quality of having parts on either side or half that match or are the same size or shape

symmetrical /səˈme·trɪ·kəl/ *adj* ***geometry*** ○ *Many types of triangles are symmetrical.*

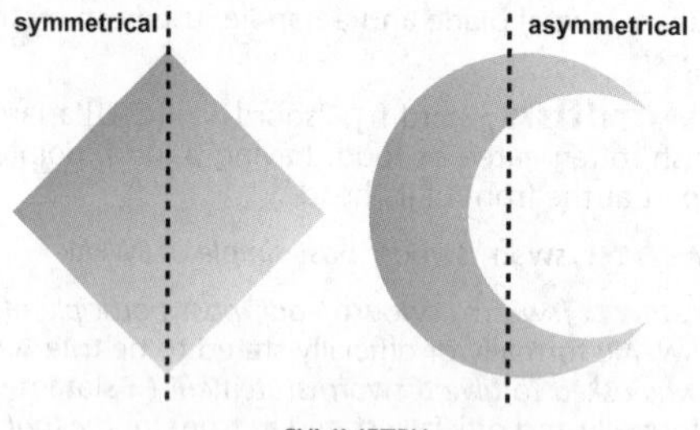

SYMMETRY

sympathy UNDERSTANDING /ˈsɪm·pə·θi/ *n* [U] a feeling or expression of understanding and caring for someone else who is suffering or has problems that have caused unhappiness ○ *When Robert died, I sent a letter of sympathy to his wife.*

sympathetic /ˌsɪm·pəˈθet̬·ɪk/ *adj* **1** showing, esp. by what you say, that you understand and care about someone's problems or suffering ○ *He suffers from back trouble too, so he was sympathetic.* **2** A sympathetic character in a book or movie is one whose actions are understandable and who is therefore likable.

sympathize /ˈsɪm·pəˌθɑɪz/ *v* [I] to listen to someone who has a problem and show that you understand and care ○ *I know what it's like to have migraine headaches, so I do sympathize with you.*

USAGE

sympathetic

Be careful not to use **sympathetic** when you simply want to say that someone is **nice**, **friendly**, or **kind**. Remember that if you say someone is **sympathetic**, you mean that this person understands your problems.

I explained to the teacher that I had been ill, but she wasn't sympathetic at all.

~~*I met some very sympathetic people while I was in Montana.*~~

I met some very nice people while I was in Montana.

SUPPORT /ˈsɪm·pə·θi/ *n* [U] a feeling or expression of support and agreement ○ *She tends to be in sympathy with the left wing of the party.* ○ [pl] *On the subject of wilderness, her sympathies were clearly pro-environmental.*

sympathetic /ˌsɪm·pəˈθet̬·ɪk/ *adj* ○ *We are sympathetic with that point of view and have the same goals.*

sympathize /ˈsɪm·pəˌθɑɪz/ *v* [I] ○ *I sympathize with your position that it would be irresponsible to lower taxes now.*

sympathizer /ˈsɪm·pəˌθɑɪ·zər/ *n* [C] ○ *a suspected communist sympathizer*

WORD FAMILY sympathy

Nouns	sympathy sympathizer	*Adjectives*	sympathetic unsympathetic
Verbs	sympathize		

symphony /ˈsɪm·fə·ni/ *n* [C] ***music*** a long piece of music usually in four parts and played by an ORCHESTRA (= large group playing different instruments)

symptom /ˈsɪm·təm/ *n* [C] **1** any feeling of illness or physical or mental change that is caused by a disease ○ *Muscle aches and fever are symptoms of the flu.* **2** A symptom is also a situation or problem that seems to represent a more serious and general problem: *This endless debate is a symptom of our lack of confidence.*

synagogue /ˈsɪn·əˌɡɑɡ/ *n* [C] a building in which people of the Jewish religion worship and study

synapse /ˈsɪn·æps, sɪˈnæps/ *n* [C] ***biology*** the point at which electrical signals move from one nerve cell to another

synapsis /səˈnæp·səs/ *n* [U] ***biology*** the joining of CHROMOSOMES from each parent during the first stage of cell division

sync /sɪŋk/ *n* [U] *infml* a state in which things happen at the same time or in the same way, or are suited to each other ○ *The president and Senate majority leader are* **in sync** (= think the same way) *on the big issues.* ○ *She found that the job was* **out of sync** (= not a good match) *with her principles, and she had to leave.*

synchronize /ˈsɪŋ·krəˌnɑɪz/ *v* [T] **1** to cause something to happen in a planned way at exact times ○ *The traffic lights were synchronized to allow cars to go at 30 mph and not have to stop for a red light.* **2** If you synchronize clocks or watches, you change them so that they all show the same time.

syncline /ˈsɪn·klɑɪn/ *n* [C] ***earth science*** a fold in layers of rock in the earth's surface which curves down ○ Compare ANTICLINE

syncopation /ˌsɪŋ·kəˈpeɪ·ʃən/ *n* [U] ***music*** musical rhythm in which the emphasis is not on beats that are normally emphasized

syndicate /ˈsɪn·dɪ·kət/ *n* [C] a group of people or companies that join together in order to share the cost of a business operation, such as the buying and publishing of newspaper stories, photographs, etc.

syndicated /ˈsɪn·dəˌkeɪṭ·əd/ *adj* [not gradable] (of articles and photographs) sold to different newspapers and magazines for publishing, or (of television or radio programs) sold to different stations ○ *Her syndicated column appears in over 150 newspapers.*

syndrome /ˈsɪn·droʊm, -drəm/ *n* [C] **1** a combination of medical problems that commonly go together and that show the existence of a disease **2** Syndrome is often used in the names of diseases: *chronic fatigue syndrome*

synonym /ˈsɪn·əˌnɪm/ *n* [C] ***English*** a word or phrase that has the same or nearly the same meaning as another word or phrase ○ *Pleasant and agreeable are synonyms.* ○ Compare ANTONYM

synonymous /səˈnɑn·ə·məs/ *adj* [not gradable] ***English*** **1** (of words) having the same or nearly the same meaning **2** If you say that one thing is synonymous with another, you mean that the two things are so closely connected in most people's minds that one suggests the other: *The name of Alfred Hitchcock is synonymous with movie thrillers.*

syntax /ˈsɪn·tæks/ *n* [U] ***grammar*** the grammatical arrangement of words in a sentence

synthesis /ˈsɪn·θə·səs/ *n* [C/U] *pl* **syntheses** the act of combining different ideas or things to make a whole that is new and different from the items considered separately ○ [C] *His latest album is a synthesis of African and Latin rhythms.*

synthesize /ˈsɪn·θəˌsɑɪz/ *v* [T] ***chemistry*** ○ *The chemical compound was first synthesized in England in 1874.*

synthesizer /ˈsɪn·θəˌsɑɪ·zər/ *n* [C] an electronic instrument used to reproduce, combine, and vary sounds, esp. of musical instruments or voices

synthetic /sɪnˈθeṭ·ɪk/ *adj* of or relating to products made from artificial substances, often copying a natural product ○ *synthetic sweeteners* ○ *a synthetic fiber*

syphilis /ˈsɪf·ə·ləs/ *n* [U] a disease caught during sexual activity

syphon /ˈsɑɪ·fən/ *n* [C] SIPHON

syringe /səˈrɪndʒ/ *n* [C] a tube for collecting blood or other liquids or for putting liquids into the body usually through a needle that can be put under the skin ○ *As a diabetic, she uses a syringe to inject herself with insulin.*

syrup /ˈsɜr·əp, ˈsʌ·rəp, ˈsɪr·əp/ *n* [U] a sweet, sometimes thick liquid made by dissolving sugar in water, to which flavoring is often added

system **SET** /ˈsɪs·təm/ *n* [C] **1** a set of connected items or devices that operate together ○ *the system of interstate highways* ○ *We're having a new computer system installed.* **2** In the body, a system is a set of organs or structures that have a particular job to do: *the digestive system*

systemic /sɪsˈtem·ɪk/ *adj* relating to or involving a whole system ○ *The problems are systemic and will only worsen.*

METHOD /ˈsɪs·təm/ *n* [C] **1** a way of doing things; a method ○ *My assistant will explain the system for filing a medical claim.* ○ *Under the US legal system, an accused person is innocent until proven guilty.* **2** A system is also a particular method of counting, measuring, or weighing things: *the metric system*

systematic /ˌsɪs·təˈmæṭ·ɪk/ *adj* using an organized method that is often detailed ○ *In his typically systematic way, he laid out the pros and cons in nine numbered paragraphs.*

systematically /ˌsɪs·təˈmæṭ·ɪ·kli/ *adv* ○ *They systematically analyze all the evidence.*

WORD FAMILY system			
Nouns	system	*Adverbs*	systematically
Adjectives	systematic		

systole /ˈsɪs·tə·li/ *n* [C] ***biology*** the part of a heart's action where it pushes blood out

systolic /sɪsˈtɑl·ɪk/ *adj* [not gradable]

S

T t

T, t /tiː/ *n* [C] *pl* **T's, Ts, t's, ts** the 20th letter of the English alphabet

tab **SMALL PIECE** /tæb/ *n* [C] **1** a small piece of material on a box, can, or container that is pulled to open it **2** A tab is also a small piece of paper or plastic attached to a paper or file so it can be found easily.

AMOUNT CHARGED /tæb/ *n* [C] an amount charged for a service or for a meal in a restaurant ○ *He offered to pick up the tab for lunch* (= pay for it).

tabernacle /ˈtæb·ərˌnæk·əl/ *n* [C] a place of religious worship ○ *We stopped for a prayer meeting at a tabernacle.*

table **FURNITURE** /ˈteɪ·bəl/ *n* [C] **1** a piece of furniture that has a flat top supported by legs ○ *We ate our meals sitting around a large dining room table.* **2** The table also means all the people at a table: *The whole table had a very good time.*

INFORMATION /ˈteɪ·bəl/ *n* [C] **1** an arrangement of facts and numbers, usually in rows on a page, that makes information easy to understand **2** A **table of contents** is a list of what is in a book.

tabulate /ˈtæb·jəˌleɪt/ *v* [T] to arrange facts, numbers, or other information in the form of a table ○ *We plan to tabulate the findings of our survey.*

Student	Occupation	Phone #
John Park	fireman	555-8978
Sue Miller	baker	555-3442
Tom Smith	actor	555-0211

TABLE

NOT DISCUSS /ˈteɪ·bəl/ *v* [T] to leave something for discussion or consideration at a later time ○ *We'll have to table these last two items until our next meeting.*

IDIOM with table

• **on the table** being discussed or considered ○ *There are several important issues on the table.*

tablecloth /ˈteɪ·bəlˌklɔːθ/ *n* [C] a piece of cloth or paper used to cover a table, esp. during a meal

tablespoon /ˈteɪ·bəlˌspuːn/, *abbreviation* **tbsp.** *n* [C] a large spoon used for measuring or serving food, or the amount this spoon holds ○ *Add three tablespoons of butter.*

tablet **MEDICINE** /ˈtæb·lət/ *n* [C] a small, round, solid object made of medicine; a pill ○ *aspirin tablets*

STONE /ˈtæb·lət/ *n* [C] a piece of stone or other hard material used for writing, esp. in ancient times ○ *The archaeologists found six tablets recording business transactions from over three thousand years ago.*

PAPER /ˈtæb·lət/ *n* [C] sheets paper that have been fastened together at one edge, used for writing or drawing; a PAD ○ *His pen swept across his drawing tablet.*

table tennis, *trademark* **Ping-Pong** *n* [U] a game played on a large table where players at each end hit a small, light ball over a low net

tabloid /ˈtæb·lɔɪd/ *n* [C] a type of newspaper that has smaller pages, many pictures, and short reports ○ *The tabloids often attract readers with sensational headlines.*

taboo /təˈbuː, tæ-/ *n* [C] *pl* **taboos** something that is avoided or forbidden for religious or social reasons ○ *Dealing with mental illness is a sensitive issue, with a lot of taboos.*

taboo /təˈbuː, tæ-/ *adj* [not gradable] ○ *The article analyzes the ways in which English speakers deal with taboo words.*

tacit /ˈtæs·ət/ *adj* [not gradable] understood without being expressed directly ○ *He gave tacit approval to the plan.*

taciturn /ˈtæs·əˌtɜrn/ *adj fml* usually speaking very little ○ *He was always quiet, reserved, and taciturn.*

tack **NAIL** /tæk/ *n* [C] a short, sharp nail with a wide, flat end, or a THUMBTACK

tack (up) /ˈtæk (ˈʌp)/ *v* [T] ○ *We tacked up a few decorations for the party.*

WAY OF DEALING /tæk/ *n* [C] one of several possible ways of dealing with something ○ *When this tack didn't work, I tried another.*

PHRASAL VERB with tack

• **tack on** *something* [M] to add something extra ○ *They tacked an additional 18% on the bill as a service charge.*

tackle **KNOCK DOWN** /ˈtæk·əl/ *v* [T] to catch and knock down someone who is running, esp. in the game of football ○ *All four players were unable to tackle the quarterback before he scored a touchdown.*

tackle /ˈtæk·əl/ *n* [C] an act of knocking someone down, or a football player who is supposed to do this ○ *A flying tackle brought him down.* ○ *He's an offensive/defensive tackle.*

ATTACK /ˈtæk·əl/ *v* [T] to attack or to deal with something ○ *There are many ways of tackling this problem.*

EQUIPMENT /ˈtæk·əl/ *n* [U] the equipment used in fishing or to lift or raise things on a ship

tacky **STICKY** /ˈtæk·i/ *adj* [*-er/-est* only] (of a substance) sticky ○ *I left a fingerprint in the tacky paint.*

CHEAP /ˈtæk·i/ *adj* [*-er/-est* only] *infml, disapproving* cheap in quality or design ○ *She reads those tacky romance novels.*

taco /ˈtɑk·oʊ/ *n* [C] *pl* **tacos** a folded TORTILLA (= thin, flat bread) filled with meat, cheese, or salad vegetables, that is fried and served with various sauces

tact /tækt/ *n* [U] the ability to say or do things in such a way that you do not make anyone unhappy or angry ○ *The editors of this book have shown tact and good sense in their selections.*

tactful /ˈtækt·fəl/ *adj* ○ *You were very tactful about the awful meal my mother fixed.*

tactfully /ˈtækt·fə·li/ *adv* ○ *I tried to say as tactfully as I could that she was totally wrong.*

tactic /ˈtæk·tɪk/ *n* [C usually pl] **1** a specific action intended to get a particular result ○ *Oliver's clumsy tactics doomed the plan from the start.* **2** Tactics is the science of planning the arrangement and use of military forces and equipment in war.

tactical /ˈtæk·tɪ·kəl/ *adj* [not gradable] **1** *He made a tactical error in agreeing to the debates.* **2** Tactical military operations or weapons are used to achieve specific goals.

tad /tæd/ *n* [U] *infml* a little bit; a small amount ○ *Those French fries were a tad greasy.*

tadpole /ˈtæd·poʊl/ *n* [C] a recently born creature with a large head, long tail, and no arms or legs, which lives in water and develops into a FROG or TOAD

tag SIGN /tæg/ *n* [C] a small piece of paper, cloth, or metal attached to an item and containing information about it ○ *Did you check the price tag on that sweater?*

tag /tæg/ *v* [T] **-gg-** ○ *The items are tagged and stacked on shelves.*

GAME /tæg/ *n* [U] a game for children in which one child chases the others and tries to touch one of them, who then is the one who chases the children

tag /tæg/ *v* [T] **-gg-** ○ *I tagged you, now you're it!*

PHRASAL VERB with tag

• **tag along** *infml* to go somewhere with a person or group of people, esp. when you have not been invited ○ *James doesn't want his little brother to tag along.*

tag sale *n* [C] a GARAGE SALE

tail BODY PART /teɪl/ *n* [C] a part of the body of an animal attached to the base of the back, or something similar in shape or position ○ *The dog greeted us, wagging its tail.* ○ *The comet's tail glowed in the night sky.*

FOLLOW /teɪl/ *v* [T] *infml* to secretly follow and watch someone ○ *FBI agents tailed him for a month.*

tail /teɪl/ *n* [C] *infml* ○ *Police put a tail on the suspect as he left the airport.*

PHRASAL VERB with tail

• **tail off** to become gradually less or smaller ○ *Profits tailed off in the last half of the year.*

tailback /ˈteɪl·bæk/ *n* [C] a football player who stands farthest away from the ball at each play and who sometimes runs with the ball

tail end *n* [C] the final part of something ○ *the tail end of the evening*

tailgate DRIVE CLOSE /ˈteɪl·geɪt/ *v* [I/T] to follow very closely behind another vehicle

CAR DOOR /ˈteɪl·geɪt/ *n* [C] a door at the back of a vehicle that opens down for loading

tail light *n* [C] either of the the two red lights on the back of a vehicle

tailor CLOTHES MAKER /ˈteɪ·lər/ *n* [C] someone whose job is to make, repair, and adjust clothes

tailored /ˌteɪ·lərd/, **tailor-made** /ˌteɪ·lərˈmeɪd/ *adj* [not gradable] ○ *a tailored suit* ○ *Her clothes fit perfectly – they must be tailor-made.*

ADJUST /ˈteɪ·lər/ *v* [T] to adjust something to suit a particular need or situation ○ *Their services are tailored to clients' needs.*

tailpipe /ˈteɪl·pɑɪp/ *n* [C] the pipe at the back end of a vehicle that carries gases away from the engine

tails /teɪlz/ *pl n* the side of a coin that does not have an image of a head on it ○ Opposite: HEADS

tailspin /ˈteɪl·spɪn/ *n* [C] a sudden fall that cannot be controlled ○ *The plane went into a tailspin and crashed.* ○ *Events in Asia sent the stock market into a tailspin.*

tail wind *n* [C] a wind blowing from behind ○ *Flights from America to Europe usually have the help of a strong tail wind.*

taint /teɪnt/ *v* [T] to damage the quality, taste, or value of something ○ *Bacteria had tainted the meat.* ○ *His reputation was permanently tainted by the scandal.*

taint /teɪnt/ *n* [U] ○ *The taint of scandal followed him for years.*

tainted /ˈteɪnt·əd/ *adj* ○ *tainted seafood* ○ *tainted election results*

take MOVE /teɪk/ *v* [T] *past simp.* **took**, *past part.* **taken** to move something or someone from one place to another ○ *Please, take me with you!* ○ *It may rain, so take your umbrella.* ○ *The suitcases were taken to Madrid by mistake.* ○ *I thought I'd take her some chocolates.* ○ *I take home about $200 a week.*

➤ Usage: **bring or take?** at BRING TAKE

REMOVE /teɪk/ *v* [T] *past simp.* **took**, *past part.* **taken** **1** to remove something ○ *Here's your pen – I took it by mistake.* ○ *A radio was taken from the car.* **2** To **take** *someone's* **life** is to kill someone: *The fire took her life.*

ACCEPT /teɪk/ *v* [T] *past simp.* **took**, *past part.* **taken** to accept something, or to receive something willingly ○ *I tried to phone him, but he refused to take my call.* ○ *Does this restaurant take credit cards?* ○ *Take this medicine three times a day.* ○ *I can take three more people in my car.* ○ *It's a girls' school that has now started taking boys.* ○ *Bob took a lot of criticism for his decision.* ○ *I refuse to take responsibility for what's happened.*

taker /ˈteɪ·kər/ *n* [C usually pl] ○ *But now at 60 years old, she found no takers for her labor.*

THINK OF /teɪk/ *v* [T] *past simp.* **took**, *past part.* **taken** **1** to think of someone or understand something in a particular way; PERCEIVE ○ [+ *to infinitive*] *I took*

T

him to be more honest than he really was. ○ *The police are taking the robberies very seriously.* ○ *In the dim light I could have taken them for brothers.* ○ *I'm not going to forge his signature! What do you take me for?* **2** Take is sometimes used to introduce an example of what you mean: *It's been really busy. Take last week – we had meetings every day.*

take /teɪk/ *n* [C] ○ *What's your take on the new proposals for new health care?*

HOLD /teɪk/ *v* [T] *past simp.* **took,** *past part.* **taken** to hold something ○ *He took my arm and led me to my seat.* ○ *Can you take this bag while I open the door?*

CATCH /teɪk/ *v* [T] *past simp.* **took,** *past part.* **taken** to catch, win, or get possession of something ○ *Rebels ambushed the train and took several prisoners.* ○ *My roses took first prize at the flower show.*

NEED /teɪk/ *v* [T] *past simp.* **took,** *past part.* **taken 1** to have as a necessary condition; need ○ *Parachuting takes a lot of nerve.* ○ *I take a size 9 shoe.* ○ *Transitive verbs take a direct object.* ○ *It didn't take much persuasion to get her to go with us.* ○ *How long does this paint take to dry?* ○ *Broken bones always take time to mend.* **2** If something **takes forever**, it happens very slowly: *In rush-hour traffic, it takes forever to get home.*

ACT /teɪk/ *v* [T] *past simp.* **took,** *past part.* **taken 1** to do something ○ *I've started taking piano lessons.* ○ *The government urged both sides to take steps to end the strike.* **2** Take is used with many nouns to make a verb phrase: *We can't delay any longer – we have to take action* (= to act). ○ *In the evening I like to take a walk* (= to walk). ○ *If you're tired, you need to take a nap* (= to sleep). **3** to **take effect** means to start working ○ *The medicine should take effect quite quickly.* **4** If you **take turns**, you and other people do the same thing, one after the other: *The mothers in our group take turns driving the children to school.*

taker /ˈteɪ·kər/ *n* [C usually pl] ○ *Census takers use a mathematical formula and apply it to the overall locality.*

MEASURE /teɪk/ *v* [T] *past simp.* **took,** *past part.* **taken** to measure something ○ *Better take the baby's temperature – she may have a fever.*

REACT /teɪk/ *v* [T] *past simp.* **took,** *past part.* **taken 1** to have or cause to have a particular feeling or opinion ○ *He takes little interest in current events.* ○ *She takes offense too easily.* **2** To **take** *someone* **by surprise** means to do something that is completely unexpected: *His sudden proposal took her totally by surprise.*

CHEAT /teɪk/ *v* [T] *past simp.* **took,** *past part.* **taken** *infml* to cheat someone ○ *You paid $500 for that thing? I think you got taken.*

WRITE /teɪk/ *v* [T] *past simp.* **took,** *past part.* **taken** to write information provided by someone or something ○ *Take notes as you read.* ○ *Journalists took down every word he said during the interview.*

PHOTOGRAPH /teɪk/ *v* [T] *past simp.* **took,** *past part.* **taken** to make a photograph of someone or something ○ *We took lots of pictures of the new baby.*

TRAVEL ON /teɪk/ *v* [T] *past simp.* **took,** *past part.* **taken** to travel on something to get from one place to another ○ *I always take the train.* ○ *Take the road on the left to get to my house.*

FILM /teɪk/ *n* [C] the filming of a small part of a movie ○ *That scene needed ten takes before they got it right.*

MONEY /teɪk/ *n* [U] the amount of money received from an activity ○ *The box office take has been huge for the new show.*

WORD FAMILY take

Nouns		Verbs	
	take taker undertaking		take overtake undertake

IDIOMS with take

• **not take** *something* **lying down** to complain about a situation rather than accepting it ○ *I can't take that criticism lying down.*

• **take a deep breath** to pause ○ *I think we all need to stop the arguments, take a deep breath, and remember why we came here.*

• **take a dim view of** *something* to disapprove of something ○ *Most bosses take a dim view of long lunches.*

• **take advantage of** *something* to use an opportunity to achieve results, sometimes in an unfair way ○ *Let's take advantage of the good weather and go to the beach.*

• **take advantage of** *someone* to use someone's weakness to improve your situation ○ *Don't you realize that he's taking advantage of you and your money?*

• **take a hike** *infml* go away ○ *This is my property – take a hike!* ○ **USAGE**: Used to rudely tell someone to leave.

• **take a hint, take the hint** to understand or do something that is communicated indirectly ○ *I've tried to get him to leave, but he can't take a hint.*

• **take a joke** to be able to laugh at jokes or tricks about you ○ *Don't be mad – can't you take a joke?*

• **take a shine to** *infml* to begin to like someone very much ○ *I think he's taken a shine to your sister.*

• **take a turn for the worse** to become worse ○ *Her health took a turn for the worse last year.*

• **take** *someone/somewhere* **by storm** to be suddenly extremely successful in a place or popular with someone ○ *As everyone knows, the Beatles took the US by storm.*

• **take care (of yourself)** *infml* goodbye ○ *"See you next month." "Yeah, take care."* ○ **USAGE**: Usually said as part of ending a conversation. ○ Compare TAKE IT EASY

• **take care of** *someone/something* **1** to be responsible for someone or something ○ *I have to take care of my little sister this afternoon.* **2 Take care of** *something* also means to do whatever needs to be done in a situation ○ *I was hoping a little money would take care of the problem.*

• **take charge (of** *something***)** to accept responsibility for something and have control over it ○ *She took charge of the project and made sure it was finished on time.*

• **take** *something* **for granted** to never think about something because you believe it will always be

T

available or stay exactly the same ○ *I took it for granted that I would find the perfect job.* ○ *It's easy to take your parents for granted.*

• **take heart** to feel encouraged ○ *Take heart. You'll be done soon, and you won't have to think about this paper ever again.*

• **take hold**, **take root** to become established ○ *The economic recovery is just beginning to take hold now.* ○ *Fascism has never taken root in the United States.*

• **take** *something* **in** *(your)* **stride** to calmly deal with something unpleasant and not let it have an effect on you ○ *Somehow the kids took all the confusion in stride.*

• **take** *something* **into account** to consider or remember something when judging a situation ○ *The report does not take into account the problems of people who do not speak English.*

• **take issue with** *someone/something* to disagree strongly with someone or something ○ *I take issue with parents who push their children too hard.*

• **take it easy 1** rest, relax, or be calm ○ *You'd better take it easy until you feel better.* ○ *Take it easy – don't get mad.* **2** *infml* You can say **take it easy** to someone when you say goodbye: *Ok, take it easy, you guys. I'll see you soon.* ○ Compare TAKE CARE (OF YOURSELF)

• **take it or leave it** either accept something without any change or refuse it ○ *I'll give you $40 for the bike – take it or leave it.*

• **take its toll**, **take a toll** to cause harm or suffering ○ *The constant stress takes its toll on emergency room workers.*

• **take it upon** *yourself* **to** *do something* to accept responsibility for something without being asked to ○ *He took it upon himself to personally thank each person at the meeting.*

• **take notice (of** *something***)** to give something your attention ○ *Voters are beginning to take notice of him as a serious candidate.*

• **take (great) pains to** *do something* to try very hard to so something ○ *He took great pains to dress well for the occasion.*

• **take part in** *something* to be actively involved in something with other people ○ *All the children took part in the Thanksgiving play.*

• **take** *your* **pick** choose any one you want ○ *You can take your pick of any dessert on the cart.*

• **take place** to happen ○ *The story takes place in the 18th century.*

• **take sides** to support one person or opinion over another ○ *My mother never took sides when my brother and I argued.*

• *something* **takes the cake** *infml* something is the most extreme example ○ *I've had some pretty bad injuries, but this one takes the cake.*

• **take stock (of** *something***)** to examine a situation carefully ○ *After the storm homeowners came out to take stock of the damage.*

• **take the bull by the horns** to deal with a difficult situation in a very direct way ○ *I took the bull by the horns and confronted him about his mistreatment of the workers.*

• **take the initiative** to be the first one to do something, esp. to solve a problem ○ *Don't be afraid to take the initiative and say what you think.*

• **take the plunge** to decide to do something, esp. after thinking about it for a long time ○ *They took the plunge and got married last month.*

• **take the time to** *do something* to spend enough time to do something well or carefully ○ *She didn't even take the time to say goodbye.* ○ **USAGE**: Often used to show you are annoyed because someone did not do something well or carefully.

• **take the wraps off** *something* to let people know about something that has been secret ○ *Today the company takes the wraps off their newest product, a drug that they have spent millions of dollars developing.*

• **take** *your* **time** to not hurry ○ *He took his time before answering the question.*

• **take** *someone* **to task for** *something* to criticize someone ○ *My professor took me to task for not citing my sources correctly.*

• **take** *something* **with a grain of salt** to understand that something is likely to be untrue or incorrect ○ *I've seen the article, which I take with a grain of salt.*

• **take** *someone's* **word for it** to believe that what someone is saying is true ○ *If she says she's sick, you have to take her word for it.*

PHRASAL VERBS with take

• **take after** *someone* to be like or to look like another family member or part of the family ○ *Most of my children take after my husband.*

• **take apart** *something* [M] to separate the parts of something so that they are not together ○ *I like to take things apart to see how they work.*

• **take away** *something* [M] to remove or subtract something ○ *Take these chairs away – we don't need them.* ○ *Twelve take away four equals eight.*

• **take back** *something* **UNDO** [M] **1** to receive or accept something that you previously sold, offered, or gave away ○ *If you're not satisfied with your purchase, we'll take it back and refund your money.* **2** If you take back something you have said, you admit that it was wrong: *I said she was lying, but I take it back.*

• **take** *someone* **back REMEMBER** to make someone remember or learn about an earlier period in time ○ *These athletes take us back to our youth and make us remember that we always dreamed of doing the things that they do.*

• **take down** *something* **REMOVE** [M] to remove something that was previously put up or put in place ○ *It must be time to take down the holiday decorations.*

• **take down** *someone* **DEFEAT** [M] to defeat or kill someone, or to stop someone from causing harm ○ *The Indiana Pacers took down Cleveland, 80–74.*

• **take down** *something* **WRITE** [M] to write something that you are looking at or listening to ○ *I can take down the messages that come in.*

• **take in** *something* **UNDERSTAND** [M] to completely understand the meaning or importance of something ○ *I had to read the letter twice before I could take it all in.*

• **take in** *someone* **SHELTER** [M] to provide a place for someone to live or stay ○ *His aunt took him in when he first came to the city.*

T

•**take in** *something* **SEE** to go to see something of interest ○ *to take in a movie* ○ *We drove around the island and took in all the sights.*
•**take in** *someone* **DECEIVE** [M] to deceive or trick someone ○ *Do you think the teacher was taken in by your excuse?* ○ *That sales pitch totally took us in.*
•**take in** *something* **MAKE SMALLER** [M] to make clothes smaller ○ *These pants fit much better since I had them taken in.* ○ Opposite: LET OUT **WIDEN**
•**take in** *something* **RECEIVE** [M] to receive money from sales ○ *The show took in $100,000.*
•**take off LEAVE 1** (of an aircraft) to leave the ground and fly ○ *The plane took off on time.* **2** *infml* To take off is also to leave suddenly: *When he saw me coming, he took off in the other direction.* ○ Related noun: TAKEOFF **AIRCRAFT**
•**take** *something* **off REMOVE** [M] to remove or get rid of something ○ *He took off his shirt and shoes and jumped in the lake.* ○ *After the poisoning scare, the product was taken off the market.*
•**take off** *something* **BE ABSENT** [M] to use a period of time for a purpose that is different from what a person usually does ○ *I've decided to take next semester off and travel and write.*
•**take off BECOME POPULAR** to suddenly become popular or successful ○ *The new product really took off among teens.*
•**take on** *something* **BEGIN** [M] to begin to have, use, or do something ○ *A chameleon takes on the color of its surroundings.* ○ *Her voice took on a troubled tone.*
•**take on** *someone/something* **FIGHT** [M] to fight or compete against someone or something ○ *I'll take you on in a game of chess.* ○ *You have to be brave to take on a big corporation in court.*
•**take out** *something* **GET** [M] to arrange to get something from a company, bank, etc. ○ *I'm going to take out a life insurance policy.* ○ *He had to take out a loan to pay his taxes.*
•**take out** *someone* **BRING** [M] to go with someone to a restaurant, theater, performance, etc. and pay for everything ○ *Our boss took us out for dinner.*
•**take out** *something/someone* **RID** [M] to get rid of something by removing it ○ *Take out the seeds before you slice the papaya.*
•**take** *something* **out on** *someone* to make someone else suffer or be responsible for your own mistakes, anger, sadness, etc. ○ *Don't take it out on me – I'm not your boss!*
•**take over** *(something)* [M] to get control of something, or to do something instead of someone else ○ *He's taken over the spare bedroom for his model railroad.* ○ *She took over management of this department last winter.* ○ *They made changes the minute they took over.* ○ Related noun: TAKEOVER
•**take** *someone* **through** *something* **GIVE INFORMATION** to give someone information about something ○ *Greene's essay takes the reader through the events leading up to the disaster.*
•**take** *something* **through** *something* **CONTINUE DOING** to continue doing something during a period of time ○ *Without a fee, the defense attorney took his case through two trials, finally winning in the Ohio Supreme Court.*
•**take to** *something/someone* **LIKE** to like something or someone ○ *We took to our new neighbors very quickly.* ○ *He didn't take kindly to the manager's insisting that he leave the restaurant.* ○ *The children have really taken to tennis.*
•**take to** *something* **START A HABIT** to start to use or do something as a habit ○ *She's taken to walking along the beach after work.*
•**take to** *somewhere* **GO** to go to or escape to a place ○ *The plane took to the air right on time.* ○ *Thousands of people took to the streets to demand a new election.*
•**take up** *something* **BEGIN** [M] to begin to do something ○ *I'm not very good at golf – I only took it up recently.*
•**take up** *something* **DISCUSS** [M] to discuss or manage something ○ *The school plans to take the matter up with the parents.*
•**take up** *something* **FILL** [M] to fill space or time ○ *This desk takes up too much room.* ○ *My day is completely taken up with meetings.*
•**take up** *something* **SHORTEN** [M] to shorten clothes ○ *This skirt is too long – I'll have to take it up.*
•**take** *someone* **up on** *something* to accept an offer or invitation from someone ○ *I think I'll take him up on his offer of a free ticket.*
•**take up with** *someone* **BECOME FRIENDLY** to become friendly with or spend time with someone ○ *She's recently taken up with a strange group of people.*
•**take** *something* **up with** *someone* **DISCUSS** [M] to begin discussing a subject with someone ○ *You'll have to take this up with the head of the department.*

taken /ˈteɪ·kən/ *past participle of* TAKE

takeoff COPY /ˈteɪ·kɔːf/ *n* [C] a humorous copy of the speech, manner, or style of someone, esp. someone famous ○ *He does a great takeoff of Kermit the Frog.*
AIRCRAFT /ˈteɪ·kɔːf/ *n* [C] the moment when an aircraft leaves the ground and starts to fly ○ *Night takeoffs and landings are banned at this airport.* ○ Related verb: TAKE OFF **LEAVE**

takeout /ˈteɪ·kɑʊt/, **carryout** *n* [C/U] a meal bought at a store or restaurant and taken somewhere else to be eaten ○ [U] *Let's have Chinese takeout for dinner tonight.*

takeover /ˈteɪˌkoʊ·vər/ *n* [C] an act of taking control of something ○ *Huge corporate takeovers were the big financial news this year.* ○ Related verb: TAKE OVER

talcum powder /ˈtæl·kəmˌpɑʊd·ər/, **talc** /tælk/ *n* [U] a powder for the skin that makes it feel smooth or keeps it dry

tale /teɪl/ *n* [C] a story or report, esp. one that is invented or difficult to believe ○ *a fairy tale* ○ *His life story makes a pretty remarkable tale.*

talent /ˈtæl·ənt/ *n* [C/U] a special natural ability to do something well, or people who have this ability ○ [C] *His talents are being wasted in that job.* ○ [U] *The baseball scouts are looking for new talent.*
talented /ˈtæl·ənt·əd/ *adj* ○ *A very young and talented violinist was the guest soloist.*

talk /tɔːk/ *v* [I/T] to say words aloud, usually to give or exchange information; to speak ○ [I] *I*

T

talked with Carol on the phone yesterday. ○ [I] *We talked about books.* ○ [T] *The candidates want to talk taxes* (= discuss this subject).

talk /tɔːk/ *n* [C/U] **1** [U] *Talk won't get us anywhere.* ○ [C] *I had a talk with my boss.* ○ [C] *Sarah gave a talk* (= a speech before a group of people) *on skyscrapers.* ○ [U] *I've heard talk of a layoff* (= unofficial information about it). **2** Talks are official discussions between organizations or countries: [C] *Contract talks between the airline and the union began today.*

talker /ˈtɔː·kər/ *n* [C] ○ *I'm not much of a talker* (= a person who is comfortable speaking).

USAGE

talk

When you use **talk** and are describing a particular subject remember to use the preposition **about**.

Let's talk about our vacation plans.

I didn't know what to talk about.

~~*I didn't know what to talk.*~~

USAGE

speak a language, not **talk**

Remember that you **speak** a language. You do not **talk** it.

She speaks excellent French.

~~*She talks excellent French.*~~

WORD FAMILY talk

Nouns	talk talker talks	*Adjectives* *Verbs*	talkative talk

WORD CHOICES talk

The most common alternatives are **speak** and **say.**

*Could you **speak** more quietly, please?*

*I couldn't hear what they were **saying**.*

The verb **chat** or the expression **have a chat** are often used if a person is talking with someone in a friendly, informal way.

*We were just **chatting** about the party on Saturday.*

*Give me a call and we'll **have a chat**.*

If people talk for a long time about things that are not important, the verb **chatter** is sometimes used.

*They spent the morning **chattering** away.*

If people talk for a long time about things that are important, the verb **discuss** can be used.

*We need to **discuss** arrangements for next week.*

If someone talks about something too much in an annoying way, you can use the expression **go on (and on).**

*He's always **going on and on** about how much he hates his work.*

If someone talks quietly so that their voice is difficult to hear, often because they are complaining about something, then the verbs **mumble** and **mutter** are used.

*She walked past me, **muttering** to herself.*

*He **mumbled** something about it being a waste of time.*

The verb **whisper** is used when someone talks extremely quietly so that other people cannot hear.

*What are you two girls **whispering** about?*

IDIOMS with talk

• **talk about** *something* here is an extreme or surprising example ○ *Talk about hot – it's 97 today.* ○ *Talk about money – all these people were earning seven figure salaries.* ○ **USAGE:** Used to emphasize what you are saying.

• **talk shop** to talk about your job when not at work ○ *She was sitting at a table with people from work, talking shop.*

• **talk some sense into** *someone* to help someone to think about a situation in a reasonable way ○ *She won't listen to me – can you try to talk some sense into her?*

• **talk the talk** *infml* to say something in a way that appears to be true or real ○ *She's only been practicing law for three years, but she sure can talk the talk.* ○ Compare WALK THE WALK at WALK **IDIOMS**

• **talk tough** to speak in a way that makes other people fear you ○ *The president talks tough but then doesn't do anything.*

PHRASAL VERB with talk

• **talk back** to answer someone in a rude way ○ *Don't talk back to your teacher.*

• **talk down** *someone* **PERSUADE** [M] to persuade people that they are wrong or that they should not act ○ *Just as soon as the President voiced his dissent, his advisors talked him down.*

• **talk down** *something* **LESSEN IMPORTANCE** [M] to tell people that something is not important or interesting ○ *Bonds is doing everything possible to talk down his achievements.*

• **talk down to** *someone* to speak to someone in a simple way, as if the person cannot understand things as well as you can ○ *Our history teacher never talks down to us.*

• **talk** *someone/yourself* **into** *something* to persuade someone to do something, or to decide to do something ○ *I tried to talk her into ordering ice cream.*

• **talk out** *something* [M] to discuss the details of something ○ *They've been talking out their problems.*

• **talk** *someone/yourself* **out of** *something* to persuade someone not to do something, or to decide not to do something ○ *I talked him out of running on his sore ankle.*

• **talk over** *something* [M] to discuss something ○ *We should get together and talk this over.*

• **talk up** *something/someone* [M] to speak in a positive way about something or someone in order to persuade others ○ *The candidate talked up his own plan to provide coverage for 27 million uninsured Americans.*

T

talkative /ˈtɔː·kət̬·ɪv/ *adj* talking a lot ○ *Cynthia is lively and talkative.*

talk radio *n* [U] a type of radio program on which events and people in the news are discussed and listeners call to talk

talk show *n* [C] a television or radio program on which guests, usually famous people, are asked questions about themselves

tall VERY HIGH /tɔːl/ *adj* [-*er*/-*est* only] of more than average height ○ *She's tall and slim.* ○ *The Sears Tower is taller than the Empire State Building.* ○ Opposite: SHORT LENGTH

THIS HIGH /tɔːl/ *adj* [-*er*/-*est* only] of a particular height ○ *Four of her friends are six feet or taller.*

tall order *n* [C] a request that is difficult to fulfill ○ *Asking me to be charming at 7 a.m. is a pretty tall order.*

tall tale *n* [C] a story that may or may not be true, but that contains details that are hard to believe

tally COUNT /ˈtæl·i/ *n* [C usually sing] a record or count of a number of items ○ *The final tally was 21 for and 16 against.*
tally /ˈtæl·i/ *v* [I/T] ○ [T] *The judges are tallying the scores.* ○ [T] *Zolga tallied* (= scored) *16 points.* ○ [M] *She tallies up our expenses each month.*

AGREE /ˈtæl·i/ *v* [I/T] to match or agree ○ [T] *I need to finish tallying the receipts.* ○ [I] *His statement doesn't tally with the other witnesses'.*

Talmud /ˈtɑl·mʊd, ˈtæl·məd/ *n* [U] the collection of Jewish laws and traditions relating to religious and social matters

talon /ˈtæl·ən/ *n* [C usually pl] a sharp nail on the foot of a bird that it uses esp. when hunting animals

tambourine /ˌtæm·bəˈriːn/ *n* [C] a small drum with metal disks around its frame that make a ringing sound, and which is played by holding it in one hand and hitting it with the other or by shaking it

tame /teɪm/ *adj* **1** (esp. of animals) not wild or fierce, either naturally or because of training or long involvement with humans ○ *Their goats seem very tame.* **2** If an entertainment is tame, it is not very exciting.
tame /teɪm/ *v* [T] ○ *He tames wild horses.*

tamper /ˈtæm·pər/ *v* [I] to touch or change something without permission or without enough knowledge of how it works ○ *Don't tamper with the boiler.*

tampon /ˈtæm·pɑn/ *n* [C] a small cylinder of cotton or other material which a woman uses to absorb her menstrual blood

tan COLOR /tæn/ *adj, n* [U] **-nn-** (of) a light brown or yellow-brown color ○ *a tan jacket*

SKIN /tæn/, **suntan** *n* [C usually sing] the darker skin that white people often get from being in the sun ○ *Ann's sundress shows off her tan.*
tan /tæn/, **tanned** *adj* **-nn-** ○ *a tanned face*
tan /tæn/ *v* [I] **-nn-** ○ *Judy tans easily.*

CHANGE INTO LEATHER /tæn/ *v* [T] **-nn-** to change an animal skin into leather by wetting it with special chemicals

tandem /ˈtæn·dəm/ *n* [C] **1** two people or pieces of equipment that work together to achieve a result, or a team of two people or animals ○ *Several races were held, including one for father-and-son tandems.* **2** A tandem is also a bicycle built for two people. **3** If something is done **in tandem**, two people develop or work on it together or during the same period of time: *This director and composer have worked in tandem on several films.*

tang /tæŋ/ *n* [U] a pleasantly strong taste or smell ○ *the tang of sea air*
tangy /ˈtæŋ·i/ *adj* ○ *the tangy taste of garlic*

tangent DIFFERENT SUBJECT /ˈtæn·dʒənt/ *n* [C] a subject or activity that is different than the one you are talking about or doing ○ *We were talking about exercise and got off on a tangent.*
tangential /tænˈdʒen·tʃəl/ *adj* ○ *a tangential issue*

MATH /ˈtæn·dʒənt/ *n* [C] **1** ***trigonometry*** in a triangle that has one angle of 90°, the RATIO (= comparison) of the length of the side opposite an angle less than 90° divided by the length of the shorter of the two sides that are next to the angle **2** ***geometry*** A tangent is also a line that touches a curve or solid at a particular point. ➤ Picture: **circle**

tangerine /ˌtæn·dʒəˈriːn/ *n* [C] a type of orange that is small and has a thin skin

tangible /ˈtæn·dʒə·bəl/ *adj* real and able to be shown or touched ○ *Drivers will see tangible improvements on major roadways.*

tangle /ˈtæŋ·gəl/ *n* [C] a messy mass of things ○ *She pulled the tangle of wires out of the box.* ○ *Her hair was in a tangle.*
tangle /ˈtæŋ·gəl/ *v* [I/T] ○ [T] *I tangled the cables and don't know which is which.* ○ [I] *Her hair tangles easily.* ○ [M] *Who tangled these wires up?*
tangled /ˈtæŋ·gəld/ *adj* ○ *She ran a hand through her tangled hair.* ○ *The whole issue is getting too tangled* (= confused).

IDIOM with **tangle**

• **tangled up in** *something* involved in something bad ○ *I was not about to get tangled up in their argument.*

PHRASAL VERB with **tangle**

• **tangle with** *someone* to disagree or fight with someone ○ *She's not afraid to tangle with her father.*

tango /ˈtæŋ·goʊ/ *n* [C] *pl* **tangos** a dance of Latin American origin for two people, or the music for this dance

tangy /ˈtæŋ·i/ *adj* ○ See at TANG

tank CONTAINER /tæŋk/ *n* [C] a container that holds liquid or gas ○ *a water tank* ○ *fuel/gas/oxygen tanks* ○ *a fish tank*

tanker /ˈtæŋ·kər/ *n* [C] a ship, aircraft, or truck built to carry liquids or gases ○ *an oil tanker* ○ *We watched a tanker coming into the harbor.*

VEHICLE /tæŋk/ *n* [C] an enclosed military vehicle that travels on metal belts turned by wheels and is armed with large guns

PHRASAL VERBS with tank

• **tank up** *(something)* **FILL VEHICLE** [M] *infml* to fill the fuel container of a car ○ *Dad asked me to tank the car up.*

tankard /ˈtæŋ·kərd/ *n* [C] a large drinking cup with a handle and usually a lid, mainly used for drinking beer

tank top /ˈtæŋk ˈtɑp/ *n* [C] a type of shirt that covers the upper part of the body but not the arms and is pulled on over the head

tantalize /ˈtænt·əlˌɑɪz/ *v* [T] to excite or attract someone by offering or suggesting something that is unlikely to be provided or is not enough ○ *Her paintings tantalize the eye.*

tantalizing /ˈtænt·əlˌɑɪ·zɪŋ/ *adj* ○ *a tantalizing question*

tantamount /ˈtænt·əˌmɑʊnt/ *adj* equal ○ *Her silence was* **tantamount to** *an admission of guilt.*

tantrum /ˈtæn·trəm/ *n* [C] a sudden period of extreme anger ○ *My mom would throw a tantrum if I wouldn't eat.*

tap HIT /tæp/ *v* [I/T] **-pp- 1** to hit something lightly and quickly, or to make a sound by doing this ○ [T] *She tapped the back of his hand.* ○ [I] *Casey is tapping away at his computer.* **2** To tap is also to TAP-DANCE.

tap /tæp/ *n* [C] ○ *She gave him a tap on the shoulder.* ○ *There was a tap at the door.*

DEVICE /tæp/ *n* [C] **1** a device that controls the flow of liquid, esp. water; a FAUCET ○ *Please turn off the tap.* **2** Beer that is **on tap** is served from a BARREL (= large container) through a tap.

OBTAIN /tæp/ *v* [I/T] **-pp-** to obtain or make use of something ○ [T] *Their try to tap the students' natural abilities.* ○ [I] *I can tap into computers all over the world.*

TELEPHONE /tæp/ *n, v* **-pp-** a WIRETAP

IDIOM with tap

• **on tap** available ○ *There are several new movies on tap this weekend.*

PHRASAL VERBS with tap

• **tap out** *something/someone* **USE UP** [M] to use everything that is available, or to get all the money that you can from someone ○ *After paying our daughter's college tuition, we're tapped out.*

• **tap out** *something* **USE KEYS** [M] to use a computer or other device to write text ○ *He tapped out the chapters on a home computer.*

tap-dance /ˈtæp·dæns/ *v* [I] to dance wearing shoes with metal pieces attached to the bottoms to make a rhythmic sound

tap dance /ˈtæp·dæns/ *n* [C] ○ *She does a tap dance with no music.*

tap dancing /ˈtæp ˌdæn·sɪŋ/ *n* [U] ○ *I took tap dancing when I was little.*

tape Ⓐ **STICKY MATERIAL** /teɪp/ *n* [U] a long, narrow strip of plastic, cloth, or paper that is sticky on one side and is used to attach things ○ *masking/duct tape* ○ *packing/electrical tape* ○ *(trademark) Scotch tape*

tape Ⓐ /teɪp/ *v* [T] ○ *I taped a note on her door.* ○ *He taped the pages back together.*

RECORDING MATERIAL /teɪp/ *n* [C/U] a long, narrow strip of plastic or thin metal used to record and play sound or sound and pictures; a CASSETTE or VIDEOTAPE ○ [C] *Did you make a tape of Tyler's concert?* ○ [U] *Is that movie available on tape yet?*

tape Ⓐ /teɪp/ *v* [T] ○ *This song was taped* (= recorded) *live in concert.*

STRIP /teɪp/ *n* [C] a long, narrow strip of cloth, paper, or thin metal ○ *a tape measure*

tape deck *n* [C] a machine that plays and may also record sound on TAPE

tape measure *n* [C] a long strip of plastic, thin metal, or cloth that is marked in units for measuring and can be rolled up to be stored ○ Compare RULER

taper /ˈteɪ·pər/ *v* [I/T] to become gradually narrower ○ [T] *The drill bit is tapered on one end.*

PHRASAL VERB with taper

• **taper off** to become smaller in size or less in degree ○ *Mortgage rates may taper off in the spring.* ○ *The rain will taper off by morning.*

tape recorder *n* [C] a machine that is used for playing and recording sound

tapestry /ˈtæp·ə·stri/ *n* [C/U] a strong cloth with colored threads woven into it to create a picture or design, usually hung on a wall or used to cover furniture ○ [C] *Mitchell creates tapestries that depict river landscapes.*

tapeworm /ˈteɪp·wɜrm/ *n* [C] a PARASITE (= animal that lives in another organism and feeds from it) that sometimes lives inside the bowels of humans and other animals

taps /tæps/ *pl n* a musical signal played at military funerals and in the evening to tell soldiers that lights are to go off ○ *We heard the bugle playing taps.*

tap water *n* [U] the water that comes into houses and other buildings from the local water system

tar SUBSTANCE FOR ROADS /tɑr/ *n* [U] a black substance, sticky when hot, used esp. for making roads

tar /tɑr/ *v* [T] **-rr-** ○ *They'll be tarring our street this week.*

SUBSTANCE IN SMOKE /tɑr/ *n* [U] a substance in tobacco smoke that causes harm to the lungs

tarantula /təˈræn·tʃə·lə/ *n* [C] a type of large, hairy SPIDER (= creature with eight legs), some of which have a painful bite

T

tardy /ˈtɑrd·i/ *adj* late in happening or arriving ○ *a tardy payment/delivery* ○ *You were tardy for school twice in the last week.*

target Ⓐ **INTENDED RESULT** /ˈtɑr·gət/ *n* [C] a result or situation that you intend to achieve ○ *We met our sales target for the year.* ○ *Your calculations were* **on target** (= accurate).

target Ⓐ /ˈtɑr·gət/ *v* [T] to intend to achieve an effect or purpose, or to direct toward a particular person or group ○ *The candidate's ads target conservative, middle-class voters.*

OBJECT AIMED AT /ˈtɑr·gət/ *n* [C] **1** an object aimed and fired at during shooting practice, often a circle with a pattern of rings, or any object or place at which arrows, bullets, bombs, and other MISSILES are aimed ○ *I missed the target.* ○ *The plane passed over the target.* **2** A target is also a person or group attacked in some way: *The president was the main target of the senator's speech.*

target Ⓐ /ˈtɑr·gət/ *v* [T] ○ *It is unfortunate that children have been targeted by so much advertising on TV.*

target practice *n* [U] the activity of shooting at TARGETS (= circles with colored rings around them) in order to improve your skill

tariff /ˈtær·əf/ *n* [C] ***social studies*** a government charge on goods entering or leaving a country ○ *import tariffs*

tarmac /ˈtɑr·mæk/ *n* [U] an area of ground covered with a hard surface, esp. the areas of an airport where aircraft park, land, and take off ○ *The plane was damaged on landing when it slid off the tarmac.*

tarnish /ˈtɑr·nɪʃ/ *v* [I/T] **1** (of metal surfaces) to become less bright or a different color ○ [I] *Silver tarnishes easily.* **2** If something tarnishes your opinion of someone or something, you no longer believe the person is as good as you had thought: [T] *The scandal has tarnished the agency's reputation.*

tarot /ˈtær·oʊ/ *n* [U] a set of cards with pictures on them that represent different parts of life and that are believed to show what will happen in the future

tarp /tɑrp/, **tarpaulin** /tɑrˈpɔː·lən, ˈtɑr·pə-/ *n* [C] a large piece of waterproof cloth or plastic that is used as a cover ○ *We hung a tarp above the picnic table to keep it dry if it rains.* ○ *A tarp was draped over the boxes.*

tar paper *n* [U] heavy paper covered with TAR that is sometimes used to protect buildings from rain

tarry /ˈtær·i/ *v* [I] *dated* to stay somewhere longer than you should ○ *The boy tarried awhile.*

tart **SOUR** /tɑrt/ *adj* tasting sour ○ *I like tart, firm apples, like Granny Smiths.*

FOOD /tɑrt/ *n* [C] a small pastry with a usually sweet filling and no top ○ *fruit tarts* ○ *I ordered the blueberry tart.*

tartan /ˈtɑrt·ᵊn/ *n* [C] a cloth woven in a pattern of different colored straight strips crossing each other at 90 angles, or the pattern itself; PLAID ○ *a tartan kilt*

tartar /ˈtɑrt·ər/ *n* [U] a hard yellow or brown substance that forms on the teeth ○ *I use a toothpaste that removes tartar.*

tartar sauce *n* [U] MAYONNAISE (= a cold, thick, creamy sauce) containing small pieces of herbs and vegetables, usually eaten with fish

Taser /ˈteɪ·zər/ *n* [C] *trademark* a special gun used by police to stop criminals by making them temporarily unable to move

task Ⓐ /tæsk/ *n* [C] a piece of work to be done, esp. one done regularly, unwillingly, or with difficulty ○ *Our first task after we moved was to find a doctor.* ○ *Making these pastries is no easy task.* ○ *They face the daunting task of rebuilding their economy.*

task force *n* [C] a group of people working together to do a particular job, esp. to solve a problem

taskmaster /ˈtæskˌmæs·tər/ *n* [C] someone who gives others a lot of work to do and expects them to work hard ○ *Our new teacher is a tough taskmaster.*

tassel /ˈtæs·əl/ *n* [C] a group of short strings or cords held together at one end and used as a hanging decoration esp. on hats, curtains, and furniture

taste **FLAVOR** /teɪst/ *n* [C/U] **1** a flavor and feeling produced by food or drink in your mouth that tells you what it is and lets you appreciate it, or the ability to have this feeling ○ [U] *Sugar has a sweet taste and lemons have a sour taste.* ○ [U] *I've lost my taste for* (= stopped enjoying the taste of) *spicy foods.* **2** A taste is also a small amount: [C usually sing] *Have a taste of this sauce and tell me if it's too salty.* ○ [C usually sing] (*fig.*) *I had a taste of* (= I briefly experienced) *factory work last summer, and I didn't like it at all.*

taste /teɪst/ *v* ○ [L] *Coffee always tastes good in the morning.* ○ [I always + adv/prep] *This tastes as if/as though/like it has pepper in it.* ○ [T] *I hope you can taste the garlic.* ○ [T] *Taste* (= try a little of) *this and tell me if you like it.*

tasteless /ˈteɪs·tləs/ *adj* (of food) not producing any flavors or feeling in the mouth that tells you what is being eaten ○ *The soup was watery and tasteless.*

tasty /ˈteɪ·sti/ *adj* (of food) producing a pleasant flavor and feeling in the mouth when eaten ○ *a tasty meal/dessert*

JUDGMENT /teɪst/ *n* [C/U] **1** a person's ability to judge and appreciate what is good and suitable, esp. in art, beauty, style, and behavior ○ [U] *Barbara has good/poor taste in clothes.* **2** Taste is also a person's liking for or appreciation of something: [C] *My son and I have very different tastes in music.*

tasteful /ˈteɪst·fəl/ *adj* showing good judgment, esp. in style ○ *a tasteful Oriental rug*

tasteless /ˈteɪs·tləs/ *adj* showing such bad judgment as to be offensive ○ *They received hundreds of complaints after he told a tasteless joke on TV.*

tastefully /ˈteɪst·fə·li/ *adv*

WORD FAMILY taste			
Nouns	taste distaste	*Adjectives*	tasteful distasteful tasteless tasty
Verbs	taste		
Adverbs	tastefully		

taste bud *n* [C usually pl] any of a large group of cells found mostly on the tongue that allow different tastes to be recognized

tatters /ˈtæt̬·ərz/ *pl n* torn pieces ○ *His clothes were* **in tatters** (= torn apart).

tattered /ˈtæt̬·ərd/ *adj* (of cloth) damaged by continuous use or age, esp. torn in strips ○ *old tattered flags*

tattoo /tæˈtuː/ *n* [C] *pl* **tattoos** a permanent picture, pattern, or word on the surface of skin, created by using needles to put colors under the skin

tattoo /tæˈtuː/ *v* [T] *pres. part.* **tattooing**, *past* **tattooed** ○ *An eagle was tattooed on his chest.*

taught /tɔːt/ *past simple and past participle of* TEACH

taunt /tɔːnt, tɑnt/ *v* [T] to try to make other people angry or upset by insulting them, laughing at them, etc. ○ *The movie is about a criminal who taunts the police with phone calls.*

taunt /tɔːnt, tɑnt/ *n* [C] ○ *At school, he had received jeers and taunts because of his size.*

Taurus /ˈtɔːr·əs/ *n* [C/U] the second sign of the ZODIAC, covering the period April 20 to May 20 and represented by a BULL, or a person born during this period

taut /tɔːt/ *adj* stretched tightly; tight ○ *She tightened the strings of the guitar to make them taut.* ○ (*fig.*) *The story is a taut* (= exciting, with fast action) *psychological drama.*

tavern /ˈtæv·ərn/ *n* [C] a place where alcoholic drinks are sold and drunk

tawdry /ˈtɔː·dri, ˈtɑ·dri/ *adj* showy, cheap, and of poor quality ○ *tawdry jewelry/furnishings*

tawny /ˈtɔː·ni, ˈtɑn·i/ *adj* [*-er/-est* only] of a light yellow-brown color, like that of a lion ○ *tawny fur*

tax MONEY /tæks/ *n* [C/U] ***social studies*** **1** (an amount of) money paid to the government, usually a percentage of personal income or of the cost of goods or services bought ○ [C] *income/sales/Social Security tax* ○ [C] *a property/gasoline tax* ○ [U] *The senator proposed a tax increase/cut.* **2** ***social studies*** A **tax refund** is money returned to you from the government because you have paid more than you needed to for a particular year.

tax /tæks/ *v* [T] ○ *He maintained that corporations were not being taxed enough.*

taxable /ˈtæk·sə·bəl/ *adj* [not gradable] (of income) that must be included in calculating the percentage you have to pay the government

taxation /tækˈseɪ·ʃən/ *n* [U] the process by which the government of a country obtains money from its people in order to pay for its expenses

NEED EFFORT /tæks/ *v* [T] to be difficult for someone or use too much of something ○ *All he has to do is wash a few dishes – that shouldn't tax him too much.* ○ *Round-the-clock nursing care severely taxed her resources.*

taxing /ˈtæk·sɪŋ/ *adj* needing too much effort ○ *After the surgery, I couldn't do anything too taxing for a while.*

WORD FAMILY tax			
Nouns	tax taxation	*Adjectives*	taxable taxing
Verbs	tax		

tax break *n* [C] a change in law that results in the opportunity to pay less in taxes ○ *With this change, high-income people will get a tax break.*

tax-deductible *adj* [not gradable] allowed to be subtracted from your income when you calculate your taxes

tax-exempt *adj* [not gradable] not considered as part of your income when you calculate your taxes ○ *tax-exempt municipal bonds*

taxi VEHICLE /ˈtæk·si/, **taxicab** /ˈtæk·siːˌkæb/, **cab** *n* [C] a car with a driver whom you pay to take you where you want to go ○ *The buses weren't running, so we took a taxi.*

MOVE /ˈtæk·si/ *v* [I] **taxis**, *pres. part.* **taxiing**, *past* **taxied** (of an aircraft) to move slowly on the ground ○ *After a half-hour delay, our plane taxied to the runway for takeoff.*

taxpayer /ˈtæksˌpeɪ·ər/ *n* [C] a person who pays taxes ○ *$130 million of taxpayers' money will be needed to build the new stadium.*

tax return *n* [C] a document on which you report your income each year to calculate your taxes

tax shelter *n* [C] a financial arrangement by which a person can avoid paying the government the usual percentage of money earned from investments or income

TB *n* [U] *abbreviation for* TUBERCULOSIS

tbsp. *n* [C] *pl* **tbsp.** *abbreviation for* TABLESPOON ○ *Add 1 tbsp. sugar.*

TD *n* [C] *abbreviation for* TOUCHDOWN FOOTBALL GOAL

tea /tiː/ *n* [C/U] **1** the dried and cut leaves of esp. the tea plant, or a drink made by pouring hot water onto these ○ [U] *I'd love a nice cup of hot tea.* ○ [C] *We have a variety of herbal teas.* **2** *Br* Tea is also a light meal eaten in the late afternoon or early evening.

tea bag *n* [C] a small amount of tea leaves in a thin paper bag

teach /tiːtʃ/ *v* [I/T] *past* **taught** **1** to instruct or train someone or give someone knowledge of something ○ [I] *I taught for a few years before becoming a lawyer.* ○ [T] *He taught his children English/taught English to his children.* **2** To **teach school** is to have a job instructing children in a school.

T

teacher /ˈtiː·tʃər/ *n* [C] a person who instructs or trains others, esp. in a school ○ *an English/math/kindergarten teacher*

teaching /ˈtiː·tʃɪŋ/ *n* [C/U] ○ [U] *I enjoy teaching, but it can be exhausting.* ➤ Usage: **learn, teach, or study?** at LEARN

WORD FAMILY teach

Nouns	teacher teaching teachings	*Verbs*	teach

WORD CHOICES teach

Instruct can sometimes be used instead of "teach."

His job is to ***instruct*** *people in the use of the gym equipment.*

Train can be used when you are teaching people how to do a job or activity.

She ***trains*** *new hairdressers.*

If someone teaches special classes in sports or a school subject, especially to one person or a small group, you could use the verb **coach**.

She ***coaches*** *students in French.*

He ***coaches*** *young football players.*

Tutor could also be used when talking about teaching a school subject to one person or a small group.

She ***tutors*** *students in French.*

Educate means "to teach someone, especially using the formal system of school or college."

How much does it cost to ***educate*** *a child privately?*

IDIOM with teach

• **teach** *someone* **a lesson** to show someone, as a result of experience, what should not be done in the future ○ *I sat in the sun all day at the beach and got a terrible sunburn – it really taught me a lesson.*

teachings /ˈtiː·tʃɪŋz/ *pl n* an accepted set of beliefs, esp. religious beliefs ○ *the teachings of the Buddha/Koran/Catholic Church*

teak /tiːk/ *n* [U] the wood of a tree that grows in hot areas of the world, often used in furniture ○ *a teak table*

T

team Ⓐ /tiːm/ *n* [C] **1** a number of people who act together as a group, either in a sport or in order to achieve something ○ *a baseball/basketball/football team* ○ *the legal/medical team* ○ *My favorite team is the New York Giants.* **2** A team is also two or more horses or other animals working together to pull a load: *a team of oxen*

team Ⓐ /tiːm/ *v* [I] to act together to achieve something ○ *Lang teamed with Draper to develop the vaccine.* ○ *Williamson and Erving teamed to give the Nets another championship.*

PHRASAL VERB with team

• **team up** (of a person or group) to join another person or group, esp. in order to work together to do something ○ *50 Cent and Jim Sheridan will team up on a new film.*

teammate /ˈtiːm·meɪt/ *n* [C] a player on someone's team

team player *n* [C] a member of a group who tries to do what is good for the group rather than what is good for just himself or herself

team spirit *n* [U] a feeling of belonging together that the members of a group have toward others in the group

teamster /ˈtiːm·stər/ *n* [C] someone who drives a TRUCK as a job

teamwork /ˈtiːm·wɜrk/ *n* [U] the combined actions of a group of people working together effectively to achieve a goal

teapot /ˈtiː·pɑt/ *n* [C] a container with a handle and a SPOUT (= tube-shaped opening) for making and serving tea

tear **EYE LIQUID** /tɪr/ *n* [C usually pl] **1** a drop of salty liquid that flows from the eye when it is hurt or as a result of strong emotion, esp. unhappiness or pain ○ *By the end of the movie I had tears in my eyes* (= I was ready to cry). ○ *The boy had lost his money and was* **in tears** (= crying). **2**

tearful /ˈtɪr·fəl/ *adj* with tears of sadness ○ *The school year ended with tearful farewells to favorite teachers and best friends.*

PULL APART /ter, tær/ *v* [I/T] *past simp.* **tore**, *past part.* **torn** to pull or be pulled apart or away from something else, or to cause this to happen to something ○ [T] *I caught my shirt on a nail and tore the sleeve.* ○ [T] *I tore a hole in my sleeve.* ○ [T] *Several pages had been torn out of the book.* ○ [M] *She tore off a strip of bandage and wrapped it around the wound.* ○ [M] *He angrily tore the letter up* (= into small pieces). ○ [M] *They tore down* (= destroyed) *the old building.* ○ [M] (*fig.*) *The political situation threatened to tear the country apart.*

tear /ter, tær/ *n* [C] ○ *There's a tear in the lining of my coat.*

HURRY /ter, tær/ *v* [I always + adv/prep] *past simp.* **tore**, *past part.* **torn** *infml* to move very quickly; to RUSH ○ *She was late and went tearing around the house looking for her car keys.*

WORD FAMILY tear

Nouns	tear	*Adverbs*	tearfully
Adjectives	tearful		

PHRASAL VERBS with tear

• **tear apart** *something/someone* [M] to severely criticize something or someone ○ *The critics tore apart his first novel, but he never gave up.*

• **tear** *someone/yourself* **away** to persuade someone to leave with difficulty, or to find it difficult to leave ○ *We were having such a good time that I had trouble tearing myself away from the party.*

• **tear into** *something/someone* **ATTACK** to attack or criticize someone or something violently ○ *He tore into the witnesses and exposed inconsistencies.*

• **tear into** *something* **DO ENTHUSIASTICALLY** to start doing something with energy and enthusiasm ○ *I'd love to see John Amos tear into the meaty role of the president.*

• **tear off** *something* [M] to quickly remove clothes ○ *She tore off her apron and ran into the living room.*

tear gas *n* [U] a gas that hurts the eyes and produces tears, and is used sometimes by police to control crowds

tearjerker /ˈtɪrˌdʒɜr·kər/ *n* [C] *infml* a book, movie, or other story that makes people cry or feel sad

tease /tiːz/ *v* [I/T] to intentionally annoy a person or animal by saying something that is not true or pretending to do something, often in a playful way ○ [T] *Don't tease the dog by showing her the treat if you're not going to give it to her.* ○ [I] *I was only teasing* (= joking), *I didn't mean anything by it.*

tease /tiːz/ *n* [C] a person who likes to annoy other people by saying false things or pretending to do something

WORD CHOICES tease

If someone is teasing a person as a joke by telling that person something that is not true, you could use the verbs **joke** or, in informal English, **kid**.

*I've lost your passport. Only **joking**!*

*I'm sorry I forgot to get you a birthday present. Only **kidding**!*

You can also use the informal phrase **pull** ***someone's*** **leg**.

*Is that really your car or are you **pulling my leg**?*

If someone is teasing a person in a friendly way, you can use the verb **rib**.

*His brothers were **ribbing** him about his new girlfriend.*

If someone is teasing a person in order to upset him or her, the phrase **make fun of** is often used.

*The other children **made fun of** him because he wore glasses.*

If someone is teasing a person in order to upset him or her, you could in more formal situations use **mock** or **ridicule**.

*It was not unusual for our greatest inventors to be **mocked** and thought crazy.*

*She didn't say what she thought for fear of being **ridiculed**.*

teaspoon /ˈtiːˌspuːn/, *abbreviation* **tsp.** *n* [C] a small spoon used to put sugar in coffee or tea and for eating or measuring food, or the amount this spoon holds

teat /tiːt, tɪt/ *n* [C] the raised part of the female breast of a mammal through which an animal takes its mother's milk; a NIPPLE

technical Ⓐ /ˈtek·nɪ·kəl/ *adj* involving or needing special skills or knowledge, esp. in science or ENGINEERING (= the design and building of machines, equipment, and structures) ○ *The computer company ran into some last-minute technical problems with its new disk drives.*

technician /tekˈnɪʃ·ən/ *n* [C] a worker trained with special skills or knowledge, esp. in how to operate machines or equipment used in science ○ *an X-ray technician* ○ *a laboratory technician* ➤ Confusables: **technique or technical?** at TECHNIQUE

WORD FAMILY technical

Nouns	technicality technicality technician technique	*Adjectives* *Adverbs*	technical technically

technically Ⓐ /ˈtek·nɪ·kli/ *adv* according to rules or to the law ○ *Technically, lampreys are fish, though they are seen by many as snake-like monsters.*

technicality /ˌtek·nɪˈkæl·ət̬·i/ *n* [C] a decision based only on a specific rule or rules and not on any other consideration ○ *The case was dismissed on a technicality and will be retried at a later date.*

Technicolor /ˈtek·nɪˌkʌl·ər/ *n* [U] *trademark* a method of making movies in color, or the colors typically produced by this method

technique Ⓐ /tekˈniːk/ *n* [C/U] **1** a way of performing a skillful activity, or the skill needed to do it ○ [C] *New surgical techniques are constantly being developed.* ○ [U] *The violinist's technique was flawless.* **2** A technique is also a way of doing anything that involves planning: [C] *She devised numerous techniques for annoying her father.*

CONFUSABLES

technique or technical?

A **technique** is a particular way of doing an activity. Do not confuse it with **technical**, which is an adjective usually describing the knowledge, machines, or methods used in science or industry.

It's a math textbook and it includes a lot of technical terms.

~~*It's a math textbook and it includes a lot of technique terms.*~~

technology Ⓐ /tekˈnɑl·ə·dʒi/ *n* [C/U] ***social studies*** **1** the methods for using scientific discoveries for practical purposes, esp. in industry ○ [U] *computer/medical/space technology* **2** Technology is also a particular method by which science is used for practical purposes: [C] *Dairy producers are experimenting with new technologies to reduce the cholesterol in milk.*

technological Ⓐ /ˌtek·nəˈlɑdʒ·ɪ·kəl/ *adj* ○ *We live in an era of rapid technological change.*

technologically Ⓐ /ˌtek·nəˈlɑdʒ·ɪ·kli/ *adv* ○ *The new cars will be energy efficient, environmentally friendly and technologically advanced.*

WORD FAMILY technology

Nouns	technology	*Adverbs*	technologically
Adjectives	technological		

T

tectonic plate /tek'tɑn·ɪk 'pleɪt/ *n* [C] ***earth science*** one of the parts of the earth's surface that move in relation to each other

teddy bear /'ted·iː ˌber, -ˌbær/ *n* [C] a soft toy bear

tedious /'tiːd·iː·əs/ *adj* boring and tiring, esp. because long or often repeated ○ *tedious work/tasks* ○ *Learning a new computer program can be a tedious process.*

tee /tiː/ *n* [C] in golf, the place where you begin to hit the ball at each HOLE (= area of play), or the small stick that holds the ball up so that you can hit it easily

PHRASAL VERBS with tee

•**tee off** **GOLF** to begin a game or a hole in golf ○ *The players teed off more than 90 minutes late because of heavy rains that made the course soggy.*

•**tee** *someone* **off** **ANGER** [M] *slang* to make someone very angry ○ *It really tees me off when she won't listen to me.*

teem /tiːm/ *v* [I] to rain heavily ○ *You can't go out without an umbrella – it's teeming out there.*

PHRASAL VERB with teem

•**teem with** *something* to contain large numbers of something, esp. animals or humans ○ *a river teeming with trout* ○ *Belmont Avenue teems with activity on a typical weekday.*

teeming /'tiː·mɪŋ/ *adj* [not gradable] filled with the activity of many people or things ○ *He was enchanted by the teeming streets and outdoor markets in the village.*

teenager /'tiː ˌneɪ·dʒər/, *short form* **teen** /tiːn/ *n* [C] a person who is 13 through 19 years old

teenage /'tiː·neɪdʒ/, **teenaged** /'tiː·neɪdʒd/, *short form* **teen** /tiːn/ *adj* [not gradable] ○ *They have two teenage sons.*

teens /tiːnz/ *pl n* **1** the years when you are 13 through 19 years old ○ *He hosted his own radio show while still in his teens.* **2** The teens are also the numbers 13 through 19: *Temperatures today will range from the teens to the twenties in the northeast.*

teeny /'tiː·ni/ *adj* [-er/-est only] *infml* small or little ○ *a teeny baby* ○ *I can't help thinking you're a teeny bit jealous.*

teepee /'tiː·piː/ *n* [C] a TEPEE

tee shirt /'tiː·ʃɜrt/ *n* [C] a T-SHIRT

teeter /'tiːt̬·ər/ *v* [I always + adv/prep] to appear to be about to fall while moving or standing ○ *They teetered around the room like two toddlers, helpless with laughter.* ○ *(fig.) The city is teetering on the brink/edge of* (= dangerously close to) *a financial calamity.*

teeter-totter /'tiːt̬·əˌtɑt̬·ər/ *n* [C] a SEESAW

teeth **TOOTH** /tiːθ/ *pl of* TOOTH

POWER /tiːθ/ *pl n* effective force or power ○ *This committee can make recommendations but it has no real teeth to enforce them.*

teethe /tiːð/ *v* [I] (of a baby or small child) to grow teeth ○ *The baby was often cranky because she was teething.*

Teflon /'tef·lɑn/ *n* [U] *trademark* a chemically-produced substance that is put on the inside of cooking pans to keep food from sticking

tel. *n* [C] *abbreviation for* TELEPHONE ○ **USAGE:** Used esp. in writing.

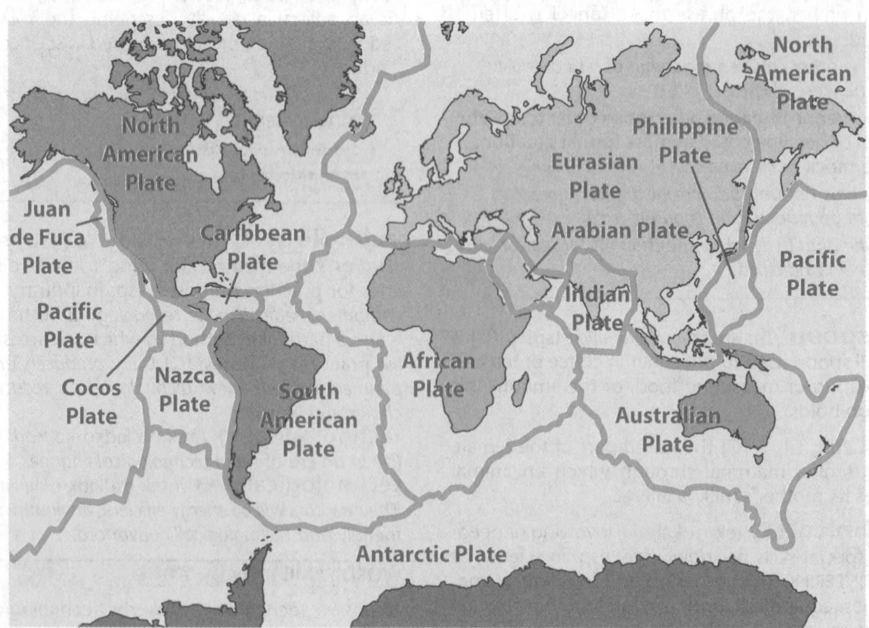

TECTONIC PLATES

telecom /ˈtel·əˌkɑm/ *n* [C] a TELECOMMUNICATIONS company (= one that provides telephone and related services) ○ *Nearly every company involved in telecom is adopting Internet telephony technology in some way.*

telecommunications /ˌtel·ə·kəˌmjuː·nəˈkeɪ·ʃənz/ *pl n* the sending and receiving of messages by computer, telephone, radio, and television, or the business of doing this

telecommuting /ˈtel·ə·kəˌmjuːt̬·ɪŋ/ *n* [U] the activity of working for a company but staying at home and communicating with an office by computer and telephone
telecommuter /ˈtel·ə·kəˌmjuːt̬·ər/ *n* [C] ○ *There are now millions of telecommuters with virtual offices.*

telegram /ˈtel·əˌɡræm/, **wire** *n* [C] a message sent by TELEGRAPH

telegraph /ˈtel·əˌɡræf/ *n* [U] a method of sending and receiving messages by electric signals that was used in the past, or the equipment used to do this
telegraph /ˈtel·əˌɡræf/, **wire** *v* [T] ○ *Reporters telegraphed details of the trial to their editors.*

telemarketing /ˈtel·əˌmɑr·kət̬·ɪŋ/ *n* [U] the selling of goods or services by telephone

telepathy /təˈlep·ə·θi/ *n* [U] communication with another person by thinking rather than by using words or other signals

telephone /ˈtel·əˌfoʊn/, **phone** *n* [C/U] a device for speaking to someone in another place by means of electrical signals ○ [C] *Your telephone is ringing.* ○ [U] *I tried to reach her by telephone.*
telephone /ˈtel·əˌfoʊn/ *v* [T] ○ *Palmer telephoned her attorney.*

USAGE

telephone and phone

Telephone and **phone** are both used to mean the device.

Can I use your phone/telephone, please?

People usually use **phone** or **call** for the verb meaning "to use a phone."

I'll phone you this evening.

I'll call you later.

When the phone rings, you **pick** it **up**, **answer** it, or **get** it.

Can you get the phone?

When you finish a phone call, you **hang up**.

Don't hang up – I can explain everything!

telephone book *n* [C] a PHONE BOOK

telephone number *n* [C] a PHONE NUMBER

telephone pole, **utility pole** *n* [C] a tall pole to which telephone or electrical wires are attached

telescope DEVICE /ˈtel·əˌskoʊp/ *n* [C] a cylindrical device that you look through to make objects that are far away look nearer and bigger
telescopic /ˌtel·əˈskɑp·ɪk/ *adj* [not gradable] ○ *My camera's telescopic lens lets me take great close-ups.*

SHORTEN /ˈtel·əˌskoʊp/ *v* [T] to shorten something ○ *Redford telescoped decades of history into a two-hour TV show.*

telethon /ˈtel·əˌθɑn/ *n* [C] a long television show broadcast to collect money for a CHARITY (= an organization that helps people)

televise /ˈtel·əˌvɑɪz/ *v* [T] to broadcast an event or show on television ○ *The game will be televised live from Cincinnati.*
televised /ˈtel·əˌvɑɪzd/ *adj* [not gradable] ○ *a televised speech*

television /ˈtel·əˌvɪʒ·ən/, *abbreviation* **TV** *n* [C/U] **1** a large box with a viewing screen which receives electrical signals and changes them into moving pictures and sound ○ [C] *Most homes have televisions.* **2** Television is also the programs that you watch, or the business of broadcasting them: [U] *Is there anything interesting on television tonight?* ○ [U] *Your problem is that you watch too much television.*

USAGE

television

Be careful to say **on** television when you are talking about the programs that you watch.

There's never anything worth watching on television.

~~*There's never anything worth watching in television.*~~

Be careful to choose the correct verb with television. You **watch** television. You do not **look** television.

Most children watch too much television.

~~*Most children look too much television.*~~

tell SAY /tel/ *v* [I/T] *past* **told** to say something to someone, esp. to give instructions or information; report ○ [T] *Can you tell me how to get to the bus station?* ○ [I] *She told about her travels overseas.* ➤ Usage: **say or tell?** at SAY SPEAK

USAGE

tell

Remember to use the preposition **about** in the phrase **tell** *someone* **about** *something.*

Tell me about your trip – where did you go?

~~*Tell me your trip – where did you go?*~~

WORD CHOICES tell

See also: **say**

Let someone know is a common phrase that means the same as "tell."

***Let me know** if you'd like to come.*

The verb **give** can be used when you tell someone some information.

*Can you **give** the message to Jo?*

*He **gave** me a few details of what had happened.* ➤

Inform or **notify** can be used when someone tells a person some facts, especially in an official situation.

The names of the injured will not be released until their relatives have been ***informed*** *of the accident.*

The school is required to ***notify*** *parents if their children fail to arrive at school.*

If someone tells a person official information, you could, in formal English, use the verb **advise.**

They were ***advised*** *of their rights.*

The verbs **relate** and **recount** are used in formal English when someone tells a story or talks about a series of events that have happened.

She ***related*** *the events of the previous week to the police.*

He ***recounted*** *his adventures since he had left home.*

The phrasal verb **pass something on** can be used when you tell someone something that another person has told you.

John told me they were getting engaged but please don't ***pass it on*** *to anyone else.*

If someone tells something to a lot of people, the phrase **spread the word** is sometimes used.

I've arranged the meeting for next Tuesday so if you see anyone, ***spread the word.***

If you tell someone some bad news which will affect them, you could use the phrase **break the news.**

I didn't want to be the one to ***break the news*** *to him.*

SHOW /tel/ *v* [T] *past* **told** to show or give information in ways other than talking ○ *This light tells you when the battery is low.*

ORDER /tel/ *v* [T] *past* **told** to order someone to do something ○ *I told you to be home by eleven.*

KNOW /tel/ *v* [I/T] *past* **told** to know or recognize ○ [I] *It's hard to tell which is better.* ○ [T] *It's easy to tell a robin by its red breast.* ○ [+ (*that*) clause] *I could tell that you were unhappy.* ○ [T] *This one is supposed to be better, but how can you tell the difference?*

T

IDIOMS with tell

• **I'm telling you, I'll tell you** believe me when I say this ○ *I'm telling you, he's the best player in the American League.* ○ *We've been waiting a long time for this, I'll tell you.* ○ **USAGE:** Used to emphasize what you are saying.

• **tell it like it is** to describe a situation honestly without avoiding any unpleasant details ○ *I want a newspaper that tells it like it is, without any opinion or political bias.*

• **tell me about it** *infml* I feel the same way or I have had the same experience ○ *"He's driving me crazy with his bad jokes." "Tell me about it!"*

• **tell** (*someone*) **the truth** to speak honestly ○ *Ok, tell me the truth, did you take her purse?*

• **(I) tell you what** I will make you this offer ○ *I tell you what, we'll pay for your plane ticket.*

• **tell time** to be able to read the time from a clock ○ *Has Adam learned to tell time yet?*

• **to tell** (*you*) **the truth** I have to admit ○ *To tell the truth, I couldn't hear a word he said.*

PHRASAL VERBS with tell

• **tell** *someone/something* **apart** to recognize the difference between people or things that are similar ○ *Many people have a hard time telling less expensive perfumes apart.*

• **tell off** *someone* [M] to criticize someone angrily ○ *Rob told off his boss, then quit.*

• **tell on** *someone infml* to give information about someone's bad behavior or secrets ○ *If you don't stop hitting, I'm going to tell on you.*

teller /ˈtel·ər/ *n* [C] a person in a bank who receives and pays out money to customers

telltale /ˈtel·teɪl/ *adj* important because of showing information ○ *These are some of the telltale signs of termites.*

telophase /ˈtel·əˌfeɪz, tiː·lə-/ *n* [U] ***biology*** the last stage in cell division

temp /temp/ *n* [C] *infml* a person employed to work temporarily for a business

temp /temp/ *v* [I] *infml* ○ *I temped for a long time.*

temper STATE /ˈtem·pər/ *n* [C/U] **1** the state of your mind or feelings ○ [C] *John has a bad temper.* **2** Temper is also strong emotion, esp. anger: [U] *a fit of temper* ○ [C] *You need to learn to control your temper.* **3** A temper tantrum is a sudden show of great anger.

LESSEN /ˈtem·pər/ *v* [T] to lessen the force or effect of something ○ *Perhaps you should temper your language.*

temperament /ˈtem·prə·mənt/ *n* [C/U] the emotional character or state of mind of people or animals, as shown in their behavior ○ [C] *Their temperaments are very different.* ○ [U] *Trudy has the nicest temperament of all our dogs.*

temperamental /ˌtem·prəˈment·əl/ *adj* [not gradable] **1** expressive of your emotional character ○ *a temperamental young man* **2** If a machine is temperamental, it sometimes works and sometimes does not: *Our VCR can be temperamental.*

temperance /ˈtem·pə·rəns/ *n* [U] ***social studies*** the habit or practice of avoiding extremes of behavior, esp. not drinking too much alcohol

temperate /ˈtem·pə·rət/ *adj* [not gradable] not extreme; within a middle range ○ *The climate here is pretty temperate.*

temperature /ˈtem·pə·rə·tʃər, -ˌtʃʊr/ *n* [C/U] **1** the measured amount of heat in a place or in the body ○ [C] *Temperatures should reach the 50s today.* ○ [U] *An increase in temperature is normal.* **2** A temperature is also a fever: [C] *You have a temperature.*

tempest /ˈtem·pəst/ *n* [C] a violent storm

IDIOM with tempest

• **tempest in a teapot** something of no importance that causes a great deal of excitement or trouble ○ *It seemed like an innocent remark, but it set off a tempest in a teapot.*

tempestuous /tem'pes·tʃə·wəs/ *adj* violently emotional ○ *They finally broke up, ending their tempestuous relationship.*

template /'tem·plət/ *n* [C] a shape made of metal, plastic, or paper which is used to make copies or to help someone cut something accurately ○ *The use of templates is crucial to stone carving.*

temple BUILDING /'tem·pəl/ *n* [C] a building used for religious worship

PART OF HEAD /'tem·pəl/ *n* [C] the flat area at each side of the upper part of the face

tempo /'tem·poʊ/ *n* [C/U] *pl* **tempos** **1** the speed of a movement or activity ○ [U] *Tracy likes the tempo of city life.* **2** ***music*** Tempo is also the speed at which music is played, sometimes written as a number at the beginning of a piece: [C] *It sounded like they were playing at different tempos.*

temporary Ⓐ /'tem·pəˌrer·i/ *adj* [not gradable] not lasting or PERMANENT ○ *a temporary condition* ○ *a temporary contract*

temporarily Ⓐ /ˌtem·pə'rer·ə·li/ *adv* [not gradable] ○ *The player was temporarily suspended from the tournament.*

WORD CHOICES temporary

The phrase **for now** can be used to say that something should happen or be done now but can be changed later.

Just put everything on the table ***for now*** *– I'll sort it all out later.*

The adjective **disposable** can be used to describe objects which are intended to be used temporarily and then thrown away.

I bought a ***disposable*** *camera at the airport.*

If something is temporary and low quality, you can say that it is **makeshift**.

We built a ***makeshift*** *shelter under the trees.*

The adjective **short-lived** can be used instead of temporary when it means "lasting for a short time."

I had a few relationships in college, most of which were fairly ***short-lived****.*

The adjectives **provisional** or **interim** can be used when something is temporary because it is likely to change soon.

After the war, a ***provisional*** *government was set up.*

This is only an ***interim*** *solution.*

The adjective **acting** is often used to describe someone who does a job temporarily while the person who usually does it is not there.

He'll be the ***acting*** *director until they appoint a permanent one.*

tempt /temt/ *v* [T] to encourage someone to want to have or do something, esp. something wrong ○ *I'm trying to diet – don't tempt me with that cake!*

temptation /tem'teɪ·ʃən/ *n* [C/U] ○ [U] *It's not easy to resist temptation.* ○ [C] *Ice cream is always a real temptation for me.*

tempting /'tem·tɪŋ/ *adj* [not gradable] ○ *Any free offer is always tempting.*

IDIOM with tempt

• **tempt fate** to take a foolish risk because you depend too much on luck ○ *Leaving your door unlocked is just tempting fate.*

ten /ten/ *number* **1** 10 ○ *The twins are ten.* ○ *a ten-seat minivan* **2** Ten can also mean ten o'clock.

tenth /tenθ/ *adj, adv, n* [C] **1** *My sister spoke tenth, right after me.* ○ [C] *It was the tenth of May.* **2** A tenth is one of ten equal parts of something.

tenacious /tə'neɪ·ʃəs/ *adj* [not gradable] unwilling to accept defeat or stop doing or having something ○ *Seles is a tenacious opponent – she never gives in.*

tenacity /tə'næs·əṭ·i/ *n* [U] ○ *They cling with admirable tenacity to their traditions.*

tenant /'ten·ənt/ *n* [C] a person who rents a room, a building, or land ○ *For years, they were tenants on my father's property.*

tend BE LIKELY /tend/ *v* [I] to be likely to happen or to have a particular characteristic or effect ○ *We tend to eat at home.* ○ *Children tend to be like their parents.*

tendency /'ten·dən·si/ *n* [C] ○ *She has a tendency to work late.* ○ *There's a growing tendency to try kids as adults.*

CARE /tend/ *v* [T] to care for something or someone ○ *He carefully tends his garden all summer.*

tender GENTLE /'ten·dər/ *adj* gentle, caring, or sympathetic ○ *He gave her a tender kiss.*

PAINFUL /'ten·dər/ *adj* easily hurt; painful ○ *My arm was very tender after the injection.*

SOFT /'ten·dər/ *adj* (of food) easily cut or chewed ○ *My steak was juicy and tender.*

tenderize /'ten·dəˌrɑɪz/ *v* [T] ○ *Certain ingredients and cooking methods tenderize tough foods.*

YOUNG /'ten·dər/ *adj* [not gradable] young and not experienced ○ *At the tender age of 17, he joined the army.*

OFFER /'ten·dər/ *v* [T] to offer something, usually in writing, or to make an offer in writing to do something ○ *The Secretary wants to leave but has not yet tendered his resignation.* ○ *This is the richest contract ever tendered to a baseball player.*

tender /'ten·dər/ *n* [C] a formal offer, esp. to buy something

tenderhearted /'ten·dər'hɑrṭ·əd/ *adj* gentle and caring ○ *He was extremely tenderhearted with little children.*

tendon /'ten·dən/ *n* [C] ***biology*** a strong cord that connects a muscle to a bone and allows movement, esp. of the arms, legs, and head

tendril /'ten·drəl/ *n* [C] a thin stem of a plant that twists and curls, or anything similar, such as a curl of hair

T

tenement /ˈten·ə·mənt/ *n* [C] a type of apartment building, esp. one with many small apartments that is in a poor area

tenet /ˈten·ət/ *n* [C] a principle that is an accepted belief of a particular group ○ *A major tenet of the women's movement has been that society needs their talents.*

tennis /ˈten·əs/ *n* [U] a game played on a specially marked playing area in which two or four people use RACKETS to hit a small ball across a center net

tennis shoe *n* [C] a SNEAKER, esp. one designed especially for playing tennis

tenor VOICE /ˈten·ər/ *n* [C] a man's singing voice in the highest range, or a person or musical instrument with this range

CHARACTER /ˈten·ər/ *n* [U] the character or usual pattern of something ○ *Suddenly the tenor of the meeting changed, and people started insulting each other.*

tense Ⓐ ANXIOUS /tens/ *adj* **1** anxious, unable to relax, or causing anxiety ○ *She was very tense as she waited for the interview.* ○ *The family was faced with a tense financial situation.* **2** If a situation is tense, it causes feelings of worry or anxiety.

tension Ⓐ /ˈten·tʃən/ *n* [U] **1** anxiety and worry ○ *The tension was unbearable as we waited for our exam results.* **2** Tension is also an anxious situation of anger and lack of trust between two groups of people.

tensely Ⓐ /ˈten·sli/ *adv*

STIFF /tens/ *adj* tight and stiff ○ *Relax! Why are you so tense?*

tense Ⓐ /tens/ *v* [I/T] ○ [T] *He tensed his body just before diving from the high board.* ○ [I] *She tensed up as the car went faster and faster.*

tension Ⓐ /ˈten·tʃən/ *n* [U] ○ *We need more tension in the wires, so pull them tighter.*

tensely Ⓐ /ˈten·sli/ *adv*

VERB FORM /tens/ *n* [C] ***grammar*** any of the forms of a verb which show the time at which an action happened ○ *"I sing" is in the present tense and shows action happening now, and "I will sing" is in the future tense, showing action that will happen later.*

tent /tent/ *n* [C] a movable shelter, usually made of a strong cloth supported by poles and held in position by ropes fixed to the ground ○ *We pitched our tents near the stream.*

tentacle /ˈtent·ɪ·kəl/ *n* [C] a long, thin, arm of some sea animals, such as the OCTOPUS and JELLYFISH

tentative /ˈtent·ət̬·ɪv/ *adj* not certain or confident ○ *We have tentative plans to go to Hawaii in February.*

tentatively /ˈtent·ət̬·ɪv·li/ *adv* ○ *We have tentatively agreed to buy that house.*

tenth /tenθ/ *adj, adv, n* See at TEN.

tenuous /ˈten·jə·wəs/ *adj* weak, unimportant, or in doubt ○ *The aging dictator's hold on power is tenuous.*

tenure /ˈten·jər/ *n* [U] the period of time when someone holds a job, esp. an official position, or the right to keep a job permanently ○ *During his tenure as mayor, relations with the police department worsened.* ○ *Michelle has tenure in her new teaching position.*

tepee, **teepee, tipi** /ˈtiː·piː/ *n* [C] a type of round tent made from animal skins and supported by a frame of poles, used by some American Indians

tepid /ˈtep·əd/ *adj* [not gradable] (of liquid) not very warm, or (of feelings or actions) not very strong ○ *There is only tepid support in Congress for the proposal.*

tequila /təˈkiː·lə/ *n* [C/U] a strong alcoholic drink originally from Mexico

term TIME /tɜrm/ *n* [C] **1** a period of time during which something lasts ○ *Watson's term as chairman expired last month.* ○ *He served a prison term for robbery.* ○ *This budget plan is good for the long term but it hurts in the short term.* **2** A term can be one of the periods into which a year is divided at a school or college: *I'm taking computer programming during the fall term.*

EXPRESSION /tɜrm/ *n* [C] **1** a word or phrase used in relation to a particular subject ○ *Erikson is said to have coined the term "identity crisis."* **2** ***mathematics*** A term is also any number, VARIABLE (= symbol), or PRODUCT (= result of mutiplying). ○ See also: TERMS

term /tɜrm/ *v* [T] ○ *None of the problems was termed serious.*

terminal Ⓐ DEADLY /ˈtɜr·mən·əl/ *adj* [not gradable] (of a disease or illness) leading to death ○ *His mother has a terminal illness.*

terminally /ˈtɜr·mən·əl·i/ *adv* [not gradable] ○ *terminally ill cancer patients*

BUILDING /ˈtɜr·mən·əl/ *n* [C] the place where a train, bus, aircraft, or ship begins or ends a trip, or the building used by passengers who are arriving or leaving ○ *Your flight leaves from Terminal 3.*

ELECTRICITY /ˈtɜr·mən·əl/ *n* [C] a point at which a connection can be made to an electrical CIRCUIT (= system through which electricity flows)

COMPUTER /ˈtɜr·mən·əl/ *n* [C] a piece of equipment used for communicating with a computer, esp. a KEYBOARD and screen

terminal moraine *n* [C] ***earth science*** the large mass of rocks and dirt that is left by a melting GLACIER (= large mass of ice) at its farthest point of movement

terminate Ⓐ /ˈtɜr·məˌneɪt/ *v* [I/T] *fml* **1** to end or stop, or to cause something to end or stop ○ [I] *Trains that used to terminate in Hoboken now run into New York.* ○ [T] *It sounded like she was trying to terminate the conversation.* **2** An employee who is terminated no longer has a job: [T] *Employees can be terminated if they miss too much work without good reason.*

termination Ⓐ /ˌtɜr·məˈneɪ·ʃən/ *n* [C/U] ○ [U] *The contract provides for termination after two years.*

terminology /ˌtɜr·məˈnɑl·ə·dʒi/ *n* [U] special words or expressions used in relation to a particular subject or activity ○ *sports terminology* ○ *scientific terminology*

termite /ˈtɜr·mɑɪt/ *n* [C] a small, pale insect that eats wood

term paper *n* [C] the main report written by a student for a particular class

terms /tɜrmz/ *pl n* **1** the conditions that are part of an agreement or arrangement, or the features of an activity or idea ○ *He violated the terms of the agreement.* ○ *She considers results in purely economic terms.* ○ *I want to leave this job on my own terms.* **2** If two people are on good/bad/friendly terms, they have a good/bad/friendly relationship with one another: *He was on good terms with important people in Brazil.* ○ See also: TERM WORD

IDIOM with terms

• **in terms of** *something* in relation to something ○ *We try to do what is best for our customers in terms of the quality of our products.*

terrace /ˈter·əs/ *n* [C] a flat area outside a building, often with a stone floor, or a narrow, flat strip of land on the slope of a hill that is used for growing crops

terra cotta /ˌter·əˈkɑt̬·ə/ *n* [U] hard, baked, red-brown clay ○ *terra-cotta tiles*

terra firma /ˌter·əˈfɜr·mə/ *n* [U] dry or solid land, when compared with the sea or air ○ *He stepped off the ladder onto terra firma.*

terrain /təˈreɪn/ *n* [U] an area of land, esp. when considering its natural features ○ *rugged mountain terrain*

terrestrial /təˈres·triː·əl/ *adj* [not gradable] ***earth science*** relating to the planet earth, or living or existing on the land rather than in the sea or air ○ *Newton investigated terrestrial and celestial motion.* ○ *marine and terrestrial environments*

terrible /ˈter·ə·bəl/ *adj* very unpleasant or serious or bad ○ *I saw terrible things happen.* ○ *My mother was a terrible cook.*

terribly /ˈter·ə·bli/ *adv* **1** (usually about something bad or unpleasant) very much ○ *I'm terribly disappointed I couldn't be there.* **2** Sometimes terribly is used to emphasize something good: *I'm terribly excited about tonight's show.*

terrier /ˈter·iː·ər/ *n* [C] any of several types of small, active dogs

terrific VERY GOOD /təˈrɪf·ɪk/ *adj* very good or enjoyable ○ *Kate looks absolutely terrific tonight.*

VERY GREAT /təˈrɪf·ɪk/ *adj* used to emphasize the great amount or degree of something ○ *This book has had a terrific influence on me.*

terrifically /təˈrɪf·ɪ·kli/ *adv* ○ *That's not a terrifically good idea.*

terrify /ˈter·əˌfɑɪ/ *v* [T] to frighten someone severely ○ *His looks are enough to terrify anyone.*

terrified /ˈter·əˌfɑɪd/ *adj* ○ *She's always been terrified of spiders.*

terrifying /ˈter·əˌfɑɪ·ɪŋ/ *adj* ○ *a terrifying experience*

territory /ˈter·əˌtɔːr·i, -ˌtoʊr·i/ *n* [C/U] an area of land, sea, or space, esp. when it belongs to or is connected with a particular country, person, or animal ○ [U] *Maryland gave up territory to form Washington, DC.* ○ [C] *The UN is sending aid to the occupied territories.*

territorial /ˌter·əˈtɔːr·iː·əl, -ˈtoʊr-/ *adj* [not gradable] ○ *He served as territorial governor.* ○ *Some animals are territorial* (= they defend particular areas against other animals).

IDIOM with territory

• **go with the territory, come with the territory** to be part of a particular activity ○ *Criticism goes with the territory in politics.*

terror /ˈter·ər/ *n* [C/U] **1** extreme fear, or violent action that causes fear ○ [U] *She was screaming in terror as the flames got closer.* ○ [C] *You can't hide from the terrors of the world.* **2** A terror is also a child who behaves badly and is difficult to control: [C] *My brother is a little terror.*

terrorize /ˈter·əˌrɑɪz/ *v* [T] ○ *Wild dogs terrorized the neighborhood.*

terrorism /ˈter·əˌrɪz·əm/ *n* [U] ***social studies*** violent action for political purposes

terrorist /ˈter·ə·rəst/ *n* [C]

terse /tɜrs/ *adj* using few words ○ *He was shouting terse orders for vehicles to pull over.*

tersely /ˈtɜr·sli/ *adv* ○ *"Storm coming," he said tersely.*

TESL /ˈtes·əl/ *n* [U] *abbreviation for* teaching English as a second language

TESOL /ˈtiː·sɑl, -sɔːl/ *n* [U] *abbreviation for* teaching English to speakers of other languages

test /test/ *n* [C] **1** a set of questions or practical activities that show what someone knows or what someone or something can do or is like ○ *a spelling test* **2** A test is also a medical examination of part of your body or of something from your body: *an eye test* ○ *a DNA test* **3** A test is also an act of using something to find out whether it is working correctly or how effective it is: *a safety test*

test /test/ *v* [T] **1** *Multiple-choice questions tested the students' knowledge.* ○ *We test every component we make.* **2** To test people or things can also be to present them with a situation which shows how good they are at dealing with difficulties: *His generation was tested by a world war.*

tester /ˈtes·tər/ *n* [C] **1** someone who tests something, esp. a new product ○ *Our 11-year-old tester pronounced the gadget "very cool."* **2** A tester is also a device or machine that performs tests ○ *a battery tester*

testing /ˈtes·tɪŋ/ *n* [U] ○ *Statewide testing begins this fall.*

IDIOMS with test

• **stand the test of time, withstand the test of time** to work well over a long period of time ○ *The US Constitution has withstood the test of time.*

• **test the water(s)** to find out whether something is likely to be successful before you do or try it ○

T

Candidates like to test the waters before running for office.

testament /ˈtes·tə·mənt/ *n* [C/U] **1** proof of something ○ [C usually sing] *He is a walking testament to the value of hard work.* **2** A testament is also a WILL DEATH PLAN.

test ban *n* [C] an agreement between countries to stop testing nuclear weapons

test case *n* [C] a case in a court that establishes principles which are used to decide other similar cases in the future

test-drive /ˈtes·drɑɪv/ *v* [T] *past simp.* **test-drove**, *past part.* **test-driven** to drive a car that you are considering buying in order to see if you like it

test drive /ˈtes·drɑɪv/ *n* [C] ○ *We went for a test drive in the new Toyota.*

testicle /ˈtes·tɪ·kəl/ *n* [C] *pl* **testicles, testes** either of the two round male sex organs that produce sperm and are enclosed in the SCROTUM (= bag of skin) near the PENIS

testify /ˈtes·tə͵fɑɪ/ *v* to speak seriously about something, esp. to tell what you know about a case in a court of law after you have officially promised to tell the truth ○ [I] *Elizabeth testified before a grand jury.* ○ [+ *that* clause] *One witness testified that she saw the thief running away.*

testimony /ˈtes·tə͵moʊ·ni/ *n* [C/U] a spoken or written statement that something is true, esp. one given in a court of law, or the act of giving such a statement ○ [U] *The value of their testimony is questionable.*

testosterone /tesˈtɑs·tə͵roʊn/ *n* [U] ***biology*** a male HORMONE (= chemical substance produced in the body) that causes growth and body changes in older boys

test pilot *n* [C] someone whose job is to fly new aircraft in order to make sure that they work correctly

test tube *n* [C] ***science*** a small glass tube with one closed end that is used in some scientific experiments

TEST TUBE

testy /ˈtes·ti/ *adj* lacking patience and feeling upset ○ *My wife gets testy if we don't have dessert.*

tetanus /ˈtet·ᵊn·əs/ *n* [U] an infectious disease that causes the muscles esp. around the mouth to become stiff

tête-à-tête /͵tet̬·əˈtet, ͵teɪt̬·əˈteɪt/ *n* [C] a private conversation between two people ○ *a romantic tête-à-tête*

tether /ˈteð·ər/ *n* [C] a rope, chain, or other device used to attach a person or animal to a fixed object

tether /ˈteð·ər/ *v* [T] ○ *Asthma kept him tethered to an oxygen tank.*

tetrad /ˈte·træd/ *n* [C] ***biology*** a group of four cells produced during cell division

tetrahedron /͵te·trəˈhiː·drən/ *n* [C] *pl* **tetrahedrons, tetrahedra** ***geometry*** a solid shape with four flat, triangular surfaces of equal size ➤ Picture: **solid**

Tex-Mex /ˈtekˈsmeks/ *adj* [not gradable] referring to the Mexican-American culture existing in Texas and the southwestern US ○ *In Texas the food is all Tex-Mex cooking and barbecue.*

text Ⓐ **WRITING** /tekst/ *n* [C/U] written or printed material ○ [U] *The text is based on Irish legends.*

textual Ⓐ /ˈteks·tʃə·wəl/ *adj* [not gradable] relating to written or printed material ○ *textual errors/analysis*

SEND /tekst/ *v* [T] to send a TEXT MESSAGE ○ *If I texted him and didn't see a response within 15 minutes, I would worry.*

textbook BOOK /ˈteks·bʊk/ *n* [C] a book that provides reading and exercises for a school or college course ○ *medical textbooks*

TYPICAL /ˈteks·bʊk/ *adj* [not gradable] usual or typical ○ *The group's rise to stardom is a textbook case of how to make it in the recording industry.*

textile /ˈtek·stɑɪl, ˈteks·təl/ *n* [C] a cloth, esp. one that is woven ○ *Imports of textiles rose last year.*

text message *n* [C] a short message you send to someone's CELLULAR PHONE by pushing buttons for letters on your phone ○ *Customers can also get text messages alerting them of traffic tie-ups.*

text messaging *n* [U]

texture /ˈteks·tʃər/ *n* [C/U] **1** the quality of something that can be known by touch, or the degree to which something is rough or smooth or soft or hard ○ [U] *Wall hangings add texture to a room.* ○ [C] *She uses unique colors and textures in her paintings.* **2** ***art*** The texture of a work of art is the features of the surface of it, which comes from the materials used to make it. **3** ***music*** The texture of a piece of music is a feature of the way it sounds, based on how the different instruments mix their parts and the speed at which they play.

textured /ˈteks·tʃərd/ *adj* ○ *textured fabrics* ○ (*fig.*) *The book is a richly textured re-creation of life in the early 1900s* (= it has a lot of detail).

than /ðæn, ðən/ *prep, conjunction* **1** used to join two parts of a comparison ○ *My brother's older than you.* ○ *You're earlier than usual.* **2** Than is used with more or less to compare numbers or amounts: *He wrote more than 20 books.* ○ *He spent less than a year there.*

thank /θæŋk/ *v* [T] **1** to express appreciation to someone for something the person has done ○ *Don't thank me, thank my father – he paid for it.* **2** *disapproving* If you thank someone for something bad, you mean that the person is responsible for it: *You can thank John for this disaster.*

thankful /ˈθæŋk·fəl/ *adj* pleased or grateful ○ [+ *that* clause] *I was thankful that school was over.*

thankfully /ˈθæŋk·fə·li/ *adv* ○ *It's been hard work, but thankfully it's finished.*

thankless /ˈθæŋ·kləs/ *adj* unlikely to be appreciated ○ *a thankless task* ○ **USAGE**: usually said about a job or some work

thanks /θæŋks/ *pl n* **1** appreciation and pleasure because of something that has been done for you ○ *I want to offer a word of thanks to all those who helped.* **2 Thanks to** means because of: *Thanks to Sandy, I found this great apartment.*

WORD FAMILY thank			
Nouns	thanks	*Verbs*	thank
Adjectives	thankful thankless	*Adverbs*	thankfully

IDIOM with thank

• **thank God**, **thank goodness** I am happy that something bad has been avoided or has finished ○ *Spring is coming at last, thank goodness.*

Thanksgiving /θæŋksˈgɪv·ɪŋ/, **Thanksgiving Day** *n* [C/U] a national holiday on the fourth Thursday in November in the US and on the second Monday in October in Canada, when families get together for a big meal and express their appreciation for life, health, etc.

thank you, *infml* **thanks** *exclamation* used to express appreciation to someone for offering or giving you something, for helping you, or for asking how you are feeling ○ *Thank you for calling.* ○ *Thanks for cleaning up.* ○ *"How are you?" "Fine, thank you."*

thank you /ˈθæŋ·kjuː/ *n* [C] something you say or do to express your appreciation for something ○ *You deserve a big thank you.* ○ *He wrote a thank you note to his grandmother for the birthday present.*

that SOMETHING NOT HERE /ðæt, ðət/ *pronoun, adj* [not gradable] *pl* **those 1** used to refer to a person, object, event, etc., separated from the speaker by distance or time, or to something that has been referred to before, or to point to a particular thing ○ *This peach isn't ripe – can I have that one* (= the one farther away) *on the table?* ○ *Put that box* (= the particular box referred to) *down before you drop it.* ○ *Where's that pen* (= the one I was using earlier)*?* ○ *If she could play like that* (= the way she is now playing) *every day, she'd be a star.* ○ *She called him an imbecile, and at that* (= immediately after that) *he stormed out of the room.* **2** That is also used to make a connection with an earlier statement: *My usual train was canceled. That's why I'm late.* ○ *I didn't know she'd been so ill. That's terrible.* **3** You say **that is** when you want to give further details or be more exact about something: *I should be there by seven, that is, unless there's a lot of traffic.* ○ Compare THIS THING REFERRED TO

INTRODUCING A CLAUSE /ðæt, ðət/ *conjunction* used to introduce a clause reporting something or giving further information, although it can often be omitted ○ *She said (that) she'd pick up Michael after work.* ○ *It's possible (that) there'll be a job opening in a few weeks.* ○ *It was so dark (that) I couldn't see anything.* ➤ Usage: **which, who, or that?** at WHICH USED TO REFER

USED TO REFER /ðæt, ðət/ *pronoun* used to show what particular thing is being referred to ○ *Have you been to the new restaurant that just opened?* ○ *That's the guy I was talking about.* ➤ Usage: **this/these or that/those?** at THIS THING REFERRED TO

AS MUCH /ðæt, ðət/ *adv* [not gradable] as much as suggested ○ *It cost at least that much, if not more.* ○ *The movie really wasn't that good* (= was not very good).

IDIOMS with that

• **that's (about) it**, **that's that** *infml* there is no more to be said or done ○ *OK everybody, I think that's it. You can all go home.* ○ *We talked about the election – that was about it.* ○ *I won't agree to it and that's that.*

• **that's life** you have to accept what happens, even if it is not exactly what you wanted ○ *I've had some good jobs and some not so good, but that's life.*

• **that's more like it** *infml* that is an improvement ○ *Try again and see if you can do better – yes, that's more like it.*

that'd /ˈðæṱ·əd/ *contraction of* that would or that had ○ *That'd* (= That would) *be nice, don't you think?* ○ *When it happened, I didn't realize that'd* (= that had) *been the reason.*

that'll /ˈðæṱ·əl/ *contraction of* that will ○ *I don't think that'll be happening next year.*

that's /ðæts/ *contraction of* that is or that has ○ *That's* (= That is) *just my opinion.* ○ *That's* (= that has) *got to be the dumbest thing I've ever seen.*

thaw /θɔː/ *v* [I] to cause something frozen and hard to become warmer and often softer or liquid ○ *Remove the meat from the freezer and let it thaw.* ○ *It may take a couple of hours to thaw out.*

thaw /θɔː/ *n* [C usually sing] **1** a period of warmer weather when snow and ice begin to melt ○ *With the spring thaw, the rivers and lakes swelled.* **2** A thaw is also a change to a friendlier attitude esp. between people or countries that were enemies: *It was hoped that the agreement to exchange athletes would lead to a thaw in relations between the two countries.*

the PARTICULAR /ðiː, ðə/ *definite article* **1** used before a noun to refer to a particular thing because it is clear which thing is intended ○ *I just bought a new shirt and tie. The shirt was expensive, but the tie wasn't.* ○ *There's someone at the front door.* ○ *I'll pick you up at the airport at 6 o'clock.* **2** "The" is used before some nouns to refer to a type of activity or thing intended: *Let's go to the movies.* **3** "The" is used to refer to things or people when only one exists at any one time: *the Statue of Liberty* **4** "The" is also used before superlatives and other words, such as first or only or numbers: *What's the highest mountain in North America?* ○ *She's leaving on the 24th of May.* **5** "The" can mean each or every: *My car gets 30 miles to the gallon.* **6** When used before some adjectives, "the" changes the adjective into a noun to refer to all of what is described: *the homeless/poor/rich* **7** You can use "the" before a singular noun to refer to all the

T

things or people represented by that noun: *Nicole is learning to play the piano.* **8** You use "the" before numbers that refer to periods of 10 years: *the 1930s*

YOUR /ðiː, ðə/ *definite article* used instead of your, my, his, her, etc. ○ *He tapped me on the* (= my) *shoulder.* ○ *How are Grace and the* (= her) *kids?*

ENOUGH /ðiː, ðə/ *definite article* enough ○ *He hasn't got the experience for this kind of work.*

theater **BUILDING**, **theatre** /ˈθiː·əṭ·ər, θiːˈeṭ·ər/ *n* [C] a building, room, or outside structure with rows of seats, each row usually higher than the one in front, from which people can watch a performance, a movie, or another activity ○ *Lincoln Plaza Cinema has five movie theaters.*

PERFORMING ARTS, **theatre** /ˈθiː·əṭ·ər, θiːˈeṭ·ər/ *n* [U] the art or activity of writing and performing plays, or the public performance of plays ○ *We have tickets to the theater tonight* (= to watch a performance).

theatrical /θiːˈæ·trɪ·kəl/ *adj* **1** *theatrical performances* **2** Theatrical also means intended to attract attention, as if acting in a play: *He threw out both arms to greet me in a theatrical gesture.*

theft /θeft/ *n* [C/U] the act of taking something that belongs to someone else and keeping it; stealing ○ [U] *car theft*

their /ðer, ðær, ðər/ *pronoun* [pl] **1** belonging to or connected with them; the possessive form of they, used before a noun ○ *It was their money, and they could spend it as they liked.* **2** *infml* Their is also used to refer to a person whose sex is not known: *Someone forgot to take their umbrella.*

theirs /ðerz, ðærz/ *pronoun* [pl] belonging to them, or that which belongs to them ○ *Here's my car. Where's theirs?*

them /ðem, ðəm/ *pronoun* [pl] **1** the things or people being spoken about, who have already been mentioned; the objective form of they ○ *I lost my keys and I can't find them anywhere.* **2** Them is also used to refer to a person whose sex is not known: *As each person arrives, we ask them to fill out a form.*

T

thematic Ⓐ /θiːˈmæṭ·ɪk/ *adj* based on a subject or group of subjects ○ *The author has adopted a thematic rather than a chronological approach to the French Revolution.*

thematically Ⓐ /θiːˈmæṭ·ɪk·li/ *adv*

theme Ⓐ **SUBJECT** /θiːm/ *n* [C] **1** topic of discussion or writing ○ *The theme of the conference was the changing role of women in modern society.* **2** ***literature***, ***art*** A theme is also the main idea of a work of literature or art.

MUSIC /θiːm/ *n* [C] **1** a short, simple tune on which a piece of music is based **2** ***music*** **Theme and variation** is a musical form in which a theme is played and then repeated several times with small changes in interesting ways.

theme music *n* [U] music that is written for and played during a particular television program or movie ○ *From down the hall the theme music of the network news blared from Nana's TV.*

theme park *n* [C] a large, permanent area for public entertainment, with amusements, rides, food, etc., all connected with a single subject

theme song *n* [C] a piece of music from a television show, movie etc. that is remembered as the music that represents that show or movie

themselves /ðemˈselvz, ðəm-/ *pronoun* [pl] **1** the people being spoken about, the reflexive form of they ○ *The girls made themselves sandwiches for lunch.* **2** Themselves is sometimes used to emphasize the subject or object of a sentence: *The police themselves apologized for overreacting.* **3** If people do something **(all) by themselves**, they do it alone or without help from anyone: *The children set up the tent all by themselves.* ○ *They were left by themselves.* **4** If people have something **to themselves**, they have it for their own use only: *When their youngest child went off to college, they had the whole house to themselves.*

then **TIME** /ðen/ *adj, adv* [not gradable] at that time (in the past or in the future) ○ *She was then sixteen years old.* ○ *Soon the sun will go down, and then it will be time to go.*

NEXT /ðen/ *adv* [not gradable] next or after that ○ *He smiled, then turned to me and nodded.*

IN ADDITION /ðen/ *adv* [not gradable] in addition ○ *We both want to go, and then there's Carmen, so we need three tickets.*

AS A RESULT /ðen/ *adv* [not gradable] as a result; in that case; also used as a way of joining a statement to an earlier piece of conversation ○ *Why don't you call them to tell them we'll be late? Then they won't worry.* ○ *If I don't hear from you by Friday, then I'll assume you're not coming.*

IDIOMS with then

• **then again** *infml* but after thinking about it ○ *It would be fun to see them – then again, I don't really have the time.*

• **then and there** *infml* immediately ○ *She walked in and I decided to tell her then and there.*

theocracy /θiːˈɑk·rə·si/ *n* [C] ***politics & government*** government that is controlled by religious leaders, or a country with such a government

theology /θiːˈɑl·ə·dʒi/ *n* the study of religion and religious belief, or a set of beliefs about a particular religion

theologian /ˌθiː·əˈloʊ·dʒən/ *n* [C] a person who studies or is a specialist in religion ○ *a Catholic/Protestant theologian*

theological /ˌθiː·əˈlɑdʒ·ɪ·kəl/ *adj* ○ *The minister had attended the Princeton Theological Seminary.*

theorem /ˈθɪr·əm/ *n* [C] ***mathematics*** a statement that can be shown to be true

theoretical Ⓐ /ˌθiː·əˈreṭ·ɪ·kəl/ *adj* based on theory or on possibilities ○ *The president does not want to answer any theoretical questions.*

theoretically Ⓐ /ˌθiː·əˈreṭ·ɪ·kli/ *adv*

theory Ⓐ /ˈθɪr·i, ˈθiː·ə·ri/ *n* [C/U] something suggested as a reasonable explanation for facts, a condition, or an event, esp. a systematic or scientific explanation ○ [U] *Adele took a course in modern political theory.* ○ [C] *I have a theory* (= an opinion) *about why everybody in the city is in such a hurry.*

theorist Ⓐ /ˈθɪr·əst, ˈθiː·ə·rəst/ *n* [C] someone who develops ideas that explain events or behavior ○ *a political theorist*

theorize /ˈθiː·əˌrɑɪz/ *v* [I] to suggest an explanation for something ○ *Investigators theorized that ice had built up on the wings of the plane, causing it to stall soon after takeoff.*

WORD FAMILY theory			
Nouns	theory	*Verbs*	theorize
Adjectives	theoretical	*Adverbs*	theoretically

IDIOM with theory

• **in theory** possibly ○ *They could, in theory, have been paid twice if someone hadn't caught the error.*

therapeutic /ˌθer·əˈpjuːt̬·ɪk/ *adj* having a healing effect; tending to make a person healthier ○ *For arthritis sufferers, moderate exercise is therapeutic.*

therapy /ˈθer·ə·pi/ *n* [C/U] treatment to help a person get better from the effects of a disease or injury ○ [U] *With physical therapy, you should eventually be able to walk again.*

therapist /ˈθer·ə·pəst/ *n* [C] ○ *a physical/speech therapist*

there PLACE /ðer, ðær/ *adv* [not gradable] in, at, or to that place ○ *Put the chair there.* ○ *The museum was closed today, so we'll go there tomorrow.*

INTRODUCING A SENTENCE /ðer, ðær/ *pronoun* used to introduce sentences, esp. before the verbs be, seem, and appear ○ *There's someone on the phone for you.* ○ *There will be plenty of time to pack tomorrow.*

IDIOMS with there

• **there's no (such thing as a) free lunch** there is always a cost for something you want ○ *In return for extra profit, investors take on additional risk, proving that there is no such thing as a free lunch.*

• **there's no telling** it is not possible to know ○ *There's no telling how her parents will react to the news.*

thereafter /ðerˈæf·tər, ðær-/ *adv* [not gradable] continuing on from a particular point in time, esp. after something else has stopped happening ○ *For the first month you'll be working here, and thereafter in Chicago.*

thereby Ⓐ /ðerˈbɑɪ, ðær-/ *adv* [not gradable] because of this; as a result of this action ○ *They had failed to agree to a settlement, thereby throwing 250 people out of work.*

there'd /ðerd, ðærd/ *contraction of* there would or there had ○ *She assured me there'd* (= there would) *be a practice this morning.* ○ *They put up the sign because there'd* (= there had) *been an incident in the past.*

therefore /ˈðer·fɔːr, ˈðær-, -foʊr/ *adv* [not gradable] as a result; because of that; for that reason ○ *We were unable to get funding and therefore had to abandon the project.*

therein /ðerˈɪn, ðær-/ *adv fml* in or into a particular place, thing, or condition ○ *Therein lies the risk* (= Here is the risk).

thereof /ðerˈʌv, ðær-/ *adv fml* from that cause, or of that ○ *The fund pays for tuition and books, or a portion thereof.*

there's /ðerz, ðærz/ *contraction of* there is or there has ○ *There's* (= There is) *no place like home.* ○ *There's* (= There has) *never been such an exciting election as this.*

thermal /ˈθɜr·məl/ *adj* **1** of, connected with, or preserving heat **2** Thermal underwear is underwear that has been specially designed to keep you warm.

thermodynamics /ˌθɜr·moʊˌdɑɪˈnæm·ɪks/ *n* [U] ***physics*** the part of physics that deals with the relationship between heat and other types of energy

thermometer /θərˈmɑm·ət̬·ər, θəˈmɑm-/ *n* [C] a device used for measuring temperature, esp. of the air or in a person's body

thermos /ˈθɜr·məs (ˈbɑt̬·əl)/ *n* [C] a special bottle that keeps liquids hot inside two layers of glass

thermostat /ˈθɜr·məˌstæt/ *n* [C] a device that controls the temperature of a system by automatically switching the supply of heat or cool air on and off when the temperature becomes too cool or too hot

thesaurus /θəˈsɔːr·əs/ *n* [C] *pl* **thesauri, thesauruses** a book or electronic text that helps you find words with similar meanings esp. by listing them together

these /ðiːz/ *pl of* THIS THING REFERRED TO

IDIOM with these

• **these days** *infml* now ○ *I used to talk to my sister every night. These days, we hardly speak to each other.*

thesis Ⓐ /ˈθiː·səs/ *n* [C] *pl* **theses 1** a piece of writing involving original study of a subject, esp. for a college or university degree ○ *a master's thesis* **2** A thesis is also the main idea, opinion, or theory of a speaker or writer, who then attempts to prove it: *His thesis was that World War I could have been avoided.*

they /ðeɪ/ *pronoun* [pl] **1** the things or people being spoken about, who have already been mentioned ○ *Where are my glasses? They were on the table a minute ago.* ○ *They* (= People who know) *say we're going to get some rain.* **2** They is also used to refer to a person whose sex is not known: *"There is someone on the phone for you." "What do they want?"*

they'd /ðeɪd/ *contraction of* they had or they would ○ *They'd* (= They would) *come if you asked them to.* ○ *They'd* (= They had) *better be here on time.*

they'll /ðeɪl, ðel/ *contraction of* they will or they shall ○ *They'll be in Baltimore for the next few days.*

they're /ðer, ðər/ *contraction of* they are ○ *They're taking attendance.*

they've /ðeɪv, ðəv/ *contraction of* they have ○ *They've always paid their bills promptly in the past.*

thick DEEP /θɪk/ *adj* [*-er/-est* only] having a large distance from one side of something to the opposite side ○ *a thick book/steak* ○ *The walls are a foot thick.*

thickly /ˈθɪk·li/ *adv* ○ *thickly carpeted floors*

thickness /ˈθɪk·nəs/ *n* [C/U]

CLOSE TOGETHER /θɪk/ *adj* [*-er/-est* only] (of particular things) close together with little space between them ○ *a thick fog* ○ *She had wonderful, thick, brown hair.*

NOT FLOWING /θɪk/ *adj* [*-er/-est* only] **1** (of a liquid) not flowing easily ○ *thick gravy/soup* **2** *fig.* If your voice is thick, it is lower than usual and not as even, usually because you are feeling a strong emotion: *Tony could hardly speak, and when he did his voice was thick with emotion.*

thicken /ˈθɪk·ən/ *v* [T] ○ *Thicken the gravy with a little flour.*

WORD FAMILY thick

Nouns	thickness	*Verbs*	thicken
Adjectives	thick	*Adverbs*	thickly

thicket /ˈθɪk·ət/ *n* [C] an area of trees and bushes growing closely together

thick-skinned *adj* not easily hurt by criticism

thief /θiːf/ *n* [C] *pl* **thieves** a person who steals ○ *The thieves stole $10,000 and several pieces of jewelry.*

thigh /θɑɪ/ *n* [C] the part of a person's leg below the hip and above the knee

thimble /ˈθɪm·bəl/ *n* [C] a small, hard cover, shaped like a cup, that fits over the end of a finger to help you push a needle through material when sewing

thin NOT DEEP /θɪn/ *adj* [*-er/-est* only] **-nn-** having a small distance from the top to the bottom side ○ *thin summer clothing* ○ *The statue is coated with a thin layer of gold.*

thinly /ˈθɪn·li/, **thin** /θɪn/ *adv* ○ *Thinly sliced cheese is good for sandwiches.*

NOT FAT /θɪn/ *adj* [*-er/-est* only] **-nn-** having little extra flesh on the body ○ *thin arms/legs* ○ *a thin face* ○ *Models must be tall and thin.*

WORD CHOICES thin

Skinny or **scrawny** are words that mean "very thin" and are usually used when you disapprove.

You should eat more. You're much too ***skinny****.*

He hated his ***scrawny*** *legs.*

Slim or **slender** can be used when someone is thin in an attractive way.

He was tall, very ***slim****, with pale, deepset hazel eyes.*

He put his arms around her ***slender*** *waist.*

If a woman is short and thin in an attractive way, you could describe her as **petite**.

She was a ***petite*** *woman with long blonde hair.*

Emaciated is a formal word that you could use to describe someone who is thin and weak, especially because of illness or extreme hunger.

Emaciated *refugees streamed into neighboring countries.*

Gaunt can be used when someone looks thin and ill.

He looked at her tired and ***gaunt*** *face.*

Bony can be used about parts of someone's body when they are very thin.

long ***bony*** *fingers*

FEW /θɪn/ *adj* [*-er/-est* only] **-nn-** having only a few of something covering an area; not dense ○ *His hair is thin on top.* ○ *Where there is little rain, grass and trees get thinner.*

thin /θɪn/ *v* [I/T] **-nn-** ○ [I] *Traffic thins out after seven o'clock.* ○ [T] *An improving economy helped thin unemployment lines.*

FLOWING EASILY /θɪn/ *adj* [*-er/-est* only] **-nn-** (of a liquid) flowing easily ○ *We began dinner with a thin but tasty soup.*

thinner /ˈθɪn·ər/ *n* [C] a substance that makes a liquid flow more easily ○ *Paint thinner comes in gallon cans.* ○ *Aspirin is an effective blood thinner.*

WEAK /θɪn/ *adj* [*-er/-est* only] **-nn-** lacking force or substance; weak ○ *a thin, metallic tone* ○ *I thought the plot was a bit thin.* ○ *We slept poorly that night in the thin mountain air.*

thinly /ˈθɪn·li/ *adv* ○ *It was a thinly disguised attempt to gain control.*

WORD FAMILY thin

Nouns	thinner	*Verbs*	thin
Adjectives	thin	*Adverbs*	thinly

IDIOM with thin

• **vanish into thin air**, **disappear into thin air** to disappear suddenly and completely ○ *The ship simply vanished into thin air.*

thing OBJECT /θɪŋ/ *n* [C] **1** a device, product, or part of nature that is not named ○ *There's a new thing that seals plastic bags.* ○ *There are some nice things in the stores on sale right now.* **2 Your things** are your small personal possessions: *Get your things together and we'll leave.*

ANY POSSIBILITY /θɪŋ/ *n* [C] **1** an event, thought, subject of discussion, or possibility ○ *A strange thing happened on my way to work today.* ○ *I have a few things to bring up at the next meeting.* ○ *Don't* *worry about a thing – it's all under control.* **2** Things can refer to a situation in general: *Things have been going really well for us this year.*

PERSON/ANIMAL /θɪŋ/ *n* [C] a person or animal ○ *When did you eat last, you poor thing?* ○ **USAGE:** This is used to refer to a person or animal affectionately or sympathetically.

IDIOM with thing

• **the thing is** *infml* this is the subject you have to consider ○ *The thing is, my car broke down, so how can I drive?*

thingamajig /ˈθɪŋ·ə·məˌdʒɪɡ/, **thingy** /ˈθɪŋ·i/ *n* [C] *infml* (esp. in spoken English) a thing, the name of which has been forgotten ○ *He stood there holding this thingamajig.*

think HAVE OPINION /θɪŋk/ *v* [I/T] *past* **thought** to have or to form an opinion or idea about something ○ [T] *"Do you think this is the right address?" "I don't think so."* ○ [I] *It doesn't make much sense when you think about it.* ○ [I/T] *Cloning animals has happened sooner than anyone thought (it would).* ○ [T] *I always thought he was a bit weird.* ○ [I] *What do you think of my new hat?* ○ [I] *I'll always think of him as someone I can rely on.* ○ [+ (that) clause] *I think (that) I'd better go now.* ○ *I still* **think of** *my***self as** (= believe I am) *her friend.*

thinking /ˈθɪŋ·kɪŋ/ *n* [U] the process of forming an opinion or idea about something, or the opinions or ideas formed by this process ○ *I feel that his thinking is outdated in some ways.* ○ *Several new books have changed my thinking about terrorism.*

USE REASON /θɪŋk/ *v* [I] *past* **thought** to use your mind to understand matters, make judgments, and solve problems ○ *I'll have to think about this.* ○ *She was thinking about running for the Senate.* ○ *I can't think of anything to say right now.*

thinker /ˈθɪŋ·kər/ *n* [C] ○ *He's a creative thinker and a good administrator.*

thinking /ˈθɪŋ·kɪŋ/ *n* [U] ○ *I've done some serious thinking about our relationship.* ○ *Thinking, for me, is hard work!*

USAGE

think about or think of?

Think about *someone/something* means to have thoughts in your mind about a person or thing, or to consider them.

I was thinking about my mother.

I thought about the question before answering.

~~*I thought the question before answering.*~~

What do you think of/about *someone/something***?** is also used when asking someone to give their opinion.

What do you think of/about the color?

~~*What do you think the color?*~~

Think of *doing something* means to consider the possibility of doing something.

We are thinking of having a party.

~~*We are thinking to have a party.*~~

WORD CHOICES think

See also: **believe**

If you are thinking about a possibility or about making a decision, the verb **consider** is often used.

Don't make any decisions before you've ***considered*** *the matter.*

If someone spends a lot of time thinking about something in a serious way, you can use the verbs **contemplate**, **ponder**, or **mull over**.

He lay in a hospital bed ***contemplating*** *his future.*

She sat back for a minute to ***ponder*** *her next move in the game.*

I need a few days to ***mull*** *things* ***over*** *before I decide.*

Reflect is a formal word that means "to think carefully, especially about possibilities and opinions."

I spent a lot of time ***reflecting*** *on what he'd said.*

If you think about something anxiously for a long time, you could use the verb **agonize**.

She ***agonized*** *for days about whether she should take the job.*

Brood or **dwell on** are used when someone thinks about something for a long time in a way that makes that person unhappy.

She sat ***brooding*** *in her room for days after she and Gary split up.*

There's no point in ***dwelling on*** *the past.*

If you suddenly think about something, you can say that something **crosses your mind** or that something **strikes you**.

The thought suddenly ***crossed my mind*** *that I might not see him again.*

It's just ***struck me*** *that I haven't paid you yet for the tickets.*

If you are thinking very hard to remember something or to find a way to do something, you can use the phrase **rack your brain**.

I've been ***racking my brain*** *all day but I can't remember where I put my keys.*

If you think again about something in order to change or improve it, you can use the verbs **rethink** or **reconsider**.

Her family's disapproval made her ***rethink*** *her plans.*

He was ***reconsidering*** *whether to accept or not.*

REMEMBER /θɪŋk/ *v* [I always + adv/prep] *past* **thought** to remember or imagine ○ *I can't stop thinking about her.* ○ *I can picture her, I just can't think of her name.* ○ *Think back to the early days of the Civil War.*

WORD FAMILY think

Nouns	think rethink thinker thinking	*Adjectives* *Verbs*	unthinkable think rethink

T

IDIOMS with think

• **not think much of** *someone/something* to have a low opinion of someone or something ○ *I don't think much of this techno music.*
• **not think straight** to be unable to use your mind in an effective way ○ *I was so tired, I couldn't think straight.*
• **think better of** *something* to decide that something is not a good idea ○ *He considered quitting college but thought better of it.*
• **think for** *yourself* form opinions and solve problems without depending on other people's ideas ○ *She's intelligent and can think for herself.*
• **think long and hard** to take the time needed to understand something before making a decision about it ○ *I thought long and hard about it, and decided that I wouldn't have the operation.*
• **think nothing of** *something*, **not think twice about** *something* to find it easy to do something ○ *When I was younger, I thought nothing of running 20 miles a week.*
• **think on** *your* **feet** to think and react quickly, esp. having good answers ready ○ *When you're called on in class, you have to be able to think on your feet.*
• **think the world of** *someone/something*, **think highly of** *someone/something* to have a very high opinion of someone or something ○ *I think the world of my niece – she's a smart, loving girl.* ○ *His professors at Columbia think very highly of him.*
• **think twice** to consider something more carefully ○ *You might want to think twice before buying an insurance policy from them.* ○ **USAGE**: Often used as a warning.

PHRASAL VERBS with think

• **think** *something* **over/through** [M] to consider something carefully ○ *They've made me a good offer, but I'll have to think it over.* ○ *We can't make a decision until we've thought through the different possibilities.*
• **think up** *something* [M] to invent a plan or solution ○ *Just give him five minutes and he'll think up an excuse.*

think tank *n* [C] an organization whose work is to study specific problems and suggest solutions, often with a particular political view

T

thin-skinned *adj* easily hurt by criticism

third /θɜrd/ *adj, adv, n* [C] **1** (a person or thing) coming immediately after the second and before all others ○ *My horse finished third in the race.* ○ [C] *They were married on the third of November.* **2** A third is one of three equal parts of something. ○ Related Number: THREE

third base, *short form* **third** *n* [C usually sing] the third place a baseball player has to touch in order to score, or the position near this place played by a member of the team in the field

third-class, **third class**, **third-rate**. **third rate** *adj* of low quality ○ *The company is earning third-rate profits.*

third degree *n* [U] severe questioning of someone to find out as much as you can ○ *We gave the babysitter the third degree before we hired her.*

third-degree burn *n* [C] the most serious type of burn on the skin

third party POLITICAL GROUP *n* [C] ***social studies*** any political PARTY (= organization to get people elected) that is not as big or as influential as the two main parties

PERSON *n* [C] a person who is not one of the two main people involved in an argument or legal case

third person *n* [U] ***grammar*** the form of pronouns and verbs that people use when speaking or writing about other people ○ *"He," "him," and "his" are third person singular pronouns, and "they," "them," and "their" are third person plural pronouns.* ○ *Novels are usually written in the third person.* ○ Compare FIRST PERSON; SECOND PERSON

third rail *n* [C] a metal bar, running parallel with train tracks, that supplies electricity to some types of trains

Third World *n* [U] ***world history*** the countries in the world whose economies are least developed

thirst /θɜrst/ *n* [U] **1** the need or desire to drink something, esp. water ○ *He took a long drink of water to quench his thirst.* **2** A thirst is also a strong desire for something: *She slaked her thirst for knowledge by reading everything she could.*

thirsty /ˈθɜr·sti/ *adj* ○ *She was very thirsty but took only a few sips of water.* ○ (fig.) *Always thirsty for power, he would do anything to get it.*

WORD FAMILY thirst			
Nouns	thirst	*Adverbs*	thirstily
Adjectives	thirsty		

thirteen /θɜrˈtiːn/ *number* 13 ○ *The bus has thirteen seats for passengers.* ○ *a thirteen-story building*

thirteenth /θɜrˈtiːnθ/ *adj, adv, n* [C] **1** *He came in thirteenth in the marathon.* ○ [C] *The baby was born on the thirteenth of May.* **2** A thirteenth is one of thirteen equal parts of something.

thirty /ˈθɜrţ·i/ *number* 30 ○ *There are thirty students taking this course.* ○ *a thirty-mile journey*

thirties, **30s**, **30's** /ˈθɜrţ·iz/ *pl n* the numbers 30 through 39 ○ *My sisters are in their thirties* (= between 30 and 39 years old). ○ *The temperature is expected to be in the thirties* (= between 30° and 39°) *tomorrow.* ○ *These dresses were fashionable in the thirties* (= between 1930 and 1939).

thirtieth /ˈθɜrţ·iː·əθ/ *adj, adv, n* [C] **1** *Ashley's having a party to celebrate her thirtieth birthday.* ○ [C] *Today is the thirtieth of September.* **2** A thirtieth is one of thirty equal parts of something.

this THING REFERRED TO /ðɪs/ *adj, pronoun pl* **these 1** used for a person, object, or thing to show which one is referred to or has been referred to before ○ *This book is mine – yours is over there.* ○ *Try on these sunglasses to see how you look in them.* ○ *If you wear the scarf like this, it will look better.* ○ (infml) *So I said to this guy, "Do I know you?"* **2** This also refers to something that is nearest to the speaker in time and sometimes in space: *I've got to see the doctor again this Thursday.* ○ *By this time tomorrow, I'll be in Paris.* **3** People say **this is** to introduce someone: *Harry, this is Joan.* **4 This minute** or **this second** means now: *It doesn't have to be done this minute, but it should be done before lunch.* ○ Compare THAT SOMETHING NOT HERE

USAGE

this/these or that/those?

Use **this** or **these** to talk about people and things that are close to the speaker in space or time.

This is Sarah, who will be working with us for a few months.

Do you like these earrings I'm wearing?

Use **that** or **those** to talk about people and things that are further away from the speaker in space or time.

That girl over there is called Sarah.

I liked those earrings you wore last night.

AS MUCH /ðɪs/ *adv* [not gradable] as much as shown, or to a particular degree ○ *Can you jump this high?* ○ *She's never been this late before.*

IDIOMS with this

• **in this day and age** now, as opposed to an earlier time ○ *How do the police handle such disputes in this day and age?*

• **this side of** *somewhere infml* between here and the place mentioned ○ *This is the best pizza I've tasted this side of Chicago.*

thistle /ˈθɪs·əl/ *n* [C] a wild plant with sharp, pointed leaves and, typically, purple flowers

thong /θɔːŋ, θɑŋ/ *n* [C] **1** a light shoe, often made of rubber, consisting of a flat bottom attached to the foot by a narrow strap that fits between the big toe and the toe next to it **2** A thong is also a narrow strip of material used to fasten something or worn for swimming or as underwear.

thorn /θɔːrn/ *n* [C] a small, sharp, pointed growth on the stem of a plant ○ *Rose bushes have thorns.*

thorny /ˈθɔːr·ni/ *adj* [*-er/-est* only] **1** *Roses are thorny shrubs.* **2** A thorny problem is one that is full of difficulties: *The thorny issue of illegal immigration remains unresolved.*

IDIOM with thorn

• **thorn in** *your* **side**, **thorn in the side of** *someone* someone or something that continually causes problems for you ○ *Money problems have been a thorn in our side since the day we got married.* ○ *Health inspectors are a thorn in the side of most restaurants.*

thorough COMPLETE /ˈθɜr·oʊ, ˈθʌ·roʊ/ *adj* with nothing left out or omitted; complete ○ *The district attorney's office conducted a thorough investigation.* ○ *The doctor gave him a thorough medical examination.*

thoroughly /ˈθɜr·ə·li, ˈθʌ·rə-/ *adv* ○ *The drug was thoroughly tested before being put on the market.*

thoroughness /ˈθɜr·ə·nəs, ˈθʌ·rə-/ *n* [U] ○ *You can rely on the thoroughness of his research.*

VERY GREAT /ˈθɜr·oʊ, ˈθʌ·roʊ/ *adj* [not gradable] (used for emphasis) very great ○ *The meeting was a thorough waste of time.*

thoroughly /ˈθɜr·ə·li, ˈθʌ·rə-/ *adv* ○ *The movie left me thoroughly confused about its real meaning.* ○ *We thoroughly enjoyed the movie.*

thoroughbred /ˈθɜr·əˌbred, ˈθʌ·rə-/ *n* [C] a horse with good qualities typical of a particular breed and with parents that are officially recognized as being the same breed

thoroughfare /ˈθɜr·əˌfer, ˈθʌ·rə-, -ˌfær/ *n* [C] a road that connects to other roads ○ *I live right on the main thoroughfare.*

those /ðoʊz/ *pl of* THAT SOMETHING NOT HERE ○ *Those of you who would like to come with us should sign up now.* ○ *Those houses are huge.*

IDIOM with those

• **those were the days** life was better in the past ○ *"Do you remember when ice cream cones used to cost 50 cents?" "Yeah, those were the days!"*

thou /ðɑʊ/ *pronoun old use* you ○ *Thou shalt* (= You shall) *not kill.*

though /ðoʊ/ *conjunction* despite the fact that; although ○ *There's a chance he'll recover, though the doctors can't say for certain.* ○ *Even though I was very young, I remember a little about the war.*

though /ðoʊ/ *adv* despite this ○ *He felt a little guilty about being overpaid, though he wasn't about to give it back.*

thought THINK /θɔːt/ *past simple and past participle of* THINK

THINKING /θɔːt/ *n* [C/U] the act of thinking about something to form ideas and opinions, or an idea or opinion produced by thinking ○ [U] *I have given this matter considerable thought.* ○ [C] *Do you have any thoughts on what we should do now?* ○ [C] *That fact never entered my thoughts.* ○ [U] *His early religious training helped to shape his thought.* ○ [C] *It's just a thought, but since it's such a beautiful day, why don't we go for a drive?* ○ [U] *The very thought of standing up in front of an audience scares me to death.*

thoughtful /ˈθɔːt·fəl/ *adj* **1** tending to think seriously about things ○ *You're looking very thoughtful – what's on your mind?* **2** Thoughtful also means showing care and consideration in how you treat other people: *"Oh, how thoughtful of you," Dina said, opening the gift.*

thoughtfully /ˈθɔːt·fə·li/ *adv* ○ *He answers questions thoughtfully* (= after thinking seriously).

thoughtfulness /ˈθɔːt·fəl·nəs/ *n* [U] ○ *She was surprised by the thoughtfulness* (= kindness) *of people who wanted to help her.*

thoughtless /ˈθɔːt·ləs/ *adj* not showing care for others ○ *I'm sorry I was late – it was thoughtless of me not to call.*

T

thoughtlessly /ˈθɔːt·lə·sli/ *adv* ○ *He thoughtlessly made an unkind remark about her mother.*

WORD FAMILY thought			
Nouns	thought thoughtfulness	*Adverbs*	thoughtfully thoughtlessly
Adjectives	thoughtful thoughtless		

thousand /ˈθɑʊ·zənd/ *number* 1000 ○ *A thousand people came to the game.* ○ *a thousand-dollar ring*

thousandth /ˈθɑʊ·zənθ/ *adj, adv, n* [C] **1** *You are our one thousandth customer.* **2** A thousandth is one of a thousand equal parts of something.

thrash /θræʃ/ *v* [I/T] **1** to make a series of wild, violent movements ○ [I] *The startled animal thrashed around in the stall.* **2** To thrash a person or animal means to hit the person or animal hard and repeatedly: [T] *He hit me once, and if you hadn't come along, he would have thrashed me.* **3** *fig.* To thrash also means to defeat badly: [T] *Atlanta thrashed New York, 119-87.*

PHRASAL VERB with thrash

• **thrash out** *something* [M] to discuss a problem completely in order to solve it ○ *These issues will be thrashed out in court.*

thread FIBER /θred/ *n* [C/U] **1** a very thin twisted string of esp. cotton or silk, used mostly for sewing ○ [U] *It takes practice to use a needle and thread well.* ○ [C] *There's a loose thread on your dress.* **2** A thread is also something continuous that connects different ideas or thoughts together: [C] *A common thread runs through their various experiences.* ○ [U] *A ringing phone interrupted the thread of her story.*

thread /θred/ *v* [T] to put thread through the hole in a needle, or to put something narrow through a small opening ○ *to thread a needle* ○ *He threaded a thin strip of tape through the machine.* ○ (*fig.*) *She threaded her way through the crowd* (= moved along a narrow path to go around people in her way).

TWISTING CUT /θred/ *n* [C] a continuous cut that twists around the outside of a screw or around an opening, as on a pipe ○ *The threads are worn, and I can't tighten the screw.*

threadbare /ˈθred·ber, -bær/ *adj* (of material) looking worn and thin from much use ○ *Her clothes were faded and threadbare.*

threat PROMISE TO HURT /θret/ *n* [C] a statement that someone will be hurt or harmed, esp. if the person does not do something in particular ○ *She was fired after making threats to her co-workers.*

threaten /ˈθret·ᵊn/ *v* [I/T] ○ [I] *They threatened to drop him from the team if he didn't come to practice.* ○ [T] *Don't threaten me!*

threatening /ˈθret·ᵊn·ɪŋ/ *adj* ○ *She received several threatening phone calls after her appearance on television.*

UNWANTED POSSIBILITY /θret/ *n* [C/U] the possibility that something unwanted will happen, or a person or thing that is likely to cause something unwanted to happen ○ [U] *A threat of rain is in today's forecast.* ○ [U] *The boundary dispute raised the threat of war.*

threaten /ˈθret·ᵊn/ *v* [T] to warn of something unpleasant or unwanted ○ *She threatened legal action against the newspaper.* ○ *Because of continuing drought, millions are threatened with starvation.*

threatening /ˈθret·ᵊn·ɪŋ/ *adj* ○ *Threatening skies meant a storm was coming.*

WORD FAMILY threat			
Nouns	threat	*Verbs*	threaten
Adjectives	threatening	*Adverbs*	threateningly

three /θriː/ *number* **1** 3 ○ *Ann-Marie has three children.* ○ *a three-bedroom house* **2** Three can also mean three o'clock. ○ Related Number: THIRD

three-dimensional Ⓐ, *abbreviation* **3-D** *adj* ***art*** having or appearing to have height, length, and width ○ *a three-dimensional computer image*

threesome /ˈθriː·səm/ *n* [C] *infml* three people as a group ○ *These guys do as good a job as any threesome in broadcasting.*

thresh /θreʃ/ *v* [T] to remove the seeds of crop plants by hitting, using either a machine or a hand tool

threshold STARTING POINT /ˈθreʃ·hoʊld/ *n* [C/U] a point at which something starts ○ [C] *a low threshold for pain* ○ [U] *We are on the threshold of a new era.*

ENTRANCE /ˈθreʃ·hoʊld/ *n* [C] the part of a floor at the entrance to a building or room ○ *It's traditional for a man to carry his bride over the threshold.*

threw /θruː/ *past simple of* THROW

thrift /θrɪft/ *n* [C/U] *dated* **1** the careful use of money, esp. by avoiding waste ○ [U] *Trina learned thrift from her mother.* **2** *dated* A thrift is also a type of bank.

thrifty /ˈθrɪf·ti/ *adj* ○ *They have plenty of money now, but they're still thrifty.*

thrift store, **thrift shop** *n* [C] a store that sells used things such as clothes, books, and furniture

thrill /θrɪl/ *n* [C] a feeling of great excitement and pleasure ○ *It gave me a thrill to see her again after so many years.*

thrill /θrɪl/ *v* [I/T] ○ [T] *Just standing next to him thrilled her.*

thrilled /θrɪld/ *adj* extremely pleased ○ *My parents weren't too thrilled when they found out.*

thriller /ˈθrɪl·ər/ *n* [C] a book, play, or movie that has an exciting and frightening story

thrilling /ˈθrɪl·ɪŋ/ *adj* very exciting ○ *a thrilling adventure*

thrive /θrɑɪv/ *v* [I] to grow, develop, or be successful ○ *She seems to thrive on hard work.*

thriving /ˈθrɑɪ·vɪŋ/ *adj* very healthy or successful ○ *The dog is thriving in its new home.*

throat /θroʊt/ *n* [C] the front of the neck, or the space inside the neck down which food and air can go ○ *A cop grabbed him around the throat.* ○ *I have a sore throat.* ○ *He cleared his throat and started speaking.*

throaty /ˈθroʊţ·i/ *adj* having a low sound ○ *a throaty voice/laugh*

throb /θrɑb/ *v* [I] **-bb-** to produce a regular, forceful beat ○ *His head throbbed with pain.*

throb /θrɑb/ *n* [C/U] ○ [U] *We could feel the throb of the music from the party upstairs.*

throes /θroʊz/ *n* difficulties or pain ○ *He was* **in the throes of** *despair after losing his job.*

throne /θroʊn/ *n* [C] a special chair used by a king or queen, or the condition of being such a ruler ○ *He is heir to the throne.*

throng /θrɔːŋ/ *n* [C] a large group of people ○ *A huge throng had gathered around the speaker.*

throng /θrɔːŋ/ *v* [I/T] ○ [T] *The narrow streets were thronged with tourists.* ○ [I always + adv/prep] *Reporters thronged around her.*

throttle CONTROL /ˈθrɑţ·əl/ *n* [C] a device that controls how much fuel goes into an engine

PRESS THROAT /ˈθrɑţ·əl/ *v* [T] to try to kill someone by pressing the throat so that the person cannot breathe ○ *I'm so mad I could throttle him.*

through ACROSS /θruː/ *adj, adv* [not gradable] **1** from one side or end to the other, from one part to another, or from the beginning to the end ○ *We drove through the tunnel* ○ *We took a shortcut through the woods.* ○ *Have you read the report all the way through?* **2** If you drive through a red light or stop sign, you do not stop at it.

FINISHED /θruː/ *adj, adv* [not gradable] finished or completed ○ *Are you through with that book?* ○ *My girlfriend says we're through* (= our relationship is over).

DURING /θruː/ *adj, adv* [not gradable] during a period of time, esp. from the beginning to the end ○ *We sat through two lectures and then left.* ○ *She had just enough energy to get through the day.* ○ *I work Tuesdays through Saturdays* (= each day during this period).

AS A RESULT /θruː/ *prep* as a result of ○ *Bob learned of the contract through a story in the newspaper.*

USING /θruː/ *prep* by; using ○ *Schools are financed through property taxes.*

IDIOMS with through

• **fall through the cracks, slip through the cracks** to not be noticed or dealt with ○ *Little details often fall through the cracks.* ○ *Too many young people slip through the cracks in the health system.*
• **through and through** completely ○ *My mother is Italian through and through.*
• **through thick and thin** in good times and bad times ○ *My brother has stuck with me through thick and thin.*

throughout /θruːˈaʊt/ *adj, adv* [not gradable] in every part, or during the whole period of ○ *Grass grows throughout the world.* ○ *She was calm throughout her visit to the dentist.*

throughway /ˈθruː·weɪ/ *n* [C] a THRUWAY

throw SEND THROUGH AIR /θroʊ/ *v* [I/T] *past simp.* **threw**, *past part.* **thrown** to send something through the air, esp. by a sudden movement of the arm ○ [T] *Throw me the ball./Throw the ball to me.* ○ [I] *I didn't throw as well as I expected to.* ○ [T] *He was thrown from his motorcycle.*

throw /θroʊ/ *n* [C] ○ *She timed her throw so the ball reached the base when he did.*

WORD CHOICES throw

Toss, and in informal English, **chuck** can be used when someone throws something in a careless way.

She ***tossed*** *the keys into her bag and went out.*

He read the letter and ***chucked*** *it into the trash can.*

If someone throws something somewhere with a lot of force, you could use the verbs **fling** or **hurl**.

He crumpled up the letter and ***flung*** *it into the fire.*

In a fit of temper he ***hurled*** *the book across the room.*

Lob is used when someone throws something in a high curve.

The boys spent an hour ***lobbing*** *stones into the lake.*

If someone **pelts** a person or thing, they throw a lot of things at that person or thing very quickly.

They ***pelted*** *each other with snowballs on the way home from school.*

MOVE QUICKLY /θroʊ/ *v* [T] *past simp.* **threw**, *past part.* **thrown** to move something quickly or with a lack of attention, or to cause someone or something to move quickly ○ *He threw the switch and the lights came on.* ○ *He grabbed the snake and threw it to the ground.* ○ [M] *They threw up their hands to protect themselves from the hail.* ○ [M] *He threw his head back and laughed.* ○ [M] *Throw a few peppers in the pot.*

CONFUSE /θroʊ/ *v* [T] *past simp.* **threw**, *past part.* **thrown** *infml* to confuse someone ○ *That question really threw me at first.*

IDIOMS with throw

• **throw a party** to have a party ○ *Janelle threw a party for Brad's 18th birthday.*
• **throw** *someone* **for a loop** to completely surprise someone ○ *When she told me she was married, it really threw me for a loop.*
• **throw** *someone* **in jail** to put someone in prison
• **throw in the towel** to admit that you are defeated or cannot do something any more ○ *Jim beat me for the fourth time, so I threw in the towel.*
• **throw** *yourself* **into** *something* to do something enthusiastically ○ *She's thrown herself into this new job.*
• **throw money at** *something* to spend a lot of money because you believe that only money can solve a problem ○ *Many people agree that throwing money at our schools has not produced good results.*
• **throw the book at** *someone* to punish someone as severely as possible ○ *The judge was not lenient – he threw the book at him.*

T

•**throw** *your* **weight around** to use your position or influence unfairly to get what you want ○ *His teammates didn't appreciate how he threw his weight around.*

PHRASAL VERBS with **throw**

•**throw away** *something* [M] to get rid of something by treating it as garbage ○ *When are you going to throw away those old magazines?* ○ Related adjective: THROWAWAY

•**throw in** *something* [M] *infml* to include something extra when selling something ○ *I bought a new sofa and they threw in a chair.*

•**throw on** *something* [M] *infml* to quickly put clothes on ○ *She threw on her jacket.*

•**throw off** *something* **REMOVE CLOTHES** [M] *infml* to quickly remove clothes ○ *He threw off his shirt.*

•**throw off** *something/someone* **CONFUSE** [M] to cause an amount to be wrong or a person to be confused ○ *They left very rich people out of the study so their spending would not throw off the results.* ○ *A busy morning can throw off my entire daily schedule.*

•**throw out** *something* **GET RID OF** [M] to get rid of something by treating it as garbage ○ *Throw it out!* ○ *I threw out everything we didn't eat.*

•**throw out** *someone* **FORCE TO LEAVE** [M] to force someone to leave a place ○ *I threw him out of my house.*

•**throw together** *something/someone* [M] to suddenly put people or things in one place without much planning ○ *We were thrown together at a conference.* ○ *I just threw the cake together at the last minute* (= made it quickly).

•**throw up** *(something)* [M] to vomit ○ *He threw up all over his shoes.* ○ *I fed the baby some fruit, but she threw it up.*

throwaway /ˈθroʊ·əˌweɪ/ *adj* [not gradable] designed to be used only once and then gotten rid of ○ *Throwaway cameras are light, compact, cheap, and simple.* ○ Related verb: THROW AWAY

throwaway line *n* [C] a remark that sounds unimportant because of the way the speaker says it

throwback /ˈθroʊ·bæk/ *n* [C] something that is like a thing from an earlier time ○ *This year's styles are throwbacks to the fashions of the 1940s.*

thrown /θroʊn/ *past participle of* THROW

thrush /θrʌʃ/ *n* [C] any of a large family of singing birds that includes the ROBIN

thrust /θrʌst/ *v* [always + adv/prep] *past* **thrust** to push suddenly and strongly ○ [T] *She thrust the money into his hand.* ○ [I] *He thrust at me with a stick.*

thrust /θrʌst/ *n* [C/U] **1** [C] *a sword thrust* ○ [C] *(fig.) The thrust* (= main point) *of her argument was the schools need improvement.* **2** ***physics*** Thrust is also the force produced by an engine that pushes in one direction.

thruway, throughway /ˈθruː·weɪ/ *n* [C] a wide road for fast-moving traffic, with a limited number of places where drivers can enter and leave it; an EXPRESSWAY ○ *the New York State Thruway*

thud /θʌd/ *n* [C] a sound made when something heavy hits a hard surface ○ *the thud of boots on the stairs*

thud /θʌd/ *v* [I always + adv/prep] **-dd-** ○ *Her bag thudded to the floor.*

thug /θʌg/ *n* [C] a man who acts violently, esp. a criminal ○ *Some thugs smashed his windows.*

thumb /θʌm/ *n* [C] the short finger that is at an angle to the other fingers ○ *How did you cut your thumb?*

thumb /θʌm/ *v infml*

IDIOMS with **thumb**

•**(give a/the) thumbs down** a sign of disapproval or opposition ○ *We applied for a loan, but the bank gave us the thumbs down.*

•**(give a/the) thumbs up** a sign of approval or support ○ *Legislators gave the thumbs up to new tax credits.*

•**thumb** *your* **nose at** *someone/something* to show a lack of respect toward someone or something ○ *Most pedestrians thumb their noses at jaywalking laws.*

PHRASAL VERB with **thumb**

•**thumb through** *something* to turn the pages of a book or magazine quickly and read only small parts ○ *I was thumbing through a magazine in the doctor's office.*

thumbnail ON FINGER /ˈθʌm·neɪl/ *n* [C] the nail on the thumb

SMALL PICTURE /ˈθʌm·neɪl/ *n* [C] a small copy of a larger picture on a computer, shown in this way to allow more to be seen on the screen ○ *You can choose whether you would like to view your photos as thumbnails or in a slide show.* ○ *thumbnail images*

/ˈθʌm·neɪl/ *adj* [not gradable] shorter or smaller than the usual length or size ○ *a thumbnail profile of the author* ○ *He gave a thumbnail sketch* (= a short description) *of life in Moscow in the 1960s.*

thumbtack /ˈθʌm·tæk/ *n* [C] a short, sharp pin with a flat, round top that can be pushed into soft wood or other material

thump /θʌmp/ *v* [I/T] to hit something, making a soft, heavy noise ○ [T] *He thumped his chest.*

thump /θʌmp/ *n* [C] ○ *I heard a thump upstairs.*

thunder /ˈθʌn·dər/ *n* [U] the sudden, loud noise that comes after a flash of lightning ○ *a clap of thunder*

thunder /ˈθʌn·dər/ *v* [I] ○ *The sky grew dark and it started to thunder.* ○ *The horses thundered past* (= moved making a lot of noise), *shaking the house.*

thunderous /ˈθʌn·də·rəs/ *adj* very loud ○ *thunderous applause*

thunderbolt /ˈθʌn·dərˌboʊlt/ *n* [C] a flash of lightning, esp. with the sound of thunder

thunderclap /ˈθʌn·dərˌklæp/ *n* [C] a single, loud sound of thunder

thundercloud /ˈθʌn·dərˌklɑʊd/, **thunderhead** /ˈθʌn·dərˌhed/ *n* [C] a large, dark cloud

thunderstorm /ˈθʌn·dərˌstɔːrm/ *n* [C] a rain storm with thunder and lightning

Thursday /ˈθɜrz·di, -deɪ/, *abbreviation* **Thur.**, *abbreviation* **Thurs.** *n* [C/U] the day of the week after Wednesday and before Friday

thus /ðʌs/ *adv* [not gradable] *fml* in this way, or with this result ○ *This plan will reduce waste, and thus cut costs.*

IDIOM with thus

• **thus far** until now ○ *We haven't had any problems thus far.*

thwart /θwɔːrt/ *v* [T] to stop something from happening or someone from doing something ○ *The city council thwarted his reform efforts.*

thyme /tɑɪm/ *n* [U] an herb with sweet-smelling leaves that is used to flavor foods in cooking

thyroid (gland) /ˈθɑɪ·rɔɪd (ˌglænd)/ *n* [C] ***biology*** a GLAND (= organ) in the front of the neck that helps to control growth and chemical processes in the body

thyroid-stimulating hormone *n* [C usually sing] ***biology*** TSH.

thyroxine /θɑɪˈrɑk·siːn, -sən/ *n* [U] ***biology*** the main chemical produced in the body by the THYROID (GLAND) (= organ in the neck), which increases the METABOLISM (= changing of food into energy) and in this way, makes the body grow and develop

tiara /tiːˈær·ə, -ˈer·ə, -ˈɑr·ə/ *n* [C] a piece of jewelry worn on the head by a woman at very formal social occasions

tic /tɪk/ *n* [C] a sudden, small, uncontrollable movement, esp. of the face ○ *He developed a tic when he was nervous.*

tick MAKE SOUND /tɪk/ *v* [I] to make a quiet, short, regularly repeated sound like that made by a clock ○ *That clock ticks too loudly.*
tick /tɪk/ *n* [C] ○ *I could hear the ticks of the passing seconds.*
ticking /ˈtɪk·ɪŋ/ *n* [U] ○ *the ticking of a clock*
ANIMAL /tɪk/ *n* [C] any of several types of very small animals that suck the blood of other animals

PHRASAL VERBS with tick

• **tick off** *something* **LIST** [M] to name items in a list ○ *She ticked off six reasons for saying no.*
• **tick off** *someone* **MAKE ANGRY** [M] *infml* to make someone angry ○ *Bad service in a restaurant ticks him off.*

ticket PROOF OF PAYMENT /ˈtɪk·ət/ *n* [C] a small card that shows that the person holding it has paid for an activity ○ *a train/movie ticket* ○ *an airline ticket* ○ *Have you bought your ticket yet?*
LEGAL NOTICE /ˈtɪk·ət/ *n* [C] an official piece of paper that tells someone that a traffic law has been broken ○ *a speeding/parking ticket* ○ *Carla got a ticket for making a U-turn on a bridge.*
ticket /ˈtɪk·ət/ *v* [T] ○ *Charles was ticketed for speeding.*
POLITICAL GROUP /ˈtɪk·ət/ *n* [C] a group of people from one political party who are trying to get elected at one time ○ *She's running on the Democratic and Independent tickets.*

tickle /ˈtɪk·əl/ *v* [T] to touch someone in a way that causes a slightly uncomfortable physical feeling which makes you laugh ○ *She tickled his feet.*
tickle /ˈtɪk·əl/ *n* [C] A tickle in your throat is an unpleasant feeling that might make you cough.
ticklish /ˈtɪk·ə·lɪʃ/ *adj* **1** *Are you ticklish* (= Do you laugh if someone tickles you)? **2** A ticklish situation is one that needs to be dealt with carefully.

IDIOM with tickle

• **tickled pink, tickled to death** *infml* very pleased ○ *I was tickled pink to be invited.*

tick-tack-toe, **tic-tac-toe** /ˌtɪkˌtækˈtoʊ/ *n* [U] a game in which two players take turns putting O's or X's in a pattern of nine squares, trying to get three O's or X's in a straight line

tidal wave *n* [C] an extremely large wave caused by violent movement of the earth under the sea

tidbit /ˈtɪd·bɪt/ *n* [C] a small piece of interesting information, or a small item of food ○ *We learned all sorts of historical tidbits.* ○ *She feeds her dog tidbits from the dinner table.*

tide /tɑɪd/ *n* [C] **1** the rise and fall of the sea that happens twice every day ○ *high/low tide* **2** A tide is also any large change in something, esp. an increase in the amount of something: *The tide of public opinion is turning against the president.*
tidal /ˈtɑɪd·əl/ *adj* connected with, or influenced or powered by, the rise and fall of the sea ○ *a tidal river*

PHRASAL VERB with tide

• **tide** *someone* **over** to supply someone with something that is lacking for a short period ○ *Can you lend me some money to tide me over till next month?*

tidy NEAT /ˈtɑɪd·i/ *adj* (of appearance or behavior) neat ○ *a tidy house*
LARGE /ˈtɑɪd·i/ *adj* (of amounts of money) large ○ *He made a tidy sum/profit.*

tie FASTEN /tɑɪ/ *v* [I/T] *pres. part.* **tying**, *past* **tied** to fasten together two pieces of string or other long, thin material, or to hold together with string, rope, etc. ○ [I] *This dress ties at the back.* ○ [T] *She tied the ribbon in a bow/knot.*
tie /tɑɪ/, **necktie** *n* [C] **1** a long, thin piece of material worn esp. by men which fits under a shirt collar, is tied in a knot, and hangs down the front of the shirt ○ *a silk tie* **2** A tie is also any piece of string, plastic, etc., used to hold together something: *Can you find the ties for the garbage bags?*
FINISH EQUAL /tɑɪ/ *v* [I] *pres. part.* **tying**, *past* **tied** to finish at the same time or score the same number of points as someone or something else in a competition ○ *Jane and I tied for first place.* ○ *The score is tied (up) at 3 to 3.*
tie /tɑɪ/ *n* [C] ○ *It's a tie for first place.*
CONNECTION /tɑɪ/ *n* [C] a connection or relationship between people, or a connection a person has

T

with a place, interest, activity, etc. ○ *a tie to the past* ○ *Gray had close ties with other powerful politicians.* ○ *He is a businessman and developer with strong ties to Beijing.*

WORD FAMILY tie			
Nouns	tie	*Verbs*	tie untie

IDIOM with tie

• **tie the knot** to get married ○ *So when are you two going to tie the knot?*

PHRASAL VERBS with tie

• **tie down** *someone/something* **HOLD IN PLACE** [M] to hold someone or something in place with ropes ○ *Tie down anything that might blow away in the storm.*
• **tie down** *someone* **LIMIT** [M] to limit someone's freedom ○ *Family obligations tied him down.*
• **tie** *something* **in with** *something* to show that something is connected to something else ○ *Our dance teacher showed us the turn, then tied it in with the basic step.*
• **tie** *something* **to** *something* **CONNECT** to show how one thing is connected to another ○ *Researchers have tied the increase in asthma to certain types of pollution.*
• **tie** *someone* **to** *something* **UNABLE TO LEAVE** to force someone to stay in a place ○ *Her work ties her to the east coast.*
• **tie up** *something* **HOLD** [M] to hold something with string or rope ○ *Tie your newspapers up with string.* ○ *Thieves tied up the night watchman.*
• **tie up** *something* **LIMIT MOVEMENT** [M] to limit someone's or something's movement or use ○ *It's a good investment, but your money will be tied up for a long time.* ○ *Sorry I'm late – I got tied up in traffic.* ○ Related noun: TIE UP TOO MANY THINGS

tie-breaker *n* [C] an additional competition among competitors who have finished with equal scores

tier /tɪr/ *n* [C] one of several layers or levels ○ *We sat in one of the upper tiers of the stadium.*

tie-up **COMBINING** *n* [C] an agreement that combines two companies ○ *A tie-up between the two air carriers is likely to be approved.*

STOP *n* [C] a stop caused by having too many things come or happen together ○ *An overturned truck caused a huge traffic tie-up.* ○ Related verb: TIE UP LIMIT MOVEMENT

tiff /tɪf/ *n* [C] *infml* a slight argument ○ *We had a little tiff over whose turn it was to walk the dog.*

tiger /ˈtɑɪ·gər/, *female* **tigress** /ˈtɑɪ·grəs/ *n* [C] a large, wild cat that has yellow-orange fur with thick lines of black fur

tight **FIRMLY TOGETHER** /tɑɪt/ *adj, adv* [*-er/-est* only] **1** (held or kept together) firmly or closely ○ *You have to wrap the bandage tight enough so that it really supports your ankle.* ○ *Make sure the door is shut tight* (= completely closed) *before you leave.* **2** Clothes that are tight fit the body closely, sometimes so closely that they are uncomfortable: *She wore a tight black skirt.* ○ *These shoes feel a bit tight.* **3** If you say about two people that they are tight, you mean they are close friends.

tightly /ˈtɑɪt·li/ *adv* ○ *Dorothy held her dog tightly so he wouldn't run after them.*

tighten /ˈtɑɪt·ᵊn/ *v* [I/T] ○ [T] *You've got to tighten the laces of your ice skates.* ○ [I] *His arms tightened around her.*

LIMITED /tɑɪt/ *adj* [*-er/-est* only] (esp. of time or money) available in limited amounts ○ *Arnold has a very tight schedule today and I don't know if he can see you.* ○ *We're on a tight budget and can't afford to eat out much.* ○ *Parking is very tight on weekdays around here.*

tighten /ˈtɑɪt·ᵊn/ *v* [T] to make something less easily available ○ *The government plans to tighten credit and slow the growth of the money supply.*

CONTROLLED /tɑɪt/ *adj* strongly controlled ○ *Security was tight at the meeting between the two leaders.*

tighten /ˈtɑɪt·ᵊn/ *v* [T] ○ *Security was tightened at US embassies around the world.* ○ *The government moved to tighten the rules on toxic substances in the air.* ○ [M] *Our team will have to tighten up its defense if we want to win.*

tightly /ˈtɑɪt·li/ *adv* ○ *Her decision to run for office was a tightly held secret.*

DIFFICULT /tɑɪt/ *adj* **1** (of situations) difficult or hard to deal with ○ *We were in a tight financial situation.* ○ *I was in a tight spot* (= difficult situation) *and wasn't sure what I should do.* **2** In a competition, tight means close, with the competitors almost even: *He was involved in a very tight race for governor.*

WORD FAMILY tight			
Adjectives	tight	*Adverbs*	tight tightly
Verbs	tighten		

IDIOM with tight

• **tighten** *your* **belt** to spend less money ○ *Many small businesses are tightening their belts because of the slow economy.*

tight-fisted *adj infml* unwilling to spend money

tight-lipped *adj* refusing to say very much about something ○ *He remained tight-lipped about whether the union would declare a strike.*

tightrope /ˈtɑɪt·roup/ *n* [C] a stretched wire or rope fixed above the ground that skilled people walk across, esp. in a CIRCUS performance

tights /tɑɪts/ *pl n* **1** a piece of clothing made of a material that stretches to cover the body below the waist, including the legs, worn esp. by dancers and people doing physical exercises ○ *Ballet students should wear a leotard and tights.* **2** *Br* Tights are also PANTYHOSE.

tightwad /ˈtɑɪt·wɑd/ *n* [C] *disapproving* a person who is not willing to spend money

tile /tɑɪl/ *n* [C] a flat, thin, usually square piece of baked clay, plastic, or other material used for covering floors, walls, or roofs ○ *a tile floor* ○ *ceiling tiles*

tile /tɑɪl/ *v* [T] ○ *We're going to tile the bathroom ourselves.*

till UNTIL /tɪl, təl, tᵊl/ *prep, conjunction* up to (the time that); until ○ *Tell him to take it easy till we get there.*

PREPARE LAND /tɪl/ *v* [T] to prepare and use land for growing crops ○ *to till the soil*

MONEY CONTAINER /tɪl/ *n* [C] a DRAWER where money is kept in a store ○ (*fig.*) *We suspected him of dipping into the till* (= stealing money from the store).

tilt /tɪlt/ *v* [I/T] **1** to cause something to move into a sloping or uneven position, or to be in this position ○ [T] *He tilted his chair back and put his feet up on the desk.* ○ [T] *The woman tilted her head back, laughing at something Pascal had just said.* **2** *fig.* Something that tilts toward/away from something increases or lessens its support for it: [I] *UN spending has tilted away from development toward relief, O'Reilly says.*

tilt /tɪlt/ *n* [C usually sing] ○ *The house was on a tilt* (= not horizontal).

timber /ˈtɪm·bər/ *n* [C/U] wood from trees that is used for building, or trees grown for this use ○ [U] *The houses were constructed of timber and whitewashed clay.*

timbre /ˈtæm·bər, ˈtɪm·bər, ˈtɑm·brə/ *n* [C] ***music*** a feature of sound in music that is produced by a particular instrument or voice

time MEASURE OF EXISTENCE /tɑɪm/ *n* [U] **1** the seconds, minutes, hours, days, weeks, months, years, etc., in which existence is measured, or the past, present, and future considered as a whole ○ *I really don't have time to call her today.* ○ *The children spent most of their time outdoors.* ○ *We'd save time* (= It would be quicker) *if we didn't have to pick up Bobby on the way.* **2** If you waste time, you do not make good use of the amount of time available to you.

PARTICULAR PERIOD /tɑɪm/ *n* [C/U] **1** a particular period of seconds, minutes, hours, days, weeks, months, years, etc., during which something has been happening or is needed or available ○ [U] *The kids are well-behaved most of the time.* ○ [C] *She was very lonely at that time.* ○ [C] *They talked for a long time.* ○ [U] *She spent most of her free time listening to music.* ○ [C] *It's unusual to get snow at this time of year.* ○ [U] *Those kids are over here all the time* (= often or continuously). **2** If you pass time, you do something while waiting for something else to happen: [U] *While he was waiting, Joe passed the time looking through magazines.* **3** Your time in a race is the number of seconds, minutes, and hours you take to complete it: [C] *The track was soft, and the times were slow.*

time /tɑɪm/ *v* [T] to measure the seconds, minutes, and hours for something to happen or someone to do something ○ *We ran two miles and were timed at 12 minutes and 30 seconds.* ○ *You've got to time the roast or it will get overdone.*

MEASUREMENT ON A CLOCK /tɑɪm/ *n* [C/U] **1** a particular moment in the day, as expressed in hours and minutes and shown on a clock, or a particular point in the day, week, month, or year ○ [U] *What time is it?* ○ [U] *What time do you finish work?* ○ [U] *He's teaching his daughter to tell time* (= to recognize what particular point in the day it is by looking at a clock). ○ [C] *I catch the train at the same time every day.* ○ [U] *Parking is not allowed here at any time* (= ever). **2** Time is also used to refer to the system of recording hours used in different parts of the world: [U] *Mountain Standard Time* ○ [U] *daylight saving time*

time /tɑɪm/ *v* [T] to arrange for something to happen at a specific moment ○ *We timed our arrivals at the airport so that we could meet and share a taxi to the city.*

timer /ˈtɑɪ·mər/ *n* [C] a device that starts or stops something at a set time or that makes a sound after a particular amount of time has passed ○ *He set the timer on the VCR to start recording at 11:30.*
➤ Usage: **hour or time?** at HOUR

SUITABLE POINT /tɑɪm/ *n* [C/U] **1** a point of the day, week, month, or year that is suitable for a particular activity, or at which something is expected to happen ○ [U] *We had enjoyed our visit, but now it was time to go home.* ○ [U] *Put away your toys, Leni, it's time for bed.* ○ [C] *The times for meals are listed on the schedule.* ○ [U] *This is no time* (= not a suitable moment) *to change your mind.* **2** To be **in time** for something is to arrive at the right moment, before it is too late to do something ○ *We arrived just in time for the show* ○ *I'm glad you got here in time to see Julie before she goes.* ○ *The plane is expected to arrive* **on time** (= when scheduled).

timely /ˈtɑɪm·li/ *adj* given or made available at a suitable moment, esp. now ○ *timely advice*

timing /ˈtɑɪ·mɪŋ/ *n* [U] the ability to choose the right moment to do or say something, or the time when something happens ○ *The difference between a joke told well and a joke told badly is the timing.* ○ *The timing of the airline strike was bad for our vacation plans.*

OCCASION /tɑɪm/ *n* [C] an occasion or period, or the experience connected with it ○ *This is a time to be serious.* ○ *There were times when he almost gave up, but somehow he managed to survive.* ○ *We visit my mother a few times a year.* ○ *She takes the medicine three times a day.* ○ *He was holding down three jobs at the same time.* ○ *We had a good time at the party.*

HISTORICAL PERIOD /tɑɪm/, **times** *n* [C] **1** a period in history ○ *Indians since ancient times have ground their corn by hand.* **2** Something or someone who is before your time happened or existed before you were born or were old enough to remember: *The Beatles were way before my time.*

WORD FAMILY time

Nouns	time overtime timer timing	*Adjectives*	timeless timely overtime untimely
Verbs	time overtime		

T

IDIOMS with time

- **at a time** during any one period ○ *I can only do one thing at a time.*
- **do time, serve time** to spend a certain period in prison ○ *He did time in a California prison.*
- **the time is ripe** the conditions are good ○ *The time is ripe for buyers looking for a bigger house.*
- **time after time** again and again; repeatedly ○ *We've been hearing the same news story time after time.*
- **time and (time) again** very often ○ *I've told you time and time again to lock both doors before you leave.*
- **time flies** a certain period has passed surprisingly quickly ○ *Time flies when you're having fun.*
- **time is on *someone's* side** someone will do better by waiting ○ *Your parents think time is on their side, and that you'll stop asking if they're patient.*
- **time on *your* hands** a period when you have nothing you must do ○ *Now that she was retired, Mary found that she had a lot of time on her hands.*
- **times have changed** the situation is different now from the way it was in the past ○ *Times have changed and many more women now have executive jobs than in the past.*
- **time's up** *infml* an activity is finished ○ *OK, everyone, time's up – hand in your tests.*
- **time will tell** you will discover in the future what the result of a present situation is ○ *Time will tell whether we made the right decision.*

time and a half *n* [U] payment for work that is 50 percent more than the usual rate

time bomb *n* [C] **1** a bomb attached to a device that will make it explode at a particular time **2** A time bomb is also a developing situation that will cause serious problems in the future if it is not stopped: *He has the kind of nasty attitude toward management that is a time bomb in any work situation.*

time clock *n* [C] a clock that employees use to record the time when they arrive at and leave work

time-honored *adj* considered important because of having existed for many years ○ *Family Thanksgiving dinners are a time-honored tradition.*

T

timeless /ˈtɑɪm·ləs/ *adj* lasting forever; never showing the effects of aging ○ *That song stands out as a timeless classic.*

timeline /ˈtɑɪm·lɑɪn/ *n* [C] **1** a plan or idea of how much time something will or should take ○ *Despite the short timeline, supporters gathered enough signatures to get the measure on the ballot.* **2** A timeline is also a written representation of a period of time, usually a line, that shows the order in which related events happened.

timely /ˈtɑɪm·lɪ/ *adj* ○ See at TIME SUITABLE POINT

timeout /ˈtɑɪmˈɑʊt/ *n* [C] a short official pause during a game when the players plan what to do next

timer /ˈtɑɪ·mər/ *n* ○ See at TIME MEASUREMENT ON A CLOCK

times MULTIPLIED BY /tɑɪmz/, *symbol* × *prep* multiplied by ○ *Two times two equals four.*

AMOUNT /tɑɪmz/ *prep* used to show the difference in amount of two things, by multiplying one of them by the stated number ○ *She earns five times as much as I do.*

time signature *n* [C] ***music*** two numbers in written music that show how many beats are in a BAR (= part of a piece of music) and which note gets one beat ○ *If the time signature is 3/4, there are three beats to a measure and a quarter note gets one beat.* ➤ Picture: **notation**

timetable /ˈtɑɪm ˌteɪ·bəl/ *n* [C] a list of the times when particular activities or events will happen; schedule ○ *An election is expected in one or two years, although no timetable has been announced.*

time zone *n* [C] one of 24 parts that the world is divided into so that different places can set their clocks correctly

timid /ˈtɪm·əd/ *adj* easily frightened; not brave or confident ○ *She was timid about swimming in deep water.* ○ Opposite: BOLD BRAVE

timidly /ˈtɪm·əd·li/ *adv* ○ *She sang timidly but sweetly.*

timidity /təˈmɪd·ət̬·i/ *n* [U] ○ *A shaky voice revealed his timidity.*

timing /ˈtɑɪ·mɪŋ/ *n* [U] ○ See at TIME SUITABLE POINT

tin /tɪn/ *n* [C/U] a soft, silver metal that is often combined with other metals or used as a layer to protect various metals

tin can *n* [C] a CAN CONTAINER

tinder /ˈtɪn·dər/ *n* [U] a substance that burns easily, such as paper or thin sticks of wood, used to light fires

tinderbox /ˈtɪn·dər ˌbɑks/ *n* [C] a situation or place where sudden violence is likely ○ *The press seems to encourage violence in an area that is already a tinderbox.*

tinfoil /ˈtɪn·fɔɪl/ *n* [U] FOIL METAL SHEET

tinge /tɪndʒ/ *v* [T] to add a slight amount of color or a quality to something ○ *The sunset tinged the sky red.*

tinge /tɪndʒ/ *n* [C] ○ *The flowers are purple with tinges of pink.*

tingle /ˈtɪŋ·gəl/ *v* [I] to have a slight stinging feeling ○ *Her skin tingled after swimming in the cold, salty water.*

tingle /ˈtɪŋ·gəl/ *n* [C/U] ○ [C usually sing] *I often get a tingle in my toes when they're cold.*

tinker /ˈtɪŋ·kər/ *v* [I always + adv/prep] to make small changes in something, because you hope to improve or fix it ○ *Chuck tinkers with the car's engine all the time.*

tinkle /ˈtɪŋ·kəl/ *v* [I] **1** to make light, ringing sounds ○ *The wind chimes tinkled in the breeze.* **2** *a child's word* Tinkle also means to excrete urine.

tinkle /ˈtɪŋ·kəl/ *n* [C usually sing] ○ *We heard the tinkle of ice as he stirred the lemonade.*

tinny /ˈtɪn·i/ *adj* (of sound) weak and high; lacking a full sound ○ *The music sounded good even on the TV's tinny speakers.*

tinsel /ˈtɪn·səl, -zəl/ *n* [U] thin strips of a shiny material used as decoration, esp. on Christmas trees

tint /tɪnt/ *v* [T] ***art*** to color something slightly
tint /tɪnt/ *n* [C] **1** ***art*** a variety of a color, or a pale color ○ *Here, the ocean is gray with a blue tint.* **2** A tint is also a substance used to change slightly the color of something, esp. hair or paint.

tiny /ˈtɑɪ·ni/ *adj* [-er/-est only] extremely small ○ *Just trim a tiny bit off my hair, please.*

tip END /tɪp/ *n* [C] the pointed end of something ○ *The tip of the cat's tail is white.* ○ *She has a house on the western tip of the island.*

INFORMATION /tɪp/ *n* [C] a useful piece of information or advice, esp. something secret or not generally known ○ *She gave me some helpful gardening tips.* ○ *Acting on a tip, the police arrested most of the smugglers.*

LEAN /tɪp/ *v* [I/T] **-pp-** to lean to one side, or to cause something to lean to one side ○ [T] *She tipped the umbrella to keep the sun off the picnic table.*

FALL OVER /tɪp/ *v* [I/T] to fall or turn over, or to cause something to fall or turn over ○ [I] *If everyone sits on one side of the boat, it will tip (over).*

PAY /tɪp/ *v* [I/T] **-pp-** to give money to someone for service which is in addition to the amount being charged ○ [T] *He tipped the porter generously.*
tip /tɪp/ *n* [C] ○ *"That guy didn't bother to leave a tip," the waitress said disgustedly.*

IDIOMS with tip

• **on the tip of** *your* **tongue** about to be said if you can remember it ○ *I know her – her name is on the tip of my tongue, but it won't come to me.*
• **the tip of the iceberg** a small and known part of something much larger and unknown ○ *As with many injuries, the damage we can see is only the tip of the iceberg.*
• **tip the balance**, **tip the scales** to cause a change, esp. in making something more likely to happen ○ *Introducing new fish to the lake tipped the balance and made it very hard for the trout that were already living there.*

PHRASAL VERB with tip

• **tip off** *someone* [M] to give secret information to someone, or to give someone information without intending to ○ *Apparently the mob leaders were tipped off that police were watching them.* ○ *Moving strike aircraft within range could have tipped off the bad guys.* ○ Related noun: TIP-OFF

tipi /ˈtiː·piː/ *n* [C] a TEPEE

tip-off *n* [C] *infml* a warning or information that something may happen ○ *He began cutting classes – a tip-off that he was in trouble.* ○ Related verb: TIP OFF

tipsy /ˈtɪp·si/ *adj infml* slightly drunk

tiptoe /ˈtɪp·toʊ/ *v* [I always + adv/prep] to walk with your heels raised off the ground ○ *She tiptoed out of the room so she wouldn't wake him.*
tiptoe /ˈtɪp·toʊ/ *n* [C] ○ *He had to stand on his tiptoes to reach the shelf.*

tiptop /ˈtɪp·tɑp/ *adj* [not gradable] *infml* excellent; perfect ○ *He swam a mile every day and kept himself in tiptop shape.*

tirade /tɑɪˈreɪd, ˈtɑɪ·reɪd/ *n* [C] an angry speech, often lasting a long time, that expresses strong disapproval ○ *My father's tirades against politicians were famous.*

tire LOSE ENERGY /tɑɪr/ *v* [I/T] **1** to cause someone to lose energy, or to be without energy ○ [I] *Weakened by the infection, he tires easily.* ○ [T] *Running tired her.* ○ [M] *Going up all those stairs tires me out.* **2** To **tire of** something is to become bored with it: *Viewers never tire of nature programs.*
tired /tɑɪrd/ *adj* [not gradable] **1** *I had been up all night with the baby and was really tired.* **2** If you are **tired of** something, you are bored or annoyed by it: *I'm tired of cleaning up after you.*
tireless /ˈtɑɪr·ləs/ *adj* [not gradable] not stopping or taking a rest from something ○ *a tireless woman*
tirelessly /ˈtɑɪr·lə·sli/ *adv* ○ *He worked tirelessly to improve the local schools.*
tiring /ˈtɑɪ·rɪŋ/ *adj* [not gradable] causing you to feel you have no energy ○ *Dad had a tiring day at work.*

USAGE

tired of or tired from?

If you are **tired of** *something* or **tired of** *doing something*, you are bored or annoyed by it.

I'm tired of hearing his awful jokes.

If you are **tired from** *something*, you want to rest because of it.

He was tired from the long trip.

~~*He was tired of the the long trip.*~~

WORD CHOICES tire

If someone is extremely tired, you can say that the person is **exhausted** or **worn-out**.

I'm too ***exhausted*** *to take the dog for a walk tonight.*

By the time I got home, I was completely ***worn out.***

You can describe someone who is tired because he or she has been working very hard as **burned out** or **drained**.

He was completely ***burned out*** *after a full week of performances.*

I'd worked a twelve-hour day and was absolutely ***drained.***

If someone is tired and wants to go to sleep, you can describe them as **drowsy** or **sleepy**.

The heat had made me ***drowsy/sleepy.***

T

WHEEL /tɑɪr/ *n* [C] a rubber ring, usually filled with air, that fits around the wheel of a car, bicycle, or other vehicle ○ *Most cars now have radial tires.*

WORD FAMILY tire			
Nouns	tire	*Adjectives*	tired
Verbs	tire		tireless
Adverbs	tirelessly		tiresome
			tiring

tiresome /ˈtɑɪr·səm/ *adj* [not gradable] tiring, annoying, or boring ○ *It's getting a little tiresome, listening to you complain.*

tissue PAPER /ˈtɪʃ·uː/ *n* [C] a piece of soft, thin paper which absorbs liquids ○ *He wiped his nose with a tissue.*

CELLS /ˈtɪʃ·uː/ *n* [U] ***biology*** a group of related cells that forms larger parts of animals and plants

tissue paper, *short form* **tissue** *n* [U] light, thin paper used for wrapping things, esp. things inside packages

titanium /tɑɪˈteɪ·niː·əm, tə-/ *n* [U] a hard, silver-colored metal that is used esp. for making other metals stronger

tit for tat /ˈtɪt·fərˈtæt/ *n* [U] something, esp. something annoying or unpleasant, done to someone because that person has done the same thing to you ○ *She would not continue to fight, and rejected returning tit for tat.*

titillate /ˈtɪt̬·əlˌeɪt/ *v* [I/T] to cause someone to feel pleasantly excited ○ [T] *We were titillated by the promise of things to come.*

titillating /ˈtɪt̬·əlˌeɪt̬·ɪŋ/ *adj* ○ *They attend get-rich seminars with titillating titles like "Turn an Ugly House into a Pot of Gold."*

title NAME /ˈtɑɪt̬·əl/ *n* [C] the name of a book, movie, play, song, or work of art ○ *The book is an index to song titles.*

title /ˈtɑɪt̬·əl/ *v* [T] ○ *He titled his autobiography "Beneath the Underdog."*

RANK /ˈtɑɪt̬·əl/ *n* [C] a word or phrase that shows a person's rank or job ○ *Her job title is director of human resources.*

SPORTS PRIZE /ˈtɑɪt̬·əl/ *n* [C] a prize or public statement showing that someone is the best in a particular sport or competition ○ *She won her third straight title in speed skating.*

LEGAL RIGHT /ˈtɑɪt̬·əl/ *n* [U] *law* the legal right to own something, esp. a piece of land or a building ○ *That little paper is your title to the car, so don't lose it.*

WORD FAMILY title			
Nouns	title	*Adjectives*	titled
	subtitle	*Verbs*	title
	entitlement		entitle
			subtitle

title page *n* [C] a page at the front of a book giving the name of the book and its writer and PUBLISHER

title role *n* [C] the main character in a play or movie whose name is in its title ○ *Brando played the title role in "The Godfather."*

title track *n* [C] the piece of music on a recording that has the same name as the recording itself

titrate /ˈtɑɪ·treɪt/ *v* [T] ***chemistry*** to measure how much of a substance is in a liquid by adding it to measured amounts of another substance which reacts to it, for example, by making it change color

titration /tɑɪˈtreɪ·ʃən/ *n* [U] ***chemistry***

titter /ˈtɪt̬·ər/ *v* [I] to laugh in a nervous and quiet way ○ *Some kids tittered at the boys who were making faces in class.*

titter /ˈtɪt̬·ər/ *n* [C] ○ *There were titters from the audience but no big laughs.*

tizzy /ˈtɪz·i/ *n* [C usually sing] *infml* a state of excitement or confusion ○ *She's in a tizzy because she locked her keys in the car.*

TNT /ˌtiːˌenˈtiː/ *n* [U] a powerful explosive

to INFINITIVE /tuː, tʊ, tə/ *prep* **1** used before a verb showing that it is in the infinitive ○ *She agreed to help.* ○ *I asked her to finish by Friday.* ○ *I need to eat something.* ○ *I'd love to visit New York.* ○ *I want to go now.* **2** "To" followed by an infinitive is used after adjectives: *It's not likely to happen.* ○ *I was afraid to tell her.* **3** "To" followed by an infinitive is used after nouns: *He has the ability to do two things at once.* **4** "To" followed by an infinitive can begin a clause: *To be honest* (= Speaking honestly), *I prefer the gray skirt.* **5** "To" followed by an infinitive can be used to express requests or orders: *Is it possible to have tea instead?* ○ *You're not to go there by yourself.* **6** "To" followed by an infinitive is used after "how," "what," "when," "where," "whether," "which," "who," "whom," or "whose": *I don't know what to do.* ○ *Can you tell me how to get there?* **7** "To" followed by an infinitive is used after "enough": *I was close enough to touch him.*

INSTEAD OF VERB /tuː, tʊ, tə/ *prep* used instead of a verb clause when answering questions ○ *"Would you like to go to the movies tonight?" "Yes, I'd love to."*

FOR /tuː, tʊ, tə/ *prep* for the purpose of doing something ○ *I asked Helen out to dinner.*

SHOWING DIRECTION /tuː, tʊ, tə/ *prep* **1** in the direction of or as far as ○ *We went to Montreal last year.* ○ *I'm going to the bank.* ○ *We were in mud up to our ankles.* **2** "To" can be used to show the position of something or someone in relation to something or someone else: *We came face to face in the elevator.* ○ *The Rocky Mountains are to the west of the Great Plains.* **3** "To" can show something is on or around something: *Can you tie the dog's leash to the fence?*

BETWEEN /tuː, tʊ, tə/ *prep* used in phrases that show a range of things or a distance between places ○ *There must have been 30 to 35 people there.* ○ *We got two to three inches of snow at home.*

○ *Read pages 10 to 25.* ○ *It's two to three hundred miles from Boston to Washington.*

RECEIVING /tuː, tʊ, tə/ *prep* used for showing who receives something or who experiences an action ○ *I told that story to Glen.* ○ *Who's the letter addressed to?*

IN CONNECTION WITH /tuː, tʊ, tə/ *prep* in connection with ○ *They exercise to music.* ○ *What was their response to that news?*

COMPARED WITH /tuː, tʊ, tə/ *prep* compared with ○ *Paul beat me three games to two.* ○ *I scored 80 to Talia's 90.*

UNTIL /tuː, tʊ, tə/ *prep* **1** until a particular time, state, or condition is reached ○ *It's only two weeks to your birthday.* ○ *We're open daily from 2 to 6 p.m.* ○ *My shirt was torn to shreds.* **2** "To" is used, when giving the time, to mean minutes before the stated hour: *It's twenty to six.*

CAUSING /tuː, tʊ, tə/ *prep* causing a particular feeling or effect in someone ○ *To my great relief, she decided against going.*

CONSIDERED BY /tuː, tʊ, tə/ *prep* considered by ○ *Does this make any sense to you?* ○ *Fifty dollars is very little to him.*

MATCHING /tuː, tʊ, tə/ *prep* matching or belonging to ○ *the top to a bottle* ○ *the keys to my apartment* ○ *There is a funny side to everything.*

FOR EACH /tuː, tʊ, tə/ *prep* for each of; PER ○ *This car gets about 30 miles to the gallon.*

toad /toʊd/ *n* [C] a small animal, similar to a FROG, that has dry, brown skin and lives mostly on land

toadstool /ˈtoʊd·stuːl/ *n* [C] a MUSHROOM (= plant), esp. a poisonous one

to and fro /ˌtuː·ən ˈfroʊ/ *adv* [not gradable] in one direction and then in the opposite direction ○ *Outside my door I could hear people walking to and fro.*

toast **BREAD** /toʊst/ *n* [U] sliced bread that has been made brown by being put near a high heat ○ *buttered toast*

toast /toʊst/ *v* [T] ○ *Would you like me to toast your bagel?*

toaster /ˈtoʊ·stər/ *n* [C] an electric device for making toast

DRINK /toʊst/ *n* [C] a short speech in honor of someone or in celebration of something, followed by everyone present taking a drink ○ *Ted raised his glass and proposed a toast "to absent friends."*

toast /toʊst/ *v* [T] ○ *At midnight, we toasted the New Year.*

toasty /ˈtoʊ·sti/ *adj* warm and comfortable ○ *You must feel nice and toasty sitting in front of the fire.*

tobacco /təˈbæk·oʊ/ *n* [U] a type of plant, or the dried leaves of this plant which are prepared and smoked in cigarettes, pipes, or CIGARS, or sometimes chewed

toboggan /təˈbɑɡ·ən/ *n* [C] a piece of equipment used for sliding over snow and ice which consists of long, thin boards fixed together that curve up at the front

today /təˈdeɪ/ *adv* [not gradable] **1** on this day ○ *What's the date today?* ○ *We could go today or tomorrow.* **2** Today can also be used more generally to mean now rather than in the past: *People are more worried today than ever before.*

today /təˈdeɪ/ *n* [U] ○ *Today is even hotter than yesterday!*

toddle /ˈtɑd·əl/ *v* [I] (esp. of a young child) to walk awkwardly with short steps ○ *Our two-year-old toddled after his puppy.*

toddler /ˈtɑd·lər/ *n* [C] a young child, esp. one just learning to walk ○ *Are these toys suitable for toddlers?*

toe /toʊ/ *n* [C] **1** any of the five long, thin parts at the end of the foot, similar to the fingers of the hand ○ *I broke a toe when I caught my foot in a door.* **2** Toe also refers to the end of a shoe or sock: *That sock has a hole in the toe.*

IDIOMS with toe

• **on *your* toes** aware and energetic as a result of being busy and challenged ○ *Teaching four different subjects keeps you on your toes.*
• **toe the line** to do what you are expected to do without causing trouble for anyone ○ *If you want to get ahead, you'd better learn to toe the line.*

TOEFL /ˈtoʊ·fəl/ *n* [U] *abbreviation for* Test of English as a Foreign Language (= a test for people learning English)

toehold /ˈtoʊ·hoʊld/ *n* [C] a starting point in a job or other opportunity from which you can advance ○ *The young person who gets a toehold in that business will do well.*

toenail /ˈtoʊ·neɪl/ *n* [C] the nail of any of the toes

toe-to-toe *adj, adv* directly opposing or competing with each other ○ *We don't have to go toe-to-toe with our competitors in every market.*

tofu /ˈtoʊ·fuː/, **bean curd** *n* [U] a soft, pale food with little flavor, but high in PROTEIN, that is made from SOYBEANS

together **WITH THE OTHER** /təˈɡeð·ər/ *adv* [not gradable] (of two people or things) each with the other, or (of more than two) as a group ○ *We've worked together before.* ○ *Sara and I were at college together.* ○ *Add these figures together.* ○ *We should all get together for lunch.* ○ *Jim and Mary live together.*

togetherness /təˈɡeð·ər·nəs/ *n* [U] the feeling of being friendly and close with other people ○ *The project encourages family pride and togetherness.*

AT THE SAME TIME /təˈɡeð·ər/ *adv* [not gradable] at the same time ○ *All the guests arrived together.*

COMBINED /təˈɡeð·ər/ *adv* [not gradable] **1** in a combined condition ○ *Together, they must earn over $80,000 a year.* ○ *I'll get my things together so we can leave.* ○ *You mix the eggs and sugar together before adding milk.* **2** If things go together, they

T

are attractive when combined: *Do purple and pink go together?* ○ *Those pants and jacket go well together.*

ORGANIZED /tə'geð·ər/ *adj* [not gradable] *infml, approving* organized, confident, and able to do whatever you decide to do ○ *I just feel like the men have it more together than the women here do.*

PHRASAL VERB with together

• **together with** *someone/something* in addition to someone or something ○ *The cost of food together with drinks and prizes made it an expensive party.*

toil /tɔɪl/ *n* [U] hard and tiring work ○ *He rested from the backbreaking toil of putting in fences.*
toil /tɔɪl/ *v* [I] ○ *Walter toiled in obscurity while his boss took the credit.*

toilet /'tɔɪ·lət/ *n* [C] a device into which people excrete waste, esp. a bowl-shaped device with a seat that has a hole in it, or a BATHROOM ○ *I couldn't get the toilet to flush.*

USAGE

toilet, bathroom, or restroom?

Toilet is more often used to refer to the device into which people excrete than to the room where the device is. **Bathroom** is the usual word for the room with a toilet, especially in someone's home. In public places, rooms with toilets are often called **restrooms** or the **women's/ladies' room** and **men's room.**

toilet paper, **toilet tissue** *n* [U] soft paper that people use to clean themselves after using the toilet

toiletries /'tɔɪ·lə·triːz/ *pl n* soaps, SHAMPOOS, TOOTHPASTE, and other items used to keep yourself clean

token **SYMBOL** /'toʊ·kən/ *n* [C] something you give to someone or do for someone to express your feelings or intentions ○ *It isn't a big present – it's just a token of thanks for your help.*
token /'toʊ·kən/ *adj* [not gradable] small or limited but having a symbolic importance ○ *a token fee* ○ *a token gesture of goodwill*

DISK /'toʊ·kən/ *n* [C] a round, metal or plastic disk which is used instead of money in some machines ○ *subway tokens*

told /toʊld/ *past simple and past participle of* TELL

IDIOM with told

• **told you (so)** what I said before was correct ○ *"I should never have lent him the money." "I told you so."* ○ **USAGE:** Used to remind someone that you were right and they were wrong.

tolerable /'tɑl·ə·rə·bəl/ *adj* of a quality that is acceptable but not wonderful ○ *A job in a theme park is tolerable only if you're young.*
tolerably /'tɑl·ə·rə·bli/ *adv* to a limited or reasonable degree ○ *I was tolerably good at sports.*

tolerance **ACCEPTANCE** /'tɑl·ə·rəns/, **toleration** /ˌtɑl·ə'reɪ·ʃən/ *n* [U] willingness to accept behavior and beliefs that are different from your own, even if you disagree with or disapprove of them ○ *religious/racial tolerance* ○ *There is zero tolerance of violence at this school – if you're caught fighting, you'll be suspended.*
tolerant /'tɑl·ə·rənt/ *adj* ○ *Working with young people helps me be a little more tolerant.*
tolerate /'tɑl·əˌreɪt/ *v* [T] ○ *They don't have the best service, but I tolerate it because I love their food.*

ABILITY TO BEAR /'tɑl·ə·rəns/ *n* [U] the ability to bear something unpleasant or annoying, or to keep going despite difficulties ○ *I don't have much tolerance for hot, humid weather.*
tolerant /'tɑl·ə·rənt/ *adj* ○ *Some grasses are very tolerant of drought.*
tolerate /'tɑl·əˌreɪt/ *v* [T] ○ *Athletes often have to tolerate a lot of pain.*

toll **MONEY** /toʊl/ *n* [C] an amount of money that you have to pay to travel along some main roads, to cross bridges, etc., or to make telephone calls over long distances ○ *They're raising the bridge toll to $5.00.* ○ *The number you dialed is a toll call – please deposit an additional fifty cents.*

SUFFERING /toʊl/ *n* [U] a high degree of suffering or damage ○ *In addition to the physical destruction caused by the flooding, the emotional toll on its victims was immense.*

RING /toʊl/ *v* [I/T] (of a large bell) to ring slowly and repeatedly, or to cause a large bell to ring in this way ○ [I] *The town hall bell tolled at noon.*

tollbooth /'toʊl·buːθ/ *n* [U] a small, enclosed room on a road, bridge, etc., where a person collects money from drivers as they enter or leave

toll-free *adj* [not gradable] (of telephone calls) free for the person making the call

tomahawk /'tɑm·əˌhɔːk/ *n* [C] a small fighting AX (= tool with a blade) used by American Indians

tomato /tə'meɪt̬·oʊ, *New Eng and eastern Virginia also* -'mɑːt̬-/ *n* [C] *pl* **tomatoes** a juicy, red fruit eaten raw, esp. in salads, or cooked as a vegetable ○ *tomato sauce/soup*

tomb /tuːm/ *n* [C] a structure or underground room where someone, esp. an important person, is buried

tomboy /'tɑm·bɔɪ/ *n* [C] a girl who dresses and acts like a boy, esp. in playing physical games that boys usually play

tombstone /'tuːm·stoʊn/, **gravestone** /'greɪv·stoʊn/, **headstone** /'hed·stoʊn/ *n* [C] a cut stone with writing on it that marks where a dead person is buried

tomcat /'tɑm·kæt/ *n* [C] a male cat

tome /toʊm/ *n* [C] a large, heavy book

tomfoolery /tɑm'fuː·lə·ri/ *n* [U] foolish, often playful, behavior

tomorrow /tə'mɑr·oʊ, -'mɔːr-/ *adv* [not gradable] on the day after today ○ *He said he'll call tomorrow after work.*

tomorrow /tə'mɑr·oʊ, -'mɔːr-/ *n* [C/U] **1** [U] *Tomorrow's meeting has been postponed.* **2** If you say you will see someone tomorrow night/evening/ etc., you mean you will see that person on the night/evening/etc. of the next day: [U] *I've arranged to see Rachel tomorrow morning/afternoon.* **3** Tomorrow can also mean the future: [U] *Today's problem child may be tomorrow's criminal.*

ton /tʌn/ *n* [C] **1** a unit of measurement of weight equal to 2000 pounds or about 907 kilograms **2** *infml* A ton or tons of something is a very large amount: *I've got a ton of homework to do tonight.*

tone VOICE EXPRESSION /toʊn/ *n* [U] a quality in the voice, esp. one that expresses the speaker's feelings, often toward the person being addressed ○ *His tone was apologetic.*

MOOD /toʊn/ *n* [U] **1** the mood or general feeling of something ○ *The tone of his remarks was confident and reassuring.* **2** ***literature*** The tone of a piece of writing expresses the writer's attitude toward the subject or the reader: *The angry tone of this essay reveals her feelings about the war.*

SOUND /toʊn/ *n* [C usually sing] a musical, mechanical, or voice sound on one note ○ *If you wish to leave a message, please wait until after the tone.*

MUSICAL QUALITY /toʊn/ *n* [C/U] ***music*** **1** the quality of sound of a musical instrument or singing voice **2** A tone is also a STEP MUSIC.

tonal /'toʊn·əl/ *adj* [not gradable] ***music*** organized based on a particular note and the relationship of other notes to it

tonality /toʊ'næl·ət̬·i/ *n* [C] ***music*** a particular musical SCALE or KEY

FIRM QUALITY /toʊn/ *n* [U] (esp. of muscles) the quality of being healthy and firm ○ *Swimming helps to develop good muscle tone.*

COLOR /toʊn/ *n* [C] ***art*** a feature of color related to its brightness or the amount of light it reflects

PHRASAL VERB with **tone**

• **tone down** *something* [M] to make something less forceful or offensive ○ *The foul language in the original play has been toned down for television.*

tone-deaf *adj* [not gradable] not able to recognize different notes or sing tunes accurately

tone poem *n* [C] ***music*** a piece of music for instruments that represents a particular story, image, or mood

tongs /tɔːŋz/ *pl n* a device, often U-shaped, having long sides for picking up objects without touching them, used by pressing or moving the sides together until the free ends hold the object ○ *She moved the smoldering logs around in the fireplace with a set of tongs.*

tongue MOUTH PART /tʌŋ/ *n* the movable part in the mouth that is used in tasting and swallowing food and, in people, in producing speech

LANGUAGE /tʌŋ/ *n* [C] a language ○ *McAdam could speak the Eskimo tongue, too.*

tongue-in-cheek *adj* intended to be understood as a joke, although often seeming serious ○ *He made some tongue-in-cheek comment about being very busy cleaning his house.*

tongue-lashing *n* [C usually sing] an act of severe criticism ○ *The mayor's public tongue-lashing of a member of his own party was a shock.*

tongue-tied *adj* having difficulty in speaking, usually because of being nervous ○ *I was practically tongue-tied.*

tongue twister *n* [C] a name or set of words that are difficult to pronounce

tonic /'tɑn·ɪk/ *n* [C] **1** a liquid medicine intended to make you feel better generally rather than treating a particular health problem **2** A tonic is also anything that makes you feel better: *Seeing his grandchildren was the perfect tonic for him.*

tonic (water) /'tɑn·ɪk ('wɔːt̬·ər, 'wɑt̬-)/ *n* [C/U] flavored, bubbly water usually added to alcoholic drinks

tonight /tə'nɑɪt/ *n* [U] (during) the night of the present day ○ *The game will be shown on TV beginning at 8 o'clock tonight.*

tonsils /'tɑn·səlz/ *pl n* the two small, soft organs at the back of the mouth

Tony /'toʊ·ni/ *n* [C] one of a set of prizes given each year to the best plays and for special achievements in the theater

too MORE /tuː/ *adv* [not gradable] more than is needed or wanted; more than is suitable or enough ○ *The sofa is too big for this room.* ○ *The apartment was nice but it was just too expensive.* ○ *This dress is too large for me – I'll need a smaller size.*

VERY /tuː/ *adv* [not gradable] very, or completely ○ *I'm not too sure I want to go out tonight.*

ALSO /tuː/ *adv* [not gradable] (esp. at the end of a sentence) in addition; also ○ *Bring your tennis racket, and your bathing suit, too.*

IDIOMS with **too**

• **(that's) too bad 1** I am sorry ○ *"I failed the test." "Oh, that's too bad – can you take it again?"* **2 Too bad** is sometimes used to say you do not care: *"He says he's sorry and he won't do it again." "Too bad – he's not getting another chance with me."*

• **(it's) too bad that** it is sad that ○ *It's too bad that more parents don't know how much reading to children can help them.*

• **too good to be true** so good in a way that is difficult to believe ○ *Her new job sounds too good to be true.*

took /tʊk/ *past simple of* TAKE

tool /tuːl/ *n* [C] **1** a piece of equipment that you use to help you do a job, esp. something that you use with your hands to make or repair something ○ *The only tools you need for this job are a hammer and a screwdriver.* **2** A tool is also anything that helps you to do something you want to do: *We believe the new law will be an effective tool in fighting poverty.*

T

toonie /ˈtuː·ni/ *n* [C] *Cdn, infml* a Canadian coin worth two dollars

tooth /tuːθ/ *n* [C] *pl* **teeth** any of the hard, white objects in the mouth that are used for biting and chewing food

toothy /ˈtuː·θi/ *adj* showing a lot of your teeth ○ *a toothy grin/smile*

toothache /ˈtuːθ·eɪk/ *n* [C] a pain caused by something being wrong with one of your teeth

toothbrush /ˈtuːθ·brʌʃ/ *n* [C] a small brush with a long handle that you use to clean your teeth

toothpaste /ˈtuːθ·peɪst/ *n* [C/U] a thick, creamy substance that you put on a TOOTHBRUSH to clean your teeth

toothpick /ˈtuːθ·pɪk/ *n* [C] a small pointed piece of wood or plastic that is used to clean the teeth, esp. after meals

top **HIGHEST PART** /tɑp/ *n* [C] the highest point, place, or part ○ *We set out for the top of the mountain at daybreak.* ○ Opposite: BOTTOM LOWEST PART

top /tɑp/ *adj* [not gradable] ○ *The pages are numbered on the top, right-hand corner.*

top /tɑp/ *v* [T] **-pp-** to be more than ○ *The school building fund now tops $180,000.*

topping /ˈtɑp·ɪŋ/ *n* [C] a food substance put on top of other food to give extra flavor or as a decoration ○ [C] *You can get pizza with six different choices of toppings.*

UPPER /tɑp/ *adj* [not gradable] in the highest or upper part ○ *She tripped over the top step and nearly fell.* ○ *The book was on (the) top of the table* (= on the upper surface of the table).

top /tɑp/ *n* [C] a piece of clothing worn esp. by women on the part of the body above the waist ○ *I'm looking for a matching top to go with this skirt.*

BEST /tɑp/ *adj, adv* [not gradable] **1** (in the position of being) at the highest level of importance, achievement, or success; best ○ *It was rated among the ten top universities in the nation.* ○ *She's one of the top executives in the fashion industry.* ○ *As a chess player, he's among the top 10% in the country.* **2** Top is used with many different words to mean best: *top-ranked athletes* ○ *top-rated bonds* ○ *top-seeded tennis players*

top /tɑp/ *n* [U] ○ *At forty he was at the top of* (= one of the leaders of) *his profession.*

top /tɑp/ *v* [T] **-pp-** to make something more or better ○ *"They've offered me $1000." "I'm afraid we can't top* (= offer more than) *that."*

tops /tɑps/ *adj* [not gradable] ○ *She is tops* (= excellent) *in her field.*

LID /tɑp/ *n* [C] a cover or lid used to close a container ○ *a bottle top*

TOY /tɑp/ *n* [C] a toy with rounded sides that you can spin on a point at its bottom

WORD FAMILY top

Nouns	top topping	*Adjectives*	top topmost
Verbs	top		

IDIOMS with top

• **at the top of** *your* **lungs** very loudly ○ *She shouted his name at the top of her lungs, but there was no answer.*

• **on top** in the best or most successful position ○ *She came out on top in every race.*

• **on top of** *something* **1** in control of a situation and aware of changes ○ *The stock market has been unpredictable, and you really have to stay on top of things.* **2 On top of** is also used to mean in addition to, esp. something unpleasant ○ *We missed the bus, and on top of that it started raining.*

• **on top of the world** very happy ○ *She was feeling on top of the world after winning the tennis tournament.*

• **to top it (all) off, topping it (all) off** to add something else unusually good or bad to a situation that is already unusual ○ *Topping it all off, they found themselves locked out of their own house.e*

PHRASAL VERBS with top

• **top off** *something* **COMPLETE** [M] to make something complete or satisfying ○ *A fabulous cherry pie topped off the meal.*

• **top off** *something* **CONTAINER** [M] fill a container completely ○ *Sean filled his glass and then topped off Ed Carey's.*

top-drawer, top drawer *adj* [not gradable] of very high quality ○ *She brought together a team of top-drawer designers and engineers.*

top-flight *adj* [not gradable] of the best quality or at the highest level ○ *He wasn't considered a top-flight manager.*

top-heavy *adj* having more weight in the higher part than in the lower part and so tending to fall easily ○ *If you stand up in such a small boat, you make it top-heavy, and it can turn over easily.* ○ (fig.) *The organization was top-heavy with vice presidents.*

topic Ⓐ /ˈtɑp·ɪk/ *n* [C] a subject that is written about, discussed, or studied ○ *We must pick topics for our research papers by next week.*

topical Ⓐ /ˈtɑp·ɪ·kəl/ *adj* relating to matters of importance at the present time ○ *It was an interesting discussion of topical issues in medicine.*

topmost /ˈtɑp·moʊst/ *adj* highest ○ *We sat on the topmost step and waited.*

top-notch *adj* [not gradable] excellent; of very good quality ○ *His level of fitness will have to be top-notch for him to play professional basketball.*

topography /təˈpɑg·rə·fi/ *n* [U] ***earth science*** the natural features of land, esp. the shape of its surface, or the science of mapping those features ○ *Volcanoes have sculpted the topography of the island.* ➤ Picture: **gulf; island; isthmus; lagoon; peninsula**

topographical /ˌtɑp·əˈgræf·ɪ·kəl/ *adj* [not gradable] ***earth science*** ○ *Borden drew the first topographical map of Texas.*

topographer /təˈpɑg·rə·fər/ *n* [C] ***earth science*** a person who maps the surface features of land

topographic /ˌtɑp·əˈɡræf·ɪk/ *adj* [not gradable] ***earth science***

topple /ˈtɑp·əl/ *v* [I/T] **1** to lean forward and fall ○ [T] *A large tree was toppled by the wind.* **2** If a government topples, it is forced from power: [T] *The government toppled after several large public demonstrations.*

top-secret, **top secret** *adj* [not gradable] very secret and not to be told or shown to anyone apart from a special group of people

topsoil /ˈtɑp·sɔɪl/ *n* [U] ***earth science*** the layer of earth in which plants grow ○ *rich topsoil*

topsy-turvy /ˌtɑp·siːˈtɜr·vi/ *adj infml* confused, or lacking organization; UPSIDE DOWN ○ *Things are so topsy-turvy at work these days.*

Torah /ˈtɔːr·ə, ˈtoʊr·ə, ˈtɔɪ·rə/ *n* [U] the holy writings of the Jewish religion, esp. the first five books of the Old Testament

torch /tɔːrtʃ/ *n* [C] **1** a stick that burns at one end and is held at the other end and is used esp. as a light ○ *Which athlete will carry the Olympic torch into the stadium?* **2** *fig.* The torch is the basic responsibilities and characteristics of a group, organization, or society, esp. when someone new takes control: *After he retired, the torch passed to his daughter, who now runs the organization.* **3** A torch is also a BLOWTORCH.

torch /tɔːrtʃ/ *v* [T] *infml* to burn something intentionally and usually illegally ○ *They torched the warehouse and ran.*

torch song *n* [C] a song about love or about people in love

tore /tɔːr, toʊr/ *past simple of* TEAR

torment /ˈtɔːr·ment/ *n* [C/U] great mental or physical suffering, or something that causes such pain ○ [U] *After three days of torment, she went to a dentist.* ○ [C] *That child acts like it's a torment to see me.*

torment /tɔːrˈment, ˈtɔːr·ment/ *v* [T] ○ *The cows were tormented by flies.*

torn /tɔːrn, toʊrn/ *past participle of* TEAR

IDIOM with **torn**

• **torn between** *something* **and** *something* finding it very difficult to choose between two possibilities ○ *She's torn between her loyalty and her desire to tell the truth.*

tornado /tɔːrˈneɪd·oʊ/, *infml* **twister** *n* [C] *pl* **tornadoes**, **tornados** a dangerous storm which is a spinning cone of wind that destroys anything in its path as it moves across the ground

torpedo /tɔːrˈpiːd·oʊ/ *n* [C] *pl* **torpedoes** a bomb designed to travel under water which explodes when it hits something ○ *No one on the ship saw the torpedo coming, not even the men on watch.*

torpedo /tɔːrˈpiːd·oʊ/ *v* [T] **torpedoes**, *pres. part.* **torpedoing**, *past* **torpedoed** ○ *The ship was torpedoed by a submarine.* ○ *(fig.) In fact, both sides torpedoed the ceasefire* (= destroyed its chances for success).

torque /tɔːrk/ *n* [U] ***physics*** a force that causes something to turn, or the power of such a force

torr /tɔːr/ *n* [C] ***physics*** a unit for measuring pressure

torrent /ˈtɔːr·ənt, ˈtɑr-/ *n* [C] a large stream of water that moves very fast ○ *Heavy storms turned the river into a raging torrent.* ○ *(fig.) The TV station received torrents of angry letters* (= many of them).

torrential /təˈren·tʃəl/ *adj* [not gradable] ○ *The torrential rains caused mud slides.*

torrid HOT /ˈtɔːr·əd, ˈtɑr-/ *adj* [not gradable] (of weather) extremely hot ○ *Summers in the tropics are torrid.*

POWERFUL /ˈtɔːr·əd, ˈtɑr-/ *adj* [not gradable] involving very powerful emotions

PERFORMING WELL /ˈtɔːr·əd, ˈtɑr-/ *adj* [not gradable] performing or doing something extremely well ○ *He kept up his torrid hitting pace with a sixth homer in eight days.* ○ *After a couple of months of torrid sales, business began to settle down.*

torso /ˈtɔːr·soʊ/ *n* [C] *pl* **torsos** the main part of the human body without the head, arms, or legs

tort /tɔːrt/ *n* [C] an act of injury or damage to a person or property that is covered by a law, so that the person can start a court action ○ *The company has an army of tort lawyers ready to back up its demands.*

tortilla /tɔːrˈtiː·ə/ *n* [C] a thin, flat, round bread made of corn or wheat flour and baked on top of a stove ○ *I could eat tortillas filled with cheese every day.*

tortilla chips *pl n* small fried pieces of a TORTILLA, often eaten with a spicy sauce

tortoise /ˈtɔːrt̬·əs/ *n* [C] a TURTLE, esp. one that lives only on land

tortoiseshell /ˈtɔːrt̬·əsˌʃel/ *n* [U] the hard shell of a TURTLE that has attractive brown and yellow patterns, or plastic made to look like this shell ○ *a tortoiseshell barrette* ○ *tortoiseshell eyeglass frames*

tortuous /ˈtɔːr·tʃə·wəs/ *adj* full of twists and turns; not straight or direct ○ *His so-called shortcut turned out to be tortuous and slow.*

torture /ˈtɔːr·tʃər/ *n* [C/U] **1** an injury or severe mental pain ○ [C] *All drivers suffer the tortures of traffic and bad weather.* **2** Torture is also the act of injuring someone or making someone suffer in an effort to force that person to do or say what you want to be done or said: [U] *The museum has many examples of instruments of torture.*

torture /ˈtɔːr·tʃər/ *v* [T] ○ *She was tortured by the memory of their last argument.*

Tory /ˈtɔːr·i, toʊr·i/ *n* [C] **1** ***politics & government*** a member of the main CONSERVATIVE political party in Canada **2** ***politics & government*** A Tory is also a member of the main CONSERVATIVE political party in Great Britain. **3** ***US history*** During the American Revolution, a Tory was a person who supported the British government: LOYALIST. ○ Compare WHIG

toss /tɔːs/ *v* [T] **1** to throw gently or easily ○ *He tossed his dirty clothes on the floor.* ○ *Matthew tossed the ball to his brother.* **2** When you toss food, you gently mix small pieces of it together or with a sauce: *I tossed the salad.* **3** If you toss your hair or your head, you move it suddenly: *The girl tossed her hair out of her eyes.* **4** If you **toss a coin**, you choose between two possibilities by throwing a coin into the air and letting each side represent one of the possibilities, then accepting the possibility represented by the side that lands facing up: *We tossed to see who would go first.*

toss /tɔːs/ *n* [C] ○ *"I don't care," she replied with a toss of her head.*

IDIOM with toss

• **toss (and turn)** to move around restlessly while sleeping or trying to sleep ○ *I was tossing and turning all night.*

PHRASAL VERBS with toss

• **toss around** *something* [M] to discuss possibilities or new ideas with a group of people ○ *Some of us have been tossing around suggestions for improving the show.*

• **toss off** *something* [M] to do something quickly, easily, and almost without paying attention ○ *No one knew she could toss off a performance as subtle and soulful as this.*

• **toss out** *something* [M] to remove something ○ *She tossed out my old chair.* ○ *The case was finally tossed out of court.*

toss-up *n* [C] a situation in which two possibilities are equally likely ○ *It was a toss-up who would win, right to the end of the game.*

tot /tɑt/ *n* [C] a small child ○ *The tiny tot was trying so hard to keep up with his brother.*

total AMOUNT /ˈtoʊt̬·ᵊl/ *n* [C] **1** the whole amount ○ *Add these up and give me the total.* ○ *We paid a total of $473.* **2 In total** means including everything added together: *Last week 45 people in total came to the senior center.*

total /ˈtoʊt̬·ᵊl/ *adj* [not gradable] ○ *Total grain exports have increased.*

total /ˈtoʊt̬·ᵊl/ *v* [T] **-l-, -ll-** ○ *This history series totals twelve volumes in all.*

COMPLETE /ˈtoʊt̬·ᵊl/ *adj* [not gradable] complete or extreme ○ *Negotiations had to be held in total secrecy.*

totally /ˈtoʊt̬·ᵊl·i/ *adv* ○ *This book is totally different from her last one.*

DESTROY /ˈtoʊt̬·ᵊl/ *v* [T] to destroy something completely ○ *She didn't total the car, but she did a lot of damage.*

totalitarian /toʊˌtæl·əˈter·iː·ən/ *adj* [not gradable] ***world history*** of or relating to a government that has almost complete control over the lives of its citizens and does not permit political opposition

totalitarianism /toʊˌtæl·əˈter·iː·əˌnɪz·əm/ *n* [U] ***world history*** the belief that a government should have total power over its citizens

tote /toʊt/ *v* [T] *infml* to carry something with you ○ [M] *Tommy always totes around his cell phone.*

tote bag *n* [C] a bag, usually made of cloth, with handles and an open top

totem /ˈtoʊt̬·əm/ *n* [C] an object that is a symbol for a group of people ○ *They thought of him as a good-luck totem.*

totem pole *n* [C] a wooden pole with symbols cut or painted on it which is connected esp. with American Indians of the Northwest

totter /ˈtɑt̬·ər/ *v* [I] to move or walk in a way that looks as if you are about to fall ○ *She tottered down the stairs.*

touch USE FINGERS /tʌtʃ/ *v* [I/T] **1** to put the fingers or hand lightly on or against something ○ [I] *That paint is wet, so don't touch.* **2** *infml* If you cannot touch something, you are not allowed to have or use it: [T] *She can't touch the money from her father until she's 21.* **3** *infml* If you say you do not touch something, you mean that you do not drink or eat it: [T] *I never touch candy.*

touch /tʌtʃ/ *n* [C/U] **1** the ability to know what something is like by putting your hand or fingers on it ○ [U] *This cloth is soft to the touch.* **2** A touch is an act of putting your hand or fingers briefly on something to operate it: [C] *At a touch of the button, the door opened.*

BE CLOSE /tʌtʃ/ *v* [I/T] **1** to be so close together that there is no space between ○ [T] *Don't let the back of the chair touch the wall.* ○ [I] *Push the bookcases together until they touch.* **2** If one thing does not touch something similar, it is not as good as the other thing: [T] *Her cooking can't touch her sister's.*

touch /tʌtʃ/ *n* [U]

CAUSE FEELINGS /tʌtʃ/ *v* [T] to cause someone to feel sympathetic or grateful ○ *Your kindness has touched my family.*

touched /tʌtʃt/ *adj* ○ *She was touched by the letters and cards sent by people she didn't even know.*

touching /ˈtʌtʃ·ɪŋ/ *adj* ○ *Many find stories about cats more touching than any human stories.*

SKILL /tʌtʃ/ *n* [U] a skill or special quality ○ *He seems to be losing his touch at poker.* ○ *The flowers were a nice touch.*

SMALL AMOUNT /tʌtʃ/ *n* [C] a small amount ○ *There was a touch of regret in her voice.* ○ *I had a touch of flu yesterday.*

WORD FAMILY touch

Nouns	touch	*Adjectives*	touched
Verbs	touch		untouched
			touching
Adverbs	touchingly		touchy

IDIOMS with touch

• **in touch (with** *someone***)** seeing someone or communicating with someone regularly ○ *We kept in touch for a while after college.* ○ *We stay in close touch with the New York office.* ○ Compare LOSE TOUCH (WITH SOMEONE) at LOSE IDIOMS

• **in touch (with** *something***)** having recent knowledge of a subject ○ *I try to stay in touch with the modern music scene.*

• **touch base (with** *someone***)** to talk briefly with someone ○ *I'll touch base with him later to tell him about the meeting.*
• *someone* **wouldn't touch** *something* **with a ten-foot pole** someone does not want to be involved with something in any way ○ *I wouldn't touch that car with a ten-foot pole – it's a gas guzzler.*

PHRASAL VERBS with touch

• **touch down** to land at an airport ○ *The flight touched down on time.* ○ Related noun: TOUCHDOWN AIRCRAFT
• **touch off** *something* [M] to start a fight or violent activity, or to cause a fire or explosion ○ *Plans for a new airport touched off a storm of protest.* ○ *Brown's raid touched off the Civil War.* ○ *Wind-blown wires touched off the blaze.*
• **touch on** *something* to speak briefly about something ○ *Of course, we only touched on how much I would be paid.*
• **touch up** *something* [M] to improve something with small changes ○ *I had to touch up the paint job on my car.*

touch-and-go *adj* having an uncertain, and possibly bad result ○ *At one point, the operation was touch-and-go.*

touchdown FOOTBALL GOAL /ˈtʌtʃ·dɑʊn/, *abbreviation* **TD** *n* [C] (in football) the act of scoring six points by carrying or catching the ball behind the other team's goal line ○ *He scored three touchdowns early in the game.*

AIRCRAFT /ˈtʌtʃ·dɑʊn/ *n* [C] the moment when an aircraft or spacecraft lands ○ *High winds delayed the space shuttle's touchdown.* ○ Related verb: TOUCH DOWN

touching /ˈtʌtʃ·ɪŋ/ *adj* ○ See at TOUCH CAUSE FEELINGS

touchstone /ˈtʌtʃ·stoʊn/ *n* [C] a basic principle for judging quality ○ *Perfect service is the touchstone of a fine restaurant.*

touchy /ˈtʌtʃ·i/ *adj* [*-er/-est* only] **1** easily angered or made unhappy ○ *She's touchy about people borrowing her books.* **2** A touchy subject or situation is one that must be dealt with carefully: *Politics can be a very touchy subject in some families.*

tough STRONG /tʌf/ *adj* [*-er/-est* only] **1** not easily broken, weakened, or defeated; strong ○ *These toys are made of tough plastic.* ○ *You have to be tough to be successful in politics.* ○ *The police are getting tougher on illegal parking.* **2** Results or actions that are tough are severe and determined: *Tough new safety standards for cars are being introduced this week.*

toughen /ˈtʌf·ən/ *v* [T] ○ *They're going to toughen civil rights laws.*

toughness /ˈtʌf·nəs/ *n* [U] ○ *He lacks the inner toughness needed in a leader.*

DIFFICULT /tʌf/ *adj* [*-er/-est* only] **1** difficult to do or deal with ○ *They will be a tough team to beat.* ○ *We've had to make some very tough decisions.* ○ *It's going to be a tough winter.* **2** Food that is tough is difficult to cut or eat: *a tough steak*

VIOLENT /tʌf/ *adj* [*-er/-est* only] likely to be violent or to contain violence ○ *a tough guy* ○ *a tough neighborhood*

IDIOMS with tough

• **a tough act to follow** *infml* so good that whatever happens next is unlikely to seem as good ○ *The last Bond movie was my favorite – it'll be a tough act to follow.*
• **a tough row to hoe** a difficult situation to deal with ○ *The candidate has a tough row to hoe – he has limited funds, and his message is not a popular one.*
• **tough (luck)** I do not have any sympathy for your problems ○ *Anyone who misses three classes will fail, and if you don't like it, tough.*

PHRASAL VERBS with tough

• **tough out** *something* [M] *infml* to be strong during a difficult situation ○ *Should we tough it out, or should we quit now and cut our losses?*
• **toughen** *someone* **up** [M] to make someone stronger ○ *The hard work certainly toughened those boys up.*

toupee /tuːˈpeɪ/ *n* [C] a specially shaped piece of artificial hair that can be worn by a man to cover an area of his head that has no hair

tour /tʊr/ *n* [C] **1** a visit to a place or area, esp. one during which you look around the place or area and learn about it ○ *a walking tour* ○ *a sightseeing tour* **2** A tour is also a planned visit to several places to give performances: *The band is currently* **on tour** *in Australia.*

tour /tʊr/ *v* [I/T] ○ [T] *We spent a month touring France.* ○ [I] *Alanis is touring to promote her new album.*

tourist /ˈtʊr·əst/ *n* [C] a person who travels and visits places for pleasure and interest ○ *Millions of tourists visit Rome every year.*

tourism /ˈtʊrˌɪz·əm/ *n* [U] the business of providing services, such as transportation, places to stay, or entertainment, for tourists

tournament /ˈtʊr·nə·mənt, ˈtɜr-, ˈtɔːr-/, **tourney** /ˈtʊr·ni, ˈtɜr-, ˈtɔːr-/ *n* [C] a competition involving many competitors in a single sport or game ○ *a chess/golf tournament*

tourniquet /ˈtʊr·nɪ·kət, ˈtɜr-/ *n* [C] a strip of cloth that is tied tightly around an injured arm or leg to stop the flow of blood

tousled /ˈtɑʊ·zəld, -səld/ *adj* (esp. of hair) looking messy ○ *She ran her fingers through her tousled hair.*

tout /tɑʊt/ *v* [T] **1** to advertise or praise something, often to encourage its use or sale ○ *Various studies have been published touting the benefits of pre-kindergarten programs.* **2** If you tout someone's good character, knowledge, skills, achievements, etc., you praise those characteristics: *The President was in Ohio on Saturday, touting his accomplishments and urging supporters to re-elect him.*

tow /toʊ/ *v* [T] to pull a car, boat, aircraft, etc., using a rope or a chain attached to another vehicle

T

○ *The town tows abandoned cars and then fines their owners.*
tow /toʊ/ *n* [C] ○ *My car broke down and Bob gave me a tow.*

IDIOM with **tow**

• **in tow** following or going along under someone's control ○ *She arrived with her three children in tow.*

toward MOVEMENT /twɔːrd, twoʊrd, tə'wɔːrd/, **towards** /twɔːrdz, twoʊrdz, tə'wɔːrdz/ *prep* in the direction of; closer to ○ *She stood up and walked toward him.* ○ *The hurricane is heading toward Florida.*

RELATION /twɔːrd, twoʊrd, tə'wɔːrd/, **towards** /twɔːrdz, twoʊrdz, tə'wɔːrdz/ *prep* in relation to ○ *Their attitudes toward politicians have changed.*

POSITION /twɔːrd, twoʊrd, tə'wɔːrd/, **towards** /twɔːrdz, twoʊrdz, tə'wɔːrdz/ *prep* near to; just before or around ○ *Our seats were toward the back of the theater.* ○ *Harry's book will be published toward the end of the year.*

PURPOSE /twɔːrd, twoʊrd, tə'wɔːrd/, **towards** /twɔːrdz, twoʊrdz, tə'wɔːrdz/, *prep* for the purpose of (buying or achieving something) ○ *I'm saving up to buy a car, and Dad gave me some money toward it.* ○ *Government should be working toward a cleaner environment.* ○ *How much does this exam count toward our final grade?*

towel /taʊ·əl, taʊl/ *n* [C] a usually rectangular piece of cloth or paper used for drying something ○ *a bath towel* ○ *paper towels*
towel /'taʊ·əl, taʊl/ *v* [T] -l-, -ll- ○ *She toweled her hair dry.*

tower /'taʊ·ər, taʊr/ *n* [C] **1** a tall, narrow structure that either forms part of a building or stands alone ○ *a clock tower* **2** A tower is also a tall, usually metal structure used for broadcasting: *a television tower*
tower /'taʊ·ər, taʊr/ *v* [I always + adv/prep] to appear very tall or large, or to be much taller than something else ○ *As we drove on, the Rocky Mountains towered before us.* ○ *Although he's only 14, David towers over his mother.*
towering /'taʊ·ə·rɪŋ, 'taʊ·rɪŋ/ *adj* ○ *Fielder hit a towering* (= very high) *home run.* ○ *Bresson's towering* (= great) *masterpiece explores the nature of freedom.*

town /taʊn/ *n* [C/U] **1** a place where there are a lot of houses, stores, and other buildings which is smaller than a city ○ [C] *He was born in the small town of Elnora, Indiana.* ○ [U] *We stayed at the best hotel in town.* **2** Town can also mean the place where you live or work: [U] *Barbara is out of town this week.* **3** Town is also the part of a town where the main stores are: [U] *I'm going into/to town to do some shopping.* **4** Town can also refer to the people who live in the town: [C] *The whole town is hoping our team will win.*
township /'taʊn·ʃɪp/ *n* [C] (in parts of the US and Canada) a unit of local government consisting of a town and the area surrounding it

IDIOM with **town**

• **on the town** going to places of entertainment in a town or city for fun ○ *I was out on the town last night.*

town hall *n* [C] a building in which local government officials and employees work and in which public meetings may be held

townhouse /'taʊn·haʊs/, **townhome** /'taʊn·hoʊm/ *n* [C] one of a row of similar houses that are usually joined by a shared wall

townspeople /'taʊnz,piː·pəl/, **townsfolk** /'taʊnz·foʊk/ *pl n* the people who live in a particular town, considered as a group

tow truck *n* [C] a truck that has special equipment for pulling vehicles that cannot be driven

toxic /'tɑk·sɪk/ *adj* ***biology, chemistry*** poisonous, or relating to poisonous substances
toxicity /tɑk'sɪs·əţ·i/ *n* [U] the quality of being poisonous, or the degree to which something is poisonous

toxin /'tɑk·sən/ *n* [C] ***biology*** a poisonous substance, esp. one that is produced by bacteria and causes disease

toy PLAY OBJECT /tɔɪ/ *n* [C] an object that children play with ○ *a stuffed toy* ○ *a toy train/soldier*

SMALL DOG /tɔɪ/ *adj* [not gradable] (of a breed of dog) very small and kept as a pet ○ *a toy poodle*

PHRASAL VERB with **toy**

• **toy with** *something* to consider or think about something in a not very serious way, and without making a decision ○ *We're toying with the idea of going to Peru next year.*

trace Ⓐ FIND /treɪs/ *v* [T] **1** to find someone or something by searching carefully ○ *Police are trying to trace the mother of the abandoned baby.* ○ *The phone company was unable to trace the call* (= find where it came from). **2** To trace something is also to discover its cause or origin: *The outbreak of food poisoning was traced to contaminated shellfish.* ○ *They trace their family back to the early settlers.* **3** To trace something is also to describe the way it developed: *The movie traces the events leading up to the Russian Revolution.*
trace Ⓐ /treɪs/ *n* [C] a mark or sign that something happened or existed ○ *They found traces of a lost civilization in the jungle.* ○ *He vanished without a trace.*
traceable Ⓐ /'treɪ·sə·bəl/ *adj* ○ *In theory, most telephone calls should be traceable.*

DRAW /treɪs/ *v* [T] to copy a drawing, pattern, etc. by drawing its lines on a thin piece of paper that is placed over it

SLIGHT AMOUNT /treɪs/ *n* [C] a very slight amount or degree ○ *There was a trace of a smile on his face,* ○ *She speaks English without the slightest trace of an accent.*

trachea /'treɪ·kiː·ə/ *n* [C] *pl* **tracheae, tracheas** ***biology*** the tube that carries air from your throat to your lungs

track **PATH** /træk/ *n* [C] **1** a path that is narrower than a road, often with an uneven surface ○ *We walked along a muddy track at the side of the field.* **2** A track is also one or a pair of parallel metal bars on which trains travel.

MARKS /træk/ *n* [C usually pl] a mark or line of marks left on a surface, esp. the ground, by a moving animal, person, or vehicle, that shows the direction of travel ○ *deer tracks in the snow*

track /træk/ *v* [T] **1** to follow something that moves or changes by noticing marks or signs that it has left behind ○ *The study tracked the careers of 1226 doctors who trained at Harvard Medical School.* **2** If you track something messy or dirty, you leave messy or dirty marks when walking because you had something on your shoes or feet: *The kids are always tracking mud in the kitchen.*

SPORTS /træk/ *n* [C/U] **1** the sport of competitive running, or a wide, circular path that is made for this sport ○ [U] *Fall sports include football, hockey, and track.* **2** A track is also a specially prepared surface for any kind of racing: [C] *a dog/thoroughbred track*

MUSIC /træk/ *n* [C] one of several songs or pieces of music on a musical recording

IDIOMS with **track**

• **on track** developing as expected ○ *We were behind schedule on this job, but we're back on track now.*

• **on the right track** doing something correctly or well ○ *You haven't quite got the answer yet, but you're on the right track.*

• **on the wrong track** not correct about something ○ *If you suspect my son was involved, you are on the wrong track.*

PHRASAL VERB with **track**

• **track down** *someone/something* [M] to search for someone or something, often when it is difficult to find that person or thing ○ *I'm trying to track down one of my old classmates from college.*

track and field *n* [U] a group of sports that includes running, jumping, and throwing objects and that usually involves large competitions

track event *n* [C] a running race over a fixed distance ○ Compare FIELD EVENT

track meet *n* [C] a sporting competition between two or more teams, involving running races as well as jumping and throwing competitions

track record *n* [C] all of the successes and failures of a person or organization considered together ○ *We invest in large companies with an impressive track record of introducing new technology.*

tract **LAND** /trækt/ *n* [C] a large area of land, or a measured area of land ○ *The house is surrounded by vast tracts of woodland.* ○ *A new hospital will be built on the 60-acre tract.*

BODY SYSTEM /trækt/ *n* [C] a system of tubes and organs in the body that are connected and have a particular purpose ○ *the digestive/urinary tract*

WRITING /trækt/ *n* [C] *fml* a short piece of writing, esp. on a religious or political subject, that is intended to influence people's opinions

traction **HOLDING** /ˈtræk·ʃən/ *n* [U] the ability of a wheel or tire to hold the ground without sliding ○ *I reduce the air pressure in all four tires during winter for better traction on slick, icy roads.*

PULLING /ˈtræk·ʃən/ *n* [U] **1** the pulling of a heavy load over a surface, or the power used to do this **2** *medical* Traction is also a state in which an injured part of the body is gently pulled with special equipment: *His broken leg was put in a cast and was in traction.*

tractor /ˈtræk·tər/ *n* [C] a motor vehicle with large back wheels and thick tires that is used on farms for pulling heavy loads and machinery

tractor-trailer /ˌtræk·tər ˈtreɪ·lər/ *n* [C] a powerful vehicle for moving heavy loads, esp. over long distances, consisting of a separate part at the front for the driver attached to a large rectangular container on wheels

trade **BUYING AND SELLING** /treɪd/ *n* [C/U] **1** the activity of buying and selling goods and services esp. between countries ○ [U] *foreign trade* ○ [U] *a trade agreement* **2** A trade is the act of exchanging one thing for another.

trade /treɪd/ *v* [I/T] **1** to buy, sell, or exchange goods ○ [I] *For centuries, Native Americans traded with European settlers.* **2** To trade is also to exchange something: [T] *The children traded comics.* ○ [T] *The two players traded insults and nearly came to blows.* **3** If you trade something in, such as a car, you give it as part of the payment for something new: [M] *He recently traded in his Jeep for a red Mercedes.*

trader /ˈtreɪd·ər/ *n* [C] someone who buys and sells goods or services

JOB /treɪd/ *n* [C/U] **1** a job, esp. one that needs special skill and that involves working with your hands, or the type of work in which such skills are needed ○ [C] *the building trades* ○ [U] *He's an auto mechanic/electrician by trade.* **2** A trade is also any business: [C] *the book/tourist trade*

WORD FAMILY trade

Nouns	trade trader	*Verbs*	trade

PHRASAL VERB with **trade**

• **trade on/upon** *something* to use something for your own advantage, esp. unfairly ○ *He ran the kind of political campaign that trades on people's fear of crime.*

trade deficit *n* [C] ***social studies*** the economic condition that exists when a greater value of goods comes into a country than the value of goods that are sold out of the country

trademark /ˈtreɪd·mɑrk/, *symbol* ™ *n* [C] a symbol, name, design, or phrase on a product that shows it is made by a particular company

tradeoff, **trade-off** /ˈtreɪd·ɔːf/ *n* [C] **1** a balancing of two opposing situations or qualities, both of

T

which are desired ○ *The tradeoff in a democracy is between individual liberty and an orderly society.* **2** A tradeoff is also a situation in which the achieving of something you want involves the loss of something else which is also desirable, but less so: *They both had successful careers, but the tradeoff was they seldom saw each other.*

trade secret *n* [C] a piece of information about a product that is known only to the company that makes it ○ *The recipe for their ketchup is a trade secret.*

trade union *n* [C] a LABOR UNION

tradition Ⓐ /trəˈdɪʃ·ən/ *n* [C/U] a way of behaving or a belief that has been established for a long time, or the practice of following behavior and beliefs that have been so established ○ [C] *It is a western tradition for brides to wear white.* ○ [U] *The Dinka people are cattle-farmers by tradition.*

traditional Ⓐ /trəˈdɪʃ·ən·əl/ *adj* ○ *the traditional two-parent family* ○ *traditional Southern cooking* ○ *the traditional politeness of Japanese culture*

traditionalist Ⓐ /trəˈdɪʃ·ən·əl·əst/ *n* [C] someone who believes in and follows traditional ideas

traditionally Ⓐ /trəˈdɪʃ·ən·əl·i/ *adv* ○ *The Democratic Party won a seat in the Senate that has traditionally been held by a Republican.*

WORD FAMILY tradition			
Nouns	tradition	*Adverbs*	traditionally
Adjectives	traditional		

traffic MOVING THINGS /ˈtræf·ɪk/ *n* [U] the movement of vehicles or people along roads, or the movement of aircraft, trains, or ships along a route ○ *heavy/rush-hour traffic* ○ *Air traffic has increased 30% in the last decade.*

TRADE /ˈtræf·ɪk/ *n* [U] illegal trade ○ *They're trying to cut down on the traffic in exotic birds being sold illegally.*

traffic /ˈtræf·ɪk/ *v* [I] *pres. part.* **trafficking**, *past* **trafficked** ○ *He was charged with trafficking in stolen goods.*

trafficker /ˈtræf·ɪ·kər/ *n* [C] someone who is involved in illegal trade ○ *ivory traffickers*

traffic circle, **rotary** *n* [C] a place where roads meet in a circle that drivers go around to find their next road

traffic jam *n* [C] a situation of too many vehicles on a road so that they can move only very slowly or not at all

traffic light, **light**, **stoplight** /ˈstɑp·lɑɪt/ *n* [C] a set of red, yellow, and green lights that control the movement of vehicles at a point where two or more streets meet

tragedy /ˈtrædʒ·ə·di/ *n* [C/U] **1** a very sad event or situation, esp. one involving death or suffering ○ [U] *His reckless driving was bound to end in tragedy.* **2** A tragedy is also a situation or result that is bad: [C] *It's a tragedy (that) so many children are unable to get a decent education.* **3** ***literature*** In the theater, a tragedy is a serious play that ends with the death or suffering of the main character: [C] *Shakespeare's tragedies*

tragic /ˈtrædʒ·ɪk/ *adj* **1** very sad because connected with death and suffering ○ *Two men lost their lives in a tragic accident.* **2** In the theater, tragic means having to do with a TRAGEDY (= type of play having a sad ending): *a tragic actor*

tragically /ˈtrædʒ·ɪ·kli/ *adv* ○ *Tragically, the side effects of the drug were not discovered until many people had been seriously hurt by it.*

trail PATH /treɪl/ *n* [C] **1** a path through the countryside, often made or used for a particular purpose ○ *a bike/mountain/nature trail* ○ *(fig.) Presidential candidates were on the campaign trail in Mississippi yesterday.* **2** A trail is also a series of marks left by a person, animal, or thing as it moves along: *A trail of muddy footprints led across the kitchen floor.*

FOLLOW /treɪl/ *v* [I/T] **1** to follow or come behind ○ [T] *Ray trailed Kate up to the porch.* ○ [I always + adv/prep] *A string of police cars led the president's limousine and others trailed behind.* **2** In a competition, to trail is to be losing to someone: [I] *Dallas trailed 34-21 with less than seven minutes to play in the football game.* ○ [T] *Bush trailed the governor by only 4 percentage points.* ○ [I] *Though trailing in the polls, she predicted victory.*

PHRASAL VERB with trail

• **trail off** to become less in amount or loudness ○ *His voice trailed off weakly and we could not hear the rest.*

trailblazer /ˈtreɪl ˌbleɪ·zər/ *n* [C] a person who is the first to do something that other people do later ○ *She was a trailblazer as the only woman in the US Senate.*

trailer VEHICLE /ˈtreɪ·lər/ *n* [C] **1** a vehicle without an engine, often in the form of a flat frame or a container, that can be pulled by another vehicle **2** A trailer is also a house on wheels that can be moved by pulling it: *We bought a trailer for camping trips.* **3** A trailer is also a MOBILE HOME.

ADVERTISEMENT /ˈtreɪ·lər/ *n* [C] an advertisement for a movie, often showing a few, brief parts of it

train VEHICLE /treɪn/ *n* [C] a railroad engine and the connected, wheeled containers it pulls along the tracks in carrying goods or people ○ *a freight/passenger train* ○ *a commuter train*

PREPARE /treɪn/ *v* [I/T] to prepare someone or be prepared for a job, activity, or sport by learning skills or by mental or physical exercise ○ [I] *She trained as a pilot.* ○ [T] *He trains teachers to use new technology.* ○ [I] *She trained hard for the race, sometimes running as much as 60 miles a week.*

trainee /treɪˈniː/ *n* [C] a person who is learning and practicing new skills, esp. ones connected with a job ○ *We have three new trainees in the accounting department.*

trainer /ˈtreɪ·nər/ *n* [C] a person who teaches skills to people or animals to prepare them for a job, activity, or sport ○ *They showed pictures of the winning horse and its trainer.*

training /ˈtreɪ·nɪŋ/ *n* [U] **1** *We got two weeks of on-the-job training on how to conduct interviews.* **2** When you are in training for a competition, you exercise in a way that prepares you for it.

SERIES /treɪn/ *n* [C] a line of animals, people, or things moving along together, or a series of connected thoughts or events ○ *a mule/wagon train* ○ *Now I've lost my train of thought and forgot what I was going to say.*

PART OF DRESS /treɪn/ *n* [C] the part of a long dress that spreads out onto the floor behind

WORD FAMILY train			
Nouns	train trainee trainer training	*Adjectives* *Verbs*	untrained train

trainer /ˈtreɪ·nər/ *n* [C usually pl] *Br* SNEAKER

trait /treɪt/ *n* [C] **1** a characteristic, esp. of a personality ○ *Patience is one of his best traits.* **2** ***biology*** A trait is also a characteristic of an organism that is passed from parent to child.

traitor /ˈtreɪt̬·ər/ *n* [C] a person who gives away or sells secrets of his or her country, or someone who is not loyal to particular beliefs or friends ○ *Benedict Arnold was a traitor during the American Revolution.* ○ *Opponents called the mayor "a traitor to the cause."*

trajectory /trəˈdʒek·tə·ri/ *n* [C] ***physics*** the curved path an object follows after it is thrown or shot into the air, or of an object that is traveling through space ○ *The missile came in on a very low trajectory.*

tram /træm/ *n* [C] **1** an electric vehicle that is similar to a bus but travels on tracks laid along roads ○ *I hopped off the tram near the park.* **2** A tram is also a car that travels on a heavy wire up mountains or across rivers.

tramp **WALK** /træmp, trɑmp/, **tromp** /trɑmp, trɔːmp/ *v* [I/T] to walk with heavy steps ○ [I] *I've been tramping through museums all day.*

tramp /træmp/ *n* [U] ○ *We listened to the rhythmical tramp of soldiers' feet.*

POOR PERSON /træmp/ *n* [C] *dated* a person who travels around, asking for temporary work, food, or money from other people ○ *Tramps knew the houses where you got good food.*

trample /ˈtræm·pəl/ *v* [I/T] to step heavily on or crush someone or something ○ [T] *The commuter in a hurry tramples anyone who gets in the way.* ○ [I] *(fig.) An employer cannot trample on the rights of employees* (= damage or destroy them).

trampoline /ˌtræm·pəˈliːn/ *n* [C] a piece of equipment that is a sheet of strong material attached by springs to a frame, on which people jump

trance /træns/ *n* [C] a mental state between sleeping and waking in which a person does not move but can hear and understand what is being said ○ *The sound of waves lulled me into a trance.*

tranquil /ˈtræŋ·kwəl/ *adj* calm, quiet, and peaceful ○ *I lay on the dock under a tranquil blue sky.*

tranquility, **tranquillity** /træŋˈkwɪl·ət̬·i/ *n* [U] ○ *The tranquility of the forest helps me relax.*

tranquilize /ˈtræŋ·kwəˌlɑɪz/ *v* [T] ○ *Vets had to tranquilize the coyote before moving her.*

tranquilizer /ˈtræŋ·kwəˌlɑɪ·zər/ *n* [C] a drug that makes people or animals calm ○ *The veterinarian who examined the horse gave him a tranquilizer to calm him down.*

transact /trænˈzækt/ *v* [T] *fml* to do business, to buy or sell things ○ *You can transact business electronically.*

transaction /trænˈzæk·ʃən/ *n* [C] ○ *It was the biggest real estate transaction in the city's history.*

transatlantic /ˌtræn·zətˈlænt·ɪk/ *adj* [not gradable] crossing the Atlantic Ocean ○ *Newfoundland was once an important stop for transatlantic flights.*

transcend /trænˈsend/ *v* [T] to go beyond or rise above a limit, or be greater than something ordinary ○ *The group makes music that transcends traditional pop categories.*

transcontinental /ˌtrænˌskɑnt·ənˈent·əl/ *adj* [not gradable] crossing a continent ○ *Kennedy Airport handles primarily overseas and transcontinental flights.*

transcribe /trænˈskrɑɪb/ *v* [T] to make a complete written record of spoken or written words ○ *Only an expert could transcribe my notes so well.*

transcript /ˈtræn·skrɪpt/ *n* [C] a complete written copy of spoken or written words ○ *I had them send me a transcript of the program.*

transcription /trænˈskrɪp·ʃən/ *n* [U] ○ *The language of the characters in the novel is like a transcription of real criminals' talk.*

transfer Ⓐ /trænsˈfɜr, ˈtræns·fɜr/ *v* [I/T] **-rr-** **1** to move from one place, person, or position to another, or to cause someone or something to move ○ [I] *She studied for two years at Smith College, then transferred to the University of Chicago.* ○ [T] *Transfer your weight to your front foot as you swing.* **2** When property is transferred to someone, legal ownership is changed from one person to another: [T] *Franklin transferred the car to his brother.*

transfer Ⓐ /ˈtræns·fɜr/ *n* [C/U] ○ [C] *I got my money through an electronic transfer into my account.*

transferable Ⓐ /trænsˈfɜr·ə·bəl/ *adj* ○ *Prizes are not transferable except to a surviving spouse.*

transference Ⓐ /trænsˈfɜr·əns, ˈtræns·fɜr·əns/ *n* [U] **1** the transfer of ideas or methods from one situation to another **2** *fml* Transference is also the movement of something or someone from one place or position to another

transfer RNA, *abbreviation* **tRNA** *n* [U] ***biology*** a type of RNA (= chemical in all living cells) that combines with a specific AMINO ACID and carries it to the PROTEIN being made

T

transfixed /træns'fɪkst/ *adj* (of a person or animal) unable to move, usually because of great fear or interest in something ○ *The entire nation will sit transfixed in front of TV sets.*

transform Ⓐ /træns'fɔːrm/ *v* [T] to change completely the appearance or character of something or someone ○ *Computers have transformed the way work is done.* ○ *Salinas dramatically transformed the country's economy.*
transformation Ⓐ /ˌtræns·fər'meɪ·ʃən/ *n* [C/U] **1** [C] *This plan means a complete transformation of our organization.* **2** ***biology*** Transformation is also a permanent change in a cell that results when DNA comes from a different type of cell.
transformer /træns'fɔːr·mər/ *n* [C] a device that changes the characteristics of an electrical current

transfusion /træns'fjuː·ʒən/ *n* [C/U] the activity or process of putting new blood into a person's or animal's body, or an amount of blood received this way ○ [C] *He needs regular blood transfusions and a lot of medication.* ○ [C] (*fig.*) *The new prime minister brought a transfusion* (= fresh supply) *of young ideas into the government.*

transgression /trænz'greʃ·ən/ *n* [C/U] *fml* an action that breaks a law or rule ○ [C] *It is hard to keep the transgressions of famous people out of the news.*
transgress /trænz'gres/ *v* [T] *fml* ○ *He transgressed the military code of honor and paid a heavy penalty.*

transient /'træn·ʃənt, -dʒənt, -ziː·ənt/ *adj* [not gradable] **1** lasting for only a short time; TEMPORARY ○ *The weakness was transient, and soon I was feeling strong again.* **2** Transient also means staying for only a short time: *Transient workers come to pick apples and then head south to harvest other crops.*
transient /'træn·ʃənt, -dʒənt, -ziː·ənt/ *n* [C] ○ *Even transients just staying a day or two pay sales taxes.*

transistor /træn'zɪs·tər/ *n* [C] a small electronic device that controls electric current in televisions, radios, and other equipment

T

transit Ⓐ /'træn·zət, -sət/ *n* [U] the process of moving, or the movement of goods or people from one place to another ○ *Our boxes are in transit and should arrive tomorrow.*

transition Ⓐ /træn'zɪʃ·ən/ *n* [C/U] **1** the process of changing, or a change from one form or condition to another ○ [U] *It was a neighborhood in transition from Jewish to Italian with a sprinkling of Irish.* ○ [C] *Retirement is a big transition.* **2** ***literature, music*** A transition is also a link between ideas or sections in a work of literature or music.
transitional Ⓐ /træn'zɪʃ·ən·əl/ *adj* [not gradable] ○ *We're in a transitional period right now, and no one knows what to expect.*

transitive /'træn·zəṭ·ɪv, -səṭ·ɪv/ *adj* [not gradable] ***grammar*** (of a verb) having or needing an object ○ *In the sentence "The car hit a tree," "hit" is a transitive verb and "tree" is the object.* ○ Compare INTRANSITIVE

transitory Ⓐ /'træn·zəˌtɔːr·i, -ˌtoʊr·i/ *adj* [not gradable] *fml* not permanent; TEMPORARY ○ *the transitory nature of life*

translate /træn'sleɪt, 'træn·sleɪt/ *v* [I/T] **1** to change writing or speech from one language into another ○ [I] *Poetry does not translate easily.* **2** If you translate an activity, you change it into a new form or condition: [I] *The ability to talk clearly does not automatically translate into the ability to write clearly.*
translation /træn'sleɪ·ʃən/ *n* [C/U] ○ [C] *I do translations at international meetings.*
translator /træn'sleɪṭ·ər, 'træn ˌsleɪṭ·ər/ *n* [C] ○ *He is a translator at the UN.*

translocation /ˌtrænz·loʊ'keɪ·ʃən/ *n* [U] ***biology*** **1** the movement of the liquid that carries the substances that a plant needs for life and growth through the plant **2** Translocation is also the movement of a CHROMOSOME (= part of a cell that controls what an animal or plant is like) to another part of the same chromosome or to a different chromosome.

translucent /trænz'luː·sənt/ *adj* (of a substance) allowing some light to pass through ○ *The vase was made from translucent, milky glass.* ○ Compare OPAQUE; TRANSPARENT

transmit Ⓐ /trænz'mɪt/ *v* [I/T] **-tt-** to send or give something ○ [T] *Germs transmit disease.* ○ [I] *To avoid delay, transmit by fax.*
transmission Ⓐ /trænz'mɪʃ·ən/ *n* [C/U] **1** [U] *You can stop the transmission of some diseases by washing your hands often.* **2** The transmission in a vehicle is the machinery that moves power from to the engine to the wheels.
transmitter /trænz'mɪṭ·ər, 'trænz ˌmɪṭ·ər/ *n* [C] ○ *A television transmitter sends the signals that reach your TV.* ○ *She wants to do original work, not just be a transmitter of others' ideas.*

transmutation /ˌtrænz ˌmjuː'teɪ·ʃən/ *n* [C/U] ***physics, chemistry*** the process of changing one element to another, either naturally or by nuclear reaction

transparent /træn'spær·ənt, -'sper-/ *adj* **1** (of a substance) allowing light through so that objects can be clearly seen through it ○ *Those transparent plastic boxes are called jewel boxes.* **2** Transparent also means obvious: *The real reason for her leaving was so transparent, no one believed it.* ○ Compare OPAQUE; TRANSLUCENT
transparency /træn'spær·ən·si, -'sper-/ *n* [C/U] **1** [U] *This plastic has the transparency of glass.* **2** A transparency is a picture you can show on a screen: [C] *They used transparencies to show pages of the new book.*

transpiration /ˌtræn·spə'reɪ·ʃən/ *n* [U] ***biology*** the process by which water is lost through the surface of a plant

transpire /træn'spaɪr/ *v* [I] *fml* to happen ○ *A lot has transpired since we last spoke.*

transplant CHANGE ENVIRONMENT /træn'splænt/ *v* [I/T] to move someone or something,

or to be moved from one place to another ○ [T] *I transplanted those bushes to the back of the house.*
transplant /ˈtræn·splænt/ *n* [C] ○ *I'm a transplant from California.*

MOVE ORGAN /trænˈsplænt/ *v* [T] to move tissue or an organ from one person's body to another's
transplant /ˈtræn·splænt/ *n* [C] ○ *He survived a kidney transplant.*

transport Ⓐ /trænˈspɔːrt, -ˈspourt/ *v* [T] to take goods or people from one place to another ○ *The movers will transport thousands of pictures, charts, and recordings to the library.*
transport Ⓐ /ˈtræn·spɔːrt, -spourt/ *n* [C/U] **1** something that takes things, esp. soldiers or military supplies, from one place to another ○ [U] *I had to arrange for transport to get to my new assignment.* **2** ***biology*** Transport also means the movement of a chemical substance in and out of living cells.
transporter Ⓐ /trænˈspɔːrt̬·ər, -ˈspourt̬·ər/ *n* [C] a machine, a company, or a vehicle that transports things or people ○ *the country's largest shipping corporation and a major oil transporter*
transportation Ⓐ /ˌtræn·spərˈteɪ·ʃən/ *n* [U] ○ *In many cities, people depend on public transportation to get around.*

WORD FAMILY transport			
Nouns	transport transportation	*Verbs*	transport

transpose /trænˈspouz/ *v* [T] to change the order of something ○ *The total was wrong because I had transposed two numbers.*

transversal *n* [C] ***geometry*** a line that crosses two other lines

transverse wave /ˈtrænz·vɜrs ˈweɪv, ˈtræns-/ *n* [C] ***physics*** a WAVE ENERGY FORM in which the substance the wave travels through moves at an angle of 90° to the wave itself ○ Compare LONGITUDINAL WAVE

transvestite /trænzˈvesˌtɑɪt/ *n* [C] a person who wears the clothes of the opposite sex

trap **DEVICE FOR CATCHING** /træp/ *n* [C] **1** a device or hole for catching and holding things ○ *A bear was caught in the trap.* **2** A trap is also a bad situation from which it is difficult or impossible to escape: *Simply by answering the letter, Robin had fallen into a trap.*
trap /træp/ *v* [T] **-pp-** ○ *Morrison was trapped by the fire.*
trapper /ˈtræp·ər/ *n* [C] someone who catches wild animals, esp. to sell their fur

MOUTH /træp/ *n* [C] *slang* a mouth ○ *Oh, shut your trap!*

trap door *n* [C] a door in a floor or ceiling that leads to another, often hidden room ○ *In the middle of the living room was a trap door to the cellar.*

trapeze /træˈpiːz/ *n* [C] a short horizontal bar hanging from two ropes, on which ACROBATS perform ○ *I held my breath as I watched the performers on the trapeze.*

trapezoid /ˈtræ·pəˌzɔɪd/ *n* [C] ***geometry*** a flat shape with four sides, two of which are parallel ➤ Picture: **geometry**

trappings /ˈtræp·ɪŋz/ *pl n* the possessions that are typical of a situation or symbols of a position ○ *He enjoyed all the trappings of wealth.*

trash /træʃ/ *n* [U] anything that is worthless and of low quality; waste ○ *We filled three cans with trash from the garage.*
trash /træʃ/ *v* [T] *infml* ○ *I simply trash* (= destroy) *that kind of mail.* ○ *Some people seem to enjoy trashing their neighbors* (= severely criticizing them).
trashy /ˈtræʃ·i/ *adj infml, disapproving* worthless, or of low quality ○ *trashy romance novels*

trash can, **trashcan** /ˈtræʃ·kæn/, **trash bin** *n* [C] a large container for holding waste ○ *The snow had covered the trash cans along with everything else.*

trash compactor /ˈkɑmˌpæk·tər, kəmˈpæk·tər/ *n* [C] a device that crushes waste so that it fits into less space

trauma /ˈtrɔː·mə, ˈtrɑʊ-/ *n* [C/U] severe shock caused by an injury ○ [U] *She never recovered from the trauma of her mother's illness.* ○ [U] *The surgeon specialized in trauma* (= sudden, severe injury), *especially from gunshots.*
traumatic /trɔːˈmæt̬·ɪk, trɑʊ-/ *adj* ○ *The death of someone we love is a traumatic event.*
traumatize /ˈtrɔː·məˌtɑɪz, ˈtrɑʊ-/ *v* [T] ○ *She was traumatized by the fact that she was involved in a car accident.*

travel /ˈtræv·əl/ *v* [I/T] **-l-**, **-ll-** to go from one place to another on a trip, usually over a long distance ○ [I] *The train was traveling (at) about 100 miles an hour.* ○ [T] *I travel long distances as part of my job, so on vacations I like to stay close to home.* ○ [I] (*infml*) *We were doing 70 miles an hour, so the guy who whizzed past us must have really been traveling* (= going very fast).
travel /ˈtræv·əl/ *n* ○ [U] *A lot of my travel is business related.* ○ [pl] *I've met some pretty interesting people in my travels* (= trips).
traveler, **traveller** /ˈtræv·ə·lər/ *n* [C] ○ *Travelers in a hurry like these self-service machines.*

USAGE

travel, journey, or trip?

The noun **travel** is a general word which means the activity of traveling, but it does not mean a single act of traveling.

Air travel has become much cheaper.

~~*Did you have a good travel?*~~

A **trip** is a journey in which you visit a place and then usually come back again.

a business trip

his last trip to China

Journey is a more formal word for trip in American English, but in British English it is more common than trip.

He fell asleep during the train journey.

IDIOM with travel

• **travel light** to bring very few things with you when you go somewhere ○ *I like to carry my bags onto the plane, so I try to travel light.*

travel agent *n* [C] a person whose job is to find information about travel and arrange for tickets and hotel rooms
travel agency *n* [C] ○ *I called several travel agencies* (= companies of travel agents) *to compare prices before I booked a cruise.*

traveler's check *n* [C] a check that you buy from a bank or other company and that can be used as money or exchanged for the local money of a country

traverse /trəˈvɜrs, træ-/ *v* [T] to move or travel through an area ○ *Moving sidewalks traverse the airport.*

travesty /ˈtræv·ə·sti/ *n* [C] something that completely fails to do what it is intended or expected to do, and therefore seems ridiculous ○ *The police chief called the judge's ruling a travesty of justice.*

trawl /trɔːl/ *v* [I/T] to pull a large net through the sea behind a boat in order to catch fish
trawler /ˈtrɔː·lər/ *n* [C] a boat that pulls a large net behind it in order to catch fish

tray /treɪ/ *n* [C] a flat container, usually with slightly raised edges, for carrying food and drinks ○ *She set the tray down between them.*

treacherous DANGEROUS /ˈtretʃ·ə·rəs/ *adj* (of the ground or the sea) extremely dangerous, esp. because of bad weather conditions ○ *Freezing rain made driving treacherous.*
NOT LOYAL /ˈtretʃ·ə·rəs/ *adj* (of a person) guilty of deceiving someone who trusts you ○ *He was treacherous, or at least sneaky.*
treachery /ˈtretʃ·ə·ri/ *n* [U] ○ *a play about treachery and betrayal*

tread STEP /tred/ *v* [I/T] *past simp.* **trod**, *past part.* **trodden**, **trod** to put the foot down while stepping, or to step on something ○ [I] (*fig.*) *I hope I haven't trod on other people's toes by saying this.*
tread /tred/ *n* [C] **1** the sound that someone's feet make in walking ○ *I heard the heavy tread of my father overhead.* **2** A tread is also the horizontal surface on which you put your foot on a step.
PATTERN /tred/ *n* [C/U] the raised pattern on a tire that holds the vehicle to the road as it moves ○ [U] *fat tires with knobby tread*

IDIOM with tread

• **tread water** **1** to float with your head above the water's surface and your feet below you by moving your legs and arms up and down **2** To **tread water** is also to be active but without making progress or falling further behind ○ *Stock prices continued to tread water this week.*

treadmill /ˈtred·mɪl/ *n* [C] **1** a machine for exercising on which you run or walk on a strip that moves back, so that you must move at the same speed as the strip ○ *She works out on a treadmill.* **2** A treadmill is also a boring, regularly repeated activity or experience: *My life has been a treadmill lately.*

treason /ˈtriː·zən/ *n* [U] ***social studies*** the crime of helping your country's enemies or attempting to illegally remove its government ○ *In 1807, Burr was arrested and tried for treason, but he was acquitted.*

treasure /ˈtreʒ·ər/ *n* [C/U] **1** great wealth, esp. in the form of a store of gold, silver, precious stones, or money ○ [U] *Pirates are said to have buried treasure there.* **2** A treasure is also anything of great value: [C] *Jazz is America's national treasure.*
treasure /ˈtreʒ·ər/ *v* [T] If you treasure something you take good care of it because you value it highly: *I treasure these old snapshots of my grandparents.*

treasure hunt *n* [C] a game in which the players are given a series of CLUES (= pieces of information) to direct them to a hidden prize

treasurer /ˈtreʒ·ə·rər/ *n* [C] an officer who is responsible for the money in a company, government, or other organization

treasure trove *n* [C] a collection of valuable things ○ *The book was a treasure trove of information.*

treasury /ˈtreʒ·ə·ri/ *n* [U] the government department responsible for financial matters such as spending and taxes

treat DEAL WITH /triːt/ *v* [T always + adv/prep] to behave toward someone or deal with something in a particular way ○ *He treated his children badly.* ○ *She always tried to treat her students as/like adults.*
treatment /ˈtriːt·mənt/ *n* [U] ○ *He accused the governor of giving rich people special treatment.*
GIVE MEDICAL CARE /triːt/ *v* [T] to do something to improve the condition of an ill or injured person, or to try to cure a disease ○ *The hospital treats hundreds of patients a day.* ○ *The new drug may allow us to treat diabetes more effectively.*
treatment /ˈtriːt·mənt/ *n* [C/U] ○ [U] *Chronic back pain may not respond to treatment.*
PUT IN NEW CONDITION /triːt/ *v* [T] to change the condition of a substance by adding something to it or putting it through a special process ○ *The sewage is treated with chemicals before being dumped.*
treatment /ˈtriːt·mənt/ *n* [C/U] ○ [U] *The city is exploring other methods of water treatment.*
SPECIAL EXPERIENCE /triːt/ *n* [C] a special and enjoyable occasion or experience ○ *It was a real treat seeing my old friends last weekend.*
PAY FOR /triːt/ *v* [I/T] to buy or pay for something for someone ○ [T] *I'm going to treat myself to a new pair of sunglasses.*
treat /triːt/ *n* [U] ○ *You paid for the taxi, so lunch is my treat* (= I will pay).

WORD FAMILY treat			
Nouns	treat treatment mistreatment	*Adjectives* *Verbs*	untreated treat mistreat

IDIOMS with **treat**

• **treat** *someone* **like dirt** to deal with someone in a way that shows a lack of respect ○ *You shouldn't treat your little brother like dirt.*

• **treat** *someone* **with kid gloves** to deal with someone very gently or carefully ○ *These athletes grow up being treated with kid gloves, and then they don't know how the real world works.*

treatise /ˈtriːt̬·əs/ *n* [C] a formal piece of writing that deals with a particular subject ○ *a medical treatise*

treaty /ˈtriːt̬·i/ *n* [C] ***politics & government*** a written agreement between two or more countries that is formally approved and signed by their leaders ○ *Under the treaty* (= according to the agreement)*, inspections are required to see if any country is secretly developing nuclear arms.*

treble THREE TIMES /ˈtreb·əl/ *v* [I/T] *fml* to become three times greater; TRIPLE ○ [I] *My property taxes have almost trebled in the last ten years.*

MUSIC /ˈtreb·əl/ *n* [U] the higher musical notes ○ *The music was too loud, the treble rattling my eardrums.*

treble clef *n* [C] ***music*** in Western music, a sign that shows the second line of a STAFF (= the five lines on which music is written) is the note G above middle C (= the note C near the middle of the piano keys) ➤ Picture: **notation**

tree /triː/ *n* [C] a tall plant that has a wooden trunk and branches growing from its upper part ○ *a pine tree*

tree house *n* [C] a small structure among the branches of a tree ○ *My dad built us a tree house when we were little.*

trek /trek/ *v* [I always + adv/prep] **-kk-** to walk a long way or with some difficulty ○ *Many people trekked for miles to reach safety.*

trek /trek/ *n* [C] ○ *It's a long trek from the railroad station to the stadium.*

trellis /ˈtrel·əs/ *n* [C] a frame of crossed bars that supports plants as they grow, sometimes against the side of a house ○ *Roses climbed the trellises.*

tremble /ˈtrem·bəl/ *v* [I] (of your body or a part of it) to shake without your intending to, usually because you are frightened, ill, tired, or upset ○ *Grant was trembling with excitement.* ○ *Her hand trembled as she lifted her cup.*

tremble /ˈtrem·bəl/ *n* [U] ○ *There was a slight tremble in her voice as she recalled her husband.*

tremendous /trɪˈmen·dəs/ *adj* **1** great in amount, size, or degree; extremely large ○ *She is under tremendous pressure at work.* **2** *infml* Someone or something that is tremendous is extremely good: *a tremendous book/concert/athlete*

tremendously /trɪˈmen·də·sli/ *adv* ○ *a tremendously expensive house* ○ *I enjoyed your show tremendously.*

tremor BODY MOVEMENT /ˈtrem·ər/ *n* [C] a shaking movement in a person's body, usually because of fright, excitement, or illness ○ *I felt a tremor of anxiety as the plane lifted off the ground.*

EARTH MOVEMENT /ˈtrem·ər/ *n* [C] a slight EARTHQUAKE (= sudden, violent movement of the earth's surface) ○ *The tremor was centered just south of San Francisco.*

trench /trentʃ/ *n* [C] **1** a narrow channel dug into the ground ○ *I dug a trench around the tent to keep rain water from getting in.* **2** ***earth science*** A trench is also a long, deep valley at the bottom of an ocean.

trenchant /ˈtren·tʃənt/ *adj* (of something said or written) forcefully and effectively expressed, and often in few words ○ *I enjoy reading Murray's trenchant comments on the relationship between sports and society.*

trench coat *n* [C] a long, loose coat with a belt, usually made from waterproof material and similar in style to a military coat

trend Ⓐ /trend/ *n* [C] the general direction of changes or developments ○ *fashion trends* ○ *The trend is toward working longer hours for less money.*

trendy /ˈtren·di/ *adj* influenced by or expressing the most recent fashions or ideas; modern in style ○ *New York City is full of trendy shops and restaurants.*

trepidation /ˌtrep·əˈdeɪ·ʃən/ *n* [U] worry or anxiety about something that is going to happen ○ *With some trepidation, I set out to find my first job.*

trespass /ˈtres·pæs, -pəs/ *v* [I] to enter someone's property without permission ○ *I didn't realize I was trespassing on their land.*

trespasser /ˈtresˌpæs·ər, -pə·sər/ *n* [C] ○ *They have several dogs to keep trespassers out.*

trestle /ˈtres·əl/ *n* [C] a set of sloping supports holding a horizontal structure, used esp. for railroad bridges, or a bridge supported in this way ○ *The train was crossing a trestle above a river near Baltimore.*

triad /ˈtraɪ·æd/ *n* [C] ***music*** a CHORD that consists of three notes that are separated by three or four HALF STEPS

trial LEGAL PROCESS /traɪl/ *n* [C/U] **1** the examination in a court of law of the facts of a case to decide whether a person is guilty of a crime or responsible for an injury to another person ○ [C] *a criminal/civil trial* ○ [U] *The case will soon go to trial* (= begin). ○ [U] *She must still stand trial* (= be judged in a court of law). **2** If someone is **on trial**, the case in which that person's guilt is being judged has begun: *He was on trial for assault and robbery.* ○ Opposite: TRY EXAMINE IN COURT

TEST /traɪl/ *n* [C/U] a test, usually over a limited period of time, to discover how effective or suitable something or someone is ○ [C] *The agency plans to conduct clinical trials of the drug.* ○ [U] *We have the videotapes on a trial basis for one week – if we don't like them, we can send them back.*

PROBLEM /traɪl/ *n* [C] something or someone that causes anxiety or problems ○ *the trials of adolescence*

T

trial and error *n* [U] a way of achieving an aim or solving a problem by trying different methods and learning from your mistakes ○ *In a language lab, students learn by trial and error.*

triangle /ˈtrɑɪˌæŋ·gəl/ *n* [C] **1** ***mathematics*** a flat shape with three straight sides ○ *Her earrings were in the shape of triangles.* **2** ***music*** A triangle is also a musical instrument consisting of a thin metal bar having three sides, which makes a high sound when held up in the air and hit with a metal bar.

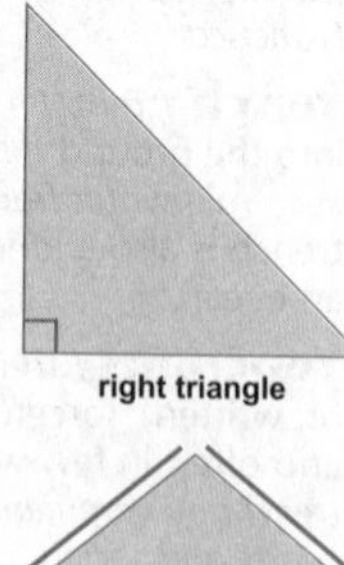

right triangle

isosceles triangle

equilateral triangle

TRIANGLES

triangular /trɑɪˈæŋ·gjə·lər/ *adj* ***mathematics*** having the shape of a triangle

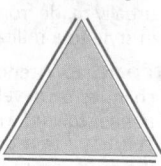

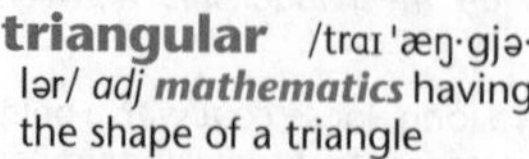

triathlon /trɑɪˈæθˌlɑn/ *n* [C] a race in which the competitors swim, ride a bicycle, and run without stopping between events ○ *He has won Hawaii's Ironman Triathlon four times.*

tribe /trɑɪb/ *n* [C] a group of people, often of related families, who live in the same area and share the same language, culture, and history ○ *She has studied Native American tribes from Mexico to Maine.*

tribal /ˈtrɑɪ·bəl/ *adj* [not gradable] ○ *tribal culture* ○ *tribal land* ○ *Tribal leaders support the proposed health center.*

tribunal /trɑɪˈbjuːn·əl/ *n* [C] a special court chosen, esp. by a government or governments, to examine a particular problem ○ *An international tribunal of judges was established to investigate alleged war crimes.*

tributary /ˈtrɪb·jəˌter·i/ *n* [C] a river or stream that flows into a larger river or lake ○ *The Misssouri River is a tributary of the Mississipi River*

tribute SHOW OF RESPECT /ˈtrɪb·juːt/ *n* [C/U] respect or admiration for someone, or a formal event at which respect and admiration are expressed ○ [U] *The memorial pays tribute to Africans brought here as slaves.* ○ [C] *There was a special tribute to Arthur Ashe by leading tennis players.*

GOOD EFFECT /ˈtrɪb·juːt/ *n* [C usually sing] something showing the benefit or positive effect of something else ○ *His ability to cook and manage a household is a tribute to the training he received from his mother.*

trick ACT OF DECEIVING /trɪk/ *n* [C] **1** an action intended to deceive, either as a way of cheating someone or as a joke or form of entertainment ○ *He showed us some card tricks.* **2 Trick or treat** is what children say on HALLOWEEN, when they dress to look frightening or amusing and visit people's homes to ask for candy: *Are your kids too old for* **trick or treating** (= visiting people's homes to ask for candy)*?*

trick /trɪk/ *v* [T] to make someone believe something that is not true, or to persuade someone to do something based on a false understanding of the facts ○ *She tricked me into telling her what I was up to.*

trickery /ˈtrɪk·ə·ri/ *n* [U] ○ *The agency used trickery, fraud, and deceit to obtain the computer software.*

tricky /ˈtrɪk·i/ *adj* ○ *He's a tricky fellow – you can't always trust him.* ○ See also: TRICKY

METHOD /trɪk/ *n* [C] a quick or effective way of doing something ○ *What's the trick to pulling out this sofa bed?*

WEAK /trɪk/ *adj* [not gradable] (of a part of the body, esp. a joint) sometimes feeling weak suddenly and unexpectedly ○ *I've had a trick knee ever since I played football.*

WORD FAMILY trick			
Nouns	trick trickery	*Adjectives*	tricky
		Verbs	trick

IDIOM with trick

• **tricks of the trade** methods that help you to do a job better or faster ○ *Journalists have to learn the tricks of the trade quickly if they want to get the good stories.*

trickle /ˈtrɪk·əl/ *v* [I] **1** (of liquid) to flow slowly and without force ○ *Blood trickled from a cut in his forehead.* **2** To trickle is also to happen gradually and in small numbers: *After the hurricane, all the telephones were out, and it was some time before reports of damage began to trickle in.*

trickle /ˈtrɪk·əl/ *n* [C] ○ *A trickle* (= small flow) *of sweat ran down his chest.* ○ *Only a trickle* (= small amount) *of goods reached the village.*

tricky /ˈtrɪk·i/ *adj* (of a piece of work or a problem) difficult to deal with and needing careful attention or skill ○ *Removing scar tissue can be a very tricky operation.* ○ See also: TRICKY at TRICK ACT OF DECEIVING

tricycle /ˈtrɑɪˌsɪk·əl/ *n* [C] a vehicle with two wheels at the back and one in front, having a seat for a rider whose feet push PEDALS around in circles to make the wheels turn ○ *Our three-year-old loves her red tricycle.*

tried /trɑɪd/ *past simple and past participle of* TRY

tried-and-true *adj* used many times in the past and proven to work well ○ *A cup of warm milk is my tried-and-true remedy for insomnia.*

trifle /ˈtrɑɪ·fəl/ *n* [C] **1** a matter or item of little value or importance **2 A trifle** means slightly or to a small degree: *He admits to being a trifle nervous before every show.*

trifling /ˈtrɑɪ·flɪŋ/ *adj* ○ *It was such a trifling sum of money to argue about.*

trigger Ⓐ START /ˈtrɪg·ər/ *v* [T] to cause something to start ○ *I triggered the smoke alarm when I burned the potatoes.* ○ *Eating chocolate can trigger a migraine headache in some people.*

GUN PART /ˈtrɪɡ·ər/ *n* [C] a part of a gun that causes the gun to fire when pressed ○ *to pull the trigger*

trigger-happy *adj* too willing to use a gun

trigonometry /ˌtrɪɡ·əˈnɑm·ə·tri/, *short form* **trig** /trɪɡ/ *n* [U] ***mathematics*** a type of mathematics that deals with the relationship between the angles and sides of triangles
trigonometric *adj* ***mathematics*** ○ *a trigonometric function*

trill /trɪl/ *n* [C] a series of quickly repeated high notes such as those sung by a bird

trillion /ˈtrɪl·jən/ *number* 1,000,000,000,000 ○ *Distances in space can be measured in trillions of miles.*

trilogy /ˈtrɪl·ə·dʒi/ *n* [C] a set of three books, plays, or movies dealing with the same characters or the same subject

trim **CUT** /trɪm/ *v* [T] **-mm- 1** to make something neater or more even by cutting a small amount off ○ *He had a neatly trimmed beard.* **2** To trim is also to reduce: *We have to trim costs by not making any unnecessary trips.*

DECORATE /trɪm/ *v* [T] **-mm-** to add decoration to something ○ *The robe was trimmed with fur.*
trim /trɪm/ *n* [U] ○ *The team's new uniforms are blue with black trim.*
trimmings /ˈtrɪm·ɪŋz/ *pl n* **1** *I want a plain black jumper with no fancy trimmings.* **2** Trimmings are also other foods that are usually served with the main dish of a meal: *For Thanksgiving, we always have turkey with all the trimmings.*

THIN /trɪm/ *adj* [-er/-est only] **-mm-** thin and appearing to be in good physical condition ○ *He was a short, trim, wiry man.*

trimester /traɪˈmes·tər/ *n* [C] **1** A trimester is any of the three, three-month periods that a human pregnancy is divided into. **2** A trimester is also any of the three periods into which the school or college year is sometimes divided.

Trinity /ˈtrɪn·ət̬·i/ *n* [U] (in many forms of Christianity) the three beings, Father, Son, and Holy Spirit, who are united as one God

trinket /ˈtrɪŋ·kət/ *n* [C] a small, decorative object or item of jewelry of little value

trinomial *n* [C] ***algebra*** a mathematical statement with three numbers or VARIABLES (= mathematical symbols)

trio /ˈtriː·oʊ/ *n* [C] *pl* **trios** three people who sing or play musical instruments together, or a piece of music written for three people ○ Compare DUET; QUARTET; QUINTET

trip **TRAVEL** /trɪp/ *n* [C] an occasion on which someone goes to a place and returns from it, or the act of traveling from one place to another ○ *a camping/shopping trip* ○ *We plan to take a trip out west later this year.* ○ *They went on a three-week trip to Europe.* ○ *Alejandro had to make a number of business trips to New York.* ➤ Usage: **travel, journey, or trip?** at TRAVEL ; **way or trip?** at WAY **ROUTE**

LOSE BALANCE /trɪp/ *v* [I/T] **-pp-** to lose your balance because your foot hits against something when you are walking or running, or to cause someone to lose his or her balance ○ [I] *He injured his ankle when he tripped over a water sprinkler while jogging.* ○ [I] *She nearly tripped on the rug.*

EXPERIENCE /trɪp/ *n* [C] *slang* a strongly felt experience ○ *What a trip this book is!*

PHRASAL VERB with trip

• **trip up** *(someone)* [M] to make a mistake or to cause someone to make a mistake ○ *I did OK on the exam except for the last question, when I got tripped up by a word I didn't understand.*

triple /ˈtrɪp·əl/ *adj* [not gradable] consisting of three parts, or three times in number or amount ○ *If he loses the case, the defendant can be required to pay triple damages.*
triple /ˈtrɪp·əl/ *v* [I/T] ○ [T] *We've tripled our output over the past two years.*

triplet /ˈtrɪp·lət/ *n* [C] one of three children born to the same mother at the same time

triplet codon *n* [C] ***biology*** CODON

triplicate /ˈtrɪp·lɪ·kət/ *n* [U] an original and two exact copies ○ *Every form was filled out in triplicate.*

tripod /ˈtraɪ·pɑd/ *n* [C] a support with three legs for a piece of equipment such as a camera ○ *Photographers set up their tripods.*

trite /trɑɪt/ *adj* done or expressed too often to be of any interest ○ *Even good acting couldn't make up for the trite story.*

tritium /ˈtrɪt̬·iː·əm, ˈtrɪʃ-/ *n* [U] ***chemistry, physics*** a RADIOISOTOPE of the gas HYDROGEN

triumph /ˈtraɪ·əmf/ *n* a complete victory or success achieved esp. after great difficulties, making the result particularly satisfying ○ [C] *The elimination of smallpox was one of medicine's greatest triumphs.*
triumph /ˈtraɪ·əmf/ *v* [I] ○ *We visited Yorktown Battlefield on the York River, where in 1781 George Washington's forces triumphed over the English army.*
triumphant /traɪˈʌm·fənt/ *adj* ○ *He made a triumphant return to the stage after several years working in television.*

trivia /ˈtrɪv·iː·ə/ *pl n* unimportant or little-known details or information ○ *This is a game for trivia buffs* (= people interested in knowing little-known facts).

trivial /ˈtrɪv·iː·əl/ *adj* having little value or importance ○ *The story spends too much time on trivial matters.*
trivialize /ˈtrɪv·iː·əˌlaɪz/ *v* [T] to make something unusual seem ordinary or unimportant ○ *My boss tends to take good ideas and trivialize them.*

tRNA /ˌtiːˌɑrˌenˈeɪ/ *n* [U] ***biology*** *abbreviation for* TRANSFER RNA

T

trod /trɑd/ *past simple and past participle of* TREAD STEP

trodden /ˈtrɑd·ən/ *past participle of* TREAD STEP

troll /troʊl/ *v* [I] to fish from a boat that is moving slowly in the water and pulling a fishing LINE (= length of string with something attached that attracts fish) behind it ○ *Many of his friends had large boats, and they frequently traveled together trolling for mackerel.*

trolley /ˈtrɑl·i/, **trolley car** /ˈtrɑl·iː ˌkɑr/, **streetcar** *n* [C] an electric vehicle that transports people, usually in cities, and goes along metal tracks in the road

trombone /trɑm ˈboʊn/ *n* [C/U] a long, BRASS musical instrument with a U-shaped piece that is slid in and out of the main part of the instrument to vary the notes and played by blowing into it, or this type of instrument generally; a HORN

tromp /trɑmp, trɔːmp/ *v* to TRAMP WALK

troop GROUP /truːp/ *n* [C] **1** a group of soldiers or police, esp. one equipped with horses **2** A troop is also an organized group of young people who are BOY SCOUTS or GIRL SCOUTS.

trooper /ˈtruː·pər/ *n* [C] a police officer belonging to a US state police force

troops /truːps/ *pl n* soldiers on duty in a large group ○ *Thousands of troops have been stationed in the region for several years.*

WALK /truːp/ *v* [I always + adv/prep] to walk or go somewhere as a group ○ *Hundreds of thousands of visitors troop through the museum every year.*

trophy /ˈtroʊ·fi/ *n* [C] **1** a prize, such as a large silver cup or bowl, given to the one who wins a competition or race **2** A trophy is also something used as a symbol of success: *Under the long high-beamed ceiling, affixed to stone walls, were the trophies – heads of a rhinoceros and an African buffalo with huge horns.*

Tropic of Cancer *n* [U] a line of LATITUDE at 23°27′ north of the equator, and the farthest north that the sun appears directly above

Tropic of Capricorn *n* [U] a line of LATITUDE at 23°27′ south of the equator, and the farthest south that the sun appears directly above

tropics /ˈtrɑp·ɪks/ *pl n* the hottest area of the earth, the area on either side of the equator reaching to 23.5 degrees to the north and south

tropical /ˈtrɑp·ɪ·kəl/ *adj* [not gradable] of or characteristic of the tropics ○ *a tropical climate* ○ *a tropical storm*

troposphere /ˈtroʊ·pəˌsfɪr, ˈtrɑp-/ *n* [U] ***earth science*** the layer of gases surrounding the earth from the surface to about 6 miles

trot /trɑt/ *v* [I always + adv/prep] **1** (of a horse or other animal with four legs) to move in a way that is slightly faster than walking **2** A person who trots runs slowly: *She trotted along behind them, determined to keep up.*

trot /trɑt/ *n* [C usually sing] ○ *The horse was moving at a slow trot.*

PHRASAL VERB with trot

• **trot out** *someone/something* [M] to show someone or something in public in order to get attention ○ *He trots out the same old jokes at every party.*

trouble DIFFICULTIES /ˈtrʌb·əl/ *n* [C/U] **1** a problem, or difficulties ○ [U] *Trouble began when he came to live with us.* ○ [C] *She thought her troubles would be over when she got a job.* ○ [U] *The patient is having trouble breathing.* **2** Trouble can also be a characteristic that is a problem or disadvantage: [C] *His trouble is that he's too impatient.* **3** Sometimes trouble is a problem or difficulty caused when a machine or system does not work as it should: [U] *I'm having trouble with my new computer.* **4** Trouble can be a cause of arguments or fights: [U] *Our brother is the source of trouble between my sister and me.* **5** Someone who is **in trouble** is in a situation that is a problem or difficulty, esp. with the law: *He would have been in real trouble if he had been caught.*

trouble /ˈtrʌb·əl/ *v* [T] to cause someone to have problems or difficulties ○ *He has been troubled by a knee injury for most of the season.*

troubled /ˈtrʌb·əld/ *adj* ○ *Peace has finally come to this troubled region after many years.*

troublesome /ˈtrʌb·əl·səm/ *adj* causing problems or difficulties ○ *His back has been troublesome for quite a while.*

USAGE

trouble or problem?

Problem means "a situation that causes difficulties and that needs to be dealt with." You can talk about **a problem** or **problems**.

Tell me what the problem is.

There's a problem with the engine.

He's having a few problems at work.

Trouble means "problems, difficulties, or worries" and is used to talk about problems in a more general way. **Trouble** is almost always uncountable so do not use the determiner "a" before it.

We had some trouble while we were on vacation.

He helped me when I was in trouble.

I had trouble with the car last night.

~~*I had a trouble with the car last night.*~~

Troubles is used to describe a related set of problems that someone has or that a country or organization has. Be careful not to use **troubles** when describing a more general group of difficulties.

The report outlines the problems caused by unemployment.

~~*The report outlines the troubles caused by unemployment.*~~

INCONVENIENCE /ˈtrʌb·əl/ *n* [U] inconvenience or effort ○ *"I'd love some coffee, if it isn't too much trouble." "Oh, it's no trouble at all."* ○ *The sweater is a bit large, but I'm keeping it because it's too much trouble to return it.*

trouble /ˈtrʌb·əl/ *v* [T] ○ *Could I trouble you to open that window?* ○ *You don't need to trouble yourself with all the details.*

WORRY /ˈtrʌb·əl/ *v* [T] to cause someone worry or anxiety ○ *What's troubling you? You seem upset.* ○ *It troubles me that she didn't tell me this sooner.*

troubled /ˈtrʌb·əld/ *adj* ○ *The children were not troubled when the dinosaurs in the movie ate up some unlucky humans.*

troubling /ˈtrʌb·ə·lɪŋ/ *adj* ○ *Perhaps most troubling is the information that some reporters have simply made up stories.*

WORD FAMILY trouble

Nouns	trouble	*Adjectives*	troubled
Verbs	trouble		troubling
			troublesome

IDIOMS with trouble

• **go to the trouble to** *do something*, **take the trouble to** *do something* to make an effort to do something ○ *If the police had gone to the trouble of looking up his record, they would not have released him.*

• **the trouble with** *someone/something* the problem with someone or something ○ *The trouble with this place is they don't care about the people who work here.*

troublemaker /ˈtrʌb·əlˌmeɪ·kər/ *n* [C] someone who causes problems for other people

troubleshooting /ˈtrʌb·əlˌʃuːţ·ɪŋ/ *n* [U] the process of solving problems, esp. complicated problems in a system ○ *He's very good at troubleshooting because he knows these computers as well as anybody.*

troubleshooter /ˈtrʌb·əlˌʃuːţ·ər/ *n* [C] ○ *An experienced politician was hired as a troubleshooter for the election campaign.*

troublesome /ˈtrʌb·əl·səm/ *adj* causing worry or anxiety ○ *The troublesome fact is that we haven't gotten much done.*

trough CONTAINER /trɔːf/ *n* [C] a narrow, open box to hold water or food for animals

LOW POINT /trɔːf/ *n* [C] a low point between two high points, as on a GRAPH or record of activity ○ *Investors have to live through stock market troughs.*

trounce /trɑʊns/ *v* [T] to defeat a competitor by a large score ○ *The Red Sox trounced the Yankees 12 to 1 in the first game.*

troupe /truːp/ *n* [C] a group of performers, such as actors or dancers, who perform and travel together

trousers /ˈtrɑʊ·zərz/ *pl n* a piece of clothing covering the lower part of the body from the waist to the foot and including separate sections for each leg; pants ○ *He had a rip in his trousers.*

trout /trɑʊt/ *n* [C] *pl* **trout** a fish found in both rivers and the sea that is a very popular food ○ *Fish farmers raise trout in refrigerated tanks.*

trowel /trɑʊ·əl, trɑʊl/ *n* [C] a small tool that has a flat, metal blade and a handle, used to spread building materials such as PLASTER or CEMENT, or a similar tool with a curved, pointed blade used to garden

truant /ˈtruː·ənt/ *n* [C] someone who is absent from school without permission

truancy /ˈtruː·ən·si/ *n* [U] ○ *Truancy is a serious problem in many schools.*

truce /truːs/ *n* [C] a temporary agreement to stop fighting or arguing, or a brief interruption in a disagreement ○ *We seemed to be arguing so much, we have declared a truce in my family.*

truck /trʌk/ *n* [C] a large vehicle with an open or covered space in the back to hold a load of goods

truck /trʌk/ *v* [T always + adv/prep] ○ *Most supplies are trucked into the city, although some come by rail or plane.*

trucker /ˈtrʌk·ər/ *n* [C] ○ *Truckers spend long periods away from home.*

trucking /ˈtrʌk·ɪŋ/ *n* [U] ○ *Railroads have lost business to trucking companies.*

truck farm *n* [C] a farm where fruits and vegetables are grown to be sold locally

truckload /ˈtrʌk·loʊd/ *n* [C] the amount a truck can carry ○ (*fig.*) *In this case, lawyers filed court papers by the truckload* (= in large amounts).

truck stop *n* [C] an area near a main road that offers fuel and food, used esp. by truck drivers

truculent /ˈtrʌk·jə·lənt/ *adj* having a bad state of mind, or behaving in a threatening manner ○ *He was a truculent bully.*

trudge /trʌdʒ/ *v* [I always + adv/prep] to walk slowly with a lot of effort, esp. on an uneven surface or while carrying something heavy ○ *We had to trudge through deep snow to get to school.*

trudge /trʌdʒ/ *n* [C] ○ *Twelve miles over rocks and hills is a long trudge for a hiker.*

true CORRECT /truː/ *adj* [-*er*/-*est* only] agreeing with fact; not false or wrong ○ *The story is actually true.* ○ [+ *that* clause] *It is true that the risk of breaking your hip increases with age.* ○ Related noun: TRUTH FACT

truism /ˈtruːˌɪz·əm/ *n* [C] a statement that is so obvious or said so often that its truth is not questioned ○ *It's a truism that preventing disease is much better than curing it.*

truly /ˈtruː·li/ *adv* ○ *Can it be truly said that he represents all the people of his country?* ➤ Confusables: **right or true?** at RIGHT CORRECT

REAL /truː/ *adj* [-*er*/-*est* only] **1** based on what is real, or actual, not imaginary ○ *His staff tried to keep the true nature of his illness a secret.* **2** Your **true love** is someone or something you love more than all others: *Her true love is music.*

truly /ˈtruː·li/ *adv* ○ *The area is truly beautiful.*

SINCERE /truː/ *adj* [-*er*/-*est* only] sincere and loyal ○ *I am lucky to have true friends.* ○ *She is one politician who remains true to her principles.*

T

truly /ˈtruː·li/ *adv* **1** sincerely ○ *I'm truly sorry about the accident.* **2** Truly is sometimes used at the end of a letter instead of sincerely: *Yours truly, Anne* ○ *Very truly yours, Joseph Logan*

HAVING NECESSARY QUALITIES /truː/ *adj* [-er/-est only] having all the characteristics necessary to be an example of a particular thing ○ *Only true deer have antlers.* ○ *This portrait is supposed to be a true likeness of Washington.*

truly /ˈtruː·li/ *adv* ○ *Tomatoes aren't truly vegetables – they're fruit.*

WORD FAMILY true			
Nouns	truism	*Adjectives*	true
	truth		untrue
	untruth		truthful
	truthfulness	*Adverbs*	truly
			truthfully

IDIOMS with true

• *someone's* **true colors** the kind of person someone really is rather than what the person seems to be ○ *I thought he was a really sweet guy, but then he got mad and showed his true colors.*

• **true enough** correct or accurate but not completely explaining something ○ *It's true enough that he had doubts about the project, but we have to look further to understand why he resigned.*

• **true to form** behaving the way other people expect someone to, based on previous experience ○ *True to form, he tried to get out of his doing any work.*

• **true to** *yourself* behaving according to your beliefs and doing what you think is right ○ *Try to remember that no matter how hard it gets, you have to remain true to yourself.*

• **true to** *your* **word** keeping a sincere promise ○ *True to his word, he paid back the money he borrowed from us.*

true-blue *adj* completely loyal to a person or belief

true-life, **true to life** *adj* realistic or based on real life ○ *true-life adventures* ○ *Some of her stories are very true to life.*

trump /trʌmp/ *v* [T] to be better than, or have more importance or power than another person or thing ○ *They operated on the assumption that money trumped everything.*

trump card *n* [C] something that gives you an advantage over others ○ *The ultimate trump card for the space program is that it is a very exciting thing.*

trumped-up /ˈtrʌmpˈtʌp/ *adj* not true; invented ○ *He was sent to prison on a trumped-up charge of armed robbery.*

trumpet INSTRUMENT /ˈtrʌm·pət/ *n* [C/U] a BRASS musical instrument that plays high notes, with keys that are pressed to vary the notes and played by blowing into it, or this type of instrument generally; a HORN

ANIMAL CALL /ˈtrʌm·pət/ *v* [I] (of an animal, esp. an ELEPHANT) to produce a loud call ○ *We heard the elephants trumpeting in the distance.*

MAKE KNOWN /ˈtrʌm·pət/ *v* [T] to make people aware of something important ○ *He's been trumpeting political reform for years.* ○ *The boys were not shy about trumpeting their successes.*

truncated /ˈtrʌŋˌkeɪt̬·əd/ *adj* [not gradable] made briefer or shorter, usually by removing a part ○ *The truncated article fit into the space allowed but made little sense.*

trundle /ˈtrʌn·dəl/ *v* [always + adv/prep] to push something on wheels, or to cause something to roll along ○ [T] *She trundled the wheelbarrow down the road.*

trundle bed *n* [C] a low bed on wheels that is stored under an ordinary bed and pulled out when it is needed ○ *We bought a trundle bed for unexpected guests.*

trunk MAIN PART /trʌŋk/ *n* [C] **1** the thick main stem of a tree, from which the branches grow **2** A person's trunk is the main part of the body, not including the head, legs, or arms.

NOSE /trʌŋk/ *n* [C] an ELEPHANT's nose, which is like a long tube that bends easily

STORAGE SPACE /trʌŋk/ *n* [C] **1** a closed space at the back of a car where things can be stored **2** A trunk is also a large, strong case used to store or transport clothes and other possessions.

trunks /trʌŋks/ *pl n* [C] very short pants, esp. worn by men for swimming ○ *He spent the summer in swim trunks and Hawaiian shirts.*

truss /trʌs/ *n* [C] a support for a building or bridge, made of wood or steel ○ *No one knows if the fire damaged the building's trusses and support beams.*

trust BELIEVE /trʌst/ *v* [I/T] to have confidence in something, or to believe in someone ○ [T] *Trust me – I would never lie to you.* ○ [T] *I was tested, but I'm not sure I trust the results.* ○ [I] *I have finally learned to trust in my own abilities.*

trust /trʌst/ *n* [U] ○ *Their relationship is based on trust and understanding.* ○ *We were obviously wrong to put our trust in her.*

trusted /ˈtrʌs·təd/ *adj* ○ *She was an old and trusted friend.*

trusting /ˈtrʌs·tɪŋ/, **trustful** /ˈtrʌst·fəl/ *adj* ○ *You shouldn't be so trusting – people will take advantage of you.*

trusty /ˈtrʌs·ti/ *adj* [-er/-est only] deserving confidence; RELIABLE ○ *So far, our trusty old car has gone 150,000 miles.*

ARRANGEMENT /trʌst/ *n* [C/U] ***social studies*** **1** a legal arrangement in which a person or organization controls property or money for the benefit of another person or organization ○ [U] *The money is being held in trust for her until she turns 21.* **2** A trust is also a group of people or organizations that controls property or money for their own benefit, or the property or money controlled by the group: [C] *The danger of trusts is that they can become very powerful.*

trustee /trʌsˈtiː/ *n* [C] a person, often one of a group, who controls property or money for the benefit of another person or an organization ○ *He was a member of the museum's board of trustees.*

HOPE /trʌst/ *v* [I/T] to hope and expect that something is true ○ [T] *I trust (that) you slept well?*

WORD FAMILY trust			
Nouns	trust distrust mistrust trustee trustworthiness	*Adjectives*	trusting trusted trusty trustworthy
		Verbs	trust distrust mistrust

trustworthy /ˈtrʌstˌwɜr·ði/ *adj* deserving of trust, or able to be trusted ○ *Not even a newspaper always gives trustworthy information.*

trustworthiness /ˈtrʌstˌwɜr·ðiː·nəs/ *n* [U] ○ *He has a well-earned reputation for absolute trustworthiness.*

trusty /ˈtrʌs·ti/ *adj* ○ See at TRUST BELIEVE

truth **FACT** /truːθ/ *n* [U] the actual fact or facts about a matter ○ *Tell the truth, now, how did the chair get broken?* ○ *We may never know the truth about what happened.* ○ Related adjective: TRUE CORRECT

QUALITY /truːθ/ *n* [U] the quality of being true ○ *I can see some truth in what she said.*

truthful /ˈtruːθ·fəl/ *adj* ○ *Are you being completely truthful?*

PRINCIPLE /truːθ/ *n* [C] *pl* **truths** a statement or principle that is generally considered to be true ○ *a scientific truth* ○ *Our system of belief is based on a few simple truths.*

IDIOMS with truth

• **in truth** actually ○ *We kept climbing but, in truth, we knew we could not reach the top of the mountain before sunset.*

• **truth is stranger than fiction** strange things often happen in real life ○ *I know it sounds unbelievable, but truth is sometimes stranger than fiction.*

try **ATTEMPT** /trɑɪ/ *v* [I/T] to make an effort to do something ○ [I] *Try to open this jar for me.* ○ [I] *You'll have to try harder.* ○ [T] *I'm trying my best.* ○ [I] *Maybe you should try getting up earlier* (= should wake earlier).

try /trɑɪ/ *n* [C] ○ *This will be her third try at an Olympic medal.* ○ *I decided to give skiing a try.*

WORD CHOICES try

Attempt is a common alternative to "try."

*I have never **attempted** to run a marathon.*

Endeavor means the same as "try" but is slightly more formal.

*Engineers are **endeavoring** to locate the source of the problem.*

Seek is a formal word that means "try."

*They **sought** to reassure the public.*

The verbs **battle**, **strive**, and **struggle** can be used when someone is trying to do something in a difficult situation.

*He was **battling** to fix the roof in the rain.*

*With limited resources, they are **striving** to make the school a better one.*

*I've been **struggling** to understand this article all afternoon.*

If someone tries very hard to do something, you can say that the person **goes to great lengths.**

*She knew that her parents would **go to great lengths** to see that she got a good education.*

TEST /trɑɪ/ *v* [T] to test something to see if it is suitable or useful, or if it will work ○ *Have you tried that new recipe yet?* ○ *I want to try scuba diving.* ○ *Try the back door* (= see if it is open).

EXAMINE IN COURT /trɑɪ/ *v* [T] *law* to examine a person accused of committing a crime in a court of law to decide if the person is guilty ○ *He was tried for fraud.* ○ See also: TRIAL LEGAL PROCESS

WORD FAMILY try			
Nouns	try	*Adjectives*	trying untried
Verbs	try		

IDIOMS with try

• **try** *your* **hand at** *something* to attempt something for the first time ○ *Mike decided to try his hand at tennis.*

• **try** *someone's* **patience** to makes someone less patient ○ *Little kids get into everything, and it can really try your patience.*

PHRASAL VERBS with try

• **try on** *something* [M] to put on clothes to see how they look or if they fit ○ *Try on those shoes.*

• **try out** **COMPETE** to compete for a position on the team or a part in the play ○ *Jim tried out for the school play.* ○ Related noun: TRYOUT COMPETITION

• **try out** *something* **USE** [M] to use something to see if it works well ○ *Lanny is trying out her new bicycle.* ○ Related noun: TRYOUT TEST USE

• **try** *something* **out on** *someone* [M] to find out what someone thinks about something ○ *I like the idea, but you should try it out on Abby.* ○ *We tried out the new song on a couple of friends, but they didn't like it.*

trying /ˈtrɑɪ·ɪŋ/ *adj* annoying; IRRITATING ○ *Most people find him very trying.* ○ *Julie's having a trying time at work lately.*

tryout **COMPETITION** /ˈtrɑɪ·ɑʊt/ *n* [C] a competition for a position on a team or a part in a play ○ *Tryouts for the team will be held next week.* ○ Related verb: TRY OUT COMPETE

TEST USE /ˈtrɑɪ·ɑʊt/ *n* [C] a test of something to see if it works well ○ *After a barefoot tryout, she concluded that the carpet passed the softness test.* ○ Related verb: TRY OUT USE

tsar /zɑr, tsɑr/ *n* [C] CZAR

TSH /ˌtiːˌesˈeɪtʃ/ *n* [C usually sing] ***biology*** *abbreviation for* thyroid-stimulating hormone (= a chemical produced in the body that causes other chemicals to be produced)

T

T-shirt, **tee shirt** /ˈtiː·ʃɜrt/ *n* [C] a type of shirt that covers the upper part of the body, has short sleeves and no collar, and is pulled on over the head ○ *He wore a T-shirt and jeans.*

tsp. *n* [C] *pl* **tsp.** *abbreviation for* TEASPOON ○ *Add 1 tsp. baking powder.*

tsunami /sʊˈnɑm·i, tsʊ-/ *n* [C] a very large and dangerous ocean wave that is caused by an EARTHQUAKE under the sea

tub **BATH** /tʌb/ *n* [C] *short form of* BATHTUB

CONTAINER /tʌb/ *n* [C] a container, esp. one used for storing food ○ *a tub of potato salad* ○ *Plant lilies in three-gallon plastic tub.*

tuba /ˈtuː·bə/ *n* [C/U] a large BRASS musical instrument that plays low notes which is played by blowing into it and has keys that are pressed to vary the notes, or this type of instrument generally

tube **PIPE** /tuːb/ *n* [C] **1** a long, hollow cylinder of plastic, metal, rubber, or glass, used for moving or containing liquids or gases ○ *a copper tube* ○ *She lay in the hospital, tubes going in and out of her.* **2** A tube is also one of the body's hollow cylindrical structures that carries air or liquid: *bronchial tubes*

CONTAINER /tuːb/ *n* [C] a cylindrical container made of soft metal or plastic which is closed at one end and has a small opening at the other, usually with a cover, and is used for holding thick liquids ○ *a tube of toothpaste/ointment*

TELEVISION /tuːb/ *n* [U] *infml* television ○ *What's on the tube tonight?*

tuberculosis /tʊˌbɜr·kjəˈloʊ·səs/, *abbreviation* **TB** *n* [U] an infectious disease that can attack many parts of the body, esp. the lungs

tuck **MAKE TIGHT** /tʌk/ *v* [T always + adv/prep] **1** to push the ends clothing or material tightly into place ○ *He tucked the sheet under the mattress.* ○ [M] *Richard needs to tuck in his shirt.* **2** If you tuck part of your body, you hold it in a particular position: *She sat with her legs tucked under her.* ○ [M] *Tuck your tummy in.*

STORE SAFELY /tʌk/ *v* [T always + adv/prep] to put something into a safe or convenient place ○ *She tucked her doll under her arm.* ○ *I found the pictures tucked away in a box.*

IDIOM with **tuck**

• **tucked away** hidden or difficult to find ○ *Van's house is tucked away at the end of the road.*

PHRASAL VERB with **tuck**

• **tuck in** *someone* [M] to cover a child in bed, esp. to make a child feel comfortable and ready to sleep ○ *I tucked the children in.*

Tuesday /ˈtuːz·di, -deɪ/, *abbreviation* **Tue.**, *abbreviation* **Tues.** *n* [C/U] the day of the week after Monday and before Wednesday

tuft /tʌft/ *n* [C] a number of short pieces of something, such as hair or grass, that grow close together or are held together at the base ○ *He had only a few tufts of hair on his chin.*

tug /tʌg/ *v* [I/T] **-gg-** to pull something quickly with force or effort ○ [T] *We tugged the sled up the hill.* ○ [I] *He had to tug hard.*

tug /tʌg/ *n* [C] ○ *She felt a tug at her sleeve.*

tugboat /ˈtʌg·boʊt/, *short form* **tug** /tʌg/ *n* [C] a boat with a powerful engine which can change direction easily and is used to pull large ships into and out of port

tug of war *n* [C usually sing] a competition in which two teams pull at opposite ends of a rope, each trying to pull the other team over a line between them, or *fig.* a fight between two people or groups

tuition /tʊˈɪʃ·ən/ *n* [U] the money paid for being taught, esp. at a college or university

tulip /ˈtuː·ləp/ *n* [C] a plant that grows from a BULB and has a large, brightly colored, bell-shaped flower on a stem, or the flower itself

tumble /ˈtʌm·bəl/ *v* [I] to fall or roll quickly and without control ○ *Rocks tumbled down the hill.* ○ *She lost her balance and tumbled into the mud.* ○ *(fig.) Stock prices tumbled* (= quickly lost a lot of value).

tumble /ˈtʌm·bəl/ *n* [C] ○ *I took a tumble and hurt my knee.*

tumbledown /ˈtʌm·bəlˌdaʊn/ *adj* (of a building) in a bad condition, esp. in a state of decay ○ *They lived in a tumbledown cottage near the railroad tracks.*

tummy /ˈtʌm·i/ *n* [C] *a child's word* a stomach ○ *My tummy hurts.*

tumor, *Cdn, Br* **tumour** /ˈtuː·mər/ *n* [C] a mass of cells in the body that grow faster than usual and can cause illness ○ *a malignant/benign tumor*

tumult /ˈtuː·mʌlt/ *n* [C/U] noise and excitement, or a state of confusion, change, or uncertainty ○ [U] *mental tumult* ○ [C usually sing] *a tumult of emotion* ○ [U] *The garden sits amid the tumult of downtown Vancouver.*

tumultuous /tʊˈmʌl·tʃə·wəs/ *adj* ○ *The honoree received tumultuous applause.*

tuna /ˈtuː·nə/ *n* [C/U] *pl* **tuna** a large fish that lives in warm seas, or its flesh eaten as food ○ [U] *a can of tuna* ○ [U] *tuna salad*

tundra /ˈtʌn·drə/ *n* [U] any of the very large, flat areas of land in northern parts of Asia, North America, and Europe where, because it is cold, trees do not grow and the earth below the surface is permanently frozen

tune **MUSICAL NOTES** /tuːn/ *n* [C] a series of musical notes, esp. one that is pleasant and easy to remember; a MELODY ○ *That's a very pretty tune.*

ADJUST INSTRUMENT /tuːn/ *v* [T] to adjust a musical instrument so the sounds produced are the correct PITCH (= degree to which the sound is high or low) ○ *Tune your guitar before you practice.*

tune /tuːn/ *n* [U] ○ *This piano is out of tune* (= the notes are too high or low). ○ *Paul just can't sing in tune* (= with correctly produced notes).

T

ADJUST SIGNAL /tuːn/ *v* [T] to move the controls on a radio or television set so that it receives programs broadcast from a particular station ○ *Tune your radio to 88.3 FM.*

tuner /ˈtuː·nər/ *n* [C] the part of a radio or television that allows you to choose the stations you want to listen to or watch

ADJUST ENGINE /tuːn/ *v* [T] to change the setting of particular parts of an engine so that it works as well as possible ○ *The engine needs tuning.*

IDIOMS with tune

• **in tune with** *someone/something* having a good understanding of someone or something ○ *He is more in tune with his players today, because he has asked them for their opinions.*

• **to the tune of** in the approximate amount mentioned ○ *We're in debt to the tune of $50,000.*

• **tuned in (to** *someone/something***)** very aware of someone or something so that you understand that person or thing well ○ *She's tuned in to all the latest fashions.* ○ *Our staff are trained to be tuned in to the needs of children.*

PHRASAL VERBS with tune

• **tune in** *(something)* [M] to turn on a radio or television ○ *Millions of viewers tuned in to learn the election results.*

• **tune out** *(something/someone)* [M] *infml* to stop paying attention to something or someone ○ *Beverly always tunes out in the middle of her music lesson.* ○ *She tends to tune out her parents' advice and make her own decisions.*

• **tune up** *something* **ADJUST** [M] to adjust something, esp. an engine, so it works as effectively as possible ○ *I haven't tuned my car up in two years.* ○ Related noun: TUNEUP

• **tune up** *(something)* **PREPARE** [M] to prepare for a performance or competition, or to adjust an instrument for playing ○ *Yards away on the infield, a marching band was tuning up.*

tuneup /ˈtuː·nʌp/ *n* [C] a set of small improvements to an engine or other device ○ *It'll actually go up to 100,000 miles before its first scheduled tuneup.* ○ Related verb: TUNE UP

tunic /ˈtuː·nɪk/ *n* [C] a piece of clothing that fits loosely over a person's body, reaching to below the waist or to the knees and often worn with a belt

tunnel /ˈtʌn·əl/ *n* [C] a long passage under or through the earth, esp. one made for vehicles ○ *The train entered the tunnel.*

tunnel /ˈtʌn·əl/ *v* [I/T] **-l-, -ll-** ○ [I] *Earthworms digest organic matter as they tunnel.* ○ [T] *The people trapped in the collapsed building had to tunnel their way out.*

turban /ˈtɜr·bən/ *n* [C] a head covering made from a long piece of cloth that is wrapped around the head

turbine /ˈtɜr·bən, -ˌbɑɪn/ *n* [C] a type of machine through which liquid or gas flows and turns a special wheel with blades in order to produce power ○ *a steam turbine*

turbulence **CONFUSION** /ˈtɜr·bjə·ləns/ *n* [U] a state of confusion and lack of order ○ *political turbulence* ○ *His songs reflect the turbulence of his times.*

turbulent /ˈtɜr·bjə·lənt/ *adj* ○ *His book discusses the turbulent years of the civil rights struggle.*

CURRENTS /ˈtɜr·bjə·ləns/ *n* [U] strong, uneven currents in air or water ○ *The plane ran into some turbulence over the Atlantic.*

turbulent /ˈtɜr·bjə·lənt/ *adj* ○ *Turbulent seas kept us from sailing.*

turf **GRASS** /tɜrf/ *n* [U] **1** a surface layer of land consisting of grass and the earth in which its roots grow ○ *Lush turf lined the river's banks.* **2** Turf is also ground cover that looks like grass: *artificial turf*

AREA /tɜrf/ *n* [U] *infml* the area that a person or group considers its own ○ *Judges feel that the courtroom is their private turf.* ○ *The fight over high-definition TV standards has been a turf war among the electronics, motion picture, and recording industries.*

turgid **TOO SERIOUS** /ˈtɜr·dʒəd/ *adj* (of speech or writing) too serious and very boring ○ *turgid prose*

SWOLLEN /ˈtɜr·dʒəd/ *adj* swollen ○ *turgid rain clouds*

turkey /ˈtɜr·ki/ *n* [C/U] a large North American bird grown for food, or the flesh of this bird ○ [C] *wild turkeys* ○ [U] *roast turkey*

turmoil /ˈtɜr·mɔɪl/ *n* [U] a state of extreme confusion, uncertainty, or lack of order ○ *Her mind was in turmoil.* ○ *She grew up in the turmoil of the 1960s.*

turn **GO AROUND** /tɜrn/ *v* [I/T] to move or cause something to move in a circle around a central point or line ○ [I] *The earth turns on its axis once every 24 hours.* ○ [T] *She turned the doorknob and opened the door.*

turn /tɜrn/ *n* [C] ○ *This little wheel will shut off the water if you give it several turns.*

CHANGE DIRECTION /tɜrn/ *v* [I/T] **1** to change the direction in which you are facing or moving, or to cause someone or something to face or move in a different direction ○ [I] *They told us to turn right at the first traffic light.* ○ [T] *Turn your head this way so that you're looking right at the camera.* ○ [I] *I turned to the person next to me and asked her what time it was.* ○ [T] *The car turned* (= went around) *the corner.* ○ [I] (*fig.*) *He felt desperate and didn't know where to turn for help.* ○ [I] *I* **turned over** (= changed how I was lying) *and tried to sleep, but quickly gave up.* **2** If you turn something or turn something over, you place the surface that was on top on the bottom: [T] *He turned the pages of a magazine.* ○ [M] *She turned the baby over onto his stomach.*

turn /tɜrn/ *n* [C] ○ *Make a left turn at the next traffic light.*

BECOME /tɜrn/ *v* **1** to become or cause to become, change, or come to be ○ [L] *The weather suddenly turned colder, and it started to rain.* ○ [I] *By mid-September, the leaves are starting to turn* (= change color). **2** A person turns a particular color when the face changes in color because the person is

T

feeling a strong emotion or feeling ill: [L] *He turned red with embarrassment.* **3** Turn is used with times and ages to show that a particular point has been reached or passed: [L] *My little girl just turned six in February.*

SWITCH /tɜrn/ *v* [always + adv/prep] to use a control to switch (a piece of equipment) on or off, or to adjust it to change the amount of what it is producing ○ [M] *Please turn off/out the lights when you leave.* ○ [M] *Who turned my computer on/off?* ○ [M] *Turn the TV down* (= make the sound quieter) *– it's too loud.* ○ [M] *Turn up the volume – I can't hear what they're saying.* ➤ Learner error: **open/close or turn on/turn off?** at OPEN READY FOR USE

OPPORTUNITY /tɜrn/ *n* [C] an opportunity or a duty to do something at a particular time or in a particular order, before or after other people ○ [+ *to* infinitive] *It's your turn to do the grocery shopping.*

TWIST /tɜrn/ *v* [T] to damage the muscles in the foot by suddenly bending it too strongly ○ *to turn your ankle*

MAKE ILL /tɜrn/ *v* [I/T] to feel that you are going to vomit, or to cause your stomach to feel this way ○ [I/T] *The stench made my stomach turn.*

WORD FAMILY turn			
Nouns	turn upturn	*Adjectives*	upturned
		Verbs	turn overturn

IDIOMS with turn

• **in turn 1** because of that ○ *Stress causes your body to release chemicals, which in turn boost blood pressure.* **2** one after the other, in order ○ *She spoke to each of the guests in turn.*

• **the turn of the century** the time when a particular century ends and another begins ○ *My great-grandfather was born at the turn of the last century.*

• **turn a profit** to begin to earn a profit ○ *He's been in business five years, but has not yet turned a profit.*

• **turn** *your* **back on** *someone/something* to ignore someone or something ○ *He said the nation had turned its back on the poor for many years.*

• **turn back the clock (on** *something***)** to change something so that it behaves or exists as it did in the past ○ *They oppose efforts to turn the clock back on civil rights.*

• **turn** *someone/something* **loose** to let people go or allow them to do what they want ○ *He turned the horse loose in the field.*

• **turn** *your* **nose up at** *something* to refuse to accept something because you feel that it is not good enough for you ○ *She turned up her nose at the job because she didn't think it had enough status.*

• **turn of events** a new development or change in a situation ○ *Salazar did not like this turn of events, but he accepted his new assignment.*

• **turn over a new leaf** to change your behavior in a positive way ○ *She turned over a new leaf and began getting to work on time.*

• **turn over in** *your* **grave** to strongly disapprove ○ *Your father would turn over in his grave if he could hear the way you are talking to me now.* ○ **USAGE:** Used to talk about the way someone who is dead would feel about a situation happening now.

• **turn the other cheek** to decide not to do anything to hurt someone who has hurt you ○ *I know it's frustrating, but it's often best to turn the other cheek. Fighting won't solve the problem.*

• **turn the tables** to change from being in a weaker position in relation to someone else to being in a stronger position ○ *The plaintiff's lawyer turned the tables this morning by producing some strong new evidence.*

PHRASAL VERBS with turn

• **turn against** *someone/something* to change from supporting to opposing someone or something ○ *A lot of his supporters turned against him.* ○ *Their idea is that the immune system turns against the body because it isn't exposed to enough germs.*

• **turn** *something* **around** to cause a situation or organization to change in a positive direction ○ *They were losing badly but they turned things around in the second half of the game.* ○ Related noun: TURNAROUND

• **turn** *someone* **away** [M] to refuse someone's request and tell that person to leave ○ *The agency turned her away because she does not have a Social Security number.*

• **turn down** *something* [M] to refuse to accept or agree to something, or to refuse someone's request ○ *The bank turned her down for a loan.* ○ *The former Joint Chiefs of Staff Chairman has turned down the job.*

• **turn in** *something/someone/yourself* **GIVE** [M] to give or return something to an authority ○ *Don't forget to turn in your papers after class.* ○ *He learned that the police were looking for him and turned himself in* (= made himself available to them).

• **turn in SLEEP** to go to your bed in order to sleep ○ *I'm getting sleepy – I think I'll turn in.*

• **turn into** *something* to change or develop from one thing to another ○ *Rain in the morning will turn into snow during the afternoon.*

• **turn** *someone* **off** [M] *infml* to cause someone to lose interest ○ *Her offensive remarks really turned me off.* ○ *The downtown has outdated architecture that might turn off some people.* ○ Related noun: TURNOFF

• **turn on** *something* **DEPEND ON** to depend on something in an important way ○ *The success of the talks turns on whether both sides are willing to compromise.*

• **turn on** *someone* **ATTACK** to attack or criticize someone suddenly ○ *He suddenly turned on me and accused me of not supporting him when he needed it.*

• **turn** *someone* **on EXCITE** *infml* to cause someone to feel excited and very interested ○ *What turns the kids on these days?*

• **turn** *someone* **on to** *something* to cause someone to be interested in something ○ *He turned me on to all sorts of music that I never would have heard otherwise.*

• **turn out RESULT** to happen or become known to happen in a particular way ○ *She assured him that everything would turn out all right.* ○ *It turns*

out (that) Ray had borrowed the money from one of his students.
• **turn out** *something* **PRODUCE** [M] to produce or make something ○ *Our factory is turning the dolls out as fast as it can.*
• **turn out** **COME** to come, appear, or be present ○ *A lot of actors turned out for the audition.* ○ Related noun: TURNOUT
• **turn out** *someone* **REMOVE** [M] to force someone to leave ○ *They turned him out of the shelter when they caught him stealing.*
• **turn over** *something/someone* [M] to give something or someone that you control to someone else ○ *Eventually he turned over control of the company to his son.* ○ *They are identifying the guilty and turning them over to civil authorities for prosecution.*
• **turn to** *someone* **GET HELP** to get help from someone ○ *You can always turn to me for help if you need it.*
• **turn to** *something* **CONSIDER** to think about or begin to consider something ○ *I think we've spent enough time on this issue – let's turn to the new business now.*
• **turn to** *something* **FIND PAGE** to open a book to a particular page ○ *Turn to page 27.*
• **turn up** *(something)* to appear or come to your attention, or to cause something to become known ○ *She said she'd let me know if anything new turned up.* ○ *A search of his office at the college turned up a wealth of evidence.*

turnabout /ˈtɜr·nəˌbɑʊt/ *n* [C] a complete change from one situation or condition to its opposite ○ *In a complete turnabout, the mayor has decided not to run for reelection.*

turnaround /ˈtɜr·nəˌrɑʊnd/ *n* [C usually sing] a positive change; improvement ○ *Business was up over 40% in a dramatic turnaround from last year.* ○ Related verb: TURN AROUND

turncoat /ˈtɜrn·koʊt/ *n* [C] a person whose support changes from one side to the opposite side; a TRAITOR

turning point *n* [C] **1** the time when a situation starts to change in an important, esp. positive, way ○ *Having the baby was a turning point in their lives.* **2** ***literature*** The turning point in a work of literature is the moment or section when the action begins to move toward the CLIMAX (= the most important or exciting part).

turnip /ˈtɜr·nəp/ *n* [C] a round, white root that is cooked and eaten as a vegetable, or the plant that produces it

turnoff **ROAD** /ˈtɜr·nɔːf/ *n* [C] a short road that leads from a large road onto a smaller one ○ *If you miss the turnoff, you'll have to go 20 miles to the next exit.*

OFFENSE /ˈtɜr·nɔːf/ *n* [C] speech, behavior, or some other thing that causes you to lose interest ○ *Younger readers find the newspaper's traditional format a turnoff.* ○ Related verb: TURN OFF

turnout /ˈtɜr·nɑʊt/ *n* [C usually sing] **1** the number of people who are present for an event ○ *Considering the rain, there was a good turnout.* **2** ***politics & government*** In an election, the turnout is the number of people who vote ○ Related verb: TURN OUT **COME**

turnover **EMPLOYEE CHANGES** /ˈtɜrˌnoʊ·vər/ *n* [U] the rate at which employees leave a company and are replaced ○ *The high turnover among day-care workers is an ongoing problem.* ○ See also: TURN OVER

PASTRY /ˈtɜrˌnoʊ·vər/ *n* [C] a piece of pastry that is folded to contain fruit within it ○ *an apple turnover*

turnpike /ˈtɜrn·pɑɪk/ *n* [C] a main road intended for fast travel, which you usually have to pay to use ○ *the New Jersey Turnpike*

turn signal *n* [C] one of the lights on a vehicle that flashes to show in which direction the driver is intending to turn

turnstile /ˈtɜrn·stɑɪl/ *n* [C] a device with waist-high horizontal bars that one person at a time can push around to enter a place, esp. a place that you pay to use ○ *More than 18 million visitors have poured through Disneyland's turnstiles.*

turntable /ˈtɜrnˌteɪ·bəl/ *n* [C] a piece of equipment with a flat, round surface that turns a record around while it is being played; a RECORD PLAYER

turpentine /ˈtɜr·pənˌtɑɪn/ *n* [U] a strong-smelling, colorless liquid used to thin paint

turquoise /ˈtɜr·kwɔɪz/ *n* [C/U] **1** a blue-green precious stone often used in jewelry **2** Turquoise is also a blue-green color.

turret /ˈtɜr·ət, ˈtʌ·rət/ *n* [C] a tall, circular structure that is part of a CASTLE or other large building

turtle /ˈtɜrt̬·əl/ *n* [C] an animal that lives in or near water, having a thick, outer shell that covers and protects its body

turtleneck /ˈtɜrt̬·əlˌnek/ *n* [C] a high, round collar that folds over on itself and covers the neck, or a piece of clothing with a collar of this type

tusk /tʌsk/ *n* [C] either of the two, long, curved teeth that stick out from the mouth of some animals, esp. ELEPHANTS and WALRUSES

tussle /ˈtʌs·əl/ *n* [C] a physical argument involving pushing and holding, usually between two people ○ *(fig.) He had numerous tussles with the law during his career as a boxer.*

tutor /ˈtuːt̬·ər/ *n* [C] a teacher paid to work privately with one student or a small group
tutor /ˈtuːt̬·ər/ *v* [T] to teach by working with one student or a small group, esp. one which needs special help ○ *Volunteers from the college tutor elementary school children in reading, mathematics, and science.*

tuxedo /tʌkˈsiːd·oʊ/, *infml* **tux** /tʌks/ *n* [C] *pl* **tuxedos** a type of black jacket, or jacket and pants, worn by men on formal occasions, usually with a BOW TIE

T

TV *n* [C] *abbreviation for* TELEVISION

twang /twæŋ/ *n* [C usually sing] **1** a ringing sound that begins suddenly and continues, gradually getting less strong, like the sound made when the string of a musical instrument is pulled and quickly released **2** A twang is also a quality of voice heard in some speakers that is related to the passing of air through the nose as they speak.

'twas, *old use* /twʌz, twɑz, twəz/ *contraction of* it was ○ *It was a sight that 'twas wonderful to see.*

tweak ADJUST /twi:k/ *v* [T] to change slightly, esp. in order to make something more effective or correct ○ *Writers and producers kept tweaking the script even as the movie was being shot.*

PULL /twi:k/ *v* [T] to pull and twist something ○ *He jumped when she tweaked his ear.*

tweed /twi:d/ *n* [U] a thick, rough material woven from wool and used in clothing, esp. suits and coats ○ *a gray tweed jacket*

tweezers /'twi:·zərz/, **tweezer** /'twi:·zər/ *pl n* a small device having two narrow, metal sides joined at one end and open at the other, used to hold or pull a small thing, such as a hair, by pressing the two sides until the open ends come together on the thing to be held ○ *He tried to get the splinter out with tweezers.*

twelfth /twelfθ/ *adj, adv, n* [C] **1** (a person or thing) coming immediately after the eleventh and before all others ○ *She finished twelfth in her age group.* ○ [C] *We will arrive on the twelfth of December.* **2** A twelfth is one of twelve equal parts of something. ○ Related number: TWELVE

twelve /twelv/ *number* **1** 12 ○ *Casey is twelve.* ○ *a twelve-volume set* **2** Twelve can also mean twelve o'clock. ○ Related number: TWELFTH

twelve-bar blues *n* [U] ***music*** the standard form of BLUES song, consisting of three parts that are each four BARs long

twelve-tone scale *n* [C] ***music*** a musical SCALE including all twelve half STEPS (= smallest differences in sound) in an OCTAVE (= series of eight notes)

T

twenty /'twent·i/ *number* 20 ○ *She's twenty years old.* ○ *a twenty-story building*

twenties, **20s**, **20's** /'twent·i:z/ *pl n* **1** the numbers 20 through 29 ○ *Temperatures were in the twenties* (= between 20° and 29°). ○ *Both of our children are now in their twenties* (= between 20 and 29 years old). **2** The twenties are the years between 1920 and 1929.

twentieth /'twent·i:·əθ/ *adj, adv, n* [C] **1** *This is our twentieth wedding anniversary.* ○ [C] *The meeting is on the twentieth of November.* **2** A twentieth is one of twenty equal parts of something.

twice /twɑɪs/ *adv* [not gradable] two times ○ *Take the medicine twice a day.* ○ *I've already asked him twice.*

twiddle /'twɪd·ᵊl/ *v* [T] to move something about between your fingers without giving it your attention ○ *She kept twiddling her necklace.*

IDIOM with twiddle

• **twiddle** *your* **thumbs** to do nothing, usually while you are waiting for something to happen ○ *She put me on hold and left me to twiddle my thumbs for ten minutes until she got back to me.*

twig /twɪg/ *n* [C] a small, thin branch of a tree or bush, esp. one removed from the tree or bush and without any leaves ○ *We gathered some dry twigs to start the fire.*

twilight /'twɑɪ·lɑɪt/ *n* [U] **1** the low level of light when it is late in the day, just before the darkness of night, or this period of the day **2** *fig.* Twilight is also any late period, when the end of something is near: *The book presents a compelling portrait of the singer in the twilight of her career.*

twill /twɪl/ *n* [U] a strong cotton cloth that has raised diagonal lines on the surface

twin /twɪn/ *n* [C] either of two children born to the same mother on the same occasion

twin /twɪn/ *adj* [not gradable] **1** *a twin brother/sister* **2** Twin is used of two things that are the same or similar: *twin engines/towers*

twin bed *n* [C] one of a set of two beds, each of which is suitable for one person

twine /twɑɪn/ *n* [U] strong string made by twisting together two or more lengths of string

twinge /twɪndʒ/ *n* [C] a sudden, brief feeling of pain ○ *When she saw the house she grew up in, she felt a twinge of sadness.*

twinkle /'twɪŋ·kəl/ *v* [I] **1** (of light) to shine brightly and then less brightly, as if quickly flashing on and off ○ *Stars twinkled in the clear night sky.* **2** Someone whose eyes twinkle has a bright, intelligent expression: *His eyes twinkled with mischief.*

twinkle /'twɪŋ·kəl/ *n* [C] ○ *We could see the twinkle of lights across the bay* ○ *I know that twinkle in your eye means trouble!*

twinkling /'twɪŋ·klɪŋ/ *adj* [not gradable] ○ *a mass of twinkling stars* ○ *twinkling eyes*

twirl /twɜrl/ *v* [I/T] to turn in a circle, or to cause something to do this ○ [I always + adv/prep] *Skaters leapt and twirled on the ice.*

twirl /'twɜrl/ *n* [C] ○ *She does a twirl to show off her pretty dress.*

twist TURN /twɪst/ *v* [I/T] **1** to turn repeatedly, or to combine thin lengths of a material by turning or wrapping ○ [I] *A river twists through the valley.* ○ [I] *Vines twisted around the trunk of the old tree.* **2** If you twist a part of your body, you hurt it by turning it awkwardly: [T] *He twisted his knee in the game on Saturday.*

twist /twɪst/ *n* [C] **1** *The path wound its way down the hill in a series of twists.* ○ *One more twist should tighten the cover.* **2** A twist can also be something that has been twisted: *She added a twist of lemon to her drink.*

twisted /'twɪs·təd/ *adj* [not gradable] ○ *He missed the first game of the season because of a twisted ankle.*

twisting /'twɪs·tɪŋ/ *adj* ○ *a twisting country road*

CHANGE /twɪst/ *v* [T] to change the meaning of facts or a statement; DISTORT ○ *You're twisting my words – that's not what I meant at all.* ○ *During the trial, lawyers twisted the truth to gain the jury's sympathy.*
twist /twɪst/ *n* [C] an unexpected change ○ *The incident was the latest twist in the story of the robbery.* ○ *Walnuts give a new twist to regular banana bread.*

WORD FAMILY twist			
Nouns	twist twister	*Adjectives*	twisted twisting
Verbs	twist		

IDIOM with twist

• **twist** *someone's* **arm** to get someone to do what you want by making it very difficult for him or her to refuse ○ *I didn't want to go to the exhibition, but Linda twisted my arm.*

twisted /ˈtwɪs·təd/ *adj* [not gradable] unusual and strange; PERVERSE ○ *The letter was clearly written by someone with a twisted mind.*

twister /ˈtwɪs·tər/ *n* [C] a dangerous wind storm; a TORNADO

twit /twɪt/ *n* [C] a person you think is stupid or foolish

twitch /twɪtʃ/ *v* [I/T] to make a short and sudden movement, or to cause part of your body to move suddenly ○ [I] *She saw his mouth twitch into a little smile that disappeared almost at once.*
twitch /twɪtʃ/ *n* [C] ○ *She signalled with a twitch of her finger.*

two /tuː/ *number pl* **twos 1** 2 ○ *Josh'll be two in February.* ○ *a two-time winner* **2** Two can also mean two o'clock. ○ Related Number: SECOND POSITION

IDIOMS with two

• **of two minds (about** *something***)**, **in two minds (about** *something***)** unable to make a decision ○ *I was of two minds about whether to invite him to the wedding.*
• *someone's* **two cents**, *someone's* **two cents' worth** someone's opinion about something, esp. when it was not asked for or wanted ○ *If the changes are going to affect me, then I want to put my two cents in.*
• **two sides of the same coin** two things that different but closely related features of one idea ○ *Rewards and punishments are two sides of the same coin – both are used to control people and neither works very well.*

two-bit /ˈtuː ˈbɪt/ *adj* [not gradable] unimportant ○ *He's just a two-bit crook.*

two-by-four, **2x4** *n* [C] a standard size for cut pieces of wood used for building, measuring about two inches thick and four inches wide

two-dimensional *adj* [not gradable] ***art*** flat, having width and length but not depth ○ *Painting is a two-dimensional art that tries to give the illusion of three dimensions.*

two-faced *adj* not to be trusted ○ *He's a two-faced cheater.*

two-piece *adj* [not gradable] made in two matching parts ○ *She was wearing a red, two-piece bathing suit.*

twosome /ˈtuː·səm/ *n* [C] two people thought of as a pair ○ *We were a twosome, best friends, and almost never played with other kids.*

two-time *v* [I/T] *infml* to deceive your husband, wife, or romantic partner by having a secret relationship with another person

two-tone *adj* [not gradable] of two different colors

two-way *adj* [not gradable] permitting movement or communication in two directions ○ *There are only a few two-way streets left in town.* ○ *This should be a two-way relationship.*

tycoon /tɑɪˈkuːn/ *n* [C] a person who has achieved great success in business and is very wealthy and powerful

tying /ˈtɑɪ·ɪŋ/ *present participle of* TIE

tyke, **tike** /tɑɪk/ *n* [C] *infml* a small child

type CHARACTERISTICS /tɑɪp/ *n* [C] the characteristics of a group of people or things that set them apart from other people or things, or people, things, or groups that share particular characteristics ○ *I'm more comfortable in jeans and T-shirts, and that type of thing.* ○ *We have makeup for all different types of skin.* ○ *Grant's my type of guy – strong and cool – but Willie's not my type at all.*
typical /ˈtɪp·ɪ·kəl/ *adj* **1** showing the characteristics of a particular kind of person or thing ○ *He looked like the typical tourist with his camera and baseball cap.* ○ *This dish is typical of Southern cooking.* **2** *disapproving* Typical also means behaving as you would expect: *"He called to say he wasn't coming." "Typical! You can't rely on Michael for anything!"*
typically /ˈtɪp·ɪ·kli/ *adv* ○ *It's a typically American town.* ○ *I typically go running at lunchtime.*
typify /ˈtɪp·əˌfɑɪ/ *v* [T] to be an example of a particular thing or kind of thing ○ *This trial typifies the problems juries face all the time.*

CONFUSABLES

typical or formal?

Don't confuse **typical** and **formal**. **Typical** means "showing the characteristics of a particular kind of person or thing." **Formal** means "serious and correct."

It was a typical season for Rodriguez.
The document was written in formal language.
~~*The document was written in typical language.*~~

WRITE /tɑɪp/ *v* [I/T] to write using a KEYBOARD ○ [I] *I never learned how to type.* ○ [T] *He typed the report yesterday.*
typing /ˈtɑɪ·pɪŋ/ *n* [U] ○ *Her typing is very accurate most of the time.*

T

typist /ˈtɑɪ·pəst/ *n* [C] ○ *Typists don't use typewriters any more, they use keyboards.*

PRINTED LETTERS /tɑɪp/ *n* [U] printed letters and symbols, or small pieces of metal with the shapes of letters and symbols on them that were used in the past in printing ○ *In big bold type, the headline announced the winner of the election.*

WORD FAMILY type			
Nouns	type typing typist	*Verbs*	typify type
		Adverbs	typically
Adjectives	typical		

PHRASAL VERBS with type

• **type in** *something* [M] to use the keys on a computer or other device to enter information ○ *How can I type in my password if I can't remember it?*

• **type out/up** *something* [M] to use a computer or a TYPEWRITER, to make a copy of something in writing ○ *Did you type up the minutes of yesterday's meeting?*

typeface /ˈtɑɪp·feɪs/ *n* [C] a FONT LETTERS

typewriter /ˈtɑɪpˌrɑɪţ·ər/ *n* [C] a machine for putting print on a page, operated with keys

typewritten /ˈtɑɪpˌrɪt·ən/ *adj* [not gradable] ○ *We found several old typewritten manuscripts in the attic.*

typhoid (fever) /ˈtɑɪ·fɔɪd/ *n* [U] an infectious disease spread by bacteria, esp. in water and food, causing fever and severe pain in the bowels

typhoon /tɑɪˈfuːn/ *n* [C] a type of violent storm with strong circular winds that happens esp. in the Pacific Ocean

typhus /ˈtɑɪ·fəs/ *n* [U] an infectious disease caused by organisms carried by LICE and causing fever, severe pain in the head, and dark red spots on the body

typical /ˈtɪp·ɪ·kəl/ *adj* ○ See at TYPE CHARACTERISTICS

typically /ˈtɪp·ɪ·kli/ *adv* ○ See at TYPE CHARACTERISTICS

typify /ˈtɪp·əˌfɑɪ/ *v* [T] ○ See at TYPE CHARACTERISTICS

typing /ˈtɑɪ·pɪŋ/ *n* [U] ○ See at TYPE WRITE

typist /ˈtɑɪ·pəst/ *n* [C] ○ See at TYPE WRITE

typo /ˈtɑɪ·poʊ/ *n* [C] *pl* **typos** a mistake made in printed material produced by a computer or a TYPEWRITER

tyranny /ˈtɪr·ə·ni/ *n* [C/U] ***social studies*** unlimited authority or use of power, or a government which exercises such power without any control or limits

tyrannical /tɪˈræn·ɪ·kəl/ *adj* ○ *American revolutionaries believed the British government was tyrannical.*

tyrannize /ˈtɪr·əˌnɑɪz/ *v* [T] ○ *In school, he was the big bully who tyrannized the whole playground.*

tyrant /ˈtɑɪ·rənt/ *n* [C] ○ *Their father was a tyrant, feared by all his children.*

tyre /tɑɪr/ *n* [C] *Br* TIRE WHEEL

T

U u

U, u /juː/ *n* [C] *pl* **U's, u's** the 21st letter of the English alphabet

ubiquitous /jʊˈbɪk·wət̬·əs, juː-/ *adj* found or existing everywhere ○ *The eel grass limpet used to be ubiquitous on the New England coast.*

udder /ˈʌd·ər/ *n* [C] the part of a cow, goat, or other animal that hangs between the back legs and produces milk

UFO /ˌjuː·efˈoʊ/ *n* [C] *pl* **UFOs** *abbreviation for* unidentified flying object (= an object seen in the sky that some people believe is a spacecraft from another planet)

ugh /ʌg/ *exclamation* the written form of the sound people sometimes use to express a strong feeling of disgust at something very unpleasant ○ *Ugh, that smells really bad!*

ugly VERY UNATTRACTIVE /ˈʌg·li/ *adj* [-er/-est only] extremely unattractive in appearance ○ *He's a really ugly dog.*

ugliness /ˈʌg·liː·nəs/ *n* [U] ○ *The city's ugliness struck me.*

UNPLEASANT /ˈʌg·li/ *adj* [-er/-est only] unpleasant and threatening or violent ○ *This policy could have some ugly consequences.*

ugliness /ˈʌg·liː·nəs/ *n* [U] ○ *He has ugliness in his heart.*

uh /ʌ, ə/, **um** /ʌm, ᵊm/ *exclamation* the written form of the sound people sometimes make when they pause in speaking, thinking of what to say next or how to say it ○ *try not to, uh, rely on my parents.*

uh-huh /ˈʌ̃·hʌ̃, ˈᵊm·hᵊm/ *exclamation infml* said to express agreement to what has just been said, or to mean yes ○ *"Did you hear what I said?" "Uh-huh."*

uh-oh /ˈʌ·oʊ/ *exclamation infml* the written form of the sound that people sometimes make when they have made a mistake or when something bad has happened ○ *Uh-oh, I think I just locked my keys in the car.*

uh-uh /ˈʌ̃·ʌ̃, ˈᵊm·ᵊm/ *exclamation infml* the written form of the sound that people sometimes make to say no ○ *"Did you do the shopping?" "Uh-uh."*

ulcer /ˈʌl·sər/ *n* [C] a sore on the skin or inside the body that will not heal without treatment ○ *a stomach ulcer*

ulterior /ʌlˈtɪr·iː·ər/ *adj* [not gradable] (of a reason) hidden or secret ○ *She had no ulterior motive for helping them out – she just wanted to do it.*

ultimate Ⓐ /ˈʌl·tə·mət/ *adj* [not gradable] **1** most important, highest, last, or final ○ *Your ultimate goal is to play the game as well as you can.* **2** Ultimate also means the best, most, or greatest of its kind: *Some people believe that he is the ultimate painter of this century.*

ultimate Ⓐ /ˈʌl·tə·mət/ *n* [U] ○ *Winning was the ultimate, because our team had never won before.*

ultimately Ⓐ /ˈʌl·tə·mət·li/ *adv* [not gradable] finally; in the end ○ *Our plans ultimately depend on the weather.*

ultimatum /ˌʌl·təˈmeɪt̬·əm/ *n* [C] a demand that a person or group do something to avoid something unpleasant ○ *The workers got an ultimatum – go back to work or face dismissal.*

ultra- /ˌʌl·trə/ *prefix* extreme or extremely ○ *ultraconservative* ○ *ultramodern*

ultrasonic /ˌʌl·trəˈsɑn·ɪk/ *adj* [not gradable] (of sound waves) too high for people to hear

ultrasound /ˈʌl·trəˌsɑʊnd/ *n* [U] sound waves that are higher than people can hear, esp. ones used to examine and treat medical problems ○ *An ultrasound scan revealed tissue damage.*

ultraviolet /ˌʌl·trəˈvɑɪ·ə·lət/ *adj* [not gradable] ***physics*** describes light at the purple end of the SPECTRUM (= set of colors into which light is separated), which cannot be seen by human beings

um /ˈʌm, ᵊm/ *exclamation* UH

umbilical cord /ʌmˈbɪl·ɪ·kəl/ *n* [C] ***biology*** the tube that connects a baby to its mother before birth and carries oxygen and food to it

umbrella /ʌmˈbrel·ə/ *n* [C] **1** a cover that protects from rain or sun, esp. waterproof material fitted on a folding frame with a handle at one end ○ *A figure carrying an open umbrella walked slowly through the rain.* **2** An umbrella is also something that includes a number of similar things: *an umbrella term* ○ *an umbrella organization*

umpire /ˈʌm·pɑɪr/, *short form* **ump** /ʌmp/ *n* [C] (in some sports) a person who controls a game and makes sure that the rules are followed

umpire /ˈʌm·pɑɪr/ *v* [I/T] ○ [T] *Who's going to umpire the game tonight?*

un- /ʌn/ *prefix* used to add the meaning "not," "lacking," or "the opposite of" to adjectives, adverbs, verbs, and nouns ○ *unaided; unalterable; unaltered; unanticipated; unappreciated; unapproachable; unassigned; unassisted; unattainable; unbiased; uncommunicative; unconfined; unconvinced; uncultured; undefined; undiminished; uneconomical; unlicensed; unmodified; unmonitored; unmotivated; unobtainable; unpublished; unregulated; unrestricted; unrestrictive; unscheduled; unstressed; unstructured; unsustainable*

UN /juːˈen/ *n* [U] *abbreviation for* United Nations (= an international organization that was established in 1945 to maintain world peace).

unabashed /ˌʌn·əˈbæʃt/ *adj* not worried about being criticized or embarrassed ○ *an unabashed critic of Congress* ○ *an unabashed supporter of the team*

unabated /ˌʌn·əˈbeɪt̬·əd/ *adj* without weakening in strength or force ○ *Their arguments continue unabated.*

unable /ʌnˈeɪ·bəl/ *adj* [not gradable] not ABLE ○ *I was unable to find a pay phone.*

unacceptable /ˌʌn·ɪkˈsep·tə·bəl/ *adj* too bad to be accepted, approved of, or allowed to continue ○ *These mistakes are unacceptable.* ○ *The proposal is unacceptable to theater owners.*

unaccompanied Ⓐ /ˌʌn·əˈkʌm·pə·niːd/ *adj* [not gradable] without anyone with you, or (of the voice or an instrument) sung or played without other musical instruments ○ *Unaccompanied teens were banned from the mall.* ○ *The kids sang an unaccompanied version of "Skylark."*

unaccountable /ˌʌn·əˈkɑʊnt·ə·bəl/ *adj* [not gradable] **1** not able to be explained or understood ○ *For some unaccountable reason, he forgot his car keys.* **2** People who are unaccountable do not have to explain their actions to anyone in authority.

unaccustomed /ˌʌn·əˈkʌs·təmd/ *adj* [not gradable] **1** (of a person) not familiar with or experienced at something ○ *She was unaccustomed to driving in heavy traffic.* **2** Unaccustomed can also mean unusual or unexpected: *His unaccustomed nervousness made us all anxious.*

unadulterated /ˌʌn·əˈdʌl·təˌreɪt̬·əd/ *adj* not spoiled or made weaker by the addition of other things ○ *She sings pure, unadulterated gospel.*

unaffected Ⓐ NOT CHANGED /ˌʌn·əˈfek·təd/ *adj* [not gradable] not influenced or changed in any way ○ *Internet access will be unaffected by the upgrade.*

SINCERE /ˌʌn·əˈfek·təd/ *adj* [not gradable] natural and sincere ○ *Her writing is very unaffected and easy to read.*

unambiguous Ⓐ /ˌʌn·æmˈbɪg·jə·wəs/ *adj* expressed in a way which makes it completely clear what is meant ○ *an unambiguous answer*
unambiguously Ⓐ /ˌʌn·æmˈbɪg·jə·wə·sli/ *adv*

un-American /ˌʌn·əˈmer·ɪ·kən, -ˈmær-/ *adj* showing opposition or a lack of support for the US and its political system ○ *It seems un-American to tell me how to run my business.*

unanimity /ˌjuː·nəˈnɪm·ət̬·i/ *n* [U] complete agreement among every member of group ○ *No one has ever suggested that there is unanimity in the party on all issues.*

unanimous /jʊˈnæn·ə·məs/ *adj* [not gradable] in complete agreement or showing complete agreement ○ *The school board was unanimous in its support for the decision.* ○ *The jury reached a unanimous verdict.*
unanimously /jʊˈnæn·ə·mə·sli/ *adv* [not gradable] ○ *Sportswriters unanimously picked him for the award.*

unannounced /ˌʌn·əˈnɑʊnst/ *adj, adv* [not gradable] sudden and unexpected ○ *Several unannounced acts made this concert special.* ○ *The President appeared unannounced.*

unanswered /ʌnˈæn·sərd/ *adj, adv* [not gradable] (esp. of a letter, question, or telephone call) not reacted to or explained ○ *She wondered why her calls went unanswered.*

unarmed /ʌnˈɑrmd/ *adj* [not gradable] not carrying or having a weapon ○ *How could an unarmed man be so frightening?*

unassuming /ˌʌn·əˈsuː·mɪŋ/ *adj* quiet and not attracting attention ○ *a shy and unassuming person* ○ *an unassuming little restaurant*

unattached Ⓐ NOT CONNECTED /ˌʌn·əˈtætʃt/ *adj* [not gradable] not joined or connected; independent

NOT MARRIED /ˌʌn·əˈtætʃt/ *adj* [not gradable] *infml* not married or involved with anyone ○ *an unattached woman*

unattended /ˌʌn·əˈten·dəd/ *adj* [not gradable] not being watched or taken care of ○ *unattended boxes and packages* ○ *unattended children*

unattractive /ˌʌn·əˈtræk·tɪv/ *adj* ugly in appearance, or unpleasant in character ○ *an unattractive room* ○ *an unattractive personality*

unauthorized /ʌnˈɔː·θəˌrɑɪzd/ *adj* [not gradable] without official permission ○ *an unauthorized biography* ○ *An unauthorized version of the software is being sold abroad.*

unavailable Ⓐ /ˌʌn·əˈveɪ·lə·bəl/ *adj* [not gradable] (of things) not able to be used or obtained, or (of people) not willing or able to be met ○ *Fresh fruit and vegetables had been unavailable for some time.* ○ *I'm sorry, the colonel is unavailable now.*

unavoidable /ˌʌn·əˈvɔɪd·ə·bəl/ *adj* [not gradable] unable to be prevented or stayed away from ○ *War is now unavoidable.*

unaware Ⓐ /ˌʌn·əˈwer, -ˈwær/ *adj* not knowing that something exists, or not having knowledge or experience of something ○ *I was unaware of the risks involved.* ○ [+ *that* clause] *Bowman was unaware that the car was gone.*

unawares /ˌʌn·əˈwerz, -ˈwærz/ *adv* suddenly and unexpectedly; without warning ○ *We were caught unawares by the fierce storm.*

unbalanced /ʌnˈbæl·ənst/ *adj* **1** emphasizing one thing or one side over another ○ *an unbalanced diet* ○ *unbalanced reporting* **2** A person who is unbalanced is mentally ill.

unbearable /ʌnˈber·ə·bəl, -ˈbær-/ *adj* [not gradable] so unpleasant or painful that you find it hard to accept ○ *We had an unbearable summer here.* ○ *The long wait was almost unbearable.*
unbearably /ʌnˈber·ə·bli, -ˈbær-/ *adv* ○ *an unbearably hot day* ○ *unbearably painful memories*

unbeatable /ʌnˈbiːt̬·ə·bəl/ *adj* [not gradable] unable to be defeated, or better than any other ○ *an unbeatable team* ○ *unbeatable pizza*

unbeaten /ʌn ˈbiːt·ən/ *adj* [not gradable] not defeated ○ *The Royals remain unbeaten after 12 games.*

unbecoming /ˌʌn·bɪ ˈkʌm·ɪŋ/ *adj* not suitable or acceptable ○ *Such conduct is unbecoming to an official.*

unbelievable SURPRISING /ˌʌn·bɪ ˈliː·və·bəl/ *adj* [not gradable] extremely surprising ○ *That little dog eats an unbelievable amount of food.*

unbelievably /ˌʌn·bɪ ˈliː·və·bli/ *adv* [not gradable] ○ *It was unbelievably stupid of you to go.*

UNLIKELY /ˌʌn·bɪ ˈliː·və·bəl/ *adj* not able to be believed because unlikely ○ *an unbelievable story/excuse* ○ *unbelievable luck*

unborn /ʌn ˈbɔːrn/ *adj* [not gradable] not yet born; in the mother's uterus ○ *an unborn child/calf*

unbounded /ʌn ˈbɑʊn·dəd/ *adj* [not gradable] very great; seeming to have no limits ○ *an unbounded commitment to excellence*

unbridled /ʌn ˈbrɑɪd·əld/ *adj* [not gradable] not controlled or limited ○ *unbridled joy/fury/greed/authority*

uncalled-for /ʌn ˈkɔːld ˌfɔːr/ *adj* [not gradable] not suitable and therefore unnecessary ○ *uncalled-for rudeness*

uncanny /ʌn ˈkæn·i/ *adj* strange or mysterious; difficult or impossible to explain ○ *He has an uncanny ability to pick a winner.* ○ *Barb's uncanny resemblance to Tia is scary.*

uncertain /ʌn ˈsɜrt·ən/ *adj* [not gradable] unclear, or not sure ○ *She faces an uncertain future.* ○ *We're uncertain of the cause of death.*

uncertainly /ʌn ˈsɜrt·ən·li/ *adv* [not gradable] not confidently or surely ○ *She looked at John uncertainly.*

uncertainty /ʌn ˈsɜrt·ən·ti/ *n* [C/U] ○ [U] *They live in uncertainty and confusion.*

unchanged /ʌn ˈtʃeɪndʒd/ *adj* not changed from an earlier time; the same as before ○ *The average combined SAT score for 2007 was unchanged from the previous year, according to results released last week.*

uncharted Ⓐ /ʌn ˈtʃɑrt̬·əd/ *adj* [not gradable] (of a place) never before described, or (of a situation) completely new ○ *New drugs lead doctors into uncharted territory.*

unchecked /ʌn ˈtʃekt/ *adj* [not gradable] not stopped or ended ○ *These problems will worsen if current trends continue unchecked.*

uncivilized /ʌn ˈsɪv·əˌlɑɪzd/ *adj* [not gradable] (of a society or country) without what is thought to be a highly developed culture and way of life, or (of a person) rude and not showing care for others ○ *uncivilized behavior*

uncle /ˈʌŋ·kəl/ *n* [C] the brother of someone's mother or father, or the husband of someone's aunt ○ *My aunt and uncle moved to Arizona when they retired.*

unclean PHYSICAL /ʌn ˈkliːn/ *adj* not clean or not pure and therefore likely to cause disease ○ *unclean water* ○ *unclean kitchens*

MORAL /ʌn ˈkliːn/ *adj* not acceptable or usable according to religious or moral standards ○ *unclean thoughts/practices*

unclear /ʌn ˈklɪr/ *adj* **1** not obvious or easy to see or know ○ [+ question word] *It's unclear what actually happened that night.* **2** A person who is unclear about something is not sure about it: *I'm unclear about a couple of things he said on the phone.*

unclearly /ʌn ˈklɪr·li/ *adv*

Uncle Sam *n* [U] the US, or a symbol for the US or its government that is pictured as a tall, thin man with a white BEARD (= hair on the face) and a tall hat wearing clothes colored like the American flag

Uncle Tom *n* [C] *disapproving* an African American who is considered to be too eager to be friendly and helpful to white Americans in authority

uncomfortable /ʌn ˈkʌm·fərt̬·ə·bəl, -ˈkʌmf·tər·bəl/ *adj* [not gradable] not COMFORTABLE or relaxed, or feeling anxiety ○ *an uncomfortable chair* ○ *She feels uncomfortable in a room full of strangers.*

uncomfortably /ʌn ˈkʌm·fərt̬·ə·bli, -ˈkʌmf·tər·bli/ *adv* ○ *an uncomfortably warm day*

uncommon NOT FREQUENT /ʌn ˈkɑm·ən/ *adj* [not gradable] not seen, happening, or experienced often ○ *It's not uncommon for someone to change jobs several times.*

uncommonly /ʌn ˈkɑm·ən·li/ *adv* ○ *an uncommonly gifted singer*

UNUSUALLY LARGE /ʌn ˈkɑm·ən/ *adj* (esp. of a human quality) unusually large in amount or degree ○ *She's a woman of uncommon kindness.*

uncompromising /ʌn ˈkɑm·prəˌmɑɪ·zɪŋ/ *adj* of a person or a person's opinions, fixed and not easily changed ○ *People are intimidated by her uncompromising ways.*

unconcerned /ˌʌn·kən ˈsɜrnd/ *adj* not worried or anxious ○ *How can you be unconcerned about how much things cost?*

unconditional /ˌʌn·kən ˈdɪʃ·ən·əl/ *adj* [not gradable] complete and not limited in any way ○ *unconditional love* ○ *He got an unconditional release from prison.*

unconfirmed /ˌʌn·kən ˈfɜrmd/ *adj* [not gradable] (of information) not proven to be true or false ○ *an unconfirmed report*

unconformity /ˌʌn·kən ˈfɔːr·mət̬·i/ *n* [C] ***earth science*** an interruption in the series of the earth's rock layers, resulting from either EROSION (= gradual loss by the effect of weather) or the failure of layers to be created

unconscionable /ʌn ˈkɑn·tʃə·nə·bəl/ *adj* unacceptable because of being too extreme ○ *It is unconscionable to say that some kids don't deserve an education.*

U

unconscious /ʌnˈkɑn·tʃəs/ *adj* [not gradable] **1** not CONSCIOUS ○ *The fall from his horse knocked him unconscious for several minutes.* **2** Unconscious feelings or actions are ones you are not completely aware of: *unconscious anxiety* ○ *There's an unconscious classification within the group.*

unconscious /ʌnˈkɑn·tʃəs/ *n* [U] *medical* (in PSYCHOANALYSIS) the part of the mind you are not aware of but which influences behavior

unconsciously /ʌnˈkɑn·tʃə·sli/ *adv* ○ *He unconsciously assumes that everyone agrees with him.*

unconstitutional Ⓐ /ˌʌnˌkɑn·stəˈtuː·ʃən·əl/ *adj* [not gradable] ***social studies*** not allowed by the CONSTITUTION (= set of political principles) of a country or organization

uncontrollable /ˌʌn·kənˈtroʊ·lə·bəl/ *adj* [not gradable] too strong or violent to be controlled ○ *an uncontrollable temper* ○ *I felt an uncontrollable desire to sit down.*

uncontrollably /ˌʌn·kənˈtroʊ·lə·bli/ *adv* ○ *He was laughing uncontrollably.*

uncontrolled /ˌʌn·kənˈtroʊld/ *adj* ○ *uncontrolled shivering* ○ *the uncontrolled spread of urban sprawl*

unconventional Ⓐ /ˌʌn·kənˈven·tʃən·əl/ *adj* different from what is usual or from the way most people do things ○ *He has an unconventional attitude toward work.*

uncountable noun /ʌnˈkɑʊnt·ə·bəl/ *n* [C] ***grammar*** a noun that has one form with no plural and names something that there can be more or less of but that cannot be counted ○ *"Heat" is an uncountable noun.* ○ **USAGE:** Uncountable nouns are marked [U] in this dictionary. ○ Compare COUNTABLE NOUN

uncouth /ʌnˈkuːθ/ *adj* of a person or a person's behavior, rude and unpleasant

uncover /ʌnˈkʌv·ər/ *v* [T] to remove what is covering something, or to discover what was hidden ○ *uncover the pot* ○ *It's the press's responsibility to uncover the truth.*

uncut /ʌnˈkʌt/ *adj* [not gradable] not made smaller or shorter, or not changed in any way ○ *an uncut book/film/play* ○ *uncut diamonds*

undated /ʌnˈdeɪţ·əd/ *adj* [not gradable] (of something written) without the day, month, and year on it ○ *an undated letter*

undaunted /ʌnˈdɔːnt·əd, -ˈdɑnt-/ *adj* [not gradable] not frightened or discouraged, despite problems or lack of success ○ *Undaunted by the cold and the rain, we continued our hike.*

undecided /ˌʌn·dɪˈsɑɪd·əd/ *adj* [not gradable] not having made a decision or judgment about something ○ *Are you still undecided about that job in San Francisco?*

undefeated /ˌʌn·dɪˈfiːţ·əd/ *adj* [not gradable] never having lost, esp. a competition, within a particular period of time ○ *The Buffaloes upset No. 1-ranked and previously undefeated Wisconsin.*

undeniable Ⓐ /ˌʌn·dɪˈnɑɪ·ə·bəl/ *adj* [not gradable] so obviously true that it cannot be doubted ○ *It is an undeniable fact that ice is cold.*

undeniably /ˌʌn·dɪˈnɑɪ·ə·bli/ *adv* [not gradable] ○ *She is undeniably brilliant.*

under **LOWER POSITION** /ˌʌn·dər/ *prep* in or to a position below or lower than (something else), often so that one thing covers the other ○ *Our dog hides under the bed whenever we have a lightning storm.* ○ *She was holding the umbrella under her arm* (= between her upper arm and the side of her chest).

under /ˈʌn·dər/ *adv* [not gradable] ○ *Several lifeguards tried desperately to reach him before he went under* (= sank below the surface of the water).

LESS THAN /ˌʌn·dər/ *prep* less than ○ *The price is still under a dollar.* ○ *Scholarship candidates must be under 21 and plan to attend college in the fall.*

under /ˈʌn·dər/ *adv* [not gradable] ○ *There is no admission charge for children six and under.*

under- /ˌʌn·dər/ *prefix* not enough ○ *The potatoes were undercooked.* ○ *Classes were too large because the school was understaffed.*

EXPERIENCING /ˌʌn·dər/ *prep* in the process of, influenced or controlled by, or according to ○ *Construction had to be done under difficult conditions.* ○ *Under current law, stores in this town can't do business on Sunday.* ○ *We liked working under her because she made us feel appreciated.* ○ *"Where can I find books on swimming?" "Look under sports* (= within the subject of sports)*."* ○ *We seemed to be under attack* (= in the process of being attacked) *by a swarm of bees.* ○ *Your request for a transfer to our Denver office is under consideration* (= being considered). ○ *I was under the impression* (= I believed) *that she was married.* ○ *I find it difficult to work under pressure* (= with this influence).

IDIOMS with under

• **under** *your* **belt** learned or succeeded in, and now a part of your experience ○ *Now that you've got the required courses under your belt, you can take some electives.*

• **under** *your* **breath** quietly so that other people cannot hear ○ *"Let's go," she muttered under her breath.*

• **under fire** being attacked with guns or with severe criticism ○ *The troops were under fire for weeks.* ○ *The president has come under fire for vetoing the bill to cut taxes.*

• **under guard** being protected or being prevented from escaping ○ *The prisoners, under armed guard, performed public service duties, such as cleaning up highways and parks.*

• **under** *your* **nose** in the place where something belongs, or in an obvious place ○ *I've been looking for my keys and they were right here under my nose all the time.*

• **under oath** having legally promised to tell the truth ○ *He was accused of lying under oath.*

• **under the influence** drunk, or having drunk some alcohol ○ *He was arrested for driving under the influence.*

• **under the sun** in existence; on earth ○ *I've tried everything under the sun to fix this lock, but I just can't get it to work.*

U

• **under the table** secretly ○ *If you want to get a good apartment, you may have to give the manager some money under the table.*
• **under the weather** not completely well ○ *I noticed that the cat was looking a little under the weather.*
• **under wraps** secret ○ *Her daily schedule is generally kept under wraps, and Dent has declined to talk about fund-raising.*

underachiever /ˌʌn·də·rəˈtʃiː·vər/ *n* [C] a person whose performance is lower than you would expect, based on that person's ability

underage /ˌʌn·dəˈreɪdʒ/ *adj* [not gradable] younger than the age at which a particular activity is legally allowed ○ *underage voters*

underarm /ˈʌn·dəˌrɑrm/ *adj* [not gradable] of or for use in the ARMPIT (= the hollow place under your arm where your arm joins your body) ○ *underarm deodorants*

underbrush /ˈʌn·dərˌbrʌʃ/, **undergrowth** /ˈʌn·dərˌgroʊθ/ *n* [U] a mass of bushes, small trees, and plants growing under the trees in woods or a forest

underclass /ˈʌn·dərˌklæs/ *n* [C] the lowest economic and social class in society, consisting of people who are considered to have few opportunities to improve themselves

underclothes /ˈʌn·dərˌkloʊðz/ *pl n* UNDERWEAR

undercover /ˈʌn·dərˌkʌv·ər/ *adj* [not gradable] working secretly to obtain information, esp. for the police ○ *an undercover cop*

undercurrent /ˈʌn·dərˌkɜr·ənt, -ˌkʌ·rənt/ *n* [C] a hidden emotion or belief that is usually negative or harmful and has an indirect effect ○ *There is an undercurrent of suspicion and even hostility in the military for their new commander-in-chief.*

undercut /ˌʌn·dərˈkʌt/ *v* [T] *pres. part.* **undercutting,** *past* **undercut 1** to weaken, damage, or cause the failure of something; UNDERMINE ○ *He's got a plan, so I don't want to undercut the effort that he has underway.* **2** To undercut is also to charge less than a competitor: *Large supermarkets can undercut their smaller rivals.*

underdog /ˈʌn·dərˌdɔːg/ *n* [C] the weaker of two competitors, or anyone not expected to win a competition ○ *He began the race for governor as the underdog.*

underestimate Ⓐ /ˌʌn·dəˈres·təˌmeɪt/ *v* [T] to think that something is less or lower than it really is, or that someone is less strong or less effective ○ *Homeowners often underestimate the cost of repairing a roof.*

underfoot /ˌʌn·dərˈfʊt/ *adv* [not gradable] under your feet as you walk ○ *The grass felt pleasant and cool underfoot.* ○ *The cat keeps getting underfoot* (= in the way).

undergo Ⓐ /ˌʌn·dərˈgoʊ/ *v* [T] **undergoes,** *pres. part.* **undergoing,** *past simp.* **underwent,** *past part.* **undergone** to experience something that is unpleasant or has a strong effect ○ *He recently underwent heart bypass surgery.*

undergraduate /ˌʌn·dərˈgrædʒ·ə·wət/ *n* [C] a student at a college or university who has not yet received a BACHELOR'S DEGREE (= the first degree given)

underground /ˌʌn·dərˈgrɑʊnd/ *adj, adv* [not gradable] **1** below the surface of the earth; below ground ○ *an underground garage* **2** Something that is done underground is secret or hidden, usually because it is not traditional or is shocking or illegal: *an underground newspaper* ○ *Officials believe the sighting of the suspect may have forced him to go underground* (= to become secret).

underground /ˈʌn·dərˌgrɑʊnd/ *n* [U] The underground is an organization that secretly works against those in power: *He was a member of the French underground in World War II.*

undergrowth /ˈʌn·dərˌgroʊθ/ *n* [U] UNDERBRUSH

underhand /ˈʌn·dərˌhænd/ *adj, adv* [not gradable] (done) by moving the arm from back to front with the hand below shoulder level and with the inner part of the hand facing forward ○ *an underhand toss*

underhanded /ˌʌn·dərˈhæn·dəd/, **underhand** /ˈʌn·dərˌhænd/ *adj* done secretly, and sometimes dishonestly, in order to achieve an advantage ○ *Shareholders sued the company, alleging an underhanded attempt to deprive them of their rights.*

underline /ˈʌn·dərˌlɑɪn/ *v* [T] **1** to draw a line under a word ○ *to underline significant parts of a text* **2** To underline is also to emphasize: *The announcement underlines IBM's newfound willingness to employ technologies developed by other companies.*

underlying Ⓐ /ˌʌn·dərˌlɑɪ·ɪŋ/ *adj* [not gradable] real but not immediately obvious ○ *The investigation focused on the underlying causes of the fire.*

underlie Ⓐ /ˌʌn·dərˈlɑɪ/ *v* [T] *pres. part.* **underlying,** *past simp.* **underlay,** *past part.* **underlain** to be a cause of or strong influence on something ○ *More fundamental economic problems may underlie last week's stock market slide.* ○ **USAGE:** said esp. of a hidden cause or influence

undermine /ˌʌn·dərˈmɑɪn/ *v* [T] to gradually weaken or destroy someone or something ○ *The incompetence and arrogance of the city's administration have undermined public confidence in government.*

underneath /ˌʌn·dərˈniːθ/ *adj, adv* [not gradable] directly under and usually hidden by (something else) ○ *The Lincoln Tunnel passes underneath the Hudson River, which separates New York from New Jersey.* ○ *When the painting was restored, an older painting was discovered underneath.*

undernourished /ˌʌn·dərˈnɜr·əʃt, -ˈnʌ·rəʃt/ *adj* not eating enough food to maintain good health

underpaid /ˌʌn·dərˈpeɪd/ *adj* paid too little money for the work you do

U

underpants /ˈʌn·dərˌpænts/ *pl n* a piece of underwear covering the area between the waist and the top of the legs ○ *a pair of underpants*

underpass /ˈʌn·dərˌpæs/ *n* [C] a passage that goes under something such as a busy road, allowing people or vehicles to go from one side to the other

underprivileged /ˌʌn·dərˈprɪv·lɪdʒd/ *adj* lacking the money and the basic social advantages that most people have; poor ○ *a summer camp for underprivileged children*

underrate /ˌʌn·dəˈreɪt/ *v* [T] to fail to recognize the importance, value, skill, power, etc., of someone or something ○ *Never underrate your opponent in a political contest.*
underrated /ˌʌn·dəˈreɪt·əd/ *adj* ○ *He is one of Hollywood's most underrated actors* (= He is much better than people think).

underscore /ˈʌn·dərˌskɔːr, -ˌskoʊr/ *v* [T] to emphasize the importance something ○ *The need for fire detectors in cargo bays was underscored by some accidents in the 1980s.*

undersecretary /ˌʌn·dərˈsek·rəˌter·i/ *n* [C] an official in a government department who is one rank below the highest official ○ *Ms. Wilkie started out as undersecretary of education, the department's No. 2 job.*

undershirt /ˈʌn·dərˌʃɜrt/ *n* [C] a type of underwear that covers the upper part of the body and is worn under a shirt

underside /ˈʌn·dərˌsɑɪd/ *n* [C] the lower or bottom side of something ○ *Mites feed on the underside of leaves.*

undersigned /ˈʌn·dərˌsɑɪnd/ *pl n* the people whose signatures appear below, usually at the end of a formal letter ○ *We, the undersigned, wish to protest the planned closing of the local library.*

understaffed /ˈʌn·dərˈstæft/ *adj* not having enough employees ○ *The facility is chronically understaffed and short of supplies.*

understand KNOW /ˌʌn·dərˈstænd/ *v past* **understood** to know the meaning of something, or to know how a person feels and why the person behaves in a particular way ○ [+ question word] *I don't understand what he means.* ○ [T] *Is there anyone here who understands English?* ○ [T] *It was so noisy I couldn't understand* (= recognize) *a word he was saying.* ○ [I] *If you choose not to come, I'll understand.* ○ [T] *He claimed that no one ever understood him* (= had any sympathy for him or knew what he was feeling). ○ [+ question word] *I understand how she feels about the loss of her dog.* ○ [T] *It is understood that* (= Everyone knows and accepts that) *you don't bring food or drinks into the library.*
understandable /ˌʌn·dərˈstæn·də·bəl/ *adj* **1** *You've got to tell a story to three-year-olds in a way that's understandable to them.* **2** If you say that something a person does is understandable, you feel that it is the way most people would behave in that situation: *Her actions are understandable when you consider how badly she was treated.*
understandably /ˌʌn·dərˈstæn·də·bli/ *adv* If you say that someone is understandably feeling a particular emotion, you mean that most people would feel the same way in that situation: *She was understandably upset when no one returned her call.*
understanding /ˌʌn·dərˈstæn·dɪŋ/ *n* [U] **1** knowledge of a particular thing ○ *He doesn't have any real understanding of mathematics.* **2** Understanding is also a feeling of kindness and caring based on knowledge, esp. of the causes of behavior: *The values he had in mind were simply family love and understanding.*
understanding /ˌʌn·dərˈstæn·dɪŋ/ *adj* sympathetic and caring ○ *an understanding friend*

WORD CHOICES understand

See also: **realize**

Comprehend is a slightly more formal way of saying "understand."

He doesn't seem to ***comprehend*** *the scale of the problem.*

The phrase **get the picture** can be used in more informal situations to mean "understand."

OK. Don't say any more. I ***get the picture.***

Follow can be used when someone understands something as it is being said.

It was so complicated I couldn't ***follow*** *what he was saying.*

If you understand something that is difficult, the verb **grasp** can be used.

I think I ***grasped*** *the main points of the lecture.*

If you understand something that you read or hear after taking time, you could use the verb **digest**.

This chapter is so difficult to ***digest.*** *I'll have to read it again later.*

Fathom can be used when someone understands something that is mysterious.

For years, people have been trying to ***fathom*** *the mysteries of the whale's song.*

If you understand a joke, the verb **get** is sometimes used.

I told him a joke, but he didn't ***get*** *it.*

BELIEVE /ˌʌn·dərˈstænd/ *v* [T] *past* **understood** to believe something is true because you have been told something that causes you to think it ○ [+ (*that*) clause] *I understand (that) the show will go on, but with a different cast.* ○ *I understood him to say* (= I believed that he said) *that the trip had been canceled.*

WORD FAMILY understand

Nouns	understanding misunderstanding	*Verbs*	understand misunderstand
Adjectives	understandable understanding	*Adverbs*	understandably

understanding /ˌʌn·dərˈstæn·dɪŋ/ *n* [C usually sing] **1** something that you have reason to believe ○ [+ *that* clause] *Ours was a generation brought up with the understanding* (= belief) *that* *science meant progress.* **2** An understanding is also an informal agreement between people: *The two sides have come to/reached an understanding about the sale of the house.*

IDIOM with understanding

• **on the understanding** according to someone's promise or statement ○ *We purchased the computer on the understanding that it could be returned within ten days.*

understate /ˌʌn·dərˈsteɪt/ *v* [T] to say that the amount or importance of something is less than it really is ○ *The company was accused of understating potential side effects of the drug.*

understated /ˌʌn·dərˈsteɪţ·əd/ *adj* not intended to be obvious ○ *The apartment was luxurious but furnished in a tastefully understated way.*

understatement /ˌʌn·dərˈsteɪt·mənt/ *n* [C/U] ○ [C] *To say I was confused is an understatement – I hadn't the slightest idea what to do.*

understudy /ˈʌn·dərˌstʌd·i/ *n* [C] an actor or other performer who learns the parts of others in a play, opera, etc., so that he or she can replace them if necessary

undertake Ⓐ /ˌʌn·dərˈteɪk/ *v past simp.* **undertook**, *past part.* **undertaken** to take responsibility for and begin doing something ○ [T] *The president directed the Department of Justice to undertake an investigation of the allegations.* ○ [+ to infinitive] *I undertook to help him learn English.*

undertaking Ⓐ /ˈʌn·dərˌteɪ·kɪŋ/ *n* [C usually sing] an effort to do something, esp. to do a large or difficult job, or the job that is done ○ *Preparing for the US national census every ten years is a massive undertaking.*

undertaker /ˈʌn·dərˌteɪ·kər/, **mortician** *n* [C] a person whose business is to prepare the dead to be buried or CREMATED (= burned) and to organize funerals

undertone CHARACTERISTIC /ˈʌn·dərˌtoʊn/ *n* [C] a quality of something that you realize exists although it is not expressed directly ○ *His remarks carried an undertone of anger.*

LOW VOICE /ˈʌn·dərˌtoʊn/ *n* [C] a low voice ○ *José muttered something to me in an undertone.*

undertow /ˈʌn·dərˌtoʊ/ *n* [C] a strong current that flows under water away from a beach at the same time as waves on the surface move toward the beach

undervalue /ˌʌn·dərˈvæl·juː/ *v* [T] to consider something to have less worth or importance than it really has ○ *The enormous stock of gold has been deliberately undervalued at about one-quarter of the market price.* ○ *I think perhaps we've undervalued your talent.*

underwater /ˌʌn·dərˈwɔːţ·ər, -ˈwɑţ-/ *adj, adv* [not gradable] under the surface of water, esp. under the surface of the sea ○ *an underwater camera* ○ *Some ducks can stay underwater for nearly two minutes.*

underway, **under way** /ˌʌn·dərˈweɪ/ *adj, adv* beginning to exist or is happening now ○ *Economic recovery is already under way.* ○ *It's time to get this project underway* (= started).

underwear /ˈʌn·dərˌwer, -ˌwær/, **underclothes** *n* [U] clothes worn next to the skin, under other clothes

underweight /ˌʌn·dərˈweɪt/ *adj* weighing less than usual ○ *The children were found to be malnourished and underweight.*

underwent /ˌʌn·dərˈwent/ *past simple of* UNDERGO

underworld /ˈʌn·dərˌwɜrld/ *n* [U] the criminal organizations and activities that exist within society

underwrite /ˈʌn·dəˌraɪt/ *v* [T] *past simp.* **underwrote**, *past part.* **underwritten** to support something that costs money by promising to pay for it, or by promising to pay if necessary to protect others who are risking their money ○ *The museum show was largely underwritten by a grant from the government of Sweden.*

undesirable /ˌʌn·dɪˈzɑɪ·rə·bəl/ *adj* not wanted or welcomed; disliked ○ *undesirable body fat*

undeveloped /ˌʌn·dɪˈvel·əpt/ *adj* (of a place or land) not built on or used for farming

undisclosed /ˌʌn·dɪˈskloʊzd/ *adj* [not gradable] not announced; kept private ○ *The Rembrandt painting was sold at auction for an undisclosed amount.*

undisguised /ˌʌn·dɪsˈɡɑɪzd/ *adj* [not gradable] (of feelings) clearly shown or expressed ○ *On the way home from the party, she said, with undisguised relief, "Well, I'm glad that's over."*

undisputed /ˌʌn·dɪˈspjuːţ·əd/ *adj* about which there is no disagreement ○ *It's an undisputed fact that women on average live longer than men.*

undivided /ˌʌn·dɪˈvɑɪd·əd/ *adj* **1** existing as a whole, not in separate parts ○ *an undivided Germany* **2** If you give someone, or if someone has, your undivided attention, you stop whatever else you are doing and listen to that person: *Just as soon as I've finished this letter, I'll give you my undivided attention.*

undo UNFASTEN /ʌnˈduː/ *v* [T] *pres. part.* **undoing**, *past simp.* **undid**, *past part.* **undone** to unfasten something that is closed or tied ○ *He undid the top button of his shirt and loosened his tie.*

undone /ʌnˈdʌn/ *adj* [not gradable] ○ *Her long hair had come undone* (= become loose).

REMOVE EFFECTS /ʌnˈduː/ *v* [T] *pres. part.* **undoing**, *past simp.* **undid**, *past part.* **undone** to remove the effects of something that happened earlier ○ *It's difficult to undo the damage caused by a father who abandons his child.*

undocumented /ʌnˈdɑk·jəˌment·əd/ *adj* not having any documents to prove that someone or something is legal ○ *undocumented immigrants/aliens/workers*

undoing /ʌnˈduː·ɪŋ/ *n* [U] the cause of a person's failure or loss of power or wealth ○ *His failure*

U

to delegate authority and his arrogance led to his undoing.

undoubtedly /ʌnˈdɑʊt̬·əd·li/ *adv* [not gradable] very likely; almost certainly ○ *It is undoubtedly one of the best movies of the year.* ○ *The highlight of the evening was undoubtedly* (= without a doubt) *the speech by the guest of honor.*

undreamed of /ʌnˈdriːmˌdʌv/, **undreamt of** /ʌnˈdremˌtəv/ *adj* [not gradable] better or greater than anyone would think possible ○ *Through the Internet, we have access to information that was undreamed of 30 years ago.*

undress /ʌnˈdres/ *v* [I/T] to remove your clothes or remove the clothes from someone else ○ [I] *She undressed quickly and took a shower.*
undressed /ʌnˈdrest/ *adj* [not gradable] ○ *The nurse said to get undressed.*

undue /ʌnˈduː/ *adj* [not gradable] more than is necessary, acceptable, or reasonable ○ *The court said the state law placed an undue burden on working mothers.*
unduly /ʌnˈduː·li/ *adv* [not gradable] ○ *He does not seem unduly concerned about the state of the economy.*

undying /ʌnˈdɑɪ·ɪŋ/ *adj* [not gradable] (of a feeling or a belief) permanent; without end ○ *undying love*

unearth DIG EARTH /ʌnˈɜrθ/ *v* [T] to find something by digging in the ground ○ *Artifacts more than 500 years old have been unearthed at the site.*
DISCOVER /ʌnˈɜrθ/ *v* [T] to discover proof or other information, often after careful searching ○ *Two amateur historians unearthed 570 documents with Mr. Lincoln's signature by sifting through the files of the national archives.*

unearthly /ʌnˈɜrθ·li/ *adj* **1** strange and mysterious, and sometimes frightening ○ *The streetlights cast an unearthly glow in the thick fog.* **2** *infml* If something happens at an unearthly hour, it happens at an unusual and unreasonable time: *I was awakened at some unearthly hour by a telephone call from Australia.*

uneasy /ʌnˈiː·zi/ *adj* uncomfortable or anxious ○ *If you travel, you know that uneasy feeling you get when you arrive in a strange city and don't have a hotel reservation.*
uneasily /ʌnˈiː·zə·li/ *adv* ○ *He stirred uneasily in his chair as she stared at him.*

U

uneducated /ʌnˈedʒ·əˌkeɪt̬·əd/ *adj* having received little education

unemployed /ˌʌn·ɪmˈplɔɪd/ *adj* [not gradable] not having a job that provides money ○ *an unemployed actor*
unemployed /ˌʌn·ɪmˈplɔɪd/ *pl n* ○ *At that time, the unemployed numbered over two million people.*
unemployment /ˌʌn·ɪmˈplɔɪ·mənt/ *n* [U] ***social studies*** the situation of not having a job that provides money, or the number of people in this situation at any time ○ *high/low unemployment* ○ *The unemployment rate was 4 percent in October.*

unemployment benefits, *short form* **unemployment** *n* [U] ***social studies*** payments made by a government to a person who has lost his or her job

unending /ʌnˈen·dɪŋ/ *adj* [not gradable] without limit or end ○ *He seemed to have an unending supply of stories.*

unequal NOT THE SAME /ʌnˈiː·kwəl/ *adj* not the same ○ *The unequal status of parent and child is recognized in law.*
UNFAIR /ʌnˈiː·kwəl/ *adj* not treating everyone the same; unfair ○ *In 1954, the Supreme Court declared that racial segregation in the public schools was unequal.*

unequivocal /ˌʌn·ɪˈkwɪv·ə·kəl/ *adj* clear and firm ○ *The answer is an unequivocal "Yes."*

unerring /ʌnˈer·ɪŋ, -ˈɜr-/ *adj* [not gradable] always right; never wrong ○ *She brings an unerring sense of timing to the role.*

unethical Ⓐ /ʌnˈeθ·ɪ·kəl/ *adj* not morally acceptable ○ *unethical business practices*

uneven NOT EQUAL /ʌnˈiː·vən/ *adj* not EVEN EQUAL ○ *The contest was uneven because one team was much stronger than the other.*
NOT FLAT /ʌnˈiː·vən/ *adj* not EVEN FLAT ○ *an uneven surface*
NOT GOOD /ʌnˈiː·vən/ *adj* varying in quality; not always good ○ *It's an uneven movie, but some of the scenes are hilariously funny.*

uneventful /ˌʌn·ɪˈvent·fəl/ *adj* without any unusual events ○ *The flight to Europe was uneventful.*

unexpected /ˌʌn·ɪkˈspek·təd/ *adj* not expected; surprising ○ *What an unexpected treat to meet you here!*
unexpectedly /ˌʌn·ɪkˈspek·təd·li/ *adv* ○ *an unexpectedly close race* ○ *A guest dropped in unexpectedly.*

unexplained /ˌʌn·ɪkˈspleɪnd/ *adj* lacking a good explanation ○ *Experts say the 747 is not noted for problems or unexplained crashes.*

unfailing /ʌnˈfeɪ·lɪŋ/ *adj* [not gradable] (of a positive quality of someone's character) showing itself at all times ○ *She was known for her unfailing good humor.*

unfair /ʌnˈfer, -ˈfær/ *adj* not FAIR RIGHT ○ *It seems unfair to tax you both where you work and where you live.*
unfairly /ʌnˈfer·li, -ˈfær-/ *adv* ○ *The company unfairly denied her medical benefits.*
unfairness /ʌnˈfer·nəs, -ˈfær-/ *n* [U]

WORD CHOICES unfair

Unjust is an alternative to "unfair."

*It seems **unjust** that people should be expected to pay twice.*

If something is unfair because it shows an unreasonable like or dislike for someone which is based on personal opinions, you could use the words **biased** or **slanted**.

*The newspaper gave a very **biased** report of the meeting.*

*The report was **slanted** in favor of the developers.*

Discriminatory is often used when something is unfair because it treats people differently because of their sex, skin color, religion, etc.

*The company has a zero-tolerance policy toward **discriminatory** practices.*

In formal English, the word **inequitable** is often used when something is unfair because it is good for some people and bad for other people.

*The current health care system is **inequitable**.*

unfaithful /ʌn ˈfeɪθ·fəl/ *adj* **1** not loyal or able to be trusted ○ *an unfaithful friend* **2** having a physical relationship with a person who is not your husband or wife

unfamiliar /ˌʌn·fə ˈmɪl·jər/ *adj* not previously experienced or known ○ *I'm unfamiliar with that word – what does it mean?*

unfasten /ʌn ˈfæs·ən/ *v* [I/T] to make looser or take apart something that fastens or is fastened ○ [T] *Cal loosened his tie and unfastened his collar.*

unfavorable CRITICIZING /ʌn ˈfeɪ·və·rə·bəl/ *adj* having or showing a negative opinion ○ *The play received generally unfavorable reviews.*

NOT HELPFUL /ʌn ˈfeɪ·və·rə·bəl/ *adj* not tending to help; not likely to lead to a positive result ○ *Unfavorable weather conditions this morning caused a postponement of the launch of the space shuttle.*

unfeeling /ʌn ˈfiː·lɪŋ/ *adj* not feeling sympathy for other people's suffering ○ *an unfeeling man*

unfettered /ʌn ˈfet̬·ərd/ *adj* not controlled, limited, or prevented by anyone ○ *The law gives the governor unfettered discretion to make these appointments.*

unfinished /ʌn ˈfɪn·ɪʃt/ *adj* not finished or complete ○ *An unfinished apartment building in North Hollywood caught fire shortly after midnight.*

unfit /ʌn ˈfɪt/ *adj* **-tt-** lacking the qualities needed or expected for something; not suitable ○ *The court ruled that she was an unfit mother and ordered that the child be placed in a foster home.*

unfold DEVELOP /ʌn ˈfoʊld/ *v* [I] (of a situation or story) to develop or become clear ○ *Events unfolded in a way that no one could have predicted.*

OPEN /ʌn ˈfoʊld/ *v* [T] to open or spread out something that has been folded ○ *She took the old wedding dress out and carefully unfolded it.*

unforeseen /ˌʌn·fər ˈsiːn, -fɔːr-/ *adj* unexpected and often unwanted ○ *Due to unforeseen circumstances, tonight's performance has been canceled.*

unforgettable /ˌʌn·fər ˈget̬·ə·bəl/ *adj* (of an experience) having such a strong effect or influence on you that you cannot forget it ○ *One unforgettable morning, we were among the elephants, perfectly situated to watch their descent to the river.*

unfortunate UNLUCKY /ʌn ˈfɔːr·tʃə·nət/ *adj* unlucky or having bad effects ○ *What happened to Monica was just a freak accident – it was very unfortunate.*

unfortunately /ʌn ˈfɔːr·tʃə·nət·li/ *adv* ○ *Unfortunately, by the time we got there the party was almost over.*

UNSUITABLE /ʌn ˈfɔːr·tʃə·nət/ *adj* (of remarks or behavior) unsuitable in a way that could cause offense ○ *It was an unfortunate remark that he later regretted.*

unfounded /ʌn ˈfɑʊn·dəd/ *adj* (of a claim or piece of news) not based on fact; UNTRUE ○ *unfounded rumors*

unfriendly /ʌn ˈfren·dli/ *adj* having an attitude or acting in a way that shows you do not like people and do not care if they like you ○ *an unfriendly person*

unfriendliness /ʌn ˈfren·dli·nəs/ *n* [U]

unfurl /ʌn ˈfɜrl/ *v* [I/T] (of a flag, sail, etc.) to become open from a rolled position, or to cause something to become open from a rolled position

ungainly /ʌn ˈgeɪn·li/ *adj* awkward in movement

ungrateful /ʌn ˈgreɪt·fəl/ *adj* not showing or expressing thanks, esp. when it is expected or deserved

unhappy NOT PLEASED /ʌn ˈhæp·i/ *adj* not feeling pleasure or satisfaction ○ *It was an unhappy time of her life.* ○ *They were unhappy about their hotel room* (= did not like it) *and asked to be moved.*

unhappiness /ʌn ˈhæp·iː·nəs/ *n* [U]

WORD CHOICES unhappy

Sad and **miserable** mean the same as "unhappy."

*I felt so **sad** after he left.*

*I just woke up feeling **miserable**.*

If someone is **upset**, that person is unhappy because something bad has happened.

*They'd had an argument and she was still **upset** about it.*

*Mike got very **upset** when I told him the news.*

If someone is **broken-hearted** or **heartbroken** that person is very sad because someone he or she loves has ended their relationship.

*She was **broken-hearted** when Richard left.*

Someone who is **devastated** or **distraught** is extremely upset.

*She was **devastated** when he died.*

***Distraught** relatives waited for word of loved ones missing after the earthquake.*

The adjectives **depressed, down,** or **low** are often used when someone is unhappy for a long time.

*She became deeply **depressed** after her husband died.*

*I've been feeling a bit **down** recently.*

*He was very **low** for months after he lost his job.*

U

NOT LUCKY /ʌn ˈhæp·i/ *adj* (of a condition or situation) not lucky ○ *We found ourselves in the unhappy situation of having had our bags, passports, and money stolen.*

unhealthy **ILL** /ʌn ˈhel·θi/ *adj* ill or appearing to be ill

HARMFUL /ʌn ˈhel·θi/ *adj* harmful to your health ○ *It's unhealthy to eat fatty foods all the time.*

unheard-of /ʌn ˈhɜrd ˌʌv, -ˌɑv/ *adj* surprising or shocking because not known about or previously experienced ○ *Price wars have sliced prices to unheard-of lows.*

unicameral legislature /ˌjuː·nɪ ˈkæm·ər·əl ˈledʒ·əˌsleɪ·tʃər/ *n* [C] ***politics & government*** a law-making body made up of one group of elected officials

unicellular /ˌjuː·nəˈsel·jə·lər/ *adj* [not gradable] ***biology*** describes a living thing that is made of only one cell

unicorn /ˈjuː·nɪˌkɔːrn/ *n* [C] an imaginary creature like a horse with a single horn growing from the front of its head

unidentified /ˌʌn·ɑɪ ˈdent·əˌfɑɪd/ *adj* [not gradable] (of a person or image of a person) whose name is not known ○ *The photo shows the two leaders shaking hands, with an unidentified woman behind them.*

unification Ⓐ /ˌjuː·nə·fəˈkeɪ·ʃən/ *n* [U] the forming of a single thing by bringing together separate parts ○ *Germany was transformed after the fall of the Berlin Wall and the unification of the country.*

uniform Ⓐ **SAME** /ˈjuː·nəˌfɔːrm/ *adj* **1** the same; not varying or different in any way ○ *The laws for adopting a child are not uniform among the states.* **2** ***physics*** Uniform means not changing in speed or power; CONSTANT.

uniformity Ⓐ /ˌjuː·nəˈfɔːr·mət̬·i/ *n* [U]

uniformly Ⓐ /ˈjuː·nəˌfɔːrm·li/ *adv* ○ *Critics were uniformly enthusiastic.*

CLOTHES /ˈjuː·nəˌfɔːrm/ *n* [C/U] a special set of clothes worn by people belonging to an organization to show others that they are members of it ○ [U] *soldiers in uniform*

uniformed /ˈjuː·nəˌfɔːrmd/ *adj* [not gradable] ○ *Only uniformed personnel are permitted to enter this building.*

unify Ⓐ /ˈjuː·nəˌfɑɪ/ *v* [T] to bring separate parts of something together so that they are one ○ *With his speech, the president sought to unify the country.*

unilateral /ˌjuːn·əlˈæt̬·ə·rəl/ *adj* [not gradable] done independently by one group or country ○ *a unilateral action*

unilaterally /ˌjuːn·əlˈæt̬·ə·rə·li/ *adv* ○ *The law is part of a disturbing trend to act unilaterally without regard to the legitimate interests of others.*

unimaginable /ˌʌn·ɪ ˈmædʒ·ə·nə·bəl/ *adj* difficult to imagine, esp. because of being very unlikely or very undesirable ○ *It was a time of drought and despair, of the Dust Bowl, of unimaginable suffering.*

unimportant /ˌʌn·ɪm ˈpɔːrt·ənt/ *adj* not important ○ *The money we lost is relatively unimportant, but the emotional stress of being robbed is hard to get over.*

unincorporated /ˌʌn·ɪn ˈkɔːr·pəˌreɪt̬·əd/ *adj* not officially part of a town or a city ○ *Bonsall is unincorporated and thus under the control of the county government.*

uninsured /ˌʌn·ɪn ˈʃʊrd/ *adj* not having any INSURANCE to pay for medical expenses or for damage or injury while driving a car ○ *The plan would provide health insurance for most Americans who now are uninsured.* ○ *uninsured motorists*

unintelligible /ˌʌn·ɪn ˈtel·ə·dʒə·bəl/ *adj* (of speech or writing) not clear enough to be understood

unintended /ˌʌn·ɪn ˈten·dəd/ *adj* not intentional; happening unexpectedly or by accident ○ *One unintended consequence of the Industrial Revolution was a rapid increase in air pollution.*

unintentional /ˌʌn·ɪn ˈten·tʃən·əl/ *adj* not planned or intended

unintentionally /ˌʌn·ɪn ˈten·tʃən·əl·i/ *adv* [not gradable]

uninterested /ʌn ˈɪn·trə·stəd, -ˈɪnt·əˌres·təd/ *adj* not excited or not wanting to become involved ○ *He's completely uninterested in sports.*

union **THINGS JOINED** /ˈjuːn·jən/ *n* [C/U] **1** the act or the state of being joined together **2** The union of two people refers to marriage.

POLITICAL UNIT /ˈjuːn·jən/ *n* [U/C] **1** ***social studies*** a political unit made up of two or more separate units such as states **2** ***US history*** In the American Civil War, **the Union** refers to the states that did not separate from the United States.

ORGANIZATION /ˈjuːn·jən/ *n* [C] ***social studies*** a LABOR UNION

unionize /ˈjuːn·jəˌnɑɪz/ *v* [I/T] ***social studies*** to form a LABOR UNION, or to organize workers into a LABOR UNION ○ [T] *We're launching a campaign to unionize workers at all major discount stores in the area.*

unique Ⓐ /jʊˈniːk/ *adj* being the only existing one of its type or, more generally, unusual or special in some way ○ *Each person's DNA is unique.*

uniquely Ⓐ /jʊˈniː·kli/ *adv* ○ *He's uniquely qualified to run this agency.*

uniqueness Ⓐ /jʊˈniːk·nəs/ *n* [U]

> **USAGE**
>
> **unique**
>
> **Unique** describes something that is special or unusual because only one example of it exists. If something is not special or important but only one of it exists, you should use the adjective **only**.
>
> *It is the only bus that goes to the airport.*
>
> ~~*It is the unique bus that goes to the airport.*~~

unisex /ˈjuː·nəˌseks/ *adj* intended for use by both males and females ○ *unisex hair salons*

unison IDIOM /ˈjuː·nə·sən/
• **in unison** together and at the same time ○ *The audience rose to its feet in unison, applauding and cheering.*

unit SEPARATE PART /ˈjuː·nət/ *n* [C] **1** a single item or a separate part of something larger ○ *The first year of the course is divided into four units.* ○ *This apartment building has 60 units* (= separate apartments). **2** A unit is also a small machine or part of a machine that has a particular purpose: *the central processing unit of a computer* **3** A unit is also a piece of furniture or equipment used as part of a set of similar or matching pieces: *a unit of a bookcase*

PEOPLE /ˈjuː·nət/ *n* [C] a group of people living or working together, esp. for a particular purpose ○ *a military unit* ○ *He's the surgeon in charge of the burn unit at the hospital.*

MEASUREMENT /ˈjuː·nət/ *n* [C] a standard measure used to express amounts ○ *An inch is a unit of length.* ○ *The dollar is the standard unit of currency in the US.*

unite /jʊˈnɑɪt/ *v* [I/T] to bring different groups or things together to become one, or to join together to become one ○ [I] *The thirteen American colonies united to form a new nation.*

unity /ˈjuː·nət̬·i/ *n* [U] **1** the state of being joined together or in agreement **2** ***writing*** Unity is also the quality of having the ideas and examples in a piece of writing clearly related to the topic and to each other

united /jʊˈnɑɪt̬·əd/ *adj*

United Church (of Canada) *n* [U] *Cdn* a large Christian church that combined several Christian churches

United Nations, *abbreviation* **UN** *n* [U] ***world history*** an international organization that was established in 1945 to maintain world peace

United States, *abbreviation* **US** *n* [U] the United States of America, a nation consisting of 50 states, all but one (Hawaii) in North America

universal /ˌjuː·nəˈvɜr·səl/ *adj* [not gradable] existing everywhere or involving everyone ○ *Congress rejected the proposal for universal health insurance.*

universally /ˌjuː·nəˈvɜr·sə·li/ *adv* ○ *Water is one of the most common and universally known substances, but researchers are still learning more about it.*

universe /ˈjuː·nəˌvɜrs/ *n* [U] everything that exists, esp. all physical matter, including all the stars and planets in space

university /ˌjuː·nəˈvɜr·sət̬·i/ *n* [C/U] a place of higher education usually for people who have finished twelve years of schooling and where they can obtain more knowledge and skills, and get a degree to recognize this ○ [U] *a university campus/professor* ○ [C] *She applied to six universities and was accepted by three.*

unjust /ʌnˈdʒʌst/ *adj* not morally right; not fair ○ *New laws will protect employees against unjust dismissals.*

unjustified Ⓐ /ʌnˈdʒʌs·təˌfɑɪd/ *adj* not able to be explained in a reasonable way; not deserved ○ *There were admittedly some unjustified delays in some Olympic projects.*

unkempt /ʌnˈkemt/ *adj* not neat or cared for; messy ○ *He needed a shave and his hair was unkempt.*

unkind /ʌnˈkɑɪnd/ *adj* not KIND ○ *He's made some very unkind remarks about his employer lately.*

unknowingly /ʌnˈnoʊ·ɪŋ·li/ *adv* without intending or realizing something ○ *Parents may unknowingly make their child feel inadequate or pressured by expecting too much of them.*

unknown /ʌnˈnoʊn/ *adj* not known, or not known to many people ○ *His whereabouts are still unknown.*

unknown /ʌnˈnoʊn/ *n* [C] a person who is not known to many people ○ *A year ago she was a virtual unknown on the figure-skating scene.*

unlawful /ʌnˈlɔː·fəl/ *adj* not according to or acceptable to the law ○ *unlawful behavior/business practices/discrimination*

unleaded /ʌnˈled·əd/ *adj* [not gradable] (of GASOLINE (= a fuel)) not containing LEAD (= a metal) ○ *Most cars today use unleaded gas.*

unleash /ʌnˈliːʃ/ *v* [T] to let happen or begin something powerful that, once begun, cannot be controlled ○ *The vice president unleashed a furious attack on leading Democratic representatives in Congress.*

unless /ənˌles, ᵊn-/ *conjunction* used to say what will or will not happen if something else does not happen or is not true; except if ○ *She won't go unless you go* (= If you do not go, she will not go either, but if you go, she will go). ○ *You can't get a job unless you've got the experience* (= You can only get a job if you have experience).

unlike DIFFERENT FROM /ʌnˈlɑɪk/ *prep* different from ○ *Unlike you, I'm not a great dancer.*

NOT TYPICAL /ʌnˈlɑɪk/ *prep* not typical or characteristic of ○ *It's unlike Debbie to be so late.*

unlikely /ʌnˈlɑɪ·kli/ *adj* not expected to happen; not LIKELY ○ [+ (*that*) clause] *It's unlikely (that) we will ever learn what happened.*

unlimited /ʌnˈlɪm·ət̬·əd/ *adj* not having a limit or highest possible amount, number, or level ○ *If you rent the car for the week, you get unlimited mileage* (= the amount you pay is not related to how many miles you drive).

unlisted /ʌnˈlɪs·təd/ *adj* [not gradable] (of a telephone number) not included in a printed list of telephone numbers available to the public

unload /ʌnˈloʊd/ *v* [I/T] **1** to remove the contents of something such as goods from a vehicle, the bullets from a gun, or the film from a camera ○ [T] *She unloaded her grocery bags from the back of the minivan.* **2** *infml* If you unload something that you no longer want, you get rid of it: [T] *Mon-*

U

aghan has said he is ready to unload his pizza business and retire to Florida.

unlock /ʌnˈlɑk/ *v* [T] to open a lock using a key, an electronic device, or a series of numbers or letters ○ *Could you unlock the door for me?*

unlucky /ʌnˈlʌk·i/ *adj* having or bringing bad luck ○ *For the unlucky people who get the flu, the health department advises: Stay home!*

unmanned /ʌnˈmænd/ *adj* [not gradable] not having or not needing people to operate or work correctly ○ *Both designs represent a new generation of unmanned aircraft, which began in the 1990s with robotic spy planes.*

unmarked /ʌnˈmɑrkt/ *adj* [not gradable] having no signs or symbols on the outside ○ *an unmarked police car*

unmarried /ʌnˈmær·iːd, -ˈmer-/ *adj* [not gradable] having no husband or wife ○ *Their youngest son is still unmarried.*

unmask /ʌnˈmæsk/ *v* [T] to show the previously hidden truth about someone or something ○ *He was unmasked as the author of the article.*

unmistakable /ˌʌn·məˈsteɪ·kə·bəl/ *adj* not likely to be confused with something else; clearly recognized ○ *There was an unmistakable smell of chocolate.*

unmitigated /ʌnˈmɪt̬·əˌgeɪt̬·əd/ *adj* (esp. of something unpleasant or unsuccessful) complete ○ *Her new business proved to be an unmitigated disaster.*

unmoved /ʌnˈmuːvd/ *adj* not feeling any emotion ○ *When the eclipse took place, no one was unmoved.*

unnamed /ʌnˈneɪmd/ *adj* [not gradable] not named, esp. in order to keep a name secret or unknown ○ *Both news stories relied on unnamed sources.*

unnatural /ʌnˈnætʃ·ə·rəl/ *adj* **1** not found in nature; artificial ○ *Nothing unnatural or polluting can be used.* ○ *The recordings have an unnatural sound.* **2** Behavior or feelings that are described as unnatural are not usual or acceptable.

unnecessary /ʌnˈnes·əˌser·i/ *adj* not needed or wanted, or more than is needed or wanted ○ *unnecessary expenses* ○ *The key to successful investing is to avoid making unnecessary errors.*
unnecessarily /ʌnˌnes·əˈser·ə·li/ *adv* ○ *I thought his explanation was unnecessarily complex.*

unnerve /ʌnˈnɜrv/ *v* [T] to make someone feel less confident and slightly frightened ○ *The long silence unnerved him.*
unnerving /ʌnˈnɜr·vɪŋ/ *adj* ○ *It's the way that he stares that I find so unnerving.*

unnoticed /ʌnˈnoʊt̬·əst/ *adj* [not gradable] not seen, or not attracting any attention ○ *She saw flaws that normally would have gone unnoticed.*

unobtrusive /ˌʌn·əbˈtruː·sɪv, -zɪv/ *adj* not noticeable; seeming to belong ○ *A good waiter is efficient and unobtrusive.*

unoccupied /ʌnˈɑk·jəˌpɑɪd/ *adj* [not gradable] without anyone in it, or not busy ○ *Are there any unoccupied seats in that row?*

unofficial /ˌʌn·əˈfɪʃ·əl/ *adj* [not gradable] not connected with or coming from a recognized office or authority ○ *We think of him as the unofficial town historian.*
unofficially /ˌʌn·əˈfɪʃ·ə·li/ *adv* ○ *Unemployment has been unofficially estimated at 70%.*

unorthodox /ʌnˈɔːr·θəˌdɑks/ *adj* (of behavior, ideas, or methods) different from what is usual or expected ○ *He has an unorthodox teaching style.*

unpack /ʌnˈpæk/ *v* [I/T] to remove things from a container ○ [T] *I haven't even unpacked my bags yet.*

unpaid /ʌnˈpeɪd/ *adj* [not gradable] owed, or without receiving payment ○ *unpaid bills* ○ *an unpaid leave of absence*

unparalleled Ⓐ /ʌnˈpær·əˌleld/ *adj* having no equal; better or greater than any other ○ *We have an unparalleled record of solid growth.*

unpleasant /ʌnˈplez·ənt/ *adj* not attractive or enjoyable or easy to like ○ *an unpleasant surprise* ○ *unpleasant memories* ○ *an unpleasant young man*
unpleasantly /ʌnˈplez·ənt·li/ *adv* ○ *Rob chuckled unpleasantly.*

unplug /ʌnˈplʌg/ *v* [T] **-gg-** to remove a plug for an electrical device from a SOCKET ○ *I unplugged the TV.*

unpopular /ʌnˈpɑp·jə·lər/ *adj* not liked or enjoyed by many people ○ *I'm not surprised the mayor is unpopular.*

unprecedented Ⓐ /ʌnˈpres·əˌdent·əd/ *adj* never having happened or existed in the past ○ *We've entered an age of unprecedented prosperity.*

unpredictable Ⓐ /ˌʌn·prɪˈdɪk·tə·bəl/ *adj* tending to change suddenly and without reason or warning, and therefore not able to be depended on ○ *unpredictable weather* ○ *The world is pretty unpredictable.*
unpredictability Ⓐ /ˌʌn·prɪˌdɪk·təˈbɪl·ət̬·i/ *n* [U]

unprepared /ˌʌn·prɪˈperd, -ˈpærd/ *adj* not ready ○ *He was completely/totally unprepared for what he saw.*

unprincipled Ⓐ /ʌnˈprɪn·sə·pəld/ *adj* having or showing no moral rules or standards of good behavior ○ *an unprincipled politician*

unproductive /ˌʌn·prəˈdʌk·tɪv/ *adj* not useful, or not creating anything ○ *We wasted three days in unproductive discussions.*

unprofessional /ˌʌn·prəˈfeʃ·ən·əl/ *adj* not showing the standard of behavior or skills that are expected of a person in a skilled job ○ *Dressing like that was very unprofessional of him.*

unprofitable /ʌnˈprɑf·ət̬·ə·bəl/ *adj* not resulting in profit ○ *unprofitable investments/businesses*

U

unprotected /ˌʌn·prəˈtek·təd/ *adj* not safe from injury, damage, or loss ○ *Many of our forests remain unprotected by environmental laws.*

unprovoked /ˌən·prəˈvoʊkt/ *adj* (esp. of an unpleasant action or remark) not caused by anything and therefore unfair ○ *Witnesses said the attack was unprovoked.*

unpublished /ʌnˈpʌb·lɪʃt/ *adj* [not gradable] **1** not published or made available for people to see ○ *Unpublished European studies show significant reductions in all the cholesterol-clogging fats.* **2** A person who is unpublished has not written anything that has been published.

unqualified WITHOUT SKILLS /ʌnˈkwɑl·əˌfɑɪd/ *adj* lacking the skills and experience needed for a particular job ○ *I liked her, but she was unqualified for the job.*

TOTAL /ʌnˈkwɑl·əˌfɑɪd/ *adj* [not gradable] not limited in any way ○ *My first attempt was an unqualified success.*

unquestionable /ʌnˈkwes·tʃə·nə·bəl/ *adj* [not gradable] not open to question or doubt; INDISPUTABLE ○ *Her achievements are unquestionable.*
unquestionably /ʌnˈkwes·tʃə·nə·bli/ *adv* [not gradable] ○ *Sakow is unquestionably the most remarkable woman writing today.*

unquestioned /ʌnˈkwes·tʃənd/ *adj* not doubted ○ *unquestioned loyalty*

unrated /ʌnˈreɪt̬·əd/ *adj* [not gradaable] not given a value in a ranking or rating system, esp. the rating system for movies that tells which ones children may watch ○ *an unrated coming-of-age tale*

unravel SEPARATE /ʌnˈræv·əl/ *v* [I/T] **-l-**, **-ll-** (of woven cloth) to separate into threads, or to separate the fibers of a thread, rope, or cloth ○ [I] *My sweater is unraveling.* ○ [I] (*fig.*) *The movie unraveled at the end* (= was not complete and satisfying).

SOLVE /ʌnˈræv·əl/ *v* [T] **-l-**, **-ll-** to solve a crime or explain a mystery ○ *You will discover what the title means as you unravel the movie's mysteries.*

unreal IMAGINARY /ʌnˈriːl/ *adj* as if imagined; strange and like a dream ○ *His face was an eerie, unreal color.*

SURPRISING /ʌnˈriːl/ *adj slang* surprising, unusual, or hard to believe ○ *We just ate and ate, and I was so full it was unreal.*

unrealistic /ˌʌnˌriː·əˈlɪs·tɪk/ *adj* not reasonable, or not likely to be achieved ○ *We're placing unrealistic demands on our schools.*

unreasonable /ʌnˈriː·zə·nə·bəl/ *adj* not based on or using good judgment; not fair ○ *It's unreasonable to expect him to work every weekend.*
unreasonably /ʌnˈriː·zə·nə·bli/ *adv* ○ *He thinks the cops acted unreasonably.*

unregulated /ʌnˈreg·jəˌleɪt̬·əd/ *adj* not controlled, esp. by laws, police, or a government department ○ *Campaign finance reform is designed to prevent large, unregulated contributions to politicians.*

unrelated /ˌʌn·rɪˈleɪt̬·əd/ *adj* **1** not having a connection ○ *His answer was completely unrelated to my question.* **2** A person who is unrelated to you is not part of your family.

unrelenting /ˌʌn·rɪˈlent·ɪŋ/ *adj* extremely determined; never weakening or ending ○ *unrelenting toughness/opposition* ○ *unrelenting neglect/pollution*

unreliable Ⓐ /ˌʌn·rɪˈlɑɪ·ə·bəl/ *adj* not to be trusted or depended on ○ *Their carpenter was totally unreliable – he never finished the job.*

unrequited /ˌʌn·rɪˈkwɑɪt̬·əd/ *adj* [not gradable] (of love) felt toward someone who does not feel the same way toward you

unresolved Ⓐ /ˌʌn·rɪˈzɑlvd, -ˈzɔːlvd/ *adj* [not gradable] (esp. of a problem or difficulty) not solved or ended ○ *The mayor's race remains unresolved.*

unresponsive Ⓐ /ˌʌn·rɪˈspɑn·sɪv/ *adj* not reacting or answering, or not reacting or answering satisfactorily ○ *The company has been unresponsive to her efforts to discuss a settlement.*

unrest /ʌnˈrest/ *n* [U] disagreements or fighting between groups of people ○ *civil/social/labor unrest* ○ *The president is cutting short an international trip because of growing unrest in his country.*

unrestrained Ⓐ /ˌʌn·rɪˈstreɪnd/ *adj* [not gradable] not limited in any way ○ *unrestrained fury* ○ *unrestrained capitalism*

unrestricted /ˌʌn·rɪˈstrɪk·təd/ *adj* not limited or controlled by rules or laws ○ *A public library must allow the town's citizens unrestricted access to its resources.*

unrivaled /ʌnˈrɑɪ·vəld/ *adj* having no equal; better than any others ○ *unrivaled beauty*

unroll /ʌnˈroʊl/ *v* [I/T] to open and become flat from a rolled position, or to cause something to do this ○ [T] *She unrolled a bolt of silk for us to look at.*

unruly /ʌnˈruː·li/ *adj* difficult to control or manage ○ *Her unruly behavior caused chaos in class.*

unsafe /ʌnˈseɪf/ *adj* dangerous, or at risk ○ *The bridge is closed because it's unsafe.* ○ *Carol feels unsafe in planes.*

unsaid /ʌnˈsed/ *adj* [not gradable] not spoken, although thought of or felt ○ *Some things are better left unsaid.*

unsanitary /ʌnˈsæn·əˌter·i/ *adj* dirty, esp. in a way that is dangerous to health ○ *unsanitary conditions*

unsatisfactory /ˌənˌsæt̬·əsˈfæk·tə·ri/ *adj* not good, or not good enough ○ *Jacob's answers were unsatisfactory.*

unsaturated /ʌnˈsætʃ·əˌreɪt̬·əd/ *n* [not gradable] ***chemistry*** **1** containing less of a substance than can be absorbed, and therefore not in a state of balance **2** Unsaturated also describes a HYDROCARBON in which the carbon atoms do not join as many HYDROGEN atoms as possible.

U

unsavory /ʌnˈseɪ·və·ri/ *adj* unpleasant or morally offensive ○ *He has a history of unsavory business dealings.*

unscathed /ʌnˈskeɪðd/ *adj* without injuries or damage being caused ○ *I came away from the accident unscathed, but the car got badly damaged.*

unscrew /ʌnˈskruː/ *v* [T] to remove the lid or top from something by twisting it, or to remove screws from something ○ *Unscrew the gas cap.*

unscrupulous /ʌnˈskruː·pjə·ləs/ *adj* willing to lie or cheat to succeed ○ *an unscrupulous salesman*

unseasonable /ʌnˈsiː·zə·nə·bəl/ *adj* (of weather) not usual for the time of year ○ *We had an unseasonable warm spell in January.*

unseat /ʌnˈsiːt/ *v* [T] to remove someone from a powerful job, esp. a job to which a person is elected ○ *She has a good chance to unseat the governor.*

unseemly /ʌnˈsiːm·li/ *adj* not suitable or polite ○ *unseemly language* ○ *unseemly haste* ○ *unseemly behavior*

unseen /ʌnˈsiːn/ *adj, adv* not seen or not able to be seen ○ *She found the door open and slipped into the house unseen.*

unselfish /ʌnˈsel·fɪʃ/ *adj* caring about or generous toward others ○ *He's an unselfish player who puts team goals first.*

unsettled CHANGEABLE /ʌnˈset̬·əld/ *adj* tending to change suddenly; not having a regular pattern ○ *Things are unsettled in the state's political arena.* ○ *The forecast is for unsettled weather, with more snow to come.*

unsettling /ʌnˈset·lɪŋ, -ˈset̬·əl·ɪŋ/ *adj* ○ *A rise in unemployment has an unsettling effect on the stock market.*

ANXIOUS /ʌnˈset̬·əld/ *adj* anxious and worried; unable to relax ○ *She was feeling unsettled the entire morning before her interview.*

unsettling /ʌnˈset·lɪŋ, -ˈset̬·əl·ɪŋ/ *adj* ○ *I received the unsettling news that I may lose my job next month.*

unsightly /ʌnˈsɑɪt·li/ *adj* not pleasing to see; UNATTRACTIVE ○ *The garden was full of unsightly weeds.*

U

unskilled /ʌnˈskɪld/ *adj* (of people) without any particular work skills, or (of work) not needing any particular skills ○ *Unskilled workers may lose their jobs.*

unsolicited /ˌʌn·səˈlɪs·ət̬·əd/ *adj* not asked for ○ *The proposed law would force senders of unsolicited e-mail to provide a valid return address.*

unsolved /ʌnˈsɑlvd, -ˈsɔːlvd/ *adj* not solved or explained ○ *The detective has spent seven years investigating the unsolved crime.*

unsophisticated /ˌʌn·səˈfɪs·təˌkeɪt̬·əd/ *adj* not complicated, not educated, or without a good understanding of culture ○ *He's an unsophisticated man, but he has been very successful in business.*

unsound NOT ACCEPTABLE /ʌnˈsɑʊnd/ *adj* (esp. of activities) not suitable or acceptable ○ *He was involved in unsound banking practices.*

WEAK /ʌnˈsɑʊnd/ *adj* (esp. of a building) in bad condition and likely to fall down or fail ○ *The bridge is structurally unsound.*

unspeakable /ʌnˈspiː·kə·bəl/ *adj* too bad or shocking to be described or expressed ○ *unspeakable crimes*

unspecified Ⓐ /ʌnˈspes·əˌfɑɪd/ *adj* [not gradable] not stated or described in detail ○ *The company was sold for an unspecified amount.*

unspoken /ʌnˈspoʊ·kən/ *adj* [not gradable] not stated, although thought, understood, or felt ○ *We have an unspoken agreement to share the housework.*

unstable Ⓐ /ʌnˈsteɪ·bəl/ *adj* **1** not firm and therefore not strong, safe, or likely to last ○ *It is a poor and politically unstable country.* **2** An unstable person suffers from sudden and extreme changes of mental state: *He's emotionally unstable – you never know how he'll react.*

unsteady /ʌnˈsted·i/ *adj* moving or changing, or not firm ○ *She's been sick, and she's still a bit unsteady on her feet.*

unstoppable /ʌnˈstɑp·ə·bəl/ *adj* continuous, or unable to be stopped ○ *The band was enjoying what seemed to be an unstoppable rise in popularity.*

unsuccessful /ˌʌn·səkˈses·fəl/ *adj* not ending in success, or not achieving success ○ *After writing three unsuccessful plays, Miller finally had a hit.*

unsuccessfully /ˌʌn·səkˈses·fə·li/ *adv* ○ *Howard's been unsuccessfully looking for an affordable apartment.*

unsuitable /ʌnˈsuːt̬·ə·bəl/ *adj* not right for a particular person, situation, or occasion ○ *Parts of this movie may be unsuitable for children.*

unsung /ʌnˈsʌŋ/ *adj* [not gradable] not noticed or praised for doing hard work, being brave, or achieving results ○ *A teacher is often the unsung hero of a great writer's success.*

unsure /ʌnˈʃʊr/ *adj* **1** in doubt, or not certain ○ [+ question word] *Officials were unsure who was in control of the city.* **2** If you are unsure of yourself, you are not confident: *He has been unsure of himself ever since he failed to get that job.*

unsuspecting /ˌʌn·səˈspek·tɪŋ/ *adj* trusting; not aware of any danger or harm ○ *The fish sometimes leap into the air and smack into unsuspecting boaters.*

unswerving /ʌnˈswɜr·vɪŋ/ *adj* (esp. of trust or a belief) always strong; never weakening ○ *unswerving support*

untangle /ʌnˈtæŋ·gəl/ *v* [T] to remove the knots from a mass of string, wire, hair, etc. and separate the different threads ○ *I spent ages trying to untangle Rosie's hair.* ○ (fig.) *It took years to untangle the facts of the case* (= make them clear and understood).

untapped /ʌnˈtæpt/ *adj* [not gradable] (of a supply of something valuable) not yet used or taken advantage of ○ *The country's forests are largely untapped resources.*

untenable /ʌnˈten·ə·bəl/ *adj* not able to be supported or defended against criticism, or no longer able to continue ○ *The position of the players' union has become untenable.*

unthinkable /ʌnˈθɪŋ·kə·bəl/ *adj* too shocking or unlikely to be imagined as possible ○ *A world without music would be unthinkable.*

IDIOM with **unthinkable**

• **the unthinkable** something that is very unlikely or undesirable ○ *The president's car did the unthinkable – it stopped at a red light.*

untidy /ʌnˈtɑɪd·i/ *adj* not neat or well-arranged ○ *an untidy yard*

untie /ʌnˈtɑɪ/ *v* [T] *pres. part.* **untying**, *past* **untied** to unfasten a knot or something tied ○ *I had to help her untie her shoelaces.*

until TIME /ənˌtɪl, ʌn-, ᵊn-/, **till** *prep, conjunction* up to the stated time ○ *I was up until 3 a.m.*

DISTANCE /ənˌtɪl, ʌn-, ᵊn-/, **till** *prep, conjunction* as far as ○ *Stay on the bus until 57th Street and then walk one block west.*

IDIOM with **until**

• **not until** not before a stated time or event ○ *Don't move until I tell you.*

untimely /ʌnˈtɑɪm·li/ *adj* (of something bad) happening unexpectedly early or at a time which is not suitable ○ *A love of fast cars led to his untimely death at the age of 34.*

untiring /ʌnˈtɑɪ·rɪŋ/ *adj* (esp. of qualities such as energy, interest, and enthusiasm) never weakening ○ *Without Tony's untiring enthusiasm, this campaign would not have succeeded.*

unto /ˌʌn·tə, ˈʌn·tuː/ *preposition old use* to ○ *Now someone has done unto you what you have been doing to others.*

untold /ʌnˈtoʊld/ *adj* [not gradable] so great in amount or level that it can not be measured or expressed in words ○ *The software saves the company untold thousands in paper and labor.*

untouchable /ʌnˈtʌtʃ·ə·bəl/ *adj* [not gradable] not able to be punished, criticized, or changed in any way ○ *His home run record remained untouchable.*

untouched /ʌnˈtʌtʃt/ *adj* [not gradable] **1** not changed or spoiled in any way ○ *These prewar apartment buildings have been virtually untouched since they were built.* **2** If food is untouched, it has not been eaten: *She left her dinner untouched.*

untoward /ʌnˈtwɔːrd, -ˈtwoʊrd, -təˈwɔːrd/ *adj* [not gradable] not expected, not convenient, or not suitable ○ *I was nervous about what he might do, but nothing untoward happened.*

untreated WITHOUT MEDICINE /ʌnˈtriːt̬·əd/ *adj* not given medical treatment ○ *Depression is a very treatable disease but if left untreated it can be deadly.*

NOT PROCESSED /ʌnˈtriːt̬·əd/ *adj* not changed, improved, or made safe by a special process ○ *untreated wood/fabric* ○ *Up to 80 times a year, the untreated overflow from the factory is dumped into the river.*

untrue /ʌnˈtruː/ *adj* [not gradable] not true; false ○ *Her remarks were irresponsible and untrue.*

unused /ʌnˈjuːzd/ *adj* [not gradable] not being used at present, or never having been used ○ *The stationary exercise bike sits unused in the basement.*

unused to /ʌnˈjuːs·tə, -ˌtuː/ *adj* [not gradable] not familiar with (a particular habit or experience) ○ *If you're unused to exercise you'll find your joints ache the next day.*

unusual /ʌnˈjuː·ʒə·wəl/ *adj* different from what is usual or expected ○ *I was actually on time, which is unusual for me.*

unusually /ʌnˈju·ʒə·wə·li/ *adv* [not gradable] in a way or to a degree that is different from what is usual or expected ○ *We had unusually warm weather in December.* ○ *There is no evidence of unusually high rates of disease.*

WORD CHOICES unusual

See also: **different, special, strange**

Uncommon or **rare** can be used instead of "unusual" when saying that something is unusual because it does not happen or exist very often.

*It's not **uncommon** for people to become ill when they travel.*

*This is a **rare** opportunity to see inside the building.*

If something is unusual because it is different from the way most people do things, the adjective **unconventional** can be used.

*I had a very **unconventional** childhood.*

Unique is used when something only happens once or only one of a particular thing exists.

*This is your chance to own a **unique** piece of jewelry.*

Exotic can be used for describing things which are unusual and exciting, especially because they relate to a foreign country.

*The room was decorated with **exotic** flowers.*

If something is unusual in an interesting and slightly odd way, you can use the words **quirky** or **offbeat**.

*He has a very **quirky** sense of humor.*

*The movie is an **offbeat** romantic comedy.*

If a person is very unusual in a nice way, you can say that he or she is **one of a kind**.

*He was truly **one of a kind**, and will be missed greatly.*

unveil /ʌnˈveɪl/ *v* [T] to make something secret known ○ *The president's new policy was unveiled at the press conference.*

unwanted /ʌnˈwɔːnt·əd, -ˈwɑnt-, -ˈwʌnt-/ *adj* [not gradable] not desired or needed ○ *Charities*

U

such as Computers for Schools are happy to take unwanted computers.

unwarranted /ʌn ˈwɑr·ənt·əd, -ˈwɔːr-/ *adj* [not gradable] lacking a good reason; unnecessary ○ *They denounced the investigation as an unwarranted interference with their business.*

unwelcome /ʌn ˈwel·kəm/ *adj* not wanted or desirable ○ *Dogs stand watch for unwelcome visitors to the estate.*

unwieldy DIFFICULT TO MOVE /ʌn ˈwiːl·di/ *adj* [not gradable] (of an object) difficult to move or handle because it is heavy, large, or a strange shape

NOT EFFECTIVE /ʌn ˈwiːl·di/ *adj* [not gradable] (of a system) difficult to manage, usually because it is too big or badly organized ○ *an unwieldy bureaucracy*

unwilling /ʌn ˈwɪl·ɪŋ/ *adj* not wanting to do something ○ [+ *to* infinitive] *The bank was unwilling to lend her money.*

unwillingly /ʌn ˈwɪl·ɪŋ·li/ *adv* [not gradable]

unwillingness /ʌn ˈwɪl·ɪŋ·nəs/ *n* [U]

WORD CHOICES **unwilling**

If someone is unwilling to do something you can say formally that the person is **loath to** do it.

I was ***loath to*** *spend all the money at once.*

The verb **balk** can be used when someone is unwilling to do something or unwilling for something to happen.

The governor ***balked*** *at a proposal to raise the state sales tax.*

Reluctant can be used when someone is unwilling to do something and therefore is slow to do it.

I was ***reluctant*** *to leave because I was having such a good time.*

If someone is unwilling to do something but does it anyway, you can say that the person does it **grudgingly** or **under protest**.

He ***grudgingly*** *agreed to a meeting.*

He did pay but ***under protest.***

unwind UNFASTEN /ʌn ˈwɑɪnd/ *v* [T] *past* **unwound** to unfasten something that is wrapped around an object ○ *to unwind string*

RELAX /ʌn ˈwɑɪnd/, **wind down** *v* [I] *past* **unwound** to relax after a period of work or anxiety ○ *I'm just going to watch some TV and unwind.*

unwise /ʌn ˈwɑɪz/ *adj* not showing good judgment or understanding of a situation ○ *We made several unwise investments and lost quite a bit of money.*

unwisely /ʌn ˈwɑɪz·li/ *adv* [not gradable]

unwitting /ʌn ˈwɪţ·ɪŋ/ *adj* [not gradable] without knowing or planning ○ *The harmful radiation tests were performed long ago on unwitting subjects.*

unwittingly /ʌn ˈwɪţ·ɪŋ·li/ *adv* [not gradable]

unworkable /ʌn ˈwɜr·kə·bəl/ *adj* (of a plan or a system) not practical or able to operate effectively ○ *The budget was considered unworkable and had to be revised.*

unwritten /ʌn ˈrɪt·ən/ *adj* [not gradable] **1** not written **2** An unwritten law/rule is one that does not exist officially, but which people generally accept and obey: *There's an unwritten rule at work that you don't wear jeans.*

unwritten constitution *n* [C] ***politics & government*** the laws, legal decisions, and customs that govern a country that does not have a CONSTITUTION (= a set of political principles) in a single written document

unyielding /ʌn ˈjiːl·dɪŋ/ *adj* [not gradable] not giving up control or responsibility for (something) as a result of influence or persuasion ○ *The economist showed an unyielding commitment to tough financial stability.*

unzip /ʌn ˈzɪp/ *v* [T] **-pp-** to open the ZIPPER (= a fastener consisting of two rows of metal or plastic teeth) on something

up HIGHER /ʌp/ *adv* [not gradable] toward a higher position, or toward a higher value, number, or level ○ *Pick up your clothes and put them away.* ○ *We need to push sales figures up higher next quarter.* ○ *The kids were jumping up and down on the bed.*

up /ʌp/ *prep* ○ *We followed the others up the stairs.*

up /ʌp/ *adj* [not gradable] ○ *Take the up escalator to the housewares department.* ○ *Gas prices are up* (= have increased).

up /ʌp/ *v* [T] **-pp-** *infml* to increase the amount or level of something ○ *We won't be able to make a profit unless we up our prices.*

up /ʌp/ *n infml*

VERTICAL /ʌp/ *adv* [not gradable] in or into a vertical position ○ *She jumped up to answer the phone.* ○ *They put up* (= built) *the house in a matter of weeks.*

TOP /ʌp/ *adv* [not gradable] in a high position; at the top ○ *They moved to a house up in the hills.*

up /ʌp/ *prep* at the top of ○ *His house is up the hill.*

ALONG /ʌp/ *prep* (farther) along ○ *There's a coffee shop just up the street.*

INCREASINGLY /ʌp/ *adv* [not gradable] to a greater degree; in order to increase ○ *The afternoon sun really heats up this room* (= increases the heat in this room). ○ *Please speak up* (= louder) *– I can't hear you.*

OUT OF BED /ʌp/ *adj, adv* [not gradable] out of bed ○ *What time did you get up?*

INTO EXISTENCE /ʌp/ *adv* [not gradable] into existence, view, or consideration ○ *I didn't hesitate to bring up the salary issue.* ○ *Something came up at the office and I had to work late.*

up /ʌp/ *adj* [not gradable] ○ *What's up* (= What is happening or What is wrong)*?*

EQUAL /ʌp/ *adv* [not gradable] so as to be equal in quality or achievement ○ *It's impossible to keep up with all the new computer developments.*

NEAR /ʌp/ *adv* [not gradable] very near ○ *He walked right up to me and introduced himself.* ○ *The cop pushed me up against the wall.*

TOGETHER /ʌp/ *adv* [not gradable] in a state of being together with other similar things ○ *Gather up your things – it's time to go.* ○ *She added up the numbers in her head.*

TIGHTLY /ʌp/ *adv* [not gradable] tightly or firmly in order to keep something safe or in position ○ *Tie the boat up at the dock.* ○ *You'd better bundle up* (= wear warm clothes) *– it's cold outside.*

IN OPERATION /ʌp/ *adj* [not gradable] (of a system or machine, esp. a computer) operating, esp. in its usual way ○ *The new inventory system should be up and running by the end of the month.*

SMALLER /ʌp/ *adv* [not gradable] made smaller in area or amount, esp. by cutting or dividing ○ *Cut the cheese up into bite-size pieces.* ○ *They broke the company up into three separate units.* ○ *He folded up the newspaper and put it in his briefcase.*

AGE /ʌp/ *adv* [not gradable] to a greater age ○ *She wants to be a singer when she grows up.*

INTENDED /ʌp/ *adj* [not gradable] intended, suggested, or being considered ○ *The house at the end of our street is up for sale.* ○ *Ray's up for promotion.*
up /ʌp/ *adv* [not gradable] ○ *They put the building up for sale* (= offered it for sale).

INTO IMPROVED POSITION /ʌp/ *adv* [not gradable] into an improved position or state ○ *By the third lap, Simms had moved up into second position.*
up /ʌp/ *n*

ENDED /ʌp/ *adj, adv* [not gradable] finished, or to an end, finish, or state of being completed ○ *Finish up your breakfast – it's almost time for school.* ○ *My time is almost up on the parking meter.*

TOWARD NORTH /ʌp/ *adv* [not gradable] toward the north ○ *She comes up from Washington about once a month.*

IDIOMS with up

• **on the up and up** honest and fair to everyone ○ *There is skepticism among many voters that the election is going to be conducted on the up and up.*
• **up and about, up and around** *infml* feeling well enough to get out of bed and move around
• **up and** *do something* to do something that is unexpected or different ○ *After 20 years of marriage, she up and left him.*
• **up for grabs** available ○ *The job was still up for grabs.*
• **up in arms** angry or upset ○ *The union is up in arms over the reduction in health benefits.*
• **up in the air** uncertain and with an unknown result ○ *The whole future of the project is still up in the air.*
• **up the creek, up a creek** *infml* in a difficult situation ○ *If any more people quit, we'll really be up the creek.*
• **up to par** feeling or performing as good as usual, with nothing wrong ○ *Jenny had not been up to par physically and did not come close to winning a medal.*
• **up to scratch** as good as the usual standard ○ *The last few episodes of the TV program haven't been quite up to scratch.*
• **up to snuff** good enough ○ *Her work isn't up to snuff.*
• **up to speed** performing at a desirable level ○ *It took me a while to get up to speed after the flu.*
• **up till, up to, up until** until ○ *Up to yesterday, we had no idea where the child was.*

up-and-coming *adj* likely to achieve success in the near future ○ *Tatiana is an up-and-coming young actress.*

up and down *adv* in one direction and then in the opposite direction, esp. repeatedly ○ *The dog was running up and down the path.*

upbeat /ʌpˈbiːt/ *adj* full of hope, happiness, and good feelings ○ *The mood is upbeat at Shaw's campaign headquarters tonight.*

upbringing /ˈʌpˌbrɪŋ·ɪŋ/ *n* [C usually sing] the way in which someone is treated and trained as a child ○ *Who can argue with the healthy upbringing of happy children?*

upcoming /ˈʌpˈkʌm·ɪŋ/ *adj* [not gradable] happening soon ○ *Party officials met to nominate candidates for the upcoming election.*

update /ʌpˈdeɪt/ *v* [T] **1** to make something more accurate and suitable for use now by showing new facts or conditions ○ *The school's budget is updated annually.* ○ *When you move, don't forget to update your mailing address.* **2** To update is also to make something more modern: *The old procedures need to be updated and streamlined.*
update /ˈʌp·deɪt/ *n* [C] new or more accurate information based on new facts or conditions ○ *You can get hourly news updates on the Internet.*

upfront **CLEAR** /ʌpˈfrʌnt/ *adj, adv* [not gradable] speaking or behaving in a way that makes your intentions and beliefs clear ○ *She's very upfront about her feelings.*

IN ADVANCE /ʌpˈfrʌnt/ *adj, adv* [not gradable] paid or obtained in advance ○ *The roofer wants 20% of the money upfront.*

upgrade /ʌpˈgreɪd/ *v* [T] to improve the quality or usefulness of something, or to raise something or someone to a higher position or rank ○ *If you want to raise rents, you have to upgrade the housing first.* ○ *They're spending more than $4 million next year to upgrade computer systems.* ○ *In 1992 the college was upgraded to a university.* ○ *We were upgraded from tourist to business class on our flight to London.*

upheaval /ʌpˈhiː·vəl/ *n* [C/U] (a) great change, causing or involving difficulty or trouble ○ [U] *The long garbage strike in 1970 caused much political upheaval.*

uphill /ʌpˈhɪl/ *adj, adv* **1** leading to a higher place on a slope ○ *The runners began the uphill climb to the finish line.* ○ *As we started driving uphill, the car made a strange noise.* **2** *fig.* Uphill can also mean difficult and needing a large amount of effort: *Recovering from the accident will be an uphill battle for her, but she's doing well.*

uphold /ʌpˈhoʊld/ *v* [T] *past* **upheld** to defend or maintain a principle or law, or to state that a

U

decision that has already been made, esp. a legal one, is correct ○ *The Supreme Court upheld California's term limit measure.*

upholster /ə'poʊl·stər/ *v* [T] to fill a seat, chair, or SOFA with a suitable material and cover it with cloth
upholstery /ə'poʊl·stə·ri/ *n* [U] the cloth and other materials used in upholstering furniture, or the process of using them

upkeep /'ʌp·kiːp/ *n* [U] the process or cost of keeping something, such as a building, in good and usable condition ○ *It costs the landlord about $2000 a month just for upkeep.*

uplifting /ʌp'lɪf·tɪŋ/ *adj* [not gradable] positive in a way that encourages the improvement of a person's mood or spirit ○ *uplifting words/music*

upon /ə'pɑn, ə'pɔːn/ *prep* **1** on ○ *That depends upon the circumstances.* ○ *She insisted upon knowing the truth.* **2** Upon can be used to show that something happens soon after, and often because of, something else: *Upon hearing the good news, we all congratulated Murphy.*

upper /'ʌp·ər/ *adj* [not gradable] at a higher position or level (than something else), or being the top part of something ○ *Our company occupied the three upper floors of the building.*
upper /'ʌp·ər/ *n* [C] the top part of a shoe

uppercase /ˌʌp·ər'keɪs/ *n* [U] ***writing*** the large form of letters when they are printed or written; capital letters ○ Compare LOWERCASE
uppercase /ˌʌp·ər'keɪs/ *adj* [not gradable]

upper class *n* the group of people who have the highest position and the most social and economic influence in a society

uppermost /'ʌp·ərˌmoʊst/ *adj, adv* [not gradable] in the highest position, or most important ○ *Her health is uppermost in my mind.*

uppity /'ʌp·əţ·i/ *adj disapproving* acting in a way that is too confident for someone in your social class or for your young age ○ *I was just an uppity kid.*

upright **STRAIGHT** /'ʌp·rɑɪt/ *adj, adv* [not gradable] (standing or being) vertical and as straight as possible ○ *He stood upright.*
MORAL /'ʌp·rɑɪt/ *adj* honest, responsible, and moral ○ *an upright young man*

uprising /'ʌpˌrɑɪ·zɪŋ/ *n* [C] an act of opposition by many people, sometimes using violence, against those who are in power

uproar /'ʌp·rɔːr, -ˌroʊr/ *n* [C/U] loud complaints esp. by angry people, or a noisy state of confusion ○ [C] *There was an uproar over the proposed rent increases.*

uproot **PULL** /ʌp'ruːt/ *v* [T] to pull a plant including its roots out of the ground
REMOVE /ʌp'ruːt/ *v* [T] to remove someone from his or her home or usual surroundings ○ *He had been with the team six years and didn't wish to uproot his family to play in a different city.*

ups and downs *pl n* good and bad things that happen to someone or something during a period ○ *the ups and downs of marriage*

upscale /'ʌp·skeɪl/ *adj* characteristic of or suitable for the wealthy ○ *an upscale residential neighborhood* ○ *an upscale restaurant*

upset **WORRY** /ʌp'set/ *v* [T] *pres. part.* **upsetting,** *past* **upset** to make someone worried, unhappy, or angry ○ *The governor's veto upset a lot of people.*
upset /ʌp'set/ *adj* ○ *Mom gets really upset if we don't call and tell her where we are.* ○ *She was very upset about losing her wallet.*
upsetting /ʌp'set·ɪŋ/ *adj* ○ *an upsetting remark*
CHANGE /ʌp'set/ *v* [T] *pres. part.* **upsetting,** *past* **upset** to change the usual or expected state or order of something in a way that stops it from happening or working ○ *The airline strike could upset our vacation plans.*
upset /'ʌp·set/ *n* [C] (in sports) a surprising victory by a person or team that was expected to lose
FEEL ILL /ʌp'set/ *v* [T] *pres. part.* **upsetting,** *past* **upset** to make your stomach feel bad ○ *an upset stomach*

WORD FAMILY upset			
Nouns	upset	*Adjectives*	upset upsetting
Verbs	upset		

upshot /'ʌp·ʃɑt/ *n* [C usually sing] something that happens as a result of other actions, events, or decisions ○ *The upshot of the discussions was that no one will be laid off.*

upside /'ʌp·sɑɪd/ *n* [U] the positive part of a situation ○ *It's too bad we can't go until Thursday, but the upside is that we get to stay through the weekend.* ○ Compare DOWNSIDE

upside down *adj, adv* [not gradable] having the part that is usually at the top turned to be at the bottom ○ *He put the pots upside down on a dish towel to let them dry.*

upstage /ʌp'steɪdʒ/ *v* [T] to take people's attention away from someone and make them listen to or look at you instead ○ *The mayor doesn't like to be upstaged by his subordinates – he likes to make all the public announcements.*

upstairs /'ʌp'sterz, -'stærz/ *adj, adv* [not gradable] toward or on the higher floor or floors of a building

upstanding /ʌp'stæn·dɪŋ/ *adj approving* behaving in a moral way ○ *She is an upstanding member of the community.*

upstart /'ʌp·stɑrt/ *adj* [not gradable] new and not experienced ○ *Upstart airlines like Southwest are competing today with the established carriers like Delta.*

upstate /ʌp'steɪt/ *adj, adv* to or in the northern part of a state ○ *She came to New York from a small town upstate because she wanted to be a dancer.*

upstream /ʌpˈstriːm/ *adj, adv* [not gradable] against the current toward the starting point of a river ○ *Rowing upstream was hard going.* ○ Compare DOWNSTREAM

upsurge /ˈʌp·sɜrdʒ/ *n* [C] a sudden or large increase ○ *Department stores report a recent upsurge in credit-card fraud.*

upswing /ˈʌp·swɪŋ/ *n* [C] an increase or improvement ○ *Many analysts are predicting an upswing in the economy.*

uptight /ˈʌpˈtɑɪt/ *adj infml* nervous, anxious, or worried ○ *I was really uptight about the interview, but it went fine.*

up to ALMOST EQUAL /ˈʌp·tə/ *adv* less than or equal to, but not more than, a stated value, number, level, or time ○ *Research suggests that up to half of those who were prescribed the drug suffered side effects.* ○ *You have up to ten minutes.*

RESPONSIBILITY /ˌʌp·tə/ *prep* being the responsibility of (someone) ○ *The decision is up to you.* ○ *If it were up to me, I'd do it.*

DOING /ˌʌp·tə/ *prep* doing (something that might be bad or illegal), often secretly ○ *When it's so quiet, I think the kids are up to something.*

up-to-date *adj* having the most recent information, or using the newest methods or tools ○ *We go to a lot of trouble to keep our database up-to-date.*

up-to-the-minute *adj* containing the very latest information or being the newest ○ *up-to-the-minute news reports*

uptown /ʌpˈtɑʊn/ *adj, adv* [not gradable] in or toward the northern part of a city or town ○ *We could walk uptown or we could take the train.*

upward /ˈʌp·wərd/, **upwards** /ˈʌp·wərdz/ *adv* [not gradable] from a lower to a higher position, level, or value ○ *Tachi glanced upward to the stars.* ○ *The stock market charged upward yesterday.*

upward /ˈʌp·wərd/ *adj* [not gradable] ○ *It was an upward climb to the campsite.*

upwind /ʌpˈwɪnd/ *adj, adv* in the direction from which the wind is blowing ○ *Stay upwind of the fumes if you can.* ○ Opposite: DOWNWIND

uranium /jʊˈreɪ·niː·əm/ *n* [U] ***physics*** a heavy metal that is RADIOACTIVE and is used in the production of nuclear power and nuclear weapons

Uranus /ˈjʊr·ə·nəs, jʊˈreɪ·nəs/ *n* [U] the planet seventh in order of distance from the sun, after Saturn and before Neptune ➤ Picture: **solar system**

urban /ˈɜr·bən/ *adj* of or in a city or town ○ *Many Americans were leaving the farm for the promise of urban life.* ○ *Over 82% of Texans live in urban areas.* ○ Compare RURAL

urbane /ɜrˈbeɪn/ *adj* having an understanding of the world and showing experience and confidence ○ *urbane conversation/pleasures* ○ *His urbane manners impressed me.*

urbanization /ˌɜr·bə·nəˈzeɪ·ʃən, -nɑɪˈzeɪ-/ *n* [U] ***social studies*** the process of becoming more like a city

urban renewal *n* [U] the replacement of buildings in a city, esp. of whole neighborhoods of housing

urban sprawl *n* [U] the spread of a city into the area surrounding it, often without planning ○ *Huge tourist attractions have produced choking urban sprawl.*

urchin /ˈɜr·tʃən/ *n* [C] *dated* a small child who is badly dressed and dirty ○ *urchins playing in the street*

urea /jʊˈriː·ə/ *n* [U] ***biology*** a colorless substance found in urine

urethra /jʊˈriː·θrə/ *n* [C] *medical* a tube in mammals that carries urine out of the body, and also carries sperm in males

urge ADVISE /ɜrdʒ/ *v* [T] to encourage someone strongly to do something or to ask that something be done ○ *Party leaders urged her to run for Congress.*

DESIRE /ɜrdʒ/ *n* [C] a strong desire or need ○ *a human/natural urge* ○ *Sometimes I get an urge to go swimming at lunchtime.*

PHRASAL VERB with urge

• **urge** *someone* **on** [M] to encourage someone ○ *His parents urge him on to greater and greater accomplishments.*

urgent /ˈɜr·dʒənt/ *adj* needing immediate attention ○ *The plumbing in this building is in urgent need of repair.*

urgency /ˈɜr·dʒən·si/ *n* [U] ○ *There was a sense of urgency in her voice.*

urgently /ˈɜr·dʒənt·li/ *adv* ○ *Flood victims urgently need medical care.*

WORD FAMILY urgent			
Nouns	urgency	*Adverbs*	urgently
Adjectives	urgent		

uric acid /ˈjʊr·ɪk ˈæs·əd/ *n* [U] ***biology*** **1** an acid that is produced during METABOLISM (= the processes by which a living thing uses food for energy and growth) and is removed from the body in the urine **2**

urine /ˈjʊr·ən/ *n* [U] ***biology*** liquid waste excreted by people and animals

urinate /ˈjʊr·əˌneɪt/ *v* [I] to excrete urine

urinal /ˈjʊr·ən·əl/ *n* [C] a device to urinate in, used by men and boys and usually attached to a wall

URL *n* [C] *abbreviation for* uniform resource locator (= the address of a page on the Internet) ○ *There you can type in a company's URL to search for records and complaints.*

urn /ɜrn/ *n* [C] a large, round container from which coffee or tea is served, or a decorative container, esp. one that holds the ASHES of the body

U

of a dead person after it has been CREMATED (= burned)

us /ʌs, əs/ *pronoun* [pl] the person speaking with other people included; the form of "we" that follows the verb ○ *Thanks for giving us a lift to the airport.*

US /ˌjuː ˈes/ *n* [U] *abbreviation for* United States ○ *a US citizen*

USA /ˌjuː ˌes ˈeɪ/ *n* [U] *abbreviation for* United States of America.

usage **USE OF WORDS** /ˈjuː·sɪdʒ, -zɪdʒ/ *n* [C/U] the way in which words are used by the people who speak and write a particular language, or an example of such use ○ [C] *We use African-American, which is the current preferred usage.*

USE OF THINGS /ˈjuː·sɪdʒ, -zɪdʒ/ *n* [U] the use of something, the way in which it is used, or how much it has been used ○ *The study tracks credit card usage over the last ten years.*

USB *n* [C] *abbreviation for* universal serial bus (= a type of computer connection that is used for printers and many other devices) ○ *I plugged my digital camera into the USB port and the operating system instantly recognized it.*

use **PUT INTO SERVICE** /juːz/ *v* [T] to put something into your service for a purpose ○ *Do you know how to use a computer?* ○ *We could use your help.* ○ *She uses so many big words, it's hard to understand her.*

use /juːs/ *n* [C/U] **1** [C] *There are so many uses for computers in the classroom.* ○ [U] *We need to look closely at our energy use and its environmental impact.* ○ [U] *Do you have any use for these old magazines?* ○ [U] *After her stroke, she lost the use of her left arm.* **2** If someone or something is of no use, it cannot be of help: [U] *There's no use paying for a permit if you won't need it.* ○ [U] *He was of no use to us because he couldn't work every day.*

usable /ˈjuː·zə·bəl/ *adj* ○ *The house needs a lot of work to make it usable.*

useful /ˈjuːs·fəl/ *adj* helping you to do or obtain something ○ *Your advice was very useful, saving me a lot of time.*

usefully /ˈjuːs·fə·li/ *adv* ○ *I was usefully occupied packing dishes all morning.*

usefulness /ˈjuːs·fəl·nəs/ *n* [U] ○ *There is no question of the usefulness of aspirin.*

U

useless /ˈjuː·sləs/ *adj* of no value; worthless ○ *With dead batteries, the flashlight was useless.*

user /ˈjuː·zər/ *n* [C] ○ *a library/computer user* ○ *The number of cell phone users has grown tremendously.*

WORD CHOICES use

See also: **valuable**

If something is useful because it helps you do or achieve something, you can describe it as **helpful** or **valuable**.

*They gave us some really **helpful** advice.*

*He was able to provide the police with some **valuable** information.*

The adjective **invaluable** means "extremely useful."

*The Internet is an **invaluable** resource for teachers.*

An activity which is useful but requires a lot of effort is sometimes described as **worthwhile**.

*It's a difficult course but it's very **worthwhile**.*

Something which is useful because it is simple to use is often described as **handy**.

*That's a **handy** little gadget.*

If speech or writing contains a lot of useful information, you can describe it as **informative** or **instructive**.

*It's an interesting and highly **informative** book.*

MAKE IT LESS /juːz/ *v* [T] to reduce the amount of something ○ *We have used all the funds in that account.*

ACT SELFISH /juːz/ *v* [T] to be friendly toward someone for your own advantage or purposes ○ *She used him to help her get into movies and then discarded him.*

WORD FAMILY use

Nouns	usage	*Adjectives*	reusable
	use		used
	misuse		unused
	usefulness		usable
	user		useful
Verbs	use		useless
	misuse	*Adverbs*	usefully
	reuse		

IDIOM with use

• **in use** being used ○ *Is the washing machine in use right now?*

PHRASAL VERB with use

• **use up** *something* [M] to use all of something, so that nothing is left ○ *Have we used up all of the paper towels?*

used /juːzd/ *adj* [not gradable] already owned or put to a purpose by someone else; not new ○ *We're looking for a used car in good condition.*

IDIOM with used

• **used to** *(doing) something* familiar with a condition or activity ○ *We were used to a cold climate, so the weather didn't bother us.* ○ *She's used to working hard.*

used to /ˈjuːs·tə, -tʊ, -ˌtuː/ *modal verb* done or experienced in the past, but no longer done or experienced ○ *I used to eat meat, but now I'm a vegetarian.* ○ *We don't go to the movies now as often as we used to.*

user-friendly *adj* easy for people to work with ○ *This software is very user-friendly.*

usher /ˈʌʃ·ər/ *v* [T always + adv/prep] to show someone where to go or where to sit ○ [T] *The guard ushered the jury members into the courtroom.*

usher /ˈʌʃ·ər/ *n* [C] ○ *The usher showed us to front-row seats.*

PHRASAL VERB with usher

• **usher** *someone/something* **in** [M] to welcome someone, or signal the beginning of something ○ *The party was an elegant way to usher in the new year.*

usual /ˈjuː·ʒə·wəl/ *adj* [not gradable] happening or done most of the time; ordinary ○ *I'll put the keys in the usual place.* ○ *If you can believe it, the food was worse than usual.*

usually /ˈjuː·ʒə·wə·li/ *adv* [not gradable] ○ *He usually gets home from work at about six.*

usurp /jʊˈsɜrp, -ˈzɜrp/ *v* [T] *fml* to take power or control of something by force or without the right to do so ○ *Some senators fear the organization will usurp congressional power.*

utensil /jʊˈten·səl/ *n* [C] a device or tool having a particular use, esp. in a kitchen ○ *We packed plates, cups, napkins, and eating utensils for the picnic.*

uterine /ˈjuː·ţ·ə·rən, -ˌrɑɪn/ *adj* [not gradable] *medical* of or relating to the uterus ○ *uterine cancer*

uterus /ˈjuː·ţ·ə·rəs/ *n* [C] ***biology*** the organ in the body of a woman or other female mammal in which a baby develops before birth; WOMB

utility Ⓐ **USEFULNESS** /juːˈtɪl·əţ·i/ *n* [U] ability to satisfy a particular need; usefulness ○ *Its basic utility lies in being able to drive where other vehicles can't go.*

PUBLIC SERVICE /juːˈtɪl·əţ·i/ *n* [C] a supply of gas, electricity, water, or telephone service to homes and businesses, or a business that supplies such services ○ *a utility bill* ○ *After I call the movers, I'll call to have the utilities turned on.*

utility pole *n* [C] a TELEPHONE POLE

utilize Ⓐ /ˈjuː·ţ·əlˌɑɪz/ *v* [T] to make use of something ○ *The library's great collection allowed me to utilize many rare sources.*

utilization Ⓐ /ˌjuː·ţ·əl·əˈzeɪ·ʃən/ *n* [U] the use of something

utmost /ˈʌt·moʊst/ *adj* [not gradable] greatest or most or farthest ○ *Speed was of the utmost importance.*

utmost /ˈʌt·moʊst/ *n* [U] the most or best that is possible ○ *He's doing his utmost to disrupt the proceedings.*

utopia /jʊˈtoʊ·piː·ə/ *n* [C/U] ***social studies*** a perfect society in which everyone is happy ○ [U] *The idea of America as utopia has recurred throughout our history.* ○ [C] *When plans to rebuild the neighborhood were first announced, I'd been hoping for a utopia.*

utopian /jʊˈtoʊ·piː·ən/ *adj* ***social studies*** having the characteristics and organization of a perfect society ○ *a utopian vision* ○ *utopian communities*

utter **COMPLETE** /ˈʌţ·ər/ *adj* [not gradable] complete or extreme ○ *What an utter fool I was!*

utterly /ˈʌţ·ər·li/ *adv* ○ *She felt isolated and utterly alone.*

SAY /ˈʌţ·ər/ *v* [T] to say something or make a sound with your voice ○ *She sat through the entire meeting and didn't utter a word.*

utterance /ˈʌţ·ə·rəns/ *n* [C] *fml* ○ *We hope their utterances will be matched by their actions.*

U-turn **180 DEGREE TURN** *n* [C] a turn like a U, made by a vehicle to go back in the direction from which it came ○ *I was making a U-turn into the southbound lanes.*

CHANGE OF OPINION *n* [C] a complete change from one opinion or plan to an opposite one

U

V v

V LETTER, **v** /viː/ *n* [C] *pl* **V's, Vs, v's, vs** the 22nd letter of the English alphabet

NUMBER, **v** /viː, faɪv/ *number* the ROMAN NUMERAL for the number 5

vacant EMPTY /ˈveɪ·kənt/ *adj* [not gradable] (of a place) not being lived in or used, or (of a job or office) available for someone to do ○ *We have three vacant apartments in our building.*
vacancy /ˈveɪ·kən·si/ *n* [C] a place or position that is available ○ *The motel was full – we saw the "No Vacancy" sign.* ○ *These companies have a lot of vacancies* (= jobs) *to fill, and they pay well.*

NOT AWARE /ˈveɪ·kənt/ *adj* not showing much awareness or interest in the world around you ○ *There was a sad, vacant look in his eyes.*

vacate /ˈveɪ·keɪt, veɪˈkeɪt/ *v* [T] to leave a place or position ○ *When he left the university, he had to vacate his university-provided housing.*

vacation /veɪˈkeɪ·ʃən, və-/ *n* [C/U] a period of time to relax or travel for pleasure instead of doing your usual work or school activities ○ [C] *The family had just left for a vacation in the Bahamas.* ○ [U] *We always went on vacation in August.*
vacation /veɪˈkeɪ·ʃən, və-/ *v* [I always + adv/prep] ○ *He was vacationing in San Francisco.*
vacationer /veɪˈkeɪ·ʃə·nər, və-/ *n* [C] ○ *Tourists and winter vacationers are now key to the economy.*

vaccine /ˈvæk·siːn, vækˈsiːn/ *n* [C] a special substance that you take into your body to prevent a disease, and that contains a weakened or dead form of the disease-causing organism
vaccinate /ˈvæk·səˌneɪt/ *v* [T] ○ *Our children have been vaccinated for measles and other childhood diseases.*
vaccination /ˌvæk·səˈneɪ·ʃən/ *n* [C] ○ *Most states require all children to receive the vaccination before beginning elementary school.*

vacillate /ˈvæs·əˌleɪt/ *v* [I] to be unable to decide something and esp. to continue to change opinions ○ *The president continues to vacillate over foreign policy.*

vacuole /ˈvæk·jəˌwoʊl/ *n* [C] ***biology*** a space inside a living cell, often containing a liquid ➤ Picture: **cell**

vacuous /ˈvæk·jə·wəs/ *adj* not showing purpose, meaning, or intelligence; empty ○ *To seem real to your readers, your characters must not be vacuous, but complex human beings with ordinary difficulties and goals.*

vacuum /ˈvæk·juːm, -jʊ·əm/ *n* [C] ***physics*** a space without any gas or other matter in it, or a space from which most of the air or gas has been removed ○ *Edison knew that he had to create a vacuum inside the lightbulb.* ○ *(fig.) No marriage exists in a vacuum* (= in a situation where nothing else has any influence).

vacuum /ˈvæk·juːm, -jʊ·əm/ *v* [I/T] to clean something by using a VACUUM CLEANER ○ [T] *Then I vacuumed the carpet.*

vacuum bottle *n* [C] a THERMOS

vacuum cleaner, *short form* **vacuum** *n* [C] a piece of electrical equipment that sucks dirt from floors and other surfaces

vagina /vəˈdʒɑɪ·nə/ *n* [C] the part of the body of a woman or other female mammal that connects the outer sex organs to the uterus
vaginal /ˈvædʒ·ən·əl/ *adj* [not gradable]

vagrant /ˈveɪ·grənt/ *n* [C] a person who has no home or job and who moves from place to place

vague /veɪg/ *adj* [-*er*/-*est* only] **1** not clearly stated, described, or explained, or not clearly seen or felt ○ *She had a vague feeling that something had gone terribly wrong.* ○ *I have only a vague memory of the house where I lived as a child.* **2** A person who is vague is not able or does not wish to state, describe, or explain something clearly: *Officials were vague about the ship's location.*
vaguely /ˈveɪ·gli/ *adv* ○ *She stood in silence for several minutes, only vaguely aware of the people around her.*

vain UNSUCCESSFUL /veɪn/ *adj* [-*er*/-*est* only] unsuccessful or useless; failing to achieve a purpose ○ *a vain attempt to avoid responsibility* ○ *Employers clearly hoped that the workers would stay longer, but their efforts were largely in vain* (= unsuccessful).

SELFISH /veɪn/ *adj* [-*er*/-*est* only] too proud of yourself, esp. in your appearance or achievements ○ Related noun: VANITY

valedictorian /ˌvæl·əˌdɪkˈtɔːr·iː·ən, -ˈtoʊr-/ *n* [C] a student, usually the one who has the best school record in a group of students, and who makes a speech at the group's GRADUATION ceremony (= ceremony to recognize their studies are completed)

valence /ˈveɪ·ləns/ *n* [C] ***chemistry*** the ability of an atom to combine with other atoms, measured by the number of ELECTRONS it will lose, add, or share

valentine /ˈvæl·ənˌtɑɪn/ *n* [C] someone you love or admire affectionately

valentine card, *short form* **valentine** *n* [C] a decorative card given on VALENTINE'S DAY to someone that you admire or love ○ *Schoolteachers get lots of valentine cards from their first-graders on Valentine's Day.*

Valentine's Day *n* [C] February 14th, when people give small presents, chocolate candy, flowers, or cards to someone they admire or love.

valet /væˈleɪ, ˈvæl·eɪ/ *n* [C] (esp. in the past) the personal male servant of a wealthy man, or (in the present) an employee of a restaurant or hotel, who puts your car in a parking space for you ○ *Valet parking is available for our customers.*

valiant /ˈvæl·jənt/ *adj* brave or determined, esp. when conditions are difficult or dangerous ○ *The team made a valiant effort to take the lead in the third quarter, but they were too far behind.*

valid Ⓐ /ˈvæl·əd/ *adj* **1** based on truth or reason; able to be accepted ○ *The money was gone, and the only valid conclusion was that someone had stolen it.* **2** A valid document is legally acceptable, usually because it has been done according to official rules: *You must have a valid driver's license to drive a car.*
validate Ⓐ /ˈvæl·əˌdeɪt/ *v* [T] to make something officially acceptable or approved ○ *A signature is one of the ways you validate checks and contracts.*
validation Ⓐ /ˌvæl·əˈdeɪ·ʃən/ *n* [U] ○ *External validation of the teachers' assessments is recommended.*
validity Ⓐ /vəˈlɪd·ət̬·i/ *n* [U] ○ *Some experts questioned the validity of the president's ideas.*
validly Ⓐ /ˈvæl·əd·li/ *adv*

valley /ˈvæl·i/ *n* [C] an area of low land between hills or mountains, often with a river or stream running through it

valor, *Cdn, Br* **valour** /ˈvæl·ər/ *n* [U] *fml* great bravery ○ *Six members of the platoon already have been recommended for medals of valor.*

value IMPORTANCE /ˈvæl·juː/ *n* [U] importance, worth, or benefit ○ *They discussed the value of having cameras in the courtroom.* ○ *The value of the thing* (= its worth in money) *was probably only a few dollars but it had great sentimental value.*
value /ˈvæl·juː/ *v* [T] to consider something as important and worth having ○ *I value his friendship more than I can ever say.*
valuable /ˈvæl·jə·wə·bəl, -jə·bəl/ *adj* important, useful, or beneficial ○ *Niekro was named the most valuable player in baseball.* ○ *They perform valuable services for poor, rural women.*

WORD CHOICES value

See also: **useful**

If something is valuable because it helps you do or achieve something, you can describe it as **helpful** or **useful**.

They gave us some really ***helpful*** *advice.*

She made a really ***useful*** *contribution to the project.*

Something which is valuable because it produces useful results may be described as **constructive**, **productive**, or **fruitful**.

It was a very ***constructive*** *discussion.*

We had a very ***productive*** *meeting and dealt with a lot of problems.*

It was a ***fruitful*** *partnership for both organizations.*

An activity which is valuable but requires a lot of effort is sometimes described as **worthwhile**.

It's a difficult course but it's very ***worthwhile.***

If speech or writing contains a lot of valuable information, you can describe it as **informative** or **instructive**.

It's an interesting and highly ***informative*** *book.*

MONEY /ˈvæl·juː/ *n* [C/U] the amount of money that can be received for something; the worth of something in money ○ [C] *a decline in property values* ○ [U] *The value of the dollar fell against the mark and the yen yesterday.*
value /ˈvæl·juː/ *v* [T] to state the worth of something ○ *The painting was valued at $450,000.*
valuable /ˈvæl·jə·wə·bəl, -jə·bəl/ *adj* worth a lot of money ○ *ABC's valuable radio and TV licenses are up for renewal.*
valuables /ˈvæl·jə·wə·bəlz, -jə·bəlz/ *pl n* small objects, esp. jewelry, that can be sold for a lot of money ○ *You may store your valuables in the hotel safe while you are here.*
valuation /ˌvæl·jəˈweɪ·ʃən/ *n* [C] the act of saying how much something is worth ○ *When Wall Street finally realized its dot-com valuations were off by 90% to 100%, the stock market damage was spectacular.*

NUMBER /ˈvæl·juː/ *n* [C] ***mathematics*** the number or amount that a letter or symbol represents

ART /ˈvæl·juː/ *n* [C] ***art*** the degree of light or darkness in a color, or the relation between light and shade in a work of art

WORD FAMILY value

Nouns		Adjectives	
	valuables		valuable
	value		invaluable
	values	Verbs	value
	valuation		undervalue

value judgment *n* [C] a personal opinion about whether something is good or bad

values /ˈvæl·juːz/ *pl n* the principles that help you to decide what is right and wrong, and how to act in various situations ○ *The political platform is based on traditional values associated with the rural South.*

valve /vælv/ *n* [C] a device that controls the flow of air or liquid from one place to another ○ *a heart valve* ○ *The explosion apparently was caused by a faulty gas valve.*

vampire /ˈvæm·pɑɪr/ *n* [C] an imaginary creature, said to be a dead person returned to life, who sucks blood from people at night

van /væn/ *n* [C] a box-shaped road vehicle of medium size ○ *a delivery van*

vandal /ˈvæn·dəl/ *n* [C usually pl] a person, often in a group, who intentionally damages public or private property
vandalism /ˈvæn·dəlˌɪz·əm/ *n* [U] ○ *The mayor promised to crack down on vandalism.*

V

vandalize /ˈvæn·dᵊlˌɑɪz/ *v* [T] ○ *The teenager was accused of vandalizing cars.*

vanguard /ˈvæŋ·gɑrd/ *n* [U] **1** the front part of a group of people who are moving forward, esp. an army **2** The vanguard is also the people who are making changes or new developments in something: *These craftspeople are in the vanguard in the art of modern furniture design.*

vanilla /vəˈnɪl·ə, -ˈnel·ə/ *n* [U] a substance made from the seeds of a plant, used to give flavor to sweet foods ○ *vanilla yogurt*

vanish /ˈvæn·ɪʃ/ *v* [I] to disappear or stop existing, esp. suddenly ○ *Her smile vanished.*

vanishing point *n* [U] ***art*** the point in a drawing or painting where parallel lines seem to meet at a far distance ➤ Picture: **perspective**

vanity /ˈvæn·ət̬·i/ *n* [U] the personal characteristic of being too proud of and interested in yourself, esp. in your appearance or achievements ○ Related adjective: VAIN SELFISH

vanquish /ˈvæŋ·kwɪʃ, væn-/ *v* [T] to defeat completely ○ *Smallpox, a once deadly disease, has now been vanquished.*

vantage point /ˈvænt·ɪdʒˌpɔɪnt/ *n* [C] **1** a place that provides a good view ○ *From our vantage point atop the mountain, we could see the whole city below.* **2** A vantage point is also a way of thinking or a set of opinions based on your particular situation: *Recently, I asked him from his vantage point how the media have changed over the years.*

vapor, *Cdn, Br* **vapour** /ˈveɪ·pər/ *n* [C/U] ***chemistry*** a gas that escapes from a liquid or solid, esp. as a result of heating ○ [U] *Warm air is able to hold more water vapor than cold air.*

vaporize /ˈveɪ·pəˌrɑɪz/ *v* [I/T] ***chemistry*** to turn from a solid or liquid into a gas, or to cause this to happen ○ [I] *When water boils, it vaporizes.*

vaporization /ˌveɪ·pə·rəˈzeɪ·ʃən/ *n* [U] ***chemistry*** the process of changing from a solid or liquid into a gas

variable Ⓐ **CHANGING** /ˈver·iː·ə·bəl, ˈvær-/ *adj* likely to change, or showing change or difference as a characteristic ○ *Our weather is very variable in the spring.*

variable Ⓐ /ˈver·iː·ə·bəl, ˈvær-/ *n* [C] something that can change, esp. in a way that cannot be known in advance ○ *Among the variables that could prevent us from finishing the building by June are the weather and the availability of materials.*

variability Ⓐ /ˌver·iː·əˈbɪl·ət̬·i, ˌvær-/ *n* [U] ○ *There is a lot of variability between brands.*

variably Ⓐ /ˈver·iː·ə·bli, ˈvær-/ *adv*

SYMBOL /ˈver·iː·ə·bəl, ˈvær-/ *n* [C] ***mathematics*** a letter or symbol that represents any of a set of values

variance Ⓐ /ˈver·iː·əns, ˈvær-/ *n* [C] permission to do something differently from the official or usual way ○ *He requested a variance to build an addition to his house.*

IDIOM with variance

• **at variance** *fml* different ○ *The official census count was at variance with the count we had made.*

variant Ⓐ /ˈver·iː·ənt, ˈvær-/ *n* [C] something that differs slightly from other similar things ○ *There are four variants of malaria, all transmitted to humans by mosquitoes.*

variation /ˌver·iːˈeɪ·ʃən, ˌvær-/ *n* [C/U] ○ See at VARY

varicose veins /ˈvær·əˌkoʊs ˈveɪnz/ *pl n* a condition in which the tubes that carry blood, esp. those in the legs, are swollen and can be seen on the skin ○ *Pregnant women often get varicose veins.*

varied /ˈver·iːd, ˈvær-/ *adj* having or showing many different types, or changing often ○ *The varied symptoms included severe muscle pain, headaches, and dizziness.*

variety **DIFFERENCE** /vəˈrɑɪ·ət̬·i/ *n* [U] the characteristic of frequently changing, or of including many different types or things ○ *The markets offer a variety of fresh fruits and vegetables.* ○ *You can get magazines there that have a little bit more variety.*

TYPE /vəˈrɑɪ·ət̬·i/ *n* [C] a type, esp. one among a group of things that share general features and differ in some details ○ *Several different varieties of sparrows live around here.*

various /ˈver·iː·əs, ˈvær-/ *adj* [not gradable] several and different ○ *He underwent various treatments for the disease, none of them successful.* ○ *We enjoy eating in various types of restaurants.* ○ *After holding various jobs in different states, he settled in Oregon and opened a law office in Portland.*

variously /ˈver·iː·ə·sli, ˈvær-/ *adv* [not gradable] in several different ways or at several different times ○ *Studies variously put the US homeless population today at a high of 2 million and a low of 230,000.*

varnish /ˈvɑr·nɪʃ/ *n* [C/U] a clear liquid that you can put on a wooden surface, to protect it and give it a shiny, attractive appearance after drying ○ [U] *The wood can be stained any color and then sealed with a coat of varnish.*

varsity /ˈvɑr·sət̬·i/ *n* [C usually sing] one of the main sports teams at a university, college, or school ○ *He was hoping to make the varsity next year.*

varsity /ˈvɑr·sət̬·i/ *adj* [not gradable] ○ *Eight varsity players will return to the football team next season.*

vary Ⓐ /ˈver·i, ˈvær·i/ *v* [I/T] to change in some way, or to cause similar things to differ ○ [I] *The value of stocks will vary from month to month.* ○ [T] *My husband varies the vegetables he plants each year.*

variation Ⓐ /ˌver·iːˈeɪ·ʃən, ˌvær-/ *n* [C/U] **1** change in quality, amount, or level ○ [U] *The variation in the price during the past month is startling.* **2** A variation also is a difference, or a thing that differs slightly from another of its type: [C] *Her movies are all variations on the same theme.*

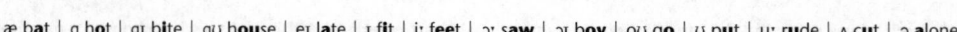

WORD FAMILY vary			
Nouns	variable variance variant variation variety	*Adjectives*	variable varied various varying invariable
Verbs	vary	*Adverbs*	invariably variously

vascular /ˈvæs·kjə·lər/ *adj* [not gradable] ***biology*** containing VEINS (= thin tubes that carry blood in animals and other liquid in plants)

vase /veɪs, veɪz, vɑz/ *n* [C] a container for holding flowers or for decoration ○ *Please put this vase of flowers on the table.*

vasectomy /vəˈsek·tə·mi, veɪˈzek-/ *n* [C/U] the medical operation of cutting the tubes through which a man's SEMEN (= liquid containing sperm) move, in order to make him unable to make a woman pregnant

vassal /ˈvæs·əl/ *n* [C] ***world history*** a person in the Middle Ages who promises to be loyal to a LORD (= a man of high social rank) who will protect him or her

vast /væst/ *adj* [-*er*/-*est* only] extremely large ○ *The vast majority of our students – nearly 90 percent – graduate within four years.*
vastly /ˈvæs·tli/ *adv* ○ *I think the original movie was vastly superior to the remake.*

vat /væt/ *n* [C] a large container for mixing or storing liquids, esp. as used in industry ○ *The grapes are crushed in deep wooden vats.*

vault ARCH /vɔːlt/ *n* [C] a type of arch that supports a roof or ceiling, esp. in a church or public building, or a ceiling or roof supported by several of these arches

ROOM /vɔːlt/ *n* [C] **1** a room, esp. in or under the ground floor of a large building, that is used to store things safely ○ *The museum keeps many of its treasures in temperature-controlled storage vaults.* **2** In a bank, a vault is where money, jewelry, important documents, etc., are locked for protection.

JUMP /vɔːlt/ *v* [I/T] **1** to jump over something ○ [I/T] *He vaulted (over) the gate.* **2** To vault is also to move someone suddenly to a much higher or more important position: [T] *The speech vaulted him into the national spotlight.*

vaunted /ˈvɔːnt·əd, ˈvɑnt-/ *adj* [not gradable] praised too frequently ○ *His much vaunted new plan has serious weaknesses.*

VCR /ˌviː·siːˈɑr/, **videocassette recorder** *n* [C] a machine that can record pictures and sounds from a television onto VIDEOTAPE, and on which videotapes can be played ○ *They have a sale on VCRs and CD players.*

VD *n* [U] *abbreviation for* VENEREAL DISEASE

veal /viːl/ *n* [U] meat from very young cattle

vector /ˈvek·tər/ *n* [C] ***physics*** **1** a representation of something that has both direction and size, usually an arrow whose direction represents direction and length represents size **2** ***physics*** A **vector quantity** is something that can be represented by a vector.

veep /viːp/ *n* [C] *infml* a VICE PRESIDENT, esp. the vice president of the US

veer /vɪr/ *v* [I] to suddenly change direction ○ *The officer saw the car veer off the side of the road.*

vegetable /ˈvedʒ·tə·bəl, ˈvedʒ·əṭ·ə-/ *n* [C] **1** a plant that is used as food, or the part of a plant, such as a root, stem, or flower, that is used as food ○ *For vegetables, we eat a lot of broccoli, spinach, and corn.* **2** A person may be called a vegetable if the person is completely unable to move and to react, usually because of brain damage.

WORD FAMILY vegetable			
Nouns	vegetable vegetarian vegetarianism	*Adjectives*	vegetarian

vegetarian /ˌvedʒ·əˈter·iː·ən/ *n* [C] a person who does not eat meat for health or for religious or moral reasons ○ *Some vegetarians avoid eggs and dairy products as well as meat.*
vegetarian /ˌvedʒ·əˈter·iː·ən/ *adj* [not gradable] ○ *a vegetarian diet*
vegetarianism /ˌvedʒ·əˈter·iː·əˌnɪz·əm/ *n* [U]

vegetate /ˈvedʒ·əˌteɪt/, *slang* **veg (out)** /ˈvedʒ ˈɑʊt/ *v* [I] to live or spend time in a way that lacks physical and mental activity and effort ○ *The children just vegetate in front of the TV all morning.*

vegetation /ˌvedʒ·əˈteɪ·ʃən/ *n* [U] ***biology*** plants in general, or the plants that are found in a particular area
vegetative /ˈvedʒ·əˌteɪṭ·ɪv/ *adj* [not gradable]

vehement /ˈviː·ə·mənt/ *adj* expressing very strong feelings, or showing great energy or force ○ *They are killing some of the birds, to the vehement protests of animal-rights groups.*
vehemently /ˈviː·ə·mənt·li/ *adv* ○ *The defense counsel vehemently objected.*

vehicle Ⓐ MACHINE /ˈviːˌhɪk·əl, ˈviː·ɪ·kəl/ *n* [C] something used to transport people or goods, esp. something used on land or roads ○ *an underwater vehicle* ○ *The snow stranded hundreds of vehicles on an interstate highway.*
vehicular /viːˈhɪk·jə·lər/ *adj* [not gradable] ○ *Pedestrian and vehicular traffic in the neighborhood have both increased.*

WAY /ˈviːˌhɪk·əl, ˈviː·ɪ·kəl/ *n* [C usually sing] a way of achieving something ○ *Many say Morse code is an outdated vehicle for communication in today's high-tech world.* ○ *She used her celebrity status as a vehicle to run for political office.*

veil /veɪl/ *n* [C] a piece of thin material worn to protect or hide the face or head ○ *The bride wore a veil made of French lace.* ○ *(fig.) A veil of secrecy*

V

surrounded the appointment of the new college president.

veil /veɪl/ *v* [T] ○ *In that country, women are veiled when they go out in public.*

veiled /veɪld/ *adj* (of statements, opinions, or intentions) not direct or clearly expressed ○ *He took the comment as a veiled threat.*

vein TUBE /veɪn/ *n* [C] ***biology*** **1** a tube that carries blood to the heart from the other parts of the body **2** A vein is also any of the many small tubes in the leaves of plants that carry SAP (= liquid containing a plant's food). ○ Compare ARTERY TUBE

LAYER /veɪn/ *n* [C] a layer of a substance in a crack in rocks or earth ○ *a vein of iron ore*

MOOD /veɪn/ *n* [U] a style or a temporary mood ○ *She published many novels and stories in the romantic vein then popular.*

Velcro /ˈvel·kroʊ/ *n* [U] *trademark* special cloth material having two rough surfaces that stick together when pressed, used for fastening clothing and other objects

velocity /vəˈlɑs·əṭ·i/ *n* [C] ***physics*** the speed at which something is traveling ○ *The wind velocity recorded at the airport was 78 miles per hour at 4 p.m.*

velour /vəˈlʊr/ *n* [U] a cloth similar to VELVET with a soft surface

velvet /ˈvel·vət/ *n* [U] a cloth with a soft, furry surface

velvety /ˈvel·vəṭ·i/ *adj* soft, like velvet ○ *She patted the dog's velvety ears.*

vena cava /ˌviː·nə ˈkeɪ·və/ *n* [C] *pl* **venae cavae** ***biology*** one of the two very large VEINS (= tubes that carry blood) that take blood without oxygen to the heart

vendetta /venˈdeṭ·ə/ *n* [C] a strong desire to harm a person or group, often because of political reasons or feelings of hate ○ *They accused the special prosecutor of carrying on a vendetta against the White House.*

vending machine /ˈven·dɪŋ·məˌʃiːn/ *n* [C] a machine you put money into to buy small items such as packages of food, candy, and drinks

vendor /ˈven·dər/ *n* [C] **1** a person or company that sells goods or services ○ *Our company deals with many vendors of women's clothing.* **2** A vendor is also a person who sells food or goods on the street: *a hot dog vendor* ○ *a street vendor*

veneer /vəˈnɪr/ *n* [C/U] **1** a thin layer of decorative wood or other material used to cover a cheaper or less attractive material ○ [C] *It's a pine table with a mahogany veneer.* **2** A veneer is also something that hides something unpleasant or unwanted: [U] *He had a veneer of sophistication but was really just a bully.*

venerate /ˈven·əˌreɪt/ *v* [T] to honor or have great respect for a person or thing ○ *The American writer Mark Twain has been venerated for almost a century.*

venerable /ˈven·ə·rə·bəl/ *adj* respected, esp. because of long experience or age ○ *The venerable American jeweler, Tiffany & Company, appointed a new president.*

venereal disease /vəˈnɪr·iː·əl/, *abbreviation* **VD** *n* [C/U] a disease caused or spread by sexual activity with another person

venetian blind /vəˌniː·ʃənˈblaɪnd/ *n* [C] a set of narrow, horizontal pieces of wood, plastic, or metal that cover a window and can be raised or set at different angles to block light from the outside or let it in

vengeance /ˈven·dʒəns/ *n* [U] an action against someone to punish that person for having hurt you ○ *She cried out for vengeance.*

vengeful /ˈvendʒ·fəl/ *adj fml* desiring to hurt someone, often violently, in order to punish that person for having hurt you ○ *We are not vengeful people but we want justice.*

venison /ˈven·ə·sən/ *n* [U] the flesh of a deer used as meat

Venn diagram /ˈven ˌdɑɪ·əˌɡræm/ *n* [C] ***mathematics*** a drawing of circles that partly cross and cover each other, in which each circle represents a set and an area where they cross contains parts belonging to more than one of the sets

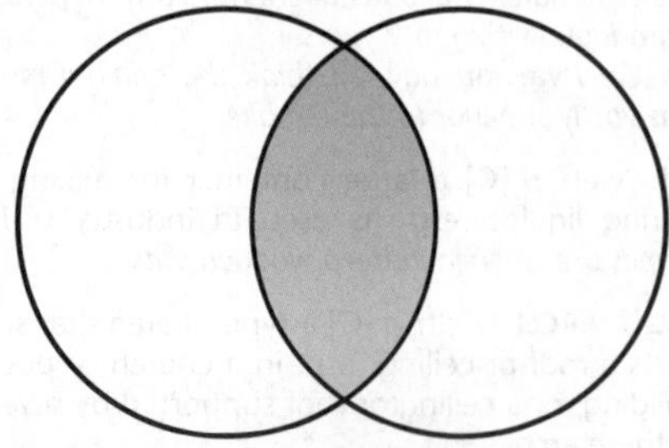

VENN DIAGRAM

venom /ˈven·əm/ *n* [U] a poisonous liquid produced by some snakes, insects, and SPIDERS when they bite ○ (*fig.*) *His diary was full of venom and hate for everyone in authority.*

venomous /ˈven·ə·məs/ *adj* ○ *a venomous snake/spider*

vent OPENING /vent/ *n* [C] an opening that allows air, smoke, or gas to escape or enter an enclosed space ○ *The residents of the basement apartment ran outside after smelling smoke coming through a vent.*

EXPRESS FEELINGS /vent/ *v* [T] to express a negative emotion forcefully ○ *Walking relieves a lot of tension and it's a good way to vent frustration.*

ventilate /ˈvent·əlˌeɪt/ *v* [T] to cause fresh air to enter and move around an enclosed space ○ *Public buildings must be safe, clean, well lighted, and properly ventilated.*

ventilation /ˌvent·əlˈeɪ·ʃən/ *n* [U]

ventricle /ˈven·trɪ·kəl/ *n* [C] ***biology*** each of the two main spaces in the heart, left and right

venture /ˈven·tʃər/ *n* [C] an activity or plan of action, often in business, that involves risk or uncertainty ○ *His most recent business venture ended in bankruptcy.*
venture /ˈven·tʃər/ *v* [I/T] **1** to risk going somewhere or doing something that might be dangerous or unpleasant ○ [I always + adv/prep] *He wanted to venture into the mountainous wilderness of the countryside.* **2** *fml* To venture something is to attempt it when you are likely to be wrong or to be criticized: [T] *I wouldn't venture an opinion about that.*

venue /ˈven·juː/ *n* [C] the place where a public event or meeting happens ○ *They changed the venue at the last minute because they realized the meeting room would have been much too small.*

Venus /ˈviː·nəs/ *n* [U] the planet second in order of distance from the sun, after Mercury and before the earth ➤ Picture: **solar system**

veranda, **verandah** /vəˈræn·də/ *n* [C] a raised, open area, often covered, attached to the front or side of a house, esp. common in the southern US ○ *I went up the walk onto the big veranda and knocked on the door.*

verb /vɜrb/ *n* [C] ***grammar*** a word or phrase that describes an action, condition, or experience ○ *"Run," "keep," and "feel" are all verbs.*

verbal SPOKEN /ˈvɜr·bəl/ *adj* [not gradable] spoken rather than written ○ *Our apartment lease is really just a verbal agreement.*
verbally /ˈvɜr·bə·li/ *adv* ○ *The judge then verbally agreed to the attorney's request.*
RELATING TO WORDS /ˈvɜr·bəl/ *adj* [not gradable] ***grammar*** having to do with or using words ○ *The children were tested for their physical coordination and verbal skills.*

verbatim /vərˈbeɪt̬·əm/ *adj, adv* [not gradable] using exactly the same words that were originally used ○ *Speeches were reported verbatim and often ran to several columns.*

verdict /ˈvɜr·dɪkt/ *n* [C] **1** a decision by a JURY as to whether someone is guilty after having heard the facts given at a trial ○ *The jury reached/returned a verdict of not guilty after six hours of deliberation.* **2** A verdict is also any judgment or opinion given after considering the facts of a situation: *City planners think it's a good idea to ban traffic from downtown streets, but the public's verdict is that it's a stupid idea.*

verge /vɜrdʒ/ *n* [C] the edge, border, or limit of something

IDIOM with verge

• **on the verge of** *something* very near to doing or experiencing something ○ *He was on the verge of saying something but stopped and shook his head.*

PHRASAL VERB with verge

• **verge on** *something* to come close to being or becoming the stated thing ○ *Some parts of the biography verge on the trivial, and the book would be much better if it were much shorter.*

verification /ˌver·ə·fəˈkeɪ·ʃən/ *n* [C/U] the process of testing or finding out if something is true, real, accurate, etc. ○ *I've never asked for verification of his resume.*

verify /ˈver·əˌfɑɪ/ *v* [T] to make certain or prove that something is true or accurate ○ *The report could not immediately be verified.* ○ [+ (*that*) clause] *Tests verified (that) Beck had torn a shoulder muscle.*

verisimilitude /ˌver·ə·səˈmɪl·əˌtuːd/ *n* [U] ***literature*** the quality of appearing realistic or true

veritable /ˈver·ət̬·ə·bəl/ *adj* [not gradable] (used to emphasize how great or unusual something is by comparing it to something else) ○ *If current projections hold, Montgomery County will experience a veritable explosion in its school-age population* (= it will have many more students).

vermin /ˈvɜr·mən/ *pl n* small animals and insects that are harmful or annoying and are often difficult to control ○ *She reported an infestation of vermin, including rats, in the basement of the apartment house.*

vernacular /vərˈnæk·jə·lər, vəˈnæk-/ *n* [C/U] the form of a language commonly spoken by the people of a particular region or by a particular group, esp. when it is different from the standard language ○ [U] *Much of his poetry derives from the American pop vernacular.*
vernacular /vərˈnæk·jə·lər, vəˈnæk-/ *adj* ○ *a vernacular expression*

versatile /ˈvɜr·sət̬·əl/ *adj* (of people) able to do many different things or to adjust to new conditions, or (of things) able to be used for many different purposes ○ *He was a versatile guitarist, and recorded with many leading rock bands.* ○ *It is an especially versatile insecticide known to control a range of insects.*
versatility /ˌvɜr·səˈtɪl·ət̬·i/ *n* [U] ○ *Daniels possesses the versatility to play right and left end and tackle.*

verse /vɜrs/ *n* [C/U] ***literature*** **1** writing that is arranged in a rhythmic pattern; poems ○ [U] *She has a talent for writing humorous verse.* **2** A verse is also one of the parts into which a poem or song is divided: [C] *We'll sing only the first and last verses.* **3** A verse is also one of the short parts into which the Bible is divided.

versed /vɜrst/ *adj* prepared by having knowledge or experience of something ○ *He was well versed in all branches of the field and published extensively.*

version Ⓐ /ˈvɜr·ʒən/ *n* [C] **1** a particular form of something that varies from other forms of the same thing ○ *They're producing several versions of the TV commercial to see which one works best.* **2** A version can also be a TRANSLATION: *Originally published in German, it was published in New York in an English-language version.* **3** Someone's version of an event is that person's description of it: *Her version of the accident was completely different from that given by the driver of the other car.*

versus /ˈvɜr·səs/, *abbreviation* **vs.**, *prep* (used to show the names of two teams or sides) against ○

The next soccer match is Mexico versus the United States. ○ *(fig.) It was a question of artistic integrity versus love of money, and money won.*

vertebra /ˈvɜrţ·ə·brə/ *n* [C] *pl* **vertebrae** *medical* one of the small bones that form the SPINE (= the line of bones down the middle of the back)

vertebrate /ˈvɜrt·ə·brət/ *n* [C] ***biology*** an animal that has a SPINE (= bone down the center of the back)

vertebrate /ˈvɜrt·ə·brət/ *adj* [not gradable]

vertex *n* [C] *pl* **vertexes, vertices** ***geometry*** the point where two lines meet to form an angle, or the point that is opposite the base of a shape

vertical /ˈvɜrţ·ɪ·kəl/ *adj* standing or pointing straight up or at an angle of 90 to a horizontal surface or line ○ *Water that had leaked from above formed a vertical line down one wall.* ○ Compare HORIZONTAL

vertigo /ˈvɜrţ·ɪˌgoʊ/ *n* [U] *medical* a feeling that everything is spinning around, causing you to be unable to balance and therefore to fall

verve /vɜrv/ *n* [U] a lot of energy and enthusiasm ○ *She expressed herself with verve and wit.*

very EXTREMELY /ˈver·i/ *adv* [not gradable] (used to add emphasis to an adjective or adverb) to a great degree, or extremely ○ *I was working very hard, but I enjoyed it.* ○ *It's very easy to find our house.* ○ *She was a very good teacher.* ○ *People didn't like him very much.*

EXACT /ˈver·i/ *adj* [not gradable] (used to add emphasis to a noun) exact or particular ○ *I'd heard stories about him and now here he was, the very person I now accompanied.* ○ *This very moment was what he had been waiting for.* ○ *He found the missing paper at the very bottom of the pile.*

IDIOM with very

• **very well** likely ○ *Stress could very well have triggered the attack.*

vesicular /vəˈsɪk·jə·lər/ *adj* [not gradable] ***earth science*** describes rock that contains holes made by gas escaping from cooling LAVA

vessel SHIP /ˈves·əl/ *n* [C] a large boat or ship ○ *A scattering of vessels anchored in the harbor.*

CONTAINER /ˈves·əl/ *n* [C] a container used to hold liquids ○ *We used bowls, pots, bottles, pitchers – any vessels we could find.*

V

TUBE /ˈves·əl/ *n* [C] a tube that carries liquid, esp. blood, through the body ○ *Blood clots clogged the vessels.*

vest CLOTHING /vest/ *n* [C] **1** a piece of clothing like a coat without sleeves that reaches to the waist ○ *My grandfather always wore his vest buttoned up.* ○ *The state requires that there be a life vest for each person in the boat.* **2** *Br* A vest is an UNDERSHIRT.

GIVE POWER TO /vest/ *v* [T] *fml* to give someone or something the power to do something ○ *Political power is now vested in an elected parliament.*

vested interest *n* [C] **1** an interest in influencing something so that you can continue to benefit from it ○ *She said the port has a vested interest in protecting the community's environment.* **2** A vested interest is also a person or group who has this type of relationship with something: *The British vested interests didn't regulate their own industries, as the Chinese state firms do.*

vestibule /ˈves·təˌbjuːl/ *n* [C] a room just inside a house or building, through which you enter the building ○ *In the school's vestibule is a sign reading, "Enter here and find a friend."* ○ *You can hang your coat in the vestibule.*

vestige /ˈves·tɪdʒ/ *n* [C] a small part left from something larger and more important, esp. one that is no longer used ○ *Vestiges of ancient settlements can be seen in the caves.*

vet MILITARY PERSON /vet/ *n* [C] *short form of* VETERAN (= a person who was in the military)

ANIMAL DOCTOR /vet/ *n* [C] *short form of* VETERINARIAN

EXAMINE /vet/ *v* [T] **-tt-** to study something, or to examine a person's record to see that it is acceptable or accurate ○ *All agencies must carefully vet new workers.* ○ *Before we signed this contract, our lawyer vetted it.*

veteran EXPERIENCED PERSON /ˈveţ·ə·rən, ˈve·trən/ *n* [C] a person who has had a lot of experience in a particular activity or job ○ *Ms. Beasly is one of our veterans – she has been teaching here for over 20 years.*

MILITARY PERSON /ˈveţ·ə·rən, ˈve·trən/, *short form* **vet** *n* [C] a person who was once a member of the armed forces

Veterans Day *n* [C] a legal holiday on November 11, or the day nearest November 11 that is not a Saturday or Sunday, in honor of members of the armed forces who fought for the US in wars

veterinarian /ˌveţ·ə·rəˈner·iː·ən, ˌve·trəˈner-/, *short form* **vet** *n* [C] a person trained in the medical treatment of animals ○ *He is the chief veterinarian for the zoo and deals with all kinds and sizes of animals.*

veterinary /ˈveţ·ə·rəˌner·i, ˈve·trəˌner·i/ *adj* [not gradable] ○ *The practice of veterinary medicine has become very sophisticated.*

veto /ˈviːţ·oʊ/ *n* [C/U] *pl* **vetoes** ***politics & government*** the power to refuse to allow something to be done, or such a refusal ○ [C] *The president has promised a veto if Congress passes that bill.* ○ [U] *The mayor will have no veto over zoning.*

veto /ˈviːţ·oʊ/ *v* [T] **vetoes**, *pres. part.* **vetoing**, *past* **vetoed** ***politics & government*** to refuse to allow something to be done ○ *The governor said she would veto the bill unless certain parts were changed.* ○ *Cory wanted to drive the car, but her mom vetoed it.*

vex /veks/ *v* [T] to cause someone to feel annoyance or trouble ○ *The question that vexes Ben the most is, "Why me?"*

vexed /vekst/ *adj* troubling and difficult ○ *a vexed question*
vexing /ˈvek·sɪŋ/ *adj* ○ *Rising gas prices are a vexing problem.*

via Ⓐ /ˌvɑɪ·ə, ˌviː·ə/ *prep* by way of, or by use of ○ *I sent the application papers via fax.*

viable /ˈvɑɪ·ə·bəl/ *adj* able to exist, perform as intended, or succeed ○ *The company had to seek other ways to remain viable.* ○ *He would be a viable candidate for any office he wanted to run for.*
viability /ˌvɑɪ·əˈbɪl·ət̬·i/ *n* [U] ○ *She's going to have to cut costs to maintain the viability of her business.*

viaduct /ˈvɑɪ·əˌdʌkt/ *n* [C] a high bridge that carries a road or railroad over an area that is difficult to cross, such as a deep valley, very wet land, or the steep side of a hill ○ *An ancient Roman viaduct crosses the valley.*

vial /ˈvɑɪ·əl, vɑɪl/ *n* [C] a small bottle used to hold a liquid ○ *The store gave away vials of their new perfume.*

vibes /vɑɪbz/ *pl n slang* the feeling you get from being in a particular place or situation or from being with a particular person ○ *I'm afraid to go there – that place has bad vibes.*

vibrant /ˈvɑɪ·brənt/ *adj* energetic, bright, and full of life or excitement ○ *The city is youthful, vibrant – an exciting place.* ○ *Flowers of vibrant colors were on each table.*

vibrate /ˈvɑɪ·breɪt/ *v* [I/T] to move quickly backward and forward, or to cause something to shake ○ [I] *Musical sounds are produced when the strings of the piano vibrate.* ○ [I] *A thundering boom made the windows vibrate.*
vibration /vɑɪˈbreɪ·ʃən/ *n* [C/U] ○ [C] *We felt the earthquake's vibrations 120 miles away!*

vicarious /vɑɪˈker·iː·əs, -ˈkær-/ *adj* experienced by reading or watching someone else do something ○ *This disaster movie will provide you with plenty of vicarious thrills.*

vice MORAL FAULT /vɑɪs/ *n* [C] **1** a moral fault or weakness in a person's character ○ *His virtues far outnumber his vices.* **2** Vice is also immoral behavior. ○ Compare VIRTUE GOODNESS

TITLE /vɑɪs/ *prefix* used as part of a title to show the rank of an officer or official of a company or organization, immediately below a president or CHAIRPERSON ○ *a vice principal* ○ *Vice Premier Zhu Rongji* ○ *He served as vice chairman of the federal reserve.* ○ *There are three vice presidents in that company.*

vice president, *abbreviation* **VP** *n* [C] **1** the elected official immediately below the president who is elected with the president every four years **2** A vice president is also a high-ranking employee in a company, usually one of several, in charge of a particular department: *This is Jeff Walton, our VP of Finance.*

vice versa /vɑɪsˈvɜr·sə, ˌvɑɪ·səˈvɜr-/ *adv* (of an opposite) being also true ○ *With this software, descriptions can replace names and vice versa.*

vicinity /vɪˈsɪn·ət̬·i/ *n* [U] the area immediately surrounding something ○ *There are many stores in the vicinity where she can shop.* ○ *An area of low pressure off the southeast coast will keep some rain showers in the vicinity of the coastline.*

IDIOM with vicinity

• **in the vicinity of** *something* approximately the stated amount: *The price for a house here is in the vicinity of $450,000.*

vicious /ˈvɪʃ·əs/ *adj* (of an act) intending to hurt badly, or (of a person or animal) likely to be violent ○ *I don't believe he is a vicious dog.* ○ *The few who disagreed became the targets of vicious written attacks on the Internet.*

vicious circle, **vicious cycle** *n* [C] a situation in which one problem causes another one, making the original problem impossible to solve ○ *In a kind of vicious circle, girls did not study science because other girls didn't study science, even though they were good at it.*

victim /ˈvɪk·təm/ *n* [C] a person who has suffered the effects of violence or illness or bad luck ○ *an accident victim* ○ *She's just a victim of circumstances beyond her control.*
victimize /ˈvɪk·təˌmɑɪz/ *v* [T] ○ *One survey showed the number of companies victimized by computer theft rose to 83 percent this year.*
victimization /ˌvɪk·tə·məˈzeɪ·ʃən/ *n* [U] ○ *National reports of victimization show a decline in certain kinds of crime.*
victimless /ˈvɪk·təm·ləs/ *adj* [not gradable] (of a crime) lacking a victim, or thought not to involve a victim ○ *Tax cheating is not a victimless crime.*

victor /ˈvɪk·tər/ *n* [C] the one who wins a competition, election, war, etc. ○ *The victor in the 1996 presidential election was Bill Clinton.*

Victorian /vɪkˈtɔːr·iː·ən/ *adj* **1** relating to the period 1837 to 1901, when Victoria was Queen of England **2** A thing can be called Victorian if it was made during this period, or in the style of this period: *My great-grandparents had a huge Victorian house in Paris, Texas.*

victory /ˈvɪk·tə·ri, -tri/ *n* [C/U] the act or an example of winning a competition or war ○ [U] *A goal in the last half minute assured victory and the World Cup for the Mexicans.*
victorious /vɪkˈtɔːr·iː·əs, -ˈtoʊr-/ *adj* [not gradable] ○ *The city honored the victorious general with a huge parade.*

video /ˈvɪd·iːˌoʊ/ *n* [C/U] *pl* **videos** **1** a series of recorded images which are shown on television or viewed on a screen ○ [U] *digital video* ○ [U] *The system transmits voice, data, and video between soldiers and command centers.* **2** A video is also a VIDEOTAPE: [C] *We watched two videos – both new films.*
video /ˈvɪd·iːˌoʊ/ *adj* [not gradable] ○ *The CD-ROM includes video clips.* ○ Compare AUDIO

video camera *n* [C] a camera that records moving pictures and often sound on a VIDEOTAPE ○ *Video cameras are used as security devices for ATMs.*

videocassette /ˈvɪd·iː ˌoʊ·kəˌset/, *short form* **video** /ˈvɪd·iː ˌoʊ/ *n* [C] a VIDEOTAPE

videocassette recorder *n* [C] a VCR

video game *n* [C] a game in which the player controls moving pictures on a television screen by pressing buttons or moving a short handle ○ *The best video games involve using your imagination to solve problems.*

videotape /ˈvɪd·iː·oʊˌteɪp/, *short form* **video,** *short form* **tape** *n* [C] a long, narrow, magnetic strip inside a rectangular plastic container which records sounds and moving images that can be heard and seen on a television, or a recording of images and sounds ○ *I bought the videotape of "Jurassic Park" for the kids.* ○ *He watches videotapes of his performances so he can see what needs work.*
videotape /ˈvɪd·iː·oʊˌteɪp/, *short form* **tape** *v* [T] ○ *Why don't you videotape the ballgame so you can watch it later?*

vie /vɑɪ/ *v* [I] *pres. part.* **vying,** *past* **vied** to compete ○ *Several companies are vying for the contract to build the new hospital.*

view SIGHT /vjuː/ *n* [C/U] what you can see from a particular place, or the ability to see from a particular place ○ [U] *She turned a corner and disappeared from view.* ○ [C] *Our room had spectacular views of the mountains.*
view /vjuː/ *v* [T] ○ *The President viewed the hurricane damage from a helicopter.*
viewer /ˈvjuː·ər/ *n* [C] ○ *Millions of viewers watch the Super Bowl on TV every year.*

USAGE
view or sight?

When you use **view** to talk about things that you can see, it describes the range of things you can see or how much you can see from a place. A **view** is often pleasant.

We had a wonderful view of the mountains from the aircraft.

~~*We had a wonderful sight of the mountains from the aircraft.*~~

Sight means something particular that you can see, or the ability to see.

The garden is a beautiful sight in spring.
The sight of blood makes me feel sick.
~~*The view of blood makes me feel sick.*~~
He lost his sight in an accident.
~~*He lost his view in an accident.*~~

OPINION /vjuː/ *n* [C] a way of looking at something; an opinion ○ *It's our view that it's time we did something and stopped just talking!* ○ *He takes a pessimistic view of our chances of success.* ○ *The meeting was an opportunity for the two leaders to exchange views.*

view /vjuː/ *v* [T] to look at or consider something ○ *How do you view your chances of getting that job?*

WORD FAMILY view

Nouns		Verbs	
	view		view
	overview		preview
	preview		review
	review		
	reviewer		
	viewer		

IDIOMS with view

• **on view** placed where the public can see it ○ *Plans for the new design of the park are on view in the library this week.*
• **in view of** *something* because of, or considering something ○ *In view of the late hour, we'll have to put off that discussion until our next meeting.*

viewpoint /ˈvjuː·pɔɪnt/ *n* [C] a POINT OF VIEW

vigil /ˈvɪdʒ·əl/ *n* [C] a period of staying awake to be with someone who is ill or to call public attention to something ○ *The boy's parents kept a long vigil in his hospital room.* ○ *A candlelight vigil on the steps of the courthouse was held to protest the verdict in this trial.*

vigilant /ˈvɪdʒ·ə·lənt/ *adj* being very careful to notice things, esp. signs of danger ○ *Security personnel need to be more vigilant in checking bags and packages.*
vigilance /ˈvɪdʒ·ə·ləns/ *n* [U] ○ *The vigilance of a mother fox protects her young from danger.*

vigilante /ˌvɪdʒ·əˈlænt·i/ *n* [C] a person who forces obedience to the law without legal authority to do so, or a member of a group that decides to force obedience to the law without official authority

vigor, *Cdn, Br* **vigour** /ˈvɪg·ər/ *n* [U] strength, energy, or enthusiasm ○ *After vacation, she returned to work with renewed vigor.*
vigorous /ˈvɪg·ə·rəs/ *adj* ○ *a vigorous debate/campaign* ○ *He still walks with vigorous steps.*
vigorously /ˈvɪg·ə·rə·sli/ *adv* ○ *Don't exercise too vigorously at first.*

vile /vɑɪl/ *adj* **1** evil or disgusting ○ *He responded with the vilest language imaginable.* **2** Vile also means very bad or unpleasant: *a vile mood/temper*

vilify /ˈvɪl·əˌfɑɪ/ *v* [T] *fml* to say or write unpleasant things about someone or something, in order to cause other people to have a bad opinion of that person or thing ○ *He claimed he was unfairly vilified by the press.*

villa /ˈvɪl·ə/ *n* [C] a large house, usually in a rural area or near the sea

village /ˈvɪl·ɪdʒ/ *n* [C] **1** a group of houses, stores, and other buildings which is smaller than a town ○ *We live just outside the village of Larchmont.* **2** A village is also the people who live in a village: *The whole village came out for the parade.*
villager /ˈvɪl·ɪ·dʒər/ *n* [C] a person who lives in a village

villain /ˈvɪl·ən/ *n* [C] a bad person who harms other people or breaks the law, or a cruel or evil character in a book, play, or film ○ *In her version of the story, Hoover emerges as the villain.*

villus /ˈvɪl·əs/ *n* [C] *pl* **villi** ***biology*** one of many small parts like fingers on the inside surface of the smaller part of the INTESTINES (= tube in the body where food goes after the stomach), through which the food is absorbed

vinaigrette /ˌvɪn·əˈgret/ *n* [U] a sauce made from oil and vinegar, used esp. on salad

vindicate /ˈvɪn·dəˌkeɪt/ *v* [T] to show something to have been right or true, or to show someone to be free from guilt or blame ○ *The decision to include Morris on the team was vindicated when he scored three touchdowns.*

vindication /ˌvɪn·dəˈkeɪ·ʃən/ *n* [C/U] ○ [U] *They are hoping for vindication in court.*

vindictive /vɪnˈdɪk·tɪv/ *adj* having or showing a desire to harm someone because you think that the person has harmed you; unwilling to forgive ○ *She was immature, spiteful, even vindictive at times.*

vine /vɑɪn/ *n* [C] a type of plant that climbs or grows along the ground and has a twisting stem ○ *a grape vine* ○ *pea vines*

vinegar /ˈvɪn·ɪ·gər/ *n* [U] a strong-tasting liquid made esp. from FERMENTED (= chemically changed) wine, apple juice, etc., that is used for flavoring or preserving food ○ *Would you like oil and vinegar on your salad?*

vineyard /ˈvɪn·jərd/ *n* [C] a piece of land on which GRAPEVINES are grown (= plants that produce small round fruits used for making wine)

vintage **WINE** /ˈvɪnt·ɪdʒ/ *n* [C] the wine made in a particular year, or a particular year in which wine was made

vintage /ˈvɪnt·ɪdʒ/ *adj* [not gradable] (of wine) of high quality that was made in a particular year, and that can be kept for several years in order to improve it ○ *vintage champagne*

HIGH QUALITY /ˈvɪnt·ɪdʒ/ *adj* [not gradable] (esp. of something old) of high quality and lasting value, or showing the best characteristics typical of the person who created it ○ *a vintage pistol/airplane/car* ○ *"Sophisticated Lady" is vintage Duke Ellington.*

USED /ˈvɪn·tɪdʒ/ *adj* [not gradable] used but of good quality ○ *vintage clothing*

vinyl /ˈvɑɪn·ᵊl/ *n* [U] strong plastic that can be bent and that is used to make floors, furniture, clothing, etc. ○ *vinyl flooring/upholstery* ○ *a vinyl raincoat*

viola /viːˈoʊ·lə/ *n* [C/U] a wooden musical instrument with four strings, slightly larger than a VIOLIN, which a player holds against his or her neck and plays with a BOW (= stick with hairs attached to it), or this type of instrument generally

violate Ⓐ /ˈvɑɪ·əˌleɪt/ *v* [T] **1** to break or act against something such as a law, agreement, or principle, or to not respect something that should be treated with respect ○ *The planes appear to have deliberately violated the cease-fire agreement.* **2** Someone who violates a place or situation goes where the person is not wanted or does something the person should not do: *Questions of this kind violate my privacy.*

violation Ⓐ /ˌvɑɪ·əˈleɪ·ʃən/ *n* [C/U] ○ [C] *a traffic violation* ○ [C] *The invasion constitutes a violation of international law.* ○ [U] *They had not acted in violation of the rules.*

violator /ˈvɑɪ·əˌleɪt̬·ər/ *n* [C] ○ *Violators can be fined up to $500.*

WORD FAMILY violate			
Nouns	violence violation violator	*Adjectives*	violent nonviolent
		Adverbs	violently
Verbs	violate		

violence /ˈvɑɪ·ə·ləns/ *n* [U] extremely forceful actions that are intended to hurt people or are likely to cause damage ○ *racial/ethnic/domestic violence* ○ *She was concerned about the amount of violence on television.* ○ *The storm turned out to be one of unexpected violence.*

violent /ˈvɑɪ·ə·lənt/ *adj* **1** using or involving force to hurt or attack ○ *violent crime* ○ *The police are concerned about the possibility of violent behavior at the demonstration.* **2** A violent death is one that is caused suddenly and unexpectedly by the use of physical force, esp. murder. **3** Violent can mean very strong: *a violent explosion* **4** A violent person or attitude is one that expresses great anger.

violently /ˈvɑɪ·ə·lənt·li/ *adv* **1** in a forceful way that causes people to be hurt **2** Violently can mean strongly or extremely: *They are violently opposed to the plans.*

WORD CHOICES violence

If someone is angry and violent, you could describe that person as **aggressive**.

*She was very **aggressive** toward the TV reporters.*

Ferocious and **savage** both mean "fierce and violent."

*a **ferocious/savage** dog*

Brutal can be used when someone is violent, cruel, and does not seem to have any feelings for people.

*He was jailed for the **brutal** crime.*

You could use **vicious** if someone is violent and seems to want to hurt someone very badly.

*It was a **vicious** crime.*

Bloody or **gory** can be used about things which are violent and involve a lot of blood.

*She refuses to watch **gory** horror movies.*

violet **COLOR** /ˈvɑɪ·ə·lət/ *adj, n* [U] (of) a color that is between blue and purple ○ *violet ink* ○ [U] *Violet is too dark for the walls of this room.*

PLANT /ˈvɑɪ·ə·lət/ *n* [C] a small plant with pleasant-smelling purple, blue, or white flowers

violin /ˌvɑɪ·ə'lɪn/ *n* [C/U] a small, wooden musical instrument with four strings that a player holds against his or her neck and plays with a BOW (= stick with hairs attached to it), or this type of instrument generally

VIP /ˌviː ˌɑɪ 'piː/ *n* [C] *abbreviation for* very important person (= a person who is treated better than ordinary people because of being famous or influential in some way) ○ *We were given the full VIP treatment.*

viper /'vɑɪ·pər/ *n* [C] a small, poisonous snake ○ *The vipers slithered and hissed.*

viral /'vɑɪ·rəl/ *adj* [not gradable] ○ See at VIRUS SMALL ORGANISM

virgin /'vɜr·dʒən/ *n* [C] someone who has never had sex
virgin /'vɜr·dʒən/ *adj* [not gradable] **1** *a virgin bride* **2** Virgin can be used of forests and areas of land that have not yet been cultivated or used by people: *a virgin forest* ○ *Antarctica is virgin territory.*
virginity /vər'dʒɪn·əṭ·i/ *n* [U]

Virgo /'vɜr·goʊ, 'vɪr-/ *n* [C/U] *pl* **Virgos** the sixth sign of the ZODIAC, covering the period August 23 to September 22 and represented by a young woman, or a person born during this period

virile /'vɪr·əl, -ɑɪl/ *adj* (of a man) full of strength, power, and energy in a way that is considered sexually attractive ○ *The ads show virile young men playing on the beach.*

virtual Ⓐ /'vɜr·tʃə·wəl/ *adj* [not gradable] almost, but not exactly or in every way ○ *She was a virtual unknown before this movie.* ○ *Snow brought Minneapolis to a virtual standstill yesterday.*
virtually Ⓐ /'vɜr·tʃə·wə·li/ *adv* [not gradable] ○ *Unemployment in this part of the country is virtually nonexistent.*

virtual reality *n* [U] a set of images and sounds produced by a computer that seem to represent a real place or situation

virtue GOODNESS /'vɜr·tʃuː/ *n* [C/U] a good moral quality in a person, or the general quality of goodness in a person ○ [C] *Patience is a virtue.* ○ Compare VICE MORAL FAULT
virtuous /'vɜr·tʃə·wəs/ *adj* possessing good moral qualities ○ *I've been up working since six o'clock this morning so I'm feeling very virtuous.*

ADVANTAGE /'vɜr·tʃuː/ *n* [C/U] an advantage or benefit ○ [C] *Caution is a useful virtue.*

IDIOM with virtue

• **by virtue of** *something* as a result of something ○ *They were excluded from voting by virtue of being too young.*

virtuoso /ˌvɜr·tʃə'woʊ·soʊ, -zoʊ/ *n* [C] *pl* **virtuosos** a person who is extremely skilled at something, especially at playing an instrument or performing ○ *Famous mainly for his wonderful voice, Cole was also a virtuoso on the piano.*

virtuoso /ˌvɜr·tʃə'woʊ·soʊ, -zoʊ/ *adj* [not gradable] ○ *The world's greatest tenor treated us to a virtuoso display of his abundant talent.*

virulent ACTING QUICKLY /'vɪr·jə·lənt/ *adj* (of a disease) dangerous and spreading quickly, or (of poison) having an effect very quickly ○ *a virulent strain of flu*

FULL OF HATE /'vɪr·jə·lənt/ *adj* fierce and full of hate ○ *virulent speech* ○ *Several newspapers mounted virulent attacks.*

virus SMALL ORGANISM /'vɑɪ·rəs/ *n* [C] **1** ***biology*** a very small organism that causes disease in humans, animals, and plants **2** A virus is also a disease caused by a virus: *She's had a virus for several days.*

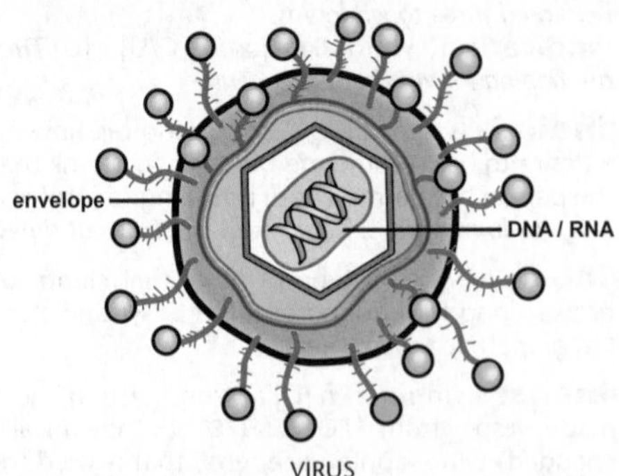

VIRUS

viral /'vɑɪ·rəl/ *adj* [not gradable] ***biology*** relating to or caused by a virus

COMPUTER PROBLEM /'vɑɪ·rəs/ *n* [C] a hidden set of instructions in a computer program that is intended to introduce faults into a computer system or cause it to perform actions that were not planned

visa /'viː·zə, -sə/ *n* [C] an official document or mark made in a PASSPORT that allows you to enter or leave a particular country ○ *an entry/exit visa*

vis-a-vis /ˌviː·zə'viː, -sə-/ *prep* in relation to, or in comparison with ○ *Later I asked him more directly about government's role vis-a-vis the environment.*

visceral /'vɪs·ə·rəl/ *adj* based on emotional reactions rather than on reason or thought ○ *He has a visceral feel for our problems.*

visceral muscle, **smooth muscle** *n* [C] ***biology*** any of the muscles that work automatically and are found in the organs of the body such as the stomach and lungs

viscous /'vɪs·kəs/ *adj* (of a liquid) thick and sticky; not flowing easily ○ *viscous oil*

vise /vɑɪs/ *n* [C] a tool having two flat sides that can be moved closer together to hold something firmly while it is being worked on ○ *After gluing both surfaces of the wood, clamp it in a vise to dry.*

viselike /'vɑɪs·lɑɪk/ *adj* [not gradable] very tight and strong ○ *a viselike handshake*

visible Ⓐ /'vɪz·ə·bəl/ *adj* **1** able to be seen ○ *There are few visible signs of her recent illness.* ○ *The* *comet is visible to the naked eye as a fuzzy ball in the western sky.* **2** Visible also means able or tending to attract public attention: *In a very short time, she became a highly visible environmental spokesperson.*

visibly Ⓐ /ˈvɪz·ə·bli/ *adv* in a way that is easily seen; obviously ○ *Earl became visibly upset.*

visibility Ⓐ /ˌvɪz·əˈbɪl·ət̬·i/ *n* [U] the degree to which objects that are far away can be seen outside, as influenced by weather conditions ○ *There will be reduced visibility because of the fog.*

vision Ⓐ **SIGHT** /ˈvɪʒ·ən/ *n* [U] the ability to see ○ *good/impaired/blurred vision*

MENTAL IMAGE /ˈvɪʒ·ən/ *n* [C] **1** an imagined mental image of something ○ *We lack a vision of what love really is.* **2** A vision can also be something seen in a dream or as a result of a religious experience.

VIEW OF THE FUTURE /ˈvɪʒ·ən/ *n* [U] the ability to imagine how a country, society, industry, etc., will develop in the future and to plan in a suitable way ○ *The theater's director is a woman of great artistic vision.*

visionary /ˈvɪʒ·əˌner·i/ *n* [C] ○ *She was a social reformer, a true visionary.*

visit /ˈvɪz·ət/ *v* [I/T] to go to a place in order to experience it, or to go to a person in order to spend time together ○ [T] *We visited a few galleries while we were in New York.* ○ [T] *When are we going to visit Grandma?* ○ [I] *She's not staying here – she's just visiting for the afternoon.*

visit /ˈvɪz·ət/ *n* [C] ○ *I think I'll pay a visit to the barbershop while I'm in town.* ○ *We had a visit from the fire inspector last week.*

visitation /ˌvɪz·əˈteɪ·ʃən/ *n* [C/U] **1** the act of visiting, or a visit ○ [U] *The hospital has strict rules about visitation.* **2** *law* Visitation is the act of a DIVORCED parent spending time with a child he or she no longer lives with at agreed times and according to agreed conditions.

visitor /ˈvɪz·ət̬·ər/ *n* [C] ○ *Every summer, this tiny fishing village receives thousands of visitors.* ➤ Usage: **meet, see, visit, or get to know?** at MEET COME TOGETHER

WORD FAMILY visit			
Nouns	visit visitor visitation	*Verbs*	visit revisit

visiting hours *pl n* the time period when you can visit someone, esp. in a hospital or prison

visor /ˈvɑɪ·zər/ *n* [C] **1** a curved piece of stiff material that is worn above the eyes to protect them from the sun **2** A visor is also a movable part of a HELMET (= hard head cover) that can be pulled down to cover the face.

vista /ˈvɪs·tə/ *n* [C] a view from a high position ○ *After a hard climb, we were rewarded by a vista of rolling hills.*

visual Ⓐ /ˈvɪʒ·ə·wəl/ *adj* relating to seeing ○ *These animals have excellent visual ability/acuity.*

visually Ⓐ /ˈvɪʒ·ə·wə·li/ *adv* ○ *a visually stunning production* ○ *Guide dogs improve the lives of the visually impaired.*

visualize Ⓐ /ˈvɪʒ·ə·wəˌlɑɪz/ *v* [T] to imagine or remember someone or something by forming a picture in your mind ○ *I was so surprised when I saw him – I'd visualized someone much older.*

visualization Ⓐ /ˌvɪʒ·ə·wə·ləˈzeɪ·ʃən/ *n* [C/U]

visual arts *pl n* the arts of drawing, painting, SCULPTURE, PHOTOGRAPHY, etc.

vital /ˈvɑɪt̬·əl/ *adj* necessary or extremely important for the success or continued existence of something ○ *The existence of a strong opposition is vital to a healthy democracy.* ○ *The kidneys play a vital role/part in removing waste from the blood.* ○ [+ *that* clause] *It's vital that you respond at once.*

vitally /ˈvɑɪt̬·əl·i/ *adv* ○ *It's vitally important that we get there by tomorrow.*

vitality /vɑɪˈtæl·ət̬·i/ *n* [U] energy and strength ○ *youthful vitality* ○ *The new factory should improve the economic vitality of the region.*

vital signs *pl n medical* your body temperature and the rate at which you are breathing and your heart is beating

vital statistics *pl n* a group of official facts that include the number of births, deaths, and marriages in a particular place, or the ages and races of the people that live there

vitamin /ˈvɑɪt̬·ə·mən/ *n* [C] ***biology*** any of a group of natural substances that are necessary in small amounts for growth and good health and that are obtained from food

vitriolic /ˌvɪ·triːˈɑl·ɪk/ *adj* intentionally unkind or causing hurt ○ *He launched a vitriolic attack on the senator, accusing him of shielding corrupt friends.*

vivacious /vəˈveɪ·ʃəs, vɑɪ-/ *adj* (esp. of a woman or girl) full of energy and enthusiasm ○ *Judy Garland was bright and vivacious, with a vibrant singing voice.*

vivid /ˈvɪv·əd/ *adj* brightly colored or (of descriptions or memories) producing clear, powerful, and detailed images in the mind ○ *vivid colors* ○ *vivid memories*

vividly /ˈvɪv·əd·li/ *adv* ○ *The author vividly describes his early life on the farm.*

vivisection /ˌvɪv·əˈsek·ʃən/ *n* [U] the cutting into or other use of living animals in tests for the purpose of increasing medical knowledge

V-neck *adj* [not gradable] (of clothing) having a V-shaped neck opening at the front ○ *She wore a blue, V-neck sweater.*

vocabulary /voʊˈkæb·jəˌler·i/ *n* [C/U] ***English*** all the words used by a particular person, or all the words that exist in a particular language or subject ○ [C] *Reading helps to improve your vocabulary.*

vocal **OF THE VOICE** /ˈvoʊ·kəl/ *adj* [not gradable] relating to or produced by the voice, either in singing or speaking ○ *vocal music*

vocal /ˈvoʊ·kəl/ *n* [C usually pl] the singing in a piece of popular music ○ *At times his vocals were drowned out by the audience singing along.*

vocalist /ˈvoʊ·kə·ləst/ *n* [C] a person who sings, esp. with a group that plays popular music

vocalize /ˈvoʊ·kəˌlɑɪz/ *v* [I/T] to sing, speak, or make sounds ○ [I] *She studied how often infants vocalized.*

vocally /ˈvoʊ·kə·li/ *adv* [not gradable]

OFTEN HEARD /ˈvoʊ·kəl/ *adj* often expressing opinions and complaints in speech ○ *He is emerging as his party's most vocal critic of the president.*

vocal cords *pl n* a pair of folds at the upper end of the throat that produce sound when air from the lungs moves over them

vocation /voʊˈkeɪ·ʃən/ *n* [C] a type of work that you feel you are suited to doing and to which you give much of your time and energy ○ *It wasn't until "The North American Review" published his story that he embraced writing as a vocation.*

vocational /voʊˈkeɪ·ʃən·əl/ *adj* [not gradable] providing skills and education that prepare you for a job ○ *vocational education/training* ○ *The school offers vocational programs in welding, electrical work, and building maintenance.*

vociferous /voʊˈsɪf·ə·rəs/ *adj* repeatedly and loudly expressing your opinions and complaints, or (of demands, complaints, etc.) expressed in this way ○ *a vociferous critic of foreign policy* ○ *vociferous objections*

vociferously /voʊˈsɪf·ə·rə·sli/ *adv* ○ *He protested vociferously, but to no avail.*

vodka /ˈvɑd·kə/ *n* [C/U] a colorless, alcoholic drink made from any of various grains or potatoes

vogue /voʊg/ *n* [C/U] the state of being popular or fashionable for a period of time ○ [U] *Bowling has come back in vogue.*

voice **SOUNDS** /vɔɪs/ *n* [C/U] the sound made when people speak or sing, or the ability to make such a sound ○ [C] *She spoke in a low, soft voice, and I had to ask her to speak louder.* ○ [C] *I heard the murmur of voices.* ○ [C] *I've been talking so much that my voice is getting hoarse.* ○ [U] *I've got a cold and I'm losing my voice* (= becoming unable to speak).

OPINION /vɔɪs/ *n* [C/U] an expression of opinion, or the right to express an opinion ○ [C] *The senator added his voice to the protest.* ○ [U] *The kids want to have a voice in where we go on our vacation.*

voice /vɔɪs/ *v* [T] to express esp. an opinion or feeling ○ *Opponents also voiced concern about the potential traffic produced by the project.*

GRAMMAR /vɔɪs/ *n* [C] ***grammar*** the relationship between the subject of the verb and the action described by the verb, or the forms of a verb that show this relationship ○ Compare ACTIVE VOICE; PASSIVE VOICE

voice mail *n* [C/U] a telephone system that records messages from people who call, or a message on such a system

void **EMPTY SPACE** /vɔɪd/ *n* [C] a space with nothing in it ○ *Some parents use television to fill the void they have created by not spending enough time with their kids, he said.*

UNACCEPTABLE /vɔɪd/ *adj* [not gradable] having no legal authority and therefore unacceptable ○ *The original version of her will was declared void.*

void /vɔɪd/ *v* [T] to remove the legal force from an agreement or contract ○ *I'll just void the check and pay you in cash.*

VoIP *n* [U] *abbreviation for* voice over Internet protocol (= a system that allows you to use your computer as a telephone, and your Internet connection as a telephone line) ○ *Most VoIP services have the ability to transfer your current phone number to your new service.*

vol. *n* [U] *abbreviation for* VOLUME **SPACE**

volatile /ˈvɑl·ət̬·əl/ *adj* **1** likely to change suddenly and unexpectedly, or suddenly violent or angry ○ *It was a volatile situation, and the police handled it well.* ○ *The stock market was highly volatile in the early part of the year.* **2** ***chemistry*** If a substance, esp. a liquid, is volatile, it will change easily into a gas: *volatile chemicals*

volatility /ˌvɑl·əˈtɪl·ət̬·i/ *n* [U] ○ *Volatility in wheat on Wednesday resulted in a single-day trading record in Kansas City.*

volcano /vɑlˈkeɪ·noʊ, vɔːl-/ *n* [C] *pl* **volcanoes, volcanos** a mountain made from burned materials that may throw out hot rocks and LAVA (= hot liquid rock) from a hole in its top

volcanic /vɑlˈkæn·ɪk, vɔːl-/ *adj* [not gradable] ○ *volcanic ash/rock*

volition /vəˈlɪʃ·ən, voʊ-/ *n* [U] *fml* the power to make your own decisions ○ *It was announced that he resigned of his own volition* (= because he chose to)*, but I believe he was forced out.*

volley **WEAPONS FIRE** /ˈvɑl·i/ *n* [C] **1** a large number of bullets or arrows fired at the same time **2** A volley is also a lot of things done or said at the same time: *a volley of questions*

SPORTS SHOT /ˈvɑl·i/ *n* [C] (in tennis and other sports) a hit to return a ball before it touches the ground ○ *I was ahead in the first game, but then hit a bad volley and a bad forehand.* ➤ Usage: **basket or basketball?** AT BASKET **GOAL**

volleyball /ˈvɑl·iːˌbɔːl/ *n* [U] a game in which two teams use their hands to hit a large ball from one side of a high net to the other, without allowing the ball to touch the ground

volt /voʊlt/ *n* [C] ***physics*** the standard unit used to measure how strongly an electrical current is sent around an electrical system ○ *Many household appliances run on a current of 120 volts.*

voltage /ˈvoʊl·tɪdʒ/ *n* [C] ***physics*** ○ *high/low voltage*

voltaic cell /voʊlˈteɪ·ɪk ˈsel/ *n* [C] ***chemistry*** a device that produces electricity by a chemical reaction

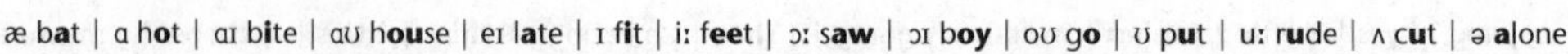

voltmeter /ˈvoʊltˌmiːt̬·ər/ *n* [C] ***physics*** a device that measures differences in electric POTENTIAL between two points

volume Ⓐ **SPACE** /ˈvɑl·jəm, -juːm/ *n* [C/U] an amount of space having length, height, and width ○ [C] *You need a big air conditioner to cool a large volume of space.* ○ [U] *About 8 percent of the total volume of garbage is plastic packaging.*

AMOUNT /ˈvɑl·jəm, -juːm/ *n* [C usually sing] the number or amount of something having a lot of units or parts ○ *The main difficulty with teaching is the sheer volume of work.* ○ *The system could not handle the volume of electronic mail.* ○ *We are looking for a high volume of sales.*

SOUND LEVEL /ˈvɑl·jəm, -juːm/ *n* [U] the level of sound produced by a television, radio, etc., or the switch or other device controlling this ○ *Could you turn the volume down, please – I'm trying to sleep.*

BOOK /ˈvɑl·jəm, -juːm/ *n* [C] a book, esp. one book in a set of related books ○ *a slim volume of poetry* ○ *I'm missing the last volume of the set.*

voluntary Ⓐ /ˈvɑl·ənˌter·i/ *adj* [not gradable] done, made, or given willingly, without being forced or paid to do it ○ *Employees can make voluntary contributions to the savings plan of up to 25% of their earnings.* ○ *Karyn leads after-school workshops that students attend on a voluntary basis.*
voluntarily Ⓐ /ˌvɑl·ənˈter·ə·li/ *adv* ○ *She voluntarily gave up her lunch break to supervise the lab.*

volunteer Ⓐ /ˌvɑl·ənˈtɪr/ *n* [C] a person who does something, esp. for other people or for an organization, willingly and without being forced or paid to do it ○ *The charity relies on volunteers to run the office and answer the phones.*
volunteer Ⓐ /ˌvɑl·ənˈtɪr/ *adj* [not gradable] ○ *a volunteer fireman* ○ *I do volunteer work for the American Lung Association.*
volunteer Ⓐ /ˌvɑl·ənˈtɪr/ *v* [I/T] ○ [+ *to* infinitive] *During the emergency a lot of people volunteered to work through the night.* ○ [T] *Three physicians volunteered their services.*

voluptuous /vəˈlʌp·tʃə·wəs/ *adj* (esp. of women) having a full, curving shape

vomit /ˈvɑm·ət/ *v* [I/T] to empty the contents of the stomach through the mouth, usually in explosive bursts
vomit /ˈvɑm·ət/ *n* [U] food or other matter that has come up from the stomach through the mouth
vomiting /ˈvɑm·ət̬·ɪŋ/ *n* [U] ○ *It causes a range of ailments, including headache and vomiting.*

voodoo /ˈvuːd·uː/ *n* [U] a religion involving magic that began in Africa and developed in Haiti

voracious /vəˈreɪ·ʃəs, vɔː-/ *adj* needing a lot of something to be satisfied ○ *Wolves are voracious eaters.* ○ *As a child, I had a voracious appetite for books.*

vortex /ˈvɔːr·teks/ *n* [C] *pl* **vortices** ***earth science*** a mass of air or water that spins around very fast and pulls objects into its empty center

vote /voʊt/ *v* [I/T] ***social studies*** to express your choice or opinion as one member of a group in order to decide a matter of importance to the whole group or to elect someone to an office ○ [I] *I voted early this morning just after the polls opened.* ○ [I] *In a democracy, all adult citizens have the right to vote.* ○ [I] *Local residents have twice voted against raising property taxes.* ○ [I] *Who did you vote for in the last election?* ○ [+ *to* infinitive] *A majority of workers voted to accept the offer of an 8% pay raise.* ○ [T] *She was voted best director at the Cannes Film Festival.*
vote /voʊt/ *n* [C/U] ○ [C] *She won a majority of the votes, 15 to 13, and was declared the winner.* ○ [U] *Opponents of the measure called Thursday's vote a setback.* ○ [C] *She cast her vote* (= voted) *for Gillespie.* ○ [C] *We called a meeting in order to take a vote on the issue.* ○ [U] *In some countries women still don't have the vote* (= are not allowed to vote in elections).
voter /ˈvoʊt̬·ər/ *n* [C] ***social studies*** a person who votes, or a person who has the legal right to vote ○ *Voters are interested in issues that affect their pocketbooks, he said.*

WORD FAMILY vote			
Nouns	vote voter	*Verbs*	vote

vote of confidence *n* [C] a vote to show support, esp. for a government or political leader ○ *(fig.) Richardson said that foreign investment amounts to a vote of confidence in the basic soundness of the U.S. economy.*

vouch for *something/someone* /ˈvɑʊtʃ·fər, -fɔːr/ *phrasal verb* to support the truth of something or the good character of someone, based on your knowledge or experience ○ *Our accountant will vouch for the accuracy of the financial report.* ○ *I've known him for years and can vouch for his honesty.*

voucher /ˈvɑʊ·tʃər/ *n* [C] a piece of paper that is a record of money paid or one that can be used to pay for particular goods or services ○ *Just present your travel voucher to the airline ticket agent, and she will give you the tickets.*

vow /vɑʊ/ *v* to make a firm promise or decision to do something ○ [+ (*that*) clause] *They vowed (that) they would never forget her kindness.* ○ [+ *to* infinitive] *After my illness I vowed to exercise every day.*
vow /vɑʊ/ *n* [C] ○ *They exchanged marriage vows in a Manhattan courthouse.*

vowel /ˈvɑʊ·əl, vɑʊl/ *n* [C] ***writing*** **1** a speech sound produced by human beings when the breath flows out through the mouth without being blocked by the teeth, tongue, or lips **2** A vowel is also a letter that represents a sound produced in this way: *The vowels in English are a, e, i, o, u, and sometimes y.* ○ Compare CONSONANT

voyage /ˈvɔɪ·ɪdʒ, ˈvɔː·ɪdʒ/ *n* [C] a long trip, esp. by ship ○ *Christopher Columbus brought cattle on his second voyage to America in 1493.*

VP *n* [C] *abbreviation for* VICE PRESIDENT

vs. *prep for abbreviation for* VERSUS

vulgar **NOT SUITABLE** /ˈvʌl·gər/ *adj* not polite or socially acceptable; not suitable or acceptable in style ○ *His manners were coarse and vulgar.*

RUDE /ˈvʌl·gər/ *adj* rude or offensive, esp. because referring to sex ○ *The movie is rated PG and has a few mildly vulgar jokes.*

vulgarity /vʌlˈgær·əţ·i/ *n* [C/U] ○ [U] *His comedy routine contains some vulgarity.*

vulnerable /ˈvʌl·nə·rə·bəl/ *adj* able to be easily hurt, influenced, or attacked ○ *Older people are especially vulnerable to cold temperatures even inside their homes.* ○ *He casts himself as a naive, vulnerable young poet.*

vulnerability /ˌvʌl·nə·rəˈbɪl·əţ·i/ *n* [U]

vulture /ˈvʌl·tʃər/ *n* [C] **1** a large bird that eats the flesh of dead animals **2** A vulture is also someone who is eager to get some advantage from other people's difficulties or weaknesses.

vying /ˈvɑɪ·ɪŋ/ *present participle of* VIE

W w

W, **w** /ˈdʌb·əl·juː/ *n* [C] *pl* **W's, Ws, w's, ws** the 23rd letter of the English alphabet

W. *adj, n* [U] *abbreviation for* WEST or WESTERN

w *n* [C] *abbreviation for* WATT

wacko /ˈwæk·oʊ/ *n* [C] *pl* **wackos** *slang* a person whose behavior is strange

wacky /ˈwæk·i/ *adj slang* strange in a pleasing and exciting or silly way ○ *The film has a wacky originality that is appealing.*

wad /wɑd/ *n* [C] a number of thin pieces of something pressed together, or something pressed into a lump ○ *a wad of bills/cash* ○ *a wad of chewing gum*
wad /wɑd/ *v* [T] **-dd-** to fold or press together something to form a mass ○ *He wadded his towel into a ball.*

waddle /ˈwɑd·əl/ *v* [I] to walk with short steps, swinging the body from one side to the other, like a DUCK (= a bird with short legs that lives by water)

wade /weɪd/ *v* [I always + adv/prep] to walk into or through an area of water that is not very deep ○ *We waded across the stream.* ○ *They come to the creek and waded in to drink.*

PHRASAL VERBS with wade

• **wade in** to start to do something in a forceful and determined way ○ *If there's a problem, she'll wade in without hesitation and try to solve it.*
• **wade through** *something* to spend a lot of time and effort doing something boring or difficult ○ *Some readers will not want to wade through the details of how the data were gathered and analyzed.*

wading pool *n* [C] an artificial pool only a few inches deep that small children can play in

wafer /ˈweɪ·fər/ *n* [C] a very thin, dry cookie that is often sweet and flavored ○ *chocolate wafers*

waffle CAKE /ˈwɑf·əl/ *n* [C] a thin, light cake, the surface of which is formed into a pattern of raised squares, often eaten for breakfast
NOT DECIDE /ˈwɑf·əl/ *v* [I] to keep changing your decisions about something so that no clear decision is made ○ *This administration has a tendency to waffle on important questions.*

waft /wɑft, wæft/ *v* [I/T] to move gently through the air, or to cause this to happen ○ [I always + adv/prep] *A warm breeze wafted through the city.*

wag /wæg/ *v* [I/T] **-gg-** (esp. of a tail or finger) to move from side to side or up and down, usually quickly and repeatedly, or to cause this to happen ○ [T] *When she came in, the dog sprang to its feet and wagged its tail.*

wage MONEY /weɪdʒ/ *n* [U] an amount of money that is paid to an employee, esp. for each hour worked ○ *an hourly wage*
wages /ˈweɪ·dʒəz/ *pl n* the money earned by an employee, esp. when paid for the hours worked ○ *He was notorious for being anti-union and for paying low wages.* ➤ Usage: **pay, wage, salary, or income?** at PAY GIVE EARNINGS
FIGHT /weɪdʒ/ *v* [T] to begin and continue a war, a fight, or a plan to achieve something ○ *A desperate medical battle is being waged against the virus.*

wage earner *n* [C] a person who works at a job for money, esp. to support a family

wager /ˈweɪ·dʒər/ *n* [C] an agreement to risk money on the unknown result of an event in the hope of winning more money than you have risked, or the amount of money risked; a BET
wager /ˈweɪ·dʒər/ *v* **1** [T] *Over $2 million was wagered.* **2** To wager is also to suggest as a likely idea: [+ *that* clause] *I would wager that not one person in ten could tell an expensive wine from a cheaper one.*

wagon /ˈwæg·ən/ *n* [C] a vehicle with four wheels, which must be pulled or pushed ○ *European settlers journeyed across America in covered wagons.*

waif /weɪf/ *n* [C] a child or animal without a home or enough care ○ *a poor little waif*

wail /weɪl/ *v* to make a long, high cry, usually because of pain or sadness, or to make a sound like this ○ [I] *The four babies were wailing in unison.* ○ [I] *Air-raid sirens wailed.* ○ [+ *that* clause] (*fig.*) *Investors wailed* (= complained) *that interest rates were skyrocketing.*
wail /weɪl/ *n* [C] ○ *The wail of the siren woke me up.*

waist /weɪst/ *n* [C] the part of the body above and slightly narrower than the hips ○ *These jeans are too tight around my waist.*

waistline CLOTHING PART /ˈweɪst·lɑɪn/ *n* [C] the part of a piece of clothing that covers the waist
PERSON'S SIZE /ˈweɪst·lɑɪn/ *n* [C] the measured size of your waist ○ *When he went off his diet, his waistline started to grow.*

wait /weɪt/ *v* [I/T] **1** to allow time to go by, esp. without doing much, until something happens or can happen ○ [I] *I waited in the car.* ○ [I] *Wait here for me – I'll be back in a minute.* ○ [I] *The dentist kept me waiting for ages.* ○ [+ to infinitive] *Several people are waiting to use the phone.* ○ [T] *Please get in line and wait your turn like everyone else.* **2** If something waits, it is being delayed or is ready: [I] *The meeting will have to wait until tomorrow.* ○ [I] *An envelope was waiting for me when I got home.*
wait /weɪt/ *n* [U] ○ *We had a three-hour wait at the airport.* ➤ Usage: **attend or wait/expect?** at ATTEND

USAGE
wait
Remember to use the preposition **for** when you are talking about waiting until someone comes or something happens. ➤

W

We're still waiting for the results of the test.
~~*We're still waiting the results of the test.*~~
I'll wait for you outside.
~~*I'll wait you outside.*~~

USAGE

wait or expect?

When you **wait**, you allow time to go by, especially while staying in one place, until a person or thing arrives or is ready.

I waited twenty minutes for the bus.
She's waiting for her exam results.

When you **expect** something, you think that it will happen.

I'm expecting the bus to arrive in about five minutes.
She expected to do well on the exam.
~~*She waited to do well on the exam.*~~

WORD CHOICES wait

In formal English **await** means the same as "wait for."

*We are **awaiting** the committee's decision.*

If people are waiting in a place, usually for no obvious reason, you can use the phrasal verb **hang around** or the verb **loiter**.

*There were a lot of teenagers **hanging around/loitering** outside the store.*

If people are waiting in a line to buy something, the verb **line up** is used.

*People were **lining up** for tickets.*

Stay and **remain** (*slightly formal*) are used when someone waits in a place until something else happens.

***Stay** there until I get back.*
*Please **remain** in your seats until the plane has come to a complete stop.*

If you want to tell someone to wait, you can use the phrase **hang on**.

***Hang on**, I'll be ready in a minute.*

IDIOMS with wait

• **wait a minute**, **wait a second** used for getting someone's attention, or when you suddenly think of something important ○ *Wait a minute – I know what we can do.*

• **wait and see** to be patient until you see what happens ○ *No decision will be made until next year, so you'll just have to wait and see.*

• **wait on** *someone* to serve someone ○ *She waited on customers all day at the department store.*

• **wait out** *someone or something* to wait and do nothing until something happens or ends ○ *We'd better wait out the storm before we start out on our trip.*

• **wait (on) tables** to serve meals to people in a restaurant ○ *She waited tables to pay for college.*

waiter /ˈweɪt̬·ər/, *female* **waitress** /ˈweɪ·trəs/ *n* [C] a person whose job is to serve meals to people in a restaurant ○ *A waiter came to the table to take our order.*

waiting list *n* [C] a list of people who asked for something that is not available now but that might be in the future ○ *The flight is full, but I can put you on the waiting list in case someone cancels.*

waiting room *n* [C] a room where people can sit while waiting, as in a bus station or a doctor's office

waive /weɪv/ *v* [T] to not demand something you have a right to or not cause a rule to be obeyed ○ *The bank waived the charge, because the mistake was their fault.*

waiver /ˈweɪ·vər/ *n* [C] **1** a document that prevents or allows an action that is different from the usual thing ○ *Applicants pay a $30 to $40 entry fee; fee waivers are available.* **2** If a sports player is on waivers he is leaving one team and joining another. ○ *The Coyotes have claimed center Joel Perrault on waivers from the St. Louis Blues.*

wake STOP SLEEPING /weɪk/ *v* [I/T] *past simp.* **woke, waked,** *past part.* **woken, waked** to become awake and conscious after sleeping, or to cause someone to stop sleeping ○ [I] *Did you wake at all during the night?* ○ [T] *The noise of the storm woke the kids.*

waken /ˈweɪ·kən/ *v* [I/T] ○ [T] *He tried to waken her, but she didn't stir.*

WATER /weɪk/ *n* [C] an area of water whose movement has been changed by a boat or ship moving through it ○ (*fig.*) *The storm left a massive amount of destruction in its wake.*

GATHERING /weɪk/ *n* [C] a gathering held before a dead person is buried, at which family and friends talk about the person's life

IDIOM with wake

• **wake up to** *something* to become aware of something ○ *I wish Dad would wake up to the fact that I'm no longer a kid.*

PHRASAL VERBS with wake

• **wake up** *(someone)* STOP SLEEPING [M] to cause someone to stop sleeping ○ *I get up, shower, go to school, go home, sleep, wake up, and do it all over again.* ○ *If you cry you'll wake your brother up.*

• **wake up** *someone* CAUSE ATTENTION [M] to make someone notice a situation and do something about it ○ *There is nothing like a disaster to wake people up.*

wake-up call MORNING CALL *n* [C] a telephone call or signal to wake you in the morning, typically in a hotel

SHOCKING EVENT *n* [C] a shocking event that changes the way many people think ○ *Fish and Game officials got a wake-up call in a survey on wildlife-related issues.*

walk /wɔːk/ *v* [I/T] **1** to move along by putting one foot in front of the other, or to move a distance in this way ○ [I] *I walked home.* ○ [I] *We just walked past a famous actress.* ○ [I] *They walked all around*

Chinatown. ○ [I] *I walk to work every morning.* ○ [T] *It's not that far – you can walk it in half an hour.* ○ [T] *We must have walked miles today.* **2** To walk someone to a particular place is to walk with the person until the place has been reached: [T] *He offered to walk her home.* **3** To walk an animal, esp. a dog, is to bring it outside with you to walk.

walk /wɔːk/ *n* [C] ○ *He went for/took a walk around the block.*

walker /ˈwɔː·kər/ *n* [C] **1** *She's a very fast walker.* **2** A walker is also a metal frame to help people who have difficulty walking, by using it to support them as they move it in front of them.

USAGE

walk or go on foot?

The expression **go on foot** means the same thing as **walk**, and is usually used when you are describing how you get somewhere.

How do you get to school? I go on foot/I walk.

WORD CHOICES walk

If someone walks somewhere very quickly in a determined way, you could use the verbs **stride** or **march**.

*She **strode/marched** purposefully up to the desk and demanded to speak to the manager.*

Stroll, **wander**, and **amble** can be used when someone walks in a slow and relaxed way.

*We **strolled/wandered** along the beach.*

*She **ambled** down the street, looking in store windows.*

If someone is walking slowly because he or she is tired or bored, you could use the verb **plod**.

*We **plodded** on until we reached the cottage.*

Pace is used when someone walks in one direction and back in the other direction several times because the person is anxious.

*He **paced** up and down the hospital corridor waiting for news.*

If someone is walking in a very confident way, especially when you find it annoying, you could use the verb **swagger**.

*He was **swaggering** around like he owned the place.*

Stagger can be used when someone walks in a very unsteady way.

*He **staggered** under the weight of all our luggage.*

To say that someone walks somewhere very quietly, you could use the verbs **creep** or **tiptoe**.

*Someone was **creeping** around outside the window.*

*He waited until the baby was asleep and **tiptoed** out of the room.*

Hike and **trek** can be used when someone walks a long way in the countryside.

*They **hiked** through Mount Rainier National Park.*

*They spent the day **trekking** through forests.*

IDIOMS with walk

• **walk the walk** to show that something is true by your actions rather than your words ○ *We're at this meeting because we're environmentalists who walk the walk.* ○ Compare TALK THE TALK at TALK IDIOMS

• **walks of life** various levels of social position or achievement ○ *In my work I see people from all walks of life.*

PHRASAL VERBS with walk

• **walk all over** *someone* to be unkind to someone and treat that person without respect ○ *You shouldn't let him walk all over you like that.*

• **walk away/off with** *something* to win something easily ○ *The German soccer team is once again favored to walk away with the championship.*

• **walk off with** *something* to take something without asking ○ *Who walked off with my drink?*

• **walk out 1** to leave an event before it is finished because you are not enjoying it or because you do not agree with it ○ *It was such a bad movie that I felt like walking out in the first fifteen minutes.* **2** If workers walk out, they go on STRIKE (= stop working at their jobs in order to express a complaint) : *Airline pilots are threatening to walk out next week.* ○ Related noun: WALKOUT

• **walk out on** *someone/something* to suddenly end your relationship or involvement with someone ○ *You can't afford to walk out on your job.*

• **walk** *(someone)* **through** *something* to practice something, or to show someone how to do something from beginning to end ○ *They can walk you through the process one more time, to give you some practice and confidence.*

walkie-talkie /ˌwɔː·kiː ˈtɔː·ki/ *n* [C] a small radio held in the hand and used for both sending and receiving messages

walk-in LIKE A ROOM *adj* [not gradable] large enough for a person to enter and walk around in ○ *a walk-in closet*

WITHOUT PLANNING *adj* [not gradable] allowing people to come without planning to do so in advance ○ *The walk-in clinic is slowly getting busy.*

walk-in *n* [C] ○ *Although the restaurant will take walk-ins, reservations are recommended.*

walkout /ˈwɔː·kɑʊt/ *n* [C] the act of leaving a place to show that you are unhappy, or (of workers) the act of stopping work because of a disagreement with management ○ *Some people who were unhappy with the changes staged a walkout during the meeting.* ○ *The airline barely averted a walkout by flight attendants this past June.* ○ Related verb: WALK OUT

walk-up *n* [C] a building with four or more floors and no ELEVATOR (= device for taking people from one floor to another), or an apartment on an upper floor in such a building

wall /wɔːl/ *n* [C] **1** a vertical structure that divides or encloses something ○ *The walls of the fortress*

W

were more than eighteen inches thick. ○ *We'd like the walls painted white.* **2** A wall of people or things is a mass of them formed in such a way that you cannot get through or past them.

wallboard /ˈwɔːl·bɔːrd, -boʊrd/ *n* [U] a large, thin, rectangular piece of building material used to make the walls inside some buildings

wallet /ˈwɑl·ət/ *n* [C] a small, folding case for paper money, CREDIT CARDS (= plastic cards you use to buy things), and other cards that you want to carry with you ○ *a leather wallet*

wallop /ˈwɑl·əp/ *v* [T] *infml* to hit someone or something hard ○ *Floyd can wallop high pitches as well as low ones.*

wallow /ˈwɑl·oʊ/ *v* [I] **1** (esp. of animals) to lie or roll about slowly in deep, wet earth, sand, or water ○ *The pig wallowed in the mud.* **2** *fig.* To wallow in an emotion or situation is to stay in that state without trying to change: *He was not a fellow to shed tears, or wallow in self-pity.*

wallpaper /ˈwɔːlˌpeɪ·pər/ *n* [C/U] a type of decorative paper sometimes used to cover the walls of a room instead of painting them ○ [U] *We found some beautiful wallpaper with an orange floral pattern.*

wallpaper /ˈwɔːlˌpeɪ·pər/ *v* [T] ○ *We decided to wallpaper Annie's bedroom.*

Wall Street *n* [U] a street in New York City that represents the financial center of the US ○ *On Wall Street today, stocks closed higher.*

wall-to-wall *adj* covering the whole floor ○ *wall-to-wall carpeting*

walnut /ˈwɔːl·nət, -nʌt/ *n* [C/U] a nut with a hard shell, the tree that produces these nuts, or the wood from the tree

walrus /ˈwɔːl·rəs/ *n* [C] a sea mammal, similar to a SEAL (= a large, fish-eating animal) but larger and with two very long teeth that stick out from the mouth

waltz DANCE /wɔːlts/ *n* [C/U] a type of dance that includes a repeating movement of three steps, or a piece of music written for this style of dancing

waltz /wɔːlts/ *v* [I] ○ *Several couples were waltzing around the floor.*

WALK /wɔːlts/ *v* [I always + adv/prep] *infml* to walk somewhere quickly and confidently ○ *Glen waltzed in an hour late as though nothing were wrong.*

W

wan /wɑn/ *adj* (of a person's face or expression) pale, tired, or weak ○ *a wan smile*

wand /wɑnd/ *n* [C] a thin stick waved by a person who is performing magic ○ *a magic wand*

wander /ˈwɑn·dər/ *v* [I/T] **1** to walk around slowly in a relaxed way or without any clear purpose or direction ○ [T] *The lost child wandered the streets for hours.* ○ [I] *We spent the morning wandering around the old part of the city.* **2** If your mind or your thoughts wander, you stop thinking about what you should be giving your attention to and start thinking about other matters: [I] *As he droned on, my mind began to wander.*

wane /weɪn/ *v* [I] to weaken in strength or influence ○ *By the late 70s, the band's popularity was beginning to wane.*

wangle /ˈwæŋ·gəl/ *v* [T] to succeed in obtaining or doing something by not being completely honest in persuading someone to allow it ○ *I wangled an expense-account trip to New York.*

wanna /ˈwɑn·ə, ˈwʌn·ə, ˈwɔː·nə/ *v* [T] *not standard* (spelled the way it is often spoken) want to ○ *I wanna be a rock star.*

wannabe /ˈwɑn·ə·bi, ˈwʌn·ə-, ˈwɔː·nə-/ *n* [C] *infml* a person who wants to be like someone else, esp. someone famous, or who wants to be thought of as famous ○ *She's a pop singer wannabe.*

want DESIRE /wɑnt, wʌnt, wɔːnt/ *v* [I/T] **1** to feel that you would like to have something or would like something to happen ○ [T] *Who wants ice cream?* ○ [T] *I want the cold weather to end.* ○ [I] *She wanted to get new shoes.* ○ [T] *I don't want him talking about me.* ○ [I] *I've been wanting to thank you for helping me.* **2** If you are wanted, someone wishes to see or talk with you: [T] *Harry! You're wanted on the phone.*

wanted /ˈwɑnt·əd, ˈwʌnt-, ˈwɔːnt-/ *adj* being searched for by the police ○ *He was one of the ten most wanted criminals in America.*

> **GRAMMAR**
>
> **want**
>
> Remember to use the infinitive **to** in the expression **want *something/someone* to *do something***. You cannot use **that** plus a verb clause after **want**.
>
> *I just want him to enjoy himself.*
>
> ~~*I just want that he enjoy himself.*~~
>
> *They don't want the summer vacation to end.*
>
> ~~*They don't want that the summer vacation end.*~~

NEED /wɑnt, wʌnt, wɔːnt/ *v* [I/T] to need something ○ [I] *You want to be careful to stay out of the sun.*

want /wɑnt, wʌnt, wɔːnt/ *n* [C/U] ○ [C] *A cat's wants are few – food and companionship.*

wanting /ˈwɑnt·ɪŋ, ˈwʌnt-, ˈwɔːnt-/ *adj* ○ *It was a perfect party – nothing was wanting* (= missing).

WORD FAMILY want

Nouns	want	*Adjectives*	wanted
Verbs	want		wanting unwanted

PHRASAL VERB with want

- **want for** *something* to lack something you need ○ *We didn't have much, but we never wanted for food.*

want ad *n* [C] a CLASSIFIED AD

wanton /ˈwɑnt·ən, ˈwɔːnt-/ *adj* causing harm or acting without showing care for others, often intentionally ○ *He displayed a wanton disregard for the facts.*

war /wɔːr/ *n* [C/U] **1** armed fighting between two or more countries or groups, or a particular example of such fighting ○ [C] *Can any country fight two wars at the same time?* ○ [U] *War is something to avoid.* ○ [U] *Several nations were at war.* **2** A war can also be any situation in which there is strong competition between opposing sides or a joint effort against something harmful: [C] *Airlines engage in fare wars to attract new customers.* ○ [U] *It sometimes seems like the war on cancer has stalled.*

warring /ˈwɔːr·ɪŋ/ *adj* [not gradable] fighting a war or as if fighting a war ○ *Warring groups roamed the countryside, making travel very dangerous.* ○ *Warring camps inside the Democratic party weaken it.*

warlike /ˈwɔːr·lɑɪk/ *adj* suited to or liking war, or threatening, as if going to fight ○ *a warlike mood* ○ *a warlike speech*

WORD FAMILY war			
Nouns	war	*Adjectives*	prewar
	warfare		postwar
	warrior		warring
			warlike

warble /ˈwɔːr·bəl/ *v* [I] to sing as a bird does with a sound that rises and falls ○ *This morning it seemed as if every bird began to warble at once.*

war chest *n* [C] *infml* money that has been collected or saved to pay for something, esp. a long fight achieve something ○ *The candidates are gathering money for their election war chests.*

war crime *n* [C] ***world history*** an act, such as harming prisoners or children, that is against the agreed international rules of war

ward **HOSPITAL ROOM** /wɔːrd/ *n* [C] a large room in a hospital which is used for treating people with similar illnesses or conditions ○ *the pediatric/maternity ward*

PERSON /wɔːrd/ *n* [C] *law* a person, esp. a child, who is legally under the protection or care of another person or of a court or government ○ *The agency serves youths who are wards of the state.*

AREA /wɔːrd/ *n* [C] a political division within a city ○ *the fifth ward*

PHRASAL VERB with ward

• **ward off** *someone/something* [M] to keep someone or something away or prevent something from happening or harming you ○ *He used his umbrella to ward off the fierce sun.*

warden /ˈwɔːrd·ən/ *n* [C] a person who is in charge of a prison

wardrobe /ˈwɔːr·droʊb/ *n* [C] **1** the clothes that a person owns, or a particular type of clothes that a person owns ○ *She has a different wardrobe for every occasion.* **2** A wardrobe is also a piece of furniture where clothes are kept.

warehouse /ˈwer·hɑʊs, ˈwær-/ *n* [C] *pl* **warehouses** **1** a large building used for storing goods ○ *Textbooks are sent right from the warehouse to the schools.* **2** A warehouse is also a type of large store where goods are sold at a reduced price.

warehousing /ˈwer ˌhɑʊ·zɪŋ, ˈwær-/ *n* [U] ○ *The buildings will be used for warehousing and distribution.*

wares /werz, wærz/ *pl n* items offered for sale, or a company's goods ○ *More than 40 dealers in furniture, art, and silver will display their wares.*

warfare /ˈwɔːr·fer, -fær/ *n* [U] the activity of fighting a war or strongly competing, esp. with reference to the type of weapons used or to the way the fighting is done ○ *psychological/nuclear warfare* ○ *economic warfare*

war games *pl n* practices held by armed forces to test new equipment and test plans for fighting

warhead /ˈwɔːr·hed/ *n* [C] the end of a bomb or MISSILE that contains explosives

warily /ˈwer·ə·li, ˈwær-/ *adv* See at WARY.

warlike /ˈwɔːr·lɑɪk/ *adj* ○ See at WAR

warlord /ˈwɔːr·lɔːrd/ *n* [C] a military leader who controls a country or, more frequently, an area within a country, esp. when the central government is not in control

warm **HIGH TEMPERATURE** /wɔːrm/ *adj* [*-er/-est* only] **1** having a fairly high temperature, but not hot ○ *Warm bread always tastes better.* ○ *Just let me sit in the sun so I can get warm.* **2** Warm clothes or covers keep out the cold and make you feel comfortable: *a warm winter coat* ○ *a warm woolen hat and mittens*

warm /wɔːrm/ *v* [I/T] to rise to a higher temperature, or to cause something to rise to a higher temperature ○ [T] *He rubbed his hands together to warm them.* ○ [I] *The water in the kettle warms quickly.*

warmly /ˈwɔːrm·li/ *adv* ○ *He was warmly dressed in a heavy overcoat and a fur hat.*

warmth /wɔːrmθ/ *n* [U] ○ *She laid down on the sand and enjoyed the warmth of the sun.* ○ *The dogs huddled together for warmth.*

FRIENDLY /wɔːrm/ *adj* [*-er/-est* only] friendly and affectionate ○ *Grace is a warm, caring woman.*

warmly /ˈwɔːrm·li/ *adv* ○ *He shook my hand warmly.*

warmth /wɔːrmθ/ *n* [U] ○ *He brought warmth and wisdom to his work with children.*

COLORS /wɔːrm/ *adj* ***art*** (of colors) light and bright, and esp. containing red, yellow, or orange

W

WORD FAMILY warm			
Nouns	warmth	*Verbs*	warm
Adjectives	warm	*Adverbs*	warmly

PHRASAL VERBS with warm

• **warm up** *something* **HEAT** [M] to make something hotter ○ *I can warm up the leftover soup for lunch.* ○ *We warmed the rolls up in the oven.*

•**warm up** *(something)* **PRACTICE** [M] **1** to exercise or practice in order to prepare for something that takes a lot of effort ○ *Ballet dancers have to warm up before performing.* ○ *A new pitcher is warming up in the bullpen.* ○ *She warms up her voice by singing scales.* **2** If you warm up a car, you let the engine get warm enough to work well. ○ Related noun: WARMUP
•**warm up to** *someone/something* to begin to like or enjoy someone or something ○ *She was not a person who was easy to warm up to.*

warm-blooded *adj* [not gradable] having a warm body temperature that stays the same ○ Compare COLD-BLOODED

warm-hearted *adj* kind and affectionate ○ *He was a warm-hearted man who helped me when I needed a friend.*

warmup /ˈwɔːr·mʌp/ *n* [C] a period of exercise or practice to prepare for something ○ *He injured his knee during pregame warmups.* ○ *I bought an exercise video, but I never got further than the warmup exercises.* ○ Related verb: WARM UP **PRACTICE**

warn /wɔːrn/ *v* [I/T] to make someone aware of a possible danger or problem so that it can be avoided ○ [T] *I warned her not to waste her money on that movie.* ○ [T] *We'd been warned that we should lock our cars in the parking lot.* ○ [I] *The radio warned all day of the bad weather coming.*
warning /ˈwɔːr·nɪŋ/ *n* [C/U] notice of a possible danger or problem, so that it can be prevented or avoided ○ [C] *Flood warnings were issued by the National Weather Service.* ○ [U] *The earthquake struck without warning while the city was asleep.*

PHRASAL VERB with warn

•**warn** *someone* **off** *(something)* [M] to tell someone not to do something because of danger or some other reason ○ *A series of flares had been placed along the pavement to warn off motorists.*

warning sign *n* [C] an early signal that something bad or dangerous might happen ○ *You should know the warning signs of a stroke.*

warp **BEND** /wɔːrp/ *v* [I/T] (of a surface or hard material) to bend or twist so that the surface is no longer flat or straight ○ [T] *Water poured in, ruining carpets, warping walls, destroying wiring.*
warped /wɔːrpt/ *adj* ○ *Galaxy ESO 510-G13, about 100,000 light-years across, is unusual because it's warped rather than perfectly flat.*

MAKE WRONG /wɔːrp/ *v* [T] to cause something or someone to no longer do what is usual or right ○ *The novel is an appraisal of how totalitarianism can warp a society.*
warped /wɔːrpt/ *adj* ○ *a warped vision of the future* ○ *a warped character*

warpath **IDIOM** /ˈwɔːr·pæθ/
•**on the warpath** angry and ready to argue or fight ○ *I told my friends to watch out because my mother was on the warpath.*

warplane /ˈwɑr·pleɪn/ *n* [C] an armed military aircraft ○ *Fifty new warplanes were delivered to the army.*

W

warrant **MAKE NECESSARY** /ˈwɑr·ənt, ˈwɔːr-/ *v* [T] *fml* to make a particular action necessary or correct, or to be a reason to do something ○ *His injury was serious enough to warrant an operation.* ○ *I can see circumstances in which these types of investigations would be warranted.*

DOCUMENT /ˈwɑr·ənt, ˈwɔːr-/ *n* [C] an official document approved by an authority, esp. a judge, which gives the police permission to do certain things ○ *a search warrant* ○ *an arrest warrant*

warranty /ˌwɑr·ən ˈtiː, ˌwɔːr-/ *n* [C/U] a written promise by a company to repair or replace a product that breaks within a fixed period of time or do again a piece of work that is not satisfactory ○ [C] *a five-year warranty* ○ [U] *I've had problems with the car, but it's still under warranty.*

warring /ˈwɔːr·ɪŋ/ *adj* See at WAR.

warrior /ˈwɔːr·jər/ *n* [C] a person who has experience and skill in fighting, esp. as a soldier ○ *The Apache chief Geronimo had a reputation as a fearless warrior.*

warship /ˈwɑr·ʃɪp/ *n* [C] a boat equipped with guns and other weapons of war

wart /wɔːrt/ *n* [C] a small, hard lump that grows on the skin and is caused by a virus

IDIOM with wart

•**warts and all** including all faults and unpleasant facts ○ *She's anxious to tell her story, warts and all.*

wartime /ˈwɑr·tɑɪm/ *n* [U] a period of armed fighting between two countries ○ *During wartime, everyone's life changes a lot.*

wary /ˈwer·i, ˈwær·i/ *adj* careful because you do not completely trust someone or something or are not certain about what you should do ○ *Teachers are often wary of standardized tests.*
warily /ˈwer·ə·li, ˈwær-/ *adv* ○ *Ted warily eyed the stranger.*

was /wʌz, wɑz, wəz/ *past simple of* BE

wash **CLEAN** /wɑʃ, wɔːʃ/ *v* [I/T] to make something or yourself clean, or to become clean, using water and usually soap ○ [T] *Alex washed his face and combed his hair.* ○ [T] *I hate washing dishes.*
wash /wɑʃ, wɔːʃ/ *n* [C/U] an act of washing, or clothing, sheets, and other cloth items being cleaned together ○ [C usually sing] *I went days without a wash or a change of clothes.* ○ [U] *She did a load of wash and hung it up to dry.*
washable /ˈwɑʃ·ə·bəl, ˈwɔː·ʃə-/ *adj* [not gradable] **1** able to be cleaned in water without damaging the material ○ *Are these pants washable?* **2** If a type of material or a piece of clothing is machine-washable, it can be cleaned in a WASHING MACHINE.
washer /ˈwɑʃ·ər, ˈwɔː·ʃər/ *n* [C] a WASHING MACHINE ○ See also: WASHER
washing /ˈwɑʃ·ɪŋ, ˈwɔː·ʃɪŋ/ *n* [U] the act of cleaning clothes, or cloth items being washed together ○ *He does his own washing and ironing.*

WORD CHOICES wash

Rinse is used when you wash something in water to remove the soap or dirt from it.

*She **rinsed** the cloth in the sink.*

If you wash something using soap, water, and a stiff brush, you could use the verb **scrub**.

*He tried to **scrub** the pen marks off the wall.*

Soak is used when you wash something by leaving it in some water for a long time.

*She **soaked** the T-shirt overnight to get rid of the stains.*

When you wash yourself, you can say that you **bathe**.

*I'll just **bathe** and then I'll be ready.*

FLOW /wɑʃ, wɔːʃ/ *v* [I/T] **1** (esp. of water) to flow or to cause to flow, often carrying something along ○ [I] *Waves washed against the boat.* ○ [T] *Heavy rains always wash the sand down the hill.* **2** If something is washed away, it is carried off by heavy rain or a flood: [M] *Even trees and cars were washed away in this flood.* **3** If something washes up or washes ashore, water has moved it there: [M] *That storm washed a lot of crabs up on the shore.*

NO CHANGE /wɑʃ, wɔːʃ/ *n* [C usually sing] an event or situation in which positive and negative things balance each other ○ *I sold my car for about what it cost me, so it was a wash.*

WORD FAMILY wash

Nouns	wash washer washing	*Adjectives* *Verbs*	washable wash

IDIOMS with wash

• **doesn't wash**, **won't wash** to be unacceptable ○ *Don't think you can get credit without doing the work – that doesn't wash around here.*

• **wash** *your* **hands of** *someone or something* to refuse to have anything more to do with someone or something ○ *You can't start a fight and then just wash your hands of it*

PHRASAL VERBS with wash

• **wash down** *something* [M] **1** to clean something by causing water to flow over it ○ *I took the hose and washed down the front porch.* **2** *infml* If you wash down food, you drink something after eating it: *She was eating bread and cheese and washing it down with iced tea.*

• **wash off** *(something)* [M] to remove something with flowing water, or to come off after you do this ○ *She could hardly wait to wash the dirt off.* ○ *I don't know if this paint will wash off.*

• **wash out** *(something)* **BE REMOVED** [M] to remove something by washing, or to disappear after washing ○ *I hope this stain will wash out.* ○ Related adjective: WASHED-OUT

• **wash out** *something* **BE DESTROYED** [M] (esp. of bad or violent weather) to cause something to fail, stop, or be destroyed ○ *Rain washed tonight's game out.* ○ *The storm washed out roads and bridges.*

• **wash up CLEAN HANDS** to clean your hands, esp. before a meal ○ *She told the children to wash up for dinner.*

• **wash up APPEAR NEAR WATER** [M] to appear on land because the ocean or a river or lake left it there ○ *Spilled oil has washed up on beaches behind the wreck.*

washable /ˈwɑʃ·ə·bəl, ˈwɔː·ʃə-/ *adj* ○ See at WASH CLEAN

washcloth /ˈwɑʃ·klɔːθ, ˈwɔːʃ-/ *n* [C] a small cloth used with soap and water to clean your face and body

washed-out /wɑʃtˈɑʊt, wɔːʃt-/ *adj* **1** lacking color or appearing old as a result of being washed over and over again ○ *a pair of washed-out jeans* **2** Someone who looks washed-out looks pale and tired. ○ Related verb: WASH OUT BE REMOVED

washed-up /ˈwɑʃtˈʌp, ˈwɔːʃt-/ *adj* [not gradable] *infml* no longer suitable for or able to do what you did in the past ○ *a washed-up comic*

washer /ˈwɑʃ·ər, ˈwɔː·ʃər/ *n* [C] a flat ring of metal, rubber, or plastic that is used to make a tighter connection between two pieces or parts of something ○ See also: WASHER at WASH CLEAN

washer-dryer *n* [C] a unit that contains two machines, one for cleaning clothes, sheets, etc., and another for drying them

washing /ˈwɑʃ·ɪŋ, ˈwɔː·ʃɪŋ/ *n* [U] ○ See at WASH CLEAN

washing machine *n* [C] a machine for washing clothes, sheets, and other cloth items

washout /ˈwɑʃ·ɑʊt, ˈwɔː·ʃɑʊt/ *n* [C usually sing] *infml* a complete failure ○ *The dance was a washout – only three people showed up.*

washroom /ˈwɑʃ·ruːm, ˈwɔːʃ-, -rʊm/ *n* [C] a bathroom

wasn't /ˈwʌz·ənt, ˈwɑz-/ *v contraction of* was not ○ *I wasn't hungry so I didn't eat.*

wasp /wɑsp, wɔːsp/ *n* [C] a flying insect that is able to sting repeatedly

WASP /wɑsp, wɔːsp/ *n* [C] *abbreviation for* white Anglo-Saxon protestant (= a white, Protestant American whose family originally came from northwestern Europe)

waste BAD USE /weɪst/ *n* [U] a bad use of something valuable that you have only a limited amount of ○ *a waste of time/money* ○ *a waste of talent/ability* ○ *I felt like being there was just a waste.*

waste /weɪst/ *v* [T] to use something without care or thought ○ *Why should I waste my time on her?* ○ *You're just wasting your money buying that stuff.*

wasteful /ˈweɪst·fəl/ *adj* ○ *wasteful spending* ○ *a wasteful use of resources*

UNWANTED MATTER /weɪst/ *n* **1** unwanted matter or material of any type, esp. what is left after use ○ [C] *hazardous/toxic wastes* ○ [U] *Most people don't recycle kitchen waste.* **2** ***biology*** Human waste is excrement. **3** Waste disposal is the process

W

or system for getting rid of unwanted material by burying it, burning it, or dropping it in the sea.

WORD FAMILY waste			
Nouns	waste	*Verbs*	waste
Adjectives	waste wasteful	*Adverbs*	wastefully

IDIOMS with waste

• **waste** *your* **breath** to say something that will likely be ignored ○ *Don't waste your breath arguing with him.*

• **waste no time** to immediately begin an activity ○ *Caroline wasted no time in tackling her new responsibilities.*

• **wasted on** *someone* to not be appreciated by someone ○ *Your excellent cooking will be wasted on them.*

PHRASAL VERB with waste

• **waste away** (of a person or animal) to gradually get thinner and weaker, esp. from disease or lack of food ○ *It was hard to watch her waste away.*

wastebasket /ˈweɪstˌbæs·kət/ *n* [C] a container to hold paper or other small things you want to get rid of

wasteland /ˈweɪst·lænd/ *n* [C] **1** a large area of land that has not been developed, usually because it cannot be easily used ○ *Rain forests are being transformed into barren wasteland.* **2** A wasteland can also be anything that seems to lack positive qualities: *Television is a vast wasteland.*

wastewater /ˈweɪstˌwɔːt̬·ər, -ˌwɑt̬·ər/ *n* [U] water that is not clean because it has already been used in homes, businesses, factories, etc. ○ *The facility pumped fuel for 101 days before the wastewater pipe leak was detected.*

watch SMALL CLOCK /wɑtʃ, wɔːtʃ/ *n* [C] a small clock usually worn on a strap around the wrist, or sometimes carried in a pocket ○ *She looked at her watch and said, "It's a quarter to five."*

LOOK AT /wɑtʃ, wɔːtʃ/ *v* to look at something for a period of time ○ [T] *He spent the evening watching an old movie on TV.* ○ [+ to infinitive] *The police were watching to see who left the house.* ○ [T] *Do you want me to watch the kids* (= notice what they are doing and care for them) *when you go out?*

watch /wɑtʃ, wɔːtʃ/ *n* [C/U] **1** [U] *The prison guards kept a close watch on him.* **2** Watch is also a period during which someone is responsible for guarding or looking around to be sure that property or people are safe, or the person who is responsible: [C] *The soldiers on the night watch had to be careful not to fall asleep.*

watcher /wɑtʃ·ər, wɔː·tʃər/ *n* [C] someone who is interested in the developments and changes of a particular thing ○ *But the real growth, industry watchers say, will come in the corporate and personal jet sector.*

watchful /ˈwɑtʃ·fəl, ˈwɔːtʃ-/ *adj* giving careful attention so as to notice what is happening and be prepared for something that might happen ○ *If you invest heavily in the stock market, you have to stay watchful and be ready to move your money quickly.*

BE CAREFUL /wɑtʃ, wɔːtʃ/ *v* [T] to be careful of something ○ *We have to watch our bank account to make sure there's enough money in it to pay our credit card bills.* ○ *I've got to start watching my weight* (= be careful not to become fat). ○ *The sign says "Watch for* (= be careful of) *falling rocks."*

WORD FAMILY watch			
Nouns	watch watcher	*Adjectives*	watchful
		Verbs	watch

IDIOMS with watch

• **watch out** used for warning someone of danger or an accident that seems likely to happen ○ *Watch out for that last step – it's a lot steeper than the others.*

• **watch** *your* **step** to be careful about how you behave ○ *He'll have to watch his step if he wants to keep his job.*

PHRASAL VERB with watch

• **watch over** *someone* to protect people and make certain that they are safe ○ *She had to watch over four young children and take care of a sick husband.*

watchdog ORGANIZATION /ˈwɑtʃ·dɔːg, ˈwɔːtʃ-/ *n* [C] a person or organization responsible for making certain that companies or other organizations maintain standards and do not act illegally ○ *a watchdog agency/organization*

DOG /ˈwɑtʃ·dɔːg, ˈwɔːtʃ-/ *n* [C] a dog trained to protect a place

water /ˈwɔːt̬·ər, ˈwɑt̬-/ *n* [U] **1** a clear, colorless liquid that falls from the sky as rain and is necessary for animal and plant life ○ *a drink/glass of water* ○ *bottled/tap water* ○ *cold/hot water* ○ *I'm boiling water to make some more coffee.* **2** The water often refers to an area of water, such as the sea or a lake: *The water's much warmer today – are you coming for a swim?* **3** Waters is an area of natural water, such as a part of the sea: [pl] *coastal waters*

water /ˈwɔːt̬·ər, ˈwɑt̬-/ *v* [I/T] **1** to provide water to a plant or animal ○ [T] *I've asked my neighbor to water the plants while I'm away.* **2** When your eyes water, they produce tears but not because you are unhappy: [I] *The icy wind made his eyes water.* **3** If your mouth waters, it produces a lot of SALIVA, usually because you can see or smell food that you would like to eat: [I] *The smell of that bread is making my mouth water.*

watery /ˈwɔːt̬·ə·ri, ˈwɑt̬-/ *adj* having a lot of or too much water ○ *The soup was thin and watery.*

WORD FAMILY water			
Nouns	water	*Adjectives*	underwater waterproof watery
Verbs	water		
Adverbs	underwater		

IDIOM with water

• **water under the bridge** something that happened in the past and cannot now be changed ○

Yes, we did have our disagreements, but that's water under the bridge.

PHRASAL VERB with water

•**water down** *something* [M] to make something weaker or less effective ○ *The law was watered down after it failed to pass the legislature the first time.*

waterbed /ˈwɔːt̬·ər ˌbed, ˈwɑt̬·ər-/ *n* [C] a bed in which the MATTRESS (= the part you lie on) is a container filled with water

water bird *n* [C] any kind of WATERFOWL

watercolor, *Cdn, Br* **watercolour** /ˈwɔːt̬·ər ˌkʌl·ər, ˈwɑt̬-/ *n* [C] ***art*** a paint that is mixed with water to create pictures, or a picture made with this paint ○ *The art gallery is having a show of early 20th-century American watercolors.*

water cycle *n* [U] ***biology*** the way that water is taken up from the sea, rivers, SOIL, etc. and then comes back down as rain or snow

waterfall /ˈwɔːt̬·ər ˌfɔːl, ˈwɑt̬·ər-/ *n* [C] water from a river or stream falling over an edge of rock to a much lower level

water fountain *n* [C] a device in a public place that allows anyone to drink water without a cup by pushing a button and drinking from a stream of water that comes out

waterfowl /ˈwɔːt̬·ər ˌfɑʊl, ˈwɑt̬·ər-/ *n* [C/U] the types of birds that live on or near rivers, lakes, or the ocean

waterfront /ˈwɔːt̬·ər ˌfrʌnt, ˈwɑt̬·ər-/ *n* [C] a part of a town next to an area of water such as a lake, a river, or the ocean

water main *n* [C] a large underground pipe that supplies water to buildings in an area of a city or town

watermelon /ˈwɔːt̬·ər ˌmel·ən, ˈwɑt̬-/ *n* [C/U] a large, round or oval-shaped fruit with dark green skin, sweet, watery, pink or yellow flesh, and a lot of black seeds

water polo *n* [U] a game played in water in which two teams try to get the ball into the other team's goal

waterproof /ˈwɔːt̬·ər ˌpruːf, ˈwɑt̬-/ *adj* not allowing water to go through ○ *waterproof boots*

water-repellent, **water-resistant** *adj* able to keep rain from being absorbed

watershed BIG CHANGE /ˈwɔːt̬·ər ˌʃed, ˈwɑt̬-/ *n* [U] an event or period that is important because it represents a big change and the start of new developments ○ *a watershed event/moment* ○ *The discovery of penicillin was a watershed in the history of medicine.*

AREA /ˈwɔːt̬·ər ˌʃed, ˈwɑt̬-/ *n* [C] ***earth science*** a high area of land where rain collects, some of it flowing down to supply rivers, lakes, etc., at lower levels

waterskiing /ˈwɔːt̬·ər ˌskiː·ɪŋ, ˈwɑt̬·ər-/ *n* [U] a sport in which you are pulled along the surface of a lake or ocean by a boat while balancing on a pair of SKIS fastened to your feet

water supply *n* [C] the water that is provided and treated for a particular area ○ *When we don't get enough rainfall, we have to worry about our water supply.*

water table [C] ***earth science*** the layer below the earth's surface where water is found

watertight /ˈwɔːt̬·ər ˌtɑɪt, ˈwɑt̬-/ *adj* having no openings to allow the passage of water ○ *They're doing some repairs on the church to make the roof watertight.*

waterway /ˈwɔːt̬·ər ˌweɪ, ˈwɑt̬·ər-/ *n* [C] a regularly used route used by boats, such as a river or channel

waterworks SUPPLY SYSTEM /ˈwɔːt̬·ər ˌwɜrks, ˈwɑt̬·ər-/ *n* [C] a system of buildings and pipes in which a public supply of water is stored and cleaned and from which it is sent out

CRYING /ˈwɔːt̬·ər ˌwɜrks, ˈwɑt̬·ər-/ *n* [U] *infml* crying ○ *The show ended, and then the waterworks started.* ○ *Whenever she gets frustrated or angry, she* **turns on the waterworks** (= starts to cry).

watery /ˈwɔːt̬·ə·ri, ˈwɑt̬-/ *adj* ○ See at WATER

watt /wɑt/, *abbreviation* **w** *n* [C] ***physics*** the standard measure of electrical power ○ *a 60-watt bulb*

wave MOVE /weɪv/ *v* [I/T] **1** to raise your hand and move it from side to side as a greeting, or to get someone's attention or give information ○ [I] *She leaned out the window and waved (good-bye).* ○ [M] *As soon as we showed our papers as journalists, the policeman waved us in* (= moved his hand to allow us to go in). **2** If you wave something or something waves, you move it from side to side while holding it in the hand, or something else moves it in this way: [T] *He was very excited and rushed into the room waving a piece of paper.* ○ [I] *Flags waved in the breeze.*

wave /weɪv/ *n* [C] ○ *She looked at him for a long time, and then, with a wave of her hand, she was off.*

WATER MOVEMENT /weɪv/ *n* [C] **1** a raised movement of water rolling across the surface esp. of the sea ○ *We were so close we could hear the waves breaking on the beach.* **2** A wave is also a sudden increase in an activity or in the strength of a condition or feeling: *A wave of emotion swept through her as she visited her home town.*

ENERGY FORM /weɪv/ *n* [C] ***physics*** the continuous, repeating pattern in which some types of energy, such as sound, light, and heat, are spread or carried ○ *electromagnetic waves*

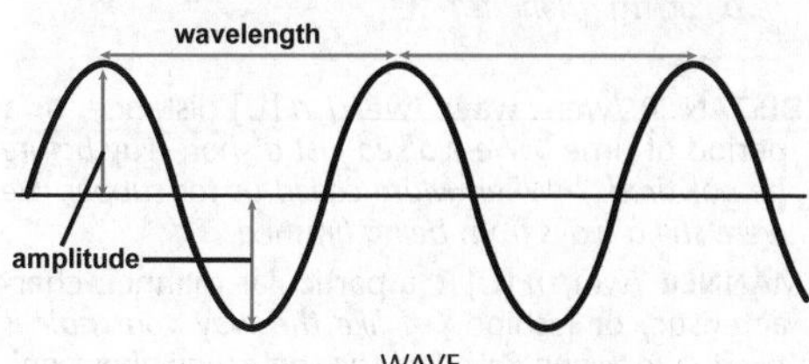

WAVE

W

wavelength /ˈweɪv·leŋθ, -lenθ/ *n* [C] ***physics*** **1** the distance between two waves of energy **2** A wavelength is also the length of the radio wave used by a particular radio station for broadcasting.

waver /ˈweɪ·vər/ *v* [I] **1** to begin to doubt or lose your determination to do something ○ *He never wavered as the leading voice of African-Americans' call for freedom and equality.* **2** If you waver between two possibilities, you have difficulty deciding between them: *She wavered between believing him and thinking that he was lying.*

wavy /ˈweɪ·vi/ *adj* curving in shape, or having a series of curves ○ *Jasmine's got wavy blond hair.*

wax SUBSTANCE /wæks/ *n* [U] a solid, fatty substance that softens and melts at a low temperature ○ *Candle wax dripped on the tablecloth.*

wax /wæks/ *v* [T] to put a thin layer of wax on the surface of something ○ *I just waxed the floor, so don't go in there yet.*

waxy /ˈwæk·si/ *adj* having the appearance of or feeling like wax ○ *He had a waxy complexion and looked ill.*

APPEAR LARGER /wæks/ *v* [I] (of the moon) to gradually appear larger and increasingly round ○ *(fig.) Such controversies have waxed and waned* (= become stronger and weaker) *but continue to this day.*

BECOME /wæks/ *v* [L] *fml* to become ○ *Brad waxed eloquent on the subject of free enterprise.*

wax paper, **waxed paper** *n* [U] paper that has a thin layer of wax on it and is used for wrapping food

way ROUTE /weɪ/ *n* [C] **1** a route or path to follow in order to get to a place ○ *Do you know the way to the train station?* **2** If you don't know your way, can't find your way, or have lost your way, you are not sure or do not know how to get where you want to go: *I don't really know my way around town yet.* **3** Way also means street: *Our office is at 17 Harbor Way.* **4** Way can mean the direction, position, or order of something: *The numbers should be the other way around – 71, not 17.* **5** Your way can also be the progress of your life: *He made his way from sales assistant to head of sales.*

> **USAGE**
>
> **way or trip?**
>
> **Way** refers only to the route that you take to get from one place to another.
>
> *Is there another way out of here?*
>
> *I must get a paper on my way home.*
>
> To talk more generally about the length of the route or the time it takes, use the word **trip**.
>
> *a car/train/long trip*

DISTANCE /weɪ/, **ways** /weɪz/ *n* [U] distance, or a period of time ○ *We walked just a short way before he got tired.* ○ *When Mom called us for supper, we were still a ways from being finished.*

MANNER /weɪ/ *n* [C] **1** a particular manner, characteristic, or fashion ○ *I like the way your hair is fixed.* ○ *Jack and Beth feel the same way about animals.* ○ *There is no way I can leave her.* ○ *They don't write songs the way they used to.* **2** Your way is also the ability to do things in the manner you want: *My little sister gets furious if she doesn't get her way.*

> **USAGE**
>
> **way or method/means of?**
>
> **Way** in this sense is used on its own or followed by **to do** *something* or **of** and a present participle (**-ing** form).
>
> *You can get there in a number of ways.*
>
> *What's the best way to get there?*
>
> *What's the best way of getting there?*
>
> **Method of** or **means of** are not used on their own, and are followed by a noun.
>
> *What method of transportation do you use?*
>
> *We had no means of communication.*
>
> ~~*We have no way of communication.*~~

FAR /weɪ/ *adv* [always + adv/prep; not gradable] *infml* **1** (used for emphasis) far or long ○ *That skirt's way too much money.* ○ *Come on now, Alexander, it's way past your bedtime.* **2** *slang* Way can also mean very: *That car is way cool!*

WORD FAMILY way

Nouns	causeway	*Adjectives*	halfway
	freeway		one-way
	highway		out-of-the-way
	subway		two-way
	thruway	*Adverbs*	halfway
	way		midway
			one-way

IDIOMS with way

• **by the way** used for introducing a statement or subject that may not be directly related to the subject being discussed ○ *By the way, I heard that Phyllis may be moving to Dallas.*

• **in a way** considered in a particular manner ○ *In a way, I hope he doesn't win.*

• **in the way** in a position that prevents something from happening or someone from moving ○ *Work often gets in the way of my social life.* ○ *It's a small street, and he parked right in the way.*

• **on its way** **1** happening or arriving soon ○ *They have three kids, and another on the way.* ○ *My school is well on its way to a championship.* ○ *We're on our way from Logan, and should be there soon.* **2** If you are **on** *your* **way** you are leaving: *Give me a kiss and I'll be on my way.*

• **the way things are**, **the way things stand** given the situation as it is now ○ *The way things stand, I cannot continue to work.*

• **way of life** the manner in which a person or society usually lives ○ *Sleeping in hotels three or four nights a week is not an ideal way of life.*

wayward /ˈweɪ·wərd/ *adj* not behaving or moving as expected ○ *He was a wayward kid.* ○ *A wayward ball bounced into the yard.*

we PEOPLE /wiː, wɪ/ *pronoun* [pl] **1** the person speaking and one or more others ○ *If you don't hurry up we won't be on time.* **2** We can be used by

W

a speaker or a writer to refer to the listener or person reading and the person speaking or writing: *We have to get started now if we're going to finish this afternoon.* **3** We can also mean you: *Now everyone, we don't want to be late, do we?*

ALL PEOPLE /wiː, wɪ/ *pronoun* [pl] all people; everyone ○ *We live on planet earth.*

weak NOT STRONG /wiːk/ *adj* [*-er/-est* only] **1** lacking strength or energy, or likely to stop working or break ○ *After having been so sick, it's not surprising you still feel weak.* ○ *That old chair is very weak and needs gluing.* **2** A drink that is weak lacks flavor: *The coffee was weak and tasteless.* **3** A weak link is the part of something that is most likely to break: *This year, the team's only weak link is that third baseman.*

weaken /ˈwiː·kən/ *v* [I/T] ○ [I] *The country's economy continues to weaken.* ○ [T] *Long exposure to vibration can weaken aircraft parts.*

weakly /ˈwiː·kli/ *adv* ○ *"I'm feeling a little better now," he said weakly.*

weakness /ˈwiːk·nəs/ *n* [C/U] **1** [U] *The building's collapse was caused by weakness in several beams.* **2** Weakness is also a fault in someone's character: [U] *Is crying always a sign of weakness?* **3** A weakness is also a strong liking for something: [C] *She admitted to a weakness for desserts.*

WORD CHOICES weak

If someone is physically weak because of being small, you could describe that person as **puny** or a **weakling.**

*He was **puny** as a child.*

*It would take more than a few exercises to turn a ninety-pound **weakling** into a heavyweight boxer.*

If someone is physically weak because of being old or ill, you could use the adjective **frail.**

*a **frail**, gray-haired lady*

If someone is weak and could easily be hurt, you can describe them as **defenseless** or **vulnerable.**

*a small **defenseless** child*

*The disease most often affects **vulnerable** people such as children and the elderly.*

BELOW STANDARD /wiːk/ *adj* [*-er/-est* only] below standard; not good enough ○ *He was always weak in languages but strong in science.*

WORD FAMILY weak

Nouns	weakling, weakness	Verbs	weaken
Adjectives	weak	Adverbs	weakly

weak acid *n* [C] ***chemistry*** an acid with a PH of 5 or 6 whose MOLECULES do not break down into smaller molecules or atoms in water

weak base *n* [C] ***chemistry*** a BASE whose MOLECULES do not break down into smaller molecules or atoms in water

weak force *n* [C/U] ***physics*** a reaction between PARTICLES (= very small pieces of matter) that causes some RADIOACTIVE substances to break down

weakling /ˈwiː·klɪŋ/ *n* [C] someone who is weak, either physically or in character ○ *Exercise can turn a weakling into a big, tough guy.*

wealth MONEY /welθ/ *n* [U] a large amount of money and other valuable possessions ○ *His wealth is so great that money doesn't mean much to him.*

wealthy /ˈwel·θi/ *adj* ○ *Natural resources and a well-trained workforce make a country wealthy.*

LARGE AMOUNT /welθ/ *n* [U] a large amount ○ *Jim has a wealth of teaching experience.*

wean /wiːn/ *v* [T] to cause a baby or young animal to stop feeding on its mother's milk and to eat other foods ○ *She started to wean her baby at six months.*

weapon /ˈwep·ən/ *n* [C] an object used in fighting or war, such as a gun or a bomb, or something used against someone ○ *The walls were decorated with swords, axes, and other medieval weapons.* ○ *Even laughter can be used as a weapon.*

weaponry /ˈwep·ən·ri/ *n* [U] weapons generally, or a particular type of weapons ○ *Precision air weaponry has revolutionized warfare.*

wear COVER THE BODY /wer, wær/ *v* [T] *past simp.* **wore**, *past part.* **worn** **1** to have clothing or jewelry on your body ○ *He wears glasses for reading.* ○ (*fig.*) *The prisoner wore a confident smile throughout the trial.* **2** To wear your hair in a particular style is to have it arranged in a certain way: *She wears her hair in a ponytail.*

wear /wer, wær/ *n* [U] clothes designed for a particular use or of a particular type ○ *She designed sportswear and very elegant evening wear.*

WEAKEN /wer, wær/ *v* [I/T] *past simp.* **wore**, *past part.* **worn** to make something become weaker, damaged, or thinner because of continuous use ○ [I] *My favorite shirt wore at the collar.* ○ [T] *I wore a hole in my favorite sweater.* ○ [M] *Wind and water slowly wore away the mountain's jagged peak, making it round.*

wear /wer, wær/ *n* [U] ○ *I've gotten a lot of wear out of this coat.*

WORD FAMILY wear

Nouns	wear, underwear	Verbs	wear

IDIOM with wear

• **wear the pants** to be the person in a relationship who makes the decisions ○ *Lisa certainly wears the pants in that family.*

PHRASAL VERB with wear

• **wear off** to stop having an effect or influence ○ *The vaccine wears off after 10 years.*

• **wear** *someone* **out** MAKE TIRED [M] to make someone very tired by demanding a lot of that person's work or attention ○ *He wears me out with his constant complaining.* ○ Related adjective: WORN OUT EXTREMELY TIRED

W

• **wear out** *something* **USE REPEATEDLY** [M] to use something so much or for so long that it is no longer usable ○ *I read that book over and over till I wore it out.* ○ Related adjective: WORN OUT **NOT USABLE**

wear and tear *n* [U] the damage that comes from ordinary use ○ *Most tires will last for four years with normal wear and tear.*

wearisome /ˈwɪr·iː·səm/ *adj* [not gradable] causing a person to be tired; boring ○ *A long project becomes wearisome and loses its excitement for me.*

weary /ˈwɪr·i/ *adj* very tired, esp. from hard work ○ *Even my brain is weary tonight!*
wearily /ˈwɪr·ə·li/ *adv* ○ *I dragged myself wearily out of bed.*
weariness /ˈwɪr·iː·nəs/ *n* [U] ○ *My weariness was so great, I couldn't even answer the telephone.*

weasel /ˈwiː·zəl/ *n* [C] a small mammal with reddish brown fur and a long body, which feeds on small animals such as mice and birds

PHRASAL VERB with weasel

• **weasel out (of** *something***)** *infml* to escape responsibility for something ○ *My roommate always tries to weasel out of doing the dishes.*

weather **AIR CONDITIONS** /ˈweð·ər/ *n* [U] the conditions in the air at a particular time, such as wind, rain, or temperature ○ *I always wear gloves in cold weather.* ○ *Expect some nasty weather tomorrow, possibly even a thunderstorm.*
weather /ˈweð·ər/ *v* [I/T] to change in color or form over a period of time because of the effects of sun, wind, rain, or other conditions in the air ○ [I] *The yellow paint will weather to a grayish white.*
weathered /ˈweð·ərd/ *adj* ○ *The wall was made from rounded, weathered stones.*
weathering *n* [U] ***earth science***

LIVE THROUGH /ˈweð·ər/ *v* [T] to live through a difficult situation or a problem ○ *She's weathered a few professional setbacks this year.*

IDIOM with weather

• **weather the storm** to be able to continue doing something despite serious problems ○ *Will the ambassador be able to weather the storm caused by his remarks?*

weather-beaten *adj* not having been protected from sun, wind, or rain and so marked or damaged by them ○ *The fisherman had a weather-beaten face.*

W

weather forecaster *n* [C] a person whose job is to report what the weather will be in the near future

weathering /ˈweð·ə·rɪŋ/ *n* [U] ***earth science*** the processes by which rock is broken into smaller pieces by the action of the weather

weatherman /ˈweð·ərˌmæn/ *n* [C] a man whose job is to report the weather on television or radio

weave **MAKE CLOTH** /wiːv/ *v* [I/T] *past simp.* **wove, weaved,** *past part.* **woven, weaved** **1** to make cloth by repeatedly passing a single thread in and out through long threads on a LOOM (= special frame) ○ [T] *How long does it take to weave three yards of cloth?* **2** You can also weave dried grass, leaves, and thin branches into hats, containers, and other items.
weave /wiːv/ *n* [C] the way in which cloth has been woven ○ *The blanket has a loose weave.*

MOVE /wiːv/ *v* [always + adv/prep] *past* **weaved** to frequently change direction while moving forward, esp. to avoid things that could stop you ○ [I] *The taxi weaved through traffic to get us to the airport.*

web **NET** /web/ *n* [C] *short form of* COBWEB ○ *A spider's web hung in a corner of the window.* ○ See also: COBWEB

SKIN /web/ *n* [C] the skin connecting the toes of some water birds and animals which helps them to swim
webbed /webd/ *adj* ○ *Ducks, gulls, and frogs all have webbed toes.*

Web /web/ *n* [U] *short form of* WORLD WIDE WEB ○ *Can you log onto the Web?*

weblog /ˈweb·lɔːg, -lɑg/, *short form* **blog** /blɔːg, blɑg/ *n* [C] a WEBSITE on which one person or group puts new information regularly, often every day

website /ˈweb·sɑɪt/ *n* [C] a place on the INTERNET with one or more pages of information about a subject ○ *His fans created a website, giving every detail of his private life.*

wed /wed/ *v* [I/T] *past* **wedded, wed** to marry someone ○ [I] *They are planning to wed in June.*
wedded /ˈwed·əd/ *adj* [not gradable] ○ *a wedded couple*
wedding /ˈwed·ɪŋ/ *n* [C] ○ *Rosie's wedding is in July.* ○ *She had an elegant wedding dress.*

IDIOM with wed

• **wedded to** *something* **1** believing strongly in something ○ *He remains wedded to the free-enterprise system.* **2** If something is **wedded to** something else, the two are closely connected: *San Diego's economy is wedded to the military.*

Wed. *n abbreviation for* WEDNESDAY.

we'd /wiːd/ *contraction of* we had or we would ○ *By then, we'd heard the same story six times.*

wedge /wedʒ/ *n* [C] a piece of wood, metal, or other material with a pointed edge at one end and a wide edge at the other, used to keep two things apart or, when forced between two things, to break them apart ○ *A wedge under the door kept it open.*
wedge /wedʒ/ *v* [T] ○ *He wedged the window open with a screwdriver.*

wedlock /ˈwed·lɑk/ *n* [U] the state of being married

Wednesday /ˈwenz·di, -deɪ/, *abbreviation* **Wed.** *n* [C/U] the day of the week after Tuesday and before Thursday

wee /wiː/ *adj* [not gradable] very small; little ○ *It may make you feel awkward to give a wee gift and get a whopper back in return.* ○ *They can't party till* **the wee hours** (= the hours starting at one o'clock in the morning) *and sack out till noon.*

weed /wiːd/ *n* [C] any wild plant that grows in a garden or field where it is not wanted ○ *My garden is overrun with weeds.*

weed /wiːd/ *v* [I/T] to remove wild, unwanted plants ○ [I] *I weeded all afternoon.*

PHRASAL VERB with **weed**

• **weed out** *someone/something* [M] to get rid of people or things that are not wanted ○ *The administration plans to weed out failed programs.*

week /wiːk/ *n* [C] a period of seven days, either from the beginning of Sunday to the end of Saturday or from the beginning of Monday to the end of Sunday ○ *next/last week* ○ *We go to the movies about once a week.*

weekly /ˈwiː·kli/ *adj, adv* [not gradable] happening or appearing every week ○ *a weekly magazine* ○ *We go to the city weekly.*

weekly /ˈwiː·kli/ *n* [C] ○ *I subscribe to several weeklies* (= magazines or newspapers that are published once a week).

WORD FAMILY **week**			
Nouns	week midweek weekday weekend weeknight work week	*Adjectives* *Adverbs*	weekly midweek weeklong weekly midweek

IDIOMS with **week**

• **a week ago (this)** last week on ○ *The problem with the TV started a week ago Monday.*

• **a week from** in one week following ○ *The first performance of the play is a week from tomorrow.*

• **week after week, week in, week out** for many weeks, for a long time, or usually ○ *I get up very early, week in, week out.*

weekday /ˈwiːk·deɪ/ *n* [C] any day of the week except Saturday or Sunday ○ *The bank is open from 8 a.m. to 4 p.m. on weekdays.*

weekend /ˈwiːk·end/ *n* [C] Saturday and Sunday, when many people do not work ○ *Do you have anything planned for the weekend?*

weeklong /ˈwiːkˈlɔːŋ/ *adj* [not gradable] lasting one week ○ *They open weeklong talks in New Zealand on Tuesday, aimed at reaching a settlement.*

weeknight /ˈwiːk·nɑɪt/ *n* [C] the night of any day of the week except Saturday and Sunday

weep /wiːp/ *v* [I/T] *past* **wept** to cry tears ○ [I] *I could hear someone weeping.*

weigh SHOW WEIGHT /weɪ/ *v* to be pulled toward the earth with a particular force that can be measured, or to measure this force in an object; to show an amount of weight ○ [L] *The baby weighed six pounds, ten ounces at birth.* ○ [L] *This table weighs a lot.* ○ [T] *She weighs herself every morning.*

INFLUENCE /weɪ/ *v* [I always + adv/prep] to have an influence ○ *The factor that weighed most heavily in her favor was her record of success as a lawyer.*

CONSIDER /weɪ/ *v* [T] to consider something carefully, esp. by comparing facts or possibilities, in order to make a decision ○ *The judge told the jury to weigh the facts and the evidence.* ○ *You have to weigh the advantage of early graduation against the disadvantage of being younger than everyone else.*

WORD FAMILY **weigh**			
Nouns	weight weightlessness	*Adjectives*	overweight underweight
Verbs	weigh outweigh		weighted weightless weighty

IDIOM with **weigh**

• **weigh a ton** to be very heavy ○ *This suitcase weighs a ton.*

PHRASAL VERBS with **weigh**

• **weigh down** *someone/something* [M] to make it difficult for someone or something to move by giving that person or thing a heavy load to carry ○ *She checked her bags because she didn't want to be weighed down.* ○ (fig.) *She was weighed down* (= made tired and worried) *by the aches and pains of old age.*

• **weigh in** GIVE OPINION to give an opinion or enter a discussion or argument ○ *The senator weighed in with a blistering attack on welfare cheats.*

• **weigh in** MEASURE to measure how heavy someone is, esp. before a competition ○ *The boxers both weighed in at 162 pounds.*

• **weigh on** *something* to make someone feel nervous or worried ○ *Problems at work are weighing on him.*

weight HOW HEAVY /weɪt/ *n* [C/U] **1** a quality of an object that is a measure of the force by which the earth attracts it, or an object considered as having this quality ○ [U] *The maximum weight the bridge can support is 15 tons.* ○ [U] *You've lost some weight since the last time I saw you.* ○ [U] *I don't want to put on weight* (= become heavier). ○ [C] *When lifting a heavy weight, keep your back straight and bend your knees.* **2** A weight is also a piece of metal whose force toward earth has been measured, and by which you can measure other objects: [C] *a one-pound weight* **3** A weight is also sports equipment, esp. a piece of metal attached to each end of a bar or to a special machine that you move or lift to strengthen your muscles: [C] *He lifts weights.*

weightless /ˈweɪt·ləs/ *adj* being in a state in which GRAVITY (= the force by which the earth attracts objects) does not cause movement of objects ○ *The astronauts are weightless in space.*

weightlessness /ˈweɪt·lə·snəs/ *n* [U]

INFLUENCE /weɪt/ *n* [U] influence ○ *Her word carried weight with her neighbors.*

weighted /ˈweɪţ·əd/ *adj* given an influence that would not happen naturally ○ *Roche's, the most heavily weighted stock in the Swiss Market Index, has climbed 25 percent since Jan. 3.*

W

weighty /ˈweɪt̬·i/ *adj* important and serious ○ *They discussed weighty topics like arms control, the Middle East, and the federal budget deficit.*

IDIOM with **weight**

• **weight off** *your* **mind** a worry that you had but that is now gone ○ *It was a weight off my mind, knowing she arrived home safe.*

weighted /ˈweɪt̬·əd/ *adj* ***science*** of information being studied, having a value attached to show its importance compared with all the information being studied

weightlifting /ˈweɪtˌlɪf·tɪŋ/ *n* [C] the activity of lifting heavy bars to strengthen the muscles, either for exercise or in a competition
weightlifter /ˈweɪtˌlɪf·tər/ *n* [C] ○ *The 5-foot-9, 200-pound weightlifter had a Superman logo tattooed on his left arm.*

weird /wɪrd/ *adj* [*-er/-est* only] strange and different from anything natural or ordinary ○ *She is a little weird in the way she dresses, I have to admit.*

weirdo /ˈwɪrd·oʊ/ *n* [C] *pl* **weirdos** *slang* a person who you think is strange and who makes you uncomfortable ○ *That guy is a real weirdo.*

welcome MEET /ˈwel·kəm/ *v* [T] to meet or speak to someone in a friendly way when the person comes to the place where you are ○ *We went next door to welcome our new neighbors.* ○ *The prime minister of Canada welcomed the president warmly.*
welcome /ˈwel·kəm/ *exclamation* ○ *Welcome! Come on in.* ○ *Welcome home!*
welcome /ˈwel·kəm/ *n* [C] ○ *We were given a warm welcome.*
welcome /ˈwel·kəm/ *adj* If you tell people they are welcome, you are telling them that you will be happy to have them visit you: *You'll always be welcome here.*

SUPPORT /ˈwel·kəm/ *v* [T] to be pleased about or support something ○ *Baseball fans welcomed the end of the players' strike.* ○ *She welcomed the opportunity to explain herself.*
welcome /ˈwel·kəm/ *adj* **1** *The cool weather was a welcome change.* ○ *You're welcome to the pie* (= you can have it). **2** "You're welcome" is a polite answer when someone thanks you: *"Thanks for taking care of our cat." "You're welcome."*

WORD FAMILY **welcome**			
Nouns	welcome	*Adjectives*	welcome
Verbs	welcome		unwelcome

weld /weld/ *v* [I/T] to join pieces of metal together permanently by melting the parts that touch, or to join one piece of metal to another in this way ○ [T] *Iron spikes were welded to the railing around the embassy.*
weld /weld/ *n* [C] ○ *A weld on the base of the chair had broken.*
welder /ˈwel·dər/ *n* [C] ○ *He works as a welder.*

welfare Ⓐ HEALTH AND HAPPINESS /ˈwel·fer, -fær/ *n* [U] physical and mental health and happiness ○ *We were concerned for our parents' welfare when we heard about the storm in Florida.*

HELP /ˈwel·fer, -fær/ *n* [U] ***social studies*** help given, esp. money, by a government to people who are poor and who do not have jobs ○ *welfare benefits* ○ *The family had to go on welfare.*

welfare state *n* [C] a political system in which the government pays for health care and other social benefits for its citizens, or a nation that operates under this system

well HEALTHY /wel/ *adj comparative* **better**, *superlative* **best** healthy ○ *I don't feel well.* ○ *I feel better now.*
wellness /ˈwel·nəs/ *n* [U] the condition of being healthy ○ *The book promotes wellness through diet and exercise.*

EXCLAMATION /wel, wəl/ *exclamation* used to introduce something you are about to say, or to connect one statement with the next, or to show doubt or disagreement, annoyance, surprise, or understanding ○ *Well, what happened next?* ○ *He started yelling at me, and well, I was scared at first.* ○ *Well, what are you going to do now that you've lost your job?* ○ *Oh well, there's not much we can do about it now.*

IN A GOOD WAY /wel/ *adv comparative* **better**, *superlative* **best** in a good way; to a high or satisfactory standard ○ *The car was well designed.* ○ *She manages people very well.* ○ *I can't sing as well as Jessica* (= She sings better). ○ *His point about reducing waste is well taken* (= accepted as a fair criticism). ○ *The two hours of discussion was time well spent* (= it was a useful discussion). ○ *I want to congratulate you on a job well done.*

TO A GREAT DEGREE /wel/ *adv comparative* **better**, *superlative* **best** **1** to a great degree; much or completely ○ *I know her well.* ○ *Put in two eggs and stir well.* ○ *He sent away for tickets well in advance* (= very early). ○ *I knew perfectly well what time it was.* ○ *I knew her pretty well when I lived in Iowa City.* **2** Well is used with some prepositions and adverbs for emphasis: *Keep the children well away from the edge of the pool.* ○ *It costs well over $100.* **3** Well is used with a few adjectives for emphasis: *The museum is well worth a visit.*

REASONABLY /wel/ *adv* [not gradable] with good reason ○ *I couldn't very well say no.*

HOLE /wel/ *n* [C] a deep hole in the ground from which water, oil, or gas can be obtained ○ *an oil well* ○ *well water*

COME TO SURFACE /wel/ *v* [I] (of a liquid) to come to the surface or into view ○ *As she read the letter, tears welled in her eyes.* ○ *(fig.) He could feel the anger well up inside him.*

IDIOM with **well**

• **well done** used for praising someone who has achieved something ○ *"I passed the test for my drivers license." "Well done!"* ○ See also: WELL-DONE

we'll /wiːl, wɪl/ *contraction of* we shall or we will ○ *We'll be there tomorrow.*

well-advised *adj* showing good judgment ○ *You would be well-advised to reserve a room in advance.*

well-balanced *adj* having the right amounts of all the different parts that make up something

○ *It's important to give your kids healthy well-balanced meals, including all the food groups.*

well-behaved *adj* behaving in a way that is considered correct ○ *a well-behaved boy*

well-being *n* [U] the state of feeling healthy and happy ○ *Seeing her grandchildren gave her a sense of well-being.*

well-built *adj* having an attractive, strong body

well-done *adj* (of meat) cooked all the way through ○ *a well-done steak* ○ See also: WELL DONE at WELL IDIOMS

well-dressed *adj* wearing or usually wearing attractive and stylish clothes

well-educated *adj* having had a good or a high level of education

well-founded *adj* based on facts or good reasons ○ *Her fears were well-founded.*

well-groomed *adj* having a neat, clean appearance

well-heeled *adj* wealthy ○ *The village has become a summer retreat for well-heeled city dwellers.*

well-informed *adj* having a lot of knowledge ○ *Marilyn is well-informed about the stock market.*

well-kept *adj* taken care of in a proper way that people notice ○ *She lives in a neighborhood of well-kept lawns and relatively little crime.*

well-kept secret *n* [C] information that very few people know ○ *It was a well-kept secret that the old system was biased in favor of homeowners.*

well-known *adj* known or recognized by many people ○ *The book is by a well-known historian.*

well-liked *adj* liked by many people

well-mannered *adj* behaving in a pleasant and polite way ○ *The other visitors were too well-mannered to complain.*

well-meant *adj* intended to be helpful or kind, although not always having a good effect

wellness /ˈwel·nəs/ *n* ○ See at WELL HEALTHY

well-nigh *adj* almost ○ *Once you get behind, it is well-nigh impossible to catch up.*

well-off *adj* wealthy

well-read *adj* having read many important books

well-rounded *adj* having or providing experience and knowledge in a number of different areas ○ *Some experts say that home-schooled children may not receive a well-rounded education.*

well-thought-of *adj* respected by many people for quality, ability, moral character, etc. ○ *He was well-thought-of as a foreign-policy expert.*

well-timed *adj* happening or made to happen at a particularly suitable time ○ *Her appearance was well-timed to coincide with the arrival of the president.*

well-to-do /ˌwel·təˈduː/ *adj* showing signs of being successful; rich ○ *It was a well-to-do neighborhood of large, single-family homes with big backyards.*

well-versed *adj* having a lot of knowledge about something ○ *He was well-versed in the history of space flight.*

well-wisher *n* [C] a person who encourages or supports someone ○ *Hundreds of well-wishers surrounded the team.*

welt /welt/ *n* [C] a raised, red area of skin usually caused by being hit

welter /ˈwel·tər/ *n* [U] a large number of things in confusion or disorder ○ *The report was issued amid a welter of conflicting evidence.*

went /went/ *past simple of* GO

wept /wept/ *past simple and past participle of* WEEP

were /wɜr, wər/ *past simple of* BE

we're /wɪr, wər, wiːr/ *contraction of* we are ○ *We're ready now.*

weren't /wɜrnt, wərnt/ *contraction of* were not ○ *They weren't outside.*

werewolf /ˈwɪr·wʊlf, ˈwer-, ˈwɜr-/ *n* [C] *pl* **werewolves** an imaginary creature in stories that is a person who changes into a WOLF (= wild animal) when the moon is a complete circle

west /west/, *abbreviation* **W.** *n* [U] the direction where the sun goes down in the evening that is opposite east, or the part of an area or country which is in this direction ○ *The points of the compass are north, south, east, and west.* ○ *The sun sets in the west.*

west /west/, *abbreviation* **W.** *adj, adv* [not gradable] ○ *the west coast* ○ *The town is west of here.*

westerly /ˈwes·tər·li/ *adj* toward or near the west ○ *a westerly wind*

western /ˈwes·tərn/, *abbreviation* **W.** *adj* [not gradable] ○ *Grand Rapids is in the western part of Michigan.*

western /ˈwes·tərn/ *n* [C] a movie based on stories about life in the part of the US west of the Mississippi River when white people began going there to live in the 19th century

westerner /ˈwes·tər·nər, -tə·nər/ *n* [C] a person from the western part of a country, or (in the US) a person from the part of the country west of the Mississippi River

westward /ˈwes·twərd/ *adj* [not gradable] toward the west ○ *a westward route*

westward /ˈwes·twərd/, **westwards** /ˈwes·twərdz/ *adv* [not gradable] toward the west ○ *The clouds drifted westward.*

WORD FAMILY west

Nouns	west western westerner	*Adjectives*	westerly western westward
Adverbs	west westward		

IDIOM with west

•**the West** **1** the part of the US west of the Mississippi River ○ *The museum grounds contain an Indian tepee and a large, heavy wagon used by early 19th-century settlers of the West.* **2** North America and the countries in the western part of Europe are also referred to as **the West**: *The West must make a commitment to Africa to help find solutions to the continent's problems.*

West Coast *n* [U] (in the US) the part of the country near the Pacific Ocean

westernize, **Westernize** /ˈwes·tərˌnɑɪz/ *v* [I/T] ***world history*** to fill with qualities typical of a western region, esp. Western Europe and America

westernization, **Westernization** /ˌwes·tər·nəˈzeɪ·ʃən/ *n* [U] ***world history*** ○ *The process of westernization in China is spreading rapidly.*

wet /wet/ *adj* [*-er/-est* only] **-tt-** **1** with liquid in, on, or around something; not dry ○ *I stepped in a puddle of water and got my shoes wet.* **2** If paint, ink, etc., is wet, it has not had time to dry. **3** Wet weather is weather with rain.

wet /wet/ *v* [T] *pres. part.* **wetting**, *past* **wet, wetted** **1** *Wet a sponge and wipe off the table.* **2** A person, esp. a child, who wets something causes it to become wet by urinating: *He still sometimes wets his bed.*

wetness /ˈwet·nəs/ *n* [U] ○ *A lot of the wetness will evaporate before the rain reaches the plant's roots.*

wetlands /ˈwet·ləndz, -lændz/, **wetland** /ˈwet·lənd, -lænd/ *pl n* an area of land that is naturally wet ○ [U] *Thousands of acres of wetlands are destroyed every year by development.*

we've /wiːv/ *contraction of* we have ○ *It's been over a year since we've done that.*

whack /hwæk, wæk/ *v* [T] to give someone or something a hard, noisy hit ○ *He whacked his newspaper on the back of the chair as he talked.*

whack /hwæk, wæk/ *n* [C] ○ *She gripped her racket with both hands and gave the ball a hard whack.*

whale /hweɪl, weɪl/ *n* [C] a very large sea mammal

IDIOM with whale

•**a whale of a** **1** a large amount of something ○ *A whale of a lot of other people were there, too.* **2** If something is **a whale of a** thing, it is a very good thing: *Perry's done a whale of a job for us.*

wham /hwæm, wæm/ *exclamation infml* used to suggest the sound of a sudden hit, or to signal that something sudden and unexpected happened ○ *All of a sudden, wham, I couldn't leave my house, except to go to school.*

wharf /hwɔːrf, wɔːrf/ *n* [C] *pl* **wharves, wharfs** a raised, level structure built beside the edge of the sea or a river, where ships can be tied and goods unloaded

what QUESTION /hwʌt, wʌt, hwɑt, wɑt, hwət, wət/ *pronoun, exclamation* **1** used to introduce general questions ○ *What did the teacher say?* ○ *What is the capital of Nevada?* **2** As an adjective, what can refer to people or things: *What time is it?* ○ *I don't know what children she was talking about.* **3** What may be used to show that you did not hear something and to ask that it be repeated: *"Humphrey Jones called." "What (was that)?" "I said Humphrey Jones called."* ➤ Usage: **how or what?** at HOW

USAGE

what

People do say **what** when they have not heard what someone has said and want them to repeat it, but it is more polite to say **excuse me, I beg your pardon, pardon,** or **pardon me.**

"It's ten o'clock." "Pardon?" "I said it's ten o'clock."

THAT WHICH /hwʌt, wʌt, hwɑt, wɑt, hwət, wət/ *pronoun* the thing which; that which ○ *I really didn't know what to say.* ○ *What annoyed me was her attitude.* ○ *I hope you like the sweater – it's what you asked for.*

OPINION /hwʌt, wʌt, hwɑt, wɑt, hwət, wət/ *pronoun* used to introduce your opinion ○ *"She can't come." "What a pity* (= I am sorry to hear that)*!"*

IDIOMS with what

•**what about** used for asking for an opinion about something ○ *What about Laurie – should we invite her?*

•**what do you know** used for expressing surprise ○ *Well, what do you know? The flight arrived on time.*

•**what do you say** *infml* used for making a suggestion ○ *What do you say we sell the car?*

•**what for** used for questioning the purpose of or reason for an action or plan ○ *"We really need a bigger car." "What for? The one we have seems big enough to me."*

•**what if** used for asking what action to take if a particular thing should happen ○ *What if our plane is delayed and we can't make the connection?*

•**what makes** *someone* **tick** the reason you behave as you do ○ *I've never been able to understand what makes him tick.*

•**what on earth** used for showing surprise ○ *What on earth is going on in there?*

•**what** *someone* **says goes**, **whatever** *someone* **says goes** whatever a particular person says must be obeyed ○ *I don't agree with the boss either, but what he says goes.*

•**what the heck** used for showing anger or surprise ○ *What the heck are you doing to my car?*

•**what's eating** *someone infml* used for asking what is worrying or annoying someone ○ *What's eating Bobby? He hasn't said anything all night.*

•**what's more** more importantly ○ *The decorations were beautiful and, what's more, the kids made them themselves.*

•**what's the matter** used for asking someone if there is a problem ○ *You look worried – what's the matter?*

•**what's up** *infml* used for asking how someone is doing or how the person has been spending time ○ *"Hi, Chuck, what's up?" "Nothing much."*

W

whatchamacallit /ˈhwʌtʃ·ə·məˌkɔː·lət, ˈwʌtʃ-, ˈhwɑtʃ-, ˈwɑtʃ-/ *n* [C] (used when you cannot remember or do not know the name of something) an object ○ *My whatchamacallit is broken – the thing that controls the oven temperature.*

whatever SOMETHING UNKNOWN /hwʌṭˈev·ər, wʌṭ-, hwɑṭ-, wɑṭ-/ *pronoun* something whose particular nature or type you do not know ○ *Whatever happens, you'll be all right.* ○ *You seem to criticize me whatever I do.*

ANYTHING /hwʌṭˈev·ər, wʌṭ-, hwɑṭ-, wɑṭ-/ *pronoun* anything or everything ○ *Give him whatever he wants.*

NOT IMPORTANT WHAT /hwʌṭˈev·ər, wʌṭ-, hwɑṭ-, wɑṭ-/ *adv* [not gradable] used to say that something is not important or makes no difference ○ *"Can I dress casually or do I have to dress up?" "Whatever."*

what's /hwʌts, wʌts, hwɑts, wɑts/ *contraction of* what is or what has ○ *What's* (= What is) *that stuff on your forehead?* ○ *They want a list of what's* (= what has) *been stolen.*

whatsoever /ˌhwʌt·soʊˈev·ər, ˌwʌt-, ˌhwɑt-, ˌwɑt-/, **whatever** *adv* [not gradable] used after a negative phrase to add emphasis to the idea that is being expressed ○ *He has no respect for authority whatsoever.*

wheat /hwiːt, wiːt/ *n* [U] a plant whose yellow-brown grain is used for making flour, or the grain itself

wheedle /ˈhwiːd·əl, ˈwiːd-/ *v* [I/T] to try to persuade someone to do something or to give you something by using your charm and by repeatedly asking in a way that would make refusal embarrassing ○ [T always + adv/prep] *He wasn't going to tell me but I wheedled it out of him.*

wheel ROUND OBJECT /hwiːl, wiːl/ *n* [C] **1** a circular object, connected at the center to a bar, that is used for making vehicles or parts of machines move ○ *the wheel of a bicycle* **2** The wheel refers to a STEERING WHEEL (= wheel in a vehicle that you turn to make the vehicle go left or right): *I never feel safe with Richard behind the wheel* (= driving). ○ *Would you mind taking the wheel* (= driving) *for a couple of hours?*

wheel /hwiːl, wiːl/ *v* [T always + adv/prep] to push or pull an object with wheels under it ○ *She was wheeling a stroller in the park.*

CHANGE DIRECTION /hwiːl, wiːl/ *v* [I always + adv/prep] to turn around quickly ○ *She wheeled around and slapped his face.*

wheelbarrow /ˈhwiːlˌbær·oʊ, ˈwiːl-/ *n* [C] a movable container with a wheel at the front and two handles at the back, used esp. for moving building materials and in gardening

wheelchair /ˈhwiːl·tʃer, ˈwiːl-, -tʃær/ *n* [C] a chair on wheels that people who are unable to walk use for moving around

wheeling and dealing *n* [U] an attempt to make a deal or get an advantage by using complicated and sometimes dishonest or unfair methods ○ *There was a lot of behind-the-scenes political wheeling and dealing going on.*

wheeze /hwiːz, wiːz/ *v* [I] to make a noise while breathing because of some breathing difficulty ○ *Since I started exercising regularly, I no longer wheeze when I run for a train.*

when AT WHAT TIME /hwen, wen, hwən, wən/ *conjunction, adv* [not gradable] at what time; at the time at which ○ *When is supper going to be ready?* ○ *When did the American Civil War begin?* ○ *I was just getting into the shower when the phone rang.*

CONSIDERING THAT /hwen, wen, hwən, wən/ *conjunction* considering the fact that ○ *I can't really call myself a vegetarian when I eat fish.*

USAGE

when or if?

In conditional sentences **when** is used to describe a situation that is always true or a situation that you are sure will happen in the future.

I always get migraines when it's this hot.

When I finish school, I'm going to go to college.

If is used to describe a possible situation.

It would be better for the environment if everyone went by bicycle.

~~*It would be better for the environment when everyone went by bicycle.*~~

ALTHOUGH /hwen, wen, hwən, wən/ *conjunction* despite the fact that ○ *He says he hasn't got any money when the truth is he's got plenty.*

whenever EVERY TIME /hwenˈev·ər, wen-, hwən-, wən-/ *conjunction* every or any time ○ *I'm embarrassed whenever I think about it.* ○ *I try to let the kids out to play whenever possible.*

NOT IMPORTANT WHEN /hwenˈev·ər, wen-, hwən-, wən-/ *conjunction, adv* [not gradable] used to say that the time something is done is not important or makes no difference ○ *"Will it be okay if we meet tomorrow instead of today?" "Sure, whenever."*

where /hwer, wer, hwær, wær/ *conjunction, adv* [not gradable] **1** to, at, or in what place ○ *Where did she go to college?* ○ *I forget where I put the car keys.* ○ *I read it somewhere – I don't know where* (= the exact place). **2** Where can be used to mean at what stage: *You reach a point where you just want to get the thing finished.*

IDIOMS with where

- **where** *someone is* **coming from** the feelings someone has that cause that person to have a particular opinion ○ *I don't agree with you entirely, but I understand where you're coming from.*
- **where to turn** what to do or whom to ask for help ○ *She had no money and didn't know where to turn for help.* ○ Compare WHICH WAY TO TURN at WHICH IDIOMS

whereabouts /ˈhwer·əˌbaʊts, ˈwer-, ˈhwær-, ˈwær-/ *pl n* the place where a person or thing is ○

W

Moreno's whereabouts are unknown, but some people think he is in Panama.

whereabouts /ˈhwer·əˌbɑʊts, ˈwer-, ˈhwær-, ˈwær-/ *adv* [not gradable] in what place; where ○ *Whereabouts is your office?*

whereas Ⓐ /hwerˈæz, wer-, hwær-, wær-/ *conjunction* compared with the fact that; but ○ *In Los Angeles, a chief cause of this pollution is paved-road dust, whereas in San Diego, it's smoke from fireplaces.*

whereby Ⓐ /hwerˈbɑɪ, wer-, hwær-, wær-/ *conjunction* by which way or method ○ *They've set up a plan whereby you can spread the cost over several months.*

wherein /hwerˈɪn, wer-, hwær-, wær-/ *conjunction* in which, or in which part ○ *The industry will have a situation wherein many companies will be unable to afford to stay in business.*

whereupon /ˈhwer·əˌpɑn, ˈwer-, ˈhwær-, ˈwær-, -əˌpɔːn/ *conjunction* immediately after which ○ *We went home for coffee, whereupon Viv became violently ill.*

wherever /hwerˈev·ər, wer-, hwær-, wær-/ *conjunction, adv* [not gradable] **1** to or in any or every place ○ *We can go wherever you like.* **2** Wherever can also mean in all types of situations: *We try to save money wherever possible, for instance by using coupons when we buy groceries.*

wherewithal /ˈhwer·wɪˌðɔːl, ˈwer-, ˈhwær-, ˈwær-, -ˌθɔːl/ *n* [U] the money necessary for a particular purpose ○ *Most people don't have the wherewithal to hire the best lawyers.*

whet IDIOM /hwet, wet/

• **whet** *your* **appetite** **1** to make you hungry ○ *The smell of the turkey roasting on Thanksgiving always whets my appetite.* **2** *fig.* If something you experience **whets** *your* **appetite**, it increases your interest in it or desire for it: *I read a short story he wrote, and it whetted my appetite for more.*

whether /ˈhweð·ər, ˈweð-/ *conjunction* (used to refer to one or more possibilities or to express uncertainty) if ○ *I didn't know whether he was too busy or (whether) he just didn't want to see me.* ○ *I wasn't sure whether (or not) you'd like it.*

IDIOM with **whether**

• **whether or not** used for saying that it is not important which of two possibilities is true ○ *Whether or not you like it, I'm going out tonight.* ○ *Whether he wants to or not, he'll have to clean his room.*

W

whew, **phew** /hjuː, fjuː/ *exclamation* an expression that shows you are surprised, tired, or RELIEVED (= happy that something worrying you is not going to happen)

which QUESTION /hwɪtʃ, wɪtʃ/ *pronoun, adj* [not gradable] (used in questions and statements having a limited number of possibilities) what one or ones ○ *Which train do you want to take – the one in the morning or the one in the afternoon?* ○ *She had trouble deciding which of her dresses to wear to the party.* ○ *She speaks Spanish or Portuguese, but I've forgotten which.*

USED TO REFER /hwɪtʃ, wɪtʃ/ *pronoun* used to show what particular thing is being referred to ○ *It was a subject which he had never thought much about.* ○ *The club to which he belonged had just become too expensive.*

USAGE

which, who, or that?

Use **who** to refer to a person.

That boy who is wearing the red coat is called Paul.

~~*That boy which is wearing the red coat is called Paul.*~~

Use **that** to refer to either a person or a thing.

The information that you provide must be accurate.

Isn't she the woman that you met yesterday?

In some sentences, you can omit **that**.

This is the shirt I bought yesterday.

Use **which** to refer to a thing, but not a person.

The restaurant which is next to the pub is really good.

~~*The restaurant who is next to the pub is really good.*~~

That is used to introduce a phrase giving necessary information in a sentence. **Which** is usually used to introduce a phrase giving extra information in a sentence.

Jeanne is the girl that I love.

Jeanne, which is my girlfriend's name, is sitting across the room.

You must also use **which**, not **that**, after a preposition when talking about a thing.

Seal the envelope in which you have placed the documents.

ADDS INFORMATION /hwɪtʃ, wɪtʃ/ *pronoun* used to add extra information about something mentioned earlier, in writing following a comma ○ *She said it would be done by March, which I doubt.* ○ *The training, for which you will be paid, takes four weeks.*

IDIOMS with **which**

• **which is which** each person or thing separately ○ *The twins look so much alike I'm surprised anyone can tell which is which.*

• **which way to turn** what to do or whom to ask for help ○ *Economic uncertainty left many companies not knowing which way to turn.* ○ Compare WHERE TO TURN at WHERE IDIOMS

whichever /hwɪtʃˈev·ər, wɪtʃ-/ *pronoun, adj* [not gradable] used to say that among various possibilities, there is no important difference or that you are free to choose the one you like ○ *We can go either Thursday or Friday, whichever is best for you.* ○ *Taxpayers could take their choice between the standard deduction and itemizing, and use whichever produced a better result.* ○ *It's going to be expensive whichever way you do it.*

whiff /hwɪf, wɪf/ *n* [C] a smell that you notice briefly ○ *I got a whiff of perfume as she walked by.* ○ *(fig.) A whiff of scandal was in the air.*

Whig /hwɪɡ, wɪɡ/ *n* [C] **1** ***US history*** an American during the Revolutionary War who wanted independence from Britain. ○ Compare LOYALIST **2** ***US history*** A Whig is also a member of a political party in the United States in the early 19th century that believed CONGRESS LAW MAKERS should have more power than the president and that supported business and economic development. **3** ***world history*** A Whig is also a member of a political party in Britain from the 17th to the 19th century which wanted to limit the power of the king and queen.

while LENGTH OF TIME /hwɑɪl, wɑɪl/ *n* [U] a length of time ○ *He only had to wait a short while.* ○ *It was a while before any waiter took their order.* ○ *That happened a while ago* (= did not happen recently). ○ *I haven't seen him for a while* (= a long time). ○ *She's getting dressed, and she'll be ready in just a little while* (= soon).

DURING /hwɑɪl, wɑɪl/ *conjunction* during the time that, or at the same time as ○ *I read it while you were drying your hair.* ○ *"I'm going to the post office." "While you're there can you get me some stamps?"*

ALTHOUGH /hwɑɪl, wɑɪl/ *conjunction* despite the fact that; although ○ *While I know he's not perfect, I do like him.*

BUT /hwɑɪl, wɑɪl/ *conjunction* compared with the fact that; but ○ *Tom is very outgoing, while Ken's shy and quiet.*

PHRASAL VERB with **while**

• **while away** *something* [M] to spend time in a relaxed way, sometimes when waiting for something else to happen ○ *I used to knit a lot when I was pregnant just to while away the time.*

whim /hwɪm, wɪm/ *n* [C] a sudden desire or idea ○ *The whims of rock stars can be hard to satisfy.*

whimper /ˈhwɪm·pər, ˈwɪm-/ *v* [I] to cry, making small, weak sounds ○ *She whimpered pathetically.*

whimper /ˈhwɪm·pər, ˈwɪm-/ *n* [C] ○ *There wasn't a whimper of complaint from anyone.*

whimsical /ˈhwɪm·zɪ·kəl, ˈwɪm-/ *adj* **1** unusual and using imagination ○ *The songs have a whimsical charm.* **2** Whimsical also describes actions that change suddenly and for no obvious reason: *Unfortunately, his decisions are often whimsical.*

whimsy /ˈhwɪm·zi, ˈwɪm-/ *n* [C/U] something playful and amusing ○ [U] *The second book is as full of happy whimsy as the first.*

whine /hwɑɪn, wɑɪn/ *v* [I] to make a high, complaining sound, or to complain continually ○ *If you don't stop whining, we won't go at all!*

whine /hwɑɪn, wɑɪn/ *n* [C usually sing] ○ *(fig.) The whine of Tracey's hair dryer wakes me every morning.*

whinny /ˈhwɪn·i, ˈwɪn·i/ *v* [I] (of a horse) to make a soft sound, like a gentle NEIGH

whip STRAP /hwɪp, wɪp/ *n* [C] a piece of leather or rope fastened to a stick, used to train and control animals or, esp. in the past, to hit people ○ *The trainer cracked his whip, and the lions sat in a circle.*

whip /hwɪp, wɪp/ *v* [T] **-pp-** ○ *(fig.) Dallas whipped Buffalo 52 to 17* (= beat them by this score).

whipping /ˈhwɪp·ɪŋ, ˈwɪp-/ *n* [C] a beating, esp. with a whip

MOVE QUICKLY /hwɪp, wɪp/ *v* [always + adv/prep] **-pp-** to bring or take (something) quickly, or to move quickly ○ [M] *They whipped my plate away before I'd even finished.* ○ [M] *Bill whipped out his harmonica.* ○ [I] *The wind whipped around the corner of the building.*

BEAT FOOD /hwɪp, wɪp/ *v* [T] **-pp-** to beat cream, eggs, potatoes, etc., with a special utensil in order to make it thick and soft ○ *I still need to whip the cream for the pie.*

POLITICS /hwɪp, wɪp/ *n* [C] an elected representative of a political party in a LEGISLATURE whose job is to gather support from other LEGISLATORS (= law makers)for particular legislation and to encourage them to vote the way their party wants them to

IDIOM with **whip**

• **whip** *someone or something* **into** *something* to make someone behave in a particular way ○ *He whipped the crowd into a frenzy.*

PHRASAL VERBS with **whip**

• **whip up** *someone/something* **CAUSE EMOTION** [M] to cause or encourage a strong feeling or reaction in someone or something ○ *I couldn't whip up any enthusiasm for the assignment.*

• **whip** *something* **up** **MAKE SOMETHING** [M] to make something very quickly ○ *He whipped up a really good dinner.*

whiplash /ˈhwɪp·læʃ, ˈwɪp-/ *n* [U] a neck injury caused by a sudden movement forward and back of the head, as in a car accident

whipping boy *n* [C] someone who is blamed or punished for the faults and mistakes of others

whir /hwɜr, wɜr/, **whirr** *v* [I] **-rr-** (esp. of machines) to make a soft, continuous sound like a wheel turning very quickly ○ *I could hear the dishwasher whirring in the kitchen.*

whir /hwɜr, wɜr/ *n* [C usually sing] ○ *There was a whir of wings as the ducks rose up into the air.*

whirl /hwɜrl, wɜrl/ *v* [I/T] to cause something to spin ○ [I] *The wind came up and the snow began to whirl around us.*

whirl /hwɜrl, wɜrl/ *n* [C] ○ *The dance was an exciting, dizzy whirl.*

whirlpool **CIRCULAR CURRENT** /ˈhwɜrl·puːl, ˈwɜrl-/ *n* [C] water that moves in a powerful, circular current, sucking into its center anything that floats near it

POOL WITH CURRENTS /ˈhwɜrl·puːl, ˈwɜrl-/ *n* [C] an artificial pool with currents of water flowing through it ○ *Some health clubs have whirlpools and steam rooms.*

whirlwind **STORM** /ˈhwɜrl·wɪnd, ˈwɜrl-/ *n* [C] **1** a storm with strong winds that move in a circle **2** People sometimes use whirlwind to describe a situation that happens suddenly and that is full of lots of quickly changing or confusing activity: *The film created a whirlwind of controversy.*

HAPPENING QUICKLY /ˈhwɜrl·wɪnd, ˈwɜrl-/ *adj* [not gradable] happening or developing very quickly ○ *a whirlwind tour*

whisk **REMOVE** /hwɪsk, wɪsk/ *v* [T always + adv/prep] to take away or remove something or someone quickly ○ *A limo whisked us off to dinner.* ○ *The horse whisked flies from its back with its tail.*

BEAT FOOD /hwɪsk, wɪsk/ *v* [T] to beat eggs, cream, or other liquid with a utensil that adds air to the food, making it light ○ *Whisk the vanilla into the batter.*

whisk /hwɪsk, wɪsk/ *n* [C] a wire kitchen utensil that you use for beating a mixture

whisker /ˈhwɪs·kər, ˈwɪs-/ *n* [C] one of the long, stiff hairs that grow near the mouth of a cat, mouse, or other mammal ○ *The cat carefully cleaned the milk off its whiskers.*

whiskers /ˈhwɪs·kərz, ˈwɪs-/ *pl n* the hair that grows on a man's face; BEARD

whiskey, **whisky** /ˈhwɪs·ki, ˈwɪs-/ *n* [C/U] a strong, pale brown, alcoholic drink made from grain

whisper /ˈhwɪs·pər, ˈwɪs-/ *v* [I/T] to say something very quietly, using the breath but not the voice ○ [I] *What are you girls whispering about?*

whisper /ˈhwɪs·pər, ˈwɪs-/ *n* [C] ○ *They spoke in whispers, not wanting anyone to hear them.*

whistle /ˈhwɪs·əl, ˈwɪs-/ *v* [I/T] to make a musical sound by forcing the breath through a small passage between the lips or through a special device ○ [I] *I whistled to my dog and she came running back.* ○ [I] (*fig.*) *The wind whistled through the trees.*

whistle /ˈhwɪs·əl, ˈwɪs-/ *n* [C] **1** *I lay in bed and listened to the whistles of trains across the river.* **2** A whistle is also a device that makes a loud, high sound when you blow into it.

whistle-blower *n* [C] a person who tells someone in authority about something illegal that is happening, esp. in a business or government

white **COLOR** /hwɑɪt, wɑɪt/ *adj, n* [C/U] **1** (of) a color like that of snow, milk, or bone ○ *white hair* ○ *a white shirt* ○ [C] *We used a bright white on the ceilings.* **2** The white of an egg is the part of an egg that becomes white when cooked.

whiten /ˈhwɑɪt·ən, ˈwɑɪt-/ *v* [I/T] to make something whiter, or to become whiter ○ [T] *This toothpaste is supposed to whiten your teeth.*

PALE SKIN /hwɑɪt, wɑɪt/ *adj* [-er/-est only] belonging to a race whose skin is pale in color; CAUCASIAN ○ *There were many white faces in the crowd.*

W

WORD FAMILY white

Nouns	white	*Verbs*	whiten
Adjectives	white		

white blood cell *n* [C] ***biology*** a cell in the blood that has no red color and is involved in fighting infection ○ Compare RED BLOOD CELL

whitecaps /ˈhwɑɪt·kæps, ˈwɑɪt-/ *pl n* waves blown by the wind that are white at their tops

white-collar *adj* [not gradable] connected with a job in an office ○ *These days, few white-collar workers actually wear white shirts.* ○ Compare BLUE-COLLAR

white flag *n* [C] a white cloth that is a symbol of defeat or of giving up on something

White House *n* [U] the official home and offices of the president of the US ○ *The White House has scheduled a news conference.*

white lie *n* [C] a lie that is about a subject that is not very important, or one that is told to be polite or kind

white meat *n* [U] meat, usually from a bird, that is light in color when cooked ○ Compare RED MEAT

White Pages *pl n* a book that lists the names, addresses, and telephone numbers of the people and businesses in a city or area ○ Compare YELLOW PAGES

whitewash /ˈhwɑɪt·wɑʃ, ˈwɑɪt-, -wɔːʃ/ *n* [C/U] **1** paint made from water and white powder which is used esp. on walls and ceilings **2** A whitewash is something that hides a wrong or illegal action: [C] *He called the report a whitewash.*

whitewash /ˈhwɑɪt·wɑʃ, ˈwɑɪt-, -wɔːʃ/ *v* [T] ○ *whitewashed houses* ○ *He's whitewashing the fence.*

white water, **whitewater** /ˈhwɑɪtˌwɔːt̬·ər, ˈwɑɪt-, -ˌwɑt̬·ər/ *n* [U] water in a river that flows quickly and has a lot of bubbles ○ *white-water rafting*

whittle /ˈhwɪt̬·əl, ˈwɪt̬-/ *v* [I/T] to slice thin pieces from a piece of wood, or to form something from wood by slicing pieces off it ○ [I] *He likes to whittle.*

IDIOM with whittle

• **whittle away (at)** *something*, **whittle** *something* **down** to gradually make something smaller or less important ○ *We've whittled away at our debts.* ○ *By halftime their lead had been whittled down to two points.*

whiz **EXPERT** /hwɪz, wɪz/ *n* [C] *infml* a person with a very high level of skill or knowledge in a particular area ○ *Everyone knows at least one computer whiz.* ○ *Jo was one of those whiz kids who are millionaires by the time they're 25.*

MOVE FAST /hwɪz, wɪz/ *v* [I always + adv/prep] **-zz-** to move very fast ○ *He whizzed through the job but made lots of mistakes.*

who **ASKING** /huː/ *pronoun* used esp. in questions to ask which person or people, or to ask someone's name ○ *Who did this?* ○ *Who's she?* ○ **USAGE**: In formal speech or writing, "whom" is the form of "who" used when it is the object of a verb or preposition.

ADDING INFORMATION /huː/ *pronoun* used as the subject or object of a verb when referring to a particular person or when adding information about a person just mentioned ○ *The other people who live in the house are really friendly.* ○ *This is Frank, who I told you about.* ○ **USAGE**: In formal speech or writing, "whom" is the form of "who" used when it is the object of a verb or preposition. ➤ Usage: **which, who, or that?** at WHICH USED TO REFER

IDIOMS with who

• **who cares** used for showing you are not interested in something ○ *"There's a dorm meeting tonight." "Who cares?"*
• **who needs** *something* used for saying you do not want something ○ *More junk mail! Who needs it?*
• **who would have thought** used for showing surprise at a piece of information ○ *She's written two novels since graduating? Who'd have thought?*

whoa /hwoʊ, woʊ/ *exclamation* used to tell a person or a horse to stop or slow down, or to express surprise ○ *Whoa! Not so fast.*

who'd /huːd/ *contraction of* who would or who had ○ *Who'd* (= Who would) *have thought we'd be married for this long?* ○ *It's about a boy who'd* (= who had) *been around the world.*

whodunit /huːˈdʌn·ət/ *n* [C] *infml* a story, book, or movie about a mystery and its solution

whoever **PERSON** /huːˈev·ər/ *pronoun* the person who ○ *Whoever broke the window will have to pay for it.* ○ **USAGE:** In formal speech or writing, "whomever" is the form of "whoever" used when it is the object of a verb or preposition.

ANYONE /huːˈev·ər/ *pronoun* any person who ○ *The picketers were shouting at whoever entered the building.* ○ *Whoever they are, I don't want to see them!* ○ **USAGE:** In formal speech or writing, "whomever" is the form of "whoever" used when it is the object of a verb or preposition.

WHAT PERSON /huːˈev·ər/ *pronoun* (used in place of who for emphasis in questions) what person or persons ○ *Whoever would believe such a ridiculous story?*

whole /hoʊl/ *adj* [not gradable] **1** all of something; the full amount ○ *Painting the two rooms will take the whole day.* ○ *He cooked a meal for the whole school.* **2** Whole can also mean in one piece: *You can eat the fruit whole or cut it up.* **3** *infml* Whole can also be used to emphasize something: *I've got a whole lot to do this afternoon.*
whole /hoʊl/ *n* [C/U] all of the parts of something considered together as one thing, or all of something ○ [C] *Two halves make a whole.* ○ [U] *She'll be away the whole of next month.*
wholly /ˈhoʊl·li/ *adv* completely ○ *I didn't think her explanation was wholly truthful.*

USAGE

the whole or the whole of?

No preposition is necessary after **whole** when it is followed by a general word or phrase.

I lived in Germany for the whole year.

The preposition "of" is needed before a more particular word or phrase.

I lived in Germany for the whole of 1999.

~~I lived in Germany for the whole 1999.~~

WORD FAMILY whole

Nouns	whole	*Adjectives*	whole
Adverbs	wholly		wholesome
			unwholesome

IDIOMS with whole

• **the whole bit, the whole shebang, the whole thing** everything related to an activity or idea ○ *He's got a fancy stove, gourmet cookware, the whole shebang.* ○ *I fell asleep and missed the whole thing.*
• **on the whole** generally ○ *On the whole, I prefer classical music.*

wholehearted /ˈhoʊlˈhɑrt̬·əd/ *adj* completely enthusiastic ○ *I'd like to thank all of you for your wholehearted support of this event.*

whole note *n* [C] *music* a note that is typically played for four times the length of a QUARTER NOTE ➤ Picture: **notation**

whole number *n* [C] *mathematics* a number, such as 1, 17, or 3126, that has no FRACTIONS and does not contain a DECIMAL POINT; an INTEGER

wholesale **SELLING** /ˈhoʊl·seɪl/ *n* [U] the activity of selling goods, usually in large amounts, to businesses which then sell them to the public ○ Compare RETAIL
wholesale /ˈhoʊl·seɪl/ *adj, adv* [not gradable] ○ *wholesale prices* ○ *Do you sell wholesale?*
wholesaler /ˈhoʊlˌseɪ·lər/ *n* [C]

COMPLETE /ˈhoʊl·seɪl/ *adj* involving everyone or everything; complete ○ *What the system needs is wholesale reform.*

wholesome /ˈhoʊl·səm/ *adj* good for you, and likely to benefit you physically, morally, or emotionally ○ *Wholesome food helps keep you healthy.* ○ *This movie is wholesome family entertainment.*

whole step *n* [C] *music* the largest difference in sound between two notes that are next to each other in a musical SCALE (= series of notes)

whole wheat *adj* [not gradable] made from whole grains of wheat ○ *whole wheat bread*

who'll /huːl/ *contraction of* who will ○ *Who'll be at your party?*

whom **ADDING INFORMATION** /huːm/ *pronoun* used as the object of a verb or after a preposition when referring to a particular person or when adding information about a person just mentioned ○ *The Kenyans have three runners in the race, any of whom could win.* ○ *He took out a photo of his son, whom he adores.*

USAGE

who or whom?

The pronoun **whom** is very formal and most people use **who** instead.

Who did you invite?

Whom is often used after a preposition.

The manager submitted a list of workers, one of whom was African-American. ➤

Some people avoid using **whom** by putting the preposition toward the end of the sentence and using **who** instead, especially in speech and in less formal writing.
Who did you go out with last night?
With whom did you go out last night?

ASKING /huːm/ *pronoun* used esp. in questions as the object of a verb or after a preposition, when asking which person or people, or when asking what someone's name is ○ *Of whom can it truly be said that they have never been dishonest?*

whomever /huːˈmev·ər/ *pronoun* WHOEVER ○ *Give it to whomever you please.* ○ **USAGE**: In informal speech and writing, "whoever" is more often used. "Whomever" is more often used immediately after prepositions than in other positions.

whoop /huːp, hʊp, hwuːp, hwʊp/ *v* [I/T] to shout loudly and in an excited way ○ [I] *I was so happy it was hard not to whoop out loud.*
whoop /huːp, hʊp, hwuːp, hwʊp/ *n* [C] ○ *Jake let out a whoop of triumph.*

IDIOM with whoop

•**whoop it up** to enjoy yourself in a noisy and enthusiastic way ○ *The crowd whooped it up when he made a hole in one.*

whoops /hwʊps, wʊps, wuːps/ *exclamation* OOPS

whopper /ˈhwɑp·ər, ˈwɑp-/ *n* [C] *infml* **1** something that is much bigger than the usual size ○ *Your monthly payment is a whopper.* **2** A whopper is also a big lie: *Fishermen are supposed to tell the biggest whoppers.*
whopping /ˈhwɑp·ɪŋ, ˈwɑp-/ *adj infml* ○ *The mayor was elected by a whopping majority.*

who're /huː·ər, hʊr/ *contraction of* who are ○ *The film begins with a young couple, who're just about to get married.*

who's /huːz/ *contraction of* who is or who has ○ *Who's* (= Who is) *coming over tonight?* ○ *This is Bob, who's* (= who has) *kept our software running.*

whose /huːz/ *pronoun* **1** used to ask which person owns or is responsible for something, or to say who is responsible for something ○ *Whose bag is this?* ○ *I don't care whose fault it is.* **2** Sometimes whose refers to a thing, not a person: *That's the house whose kitchen is painted purple.*

who've /huːv/ *contraction of* who have ○ *I know people who've found homes on the Internet.*

W

why /hwɑɪ, wɑɪ/ *conjunction, adv* [not gradable] for what reason ○ *Why do you like living in Paris?* ○ *She'll ask why you don't have your homework.*

IDIOM with why

•**why not 1** used for making a suggestion ○ *If you're so unhappy, why not leave?* **2 Why not** is also used for expressing agreement: *"Do you want Italian food tonight?" "Sure, why not."*

wick /wɪk/ *n* [C] a piece of string in the center of a candle, or a similar part of a light, which supplies fuel to a flame

wicked /ˈwɪk·əd/ *adj* **1** morally wrong and bad ○ *He was a wicked, ruthless, and dishonest man.* **2** Wicked can also mean slightly bad, but in an attractive way: *She has a wicked sense of humor.* **3** *slang* Wicked also means extreme: *The demands of fund-raising are wicked.*

wicker /ˈwɪk·ər/ *adj* [not gradable] made of very thin pieces of wood twisted together ○ *a wicker basket*

wide FAR FROM SIDE TO SIDE /wɑɪd/ *adj* [*-er/-est* only] **1** far from one side to the other, esp. in comparison with length from top to bottom, or being a particular distance across ○ *a wide window* ○ *a wide yard* ○ *The bay is 15 miles wide here.* **2** Wide open spaces are land with no buildings on it. ○ Related noun: WIDTH
widen /ˈwɑɪd·ən/ *v* [I/T] ○ [I] *After it passes through town, the road widens.*

MANY OR MUCH /wɑɪd/ *adj* [*-er/-est* only] covering a large area, or including many types of things ○ *They sell a wide range of skin-care products.* ○ *The candidate has wide support* (= the support of many people).
widely /ˈwɑɪd·li/ *adv* by many ○ *French was widely spoken there.*
widen /ˈwɑɪd·ən/ *v* [I/T] ○ [T] *Let's widen the discussion by listening to people with other points of view.*

COMPLETELY /wɑɪd/ *adv* [*-er/-est* only] to the greatest degree possible; completely ○ *I was wide awake.* ○ *The dentist said, "Open wide."*

WORD FAMILY wide

Nouns	width	*Verbs*	widen
Adjectives	wide	*Adverbs*	wide
			widely

IDIOM with wide

•**wide open to** *something*, **wide open for** *something* likely to be influenced by something ○ *I'm wide open to suggestions.*

widespread Ⓐ /ˈwɑɪdˈspred/ *adj* existing or happening in many places or among many people ○ *Minnesota has experienced widespread flooding.*

widow /ˈwɪd·oʊ/ *n* [C] a woman whose husband has died and who has not married again
widower /ˈwɪd·ə·wər/ *n* [C] a man whose wife has died and who has not married again
widowed /ˈwɪd·oʊd/ *adj* [not gradable] having lost a husband or wife through death ○ *My widowed uncle lives upstairs.*

width /wɪtθ, wɪdθ/ *n* [C/U] the distance across something from one side to the other ○ [C] *The shoes are available in three widths.* ○ Related adjective: WIDE DISTANT FROM SIDE TO SIDE ○ Compare LENGTH DISTANCE

wield /wiːld/ *v* [T] to have or use power, authority, or influence, or to hold and use a weapon ○ *Under the new city charter, the mayor wields most of the power.*

wife /wɑɪf/ *n* [C] *pl* **wives** the woman to whom a man is married; a married woman ○ Compare HUSBAND

Wi-Fi /ˈwɑɪ ˈfɑɪ/ *n* [U] *trademark* a method of connecting a computer to the INTERNET or to another computer without using wires ○ *The mayor said his administration would look at making Wi-Fi available citywide at little or no charge.*

wig /wɪɡ/ *n* [C] a covering of hair that can be removed and is worn on the head to hide a lack of hair or to cover your own hair ○ *a blond wig* ○ Compare TOUPEE

wiggle /ˈwɪɡ·əl/ *v* [I/T] to move up and down or from side to side with small, quick movements, or to cause this to happen ○ [T] *He wiggled the handle but nothing happened.*

wiggle /ˈwɪɡ·əl/ *n* [C] ○ *The little boy gave his loose tooth a wiggle.*

wigwam /ˈwɪɡ·wɑm/ *n* [C] a cone-shaped tent made and lived in, esp. in the past, by American Indians in the eastern US

wiki /ˈwɪk·i/ *n* [C] a place on the INTERNET where anyone can add new information, or change information that is already there ○ *However, staffers who need to regularly update content prefer a wiki because it is simple to use and edit.*

wild NATURAL /wɑɪld/ *adj, adv* [*-er/-est* only] living or growing independently of people, in natural conditions, and with natural characteristics ○ *wild turkeys* ○ *These herbs grow wild.*

wild /wɑɪld/ *n* [U] places that have few towns or roads, are difficult to get to, and lack conveniences ○ *In Kenya we saw elephants and lions in the wild.*

NOT CONTROLLED /wɑɪld/ *adj* [*-er/-est* only] **1** extreme or violent and not controlled ○ *He led a wild life.* ○ *When I told him what I'd done, he went wild* (= became angry). ○ *I'll make a wild guess* (= one not based on careful thought). **2** *slang* Wild also means excellent, special, or unusual: *The music they play is just wild.* **3** Your wildest dreams are your hopes or thoughts about the best things that could happen in your future: *Never in my wildest dreams did I think I'd win.*

wildly /ˈwɑɪl·dli/ *adv* ○ *He danced wildly for hours.*

wild /wɑɪld/ *adv* [*-er/-est* only] ○ *The teacher left the room, and the kids ran wild* (= were not controlled).

WORD FAMILY wild			
Nouns	wild	*Adverbs*	wildly
Adjectives	wild		

IDIOM with wild

• **wild about** *something* to like something a lot ○ *I'm not wild about apples.*

wild card ANY VALUE *n* [C] (in some card games) a card that can be used instead of any other ○ (*fig.*) *Undecided voters are this election's wild card.*

CHANCE TO PLAY *n* [C] (in sports) an extra opportunity to qualify for a CHAMPIONSHIP competition

wilderness /ˈwɪl·dər·nəs/ *n* [C usually sing] an area of land that has not been farmed or had towns and roads built on it, esp. because it is difficult to live in as a result of its extremely cold or hot weather or bad earth ○ *Large parts of Canada are still wilderness.*

wildfire /ˈwɑɪld·fɑɪr/ *n* [C] a powerful fire that burns out of control across a large area ○ *Wildfires destroyed thousands of acres across Oregon.*

wildflower /ˈwɑɪld ˌflɑʊ·ər, -ˌflɑʊr/ *n* [C] any flower that grows without having been planted by people

wildlife /ˈwɑɪld·lɑɪf/ *n* [U] animals that live independently of people, in natural conditions ○ *Wildlife in the area includes deer, bears, and raccoons.*

wiles /wɑɪlz/ *pl n* skill and ways of tricking people into doing what you want ○ *He'll need to use all his unusual methods and screwball wiles to complete his mission.* ○ Related adjective: WILY

will FUTURE /wɪl, wəl/ *modal verb* **will** used only with the base forms of verbs when referring to the future ○ *Claire will be five years old next month.* ○ **USAGE:** The negative contraction is WON'T. ○ See also: SHALL

INTENTION /wɪl, wəl/ *modal verb* **will**, *past simp.* **would** used to express your intentions ○ *This time I will learn from my mistakes.* ○ **USAGE:** The negative contraction is WON'T.

REQUEST /wɪl, wəl/ *modal verb* **will**, *past simp.* **would** **1** used to ask or tell someone to do something ○ *Will you give me her address, please?* ○ *You will do it because I said so!* **2** Will can be used as a polite way of inviting someone to do something, or of offering someone something: *Will you come in?* ○ **USAGE:** The negative contraction is WON'T.

CAN /wɪl, wəl/ *modal verb* **will**, *past simp.* **would** used to refer to what is possible; to be able to do something ○ *This car will seat six people comfortably.* ○ **USAGE:** The negative contraction is WON'T.

ACCEPTANCE /wɪl, wəl/ *modal verb* **will**, *past simp.* **would** used to say that behavior which usually happens is acceptable because it is expected ○ *Boys will be boys.*

MENTAL POWER /wɪl/ *n* [C/U] **1** the mental power used to control and direct your thoughts and actions, or a determination to do something, despite any difficulties or opposition ○ [C] *He'll need an iron will to stick to that diet.* ○ [U] *After six months in the hospital, she lost the will to live* (= the desire and determination to stay alive). **2** Someone's will is also what the person wants to happen: [U] *I went there against my will.*

will /wɪl/ *v* [T] to try to make something happen by using your thoughts ○ *She willed herself to remain optimistic.*

DEATH PLAN /wɪl/ *n* [C] your official statement of what should be done with your money and property after you die ○ *Your will isn't valid until you sign it.*

will /wɪl/ *v* [T] to officially arrange for someone to receive part or all of your money or property after your death ○ *She willed the house to her brother.*

IDIOMS with will

• **at will** when you want to ○ *Some actors can cry at will.*

•**will have** used for referring to the past from a point in the future ○ *By the time we get there, Jim will have left.*

willful /ˈwɪl·fəl/ *adj* (of something bad) done intentionally, or (of a person) determined to do exactly as you want, even if you know it is wrong ○ *I think he showed a willful disregard for safety.*

willing /ˈwɪl·ɪŋ/ *adj* not opposed to doing something; ready or eager to do something ○ *If you're willing to fly on Thursday you can get a cheaper ticket.*
willingly /ˈwɪl·ɪŋ·li/ *adv* readily and enthusiastically ○ *I willingly babysit for my granddaughter.*
willingness /ˈwɪl·ɪŋ·nəs/ *n* [U] ○ *She shows a willingness to work hard.*

WORD FAMILY willing			
Nouns	willingness unwillingness	*Adverbs*	willingly unwillingly
Adjectives	willing unwilling		

willow (tree) /ˈwɪl·oʊ (ˈtriː)/ *n* [C] a tree that usually grows near water and has long, thin branches that hang down

willowy /ˈwɪl·ə·wi/ *adj* (esp. of a woman) graceful and thin, with long arms and legs ○ *a willowy figure*

willpower /ˈwɪlˌpaʊ·ər/ *n* [U] the ability to control your own thoughts and behavior, esp. in difficult situations ○ *Staying on a diet takes a lot of willpower.*

willy-nilly /ˌwɪl·iˈnɪl·i/ *adv* [not gradable] suddenly and without planning or order ○ *Her words tumbled out all willy-nilly.*

wilt /wɪlt/ *v* [I] (of a plant) to become weak and begin to bend toward the ground, or (of a person) to become weaker, tired, or less confident ○ *Put the flowers in water before they wilt.*

wily /ˈwɑɪ·li/ *adj* quick to think of things, having a very good understanding of situations and possibilities, and often willing to use tricks to achieve an aim ○ *a wily hunter* ○ Related noun: WILES

wimp /wɪmp/ *n* [C] *infml, disapproving* a person who is not strong, brave, or confident ○ *I always thought he was a wimp.*

win /wɪn/ *v* [I/T] *pres. part.* **winning,** *past* **won** to defeat a competitor, or to achieve first position or get a prize in a competition ○ [I] *Did they win last night?* ○ [T] *Our team won the game!*
win /wɪn/ *n* [C] ○ *It was the team's sixth win this season.*
winner /ˈwɪn·ər/ *n* [C] **1** *The winner of this game will play Gigante in the semifinals.* **2** *infml* In sports, a winner is also a goal or point that causes a person or a side to win a game: *Eaves scored the winner in the final seconds of the game.* **3** *infml* A winner is also something that is extremely successful and popular: *That chocolate cake was a winner.*
winning /ˈwɪn·ɪŋ/ *adj* **1** *It's nice to be on the winning side for a change!* **2** If someone has a winning smile or way of behaving, it is friendly and tends to make people like that person: *I'm sure Anna, with her winning ways, can persuade him.*

W

USAGE
win or beat?
You **win** a game or competition.
Who do you think will win the football game?
You **beat** a person or a team you are playing against.
We beat both teams.
~~*We won both teams.*~~

WORD FAMILY win			
Nouns	win winner winnings	*Adjectives*	winning
		Verbs	win

PHRASAL VERBS with win

•**win out** to succeed after a lot of difficulty ○ *The more cautious approach won out.* ○ *Greed won out over principles.*
•**win** *someone* **over** [M] to succeed in getting someone's support or agreement, esp. when the person was previously opposed to you ○ *He had some good ideas, but failed to win over Congress.*

wince /wɪns/ *v* [I] to tighten the muscles of the face briefly and suddenly in a show of pain, worry, or embarrassment ○ *She cut her finger, but didn't even wince.*
wince /wɪns/ *n* [C usually sing] ○ *He sat down with a wince, rubbing his injured left knee.*

winch /wɪntʃ/ *n* [C] a machine that lifts heavy objects by turning a chain or rope around a tube-shaped device
winch /wɪntʃ/ *v* [T] ○ *He winched the crate off the truck.*

wind MOVEMENT OF AIR /wɪnd/ *n* [C/U] the movement of air outside, esp. when strong enough to be felt ○ [U] *The wind is so strong that it's hard to keep an umbrella up.* ○ [C] *We expect light winds from the west today.*
windy /ˈwɪn·di/ *adj* ○ *It will be wet and windy for most of the week.*

BREATH /wɪnd/ *n* [U] breath or the ability to breathe ○ *She ran so hard that it took her a few seconds to get her wind (back) before she could speak.*
winded /ˈwɪn·dəd/ *adj* having difficulty breathing, usually because you have just done some physical activity that caused you to breathe too quickly ○ *He was overweight and out of shape, and he got winded easily.*

TWIST /wɑɪnd/ *v* [I/T] *past* **wound 1** to twist something around something else or turn something in a circle ○ [T] *She wound the string around the spool.* **2** To wind a mechanical device is to cause it to work by turning a key or handle.

TURN /wɑɪnd/ *v* [I always + adv/prep] *past* **wound** (of a road, path, or river) to follow a route that turns repeatedly in different directions ○ *The river winds through the valley.*

winding /ˈwɑɪn·dɪŋ/ *adj* ○ *a winding road*

PHRASAL VERBS with **wind**

•**wind down** *(something)* [M] to end gradually or in stages, or to cause something to end in this way ○ *The storm finally began to wind down after four hours of heavy rain.* ○ *Temple University is winding down its 14th consecutive losing season.*

•**wind up** *(something)* **FINISH** [M] to end something ○ *We should be able to wind (things) up by 10 o'clock.*

•**wind up** **BECOME** to come to be in a particular situation or condition, esp. a bad one ○ *If you aren't careful lifting weights, you could wind up hurting yourself.*

windchill /ˈwɪnd·tʃɪl, ˈwɪn-/ *n* [U] the effect that wind has on how cold the air feels ○ *It's 15 degrees outside, but with the windchill factor it feels like minus five.*

windfall /ˈwɪnd·fɔːl/ *n* [C] an amount of money that you receive unexpectedly ○ *The Belridge School, after receiving a financial windfall, purchased computers for all students and teachers.*

wind instrument *n* [C] a musical instrument whose sound is produced by blowing ○ *Saxophones, clarinets, and flutes are wind instruments.*

windmill /ˈwɪnd·mɪl/ *n* [C] a building or structure with large blades on the outside that, when turned by the force of the wind, provide electrical or mechanical power

window **OPENING** /ˈwɪn·doʊ, -də/ *n* [C] **1** an opening in the wall of a building or vehicle, usually covered with glass, to let light and air in and to allow people inside to see out ○ *to open/close a window* ○ *From her bedroom window she could see a lovely garden.* **2** In a store, a window is the large glass-covered front behind which goods for sale are usually shown: *We walked along Fifth Avenue, looking in the shop windows.* **3** A window is also a period when there is an unusual opportunity to do something: *If a window of opportunity presents itself, I'd be a fool not to take advantage of it.*

COMPUTER /ˈwɪn·doʊ, -də/ *n* [C] an area of a computer screen that shows a particular type of information

window dressing *n* [U] *disapproving* a person or thing that is used to make an activity appear more important or attractive than it really is

windowpane /ˈwɪn·doʊˌpeɪn, -də-/ *n* [C] a single piece of glass in the window of a building

window shade *n* [C] a cover that can be pulled over a window to block the light or to keep people from looking in

window-shopping *n* [U] the activity of looking at products in store windows without buying them

window-shop *v* [I]

windowsill /ˈwɪn·doʊˌsɪl, -də-/ *n* [C] a shelf formed by the bottom part of the frame of a window

windpipe /ˈwɪnd·pɑɪp/ *n* [C] the tube in the body that carries air that has been breathed in from the upper end of the throat to the lungs

windshield /ˈwɪnd·ʃiːld/ *n* [C] the window at the front of a car or other four-wheeled vehicle

windshield wiper *n* [C] a blade with a rubber edge that cleans rain or snow off a car window

windsurfing /ˈwɪndˌsɜr·fɪŋ/ *n* [U] the activity of sailing over water while standing on a narrow board and holding onto a sail

windswept /ˈwɪnd·swept/ *adj* (of places) open to and not protected from strong winds ○ *We drove along the windswept coast of Big Sur in Southern California.*

windward /ˈwɪn·dwərd/ *adj, adv* ***earth science*** toward or turned toward the direction from which the wind is blowing

windy /ˈwɪn·di/ *adj* ○ See at WIND **MOVEMENT OF AIR**

wine /wɑɪn/ *n* an alcoholic drink made from GRAPES, or less commonly an alcoholic drink made in a similar way but from other fruits ○ [U] *a glass of red/white wine* ○ [C] *California wines*

winery /ˈwɑɪ·nə·ri/ *n* [C] a place that makes wine and also usually grows its own GRAPES

IDIOM with **wine**

•**wine and dine** *someone* to entertain someone with food and drink, esp. expensive food and drink ○ *They wine and dine clients in festive tents, promoting their image of achievement and success.*

wing **STRUCTURE FOR FLYING** /wɪŋ/ *n* [C] one of the movable, usually long and flat, parts on either side of the body of a bird, insect, or BAT that it uses for flying, or one of the long, flat, horizontal structures that stick out on either side of an aircraft ○ *The duck flapped its wings and took off.* ➤ Picture: **insect**

POLITICAL GROUP /wɪŋ/ *n* [C] a group within a political party or organization whose beliefs are in some way different from those of the main group ○ *She's in the conservative wing of the party.*

PART OF BUILDING /wɪŋ/ *n* [C] a section of a large building that connects to a side of the main part ○ *His office is in the west wing of the White House.*

wings /wɪŋz/ *pl n* the sides of a stage which cannot be seen by the people watching the play

wingspan /ˈwɪŋ·spæn/ *n* [C] the distance between the ends of the wings of a bird or aircraft ○ *Some eagles have a wingspan of over seven feet.*

wink /wɪŋk/ *v* [I] to close one eye briefly as a way of greeting someone or of showing that you are not serious about something you have said ○ *He winked when he said it.*

wink /wɪŋk/ *n* [C]

PHRASAL VERB with **wink**

•**wink at** *something* to pretend that you do not notice something that is wrong ○ *During the holiday, parking violations were winked at.*

winner /ˈwɪn·ər/ *n* [C] ○ See at WIN

winnings /ˈwɪn·ɪŋz/ *pl n* an amount of money won ○ *What are you going to spend your winnings on?*

winnow /ˈwɪn·oʊ/ *v* [T] to reduce a large number of people or things to a much smaller number by judging their quality ○ *The six architects chosen to compete for the commission were winnowed from an original list of 27.*

winsome /ˈwɪn·səm/ *adj* charming and attractive in a simple way ○ *She opened her eyes and gave her mother a winsome smile.*

winter /ˈwɪnt·ər/ *n* [C/U] the season when the weather is coldest between fall and spring, lasting from November to March north of the equator and from May to September south of the equator ○ [C] *last/next/this winter* ○ [U] *My grandparents often vacation in Florida for part of the winter.*
wintry /ˈwɪn·tri/ *adj* typical of winter's cold, windy, and snowy weather ○ *You'll definitely need snow tires on your car for the wintry weather around here.*

WORD FAMILY winter			
Nouns	winter	*Adjectives*	wintry

wintertime /ˈwɪnt·ər ˌtɑɪm/ *n* [C] the season of winter ○ *This lake becomes a skating rink in the wintertime.*

win-win *adj* [not gradable] having a benefit for everyone that is involved, or a benefit for one person or group no matter what the result is ○ *State officials claim it's a win-win situation for property owners and taxpayers.*

wipe /wɑɪp/ *v* [T] to slide something over the surface of something else, in order to remove dirt, food, or liquid ○ *Please wipe your feet before you come into the house.* ○ *She gently wiped and cleaned her scraped knee.* ○ [M] *Just take the sponge in the sink and wipe the table off.*
wiper /ˈwɑɪ·pər/ *n* [C] a WINDSHIELD WIPER ○ *One of our wipers is stuck.*

PHRASAL VERB with wipe

• **wipe out** *something* [M] to destroy something completely or cause something to be completely lost ○ *Poor investments wiped out most of his earnings.*

W

wire METAL THREAD /wɑɪr/ *n* [C/U] thin metal that can be bent, used in a stiff form in fences and in a form more easily shaped for fastening things or for carrying electric currents ○ [C] *telephone wires* ○ [U] *There was a six-foot high wire fence around the playground.*
wire /wɑɪr/ *v* [T] **1** connected or fastened by wire ○ *Our building is wired for cable TV.* **2** A person or place that is wired is secretly equipped with an electric device that records sounds such as conversations: *Wired by the FBI, he began recording meetings with Chicago officials.*
wiring /ˈwɑɪr·ɪŋ/ *n* [U] the system of wires in a building that carry electricity ○ *Faulty electrical wiring could cause a fire.*
wiry /ˈwɑɪr·i/ *adj* If hair or fur is wiry, it is stiff and not soft. ○ See also: WIRY

SEND MESSAGE /wɑɪr/ *v* [T] *dated* to send a message or money by TELEGRAPH ○ *My father wired me $300.*
wire /wɑɪr/ *n* [C] *dated* a TELEGRAM

WORD FAMILY wire			
Nouns	wire wireless wiring	*Adjectives* *Verbs*	wireless wiry wire

wireless /ˈwɑɪr·ləs/ *adj* [not gradable] not needing wires to make a connection or to communicate ○ *They have a plan to link 9,700 office buildings to the Net via a high-speed wireless network.*
wireless /ˈwɑɪr·ləs/ *n* [U] **1** broadcasting or computer communication that does not use wires ○ *If you've been waiting to jump into wireless, the water is safe.* **2** *dated, Cdn and Br* A wireless is also a radio.

wiretap /ˈwɑɪr·tæp/ *v* [I/T] **-pp-** to secretly listen to people by connecting a listening device to their telephone, or to attach a listening device to a telephone for this purpose ○ [T] *The court gave permission to have his phone wiretapped to gather evidence.*
wiretap /ˈwɑɪr·tæp/ *n* [C] ○ *The government put a wiretap on his phone.*

wiry /ˈwɑɪr·i/ *adj* (of a person) thin but strong ○ *He was a wiry man 5 feet 10 inches tall and weighing 145 pounds.* ○ See also: WIRY at WIRE METAL THREAD

wisdom /ˈwɪz·dəm/ *n* [U] **1** the ability to make good judgments based on what you have learned from your experience, or the knowledge and understanding that gives you this ability **2** Wisdom also means the quality of being a good judgment: *I question the wisdom of separating a child from his brothers and sisters whatever the circumstances.*

wisdom tooth *n* [C] any of the four teeth at the back of the JAW that are the last to develop

wise /wɑɪz/ *adj* [-*er*/-*est* only] having or showing good judgment, or the ability to make good judgments, based on what you have learned from your experience ○ *a wise man/woman* ○ [+ *to* infinitive] *They decided that it was wiser to wait until they were making a little more money before buying a house.*
wisely /ˈwɑɪz·li/ *adv* ○ *Spend your money wisely.*

IDIOM with wise

• **wise to** *something* *infml* aware of a situation or way of doing something, esp. one that is dishonest ○ *He calls in sick almost every Monday with some phony story – I'm wise to him.*

PHRASAL VERB with wise

• **wise up** *infml* to begin to understand the truth about an unpleasant situation or a fact ○ *It's time that Congress wised up to the fact that most citizens do not trust politicians.*

-wise /ˌwɑɪz/ *suffix* relating to ○ *Moneywise, of course, I'm much better off than I used to be.*

wisecrack /ˈwɑɪz·kræk/ *n* [C] a remark that criticizes someone or something in a humorous way

wish DESIRE DIFFERENT SITUATION /wɪʃ/ *v* [+ (*that*) clause] to desire some situation that is different from the one that exists ○ *I wish (that) I didn't have to go to work today.* ○ *She wished she could afford a new car.* ○ *I wish I hadn't eaten so much.*

EXPRESS DESIRE /wɪʃ/ *v* [I/T] to hope that you will get something or that something will happen ○ [I] *I was wishing for summer so hard I could almost make it happen at that moment.*

wish /wɪʃ/ *n* [C] ○ [+ *that* clause] *It was his greatest wish that one of his children would become a scientist.* ○ *Close your eyes and make a wish.*

WANT SOMETHING /wɪʃ/ *v fml* to want something, or want to do something ○ [+ *to* infinitive] *If you wish to volunteer to work in the museum, please indicate what department you are interested in.*

wish /wɪʃ/ *n* [C] ○ [+ *to* infinitive] *His greatest wish is to become a famous writer.*

EXPRESS KIND FEELINGS /wɪʃ/ *v* [T] to express kind feelings for someone on a particular occasion ○ *Don't forget to wish her a happy birthday.* ○ *I'm off for the interview now – wish me luck.* ○ *His old teammates wished him well* (= hoped that he did well).

wishes /ˈwɪʃ·əz/ *pl n* ○ *When you see Joyce, please give her my best wishes.*

IDIOM with wish

• **wouldn't wish** *something* **on anyone**, **wouldn't wish** *something* **on** *someone's* **worst enemy** used for saying you would not want anyone to experience something very bad ○ *Having the flu was awful – I wouldn't wish it on anyone.*

PHRASAL VERB with wish

• **wish away** *something* [M] to do nothing and hope that a problem will disappear ○ *Some people seem to think if they wish the disease away, then it will go away.*

wishful thinking /ˈwɪʃ·fəl ˈθɪŋ·kɪŋ/ *n* [U] the imagining of an unlikely future event or situation that you wish were possible ○ *We talked about buying a house someday, but right now it's just wishful thinking.*

wishy-washy /ˈwɪʃ·iː ˌwɑʃ·i, -ˌwɔː·ʃi/ *adj* lacking in firm ideas, principles, or the ability to make a decision ○ *He's got TV ads accusing Dole of being wishy-washy on the issues.*

wisp /wɪsp/ *n* [C] a delicate, thin, and sometimes twisting piece or line of something ○ *Rita brushed back the stray coppery wisps of hair escaping her braid.* ○ *A wisp of smoke from the campfire curled in the air.*

wistful /ˈwɪst·fəl/ *adj* sad and thinking about something that is impossible or past ○ *She cast a wistful glance at the bridal gowns in the window.*

wistfully /ˈwɪst·fə·li/ *adv* ○ *She spoke wistfully of their early years together.*

wit /wɪt/ *n* [C/U] the ability to use words in an amusing and intelligent way, or a person who has this ability ○ [U] *The warmth and wit of her literary style bring the subject to life.*

witty /ˈwɪt̬·i/ *adj* using words in an amusing and intelligent way; full of wit ○ *a witty remark* ○ *I think she's one of the wittiest comics on television.* ○ **USAGE:** A witty remark is a WITTICISM.

witch /wɪtʃ/ *n* [C] a woman who is believed to have magical powers and, esp. in stories, uses them to help or harm people ○ Compare WIZARD

witchcraft /ˈwɪtʃ·kræft/ *n* [U] the use of magic, esp. in stories, to help or harm people

witch hunt *n* [C] *disapproving* an attempt to find and punish people whose opinions are not popular

with TOGETHER /wɪð, wɪθ/ *prep* used of people or things that are together or doing something together ○ *She's in the kitchen with Dad.* ○ *He's an impossible person to work with.* ○ *I think I'll have some ice cream with my pie.* ○ *I'll be with you* (= I will give you my attention) *in a moment.* ○ *She's been with the magazine* (= working for it) *for two years.*

USING /wɪð, wɪθ/ *prep* using (something) or by means of (something) ○ *I bought it with my gift certificate.* ○ *The label on the box says, "Handle with care."* ○ *He caught the crabs with a large net.*

HAVING /wɪð, wɪθ/ *prep* **1** having or possessing (someone or something) ○ *I'd like a room with an ocean view.* ○ *He's married with three children.* ○ *The doctor spoke with a German accent.* ○ *We're a multinational company with offices in London, Paris, and New York.* ○ *With a little luck, we should be back in time for dinner.* ○ *Both their children graduated with degrees in economics.* **2** With can also mean including: *With your contribution, we have a total of $450.*

RELATING TO /wɪð, wɪθ/ *prep* relating to or in the case of (a person or thing) ○ *How are things with you?* ○ *That has nothing to do with the subject.* ○ *Her books are popular with teenage girls.* ○ *He's very careless with his money.* ○ *The trouble with this skirt is that it wrinkles too easily.* ○ *What's the matter with her?*

CAUSED BY /wɪð, wɪθ/ *prep* because of or caused by (something) ○ *He was trembling with fear.* ○ *She's at home with a bad cold.* ○ *His confidence was bolstered with the support of a lot of friends and relatives.* ○ *With all the excitement and confusion, I forgot to say goodbye to her.*

AGAINST /wɪð, wɪθ/ *prep* against (something) ○ *The company faces a long battle with the software giant.* ○ *I always end up arguing with him about politics.*

SUPPORTING /wɪð, wɪθ/ *prep* supporting (someone or something) ○ *If you want to go for a promotion, I'll be with you all the way.* ○ *Where do you stand on this issue – are you with us or against us?*

DESPITE /wɪð, wɪθ/ *prep* despite (something) ○ *With all her faults, she's still one of the best teachers we've ever had.*

AND /wɪð, wɪθ/ *prep* and; followed by ○ *I'd like a hamburger and French fries with a small salad.* ○ *Two* *hundred dollars is payable immediately, with a further $100 payable on delivery.*

IDIOMS with with

•**with a vengeance** using a lot of effort, energy, or time ○ *She works out every day with a vengeance.*
•**with all due respect** used for expressing polite disagreement ○ *I've been thinking about what you said and, with all due respect, I think you're mistaken.*
•**with all my heart** completely ○ *I love you with all my heart.*
•**with child** *fml* pregnant ○ *The painting is of a woman with child.*
•**with** *your* **eyes closed** very easily ○ *I can find your house with my eyes closed.*
•**with flying colors** very easily ○ *She passed the exam with flying colors.*
•**with it** to be aware of popular ideas and fashions ○ *She reads all the style magazines and thinks she's really with it.*
•**with open arms** in a very friendly way
•**with the naked eye** without using any special device for making images larger ○ *We live miles away, but on a clear night, you can see the city skyscrapers with the naked eye.*

withdraw /wɪð'drɔː, wɪθ-/ *v* [I/T] *past simp.* **withdrew**, *past part.* **withdrawn** to take something back, or to remove something ○ [T] *He asked that his name be withdrawn from nomination for a Golden Globe Award.* ○ [T] *Democrats threatened to withdraw* (= stop giving) *their support of the tax bill.* ○ [T] *I have to withdraw* (= take out) *some money from an ATM machine.*
withdrawal /wɪð'drɔː·əl, wɪθ-/ *n* [C/U] **1** [C] *a troop withdrawal* ○ [C] *He had made several large withdrawals from his bank account* (= He had taken out a lot of money). ○ [C] *Her sudden withdrawal from the competition surprised everyone.* **2** Withdrawal also means the physical and mental effects experienced when a person stops using a drug.
withdrawn /wɪð'drɔːn, wɪθ-/ *adj* (of a person) preferring to be alone and taking little interest in other people ○ *During the winter, she became depressed and withdrawn.*

wither /'wɪð·ər/ *v* [I/T] to become, or cause something to become, weak, dry, and smaller ○ [T] *Hot, dry weather withered the peanut crop in the southeast.* ○ [I] (*fig.*) *Public interest in the scandal will not wither away any time soon.*

withering /'wɪð·ə·rɪŋ/ *adj* expressing strong criticism ○ *She delivered a withering attack on the book and its authors.*

W

withhold /wɪθ'hoʊld, wɪð-/ *v* [T] *past* **withheld** to refuse to give something, or to keep back something ○ *Has the government been withholding crucial information?* ○ *The governor said he would withhold judgment until he receives the committee's report.*

within /wɪð'ɪn, wɪθ-/ *prep, adv* [not gradable] inside or not beyond (a particular area, limit, or period of time) ○ *Most Californians live within 20 miles of the coast.* ○ *The tickets should reach you within a week.* ○ *The company has always acted within the law* (= legally).

IDIOMS with within

•**within an inch of** *something* very close to something ○ *She came within an inch of losing her life.*
•**within limits** if you follow certain rules ○ *We can wear what we like to work, within limits.*
•**within reason** if you use good judgment ○ *You can say whatever you like, within reason.*

without /wɪð'ɑʊt, wɪθ-/ *prep, adv* [not gradable] not having or doing (something), or not having the use or help of (someone or something) ○ *He came out without a coat.* ○ *He looks younger without the moustache.* ○ *Thanks for your help – I couldn't have done it without you.* ○ *You shouldn't drive for more than three hours without taking a break.* ○ *That was without (a) doubt/without question* (= certainly) *the best vacation I've ever had.* ○ *When you have no money, you just have to learn to do without.*

IDIOMS with without

•**without fail** in every case, or for certain ○ *She takes a walk every morning without fail.*
•**without further ado** with no more delay ○ *And now, without further ado, here is our special guest speaker.*

withstand /wɪθ'stænd, wɪð-/ *v* [T] *past* **withstood** to receive without being changed or damaged by something powerful; bear ○ *The building has to be strong enough to withstand severe winds and storms.* ○ *Coaches have to be tough to withstand the constant pressure to win.*

witness PERSON WHO SEES /'wɪt·nəs/ *n* [C/U] **1** a person who sees an event happening, esp. a crime or an accident ○ [C] *According to witnesses, the car used in the robbery was a green van with Pennsylvania license plates.* **2** Someone who is witness to something sees it: [U] *She was witness to the tragic event.* **3** If you are a witness, you are asked to be present at a particular event and to SIGN (= write you name on) a document in order to prove that things have been done correctly: [C] *The will has to be signed by two witnesses.*
witness /'wɪt·nəs/ *v* [T] **1** to see something happen ○ *We were there at the time and witnessed the accident.* ○ *The university has witnessed* (= experienced) *quite a few changes over the years.* **2** Witness also means to show or give proof of something: *The program aroused strong feelings, as witnessed by the number of letters the station received.* ○ *Rock music is becoming a health problem – witness the loss of hearing* (= for proof, look at the loss of hearing) *in some of our youth.* **3** If you are asked to witness an event, you are asked to be present at it and sign your name to prove that things have been done correctly.

PERSON IN COURT /'wɪt·nəs/ *n* [C] a person in a law court who promises to tell the truth and answers questions about something that was seen or is known ○ *defense/prosecution witnesses* ○ *Five witnesses are expected to testify at the trial today.*

IDIOM with witness

• **bear witness to** *something* to show or prove something ○ *The latest sales figures bear witness to the success of our advertising campaign.*

witness stand *n* [C] a raised place, usually near the judge, where someone who is giving information about a case sits

wits /wɪts/ *pl n* practical intelligence or understanding ○ *She's learned to survive on her wits.*

IDIOMS with wits

• **at** *your* **wits' end** so worried, confused, or annoyed that you do not know what to do next ○ *She was at her wits' end trying to figure out how to control her 14-year-old son.*
• **frighten** *someone* **out of** *their* **wits, scare** *someone* **out of** *their* **wits** to cause extreme fear in someone ○ *That strange noise during the night scared me out of my wits.*
• **have** *your* **wits about** *you*, **keep** *your* **wits about** *you* to think and react quickly when something dangerous or difficult happens unexpectedly ○ *She managed to keep her wits about her and escaped unharmed.*

witticism /ˈwɪt̬·əˌsɪz·əm/ *n* [C] a remark that is WITTY (= both intelligent and amusing)

witty /ˈwɪt̬·i/ *adj* ○ See at WIT

wives /wɑɪvz/ *pl of* WIFE

wiz /wɪz/ *n* [C] *infml* a WIZARD (= skilled person) ○ *Adele is a wiz at fixing computer problems.*

wizard /ˈwɪz·ərd/ *n* [C] **1** a man who is believed to have magical powers and, esp. in stories, uses them to help or harm people ○ Compare WITCH **2** *approving* You might call someone a wizard who has great skill or who manages to do something that is extremely difficult: *a financial wizard*

wizened /ˈwɪz·ənd/ *adj* having dry skin showing many lines, esp. because of old age ○ *a wizened old man*

WMD *n* [C] *abbreviation for* weapons of mass destruction (= weapons, such as chemicals, poisons, and nuclear bombs, that can kill many people very quickly)

wobble /ˈwɑb·əl/ *v* [I/T] to shake or move from side to side in a way that shows a lack of balance, or to cause something to do this ○ [I] *The table wobbles because its legs are uneven.*
wobbly /ˈwɑb·li, -ə·li/ *adj* ○ *a wobbly ladder* ○ *I was still weak, and my legs felt a little wobbly.*

woe /woʊ/ *n* [U] *fml* **1** bad troubles causing much suffering ○ *She poured out her tale of woe.* **2** Woes are great problems or troubles: *The country has been beset by economic woes for the past few years.*

woefully /ˈwoʊ·fə·li/ *adv* (of a bad situation) extremely; very ○ *Medical resources were woefully inadequate during the emergency.* ○ *The staff was woefully underpaid and thoroughly demoralized.*
woeful /ˈwoʊ·fəl/ *adj* very bad, or (of something bad) very great or extreme ○ *They displayed a woeful ignorance of the safety rules.*

wok /wɑk/ *n* [C] a large, bowl-shaped pan used for frying food quickly in hot oil

woke /woʊk/ *past simple of* WAKE STOP SLEEPING

woken /ˈwoʊ·kən/ *past participle of* WAKE STOP SLEEPING

wolf ANIMAL /wʊlf/ *n* [C] *pl* **wolves** a wild animal of the dog family

EAT /wʊlf/ *v* [T] *infml* to eat a large amount of food very quickly ○ *He wolfed down lunch in five minutes.*

IDIOM with wolf

• **a wolf in sheep's clothing** someone or something that seems to be good but is actually not good at all ○ *My grandfather was a wolf in sheep's clothing – he looked like a sweet old man, but he was really mean.*

woman /ˈwʊm·ən, *Southern also* ˈwʌm-/ *n* [C] *pl* **women** an adult female human being ○ *Our chief of police is a woman and our mayor is a woman, too.* ○ *She is an active, elderly woman.* ○ *More men than women suffer from high blood pressure.*
womanhood /ˈwʊm·ən ˌhʊd/ *n* [U] the state of being a woman ○ *The girl had matured into womanhood.*
womanly /ˈwʊm·ən·li/ *adj* having qualities thought typical of a woman

WORD FAMILY woman			
Nouns	woman womanhood	*Adjectives*	womanly

IDIOM with woman

• **the woman in the street** a woman or women who think like most other people ○ *What does the woman in the street want from a fashion magazine?* ○ Compare THE MAN IN THE STREET at MAN IDIOMS

womankind /ˈwʊm·ən ˌkɑɪnd/ *n* [U] the female part of the human race ○ *We're talking about womankind, not about men!*

woman-to-woman *adj, adv* direct and honest and done as equals ○ *I want to talk to you, woman-to-woman.* ○ Compare MAN-TO-MAN

womb /wuːm/ *n* [C] the organ of a woman or other female mammal in which a baby develops before birth; uterus

women /ˈwɪm·ən/ *pl of* WOMAN

women's room *n* [C] a LADIES' ROOM

won /wʌn/ *past simple and past participle of* WIN

wonder QUESTION /ˈwʌn·dər/ *v* to think about things in a questioning and sometimes doubting way ○ [I] *I often wonder about those kids.* ○ [+ question word] *I wonder what he is doing here.* ○ [I] *Don't you ever wonder if she's happy?*

SURPRISE /ˈwʌn·dər/ *n* [C/U] a feeling of great surprise and admiration, or someone or something that causes such feelings ○ [U] *People simply stared at her in wonder.* ○ [C] *She's a wonder!* ○ [U] *If you* *didn't study, no wonder you failed the test.* ○ [C] *Among the wonders of medicine is anesthetic.*

WORD FAMILY wonder			
Nouns	wonder	*Verbs*	wonder
Adjectives	wonderful	*Adverbs*	wonderfully

IDIOM with wonder

• **it's a wonder** it is surprising ○ *After having so many problems with the house, it's a wonder they stayed.*

wonder drug *n* [C] *infml* an extremely effective medicine ○ *Aspirin has often been called a wonder drug, partly because it is powerful and effective for many health problems.*

wonderful /ˈwʌn·dər·fəl/ *adj* extremely good ○ *Becoming a father was the most wonderful experience of my life.*
wonderfully /ˈwʌn·dər·fə·li/ *adv* ○ *I took a vacation and feel wonderfully rested.*

wonk /wɔːŋk, wɑŋk/ *n* [C] *slang* a person who likes to think about or study something and spends a great amount of time doing it ○ *He's a policy wonk and will talk for hours about solutions to problems.*

won't /woʊnt/ *contraction of* will not ○ *You won't believe this, but that cactus is a member of the lily family.* ○ *Won't you come in?* (= Will you please come in?)

wont /wɔːnt, woʊnt/ *n* [U] (used after a possessive) habit or custom ○ *Mr. Rivers, as is his wont, has asked some difficult questions.*
wont /wɔːnt, woʊnt/ *adj* [+ *to* infinitive] ○ *They were wont to use the word "inspiration" too much* (= this was their habit).

woo /wuː/ *v* [T] **woos,** *pres. part.* **wooing,** *past* **wooed 1** to try to persuade someone to support you ○ *A candidate must woo voters by making them feel important.* **2** *dated* To woo someone is to try to persuade that person that you are a good person to marry.

wood HARD MATERIAL /wʊd/ *n* [C/U] the hard substance that forms the inside part of the branches and trunk of a tree, used to make things or as a fuel ○ [C] *He makes tables and other things from different kinds of wood.*
wooden /ˈwʊd·ən/ *adj* [not gradable] ○ *They ate at a long wooden table.*
GROUP OF TREES /wʊd/ *n* [C] WOODS ○ *Beyond them lay a dense wood.*

WORD FAMILY wood			
Nouns	wood woods	*Adjectives*	wooded wooden

woodchuck /ˈwʊd·tʃʌk/ *n* [C] a GROUNDHOG

woodcut /ˈwʊd·kʌt/ *n* [C] a picture printed from a pattern cut into the surface of a block of wood ○ *Long ago, woodcuts were used by printers for illustrations.*

wooded /ˈwʊd·əd/ *adj* ○ See at WOODS

wooden WOOD /ˈwʊd·ən/ *adj* [not gradable] ○ See at WOOD HARD MATERIAL
AWKWARD /ˈwʊd·ən/ *adj* stiff and awkward, or lacking expression ○ *She's a wooden speaker.*

woodland /ˈwʊd·lənd, -lænd/ *n* [C] an area of land on which many trees grow

woodpecker /ˈwʊd ˌpek·ər/ *n* [C] a bird with a strong beak that it hammers into tree trunks to find insects to eat

woods /wʊdz/, **wood** /wʊd/ *pl n* an area of land covered with a thick growth of trees ○ *Shaded from the sun, the woods were cool and quiet.*
wooded /ˈwʊd·əd/ *adj* ○ *The house stood on a wooded hillside.*

woodshed /ˈwʊd·ʃed/ *n* [C] a small building where wood used as fuel is stored

wood stove, woodstove /ˈwʊd ˈstoʊv/, **wood-burning stove** *n* [C] a stove for heating or cooking that uses wood for fuel

woodwind /ˈwʊd·wɪnd/ *n* [C/U] a type of musical instrument that is played by blowing over a REED ○ [U] *The recording has some nice woodwind parts.* ○ [C] *She uses keyboards and woodwinds.*

woodwork /ˈwʊd·wɜrk/ *n* [C] anything made of wood inside a building, esp. the wood around the edges of doors, windows, and floors

woodworking /ˈwʊd ˌwɜr·kɪŋ/ *n* [U] the activity of making objects, esp. furniture, from wood

woof /wʊf/ *n* [C] the noise that a dog makes when it BARKS

wool /wʊl/ *n* [U] the soft, curly hair from sheep, or thread or cloth made from this ○ *I bought some fine wool to knit a baby sweater.*
woolen /ˈwʊl·ən/, **wool** /wʊl/ *adj* [not gradable] ○ *She lay under a red woolen blanket.*
woolens /ˈwʊl·ənz/ *pl n* clothes made from wool ○ *I wear woolens a lot.*

WORD FAMILY wool			
Nouns	wool woolens	*Adjectives*	woolen wooly

woozy /ˈwuː·zi/ *adj infml* slightly weak and confused and likely to fall ○ *This medicine may make you woozy.*

word LANGUAGE UNIT /wɜrd/ *n* [C] a single unit of language that has meaning and can be spoken or written ○ *The word "environment" means different things to different people.* ○ *She spoke so fast I couldn't understand a word* (= anything she said).
word /wɜrd/ *v* [T always + adv/prep] to choose the words with which to express something ○ *His description was carefully worded to cover various possibilities.*
worded /ˈwɜrd·əd/ *adj* [not gradable] ○ *a strongly worded letter*

wording /ˈwɜrd·ɪŋ/ *n* [U] the exact choice of words ○ *The wording of the agreement was too vague.*

wordy /ˈwɜrd·i/ *adj* containing too many words ○ *Your memo is too wordy – make it short and to the point.*

BRIEF STATEMENT /wɜrd/ *n* [C usually sing] a brief discussion or statement ○ *Could I have a word with you?* ○ *Let me give you a word of advice.* ○ *Tell us what happened* **in your own words** (= say it in your own way).

NEWS /wɜrd/ *n* [U] news or a message ○ *We were excited when word of the discovery reached us.*

PROMISE /wɜrd/ *n* [U] a promise ○ *You have my word – I won't tell a soul.* ○ *She wouldn't give me her word if she didn't mean to keep it.*

ORDER /wɜrd/ *n* [C usually sing] an order or request ○ *If you want me to leave, just say/give the word.*

WORD FAMILY word

Nouns	word wording	*Adjectives*	worded wordy
Verbs	word		

IDIOMS with word

• **breathe a word, say a word** to tell a secret ○ *Don't breathe a word of this to anyone.* ○ *I promise not to say a word to Dad about it.*

• **man of *his* word, woman of *her* word** people who do what they say they will do ○ *He is obviously a man of his word, a man of integrity.*

• **the word is** it has been reported but is not certain ○ *The word is that the boss is retiring soon.*

• **word for word** exactly as spoken or written ○ *She copied it word for word from the encyclopedia.*

• **word of mouth** by someone telling you ○ *Students discovered the center by word of mouth.*

word processing *n* [U] the act of putting documents, letters, and other texts in electronic form on a computer

word processor *n* [C] a computer program that is used for preparing documents and letters

wore /wɔːr, woʊr/ *past simple of* WEAR

work DO A JOB /wɜrk/ *v* [I/T] to do a job, esp. a job you do to earn money ○ [T] *She works long hours.* ○ [T] *Richie worked the night shift.* ○ [I] *Designers worked with the director.* ○ [I] *Mike works for a computer company.* ○ [I] *Medics were working on him for an hour.* ○ [I] *She worked on the project with Luce.* ○ [I] *Anna works well with others.* ○ [I] *I have to work on Saturday.*

work /wɜrk/ *n* [U] the use of effort to do or make something that has value, and for which you are usually paid ○ *outdoor/office/manual work* ○ *Steve's out of work again* (= not employed).

worker /ˈwɜr·kər/ *n* [C] a person who is paid for using effort to do something ○ *clerical/factory/farm workers* ○ *skilled/unskilled workers*

working /ˈwɜr·kɪŋ/ *adj* [not gradable] **1** *Employees are unhappy with working conditions.* **2** A working person is employed: *working mothers*

CONFUSABLES

work or job?

Work is something you do to earn money. Remember that this noun is uncountable.

She enjoys her work in the hospital.
He's looking for work.
~~*He's looking for a work.*~~

Job is used to talk about the particular type of work activity you do.

He's looking for a job in computer programming.
Teaching must be an interesting job.
~~*Teaching must be an interesting work.*~~

FORCE /wɜrk/ *n* [U] ***physics*** force used on an object multiplied by the distance it moves the object, measured in JOULES

PLACE /wɜrk/ *n* [U] the place where a person regularly goes to do his or her job ○ *I had to leave work early.* ○ *Does it take long to commute to work?*

PERFORM AS INTENDED /wɜrk/ *v* [I/T] to perform as intended or desired, or to cause something to do what it was intended to do ○ [I] *The medicine ought to work right away.* ○ [I] *Our plan worked perfectly.* ○ [T] *I don't know how to work this computer.* ○ [T] *He knows how to work the system* (= get what he wants from it).

workable /ˈwɜr·kə·bəl/ *adj* likely to do or achieve what is intended ○ *a workable plan/solution*

working /ˈwɜr·kɪŋ/ *adj* [not gradable] **1** *The mechanic finally got the car back in working order.* **2** If you have a working knowledge of something, you have enough practical experience to be able to use it or do it: *a working knowledge of English*

workings /ˈwɜr·kɪŋz/ *pl n* the way something, such as an organization or machine, does what it is intended to do ○ *Powerful microscopes reveal the inner workings of cells.*

works /wɜrks/ *pl n* the parts of a machine, esp. the parts that move ○ See also: WORKS

OBJECT /wɜrk/ *n* [C] an object produced as a result of effort, esp. something intended to be art ○ *The museum is showing works by 20th-century artists.*

work /wɜrk/ *v* [T] to shape something with your hands ○ *She carefully works the clay.*

HAVE EFFECT /wɜrk/ *v* [I always + adv/prep] (of a condition or fact) to have an effect, esp. one that either helps or causes difficulties ○ *Time was working against us.* ○ *Jimmie has a lot working in his favor.*

WORD FAMILY work

Nouns	work works workaholic worker workings overwork	*Adjectives*	workable unworkable overworked working
		Verbs	work rework overwork

IDIOMS with work

• **at work** doing a job ○ *Bob's at work on that software.*

• **in the works** in the process of being done ○ *Salary increases are already in the works.*
• **work like a dog** to work very hard ○ *You can work like a dog and still not make ends meet.*
• **work the land, work the soil** to grow crops, esp. as a job ○ *He's the fourth generation of his family to have worked the land.*
• **work** *your* **way up** to achieve a better position within the organization you work for ○ *She quickly worked her way up to vice president.*
• **work wonders** to cause improvements or have a very good effect ○ *A little flattery can work wonders.* ○ Compare DO WONDERS FOR SOMETHING/SOMEONE at DO **IDIOMS**

PHRASAL VERBS with **work**

• **work out** *something* **AGREE TO** [M] to agree to or arrange something, esp. after discussion ○ *Committee members met today to work out a compromise.*
• **work out** *something* **DISCOVER** [M] to discover an answer, develop an idea, or calculate an amount ○ *You can use a calculator to work out the solution.* ○ *She works out each scene on paper.*
• **work out HAPPEN** (of a situation) to happen or develop in a particular, esp. a satisfactory, way, or (of a person) to be suitable for a particular situation ○ *Nothing was working out right.* ○ *Is your new assistant working out OK?*
• **work out EXERCISE** to exercise in order to improve health, strength, or physical appearance, or to improve your skill in a sport ○ *I work out on my stationary bike.* ○ Related noun: WORKOUT
• **work through** *something* [M] to manage a problem that has many different parts step by step ○ *There are a lot of details we need to work through.*
• **work up** *something* **BRING INTO BEING** to bring something into existence, esp. gradually or in stages ○ *I can't work up any enthusiasm for this plan.* ○ *You went running and barely worked up a sweat.*
• **work** *someone/yourself* **up MAKE UPSET** to make yourself or another person excited or upset ○ *You've worked yourself up over nothing.*
• **work up to** *something* to reach a goal by increasing the difficulty of something every time you practice it ○ *Start by jogging for five minutes and slowly work up to a half hour.*

workaholic /ˌwɜr·kəˈhɔː·lɪk, -ˈhɑl·ɪk/ *n* [C] a person who works a lot of the time and finds it difficult not to work

workbench /ˈwɜrk·bentʃ/ *n* [C] a strong, solid table on which you can work with tools, wood, small machines, etc.

W

workday /ˈwɜrk·deɪ/ *n* [C] a day on which most people do a job for money, or the amount of time each day a person spends doing his or her job

work ethic *n* [U] the belief that work is valuable as an activity and is morally good

workfare /ˈwɜrk·fer, -fær/ *n* [U] a government program under which people who receive WELFARE (= money from the government) and are able to work must work

work force, workforce /ˈwɜrk ˈfɔːrs/ *n* [U] the people available to work or actually employed in a particular area, industry, or company

working class *n* [C usually sing] the group of people in society who use physical skills in their jobs and are usually paid by the hour ○ *a working-class neighborhood/family*

workload /ˈwɜrk·loʊd/ *n* [C usually sing] an amount of work that a person is expected to do

workman /ˈwɜrk·mən/ *n* [C] *pl* **-men** a man who uses physical skill and especially his hands in doing his job
workmanlike /ˈwɜrk·mənˌlɑɪk/ *adj* done with skill ○ *The soft-spoken Congressman has carried out his duties in workmanlike fashion.*
workmanship /ˈwɜrk·mənˌʃɪp/ *n* [U] the skill with which something was made or done ○ *The city spent $50,000 to repair shoddy workmanship on the sidewalks.*

work of art *n* [C] *pl* **works of art** an object made by an artist, esp. a picture or statue

workout /ˈwɜr·kɑʊt/ *n* [C] a period of physical exercise ○ *After a one-hour workout, Sam felt good.* ○ Related verb: WORK OUT **EXERCISE**

workplace /ˈwɜrk·pleɪs/ *n* [C] a place where people do their jobs

works /wɜrks/ *pl n infml* all the extra things that may be offered with something ○ *This camera came with a carrying case, zoom lens, tripod – the works.* ○ See also: WORKS at WORK **PERFORM AS INTENDED**

workshop ROOM WITH TOOLS /ˈwɜrk·ʃɑp/ *n* [C] a space in a building equipped with tools and often machines for making or repairing things
MEETING WITH PURPOSE /ˈwɜrk·ʃɑp/ *n* [C] a meeting in which people discuss and show how to do a job or perform an activity, so that everyone can learn ○ *a teacher-training workshop*

workstation /ˈwɜrkˌsteɪ·ʃən/ *n* [C] an area in a place of business where one person works at a computer, or the computer itself

workweek, work week /ˈwɜrk·wiːk/ *n* [C] **1** the days or hours that a person spends working during one week ○ *Many offices operate on a thirty-five hour workweek.* **2** Workweek also means Monday through Friday, when most people are working.

world THE EARTH /wɜrld/ *n* [U] **1** the planet on which human life has developed, esp. including all people and their ways of life ○ *People from all over the world will be attending the conference.* ○ *The rapid growth of computers has changed the world.* **2** The world can also mean the whole physical universe: *The world contains many solar systems, not just ours.*
WHOLE AREA /wɜrld/ *n* [C] all of a particular group or type of thing, such as countries or animals, or a whole area of human activity or understanding ○ *the animal/plant world* ○ *the business world* ○ *the world of entertainment* ○ *In the world of politics, the president's voice is still the most powerful in the nation.*

LARGE DEGREE /wɜrld/ *n* [U] a large degree; a lot ○ *There's a world of difference between the two hotels.*
worlds /ˈwɜrldz/ *pl n* ○ *The two men are worlds apart* (= completely opposed) *in their political views.*

WORD FAMILY world			
Nouns	world worlds underworld	*Adjectives*	worldly unworldly worldwide
Adverbs	worldwide		

IDIOMS with **world**

• **in a world of *your* own** not giving much attention to what is happening around you, because you are thinking about something else ○ *He won't hear you – he's off in a world of his own.*
• **in the world** in any conditions; of all possible things ○ *What in the world are you doing in the closet?* ○ *How in the world does this amazing thing work?* ○ Compare ON EARTH at EARTH IDIOM
• **man of the world, woman of the world** someone who has a lot of experience of life and can deal with most situations ○ *They would grow up to be true women of the world, educated and experienced in magnificent ways.*

world-class *adj* [not gradable] among the best in the world ○ *a world-class athlete*

world-famous *adj* known to many people in the world ○ *a world-famous actress*

worldly PHYSICAL /ˈwɜrl·dli/ *adj* having to do with physical things and ordinary life ○ *worldly success* ○ *She lost all her worldly possessions in the fire.*
EXPERIENCED /ˈwɜrl·dli/ *adj* experienced in the ways of the world ○ *He's older and more worldly than the other students in his class.*

world power *n* [C] a country that has enough economic, military, and political strength to influence events in many other countries

World Series *n* [C] a set of baseball games played each year between the two best teams in the US and Canada

worldwide /ˈwɜrlˈdwɑɪd/ *adj, adv* [not gradable] existing or happening in all parts of the world ○ *a worldwide recession* ○ *Their worldwide sales were growing by 20% a year.* ○ *The rock group has sold six million copies of the album worldwide.*

World Wide Web, *abbreviation* **WWW** *short form* **Web** *n* [U] an information network of text, pictures, and sound that people have access to when they use the INTERNET

worm ANIMAL /wɜrm/ *n* [C] a small animal with a long, narrow, soft body without legs or bones
MOVE SLOWLY /wɜrm/ *v* [T always + adv/prep] to move slowly or carefully through a crowd or tight space ○ *He wormed his way through the crowd as quickly as he could.* ○ (fig.) *He was a distant relation who wormed his way into the confidence of the family.*

worn /wɔːrn, woʊrn/ *past participle of* WEAR

worn out NOT USABLE, **worn-out** *adj* no longer usable because of too much use ○ *The city is looking for a place to dump its worn-out equipment.* ○ Related verb: WEAR OUT USE REPEATEDLY
EXTREMELY TIRED, **worn-out** *adj* extremely tired ○ *They were worn out after their long walk.* ○ Related verb: WEAR OUT MAKE TIRED

worrisome /ˈwɜr·iː·səm, ˈwʌ·riː-/ *adj* causing worry ○ *The possibility of fire is especially worrisome for people who live on the edge of the forest.*

worry /ˈwɜr·i, ˈwʌ·ri/ *v* [I/T] to think about problems or unpleasant things that make you anxious, or to make someone feel anxious ○ [I] *If you get a monthly train ticket, you won't have to worry about buying a ticket every day.* ○ [I] *My mother always worries about me when I don't come home by midnight.* ○ [I] *"Will you be all right walking home?" "Don't worry – I'll be fine."* ○ [+ *that* clause] *She worried that she might not be able to find another job.* ○ [T] *A lot of things worried him about his roommate.*
worry /ˈwɜr·i, ˈwʌ·ri/ *n* [C/U] ○ [C] *Fortunately, right now we don't have any worries about money.*
worried /ˈwɜr·iːd, ˈwʌ·riːd/ *adj* ○ *We were very worried when he did not answer his phone.* ○ *She had a worried look on her face.*

USAGE
worry

Remember to use the preposition **about** after the verb **worry** when decribing the things that make someone anxious.

They were all worried about their jobs.
~~*They were all worried for their jobs.*~~

WORD FAMILY worry			
Nouns	worry	*Adjectives*	worried unworried worrisome
Verbs	worry		

WORD CHOICES worry

Fret can be used instead of worry.
*Don't **fret**. I'm sure she'll be OK.*

If someone is worrying about something, you can say that the person is **concerned** about it.
*Aren't you **concerned** that she might tell someone?*

In formal English, you can use **perturbed** to describe someone who is worrying.
*He didn't seem unduly **perturbed** by the news.*

Anxious or **apprehensive** can be used when someone is worrying about something that might happen in the future.
*All this waiting is making me **anxious**.*
*He's a bit **apprehensive** about living away from home.*

If someone is worrying so much that he or she is very upset and does not know what to do, you could use the word **frantic** or say that the person is **at his/her wits' end**.
*Where on earth have you been? I've been **frantic**.* ➤

*I've been **at my wit's end** wondering where you've been.*

The phrase **on *your* mind** is used when someone is thinking and worrying about something a lot.

*I've got a lot **on my mind** at the moment.*

The idiom **lose sleep over** something can also be used to say that someone is worrying about something.

*It'll be OK. Don't **lose** any more **sleep over** it.*

worse /wɜrs/ *adj* more unpleasant, difficult, or severe than before or than something else; *comparative of* BAD ○ *Annette may be bad at math, but Bill is even worse.* ○ *If this sore throat gets any worse, I'll have to see a doctor.*
worse /wɜrs/ *adv comparative of* BADLY ○ *The storm grew worse.* ○ *Walking only made the cough worse.*
worse /wɜrs/ *n* [U] ○ *"How was the movie?" "I've seen worse."*
worsen /ˈwɜr·sən/ *v* [I/T] ○ [I] *The next day his fever went up and his condition worsened.*

IDIOM with worse

• **worse off** in a less satisfactory or less successful situation ○ *If you keep borrowing money to pay off your debts, you'll be even worse off than you are now.*

worship PRAY /ˈwɜr·ʃəp/ *v* [I/T] **-p-, -pp- 1** to pray to God or a god ○ [I] *They went on a pilgrimage to India to worship at the holy Buddhist shrines there.* **2** To worship is also to go regularly to a place for religious ceremonies: [I] *They work for the same company, socialize together, and worship at the same church.*
worship /ˈwɜr·ʃəp/ *n* [U] **1** *The law would allow workers to take either Saturday or Sunday off as a day of worship.* **2** A house/place of worship is a building for religious ceremonies and prayer.
worshiper, worshipper /ˈwɜr·ʃə·pər/ *n* [C] ○ *By noon, worshipers had begun streaming out of the cathedral.*

ADMIRE /ˈwɜr·ʃəp/ *v* [T] to feel a lot of love and admiration for someone or something ○ *As kids, we worshiped our Aunt Martha, who let us sleep late and took us to great places.*
worshiper, worshipper /ˈwɜr·ʃə·pər/ *n* [C] ○ *(fig.) Sun worshipers were at the beach all day long.*

worst /wɜrst/ *adj, adv* of the lowest quality, or the most unpleasant, difficult, or severe; *superlative of* BAD and BADLY ○ *That was the worst meal I've ever eaten.*
worst /wɜrst/ *n* [U] ○ *None of my brothers were very good in sports, but I was easily the worst.*

IDIOM with worst

• **at worst** in the worst possible case ○ *There's no harm in applying for the job – at worst, they'll turn you down.*

worst-case *adj* [not gradable] (of situations) as bad as possible ○ *Emergency services need to be prepared for a worst-case scenario.*

worsted /ˈwɜr·stəd, ˈwʊs·təd/ *n* [U] a type of woolen cloth used to make clothes

worth MONEY /wɜrθ/ *n* [U] **1** the amount of money that something can be sold for ○ *The estimated worth of her jewels alone is about $30 million.* **2** A particular amount of money's worth of something is the amount of money that it costs: *$20 worth of gasoline*
worth /wɜrθ/ *adj* [not gradable] **1** having a value in money of ○ *They're asking $10,000 for the car, but I don't think it's worth that much.* ○ *It is an expensive restaurant, but for special occasions it's worth it* (= the value of what you get is equal to the money spent). **2** If a person is worth a particular amount of money, the person has that amount or owns things that would cost that amount: *She must be worth at least half a million.*
worthless /ˈwɜrθ·ləs/ *adj* having no value in money ○ *Now that the company has gone bankrupt, your contract is worthless.*
worthlessness /ˈwɜrθ·lə·snəs/ *n* [U]

IMPORTANCE /wɜrθ/ *n* [U] the importance or usefulness of something or someone ○ *a sense of personal worth* ○ *Some people are modest to the point of not realizing their true worth.*
worth /wɜrθ/ *adj* [not gradable] important or useful enough to have or do ○ *There are only two things worth reading in this newspaper – the TV listings and the sports page.* ○ *I don't think it's worth talking about any more.*
worthless /ˈwɜrθ·ləs/ *adj* unimportant or useless ○ *Examples of this artist's early works reminded me that he was not worthless, as some reviewers seemed to feel.*
worthlessness /ˈwɜrθ·lə·snəs/ *n* [U] ○ *Feelings of worthlessness overwhelmed him.*

GRAMMAR

worth

When the adjective **worth** is followed by a verb, the verb is always in the present participle (the **-ing** form).

Do you think it's worth asking Patrick first?

~~*Do you think it's worth to ask Patrick first?*~~

AMOUNT /wɜrθ/ *n* [U] an amount of something that will last a stated period of time or that takes a stated amount of time to do ○ *We got a week's worth of diapers at the supermarket.* ○ *When the computer crashed, we lost six month's worth of work.*

WORD FAMILY worth

Nouns	*Adjectives*
worth	worth
worthlessness	worthless
	worthwhile
	worthy
	unworthy

IDIOMS with worth

• **worth it** enjoyable or useful despite the effort you made ○ *It was a long climb to the top of the hill, but the view from the top was worth it.*

• **worth** *your* **while** important, useful, or satisfying enough to be worth the effort you make ○ *It would be worth your while to see if you can still get tickets to the show.*

worthwhile /wɜrθˈhwɑɪl, -ˈwɑɪl/ *adj* useful, important, or helpful enough to be a suitable reward for the money or time spent or the effort made ○ *She considers teaching a worthwhile career.*

worthy **DESERVING RESPECT** /ˈwɜr·ði/ *adj* deserving respect, admiration, or support ○ *a worthy goal/project* ○ *It was a worthy cause, and we were glad to make a contribution.* ○ *She soon proved herself worthy of the trust we placed in her.*

DESERVING /ˈwɜr·ði/ *adj* deserving or suitable for ○ *Each of the ten chapters is worthy of a separate book.* ○ *After viewing the damage, the president decided that the area was worthy of federal disaster relief.*

would **FUTURE** /wʊd, wəd/ *modal verb* used to refer to future time after a verb in the past tense ○ *He said he would see his brother tomorrow.* ○ *They hoped they would go to France for their next vacation.*

INTENTION /wʊd, wəd/ *modal verb* used to express an intention or plan after a verb in a past tense ○ *He said he would love her forever.* ○ *They promised that tomorrow they would help.*

REQUEST /wʊd, wəd/ *modal verb* used as a form of will in requests and offers ○ *"Would you like some cake?" "Yes, I would."* ○ *Would you pick up a newspaper on your way home?*

WILL /wʊd, wəd/ *past simple of* WILL **CAN** ○ *The car wouldn't start this morning.*

POSSIBLE /wʊd, wəd/ *modal verb* **1** used to refer to a possibility or likelihood ○ *I would hate to miss the show.* **2** Would is used with if in sentences that show what will happen if something else happens: *What would you do if you lost your job?*

ALWAYS /wʊd, wəd/ *modal verb* used to suggest that in the past something happened often or always ○ *In summer my dad would sit on the back porch after supper and read the newspaper.*

would-be *adj* [not gradable] wanting or trying to be ○ *a would-be artist/politician*

wouldn't /ˈwʊd·ᵊnt/ *contraction of* would not ○ *He wouldn't say yes and he wouldn't say no.*

would've /ˈwʊd·əv/ *contraction of* would have ○ *I would've believed you until you started laughing.*

wound **WIND** /wɑʊnd/ *past simple and past participle of* WIND

INJURY /wuːnd/ *n* [C] a hurt or injury to the body, such as a cut or tear in the skin or flesh ○ *a puncture wound* ○ *He had a deep wound in his arm and had lost a lot of blood.*

wound /wuːnd/ *v* [T] ○ *Several people were wounded by falling rocks.*

HURT FEELINGS /wuːnd/ *v* [T] to hurt the feelings of someone; upset ○ *He totally ignored her, and she was deeply wounded.*

wove /woʊv/ *past simple of* WEAVE **MAKE CLOTH**

woven /ˈwoʊ·vən/ *past participle of* WEAVE **MAKE CLOTH**

wow /wɑʊ/ *exclamation infml* used to show surprise or pleasure ○ *Wow! Did you hear that noise?*

wrangle /ˈræŋ·gəl/ *v* [I] to argue, often in a noisy or angry way ○ *We have been wrangling with the management for weeks over parking spaces for employees.*

wrap /ræp/ *v* [T] **-pp- 1** to cover something or someone with paper, cloth, or other material ○ *She wrapped the present and tied it with a ribbon.* ○ *Wrap the chicken in foil and cook it for two hours.* ○ *If you wrap yourself in this blanket, you will stay warm.* **2** If you wrap your fingers or arms around something, you hold it tightly: *She sat back in her chair and wrapped her arms around her knees.*

wrap /ræp/ *n* [C/U] **1** a piece of clothing that a person, esp. a woman, wears around the shoulders to keep warm or as a stylish addition to a suit, coat, etc. ○ [C] *a silk/woolen wrap* **2** Wrap is material that is used to cover or protect something, such as food: [U] *Put some plastic wrap around the leftover meat.*

wrapper /ˈræp·ər/ *n* [C] a piece of paper or plastic that has been used to cover something ○ *a candy wrapper*

IDIOM with wrap

• **wrap** *someone* **around** *your* **little finger** to easily persuade someone to do what you want that person to do ○ *She could wrap her father around her little finger.*

PHRASAL VERBS with wrap

• **wrap up** *something/someone* **COVER** [M] to cover something or someone with paper, cloth, or other material ○ *A woman held the baby wrapped up in a cloth.* ○ *You don't have to finish the candy – we can wrap it up and save it for later.*

• **wrap up** *something* **FINISH** [M] to complete or finish something ○ *It's getting late – let's wrap it up.* ○ *She wrapped up a deal just before she left on vacation.*

wraparound /ˈræp·əˌrɑʊnd/ *adj* [not gradable] **1** (of clothing) made so that it can be tied around the body ○ *She wore a blue wraparound skirt.* **2** Wraparound also means curving around in one continuous piece: *wraparound sunglasses* ○ *a wraparound windshield*

wrapping paper *n* [U] decorated paper that is used to cover presents

wrath /ræθ/ *n* [U] *fml* extreme anger ○ *He left home to escape his father's wrath.*

W

wreak /riːk, rek/ *v* [T] *past* **wreaked, wrought** to cause something to happen in a violent way ○ *Uncontrolled financial markets continue to wreak one disaster after another.* ○ *Changes in the climate have wreaked/wrought havoc with the region's usual weather pattern.*

wreath /riːθ/ *n* [C] *pl* **wreaths** a ring made of flowers and leaves or EVERGREENS (= plants that are

green all year) ○ *The bride wore a wreath of flowers on her head.*

wreck /rek/ *v* [T] to destroy or badly damage something ○ *The explosion wrecked one house and shattered nearby windows.* ○ *A prison record would wreck his chances of becoming a lawyer.*

wreck /rek/ *n* [C] **1** a vehicle or ship that has been destroyed or badly damaged **2** A wreck can also be something that is badly in need of repair: *We bought this old wreck of a house and fixed it up.* **3** A person who is described as a wreck is in bad physical or mental condition: *Coping with three kids and a mother in the hospital, she's a nervous wreck.*

wreckage /ˈrek·ɪdʒ/ *n* [U] what is left of something badly damaged ○ *Safety experts were studying the wreckage to find out what caused the crash.*

wren /ren/ *n* [C] a very small brown bird

wrench TWIST /rentʃ/ *v* [T] **1** to pull and twist something suddenly or violently away from a fixed position ○ *The ball was wrenched from his hands by another player.* **2** If you wrench part of your body, such as your arm or knee, you twist it badly and injure it: *He wrenched his back while digging in the garden.*

wrenching /ˈren·tʃɪŋ/ *adj* extremely stressful ○ *It was the most wrenching decision of the President's life.*

TOOL /rentʃ/ *n* [C] a tool for holding and turning objects ○ *an adjustable wrench*

wrest /rest/ *v* [T] *fml* to obtain something with difficulty, effort, or violence ○ *Shareholders will try to wrest control of the company from the current management.*

wrestle /ˈres·əl/ *v* [I/T] to fight with someone by holding and trying to throw that person to the ground, or to do this as a sport ○ [I] *He wrestled for Iowa State University.*

wrestler /ˈres·lər/ *n* [C] ○ *professional wrestlers*

wrestling /ˈres·lɪŋ/ *n* [U] a sport in which you use your arms and legs, or sometimes the arms only, to try to force the other competitor to the ground and hold that person there for a short time

PHRASAL VERB with wrestle

• **wrestle with** *something* to try to solve a difficult problem or make a difficult decision ○ *He wrestled with the problem for several weeks, not sure what to do.*

wretch /retʃ/ *n* [C] someone who has suffered a lot and deserves sympathy ○ *The poor wretches had no chance to survive.*

W

wretched /ˈretʃ·əd/ *adj* **1** unhappy or extremely sad ○ *He looked so ill and wretched as he spoke that he made me feel wretched myself.* **2** Something described as wretched is very bad or of poor quality: *Workers lived in wretched, overcrowded shacks.*

wriggle /ˈrɪg·əl/ *v* [I/T] to make small quick movements with the body, turning from side to side ○ [I] *Somehow he twisted himself about and wriggled free of Farkas's grip and danced away.*

wring /rɪŋ/ *v* [T] *past* **wrung** to twist something by holding it tightly and turning your hands in opposite directions ○ [M] *She wrung out the shirt and hung it up to dry.*

IDIOMS with wring

• **wring** *something* **from** *someone*, **wring** *something* **out of** *someone* to force or persuade someone to give or tell you something ○ *Congress is seeking to wring concessions from a weakened President.*

• **wring** *your* **hands** to be anxious or worried about something but not do anything about it ○ *We should do something to help rather than just wringing our hands about it.*

• **wring** *someone's* **neck** used for emphasizing that you are very angry at someone ○ *I could wring her neck for getting me in such trouble.*

wrinkle /ˈrɪŋ·kəl/ *n* [C] a small line in the skin, or a small fold in cloth ○ *You need to iron out the wrinkles in your skirt.* ○ (fig.) *We still need to iron out a few wrinkles* (= slight problems) *in our agreement.*

wrinkle /ˈrɪŋ·kəl/ *v* [I/T] ○ [I] *If you don't pack the dress carefully, it will wrinkle.*

IDIOM with wrinkle

• **wrinkle** *your* **nose** to show surprise, uncertainty, or disgust at something ○ *"Oooh, yuck!" 7-year-old Pamela says, wrinkling her nose as she wipes gooey paste from her fingers onto her sweat pants.*

wrist /rɪst/ *n* [C] the narrow part of the arm above the hand that can bend to move the hand in different directions ○ *He developed strong wrists playing baseball.*

wristwatch /ˈrɪst·wɑtʃ, -wɔːtʃ/ *n* [C] a watch that is worn on the wrist

writ /rɪt/ *n* [C] *law* a legal document from a court of law which orders someone to do something or not to do something

write /rɑɪt/ *v* [I/T] *past simp.* **wrote**, *past part.* **written** **1** to create something for other people to read or use, such as a book, poem, letter, or piece of music ○ [T] *to write a poem/a story/a textbook* ○ [T] *They wrote some of the best songs of the 70s.* ○ [T] *They have written computer software to handle our sales records.* ○ [T] *Hammond wrote a letter to his mother/wrote his mother a letter.* ○ [I] *He writes well and is always a pleasure to read.* **2** To write is also to put letters, words, numbers, or symbols on a paper, screen, or other surface using a pen, pencil, KEYBOARD (= the keys of a computer), etc.: [T] *Please write your name on the dotted line.* **3** Someone whose job is to write creates articles, stories, or books to be published: [I] *She writes for the New York Times.* **4** To write also means to express an idea or opinion in an article, book, etc.: [+ *that* clause] *He writes that our highways are getting safer.*

writer /ˈrɑɪt̬·ər/ *n* [C] a person who writes articles, books, etc., to be published ○ *a sports writer* ○ *a well-known writer of children's books*

writing /ˈrɑɪt̬·ɪŋ/ *n* [U] **1** a person's style of forming letters and words with a pen or pencil, or something written ○ *Do you recognize the writing on the envelope?* ○ *There was writing in the margins* *of many pages in the book.* **2** Writing is also articles, poems, books, etc.: *fiction/nonfiction writing* ○ *travel writing* **3** Writing is also the activity of creating stories, poems, or articles: *He talked about the experience of teaching writing through interactive television.*

writings /ˈrɑɪt̬·ɪŋz/ *pl n* the written works of a person ○ *the writings of Abraham Lincoln*

> **GRAMMAR**
>
> **write**
>
> The verb **write** has two "t's" in its past participle **written**. All other forms have a single "t."
>
> *I write English better than I speak it.*
>
> *She writes very well.*
>
> *We wrote him a letter when he was in hospital.*
>
> *I am writing English now.*
>
> *They have written a song together.*
>
> ~~*I am writting English now.*~~
>
> Remember to use the correct grammar after **write**. You can **write to *someone*** or, in informal contexts, **write *someone***.
>
> *Pam wrote to me last week.*
>
> *Rachel wrote me last week.*
>
> If **write** is followed by two objects, do not use a preposition.
>
> *Jane wrote me a letter last week.*

WORD FAMILY write

Nouns	writer writing rewrite writings	*Adjectives* *Verbs*	unwritten write rewrite

IDIOM with write

• **in writing** in the form of a document, printed or written on paper ○ *We need to have your offer in writing before we can respond to it.*

PHRASAL VERBS with write

• **write down** *something* [M] to record information on paper ○ *If I don't write it down, I'll forget it.*

• **write in** *someone* **VOTE** [M] (when voting in an election) to give the name of someone who is not officially listed as your choice ○ Related adjective: WRITE IN

• **write in SEND MESSAGE** to send a letter or an E-MAIL message to make a request or a statement, esp. to an organization or business ○ *A lot of consumers write in and get nothing in response.*

• **write off** *something* **LOSE MONEY** [M] to accept that a debt will not be paid or that money has been lost ○ *Last year the bank wrote off $17 million in bad debts.* ○ Related noun: WRITE-OFF

• **write off** *someone/something* **CONSIDER UNIMPORTANT** [M] to decide that someone or something is not suitable or good enough to be successful ○ *When he lost the election for governor, some observers wrote him off as a future candidate, but they were proven wrong.*

• **write out** *something* [M] to write something on paper with all the necessary details ○ *Write the check out to me.*

• **write up** *something/someone* [M] **1** to record something completely on paper or on a computer, often using notes that you have made ○ *We have to write up the lab report for chemistry.* **2** To write up something or someone is also to write an article or report about that thing or person that is then published: *My sister was written up in the school newspaper.* ○ Related noun: WRITE-UP

write-in *adj* [not gradable] relating to a person whose name is not on a BALLOT (= voting paper) but who wants to be elected ○ *He got 32 write-in votes to Mr. Rose's 16.* ○ *They were running a last-minute write-in campaign.* ○ Related verb: WRITE IN VOTE

write-off *n* [C] a change in a company's accounts when it has lost money ○ *After write-offs, taxes, and government transfers were deducted, the phone company found itself deeply in debt.* ○ Related verb: WRITE OFF LOSE MONEY

write-up *n* [C] a report or article that makes a judgment about something, such as a play or movie ○ *I liked the show and gave it a good write-up in the college magazine.* ○ Related verb: WRITE UP

writhe /rɑɪð/ *v* [I] to make twisting movements with the body, esp. because you are feeling strong emotion ○ *He writhed in agony at the thought.*

written /ˈrɪt·ᵊn/ *past participle of* WRITE

wrong NOT CORRECT /rɔːŋ/ *adj* not correct or not accurate ○ *Three of your answers were wrong.* ○ *That clock is wrong – it's 12:30, not 12:15.* ○ *I dialed the wrong number.* ○ Opposite: RIGHT CORRECT

wrong /rɔːŋ/ *adv* [not gradable] ○ *It doesn't work – what am I doing wrong?*

wrongly /ˈrɔːŋ·li/ *adv* [not gradable] ○ *He was wrongly accused of the crime.*

wrong /rɔːŋ/ *n*

> **WORD CHOICES wrong**
>
> **Incorrect** is an alternative to "wrong" when information or facts are wrong.
>
> *The information on the website is **incorrect**.*
>
> A formal word which means "wrong" is **erroneous**.
>
> *No one could explain how the **erroneous** information had gotten into the report.*
>
> If facts are not completely correct or exact, you can use the adjective **inaccurate**.
>
> *Their estimation of the cost was wildly (= extremely) **inaccurate**.*
>
> **False** or **mistaken** can be used when an idea or belief is wrong.
>
> *The title gives a **false** impression of what the movie is about.*
>
> *I went there in the **mistaken** belief that it would help.*
>
> You can also use **mistaken** to describe a person who is wrong about something. ➤

*You're **mistaken** if you believe we've discovered nothing of value.*

NOT SUITABLE /rɔːŋ/ *adj* not suitable or desirable, or not as it should be ○ *It was the wrong time to ask for a raise.* ○ *She was just the wrong person for the job.* ○ Opposite: RIGHT **SUITABLE**

IMMORAL /rɔːŋ/ *adj* [not gradable] not morally acceptable ○ *He believes that censorship is wrong.* ○ Opposite: RIGHT **MORAL RULE**

wrong /rɔːŋ/ *n* [C/U] behavior or an act that is morally unacceptable; evil or an evil act ○ [U] *She has a keen sense of right and wrong.* ○ [C] *It's impossible to exaggerate the wrongs caused by slavery.*

TREAT UNFAIRLY /rɔːŋ/ *v* [T] **1** to treat someone in an unfair or unacceptable way ○ *He felt he had been wronged, but everyone else blamed him for what happened.* **2** To wrong someone is also to judge someone unfairly and express uncertainty about that person's character: *That reporter wronged her, saying she was an unfit mother.*

wrongful /ˈrɔːŋ·fəl/ *adj* [not gradable] unfair or illegal ○ *He has suffered terribly, after 15 years of wrongful imprisonment.*

NOT WORKING /rɔːŋ/ *adj* [not gradable] not working correctly ○ *Something's wrong with the dishwasher – it's leaking again.*

WORD FAMILY wrong

Nouns	wrong	*Verbs*	wrong
Adjectives	wrong wrongful	*Adverbs*	wrong wrongly wrongfully

IDIOMS with wrong

• **in the wrong** responsible for something bad ○ *We had a green light, so she was clearly in the wrong when she hit us.*

• **in the wrong place at the wrong time** in a situation where something bad happens to you because you are unlucky, not because you do anything wrong ○ *A storm can come up, and if you are in the wrong place at the wrong time, you could get hurt.*

wrongdoing /ˈrɔːŋˌduː·ɪŋ/ *n* [U] bad or illegal behavior ○ *Investigators found no evidence of wrongdoing.*

wrongheaded /ˈrɔːŋˈhed·əd/ *adj* unsuitable and likely to bring bad results if continued ○ *It seems wrongheaded to me to spend public money on private schools.*

wrote /roʊt/ *past simple of* WRITE

wrought **CAUSED** /rɔːt/ *past simple and past participle of* WREAK

MADE /rɔːt/ *adj* [not gradable] *fml* brought into being; made ○ *She's modest about what she has wrought.*

wrought iron /rɔːt̬ ˈɑɪ·ərn/ *n* [U] a type of iron that can be shaped ○ *a wrought-iron gate*

wrung /rʌŋ/ *past simple and past participle of* WRING

wry /rɑɪ/ *adj* [*-er/-est* only] showing that you find a bad or difficult situation slightly amusing ○ *a wry smile* ○ *a wry sense of humor*

WWW *n* [U] *abbreviation for* WORLD WIDE WEB.

X LETTER, x /eks/ *n* [C] *pl* **X's, Xs, x's, xs** the 24th letter of the English alphabet

NUMBER, x /eks, ten/ *number* the ROMAN NUMERAL for the number 10

x /eks/, **X** *n* [U] used to represent a number, or the name of person or thing, that is not known or stated ○ *If 2x = 8, then x = 4.*

X-axis /ˈeks ˌæk·səs/ *n* [C] *pl* **X-axes** ***mathematics*** a horizontal line that forms one side of a COORDINATE PLANE (= region formed by two number lines)

Xerox /ˈzɪr·ɑks/ *n* [C] *trademark* a copy of a document or other piece of paper with writing or printing on it made by a machine that uses a process similar to that for making photographs ○ *I can give you a Xerox of the letter if you like.*

Xerox /ˈzɪr·ɑks/ *v* [T] ○ *Would you Xerox six copies of the report, please?*

XL /ˈek·strə ˈlɑrdʒ/ *adj* [not gradable] *abbreviation for* extra large; used esp. on clothing to show its size

Xmas /ˈkrɪs·məs, ˈek·sməs/ *n* [U] *abbreviation for* CHRISTMAS.

X-rated *adj* [not gradable] (of movies, electronic images, books, magazines, etc.) containing very rude language or pictures or information about sex that is generally considered offensive

X-ray /ˈeks·reɪ/ *n* [C] **1** a type of RADIATION (= energy in movement) that can go through many solid substances, allowing hidden objects such as bones in the body to be photographed **2** An X-ray is also a photograph of a part of the body made by using X-rays: *Fortunately the X-rays showed no broken bones.*

X-ray /ˈeks·reɪ/ *v* [T] ○ *All luggage has to be X-rayed before you can board the plane.*

xylem /ˈzɑɪ·ləm, -lem/ *n* [U] ***biology*** the plant tissue that carries water from the roots to the leaves and gives strength to the stem or trunk

xylophone /ˈzɑɪ·ləˌfoʊn/ *n* [C/U] a musical instrument of flat, wooden bars of different lengths that produce notes when hit with sticks

X

Y y

Y, y /waɪ/ *n* [C] *pl* **Y's, Ys, y's, ys** the 25th letter of the English alphabet

ya /jə/ *pronoun not standard* (spelled the way it is often spoken) you ○ *He greeted me with "How ya doin'?"*

yacht /jɑt/ *n* [C] a large and usually expensive boat, used for racing or for traveling around for pleasure ○ *Now he's had to sell his yacht, his place in the Bahamas, his wife's diamonds.*

yacht club *n* [C] a private organization for people who own expensive boats ○ *the New York Yacht Club*

yak ANIMAL /jæk/ *n* [C] a type of cattle with long hair and long horns, found mainly in Tibet

TALK /jæk/ *v* [I] **-kk-** *infml* to talk for a long time about unimportant matters or without achieving anything

y'all /jɔːl, jəˈɔːl/ *pronoun regional US* YOU-ALL

yam /jæm/ *n* [C] a SWEET POTATO

yank /jæŋk/ *v* [T] to pull something forcefully with a quick movement ○ *They yanked open the screen door to run into the kitchen for cookies.*

yank /jæŋk/ *n* [C] ○ *She gave a yank to the reins and the horse stopped.*

Yankee /ˈjæŋ·ki/ *n* [C] *regional US* (used mainly in the South) an American who comes from the northern US

yap /jæp/ *v* [I] **-pp-** **1** (of a small dog) to make short, high sounds **2** *disapproving slang* (of a person) To yap is to talk: *If you weren't so busy yapping you wouldn't have missed our exit.*

yard MEASUREMENT /jɑrd/, *abbreviation* **yd.** *n* [C] a unit of measurement of length equal to 3 feet or approximately 0.914 meter

LAND AROUND HOUSE /jɑrd/ *n* [C] a piece of land surrounding a house, usually grassy land with trees and other plants ○ *The kids are playing in the yard out back.*

LAND NEXT TO BUILDING /jɑrd/ *n* [C] an area of ground next to a building that is used for a particular, usually business, purpose ○ *a boat yard* ○ *a lumber yard*

yard sale *n* [C] A GARAGE SALE

yardstick /ˈjɑrd·stɪk/ *n* [C] a way of measuring how good, accurate, or effective something is ○ *A high salary isn't the only yardstick for success.* ○ *The only valid yardstick for measuring traffic safety is deaths per miles driven.*

yarmulke /ˈjɑm·ə·kə, ˈjɑr·məl·kə/ *n* [C] a small, circular cover for the head worn by some Jewish men, esp. at religious ceremonies

yarn THREAD /jɑrn/ *n* [U] thick thread used for making cloth or for making a piece of clothing esp. by KNITTING

STORY /jɑrn/ *n* [C] a story, usually a long one with a lot of excitement or interest ○ *a boys' adventure yarn*

yawn /jɔːn/ *v* [I] to open the mouth wide and take in and let out a deep breath without conscious effort, usually when you are tired or bored ○ *She yawned, covering her mouth with her hand.*

yawn /jɔːn/ *n* [C] ○ *It had been an especially long day, she thought, barely stifling a yawn.*

Y-axis /ˈwɑɪ ˌæk·səs/ *n* [C] *pl* **Y-axes** ***mathematics*** a vertical line that forms one side of a COORDINATE PLANE (= region formed by two number lines)

yd. *n* [C] *pl* **yd.** *abbreviation for* YARD MEASUREMENT

ye /jiː/ *pronoun old use* you ○ *Seek and ye shall find.*

yeah /jeə, jæə/ *adv* [not gradable] *infml* (spelled the way it is often spoken) yes ○ *"Will you drive?" "Yeah, sure."*

year /jɪr/ *n* [C] **1** any period of twelve months, or a particular period of twelve months beginning with January 1 ○ *last/next year* ○ *She brought along her eight-year-old daughter.* ○ *My parents have been married for 30 years.* ○ *Richard earned his degree in the year 1995.* ○ *You can get cheaper fares now, so it's a good time of year to travel abroad.* **2** In a school, a year refers to the part of the year during which courses are taught: *September is the start of the new academic year.* ➤ Usage: **x years old or x-year-old?** AT OLD AGE

yearly /ˈjɪr·li/ *adj, adv* [not gradable] ○ *A yearly subscription costs $25.* ○ *Members receive a newsletter twice yearly* (= two times each year).

WORD FAMILY year

Nouns	year	*Adverbs*	yearly
Adjectives	yearly		

IDIOMS with year

• **in years** in a long period of time ○ *We haven't seen Marie in years.*

• **year in and year out, year in, year out** continuously for many years ○ *Year in and year out, he has been one of the best players in baseball.*

yearbook /ˈjɪr·bʊk/ *n* [C] a book that is published every year by a school or other organization to give facts about the events and achievements of the previous year

yearlong /ˈjɪrˈlɔːŋ/ *adj* [not gradable] lasting one year, or one school year ○ *The course is a standard yearlong introduction to Western civilization.*

yearn /jɜrn/ *v* [I] to desire something strongly, esp. something difficult or impossible to obtain ○ [+ *to* infinitive] *Joy yearns to earn enough money from her job as a doctor's assistant for her to become independent.*

yeast /jiːst/ *n* [U] a type of FUNGUS (= simple organism) that is used in making alcoholic drinks such as beer and wine, and in making bread RISE (= swell) and become soft

yell /jel/ *v* [I/T] to shout words or make a loud noise, often when you want to get someone's attention or because you are angry, excited, or in pain ○ *"Come back," they yelled.* ○ [I] *Snyder heard a woman yell for help.*
yell /jel/ *n* [C] ○ *We all let out a yell of satisfaction.*

yellow /ˈjel·oʊ/ *adj, n* [C/U] (of) a color like that of a lemon ○ *yellow roses* ○ *sweet yellow corn*

yellow jacket *n* [C] a black and yellow flying insect that stings

yellow pages *n* [U] a telephone book or part of one that is printed on yellow paper and contains telephone numbers and advertisements for businesses

yelp /jelp/ *v* [I] to make a sudden, short, high sound, usually when in pain ○ *He screwed up his face and yelped in pain.*
yelp /jelp/ *n* [C] ○ *She let out a yelp of fear.*

yen /jen/ *n* [C usually sing] *infml* a strong but often sudden and temporary desire ○ *That day she had a yen for pizza.*

yep /jep, jʌp/ *adv infml* (spelled the way it is often spoken) yes ○ *"Should we go?" "Yep."*

yes /jes, jeə, jæə/ *adv* [not gradable] **1** used to express approval, willingness, or agreement ○ *"Would you like a glass of water?" "Yes, please."* ○ *"Is Chambers Street in this direction?" "Yes, just keep going and you'll come to it."* ○ *If you would say yes* (= agree), *you'd save us all a lot of trouble.* **2** Yes can be used to show that you are ready to listen to someone or to answer someone's request for information: *"Daddy." "Yes, what do you want, honey?"*
yes /jes/ *n* [C] ○ *The answer is yes.*

IDIOM with yes

• **yes, sir** used for expressing strong agreement ○ *He asked if he could talk to me, and I said, "Yes, sir."*

yesterday /ˈjes·tər·di, -deɪ/ *adv* [not gradable] on the day before this day ○ *We got back from our vacation yesterday.* ○ *Yesterday I started exercising seriously.*
yesterday /ˈjes·tər·di, -deɪ/ *n* [U] ○ *"Is that today's paper?" "No, it's yesterday's."*

yet NOW/THEN /jet/ *adv* [not gradable] (used in negative statements and questions) at this time or at that time; now or then ○ *"Is dinner ready?" "Not yet."* ○ *Has Janet finished her homework yet?* ○ *He had not yet decided what to do.*

IN THE FUTURE /jet/ *adv* [not gradable] in the future; still ○ *The best was yet to come.*

DESPITE THAT /jet/ *conjunction, adv* [not gradable] despite that ○ *Melissa was not doing well in her physics course, yet overall she had a B average.*

IN ADDITION /jet/ *adv* [not gradable] (used esp. when describing a long process or an event in a series) in addition; once more ○ *The governor commissioned yet another study.* ○ *She didn't want to explain yet again why she was disappointed.*

EVEN NOW /jet/ *adv* [not gradable] even at this stage or time ○ *We may yet succeed – you never know.*

yield PRODUCE /jiːld/ *v* [T] to supply or produce something positive such as a profit, an amount of food, or information ○ *Some mutual funds are currently yielding 15% on new money invested.*
yield /jiːld/ *n* [C usually pl] a profit or an amount esp. of a crop produced ○ *Over the past 50 years, crop yields have risen steadily in the US.*

GIVE UP /jiːld/ *v* [I/T] **1** to give up the control of or responsibility for something, often because you have been forced to ○ [T] *to yield power* **2** If something yields information, it provides it: *A letter found by the FBI last week may yield new clues.* **3** If you yield to something, you accept that you have been defeated by it: [I] *It's easy to yield to the temptation to borrow a lot of money.* **4** To yield to traffic coming from another direction is to wait and allow it to go first.

y'know /jəˈnoʊ/ *contraction of* you know ○ See at YOU IDIOMS

yo /joʊ/ *exclamation infml* used as a spoken greeting, or to get someone's attention ○ *Yo, check it out!*

yodel /ˈjoʊd·əl/ *v* [I] to sing by making a series of fast changes between the natural voice and a much higher voice
yodel /ˈjoʊd·əl/ *n* [C]

yoga /ˈjoʊ·gə/ *n* [U] a set of physical and mental exercises that are intended to give control over the body and mind

yogurt, **yoghurt** /ˈjoʊ·gərt/ *n* [U] a thick, liquid food made from milk with bacteria added to it, that is slightly sour but is sometimes made sweet and flavored with fruit

yoke /joʊk/ *n* [C] **1** (esp. in the past) a wooden bar fastened over the necks of two animals, esp. cattle, and connected to a vehicle or load that they are pulling **2** *fig.* Yoke can also refer to something that unfairly limits freedom: *the yoke of slavery*

yokel /ˈjoʊ·kəl/ *n* [C] a person who lives in an area far from cities, is not familiar with city ways, and is therefore considered slightly stupid ○ **USAGE:** This word is offensive

yolk /joʊk/ *n* [C/U] ***biology*** the yellow middle part of an egg, which provides food for a developing animal

Yom Kippur /ˌjoʊm·kəˈpʊr, ˌjɔːm-; jɑmˈkɪp·ər/, **Day of Atonement** *n* [U] a Jewish holy day in September or October

yonder /ˈjɑn·dər/ *adj, adv* [not gradable] *dated* in the place or direction shown; over there ○ *She lives in that town yonder.*

you PERSON/PEOPLE /juː, jə/ *pronoun* the person or people spoken to ○ *You look nice.* ○ *I love you.* ○ *Are you two ready?*

PEOPLE GENERALLY /juː, jə/ *pronoun* people in general; anyone ○ *How do you get this thing to start?*

IDIOMS with you

• **you bet** yes, I agree ○ *"You will pick up Alice after school, won't you?" "You bet."*
• **you can say that again** I completely agree with you ○ *"It's hot!" "You can say that again."*
• **you can't miss it** it is easy to find ○ *To get to the mall, go to the next traffic light and make a left – you can't miss it.*
• **you can't win them all, you win some, you lose some** no person can always succeed ○ *"I was sorry to hear that someone else got the job." "Oh well, you can't win them all."*
• **you know, y'know 1** *infml* used as a pause while speaking or while thinking of what to say next or how to say it ○ *She was cleaning the house, you know, when the phone rang.* **2** *infml* Some people say **you know** or **(y'know)** at the end of a statement to make sure the person they are talking to understands: *It didn't have to happen that way, you know?*
• **you know something, you know what** *infml* used before giving an opinion or a piece of information ○ *You know what? I think it's time to go home.*
• **you mean** used as part of a question when you are not sure of the facts or are expressing surprise ○ *"They all showed up." "You mean the entire family?"*
• **you name it** anything ○ *Coke, ginger ale, root beer – you name it, I've got it.*
• **you never can tell, you never know** there is no way of knowing or being certain, esp. about the future ○ *It sounds like a nice place to live, but you never can tell – we may end up hating it.*
• **you said it** I agree with you, but I did not want to be the person to say what you said ○ *"It was stupid of me to lend him that money." "You said it."*
• **(do) you see what I mean** do you understand what I am trying to explain ○ *You have to hold the bar down while you lock it – do you see what I mean?*
• **you're telling me** used for expressing strong agreement with something someone just said ○ *"Stephen's in a really bad mood today." "You're telling me!"*
• **you're welcome** used as a polite answer when someone thanks you for something ○ *"Thanks for returning the video." "You're welcome!"*

you-all, y'all /juːˈɔːl, jəˈɔːl, jɔːl/ *pronoun regional US* you ○ *Do you-all want some coffee before you leave?* ○ **USAGE**: You-all is a normal part of polite speech in the southeast of the US, and usually refers to more than one person.

you'd /juːd, jʊd, jəd/ *contraction of* you had or you would ○ *You'd* (= You would) *be warmer in your black jacket.* ○ *It happened just after you'd* (= you had) *left the room.*

you'll /ˈjuː·əl, jʊl, jəl/ *contraction of* you will or you shall ○ *I don't know if you'll like it.*

young /jʌŋ/ *adj* [-er/-est only] (esp. of something living) at an early stage of development or existence; not old ○ *Young children should not be left alone at home.* ○ *I work with wonderful young people mostly in their late teens.* ○ *The new law creates a new driver's license for those as young as 14.*

young /jʌŋ/ *pl n* **1** *Society can provide the young with valuable opportunities to help their communities.* **2** Young are the babies of an animal: *The bird flew back to the nest to feed her young.*

WORD FAMILY young

Nouns	young	*Adjectives*	young
	youngster		youthful
	youth		
	youthfulness		

youngster /ˈjʌŋ·stər/ *n* [C] a young person ○ *The program was designed to find summer jobs for city youngsters ages 14 to 21.*

your BELONGING TO YOU /jʊr, joʊr, jɔːr, jər/ *pronoun* belonging to or connected with the person or people being spoken to; the possessive form of you ○ *Is this your umbrella?* ○ *Let's take your car because it has more room than mine.*

OF PEOPLE GENERALLY /jʊr, joʊr, jɔːr, jər/ *pronoun* belonging to or connected with any person or people generally ○ *Exercise is good for your health.*

IDIOM with your

• **in your face** *slang* behaving or done in a direct, often rude way that is annoying and cannot be ignored ○ *If you don't tell them to get lost, they'll be back in your face faster than you know it.*

you're /ˈjuː·ər, jər, jʊr, joʊr, jɔːr/ *contraction of* you are ○ *You need to wear seat belts when you're in the car.*

yours /jʊrz, joʊrz, jɔːrz, jɜrz/ *pronoun* belonging to or connected with the person or people being spoken to, or that which belongs to you ○ *Our apartment isn't as large as yours, but it suits us.* ○ *I've got something of yours* (= that belongs to you).

yourself /jərˈself/ *pronoun pl* **yourselves 1** the person or people being spoken to; the reflexive form of you ○ *Be careful with that knife or you'll cut yourself.* **2** Yourself is sometimes used to emphasize the subject of the sentence: *Did you girls actually raise this money yourselves?* **3** If you do something **(all) by yourself**, you do it alone or without help from anyone: *You're old enough to take the bus by yourself, aren't you, Joyce?* **4** If you have something **(all) to yourself**, you have it for your use only: *Now that Neil and Sam are away, you've got the whole house to yourself.*

yours truly *n* [U] *humorous* me ○ *You heard Michael and yours truly talking just a few minutes ago.*

youth /juːθ/ *n* [C/U] **1** the period of your life when you are young, or the state of being young ○ [U] *I was a good football player in my youth.* **2** Youth also refers to young people in general: [U] *It's quite a job, training the youth of the country to be mature, responsible citizens.* **3** A youth is a boy or a young man: [C] *Our organization helps to shape character, citizenship, and fitness in these youths.*

youthful /ˈjuːθ·fəl/ *adj* characteristic of young people, or relating to the period of life when you are young ○ *Her youthful enthusiasm always makes her seem ageless.*

youthfulness /ˈjuːθ·fəl·nəs/ *n* [U]

you've /juːv, jəv/ *contraction of* you have ○ *You've told me that story at least twice before.*

yo-yo /ˈjoʊ·joʊ/ *n* [C] *pl* **yo-yos** a toy consisting of a circular object that can be made to roll down and up a string that is tied to your hand if you spin the object and move your hand quickly at the same time
yo-yo /ˈjoʊ·joʊ/ *adj* [not gradable] *fig.* characterized by large and sudden changes from one condition to another ○ *Research on yo-yo dieting indicates that going on and off diets repeatedly will make weight control difficult in the long run.*

yucca /ˈjʌk·ə/ *n* [C] a plant with long, stiff leaves on a thick stem and sometimes with white, bell-shaped flowers

yuck /jʌk/ *exclamation* an expression of disgust ○ *"Do you want to hold the snake?" "Yuck, no thanks."*
yucky /ˈjʌk·i/ *adj infml* disgusting or unpleasant ○ *My daughter says broccoli is yucky and refuses to eat it.*

yule /juːl/ *n* [U] *esp. old use* Christmas.

yummy /ˈjʌm·i/ *adj infml* (of food) tasting extremely good ○ *The chocolate cake was yummy.*

yup /jʌp/ *adv infml* (spelled the way it is spoken) yes ○ *"Can you see it?" "Yup, there it is."*

yuppie /ˈjʌp·i/ *n* [C] *esp. disapproving* a young, educated person who lives in a city and is successful in business, and who has a life style that involves spending a lot of money ○ *Once the yuppies started moving in, rents went way up.*

Z z

Z, **z** /ziː, *Cdn often* zed/ *n* [C] *pl* **Z's, Zs, z's, zs** the 26th and last letter of the English alphabet

zany /ˈzeɪ·ni/ *adj* surprisingly different and a little strange, and therefore amusing and interesting ○ *He was responsible for the zany Sesame Street puppet characters loved by children worldwide.*

zap **DESTROY** /zæp/ *v* [T] **-pp-** *infml* **1** to destroy or attack something suddenly, esp. with electricity, RADIATION, or another form of energy ○ *The salon uses lasers to zap unwanted hair.* **2** To zap something is also to cook or heat it in a MICROWAVE: *Do you want that meatloaf cold, or should I zap it?*

GO QUICKLY /zæp/ *v* [T] **-pp-** *infml* to move something quickly ○ *You can zap files straight to the printer from a PDA or laptop.*

zeal /ziːl/ *n* [U] great enthusiasm or interest ○ *religious zeal* ○ [+ to infinitive] *In his zeal to get his work finished on time, he made a lot of mistakes.*

zealous /ˈzel·əs/ *adj* enthusiastic and eager ○ *He thought the reporters were too zealous in their attempts to get into the event.*

zebra /ˈziː·brə, *Cdn often* ˈzeb·rə/ *n* [C] an African wild animal that looks like a horse but has black and white or brown and white lines on its body

zed /zed/ *n* [C] *Br, Cdn* the last letter of the English alphabet; Z

Zen /zen/ *n* [U] a religion that is a form of Buddhism developed in Japan

zenith /ˈziː·nəθ, *Cdn often* ˈzen·əθ/ *n* [C] the best, highest, or most successful point or time ○ *Their popularity reached its zenith in the mid-1990s.*

zero **NUMBER** /ˈzɪr·oʊ, ˈziː·roʊ/ *number pl* **zeros, zeroes** 0

NOTHING /ˈzɪr·oʊ, ˈziː·roʊ/ *n* [U] nothing; not anything ○ *Visibility in the fog was just about zero.*

zero /ˈzɪr·oʊ, ˈziː·roʊ/ *adj* [not gradable] not any or no ○ *The economy showed zero growth in the first quarter of this year.*

PHRASAL VERB with zero

•**zero in (on** *something/someone***)**, **zeroing, zeroed** **1** to direct all your attention to one thing ○ *We've zeroed in on the real problem – we don't save enough money.* **2** If you zero in a weapon, you aim it directly at something you want to hit: *Computers help the pilots to zero in on their targets.*

zero-sum *adj* [not gradable] having a result in which one person loses as much as another benefits

zest /zest/ *n* [U] enthusiasm and energy ○ *She's over 80, but she still has an amazing zest for life.*

zigzag /ˈzɪg·zæg/ *v* [I] **-gg-** to move by going first in one direction and then in a different direction, and continuing in this way ○ *We zigzagged through the crowds of tourists in the museum.*

zilch /zɪltʃ/ *n* [U] *infml* nothing ○ *Tom knew zilch about sports.*

zillion /ˈzɪl·jən/ *n* [C] *infml* an extremely large number or amount ○ *There were zillions of people to help you, all the time.*

zinc /zɪŋk/ *n* [U] a blue-white metal used esp. in combination with other metals or for covering other metals to protect them

zinfandel /ˈzɪn·fənˌdel/ *n* [C/U] a dry, red wine made in California, or the GRAPES that it comes from

Zionism /ˈzɑɪ·əˌnɪz·əm/ *n* [U] ***world history*** an international political and religious movement that supported establishing an independent Jewish state in Palestine and that supports the modern state of Israel

zip **FASTEN** /zɪp/ *v* [T] **-pp-** to fasten a bag, clothing, etc. with a ZIPPER ○ [T] *I've got so much stuff in this bag, I can't zip it shut.* ○ [M] *You have to help the kids zip their coats up.*

MOVE FAST /zɪp/ *v* [I always + adv/prep] **-pp-** to travel very fast ○ *Messengers on bicycles zipped fearlessly through the capital's traffic.*

zip /zɪp/ *n* [U] *infml* something that creates a feeling of energy or excitement ○ *Add pepper to give a little zip to the sauce.*

zip code, **ZIP code** *n* [C] a series of numbers that forms part of an address in the US and is used to help organize mail for delivery

zipper /ˈzɪp·ər/ *n* [C] a device for fastening together an opening in clothes, bags, etc., and consisting of two rows of little metal or plastic parts that can be locked together by sliding another part over them

zodiac /ˈzoʊd·iːˌæk/ *n* [C/U] an area of the sky in which the positions of the sun, moon, stars, and planets are believed in ASTROLOGY to influence human behavior, and which is divided into twelve equal sections

zombie /ˈzɑm·bi/ *n* [C] **1** someone who moves around as if unconscious and being controlled by someone else ○ *I was so tired, I walked around like a zombie.* **2** (in stories, movies, etc.) A zombie is a dead person brought back to life without the ability to speak or move easily.

zone /zoʊn/ *n* [C] an area, esp. one that has different characteristics from the ones around it or is used for different purposes ○ *a construction/work/flood/combat/war zone* ○ *He was charged with driving 75 mph in a 55 mph zone.*

zone /zoʊn/ *v* [T] to set rules for the use of land or for the types of structures that can be built on it ○ *The land is now zoned for single-family homes on two-acre plots.* ○ *This area was originally zoned commercial.*

zoning /ˈzoʊ·nɪŋ/ *n* [U] the act of setting rules for the use of land and the types of structures that can be built on it ○ *The town's new zoning establishes a height limit of eight stories on any new building.* ○ *San Francisco has strict zoning laws to preserve neighborhoods.*

zoo /zuː/ *n* [C] *pl* **zoos** an area in which animals, esp. wild animals, are kept so that people can go and look at them ○ *The children love to visit the elephants at the zoo.*

zoology /zoʊˈɑl·ə·dʒi, zəˈwɑl-/ *n* [U] the scientific study of animals
zoological /ˌzoʊ·əˈlɑdʒ·ɪ·kəl/ *adj* [not gradable] ○ *zoological research*

zoom /zuːm/ *v* [I] *infml* **1** to move very quickly ○ *Cars and trucks zoom past.* **2** If costs, sales, etc., zoom, they increase quickly: *In two months the magazine's circulation zoomed to 26,000.*

PHRASAL VERBS with zoom

• **zoom in** to adjust a camera to make a person or thing being photographed appear larger or closer ○ *At the beginning of the movie, the camera zooms in to show two people sitting by the side of a river.*
• **zoom out** to adjust a camera to make a person or thing being photographed appear smaller or farther away ○ *Zoom out and aim at Uncle Dave flipping burgers on the grill.*

zooplankton /ˌzoʊ·əˈplæŋk·tən/ *pl n* ***biology*** very small animals that float near the surface of water

zucchini /zʊˈkiː·ni/ *n* [C/U] *pl* **zucchini, zucchinis** a long, thin vegetable with a green or yellow skin that is usually cooked before being eaten

zygote /ˈzaɪ·goʊt/ *n* [C] ***biology*** the cell that will develop into a baby person or animal and that is created when a male and female GAMETE (= cell from each parent) unite

Z

Reference pages

Geographic names

This list shows the spellings for the names of countries, regions, continents, seas, and oceans that you may see when you are reading English. Each name is followed by the adjective that you use when talking about the noun (e.g. **Belgium** is a country in Europe. **Belgian chocolate** comes from Belgium). Usually, the word meaning "a person from this country" is a noun that is exactly the same as the adjective (so someone from **Belgium** is a **Belgian**). If the word for a person is different from the adjective, it is shown in the list below after the adjective (e.g. **Finland**, **Finnish**, **Finn**).

To talk about more than one person from a country, just add *s* (e.g. one **Belgian**, two **Belgians**), except for words ending in *-ese* or *-s*, which stay the same (e.g. **Chinese**, **Swiss**) and words ending in *-man* or *-woman*, which change to *-men* or *-women* (e.g. one **Irishman**, two **Irishmen**).

This list is only here to help you with spelling and reading. Not all of these words are names of countries. Some of them are continents or regions. If a name is included or not included here, that does not mean that it is or is not an official country. The list also includes some old names of countries, because you may still find these names when your are reading.

Name	*Adjective*	*Person*
Afghanistan	Afghan	
Africa	African	
Alaska	Alaskan	
Albania	Albanian	
Algeria	Algerian	
Andorra	Andorran	
Angola	Angolan	
Antarctica	Antarctic	
Antigua and Barbuda	Antiguan	
the Arctic	Arctic	
Argentina	Argentine/Argentinian	
Armenia	Armenian	
Asia	Asian	
the Atlantic	Atlantic	
Australia	Australian	
Austria	Austrian	
Azerbaijan	Azerbaijani	Azeri
the Bahamas	Bahamian	
Bahrain	Bahraini	
the Balkans	Balkan	
the Baltic	Baltic	
Bangladesh	Bangladeshi	
Barbados	Barbadian	
Belarus	Belorussian	
Belgium	Belgian	
Belize	Belizean	
Benin	Beninese	
Bermuda	Bermudan	
Bhutan	Bhutanese	
Bolivia	Bolivian	
Bosnia-Herzegovina	Bosnian	
Botswana	Botswanan	Motswana (*singular*)/Batswana (*plural*)
Brazil	Brazilian	

Name	*Adjective*	*Person*
Brunei	Bruneian	
Bulgaria	Bulgarian	
Burkina Faso	Burkinabe	
Burma	Burmese	
Burundi	Burundi	Burundian
Cambodia	Cambodian	
Cameroon	Cameroonian	
Canada	Canadian	
Cape Verde	Cape Verdean	
the Caribbean	Caribbean	
the Cayman Islands	Cayman Island	Cayman Islander
the Central African Republic	Central African	
Central America	Central American	
Chad	Chadian	
Chile	Chilean	
China	Chinese	
Colombia	Colombian	
Comoros	Comoran	
the Democratic Republic of Congo	Congolese	
Costa Rica	Costa Rican	
Côte d'Ivoire	Ivorian	
Croatia	Croatian	Croat
Cuba	Cuban	
Cyprus	Cypriot	
the Czech Republic	Czech	
Denmark	Danish	Dane
Djibouti	Djiboutian	
Dominica	Dominican	
the Dominican Republic	Dominican	
East Timor	East Timorese	
Ecuador	Ecuadorian	
Egypt	Egyptian	
El Salvador	Salvadoran	
England	English	Englishman/Englishwoman
Equatorial Guinea	Equatorial Guinean	
Eritrea	Eritrean	
Estonia	Estonian	
Ethiopia	Ethiopian	
Europe	European	
Fiji	Fijian	
Finland	Finnish	Finn
France	French	Frenchman/Frenchwoman
Gabon	Gabonese	
Gambia	Gambian	
Georgia	Georgian	
Germany	German	
Ghana	Ghanaian	
Gibraltar	Gibraltarian	
Greece	Greek	
Greenland	Greenlandic	Greenlander

Name	*Adjective*	*Person*
Grenada	Grenadian	
Guatemala	Guatemalan	
Guinea	Guinean	
Guinea-Bissau	Guinea-Bissauan	
Guyana	Guyanese	
Haiti	Haitian	
Holland/the Netherlands	Dutch	Dutchman/Dutchwoman
Honduras	Honduran	
Hong Kong	Hong Kong	
Hungary	Hungarian	
Iceland	Icelandic	Icelander
India	Indian	
the Indian Ocean	Indian Ocean	
Indonesia	Indonesian	
Iran	Iranian	
Iraq	Iraqi	
Ireland	Irish	Irishman/Irishwoman
Israel	Israeli	
Italy	Italian	
Ivory Coast	Ivorian	
Jamaica	Jamaican	
Japan	Japanese	
Jordan	Jordanian	
Kazakhstan	Kazakh	
Kenya	Kenyan	
Kiribati	Kiribati	
Kuwait	Kuwaiti	
Kyrgyzstan	Kyrgyz	
Laos	Laotian	
Latvia	Latvian	
Lebanon	Lebanese	
Lesotho	Sotho	Mosotho (*singular*)/Basotho (*plural*)
the Levant	Levantine	
Liberia	Liberian	
Libya	Libyan	
Liechtenstein	Liechtenstein	Liechtensteiner
Lithuania	Lithuanian	
Luxembourg	Luxembourg	Luxemburger
Macedonia	Macedonian	
Madagascar	Malagasy	
Malawi	Malawian	
Malaysia	Malaysian	
the Maldives	Maldivian	
Mali	Malian	
Malta	Maltese	
the Marshall Islands	Marshallese	Marshall Islander
Mauritania	Mauritanian	
Mauritius	Mauritian	
the Mediterranean	Mediterranean	
Melanesia	Melanesian	

Name	*Adjective*	*Person*
Mexico	Mexican	
Micronesia	Micronesian	
Moldova	Moldovan	
Monaco	Monégasque	
Mongolia	Mongolian	
Montserrat	Montserratian	
Morocco	Moroccan	
Mozambique	Mozambican	
Myanmar	Burmese	
Namibia	Namibian	
Nauru	Nauruan	
Nepal	Nepalese	
the Netherlands/Holland	Dutch	Dutchman/Dutchwoman
New Zealand	New Zealand	New Zealander
Nicaragua	Nicaraguan	
Niger	Nigerien	
Nigeria	Nigerian	
North America	North American	
North Korea	North Korean	
Norway	Norwegian	
Oman	Omani	
the Pacific	Pacific	
Pakistan	Pakistani	
Palestine	Palestinian	
Panama	Panamanian	
Papua New Guinea	Papua New Guinean	
Paraguay	Paraguayan	
Persia	Persian	
Peru	Peruvian	
the Philippines	Philippine	Filipino
Poland	Polish	Pole
Polynesia	Polynesian	
Portugal	Portuguese	
Puerto Rico	Puerto Rican	
Qatar	Qatari	
Quebec	Quebecois	
the Republic of Congo	Congolese	
Romania	Romanian	
Russia	Russian	
Rwanda	Rwandan	
Samoa	Samoan	
San Marino	Sanmarinese	
São Tomé and Príncipe	São Toméan	
Saudi Arabia	Saudi	
Scandinavia	Scandinavian	
Scotland	Scottish	Scot/Scotsman/Scotswoman
Senegal	Senegalese	
the Seychelles	Seychelle	Seychellois
Siberia	Siberian	
Sierra Leone	Sierra Leonean	
Singapore	Singaporean	

Name	*Adjective*	*Person*
Slovakia	Slovak	
Slovenia	Slovenian	Slovene
the Solomon Islands	Solomon Islander	
Somalia	Somali	
South Africa	South African	
South America	South American	
South Korea	South Korean	
Spain	Spanish	Spaniard
Sri Lanka	Sri Lankan	
St. Kitts and Nevis	Kittsian	
St. Lucia	St. Lucian	
St. Vincent and the Grenadines	Vincentian	
Sudan	Sudanese	
Suriname	Surinamese	Surinamer
Swaziland	Swazi	
Sweden	Swedish	Swede
Switzerland	Swiss	
Syria	Syrian	
Tahiti	Tahitian	
Taiwan	Taiwanese	
Tajikistan	Tajik	
Tanzania	Tanzanian	
Thailand	Thai	
Tibet	Tibetan	
Togo	Togolese	
Tonga	Tongan	
Trinidad and Tobago	Trinidadian	
Tunisia	Tunisian	
Turkey	Turkish	Turk
Turkmenistan	Turkmen	
Tuvalu	Tuvaluan	
Uganda	Ugandan	
Ukraine	Ukrainian	
the United Arab Emirates	Emirian	
the United Kingdom	British	Briton
the United States of America	American	
Uruguay	Uruguayan	
Uzbekistan	Uzbek	
Vanuatu	Vanuatuan	
Vatican City	Vatican	
Venezuela	Venezuelan	
Vietnam	Vietnamese	
Wales	Welsh	Welshman/Welshwoman
Western Sahara	Sahrawi/Sahrawian	Sahrawi
Yemen	Yemeni	
Yugoslavia	Yugoslav	
Zaire	Zairean	
Zambia	Zambian	
Zimbabwe	Zimbabwean	

Irregular Verbs

Infinitive	*Past Simple*	*Past Participle*
arise	arose	arisen
awake	awoke, awaked	awoken, awaked, awoke
be	was/were	been
bear	bore	borne
beat	beat	beaten
become	became	become
befall	befell	befallen
begin	began	begun
behold	beheld	beheld
belie	belied	belied
bend	bent	bent
bet	bet	bet
bid	bade, bid	bid, bidden
bind	bound	bound
bite	bit	bitten
bleed	bled	bled
blow	blew	blown
break	broke	broken
breed	bred	bred
bring	brought	brought
broadcast	broadcast, broadcasted	broadcast, broadcasted
build	built	built
burn	burned, burnt	burned, burnt
burst	burst	burst
buy	bought	bought
cast	cast	cast
catch	caught	caught
choose	chose	chosen
cling	clung	clung
come	came	come
cost	cost	cost
creep	crept	crept
cut	cut	cut
deal	dealt	dealt
dig	dug	dug
dive	dived, dove	dived
draw	drew	drawn
dream	dreamed, dreamt	dreamed, dreamt
drink	drank	drunk
drive	drove	driven
dwell	dwelled, dwelt	dwelled, dwelt
eat	ate	eaten
fall	fell	fallen
feed	fed	fed
feel	felt	felt

Infinitive	*Past Simple*	*Past Participle*
fight	fought	fought
find	found	found
flee	fled	fled
fling	flung	flung
fly	flew	flown
forbid	forbade	forbidden
forecast	forecast, forecasted	forecast, forecasted
foresee	foresaw	foreseen
forget	forgot	forgotten
forgive	forgave	forgiven
forgo	forwent	forgone
forsake	forsook	forsaken
freeze	froze	frozen
get	got	got, gotten
give	gave	given
go	went	gone
grind	ground	ground
grow	grew	grown
hang	hung, hanged	hung, hanged
have	had	had
hear	heard	heard
hew	hewed	hewed, hewn
hide	hid	hidden
hit	hit	hit
hold	held	held
hurt	hurt	hurt
input	input, inputted	input, inputted
interweave	interwove	interwoven
keep	kept	kept
kneel	knelt, kneeled	knelt, kneeled
knit	knitted, knit	knitted, knit
know	knew	known
lead	led	led
leap	leaped, leapt	leaped, leapt
leave	left	left
lend	lent	lent
let	let	let
lie	lay, lied	lain, lied
light	lit, lighted	lit, lighted
lip-read	lip-read /ˈlɪp·red/	lip-read /ˈlɪp·red/
lose	lost	lost
make	made	made
mean	meant	meant
meet	met	met
mimic	mimicked	mimicked
mislay	mislaid	mislaid
mislead	misled	misled
mistake	mistook	mistaken

Infinitive	*Past Simple*	*Past Participle*
misunderstand	misunderstood	misunderstood
mow	mowed	mowed, mown
offset	offset	offset
outdo	outdid	outdone
outgrow	outgrew	outgrown
outrun	outran	outrun
overcome	overcame	overcome
overdo	overdid	overdone
overeat	overate	overeaten
overhang	overhung	overhung
overhear	overheard	overheard
override	overrode	overridden
overrun	overran	overrun
oversee	oversaw	overseen
overshoot	overshot	overshot
oversleep	overslept	overslept
overtake	overtook	overtaken
overthrow	overthrew	overthrown
partake	partook	partaken
pay	paid	paid
plead	pleaded, pled	pleaded, pled
prove	proved	proved, proven
put	put	put
quit	quit	quit
read	read /red/	read /red/
rebuild	rebuilt	rebuilt
remake	remade	remade
rend	rent	rent
repay	repaid	repaid
rerun	reran	rerun
rethink	rethought	rethought
rewrite	rewrote	rewritten
rid	rid	rid
ride	rode	ridden
ring	rang	rung
rise	rose	risen
run	ran	run
saw	sawed	sawn, sawed
say	said	said
see	saw	seen
seek	sought	sought
sell	sold	sold
send	sent	sent
set	set	set
sew	sewed	sewn, sewed
shake	shook	shaken
shear	sheared	sheared, shorn
shed	shed	shed

Infinitive	*Past Simple*	*Past Participle*
shine	shone	shone
shoe	shod, shoed	shod, shoed
shoot	shot	shot
show	showed	shown
shrink	shrank	shrunk
shut	shut	shut
sink	sank	sunk
sit	sat	sat
slay	slayed, slew	slain
sleep	slept	slept
slide	slid	slid
sling	slung	slung
slink	slunk	slunk
slit	slit	slit
smell	smelled	smelled
sneak	sneaked, snuck	sneaked, snuck
sow	sowed	sown, sowed
speak	spoke	spoken
speed	sped, speeded	sped, speeded
spend	spent	spent
spin	spun	spun
spit	spat	spat
split	split	split
spoil	spoiled, spoilt	spoiled, spoilt
spring	sprang	sprung
stand	stood	stood
steal	stole	stolen
stick	stuck	stuck
sting	stung	stung
stink	stank, stunk	stunk
strew	strewed	strewn, strewed
stride	strode	strode
strike	struck	struck, stricken
string	strung	strung
strive	strove, strived	striven, strived
sublet	sublet	sublet
swear	swore	sworn
sweep	swept	swept
swell	swelled	swollen, swelled
swim	swam	swum
take	took	taken
teach	taught	taught
tear	tore	torn
tell	told	told
think	thought	thought
throw	threw	thrown
thrust	thrust	thrust
tread	trod	trodden, trod

Infinitive	*Past Simple*	*Past Participle*
typecast	typecast	typecast
undercut	undercut	undercut
undergo	underwent	undergone
underlie	underlay	underlain
underwrite	underwrote	underwitten
understand	understood	understood
undertake	undertook	undertaken
undo	undid	undone
unwind	unwound	unwound
wear	wore	worn
weave	wove, weaved	woven, weaved
wed	wedded, wed	wedded, wed
weep	wept	wept
wet	wet, wetted	wet, wetted
win	won	won
wind	wound	wound
withdraw	withdrew	withdrawn
withhold	withheld	withheld
withstand	withstood	withstood
wreak	wreaked	wreaked
wring	wrung	wrung
write	wrote	written

Prefixes

ante- before or in front of

anti- **1** opposed to or against **2** preventing or destroying

auto- **1** operating without being controlled by humans **2** self

bi- two

centi-, **cent-** hundred

co- with or together

contra- against or opposite

counter- opposing or as a reaction to

cross- **1** across **2** including different groups or subjects

cyber- involving, using, or relating to computers, especially the Internet

de- to take something away

dis- not or the opposite of

e- electronic, usually relating to the Internet

eco- relating to the environment

en- **1** used to form verbs which mean to put into or onto something **2** used to form verbs which mean to cause to be something

Euro- relating to Europe

ex- from before

extra- outside of or in addition to

geo- of or relating to the earth

hyper- having a lot of or too much of a quality

ill- in a way which is bad or not suitable

in-, **il-**, **im-**, **ir-** not

inter- between or among

intra- within

kilo- a thousand

mega- (*infml*) extremely

micro- very small

mid- in the middle of

milli- a thousandth

mini- small

mis- not or badly

mono- one or single

multi- many

neo- new

non- not or the opposite of

omni- everywhere or everything

out- more than or better than

over- too much

photo- connected with or produced by light

poly- many

post- after or later than

pre- before or earlier than

pro- supporting

pseudo- false

psycho- of the mind or mental processes

quasi- partly

re- again

retro- looking at or copying the past

self- of or by yourself or itself

semi- half or partly

socio- relating to society

sub- **1** under or below **2** less important or a smaller part of a larger whole

super- extremely or more than usual

tele- **1** over a long distance **2** done by telephone **3** on or for television

thermo- relating to heat or temperature

trans- **1** across **2** showing a change

tri- three

ultra- extremely

un- not or the opposite of

under- **1** not enough **2** below

Suffixes

-**able**, -**ible** changes a verb into an adjective meaning "able to be"

-**age** **1** makes a noun meaning "a collection of" **2** changes a verb into a noun meaning "the action (of the verb)"

-**al** **1** changes a noun into an adjective meaning "relating to" **2** changes a verb into a noun meaning "the action (of the verb)"

-**an**, -**ian** **1** makes a noun meaning "a person of or from" **2** makes an adjective meaning "belonging to" or "like"

-**ance**, -**ancy** makes a noun meaning "an action, condition, or characteristic"

-**ation**, -**ion** changes a verb into a noun meaning "the action, or the result of the action (of the verb)"

-**centric** makes an adjective meaning "having as the most important thing"

-**ed** makes an adjective meaning "having" or "characteristic of"

-**ee** **1** changes a verb into a noun meaning "someone who benefits from or receives" **2** makes a noun meaning "like"

-**en** changes an adjective into a verb meaning "to become" or "to make something become"

-**ence**, -**ency** makes a noun meaning "an action, condition, or characteristic"

-**er**, -**or** changes a verb into a noun meaning "someone who does (something)"

-**esque** makes an adjective meaning "like"

-**ful** **1** changes a noun to an adjective meaning "full of" **2** changes a noun to an adjective meaning "having a particular characteristic"

-**hood** makes a noun meaning "the condition of"

-**ian** **1** makes a noun meaning "a person who does (something)" **2** makes an adjective meaning "belonging to"

-**ible**, -**able** changes a verb into an adjective meaning "able to"

-**ical** changes a noun ending in *-y* or *-ics* to an adjective meaning "relating to"

-**ing** makes an adjective meaning "making someone feel something"

-**ion**, -**ation** changes a verb to a noun meaning "the action, or the result of the action (of the verb)"

-**ish** **1** makes an adjective meaning "slightly" or "approximately" **2** makes an adjective meaning "similar to"

-**ist** **1** makes a noun meaning "a person who does something" **2** makes a noun and an adjective meaning "someone with a particular set of beliefs"

-**ive** changes a verb to an adjective meaning "having a particular characteristic or effect"

-**ize** changes an adjective to a verb meaning "to cause to be or become"

-**less** changes a noun to an adjective meaning "without"

-**like** changes a noun to an adjective meaning "similar to"

-**ly** **1** changes an adjective into an adverb meaning "in this way" **2** makes an adjective and an adverb meaning "every" **3** changes a noun into an adjective meaning "like"

-**ment** changes a verb into a noun meaning "the action or its result"

-**ness** changes an adjective into a noun meaning "the characteristic or condition"

-**ology** makes a noun meaning "the study of "

-**or**, -**er** changes a verb to a noun meaning "someone who does (something)"

-**ous** changes a noun into an adjective meaning "having that characteristic"

-**phile** makes a noun meaning "enjoying or liking (something)"

-**proof** makes an adjective meaning "protecting against" or "not damaged by"

-**ridden** makes an adjective meaning "full of"

-**ship** makes a noun meaning "in the condition" or "having the characteristic"

-**speak** used to form nouns meaning "the special language used in a particular subject area or business"

-**ward(s)** makes an adverb meaning "toward the direction"

-**wise** changes a noun into an adverb meaning "relating to "

-**y** changes a noun into an adjective meaning "having a lot of"

Punctuation

Punctuation mark	Use
capital letter	• the first letter of a sentence country, nationality, language religion person's name and title organization name trademark day, month • the first letters of some words in the titles of books, magazines, stories, poems, movies, art works, etc. • some letters in some abbreviations (*Mrs., TV*)
, comma	• in a sentence between parts of a sentence before *and, or,* and *but* beginning a clause before and after a phrase that gives information before an introductory word or phrase to separate quoted speech • at the end of each item in a list
. period	• at the end of a sentence • after initials • after an abbreviation • after a number or letter at the beginning of each new item of an outline or of a list arranged in a column
; semicolon	• in a compound sentence, before a clause that does not begin with *and, or,* or *but* • between items in a list when one or more of the items contains a comma
: colon	• in a sentence before a statement before a part of a compound sentence that explains more about the main part • before the items in a list or series • following an introductory phrase • in a title that has two parts, before the second part
? question mark	• at the end of a sentence that asks a question
! exclamation point	• at the end of a sentence to show strong emotion, sudden importance, or loud sound
’ apostrophe	• to form the possessive before an *s* added to a singular noun or pronoun following an *s* or *z* that ends a singular noun following the *s* of a plural noun • in a contraction or other short form of a word to show the place where letters have been left out (*we're* for *we are*; *'night* for *good night*) • in a date, to show that the first part of the date is missing (*'04* for *2004*)

Punctuation mark	Use
- hyphen	• to combine two or more words into one word • between a prefix and a proper noun
– dash	• in a sentence before and after a word or phrase that gives extra information to replace a semicolon or colon in informal writing
" " quotation marks	• to show words are a quotation and were written or spoken by someone else • to show a word or phrase is being used in an unusual or particular way • for the titles of short works such as a poem, article, or chapter of a book
' ' single quotation marks	• to show a quotation within another quotation • in areas such as psychology, to show a word or phrase is being used in an unusual or particular way
( ) parentheses	• in a sentence, to give extra information • around a number or letter before each item of a list in a sentence or paragraph
[ ] brackets	inside of parentheses, around extra information

Literary terms, forms, and techniques

Poetry Terms

allegory a work in which characters and events represent particular qualities

allusion a reference to a familiar literary or cultural figure or event

ambiguity unclear meaning

assonance the use of similar sounds in two or more words

ballad a poem that tells a story, often one that is sung

blank verse a style of writing poems without using RHYME

couplet two lines in a poem with the same METER (= rhythm) and RHYME

dramatic monologue a poem written as a long speech to an unseen listener

elegy a sad poem remembering someone who has died

epic a long poem about events in the past that tells the story of a HERO

free verse a style of writing poems without regular rhythm or RHYME

hyperbole the use of language to make something seem more than it is

iambic pentameter a METER (= rhythm) in lines of ten syllables

metaphor an expression that gives a description by referring to something with similar characteristics

meter the rhythm of a poem produced by the arrangement of syllables

ode a poem that deals with thoughts and feelings about an idea or subject

onomatopoeia the sound something makes used as the word to describe it

poem a piece of writing in which the words suggest images and ideas and often follow a particular rhythmic pattern; a POET writes poems

prose poem a poem written in sentences with a poem's rhythm and images

rhyme the same final sound of words at the ends of lines in a poem

sonnet a poem that has 14 lines and a particular pattern of RHYME

stanza a related group of lines

verse one of the parts into which a poem or song is divided

Literature Terms

analogy a comparison of different things to show their similarities

anecdote a brief story involving a particular person

atmosphere the mood or feeling produced by a piece of writing

autobiography the story of a person's life, written by that person

biography the story of a person's life, written by another person

conflict the forces that oppose each other in a story

essay a short piece of writing on a particular subject

fable a story that tells a moral truth, in which the characters are animals

fairy tale a traditional story that involves imaginary creatures and magic

folktale a traditional story

foreshadowing the use of details that will take on more meaning later in a story

genre a particular subject or style

irony a writing style where what is said is different from what is meant

legend an old story from ancient times or about a famous event or person

monologue a long speech by one person

moral a lesson that can be learned from a story

myth a traditional story about gods or characters with special powers that explains a belief or natural event

narrative a story of description; a NARRATOR tells a story

novel a long invented story; a NOVELIST writes novels

plot the plan or main story

point of view how and by which character an imaginary story is told; or the attitudes of the writer of a true story

preface an introduction to a piece of writing

prologue a beginning part that introduces the story, play, or poem

prose writing in sentences and paragraphs

rhetoric the art of speaking and writing effectively

short story a short invented story

The planets

Mercury
Venus
Earth
Mars
Jupiter
Saturn
Uranus
Neptune

Mohs scale of mineral hardness

The following scale was developed by Friedrich Mohs in 1812. It is used to compare the hardness of minerals – the higher the number on the scale, the harder the mineral is. The scale does not show how much harder one mineral is than another, just that each one listed is harder than the one before it.

A harder mineral can always scratch the surface of a mineral that is less hard or equally hard. To use the scale, you need to have available some of the minerals listed here. You can then scratch an unknown mineral with one of these to see which is harder. For example, if an unknown mineral can scratch topaz, it has a hardness of 8 or higher. If they can scratch each other, it has a hardness of 8.

1. talc
2. gypsum
3. calcite
4. fluorite
5. apatite
6. feldspar
7. quartz
8. topaz
9. corundum (ruby or sapphire)
10. diamond

Geologic time

Era	*Period*		*Epoch*	*number of years ago*	
Cenozoic	Quaternary		Holocene (Recent)	11,000	Ice Age ends
			Pleistocene	1.6 million	Great Lakes formed by glaciers; Ice Age
	Tertiary		Pliocene	5 million	land bridge forms between North and South America
			Miocene	24 million	forests decrease; grass covers large plains
			Oligocene	38 million	Alps and Himalayas rise; widespread forests
			Eocene	55 million	flowering plants widespread; tropical and subtropical forests spread
			Paleocene	66 million	flowering plants spread
Mesozoic	Cretaceous		Late Early	138 million	chalk deposits form; flowering plants appear; dinosaurs disappear
	Jurassic		Late Middle Early	205 million	low, wet land areas and dinosaurs widespread
	Triassic		Late Middle Early	240 million	thick conifer forests and dinosaurs appear
Paleozoic	Permian		Late Early	290 million	Northern Hemisphere deserts; Southern Hemisphere glaciers
	Carboniferous	Pennsylvanian	Late Middle Early	320 million	tropical forests widespread (from which coal formed); large inland seas form
		Mississippian	Late Early	360 million	shallow seas and low, wet land areas widespread
	Devonian		Late Middle Early	410 million	shallow seas
	Silurian		Late Middle Early	435 million	
	Ordovician		Late Middle Early	500 million	
	Cambrian		Late Middle Early	570 million	
Precambrian	Proterozoic		Neoproterozoic Mesoproterozoic Paleoproterozoic	2000 million	
	Archean			3800 million	liquid water appears

Periodic table of the elements

	1	2	3	4	5	6	7	8	9	10	11	12	13	14	15	16	17	18
1	1 H hydrogen																	2 He helium
2	3 Li lithium	4 Be beryllium											5 B boron	6 C carbon	7 N nitrogen	8 O oxygen	9 F fluorine	10 Ne neon
3	11 Na sodium	12 Mg magnesium											13 Al aluminum	14 Si silicon	15 P phosphorus	16 S sulfur	17 Cl chlorine	18 Ar argon
4	19 K potassium	20 Ca calcium	21 Sc scandium	22 Ti titanium	23 V vanadium	24 Cr chromium	25 Mn manganese	26 Fe iron	27 Co cobalt	28 Ni nickel	29 Cu copper	30 Zn zinc	31 Ga gallium	32 Ge germanium	33 As arsenic	34 Se selenium	35 Br bromine	36 Kr krypton
5	37 Rb rubidium	38 Sr strontium	39 Y yttrium	40 Zr zirconium	41 Nb niobium	42 Mo molybdenum	43 Tc technetium	44 Ru ruthenium	45 Rh rhodium	46 Pd palladium	47 Ag silver	48 Cd cadmium	49 In indium	50 Sn tin	51 Sb antimony	52 Te tellurium	53 I iodine	54 Xe xenon
6	55 Cs cesium	56 Ba barium	(57–71)	72 Hf hafnium	73 Ta tantalum	74 W tungsten	75 Re rhenium	76 Os osmium	77 Ir iridium	78 Pt platinum	79 Au gold	80 Hg mercury	81 Ti thallium	82 Pb lead	83 Bi bismuth	84 Po polonium	85 At astitine	86 Rn radon
7	87 Fr francium	88 Ra radium	(89–103)	104 Rf rutherfordium	105 Db dubnium	106 Sg seaborgium	107 Bh bohrium	108 Hs hassium	109 Mt meitnerium	110 Ds darmstadtium	111 Rg roentgenium							

lanthanoids	57 La lanthanum	58 Ce cerium	59 Pr praseodymium	60 Nd neodymium	61 Pm promethium	62 Sm samarium	63 Eu europium	64 Gd gadolinium	65 Tb terbium	66 Dy dysprosium	67 Ho holmium	68 Er erbium	69 Tm thulium	70 Yb ytterbium	71 Lu lutetium
actinoids	89 Ac actinium	90 Th thorium	91 Pa protactinium	92 U uranium	93 Np neptunium	94 Pu plutonium	95 Am americium	96 Cm curium	97 Bk berkelium	98 Cf californium	99 Es einsteinium	100 Fm fermium	101 Md mendelevium	102 No nobelium	103 Lr lawrencium

= hydrogen   = nonmetals

Biological classification of organisms

To better understand and study the more than 1.5 million different types of creatures on earth, CLASSIFICATION (= grouping) systems have developed. The most commonly used classification system organizes all living organisms into five large groups called kingdoms.

Kingdom	*Characteristics*	*Examples of Organisms*
Monera	simple, single-cell forms	bacteria; blue-green algae
Protista	single-cell forms in some ways plant- or animal-like	protozoa such as amoebas and paramecia; algae
Fungi	single- or multi-cell, often threadlike forms that absorb food	mushrooms; yeast; mold
Plant	complex, multi-celled organisms that use light for growth and energy through PHOTOSYNTHESIS and cannot move about	moss; ferns; trees; grains; flowering plants
Animal	complex multi-celled organisms that take in food to the stomach and are able to move themselves about	worms; insects; fish; frogs; reptiles; birds; mammals, including humans

Each kingdom is further divided into smaller and smaller groups with more closely related members, placing each organism in a specific PHYLUM, CLASS, ORDER, FAMILY, GENUS, and SPECIES.

Math and science symbols

$+$	plus/add
$-$	minus/subtract
$\div$	divide
$/$	divide
$\times$	multiply/times
$\cdot$	multiply/times; scalar product of vectors
$=$	equals/equal to
$\equiv$	identical to
$\neq$	not equal to
$\approx$	approximately equal to
$>$	greater than
$\geq$	greater than or equal to
$\gg$	much greater than
$<$	less than
$\leq$	less than or equal to
$\ll$	much less than
$\pm$	plus or minus; error margin
$\mp$	minus or plus
$\surd$	square root

SI units

The International System of Units (SI Units) is used worldwide for scientific measurements. The system is made up of seven base units and derived units. Many of the units are the same as those in the metric system of measurement. The SI units commonly used in school science content areas include the base units and the derived units shown below.

SI Base Units

Quantity	*Unit*	*Abbreviation*
length	meter	m
mass	kilogram	kg
time	second	s
electric current	ampere	A
temperature	kelvin	K
amount of substance	mole	mol
luminance intensity	candela	cd

Prefixes Commonly Added to SI Units

Prefix	*Symbol*	*Represents*	*Prefix*	*Symbol*	*Represents*
deca, deka	da	10 (10^1)	deci	d	0.1 (10^{-1})
kilo	k	1,000 (10^3)	centi	c	0.01 (10^{-2})
mega	M	1,000,000 (10^6)	milli	m	0.001 (10^{-3})
giga	G	1,000,000,000 (10^9)	micro	µ	0.000001 (10^{-6})
tera	T	1,000,000,000,000 (10^{12})	nano	n	0.000000001 (10^{-9})

SI Units Used in Science Classes

Quantity	*Unit*	*Symbol*
frequency	hertz	Hz
force	newton	N
pressure	pascal	Pa
energy	joule	J
power	watt	W
electrical current	ampere	A
quantity of electricity	coulomb	C
electrical potential	volt	V
electrical resistance	ohm	Ω

Weights and measures

Metric

Length

10 millimeters	=	1 centimeter
10 centimeters	=	1 decimeter
10 decimeters	=	1 meter
10 meters	=	1 decameter
10 decameters	=	1 hectometer
10 hectometers	=	1 kilometer

Area

100 square millimeters	=	1 square centimeter
10,000 square centimeters	=	1 square meter
100 square meters	=	1 are
100 ares	=	1 hectare
10,000 square meters	=	1 hectare
100 hectares	=	1 square kilometer

Volume

1,000 cubic millimeters	=	1 cubic centimeter
1,000 cubic centimeters	=	1 cubic decimeter
1,000 cubic decimeters	=	1 cubic meter
1 million cubic centimeters	=	1 cubic meter

Capacity

10 milliliters	=	1 centiliter
10 centiliters	=	1 deciliter
10 deciliters	=	1 liter
1,000 liters	=	1 cubic meter

Mass

10 milligrams	=	1 centigram
1,000 milligrams	=	1 gram
1,000 grams	=	1 kilogram
1,000 kilograms	=	1 metric ton

US System

Length

12 inches	=	1 foot
3 feet	=	1 yard
5.5 yards	=	1 rod
40 rods	=	1 furlong
8 furlongs	=	1 mile
5,280 feet	=	1 mile
1,760 yards	=	1 mile

Area

144 square inches	=	1 square foot
9 square feet	=	1 square yard
30.25 square yards	=	1 square rod
4,840 square yards	=	1 acre
640 acres	=	1 square mile
1 square mile	=	1 section
36 sections	=	1 township

Mass

16 ounces	=	1 pound
14 pounds	=	1 stone
100 pounds	=	1 hundredweight (cwt)
20 cwt	=	1 ton
2,000 pounds	=	1 ton

Capacity

16 fluid ounces	=	1 pint
4 gills	=	1 pint
2 pints	=	1 quart
4 quarts	=	1 gallon
8 pints	=	1 gallon

Volume

1,728 cubic inches	=	1 cubic foot
27 cubic feet	=	1 cubic yard

Temperature

Fahrenheit	Celsius	Kelvin	
212	100	373	Boiling point of water at sea level
194	90	363	
176	80	353	
158	70	343	
140	60	333	
122	50	323	
104	40	313	
86	30	303	
68	20	293	Average room temperature
50	10	283	
32	0	273	Melting (freezing) point of ice (water) at sea level
14	–10	263	
–4	–20	253	
–22	–30	243	
–40	–40	233	
–58	–50	223	

Time

60 seconds	=	1 minute
60 minutes	=	1 hour
24 hours	=	1 day
28–31 days (month dependent)	=	1 month
12 months	=	1 year
10 years	=	1 decade
10 decades / 100 years	=	1 century
10 centuries	=	1 millennium